africa
on a shoestring

David Else, Kevin Anglin, Becca Blond, Jean-Bernard Carillet, Tione Chinula, Jane Cornwell, Pascale de Lacoudraye, Matt Fletcher, Anthony Ham, Abigail Hole, Alex Landragin, Tom Parkinson, Gemma Pitcher, Liza Power, Nick Ray, Noo Saro-Wiwa, Nicola Simmonds, Vincent Talbot

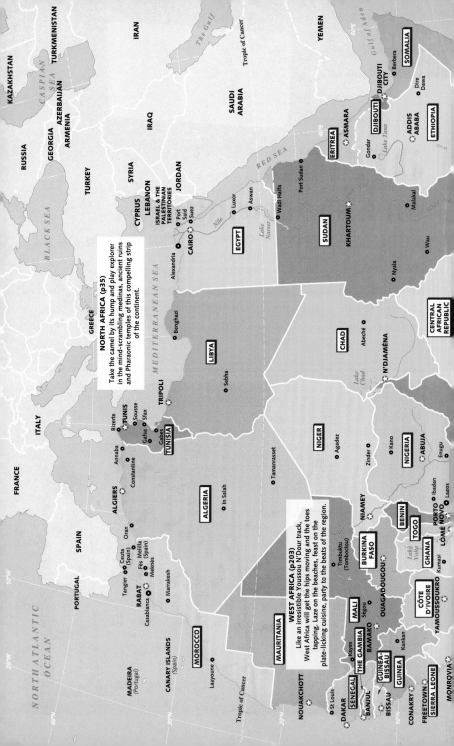

NORTH AFRICA (p35)
Take the camel by its hump and play explorer in the mind-scrambling medinas, ancient ruins and Pharaonic temples of this compelling strip of the continent.

WEST AFRICA (p203)
Like an irresistible Youssou N'Dour track, West Africa will get the hips moving and the toes tapping. Laze on the beaches, feast on the plate-licking cuisine, party to the beats of the region.

KAZAKHSTAN
TURKMENISTAN
IRAN
YEMEN
SOMALIA
Berbera
DJIBOUTI CITY
DJIBOUTI
Dire Dawa
ADDIS ABABA
ETHIOPIA
ERITREA
ASMARA
Gondar
Lake Tana
Port Sudan
Malakal
KHARTOUM
SUDAN
Wau
Nyala
CENTRAL AFRICAN REPUBLIC
Abéché
CHAD
N'DJAMÉNA
Lake Chad
Zinder
Kano
NIGERIA
ABUJA
Enugu
Ibadan
Lagos
PORTO NOVO
BENIN
LOMÉ
TOGO
GHANA
Kumasi
CÔTE D'IVOIRE
YAMOUSSOUKRO
Lake Volta
Agadez
NIGER
NIAMEY
Tamanrasset
BURKINA FASO
OUAGADOUGOU
Timbuktu (Tombouctou)
In Salah
ALGERIA
MALI
Ségou
BAMAKO
Kankan
GUINEA
CONAKRY
FREETOWN
SIERRA LEONE
MONROVIA
GUINEA-BISSAU
BISSAU
THE GAMBIA
BANJUL
SENEGAL
DAKAR
Kayes
St Louis
NOUAKCHOTT
MAURITANIA
Laayoune
Tropic of Cancer
MOROCCO
CANARY ISLANDS (Spain)
MADEIRA (Portugal)
NORTH ATLANTIC OCEAN
Marrakesh
Casablanca
RABAT
Meknès
Fés (Spain)
Tangier
Ceuta (Spain)
Melilla (Spain)
Oran
PORTUGAL
SPAIN
ALGIERS
Constantine
Annaba
TUNISIA
Gafsa
Gabès
Sousse
Sfax
Bizerte
TUNIS
TRIPOLI
Sebha
LIBYA
Benghazi
ITALY
FRANCE
GREECE
MEDITERRANEAN SEA
BLACK SEA
CASPIAN SEA
RUSSIA
GEORGIA
ARMENIA
AZERBAIJAN
TURKEY
CYPRUS
SYRIA
LEBANON
ISRAEL & THE PALESTINIAN TERRITORIES
JORDAN
IRAQ
SAUDI ARABIA
The Gulf
Tropic of Cancer
Alexandria
CAIRO
Port Said
Suez
Luxor
Aswan
Wadi Halfa
EGYPT
Nile
Lake Nasser
RED SEA
Gulf of Aden
Tropic of Cancer

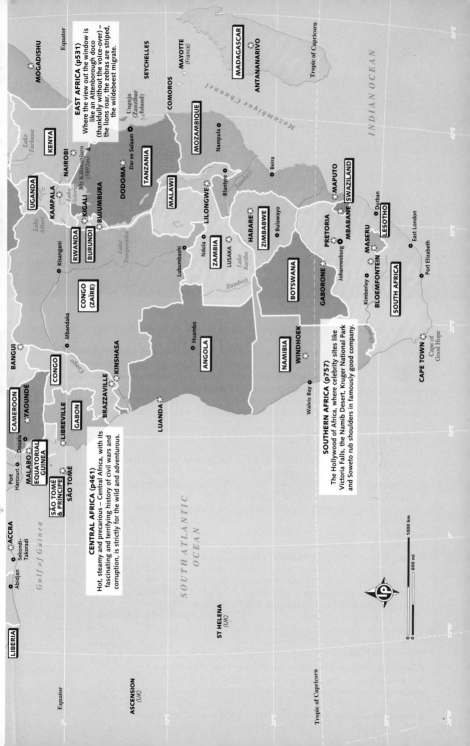

EAST AFRICA (p531)
Where the view out the window is like an Attenborough doco (thankfully without the voice-over) – the lions roar, the zebras are striped, the wildebeest migrate.

CENTRAL AFRICA (p461)
Hot, steamy and precarious – Central Africa, with its fascinating and terrifying history of civil wars and corruption, is strictly for the wild and adventurous.

SOUTHERN AFRICA (p757)
The Hollywood of Africa, where celebrity sites like Victoria Falls, the Namib Desert, Kruger National Park and Soweto rub shoulders in famously good company.

LIBERIA

MOGADISHU

Equator

KENYA

UGANDA
NAIROBI
KAMPALA

RWANDA
KIGALI
BURUNDI
BUJUMBURA

SEYCHELLES

MAYOTTE
(France)

COMOROS

MADAGASCAR

ANTANANARIVO

Tropic of Capricorn

Mt Kilimanjaro
(5892m)

DODOMA
Dar es Salaam
TANZANIA

Lake
Turkana

MOZAMBIQUE
Nampula

Mozambique Channel

INDIAN OCEAN

50°E

40°E

Lake
Victoria

Kisangani

Lake
Albert

Lake
Tanganyika

MALAWI
LILONGWE

Blantyre

Beira

Ungula
(Zanzibar
Island)

CONGO
(ZAÏRE)

Lubumbashi

Ndola

ZAMBIA
LUSAKA

Lake
Kariba

Zambezi

ZIMBABWE
HARARE
Bulawayo

MAPUTO
MBABANE
SWAZILAND
Durban

PRETORIA
MASERU
LESOTHO
East London

BOTSWANA

GABORONE
Johannesburg
BLOEMFONTEIN
Kimberley
Port Elizabeth

SOUTH AFRICA

BANGUI

CAMEROON
YAOUNDÉ

CONGO

GABON
LIBREVILLE

BRAZZAVILLE
KINSHASA

Mbandaka

Congo

Huambo

ANGOLA

LUANDA

NAMIBIA
WINDHOEK

Walvis Bay

Orange

CAPE TOWN
Cape of
Good Hope

ACCRA
Sekondi-
Takoradi
Abidjan

Port
Harcourt
Douala

MALABO
EQUATORIAL
GUINEA

SÃO TOMÉ
& PRÍNCIPE
SÃO TOMÉ

Gulf of Guinea

30°E

20°E

10°E

0°

10°W

SOUTH ATLANTIC
OCEAN

ST HELENA
(UK)

ASCENSION
(UK)

Equator

Tropic of Capricorn

30°S

20°S

10°S

0°

1000 km

600 mil

lonelyplanet

30°W

Responsible Travel

One of the joys of travel is leaving responsibilities behind, so who really wants to think about responsible travel? But responsibility clings to us like a good backpack, and no matter how carefully we travel, we still have an impact on the communities and natural habitats we visit.

Being a responsible traveller doesn't mean you have to get depressed and angry, walk everywhere and live on bread and lentils. It simply means that you should ask questions, and get a better insight into Africa, its peoples and problems, so as to lessen your impact on the continent. Throughout this book we recommend ecotourism operations (businesses that help preserve natural environments and their communities through tourism) where they exist.

TIPS TO KEEP IN MIND

- **Respect local traditions** Dress appropriately when visiting mosques and churches.
- **Learn the lingo** Learn a few words of the local languages of the countries you are visiting.
- **Spend at the source** Buy crafts directly from artisans themselves.
- **Ask before taking someone's photo** Some people have strong beliefs about photography. Always ask permission.
- **Rein in your consumption** Don't take endless showers; turn off that fan, light or tap; avoid using fires.
- **Hire responsible guides** Choose a guide with a good reputation who will respect the environment and communities you'll visit.
- **Don't give to kids** Giving pens, money or sweets to children encourages begging – instead, donate money to organisations that help the areas you are visiting.
- **Don't pollute the environment** Be sure to observe and comment on polluting practices of hotels and restaurants.
- **Don't litter**
- **Support local enterprises**

WEB RESOURCES

- **www.planeta.com** Ron Mader's outstanding ecotourism website
- **www.ecotourism.org** Links to businesses devoted to ecotourism
- **www.tourismconcern.org.uk** Operates several schemes for the benefit of Africans working in tourism
- **www.transitionsabroad.com** Focuses on immersion and responsible travel

Contents

The Authors

DAVID ELSE
Coordinating Author

David has travelled, trekked, worked and written all over Africa: from Cairo to Cape Town, from Zanzibar to Senegal – via most of the bits in between. Highlights include crossing the Sahara, canoeing the Zambezi, trekking on Kilimanjaro, tracking gorillas in Congo and watching elephants in Kenya. Lowlights include a two-week 400km truck-ride in Sudan, surviving on nothing but onions. Based on these experiences, David has written several guidebooks including previous editions of Lonely Planet's *West Africa*, *Trekking in East Africa* and *Southern Africa*.

KEVIN ANGLIN
Cameroon, Côte d'Ivoire, Equatorial Guinea, Gabon, São Tomé & Príncipe

Kevin spent two years as a Peace Corps volunteer in Fougamou, Gabon, teaching English at the local secondary school and studying French at the prestigious La Dakaroise Bar-Dancing. From there, a trip through Africa, Europe and Asia landed him in Lonely Planet's office in Oakland, California, where he has worked as an editor and author.

BECCA BLOND
Botswana, Namibia, South Africa

Becca got the African travel bug during a college semester studying in Zimbabwe in 1998. Since then she's returned to the continent three times. She has also seen Southeast Asia, Western Europe and the United States. This was Becca's first assignment for Lonely Planet. She travelled more than 15,000km in two months, ran out of petrol a few times and almost hit an elephant. When not writing for Lonely Planet she lives at the base of the Colorado Rocky Mountains, skis often and freelances for the *Denver Post*.

JEAN-BERNARD CARILLET
Djibouti, Eritrea, Ethiopia

A Frenchman based in Paris, Jean-Bernard found himself discussing in French the art of grazing cattle with Afar nomads in Lake Abbe (Djibouti) – a surreal experience in a no less surreal landscape. When he is not checking out Addis Ababa's cheerful nightlife, chewing qat or questioning the sense of life in eerie Dankalia (Eritrea), he spends part of his time diving in aqua lagoons in the Bahamas or French Polynesia.

MATT FLETCHER
Guinea-Bissau, Liberia, Sierra Leone, Somalia

Matt's travelling life started with an under-funded beer-and-train-station tour of Europe until, on emerging from art college, he fled to Africa. Matt wandered through remote parts of the Rift Valley, lost money gambling at the Maralal International Camel Derby, lounged on Africa's best beaches in Mozambique and let fascinating, baffling Africa get under his skin. He has returned frequently, contributing to Lonely Planet's *Morocco*, *Kenya*, *West Africa*, *Trekking in East Africa* and the *Unpacked* anthology. Matt also wrote the front chapters and Transport chapter.

ANTHONY HAM
Lesotho, Morocco, Swaziland

Anthony had dreamed of seeing Africa since he was a young boy. His first visit was quite a shock as 10-hour journeys to travel 100km and heat-driven inertia made him wonder why he'd come. As soon as he left he started planning his return. Now drawn by Africa's wonderfully diverse people, its open spaces and musical heritage, he leaves home in Madrid at least once a year bound for an extended stay in Africa. Anthony's favourite projects for Lonely Planet have included *Africa*, *West Africa* and writing the 1st edition of *Libya*.

ABIGAIL HOLE Egypt, Mali, Mauritania, Tunisia

Before working as a regular writer for Lonely Planet, Abigail was employed as an editor, prior to which she had travelled extensively in Africa and Asia, and lived and worked in Hong Kong for three years. Her travels have taken her from China to the Channel Islands, but she counts those for this book as the most entertaining and unpredictable.

ALEX LANDRAGIN Burkina Faso, The Gambia, Guinea, Senegal

Spurred by a long-standing curiosity about West African history and cultures, Alex has barely stopped raving about the region since, in particular about the joys of travel by motorscooter. Previously, Alex authored in Australia and France and worked in Lonely Planet HQ. He's currently writing a novel.

TOM PARKINSON Algeria, Chad, Niger, Nigeria, Sudan

Tom's first trip to Africa was a five-week social call to Tanzania while still a student; Lonely Planet subsequently sent him to Morocco and Kenya before plunging him into the depths of the Sahara, where he experienced Nigerien night driving, crotchety camels, all-in hospitality and the odd whiff of tear gas. Tom's other travels have taken him halfway around Europe and lured him further afield to Bali. When not abroad he can be found in any of several dozen pubs around the UK, or on someone's sofa 'researching' godawful TV.

GEMMA PITCHER Kenya, Mozambique, Tanzania

Gemma Pitcher spent her childhood with her nose buried in books with titles like *Safari Adventure* and *Across the Dark Continent*, prompting her to disappear to Africa at 17. She later returned to the UK to read English at Exeter University, and after a spell as a safari consultant moved back to East Africa to become a freelance travel writer. Going on the road in Mozambique, Tanzania and Kenya helped hone her talent for sleeping in ridiculous positions on absolutely any form of public transport.

NICK RAY Burundi, Rwanda, Uganda

Nick has travelled in many African countries over the years, but finds Burundi, Rwanda and Uganda to be small but perfectly formed. He has covered them in some depth for Lonely Planet's *East Africa* and relished the chance to return for another round of towering volcanoes, plentiful primates and blessed beers from Kampala to Kigali. He has contributed to more than a dozen titles for Lonely Planet including *Britain; Cambodia; Cycling Vietnam, Laos & Cambodia; Indonesia*; and *Southeast Asia on a shoestring*.

NOO SARO-WIWA Benin, Ghana, Madagascar, Togo

Born in West Africa but raised outside the region, Noo couldn't resist the chance to quit her TV news job and explore this amazing continent. Her research for this edition reminded her that Africa can't be displayed in a glass cage or fully captured in a book: you have to live and breathe its culture first hand in order to understand it and fall in love with it.

NICOLA SIMMONDS
Angola, Central African Republic

Nicola has worked in and backpacked around Indonesia, India, Europe, Japan and Central and South America. She currently lives in Angola. Her time in the region mastering water shortages, African bureaucracy and postwar chaos put her in an ideal position to cover Angola and CAR.

TIONE CHINULA & VINCENT TALBOT
Malawi, Zambia, Zimbabwe

Tione is Malawian born and bred, while Vincent grew up in France and Tahiti. Vincent first discovered Africa when his parents were posted to Cameroon. The couple met under the Tahitian sun and were married in Malawi in 2001. They now live on the Pacific island of New Caledonia. Tione and Vincent updated Lonely Planet's *Zimbabwe* guidebook; this was their second trip to Southern Africa for Lonely Planet.

CONTRIBUTING AUTHORS

Jane Cornwell wrote the special section The Music of Africa. Jane is an Australian-born, London-based journalist writing on music for publications including the *Evening Standard*, *Guardian*, *Songlines* and *Jazzwise*. Her articles also appear regularly in the *Australian*. She holds a postgraduate honours degree in anthropology and has worked for the Institute of Contemporary Arts, Real World Records, Womad and Sydney's Ignite Festival. Her favourite African album is Fela Kuti's *Underground System*.

Pascale de Lacoudraye updated the Congo and Congo (Zaïre) chapters. Originally from the Seychelles, Pascale lived in Brazzaville and worked as a correspondent for the BBC.

Dr Caroline Evans wrote the Health chapter. Caroline studied medicine at the University of London and completed General Practice training in Cambridge. She is the medical adviser to Nomad Travel clinic, a private travel health clinic in London, and also a GP specialising in travel medicine. She has been an expedition doctor for Raleigh International and Coral Cay expeditions.

Liza Power updated the Libya chapter. Liza developed her travel addiction at the age of 20 during a six-month trip around South America. Working as a travel writer for the *Age* newspaper in Australia, life has taken Liza from Kyrgyzstan to Colombia and from Mali to Sarajevo, with lazy days in the Caribbean in between. She's currently completing a degree in anthropology in the hope of studying under a sorko in Niger.

Destination Africa

Men in the Merzouga dunes (p198), Morocco

Africa rocks. No other continent comes even close to it in terms of scale, diversity or sheer impact. Sure, things are a little tricky in some areas, but Africa offers a travel experience a thousand miles from the well-backpacked, temple-lined tourist trails of Southeast Asia and cash-driven theme parks of Australasia or Europe. Africa is the place for adventurous travel. It's a place where much of the joy is in the journey itself, where stunning geography rules the roost, where the beaches make you want to laze around for weeks and where raucous all-night partying is a cultural experience and an adventure sport. Wondrous architecture awaits your gaze in mind-scrambling medinas of the Maghreb, on the fringes of the Sahara and beside the beautiful Indian Ocean coast. And Africa is, of course, the ultimate wildlife destination – where else can roaring lions keep you awake at night and elephants wander through your camp site?

Africa can be challenging. In fact, it can be pain in the arse at times. But the honesty and vitality of spirit shown by African people is second to none; these folk are, by and large, hospitable, ceaselessly cheerful and gregarious. On the average African street you'll be met by music and noisy stallholders, and you'll find the roads jammed with people, carts and vehicles.

Don't believe the hype: Africa is not a total basket case full of civil war, plague, famine and lawlessness. Despite the occasional hardship or logistical disaster, it's a fantastic, enlightening, surprising and intriguing continent.

Travellers on a canoe safari, Zambezi River (p900), Zimbabwe

HIGHLIGHTS

BEST NATURAL SPECTACLES

Victoria Falls ▪ feel the mighty spray from the wettest of the world's natural wonders (p815 & p910)

Sossusvlei ▪ let your jaw drop amid towering red dunes (p847)

Aïr Mountains & Ténéré Desert ▪ witness camel trains, wild geology and classic Saharan landscape (p295)

Parc National de Ranomafana ▪ explore this truly amazing park for lemur-lovers and hiking fiends (p743)

Atlas Mountains ▪ tackle these big, bruising mountains (p187)

BEST ACTIVITY SPOTS

Zambezi River ▪ spot wildlife while peacefully canoeing or pump up the volume rafting down class V white-water rapids (p815 & p910)

Simien Mountains ▪ trek fractured mountains and plateaus (p688)

Sinai ▪ enjoy diving, water sports, mountain trekking and more (p72)

Agadez ▪ launch your desert exploration from this ancient town (p292)

Drakensberg Range ▪ grab a horse or walking boots and get into it (p972)

Zebras, Etosha National Park (p851), Namibia

BEST WILDLIFE EXPERIENCES

Serengeti ▪ witness the July to November wildebeest migration (p612)
Etosha National Park ▪ go zebra-spotting on the Etosha pan (p851)
Parc National de l'Isalo ▪ track several species of lemur among extra-ordinary landscapes (p745)
Red Sea ▪ dive with thresher sharks and scalloped hammerheads off Ras Mohammed (p73)
Bwindi Impenetrable National Park ▪ see the remarkable mountain gorillas (p558)

BEST CULTURAL ENCOUNTERS

Marrakesh ▪ enjoy getting lost in this complex North African city (p187)
Masai Mara National Reserve ▪ walk with Maasai warriors through *Out of Africa* landscapes (p654)
Leptis Magna ▪ wander Roman ruins that bring history back to life (p102)
Kumasi ▪ get blown away by the sheer richness of the Ashanti cultural and architectural heritage (p384)
Gerewol Festival ▪ check out the talent at the famous male-only cattle-herders' beauty contest (p295)

Fishermen with traditional outriggers, Zanzibar (p598), Tanzania

BEST HANG-OUTS

Cape Maclear laze around on Lake Malawi and draw in the bleary backpacker scene (p796)

Cintsa answer the sirenlike call of Buccaneer Backpackers (p964)

Kribi chill out, wind down, eat fresh seafood and ease away the rigours of West African travel (p444)

Zanzibar hang out with locals, seaweed farmers and fishermen (p598)

Chefchaouen lay back in this beautiful hill town (p165)

BEST SPOTS OFF THE BEATEN TRACK

Querimba Archipelago explore beautiful, isolated coral islands with a Portuguese and Arabic legacy (p773)

Kakamega Forest enjoy sun-dappled rainforest walks among birds and monkeys (p654)

Canal des Pangalanes boat along this obscure waterway (p750)

West Caprivi Strip the grass really is greener post-Unita (p855)

Arquipélago dos Bijagós breathtakingly beautiful and packed with unique wildlife – what does the beaten track look like? (p322)

ITINERARIES

TOP TO BOTTOM

If you dream of travelling from the very top to the very bottom – rejoice, it can be done. Catch the ferry or fly into **Tunisia** (p107), then head east past the ancient archaeological joys of **Libya** (p94) to **Egypt** (p36) where the classic Cairo to Cape Town trail begins. After Egypt's treasures it's smooth sailing across Lake Nasser to **Sudan** (p80) then east into the Ethiopian highlands. From **Ethiopia** (p674) it's a rough truck journey down to Kenya.

An alternative northern launching point is **Morocco** (p146), where the popular Western Sahara Route leads south to **Mauritania** (p204), via Gueguarat (southern Morocco). There's no public transport for the 460km desert crossing, but there are loads of hitching opportunities. The latest reports from travellers suggests that it might be possible to take a 'desert taxi' between Dakhla (southern Morocco) and Nouâdhibou (Mauritania). Once in Mauritania, West Africa is yours (see French Footsteps, p17).

Many travellers avoid the long haul from Cairo, preferring to concentrate on the classic jaunt from Nairobi to Cape Town – **Kenya** (p630), **Tanzania** (p583), **Malawi** (p776), **Zambia** (p801; especially for South Luangwa National Park), Victoria Falls, **Botswana** (p863) then down to **South Africa** (p941), sometimes via **Namibia** (p831; but like Botswana, it's expensive). **Zimbabwe** (p888) is being given a wide berth by most travellers and now that tourism is booming in southern **Mozambique** (p758), many head there from Malawi.

How long?
1 year
When to go?
Dec-Dec
Budget?
US$10-30 per day

At least 11,500km, including short cuts, and about double that if you kick off in Morocco with an amazing December desert crossing, hit Cairo in March and Cape Town for the southern spring in September.
Go on, spend a year in Africa.

Alternatively, reverse this route using a cheap car bought in **South Africa** (p941) – you don't need a 4WD to explore Southern and East Africa.

MAGHREB MEANDER

Loads of shoestringers get their first African experiences travelling across North Africa. The region is accessible, you can move easily east to west and the historical and cultural treasures are immense. Think about grabbing a cheap package deal to **Egypt** (p36), or a charter flight to a resort in Sinai (on the Red Sea coast), then make for the Nile, where a huge number of ancient temples and remarkable archaeological sites lie between Luxor and Aswan.

Up in Cairo the Pyramids of Giza are a wonder of the ancient world, but the Egyptian Museum is just as incredible. Further north, in the Mediterranean port of Alexandria, head for **Libya** (p94) which is 'opening up', but travel arrangements should still be made though a tour company. Libya's Leptis Magna offers remarkable Roman ruins, and Ghat and the Jebel Acacus region feature prehistoric rock art and stunning desertscapes. In **Tunisia** (p107), check out the Berber Ksour (fortified granaries) around Tataouine and cross the desert to Tozeur before heading north to the wonders of Tunis.

The Tunisia–**Algeria** (p135) border is open, and although northern Algeria can still be dangerous the dramatic Tassili N'Ajjer and Hoggar southern desert regions are popular with tourists. The Algeria–**Morocco** (p146) border is closed, so from Algiers fly to Casablanca, the perfect launching pad for Moroccan exploration – taking the train to labyrinthine medinas of Marrakesh or Fès is a good way to start.

How long?
4 months
When to go?
Nov-May
Budget?
US$15-40 per day

Casablanca and Cairo may be just 3800km apart as the crow flies, but the stunning history and vibrant culture of North Africa will easily eat up four months.

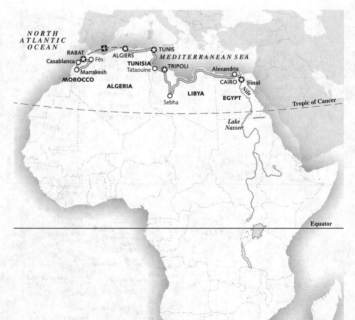

FRENCH FOOTSTEPS

Flights into **Senegal** (p216) are cheap, so while West Africa is crammed with many interesting countries, Senegal is a good place to start (not least because of Dakar's vibrant nightlife, the beautiful colonial architecture in St-Louis, the Parc National du Niokolo-Koba and the Siné-Saloum Delta). Most people then head southeast to **Guinea** (p326).

After checking out some fine beaches, Guinea's pumping music scene and the beauty of walking in the Fouta Djalon highlands, it's easy to cut up into **Mali** (p256) by shared taxi.

The vast, ornate mud mosque in Djenné, the vibrant port at Mopti, trekking in the fascinating Dogon Country, and the legendary desert outpost of Timbuktu are among the highlights along the Niger River (which leads into the desert country of **Niger**; p283). Camels and Tuareg nomads are found in Agadez, Niger's premier ancient city, while the desert scenery of the Aïr Mountains and Ténéré Desert leave powerful memories.

From Niger you have a couple of options: south through **Nigeria** (p423) to **Cameroon** (p436); or southwest to **Burkina Faso** (p302) and on to **Ghana** (p368), a gem of a country, and an English-speaking one.

Ghana's national parks are excellent, but the beaches and colonial coastal forts on the Gulf of Guinea draw the most travellers. Flights out of Accra (Ghana) to the rest of Africa, Europe and North America are cheap.

Side trips from this itinerary are many and varied – **Mauritania** (p204), **Guinea-Bissau** (p317) and **The Gambia** (p241) can be added from Senegal, while **Togo** (p393) and **Benin** (p408) can be visited later.

How long?
6 months
When to go?
Oct-May
Budget?
US$10-30 per day

Say *adieu* to six months when you embark on this epic 9000km-plus road trip. Journey from tropical beach to Sahara desert – and back again.

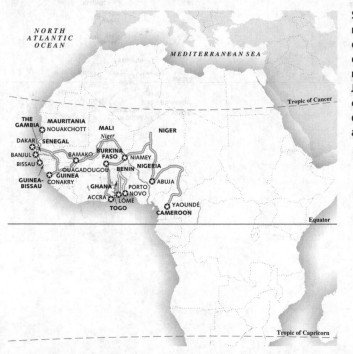

SWAHILI SAFARI

Many shoestringers choose to concentrate on East Africa, but few spend all their time hanging out with lions and zebras. Fly into **Kenya** (p630; Nairobi may be daunting, but it's cheap), explore the Central Highlands around Mt Kenya and then head east to the palm-fringed beaches, coral reefs and coastal communities (Lamu is a must) on the Indian Ocean.

Head south into **Tanzania** (p583) to drink in the Swahili culture and history of Zanzibar, then move on to Arusha; all sorts of activities can be arranged here including 4WD safaris to the Ngorongoro Crater and Serengeti National Park or trekking trips (up Mt Kilimanjaro and in the crater highlands).

However, don't discount southern and central Tanzania, where national parks like Mukumi National Park are located. From west of Lake Victoria you can move up through **Rwanda** (p532; still recovering, but a great place to see mountain gorillas) or directly into western **Uganda** (p546). On the lake the Ssese Islands are a good place to chill out; there's fantastic white-water rafting at Jinja; and Murchison Falls National Park is a gem.

From Uganda, cut back east to explore western and northwest **Kenya** (p630), perhaps starting with a trip north to remote Lake Turkana. Arrange (in Nairobi) your safari to the Masai Mara National Park in advance. Adventurous jaunts to **Ethiopia** (p674), **Eritrea** (p709) or northern **Mozambique** (p758; which has some fantastic outlying islands) are also possible – head to Lake Malawi for some laid-back beach time.

How long?
7 months
When to go?
Jun-Mar
Budget?
US$15-20 per day

Set aside at least three months for this 3800km jaunt around *Out of Africa* country, then add another month to lounge on a Swahili island plus another three for exploring Ethiopia, Mozambique and Malawi.

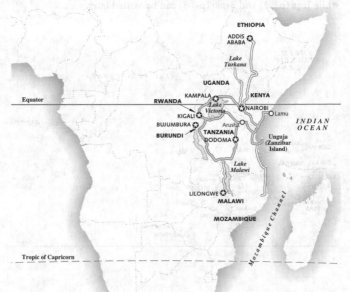

Getting Started

There are no hard and fast rules for travelling in Africa. Climate, behaviour and customs all vary from the top to the bottom of the continent – cruising the beaches of Cape Town in January wearing a T-shirt and thongs is fine, but is way out of place in the souqs (markets) of Tripoli where your attire will offend (and anyway, January's cold up there). See Responsible Travel on p4 for more information. The following section tells you what you need to know before you go (see also the Africa Directory from p992). But remember: nothing can quite prepare you for the wave of sights, sounds and smells that'll whack you in the face once you step onto African soil.

WHEN TO GO

The equator cuts Africa in half, which not only means that water goes in opposite directions down the plughole in the north and the south, but the continent experiences huge climatic variation. Although it's always the perfect time to visit there somewhere, watch out for the wet or rainy

See Seasons in the Fast Facts box of each country chapter for more information.

WHAT TO TAKE?

We guess you know to take things like a backpack, toothbrush and spare underwear. Here are a few more items to consider:

- **Backpack cover** – your friend on the road. Get a strong sack or rainproof bag to cover your pack; on bus trips it'll be tied on the roof and otherwise defenceless to dust, rain and chicken droppings.
- **Camping gear** – if you're planning on camping, bring everything you need: a tent, sleeping mat, stove etc.
- **Cash** – you can't go wrong with a wad of cash in your pocket (or, better, strapped about your person). Travellers cheques and ATM cards are good too, but not always viable.
- **Medicine** – general first-aid gear and all sorts of pills and potions are available without prescription, but it's a good idea to have some with you, particularly anti-diarrhoea pills (you will need these at some point); malaria prevention pills are a must. See Health chapter (p1028).
- **Mosquito net & repellent** – absolutely essential. The best way to avoid malaria is by not getting bitten and the nets in many African hotels are more hole than net. Insect repellents (although not insects) are difficult to find; smoky mosquito coils are readily available.
- **Photocopies of important documents** – definitely; photocopy your passport data pages (and those with relevant visas), tickets and travellers cheques, and pack them separately from the originals.
- **Rain gear** – you can pick up cheap raincoats nearly everywhere, or bring a breathable jacket from home.
- **Sleeping bag** – even if you're not camping, a sleeping bag is vital for trekking and is useful when you join an organised safari (where tents are provided); most backpackers lodges and local guesthouses have bedding but a sleeping bag is always useful.
- **Sun hat & protection** – standard issue for travel in Africa; don't underestimate the power of the sun and don't rely on buying sunscreen locally.
- **Water purifier** – bottled water is available everywhere, but the plastic bottles are an environmental nightmare; tap water is fit to drink in many major towns, but bringing purifying tablets or solution (and ideally a water filter) makes good sense.

season, which can cause all sorts of chaos: sudden, torrential downpours can turn dirt roads into rivers or bogs (curtailing travel to some regions) and parts of some towns and cities into boating lakes.

Late-October to February is a great time to visit the Sahara and arid Central Africa (although be prepared for cold nights) and you can also enjoy the warm summer days of Southern Africa or beachcomb along the West African coast. However, Madagascar gets swiped by the occasional cyclone at this time of year, so visit between April and October.

By around January or February, East African wildlife is concentrated around diminishing water sources and is therefore easier to spot. In contrast, the usually arid lands of North Africa spring into life between March and May.

More information and climate charts for Africa can be found in the Africa Directory (p997).

COSTS & MONEY

Africa can be as cheap or expensive as you want it to be. Travelling around like a maniac is going to cost much more than taking time to explore a small region slowly and in depth. Moving slowly certainly gives you the time to sniff out bargains and also reduces the number of times you'll turn up in a town dog-tired and fall into the nearest hotel or bar no matter the cost.

Africa is thought of as expensive among some budget travellers, but you can still scrape around for under US$15 per day. For a degree of luxury, such as a toilet in your room (sometimes a smelly mixed blessing), shoot for US$25. Things can get quite expensive in bigger cities and some countries – for example, Zambia, Botswana and Namibia tend to go for low-impact, high-cost tourism, although there are some backpacker options.

The actual cost of living (food, transport, etc) varies only a little around the continent, but travellers commonly blow big chunks of their wedge on car hire (which can cost US$30 to US$100 per day), internal flights and partying. Others blow their cash by going on safari, doing a course in Swahili, Hausa or another useful African language, camel trekking, undertaking a PADI open-water diving course, climbing a big impressive mountain, or taking a 4WD desert trip.

For more on money issues, see Money in the Africa Directory (p1004). The Fast Facts boxes in the country chapters provide more-specific country budgets. For this book, the budget amount covers the cost of three meals, one attraction or activity, two beers, one night's accommodation and about 100km on public transport.

HOW MUCH?

dorm bed US$1.50-10

500ml beer US$0.50-1.25

foodstall meal US$0.80-8

hotel double US$4.50-40

Internet per hr US$0.75-3

newspaper US$0.10-0.50

soft drink US$0.25-1

200km bus US$2.50-5

LIFE ON THE ROAD

Shortly after dawn, many locals are already out and about. But most travellers take a little longer to stir and think about breakfast, which usually means an omelette, egg sandwich or stodge-powered oily donut (they're much better dipped into milky tea). Breakfasts are often poor value in hotels – unless banana pancakes are on the menu, of course – so head to a roadside restaurant or street stall, where local chat comes free.

Thinking about African public transport? Then think time, patience and stamina. New roads are constantly being built, but both the dirt and tar varieties can be truly terrible; expect a few long, torturous journeys. In most areas public transport varies in quality (much like the onboard entertainment – sometimes action videos, sometimes escaped chickens) and rarely leaves or arrives on time. There are only a few interesting places you cannot reach by public transport, but you'll sometimes need to wait a few days for a rickety bus, truck or pick-up.

Accommodation across Africa is variable. Clued-up backpacker hostels with dorms and Internet connections are in short supply, but there are a few sweet, welcoming places that attract shoestringers like bees to honey.

Most budget accommodation is in small local hotels. 'Shabby' springs to mind far too often, but there are usually a couple of good, clean places offering singles or doubles in each town. See p992 for more information.

CONDUCT

It's hard to generalise about appropriate behaviour for travel in Africa. Certainly, traditional values remain strong and vibrant across the continent, even when they're masked with a veneer of Westernisation (in East Africa, a Maasai *moran* (warrior) may dress in trousers and shirt in town and then change into traditional loincloth and blanket once he's home).

By and large Africans are easy-going and polite. Your social gaffes are usually forgiven and are more likely to cause confusion and amusement than offence. At the same time, good manners are respected and many people will think you most rude if you don't say hello and inquire after their health before asking them when the next bus is going to leave. That's why it's useful to learn a few local greetings (see p1039), although in some African societies these initial exchanges can go on for minutes, and you'll inevitably have to switch back to English or French.

Shaking hands is a big deal in most African countries. Men who know each other well will often clasp each others' hands for many minutes, with much enthusiasm. There are more than a few styles of shake: in some places shakers link thumbs in the clasp, others touch their right elbow with the left hand during the shake or touch their hearts with the right hand after releasing the clasp. You'll soon pick it up. Local women don't usually have their hands shaken, but foreign women are sometimes treated as honorary blokes – see Women Travellers in the Africa Directory (p1012) for more information.

Africans operate with a smaller area of personal space than most Westerners, which can feel odd at first. You will find there are few queues in Africa – just scrums.

DO

- Learn to use the local language – a little goes a long way.
- Interact with local folks; don't hide in backpacker ghettos.
- Share your food and drink with local people on long journeys.
- Respect local customs and superstitions.
- Get off the beaten track; people can be more warm and welcoming.
- Tread lightly; leave little lasting evidence of your visit.

DON'T

- Undermine the authority of elders and officials; treat them politely and with respect.
- Insult touts and hustlers, no matter what the provocation.
- Stumble around drunk.
- Camp on or wander across private land; ask permission first.
- Use your left hand for eating or passing anything on.
- Partake in public displays of love and affection.

Travellers to remote areas are treated pretty much as curiosities, so your habits and dress will often be a source of considerable amusement.

Hospitality towards travellers is common, and only in a few tourist destinations (such as Egypt and Morocco) does it come with a catch, where travellers are sometimes exploited for income or hustled for money by people they believed to be their friends.

Dress

Urban hipsters in Dakar or Nairobi may like their clubbing gear, but African society is generally conservative in outlook. It's inappropriate to wear immodest and revealing clothes. Being meeting-granny neat will help your cause when applying for visas, crossing borders or otherwise dealing with authorities. On the road, T-shirts and shorts are just about OK in major tourist areas, but revealing tops or bottoms are unacceptable almost everywhere except on tourist-only beaches. Extra care is needed in rural areas and Muslim countries, where women should keep shoulders covered and wear long skirts or loose trousers.

'Being meeting-granny neat will help your cause when applying for visas, crossing borders or otherwise dealing with authorities.'

Meals

Travellers often get the royal treatment when invited to eat in African homes. A bowl of water is passed before dinner so hands can be washed (remember it's the right hand that's used to eat!). If you're really struggling, a plate and cutlery may appear. In most societies it's impolite to scoff food or take the last handful from the bowl; leave a little food on your plate – it shows satisfaction. Water or homebrew beer is sometimes drunk communally, but it's not customary to share coffee, tea or bottled drinks.

See Food & Drink in the Africa Directory (p1001) for information.

Giving Gifts

You should expect a few requests from locals for you to give them your flashier travel items, clothing or other gifts, but a polite knock-back isn't considered rude. Indeed, foreigners can be seen as a soft touch and the guilt-driven redistribution of goods can erode well-established values, distort perceptions of visitors and, in extreme cases, create communities of people likely to greet travellers with their hands outstretched. On the other hand, if you're offered a gift, don't feel guilty about accepting it – to refuse may bring shame on the giver. A reciprocal gift is obviously good form. Accept a gift with both hands and a slight bow, or with the right hand while using the left to touch your right elbow.

Taking Photographs

Always, always ask permission before taking photos, and respect an individual's right to privacy. Many Muslim women feel very strongly about having their photographs taken by strangers. Likewise, some tribal peoples get really irritated with being constantly photographed. This doesn't necessarily mean photography is banned, it just means that it's going to cost you, which is fair enough; negotiate a fee when asking permission.

Religion

Respect should be shown to all places of worship. Most Christian churches are open to travellers, as are some (but far from all) mosques. In Islamic countries, care should also be taken when visiting shrines and other holy sites. It's harder to navigate Africa's traditional religions: many of these involve a series of taboos, secret societies and sacred places. Always consult local people before exploring rural areas.

Snapshots

'The darkest thing about Africa has always been our ignorance of it.'
*George HT Kimble, 'Africa Today: The Lifting Darkness', Reporter
(15 May 1951)*

CURRENT EVENTS

Read the Western press for any length of time and you'd be forgiven for thinking that it will be the Four Horsemen of the Apocalypse meeting you off the plane. Civil war, famine, lawlessness and rampant corruption in Africa are all-too-common headlines, but hey, there are a *few* reasons to be cheerful.

The relentless spread of democracy continues across Africa. It's true that Western donor nations, the International Monetary Fund (IMF) and the World Bank do some serious arm twisting, and many countries are democracies in name only, but Ghana, Senegal, Mali, Botswana, South Africa and most recently (and somewhat surprisingly) Kenya are potential role models for democratic government.

Other good news is the introduction of the Heavily Indebted Poor Countries Initiative (HIPCI), which has reduced short-term debt repayments for dozens of African countries. However, many nations still pay the equivalent of their annual health budgets to banks, governments, the IMF and other lenders each year, so the campaign for total debt cancellation continues (see www.jubileedebtcampaign.org.uk).

In 2002 the African Union (AU; the former OAU and now an optimistic copy of the European Union, the EU) and the New Partnership for Africa's Development (Nepad) were launched. These home-grown initiatives aim to give Africa a collective kick up the butt by modernising African governance and creating a more business-friendly environment. Nepad is more direct (and realistic) in this regard, and has multibillion-dollar targets for inward investment as well as initiatives for democratic reform, free trade, conflict resolution and infrastructure improvements. Post-apartheid South Africa, which continues to flex its political and economic muscles around the continent, is a prime mover in both initiatives.

Regional free-trade agreements are established across the continent, but trade with the EU and USA remains horribly skewed against Africa, thanks largely to massive agricultural subsides in Europe and the USA, and powerful multinationals. What's more, lurking in the shadows of lofty ideals about an 'African renaissance' is the sad, depressing fact that comically inept governance and the outright theft of land, resources and money by corrupt regimes continues apace across the continent.

Pointless wars remain 'popular'; as one country manages to raise its game, so another becomes seemingly intent on flushing its immediate future down the toilet. Many more people have died in the recent conflict in Congo (Zaïre) than during the whole of WWII, but you'll struggle to get any details about this in the Western media. Natural resources (the

Focus on Africa (www.bbc.co.uk/world service/focusonafrica) and Jeune Afrique (www.jeuneafrique.com in French) will keep you bang up to date on African current events. Alternatively log on to www.allafrica.com, www.bbc.co.uk, www.newafrica.com or www.afrika.no.

Africa has plenty of cheap guns thanks to Cold War conflicts and other wars. An AK-47 can cost as little as US$6. There was a time in northern Kenya when you could exchange an AK-47 for a loaf of bread.

REASONS TO BE CAREFUL

While researching this book, some authors noticed an increase in local resentment being directed towards US and European governments. These governments are widely perceived as self-serving hypocrites, and this is not just in the Muslim countries where you can buy Osama Bin Laden posters and T-shirts at the market. Keep an eye on current events.

DIAMONDS ARE A DICTATOR'S BEST FRIEND

The smuggling and illegal trade of diamonds has funded conflicts in Central, Southern and West Africa. In an effort to curb the trade in so-called conflict diamonds, the Kimberley System came into force in 2002. The system aims to impose a method of authentication for all diamonds. Critics of the system suggest that administrative processes and domestic legislation in the USA (which buys 65% of the world's diamonds) need to be strengthened for the scheme to work.

After examining complex parts of human DNA from across the globe, one group of researchers has concluded that the whole of humanity outside of Africa is descended from just one African lady who lived over 10,000 generations ago.

cause of many protracted civil wars) continue to be exploited to the detriment of locals and the enrichment of foreign interests and African elites. Western governments and multinational companies may have buckets of blood on their hands, but Africa's people have been also repeatedly let down by their leaders. No wonder that immigration is on the minds of many Africans.

HISTORY

African history is a massive and intricate subject. We can't possibly give a comprehensive account here, but have aimed to provide a short explanation of the overriding trends. For country-specific histories see the individual country chapters.

Origins & Migrations

Africa is the birthplace of humanity. Current thinking is that once upon a time humans and modern apes had a common ancestor, but between five million and 10 million years ago *Australopithecines* (commonly known as 'ape men') branched off, or rather let go of the branch, and walked on two legs down a separate evolutionary track. This lead to *Homo habilis* around 2.4 million years ago, *Homo erectus* some 1.8 million years ago and in the final break from hairy, dim-witted hominids, *Homo sapiens* (modern humans) around 200,000 years ago.

Architectural relics are pretty thick on the ground in North Africa, but the lack of ancient buildings in sub-Saharan Africa has nothing to do with a lack of history or culture. It's more to do with the selection of building materials – mud and wood just don't last as long as stone.

A 'break out' from Africa into the wider world took place around 100,000 years ago, at a time when early African communities were divided into five main racial groups: the small and light San in East and Southern Africa; the thick-set Negroid peoples in the West; the thin and tall Nilo-Saharans of the middle Nile Valley; and the diminutive pygmies living in the rainforested Congo Basin. It's thought that North Africa was originally populated by peoples (including Berbers and Egyptians) who developed in the Middle East and then 'came back' to Africa.

The period from 32,000 BC to 16,000 BC was pretty dry, relatively speaking, but between 14,000 BC and 9500 BC things took a turn for the wetter, and the Sahara and North Africa became verdant and well-watered. It was in these green and pleasant lands that the first moves away from hunter-gathering to farming and sedentary communities were made, bright ideas possibly introduced from Asia.

TIMELINE

2755–2255 BC: Pharaohs of Egypt oversee Pyramids of Giza; huge advances in navigation, astronomy & medicine

1339–51: The Black Death kills 25% of Africa's population

1593: Portuguese build Fort Jesus in Mombasa (Kenya); garrison subsequently massacred in 1631

3000 BC	100 AD	1300	1500	1600	1700	1830

639: Islam sweeps through North Africa, displacing Christianity

1510: First African slaves shipped to Spanish colonies in South America

1834: Slavery abolished in British Empire; French do the same 13 years later

By 2500 BC the rains began to fail and the sandy barrier between North and West Africa became the Sahara we know today. People began to move south towards the Gulf of Guinea, which had a huge impact on the populations on the coast. Iron smelting technology (introduced between 600 BC and 300 BC) provided an impetus and by 100 BC Bantu peoples had reached East Africa; by AD 300 they reached Southern Africa.

Empires
African societies were developing complex empires and civilisations while Europeans were still chasing after wild animals with clubs. Many of these empires were small and short-lived, but others were truly great and had an influence on both Asia and Europe. Arguably the greatest was the first, Ancient Egypt. Formed through an amalgamation of already organised states around 3100 BC, it achieved an amazing degree of cultural and social sophistication. God-like Pharaohs sat atop a highly stratified social pyramid, and amazing public buildings (such as the Pyramids of Giza) were constructed. The good times lasted 2700 years, until Egypt was overrun by the Nubian Empire, then by the Assyrians, Persians, Alexander the Great and finally the Romans. However, the Nubians retained control of a great swath of the Lower Nile Valley despite getting a spanking from the Ethiopian empire of Aksum around AD 500. Legend has it that Aksum, which was possibly Jewish in origin and controlled much of Sudan and southern Arabia at the height of its powers, supposedly held the Ark of the Covenant.

The unbroken dynasty of Ethiopian rulers of the Aksum Empire began with the son of the Queen of Sheba in 1000 BC and lasted until 1974 when the 237th emperor, the famous Haile Selassie, was deposed.

CARTHAGE & NORTH AFRICA
Established in Tunisia by the Phoenicians (who hail from Tyre in modern-day Lebanon), Carthage controlled much of the Mediterranean trade by the 6th century BC. Unfortunately their Roman rivals razed it to the ground and enslaved its population in 146 BC. A host of foreign armies swept across North Africa in the succeeding centuries, but it was the Arabs who had a lasting impact, introducing Islam around AD 670.

WEST AFRICAN POWERS
Based on gold mining and Saharan salt mines, three hugely wealthy West African empires arose in present-day Mali. The Ghana Empire flourished from AD 700 to 1000 and was followed by the Mali Empire (around AD 1250 to 1500), which once stretched from the coast of Senegal to Niger, and the Songhai Empire (AD 1000–1591). Organised systems of governance and Islamic centres of scholarship and learning were cultivated until Morocco invaded in 1591.

Mansa Kankan Musa presided over the incredibly wealthy Mali Empire (1312–37). It's said that he possessed a nugget of gold so large you could tether a horse to it. When on pilgrimage to Mecca in 1324, Musa's entourage was made up of 60,000 people (including 14,000 slave girls) and 100 camels each laden with 135kg of gold.

GREAT ZIMBABWE
Attaining power and wealth through trading gold and ivory with Swahili traders from the 11th century, Great Zimbabwe (also called Mwene Mutapa or Monomotapa) was a triumph for 400 years. A great stone city

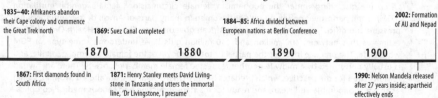

1835–40: Afrikaners abandon their Cape colony and commence the Great Trek north

1869: Suez Canal completed

1884–85: Africa divided between European nations at Berlin Conference

2002: Formation of AU and Nepad

1870   1880   1890   1900

1867: First diamonds found in South Africa

1871: Henry Stanley meets David Livingstone in Tanzania and utters the immortal line, 'Dr Livingstone, I presume'

1990: Nelson Mandela released after 27 years inside; apartheid effectively ends was constructed in the south of modern-day Zimbabwe, but by the 16th century it had exhausted local natural resources and collapsed.

Colonialism & Slavery

There has always been slavery in Africa (slaves were often the by-products of war), but after Portuguese ships arrived off the West African coast around 1450, with a view to circumventing the trans-Saharan gold trade, slaving turned into an export industry. The Europeans soon saw how African slavery worked and were impressed with how the system helped fuel agricultural production. They figured that slaves would be just the thing for their huge American sugar plantations. At the same time, African leaders realised they could extend their kingdoms by waging war and getting rich trading with Europeans, whose thirst for slaves (and gradual insistence that slaves be exchanged for guns) created a vicious circle of conflict.

Exact figures are impossible to establish, but from the end of the 15th century until around 1870 (when the slave trade was abolished) up to 20 million Africans were enslaved. Perhaps half died en route to the Americas; millions of others perished in slaving raids.

The trans-Atlantic slave trade gave European powers a huge economic boost, while the loss of farmers and tradespeople, as well as the general chaos, made Africa an easy target for colonialism. Colonisation really began around 1850 – until then European powers had contented themselves with coastal bases. At the Berlin Conference of 1884 to 1885 most of the Africa was split neatly into colonies. France and Britain got the biggest swaths, with Germany, Portugal, Italy, Spain and Belgium picking up bits and pieces.

Forced labour, heavy taxation and swift and vengeful violence for any insurrection were all characteristics of the colonial administrations. African territories were essentially organised to extract cheap cash crops and natural resources for use by the colonial power. Industrial development was not a priority and the effects of colonialism and slavery continue to disadvantage the continent. Despite independence, a process that started in the 1950s, Africa remains at the mercy of external forces (weather, global markets, former colonial powers, multinationals).

THE CULTURE

Africa is the most ethnically and linguistically diverse continent on earth. Over the last 100 years it has experienced enormous cultural change with a number of factors, not least colonialism, globalisation and foreign (especially American) culture, leading to a general Westernisation of society – Africans have become more sedentary, and large urban populations have emerged.

> Slavery on the east coast was on a smaller scale than that of West Africa, but the slave markets of Zanzibar and Ilha de Moçambique thrived nevertheless. Close to 600,000 slaves passed through Zanzibar between 1830 and 1873, mostly destined for the Indian subcontinent, Arabia and French colonies in Réunion and Mauritius.

> In Africa, slaves led similar lives to many other poor men and women, but they had even fewer rights. By contrast, slaves in the Americas could expect just a few years of hard, brutal servitude.

FEMALE GENITAL MUTILATION

Often masquerading under the euphemism 'female circumcision', female genital mutilation (FGM) is still performed on young girls and women in many parts of Africa, despite international pressure and official opposition from many African governments. The World Health Organization estimates that between 100 million and 130 million girls have undergone some type of FGM worldwide. The practice involves the partial or total removal of the female external genitalia, and is usually performed by a midwife or other respected female member of society. There are myriad reasons cited for the practice, which predates Islam. In many societies, an 'altered' woman is seen as chaste, honourable and clean, and ready for marriage. Infection and serious medical complications are common.

AIDS

It's impossible to overstate the impact that HIV/AIDS is having on Africa. Within the last 24 hours around 5500 Africans were killed by HIV/AIDS. One in five African adults is infected – in some parts of East and Southern Africa, it's one in three. There are many possible reasons why HIV/AIDS has taken such a hold in Africa compared with other parts of the world. Collective denial of the problem, migration in search of work and to escape wars and famine, a general lack of adequate healthcare and prevention programmes, and social and cultural factors – in particular the low status of women in many African societies – are all believed to have played a role in the rapid spread of the disease. But in some countries, such as Senegal and Uganda, vigorous education programmes have slowed the spread.

The personal, social and economic costs associated with the disease are devastating. The Joint United Nations programme on HIV/AIDS (UNAIDS) estimates that there will be 42 million orphans by 2010, many of whom will end up on the street as nihilistic little crime waves. Some observers believe that HIV/AIDS is causing societal breakdown in some places – certainly, AIDS orphans became child soldiers in Sierra Leone, Liberia, Congo and Uganda.

In 2003 US President George W Bush pledged US$15 billion towards fighting AIDS in Africa and the Caribbean, but the cash may not be available to any organisation that promotes or condones abortion. Drug treatments that are available in the West to increase the lifespan of AIDS sufferers and reduce the risk of HIV-infected women passing the infection on to their unborn babies are still out of the reach of most Africans (Brazil has managed to halve AIDS deaths by making such drugs free at the point of use).

HIV/AIDS predominantly hits the most productive members of society – young adults. This has a huge impact on family income, food production and local economies in general, and large parts of Africa face the loss of a significant proportion of entire generations. The result: a population age profile that no longer resembles the usual pyramid, but rather an hourglass – a world of orphans and the elderly.

AIDS Facts

- Scientists think that HIV/AIDS leapt the species barrier from chimpanzees to people some 70 years ago.
- 30 million Africans are infected with HIV.
- 17 million Africans have died since the start of the epidemic; 2.4 million died in 2002.
- Average life expectancy in Africa has fallen since 1980, from 48 to 47; Zambia's is down to 38.
- In Botswana a 15-year-old boy has an 80% chance of dying of AIDS.
- More women than men are infected and it's women who do most agricultural work in Africa.

Urbanisation is common in Africa, although some young men from rural areas are short-term migrant workers, using their wages to set themselves up back home. Women form the backbone of African families, institutions that provide an excellent support network, but one that's being sorely tested by the AIDS epidemic and is often upset if all the men work away. Women usually tackle the lion's share of agricultural work and in some nations sexual equality is enshrined in law. Sadly, on the ground, equal rights are some way off and women are often treated as second-class citizens. Families sometimes deny girls schooling, although education is valued highly by most Africans.

In many nations, sport (usually football, which is played and followed everywhere) successfully illustrates a post-colonial sense of national belonging, but this often co-exists with the ethnically specific identities, beliefs and values important to many. In sub-Saharan Africa there's a distinctive philosophy concerning the importance of extended

Interested in how the World Bank and the IMF influence developing countries? Look for *Tropical Gangsters*, Robert Klitgaard's account of his efforts to modernise Equatorial Guinea's economy.

CONTEMPORARY FOLKTALES

Nigerian authors dominate the English-speaking West African literature scene and some, like Amos Tutuola, have adapted African folklore into their own works. Penned by Tutuola, *The Palm-Wine Drinkard* is a rather grisly tale of a man who enters the spirit world in order to find his palm wine supplier. Another of his works, *My Life in the Bush of Ghosts*, offers similar miraculous themes and features a boy who gets trapped in the spirit world. *Things Fall Apart* by Chinua Achebe is a more contemporary but deeply symbolic tale about a man's rise and fall at the time colonialism arrived in Africa.

---

families, traditional practices and respect for elders. North Africans generally share these principles, but Arabic and Islamic traditions are also strong.

Art & Craft

Traditionally, African art and craft is not divided neatly into sculpture, painting and 'craft', but rather is a part of the religious, cultural and practical life of the community.

In the West, arts and craft traditions are constantly evolving and changing in appearance (take the movement over 500 years from Renaissance to Impressionist and postmodern styles, for example), but the same variation and adaptation did not occur within the African visual arts until Western influences came to bear. Change came very, very slowly and maintaining a constant tradition (that is, reproducing what had gone before) was always the most important thing to African culture.

Traveller's Literary Companion – Africa edited by Oona Strathern, *Unwinding Threads: Writing by Women in Africa* by Charlotte H Bruner, *The Book of African Stories*, edited by Stephen Gray, and *Penguin Book of Modern African Poetry* edited by Moore and Beier provide a very useful literary background.

It's still largely true that no special value is placed upon an 'antique' object in Africa – if it's old and ragged, it's time to make a new one. Traditional African art and craft consists of ceremonial masks, figures related to ancestral worship, fetishes (which protect against certain spirits), weapons, furnishings and everyday utensils. All kinds of materials are used (including bronze casting in some regions) and great skill can also be seen in the production of textiles, basketry and leatherwork.

Westernisation and tourism have all greatly affected African art and craft. Considerable effort now goes into producing objects for sale rather than traditional use, and popular styles in one part of Africa are widely mimicked elsewhere.

In North Africa, ancient Arabic and Islamic traditions have produced some very fine art (ceramics and carpets are particularly beautiful and refined), as well as some phenomenal architecture; in the Sahara, Tuareg silver jewellery is unique and beautiful.

But it's arguably West Africa that produces the most amazing art: Nigeria and Benin have long been associated with fine bronze sculptures and carvings, and the Ashanti people of Ghana are renowned for fine textiles and gold sculptures.

In East Africa the Makonde people of Mozambique produce excellent, widely copied, figures and totems.

There are also some wonderful African takes on Western traditions of painting and sculpture. Recycling everyday materials into interesting objects is another contemporary trend.

Literature

Swahili (East Africa), Hausa (Nigeria) and Amharic (Ethiopia) contemporary cultures have had a written literary history for a few centuries, and in North Africa the writings of Islamic scholars and academics provides almost 1500 years of African historical background and endless reams of prose and poetry. Evidence of ancient written languages has been found in modern-day Ethiopia and Egypt, but sub-Saharan Africa's rich, multi-layered literary history was almost entirely oral.

Folk tales, poems, proverbs, myths, historical tales and (most importantly) tribal traditions were passed down through generations by word of mouth. Some societies have specific keepers of history and storytelling, but in many cases stories are sung or tales performed in a form of theatre. As a result, little of Africa's rich literary history was known to the outside world until relatively recently. However, African writers and academics across the continent are collecting and conserving Africa's disappearing oral heritage and there are a few collections of Africa tales and proverbs available.

Modern-day and 20th-century African literature has been greatly influenced by colonial education and Western trends. Some African authors have made an effort to use traditional structures and folk tales in their work, while others write of the contemporary hardships of Africans and the fight to shake off the shackles of colonialism, using Western-influenced narrative methods (and penning their works in English, French or Portuguese).

If you are interested in corruption, leopard-skin hats and pink Champagne (and who isn't?), then get yourself a copy of Michela Wrong's excellent book about Mobutu, *In the Footsteps of Mr Kurtz*.

Religion

Roughly put, North Africa, West and Central Africa close to the Sahara and much of the East African coast is Islamic; East and Southern Africa and the rest of the continent are predominantly Christian. If statistics are to be believed, 40% of Africans are Muslim and 50% Christian. Accordingly, around 10% of Africans follow traditional African beliefs, but these are pretty loose figures as many people combine traditional African beliefs with Islam or Christianity, and the level of belief in African religions is usually underestimated.

Until quite recently, there were Jewish populations in Ethiopia and North Africa, but the majority of Jews have since moved to Europe, the USA or Israel. Hindus and Sikhs are found in pockets across the continent where immigrant populations arrived from the Indian subcontinent during the colonial era.

Christian missionaries were at the forefront of African exploration and colonisation, and today both Islamic and Christian missionaries are hunting for souls in Africa. On the fringes there's an ugly mix of the puritanical Islamic sect Wahabi (exported from Saudi Arabia) and US-style evangelical Christianity.

RELIGION AFRICAN STYLE

The region's traditional religions are generally animist, and most centre around ancestor worship, spirits of natural phenomenon and ritual objects. Most acknowledge the existence of a supreme deity with whom communication is possible through intercession of the ancestors and who can be angered through certain behaviour or breaking of taboos. Among the Oromo of Ethiopia and several other tribes, there is little or no tradition of ancestor worship; the supreme deity is the sole focus of devotion.

The practice of traditional medicine is closely intertwined with traditional religion. Practitioners use divining implements, totems, prayers, chanting and dance to facilitate communication with the spirit world. The practice of geomancy and taboo is most pronounced in Madagascar, which has a remarkable, multilayered belief system.

ENVIRONMENT

Africa's ancient lands host many geographical marvels and most of them sit on the vast plateau of the interior that covers East and Southern Africa (this plateau is highest in Ethiopia, much of which sits between 2000m and 3000m above sea level).

Mt Kilimanjaro (5895m) in Tanzania and Lake Assal (153m below sea level) in Djibouti are the highest and lowest points in Africa.

The plateau drops down to some of Africa's great beaches via dramatic escarpments, and there are some stunning reefs and coral islands along the eastern coast.

The great mountain ranges of Africa are confined to the northeast (the Atlas Mountains), Southern Africa (the Cape Ranges) and East Africa (the Rwenzori Mountains of Uganda and Congo). Experiencing the wildlife, landscapes and people of these mountains can make your spirit sing, but the continent's highest peaks are the classic, stand-alone, dormant volcanoes of East Africa – such as Mt Kenya and Mt Kilimanjaro.

For the complete low-down on the continent's wildlife, grab a copy of Lonely Planet's *Watching Wildlife East Africa* and *Watching Wildlife Southern Africa*.

The Nile and Congo Rivers dominate Africa's hydrology, but the Niger (West Africa), Zambezi and Orange (Southern Africa) Rivers are no slouches either – all offer potential for waterborne adventures (particularly the Nile in Uganda and the Zambezi below Victoria Falls in Zimbabwe). Africa's great lakes offer huge potential for interesting travel and nothing can compare to slow-moving boat travel through Africa's great swamps and wetlands – try the Okavango Delta or Niger Inland Delta.

The geological fault lines, soda lakes, escarpments and volcanoes of East Africa's Great Rift Valley, which stretches from Eritrea down into Mozambique, provide a tremendous backdrop to one of the great wildlife habitats of the world.

If that's not your bag try the Sahara, the world's largest contiguous desert, which occupies a quarter of the continent. Other major deserts include the Namib and Kalahari of Botswana and Namibia. All three can be visited by travellers in search of dusty, thirsty adventure.

Wildlife & Habitat

Africa is a powerhouse of evolution, and East and Southern Africa have a clutch of wildly popular parks showcasing some of the greatest wildlife spectacles on earth. Lions lounge lazily under umbrella acacia, the savanna trees that provide that classic image of Africa and seasonal food for elephants and giraffes. Leopards prefer to lounge in the boughs of large, riverine trees (probably plotting against noisy, squabbling baboons, a favourite snack).

A budget safari in East or Southern Africa is your big chance to tick off the Big Five, but if cash is tight, concentrate on spotting smaller mammals such as mongooses, porcupines and honey badgers outside the parks – it can be just as exciting as watching a lion from a minibus window with 47 other tourists.

Bush savanna provides cover for numerous antelope species, while well-wooded areas are packed with primates, including vervet monkeys (the cheeky opportunists will raid your car or tent) and beautiful colobus monkeys with flowing hair and tails. Drought-resistant baobabs (weird-looking with a vast trunk and stunted, root-like branches) and sausage trees (with, not unsurprisingly, sausage-shaped fruit) are found on the drier fringes of the savanna, the haunt of bat-eared foxes (whose big ears detect termites far beneath the soil). Hippos and ruthless Nile crocodiles (two of Africa's biggest people-killers after mosquitoes) are found in deceptively inviting rivers and lakes across sub-Saharan Africa.

In Africa every conceivable ecological niche is packed with life; you could visit mountain gorillas in the rainforests of Uganda or Rwanda; track desert elephants through semidesert in Burkina Faso and Mali; look for chimpanzees in the hills of Senegal, Guinea and Tanzania; dive with great white sharks off the coast of South Africa or just sit back and enjoy the blooming deserts of Botswana and Namibia after the year's first rains.

Spend some serious time in Africa and you may become more interested in birds than mammals. There are over 1700 species to see and it's often bird-watchers who get the most out of Africa's national parks.

Ninety per cent of Africa's primary rainforest is found in the Congo Basin

National Parks

With over 500,000 sq km of land protected (an amazing feat, even though enforcement is at times lacklustre), some really cracking national parks are found across Africa. By and large the parks in East and Southern Africa are the most organised and exciting, but in the North and West some classic landscapes have also been protected.

In the past, Africans have been kicked off their land to make way for wildlife reserves and national parks. Understandably, this didn't usually go down well, but thankfully community-based conservation is now all the rage: experts have woken up to the fact that conservation is not going to work in the long term unless local people can see real benefits.

Global Witness (www.globalwitness.org) publishes many reports on human rights' abuses and the exploitation of natural resources in Africa; also worth checking out are Human Rights Watch (www.hrw.org) and Amnesty International (www.amnesty.org).

Environmental Issues

Cripes, where do you start? The continent's rapidly growing population has led to soil erosion, declining soil fertility, deforestation, desertification, water pollution and loss of biodiversity. Things are going to get worse, too, as Africa's population may more than double (to two billion) in the next 50 years. Wars, poor governance and corruption are all adding to the environmental destruction. Logging, mineral and oil extraction don't exactly improve biodiversity, regardless of whether it's locals or multinationals sucking up resources. The state of West and Central Africa's primary rainforest remains a concern, but pockets of temperate forest are getting the chop all over Africa not only for timber, but also for firewood and to be cleared for agricultural land. The Sahara is expanding at an alarming rate (up to 500m a year in some places), thanks to a whole combination of factors – not the least of these chronic overgrazing, deforestation and climate change.

Large-scale conservation measures are not common in Africa. However, across the continent, governments and aid agencies are instituting projects, many of them community based, aimed at tackling problems on a local level. Travellers can help too: take measures to reduce personal environmental impact while you're in Africa (for more information see Responsible Travel on p7).

Africa Rainforest and River Conservation (ARRC; www.africa -rainforest.org) has taken rather extreme measures to protect wildlife in a troubled corner of Central African Republic (CAR) that has been plagued by poachers: hired mercenaries have set up an anti-poaching unit along the Chinko River, where ARRC hopes to establish a national park.

MADAGASCAR'S NATURAL THEME PARK

If you've had enough of shooting the wildlife in East Africa's wildlife parks (with a camera, that is), head to Madagascar. Isolated for millions of years, Madagascar's weird and wonderful wildlife has cantered off on a different evolutionary tangent. In glorious isolation, many lemurs (ancient, dim-witted primates), baobabs, aloe plants, chameleons and birds evolved before humans arrived 2000 years ago and messed up the ecological balance.

The Music of Africa by Jane Cornwell

Jane Cornwell is an Australian-born, London-based journalist writing on music for publications including the *Evening Standard*, *Guardian*, *Songlines* and *Jazzwise*. Her articles also appear regularly in the *Australian*. She holds a postgraduate honours degree in anthropology and has worked for the Institute of Contemporary Arts, Real World Records, Womad and Sydney's Ignite Festival. Her favourite African album is Fela Kuti's *Underground System*.

Musician by a Wassu Stone Circle (p253), The Gambia

They don't call Africa the 'motherland' for nothing. The continent has a musical history that stretches back further than any other – it's a history as vast and varied as its range of rhythms, melodies, musical textures and overlapping sources and influences. Here, music – traditional and contemporary – is as vital to communication and storytelling as the spoken word. It helps keep cultures alive. As a political tool, too, its lyrics and associations can wield immense power. Just as musicians are regularly expelled from the likes of Algeria, Uganda and Zimbabwe for their political beliefs (Paris in particular is full of exiled African artists), there are others (such as the Senegalese superstar Baaba Maal) whose popularity African leaders are forever trying to cash in on.

THE CONTINENTAL PULSE

Without African music there would be no blues, reggae or – some say – rock. Let alone Puerto Rican salsa, Brazilian samba, Trinidadian soca or any of the innumerable genres that have roots in Africa's timeless sounds. African music has inevitably been affected by the West as well. Jazz, soul and classical music helped form the Afro-Beat of the late great Nigerian legend Fela Kuti, and it continues to develop courtesy of his technology-friendly son, Femi. In Ghana, electric guitars are now the mainstay of the dance music known as highlife, which is in danger of being overshadowed by hip-life (hip-hop plus highlife) and techno-pop, because the country has very few live venues worth performing in. Senegal's all-pervasive *mbalax* rhythms mix traditional percussion with plugged-in salsa, reggae and funk, although it's local hip-hop acts such as Daara J, Djollof and Pee Froiss who really appeal to the kids.

PRESS PLAY

Like many African artists who are hugely popular in the West – the Congo's Papa Wemba, say, or Mali's Salif Keita – Youssou N'Dour works in a double market, making different mixes of the same songs for home and abroad or recording cassette-only albums for local consumption. Across Africa, cassettes proliferate and piracy is such a problem that some artists even write songs about it. You won't find many CDs for sale on the street, but you will find endless cassette stalls. If you're looking for a club or gig *sans* tourists, it can't hurt to ask a cassette stallholder. They might send you to a posh hotel, or they might send you to a dingy club in the suburbs. Inevitably, it'll be an experience. Getatchew Mekuria, the splendid 80-something Ethiopian saxophonist and clarinettist, occasionally plays the lounge at the Addis Ababa Sheraton, so you never know what might happen.

TURN IT UP

What's hot in Africa right now? Just about everything, really, but there are distinct musical trends too important to ignore. Let's look north – in Algeria it's rai, a danceable phenomenon unleashed on the West via Paris-based stars including Khaled, Faudel and sometime Sting collaborator Cheb Mami, along with the street-style pop known as *chaabi* – both Cheb Hassan and Keira are worth checking out. In Egypt, it's best to acknowledge the late Umm Kolthum as the greatest singer in the Arab world. Everyone else does, and her stern, dramatic presence is everywhere. There's also *chaabi* (they spell it *shaabi*) in Egypt and Morocco, as well as an Arabic techno pop known as *al-jil*, both jostling in a music scene simply too diverse to cover here. Morocco's *gnawa* healing music – stringed instruments, hand clapping and singing in unison – hijacks Essaouria each June during the massive Gnawa & World Music Festival.

Across West Africa the haunting vocals of the griots and jalis, the oral historians-cum-minstrels, are ubiquitous (see p219). In Senegal, Youssou N'Dour's *mbalax* style blew away the big dance orchestras that came before it, although some orchestras – most notably Orchestra Baobab – are making steady comebacks. Mali's Arabic-flavoured *wassoulou* rhythms has champions in female singers such as Oumou Sangaré and Sali Sidibé. Still in Mali, the blues guitar of Ali Farke Touré takes some beating, though the palm wine music of tropical Sierra Leone – all light, airy guitar riffs and traditional beats – comes close. The furious percussion of Nigerian *juju*, a Yoruba dance rhythm popularised in the 1970s

RECOMMENDED LISTENING

El Sett (The Lady) by Umm Kolthum (2002)

Fight to Win by Femi Kuti (2001)

Indestructible Beat of Soweto Volume One by various artists (1985)

Juju Music by King Sunny Adé (1982)

Khaled by Khaled (1992)

Nothing's In Vain by Youssou N'Dour (2002)

by rivals Commander Ebenezer Obey and King Sunny Adé (who's still in top form), has been elbowed out by *fuji* (think *juju* without guitars) and awaits a predicted boom in, er, *juju-fuji* fusion. In Cameroon they're either shaking it to *makossa*, the horn-fuelled style as popularised by Manu Dibango, or whooping it up to the guitar-based *bikutsi*.

Soukous rules in the heartlands of Congo (Zaïre) and Congo, where it grew out of the Cuban rumba that made its way back across the Atlantic in the early 20th century and became an upbeat dance style. Papa Wemba, who splits his time between the Congo and Paris, remains soukous' best-known exponent.

To the east – in Mozambique the locals sway to the sounds of *marrabenta*; Ghorwane, Eyuphuro and newcomers K10 are three such roots-based urban dance bands. A similar scene exists in Tanzania, where the steady, melodic rhythms and political, philosophical lyrics of Remmy Ongala and his Orchestre Super Matimila get people thinking as well as grooving. Kenya's *benga* guitar style is that instrument's adaptation of the country's traditional rhythms. Along the Indian Ocean coast and on the island of Zanzibar, poetic Arab/African *taarab* music is enjoying a renaissance – look out for cassettes by World of Music, Arts & Dance (Womad) festival favourite Bi Kidude.

Heading south, Angola boasts its own merengue, samba and an accordion-fuelled dance music called *rebita*; down in Zimbabwe they're listening to the life-enhancing *tuku* sounds of Oliver Mtukudzi or playing the mbira (thumb-piano) based music known as *chimurenga*. South Africa's gigantic recording industry rivals that of Europe and America, embracing everything from the mbaqanga (township jive) of the Mahotella Queens and Johnny Clegg to kwela pennywhistle music, neotraditional styles (Zulu, Shangaan, Sotho, Pedi) and the Zulu *iscathamiya* call-and-response singing as popularised by Ladysmith Black Mambazo. Not to mention jazz, gospel, soul, pop, reggae, funk, rock and all points in between.

In Africa, music is more than a way of life. It's a force. 'Politics can be strengthened by music,' Nelson Mandela once observed, 'but music has a potency that defies politics.'

NORTH AFRICA

Africa is the Mother of Civilisation and North Africa her regal head. It's a geographical showcase of the powers of the mind: intelligence, imagination and spirituality. To travel here is to take a trip through the senses, to knock yourself out with information-and-visual overload: mystery, history, carpets, camels, tea, traffic, trinkets and those hellish saviours, taxis. Submerge yourself in bazaars and the truly bizarre. Smell the spice, breathe the bedlam, rock those kasbahs. Your sense of personal space will be assaulted, expanded and redefined for there is, in turn, too little and too much of it.

After the city chaos of Cairo and Marrakesh, sensational mountains and craggy canyons dwarf you, before pyramids and gigantic temples blow your mind. Be seduced by Arabic Africa: minarets of mosques, mazes of medinas and the warm effusiveness of the Arabs themselves. But despite their hospitality, this will not feel like home: you land in a world where time has never mattered – and so what was still is, and the future will be absorbed. Take your sunglasses and sense of fun but leave your watch at home. Time here ticks at a very different pace. Drift on the Nile in a felucca, dive the Red Sea coral reefs and Libya's ancient sunken port of Apollonia. Cruise seas of scorching Sahara sand in four-wheel (or four-legged) drives and stop–revive–survive at spring-fed oases. At sunset, planets of pink and orange dunes will fold you into their silence – the perfect place to safari and sleep.

For 3000 years North Africa has been a Mecca for conquerors and colonists, all of whom have left their mark. This influx of foreigners has never stopped, with academics and historians wanting to solve its riddles, artists wanting to capture its spirit, and travellers and Hollywood filmmakers wanting out-of-this-world locations. For out of this world it is.

Egypt

HIGHLIGHTS

- **Cairo** Pyramids, Egyptian Museum, culture and chaos (p43)
- **Red Sea** Colourful coral, abundant fish and a laid-back vibe (p70)
- **Luxor** Extraordinary ancient splendour (p54)
- **Aswan** Nile-side town with a sense of Nubia (p58)
- **Sinai** Canyons, mountains and monastic life (p72)
- **Off the beaten track** Western Desert exploration on the back of a camel (p62)

FAST FACTS

- **Area** 1,001,450 sq km
- **ATMs** in all large towns
- **Borders** Libya, can be crossed over land; Sudan by ferry; Israel & the Palestinian Territories at Taba (safest) or Rafiah (not recommended)
- **Budget** US$10 per day
- **Capital** Cairo
- **Money** Egyptian pound; US$1 = E£6 (600 piastres)
- **Language** Arabic
- **Population** 65 million
- **Seasons** hot and dry year round, cool in the north (Dec–Feb), rainy on north coast (Dec–Feb)
- **Telephone** country code ☎ 20; international access code ☎ 00
- **Time** GMT/UTC + 2
- **Visas** US$15 at any port entry other than Taba and Rafiah

As if determined to impress on every level, Egypt doesn't miss a trick: from pharaonic monuments – the pointed perfection of the Pyramids – so iconic you can scarcely believe that they exist, to the enormous drifted voids and bizarre contortions of the Western Desert; from the dreamy progress of the Nile to the pinnacles of Islamic art; from biblical mountaintops to temples that seem to have grown from the desert; from faded colonial elegance to crumbling Christian monasteries; and from long pale-sand stretches of coast to the depths of the jewel-coloured life of the Red Sea.

Among all this natural and created splendour teems the glorious tangled mayhem and intrigue of the everyday, from the voice of an Arabic diva to a shopkeeper's witty retort; from the pale flow of long robes to the fierce white of a felucca sail; from the wail of the muezzin (call to prayer) to the gurgle of a *sheesha* (water pipe) and from the jumble of the souqs to the meandering progress of a ferry at dusk.

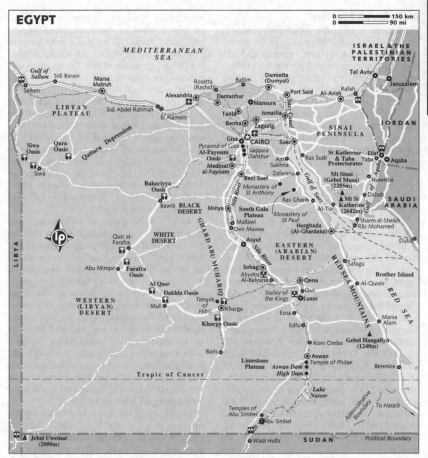

EGYPT

| 0 | 150 km |
| 0 | 90 mi |

MEDITERRANEAN SEA

ISRAEL & THE PALESTINIAN TERRITORIES

Gulf of Sallum
Sidi Barani
Sallum
Marsa Matruh
LIBYAN PLATEAU
Sidi Abdel Rahman
El Alamein
Alexandria
Rosetta (Rashid)
Baltim
Damietta (Dumyat)
Damanhur
Tanta
Mansura
Port Said
Al-Arish
Rafah
Tel Aviv
Jerusalem
Benha
Ismailia
Zagazig
JORDAN
SINAI PENINSULA
Suez Canal
Siwa Oasis
Qara Oasis
Siwa
Qattara Depression
Giza
Pyramid of Giza
CAIRO
Suez
Al-Fayoum Oasis
Saqqara
Dahshur
Medinat al-Fayoum
Ain Sukhna
Ras Sudr
St Katherine & Taba Protectorates
Eilat
Taba
Aqaba
SAUDI ARABIA
Bahariyya Oasis
Beni Suef
Zafarana
Mt Sinai (Gebel Musa) (2285m)
Nuweiba
Dahab
BLACK DESERT
Bawiti
Minya
Monastery of St Anthony
Ras Gharib
Mt St Katherine (2642m)
WHITE DESERT
Qasr al-Farafra
South Gala Plateau
Mallawi
Deir Mawas
Monastery of St Paul
Al-Tor
Hurghada (Al-Ghardaka)
Sharm el-Sheikh
Rás Mohamed
Duba
Abu Minqar
Farafra Oasis
Asyut
EASTERN (ARABIAN) DESERT
Safaga
Brother Island
Al Qasr
Dakhla Oasis
Sohag
Abydos
Al-Balyana
Qena
Qus
Al-Quseir
RED SEA MOUNTAINS
RED SEA
WESTERN (LIBYAN) DESERT
Mut
Temple of Hibis
Kharga
Valley of the Kings
Luxor
Esna
Marsa Alam
Kharga Oasis
Edfu
Gebel Hangaliya (1240m)
Baris
Kom Ombo
Aswan
Temple of Philae
Berenice
Limestone Plateau
Aswan Dam
High Dam
Tropic of Cancer
Lake Nasser
Temples of Abu Simbel
Abu Simbel
Administrative Boundary
To Halaib
Jebel Uweinat (2000m)
Wadi Halfa
SUDAN
Political Boundary
LIBYA
GHARD ABU MUHARIQ

HISTORY

The history of Egypt is inextricably linked to the Nile. Its regular rhythms made Egypt's great civilisations and development possible. But it has been a long time since the resources around the river alone were able to sustain the most populous country of the Arabic world.

Life on the Nile

Recorded history stretches back at least 6000 years, beyond the time of the pharaohs. The country developed into two important states, one consisting of the Upper Nile Valley, which stretched north to the delta, and another consisting of the delta itself. The unification of these two states by Menes in about 3000 BC set the scene for the greatest era of ancient Egyptian civilisation. During the Old Kingdom – from the IV to the VI dynasties, trade developed and building flourished – but power gradually became decentralised. Internal struggles continued and the country once again split, but was reunified in around 2050 BC, ushering in the Middle Kingdom. More than 30 dynasties, 50 rulers and 2700 years of indigenous (and occasionally, foreign) rule passed before Alexander the Great ushered in a long, unbroken period of foreign domination in 332 BC. The ruined cities and monuments that these dynasties left – remarkably preserved thanks to the desert climate – are testament to their inventiveness and vitality.

EGYPT

Rule Like an Egyptian

From time to time the dynasties collapsed, due to decadence, religious conflicts and invasion – the Assyrians, Persians and Ma cedonians all conquered Egypt in their time – but the strength of the Egyptian culture meant that it tended to absorb its conquerors. Even after Alexander's conquest, the rulers that followed (the Ptolemies) were more Egyptian than Greek.

The Ptolemies ruled Egypt for 300 years until the defeat of Mark Antony's navy by the Romans in 31 BC and the subsequent suicide of Antony and Cleopatra. Egypt became a backwater of the Roman Empire and remained so until taken by the armies of Islam in AD 640. In the centuries that followed, Cairo became one of the greatest centres of Islamic culture and learning.

In the early 16th century Egypt became part of the huge Ottoman Empire. However, as the vitality of this empire waned, Egypt gained autonomy under the rule of a headstrong local ruler, Mohammed Ali. He and his successors hoped to make Egypt economically independent. The greatest of his projects was the Suez Canal. Mismanagement bankrupted the country, however, and by 1882 the British and French had taken control of its finances. When war broke out in 1914, Egypt was made a British protectorate. In 1922 the country once again became an independent state. The nationalist Wafd party were in power, but the king retained control and had British backing. The British kept control of all the important institutions and the Suez Canal. During WWII Egypt was an important base for the British, and the government provided their support on the understanding that they would receive full independence once the war was over. After the war, the Wafd demanded that British troops leave and the resulting situation led to riots and strikes.

War & Peace

The Wafd won Egypt's first democratic elections, and Nahas Pasha became prime minister. King Farouk, however, dismissed Nahas in 1952, which led to more anti-British riots and clashes between the public and the army. King Farouk was forced to abdicate and the ensuing coup led to the establishment of the modern state by Colonel Abdel Nasser. In 1959, the British and French attracted widespread condemnation when they tried to take control of the Suez Canal during the Suez Crisis. Nasser was a consummate politician, able to attract the aid he needed for the construction of the Aswan Dam and procure weapons to fight Israel.

The wars with Israel (the first in 1948 and the second in 1967) devastated the country's economy and the second resulted in the closure of the Suez Canal and the occupation of Sinai by the Israelis. It was Anwar Sadat, Nasser's successor, who was instrumental in reaching a peace treaty, the Camp David Agreement, with Israel in 1978 despite condemnation by every other Arab state. Egypt recovered Sinai and moved closer to the USA.

Sadat's willingness to talk peace cost him his life. He was assassinated in 1981 by members of the radical group Islamic Jihad. Since then, leadership has been in the hands of Hosni Mubarak, who has maintained a pragmatic attitude towards regional politics, rehabilitating Egypt in the Arab world. Maintaining Egypt's role as a peace broker between Israel and the rest of the Arabs, Mubarak has also reduced tensions on his western front, normalising relations with Libya. The situation in the south has been less happy, with arguments flaring between Cairo and Sudan over possession of the disputed Halaib region and the alleged harbouring of Islamist militants.

On the domestic front, Mubarak's regime appears to have won the battle against its greatest foe, the violent Islamist opposition that led to the death of more than 1200 people, including numerous foreign travellers, between 1993 and 1999. But while the violence has ebbed, a high price has been paid in terms of human rights and political freedoms. Many of the economic and social factors that led to the bloodshed – such as unemployment, the burgeoning population, overtaxed resources and falling living standards – remain. However, the country is on a slow but steady climb, performing an impressive balancing act between the Arab nations and the aid-providers in the West.

THE CULTURE

Egyptians are wry and sarcastic, with a gift for the one-liner and a well-developed sense of the ridiculous. Perhaps the difficulties of everyday life forces refuge in humour.

In some ways, little has changed for a very long time. Over half the population lives in the countryside, where traditional conservatism dominates. The men wear *galabayas* (long, loose robes), the women *abbeyas* (long gown), they eat *fuul* (fava beans, usually cooked with oil and lemon) and everything is *in sha' Allah* (God's will). Large families are the norm, and women take care of the home and more often than not lack education and rights. Agriculture still employs about a third of the workforce, but this is changing as the land fails to give people a living, and most people try to make ends meet with several jobs. However, there's also a more Westernised urban upper class who have a disproportionate influence due to their wealth and position.

The country is 90% Muslim. As Islam forbids the worship of idols, it is ironic that Egyptians live among the relics of some of the biggest exercises in idolatrous glorification the world has ever seen – and goes some way to explaining their nonchalance towards these riches.

People

People might claim to be descended from the pharaohs, but the bloodline has been seriously diluted by centuries of intermarriage with invaders. Most significant of these were the 4000 Arab horsemen who invaded in the 7th century. After this there was a lot of Arab migration and intermarriage with the indigenous people who had peopled the Nile for millennia. The Ottoman Turks who moved in from the 16th to 18th centuries also intermarried. About 10% of the population are Coptic Orthodox Christians. The Copts are often thought to be more direct descendents of the ancient Egyptians as intermarriage is rare in this community. Besides the Egyptians, there are several indigenous groups with ancient roots. The largest is descended from the Hamito-Semitic race that has peopled the Nile for millennia. Also included in this group are the Berbers, a minority group who settled around Siwa in the Western Desert.

Another group, the truly Arab element, is made up of the Bedouin Arab nomads who migrated from Arabia. Nearly 500,000 Bedouin survive in the harshest, most desolate parts of the Western and Eastern Deserts and Sinai. Despite being the country's most isolated population group, with the inevitable influx of outsiders into their domains the Bedouin are becoming more settled and less self-sufficient, clutching mobile phones as they crouch around the campfire.

The Nubians are the original people of Nubia, the region located between Aswan in the south and Khartoum in Sudan. Their traditional way of life – based on agriculture, fishing and the transport of goods along the Nile – existed virtually unchanged until the Aswan and High Dams were built. As the waters rose, the Nubians' homeland was consumed.

ARTS

Chief musical icon, in a country where music is woven into everyday life, is Umm Kolthum, classical music queen: the streets used to become deserted at the time of her monthly live broadcast on the radio. Her male counterparts were Abdel Halim Hafez and Farid al-Attrache, but they never attracted the same devotion. A low-rent extreme developed in the 1970s, starting with Ahmed Adawiyya – he spawned *al-jeel* (the generation) and *shaabi* (popular), both forms of tacky, repetitive, highly disposable pop. Shaabi is the cruder form and lyrics are frequently satirical or political. Today, Amr Diab is the most popular male star, with slickly produced sing-along sounds. Egypt no longer produces all the greatest names in Arabic music, despite its legacy.

Somewhat ignored locally, but fêted abroad, Nubian music is a warm sound, with simple melodies. The most famous exponent is Ali Hassan Kuban.

Nobel prize-winner Naguib Mahfouz is revered in the Arabic world for his profound ability to capture Egyptian life and language. His masterpiece is considered *The Cairo Trilogy*. His 1956 work *Children of the Alley* is still banned in Egypt; many regard it as blasphemous, and a savage knife attack in 1994 nearly ended Mahfouz' writing career. Nawal al-Saadawi is well known abroad, her works include *Woman at Point Zero* and *The Hidden Face of Eve* (banned in Egypt). Salwa Bakr also tackles taboo subjects; she writes in English and her *The Map of Love* was shortlisted for the prestigious Booker Prize.

ENVIRONMENT

Egypt's central feature is the Nile Valley. To the east is the Eastern (Arabian) Desert, a barren plateau bounded on its eastern edge by high mountains. To the west is the Western (Libyan) Desert, a plateau punctuated by diverse geological formations and luxuriant oases.

Separated from the rest of Egypt by the Gulf of Suez, terrain in Sinai extends from the jagged mountain ridges, which include Mt Sinai (Gebel Musa) and Mt St Katherine (Gebel Katerina – the highest in Egypt at 2642m), in the south to desert coastal plains and lagoons in the north.

Environmental awareness has been a luxury that traditionally few Egyptians have been able to afford. Air pollution in Cairo is among the world's worst. Population density is another problem, with the country's infrastructure stretched to the limit. Migrating birds en route from Europe to Africa are being killed in Egypt in massive numbers; waterfowl are hunted in protected wetland breeding areas; and ivory and other illegal animal products are traded in shops. The coral reefs of the Red Sea are under enormous threat from irresponsible tourism and opportunistic development. Freshwater lakes, such as Lake Manzala in the Nile Delta, are being poisoned by industrial and agricultural toxins.

On a positive note, the government has started to take action. There are regulations in place in Cairo aimed at addressing industrial pollution. Additionally there are currently 21 protected areas throughout Egypt and 19 more have been proposed. The national parks in southern Sinai are the most developed, with visitor centres and rangers, but resources are limited so there is still a lag between regulation and enforcement. But at least the situation is getting recognition, and there is hope that some of Egypt's most fragile areas will be preserved for the future.

TRANSPORT

GETTING THERE & AWAY

Air

Egypt's international and national carrier is EgyptAir. It's neither particularly good nor cheap.

All the major European airlines fly direct to Cairo; some of the better deals can be found in London (around US$240 return). It's worth checking prices of charter flights to Cairo, Sinai, Luxor or Aswan. Leaving Egypt, there are rarely spectacular deals from Cairo. Flying from Cairo to Tunisia, Morocco or Sudan costs around US$300 one way, while to Israel it's US$185.

Boat

JORDAN & SAUDI ARABIA

There are daily car ferries (1st/2nd/deck, US$38/34/32, 3½ hours) and a catamaran (1st/2nd US$50/45, 1½ hours) between Nuweiba in Sinai and Aqaba in Jordan. The catamaran is much more reliable. Arrive with some time to spare to go through formalities before getting on the boat. Once on board, you'll be asked to hand over your passport, but don't worry, you'll get it back later. Most nationalities can get a visa on arrival in Jordan, but check this before you travel. Likewise, passport officials will issue you an Egyptian visa at the port or on the boat.

There are also boats between Suez and Amman in Saudi Arabia (US$50, 20 hours, 8pm daily) and between Hurghada and Duba (US$35, three hours).

SUDAN

A ferry chugs along Lake Nasser between Egypt and Sudan. It leaves from the port near the Aswan Dam (about 20km south of Aswan) at about 4pm every Monday bound for Wadi Halfa (1st/2nd US$195.50/120, 24 hours). First class entitles you to a meal and a bed in a small cabin. Second-class passengers fight for seats. You should arrive a few hours before the departure time, to be ushered through all the customs and passport formalities. Meals, tea and soft drinks can be bought on board but you should bring water and snacks. Tickets can be bought at the **Nile Navigation Company** (☎ 097-303 348; Sharia Abtal Al-Tahrir; ⏰ 8am-2pm Sat, Sun, Tue & Wed). It's worth reserving your ticket in advance. Note that you must have a Sudanese visa to get a ticket.

Land

ISRAEL & THE PALESTINIAN TERRITORIES

There are two main places to cross the border between Egypt and Israel – at Taba and at Rafiah. You can take a bus from Cairo to Taba (US$8, 8½ hours, four daily); a shared taxi (US$11 per person, 6½ hours) is quicker, but you'll have to bargain hard. There are also buses (US$1.50, one hour) from Nuweiba to Taba. See the Taba section for more information on the town (p75).

From here, you walk through to Israel. The border is open 24 hours and immigration formalities take about 30 minutes. Once over, you can catch a shared taxi to Eilat, where there are frequent buses to Tel Aviv and Jerusalem. Coming the other way, you can get a 14-day permit that allows you into part of Sinai, if you haven't got a visa; but note there is an Egyptian consulate in Eilat.

Due to the trouble along the Gaza Strip, the crossing at Rafiah is not recommended.

LIBYA
There are direct buses running to Benghazi from Cairo (US$100, 36 hours) and Alexandria (US$60, 12 hours). There are also long-distance buses that go direct to Tripoli from Cairo (US$189, 48 hours, Monday and Thursday 8am) and Alexandria.

The border crossing of Amsaad is 12km west of Sallum. Service taxis run up the mountain between Sallum and the Egyptian side of the crossing for about US$0.50. Once you get through passport control and customs on both sides (you can walk through), you can get a Libyan service taxi on to Al-Burdi. From there you can get buses on to Tobruk and Benghazi, though it's less hassle to get a direct bus. From Sallum, there are buses for Marsa Matruh (US$1, four hours, three daily), which go on to Alexandria (US$4, nine hours). Note you can't get a Libyan visa on the border.

GETTING AROUND
Air
EgyptAir is the main domestic carrier. Domestic air fares are expensive even by international standards. The fare from Cairo to Aswan is US$165; to Kharga US$135; to Hurghada or Mut US$125; to Luxor US$120 and Marsa Matruh US$100.

Air Sinai (EgyptAir by another name) has flights from Cairo to Taba (Ras an-Naqb airport; winter only) and to Sharm el-Sheikh (all year round).

Bicycle
Bicycles are a practical way of getting around a town and its surrounding sites. In most places, particularly Luxor and Siwa, you can rent bicycles; prices start at around US$1 per day.

Boat
The felucca, the ancient sailing boat of the Nile, is still the most common means of transport up and down the river. The three-day trip between Aswan and Edfu is highly recommended. Continued police restrictions on travel in the south mean that felucca trips cannot go further north than Kom Ombo.

You can also take shorter trips – just for a few hours. It's best at sunset, but don't let that stop you going at other times of the day.

Hitching
It is easy to hitch in Egypt, but drivers are used to being paid for giving you a ride. You probably won't save much money by hitching, but it can be a good way to meet people. Obviously, women should be cautious about hitching.

Local Transport
Buses service just about every city, town and village in Egypt. Intercity buses, especially on shorter runs and in Upper Egypt, tend to become quite crowded, and you'll be lucky to get a seat.

Deluxe buses travel between some of the main towns. They are fast and comfortable, with air-con (it doesn't always work), toilet and, unfortunately, nonstop, noisy video. It's worth making a reservation in advance to secure a seat.

Travelling by service taxi (shared taxi; usually Peugeot 504s, also called *bijous*) is the fastest way to go from city to city. They travel on set routes and in most places congregate near bus and train stations. Each driver waits with his taxi until it's full. Fares tend to be a little higher than on the buses.

Minibuses are built to take 12 people. More often than not they cram in as many as 22 people. These run on fewer routes than the service taxis, and cost about the same.

Even though there have been no terrorist acts in Egypt since the 1997 Luxor massacre, the authorities are leaving nothing to chance, and tourist buses and taxis must travel in a convoy, with a police escort, between Aswan and Luxor or Abu Simbel. These convoys set off at certain times of day – you can find out when locally.

Train

Trains travel along more than 5000km of track to almost every major city and town in Egypt from Aswan to Alexandria. A timetable for the main destinations is updated every year and is occasionally actually available for a small fee.

Trains range from luxury wagons-lits (sleeping cars) services that run between Cairo, Luxor and Aswan (US$50) to rattling old 3rd-class museums, packed to the hilt. Student discounts of up to 50% are available for holders of International Student Identification Cards (ISIC). Keep in mind that due to police restrictions in Upper Egypt, foreigners are only allowed to travel on certain trains; you can get around this by buying your ticket on the train.

CAIRO

☎ 02 / pop 16 million

In Arabic, both Cairo and Egypt are known by the same name, Masr.

Cairo *is* Egypt, a top-heavy capital that dominates the country as it dominates Arabic culture. The city itself is thriving, seething, exhilarating, brilliant chaos, with madcap traffic, a soundtrack of hooters and the clackity-clack of dominoes, the bright glare of shoe-stuffed shopfronts, and rows of men sucking on scented hookahs.

Actually a crammed collection of districts that merge together to take you over and wring you out, there is layer upon layer to explore, including Coptic Cairo, Islamic Cairo, Giza and Downtown. At times it's a Middle-Eastern Manhattan, at others an ancient warren of backstreets; Art-Deco heaviness gives way to arena-sized mosques. The past lives on here as an incidental feature of the present. You will step into wood-polished, dirt-caked lifts like stepping back in time, you'll see people living among the mausoleums of the dead, and see the world's most famous monuments, the Pyramids, edged by the city's relentless, hungry sprawl.

ORIENTATION

Bus No 356 runs from the airport to the main bus station (Turgoman Garage); there is also a stop behind the Egyptian Museum, from Midan Abdel Moniem Riad. Local bus No 400 also goes to the airport from here.

A taxi from the airport costs about US$5, while going to the airport should cost no more than US$3.50. Midan Tahrir is the centre of town, and to the northeast is Downtown, centred on Sharia Talaat Harb, a noisy, busy commercial district that's glaring with light and thronged with people until at least midnight. It's where you'll find most of the cheap eateries and budget accommodation. Midan Ramses, location of the city's main train station, is to the north. Heading east, Downtown ends at Midan Ataba and Islamic Cairo takes over, with the great bazaar of Khan al-Khalili at its centre.

The wealthy enclave of Zamalek sits in the middle of the Nile, site of many of Cairo's Western-style bars and restaurants. On the west side of the Nile are the residential areas of Mohandiseen, Doqqi and Giza.

INFORMATION
Bookshops
American University in Cairo Bookstore (Map p48; Sharia Mohammed Mahmud)
Anglo-Egyptian Bookshop (165 Sharia Mohammed Farid)
Diwan (Map p44; Sharia 26th of July, Zamalek)
Lehnert & Landrock (Map p48; 44 Sharia Sherif)

Internet Access
Cairo has an ever-burgeoning number of cybercafés, open long hours and charging about US$0.75 per hour. Some central cafés:
4U Internet (Map p48; Midan Talaat Harb)
First Insurance Net (Map p48; 1 El Bostan El Saedy St)
Interclub (Map p48; 12 Sharia Talaat Harb)

Medical Services
The **Anglo American Hospital** (Map p44; ☎ 735 6162; Sharia Hadayek al-Zuhreyya) is located in Gezira.

Money
There are banks, foreign exchange bureaus and ATMs all over town, but it's worth knowing that the Banque Masr exchange offices at the Nile Hilton and Helnan Shepherd's on the Corniche are open 24 hours, as are the airport money-changing booths. All the big hotels have ATMs.

Branches of **Amex** (Map p48; ☎ 574 7991; 15 Sharia Qasr el-Nil) and **Thomas Cook** (Map p48; ☎ 574 3955; 7 Sharia Mahmoud Bassiouni) are dotted about the city centre.

Post

Cairo's **main post office** (Midan Ataba; 🕙 8am-8pm Sun-Thu, 8am-1pm Fri) has a poste restante down the side street to the right of the main entrance.

Tourist Offices

Cairo's main **tourist information office** (Map p48; ☎ 391 3454; 5 Sharia Adly; 🕙 8am-8pm) is near Midan Opera. The staff are quite helpful, though you might feel you're disturbing them from the day's real business of reading the papers and watching TV.

Travel Agencies

The area around Midan Tahrir is teeming with travel agents selling air tickets to all parts of the world. **Panorama Tours** (☎ 359 0200; www.eptours.com; 4 Road 79) is a reputable, cheap agency, near Ma'adi metro station, out in the suburbs. You can book over the phone, and the English-speaking staff will courier tickets to you.

SIGHTS & ACTIVITIES
Pyramids of Giza & the Sphinx

The sole survivor of the Seven Wonders of the World, the **Pyramids of Giza** (admission to grounds US$3.50, camera US$1.50, video US$15; 🕙 8am-5pm May-Oct, 8am-4pm Nov-Apr) still live up to more than 4000 years of hype. Their extraordinary shape, geometry and age render them somehow alien constructions, rising out of the desert. More than this, they fascinate us because of the mysteries associated with them – why were they built like this? Why was so much effort lavished on them and what do they mean? Evidence shows that tens of thousands of people worked on the tombs – and that they were not slaves, but a highly trained workforce. These incredible mausoleums were not built out of a morbid fascination with death, but out of a love of, and belief in, eternal life, and a desire to be at one with the cosmos. The pharaoh connected the world's mortal with the divine, and so was honoured in life and worshipped in death. A pyramid was the apex of a much larger funerary complex that provided a place of worship, as well as a reminder of the absolute power of the gods. The complexes of Khufu (dedicated to Cheops), Khafre (dedicated to Chephren) and Mycerinus, who were father, son and grandson, included a pyramid – the tomb

and repository for all the stuff needed for the afterlife – a funerary temple, pits for the storage of solar barques (boats), a valley temple on the banks of the Nile and a causeway from the river to the pyramid.

Cheops and Chephren's pyramids are the largest, and have stood for 46 centuries. Originally all three were encased in polished white limestone and would have gleamed like crystals. But until the 19th century, builders happily helped themselves to the limestone to build palaces and mosques. Along the eastern and southern sides of Khufu are five long pits that once contained the boats that brought the mummies across the Nile to the valley temple and were then buried to provide transport in the next world. The **Solar Barque Museum** (admission US$1.50; 🕙 8am-5pm May-Oct, 8am-4pm Nov-Apr) contains an ancient cedar-wood barque, possibly the oldest boat in existence.

Admission to the larger Pyramids costs US$7 and only 300 tickets are sold per day, half released at 8am and half at 1pm. To the smallest pyramid the fee is US$1.50, but there's not a lot to see. They close on a rotating basis to allow for restoration work.

The **Sphinx** sits nearby. Mystery surrounds this 50m-long feline character, carved from a single block of stone. Known in Arabic as Abu al-Hol (Father of Terror), the Sphinx is the centrepiece of the nightly **sound-and-light performances** (admission US$9); one reader suggested eating at a restaurant opposite, from where you get a view of the show for free.

There are swarms of visitors to the site, attended by swarms of camel and horse touts, but they fail to destroy the wonder. If you want a peaceful view of the pyramids, it's best to take a **horse ride** in the area at around 5pm – you won't see them close up, but it can be a lot more atmospheric than battling around close to the monuments. Horses cost US$3.50 per hour, camels US$5.

A taxi from Midan Tahrir should not cost more than US$1.50. Buses and minibuses to the pyramids cost US$0.15 and can be found in the area close to the Ramses Hilton Hotel (ask for 'Haram' and somebody will point out the place). Far more comfortable is the air-conditioned bus No 355 (US$0.30), which picks up from the bus station behind the Egyptian Museum. For the return journey, buses and minibuses pick up from the junction of the Pyramids Rd and the desert road

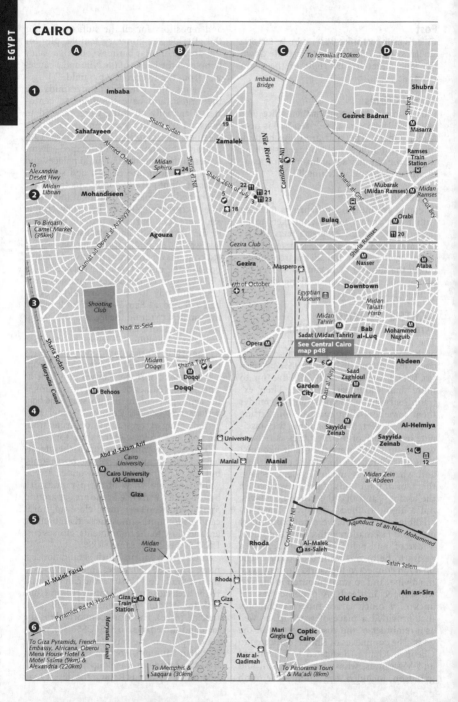

CAIRO

A **B** **C** **D**

1

To Ismailia (120km)

Imbaba
Imbaba Bridge
Shubra

Sahafayeen
Shana Sudan
Geziret Badran
Shubra
Masarra

Zamalek
Nile River
Corniche el-Nil
Ramses Train Station

2

Ahmed Orabi
Midan Sphinx
Shana el-Nil
Shana 26th of July
2
Shana al-Gaysh
Mubarak (Midan Ramses)
Midan Ramses

To Alexandria Desert Hwy
Midan Libnan
24
22
21
5
3
23
26
Orabi

Mohandiseen
18
20

Agouza
Gezira Club
Bulaq

To Birqash Camel Market (35km)
Gamal ad-Dowal al-Arabiyya

3

Shooting Club
Gezira
Maspero
Shana Ramses
Nasser
Ataba

6th of October
1
Egyptian Museum
Downtown

Nadi as-Seid
Midan Talaat Harb

Sadat (Midan Tahrir)
See Central Cairo map p48
Midan Tahrir
Bab al-Luq
Mohammed Naguib

Shana Sudan
Opera
Abdeen

Midan Doqqi
Shana Tahrir
4
7
6
Saad Zaghloul

4

Behoos
Doqqi
Doqqi
13
Garden City
Mounira

Qasr al-Ainy

Abd al-Salam Arif
University
Sayyida Zeinab
Al-Helmiya

Cairo University
Manial
Manial
Sayyida Zeinab
14
12

Cairo University (Al-Gamaa)
Giza

5

Maryutia Canal
Shana al-Giza
Midan Zein al-Abdeen

Midan Giza
Rhoda
Al-Malek as-Saleh
Aqueduct of an-Nasr Mohammed

Salah Salem

6

Al-Malek Faisal
Rhoda
Ain as-Sira

Pyramids Rd (Al-Haram)
Giza Train Station
Giza
Giza
Old Cairo

To Giza Pyramids, French Embassy, Africana, Oberoi Mena House Hotel & Motel Salma (9km) & Alexandria (220km)
Mari Girgis
Coptic Cairo

To Memphis & Saqqara (30km)
Masr al-Qadimah
To Panorama Tours & Ma'adi (8km)

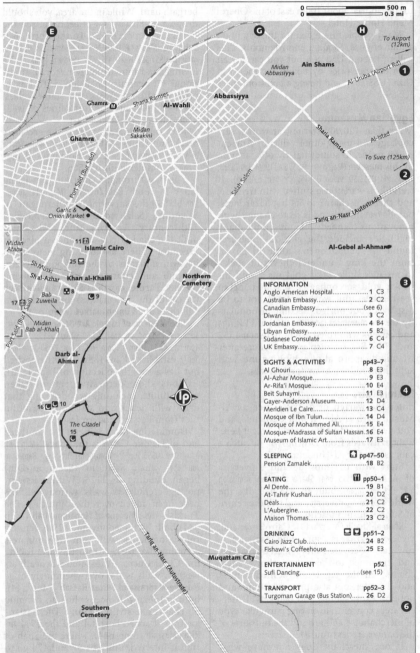

0 — 500 m
0 — 0.3 mi

To Airport (12km)

Midan Abbassiyya   Ain Shams

Al-Uruba (Airport Rd)

Ghamra M   Sharia Ramses   Al-Wahli   Abbassiyya

Sharia Ramses   Al-Istad

Ghamra   Midan Sakakini

To Suez (125km)

Salah Salem

Tariq an-Nasr (Autostrade)

Garlic & Onion Market ●

Midan Ataba

11   Islamic Cairo

Al-Gebel al-Ahmar

25

Sh Muski
Sh al-Azhar   Khan al-Khalili

Northern Cemetery

Bab Zuweila

8

17   9

Midan Bab al-Khalq

Darb al-Ahmar

16   10

The Citadel
15

Muqattam City

Tariq an-Nasr (Autostrade)

Southern Cemetery

INFORMATION
Anglo American Hospital.....................1 C3
Australian Embassy.............................2 C2
Canadian Embassy........................(see 6)
Diwan...3 C2
Jordanian Embassy..............................4 B4
Libyan Embassy...................................5 B2
Sudanese Consulate 6 C4
UK Embassy 7 C4

SIGHTS & ACTIVITIES   pp43–7
Al Ghouri..8 E3
Al-Azhar Mosque................................9 E3
Ar-Rifa'i Mosque...............................10 E4
Beit Suhaymi.....................................11 E3
Gayer-Anderson Museum...................12 D4
Meridien Le Caire...............................13 C4
Mosque of Ibn Tulun.........................14 D4
Mosque of Mohammed Ali.................15 E4
Mosque-Madrassa of Sultan Hassan...16 E4
Museum of Islamic Art.......................17 E3

SLEEPING   pp47–50
Pension Zamalek................................18 B2

EATING   pp50–1
Al Dente..19 B1
At-Tahrir Kushari...............................20 D2
Deals...21 C2
L'Aubergine.......................................22 C2
Maison Thomas..................................23 C2

DRINKING   pp51–2
Cairo Jazz Club..................................24 B2
Fishawi's Coffeehouse........................25 E3

ENTERTAINMENT   p52
Sufi Dancing...............................(see 15)

TRANSPORT   pp52–3
Turgoman Garage (Bus Station)........26 D2

to Alexandria, about 100m east of the Oberoi Mena House Hotel.

Many people hire a taxi for the day to do a tour of Giza, Saqqara and Memphis. This will cost about US$18 – but you can get an even cheaper price by taking the metro to Giza (US$0.07), and hiring a taxi from there (US$9).

Egyptian Museum

More than 120,000 statues, artworks, sarcophagi and many other relics of Ancient Egypt reside, in somewhat chaotic fashion, in this **museum** (Map p48; ☎ 575 4319; Midan Tahrir; admission US$3.50, video US$15; ☽ 9am-6.45pm). It feels like a warehouse stuffed with treasure, and there's a charm to its haphazardness, but it's frustrating and is set to change, with renovations planned. The museum's many highlights include the glorious treasures found in Tutankhamen's tomb in Luxor, from the king's underclothes and socks, to his incredible 11kg gold mask and his 110kg gold sarcophagus. It's amazing to see the beautiful work, created not to be displayed, but buried. Second in popularity are the **mummies** (admission US$7) of 11 kings and queens who ruled Egypt between 1552 and 1069 BC, on display once more after Islamic disapproval of exhibiting the dead kept them hidden away for 15 years.

Islamic Cairo

Enter the warren of districts such as Al-Muski, Darb al-Ahmar and Gamaliya, and you step into a different world. To get here, walk eastwards from Downtown, or catch a cab, asking for Al-Hussein.

Start with the mosque and university of **Al-Azhar** (Map p44; Sharia al-Azhar; admission free; ☽ 7am-10pm), built in AD 970. It's the world's oldest university and still the centre of Sunni Muslim teaching today.

Khan al-Khalili (Map p44), Cairo's frenetic, vivacious bazaar is a sprawling mass of narrow, canvas-covered alleys lined by markets and crammed-to-the-ceiling shops. Merchants sell the regulation stuffed camels and alabaster, but also precious stones and potions, exotic lamps and blankets. Different areas concentrate on one particular type of merchandise and around the outskirts of the bazaar are less-touristed streets.

If one merchant does not have what you're after, he'll know someone who does –

bargain hard. While in the area, you should drop in at Fishawi's Coffeehouse, see the Drinking section (p52). To the north, **Beit Suhaymi** (Map p44; Darb Al-Asfur; admission US$3.50, camera US$1.50, video US$15; ☽ 9am-4pm) is a lovingly and immaculately restored, traditional 17th-century mansion, with lots of olive wood, latticework and stained glass. It's a glimpse into the formalities of well-heeled family life in the past.

Back on Sharia al-Azhar is the exquisite black-and-white **Al-Ghouri** (Map p44; Sharia al-Azhar; admission free), a mausoleum and madrassa complex built in 1505.

You pass through a labyrinth of twisting lanes to reach **Bab Zuweila** (Map p44; admission US$1.50) the surviving southern gate of Saladdin's (Salah ad-Din – the renowned 12th-century Ayyubid ruler, who also built the citadel) city and once a place of execution. There are amazing views from its twin minarets of the surrounding city hubbub and countless minarets spiking the sky. Farther north is **Sharia an-Nahaseen** (Street of the Tentmakers) and farther on still the **Garlic & Onion market** (Map p44).

The **Museum of Islamic Art** (Midan Bab al-Khalq; admission US$2.50, camera US$1.50, video US$15; ☽ 9am-4pm, closed 11.30am-1.30pm Fri Oct-Apr, 12.30-2pm May-Sep), established in 1881, is little visited but has a superb collection of Islamic art. Exhibits show decorative pattern taken to its limits, including woodcarving that drips with detail, and startlingly beautiful tiles from Persia (modern Iran).

Dominating the skyline at the southern end of Islamic Cairo is the **Citadel** (Map p44; admission US$3.50; ☽ 8am-5pm Oct-May, 8am-6pm Jun-Sep) which Saladdin (Salah ad-Din) began building in 1176. Within its imposing crenulated walls various edifices have been added over the centuries. The Turkish-style **Mosque of Mohammed Ali** (Map p44) built by the eponymous 19th-century ruler, dominates, with 86m-high minarets zooming like rockets into the sky. Facing the Citadel across the square beneath its western walls is the overwhelmingly huge **Mosque-Madrassa of Sultan Hassan** (Map p44), built in 1362, with incense holders hanging on chains like stylized rain, a Dickensian-looking attached hospital and the 1911 **Ar-Rifa'i Mosque** (Map p44), where the Shah of Iran is interred. Bus Nos 57 and 174 go to the Citadel from Midan Ataba.

About 1km southwest of Sultan Hassan, along Sharia Saliba, is one of the largest mosques in the world – 6.5 hectares in size. It's the **Mosque of Ibn Tulun** (Map p44) the 9th-century commander sent to rule in the name of Baghdad, but who instead established his own dynasty. The mosque was built in AD 879. Admission is free, but donations are welcomed and baksheesh is needed to see the Shah's tomb.

Close to Ibn Tulun is the **Gayer-Anderson Museum** (Map p44; admission US$2.60; ⏷ 8am-4.30pm), consisting of two 16th-century houses restored by a British major, John Gayer-Anderson, between 1935 and 1942, and then bequeathed to Egypt. The puzzle of rooms is exquisitely decorated and stuffed with artefacts. It was the location for some Roger Moore eyebrow-raising in *The Spy Who Loved Me*.

To the east of Khan al-Khalili is the **Northern Cemetery** (Map p44), half of an enormous necropolis known as the City of the Dead. Mamluk sultans built huge mausoleums here, meant not only as tombs, but also as places for entertaining. People began to squat there in the 14th century, leading to the situation today, where the dead and living coexist side by side.

SPLURGE!

The rooms might be out of reach, but you could always splash out on a swim at the former royal hunting lodge **Oberoi Mena House Hotel** (☎ 3833 222; Pyramids Rd), where you can spend the day floating in the large pool with a view of the pyramids. If you reserve a two-person cabana it costs US$26. Or dive into the Nile-side pool at the **Meridien Le Caire** (Map p44; ☎ 362 1717; US$11; Roda Island).

Old Cairo

Old Cairo is the ancient seat of the Coptic Christian community, and the cobbled streets and cluster of churches have a sense of Jerusalem. It was here that Cairo was born: it's believed that there has been a settlement in the area, known in Arabic as Masr al-Qadima, since the 6th century BC. The Romans established a fortress called Babylon-in-Egypt in the 2nd century – it was a provincial city to Alexandria's capital until the Islamic conquest, when the Arabic conquerors decided to rule from here. Today it is a kernel of calm, a walled enclave seemingly immune to the external burgeoning chaos that it spawned.

The **Coptic Museum** (Sharia Mar Girgis; admission US$2.50; ⏷ 9am-5pm) houses intricate mosaics, manuscripts, tapestries and other Christian artwork in elaborately decorated rooms that are half the attraction.

The **Hanging Church** (Al-Muallaqa; Kineeset al-Muallaqa; Sharia Mar Girgis; admission free; ⏷ Coptic mass Fri 8-11am, Sun 7-10am) is the centre of Coptic worship, so-called because it is built above the Water Gate of Roman Babylon – in the baptistery you can peer down through a gloomy panel and try to make out the gate; or look out of the window for a better view. Among the other churches and monasteries here, **St Sergius** (Abu Serga; ⏷ 8am-4pm) is supposed to mark one of the resting stops of the Holy Family on its flight from King Herod.

The easiest way to get to Old Cairo from Midan Tahrir is by metro to Mari Girgis station (US$0.07, every few minutes). A more exciting way is to take a river bus (US$0.15, one hour, half-hourly 6.30am to 3.45pm) from Maspero Terminal near the Radio and TV Building.

Felucca Rides

Feluccas are the ancient broad-sail boats that dot the length of the Nile. A lovely thing to do in Cairo is to take an hour-long cruise from the mooring point on the Corniche, south of Tahrir Bridge; take a picnic and some beers. A boat and captain cost around US$5 per hour.

SLEEPING
Hostels

Downtown, from Midan Tahrir to Sharia 26th of July, is bursting with budget possibilities. It's central, close to many sights and packed with places to eat. Many of the following include breakfast, but don't expect more than a roll and a cuppa.

Pension Roma (Map p48; ☎ 391 1088, 169 Sharia Mohammed Farid; s/d/tr US$5.50/6/10) This is the most charming budget option. It has rooms with character, shiny hardwood floors and antique furniture. There's also a cosy lounge with TV. Book ahead.

Dahab Hotel (Map p48; ☎ 579 9104; Sharia Mahmoud Bassiouni 26; s/d/tr US$3.50/4.50/5, with shower

EGYPT

CENTRAL CAIRO

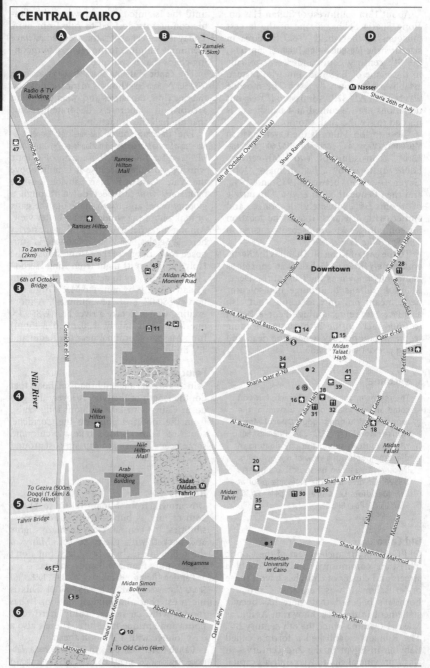

A | B | C | D

To Zamalek
(1.5km)

1

Radio & TV
Building

Corniche el-Nil

47

2

Ramses
Hilton
Mall

M Nasser

Sharia 26th of July

6th of October Overpass (Galaa)

Sharia Ramses

Abdel Khalek Sarwat

Abdel Hamid Said

Maaruf

Ramses Hilton

To Zamalek
(2km)

46

6th of October
Bridge

43

Midan Abdel
Moniem Riad

Corniche el-Nil

3

23

Downtown

Champollion

Sharia Talaat Harb

Buca al-Gedida

28

4

Nile River

42

11

Sharia Mahmoud Bassiouni

14

8 $

15

Midan
Talaat
Harb

Qasr el-Nil

Sheriffein

13

34

Sharia Qasr el-Nil

2

41

6 @

38

39

16

31

32

Sharia Talaat Harb

Sharia

Yousef El Gendi

Huda Shaarawi

18

Al-Bustan

Midan
Falaki

Nile
Hilton

5

Nile
Hilton
Mall

20

Arab
League
Building

Sadat
(Midan
Tahrir)

Midan
Tahrir

Sharia at-Tahrir

30

26

To Gezira (500m),
Doqqi (1.6km) &
Giza (4km)

Tahrir Bridge

35

Falaki

Mansour

Mogamma

American
University
in Cairo

1

Sharia Mohammed Mahmoud

45

6

5

Midan Simon
Bolivar

Abdel Khader Hamza

Qasr al-Ainy

Sheikh Rihan

Sharia Latin America

10

To Old Cairo (4km)

Lazoughli

EGYPT

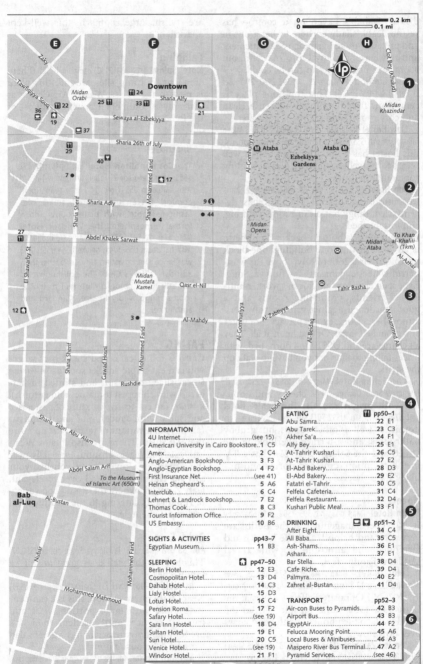

0.2 km
0.1 mi

Downtown

Midan Orabi
Tawfiqiyya Souq
Zaki
Midan Khazindar

Clot Bey (Khulud)

Sharia Alfy
Sewaya al-Ezbekiyya
Sharia 26th of July

Ataba · Ataba

Ezbekiyya Gardens

Sharia Adly
Sharia Sherif
Sharia Mohammed Farid

Abdel Khalek Sarwat
El Shawarby St

Midan Opera

Midan Ataba

To Khan al-Khalili (1km)

Al-Azhar

Tahir Basha

Midan Mustafa Kamel
Qasr el-Nil

Al-Mahdy
Mohammed Farid
Gawad Hosni

Rushdie

Al-Gomhuriyya
Al-Zahhiyya
Al-Beidaq

Mohammed Ali

Sharia Sherif
Sharia Sabri Abu 'Alam

Abdel Salam Arif
To the Museum of Islamic Art (650m)

Bab al-Luq
Al-Bustan

Nubar

Abdel Aziz

Mohammed Farid
Mohammed Mahmoud

INFORMATION	
4U Internet	(see 15)
American University in Cairo Bookstore	1 C5
Amex	2 C4
Anglo-American Bookshop	3 F3
Anglo-Egyptian Bookshop	4 F2
First Insurance Net	(see 41)
Helnan Shepheard's	5 A6
Interclub	6 C4
Lehnert & Landrock Bookshop	7 E2
Thomas Cook	8 C3
Tourist Information Office	9 F2
US Embassy	10 B6

SIGHTS & ACTIVITIES	pp43–7
Egyptian Museum	11 B3

SLEEPING	pp47–50
Berlin Hotel	12 E3
Cosmopolitan Hotel	13 D4
Dahab Hotel	14 C3
Lialy Hostel	15 D3
Lotus Hotel	16 C4
Pension Roma	17 F2
Safary Hotel	(see 19)
Sara Inn Hostel	18 D4
Sultan Hotel	19 E1
Sun Hotel	20 C5
Venice Hotel	(see 19)
Windsor Hotel	21 F1

EATING	pp50–1
Abu Samra	22 E1
Abu Tarek	23 C3
Akher Sa'a	24 F1
Alfy Bey	25 E1
At-Tahrir Kushari	26 C5
At-Tahrir Kushari	27 E2
El-Abd Bakery	28 D3
El-Abd Bakery	29 E2
Fatatri el-Tahrir	30 C5
Felfela Cafeteria	31 C4
Felfela Restaurant	32 D4
Kushari Public Meal	33 F1

DRINKING	pp51–2
After Eight	34 C4
Ali Baba	35 C5
Ash-Shams	36 E1
Ashara	37 E1
Bar Stella	38 D4
Cafe Riche	39 D4
Palmyra	40 E2
Zahret al-Bustan	41 D4

TRANSPORT	pp52–3
Air-con Buses to Pyramids	42 B3
Airport Bus	43 B3
EgyptAir	44 F2
Felucca Mooring Point	45 A6
Local Buses & Minibuses	46 A3
Maspero River Bus Terminal	47 A2
Pyramid Services	(see 46)

US$5/6/7) Dahab's haven on a rooftop has restful, leafy, shady corners to hang out in and pretend you're in a beachside settlement and nowhere near any Cairo mayhem, but rooms are a bit boxy and can be cold.

Sara Inn Hostel (Map p48; ☎ 392 2940; 21 Yousef El Gendi; s/d US$3.50/5) This top-floor place is central and friendly with no-nonsense, clean and cosy rooms, and plenty of hot water.

Lialy Hostel (Map p48; ☎ 575 2802; 3rd fl, 8 Midan Talaat Harb; s/d US$5/7.50) With clean, small rooms, this hostel has a good location and is well set up for travellers; there's a pleasant sitting room and no hustle.

Sun Hotel (Map p48; ☎ 773 0087, 9th fl, 2 Sharia Talaat Harb; dm/s/d US$2/5/7) The Sun has decent-sized, dingy but clean rooms with big, comfortable beds.

The real rock-bottom backpacker ghetto is all contained in one building, one block north of Sharia 26th of July, above the wonderfully hectic, vibrant Tawfiqiyya Souq. Expect an elevator that doesn't work, multi-legged friends, crumbling rooms and a good hardened-against-grunge travellers' atmosphere. Don't expect privacy, hot water and clean bed linen. Or bed linen at all. They all charge around US$1 for a dorm bed, with prices falling the farther you have to walk up the stairs.

The **Sultan Hotel** (Map p48; ☎ 577 2258; 1st fl, Tawfiqiyya Souq, Downtown) is cheery and popular, with bright murals; the **Venice Hotel** (☎ 574 1171; s/d US$2.50/3.50) has clean-ish dorms, as well as other rooms, but grubby bathrooms, and a terrace overlooking the street; and the **Safary** (☎ 577 8692) has a TV in the reception, crowded dorms and unlikely PVC sheets.

Hotels

Berlin Hotel (Map p48; ☎ 395 7502; 2 El Shawarby St; ✕) The management at the Berlin are very nice and helpful, and the hotel is old fashioned and atmospheric, with a real 'Addams Family' feel.

Lotus Hotel (Map p48; ☎ 575 0966; www .lotushotel.com; 12 Sharia Talaat Harb; s/d with bathroom US$13/17; ✕) Opposite Felfela Cafeteria, the Lotus is a 1950s time capsule – from the floral walls to the phones – with good views over downtown.

Pension Zamalek (Map p44; ☎ 735 9318; 6 Sharia Salah El Din; s/d US$10/14) If you'd like to stay in the salubrious Zamalek quarter, there are stylish, large rooms in this well-kept apartment.

Camping

Motel Salma (☎ 384 9152; camping US$2) There aren't many camp sites around; this place is next to the Wissa Wassef Art Centre at Harraniyya, south of Giza, with a glimpse of the Pyramids.

SPLURGE!

The **Cosmopolitan Hotel** (Map p48; ☎ 392 3663; Sharia el-Kady el-Fahel, off Qasr el-Nil; s/d with bathroom US$47/60; ✕) is a leap up in comfort. It's an understated, smart, old-fashioned hotel with plain rooms and a formal atmosphere. The **Windsor Hotel** (Map p48; ☎ 591 5277; Sharia Alfy; s/d US$30/35, with bathroom US$35/45, deluxe US$45/55; ✕) was once the Egyptian Royals' baths, then a British Officer's Club. The polished-wood bar still has a colonial club feel to it. The rooms range wildly in size, standard and ambience.

EATING

Cairo is full of cafés and snack bars where you can eat staple snacks such as *shwarma* (meat sliced off a spit and stuffed in flat-bread with chopped tomatoes and garnish), *kushari* (an eat-to-live mixture of pasta, rice and spicy lentil sauce), *fuul* and *ta'amiyya* (an Egyptian variant of felafel) for no more than US$0.30. There are also lots of Western fast-food places around, especially near the American University. If you like your *sheesha* chichi, then head over to elegant, leafy Zamalek, where there is a good variety of restaurants catering to the wealthy local and expat clientele.

Quick Eats

Abu Samra (Map p48; Tawfiqiyya Souq; dishes US$0.07) This hole-in-the-wall does great *ta'amiyya* sandwiches.

At-Tabie Ad-Domyati (31 Sharia Orabi; dishes US$1) Near Orabi metro station, this is a canteen-style place with large portions, fast and friendly service, and excellent food. It's predominantly vegetarian, has a great salad bar and delicious *ta'amiyya*.

At-Tahrir Kushari (dishes US$1) Midan Tahrir (Map p48; Sharia at-Tahrir); Midan Talaat Harb (Map p48; Sharia Abdel

Khalek Sarwat) It's got noodles, rice, lentils and a spicy tang, all mixed together – what else could you want: these two branches serve up big portions of good *kushari*.

Kushari Public Meal (Map p48; Sharia Alfy; dishes US$1) This bright and cheerful place has mirrors and hanging lamps and serves up more of the tasty noodly stuff.

Abu Tarek (Map p48; 40 Champollion; dishes US$0.20-0.50) Thought by some to serve the city's best *kushari*: you might have to queue, but it's worth it.

Akher Sa'a (Map p48; 8 Sharia Alfy; dishes US$0.20; ✆ 24hr) This very popular place has a good but limited menu. It serves *fuul* and *ta'amiyya*, and there's a restaurant next door. The menu is limited but good. The sign's in Arabic – it's next door to a Christian bookshop.

Felfela Cafeteria (Map p48; dishes US$0.15-1) Just around the corner from the main restaurant, this has more *kushari* and various sandwiches.

Fatari el-Tahrir (Map p48; 165 Sharia at-Tahrir, dishes US$2; ✆ 24hr) This place whips up sweet or savoury *fiteer* (Egyptian pizza).

El-Abd Bakery (Map p48) Midan Talaat Haab (35 Talaat Haab); Midan Orabi (cnr Sharias 26th of July & Sherif) The delectable pastries here are signalled by the crowds around each branch.

Restaurants Alfy Bey (Map p48; ✆ 577 713 888; 3 Sharia Alfy; dishes US$0.50-9) This place is old-fashioned and feels highly respectable, with waiters in waistcoats.

L'Aubergine (✆ 735 6550; 5 Sayyed al-Bakry, Zamalek; dishes US$3-5) With an inventive, constantly changing, vegetarian menu, L'Aubergine has an elegant, comfortable ambience, sandwiched between restaurants and galleries in Cairo's SoHo. Alcohol is served.

Felfela Restaurant (Map p48; ✆ 392 2833; 15 Sharia Hoda Shaarawi, dishes from US$0.50) The décor in this place, off Sharia Talaat Harb, is like a love-in between the bar from *Cheers* and a tropical rainforest. The best dishes are the simple ones – try the *fuul*, *ta'amiyya*, salads and *baba ghanoug* (eggplant and tahini dip). Alcohol is served.

Maison Thomas (Map p44; ✆ 419 2914; 157 Sharia 26th of July, Zamalek; dishes US$3) A continental-style deli, this place has the best pizza in Cairo.

Al Dente (✆ 735 9117; 26 Bahgat Aly, Zamalek; dishes US$1-1.50) This is a tiny Italian place with huge portions of pasta, popular with

American University in Cairo students from the nearby hostel.

DRINKING & CLUBBING

Despite the crammed, carnival atmosphere on the city streets at night, it's not packed with late-night drinking and dancing places – though this has improved in recent years and those that do exist are a laugh. Check the weekly *Cairo Times* (US$0.50) for entertainment listings.

Cafe Riche (Map p48; ✆ 392 9793; 17 Sharia Talaat Harb; ✆ to midnight) With a lovely old-colonial, polished-wood interior, this is perfect for a relaxed drink. It's popular with expats and serves good food.

Bar Stella (Map p48; cnr Sharias Hoda Shaarawi & Talaat Harb; ✆ to midnight) This is a local, spit-and-sawdust, men-heavy haunt, with lots of small tables: it's the kind of place where you might weep into your beer while smoking 40 cigarettes.

Deals (Map p44; ✆ 736 0502; 2 Maahad al-Swissry, Zamalek; ✆ to 2am) A tiny Western-style pocket of a bar, which does get rather rammed and raucous.

Windsor Hotel (Map p48; 19 Sharia Alfy) A former gentleman's club, the Windsor retains its colonial feel – a spacious place with books, sofas and floorboards. Single women would feel comfortable here.

Ali Baba (Map p48; Midan Tahrir; ✆ to midnight) This place is recommended for its upstairs window-table spot, overlooking the chaos of the centre.

Palmyra (Map p48; off Sharia 26th of July; ✆ 1am-4am) Palmyra mainly features belly dancers, and has the feel of a strip club – without the stripping. Men throw money at the stage and occasionally get up on it to dance – it's an entertaining slice of life.

After Eight (Map p48; ✆ 574 0855; 6 Sharia Qasr el-Nil; minimum charge US$6; ✆ to 4-5am) At this excellent place, journalists, expats and moneyed Egyptians shake their thing, with sometimes good, sometimes alarming results. The small dance floor gets busy to a party mixture of trashy Arabic and Western pop. There's often fantastic live Arabic or salsa music.

Cairo Jazz Club (✆ 345 9939; 197 Sharia 26th of July, Agouza; minimum charge US$4.50; ✆ 7pm-2am) This has live jazz, blues or rock every night of the week, and a great atmosphere.

Africana (Pyramids Rd; admission US$4.50; ✆ midnight-5am) This is something different, a big seedy

EGYPT

place that plays sub-Saharan sounds, where African students and refugees come to let off steam, accompanied by lots of working women. The odd fight is greeted with serene indifference. Admission includes one beer.

Ahwas

The gurgle of waterpipes from Cairo's many fine *ahwas* (coffeehouses) are the life-breath of the city, and there are no better places to sit, watch the world go by and set it to rights. They are normally male preserves, but some have a mixed crowd, such as these listed, so women will feel comfortable too.

Fishawi's Coffeehouse (Map p44; Khan al-Khalili) This coffeehouse is an ornate piece of the past which shrugs off its potential as a tourist-swamped heritage experience and remains an authentic, charismatic *ahwa*. There are huge, dusty, ornate mirrors, blackened chandeliers and tables that spill into the narrow alleyways. Fishawi's claims to have been open 24 hours for the last 200 years, but it does close in the mornings during Ramadan.

Ashara (Map p48) Spilling across a pedestrianised street behind the Grand Hotel, this is a bright, clean, hubbub of a place, with streams of hawkers selling everything from packets of tissues to stuffed birds and rabbits.

Ash-Shams (Map p48; btwn Sharia 26th of July & Tawfiquiyya Souq) This coffeeshop is crammed into an alleyway, decorated with brilliantly garish kitsch paintings and close to the backpackers ghetto.

Zahret al-Bustan (Map p48; off Sharia Talaat Harb) In another alley, among shrubs, this was once the haunt of writers and intellectuals, but they've been replaced by assorted smooth-talking scamsters. You will never receive so many offers of instant friendship: it's an entertaining hang out, but don't let yourself be reeled in.

ENTERTAINMENT

If you'd like to see some dervishes whirl, head to the marvellous **sufi dancing** (Map p44; ☎ 510 0823; Sarayat Al Gabal Theatre, Citadel Complex, Islamic Cairo; admission free; 7pm Sat, Mon & Wed). Sufis are adherents of a Muslim mystical order that emphasises dancing as a spiritual experience. Arrive early, especially in winter.

GETTING THERE & AWAY
Air

The main sales office of **EgyptAir** (Map p48; ☎ 390 3444; Sharia Adly) is just one of a number of offices around town.

Bus

The main bus station is the **Turgoman garage** (off Sharia al-Gisr, Bulaq), in the densely populated area roughly bounded by Sharia 26th of July and Sharia al-Galaa. From here you can get buses to anywhere in the country.

Destination	Price	Duration	Frequency
Alexandria	US$3.50	3hr	hourly
Aswan	US$10	12hr	1 daily
Bahariyya	US$3.50	5hr	2 daily
Dahab	US$10-13	9hr	4 daily
Dakhla	US$8.50	10hr	1 daily
Farafra	US$6	8hr	2 daily
Hurghada	US$8.50	6½hr	hourly
Kharga	US$8	10hr	3 daily
Luxor	US$10	11hr	1 daily
Marsa Matruh	US$5	5½hr	4 daily
Port Said	US$2.50	3hr	hourly
St Katherine's Monastery	US$10	6hr	1 daily
Sharm el-Sheikh	US$9	6hr	11 daily

Train

All trains leave from **Ramses train station** (Midan Ramses). The wagon-lit sleeper to Luxor and Aswan leaves at 8pm, arriving in Luxor at 5am and in Aswan at 9.30am. For either destination it costs US$50 one way in a comfortable sleeper compartment. There is no student discount. Most travellers take the ordinary trains, which are comfortable enough not to make the journey a hardship.

Tickets for 1st/2nd-class seats on the two other trains foreigners are allowed to take to Luxor (US$2.50/2) and Aswan (US$3/2) must be bought from the ticket office beside platform 11. The trains depart at 7.30am and 10pm. In both cases it's best to buy your tickets a day or so before to be assured of a seat.

GETTING AROUND
Boat

River buses ply the Nile, and are a particularly nice way to get to Old Cairo (US$0.15, 50 minutes, half-hourly 6.30am to 3.45pm). They leave from the **terminal** (Map p48; Corniche el-Nil, Maspero).

Bus

Buses are a cheap way to get around, but they can get ridiculously crowded at times. Cairo's **main station** (Map p48; Midan Abdel Moniem Riad) is behind the Egyptian Museum. Fares for buses are very cheap – usually US$0.08. Minibus fares cost slightly more. The numbers are sometimes in Arabic numerals only, so it pays to learn them. Bus No 355 goes to the pyramids (US$0.15).

Metro

The metro is efficient, cheap and, outside rush hours, not too crowded; carriages at the front are reserved for women only. You are most likely to use the metro if you're going down to Old Cairo (Mari Girgis station) or to Giza. A short-hop ticket (up to nine stations) costs US$0.08.

Taxi

Taxis in Cairo are cheap enough to fit into your shoestring lifestyle. From Midan Tahrir to Midan Ramses it costs around US$0.50, from Midan Tahrir to the Citadel it's about US$0.75, from Downtown to Khan al-Khalili or Zamalek it costs about US$0.50.

The best way to pay the proper fare is to know it beforehand and not to raise the subject of money at all, just hand the driver the sum at your destination. Make sure you have the correct change, because it's impossible getting it back from drivers. If the driver starts to talk money once you get in, just state a fair price and if they don't accept, get out and take another car. When you pay, sometimes the driver will demand more and yell – or he might refuse to accept what you give him. Just pay and walk away – it's all bluster.

Tram

Cairo's trams are very slow and are rarely used.

AROUND CAIRO

MEMPHIS & SAQQARA

Memphis (admission US$2, camera US$0.30, video US$4.50), 24km south of Cairo, is not the birthplace of rock'n' roll, but a former Pharaonic capital, one of the greatest cities of the ancient world and believed to have been founded in 3100 BC. The city remains are sparse, but the outdoor museum has some impressive remnants, such as an alabaster sphinx and a statue of Ramses II that lies on its back, huge and Gulliver-like, prone in a shed.

A few kilometres away is **Saqqara** (admission US$3.50, camera US$0.75, video US$4; 8am-4pm Nov-Apr, 8am-5pm May-Oct), once Memphis' necropolis, which is a vast desert site strewn with pyramids, temples and tombs. The star attraction there is the **Step Pyramid** of Zoser, the first attempt at pyramid building, constructed around 2650 BC, with a broad hypostyle hall nearby. There are some beautifully painted **nobles' tombs** (US$1.50), including Masturba of Ti and the Tomb of Ptahhotep. The **Serapeum** contains the tombs of sacred Apis bulls, and consists of small galleries containing huge black sarcophagi.

The best way to get here is via taxi, possibly taking in the Pyramids of Giza as well. See that section (p43) for details of prices.

BIRQASH CAMEL MARKET

On the edge of the Western Desert, 35km northwest of Cairo, the **Camel Market** (Souq al-Gamaal; admission US$1) is a fascinating half-day trip from Cairo. However, like all Egypt's animal markets, it's not for animal lovers or the faint-hearted. Hundreds of camels are sold here every day, most having been brought up the 40 Days Road from western Sudan (and it shows). The market is liveliest on Friday and Monday mornings, from about 6am to 9am.

You can get to the market by taking a taxi (US$1) to the site of the old camel market at Imbaba, one of Cairo's western suburbs, from where minibuses shuttle back and forth along the dusty, date-palm and orange-grove dotted route to Birqash. Alternatively, on Friday only, the Sun Hotel (see Cairo's Sleeping section, p50) organises a minibus tour (US$3.50 per person; minimum five people) departing at 7am. A taxi there and back costs around US$12; make sure to negotiate waiting time.

NILE VALLEY

The Nile is the world's longest river, cutting through 6680km of Africa. It is Egypt's artery, and all that is important is clustered along its banks on the country's only fertile land – as it has been for thousands of years.

EGYPT

LUXOR
☎ 095 / pop 421,500

Built on and around the 4000-year-old site of ancient Thebes, contemporary Luxor is a curious but comfortable mix of provincial country town and staggering ancient splendour. The concentration of monuments is extraordinary: they tower incongruously above the buzz of everyday city life. The East Bank is a moderately busy town, while on the West Bank, lush green fields taper off into parchment-coloured, folding cliffs – the Valley of the Kings.

Luxor also has the dubious distinction of being Egypt's hassle capital. Whether this gets annoying seems to be largely a matter of luck. It's worth keeping in mind that people are only trying to make a living.

Orientation
What most visitors today know as Luxor is actually three separate areas: the town of Luxor itself, the village of Karnak a couple of kilometres to the northeast (both on the East Bank of the Nile) and the Valley of the Kings and the other monuments of ancient Thebes on the West Bank.

Luxor is the main accommodation centre. It has only three main thoroughfares: Sharia al-Mahatta runs between the train station and the gardens of Luxor Temple; the Corniche runs along the river; and Sharia al-Karnak runs parallel to it and out towards Karnak.

Information
The main **tourist office** (☎ 372 215; ☺ 8am-9pm) is next to the New Winter Palace Hotel. You can leave messages for other travellers here. The main banks have branches on or near the Corniche and a number of them have ATMs. **Amex** (☎ 372 862) and **Thomas Cook** (☎ 372 196) have offices at the Old Winter Palace Hotel.

There's a main **post office** (Sharia al-Mahatta) and a **branch office** (tourist office). There's a central **telephone office** (Sharia al-Karnak; ☺ 24hr) and another branch below the resplendent entrance of the Old Winter Palace Hotel.

There are a growing number of Internet cafés in Luxor, all of which charge around US$1 per hour.

Aboudi Internet (Tourist Bazaar; Corniche el-Nil)
Mantel Computer & Internet (off Sharia Medina al-Manawara)
Rainbow Internet (Sharia Yousef Hassan)

Sights & Activities
EAST BANK
The most overwhelming of the East Bank sites are the **Temples of Karnak** (admission US$3.50, video US$4.50; ☺ 6am-4.30pm Nov-Apr, 6am-6.30pm May-Oct). This is a complex of sanctuaries, temples, obelisks and statuary that was worked on and added to for over 1500 years. Everything is on a gigantic scale and wandering here makes you feel as if you've been shrunk. Its Great Hippostyle Hall covers 6 sq km and is a forest of 134 colossal stone pillars.

Karnak's camp, epic **sound-and-light show** (admission US$5) is well worth seeing to walk among the temples at night and to hear booming lines like, 'and the waters of the Nile spurt from my sandals'. There are three to four performances per night in English, French, German, Japanese, Italian, Spanish and Arabic.

There are local minibuses that run to the temples from the bus station in the centre of Luxor (US$0.07).

The town centre bustles around the stately splendour of **Luxor Temple** (Sharia al-Bahr; admission US$3.50; ☺ 6am-9pm Nov-Apr, 6am-10pm May-Oct) built by Pharaoh Amenophis III. It was added to over the centuries by Tutankhamen, Ramses II, Alexander the Great and the Arabs, who built a mosque in one of the interior courts.

Luxor Museum (Corniche el-Nil; admission US$4.50; ☺ 9am-1pm & 4-9pm Nov-Mar, 9am-1pm & 4-10pm Apr-Oct) has a fine, strikingly lit collection of relics from the Theban temples and necropolis, including sandals, model boats and gilt-decorated figures from Tutankhamen's tomb.

The **Mummification Museum** (Corniche el-Nil; admission US$3; ☺ 9am-1pm & 4-9pm Nov-Mar, 9am-1pm & 4-10pm Apr-Oct) is a small, well-laid out exhibit explaining how corpses were preserved, complete with 'how to' mummification diagrams, brain-scraping spatulas and the mummy of a 21st-dynasty high priest, who looks remarkable for his age.

WEST BANK
The West Bank houses some of Ancient Egypt's most extraordinary monuments. Admission to a group of three of the minor sites costs US$2, while the most impressive attractions have separate admission fees. You can buy tickets at the ticket office. On

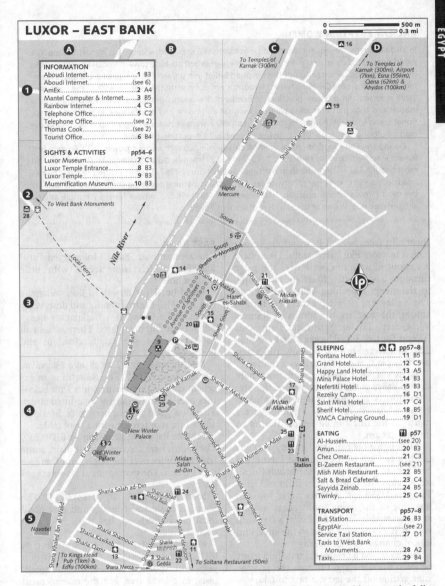

LUXOR – EAST BANK

| 0 | 500 m |
| 0 | 0.3 mi |

INFORMATION
Aboudi Internet..........................1 B3
Aboudi Internet.....................(see 6)
AmEx..2 A4
Mantel Computer & Internet.......3 B5
Rainbow Internet......................4 C3
Telephone Office.......................5 C2
Telephone Office...................(see 2)
Thomas Cook........................(see 2)
Tourist Office............................6 B4

SIGHTS & ACTIVITIES pp54–6
Luxor Museum..........................7 C1
Luxor Temple Entrance..............8 B3
Luxor Temple............................9 B3
Mummification Museum.............10 B3

SLEEPING pp57–8
Fontana Hotel...........................11 B5
Grand Hotel.............................12 C5
Happy Land Hotel.....................13 A5
Mina Palace Hotel....................14 B3
Nefertiti Hotel..........................15 B3
Rezeiky Camp..........................16 D1
Saint Mina Hotel......................17 C4
Sherif Hotel.............................18 B5
YMCA Camping Ground.............19 D1

EATING p57
Al-Hussein............................(see 20)
Amun.......................................20 B3
Chez Omar...............................21 C3
El-Zaeem Restaurant.............(see 21)
Mish Mish Restaurant...............22 B5
Salt & Bread Cafeteria..............23 C4
Sayyida Zeinab.........................24 B5
Twinky....................................25 C4

TRANSPORT pp57–8
Bus Station...............................26 B3
EgyptAir..............................(see 2)
Service Taxi Station..................27 D1
Taxis to West Bank
Monuments..........................28 A2
Taxis.......................................29 B4

To Temples of Karnak (300m)

To Temples of Karnak (300m), Airport (7km), Esna (55km), Qena (62km) & Abydos (100km)

To West Bank Monuments

Nile River

Local Ferry

Corniche el-Nil

Sharia al-Karnak

Sharia Nefertiti

Hotel Mercure

Souqs

Sharia el-Montazah

Souqs

Sharia el-Matafy

Sharia Yusef Hassan

Midan Hassan

Haret es-Sahabi

Avenue of Sphinxes

Sharia Souq

Sharia al-Bahr

Sharia al-Karnak

Sharia Cleopatra

Sharia al-Mahatta

Sharia Rames

Midan al-Mahatta

Train Station

New Winter Palace

Old Winter Palace

El-Corniche

Sharia Mohammed Farid

Midan Salah ad-Din

Sharia Ahmed Orabi

Sharia Abdel Moneim al-Adasi

Sharia Ahmed Orabi

Sharia Mohammed Farid

Sharia Salah ad-Din

Sharia Ahad

Sharia Badr

Novotel

To Kings Head Pub (1km) & Edfu (100km)

Sharia Khaled Ibn al-Walid

Sharia Shamouz

Sharia Kawkeb

Sharia Qamr

Sharia Medina al-Manawara

Sharia Mishmish

Sharia Television

Sharia Mecca

Sharia Gedda

To Soltana Restaurant (50m)

the way you'll pass the looming, 18m **Colossi of Memnon**, backdrop for a billion snaps, and the remains of an enormous complex that continues to be excavated.

Near the ticket office is the magnificent temple complex of **Medinat Habu**, with its animated, frozen walls, at the foot of mountains, a sleepy village nestled against it.

Towards the less-visited but wonderfully decorated **Tombs of the Nobles** is the **Ramesseum,** with beautiful friezes, and a massive statue of Ramses II (once 17.5m high) lying in pieces on the ground, like an illustration of pride before a fall.

The spectacular **Deir al-Bahri** (Temple of Hatshepsut; admission US$2) seems to grow out of the

---

ANCIENT EGYPTIAN WOMEN

In ancient Egypt, the equal balance of power between men and women was almost unique in a world dominated by masculine strength. This enlightened attitude toward sexual equality was in many ways a logical extension of the Egyptian belief in a universe made up of a complete male-female duality. As the Greek historian Herodotus noted on a trip to Egypt in c 450BC, the Egyptians 'have reversed the ordinary practices of mankind'. Herodotus described how women 'attended market and took part in trading whereas men sat and home and did the weaving'. In one exceptional scene in an Old Kingdom tomb at Saqqara, a woman steers a cargo ship while telling the man who brings her food 'Don't obstruct me while I am putting to shore!'

During the Old Kingdom, royal women clearly wielded tremendous power, with Egypt's first female king Neithikret (or Nitocris; c 2148–2144 BC) remembered as 'braver than all the men and most beautiful of all the women of her time'. Sobeknefru (c 1787–1783 BC) wore the royal nemes headcloth and kilt over her otherwise female dress, something repeated three centuries later by the most famous female pharaoh, Hatshepsut (c 1473–1458 BC), whose funerary temple at Deir al-Bahri (see p55) is one of the wonders of ancient Egypt.

---

sheer cliff faces behind it, with long colonnaded terraces like bared teeth. From here it's about 45 minutes' walk over the ridge through a dramatic Martian landscape, to the steep, scorching **Valley of the Kings**. The valley encloses 62 excavated tombs; among the best are the tombs of Ramses VI, Queen Tawsert/Sethnakt, Tuthmosis III and Saptah. **Tutankhamen's Tomb** (admission US$7), discovered in 1922 by Howard Carter, is pretty plain and not worthy of the fee.

There's a long walking trail from here to the **Valley of the Queens**, where the star attraction is the **Tomb of Nefertari** (admission US$15), whose stunning wall paintings are hailed as the finest in all Egypt. Tickets go on sale at 6am.

Although you can get here by taxi via the bridge 7km to the south of Luxor, the best way to get here is via the *baladi* (local) ferry below the Corniche in front of Luxor Temple (US$0.15). Alternatively, you can hire one of the many motorboats waiting at the waterside for US$1. Bring water with you, as it's expensive close to the sites, and lots of change for baksheesh.

However, you'll need some transport to get between the sites, and this you can arrange after getting off the ferry; a taxi to take you around the sites will cost around US$8. Alternatively, hire a bike (US$1.50 per day). This is a great way to see the area, just bear in mind it gets very hot and don't push yourself.

Sleeping

There's lots of competition in Luxor and thus some excellent choices.

EAST BANK

The area around Sharia Mohammed Farid and Sharia Television teems with little budget hotels.

Grand Hotel (☎ 382 905; off Sharia Mohammed Farid; s/d US$1/2) Clean, friendly and deservedly popular, the Grand is a backpacker hangout serving big breakfasts. There is a small rooftop terrace with comfy cushions and great views.

Nefertiti Hotel (☎ 372 386; off Sharia al-Karnak; s/d with bathroom US$5/7; 🖳) The Nefertiti is an excellent choice: very clean rooms with balconies overlooking a narrow café-lined street. There's a good atmosphere, nice breakfast and a fine roof terrace with a pool table.

Fontana Hotel (☎ 380 663; dm/s/d US$1/1.50/2) The rooms here are smartish, if plain, some with balconies over the street, and there's a roof garden. The management is sometimes pushy.

Sherif Hotel (☎ 370 757; s/d US$1.50/2.50) The Sherif is basic and friendly and in a good local neighbourhood, but the school next door is noisy.

Happy Land Hotel (☎ 371 828; Sharia Qamr; dm US$1, s/d with bathroom US$4/5) This is a bit of a gem, with spotless rooms and good breakfasts, in a local area, but the management can be pushy. Bike hire is available (US$1.50 per day).

Saint Mina Hotel (☎ 375 409; off Sharia Ramses; s/d US$3.50/5, with bathroom US$4.50/6) Friendly, with small, modern rooms, the Saint Mina is tucked away near the station.

Mina Palace Hotel (☎ 372 074; s/d with bathroom US$10/12) The rooms here are a bit run-down, but they have glorious river views. There's a turbaned guardian loitering about on every floor.

YMCA (☎ 372 425; Sharia al-Karnak; camping US$1) This camping ground is basic, but quite green and shady.

Rezeiky Camp (☎ 381 334; www.rezeikycamp.com; Sharia al-Karnak; camping US$1.50, parking US$1.50) Just up the road, this is a more upmarket, well-set-up option, with a small pool and relaxing restaurant where you can buy beer.

WEST BANK

The West Bank has some peaceful, characterful options, and the best restaurants are nearby.

Habu Hotel (☎ 372 677; s/d US$4/8) This could have been a lovely hotel: the views are spectacular, and there's an arched terrace, but it's run-down with not-that-comfortable rooms and not-that-clean bathrooms. It's opposite Medinat Habu.

Marsam Hotel (Sheikh Ali's; ☎ 372 403; s/d US$4.50/9, with bathroom US$7/14) This place has character, with clean and simple, mud-walled, high-ceilinged rooms. It's popular with travellers and archaeologists. There's also a shady terrace restaurant (meals around US$3).

Abul al-Kasem Hotel (☎ 012-272 8999; Sharia Wadi al-Melouk; s/d US$3.50/7) Near the Temple of Seti I, rooms here are a little scruffy these days, but it has a pleasant courtyard and the family is friendly – they live in a block next door, all 60 of them.

Al-Gezira Hotel (☎ 310 034; d with bathroom US$9) Gezira is near the river, and has calm rooms with balconies and Nile views. There's a lovely roof terrace and garden, and excellent food (meals US$3.50) and beer.

Nour El Qurna (☎ 311 430; d with bathroom US$12) Surrounded by a palm grove, this is an unusual, atmospheric little hotel. It has cosy, romantic rooms, veiled with mosquito nets, and colourful tiled bathrooms. There's a shady garden restaurant (meals around US$3).

Eating
EAST BANK

There are a few budget dining places on or close to Sharia al-Mahatta, as well as the northern end of Sharia Television.

Salt & Bread Cafeteria (Midan al-Mahatta; dishes US$0.30-2) This is a good place to snack on simple food while waiting for a train.

Sayyida Zeinab (Sharia Television; dishes US$0.30) This is one of Luxor's best *kushari* joints, with large portions.

Mish Mish Restaurant (☎ 380 407; Sharia Television; dishes US$0.30-2) Mish Mish is a small place with some unusual dishes and a version of pizza too.

Soltana Restaurant (☎ 012-451 2949; Sharia Television; dishes US$1-2) This is even smaller, and does a *bram* (vegetable stew) served in a steaming clay pot.

Chez Omar (Midan Hassan; dishes US$1-2) This is a small green oasis in the town centre, with tasty, basic Egyptian food.

El-Zaeem Restaurant (Midan Hassan; dishes US$0.40-1) Next door to Chez Omar, this place is a buzzing alfresco *kushari* and snack joint.

Kings Head Pub (Sharia Khaled ibn el-Walid; dishes US$1.50-5; ⏰ 24hr) One of Luxor's most popular restaurant-bars, this place is English through and through – without the ludicrous licensing laws. There's authentically dispiriting English grub and a wide selection of beer on tap.

Twinky (El Mansheya St) This bakery serves up extremely good sweets.

Al-Hussein (Sharia al-Karnak; dishes US$0.30-6) and nearby **Amun** (Sharia al-Karnak; dishes US$0.30-6) are two longstanding travellers' favourites, next door to each other, with similar menus and unremarkable but reliable food. Each has a partially outside area that's a nice place to sit.

WEST BANK

Over on the West Bank there are some excellent restaurant options.

Tutankhamun (☎ 310 118; Al-Gezira; dishes US$1.50-5) This place by the ferry landing offers good food cooked in traditional clay pots.

Nile Valley Restaurant (☎ 311 477; Al-Gezira; dishes US$1.50-6) A smart place with a rooftop overlooking the street that has been recommended by travellers.

Restaurant Mohammed (☎ 311 014; dishes US$2.50) This place is near the ticket office. It's Luxor's serenest restaurant: good, home-cooked lamb kofta, vegetables and salads with home-made cheese are served in an idyllic, dappled garden, with attendant birdsong and cats.

Getting There & Away

The bus station is on Sharia al-Karnak. There are services to Cairo (US$9, 10 hours, one daily), Aswan (US$1.50, three hours, five daily), Asuyut (US$2, five hours, one daily), Hurghada (US$3.50, five hours, four daily), all of which go on to Suez (US$6, eight hours). Convoys to Hurghada leave at 2pm and 6pm, while to Aswan they leave at 7am, 11am and 3pm.

The wagon-lit train heading for Cairo leaves at about 8pm (US$50; nine hours), and other services leave at 9.15am, 9.15pm and 11.10pm. Trains going to Aswan (three hours) leave at 7.15am, 9.30am and 5.15pm.

Getting Around
It's a really good idea to hire a bike in Luxor (US$1 to US$1.50 per day), not only to get to the sights, but also to whiz away from touts.

Hantours, also known as calèches, are horse-drawn carriages that are popular tourist vehicles in town. You'll need to agree on a price before you set off. A short journey should cost around $US1.

AROUND LUXOR
Abydos
☎ 093
According to mythology, the head of the god Osiris was buried here after his brother Seth killed him, and so **Abydos** (admission US$2; ⏲ 7am-5pm May-Oct, 7am-4pm Nov-Apr) became the most important site of his worship – a place of pilgrimage – and *the* place to be buried in Ancient Egypt. It has an air of mystery and an almost tangible sense of ancient pomp. The **Cenotaph Temple of Seti I** is one of Egypt's most beautiful and complete temples. It honours seven gods, including Osiris and the deified pharaoh himself. To the northwest lies the **Temple of Ramses II**, built by Seti's son, with brightly coloured reliefs.

There is heavy security in this area: you are likely to get a police escort on arrival and unlikely to be allowed to stay in nearby Al-Balyana, though there are a couple of hotels here should the situation change.

Abydos is about 100km from Luxor. There's a convoy from Luxor at 8am, 2pm and 6pm. A return taxi from Luxor will cost US$45.

Buses from Luxor to Qena, 91km east of the site, leave at 6.30am, 8am and 10.30am (40 minutes), and trains and buses from Asyut, Sohag, Qena and farther afield stop at Al-Balyana, 10km from the site, from where service taxis and minibuses go to the

temple complex (US$1). You are unlikely to be allowed to leave the train station without a police escort.

There's also a train from Luxor to Al-Balyana (1st/2nd US$4.50/3, three hours, three daily).

Edfu
The Greek-built **Temple of Horus** (admission US$3.50, video US$9; ⏲ 7am-4pm Nov-Apr, 7am-5pm May-Oct) at Edfu is the best-preserved temple in Pharaonic style, with the same plan, scale and decoration, right down to the Egyptian clothes worn by the Greek Pharaohs in the friezes. It's evocative – one of the most complete of Egypt's ancient temples, dedicated to the falcon-headed son of Osiris. Its massive walls are smothered in meaning and the marvellous state of preservation has helped fill in a lot of gaps about the architecture it imitates.

There is a cheap **hotel** in Edfu, near the temple, which is scrubby but famous for its good breakfast, and also a couple of small **eateries** near the square.

There are frequent bus connections to Edfu from Luxor (US$1, two hours) and Aswan (US$0.50, 1½ hours), and you can get here by felucca (see p61 for more information) or train (most trains between Cairo and Luxor continue on to here). However, the train station is about 4km away, so you'll have to charter a covered pick-up truck (US$1) to the site.

ASWAN
☎ 097 / pop 36,300
Aswan sits on the bank of a particularly beautiful stretch of the Nile, a dark blue swathe of water surrounded by dense palms and butterscotch islands. The river often seems to turn to glass, sliced by graceful white felucca sails. Wandering around the backstreets, the town appears stuck in another time – with stacks of bread and raw cotton, and men in spotless *galabiyyas* playing dominoes. Aswan also has one of Egypt's most colourful **souqs**, well worth getting lost in.

Egypt's southernmost city has been many things – a garrison town, the gateway to Africa and the now inundated land of Nubia (see People on p39 for further details), a prosperous stop on the ancient caravan routes and, today, a popular winter

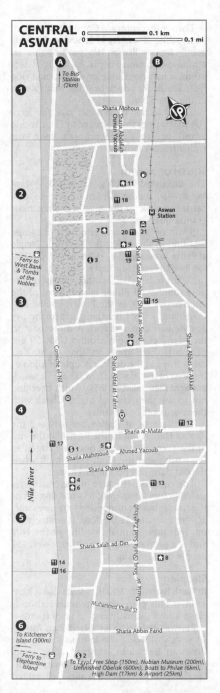

resort. The legacy of Nubia is strong here and Nubian culture lends the place a different atmosphere from elsewhere. Many travellers find Aswan one of the highlights of their stay, and it's the best base from which to visit the awesome temple complex at Abu Simbel.

Information
The very helpful **tourist office** (☎ 312 811; ⏰8am-3pm & 6-8pm Nov-Apr, 8am-3pm & 6-9pm May-Oct) is by the train station. There are lots of exchange places along the Corniche, including **Banque Misr**, with an ATM, and a branch of **Thomas Cook** (☎ 306 839; 59 Ablal El-Tahrir St). There are a few Net cafés around town, the best of which is **Aswanet Internet Cafe** (☎ 317 332; Kelylany Hotel, 25 Sharia Keylany), which charges US$1 per hour.

Sights & Activities
South of the town centre is the large and fascinating **Nubian Museum** (☎ 319 222; admission US$3, camera US$1.50, video US$15; ⏰9am-1pm & 5-9pm) detailing the disrupted history, art and culture of the Nubians – 60,000 people had to move because of the construction of the High Dam and Aswan Dam. Its many highlights include delicate, smooth, 6000-year-old bowls, the stunning sculpture of a 25th-dynasty Kushite Amun priest – who looks as if he's been asked to hold still for a minute – amazing silver crowns and

impressive photos of the moving of Abu Simbel to make way for the dam.

If you'd like a **swim**, it's inadvisable to leap in the Nile because of bilharzia (see the Health chapter, p1034), but most of the upmarket hotels have pools you can use, including the Nile-side **Isis Hotel** (☎ 324 744; Corniche el-Nil; nonguests US$2).

The easiest way to visit the sights south of Aswan is as part of a tour (they are often included in the Abu Simbel trip).

NILE ISLANDS

No visit here would be complete without at least an hour sailing around the islands in a **felucca**, one of Egypt's famous canvas-sailed boats. Prices depend on how the season is going, but you can bargain for around US$2 per hour. You won't have any trouble finding a felucca captain, they hang around the riverbank, particularly around Aswan Moon Restaurant. Highly recommended is the longer journey to Edfu (see Getting There & Away, p61).

Once the core of what is now Aswan, **Elephantine Island** is characterised by its huge grey (elephantlike?) boulders. There are many Nubian families here. At the southern end of the garden, the **Aswan Antiquities Museum** (admission US$1.50; ☒ 8.30am-6pm May-Oct, 8am-5pm Nov-Apr) includes many ancient artefacts discovered in Nubia and Aswan, such as 6000-year-old combs. In its attractive flower and spice gardens, ongoing excavations have revealed the ruins of Yebu (a small town), temples, a small pyramid, fortifications and a Nilometer.

Kitchener's Island (admission US$1; ☒ 8am-5pm) is a flourishing botanic garden, established by Lord Kitchener. It's a very English imposition of order and an appealing place to wander, against the contrast of the curvaceous caramel-coloured riverside.

WEST BANK

Over on the West Bank, the elaborate **Mausoleum of the Aga Khan** is modelled on Fatimid tombs in Cairo (which are complex domes built on cubes). It's closed to the public. South of the mausoleum, pocking the high cliffs, the **Tombs of the Nobles** (admission US$2, camera US$1, video US$15; ☒ 7am-4pm Nov-Apr, 7am-5pm May-Oct) are local Old and Middle Kingdom dignitaries' tombs with a view. A ferry for the tombs leaves from the Corniche (US$0.03).

The 6th-century Coptic Christian, fortresslike **Monastery of St Simeon** (admission free; ☒ 8am-4pm Nov-Apr, 7am-5pm May-Oct) is an atmospheric, isolated place among desert sands, a half-hour hike or short camel ride from the felucca dock near the Mausoleum of the Aga Khan.

To get to the West Bank, take the ferry (US$0.03) from the Corniche to Elephantine Island, or you can incorporate your visit with a felucca tour.

SOUTH OF ASWAN

The **Unfinished Obelisk** (admission US$2; ☒ 7am-4pm Nov-Apr, 7am-5pm May-Oct) is a huge discarded obelisk on the edge of the northern granite quarries.

South of Aswan and relocated to escape flooding in the 1960s, the romantic **Temple of Philae** (admission US$3; ☒ 7am-5pm May-Oct, 7am-4pm Nov-Apr) was dedicated to Isis, who found the heart of her slain brother, Osiris, on the now submerged Philae Island. Most of the temple was built by the Ptolemies and Romans, and early Christians turned the hypostyle hall into a chapel. A motorboat to the island costs from around US$0.50 per person if there are more than eight. You catch these at the dock, a couple of kilometres east of the Aswan Dam. There's a **sound-and-light show** (admission US$5), worth checking out to see the island at night. Check with the tourist office for times.

The Temple of Philae lies between the Aswan Dam, built by the British at the end of the 19th century and once the largest in the world, and the High Dam, built when the old dam was no longer enough.

The colossal structure of the controversial **High Dam** (admission US$1) is not that exciting to see, but its dimensions are awesome: 3600m long and 111m deep. It controls the unpredictable annual flooding of the Nile and is a source of hydroelectric power; 451 people died making it.

Sleeping

HI Youth Hostel (☎ 302 313; 96 Sharia Abtal at-Tahrir; dm US$1) This place near the train station is clean and it's usually easy to get a room.

Rosewan Hotel (☎ 304 497; off Sharia Abtal at-Tahrir; s/d US$1.50/3.50, with bathroom US$2/4) The Rosewan has clean, simple, rather small rooms. It is run by Farouk Nasser, a self-taught painter and all-round character, whose funky artwork decks the walls, and there's a restaurant (see below).

Marwa Hotel (no phone; off Sharia Abtal at-Tahrir; dm US$1) Tucked away off an alley, this is popular and one of the cheapest in town.

Nubian Oasis Hotel (☎ 312 126; 234 Saad Zaghloul St; d US$1.50, with bathroom US$3.50; ✂) This is a popular travellers haunt, with good, plain, clean rooms. There's a large lounge area and a roof garden where you can sit and drink beer.

Keylany Hotel (☎ 317 332; 25 Sharia Keylany; d US$4.50; ✂) In the souq, this excellent place has rooms with fans, pine furniture and spotless bathrooms.

Happi Hotel (☎ 314 115; Sharia Abtal at-Tahrir; s/d with bathroom US$8.50/12; ✂) Happi is a good, popular and central hotel, with smart rooms, TVs and Nile views.

Hathor Hotel (☎ 314 223; Corniche el-Nil; s/d with bathroom US$4/6; ✂) Smart, small rooms are to be had at this good-value option. It has a rooftop, with a pint-sized pool and great views, perfect for sitting and drinking beer.

El Salam Hotel (☎ 308 435; Corniche el-Nil; s/d with bathroom US$5/7; ✂) Next door to the Hathor, this is an attractive, welcoming old French-style place with shuttered balconies overlooking the street or the Nile.

Eating & Drinking

Restaurant Derwash (Sharia Saad Zaghloul; dishes US$1-2) On the south side of the square in front of the station, this place serves up chicken, rice and vegetable dishes, and has been recommended by travellers.

El Madina Restaurant (Sharia Saad Zaghloul; dishes US$0.50-3.50) This bright-and-breezy place, popular with travellers and locals, dishes out a range of standards, including a vegetarian meal.

Rosewan Restaurant (off Sharia Abtal at-Tahrir) This was due to open at the time of research and looked promising, with paintings on the walls, tables made from terracotta water vessels, and traditional dishes.

Al-Sayyida Nefissa (dishes US$1) This is an excellent eatery, tucked away in a side alley in the heart of the souq. Meals, for instance the tasty vegetarian array, or kofta, are good value. There are outside tables, and it is very relaxed.

Akl Restaurant (dishes US$1) Just in front of Al-Sayyida Nefissa, this hole-in-the-wall does a good lunch spread and is very popular with locals.

Koshari Al Sedk & Alamana (off Sharia Abtal at Tahrir; dishes US$0.30) This does the noodle-rice-spice thing in a small, clean cafeteria.

Al-Masry Restaurant (☎ 302 576; Sharia al-Matar; dishes US$4-5) An Aswan institution, Al-Masry is a smartish set-up serving kebabs and kofta with salads and dips.

Aswan Moon Restaurant (☎ 316 108; Corniche el-Nil; dishes US$1-2.50) A lovely tented barge on the Nile – the nicest of the Corniche options, Aswan Moon serves good food and has a section for smoking *sheesha*. Alcohol is served too.

Emy Restaurant (Corniche el-Nil; dishes US$1-2.50) Next door, the deck here has blissful views and luscious fruit cocktails.

Isis Hotel (Corniche el-Nil) This is another good place for a riverside *sheesha* and beer.

Ismoay (Sharia Abtal at-Tahrir) This gleaming bakery does a great array of sticky cakes and pastries.

Egypt Free Shop (Corniche el-Nil) You can buy wine or beer here to take on your felucca trip or sup on your rooftop.

Getting There & Away
BUS & SERVICE TAXI

At the time of writing the police in Aswan were allowing only four foreigners per bus on services out of Aswan, as part of the security measures that have been in place since 1997, see Dangers & Annoyances (p77) for details. The bus station is about 2km north of town – you can catch a minibus heading along the Corniche (US$0.07). Buses go to Cairo (US$9, 12 hours), Edfu (US$1, two hours), Luxor (US$1.50, four hours, six daily), Hurghada (US$6, seven hours, four daily) and Suez (US$9, 12 hours, six daily).

Foreigners are not permitted to take service taxis to other towns. The best way around this is to get a group of people to hire a taxi at the stand across the train tracks and plan to leave in time to catch one of the daily police convoys. One leaves at 8am and stops at Kom Ombo or Edfu for one hour, the other heads direct to Luxor at 1.30pm. The tourist office will be able to advise you on the latest information.

FELUCCA

Highly recommended is the felucca trip downstream from Aswan to Edfu – it's an opportunity to see the river life and a beautiful relaxing trip that takes about two or three days. There's no shortage of captains or touts along the Corniche trying to sell rides. Get a group of people (a comfortable number is six; more than eight is a tight squeeze) and the charge is around US$9 per person to Edfu, with all food included. Note that police restrictions prevent foreigners from going north of Edfu by felucca.

TRAIN

There's a handful of trains running daily between Cairo and Aswan, although only three of them can officially be used by foreigners. The most expensive (about US$50) is the wagon-lit train that departs at 6.30pm. Express trains to Cairo leave at 6am, 6pm and 8pm (1st/2nd class US$13/7). There are trains to Luxor (US$4.50/2.50, four hours) at 6pm and 8pm.

Other trains to Luxor leave at 7.30am, noon, 4pm and 9pm – foreigners are not supposed to travel on these, so if you do you must buy your ticket on the train.

ABU SIMBEL

☎ 097

Self-effacing Ramses II outdid himself at the **Great Temple of Abu Simbel** (admission US$6; ☻ 7am-4pm Nov-Apr, 7am-5pm May-Oct). His four statues fronting the temple have a cartoonish hugeness – they are more than 20m tall. The temple was discovered by chance in 1813 by Swiss explorer Jean-Louis Burkhardt – only one head was poking above the sand – a marvellous scene, like Charlton Heston spotting the Statue of Liberty in *Planet of the Apes*.

The vast wonder of this piece of mammoth architecture is matched by Unesco's amazing feat – cutting up and moving it to escape the rising waters of Lake Nasser in the 1960s, at a cost of US$40 million.

The temple was dedicated to the gods Ra-Harakhty, Amun, Ptah and the deified pharaoh himself. The tremendous egos in stone stood to show his power and warn the southern tribes what they were up against. Smaller statues show the king's mother, Queen Tuya, his wife Nefertari and some of their children. The other temple at the Abu Simbel complex is the rock-cut **Temple of Hathor**, fronted by six massive standing statues 10m high. Four represent Ramses and the other two his beloved wife, Nefertari.

A **sound-and-light show** (admission US$8.50) takes place nightly, but if you want to see it you'll have to stay overnight – there are several hotels near the site, but they are pricey. For show times contact the Aswan tourist office.

There is a convoy from Aswan to Abu Simbel at around 4am; you have to book transport through a tour agency or your hotel, all of which run minibus tours. You can either take a tour to Abu Simbel only (US$5), which will finish about midday or go for a longer tour taking in other sights, including the Unfinished Obelisk, the Temple of Philae, and the High Dam (US$7), finishing at about 3pm. These are a great, hassle-free way to get to Abu Simbel and the other sights, and even the early morning drive through the desert is something special.

WESTERN DESERT

Forming the northeast section of the great Sahara, the Western (Libyan) Desert starts on the banks of the Nile and continues into Libya, covering 2.8 million sq km. The landscape is bizarre, beautiful and stark, the emptiness tinged with light, changing from a rolling, immobile sand sea to rocky, red-topped mountains with custard sand drifts, to strange blasted chalk-white rock shapes. An entirely different Egyptian experience can be had exploring this desert and its isolated oasis towns.

Sealed roads link the five main oases, four of them (Kharga, Dakhla, Farafra and Bahariyya) in a long loop from Asyut around to Cairo, making this a possible return journey if you've travelled down the Nile Valley from Cairo to Luxor or Aswan. Siwa is normally reached from the north via the sealed road running down from the coast west of Alexandria. All the oases can be reached by public transport.

Siwa is also linked by a rotten road to Bahariyya, but no public transport uses this route as yet.

All the oases have tour operators eagerly offering **desert treks**; a 4WD trip for two days and one night for five people, costs US$75 to US$90, while a **camel safari** will cost around US$15 to US$20 per person for one day and one night.

KHARGA OASIS

☎ 092 / pop 57,800

Kharga is the largest of the oases, and is surrounded by antiquities. About 240km south of Asyut, the town itself is not that interesting, but untouristed, and has an excellent **Antiquities Museum** (Sharia Gamal Abdel Nasser; admission US$3.50, camera US$1.50; ☺ 8am-4pm). This includes wonderful surprised-looking golden mummy masks, 4000-year-old clay toys and beautiful Coptic wooden friezes (AD 4–6).

Two kilometres to the north of town you'll find the **Temple of Hibis** (admission US$3.50; ☺ 8am-6pm May-Oct, 8am-5pm Nov-Apr) built for the god Amun by the Persian emperor Darius I. Nearby are the early **Christian tombs** of Al-Bagawat, a crumbling, sand-drenched necropolis, and to the south are the hilltop Roman fortresses of **Qasr al-Ghueita** and **Qasr az-Zayyan**.

Kharga Oasis Hotel (☎ 921 500; Sharia Aref; camping per person US$1) You can camp in the palm-filled grounds of this friendly place, right in the centre.

Waha Hotel (☎ 920 393; Sharia an-Nabawi; s/d US$1.50/3) Another central option, the Waha is a welcoming, four-storey place with a time-less feel, and cleanish rooms with balconies.

Dar al-Bayda Hotel (☎ 921 717; off Midan Shoala; s/d/tr US$4/5/7) To the south of town, this place has rooms with balconies overlooking a dusty street and swampy bathrooms.

Al-ahram Restaurant (dishes US$0.50-2) Just next to the Waha, this place has good roast chicken and basic salads.

Buses leave Kharga from the new station at Midan Basateen, for Cairo (US$8, seven to eight hours, five daily), Asyut (US$1.50, four hours, three daily) and Dakhla (US$1.50, three hours, three daily).

Regular service taxis serve Dakhla and Asyut for about the same fares. There is a train to Luxor at around 7am Friday (3rd class US$2, seven hours); it returns to Luxor at 7am on Thursday.

DAKHLA OASIS

☎ 092

The easygoing oasis of Dakhla contains two small towns, **Mut** and **Al-Qasr**. Mut is dotted with shaded cafés, palms and men in rak-ish straw hats on bicycles and donkeys. Thirty kilometres northwest, Al-Qasr (the Fortress) is an amazing ancient town, with

narrow sand-filled streets and elaborately carved lintels against its rounded, cool mud bricks.

There's a useful **tourist office** (☎ 821 686) in Mut.

Mut has most of the hotels.

Gardens Hotel (☎ 821 577; Sharia al-Genayen, Mut; s/d with bathroom US$2/4) is friendly; the bathrooms are grubby but there's a lovely garden and rooftop that's good for watching the sunset.

Nasser's Camp (☎ 820 767; camping US$1.50, dm US$2) This is a family-run place 5km east of Mut, and has a few peasant-style rooms and a lovely relaxing area around a small pool.

Bedouin Camp (☎ 830 604; camping US$2, d US$6) About 7km north of Mut, on a desert hill-top, this camp has simple, clean rooms with dramatic views.

Al-Qasr Hotel (☎ 876 013; d US$1.50) In Al-Qasr there's this friendly hotel run by the amiable Mahmed, with big rooms, a good atmosphere and tasty meals. You can sleep on the roof for US$0.30.

It's also possible to **camp** near the dunes west of Mut or in Al-Qasr.

Mut has two good restaurants; both serve beer.

Ahmed Handy's Restaurant (☎ 820 767) With very tasty food and a terrace out front, this place is run by Nasser's brother (you can arrange lifts to his camp from here).

Abu Mohamed Restaurant (☎ 821 431) This restaurant offers excellent food and big helpings. The owner is very enthusiastic and there's Net access for US$1.50 per hour.

There are bus services to Cairo (US$6, 10 hours, three daily) via Kharga (US$1.50) and Asyut (US$3), as well as via Farafra (US$2) and Bahariyya Oasis (US$2.50).

Service taxis to Kharga, Farafra or Asyut, and minibuses to Farafra leave from the bus station, and cost about the same.

You can hire bone-rattling bikes in Mut, which are a good way to get about (US$1 per day).

FARAFRA OASIS

☎ 019

Some 300km northwest of Dakhla, Farafra is the smallest and most untouched of the oases. The main attractions of this low-key spot are palms and fruit trees bearing everything from dates to apricots, and a couple of hot springs – it's lovely to swim in **Bir Saba**, 6km to the west, at night. The oasis is surrounded by the **White Desert** (Sahra al-Beida), where gleaming white shocks of rock resemble whipped-up meringue and make weird atom-cloud formations and strange molten stones litter the custard-coloured ground. You can organise excursions here from the town.

Zwada Hotel (s/d/tr US$3.50/5/7) This place on the main road has clean, modern rooms with coloured rugs and stained-glass windows.

Al-Badawiyya Safari & Hotel (☎ 010-536 4441; s/d US$3.50/7, d with bathroom US$8) Near the Zwada, this hotel has spotless, attractive rooms – the more expensive ones are split level – and a good restaurant. The Bedouin owners also run recommended camel, walking and jeep safaris.

There is a **camping ground** on a hillock above Bir Sitta, a hot spring 6km west of town, but the site lacks shade.

Cafeteria & Restaurant Aly is a cheap eatery on the main road, while **Restaurant Samir** is another recommended place, family-run and off the main road.

Buses serve Cairo (US$7, eight hours) via Bahariyya (US$2, 2½ hours). There are buses to Dakhla (US$2.50, five hours, two daily).

Minibuses to Dakhla leave from the main street whenever they have a full load.

BAHARIYYA OASIS
☎ 018

Bahariyya is a lovely oasis, hilly, lush and thick with palms, about 185km from Farafra. Buses will bring you to Bawiti, the main village. The **tourist office** (☎ 847 3039; Main Rd; 8.30am-2pm & 7-10pm Sat-Thu & 8am-2pm Sun-Wed) is helpful. You can only change cash at the **National Bank**, by the vegetable market.

A few years ago, an ancient 6-sq-km necropolis piled high with an estimated 10,000 Graeco-Roman mummies was discovered here. The find is still being excavated, but some of the gilded cache are on show at the **Antiquities Inspectorate** (admission US$5; 8.30am-4pm). The entry fee allows you admission to seven ancient sights in the area.

The oasis is known for its natural **springs** – one of the best, Bir Ghaba, is accessible only by 4WD. Other attractions include **Gebel al-Ingleez**, or the Black Mountain, 7km to the east, and a small, but beautiful, palm-fringed **salt lake** (Buheera Malh), 4km east of town.

Ahmed's Safari Camp (☎ 802 090; d US$1.50, s/d with bathroom US$3/4) About 4km out of Bawiti,

this has a range of rooms and is a favourite among travellers and trans-Africa groups.

Sahara Camp (camping US$1, s/d US$1.50/3) With a good, very peaceful setting overlooking mountains and the oasis, this has pointy huts and a shaded flower-laden area. It's a couple of kilometres east of the town.

Paradise Hotel (☎ 802 600; s/d US$1/2) This is central and very cheap, but doesn't live up to its name, with an aura of grubbiness.

There's a **campsite** (camping US$1.50) with huts instead of tents, out at Bir Ghaba.

Popular Restaurant (☎ 802 322; dishes US$0.50-2) This is the tingling nerve centre of the village, just off the main road, with reasonable food and outside tables.

Cafeteria Rashed (dishes US$1.50) On the main road, near the petrol station, this is a family-run place serving traditional dishes and *sheesha*.

There are buses to Cairo (US$4, five hours, four daily) and to Farafra (US$2.50, two hours, two daily), that leave from opposite the Paradise Hotel.

Service taxis and minibuses go to Farafra, but it can be a long wait while they fill up.

SIWA OASIS
☎ 046

With a donkey-slow pace of life, Siwa Oasis is the most beautiful of the oases, an idyllic, mystical place. At its centre is the 13th-century shali, or fortified town, its mud-brick walls like torn and twisted paper. Siwa is famous for its dates and olives and is close to big fat dunes and large, deep-blue salt lakes, backed by mountains. It was cut off from the rest of Egypt for centuries – an asphalt road was only built from the coast in the 1980s – and has a very distinct Berber culture. Siwan women lead a very secluded life: once they are married, they only talk to men of their family, and in public they are completely cloaked in a *tarfodit*, a grey shawl which covers their face and upper body.

The helpful **tourist office** (☎ 460 2883) is across the road from the telephone office, north of the main square. There are no banks. **Siwa Oasis Net** is next to the Palm Trees Hotel and charges US$1.50 per hour.

Alexander the Great came to ask questions at the 6th-century **Temple of the Oracle**, 2km to the east, where he had it confirmed that he was a god. At the northern end of town is **Gebel al-Mawta** (admission free; 9am-

3pm), a hill honeycombed with Graeco-Roman tombs, with some beautiful tomb paintings – the best in the **Tomb of Si Amun**. One tomb has been dumped full of night-marish mummies. There are several hot springs around; worth a visit is **Fatnas Spring**, about 6km west of town, an oasis by the saltwater Lake Siwa, accessible across a narrow causeway, and **Bir Wahed**, a hot spring at the edge of the Great Sand Sea, which can be visited on a half-day excursion (US$8) offered by local guides.

Siwa has distinctive crafts on sale all around the oasis.

Yousef Hotel (☎ 460 2162; s/d US$1/1.50) This has clean, bright rooms with shuttered balconies overlooking the main square and great views. There's a kitchen.

Palm Trees Hotel (☎ 460 2304; s/d US$1.50/2, with bathroom US$3.50/5) Just off the main square, this has a lovely garden and a range of rooms, but is a bit run-down.

Alexander Hotel (☎ 460 0512) This small, spotless place near the tourist office has pleasant rooms.

SPLURGE!

Shali Lodge (☎ 4602399; Midan el-Souq; s/d/tr with bathroom US$23/30/38) is a gorgeous little hotel around a courtyard, with eight spacious rooms, simply and naturally decorated. Its **Kenooz Restaurant** (dishes US$0.50-3.50) has white cushions on the rooftop among the tops of palm trees. The food is delicious and the date milkshake divine.

Shaly Hotel (☎ 460 2203; s/d US$1/2) Next to the Shali, this is a bit shabby but the back rooms have fantastic views of the ruins.

Desert Lodge (☎ 440 8164; s/d/tr US$4/7/10) This is a lovely place, about 3km southwest of town toward the dunes – very secluded, bright and clean, with cosy rooms, a roof terrace and a pool filled with spring water. There's a smart kitchen and a vegetable garden. Meals cost US$1.50 to US$3.50.

Of the town's eateries, the most long-standing is the Abdu Restaurant, across the road from the Yousef. Other good choices nearby include the Alexander Restaurant, the old-fashioned-feeling Alexander Great Restaurant, the East West Restaurant and the Dune Restaurant, with a shady gar-den. All have similar menus featuring lentil soup, couscous, pizza, pancakes and so on (dishes US$0.50 to US$3.50).

The West Delta Bus Co station is on the main square in Siwa. There are buses which go to Alexandria at 7am and 10am (US$4.50, eight hours), stopping at Marsa Matruh (US$2, five hours). An additional daily ser-vice to Marsa Matruh leaves at 1pm.

Although there is a road linking the oases of Siwa and Bahariyya, there is no public transport between the two; to hire a taxi costs around US$90; you need an easily obtainable military permit as well.

It's a good idea to hire a bike to get around the sights; it costs around US$1 per day.

You can also take a ride on a *careta* (around US$0.30). These donkey-drawn carts with plastic awnings and wooden seats are used as local taxis.

MEDITERRANEAN COAST

The sparkling Mediterranean coastline is sparsely populated. Its main focus is the charming city of Alexandria, though it is dotted with resorts and white-sand beaches.

ALEXANDRIA
☎ 03 / pop 444,260

Alexandria stretches along a confident sweep of bay, its long waterfront backed by tall colonial buildings that give it a cosmopolitan feel. It's a city that has been through many incarnations. Established in 332 BC by Alexander the Great, it became a major trading centre and place of learning, and its legendary ancient library held 500,000 volumes, while the Pharos lighthouse was one of the Seven Wonders of the World. In the 7th century, it became a backwater when the conquering Muslims made Cairo their capital. Napoleon's arrival 11 centuries later and Alexandria's subsequent redevelopment as a major port meant renaissance, and foreigners flooded in, building the villas, squares and elegant coffeehouses that so characterise the city today, only to flood out again following the revolution of 1952. There's a sophisticated yet provincial air about contemporary Alexandria, a bustling city with a sense of nostalgia for the greatness of its

EGYPT

CENTRAL ALEXANDRIA

0 — 500 m
0 — 0.3 mi

EASTERN HARBOUR

MEDITERRANEAN COAST

To Agami & Hannoville
Beaches (17km)

To Fort
Qaitbey
(500m)

Ras
Ab-tin

Anfushi

To Chatby Youth Hostel
& Biblioteca Alexandrina (200m)
Montazah Palace & Maamoura Beach (715km)

To Sidi Gaber (4km)
& Train Station

Mahattat Masr
(Masr Train Station)

To Pompey's Pillar
& Catacombs of
Kom ash-Shuqqafa (1km)

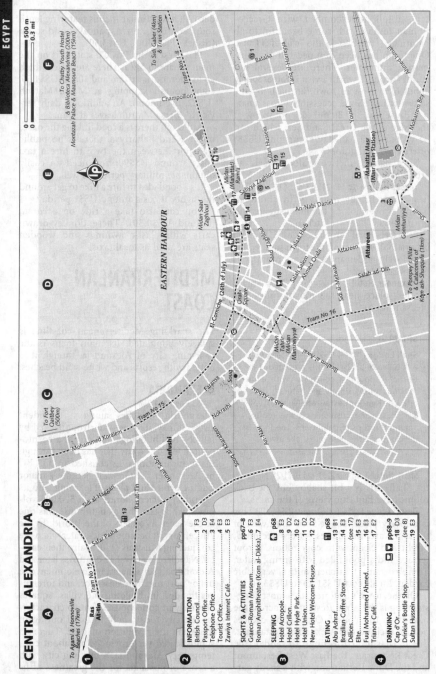

INFORMATION	
British Council	1 F3
Passport Office	2 D3
Telephone Office	3 E4
Tourist Office	4 E3
Zawiya Internet Café	5 E3

SIGHTS & ACTIVITIES	pp67-8
Graeco-Roman Museum	6 F3
Roman Amphitheatre (Kom al-Dikka)	7 E4

SLEEPING	🛏 p68
Hotel Acropole	8 E3
Hotel Crillon	9 D2
Hotel Hyde Park	10 E2
Hotel Union	11 D2
New Hotel Welcome House	12 D2

EATING	🍴 p68
Abu Ashraf	13 B1
Brazilian Coffee Store	14 E3
Délices	(see 17)
Elite	15 E3
Fuul Mohammed Ahmed	16 E3
Trianon Café	17 E2

DRINKING	🍷🎵 pp68-9
Cap d'Or	18 D3
Drinkie's Bottle Shop	(see 8)
Sultan Hussein	19 E3

past – something it seeks to rekindle with the creation of its new Biblioteca.

Orientation

Alexandria is a true waterfront city, 18km long from east to west and only about 3km wide. Its focal point is Midan Saad Zaghloul, a large square running onto the waterfront.

There are two airports: Nozha is 10km south of the city – you catch bus No 203 (US$0.04) or minibus No 703 (US$0.07) to Orabi Square, while Porg El Arab is served by buses (US$1, baggage US$0.40, one hour) according to the arrival and departure of flights. Call ☎ 485 8253 for details.

Long distance buses arrive at Sidi Gaber, 5km east of the centre, from where you can take a tram to Midan Ramla in the centre. Mahattat Masr (Masr station) is the main train terminus, 1km south of Midan Ramla.

Information

The main **tourist office** (☎ 485 1556; ☽ 8am-6pm) is at the southwest corner of Midan Saad Zaghloul, while in the streets to the south and west are the central shopping area, airline offices, restaurants and cheaper hotels.

The main **post office** is east of Midan Orabi. There is a **telephone office** (Mahattat Ramla tram station; ☽ 24hr) west of Midan Gomhuriyya.

There aren't that many Net cafés, but two reliable places are the **British Council**, which charges US$0.30 for day membership and has a good array of English papers and magazines, and **Zawiya Internet Cafe** (Sharia Dr Hassan Fadaly). Both charge US$0.75 per hour.

Sights

Biblioteca Alexandrina (☎ 483 4444; www.bibalex.org; admission US$1.50; ☽ 11am-7pm Wed-Mon, 3-7pm Fri & Sat) is an exceptional complex inspired by Alexandria's historic library – legend had it that every ship calling at the port had to hand over any manuscripts for copying (and frequently didn't get them back – a reverse of what happens with today's libraries). That library was destroyed by fire, possibly around the 3rd century, and Alexandria never really regained its cultural status, despite having been home to such literary luminaries as Lawrence Durrell, EM Forster and Constantine Cavafy. This is an attempt to change all that. It's a state-of-the-art com-

plex, not just a library, but a planetarium, science museum, manuscript museum and exhibition gallery, with changing, interesting exhibitions – its total size is 85,405 sq metres. Designed by Norwegian firm Snohetta, the main building is a huge slanted disc inspired by the rising sun; the complex falls somewhere between the Death Star from *Star Wars* and a university faculty. The library interior is beautifully realised, with soft aquarium lighting in a vast, calm hall supported by 66 columns.

You can get an idea of the splendours Alexandria must have once contained by visiting the excellent **Graeco-Roman Museum** (5 Sharia al-Mathaf ar-Romani; admission US$1; ☽ 9am to 5pm). It contains around 40,000 relics dating from as early as the 3rd century BC, including impressive mosaics, carvings and about the only historical depictions of the legendary lighthouse, in the shape of some small terracotta lanterns.

The only example of a Roman theatre in Egypt is the **Roman Amphitheatre** (Kom id-Dikka; Midan Gomhuriyya; admission US$1; ☽ 9am-5pm). Its 13 marble terraces are well preserved, and there are displays on the ongoing excavations and underwater discoveries in the harbour – a former palace has been discovered, huge statues, and blocks that may come from the legendary Pharos lighthouse.

The famed, misnamed and missable **Pompey's Pillar** (☎ 484 5800; Carmous; admission US$1; ☽ 9am-4pm) is a 30m-high column put up in AD 293. It's southwest of tram line 16.

Nearby, the **Catacombs of Kom ash-Shuqqafa** (☎ 484 5800; Carmous; admission US$1; ☽ 9am-5pm) held about 300 bodies in spooky niches and are a curious sight, their eagle and serpent carving like a horror movie set. They're in an interesting local area, about five minutes' walk from Pompey's Pillar. Follow the wall round to the right and keep going straight ahead.

The Mamluk sultan, Qaitbey, built a **fortress** (admission US$2; ☽ 9am-5pm & 5.30-8.30pm) on the foundations of the destroyed Pharos lighthouse in 1480 – if you get up close, you can see some great pillars of red granite, likely to have come from the ancient lighthouse. In the 19th century, Mohammed Ali expanded its defences, which accounts for its toy-town appearance. Take No 15 tram.

Once the summer residence of the royal family, **Montazah Palace** (admission free), a collision of Florentine and Moorish styles at the eastern extremity of the city, is now reserved for the president and his VIPs, but the lush, pine and palm-dotted gardens are a good place for a picnic. To get here flag down a minibus heading eastward along the Corniche, or catch one at Midan Gomhuriyya or on Tariq al-Horreyya.

The city **beaches** are busy and grubby, but locals flock to them in summer. Maamoura, just east of Montazah Palace, is good, but Agami and Hannoville, about 17km west of central Alexandria, are better. Buses and minibuses go there from Midan Saad Zaghloul.

Sleeping

Hotel Union (☎ 480 7312, 5th fl, 164 Sharia 26th of July; s/d US$5/7, s/d with bathroom US$7/9) This hotel is great value and friendly. Some rooms have TVs, sparkling tiled bathrooms, balconies and fantastic harbour views, and some rooms are huge.

Hotel Crillon (☎ 480 0330, 5 Sharia Adib Ishaq; s/d US$4.50/7, d with bathroom or view US$8.50) The Crillon has old-fashioned charm, stripped, polished floors and French windows with harbour views.

Hotel Hyde Park (☎ 487 5666; 8th fl, 21 Amin Fikry; s/d US$4/7.50, with bathroom US$7/11) High above Midan Ramla, the views from here are amazing and the rooms are good. There's no sign outside: it's the building on the corner of the square.

Hotel Acropole (☎ 480 5980, 4th fl, 1 Sharia Gamal ad-Din Yassin; s/d/tr US$2.50/4/5.50) Pleasant and central, with tall-ceilinged rooms, this is a good choice. Room 10, with a balcony over the square, is ideal for anyone with an Evita complex.

Chatby Youth Hostel (☎ 592 5459, 13 Sharia Port Said; dm US$2, d/tr with bathroom US$6/8) This is near the Biblioteca. It's clean, functional and popular with local students.

New Hotel Welcome House (☎ 480 6402; 5th fl, Sharia Gamal ad-Din Yassin; d US$4) This place is the best in this building; one room has a great view over the harbour. On the 4th floor, **Hotel Gamil** and **Hotel Normandie**, are shabby and a bit whiffy, and best avoided.

Eating

There are lots of places to eat along Sharia Safiyya Zaghloul. At the Midan Ramla end, near the seafront, there are a number of

cafés, juice stands, *shwarma* stands and bakeries.

Brazilian Coffee Store (Sharia Saad Zaghloul) If you're content with a croissant and good coffee, this is good and the oldest coffeeshop in the city.

Trianon Café (Metropole Hotel; 52 Sharia Saad Zaghloul; dishes US$0.50-4.50) Another of Alexandria's great coffeeshops, this is a timeless place, still buzzing with people, and with chandeliers like 19th-century spaceships. It's good for breakfast or cakes, but the coffee is criminal.

Fuul Mohammed Ahmed (317 Sharia Shakor; dishes US$0.75) This is the best place in town – perpetually packed – for a cheap, simple meal of *fuul* or *ta'amiyya*, plus all the usual accompaniments. There's also a popular takeaway section.

Elite (43 Sharia Safiyya Zaghloul; dishes US$0.15-4.50) This is what happened when a 1950s diner got crossed with a conservatory: it's another place frozen in time, with good windows for street watching. It serves dishes such as pizza and spaghetti, or you can just sit down for a beer.

Délices (☎ 486 1432; 46 Blvd Saad Zaghloul; dishes US$0.30-1.50) Old-fashioned, long mirrored and popular, this has good cakes; the *omy aly* is singled out for special praise.

On wonderful Sharia Safar Pasha, west of the centre, it's cheek-by-jowl swinging hunks of meat and *sheesha* hang-outs, unsuspecting rabbits-for-sale, and fresh fish restaurants.

Abu Ashraf (☎ 481 6597; Sharia Safar Pasha; dishes US$2) This is an excellent choice, though there are many good restaurants along here. It's an awning-covered, column-decorated restaurant, lively and friendly, and you choose your fresh fish from the catch of the day. It's served with loads of salad and freshly baked bread.

Drinking

Cap d'Or (☎ 487 5177; 4 Sharia Adib; dishes US$0.50-5; ☺ noon-3am) Stained glass-filtered light, a marble-topped bar and calamari, fish and shrimp dishes all add up to an Andalucian tapas bar sensation. You can eat or pull up a stool and have a beer.

Sultan Hussein (cnr Safiyya Zaghloul & Sultan Hussein) This airy ahwa has the requisite elderly men, but a sprinkling of women too, and big windows open to the street.

Drinkie's Bottle Shop (Mohammed Koralem) This off-licence sells large beers for US$0.50.

Getting There & Away
BUS
Long-distance buses all go from behind Sidi Gaber train station; the tram connects it with the city centre. From here there are frequent buses to Cairo (US$3.50 to US$5, 2½ hours, half-hourly), to Marsa Matruh (US$2 to US$4, five hours, hourly), to Sallum (US$4, nine hours, three daily), Siwa (US$4.50, nine hours, three daily) and Hurghada (US$9 to US$11, 10 hours, two daily). There are also daily buses to Benghazi (US$60, 12 hours) and Tripoli (US$123) in Libya.

TRAIN
Alexandria's main train terminal is Mahattat Masr (Masr station), but there is also a station at Sidi Gaber. Cairo-bound trains leave at least hourly, from about 5am to 10pm. The best trains, the Turbini or Espani (also known as the Spanish trains), depart Mahattat Masr at 7am, 8am, 2pm, 3pm, 7pm and 7.30pm (1st/2nd class US$5.50/4.50, 2½ hours). There are also trains to Marsa Matruh, but bus is a better option.

Getting Around
Tram is the best way to travel in Alexandria. Midan Ramla is the main tram station and from here lime-yellow trams go west and blue ones go east. A short trip, say from Midan Ramla to Masr train station, will cost US$0.30, while around US$0.50 is reasonable for a trip to the eastern beaches.

MARSA MATRUH
☎ 046 / pop 61,100
This large waterfront town has unfortunately unattractive buildings built around a charming bay of piercing azure Mediterranean waters and white sandy beaches. It is a popular summer destination with Egyptians, but does not see that many foreign visitors (so those who do come here tend to get a bit of attention). Most hotels and restaurants close over winter (November to March). There's a **tourist office** (☎ 493 1841; el-Corniche; ☼ 9am-3pm), one block west of Sharia Iskendariyya.

The main reason to come here is to explore the beaches, the balmiest of which are outside the town. **Cleopatra's Beach** is 14km

west of town, while the best beach, **Agiba** (meaning 'miracle'), is 24km west. A pick-up or minibus goes out to these in summer (US$0.30), otherwise you can hire a taxi for about US$8 return. However, be warned that most women head for the water fully clothed, and if you wear less the hassle will increase accordingly.

There are a few budget options around.

Ghazala Hotel (☎ 493 3519; off Sharia Iskendariyya; s/d US$1.50/3) Mr Soliman, the owner here, is a war veteran and nice chap and this is the most popular traveller stop (doesn't mean there'll be any other guests though). The visitors book seems to have become a kind of therapeutic outlet.

Hotel Hamada (☎ 493 3300; off Sharia Iskendariyya; s/d US$1.50/3) This is a very friendly, helpful place, and has basic but clean rooms with small windows.

Camping might be possible – check with the tourist office.

Asmak Hammo al-Temsah & Abdu Kofta Restaurant (Sharia Tahrir; dishes US$2) At this delicious place, you choose your fish and it's dipped in spices then served up with fine salads and breads.

New Panayotis Tourist Restaurant (Sharia Iskendariyya; dishes US$1-2) This does decent fish dishes and serves beer.

Camona Tourist Restaurant (Sharia al-Galaa; dishes US$0.30-2) Providing regular Egyptian options, such as kofta and salads, this place also serves beer and has outside tables.

Marsa Matruh's main bus station is 2km to the south of town. There are numerous buses to Alexandria (US$2.50 to US$3.50, four hours, hourly), Cairo (US$4 to US$5.50, five hours, four daily) and Siwa (US$2, five hours, three daily).

SUEZ CANAL

The Suez Canal severs Africa from Asia and links the Mediterranean with the Red Sea. It's an extraordinary sight to see supertankers appear to glide through the desert as they ply the waters. One of the greatest feats of modern engineering, the canal opened in 1869 and remains one of the world's busiest shipping routes. Its toll revenues are very important to Egyptian coffers.

The canal was in French and British hands till independence, when President Nasser

EGYPT

nationalised the waterway. The European powers promptly tried to take it by force, provoking the Suez Crisis. They withdrew following international condemnation.

The three principal cities along the canal – Port Said, Ismailia and Suez – are not really busy with travellers. Suez suffered badly in the 1967 and 1973 wars and is, above all, a transit point for tankers, pilgrims to Mecca and people travelling between Sinai and the rest of the country.

However Port Said and, to a lesser extent, Ismailia, are full of late-19th- and early-20th-century, colonial-style architecture.

PORT SAID
☎ 066 / pop 548,900

Port Said was founded in 1859. Its main attraction is the canal, with its hordes of ships, but the streets are lined by four-storey buildings with wooden balconies and verandas, like a less funky New Orleans. The town is effectively built on an island, connected to the mainland by a bridge to the south and a causeway to the west. It's a duty-free zone, and many people come here to buy designer jeans and electrical goods. There are customs controls on the way in and out of the city, and at the train and bus stations; check whether anything you buy will be subject to duties. There are numerous **banks** with ATMs. **American Online Net** (Sharia Memphis; ۞ 24hr) charges US$0.50 per hour.

Suez Canal House is a striking Moorish-style canal-side building (closed to the public). The **National Museum** (Sharia Palastine; admission US$1; ۞ 9am-4pm Sat-Thu) has a fine collection of artefacts from all stages of Egyptian history and is worth visiting. The **Military Museum** (Sharia 23rd of July; admission US$1; ۞ 9am-2pm Sat-Thu) offers some interesting relics of the conflicts over the canal.

Sleeping
Akri Palace Hotel (☎ 221 013, 24 Sharia al-Gomhurriya; s/d US$2/4) This friendly place has a 19th-century feel, both in terms of fixtures (dusty bakelite phones and tall shuttered windows) and staff. There's no hot water.

Mereland Hotel (☎ 227 020; off Shari Souq; s/d US$2/4) This modernish place has plain, no-nonsense rooms and hot water.

Youth Hostel (☎ 228 702; dm US$1.50) This has basic bunks in quite clean rooms of about 20 beds.

Eating & Drinking
Reana (Sharia al-Gomhurriya; dishes US$2-7) This is a Chinese-Korean restaurant with red tablecloths and a nice atmosphere. It serves beer.

Cecil (Sharia al-Gomhurriya) A spit-and-sawdust bar, downstairs from Reana, which is open until late.

Galal (cnr Sharias al-Gomhuriyya & Gaberti; dishes US$2-8) A popular local seafood place which serves alcohol.

Getting There & Away
There are three bus terminals, but the most useful is Mubarak Station; getting here costs US$0.50 by taxi. There are buses for Cairo (US$2.50, three hours, hourly) and for Alexandria (US$4, four hours, hourly). There are five slow trains to Cairo each day; the 2nd-class ordinary/air-con fare is US$2/3.

RED SEA COAST

Egypt's Red Sea coast stretches more than 800km, from Suez in the north to the border with Sudan in the south. Its underwater pleasures are unparalleled, though above ground it has been the victim of much development as a result.

HURGHADA
☎ 065 / pop 70,200

Once a fishing village, white-sand beaches and thrilling underwater scenery have been Hurghada's (Al-Ghardaka's) blessing and curse. Malls line the streets, where travellers escaping from unappealing complexes wander around high-street shops, showing off their tans, and checking out the *sheesha*-pipe outlets and belly-dancing outfits. It doesn't feel like Egypt and the building never seems to stop. However, put your head underwater and you can forget all this (you'll have to get away from the coast, which has been trashed by development).

The main town area, Ad-Dahar, where virtually all the budget accommodation is located, is at the northern end. South of Hurghada is the port area of Sigala and then the resort strip.

There are plenty of **banks** and ATMs, and tons of Internet cafés all over Hurghada, charging from US$0.50 to US$3.50 per hour. The cheapest and fastest is **Speednet** (Sheraton Rd). The main **post office** (Sharia an-Nasr) is in Ad-Dahar, and the **telephone exchange** (☺ 24hr) is northwest along the same road.

Sights & Activities

Most people come here to dive, snorkel and bask. Hurghada is crawling with dive clubs and agents for snorkelling trips. One popular snorkelling trip is to **Giftun Island**, which teems with marine life and costs around US$7 for gear-hire, two snorkelling stops and lunch.

There are loads of diving operators. **Subex** (☎ 547 593; Ad-Dahar), off the Corniche, is recommended for shorter trips and the **Red Sea Diving Centre** (☎ 442 960; Sigala), near the ferry terminal, is a reputable place with years of experience.

The beach has been turned into territorial segments and you can pay around US$2 for access; most hotels and restaurants can arrange this.

Sleeping

These places are all in or around Ad-Dahar.

Youth Hostel (☎ 544 989; dm US$4) This is about 5km north of Ad-Dahar on the main road, but it has spacious rooms and its own beach.

Four Seasons Hotel (☎ 549 882; Dr Said Korayem St; s/d with bathroom US$4/6; ☒) An excellent, helpful budget choice, this is friendly and smart, with balconies.

Snafer Hotel (☎ 540 260; s/d with bathroom US$3/4) In a small building behind the National Hospital, this has big, bright rooms that are good value.

Happyland Hotel (☎ 547 373; El Sheik Sebaks; s/d US$3.50/4, with bathroom US$4/6) This friendly hotel is centrally located in the souq, with clean rooms and balconies.

Hotel California (☎ 549 101; s/d with bathroom US$3/4) Just off the corniche, at its northern end, this has cleanish, good-value rooms, some worn but groovy wall paintings and a roof terrace. However, the management can be a bit frantic. And remember: you can check out any time you like, but you can never leave.

Eating

Ad-Dahar has the best range of restaurants – particularly concentrated around the seaside area. Choice budget options include the following.

Hurghada Fish Place Restaurant (☎ 549 782; Sharia an-Nasr; dishes US$1.50-6) This cheery café has a selection of simple fish dishes.

Pizzaria Tarboush (☎ 548 456; Sharia Abdel Aziz Mustafa; dishes US$1.50-3.50) A popular pizza place, this is open to the street and has lots of topping choices.

Restaurant Dandrarmy (Sharia Abdel Aziz Mustafa; dishes US$1) This corner cubby-hole has good salads, tasty *fuul* and so on.

Zeko (Main Square; dishes US$0.30-1.50) Near the mosque in Ad-Dahar's centre, this small, busy, local place does good grilled chicken, bread and salads.

El-Showihi (off el-Corniche; dishes US$1) A large, bright local restaurant with a TV, El-Showihi serves up salads, *ta'amiyya*, *fuul* and various mezze (starters).

Drinking

This is probably a good idea. Among the bland tack there are a few good places, and if it's house music you're after, Hurghada has it.

Papas (www.papasbar.com) has several incarnations. **Papas Bar** (Sharia Sheraton, Sigala) and **Papas II** (el-Corniche, Ad-Dahar) both have lots of soft-lit wood, are open to the street and popular. **Papas Beach Club** (Sigala, off Sharia Sheraton; admission US$4.50) has a boat-shaped bar, funky dance floor and a good stretch of beach that's open from the morning (US$2). Admission here includes one beer.

The **Chill** (Sigala, Sharia Sheraton) is the coolest place in Hurghada. It has dark red lanterns, good music, cushions out on the beach and daily DJs.

Café Cheers (☎ 545 200; Shedwan Golden Beach Hotel; El Corniche, Ad-Dahar; ☺ 24hr) At this haunt you can sit outside on the raised pavement, or shoot pool inside.

Getting There & Away

BOAT

International Fast Ferries (☎ 447 571; www.internationalfastferries.com) operates a high-speed luxury ferry from the old port in Sigala. The ferry runs at 8am each Tuesday, Thursday, Saturday and Sunday, or at 5am on Monday (US$32). Book ahead at the port or at any travel agent.

There are also ferries from here to Saudi Arabia; see the Transport section (p40) for details.

BUS

Superjet's terminal is near the main mosque in Ad-Dahar. It has buses to Cairo (US$7.50,

EGYPT

six hours, three daily) and Alexandria (US$22, nine hours, one daily).

The Upper Egypt Bus Co operates from the main bus station at the southern end of Ad-Dahar. It runs buses almost hourly to Cairo (US$7.50, six hours). There are also buses to Luxor (US$4, five hours) and Aswan (US$6, seven hours).

AROUND HURGHADA
Monasteries of St Anthony & St Paul

These two isolated Coptic Christian **monasteries** (🕙 9am-5pm), in the barren mountains overlooking the Gulf of Suez near Zafarana (about a third of the way from Cairo to Hurghada), were founded in the 4th century.

Neither place will take visitors during Lent. St Paul's has the fascinating, cluttered **Church of St Paul**, built in and around the cave in which the saint lived for nearly 90 years.

The monastery has separate guesthouses for men and women – you need permission from the **monasteries' Cairo residences** (☎ 02-590 0218) to stay overnight. If you can't stay in the guesthouse, you can camp in the dry riverbed nearby. Food and lodging are free, but don't abuse the hospitality.

St Anthony's, about 45km from the Red Sea coast, is more modernised. Its church has a fine collection of Coptic wall paintings. It is worth climbing the 500m up the mountain behind the monastery to see **St Anthony's Cave**, and breathtaking views.

To get to St Paul's, take a bus along the coastal road north from Hurghada and get off at the turn-off for the monastery, south of the Zafarana lighthouse. From there it's a 13km walk on a dirt track across baking desert with very little traffic – don't rely on getting a lift and take lots of water.

To get to St Anthony's, take the road inland to the Nile Valley from Zafarana and take the monastery turn-off. From there it's a 13km walk.

The easiest way to reach the monasteries is to join a tour or hire a taxi (US$55) from Hurghada.

WARNING

Despite what local tour operators may tell you, some areas of Sinai still contain land mines left from the wars with Israel. Be very wary about going off the beaten track.

SINAI

☎ 062

Sinai is a region of incredible beauty: crumpled mountains, white-sand coastline backed by palms and contorted rocks, colour-streaked desert plains and the coral reefs of the Red Sea. Wedged between Africa and Asia, Sinai's northern coast is bordered by the Mediterranean, and its southern peninsula delineated by the Red Sea gulfs of Aqaba and Suez.

It was on Mt Sinai that Moses received the Ten Commandments, but the sixth has been broken here with monotonous regularity. The area's strategic significance has made it the setting of conflict for centuries, most recently when Israel occupied the peninsula from 1967 until 1978 when, under the Camp David Agreement, it agreed to pull out.

Many mainland Egyptians have migrated here to take advantage of the exploding tourist trade, and the Bedouin, the traditional inhabitants of Sinai, are now in a minority and increasingly marginalised in their native land.

SHARM EL-SHEIKH & NA'AMA BAY

☎ 069

The south coast of the Gulf of Aqaba, between Tiran Island in the strait and Ras Mohammed, features an explosion of shimmering, vivid underwater scenery. Unfortunately it's not matched overground: Na'ama Bay is a plastic, manicured resort full of sanitized boulevards and sun-basted skin. Sharm el-Sheikh, initially developed by the Israelis, is a long-standing settlement 6km away, and feels a little more Egyptian and a little less bland. Minibuses run between the two for about US$0.50.

Diving & Snorkelling

Na'ama itself has few reefs, but the stunning Near and Middle Gardens and the even more incredible Far Garden can be reached on foot from the bay. Some of the most spectacular diving is off Ras Mohammed (see that section opposite) and in the **Strait of Tiran**. There is also good snorkelling at most of the popular coastal dive sites, including **Ras um Sid** near the lighthouse at Sharm. The deep drop-offs and strong cross currents at Ras Mohammed are not ideal for snorkelling. There are several wrecks including the prized **Thistlegorm**.

Any of the dive clubs and schools can give you a full rundown of the possibilities. Below are some of the better and more established.

Anemone (☎ 600 995)
Aquamarine Diving Centre (☎ 600 276)
Aquanaute (☎ 549 891)
Camel Dive Club (☎ 600 700)
Emperor Divers (☎ 601 734)
Red Sea Diving College (☎ 600 313)
Sinai Divers (☎ 600 697; www.sinaidivers.com)
Subex (☎ 600 100)

Sleeping

Budget places are scarce in Sharm el-Sheikh and Na'ama Bay.

Pigeon House (☎ 600 996; Na'ama Bay; s/d/tr US$12/15/18, with bathroom US$19/26/30) On the northern edge of town, this is the best of the budget options, with comfortable rooms, friendly management and good food.

Sandy Hotel (☎ 661 177; Sharm al-Maya, Sharm el-Sheikh; s/d with bathroom US$13/18) This is close to the main market in Sharm and is an attractive, Spanish-style hotel with clean rooms and a pool.

Youth Hostel (☎ 660 317; Sharm el-Sheikh; dm US$8.50) Up on the hill, this has been smartened up and offers places in three-bed rooms.

Palermo Resort (☎ 661 561; Sharm el Sheikh; s/d with bathroom US$28/33) Although rather out of the way in the cliff-top area, this has a large pool and three stars. There's a shuttle bus to the beach at Ras Um Sid.

Eating & Drinking

There are several small restaurants and cafés in the souq behind the bus station in Sharm el-Sheikh.

Safsafa Restaurant (Sharm al-Maya; Sharm el Sheikh; dishes US$1.50-7) This family-run place is popular with locals and offers very good fresh fish.

Sinai Star (☎ 660 323; Sharm al-Maya; Sharm el Sheikh; dishes US$1-7) This lively place cooks up excellent fish and you can bring your own alcohol.

Tam Tam Oriental Cafe (Ghazala Hotel, Na'ama Bay; dishes US$1.50-3) This is a laid-back place with cushions on the floor outside, serving up a mixture of mezze and antipasti.

Bus Stop Pub & Club (☎ 399 020; www.sharm events.com; Sanafir Hotel, Sharm) This bar has long

been driving the resort's nightlife; it has a red bus front and an intimate club upstairs that holds nights such as House Nation and Hits Mania.

Camel Bar (Camel Hotel, Na'ama Bay) A popular bar in the heart of town, this is a good place to hang out and practise your diving jargon.

Getting There & Away

The main bus station is on the main road halfway between Sharm el-Sheikh and Na'ama Bay, behind the petrol station. There are frequent services to Cairo (US$9, seven hours), to Dahab (US$2, 1½ hours) and on to Nuweiba (US$7) and Taba (US$8).

There's a high-speed ferry to Hurghada (US$27, 1½ hours) at 6pm daily except Friday and Wednesday. Tickets can be booked through most hotels and travel agents.

RAS MOHAMMED

Declared a **national park** (admission US$5) in 1988, the headland of Ras Mohammed is about 30km west of Sharm el-Sheikh, at the southern tip of the peninsula. Inside the park's boundaries are some of the world's most spectacular coral reef ecosystems, teeming with most of the Red Sea's 1000 varieties of fish. You can dive here; most clubs in Na'ama Bay and Sharm offer trips (see this page).

Camping is allowed only in designated areas. Permits (US$1 per person per night) are available from the visitor centre inside the park.

Take your passport with you, and remember that it is not possible to go to Ras Mohammed if you only have a Sinai permit in your passport.

DAHAB

If a cliché backpacker decided to construct heaven, it might look like the beach resort of Assalah at Dahab. Small-scale camps line a long stretch of pale sand, with restaurants jutting out over the fiercely blue water or spreading onto cushions on the beach. You could spend some time here thinking over serious things, such as which place does the best milkshakes. If lazing in the sun and milkshake-testing wears thin, it's an excellent place to do a dive course, and the bay is perfect for windsurfing.

Dahab (literally Gold) is 85km north of Sharm el-Sheikh on the Gulf of Aqaba, and there are two parts to it – in the new part, referred to by the locals as Dahab City, are the more expensive hotels, the bus station, the post and phone offices and the bank. **Assalah**, a Bedouin village, is about 2.5km north of town, although it now has more budget travellers and Egyptian entrepreneurs than Bedouins in residence. Most travellers come here simply to laze around. Please respect local sensitivities and refrain from sunbathing topless. There's dope around, but it's a lot less prevalent than it once was. Anyway, be discreet.

Information
National Bank of Egypt changes cash and travellers cheques and has an ATM on the beach. **Seven Heaven Internet Cafe** is reliable and charges US$0.50 per hour.

Sights & Activities
It only costs US$200 to do your **diving** certificate here, and there are numerous dive clubs. The following are among the better ones.
Fantasea (☎ 640 483)
Nesima (☎ 640 320)
Orca (☎ 640 020)

These places offer the full range of diving services as well as combined camel and diving safaris. Snorkellers tend to head for Eel Garden, just north of the village. You can hire **snorkelling** gear from places along the waterfront and **windsurfing** stuff from the beach near Dahab City.

Most people breathing in Dahab offer **trips into the interior** of Sinai, and camel drivers congregate along the waterfront to organise camel trips (one day, including food, from US$20).

If the sea doesn't appeal, you can lush it up at the **Nesima Resort pool** (☎ 640 320; US$3.50 per day).

Sleeping
Budget travellers head straight for Assalah, where the beach is lined with simple camps – mainly groups of huts with shared bathrooms. Prices here are always negotiable.

Auski Camp (☎ 640 474; d US$1.50) This is a much-recommended camp, with bright plain rooms, a central cushioned area, and a good beachside restaurant.

Penguin Village (☎ 640 117; s/d US$1/2) Run by cheery, helpful Jimmy, this is a basic camp

with lots of broken-china mosaic and a good beachside area.

Star of Dahab (☎ 640 130; Mashraba; s/d US$2/3.50) With small apricot-toned rooms or beehive-shaped huts, this is a long-running, cosy place.

Jasmine Pension (☎ 640 111; d with bathroom US$6-11) This is a pension rather than a camp, and the more expensive rooms, although small, have fantastic wooden balconies with sea views. The food is simply excellent here (mains US$3.50).

Eating
Jays Restaurant (Masbat; dishes US$0.50-1.50) This has an intimate, shady garden with cushions on the ground.

Al Capone (Masbat; dishes US$1-7) Very popular, this has floor cushions, fresh fish and barbecued food.

Lakhbatiba (Mashraba; dishes US$3.50-4.50) Resembling a trippy grandma's beachside kitchen, this eccentric place has really tasty food.

Tratoria Pizzeria (Masbat; dishes US$2-4) This is where you get the best pizzas on the beach.

Drinking
The beach is dotted with bars; most charge US$1 for a beer.

Crazy House (Masbat) Crazy House is the place for a game of pool or a leisurely beer.

Top Deck (Masbat) This might look like a mild-mannered ship-shaped bar/restaurant, but inside there's a please-everyone disco just waiting to get out.

Furry Cup (Blue Bay Hotel, Masbat) This is a popular, recommended divers hang-out.

New Sphinx Bar (Sphinx House, Mashraba) A relaxing, quiet bar, this is a little bit away from the Masbat scene.

Getting There & Away
The bus station is in Dahab City. The most regular connection is to Sharm el-Sheikh, (US$3, 1½ hours, six daily). There are buses to Nuweiba (US$2, 1½ hours, two daily) going on to Taba (US$5, three hours). There's a bus to St Katherine's Monastery (US$4.50, two to three hours, one daily) and to Cairo (US$10 to US$13, nine hours, four daily).

NUWEIBA
The former Bedouin village of Tarabin at Nuweiba, 87km north of Dahab, is a string of beach-hut camps, clinging to a peaceful

sandy bay backed by streaky terracotta-coloured hills. Once buzzing with Israelis, political troubles have rendered it something of a ghost resort. However, if you can embrace the deserted air rather than finding it disconcerting, it's a lovely place to get away from it all.

Nuweiba is actually divided into three parts. To the south is the port with the bus station, banks and awful hotels. A few kilometres farther north is Nuweiba City, with resort hotels and a dive centre, as well as a couple of good eateries. About 2km north of here, draped along the northern end of Nuweiba's calm bay, is Tarabin, the beachside oasis that's the main attraction.

Once again, lazing, diving and snorkelling are the prime activities.

There are lots of simple camps at Tarabin, and all serve food.

Moonland (☎ 010-612 6683; s/d US$1/2) This is set back among the jagged mountains and has lots of spaced-out huts.

Soft Beach Camp (☎ 500 675; s/d US$1/2) Set on a really good patch of beach, this is fairly clean and convenient for beachside lazing.

Blue Bus Camp (☎ 500 624; s/d US$1/2) Blue Bus is very friendly and helpful, and again has simple huts and a great beachside sitting area.

Dr Shishkebab (☎ 500 273; Bazaar, Nuweiba City; dishes US$0.50-7) A popular, sunny place, this has generous portions of tasty meat dishes and mezze.

Abu Tamer (☎ 520 273; Souq, Nuweiba Port; dishes US$0.20-1) This small *kushari* joint buzzes with locals – there are several *fuul* places nearby as well.

Buses leave for Taba (US$2, one hour, two daily), for Cairo (US$8, seven hours, four daily) and for Sharm el-Sheikh (US$3.50, two hours, four daily) via Dahab (US$2). The buses stop in Nuweiba City and also usually call in at the port; you can hail buses from the roadside or ask to be let off at Tarabin, though there is no official stop.

For boat services to Jordan, see the Transport section (p40).

AROUND NUWEIBA

Along the road to Taba and the border with Israel, desolate **beaches** are sandwiched between stunning blue waters and barren, pale-purple, blue-shadowed rocky mountains. Small-scale, tranquil camps dot this stretch of road, though the tourist developers have descended on some places.

Basata (☎ 500 481; camping US$3.50, d US$10, chalet d US$14), 23km north of Nuweiba, is the best place to stay. It's set on an amazing bay with clean white sand meeting a lovely bit of sea. Run by an Egyptian-German couple, it's a simple, clean and ecologically friendly travellers' settlement, with suitelike bamboo huts that have sections open to the view. More substantial chalets are also beautifully designed domed buildings with Moorish shutters. Evening meals (US$3 to US$4.50) are available, and you can cook in the attractive kitchen. The management organises Bedouin-run trips too.

At **Ras Shaitan** about 11km north of Nuweiba, there's **Ayash** (☎ 010-525 9109; d US$1.50), set on lunar rocks, with candlelit, simple huts looking across to distant, folded hills. A bit farther on is **Barracuda Village**, which has a series of waterfront stone huts.

TABA

The busy border crossing point into Israel is open 24 hours. There is a small post and telephone office in the 'town', along with a hospital, bakery and an EgyptAir office (often closed). You can change money at booths of **Banque du Caire** (unreliable opening hours) and **Banque Masr** (☾ 24hr), both 100m before the border, or at the Taba Hilton Hotel. See the Transport section (p40) for details of the crossing.

MT SINAI & ST KATHERINE'S MONASTERY

At a height of 2285m, **Mt Sinai** (Gebel Musa), revered as the place Moses received the Ten Commandments, towers over St Katherine's Monastery, splendidly dramatic and on a towering Old Testament scale. It is easy to hike to the top – most people take the three-hour gentle 'camel trail' and come down the 3000 Steps of Repentance, carved out by a monk. It's usual to stay in or around St Katherine's and walk up the mountain in the dark, getting to the top in time for sunrise. It's a magical experience, walking in the pitch dark, lit only by a staggering number of stars (although it's handy to have a torch too). Other people prefer to walk up during the day and see sunset. There are plenty of little huts on the route, selling tea, coffee and biscuits to keep you going. It's also possible to stay overnight at one of the huts near the top.

The mountain is part of the 4350-sq-km St Katherine Protectorate, so national park rules apply here. Temperatures can plummet to below zero in the winter, and it's cold at night at any time of year. You can hire blankets at the top (US$1).

At the foot of Mt Sinai, the ancient **St Katherine's monastery** (admission free; ☺ 9am-noon Mon-Thu & Sat) is set amid a landscape that resembles a faded biblical print, under the bleaching sun. Twenty-two Greek Orthodox monks live here, part of an order founded in the 4th century by the Byzantine empress Helena, who had a small chapel built beside what was believed to be the burning bush from which God spoke to Moses, and which is still looking remarkably healthy. The exquisite **chapel** is dedicated to St Katherine, the legendary martyr of Alexandria, who was tortured on a spiked wheel and then beheaded for her Christianity. It's filled with vivid golden icons and suspended silver lamps and incense holders. There's a **museum** (admission US$3.50), filled with beautiful illuminated manuscripts. Outside the main building is a **skull room**, full of the bones of deceased monks, divided by rank even in death.

Sleeping & Eating
Monastery Guest House (☎ 206-947 0353; dm US$20; s/d with bathroom US$35/50) St Katherine's Monastery runs this guest house, with lush, but unflashy, rooms that are not in the least monastic.

Fox Camp (☎ 470 344; s/d US$1.50/3) Run by amiable brothers, about 3km from the monastery, this is a very friendly Bedouin camp. The rooms are simple, the shower's a trickle, and there's a snug sitting room with a fire to huddle around when it gets chilly.

In the village of Al-Milga, about 3.5km from the monastery, there's a **bakery** opposite the mosque and a couple of well-stocked **supermarkets** in the shopping arcade. Behind the bakery are a few small restaurants, the most reasonable of which is **Kafeteria Ikhlas**. Near the bus stop, **Katrien Rest House** serves filling basic lunches.

Getting There & Away
There is not much public transport to St Katherine's, but there's enough.

Buses leave from Cairo (US$6, six hours, two daily), one of which goes via Dahab (US$2.50, two to three hours) and Nuweiba (US$3.50). Buses stop at the square in Al-Milga.

EGYPT DIRECTORY

ACCOMMODATION
Egypt has great value budget accommodation; it is remarkably cheap following devaluation of the pound, and you can frequently get very good basic rooms for around US$1 to US$3 per person. Watch out for security: in some cheap places the 'keys' will open any of the doors.

ACTIVITIES
The waters of the Red Sea offer some of the world's most spectacular diving. There's a plethora of dive operators in Sinai (at Na'ama Bay, Sharm el-Sheikh, Dahab and Nuweiba) and on the Red Sea coast (Hurghada). Most of the dive operators offer every possible kind of dive course, from one-day introductions (a single dive is about US$60) to open-water certification courses that last about five days and cost from US$200 to US$300 depending on the operator and location.

Alternatively, you can hire a mask, snorkel and fins from most dive centres for around US$1 per day.

Keep in mind that Egypt's reefs are protected by law and you should not touch or remove coral or any other underwater flora and fauna. Before leaping into the water, it's a good idea to become familiar with dangerous creatures, including lionfish, stonefish, barracuda and moray eels.

Away from the sea, you can head into the desert, travelling by 4WD or camel (see p62). Egypt's huge deserts have geological wonders, as well as forgotten archaeological ruins. Reasonably priced guides can be found through small hotels in the Western Desert oasis towns and in Sinai. Many operators offer treks into the Sinai interior; treks via camel, with some diving off the coast thrown in, are becoming increasingly popular.

You can also go riding around the desert near Cairo – there are lots of stables around the pyramids at Giza that offer anything from an hour to a full day's riding on horses or camels (see p43).

Boating along the Nile is a very tranquil activity, and the best places to take to the water are Cairo (see p47) and Aswan (see p60).

BUSINESS HOURS

As Egypt is a Muslim country, Friday is the main day off during the week, although most government offices and banks are shut on Saturday too. To confuse the issue, many shops close on Sunday, a hangover from colonial rule. Working hours are roughly 8am to 3pm, although shops remain open until 8pm or 9pm. During Ramadan, hours are from 10am to 1pm; most shops open from 11am until 2pm and then open again in the evening.

DANGERS & ANNOYANCES

Between 1993 and 1997, Egypt's largest Islamist opposition group, the Gama'a al-Islamiyya, targeted foreign travellers in its campaign to overthrow the government. The massacre of 58 people in Hatshepsut Temple in November 1997, however, cost the movement a huge amount of support in Egypt, and the Gama'a later announced that it was ending its campaign of violence, particularly in relation to foreigners.

Since then there have been a few sporadic attacks on policemen around the town of Minya, south of Cairo. Nevertheless, the authorities are taking no chances, and the few travellers who show up in the former trouble spots of Minya, Asyut, Sohag and Qena are often hurriedly escorted to the nearest train or bus out of town. If they are allowed to stay they will be tailed by armed policemen. All road travel between towns in Upper Egypt must be made with a police escort. This is annoying and restrictive (wandering around with guns pointing at the local populace is hardly a way to make friends) but there is no way around it at present.

EMBASSIES & CONSULATES

The countries listed below have diplomatic representation in Cairo.

Australia (Map p44; ☎ 575 0444; 11th fl, World Trade Centre, 1191 Corniche el-Nil)
Canada (Map p44; ☎ 794 3110; 5 el-Saray el-Kubra Square, Garden City)
Ethiopia (☎ 335 3693; 6 Abdel Rahman Hussein St, El-Gomhuria Sq, Mohandiseen)
France (☎ 570 3916; 29 Sharia al-Giza, Giza)

Jordan (Map p44; ☎ 348 5566; 6 Al-Shaheed Basem al-Khatib, Doqqi)
Libya (Map p44; ☎ 735 1864; 7 Sharia as-Saleh Ayoub, Zamalek)
Sudan (Map p44; ☎ 794 5043; 3 Sharia Ibrahimi, Garden City)
UK (Map p44; ☎ 794 0850; 7 Sharia Ahmed Ragheb, Garden City)
USA (Map p48; ☎ 795 7371; 5 Sharia Latin America, Garden City)

In Africa Egypt has diplomatic representation in the following neighbouring or near-neighbouring countries: Libya, Morocco, Sudan and Tunisia.

GAY & LESBIAN TRAVELLERS

Although there is something of a gay scene in Egypt, and men in the Siwa Oasis, through a quirk in the culture, actually used to marry other men until the 1940s, it has been a bleak scene in recent years. On 11 May 2001 a raid on the Queen Boat (a disco/bar) in Cairo saw 52 men arrested and many dragged through the courts. Although foreigners are extremely unlikely to suffer the same harassment as Egyptian men, it's wise to be extremely discreet about how you conduct your affairs. There's a useful website at www.gayegypt.com.

Lesbianism doesn't feature in the Egyptian public consciousness – it's best for lesbians to remain discreet as well.

HOLIDAYS

As well as religious holidays listed in the Africa Directory chapter (p1003) the principal public holidays in Egypt are as follows:
New Year's Day 1 January
Sinai Liberation Day 25 April
Labour Day 1 May
Revolution Day 23 July
1973 War 6 October

The Coptic Christian community has an Easter holiday. but this is not the same as the Western date, as the Coptic calendar is used.

MEDIA

The *Egyptian Gazette* is the dreadful English-language daily, with a Saturday issue called the *Egyptian Mail*. It does have a great feature called 'Red Handed', about crimes of passion and jilted lovers. For more heavyweight news, the weekly *Cairo Times* (Thursday) is recommended and readable. You can get most Western press in Cairo, a day or so out of date.

MONEY
Exchanging Money
Most foreign hard currencies, cash or travellers cheques can be readily changed in Egypt, at commercial banks, American Express (Amex) and Thomas Cook offices, foreign exchange bureaus and also many hotels.

Visa and MasterCard are good for cash advances from many branches of Banque Masr and the National Bank of Egypt, as well as Thomas Cook.

ATMs have become commonplace in Cairo and are also available in major tourist towns such as Alexandria, Luxor, Aswan, Hurghada and Sharm el-Sheikh. Outside the big cities and tourist hubs, cash advances can be more problematic. Excess Egyptian pounds can be exchanged back into hard currency at some banks, foreign exchange bureaus and offices of Thomas Cook and American Express.

You can use Amex, Visa, MasterCard, JCB and Eurocard at many stores.

Tipping & Bargaining
Tipping in Egypt is called baksheesh. Wages in Egypt are much lower than in Western countries, so baksheesh is regarded as a means of supplementing income. Services such as opening a door or carrying your bags warrant 50pt (US$0.07) to E£1 (US$0.15). A guard who shows you something off the beaten track at an ancient site should receive about US$0.15. Baksheesh is not necessary when asking for directions.

In hotels and restaurants, a 12% service charge is included at the bottom of the bill, but the money goes into the till rather than into the pocket of the waiter or the woman who cleaned your room. If you want to tip someone, you'll have to do so directly.

Bargaining is part of everyday life in Egypt. Almost everything is open to haggling – from hotel rooms to the fruit juice you buy at a local stand. When buying souvenirs in markets, don't start bargaining until you have an idea of the true price, and never quote a price you're not prepared to pay.

POST & TELEPHONE
The Egyptian postal system is slow but eventually most mail gets to its destination. Receiving and sending packages through customs can cause tremendous headaches but there is generally little problem with letters and postcards. They can take anything from four to 10 days to get to Europe and from one to three weeks to the USA or Australia. Postcards and letters up to 10g cost US$0.15.

Cardphones are everywhere, and you can buy phonecards (US$0.75, US$1.50 and US$3) at grocery shops, post offices and telephone offices.

You can call direct anywhere in Egypt or abroad (dial 00 and the country code). Otherwise you'll have to book a call at the desk in a state telephone office, called a 'centrale', with a three-minute minimum. The cheap rate is from 8pm to 7.59am.

RESPONSIBLE TRAVEL
Since Roman times Egypt's monuments have suffered vandalism at the hands of visitors. To preserve these sights, please behave responsibly: don't use your camera flash to illuminate paintings and don't touch them either. Do refrain from clambering over toppled masonry. Likewise, take particular care in fragile environments, such as Ras Mohammed. When exploring underwater, avoid touching anything and leave nothing behind. Don't add to Egypt's garbage problem.

At many sights, it can be annoying having guides tag along and give explanations in broken English, but remember that their pay is pathetic and they're expected to supplement their income with tips.

TOURIST INFORMATION
There are tourist offices throughout the country, and they all give out free maps and brochures (some of the latter might be out of date). How helpful the office is depends entirely on its staff – those in Aswan, Siwa, Luxor and Alexandria are particularly knowledgeable and will go out of their way to help you.

VISAS
All foreigners entering Egypt, except nationals of Malta, South Africa, Zimbabwe and Arab countries, must have a visa.

Visas can be obtained in most neighbouring countries with little fuss, and cost about US$15.

For the same price, you can get a visa on arrival in Egypt by air or sea but not by land. At Cairo airport the process is simple, depending on your passport – buy a stamp (US dollars only) from any of the bank booths just before immigration and then get it validated at passport control.

The single-entry visa is valid for presentation for three months and entitles the holder to stay in Egypt for one month. Multiple-entry visas (for three visits) are also available.

While you can't get an Egyptian visa at the border with Israel, if you're coming from Israel it is possible to visit the area of Sinai between Taba (on the Israeli border) and Sharm el-Sheikh, including St Katherine's Monastery, without a full visa. On arrival, you are issued with an entry stamp, free of charge, allowing you up to 14 days in the area.

You can get a visa on the boat from Jordan or on arrival in Nuweiba, but this can be a hassle; your best bet though is to get it from the Egyptian consulate in Aqaba or the embassy in Amman.

Visa Extensions & Re-Entry Visas

Extensions of your visa beyond the first month can be obtained for up to 12 months and cost US$1.50. You need one photograph, photocopies of your passport and a modicum of patience.

If you do not have a multiple-entry visa, it is also possible to get a re-entry visa, valid to the expiry date of your visa and any extensions. A single/multiple re-entry visa costs US$1.50/3. These are available at most passport offices, including the **Cairo passport office** (Map p48; 1st fl, Mogamma, Midan Tahrir, Cairo; ☺ 8am-2pm Sat-Thu) in the great white building on Midan Tahrir. You can also try the **Alexandria passport office** (28 Sharia Talaat Harb, Alexandria).

Note that there is a two-week grace period beyond the expiry date of your visa.

Visas for Onward Travel

Contact details for the embassies of neighbouring countries are provided in the Embassies & Consulates section (see p77 for address details).

Eritrea Visas cost US$30 and are usually issued the same day.

Ethiopia Applicants should bring two photos and a return air ticket. One-month visas cost US$69, and should be issued within 24 hours.

Jordan Visas cost from nothing for Australians to US$20 for UK and US citizens, and are usually issued the same day. You need one photo.

Libya Don't rely on getting a visa for Libya in Cairo; it's a torturous and usually unsuccessful process.

Sudan Visas take from 24 hours to a month to issue and cost US$85 for one month; you need a letter of invitation and three photos.

WOMEN TRAVELLERS

A book could be written about women travellers and their misadventures in Egypt. At the least, groping or making lewd suggestions seem to be considered by some Egyptian men as perfectly natural means of communication with an unknown foreign woman. This is because, in Egypt, sex outside marriage is taboo, so foreign women are seen as outside the strictures of Egyptian society, with tantalisingly loose morals when compared with Egyptian women. Men take the view that it's always worth a try, or just that they are compelled to harass you out of the kind of machismo that in Western countries is most commonly found on building sites. By dressing modestly and covering your hair, you may reduce such attentions, but not necessarily. Wearing a wedding ring, carrying pictures of your numerous children, ignoring obnoxious comments and avoiding eye contact are all good tips. Don't sit in the front of cabs and try to get a seat next to a woman on buses. Useful phrases in Arabic include la tilmasni (don't touch me) and harem alek (shame on you). Try not to let your desire to battle harassment lead you to knock back what can be genuine friendliness – you'll soon realise instinctively who's a pest and who's not.

Sudan

HIGHLIGHTS

- **Meroe** Sudan's best-preserved pyramids, in a stunning desert location (p89)
- **Port Sudan** Red Sea diving, quality dining and the enchanting abandoned port of Suakin (p90)
- **Dongola** Busy, friendly little town on the Nile, perfect for a relaxed stopover (p90)
- **Omdurman** Khartoum's most traditional suburb and home to the largest souq in the country (p86)
- **Off the beaten track** If it's safe, do some walking in the hills around the charming town of Kassala (p89)

FAST FACTS

- **Area** 2,505,820 sq km
- **ATMs** none
- **Borders** Egypt, Ethiopia, Chad (recent problems) open; crossing land borders to CAR, Congo (Zaïre), Kenya, Libya, Uganda not recommended; Eritrea border closed
- **Budget** US$15 to US$20 a day
- **Capital** Khartoum
- **Languages** Arabic, English
- **Money** Sudanese dinar; US$1 = SDD260
- **Population** 37 million
- **Seasons** north: wet (Jul–Sep), dry (Oct–Jun); south: wet (Apr–Nov), dry (Dec–Mar)
- **Telephone** country code ☎ 249; international access code ☎ 00
- **Time** GMT/UTC + 3
- **Visas** US$35 to US$80 for 30 days; best obtained in advance

WARNING

There is an ongoing war in the south and east of the country, and the area bordering Eritrea is also considered unsafe. Check the situation before travelling to these parts of the country.

Sudan is the largest, yet least visited, country in Africa. Although civil war has caused great devastation to the south of the country since 1956, and travel restrictions are still in force, travellers who take the opportunity to visit some of this vast nation invariably agree that despite the political problems, the Sudanese people themselves are among the friendliest in Africa, with a natural generosity that entirely belies their poverty and makes any trip worthwhile. If you can stay aware of the dangers and keep an open mind, visiting Sudan is an eye-opening and hugely fulfilling experience.

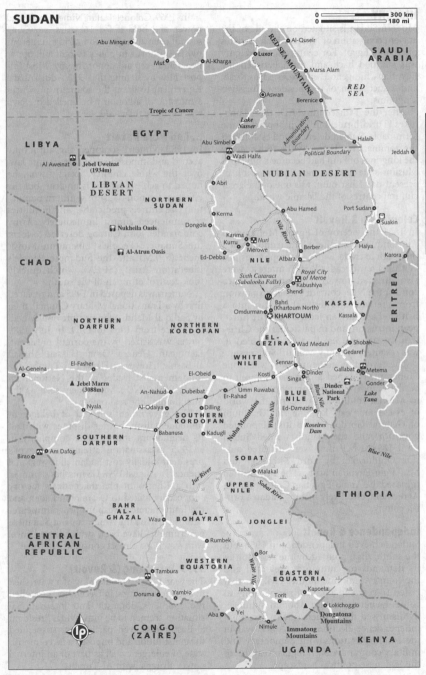

SUDAN

SUDAN

HISTORY

Modern Sudan is situated on the site of the ancient civilisation of Nubia, which predates pharaonic Egypt. For centuries, sovereignty was shuttled back and forth between the Egyptians, indigenous empires such as Kush, and a succession of independent Christian kingdoms.

After the 14th century AD, the Mame-lukes (Turkish rulers in Egypt) breached the formidable Nubian defences and established the dominance of Islam. By the 16th century the kingdom of Funj had become a powerful Muslim state and Sennar, 200km south of present-day Khartoum, was one of the great cultural centres of the Islamic world.

Colonialism & Revolt

In 1821 the viceroy of Egypt, Mohammed Ali, conquered northern Sudan and opened the south to trade, with catastrophic results. Within a few decades British interests were also directed towards Sudan, aiming to control the Nile, contain French expansion from the west and draw the south into a British–East African federation. The Euro-pean intrusion, and in particular the Chris-tian missionary zeal that accompanied it, was resented by many Muslim Sudanese.

The revolution came in 1881, when one Mohammed Ahmed proclaimed himself to be the Mahdi – the person who, according to Muslim tradition, would rid the world of evil. Four years later he rid Khartoum of General Gordon, the British-appointed governor, and the Mahdists ruled Sudan until 1898, when they were defeated out-side Omdurman by Lord Kitchener and his Anglo-Egyptian army. The British then imposed the Anglo-Egyptian Condominium Agreement, effectively making Sudan a Brit-ish colony.

Independence & Revolt

Sudan achieved independence in 1956, but the south, disappointed by the rejection of its demands for autonomy, revolted and the country sank into a bitter civil war that lasted 16 years. In a forerunner of things to come, General Ibrahim Abboud summar-ily dismissed the winners of the first post-independence elections. Ever since, war in the south, flirtations with democracy and military coups have been regular features of the Sudanese political landscape.

In 1969 Colonel Jaafar Nimeiri assumed power and held it for 16 years, surviving several coup attempts and making numerous twists and turns in policy to outflank oppo-nents and keep aid donors happy. Most im-portantly, by signing the 1972 Addis Ababa Agreement to grant the southern provinces a measure of autonomy he quelled the civil war for more than a decade.

... And More Revolt

In 1983 Nimeiri scrapped the autonomy accord and imposed *sharia*, or Islamic law, over the whole country. Exactly what he hoped to achieve by this is unclear, but the effect on the non-Muslim southern popula-tion was entirely predictable, and hostilities recommenced almost immediately. Army commander John Garang deserted to form the Sudanese People's Liberation Move-ment (SPLM) and the Sudanese People's Liberation Army (SPLA), which quickly took control of much of the south.

Nimeiri was deposed in 1985 and replaced first by a Transitional Military Council, then by Sadiq al-Mahdi, who had previously held the office from 1965 to 1969. In July 1989 power was seized by the current president, Lieutenant General Omar Hassan Ahmad al-Bashir. However, Hassan al-Turabi, the fundamentalist leader of the National Is-lamic Front (NIF), was widely seen as the man holding the real power.

The government's brand of belligerent fundamentalism, border disputes with half its neighbours and possible complicity in a 1995 assassination attempt on Egypt's president initially cost Sudan all its regional friends. In August 1998 US missiles slammed into a Khartoum pharmaceuticals factory supposedly linked to Osama bin Laden and the Iraqi chemical weapons programme; re-lations between the American and Sudanese governments have been strained ever since, with sanctions almost constantly in force.

1999: Infighting (& Revolt)

The year 1999 was something of a watershed in Sudanese politics: in December, just when the country's domestic and international situation seemed to be improving, President al-Bashir dissolved parliament, suspended the constitution and imposed a three-month state of emergency, all as part of an internal power struggle with Al-Turabi.

The subsequent elections in December 2000 were boycotted by opposition parties, giving al-Bashir an easy win, and in 2001 Al-Turabi and several members of his party were arrested after signing an agreement with the SPLA. In the meantime, countless rounds of southern peace talks in Kenya had failed, the government was accused of forcibly depopulating potential oilfields, and the death toll from the fighting and the resulting humanitarian disaster reached almost two million.

21st Century

Since the end of 2001 Sudan's general situation seems to have improved. Some surprisingly sound government policies have stabilised the economy, several ceasefire agreements have been signed in the south and demarcation discussions on the various troublesome borders are continuing. In July 2002 John Garang and President al-Bashir met for the first time to sign a memorandum of understanding in Nairobi, agreeing to a renewable cessation of hostilities and proposing a referendum on independence for the south in 2008. The ceasefire was re-extended after further talks in 2003, although sporadic fighting continues.

Anti-American sentiments were very much in evidence in Sudan at the start of the Iraq war in 2003: Khartoum's student population hit the streets in force for several days, and tensions worsened when a student was killed in one of the frequent clashes with the police.

THE CULTURE

Some 75% of Sudan's population, including around two million nomads, live in rural areas, and agriculture still employs 80% of the workforce. There are more than 550 ethnic groups; approximately 70% of the total populace is Muslim, although the south is dominated by traditional animists (25%) and Christians (around 5%). Despite their differences, hospitality is a key concept for all Sudanese, and wherever you go you'll constantly find people paying for things for you, sharing meals or even inviting you to stay in their homes!

More than a hundred languages are spoken in Sudan. Arabic is the official language, the mother tongue of about half the population (mainly in the north and centre of the country) and the common language almost everywhere. Regional languages tend to dominate in the south and the western provinces so, although English is widely spoken, it is by no means universal.

As Islamic law is strictly enforced, you won't find alcoholic drinks on sale anywhere in northern Sudan. The favoured alternative is the *chicha* or *narguila* – large water pipes used to smoke flavoured tobacco. Discreet *chicha* joints can be found in most towns.

ENVIRONMENT

Northern and western Sudan are vast, desolate areas of desert that support little life, and Nubia in the northeast is semidesert. In summer (March to July is the hottest period) there are frequent dust storms. In the south, the desert gradually gives way to savanna and rainforest on the borders with Uganda and Congo (Zaïre).

Sudan's climate ranges from hot and dry in the north to humid and tropical in the equatorial south. Any rain in the north (rarely more than 150mm per year) normally falls between July and September. In the south, annual rainfall can exceed 1000mm and usually occurs between April and November. Northern temperatures are generally high, climbing to more than 40°C in Khartoum in summer.

TRANSPORT

GETTING THERE & AWAY
Air

Sudan Airways (☎ 011-787249/780928; ☻ 8am-7pm Sun-Thu, 8.30am-noon Fri) connects Khartoum with destinations throughout Africa. There are also services from Port Sudan and Dongola to Egypt and Saudi Arabia.

Of the international airlines, **EgyptAir** (☎ 011-780064; ☻ 9am-3pm Sun-Thu, 9am-12.30pm Fri) serves Cairo, **Kenya Airways** (☎ 011-781080; www.kenya-airways.com; ☻ 9am-3pm Sun-Thu, 9am-12.30pm Fri) flies to Nairobi and **Ethiopian Airlines** (☎ 011-781884; ☻ 9am-3pm Sun-Thu, 9am-12.30pm Fri) fly to Addis Ababa.

Lufthansa (☎ 011-771322; lufthansa@sudanmail.net; ☻ 8.30am-2.30pm daily) flies frequently to Europe and the USA via Frankfurt (eg NYC); **Gulf Air** (☎ 011-775334; www.gulfairco.com) and **Emirates** (☎ 011-799473; www.emirates.com)

DEPARTURE TAX

The airport departure tax for international flights is the usual hefty US$20, payable in dollars.

connect with worldwide destinations via the Middle East.

Land

Sudan shares borders with many countries, but not all are open. Overland travel to the Central African Republic, Congo (Zaïre), Uganda and Kenya is very dangerous as it involves passing through the war zones of southern Sudan. The frontier with Eritrea is closed to travellers.

CHAD

The usual border crossing is between Al-Geneina and Abéché in Chad, but this route is frequently dangerous because of both bandits and tribal skirmishes, and you'll have more trouble getting a visa if you intend to use this route. At time of research the road from El-Fasher was closed; the more southerly route to Al-Geneina via Nyala is arguably safer, but check with your embassy before setting out. To reach El-Fasher or Nyala there's regular transport between Khartoum and El-Obeid (US$8.50, eight hours), after which you'll have to take whatever you can find to Nyala and then to the border. The El Obeid–Nyala trip will cost US$15 to US$23 (24+ hours). The Nyala–Al Geneina bus costs US$9.50 (12 hours); Al Geneina–Adré around US$3.75 (30 mins).

EGYPT

The roads between Sudan and Egypt seem to be open, but there is no bus or any public transport across the border. It's easier to go by the weekly ferry that leaves Sudan's inland port of Wadi Halfa and sails along Lake Nasser to the port near the Aswan Dam about 20km south of Aswan in Egypt. It departs Wadi Halfa on Wednesday, returning on Tuesday. The journey takes around 16 hours plus immigration time, and costs US$25/15 in 1st/2nd class. First-class passengers share two-bed cabins, whereas in 2nd class you fight for seats; prices might rise in 2004. You can buy tickets in **Wadi Halfa** (☎ 0251-22256) or in Khartoum, next to the train station.

There is also a monthly passenger ferry from Suakin to Suez (US$90, two days), via Jeddah.

ETHIOPIA

The road from Sudan to Ethiopia via the border-posts at Gallabat and Metema is officially open. There's little public transport, but some pick-ups do run between Gedaref and Gondor (five hours). Sporadic fighting along the border can make travel here dangerous.

SAUDI ARABIA

Regular ferry services run between Suakin and Jeddah (US$80, 13 hours). Tickets are available through the many travel agents in Port Sudan.

GETTING AROUND

Large areas of Sudan are currently closed to travellers. For details, see p91 and p93.

Air

Sudan Airways (☎ 011-787249/780928) flies to all of Sudan's major cities (Ed-Debba, Dongola, El-Fasher, Al-Geneina, Juba, Khartoum, Malakal, Merowe, Nyala, El-Obeid, Port Sudan, Wadi Halfa and Wau) but be prepared for last-minute schedule changes and overbooked flights. There's a domestic airport tax of US$4.

Local Transport

Sudan's major highway is the sealed road linking Khartoum with Port Sudan via Gedaref and Kassala. The routes from Khartoum to Atbara, Ed-Debbah and El-Obeid are also mostly sealed. Luxury buses run between Khartoum, Kassala and Port Sudan, and less comfortable buses run on the other sealed roads.

In the rest of the country, 'roads' are mostly desert tracks and the only public transport is very hardy 'buses' adapted from trucks. In some instances your only choice is a truck; in this case, all the passengers sit on top of the cargo and pay a fairly standard fare for the journey.

For shorter distances, and around towns, the transport of choice is Toyota pick-ups known as *boksi* (plural *bokasi*).

In many places the Souq esh-Shabi (People's Market) will serve as a pick-up/drop-off point for road transport. You should take note, however, that although the souq will be in the town centre in some places, in others it might be at the edge of town or even some 5km further out.

Fuel shortages can sometimes be a problem. Things are most likely to stop running if fuel is short, so you'll have fewer, even more crowded services.

Train

The state-run rail network, once one of the best in Africa, is sadly run-down as a result of war and lack of investment and maintenance. The only remaining passenger services are from Khartoum to Wadi Halfa and Port Sudan (via Atbara). There's also a branch line in the west from Er-Rahad to Nyala.

First-class seats are expensive but comfortable, with sleeper carriages on the Wadi Halfa run; 2nd class is bearable, and in 3rd class you really get what you paid for!

KHARTOUM

☎ 011 / pop 3 million

Built where the two Niles meet, Khartoum is one of the more modern cities in Central Africa, with paved roads, high-rise buildings and wide tree-lined boulevards. Its people are hospitable, the riverside setting is gorgeous, Internet access is dirt cheap and it's one of the safest cities in Africa for travellers – so for one reason or another most people end up liking it here.

ORIENTATION

Situated at the confluence of the White and Blue Niles, the capital has three main parts: Khartoum, Bahri (Khartoum North) and Omdurman, each separated from one other by an arm of the river. The strict grid system makes the streets of central Khartoum easy to navigate.

The short ride by taxi from the airport to the centre should cost around US$2.50, depending on the time of day.

INFORMATION

For novels and textbooks in English, try the **New Bookshop** (Map p87; ☎ 777594; Sharia Zubeir Pasha).

Basic medical services are available at **Khartoum Teaching Hospital** (Map p87; ☎ 7779500;

Sharia al-Isbitalya). Some embassies can provide a list of private doctors and clinics.

The **Sudanese-French Bank HQ** (Map p87; Sharia al-Qasr) changes travellers cheques, but couldn't accept US dollar cheques at time of writing due to US embargoes on Sudan. Private exchange offices such as **Kalsan Forex** (Map p87; ☎ 795248; Sharia Zubeir Pasha) also do money transfers for a small fee (around 1%). There is a small black market around the souq al-Arabi, but rates are no better than at the banks.

The **post office** and **Sudatel phone office** (Map p87; Sharia al-Khalifa) are housed in the same building.

Cultural Centres

British Council (Map p87; ☎ 780817; elamien.saeed@sd.britishcouncil.org; 14 Abu Sinn St)
French Cultural Centre (Map p87; ☎ 772837; Sharia Ali Dinar)
German Kulturforum (Map p87; ☎ 777833; Sharia al-Muk Nimir)

Internet Access

Hama Net (Map p87; ☎ 781496; 17th St; US$0.75 per hour)
Khartoum Internet Club (Map p87; off Sharia al-Qasr; US$1.15 per hour)
Meridien Internet (Map p87; ☎ 775970; Meridien Hotel, Sharia as-Sayed Abdul Rahman; 🕐 until midnight; US$2 per hour) The only place in town that doesn't close on Friday.
Net Café (Map p87; Sharia al-Gama'a; US$1.15 per hour) Part of the main post office complex.
University of Khartoum (Map p87; Sharia Osman Digna) Free Internet access between 8.30 and 9.30am.

SIGHTS

The **National Museum** (Map p86; Sharia el-Nil; admission US$0.20; 🕐 8.30am-6.30pm, closed noon-3pm Fri & Mon) is dwarfed by the modern buildings next to it but has some fine exhibits in its dusty halls, notably the pharaonic stone carvings and the stunning Christian frescoes.

The **Ethnographical Museum** (Map p87; Sharia al-Gama'a) was closed for renovations at time of research, but should definitely be worth a visit when it reopens.

The confluence of the **Blue** and **White Niles**, best seen from the White Nile Bridge, is a languid high point of the world's longest river. For an original perspective, try the fast-moving Ferris wheel in the **Al-Mogran Family Park** (Map p86; Sharia el-Nil; admission US$0.30). You can actually see the different colours of

SUDAN

SUDAN

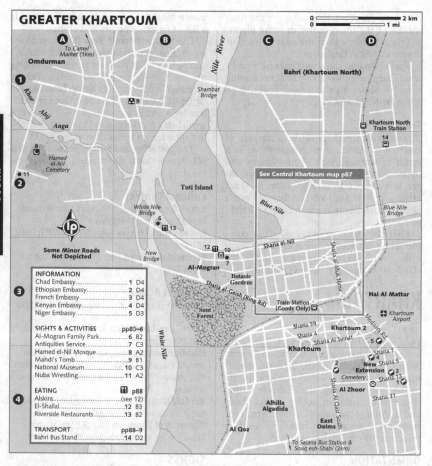

GREATER KHARTOUM

INFORMATION	
Chad Embassy	1 D4
Ethiopian Embassy	2 D4
French Embassy	3 D4
Kenyan Embassy	4 D4
Niger Embassy	5 D3

SIGHTS & ACTIVITIES	pp85–6
Al-Mogran Family Park	6 B2
Antiquities Service	7 C3
Hamed el-Nil Mosque	8 A2
Mahdi's Tomb	9 B1
National Museum	10 C3
Nuba Wrestling	11 A2

EATING	p88
Alskira	(see 12)
El-Shallal	12 B3
Riverside Restaurants	13 B2

TRANSPORT	pp88–9
Bahri Bus Stand	14 D2

the rivers from the bridge – and the waters of each Nile flow side by side before blending further downstream.

The traditional Muslim suburb of **Omdurman**, founded by the Mahdi in the 1880s, is a big attraction; the famous **souq** (Map p86) – the largest in the country – has an amazing variety of wares, and the **camel market** (Map p86) is equally spectacular.

Every Friday afternoon you can see the **Halgt Zikr**, where the local troupe of whirling dervishes stir up the dust in celebration of Allah at the **Hamed el-Nil Mosque** (Map p86). Across the road, traditional **Nuba wrestlers** (Map p86; US$0.20) go through their paces for the last two hours before sunset. They're both very friendly occasions, but you'll need

to take a taxi, as the mosque is not easy to find.

Mahdi's Tomb (Map p86), housed in a striking postwar onion-domed building, is also worth making the effort to see, although foreigners aren't allowed inside; the original was destroyed on Kitchener's orders by General Gordon's nephew 'Monkey', who, somewhat unsportingly, threw the Mahdi's ashes into the Nile!

SLEEPING

There are plenty of budget hotels in central Khartoum. All are very basic and start around US$3 a bed; for the cheapest places you'll need to read or speak a little Arabic.

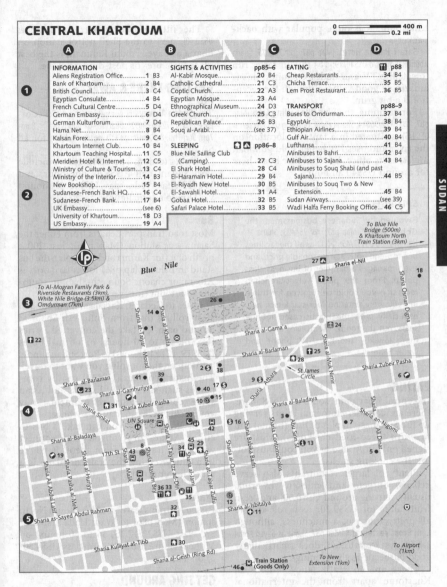

CENTRAL KHARTOUM

INFORMATION
Aliens Registration Office..........1 B3
Bank of Khartoum....................2 B4
British Council.......................3 C4
Egyptian Consulate..................4 B4
French Cultural Centre..............5 D4
German Embassy.....................6 D4
German Kulturforum.................7 D4
Hama Net............................8 B4
Kalsan Forex........................9 C4
Khartoum Internet Club..........10 B4
Khartoum Teaching Hospital....11 C5
Meridien Hotel & Internet.......12 C5
Ministry of Culture & Tourism..13 C4
Ministry of the Interior..........14 B3
New Bookshop.....................15 B4
Sudanese-French Bank HQ......16 C4
Sudanese-French Bank...........17 B4
UK Embassy.....................(see 6)
University of Khartoum...........18 D3
US Embassy.........................19 A4

SIGHTS & ACTIVITIES pp85–6
Al-Kabir Mosque...................20 B4
Catholic Cathedral.................21 C3
Coptic Church......................22 A3
Egyptian Mosque..................23 A4
Ethnographical Museum..........24 D3
Greek Church.......................25 C3
Republican Palace.................26 B3
Souq al-Arabi...................(see 37)

SLEEPING pp86–8
Blue Nile Sailing Club
  (Camping).......................27 C3
El Shark Hotel......................28 C4
El-Haramain Hotel.................29 B4
El-Riyadh New Hotel..............30 B4
El-Sawahli Hotel...................31 A4
Gobaa Hotel........................32 B5
Safari Palace Hotel................33 B5

EATING p88
Cheap Restaurants.................34 B4
Chicha Terrace.....................35 B5
Lem Prost Restaurant.............36 B5

TRANSPORT pp88–9
Buses to Omdurman...............37 B4
EgyptAir.............................38 B4
Ethiopian Airlines..................39 B4
Gulf Air..............................40 B4
Lufthansa...........................41 B4
Minibuses to Bahri.................42 B4
Minibuses to Sajana...............43 B4
Minibuses to Souq Shabi (and past
  Sajana)............................44 B5
Minibuses to Souq Two & New
  Extension.........................45 B4
Sudan Airways..................(see 39)
Wadi Halfa Ferry Booking Office...46 C5

El-Haramain (Map p87; US$3), south of the Al-Kabir mosque, and the **El-Riyadh New Hotel** (Map p87; US$4.50), located near the ring road, are both reasonable; there is also a cluster of Arabic-signed places on Sharia al-Isbitalya.

El-Sawahli Hotel (Map p87; ☎ 772544; Sharia Zubeir Pasha; tw US$12; ❄) Central, comfortable and friendly. The large rooms sport posters of lush alpine landscapes and have shared balconies overlooking the rather more prosaic streets outside.

El-Shark Hotel (Map p87; ☎ 797818; Sharia al-Gamhuriyya; s/tw US$8/9) This Greek-run place near the British Council offers just about the cheapest private rooms you'll get in

Khartoum. It is quite popular with back-packers.

Safari Palace Hotel (Map p87; ☎ 782075; Sharia Abdul Rahma; s/d US$10/19; 🕸) If your tastes run to satellite TV and dodgy en suites, this is amazingly good value, although the recep-tion's a bit grim.

For camping, the **Blue Nile Sailing Club** (Map p87; ☎ 0122-96014; Sharia el-Nil; camping US$3, bike/car US$2/5) is situated in a fantastic location on the river and uses Kitchener's old gunboat, *Melik*, as its office. You can hire boats here for around US$40 an hour.

SPLURGE!

Favoured by Sudanese businessmen, the **Gobaa Hotel** (Map p87; ☎ 784423; Sharia al-Isbitalya; s/d US$37/45; 🕸) has all the facilities of a top-end hotel at a reasonable price, and even manages a glimmer of business-class pomp. From the plush velvet-drenched reception you could be forgiven for think-ing you were entering four-star kitsch hell, especially with the plastic-cased lounge seats, but the rooms themselves are much more low-key and have TV, phone and water heater.

EATING

In central Khartoum, south of UN Square, there are countless informal joints serving up the Sudanese staples of *fuul* (beans) and *ta'amiya* (deep-fried chickpeas). Most are signed only in Arabic or you could just fol-low the cooking smells.

Plenty of larger restaurants also serve kebabs, burgers and chicken shwarma, usually starting around US$0.50, and fresh fruit juices for US$0.20. As a rule they're all pretty much of a muchness, although **Lem Prost restaurant** (Map p87; Sharia as-Sayed Abdul Rahman; shish kebabs US$0.95) does a particularly good barbecue in the evenings.

There are no really fancy options in Khartoum apart from the international hotels, but the series of riverside restau-rants between the museum and the White Nile Bridge are great places to while away an evening. The best are those close to the entrance of the Al-Mogran Family Park, **El-Shallal** (Map p86; mains around US$2-4) and **Alskira** (Map p86; mains from US$2) opposite the national museum.

The little *chicha* **terrace** (Map p87; pipes US$0.40), next to the Shell petrol station on Sharia as-Sayed Abdul Rahman, is the best place for a pre- or post-dinner smoke.

GETTING THERE & AWAY
Air

The **Sudan Airways** reservation and ticket of-fice (☎ 787249/780928; Sharia al-Gamhuriyya; ⏰ 8am-7pm Sun-Thu, 8.30am-noon Fri) sells tickets for all SA flights.

Flights to domestic destinations include Port Sudan (daily, US$70, one hour) and Wadi Halfa (Wednesday, US$80, 3½ hours) via Dongola (one hour).

Bus

Most road transport departs from either the Sajana bus station (Map p86), just 200m north of it (for Karima and Dongola), the bus stand in Bahri (Map p86) for as far north as Atbara, or chaotic Souq esh-Shabi in south-ern Khartoum (for everywhere else).

Buses to Gedaref, Kassala and Port Sudan start rolling out from Souq esh-Shabi at around 6am. To take the converted lorries (US$14, up to 20 hours) or normal buses (US$19, 12 to 14 hours) to Port Sudan simply turn up on the morning you want to travel. The luxury coaches (US$30) run by com-panies such as El SafSaf Express and Aslan serve complimentary refreshments; buy your ticket at least a day in advance.

For Wadi Halfa, you can take a bus to either Atbara or Dongola and connect with local transport from there. If you're in a hurry, taking the train or plane is a much better option.

Train

Passenger trains leave from Khartoum North station (Map p86) to Wadi Halfa (1st/2nd/3rd class US$22/17/15, 36 to 50 hours) on Monday and Atbara (1st/3rd class US$4.50/3) on Tuesday.

GETTING AROUND

Buses, minibuses and shared taxis cover most points in Khartoum. Minibuses to Omdurman and Bahri fill quickly and leave from Souq el-Arabi (US$0.10).

Taxi prices are negotiable; expect to pay around US$1 for journeys within the centre and US$2 to US$2.50 to the suburbs or Souq esh-Shabi. For shorter trips there are also

Thai-style motorised rickshaws, particularly in Omdurman. It should be no more than US$1 for a rickshaw journey; the main advantage is that they're a bit nippier than taxis and can get around unpaved streets and alleys easier (especially useful in Omdurman).

AROUND KHARTOUM

MEROE

The ancient **royal cemetery** of Meroe (not to be confused with Merowe, which lies to the northwest) is one of Sudan's most spectacular sights. The Meroitic pharaohs thrived from 592 BC until overrun by the Abyssinians in AD 350. Although nothing here compares with better-known sites in Egypt, the cluster of narrow **pyramids** in their dramatic sand-swept location is well worth a visit; sunset over the distant hills, also scattered with ruins, is quite a sight. Some well-preserved hieroglyphics are can still be seen in the tombs' antechambers, and even the graffiti here dates back centuries!

You can also visit the remains of the **Royal City** itself, although there's not a lot to see and no explanations of the ruins are provided.

Visitor permits (US$10) must be obtained from the Antiquities Service in Khartoum (Map p86), on the 2nd floor of the administration building next to the museum; a separate permit is usually required for each site. These are checked, but if you're arriving from the north and don't fancy a six-hour round-trip to Khartoum, you might be able to sort something out with the gatekeeper.

Meroe can be visited as a day trip from Khartoum, although you'll probably get there in the hottest part of the day. If you want to catch the sunset you can sleep in the desert near the pyramids (bring a sleeping bag, water and food), or you might be able to find basic accommodation in **Shendi**.

To get there, take a minibus toward Atbara from the bus station in Bahri (Khartoum North; Map p86) and ask to be let out at Al-Ahram (Pyramids). Prices are negotiable but should be about US$2.70 (three hours direct). From the road, it's a 700m walk across the sand. Coming back, flag down vehicles heading south; you might have to change in Shendi. The nearest train station is Kabushiya, 5km away through the desert.

EASTERN SUDAN

KASSALA
☎ 41 / pop 335,000
At first glance Kassala is little more than a patch of greenery in the shadow of the nearby hills, looming out of the desert 5km east of the road to Port Sudan. In more peaceful times the colourful **souq** was the town's main attraction; today, however, the region is better known for the estimated 500,000 refugees from the civil war and conflicts in Eritrea and Ethiopia housed in camps around Kassala itself.

The town is still a charming place to visit and there is some great walking in the Kassala Hills, but getting past the police checkpoint on the way into the town is becoming more difficult. You should ask about obtaining an official permit in Khartoum if you want to spend any time here.

If you do get to stay, **Toteel Hotel** (dm US$2.50-4; ☒) is a good option. Nearby, **Safa Hotel** (tw US$12-17; ☒) has a good range of rooms, with the best boasting satellite TV, fridge and mountain view.

Minibuses (US$0.10) and some of the shabbiest taxis in the world shuttle from town to Souq esh-Shabi (about 2km), where the buses/coaches to Port Sudan (US$9/11, eight hours) and Khartoum depart from.

PORT SUDAN
☎ 0311 / pop 450,000
Sudan's only major industrial port, this sprawling but surprisingly laid-back city is an excellent base for some of the Red Sea's best diving. The **dive centre** (☎ 39800; RM_Port-Sudan@Hilton.com; snorkelling/diving US$30/60) at the new Hilton Hotel is the best place to go, and will accept Visa cards.

The Bank of Khartoum off Sharia Suakin is the best bank to change money. The Hilton on Sharia Kabhashi Eissa will also change cash at bank rates.

There are several Internet cafés around town, with prices starting at US$1.15 a minute. **Salah Computer Centre** (US$1.50 per minute), next to the Al Maysara Hotel, is the most reliable.

Sleeping & Eating
Zahran Hotel (☎ 22397; s/d US$6/10) This friendly place is probably the best-value hotel in

town, certainly by Khartoum standards. The big en suite rooms often don't have water, but they're clean and generally quiet.

There are plenty of smaller hotels and *lokandas* (basic type of accommodation) around the market, offering beds from around US$2 with facilities ranging from basic to bomb site. The distinctly un-Welsh **Cardiff Hotel** (r US$2.60) is a reasonable option.

The area around the local bus station on Sharia No 2 is teeming with brightly lit cheap restaurants and juice bars, giving it a fairground atmosphere at night. For a bit of a treat, try the restaurants along the waterfront, which do a good range of meat and fish dishes and a few Western standards for around US$2.50.

Getting There & Away

Minibuses (US$0.95, one hour), shared taxis and pick-ups (US$1.50) for Suakin leave from near Sharia No 2 (a short distance south). The major bus companies serving Kassala (US$15), Khartoum and Atbara (US$12, 12 to 14 hours) have offices at Souq esh-Shabi and in the centre of town. There is also a train to Atbara every two weeks (1.30pm Thursday; 1st/3rd class US$12/8).

SUAKIN

☎ 31 / pop 32,500

Set against the picturesque backdrop of the Red Sea Hills, Suakin was Sudan's only port before the construction of Port Sudan, handling the thousands of pilgrims bound for Mecca. Abandoned in the 1930s, it became an intriguing ghost town, full of decaying **coral houses** and crumbling facades. The **ruins** (admission US$3.80, camera US$0.40), connected to the mainland by a short causeway, are fascinating to explore, and the 'modern' town also has a delightfully sleepy feel to it.

Suakin is best visited as a day trip from Port Sudan.

NORTHERN SUDAN

ATBARA

☎ 0211 / pop 105,500

Atbara was the scene of the first battle between Kitchener's advancing troops and the Mahdists, but you'd have trouble finding any modern Britons who would fight over it. These days the town is basically a

transport hub and a place to change trains for those heading to or from the north.

The best hotel in town is the **Nile Hotel** (☎ 22111; r US$8; 🏵), which has smart, clean rooms, decent food and (amazingly!) hot water in the shared showers. There are some cheaper lodges nearer the centre, but these seem decidedly reluctant to take foreigners.

The weekly trains to Wadi Halfa (1st/3rd class US$14/8) and Khartoum (1st/3rd class US$5/3) pass through here. Buses, minibuses and pick-ups also serve a wide variety of destinations, leaving from the many different stands around town. The weekly buses to Wadi Halfa cost US$19 (35 hours), while a pick-up to Karima is US$10 (12 to 14 hours, including two river crossings).

KARIMA

The town of Karima itself has little to appeal to visitors, but there are some interesting ancient sites in the area: **Jebel Barkal**, 2km south, was sacred ground for the Egyptians at the time of the 18th dynasty pharaohs, and has some well-preserved **pyramids** and a **temple complex** nearby. There are also some dilapidated pyramids across the river at Merowe and Nora.

The El-Shamalia Hotel is horribly basic (no mattresses!) but seems to be the only option in town – ask around.

There are frequent buses (at least one bus and several pick-ups daily) and *bokasi* between Karima and Dongola (US$6/8, four to eight hours).

DONGOLA

☎ 0241 / pop 18,400

Famous for its palm groves, this relaxed little town is the capital of the Northern Province; it's full of character, with plenty of friendly locals and a lovely setting on the Nile. It also boasts surprisingly good amenities, including decent Internet access. The ruins of the **Temple of Kawa**, which you reach by taking the ferry across the river, then a pick-up, are on the river's eastern bank.

Most hotels are clustered together on the main road, near the market; they might be reluctant to allow women in and often insist on police registration. **Lord Hotel & Restaurant** (☎ 23642; tr with shower US$2) is a quirky place;

a bed here comes at the same price as a standard dorm in **Haifa Hotel** (☎ 22573). **Al-Shamal Palace** (☎ 23782; shared/private toilet US$5/6) is a step up, although the rooms are a bit gloomy.

It's possible to get to Wadi Halfa from Dongola with local transport; it's a great stretch of country, with rocky hills and countless tiny villages along the Nile. You'll have to do the trip in stages, however, which can take several days, so if you're in a hurry, the quickest way is to catch the regular buses from Kerma (Sunday) or Abri (Monday and Thursday).

Buses and *bokasi* to Karima cost about US$6/8 (four to eight hours).

WADI HALFA
☎ 0251
Wadi Halfa is the nondescript transit point where the Lake Nasser steamer meets the train, plane and automobiles arriving from Khartoum.

Beds are hard to get on both the days that the ferry is in town. The small hotels near the border all charge around US$2.65 for basic dorms.

Ferry tickets can be bought from the office by the dock.

SUDAN DIRECTORY

ACCOMMODATION
Prices have risen sharply over the past few years, particularly in Khartoum – gone are the days when you could get an en suite room with satellite TV for less than US$2.

The most basic places to stay are called *lokandas*, with beds in shared rooms or courtyards, charging US$2 to US$5 per person. In simple hotels, rooms with shared bathrooms start around US$4.50, and the cheapest rooms with a private bathroom are around US$6.

In the hottest months power cuts can be long and frequent, so think twice before investing in rooms with air-con that might not do the job.

Surprisingly, some of the cheaper hotels aren't that keen on taking in foreigners, and you might be asked to register with the police before checking in – whatever time of night you arrive!

BUSINESS HOURS
Banking and office hours are 8am to 2pm; most local shops stay open late, but might close between 1pm and 5pm. Everything closes on Friday for the Muslim weekend.

Breakfast, which most people take between 9am and 10am, is a Sudanese institution – don't be surprised if that vital functionary isn't at his desk.

DANGERS & ANNOYANCES
At the time of writing, travellers' wings were severely clipped. You won't get a travel permit for anywhere south of Kosti. The provinces of Upper Nile, Blue Nile, Bahr al-Ghazal and Equatoria are all war zones, and there's sporadic fighting in Dafur. The Southern Dafur to Nyala–Al-Geneina road is generally considered safe(ish), however, Southern Kordofan (particularly the Nuba Mountains) and along Sudan's frontiers with both Eritrea and Ethiopia.

It should also be remembered that public feeling in Sudan was very much against the 2003 war in Iraq, which fuelled already considerable resentment at US foreign policy. These sentiments are very rarely directed at travellers, but American and British citizens in particular might want to keep a low profile and check Middle East developments frequently. For the latest information, check with your embassy or consulate.

EMBASSIES & CONSULATES
Sudan has diplomatic representation for several countries:
Canada (☎ 790320; Sharia 10)
CAR (Sharia 35, New Extension)
Chad (Map p86; ☎ 471084; Sharia 17, New Extension)
Congo (Zaïre) (☎ 471125; Sharia 13, New Extension)
Egypt (Map p87; ☎ 772190; Sharia al-Gamhuriyya)
Eritrea (☎ 483834; 26 Sharia 39, Khartoum 2)
Ethiopia (Map p86; ☎ 471156; Sharia 1, Khartoum 2; eekrt@hotmail.com)
France (Map p87; ☎ 471082; Sharia 13, New Extension)
Germany (Map p86; ☎ 777995; Sharia al-Baladaya)
Libya (☎ 222547; Block 18, Riyadh; PO Box 1526)
Kenya (Map p86; ☎ 460386; Sharia 1, New Extension)
Niger (Map p86; Sharia 1, New Extension)
Saudi Arabia (☎ 472583; Sharia 29, New Extension)
Uganda (☎ 797867; ugembkht@hotmail.com; Sharia Abuanja, Khartoum East)
UK (Map p87; ☎ 777105; consular.khartoum@fco.gov.uk; off Sharia al-Baladaya; ☎ 774611; Sharia Ali Abdul Latif) Currently no permanent staff.

SUDAN

FOOD & DRINK

Sudanese food isn't particularly varied – the staples are *fuul* (stewed brown beans) and *ta'amiya*, known elsewhere as falafel. Outside the larger towns you'll find very little else.

Meat dishes include *kibda* (liver), shish kebabs and *shwarma*, hunks of chicken or lamb sliced fresh from the classic roasting spit. Along the Nile you can find excellent fresh perch.

Tea is the favourite drink, served sweet as *shai saada* (black, sometimes spiced), *shai bi-laban* (with milk) or *shai bi-nana* (with mint). Also common is *qahwa turkiya* (Turkish coffee) and *jebbana*, served from distinctive clay pots and often spiked with cardamom, cinnamon or ginger. Local fresh fruit juices are excellent, although they're usually made with untreated water/ice.

GAY & LESBIAN TRAVELLERS

Homosexuality is illegal for both genders in Sudan, and the maximum penalty if convicted is death. Few travellers encounter problems, but exercising extra discretion is highly advisable.

HOLIDAYS

As well as religious holidays listed in the Africa Directory chapter (p1003), these are the principal public holidays in Sudan:
1 January Independence Day
30 June Revolution Day

INTERNET ACCESS

Internet cafés all over Khartoum offer fast connections for good prices. Reliable access is also available in Port Sudan and, increasingly, in smaller towns around Sudan.

MONEY

Sudanese money can be confusing when you first arrive. Although banknotes are in dinars (50, 100, 200, 500 and 1000), prices are quoted in the old Sudanese pounds (1 dinar = S£10). Assume that the real price is minus a zero. Just to confuse matters, some people drop the thousands, so '10 pounds' means S£10,000, ie SDD1000. If you're not sure, ask for the US dollar equivalent.

Sudan is awash with banks, but most are of little use to the traveller because they don't have exchange services. US dollars and euros are the easiest to change; outside Khartoum you'll only be able to change cash. At the mo-

ment you can't change US dollar travellers cheques anywhere because of sanctions.

PHOTOGRAPHY

Photo permits are obligatory for all foreigners. Get one from Khartoum's **Ministry of Culture & Tourism** (Map p87; Abu Sinn St). It's free but you need a passport photo. The permit expressly forbids sensitive sites, including bridges, plus 'slum areas, beggars and other defaming subjects'. Note that travellers have been arrested for taking photos of the confluence of the Blue and White Niles from the main bridge to Omdurman.

POST & TELEPHONE

Mail in and out of Sudan, like the poste restante services throughout the country, is unreliable.

International telephone calls are easy to make at post offices in Khartoum and Omdurman or private telephone offices anywhere, costing around US$1.50 a minute to Europe and Australia and US$2 a minute to the USA. You can also buy prepaid calling cards for phoneboxes (Europe US$1 per minute) or make Net2Phone Internet calls from a computer (US$0.40 per minute), although neither offer much privacy. For more info see www.net2phone.com.

VISAS & DOCUMENTS

Everyone needs a visa. The length of the application process depends largely on your nationality and in which country you apply – some visas are granted on the spot, others take up to two months with no guarantee of success.

If possible, try to get your visa before leaving home or allow yourself plenty of time once you arrive in Africa (but watch the expiry date!). Visas are usually valid for one month from the date of entry and costs range from US$35 to US$80.

Registration

You have to register within three days of arrival in Khartoum, Port Sudan or Wadi Halfa; you might also need to register in some provincial towns. In Khartoum, go to the **Aliens Registration Office** (Map p87; Sharia at-Taiyar Morad); the process costs US$19 and you need one photo and photocopies of your passport and Sudanese visa (there's a copier in the building).

Note that if you registered on entry at a land border, you do not need to pay the registration fee again in Khartoum.

Travel Permits

A travel permit is required for every journey outside Khartoum, although you can list as many towns en route as you want. Semi-official free permits are issued by the **Ministry of Culture & Tourism** (Map p87); you will need one photo. For the full version, go to the **Aliens Registration Office** (Map p87) with three photos and US$20; this might be necessary if you intend to visit Kassala.

It's a good idea to take a couple of photocopies of your permits to give to the police if they ask.

Visa Extensions

Visa extensions are issued at the **Aliens Registration Office** in Khartoum (Map p87). You need two photos and varying amounts of money and patience. The length of stay granted seems to be arbitrary.

Visas for Onward Travel

Visas for the following neighbouring countries are available from embassies in Khartoum (see p91 for address details).

Chad A one-month visa costs US$30 to US$60. You'll need two photos, a photocopy of your passport and Sudanese visa, and a letter of recommendation from your embassy. Visas are usually issued the same day.

Egypt The consulate here is not the most organised place – arrive early to beat the worst queues and be prepared for a long morning. Prices vary, and you'll need two photos plus a letter of recommendation. It's easier to pick up a tourist visa (US$15) on arrival, especially if you're flying.

Ethiopia One-month visas cost around US$60. Applications are received only on Sunday and Tuesday, and take 48 hours to process. You need three photos, a letter of recommendation, a health certificate, proof of sufficient funds and an onward air ticket, even if you intend travelling overland.

Kenya A single-entry visa valid for three months costs US$50 and is issued the same day. You need two photos and a photocopy of your passport; applications are received from 10am to noon on Mondays and Wednesdays.

Uganda Single/double-entry visas valid for up to three months cost US$30/60 (US$20/40 if you have student ID); 48-hour transit visas cost US$15.

VOLUNTEERING

The **Sudan Volunteer Programme** (SVP; ☎ 020-7485 8619; www.svp-uk.com; 34 Estelle Rd, London NW3 2JY, UK) is a charity that sends native English speakers to teach English in schools, colleges and universities in Sudan. Volunteers must pay for their own travel, but SVP will arrange subsistence, accommodation, health insurance and some on-site training.

Libya

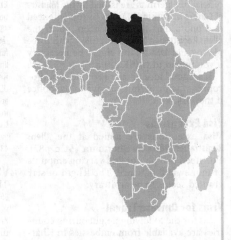

FAST FACTS

- **Area** 1,759,640 sq km
- **ATMs** in the capital, but unreliable
- **Borders** Tunisia (Ras Jedir) and Egypt (Al-Burdi) only are open to non-Libyans.
- **Budget** US$80 to US$100 a day
- **Capital** Tripoli
- **Languages** Arabic, some Italian, French and indigenous languages
- **Money** Libyan dinar; US$1 = LD1.43
- **Population** 5.5 million
- **Seasons** hot (Jun–Aug), wet (Mar & Oct), dry (at other times of the year)
- **Telephone** country code ☎ 218; international access code ☎ 00
- **Time** GMT/UTC + 1
- **Visas** US$30 to US$50 plus translation (and possibly courier) fees

WARNING

Because travel to Libya is restricted to organised tours, it remains difficult to do independent, on-the-ground research. Some parts of this chapter might be unreliable.

With one foot in Africa, another in the Arab world and a history of Italian occupation, Libya presents travellers with a somewhat beguiling façade. Although the West's image of the country remains dominated by the doctrine of Muammar Gaddafi and his larger-than-life schemes (the Great Man-Made River Project and the Organisation for African Unity are the latest), Gaddafi's revulsion for all things Western is mellowing, leaving tourism here with the potential to become big business.

Libya still suffers from the United Nations (UN) sanctions that, although lifted in May 1999, still prevent a wide range of goods (most importantly car parts and other machinery) from finding easy passage into the country. Still, the Libyan take on bush mechanics will certainly make your journey through the country all the more educational.

With a 2000km coastline, well-preserved classical ruins, prehistoric rock art and vast oceans of mesmerising desertscape, Libya offers travellers an extraordinary chance to visit a land that remains untainted by mass tourism and all that it entails.

When you finally discover the real Libya – somewhere between the tiny pages of Gaddafi's infamous *Green Book*, the palm-fringed Ubari oases, the salt-dusted ruins of Sabratha

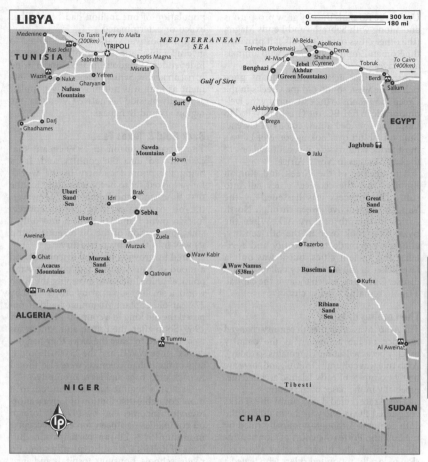

LIBYA

and Leptis Magna and the rooftop walkways of Ghadames – you will, no doubt with apple tobacco-laced pipe in hand, be besotted with what you have found.

HISTORY

As the ultimate destination of the major trans-Saharan caravan routes, and one of the key gateways from Europe to Africa, varied and violent experience has been Libya's lot throughout history. Ever since the Phoenicians set sail from Tyre, as long ago as 1000 BC, Libya's patchwork history has been one long saga of conquest and colonisation. Berbers, Jews, Greeks, Romans, Vandals and Byzantines all had their time here long before the Islamic *jihad* (holy war against infidels) swept down from Mecca and Medina in the Hejira of AD 622. In the

20th century alone, Libya has been subject to Turkey's Karamanli Pashas, the brutal Italian occupation of the 1920s and 1930s, WWII, independence, royal rule and, ultimately, Muammar Gaddafi's 1969 socialist revolution.

Way Back When

Tripoli was founded by the Phoenicians in about 500 BC, and was one of many settlements they established along the African coast. After the fall of Carthage in 146 BC, Tripoli became a Roman protectorate and later a part of the province of Africa Nova.

Under the Romans the city grew prosperous and, along with Sabratha and Leptis Magna (the other cities of the 'tripolis'), it provided the Roman Empire with grain, wild animals and slaves.

As the Phoenicians and Romans grew rich in the west, so too did the Greeks in the Green Mountains to the east. Sent by the Delphic oracle in 631 BC, the Greeks travelled to Libya and founded a new colony at Cyrene. Built on a bluff overlooking some of Libya's most fertile countryside, it constituted one of the largest cities in North Africa.

The decline of the Greek and Roman Empires saw the classical cities fall into ruin. This process was hastened by the Vandals' destructive sweep through North Africa in the 5th century AD. When the Byzantines took over in the 6th century, efforts were made to re-fortify and revitalise the ancient cities, but it was only a last flicker of life before they collapsed into disuse. Only Oea, which today is the capital, Tripoli, remains a living city.

The Coming of Islam

The Arab invasion in the 7th century changed the face of Libya forever, as the country quickly became Islamic (it remains so today). Arab rule was culturally fruitful, and there are many examples of early Islamic architecture, especially in the oases of the south.

The Arabs ruled Libya until the Turks conquered the country in the middle of the 16th century. Although nominally ruled by the Sublime Porte (the court of Constantinople), Tripoli was in fact run by a succession of locally appointed rulers who levied a toll on every Christian fleet using the Mediterranean.

Following the Napoleonic Wars, the European powers began to colonise North Africa. The Turks hastened to strengthen their control of Libya, once more ruling it directly from Constantinople.

By the 20th century, Libya was the last North African possession of the Turks; in 1911 it was taken from them by the Italians in that country's last-minute bid for colonies in Africa. The Italian period was a devastating one for the Libyan people. The Italians viewed Libya as a 'fourth shore' of Italy and embarked upon a complete 'Italianisation' programme. Between 1911 and the end of WWII, half of the indigenous

population of one million had been either exiled or exterminated.

In the postwar years Italy was forced to give up Libya, and the country became an independent kingdom in 1951 under King Idris, an ageing Senussi leader. His appointment as king was not universally popular, especially outside his native Cyrenaica, the region around Benghazi.

Back Gold & Texas Tea

The discovery of oil in 1959 meant that cash flowed into the country and, from being the poorest country in the world, Libya looked set to become wealthy for the first time since the Roman era. However, the oil companies were almost entirely foreign owned and controlled, and only a small proportion of the oil revenue found its way into the Libyan treasury.

Fired by growing political discontent and a mood of Pan-Arabism (support for Arab political union) that was sweeping the Arab world, a small group of army officers, led by 27-year-old Captain Muammar Gaddafi, deposed the old king in a coup on 1 September 1969. Soon after, the British and Americans were ordered to leave the bases they had occupied since WWII, and the 25,000 descendants of the Italian colonists were also forced to pack their bags and leave promptly.

Gaddafi's regime was committed to a more equitable distribution of Libya's enormous oil income, and by 1973 all foreign oil companies had been forced to accept a minimum 51% Libyan participation. Billions of dollars were subsequently spent on roads, schools, housing, hospitals and agriculture. Oil money also funded the US$27 billion Great Man-Made River Project that pumps water from ancient aquifers deep in the desert to the coastal areas. The water is intended to make Libya self-sufficient in food production.

It Ain't Easy Being Green

During the mid-1970s Gaddafi wrote the *Green Book*, which he claims is a radical alternative to capitalism and communism. Launching his revolution, he declared Libya to be a *jamahiriya* (which loosely translates as 'state of the masses') and set about dismantling the state apparatus and replacing it with People's Committees. In practice Libya's government is a military dictatorship.

Throughout the 1970s and 1980s Libya adopted a high international profile based on Pan-Arabism, its virulent condemnation of 'Western imperialism', its support of liberation movements around the world and its backing of military adventurism in neighbouring African countries.

What angered Western countries most was Gaddafi's support of real and so-called liberation movements, and particularly his alleged support of international terrorist organisations. This support only served to isolate Libya further from the international community. The most violent reaction came from the USA, culminating in the air strike of April 1986, which killed dozens of people including Gaddafi's adopted baby daughter.

The most serious crisis to hit Libya came following the 1988 bombing of the USA's Pan Am airliner over Lockerbie in Scotland in which 280 people were killed. Libya was accused of planting the bomb and two Libyans were named as suspects. Following Libya's denial of the charges and refusal to hand over the suspects for trial, the UN Security Council (under strong pressure from the USA) ordered an embargo on any flights in and out of the country and a ban on the sale of military equipment and related spare parts.

Libyan intelligence officer Abdelbaset Ali Mohmed al-Megrahi was convicted of the crime in a specially convened Scottish court in the Netherlands in 2001. Libyan airline official Lamin Khalifa Fhimah was acquitted in the same trial.

It wasn't until August 2003, however, that the finale of the Lockerbie tragedy was staged at UN headquarters in New York, when Britain tabled a Security Council resolution to lift 14-year sanctions against Libya. Libya accepted responsibility for the act, agreeing to pay $US2.7 billion ($A4 billion) into a fund for the victims' families.

Libya also agreed to pay Lockerbie-style compensation to the relatives of those killed in the 1989 bombing of a French airliner over Niger.

Since the lifting of sanctions, Gaddafi has been working hard to overturn Libya's 'terrorist state' image. He now styles himself as an African 'peacebroker', turning his back on his Arab neighbours to take a leading role in the aims of the Organisation for African Unity (OAU).

Right Here, Right Now

Libya is a country in transition, making the leap from a largely Bedouin society to a modern consumer society – a change that has so far resulted in an uneasy alliance of medievalism and technocracy. Although Tripoli sports sufficient bells, whistles and designer trimmings to make you feel not so far from home, outside the capital is a different case altogether.

The country's political future depends singularly on 'Brother' Gaddafi's efforts to appease Western governments. Gaddafi's recent public damning of terrorist groups and those associated with Osama bin Laden is a particularly politically savvy move, in the eyes of Western governments anyway. In the context of current difficulties in the Middle East, Libya presents travellers with an exceptionally safe and fascinating land to explore.

THE CULTURE

Libyans are both fiercely proud of their own culture and curious about what lies beyond their borders. Although initially you might be treated by locals with a degree of bemusement, differences in culture, religion and ideology won't stop you making friends here.

Libya has a population of approximately five and a half million. This figure does not include a further 500,000 expatriate workers and refugees from neighbouring Algeria, Niger and Sudan. The Libyans consider themselves to be Arab, although their ethnic heritage comprises a mixture of other races, including Turkish, Berber and sub-Saharan African. In the south, especially around Ghat and Ghadames, there are large Tuareg and Tibu communities, most of whom now live in settlements after desert nomadism was banned by the Gaddafi government.

Libya is almost 100% Sunni Muslim. Most Tripolitanians are relatively liberal in their outlook and more moderate in their religious practices, but those living outside the capital are conservative in their dress and their adherence to daily prayer. Exceptions are foreign workers, who account for the tiny number of Christians and other faiths. There is a Christian church in both Tripoli and Benghazi.

Religion is important in Libya. Don't be surprised if your journey is paused several

LIBYA

times a day to enable drivers and guides time to face Mecca and pray.

Arabic is the official language, although many Libyans know a little Italian and English. All road, shop and other public signs are in Arabic, so a working knowledge of the language is extremely useful. Outside Tripoli and Benghazi, fewer people speak a foreign language. In Ghadhames and Ghat, you might find that some older people speak French. See the Language chapter (p1039) for useful Arabic and French words and phrases.

ENVIRONMENT

There are no national parks as such in Libya, although the Jebel Acacus is the closest thing in terms of being a properly (government) managed area of land.

Libya comprises 1.75 million sq km of mostly desert terrain. Only the narrow coastal strip receives sufficient rainfall for agriculture. Nearly 90% of the population lives along this coastal strip and it is here that the two capitals, Tripoli in the west (where all the power resides) and Benghazi in the east, are situated. The northeastern part of the country, the Jebel Akhdar (Green Mountains), is the most verdant region, while the interior is largely uninhabited desert dotted with oasis towns.

Summer is very hot, with temperatures on the coast averaging 30°C, often accompanied by high humidity. Temperatures in the south often reach 50°C. In winter the coast is cool and rainy, while desert temperatures can drop below freezing at night. During April and September, the *ghibli*, a hot, dry, sand-laden wind, blows every few days. It can last anything from a few hours to several days and can make desert travel dangerous, if not virtually impossible, due to reduced visibility. Bear this in mind if your main interest is visiting the desert.

Libya has few serious environmental headaches. Far and away the biggest problem is chronic littering. Many of Libya's indigenous animals – in particular desert gazelles, houbaras and bustards – have long been hunted to virtual extinction. But increasing desertification and over-grazing have had the largest impact on their habitats. Attempts to vegetate the encroaching sand dunes has government backing, but it's a slow process. The country's chronic

water shortage has been solved in the short term by the Great Man-Made River Project, but the impact on the Saharan aquifers it drains is not discussed publicly.

TRANSPORT

GETTING THERE & AWAY
Air
Many airlines serve Tripoli (see p101):

Alitalia (www.alitalia.com)
Austrian Airlines (www.austrianair.com)
British Airways (www.british-airways.com)
Emirates (www.emirates.com)
KLM (www.klm.com)
Lufthansa (www.lufthansa.com)

You must have a return ticket before arriving in Libya and, because it's difficult extending visas, altering outbound flight dates can be tricky. Flying in and out of Tripoli is much more expensive than landing in Tunis and overlanding through the border near Sabratha. For flying into Tunis see p115.

Boat
A car ferry operated by the Libyan government shipping line did sail regularly from Tripoli to Malta and several Italian ports but has been cancelled by the government.

Land
EGYPT
You can cross into Egypt at Sallum. Frequent buses travel from Benghazi to Alexandria (US$30, 21 hours) and Cairo (US$38, 24 hours). There are also local buses to the border, where you can connect with an Egyptian bus. It is possible to get a shared taxi to and from either side of the border. Prices for these vary widely.

There are a few long-distance buses from Tripoli direct to Cairo (36 hours), but due to restrictions on individual travel, and the official need to travel with a Libyan company, you would need to do this journey with a hire vehicle. See p106 for Libyan visa information.

DEPARTURE TAX

There is a US$5 departure tax charged in Libya.

TUNISIA
The coastal border crossing with Tunisia is at Ras Jedir. Buses leave from the central bus station in Tripoli and serve Sfax, Gabès, Medenine and Tunis. They usually leave early in the morning and fill up quickly, so it is best to get there early. There are also shared taxis that leave from a stand at the central bus station near the waterfront. The fares are very low, but the driving can be erratic.

Land crossings elsewhere can be difficult at best and downright impossible at worst, particularly Chad, Sudan, Algeria and Niger. If you're hell-bent on overlanding it to these countries, you'll need to negotiate arrangements with a competent travel and tour agency in Tripoli. Some companies have begun trips into southern Algeria so bending some official rules might be possible.

GETTING AROUND
Air
Libyan Arab Airlines (☎ 333 7500; www.aaco.org) has flights between all major Libyan towns. There are two flights daily between Tripoli and Benghazi (US$23), and there are twice-weekly flights (Wednesday and Saturday) from Tripoli to Sebha (US$22), from where you can make a connection to Ghat or Ghadames. Flights from Benghazi to Sebha and Kufra are also available. All internal flights are prone to unexpected delays and cancellations.

Car
Unfortunately travellers can't hire cars in Libya unless they go through a Libyan travel company. Car hire is expensive – about US$150 per day plus insurance – but petrol is cheap.

Many tourists, particularly Italians, travel through Libya in campervans brought with them on the ferry across the Mediterranean, usually through Tunisia. This must be fully arranged through a Libyan travel company.

Local Transport
Libya's road system is sometimes excellent, smooth and fast, and other times it is rough, slow and downright dicey. Although air-con buses and yellow-and-white shared taxis (called *roumees* or *aujra*) cover most of the country, because of the restrictions on individual travel you're more likely to spend most of your time aboard 4WD vehicles.

This obviously depends on which Libyan travel company you choose to travel with.

TRIPOLI
☎ 021 / pop 2 million
With a distinctly Italian face, infectious Arabic spirit and decidedly North African disposition, Tripoli (Tarabulus) charms you within minutes. Rimmed by Mediterranean blue and blotted, somewhat comically, with gigantic billboards of the ubiquitous Gaddafi, Tripoli combines an ancient medina and flashy boutiques with a colourful marketplace and some fascinating architecture.

Most tourists zot in and out of the capital on their way to and from Sabratha and Leptis Magna, which is a shame because Tripoli is the kind of place that needs to be soaked in and enjoyed. Don't miss seeing the sun set over the harbour, and picking up a souvenir Gaddafi watch in the medina is obligatory – just make sure the hour hand doesn't get caught on his double-chin.

ORIENTATION
The centre of Tripoli is dominated by the Al-Saray al-Hamra (Red Castle), which overlooks the port, As-Sadah al-Kradrah (Green Square) and the medina gates. Streets radiate from the square in all directions with the districts of Garden City and Bin Ashour falling to the southeast, the ferry port and swish hotels to the east and the Burj al-Fateh Complex to the west.

Most of the city's historic buildings, mosques, *hammams* (steam baths) and *funduq* (inns) can be found within the walls of the Old City, along with tea house hang-outs, kooky shops and their bubbly shopkeepers ever eager to force-feed you fresh mint tea and espresso.

As all visitors to Libya must arrange their visit through a travel agent/company, airport transfers should be arranged through them, too.

INFORMATION
Internet Access
Internet is cheap and the connections are generally quite fast, for Africa anyway. Rates vary around the US$4 per hour mark. There is an Internet café (ask for directions) open until very late in the Burj al-Fateh Complex.

LIBYA

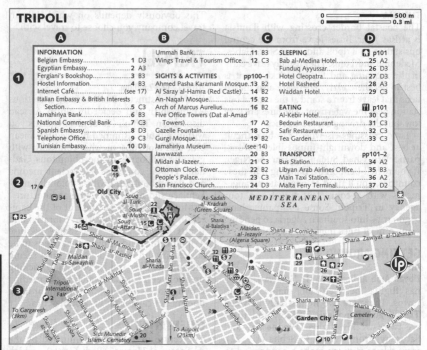

TRIPOLI

INFORMATION		
Belgian Embassy	1	D3
Egyptian Embassy	2	A3
Fergiani's Bookshop	3	B3
Hostel Information	4	B3
Internet Café	(see 17)	
Italian Embassy & British Interests Section	5	C3
Jamahiriya Bank	6	B3
National Commercial Bank	7	C3
Spanish Embassy	8	D3
Telephone Office	9	C3
Tunisian Embassy	10	D3

Ummah Bank	11	B3
Wings Travel & Tourism Office	12	C3
SIGHTS & ACTIVITIES	**pp100–1**	
Ahmed Pasha Karamanli Mosque	13	B2
Al Saray al-Hamra (Red Castle)	14	B2
An-Naqah Mosque	15	B2
Arch of Marcus Aurelius	16	B2
Five Office Towers (Dat al-Amad Towers)	17	A2
Gazelle Fountain	18	C3
Gurgi Mosque	19	B2
Jamahiriya Museum	(see 14)	
Jawwazat	20	B3
Midan al-Jazeer	21	C3
Ottoman Clock Tower	22	B2
People's Palace	23	B3
San Francisco Church	24	D3

SLEEPING	☐ p101	
Bab al-Medina Hotel	25	A2
Funduq Ayyussar	26	D3
Hotel Cleopatra	27	D3
Hotel Rasheed	28	A3
Waddan Hotel	29	C3
EATING	**▯ p101**	
Al-Kebir Hotel	30	C3
Bedouin Restaurant	31	C3
Safir Restaurant	32	C3
Tea Garden	33	C3
TRANSPORT	**pp101–2**	
Bus Station	34	A2
Libyan Arab Airlines Office	35	B3
Main Taxi Station	36	A2
Malta Ferry Terminal	37	D2

Money

The six main banks are on or near As-Sadah al-Kradrah (Green Square): Central Bank of Libya, National Commercial Bank, Commerce & Development Bank, ABC Bank Libya, Libyan Arab Foreign Bank, Sahara Bank.

They are open from 8am to 1pm on Sunday, Monday, Tuesday and Thursday plus 8am to noon and 3pm to 5pm on Saturday and Wednesday. You can also change money at the larger hotels. The favoured foreign currency is the US dollar, although some other hard currencies can be changed in banks.

Post & Telephone

Libya's postal system is a tad hit and miss. Most Tripolitanians will advise you not to send mail outside the capital and to head for post offices rather than relying on hotel reception desks to post things for you. The cost of stamps can vary widely depending on where you purchase them from. Hotels will often charge a duty on top of the official price. Letters to Europe cost US$0.35, and prices to the USA, Canada, Australia and

New Zealand are similar. Allow a week to 10 days for mail to arrive from Tripoli, longer if you post from anywhere else. DHL international courier services are also available from the larger hotels and private post offices.

The main post office is on Midan Al-Jazeer, near the former cathedral (now a mosque) at the end of Sharia Al-Magarief. There is a public telephone office in the same building and it is open 24 hours a day. Poste restante services are available in the main cities.

Both the main and private post offices offer public telephone services for local and international calls. Connections rarely cost more than US$0.70 per minute to anywhere in the world. If you're staying in a swish hotel you can call from your room, but this might cost you more.

SIGHTS & ACTIVITIES

Al Saray al-Hamra (Red Castle) houses the **Jamahiriya Museum** (☎ 3330292; off Shara Omar al-Mukhtar; ⏰ 8am-1pm; admission US$2, camera US$3.50, video camera US$7), whose four floors and 47 galleries should keep you out of trouble for several hours. It's a slightly dim and musty place, but the collections are so enormous that if you get bored in one room you're sure to find another that'll grab your attention.

This is also one of the few chances you'll get to see Roman statues with their heads intact. The Vandals left most of the stone folk at Leptis and Sabratha decapitated, making statues with heads seem a bit of a novelty here. The section of freaky two-headed animals is a little off-putting, but you can get a photo of yourself standing next to Gaddafi's baby-blue VW.

The **medina** is the best place in town to get totally lost. Its labyrinth of narrow streets and covered *souqs* (markets) sell everything from jewellery and clothes to crystal chandeliers (tough to take home) and antique furniture. There are also 38 mosques within its walls. Those well worth a visit include **Ahmed Pasha Karamanli Mosque**, built by the founder of the Turkish dynasty in the 18th century; **An-Naqah Mosque**, which is the oldest in the city; and the finely decorated **Gurgi Mosque**, the most beautiful, with 16 domes and the tallest minaret in Tripoli. The old British and French consulates can also be visited.

At the northern end of the medina is the **Arch of Marcus Aurelius**, the only Roman monument left in Tripoli.

FESTIVALS & EVENTS

Tripoli ain't the place to drink yourself silly (alcohol is strictly forbidden) but Tripolitanians do love a toe-tap, a dash of music and a long night at the bar. (Alcohol-free beers such as Becks are widely available, and chain-smoking Marlboros keeps most locals busy.)

The big events are Islamic holidays, and family gatherings such as weddings.

SLEEPING

Because individual travel is not permitted in Libya, you will need to negotiate and book all accommodation anywhere in the country through a Libyan travel company. Most of these companies have special arrangements with various hotels, and some companies even own their own hotels, so rooms will be booked accordingly.

If you are determined to travel 'on the cheap' you must brief the company you're booking through to make reservations with budget constraints in mind.

There are a few choices here in the budget range, including the YMCA and a couple of

youth hostels. Tripoli also has a number of decent hotels for the mid- to high-end market, starting at US$25 a night.

EATING & DRINKING

Fast food and snack bars aren't hard to find in Tripoli. As with any country, if you're looking for something quick and cheap head to the city bus terminal, where *shwarmas*, roast chicken, felafel sandwiches and pizzas are always served hot and fresh.

Sit-down restaurants can be pricey in Libya, and you generally don't see many women in them. Still, due to the shortage of nightclubs and other evening entertainment options, a nice dinner out is one of the best ways to see some local nocturnal life.

ENTERTAINMENT

Al Sakhra Restaurant and coffee shop has live music and bands Saturday to Thursday, and Montazah Al Ula Restaurant boasts a beautiful open-air garden where locals like to gather and chatter. The building itself once served as the house of a contessa during the Italian occupation, and was later the British governor's house in the late 1940s.

The Tripoli corniche (seaside) in the heart of Tripoli close to As-Sadah al-Kradrah (Green Square) has coffee shops, a restaurant and funfair rides. But you'll find the proper Tripoli-style fun can be found in people's homes, where the real parties go on.

GETTING THERE & AWAY
Air

Ticket prices depend largely on where you purchase your fare. The cheapest option is to fly from London on a package holiday to Djerba and then travel into Libya from there.

Most travellers are still best advised to travel to Libya via Tunisia because it is much cheaper, and there are more connections. Djerba airport, for example, has daily connections to most European ports. Sample fares (one-way fares are not applicable here because travellers won't be able to get a Libyan visa without a return ticket) are Malta to Tripoli (US$300 to US$500, return), London to Tripoli (US$570, return), Berlin to Tripoli (US$950, return) and Amsterdam to Tripoli (US$750).

Airlines with offices in Tripoli are listed on p98.

Boat

Sea Malta has cancelled its ferry service from Malta to Tripoli.

GETTING AROUND

Buses and shared taxis serving Tripoli, the suburbs and the airport can be found on the southwest side of the medina. Avoid the private black-and-white taxis, as they are hideously expensive.

NORTHERN LIBYA

LEPTIS MAGNA

Chances are you will get lumped with a guide here intent on telling you every last detail about Leptis Magna, so don't think you'll be able to skip the communal loos and the group steam rooms – and get away with it. Enduring the lengthy patter shouldn't bother you too much because this place is truly amazing.

If you have ever struggled to get your head around what a Roman city might have looked like in its heyday, Leptis Magna is the missing piece of the jigsaw. Leptis Magna is so cool that even after the rudimentary three-hour tour, you will still want to lurk around.

Originally a Carthaginian city, Leptis Magna was to become one of the most important cities in the Roman Empire, supplying grain and oil and occupying a key position on the African trade route.

During the reign of Emperor Septimius Severus (AD 193–211), Leptis Magna flourished, and many of the fine buildings seen today date from this period. Among the many buildings are a magnificent carved basilica, a theatre, a gigantic forum and baths, which are the largest outside Rome. The **Leptis Magna site** (8am to 5.30pm Tue-Sun; admission US$2, camera US$2) is about 10 minutes' drive from town.

The neighbouring town of Khoms is dull and modern, but there's a great stretch of **beach** running to it from Leptis Magna.

Sleeping

Fundk al-Khoms al-Syahi is your best bet along with Kryat al Khoms al-Syahia. Your tour operator will know where is best to stay, depending on which direction you're heading in next.

SABRATHA

Sabratha is the sister town of Leptis Magna. If you're entering the country through Tunisia, you'll visit Sabratha en route to Tripoli. Sabratha doesn't come close to Leptis Magna in most respects, although the theatre is near-perfectly preserved and is very impressive. The **site** (8am-5.30pm; admission US$2, camera US$2) is around 10 minutes' drive from the town.

Keep your ticket, as it allows you entry into the museum.

Sleeping & Eating

There is really no reason to stay here. Best to keep going until you reach Tripoli. You can buy drinks and have a sit down at Aros Al Bhar Restaurant just near the site.

BENGHAZI

☎ 061 / pop 600,000

Benghazi is the second-largest city in Libya and is situated on the eastern side of the Gulf of Sirte. It is a major commercial centre and port (the port is built around a large double harbour).

Due to extensive bombing during WWII there is now little of interest in the city itself. However, it does make a good base for touring the **Jebel Akhdar** (Green Mountains) and there are good **beaches** nearby.

There are several good **souqs** in the town, the most notable being the gold souq, known as Souq al-Jreed, and the lively Egyptian souq. All the souqs are open daily, except for Friday when most places are closed except for a handful of private high-street shops.

Sleeping & Eating

There are a range of accommodation options in Benghazi, from five-star hotels to basic bed and (shared) shower options. If you plan to spend a few days in Benghazi, it's worth having your tour operator hunt down a room in one of the plusher hotels, many of which boast beautiful ocean views and large balconies from which to enjoy the salty air and spectacular sunsets.

Until a few years ago it was quite tricky to track down a decent, and reasonably priced, meal in Benghazi. Thankfully an increase in tourism dollars to the city has translated into more dining options, although many of these remain expensive and specialise in hotel-style dishes devoid of any authentic Libyan flavour. Expect to pay at least US$10 to US$15 for a main. One of the best eating options is to head down to the waterside where at many stalls you can select your own fish and have them cooked on the spot.

For the cheapest, tastiest snacks try the various hole-in-the-wall places in the souq or on Sharia Omar ibn al-Khattab. Also in the Old Town, just off Sharia Gasr Ahmed, you will find the popular Libyan delicatessen and ice-cream parlour, Andalus.

Getting There & Away
There is one flight daily to and from Tripoli. The one-way/return fare is around US$25/50. Burak Airways, just out of Tripoli, are cheaper than Libyan Arab Airlines.

CYRENE
The most likely of the Greek cities of Cyrenaica (the Pentapolis) to appear on every other postcard, T-shirt and biscuit tray (yes, really, you can buy 'em). Cyrene is situated on the crest of a hill next to the modern village of **Shahat**, 220km east of Benghazi.

Founded in 600 BC by Greek settlers, a visit here is a must, not only for its temples but also because Cyrene is essentially a replica of Delphi. The **ruins** (☼ 8am-5.30pm Tue-Sun; admission US$6) are 2km from Shahat. They are somewhat overgrown and you'll often find yourself walking over mosaics that would be under glass if they were in Europe.

About 20km east of Shahat is the ancient port of **Apollonia**, near the village of Susah, where the ruins are now partially submerged (heaven for divers). It's a beautiful site with great swimming (although technically this is not allowed). The site is closed on Monday. To get here you can take a taxi from Shahat.

Sleeping & Eating
There is accommodation available near Cyrene as well as a resort near Apollonia. Most visitors would do Cyrene as a day trip from Benghazi. Accommodation and eating options here are limited.

Getting There & Away
Chances are you'll be on a tour bus between the ruins from Benghazi, although daily local buses and shared taxis also make the trip.

TOBRUK
The 400km drive east to Tobruk from Benghazi passes through the winding **Wadi Kuf** and along the prettiest part of Libya's coastline. **Ras Al-Hilal**, 30km east of Cyrene, is considered to be the most beautiful point on the coast.

After Derna the scenery changes dramatically, and the landscape around Tobruk turns to stony *hammada*, best described as boring-as-hell gravel desert.

SOUTHERN LIBYA

GHADHAMES
Ghadhames is touted as the Pearl of the Sahara and, although when you first arrive you'll struggle to understand how it qualifies for the title, a day spent exploring the old medina houses and their amazing rooms – adorned with hats, mirrors, miniature shrines and colourful murals – will set you straight. About 650km southwest of Tripoli and close to the borders of Algeria and Tunisia, the town is home to a number of diverse ethnic groups.

You must attend a traditional dancing and singing performance here, even if that means sitting in a room packed with schmaltzy tourists who just blew into town in an enormous tour bus. The **Ghadames Festival** is held each October. If you can possibly swing it, that's the best time to come. Dancing is often staged on dunes out in the desert, which is really spectacular. You'll also see traditional dress and instruments and competitions between different tribal groups for the best routines and tricks.

Sleeping & Eating
The best places to stay in town are private villas, such as Vila Othman Al Hashaishi and the adjoining Vila Omar. Most of these sit in the modern town although there are a few homes in the Old City where you can sleep in Technicolor chambers. When you book through a tour agency, mention that you'd prefer to stay in villas rather than one of the hotels in town.

GHAT & JEBEL ACACUS
There's not much to do in Ghat apart from wander around the Old City and

climb up to the fort which overlooks town (and is now being converted into a ritzy, novelty hotel). The only real reason to be here is the **Jebel Acacus** (Acacus Mountains) nearby, where you can see some of the most impressive **prehistoric rock art** in Africa, along with some pretty out-there desertscapes.

The town is mostly inhabited by Tuareg people, who sell handcrafted silverware and antique knives at truly outrageous prices. Still, it's worth lashing out because even the letter openers are very cool.

Tours

You will have to have booked through a tour operator to get to Ghat and they take care of the respective permits and camping arrangements.

There aren't any grocery shops in the Jebel Acacus so make sure you leave Ghat with plenty of water and food to last you for the number of days you'll be away.

Sleeping & Eating

There is only one hotel in town, the Tasili Hotel, and it's not that great. It is better to stay at Asdika Al Sahra fixed camp, or at Tin lalin fixed camp. Your tour operator will no doubt organise these in advance. Even if you have a booking, if you are travelling in the high season and you get to camp late you will end up with the crappy end of the camping spots.

The only places to eat are the fixed camp restaurants, although a couple of town cafés do sell snacks.

LIBYA DIRECTORY

ACCOMMODATION

It is difficult but not impossible to travel through Libya on the cheap. Because independent travel is not permitted, if you do wish to travel without spending a heap of dosh you will need to negotiate this firmly with a tour company before you advise them to go ahead and make bookings for you. Remember that you will always get what you pay for, so it's best to lash out a bit with a good company to ensure you'll be travelling with guides who have decent drivers, equipment and knowledge of where you're heading.

BUSINESS HOURS

Libya operates on an Islamic working week, with Friday as the day off. Thursday night is the best night to hit the town.

Business hours are 7am to 2pm in summer and from 8am to 1pm and 4pm to 6.30pm in the winter. Shops are often open until 9pm or 10pm, and government office hours are generally 8am to 2pm.

If you want to know when certain offices or buildings are open, just ask at your hotel's reception. They can make a call in advance and save you a trip to somewhere that is closed for lunch.

CUSTOMS

All pork and alcohol products are prohibited. Books, magazines and videos might be confiscated. Video cameras and personal computers must be presented at customs where their serial numbers will be recorded.

Immigration forms are in Arabic.

DANGERS & ANNOYANCES

Libya is a very safe country to travel in, and Libyans are well known for their hospitality and friendliness. Driving and the deterioration of cars are the main dangers you will encounter. It is not unusual to come across cars with only one light – or no lights at all – on the highway at night.

EMBASSIES & CONSULATES

Belgium (☎ 335 0115; Dhat al-Ahmat Tower 4, level 5, Tripoli)

Egypt (☎ /fax 660 5500; Shara al-Fat'h, Tripoli)

France (☎ 477 4891; Shara Beni al-Amar, Hay Andalus (Gargaresh), Tripoli)

Germany (☎ 333 05 54; Shara Hassan al-Mashai, PO Box 302)

Italy (☎ 333 41 31; 1 Shara Uaharan, PO Box 219)

Spain (☎ 333 32 75; Shara Abdelkader el Yazairi, PO Box 2302)

Tunisia (☎ 333 1051; Shara al-jrabah, Bin Ashour, PO Box 613)

UK (☎ 335 1084; Burj al-Fateh, level 24, Tripoli)

USA (☎ 333 7797; US interests section, c/o Belgian embassy, 1 Shara Abu Ubeida ibn al-Jarrah, PO Box 663)

Libya has embassies in Egypt and Tunisia.

FESTIVALS & EVENTS

As well as the following national holidays, Libya observes Islamic holidays (see p103).

Declaration of the People's Authority Day March
Declaration of the Jamahiriya Day 2 March
Evacuation of Foreign Military Bases Day 11 June
Anniversary of the Revolution Day 1 September
Day of Mourning 26 October

Annual festivals are held in Ghadames, Ghat, Germa, Kabaw and Houn. They're colourful, full of flash costumes and fancy dance moves and a lot of fun to see. If you want to see the brighter, lighter side of Libyan life, festivals are the way to go.

FOOD & DRINK

Libyan cuisine isn't exactly going to swipe you off your feet, but it's not bad either. Libyan soup, served at almost every meal, is a spicy version of minestrone with lamb and pasta.

Away from the coast you might come across such Saharan dishes as *ftaat*, which is made with buckwheat pancakes and layered with sauce and meat.

There is strictly no alcohol on sale in Libya – although backyard-brewed *bokha* and Tunisian rosé is not too difficult to track down.

Tea is always served sweet, and the coffee, both Arabic and espresso, is excellent. Bottled water is easily available.

INTERNET ACCESS

Internet access is not expensive (it costs about US$4 to US$8 per hour). You will find that the connections are generally quite fast in Tripoli, but not so outside the capital. There are several Internet places in Tripoli and Benghazi, although outside these two main cities you will struggle to find a connection.

MONEY

Bring your money in US dollars cash and change it in either Tripoli or Benghazi. The black market used to be big during the embargo, but these days it's not worth the trouble. Some of the largest hotels in the capital will accept the major credit cards but elsewhere you'll just get blank looks.

You can bargain with shop keepers on some (souvenir) items, but don't expect to halve their first offer because you won't get anywhere. Start at 80% of their initial price and work upwards.

PHOTOGRAPHY

The main problem with carrying a camera in Libya is that you'll have to pay extra admission charges upon entering every tourist site you visit. This can eventually make postcards a cheaper option, considering there's a US$3.50 to US$7 fee for every entry.

As with anywhere you travel, ask people for their permission before you go trigger happy, particularly in relation to women who in Libya rarely enjoy being snapped. Video cameras are fine as long as you have declared them on border entry and you're prepared to pay the requisite fees for using them at each site, usually around US$7.

There are photography shops that sell films and offer processing services in Tripoli and Benghazi.

RESPONSIBLE TRAVEL

Libyan tour operators are pretty *au fait* with low-impact travel because they appreciate that travellers don't enjoy seeing sublime desertscape cloaked in plastic wrappings. The same can't be said for Libyans generally, but there's no harm in setting a good example.

There are widespread ethnic tensions between tribal groups in Ghadames, Ghat and the Acacus. Although travellers can hardly expect to be instrumental in changing the inequalities endemic to Libyan society, attending performances of dances does help to raise the profiles of these groups and ensures that such traditions are passed on through the generations, if only for money-making purposes in the short term.

TOURS

Desert safaris and archaeological tours are available from numerous private tour operators. Desert safaris cost around US$100 per person per day fully inclusive, although prices can vary widely depending on where you want to go and the equipment and service the respective operator offers. It is easy to arrange a tailor-made itinerary, although it is worth ensuring that you discuss the fine print of your trip, right down to the models of the vehicles that will be used and the kind of meals you expect from day to day. The following tour companies are recommended:

Aiel Travel & Tour Services (☎ 061-909 2385, fax 908 0272; 7th fl, Islamic Building, Benghazi)
Bright Focus (☎ 061-909 1467; Benghazi)

Wings Travel & Tours (☎ 021-333 1855, fax 333 0881; Sharia Garnata, Tripoli)
Winzrik Travel & Tourism Services Company (☎ 021-361 1123, fax 361 1126; Sharia 1st September, Tripoli)

VISAS & DOCUMENTS

Visitors of all nationalities, except those from Arab countries and Malta, require a visa. Nationals of Israel are not admitted. Independent tourist visas are not granted. Travellers wishing to visit Libya must apply for a group tourist visa sponsored by a Libyan tour company. Journalists and single, unaccompanied women might have problems obtaining a visa. You will not get a visa if your passport has an Israeli stamp in it.

Before applying for a Libyan visa you *must* have your passport details translated into Arabic. It's essential that the translator is approved by the Jamahiriya. It's wise to have this done at a Libyan People's Bureau (or embassy) so there can be no question about the translation's authenticity.

Visas should be obtained in your home country. You cannot obtain visas in Tunisia or Egypt. If your country has no diplomatic representation you must courier your passport to one that does. This is a lengthy and very expensive process. Allow for at least six to eight weeks. Your tour operator will arrange for letters of invitation from the Libyan Government and will also oversee the processing of the visas.

Visa charges vary, but the average cost is between US$30 and US$50. Processing can take between two and four weeks, although some embassies will process 'priority' applications in less than two days. Visas are valid for the dates you specify in your application. Groups of more than five people must be accompanied by an official tourist officer for the duration of their stay.

Registration

On arrival in Libya, all foreigners have to register at the *jawwazat* (security office) within seven days. Usually your hotel or tour guide will do this for you. Registration outside the capital tends to be much faster. If you are determined to do this yourself, take along someone to translate. There is a small fee for the registration stamp.

Visa Extensions

Libyan visa extensions are possible, but difficult and time consuming to arrange. You need to visit the *jawwazat*, and again it's best to do this with someone who speaks Arabic. The costs vary widely between US$20 to US$40. Often they are not approved, and tour operators will tell you it's not worth the trouble trying to get one.

Visas for Onward Travel

Travellers are advised to apply for onward visas outside Libya where the process will be faster and much cheaper.

Tunisia

HIGHLIGHTS
- **Tataouine** Other-worldly architecture in nearby villages (p128)
- **Tozeur** Geometric brickwork, desert dunes and famous filmscapes (p130)
- **Hammams** Welcoming steam and socialising in every town (p114)
- **Dougga & Bulla Regia** Startlingly well-preserved Roman ruins (p118 & p117)
- **Best journey** The causeway straddling Chott el-Jerid, a huge salt lake (p130)
- **Off the beaten track** Cobbled, quiet, charismatic Le Kef (p118)

FAST FACTS
- **Area** 164,000 sq km
- **ATMs** in all large towns
- **Borders** Algeria closed; Libya open
- **Budget** US$15 per day
- **Capital** Tunis
- **Languages** French, Arabic
- **Money** Tunisian dinar; US$1 = TD1.3
- **Population** 9.8 million
- **Seasons** cool (Nov–Apr), warm (May–Oct)
- **Telephone** country code ☎ 216; international access code ☎ 00
- **Time** GTM/UTC + 1
- **Visas** US$8 for Australians and South Africans, available at airport; US$6.50 for others, need to apply in advance; unnecessary for Western Europeans, Americans, Canadians and Japanese

TUNISIA

This is Africa at its most Mediterranean, brimming with olives, dates and oranges. Tall blue shutters and wrought iron railings divulge Tunisia's French colonial past, but the muezzin call divides up the day. It's exotic, yet provincial, with narrow cobbled streets and gnarled men in smoky tiled cafés indulging in chat, chequers and chess. Goatherds are the main traffic in the countryside, whereas in Tunis, sunglass-wearing women-about-town swish past elderly men who are still sporting *chechias* (red felt hats).

Tunisia's northern dark moss-green hills, dotted with cypress trees and improbably preserved Roman remains, feel like its close northern neighbour, Italy. In contrast, its southern desert landscape and moulded-pod architecture are so weird that they stood in for 'a galaxy, far far away' in the *Star Wars* films – the latest contributor to this small country's imperial baggage, with a lineage that includes the Phoenicians, Romans, Ottomans and French.

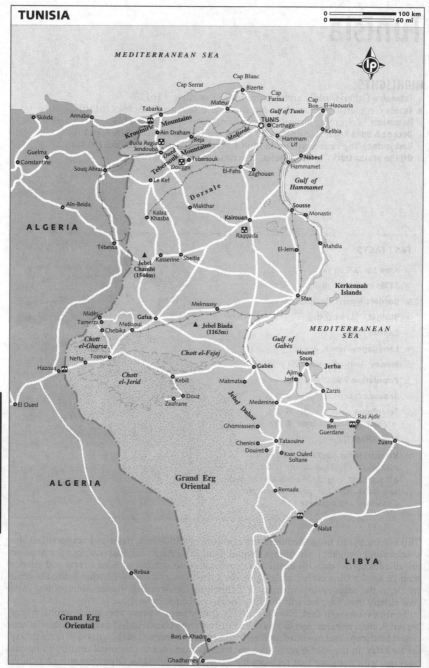

HISTORY

Fought over by successive great civilisations, today Tunisia is a pocket of serenity wedged between its troubled neighbours. Nature, luck and canny political stewardship have led to this state of calm. Its lush cultivated areas – once the breadbasket of Rome – still account for a reasonable bite of the economy, and its strategic position has long dealt it an economically viable hand.

Empires Strike Back

The Phoenicians hit the scene in around 1100 BC, and by the 6th century their capital, Carthage (just north of today's Tunis), had become the main power in the western Mediterranean. This led to inevitable conflict with the emerging Roman Empire, and 128 years of Punic Wars ensued. Carthage's legendary general, Hannibal, nearly conquered the Romans after his invasion of Italy in 216 BC, but eventually the Romans came out on top, razing Carthage, selling its population for slaves and then recreating it as a Roman city in 44 BC. Roman Tunisia boomed, creating the temple-decked city of Dougga and the extravagant El Jem colosseum.

With the Roman decline and fall in the 5th century, the Vandals saw their opportunity and captured Carthage in AD 439. Disliking the Vandals' tendency to vandalise, the local Berber population formed small kingdoms and rebelled. The Vandals were ousted by the Byzantines in AD 533, who fared little better against the Berbers.

In the 7th century the Arabs arrived from the east. Culturally these conquerors were the strongest of them all, as with them came Islam. Berber belligerence continued, but the Arabs managed to just about hang on to power until the 16th century. Following power struggles between the Turks and the Spanish, Tunisia ended up an outpost of the Ottoman Empire, and so it remained until France began to gain ground in the region. From 1881, the French spent the next 50 years trying to transform Tunisia into a European-style nation.

Bourguiba & Ben

Tunisia finally became a republic in 1957, with Habib Bourguiba as the first president, who waged jihad on poverty with one hand while distancing politics from religion with the other. He instituted a secular state, laying the groundwork for the tolerant and economically savvy structure of today, including women's rights, free education and the abolition of polygamy. However, in his final years he began to behave erratically; there was a bloodless coup in 1987 and Zine el-Abidine Ben Ali jumped into the ageing president's shoes. Ben Ali continued down similar roads to Bourguiba, and confirmed his stranglehold on power at 'elections' in 1989, 1994 and 1999 – in the last he won 99.44% of the vote.

Despite cynicism about election results and alarm at the suppression of opposition, Tunisia is one of the most stable and moderate Arab states. It has developed close ties with both the USA and Germany, which supply the bulk of its foreign aid, and carefully developed a diverse economy resting mainly on agriculture, mining, energy and manufacturing. Another big earner, tourism, has been buffeted by global events, particularly in 2002 when Djerba suffered a terrorist bomb attack in which 21 tourists died (Al-Qaeda claimed responsibility). However, security has been stepped up, tourists have returned, and Tunisia remains an incredibly welcoming, relaxed and tolerant North African country.

THE CULTURE

Despite wave after wave of invader, Tunisia has an ethnic and religious uniformity that allows for a certain social ease. Islam is pervasive yet relaxed. Tunisian life revolves around the family, the mosque, the hammam (bathhouse) and hospitality, as it has done for centuries. Strangers are readily invited into people's homes and then invited back again the next day. With typical Arabian–African generosity, people share their food and most importantly their time. Tunisians want cash to benefit their family but are not so interested in the trappings of wealth – even the souq salespitch has a take-it-or-leave-it quality. People have a strong mischievous streak and prefer not to take things too seriously. The relatively strong economy tends not to breed extremism. The level of education is high, though not necessarily matched by opportunities – count the taxi drivers with degrees.

Men sit and chat in the cafés, whereas women visit each other at home. In Tunis couples intermingle and walk arm in arm, but outside the capital women and men are largely segregated in public life.

At the same time, thanks to Habib Bourguiba, this is a proudly forward-looking nation with an egalitarian squint.

ARTS

Tunisia's national poet is Abu el-Kacem el-Chabbi; his poem *Will to Live* is taught to every school child. Not many authors have been translated into English, but Mustapha Tlili is one, and his novel *Lion Mountain* addresses the impact of progress and tourism on a remote village. Tunisian by birth, Albert Memmi lives in Paris and has written acclaimed works in French about the Jewish–North African immigrant's identity crisis.

During the colonial period, European artists began to be drawn to Tunisia, attracted by its exotic light, architecture and lifestyle. The most famous to be inspired here were Paul Klee and Auguste Macke, who visited in 1914 and produced many works inspired by what they saw.

Yahia Turki is considered the father of Tunisian figurative painting, and depicted scenes of daily life. After independence, artists such as Hédi Turki and Nja Mahdaoui began to explore the Islamic traditions of geometric decoration and calligraphy.

ENVIRONMENT

It may be small, but Tunisia packs in a range of landscapes worthy of a continent, from its northern thickly forested deep-green mountains to southern crystallised salt lakes and plump silky dunes.

In the north, the Kroumirie and Tebersouk Mountains are the easternmost extent of the High Atlas Mountains, covered with mysterious, dense forests where there's always a chance of glimpsing wild boars, jackals, mongooses and genets. Their foothills dive down to the luxuriant northern coastal plain, with its citrus and cypress trees and white-sand beaches. Further south, the country's main mountain range is the rugged, dry central Dorsale, which runs from Kasserine in the west and peters out into Cap Bon in the east. Between these ranges lies the lush Medjerda Valley, once the Roman breadbasket, fed by the country's only permanent river, Oued Medjerda. Olives cover the east coast, particularly around Sfax. South of the Dorsale, a high plain falls away to a series of huge, glittering *chotts* (salt lakes) and the silent, lonely, magnificent *erg* (sand sea) – the eastern extremity of the Grand Erg Oriental that carpets a large part of Algeria.

Tunisia's environmental headaches include the regional problem of desertification and various forms of pollution – industrial pollution, sewage disposal and litter – though many of its cities are strikingly clean. Tunisia's trawler fleet has been accused of serious overfishing and seabed degradation in the Gulf of Gabès. In the south, the huge water requirements of the tourist industry have depleted artesian water levels and dried up springs, though dam construction in the north has ensured a steady supply to most places.

TRANSPORT

GETTING THERE & AWAY
Air

There are regular flights, both scheduled and charter, from Tunisia to destinations all over Europe, but no direct flights to the Americas, Asia or Oceania.

Cheap air tickets are unobtainable in Tunisia. Tickets can be very cheap *from* Europe; last-minute deals in London may go as low as US$60 return.

Boat

Boats run from Tunis to Trapani, Naples, sometimes La Spezia, and Genoa in Italy. They also serve Marseilles in France and Bastia (Corsica). See p116 for more details.

Land
ALGERIA

There are numerous border-crossing points, and louages (shared taxis) travel between Tunis and various towns in eastern Algeria. For travellers, the southern border crossing between Nefta and El-Oued is the best bet, but check the current situation before heading for Algeria. You reach

---

DEPARTURE TAX

There is no departure tax to be paid when leaving Tunisia. The tax is included in the price of your ticket.

Nefta from Gafsa and Tozeur, and take a bus or louage from Nefta to the border post at Hazoua.

LIBYA
The coast road from Gabès to Tripoli runs via the border-crossing at Ras Ajdir. Louages make the journey from Gabès, Medenine, Sfax, Sousse and Tunis to Tripoli (US$20, 10 hours), and there are several weekly buses from the southern Tunis bus station to Tripoli (US$20, 11½ hours).

GETTING AROUND
Air
Tuninter operates internal flights from Tunis to/from Jerba, Sfax and Tozeur. Tuninter tickets can be bought from **Tunis Air** (☎ 330 100; 48 Ave Habib Bourguiba), or from any travel agent. **Tuninter** (☎ 701 717) also has a special reservations service.

Boat
There are ferries from Sfax to the Kerkennah Islands, but not many reasons to go there. A 24-hour car ferry operates on the short hop between Jorf, on the mainland, and Ajim on the island of Jerba.

Hitching
Hitching is possible down the coast to the Libyan border and as far south as Tozeur, although you may be expected to pay (the bus fare equivalent). It is more difficult, but still possible, for two people. Hitching in the north is easier away from the main tourist areas, and you'll seldom be expected to pay.

Although many people do hitch, bear in mind that it is not an entirely safe means of transport. Women should never hitch alone, and even in pairs it will be more hassle than it could possibly be worth and not necessarily safer.

Local Transport
The national bus company, Société Nationale du Transport Interurban (SNTRI), has daily air-conditioned buses between Tunis and most towns.

Advance booking is advisable, especially in summer and around important holidays. Sample one-way fares from Tunis include Sousse (US$5.50) and Jerba (from US$16 to US$18).

Local buses are handled by regional companies and go to all but the most remote villages.

Louages are large cars or minibuses. They are always white with a coloured stripe along the side, and they ply the same routes as the buses. They are usually cheaper and faster than buses and are quite safe. They leave when full – you rarely have to wait long for departure.

All towns have metered private yellow taxis. These can either be hired privately or they operate on a collective basis – they collect four passengers for different destinations. If you take a shared taxi, your fare will be much cheaper.

Train
The rail network isn't huge, but it's the best way to get to certain places. The best-serviced route is the line from Tunis to Sousse (US$4.50) and Sfax (US$7.50).

TUNIS

☎ 71 / pop 702,000

Old colonial architecture, kaleidoscope-tiled cafés, hubbly-bubbly scent, magnificent mosaics, early-morning espresso shots, lazy afternoons at boulevard tables, elderly men in red hats, women bundled in headscarves, glamorous hair-flicking city slickers – all mingle to make up this relaxing city, which mocks the frantic character of other Arabic capitals with its easy-going nonchalance. The confusing mass of the medina slides from shopfronts laden with modern tack to arched alleys of delicate Islamic splendour to vivid fruit and meat stalls. Outside, the French grid of the Ville Nouvelle spreads out and lays claim to the city as the Mediterranean hybrid that it is.

ORIENTATION
The airport is 8km northeast of the centre: a taxi will cost you around US$3, or bus No 35 (US$0.60, half-hourly 6.30am to 5.30pm) heads to Ave Habib Bourguiba, the city's main thoroughfare, which runs east–west from Lake Tunis to Place de l'Indépendance.

Ave Habib Bourguiba is lined with cafés, banks, cinemas and restaurants, and is a favourite stretch to strut up and down

TUNISIA

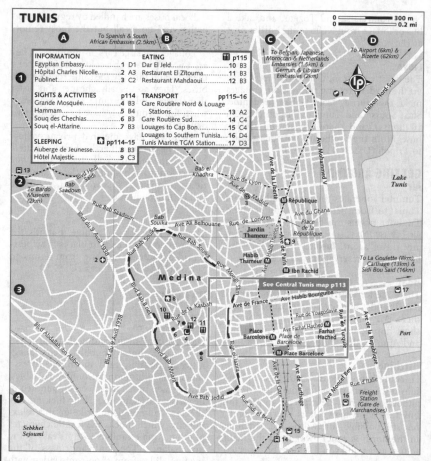

TUNIS

0 _____ 300 m
0 _____ 0.2 mi

INFORMATION
Egyptian Embassy....................1 D1
Hôpital Charles Nicolle............2 A3
Publinet...................................3 C2

SIGHTS & ACTIVITIES p114
Grande Mosquée......................4 B3
Hammam.................................5 B4
Souq des Chechias...................6 B3
Souq el-Attarine......................7 B3

SLEEPING pp114–15
Auberge de Jeunesse................8 B3
Hôtel Majestic.........................9 C3

EATING p115
Dar El Jeld.............................10 B3
Restaurant El Zitouna.............11 B3
Restaurant Mahdaoui..............12 B3

TRANSPORT pp115–16
Gare Routière Nord & Louage
Stations............................13 A2
Gare Routière Sud..................14 C4
Louages to Cap Bon...............15 C4
Louages to Southern Tunisia....16 D4
Tunis Marine TGM Station........17 D3

To Spanish & South African Embassies (2.5km)

To Belgian, Japanese, Moroccan & Netherlands Embassies (1.5km) & German & Libyan Embassies (2km)

To Airport (6km) & Bizerte (62km)

Lake Tunis

To Bardo Museum (2km)

Bab Saadoun

Bab el Khadhra

Bab Souika

Médina

Habib Thameur

Ibn Rachid

To La Goulette (8km), Carthage (13km) & Sidi Bou Saïd (16km)

See Central Tunis map p113

Place Barcelone

Farhat Hached

Place Barcelone

Port

Place de Barcelone

Freight Station (Gare de Marchandises)

Sebkhet Sejoumi

Ave Bab Jedid

---

in the evenings. The main north-south thoroughfare of the Ville Nouvelle is the street known as Ave de Carthage to the south of Ave Habib Bourguiba and as Ave de Paris to the north. Ave de Carthage runs east to Place Barcelone, hub of the Métro Léger network, and with the train station on its southern side.

The western extension of Ave Habib Bourguiba is Ave de France, which terminates in front of Bab Bhar (Porte de France), a huge arch, beyond which is the medina. The medina's two main streets lead off the western side of the square: Rue de la Kasbah, which leads to Place du Gouvernment at the other side of the medina, and Rue Jemaa Zitouna, which leads to the

Zitouna mosque at its heart. At the eastern end of Ave Habib Bourguiba a causeway carries road and light-rail traffic across to La Goulette, a port, and then north along the coast to the rich suburbs of Carthage, Sidi Bou Saïd and La Marsa.

Tunis has two bus stations. The one for northern destinations (Map p112, Gare Routière Nord de Bab Saadoun) is served by Métro Léger lines Nos 3 or 4 (Bab Saadoun station), or take No 3 bus to Ave Habib Bourguiba. Louages from the north also arrive and leave from here. The other station is for international buses and the south (Map p112, Gare Routière Sud de Bab el-Alleoua). Louages for Cap Bon leave from/arrive near here. It's a 10-minute walk north to Place

TUNISIA

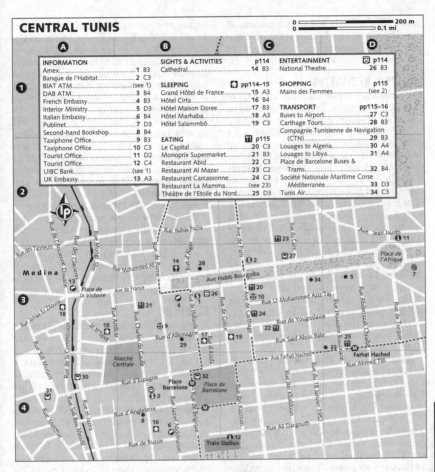

CENTRAL TUNIS

INFORMATION		SIGHTS & ACTIVITIES	p114	ENTERTAINMENT	p114
Amex	1 B3	Cathedral	14 B3	National Theatre	26 B3
Banque de l'Habitat	2 C3				
BIAT ATM	(see 1)	SLEEPING	pp114–15	SHOPPING	p115
DAB ATM	3 B4	Grand Hôtel de France	15 A3	Mains des Femmes	(see 2)
French Embassy	4 B3	Hôtel Cirta	16 B4		
Interior Ministry	5 D3	Hôtel Maison Doree	17 B3	TRANSPORT	pp115–16
Italian Embassy	6 B4	Hôtel Marhaba	18 A3	Buses to Airport	27 C3
Publinet	7 D3	Hôtel Salammbô	19 C3	Carthage Tours	28 B3
Second-hand Bookshop	8 B4			Compagnie Tunisienne de Navigation	
Taxiphone Office	9 B3	EATING	p115	(CTN)	29 B3
Taxiphone Office	10 C3	Le Capital	20 C3	Louages to Algeria	30 A4
Tourist Office	11 D2	Monoprix Supermarket	21 B3	Louages to Libya	31 A4
Tourist Office	12 C4	Restaurant Abid	22 C3	Place de Barcelone Buses &	
UIBC Bank	(see 1)	Restaurant Al Mazar	23 C2	Trams	32 B4
UK Embassy	13 A3	Restaurant Carcassonne	24 C3	Société Nationale Maritime Corse	
		Restaurant La Mamma	(see 23)	Méditerranée	33 D3
		Théâtre de l'Etoile du Nord	25 D3	Tunis Air	34 C3

Barcelone, where the train station and numerous hotels are situated, in the city centre. Métro Léger Line 1 runs from Tunis Marine to Ben Arous via Place Barcelone. Bab Alioua, one stop south of Place Barcelone, is the closest stop to Gare Routière Sud.

INFORMATION
Bookshops
There's a **second-hand bookshop** (Map p113; Rue d'Angleterre), with an English selection, where the owner will buy and exchange books.

Internet Access
Publinet (US$1 per hr) Ave Habib Bourguiba (Map p113; 28 Ave Habib Bourguiba); Ave de Madrid (Map p113; Ave de Madrid)

Money
The major banks are along Ave Habib Bourguiba. There's a branch of **American Express** (Map p113; ☎ 254 304; UIBC Bank, 156 Ave de la Liberté).

Post & Telephone
The **main post office** (Map p113; Rue Charles de Gaulle) is open daily and has a poste restante.

Taxiphone offices dot the city centre. Two of the most convenient are on Rue Jamel Abdelnasser and Ave de Paris (Map p113).

Tourist Offices
The **tourist office** (Map p113; ☎ 341 077; Place de l'Afrique; ⏰ 8am-6pm Mon-Sat, 9am-noon Sun) has a map of Tunis, a road map of Tunisia and

TUNISIA

brochures on Carthage and the medina, all free. There's another branch at the train station, open the same hours. You'll be able to find someone who speaks English.

SIGHTS & ACTIVITIES

The **medina** is a sprawling, intricate maze of passages, alleyways, overhanging bridges, souqs, small shops, big doorways and tiled cafés. An atmospheric time to explore is the early morning, before the stalls are set up and people are clustered around the coffee shops. At its heart lies the **Grande Mosquée** (Map p112; ☽ 8am-noon) – its forest of columns is scrounged from Roman Carthage. Many of the souqs concentrate on knock-down high fashion, flouncy satin-lined baskets and tourist tat, whereas others sell perfume (the Souq el-Attarine) or traditional red felt caps (Souq des Chechias), lined with dusty hat-filled shops. There is a steam-filled darkened **hammam** (Map p112; admission US$4, incl massage; ☽ men 5am-1pm, women 1-8pm).

The Ville Nouvelle has many elaborate edible-looking ornate facades, such as the meringue of the National Theatre (Ave Habib Bourguiba), and the wedding-cake Hôtel Majestic.

A must-see is the **Bardo Museum** (☎ 513 650; Ave du 2 Mars; admission US$3.50, camera US$1; ☽ 9.30am-4.30pm Tues-Sun mid-Sep–Mar, 9am-5pm Apr–mid-Sep). This magnificent collection provides a taste of ancient life, housed in a glorious palace. Huge statues, such as the 2nd-century languorously sensual Apollo, are countered by such human details as a tomb mosaic stating 'Crispina lived eight years, 10 months, 24 days and six hours'. The many incredibly well-preserved mosaics, with their images of gods feasting and farming, are absolutely stunning, and include some of Africa's oldest. It's 3km northwest of the city centre. The best way to get there is using Métro Léger line No 4 (US$0.30; see Getting Around p116) to the Bardo stop. A taxi costs US$3.

The remains of Punic and Roman **Carthage** lie northeast of the city centre and are easily reached by Tunis-Gouette-Marsa (TGM) suburban train from Tunis Marine station. Get off at Carthage Hannibal station and wander up to the top of **Byrsa Hill** for a fine view across the site. Once the city held 400,000 people and was surrounded by 13m-high walls. It's where Dido, queen of Carthage, dazzled Aeneas with her beauty

before he went off to found Italy and deserted her. You'll have to use a bit of imagination, as the ruins are scant and scattered over a wide area; they include impressive Roman baths, houses, cisterns, basilicas and streets. The **Carthage Museum** (admission to all sites US$4, camera US$1; ☽ 8.30am-5pm mid-Sep–end Mar, 8am-7pm Apr–mid-Sep) gives an idea of the site's former glories, with such wonders as monumental statuary, mosaics and extraordinary everyday stuff such as razors and kohl pots. It's next to the 19th-century deconsecrated neo-Gothic monster of a **cathedral** (admission US$1.50; ☽ same as museum) and the **Byrsa Quarter**, an excavated quarter of the Punic city, in the grounds of the museum.

A few stops further along the TGM line is the magically picturesque village of **Sidi Bou Said**, with narrow cobbled streets and whitewashed buildings with blue-painted wrought-iron, set high on a cliff above the sea. Wandering its streets can be topped only by watching the sunset from one of its cafés.

SLEEPING

There are lots of rock-bottom budget places in and around the medina, but they are mainly for male commercial travellers and have a sleazy atmosphere and a soundtrack of bodily functions. But there are a couple of exceptions. If you pay a bit more, you get a leap up in quality.

Auberge de Jeunesse (Map p112; ☎ 567 850; 25 Rue Es Saida Ajoula; dm with breakfast US$5) In the thick of the medina, this occupies the 18th-century Dar Saida Ajoula palace. It has a surfeit of regulations and management who seem to get their kicks from enforcing them: closed 10am to 2pm, a 10pm curfew and no showers between 7.30pm and 9am. However, it's still a bargain: very clean, and the large dorm has fine murals.

Grand Hôtel de France (Map p113; ☎ 326 244; hotelfrancetunis@yahoo.fr; 8 Rue Mustapha M'barek; s/d US$13/15, with shower US$18/24) This has faded elegance, airy and light, with a wooden coffinlike lift and lots of wrought iron. The best rooms are those with balcony on the top floor, with good views.

Hôtel Salammbô (Map p113; ☎ 334 252; hotel.salammbo@gnet.tn; 6 Rue de Grèce; s/d US$13/21, with bathroom US$16/23) Clean, simple rooms, some with balcony.

Hôtel Marhaba (Map p113; ☎ 354 006; 5 Rue de la Commission; s/d/tr US$7/10/12) This very popular place is just inside the medina. It's basic but fairly clean and in a good location.

Hôtel Cirta (Map p113; ☎ 321 584; 42 Rue Charles de Gaulle; s/d US$8/10, showers US$1.50) Rather grubby and dingy, with lumpy beds, this at least has some atmosphere and balconies over the street.

> **SPLURGE!**
>
> **Hôtel Maison Dorée** (Map p113; ☎ 240 632; 3 Rue el-Koufa; s/d US$21/23, with bathroom US$25/30) Maison Dorée is charming: simple and spotless with an old-fashioned formality, shuttered balconies and comfortingly 1950s furnishings.

EATING

You can buy slightly addictive spicy tuna-filled chapattis in the medina for US$1.50. For self-catering, around the **Marché Centrale** and near the Grand Hôtel de France are alluring delicatessens selling succulent olives, differing date varieties, *harissa* (spicy chilli paste) and cheeses. There's also a Monoprix supermarket (Ave Charles de Gaulle) where you can buy local wine.

Restaurant Mahdaoui (Map p112; 2 Rue Jemma Zitouna; dishes US$3-5) This place in the medina is popular, and the tables fill a narrow alley by the Grand Mosquée. The daily blackboard menu lists such dishes as couscous, fish and chicken.

Restaurant El Zïtouma (Map p112; dishes US$2.50) Around the corner from Restaurant Mahdaoui, this simple place serves simple dishes, such as pasta and tomato sauce, and has tables in a pretty alley under an arch.

Restaurant Al Mazar (Map p113; ☎ 355 077; 11 Rue de Marseilles; most mains US$4) Al Mazar has a good atmosphere, befitting a bar cunningly disguised as a restaurant. With paintings on the walls and big globe lightshades, you might think yourself in Paris if it were not for the drunken Tunisians singing. The food is excellent, with special mention going to both the *harissa* and the chocolate mousse (US$1.50).

Restaurant Carcassonne (Map p113; 8 Ave de Carthage; 4-course menu US$3.50) This is an excellent bargain, with a generous four-course menu, and it serves alcohol.

Restaurant La Mamma (Map p113; ☎ 241 256; Rue de Marseilles; dishes US$4-13) This has a red interior, plastic flowers, such dishes as barbecued octopus and occasional live musicians who look like moonlighting snooker players. It serves alcohol.

Restaurant Abid (Map p113; ☎ 257 052; 98 Rue de Yougouslavie; dishes US$2.50-4) This bright place with tiled walls serves meat and fish.

Le Capital (Map p113; ☎ 256 601; Ave Habib Bourguiba; dishes US$4-8) Overlooking the hubbub of the main drag, this place is flouncy and calm, and specialises in brochettes, meat and fish.

Théâtre de l'Etoile du Nord (Map p113; ☎ 256 242; www.etoiledunord.org; 41 Ave Farhat Hached; snacks US$1-3; set menu US$4) A funky neon-lit, spacious theatre-café-bar, this is quite unlike anywhere else in Tunis, and is where the city's artsy crowd hang out, both men and women.

> **SPLURGE!**
>
> **Dar El Jeld** (Map p112; ☎ 560 916; 5-10 Rue Dar El Jed; starters US$4.50-7, mains US$14-20, dessert US$6) This is special from the moment you knock on the grand arched doorway, which opens into an immaculately restored, elaborate 18th-century tiled and stuccoed mansion. The magnificent main dining room is in a covered central courtyard, but there are also private alcove tables around the edge that are ideal for scheming or romancing, or a spot of both. A good way to start is with the mixed hors d'oeuvres, then try delicious traditional Tunisian dishes such as *kabkabou*, fish with fresh tomatoes, capers and olives.

SHOPPING

Mains de Femmes (47 Ave Habib Bourguiba) A co-op that sells quality handicrafts at fixed prices: the profits are ploughed back into the rural communities that make them.

For perfume, tiles, *chechias*, cheap clothes, accessories and tonnes of glorious tat, head to the **medina**, and delicious foodstuffs can be found at and around the **Marché Central**.

GETTING THERE & AWAY
Air
Tuninter (☎ 701 717) flies from Tunis to/from Jerba, Sfax and Tozeur; each flight costs around US$80, but cheaper deals are sometimes available.

TUNISIA

Boat

Ferries from Europe arrive at La Goulette, at the end of the causeway across Lake Tunis. The cheapest way to reach the city from here is by TGM suburban train. A private taxi from the port to Ave Habib Bourguiba shouldn't cost more than US$5.

Tirrenia Navagazione, whose agent is **Carthage Tours** (☎ 344 066; www.carthagetours.com .tn; 59 Ave Habib Bourguiba), run boats between Tunis and Trapani (passenger/car from US$50/100, Monday), Naples (US$100/170, Sunday), and sometimes La Spezia in Italy. **Compagnie Tunisienne de Navigation** (CTN; ☎ 322 802; www.ctn.com.tn; 122 Rue de Yugoslavie) run services to/from Genoa, Italy (US$130/240) and Marseilles, France (US$170/360). **Société Nationale Maritime Corse Méditerranée** (SNCM; ☎ 338 222; www.sncm.fr; 47 Farhat Hached) run to/from Marseilles for similar prices as well as Bastia (Corsica; US$160/365).

Local Transport

Services to/from Tozeur (US$15, seven hours, five daily), Tataouine (US$18, 8½ hours, three daily), Matamata (US$13, eight hours, one daily), Jerba (US$16, eight hours, three daily), Sfax (four hours, hourly), Sousse (US$6, 2½ hours, hourly) and Tripoli (Libya; US$20, 11½ hours, several weekly) are found at the southern bus station; louages to the same destinations (except Tripoli) leave regularly nearby. At the northern bus station, services go to/from Tabarka (US$7, three hours, hourly), Ain Draham (US$7, 4½ hours, four daily), Jendouba (US$6, three hours, six daily) and Le Kef (US$7, 3½ hours, hourly) via Tebersouk. Louages for eastern Algeria leave from Rue el-Jazira and to Tripoli (Libya; US$20, 10 hours) from Place Sidi Bou Mendil at the southeast corner of the medina.

Train

The most popular route is the line from Tunis to Sousse (US$6), Sfax (US$8) and Jendouba (US$4).

GETTING AROUND
Taxi

Private taxis are cheap. It's hard to run up a fare of more than US$10. A short hop will cost less than US$1 and a longer one, such as to the Bardo, around US$2.50.

Train

The TGM rail system connects central Tunis with the northern beachside suburbs of La Goulette, Carthage, Sidi Bou Said and La Marsa (US$0.50; 5am to midnight).

Tram

The modern (Métro Léger) tram system has five routes running to various parts of the city. The useful lines are No 1 for the southern bus and louage stations, No 2 for consulates on Ave de la Liberté and Nos 3 and 4 for the northern bus and louage stations. No 4 also has a stop for the Bardo Museum. The main stations are Place Barcelone and Place de la République. Tram fares are usually around US$0.50.

NORTHERN TUNISIA

Northern Tunisia is a surprise – a rolling, darkly wooded, magnificently lush region that hasn't been much discovered by foreign tourists. Its hills allow vast views and hide the amazing Roman cities of Dougga and Bulla Regia, uncannily preserved.

TABARKA
☎ 78 / pop 13,600

Tabarka's a quiet coastal town, with an old-fashioned feel, where the cafés spill over the tree-shaded pavements. Backed by dark green mountains, it's one of the prettiest settings in Tunisia. A popular local getaway, it's free from the European invasion of many other seaside resorts. There's a small beach near the town, overlooked by a sturdy Genoese **fort** (closed to the public), and a long white-sand stretch curves away eastwards. Tabarka hosts brilliant summer music festivals: the big one is the **jazz festival** in July, but there are also Raï, Latin and world music events.

Information

The small town has a grid layout, bisected by the main street, Ave Habib Bourguiba. There are banks along Ave Habib Bourguiba in the centre, a **post office** (Ave Hedi Chaker) and **Publinet** (Route Touristique), which charges US$1 per hour.

Sleeping

Tabarka is underwhelmed with good budget accommodation.

Hôtel de Corail (☎ 673 789; Rue Tazarka; s/d US$7/12) Old-fashioned rooms with high ceilings and balconies. However, the bathrooms are a bit grubby, and there's no hot water.

Hôtel Mamia (☎ 671 058; 3 Rue de Tunis; s/d US$8/14) This place, which has rooms set around a courtyard, is clean, but the windows open only on to the courtyard so you'll have to keep your curtains drawn if you want any privacy. The management might make you feel as if you are greatly inconveniencing them by using their facilities.

Hôtel Les Mimosas (☎ 673 018; US$10/16; ✕) This elegant, good-value, three-star place has wonderful views over the bay and town. It's like a cartoon French villa with bright yellow shutters – ask for a room with a balcony as the views are impeccable. Bourguiba spent some time here. The spacious, lovely pool overlooks the panorama and is set in perfect lawns – ideal for an evening drink. The air-con doesn't work too well, however.

Eating
Restaurant Sidi Moussa (cnr Ave 7 Novembre & Ave d'Algérie; mains US$3.50) A small, very welcoming place, this restaurant offers tasty fresh fish with chips, salad and fruit.

Hôtel Novelty (☎ 670 176; 68 Ave Habib Bourguiba; set menu US$8) This has lovely seating outside, shaded by vine-covered trees, and the friendly management offer a good set menu.

Café Andalous (Ave Heidi Chaker) With chairs and tables all over the pavement, this is a classic coffee house – the elaborately tiled interior is chock-a-block with Ottoman bric-a-brac, such as spiky antlers, and men playing chequers.

Getting There & Away
The SNTRI bus station is on Rue du Peuple and has services to/from Tunis (US$6.50, three hours, six daily), Jendouba (US$2, 1½ hours, five daily), Ain Draham (US$1, 45 minutes, 11 daily) and Le Kef (US$4, three hours, two daily). Louages leave from Ave Habib Bourguiba for Ain Draham (US$1), Jendouba (US$2.50) and Tunis (US$6).

AIN DRAHAM
Ain Draham has slanted red roofs and haunted-looking houses. Gnarled trees match the café characters, and all around is the cork forest of the Kroumirie Mountains. Shops display faded cassette boxes and more carvings of stags than is strictly necessary. At an altitude of around 900m, it usually has snow in winter and offers welcome respite from the summer heat. The road between here and Tabarka snakes through huge hills, thick with trees, with vast views opening up, dappled in light – it's a great base for mountain walks.

Maison des Jeunes (☎ 647 087; dm US$4) is at the top end of town, on the road to Jendouba.

Hôtel Beauséjour (☎ 655 363; d with bathroom from US$19; three-course menu US$12) This green-shuttered former hunting lodge feels like the setting for an Agatha Christie novel. Perhaps it's the dive-bombing boars on the walls. The restaurant serves beer.

Résidence Le Pins (☎ 656 200; s/d with bathroom US$20/28) is modern and clean, with a sweeping view from the roof.

There are buses to Jendouba (US$1.50, one hour, seven daily) and to Tabarka (US$1, 45 minutes, 11 daily), Le Kef (US$2.50, three hours, nine daily) and Tunis (US$7, 4½ hours, four daily). Regular louages go to/from Tabarka and Jendouba, and occasionally Tunis.

BULLA REGIA
This remarkably well-preserved **Roman city** (admission US$1.50, camera US$1; ☼ 7am-7pm Apr-Sep, 8.30am-5.30pm Oct-Mar) is famous for its extraordinary underground villas. To escape the summer heat, the ever-inventive Romans retreated below the surface. But these are no burrows; they're the extensive, elegant homes of the moneyed. All named according to their mosaic subjects, the oldest of these structures is the 2nd-century House of Fishing, a simpler structure, but with fine mosaics. The newer villas become increasingly elaborate: most impressive is the House of the Hunt. Some of the stunning works have been removed to the Bardo Museum in Tunis, but lots remain in place, and it's an evocative experience to see them as flooring in these buildings. The most striking is found in the House of Amphitrite – of Venus and centaurs, with attendant cherubs.

Bulla Regia is about 160km west of Tunis, 9km north of Jendouba, and may be easily visited on a day trip from Tunis, Le Kef or Tabarka. If you visit en route to somewhere, you can leave your pack at the ticket office.

TUNISIA

Train to Jendouba is the best bet to/from Tunis, and there are regular buses and louages to/from Le Kef and Tabarka. A taxi from Jendouba costs US$2, or shared taxis to/from the site cost US$0.30.

LE KEF (EL KEF)

☎ 78 / pop 46,000

High in the hills, Le Kef (El Kef, Arabic for 'rock') is topped by a storybook Byzantine kasbah. Skirted by fields that are dotted with figures in woolly hats and headscarves, the city is made up of narrow, hilly, cobbled streets and blue-shuttered buildings and is centred on a scoop of park. It is one of Tunisia's best-kept secrets, with the usual men-hangin'-out-in-cafés scene and a kind and friendly atmosphere.

The city centre, set around the Place de l'Indépendance, is a 10-minute walk uphill from the bus and louage station, or US$0.20 in a shared taxi.

Information

There are several banks around Place de l'Indépendance, and a busy **post office** (Rue Hedi Chaker) nearby. **Publinet** (Place de l'Indépendance) charges US$1 per hour.

Sights

The **kasbah** (🕑 8am-5pm; admission free) dominates the city from a spur running off Jebel Dyr. It's often used as a film location. There are great views across the rolling blue-green landscape with its Tuscan trees. The structure that stands today is the latest of a string of fortresses that have occupied the site since the 5th century BC. To get there, follow the stone steps leading uphill through the old **medina** from Place de l'Indépendance. The road that flanks the kasbah leads to the well-laid-out **Musée des Arts et Traditions Populaires** (admission US$1, camera US$1; 🕑 9.30am-4.30pm mid-Sep–May 9am-1pm & 4pm-7pm Apr–mid-Sep), in a beautiful former high-ceilinged *zaouia* (a complex surrounding the tomb of a saint) dating from 1666. The museum concentrates on the culture of the region's Berber nomads, complete with tents. Below the kasbah is the beautiful 17th-century **Mosque of Sidi Boumakhlouf**, with white cupolas and a brilliantly tiled interior. Outside is an enchanting stepped area, shadowed by a single tree and dotted with café chairs.

The **Synagogue Al Ghriba** (Rue Farhat Hached) is a curiosity – there are no Jews here now, and the restored synagogue pays tribute to a part of local culture that's disappeared. As well as the restored interior, there are fragments of newspapers and old manuscripts, like relics. The caretaker will let you in; you should give him a tip.

Sleeping & Eating

All the hotels are on or around Place de l'Indépendance.

Hôtel Le Source (☎ 204 397; s/d US$12/20) This place has eccentric management. There are some attractive rooms with balconies, though the bathrooms are not always gleamingly clean. The best room has an attached bathroom and is completely tiled, with an elaborate stuccoed domed ceiling – it's the owner's pride and joy.

Hôtel Medina (☎ 204 183; 18 Rue Farhat Hached; s/d US$8/16) Basic but friendly. The beds bear a resemblance to hospital furniture, but the rooms are clean and the bathrooms cleanish.

Résidence Venus (☎ 204 695; Rue Mouldi Khamessi; s/d US$16/24 with bathroom & breakfast) This much smarter place is nestled beneath the walls of the old kasbah; it's a small, family-run pension with comfortable rooms that have heating. Prices include a good breakfast.

Restaurant Bou Maklouf (Rue Hedi Chaker; mains around US$1.50) Diagonally opposite the post office, this is welcoming and popular, and has good chicken and chips and *lablabi* (chickpea soup).

Restaurant Venus (☎ 200 355; Rue Farhat Hached; mains around US$8) The town's best restaurant, and it serves alcohol.

Getting There & Away

There are buses to/from Tunis (US$5.50 toUS$6.50, 3½ hours, hourly) – you can ask to be dropped off at the New Dougga turnoff, for Dougga (US$2.50, one hour) and to/from Jendouba (one hour, two daily).

DOUGGA

Perched above the rolling, *Sound-of-Music* landscape of the Kalled Valley and Tebersouk Mountains lies the Roman city of **Dougga** (admission US$1.50, camera US$1; 🕑 8am-7pm Apr-Sep, 8.30am-5.30pm Oct-Mar). It's incredibly complete, giving a beguiling glimpse of Roman comforts and culture – there's a powerful sense of how Romans lived their lives, flitting between the baths, the theatre and temples (21 have been identified here). The city was built on the site of ancient Thugga, a Numidian settlement, which explains why the streets are so uncharacteristically tangled. The semicircular sweep of the theatre, built in AD 188, accommodated more than 3500 spectators. Today it allows the audience beautiful views, and is used to good effect during the **Dougga Festival** in July and August. The town is dominated by the imposing, hilltop **Capitol of Dougga** (AD 166), with 10m-high walls and six mighty, show-off columns supporting the portico. Nearby are the **Licinian Baths** – their size is a further indication of the town's prosperity. A tunnel for the slaves, who kept the baths operating, is a reminder of how all this good life was maintained.

The site is 110km southwest of Tunis; Tebersouk is the closest town. It's easy to visit the site on a day trip from Tunis or Le Kef – or en route between the two; you can leave your pack at a local business. Frequent buses or louages between Tunis and Le Kef all call at Tebersouk. At the bus stop you'll find locals asking US$4 to take you the remaining 7km to the site and pick you up at a time of your choice. Alternatively, if you're coming from Le Kef, you can get off the bus at the New Dougga turn-off on the main road. From here it's a 3km walk to the ruins, but, again, locals will offer to take you there and pick you up later for US$4.

CENTRAL TUNISIA

The transition zone between north and south encompasses vibrant, quiet towns, centred on mazelike medinas. All bear the signs of historic civilisations, but El Jem is most in thrall to the past, being completely dominated by its imposing Roman colosseum. Off the east coast is the culturally intriguing, beach-fringed island of Jerba.

SOUSSE
☎ 73 / pop 155,900
Sousse has a huge medina, surrounded by sandcastle-simple, perfectly formed fortifications. The twisting, arched and cobbled streets and alleyways are packed with shops selling kiss-me-quick *chechyas* (red felt

skullcaps), lurid paintings, perfume and nougat, but the sales pitch is appealingly laidback. The long, powdered-sand beaches are attractive, if busy, and the museum is peaceful and a must-see. The continual holiday trade and large student population make it a lively place.

Information
Everything of importance is close to the main square, Place Farhat Hached, on the northeast side of the medina. The **tourist office** (☎ 225 157; Place Farhat Hached; ⏰ 8.30am-1pm & 3-5.45pm Sun-Thu & 8.30am-1.30pm Fri & Sat) is efficient and English is spoken. The **post office** (Ave de la République) is nearby. There are banks along Ave Habib Bourguiba. There's a **Publinet** (Ave Mohammed Maarouf) and a **Taxiphone office** (Place des Martyrs).

Sights
The main monuments of the medina are the **ribat**, a monastery that is more like a fortress, and the **Grande Mosquée**. Both are in the northeast corner, near Place Farhat Hached.

The **kasbah** on top of the hill contains the **Musée de Source** (☎ 7322 7256; admission TD1.6, camera US$1; ⏰ 9am-noon & 2-6pm Tue-Thu & 9am-6pm Fri-Sun). This collection is second only to the Bardo Museum in Tunis, and it displays some incredible Roman mosaics, beautifully restored and presented in buildings around courtyards, providing a glimpse of the glory of Roman life. Subjects include a swirling-haired, sad-eyed Neptune, muscular gods and lots of fish. There's no access to the kasbah from inside the medina; access is from an entrance outside the medina walls.

The flip side of Sousse's gleaming antiquities is the unexpected walled-off **red light district** in the northwestern corner of the medina.

Sleeping
The cheapest hotels are to be found in the streets around the Grand Mosquée in the northeastern corner of the medina.

Hôtel Ezzouhour (☎ 228 729; 48 Rue de Paris) The rooms here are small, but they are brightened by tiling and it's in the heart of the medina.

Hôtel Gabès (☎ 226 977; 12 Rue de Paris) This is well placed for emergency stuffed-camel purchases. It has higgledy-piggledy small

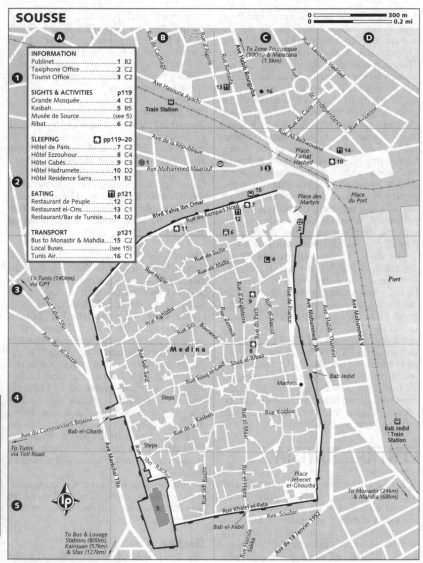

SOUSSE

0 _____ 300 m
0 _____ 0.2 mi

INFORMATION
Publinet.........................1 B2
Taxiphone Office...............2 C2
Tourist Office...................3 C2

SIGHTS & ACTIVITIES p119
Grande Mosquée................4 C3
Kasbah...........................5 B5
Musée de Source...........(see 5)
Ribat.............................6 C2

SLEEPING pp119–20
Hôtel de Paris..................7 C2
Hôtel Ezzouhour...............8 C4
Hôtel Gabés.....................9 C3
Hôtel Hadrumete..............10 D2
Hôtel Residence Sarra........11 B2

EATING p121
Restaurant de Peuple.........12 C2
Restaurant el-Ons.............13 C1
Restaurant/Bar de Tunisie...14 D2

TRANSPORT p121
Bus to Monastir & Mahdia....15 C2
Local Buses...............(see 15)
Tunis Air.......................16 C1

To Zone Touristique (100m) & Maracana (1.5km)

Train Station

To Tunis (140km) via GP1

To Tunis via Toll Road

Medina

Steps

Steps

Place des Martyrs

Place du Port

Port

Place Farhat Hached

Bab Jedid

Bab Jedid Train Station

Markets

Bab el-Gharbi

Bab el-Kebli

Place Jebenet el-Ghourba

To Monastir (24km) & Mahdia (68km)

To Bus & Louage Stations (800m), Kairouan (57km) & Sfax (127km)

rooms, some with good views. The walls are
thin here but it's fairly clean.

Hôtel Residence Sarra (☎ 227 737; Rue du
Rempart Nord; s/d US$8/16) With a family feel,
this has clean rooms opening on to a
courtyard.

Hôtel de Paris (☎ 220 564; 15 Rue du Rempart Nord;
s/d US$10/18) Just inside the medina's north

wall, this is so spic and span it's almost
clinical, with narrow modern rooms opening on to a rooftop.

Hôtel Hadrumete (☎ 226 291; Place Farhat
Hached; s/d with bathroom from US$18/26) This more
upmarket place has a fine 1950s interior.
Rooms have good views of the port and the
medina, and discounts are available.

Eating

Rue de Remada, between the train station and Ave Habib Bourguiba, has several good cheap restaurants, but there are also several good snack places dotted in the medina, particularly along Rue de Paris.

Restaurant du Peuple (☎ 226 182; Rue du Rempart Nord; dishes US$2.50-7) Just inside the medina wall, this is an excellent choice, very clean with good food, such as fresh fish. You can sit outside or in the tiled interior, and bring your own wine.

Restaurant el-Ons (Rue de Remada; dishes US$1-2) This is one of a couple of similar places on this street, offering salads and some simple main dishes.

Restaurant-Bar de Tunisie (Rue Ali Belhaouane; dishes US$3.50-7) Smart and popular, this specialises in seafood and serves booze.

Entertainment

There are several big brash discos catering to the tourist trade, such as **Maracana** (admission US$4), a giant, glitzy, bingolike hall with a big sound system, mirrors and lots of over-the-top lighting. There's lots of velvet booth seating, and it's good for a drink even if you don't fancy getting tacky on the dancefloor.

Getting There & Away

The train stations are conveniently central, making train the best way to travel. The station for Sfax and Tunis is just northwest of Place Farhat Hached, whereas trains to Monastir and Mahdia (US$1.50, 1½ hours, half-hourly), via the airport (20 minutes), leave from Bab Jedid station at the southern end of Ave Mohammed V. Watch out for pickpockets – several travellers have reported having stuff stolen here.

The bus and louage stations are at Souq el-Ahad, 1km southwest of the medina on the road to Kairouan. Buses run to/from the towns of El Jem (US$2.50, one hour, three daily), Tataouine (US$14, 6½ hours, one daily), Matmata (US$10, 5½ hours, one daily), Jerba (US$13, seven hours, one daily), Douz (US$13, seven hours, one daily), Tunis (US$5.50, 2½ hours, 10 daily), Nefta (US$12, six hours, one daily) and Tripoli (Libya; US$20, one daily Monday, Tuesday & Friday). There are louages to the same destinations for around the same fares, as well as to Kairouan (US$2.50, 1½ hours), Gabès (US$9, three hours) and Sfax (US$5, 2½ hours).

KAIROUAN

☎ 77 / pop 110,000

The old walled holy city of Kairouan encloses crumbling, white-washed, blue- and green-edged houses, some hung with birdcages and many marked by the hand of Fatima. It was here that Arabs established their first base when they arrived from the east in AD 670. The city is famous for its carpets, and woollen splashes of colour decorate most shops.

Away from the main souvenir drag, it's lovely to wander around the narrow cobbled streets and big doorways of the medina. Many local women are wrapped in the traditional Berber cream shawls, and their faces are marked with traditional tattoos.

Information

There's an **ONTT tourist office** (☎ 231 897/797 221/230 452; Place des Martyrs; ☺ 8am-5.30pm Mon-Sat, 8am-noon Sun) and a **tourist office** (Ave Ibn el-Aghlab; ☺ 8am-6pm Apr-Sep, 8am-5.30pm Nov-Mar) near the Aghlabite Basins that sells combined tickets that allow you into most of the town's attractions (US$3.50).

All the major banks are on the streets south of Place des Martyrs, and there's a **post office** (Ave de la République). Travellers can check email at **Publinet** (Ave Zama el-Belaoui) for US$1 per hour. It's open 24 hours, and there's another branch next to Hotel el Menema.

Sights

The fortlike 9th-century **Grande Mosquée** (Rue Okba ibn Nafâa; ☺ 8am-noon Tue-Sun, 8am-2pm Mon) fills up a large area of the northeastern corner of the medina. Plain on the outside, inside it is filled with a huge marble-paved courtyard surrounded by a colonnade. The prayer hall is at the southern end, and is supported by around 400 pillars – non-Muslims are not allowed in this part. A lot of the building materials, such as columns, have been taken from Roman and Byzantine buildings. On Friday it's packed with people for afternoon prayer, and a glimpse of the crowded courtyard and everyone pouring out afterwards is an arresting sight.

Other sites in the medina include the **Mosque of the Three Doors** (interior closed to non-Muslims), also 9th century, famous for the rare intertwined floral and Arabic inscriptions carved in its facade; the 14th-century

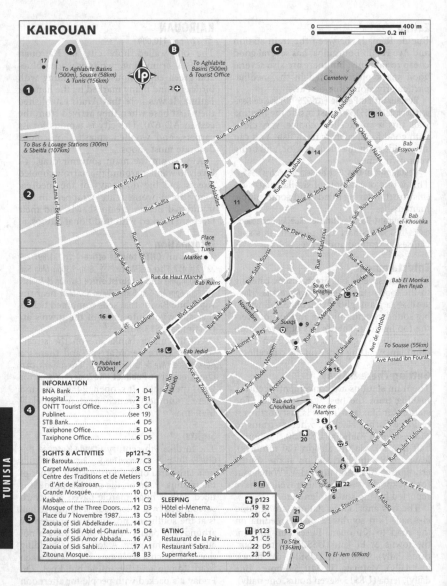

KAIROUAN

0 — 400 m
0 — 0.2 mi

Zaouia Sidi Abid el-Gharian with some fine stucco and woodwork; and the depressing one-to-avoid **Bir Barouta** where a blindfolded camel makes a small enclosed circuit to draw water from a well whose waters are said to be connected to Mecca.

Northwest of the medina is the 17th-century **Zaouia Sidi Sahab** (☼ 7.30am-6pm), tiled in luminescent colours and known as the 'barber mosque', because it contains the mausoleum of one of the Prophet's companions, Abu Zama el-Belaoui, who used to carry around three hairs from the Prophet's beard. Nearby are the **Aghlabite Basins** (☼ 8am-noon & 3-7pm Apr-Oct, 8.30am-5.30pm Nov-Mar), 9th-century reservoirs – good for a picnic.

Sleeping & Eating

Hôtel Sabra (☎ 230 263; Place des Martyrs; s/d US$9/14) Just outside Bab ech Chouhada, the main gate, this hotel overlooks a square with a lovely tree-shaded café that has school chairs. Rooms are plain and clean, and there are 24-hour hot showers.

Hôtel el-Menema (☎ 225 003; Rue Moez ibn Badiss; s/d US$8/16) Between the medina and the Aghlabite basins, this is better than it looks from the outside, but can be a bit noisy.

Restaurant Sabra (☎ 235 095; Ave de la République; mains US$1-3) A friendly, popular local eatery with a piercing bird in a cage.

Restaurant de la Paix (Ave de la République; dishes US$2-4) A rough-and-ready local favourite.

Stalls everywhere sell the Kairouan speciality, *makhroud* – honey-soaked pastry stuffed with dates.

Getting There & Away

The bus and louage stations are northwest of the medina on the road to Sbeitla, off Ave Zama el-Belaoui. Kairouan has good transport connections with the rest of Tunisia.

MAHDIA

☎ 73 / pop 44,600

Mahdia is a beguiling place, with an eccentric small-town feel, as if David Lynch–style characters could be on the cards. It's pretty, with a most lovely central **Place du Caire** filled with café seating, shaded by trees and vines, and bordered by the 18th-century **Mosque of Mustapha Hamza** (non-Muslims allowed in courtyard outside prayer times). The town dates back to the 10th century, when it was the capital of the Fatimids, a Muslim dynasty ruled by Mahdi, which dominated North Africa from AD 909 to 1171. There are lots of weaving workshops hidden away in the back streets – some of the burly artisans spend half the week fishing, the other half making silk scarves. Access to the old medina is through the massive **Skifa el-Kahla gate** – more of a tunnel – which is all that remains of the fortifications that protected ancient Mahdia. The unadorned **Grande Mosquée** (non-Muslims allowed in courtyard outside prayer times; Place Khadi en-Noamine) is a 20th-century replica of the mosque built by the Mahdi in the 10th century. The **Borj el-Kebir** (admission US$1; ☺ 9am-noon & 2-6pm) is a large fortress – there's not much left to see but the views from the ramparts are worth paying for.

Mahdia's **docks**, near the train station, were used as the seafront at Benghazi in *The English Patient*. There are two **bain maures** (hammams; ☺ men 4am-2pm & 7pm-midnight, women 2-7pm) in the centre.

Information

There is a small **tourist office** (☎ 681 098; Rue Aly Bey) just inside the medina. **Banque de Sud** (Ave Farhat Hached) changes money, as does **Banque de Tunisie** (off Rue des Fatimides).

Sleeping & Eating

There are two hotels inside the medina.

Hôtel el-Jazira (☎ 681 629, 36 Rue Ibn Fourat; s/d US$7/18) A top location with rooms overlooking the sea.

Hôtel Médina (☎ 694 664; Rue el Kaem; s/d US$7/18) A family feel, run by a distinguished black-cloaked character, and the rooms are clean.

Restaurant el-Moez (mains US$1.50) Friendly and a local favourite, with a selection of perhaps two daily specials, such as chicken or fish. The food is hearty, simple and very fresh.

Restaurant Le Lido (☎ 681 339; Ave Farhat Hached; dishes US$3-15) A leap upmarket, with tablecloths. You can sit outside, and wine and beer is served.

Getting There & Away

The train station is 500m west of the town centre, beyond the port. There are regular trains to Sousse (1st/2nd US$2.50/1.50) and one daily to Tunis (US$8/5.50, four hours). The bus and louage station are about 800m further west on the road to Sfax. There are louages to Tunis (US$6.50), Sousse (US$1.50, one hour), Sfax (US$3.50), Karaouan (US$3.50) and El-Jem (US$1.50, 30 minutes), and buses to Sfax (US$3.50, 2½ hours) and Sousse (US$1.50, 1½ hours, hourly).

EL-JEM

☎ 73 / pop 19,500

The huge honey-coloured **Roman Colosseum** (admission US$3.50, camera US$1; ☺ 7am-7pm Apr–mid-Sep & 7.30-5.30pm mid-Sep–Mar) seems to be on a different scale from the small town of El-Jem, as if it's turned up from a grander, huger place. Built nearly 2000 years ago by olive oil traders with money to burn, it showcased gladiatorial combat, executions and other such popular Roman entertainments, and it had such state-of-the-art features as a movable floor. The town was once a kind of

Roman Las Vegas, with lots of feasting and merry-making between the bloodletting. There are more than 20 El-Jem mosaics on Dionysian themes in the Bardo Museum in Tunis. Today, the town is more subdued, with lots of Obi-Wan lookalikes on mopeds and some interesting antique shops.

Admission to the colosseum also gets you into the **museum**, which is about 500m south of the train station on the road to Sfax. It houses some excavated villas of the previous, loaded locals and fine, complete mosaics, including such subjects as the coy-looking *Genius of the Year*.

Hôtel Julius (☎ 690 044; s/d US$13-16/17-26 with bathroom) Right next to the train station, this is the only hotel – and only bar – in town. It has unexciting, but comfortable and well-appointed rooms, with views of the colosseum.

Restaurant Le Bonheur (☎ 630 306; dishes US$3-6) The slogan is 'live the dream with Restaurant Le Bonheur' – depends what your dream is, but it does serve good food, such as *salade tunisienne* and *salade mechouia*.

The louage station is near the museum and serves Sfax (US$2.50, one hour), Sousse (US$2.50, 1½ hours) and Mahdia (US$1.50, 30 minutes). There are trains to/from Sfax (US$2.50, one hour, three daily) via Sousse (US$2.50, 30 minutes, three daily). You can leave your luggage at the train station for US$1.50.

SFAX
☎ 74 / pop 249,000
Sfaxiens have the reputation of being hard-working business people, and Tunisians might laugh if you tell them you're coming here. However, Tunisia's second-largest city is worth a visit partly because there are so few tourists. The medina hasn't been pret-tified for visitors, but contains blacksmith workshops and butchers as it has for cen-turies. It's surrounded by crenulated walls that could have been filched from a chil-dren's castle, dating from the 7th century. Female travellers might find the atmosphere somewhat oppressive, as local men are not so used to seeing foreign women.

Information
The **tourist office** (☎ 497 041; Ave Mohammed Hedi Khefecha) is by the port. There are lots of banks around Ave Habib Bourguiba, several

with ATMs. **Publinet** (Ave Ali Bach Hamba) charges US$1.50 per hour.

Sights
The old medina, used to represent Cairo in the film *The English Patient*, contains the major attractions. Highlights include the atmospheric old **covered souqs**, just north of the 9th-century **Grande Mosquée** (Rue de la Grande Mosquée; closed to non-Muslims) and the **Dar Jellouli Museum of Popular Traditions** (admission US$1, camera US$1; ☻ 9.30am-4.30pm Tue-Sun) housed in a very beautiful 17th-century mansion with carved wooden panelling and ornate stucco and displaying jewellery, costume and painted glass.

Sleeping
Hôtel Ennacer (☎ 211 037; 100 Rue des Notaires; s/d US$6/11) This medina place is friendly and quite clean with small, blue-shuttered rooms.

Hôtel Medina (☎ 220 354; Rue Mongi Slim; s/d US$3/6) The only real recommendation for this place in the medina is that it's cheap. Single women would feel uncomfortable here. The rooms are dingy, and there's a creepy pair of clogs in each.

Hôtel de la Paix (☎ 296 437; 10 Rue Alexandre Dumas; s/d US$6/13, with shower US$10/13; shower US$1) In the Ville Nouvelle, this hotel has tired-looking rooms, but they do have balconies.

Hôtel Alexander (☎ 221 911; 16 Rue Alexandre Dumas; s/d US$15/19) Nearby, this place has a lot more class, with comfortable, shuttered rooms.

Eating
Shop 90 (Souq el-Omrane) Ahmed serves up su-perb, delicious lablabi (US$0.50) from this market hole-in-the-wall, and is a friendly soul.

Restaurant au Bec Fin (Place 2 du Mars) Seafood is Sfax's speciality, and the Bec Fin does some good dishes amid plastic plants.

Restaurant Tunisienne (Rue Borj Ennar; mains around US$1.50) Just inside the medina, this is a brightly lit, wipe-clean place with simple dishes such as spaghetti and couscous.

Salon de Thé Chez Elle (Ave Ali Bach Hamba; cof-fee US$0.50) This is an unusual place – an all-women café (at least in the downstairs room). It features dusty Christmas decora-tions, goldfish and local women with big hair who smoke furiously.

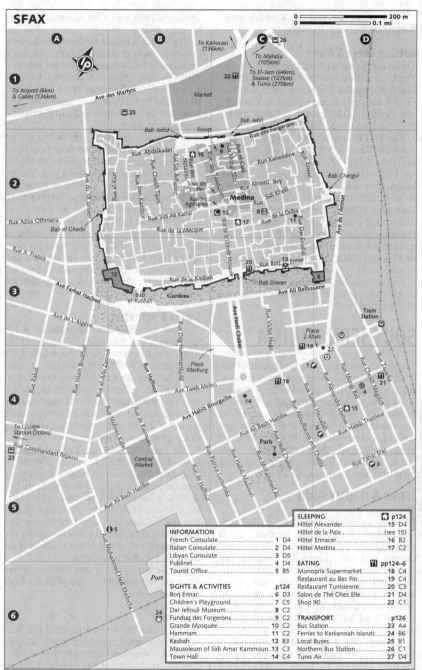

SFAX

0   200 m
0   0.1 mi

To Kairouan
(136km)

To Mahdia
(105km)

To El-Jem (64km),
Sousse (127km)
& Tunis (270km)

To Airport (6km)
& Gabès (136km)

Ave des Martyrs

Market

Bab Jedid   Souqs   Bab Jebli

Rue des Forgerons

Rue Abdelkader

Rue Kaireddine

Bab Chergui

Rue Ahmed Bey

Medina

Rue de la Driba

Rue Aziza Othmana

Bab el Gharbi

Rue de la Mecque

Rue A. France

Rue de la Kasbah

Bab Diwan

Rue Bori Ennar

Ave Farhat Hached

Bab
el-Kasbah   Gardens

Ave Ali Belhouane

Ave de L'Algérie

Train
Station

Place
2 Mars

Place
Marburg

Ave Taieb Mehiri

Ave Habib Bourguiba

Ave Ali Bach Hamba

Park

To Louage
Station (300m)

Rue Commandant Bejaoui

Central
Market

Port

TUNISIA

INFORMATION
French Consulate............... 1 D4
Italian Consulate............... 2 D4
Libyan Consulate............... 3 D5
Publinet............... 4 D4
Tourist Office............... 5 B5

SIGHTS & ACTIVITIES   p124
Borj Ennar............... 6 D3
Children's Playground....... 7 C5
Dar Jellouli Museum......... 8 C2
Funduq des Forgerons....... 9 C2
Grande Mosquée............. 10 C2
Hammam............... 11 C2
Kasbah............... 12 B3
Mausoleum of Sidi Amar Kammoun.13 C3
Town Hall............... 14 C4

SLEEPING   p124
Hôtel Alexander............... 15 D4
Hôtel de la Paix............... (see 15)
Hôtel Ennacer............... 16 B2
Hôtel Medina............... 17 C2

EATING   pp124–6
Monoprix Supermarket....... 18 C4
Restaurant au Bec Fin....... 19 C4
Restaurant Tunisienne....... 20 C3
Salon de Thé Chez Elle....... 21 D4
Shop 90............... 22 C1

TRANSPORT   p126
Bus Station............... 23 A4
Ferries to Kerkennah Islands.24 B6
Local Buses............... 25 B1
Northern Bus Station......... 26 C1
Tunis Air............... 27 D4

For self-caterers, there's a **Monoprix super-market** (Rue Aboulkacem ech Chabbi).

Getting There & Away
Trains are the most convenient way to travel. The train station is at the eastern end of Ave Habib Bourguiba. There are trains north to El-Jem, Sousse (1st/2nd US$6/4, half-hourly) and Tunis (US$10/8); south to Gabès (US$6/5.60); and west to Metlaoui (US$9/7).

The SNTRI bus station is on Rue Commandant Bejaoui. SNTRI has regular buses to Tunis (US$10, four hours, nine daily) via Douz (two daily), Sousse (US$5, two hours, two daily), Matmata (one daily), Jerba (US$9, four hours, three daily) and Tataouine (US$10, four hours, two daily). The louage station is 300m west of the bus station, and has services to all these destinations for around the same price, as well as El-Jem (US$2.50) and Tripoli (US$20, seven hours).

Ferries to the Kerkennah Islands (US$0.50, seven daily) leave from the docks on Ave Mohammed Hedi Khefecha.

SOUTHERN TUNISIA

The south leads into the bleak heat of the desert, and the landscape becomes increasingly Martian. Huge salt lakes form strange cracked white surfaces, fringed by crowded palmeraies. Fortified granaries and towns surmount barren hilltops and overlook pitted and pocked scrubland. Hot springs spout at miragelike oases deep in the desert. From rolling around on big dunes to trainspotting phantom film locations, it's all here.

JERBA & HOUMT SOUQ
☎ 75
Jerba is an island ringed by palm-lined, white-sand, resort-laden beaches. It is distinguished by its unusual whitewashed domed and soft, curved architecture. The culture here is distinct from that of the mainland: with strong Berber origins, it was also for a long time shaped by a significant Jewish community, which, since the formation of Israel, has been reduced to about 700, as former residents have migrated there.

It claims to be the Land of the Lotus Eaters described in Homer's *Odyssey*, where people lived 'drugged by the legendary honeyed

fruit' – Ulysses had a lot of trouble prising his crew away.

The island is linked to the mainland by a causeway built in Roman times, and more mundanely by 24-hour car ferries between Ajim (where Obi-Wan Kenobi had his house; see 'Top Ten *Star Wars* Locations', p129) and Jorf. The island's main town and transport hub is Houmt Souq, in the middle of the north coast.

In Houmt Souq a narrow tangle of souvenir souqs open into lazy café-lined squares. There's a **tourist office** (☎ 650 915; off Ave Habib Bourguiba; ☼ 9am-1pm & 3-6pm Mon-Thu, 9am-1pm Fri & Sat) in the middle of town and an **Office National du Tourisme Tunisien** (ONTT; ☎ 650 016; ☼ same hours) near the fort. There are also banks with ATMs and a **post office** (Ave Habib Bourguiba). **Publinet** (off Ave Abdelhamid el-Kadhi) charges US$1.50 per hour, as does **Djerba Cyber Espace** (1st floor, 135 Ave Habib Bourguiba), accessed through the arch and up the stairs. There's a **Taxiphone** office (Ave Abdelhamid el-Kadhi).

Sights & Activities
The old fort, **Borj Ghazi Mustapha** (off Blvd de l'Environment), on the beach, 500m north of town, is sturdy and square shaped, as if it's come from a well-formed bucket. It dates from the 13th century, but was extended in the 16th. An infamous massacre took place here in 1560, when the Turks captured the fort and stacked the skulls of their Spanish victims just west of it – they remained there as a menacing warning for about 300 years.

The **museum** (Ave Abdelhamid el-Kadhi) is housed in a beautiful, simple Zaouia of Sidi Zitouni (a former religious fraternity based around a marabout) with whitewashed domes, a cedar-wood painted ceiling and small courtyards. It has costumes, jewellery and cultural stuff about the Berber and Jewish communities. It's worth visiting the busy **fishing port**, about 500m north of town along Ave Habib Bourguiba.

Bain Turque (US$1; ☼ men 6am-noon, women 1-6pm; Ave Habib Bourguiba) is the place to head for a hammam.

Sleeping
Houmt Souq has some wonderful places to stay at, converted from funduqs – lodging houses for the camel caravans that stopped here in Ottoman times; the merchants stayed

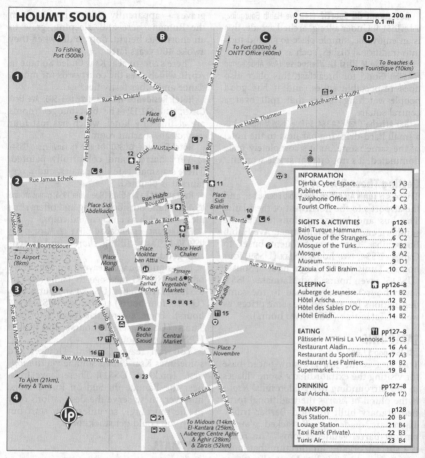

HOUMT SOUQ

INFORMATION	
Djerba Cyber Espace	1 A3
Publinet	2 C2
Taxiphone Office	3 C2
Tourist Office	4 A3

SIGHTS & ACTIVITIES	p126
Bain Turque Hammam	5 A1
Mosque of the Strangers	6 C2
Mosque of the Turks	7 B2
Mosque	8 A2
Museum	9 D1
Zaouia of Sidi Brahim	10 C2

SLEEPING	pp126–8
Auberge de Jeunesse	11 B2
Hôtel Arischa	12 B2
Hôtel des Sables D'Or	13 B2
Hôtel Erriadh	14 B2

EATING	pp127–8
Pâtisserie M'Hirsi La Viennoise	15 C3
Restaurant Aladin	16 A4
Restaurant du Sportif	17 A3
Restaurant Les Palmiers	18 B2
Supermarket	19 B4

DRINKING	pp127–8
Bar Arischa	(see 12)

TRANSPORT	p128
Bus Station	20 B4
Louage Station	21 B4
Taxi Rank (Private)	22 B3
Tunis Air	23 B4

on the top floor while their animals were housed below.

Auberge Centre Aghir (☎ 657 366; dm US$1, camp sites per person US$1.50) Camping is on the east coast. Buses from Houmt Souq to Aghir can drop you there.

Auberge de Jeunesse (☎ 650 619; 11 Rue Moncef Bey; dm with breakfast US$5) In an old funduq, this place is friendly and great value, with cool arched rooms around a flower-filled courtyard.

Hôtel Arischa (☎ 650 384; 36 Rue Ghazi Mustapha; from s/d US$9/13, with bathroom US$11/17) Another funduq, this surrounds a lovely courtyard as well. The more expensive rooms are spacious, with painted furniture and soft-coloured walls.

Hôtel des Sables d'Or (☎ 650 423; s/d with shower US$8/16) This is an immaculate townhouse around a pretty inner courtyard. It has small rooms.

Hôtel Erriadh (☎ 650 756; 10 Rue Mohammed Ferjani; s/d from US$16/21) This is an attractive, upmarket funduq with large tiled rooms.

Eating & Drinking
Restaurant Les Palmiers (Place d'Algérie; dishes US$2-4) Tasty, simple food. The interior is decorated with red cotton, and there's a TV to watch if you get bored with your companions.

Restaurant Aladin (Ave Mohammed Badra; dishes US$0.50-4) This cheery little place with small tables serves traditional dishes, such as *chorba*, and lots of seafood.

Restaurant du Sportif (147 Ave Habib Bourguiba; dishes US$1-4) Under a long, arched arcade, this is an enjoyable, simple place to sit and tuck into traditional dishes, such as couscous.

Pâtisserie M'Hirsi La Viennoise (Ave Abdelhamid el-Kadhi) Good for breakfast, this place also does respectable cakes, and it has good people-watching tables that spill over a central square.

Bar Arischa (☎ 650 384; 36 Rue Ghazi Mustapha) is a small hard-drinking bar next to the hotel of the same name. As it's completely male dominated, it's not one for single women.

Getting There & Away

There's a **Tunis Air office** (Ave Habib Bourguiba), and the airport's to the northwest of the island. The bus and louage stations are at the southern end of the main street, Ave Habib Bourguiba. There are frequent buses to Gabès (US$4, two hours), Sfax (US$9, four hours), Tunis (US$16, eight hours), Sousse (US$13, seven hours) and Matmata (US$5, seven hours). Louages head to the same destinations for around the same prices, as well as Tataouine (US$5, two hours).

TATAOUINE

☎ 75 / pop 57,800

This is a gentle town, a slow-paced base for visiting the extraordinary *ksour* villages in the surrounding dry golden hills. *Ksour* is the plural of *ksar* – the traditional fortified granary built by local Berber tribes. These are made up of stacked *ghorfas*, narrow barrel-vaulted rooms. The result is a surreal, organic architecture that looks as if it should be inhabited by trolls. It's no surprise that the makers of *Star Wars* have used these villages as sets for the films.

The best sites are a fair way from town, but can easily be reached by chartering a taxi (half day about US$16), or via local transport with luck, patience and a bit of timing (see later on this page for more details). Don't miss beautiful **Ksar Ouled Soltane**, 24km southeast of Tataouine, where the *ghorfas* rise a dizzying four storeys, reached by precarious fairytale staircases, and overlook desert scrub hills. Equally impressive are the ancient hilltop villages of **Chenini** and **Douiret**, which spill across and merge with the rocky ochre slopes, southwest of Tataouine. Chenini boasts the mysterious underground mosque, containing 5m-long

graves – apparently Christians hid from the Romans here and, sleeping, grew to an enormous height, only to die when they awoke 400 years later.

There's a festival at Ksar Ouled Soltane in April, which uses the courtyards for music, dance and other festivities.

Hôtel Résidence Hamza (☎ 863 506; Ave Hedi Chaker; s/d US$12/13) The best budget rooms are at this tiny hotel, which has just four very clean, spartan rooms.

Hôtel Essour (☎ 860 104; Rue 18 Janvier; s/d US$4/8) Very narrow and colourfully painted. There's a small café downstairs, and a restaurant is planned.

Restaurant La Medina (Rue 1 Juin 1955; mains around US$1.50) Some outside seating and offers simple meals such as chicken and chips.

Restaurant Essendabad (Rue 2 Mars; dishes US$0.50-2) Tasty, filling *chorba* and is reliably good.

Buses and louages leave from the centre of town. SNTRI buses go to Tunis (US$18, 8½ hours) via Gabès (US$5, two hours), Sfax (US$10, four hours) and Sousse (US$14, 6½ hours). There are regular louages to/from Tunis (US$16, eight hours) and Gabès (US$4.50, two hours).

You can reach Chenini, Douiret and sometimes Ksar Ouled Soltane via *camionnette* (pick-up; US$1). These leave from near the Banque du Sud on Rue 2 Mars; however, these serve the destinations only in the mornings, so unless you start out early you could get stuck there.

MATMATA

☎ 75

The Berbers of Matmata burrowed underground to escape the summer heat, and their otherworldly underground homes are set among sculpted sand hills, the colour of sawdust. This alien architecture was spotted by George Lucas as a location for the first *Star Wars* film, and a few, seemingly insignificant weeks spent shooting here in 1976 changed Matmata forever: the tour buses started trundling through and have never stopped.

Matmata boasts dozens of troglodyte pit homes, all built along the same lines: a large central courtyard, usually circular, is dug out of the soft sandstone, and the rounded rooms are then tunnelled off the perimeter.

TOP 10 STAR WARS LOCATIONS

Tunisia has the sensuous desert curves that filled out *The English Patient*, and its impressive fortifications lent an air of authenticity to *Monty Python's Life of Brian*. But it's best known for supplying the strange podlike architecture and wild desertscapes that have given the *Star Wars* canon such a powerful visual identity. The makers even left bits of sets behind – it's intriguing to learn how much was made out of plywood. Some agencies offer *Star Wars* tours; try in Tozeur, where most hotels and agencies offer *Star Wars* tours, and all charge the same reasonable prices.

- **Sidi Driss Hotel (Matmata)** The famous Sidi Driss was used for interior shots of the Lars family homestead in *Star Wars*. Bits of set are still in place here (it was used again in *Phantom Menace*, *Attack of the Clones* and *Episode IV: A New Hope*), complete with writing in black marker pen on the back. A dining room is spangled with ceiling paintings – this is where Luke tucked into blue milkshake and went head to head over the harvest with his Uncle Owen.

- **Ong Jemel (30km north of Tozeur)** This was Darth Maul's lookout in *The Phantom Menace* and the location for his and Qui-Gon's tussle, as well as lots of podrace scenes. The road here was built by *The English Patient* crew, who indulged in a lot of billowing sandblown romantic stuff in the area.

- **Mos Espa (30km north of Tozeur)** Near Ong Jemel, Mos Espa village is a construct in the middle of the desert used for the prequel films; its battered sets echoing local Berber architecture.

- **Sidi Bouhlel (east of Tozeur on the edge of Chott el-Jerid)** Nicknamed *Star Wars* Canyon, this has seen jawas parking their sandcrawlers, R2D2 trundling plaintively along, Luke attacked by Tusken Raiders, and Ben and Luke overlooking Mos Eisley. Scenes from the *Phantom Menace* and *Attack of the Clones* were filmed here too.

- **Ksar Haddada (near Tataouine)** A location for the Mos Espa slave quarters, Ksar Haddada has stunningly weird architecture, and is where Qui-Gon learned the truth about Anakin's parentage in *The Phantom Menace*. A hotel that's falling into ruin, it retains some brightly painted doors from the set.

- **Ksar Ouled Soultane (near Tataouine)** Here are more slave quarters – these are perhaps the finest example of the curious moulded courtyard-centred buildings.

- **La Grande Dune (near Nefta)** This stood in for the *Star Wars* Dune Sea, where C3PO staggered past a Krayt dragon skeleton, and if you're lucky, you might pick up some fibre-glass bones.

- **Chott el-Jerid (east of Nefta)** Here, in the first film, Luke contemplated two suns while standing soulfully at the edge of a crater, peering over these vast, dry salt flats. The landscape around its fringes doubled as Junland Wastes populated by Krayt dragons and sand people.

- **Medenine (near Tataouine)** Anakin Skywalker's *Phantom Menace* slave-quarters home is off bustling Ave 7 Novembre.

- **Ajim (Jerba)** Obi-Wan Kenobi's house exterior is about 3km out of town, while the freak-filled *Star Wars* Cantina scene was filmed in the centre (not, as many think, at the Sidi Driss).

Three have been transformed into interesting budget hotels, the most famous of which is **Hotel Sidi Driss** (☎ 240 005; s/d with breakfast US$9/18). This was the setting for the Lars family homestead in *Star Wars*, and was used for *Attack of the Clones* as well (see the boxed text). It's a major tour-group lunch date, but if you stay overnight you might be the only trog in town. It's best to eat at your hotel, as the local eateries are pretty dire.

There are regular buses and louages to/from Gabès (US$1) and one SNTRI bus to Tunis (US$14, eight hours).

DOUZ
☎ 75 / pop 27,400

Douz is an oasis at the edge of the Grand Erg Oriental. This erg, a sea of sand, fulfils all your preconceptions of how desert should be: still, silent, with great, golden drifts and strange warped shadows. Douz is the centre of desert tourism in the region, but most visitors head for the big hotels in the *zone touristique*, and the town remains laidback and friendly. Its streets lead into a central square, with fruit-laden stalls and shopfronts hung with brilliant patterned carpets. At its edge is an enormous *palmeraie* (palm grove), where more than 400,000 trees slice into the fierce sunlight.

Information

The **ONTT tourist office** (☎ 470 351; Ave Mohammed V; ❂ 8.30am-1pm & 3pm-6pm) is close to the palmeraie. **Société Tunisienne de Banque** (STB; Ave Taieb Mehiri) and **Banque de Sud** (Ave du 7 Novembre 1987) change cash and travellers cheques. **Publinet** (Rue el-Hounine) charges US$1 per hour.

Sights & Activities

Most people come to Douz to organise **camel trekking**. To appreciate the desert, it's best to take an overnight trip, which cost from US$28 per day.

The desert immediately south of Douz is crowded and not so interesting. You'll find more interesting country around **Zaafrane**, 14km southwest of Douz, as well as lots of camels and similar prices. The giant dunes of the **Grand Erg Oriental** lie some distance further south. If you want to reach the huge dunes, you'll need to take a 4WD at least for the first section. If you hire a driver and 4WD for the whole day, a guide price is US$160 per day or US$200 for an overnight trip.

Everyone in town claims to be a camel-trekking guide, but it's safer to use an agency or your hotel, or to seek advice from the tourist office.

Try to time your visit so that you're in town for the famous **Thursday market**, still an authentic market in spite of all the tour buses. Don't miss the livestock markets, where the last of Tunisia's nomadic camel herders come to trade.

The **palmeraie**, the largest in the country, is a wonderful, cool place for a stroll.

The **Sahara Festival** usually takes place in November. This is very popular with Tunisians as well as foreign tourists and has displays of traditional desert sports, colourful parades and music.

Sleeping & Eating

Desert Club (☎ 470 575; Ave 7 Novembre; camp site per person US$3) This shady camping ground is set in the palmeraie; there's hot water, and a restaurant and bar.

Hôtel 20 Mars (☎ 470 269; Rue 20 Mars; s/d US$7/10) There are hot showers here, and it's a sociable place, with lots of small courtyards and friendly service.

Hôtel de la Tente (☎ 470 468; Rue el-Hounine; s/d with breakfast US$5/10, with shower US$7/14) The rooms upstairs here are good: they open on to a sunny little terrace.

Restaurant La Rosa (☎ 471 660; Ave du 7 Novembre 1987; dishes US$2-3.50) Near the central square, this is a cosy place with some outdoor seats and simple food, such as chicken and couscous.

Restaurant Ali Baba (☎ 472 498; Ave du 7 Novembre 1987; mains around US$2.50) This friendly place is now run by the sons of Ali Baba; it's got a lovely quiet garden with a nomad tent. It's perfect for a lunch dappled in sunshine.

Getting There & Away

There are regular local buses and louages to Kebili (US$1.50, 30 minutes) and Zaafrane (US$0.30, five daily), and daily buses to Tozeur (US$5, 1½ hours) and Gabès (US$4, three hours, two daily). SNTRI has air-con services to Tunis (US$16, nine hours, two daily), either via Tozeur or via Gabès and Sfax.

TOZEUR

☎ 76 / pop 33,500

With palm tree–shaded boulevards and elaborate straw-coloured brickwork arranged in geometric patterns, Tozeur is an attractive town edged by an enormous, shady palmeraie, close to the edge of the salt lake Chott el-Jerid. This pale blue expanse has a salt-caked, salt-drifted surface, as if covered in cracked ice and piles of snow, while ringed by palms, sand and mountains. It's the largest of Tunisia's salt lakes and has a causeway running over it – this is an extraordinary journey and not to be missed.

There's a **tourist office** (☎ 450 088; Ave Abdulkacem Chebbi; ❂ 8am-noon & 3-6pm). Another tourist office is the **Syndicat d'Initiative** (☎ 462 034; Place Bab el-Hawa). There are several banks (but no ATMs) on Ave Habib Bourguiba, which is lined with souvenir shops selling the area's colourful rugs.

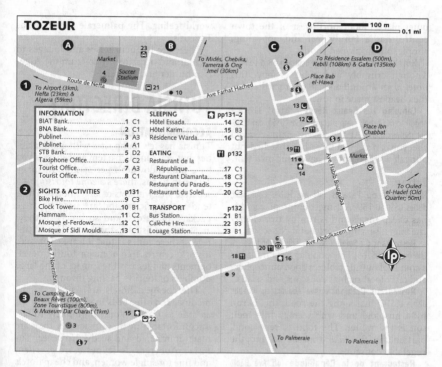

TOZEUR

INFORMATION	
BIAT Bank	1 C1
BNA Bank	2 C1
Publinet	3 A3
Publinet	4 A1
STB Bank	5 D2
Taxiphone Office	6 C2
Tourist Office	7 A3
Tourist Office	8 C1

SIGHTS & ACTIVITIES	p131
Bike Hire	9 C3
Clock Tower	10 B1
Hammam	11 C2
Mosque el-Ferdows	12 C1
Mosque of Sidi Mouldi	13 C1

SLEEPING	pp131–2
Hôtel Essada	14 C2
Hôtel Karim	15 B3
Résidence Warda	16 C3

EATING	p132
Restaurant de la République	17 C1
Restaurant Diamanta	18 C3
Restaurant du Paradis	19 C2
Restaurant du Soleil	20 C3

TRANSPORT	p132
Bus Station	21 B1
Calèche Hire	22 B3
Louage Station	23 B1

There are two **Publinets** at Route de Nefta (open 24 hours) and at Ave Abdulkacem Chebbi, both charging US$1.50 per hour.

Sights & Activities

Ouled el-Hadef, the town's labyrinthine old quarter, is well worth exploring for its unique, striking architecture and elaborately patterned relief brickwork.

The enormous **palmeraie** is best explored by bicycle, which can be hired (per hour US$5) from west of Résidence Warda on Ave Abdulkacem Chebbi. You can take a calèche ride around the palmeraie – they wait outside Résidence Warda. It should cost around US$8 for half an hour.

The **Museum Dar Charait** (☎ 452 100; Ave Abdulkacem Chebbi; admission US$2.50, camera US$1, video US$8; ☉ 8am-midnight), 1km from the town centre, has displays on arts and popular traditions, as well as some gloriously tacky tableaux that deal a bit with history and a lot with fantasy.

Excursions that can be made from Tozeur include a half-day trip via 4WD to **Ong Jemel**, a dramatic location used in both

Star Wars and *The English Patient*, Nefta (see p132 & Top Ten *Star Wars* Locations, p129), or the beautiful Berber villages of **Midés**, **Chebika** and **Tamerza**. Each half-day trip costs about US$25 – all hotels arrange tours and they seem to have made an agreement about prices, because everyone charges the same.

There's a good, welcoming **hammam** (US$1; off Ave Habib Bourguiba; ☉ men noon-6pm, women 7-11pm).

Sleeping

Hôtel Karim (☎ 454 574; 150 Ave Abdulkacem Chebbi) Opposite the *calèche* waiting area, this is a top choice, with bright tiled rooms. The roof terrace has great views across the *palmeraie*, and you can sit here and drink beer.

Résidence Warda (☎ 452 597; 29 Ave Abdulkacem Chebbi; s/d with breakfast US$13/16, with bathroom and breakfast US$12/20) This is a friendly, good-value place, with neat rooms around a courtyard and a good, central location. The rooms overlooking the street are particularly good.

Résidence Essalem (☎ 462 881; Ave l'Environment; s/d US$5/10, with shower US$6/12) This clean and

TUNISIA

quiet place, 500m northwest of the town centre, has a family feel and appealing, simple, old-fashioned rooms.

Hôtel Essada (off Ave Habib Bourguiba; s/d US$4/8) Though crumbly and a bit grubby, this hotel is set around a small courtyard and is the cheapest place in town.

Camping Les Beaux Rêves (☎ 453 331; Ave Abdulkacem Chebbi; camp site per person US$4, dm US$5, hot showers US$1) At this lovely, palm-covered site, you can sleep in three-bed thatched-hut bungalows if you don't have your own tent.

Eating

Restaurant du Paradis (off Ave Habib Bourguiba; dishes US$0.50-1.50) A tiny, quaint place, this has cheap meals and is run by two elderly charmers, serving *chorba* and couscous.

Restaurant du Soleil (☎ 235 329; Ave Abdulkacem Chebbi; dishes US$1-5) This popular restaurant has a couple of outside tables, a good atmosphere and tasty food such as couscous and salads.

Restaurant Diamanta (Ave Abdulkacem Chebbi; dishes US$1-5) Just along the road, this is run by a husband and wife team, while their son is the waiter. The food is very good, particularly the *salade mechouia* and the vegetable couscous.

Restaurant de la République (off Ave Habib Bourguiba; dishes US$1-5) With more of a touristy feel, this has outside tables in a covered area and is decorated by waterfall pictures, tiling and lamps. It serves good simple food.

Getting There & Away

The bus and louage stations are near each other just north of the road to Nefta. There are buses daily to/from Tunis (US$15, seven hours, five daily), via Kairouan (US$10, three hours) and Gafsa (US$3.50, 1½ hours), Nefta (US$1, 30 minutes, five daily), Douz (US$5, 1½ hours, one daily) and Gabès (US$8, 3½ hours, two daily). There are louages to/from Nefta, Tunis and Gabés for the same prices and to/from Kebili (US$3.50, 1½ hours).

NEFTA

pop 21,300

A sleepy oasis town slashed through with a gully, Nefta is decorated with ornately patterned ornamental beige brickwork and dotted with domes – it was a Sufi centre from the 16th century. It lies 23km west of Tozeur on the road to the Algerian border, and it's worth visiting for its end-of-the-

world feeling. The palmeraie is as huge as Tozeur's.

There are frequent buses and louages to Tozeur and occasionally to/from the Algerian border and Hazoua.

TUNISIA DIRECTORY

ACCOMMODATION

Tunisia has few camp sites with good facilities, but you can pitch a tent anywhere if you have the landowner's permission. In many Tunisian towns, there's a *zone touristiqe* – a separate area with lots of larger hotels. These tend to be pricier, and are used by large package operators, and so hotels in these areas are not listed in this book. The advantage of these zones is that it leaves Tunisia's historic centres free of major tourist developments and lessens the impact of the large numbers of tourists passing through.

The cheapest hotels are usually in the medina, and offer beds in shared rooms for as little as US$3. Women are likely to feel uncomfortable in these places as they are male-dominated and seedy. However, Tunisia's Auberges de Jeunesse are excellent and fine for single women, and cheap hotels outside the medina are usually better.

EMBASSIES & CONSULATES

The following embassies and consulates are in Tunis.

Algeria (18 Rue du Niger, 100 2 Tunis)

Australia The Canadian embassy in Tunis handles consular affairs for the Australian government.

Canada (Map p113; ☎ 104 000; 3 Senegal St)

Egypt (Map p113; ☎ 791 181; Ave Mohammed V)

France (Map p113; ☎ 245 700; Place de l'Indépendance, Ave Habib Bourguiba)

Germany (Map p113; ☎ 786 455; 1 Rue el Hamra)

UK (Map p113; ☎ 340 239; 5 Place de la Victoire)

USA (Map p113; ☎ 962 115; Zone Nord-Est de Berges du Lac)

Tunisia has embassies in Libya, Algeria, Egypt and Morocco. Details are listed in the Directory section of the relevant chapter.

FESTIVALS & EVENTS

Ksar Ouled Soltane Festival (April) Music, dance and other festivities.

Tabarka Raï Festival (May & June) Algerian musicians play al-fresco.

Tabarka Jazz Festival (July) Outdoor concerts, international stars.

Carthage International Festival (July & August) Music, dance & theatre.

Dougga Festival (July & August) Classical drama.

Carthage International Film Festival (October, odd years only; even years in Burkina Faso) Middle Eastern and African film.

Douz Sahara Festival (November) Desert sports, colourful parades and music.

FOOD

Tunisians love spicy food. The prime ingredient is *harissa*, a fiery chilli paste that is used to add zip to a range of stews and sauces. It's often eaten as an appetiser, mopped up with fresh bread. There's lots of fresh produce here, and on most menus you'll find *salade tunisienne* – a mixed salad – and *salade mechuoia* – an aubergine paste with a smokey flavour.

The national dish is couscous. Apparently there are more than 300 ways of preparing the stuff, sweet as well as savoury. A bowl of couscous served with some variety of stew costs about US$2.50 in local restaurants.

You'll find fresh French loaves everywhere, and in some places *tabouna*, traditional flat Berber bread.

Tunisians love snacks too, and tuck into variations of the *briq*, a fried, very thin pastry pocket that comes with a range of fillings (always including egg), or *chapati*, a toasted and tasty envelope, filled with a spicy tuna and egg combo.

HOLIDAYS

As well as religious holidays listed in the Africa Directory chapter (p1003), these are the principal public holidays in Tunisia:

1 January New Year's Day
20 March Independence Day
21 March Youth Day
9 April Martyrs' Day
1 May Labour Day
25 July Republic Day
3 August Public Holiday
13 August Women's Day
15 October Evacuation Day
7 November Anniversary of Ben Ali's Accession

INTERNET ACCESS

Public access to the Internet is handled by Publinet, which operates offices in all the main towns. Most charge around US$1.50 per hour. You might find it difficult to get on to Hotmail and Yahoo (see Media), though Publinet staff can sometimes suggest ways to get around this.

MEDIA

Freedom of speech is guaranteed under the constitution, but the government places strict restrictions on the media – print, broadcasting and the Internet.

MONEY

The unit of currency is the Tunisian dinar (TD), which is divided into 1000 millimes (mills). It's illegal to import or export dinars.

You can re-exchange up to 30% of the amount you changed into dinar, up to a limit of TD100. You need bank receipts to prove you changed the money in the first place.

Major credit cards such as Visa, American Express and MasterCard are widely accepted at big shops, tourist hotels, car-rental agencies and banks. ATMs are to be found in major towns and resort areas. Cash advances are given in local currency only.

POST & TELEPHONE

The Tunisian postal service is slow but reliable: allow a week to Europe and 10 days to North America, Asia and Oceania.

The telephone system is fairly modern and easy to operate. Few people have a phone at home, so there are lots of public telephones – known as Taxiphones. They accept 100-mill, 500-mill and one-dinar coins. An attempt to introduce cardphones appears to have fizzled out.

All public telephones can be used for international direct dialling. Some places advertise themselves as International Taxiphones; all it means is that the meters accept only 500-mill and one-dinar coins.

VISAS

Nationals of most Western European countries can stay up to three months without a visa – you just roll up at the port or airport and collect a stamp in your passport. Americans, Canadians, Germans and Japanese can stay up to four months. Other nationalities have to apply for a visa before travel.

TUNISIA

Australians and South Africans travelling independently can get a three-month visa at the airport for US$8. Other nationalities need to apply before they arrive; the visa costs US$7 and takes three to four weeks in person or six weeks via post, and the length of stay is up to the embassy.

Israeli nationals are not allowed into the country.

Visa Extensions

Extending a visa is a process to be avoided. Applications can be made only at the Interior Ministry on Ave Habib Bourguiba in Tunis. They cost US$2 to US$8 (payable only in *timbres fiscales*, revenue stamps) and take up to 10 days to issue. You will need two photos, and you may also need bank receipts and a *facture* (receipt) from your hotel, for starters. It'd be easier to leave the country and return to get another three-month stint.

Visas for Onward Travel

If you're planning on travelling to Algeria (inadvisable at the time of writing) or Libya (difficult) you should apply for visas in your home country.

WOMEN TRAVELLERS

Prior to marriage, Tunisian men have little opportunity to hang out with women. The expense of getting married means that, for many, this mixing of the sexes is being delayed still further. Foreign women exist outside the social structure, and are seen as a separate and enticing species. Sexual harassment is par for the course, and the tidal waves of testosterone that you may encounter can be a bit intimidating. Harassment usually takes the form of being stared at, subjected to slimy chat-ups and very occasional physical harassment – though this is not half as likely as in Egypt. You can try a few things to reduce your hassle quota: the first is by modest dressing. In remote areas, a headscarf can be useful to indicate modesty. The best policy is to ignore sexist remarks and sound effects; sunglasses are good for avoiding eye contact. It's advisable to sit next to other women on buses and louages, sit in the back seat of taxis and avoid staying in cheap medina hotels. If someone does touch you, '*Harem alek*' (Arabic for 'shame on you') is a useful phrase. However, try not to let your desire to fend off unwanted attention get in the way of genuine friendliness.

Algeria

FAST FACTS

- **Area** 2,381,745 sq km
- **ATMs** none
- **Borders** Niger, Tunisia; border with Morocco closed; crossing borders into Mali, Mauritania & Libya not advised
- **Budget** US$35 to US$40 a day
- **Capital** Algiers
- **Languages** Arabic, French, Berber
- **Money** Algerian dinar; US$1 = DA80
- **Population** 32.3 million
- **Seasons** in the north: wet (Oct–Mar), dry (Jun–Sep); south: hot (Mar–Oct), cooler (Nov–Feb)
- **Telephone** country code ☎ 213; international access code ☎ 00
- **Time** GMT/UTC + 1
- **Visas** US$40 to US$50 for one month; best obtained in advance

WARNING

Parts of Algeria remain unsafe. Travel to the northwest and the desert and mountain regions of the southeast (where a number of tourists were kidnapped in 2003) should be avoided. We did on-the-ground research in some areas in the south, but as we were unable to do on-the-ground research in large parts of the country, some information in this chapter might not be reliable. Check the situation before travelling to Algeria.

Once a popular holiday destination on a par with neighbouring Morocco, Algeria's tourist industry all but disappeared when bitter civil war broke out in 1992. After a decade of conflict the situation improved slightly, and some access to the southern Sahara region has been possible in the last couple of years. However, independent travel without a vehicle is almost nonexistent, and after the tourist abductions of 2003 (see the boxed text on p140) self-drive travellers need to be very aware of the risks involved.

This dearth of visitors is a great shame, as Algeria is one of the most fascinating countries in North Africa. The dramatic Tassili N'Ajjer and Hoggar regions are both Unesco-listed, tribal culture is very much alive, and the day-to-day hassle common to many Arab countries is conspicuously absent. Your options for travel are limited, especially as a backpacker, but a chance to see even a part of this vast nation should not be passed up.

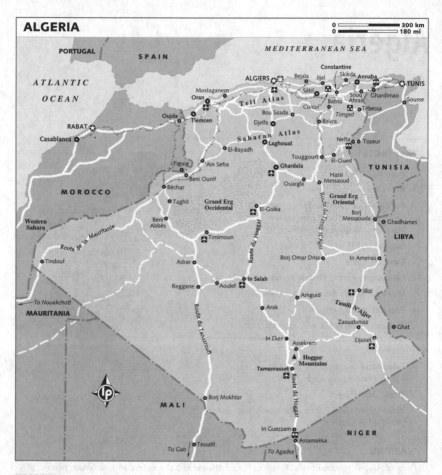

HISTORY

The modern state of Algeria is a relatively recent creation. The name was coined by the Ottoman Turks in the 16th century to describe the territory controlled by the regency of Algiers – initially a Turkish colony. The regency broke free of the Ottoman Empire (which at one stage spanned much of the Mediterranean and North Africa) and founded a military republic of unusual stability. This endured almost 300 years until spurious diplomatic problems prompted the French to invade in the 19th century.

The Barbary Coast

Before the arrival of the French, Algeria was known to Europeans as the Barbary (a corruption of Berber) Coast, notorious for the pirates who preyed on Christian shipping. The dreaded Khayr al-Din, better known as Barbarossa, was the first regent of Algiers during this period, and at one point he held no fewer than 25,000 Christian captives in the city. Piracy remained a serious problem until a Barbary fleet was defeated by the US Navy off Algiers in 1815, and it was not eradicated entirely until the French attacked Algiers in 1830 and forced the ruling *dey* (commander or governor) to capitulate. It took another 41 years for French domination of the country to become complete.

The main opposition came from the charismatic figure of Emir Abdelkader, the great hero of Algeria's nationalist movement. Abdelkader was a sherif (descendant of the Prophet) who ruled a large slice of western and central inland Algeria. His forces resisted the French for almost six years before they were defeated near Oujda in 1844; Abdelkader himself finally surrendered in 1846 and spent the rest of his life in exile, dying in Damascus in 1883.

French Rule

The French colonial authorities set about changing the face of Algeria. Local culture was actively eliminated, mosques were converted into churches and the old medinas (Arab cities) were pulled down and replaced with streets laid out in neat grids. Symbolic of the change was the conversion of the Great Mosque of Algiers to the Cathedral of St Philippe. French rule also saw large-scale appropriation of prime farming land for distribution among European settlers (known as *pieds-noirs*) – Italian, Maltese and Spanish as well as French.

The fighting that became Algeria's war of independence began on 31 October 1954 in Batna, east of Algiers, led by the newly formed Front de Libération Nationale (FLN; National Liberation Front). The struggle continued for seven years, with terror campaigns led by both native Algerians and *pied-noir* settlers; it cost at least a million Algerian lives, until French president Charles de Gaulle agreed to a referendum on independence in March 1962. The result was a resounding six million in favour and only 16,000 against.

Socialism & Democracy

FLN candidate Ahmed Ben Bella, who had once robbed a bank to fund a revolutionary group, became Algeria's first president, promising to create a 'revolutionary Arab-Islamic state based on the principles of socialism and collective leadership at home and anti-imperialism abroad'. He was overthrown in 1965 by former backer Colonel Houari Boumédienne, effectively returning the country to military rule.

Boumédienne's emphasis on industrial development at the expense of the agricultural sector was to have a major impact in later years, with the country becoming heavily dependent on food imports and migrant workers. Boumédienne died in December 1978 and the FLN replaced him

with Colonel Chadli Benjedid, who was re-elected in 1984 and 1989.

There was very little political change under Boumédienne and Chadli. The FLN was the sole political party, pursuing basically secular, socialist policies. There was little evidence of opposition until October 1988, when thousands of people took to the streets in protest against government austerity measures and food shortages. The army was called in to restore order, and between 160 and 600 people were killed.

The government reacted by pledging to relax the FLN monopoly on political power and work towards a multiparty system. The extent of the opposition became clear at local government elections held in early 1990, which produced landslide victories for the previously outlawed fundamentalist Front Islamique du Salut (FIS; Islamic Salvation Front).

The initial round of Algeria's first multiparty parliamentary elections, held in December 1991, produced another landslide for the FIS. The FLN was left looking like a political irrelevance, taking only 15 of the 231 seats. Chadli's apparent acceptance of this prompted the army to step in, replacing the president with a five-person Haut Conseil d'Etat (HCE; High Council of State) headed by Mohammed Boudiaf, a former leader of the Algerian revolution. The second round of elections was cancelled, and FIS leaders Abbas Madani and Ali Belhadj were arrested while others fled into exile.

Civil War

Boudiaf lasted barely six months before he was assassinated amid signs of a growing guerrilla offensive led by the Armed Islamic Group (Groupe Islamique Armé or GIA). He was replaced by former FLN hardliner Ali Kai, who oversaw a rapid descent towards all-out civil war before he was replaced by a retired general, Liamine Zéroual, in January 1994. Zéroual attempted to defuse the situation by holding fresh elections in 1995; however, Islamic parties were barred from the poll, and Zéroual's sweeping victory came amid widespread claims of fraud.

Hopes for peace went unfulfilled; instead, the war became even more brutal, with Amnesty International accusing both sides of massacres and other atrocities. The GIA, angered by French aid to the government, extended the war to French soil with a series of bombings and hijackings.

Eventually, government security forces began to gain the upper hand, and at the beginning of 1999 Zéroual announced that he was stepping down. New elections in April resulted in a controversial victory for establishment candidate Abdelaziz Bouteflika, a former foreign minister, who was elected unopposed after the rest of the field claimed fraud and withdrew.

Bouteflika moved quickly to establish his legitimacy by calling a referendum on a plan to offer amnesty to the rebels. War-weary Algerians responded overwhelmingly with a 98% 'yes' vote, and by the end of 1999 many groups had responded and laid down their weapons. However, elements within the GIA remained defiant, and were suspected of assassinating FIS leader Abdelkader Hachani in October 1999 in an attempt to derail the peace process.

Current Events

Since 1999 little has changed in this stand-off – GIA splinter groups continue their campaign against the government, and the army continues its own campaign against the rebels, amid accusations of brutality, executions and failure to prevent massacres. Added to this has been violent unrest among the Berber people, which led to an appeasement package from the government in 2001, and criticism of repressive attitudes towards the media (journalists can still be jailed for insulting the president).

Relations with France have improved considerably in recent years; 2003 was celebrated as the Year of Algeria in France, and President Chirac made his first official visit to the country. Many Algerians boycotted the festivities in Paris, calling it a whitewash of history and resenting any suggestion of renewed French influence after so many years of abuse.

Parliamentary elections in May 2002, won by current prime minister Ali Benflis of the FLN, were marred by violence and low voter turnout, and did little to strengthen people's faith in Algerian democracy. Four parties boycotted the vote, including two of the major Berber parties. To cap all the political problems, northern Algeria was rocked by a severe earthquake in May 2003, killing more than 2000 people.

With presidential elections due in 2004, Algeria's political future is still uncertain; Bouteflika is widely tipped for re-election, but will face some stiff opposition from Benflis, as well as the potential candidacy of Taleb and Aït Ahmed, his former opponents in the 1999 debacle. One general has even been quoted as saying that the army would not oppose an Islamic government this time round. With the Sahara kidnap drama in 2003 and renewed ambushes on soldiers in the western regions, it is clear that until the ongoing civil conflict is finally resolved, no regime will be able shake off the spectre of Algeria's violent past.

THE CULTURE

An estimated 99% of Algeria's population are Sunni Muslims; the majority are Arab–Berber and live in the north of the country. Berber traditions are best preserved in the Kabylie region southeast of Algiers, where people speak the local Berber dialect as their first language, French as their second and Arabic as their third. After sustained protests and rioting, Berber was finally recognised as an official language in 2002. The Tuareg people of the Sahara are also Berbers, but speak their own tribal language, Tamashek.

The most interesting traditional crafts here are those of the southern Saharan Tuareg, known for their intricate leatherwork and silver jewellery. In the north, as in Morocco, carpets are big business, although with less tourist custom the whole selling process is much less high-pressure.

Music is a big part of life here too, and few road journeys are complete without a constant accompaniment of distinctive wailing vocals. Algeria's contribution to world music culture is Raï, a genre that started out as subversive underground protest pop and has now spread around the Arab world; unless you can track down something live, however, chances are anything you hear here will actually be Egyptian.

As very few people depend on tourism for their income, the constant Moroccan-style street hassle you might expect to find is extremely rare in Algeria, and anyone who does accost you will usually be genuinely interested in where you come from and what you are doing. Invitations to tea can be regarded with far less suspicion than elsewhere!

ENVIRONMENT

Algeria is Africa's second-largest country after Sudan. About 85% of the country is taken up by the Sahara, and the mountainous Tell region in the north makes up the balance.

The Tell consists of two main mountain ranges: the Tell Atlas, which runs right along the north coast into Tunisia, and the Saharan Atlas, about 100km to the south. The area between the two ranges is known as the High Plateaus. The Sahara covers a great range of landscapes, from the classic S-dunes of the great ergs (sand seas) to the rock-strewn peaks of the Hoggar Mountains in the far south.

In the north, summers are hot and humid, and the winters mild and wet. In the Sahara, summer is ferociously hot with daytime temperatures seldom below 25°C, but nights can be very cold, particularly in the Hoggar region. Rainfall ranges from more than 1000mm per year in the northern mountains to zero in the Sahara. Some places go decades without a drop.

TRANSPORT

GETTING THERE & AWAY

Air

Air Algérie (☎ 742428; www.airalgerie.dz; 1 Place Maurice Audin, Algiers) serves destinations throughout North and West Africa, including Tripoli (Libya), Casablanca (Morocco), Dakar (Senegal) and Bamako (Mali). **Air France** (☎ 731610; Immeuble Maurétania, Place de Perou, Algiers) and **Khalifa Airways** (☎ 372424; 2 Ave Souidani Boudjemaâ, Algiers) mainly serve Europe, but Khalifa Airways also has a weekly flight to Johannesburg. Air Algérie and Khalifa Airways also fly daily to France, three times a week to London, two or three times weekly to Dubai and two to five times weekly to Germany. Most travel agents sell tickets for both companies.

Many tourists fly into Algeria by flying to Tamanrasset – either nonstop direct from Europe or with a change of planes at Algiers (see p141).

Boat

Algiers is currently the only advisable entry port for travellers, and the ferry terminal is near the main train station. The French company **SNCM** (☎ 021-736569; 28 Blvd Zirout-Youcef)

operates ferry services between Marseilles and Algiers once or twice a week. **Algérie Ferries** (☎ 021-423048; Gare Maritime) serves Algiers, Annaba, Béjaia and Oran from Marseille via Alicante, Spain. Tickets between Algiers and Marseilles (the most common route) cost around US$160/240 for a seat/cabin. The voyage takes about 21 hours.

Land

MALI & MAURITANIA

Algeria's southern borders are frequently closed, and there is very little transport along these routes. The road to Mauritania also passes near the disputed territory of Western Sahara (for more details on this area see the Morocco chapter, p149), which is best avoided.

MOROCCO

The border with Morocco has been closed for some time due to ongoing political disputes.

LIBYA

The main crossing points into Libya are at Bordj Messaouda and Tin Alkoum (between Djanet and Ghat). However, it is not currently advisable to use these routes.

NIGER

The border between Algeria and Niger slices through the emptiness of the central Sahara, with just one official crossing point between the sandy outposts of In Guezzam and Assamakka, on the main overland route from Tamanrasset to Agadez (the Route de Hoggar). Perhaps surprisingly, there's plenty of traffic (mainly local trucks and 4WDs, plus a few brave travellers in their own vehicles), so backpackers can find lifts, although you'll probably have to pay and do the trip in stages. If you're very lucky you might get one lift all the way.

From Tamanrasset, trucks and battered old 4WDs run to the Algeria border post at In Guezzam (US$17, nine to 12 hours plus waiting time), where you complete most of the formalities. From here you can hitch on a truck to the lonely check-point on the actual border and then to the chaotic Niger border post at Assamakka. Lifts on trucks between the border posts will cost about US$2.50 – but as it's mostly private vehicles they can ask for whatever they want. From

ALGERIA

Assamakka, numerous trucks and 4WDs head to Arlit (about US$5) and Agadez (US$8.50).

The road is sealed as far as Tamanrasset, a sandy track runs from there to Arlit, then tarmac to Agadez and beyond. Note that a 'tourist tax' of CFA1000 (US$1.60) is payable at the Niger border post. Make sure you have some CFA francs or you'll have to pay DA1000 (US$13) instead.

TUNISIA

The main border crossing is just outside Hazoua on the route between El-Oued and Tozeur. This is used by foreign travellers driving their own vehicle and the occasional overland truck, but is not currently recommended; see the boxed text.

GETTING AROUND
Air

Air Algérie (☎ 021-742428; www.airalgerie.dz) and **Khalifa Airways** (☎ 021-372424) both offer extensive domestic services at relatively low cost. Popular domestic routes include those from Algiers to Tamanrasset, Timimoun and Ghardaïa.

Hitching

Independent travel in all parts of Algeria is considered risky because of the current political situation. However, the Sahara has long been a popular region for adventurers

in their own vehicles, so backpackers have traditionally hitched rides. A great deal of patience is often required before securing a lift, especially now, as there are relatively few visitors. Most tourist vehicles are already full of passengers and kit, so drivers might be unwilling to take an extra load. You might be lucky, however, and meet a loner who's happy to offer a spare seat in return for help digging when the car gets stuck in the sand, and possibly a contribution towards fuel.

The most popular route across the Sahara is the Route du Hoggar, which runs from Ghardaïa via El-Goléa and In Salah to Tamanrasset (and then on to the border and Arlit in Niger). The road is tar all the way to Tamanrasset. Other less-used roads include the eastern Route du Tassili N'Ajjer, which runs from Hassi Messaoud to Tamanrasset across the Grand Erg Oriental, and the Route du Tanezrouft, which runs from Adrar to Borj Mokhtar near the Mali border. The latter two routes include sections of sandy track (known as *piste* in all the Sahara countries).

Local Transport

Long-distance buses are run by various regional companies, mainly in the north but also as far south as Tamanrasset. Tickets can be in great demand on less well-serviced routes, such as from In Salah to Taman-

---

SUN, SAND & SAFETY

In February 2003 the dangers of desert driving were dramatically illustrated when no fewer than 32 people disappeared in the Sahara. Several separate expeditions, mostly German and Swiss, vanished in different parts of southeast Algeria. Speculation was rife about their fate: one Algerian source even claimed they were being held illegally in a military facility and the searches were 'nothing but a sordid show aimed at impressing the media'. By March, however, it had become apparent that the travellers were in the hands of an extreme Islamist group, the Salafist.

For the next six months the kidnappers played a cat and mouse game with Algerian and German security forces. In April a message was found in the desert, saying 'We are alive'; in May 17 of the hostages were released unharmed, but a few weeks later searchers uncovered the body of one of the missing women, who had died of heatstroke.

Eventually the remaining party was tracked down to Mali, having crossed the southern Saharan border. Negotiations through the Malian government proved effective, and on 18 August the last 15 tourists finally flew home, though not to an entirely sympathetic welcome – several German politicians have demanded that the travellers be made to pay the costs of their rescue, as it was their choice to travel without a guide and put themselves in danger!

In the light of these events, independent travel in the desert areas around the Tunisia and Libya borders, Tamanrasset, Illizi and Djanet is discouraged, and the Algerian tourist industry is once again tightening its collective belt.

rasset, so you should book in advance. Fares are: In Salah to Tamanrasset (US$12), Algiers to Ghardaia (US$6), Adrar to In Salah (US$0.85), El Golea to In Salah (US$1) and Adrar to Timimoun (US$0.50).

Trucks and 4WDs carrying paying passengers are much more common means of transport in the south. Prices for 4WD are negotiable, around US$17 for a full day's driving (eg Tamanrasset to In Guezzam).

Shared taxis (louages) operate only in the north of the country. They run when full and are more expensive than buses.

Train
The northern train line connects Oran, Algiers, Constantine and Annaba. Additional lines run south from Oran to Béchar and also from Constantine to Touggourt. Many services, including to Tlemcen (for Morocco) and Tunis (Tunisia), are currently suspended.

ALGIERS

☎ 021 / pop 3.5 million

Once famed as one of the most beautiful cities in the Arabic kingdoms, Algiers (Al-Jazaïr) was never the same after years of colonial abuse, and today is little more than a modern port town. It's generally safer than you might think, with a serious police presence inside the *périphérique* (ring road), but unfortunately most points of interest are found in the kasbah or medina district. This district has been off limits to foreigners since the start of the troubles. Most people stay here just long enough to organise their transport to Tamanrasset as well as to other parts of Algeria, Africa or Europe.

ORIENTATION
The harbour is an obvious landmark; four main streets run parallel to the waterfront, changing names every 500m or so. The kasbah lies between Blvd de la Victoire and Rue Ahmed Bouzrina.

The area around the airport is one of the less safe parts of Algiers, as it lies in the suburbs outside the ring road; there are regular buses (US$0.25) but it's better to take a taxi into town (US$8). Don't let pushy locals 'share' it with you.

INFORMATION
Internet access is available in the larger hotels and in several small offices around town. There are banks all over the city centre. The **main post office** (Place Grande Poste) is at the southern end of Rue Larbi ben M'Hidi. A block away, towards the harbour, you'll find the **telephone office** (cnr Rue Asselah Hocine & Blvd Colonel Amirouche). There are several branches of **ONAT** (Office National Algérien du Tourisme; ☎ 744448; www.onat-dz.com; 126b Rue Didouche Mourad) in Algiers.

SIGHTS
Most of the buildings in the medina are of French origin, but there are some magnificent **Turkish palaces**; the main concentration is around the Ketchaoua Mosque on Rue Hadj Omar. One of the finest palaces is the **Dar Hassan Pacha**.

The distinctive abstract monstrosity dominating the skyline south of the centre is the **Martyrs' Monument**, opened in 1982 on the 20th anniversary of Algeria's independence. The **views** over the city here are the best you'll get, and there's also a convenient shopping centre nearby.

SLEEPING & EATING
Most of the cheap accommodation centres on Place Port Said on the edge of the kasbah, although few foreign visitors stay here because it is dangerous. For Algerian food, there is a stack of places between Place Emir Abdelkader and Place Port Said.

GETTING THERE & AWAY
Air
Air Algérie, Air France and Khalifa Airways cover destinations throughout the country; for their addresses see p139. Useful routes include Tamanrasset (US$60, 2½ hours, daily), Ghardaïa (US$80, one hour, daily) and Timimoun (US$80, 1½ to two hours, four times weekly).

Land
The main intercity bus station is about 800m south of Place Grande Poste on Rue de Compiégne. There are daily buses to Ghardaïa (US$6, eight hours) and El-Oued (US$4, 14 hours). The train station is on the lower level of the waterfront. Surviving services include Oran (US$8, six hours, three daily) and Annaba (US$11, 14 hours, two daily).

ALGERIA

GETTING AROUND

The four major city bus stations are at Place des Martyrs, Place Grande Poste, Place Maurice Audin and Place 1 Mai.

There are private taxis everywhere; prices are negotiable. It's US$8 from the airport, around US$3 across town.

NORTHERN ALGERIA

Very little of the northern region is currently considered safe for travellers. If things do happen to pick up, high points for visitors will include Djemila, a tiny mountain town in the stunning area around Sétif; Oran, the modern but fascinating port town made famous by Albert Camus; Batna, a charming town in an area known for its Roman ruins; and Tlemcen, the beautifully preserved gateway city for Morocco and former capital of the central Maghreb region.

EL-OUED

☎ 032 / pop 678,000

Tagged the 'Town of a Thousand Domes', El-Oued is the major town of the Souf region in the Grand Erg Oriental. Along with Touggourt it is the main port of call for people heading to or from Tunisia. Most of the buildings have **domes**, built to alleviate the summer heat.

The town is also famous for its **carpets**, which often bear the traditional cross of the Souf. The daily **souq** in the old part of town is at its most animated on Friday.

GHARDAÏA

☎ 029 / pop 340,000

Ghardaïa is actually a cluster of five towns in the river valley of the Oued M'Zab – Ghardaïa, Melika, Beni Isguen, Bou Noura and El-Ateuf. It is home to a conservative Muslim sect called the Mozabites, which broke from mainstream Islam some 900 years ago.

The area is famous for its **carpets** and for the daily **souq** in the old town. It's also worth visiting **Beni Isguen**, the religious fulcrum of the valley, 3km from central Ghardaïa. Foreigners are not allowed to enter without a guide, and not at all on Friday; it's also forbidden to wear shorts, take photos or smoke.

The cheapest hotels in the area are mostly found around Rue Ahmed Talbi, the road that crosses the river to the bus station. Camping is also possible near the river.

Air Algérie and Khalifa Airways both fly from Ghardaïa to Algiers (US$80, one hour, daily) and Tamanrasset (US$85, 1½ hours). Khalifa also serves Timimoun (US$65, 1¼ hours).

Regular buses run to Algiers (US$6, daily) via Djelfa and Reggane (US$3.50, daily) via Timimoun and Adrar.

SOUTHERN ALGERIA

Although the southern Saharan regions of Algeria are generally considered safer than the northern Algeria, safe travel possibilities are still limited for independent travellers, and most visitors fly straight to Tamanrasset.

More remote destinations favoured by travellers with their own vehicles include **Illizi**, a busy desert outpost on the fringes of the Tassili N'Ajjer; **Djanet**, home to some of the best prehistoric rock art in the Sahara; and **Beni Abbès**, a spring watered town on an escarpment overlooking an oasis in the west of the country.

If the security situation in the north improves and stabilises, overland companies might resume using the superb trans-Sahara route via Béchar and Adrar, which skirts the Grand Erg Occidental and passes through some of the most dramatic scenery in North Africa.

EL-GOLÉA

☎ 029 / pop 30,000

On the eastern edge of the Grand Erg Occidental, this little oasis town boasts some of the sweetest natural water in the whole of the Sahara – it's bottled and sold across the country.

Air Algérie has weekly flights to/from Algiers (US$80, 1¼ hours). There are regular buses to Ghardaïa, Timimoun and In Salah (US$1, four hours, daily).

TIMIMOUN

☎ 029 / pop 27,000

Timimoun is possibly *the* definitive Saharan oasis town. It is a very enchanting place, built on the edge of an escarpment with fantastic views over an ancient salt lake to the distant dunes – especially magical on a moonlit night.

Air Algérie flies here from Algiers four times weekly (US$82) and from Oran twice weekly (US$74), and daily buses go to Béchar (US$1, 9½ hours) and Ghardaïa (US$6, 11 hours).

IN SALAH
☎ 029 / pop 34,000

In Salah is the main town between El-Goléa and Tamanrasset. It has a reputation as a laid-back place. The only problem is the inescapable salty water that gives the town its name (Salah is Arabic for salt) – even the local soft drinks are made from it!

The main feature here is the **creeping sand dune**, which has effectively cut the town in two. Scramble to the top for the views over both sides.

The only hotel is the upmarket state-run Hôtel Tidikelt near the bus station.

The bus station is on the main Tamanrasset to El-Goléa road, which passes about 1km east of town. Daily buses go to Tamanrasset (US$13, 13 to 20 hours) and El Golea (US$1, four hours).

Air Algérie flies here two or three times weekly (US$87).

TAMANRASSET
☎ 029 / pop 62,500

Tamanrasset, set at the foot of the **Hoggar Mountains**, is the last major town on the route south to Niger. In recent years it has regained its former position as centre of the limited Algerian tourist industry, although, with its secure reputation shattered by the 2003 kidnap drama, its popularity seems sure to nosedive once again.

It's a surprisingly busy place with plenty of modern amenities, including several banks, two Air Algérie offices, innumerable travel agencies, including an ONAT branch, and – for some reason – dozens of barbers. The travel agencies and ONAT organise tours to Assekrem (see this page). Almost everything can be found on the main street, Ave Emir Abdelkader.

Slightly unreliable Internet access is available at **Tamtamnet** (US$1.30 per hour), across the small square in the centre of town.

The consulates of Mali and Niger are next to each other on Rue Fougani, towards the southern end of town.

Sleeping
As Tamanrasset is the only place in Algeria still geared to mass tourism, there are a few camping grounds spread out along the main road south of town. Most of these have rooms as well as tent space.

Eating & Drinking
Most restaurants in town offer the usual 'fast food' mix (whole grilled chicken US$6); but there are also plenty of pâtisseries where you can get excellent cakes and pastries for US$0.25.

Getting There & Away
Air Algérie and Khalifa Airways fly between Tamanrasset and the major northern towns (Algiers, Oran and Constantine) as well as El-Goléa, Djanet, Illizi and In Salah. The French company Point-Afrique also has very convenient weekly flights to Paris and Marseilles; see www.point-afrique.com for more.

The bus station is on the road to the north of town. By bus it can take 12 to 20 hours to In Salah (US$13). There are infrequent buses to In Guezzam, near the border with Niger (US$15, 23 hours, weekly); regular 4WDs (they leave when they're full) also cover this route (US$17, nine hours).

ASSEKREM
Seeing the incredible scenery and the sunrise in the mountains at Assekrem, about 80km northeast of Tamanrasset, is an unforgettable experience. It's hard to get here without your own vehicle but totally worth the effort. The many travel agencies in Tamanrasset operate tours to Assekrem, with some good deals available for groups. Overnight trips run by ONAT are decent value at US$80 per vehicle, but don't offer much in the way of service. Without a vehicle or a tour it would be virtually impossible to get here at all, unless you hitched a lift with another tourist group.

You could camp if you don't mind the freezing wind.

ALGERIA DIRECTORY

ACCOMMODATION
Hotels in Algeria tend to be either expensive state-run tourist hotels with good facilities or cheap, tatty places intended for local visitors. There are also some excellent

ALGERIA

camp sites in the south, particularly in Tamanrasset. The HI-affiliated network of youth hostels has branches in most towns and is generally the cheapest option, although facilities are minimal.

BUSINESS HOURS
Most businesses in Algeria keep standard opening hours (p996), but everything closes on Friday for the Islamic weekend.

DANGERS & ANNOYANCES
Safety is a major issue in Algeria; foreigners are not usually targets of violence, but the indiscriminate nature of bomb attacks on public places, such as markets and bus and train stations, makes caution extremely advisable. Anywhere north of Ghardaïa is currently considered dangerous, and the area around Algiers is a particular hot spot. Fake police roadblocks set up by armed bandits are also common on northern roads.

Even if you do not encounter any trouble, you might well find that local police will prevent you from travelling for your own safety, especially if you are alone or trying to hitch. It's almost always safer and easier to travel by air, although in January 2003 a group of unarmed men did try to hijack a domestic Air Algérie flight.

Expeditions into the Sahara pose a whole host of other problems, from fuel shortages to sandstorms and bandits (see the boxed text on p140); make sure you are adequately briefed and prepared well before departure.

In Algiers it is advisable to make use of taxis rather than wandering around on your own, and you should take care in crowded public places.

EMBASSIES & CONSULATES
Countries with diplomatic representation in Algiers include:

Australia (☎ 601965; 1 Rue Djenane Malik)
Canada (☎ 914951; 18 Mustapha Khalef St, Ben Akmoum)
France (☎ 692488; 25 Chemin Gaddrouche, Hydra)
Germany (☎ 741941; 165 Chemin Sfindja)
Italy (☎ 922330; 18 Rue Mohamed Ouidir Amellal)
Libya (☎ 921502; 15 Chemin Cheikh Bachir el-Ibrahimi, El-Biar)
Mali (☎ 691351; Cité DNC/ANP, Villa No 15, Hydra)
Mauritania (☎ 937106; 30 Rue du Vercors)
Morocco (☎ 607408; 8 Rue des Cèdres, Parc de la Reine)
Niger (☎ 788921; 54 Rue du Vercors)

Spain (☎ 922713; 46 Bis Rue Med Chabane)
Tunisia (☎ 691388; 11 Rue du Bois de Bologne)
UK (☎ 230068; 6 Ave Souidani Boudjemaâ)
USA (☎ 691425; 4 Chemin Cheikh Bachir el-Ibrahimi, El-Biar)

Algeria has diplomatic representation in the following neighbouring countries: Libya, Mali, Mauritania, Morocco, Niger and Tunisia.

GAY & LESBIAN TRAVELLERS
Homosexual sex is illegal for both men and women in Algeria, and incurs a maximum penalty of three years in jail and a stiff fine. You're unlikely to have any problems as a tourist, but some discretion is advisable.

HOLIDAYS
As well as the following national holidays, Algeria observes Islamic holidays (p1003).
Labour Day 1 May
Revolutionary Readjustment (1965) 19 June
Independence Day 5 July
National Day (Revolution Day) 1 November

INTERNET ACCESS
Access is now available throughout the north and has even reached Tamanrasset. Connections vary, but prices are generally reasonable.

MONEY
Some Algerians, especially in rural areas, might give prices in centimes rather than dinars (100 centimes equals DA1). To confuse matters further, they might also drop the thousands, so a quote of '130' means 130,000 centimes, ie DA1300.

Changing foreign currency is no problem at banks and larger hotels. Travellers cheques might be accepted in Algiers; credit cards can be used only in the international chain hotels where they still use the old fraud-friendly slip system. You'll need dinar for day-to-day expenses, although tourist-oriented businesses (hotels, airlines, tour companies) might accept US dollars.

POST & TELEPHONE
The postal system in Algeria is very slow, so it's advisable to send mail from a major town.

International phone calls can be made from any of the public Taxiphone offices found in most towns. The usual price is a flat rate of US$0.03 per unit – a 10-minute call to Europe should use around 500 units.

TOURIST INFORMATION

Tourist offices can be found in many southern towns, and are generally pretty helpful. The state-run travel agency, ONAT, organises excursions and is handy for lone travellers wanting to join a tour.

VISAS

Everyone except Moroccan and Tunisian nationals needs a visa to enter Algeria. Nationals of Israel, Malawi and Taiwan are not allowed into the country, and if you have a stamp in your passport from any of these countries your application might be rejected.

If you're getting an Algerian visa before leaving home, you need a letter from your employer or university to say you'll be coming back after your holiday and an 'invitation' to visit the country from an Algerian contact or tourist agency (available from several travel agencies in Tamanrasset). Applications lodged in Europe might also require three photos. Getting a visa en route is usually pretty straightforward in Niger, Chad and Mali.

Costs of a 30-day visa are around US$45. Some embassies ask for photocopies of your passport (and it's worth having some with you anyway).

Visa Extensions

Visa extensions can be obtained from the **Department des Estrangers** (Blvd Youssef 19A, Algiers) but are not easy to obtain.

Visas for Onward Travel

Visas for the following countries are available from embassies in Algiers (see opposite) or consuls in Tamanrasset.

Mali One-month visas cost €10 (US$11.25) and are usually issued in 24 hours. You'll need two photos.

Niger One-month visas are issued the same day, costing US$60 or €50. Three photos and three application forms are required.

Morocco

HIGHLIGHTS

- **Fès** An exceptional medieval city with bazaars, exquisite Islamic architecture and a vision of a Morocco unchanged by time (p169)
- **Marrakesh** Storytellers, exotic smells and captivating souqs make this unmissable city the bewitching soul of the country (p187)
- **Chefchaouen** A magnificent village set against a Rif mountain backdrop and the perfect place to chill out high above the clamour (p165)
- **Sahara** The desert of all deserts with opportunities to ride a camel out from Merzouga, over the sand dunes and then sleep under the stars (p198)
- **Essaouira** This delightful Atlantic fishing port with the best beach in Morocco boasts a lovely old city and a laid-back, artistic ambience (p181)
- **Off the beaten track** Trekking in the High Atlas Mountains, get away from the crowds and into a world of spectacular scenery (p193)

FAST FACTS

- **Area** 710,000 sq km
- **ATMs** throughout the country except small towns
- **Borders** Algeria closed; Mauritania open but no public transport
- **Budget** US$15 to US$20 a day
- **Capital** Rabat
- **Languages** Arabic, French, Berber
- **Money** dirham; US$1= Dh11
- **Population** 30 million
- **Seasons** hot (Jun–Aug), cold (Nov–Feb)
- **Telephone** country code ☎ 222; international access code ☎ 00
- **Time** GMT/UTC
- **Visas** 90 days, issued on entry for most nationalities

Morocco has it all. This is a land saturated with colour – the blue tiles of Fès, the red shades of Marrakesh, the earthen tones of desert kasbahs and the green of Islam in Meknès. For some, its greatest charm lies in losing yourself in the clamorous labyrinths of medieval cities. For others, watching the sun set from high on a Saharan sand dune is worth the trip on its own. Or it could be simply the fact that Morocco is spectacularly beautiful with the Atlas and Rif Mountains, picturesque coastline and some of the most stunning (and accessible) desert landscapes in North Africa.

If you tire of life on the African road, there's always the beach. Whatever your thing, chances are you'll find it in Morocco. The 'farthest land of the setting sun' (as it's known to the Arabs) is an evocative place to start your African journey.

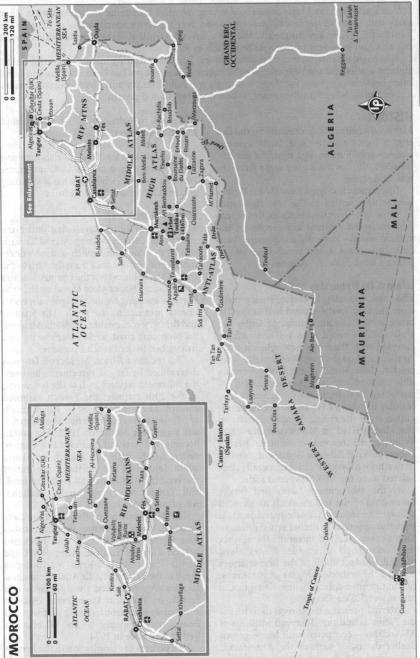

You'll also find the Moroccan people among the most hospitable on the continent. They carry with them strong traditional roots and a very modern understanding of the way the world works: King Mohammed VI may be a direct descendant of the Prophet Mohammed, but he's also president of Oudayas Surf Club in Rabat.

When you first arrive, it can be quite a shock. Full of contrasting images, colourful sights, strange smells and wild experiences, Morocco is, and always has been, a fascinating and often bewildering place. For those wanting a trip full of variety and life, Morocco provides a stimulating assault on the senses. Take a deep breath and dive in.

HISTORY

Morocco's history is dominated by the fact that it looks out over the Mediterranean and towards Europe. For much of history, however, the covetous gaze came from the other direction.

The country's origins lie with the Berber people who settled in the area thousands of years ago. Over the centuries their independent spirit outlived conquerors of the ancient world – Phoenicians, Romans, Vandals, Byzantines – and resulted in one of Africa's most colourful cultures.

Islam & Its Dynasties

The most enduring historical legacy came from the east. In the second half of the 7th century, the Islamic armies of Uqba bin Nafi al-Fihri raced across North Africa, carrying with them the new religion from Arabia. Although they were partly successful, their brutal method of governing didn't sit well with a Berber population accustomed to fighting off foreign invaders. Moulay Idriss, an Arab noble fleeing persecution from the ruling Abbasid dynasty in Baghdad, arrived in Morocco in the 780s. Winning the respect of enough Berber tribes, he established a dominant dynasty in northern Morocco. This is generally considered to be the first Moroccan state.

By the 8th century Islam had finally taken hold of the region. With its roots in a tough desert and tribal environment, it probably appealed to Berber sensibilities, so long as they received in return the respect they considered their due. Nonetheless, the independent spirit of the Berber tribes rejected the orthodox dogma of the Arabs, finding greater solace in the Kharijites, a breakaway Shi'ite sect.

External pressure from rival dynasties – the Fatimids and the Umayyad Muslims of Al-Andalus – competed with home-grown Berber dynasties such as the Almoravids and Almohads. By the 14th century, the

Merenids had their turn, leaving behind exquisite architectural landmarks.

The Medersa Bou Inania in Fès is considered the most extravagant, elaborate and perfect of the monuments built under the Merenid dynasty, while Salé has a stunning Merenid medersa as does Meknès.

European Interest

Morocco may never have come under the sway of the Ottomans (the powerful Turkish empire that controlled much of the Mediterranean and North Africa from the 14th to the early 20th centuries) but the country was still a much sought-after piece of real estate, with Portugal asserting claims and Spain always an uneasy presence to the north. The Spanish and British forces established footholds along the Moroccan coast, while Algeria to the east succumbed to the French invasions.

Like much of Africa, Morocco's fate was determined by far-off agreements between the European powers and, at the beginning of the 20th century, the French assumed control. The treaty of Fès, by which much of Morocco became a French protectorate, was signed on 30 March 1912. The sultan became a figurehead and effective control rested firmly with the French governor. Spain controlled the northern portion of the country (the coast and its hinterland) and Tangier was made an international zone (interzone) in 1923.

The Moroccan people were not amused. As usual, it was the Berber mountain tribes who reacted most strongly and remained beyond colonial control. After WWI the Berber leader Abd al-Krim marshalled a revolt in the Rif and Middle Atlas Mountains, and for five years had the Spaniards and French on the run. Spain came close to a massive and embarrassing defeat, and France only managed to end all effective Berber resistance in 1934.

The process of colonisation in the French zone was rapid. From a few thousand people before 1912, the number of foreigners living in Morocco rose to more than 100,000 by 1929.

The French contribution was threefold: roads and railways were built, the port of Casablanca was developed virtually from scratch and the political capital moved to Rabat. In the French zone, *villes nouvelles* (new towns) were built next to the old medinas. The Spaniards followed suit in their zone, but on a much more modest scale.

When WWII ended, nationalist feeling grew and the French became increasingly inflexible. Moroccans boycotted French goods and terrorist acts against the administration multiplied. The sultan, Mohammed V, sympathised with the nationalists – so much so that the French authorities in Rabat deported him to Madagascar in 1953.

Madrid's administration of the Spanish zone after the war was considerably less heavy-handed than that of the French. In fact the area even became something of a haven for Moroccan nationalists.

Independence

Mohammed V returned to Morocco in November 1955 to a tumultuous welcome and on 2 March 1956 the French protectorate formally came to an end. Shortly afterwards, Spain pulled out of the north, but hung on to the enclaves of Ceuta, Melilla and Sidi Ifni. It abandoned the last in 1970, but hasn't the least desire to give up the other two.

The sultan resumed virtually autocratic rule over an optimistic country but after becoming king in August 1957, he died suddenly in February 1961 and was succeeded by his son, Hassan II. After a series of coup attempts by radical groups apparently within the army, riots and states of emergency, general elections were finally held in 1977; supporters of the king won by a big majority.

Western Sahara

In November 1975, the extraordinary happened – 350,000 Moroccans walked over the border into the oil- and phosphate-rich territory of the former colony of Spanish Sahara. Known as the Green March (and now part of Moroccan folklore), this fulfilled long-held national dreams of incorporating the region into Morocco. First the Spanish withdrew, then the Mauritanians, but the 100,000 or

so inhabitants of the territory weren't quite so accommodating. The Popular Front for the Liberation of Saguia al-Hamra and Río de Oro (Polisario) embarked on a 16-year guerrilla war against the Moroccan invasion in an attempt to establish the Saharawi Arab Democratic Republic.

In 1991 the United Nations (UN) brokered a cease-fire on the understanding that a referendum would be held in 1992 to allow the people of the Western Sahara to decide between independence and integration with Morocco. It never happened.

Despite Morocco's many reasons for optimism, one intractable challenge to the country's stability remains the disputed territory of the Western Sahara which, sadly, has degenerated into one of Africa's most protracted conflicts. Military deployment in the region costs Morocco US$2 million per day but employs 300,000 ethnic Moroccans.

The latest proposal from UN special envoy for Western Sahara, former US secretary of state, James Baker (the first draft of the plan was released on 20 June 2001, and a second draft released on 23 May 2003), gives Western Sahara limited autonomy under Moroccan sovereignty for four years, during which time democratic institutions will be put into place to allow self-determination by the Saharawis. The plan has been rejected by Polisario, which has threatened a return to armed conflict unless a referendum is held.

Recent Times

The 1980s and 1990s were marked by economic stagnation, hardship and unrest, with government pitted against Islamist groups and radical left-wing opposition organisations. Throughout, the government maintained a moderate stance on the international stage, recognising Israel's right to exist and maintaining close ties to the West, all balanced with the need to stay close to other Arab regimes.

The last years of Hassan II's reign saw a gradual improvement in human rights and greater political openness, but he effectively remained an absolute ruler until his death on 23 July 1999, aged 70.

Since assuming power Mohammed VI has shown a more liberal hand than his father. However, despite being an obvious moderniser, and understanding that he

MOROCCO

must carry the people with him, he retains tight political control.

THE CULTURE

Moroccans cast their eye in many directions – to Europe, the economically dominant neighbour; to the east and the lands of Islam; and to its traditional Berber heartland. The result is an intoxicating blend of the modern and the traditional, liberal and conservative, hospitality and the need to make a dirham. Away from the tourist scrum, a Moroccan proverb tells the story – 'A guest is a gift from Allah'. The public domain may belong to men, but they're just as likely to invite you home to meet the family. If this happens to you, consider yourself truly privileged, but remember: keep the left hand firmly out of the communal dish and feel free to slurp your tea and belch your appreciation loudly.

In present-day Morocco *jellabas* (flowing cloaks) cover Western suits, turbans jostle with baseball caps, thumping European dance music competes with sinuous Algerian rai and mobile phones ring in the midst of perhaps the greatest of all Moroccan pastimes – the serious and exuberant art of conversation. An inherently social people, Moroccans have a heightened sense of mischief, love a good laugh and will take your decision to visit their country as an invitation to talk... and drink tea and perhaps even buy a carpet, a very beautiful carpet, from my private collection, just for the pleasure of your eyes...

With so many historical comings and goings, one sector of society holds firm. The majority of Morocco's inhabitants claim some form of Berber lineage – an ancient, resilient race that has inhabited North Africa since Neolithic times. Notoriously resistant to outside control, it would be a mistake to tell a member of this erstwhile warrior race that 'your father died in his bed' – a particularly nasty insult.

ARTS

For many first-time visitors to North Africa, Morocco is like visiting an extravagant art gallery.

MOROCCO IN MOVIES

If you feel like you've been to Morocco before but your passport says otherwise and you can't quite work out why, it's probably because Morocco is one of the greatest stars of the silver screen. Orson Welles shot much of his acclaimed *Othello* in the former Portuguese ports of Essaouira, Safi and El-Jadida, while Alfred Hitchcock chose the chaotic medinas of Marrakesh (the carpet dealers must have had a field day) for *The Man Who Knew Too Much*, which starred James Stewart and Doris Day.

Lawrence of Arabia, directed by David Lean in 1962 and starring Peter O'Toole, Alec Guinness, Anthony Quinn, Anthony Quayle and Omar Sharif, includes scenes filmed on location in the fabulous kasbah of Aït Benhaddou and contains some stupendous shots of central Morocco. In a case of art imitating life, Aït Benhaddou was even partially rebuilt for the making of *Jesus of Nazareth* in 1977.

Moroccan visuals feature strongly in Bernardo Bertolucci's *The Sheltering Sky* (1990), based on Paul Bowles' novel and starring John Malkovich and Debra Winger. At one point, we see the 80-year-old Bowles watching his characters from a Tangier café.

Other blockbusters shot on Moroccan soil include *Gladiator*, *The Man Who Would Be King*, *The Last Temptation of Christ*, *The Living Daylights*, *Asterix* and *Hideous Kinky*. This last stars Kate Winslet, is based on the novel of the same name, and captures the feel of Morocco quite well. Filming of the historical epic *Alexander the Great* in 2003 attracted foreign investment of over US$60 million.

In contrast to Western directors, who are drawn to Morocco for its exotic locations, local filmmakers are more interested in contemporary issues and, in particular, conflicts arising between ancient tradition and modern life. Good examples to watch out for include *El-Chergui* (1970), *Le Coiffeur du Quartier des Pauvres* (1985) and *Le Grand Voyage* (1980).

Morocco's most famous movie appearance of all, and the reason that Casablanca has become an exotic household name, came in *Casablanca*, starring Humphrey Bogart and Ingrid Bergman. Except for the fact that the film-makers and actors never set foot in Morocco.

Music

Invasion and cultural fusion have left behind several musical traditions in Morocco – Arab-Andalucian and Berber are the most dominant.

Berber music is not just entertainment – it's also the medium for storytelling and the passing on of oral culture from generation to generation. It can still be heard at *moussems* (pilgrimages or festivals in honour of a local saint), wedding ceremonies, public town or tribal gatherings and festivals, as well as at private celebrations and dances.

Gnawa (or *gnaoua*) music is a coming together of Berber and Arab influences, with its roots in sub-Saharan Africa. The term describes a spiritual brotherhood of descendants from slaves brought to Morocco from Central and West Africa in the late 16th century. Gnawa music is performed at public recitals known as *L'fraja* or in private trancelike rituals known as *lila* (or *derderba*), which are used to placate malevolent spirits. The surging waves of hypnotic rhythm are created by drums, a double-reed pipe known as a *ghaita* and the *nakkous* or *karkab* – percussive metal castanetlike instruments.

Probably the most famous Berber group is Master Musicians of Joujouka. The musicians were introduced to the world by Brian Jones of the Rolling Stones and have since recorded with the Rolling Stones, Robert Plant and Jimmy Page. This didn't make them great. It merely revealed their brilliance to the outside world. Based in the Rif, the group has been passing down musical tradition from father to son for over 2000 years.

Architecture

Morocco's abundant architectural treasures include mosques, *medersas* (Quranic schools), medinas and kasbahs; step inside to find the most captivating of Morocco's artistic traditions. The medersas in particular contain incredibly elaborate decoration, which includes detailed carving, *zellij* (tile work), Kufic script and *muqarna* (stalactite-like decoration used to decorate doorways and window recesses) stucco work.

Performance Art

Morocco is one of the most theatrical places in the world. Storytellers, acrobats, clowns, musicians, dancers and mime artists have been found for centuries in public squares, private houses and palaces. Djemaa el-Fna in Marrakesh is considered the cradle of popular Moroccan theatre and is a good place to watch it in action.

In contrast to Western theatre, the Moroccan *halqa* (meaning 'circle', in reference to the crowds it attracts) is itinerant, spontaneous, relies on audience participation and does not confine itself to one genre. It is a mixture of farce, tragedy and history, and is often accompanied by music and·dancing.

There are a tremendous number of other forms of Moroccan theatre, including the travelling puppet shows, poetry recitations of the Ilizlan, the itinerant Berber artists and musicians from the Middle Atlas and the 'ceremonial theatre' (which consists of ecstatic dancing and mysterious chanting) of the Zaouias.

ENVIRONMENT

The biodiversity found in Morocco is among the greatest in the Mediterranean basin. More than 40 different ecosystems have been identified in the country, home to some 4000 species of plant, over 100 species of reptile and 460 species of bird.

The first-time visitor to Morocco may be struck by the amount of green encountered in a country more popularly associated with vast stretches of desert. The remarkable forests of Morocco shelter two thirds of the country's plants and many species unique to Morocco. But the green is a cover for serious environmental problems of overgrazing, deforestation and a dangerously lowered water table. Animal extinction is another problem – the last wild Barbary lion was shot in 1936 and leopards, cheetahs, hyenas, jackals and desert foxes have all become extremely rare if not extinct.

That said, the conservation movement in Morocco is relatively well developed and there are numerous programmes (including plantation and the reintroduction of wild animal species) underway, designed to redress the damage.

Morocco is busy year-round. In summer, daytime temperatures can soar, but the cooler temperatures in the mountains and covered lanes of the medinas compensate. Summer is also the most popular time for Europeans on their holidays so things can get crowded. Average temperatures in winter hover around the 10 to 15 degree mark – cool but warmer than Europe. Spring and autumn are the best times – mild temperatures, fewer crowds and a good chance of clear skies.

TRANSPORT

GETTING THERE & AWAY
Air

Morocco is well served by air from Europe, the Middle East and West Africa. The main entry point is the Mohammed V airport 30km southeast of Casablanca. International flights also land at other cities including Rabat-Salé, Tangier, Agadir and Marrakesh.

Air France and Royal Air Maroc (RAM) are the major carriers; others include Iberia, Lufthansa Airlines, KLM-Royal Dutch Airlines, British Airways, Swissair, TAP Air Portugal, Sabena, Alitalia, Air Algérie, Royal Jordanian, EgyptAir, Tunis Air and Regional Air Lines (a small Moroccan carrier).

The standard fare from most European capitals to Morocco costs around US$400 but the cheapest return charters from Paris are: Casablanca (US$280); Agadir (US$377); Ouarzazate (US$399); and Tangier (US$399), with a maximum stay of four weeks. From Marseille to Marrakesh is US$350.

RAM has direct flights between Casablanca and South Africa (US$630 one way), Mali (US$480), Mauritania (US$420), Egypt (US$300), Tunisia (US$275) and Senegal (US$415). Flights into Algeria cost US$155/225 one way/return. There are also seasonal flights from Casablanca to Abidjan (Côte d'Ivoire) and Conakry (Guinea).

Boat

If you're coming from Europe, there are boat services to Morocco from various ports in Spain (Algeciras, Málaga, Tarifa, Almeria), France (Sète) and Italy (Genoa). The most popular route is from Algeciras to Tangier in northern Morocco. There are also frequent services from mainland Spain to Ceuta and Melilla (Spanish enclaves on the north coast of Africa, surrounded by Moroccan territory). For full details, see p1014.

Land
ALGERIA

Algeria is still in a state of de facto civil war and remains unsafe to visit. The land border between Morocco and Algeria was closed in

1994 and at the time of writing, that looks unlikely to change any time soon.

MAURITANIA

Although a UN cease-fire has kept the Western Sahara quiet since September 1991, crossing the border into Mauritania is not straightforward (though it's getting easier). In spite of this, hundreds of adventurous souls in 4WDs and on motorbikes do it every year. It won't be too long before it becomes possible to do the trip by some form of public transport.

The route into Mauritania runs from Dakhla south along the coast for 367km to Nouâdhibou on the border and then south along the coast to the Mauritanian capital Nouakchott. The route seems safe, though vehicles and small convoys, including parts of the Paris to Dakar Rally, have in the past been robbed at gunpoint along other inland routes. The only way for budget travellers to make the crossing is to head to Dakhla and hitch (expect to pay a negotiable fee).

Moroccan border formalities are now held in the basic settlement of Gueguarat, where most vehicles set up camp for the night. The border, about 15km from the settlement, is heavily mined, so stay on the piste (dirt track). It may be possible to get a Mauritanian visa at the border but you are strongly recommended to get one beforehand from Rabat.

At the time of writing there was talk of Compagnie de Transports Morocains (CTM), or possibly a private carrier, running a bus from Dakhla to the border (around Dh140, seven hours).

For the trip to Mauritania and trans-Saharan travel generally, Chris Scott's *Sahara Overland* is just about indispensable. Up to date information is also available at www.sahara-overland.com

Entering Morocco from Mauritania is possible, though you need a special permit from the Moroccan embassy in Nouakchott (p214).

GETTING AROUND
Air

If you're under 26 or a student under 30, you're entitled to between 25% and 60% off all fares. For example, the student one-way fare from Casablanca to Agadir is US$55 (US$100 full fare) and to Laayoune (Al-Uyen)

it's US$95 (US$180 full fare). Group reductions are available and children aged from two to 12 travel at half price. These discounts are normally only available through RAM.

Internal airports serviced by RAM are Agadir, Al-Hoceima, Casablanca, Dakhla (Ad-Dakhla), Essaouira, Fès, Laayoune, Marrakesh, Nador, Ouarzazate, Oujda, Rabat and Tangier. The bulk of internal flights involve making a connection in Casablanca, from where Marrakesh, Tangier and Agadir are the most popular destinations (with at least daily flights).

Local Transport
There is a good network of bus routes all over the country, except the Western Sahara region. Departures are frequent and tickets are cheap. The only real national bus company is Compagnie de Transports Morocains (CTM) but companies with smaller networks, such as Satas, are just as good. Many CTM buses are fairly modern and comfortable (though there are a few old boneshakers out there) and some 1st-class buses have videos (a mixed blessing), air-conditioning and heating (they sometimes overdo both).

Advance booking is advisable especially in smaller towns with fewer services. Main bus stations are called *gare routières*, but in many towns CTM has its own terminal. There is an official baggage charge on CTM buses (US$0.50 per piece), while on other lines baggage handlers may demand up to US$1.

Running alongside the bus services are shared taxis (*grands taxis* in French or *taxiat kebira* in Arabic). These are the workhorses of the Moroccan road – normally elderly Mercedes vehicles which you'll see belting along the highways or gathered in great flocks near bus stations. Shared taxis are a big feature of Morocco's public transport system and link towns to their nearest neighbours in a kind of 'leapfrogging' system, going from one town to another, en route to a final destination. The fixed-rate fares (listed in individual city entries) are generally a little higher than bus fares.

Petits taxis (local taxis) are equally cheap within towns, provided the driver uses the meter. Sharing these taxis is also quite common. Take note that fares rise by about 50% after 8pm.

Train
Travel by train when you can – Morocco has one of the most modern systems in Africa. You have a choice of 1st- and 2nd-class in *ordinaire* and *rapide* trains. The latter are in fact no faster, but have air-con and are more comfortable. The former are cheaper, but are usually restricted to evening services. Second-class is more than adequate on any journey.

The shuttle trains (*Trains Navettes Rapides* or TNRs) between Rabat, Casablanca and Mohammed V International Airport are fast (Rabat to Casablanca in 55 minutes plus 15 minutes to the airport) and comfortable. Fares in 2nd-class are roughly comparable to bus fares.

On long-distance night trains between Marrakesh and Tangier, couchettes are available. There are also refreshment trolleys and sometimes buffet cars.

Supratours (☎ 022 277160; 98 Blvd Mohammed V, Casablanca) runs luxury buses in conjunction with trains to destinations that are not on the train network. These include Agadir, Dakhla, Essaouira and Tetouan. You can buy combined bus-train tickets.

RABAT

☎ 037 / pop 1.5 million
As Morocco's capital, Rabat is the sort of place to which you come to transact essential business and rest from life on the African road. Cosmopolitan and devoid of the bustle for which Moroccan cities are famous, Rabat is an easy introduction to the country and to the rest of the continent.

It nonetheless has the requisite elements of any Moroccan city – an attractive medina replete with souqs, a kasbah and a burgeoning city; past and present drawn together with Arab charm and a hint of French sophistication. Much of Morocco's modern capital is precisely that – modern – so it's sometimes difficult to imagine that it has a 2500-year history. Its days of infamy are still evident in Salé, the erstwhile home of the infamous corsairs. These 17th-century pirates ranged far and wide in search of gold and slaves, and returned home to a city populated by a colourful cast of Christian renegades, Moorish opportunists, freebooters and multinational adventurers.

MOROCCO

RABAT & SALÉ

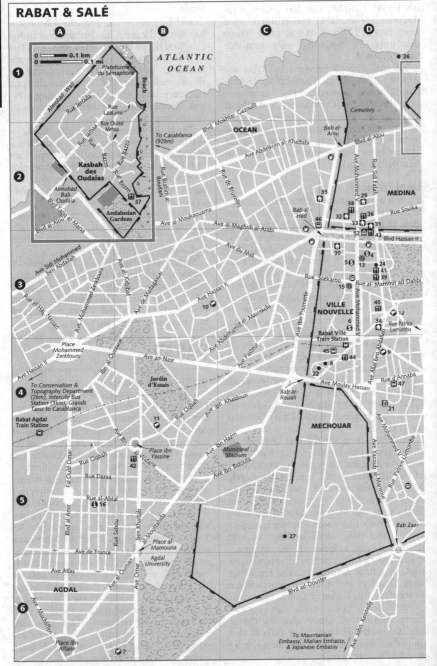

ATLANTIC OCEAN

Inset (A1–B2):
0   0.1 km
0   0.1 mi

Plateforme du Sémaphore

Beach

Almohad Wall

Rue Ierada

Rue Laalami

Rue Oulad Metaa

Rue Jamaa

Rue Bazzo

Rue Bazzo

Kasbah des Oudaias

Almohad Bab Oudaia

Blvd Tariq al-Marsa

Blvd al-Alou al-Marsa

Andalusian Gardens

37

Main map labels:

26

Cemetery

Blvd Mokhtar Gazoulit

OCEAN

Bab al-Alou

Blvd al-Alou

Ave Abdelkrim al-Khattabi

Ave Mohammed V

Rue Sidi Fatah

MEDINA

To Casablanca (92km)

Rue Brahim ar-Roudani

Rue de Bruxelles

Ave al-Moukaouama

Ave al-Maghrib al-Arabi

35

Bab al-Had

46

38   29

32   36

33   31

52   43

Blvd Hassan II

Rue Souika

Ave Sidi Mohammed ben Abdallah

Ave al-Kebibat

Ave Mohammed Zerktouni

Rue de Madagascar

Ave Hassan II

30

5 S

13

@

4

15 @

Rue Soékarno

Rue al-Mansour ad-Dahbi

24

41

39

Rue el-Haj Nassin

Rue Abdelhamid el-Marrakchi

10

Ibn al-Ouzzane

Ave an-Nasr

Ave Pasteur

VILLE NOUVELLE

40

34   14

Ave Allal ben Abdallah

Rue Patrice Lumumba

Place Mohammed Zerktouni

Ave Hassan II

Jardin d'Essais

Ave Ibn Toumerte

6

S

Rabat Ville Train Station

45

8

44

9

To Conservation & Topography Department (2km), Intercity Bus Station (3km), Grands Taxis to Casablanca

Rabat Agdal Train Station

22

Ave Moulay Hassan

Rue d'Annaba

47

Bab ar-Rouah

21

Ave Ibn Khaldoun

Ave Ibn Hazm

MECHOUAR

Ave Mohammed al-Mansour

11

Rue Oqbah

Ave Ibn Batouta

Municipal Stadium

Fal Ould Omar

Ave Ibn

Place ibn Yassine

42

Rue Oqbah

Rue Daraa

Ave Yacoub al-Mansour

Blvd al-Amir

Rue al-Abtal

16

Rue Sebou

ben Khattab

Ave al-Ouman

Place al-Mamouna

Agdal University

27

Rue Patrice Lumumba

Bab Zaer

Ave de France

Ave Omar

Ave Atlas

AGDAL

Ave Mischiften

Place ibn Affane

7

Blvd ad-Douster

To Mauritanian Embassy, Malian Embassy, & Japanese Embassy

Ave John Kennedy

MOROCCO

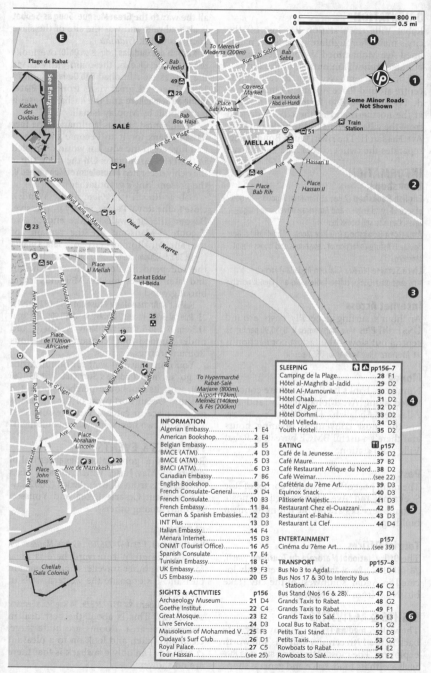

INFORMATION
Algerian Embassy....................1 E4
American Bookshop..................2 E4
Belgian Embassy......................3 E5
BMCE (ATM)..........................4 D3
BMCE (ATM)..........................5 D3
BMCI (ATM)...........................6 D3
Canadian Embassy...................7 B6
English Bookshop.....................8 D4
French Consulate-General..........9 D4
French Consulate....................10 B3
French Embassy......................11 B4
German & Spanish Embassies....12 D3
INT Plus...............................13 D3
Italian Embassy......................14 F4
Menara Internet.....................15 D3
ONMT (Tourist Office)..............16 A5
Spanish Consulate..................17 E4
Tunisian Embassy...................18 E4
UK Embassy...........................19 F3
US Embassy...........................20 E5

SIGHTS & ACTIVITIES p156
Archaeology Museum..............21 D4
Goethe Institut......................22 C4
Great Mosque........................23 E2
Livre Service.........................24 D3
Mausoleum of Mohammed V....25 F3
Oudaya's Surf Club.................26 D1
Royal Palace.........................27 C5
Tour Hassan.......................(see 25)

SLEEPING pp156-7
Camping de la Plage................28 F1
Hôtel al-Maghrib al-Jadid..........29 D2
Hôtel Al-Mamounia..................30 D3
Hôtel Chaab..........................31 D2
Hôtel d'Alger.........................32 D2
Hôtel Dorhmi.........................33 D2
Hôtel Velleda.........................34 D3
Youth Hostel.........................35 D2

EATING p157
Café de la Jeunesse.................36 F1
Café Maure...........................37 B2
Café Restaurant Afrique du Nord...38 D2
Café Weimar.......................(see 22)
Cafétéria du 7ème Art..............39 D3
Equinox Snack.......................40 D3
Pâtisserie Majestic..................41 D3
Restaurant Chez el-Ouazzani....42 B5
Restaurant el-Bahia.................43 D3
Restaurant La Clef..................44 D4

ENTERTAINMENT p157
Cinéma du 7ème Art............(see 39)

TRANSPORT pp157-8
Bus No 3 to Agdal...................45 D4
Bus Nos 17 & 30 to Intercity Bus
   Station..............................46 C2
Bus Stand (Nos 16 & 28)..........47 D4
Grands Taxis to Rabat..............48 G2
Grands Taxis to Rabat..............49 F1
Grands Taxis to Salé................50 E3
Local Bus to Rabat..................51 G2
Petits Taxi Stand.....................52 D3
Petits Taxis...........................53 G2
Rowboats to Rabat..................54 E2
Rowboats to Salé....................55 E2

MOROCCO

ORIENTATION

Rabat Ville train station lies just off the city's main thoroughfare – the wide, palm-lined Ave Mohammed V – but the intercity bus station lies 5km outside of the centre.

The main embassy area is east of the centre around Place Abraham Lincoln, Ave de Fès and Ave Bou Regreg. The medina, at the northern end of the city, is divided from the ville nouvelle by the wide and busy Ave Hassan II. The river, Oued Bou Regreg, separates the twin cities of Salé and Rabat.

INFORMATION

Bookshops

English Bookshop (7 Rue al-Yamama) A good selection of second-hand English and American novels and magazines. Can also sell books here.

American Bookshop (cnr Rue Moulay Abdelhafid & Rue Boujaad) Astute collection of new books and books about Morocco.

Livre Service (46 Ave Allal ben Abdallah) French-language guidebooks, coffee-table books and French novels.

Internet Access

An hour's surfing generally costs around US$1. **INT Plus** (Ave Mohammed V; US$0.90 per hr) is central but slow – the fastest connection is at **Menara** (Rue Soékarno; US$1 per hr).

Money

Numerous banks (with ATMs) are concentrated along Ave Mohammed V and Ave Allal ben Abdallah. The **BMCE** (☼ 8am-8pm) has the most convenient opening hours and there's a useful BMCE bureau at Rabat Ville train station.

Post

The main post office is on the corner of Rue Soékarno and Ave Mohammed V; poste restante services are on the left in the main building.

Tourist Offices

The **Office National Marocain du Tourisme** (ONMT; ☎ 037 730562; Rue al-Abtal) is inconveniently located in Agdal, southwest of the city (take bus No 3 from Blvd Hassan II).

SIGHTS & ACTIVITIES

The walled **medina** (old city) may only date back to the 17th century, but it is still worth exploring. The most interesting street is **Rue Souika** with its food, spice and general shops

all the way to the **Great Mosque. Souq as-Sebbat** is also vibrant and was the site of the slave auctions (think *Gladiator*).

Kasbah des Oudaias (admission Dh10) overlooks the Atlantic Ocean; the main entry is via the impressive Almohad **Bab Oudaia**, built in 1195. There are great views from the **Plate-forme du Sémaphore** and the kasbah houses a palace built by Moulay Ismail.

Rabat's most famous landmark is the **Tour Hassan**. Plans for it to become the largest and highest in the Muslim world crumbled in the 1755 earthquake. On the same site is the richly decorated **Mausoleum of Mohammed V**, the present king's grandfather.

Bab ar-Rouah (the Gate of the Winds), close to the Royal Palace, is very impressive. Beyond the city walls, at the end of Ave Yacoub al-Mansour, are the remains of the ancient Roman city of **Sala Colonia** (☼ 8.30am-5.30pm; admission US$0.90). It became the independent Berber city of Chellah and later still became the Merenids' royal burial ground.

Rabat's **Archaeology Museum** (☎ 037 701919; 23 Rue al-Brihi Parent; admission US$0.90; ☼ 9am-11.30am & 2.30-5.30pm Wed-Mon) is dusty and under funded but contains marvellous Roman bronzes.

You don't have to wait for South Africa to go surfing. **Oudaya's Surf Club** (☎ 037 260 683), with its clubhouse perched above the Atlantic Ocean northwest of the Kasbah is a great place to catch a wave; lessons cost US$15 for two hours, including equipment.

FESTIVALS & EVENTS

Rabat has a good **international festival of culture** in May/June, which attracts class musical acts from all over Africa (2002 saw the excellent Cesaria Evora and Youssou N'Dour, among others).

SLEEPING

Youth hostel (☎ 037 725769; 43 Rue Marassa; dm US$3.15) The green courtyard here is ideal for meeting other travellers and rooms are pleasant. It's opposite the western walls of the medina.

Hôtel d'Alger (☎ 037 724829; 34 Rue Souq Semara; s/d US$3.15/7) This is about the best deal in the medina area. Rooms are quite large, clean and quiet, and look on to a pleasant courtyard. The only drawback is that there are no showers.

Hôtel al-Maghrib al-Jadid (☎ 037 732207; 2 Rue Sebbahi; s/d US$4.50/8) More geared towards travellers, this is a good place to gather information for the trip ahead. Rooms are clean and bright and the shocking-pink walls come at no extra cost.

There are numerous other cheapies near the central market, but in a league of its own is the quite immaculate **Hôtel Dorhmi** (☎ 037 723 898; 313 Ave Mohammed V; s/d US$7.20/9). Friendly and family-run, this hotel has simple rooms which are often deservedly full.

Hôtel Chaab (☎ 037 731351; s/d US$2.70/4.50) Located in the first lane inside the medina wall between Ave Mohammed V and Rue Sidi Fatah, Chaab is one of the cheapest hotels in Rabat. It's a bit grungy and there are no showers, but rooms are set around a pleasant covered courtyard.

Hôtel Al Mamounia (☎ 037 724479; 10 Rue de la Mamounia; s/d US$6/8) Head to the ville nouvelle, and a block south of Blvd Hassan II, to reach this peaceful, airy and clean place. Some doubles have balconies.

Hôtel Velleda (☎ 037 769531; 106 Ave Allal ben Abdallah; s/d US$12/15) More expensive, this tidy, bright place on the 4th floor (there's a lift) has good views. Some rooms have toilets.

Campers should go to nearby Salé beach (p158).

EATING

Hypermarché Rabat-Salé Marjane (Route de Salé; ⏰ 7am-7pm) is just off the road to Salé, at the bottom of the hill, and if it hasn't got it, you probably can't buy it in Morocco.

The best budget bets for eating are in the medina on Ave Mohammed V, including a group of small restaurants under a common roof just off Blvd Hassan II, west of the market. You can get meat dishes or freshly fried fish, salad and the like for as little as US$2.

Café de la Jeunesse (305 Ave Mohammed V; meals US$1.80-2.70) A popular eatery in the medina where you can get a full meal of kebabs, chips, salad and bread for a pittance.

Café Restaurant Afrique du Nord (harira US$0.35, tajines US$2.35) When it comes to *tajines*, this place has the edge over Café de la Jeunesse, across the street. The *harira* (soup or broth with lentils and vegetables) is also good and cheap.

Restaurant el-Bahia (☎ 037 734504; Ave Hassan II) A pleasant restaurant built into the outside of the medina walls. You can sit in the Moroccan-style interior upstairs, in a shaded courtyard or outside on the terrace. It's also quite good value: a *tajine* costs US$2.90, brochettes (skewered meat) US$3.15.

Equinox Snack (Rue Tanta; mains US$4.50-8, set menus from US$7; ⏰ 8.30am-11pm), a friendly, relaxed place. The set menus are better value than the mains.

Restaurant Chez el-Ouazzani (☎ 037 779297; Sahat ibn Yassine; salads US$0.90, tajine US$3.15) On the edge of Agdal district, this is a great place for brochettes. The lovely *zellij* and cedar ceilings are genuine, and the place is packed with locals. Brochettes are the main things on offer, and a dozen with chips will cost you US$7. It's a lively place.

Restaurant La Clef (☎ 037 701972; Ave Moulay Youssef; mains around US$5, salads US$1.10, 3-course dinner US$6) Just south of Rabat Ville train station, La Clef is the best choice for cheap traditional Moroccan fare (the *pastilla* is very sweet). In summer, you can sit outside on the little terrace.

Café Weimar (☎ 037 732650; 7 Rue Sana'a; pizza US$5, chicken carbonara US$4.30) Located in the Goethe Institut, Weimar is a favourite of well-heeled locals and expats. The mix of German-French and Mediterranean cuisine is excellent; for example, the chicken carbonara – yes, bacon! – and pizzas are some of the best in town.

Rabat is crawling with (mainly European-style) cafés, which are great places for a morning croissant and coffee. Most of these are women-friendly; some double as bars.

Café Maure (Kasbah des Oudaias; ⏰ 9am-5.30pm; coffee & mint tea US$0.55, soft drinks & pastries US$0.65) The most pleasant by far. Set in a calm and shady spot looking out over the estuary to Salé, it's a favourite with young Moroccan courting couples. Offers a small selection of excellent Moroccan pastries.

Cafétéria du 7ème Art (coffee US$0.75) A popular open-air spot for evening coffee, housed in the Cinéma du 7ème Art.

Pâtisserie Majestic (cnr Rue Jeddah Ammane & Ave Allal ben Abdallah) Excellent, nonsmoking and women-friendly, the Majestic is great for cakes, and its bread is top-notch.

GETTING THERE & AWAY
Bus

The intercity bus station *(gare routière)* is inconveniently located 5km from the centre of town. Take a local bus (No 30) or petit

MOROCCO

taxis (US$1.35) to/from the southwest corner of the medina in the centre.

CTM (☎ 037 795124) has buses to Casablanca (US$2.70, 1½ hours, six daily), Essaouira (US$12, eight hours), Fès (US$4.70, 3½ hours, nine daily), Marrakesh (US$9, five hours) and Tangier (US$7, 4½ hours).

Train

Rabat Ville train station is near the roundabout on Ave Mohammed V. There are more than 20 trains per day to Casablanca (US$2.75, 50 minutes). Of these, about half are Trains Navettes Rapides (TNR) shuttle services that link Rabat with Casablanca's Mohammed V airport (US$6) via the city centre's Casa-Port train station.

There are also daily departures to Fès (US$7 for 2nd-class rapide, 3½ hours, eight services daily) via Meknès (US$6, 2½ hours), Tangier (US$9, 4½ hours, three services) and Marrakesh (US$10, 4½ hours, eight services). On all long-distance routes there's one late-night ordinaire train among the rapide services.

Shared taxi

Grands taxis for Casablanca (US$2.50) leave from outside the Intercity bus station. Other grands taxis for Fès (US$5.15), Meknès (US$3.75) and Salé (US$0.30) leave from near the Hôtel Bou Regreg on Blvd Hassan II.

GETTING AROUND

The main city bus station is on Blvd Hassan II. From here, bus No 16 goes to Salé and No 3 to Agdal. Bus Nos 30 and 17 run past Rabat's Intercity bus station; they leave from just inside Bab al-Had.

AROUND RABAT

SALÉ

☎ 037

Whitewashed and worlds away from Rabat, Salé is the place to experience the sights, smells and sounds of the Morocco of yesteryear and imagine the days of the corsairs, who made this town their base. The main sight inside the town's walls is the splendid **Merenid medersa** (admission US$1; ⊙ 9am-noon & 2.30-6pm), built in 1333, next to the Grande

Mosquée and containing intricately carved stucco and elegant cedar woodwork.

At Salé beach, and well signposted, is **Camping de la Plage** (camp site per person/tent US$1.40/2).

Grands taxis to Rabat (US$0.30) leave from Bab Mrisa. Bus No 16 also links the two towns or you can catch a boat across the river from just past the end of Ave de la Plage.

MEDITERRANEAN COAST & THE RIF

TANGIER

☎ 039 / pop 500,000

Tangier has seen it all before. A world-weary port at the strategic meeting point of Europe and Africa, the city has hosted every power who ever dreamed of conquering the Mediterranean. They carried in their wake writers, artists, smugglers, hustlers, money launderers, gun runners and prostitutes. If you've just arrived from Europe and think that the African light is different, Matisse thought so too. And if you feel strangely drawn to Tangier's gritty charm and whiff of intrigue, it was the inspirational muse for a host of Beat Generation writers. It's a compelling, at times overwhelming, place – a mongrel creation poised on the top of Africa, resting like an ageing libertine propped up languidly at the bar.

More than anything it's money that makes Tangier tick. Give it time, take the place head on and learn to handle the hustlers, the pickpockets, the con artists, the touts at the port and the medina's limpetlike souvenir sellers, and you'll find it a likable, lively city buzzing with energy.

Welcome to Africa.

Orientation

Like many larger Moroccan towns, Tangier is divided between the convoluted streets of the medina and the wide, ordered boulevards of the ville nouvelle. The square known as Petit Socco is the heart of the medina; the larger Grand Socco lies between the medina and the ville nouvelle.

Information

The **Librairie des Colonnes** (☎ 039 936955; 54 Blvd Pasteur) has a good selection of Francophone literature and some English novels.

TANGIER

0 _____ 500 m
0 _____ 0.3 mi

A

INFORMATION
Banks.......................................1 D3
Banque Populaire (ATM)..........2 C5
Banque Populaire (ATM)..........3 B4
BMCE (Late Bank & ATM)........4 C5
BMCE.......................................5 B4
British & Belgian Consulates......6 D6
Bureaux de Change.............(see 1)
Crédit du Maroc.......................7 C5
Crédit du Maroc.......................8 B4
Cyber Café Adam......................9 C5
Danish Consulate....................10 C5
Espace Net.............................11 B5
French Consulate....................12 B5
Italian Consulate....................13 A3
Librarie des Colonnes.............14 C5
ONMT (Tourist Office).............15 C5
Pharmacy de Paris..................16 C5
Pharmacy du Lycée.................17 C6
Pizza Web...............................18 B5
Société Générale.....................19 B4
Wafa Bank..............................20 C5

SIGHTS & ACTIVITIES   p160
Church of the Immaculate
    Conception........................21 C4
Dar el-Makhzen Museum........22 B3
Great Mosque.........................23 C4
Mohamed V Mosque...............24 A5

B

Musée d'Art Contemporain.........25 B5
Musée de la Fondation Lorin.......26 C4
Old American Legation Museum ..27 C4
Sidi Hosni Palace.......................28 C3
Spanish Cathedral......................29 A5
St Andrew's Church....................30 B5

SLEEPING   🏠 pp160–1
Hôtel Atlal...............................31 C5
Hôtel Continental.....................32 C3
Hôtel el-Muniria.......................33 C5
Pension Agadir.........................34 C4
Pension Le Détroit....................35 C5
Pension Mauritania...................36 C4
Pension Miami..........................37 C5
Pension Palace.........................38 C4
Pension Victoria.......................39 C4
Youth Hostel............................40 D5

EATING   🍴 pp161–2
Africa......................................41 C4
Agadir.....................................42 B5
Café Andalus............................43 C4
Café Central........................(see 36)
Fried-Fish Stalls........................44 C4
Hamadi....................................45 B4
Hassi Baida.........................(see 41)
Pâtisserie Charaf......................46 B4
Pâtisserie Rahmouni.................47 C5

C

Restaurant el-Khorsan..............48 B5
Restaurant Populaire Saveur......49 C5
Romero's.................................50 C5
Safarine...................................51 C5
Sandwich Cervantes.................52 C5
Tingis Café..........................(see 36)

DRINKING   🍷 p162
Dean's Bar...............................53 B4
London's Pub............................54 C6
Miami Beach............................55 D5
Morocco Palace.......................56 C5
Negresco.................................57 B5
Tanger Inn.........................(see 33)

ENTERTAINMENT   🎭 p160
Cinema Rif...............................58 B4

TRANSPORT   p162
British Airways.........................59 C5
CTM Office Bus Station.............60 C4
Ferry Company Ticket Offices....61 D3
Ferry Terminal.........................62 D3
Iberia......................................63 C5
Limadet Boat Ticket Office........64 C5
Local Buses for Train Station.....65 D5
Royal Air Maroc.......................66 B5
Transmediterranea Ticket
    Office.............................(see 64)

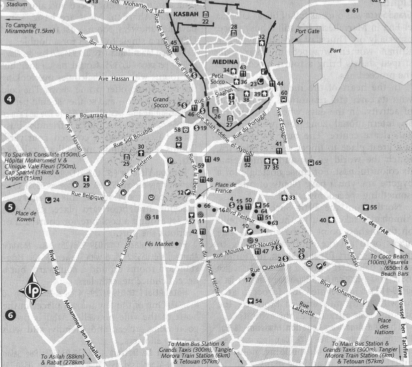

There are numerous Internet cafés in the ville nouvelle. Most charge US$1 per hour. Quality varies, but **Cyber Café Adam** (Rue ibn Rochd), **Espace Net** (16 Ave Mexique) and **Pizza Web** (15 Rue M'sallah) are recommended.

There are banks along Blvd Pasteur and Blvd Mohammed V as well as in other locations a little further from the centre of town. The BMCE on Blvd Pasteur has ATMs and an exchange booth that is open until 7pm daily.

The well-organised **main post office** (Blvd Mohammed V) is in the ville nouvelle. For **poste restante** (c/o Tangier Principle 90000), head to counter No 1.

The **Délégation Régionale du Tourisme** (☎ 039 948050; 29 Blvd Pasteur), also known as ONMT, has the usual limited range of brochures. The staff are helpful (if pushed) and speak several languages, including English, French and Spanish.

There's also a **24-hour emergency service** (☎ 039 333300) should you need a doctor.

Sights

Grand Socco was once as full of life as Djemaa el-Fna in Marrakesh. It's still a busy place, especially on Thursday and Sunday, when Riffian women wrapped in their gaily striped shawls bring a touch of colour to the proceedings.

In the heart of the medina **Petit Socco**, with its cafés and restaurants, is the focus of activity. In the days when Tangier was an international zone this was the sin and sleaze centre. The busy little square is a great place to linger over a mint tea, watch the world go by and contemplate its colourful past. For those nostalgic for a bygone era, you'll have plenty of offers of 'something special, my friend'.

North from the Petit Socco, Rue des Almohades takes you to the **kasbah**, built on the highest point of the city. The gate opens onto a large courtyard leading to the 17th-century **Dar el-Makhzen**, the former sultan's palace. It's now a **museum** (admission US$1; ☉ 9am-12.30pm & 3-5.30pm Mon, Wed, Thu, Sat & Sun, 9-11.30am Fri) devoted to Moroccan arts. As with many museums in Morocco, the building is as attractive as the exhibits.

The **Old American Legation Museum** (8 Rue d'Amerique; admission free; ☎ 10am-1pm & 3-5pm Mon-Fri), set in a fine old building, houses a superb collection of antique maps, 17th- to 20th-century paintings, and prints and drawings by (as well as photos of) various artists who either lived in or passed through Tangier. Its significance resides partly in the fact that Morocco was the first country to recognise US independence.

The **Musée de la Foundation Lorin** (44 Rue Touahine; admission free; ☉ 11.30am-1.30pm & 4-7.30pm Sun-Fri), which is housed in a former synagogue, contains an engaging collection of photographs, posters and prints of Tangier from 1890 to 1960.

Festivals & Events

In May a very successful week-long **International Festival of Amateur Theatre** brings Arabic and French-speaking theatre groups to the Cinéma Rif on Grand Socco.

TanjaJazz sets the city swinging in September with its mix of international and local jazz stars.

Sleeping

There are numerous small hotels in the medina around the Petit Socco and along Ave Mokhtar Ahardan. Most are basic, some have hot showers; rooms cost from around US$4 for a single to US$8 for a double.

Pension Mauritania (☎ 039 934677; Rue des Almohades; r per person US$3.75) Could be cleaner but the rooms with small balconies overlooking the Petit Socco offer prime views. The cold showers are free – and so they should be!

Pension Agadir (☎ 039 938084; 16 Rue de Palmier; s/d US$4.70/8, hot showers US$0.75) A friendly, busy place based around a covered courtyard. Rooms are nothing more than cell-like boxes.

Pension Victoria (☎ 039 931299; 22 Ave Mokhtar Ahardan; r per person US$2.80, hot showers US$1) One of the better options in this category. A peaceful, straightforward place, its rooms are set around a cool interior courtyard or overlook the port.

Pension Palace (☎ 039 936128; 2 Ave Mokhtar Ahardan; s/d US$3.75/8, d with shower US$12) Bog-standard rooms around a courtyard, but a decent choice nevertheless.

Hôtel Atlal (☎ 039 937299; 4 Rue al-Moutanabi; s/d US$7/12) One of the few budget places in the heart of the ville nouvelle, Atlal is pretty good value – clean and friendly, and with free hot showers.

Pension Le Détroit (☎ 039 934838; Rue Salah Eddine el-Ayoubi; s/d US$4.70/8, hot showers US$0.75)

Good value and straight down the line, this place offers clean, functional rooms.

Pension Miami (☎ 039 932900; 126 Rue Salah Ed-dine el-Ayoubi; s/d US$4.70/8, hot showers US$1) Here you'll find a similar deal to the Détroit, although if you've just arrived, don't judge Moroccan friendliness on this one. Some rooms come with balcony if not a smile.

Hôtel el-Muniria (☎ 039 935337; 1 Rue Magellan; s/d US$12/14) Further up the hill, this place is showing its age but remains an excellent choice. Fairly large rooms come with hot showers. There's a lingering nostalgic air of the 1950s, when Jack Kerouac and Allen Ginsberg stayed here. William Burroughs supposedly wrote *The Naked Lunch* in room No 9.

Camping Miramonte (☎ 039 937133; camp site per adult/child US$1.80/1.40, plus US$1.80 per tent, hot showers US$1) Some 3km west of the centre and set on a hillside in lush gardens, Miramonte is the most convenient and reliable of Tangier's camping grounds. Take a petit taxi from the town centre (US$0.70).

> **SPLURGE!**
>
> To catch a glimpse of Tangier as it once was, the **Hôtel Continental** (☎ 039 931024; hcontinental@iam.net.ma; 36 Rue dar el-Baroud; s/d US$27/34), perched above the port, is the place to go. This charmingly eccentric hotel was used for some scenes in the film version of Paul Bowles' *The Sheltering Sky*. It's a little ragged around the edges, although the rooms are gradually being redecorated and the terrace is a great place to relax and watch the activity of the port. It's very popular (so book ahead) and well signposted.

Eating

For really cheap food and self-catering head to the covered market and food stalls close to Grand Socco. There are numerous small cafés and restaurants here and around the Petit Socco offering cheap traditional fare.

Café Andalus (7 Rue du Commerce; salad US$0.50, mains from US$3.25) This one's a friendly little hole-in-the-wall, sawdust-on-the-floor place in the medina that serves up excellent cheap meals. Liver, peas and chips hits the spot if internal organs are your thing.

Agadir (21 Ave du Prince Héritier; mains US$3-3.75, set menu US$4.50) It may not look much, but

> **SPLURGE!**
>
> **Restaurant Populaire Saveur** (☎ 039 336326; set menus US$10-14) This attractive and welcoming little fish restaurant down the steps from Rue de la Liberté serves excellent set menus. This is well-crafted Moroccan home cooking and eating here is a real experience. Not to be missed.
>
> **Restaurant el-Khorsan** (☎ 039 935885; mains around US$12.10) In the El-Minzah hotel is one of Tangier's – some say Morocco's – top restaurants. It serves expensive but high-quality Moroccan food and there's often traditional dancing in the evening.

Agadir offers top-value local fare with a French twist. This is 'slow food' but the freshly cooked, succulent *tajines* more than justify the wait. Prices exclude a 10% tax.

Hamadi (2 Rue de la Kasbah; mains US$3.75-6, beer/wine from US$1.80/8) Just outside the medina walls, the Hamadi is a surprisingly reasonable palace restaurant. Sumptuous surroundings and live folk music provide the backdrop for a feast of *harira*, *pastilla* and other local delicacies.

Sandwich Cervantes (Rue Salah Eddine el-Ayoubi; sandwiches US$0.75-1.80, mains US$1.80-3.25) Downhill from Grand Socco in the ville nouvelle, this is a long-standing favourite for its well-priced – and well-stuffed – sandwiches.

Safarine (Blvd Pasteur) The *shwarmas* sandwiches (from US$1.60) take some beating. While you're waiting, nibble on a *pastilla* or *briouat* (a flaky-pastry snack) with a choice of chicken or seafood fillings.

Africa (83 Rue Salah Eddine el-Ayoubi; soups US$1, salads around US$1, mains from US$3.25, set menu US$4.70) Not far from the port, Africa dishes up straightforward meals and serves alcohol. The set menus are a bargain.

Romero's (☎ 039 932277; 12 Rue du Prince Moulay Abdallah; mains US$4.70-7) Not too fancy but with excellent service and food a cut above the norm, this is a good choice. There's plenty of fish and seafood – including a tasty seafood paella (US$6) that can be followed by luscious desserts. Don't forget the 10% tax.

Pâtisserie Rahmouni (35 Rue du Prince Moulay Abdallah) This is the place for high-quality, traditional Moroccan pastries.

If you want to watch the world go by over coffee or mint tea, try Café Central, a favourite hang-out for William Burroughs and others, and the pleasantly faded Tingis Café right on the Petit Socco. Pâtisserie Charaf off the Grand Socco serves an excellent selection of pastries and good coffee.

Drinking

Dean's Bar (Rue Amérique du Sud; beer & tapas from US$1.30) Hardly a Westerner of any repute has not propped up this bar at one time or another. South of Grand Socco, it's satisfyingly seedy and intimate.

Negresco (20 Ave Mexique; ⏰ 11am-3pm & 7-11pm) Clean and calm, Negresco is mostly a locals' bar with draught beer.

London's Pub (15 Rue al-Mansour Dahabi; beer from US$1.80; tapas until 11pm; ⏰ 6.30pm-1am) This is an excellent, well-stocked place for a civilised drink. Most nights a singer croons a mixed bag of international hits. It's by far the best bet for women too – any problems ask for Youssef, the owner!

Tanger Inn (1 Rue Magellan; beer US$1) Next to Hôtel el-Muniria, this is a tiny, kitsch place that has been lovingly maintained – one of the last reminders of the days when Tangier was an international zone. As such it's a bit of a tourist ghetto but worth investigating for the nostalgia. Be on your toes though – this area can be dodgy in the early hours.

The (now much-reduced) European gay population in Tangiers still frequents some of the beach bars south of town. Popular places include the Miami Beach and Coco Beach.

Clubbing

Pasarela (Ave des FAR) On the seafront southeast of the city centre, you'll find this large complex with several bars, an attractive garden and an outdoor swimming pool. It plays a mix of mainly Western music, heavy on the techno, and in summer (July and August) hosts live bands.

Morocco Palace (Rue du Prince Moulay Abdallah) Try this place if you're looking for quality traditional décor with live pop music (mostly contemporary Arabic covers). It's a bit sleazy with the occasional belly dancer, but the beers are relatively cheap (US$3.25) and you can dance until dawn.

Getting There & Away

BOAT

If you're heading to Europe by boat, you can buy tickets from virtually any travel agency or at the port itself. However, the port and entrance to the port can be a real hassle.

Both the Limadet and Transmediterranea offices are on Rue du Prince du Moulay Abdallah.

BUS & SHARED TAXI

The CTM office, where the buses stop, is beside the port gate. Many also pass through the main bus station (*gare routière*) on Place Jamia el-Arabia, about 2km to the south (US$0.80 by petit taxi). Departures include: Agadir (US$23, 14 hours), Asilah (US$1.40, one hour), Casablanca (US$11, six hours), Chefchaouen (US$3, three hours), Fès (US$8, six hours), Marrakesh (US$16, 10 hours), Meknès (US$7, five hours), Rabat (US$7, 4½ hours) and Tetouan (US$1.30, one hour). Cheaper bus companies operate services from the main bus station to all these destinations.

Grands taxis leave from a lot next to the main bus station. There are frequent departures to Asilah (US$1.10) and Tetouan (US$1.80), leaving when they are full.

TRAIN

The Tangier Morora station, about 6km southeast of town, is due to be replaced in 2004 with a new station in the Malabata district, roughly 3km out of town to the east.

There are daily departures (2nd-class rapide fares) to: Casablanca (US$11, 5½ hours), Fès (US$9, five hours), Meknès (US$8, four hours) as well as Rabat (US$9, 4½ hours). The overnight train to Marrakesh takes about 10 hours and costs US$26/18 for 1st/2nd class with a couchette and US$20/14 without. The same overnight service from Marrakesh arrives in Tangier at 6am, in time to catch an early ferry to Spain; to be on the safe side buy your ferry ticket in advance.

Getting Around

There's a well-organised city bus service operated by Autasa. Useful lines include No 13, from the train station via Ave des FAR to the port gate, and No 17 linking the train station and the main bus station. Route maps are posted on the bus shelters and buses run from around 6.30am to 9.30pm. There's a US$0.30 flat fare.

Petits taxis do standard journeys around town for around US$0.55.

CEUTA (SEBTA)

☎ 956 / pop 75,000

Ceuta, a Spanish enclave, is a small corner of Mediterranean Europe in Africa. It's a good place to come if you're feeling fatigued from the strains of African travel. It's not cheap so if you've just arrived in Africa, you may want to push on. Ceuta came under Spanish control in the 16th century and to this day some 70% of the inhabitants are Spanish.

Information

For Internet access try **Cyber Ceuta** (Paseo Colón) or **Indy Net Café** (6 Isabel Cabral), in the backstreets to the north of Calle Real, which charges around US$2.25 per hour.

Ceuta transacts in the euro. There are plenty of banks with ATMs and foreign-exchange facilities along the main street, Paseo de Revellín, and its continuation, Calle Camoens.

You can't miss the **Correos y Telégrafos** (main post office; Plaza de España) – it's the big yellow building off Calle Camoens in the centre of town. There are plenty of both blue and green public phones around. Direct overseas dialling is cheaper here than in Morocco.

The main **tourist office** (☎ 956 501401; 🕑 9am-3pm Mon-Fri) is located at the eastern end of Avenida Muelle Cañonero Dato. There's also a **booth** (🕑 9am-9pm) in the ferry terminal itself. Accommodation lists are available.

Don't forget that Ceuta (and Melilla) keep Spanish time, which is two hours ahead of Morocco in summer and one hour ahead in winter.

Sights

The impressive remnants of the **city walls** (admission free; 🕑 11am-2pm & 5-7pm) to the west of Plaza de Africa and the navigable, walled moat of **Foso de San Felipe** date back to Almohad times (12th century), although they were largely reconstructed by the Spaniards at the end of the 17th century.

The **Museo de la Legión** (Paseo Colón; admission free; 🕑 10am-1.30pm Mon-Fri, 10am-1.30pm & 4-6pm Sat) is perhaps the most intriguing of Ceuta's museums. Dedicated to, and run by, the Spanish Legion it holds a staggering array of military paraphernalia.

Sleeping

There is no shortage of inexpensive *pensiónes* or *casas de huéspedes* (guesthouses), some of which are identifiable only by the large blue-and-white 'CH' plaque.

Pensión Charito (☎ 956 513982; 1st floor, 5 Calle Arrabal; s/d US$14/17) If you can manage a 15-minute walk along the waterfront from the ferry terminal (look for the sign saying 'rooms'), you'll be rewarded with a clean and homely place with hot showers and a small, well-equipped kitchen.

Pensión Real (☎ 956 511449, 1 Calle Real; s/d US$23/26) Further west and also better than it looks from the outside, this *pensión* is nothing special but it's well-kept, and has hot showers and a washing machine.

Pensión La Bohemia (☎ 956 510615; 16 Paseo de Revellín; d US$23) One of the best deals in town is to be found on the 1st floor (look for the small sign in the shopping arcade). The rooms are fresh, very clean and there are piping-hot communal showers.

Eating & Drinking

There are plenty of cafés and bars serving snacks and simple meals. Things get cheaper as you head east from the town centre along Calle Real. The Pablado Marinero (Seamen's Village) development beside the yacht harbour is home to a number of reliable, if not outstanding restaurants, ranging from Italian and Chinese to burger places.

La Mar Chica (8 Plaza Rafael Gilbert; dishes US$2.75-3) This is a cheap local bar first and foremost, but does some reasonable lunch-time paella and fish dishes plus a few Moroccan staples such as *tajine* and couscous.

Club Nautico (Calle Edrisis; set menu from US$5) A simple but decent restaurant overlooking the yacht harbour. The three-course *menú del diá* (daily set menu) is a popular choice, while the luscious fish dishes will set you back the same amount on their own.

The best place to look for tapas bars is in the streets behind the post office and around Millán Astray to the north of Calle Camoens. The majority are a far cry from the male-dominated drinking establishments of Morocco. In addition to tapas, they all serve more substantial *raciones* (a larger helping of tapas) and *bocadillos* (sandwiches). You'll pay around US$1.35 for a glass of wine and upwards of US$1.20 for a *caña* (small glass) of beer. But be warned – negotiating the Morocco-Ceuta border with a stinking hangover is not a pleasant experience!

Getting There & Away

MOROCCO

The No 7 bus runs every 10 minutes or so between Plaza de la Constitución and the border (US$0.45, 15 minutes). If you want to head for the border straight from the ferry, there's a bus stop on Avenida González Tablas opposite the entrance to the ramparts.

Once over the border, there are plenty of grands taxis to Tetouan (US$1.40).

SPAIN

The **estación marítima** (ferry terminal; Calle Muelle Cañonero Dato) is 800m west of the town centre. There are frequent high-speed ferries to Algeciras.

TETOUAN

☎ 039 / pop 450,000

Tetouan's flavour is unmistakably Spanish-Moroccan. The Unesco World Heritage–listed medina – a conglomeration of cheerfully whitewashed and tiled houses, shops and religious buildings set against the brooding Rif Mountains – shows off its Andalucian heritage.

Information

There are several good Internet cafés around town, including **Cyber Primo** (6 Place Moulay el-Mehdi), **Remote Studios** (13 Ave Mohammed V) and **World Vision** (8 Rue Salah Eddine al-Ayoubi). All charge US$1 per hour.

There are plenty of banks along Blvd Mohammed V. The **BMCE** (Place Moulay el-Mehdi), has an ATM and a bureau de change that's open until 8pm daily.

The **post office** (Place Moulay el-Mehdi) is centrally located.

The **Délégation Régionale du Tourisme** (30 Ave Mohammed V) has helpful staff, most of whom speak English.

Sights

Surrounded by three mosques and four modern minarets, not to mention the Royal Palace, **Place Hassan II** links the medina to the ville nouvelle and is the showpiece of the town. The busiest entrance to the bustling medina is **Bab er-Rouah** (Gate of the Winds). There are some 20 mosques within the medina, of which the **Great Mosque** and **Saidi Mosque**, both northwest of place Hassan II, stand out. In the area towards the eastern gate, **Bab el-Okla**, are some fine houses built in the 1800s.

Just inside this gate, the excellent **Musée Marocain** (Musée Ethnographique; admission US$1; ⊙ 8.30am-noon & 2.30-4.30pm) has well-presented exhibits of everyday Moroccan and Andalucian life.

The **Archaeology Museum** (Ave al-Jazaer; admission US$1; ⊙ 8.30am-noon & 2.30-4.30pm), just off Place al-Jala, is also worth a visit for its mosaics, gardens and gravestones.

Just outside Bab el-Okla, children can learn traditional crafts such as leatherwork, woodwork and the making of *zellij* at the **Artisanat School** (admission US$1; ⊙ 8am-noon & 2.30-5.30pm Mon-Thu & Sat). Even the building itself is worth a visit for its quiet courtyard garden and palatial exhibition room.

Sleeping

Tetouan has plenty of cheap, basic pensions.

Pensión Iberia (☎ 039 963679; 5 Place Moulay el-Mehdi; s/d US$4.70/8) Excellent value, small and spick-and-span, this place has a homely atmosphere as an added bonus. The rooms come with washbasin and shared bathroom.

Hotel Victoria (☎ 039 965015; 23 Ave Mohammed V; s/d US$4.70/8) The Victoria is a similarly well-scrubbed, family-run place with only a few rooms – you'll need to book ahead. There are communal hot showers but no washbasins in the rooms.

Hôtel Cosmopolita (☎ 039 964821; 3 Rue du Prince Sidi Mohammed; s/d US$4.70/10) Another good option, the rooms here (with shared bathroom) are fairly large and some have small balconies.

Hotel Príncipe (20 Rue Youssef ben Tachfine; s/d US$6/7, with shower US$7/10) The luxury of a shower in some rooms is balanced by the absence of toilets and there's no communal shower, but it's clean and staff claim there's hot water 24 hours a day.

Hotel Nacional (☎ 039 963290; 8 Rue Mohammed ben Larbi Torres; s/d US$7/9) Although an unexciting choice, the rooms with shower and toilet are a fair price. Those with shared facilities are no cheaper.

Camping al-Boustane (☎ 039 688822; camp site per person US$1, plus US$1 per tent) Tetouan's nearest camping ground is on the beach at Martil, 8km northeast from town. It's an unusually spruce site with a good restaurant.

Eating & Drinking

Sandwich Ali Baba (19 Rue Mourakah Anual; sandwiches US$0.35-0.75, salads US$0.75, tajine US$1.40) is, together with Snack El-Yesti, one of the best places for a cheap filling meal.

Snack El-Yesfi (Rue Youseff ben Tachfine) does great baguette sandwiches with various meats, potato salad, chips and salad for US$1.50.

Restaurant Saigon (2 Rue Mohammed ben Larbi Torres; fish dishes US$2-6) Despite its name, Saigon serves good-quality fish and Moroccan fare.

Restaurant Restinga (21 Ave Mohammed V; fish dishes US$3.25-4.20, paella US$3.25, beer from US$1.10, 0.5L wine US$3.75) Not quite up to Saigon's quality or quantity, Restinga has two big advantages: a quiet, vine-covered courtyard and alcohol.

Heladería Atlas (Rue 10 Mai; orange juice US$0.35) Squeezes, mixes and shakes the best juice in town.

Getting There & Away
BUS
The bus station is at the junction of Rue Sidi Mandri and Rue Moulay Abbas. There are CTM buses to Casablanca (US$10, six to seven hours), Chefchaouen (US$1.40, 1½ hours), Fès (US$7, 5½ hours), Rabat (US$7, four to five hours) and Tangier (US$1.30, 1¼ hours).

Numerous other companies have buses to these and other destinations including

---

KIF IN THE RIF

The smoking of *kif* (marijuana) is an ancient tradition in northern Morocco. (The word stems from the Arabic word for 'pleasure'.) In the Rif Mountains, from Chefchaouen to Ketama and beyond, its cultivation is widespread; some villages grow nothing else and its cultivation is tolerated until another crop can be found that grows as successfully or profitably.

Hashish (essentially compressed *kif*) is a stronger, modern (1960s) invention developed for export. Whereas an old goatherd in the mountains will break out his *kif* pipe should you stop to chat, hashish is favoured by younger, more Westernised Riffians.

In practice, discreet possession and use is tolerated. Some travellers get away with buying small quantities for personal use. But be warned: never travel in possession of *kif* and mistrust all dealers – many double as police informers – unless you're interested in spending some time in a Moroccan prison.

Marrakesh (US$12) and Meknès (US$6, five hours).

SHARED TAXI
Grands taxis for Ceuta (US$1.40) leave from Ave Hassan II, southeast of and downhill from the bus station. The border is open 24 hours, but transport dries up after 7pm.

CHEFCHAOUEN
☎ 039 / pop 43,000
This delightful town, set on a wide valley in the Rif Mountains, has long been a favourite with travellers. It's relatively hassle-free, the air is cool and clear, there's more *kif* than you can poke a pipe at and the medina is clean, small and manageable. With its cheery white and blue houses and unique atmosphere, it's a wonderful place to chill out for a couple of days. In fact you'll probably find it hard to tear yourself away.

Information
For the Internet, try **Kouera Computer** (Ave Aba Hassan el-Mandri; ☷ 9am-1pm & 3-10pm) or **Cyber des Amis** (Ave Allal el-Fassi; ☷ 8.30am-10pm), both in the ville nouvelle. The going rate is US$0.90 per hour.

On Ave Hassan II in the ville nouvelle both BMCE and Banque Populaire can change cash and travellers cheques. They also handle cash advances on credit cards, and both have ATMs.

The **post office** (Ave Hassan II; ☷ 8.30am-12.15pm & 2.30-6.30pm Mon-Thu, 8.30-11.30am & 3-6.30pm Fri) is about 50m west of the Bab el-Ain entrance to the medina.

Sights
Chefchaouen's old blue-white **medina** is worth a wander through and it's easy to find your way around. In streets to the north and east especially, you'll still find a few tiny ground-floor rooms crowded with weaving looms.

Numerous cafés surround the shady and cobbled **Plaza Uta el-Hammam**, which is dominated by the red-hued walls of the 15th-century **kasbah** (admission US$1; ☷ 9am-1pm & 3-6.30pm Wed, Thu & Sat-Mon, 3-6.30pm Tues, 9am-noon Fri) and the **Grande Mosquée** (Great Mosque) with its unusual octagonal tower. Just off the northeast corner of the square is **Funduq Chifchu** (caravanserai), an ancient accommodation and stabling block, long used by pilgrims and travellers and still

MOROCCO

CHEFCHAOUEN

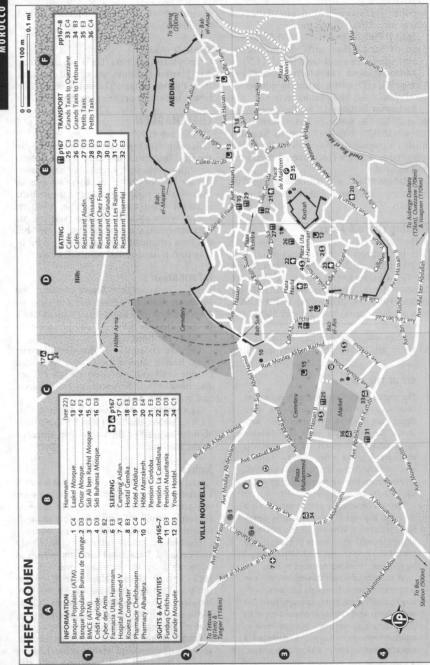

INFORMATION
Banque Populaire (ATM)...................	1 C4
Banque Populaire Bureau de Change...	2 D3
BMCE (ATM).....................................	3 C3
Crédit Agricole.................................	4 D3
Cyber des Amis.................................	5 B2
Farmacia Utaa Hammam....................	6 E3
Hospital Mohammed V......................	7 A3
Kouera Computer..............................	8 B3
Pharmacie Chefchaouen....................	9 C4
Pharmacy Alhambra..........................	10 C3

SIGHTS & ACTIVITIES pp165-7
Funduq Chitchu................................	11 D3
Grande Mosquée...............................	12 D3
Hammam...	13 C4
Laakel Mosque.................................	14 F2
Onsar Mosque..................................	15 C3
Sidi Ali ben Rachid Mosque..............	15 C3
Sidi Buhansa Mosque........................	16 D3

SLEEPING ♠♣ p167
Camping Azilan.................................	17 C1
Hostal Gernika.................................	18 E3
Hotel Andaluz..................................	19 D3
Hôtel Marrakesh...............................	20 E4
Pension Cordoba...............................	21 E3
Pensión La Castellana.......................	22 D3
Pensión Mauritania...........................	23 D3
Youth Hostel....................................	24 C1

EATING p167
Cafés...	25 C3
Cafés...	26 D3
Restaurant Aladin.............................	27 D3
Restaurant Assaada...........................	28 C3
Restaurant Chez Fouad.....................	29 E3
Restaurant Granada..........................	30 E3
Restaurant Les Raisins......................	31 C4
Restaurant Tissemlal.........................	32 E3

TRANSPORT pp167-8
Grands Taxis to Ouezzane.................	33 C4
Grands Taxis to Tetouan...................	34 B3
Petits Taxis......................................	35 E3
Petits Taxis......................................	36 C4

full on market days. A look inside is like a glance back in time.

The lively **market** in the ville nouvelle is held on Monday and Thursday.

The mountains around the town provide some excellent trekking. For more information contact the **Association des Guides du Tourisme** (☎ 062 113917; guide5@caramail.com) through the Casa Hassan hotel, Hotel Parador.

Sleeping

The cheapest hotels are in the medina.

Pensión La Castellana (☎ 039 986295; 4 Sidi el-Bouhali; US$2.80) This is the best of the bunch. Just off the western end of Plaza Uta el-Hammam, it's a major travellers' hang-out, got a great atmosphere, a fabulous roof terrace and, although some rooms are a wee bit boxy, it also has a kitchen and plenty of washing facilities. Rates include hot showers.

Hotel Andaluz (☎ 039 986034; 1 Rue Sidi Salem; r per person US$2.80, hot showers US$0.50) Equally popular and offering similar facilities to La Castellana, the Andaluz has a quiet interior courtyard; rooms on the upper floor are light and airy.

Pensión Mauritania (☎ 039 986184; 15 Rue Qadi Alami; r per person US$2.30) Also popular, the Mauritania offers dark but habitable rooms.

Pensión Cordoba (☎ 061926750; Calle Garnata; r per person US$4.70) Occupying a delightful Andalucian-style house, the rooms surround a lovely quiet courtyard (with a fire in winter) and the roof terrace looks out over the kasbah. With showers thrown in, this place is excellent value.

Hostel Guernika (☎ 039 987434; 49 Calle Ibn Askar; s/d US$4.70/10, d with shower US$13) Northeast of Plaza de Makhzen, this hostel is very comfortable. It stands out for its cheery fabrics, cats and clutter. To top it all, this Spanish-run place has one of Chefchaouen's best roof terraces – which is saying something.

Hôtel Marrakesh (☎ 039 987113; Ave Hassan II; s/d US$4.70/8, d with bathroom US$10) Outside the medina wall, this place is friendly, away from the throng, and, although it's a bit soulless, you get great views over the valley from the three bedrooms on the top floor.

On the side of the hill north of the Hôtel Asma are **Camping Azilan** (☎ 039 986979; US$1), which is very pleasant, and the **youth hostel** (☎ 039 986979), which is very basic. They're a steep 30-minute walk – just follow the signs to Hotel Asma.

Eating

Near the market are some cheap brochette-munching places (US$1.50), but the most popular places to eat in Chefchaouen are the small restaurants and cafés on Plaza Uta el-Hammam. There are often stalls selling soup (US$0.30) or snails (US$0.20 for a bowl of the slippery suckers) in the square itself or just outside Bab el-Ain.

Restaurant Granada (Rue Granata; tajine US$1.80, couscous US$1.85) Northeast of the Plaza Uta el-Hammam is this simple little place run by a cheery character who cooks a variety of dishes at reasonable prices.

Restaurant Chez Fouad (Rue Adarve Chabu; mains US$2.40) Directly opposite Restaurant Granada, Chez Fouad is similarly recommended for its hearty *tajines*.

Restaurant Aladin (Rue Targui; tajine US$2.60, pastilla US$3.25, set menu US$4.20) Just north of Plaza Uta el-Hammam is this traveller-friendly restaurant with a chilled atmosphere and delicious food (including vegetarian options). People swear by its *pastilla*.

Restaurant Assaada (Calle Abi Jancha; tajine US$1.85, set menu US$2.80) Inside Bab el-Ain and up to the left, this good restaurant draws a mostly local crowd. This friendly, family-run place has mastered the art of doing simple things well. The three-course set menu is a bargain.

Restaurant Les Raisins (7 Rue Sidi Srifi; tajine US$1.85, set menu from US$3.75) Although a bit out of the action in the ville nouvelle, this one's been pleasing the palates of locals and tourists alike for 25 years. You can choose from four set menus or the standard menu.

Restaurant Tissemlal (☎ 039 986153; 22 Rue Targui; set menu US$5.60) One of Chefchaouen's top restaurants. Not only is the food (including a delectable lemon pie) more imaginative than usual, but the place is beautifully conceived. Get here early or book.

Getting There & Away
BUS

The bus station is a 20-minute walk southwest of the medina centre. Chefchaouen can be an easy place to get to, but a difficult one to get out of – many of the CTM and other buses (especially to Fès) are 'through' services that often arrive already full. Give yourself a fighting chance and book a seat in advance at the bus station.

If you're not having any luck getting a bus to Fès (US$4.85, five hours), try for Meknès (US$4.20, five hours) or Ouezzane (US$1.70, 1½ hours). There are loads of buses and grands taxis between Meknès and Ouezzane and Fès.

SHARED TAXI
Grands taxis going to Tetouan (US$2.35) and Tangier (US$8, but difficult to get) leave from just west of Plaza Mohammed V. Other taxis heading to Ouezzane (US$2.35) and other southern and eastern destinations leave from south of the central market.

MELILLA
☎ 956 (☎ 0034 from outside Spain) / pop 60,000
Smaller and more run-down and 'Moroccan' than Ceuta, Melilla retains a fascination because of its medieval fortress. This is partly due to the fact that a third of the population is of Rif Berber origin. The town centre, with its palm trees, well-tended gardens and a number of beautifully restored Spanish-era facades, has more immediate appeal than Ceuta and the old part of town has a distinctly Castilian flavour with narrow, twisting streets, squares, gates and drawbridges.

Information
A few places offer Internet access for around US$1.35 an hour.

You'll find several banks (with ATMs) along or near Avenida de Juan Carlos I Rey. On the Moroccan side of the border you can change cash at the Crédit du Maroc. There's also a Banque Populaire with an ATM 200m further into Morocco. Melilla's moneychangers offer poor rates.

The **main post office** (Correos y Telégrafos; Calle Pablo Vallescá) is northwest of Plaza de España.

The helpful **Officiana du Turismo** (☎ 956 675444; 21 Calle Fortunyi) is in the Palicio de Congresos y Exposiciones.

Sights
The fortress of **Melilla la Vieja** (Old Melilla), also known as the Medina Sidonia, is very impressive and offers great views. Inside the walls is the **Museo de Melilla** (admission free; 🕙 10am-2pm & 5-9.30pm Tues-Sat, 10am-2pm Sun Apr-Sept, 10am-2pm & 4.30-8.30pm Tues-Sat Oct-Mar), which has a good collection of historical and architectural drawings. It also has a great terrace overlooking the city.

The main entrance to the fortress is the massive **Puerta de la Marina** (Calle General Macías). In front of the gate stands a statue of General Franco.

Sleeping & Eating
Accommodation in Melilla is expensive.

Pensión del Puerto (☎ 956 681270; 1 Calle Santiago; s/d US$11/23) This place, off Avenida General Macías, one of the cheapest, if a little rough and ready.

Hostel Residencia Rioja (☎ 956 682709; 10 Calle Ejército Español; s/d US$18/26) Expensive but still among the cheapest is this family-run hostel with clean, plain rooms, all with wash basin and shared hot showers.

Hostel Residencia Parque (☎ 956 682143; 15 Calle General Marina; s/d US$17/32) The bright, tidy rooms with TV and bathroom overlook the park. You'll need to phone ahead.

Camping de Rostrogordo (☎ 956 685262; camp site per adult from US$2.90, plus US$2.90 per tent) Two kilometres north of town and set among pine trees, it's well maintained if not exactly convenient. Prices increase by about 12% in high season.

The best area for good, cheap *bocadillos* (sandwiches) is along Calle Castelar (near the Mercado Municipal). There are also numerous bars and the odd restaurant where you can get a meal in the streets around Avenida de Juan Carlos I Rey.

The popular **Antony Pizza Factory** (1 Calle Cándido Lobera) serves good pizza, pasta and burgers for US$1.50 to US$6. **Café Rossy** (5 Calle General Prim) is good for breakfast and very popular with women. Great *bocadillos* (with delicious ham) go for upwards of US$1.40.

Of the tapas bars, particularly worth trying are **La Onubense** (5 Calle Pareja; 🕙 noon-3pm & 7pm-midnight Mon-Sat) and **Bar Aragón** (25 Calle Garcia Morato; 🕙 11am-3pm & 8.30pm-2am Wed-Mon), where things get pleasantly rowdy as the night wears on. **La Pérgola** (Calle General Marcías; 🕙 3-11pm) makes a great place for a drink in the late afternoon.

Getting There & Away
MOROCCO
The No 2 bus (marked 'Aforos') runs between Plaza de España and the Beni–Enzar border post (US$0.40) about every half hour from 7.30am to 11pm. On the Moroccan side of the border, the No 19 (usually unmarked) bus (US$0.20) and frequent

grands taxis (US$0.35) go to Nador, where you can catch onward transport.

SPAIN

Only Transmediterranea operates ferry and hydrofoil services out of Melilla. Buy your tickets at the **Transmediterranea office** (☎ 956 690902; Plaza de España), or direct at the **estación marítima** (☎ 956 681633). There are at least six ferries a week in each direction between Málaga and Almeria.

FÈS

☎ 055 / pop 1.3 million

Fès, the symbolic and cultural capital, is the Morocco you've always dreamed of – a veiled world of covered bazaars, the smell of spices, the call of the muezzin, blue tiles and jostling crowds. The medina of Fès el-Bali (Old Fès), one of the largest living medieval cities in the modern world, is beyond compare.

Orientation

There is a regular bus service (No 16) between the airport and the train station (US$0.30, 25 minutes), with departures every half hour or so. A grand taxi will cost US$11. Bus services include: No 10 Train station via Bab Guissa (northern Fès el-Bali) to Bab Sidi Bou Jida (northeastern Fès el-Bali); No 19 Train station via Ave Hassan II (both in ville nouvelle) and Bab el-Jdid (southern Fès el-Bali) to Place er-Rsif (central Fès el-Bali); No 47 Train station to Bab Bou Jeloud (Fès el-Bali). The bus station is right next to the medina.

Fès has three distinct parts: Fès el-Bali (the core of the medina) in the east (Map p170); Fès el-Jdid (containing the mellah and Royal Palace) in the centre (Map p170); and the ville nouvelle to the southwest (Map p171).

Finding your way around Fès is challenging, but not half as difficult as shaking off the legions of unofficial guides keen for your business. Official guides, available through the tourist office, charge US$11/14 for a half/full day tour.

Information

Fès Hadara (Map p170; ☎ /fax 055 740292; 24 Derb Oued Souaffine; admission including tea & cakes US$4.70), in the heart of the medina, is aimed at preserving the medina and its traditional way of life. The partially restored mansion, where plays and concerts are performed, is open to the public; it also offers tailor-made workshops in various traditional crafts.

INTERNET ACCESS

Try **Cyber la Colombe** (Map p171; Blvd Mohammed V) in the ville nouvelle and London Cyber

---

INTERVIEW WITH A FAUX GUIDE

Ahmed is one of 10 children; he has four brothers and five sisters. They live with their mother and aunt in the medina, Fès el-Bali.

Ahmed's father, a bus driver, had a heart attack one morning in 1987 at the age of 46. Ahmed, aged 15, was the eldest, so he left school in order to help his mother. He had hoped to learn the woodcarver's trade, but Dh700 had to be found each month to pay the rent.

Sometimes he helped his uncle who owned a clothes stall in the medina. Occasionally he sold cigarettes or ran errands for his neighbours and friends. Then he got to know the tourists who gave him sweets and pens, and began guiding them through the medina when they got lost. Some times he'd get tips as well, which he'd take home to his family.

Spurred on by his mother, he learnt to repeat what the official guides told the tourists – the history, the places, the stories. Later, and encouraged by his progress, he began to borrow basic school language books from his cousin Ali. Things began to improve for the family. The best times, he remembers, were always in June, July and August when he could find work among the tourists all day and sometimes in the evening too. Then, a couple of years ago, the law changed and he wasn't allowed to guide any more.

Ahmed was caught by police one day leading a German tourist to the Medersa Bou Inania in Fès. He got three months in prison. Many of his friends – the older ones – have given up guiding. Ahmed will continue. He says he can take it – he's still young, and so are his brothers and sisters who need him. What else will he do, anyway? He's never learned any other profession and there are no jobs. Prison won't kill him and, if it does, at least he's done his duty and taken care of his family.

FÈS

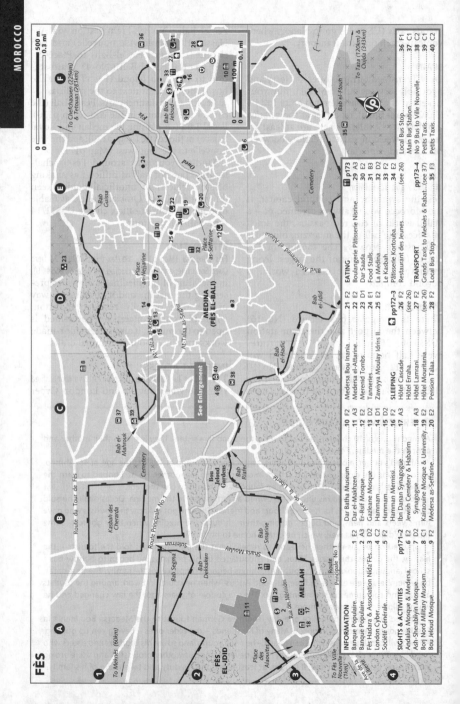

INFORMATION

Banque Populaire..........................1	E2
Banque Populaire..........................2	A3
Fès Hadara & Association Nida Fès..3	D2
London Cyber................................4	C2
Société Générale...........................5	F2

SIGHTS & ACTIVITIES pp171–2

Andalus Mosque & Medersa...........6	F2
Ash-Sherablyin Mosque..................7	D2
Borj Nord Military Museum............8	C1
Bou Jeloud Mosque.......................9	F2
Dar Batha Museum......................10	E2
Dar el-Makhzen..........................11	A3
Er-Rsif Mosque...........................12	E2
Gazleane Mosque........................13	D2
Hammam....................................14	D1
Hammam....................................15	D2
Hamam Mernissi.........................16	F2
Ibn Danan Synagogue..................17	A3
Jewish Cemetery & Habarim	
Synagogue.................................18	A3
Kairaouine Mosque & University....19	E2
Medersa as-Seffarine....................20	E2
Medersa Bou Inania.....................21	F2
Medersa el-Attarine.....................22	E2
Merenid Tombs...........................23	D1
Tanneries....................................24	E1
Zawiyya Moulay Idriss II...............25	E2

SLEEPING pp172–3

Hôtel Cascade.............................26	F2
Hôtel Erraha..............................(see 26)	
Hôtel Lamrani.............................27	F2
Hôtel Mouritania........................(see 26)	
Pension Talaa.............................28	E2

EATING p173

Boulangerie Pâtisserie Nisrine.......29	A3
Dar Saada...................................30	E2
Food Stalls..................................31	B3
La Medina...................................32	D2
Le Kasbah...................................33	F2
Pâtisserie Kortouba......................34	E2
Restaurant des Jeunes................(see 26)	

TRANSPORT pp173–4

Grands Taxis to Meknès and Rabat...(see 37)	
Local Bus Stop.............................35	F3
Local Bus Stop.............................36	F1
Main Bus Station.........................37	C1
No 9 Bus to Ville Nouvelle............38	C2
Petits Taxis.................................39	C1
Petits Taxis.................................40	C2

(Map p170), down the road from Hôtel Batha, in the medina. Most places charge US$1 per hour.

MEDICAL SERVICES

The **night pharmacy** (Map p171; ☎ 055 623493; Blvd Moulay Youssef; ☾ 9pm-6am), in the north of the ville nouvelle, is staffed by a doctor and pharmacist.

MONEY

The majority of banks (and ATMs) are in the ville nouvelle along Blvd Mohammed V, Ave de France and Ave Hassan II. In the medina, the Société Générale, immediately outside Bab Bou Jeloud, changes cash and travellers cheques.

POST

The **main post office** (Map p171; cnr Ave Hassan II & Blvd Mohammed V) is in the ville nouvelle. There's a **post office** (Map p170) in the medina near the Dar Batha Museum.

TOURIST OFFICES

The **ONMT office** (Map p171; ☎ 055 623460; Place de la Résistance) is in the ville nouvelle; the staff are well-organised and helpful. There is also a **Syndicat d'Initiative** (Map p170; ☎ 055 623460; Place Mohammed V).

Sights

The overwhelming number of sights are in the Fès el-Bali with a few in the Fès el-Jdid. You could easily spend a week exploring Fès, but allow a minimum of three days.

FÈS EL-BALI   Map p170

The incredible maze of approximately 9400 twisting alleys, 350 mosques, blind turns and souqs of the Fès el-Bali is a delightful place to get lost and found. **Bab Bou Jeloud** is a convenient entry point.

Medersa Bou Inania (☾ 8am-5pm, except prayer times) lies close to Bab Bou Jeloud. This is a stunning 14th-century medersa and an example of the Merenid building style at its most perfect. The *zellij muqarna* (plasterwork) and woodcarving are stunning, and there are excellent views from the roof.

Kairaouine Mosque (closed to non-Muslims) Towering over the heart of the city is one of the largest mosques in Morocco. Founded between AD 859 and 862, the attached **university** is one of the world's oldest and a

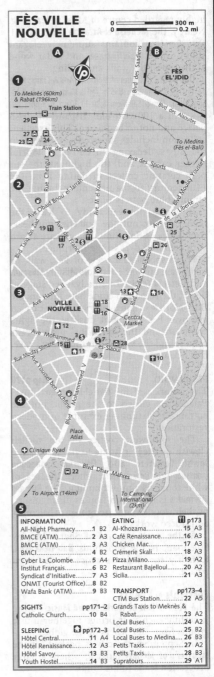

FÈS VILLE NOUVELLE

INFORMATION		EATING	🍴 p173
All-Night Pharmacy..........1 B2		Al-Khozama..................15 A3	
BMCE (ATM)..................2 A3		Café Renaissance.............16 A3	
BMCE (ATM)..................3 A3		Chicken Mac..................17 A3	
BMCI..........................4 B2		Crémerie Skali...............18 A3	
Cyber La Colombe.............5 A4		Pizza Milano.................19 A2	
Institut Français.............6 B2		Restaurant Bajelloul..........20 A2	
Syndicat d'Initiative.........7 A3		Sicilia........................21 A3	
ONMT (Tourist Office)........8 B2			
Wafa Bank (ATM)............9 B3		TRANSPORT	pp173-4
		CTM Bus Station.............22 A5	
SIGHTS	pp171-2	Grands Taxis to Meknès &	
Catholic Church.............10 B4		Rabat.......................23 A2	
		Local Buses..................24 A2	
SLEEPING	🛏 pp172-3	Local Buses..................25 B2	
Hôtel Central................11 A4		Local Buses to Medina...26 B3	
Hôtel Renaissance...........12 A3		Petits Taxis...................27 A2	
Hôtel Savoy.................13 B3		Petits Taxis...................28 B3	
Youth Hostel.................14 B3		Supratours..................29 A1	

highly regarded centre of Muslim learning. Nearby, the **Medersa el-Attarine** (admission US$1; ☻ 8.30am-6pm) contains supremely elegant stucco work, a *zellij* base, and cedar wood at the top of the walls and ceiling.

Dar Batha (Museum of Moroccan Arts & Crafts; Place de l'Istiqlal; admission US$1; ☻ 8.30am-noon & 2.30-6pm Wed, Thu & Sat-Mon, 8.30-11.30am & 3-6pm Fri) is set in a 100-year-old Hispano-Moorish palace and not to be missed. This excellent collection includes superb decoration from the city's decaying medersas, colourful Berber carpets and, the highlight, the superb ceramic collection dating from the 14th century to the present, including the famous blue pottery of Fès.

If you're not yet ready to leave the medina, seek out the **tanneries** northeast from Place as-Seffarine. The pits are awash with coloured dyes in the morning.

For a spectacular view of Fès, walk or take a taxi up to the **Borj Nord Military Museum** and **Merenid Tombs**. In an advanced stage of decay, the reason to come here mirrors the Borj Nord's original purpose – to cast an eye over Fès. Come at dusk as the lights come on and the muezzins' prayer calls echo round the valley, but for safety's sake, don't come alone.

FÈS EL-JDID   Map p170
The grounds of the **Dar el-Makhzen** (Royal Palace) are closed to the public but the entrance is a stunning example of modern restoration.

The southwest corner of the mellah (Jewish quarter) is home to the fascinating **Jewish Cemetery** and **Habarim Synagogue** (admission free; ☻ 7am-7pm), where the sea of white tombs is almost blinding. The **Rue des Mérinides** is lined with houses distinguished by their wooden and wrought-iron balconies and stucco work.

At the northern end of Sharia Moulay Suleiman, is the enormous **Bab Dekkaken**, formerly the main entrance to the royal palace.

Festivals & Events
The **Fès Festival of World Sacred Music** during June/July each year brings together music groups from all corners of the globe.

In September the city is packed for the **Moussem of Moulay Idriss II**, when a large procession leads to his tomb.

The modest **National Festival of Andalucian Music** takes place over two or three days in October/November.

Sleeping
Youth hostel (Map p171; ☎ /fax 055 624085, 18 Rue Abdeslam Serghini; dm HI members/nonmembers US$4.20/4.70, tw US$5/6; ☻ 8-10am, noon-3pm & 6-10pm) Located in the ville nouvelle, this is one of Morocco's best youth hostels. It's relatively central, welcoming and very well cared for. It also has hot showers.

In the medina, the most colourful hotels are around Bab Bou Jeloud at the entrance to Fès el-Bali.

Hôtel Erraha (Map p171; ☎ 055 633226; Place Bou Jeloud; s/d US$5/7.50) Just outside Bab Bou Jeloud, this is one of the cheapest hotels with cell-like rooms, communal cold showers and washbasins. Some rooms overlook the gate.

Hôtel Mouritania (Map p171; ☎ 055 633518; 20 Rue Serrajine; s/d US$6/9, hot showers US$1) Similarly boxy rooms, set around a central courtyard, are on offer here; the bonus is the hot showers.

Hôtel Cascade (Map p171; ☎ 055 638442; 26 Rue Serrajine; r per person US$5) Next door to Hôtel Mouritania, Cascade remains popular though it's sometimes hard to see why – it's not particularly clean and offers the occasional aggressive tout. In its favour, there are hot showers, and the two big roof terraces have unbeatable views.

Hôtel Lamrani (Map p171; ☎ 055 634411; Talaa Seghira; s/d US$6/9) Down towards the Medersa Bou Inania, Lamrani has largish rooms and cold showers.

Pension Talaa (Map p171; ☎ 055 633359; 14 Talaa Seghira; s/d US$6/14) A good choice, slightly out of the scrum, this place offers a warm welcome, hot showers and four characterless but spotless rooms.

Hôtel Savoy (Map p171; ☎ 055 620608; 16 Blvd Abdallah Chefchaouni; s/d US$5/7, hot showers US$0.50) In the ville nouvelle, reasonably spruce rooms with washbasins and hot showers are the order of the day here. Toilets are iffy and doors are locked at midnight.

Hôtel Renaissance (Map p171; ☎ 055 622193; 29 Rue Abdelkarim el-Khattabi; s/d US$5/9) This old, rather dark, cavernous place remains a popular cheapie. The rooms (some with balcony) are clean, and the communal showers have unpredictable hot water.

Hôtel Central (Map p171; ☎ 055 622333; 50 Rue Brahim Roudani; s/d US$6/11) Rooms are a cut above basic, though the communal toilets could be cleaner.

Camping International (☎ 055 731439; camp site per person US$3.75, plus US$3 per tent) The nearest campsite is 4km south of town on the Sefrou road. It's well maintained, set in large gardens and comes with a swimming pool, restaurants and a bar. Take Bus No 38 from Place Atlas.

Eating

There are many snack stands in the Bab Bou Jeloud area (Map p170), where you can get a huge sandwich stuffed with all sorts for about US$1. If you're feeling peckish down near the Kairaouine Mosque, there is a small huddle of cheap stalls between the mosque and the Medersa el-Attarine (Map p170).

In the ville nouvelle there are a few cheap eats around Blvd Mohammed V and the central market. You'll also find a good choice of sandwich places around Place Florence.

Good choices for a decent feed:

Restaurant des Jeunes (Map p170; 20 Rue Serrajine; mains US$2-3, set menu US$3.25) Under Hôtel Mouritania, it remains a popular hang-out close to the bab.

Le Kasbah (Map p170; Rue Serrajine; mains US$3.75, set menu US$7) Get here early for a seat and commanding views from the roof. The food is excellent and the four-course set menu takes some beating.

Chicken Mac (Map p171; 7 Ave Lalla Meryem; chicken & chips US$2.35) Hits the spot with its wickedly spiced-up rotisserie chicken.

Pizza Milano (Map p171; 11 Ave Lalla Meryem; pizza from US$3.30, *shwarma* US$3.30) Great for thick-crust pizza and its *shwarma* platter.

Restaurant Bajelloul (Map p171; Rue Arabie Saoudite; meals around US$2.80) Good selection of grilled meat with salad and bread.

Al-Khozama (Map p171; 23 Ave Mohammed es-Slaoui; set menu US$6, sandwiches from US$1.40) Tasty food in decent portions.

Sicilia (Map p171; ☎ 055 625265; 4 Blvd Abdallah Chefchaouni; salads from US$1.40, pizzas US$2.80-8 plus 10% service) Good for fresh salads, sandwiches and pizza.

There's a whole row of patisseries and fruit-juice bars just outside the central market. They're all good, but **Café Renaissance** (Map p171; juices from US$0.55) gets a thumbs up for its juices, while early birds should head to **Crémerie Skali** (Map p171; breakfast around US$1.80) for a hearty breakfast.

Near the Kairaouine Mosque, it's impossible to pass the Pâtisserie Kortouba (Map p170) without sampling its seductive range of goodies – just the ticket for a sugar hit while sightseeing.

SPLURGE!

The medina is the place for extravagant Moroccan meals in lavish surrounds. It would be a false economy to miss out on one of *the* great Moroccan dining experiences, and Fès is a great place to splash out on the cuisine. In addition to the usual staples, this may be the time to try *trid* (fried dough stuffed with egg and meat and covered in cinnamon and sugar), *m'choui* (whole roast lamb), or pigeon *tajine*. Both places mentioned here serve alcohol and add 10% tax to your bill.

■ **La Médina** (Map p170; ☎ 055 635857; 13 Derb el-Hammam; set menus US$11-20) The *pastilla* served here is rated among the best in Fès.

■ **Dar Saada** (Map p170; ☎ 055 637370; 21 Souq el-Attarine; mains from US$9, set menus US$14 & US$20; ☽ noon-3pm) This is a great place for sampling less standard dishes.

Getting There & Away
BUS & SHARED TAXI

CTM (☎ 055 732992) buses leave from both the CTM bus station (Map p171) near Place de l'Atlas and the main bus station (Map p170) outside Bab el-Mahrouk, northwest of Fès el-Bali.

There are daily departures to Casablanca (US$8, five hours), Rabat (US$5, 3½ hours), Meknès (US$1.40, one hour), Marrakesh (US$12, nine hours), Tangier (US$8, six hours) and Tetouan (US$7, five hours).

Grands taxis to Meknès (US$1.50) and Rabat (US$5) leave from in front of the main bus station (outside Bab el-Mahrouk) and from near the train station.

TRAIN

The train station (Map p171) is in the ville nouvelle, a five-minute walk from Place des Alaouites.

There are eight daily ordinaire/rapide departures to Casablanca (US$7/9, 4¼ hours), all of which stop at Rabat (US$5/7, 3½ hours) and Meknès (US$1/1.50, one

MOROCCO

hour). There are five direct rapide trains to Marrakesh (US$7, eight hours) and one to Tangier (US$9, five hours, every day).

Getting Around

BUS

Fès has good local bus services. Fares cost around US$0.20, although the buses are like sardine cans at times. Useful routes include:

No 9 Place Atlas (in the ville nouvelle)–near the Dar Batha Museum (Fès el-Bali)

No 12 Bab Bou Jeloud–Bab Guissa–Bab el-Ftouh (all in Fès el-Bali)

No 16 Train station–airport

No 47 Train station–Bab Bou Jeloud (Fès el-Bali)

MEKNÈS

☎ 055 / pop 200,000

Billing Meknès as the Versailles of Morocco may be overdoing it but its impressive buildings nonetheless reflect the former heart of the Moroccan sultanate. It's also quieter and more hassle-free than Marrakesh and Fès, and has a habit of imperceptibly growing on you.

Information

Among Meknès' Internet cafés, try **Carting Info** (3 Rue Menton) or **Easy Everything Internet Shop** (Zankat Accra) in the ville nouvelle. **JF Friends** (Rue Rouamzine) is in the medina. Expect to pay between US$0.40 and US$0.65 per hour.

There are banks with ATMs both in the new town (mainly on Ave Hassan II, Ave Mohammed V and Blvd Allal ben Abdallah) and the medina (Place el-Hedim and Rue Sekkakine).

The **main post office** (Place de l'Istiqlal) is in the ville nouvelle. There is also a useful **post office** (Rue Dar Smen) in the medina.

The **Délégation Régionale du Tourisme** (☎ 055 524426; Place de l'Istiqlal) is near the main post office, on Place de l'Istiqlal (also known as Place Batha). Staff are helpful, though, as usual, have nothing to hand out beyond a glossy brochure with a very basic map.

Sights

These sights are open from 9am to noon and 3pm to 6pm Wednesday to Monday and entry costs US$1.

The focus of the old city is the massive **Bab el-Mansour**, one of the most impressive monumental gateways in all Morocco

and the main entrance to Moulay Ismail's 17th-century **imperial city**. The gate faces **Place el-Hedim**, where a few storytellers and musicians gather in the evening. On the north side of the square is the **Dar Jamaï Museum**, housed in a beautiful 19th-century palace with traditional ceramics, jewellery, textiles and a funky silver *sebsi* (pipe) for smoking *kif* (marijuana).

The easiest access to the **medina** is through Bab Bernima to the west of the museum. The covered main street leads to the **Grande Mosquée** and also the 14th-century **Medersa Bou Inania** where the *zellij* (tile work) base, stucco midriff and carved olive-wood upper section of the interior walls are present in all their elegance.

For the imperial city, follow the road round from Bab el-Mansour to the **Mausoleum of Moulay Ismail** (admission free), the last resting place of the much-loved sultan who made Meknès his capital in the 17th century. The mausoleum is peaceful and beautifully displays Moroccan architecture and craftsmanship. It's also one of the few functioning Islamic monuments open to non-Muslims.

From the mausoleum, the road leads to the spectacular **Heri es-Souani**, built as an immense granary which was ingeniously designed with tiny windows, massive walls and a system of underfloor water channels that kept the temperatures cool and air circulating.

Festivals & Events

One of the largest moussems (festivals in honour of a saint) in Morocco takes place in May/June at the Mausoleum of Sidi ben Aïssa, just outside the medina walls. It's a busy festival with *fantasias* (musket-firing cavalry charges), fairs and a riot of singing and dancing.

Sleeping

Youth Hostel (☎ /fax 055 524698; dm with breakfast US$4.20, hot showers US$0.50) In a quiet residential area in the ville nouvelle, this hostel has a café, communal kitchen and washroom.

Most of the cheapest hotels are clustered together in the old city along Rue Dar Smen and Rue Rouamzine.

Hôtel Nouveau (☎ 067 309317; Rue Rouamzine; s/d US$3.75/6, hot showers US$0.50) The best choice, it has recently been retiled and is quite jolly. Rooms have washbasins and two boast views over the medina. There's

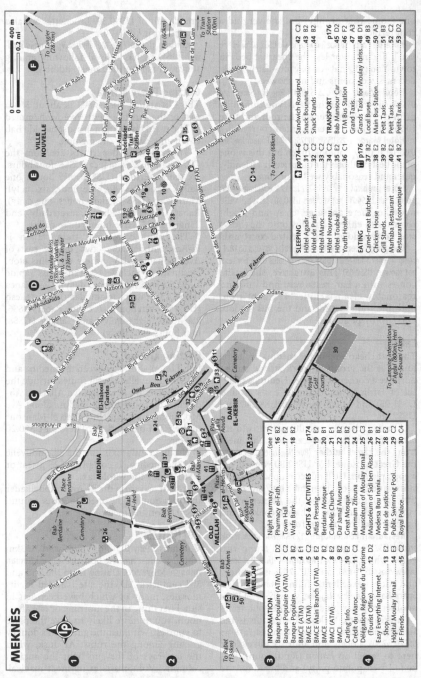

MEKNÈS

0   400 m
0   0.2 mi

one (somewhat grungy) hot shower and a roof terrace.

Hôtel de Paris (58 Rue Rouamzine; s/d US$2.80/6) Here you'll find more or less the cheapest beds in town. You get what you pay for – fairly bleak, decent-sized rooms and no showers.

Hôtel Agadir (☎ 055 530141; Rue Dar Smen; s/d US$3.75/7) Similar to the Paris, you can enjoy primitive cold shower on the roof and bare rooms around a green-painted courtyard.

Hôtel Maroc (☎ 055 530075; 7 Rue Rouamzine; s/d US$6/12) It may not look much but this is one of the best boltholes for the price. It's friendly, quiet and reasonably well maintained.

Hôtel Toubkal (☎ 055 522218; 49 Ave Mohammed V; r per person US$4.70, hot showers US$0.50) In the ville nouvelle, there are large, clean and bright rooms with either a balcony onto the (busy) street or windows onto a central courtyard.

Camping International d'Agdal (☎ 055 551828; camp site per adult/child US$1.60/1.10, plus US$1 per tent, hot showers US$0.65) This attractive, shady site comes with a bar, restaurant and café and reasonably clean facilities. It's 2km from both the train station and the bus station; US$1.10 by petit taxi.

Eating

The best cheap eats in the medina are to be found at the group of snack stands on the northwest corner of Place el-Hedim; a plate-ful of sardines, for example, costs around US$1.25, and *tajines* between US$1.40 and US$2.80.

A more adventurous alternative is to try camel meatballs. You can buy the meat from the **camel butcher** (Rue Najjarine) opposite the Great Mosque. For US$2.80 you will get a good plateful. He'll mince it up with onion, spices and parsley. Then take it to one of the little grill stands round the corner where you'll pay about US$1 to have it cooked (and have a round of bread thrown in).

Restaurant Économique (123 Rue Dar Smen; meals around US$2.35) is good for chicken *tajine* with chips while **Sandwich Rossignol** (Rue Dar Smen; sandwiches US$1-1.80, mains US$2.80) is friendly and does excellent, filling sandwiches. **Snack Bounana** (Rue Najjarine; meals US$3.75-4.20) is another popular pit stop on the souq trail.

A great-value Meknès institution is the **Marhaba Restaurant** (23 Ave Mohammed V; tajines US$2.15-2.80). Locals and tourists alike flock here to refuel on *harira* (lentil soup), *ma-koda* (fried-potato patty) and bread for the

grand sum of US$0.50. Brochettes are also available for US$1.70.

Chicken House (Ave Mohammed V; *shwarma* sand-wiches US$2.35) has a loyal following among *shwarma* (spit-grilled meat) addicts.

Getting There & Away

The **CTM station** (Ave des FAR) is about 500m east of the junction with Ave Mohammed V. The main bus station lies just outside Bab el-Khemis, west of the medina.

The following departures are from the CTM station: Casablanca (US$6, four hours, six daily); Erfoud (US$10, 8½ hours, one daily); Fès (US$1.40, one hour, six daily); Marrakesh (US$12, eight hours, one daily); Rabat (US$3.30, 2½ hours, seven daily); and Tangier (US$7, five hours, three daily).

The most convenient train station is El-Amir Abdelkader, two blocks east of Ave Mohammed V, where all trains stop. Destinations include Fès (2nd-class rapide US$1.60, one hour, nine daily); Casablanca (US$8, 3½ hours, eight daily); Marrakesh (US$15, seven hours, six daily); Rabat (US$6, 2¼ hours, eight daily); and Tangier (US$8, four hours, four daily).

Getting Around

Local buses shuttle between the medina and the ville nouvelle. Useful routes include the No 2 (Bab el-Mansour to Blvd Allal ben Ab-dallah, returning to the medina along Ave Mohammed V) and No 7 (Bab el-Mansour to the CTM bus station). There's a US$0.20 flat fare.

Urban grands taxis link the ville nouvelle and the medina. It costs US$0.25 a seat or US$1.50 for the whole taxi.

A petit taxi from the El-Amir Abdelkader train station to the medina costs around US$0.60 on the meter.

VOLUBILIS

Volubilis (entry US$1.90, ☉ 8am-sunset), 33km from Meknès, has the best-preserved **Roman ruins** in Morocco. Dating from the 2nd and 3rd centuries AD, the site is noted for its mosaics, many of which have been left in situ. First thing in the morning or late after-noon, you're more likely to have the place to yourself, with just the guardian's donkey grazing among the ruins. At dusk, when the last rays of the sun light the ancient columns, Volubilis is at its most magical, but if you stay until then make sure you pre-arrange return transport.

Among the many highlights are the **Decumanus Maximus**, the great ceremonial road built in AD 217, the **House of the Columns** and the exceptional mosaics in the **House of Venus**.

The cheapest way to get there is to take a grand taxi from Place de la Foire in Meknès to Moulay Idriss (US$0.65) and change there for Volubilis (US$0.45).

THE ATLANTIC COAST

ASILAH

After a tumultuous history of foreign occupation – by the Carthaginians, Romans, Portuguese and Spanish – Asilah has found its niche as a bijou resort town. Affluent Moroccans, the government and Europeans have poured money into gentrifying houses within the city walls. Other than the medina, the beaches to the north of town are the main attraction.

Sights

The 15th-century Portuguese **ramparts** are intact, but access is limited to the southwest corner beside the mausoleum of Sidi Ahmed El Mansour. The views are excellent. The bright **medina** is worth a wander through, but it's a little sanitised for some tastes. The streets gleam with whitewash, ornate wrought iron adorns windows and there's the occasional craft shop or workshop.

The **Centre de Hassan II Rencontres Internationales** (Hassan II International Meeting Centre) and **El-Kamra** tower are the focus of the annual **Cultural Moussem** (Cultural Festival) held in early August. They house art exhibitions throughout the year.

Several decent **beaches** stretch north of the town, while **Paradise Beach**, a local favourite, is 3km south.

Sleeping

Hôtel Marhaba (☎ 039 417144; d US$7.50) This simple, pokey hotel overlooking Place Zelaka, in front of the medina's main entrance (Bab Kasaba), is a welcome relief after the heat of the day. Hot showers are free.

Hôtel Asilah (☎ 039 417286; Ave Hassan II; s/d US$3.25/7, with shower US$10/12) Try this place for one of the best-value deals in town with small but clean rooms.

Hôtel Mansour (☎ 039 417390; fax 417533; 49 Ave Mohammed V; s/d US$10/17) and **Hôtel Sahara** (☎ 039 417185; 9 Rue Tarfaya; s/d from US$7/10) are both well-maintained and worth trying.

There are two good camping spots a few hundred metres north of town. Both are secure, have decent facilities and fill up in summer.

Camping Echrigui (☎ 039 417182) The better of the two places, this one has a café and a shop. It charges slightly more, but choices range from self-contained apartments (US$10/24 in off-peak/peak season) to tiny huts highly suited to amorous couples (US$6/10).

There's also **Camping As-Saada** (☎ 039 417317; per person/tent US$1.10/1).

Eating

There's a string of restaurants and cafés on and around Ave Hassan II, especially by the medina wall. A main course costs around US$3 and fish is the speciality. Slightly more-expensive restaurants lie across from Bab Kasaba and opposite the new harbour.

For Spanish-style fish dishes at around US$5, the lively **Casa García** (Rue Moulay Hassan ben el-Mehdi) is currently top dog, but **Restaurante Oceano Casa Pepe** (8 Place Zellaka) is snapping at its heels.

Getting There & Away

The best way to reach Asilah is by bus (US$1) or grand taxi (US$1.20) from Tangier, or by bus from Larache (US$1). Regular buses leave Asilah bound for Rabat (US$4.70), Casablanca (US$7) and Fès (US$6).

There are also trains, but the station is 1.5km north of town. It's possible to catch one of three daily services to Tangier (US$1.40), or four south-bound services to Casablanca (US$10); Fès (US$8); Marrakesh (US$16), which may require a change of train at Sidi Kacem; and Rabat (US$7.50).

CASABLANCA

☎ 022 / pop 5 million

One of Africa's most evocative names, Casablanca carries with it the resonance of a myth. The reality is somewhat less exotic. Casablanca is nothing like the movie – hardly surprising really when you consider that it was filmed entirely in Hollywood. If you come looking for the sophisticated city of Humphrey Bogart and Ingrid Bergman, you'll be disappointed. And yet, with its

MOROCCO

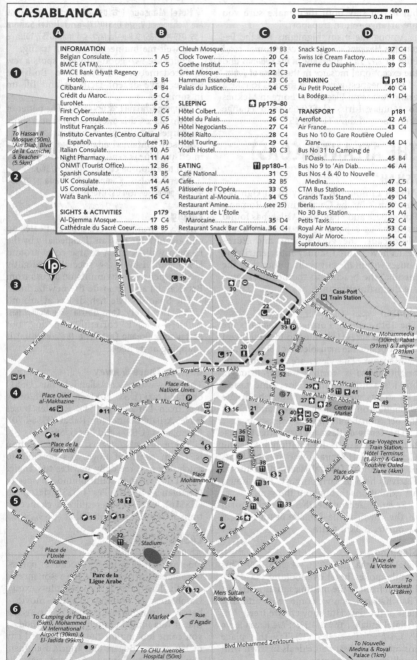

CASABLANCA

0 ——————————— 400 m
0 ——————————— 0.2 mi

INFORMATION
Belgian Consulate	1 A5
BMCE (ATM)	2 C5
BMCE Bank (Hyatt Regency Hotel)	3 B4
Citibank	4 B4
Crédit du Maroc	5 C4
EuroNet	6 C5
First Cyber	7 C4
French Consulate	8 C5
Institut Français	9 A6
Instituto Cervantes (Centro Cultural Español)	(see 13)
Italian Consulate	10 A5
Night Pharmacy	11 A4
ONMT (Tourist Office)	12 B6
Spanish Consulate	13 B5
UK Consulate	14 A4
US Consulate	15 A5
Wafa Bank	16 C4

SIGHTS & ACTIVITIES   p179
Al-Djemma Mosque	17 C4
Cathédrale du Sacré Coeur	18 B5
Chleuh Mosque	19 B3
Clock Tower	20 C4
Goethe Institut	21 C4
Great Mosque	22 C3
Hammam Essanoibar	23 C6
Palais du Justice	24 C4

SLEEPING   pp179–80
Hôtel Colbert	25 D4
Hôtel du Palais	26 C5
Hôtel Negociants	27 C4
Hôtel Rialto	28 C4
Hôtel Touring	29 C4
Youth Hostel	30 C3

EATING   pp180–1
Café National	31 C5
Cafés	32 B5
Pâtisserie de l'Opéra	33 C5
Restaurant al-Mounia	34 C5
Restaurant Amine	(see 25)
Restaurant de L'Étoile Marocaine	35 D4
Restaurant Snack Bar California	36 C4

Snack Saigon	37 C4
Swiss Ice Cream Factory	38 C5
Taverne du Dauphin	39 C3

DRINKING   p181
Au Petit Poucet	40 C4
La Bodéga	41 D4

TRANSPORT   p181
Aeroflot	42 A5
Air France	43 C4
Bus No 10 to Gare Routière Ouled Ziane	44 D4
Bus No 31 to Camping de l'Oasis	45 B4
Bus No 9 to 'Ain Diab	46 A4
Bus Nos 4 & 40 to Nouvelle Medina	47 C5
CTM Bus Station	48 D4
Grands Taxis Stand	49 D4
Iberia	50 C4
No 30 Bus Station	51 A4
Petits Taxis	52 C4
Royal Air Maroc	53 C4
Royal Air Moroc	54 C4
Supratours	55 C4

wide boulevards, public parks, fountains and imposing public buildings, Casablanca is cosmopolitan Morocco. With one eye on Africa and looking over its shoulder at Europe, Casablanca is a metaphor for modern Morocco.

A small nondescript town at the time the French arrived, 'Casa' today is a bright beacon to Moroccans looking for a better life. Impoverished economic refugees share the city with Morocco's nouveau-riche – designer sunglasses and scarcely a veiled woman to be seen.

Orientation

The heart of the city is Place des Nations Unies. From this large traffic roundabout at the southern end of the medina, the city's main streets branch out.

Casa-Port train station lies about 600m northeast of this main square, on Blvd Houphouet Boigny, while the main train station, Casa-Voyageurs, is about 2km east of the town centre off Blvd Mohammed V. The main bus station, Gare Routière Ouled Ziane, is about 4km to the southeast on Route Ouled Ziane; the far more convenient CTM bus station is about 800m east of the square on Rue Léon L'Africain.

Most of Casablanca's budget and mid-range hotels are in the area bounded by Ave des FAR, Ave Hassan II, Ave Lalla Yacout and Blvd Hassan Seghir

You can get from Mohammed V International Airport to Casablanca by train (US$0.30, 2nd class, 30 minutes). The trains leave from below the ground floor of the airport terminal building.

A **shuttle bus** (☎ 022 448376) runs from the CTM bus terminal 12 times a day (US$1, one hour). The earliest gets you to the airport at 7am; the latest leaves the airport at midnight.

Information

INTERNET ACCESS

There are several Internet cafés dotted around town. They all charge US$0.90 per hour and are open until about 10pm daily. Try **EuroNet** (51 Rue Tata) or **First Cyber** (62 Rue Allah ben Abdellah).

MEDICAL SERVICES

In the event of a medical emergency, ring **SOS Médecins** (☎ 022 444444). These private

doctors operate around the clock and can come to your hotel for about US$28. **Service d'Aide Médicale Urgente** (SAMU; ☎ 022 252525) is a private ambulance service.

There's a **night pharmacy** (cnr Place Oued al-Makhazine & Blvd d'Anfa).

MONEY

There are loads of banks (with ATMs) in Casablanca including the **Banque Marocaine du Commerce Extérieur** (BMCE; Hyatt Regency Hotel; ⏲ 9am-9pm).

POST

The **main post office** (cnr Blvd de Paris & Ave Hassan II; ⏲ 8.30am-6.30pm Mon-Fri), just north of Place Mohammed V, is the place to collect poste restante mail.

TOURIST OFFICES

The helpful **ONMT** (☎ 022 271177; 55 Rue Omar Slaoui; ⏲ 8.30am-noon & 2.30-6.30pm Mon-Fri) is south of the city centre.

Sights

Don't miss the beautiful **Hassan II Mosque**, which overlooks the ocean just west of the northern tip of the medina. Finished in 1993, it is the third-largest religious monument in the world; it can hold 25,000 worshippers and up to 80,000 more can be accommodated in the esplanades around it. Cedar wood was brought in from the Middle Atlas, marble from Agadir and granite from Tafraoute. The mosque is open to non-Muslims and there are **guided tours** (☎ 022 440448; tours adult/student US$10/5; ⏲ 9, 10 & 11am, 2pm Sat-Thu, 2.30pm in summer) in various languages.

The **medina**, although rather small when compared with others in Morocco, is definitely worth a little time and is a pleasant, bright place to stroll around.

The ville nouvelle around Place Mohammed V has some of the best examples of Mauresque architecture, a blend of French colonial and traditional Moroccan styles inspired by Art Deco. They include the **Hôtel de Ville** (Town Hall), the **Palais de Justice** (Law Courts), the **post office** and the extraordinary but shamefully neglected **Cathédrale du Sacré Cœur**.

Sleeping

Youth hostel (☎ 022 220551; fax 227677; 6 Place Ahmed el-Bidaoui; dm for HI cardholders/noncardholders US$4.20/

MOROCCO

4.50, d US$12) In the medina, just off Blvd des Almohades, is this large, comfortable and clean place with a bright café/sitting area. Rates include breakfast, hot showers and use of the kitchen facilities.

The hotels in the medina are unclassified, don't have hot showers (so use the local hammam), are seedy and cost around US$4 per person. There are a number around Rue Centrale, northwest of the clock tower, but you can do much better outside the medina for a little more.

Hôtel du Palais (☎ 022 276121; 68 Rue Farhat Hachad; s/d US$7/10, with bathroom US$13/19) Near the French consulate, it may not quite be a palace but still offers about the best value for money you'll find. Renovated rooms are clean and spacious, and some have a balcony. The communal showers are free and hot.

Near the central market and around Rue Allah ben Abdellah is a cluster of cheapies:

Hôtel Touring (☎ 022 310216; 87 Rue Allah ben Abdellah; s/d US$6/8) Big old rooms that are dim but decent (each with a balcony); shared bathrooms are clean.

Hôtel Negociants (☎ 022 314023; 116 Rue Allah ben Abdellah; s/d US$10/14) Clean, bright and popular.

Hôtel Colbert (☎ 022 314241; 38 Rue Chaoui; s/d US$5.90/7.25, with shower US$7.85/9.30, hot showers US$0.65) A good friendly choice opposite the market. Simple rooms with washbasin are a bit run down but look onto cheery interior gardens.

Hôtel Rialto (☎ 022 275122; 9 Rue Salah Ben Bouchaib; s/d US$8/12) Small, bright and well run, with a touch (just a touch) of style and a shower.

Hôtel Terminus (☎ 022 240025; 184 Blvd Bahmad; s/d US$7/12, hot showers US$0.50) Across the road from Casa-Voyageurs train station, east of the centre, Terminus is convenient if you get in late. Rooms are spacious and come with small balconies.

Camping de l'Oasis (☎ 022 234257; Ave Mermoz; camp site per person US$0.90, plus per tent US$0.90) Around 5km out on the P8 road to El-Jadida and southwest of the centre, Bus No 31 runs past this camp site.

Eating

Casablanca has the greatest variety of places to eat in Morocco

There are cheap restaurants around the clock tower entrance to the medina. Outside the medina, the best place for good,

cheap food is along Rue Chaoui. There are several rotisseries and the excellent **Restaurant Amine**, which serves large portions of freshly cooked seafood from US$3.

Opposite the market are a number of fruit and vegetable stalls (expensive) and a good delicatessen (with parma ham and pate). Fresh food is cheaper in the medina.

Restaurant de l'Étoile Marocaine (107 Rue Allah ben Abdellah; mains from US$5) This friendly place serves decent Moroccan dishes (including a delicious *pastilla* for US$6) or *Mechoui d'Agneau* (roast lamb) for US$8 in sumptuous traditional surroundings.

Restaurant Snack Bar California (19 Rue Tata; mains US$4) Food here remains good. Mains, include *tajine*, couscous and brochettes and some vegetarian dishes. It's a peaceful and relaxing place for women travellers.

Taverne du Dauphin (115 Blvd Houphouet-Boigny) For seafood, this place may not look much from the outside but the food is fresh, beautifully cooked and not overly expensive. A fish fillet costs around US$3.70 to US$9, calamari costs US$4.70 and the unbelievably delicious grilled *Crevettes royales* (Dublin prawns) costs US$4.70 per 100g (enough for a starter). If you don't fancy a full meal, pop in for a snack or relaxed drink at the bar (US$1.40 for a Flag beer).

Snack Saigon (Rue Salah Ben Bouchaib) Tiny, but a real locals' place. Prices seem to fluctuate with the mood of the waiter but on a good day you'll pay about US$2.50 for a world-class *tajine*.

The city centre is filled with French-style cafés:

Café National (cnr Rue Prince Moulay Abdallah & Ave Lallah Yacout) A beautiful example of the Art Deco style.

Pâtisserie de l'Opéra (50 Blvd du 11 Janvier) A civilised, tranquil place, great for a quiet cuppa.

For delicious home-made ice cream visit the **Swiss Ice Cream Factory** (Rue Ech-Cherie Amziane).

SPLURGE!

Restaurant Al-Mounia (95 Rue Prince Moulay Abdallah; mains from US$10) Check out this place for excellent Moroccan food in a traditional setting. Dishes include chicken *pastilla* and pigeon with raisins. There's a lovely, cool garden at the front where you can dine in the shade.

It's deservedly popular with the young and trendy.

Drinking
Central Casablanca has a large red-light district and plenty of seedy bars and cabaret places – this is a port after all. Women should be particularly careful after dark.

Au Petit Poucet (Blvd Mohammed V) is a good low-key bar and a die-hard relic of 1920s France. Antoine de Saint-Exupéry, the French author and aviator, used to spend time here.

La Bodéga (129 Rue Allah ben Abdellah; 12.30-3pm & 7pm-midnight) A Spanish-style tapas bar and restaurant. It's expensive but good fun with live music, and it's women-friendly.

Getting There & Away
BUS & SHARED TAXI
The CTM bus station is on Rue Léon L'Africain; the modern Gare Routière Ouled Ziane is the bus station for almost all non-CTM services. It's 4km from the city centre; take bus No 10 from opposite the market.

There are regular CTM departures to Agadir (US$13, nine hours, seven daily), Essaouira (US$10, seven hours, two daily), Fès (US$8, five hours, 10 daily), Marrakesh (US$7, four hours, seven daily), Meknès (US$7, four hours, 10 daily), Rabat (US$2.80, one hour, 10 daily), Tangier (US$12, six hours, four daily) and Tetouan (US$12, seven hours, two daily).

Grands taxis to Rabat (US$2.50) and Fès (US$6) leave from Blvd Hassan Seghir, near the CTM bus station.

TRAIN
Most train departures are from the Casa-Voyageurs station, 4km east of the city centre. Local bus No 30 runs to Casa-Voyageurs along Ave des FAR and Blvd Mohammed V for about US$0.25; a petit taxi from the city costs US$1.

Destinations serviced by rapide trains include Fès (US$9, 4½ hours, eight trains daily) via Meknès (US$8, 3½ hours), Marrakesh (US$7 2nd-class, three hours, seven trains daily) and Tangier (US$11, 5¾ hours, two trains daily).

The quickest and easiest way to get to Rabat (US$2.75, one hour) is by the express shuttle trains that run from Casa-Port train station. These operate hourly from around 7am to midnight.

Getting Around
Local buses (a trip costs about US$0.25) run from a terminus on Place Oued al-Makhazine, west of central Casablanca, to Ain Diab (No 9) and Place de la Victoire (No 5). Bus No 30 connects Casa-Voyageurs train station to central Casablanca. Bus No 15 runs to the Hassan II mosque.

There's no shortage of petits taxis in Casablanca; just make sure the meter is on. Expect to pay US$1 for a ride in or around the city centre.

ESSAOUIRA
044 / pop 45,000

Essaouira (Esa-weera), with its colourful fishing port, ramparts, woodcarving workshops, a magnificent sweeping beach and relaxed feel, is a magnet for artists, independent travellers and day-tripping package tourists.

Information
At the time of writing, the cheapest Internet café was **Espace Internet** (5 Ave de l'Istiqlal), at US$1 per hour. There are several banks with ATMs around Place Moulay Hassan. The main **post office** (Ave el-Moukaouama) is a five minute walk southeast. The helpful **Syndicat d'Initiative** (044 475080) is on Rue de Caire.

Sights
The fortifications of the **old city** are a mixture of Portuguese, French and Berber military architecture, and their massiveness lends a powerful mystique to the town. Inside it's all light and charm. You'll find narrow lanes, whitewashed houses with blue-painted doors, tranquil squares, pleasant cafés and artisans in tiny workshops beavering away at fragrant thuya wood.

You can walk along most of the **ramparts** on the seaward part of town and visit the two main **skalas** (forts; US$1; 8.30am-noon & 2.30-6pm). It was on these ramparts that Orson Welles filmed the dramatic opening shots of *Othello*.

The port, bustling with shipbuilders and fishing boats, is well worth a wander at any time, but try to catch the **fish auction** (Market hall; 3-5pm Mon-Sat) just outside the port gates.

The **beach** stretches some 10km down the coast to the sand dunes of Cap Sim – beware, the currents are strong and attacks

MOROCCO

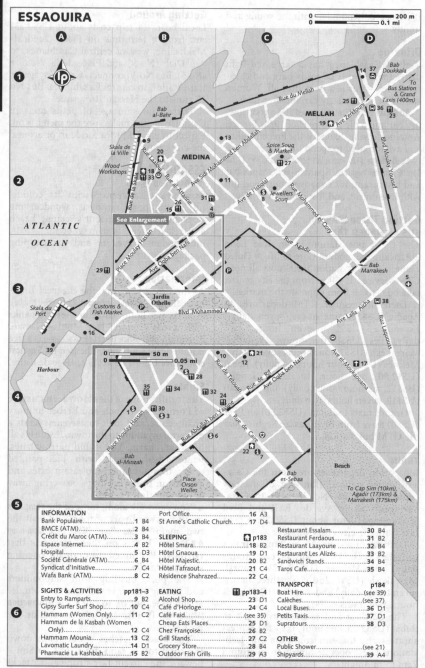

have been reported to have occurred on the beach. Free entertainment in the form of soccer and basketball matches often takes place at the town end. The beach is windy and has a strong current but is excellent for windsurfing; there are a couple of places that hire windsurfing gear.

Along the shore, **Magic Fun Afrika** (☎ 473856, 061 103777; magicfunafrika@hotmail.com; Blvd Mohammed V; ☼ 9am-6pm Mar-Dec) rents windsurfing equipment (US$17 per hour) and surfboards (US$6 per hour). It also offers kite surfing (using a kite to propel yourself; from US$20 for a one-hour course). Shops in Essaouira also rent out surfboards and all the kit. Equipment standards vary, so shop around.

Festivals & Events

The **Gnawa & World Music Festival** is a four-day musical extravaganza usually held around the third weekend in June. Concerts are held on Place Moulay Hassan and at other venues throughout town. International, national and local performers provide music ranging from gnawa to jazz and there are simultaneous art exhibitions.

A much smaller classical music festival, **Printemps des Alizés**, takes place over four days in April.

Sleeping

Hôtel Smara (☎ 044 475655; 26 Rue de la Skala; s/d US$6/9, d with sea view US$12) Newly decorated in Essaouira's trademark white and blue, the simple rooms here are grouped around a covered courtyard and all come with built-in shower and toilet. Some of the best sea views in town are those from the terrace.

Hôtel Majestic (☎ 044 474909; 40 Rue Laalouj; s/d US$7/13) Not overly friendly and needs a lick of paint, but the Majestic is saved from mediocrity by its terrace which affords one of the highest panoramas in Essaouira.

Hôtel Tafraout (☎ 044 476276; 7 Rue de Marrakesh; s/d from US$10/14) Tucked down an alley off Ave Sidi Mohammed ben Abdallah, Tafraout is very welcoming. Though aged and rather gloomy, the rooms are in reasonable shape.

Résidence Shahrazed (☎ 044 472977; 1 Rue Youssef El Fassi; s/d US$12/15) The four terrace rooms are particularly sought after in this place, just north of the tourist office. Most of the big old rooms have their own showers.

Hôtel Gnaoua (☎ 044 475234; 89 Ave Zerktouni; s/d US$14/20) Gnaoua stands out from the crowd with its smartly painted exterior. Inside is equally neat and tidy. Rooms come with (smallish) bathrooms.

Eating

The best cheap eats are en route to the port, at several outdoor fish grills offering a fabulous selection of the day's catch. Just US$2.35 will get you an excellent al-fresco lunch. A fun alternative is to buy your own fish in the market on Ave de l'Istiqlal and take it to one of the grill stands in the southern corner. It will come served up with salad and bread for an extra US$2.35.

Restaurant Les Alizés (☼ 044 476819; 26 Rue de la Skala; set menu US$7) A tiled and vaulted candle-lit salon with cosy alcoves, this draws the crowds with a winning combination of atmosphere, value for money and a warm welcome. Even if the set menu (eg soup/salad followed by couscous/fish) holds no surprises, you won't leave hungry.

There are plenty of good reasonably priced restaurants in town:

Restaurant Essalam (Place Moulay Hassan; set menu US$3.75)

Restaurant Laayoune (Rue el-Hajelli; set menus US$4.50-7)

Restaurant Ferdaous (☎ 044 473655; 27 Rue Abdesslam Lebadi; mains US$4.70, set menu US$7) Offers inventive takes on *tajines* and other local dishes.

Chez Françoise (1 Rue Hommane el-Fatouaki; salad US$3.30, lunch set menu US$6; ☼ Mon-Sat) Has a health-food feel with its cheerful tiles and scrubbed tables.

For breakfast you can't beat the cafés on Place Prince Moulay Hassan, past which boys parade with trays of cakes and pastries. You could also try **Café d'Horloge** (Place Chefchaouni) which lays on a good Moroccan breakfast (US$2.35) of *amlou* (a spread made of local argan oil, almond and honey) and crepes or bread.

For simple snacks and cheap hole-in-the-wall-type food, browse along Ave Sidi Mohammed ben Abdallah, Ave Zerktouni and just inside Bab Doukkala. On Place Moulay Hassan, three sandwich stands sell excellent baguettes stuffed with meat, salad and just about anything else for around US$1.40.

Almost a mandatory prelude to any night in Essaouira is finding a good spot to watch the sun go down. Alcohol can be bought at the shops just outside Bab Doukkala.

Getting There & Away

The bus station is about 400m northeast of the medina across an open parking lot.

CTM has buses to Agadir (US$3.75, three hours), Casablanca (US$8 to US$10, six to 7½ hours) and Marrakesh (US$4.20, 2½ hours). **Supratours** (☎ 044 472317) runs buses from near Bab Marrakesh to Marrakesh train station (US$4.70, 2½ hours) and Agadir (US$4, three hours).

Getting Around

The blue petits taxis are a good idea for getting to and from the bus station but they can't enter the medina. An alternative is to chuck your luggage into a cart at the bus station and let the guy pushing it take you directly to your chosen accommodation (about US$1 from the bus station to a hotel in the medina).

AGADIR

☎ 048 / pop 350,000

Agadir's main claim to fame is its fine crescent **beach**, which usually remains unruffled when the Atlantic winds are blustering elsewhere.

For the independent traveller, Agadir (although expensive) is well placed for trips east and south, although the reek of Ambre Solaire and the rustle of *Paris Match*, *Der Spiegel* and the *Sunday Times* fill the air. Not that it's unpleasant – it's just that it could be any resort town on the northern Mediterranean coast.

Orientation

Agadir's bus stations and most of the budget hotels are in a small area called New Talborjt in the northeast of the town. From here it's about a 15-minute walk down to Blvd du 20 Août, the main strip, which is lined with cafés and restaurants.

Information

Internet options include **Futurenet** (Ave du 29 Février) in New Talborjt and **Globenet** (33 Blvd Hassan II). Expect to pay US$1 per hour at the most.

Most banks have branches here with ATMs. There are several banks on Ave du Général kettani and on Ave du President Kennedy.

The **main post office** (Ave du Prince Moulay Abdallah; ☼ 8.30am-12.15pm & 2.30-6.30pm Mon-Thu, 8.30-11.30am & 3-6.30pm Fri, 8.30am-12.15pm Sat) is beside the town hall. There are smaller post offices on Blvd du 20 Août and in New Talborjt on Ave de 29 Février.

The helpful **ONMT tourist office** (☎ 048 846377; Place du Prince Héritier Sidi Mohammed; ☼ 8.30am-noon & 2.30-6.30pm Mon-Thu, 8.30am-11.30am & 3-6.30pm Fri) is in the market just off Ave Sidi Mohammed.

Sleeping & Eating

Hôtel Canaria (☎ 048 846727; Place Lahcen Tamri; s/d US$7/9, with shower US$8/10) One of the better crash pads in town, it has the added bonus of being near the bus station. The rooms are a notch above basic, with pine furniture and potted plants around the upstairs courtyard. Toilets are communal.

Hôtel Tamri (☎ 048 821880; 1 Ave du Président Kennedy; s/d with washbasin US$7/10) This appealing place has a cheerful plant-filled courtyard and reasonably well-kept shared facilities. Rooms along the front even have windows.

Camping ground (☎ 048 846683; per person/tent US$1.15/1.60) Agadir's camp site, on the port side of town, is largely the domain of camper vans. It's stony but liveable.

Mimi La Brochette (☎ 048 840387; Rue de la Plage; mains from US$4.65) Up at the north end of the beach towards the port, is a popular French-run place to chill out. The menu features everything from brochettes, pasta and omelettes to smoked eel and duck's gizzards – they go down a treat with raspberry sauce. There's great music here, too.

There are snack stands on Rue Yacoub el-Mansour. Nearby is a number of restaurants, notably **Restaurant Mille et Une Nuits** (Place Lahcen Tamri) and **Café Restaurant Coq d'Or** (Place Lahcen Tamri), which are very popular with travellers and night strollers. The food is good, portions are large and, strangely for Agadir, prices are reasonable – three-course set menus cost US$3.25.

If you fancy fresh fish, head to the port entrance where there are dozens of cheap seafood stalls.

Getting There & Away

CTM (☎ 048 822077) buses leave from Rue Yacoub el-Mansour three times a day for Casablanca (US$13, 10 hours) and five times daily for Marrakesh (US$7, four hours). There are daily departures to

AGADIR

0 ____ 400 m
0 ____ 0.2 mi

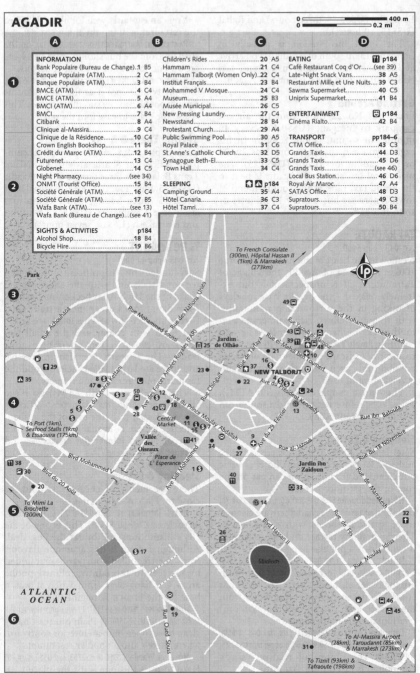

INFORMATION
Bank Populaire (Bureau de Change)..1 B5
Banque Populaire (ATM)..................2 C4
Banque Populaire (ATM)..................3 B4
BMCE (ATM)..................................4 C4
BMCE (ATM)..................................5 A4
BMCI (ATM)..................................6 A4
BMCI...7 B4
Citibank.......................................8 A4
Clinique al-Massira........................9 C4
Clinique de la Résidence...............10 C4
Crown English Bookshop.................11 B4
Crédit du Maroc (ATM)..................12 B4
Futurenet....................................13 C4
Globenet....................................14 C5
Night Pharmacy.....................(see 34)
ONMT (Tourist Office).................15 B4
Société Générale (ATM)................16 C4
Société Générale (ATM)................17 B5
Wafa Bank (ATM).....................(see 13)
Wafa Bank (Bureau de Change)...(see 41)

SIGHTS & ACTIVITIES   **p184**
Alcohol Shop...............................18 B4
Bicycle Hire................................19 B6

Children's Rides...........................20 A5
Hammam....................................21 C4
Hammam Talborjt (Women Only)..22 C4
Institut Français...........................23 B4
Mohammed V Mosque.................24 C4
Museum....................................25 B3
Musée Municipal.........................26 C5
New Pressing Laundry..................27 C4
Newsstand..................................28 B4
Protestant Church........................29 A4
Public Swimming Pool..................30 A5
Royal Palace................................31 C6
St Anne's Catholic Church.............32 D5
Synagogue Beth-El......................33 C5
Town Hall...................................34 A4

SLEEPING   **p184**
Camping Ground..........................35 A4
Hôtel Canaria..............................36 C3
Hôtel Tamri................................37 C4

EATING   **p184**
Café Restaurant Coq d'Or.......(see 39)
Late-Night Snack Vans.................38 A5
Restaurant Mille et Une Nuits....39 C3
Sawma Supermarket....................40 C5
Uniprix Supermarket...................41 B4

ENTERTAINMENT   **p184**
Cinéma Rialto..............................42 B4

TRANSPORT   **pp184–6**
CTM Office..................................43 C3
Grands Taxis................................44 D3
Grands Taxis................................45 D6
Grands Taxis.........................(see 46)
Local Bus Station........................46 D6
Royal Air Maroc..........................47 A4
SATAS Office...............................48 D3
Supratours..................................49 C3
Supratours..................................50 B4

Park

To French Consulate
(300m), Hôpital Hassan II
(1km) & Marrakesh
(273km)

Rue Achoulhaoa

Rue Mohammed Soussi

Rue des Nations Unies

Blvd Mohammed Cheikh Saadi

Rue Yacoub el-Mansour

Rue el-Mehdi ben Toumert

Rue de Tafraya

Jardim
de Olhão

NEW TALBORJT

Ave du Président Kennedy

Ave des Forces Armées Royales (FAR)

Rue Chinguiti

Rue ibn Batouta

Ave du Général Kettani

Central
Market

Ave du Prince Moulay Abdallah

Ave du 29 Février

Rue al-Jazouli

Rue du 18 Novembre

To Port (1km),
Seafood Stalls (1km)
& Essaouira (175km)

Vallée
des
Oiseaux

Place de
L' Esperance

Blvd Mohammed V

Ave Sidi Mohammed

Jardin ibn
Zaidoun

Rue de Marrakesh

Blvd du 20 Août

To Mimi La
Brochette
(300m)

Blvd Hassan II

Rue de Fès

Rue Moulay Idriss

ATLANTIC
OCEAN

Stadium

Rue Oued Souss

Rue Oued Souss

To Al-Massira Airport
(28km), Taroudannt (85km)
& Marrakesh (273km)

To Tiznit (93km) &
Tafraoute (198km)

Essaouira (US$3.75, three hours) and Rabat (US$15, 10 hours).

The main bus station is actually in Inezgane, 13km south of Agadir. If you arrive at Inezgane simply jump in a grand taxi (US$0.30) or local bus No 5 or 6 to Agadir.

Getting Around
Local bus No 22 runs from the airport car park to Inezgane (US$0.40) every 40 minutes or so until about 8.30pm. In Inezgane you can change to bus Nos 20, 24 or 28 heading for Agadir (US$0.25). The main local bus station in Agadir is next to the grand taxi rank at the southern end of town. There are buses every 10 minutes or so to Inezgane.

TAFRAOUTE
☎ 048 / pop 5000

Nestled in the heart of the Anti-Atlas, some 100km southeast of Agadir, the village of Tafraoute itself is unspectacular, but extremely relaxed – the perfect base for days of hiking in the surrounding mountains, with tranquil valleys, rich palmeraies and mud-brick Berber settlements. The enchanting **Ameln Valley** is nearby; its stunning rose-pink landscape provides days of hiking possibilities – even the journey from Tiznit is rewarding in itself.

There are a couple of banks (no ATMs), a post office, Internet café and a souq from Monday to Wednesday.

Sleeping & Eating
Hôtel Tanger (☎ 067 033073; r per person US$2.35; meals US$2.35) By the river, this hotel is basic but clean and friendly. You can eat on the roof or the 1st-floor terrace.

Hôtel Reddouane (☎ 048 800066; s/d US$3.25/4.70) Even better across the road, there are cleaner, more spacious rooms with a washbasin. There is a sunny terrace and the restaurant downstairs is a popular hang-out.

Hôtel Salama (☎ 048 800026; s/d US$11/14) Large, comfortable rooms with bathroom are the order of the day here. The hotel has some Moroccan flavour, great views from the terrace and a *salon de thé* (tea room) overlooking the market square.

Camping Les Trois Palmiers (☎ /fax 048 800038; camp site per adult/child US$0.90/0.60, plus per tent US$1.15, s/d US$6/9) This stony but relatively shady compound is just off the Tiznit road.

You can eat fairly well for about US$3 in the restaurants lining the main streets.

Restaurant Marrakech (couscous US$2.35), on the road up from the bus station, attracts a local crowd and knocks up a mean couscous.

Restaurant L'Étoile d'Agadir (tajines around US$3.30), in a pretty little spot near the post office, is equally popular for its succulent *tajines*. This is also the place to ease into the day.

Getting There & Away
Buses depart from outside the various company offices on Sharia al-Jeish al-Malaki. Trans Balady has three buses a day to Agadir (US$3.75, four hours), twice daily via Tiznit (US$2.35, three hours). Other companies also serve Casablanca (US$14, 14 hours) and Marrakesh (US$10, seven hours).

TAROUDANNT
☎ 048 / pop 60,000

Surrounded by magnificent, crenulated red-mud walls and with the snow-capped peaks of the High Atlas beckoning beyond, Taroudannt looks every inch a traditional Berber market town. The **souqs** are lively and filled with colour and the small **tanneries** are evocative reminders of bygone trades. The **ramparts** are also impressive and there are large **markets** held beyond the ramparts on Thursday and Sunday.

There are banks (with ATMs) on Place al-Alaouyine and the main post office is off Ave Hassan II, to the east of the kasbah. Internet access is available for US$1 per hour or less at **Infonet** (Ave Bir Anzarane) and **Wafanet** (Ave Mohammed V).

Sleeping & Eating
There are plenty of cheapies around, or close to, Place al-Alaouyine.

Hôtel Taroudannt (☎ 048 852416; s/d US$6/7, with bathroom & toilet US$13/15) This is one of the city's institutions and by far the best deal. Although fading, it has a unique flavour, from the tree-filled courtyard surrounded by terraces to the faintly colonial public areas – a hang-over from when it was a base for the French Foreign Legion.

Hôtel Souss (☎ 048 852397; 11 Ave Prince Héritier Sidi Mohammed; s/d US$2.35/4.70) Plain but reasonably clean boxes open onto an interior courtyard, where there's also a popular restaurant.

Hôtel el-Warda (☎ 048 852763; s/d US$2.80/4.70) Hard to miss this one – it's the place with all the *zellij* (tile work) terraces overlooking Place an-Nasr. There are basic rooms with a washbasin but no shower – you can use the hammam next door.

Hôtel Roudani (☎ 048 852219; r with/without shower US$7/3.75) You'll find one of the better options right on the square. The best rooms are on the large terrace, but don't have showers.

The best place to look for cheap snack stalls and restaurants is around Place an-Nasr and north along Avenue Bir Anzarane, where you can get traditional food such as *tajines*, *harira* and salads.

Sandwich Barcelone (Place al-Alaouyine; baguettes US$1.40) The satisfyingly fat baguettes stuffed with *kefta* (seasoned minced lamb), chips and salad and such like are difficult to walk past.

Snack El-Baraka (Ave Prince Héritier Sidi Mohammed; meals from US$1.90) This small friendly place is where locals go for chicken, *kefta* or brochettes served along with the usual accompaniments. Women tend to congregate upstairs.

Getting There & Away
CTM has one bus departing at 9pm for Casablanca (US$13, nine hours) via Marrakesh (US$8, five hours). Other companies run services throughout the day to both these cities as well as, less frequently, Ouarzazate (US$6, six hours).

All buses leave from outside Bab Zougan.

CENTRAL MOROCCO & THE ATLAS MOUNTAINS

MARRAKESH
☎ 044 / pop 900,000
The name Marrakesh conjures up images of medieval bazaars, labyrinths filled with exotic smells and the cries of hawkers, sunlit squares hidden from the outside world and a musical accompaniment to a way of life little changed in centuries. Marrakesh is all that and more. If Fès is Morocco's spiritual and cultural capital, enchanting Marrakesh is its beating heart.

Basking in the clear light of the south, Marrakesh has an entirely different feel from its sister cities to the north. It remains unmistakably more African than cosmopolitan Casablanca, it's more Moroccan than sanitised Rabat, and more Berber than proud and aloof Fès.

Marrakesh is the red city. A local Berber legend has it that when the Koutoubia Mosque was planted in the city's heart, it poured so much blood that all the walls, houses and roads were forever marked. Surrounded by the medina's earth walls and its flat-roofed houses at dusk, as the city's ramparts turn crimson with the last rays of the setting sun, you could be forgiven for never wanting to leave. Whatever else you do on this trip, don't miss it.

Information
BOOKSHOPS
For a range of English literature and English-language titles on Morocco, check out the **American Language Center bookshop** (Map p188; 3 Impasse du Moulin). For French speakers the best bookshop in town is **Charter Ahmed** (Map p188; 19-21 Ave Mohammed V) in the ville nouvelle. Also worth checking out is the **Librairie d'Art** (Map p188; 55 Blvd Mohammed Zerktouni) which has some beautiful coffee-table books on Moroccan arts.

INTERNET ACCESS
The many Internet cafés in the medina and Gueliz charge a standard US$1 per hour.

MEDICAL SERVICES
There's a **night pharmacy** (Map p188; Rue Khalid ben el-Oualid) north of Place de la Liberté in the ville nouvelle, where a doctor is also permanently available, and one on the west side of Djemaa el-Fna (Map p190). The **Red Cross clinic** (Map p190; Djemaa el-Fna; ☒ 24hr), on the opposite side of the square, can also provide basic care.

MONEY
There's no shortage of banks with ATMs, even around Djemaa el-Fna in the central medina.

Crédit du Maroc central medina (Map p190; 215 Ave Mohammed V; ☒ 8.45am-1pm & 3-6.45pm Mon-Sat); ville nouvelle (Map p188; Rue de Bab Agnaou; ☒ 8.45am-1pm & 3-6.45pm Mon-Sat) Offers after-hours exchange facilities at its branches.

POST
The **main post office** (Map p188; Place du 16 Novembre) is in the ville nouvelle. There's also a useful **post office** (Map p190; Djemaa el-Fna) on the medina's main square.

MOROCCO

MARRAKESH

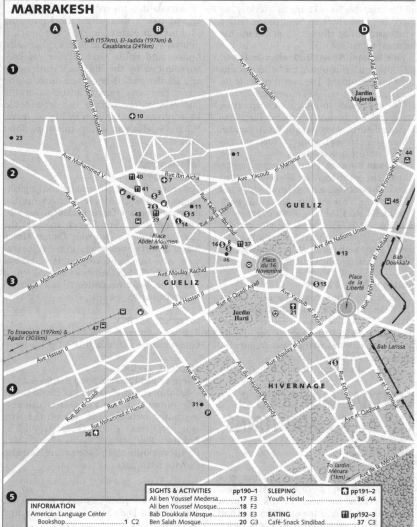

Safi (157km), El-Jadida (197km) &
Casablanca (241km)

Jardin
Majorelle

GUELIZ

GUELIZ

Place
Abdel Moumen
ben Ali

Place
du 16
Novembre

Place
de la
Liberté

Bab
Doukkala

Jardin
Harti

Bab Larissa

HIVERNAGE

To Essaouira (197km) &
Agadir (303km)

To Jardin
Ménara
(1km)

MOROCCO

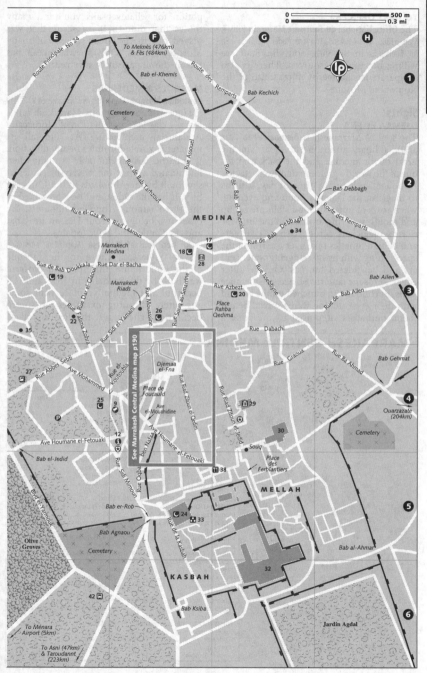

TOURIST OFFICES

The **Office National du Tourisme Marocain** (ONMT; Map p188; ☎ 044 436131; Place Abdel Moumen ben Ali, Gueliz) is in the ville nouvelle. Staff are willing but under-resourced. There is also a separate **medina tourist office**, south of the Koutoubia Mosque.

Sights

DJEMAA EL-FNA

The soul of Marrakesh is **Djemaa el-Fna** (Map p190), a huge, atmospheric square in the heart of the medina and the backdrop for one of the world's greatest nightly spectacles. Although lively at any time of day, it turns to magic in the late afternoon and evening, when rows of open-air food stalls are set up and mouth watering aromas fill the air. Musicians, magicians, acrobats, snake charmers and benign lunatics take over the rest of the space, along with hustlers, ageing water sellers and bewildered tourists. On the outer edges, kerosene lanterns ablaze, are the juice stalls. Beyond them, hunched on the ground with their eye-catching wares spread before them, herbalists sit poised to prescribe a

potion for whatever ails you (and many things that didn't). It's a scene that was played out in the great squares of many Moroccan cities. Only in Marrakesh has this medieval pageantry survived.

MOSQUES & MEDERSAS

Koutoubia Mosque (Map p188; Ave Mohammed V) This mosque is a most famous Marrakesh landmark, a classic representation of Moroccan–Andalucian architecture. At 70m tall, its minaret is visible for miles in any direction. It is particularly memorable at night when illuminated against the velvety-black desert sky. Built by the Almohads in the 12th century, it has the oldest and best preserved of the three famous Almohad minarets, the other two being the Tour Hassan in Rabat and the Giralda in Seville (Spain).

Ali ben Youssef Medersa (Map p188; admission US$1.80; ⏰ 9am-6pm) Close to the mosque of the same name, this splendid *medersa* was built by the Saadians in 1565 and is a beautiful and meditative place with some absolutely stunning examples of stucco decoration. The largest theological college

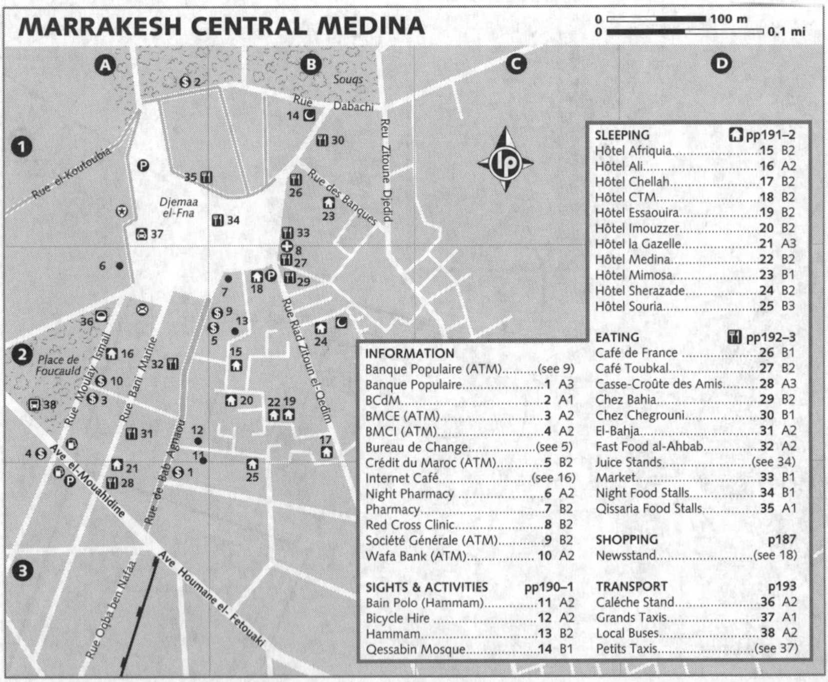

MARRAKESH CENTRAL MEDINA

in the Maghreb, it once housed up to 900 students and teachers.

MUSEUMS & TOMBS
Museum of Moroccan Arts (Map p188; Dar Si Said; admission US$1; 9-11.45am & 2.30-5.45pm Mon, Wed, Thu, Sat & Sun, 9-11.30am & 3-5.45pm Fri) Built around the 19th century and well worth a visit, this museum houses one of the finest collections in the country, including jewellery from the High Atlas, the Anti-Atlas and the extreme south; carpets from the Haouz and the High Atlas; oil lamps from Taroudannt; blue pottery from Safi and green pottery from Tamegroute; and leatherwork from Marrakesh.

Museum of Marrakesh (Map p188; Place ben Youssef; adult/child US$2.80/1; 9.30am-6pm) Inaugurated in 1997, the building is the main highlight – a beautifully restored 19th-century *riad* (traditional, lavish town house) with some very impressive *zellij* (tile work).

Saadian Tombs (Map p188; admission US$1; 8.30-11.45am & 2.30-5.45pm) Sixty-six of the Saadians, including Al-Mansour, his successors and their closest family members, lie buried under the two main structures next to the Kasbah Mosque. The tombs still convey some of the opulence and superb artistry of the Saadian aesthetic vision.

PALAIS DE LA BAHIA
Palais de la Bahia (Map p188; admission US$1; 8.30-11.15am & 2.30-5.45pm Sat-Thu, 8.30-11.30am & 3-5.45pm Fri) This rambling 19th-century structure boasts fountains, elaborate reception rooms, living quarters, pleasure gardens and numerous secluded, shady courtyards.

SOUQS
The **souqs** of Marrakesh – east of the medina near the Palais de la Bahia and at the northeast corner of the medina opposite Qessabin Mosque – are the best in Morocco. From antique lamps to Liverpool shirts, colourful carpets to cures for snoring, tea glasses to tapes of Mariah Carey, here you'll find everything you never knew you wanted and many things that you did.

'Antiques' barely an hour old can be worth every dirham as the late afternoon sunlight filters through the souq's straw roof. Even the most functional items can appear exotic when placed alongside a stunning Moroccan tile or glasswork, or accompanied by a far-off

oud (a stringed lute used in traditional music). And the most exquisite piece you've ever seen will surely be the perfect memory of this magical place. The souqs of Marrakesh may have what you have always been wanting – whether you buy it or simply soak it up, the effect is the same.

However averse you may be to the idea, you're likely at some stage to find yourself in a carpet shop, most likely owned by Mohammed, Ahmed or Hassan, who has a brother living in your country. The secret is to accept the hospitality, enjoy the ceremony and not feel in the least obliged to buy. Easier said than done – the full repertoire of the famous Moroccan sales technique is generally regarded as the most skilled, sophisticated and effective in the world. In Marrakesh, life is theatre and this is performance art at its best. As the man will tell you, looking is free; admire it for the art form that it is.

There are also plenty of opportunities to watch artisans at work fashioning slippers, weaving rugs, dyeing textiles and hammering metals. Remember that most shopkeepers take a break between 1.30pm and 3pm; Friday also tends to be a quiet day.

Festivals & Events
The **Festival of Folklore**, held each June, attracts some of the best troupes in Morocco. For performers and spectators alike, the festival is a mammoth party-cum-jam session. Around the same time, there's the famous **Fantasia**, featuring charging Berber horsemen outside the ramparts.

Sleeping
Youth hostel (Map p188; ☎ 044 447713; Rue Mohammed el-Hansali; dm US$3.75, hot showers US$0.50; 8-9am & 1-10pm) You'll need your HI membership card here. It's spotlessly clean and boasts a kitchen. There's an 11.30pm curfew.

There are many places south of Place Djemaa el-Fna in the medina. Hot showers generally cost US$0.50 to US$1 on top of the room price.

Hôtel Essaouira (Map p190; ☎ 044 443805; 3 Derb Sidi Bouloukat; s/d US$4.70/8) Among the most appealing in this category, there's a tiled central courtyard, terrace café – a good place to crash and meet other travellers – and basic but clean rooms.

Hôtel Medina (Map p190; ☎ 044 442997; 1 Derb Sidi Bouloukat; s/d US$3.75/8) Not quite as attractive as the Essaouira next door, this is still a fine choice and the painted ceilings add a nice touch.

Hôtel Imouzzer (Map p190; ☎ 044 445336; 74 Derb Sidi Bouloukat; s/d US$3.75/8) Continuing northwest along the same lane, is another cheerful, well-scrubbed and welcoming little hotel with a terrace café.

Hôtel Afriquia (Map p190; ☎ 044 442403; 45 Derb Sidi Bouloukat; s/d from US$4.70/10) This has a lovely, tree-filled courtyard and a psychedelically tiled and tiered terrace affording panoramic views (including some over Djemaa el-Fna).

Hôtel Chellah (Map p190; ☎ 044 442977; Derb Skaya; s/d US$4.70/8) Chellah stands out for its orange trees and salons; it's a nice place to chill out. It's also outside the main budget-hotel epicentre.

Hôtel Mimosa (Map p190; ☎ 044 426385; 16 Rue des Banques; s/d from US$4.70/10) Off the northeastern edge of Djemaa el-Fna, Mimosa gets top marks for its plasterwork detailing. As it's a bit off the usual tourist track, it tends not to fill up too quickly.

Hôtel la Gazelle (Map p190; ☎ 044 441112; 12 Rue Bani Marine; s/d US$7/12) Southwest of the main budget hotel area, you'll find this a spruce, friendly place. From the terrace there are fine views to the square, Koutoubia Mosque and the mountains.

Hôtel Souria (Map p190; ☎ 067 482131; 17 Rue de la Recette; d US$12) Prices are slightly above average, but it's a delightfully homy place and you get a tidy little room, either opening onto a cool and tranquil courtyard or the terrace.

Hôtel CTM (Map p190; ☎ 044 442325; Djemaa el-Fna; s/d from US$7/10) A real old institution. It's certainly in the thick of things, right on the main square, with unbeatable views from the roof and from the (noisy) front rooms. Most rooms, though, open onto an unspectacular courtyard. The communal facilities have seen better days.

Hôtel Ali (Map p190; ☎ 044 444979; hotelali@hotmail.com; Rue Moulay Ismail; dm & roof-terrace sleeping US$3.75, s/d US$10/14) Another stalwart of the budget scene, this a place where regulars swear by its cheap rates and friendly and efficient service, not to mention sweeping terrace views over the square and from the Koutoubia Mosque to the Atlas. It's got everything the traveller needs.

Hôtel Sherazade (Map p190; ☎ 044 429305; sharazade@iam.net.ma; 3 Derb Djama; s/d from US$13/18) This is a *riad*, decorated in traditional style

and run by a Moroccan–German couple. It's highly recommended, as are reservations.

Eating

In the evening, the liveliest, cheapest and most entertaining place to eat is the food stalls of the Djemaa el-Fna, one of *the* great dining experiences in Africa. By the time the sun sets, much of the square is taken over by stalls, each specialising in certain dishes and vying for your custom – the busiest are usually the best. At one you can order kebabs with salad, while at another it's fish-and-chips Moroccan style or even snails or sheep heads. Almost as soon as you've ordered, your food's in front of you with a range of accompaniments such as french fries, salad, eggplant and fried chillies. Best of all, you can eat your fill for US$2.35 or less and wash it down with a US$0.25 orange juice from a nearby juice stand.

At lunchtime, before the stalls on Djemaa el-Fna itself get going, you'll find much the same fare in the *qissaria* (the commercial centre of medina) on the north side of the square. Here several vendors sharing a central kitchen will do you a meal – such as *tanzhiyya* (similar to *tajine*), fried fish or lemon-chicken and french fries – for under US$1.80.

Chez Chegrouni (Map p190; 4-6 Djemaa el-Fna; salads US$0.50, mains around US$3.75) Probably the best cheap restaurant on the square, this one's best known for its excellent *tajines*, including a melt-in-the-mouth lamb version.

Café Toubkal (Map p190; Djemaa el-Fna; mains US$3.75-4.70, breakfast US$1.20) Another cheap-and-cheerful place offering soups, *tajines* and other staples. A breakfast of crepes with *amlou* (an argan oil, almond paste and honey spread) kicks off the day with a bang. It's to be found in the square's southeastern corner.

Chez Bahia (Map p190; Rue Riad Zitoun el-Qedim; tajines US$1.40) Dishing up some of the cheapest *tajines* in town, it's easy to fill up on *pastillas* or some of the bite-sized flaky-pastry triangles known as *briouat*.

Fast Food al-Ahbab (Map p190; Rue de Bab Agnaou; salads US$1-1.80, sandwiches US$1.80) Head here for well-stuffed *shwarma* sandwiches (spit-grilled meat or chicken) to eat in or take away. Be prepared to queue at peak times.

El-Bahja (Map p190; Rue Bani Marine; set menus from US$4.60) Tempting set menus include *tajines* and other no-nonsense hearty food. Simple, clean and friendly, it's very popular with the locals.

Casse-Croûte des Amis (Map p190; Rue Bani Marine; set menus from US$2.90) With its pretty Moroccan-style dining room, this is one of the few places in this category to bother much about décor. The warm welcome and well-priced set menus are an added bonus.

Hôtel Ali (Map p190; ☎ 044 444979; Rue Moulay Ismail; set menus from US$4.70, buffet hotel guests/non-guests US$4.70/6) Like the hotel, the attached restaurant is a major hang-out for travellers stoking up on its no-nonsense fodder.

You'll find a good selection of inexpensive eats on or around Ave Mohammed V and Blvd Mohammed Zerktouni in the ville nouvelle.

For bottom-rung local food, head for a group off Marrakesh Rue ibn Aicha, where a solid meal of rotisserie chicken or brochettes, french fries and salad will cost around US$2.80.

Café-Snack Sindibad (Map p188; 3 Ave Mohammed V; mains US$2.80) It looks a bit down-at-heel, but the food – everything from pizzas and salads to couscous, *kefta* and *tajines* – is as cheap and tasty as ever.

Snack Le Siroua (Map p188; 22 Blvd Mohammed Zerktouni; breakfast US$1.70, mains US$2.80-3.75, set menus US$4.70) This good-value option offers a range of dishes, such as chicken and preserved-lemon *tajine*, in a pleasant retro environment.

Cheap restaurants with roof terraces overlooking Djemaa el-Fna are packed to the rafters at night, but they're better for their ambience than food:

Café de France (Map p190)

Hôtel CTM (Map p190; Djemaa el-Fna)

There are several small restaurants along Rue Bani Marine and Rue de Bab Agnaou, and other eateries around Djamaa el-Fna.

Getting There & Away
BUS
The **bus station** (Map p188; Rue Mohammed el-Mallakh) is outside the city walls by Bab Doukkala, a 20-minute walk or US$1.40 taxi ride north-west from Djemaa el-Fna. CTM operates daily buses to Agadir (US$7, four hours), Fès (US$13, 8½ hours) and Casablanca (US$6, four hours). Other buses also run to Essaouira (US$3, three hours), Rabat (US$8, six hours), Tangier (US$14, 11 hours) and Zagora (US$9, eight hours). Buses to Asni (US$0.75) also leave from a dirt patch on the southern side of the medina outside Bab er-Rob.

TRAIN
The **train station** (Map p188; Ave Hassan II) lies on the western side of Gueliz. Take a taxi or city bus (Nos 3, 8, 10 and 14, among others; US$0.30) into the centre. Every day there are eight trains to Casablanca (2nd-class rapide, US$7, three hours) and Rabat (US$10, four hours). There are six direct trains to Fès (US$16, eight hours) via Meknès (US$15, seven hours) and one overnight train to Tangier (US$14).

Getting Around
The creamy-beige petits taxis around town cost between US$4.50 and US$9 per journey. They're all supposed to use their meters, but you may need to insist, especially coming from the train station.

Local buses (all fares US$2.50) run from Place de Foucauld, near Djemaa el-Fna, to the following destinations:

Nos 1 & 20 Ave Mohammed V, Gueliz.

Nos 3 & 10 Bab Doukkala, main post office, train station, Douar Laskar.

No 8 Bab Doukkala, main post office, train station, Douar Laskar.

No 11 Ave Ménara, airport.

No 14 Train station.

HIGH ATLAS MOUNTAINS
The highest mountain range in North Africa, the High Atlas runs diagonally across Morocco, from the Atlantic coast northeast of Agadir all the way to northern Algeria, a distance of almost 1000km. In Berber it's called Idraren Draren (Mountains of Mountains) and it's not hard to see why. Flat-roofed, earthen Berber villages cling tenaciously to the valley sides, while irrigated terraced gardens and walnut groves flourish below.

Trekking
One of the most popular of the endless trekking possibilities in the High Atlas is the ascent of Jebel Toubkal (4167m), North Africa's highest peak. The Toubkal area is just two hours' drive south of Marrakesh and easily accessed by local transport. It's a beautiful area and on clear days there are incredible views.

You don't need mountaineering skills to reach the summit, provided you follow the standard two-day route and don't do it in winter. You will, however, need good boots, warm clothing, a sleeping bag, food and water.

The usual starting point is the picturesque village of **Imlil**, 17km from Asni off the Tizi n'Test road between Marrakesh and Agadir. Most trekkers stay overnight in Imlil. There are a handful of basic hotels and shops to stock up on supplies.

The ONMT publishes an extremely useful booklet, *The Great Trek through the Moroccan Atlas* (1997). A more recent (2000) French-language version is *Maroc: Tourisme en Montagne et au Desert*. The booklets contain a list of guides, trekker accommodation and prices. Marrakesh's tourist office has the most reliable stock, but other tourist offices should be able to help.

You don't need a guide for the normal two-day trek, but longer treks will almost certainly require a guide and mule (to carry kit and supplies). There are *bureaux des guides* (guide offices) in Imlil, Setti Fatma, Azilal, Tabant (Aït Bou Goumez Valley) and El-Kelaâ M'Gouna, where you should be able to pick up a trained, official guide.

Official guides carry ID cards. At the time of writing guides charged US$19 and mules were US$8 per day.

JEBEL TOUBKAL TREK
Ascending Jebel Toubkal is a challenging walk, but anyone in good physical condition can get to the summit. It's not particularly steep, but it's a remorseless uphill trek all the way (an ascent of 1467m), and it can be very tiring if you haven't done any previous warm-up walks or spent time acclimatising. The first day's walk (10km, about five hours) winds steeply up through the villages of Aroumd and Sidi Chamharouch to the **Toubkal refuge** (☎ 061 695463; from US$8 depending on season). The refuge sits at an altitude of 3207m and sleeps more than 80 people.

The ascent from the hut to the summit on the second day should take about four hours and the descent about two hours. It can be bitterly cold at the summit, even in summer.

OTHER TREKS
In summer it is quite possible to do an easy one- or two-day trek from the ski resort of **Oukaïmeden** (which also has a Club Alpin Français (CAF; French Alpine Club) refuge) southwest to Imlil or vice-versa. You can get here by grand taxi from Marrakesh.

From **Tacheddirt** (where the CAF refuge charges US$4.85 for nonmembers) there are numerous trekking options. One of these is a pleasant two-day walk northeast to the village of **Setti Fatma** (also accessible from Marrakesh) via the village of **Timichi**, where there is a welcoming *gîte* (literally 'resting place'; a village house with rooms and kitchen facilities). A longer circuit could take you south to **Amsouzerte** and back towards Imlil via **Lac d'Ifni**, Toubkal, **Tazaghart** (also with a refuge and rock climbing) and **Tizi Oussem**.

Sleeping & Eating
Club Alpin Français (CAF) Refuge (Imlil; camp site per person US$0.60, plus US$1.15 per tent, dm members/nonmembers US$2/US$4.85) On the village square, this is a good, cheap place to stay. It has a common room with an open fireplace, cooking facilities (US$0.45 for use of gas), cutlery and crockery.

Hôtel el-Aïne (Imlil; ☎ 044 485625; rooftop beds US$1.80, r per person US$3.75) Fair value. Rooms are comfortable and bright, and gathered around a tranquil courtyard. Hot showers are included, but prices rise in midsummer. Below the hotel, Café de la Source serves some reasonable food.

Café Soleil (Imlil; ☎ /fax 044 485622; rooftop beds US$1.80, s/d with foam mats US$6/8) On the village square, providing spartan accommodation on beds or foam mats on the floor (hot showers included). The restaurant on the terrace is good and cheap.

Gîte d'Étape Chez Ait Idar Mohammed (☎ 044 485616; beds US$2.80, half board US$8) A simple and friendly place, it has trekking maps on the wall and a kitchen, which guests can use free of charge.

Café Imouzar just off the square has cheap, excellent eats.

Getting There & Away
There are frequent buses (US$1, 1½ hours) and grands taxis (US$1.40) to Asni from Bab er Rob in Marrakesh. Local minibuses and occasional taxis travel the final 17km between Asni and Imlil (US$1.40 to US$1.80, one hour). The dirt road to Imlil is poor but spectacular.

AÏT BENHADDOU

Aït Benhaddou is one of the most exotic and best-preserved kasbahs in the entire Atlas region. Climbing up the hill, the fairytale mud-brick village is simply beautiful, especially in the early morning or late afternoon when the light turns soft and the busloads of tourists disappear. With the Atlas Mountains to the north and the Sahara Desert to the south, it's a very special place to linger.

Sleeping & Eating

Auberge la Baraka (☎ 044 890305; s/d with shower US$4.70/8, with bathroom US$6/10) By the roadside in the centre, this auberge has clean and basic doubles. It also has a cosy restaurant, from where Berber music emanates.

Auberge Etoile Filante d'Or (☎ 044 890322; mattresses on terrace US$1.80, s/d from US$7/8, hot showers US$1) Clean, sociable and with a range of rooms, this is further along the road from Auberge la Baraka.

Auberg Café Restaurant Kasbah du Jardin (☎ 044 888019; s/d US$2.80/6) A basic but peaceful place at the far end of town, the rooms here are a steal at the price but the inner building has the aesthetic charm of a concrete barn.

Defat Kasbah (☎ 044 888020; camp site per person US$1, mattresses on roof US$2.35, d with/without bathroom US$12/8) Further away, 3km towards Tamdaght, this lovely Spanish-run place has a range of nicely decorated rooms. Bathrooms are private or communal (but clean!). There's a fine swimming pool, and a bar and restaurant.

Getting There & Away

Grands taxis run from outside Ouarzazate bus station when full (US$1.40 per person).

DRÂA VALLEY

☎ 066, ☎ 044

The Drâa Valley is one long ribbon of technicoloured *palmeraies* (oasislike areas with palm trees), earth-red kasbahs and Berber villages. It's a magical route, especially in the soft mauve light of the early evening. One of the longest rivers in Morocco, the Drâa originates in the High Atlas and winds its way through mountains and desert sands. The fertile palmeraies of the Drâa are crammed with date palms, olive and almond groves and citrus trees – although the riverside crocodiles described by Pliny in the 1st century AD are long gone.

For most people this beautiful valley is also a main route to reach the edge of the real Sahara Desert (along with the route to Erfoud).

Zagora

Largely a creation of the French, attractions at the dusty town of Zagora are limited to the famed, but somewhat battered, sign reading 'Tombouctou 52 jours' (by camel caravan) and its large Wednesday and Sunday **markets**. The spectacular **Jebel Zagora**, rising up across the other side of the river, is worth climbing up for the views.

Zagora is the last stop for banks, supermarkets (no alcohol) and Internet access (US$1.40 per hour).

Caravane Desert et Montagne (☎ 066 122312; brahim83@caramail.com) is a reliable agency which can tailor desert expeditions according to special interests.

SLEEPING & EATING

Hôtel Vallée du Drâa (☎ 044 847210; s/d US$4.20/6) This hotel is clean and friendly and has a popular restaurant.

Hôtel des Amis (☎ 044 847924; d from US$4.70) Almost next door, this one is basic, but some rooms have balconies.

Hôtel la Rose des Sables (☎ 044 847274; Ave Hassan II; s/d from US$3.75/6) Better rooms than Hôtel des Amis, but without the balconies. The upper-floor rooms are brighter and good value. There's also a good restaurant.

Hôtel la Palmeraie (☎ 044 847008, Ave Mohammed V; s/d from US$7/12) A popular one-star place with good-value rooms. The main attractions are the pool, restaurant and bar. It's possible to sleep in the Berber tent by the pool for US$3.50.

The camping grounds in town are Camping Sindbad, Camping d'Amezrou and Camping de la Montagne (off the M'Hamid road). They all charge around US$1 per person plus the same for a tent.

There are plenty of cheap restaurants over and above those at the hotels, all of which produce tasty Moroccan dishes. The popular **Restaurant Timbouctou** (Blvd Mohammed V) offers meals for around US$3.

Tinfou

About 23km south of Zagora you get your first glimpse of the Sahara at **Tinfou Dunes**, although those at Merzouga are better.

Hôtel Repos du Sables (☎ 044 848566; mattresses in Berber tent US$2.80, s/d US$6/10, meals around US$6) A kasbah with simple but comfortable rooms and a relaxed ambience. The camels parked outside can take you to the dunes, only a short walk away, for US$15.

M'Hamid

You hit the end of the road at M'Hamid, about 40km north of the Algerian border. There's not an awful lot happening here apart from camel trips. **Jew's Dunes** to the north of the village is where any overnight camel ride (US$19 per person) will lead. Most overnight camel treks end in **Erg Lehoudi**, a section of 100m-high dunes 10km northeast of town.

Sahara Services (☎ 061 776766, saharacamel@ hotmail.com) is a professionally run local outfit offering camel rides (from US$28 per day) and 4WD trips.

SLEEPING & EATING

Hôtel Sahara (☎ 044 848009; s/d with breakfast US$4.70/7; tajine US$3.75-6) The first place you'll see, this has simple rooms, communal hot showers and Western-style toilets. The hotel café serves decent meals.

Hôtel Elghizlane (☎ 044 848076; Berber tents per person US$2.80, r US$8, with shower & toilet US$12) Another option, though the rooms are a little boxy and overpriced.

Camping Hammada du Drâa (☎ 044 848086; camping per person US$0.90, Berber tents per person US$3.75) About 500m over the river to the left as you enter town and as good a choice as any for sleeping under the stars.

You can eat at your hotel or the good Restaurant Les Dunes D'Or, by the central square, next to (and owned by) Sahara Services.

Getting There & Away

A daily CTM bus travels from M'Hamid goes to Zagora (US$1.90, two hours), Ouarzazate (US$3.75, four hours) and Marrakesh (US$12, 12 hours). Minibuses run to Zagora (US$2.35) all day when full.

Other daily buses leave Zagora for Boumalne du Dadès, Casablanca, Erfoud, Marrakesh, Ouarzazate and Rabat.

THE DADÈS GORGE

☎ 044

The towering ochre-coloured cliffs and fabulous rock formations of the Dadès Gorge, just over 100km east of Ouarzazate, are among Morocco's most magnificent natural sights.

The main access to the gorge is from **Boumalne du Dadès**, a pleasant, laid-back place with a good Wednesday market. From there, a good sealed road wiggles past 63km of *palmeraies*, fabulous rock formations, Berber villages and some beautiful ruined kasbahs to Msemrir, before continuing as *piste* (dirt track) to Imilchil, in the heart of the High Atlas.

If you have plenty of time, you could easily spend several days pottering about in the gorge – watching nomads bring vast herds of goats down the cliffs to the river, fossicking for fossils and generally enjoying the natural splendour.

Sleeping & Eating
DADÈS GORGE

There are half a dozen simple hotels lining the road; all have restaurants and will let you sleep on their terrace or salon from around US$1 per person.

Hôtel Atlas Berbere (☎ 044 831742; d with/ without shower US$13/9) Close to the narrowest part of the gorge, and right on the river, is this good place built in earthen kasbah style. It has nicely decorated and homely rooms and a terrace by the riverside.

Café Mirguirne (mattresses on terrace US$1.90, r with/without view US$6/3.75) This is the first hotel, coming from Boumalne du Dadès. It's basic with a fine terrace overlooking the valley, and the restaurant is one of the cheapest.

Hôtel Restaurant Kasbah (beds in salon US$0.90, s/d from US$3.75/6, 3-course meals US$5.60) Overlooking fantastic rock formations, this attractive little place has small balconies and live music in the interior courtyard.

Hôtel la Gazelle du Dadès (☎ 044 831753; mattresses on floor US$1.40-2.30, s/d US$6/8) This good-value choice has a pleasant rooftop terrace and the clean rooms come with hot showers.

You can also camp by the river for around US$1 per person.

BOUMALNE DU DADÈS

Boumalne du Dadès has a reasonable choice of accommodation.

Hôtel Bougafer (☎ 044 831307; s/d from US$3.70/ 4.70) Across from the bus station, Bougafer has a hint of character as well as a terrace and decent restaurant.

Auberge le Soleil Bleu (☎ 044 830163; camp sites per person US$0.90, mattresses on roof US$2.80, s/d US$8/14) Located up the hill, this is the place to go for clean and cosy rooms with showers and great views.

SPLURGE!

Kasbah Tizzarouine (☎ 044 830690; tizza rouine@atlasnet.net.ma; tents/r with half board per person US$19/33) If you're tired of experiencing all the colours of Morocco from the drab interior of a budget hotel, this is a great splurge in the heart of the Atlas. It's a wonderful kasbah-style complex with superb valley views and a pool. You have the choice of comfortable rooms in the main building or troglodyte rooms built into the rock overlooking the valley; both have bathrooms and nice furnishings. It also has a decent restaurant and is a good place to hear Berber music.

Getting There & Away

The CTM office is in the centre of town. It has daily buses to Ouarzazate, Marrakesh, Tinerhir and Er-Rachidia. Trans Chihatours has daily departures for Casablanca (US$12), Erfoud (US$6), Er-Rachidia (US$4.70), Fès (US$12), Marrakesh (US$7) and Zagora (US$6).

You may have to wait a while for a grand taxi or minibus to fill up before it heads off; they head occasionally for Ouarzazate, Tinerhir and Aït Oudinar (US$0.90) at the start of the gorge.

TODRA GORGE & TINERHIR

☎ 044

The spectacular pink canyons of the **Todra Gorge** (entry US$0.50), 15km from Tinerhir, rise up at the end of a lush valley of mud-brick villages, ruined kasbahs and *palmeraies*. A massive fault in the plateau dividing the High Atlas from the Jebel Sarhro, with a crystal-clear river emerging from it, the gorge rises to 300m at its narrowest point. It's best in the morning, when the sun penetrates to the bottom of the gorge, turning the rock from rose pink to a deep ochre.

There are banks, a post office and Internet access (US$1 per hour) in Tinerhir, which has an enormous souq on Monday.

Sleeping & Eating
TODRA GORGE

Hôtel la Vallée (☎ 044 895126; s/d US$6/8) One of the best cheap hotels in the gorge, try it for nicely decorated rooms, clean common bathrooms and trekking information.

Hôtel Etoile des Gorges (☎ 044 895045; dm US$1.90, r US$4.70-10) Next door to el-Mansour, is this friendly place which offers slightly better rooms, some with a basic shower in the corner. There's a cheap terrace restaurant.

Hôtel el-Mansour (☎ 044 834213; s/d US$3.75/4.70) This intimate little hotel, just before the entrance to the gorge proper, has only four basic rooms and a common hot shower. It has a Berber-tented café outside.

Camp sites abound along the road to the gorge, about 9km from Tinerhir. You'll pay around US$1 per person and up to US$1.50 to pitch a tent.

Camping Le Soleil (☎ 044 895111; camp site per person US$1.15, plus US$1.15 per tent, r from US$8) The first one you come to and one of the best. Facilities include a good restaurant, clean hot showers, shady sites and a washing machine (around US$2 per load).

Auberge de l'Atlas (☎ 044 895046; camping per adult/child US$1/0.65, plus US$1.40 per tent, s/d US$7/9) A good site with a restaurant and Berber-tent area.

TINERHIR

Hôtel l'Oasis (☎ 044 833670; Ave Mohammed V; s/d US$3.75/8, with bathroom US$10/14) Adjacent to the Total petrol station this is a good bet. It has a rooftop restaurant with great views and comfortable good-value rooms, many with balconies.

Hôtel de l'Avenir (☎ /fax 044 834599; s/d US$6/10) If you're looking for more travellers, try this popular place back behind Ave Hassan II,

---

SPLURGE!

Hôtel Tomboctou (☎ 044 834604; tomboc tu@iam.net.ma; 126 Ave Bir Anzarane; s/d US$13/24, with bathroom & breakfast US$32/44) This is a beautiful old kasbah (built in 1944 for the local sheikh). Rooms are chic but small. Cheaper rooms are in corner towers on the roof. There's a pool in the serene courtyard, an excellent tented restaurant and the corridors are decorated with photos and models of local kasbahs.

---

near the central market area. Pleasant rooms are arranged around the sociable restaurant area. The restaurant serves a very good paella (US$4.20, two hours' notice required).

Hôtel Salam (☎ 044 835020; s/d US$2.80/6) Next to the CTM office, the Salam has dark rooms (some spacious) around an open courtyard.

Getting There & Away
In the centre of Tinerhir, buses leave from the Place Principale, off Ave Mohammed V. Privately-owned buses run to Casablanca (US$13, 3pm), Erfoud (US$2.80, 10am and 3pm), Marrakesh (US$8, five daily) via Ouarzazate (US$3.30), Meknès (US$10, six daily) Rissani (US$3.30, 6am) and Zagora (US$7, 1pm). Anything westbound will drop you in Boumalne du Dadès (US$1).

Some grands taxis head up to the Todra Gorge (US$0.70) and, on market days, you can find *camionettes* (shared taxi trucks) heading to more-remote High Atlas villages.

MERZOUGA & THE DUNES
About 50km south of Erfoud is the tiny village of Merzouga and the famous **Erg Chebbi**, Morocco's only genuine Saharan erg – one of those huge, drifting expanses of sand dunes that typify much of the Algerian Sahara.

It's a magical landscape, which deserves much more than just a sunrise glimpse. The dunes themselves are fascinating, changing colour from pink to gold to red at different times of the day in enchanting plays of light and shadow. Sometimes shallow lakes appear in spring, attracting flocks of pink flamingos and other water birds.

Merzouga itself is tiny but it does have telephone centres, general stores, a mechanic and, of course, a couple of carpet shops.

Activities
You can arrange **camel treks** from most hotels. Prices can be high, but should range from around US$10 for a couple of hours' sunrise or sunset trip, to US$24 to US$33 per person per night with meals (some places will try for up to US$50 per person). The cheaper ones often congregate in the same spot for the first night, so if you have a romantic notion of just you, the dunes and the stars, you'd be better off taking a two-day trip. Nights are cold.

Sleeping & Eating
Over 25 auberges, most built in similar kasbah style, flank the western side of Erg Chebbi to the north and south of the villages of Merzouga and Hassi Labied. Most offer half board options as there aren't any real restaurants. You can usually sleep on a mattress on or in the roof, in the salon or in a Berber tent for about US$2.35 per person. All have views of the dunes.

Kasbah Mohajut (s/d US$4.70/7, half board per person US$14) Next door to Kasbah Hôtel Aiour, Kasbah Mohajut has lovely rooms with terracotta walls and wrought-iron fittings – a steal.

Kasbah Hôtel Aiour (☎ 055 577303; r with/without bathroom US$14/9) Between the two villages this is a more upmarket place with a stylish interior, colonnaded portico and pleasant rooms.

Auberge Kasbah des Dunes (☎ 055 577287; d US$6, with bathroom from US$8) Pleasant with rooms around a cosy courtyard. They claim they'll pick you up in Rissani at no charge if you ring ahead.

Ocean des Dunes (☎ 066 911726; r US$4.70) In Hassi Labied, this place is clean and friendly with a nice restaurant.

Kasbah Le Touareg (☎ /fax 055 577215; r from US$6, r with half board per person US$14) This is slightly more upmarket with colourful rooms. The more-basic rooftop turret rooms have excellent views.

Auberge la Palmeraie (r US$4.70) South of Merzouga, is a super chilled-out place. Unfortunately none of its pink rooms face the dunes.

Getting There & Away
There are daily buses to Fès (eight hours) or Meknès (eight hours) from Rissani or Erfoud. Minivans usually run from Merzouga to Rissani and Erfoud and back between 7.30am and 9.30am – your auberge can make arrangements.

MOROCCO DIRECTORY

ACCOMMODATION
Most of the bigger cities have camp sites, often located out of town. At official sites you'll pay around US$1 per person, plus US$1 to pitch a tent.

You will find youth hostels at Asni, Casablanca, Chefchaouen, Fès, Marrakesh,

Meknès, Rabat and Tangier. If you're travelling alone, they are among the cheapest places you can stay (between US$1.80 and US$3.75 and you'll often also pay US$0.50 for use of showers).

You'll find cheap hotels of varying quality clustered in the medinas of the bigger cities. Basic singles/doubles cost from US$2.80/4.70 and showers are often cold. Many cheap hotels in the south offer a mattress on the roof terrace for around US$1.80. In one-star hotels, rooms with showers start at around US$6/12 for singles/doubles.

For the budget traveller, hammams are less an exotic one-off than an excellent respite from cold showers. Every town has one; ask your hotel for directions.

ACTIVITIES
Camel Treks & Desert Safaris
For many travellers, a camel expedition into the desert is a real highlight of a trip to Morocco. Though fairly expensive (from US$19 per person per night, all inclusive) and hard on the bottom, it's a great way to experience the drama of the landscape. You can choose to trek for anywhere between a couple of hours and a couple of weeks. Places to head for include the Drâa Valley and the dunes at Merzouga.

Trekking
Morocco is a superb destination for mountain lovers, offering a variety of year-round trekking possibilities. It's relatively straightforward to arrange guides, porters and mules for a more independent adventure. Look at paying a minimum of US$28 per person plus food. Jebel Toubkal (4167m), the highest peak in the High Atlas mountain range, tends to attract the lion's share of visitors, but great possibilities exist throughout the country.

BUSINESS HOURS
Banking hours are from 8.30am to 11.30am and 2.30pm to 4.30pm weekdays, with Friday lunch from 11.15am to 3pm. During Ramadan they're open from 9am to 3pm. Post offices are usually open similar hours to banks, but don't close until around 6pm.

Shops often close for a couple of hours in the middle of the day. Most shops, apart from grocery stores and the like, close over the weekend.

Medina souqs and produce markets in the villes nouvelles (new towns) of the bigger cities tend to wind down on Thursday afternoon and are usually dead on Friday. Souqs in small villages start early and usually wind down before the heat of the afternoon.

DANGERS & ANNOYANCES
Morocco is a comparatively safe place to travel. Plenty of fine dope may be grown in the Rif Mountains, but drug busts are common and Morocco is bad place to check out local prison conditions. Associating with Tangier's lowlife is for the initiated only.

Those disembarking (and embarking) the ferry in Tangier should expect at least some hassle from touts and hustlers trying to pull you one way or the other (usually to a hotel/ferry ticket office where they can expect a commission).

The legendary hustlers of cities like Marrakesh remain an unavoidable part of the Moroccan experience. They can smell fear so if you don't want their services, ignore their offers and try not to get your feathers ruffled.

EMBASSIES & CONSULATES
Algeria (☎ 037 765474; 46-8 Ave Tariq ibn Zayid, Rabat)
Canada (☎ 037 687400; 13 Rue Jaafar as-Sadiq, Agdal, Rabat) Also assists Australian citizens.
France (☎ 037 689700; 3 Rue Sahnoun, Agdal, Rabat)
Germany (☎ 037 709662; 7 Rue Madnine, Rabat)
Mauritania (☎ 037 656678; 266 Souissi II, OLM, Rabat)
Spain (☎ 037 768989; 3-5 Rue Madnine, Rabat)
UK (☎ 037 729696; 17 Blvd de la Tour Hassan, Rabat) Also assists citizens of New Zealand & the Republic of Ireland.
USA (☎ 037 762265; 2 Ave de Marrakesh, Rabat)

For other embassies, see the Rabat map on p154. Morocco has embassies in Spain, Mauritania and Algeria.

FESTIVALS & EVENTS
Moussems (festivals) are often held in honour of *marabouts* (local saints). These festivals are common among the Berbers and are usually held during the summer months.

Among Morocco's many festivals, highlights to watch out for are those in Rabat (May/June), Essaouira (April and June), Fès (June/July, September, October/November), Marrakesh (June), Meknès (May/June) and Tangier (May and September).

FOOD & DRINK

If you didn't come to Africa for the food, Morocco is the exception. It's superb. Influenced by Berber, Arabic and Mediterranean (particularly Spanish and French) traditions, the cuisine features a sublime use of spices and the freshest of local produce.

Typical Morrocan dishes include *tajine*, a meat and vegetable stew cooked slowly in an earthenware dish; and *couscous*, fluffy steamed semolina served with tender meat and vegetables and a spicy sauce. The preparation of couscous requires laborious effort and most cheap restaurants only serve it on Friday.

Harira, a thick soup made from lamb stock, lentils, chickpeas, onions, tomatoes, fresh herbs and spices, is usually eaten as a first course in the evening, but is a substantial and cheap meal (around US$0.30).

Pastilla, a Fès speciality, is a very rich and delicious savoury-sweet dish made from pigeon meat and lemon-flavoured eggs, plus almonds, cinnamon, saffron and sugar, encased in layer upon layer of very fine *ouarka* pastry.

Vegetarians should be OK – fresh fruit and vegetables, as well as a range of pulses such as lentils and chickpeas, are widely available. When ordering couscous or *tajine*, simply ask for your dish to be served *sans viande* (without meat).

For breakfast, *bessara* (pea soup with spices and olive oil), fresh bread and sweet mint tea is a great way to start the day.

Morocco is bursting at the seams with cafés where sipping mint tea or coffee is a serious occupation. More often than not, the café is an all-male preserve and lone females may prefer to head for the patisseries.

Beer is reasonably easy to find in the *villes nouvelles* (new towns). A bottle of local Stork or Flag beer typically costs from US$1.20 to US$1.50 in bars. Morocco produces some quite palatable wines that sell in liquor stores for as little as US$3.50 a bottle.

GAY & LESBIAN TRAVELLERS

Homosexual acts are officially illegal in Morocco – in theory you can go to jail and/or be fined. However, although not openly admitted or shown, male homosexuality remains relatively common. Regardless of your sexual orientation, discretion is the key.

Tangier was once quite a scene, and still is to a lesser extent in summer, but gay travellers follow the same itineraries as everyone else, the most popular destinations being Fès and Marrakesh. 'Gay' bars can be found here and there, but Moroccan nightlife tends to include something for everybody.

HOLIDAYS

As well as religious holidays listed in the Africa Directory chapter (p1003) the principal public holidays in Morocco include:

1 January New Year's Day
11 January Independence Manifesto
1 May Labour Day
23 May National Day
30 July Feast of the Throne
14 August Allegiance of Wadi-Eddahab
20 August Day of the King's and People's Revolution
21 August Young People's Day
6 November Anniversary of the Green March
18 November Independence Day

INTERNET ACCESS

Access is widely available, efficient and cheap (usually about US$1 an hour).

MAPS

Michelin's No 742 map of *Morocco* is the best country-specific map.

MEDIA

The French-language *l'Opinion* is perhaps the best newspaper for getting an idea of the points of contention in Moroccan society. *Libération* and *Al-Bayane* are similar. There is virtually nothing produced locally in English, although a few international newspapers and magazines are available in major cities.

There is only a handful of local AM and FM stations, the bulk of which broadcast in either Arabic or French. *Midi 1* at 97.5 FM covers northern Morocco, Algeria and Tunisia, and plays quite reasonable contemporary music. You can usually tune into Spanish radio just about anywhere in Morocco. The BBC broadcasts on 9410MHz, 12,095MHz, 15,070MHz and several other frequencies.

MEDICAL SERVICES

Large towns often have a *pharmacie de nuit* (night pharmacy), which is open from around 9pm to 9am.

MONEY

The unit of currency is the dirham (Dh), equal to 100 centimes, although in the Spanish enclaves of Ceuta and Melilla, the euro is used. Banking services are generally quick and efficient and banks often have separate bureau de change sections.

ATMs (automated teller machines, *guichets automatiques*) are a common sight – those at BMCE and Crédit du Maroc are usually your best bet.

Major credit cards are widely accepted in the main tourist centres, although their use often attracts a surcharge of around 5% from Moroccan businesses.

POST

The postal system is fairly reliable, but not terribly fast. Sending post from Rabat or Casablanca is quickest. Outgoing parcels have to be inspected by customs (at the post office) so don't turn up with a sealed parcel.

RESPONSIBLE TOURISM

Dress code is important all over Morocco, but especially in the deeply conservative hill-tribe societies. Many of the inhabitants have had little or no exposure either to modernisation from inside their country or foreign customs from without. Travellers will feel most comfortable in buttoned shirts (rather than T-shirts, which are seen by some villagers as underwear) and trousers or long skirts (rather than shorts). An effort to respect tradition will more likely attract a friendly reception, generous hospitality, reasonable prices in the souqs and help or assistance.

STUDYING

There are limited opportunities for studying Arabic in Morocco. Your best bet would be to head for the **Arabic Language Institute** (☎ 055 624850; alifez@iam.net.ma; 2 Rue Ahmed Hiba, Fès). Three-/six-week courses start from US$428/800 and individual tuition is available for US$16 per hour.

Fès Hadara (☎ /fax 055 740292; 24 Derb Oued Souaffine, Fès) offers tailor-made workshops in various traditional crafts (carpets, leatherwork, pottery, brass and copperware and jewellery); see Fès/Information (p169).

TELEPHONE & FAX

The telephone system in Morocco is excellent and privately run *téléboutiques*

(telephone offices) abound. Telephone cards (*télécartes*) for public phones are available at post offices and some newsagents/tobacconists (*tabacs*).

Note that you must dial the local three-digit area code *even if you are dialling from the same town or code area*. To dial the Spanish enclaves of Melilla and Ceuta you must first dial ☎ 0034 and then the nine-digit telephone number.

International calls from Morocco are expensive. The cheap rate (20% off) operates on weekends and public holidays, and from 8pm to 8am weekdays.

It is possible to make reverse-charge (collect) calls from Morocco, but it can involve painfully long waits in phone offices. If you want to do this, say '*Je voudrais téléphoner en PCV*' (pronounced 'peh-seh-veh' – the French expression for this service).

Most *téléboutiques* offer fax services, but they're often ridiculously expensive.

TOURIST INFORMATION

The national tourism body, **Office National du Tourisme Marocain** (ONMT; www.tourism-in-morocco.com), has offices (usually called Délégation Régionale du Tourisme) in the main cities. A few cities also have a local office called a **Syndicat d'Initiative**.

VISAS

Most visitors to Morocco are granted a 90-day stay upon entry. Exceptions include nationals of Israel, South Africa and Zimbabwe, who can apply for a three-month, single-entry visa (about US$15) or a three-month, double-entry visa (about US$25).

Entry requirements for Ceuta and Melilla are the same as for Spain.

Visa Extensions

If 90 days is insufficient, the simplest thing to do is leave (eg, travel to the Spanish enclaves) and come back a few days later. Your chances improve if you re-enter by a different route.

Visas for Onward Travel

Visas for the following neighbouring countries can be obtained in Morocco.
Algeria Still in a state of de facto civil war, Algeria remains unsafe to visit. Normal embassy operations in Rabat are hit and miss and the land border with Morocco remains closed.

Mali Visas are required for everyone except French nationals and are valid for one month, but are renewable. Two photographs and a yellow fever vaccination certificate are required and the visa is issued on the spot. The embassy is open 8.30am to 12.30pm and 1pm to 4pm, or whenever the consul is around.

Mauritania Visas for Mauritania are available from the Mauritania embassy in Rabat. One-month visas are issued the same day if you apply between 9am and 10am (get there by 8.30am). Visas cost US$10 and you need two photos.

VOLUNTEERING

Chantiers Sociaux Marocains (☎ 037 297184; ccsm@planete.co.ma; BP 456, Rabat) is a volunteer organisation with international links.

WOMEN TRAVELLERS

Prior to marriage, Moroccan men have little opportunity to meet and get to know women, which is why Western women receive so much attention. Around 70% of Morocco's population is under the age of 30 and by the end of their trip most women may think they've met every male in this group and have barely even said hello to a female. The constant attention soon becomes wearing and, no matter what tactic is employed, impossible to shake off. Wearing dark glasses is good for avoiding eye contact and a good humoured *non merci* or *la shukran* ('no thank you') is much more effective than abuse.

To avoid unwanted attention, a wedding ring may be useful. Showing a photo of your 'husband' and 'child' will help immeasurably, although the fact that you are travelling without them will attract suspicion. Counter this by saying you will be meeting them at your next destination.

As for those times you do want to be alone, you can try to brazen it out in a café or look for the ever-increasing number of places accustomed to having the business of single Moroccan women. The upper floor of a *salon de thé* (tea room) or any trendy pizzeria-style café is a good bet. Women-only *hammams* (traditional bathhouses – always men-only or women-only) are good male-free zones for a relaxing reprieve. Hotel terraces too can be extremely relaxing and hassle-free – you can even get breakfast there.

Women travelling with male companions are likely to encounter a different problem altogether – being invisible, or questions (to the male) of the 'what's her name?' variety.

WEST AFRICA

West Africa is testimony to our need for creative expression. In this rough and often feature-less region, beauty is mostly artificial. Its people turn dust to magic from which they colour their world, plants become melodious instruments, and from West African souls stem song and rhythm. Music is in their blood, drumbeats in their hearts, and just as they breathe they sing. Street celebrations explode spontaneously here and everyone's invited.

The unpredictable and, at times, primitive conditions of West Africa are what Western travellers find so enticing. But even in the most desolate and inhospitable of places, you will be welcomed by its hosts and come to know their strength, grace and endurance. West Africa is home to a tremendous number of tribes and cultures, and many of them coexist harmoniously. Others war.

Check out Africa's biggest market in Nigeria, marvel at the handmade mud mosque in Mali's medieval Djenne, and weave through the winding streets of the legendary Timbuktu. Away from the cities, catch a wrestling match in The Gambia or paddle a pirogue to the mysti-cal Wassu Stone Circles. Festivals are frequent in the wild, wild West, and everywhere markets burst at the seams. Boogie all night with new best friends in Senegal – eating delicious street food and drinking great beer as you go – then recover all day on a sun-soaked beach.

Magic and music are the life-force of this land. See the masks and stilt dancing of the Dans in Côte d'Ivoire and, if you dare, go to Lac Togo – headquarters of the cult of voodoo. It's these ancient rituals that spiritually connect the people to their gods, their ancestors and their tribes. A good life here is about avoiding bad luck, and magic is the answer. It's this same magic that will connect you to the people and your soul to West Africa.

Mauritania

HIGHLIGHTS

- **The Sahara** An empty dune sea stretching out from Chinguetti (p213)
- **Chinguetti** A once-great Saharan city, where crumbling golden buildings house ancient libraries (p213)
- **Ouadâne & Terjît** Two desert oases – one an ancient city and the other a palm-tree–filled gorge (p214)
- **Off the beaten track** Banc d'Arguin National Park offers bird-watching along a desert coast (p213)

MAURITANIA

FAST FACTS

- **Area** 1,030,700 sq km
- **ATMs** none
- **Borders** Morocco, Mali, Senegal open; Algeria inadvisable
- **Budget** $20 per day
- **Capital** Nouakchott
- **Languages** Arabic (Hassaniya), French
- **Money** Ouguiya; US$1 = UM276
- **Population** 2.754 million
- **Seasons** very hot (Apr–Oct); hot (Dec–Mar)
- **Telephone** country code ☎ 222; international access code ☎ 00
- **Time** GMT/UTC
- **Visas** US$25/45 one month/three months; visas available on Morocco border

In this mysterious, wild, confounding country resources are scarce and sand is plentiful. Among the vast, blank shifting dune-fields and strange, flat-topped mountain ranges, the only fertile land is found in the oases and along a narrow strip bordering the Senegal River. There are not many roads. Set in this severe landscape is a deeply traditional Islamic republic, inhabited by warm, yet reserved, humorous people, measuring out endless amounts of hospitality in glasses of tea-with-ten-sugars.

Mauritania offers naked scenery, endless views, forgotten towns, weird journeys along nonexistent roads, the world's longest train, timeless tea-rituals in nomadic tents, and a stunning coast where the Sahara meets the sea. It has a desolate magnetism for travellers who like adventure and for wild-eyed desert-heads who should probably know better.

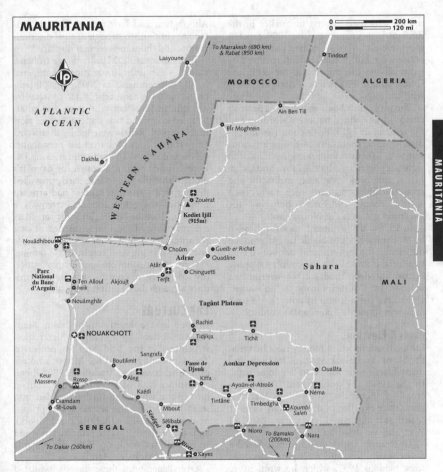

MAURITANIA

0 ____ 200 km
0 ____ 120 mi

ATLANTIC
OCEAN

To Marrakesh (690 km)
& Rabat (850 km)

Laayoune

Tindouf

MOROCCO

ALGERIA

Aïn Ben Tili

Bîr Moghrein

Dakhla

W E S T E R N   S A H A R A

Zouérat
Kediet Ijill
(915m)

Nouâdhibou

Choûm

Guelb er Richat

Adrar   Ouadâne

Sahara

Atâr

Parc
National
du Banc
d'Arguin

Ten Alloul
Iwik

Akjoujt

Terjît

Chinguetti

MALI

Nouâmghâr

Tagânt Plateau

Rachid

NOUAKCHOTT

Tidjikja

Tichit

Sangrafa

Boutilimit

Passe de
Djouk

Aoukar Depression

Oualâta

Keur
Massene

Rosso

Aleg

Kiffa

Ayoûn-el-Atroûs

Néma

Diamdam
St-Louis

Kaédi

Tintâne

Timbedgha

Koumbi
Saleh

Mbout

Nioro

To Bamako
(200km)

Nara

SENEGAL

Sélibabi

To Dakar (260km)

Sénégal

River

Kayes

MAURITANIA

HISTORY
Camels & Castes
Mauritania has a uniquely nomadic history
and heritage. The area has been inhabited
since ancient times, but when the camel was
introduced to Morocco in the 3rd century,
Berbers began to roam southward. This was
the beginning of the great Saharan trade
routes. The pickings in gold, slaves and
salt were so rich here that the Marrakesh-
based Islamic Almoravid dynasty took notice. In 1076 they defeated the dominant
Empire of Ghana, which covered much of
modern-day Mauritania.

Their descendants ruled over the area,
struggling periodically with Arabian nomads,
until they were defeated by the Arabs in 1674.

The Berber–Arab cultural mix formed a rigid
caste system that's still intact today.

Colonialism, Independence & War
Europe showed little interest until the 19th
century, when France took control of the
country, and concentrated mainly on playing factions off against each other. The Islamic Republic of Mauritania was declared
in 1960, under Mokhtar Ould Daddah, the
republic's first and last civilian leader. The
French wanted to prevent the country's ab-
sorption by newly independent Morocco.

In Ould Daddah's early years, opposition first came from the black southerners
when he decided to make Arabic, along with
French, an official language. Then trade

unions protested against inequality in the Zouérat iron ore mines (the 3000 expatriates there earned two-thirds of the country's entire wage bill). Ould Daddah survived by nationalising the mines and replacing the Communauté Financière d'Afrique (CFA) with the *ouguiya*.

The very sandy Spanish Sahara (a Spanish colony) was divided between Morocco and Mauritania in 1975. Both countries immediately found themselves fighting a vicious war with Saharawi Polisario guerrillas, who were supported by Algeria, Libya and Cuba. Mauritania was incapable, militarily and economically, of fighting such a war, even with Moroccan and French help, and the guerrillas got as far as Nouakchott.

In 1978 a new regime took over, headed by Mohamed Khouna Haidallah. After much dithering, the government renounced its territorial claims. With the country slipping further into debt, Haidallah was overthrown in 1984 by Colonel Maaouya Sid'Ahmed Ould Taya (who is still in power). He took measures to pacify Mauritania's creditors.

Riots & Elections

Ethnic tensions led to bloody riots between the Moors and black Africans in 1989, and many blacks were forced to flee to Senegal. In the 1990s the government became increasingly extremist. Many black Mauritanians were expelled or disappeared. In 1991 Mauritania supported Iraq during the Gulf War, and aid dried up.

To counter criticism, Taya introduced a new constitution, and multiparty elections were held in 1992, which he won. More elections were held for the National Assembly (Majlis al-Watani) in 1996, which resulted in one opposition seat. In the 1997 presidential elections, Taya won with a suspicious 97% majority. Elections have been boycotted by opposition groups who, curiously enough, cite massive vote-rigging.

Mauritania commenced diplomatic relations with Israel in 1995 to curry international favour. Following Iraqi criticism, Mauritania cut ties with Iraq in 1999.

Exile & Survival

In 2000 Senegalese citizens were expelled – the government believes the Senegalese are illegally diverting water from the Senegal River and supporting the black southerners.

Although attacks have ceased, black Mauritanians continue to struggle against discrimination, and thousands remain displaced.

Inequalities aside, Mauritania is a troubled nation – survival is increasingly hampered by the environment. In 2003, 750,000 people were facing food crisis after consecutive drought. In June that year, there was an attempted coup and two days of violent riots in the capital. Rebels were led by disaffected army chiefs. They took over the presidential palace and several TV and radio stations, but were crushed within a couple of days. It's thought that the war in Iraq partly provoked the uprising – the government had arrested numerous suspected Islamic extremists a couple of months before, and this served as a trigger. Other factors were discontent over Mauritanian relations with Israel and the US, and the suffering as a result of the famine. Perhaps the ongoing offshore oil exploration (by foreigners, of course) will one day produce a crutch for Mauritania's economy.

THE CULTURE

Defined by the desert and by Islam, Mauritanian society has a complex hierarchical structure that has held firm for centuries. The dominant group is the Moors, who are proud, reserved and traditional. For them, appearance is all. Moor families are grouped into tribes, which are further divided into strict hierarchies: the warriors and priests, made up of the Bidan (light-skinned Moors), and the artisans, *griots* (storytellers) and servant classes, made up of the descendants of enslaved blacks, or Haratines.

Over generations these slaves assimilated Moorish culture, and today 60% of the population is of mixed ancestry. Society may be more mixed, but slavery continues. It was finally declared illegal in 1981, but little is done to enforce this. Meanwhile, down in the south, the black Fulani and Tukulor tribes, living along the river, have more in common with their Senegalese and Malian neighbours than with the people of the north, and are treated as third-class citizens. The southerners are grouped into hierarchies similar to those of the Moors.

However rigid Mauritania's social system, it's been shaken by massive migration: droughts have forced nomads to stop moving, and more than half the population is now urban (it was 4% in 1960).

And despite the divisions, Mauritanians are united by Islam, and by a hospitality that's both generous and dutiful: people will always share their food with you, invite you into their homes and make sure you're topped up with tea.

ARTS

Mauritanian arts are a fine fusion of Islamic and African traditions, both in crafts – such as silver inlaid wooden chests, beads, colourful leatherwork and tie-dyed cloth – and in music. Singers are powerful and rhythms repetitive. Diva Dimi Mint Abba combines Arabic melodies and African percussion to stunning effect.

As far as film goes, Med Hondo made the controversial *Soleil O*, about colonialism (1970), and his *Sarraounia* (1987) is an epic about an African queen. Abderrahmane Sissako landed the top prize at FESPACO 2003, Africa's biggest film festival, for his poignant *Hermakano* (Waiting for Happiness) set in Nouâdhibou.

ENVIRONMENT

Mauritania is being eaten by the desert which covers nearly 75% of its surface. Overgrazing, deforestation and drought all contribute to desertification. This has encroached on animal life as well as humans, and fauna is limited to the occasional gazelle and camels.

Some foreign fishing boats catch 400 tonnes of small fish on a good day. Concerns about overfishing are ignored – Mauritania needs cash, and a recent agreement allowed vessels to increase 30% in the size. Sawfish have completely disappeared, and the catch of octopus has halved in recent years.

The coastal Parc National du Banc d'Arguin is home to extraordinary bird populations: more than two million sandpipers have been recorded in winter. The flood plains of the Senegal River also provide an ideal habitat for breeding birds.

TRANSPORT

GETTING THERE & AWAY
Air

Point Afrique (in France ☎ 08 20 00 01 54; www.point-afrique.com) is a cooperative that runs a wonderful service with the aim of encouraging tourism – cheap charter flights from

DEPARTURE TAX

This is usually included in the price of your air ticket, but costs around US$2 to other African countries and US$3.50 elsewhere.

France to unusual destinations in Africa. It flies between Paris and Marseilles and Atâr (US$200 to US$250) from the end of October to early May. From the end of December to early May it flies to/from Nantes for the same price.

Air Mauritanie (☎ 525 2216; www.airmauritanie.mr) flies between Nouakchott and Paris, Abidjan (Côte d'Ivoire), Bamako (Mali), Banjul (The Gambia), Dakar (Senegal), Casablanca (Morocco), Pointe-Noire (Congo), Cotonou (Benin), Lomé (Togo) and Las Palmas (Canary Islands). You can also fly to/from Paris on **Air France** (www.airfrance.com) or **Royal Air Maroc** (www.royalairmaroc.com), or to Paris via Tunis on **Tunis Air** (www.tunisair.com).

Land
MALI

You can take a battered bush taxi, truck or *bâché* (pick-up truck) along the 1100km tarred Route d'Espoir (Road of Hope) from Rue de l'Indépendance in Nouakchott to Néma (US$26, two days, daily) via Tintâne or Ayoûn-el-Atroûs (US$19, 12 to 15 hours) and stopping the night at Tintane or Ayounel-Atrous. From Néma you can get a bush taxi or *bâché* to Nara or Nioro (US$12, daily) and then from Nara or Nioro to Bamako. The Nioro road is better. The journey to/from Bamako can be done in three days, if you're lucky.

There are bush taxis and *bâchés* to/from Sélibabi between Nouakchott and Sélibabi (US$19, two days, daily), and battered 4WDs travel between Sélibabi and Kayes (US$12, six hours, daily) – a bumpy ride. They usually head off late in the afternoon, so you will arrive in Sélibabi late in the evening and have to stay overnight; be warned, there are no hotels in Sélibabi so you will need to stay with a local or camp. You will pick up transport to Nouakchott the following day.

Only the Route d'Espoir and some sections of the Nioro to Bamako road are paved, so these routes are impassable during the wet season.

MAURITANIA

MALI TO MAURITANIA OVERLAND *Abigail Hole*

We reached the Mauritanian border post around midnight: a thatched hut, a roaring fire and a roasting goat. Mali blues echoed in the pitch dark. I got out, dazed from my sleepy head rebounding off the truck interior. I talked to one of the driver's helpers. In the dark I couldn't see his face, just the outline of his turban. 'You know *nobody* in Sélibabi?' he asked, and added, 'You must stay with us.'

'Us' turned out to be the driver's family, and I stayed at their house, or rather (since it was too small), out in the yard where they laid out a mat for me, among the chickens and goats. The next day they gave me breakfast, then lunch. When I offered them some money, they laughed and said, 'No, this is Africa.'

Transport to Nouakchott, a battered pick-up, reputedly left in the afternoon. A group gathered around it – too many for all to get in, but no-one seemed to register this, so we all did a mad Dantesque scramble and I ended up in the middle, every limb trapped. There were about 40 in the back, adults, children and babies, all pinned among each other, like a highly evolved game of Twister. The driver chose this moment to ask for our tickets before driving at a leisurely pace to get petrol. We left as night fell.

Every so often the police stopped us. Seeing me there, they'd shine a torch in my face and ask the pertinent question: 'What are you *doing* here?'

'I'm a tourist,' I'd say, feeling absurd.

MOROCCO

The convoy days are over, and there are buses between Dakhla and Nouâdhibou (US$77, twice weekly, 12 to 16 hours).

Coming from the north, it's easy to hitch a ride with other travellers from a Dakhla *campement* (guesthouse) – people usually charge US$20 to US$40 per person. It's a challenging drive through the desert, and drivers are usually happy to take people along to cover the costs of a guide and to help with digging the vehicle out of the sand. The route is an adventure – a first taste of the desert, like a scene from *Mad Max*, scattered with car wrecks and people appearing from nowhere. There's less traffic from south to north, but it's possible to get a lift this way too.

You could also club together with other travellers and arrange a bush taxi for the journey for around US$70 per person.

SENEGAL

Bush taxis run regularly from Nouakchott to Rosso (US$19, three hours). Expect hassle at the border (insist on receipts for all payments), although car owners get most of it as everyone tries for a piece of the pie. Note that the border is open on the Mauritanian side only from 8am to noon and 3pm to 6pm. You take a ferry or pirogue (dugout canoe) across the Senegal River (US$1), then complete the immigration formalities in a shack. There are plenty of minibuses from here to St Louis (five hours) and buses to Dakar.

GETTING AROUND
Air
Air Mauritanie flies between Nouakchott (see p211) and regional cities.

Local Transport
Mercedes, Peugeot 504s and 4WD share-taxis (the latter known as bush taxis), Land Rovers, minibuses and *bâchés* (pick-up trucks) are the various forms of public transport in Mauritania. Expect long, hot, dusty, crowded trips, with frequent prayer and tea stops. Prices vary according to the vehicle, with Mercedes being the costliest and *bâchés* the cheapest. It's more expensive to sit in the front. It can be a long wait for your vehicle to fill up with passengers.

If you want to hire private transport, a 4WD and driver, seating around four to six, costs around US$50 per day.

Train
Mauritania boasts the longest, slowest, dustiest **train** (www.snim.fr) in the world, trundling 675km between the port of Nouâdhibou and the iron ore mines of Zouérat, deep in the desert. The train is usually about 2.5km long and is made up of open-topped wagons. You can ride in these for free – an atmospheric journey through the desert – but

cover your pack with a bag and wear warm clothes that you don't mind wrecking – you will be covered by black dust. Alternatively, there's a passenger car – 40 times older and sandier than any train carriage you've seen before. Prepare for a stampede to get on, though there's usually space for everyone. Even in the passenger car, take a scarf to wrap around your face and warm clothes – it gets cold at night. You'll share the trip with local people, who pass the time with singing, praying and tea-making.

See the Nouâdhibou section (p213) for fare information.

NOUAKCHOTT

pop 661,400
Nouakchott was hastily slung together at independence in 1960. Constructed for 200,000 people, the population has since trebled, as recurrent droughts have forced people citywards. A place with a sense of the desert, it veers between grand, brand-new mansions, breeze-block buildings and shanty towns. The broad streets are buried in grey sand and the city has a curiously still atmosphere. Yet it's friendly and laid-back, perhaps induced by the belting sun. Most men wear pale indigo *galabiyyas* – long robes the colour of a hard sky. While strolling the streets you'll see the occasional 'Coiffeur Bin Laden' or 'Epicerie Saddam Hussein'.

ORIENTATION
The airport is 3km northeast of the centre. A taxi should cost only US$1. Garage Rosso, for transport to/from the Senegal border, is 6km to the south, transport to/from Mali is based near the Mosquée Marocain, and Garage Nouâdhibou for transport north is 3km to the west. Garage Atâr, for transport to/from Atâr, is 3km north of the airport.

Nouakchott is sprawling, but the centre is walkable. The main streets are Ave Abdel Nasser running east–west and Ave Kennedy running north–south. **Bana-Blanc** (Ave du Général de Gaulle), a supermarket, is a handy landmark that everyone seems to know.

INFORMATION
Internet Access
@yber Café (Rue Mohammed el Habib; US$0.50 per hr)
Cyber Café (Ave Kennedy; US$1 per hr)

Medical Services
There's a **hospital** (☎ 525 2132; off Ave Abdel Nasser) near the centre of town.

Money
There are lots of moneychangers around the Marché Capital. Most hotels will arrange exchange, too.

Post & Telephone
The post office in Nouakchott is open daily and has a poste restante.

There are lots of telephone offices around town; several are marked on the map.

DANGERS & ANNOYANCES
Nouakchott is a relatively safe city, but take normal precautions. It's inadvisable to walk along the beach at night – muggings are common. If you're a lone female, avoid getting into a shared taxi with two or more men in it.

SIGHTS & ACTIVITIES
Around 5pm the fishing boats come in to the **Port de Pêche**, a colourful, timeless sight. The nearby **beach** is also good. For a singular experience, head here on a Friday afternoon when there's **drag racing** with 4WDs. A taxi costs US$1 from town, or you could hitch if you're not alone.

The Saudi-constructed **Mosquée Saudique** (Rue Mamadou Konaté; non-Muslims not permitted inside) is vast and stunning.

The **National Museum** (Rue Mohamed el Habib; admission free; ☉ 8am-2pm Sat-Thu) is a tribute to the harsh romance of nomadic culture, although the black southerners are not mentioned.

If you want a swim, **Hôtel Mercure** (☎ 529 5050; Ave Abdel Nasser; US$6/2 adult/child) has a good pool.

SLEEPING
Budget places are all conveniently situated around the centre.

Auberge de Jeunesse l'Amitié (☎ 525 4419; off Rue Mamadou Konaté; dm US$4) Run by personable brothers, this is a recommended, helpful, homey youth hostel, although not overwhelmingly clean. It has four-bed rooms, hot water, a kitchen and parking.

Auberge La Dune (☎ 525 6274; Ave Kennedy; s/d/tr US$10/20/28, with bathroom US$12/23/30) With clean, bright rooms in a leafy setting, this is a good, popular choice. There's a cheery little café.

MAURITANIA

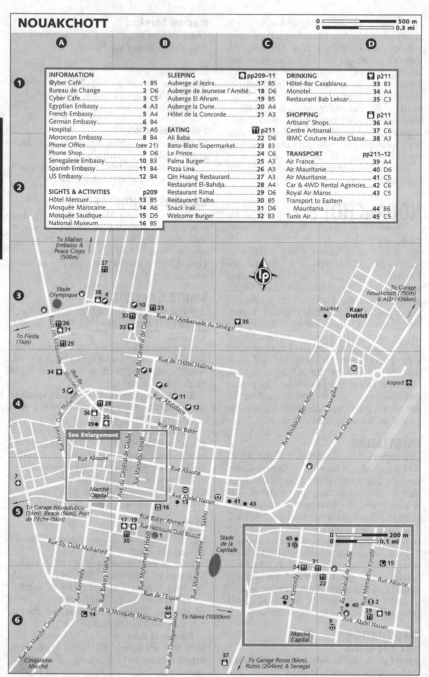

NOUAKCHOTT

0 — 500 m
0 — 0.3 mi

INFORMATION
@yber Café..............................1 B5
Bureau de Change....................2 D6
Cyber Cafe..............................3 C5
Egyptian Embassy......................4 A3
French Embassy.........................5 A4
German Embassy........................6 B4
Hospital...................................7 A5
Moroccan Embassy.....................8 B4
Phone Office.........................(see 21)
Phone Shop.............................9 D6
Senegalese Embassy..................10 B3
Spanish Embassy......................11 A4
US Embassy.............................12 B4

SIGHTS & ACTIVITIES p209
Hôtel Mercure..........................13 B5
Mosquée Marocaine.................14 A6
Mosquée Saudique...................15 D5
National Museum......................16 B5

SLEEPING pp209–11
Auberge al Jezira.....................17 B5
Auberge de Jeunesse l'Amitié... 18 D6
Auberge El Ahram....................19 B5
Auberge la Dune......................20 A4
Hôtel de la Concorde...............21 A3

EATING p211
Ali Baba.................................22 D6
Bana-Blanc Supermarket...........23 B3
Le Prince................................24 C6
Palma Burger...........................25 A3
Pizza Lina...............................26 A3
Qin Huang Restaurant...............27 A3
Restaurant El-Bahdja................28 A4
Restaurant Rimal......................29 D6
Restaurant Taiba.....................30 B5
Snack Irak...............................31 D6
Welcome Burger.......................32 B3

DRINKING p211
Hôtel-Bar Casablanca...............33 B3
Monotel.................................34 A4
Restaurant Bab Leksar..............35 C3

SHOPPING p211
Artisans' Shops........................36 A4
Centre Artisanal......................37 C6
IBMC Couture Haute Classe......38 A3

TRANSPORT pp211–12
Air France...............................39 A4
Air Mauritanie........................40 D6
Air Mauritanie........................41 C5
Car & 4WD Rental Agencies......42 C6
Royal Air Maroc......................43 C5
Transport to Eastern
  Mauritania............................44 B6
Tunis Air................................45 C5

To Malian
Embassy &
Peace Corps
(500m)

Stade
Olympique

To Fiesta
(1km)

Rue de l'Ambassade du Sénégal

Market   Ksar
District

To Garage
Nouakchott (750m)
& Atâr (436km)

Rue de l'Hôtel Halima

Airport

Rue Abdallaye

Rue du Nord

Rue Amrou Ould Mohamed

Ave Boubacar Ben Amer

Ave Bourgiba

Rue Chary

Rue Abou Baker

See Enlargement

Rue Alioune

Ave du Général de Gaulle

Rue Mamadou Konaté

Rue Alioune

Marché
Capital

Ave Abdel Nasser

To Garage Nouâdhibou
(3km), Beach (5km), Port
de Pêche (5km)

Rue Baker Ahmed

Rue Hennoune Ould Bouccif

Rue Mohamed el Habib

Sakho

Stade
de la
Capitale

Rue Ely Ould Mohamed

Ave Kennedy

Rue Bakary Hakha

Rue de l'Espoir

Rue Mohamed Lemine

Rue de l'Indépendance

To Néma (1000km)

Rue de la Mosquée Marocaine

Rue du Marché Cinquième

Cinquième
Marché

To Garage Rosso (6km),
Rosso (204km) & Senegal

0 — 200 m
0 — 0.1 mi

Ave Kennedy

Ave du Général de Gaulle

Rue Mamadou Konaté

Rue Alioune

Ave Abdel Nasser

Marché
Capital

Hôtel de la Concorde (☎ 525 6525; Route des Ambassades; dm US$5.50, d with bathroom US$15) Formerly the Petit Paris, it's debatable whether the shady reputation has changed with the name, but the Concorde is clean, calm and tree-shaded.

Auberge Al Jezira (☎ 529 2530; off Rue Hennoune Ould Bouccif; d with bathroom US$19) Al Jezira has bright mural-painted halls and large, airy rooms with balconies upstairs.

Auberge el-Ahram (Rue Hennoune Ould Bouccif; s/d with bathroom US$12/23) Run by a friendly family, these rudimentary rooms are good value in a friendly neighbourhood.

EATING

Nouakchott has loads of places for a snack attack and a refreshing variety of restaurants.

Restaurant El Bahdja (☎ 630 5383; off Route des Ambassades; dishes US$1-12) A delicious Moroccan place, this is smart, with gingham tablecloths. A beer costs US$4.50.

Restaurant Rimal (☎ 525 4832; Ave Abdel Nasser; dishes US$1.50-3.50) This has good fish brochettes (US$3.50) and a secluded, shrub-shrouded sitting-out-front area.

Pizza Lina (☎ 258 662; Route des Ambassades; dishes US$5) Popular with expats, Pizza Lina has fine pizzas, exposed brick walls and video screens showing some choice Arabic pop videos. It's US$4.50 for a beer.

Restaurant Taiba (off Rue Hennoune Ould Bouccif; dishes US$1) With a couple of daily choices, this is a small neighbourhood cheapie, where you sit on the floor.

Fast food, such as burgers or *shwarma* (slivers of meat served in pitta bread), costs around US$1; try **Welcome Burger** (Rue de l'Ambassade du Sénégal), **Palma Burger** (Route des Ambassadors) or **Le Prince**, **Ali Baba** and **Snack Irak** on Rue Alioune.

SPLURGE!

Mauritanian Mexican, **Fiesta** (☎ 529 3328; off Rue de l'Ambassade du Sénégal; dishes US$4.50-9) has seats in a lush garden, on the roof terrace or the plain, blanket-decorated inner room. The food's fab. Try the tacos. For some authentic Eastern eats, **Qin Huang Restaurant** (☎ 524 1107; off Rue de l'Ambassade du Sénégal; dishes US$4-8) is sparkling clean, with red lanterns, and eager-to-please management who rush out to greet you.

There are food stalls at the **Port de Pêche**; try some peanut brittle or a *toubab* (white person) coffee.

DRINKING

Nouakchott is not a place to head for nightlife, but this is what gives its few options their particular charm. Thursday and Friday are the big nights.

Restaurant Bar Leksar (Rue de l'Ambassade du Sénégal; beer US$6) A proper, darkened bar that you can even prop up. It has video screens and vaguely Eastern arches. The food's good, too (dishes US$4).

Hotel-Bar Casablanca (off Ave du Général de Gaulle; admission US$4-7; ☾ to 5am) After leaving Leksar, come down to Casablanca. This quasi-club plays Arabic, hip-hop and Senegalese tunes. Admission is free if you eat here, or you could pay the admission and get a free drink.

Monotel (Route des Ambassades; US$4-7; ☾ to 6am) A hotel club, this plays hip-hop and Senegalese music.

SHOPPING

Marché Capital (Grand Marché) A big Moor socialising spot, with blaring Arabic music and beautiful Mauritanian crafts, including delicate narrow pipes, silver-inlaid boxes, *galabiyyas*, *malafas* (brilliantly dyed, crinkled-cotton veils), *gris-gris* (charms), such as dried frogs, and henna decoration (US$4 to US$7).

Cinquième Marché (Rue du Marché Cinquième) Just as good but entirely different. It's a full-on, funky African market – a sprawling mass of hawkers, squawking chickens, tailors, bead-sellers, vegetables, and more.

IBMC Couture Haute Classe (☎ 631 7090; Rue de l'Ambassade de Sénégal; shirt, skirt or trousers US$4-8) Superb tailors, particularly if they have got something to copy (like the shirt you wrecked on the iron-ore train). Bring fabric.

Artisans' shops (Route des Ambassadors) sell silverwork and inlaid stuff.

The **Centre Artisanal** (Artisans' Centre; Rosso Rd) is obscure but has a good choice of silver.

GETTING THERE & AWAY

Air Mauritanie flies between Nouakchott and Nouâdhibou, Atâr, Néma, Tidjikja and Zouérat, among other places.

Numerous vehicles ply the tar road between Garage Nouakchott and Atâr (US$6 to US$12, five hours). See the Nouâdhibou

MAURITANIA

section (opposite) for details of the coastal route to Nouâdhibou.

If you want to hire a car or 4WD, there are agencies clustered around the junction of Aves Abdel Nasser and Kennedy.

GETTING AROUND

The city centre is small enough to be walkable, but to get further afield, taxis are cheap and plentiful. For example a taxi to Garage Nouakchott or to Port de Pêche will set you back around US$1. If you're not alone, you could try hitching. You can catch crowded collective minibuses from around the Marché Capita, which head out to Cinquième or Garage Nouâdhibou (US$0.30) among other places; you'll need to stop one and check the destination.

AROUND MAURITANIA

Mauritania is a vast country, but much of it is off-limits to visitors unless you happen to have a fully-equipped expedition vehicle or a couple of camels. We've listed the more accessible places, roughly from north to south.

NOUÂDHIBOU

pop 80,400

Nouâdhibou is surrounded by the world's richest fishing area. Offshore is always teeming with boats, alongside a series of bleak wrecks. Ironically, the EU owns the fishing rights (sold to finance the national debt), local fishing crews get what's left over (not much), and Mauritanians end up buying expensive imported canned fish that originated in their own waters.

This is the first place people hit after the rough road from Morocco, and thousands of sailors pass through. It seems to be defined by this transient population, which accounts for its insubstantial feel.

The town has a sleepy **central market**, featuring tailors whipping up *galabiyyas* and women selling wigs and other beautifying bits and pieces.

There are some beautiful deserted **beaches** nearby, backed by wind-sculpted pale golden cliffs, including pristine **Cape Blanc**, 15km from town.

Don't go any further west than the train line – this area is part of the disputed Western Sahara and is dotted with land mines.

Orientation & Information

The 'station' is about 2km south of town, and Garage Nouâdhibou is about 2km north. The town is centred on Blvd Médian, with the market to the east.

Overlanders must get their passports stamped at the **sûreté** (☎ 574 5072; ☉ 8am-noon Thu, 8am-2.30pm Sun-Wed). If you have a vehicle, you usually have to buy insurance (US$29 for two weeks).

Auberges provide exchange, or there are bureaux de change along Blvd Médian. Internet cafés include **Cyber Éspace** (Blvd Médian; US$1 per hour) and **SIG Cyber** (US$1.50 per hour), opposite Hôtel de Ville.

Sleeping

There's a good selection of places to stay, all set up for overland drivers.

Camping Abba (☎ 574 9887; auberge.abba@cara mail.com; Blvd Médian; camping US$3.50, dm US$4.50, s/d with bathroom US$7/9) This sociable place has clean rooms with hot water leading off a good-for-hanging-out, high-ceilinged lounge, with kitchen. Staff are helpful and can recommend guides.

Camping Bale du Lévrier (☎ 574 6536; Blvd Médian; dm US$6) A clean place, with small rooms around a sheltered courtyard. There's a small communal area and hobs, and it also has the advantage of being next to the Clair de Lune pâtisserie.

Auberge Sahara Chez Momo & Artoro (☎ 574 6216; off Blvd Médian; dm US$6) This has three four-bed rooms and a roomy kitchen. The roof terrace is ideal for a barbecue, or you can sleep on it (US$4).

Eating

Clair de Lune (dishes US$0.50-1.50; Blvd Médian) This popular, gleamingly clean pâtisserie has proper coffee, melt-in-the-mouth pastries and some tables.

Hogar Canario (off Bvld Maritime; dishes US$4.50-6) Nouâdhibou's funkiest restaurant has a charming Spanish owner, excellent food and mean G&Ts.

Restaurant Merou (Blvd Médian; dishes US$6-10) Merou has a smartish air and recommended food, particularly the fish. There's a cosy bar frequented by incongruously glamorous women (this is a port, after all).

Restaurant de l'Oiseau du Paradis (dishes US$3-6) One of several similar-standard Chinese restaurants (catering to Korean sailors), this has a telephone-directory menu and authentic food. The fish cooked with lemon is tasty, and beer costs US$4.50.

You can eat *tiéboudienne* (fish stew) and *yassa* (Senegalese chicken) in local holes in the wall (US$1). Try **Chez Astou** (Rue de la Galérie Mahfoud), with 'fast food' painted on the outside, or friendly, Gambian-run **Restaurant Mourabitoune** (Rue de la Galérie Mahfoud).

You can buy fresh seafood at the **fish market** (Blvd Maritime) and cook it at your camp.

Getting There & Away

Vehicles run from Nouakchott's Garage Nouâdhibou along the sandy coast road to Nouâdhibou (US$12 to US$19; 12 to 24 hours, four daily Monday, Thursday and Saturday, two on other days). Most of the route is due to be tarred by 2004. Until then, a guide is advisable for this challenging tide-dependent, desert–beach–scrubland trip. The guide fee is US$230, but if you travel in a convoy you can split it. You have to pay the national park admission (see following) on the way.

Trains between Nouâdhibou and Zouérat (US$9/4 in 1st/2nd, 18 hours) go via Choûm (US$6/3, 12 hours), where bush taxis meet the train to take you to Atâr (US$4.50, four hours). In 1st class you get a grubby couchette. There are several trains daily, but the one with a passenger car departs Nouâdhibou daily at 2.50pm and Choûm at 5.40pm.

Some drivers can put their vehicle on the train (the *piste*, or track, on this route is terrible) but only on Monday or Saturday. Nouâdhibou to Choûm costs US$46/105 per car/truck.

PARC NATIONAL DU BANC D'ARGUIN

Along 180km of desert coast, dotted with small islands, the **park** (admission per person/vehicle US$3/1.50), is home to millions of birds – including spoonbills, pelicans and flamingos. The nesting season is April to July and October to January. Its remoteness keeps it off the beaten track. It's 235km south of Nouâdhibou: bush taxis go to Ten Alloul from Nouâdhibou (US$12 to US$19), where you can hitch 12km to **Iwik**. Here you can hire boats (US$60 per day), and there's a **campement** (dm US$3.50, d US$12). The **park's head office** (☎ 525 8541; Blvd Médian, Nouâdhibou) can provide information.

ATÂR

pop 30,900

Atâr is a gentle, modern, sand-drenched, palm-dotted town and a good base for exploring the Adrar, Mauritania's most sight-packed region, which has prehistoric landscapes and melted-looking mountains, ancient Saharan caravan towns, desert dunes and oases.

In the town centre is an interesting but pricey **artisans' market**. Other services include a couple of Internet cafés.

There are lots of well-kept camps, or you could also ask at restaurants about rooms with local families.

Camping Bab Sahara (☎ 647 3966; off Route de Azougui; dm US$4.50-6; parking US$0.50-6) This Dutch–German-run place is the best in town – well kept, with a good outdoor restaurant, a library and tents or spacious sitting-room-style four-bed huts.

Hôtel Dar Salaam (☎ 546 4622; Route de Chinguetti; dm US$10, d US$19) This clean, friendly place has pod-shaped huts and lots of communal sitting areas.

Auberge Monod (☎ 546 4595; Route de Chinguetti; dm US$4.50) This place has a good dorm opening on to a rooftop and is in the centre of town.

Restaurant Jour-Nuit Marocain (Route de Chinguetti; dishes US$1) Run by a cheerful Moroccan, this has street-side tables and good camel sandwiches.

Restaurant Le Tata (off Route de Chinguetti; dishes US$1) has good *mafe* (Senegalese vegetables) and great beans.

See the Nouakchott section (p211) for flight information and the Nouâdhibou section (left) for information on getting here by train and bush taxi.

Bush taxis go to Chinguetti (US$4 to US$6, two hours, twice daily) from Garage Chinguetti, which is off the Route de Chinguetti. Transport to Ouadâne (US$6 to US$8, four hours) is irregular, inquire at Garage Chinguetti. The main *gare routière* is near the roundabout. Transport goes to/from Nouakchott (US$6 to $13, seven hours) and Choûm (US$4.50 to $8, four hours, two to four daily).

CHINGUETTI

A dramatic, 80km journey from Atâr through blackened-copper mountains will lead you to Chinguetti. This sleepy date-palm oasis, once a splendid Saharan trading city, is the seventh holiest city of Islam, situated at the edge of rolling dunes that fill the horizon.

Chinguetti is Mauritania's biggest tourist destination – with direct charter flights from Paris to Atâr. It's the most accessible of the desert towns and a popular starting point for desert treks. Life partly revolves around the twice weekly influx of money-bearing tourists. Despite the regular appearance of large groups, and the array of facilities for tourists, the town remains sleepy and is a good place to settle for at least a few days.

Several family **bibliothèques** contain ancient Islamic manuscripts. All *auberges* can arrange desert treks (US$19 per day).

Chinguetti is cheek-by-jowl *campements*, all of which serve food.

Auberge La Rose des Sables (larosedesables@caramail.com; New Town; dm US$4.50; dishes US$4) Run by the amiable Cheikh, this is a well-kept place with charm and good food.

Auberge Bien Être (Old Town; s/d US$4.50/9) The oldest *campement*, this is well run and has a nomad tent in the lovely yard.

Some cheaper but starker places include Auberge des Oasis, with a garden courtyard, and popular Auberge Zarga.

OUADÂNE

The ruins of the ghost city of Ouadâne are dissolving into the hillside. It's 120km northeast of Chinguetti, surrounded by palms and desert, and arriving after a trip to the middle of nowhere you may wonder what possessed anyone to build a city here. The crumbling old quarter, Le Ksar al Kiali, is now surmounted by the new town.

There are four *campements* here, all good, each charging US$4.50 per person. **Auberge Vasque Ouadâne** is unique – it's run by a woman.

For transport details, see Atâr (p213). You can travel between Chinguetti and Ouadâne by camel (there's no public transport); this takes six days (US$19 per day).

TERJÎT

At this lush oasis, 40km from Atâr, date palms pack a narrow canyon, around cool- and warm-water pools. You can stay at **Oasis Touristique de Terjît** (dm US$6) in a tent by the stream, at night lit by stars and fireflies.

To get here from Atâr, take any transport towards Nouakchott, and then hitch the 13km from the turnoff.

MAURITANIA DIRECTORY

ACCOMMODATION

There's plenty of inexpensive accommodation in Mauritania, much of it aimed at overland drivers, so often there'll be secure parking – but most don't have hot water. It's often cheapest to sleep on the rooftop. Locals will frequently offer you a bed, and many restaurants will let you sleep on the floor if you buy a meal. Camping in the desert is legal.

CUSTOMS

As Mauritania is an Islamic republic, importing alcohol is prohibited.

EMBASSIES & CONSULATES

The following embassies and consulates are in Nouakchott.

Canada (☎ 529 2697; Av Charles de Gaulle)
Egypt (☎ 525 2192; Villa 468, Rue de l'Ambassade de Senegal)
France (☎ 525 1740; Rue Ahmed Ould Mohamed)
Germany (☎ 525 1729; Rue Abdallaye)
Mali (☎ 525 4081; Rue Mamadou Konaté)
Morocco (☎ 525 1411; Av du Général de Gaulle)
Senegal (☎ 525 7290; Av de l'Ambassade du Sénégal)
Spain (☎ 525 2080)
UK (☎ 525 1756)
USA (☎ 525 2660; Rue Abdallaye)

Mauritania has diplomatic representation in Mali, Senegal and Morocco.

HOLIDAYS

As well as religious holidays listed in the Africa Directory chapter (p1003), these are the principal public holidays in Mauritania:
1 January New Year's Day
26 February National Reunification Day
1 May Workers' Day
25 May African Liberation Day
10 July Army Day
28 November Independence Day
12 December 1984 Coup Anniversary

MAPS

The IGN 1:2,500,000 is good but the scale is small; 1:500,000 and 1:200,000 maps are available from **Espace IGN** (☎ 01 43 98 85 10; www.ign.fr; 107 rue de la Boétie).

MEDIA

Papers are withdrawn if anything in them is deemed anti-Islamic or a threat to national security. Newspapers in French include *Horizon* and *Chaab* (government-owned) and *L'Eveil-Hebdo* (privately owned). You can tune into Radio France International on FM.

MONEY

Credit cards are pretty useless. Nouakchott bureaux de change stay open longer than the banks and offer better rates, but most people change their money on the black market.

US dollars and euros are the preferred currencies.

You might have to complete a currency declaration at the border, although this is increasingly rare – if you do, don't declare all your cash if you intend to use the black market.

RESPONSIBLE TRAVEL

As this is a Muslim country, it's important that both men and women dress appropriately. Wearing shorts will make you the talk of the town. Displays of affection in public are another way to give travellers a bad name.

Water is scarce here – use it sparingly. Make sure you carry all your rubbish away with you.

People regard hospitality as an important duty, and you might be offered accommodation. Often they won't accept payment, so it's good to give them a gift in return instead.

TELEPHONE

It's easy to make direct-dial international phone calls (US$3 per minute to the USA or Europe).

VISAS

Most travellers from Europe, the Americas and Australasia need visas. Citizens of France and Italy don't require visas. Month-long visas cost about US$25. You'll need two photos, and might need to produce a yellow fever vaccination certificate and a return air ticket.

It is difficult to get a visa extended, so if you do want to prolong your stay it's best to leave the country and apply for another, or get a visa on the border where they are available.

Visas for Onward Travel

Visas can be obtained for the following countries in Nouakchott (see embassy details opposite). You'll need two photos.

Burkina Faso, Côte d'Ivoire & Togo Available from the French embassy, 30-day visas cost US$30 (48 hours to issue).

Mali 30-day visas cost US$30 (expect approximately a 24-hour turnaround).

Senegal 30-day visas cost US$15 (these usually take around 48 hours).

VOLUNTEERING

Schools in Chinguetti would love to have English speakers come into the classroom – all they need to do is talk to the English teacher. For French speakers, there is also a small school in Tindiwali, a small oasis about 2km from Chinguetti, that wants to bring in foreigners to help with classes. For details, visit the Peace Corps Bureau in Atâr (opposite Pharmacy Tungad).

WOMEN TRAVELLERS

Women travellers are treated respectfully, though proposals of marriage are comically common. You might get the odd bit of sexual harassment, but it's nothing in comparison with North African countries such as Morocco and Egypt. It's wise to dress modestly. Many men are not supposed to touch Western women at all, so don't offer to shake hands.

Senegal

HIGHLIGHTS

- **Dakar's markets** Colour, culture and chaos – soak it up! (p226)
- **St-Louis** This former capital has barely changed since the colonial era (p228)
- **Ile de Gorée** A beautiful tribute to the memory of 20 million slaves (p227)
- **Parc National du Niokolo-Koba** The jewel in the crown of Senegal's national parks (p232)
- **Best journey** A pirogue trip through a stunning network of waterways in the Siné-Saloum Delta (p233)
- **Off the beaten track** Casamance's pristine beaches and lush hinterland (p233 & p237)

FAST FACTS

- **Area** 197,000 sq km
- **ATMs** in major towns (Dakar, St-Louis, Ziguinchor and Kaolack) and some beach resorts
- **Borders** The Gambia, Guinea, Guinea-Bissau, Mali and Mauritania; all borders open from dawn to dusk
- **Budget** US$20 to US$30 a day
- **Capital** Dakar
- **Languages** French, Malinké, Pulaar (Fula), Susu
- **Money** West African CFA; US$1 = CFA600
- **Population** 10.6 million
- **Seasons** dry (Dec–Mar), hot (Mar–May), wet (Jun–Nov)
- **Telephone** country code ☎ 221; international access code ☎ 00
- **Time** GMT/UTC
- **Visas** required by all except nationals of Canada, the European Union, Israel, Japan, Norway, South Africa and USA

Senegal: the all-singing, all-dancing extravaganza with a contagious and constantly restless beat. The country's seductiveness has made it West Africa's number one travel destination, and it's easy to see why. The capital Dakar is the kind of city that activates the adrenal glands, while in contrast St-Louis is a kind of elegant old colonial lady who dreams of long-ago aviation heroes in safari suits. The endless golden beaches can be enjoyed from sleepy fishing villages or plush Western-style resort towns, and the national parks rank

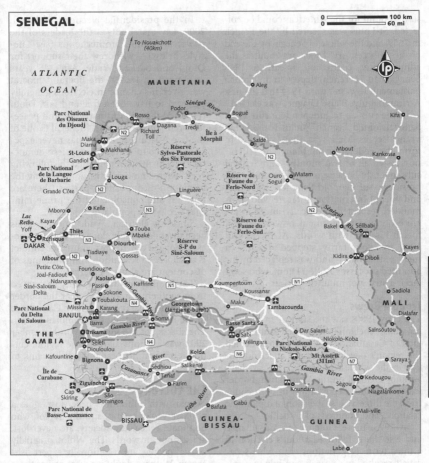

SENEGAL

To Nouakchott
(40km)

ATLANTIC
OCEAN

MAURITANIA

0   100 km
0   60 mi

among the region's best. Down south, Casamance is like a troubled movie starlet, desired and pitied by everyone. Wherever you go, the Senegalese people constantly amuse and occasionally even exasperate with their boundless wit, smooth talking charm and irrepressible will to connect.

HISTORY

Proud, optimistic, dynamic, democratic and economically booming, Senegal at first glance seems to have a lot going its way, especially when seen in its regional context. Throw in words like rural exodus, urban poverty, social and economic inequality, mass unemployment, juvenile delinquency, drug abuse and southern separatism, however, and a different picture begins to emerge. The truth is Senegal is all of these things.

Auspicious Beginnings

Senegal has been occupied for 15,000 years or more and was part of the empire of Ghana in the 8th century and the Djolof kingdom, in the area between the Senegal River and modern-day Dakar, during the 13th and 14th centuries. In the early 16th century, Portuguese traders made contact with coastal kingdoms, they were the first in a long line of 'interested' foreigners: the British, French and Dutch soon followed jostling for control of strategic points where slaves bound for the Americas could be collected. St-Louis was secured by the French in 1659, and the whole of Senegal by the end of the 19th century. Dakar was built as the administrative centre, and as early as 1848 Senegal had a (French) deputy in the French parliament. It wasn't until 1914 that the first African deputy, Blaise Diagne, was elected.

In the run-up to independence in 1960, Senegal joined French Sudan (or Soudan Francaise, as Mali was then known) to form the Federation of Mali. The federation lasted all of two months, and Senegal subsequently became a republic under the presidency of Leopold Senghor, a socialist and poet of international stature who commanded respect domestically and abroad. His economic management, however, didn't match his way with words. At the end of 1980, he voluntarily stepped down – a mark of the man – and was replaced by his anointed successor Abdou Diouf, who soon faced a string of mounting crises.

Trouble Brews

The early 1980s saw the start of an ongoing separatist rebellion in the prized southern region of Casamance that has severely dented the region's development and affected tourism in the whole country. Seven years later a minor incident on the Mauritanian border led to riots and deportations in both countries, the three-year suspension of diplomatic relations, and hundreds of casualties.

In 1993, more violence, in Casamance and elsewhere, followed Diouf's election to a third term. Negotiations with rebel separatists resulted in a ceasefire in July that collapsed three years later. Tensions mounted in other parts of the country as a result of austerity measures introduced by the government, such as utilities privatisations and the halving of the value of the CFA franc, designed to put an end to the long-term shrinking of the economy. In February 1994 the government, made increasingly paranoid by civil unrest, arrested opposition leader Abdoulaye Wade on charges of sedition, however it could barely contain the reaction to his incarceration and he was released three months later. Although the economy has since grown at an average annual rate of 5%, there is little evidence the benefits are trickling down. For the vast majority of Senegalese, life is still a struggle.

In the presidential elections of March 2000, key marabouts – the leaders of the powerful Islamic brotherhoods (see Lifestyle, below) – withdrew their support for Diouf and backed Wade. After 25 years as opposition leader, the liberal-democrat was given his chance in elections generally believed to have been free and fair. Diouf respected the will of the people and peacefully relinquished power. (Senegal is one of the few African states that has never experienced a coup d'état.) Senegalese democracy was further strengthened the following year, when a new constitution allowing the formation of opposition parties (there are now 65) and consolidated the prime minister's role was popularly approved.

Since his election, Wade's progress has been disappointingly slow: the reform process is bogged down, the Casamance conflict is no closer to resolution and rumblings of discontent are already emerging.

The conflict's centre of gravity has moved from southern Casamance, near the border with Guinea-Bissau, to northern Casamance in the region abutting the Gambian border. The sinking of the Joola ferry in November 2002 was a painful blow to the region, cutting it off from its best and quickest link to the capital.

THE CULTURE

'A man with a mouth is never lost,' goes a popular Wolof saying, and the Wolof, who dominate Senegalese society, are never lost, at least not for words. The Wolof, originally coastal people, are traditionally expert fishermen. Without doubt it's what makes them such skilful navigators of the mouth; perhaps it explains why they are so enamored of the art of conversation. Senegal is a society in a constant state of communication, verbal, musical and physical. The words flow endlessly, the storytellers are always a step ahead of their audience, and the truth is rarely allowed to get in the way of a good story.

Lifestyle

Senegalese society is conservative, heavily reliant on tradition, and overwhelmingly Muslim. It has its own unique version of Islam that blends traditional beliefs with a reliance on the priesthood and veneration of saints. Virtually all adherents belong to one of five brotherhoods, the two principal ones being the Mourides, based in Touba and Diourbel, and the Tidjanes, based in Kaolack and Tivaouane.

Marabouts, or Islamic holy men, play a central role in social life. They not only head the brotherhoods, thus wielding enormous political power (they are widely believed to hold the power to cast the fate of the country's top politicians), they are often called on as healers, advisers and casters of spells, giving them a position of unparalleled eminence.

People

Estimates put the current population at around 10.6 million. About 85% are Muslim and Wolof is the lingua franca.

The dominant ethnic group is the Wolof (about 35% of the population), who live mostly in the central area, north and east of Dakar and along the coast. The Sérèr (17%) also live in the central regions, while the Fula (12%), also called Fulbe and Peul, live throughout northern and eastern Senegal. Other groups include the Tukulor in the north; the Malinké or Mandinka in the areas bordering The Gambia; and the Diola (also called Jola), who live almost exclusively in the Casamance.

ARTS

Senegal is world-renowned for its music. Once-dominant, salsa has been overshadowed by a variety of popular musical forms, particularly the high energy *mbalax*

dance music, whose most famous exponent is Youssou N'Dour. Mbalax blends traditional percussion with Latin sounds and a pop sensibility. Senegal also has a distinguished literary tradition, whose pre-eminent figure is Senegal's former President Senghor.

SPORT

The Senegalese are mad about sport, so don't be surprised to see joggers, often running barefoot along the beach or congested Dakar thoroughfares. Traditional wrestling is popular – bouts are staged most weekends in Dakar – but football (soccer) reigns supreme. Senegal's march to the 2002 World Cup quarter finals – knocking over France, former colonial masters and the reigning champions, in the process – was a huge achievement not just for the country but for the whole continent. It's a good idea to bring a deflated soccer ball and small pump with you. Fill it, and players will come.

ENVIRONMENT

Senegal consists mainly of flat plains, cut by three major rivers: the Senegal River in the north, which forms the border with Mauritania; the Gambia River in the middle, which is surrounded by the small country of The Gambia; and the Casamance River in the south, which gives its name to the surrounding Casamance area, a fertile zone of forest and farmland.

THE RHYTHM OF LIFE

Among many West African cultures, music is not just a decorative entertainment; it's the manifestation of a divine spirit. Little wonder, then, that singing, dancing and the playing of traditional instruments such as the kora, a kind of cross between a harp and a lute, have assumed the stature of an act of veneration that reinforces the music's emphasis on physical pleasure and joy.

But not just anyone can pick up a kora and start strumming: the playing of traditional music, as opposed to popular forms, is reserved for the *griots*, otherwise known as *jalis* or *gawlos*, a caste into which one can only be born. Griots play a crucial, complex social role, but enjoy a relatively low social status: alongside the *forgerons* (smiths), who through the use of fire have the quasi-mystical ability to change the shapes of metal objects, they rank among the artisans, just one level above the descendants of slaves. Griots are the custodians of the past in a culture that's oral rather than written. It's this knowledge of the past, combined with their musical prowess, that can make them alternately objects of respect, derision and fear.

Once translators and diplomats to the royal courts, today they are akin to singing historians and genealogists, invited to the most important social events such as weddings and naming ceremonies and lavishly paid to recite epics and family histories – the equivalent, perhaps, of a librarian, a gossipy grandmother and a sidewalk folksinger rolled into one.

The best time to travel in Senegal is between November and March, when it's cool and dry. At this time the harmattan, a dry, dusty wind, blows off the Sahara, and the skyline may be hazy. In northern and central Senegal the rainy season is July to September; in Casamance it is June to early October.

National Parks

The only place to see large animals in Senegal is in Parc National du Niokolo-Koba. There are very few protected areas.

Other national parks are in coastal regions (including the Saloum Delta, the Langue de Barbarie and the Parc National des Oiseaux du Djoudj) and are noted for their bird-watching.

Environmental Issues

Desertification is the greatest problem facing Senegal, especially in the north of the country, site of overgrazing and small-scale timber harvesting outside of the irrigated areas.

There is also intense competition between pastoralists and nomadic herders for both water and land resources. The farmers have begun to move into the marginal areas that were once the preserve of Fulani pastoralists and their cattle, sheep and goats. The farmers have a limited understanding of the nature of the new environment, and chop out drought-resistant species (which are eaten but not overgrazed by stock) to replace them with peanuts, a cash crop introduced by the French in the 19th century. The peanut is not a friend of the soil – when harvested, the whole plant is removed and no organic matter is left. When the harmattan wind lashes the soil, the loose sand is blown away. Meanwhile, pastures well understood by the Fulani herders continue to diminish.

TRANSPORT

GETTING THERE & AWAY
Air

For flying between Europe and Senegal you have a wide choice of airlines, including Air France and Alitalia. Fares from London start at US$350 return, rising another US$100 in the high season (October to May).

The departure tax is US$20 or CFA10,000, but most airfares already have that included in the price.

Land
THE GAMBIA

From Dakar there are minibuses (US$5) and taxi-brousse (bush taxis; US$10) south to Barra in The Gambia. (See the Getting Around section following for an explanation of these transport options.) From Barra the ferry crosses to Banjul (US$0.30). The journey takes five to seven hours depending on your luck with connections and the ferry (the last ferry crosses at 7pm).

From southern Senegal, bush taxis (US$4, five hours) and buses (US$3.50, five hours) run regularly between Ziguinchor and Serekunda (which is west of Banjul in The Gambia), and bush taxis run between Kafountine and Brikama (US$2, two hours).

In eastern Senegal, bush taxis go from Tambacounda to Vélingara (US$3, three hours), and then from Vélingara to Basse Santa Su (US$1, one hour).

GUINEA

The best place to pick up transport to Guinea is Tambacounda in eastern Senegal, where bush taxis ply the route to Labé (US$27, about 24 hours). Most traffic passes via Diaoubé (Senegal) and Koundara (Guinea), where you may have to change, and some goes via Kedougou (Senegal). Some vehicles travel the whole route between Dakar and Koundara (US$34, about 25 hours).

GUINEA-BISSAU

Bush taxis leave every morning from Ziguinchor to Bissau via the border post at São Domingos and Ingore (US$6.50, about six hours). The road is paved but crosses two rivers, which can cause delays; start early. There are pirogues (dugout canoes) if the ferries aren't operating, but you'll need to change transport on the other side of the river if you take a pirogue (you may not have a choice as the ferries are frequently out of action).

The route between Ziguinchor and Bissau via Canchungo is not viable as there is no longer a ferry between São Domingos and Cacheu.

MALI

The usual way to travel from Senegal to Mali is on the Dakar–Bamako international express train, which departs from Dakar at around 10am on Wednesday and Saturday, and takes 30 to 35 hours to reach Bamako.

Large, comfortable 1st-class seats can be reserved in advance; 2nd class is more crowded with less comfortable seating. All classes have air-con. From Dakar to Bamako, 1st/2nd class fares are US$56/41, and *couchettes* (two-person compartments) cost US$83 per person. From Dakar to Kayes, fares in 1st/2nd class are US$32/24. There are two trains on this route: the Senegalese-operated train usually leaves Dakar on Wednesday and is markedly superior to, safer than, and about 15% more expensive than its Malian counterpart, which usually leaves Dakar on Saturday.

You can buy tickets the day before the train departs, and reserve a seat in couchette and first class. To be sure of a seat in 2nd class, get to the train about two hours before it leaves. The train has a bar and restaurant car, and you can buy cheap food at stations along the way.

At each border post you have to get your passport stamped. An inspector on the train may take it, but you still have to collect it yourself by going to the office at the border post. Nobody tells you this. So if your passport is taken, ask where and when you have to go to collect it. You may need a stamp at the police station in Kayes too, but this seems fairly arbitrary. Watch out for thieves on the train, especially at night.

If you prefer to skip the train, from Tambacounda minibuses and bush taxis run 180km along a new highway to Kidira (US$4/6.50, three hours). Crossing the road bridge at Kidira leads to Doboli, in Mali, from where bush taxis to Kayes cost US$4.

MAURITANIA
Bush taxis run regularly from Dakar to the main border point at Rosso (US$7.50, from St-Louis US$1.50). A pirogue across the river costs US$1 per person. From immigration it's 500m to the gare routière, where bush taxis run to Nouakchott. The whole journey can be done in a day if you leave early.

GETTING AROUND
Air
Air Senegal has daily flights from Dakar to Ziguinchor (US$71, one way), continuing to Cap Skiring twice weekly. There's one weekly flight to Tambacounda. A hint: confirm, and then confirm again.

Local Transport
The main routes between Dakar, Kaolack, Ziguinchor and other large towns are covered by *grand cars* (buses) carrying 30 to 40 people, and good quality *petit cars* (minibuses), with 15 to 25 seats. On many routes you also find more rustic minibuses (sometimes rather misleadingly called *car rapides*). They are battered, slow, crowded and worth avoiding if possible.

Your other option for long-distance travel is a bush taxi, or *taxi-brousse*. On the main routes these are usually Peugeot 504s with three rows of seats; they are safe and reliable. On rural routes, bush taxis are pick-ups (sometimes called *bâchés*), which seat about 12 people on benches. Fares are reasonable. Buses cost about one-third less than bush taxis, and minibuses are somewhere in between. There's normally an extra, negotiable charge for luggage (about 10% of the bill).

Each town has a *gare routière* where these vehicles wait for passengers. By repeating the name of your destination, you'll find transport without a problem, so you can ignore the touts, who gain a commission for scouting for passengers.

Train
There is a twice-weekly service (Wednesday and Saturday) from Dakar to Thiès and Tambacounda (and on to Bamako in Mali). For Tambacounda, the fare in 1st/2nd class is US$20/15, but it's wiser to take a bus, bush taxi or minibus.

DAKAR

pop 2 million
Relentless and complex, Dakar is a giant termite nest, tough on the outside and teeming with life on the inside. It's an uncut jewel where grinding poverty rubs shoulders with the jetset, the cosmopolitan centre of power where expats, French military types and the local glitterati take bites out of each other, and the peninsular magnet where everyone's a hustler and hard-luck stories are the common currency. Life is often cheap in Dakar and the cost of living is invariably high – just being here raises your metabolic rate. Love it or loathe it, it provides all the atmosphere, colour, scents and activity an African city has to offer. Dakar is the real deal.

SENEGAL

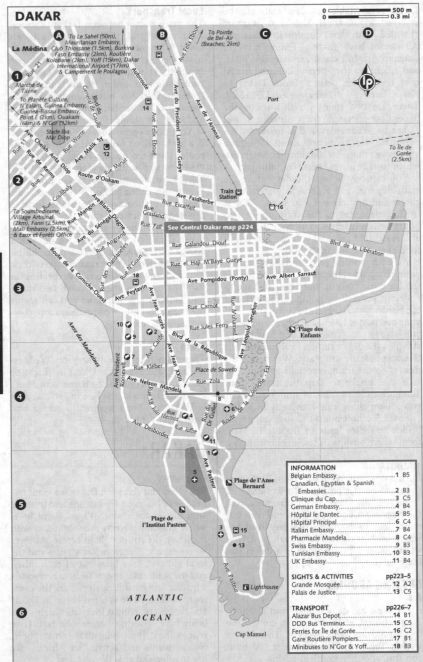

DAKAR

0 ————— 500 m
0 ————— 0.3 mi

ATLANTIC OCEAN

Cap Manuel

INFORMATION
Belgian Embassy 1 B5
Canadian, Egyptian & Spanish
    Embassies 2 B3
Clinique du Cap 3 C5
German Embassy 4 B4
Hôpital le Dantec 5 B5
Hôpital Principal 6 C4
Italian Embassy 7 B4
Pharmacie Mandela 8 C4
Swiss Embassy 9 B3
Tunisian Embassy 10 B3
UK Embassy 11 B4

SIGHTS & ACTIVITIES   pp223–5
Grande Mosquée 12 A2
Palais de Justice 13 C5

TRANSPORT   pp226–7
Alazar Bus Depot 14 B1
DDD Bus Terminus 15 C5
Ferries for Île de Gorée 16 C2
Gare Routière Pompiers 17 B1
Minibuses to N'Gor & Yoff 18 B3

ORIENTATION

A massive square called Place de l'Indépendance (usually simply called the 'Place') is the city's heart. From here, major streets lead in all directions, including Ave Leopold Senghor (which passes the Palais Présidentiel) and Ave Pompidou, the main street, which leads west to Marché Sandaga. From here, Ave du President Lamine Guéye goes north to Gare Routière Pompiers and the auto-route, which leads inland.

The train station is 3km north of Place de l'Indépendance, and the airport is 19km north of the town centre.

INFORMATION
Bookshops

Librairie Aux Quatre Vents (Map p224; ☎ 821 8083; Rue Félix Faure)

Librairie Clairafrique (Map p224; Place de l'Indépendance)

Cultural Centres

The **American Cultural Center** (Map p224; ☎ 823 1185; Ave Léopold Senghor) and the **British Council** (Map p224; ☎ 822 2015; Blvd de la République) both have libraries. The **French Cultural Centre** (Map p224; ☎ 823 0320; Rue Gomis) has a lively cultural programme throughout the year.

Internet Access

There are many Internet cafés in Dakar. One of the best is **Afriser** (Map p224; Ave Allès Delmas; per hr US$0.80), north of the Place.

Media

Free listings magazines, *Dakar Tam Tam* and *L'Avis*, are available from major hotels and travel agencies. They include details of restaurants, travel agencies, hospitals, embassies and entertainment venues.

Medical Services

For emergencies, try the **Hôpital Principal** (Map p222; ☎ 839 5050; Ave Léopold Senghor). Nearby, **Pharmacie Mandela** (Map p222; ☎ 821 2172) is one of several 24-hour pharmacies. For minor injuries and illnesses, seek out a consular recommendation.

Money

On the western side of the Place are three banks, **CBAO** (Map p224) with ATM accepting both Visa and MasterCard-linked cards, **BICIS** (Map p224) and **Citibank** (Map p224). CBAO has the quickest service. The **Bureau de Change** (Map p224; Ave Allès R Delmas) offers slightly better rates. Among the vultures hovering outside the banks on the Place are black market traders – careful they don't short-change (or rob) you.

Post & Telephone

Other than the **main post office** (Map p224; PTT; Blvd el Haji Djily Mbaye; ☒ Mon-Sat, closed at lunch time), there's also a small PTT at the east end of Ave Pompidou.

For phone calls, try **Sonatel** (Map p224; Rue Wagane Diouf & Blvd de la République; ☒ 7am-11pm), Senegal's internal phone service. There are also many private **télécentres**, some of which have also have Internet access.

Travel Agencies

Senegal Tours (Map p224; ☎ 839 9900; Place de l'Indépendance) is an American Express agent, makes flight reservations and sells tours.

Also recommended for tours, information and bookings and are **M'boup Voyages** (Map p224; ☎ 821 8163; Place de l'Indépendance), where some staff speak English, and **Nouvelle Frontières** (Map p224; ☎ 823 3434; 3 Blvd de la République).

DANGERS & ANNOYANCES

Dakar has a bad reputation for muggings, scams and petty theft such as pickpocketing, frequently in broad daylight, especially around beaches, markets, central city banks and any crowded areas. Less worrying, but equally annoying, are street traders and hustlers. Deal with them either by ignoring them or replying with a firm but polite *non merci*.

SIGHTS & ACTIVITIES

The **IFAN Museum** (Map p224; Institut Fondamental d'Afrique Noir; Place de Soweto; admission US$3.50; ☒ 8am-12.30pm & 2-6.30pm) has an impressive collection of masks, statues, musical instruments and agricultural implements from all over West Africa. A return visit, after experiencing West Africa first-hand, is rewarding. The **Assemblée Nationale** is next door.

Five blocks south, the white **Palais Présidentiel** (Map p224; Ave Leopold Senghor) dates from 1907 and is surrounded by sumptuous gardens (the resplendent guards occasionally permit photos).

Also out of the city centre is the **Grande Mosquée** (Map p222; Ave Malik Sy), built in 1964 with

CENTRAL DAKAR

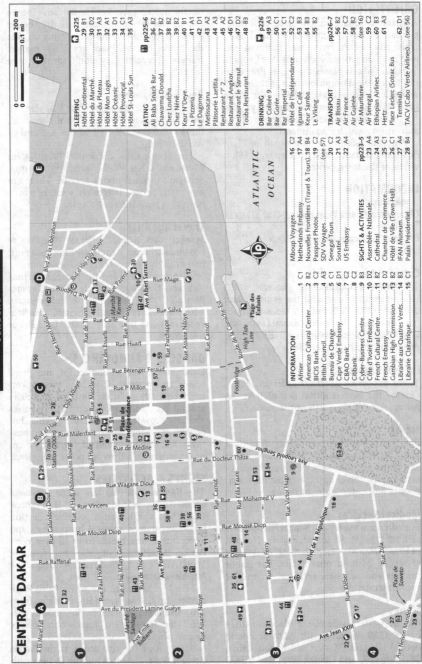

SENEGAL

INFORMATION	
Afriser	1 C1
American Cultural Center	2 B2
BICIS Bank	3 C2
British Council	4 A3
Bureau de Change	5 C1
Cape Verde Embassy	6 D1
CBAO Bank	7 C2
Citibank	8 C2
Cyber-Business Centre	9 B3
Côte d'Ivoire Embassy	10 D2
French Cultural Centre	11 B2
French Embassy	12 D2
Gambian High Commission	13 B2
Librairie aux Quatres Vents	14 B3
Librairie Clairafrique	15 C1
Mboup Voyages	16 C2
Netherlands Embassy	17 A4
Nouvelles Frontières (Travel & Tours)	18 B4
Passport Photos	19 C2
SDV Voyages	(see 57)
Senegal Tours	20 C2
Sonatel	21 A3
US Embassy	22 A4

SIGHTS & ACTIVITIES	pp223–5
Assemblée Nationale	23 A4
Cathedral	24 A3
Chambre de Commerce	25 C1
Hôtel de Ville (Town Hall)	26 C1
IFAN Museum	27 A4
Palais Présidentiel	28 B4

SLEEPING	p225
Hôtel Continental	29 B1
Hôtel du Marché	30 D2
Hôtel du Plateau	31 A3
Hôtel Mon Logis	32 A1
Hôtel Océanic	33 D1
Hôtel Provençal	34 C1
Hôtel St-Louis Sun	35 A3

EATING	pp225–6
Ali Baba Snack Bar	36 B2
Chawarma Donald	37 B2
Chez Loutcha	38 B2
Chez Néné	39 B2
Keur N'Deye	40 B1
La Pizzeria	41 A1
Le Dagorne	42 D1
Metissacana	43 A2
Pâtisserie Laetitia	44 A3
Restaurant '?' 2	45 A2
Restaurant Angkor	46 D1
Restaurant le Sarraut	47 D2
Touba Restaurant	48 B3

DRINKING	p226
Bar Colisée 9	49 A3
Bar Gorée	50 C1
Bar l'Imperial	51 C1
Hôtel de l'Indépendance	52 C2
Iguane Café	53 B3
Keur Samba	54 B3
Le Viking	55 B2

TRANSPORT	pp226–7
Air Bissau	56 B2
Air France	57 C2
Air Guinée	58 B2
Air Mauritanie	(see 16)
Air Senegal	59 C2
Ethiopian Airlines	60 B3
Hertz	61 A3
Place Leclerc (Sotrac Bus Terminal)	62 D1
TACV (Cabo Verde Airlines)	(see 56)

its landmark minaret, floodlit at night. The mosque is closed to the public, but it's worth coming here anyway because the area around it, called **La Médina**, while not picturesque, is a bustling place that contrasts sharply with the sophisticated central city. Travellers are rare here and you won't be hassled.

The fishing village of **Soumbédioune** (Map p222), west of the city centre, is where pirogues beach at dusk, and is well worth a visit, as are the private beaches of Bel-Air, **Plage Monaco** (Map p222) and **Plage Voile d'Or** (Map p222), 3km northeast of the city, which are fenced and have bars, restaurants and cabins. There is a US$1 entry fee to either beach. At the other beaches near central Dakar you run a high risk of being robbed. Better are the beaches at **N'Gor**, 13km northwest of Dakar (and the nearby Pointe des Almadies), and **Yoff**.

Top-end hotels have pools that can be enjoyed for a fee. The pool at the Hôtel de l'Indépendance charges US$5 for its facilities, which include a great view of Dakar, or it's free with a meal.

SLEEPING

Good, cheap accommodation is hard to find in Dakar. It's worth deciding in advance on your first night's accommodation, or booking in advance if you can (even if it means going above your normal budget for a night or two), and going directly there without wandering the streets with a backpack. You can always look for somewhere cheaper the next day. If you'll be in Dakar for a week or more, think about staying in Yoff or on Île de Gorée: what you lose in time spent getting in and out of town you'll save in money and enjoyment.

Hôtel Continental (Map p224; ☎ 822 1083; 10 Rue Galandou Diouf; s/d US$20/22) Perhaps the best in the budget category, the Continental is decent and friendly and has a wide choice of rooms.

Hôtel Provençal (Map p224; ☎ 822 1069; 17 Rue Malenfant; s/d US$17/21) Near the Place, this central and quiet place has good-value, airy upstairs rooms with washbasins.

Hôtel du Marché (Map p224; ☎ 821 5771; 3 Rue Parent; s/d US$19/20) Boasts a lovely back patio and large, airy rooms.

Hôtel Oceanic (Map p224; ☎ 822 2044, fax 821 5228; 9 Rue du Thann; s/d with bathroom US$35/42; 🖳) Homely and with large, clean rooms with small balconies. There's a bar/restaurant downstairs.

Campement le Poulagou (Map p222; ☎ 8202347; s/d US$10/20, half board US$14.70/29.40) Outside the city centre, near the airport in Yoff village and only 100m from a beach, this camp site has basic doubles and triples. Ask the owner if he can pick you up from the airport; to get there from the city centre take DDD bus No 8 to Yoff; it is at the end of a small road off the main road.

Also recommended are two mid-range places, the comfortable **Hôtel du Plateau** (Map p224; ☎ 823 4420; fax 822 5025; 62 Rue Jules Ferry; s/d US$40/44); and the more attractive **Hôtel St-Louis Sun** (Map p224; ☎ 822 2570; 68 Rue Félix Faure; s/d US$38/48), where a pleasant courtyard features two gorgeous palm trees.

EATING

Senegal stakes a healthy claim to being West Africa's culinary capital. On street corners are stalls selling bread with various fillings – butter, chocolate spread, mayonnaise, sardines. Next to the stalls, particularly along Rue Assane Ndoye, women cook rice and sauce in big pots, and serve meals for around US$1. Lebanese *shwarmas* (grilled meat wrapped in bread) are sold throughout the city.

Pâtisserie Laetitia (Map p224; cnr Blvd de la République & Rue Mohamed V; 🕑 Mon-Sat & Sun mornings) A recommended bakery which serves good coffee and pastries from US$1.

Chawarma Donald (Map p224; Ave Pompidou; mains US$1.20-2.50) A good place to buy filling *shwarmas* and *fajayas* (similar to samosas). The food is just as good at the **Ali Baba Snack Bar** across the street, but you pay a bit extra for the classier setting.

For African food in pleasant surroundings, the best-value places are: **Chez Néné** (Map p224; cnr Rue Assane Ndoye & Rue Mohamed V; mains US$2-3.50); and **Restaurant '?' 2** ('Restaurant Point d'Interrogation'; Map p224; near cnr Rue Assane Ndoye & Rue Gomis; mains from US$2).

Touba Restaurant (Map p224; Rue Gomis; mains from US$2) A neighbourhood joint with *mafé* (groundnut sauce), *poisson riz* (fish and rice) and chicken on the menu.

Metissacana (Map p224; 30 Rue de Thiong; mains US$3-5.60) This is a great place to eat barbequed meat. There is a downstairs restaurant, an upstairs open-air patio and a bar.

Chez Loutcha (Map p224; ☎ 821 0302; 101 Rue Moussé Diop; mains US$4-7) A smarter restaurant and one with a deservedly popular reputation, it caters for all tastes with a menu that includes Cap

SENEGAL

Verdean, Senegalese, regional and European specialties, and the servings are huge.

Keur N'deye (Map p224; ☎ 821 4973; 68 Rue Vincens; mains around US$5, set menus from US$8) Another smart establishment, there are occasional performances by griot kora musicians.

Other eateries worth checking out include: **La Pizzeria** (Map p224; 47 Rue el Hadj Abdoukarim Bourgi; mains US$5.60-6) for excellent pizza and pasta; **Restaurant Le Sarraut** (Map p224; Ave Albert Sarraut; 3-course meal US$11) for good French cuisine; and **Restaurant Angkor** (Map p224; Rue Dagorne; mains US$4-6) for good-value Chinese food (despite the name).

SPLURGE!

Especially recommended is **Le Dagorne** (Map p224; cnr Rue Dagorne & Rue Parent; mains US$8-16) near Marché Kermel, with a bustling, energetic atmosphere inside, and courtyard seating outside. The superb menu is well worth the splurge.

DRINKING

Bar L'Impérial (Map p224; Place de l'Indépendance; 🕙 10am-3am) At the northern end of the Place, this is a stylish place for a quiet ale.

Bar Colisée 9 (Map p224; cnr Ave du President Lamine Guéye & Rue Félix Faure; 🕙 10am-3am) Another smart place on a strip that features several watering holes.

Bar Gorée (Map p224; 🕙 10am-3am) Almost opposite the Gorée ferry wharf, has cheap beer, snacks and music. It's popular with sailors and anyone who wants a good time without busting the bank.

Le Viking (Map p224; 🕙 10am-3am) One of several watering holes along Ave Pompidou, this is a Western-style sports bar.

The main hotels all have bars. They're more expensive, less interesting and feel a little safer – the best of them is the rooftop bar at **Hôtel de l'Indépendance** (Map p224; Place de l'Indépendance).

CLUBBING

Dakar is one of the best cities in West Africa for live music and clubbing. Admission on the most popular nights is usually US$4 to US$5.

Club Thiossane (Map p222; ☎ 824 6046; Sicap Rue 10; 🕙 9pm-6am) A hot, crowded place in La Médina owned by international music star

Youssou N'Dour. He often performs here. It's hard to find it but taxi drivers know it.

Le Sahel (Map p222; ☎ 821 2118; Centre Commercial Sahm; 🕙 9pm-6am) Similar to Thiossane and just as popular, it's about 3km north of Marché Sandaga.

Planète Culture (Map p222; Ave Cheikh Anta Diop, Point E; 🕙 Mon-Sat) Owned by a local band it specialises in live acoustic music.

N'galam (Map p222; Ave de l'Est, Point E) Also in Point E, this is a club that only gets going just before dawn. It's popular with locals and plays great Senegalese music.

There are several clubs in the central city. **Keur Samba** (Map p222; 13 Rue Jules Ferry) is a Western-style club; while Iguane Café, opposite, is smaller, cosier and more popular.

ENTERTAINMENT

Traditional Senegalese wrestling matches (les lutes, in French) are held most weekends during the dry season (less often during Ramadan), starting around 4pm, at or near the large **Stade Iba Mar Diop** (Map p222; Route d'Ouakam, La Médina). Matches last only a few minutes, until one contestant forces the other to the ground, but there can be many fights and the event can go on for hours. Every section of town has its heroes – the event can be very lively.

SHOPPING

Dakar has two major markets. Both are very lively, deservedly popular with travellers and thus magnets for tourist leeches. Ignore them; if you can't, hire one as a guide.

Marché Kermel (Map p224) East of the Place towards the port, this market is in a smart new hall built after a 1993 fire, and is more touristy.

Marché Sandaga (Map p224; cnr Ave Pompidou & Ave du President Lamine Guèye) Large and with more fruit and fewer souvenirs. The choice of fabric provides the main attraction.

Village Artisanal (Map p222) For souvenirs, Soumbédioune's Artisanal, on the Corniche-Ouest, caters for the traveller trade, but prices are high and the work is nothing special.

GETTING THERE & AWAY
Air

For a one-way flight back to Europe, **Nouvelles Frontières** (☎ 823 3443; Ave Pompidou), sometimes has cheap seats on charter flights for around US$400.

For flights between Dakar and other destinations in West Africa there's a wide choice, including Abidjan (US$285 one way), Accra (US$45 one way), Bamako (US$135 one way), Banjul (US$8 one way), Bissau (US$165 one way), Cape Verde (US$22 one way to Praia), Conakry (US$135 one way), Niamey (US$43 one way) and Nouakchott (US$13 one way). Most airline offices are on or near the Place de l'Indépendance in Dakar, but it can be easier to use a travel agency; compare prices before buying.

Local Transport

Road transport for long-distance destinations leaves from Gare Routière Pompiers off Ave Malik Sy, 3km north of the Place (a taxi should cost around US$1.50). To Ziguinchor costs about US$1 by bush taxi (one hour) or US$8 by minibus (11 hours), all vehicles leave before noon. Bush taxis/minibuses go to M'bour (US$2/1.80), Kaolack (US$4.50/2.50), St-Louis (US$5/4), Tambacounda (US$11/8), and the Gambian town of Barra (US$10/5).

Local transport for nearer towns, such as Thiès (US$1.50) and Rufisque (US$1), occasionally terminate at Gare Routière Kolobane, about 2km further away from the city centre on the other side of the autoroute.

Train

Dakar's train station is 500m north of Place de l'Indépendance. For more information on Senegal's trains, see the Transport section on p221.

GETTING AROUND
Bus

Travel around Dakar on the Dakar Dem Dikk (DDD) bus network costs between US$0.20 and US$0.30 depending on the length of the ride. If there is no DDD bus, consider the privately owned white minibuses, which follow the same routes. Useful DDD routes include: No 5 to Guédiawaye; No 6 to Cambérene; No 7 to Ouakam; No 8 to Yoff and the airport; No 9 to Liberté VI, No 15 to Rufisque; and No 16 to Malika. Buses for destinations east of Dakar leave from the terminal on Blvd de la Libération; other lines terminate at the old Palais de Justice, near the tip of Cap Manuel (Map p222).

DDD city bus No 8 goes to the city centre and stops only a few hundred metres

from the airport; these run between 6am and 9pm.

Car

You may consider teaming up with other backpackers and hiring a car to reach places around Dakar that aren't served by public transport, but rental is not cheap. Hertz and Avis, for example, charge from US$3 a day plus US$0.3 per kilometre, US$6.5 per day for insurance and 20% tax for their most compact cars. Some smaller outfits have cheaper deals available. The cheapest of them is **Assurcar** (☎ 823 7251), which charges US$17 per day for a Peugeot 204, plus US$0.2 per kilometre.

Taxi

Dakar's taxis have meters but they are rarely used, so you must agree on a price before you get in (as the locals do). Short trips (such as from Place de l'Indépendance to Gare Routière Pompiers) should cost under US$2.50. The official taxi rates for trips from Leopold Senghor international airport (formerly Dakar-Yoff) into the city centre are posted in the arrivals hall – US$5 during the day and about US$6 from midnight to 6am. Going to the airport, you can sometimes get a taxi for around US$4.

When arriving at the airport, insist on hauling your own luggage and choosing your own taxi.

AROUND DAKAR

ILE DE GORÉE

The 28-hectare Ile de Gorée has retained a lively sense of community despite an ongoing facelift and the flood of money that's poured in since it was listed as a World Heritage Site by Unesco. It's a superbly mellow place, with colonial-style houses, trailing bougainvillea, a small beach with pirogues parked on the sand, cheap food and accommodation, no roads, no cars or bikes and only a few hustlers. Although it's busy at weekends, it's the perfect place to wander around, and its proximity to Dakar makes it a recommended alternative to staying in the central city.

If you hire one of the guides who hover around the Dakar port terminal, expect to pay about US$4 for half a day (it's essential to agree on the price first).

SENEGAL

On a rocky plateau at the far end of the island there is an old fort called **Le Castel** (inhabited by a group of hippyish Baye Fall disciples), with fortifications and great views of the island and back across to Dakar. The nearby cliffs featured in the movie *The Guns of Navarone*.

Sights & Activities

Gorée's status as one of the busiest slave centres in West Africa during the 18th and 19th centuries is debatable – The Gambia's Jufureh and Ghana's slave forts are undoubtedly more authentic. Even so, a visit to the famous **Maison des Esclaves** (The Slave House; admission US$0.50), brings slavery's inhumanity to life, and the excellent **IFAN Historical Museum** (admission US$0.30; ☼ 10am-1pm & 2.30-6pm Tue-Sat) in the Fort d'Estrées at the north end of the island, and the **Musée de la Femme** (admission US$0.50; ☼ 10am-5pm Tue-Sun) are also recommended. All museums close on Monday.

There's also a small **tourist market**, just behind the row of bars and restaurants, where the bargaining is slightly more relaxed than in Dakar.

Sleeping & Eating

As you come off the ferry you'll see several small bars and restaurants around the small port. These all serve meals for around US$5. Ask at any of these places about renting a room with locals. The going rate is US$13 per night, but bargaining may lower the price a little.

The cheapest official place, and also the tourist office, is the **Syndicat d'Initiative** (☎ 822 9703; s/d US$16/24). It wasn't offering accommodation at the time of writing, but this is subject to change. Very good value is **Asao** (☎ 821 8105; Rue St-Joseph; d US$16), with three beautiful rooms, for two, three (US$32, with a terrace) and four people (US$40, with a living room).

The stylish **Auberge Keur Beer** (☎ 821 3801; 1 Rue du Port; s/d US$30/37, with bathroom US$37/41) has comfortable double rooms that include breakfast. At the charming **Hostellerie du Chevalier de Boufflers** (☎ 822 5364; mains US$6-10), rooms cost about the same but are more airy.

Getting There & Away

From Dakar the *chaloupe* (ferry) to Gorée leaves every one to two hours from the dock

area between 6am and 11pm. The dock area is a 10-minute walk north of the 'Place'. The ferry trip across takes two minutes and costs foreigners US$8 for a return trip.

LAC RETBA

Dakar tour companies call Retba 'Lac Rose' because of a pink colouring caused by a high mineral and salt content which makes for very buoyant swimming. It's a popular Dakarois picnic spot attracting tour groups and, inevitably, souvenir sellers, and has achieved notoriety in modern times as the terminus of the annual Paris–Dakar motor rally.

British-run **Bonaba Café** (☎ 638 7538; half board US$15) is the best place to stay and eat: to get there, walk over the dunes away from the tourists for 2km, keeping the water on your right or hire a pirogue from the salt village for US$5. A kid will take you there for a small fee.

Take a No 11 DDD bus or a minibus from Dakar to Malika or Keur Massar, and a bush taxi or minibus from there to Niaga (US$0.50). Then it's a 5km walk. Or you could spend US$32 on a round trip by taxi.

NORTHERN SENEGAL

ST-LOUIS
pop 150,000

No city oozes faded colonial charm more than St-Louis, making it one of Senegal's highlights and a welcome sight for overlanders descending from Mauritania. At the mouth of the Senegal River, the city is in three parts: the area called Sor, on the mainland; the old town on an island with most of the colonial buildings, the site of the former colonial capital; and part of the Langue de Barbarie Peninsula. You reach the island on the 500m-long **Pont Faidherbe**, originally built to cross the Danube but shipped here in 1897. Two smaller bridges link the island to **Guet N'Dar**, a lively African fishing community on the peninsula. About 3km north of Guet N'Dar is the Mauritanian border, which is a restricted area.

Information

The helpful Syndicat d'Initiative **tourist office** (☎ 961 2455; Rue Milles Lacroix; www.saintlouisdusenegal.com) provides all kinds of information.

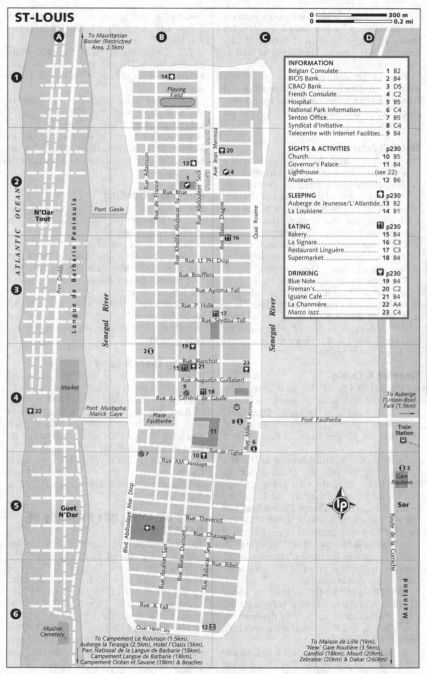

ST-LOUIS

| | 0 | 300 m |
| | 0 | 0.2 mi |

INFORMATION
Belgian Consulate	1	B2
BICIS Bank	2	B4
CBAO Bank	3	D5
French Consulate	4	C2
Hospital	5	B5
National Park Information	6	C4
Sentoo Office	7	B5
Syndicat d'Initiative	8	C4
Telecentre with Internet Facilities	9	B4

SIGHTS & ACTIVITIES p230
Church	10	B5
Governor's Palace	11	B4
Lighthouse	(see 22)	
Museum	12	B6

SLEEPING p230
| Auberge de Jeunesse/L'Atlantide | 13 | B2 |
| La Louisiane | 14 | B1 |

EATING p230
Bakery	15	B4
La Signare	16	C3
Restaurant Linguère	17	C3
Supermarket	18	B4

DRINKING p230
Blue Note	19	B4
Fireman's	20	C2
Iguane Café	21	B4
La Chanmière	22	A4
Marco Jazz	23	C4

SENEGAL

Map labels:
To Mauritanian Border (Restrictred Area; 2.5km)

Playing Field

N'Dar Tout

ATLANTIC OCEAN

Langue de Barbarie Peninsula

Ave Dodds

Pont Geole

Senegal River

Rue Adamson
Rue de France
Rue Brue
Rue Abdoulaye Seck
Ave Jean Mermoz
Rue Khalifa Ababacar Sy
Rue Blaise Diagne
Quai Roume
Rue Lt PH Diop
Rue Boufflers
Rue Aynima Fall
Rue P Holle
Rue Seydou Tall
Rue Blanchot
Rue Augustin Guillabert
Rue du Général de Gaulle
Place Faidherbe
Pont Mustapha Malick Gaye

Market

Senegal River

To Auberge l'Union-Bool Falé (1.5km)

Pont Faidherbe

Rue Milles Lacroix
Rue de l'Eglise
Rue AM Javouye

Train Station

Gare Routière

Sor

Guet N'Dar

Blvd Abdoulaye Mar Diop
Rue Ibrahim Sarr
Rue Blaise Dumont
Rue Babacar Seye
Rue Thevenot
Rue Chassagnol
Rue Ribet
Rue A Fall

Route de la Corniche

Mauritania

Muslim Cemetery

Quai Henri Jay

To Campement Le Robinson (1.5km),
Auberge la Teranga (2.5km), Hotel l'Oasis (3km),
Parc National de la Langue de Barbarie (18km),
Campement Langue de Barbarie (18km),
Campement Océan et Savane (18km) & Beaches

To Maison de Lille (1km),
'New' Gare Routière (3.5km),
Gandiol (18km), Mouit (20km),
Zebrabar (20km) & Dakar (260km)

St-Louis hosts a **blues festival** in January or February and a **jazz festival** in May. **Les Fanals**, an historic festival of decorated lanterns, is held around Christmas as well as the jazz festival.

You can get online at several places, the most up-to-date being the **Sentoo office** (Blvd Abdoulaye Mar Diop; per hr US$0.80). For round-the-clock cash fixes, there's a CBAO ATM on the island.

Sights & Activities

On St-Louis Island, local guides will take you up onto the roof of the **post office** (Rue du Général de Gaulle) for a small fee, from where you get good views of the bridge and the city. Nearby is the old **governor's palace**, which was a fort during the 18th century, and is now a government building. The **museum** (admission US$0.80; ⊙ 9am-noon & 3-6pm) at the southern tip of the island has some fascinating old photos of St-Louis and some woodcarvings.

The setting out of the pirogues at dusk from Guet N'Dar's dirty beach is unforgettable, but doesn't happen every day. There is a **Muslim cemetery** south of the village, where each grave is draped with a fishing net, and further south down the peninsula are some better **beaches**.

Sleeping & Eating

Maison De Lille (☎ 961 1135; s/d US$8/16), 2km south of the mainland, is one of the cheapest places, but a little further on **Campement Le Robinson** (☎ 961 4221; s/d US$16/20), right on the beach of the peninsula, is more attractive.

In town, the friendly **Auberge de Jeunesse** (L'Atlantide; ☎ 961 2409; Rue Abdoulaye Seck; dm US$8.80) has a friendly vibe going on opposite the French consulate, while on the mainland at the **Auberge L'Union-Bool Falé** (☎ 961 3852; rooftop beds US$4; d from US$8) the price of a rooftop mattress is as cheap as it gets. **Auberge la Teranga** (☎ 961 5050; s/d US$8/14) on the Langue de Barbarie is aimed at backpackers, with great views of the area from the rooftop restaurant/bar.

Hôtel l'Oasis (☎ 961 4232; s/d US$17/26), about 4km south of the city centre, is right on the edge of a beautiful and mostly deserted St-Louis beach, and the restaurant serves up a tasty shrimp baguette.

At the island's northern tip is **La Louisiane** (☎ 961 4221; s/d with bathroom US$25/30), a good

mid-range option with well-appointed rooms and an excellent **restaurant** (mains from US$4.85).

For cheap eats, try the shwarma joints on Ave Blaise Daigne, and there's a good **bakery** (Rue Khalifa Ababacar Sy) under the Hotel du Palais.

For more substantial fare, **La Linguère** (Ave Blaise Diagne; mains from US$1.50) is good-value local fare. *Tiéboudienne* (fish stew) is a speciality here. On the same street, **La Signare** (☎ 961 1932; menu du jour US$11; ⊙ Thu-Tue) is reputed to be one of the finest restaurants on the island.

Drinking & Clubbing

For a cheap drink and a chat with a local or two, try **Fireman's** (Ave Jean Mermoz), just north of the Centre Culturel.

St-Louis is renowned for its jazz. A good venue to sample some tunes is **Marco Jazz** (Quai Roume); the **Blue Note** (Rue Abdoulaye Seck) and **Iguane Café** (Rue Abdoulaye Seck) are two of the hipper places in town.

La Chaumière (Guet N'Dar beach) is a bar and nightclub popular with locals as well as travellers, and probably the best spot for a boogie in St-Louis.

Getting There & Away

The old *gare routière* is on the mainland (Sor), 100m south of Pont Faidherbe. There is a new gare, absurdly located 4.5km south of here, but at the time of writing drivers were boycotting it. It may be in use when you pass by, in which case a taxi to the island should cost about US$1.40.

The train station is World Heritage listed but trains to Dakar are sporadic. Bush taxis and minibuses are the go (US$5/4, 3½ hours).

PARC NATIONAL DE LA LANGUE DE BARBARIE

This **national park** (admission US$3.20; ⊙ 7am-dusk daily), 20km south of St-Louis, covers the southern tip of the Langue de Barbarie Peninsula and a section of the mainland on the other side of the river's mouth. It's easier to reach than Djoudj, and almost as good, but without the volume and variety of bird life. A guided tour costs US$12 for one or two people (US$5.6 per additional person). The best way to experience the park is by boat.

In a great position at the southern end of the Langue de Barbarie are two campements. They are outside the park, across the river from Gandiol. The smart **Campement Langue de Barbarie** (☎ 961 1118; s/d US$17/24) is managed by Hôtel de la Poste in St-Louis. Further along is the relaxed **Campement Ocean et Savane** (☎ 961 1259; s/d US$25/34) with beds in large Mauritanian-style tents; book at Hôtel de la Résidence in St-Louis.

Across the river, near the village of Mouit, 20km south of St-Louis and 2km south of Gandiol, is **Zebrabar** (☎ 638 1862; camping US$3, s/d huts US$10/15), a Swiss-run and very friendly campement that's quite a hit with overland drivers.

Most people reach the park on a trip organised by one of the hotels or tour companies in St-Louis. However, it is possible to get a bush taxi to Gandiol, from where you can enter the park by pirogue.

PARC NATIONAL DES OISEAUX DU DJOUDJ

From November to April, some three million birds migrating south from Europe stop here, because it's one of the first places with permanent water south of the Sahara. The **park** (☎ 963 8706; per person/car US$3/8; ☼ 7am-dusk) is one of the most important bird sanctuaries in the world, and almost 30species have been recorded. Pink flamingos, pelicans, ducks and waders are most plentiful.

At the park headquarters you can stay at the **station biologique** (s/d US$10/21), which is mainly for research groups, but it's also open to the public.

The park is 25km off the main road and there's no public transport, so most people take an excursion organised by one of the hotels or tour companies in St-Louis. Rates for day trips vary, starting at US$42 for one person alone and dropping to US$32 per person for three people. Otherwise hiring a taxi for four hours costs around US$12. Once in the park, pirogue tours cost US$6 per person; they are useful because much of the park is inundated with water.

The park is best seen in season (November to April) by pirogue (US$6 per person for a two-hour trip). If you want a guide, you can arrange this in St Louis. Most charge around US$6.5 for a full day, and will also arrange a vehicle (US$32 for up

to about five people). You pay your park entrance fees on top of this.

CENTRAL SENEGAL

KAOLACK

Kaolack (**ko**-lack), between Dakar and Tambacounda, is a busy transport hub and a handy gateway to the Siné-Saloum Delta. It's a more active city than sleepy St-Louis or Ziguinchor, and worth visiting for a day or two.

The city has a beautiful large **mosque**, decorated in the Moroccan style, and the second largest **covered market** in Africa (after Marrakesh), with Sudanese-style arches and arcades. There's not much hassle; it's a place to soak up the atmosphere.

The CBAO and SGBS banks have ATMs.

The tranquil **mission catholique** (☎ 941 2526; Rue Merleau-Ponty; dm/s US$3.20/8), in the southwest part of town, has spotless dorms and singles, but no sharing is allowed. Nearby, Caritas (an aid organisation) has **Chambres de Passage** (☎ 914 2730; s/d US$16/24).

For cheap eats there are several nameless gargottes (cheap restaurants) near the gare routière, and there is street food at the market.

For snacks and meals try the Lebanese-run **Chez Mariam** in the northeast part of the city centre near Rue Cheikh Tidiane Cherif. **Chez Du Du** (mains US$2.50-3.50) is similar.

Transport leaves from Gare Dakar, about 2km northwest of the city centre, for Dakar (US$4, three hours by bush taxi) and northern and western towns. From Gare Sud, also known as Gare Nioro, on the southeast side of the city centre, transport goes to Ziguinchor, Tambacounda and the Gambian border post of Karang (US$3.2 by bush taxi, two hours).

TAMBACOUNDA

Tambacounda is a major crossroads on the routes between Senegal, Mali, Guinea and The Gambia. The town, which lies in hot savanna country full of baobab trees, is also a jumping-off point for Niokolo-Koba National Park.

An old backpacker fave is **Chez Dessert** (☎ 981 1642; s US$5), about 1km south of the town centre. The rooms are basic, and there's a guest kitchen. Nearby is **Hôtel Niji**

(☎ 981 1259; s/d from US$18/22; ❄), where the rooms are OK and have bathrooms. You pay more for the rooms with air-con.

There are plenty of gargottes at the gare routière, south of town. For cheap drinks or meals (US$1 to US$3) try one of the small restaurants, such as Chez Francis.

There are two gare routières: Gare Kidira, on the eastern side of town, for vehicles towards Mali; and the larger Gare Dakar, on the southern outskirts of town, for most other destinations, including Niokolo-Koba. Bush taxis cost US$12 to Dakar (six hours).

By train, there is a twice-weekly service to/from Dakar and to/from Bamako in Mali. The fare to Dakar is US$20/15 for 1st/2nd class.

PARC NATIONAL DU NIOKOLO-KOBA

Niokolo-Koba, covering about 900 sq km in the southeast, is Senegal's major national park, a World Heritage site and an international biosphere reserve. Home to 35 bird and eight mammal species, it's had a facelift in recent years, but poaching remains a problem. It's very beautiful, with lush and varied vegetation. Residents include elephants, lions, leopards and the giant derby eland, although you shouldn't bet on seeing them. You are likely, however, to see hippos, crocodiles, waterbuck, bushbuck, kob, baboons, buffaloes, monkeys (green and hussar), warthogs, roan antelopes and hartebeest.

The best time to come is between December and May (the dry season), but some park tracks are not cleared until a month after the rains have ended, so don't take anything for granted. For information, visit the park headquarters in Tambacounda, where you might be lucky and find a lift. Entrance costs US$3.2 per person and US$8 per car. Hiring a guide (US$10) is obligatory.

Camping is permitted in the park but you must be fully self-sufficient, which includes wheels. Otherwise, there's **Dar-Salam Campement** (☎ 981 2575; tents/bungalows with bathroom US$5/ 10) at the park entrance or the ugly **Hôtel de Simenti** (bungalows US$11). Camp du Lion is 6km east of Simenti, in a beautiful location on the Gambia River. Huts are US$11.50, tent sites US$5, meals US$6. It's reachable by ordinary car and there's a 4WD for excursions.

You must have a vehicle to enter the park, and walking is not allowed anywhere, but it

is possible for animal and bird enthusiasts without a car to visit, most conveniently if they organise a group tour from Tambacounda, which means renting a bush taxi for a day or two, buying all provisions and paying park fees and accommodation on site. This can be organised either through the hotel or at the gare routière.

PETITE CÔTE & SINÉ-SALOUM DELTA

The 150km Petite Côte stretches south from Dakar and is one of Senegal's best beach areas. Along the coast where the seasonal Siné and Saloum Rivers meet the tidal waters of the Atlantic Ocean is the Siné-Saloum Delta. This stunning 180-sq-km delta boasts mangrove swamps, lagoons, forests and sand islands, about 40% of which forms the Parc National du Delta du Saloum.

M'BOUR

This is the main town on the Petite Côte, about 80km south of Dakar. A few kilometres to the north is **Saly-Portugal**, a strip of big ocean-front hotels, packed with European travellers during winter.

The **Centre Touristique Coco Beach** (☎ 957 1004; d with bathroom US$20; ❄) proves that looks can be deceiving – the rooms are good value.

Another popular place is the friendly and colourful **Le Bounty** (☎ 957 2951; s/d US$24/30), a few blocks south of Coco Beach, along the sandy street that is closest to the water.

Near the market and taxi park are several small gargottes. For meals try **Restaurant Luxembourg** (mains US$3-6), near the market, while around the corner is a snack bar with schwarmas for US$1.

A bush taxi from M'Bour to Dakar is US$1.50, and from M'Bour further down the Petite Côte, to Joal-Fadiout, is US$1.8 and US$2.20.

JOAL FADIOUT

The twin villages of Joal and Fadiout (also spelt Fadiouth) are south of M'Bour at the end of the tar road. Joal is on the mainland, while Fadiout is on a small island made of oyster and clamshells that have accumulated over the centuries, reached by an old wooden bridge. This place is on the tour circuit, and is plagued by touts. The villages of Palmarin and Djifer, further south in the Siné-Saloum Delta, are pleasant alternatives.

In Joal, the best place to put your feet up is **Relais 114** (☎ 957 6114; d US$12), also called Chez Mamadou Balde, which serves meals for around US$5.

NDANGANE

This is the northernmost village bordering the Parc National du Delta du Saloum and has developed into a thriving traveller centre. From here you can take a pirogue to any point in the delta.

There are five unpretentious bungalows at **Chez Mbake** (☎ 936 3985; s/d US$8/16); otherwise, on a dirt track near the junction, the **Annacardiers** (☎ 949 9313; s/d US$12/24) has clean, good-value rooms with fan and bath.

Across from Ndangane is **Mar Lodj**, a perfect getaway and superb bird-watching locale. Of the three associated **campements** (s/d US$17/31, less in low season) lining the shore, Nouvelle Vague is the best value, with six of the 1 new bungalows overlooking the river. Pickup from Ndangane is free, and breakfast is included.

To get to Ndangane, take any bus between Kaolack and M'bour and alight at Ndiosomone, where bush taxis do the shuttle to Ndangane (US$2.50). A pirogue across to Île de Mars costs about US$0.50, but you may have to charter a boat for US$6.50.

DJIFER

Djifer is on the western edge of the delta at the tip of a narrow spit of land called the Pointe de Sangomar. You can hire a pirogue here and reach the beautiful islands of **Guior** and **Guissanor**. The campements listed here can arrange boat trips around the delta for about US$24 to US$32 per boat.

Superb **Campement Pointe de Sangomar** (☎ 835 6191; d US$10) has bungalows with open-air shower, and the quiet **Campement la Mangrove** (bungalows US$8) is 2km north of the village and has basic huts with breakfast included.

PALMARIN

In Palmarin, a few kilometres north of Djifer, the community-owned **Campement de Palmarin** (s/d US$8/14) has slightly weather-beaten thatched huts on a sandy beach under the coconut palms.

Palmarin and Djifer are reached from M'Bour, via Joal-Fadiout; Joal to Palmarin costs US$1.10.

FOUNDIOUGNE

West of Kaolack, Foundiougne (**foun**-dune) is easy to reach, and another good place for pirogue trips around the delta. Ismaila, the resident boatman at **Campement Le Baobab No 1** (☎ 948 1708; half board US$16), offers pirogue trips to **Ile aux Oiseaux** (great for bird-watching) for about US$4 per half day for the boat.

The **Campement Le Baobab No 2** (☎ 948 1262; s/d US$13/23), also called Chez Anne-Marie, is a friendly place that serves meals for about US$4.

Overlooking the river, **Saloum Saloum** (☎ 948 1269; r for up to 3 people US$24) is friendly and good value.

A bush taxi from Kaolack to Passi (en route to Karang, the Gambian border post) is US$1, and from Passi to Foundiougne is less than US$1. You can also go from Fatick (on the M'Bour to Kaolack highway) to Dakhonga, taking a ferry across to Foundiougne.

MISSIRAH & PASSI

Missirah is a small village south of Toubakouta, and is the most convenient point of entry to the **Parc National du Delta du Saloum**. The park's headquarters is 6km from Missirah; entry to the park is US$3. About 2km west of Missirah, the **Gîte de Bandiala** (☎ 948 7735; half/full board US$21/28) is a great base for exploration of this part of the delta. Pirogue trips, fishing and photo safaris are available.

South of Kaolack on the road to Toubakouta, Passi is renowned for its huge traditional market.

To reach Missirah, get off your minibus at the village of Santhiou el Haji (80km from Kaolack) and walk 8km along a sandy track through the forest, or take a bush taxi from Toubakouta for US$0.50.

CASAMANCE

If travellers exercise their common sense and better judgment, Casamance, the region of Senegal south of The Gambia, is a rewarding destination. A well-watered, fertile area populated by non-Muslim Diola (Jola) people, it clings to its distinct identity

SENEGAL

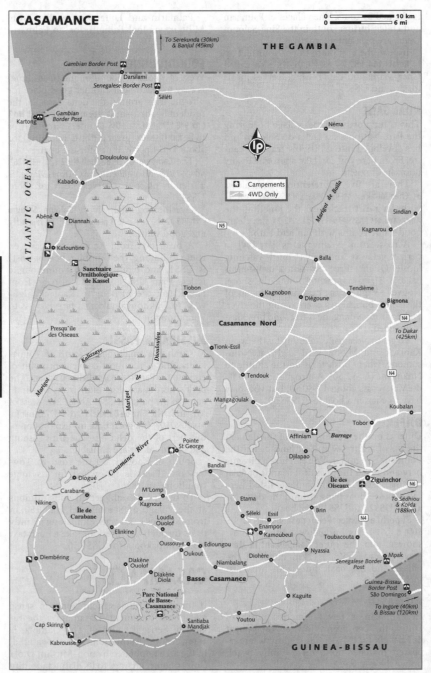

CASAMANCE

0 — 10 km
0 — 6 mi

THE GAMBIA

To Serekunda (30km)
& Banjul (45km)

Gambian Border Post
Darsilami
Senegalese Border Post
Séléti

Néma

Kartong
Gambian
Border Post

Diouloulou

Kabadio

N5

Marigot de Baïla

Sindian

Kagnarou

Abéné
Diannah

Kafountine

Baïla

Sanctuaire
Ornithologique
de Kassel

Tiobon

Kagnobon
Diégoune

Tendième

Bignona

N4

To Dakar
(425km)

Campements
4WD Only

Casamance Nord

Presqu'île
des Oiseaux

Tionk-Essil

N4

Tendouk

Mangagoulak

Koubalan

Tobor

Affiniam
Barrage

Pointe
St George

Djilapao

Dioubélong

Casamance River

Bandial

Île des
Oiseaux

Ziguinchor

N6

Diogué

Carabane

M'Lomp

Etama

Brin

To Sédhiou
& Kolda
(188km)

Nikine

Île de
Carabane

Kagnout

Séléki

Essil

Elinkine

Loudia
Ouolof

Enampor
Kamoubeul

Toubacouta

Oussouye
Edioungou

Diohère

Nyassia

Mpak

Diembéring

Oukout

Niambalang

Senegalese Border
Post

Diakène
Ouolof

Basse Casamance

Guinea-Bissau
Border Post
São Domingos

Diakène
Diola

Parc National
de Basse-
Casamance

Kaguite

To Ingore (40km)
& Bissau (120km)

Cap Skiring

Santiaba
Mandjak

Youtou

Kabrousse

GUINEA-BISSAU

ATLANTIC OCEAN

SENEGAL

Kalissaye

Marigot

de

Marigot

WARNING

Rebels from the Mouvement des Forces Démocratique de la Casamance (MFDC) have fought an ongoing separatist struggle against the Senegalese government since 1982. The conflict is more of a sporadic series of skirmishes rather than a war, and is complicated by Gambian and Guinean meddling. Its politics are a tangled mess, and a resolution is as far away as ever. What's changed is the geography of the conflict. In recent years, the border between Senegal and Guinea-Bissau, where rebel activity had long been concentrated, has been shored up, and it now seems that the rebels are using The Gambia as a base. As a result, their targets are tending to be in northern Casamance. The *Joola* ferry disaster in late 2002 has complicated the tragedy: rebel activity makes road transport insecure for people and cargo, and without a reliable ferry link, Casamance is more isolated than ever.

Because Casamance is a conflict zone, travellers must obtain reliable and up-to-date information on the latest developments and no-go areas to minimise any risk to their security, especially before heading off into remote Casamance.

so tenaciously that a separatist movement has existed here since the 1950s. Dakar won't let go of its most precious jewel, and as a result there is a crippling conflict with no end in sight. See the Warning boxed text (above) for more information. The military presence is strong, with roadblocks and searches common, but it hasn't brought an end to sporadic clashes. Moreover, the sinking in September 2002 of the *Joola* ferry has affected the whole region. Many of the more than 200 victims were students and merchants from Casamance, and their loss will be felt for many years.

Despite the sad background, The Casamance is perfect for touring on foot, bicycle or pirogue. You can stay at some of the village-run campements (called Campements Rurals Integrés or CRIs), which provide simple accommodation for visitors and raise money for local projects. Standard prices apply: a bed (with mosquito net) is US$5, breakfast is US$3, and a three-course lunch or dinner is US$4. Most CRIs have clean rooms, oil lamps, and showers and toilets with running water, but at the time of writing only four were open to travellers due to the recent downturn in tourism: Affiniam, Enampor, Pointe St George and Kafountine. There are also privately owned campements in the Casamance, offering similar facilities and prices.

ZIGUINCHOR
pop 206,000
Ziguinchor is a river town and the capital of the Casamance. Nowadays there's a wistful sadness about the place – hardly anyone in

town didn't lose a loved one in the *Joola* tragedy. Ziguinchor isn't just a traveller convenience, however. It has its charms, and is worth a visit for a couple of days. The **Marché St-Maur** and **Centre Artisanal** are both well worth visiting.

Banks include the CBAO at the junction of Rue de France and Rue Javelier, where you can get an advance on a credit card, and the SGBS, at the back of which is an ATM accepting both Visa and MasterCard.

The Guinea-Bissau **consulate** (☎ 991 1046; Rue de France), near Hôtel du Tourisme, is open weekday mornings. Visas cost US$8 and are issued on the spot (bring one photo).

Sleeping
One of the cheapest places in town is **Auberge Kadiandou** (☎ 991 1071; d US$7, with bathroom US$10) near the gare routière.

About 3km west of the city centre on the road to Cap Skiring are a couple of cheap campements. The better one is **Auberge Aw-Bay** (☎ 936 8076), which charges standard CRI prices. It has clean bathrooms and a good restaurant.

SPLURGE!

The upmarket **Hôtel le Flamboyant** (☎ 991 2223; Rue de France; s/d US$21/24; 🛏 🐕) in the heart of town is unbeatable value. Spotless rooms have satellite TV and a bar fridge, and just outside the door is the pool. Across the road are run by the same people is the **Hôtel du Tourisme** (s/d US$11/13), a long-time favourite, with a popular bar and restaurant.

Friendly **Hôtel le Bel Kady** (☎ 991 1122; s/d US$4/5), near Marché St Maur, has basic rooms that can get hot in summer. The restaurant is good value.

Also recommended is the **Relais de Santhiaba** (☎ 991 1199; s/d US$9/12, with bathroom US$15/21; ✜) which has spartan, but clean, rooftop rooms.

Overlooking the river, **Hôtel le Perroquet** (☎ 991 2329; s/d US$14/19) is beautifully located in Rue du Commerce, next to the ferry terminal.

Eating, Drinking & Clubbing

On Ave Lycée Guignabo, in the area of Marché St Maur, are several cheap cafés, bars and gargottes.

For fresh bread and cakes, the pâtisserie on Rue Javelie is good value, but get there early.

A good-value local eatery on the waterfront is **Le Palmier** (Rue du Commerce; mains US$1). **Le Mansah** (Rue Javelier; mains from US$3) serves big meals, including tiéboudienne with chips.

Le P'tit Bedon (☎ 991 2653; Ave Emile Badiane; mains US$7) is reputed to be Ziguinchor's finest restaurant.

The **Bar Malila** (Rue Javelier) with its Bob Marley overtones is friendly and a good spot for a beer. Nearby **Le Kassa** (Rond-Point Jean Paul II) is a bar-restaurant popular with locals. The place to go for good music is the nightclub at the **Hôtel Bombalong** (Rue du Commerce). If it is jam-packed go to the **Rubis** (Rue de Général de Gaulle), just east of the city centre.

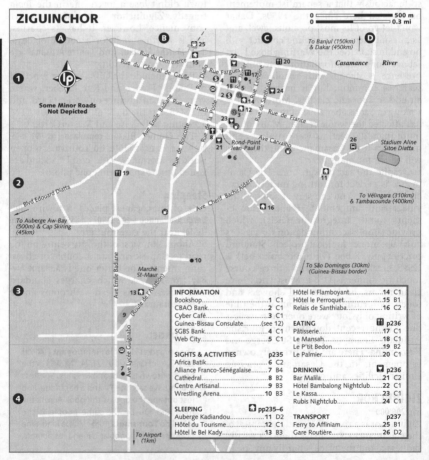

INFORMATION		
Bookshop	1	C1
CBAO Bank	2	C1
Cyber Café	3	C1
Guinea-Bissau Consulate	(see 12)	
SGBS Bank	4	C1
Web City	5	C1

SIGHTS & ACTIVITIES	p235	
Africa Batik	6	C2
Alliance Franco-Sénégalaise	7	B4
Cathedral	8	B2
Centre Artisanal	9	B3
Wrestling Arena	10	B3

SLEEPING	pp235–6	
Auberge Kadiandou	11	D2
Hôtel du Tourisme	12	C1
Hôtel le Bel Kady	13	B3
Hôtel le Flamboyant	14	C1
Hôtel le Perroquet	15	B1
Relais de Santhiaba	16	C2

EATING	p236	
Pâtisserie	17	C1
Le Mansah	18	C1
Le P'tit Bedon	19	B2
Le Palmier	20	C1

DRINKING	p236	
Bar Malila	21	C2
Hotel Bambalong Nightclub	22	C1
Le Kassa	23	C1
Rubis Nightclub	24	C1

TRANSPORT	p237	
Ferry to Affiniam	25	B1
Gare Routière	26	D2

Getting There & Around

Air Senegal flies between Dakar and Ziguinchor (US$71 one way).

The gare routière is 1km east of the city centre. The fare to Dakar is US$10.50/8 by bush taxi/minibus (10/11 hours). Transport to Casamance villages also leaves from here.

To get anywhere around town by private taxi costs US$0.50. For around town, or for touring the Casamance in relaxed style, bicycles can be hired from the Relais de Santhiaba or Campement ZAG. Decent mountain bikes (vélos tout terrain) cost US$9.5 per day, and old steel bicycles cost US$4.

AFFINIAM

On the north bank of the Casamance River, opposite Ziguinchor, this village contains a splendid impluvium – a large, round mud house with a funnel-shaped roof. In times of war, people would shut themselves inside the impluvium for safety. Rainwater would be funnelled into a large tank in the courtyard at centre of the house.

The impluvium is also the **campement**, and you can stay for standard CRI prices.

To get to Affiniam from Ziguinchor, take the public ferry, which runs three times weekly. It stops at the Affiniam landing (about 1km from the campement) for one hour, then returns. The fare is less than a dollar.

OUSSOUYE

About halfway between Ziguinchor and Cap Skiring, sleepy Oussouye (**ou**-sou-yeh) is the main town in the Basse (Lower) Casamance area, and a good base for visiting the region. Bicycles can be hired on the main street. Oussouye has been affected by rebel activity in recent years – check on the latest before you go.

The well-run **village campement** is 1km north of town on the old dirt road that leads northwest towards Elinkine. It is a fascinating example of local mud architecture. Rooms and meals are standard CRI prices.

Auberge du Routard (☎ 993 1025; d US$5), 500m from town, has nice bungalows and costs a bit more than a CRI; the food is very good here. About 300m further is **Campement Emanaye Oussouye** (☎ 933 1004; s/d US$8/10), which has better quality, mud hut rooms in rice fields.

AROUND OUSSOUYE
Parc National de Basse-Casamance

This national park is 10km southwest of Oussouye. It has several vegetation zones, including forest, open grassland, tidal mud flats and mangrove swamps, and animals including red colobus monkeys and duikers. The park has a good network of roads, white sandy trails and several miradors (lookouts).

Unfortunately the park has been closed for a number of years for security reasons, and may remain so because of land mines. Check the situation before you go, and stick to the trails.

Elinkine & Île de Carabane

Elinkine is a busy fishing village at the end of the tar road northwest of Oussouye and a jumping-off point to Île de Carabane (sometimes spelt Karabane), which is a really cool place to relax and just hang out. On the island, you can still see the Breton-style **church**, with dusty pews and crumbling statues. Along the beach is an old **cemetery** with settlers' graves from the 1840s, now covered in sand.

On Carabane, **Campement Barracuda** (☎ 659 6001; half board US$12; meals US$5) caters mainly to anglers and has a lively bar. More tranquil than the Barracuda is the arty and carefree **Campement Badji Kunda** (dm US$4, full board US$18), 1km further along the beach, where rooms are solar-powered. The comfortable rooms at **Chez Helena** (☎ 652 1772; d/half board US$7/10) are a real bargain.

Excellent **Hôtel Carabane** (☎ 633 1782; s/d US$18/26), on the beach between the two campements, used to be a mission, and the chapel is now the bar!

Elinkine can be reached by minibus from Ziguinchor (US$1.30, two hours, two daily), and occasionally bush taxis too. Carabane can be reached by pirogue from Elinkine (US$1.30, around three minutes).

CAP SKIRING

The beaches at Cap Skiring are some of the finest in Africa. This is where you'll find most of Senegal's traveller hotels, and several cheap campements too. If you want a few days of easy beach life, this is the place; if you want an African experience, keep movin'.

There's a row of campements about 1km from the village, near Ziguinchor Junction, all reached by walking south from the junction

SENEGAL

for 100m, then turning right down a dirt road for 200m towards the ocean.

There's the friendly **Auberge de la Paix** (d US$5, with bathroom US$10), which is popular but slightly tatty; the good-value **Campement Le Bakine** (☎ 641 5124; d/half board US$5/11) has simple rooms and a creative vibe that draws artists and their muses; and the small and relaxed **Campement Chez M'Ballo** (☎ 936 9102; d US$7, with bathroom US$11).

Up the scale a bit is the **Auberge le Palmier** (d with bathroom from US$16; ⊠)) in Cap Skiring village, where the bar/restaurant serves a selection of French and Senegalese dishes.

There are cheap gargottes in the village serving meals from US$1. Or try **Mamans** (meals US$0.80) restaurant, a few metres back from the main street, with its friendly atmosphere and good-value food.

Air Senegal flies to Cap Skiring from Dakar for around US$96 one way. Bush taxis and minibuses (US$2/1.60) regularly ply the route between Ziguinchor and Cap Skiring.

AROUND CAP SKIRING
Diembéring

If Cap Skiring is too frantic for you, head for Diembéring (**jem**-bay-ring), 9km north, which has a genuine African feel and a beach that is hassle-free.

The peaceful **Campement Asseb** (☎ 993 3106) at the entrance to the village has bungalows and meals at CRI prices.

Diembéring is easily reached from Ziguinchor by private taxi (US$8 each way) or by daily minibus (it passes through Cap Skiring at 5pm). Otherwise you can cycle from Cap Skiring – hard work on sandy tracks.

Enampor

Enampor is 23km southwest of Ziguinchor. The **village campement** is an impluvium, and is worth a visit even if you're not staying here. There are other such houses in the Casamance, but this is a good example. To sleep and eat here you pay standard CRI prices. The manager will show you around for a small fee.

There's a daily minibus to Enampor from Ziguinchor for less than a dollar.

KAFOUNTINE & ABÉNÉ

In the far northwest corner of the Casamance, these two villages were until recently

among the most laidback places on the planet. Drought and local rebel activity have strung tempers a little higher than usual, but the beaches are still stunning and the surrounding countryside worth exploring – once you've checked on the security situation, of course. Kafountine is a large village only 15km down the beach from the Gambian border, not far from the southern end of the tar road that runs south from Diouloulou. Abéné is a smaller place, about 6km further up the coast and 9km from the border.

Sleeping & Eating

Most places to stay are a few kilometres beyond Kafountine, near the beach. Best is the recommended, beautifully located **Esperanto** (bungalows/half board US$12/20) between the beach and a creek. A little to the south, set in woodland, is **Kale Diang** (☎ 936 9519; d with bathroom US$5; meals US$3-5; ⊠ Oct-Jun), where the rooms are cheaper, the ambience is peaceful and the food is a wonder. In the village try one of the excellent lunches at **Satang Jabang**, a women's vocation training school, or one of the cheap eateries in the market.

In Abéné village is the tidy **Campement la Belle Danielle** (☎ 936 9542; d/half board US$4/10) where the friendly Konte brothers also hire bikes. From the village it's 2km along a sandy track to the beach and the more upmarket Italian-run **Campement le Kossey** (d/half board US$8/16) where comfortable bungalows are set in a beautiful garden.

Getting There & Away

A minibus to Kafountine from Ziguinchor costs US$3.2 (four hours) and from Serekunda in The Gambia it costs US$2.5 (three hours). Abéné can be reached by any transport going to Kafountine, although the village is 2km off the main road, and the beach a further 2km, which you'll have to walk.

SENEGAL DIRECTORY

ACCOMMODATION

Senegal has a very wide range of places to stay, from the top-class hotels at the coastal resorts to dirty dosshouses in Dakar, plus pleasant *campements* (guesthouses) in the rural areas. All hotels and campements charge US$1 per person tourist tax. This may or may not be included in the price. Some hotels charge by the room, and it makes no difference to the price (apart from the tourist tax) whether you're alone or with somebody.

BUSINESS HOURS
Businesses and government offices are open 8am to noon and 2.30pm to 6pm Monday to Friday and 8am to noon on Saturday. Banks close a little earlier in the afternoon, and only some banks are open Saturday mornings. The bank at Léopold Senghor International Airport is open until midnight.

DANGERS & ANNOYANCES
There are two main dangers you may encounter: civil unrest in Casamance and Dakar street crime. See the Casamance section (p235) for more details.

In Dakar, don't let vendors or anyone else slow you down on the streets: reply to their advances if you want but keep walking. At night, exercise common sense: stay away from dark alleys and the beaches. Rely on taxis and avoid wearing expensive jewellery, watches or 'bum bags'. See the Dakar (p223) section for more details.

Of less concern are the hustlers and guides who can be hard to shake and have an endless bag of tricks up their sleeves, including emotional blackmail. Favourite lines include 'Don't you remember me from...' and 'You're not racist like the others'.

Above all, realise that these approaches can be managed, and don't allow paranoia to cloud your opportunity to meet the beautiful Senegalese, a genuinely friendly people.

EMBASSIES & CONSULATES
Countries with diplomatic representation are dispersed throughout Dakar; some are in the Point E neighbourhood, 5km northwest of the city centre via bus No 7 or 12.
Burkina Faso (Map p222; ☎ 827 9509; Lot 1 Liberty VI Extension)
Canada (Map p222; ☎ 823 9290; 45 Blvd de la République)
Cape Verde (Map p224; ☎ 821 3936; 3 Blvd el Haji Djily Mbaye)
Côte d'Ivoire (Map p224; ☎ 821 3473; 2 Ave Albert Sarraut)
France (Map p224; ☎ 839 5100; 1 Rue Assane Ndoye)

The Gambia (Map p224; ☎ 821 7230; 11 Rue de Thiong)
Germany (Map p222; ☎ 823 2519; 2 Ave Pasteur)
Guinea (Map p222; ☎ 824 8606; Rue 7, Point E)
Guinea-Bissau (Map p222; ☎ 824 5922; Rue 6, Point E)
Mali (Map p222; ☎ 894 6950; 23 Route de la Corniche Ouest, Fann)
Mauritania (Map p222; ☎ 822 6238; Rue 37, Kolobane)
Netherlands (Map p224; ☎ 823 9483; 37 Rue Kléber)
UK (Map p222; ☎ 823 7392; 2 Rue du Dr Guillet)
USA (Map p224; ☎ 823 3424; Ave Jean XXIII)

For details on getting visas for neighbouring countries, see p240. It's worthwhile to note that most embassies close late morning or early afternoon Monday to Friday, so set off early – Dakar's snarling traffic jams can be a drag.

In West Africa, Senegal has embassies in Burkina Faso, Cape Verde, Côte d'Ivoire, The Gambia, Guinea-Bissau, Guinea, Mali and Mauritania.

FESTIVALS & EVENTS
The Grand Magal pilgrimage and festival is held annually 48 days after the Islamic New Year to celebrate the return from exile of the founder of the Mouride Islamic brotherhood.

The Paris–Dakar car rally traditionally ends at Lac Retba in the middle of January.

Refer to the St-Louis section (p230) for details on the city's music festivals.

FOOD & DRINKS
Senegal has some of the finest cuisine in West Africa. Common dishes include *tiéboudienne* (chey-**bou**-jen), which is rice baked in a thick sauce of fish and vegetables with pimiento and tomato; *yassa poulet* or *poisson yassa* (marinated and grilled chicken or fish); *mafé* (peanut-based stew); and *bassi-salété* (millet covered with vegetables and meat).

Senegalese beer is also good. Gazelle is cheapest, while Flag is a stronger and better quality brew. The reddish *bissap*, made from bissap flowers, is a popular, very sweet nonalcoholic drink.

INTERNET ACCESS
Internet cafés have become a common sight in Senegal's towns, and Internet access is sometimes available in smaller towns and villages on the travel map. Surfing costs about US$1.6 per hour.

SENEGAL

HOLIDAYS

As well as religious holidays listed in the Africa Directory chapter (p1003) the principal public holidays in Senegal are:

1 January New Years Day
4 April Independence Day
1 May Workers Day
15 August Assumption

MAPS

The locally produced *Carte du Senegal* (1: 912,000) is the best and cheapest available map, and includes an excellent street map of Dakar. It's hard to find outside Senegal.

MONEY

The unit of currency is the West African CFA franc. As in most West African countries, carry euros, especially in cash (the CFA franc is pegged to the euro).

Cashing travellers cheques is easy in Dakar, but a little more of a hassle elsewhere if they are not in euros.

PHOTOGRAPHY & VIDEO

Senegal doesn't require the purchase of a photography permit, although snapping military installations, airports or government buildings may nevertheless raise official eyebrows.

POST & TELEPHONE

Senegal's postal service is reliable and inexpensive for letters. The poste restante in Dakar is slow, unreliable, holds letters for only three days and charges US$0.50 per letter.

The telephone service is reasonable, and international connections are good. Calls from public Sonatel offices cost about US$1

per minute to Europe (less to France) and slightly more to the USA and Australia. Rates are cheaper late at night and on the weekend. Dakar has private *télécentres*, usually open until late evening, for phone calls, telexes and faxes.

Mobile phones are easily connected to one of two local GSM networks with the purchase of a SIM card. There are no area codes in Senegal.

VISAS & DOCUMENTS
Visas

Visas for up to nine days are required by all except nationals of the European Union (member states of 2003, not candidate nations), USA, Canada, Norway, South Africa, Israel, Japan and several other (mainly African) countries. Australians and New Zealanders require visas.

Visas for Onward Travel

You can get visas for other African countries in Dakar. Each requires one to four photos. For contact details, see p239.

Burkina Faso Visas cost US$21, take two days and require three photos.

The Gambia Three-month visas cost US$24. If you come early, you can get the visa by 2.30pm, otherwise within 24 hours. Seven-day visas to The Gambia are available at the border, but they are expensive.

Guinea Visas cost US$33 and are issued in 24 hours if you're lucky.

Guinea-Bissau One-month visas cost US$17 and are issued in 24 hours in Dakar. At the consulate in Ziguinchor they are issued on the spot for US$8.

Mali One-month visas cost US$12 and take 48 hours to issue.

Mauritania Three-month visas cost between US$2 and US$7 depending on nationality and are issued the same day. A *note verbal* (letter of introduction) may be required. You can pick up your visa in the afternoon.

The Gambia

HIGHLIGHTS

- **Serekunda** There's a beach – and a beach bar – for every taste in The Gambia (p248)
- **Abuko** Home to 250 bird species, this 105-hectare nature reserve is easily accessible from the main travel spots (p252)
- **Raging** The Gambia's clubs rage until dawn – head to Kololi for the glitz and to Serekunda for the African beats (p251)
- **Gunjur** This southern fishing village is a haven compared with its northern cousins; and you can learn to drum here too (p252)
- **Off the beaten track** Cruise down the Gambia River with an amazing array of birdlife for company (p253)

FAST FACTS

- **Area** 11,295 sq km
- **ATMs** at banks in Banjul, on the Atlantic Coast, in Serekunda and at the airport
- **Borders** Senegal (The Gambia is surrounded by Senegal)
- **Budget** US$10 to US$20 a day
- **Capital** Banjul
- **Languages** English, Mandinka, Wolof, Fula
- **Money** dalasi; US$1 = D26
- **Population** 1.4 million
- **Seasons** dry (Nov–Apr), hot (May–Jun), wet (Jul–Oct)
- **Telephone** country code ☎ 220; international access code ☎ 00
- **Time** GMT/UTC
- **Visas** cost US$25 to US$45, but are not required by citizens of the British Commonwealth, Scandinavian countries, Belgium, Germany, Netherlands and Spain

THE GAMBIA

One of the globe's most oddly shaped countries, The Gambia is also the perfect introduction to travelling in Africa: a narrow stretch of land, 500km long and only 25km to 50km wide, completely surrounded by Senegal – except, that is, for the sea and the famous long, white, sandy beaches. Sun seekers can limit themselves to the coast and still enjoy countless restaurants and bars, nature reserves, Serekunda's bustle, Banjul's faded elegance, and nightlife to keep them dancing until dawn. Those wishing to get their toes wet upriver will find unspoilt traditional villages, ancient stone circles, bustling riverfront markets and utterly charming people.

THE GAMBIA

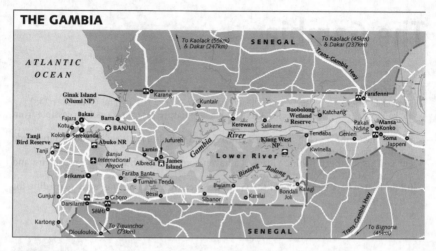

HISTORY

The Gambia's reliance on tourism means that political stability and a semblance of democracy are crucial to its economic prospects. President Jammeh's leanings are autocratic; posters on the walls of government buildings show his portrait and the slogan, 'In Jammeh We Trust'. Before Tourism and foreign aid keep the country afloat, but in recent years global insecurity and airline turmoil have hit the tourist industry hard, and Gambians will be praying that their trust in Jammeh is well placed.

First Contact

The empires of Ghana (5th to 11th centuries) and Mali (13th to 15th centuries) extended their influence over the region that is now The Gambia, so imperial domination was nothing new by 1456, when Portuguese navigators landed on James Island. Without establishing a settlement, the newcomers monopolised trade along the West African coast throughout the 15th and 16th centuries, exchanging salt, iron, pots and pans, firearms and gunpowder for ivory, ebony, beeswax, gold and slaves.

Baltic Germans first built a fort on James Island in 1651, and were displaced in 1661 by the British, who found themselves under constant threat from French ships, pirates and African kings. New forts were built at Barra and Bathurst (now Banjul), at the mouth of the Gambia River, to control the movement of ships. Fort James continued to

be an important collection point for slaves until the abolition of slavery in 1807.

The British continued to extend their influence further upstream until the 1820s, when the territory was declared a British protectorate ruled from Sierra Leone. In 1888 Gambia became a crown colony, by which time the surrounding territory of Senegal had fallen into French custody.

The Gambia, long considered dead weight by its colonial masters, who had tried to trade it to another colonial power, became self-governing in 1963. However, the British considered independence to be economically and politically impractical, and a possible merger with Senegal was considered. Nevertheless, independence came in 1965. Gambia became The Gambia, Bathurst became Banjul, and David Jawara, leader of the People's Progressive Party, became Prime Minister Dawda Jawara.

Benign Neglect

High groundnut prices and the advent of package tourism led to something of a boom in the 1960s. Jawara consolidated his power, which was built on a complex web of patronage rather than genuine popular support, and became president when The Gambia became a fully fledged republic in 1970. As groundnut prices fell in the 1980s, and tourism revenues did not trickle down the economic scale, two coups were hatched – but thwarted with Senegalese assistance. This cooperation led to the 1982 confederation of the two countries

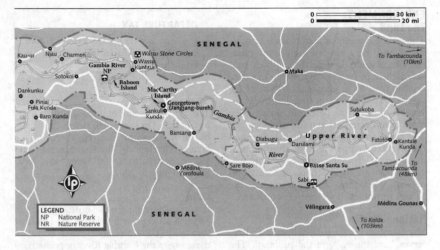

under the name of Senegambia, reportedly the first step to unification, but the union had collapsed by 1989. Meanwhile, corruption increased, economic decline continued and popular discontent rose. Finally, in July 1994, Jawara was overthrown in a reportedly bloodless coup led by Lieutenant Yahya Jammeh. Jawara escaped to exile in Senegal.

After a brief flirtation with autocracy, the 30-year-old Jammeh bowed to international pressure, inaugurated a Second Republic and contrived to win the September 1996 presidential election comfortably. Jammeh's democratic impulses are a convenience, and there is reportedly corruption at the highest levels, as democratic watchdogs, human-rights groups and what little free press and genuine political opposition remain inside the country will attest. Nevertheless, the president's sense of theatrics, his ambitious public works program and the climate of stability lend him wide appeal.

THE CULTURE
The National Psyche
The Gambia's high aspirations are matched by an equally well-developed sense of realism. The apocryphal story of the country's origins help explain why its people are so laid-back: the borders were fixed when an English gunship sailed up the Gambia River and fired cannonballs port and starboard – the border was drawn where the cannonballs fell. Few countries better typify the artifice of the postcolonial nation-state.

The grim realities of politics and economics, such as the ups and downs of tourism, are the ultimate theatre of the absurd – best taken with a fistful of salt.

Lifestyle
Modern Gambian life consists of the scramble to make ends meet and get ahead, tempered by the pleasures of family, the obligations of community and a genuine concern for others' welfare. Further upriver, an alternative reality emerges, one that is poorer and more isolated. Opportunities may be thinner on the ground, but the rhythms of river life are calmer and more dignified.

People
The Gambia is one of Africa's most densely populated countries. Twenty per cent of the population lives in Banjul, Serekunda and Brikama. About 90% are Muslims. The main ethnic group is the Mandinka (Mandingo), who comprise about 40% of the total population. They are mostly involved in farming and fishing, and have a strong musical tradition.

Other large groups include the Fula and Wolof, mainly farmers and traders who control a great deal of commerce in the region. A small but significant group is the Aku, found only in The Gambia, who are mostly descendants of freed slaves brought from Sierra Leone in the early 19th century. In colonial times many Aku were employed in the civil service.

THE GAMBIA

ENVIRONMENT
The Land
The main geographical feature is the Gambia River, and there are few significant variations in altitude or vegetation, which consists largely of savanna and saline marshes. Baobab trees are a significant feature of the savanna. The dry season stretches from November to April (the best time to visit). The main rains occur between July and October. The heat can be relentless in March, when the average temperature is around 36°C most days. Despite ongoing education programs, particularly in schools, deforestation presents a real threat to The Gambia as the Sahara continues to creep ever southward.

National Parks
The Gambia has six national parks and reserves, covering 3.7% of the landmass. The four most accessible and interesting – Abuko, Kiang West, Gambia River and Tanji – are mentioned in this chapter.

Environmental Issues
The most visible environmental problem is beach erosion on the Atlantic coast, but The Gambia's fishing villages also face dwindling stocks as a result of overfishing, while a fall of 30% in annual rainfall over 30 years, probably caused by deforestation, means drought is becoming an ever-present threat.

TRANSPORT

GETTING THERE & AWAY
Air
SN Brussels Airlines is the only airline that flies between The Gambia and Europe. There are also numerous cheap charter flights, as The Gambia is popular with European package tourists between November and April. The leading charter holiday operator is the British-based **Gambia Experience** (☎ 023-80730888).

Regional airlines serving The Gambia include Ghana Airways, Air Guinée, Bellview, Gambia International Airline and Air Senegal International. The latter two link Banjul with Dakar (Senegal); one-way fares are about US$45. Most airlines have their offices in central Banjul or in Fajara. Shop around the airlines, as prices can vary considerably.

> **DEPARTURE TAX**
>
> The departure tax is US$7, payable in hard currency. Some charter flights include the tax in the ticket price.

Boat
The Gambia is surrounded on three sides by Senegal. On the fourth side is the ocean, but at the time of research, there was no boat service linking The Gambia and Senegalese destinations, following the *Joola* ferry tragedy in 2002.

Land
If you're heading to the northern part of Senegal, an express bus leaves for Dakar at 9am daily (US$4, five hours) from Barra, on the shore of the Gambia River opposite Banjul. A slower bus leaves between 10am and noon. Minibuses and bush taxis run regularly between Barra and the border at Karang (US$1.60), from where travellers can climb into Dakar-bound bush taxis and minibuses (US$2.50 to US$4, six to nine hours).

If you're heading for southern Senegal, minibuses and bush taxis leave frequently from Serekunda *garage* (bus and taxi station); the fare for the five-hour trip to Ziguinchor is about US$4. Transport also goes from Brikama to Ziguinchor. You might have to change vehicles at the border. The road is rutted and potholed, particularly from the border to Ziguinchor.

At the far-eastern tip of The Gambia, bush taxis run from Basse Santa Su to Vélingara for US$1.40, and from there bush taxis go to Tambacounda (when they're full) for US$2.30.

GETTING AROUND
Boat
River Gambia Excursions (☎ 497603; mosa@qanet .gm) runs a passenger-boat service along the Gambia River between Tendaba and Georgetown, but the trip can be taken from the Georgetown end only as part of a 14-day tour. From the Georgetown end, the trip is generally only possible as part of a 14-day tour. However, it can be taken this way for about US$46 all-inclusive. Sometimes it even runs between Basse Santa Su and Georgetown; contact the operator for more information.

A high-speed riverboat linking Banjul and Georgetown has just begun operating: call **Pleasuresports** (☎ /fax 462125).

Local Transport

Frequent GPTC (government) buses run between Banjul and Basse Santa Su, as do bush taxis and minibuses. Upcountry services often require a change of vehicle at Soma. Fares are reasonable: for example, to travel the length of the country from Banjul to Basse Santa Su by bus costs US$3, or US$3.50 on the express. Shared taxis are to be found only in the Banjul and Atlantic Coast resorts area, and fares are comparable with bus fares.

Wherever you go, by bush taxi or minibus, there's usually a baggage charge of a few dalasi.

BANJUL

pop 50,000

Banjul's one of those rare African capitals: a small town on the margins of the national pulse, with a relatively peaceful, village-like atmosphere. Founded in 1816 as Bathurst, the island settlement quickly became the centre of the small, neglected colony. With no room to expand, Banjul has taken on a quaint air of decaying colonial elegance, with peeling paint and potholed streets. It's not without its charm. Banjul has a life of its own that is distinctly African, and is a great contrast to Serekunda, the nation's real centre of gravity, and the coastal resorts, where travellers should find most of the conveniences they require.

Banjul International Airport's main runway was partly built by NASA as an emergency runway for space shuttles.

ORIENTATION

The airport, about 20km from the city centre. A private-hire taxi from the airport to Banjul costs US$4. Drivers keep to the official fares (listed on the wall at the taxi rank), so bargaining is not required. Going to the airport, you should get at least 30% off this price.

INFORMATION

Internet Access

For international telephone and Internet access in Banjul, **Roots Enterprises Internet Café**

(July 22 Dr) has a couple of cramped terminals and charges an expensive US$0.90 for 10 minutes.

Money

Banks in Banjul include **Standard Chartered** (☎ 221681; Ecowas Ave) and **BICIS** (11A Liberation St). Some banks have ATMs. Black-market moneychangers can be found around July 22 Square. They offer about 5% more than official rates.

Post & Telephone

The **main post office** (Russell St; ☼ 8am-4pm Mon-Sat) is next door to the **Gamtel** office (☼ 8am-11.30pm).

Travel Agencies

The **Banjul Travel Agency** (☎ 228473; Ecowas Ave) handles flights on most airlines and is quite efficient.

DANGERS & ANNOYANCES

The Barra ferry is rife with pickpockets, and tourists are easy prey at the ferry terminals and the Albert Market. There's no street lighting at night, so take care not to fall into an open drain or sewer.

SIGHTS & ACTIVITIES

In Banjul, the **National Museum** (July 22 Dr; admission US$1; ☼ 8am-4pm Mon-Thu, 8am-1pm Fri & Sat) is perhaps worth a visit for its history and ethnology exhibits, which are all well labelled and explained in detail.

There are good views from the balcony of **Arch 22** (July 22 Dr; admission US$0.40; ☼ 9am-11pm), a massive gateway at the city's entrance, built to celebrate the military coup of 22 July 1994. The fountain is empty, but thirsts are slaked at the small café here.

Taking a **pirogue trip** through the creeks and mangrove swamps around Banjul is a popular activity for many travellers. You can either team up with some other people and ask one of the tour companies to arrange your trip, or you can find a local pirogue operator and arrange it all yourself. Ask on the mainland side of Denton Bridge, where the highway between Banjul and Serekunda crosses the creek (ask the bus driver to drop you off). Expect to pay about US$6 for a motorised pirogue, less for a paddled pirogue, and try to organise the trip beforehand.

THE GAMBIA

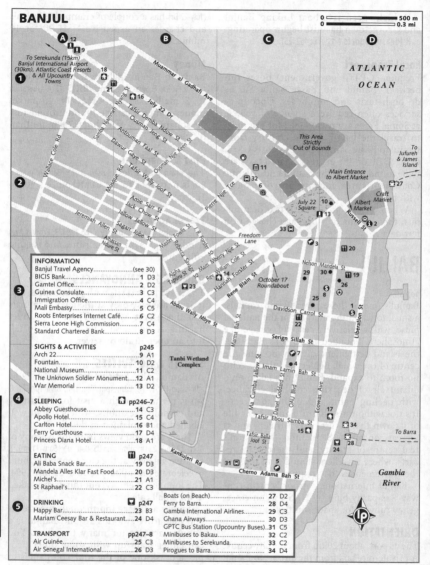

BANJUL

0 — 500 m
0 — 0.3 mi

ATLANTIC OCEAN

This Area Strictly Out of Bounds

To Jufureh & James Island

Main Entrance to Albert Market

Albert Market

Craft Market

July 22 Square

Freedom Lane

October 17 Roundabout

Tanbi Wetland Complex

To Barra

Gambia River

INFORMATION
Banjul Travel Agency............(see 30)
BICIS Bank...................................1 D3
Gamtel Office.............................2 D2
Guinea Consulate.......................3 C3
Immigration Office.....................4 C4
Mali Embassy..............................5 C5
Roots Enterprises Internet Café...6 C2
Sierra Leone High Commission....7 C4
Standard Chartered Bank............8 D3

SIGHTS & ACTIVITIES   p245
Arch 22.......................................9 A1
Fountain....................................10 D2
National Museum.......................11 C2
The Unknown Soldier Monument..12 A1
War Memorial...........................13 D2

SLEEPING   pp246–7
Abbey Guesthouse....................14 C3
Apollo Hotel.............................15 C4
Carlton Hotel............................16 B1
Ferry Guesthouse......................17 D4
Princess Diana Hotel.................18 A1

EATING   p247
Ali Baba Snack Bar...................19 D3
Mandela Alles Klar Fast Food....20 D3
Michel's....................................21 A1
St Raphael's.............................22 C3

DRINKING   p247
Happy Bar................................23 B3
Mariam Ceesay Bar & Restaurant..24 C4

TRANSPORT   pp247–8
Air Guinée................................25 C3
Air Senegal International...........26 D3

Boats (on Beach)......................27 D2
Ferry to Barra...........................28 D4
Gambia International Airlines....29 C3
Ghana Airways.........................30 D3
GPTC Bus Station (Upcountry Buses)..31 C5
Minibuses to Bakau..................32 C2
Minibuses to Serekunda............33 C2
Pirogues to Barra.....................34 D4

SLEEPING

Princess Diana Hotel (☎ 228715; July 22 Dr; r US$9-14; ❄) Also known as the Kantora Hotel, this place is good value. The best rooms are on the 2nd floor.

Carlton Hotel (☎ 228670; July 22 Dr; s/d US$14/16) A few doors down from the Princess Diana, this place is a step up in price and quality,

although reception has a reputation for iciness.

Apollo Hotel (☎ 228184; Tafsir Ebo Samba St; s/d US$8/11) Once elegant but now somewhat faded and lacking in soul. The rooms are adequate and it's the best option close to the port.

Abbey Guesthouse (☎ 225228; 38 Rev William Cole St; d US$3-6) This friendly place occupies the former German consulate in the old part of Banjul. The rooms are big, clean and oh-so-basic, and can sleep one to three people.

Ferry Guesthouse (☎ 222028; Liberation St; s/d US$10/12) The cheapest option, and conveniently located opposite the ferry terminal. Rooms are rented by the hour as well as by the night. You can also get a dirty mattress on the floor for US$4.

EATING

Street food stalls are plentiful in Liberation St, particularly around the ferry terminal and the market in Banjul.

Ali Baba Snack Bar (☎ 224055; Nelson Mandela St; 🕑 9am-5pm; dishes from US$0.50) Famous for its *shwarma* (meat sliced off a spit and stuffed in a pocket of pita-type bread with chopped tomatoes and garnish), this place has a good range of cheap meals and is popular with travellers.

Mandela Alles Klar Fast Food (☎ 223455; Ecowas Ave; dishes from US$1; 🕑 until 9pm) Around the corner from Ali Baba. Excellent fish and chips cost US$2.50.

Michel's (☎ 223108; 29 Independence Dr; dishes US$1-6) Good for a real meal. Michel's serves a variety of cuisines at great prices, and the service is excellent.

St Raphael's (☎ 226324; 17 Davidson Carrol St; dishes from US$1) Also recommended.

DRINKING

It's difficult to find a place for a drink in Banjul these days, as the nightlife is entrenched in the resorts along the Atlantic Coast.

Mariam Ceesay Bar & Restaurant (☎ 226912; Liberation St; 🕑 10am-7.30pm) At the ferry terminal, Mariam's has a colourful clientele of fishermen, wharfies and ferry workers.

Happy Bar (Rev William Cole St; 🕑 11am-late) Go there only if you're happy, as it's a condition of entry. At least pretend – once inside, cheap beer, happy regulars and the good Gambian and Ghanaian food should do the trick.

GETTING THERE & AWAY
Boat

Ferries run between Banjul and Barra, on the northern bank of the river (US$0.40, about 30 minutes). The ferries are supposed to run every hour or two between 7am and 7pm, but there are frequent delays. Small, dangerously overcrowded pirogues also make the crossing.

Bus

Government (GPTC) buses from Banjul to Georgetown and Basse Santa Su, and major destinations in between, leave from the bus station on Cherno Adama Bah St in Banjul and another station in Serekunda. There are several services daily – regular buses cost US$3 (seven hours); express buses leave at 8am and cost US$0.50 more (five to six hours). Demand for this service is high. It's best to go to the Banjul bus station the day before to check times; ask the helpful attendants at the small blue shed across the road from where the buses load and unload. Reservations are not possible, but the regular buses are rarely full.

Local Transport

Bush taxis and minibuses to upcountry destinations south of the river and to southern Senegal leave from the *garage* in Serekunda. Bush taxis to the northern border with Senegal (from where you can get transport to Dakar) and along the northern side of the river leave from Barra.

GETTING AROUND
Local Transport

For getting around Banjul and the Atlantic Coast resorts, minibuses and shared taxis are cheap and frequent. There are no buses to/from the airport itself, but minibuses running along the main road between Serekunda and Brikama pass the turn-off, 3km from the airport.

In Banjul, minibuses to Bakau leave from opposite the Shell petrol station on July 22 Dr, and to Serekunda from any of the roads off MacCarthy Square, although you'll have no problem picking one up anywhere on July 22 Dr.

Shared taxis are yellow taxis on a route designated by the first customer in the car. They operate on all major roads and need to be flagged down (if a half-full taxi stops for you, then it's a shared taxi); ask the driver if he is going to/near your destination. Most minibus and shared-taxi trips cost US$0.20.

Taxi

A short ride across town in a private taxi (known as a 'town trip') should cost about US$1. Bargaining is definitely required, although some drivers will not even consider the trip worth their while unless you pay a

THE GAMBIA

very inflated price. As a rough guide: from Banjul to Bakau costs about US$2.80; to Serekunda, US$3; to Fajara, US$3.20; and to Kotu Strand, US$3.50.

SEREKUNDA & THE ATLANTIC COAST

pop 260,000

Chaotic, splitting-at-the-seams Serekunda is by far the nation's largest urban centre and is a truer reflection of Gambian rhythms than sedate Banjul. Most people who work in Banjul live here. The nearby Atlantic Coast resorts of Bakau, Fajara, Kotu Strand and Kololi are where the package tourists flock, and amid the tawdriness of the ganja peddlers, sex tourism and eroding beaches there are some lovely spots, good nightlife and a healthy dose of genuine hospitality.

ORIENTATION

Running north–south, Bakau, Fajara, Kotu Strand and Kololi are a string of former fishing villages that now cater primarily to tourism. Serekunda, a couple of kilometres inland, is a real city, and Westfield Junction is the hub of its wheel.

A taxi from the airport, about 20km from the city centre, is US$6 to Serekunda and US$6.50 to Bakau and Fajara.

INFORMATION

Bookshops

Timbooktoo (☎ 494345; cnr Kairaba Ave & Garba Jahumpa Rd, Fajara; ☽ Mon-Fri 9am-6pm, Sat 10am-1pm) is the best English-language bookshop in the region.

Internet Access

There are now dozens of cybercafés in this area, especially along Kairaba Ave. Quantum Net branches are cheap and relatively quick; Gamtel branches are as slow as a wet week. Prices hover around US$1 per hour.

Medical Services

In Serekunda, **Westfield Clinic** (☎ 398448; off Sukuta Rd) is the place for medical emergencies. On the coast, try the British-run **Medical Research Council** (MRC; ☎ 495446; off Atlantic Rd) in Fajara.

Money

Among the many banks in the area (there are a few around Westfield Junction), Standard Chartered is open on Saturday morning. Some foreign exchange bureaus offer slightly better rates, as do moneychangers; the latter gather at Westfield Junction, but be discreet, know the rate you want and count your change. ATMs in Bakau, Kololi and at the Shell petrol station on Kairaba Ave accept Visa-affiliated cards only.

Post & Telephone

The post office is just off Kairaba Ave, halfway between Fajara and Serekunda. There is a rash of Gamtel offices and private telecentres, especially in Serekunda.

Tourist Offices

Until the Gambia Tourist Authority makes good its promise to set up information booths along the coast, hotels are the best source of information.

Travel Agencies

Most travel agencies are on Kairaba Ave. Shop around because most agencies represent an airline or two. A good start is **Olympic Travel** (☎ 497204; Garba Jahumpa Rd).

DANGERS & ANNOYANCES

The constant hustling by 'bumsters' (touts and hustlers) reached such a level in recent years that the police had to crack down on them forcefully; they were felt to be detracting from the country's international reputation. As a result, there's been a vast improvement. Crime rates are low, but crime does happen, especially around nightclubs late at night.

SIGHTS & ACTIVITIES

In Bakau, the **Botanical Gardens** (northeastern end of Atlantic Rd; ☽ dawn-dusk) are a peaceful, shady, slightly dilapidated haven, good for spotting birds and watching the fishermen go about their business.

You can get up close and personal with a croc at the **Kachikaly Crocodile Pool** (Bakau village; admission US$0.50; ☽ 9am-6pm), a sacred site for the local people and perhaps for tourists, too, judging by their numbers.

Bijilo Forest Park (admission US$0.90; ☽ 8am-6pm) is a small reserve on the Atlantic Coast at Kololi and is easy to reach by taxi, minibus or bicycle. To see various species of monkeys

SEREKUNDA & THE ATLANTIC COAST

0 — 1 km
0 — 0.5 mi

INFORMATION
Castle Exchange Bureau................1 A4
Chez Awa Exchange Bureau......(see 36)
Discount Travel.............................2 C5
Gamtel Office................................3 A4
Gamtel Office................................4 C6
Gamtel Office...........................(see 57)
Guinea-Bissau Embassy.................5 C4
Internet Café.................................6 C4
Mauritanian Consul General.........7 C4
Mauritanian Consulate..................8 A6
Medical Research Council..............9 C4
Official Tourist Guides.............(see 32)
Olympic Travel.........................(see 11)
Pharmacy...................................10 C4
Quantum Net Internet Café.........11 C4
Senegalese High Commission......12 C5
Standard Chartered Bank...........(see 5)
Swedish & Norwegian Consuls... 13 D4
Telephone..................................14 C4
Telephone..................................15 C5
Timbooktoo Bookshop............(see 11)
UK High Commission..................16 B4
US Embassy.................................17 C5
Westfield Clinic (Hospital)...........18 A4

SIGHTS & ACTIVITIES   pp248–50
Alliance Française-Gambienne..... 19 C6
Arena Babou Fatty (Wrestling
    Area)......................................20 C6
Bijilo Forest Park Headquarters...21 A6
Botanic Gardens.........................22 D3
Catholic Church..........................23 D4

Fajara Watersports Centre........(see 43)
Mosque......................................24 C5
Water Tower...............................25 C5

SLEEPING   p250
Bakau Guesthouse......................26 D4
Cape Point Hotel........................27 D3
Croc's Guesthouse......................28 D4
Fajara Guest House.....................29 B4
Friendship Hotel.........................30 D4
Green Line Motel........................31 C6
Kairaba Hotel.............................32 A6
Kanifeng YMCA Hostel...............33 C5
Kololi Inn & Tavern.....................34 B6
Praia Motel.................................35 C6
Romana Hotel............................36 D4
Senegambia Hotel..................(see 32)

EATING   pp250–1
Amsterdam Café.........................37 B6
Baobab Sunshine Bar..................38 D4
Buggerland.................................39 D4
Eddie's Bar & Restaurant.............40 B4
Golden Bamboo..........................41 B5
Safe Way Afra King.....................42 C4
Sailor...43 B5

Sen Fast Food........................(see 1)
St Mary's Food & Wine
    Supermarket..........................44 D4

DRINKING   p251
911 Nightclub........................(see 27)
Bobby's Choice..........................45 C6
Dolphin Bar & Restaurant......(see 32)
Joker's.......................................46 A5
Kumba's Bar..........................(see 36)
Laconda International Pub...........47 D4
Spy Bar......................................48 A6
Waaw Nightclub.........................49 A6

SHOPPING   p251
African Living Art Centre.............50 C4

TRANSPORT   pp251–2
AB Rent-a-Car........................(see 32)
Garage (Bus & Taxi Station).........51 C6
GPTC Bus Depot.........................52 D5
Green Taxi Rank.........................53 A5
Minibuses to Banjul & Serekunda..54 C4
Minibuses to Banjul....................55 C6
Minibuses to Banjul....................56 A4
Taxis..57 C4

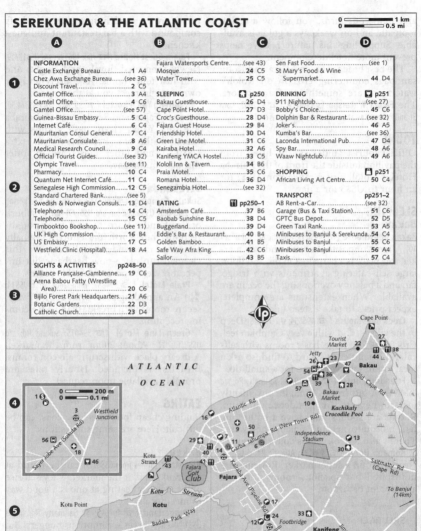

THE GAMBIA

and numerous birds, you follow a 4.5km footpath, and on weekdays a guide is available. Supporting this nature reserve helps prevent more hotel development.

The best beaches are in Fajara and Kotu; sandbags countering erosion on Kololi's waterfront are something of an eyesore. The **Fajara Watersports Centre** (☎ 912002; Kotu Strand) rents water-sports equipment.

TOURS
Official tourist guides can be hired from the pavilion outside the front of the Kairaba Hotel in Kololi. Prices range from US$1 for an hour to US$3 for a day.

SLEEPING
Bakau
Bakau Guesthouse (☎ 495059; Atlantic Rd; s/d US$6/10) Almost opposite the fruit-and-veg market, this place is a bargain. On the 2nd floor, large self-catering apartments with fridge, fan and a balcony overlooking the ocean are available. When extensions are complete, expect prices to take a steep hike.

Croc's Guesthouse (☎ 496654; s/d US$6/8) Deep in the village, and with a very Gambian feel, Croc's has four large, basic rooms with self-catering facilities. It's hard to find, so ask a local kid to take you there for a small tip.

Friendship Hotel (☎ 495830; off Saitmatty Rd; s/d US$10/12) A gift from China, inconveniently located next to Independence Stadium. Rooms are spotless and have a bathroom, fan, mosquito net and reliable hot water. There's also a pool, tennis court and gym.

Romana Hotel (☎ 495127; Atlantic Rd; d US$13) Near Maroun's supermarket, Romana has uninspired but spacious rooms with fan and decent bathroom.

> **SPLURGE!**
>
> **Cape Point Hotel** (☎ 495005; d US$20-23, apartments US$27; 🏊) Worth trying when you want something more upmarket and if you don't suffer from package-tourist snobbery.

Fajara & Kololi
Budget accommodation is hard to find in this area.

Kololi Inn & Tavern (☎ 463410; s/d US$6/8) About 1.5km in from the coast. Colourful

rooms in thatched huts are set in a leafy compound with a bar-restaurant and guest kitchen.

Fajara Guest House (☎ /fax 496122; s/d US$13/19) Newly renovated, lovely and bright, and with just four rooms. Ask nicely and the owner might meet you at the airport.

Kanifeng YMCA Hostel (☎ 392647; s/d US$3/4.50) Between Fajara and Serekunda, off Kairaba Ave, the Y has clean, basic rooms with shared bathroom. Breakfast is an extra US$0.50, and other meals are on offer throughout the day.

Serekunda
Sukuta Camping (☎ 994149; camp site per person US$2.50 plus US$1 per car, s/d US$7/9) In a suburb of Serekunda. Hard to find (ring for directions) but worth the effort. Originally aimed at overlanders and campers, this German-run place now has basic but impeccably clean and comfortable rooms.

Praia Motel (☎ 394887; Mme Jout St; r US$14; 🏊) An appealing place with cool, private, secure rooms with breakfast and a welcoming reception.

Green Line Motel (☎ 394015; Sukuta Rd; s/d US$8/12; 🏊) About 200m from the market. A dreary place with scruffy air-con rooms. Breakfast is included. Hourly rates are probably available upon request.

EATING
Finding cheap food along the coast can be difficult. Here are some suggestions.

Bakau
Rice stalls (dishes from US$0.30) can be found at taxi ranks and at the market. They sell rice and sauce, and eating at one is a good way to meet locals.

Buggerland (☎ 497697; 52 Saitmatty Rd; meals US$1.20-2.50) Serves scrumptious buggers! But the fish and chips are the highlight of the menu.

Kumba's Bar (☎ 496123; Atlantic Rd; dishes from US$2; 🕙 10am-2am) Another charming budget option, near the GSC Supermarket.

Baobab Sunshine Bar (☎ 931800; snacks from US$1) Right on the beach and out of the way. Friendly and utterly charming. Here fish and chips cost US$2.30 and a JulBrew beer is US$0.80.

St Mary's Food & Wine (Cape Point Rd) is the supermarket for self-caterers.

Fajara

Eddie's Bar & Restaurant (off Kairaba Ave; dishes US$1.50-3) This local favourite serves local dishes such as *benechin* (rice baked in a thick sauce of fish and vegetables) for around US$3, as well as European fare.

Golden Bamboo (☎ 494213; dishes US$2-4) This place is tucked away in Fajara's backstreets, but worth finding for good-value Western-style Chinese food.

SPLURGE!

In the resort areas, there are many specialist restaurants, although none are cheap. Most of the upmarket hotels offer all-you-can-eat **buffets** in the US$10 to US$15 range.

Kotu & Kololi

Sailor (☎ 460521; dishes US$1.50-5; ✆ 9am-midnight) In Kotu, this is recommended by readers as the pick of the beach bars.

Dolphin Bar & Restaurant (☎ 460929; dishes US$2-6) Near the entrance to Kairaba Hotel. A favourite tourist hang-out in the middle of the Kololi action.

Amsterdam Café (☎ 461805; dishes US$1.50-2.50) Halfway to Serekunda, way off the beaten track and a great place to meet locals.

Serekunda

In Serekunda, the best place for cheap food is around the market and bus station, where there are several streets full of bars, cafés serving drinks and bread, and Senegalese-style *gargottes* (cheap restaurants) offering basic rice dishes.

Sen Fast Food (☎ 372792; Kairaba Ave; meals from US$0.50. ✆ until dusk) Near Westfield Junction, Sen is good value for light meals.

Safe Way Afra King (☎ 391360; Mosque Rd; dishes from US$1; ✆ 5pm-midnight) Lists 'cowfoot' among its African temptations.

DRINKING

There's no shortage of places to have an ale or three: here are just a couple of suggestions.

Laconda International Pub (☎ 495945; 21 Old Cape Rd, Bakau; ✆ evening-2am) Good for the Gambian pub experience or a cheap beer. The atmosphere is 'reggae on the rocks'.

Bobby's Choice (✆ noon-late) Opposite the Serekunda market. Another local with a good outlook.

CLUBBING

Cover charges vary according to the venue and the night: expect to pay between US$1 and US$3.

Joker's (Westfield Junction, Serekunda; open 6pm-late) Buzzes on Friday and Saturday nights playing *mbalax* (a Senegalese music style) and reggae – a real local hang-out.

911 Nightclub (Westfield Junction, Serekunda; ✆ 6pm-late) Near Cape Point Hotel, attracts locals and tourists.

Spy Bar (Badala Park Way, Kololi; ✆ 6pm-late) The Gambia's biggest club, it has four bars, a poolroom and an outdoor garden area.

Waaw Nightclub (Badala Park Way, Kololi; ✆ 6pm-late) The current pick among the trend pundits.

ENTERTAINMENT

In Serekunda, traditional wrestling matches are popular events with tourists and locals. The 'arena', known formally as Arena Babou Fatty, off Sukuta Rd, is a vacant lot about 1km southwest of the market. Matches take place between 5pm and 7pm on most Sundays (except during Ramadan). The entry fee is US$1.

SHOPPING

African Living Art Centre (☎ 495131; Garba Jahumpa Rd) A gallery, museum, café, orchid garden, private residence and hair salon rolled into one. It's a refreshing change from the countless souvenir stalls along the coast.

Bakau market (Atlantic Rd; ✆ 6am-5pm) Fresh produce and more souvenirs than you care to imagine.

Serekunda market (cnr Sukuta & Mosque Rds; ✆ 6am-5pm) The African real deal, where you *can* find just about anything you care to imagine.

GETTING THERE & AWAY
Local Transport

Bush taxis and minibuses bound for all destinations in The Gambia leave from the *garage*, which is inconveniently located in the middle of Serekunda market. Southern destinations include Tanji, Brikama (both US$0.20) and Gunjur (US$0.30).

GETTING AROUND
Bicycle & Moped

Many of the major beach hotels rent out bicycles and mopeds, and there are also several private outfits with bikes to rent. Cycling is a great way to see this flat country. You can always put your bike on top of a bush taxi if you get tired. Prices start at around US$4 per day for a bicycle; moped prices are negotiable. Bargain hard.

Local Transport
Shared taxis are plentiful, and fares around the resort area and Serekunda range from US$0.10 to US$0.30. Green 'tourist' taxis are parked in ranks dotted along the coast; they're safe but expensive – a fare from Bakau to Kololi is US$5, for example. You're better off negotiating a price with a yellow shared taxi, which could be two-thirds cheaper or even less.

AROUND BANJUL & SEREKUNDA

ABUKO NATURE RESERVE
Abuko Nature Reserve (☎ 472888; admission US$1.50; ⏰ 8am-7pm) is rare among African wildlife reserves: it's easy to reach, being only 20km south of Banjul; you don't need a car to go in; and it's well managed. It also has an amazing diversity of vegetation and animals.

More than 250 bird species have been recorded in its 105 hectares, making it one of the region's best bird-watching haunts. Take some food and plenty to drink, and sit in one of the cosy hides and watch the birds pass. Morning's best – gates open at 6.30am for bird-watchers.

To get here, take a private yellow taxi (expensive at US$10) or a minibus headed for Brikama from Banjul or Serekunda (cheap at US$0.40). The reserve is signposted.

TANJI
The village of Tanji is a tranquil, friendly spot. It's easy to explore on a day trip from the hectic Atlantic Coast resorts, although it's worth spending a couple of days here.

Tanji Bird Reserve (admission US$1.50), 3km north of Tanji village, is in an area of lagoons, dunes, palms, dry woodland and coastal scrub that attracts an excellent range of birds. The reserve is also an important turtle breeding area.

About 2km south of the village is the engaging **Tanji Village Museum** (☎ 371007; admission US$1), which has huts of various eth-

nic designs, displays of traditional artefacts and a nature trail. There is a simple **hostel** (d US$6) here.

In the village, comfortable bungalow accommodation is available at **Paradise Inn** (☎ 414013; d US$10), a 25-minute walk from the main road.

Tanji village is a short minibus ride (US$1) from Serekunda *garage*.

GUNJUR
This small magical fishing village, about 30km south of Serekunda, is the antithesis of the beach resorts around Banjul (ie less crowded and less commercial). There is safe swimming about 100m away. Also nearby is a shallow lagoon that is home to a wide variety of migratory birds, and a patch of original forest is just behind.

The **Sankule Beach** (☎ 486065; s/d with bathroom US$8/12) has the best setting of the hotels and a good backpacker vibe. Camping is OK, and drumming lessons are available.

Minibuses from Serekunda (US$3) ply the southern coastal route as far as Gunjur.

LOWER GAMBIA RIVER

JUFUREH, ALBREDA FORT & JAMES ISLAND
When Alex Haley, the American author of *Roots*, dubiously traced his origins to **Jufureh**, a village about 25km from Barra, the place quickly became a kind of back-to-the-origins theme park. The fuss is dying down, but Jufureh is still overrated. Nearby are **Albreda Fort** and **James Island**, although there isn't much left of the fortress that once stood there.

Behind the museum in Albreda, the **Home at Last Motel** (s/d US$4/6) is cheap and clean.

To get to Jufureh from Banjul, take an early ferry to Barra, dodge the touts and find a bush taxi (US$1) – or take an organised tour.

KIANG WEST NATIONAL PARK
Also called **West Kiang** (admission US$1.50), this area of bush and riverine forest on the southern bank of the Gambia River, about 150km by road from Banjul, is a refuge for several species of monkeys and antelopes, as well as many types of birds. It's the biggest and most important national park in

the country, a great place to spot animals and go bird-watching.

Most people stay at nearby **Tendaba Camp** (☎ 541024; bungalows US$6, with bathroom US$7; meals from US$3), which is about 5km north of the main highway, and reach the park by 4WD or organised boat trip. It was the country's first inland tourist hotel, and is easily accessible by car. Otherwise, you will have to take a tour from Tendaba.

UPPER GAMBIA RIVER

GEORGETOWN
Georgetown is a sleepy, crumbling former colonial administrative centre, and is a fine place to soak up the atmosphere for a couple of days. It is situated on the northern edge of MacCarthy Island in the Gambia River, about 300km upstream from Banjul. Georgetown was originally called Jangjang-bureh. The old name is slowly being revived, but most people still call it Georgetown. The tranquil island is 10km long and 2.5km wide, mostly covered with fields of rice and groundnuts.

Sleeping & Eating
Government Resthouse (s/d US$4/8) Just off the main street. Good, clean rooms with hot-water showers.

Alaka-bung Lodge (☎ 676123; Owens St; s/d US$3.50/7) At the other end of the main street. Better value, friendly and recently renovated. In addition to dusty, double-thatched huts with shower and clean shared toilets, it has Georgetown's only email access.

Baobolong Camp (☎ 676133; s/d US$6/12) East of town and a step up. It has double chalets with fan and bathroom.

Jangjang-bureh Camp (☎ 676182; s/d US$6/12) Beautifully located on the northern side of the river in the Lamin Koto area. It has good bungalows and also hires kayaks.

Chop houses (cheap local-style restaurants) can be found near the market and the ferry.

Bendula Restaurant & Bar (on the main street opposite the school) Bendula has cheap, filling meals; *benechin* is US$3 and fish and chips cost US$2.

The lodges all serve reasonable meals. If you are after a cold beer, you can't go wrong at Tida's Bar. Ask a local for directions.

Getting There & Away
MacCarthy Island can be reached by ferry from either the southern or northern bank of the river. The southern ferry is reached by turning off the main Banjul to Basse road. Some buses go there, but on the super-express bus you have to get off at Bansang and take a bush taxi back to the ferry (US$0.50). The southern ferry costs US$0.10 for passengers, then bush taxis take you across the island to Georgetown (US$0.50), or you can walk (5km).

GAMBIA RIVER NATIONAL PARK
A few kilometres southwest of Kuntaur (northwest of Georgetown) is the **Gambia River National Park**. You will find a primate research project here, but casual visitors are not allowed, as tourism interferes with primate rehabilitation efforts. Touring the river is pleasant enough, though, and you can cruise the river in a boat, which can be hired in Kuntaur; prices start at about US$10 for a trip of three- or four-hour duration – though this might take some expert negotiation!

WASSU STONE CIRCLES
About 25km northwest of Georgetown near the town of Kuntaur are the **Wassu Stone Circles** (admission US$0.50), which archaeologists believe are burial sites constructed about 1200 years ago. Each stone weighs several tonnes and is between 1m and 2.5m in height. (The National Museum in Banjul, p245, has more information.)

Bush taxis from Georgetown's northern bank (US$0.50) will drop you near Wassu village.

BASSE SANTA SU
At the end of the sealed road, Basse Santa Su, more commonly called Basse, is The Gambia's most easterly town of any size and is the liveliest upcountry settlement. It is the only upcountry town with a bank. The riverside market revs up on Thursday, and the waterfront, which has many old shops, is fascinating. It's also refreshingly free of hassle.

Sleeping & Eating
Falladu Camp (☎ 668743; s/d US$9/17) On the north bank 100m east of the ferry landing, this is by far the best option in Basse. It has clean, comfortable bungalows, a great

kitchen, a pool, a free ferry service and (the downside) caged monkeys.

Basse Guesthouse (d US$4) The best of a bad lot of cheap places. It's friendlier and a bit cleaner than some. On the central square.

Apollo Hotel (☎ 668659; r US$4) On the main street. Basic and grimy.

There are several tea shacks around the bush-taxi park, and there's street food in the market.

Cheap restaurants include **Fatu's Chop Shop** (dishes from US$0.30) beside the *garage*, and in town **Abdoulie's International Diner** (☺ 7am-late) is one of the places serving good meals for under US$1.

Traditions (dishes US$0.50-US$1.50, ☺ lunch only) On the waterfront, this is a good place to eat lunch; serves sandwiches, snacks and omelettes. You can also camp here for US$2.

Entertainment
The Kassoumai Nightclub has cold beer and loud music on most weekends.

Getting There & Away
Buses between Banjul and Basse leave throughout the day, and minibuses and bush taxis run between Basse and Bansang, Georgetown and Soma. A minibus from Basse to Georgetown costs US$1.25. The ferry to the Gambia River's northern bank costs US$0.10 per passenger. There are also smaller boats making the crossing.

THE GAMBIA DIRECTORY

ACCOMMODATION
In Banjul and the nearby Atlantic Coast resorts of Bakau, Fajara, Kotu Strand and Kololi there's a very wide choice of places to stay, ranging from simple hostels to international-standard hotels. Upcountry, there are a few smart tourist lodges, but your choice is normally limited to basic local-style rest-houses.

DANGERS & ANNOYANCES
Petty thefts and more serious muggings have increased in the Banjul city centre, Serekunda and on the beaches around Bakau and Fajara. However, these areas are still surprisingly safe given the level of tourism along the Atlantic Coast. Avoid walking around these places at night – catch a taxi instead.

Many visitors complain about the beach boys (known as 'bumsters') who wait outside hotels and offer tourists anything from souvenirs to drugs and sex. It's best to ignore these guys completely (presuming you don't want any of their services); don't even shake hands or try to explain that you want to be on your own. Verbal abuse is their usual response, but it's all hot air.

The beaches around the Atlantic Coast resorts can be a hassle, with scantily clad package tourists strolling around the nearby villages with their bumster guides, showing little regard for local sensibilities.

EMBASSIES & CONSULATES
Countries with diplomatic representation in The Gambia:

Guinea (☎ 226862; top fl, 78A Daniel Goddard St, Banjul)
Guinea-Bissau (☎ 228134; Atlantic Rd, Bakau)
Mali (☎ 226942; VM Company Ltd, Cherno Adamah Bah St, Banjul)
Mauritania (☎ 461048)
Senegal (☎ 373752) Located one block west of Kairaba Ave in Fajara, behind the mosque not far from the US embassy
Sierra Leone (☎ 228206; 67 Daniel Goddard St, Banjul)
UK (☎ 495133; 48 Atlantic Rd, Fajara)
USA (☎ 392856; Kairaba Ave, Fajara)

In Africa, The Gambia has diplomatic representation in Côte d'Ivoire, Ghana, Guinea-Bissau, Nigeria, Senegal and Sierra Leone.

FOOD & DRINK
In every town there are usually several street stalls and at least one cheap chop house. Prices are around US$1 for *domodah* (peanut stew with rice) or *benechin*. Around the resorts, countless restaurants serve cheap African and Western fare.

JulBrew, the local beer, is refreshing. Local palm wine and various 'fire-waters' (made from distilled sugar cane or rice) are also available, especially in upcountry areas.

HOLIDAYS
As well as religious holidays listed in the Africa Directory chapter (p1003), these are the principal public holidays in The Gambia:

1 January New Year's Day
18 February Independence Day
1 May Workers' Day
15 August Assumption

INTERNET ACCESS

There are Internet cafés in Banjul and in all of the resorts. Rates are around US$1 per hour or less. Expect connections to be slow. Upcountry, access is harder to find.

MONEY

Theoretically, the dalasi was set to be scrapped in 2003 in favour of an ambitious West African scheme for a single monetary zone in the region to be implemented in two phases. In practice, the scheme is already running way behind schedule, and the dalasi is still alive and kicking.

The unit of currency is the dalasi (D), which equals 100 bututs. There are no restrictions on its import or export, and its value has declined markedly in recent times.

There are moneychanging bureaus on the Atlantic Coast that usually offer slightly better rates than the banks and don't charge commission. In Banjul and Serekunda, black-market moneychangers offer about 5% more than official rates. You will also find them at the borders and at towns along the Trans-Gambia Hwy.

If you've come in from Senegal and have no dalasi, Communauté Financière Africaine (CFA) francs are accepted for many items, including bush taxis.

TELEPHONE

The telephone system is handled by Gamtel, which has offices and kiosks in Banjul, Bakau, Serekunda and most upcountry towns, where you can dial direct overseas 24 hours a day. The lines are good, and calls to Europe cost about US$7.50 for three minutes at peak times (7am to 6pm). There are many private telecentres offering better rates. There are no area codes in The Gambia.

VACCINATION CERTIFICATES

A yellow-fever vaccination certificate is required of travellers coming from an infected area.

VISAS

Visas are required by all except nationals of the Commonwealth countries and a few others such as Belgium, Canada, Denmark, Finland, Germany, the Netherlands, Norway, Spain and Sweden. The cost varies between US$25 and US$45; visa extensions are US$17.

Those who don't need visas are given a stay permit at the border or airport, which can range from 24 hours to a month. This can be extended free of charge at the **immigration office** (☎ 228611; OAU Blvd, Banjul; ☯ 8am-4pm Mon-Fri) in Banjul.

Visas for Onward Travel

Banjul is a good place to get visas for other West African countries, as the city centre is small and easy to walk around, although some embassies are also in Bakau and Fajara on the Atlantic Coast (see opposite for addresses). When you apply for any of the visas below, you'll need one or two photos. Most embassies are open from 9am to 1pm and 2pm to 4pm weekdays.

Visas for the following neighbouring countries can be obtained in Guinea. See opposite for embassy and consulate information.

Guinea Three-month, single-entry visas are issued for US$40 the same day if you come in the morning. The consulate is open weekdays and is also sometimes open on Saturday morning.

Guinea-Bissau One-month, single-entry visas are issued for US$10, and six-month, multiple-entry visas are US$34; the process takes a few hours. (Guinea-Bissau visas are also available on the spot at the consulate in Ziguinchor, Senegal, for US$8.) The embassy is open in the morning only.

Mali The consulate here does not issue tourist visas. For visas, the closest embassy is in Dakar, Senegal.

Mauritania One-week/one-month visas are issued for about US$30/46 in 24 hours. A letter of introduction from your embassy is required.

Senegal One-month, multiple-entry visas take 24 hours to issue and cost US$8. New Zealanders, for some unknown reason, wait a long period for Senegalese visas.

THE GAMBIA

Mali

HIGHLIGHTS

- **Bamako** Live music at one of the capital's open-air clubs (p267)
- **Dogon Country** The red-rock Mars-like landscape and other-worldly culture of the Dogon (p275)
- **Djenné** Vibrant market and the organic curves of the world's largest mud building (p269)
- **Best journey** From Mopti to Timbuktu by boat along the desert-edged Niger, with bird and hippo-spotting (p262)
- **Off the beaten track** Desert trails among Hombori's hulking, rocky outcrops (p274)

FAST FACTS

- **Area** 1,240,140 sq km
- **ATMs** one, in Bamako
- **Borders** Algeria, Burkina Faso, Côte d'Ivoire, Guinea, Mauritania, Niger, Senegal; for Algeria and Côte d'Ivoire check the situation before travelling
- **Budget** US$20 per day
- **Capital** Bamako
- **Languages** French, Bambara
- **Money** West African CFA; US$1 = CFA600
- **Population** 10.5 million
- **Seasons** cool (Oct–Feb), hot (Apr–Jun), wet (Jul–Aug)
- **Telephone** country code ☎ 223; international access code ☎ 00
- **Time** GMT/UTC
- **Visas** US$30/80 one month/three months; not available on borders

Mali moves to a powerful soundtrack, a tangle of music, song and epic poetry. The pounding sun slows everything down, and only the music – simultaneously mournful and celebratory – transcends the muffling heat. The Niger River, a mass of pale ochre water, is the country's lifeline and flows through the desert like a contradiction, punctuated by slim wooden boats, like brushstrokes. Baked-mud towns and villages cling to its edges, populated by a cacophony of bright colours, men and women in regal *boubous* (long robes), crowned

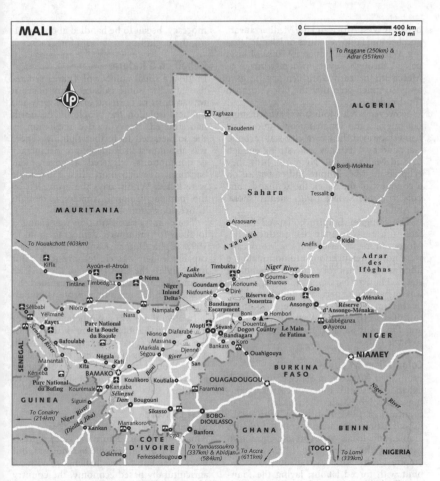

MALI

| 0 | | 400 km |
| 0 | | 250 mi |

To Reggane (250km) & Adrar (351km)

ALGERIA

Taghaza

Taoudenni

Bordj-Mokhtar

S a h a r a   Tessalit

MAURITANIA

To Nouakchott (403km)   Araouane

A z a o u â d   Anéfis   Kidal

Kiffa   A d r a r   d e s   I f ô g h a s

Ayoûn-el-Atroûs   Lake   Faguibine   Timbuktu   Niger River   Gourma-   Bourem

Tintâne   Timbedgha   Néma   Goundam   Korioumé   Rharous   Gao

Niger   Niafounké   Diré   Réserve de   Gossi   Ansongo   Ménaka

Sélibabi   Niger   Inland   Delta   Bandiagara   Boni   Hombori   Réserve

Yélimané   Nioro   Nara   Nampala   Escarpment   Douentza   d'Ansongo-Ménaka

Kayes   Parc National   Diafarabé   Mopti   Sévaré   Dogon Country   Le Main   Labbéganza

Senegal River   de la Boucle   Niono   Massina   Bandiagara   Koro   de Fatima   Ayorou

Bafoulabé   du Baoulé   Markala   Djenné   Bankass   NIGER

Manantali   Négala   Kati   Ségou   River   San   NIAMEY

Kéniéba   Kita   BAMAKO   Koulikoro   Koutiala   Ouahigouya

Parc National   Kangaba   Bani   BURKINA

du Bafing   Siguiri   Sélingué   Bougouni   Faramana   OUAGADOUGOU   FASO

GUINEA   Kourémalé   Dam   Niger River

To Conakry   (214km)   Niger River   Sikasso   BENIN

(Djoliba Jiba)   Manankoro   BOBO-   GHANA

Kankan   Pogo   DIOULASSO   NIGERIA

CÔTE   Banfora

D'IVOIRE   *To Yamoussoukro*   *To Accra*   TOGO   *To Lomé*

Odiénné   Ferkessédougou   *(337km) & Abidjan*   *(611km)*   *(339km)*

(584km)

by magnificent turbans. Mali is home not only to Dogon Country's amazing tribal villages, embedded into a dramatic escarpment, but also to mysterious, intangible Timbuktu. At night, most towns are plunged into darkness, and children chant the Quran under street-lamps. It's poor – one of the world's poorest countries – and battles against the dust but has a magnificent pride, humour and vibrancy that make it one of West Africa's greatest destinations.

HISTORY

Although inhabited by humans since before the Sahara Desert existed, Mali's history kick-starts in the 4th century with a succession of mighty ancient African empires, powered by the cross-Saharan trade in gold, slaves and salt. The first, the Empire of Ghana, covered much of present-day Mali and Senegal, but in 1076 was destroyed by marauding Muslim Almoravids from Mauritania.

Golden Years

In the 13th century, Sundiata Keita founded the Empire of Mali and converted to Islam as a friendly gesture to his northern trading partners. By the next century the empire stretched from the Atlantic to the borders of present-day Nigeria and controlled nearly all trans-Saharan trade. Its great commercial cities – Djenné and Timbuktu – grew fat on the transport of gold, salt and other goods

MALI

between West Africa and the Mediterranean, and became famous centres of Islamic leaning. When the Mali emperor Mansa Moussa passed through Egypt on a pilgrimage to Mecca in the early 14th century he gave away so much gold that the price slumped for decades.

However, while Moussa was away dishing out nuggets, the Songhaï people in the east had established their own city-state around Gao, and by 1400 they were strong enough to raid Mali's capital, Niani. In 1464 they eclipsed the Mali Empire and embarked on a conquest of the Sahel, the semiarid zone bordering the Sahara (*sahel* means 'shore' in Arabic).

The Songhaï Empire collapsed in the late 16th century after being attacked by Moroccan mercenaries, but the Moroccans were not powerful enough to dominate the huge area, and it broke up into squabbling states. The Bambara empires of Ségou and Kaarta had a brief period of dominance, but by this time European ships were beginning to sail directly to the West African coast, and the trans-Saharan trade routes began to fizzle out.

Colonialism & Coups
From their first base in Senegal, the French expanded eastward into West Africa, gaining control of Mali (then called Soudan Français) in 1898. Plantations were established, mainly groundnuts, cotton and gum arabic, and locals were press-ganged into gathering the crops. The 1200km trans-empire Dakar–Bamako train line was also built with forced labour; laying the foundations for nationalist sentiment and later rebellion.

In 1960 Soudan Français became the Republic of Mali. Modibo Keita, the first president, enthusiastically and unsuccessfully pursued one-party state socialism, creating state corporations that haemorrhaged money. In 1968 Keita was overthrown in a bloodless military coup led by Moussa Traoré. Over the next 20 years his relentless austerity measures and rampant corruption encouraged five coup attempts and numerous strikes, often violently suppressed. Continual food shortages were conveniently blamed on droughts, but were due largely to government mismanagement and corruption. Phrases like 'multiparty de-

mocracy' began to be bandied about, spelling the beginning of the end for Traoré.

Rebellion & Reform
In 1990 a small number of Tuareg separatists attacked some isolated army posts; it was an uprising born out of the poverty and political isolation the people of the north had suffered. Heavy-handed retaliation by the soldiers led to further fighting. There was also unrest in Bamako; pro-democracy demonstrations triggered a government backlash in which more than 150 people were killed. Within days the army, led by the popular Colonel Amadou Toumani Touré, took control.

The country's constitution was changed to allow for multiparty democracy, and in 1992 Alpha Oumar Konaré, a respected, capable leader, was elected president. But in the 1990s the CFA (franc of the African financial community) was devalued by 50%, which led to rioting, protests and an attempted coup.

In 1996 there was a symbolic burning of weapons in Timbuktu to mark the end of the four-year Tuareg insurgency in Mali. Konaré and his party were re-elected in 1997, though the elections were marred by irregularities and opposition parties withdrew.

21st Century
In 2002 former general and national hero Amadou Toumani Touré was elected president. ATT has his people behind him, but faces some enormous challenges. With an agriculturally based economy, the country is dependent on rain and aid for the welfare of its people. Two out of every three people live below the poverty line, and infant mortality is 10%, one of the world's highest. Crops failed in 2003, and the situation was countered only by emergency aid. The civil war in Mali's biggest trading partner, Côte d'Ivoire, has hit Mali hard, and many expat Malians and refugees have been forced north.

However, Mali has a positive basis on which to build. The government is stable and popular and continues to try to clamp down on corruption; it enjoys some of the greatest media freedom in Africa; and its diverse population live in a harmony that's rare in this part of the world.

THE CULTURE

Conscious of their heritage at the core of former great African empires, the Malian people are loud and proud – every family can boast of heroic ancestry. Mali is about 80% Muslim, but traditional animist beliefs continually entangle with the Quran; *marabouts* (Islamic teachers) hold a position somewhere between holy teacher, soothsayer and headmaster.

Hospitable, warm, tolerant, flirtatious, direct, expansive and loving a laugh: this is a Muslim country that likes to party. It likes to show off, too – dressing with exuberant magnificence, in prints of anything from mobile phones to ice cream. Rather than get riled about the cultural divides between complex tribal groups and hierarchical castes, people poke fun at them. The main groups are the urbane Mande (Bambara, Malinke, Soninke), around half the population, in the region around Bamako and Ségou; the Fulani (Peul), with their chivalrous moral code; the proud, nomadic Tuareg in the north and Songhai around Gao; the Bozo, river people; the hard-working Bobo from the inland Delta; and the Dogon, who are dedicated farmworkers. But people travel a lot from these stereotypes, and even change their names just to promote neighbourliness. Whatever your tribal moniker, social completeness is reliant on child-bearing. Women form the family backbone, and they're strong and revered, though polygamy and genital mutilation are still the norm. It's a society where tradition holds strong, though mobile phones are becoming more alluring than *marabouts*.

ARTS
Art

Carvings have been produced for centuries for particular functions – religious, magical or practical (art for art's sake is a relatively recent development). Bambara woodcarvings tend to be angular, while their masks are bold and solid – the most famous is the *chiwara*, a headpiece resembling an antelope, used in ritual dances. The Bozo produce masks as well, such as the *saga*, the representation of a sacred ram. The Dogon are famous for their carved doors (depicting their view of history), their sculpture and their masks – carved headdresses are used in elaborate ceremonies. Expressive marionettes are produced by various communities. *Bogolan* (handpainted mudcloth) is a craft centred around the area north and east of Bamako.

Film

Mali's best-known filmmaker is Souleymane Cissé, who made *Yeelen* (1987), the beautifully shot story of a father-son struggle that explores the world of magic. It won the Jury Prize at Cannes. Assane Kouyaté's *Kabala*, about a village's responses to the loss of a well, won five prizes at FESPACO, Africa's biggest film festival, in 2003.

Je Chanterai pour Toi (2002) is worth seeking out, a *Buena Vista*–style piece about musician Boubacar Traoré.

BEAN-EATING JOKING COUSINS

'What's your name?'

'Coulibaly. What's yours?'

'Traoré. What are you doing, you bean eater?'

'I eat beans! What do you mean, Traoré? You are my slave.'

Silliness in Mali has a serious function. A system of *cousinage* or 'joking cousins' exists, which is a historical relationship between different families and ethnic groups. Every family name or ethnic group has certain counterpoints, and when two people meet, on learning that their surnames denote them joking cousins, then they can insult each other – with historical references, ethnic stereotyping or just plain old silly comments – without fear of giving offence. There is a certain protocol about this: people know not to breach certain rules, and the insults tend to have a similar content. This practice eases social interaction and tensions, and the relationship cuts across status, age and gender. Over centuries of Malian history, people's ancestors have subjugated and enslaved, and then themselves been enslaved and subjugated. Through this system familial and tribal bonds are acknowledged and laughed about, helping to maintain goodwill, break ice and ridicule animosity.

Music

Malian culture has given rise to a superb, bewitching music tradition: it is not a form of entertainment but part of the fabric of life. At the heart of this tradition are the poets, musicians and historical storytellers known as *griots* (pronounced gri-ohs, also known as *jalis*; see 'The Rhythm of Life' on p219 of the Senegal chapter for an explanation of their complex role). As important as the vocal expression of history is the playing of traditional instruments, such as the *kora*, a 21-stringed instrument with a sound between a harp and a lute. The art and the instruments are passed from generation to generation, as with the innovative master Toumani Diabaté and his father Sidiki Diabaté, and 70 generations of *kora* players before them.

Typical *griot* surnames are Diabaté, Kouyaté, Sissoko and Koité, and among the best known are Kandia Kouyaté, Habib Koité, Mariam Koyaté, Ami Koita, Fanta Damba and Tata Bambo Kouyaté. Most famous of all is Salif Keita, who's not even from the *griot* caste but a direct descendant of Sundiata Keita, the founder of the 13th-century Mali empire. Already different as an albino, Keita defied his lineage to follow a musical career. Boubacar 'Kar Kar' Traoré is a veteran from Kayes who also broke with tradition, as did silver-voiced Rokia Traoré.

The most popular female singer is Oumou Sangaré, from Wassoulou in the south, who champions women's rights in her songs. Other stylistically similar stars include Sali Sidibé and Kagbe Sidibé.

Legendary, enigmatic guitarist Ali Farka Touré is from the east, and his distinctive sound marries Malian tradition with his interpretation of the American blues, a coupling that works so seamlessly that it points to the blues' origins – born partly out of the music of African slaves working in the Mississippi Delta.

Today, more cross-fertilisation has brought Malian music to a different audience: Damon Albarn, of British band Blur, collaborated with Toumani Diabaté and Afel Bocoum, among others, to make *Mali Music*, and Ry Cooder made *Talking Timbuktu* with Ali Farka Touré.

ENVIRONMENT

Mali is West Africa's largest country. The barren blankness of the Sahara covers the northern half of the country, whereas in the south there is usually enough rainfall to grow crops without irrigation. The west is a woody, hilly extension of the Futa Djalon highlands of Guinea, while the semiarid Sahel zone depends largely on the flooding of the Niger, which sweeps in a great arc for more than 1600km through the country.

Major environmental issues are the usual suspects of deforestation, overgrazing and desertification. Problems have been exacerbated by repeated droughts, forcing nomads and rural workers to the cities in search of work.

Much of Mali's wildlife has been hunted out of existence. However, there are birds, such as crowned cranes and pied kingfishers, and hippos along the Niger. Between Mopti and Gao is the Réserve de Douentza, through which a herd of huge desert elephant migrates.

TRANSPORT

GETTING THERE & AWAY
Air

Most flights from Europe to Mali cost around US$750 to US$950 return, and airlines include Air France, Ethiopian Airlines, Royal Air Maroc and Air Mauritanie. Point Afrique, flying from Paris and Marseilles to Gao, Timbuktu or Bamako, is a charter company that provides great bargains to out-of-the-way places, with flights costing around US$450 return.

Boat
GUINEA

A privately run passenger barge departs from Jukuroni (upstream from Bamako) for Kankan between July and November, or when the river is high enough (four days there, three days back).

Land
BURKINA FASO

The main border-crossing is at Faramana. There are buses between Bamako and Bobo-Dioulasso (US$15 to US$24, 15 hours, daily),

---

DEPARTURE TAX

Departure tax is included in the price of an air ticket.

running via Ségou and Faramana. Some buses go all the way from Bamako to Ouagadougou (US$26, 20 to 24 hours). Many travellers do the journey in stages: Bamako to Sikasso (US$3 to US$7, six hours), then to Bobo-Dioulasso (US$6, four hours). All bus traffic towards Burkina leaves from Sogoniko *gare routière* (bus station) in Bamako.

You can also get to Bobo-Dioulasso by bus from Ségou (US$10, 11 hours, daily) and Mopti (US$11, 15 hours, daily).

If you're in Mopti or Dogon Country and heading for northern Burkina Faso, there are bush taxis between Mopti and Bankass (US$4.50, three hours) and from Bankass to the border-post at Koro (US$2.50, two hours, daily), and a bus between Koro and Ouagadougou (US$8, seven hours, daily).

CÔTE D'IVOIRE
At the time of writing, transport to the Côte d'Ivoire had diminished because of the civil war. However, buses might go from Sogoniko *gare routière* in Bamako to Abidjan (US$31, 36 to 48 hours, three weekly).

GUINEA
The main route to Guinea is from Bamako to Conakry (US$39, 24 hours, daily), via the border at Kourémalé. Between Bamako and Kankan there are buses (US$14, 24 hours) on Thursday, Sunday and Monday from Bamako's *gare routière* at Djikoroni-Para (3km from the centre) and Sogoniko (6km south of the centre).

There are bush taxis from Bamako to Kankan (US$19), departing from the *gare routière* at Djikoroni-Para and Sogoniko on Thursday, Sunday and Monday.

MAURITANIA
Trucks leave from Bamako's Marché Medina, in the Hippodrome, for Nioro (US$15, 12 hours) and from Nioro over the border to Ayoûn el Atroûs (US$26, 12 hours). From Ayoûn el Atroûs you can get transport along the tar road to Nouakchott. The whole journey takes about three days.

If you're in Kayes, in the far west of Mali, daily bush taxis run from Kayes Ndi, on the north side of the river, to Nioro (US$9) from where you can reach Ayoûn el Atroûs. Battered 4WDs head to Sélibabi (US$9 to US$13, daily) from another station (from Kayes Ndi walk westwards for around 200m).

The *pistes* (dirt tracks) from Kayes are best travelled between November and February, and are impassable during the wet season. Even in the dry season it can be a very bumpy ride. At the border your passport might be taken for stamping, in which case check from where and when you'll have to collect it.

NIGER
The main route is from Gao to Niamey, via the border crossing at Labbéganza. Niger's national bus line (SNTN) makes the trip (US$15, 20 to 30 hours, twice weekly) as does CTR (US$14). You'll inevitably end up sleeping at one of the border posts. The road from Gao to Ansongo is really bad, and it doesn't get much better on the Niger side of the border.

SENEGAL
The most common route between Mali and Senegal is the Bamako to Dakar train – despite its being notoriously knackered.

The train (US$90/60/45 in couchette/1st/2nd class, two days) *in principle* departs Bamako at 9.15am and Kayes at 7.40pm on Saturday, and arrives in Bamako some time on Sunday. If you catch the train in Kayes, the fare to Dakar is US$60/35/25. Comfortable couchettes or large first-class seats can be reserved in advance; second class has adequate seating. There's a dining car, and you can buy cheap food en route.

The train crosses the border between Kayes and Tambacounda. The Mali and Senegal border posts are about 10km apart. At each border post you must leave the train for your passport to be stamped. Alternatively, it might be taken by a train inspector – if so, check where and when you'll have to collect it. You might need a stamp at the Kayes police station, too, but this seems fairly arbitrary. Beware of thieves on the train, especially at night.

If you miss the train to Senegal, there's a bus from Kayes direct to Dakar (US$22, twice weekly).

Bush taxis leave regularly from Kayes to the Mali side of the border at Diboli (US$5, two hours). From here you walk across the bridge to the small town of Kidira, from where minibuses run to Tambacounda. To catch a taxi in Kayes, head to Blvd de l'Indépendance, 2km west of the centre. There's also a bus to Dakar (US$22, 24 hours) on Saturday and Wednesday at 2pm.

GETTING AROUND

Air

Internal flights are operated by **Air Mali** (AKA Air Maybe; ☎ 222 8439)) and **Société Transport Aérienne** (STA; ☎ 223 8339). Both operate flights twice weekly between Bamako and Timbuktu, stopping at Mopti occasionally, as well as to Kayes.

Double-check the status and time of your flight the day before.

Boat

PASSENGER BOAT

Large passenger boats, operated by Comanav, ply the Niger between Koulikoro (60km northeast of Bamako) and Gao, via Mopti, Korioumé (for Timbuktu) and several other riverside towns. They run from August to mid-December, when the river is high. It takes about a week each way: Koulikoro to Mopti should take three days and Mopti to Gao should take four days, but schedules are unreliable and the journey along each section can take twice as long. Expect a floating mass of jostling humanity. Luxe and first class consist of two-berth cabins; second is a four-berth cabin; third is either an eight-berth or 12-berth cabin (although you can sleep and hang out on the upper deck); and fourth class is in the packed and basic lower deck (which even the most hardened travellers rate as the pits). Whatever class you're in, it'll be sweltering and the toilets will be flooded. You can buy tickets at Comanav in Bamako (p267), Mopti, Timbuktu and Gao.

Except in fourth class, meals are included in the fare. The food is bland, but you can buy extra supplies on the way. Beer, soft drinks and bottled mineral water can be bought on the boat, but sometimes run out.

Passenger boat fares in US$ include:

Section	Cabine Luxe	1st	2nd	3rd	4th
Koulikoro–Ségou	155	36	26	16	4
Ségou–Mopti	150	80	55	35	8
Mopti–Korioumé	120	65	50	30	6.50
Korioumé–Gao	150	65	60	35	8

PIROGUE & PINASSE

There are also more traditional riverboats. Pirogues (small dugout canoes) are motor-ised, punted or paddled. Pinasses tend to be larger, motorised and faster than pirogues. They may also have a simple cabin. Both can travel even when the water is low. The most popular routes are Mopti to Djenné and from Mopti to Korioumé (for Timbuktu) – see the Mopti section (p269) for details.

Bus

Several private bus companies run vehicles between main towns, including Bittar Transport (the most reliable company), Somatra (the next best), Bani Transport and Binke Transport. Booking in advance should ensure a seat.

Local Transport

Because buses are better and cheaper, there are not many bush taxis on the main long-distance routes. However, on shorter routes, such as Mopti to Djenné, they are the best (or only) overland option. Luggage costs around 5% of the fare.

BAMAKO

pop 935,400

Under the bleaching sun, with broad, dusty boulevards lined by low-rise buildings and beaten-up cars, and table football on every corner, Bamako feels like an endless market. Magnificently dressed women balance trays with wild piles of carrots on their heads, or heaps of exultant fabrics, and crouch selling henna or second-hand plastic bottles. Open sewers flank the roads. At traffic lights hawkers offer motorists the kind of thing you might want on a journey: a plastic toy, a caged bird or a brace of guinea fowl. There are more phone-card sellers here than anywhere else on earth, it seems. Quran-school boys sing harmonies as they beg. At prayer time the streets fill with the kneeling faithful. It's colourful, friendly and surprisingly relaxing. And it's one of the best places in West Africa to hear live music.

ORIENTATION

Bamako city centre is on the north bank of the Niger, focused on the triangle formed by the Ave Modibo Keita, Blvd du Peuple and the train tracks. South of Ave Modibo Keita is Square Lumumba, leading into Pont des Martyrs, which in turn leads to Route de Ségou – the main route out of town.

Taxis from Sénou International Airport (17km to the southwest) to the city centre cost about US$13, so try to share one. Getting to the airport from the city centre, you can take a *dourouni* from Square Lumumba or Gare de Ryda to the major road junction at the southern end of Route de Ségou (US$0.20). From there you can get a taxi to the airport for US$3.50.

The train station is at the heart of the city, off Rue Baba Diarra. The main bus hub is Sogoniko *gare routière*, 6km south of the city centre, just off the Route de Ségou. It's US$3.50 by taxi between Sogoniko and the city centre, or you could catch a *dourouni* (minibus; US$0.20) – they regularly pass along the Route de Ségou.

INFORMATION
Cultural Centres
The **Centre Culturel Français** (☎ 222 4019; Ave de l'Indépendance) has a decent library and puts on good events and concerts.

For details of embassies in Bamako, see p281. For details on getting visas for neighbouring countries, see the Visas for Onward Travel section in the Mali Directory (p282).

Internet Access
There are numerous Internet cafés, the best of which are as follows:
Cybercafé Companet (Ex Immeuble Somiex, Face Tribunal; US$1.50 per hr)
Smint (Ave de la Nation; US$1.50 per hr)

Medical Services
Clinique Guindo (☎ 222 2207; 19 Rue 18, Badala-bougou Estate) This is a recommended clinic.
Hôpital Gabriel Touré (☎ 222 2712, Ave van Vollenhoven) Your best bet for accident and emergency.

Money
There's a thriving black market outside the banks, where you can change travellers cheques and cash. This can be quicker and more convenient, but count what you're getting carefully. Nonbank rates are OK for euros but dismal for dollars, and are much better for cash. You can also change money at supermarkets and upmarket cafés.
BDM (☎ 222 2040; Ave Modibo Keita) Fast service; gives Visa and Mastercard cash advances.
BICIM (☎ 222 5111; Immeuble Nimagala, Bvld du Peu-

ple) Not only changes cash and travellers cheques (slowly) but also has Mali's only ATM.
BIM (☎ 222 5089; Ave de l'Indépendance) Cash and travellers cheques may be changed here.

Post & Telephone
The **Main Post Office** (Rue Karamoko Diaby) has a poste restante facility, but this is reliable for letters only.

There are loads of *cabines téléphoniques* (telephone offices) around; some are marked on the map.

Tourist Offices
Office Malien du Tourisme et l'Hôtellerie (☎ 222 5673, 0matho; ⌚ 9am-4pm Mon-Fri), near the end of Rue Mohammed V, gives out a free map and the employees are friendly – but ignore them if they try to encourage you to take a guide. No English is spoken.

Travel Agencies
For air tickets try the following:
ESF (☎ 222 5144; www.esf-travel.com; Place du Souvenir) English-speaking.
TAM Voyages (☎ 222 9200; Square Lumumba)

DANGERS & ANNOYANCES
Bamako is a pretty safe city, but there are a few areas where you should watch your back. Around the station, near the Maison des Jeunes de Bamako and near the riverbanks are areas where people have been mugged and which should be avoided at night. If your train arrives at night, stay in the station (or the foyer of the station hotel) until morning or take a taxi to your hotel.

SIGHTS & ACTIVITIES
The capital's many markets are a sea of stalls, colour and everyday entertainment. The **Grand Marché** (Rue Mohammed V) pulsates through the central pavements, packed with fabrics, potions, dried fish and plastic jars. Abutting the **Grande Mosquée**, the **Maison des Artisans** (Blvd du Peuple) is wall-to-ceiling woodcarving, with instruments, games, jewellery, beads and leather all for sale. All around the shops you can see artisans at work, stretching out skins, carving or sewing. Next door is the **Institut National des Artes** (admission free; Blvd du Peuple), where there's usually an exhibition of young sculptors' or painters' work. Another place to see artisans' work is the lesser-known **Village des Antiquares** (Marché Golonina).

BAMAKO

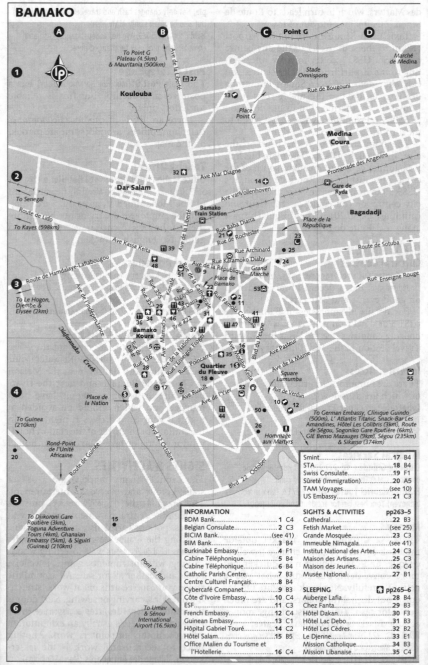

To Point G
Plateau (4.5km)
& Mauritania (500km)

Marché
de Medina

Point G

Stade
Omnisports

Koulouba

Rue de Bougouni

Place
Point G

Medina
Coura

Ave Mar Diagne

Promenade des Angevins

Gare de
Ryda

Dar Salam

Ave vanVollenhoven

Bagadadji

To Senegal

Route de Lido

Bamako
Train Station

Place de la
République

To Kayes (598km)

Rue Baba Diarra

Ave Kassa Keita

Rue de Rochester

Route de Sotuba

Rue Archinard.

Rue Enseigne Rouge

Route de Hamdalaye-Lafiabougou

Ave de la République

Rue Karamoko Diaby

Grand
Marché

Place de
Bamako

To Le Hogon,
Djembe &
Elysee (2km)

Bamako
Koura

Quartier
du Fleuve

Square
Lumumba

To Guinea
(210km)

Ave de l'Yser

Ave Ruault

Ave de Verdun

Rond-Point
de l'Unité
Africaine

Place de
la Nation

Hommage
aux Martyrs

To German Embassy, Clinique Guindo
(500m), L' Atlantis Titanic, Snack-Bar Les
Amandines, Hôtel Les Colibris (3km), Route
de Ségou, Sogoniko Gare Routière (6km),
GIE Benso Mazauges (9km), Ségou (235km)
& Sikasso (374km)

To Djikoroni Gare
Routière (3km),
Toguna Adventure
Tours (4km), Ghanaian
Embassy (5km), & Siguiri
(Guinea) (210km)

To Umav
& Sénou
International
Airport (16.5km)

Blvd 22 Octobre

Pont du Roi

INFORMATION	
BDM Bank	1 C4
Belgian Consulate	2 C3
BICIM Bank	(see 41)
BIM Bank	3 B4
Burkinabé Embassy	4 F1
Cabine Téléphonique	5 B4
Cabine Téléphonique	6 B4
Catholic Parish Centre	7 B3
Centre Culturel Français	8 B4
Cybercafé Companet	9 B3
Côte d'Ivoire Embassy	10 C4
ESF	11 C3
French Embassy	12 C4
Guinean Embassy	13 C1
Hôpital Gabriel Touré	14 C2
Hôtel Salam	15 B5
Office Malien du Tourisme et l'Hotellerie	16 C4

Smint	17 B4
STA	18 B4
Swiss Consulate	19 F1
Sûreté (Immigration)	20 A5
TAM Voyages	(see 10)
US Embassy	21 C3

SIGHTS & ACTIVITIES	pp263–5
Cathedral	22 B3
Fetish Market	(see 25)
Grande Mosquée	23 C3
Immeuble Nimagala	(see 41)
Institut National des Artes	24 C3
Maison des Artisans	25 C3
Maison des Jeunes	26 C4
Musée National	27 B1

SLEEPING	pp265–6
Auberge Lafia	28 B4
Chez Fanta	29 B3
Hôtel Dakan	30 F3
Hôtel Lac Debo	31 B3
Hôtel Les Cèdres	32 B2
Le Djenne	33 E1
Mission Catholique	34 B3
Mission Libanaise	35 C4

MALI

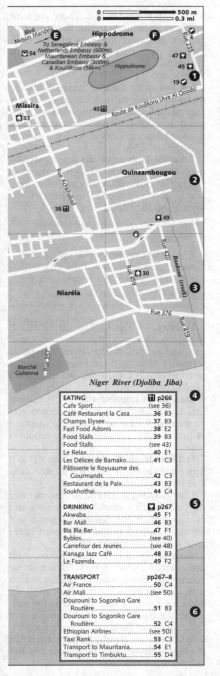

0   500 m
0   0.3 mi

Blvd Nelson Mandela
E   **Hippodrome**   **F**
Rue 235
To Senegalese Embassy & Netherlands Embassy (600m), Mauritanean Embassy & Canadian Embassy (800m) & Koulikoro (58km)
54
47
45
19
Hippodrome
Missira
33
40
Route de Koulikoro (Ave Al Qoods)
Quinzambougou
Rue Achkhabad
38
49
Rue 420
Bankoni (creek)
Rue 459
30
Niaréla
Rue 376
Rue 419
Rue 357
Marché Golonina
Niger River (Djoliba Jiba)

EATING	p266
Cafe Sport	(see 36)
Café Restaurant la Casa	36 B3
Champs Elysee	37 B3
Fast Food Adonis	38 E2
Food Stalls	39 B3
Food Stalls	(see 43)
Le Relax	40 E1
Les Délices de Bamako	41 C3
Pâtisserie le Royuaume des Gourmands	42 C3
Restaurant de la Paix	43 B3
Soukhothai	44 C4

DRINKING	p267
Akwaba	45 F1
Bar Mali	46 B3
Bla Bla Bar	47 F1
Byblos	(see 40)
Carrefour des Jeunes	(see 48)
Kanaga Jazz Café	48 B3
Le Fazenda	49 F2

TRANSPORT	pp267–8
Air France	50 C4
Air Mali	(see 50)
Dourouni to Sogoniko Gare Routière	51 B3
Dourouni to Sogoniko Gare Routière	52 C4
Ethiopian Airlines	(see 50)
Taxi Rank	53 C3
Transport to Mauritania	54 E1
Transport to Timbuktu	55 D4

The **Fetish Market** (Route de Sotuba) is where people with a problem can stock up on dried dead stuff: shrunken monkey heads, lizards and so on, as they have been directed by the *marabout* (holy man). The sad stalls are a salutary indication of the faith some place in magic. The very local, refreshingly hassle-free **Marché de Médina** is like a commercial shanty town – its stalls forming street upon street across the rough ground, piled high with bouncing fabrics, flip-flops, garlic, goats, beads, buckets and any size screw that you could want. You can get your hair braids or henna decorations here, and there's a whole section of tailors whirring.

The **Musée National** (Ave de la Liberté; admission US$1.50; 9am-6pm Tue-Sun), north of the city centre, had a big refurbishment in 2003. It has some amazing masks, including a multistorey Dogon one inspired by a block of flats. There are also hats and loincloths belonging to the mysterious Tellum, the small people who once inhabited the Bandiagara escarpment.

For a quiet walk and a stunning panorama, head to **Point G**, a plateau above Bamako. The path starts near the museum. About halfway along this road, you will see a sign that says 'Point de Vue Touristique' – follow the track for 1km.

To cool off, head to the lung-shaped pool at **Hôtel Salam** (222 1200), where you can bask the day away for US$6.

Enquire at the **Carrefour des Jeunes** (Ave de l'Oyako) about drumming or dancing lessons – see the Clubbing section on p267.

SLEEPING

The central district, Bamako Koura, is the convenient backpackerville, complete with shabby but personable places to stay, good street food, cheap restaurants, travellers and hangers on.

Mission Catholique (227761; Rue Ousamane; dm US$4.50, tw/tr US$14) This, the best budget option, is clean and peaceful, and the nuns are nice. It's often full. You can check in from 7.30am to 1pm and 4pm to 10pm Monday to Saturday, and 5pm to 10pm Sunday.

Mission Libanaise (223 5094; Rue Poincarré; dm US$4.50, s/d with bathroom US$10/14) The dorm resembles an aircraft hangar, the tin-box doubles are overpriced, and the shared bathrooms are swampy, but this rundown former mission is popular with backpackers and overland drivers. In the tranquil yard

MALI

you can have a beer and a most-grizzled-traveller contest.

Chez Fanta (300 Rue 357; dm US$7) Madame Fanta is a redoubtable character who cleans the small dorm ferociously. There's no sign, but ask locals for directions when you get close.

Auberge Lafia (☎ 223 2699; off Ave de la Nation; dm US$7, d US$14-20) This small place is in a good local area, with a family feel, but it can get very hot if the fan isn't working, and there are a few guides hanging around.

GIE Benso Mazauges (☎ 269 0194; djigiya@yahoo .com; 451 Rue 416; s US$8-12, d US$14-21) A calm haven, 9km from the centre, this French-run place has well-kept rooms, a roof terrace and meals for around US$2. Profits go back into the local community. Take a *dourouni* (US$0.20) and ask for Magnambougou Projet.

Hôtel Les Cèdres (☎ 222 7972; Ave Mar Diagne, Dar Salam; r with fan US$17; 😎) Les Cèdres has shaken off its shady past, and has good-value rooms and an attractive courtyard bar-restaurant.

Hôtel Lac Debo (☎ 222 9635; cnr Ave Modibo Keita & Ave de la Nation; s/d US$20/27) This is a bit of a dump, but friendly and central. The rooms with balconies are best.

Hôtel Les Colibris (☎ 222 6637; off Route de Ségou; d with bathroom US$34; 😎) With a serene, relaxing pool and mango-tree-shaded garden, this is a good choice with sunny rooms. It's 3km south of the bridge.

Hôtel Dakan (☎ 221 9196; south of Route de Sotuba, Niaréla; s/d with bathroom US$29/34; 😎) The Dakan's fairly spruce rooms surround a leaf-shaded garden, but the nearby road is noisy. Breakfast is included.

SPLURGE!

Bamako's most charismatic hotel is **Le Djenné** (☎ 221 9196; off Ave de la Liberté; s/d with bathroom US$36/51/60; 😎). It's not plush but it's comfortable, with simple, African decoration. The cheapest rooms have a slight corridor vibe, but the better ones are spacious and relaxing, with lots of mosquito-net-veiled atmosphere.

EATING

Cheap street food, mainly beef brochettes, fried plantains and beans, is sold all over

town from around sunset. There are some excellent stalls next to the Restaurant de la Paix and near the Kanaga Jazz Café. Pleasing patisseries and good restaurants are dotted all over Bamako Koura and Hippodrome.

Les Délices de Bamako (Immeuble Nimagala; Rue Famolo Coulibaly; dishes US$1.50-7) Big, cheery and relaxed, this has a vaguely common-room atmosphere and serves everything from breakfast to dessert. Cakes cost from US$0.50 to US$1.

Pâtisserie le Royaume des Gourmands (Ave Modibo Keita; dishes US$1.50-5) This is a cake-shop verging on greatness, with real coffee, fresh orange juice and good salads. Pastries cost from US$0.50 to US$1.

SPLURGE!

It's time for Thai. **Soukhothai** (☎ 222 2448; Rue 311, Quartier du Fleuve; dishes US$4.50-17) has good service and is cosy, and the food's delicious.

Le Relax (Route de Koulikoro; dishes US$1.50-7) Popular with expats, this has dusty canopies and is open to the street. The pâtisseries are great, and the main courses are usually tasty. It's also open late and serves alcohol (wine US$13).

Snack-Bar Les Amandines (☎ 222 1171; 622 Ave de l'Oua; dishes US$2.50) What is it with expats and patisseries? You can ponder the question at this swanky, popular, creamy-canopied joint.

Fast Food Adonis (Rue Achkabad; dishes US$1.50-5) This place has the ambience of a kebab shop and serves up delicious felafel.

Champs Elysee (☎ 223 7572; Rue l'Enseigne Froger; dishes US$4.50) This small white-painted and mirrored place has delicious Russian and Lebanese food (the *capitaine* brochettes are good), and occasional karaoke.

Bargain places in Bamako Koura, with dishes around US$1 to US$1.50, are old favourite Café Restaurant de la Casa, which is welcoming and a big travellers' hangout, and Café Sport, a colourful hole in the wall, where the outside tables are a prime spot for a cold beer. Both are opposite the Mission Catholique. Nearby **Restaurant de la Paix** (Rue Bagayoko; dishes US$1) is Senagalese-run and another friendly joint.

MALI

DRINKING & CLUBBING

There's lots of live music around town – in about every neighbourhood club at the weekend. Check the clusters to the west of town, to the east, in the Hippodrome area and just to the south of the river. Places are in their prime from around midnight, and keep going till around 5am or so. A beer costs from US$1.50 to US$3.50. Admission is free unless otherwise stated.

Le Hogon (☎ 223 0760, N'Tomi Korobougou; admission US$1) Where to head if you like dancing under the stars to virtuoso musicians and drinking beer. On Friday, at around midnight, Toumani Diabaté (see the Music section on p260) takes to the stage.

Djembe (Lafiabougou) A fantastic, sultry, partly open-air, live music venue, this is near Le Hogon. *Griots* and regular Guinean bands are a feature.

Elysée (Ancienne Route de Kati) Another winner in the west, this is on a tropical trip, with a grass-woven roof, glitter balls, Afro jazz, traditional Malian music and a packed dance-floor.

Bla Bla Bar (Rue 235, Hippodrome) Long the place to be seen, the Bla Bla is mostly open air, set in a strip of restaurants. Spot the faces at Byblos later.

Carrefour des Jeunes (Ave de l'Oyako) This place has a youth-club feel, with its open-air auditorium and low stage, sometimes trod by such stars such as Ali Farka Touré (see the Music section on p260). The admission price depends on the act.

Kanaga Jazz Café (Ave de l'Oyako) Just next door to Carrefour des Jeunes, this place has a terrace that's another great place to see live bands.

La Fazenda (Route de Sotuba) A laid-back local haunt with an open-air courtyard and low chairs, a funky inner bar, regular live musicians and food (meals around US$1.50).

Akwaba (Rue 235, Hippodrome) This open-air salsa place has occasional live bands.

SPLURGE!

The popular **Byblos** (Route de Koulikoro; admission US$8.50) is a special hit with male expats and glammed-up hookers. Admission (which includes two drinks) can be bargained down or avoided, particularly if you're female.

Bar Mali (Ave Mamadou) A serious spit-and-sawdust drinking den (read 'brothel').

L'Atlantis (off Ave de l'Oua, Badalabougou Estate; admission US$8.50; ☺ Fri-Sun) This busy club has a recommended garden bar next door, **Titanic** (admission US$2.50; ☺ Fri-Sun), with live music.

GETTING THERE & AWAY
Air

There are numerous airlines that fly in and out of Bamako. These include the local and unreliable **Air Mali** (☎ 222 8439) as well as **Société Transport Aérienne** (STA; ☎ 223 8339). Both fly from Bamako to Mopti (US$111) and Timbuktu (US$165). Mopti to Timbuktu costs US$112. Twice weekly Air Mali flies to Kayes, while STA flies there four times weekly (US$97).

Foreign carriers:

Air France (☎ 222 2212; www.airfrance.com)
Air Mauritanie (☎ 222 6750; www.airmauritanie.mr)
Ethiopian Airlines (☎ 222 6036; www.flyethiopian.com)
Point Afrique (☎ 223 5470; www.point-afrique.com)
Royal Air Maroc (☎ 221 6105; www.royalairmaroc.com)

Royal Air Maroc flies between Bamako and either Casablanca or Rabat (Morocco), and Société Transport Aérienne (STA) flies between Bamako and Abidjan (Côte d'Ivoire; US$150) and Dakar (Senegal; US$285).

Boat

Passenger boats run between Koulikoro (60km northeast of Bamako) and Gao, via Mopti and Timbuktu. To make a booking, go to **Comanav** (☎ 222 3802) on the riverbank, west of Pont des Martyrs. Ask the Comanav staff about transport between Bamako and Koulikoro.

For further details and fares, see the Transport section (p262).

Bus

Most long-distance buses go from Sogoniko *gare routière*, about 6km south of the centre. It's advisable to make a reservation.

Bittar Transport have services that go to Gao (US$24, 17 hours, twice weekly), Mopti/Sévaré (US$12, six hours, four daily), Ségou (US$4.50, three hours, hourly 7am to 7pm), Bobo-Dioulasso (Burkina Faso; US$24, daily), Sikasso (US$3.50, six hours, every two hours 8am to 8pm) and Koro (US$18, twice weekly).

MALI

Somatra are also good, and have services to Ségou, Mopti and Bobo-Dioulasso for similar prices. Both Bittar Transport and Somatra have separate stations near the Sogoniko *gare routière*.

Federation Nationale des Transports (☎ 222 9818) at the *gare routière* is a cooperative of many different companies. It runs services to Abidjan (Côte d'Ivoire; US$26), Sikasso (US$7), Gao (US$22), Mopti (US$12), Djenné (US$12), Ségou (US$4.50) and Bobo-Dioulasso (US$15).

Local Transport

Trucks to Timbuktu leave about weekly from an office by Marché Golonina. It takes two to three arduous days (US$26 to US$34).

Train

For train services west to Kayes and on to Dakar (Senegal) see Transport (p261).

GETTING AROUND

All taxis in Bamako are yellow. Those with a 'taxi' sign are shared taxis. A short journey, for example from Hippodrome to Bamako Koura, will cost around US$1, while from Bamako Koura to Sogoniko will cost around US$2.50. A shared taxi costs around US$0.50 for a short hop and US$1 to Sogoniko.

Dourounis (also called *soutramas*) are green vans that zip around town to a multitude of destinations (US$0.20). Their main gathering points are Square Lumumba and the Gare de Ryda. For Sogoniko, you can take a *dourouni* from Square Lumumba or Ave Kassa Keita.

NIGER RIVER ROUTE

For most visitors, a journey through Mali means following the course of the great Niger River as it winds its way through the southern skirt of the Sahara. You can go mostly by road, but sometimes by boat on the river itself, branching off at key points to see such wonders as Dogon Country. The places in this section are listed from west to east.

SÉGOU

pop 100,200

Ségou is graceful, lazy and balanzan-tree-lined, with wide avenues and a Monday market that jumps with colour along the sleepy waterfront. The Niger is a broad, blue-green, calm swathe here, slashed with wooden boats and edged by Bozo and pottery villages that you can visit via pirogue. Ségou is also an artisan centre, and there are lots of stalls where you can bag that *bogolan* (mud painting).

Information

BDM (Blvd de l'Indépendance) changes cash and travellers cheques. The **telephone exchange** (Blvd de l'Indépendance) has fast Internet connections (US$2.50 per hour).

Sleeping

Hôtel Djoliba (☎ 232 1572; www.segou-hotel-djoliba.com; dm US$7-9, d US$29) Conveniently central and sparkling clean, this has a European feel. There's one 10-bed and one four-bed backpacker dorm, though it's a long way to the bathroom from the latter. Excellent meals cost from US$3.50 to US$10.

Grand Hôtel de France (☎ 232 0315; d US$12) is central, though more accustomed to prostitutes than budget travellers. It has simple, dingy rooms set around a pleasant courtyard.

Delta Hôtel (☎ 232 0272; d US$17-28) is about 2km out off the main road to Bamako. It has a big veranda and a great garden, complete with model deer. The rooms are spacious and have hot water.

Eating & Drinking

There are some cheap eateries at the *gare routière*, and food stalls around the Grand Marché area.

Le Golfe (☎ 232 0698; dishes US$0.50-4) A small but good people-watching spot, with dusty-plant-sheltered tables, Le Golfe serves up good, simple food from omelettes to *capitaine* (local fish) and beer.

Hôtel-Restaurant Balely Agne (Route de Mopti; dishes US$0.50-1) *Riz sauce* (rice and sauce), served outside under a shady shelter, is tasty and plentiful here, and the fish is particularly good. It's 3.5km along Route de Mopti.

Ariane (dishes US$1.50-4.50) Near Hotel Joliba, this garden restaurant serves fine platefuls.

There's also Mombasa, an open-air disco that plays African and salsa music. It's busy on weekends but is always good for beers till the early hours.

Getting There & Away

Somatra has its own *gare routière* (east of the centre) and runs buses to/from Bamako (US$3.50, three hours, hourly), Sikasso (US$6, daily) and Bobo-Dioulasso (Burkina Faso; US$10, 11 hours, daily).

Binke's buses depart from a station 2km east of the town, and go to/from Mopti (US$8, six hours, two daily), Douentza (US$12, seven hours, two daily), Gao (US$15, 12 hours, one or two daily) and regularly to/from Bamako (US$4.50, three hours).

Bittar Transport's buses leave from the main *gare routière* east of the centre, and go to/from Bamako (US$3.50, hourly), Mopti (US$8, six hours, three daily), Gao (US$14, 11 hours, twice weekly) and Bobo-Dioulasso (US$10, daily).

DJENNÉ
pop 21,200

Smooth, monochromatic, mud buildings line the streets of the ancient trading city of Djenné, which appears to have changed little since its 15th- and 16th-century heyday. It's centred on the **Grande Mosquée**, the world's largest mud-brick structure, whose curved and spiky hugeness resembles a hallucination rather than a building. Non-Muslim visitors aren't allowed inside since some insensitive behaviour by a Western fashion photographer, but you can get a good view from a nearby rooftop.

On Monday, the **Grand Marché** fills the city with an onslaught of colour – from brilliant clothing to plastic buckets – contrasting with the quiet tones of its walls. It's advisable to stay at least a night to watch the buildings bathed in dusk. There are impressive Moroccan-decorated houses in the oldest part of the city.

To tour the town's narrow alleyways, consider hiring a guide (US$3.50 for a few hours), as you will get less hassle and see more.

Sleeping & Eating

Many people visit Djenné for the day from Mopti, but staying over for a night or two is a better way to appreciate the atmosphere of this ancient trading centre.

Restaurant Kita Kouraou (☎ 420138; d US$9) This tiny place is centred on a small bird-cage-hung courtyard. It has seven basic but good rooms with a single large, clean bathroom. Tasty meals (US$3.50) are served on the small veranda.

Chez Baba (d US$11) There are rudimentary, dusty rooms leading off a walkway, but the outlook over the mosque and the city from the roof terrace, where you can sleep for US$4.50, is excellent. The restaurant is deservedly popular, with *riz sauce* for US$2.50.

Hotel Tapana (☎ 420527; d with bathroom US$13) Out of the centre, this place has spacious but ramshackle rooms, which enclose a courtyard with a well.

Getting There & Away

Most transport arrives and departs on Monday. From Bamako, there are a few buses to Djenné (US$10) per week from Sogoniko, and a bus returns to Bamako on Monday.

From Mopti, there are regular bush taxis for Djenné (US$3 to US$3.50, four hours). It costs US$5/8 by pirogue/pinasse (two days/one day) between Mopti and Djenné.

MOPTI
pop 112,700

At Mopti's heart lies a thriving port, its large loop filled with elegant wooden boats, like sleek upturned moustaches. A daily market bustles around its edge, busy with hair-braiding, bicycle washing and boat building, and trading fish, beads, cloth and stacked biblical-style slabs of salt that glisten like marble. Mopti's a good place to meet locals and other travellers and to arrange a river trip to Djenné or Timbuktu, and although it has more than its fair share of touts, they tend to leave you alone after your first day or two in town.

Information

BIM (Blvd de l'Indépendance) changes cash and travellers cheques, as do some tour companies. **Cyber Café** (Ave de l'Indépendance) charges US$4 per hour.

Sights

Mopti's busy **port** is fascinating. The impressive **Grande Mosquée** (Ave de l'Indépendance) was built in 1935. Non-Muslims are not allowed inside – it is best seen from a nearby rooftop.

The **Marché des Souvenirs**, in the centre, is Craft Central, with carpets, beads, silver jewellery, masks, pottery and tailors slicing into

MALI

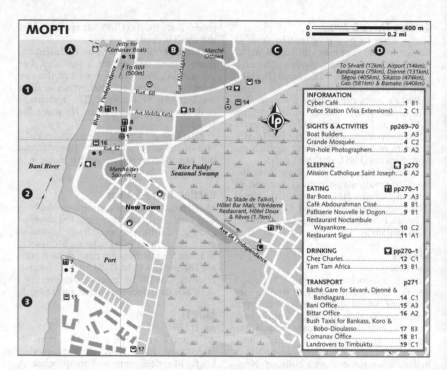

brilliant cloth. Mopti is where to buy eye-candy Fulani wedding blankets – the sellers walk around with stacks on their heads.

Along Rue 62 there is a row of **pin-hole photographers**. It's worth having your photo taken just to watch the process.

Sleeping

Mission Catholique Saint Joseph (Blvd de l'Indépendance; dm/d US$4.50/9) Superbly located, this is calm, clean and quiet, with a good rooftop. It's also a great place to meet other travellers.

Hôtel Doux Rêves (☎ 430490; dm US$5; s/d US$12/16, with bathroom US$17/20) In the oldest quarter, a little away from the action near Stade Taïkiri, Doux Rêves is smart and clean. There's live music on Tuesday and Saturday evening, and it's run by an association to support young single mothers. They also run the Yérédemé Restaurant nearby (see Eating & Drinking, next).

Hôtel Bar Mali (Rue 157, Gungal; dm/s/d US$7/9/10) A dark, grubby warren and hooker hangout, this place has a gothic charm and caricature sleaziness that makes it feel like a film set – unfortunately it's not.

Eating & Drinking

Yérédemé Restaurant (dishes US$1-4.50) This place, opposite Stade de Taïkiri, serves good food in a shady courtyard, and has a tailoring service.

Pâtisserie Nouvelle le Dogon (Ave de l'Indépendance) You might have to visit this pâtisserie several times to try all their cakes.

Café Abdourahman Cissé (Ave de l'Indépendance) This cubby-hole serves good egg sarnies (US$0.50).

Restaurant Noctambule Wayankore (off Ave de l'Indépendance; dishes US$1-1.50) This Nigerian-run place does simple meals (two eggs US$0.50) in plain, clean surroundings.

Restaurant Sigui (Blvd de l'Indépendance; dishes US$1.50-5) Upmarket Sigui has a waterfront terrace and garden, African and European dishes, and beer.

Bar Bozo (port; dishes US$1.50-5) The Bozo juts out over the end of the port, with brilliant river views; it's perfect for a sunset beer.

At the back of Marché Ottawa, Chez Charles is little more than a trestle table in the dark, a secret market speakeasy, and worth seeking out as it'll be nothing like you expect. Beers are cheap, and the locals are friendly.

Tam Tam Africa (☼ 8pm-3am Thu-Sat) Tam Tam is Mopti's hot nightspot, with mixed African and Western music. There's also a good **restaurant and garden bar** (dishes US$1-4.50) that's open daily.

Food stalls cluster around the *gare routière*, the entrance to town and the waterfront.

Getting There & Away
BUS
Bittar (Bvd de l'Indépendance) has buses to/from Bamako (US$12, three daily) via Ségou (US$7.50). Bani (near port) runs buses to/from Gao (US$10, daily) via Douentza (US$5, three hours) and Bamako (US$7, eight hours) via Ségou (US$10, six hours). These buses run to/from the Bittar and Bani offices, not the *gare routière*.

BOAT
Pirogue and pinasse trips are popular from Mopti. You can travel to Djenné on the Bani River by pirogue/pinasse (US$5/8, two days/one day) or to Korioumé (for Timbuktu). This latter trip – along the pale luminous swell of the Niger banked by sand dunes, passing boats with rice-bag sails, makeshift villages, waving people and wading fishermen – is a highlight for many travellers. You can travel by large, laden cargo pinasse (about US$15, three days to two weeks), but this can be slow. A more serene, comfortable and quicker option is to get a group together and hire a tourist pinasse (about US$35, three days). Either way, all meals should be included, but you'll need to take your own drinking water. You sleep on the riverbank or in the boat – nights are magical, silent and starlit, but also cold, so pack a blanket or sleeping bag. To sort out your trip, you'll need to negotiate with a pirogue operator or tout – there is no shortage of them around town. You can either ask around along the riverbank to compare prices, or speak to one of the many who hang around Bar Bozo.

Large passenger boats travel between Mopti and Koulikoro (60km northeast of Bamako), Ségou Korioumé and Gao. You can buy tickets from the **Comanav office** (Bvd de l'Indépendance). For further details and fares, see the Transport section (p262).

LOCAL TRANSPORT
Bush taxis to/from Bankass (US$5, 2½ hours), Koro (US$6, 3½ hours) and Bobo-Dioulasso (Burkina Faso; US$11, 15½ hours) leave from south of the port. Bush taxis leave Baché Gare for Djenné (US$3, four hours, one or two daily, except Monday when there are more) and Sévaré (US$0.50, a few times per hour) leave when full.

Four-wheel drives to Timbuktu leave from near the *gare routière* (see Timbuktu p274 for details).

SÉVARÉ
For many people, Sévaré is just a junction town and jumping-off point for Mopti, a more famous destination just 12km away, north of the main road. But Sévaré is a laid-back town, with broad copper-dust-coloured streets, night-time socialising under street lamps and a busy bazaar. It's an appealing, restful alternative to staying in Mopti.

BNDA (Route de Mopti) changes cash and travellers cheques, and is quicker than the bank in Mopti. **Farafina Tigne** (Route de Bamako) has Internet access (US$4.50 per hour).

Galerie Farafina Tigne (☎ 420449; Route de Bamako) has a bead museum upstairs and live music on Saturday from around 4pm.

Sleeping & Eating
Sévaré offers classier accommodation than Mopti.

Mac's Refuge (☎ 242 0621; d US$12, with bathroom US$14) Mac's has rooms decorated with tribal themes, a small pool (nonguests US$2.50) and to-die-for breakfasts. Popular with the missionary set, this comfortable haven pays attention to detail, and Mac is a fount of knowledge about the region. There's an excellent reference library, a delicious, sociable three-course evening meal is provided, and bike hire is available.

Maison de Artes (377 Rue 106; dm US$7, d US$17, s/d with bathroom US$13/20) Run by an English–Dogon couple, this is a lovely place, thoughtfully decorated and clean. It's set around a garden-courtyard. Rooms have fans, although they still can become stuffy.

There are good, cheap eats in Sévaré.

Chez Fofana (dishes US$1) A street stall opposite the Mobil garage where a big man sells big portions.

MALI

La Gargote – Chez Tante Therese Togo (dishes US$1.50) This is a small hole-in-the-wall – another good place for a cheap meal.

La Source, next to the Mobil garage, is the place for a cold beer.

> **SPLURGE!**
>
> The best place to give your stomach a treat in Sévaré is the **Teranga** (dishes US$1-6), a Senegalese restaurant with delicious *capitaine* brochettes, set in a leafy garden, with a great terrace lit by coloured neon sticks. A small/large beer is US$1/1.50.

Getting There & Away

Sévaré is a transport hub. Buses leave the *gare routière* regularly for Ségou (US$8, four hours), Bamako (US$10, six hours), Douentza (US$4.50, 1½ hours), Hombori (US$6, 3½ hours), Gao (US$10, six hours) and Sikasso (US$8.50, seven hours).

Minibuses leave from outside the main station to Bandiagara (US$2.50, two hours), Djenné (US$3.50, four hours), Bankass (US$4.50, 2½ hours), Koro (US$6, 2½ hours) and Mopti (US$0.50).

TIMBUKTU
pop 35,300

Synonymous with nowhere, this dust-swirling city is still hard to reach, but its isolation creates only part of its mystery. Lost on the edge of the desert, Timbuktu (called Tombouctou in Mali) is a sprawl of unprepossessing flat-roofed buildings with winding streets and alleyways. It's mystical but unimpressive, and travellers, having struggled to reach the talismanic town, are often disappointed. Heavy doors are decorated with brass studs and surrounded by ornate frames. The streets are drowned in sand; even the bread, made in anthill-shaped outdoor ovens, crunches with it.

From its beginnings as a remote Tuareg settlement – one story goes that the old woman in charge was called 'Bouctou' meaning 'large navel', while 'Tim' means 'well' – by the 15th century it had become a major trading city and a famous Islamic centre. The Tuaregs run the show here, and billowing indigo robes and dramatic, mouth-masking turbans are the dress of choice. Now this distant place has the addi-tion of occasionally bewildered visitors with attendant would-be guides and souvenir-sellers.

Information

The **Bureau Regionale du Tourisme** (☎ 922086; Blvd Askia Mohamed; ☽ 7.30am-4pm) has a list of guides. BDM and BNDA, on Route de Korioumé, change cash and travellers cheques. **Telecentre Polyvalents** (Route de Korioumé) charges US$2.50 per hour for Net surfing.

Sights & Activities

A US$9 tourist tax allows you admission to Djinguereber and the museum, and you get a souvenir stamp in your passport. It's not compulsory, however. If you do not fancy paying but want the stamp, the police at Place l'Indépendance will put that all-important Timbuktu mark in your passport for US$1.50.

The **Djinguereber** (Blvd Askia Mohamed; admission US$4.50) is West Africa's oldest existing mosque. Spanish-designed and built by 500 masons in the 14th century, it has 275 huge, rough-hewn pillars and the sense of a storehouse, shot through with light. There are two other mud-brick mosques: **Sankoré** is Timbuktu's renowned, 16th-century university, with 25,000 students. There's also the 15th-century **Sidi Yahaya**.

The **Ethnological Museum** (admission US$1.50; ☽ 9am-2pm Mon-Fri), near Sidi Yahaya Mosque, gives an insight into Tuareg life and has Bouctou's well (she of the big belly-button). As elsewhere, the exhibits are covered in a fine layer of sand.

Centre des Recherches Historiques Ahmed Baba (Cedrhab; ☎ 921081; Rue de Chemnitz; admission US$1.50; ☽ daily), to the east of the post office, has an extraordinary collection of ancient *tarikh* (documents) chronicling the history of Mali.

The crumbling houses of such 19th-century explorers as **René Caillié** and **Gordon Laing**, and of **DW Berky**, leader of the first American trans-Saharan expedition, bear plaques. At the house of **Heinrich Barth** (admission US$1.50; ☽ 8am-6pm), one of the more culturally sensitive explorers, there's a pint-sized but interesting museum.

The **Marché Artisanal** (Blvd Askia Mohamed) sells Tuareg crafts.

Desert **camel treks** cost around US$17 per day and one night, food included. You can

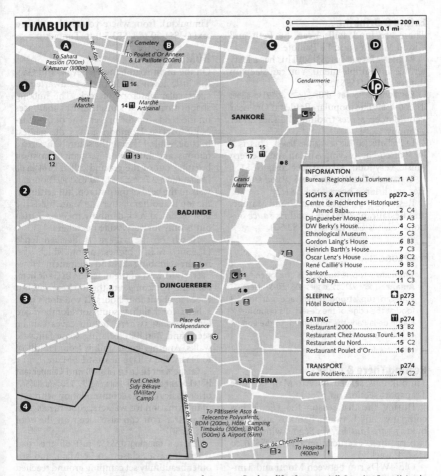

TIMBUKTU

0 —————— 200 m
0 —————— 0.1 mi

To Sahara Passion (700m) & Amanar (800m)

Cemetery

To Poulet d'Or Annexe & La Paillote (200m)

Gendarmerie

Petit Marché

SANKORÉ

Marché Artisanal

Grand Marché

BADJINDE

DJINGUEREBER

Place de l'Indépendance

Fort Cheikh Sidy Békaye (Military Camp)

SAREKEINA

To Pâtisserie Asco & Telecentre Polyvalents, BDM (200m), Hôtel Camping Timbuktu (300m), BNDA (500m) & Airport (6km)

Rue de Chemnitz

To Hospital (400m)

INFORMATION	
Bureau Regionale du Tourisme	1 A3

SIGHTS & ACTIVITIES	pp272–3
Centre de Recherches Historiques Ahmed Baba	2 C4
Djinguereber Mosque	3 A3
DW Berky's House	4 C3
Ethnological Museum	5 C3
Gordon Laing's House	6 B3
Heinrich Barth's House	7 C3
Oscar Lenz's House	8 C2
René Caillié's House	9 B3
Sankoré	10 C1
Sidi Yahaya	11 C3

SLEEPING	p273
Hôtel Bouctou	12 A2

EATING	p274
Restaurant 2000	13 B2
Restaurant Chez Moussa Touré	14 B1
Restaurant du Nord	15 C2
Restaurant Poulet d'Or	16 B1

TRANSPORT	p274
Gare Routière	17 C2

also take short sunset or evening trips, for just a few hours. These will cost only around US$5 per person. You won't get out to large dunes if you take a short trip – you'll need at least a few days or to combine your camel ride with some 4WD action. You can also take **4WD excursions** to such places as Agouni (35km away), where salt caravans muster before entering Timbuktu; with guide, driver and food it'll cost from US$125 per vehicle for a day.

Sleeping

Timbuktu accommodation is pricey. Some locals offer places to stay – usually a mattress on a rooftop costing around US$2.50 – they'll find you before you find them.

Poulet d'Or Annexe (off Rue des Etats Unis; dm US$2.50; dishes US$1-4.50) A small, mud-walled, sand-floored place, this has bucket showers and squat toilets. Simple but tasty meals are available.

Hôtel Camping Timbuktu (☎ 924032; Route de Korioumé; camp site US$5, d US$9, with bathroom US$10) Rundown rooms are balanced by a damn fine breakfast.

Sahara-Passion (near Flame de la Paix; ☎ 921394; dm US$5-9, s/d US$17/20) This is a tranquil place, with an airy dorm and plain rooms.

Hôtel Bouctou (☎ 921012; s/d US$15/22, with bathroom US$24/30; ⚡) Rooms here are simple and perhaps a little overpriced, but the back terrace is good for a beer. It's quite popular with groups.

MALI

Eating & Drinking

There are food stalls near the Petit and Grand Marchés and La Paillote.

Pâtisserie Asco (dishes US$1.50) This has a leafy terrace and simple menu. You can sleep on the roof here (US$3.50).

Restaurant Poulet d'Or (☎ 921913; dishes US$1.50-4.50) The popular Poulet d'Or, near Petit Marché, serves traditional dishes under a canopy.

La Paillote (off Rue des Nations Unies) This is a local disco-bar, playing African and Western music, very loud. A large beer costs US$1.

Restaurant Chez Moussa Touré (Marché Artisanal) Has small/large beers for US$1/2.

Restaurant du Nord, near Grand Marché, and Restaurant 2000 are good *riz sauce* options (dishes US$1.50 to US$3.50).

> **SPLURGE!**
>
> Timbuktu's top restaurant is the open-air **Amanar** (☎ 921285; dishes US$1.50-5). Here you can sup strong drinks and eat fine food at the edge of the desert. It's opposite Flame de la Paix, the monument to the end of the Tuareg rebellion.

Getting There & Away

Timbuktu is served by Air Mali (see the Transport section on p260).

During the dry season the Djedje bus company runs between Bamako and Timbuktu's *gare routière*, via Ségou, which takes two or three excruciating days (US$26 to US$34; weekly).

Old 4WDs run between Mopti and Timbuktu (US$20 to US$26, 12 to 24 hours, twice weekly), a long, hot trip through the desert; breakdowns are common – take plenty of water. Many travellers group together and hire a 4WD with driver themselves (aim for around US$220).

The best way to get here is by boat, an unforgettable trip along the dune-edged, opaque swell of the Niger to Koulikoro (60km northeast of Bamako), Ségou, Mopti and Gao. For further details and fares, see the Transport section (p262).

Hiring a tourist pinasse from Mopti is a good option (US$26 to US$34, three days). If you get a place on a cargo pinasse, it'll be cheaper (US$13) but slower. Take lots of water. You disembark at Korioumé (18km from Timbuktu), from where you catch a shared taxi (US$1.50 to US$3.50) to Timbuktu.

HOMBORI

On the main road between Sévaré and Gao, the little town of Hombori is dwarfed by spectacular outcrops of rock. The hulking shapes turn red at sunset, just as the buses on the road stop for prayer. The old, picturesque part of Hombori covers the nearest hillside, while 11km to the south is the area's famous and holy site – a giant formation bursting out of the ground called **Le Main de Fatima** (Hand of Fatima; tourist tax US$2.50). You can walk to the base of the outcrop, but getting to the top is another matter: 'Le Main' holds the best technical rock climbing in West Africa but is only for very skilled climbers.

North of the village is **Hombori Tondo** (1155m), Mali's highest point, which also requires climbing skill and equipment. However, southwest of the massif is **La Clé de Hombori**, and you can get to the top here without ropes in about four hours. If you don't have a head for heights, south of Hombori are **Fada**, **Barcousi** (where Tellum caves can be seen) and **Wari Hills**, offering some fantastic walks. Another good walk is from Hombori to Daari, the village nearest Le Main.

Campement Le Le Le (d US$9) and **Campement Hôtel Mangou Bagni** (camping US$3.50; s/d US$5/7) offer basic, clean accommodation with lots of information for walkers, good meals, and bike hire. You can also sleep on the roof (US$3.50).

There's **camping** (US$3.50) just off the road where it passes closest to Le Main, and another beautifully set camping ground reached by walking south of Fatima's northern-most finger.

Most transport is on Tuesday, which is Hombori's market day. Buses cost US$2.50 to/from Douentza, US$5 to/from Gao and US$4.50 to/from Mopti.

GAO

pop 38,300

There's a wild frontier feel about Gao. Like Djenné, it was once a prosperous Sahelian trading city that flourished during the 15th and 16th centuries. In more recent times, the town was a fixture for trans-Saharan overland drivers, but the Tuareg rebellion in the early 1990s and events in Algeria have effectively closed this route, which means that far fewer visitors pass through. More than most cities this one feels underemployed: a lot of tea drinking goes on. Nevertheless the town has a vibrant port and markets, is a centre of Tuareg and Songhaï culture, and has a striking 15th-century mud mosque.

Information
Both BDM, near Grand Marché, and **BNDA** (Place de l'Indépendance) change cash and travellers cheques.

Sights & Activities
Tomb of the Askia (admission US$1.50) houses the remains of Askia Muhammed Touré beneath an impressive mosque that resembles a termite mound pronged with wild sticks.

Musée du Sahel (admission US$1.50; ⊗ 7.30am-12.30pm & 4-6pm Sun & Tue-Fri) gives excellent background to the proud Songhaï and Tuareg cultures and includes an inventive mosquito net.

The two good **markets** and the busy **waterfront** are worth checking out – you can cross the river in a pirogue (US$0.05) and hang out on the 'beach'. A three-hour **pirogue trip** to the dunes costs around US$17 per boat. You can also explore the desolate surrounding desert-scape on a **camel trek**, costing around US$17 per day and one night.

Sleeping
Auberge Askia (d US$17, with bathroom US$20) Run by a friendly ex-guide, this is signposted off the main road, and has big bare rooms and a large grassy courtyard.

Camping Bangu (tents US$4.50, d US$10; dishes US$1-2.50) A good choice with a variety of accommodation, an Association des Femmes cooperative shop and excellent food; this also has the cheapest rooftop sleeping in town (US$2.50).

Chez Michel/Escale Saneye Auberge (☎ 282 0483; dm US$10) Next door to Camping Bangu, Chez Michel has an airy, clean, attractive dorm with mud walls. It's a good place for a rooftop snooze (US$4.50).

Camping Yurga (dm & camping US$5) Run by a nice elderly man, Yurga has rough-and-ready rooms with mud bed bases. It's about 4km south of town.

Sahara-Passion (☎ 282 0187; s/d US$20/25) On the way to the airport, popular Sahara Passion is well run, with an attractive garden and rooms that actually have some decoration.

Hôtel Atlantide (☎ 282 0130; d with bathroom US$17) Near the Grand Marché, the Atlantide is the only central option. An attractive old colonial building, it's rundown and audaciously overpriced.

Eating & Drinking
There are food stalls around the market selling grilled meat, egg sarnies and spicy sausages.

Restaurant Source du Nord (☎ 282 0355; dishes US$1.50-6) Small, central and popular, this place does hearty *riz sauce*.

Restaurant de l'Amitié (dishes US$1.50-6) Behind the museum, this is a restful garden restaurant, with excellent simple fish dishes.

Gao has an impressive array of seedy bars.

Chez Michel/Escale Saneye Auberge (☎ 282 0483) Snug bar huts outside.

Bar l'Oasis is definitely the dustiest; dark, mildly sleazy, and plays good reggae.

Baji Nightclub is busy on Saturday; other nights it's just a courtyard with a palm tree. A relaxing place for a drink.

Getting There & Away
Bittar Transport (☎ 282 0275) runs buses to/from Bamako (US$24, 18 to 24 hours, four daily). **Binke Transport** (☎ 2820291) also runs to Bamako (US$20, two daily), as does Bani Transport (US$14, daily). All travel via Hombori (US$5, two hours), Douentza (US$5, five hours), Sévaré (US$8.50, seven hours) and Ségou (US$12, 18 hours).

Gao is north of the river, and to reach it you have to cross by ferry. If you arrive at the river crossing after 6pm you'll have to sleep there overnight.

Boats operated by Comanav travel along the river to Koulikoro (60km northeast of Bamako), Ségou, Mopti and Korioumé. For further details and fares, see the Transport section (p262).

DOGON COUNTRY

The land of the Dogon people (Pays Dogon in French) resembles Hobbiton, with villages like scattered rocks, granaries with witch-hat straw roofs, shocked-looking baobab trees and perfect, small fields spread across unlikely, inhospitable terrain. Mud houses huddle around the copper-red, cracked

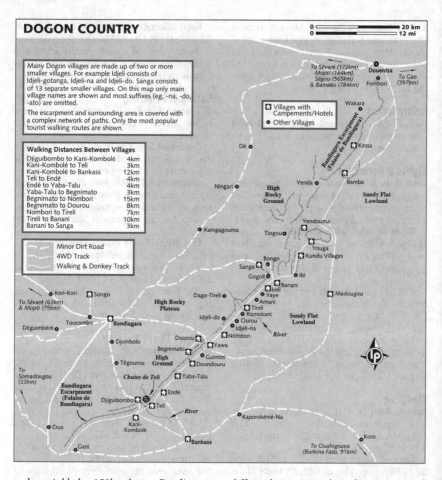

DOGON COUNTRY

0 ――――― 20 km
0 ――――― 12 mi

Many Dogon villages are made up of two or more smaller villages. For example Idjeli consists of Idjeli-gotanga, Idjeli-na and Idjeli-do. Sanga consists of 13 separate smaller villages. On this map only main village names are shown and most suffixes (eg, -na, -do, -ato) are omitted.

The escarpment and surrounding area is covered with a complex network of paths. Only the most popular tourist walking routes are shown.

Villages with Campements/Hotels
● Other Villages

Walking Distances Between Villages
Djiguibombo to Kani-Kombolé	4km
Kani-Kombolé to Teli	3km
Kani-Kombolé to Bankass	12km
Teli to Endé	4km
Endé to Yaba-Talu	4km
Yaba-Talu to Begnimato	3km
Begnimato to Nombori	15km
Begnimato to Dourou	8km
Nombori to Tireli	7km
Tireli to Banani	10km
Banani to Sanga	3km

Minor Dirt Road
4WD Track
Walking & Donkey Track

To Sévaré (172km), Mopti (184km), Ségou (565km) & Bamako (784km)
Douentza
To Gao (397km)
Fombori
Wakara
Bandiagara Escarpment (Falaise de Bandiagara)
Dé
Kassa
Ningari
High Rocky Ground
Yenda
Bamba
Sandy Flat Lowland
Kanigagouma
Tiogou
Yendouma
Youga
Kundu Villages
Bongo
Ibi
Sanga
Gogoli
Banani
Tireli
Yaye
Amani
Daga-Tireli
Madougou
High Rocky Plateau
Idjeli-do
Tireli
Komokani
Ourou
Idjeli-na
Sandy Flat Lowland
Kori-Kori
Songo
To Sévaré (63km) & Mopti (75km)
Toucombo
Bandiagara
Déguimbéré
Djombolo
Dourou
Yawa
Nombori
River
Begnimato
Guimini
To Somadougou (33km)
Tégourou
High Ground
Doundouru
Chutes de Teli
Yaba-Talu
Bandiagara Escarpment (Falaise de Bandiagara)
Endé
Djiguibombo
Teli
River
Kaporokénié-Na
Koro
Kani-Kombolé
Ouo
Gani
Bankass
To Ouahigouya (Burkina Faso, 91km)

and wrinkled, 150km-long Bandiagara Escarpment (Falaise de Bandiagara), and ancient dwellings pockmark the cliff face. The Dogon have a unique cosmology, and villages are protected by fetishes. These are sacred places – usually mud mounds, often covered with porridge. Funerals, at which dances are performed with masks and stilts, are celebrated with far more fervour than weddings.

The Dogon are believed to have arrived at the escarpment around 1500, when it was occupied by the Tellem (described in Dogon tradition as short, red-skinned people), who lived in cliff-face dwellings. One theory is that they could fly or had magical powers; another is that creepers covered the cliffs in those wetter days, forming natural ladders. The Tellum were forced away by the Dogon, but their architecture remains and is used to bury Dogon dead.

African warlords frequently attacked the Dogon, keeping them living defensively around the escarpment, and in 1920 the French conquered the region. Fortunately, all the raiders had little impact on Dogon culture. The Dogon are famous for their woodcarving – particularly small fetishes and granary doors. These artefacts have been plundered by a more recent invader: the tourist. Much work is produced today specifically for the tourist market. Ensure that what you buy is new and that you are not depriving the Dogon of their heritage.

TREKKING

The best way to see Dogon Country is to trek around it, for anything between two days and three weeks, walking from village to village along ancient tracks, sometimes above the escarpment, sometimes below the escarpment, and sometimes zigzagging along the escarpment.

You can find food and accommodation in the villages (for a small fee), and guides are available to show you the way (see the Guides section, below right). Daily distances are usually short, allowing enough time to appreciate the people and the landscape, while avoiding the midday heat.

The main gateway villages to Dogon Country are Bandiagara, Bankass, Sanga and Douentza – see the Dogon Gateways section (p278) for details.

From Bandiagara and Bankass you need to arrange transport to a village on the escarpment, such as Djiguibombo, Kani-Kombolé, Endé or Dourou. You can arrange to charter a bush taxi or hire a moped and driver – either through a local guide or ask at a *campement*. From Bandiagara you can also reach Sanga, itself within walking distance of the escarpment edge. From Douentza you can reach the far northern end of the escarpment.

From March to May it's fiercely hot, though early in the morning is OK for walking. From June to September is the rainy season – not a popular time to visit – but downpours are short, the air is clear, and the waterfalls and flowers are spectacular. November to February is the best time to trek, though temperatures are still higher than 30°C. December and January are the busiest months.

The unusual Dogon calendar has five days per week (although villages on the plateau tend to keep a seven-day week), with once-weekly markets. These are amazingly lively and colourful, and, an opportunity for beer drinking. You should definitely try to catch one during your trek.

Accommodation & Equipment

There are *campements* (basic resthouses, not camp sites) in the large villages, while in smaller ones you'll stay with a family, usually on the rooftop under a shed of stars. This is a wonderful experience, particularly in the early morning, as the sunlight hits the top of the cliffs and you listen to the sounds of the village stirring around you.

Travel light! Essentials include a good hat and a water bottle, as it can get extremely hot on the escarpment and trekkers are at risk of heatstroke and serious dehydration. You should carry at least 1L of water while walking. Filter and purify well-water before you drink it. Also bring a blanket or sleeping bag for the predawn chill, torch (flashlight) for pitch-black nights, and mosquito repellent.

Costs

Visitors to Dogon Country must pay. Fees are reasonable, and provide the local people with a much-needed source of income. The US$1 fee to enter a village allows you to take photos of houses and other buildings (but not of people – unless you get their permission) and to visit nearby cliff dwellings. To sleep at a village costs from US$1.50 to US$4.50. Villages provide simple food – chicken or peanut sauce and couscous or rice (around US$1.50 per meal). At larger villages you can buy mineral water, beer and soft drinks. Kola nuts are sought after by villagers, and you'll probably want to take some to give to the elders you meet.

Most guides offer all-inclusive tours that include all transport, fees, food, accommodation and so on. The fee ranges from US$17 to US$30 per person per day depending on the size of the group and the length of the trip. This includes the guide's food and accommodation, but excludes extra drinks and water. Some negotiation is essential.

From Bandiagara, a taxi to a local trailhead will cost from US$17 to US$34. From Bankass to Endé or Kani-Kombolé (12km), you can hire a horse and cart for between US$5 and US$9, or save money by walking this section. Douentza is 5km from the first Dogon village, at the foot of the northern part of the escarpment – but the villages at this end are spread out and the landscape less interesting.

Guides

Guides are not essential, but will help you get the most out of Dogon Country. They show you the route, help with translation (as few Dogon speak French, let alone English), find accommodation and food, stop you stumbling over sacred sites, and take you to abandoned cliff dwellings. They'll also help you observe such etiquette as the distribution of kola nuts and can explain the Dogon culture.

It is best to hire your guide in one of the gateway towns to Dogon Country (eg Bandiagara, Bankass or Sanga) rather than in Mopti or Bamako – although tour operators can be useful if you're planning a long trek with a large group. **Toguna Adventure Tours** (☎ 223 7853; ACI 2000, Hamdallaye, Bamako) is run by a Dogon–American couple, and provides a shoestring tour to Dogon Country.

When choosing a guide, write down all the expenses and your proposed itinerary, to make sure you both know what is expected. Make sure it's clear who will be paying for the guide's food and lodging. Ask questions about market days, history, festivals and so on, to see if they know their stuff, and get recommendations from other travellers. Some hotels, such as Mac's Refuge in Sévaré (p271) or the Mission Culturelle in Bandiagara (see below, right), have lists of good guides.

Routes

The options for hiking and trekking in Dogon Country are endless, but first you need to decide what part of the escarpment to visit. The central area between Dourou and Banani is the most spectacular, but also receives the most visitors, especially the villages of Gogoli and Ireli, which are easily reached from Sanga. The area north of Banani sees far fewer visitors, but the landscape is less striking. The southern section from Dorou to Djiguibombo is also very beautiful, and again popular. The far south of the Dogon, between Kani-Kombolé and Nombori, is more tranquil but less dramatic. To put all this in a cultural perspective, Islam is stronger towards the south, whereas animist traditions are most evident in the north.

The following are some three- or four-day treks, all of which may be lengthened, shortened, combined or done in reverse. See Dogon Country map (p276) for distances between villages.

SOUTHERN VILLAGES

From **Bandiagara** you could head to **Djigui-bombo**, then walk to picturesque **Teli** (first night), near a waterfall, and visit **Kani-Kombolé** with its interesting mosque. Next you could trek to pretty **Endé**, also near a waterfall. From here you could either head

to **Begnimato** (second night) for a panorama of the plains, then up the escarpment to **Dourou**, with more great plains views. You could add an extra day by diverting to **Nombori**, an enchanting village. You could, alternatively, start in **Bankass** and walk to **Kani-Kombolé**, **Teli** or **Endé**, then to **Dourou**.

CENTRAL VILLAGES

Another excellent route is to start at **Dourou**, then head to **Nombori** (first night), then to beautiful **Tireli** (second night). Next walk up on to the red-rock plateau to see **Daga-Tireli**, which has fields around a dam, then head down to **Amani**, with its sacred crocodile pool, and on to **Ireli** (third night), a classic cliff-foot village. Next scramble up the plateau to **Gogoli** and then across to **Sanga**.

NORTHERN VILLAGES

A good route from **Sanga** goes to **Banani**, then to the **Kundu villages** (first night), which stretch from top to bottom of the escarpment, then **Youga** (second night), followed by **Yendouma** (third night). These are strongly animist villages that are set around a separate hill. Finally walk up to **Tiogou** and return over the plateau to **Sanga**.

FAR-NORTHERN VILLAGES

From **Douentza**, you could walk to **Fombori**, then head up the escarpment to **Wakara** (first night), one of the area's highest villages, then to **Kassa** (second night) with its numerous springs, and then **Bamba**.

DOGON GATEWAYS
Bandiagara

Bandiagara is a quiet, dusty town, at night lit by stars rather than electricity. It's well used to people passing through. Market days are Monday and Friday, but it's liveliest on Monday. The town is 75km east of Mopti and 20km from the top of the escarpment. **Mission Culturelle** (☎ 420263) staff provide cultural information and can recommend guides.

Hôtel Satimbe (☎ 242 0378; d US$10; dishes US$1.50-5) is the most appealing budget place – a gentle oasis set around a restful courtyard.

Auberge Kansaye (☎ 420461; d US$5; dishes US$1-4.50) is well located by the (usually dried-up) river. This Rasta-run joint has cheery reggae paintings in the reception and beds in spartan rooms, and is a popular travellers' hangout.

Hôtel le Village (☎ 420331; d US$14), on the Mopti road, has simple rooms with mosquito nets around a goat-filled yard.

Toguna Hotel (☎ 242378; d with bathroom US$17; dishes US$0.50-6), 4km west of town, is shady, leafy and calm. Rooms have bright wall paintings. There is also a bar and meals.

Bar Petit Coin (dishes US$3.50) is the best restaurant. You can sit out front, in the back courtyard or in the strangely lit rooms. There are tasty dishes such as spaghetti bolognaise with an African twist (goat).

For good *riz sauce* (US$1), try Restaurant Ogotungo, a cute hole-in-the-wall, near the bus stop, or Chez Tandou, off the Sévaré road. Good places to grab a beer or find guides are Le Terminus, Galaxie or Hôtel le Village.

There are regular bush taxis to/from Sévaré (US$2.50, two hours). It is easier to get to Bankass from Mopti as there are not many bush taxis between Bankass and Bandiagara. You could also get a group of five to seven travellers together and charter a bush taxi to/from Bankass. You can arrange transport via bush taxi or moped to the escarpment through a local guide or campement.

Bankass

Bankass, which has a smooth-mud mosque and wide, red dust-coated streets, makes Bandiagara look like a bustling hub. Located 120km from Mopti and 12km from the escarpment, Bankass is a good starting point for a trek, especially if you're coming from Burkina Faso. Most of the accommodation is near the junction of the main road to Bandiagara.

Camping Hogon (d US$9) has circular, cleanish rooms. The large yard is filled with attractive wood carvings.

Hôtel Togona (d US$9) is a half-asleep place, near Hogon, and has small, dark rooms around a peaceful courtyard.

Gargotte Dogon Italienne (dishes around US$1.50) is indeed Italian-run. It serves delicious fish soup and very good millet beer, brewed with honey. Food is served in a shady garden, and some rooms were being built when we visited.

For plentiful, good *riz sauce* try **Restaurant-Bar Bintou Diarra** (dishes US$0.25), a grand name for this shack on the main road, to the right as you come into town.

The *campements* also serve food.

There are regular bush taxis to/from Mopti (US$5, 2½ hours) and daily bush taxis to/from Koro (US$2, two hours).

To get to the escarpment, arrange a bush taxi, moped or donkey cart through a *campement* or local guide.

Sanga

Sanga (also spelt Sangha) is strongly animist, packed with sacred spots, and has one of the region's biggest markets (every five days).

Actually a conglomeration of several smaller Dogon villages, it's 43km northeast of Bandiagara.

Hôtel Femme Dogon (d US$26) is a well-run and long-running hotel. Femme Dogon has airy rooms with mosquito nets, clean bathrooms and a serene sitting-out area.

Hôtel Guirouyam (d US$17), off the Bandiagara road, feels a bit out on a limb, but the big, brown-walled bar at this place serves hearty food. The rooms carry on the brown theme, but they are clean, and it is the cheaper place to sleep on the roof (US$2.50).

A lovely place to eat, **Le Grand Castor Dogon** (dishes US$2.50-4.50) has a flower-laden terrace.

There's no regular transport to/from Bandiagara, but a patient hitcher might be able to get here. Alternatively, hire a *mobylette* (moped) and rider for US$13 or US$17 (with petrol). If you get a group together, you could rent a 4WD (US$70 per day) or a bush taxi (US$26).

The best day for transport is market day, when you can pay US$2.50 per person in a shared taxi.

Douentza

Douentza is a quiet place with not much to it, but it's close to some dramatic scenery. It's only a 5km walk to the first Dogon village near the base of the escarpment, but there are long stretches between the others in the less-visited northern area.

Auberge Gourma (☎ 452031; d US$8) has rooms around a garden and is a big guide hangout.

Chez Jerome (☎ 245 2052; tents US$9; dishes US$4.50) has beds in kerosene-lit tents and excellent food, and can also help with exploring the region.

Daily buses between Bamako (US$14, eight hours) and Gao (US$5, five hours) stop here. They all call at Hombori (US$2.50, 1½ hours) as well as Sévaré and Ségou.

SOUTHERN MALI

SIKASSO
pop 125,500

The old town of Sikasso lies at the centre of Mali's lushest region. It's surrounded by crop-fields and groves of mango trees, and life revolves around the colourful and wonderfully chaotic market. Kéné Arts sells local Senoufo artisans' wares (old and new) at fixed rates.

Sleeping & Eating

Hôtel Lotio (☎ 621001; d US$7) This is the best of the cheapies in the centre. 'Chambre de passage' is advertised here (that's room rental by the hour). But rooms are reasonably clean.

Hôtel Solo-Khan (☎ 620564; s/d with bucket shower US$5/7) This hotel, at the gare routière, has bare, grimy, small rooms and is for real cheapskates.

Hôtel Mamelon (☎ 620044; d US$26; 🕵) Mamelon is much more balmy and central, with well-kept rooms and colonial charm.

Restaurant Bar Chez Les Amis (☎ 262 0955; dishes US$0.50-2.50) We're told that the brochettes (US$0.50) here are Mali's finest and the couscous (US$1.50) is fantastic. Service is slow, but you pass the time sitting under the mango trees watching outdoor TV with a large beer (US$1.50). It's between Wayerma I and Wayerma II quarters.

Other good cheap places are **Restaurant Kenedougou** (dishes from US$0.50), which is quite smart, with frilled tablecloths, or small, cosy **Le Vielle Marmite** (dishes US$1-1.50).

There's lots of street food at the Sunday market.

GUIDE TO GUIDES

One of the effects of Mali's high unemployment is that many young men try their luck as guides. You might first encounter them at the airport, and in your first few days, hopefuls might loiter around your hotel. A guide around Mali is unnecessary. It's best to hire a guide for the Dogon locally. Don't ever pay any money in advance, however convincing the spiel.

Getting There & Away

Buses go to/from Bamako (US$7, six hours, five daily), regularly to/from Bobo-Dioulasso (US$6, four hours) and on to Ouagadougou (Burkina Faso; US$17, 12 hours). At the time of research services to/from Côte d'Ivoire had ceased.

WESTERN MALI

KAYES
pop 86,500

On the Senegal River, Kayes has a frantic, vibrant market and wooden-balconied buildings. Not many travellers do more than pass through, but it's worth a stop. The town is hassle-free and you can take a pinasse trip (US$1 per person one way) along the vibrant Senegal River to the **Fort de Médine**, a crumbling colonial defence post about 15km upstream.

Sleeping & Eating

Hôtel Municipal (☎ 521947; Rue 18; s/d US$7/10) A good-value place to stay, with stark, cleanish rooms adjoining a restful garden here.

Centre d'Accueil de Jeunesse (camping US$3.50; s/d US$9/13) This place near the train station isn't too bad, and you can always drink your way through it at the bar. Rooftop sleeping costs US$3.50.

There are loads of food stalls outside the train station or in the market.

Getting There & Away

There's an airport 5km northeast of the town with regular flights to/from Bamako.

An unreliable train leaves for Bamako at 7.15am on Tuesday and Wednesday and at 7.45pm on Sunday (US$19/12 in 1st/2nd class, 14 hours).

See the Transport section (p261) for information on travelling to Mauritania and Senegal.

MALI DIRECTORY

ACCOMMODATION

Accommodation in Mali is relatively expensive, compared to other countries in the region. Cheaper places are often very grimy and unappealing (and might double as brothels), but there are smart hotels in Bamako and larger towns. Between these extremes you'll find *campements* (a basic hotel, not necessarily a camp site), where accommodation is simple but adequate and sometimes good value. There's at least one in every town.

Often the cheapest and most atmospheric way to sleep is on a *campement* or hotel rooftop – in Dogon Country it might be the only option, so a blanket or light sleeping bag, as well as mosquito repellent, will be useful. It usually costs from US$1.50 to US$4.50.

ACTIVITIES
Trekking is possible along the Bandiagara escarpment in Dogon Country (p277). Hombori offers some spectacular hiking as well as outstanding sandstone rock-climbing (p274). Camel trekking is all the rage around Timbuktu (p272) and Gao (p275).

DANGERS & ANNOYANCES
Mali is a relatively safe country – of course, if you flaunt your wealth, there might be someone who wants to lighten your load. There have been various instances of banditry on the Timbuktu to Gao route and in the northeast. Newer 4WD vehicles are popular items to steal, so look on the bright side when you can't hitch in a comfy car and have to go by beaten-up bus.

Scams to watch out for include men who initiate a discussion about Malian politics, then turn out to be secret police looking for a large fine for subversion; and an invitation to a party where 'joints' are in evidence – police turn up and you're in line for another 'fine'.

EMBASSIES
Mali has diplomatic representation in the following neighbouring or nearby countries: Senegal, Niger, Mauritania, Côte d'Ivoire and Ghana. Details are listed in the capital city section of the relevant country chapter. The following embassies and consulates are in Bamako:

Belgium (☎ 222 3875; Place du Souvenir)
Burkina Faso (☎ 221 3171; off Route de Koulikoro)
Near the Hippodrome, about 3km east of the city centre.
Côte d'Ivoire (☎ 221 2289; Square Lumumba)
France (☎ 221 3141; Square Lumumba)
Germany (☎ 222 3299; Ave de Farako, Badalabougou)
Guinea (☎ 222 3007; Immeuble Saibou Maiga, Quartier du Fleuve)

Mauritania (☎ 221 4815; Rue 218, Hippodrome, off Route de Koulikoro)
Senegal (☎ 221 8273; Rue 287, Hippodrome)
UK (British Embassy Liaison Office c/o Canadian Embassy; ☎ 227-36-74; Route de Koulikoro Hippodrome)
USA (☎ 222 3833; cnr Rue Mohamed V & Rue de Rochester)

FESTIVALS & EVENTS
Festival au Désert Timbuktu Come January, Malian and international music stars play in the desert.
Fête des Masques Held in Dogon Country in April/May, this festival celebrates the dead and harvests.
Crossing of the Cattle Diafrabe Held in December, this is a Fulani celebration of river crossing.

HOLIDAYS
As well as religious holidays listed in the Africa Directory chapter (p1003), these are the principal public holidays in Mali:
1 January New Year's Day
20 January Army Day
1 May Labour Day
25 May Africa Day
22 September Independence Day

MAPS
The IGN 1:2,000,000 is good. IGN's 1: 500,000 and 1:200,000 maps are available from **Espace IGN** (☎ 01 43 98 85 10; www.ign.fr; 107 Rue de la Boétie, Paris).

MEDIA
The Malian media is among Africa's freest. Various dailies are available in French in Bamako and other large towns. *Le Soir* and *Le Malian* are among the best. French newspapers, such as *Le Figaro* and *Le Monde*, are widely available, and Bamako hawkers will also often have US publications such as *Time* and *Newsweek*.

MONEY
Commissions vary according to the currency and whether you are changing cash or travellers cheques, but they are invariably high, and at many banks the process is slow. Euros are the best currency to carry – the rates are always better, and many banks won't even change dollars.

Some large hotels in the main towns change travellers cheques – with high commissions. You'll need your purchase receipts. There's a lonely ATM at BICIM in Bamako for Visa cardholders. Many banks transfer money via Western Union.

MALI

POST & TELEPHONE

Letters posted from regional capitals to destinations outside Africa generally arrive, but parcel post can be unreliable. Postcards to Europe and North America cost US$0.50 and letters US$1. The poste restante service in Bamako is reliable for letters.

There are many private télécentres in Bamako where you can make international calls. You can also make calls with Sotelma (the national telephone company) cardphones in the major centres; international calls are expensive. There are no area codes.

RESPONSIBLE TRAVEL

Greetings are important *herem*, so remember it's impolite to ask for directions without first saying hello and enquiring after the person's health. Mali is a Muslim country so don't wander around exposing lots of flesh or displaying affection in public. Shorts look offensive or silly anywhere but Dogon Country.

Malian artefacts have become much sought-after, with the result that Dogon granary doors now rarely grace granaries. Buying newly carved pieces will avoid plundering Mali's heritage and help artisans.

Mali's schools are desperate for materials: exercise books, biros, crayons and pencils. Rather than handing out pens or sweets on the street, you can really make a difference by making donations to local schools. Even **Bamako University** (☎ 678 5573; Bagadadji, 601 Rue 508, Bamako) is short of books: it's crying out for English classics by such authors as Jane Austen and George Orwell.

Donating medicines to medical centres is dodgy – it's illegal to use medicines that don't conform to French standards, so anything unusable will get thrown out and risks being misused. Good items to donate are bandages and dressings; these you can give to any village community centre, or

take them to the **Catholic Parish Centre** (Bamako; ☯ Tue, Thu & Sat morning) opposite the cathedral. This respected organisation visits Bamako prison, and needs dressings for prisoners' wounds. Another good item to donate is spectacles (even just the frames); contact Mr Moumouni Diarra at **UMAV** (☎ 220 3267; Faladie, Bamako) near the airport in Bamako – this organisation can adapt old glasses for people who cannot afford new pairs.

VISAS

Visas are required for all visitors except French nationals and cost US$30/80 for one month/three months; they are not available at the border.

Visa Extensions

One-month extensions cost US$9 and are easy to get at the *sûreté* building in Bamako or Mopti police station in Ave de l'Indépendance. You'll need two photos.

Visas for Onward Travel

You can get visas for the following neighbouring countries in Bamako (see p281 for address details). You'll need two to four photos.

Burkina Faso Three months US$23; issued same day.
Côte d'Ivoire Three months US$90; available within three days.
Guinea One month US$34; issued within 24 hours.
Mauritania One month US$24; issued same day.
Senegal One month/three months US$5/12; issued within 24 hours.

VOLUNTEERING

Secondary schools all have English teachers keen to practise their English. In Sévaré, for example, teachers have regular meetings just to speak in English. If you would like to help teachers with some conversational practice, contact any local school.

Niger

HIGHLIGHTS

- **Agadez** Mud minarets, swarming markets and nomads, nomads all around in Niger's No 1 ancient city (p292)
- **Aïr Mountains & Ténéré Desert** See some of the best scenery in West Africa from the back of camel; a vast slice of real Sahara, pure, simple and surprisingly spectacular (p295)
- **Niamey** Not the city itself but the Niger River nearby, perfect from a pirogue at sunset (p289)
- **Best journey** The tough but stunning stretch from Arlit to Tamanrasset, Algeria (p286)
- **Off the beaten track** If it's safe, venture past the forgotten salt town of Bilma into the forbidding and remote Plateau du Djado (p295)

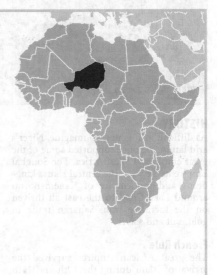

FAST FACTS

- **Area** 1,267,000 sq km (roughly five times the size of the UK)
- **ATMs** none
- **Borders** Algeria, Mali, Burkina Faso, Benin, Nigeria, Chad; land crossing into Libya not recommended
- **Budget** US$15 to US$20 a day
- **Capital** Niamey
- **Languages** French, Hausa, Djerma, Fulani, Tamashek
- **Money** West African CFA franc; US$1 = CFA600
- **Population** 10.5 million
- **Seasons** hot & dry (Sep–Jun), wet (Jul–Aug)
- **Telephone** country code ☎ 227; international access code ☎ 00
- **Time** GMT/UTC + 1
- **Visas** US$35 to US$50; easily obtained in Algeria, Benin & Chad

Niger is one of the few Saharan countries that still receives regular groups of travellers, drawn by the romance of the desert and the exotic allure of towns like Agadez and Zinder. The transport infrastructure is healthy, the people are very friendly and even the police are much less trouble than you will have been led to believe. Niger is expensive compared with some other West African countries, but the whole experience of travelling here is worth every centime spent and every gallon of sweat shed in summer. As they say locally, if you don't come to Niger, it's as if you haven't visited the Sahara at all.

NIGER

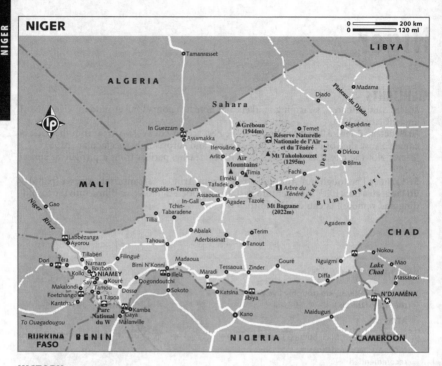

HISTORY

As difficult as it is now to imagine, Niger's arid landscape once supported some of the great empires of West Africa. The Songhaï Empire in the west, the central Hausa kingdoms and the empire of Kanem-Bornu around Lake Chad to the east all thrived on the lucrative trans-Saharan trade in gold, salt and slaves.

French Rule

The great African empires survived the arrival of Islam during the 10th and 11th centuries, but not that of the Europeans in the 19th. After the first explorers, soldiers poured into the country as part of France's West African project. Encountering stronger-than-expected resistance from local inhabitants, the invaders quickly lost patience and laid waste to much of southern Niger to assure French control. Despite these overwhelming shows of force, Tuareg revolts in the north continued, culminating in the siege of Agadez in 1916–17.

Niger, like its neighbour Chad, did not get the best deal under the colonial system,

with minimal investment and maximum interference. The French administration selectively cultivated the power of traditional chiefs, whose abuses were tolerated, if not encouraged, as a form of control. The replacement of local currency with the French franc (in which taxes had to be paid) drove many agricultural workers from their farms and into the cities in search of work, and the enforced shift from subsistence farming to cash crops further cemented French dominance by reorienting trade away from traditional trans-Saharan routes.

1960: Independence

Niger's first president, Hamani Diori, ensured a seamless transition to local rule by establishing a repressive one-party state. Social unrest and the devastating Sahel drought from 1968 until 1974 proved to be his undoing, and when large stores of food were discovered in the homes of government ministers in 1974, the would-be dictator was swiftly deposed by Lt Gen Seyni Kountché, who remained in power at the head of a military council until his death in 1987.

In 1990 students at Niamey University staged a demonstration calling for democratic reform. Several people were killed when security forces opened fire and the ensuing public outcry forced a reluctant President Ali Saïbou to convene a national conference in July 1991. An interim government was subsequently appointed to govern until elections could be held.

The Tuareg Rebellion
The small but active Tuareg population in Niger, frustrated at continually being marginalised as an insignificant minority, did not wait for these elections to address their grievances. In 1992 a raid on a police post in the small Sahel town of Tchin-Tabaradene incurred brutal police reprisals, which in turn sparked a protracted conflict that spread throughout the north, claiming hundreds of lives and effectively destroying the fledgling tourist industry.

While demands for autonomy were never accepted, some significant concessions were made, and the situation was finally resolved in 1995 with a peace accord between the government and Tuareg representatives; despite this, some rebel groups remained active as late as 1998.

Coups & Elections
Niger's first multiparty elections were held in 1993, when Mahamane Ousmane became the country's first Hausa head of state (power having been previously held by the Djermas people). His reign was short-lived: a military junta, led by Colonel Ibrahim Bare Mainassara, staged a successful coup in January 1996. Elections held in July were won by Mainassara – hardly surprising given that he dissolved the independent election commission and put his four main opponents under house arrest.

In April 1999, against the backdrop of widespread strikes and economic stagnation, Mainassara was killed by the commander of the presidential guard. The leader of the coup, Major Daouda Mallam Wanke, quickly set about a return to democratic rule. In peaceful elections in October and November 1999 Mamadou Tandja was elected with over 59% of the vote, and forged a coalition in the National Assembly with supporters of former president Ousmane.

Current Events
With elections due in 2004, government in Niger seems to be functioning smoothly and moderately, and so far the nation can take pride in the impressively swift transition from military to democratic rule. However, civil unrest among students and soldiers in particular are ever-present, and the economic situation is a constant worry.

Negative GDP growth since 1990, a heavy reliance on imports, shrinking arable land and falling uranium export prices have all helped to impoverish Niger. Over 60% of the population lives on less than US$1 a day, and in 2002 Niger still languished in second-to-last place on the UN's Human Development Index; it is hoped that World Bank loans and IMF aid and debt relief amounting to US$300 million, announced in 2000, will improve matters. Even so, the task that confronts the government is enormous, and many people are looking to tourism as a potential economic saviour.

THE CULTURE
There are five principal tribal groups: the southern Hausa (about 55% of the population); the Songhaï-Djermas in and around Niamey (22%); the pastoral Peul-Fulani (10%), including the well-known Wodaabe from west of Agadez; the Tuareg in the north (8%); and the Kanouri close to Lake Chad. Around 20% of the population remains nomadic, and 90% is involved in the agricultural sector.

French is the official language and is spoken by almost everyone, except in some rural areas. Each tribal group has its own customs and language but the high proportion of subsistence-level communities means most people cannot read or write any language (literacy stands at a shockingly low 15%).

Over 80% of the population is Muslim. While non-Islamic pastimes such as drinking and gambling are common, dress is taken very seriously and foreign women in particular should wear modest clothing.

Nigeriens have two main national obsessions: *la lutte traditionelle* (traditional wrestling), which eclipses all other spectator sports here and fosters great rivalries between towns, and table football, which you'll constantly see being played on battered old tables in the streets of most towns. Even if you don't share these enthusiasms,

NIGER

it's worth getting involved enough to have a conversation about one or the other.

ENVIRONMENT

Much of Niger is taken up by the sandy, rocky expanses of the Sahara, with most of the remainder lying in the Sahel (the dry savanna area south of the desert). The Aïr Mountains in the north rise to 2000m and can be surprisingly green in places; vegetation elsewhere in the north is sparse or nonexistent, gradually merging into scrub in the Sahel and into lightly wooded grassland in the extreme south.

The Niger, Africa's third-longest river, winds its way through the southwest corner and is the country's only permanent body of water. Lake Chad, in the southeast, is now dry on the Niger side.

The climate is hot and dry except for a brief rainy period. Most of the country receives less than 500mm of rain per year. November to January are the coolest months.

Desertification is Niger's most serious environmental problem, as only 3% of the land is arable. In particular, the introduction of high-density farming under the French put paid to traditional fallow periods, which had previously preserved the fragile ecological balance. There have been concerted but small attempts at reafforestation; sadly, well-meaning well-digging programmes have intensified overgrazing, with an increase in livestock contributing to the denuding of the landscape.

TRANSPORT

GETTING THERE & AWAY

Air

Various national airlines serve points throughout West and Central Africa, including:

Air Algérie (☎ 733156; Immeuble El-Nasr, Rue de Gaweye) For Algiers.

Air Burkina (☎ 737067; Rue de Gaweye) For Ouagadougou.

Air Niger International (☎ 734179; 3-5 Rue du Président Heinrich Lubké) For Cotonou and Abidjan.

Royal Air Maroc (☎ 732853; Immeuble El-Nasr) For Casablanca.

Land

All Niger's borders were open at the time of research; however, land crossings into

---

DEPARTURE TAX

Departure tax is around US$4.50/$15 for West Africa/international flights, although it's usually included in the price of the ticket.

Libya are dangerous and highly inadvisable for travellers (see p299), although some public transport does exist.

ALGERIA

The tough desert route from Agadez to Tamanrasset has opened up to travellers in recent years, but the problems in Algeria in 2003 (see the boxed text on p140) make caution highly advisable. From Agadez, take a bus or *taxi-brousse* (bush taxi) to Arlit, from where there should be various forms of transport heading to the shambolic border post at Assamakka. You'll then need to hitch or pay for a lift to the Algerian side and on to the frontier town of In Guezzam, where you can find transport for Tamanrasset. For more details see the Algeria chapter (p143).

BENIN

The national bus company **SNTV** (☎ 723020) has a weekly service from Niamey to Cotonou, leaving on Friday and returning on Sunday. The journey takes 13 to 15 hours and costs roughly US$22. Most travellers do this trip in stages though: minibuses and *taxis-brousses* run from Niamey's Wadata Autogare as far as the border town of Gaya (US$7, four hours); a motorcycle taxi then takes you across the Niger River to the town of Malanville. Alternatively, you can take a *taxi-brousse* direct to Malanville from the town of Dosso (halfway between Niamey and Gaya). See Benin (p421) for transport options from Malanville.

BURKINA FASO

Regular SNTV buses operate direct between Niamey and Ouagadougou (US $12.50, 13 hours). Alternatively, minibuses and *taxis-brousses* run from Niamey to the Burkina Faso border at Foetchango (US$3.50, two hours) – but they don't cross the border, whatever the driver says. From Foetchango, taxis run to the town of Kantchari, from where there are minibuses to Ouagadougou.

CHAD
The main route between Niger and Chad is a sandy track looping round to the north of Lake Chad from Zinder via Nguigmi and Mao to N'Djaména. Zinder to N'Djaména can be a slog of up to a week. You can trim this to three days, but it's more expensive.

The small town of Nguigmi is the departure point for all transport to Chad; to get there from Zinder take the twice-weekly SNTV bus (US$13) or one of the frequent minibuses and *taxis-brousses* via Diffa (US$12.50 to US$13.50).

The quickest way across the border is with one of the passenger-carrying 4WDs that run frequently to Mao (US$25, around 12 hours); there you can hook up with similar vehicles heading to N'Djaména for about the same price. Cheaper public transport in the form of small vehicles (trucks, pickups etc) and big lorries is readily available, but you'll probably have to do the journey in stages, via Massakori and Nokou, which can take up to a week if you're unlucky. Costs start at around US$8.50 for one section of the journey.

Get your passport stamped in Nguigmi and Mao (where you'll be asked for US$5) as well as at the borders, and remember that Chad uses Central African Communauté Financièr Africaine (CFA) francs; you should be able to change leftover West African CFA unofficially at a rate of one to one.

MALI
Two SNTV buses per week make the direct run from Niamey to Gao (US$20). The journey rarely takes less than 30 hours and usually involves sleeping at the border.

Alternatively, you can make the journey in stages by *taxi-brousse* (in Niamey trucks leave from Rond-point Yantala or *taxis-brousses* from Wadata Autogare) and consider breaking the trip in Tillabéri or Ayorou en route to the border town of Labézanga. Across the border you'll have to take whatever you can find going north, which won't be much more than a handful of *taxis-brousses* and private vehicles. It's worth considering travelling via Burkina Faso instead. From July to September the route is very muddy and the whole trip can be a nightmare. Take plenty of drinking water.

NIGERIA
The main departure towns for Nigeria are Zinder, Birni N'Konni and Maradi. Minibuses and *taxis-brousses* from Zinder go either direct to Kano (US$4/5) or as far as the border. From Birni N'Konni you can go to Sokoto (US$3.25), but this route is heavily potholed, there are umpteen checkpoints along the way, and the Nigerian border officials have been known to give travellers a hard time. The other routes are from Maradi to Katsina and from Dosso to Sokoto via Gaya on the Benin border.

Expect to spend some time (and money) at the Nigeria border point wherever you cross.

GETTING AROUND
Air
Until Agadez airport reopens, there are no scheduled internal flights operating in Niger. There may, however, be charter flights (see p292).

Local Transport
SNTV (☎ 723020), the government bus service, is the most expensive mode of transport. It's surprisingly professional and the buses are relatively comfortable and quite quick. You can buy your tickets a day or more in advance. The main competition comes from the private company **EHGM** (☎ 743716), sometimes known as Maïssagé ('sideburns' – after the owner's facial hair), which covers most of the same routes with comparable buses at significantly cheaper rates.

Taxis-brousses, usually Peugeot 504s, cover all the major routes and are more frequent than the SNTV buses, although they cost around the same. They also tend to take longer, make unscheduled detours and break down periodically. They only leave when full (eight people) and can get pretty cramped.

Minibuses and trucks are the cheapest option but it's definitely a case of getting what you pay for, particularly on long trips. The Niamey to Agadez journey has been known to take a nightmarish 42 hours!

There are good sealed roads from Niamey to Arlit (via Agadez) in the north, to Diffa in the far east, and to the Burkina Faso border. The road between Agadez and Zinder is sealed except for a 100km stretch of desert near Aderbissinat, which slows the journey considerably.

NIAMEY

INFORMATION
Agence Ténéré Voyages.................1 B3
American Cultural Center.............2 C4
Bank of Africa..........................(see 30)
Beninese Embassy.......................3 B3
BIA-Niger Bank..........................4 A5
Canadian Embassy......................5 C2
Centre Culturel Franco-Nigérien...6 C4
Centre Culturel Oumarou Ganda...7 F4
Centre Nigérien de Promotion
   Touristique.............................8 A6
Chadian Embassy........................9 B3
Clinique de Gamkalé..................10 D6
Cyberéspace..............................(see 6)
Eco Bank.................................11 D5

French Consulate.......................12 C4
German Embassy........................13 B4
Hospital....................................14 C4
Informanet................................15 A6
Net.com....................................16 A5
Niger-Car Voyages.....................17 D5
Nouvelle Poly-Clinic Pro-Santé..18 B3
Pharmacie du Grand Marché......19 B5
Pharmacie El Nasr..................(see 28)
Photo-adc.................................20 A5
Satguru Travels & Tours.............21 A5
Sonibank...................................22 A5

SIGHTS & ACTIVITIES   p290
Artisan Workshops.................(see 32)
Assemblée Nationale..................23 B5
Cathedral..................................24 C4
Grand Marché...........................25 B5
Grande Mosquée.......................26 E4
Hôtel de Ville............................27 A5

Immeuble El Nasr.......................28 A6
Immeuble Sonara I.....................29 A6
Immeuble Sonara II....................30 A6
Marché de Wadata.....................31 F5
Musée National..........................32 C4
Palais des Congrès.....................33 C4
Petit Marché..............................34 A5
Presidential Palace.....................35 B4
Stade de la Lutte Traditionelle
   (Traditional Wrestling)..........36 F4
Zoo.....................................(see 32)

SLEEPING   p291
Camping Touristique (Yantala
   Camping)............................37 A2
Hôtel le Dé................................38 C5
Hôtel Le Sahel...........................39 D5
Hôtel Maourey..........................40 A5
Hôtel Moustache.......................41 E4
Mission Catholique....................42 C4

To Malian Consulate (1.2km),
Tillabéri (114km), Ayorou (198km)
& Mali Border (237km)

Rond-point Yantala

Blvd du Sni et Maïnar
Blvd de Mali Béro

To French Embassy
(150m), US Embassy
(300m) & Nigerian
& Algerian
Embassies (1.3km)

Ave de la Jeunesse

Yantala

Ave de la Gaulle
Blvd de la République
Rue des Dallois
Ave du Fleuve Niger
Ave du Général de Gaulle

Blvd de l'Indépendance

Corniche de Yantala

Niger River

Plateau

Place Nelson Mandela

Ave Mitterand

Ave de la Maine

Rue Martin Luther King (Q)

Stadium

Blvd de l'Indépendance

Rue de Kabadoria

Blvd de la Liberté

Rue du Sénégal

Rue du Togo

Rue de Gaweye

Rue du Maroc

Kennedy Bridge

Rond-point Kennedy

See Enlargement

To University &
Gare Routière for
Burkina Faso (1km), Say (56km)
& Ouagadougou (500km)

Rue du Sahel

Gamkalé

Ave de l'Afrique (Route de Gamkalé)

Corniche de Gamkalé

Niger River

Rond-point Maourey

Ave Quebkè
Rue de Coulibaly Kalleye

Blvd de la Liberté

Rue de Copro

Ave de la Maine

Place de la République

Rue Nasser
Rue de l'Ass
Stadium

Rue du Gaweye
Rue du Président Henri Luber
Rue de la Grande Poste
Rue du Stade
Rue du Maroc

Place Monteil
Ave de l'Amitié

Rue du Grand Hôtel
Rond-point Grand Hôtel
Rue du Terminus

0   200 m
0   0.1 mi

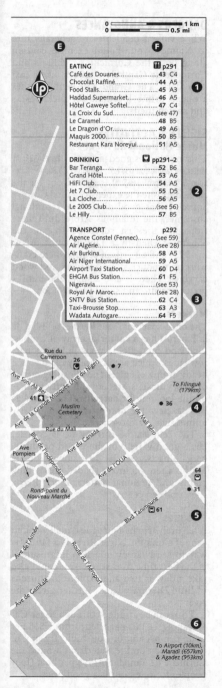

Rue du
Cameroon
26
7
Ave Soni Ali Ber
Ave de la Grande Mosquée (Ave du Niger)
41
Muslim
Cemetery
Rue du Mali
Blvd de Mali Béro
To Filingué
(179km)
36
Blvd du Canada
Ave du Canada
Ave
Pompiers
Blvd de l'Indépendance
Ave de l'OUA
Rond-point du
Nouveau Marché
64
31
Ave de l'Armée
Blvd Tanimoune
61
Route de l'Aéroport
Ave de Gainkalé
To Airport (10km),
Maradi (657km)
& Agadez (953km)

NIAMEY

pop 750,000

Niamey is first and foremost a very hot place – temperatures can hit 45°C in summer, and the desert sands of the Sahara lap at the city's edge. It was made capital of Niger in 1926 and the city's population has swelled considerably, from a modest 2000 inhabitants in 1940 to the current 750,000 or so. Infrastructure has struggled to keep pace with such rapid growth; even the deceptive modernity of the city centre, paid for by the 1970s uranium boom, is not enough to conceal the desperate poverty of the suburbs. Despite this, the city is often more pleasant than you'd expect, with leafy suburbs, modern amenities, and some areas of pure Sahelian charm. Relax by the cooling Niger River at sunset and you'll find it hard not to forgive Niamey its faults.

ORIENTATION

At first glance Niamey's geography can be confusing, particularly as street names change frequently, but once you get an idea for how things link up it's actually fairly easy to get around. The key road in the centre is Rue de Coulibally Kalleye (which becomes Rue de Gaweye) and most things can be found in the area between its intersections with Rue de la Copro (which becomes Rue de la Grande Poste) and Rue du Président Heinrich Lubké. The Plateau district is west of the city centre, up Av de la Mairie or Av Mitterand.

Taxis from the airport, 12km from the city centre, charge around US$8 initially but it is possible to get a fare as low as US$4, depending on your bargaining skills and the time of day. Alternatively, walk 150m to the highway and hail a shared taxi (US$0.40).

Shared taxis from the SNTV bus station may try and charge you US$1.65 to the centre; unless it's very early or late, the ride shouldn't actually cost more than US$0.60.

INFORMATION
Cultural Centres

American Cultural Center (☎ 733179; Av du Général de Gaulle) Closed more often than it's open.
Centre Culturel Franco-Nigérien (☎ 734240; www.ccfn.ne; Rue du Musée; ⏰ 9am-12.30pm & 3.30-6.30pm Mon-Sat) Public Internet access, an extensive

library and a busy schedule of nightly films (US$0.85) as well as exhibitions and live performances.

Centre Culturel Oumarou-Ganda (☎ 740903; Blvd de Mali Béro) Activities are advertised in *Le Sahel* newspaper.

Internet Access

Informanet (Rond-point Grand Hôtel; US$1.65 per hr) Similar set up to Net.Com.

Net.Com (Rue de Gaweye; US$2 per hr) Good deals for longer periods.

Photo-adc (Rond-point Maourey; US$0.04 per min) Excellent Japanese-run place with the best machines, open late.

Medical Services

Clinique de Gamkalé (☎ 732033; Corniche de Gamkalé; ⏰ 8.30am-12.30pm & 3.30-6.30pm Mon-Fri, 8.30am-12.30pm Sat)

Nouvelle Poly-Clinic Pro-Santé (☎ 722650; Av du Général de Gaulle; ⏰ 24hrs)

Pharmacie el-Nasr (Immeuble El-Nasr, Rue de Gaweye)

Money

Bank of Africa (Immeuble Sonara II)

BIA-Niger (Rue de Gaweye) The best option for most exchange transactions.

Eco Bank (Blvd de la Liberté; ⏰ 8.30am-5.30pm Mon-Fri, 9am-1pm Sat)

Post

The main **post offices** are in the centre of town (on Rue de la Grande Post) and on Place Nelson Mandela in the Plateau district. Poste restante at the latter is generally good.

Tourist Office

The **Centre Nigérien de Promotion Touristique** (CNPT; ☎ 732447; Rue du Président Heinrich Lubké; ⏰ 7.30am-noon & 3-6pm Mon-Fri) has very limited resources, though it does offer colour brochures on Niger and the Parc National du W, and also sells a tourist map of Niamey (US$4.90).

Travel Agencies

Niger-Car Voyages (☎ 732331; nicarvoy@intnet.ne; Av de l'Afrique) and the **Agence Ténéré Voyages** (☎ 732661; atv@intnet.ne; Av de Zarmakoye) are among the best travel agencies in Niamey. These are primarily tour agencies but also arrange flights and river boats. **Satguru Travels & Tours** (☎ 736931; stts-nim@intnet.ne; Rue de la Copro) is a good one-stop shop for airline tickets.

DANGERS & ANNOYANCES

While violent incidents are generally rare in Niamey, you should exercise caution along both the Corniche de Yantala and Corniche de Gamkalé – always take a taxi after dark. The Grand and Petit Marchés are also prime locations for pickpockets and snatch thefts.

SIGHTS & ACTIVITIES
Musée National du Niger

This nicely designed **museum** (☎ 734321; Av Mitterand; admission US$1.65, camera US$0.80; ⏰ 8am-noon & 4-6.30pm Tues-Sun) is spread out on the slope opposite the expensive Hôtel Gaweye Sofitel. It has good displays of traditional costumes, the infamous Arbre du Ténéré (formerly the last surviving tree of the Sahara – felled by a Libyan truck driver in 1973) and an artisan centre where craftworkers produce silver jewellery and wood carvings. There is also a small zoo but it's pretty horrific and should be avoided.

Markets

The once-spacious **Grand Marché** (off Blvd de la Liberté) has a colourful array of clothes, food and household goods lining its narrow lanes, which are invariably filled with a heady aroma of spices and a jostling crowd of kids, chickens, traders and hefty mamas on the lookout for bargains. The **Marché de Wadata**, near the *autogare*, has a similarly unmistakable atmosphere.

The **Petit Marché** (off Av de la Mairie) has a good variety of shops and products; bargaining is essential. Just along Av de la Mairie, there's a lovely shaded area selling plants and regional **pottery**, much like a cheap garden centre.

Pirogues

A leisurely trip in a pirogue (small wooden canoe) along the Niger River is a fantastic way to see Niamey in a new light; sunset is the best time to cast off. You could also take a day or two and explore the dozens of little Djerma villages further along the river.

Trips can be arranged through Niger-Car Voyages (see this page, left) from US$8 per hour per person, or you could try any of the boatmen on the waterfront around the Corniche de Yantala – US$8 per boat (four people) for one hour is a good price.

SLEEPING

There is a shocking lack of budget accommodation in Niamey, even compared with other West African capitals.

Mission Catholique (☎ 733203; s US$10) Quite literally the only cheap place anywhere near the centre of town. The rooms are good but it's often full and only single beds are available; if you're really desperate they may be able help you out with a bed elsewhere.

Hôtel Maourey (☎ 732850; Rond-point Maourey; s/d US$34/43; ⚡) Situated very centrally, the Maourey is a slightly shabby but characterful place with strangely shaped rooms (some with balconies) and corduroy furniture. It doesn't have all the top-end trimmings of the Hôtel Le Sahel, but the staff are friendly and the small restaurant is open all day.

Camping Touristique (☎ 754489; Blvd des Syet Mamar; camping US$3) Also known as Yantala Camping, Niamey's only camp site is 4km from the town centre and feels closer to Mali than Niamey. It's a big site with plenty of shade (and dust), plus a restaurant and bar. Semiregular shared taxis (US$0.35) and buses run into town.

The only other options for budget travellers are distinctly dubious. **Hôtel Moustache** (☎ 733378; Av Soni Ali Ber; r US$6-13; ⚡), east of the centre, is notoriously seedy and not suitable for women. If you're truly stuck, the barman at **Hôtel le Dé**, a run-down pastis joint off Rue du Maroc, may be able to fix you up with a local family.

SPLURGE!

Hôtel Le Sahel (☎ 732431; Rue du Sahel; s/d US$30/34; ⚡) This excellent tourist-class hotel is about the cheapest you'll get if the Mission Catholique is full and you don't fancy any of the dodgier options listed. The riverside location is superb, it's crammed with facilities and you even get satellite TV; however, it's some way out of town in a secluded area, and you shouldn't walk here after dark.

EATING

Good, cheap **food stalls** proliferate in the streets around the two markets, at Rondpoint Yantala and at the Wadata Autogare.

There are also plenty of lively if simple restaurants in the centre of town doing cheap food for around US$0.75. **Restaurant Kara Noreyui**, near Hôtel Maourey, is a decent little Senegalese place; **Cafe des Douanes** (Av de l'Uranium), next to the Customs building, sports traditional thatch and quite a peaceful atmosphere. **Maquis 2000**, off Rue du Maroc, is more expensive (mains around US$3.50) but does some excellent Ivorian cuisine.

SPLURGE!

Le Dragon d'Or (☎ 734123; Rue du Grand Hôtel; mains from US$4) This superb Chinese restaurant is worth every centime you pay, which, with over 200 items to choose from, will often be more than you intended. The pleasant garden with its red Chinese lanterns is superb on a warm Sahelian night, and vegetarians in particular will appreciate every mouthful.

Le Caramel (Rue de la Copro) is a café/pâtisserie offering a limited selection of pastries for breakfast (from 6am), including croissants for US$0.25.

For a spot of European sophistication, the restaurants in the larger hotels are generally good, if a touch pricey; **Le Croix du Sud** (☎ 722710; Av Mitterand; mains from US$8), in the Hôtel Gaweye Sofitel, is easily the best of its kind, and the hotel also does a Sunday jazz brunch. The scarcity of chocolate in Niger makes a visit to **Chocolat Raffiné**, near the Petit Marché, something of a rare indulgence.

The larger branch of **Haddad Supermarket** (Av de la Mairie) is the place to go for cheese, chocolate and other imported French treats (Carte d'Or ice cream!).

DRINKING

There are dozens of cheap spit'n'sawdust-type bars scattered around town, serving the usual bottled beers for around US$0.80; most also do cheap food. **Le Hilly** (Rue de la Copro) blasts out African music in the evenings, while **Bar Teranga**, off Rue du Maroc, has some great outdoor tables in the garden.

For a sunset drink, it's hard to beat the view over the Niger from the riverside bars of **Hôtel Le Sahel** (Rue du Sahel) and the nearby **Grand Hôtel**.

French expats and NGO workers seem to favour the upstairs terrace of **La Cloche** (Rue du Président Heinrich Lubké), which has a big TV screen, pool and table football.

Nearby, there is a lively strip of nightclubs on the corner of Rue de Gaweye; **HiFi** and **Le 2005** are both popular venues. Further from the centre, **Jet 7** (☎ 732626; Corniche de Gamkalé) holds special events and stays open until dawn at weekends for the serious party people. Entry is around US$4 *avec conso* (including one drink), more on weekends. They're all chaotic, upfront places and can be a good laugh, but be warned – drinks are usually the same price as admission.

GETTING THERE & AWAY
Air
From the airport just outside of Niamey, various national airlines serve points throughout West and Central Africa including Abidjan (US$267, four weekly), Algiers (US$35, three hours, weekly), Casablanca (US$450, five hours, weekly), Cotonou (US$185, twice weekly) and Ouagadougou (US$170, one hour, four weekly). See p286 for contact details of airlines operating these flights.

The private charter carrier **Fennec** (☎ 737535; Agence Constel, Rue du Président Heinrich Lubké) may offer flights to Kano. **Nigeravia** (☎ 733590; Grand Hôtel) may also offer charter flights; look for notices pasted around Niamey.

Local Transport
From the **SNTV bus station** (☎ 723020; sntv@intnet .ne; Corniche de Yantala; ☯ 7.30am-12.30pm & 3.30-6.30pm Mon-Fri, 8-9am Sat, 8am-noon Sun) five buses a week run to Arlit (US$30, 15 hours) via Agadez (US$25, 12 hours) and Tahoua (US$15, eight hours), and there is a daily service to Zinder (US$20, 14 hours) via Maradi (US$15, nine hours). All buses pass through Dosso (US$4, two hours) and Birni N'Konni (US$11, six hours).

EHGM buses (☎ 743716; Blvd Tanimoune) serve the same routes slightly less frequently from their terminus near the Wadata Autogare; to Agadez costs US$20 and Zinder US$18.

The **Wadata Autogare** has daily minibus and *taxi-brousse* departures for most destinations around the country. Minibuses for Agadez/Zinder cost US$25/18.

GETTING AROUND
Shared taxis to just about anywhere within Niamey cost US$0.35, though you'll usually have to negotiate. A taxi to yourself shouldn't cost more than US$1.65. If you can work out where the many public minibuses are actually going, a ride should cost US$0.15.

NORTHWEST NIGER

TAHOUA
pop 40,000
This friendly Hausa town is a convenient overnight stop for vehicles travelling between Agadez and Niamey. The dynamic Sunday **market** is quite something.

Accommodation in Tahoua has become unreasonably expensive recently, although it's still nothing on Niamey.

Bungalows de Tahoua (☎ 610553; r US$10-15; ☒) The cheapest place in town, this is a collection of round huts next to the Jardin Publique. It's OK, but the carpets breed mosquitoes.

Hôtel l'Amitié (☎ 610153; r US$20; ☒) Nearer the SNTV station, it offers clean but distinctly underwhelming rooms. It's a good location and the grounds are nice, but at this price they're really taking the mick.

There are plenty of **food stalls** opposite the entrance to the *autogare*. The informal **Restaurant Les Délices**, next to the Bungalows, has a lovely setting in the Jardin Publique; you can eat well for under US$3 here, and even get a choice of beer (US$0.80).

The shaded terrace of the tiny **Maquis de la Paix**, further north, is a great place to have a cold drink and watch the lizards.

AGADEZ
pop 122,000
One of the great ancient trading towns of the Sahara, Agadez is the first (and often only) destination on most people's lists when they visit Niger. Its sandy streets, distinctive mud-brick architecture and lively population of Tuareg people make for a fascinating experience, and a few days here, combined with forays into the Aïr Mountains or the forbidding Ténéré Desert, can be a real high point of any trip to Western Africa.

Information
You should register with the *commissariat* (police) on arrival, to get your passport stamped. Politely refuse any requests for a *cadeau* (a 'gift', ie bribe). For travellers who are heading north, the **Algerian Consulate** is

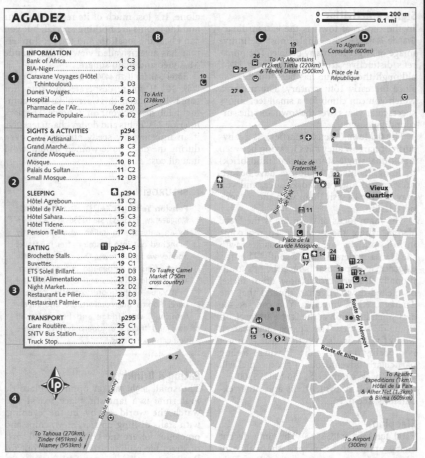

AGADEZ

0 — 200 m
0 — 0.1 mi

INFORMATION
Bank of Africa...........................1 C3
BIA-Niger.................................2 C3
Caravane Voyages (Hôtel
   Tchintoulous)........................3 D3
Dunes Voyages.........................4 B4
Hospital..................................5 C2
Pharmacie de l'Aïr...................(see 20)
Pharmacie Populaire.................6 D2

SIGHTS & ACTIVITIES   p294
Centre Artisanal.......................7 B4
Grand Marché...........................8 C3
Grande Mosquée.......................9 C2
Mosque...................................10 B1
Palais du Sultan.......................11 C2
Small Mosque..........................12 D3

SLEEPING   p294
Hôtel Agreboun.......................13 C2
Hôtel de l'Aïr..........................14 D3
Hôtel Sahara...........................15 C3
Hôtel Tidene...........................16 D2
Pension Tellit..........................17 C3

EATING   pp294–5
Brochette Stalls.......................18 D3
Buvettes.................................19 C1
ETS Soleil Brillant....................20 D3
L'Elite Alimentation..................21 D3
Night Market...........................22 D2
Restaurant Le Pilier..................23 D3
Restaurant Palmier..................24 D3

TRANSPORT   p295
Gare Routière..........................25 C1
SNTV Bus Station....................26 C1
Truck Stop..............................27 C1

To Algerian
Consulate (600m)
To Aïr Mountains
(12km), Timia (220km)
& Ténéré Desert (500km)
Place de la
République

To Arlit
(238km)

Place de
Fraternité

Rue de Sultanat
de l'Aïr

Vieux
Quartier

Place de la
Grande Mosquée

To Tuareg Camel
Market (750m
cross country)

Route de l'Aéroport

Route de Bilma

To Agadez
Expeditions (1km),
Hôtel de la Paix
& Alher.Net (1.3km)
& Bilma (605km)

Route de Niamey

To Tahoua (270km),
Zinder (451km) &
Niamey (953km)

To Airport
(300m)

northeast of the centre, 600m from Place de
la République.

Internet access is available at **Alher.Net** (Route
de Bilma; US$0.20 per min), next to the posh Hôtel de
la Paix; it's pretty fast once it gets going, but
takes time to establish a connection.

The **Bank of Africa** and **BIA-Niger**, opposite
the Grand Marché, change cash and travellers cheques quickly and easily.

The **post office** (☼ 8am-noon & 3-5pm Mon-Fri) is
opposite the SNTV bus station. There are
private **telephone offices** all over town.

TRAVEL AGENCIES
There are literally dozens of travel agencies
around town, from big professional operations to independent one-man outfits.

Recent slow-downs in tourist numbers
means that competition is quite fierce, and
everyone seems willing to take you out into
the desert at a moment's notice. There's
no need to be too wary of most wannabe
guides, but bargain hard and never hand
over the full amount until the end of the
trip. It's a good idea to get recommendations from other travellers if you can, but
the following larger companies have good
reputations:
Agadez Expeditions (☎ 440170; az-tours@intnet.ne;
Route de Bilma)
Caravane Voyages (☎ 440459; Hôtel Tchintoulous,
Route de l'Aéroport)
Dunes-Voyages (☎ 440372; www.dunes-voyages.com;
Route de Niamey)

Sights & Activities

In the centre of town is the extraordinary **Grande Mosquée**, the single most definitive image of Niger for many people. The minaret's distinctive structure dates from 1844, although the mosque has been on this site since the early 16th century. The minaret, which you can climb for a small fee, enjoys spectacular views over the town and the surrounding desert.

The **Old Town** (Vieux Quartier), is a labyrinth of narrow alleyways weaving between traditional single-storey *banco* (mud-brick) buildings. Some of the houses have beautifully carved and painted facades, and you may be able to visit them with the owner's permission.

The main focus of town life is the **Grand Marché**, where the nomadic Tuareg come in from outlying areas to do business with the Hausa traders from the south. The **croix d'Agadez** is a popular souvenir; it's traditionally a silver cross (now often nickel or melted-down Algerian dinars) that the Tuareg used as currency. You can see the craftsmen in action at the **Centre Artisanal**, off Route de Niamey. The Tuareg **camel market**, west of town, is also worth a visit – sunset is probably the best time. If you're feeling particularly adventurous, a good camel will set you back around US$450 to US$500.

For details of camel treks and other excursions, see p295.

Sleeping

Hôtel Agreboun (r US$6.50-8) The only decent cheap option in town, past the walled-in Place de la Fraternité, west of Route de l'Aéroport. The concrete rooms are a bit bunkerlike with some dodgy electrics, but they're spacious and stay cool during the day; prices may be negotiable when it's not busy, so you could get a room with shower for the price of one without.

Hôtel Tidene (☎ 440258; Place de Fraternité; s/d US$16/25; ✖) If you want decent facilities without blowing a fortune, the Tidene is the place to go – its bright, clean rooms are better value than some of the more expensive places around, and there's an excellent restaurant and bar. It can fill up with tour groups at busy times.

Hôtel de l'Aïr (☎ 440109; Place de la Grande Mosquée; r US$16-25; ✖) Formerly the Sultan's Palace, and worth visiting for the architecture

alone. It's lost much of its regal splendour and the rooms are nothing special, but you can't beat the location, and the rooftop terrace has an unrivalled view of the Grande Mosquée and main square.

Hôtel Sahara (☎ 440480; Route de Bilma; r from US$9; ✖) If you're desperate and stuck for somewhere cheap, this warrenlike dive-cum-nightclub may be your only choice. The dark interior, UV lights and dodgy characters give it an unbelievably seedy atmosphere even during the day – lone women should avoid it at all cost.

SPLURGE!

Pension Tellit (☎ 440231; Place de la Grande Mosquée; tw US$30-33, ste US$36-46; ✖) Run by an enterprising Italian who apparently branched out into hostelry after his travel agency was shut down, this charming little hotel offers an appealing mix of modern and traditional styles and is probably the best value of the more expensive options here. Rooms are comfortable and nicely furnished, with fridge and hot water all day, and there's a superb terrace where you can take meals.

Eating & Drinking

The small **night market** opposite Place de Fraternité is a fantastic place to eat and watch the world go by in the evening, with stalls dishing up rice, stew, chips and omelettes for around US$0.75 and all sorts of street life milling around – look out for the local medicine men with their carts and loudspeakers. There are also plenty of **brochette stalls** (US$0.15 each) further down Route de l'Aéroport and a string of basic but friendly **buvettes** (small cafés) near the *gare routière* (mains from US$0.75).

For a more formal meal, **Restaurant Palmier** (Route de l'Aéroport; mains around US$1.50) is popular with travellers and tour groups and does the usual standards.

Imported treats from France and the Middle East are available from **L'Elite Alimentation** and **ETS Soleil Brillant** supermarkets on the main road.

Finding a beer in Agadez can be surprisingly hard work – there are few local bars in the centre and the hotels frequently run dry. The only place with a reliable supply seems to be the five-star **Hôtel de la Paix** (Route de Bilma), which charges a shocking US$1.65 per bottle.

SPLURGE!

Restaurant Le Pilier (☎ 440231; Route de l'Aéroport; mains from US$4) Once again the Italians show how it's done – this top-class restaurant is run by the same family as the Pension Tellit, and has been successful enough to open branches in Niamey and Ouagadougou. The food is superb, especially the homemade ice cream, and the traditional semiopen design turns a meal here into a pretty special experience.

Getting There & Away

Agadez airport, south of town, has been closed for repairs since 1999; when it does finally reopen, flights to domestic destinations, as well as to Algeria, Chad and France, should be available.

From its station in the northern part of town, SNTV runs five buses per week to Niamey (US$25, 12 hours), via Tahoua (US$11, six hours), and a weekly service to Zinder (US$10.60, 10 hours).

A motley selection of minibuses, *taxis-brousses* and Toyota 4WDs covers these and other destinations such as Arlit (US$4.25, 3½ to four hours) and Assamakka (US$8, 12 hours), leaving from the dusty *gare routière*, next to the SNTV office. Slow, cheap rides can also be found at the truck stop just opposite.

AÏR MOUNTAINS & TÉNÉRÉ DESERT

Northeast of Agadez are the remote and exotic **Aïr Mountains**, scattered with hospitable Tuareg villages, lush valleys and rough,

stony mountains rising out of the Sahara. The best way to see this fascinating region is by camel – while the whole range takes up an area the size of Switzerland, you can see a wide range of scenery on even a short trip out of Agadez. With a bit more time, you can make it to the dark volcanic peak of **Mt Bagzane** (2022m), the lovely oasis towns of **Timia** and **Iferouâne**, or the stunning 400m sand dunes at **Temet**. The mountains also conceal some of the best sites in the Sahara for Neolithic **rock art**.

The **Ténéré Desert**, 500km from Agadez as the crow flies, often receives the label of the Sahara's most beautiful region, thanks to its thousands of square kilometres of towering sand dunes. It really is the classic image of endless empty desert, scattered sparingly with cave paintings, dinosaur fossils and car wrecks, and only the truly adventurous make it out here on their own. The town of **Bilma**, at the end of one of the great desert salt routes, is one of the most isolated settlements on earth.

Agadez is an excellent place in which to organise **camel** or **4WD expeditions** to these areas. Typical costs are around US$25 per person per day for a short camel trek or US$95 per day for a 4WD (for the whole car). The Ténéré is the most inaccessible area (therefore the most expensive), and you are required to take along at least two vehicles in case one breaks down. Most operators offer good package deals and are amenable to bargaining – if you can get a group together, costs come down dramatically.

ARLIT

This small, lively town has enjoyed an increase in visitors since the route to/from Algeria reopened, but tourists, and drivers in particular, are still enough of a novelty

---

CURE SALÉE

The Agadez region is renowned for its festivals, the most important of which is the **Cure Salée**. This intriguing event is held in August or September after the rains, somewhere to the west of Agadez. In a ceremony called the Gerewol, young men of the nomadic Peul-Fulani group adorn and beautify themselves so that only the most obstinate female can resist them. With luck, each will find a wife – a woman brave enough to move forward and demand his services, at least for a night. The virility test, the Soro, is another story altogether, requiring initiates to be beaten with big sticks while maintaining an inane grin. It is difficult for outsiders to witness the events themselves, but if you're in the region around this time you will undoubtedly run into plenty of spectacularly garbed nomads preparing for their big day.

to get the attention of seemingly everyone in town.

Hôtel Temesna (☎ 452330; r US$6.50) is the best place to stay, though the rooms are shabby and the air-con is a joke; it also functions as a bar, nightclub and social centre.

SOUTHWEST NIGER

DOSSO

Formerly an important religious centre, Dosso is now essentially a crossroads town, with roads running south to Benin and west to Nigeria. It's not a bad place but you'd have to look hard to find a reason to stay here.

Hôtel Djerma (☎ 650206; Place de l'Unité; r from US$20; ✗) is a bit pricey but tries hard and is easily the best option in town. Cheaper options include **Sous les Palmiers** (dm US$5.70), off the main road, and **Auberge du Carrefour** (☎ 650017; r US$7-10; ✗), near the *gare routière*.

At night, the road to Niamey is alive with gas lanterns, diesel fumes and the smell of **street food**. Lovers of eccentricity should head to the **Chez Rita** restaurant, near the Grand Marché.

As well as the frequent intercity buses, there are plenty of minibuses and *taxis-brousses* for local destinations from around the main roundabout. A taxi to Gaya, for Benin or Nigeria, should cost around US$3.25.

PARC NATIONAL DU W DU NIGER

This magnificent national park on the western bank of the Niger gets its unusual name from the double bend in the Niger River at the park's northern border. It straddles three countries: Niger, Benin and Burkina Faso. Wildlife is scarcer here than in East or Southern Africa, but you will see a variety of animals, including many bird species – perhaps 300 – between February and May.

The park is open from early December to laté May; the entrance fee is US$6.50 and a free map is provided. An obligatory (and useful) guide charges about US$7.50 per person.

The **camp site** (per person US$3.25) is just before the park entrance, overlooking the Tapoa River. The only other option is the expensive half board bungalows at **Hôtel de la Tapoa** (s/d US$30/45; ✗), which can be reserved through Niger-Car Voyages in Niamey (see p290).

It's hard to get here by public transport; the three-hour drive from Niamey to the park entrance at La Tapoa is very rough going, and without your own vehicle you'll have problems getting around the park anyway. Consider doing a tour from Niamey through Niger-Car Voyages. Expect to pay around US$70 per person, per day.

SOUTHEAST NIGER

BIRNI N'KONNI

Often known simply as Konni, this is very much a border town, with little of interest for casual visitors. Cheap Nigerian petrol, food and naira (Nigerian currency) can all be found along the busy main drag.

You won't find much variety here. **Hôtel Kado** (☎ 296; r US$10.60-16; ✗), near the *gare routière*, is about the best you'll get, and has some cheaper rooms with fan. For those on tighter budgets, **Hôtel Wadata** (r US$3), one block south, offers very basic accommodation.

Camping and rooms are available at the **Relais-Camping Touristique** (☎ 338; camping US$2.50, d US$9.75), 2km west of town on the Niamey road.

There are plenty of **food stalls** along the main street and in the *gare routière*, selling rice, meat and sauces. **Restaurant Teranga** and **Maquis 2001**, on the main street, may be worth a look for a sit-down meal (mains around US$0.75).

SNTV buses pass through Birni N'Konni on its Niamey–Zinder (US$12) and Niamey–Agadez routes. They're usually full, so you'll probably have to stand once on board.

Taxis-brousses and minibuses also run to Maradi and other local destinations.

MARADI
pop 70,000

Maradi is the commercial and industrial capital of Niger, with more than the usual quota of international aid organisations and an excellent **market** on Monday and Friday. It's also a staunchly conservative religious centre with a vocal Muslim majority, whose bully tactics in recent years have had a profound impact and made headlines throughout the country.

The town is not the most engaging place for visitors, but there is a good **Centre Artisanal** on the main road north, and the

Maison des Chefs at Place Dan Kassawa is a fine example of Hausa architecture.

Internet access is available at **Sareli Informatique** (Route de l'Aéroport; US$0.25 per min).

Sleeping

Hôtel Liberté (☎ 410380; s from US$5.40, d US$7.80-12.20; ⌘) The cheapest singles here are little more than dodgy closets, but the doubles with fan are not bad value, despite the clanging metal doors and noisy cooking right outside (mains from US$0.75). A good location southwest of the market makes this the best option in town.

Hôtel Larewa (☎ 410813; d US$8-15; ⌘) The leafy courtyard makes this a nice place to stay, but it's a fair hike north of the centre, convenient for the EHGM bus station but very little else. The air-con rooms are overpriced.

Hôtel Jangorzo (☎ 410140; Route de l'Aéroport; s/d/ste US$22/26/49; ⌘) Basically a mid-range tourist hotel, the Jangorzo also has a few cell-like singles for US$9.

SPLURGE!

Maradi Guest House (☎ 410754; d US$49-57; ⌘) To listen to the management you'd think that the clientele of this well-signposted little hideaway was largely made up of guidebook writers, and judging by the number of recommendations it gets, they might just be right. Either way, it's a charming place with excellent facilities, somehow resembling a Kenyan safari lodge, and knocks the socks off just about anything you'll find elsewhere in Niger. You'll find it about 2km southeast of the centre – follow the large signs leading from the main road.

Eating & Drinking

Street food abounds near the central market and *gare routière*; Restaurant Excellence, in the Jardin Publique, is a great place to eat on a warm night (mains around US$1.25).

Most of Maradi's nightlife has been eradicated thanks to hardline Muslim activists, but Bar-Restaurant Prestige, west of the Jardin Publique and not far from Hôtel Liberté, still serves up beer (US$0.75) and live music most nights.

Getting There & Away

The daily SNTV buses between Niamey and Zinder pass through Maradi (to Niamey is US$15 and takes nine hours; to Zinder is US$6, three hours). EHGM buses (Niamey US$13.20, Zinder US$5) run four times weekly from the station off Route de Niamey, north of town.

Taxis-brousses to Zinder (US$5) fill up much quicker than minibuses (US$4, five hours).

ZINDER

pop 80,000

Zinder, the capital of Niger until 1926, is one of the country's traditional market towns and has a lot in common with Agadez; indeed, thanks to the lack of travellers here, many people find they prefer Zinder's relaxed atmosphere to that of its larger northern counterpart.

Information

The **Centre Culturel Franco-Nigérien** (☎ 510535; ccfnz@intnet.ne; Rue du Marché) has regular film screenings, theatre and dance performances as well as a popular terrace bar-restaurant, and is a great place to meet Zinder's friendly community of volunteer workers.

Internet access is available at the **Abani Telecentre** (☎ 510157; Av des Banques; US$0.25 per min).

Sights & Activities

The highlight of any visit to Zinder is a wander through the mazelike traditional quarters of **Zengou** and **Birni**, where people still live in the old mud-brick houses with their castellated walls and coloured *banco* facades. There is an ongoing project to restore more of these dwellings and teach the people who live in them how to preserve them. Birni also boasts the **Sultan's Palace** (still inhabited by the current Sultan) and the spectacular **Grande Mosquée**.

The **Grand Marché** (Blvd de l'Hippodrome) is one of the best markets in West Africa; on Thursday it's filled with a diverse mix of people from outlying villages.

The **Musée Regional de Zinder** (Av de la République; admission US$1.60; ⌣ 8am-noon & 3-6pm Tues-Sun) is a nice example of Hausa geometric design, and has a wonderful wooden door from the Sultan's Palace.

For something a bit less worthy, the regular weekend **horse races** at the Hippodrome

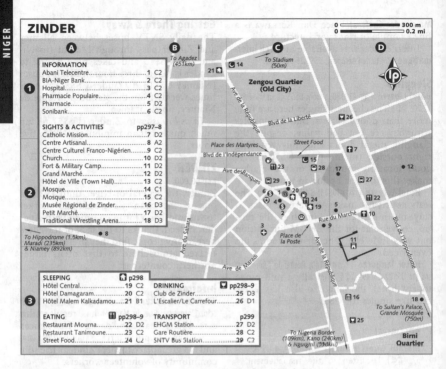

ZINDER

0 — 300 m
0 — 0.2 mi

To Agadez (451km)
To Stadium (50m)
Zengou Quartier (Old City)
Ave de la République
Blvd de la Liberté
Place des Martyres
Blvd de l'Indépendance
Street Food
Ave des Banques
Ave du Sahara
To Hippodrome (1.5km), Maradi (235km) & Niamey (892km)
Ave de Maradi
Rue du Marché
Place de la Poste
Ave de la République
Blvd de l'Hippodrome
To Sultan's Palace, Grande Mosquée (750m)
To Nigeria Border (109km), Kano (240km) & Nguigmi (398km)
Birni Quartier

(Av de Maradi), west of town, are a hotbed of healthily secular gambling.

Sleeping

Hôtel Malam Kalkadamou (☎ 510570; Av de la République; s/d/tw US$5.40/7/10.25; ☒) The cheapest and thus best option in town, this appealing little place is some distance from the centre but has great views over the traditional terraces of the Zengou district.

Hôtel Central (Av de la République; r US$11.25-15.50; ☒) Known to the French here as the hotel 'le plus merdique' in town (get a dictionary), the Central isn't as bad as all that but the bathrooms are pretty shady and it's definitely overpriced.

Hôtel Damagaram (☎ 510069; Av de la République; s/d/tw US$27/33/37; ☒) The only other option in the centre. The rooms are large and comfortable, it's friendly and the shady interior courtyard bar-restaurant is great; only the hefty price tag lets it down.

Note that the water supply in Zinder usually only functions before 8.30am and between 3pm and 6.30pm due to severe shortages.

Eating & Drinking

There aren't a lot of restaurants in Zinder outside the hotels. The main competition is between **Restaurant Tanimoune** (Av de la République), which has an excellent balcony overlooking the street, and **Restaurant Mourna** (Rue du Marché), with a tiny Chinese-styled patio tucked away in its own compound, with TV in the evening. Both have impressively extensive and varied menus with mains from US$1.65; the Cantonese rice at these establishments makes a nice change from the usual riz sauce.

The best place for street food is the dirt square in front of Hôtel Central.

There is a surprising amount of nightlife tucked away outside the centre of town, frequented by locals and expats alike, and it's worth asking around to see what's hot. Try the unsigned bar known as either L'Escalier or Le Carrefour, off Blvd de l'Hippodrome – it's rowdy and appealingly eccentric, with occasional local music inflicted on a core crowd of hard drinkers and prostitutes.

Much calmer and favoured by expats, the **Club de Zinder** (Av de la République) serves rare treats such as lasagne and ham-and-Gruyère toasties along with the beer. It stays open until 2am at weekends, and also has a pool, pool table and *pétanque* (bowls) pitch; visitors are welcome but only members can order anything. Many of the regulars (especially the younger ones) are generally quite happy to order on behalf of visitors if asked nicely.

Getting There & Away
Daily SNTV buses leave for Niamey at 6am (US$20, 14 hours); there are also buses to Arlit via Agadez (US$10.60, 10 hours, Saturday) and Nguigmi (US$12.85, overnight, Monday and Friday). EHGM runs similar services from its own station, but only goes as far east as Diffa (US$10, up to 12 hours) once a week (Thursday).

Taxis-brousses and minibuses leave from the *gare routière* near the Petit Marché.

DIFFA
This small administrative town is of very little interest to most travellers, but anyone heading to Nguigmi and Chad may have to stop here; the SNTV bus often parks here for the night as it's not supposed to travel after 6.30pm. It could be worth stocking up on supplies here – if you haven't already – as you'll find some pretty imaginative prices for essential items further down the road.

If you don't fancy sleeping on the bus, **Hôtel Kandari** (r US$12-22; ✿), behind the petrol station on the main road, has reasonable rooms with plywood doors and a courtyard bar.

NIGER DIRECTORY

ACCOMMODATION
Accommodation in Niger is relatively expensive and rooms in many of the cheaper hotels can be pretty dubious. Prices usually depend on whether a room has en suite and/or air-con rather than the number of occupants. Camping is possible in Niamey, Agadez and Birni N'Konni, but the camp sites can be bleak places.

Many mid-range places, particularly in the popular tourist towns, add a *taxe de séjour* (tourist tax) of US$0.50 to US$0.80 per person, per day.

BUSINESS HOURS
Banking hours are 8am to 11.30am and 3.30pm to 5pm Monday to Friday; most other businesses and offices open 7.30am to 12.30pm and 3.30pm to 6.30pm, though many foreign embassies are only open in the morning. Shop hours vary, but most places open early and close for the afternoon, due to the heat; you'll find it difficult to get a sit-down meal between 2pm and 7pm.

DANGERS & ANNOYANCES
On the whole, Niger is relatively safe. In both Niamey and Agadez scams, theft and armed hold-ups do occur, but it's unlikely that you'll encounter any major problems. The most common minor annoyance comes from local kids, who invariably demand *cadeaux* (gifts) and may even chase you down the street in their enthusiasm.

While the Tuareg rebellion ended in 1995, armed banditry still sometimes occurs in the far north. The Libyan border is extremely dangerous (three Italian travellers were killed by a mine in 2002), and the areas around the Algerian border and the northern section of the road between Zinder and Agadez can also be dodgy. The latter is generally safe during daylight hours, and the SNTV bus travels with a loosely defined military convoy, but travel should be avoided at night. Check with the US embassy in Niamey (p300) for the most recent information.

EMBASSIES & CONSULATES
The following embassies and consulates are found in Niamey:
Algeria (☎ 723583; Blvd de la République)
Benin (☎ 722860; Rue des Dallois)
Canada (☎ 733686; off Blvd de Mali Bero, Yantala)
Chad (☎ 753464; Av du Général de Gaulle)

HARMATTAN WINDS

The harmattan winds that blow the dust in off the Sahara can cause respiratory problems, though usually nothing worse than a nasty cough. Visibility can also be poor, as little as 50m. It's a good idea to follow the Tuaregs' lead and cover your mouth and nose when travelling. The worst times are from January to April.

France embassy (☎ 722431; www.ambafrance.ne; Blvd de la République); consulate (☎ 722722; Place Nelson Mandela, Plateau)
Germany (☎ 722534; 71 Av du Général de Gaulle)
Mali (☎ 754290; www.gsi-niger.com/consulat-mali; off Blvd de li'Indépendance)
Nigeria (☎ 732410; Blvd de la République)
USA (☎ 722640; Blvd de la République)

Niger has diplomatic representation in Algeria, Benin, Chad and Nigeria.

FOOD & DRINK

You'll find all the usual West African staples here, with rice or couscous and peanut sauce forming a key component of the local diet. Brochettes, grilled chicken, steak, chips and omelettes are also common, and you can get some excellent fish along the Niger River.

Tea is the daytime drink of choice; the nomadic Tuareg also have their own brew, so-called 'desert tea', which is drunk strong and sugared in small glasses. Most bars stock French Flag beer and the superior Bière Niger (BN), as well as the occasional canned import lager.

HOLIDAYS

As well as religious holidays listed in the Africa Directory chapter (p1003) the principal public holidays in Niger are:

1 January New Year's Day
24 April Day of Concord
1 May Labour Day
3 August Independence
5 September Settlers Day
18 December Republic Day

INTERNET ACCESS

Good Internet access is widely available and reasonably priced in Niamey; elsewhere it is less reliable and rates can be extortionate.

MONEY

The euro is the most convenient form of currency to carry with you as it can be easily exchanged in most towns; cash exchanges are usually commission-free. Travellers cheques are difficult to change outside Niamey – the BIA-Niger Bank charges 2% commission and sometimes also does Visa cash advances, but don't count on this.

Whenever you change money, ask for as many CFA1000 notes as possible as no-one ever has change. Stow it carefully on your person – petty thieves lurk outside some banks ready to snatch and run.

PHOTOGRAPHY

A photo permit from the Ministry of the Interior is supposedly required, but no-one ever seems to check this. Avoid photographing government or military buildings, bridges (particularly the Kennedy Bridge in Niamey) and people bathing in rivers.

POST & TELEPHONE

Postal services outside Niamey are unreliable. International telephone services are OK although it sometimes takes time to get a line. Private telephone offices generally charge a fixed rate of US$0.20 per unit; all calls are cheaper at weekends.

TOURIST INFORMATION

The only functioning tourist office in Niger is the CNPT in Niamey (p290), although there are plans to open a private information office and visitor centre in Agadez.

VISAS

Visas are required for all visitors except nationals of some West African countries. Visas are normally issued within 24 hours for a stay of up to one month and cost between US$35 and US$50.

Niger has few embassies around the world so getting a visa requires some planning. In Africa, visas are most easily obtained in Benin (Cotonou and Parakou), Algeria and Chad. You may be able to get a visa at the border on entry, but this requires the goodwill of the border guards. Your chances are best if you're coming from Mali or Burkina Faso.

In Agadez and Arlit you'll probably be asked to report to the *commissariat* (police) if you stay overnight. They'll give you a free *vu au passage* stamp in your passport that may save you some hassle later on.

Visa Extensions

Visa extensions of one month are available in 24 hours from the *sûreté* (police station) on Place de la République in Niamey for US$13. You need two photos.

Visas for Onward Travel

Visas for the following neighbouring countries can be obtained in Niger. See p299 for embassy and consulate information.

Algeria The consulate in Agadez is your best bet: single-entry visas for up to a month cost around US$37, depending on nationality, and require three photos. They can be issued inside a week but it's best to start the process as early as possible.

Benin Single-entry/three-month visas cost US$20/32 and are usually issued within 24 hours. You'll need two photos and a photocopy of your passport.

Burkina Faso Visas are issued within 24 hours by the French consulate on Place Nelson Mandela. Costs start at US$26 for up to 30 days; applications require one photo and a copy of your passport.

Chad The embassy charges US$24.50 for visas of 30 days or so (you'll need to specify your exact length of stay, so allow a margin for error). They're usually valid for three months and should be issued the same day. You'll need three photos.

Mali A one-month visa, which is valid for six months from the date of issue, costs around US$32.50 and can usually be processed right on the same day. You will also need two photos.

Nigeria One-month visas are usually issued within 24 hours and can cost anything between US$10 and US$45!

Burkina Faso

HIGHLIGHTS

- **Bobo-Dioulasso** A charming town with some excellent attractions and a convenient base for side trips in Southern Burkina Faso (p311)
- **Ouagadougou** The most relaxed capital city you're ever likely to visit; the locals also love to put on a party (p307)
- **Gorom-Gorom's market** Mingle with people who have come from far and wide to shop at the famous Thursday market (p314)
- **Pics de Sindou (Sindou Peaks)** Discover the excellent hiking opportunities in the other-worldly landscape of these rock escarpments (p313)
- **Off the beaten track** The Karfiguéla waterfalls are most spectacular in the rainy season but best for swimming in the dry (p313)

FAST FACTS

- **Area** 274,100 sq km
- **ATMs** Ouagadougou has two ATMs linked to the Visa network
- **Borders** Mali, Niger, Togo and Ghana open to 5.30pm; border crossing at Niangoloko for Côte d'Ivoire closed at the time of research due to the civil war
- **Budget** US$15 to US$20 a day
- **Capital** Ouagadougou
- **Languages** French, Dioula, Moré, Fula, Gourmantché, Gourounsi
- **Money** West African CFA; US$1 = CFA600
- **Population** 12.6 million
- **Seasons** wet (Jun–Oct), dry (Nov–Feb), hot (Mar–Jun)
- **Telephone** country code ☎ 226; international access code ☎ 00
- **Time** GMT/UTC
- **Visas** US$16 to US$40; required by all nationalities, two photos needed

Between Sahelian empires and coastal kingdoms, between Muslim and animist Africa, between Saharan desertscapes and southern waterfalls, Burkina Faso weaves many of Africa's diverging strands into a fascinating and thoroughly seductive fabric. In the markets, turbaned traders on camels mix with farmers on donkey-drawn carts in a colourful swirl of diverse ethnic groups. The spell is probably the effect of the legendary Burkinabé openness combined with the dazzling light and the overarching sense of space.

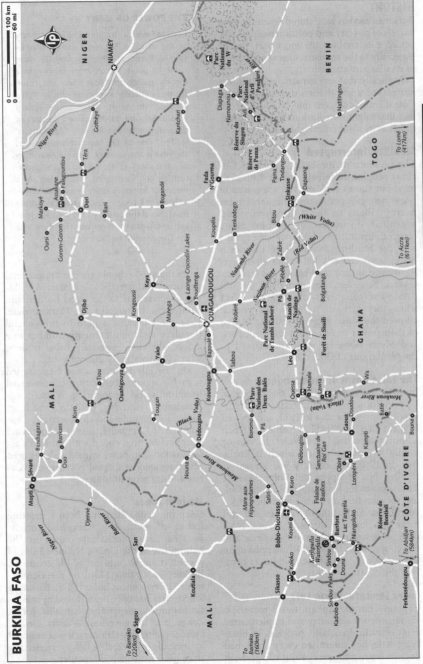

BURKINA FASO

BURKINA FASO

HISTORY

Burkina Faso has long stared down the twin barrels of poverty and political malpractice, yet kept its cool for the most part, thanks especially to the industriousness and ability of its diaspora community.

Ironically, that very expatriate community has played a key though unwitting role in Côte d'Ivoire's descent into civil war, a conflict that might hurt Burkina Faso almost as much as its southern neighbour.

Stability, Interrupted

The presence of the Bobo, Lobi and Gurunsi peoples dates back to the 13th century, but things took off when a group of horsemen galloped across the Sahel from nearby Ghana in the 15th century and organised themselves an empire along classical, institutional lines, which explains why the Muslim advance from the north made fewer inroads here than elsewhere. Resistance against the French was less successful, however: they employed the old divide-and-conquer trick to great effect when they arrived in 1897. The French allowed the Mossi kings to retain a vestige of their power in return for their support, and Mossi labourers were conscripted to the plantations of Côte d'Ivoire.

The False Dawn of Independence

In 1919 the French created the colony of Upper Volta for administrative convenience, scrapped the idea in 1932, and revived it again after WWII. Sixty years of French administration had Upper Volta clamouring loudly for independence, which it finally won in 1960. The country was known as the Republic of Upper and Volta. Maurice Yaméogo was the inaugural president; it took just six years for him to end up in the clink – corruption and authoritarianism did not make him popular. Between 1966 and 1982, there were two periods of military rule and five coups, in the last of which stepped up to the microphone a young, ambitious, reformist military star.

Enter Sankara, Stage Left

Captain Thomas Sankara was a maverick. He renamed the country and implemented a set of radical socialist policies. In blitz-krieg style, he immunised every child, had doctors trained for every rural village, built

---

THE POWER OF MANY

Burkina Faso is a strange name for a country by any standard. The name was adopted by former President Thomas Sankara, who came to power as an army captain in a bloody putsch in 1982 when the country was officially known as Upper Volta. Although he usurped power by violent means, Sankara quickly gained the sort of popularity reserved for very few national leaders. One of his populist reforms was to rename the country: Burkina Faso literally translates as 'Homeland of the Incorruptible', or 'Country of Honest Men'. As a means of fostering unity among an ethnically diverse people, the name was coined from two of the country's most widely spoken languages: the Moré word for 'pure' and the Dioula word for 'homeland'.

---

more than 350 schools, reduced ministerial privileges and overspending, started building a railway line to the Niger border, and painted Ouagadougou a non-Marxist white. He rapidly became a hero to the general populace and public enemy number one among the elite, especially tribal leaders, who felt increasingly undermined.

On the international scene, Sankara led with his mouth, cultivating controversial friendships and denouncing Western imperialism. Predictably, he didn't last long. Sankara's comrade and close adviser, Captain Blaise Campaoré, staged a successful coup in 1987 that ended with Sankara's assassination. Campaoré immediately restored the status quo, reinstated government salaries and cut food subsidies.

Modern Times

Since the coup, there has been a growing feeling of malaise in Burkinabé society. Burkina Faso consistently ranks in the bottom five of the United Nations index of poorest countries, and out of 146 countries, Burkina Faso ranks 143rd on the Gender-related Development Index (GDI). Nostalgia for Sankara has only been stoked by the assassination of independent journalist Norbet Zongo, and the government drifts. On the upside, multiparty democracy was restored in principle in 1992, although every election since has been widely discredited.

In the 1990s, relations with Côte d'Ivoire deteriorated as expatriate Burkinabé became the political scapegoat for Côte d'Ivoire's political problems. Burkina Faso is heavily dependent on its southern neighbour, and the economy, especially in the south, has taken a blow following the closure of the borders.

THE CULTURE
The National Psyche
Burkina Faso is a curious mix of conservative family values and progressive aspirations for social justice, founded on a survival instinct tempered by a deep faith in family as the social cornerstone and interconnectedness as a way of life. It explains the resilience, the easy-going pride, the openness to outsiders, and the lack of hidden agendas. Usually, the agenda is right there on the surface: the people of Burkina Faso, ignored and isolated, love to connect, in all humility. They rarely take anything personally, rarely sell out their dignity and are grateful for any reciprocated effort. It's a way of getting by.

Lifestyle
There is a handful of sizable Burkinabé towns with all mod cons, but home is where the heart is, and the village is the country's beating heart. Loyalty to the family is an irrepressible duty, and great are the lengths a Burkinabé will go to in order to feed his or her younger siblings. Families are large – the fertility rate (the number of children per woman) is 6.8 – which creates all kinds of inheritance problems.

People
Burkina Faso is one of the most densely populated of the Sahel countries, with 12.6 million people in 274,100 sq km (that is, 46 people per sq km). Important ethnic groups include the Mossi, Bobo, Dioula, Gourmantché, Peul and Lobi. About 50% of the population is Muslim, around 40% animist and 10% Christian. French is the official language and is spoken by most Burkinabé. Major African languages are Moré, Dioula, Gourma, Fulfuldé and Lobiri.

ARTS
Each ethnic group in Burkina Faso has its own artistic style, and the work of the Mossi, the Bobo and the Lobi are the best known.

The Mossi are famous for their tall antelope masks, the Bobo for their butterfly masks and the Lobi for their figurative sculptures.

Burkina Faso's film makers and musicians are well known throughout West Africa, and of course music is especially prevalent – it's everywhere and it's usually very good.

ENVIRONMENT
The Land
Burkina Faso is an arid, landlocked country with semidesert in the north and wooded savanna in the south (yet it is a signatory to the Law of the Sea). Three major rivers, the Mouhoun, Nakambé and Nazinon, water the plains, but settlement in the valleys is sparse owing to the prevalence of river blindness and malaria.

There is a short rainy season between March and April, particularly in the southwest, and a long rainy season from May to October. From November to mid-February it is dry and temperatures are moderate, although the dusty harmattan (seasonal Saharan wind) can be unpleasant.

National Parks
There are some great parks and reserves around the country featuring a diverse array of fauna; unfortunately most are inaccessible without your own wheels. Seasonal passes (valid from 15 December to 31 May) cost US$8 (US$1.60 for locals) and can be obtained at the parks and reserves themselves. A very expensive photo permit (US$80) is required for visitors wishing to photograph animals, but this requirement is rarely enforced.

Environmental Issues
Some estimates place GNP loss owing to environmental damage at 9% annually. One of its most visible aspects is deforestation: wood accounts for 94% of the country's energy consumption, and carts laden with it are a common sight on roads approaching the capital. This private and commercial logging, combined with slash-and-burn agriculture and free-range grazing of animals, has exacerbated desertification, particularly in the north, and diminished the land's carrying capacity. The success of small-scale projects that address these issues, such as education about traditional farming practices, which are usually carried out by nongovernmental

organisations, has prompted their export to other Sahelian countries.

TRANSPORT

GETTING THERE & AWAY
Air
Airlines servicing Burkina Faso:

Air Algérie (☎ 312301)
Air Burkina (☎ 315325) Offers student discounts on international routes.
Air France (☎ 306065)
Air Ivoire (☎ 306207)
Ghana Airways (☎ 304146)

Land
Public-transport services exist between Burkina Faso and all surrounding countries, except, at the time of writing, for a temporary cessation of services to and from Côte d'Ivoire. Your choice might be bus, minibus or 'bush taxi' (also known as *taxi-brousse* or *sept-place*), usually a Peugeot station wagon.

BENIN
The main border crossing is at Porga, the nearest town on the Beninese side to the border on the way to Tanguieta. A Sotrao bus runs each Sunday from Ouagadougou to Tanguiéta (US$8) in the northwest corner of Benin. Or you can do the trip in stages: there's an STMB bus connection (US$4, four hours, twice daily) between Ouagadougou and Fada N'Gourma; then from Fada N'Gourma to the border, minibuses and bush taxis (US$5) are infrequent and fill up slowly. From the border, minibus transport is scarce along the dirt road to Tanguiéta (US$4), except on market day (Monday), but once in Tanguiéta there's at least one bush taxi per day to Natitingou.

Benin time is one hour ahead of Burkina Faso time.

CÔTE D'IVOIRE
Before the closure of the borders, several companies operated popular services for

---

DEPARTURE TAX

The international departure tax is about US$13, although it is normally included in the ticket price.

Burkinabé workers from Ouagadougou to Ferkessédougou (US$10, 12 hours), Bouaké, Yamoussoukro and Abidjan (US$24, up to 24 hours). Services might resume if the troubles in Côte d'Ivoire cease.

GHANA
The main border between Burkina Faso and Ghana is at Hamale. The Ghanaian company **VanefSTC** (☎ 308750) has a bus every Monday, Wednesday and Friday from the main *gare routière* (bus station) in Ouagadougou to Accra (US$16) via Tamale and Kumasi. Book ahead and report two hours before the 8.30am departure time. There's also a Sotrao bus to Pô (US$1.80, twice daily), 15km from the Ghanaian border, from where there are bush taxis to the border and on to Bolgatanga in Ghana.

MALI
The main routes from Burkina to Mali are via Bobo-Dioulasso and Sikasso, or via Bobo-Dioulasso, Koutiala and Segou. **STBF** (☎ 312 795) has buses to/from Ouagadougou to Bamako via Bobo-Dioulasso (US$22, 12 hours, twice daily); book well ahead.

There are Sans Frontière and Sotrakof buses from Bobo-Dioulasso to Bamako (US$13, 15 hours, daily) via Ségou (US$10, 12 to 15 hours, daily). If you're heading for Mopti, from Bobo bush taxis (US$13, 12 to 15 hours) leave either early morning or early evening, but they can take all day to fill.

If you're in northern Burkina, you can reach Mopti from Ouahigouya, via Bankas (a jumping-off point for Dogon Country). Take the 10am Sogebaf bus from Ouahigouya to Koro (US$4, two to four hours, daily), and to connect by bush taxi to Bankass and onward to Mopti. Saturday is the best day to make the crossing.

NIGER
Sotrao buses run from Ouagadougou to Niamey (US$12, 12 to 14 hours, Wednesday and Friday); book in advance. Sans Frontière, CTI and STMB are among those with a 7am service to Kantchari (US$8, daily), from where there's intermittent transport across the border and on to Niamey.

Minibuses from Ouagadougou to Niamey (US$15, 11 to 14 hours) leave from the petrol stations immediately north of the Zaka in Ouagadougou. Leave Ouagadougou early or you won't make it to the border before it closes at 5.30pm.

Niger time is one hour ahead of Burkina Faso.

TOGO
There are no bus services linking Burkina Faso and Togo directly – it's best to travel via Accra (Ghana). Bush taxis ply the almost 1000km of tar road between Ouagadougou and Lomé (US$24, 36 hours), via the border at Sinkasse. It's cheaper to do the trip in stages, as bush taxis in Togo are cheaper. Take a minibus to Bitou, 40km from the border (US$7), then from there to Dapaong (US$1). Expect a thorough luggage search at the border, which closes at 6.30pm.

GETTING AROUND
Air
Air Burkina has at least three flights a week between Ouagadougou and Bobo-Dioulasso (US$46 one way).

Local Transport
Buses are the most reliable and comfortable form of local transport. All forms of transport except express buses (which actually leave on time) take a long time to fill. Buses are almost always cheaper than bush taxis; most leave from their own offices.

Minibuses and bush taxis cover routes between major towns as well as the outlying communities that large buses don't serve. They leave from the *gares routières* mostly in the morning. The minibuses tend to be cheaper and take longer to fill up.

Train
All train services in Burkina Faso were suspended at the time of writing.

OUAGADOUGOU

pop 1.275 million

Ouagadougou (or Ouaga, as it is sometimes called) seems unremarkable at first, but it has a charm all its own. The friendliness and good humour of the locals has something to do with it and, by the standards of other major West African urban centres, this is one city that has not yet grown too big for its boots. This city also has a penchant for festivals. It suggests that the residents (Ouagadougourians?) are pretty good at enjoying themselves, not at the frenetic pace of other, better-known party places, but at a gentler rhythm that many visitors find, to their pleasant surprise, all the more seductive.

ORIENTATION
Ouagadougou's airport is dangerously close (2km) to the city centre. Much to the distress of local taxi drivers, the airport is very much the hub of the urban grid.

To the east of Place des Nations Unies is the administrative and legislative neighbourhood, replete with the Presidential Palace, Parliament and various embassies. On the other side, and heading south, is the beating heart of the city, with markets, hotels cheap and upmarket, cinemas, nightclubs and so on.

INFORMATION
Bookshops
Librairie Diacfa (Rue de l'Hôtel Ville), facing the Grand Marché, carries a wide range of magazines, newspapers (including a few in English) and stationery items.

Cultural Centres
The **Centre Culturel George Méliès** (☎ 306997; Ave Nelson Mandela) hosts French-language cultural events throughout the year.

Internet Access
A number of Internet cafés have popped up all over Ouaga. The best of a slow bunch is **Éspace Internet** (☎ 306060; Av Léo Frobenius; ⊗ 8.30am-noon & 2-6pm Mon-Fri, Sat 9am-noon) at the ONTB office.

Medical Services
Hôpital Yalgado (Ave d'Ourbritenga) is Ouaga's largest hospital; for a good pharmacy try **Pharmacie Diawara** (Rue de la Chance). In the case of a medical emergency seek a recommendation through your embassy or a top-end hotel.

Money
Ecobank (cnr Aves Agostina Neto & de la Résistance; ⊗ Mon-Fri 8am-4pm & Sat 8am-1pm) gives the best exchange rates on travellers cheques, and is a hassle-free bank (provided you get there early in the day). There are BICIAB ATMs dispensing cash against a Visa card around

BURKINA FASO

BURKINA FASO

OUAGADOUGOU

0 —— 500 m
0 —— 0.3 mi

INFORMATION		SIGHTS & ACTIVITIES	p309	Nabonswende........................41 C6
Armelle Voyages........................1 C5		Cathedral..............................22 B6		Restaurant Café Riale.............42 B5
BCEAO Bank (Central Bank)......2 A5		Fespaco Office........................23 C4		Sindabad's.............................43 B5
BIB Bank................................3 B4		Grande Mosquée....................24 B5		
BICIAB...................................4 C5		Hôtel Relax............................25 B4		DRINKING p310
Canadian Embassy....................5 C5		Maison du Peuple.............(see 29)		Jimmy's Discotheque.............44 C6
Centre Culturel George Méliès...(see 51)		Ministries..............................26 D4		Maquis Pili-Pili..................(see 44)
Centre d'Art Artisanal National...6 B4		Moro-Naba Palace..................27 B6		Sahel's..................................45 C6
Danish Embassy....................(see 5)		Mosque.................................28 B5		Zaka....................................46 B5
Ecobank.................................7 C5		Musée National......................29 B4		
Espace Internet....................(see 18)		ONAC Building...................(see 18)		ENTERTAINMENT p310
French Embassy & Consulate.....8 D4		Palais Présidentiel...................30 D4		Ciné Burkina......................(see 43)
Ghanaian Embassy....................9 D4				Ciné Neerwaya......................47 A4
Hôpital Yalgado....................10 D3		SLEEPING pp309–10		Ciné Oubri............................48 B5
Institut Géographique du Burkina		Centre d'Accueil des Soeurs		
(IGB)....................................11 C4		Lauriers................................31 B6		TRANSPORT pp310–11
Italian Embassy......................12 D3		Fondation Charles Dufour.......32 B5		Air Algerie............................49 C5
Ivoirien Embassy....................13 D5		Hôtel de la Paix.....................33 B6		Air Burkina...........................50 B5
L'Agence Tourisme.................14 B5		Hôtel de l'Indépendance........34 C4		Air France.............................51 B4
Librairie Diacfa......................15 B5		Hôtel Delwendé....................35 B4		BFCI/Sans Frontières Bus
Netherlands Embassy..............16 C5		Hôtel Idéal............................36 B5		Station................................52 A6
Onatel..................................17 B4		Hôtel Le Pavillon Vert............37 B4		Bush Taxis.............................53 B5
ONTB (Tourist Office).............18 C5				CTI Buses..............................54 B4
Pharmacie Diawara.................19 B5		EATING p310		Ghana Airways......................55 C6
Photography Permits............(see 18)		Café Chez Salif......................38 B5		Sotrao Buses.........................56 A4
US Embassy...........................20 D5		Café Étalon...........................39 C6		STC Ticket Office...................57 C5
Éspace Internautes................21 B5		Le Verdoyant........................40 C4		STMB Bus Station..................58 A4

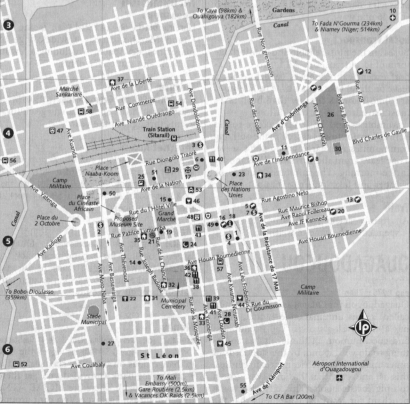

the clock on Ave Nkrumah, Ave Loudun and Ave Yennenga.

Post
The main post office and the Onatel office are just west of Place des Nations Unies on Ave de la Nation.

Tourist Offices
The **tourist office** (ONTB; ☎ 306060, ONAC Bldg, Ave de la Résistance du 17 Mai) sometimes has maps of Ouagadougou for sale. A better bet for maps is the **Institut Géographique Burkinabé** (IGB; Ave de l'Indépendance), near the Sûreté, which sells Ouagadougou maps (US$2.50) and country maps.

Travel Agencies
Recommended for reliability and service among travel agencies offering tours around Burkina Faso are **L'Agence Tourisme** (☎ 318443; Hôtel Les Palmiers, Rue Joseph Badoua) and **Vacances OK Raids** (☎ 382749). For air tickets, try **Armelle Voyages** (☎ 311760; Ave Léo Frobenius).

DANGERS & ANNOYANCES
Most resident expats walk the streets at night without qualms, although it is, of course, prudent to watch your back, particularly on Ave Yennenga and the southern stretches of Rue Joseph Badoua. There have recently been a few reports of muggings (some even in daylight and, occasionally, at knifepoint) of bag-carrying travellers, so carry as little as you need, never carry a bag after dark and walk with people you know. After 10pm always take a taxi. Should you have a problem, contact the police at the **Commissariat Central** (☎ 306271).

SIGHTS & ACTIVITIES
The **Musée National** (☎ 330637; Ave de la Nation; admission US$1.50; ☺ 9am-noon & 3.30-6pm Mon-Sat) had been closed for some time when this book was researched, awaiting its move to new premises. Head instead to the **Maison du Peuple** (Ave de Nelson Mandela), which houses a small but interesting collection of masks – particularly useful if you're planning to buy one yourself.

Nonguests can use the swimming pools at the **Hôtel Relax** (☎ 313233; Ave de la Nation) and **Hôtel de l'Indépendance** (☎ 306060; Ave de la Resistance du 17 Mai) for US$2.50.

FESTIVALS & EVENTS
Ouaga's festivals include the **Pan-African Film Festival** (Fespaco; ☎ 307538; www.fespaco.bf), held in late February in odd-numbered years (it's held in Tunis in even-numbered years); the **International Theatre and Puppetry Festival** (Festival International de Théâtre et de Marionette de Ouagadougou, or FITMO), also held in odd-numbered years in October or November; the International Festival of Theatre for Development, held in even-numbered years in February or March; the Salon International de l'Artisanat (SIAO), the largest commercial exhibition of African craft in the world, held in September and October of even-numbered years; the Festival 'Jazz à Ouaga' is held annually in March and April; and a book fair occurs irregularly.

SLEEPING
Budget accommodation options in Ouagadougou are all in the centre of town. They are close to all the lively part of town with its bars clubs and cinemas.

Hôtel Delwendé (☎ 308757; Rue Patrice Lumumba; s/d US$12-18; ☒) The best budget-range hotel in the centre, the Delwendé has clean rooms, a bar and a wide balcony overlooking the street.

Fondation Charles Dufour (☎ 303889; Rue de la Chance; dm/s/d US$5/8/10) Facing the Cimetière Municipal. The atmosphere here is best described as grubby but friendly. Most beds have mosquito nets, and there's a kitchenette and secure parking. If it's full, you can sleep on a mattress on the floor or camp in the tiny garden (US$3.20). Many guests stay here because of its friendliness and because proceeds go to a local orphanage.

Centre d'Accueil des Soeurs Lauriers (☎ 306490; dm/s/d US$5/6/10). Set in a calm garden in the cathedral compound, this nun-run mission has spotless rooms with shared facilities for men and women. Breakfast is just US$0.80.

Hôtel de la Paix (☎ 335283; Ave Yennenga; s/d US$9/11, d with bath US$17; ☒) One of several cheap hotels on Ave Yennenga, Hôtel de la Paix is friendly and has acceptably clean rooms that tend to stay warm at night.

Hôtel Idéal (☎ 306502; Ave Yennenga; s/d US$10/11) A little further on, the Idéal has well-ventilated rooms that verge on being overpriced. There is also a restaurant, and the staff are friendly.

Hôtel Le Pavillon Vert (Ave de la Liberté; ☎ 310611; r with fan & shared bath US$8-26; ✕) A mellow hotel a couple of kilometres northwest of the centre, which attracts travellers with its large, airy air-con rooms. There's a pricey outdoor French restaurant that serves a variety of tempting dishes from US$2.50.

EATING

Ouagadougou has a number of 'squares' where customers are served cheap eats under *paillottes* (straw awnings), and countless street stalls selling rice-based dishes and *brochettes* (kebabs).

There are many inexpensive street stalls near Aves Yennenga and Loudun. **Restaurant Café Riale** (☎ 314430; Ave Yennenga; dishes US$1.60-4.85) is recommended for its *sauce yassa* (grilled chicken in a sauce of lemon and onion; US$3.20).

Nearby, the tidy **Café Chez Salif** (Ave Yennenga; dishes from US$0.60) serves *riz sauce* (rice with sauce) for US$0.80, and other spaghetti and meat dishes even less. **Nabonswende** (Rue du Dr Gournisson; meals from US$0.40; ✕ early-dusk) sells yogurt and spiced meat sandwiches.

Café Etalon (Ave Yennenga; dishes from US$0.80; ✕ noon-11pm) is another typically Burkinabé diner: cheap meals, rustic setting, friendly ambience – and the cuisine is remarkably good. In the city centre, behind Ciné Burkina, **Sindabad's** (Ave Loudun; dishes US$1.20-4) has a variety of sandwiches, snacks and more substantial dishes, including Lebanese cuisine and other international selections.

SPLURGE!

For a more luxurious dining experience, try the pleasant **Le Verdoyant** (☎ 315407; Ave Dimdolobsom; dishes US$4-6; ✕ noon-11pm Tue-Thu), a popular place that serves good pizza in a pleasant outdoor setting.

DRINKING

In Ouagadougou, the line between a bar and a nightclub is blurred. In neighbourhood bars, the focus is not on the drinking but on the music.

In the city centre, drop by the **Zaka** (☎ 315312; Carrefour de la Rue de l'Hôtel de Ville; ✕ noon-1am) for a draught beer and nightly live music. There's a US$0.80 cover charge at weekends.

One of the liveliest places is **Sahel's** (Ave Loudun; ✕ until late), which has good drumming and live music under the stars every night, with no cover charge.

In contrast, **Jimmy's Discotheque** (☎ 313364; Ave Nkrumah; ✕ until late) is a conventional – if slightly passé – nightclub catering to the expat scene and is expensive, with a cover charge of US$4. Next door, **Maquis Pili-Pili** (☎ 313364; Ave Nkrumah) has live blues music at weekends and also serves food. Nearby, **New Jack** (☎ 315316; Ave Nkrumah) is cast in the same mould as Jimmy's.

ENTERTAINMENT

In addition to the Centre Culturel, there are two other indoor, air-conditioned cinemas: **Ciné Burkina** (Rue du Dr Gournisson) and **Ciné Neerwaya** (☎ 317272), off Ave Kuanda. Tickets are cheaper at outdoor cinemas, such as **Ciné Oubri** (Rue Patrice Lumumba), but the seats are harder.

SHOPPING

The **Grand Marché Rood Wooko** (Rue Patrice Lumumba; ✕ 7am-5pm) is a concrete monolith that speaks volumes about faded post-independence optimism. Nonetheless, it pumps with civic life and is the heart and soul of the town. There are some good craft stalls upstairs. Another place for crafts is the **Centre d'Art Artisanal National** (National Centre for Artisanal Art; Ave Dimdolobsom; ✕ 8am-6pm Mon-Sat), where you can watch artists working with bronze, wood and pottery. Prices here are fixed and high.

GETTING THERE & AWAY

The main *gare routière* for bush taxis and minibuses to destinations throughout Burkina Faso is about 4km south of the city centre, on the southern side of the airport. Take a shared taxi or bus No 3 along Ave Bassawarga. Most buses leave from the relevant company depot rather than the *gare routière*.

GETTING AROUND

There are several bus lines running through the city. Destinations and stops are clearly marked; most routes cross Ave de la Nation at some point. The base fare is US$0.15.

If you need a car to get around, several hotels in Ouagadougou have rental agencies; it's cheaper to hire a car with a driver than to self-drive. Try **Vacances OK Raids** (☎ 382749) for the best price, typically about US$32 per day for a small car.

Shared taxis around town cost US$0.30 for a short ride, or US$0.60 after 10pm. Private taxis charge at least US$1. To the airport, the fare is US$1.70; orange metered taxis (☎ 343838) are more expensive.

SOUTHERN BURKINA FASO

BOROMO

Halfway between Ouagadougou and Bobo-Dioulasso, Boromo is a good jumping-off point for **Parc National des Deux Balés**. There are several areas within 10km of Boromo where elephant sightings are common.

The only place to stay in Boromo is the **Relais Touristique** (☎ 440684; s/d US$6/7, with air-con US$9/11; ❄), where the staff are very helpful and will assist in arranging your visit to the park. Closer to the action is the **Campement Le Kaicedra** (☎ 212691; campsite per person US$3, d US$29), well situated for elephant-gazing. If you ask nicely, you will be picked up from the bus station.

To get there, take a bus or bush taxi (US$3.20, three hours) from either Ouaga or Bobo.

BOBO-DIOULASSO

pop 230,000

Burkina Faso's second-largest city, Bobo (as it's usually tagged) is a pleasant, relaxing place, as well as a good base for exploring the region. During late March or early April in even-numbered years, Bobo hosts the **Semaine Nationale de la Culture**, a festival featuring music, dance and theatre performances.

Information

The **tourist office** (ONTB; ☎ 771986; Ave de l'Unité; ⏰ 7am-12.30pm & 3-5.30pm Mon-Fri) is helpful and has some written material on offer, too.

Ecobank changes US dollar and euro travellers cheques, but charges commission and requires proof of purchase. You can draw money from a Visa card at BICIAB.

The poste restante in Bobo-Dioulasso charges US$0.80 per collected letter. There are many Internet cafés, including **Intelec** (☎ 972520; Ave Ouédraogo; ⏰ 7am-8pm Mon-Sat,

noon-8pm Sun), which charges US$3.20 per 15 minutes.

The bookshop **Librairie Socifa** (Rue Joffre), near the Grand Marché, sometimes has maps of Burkina Faso in stock.

Hôpital Sourou Sanou (Ave de l'Indépendance) near Place de la Nation provides medical facilities; there is an adjoining pharmacy.

Danger & Annoyances

For your personal security, it's best to avoid walking by the river, as it has been a favoured locale of some local thieves in the past. Don't trust 'guides' who offer to take you.

Sights & Activities

Bobo's **Grande Mosquée** is a beautiful example of Sahelian architecture and the number-one sight in town. Although at the time of research entrance was forbidden to non-Muslims, its exterior is still a breathtaking sight. The **Grand Marché** has some good bargains, including beads, carvings and cloth, although throwing off the sales pitches can be tough.

Bobo's small but interesting **Musée Provincial du Houët** (Place de la Nation; admission US$1.60; ⏰ 8.30am-noon & 3.30-6pm Tues-Sat, 9am-1pm Sun) has a display of regional artwork and full-scale examples of traditional buildings.

Out of town and not too hard to find by car or motorcycle are **La Guingette** swimming hole (14km west) and the scenic Bobo villages of **Koumi** (15km west) and **Koro** (entrance fee with guide US$1.60), 12km east.

Sleeping

Campement Le Pacha (☎ 980954; camp site per person US$3; s/d US$9/11, with air-con US$16/12; ❄) This clean and friendly place 3km west of the centre, near the Autogare des Fruits, has clean rooms with mosquito net, fan and shared facilities. There is also a pleasant but pricey garden restaurant.

Casa Africa (☎ 980157; Rue 9.46; camping US$3; s/d US$7/9, with bathroom US$8/10) Set in a leafy compound on the western edge of town. The ventilated singles/doubles with mosquito net are decent. There is also a restaurant serving meals from US$1.60. A shared taxi from the centre costs US$0.30.

Hotel Renaissance (☎ 982331; Ave de la République; d with fan US$7, with bathroom US$10, with air-con US$19; ❄) The balcony rooms are good value, and the central location is hard to beat.

BURKINA FASO

BOBO-DIOULASSO

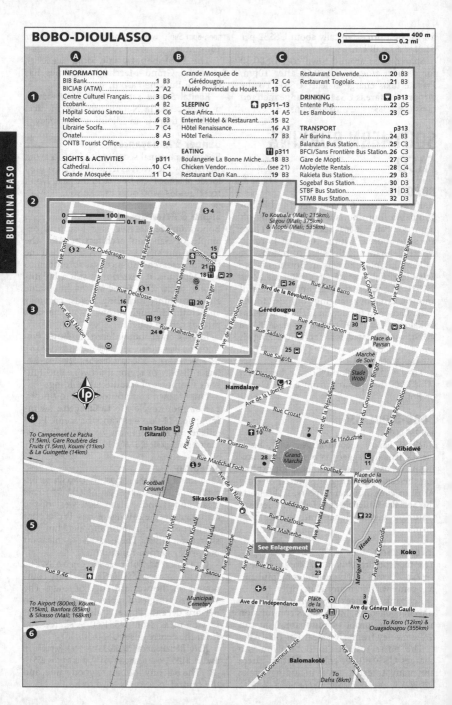

INFORMATION		
BIB Bank	1	B3
BICIAB (ATM)	2	A2
Centre Culturel Français	3	D6
Ecobank	4	B2
Hôpital Sourou Sanou	5	C6
Intelec	6	B3
Librairie Socifa	7	C4
Onatel	8	A3
ONTB Tourist Office	9	B4

SIGHTS & ACTIVITIES		p311
Cathedral	10	C4
Grande Mosquée	11	D4

Grande Mosquée de		
Gérédougou	12	C4
Musée Provincial du Houët	13	C6

SLEEPING		pp311–13
Casa Africa	14	A5
Entente Hôtel & Restaurant	15	B2
Hôtel Renaissance	16	A3
Hôtel Teria	17	B3

EATING		p311
Boulangerie La Bonne Miche	18	B3
Chicken Vendor	(see 21)	
Restaurant Dan Kan	19	B3

Restaurant Delwende	20	B3
Restaurant Togolais	21	B3

DRINKING		p313
Entente Plus	22	D5
Les Bambous	23	C5

TRANSPORT		p313
Air Burkina	24	B3
Balanzan Bus Station	25	C3
BFCI/Sans Frontière Bus Station	26	C3
Gare de Mopti	27	C3
Mobylette Rentals	28	C4
Rakieta Bus Station	29	B3
Sogebaf Bus Station	30	D3
STBF Bus Station	31	D3
STMB Bus Station	32	D3

Entente Hotel (☎ 971205; Rue du Commerce; d US$11, with air-con $17; ❄) and **Hôtel Teria** (☎ 971972; Ave Alwata Diawara; s/d with fan & bathroom US$12/15, with air-con US$24/28; ❄), both in the heart of town, are comfortable, upmarket choices.

Eating
There is a restaurant in the *paillotte*-shaded garden of the Entente Hotel, which has a small but good selection of African food.

Restaurant Togolais (Rue du Commerce; dishes from US$0.80) Across the street from Entente, this serves inexpensive *riz* sauce and other dishes scooped from cauldrons. Out the front a guy grills chickens for US$2.40.

Restaurant Dan Kan (Rue Malherbe; meals US$3.20) Not far from the Onatel office, Dan Kan is good value. Vegetarians will be grateful for its range of salads.

Restaurant Delwendé (Rue Delafosse; meals from US$0.80) Recommended for its large African menu at reasonable prices.

For excellent brioche, try **Boulangerie La Bonne Miche** (Ave du Gouverneur Binger).

Drinking & Entertainment
Near Place de la Nation, **Les Bambous** (☎ 982931; Ave du Gouverneur Binger) has nightly live traditional music. **Entente Plus** (Ave de la Révolution) was the locals' favourite nightclub at the time of writing.

Getting There & Away
STMB, Sans Frontière, STBF and Sogebaf each run several daily services to Ouaga (US$8, five hours), although it's worth buying tickets in advance to take the 10am and 2pm STMB air-con services (US$11 and US$13 respectively).

Rakieta has several departures daily to Banfora (US$1.80, 1½ hours, 10 daily), Gaoua (US$6, five hours, three daily) and Ouagadougou (US$8).

Minibuses and minor bus companies congregate at Autogare des Fruits west of town. With luck, there are daily departures for Ouagadougou (US$10), Ferkessédougou (US$10) and Bamako (US$13).

For air services to and from Bobo, see p307.

Getting Around
A shared taxi from the market to the Autogare des Fruits costs US$0.30 (US$0.80 in a private taxi).

If you want to visit neighbouring villages, you can rent a *mobylette* (moped) or motorbike (US$6/10 per day plus petrol) near the Grand Marché.

BANFORA
Banfora is a quiet town in a gorgeous area, ideal for exploring by rented bike or moped. The **Cascades de Karfiguéla** are about 12km northwest of town. These waterfalls are worth a look at any time, but are best in the rainy season. The **Dômes de Fabedougou**, an escarpment-type formation not far from the waterfalls, is potentially good for rock climbing.

About 10km west of Banfora is **Lac Tengréla**, which is home to hippos and interesting birdlife. A trip in a pirogue (traditional canoe) costs about US$2.

About 40km from Lac Tengréla is the town of **Douna**, which is close to some interesting rock formations, **Pics de Sindou** (Sindou Peaks), and to villages reminiscent of those in Mali's Dogon region. To get to Douna you'll need to hire a motorcycle or private car.

With a shady courtyard and a restaurant, the **Hôtel le Comoé** (☎ 880151; Rue de la Poste; s/d US$10/12, with air-con & bathroom US$19/22; ❄), at the southern edge of town, is best value.

Hôtel Fara (☎ 880117; off Route de Bobo; s/d US$11/12, d with air-con S$15; ❄) is more central, just behind the *gare routière*.

Le Flamboyant (Route de Bobo) is a recommended, good-value eatery.

Rakieta has hourly connections to Bobo-Dioulasso (US$1.80, 1½ hours, 10 daily). STMB, Sogebaf and Sotrakof also serve this route, as well as Ouagadougou. Each company has a station near the market.

Minibuses and bush taxis leave from the *gare routière*, north of the centre.

A shared taxi from the market to the *gare routière* costs US$0.30 (US$0.80 in a private taxi). It's a half-hour walk. Bicycles (US$4 per day) and *mobylettes* (US$7) can be rented at the market. Alternatively, ask at your hotel about the possibility of a private rental deal.

GAOUA
Gaoua is a good base for exploring Lobi Country. Its nightclubs will please musical purists, and it has a small **Musée de Poni** (☎ 870169; admission US$1.80) displaying Lobi pottery, masks and houses.

BURKINA FASO

The surrounding region has many picturesque villages, built in distinctive Lobi architectural style, such as **Doudou**, 14km from Gaoua. In **Loropéni**, 39km to the west, are ancient stone ruins of unknown origin. The local Gan people call the site *'la maison de refuge'* ('house of refuge').

About 8km northwest of Loropéni in Obiré is the **Sanctuaire du Roi Gan**, the Gan king's residence.

Just behind the market, **Hôtel de Poni** (☎ 870200; d US$7) has simple rooms and a dirty bar.

A step up in luxury is the **Hôtel Hala** (☎ 870121; d US$16, with air-con US$29; ✗), about 1.5km north of the centre, which has spotless rooms.

For cheap eats, La Porte Ouverte offers African fare.

Rakieta goes to Banfora (US$4.85, three hours, twice daily) and Bobo-Dioulasso (US$6, four hours, three times daily). Some minibuses also leave from the *gare routière*, but make sure to get there early.

FADA N'GOURMA

Fada N'Gourma is a convenient overnight stop for those travelling to/from Niger or Benin. Bush taxis in all directions take a long time to fill up; for Benin, you might have to wait several days.

The best place to stay is the **Auberge Yemmamma** (☎ 770039; s/d with fan & bath US$8/9, with air-con US$10/11; ✗), opposite the market. The outdoor bar-restaurant is the most popular eatery in town, with meals starting from US$2.40.

Le Campement (s/d US$3.20/4), opposite the *gare routière*, is Fada's cheapest option and is conveniently located opposite the *gare routière*.

NORTHERN BURKINA FASO

DORI

Known for its prized woollen blankets, Dori, in the northeast of the country, has a small, daily **market** made interesting by the Tuareg, Peul, Songhaï and other ethnic groups of the region. Roughly 35km southwest lies **Bani** with its distinctive series of mosques with fingerlike minarets reaching

for the sky. Also nearby is **Gorom-Gorom** and its colourful market.

Auberge Populaire (r with shared bath $6) This place, just north of the market, has no-frills rooms. The bar can be noisy. It's on the road to Gorom-Gorom, and is also known as Chez Tanti Véronique.

Hebergement de Dori (☎ 660341; d with fan & bath US$6, with air-con US$17; ✗) A fair hike from the *gare routière*, and its sanitation leaves something to be desired. At least it's quiet.

Café La Joie de Vivre has cheap meals like *riz gras* (rice with meat sauce) and spaghetti for around US$0.50.

STMB and Sogebaf both have a service between Ouagadougou and Dori (US$6, five hours, twice daily).

GOROM-GOROM

Gorom-Gorom has one of the most ethnically diverse and colourful **markets** in Burkina Faso. There's a camel market here, as well as Tuareg leather and jewellery merchants. Held every Thursday, it gets into full swing around 11am. A 'tourist tax' of US$1.60 is payable at the *commissariat* (police station) upon entering the town, and a US$8 photo permit must also be bought by those planning to take pictures, although it's seldom enforced.

Transport is scarce. The road from Ouagadougou to Gorom-Gorom is sealed as far as Kaya, unsealed but in decent condition to Dori, and brutal from there onwards. The road from Kaya is often washed out for several weeks during the rainy season.

If the **Auberge Populaire** (r US$4.85) is too grubby you can pitch a tent here. There is neither electricity nor running water.

The only other option is the shabby but comparatively luxurious **Campement Hôtelier** (☎ 660144; camp site per person US$3.20, s/d US$10/11), where there are frequent water and electricity cuts, as well as mediocre meals.

The best connections to/from Ouagadougou (US$6, seven hours) are with Sogebaf, CTI and ZGR. They leave Ouaga Monday, Wednesday and Saturday and return the following day, leaving at 2pm on market day. Bush taxis head for Dori (US$3.20, two hours) at 7pm after the market.

OUAHIGOUYA

If you're heading for Dogon Country in Mali, the most direct route from Ouagadougou is through Ouahigouya, Burkina Faso's fourth-largest city.

In the centre, **Plan International** (Ave de Mopti; dm US$4.85) has basic mattresses and mosquito nets.

Southeast of town, near the Djibo road, the friendly **Colibri** (☎ 550787; d with fan/air-con & bathroom US$8/14; ⌧) is a 1km hike east of the town centre, but the friendly welcome makes it worth the effort.

STAF, STMB and Sogebaf run services between Ouaga and Ouahigouya almost hourly (US$4, five hours). Bush taxis run the same route, but are slower and more expensive.

BURKINA FASO DIRECTORY

ACCOMMODATION

Expect to pay anywhere between US$5 and US$8 for basic accommodation, which usually consists of a room with fan and shared bathroom and a breakfast of bread, jam and coffee. Camping fees are between US$2 and US$3.

There's a *taxe de séjour* charged per night at places to stay. It varies according to the standard of accommodation, beginning at US$0.30 per person per night for the cheapest places. A once-off *taxe communal* of US$1.60 is also supposed to be charged, but is often not enforced. Sometimes these taxes are included in the prices, sometimes not, so it's best to check.

BUSINESS HOURS

Businesses are open from 7.30am to noon and 3pm to 5.30pm weekdays and 9am to 1pm Saturday. Banking hours are from 7.30am to 11am and 3.30pm to 5pm weekdays, and Ecobank is also open from 9am to 12.30pm Saturday.

DANGERS & ANNOYANCES

Police roadblocks and baggage searches occasionally delay a journey. Burkina Faso is relatively safe, but crime isn't unknown, particularly around major markets, cinemas and *gares routières*, where it's usually confined to petty theft and pickpocketing. In Ouagadougou, watch your valuables. At night either take a taxi or walk in a group.

EMBASSIES & CONSULATES

For details on getting visas for neighbouring countries, see p316. Embassies and consulates in Ouagadougou:

Canada (☎ 311894; Rue Agostino Neto)
Côte d'Ivoire (☎ 3182280; Ave Raoul Follereau)
Denmark (☎ 313192; Rue Agostino Neto)
France (☎ 306774; Ave de l'Indépendance)
Germany (☎ 306731; Rue Joseph Badoua)
Ghana (☎ 301701; Ave d'Oubritenga)
Italy (☎ 308694; Rue 4.69)
Mali (☎ 381922; 2569 Ave Bassawarga)
Netherlands (☎ 361582; Ave Kwame Nkrumah)
USA (☎ 306723; Ave Raoul Follereau)

The Canadian embassy in Ouagadougou handles British and Australian affairs. Benin and Niger have no diplomatic representation in Burkina Faso, not even through the French embassy.

There are Burkinabé embassies in Côte d'Ivoire, Ghana, Mali, Morocco and Senegal. Details are listed in the capital city section of the relevant country chapter. Where there's no diplomatic representation, visas can usually be obtained from French embassies or consulates.

FESTIVALS & EVENTS

See the Ouagadougou (p309) and Bobo-Dioulasso (p311) sections for details.

FOOD & DRINK

Tô is the millet or sorghum-based *pâté* eaten as a staple in Burkina Faso. Also widely eaten are *riz sauce* (rice with sauce) and *riz gras* (rice with meat sauce). In larger towns, many people start the day with bread and *yaourt* (yogurt, often vanilla-flavoured) at street-side coffee stalls. Burkina Faso is well known for its *pintade grillé* (grilled guinea fowl) and *poisson grillé* (grilled fish), available in larger towns.

There are countless street stalls selling rice-based dishes and *brochettes*: (skewered barbecued meats and sometimes offal – ask for *viande* if you want meat), best eaten served in a crusty bun, ideally with barbecued onion and an oily sauce. It should cost around US$0.80.

HOLIDAYS

As well as religious holidays listed in the Africa Directory chapter (p1003), these are the principal public holidays in Burkina Faso:

1 Janurary New Year's Day
8 March Women's Day
1 May Labour Day
4 August Revolution Day
5 August Independence Day
15 October Anniversary of Sankara's overthrow
1 November All Saints Day

INTERNET ACCESS

There are plenty of Internet cafés in Ouaga-dougou, Bobo-Dioulasso and Ouahigouya, most of which will require patience.

MAPS

Burkina Faso (1:1,000,000), a map published by the French-based Institut Géographique National, is the most widely available. It's sold at the **Institut Géographique du Burkina** (IGB; ☎ 324823) on Ave de l'Indépendance in Ouagadougou, or in many European bookshops.

MONEY

The unit of currency in Burkina Faso is the West African Communauté Financière Africaine (CFA) franc, and it's best to arrive laden with euros – it's hard to exchange anything else outside Ouagadougou and Bobo. The cost of living is considerably higher than in Ghana, and slightly lower than in neighbouring countries in the West African CFA zone. Determined bargaining is expected for souvenirs and cultural artefacts, and moderate bargaining can take the edge off taxi prices, but most other prices are fixed.

Banks generally require proof of purchase to change travellers cheques, so keep receipts in a safe place. Euros are the most sought-after currency. BICIAB's ATMs throughout the country give cash advances on Visa cards; otherwise, credit cards are practically redundant. The black market doesn't offer much advantage over banks.

PHOTOGRAPHY & VIDEO

A photo permit is required in Burkina Faso, although this requirement is rarely enforced. Free permits are issued on the spot by the secretariat of the **Office National du Tourisme du Burkina** (ONTB; ONAC Bldg, Ave Ouédraogo, Ouagadougou; ⌚ 7am-12.30pm & 3-5.30pm Mon-Fri). Even with this permit, don't photograph anything associated with the military or the police and always ask citizens first before photographing them. A separate permit is required if you wish to photograph animals in national parks.

POST & TELEPHONE

Ouagadougou's **poste restante** (⌚ 7.30am-12.30pm & 3-5pm Mon-Fri) charges CFA500 per collected letter and will hold mail for one month. There is also a poste restante in Bobo-Dioulasso.

International phone calls can be made easily from telecommunications centres (Onatel) in large towns from 7am to 10pm daily. Rates are US$4 to US$6.40 for three-minute calls to Europe, the USA and Australia. You can also send/receive faxes here for about US$1.30 per received page. There are no regional area codes.

TOURIST INFORMATION

The Office National du Tourisme Burkinabé, or ONTB, has accommodating offices centrally located in Ouaga and Bobo.

VISAS

Visas are required for all. You can buy a tourist visa at Ouagadougou airport for US$16 and two photos, and most land border posts also issue visas on arrival. Burkinabé embassies can issue multiple-entry visas valid for three months, also requiring two photos. In countries without diplomatic representation, the French embassy will normally issue visas on Burkina Faso's behalf. Typical costs are around US$25 to US$40.

Visas for Onward Travel

Note that Benin and Niger have no diplomatic representation in Burkina Faso, not even through the French embassy.

Travellers to Benin can buy a 48-hour visa at the border post for US$16. It is possible to buy a visa at the Niger border, although the immigration officials may penalise you for your lack of planning; the visa is short-term and will require an extension in Niamey.

Visas for the following neighbouring countries can be obtained in Burkina Faso. See p315 for embassy and consulate information.

Ghana One-month visas cost US$20, require four photos and are issued within 24 hours, between 8am and 2pm Monday to Friday.
Mali One-month visas cost US$32, require two photos and are issued within 24 hours, between 8.30am and noon, and 2pm to 5pm Monday to Friday.
Togo The French consulate will issue 48-hour visas for Togo within 24 hours for US$27 plus two photos.

Guinea-Bissau

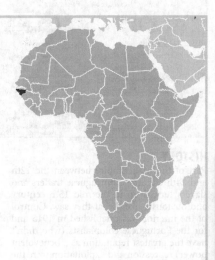

FAST FACTS

- **Area** 36,125 sq km
- **ATMs** none
- **Borders** Guinea (Kandika open); Senegal (Salikenie and Pirada open, São Domingos open but not recommended)
- **Budget** US$25 to US$30 per day
- **Capital** Bissau
- **Languages** Portuguese, Crioulo (a mix of Portuguese and African), Wolof and Fula
- **Money** Central African CFA; US$1 = CFA600
- **Population** 1.3 million
- **Seasons** dry & cool (late Nov–Feb), wet & hot (Mar–early Nov)
- **Telephone** country code ☎ 245; international access code ☎ 00
- **Time** GMT/UTC
- **Visas** US$45 for 30 days; must be obtained in advance.

WARNING

The situation in Guinea-Bissau has greatly improved since the end of the civil war. However we were not able to do on-the-ground research, so some information in this chapter may not be reliable. It is still important to seek reliable advice before travelling to Guinea-Bissau.

Tiny, verdant and fractured by rivers, creeks and estuaries, Guinea-Bissau is something of a gem, far enough off the beaten track to keep things 'select', but with some fantastic stuff waiting for those prepared to seek it out. Some travellers think that tourism here begins and ends with the Arquipélago dos Bijagós, a cluster of beautiful offshore islands that have a unique culture and fantastic marine and animal life. While it's true that they *are* pretty amazing, on the mainland await sleepy old colonial towns, quiet beaches and wonderful sacred rainforests.

The flip side is that Guinea-Bissau is not a well-developed nation even by African standards; it's gut-wrenchingly poor in fact. Badly served by its recent leaders, there's many a nervous government travel warning about Guinea-Bissau thanks to huge economic and political problems, a hangover from the 1998–99 civil war. Still, the country remains peaceful and it's people some of the most unconditionally hospitable in West Africa.

GUINEA-BISSAU

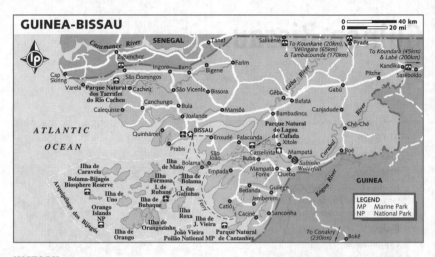

HISTORY

Part of the Mali Empire between the 12th and 14th centuries, Portuguese traders and slavers turned up in the mid-15th century and obviously liked what they saw. Control of the interior was established in 1915 and for the Portuguese colonialists (who didn't have the greatest reputation as a benevolent power) repression and exploitation were the order of the day; if you were a peasant, you planted groundnuts – like it or not. In the 1950s and '60s Portuguese Guinea (as it was then called) remained undeveloped and under the iron fist of Portugal's far-right dictator Antonio de Oliveira Salazar. Not unsurprisingly the African Party for the Independence of Guinea and Cape Verde (PAIGC) was created and fought the Portuguese from 1961 until the early 1970s, one of Africa's longest colonial wars. The PAIGC were pretty hot as African revolutionary armies go, and by the early 1970s elections were being held in liberated territory, which amounted to over half the country. In 1973 the leader of the PAIGC, Amílcar Cabral, was assassinated in Guinea, but by early 1974 independence was finally achieved.

Viva a Revolução

Many of the PAIGC's leaders came from the Cape Verde islands and the party was committed not only to the liberation of Guinea-Bissau and Cape Verde, but the unification of the two. However, this idea got canned in 1980 after a coup brought João

Bernardo Vieira to power. He was a determined character who tackled the country's enormous problems with some intelligence and sensitivity, traits he offset with a large slab of Marxism and a highly repressive system of governance. Ever the pragmatist, Vieira ditched hardcore socialism in 1986 and allowed other political parties in 1991, and over the next three years Vieira skirted around three coup attempts and scraped through a presidential election.

Self-Destruction

In 1997 Guinea-Bissau joined the West African franc (CFA) zone and economic uncertainty, nationwide strikes and allegations of massive corruption led to widespread unrest. This was followed neatly in 1998 by a military coup led by Ansumane Mane, the former head of the armed services who'd been implicated in supplying weapons to separatist rebels in Casamance, Senegal. Guinea-Bissau descended into civil war. 'Peacekeeping' troops from Senegal and Guinea waded in on the side of Vieira's government and the people of the countryside were caught in the middle. Vieira was overthrown in May 1999, but the rebels held elections the following year and the rather erratic Kumba Yalá was sworn in as president. However, the military meddling didn't stop and eventually led to conflict between Mane and troops loyal to the new government. Mane came off the worse, killed in a gun battle (and you can't get much worse than that) and slowly things calmed down in this land of only 1.3 million people.

Bobble Hats & Confusion

Yalá has had a very chequered presidential career. He has pledged to promote national reconciliation, balanced budgets and agricultural production, but is renowned for firing judges, ministers and whole swathes of civil servants, and reacting badly to criticism (journalists have been arrested). In October 2001 he addressed a press conference (sporting his trademark red bobble hat) and declared that he'd just foiled a coup, which many suspect never happened. Then in November 2002 he accused parliament of sabotage and installed a caretaker government. Elections scheduled for 2003 were repeatedly postponed, but Yalá subsequently appointed a critical journalist into his cabinet and then decided that the capital should be moved 200km southeast to Buba! Many observers muttered that Yalá might be mentally ill and predictably enough he was removed by a bloodless coup in September 2003, shortly after he again cancelled presidential elections.

The military quickly installed a civilian transitional government headed by businessmen Henrique Rosa, but Guinea-Bissau remains in a deep hole, and it's not milk and honey that's filling it. At the time of writing it was hoped that elections would take place by early 2004, but the country was an economic disaster area; government employees hadn't been paid for some time and substantial infrastructure destroyed in the 1998–99 civil war had not been rebuilt.

THE CULTURE

The two biggest cultural groups are the coastal- and southern-dwelling Balante and the Fula in the north. The Manjaco (or Manjak), Papel, Fulup and Mandinka (or Mande) peoples are also present, along with Portuguese and Lebanese traders and quite a few *mestizos*, folks of mixed European and African descent. Guinea-Bissau's islands are the domain of the Bijago who have some pretty interesting customs, including the practice of taking their dead to another island for burial so that their spirits do not haunt the living.

About 55% of Guinea-Bissau's population follow African religions, while 40% are Muslim and a small proportion Christian.

ENVIRONMENT

Much of the country is low lying with a fractured coastline consisting of numerous creeks, estuaries, islands and mangrove swamps, often backed by forest that gives way to savanna in the east and green hills on the Guinean border.

Guinea-Bissau's important, threatened (by rice farming) mangroves are protected by Parque Natural dos Tarrafes do Rio Cacheu and the embryonic Parque Natural de Cantanhez, which will also protect several sacred forests. Near Buba, Parque Natural do Lagoa de Cafada protects a wetland area, but of most interest (and accessibility) to travellers is the Unesco Bolama-Bijagós Biosphere Reserve which covers part of the Arquipélago dos Bijagós. However, while this may sound pretty good and the potential for fantastic primate viewing (including chimpanzees) and birdwatching is huge, tourist facilities in the parks are limited, verging on nonexistent.

Guinea-Bissau is generally hot and humid, but the rainy season (which is very heavy on the coast) runs from June to October. The coolest months are December and January; April and May are hideously hot and humid. Travelling is sweetest in the months after the rains, despite 30°C+ temperatures.

TRANSPORT

GETTING THERE & AWAY
Air

Most visitors arriving by air fly to Dakar (Senegal) and then take a short hop to Bissau from there – **Air Senegal International** (www.air-senegal-international.com) has flights for around US$165 one way. Still, check out the direct flights from Lisbon (Portugal) with **TAP** (www.tap-airportugal.pt); connections to/from North America and Europe are easy. Alternatively, get to Cape Verde from the US and Europe and then make the hop to Bissau with Transportes Aereas Cape Verde (TACV).

Air Bissau (TAGB) has services to a limited number of destinations in West Africa. These include Conakry (Guinea) and Banjul

(The Gambia), while Aeroservices fly from Dakar to Ilha de Bubaque every Saturday (US$350).

Departure tax is US$20.

Land
GUINEA
The usual route goes via Gabú crossing at Kandika and continuing through Koundara to Labé. Transport between Koundara and Gabú is chancy so aim to catch traffic heading to the Sunday market at Saréboïdo (Guinea). Think three days.

The ferry and other boats usually servicing the Arquipélago dos Bijagós sometimes venture down to Conakry and it would be surprising if there wasn't other boat traffic hopping down the coast; enquire in Bissau.

SENEGAL
Current government travel advice states that you should avoid Guinea-Bissau's northwest border, including the crossing at São Domingos, which is a pain in the arse, because this is the quickest and easiest way into Senegal with daily bush taxis along the tarred road via Bula and on to Ziguinchor (Senegal).

Alternative (and recommended) routes cross further east at Salikenie or go via Gabú (from where there's sometimes a bush taxi to Tambacounda, Senegal) and cross at Pirada.

There are doubtless adventurous sea routes into Senegal from the islands to southern Casamance.

GETTING AROUND
Aeroservices have a limited service into the Arquipélago dos Bijagós, but planes can be chartered; make reservations at Guiné Tours in Bissau.

Bissau's main sealed roads stretch out from the capital east to Gabú and up to the São Domingos border crossing. Other roads can be utterly impassable in the rainy season and highly tedious the rest of the time. There are few river bridges so traffic is at the mercy of ferries, which can delay journeys especially if the river ferry is stuffed and you have to use a dugout canoes to cross.

Public transport consists of minibuses and Peugeot 504 bush taxis on the main routes, and pick-ups (kandongas) on rural routes. It's best to hit the road before 8am; fares are cheap, but baggage is 10% extra.

Rodofluvial operates ferries into the Arquipélago dos Bijagós from Bissau port, but their services seem to be getting fewer. There are also smaller boats and canoas (motorised canoes) out to the islands and along the coast from Port Bandim and Port de Canoa in Bissau.

Many of the bigger hotels in Bissau can arrange motorboat hire; budget option Casino Galeon is a good place to start, but expect to pay US$100 to US$180 per boat per day.

BISSAU

Bissau is a stark contrast to the craziness and chaos of most West African capitals. The city has a not-unpleasant, laid-back, small-town feel, but the war and subsequent economic malaise has a lot to do with the lack of hassle, hustle and bustle. Sightseeing is not going to take long; you could gawp at the debris of war, the destroyed French Cultural Centre and presidential palace, and check out some interesting 19th-century buildings, but that's about it. Bissau is one of the poorest capitals in West Africa – a place where electricity is a pretty hit-and-miss affair – but as a staging post to further adventures it's quite agreeable, especially if you tune into the vibrant local music scene.

ORIENTATION
The wide Avenida Amílcar Cabral runs between the port and the Praça dos Heróis Nacionais and is crossed halfway by Rua Eduardo Mondlane; most facilities and attractions are concentrated around these two streets. Avenida de 14 Novembro leads northwest to the main paragem (bus and taxi park) and to the international airport 10km away at Bissalanca; catch a taxi for US$4 or walk 200m to the start of Avenida de 14 Novembro and take a minibus.

INFORMATION
Medical Services
Hospital Simão Mendes (☎ 212861; Avenida Pansau Na Isna) Has scarily limited facilities.

Pharmacie Moçambique (☎ 205513; off Rua de Angola) The best pharmacy.

Money
BAO (Avenida Amílcar Cabral) is the best bank to change cash, but also try the forex bureaus

near Mercado Central and **Mavegro Supermarket** (Rua Eduardo Mondlane), which apparently changes cash and travellers cheques at good rates.

Post & Telephone
The main post office is on Avenida Amílcar Cabral. You can phone from here, the public phone office nearby or from phonecard booths outside. The post office also offers Internet access.

Tourist Offices
Travel agencies are often a better bet than **Ministério do Comércio e Turismo** (☎ 202195; off Avenida Pansau Na Isna).

Travel Agencies
The following agencies can organise flights and tours, and have plenty of tourist information.
Agencia de Viagem et Turismo (☎ 213709; odyssetours@sol.gtelecom.gw; Bissau Hotel, Avenida de 14 Novembro)
Guiné Tours (☎ 214344; guine-tours@ sol.gtelecom.gw; Avenida Amílcar Cabral)

SIGHTS
There are meagre pickings here folks. **Museu Nacional** (Avenida 14 de Novembro; ☯ 8am-1.30pm Mon-Fri) has *some* interesting indigenous artefacts, but it's probably more fun wandering past the pastel-coloured **old Portuguese buildings** at the southern end of Avenida Amílcar Cabral or through the **Mercado Centrale** (central market). The imposing **Pidjiguiti monument**, set back from the docks, is dedicated to the 50 or so Bissau dock workers who were killed during a strike on 3 August 1959, a massacre that helped firm up the independence movement. Sadly **Fortaleza d'Amura**, a huge Portuguese fort and significant landmark is closed to visitors.

For a glimpse of rural village life, take a canoa across the estuary to **Enxudé**. Sadly the nearest **beaches** are over 20km away past the airport; they're not of Caribbean standard.

FESTIVALS & EVENTS
If you're in the country during February, enquire about Bissau's carnival; it's a pretty colourful event full of processions, papiermâché masks and cultural events.

SLEEPING
Bissau is not blessed with kicking budget options, so you'll need to splash the cash and stay at somewhere like **Casino Galeon** (☎ 201548; Praça Ché Guevara; d US$18); you can arrange motor boat hire for trips to the islands at **Hotel Ta-Mar** (☎ 214876; cnr Avenida 12 de Setembro & Rua 2; d US$20) or **Pensão Centrale** (☎ 201232; Avenida Amílcar Cabral; d US$25). If you're feeling flush stay at **Hotel do 24 de Setembro** (☎ 221033/34; hotel24setembro@bissau.net; Estrada de Santa Luzia; r US$50-110).

EATING
Street food is hard to come by in Bissau. The port is a reasonable hunting ground and look out for stalls selling *riz gras* (rice with a greasy sauce) and simple fish dishes (US$1 to US$2). If you're after a restaurant try **Santa Rosa** (Avenida Domigos Ramos; meals US$1.50-4) for *shwarmas* and some great roast chicken; **Papa Louca Fast Food** (Avenida Francisco Mendes; dishes US$2-6) for fast food African style; and the fine, **Senegalese Restaurant Magui** (Rua Vitorino Costa; meals US$1.50-4). **Guiné-Serviço** (Rua Justino Lopes) and **Fortaleza d'Amura Café** (opposite fort), are both good for cheap espresso and sandwiches.

DRINKING & CLUBBING
You could cruise the area around Hotel Caracol or try **Briso do Mar** (Avenida de 3 Augusto) and the almost chic **Bar Galeon** (Praça Ché Guevara) which are popular drinking holes. **Bar Ninho de Pilun** (Avenida Naceos Unis) is not bad and close by is **Centro Cultural Mansa Flama**. The latter is pretty earthy, but a great place to hear good contemporary local artists; nights here tend to go on and on. **Tropicana** (Rua Justino Lopes) and **Black & White** (Avenida 14 de Novembro) are two other kicking local clubs. **X-Club** (Rua Osvaldo Vieira) and Capital are much plusher, more expensive and quite Portuguese.

GETTING THERE & AWAY
Boat
Ferries to Ilha de Bubaque are operated by **Rodofluvial** (☎ 212350; Avenida de 3 de Agosto). There are also some services up the Gêba River. Also check out the Arquipélago dos Bijagós entry (p322).

Local Transport
All minibuses and bush taxis leave from the *paragem* (bus station) off Avenida de 14 Novembro. Twice daily minibuses go to

GUINEA-BISSAU

Bafatá (US$3, approximately three hours) and to Gabú (US$4, four hours) among other destinations.

GETTING AROUND

Small blue-and-yellow minibuses *(toca-toca)* and blue-and-white shared taxis run around the city to set routes; most rides cost around US$0.30 to US$0.50.

Private taxis are reasonably common around town, but dry up after midnight – head to the more expensive hotels if you can't find one.

THE MAINLAND

GABÚ

In the east, 200km from Bissau, Gabú is a lively trading town and the country's major transport hub outside Bissau. It's pretty likely that you will pass through this Fula-influenced town if you're heading to Guinea or Senegal. There's not much to see, but the bustling market is worth exploring.

There are a few places to stay in and around town, and there is some good street food (mostly rice dishes and roast meat) as well as cheap cafés around the market.

There are minibuses to and from Bissau (US$4, four hours). If you're heading for Guinea or Senegal, see Getting There & Away (p319).

BAFATÁ

If you want to break your journey in or out of Guinea-Bissau, the pleasant old colonial town of Bafatá is not a bad place to do it. There are a few accommodation options, and they may be able to arrange wildlife-viewing trips in the surrounding country-side and forest, where antelope and primates are commonly seen.

Minibuses run twice daily between Bafatá and Bissau (US$3).

BUBA

Buba is a lively junction town on the Gêba River and the surrounding area was once something of a colonial tourist playground. Sitting at the heart of Parque Natural do Lagoa de Cafada, pockets of forest, rapids, waterfalls (the nearest of which lie on the Corubal River) and river-side swimming beaches are all found close by. However,

the wildlife is arguably better further south near Jemberem, which borders the primary rainforest of **Parque Natural de Can-tanhez**. Here the local women's association has set up the small and inexpensive Racá Banana Guesthouse and guides can be arranged for trips to see the huge range of birds, primates (including chimpanzees) and other wildlife in the nearby sacred forest.

The easiest way to get to this region is to take a canoa across from Bissau to Enxudé and then pick up a bush taxi from there. Alternatively take a bush taxi/hitch the long way round via Bambadinca.

ARQUIPÉLAGO DOS BIJAGÓS

This archipelago is a real gem, a group of wild, remote islands with delicate and rare environments (rainforest, reef and man-groves) and renowned for their many rare bird and plant species. The area has been declared a Unesco International Biosphere Reserve, but remains rarely visited. Several islands are uninhabited, while others home to small fishing communities – the islands we describe here make up just the tip of a rather large, hot and humid iceberg. If you really want to get off the beaten track (and the wildlife of the southern and western islands will take your breath away) you'll need to put your faith in Bijagós boat traf-fic and hospitality. You'll also need a tent and camping gear; a bike would be handy too. Exploring these islands is certainly a worthy adventure.

ILHA DE BOLAMA

This is the closest island to Bissau and the main town, also called Bolama, has been a good illustration of fading colonial glory since 1941 when the capital was moved from here to Bissau. The beach about 4km south of the town is good, although the ones at the southwestern end of the island, about 25km from Bolama, are reckoned to be better. Down here you are going to have paradise to yourself. **Residencial Rui Ramos** (☎ 811136; close to the port; d US$18) is the only place to stay and the island's only restau-rant, **Mercearia Bar** (Cantinho da Pedra; grilled fish

US$1-2) is nearby. Local people may also offer a place to stay and eat.

There's no longer a ferry to Bolama so the choices are: take a weekend canoa from Port de Canoa in Bissau; find a captain of a cheap fishing boat; hire a safe, but expensive fishing boat; or get a canoa to Enxudé, then a bush taxi to São João and then a canoa across the narrow channel to Bolama.

ILHA DE BUBAQUE

Ilha de Bubaque is at the centre of the archipelago and Guinea-Bissau's tourist industry (such as it is). It's a delightful place to pass a few days or weeks, not that there's a whole bundle of things to do apart from take boat rides to nearby islands, walk through the forest, palm groves and fields, or lounge on the beaches.

Bubaque town (well, it's a village really) has a market, a bakery, a selection of accommodation, some small cafés, a post office and the small **Casa do Ambiente e da Cultura**, which has displays on local people and the islands' wildlife.

Around the port/market area are several places for cheap eats (fish and rice with sauce) and most of the places to stay serve food. Simple lodgings can be found at **Chez Raoul Rooms** (Pension Meda-Njun; d US$8), which reportedly has the best food in town, **Pensão Cadjoco** (☎ 821185; 200m southwest Cruz Pontes; d US$9) and **Chez Titi** (s/d US$9/18).

More expensive, but often recommended, is **Hotel Epicuro** (☎ 00871-763 094835; 18km south of Bubaque; d US$36), which sits on the island's best beach, Praia da Bruce.

Before you go to any beach, check the tides. When the tide is low the sea is a long way out and you'll have to wade through thigh-deep mud before you can swim. If you want to be a big-game fisherman, a few top-end hotels can arrange trips, but most people take it easy and drink the place in.

Aeroservices flies from Bissau (US$90, 15 minutes) every Saturday; the plane originates in Dakar. Flights can also be chartered; make reservations at **Guiné tours** (☎ 214344; guine-tours@sol.gtelecom.gw) in Bissau. The **Rodofluvial ferry** (☎ 212350; Avenida do 3 de Agosto) leaves Bissau Friday and returns Sunday (US$4.50, five to six hours). The *Téamanhá*, which is less ferry and more canoa, leaves from Port Bandim in Bissau during the week. Smaller

canoas make the trip, but the overloaded journeys can be tricky (having passengers bailing out is not uncommon).

ILHA DE GALINHAS

Galinhas is a small island between the islands of Rubane and Bolama, about 60km south of Bissau.

Hotel Ambancana (☎ 215555; US$14-18) The only accommodation on the island and thankfully pretty darn good, with bungalows that have great beach/sea views. Meals cost US$5. Come for a weekend, stay a week.

The hotel's boat *Amor* goes from Bissau to Galinhas (US$9 return) on Thursday or Friday and returns Sunday. You might get lucky getting transport from Bubaque (fish around the port), but transfers can also be arranged through the hotel.

ILHA DE ORANGO

West of Bubaque is Ilha de Orango, which, along with several other islands, forms part of the **Orango Islands National Park**. The vegetation is mainly palm groves and light woodland, with significant areas of mangrove and mud flats exposed at low tide. The park's inhabitants include rare saltwater species of hippo and crocodile, and the area is particularly good for birds. This is also one of the largest green and Ridley turtle nesting sites on the West African coast.

The obvious base for visiting the park and exploring this part of the archipelago is the good-quality **Orango Parque Hotel** (☎ 00871-761 273221; orangotel@sol.gtelecom.gw; s/d US$18/32, meals US$9) near the village of Eticoga on the west coast. There are a couple of hotels nearby. Also reportedly open is **Chez Frédérico** (d US$50) and there are some cheap huts for rent at the park headquarters, where birdwatching and fishing trips can be arranged.

As for transport, contact the hotel or get to Bubaque and sort out canoa transport from there (you might have to hop through a few islands first).

GUINEA-BISSAU DIRECTORY

ACCOMMODATION

The choice of budget accommodation is limited, especially in the capital. In fact, the only cheap places are dodgy flop houses where rooms are rented by the hour. Even where there are a few good, clean, comfortable deals (and they're not that common) you're still looking at around US$10 a night.

DANGERS & ANNOYANCES
Despite the fact that Guinea-Bissau is a very safe and laid-back country it has not fully recovered from the 1998–99 conflict and the recent coup (albeit bloodless) has added to political and economic woes. It's wise to avoid all political gatherings and keep an eye on the news. Also be careful about taking photographs; travellers have been arrested for taking pictures in Bissau's Mercado Central! The crime rate may be low, but take the usual precautions.

Avoid Guinea-Bissau's northwest border area, which adjoins the western portion of the Casamance region of Senegal where separatist guerrillas are active. This warning includes the popular border crossing at São Domingos.

Don't expect a reliable electricity supply anywhere.

EMBASSIES & CONSULATES
Most embassies shut up shop during the 1998–99 conflict and few have deemed it worth reopening yet. Countries that still have diplomatic representation in Bissau include:

France (☎ 201312, fax 201285; cnr Avenida 14 de Novembro & Avenida do Brazil)
Gambia (☎ 251099; Avenida 14 de Novembro)
Guinea (☎ 212681; Rua Marien Ngouabi)
Portugal (☎ 211261; fax 20 12 69; 6 Rua de Lisboa)
Senegal (☎ 212944; southwest of Praça dos Heróis Nacionais)
UK & Netherlands (honorary consul; ☎ 201224; fax 201265; Mavegro supermarket, Rua Eduardo Mondlane)

Germans will certainly be looked after by the French embassy, which probably is where all other Western nationals should head in time of crisis. For less serious incidents the British honorary consul may be a good bet for Australians and Kiwis.

Guinea-Bissau has diplomatic representation in the following neighbouring or near-neighbouring countries: The Gambia, Guinea and Senegal (there's also a handy consulate in Ziguinchor, Casamance, southern Senegal).

FOOD & DRINK
Street food can be surprisingly hard to find. Even coffee and bread stalls take some determined tracking down.

Local brews include palm wine, as in many other West African countries. For a stronger home-brew, you may be offered *caña* (rum). You may also come across *caña de cajeu* (cashew rum), equally strong, and made not from the nuts, but from the fruit that surrounds them.

HOLIDAYS
As well as religious holidays listed in the Africa Directory chapter (p1003), these are the principal public holidays in Guinea-Bissau:
1 January New Year's Day
20 January Death of Amílcar Cabral
8 March International Women's Day
1 May Labour Day
3 August Pidjiguiti Day
24 September Independence Day
14 November Movement of Readjustment

INTERNET ACCESS
There are a handful of Internet cafés dotted around Bissau, but Internet use is pretty far from common.

MONEY
The unit of currency is the West African franc (CFA), but euros are the cash to carry (even the mighty US dollar can be difficult to shift). Thick wedges of cash it must be, because travellers cheques and credit cards are pretty useless.

Forex bureaus and some expensive shops are the best places to change cash. However, outside of Bissau changing cash can be a big problem, although hotel bills can sometimes be paid in euros.

POST & TELEPHONE
The postal service out of the country and international phone connections are quite good, but the poste restante is unreliable.

International telephone calls are best made in Bissau, where phonecards (buy them from the main post office) are the best way to go. Calls are expensive and there are phone booths outside on the street.

VISAS
Visas are required by all visitors except nationals of most West African countries.

They must be obtained in advance and usually cost US$45 for 30 days.

Visa Extensions

Extensions can be easily obtained at the **Serviço de Estrangeiros** (Ave de 14 Novembro), opposite Mercado Bandim behind the immigration office in Bissau.

A 45-day visa extensions costs a mere US$3.50 and is often available the same day if you get there early.

Visas for Onward Travel

Visas are available from embassies in Bissau (see opposite):

Gambia Visas cost between US$25 and US$45; visa extensions are US$17.

Guinea Visas cost between US$25 and US$50 and are usually for a one-month stay.

Senegal Visas are required for all foreigners, except nationals of Denmark, France, Germany, Ireland, Italy, Luxembourg, the Netherlands, South Africa, the UK and the US, who may visit for up to 90 days without a visa.

Guinea

HIGHLIGHTS

- **Conakry** Why Guinean music doesn't win more international accolades is a mystery – the music scene in Conakry sparkles (p330)
- **Îles de Los** A relaxing tropical getaway, these islands are just 10km southwest of Conakry (p332)
- **Fouta Djalon** The rolling green landscape makes this the coolest place in the region to go walking, literally (p335)
- **Off the beaten track** Kissidougou's gentle surrounding landscape is perfect for pedal pushers (p337)

FAST FACTS

- **Area** 246,000 sq km
- **ATMs** none at all
- **Borders** Senegal, Mali, and Guinea-Bissau open dawn to dusk; border with Liberia and Sierra Leone intermittently closed; border with Côte d'Ivoire closed at the time of research
- **Budget** US$10 to US$20 a day
- **Capital** Conakry
- **Languages** French, Malinke, Pulaar (Fula), Susu
- **Money** Guinean franc; US$1 = GFr2057
- **Population** 7.78 million
- **Seasons** dry (Dec–May), wet (Jun–Nov)
- **Telephone** country code ☎ 224; international access code ☎ 00
- **Time** GMT/UTC
- **Visas** required for all except residents of Economic Community of West Africa States (Ecowas); must be bought before arrival

---

Geography is a mistress both cruel and kind to Guinea. Cruel because this country is something of an overlander dead end, surrounded by six other countries, four of which are at or emerging from civil war. On the other hand, Guinea is naturally blessed – hence the bottomless love Guineans have for their country and their mystification and anger that it continues to be among the poorest countries in the world. For travellers there are plenty of attractions: the hot, humid coast with its top-notch islands and beaches; the cool beauties of the Fouta Djalon plateau; the arid Sahelian landscape of the east; and the teeming greenery of the dense southern forests.

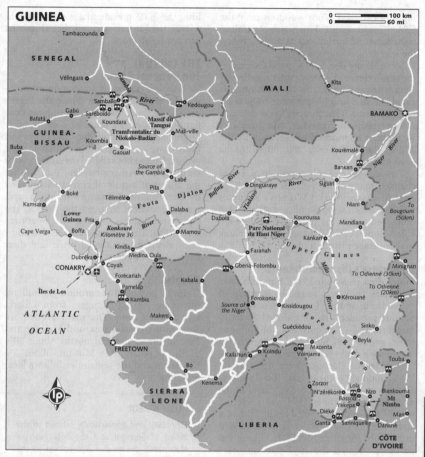

HISTORY

Guinea's story is one that is tragically familiar: the post-independence promise of a socialist utopia, the slide down the slippery slope to xenophobic isolation and murderous cultural revolution, and more recently the transformation into ramshackle klepto-capitalism. While prosperous countries turn away handfuls of asylum seekers, Guinea is home to around 700,000 refugees from neighbouring countries (one in 10 people in Guinea is a refugee), and this number just keeps growing.

As the current regime slips into senility, Guineans have their hearts in their mouths: is life set to improve at last, or is chaos just around the corner?

Poverty in Liberty

Guinea was part of the Mali empire, which covered a large part of western Africa between the 13th and 15th centuries. From the mid-1400s, Portuguese and other European traders settled Guinea's coastal region, and the country eventually became a French colony in 1891.

The end of French West Africa began with Guinea. It was granted independence in 1958 under the leadership of Sekou Touré, who rejected a French offer of membership in a commonwealth and demanded total independence, declaring: 'We prefer poverty in liberty to riches in slavery'. French reaction was swift: financial and technical aid was cut off, and there was a massive

GUINEA

flight of capital. Guinea withdrew from the CFA (Communauté Financière Africaine) franc zone and introduced its own currency, the syli.

Sekou Touré decided to model Guinea on the revolutionary Chinese pattern, collectivising farms and industries. It was an unmitigated disaster, and his paranoia triggered a reign of terror. 'Conspiracies' were detected in one group after another, and dissidents were either imprisoned or executed. By the end of the 1960s, over 250,000 Guineans lived in exile.

Towards the end of his presidency, Touré changed many of his policies. A major influence was the Market Women's Revolt of 1977, in which several police stations were destroyed and some local governors were killed, as part of the fight against state plans to discourage private trade.

Democracy's Disappointments

Touré died in March 1984. A month later a military coup was staged by a group of colonels, including Lansana Conté, who became president. He introduced austerity measures and a new currency, the Guinean franc, and in 1991 he bowed to pressure to introduce a multiparty political system.

Presidential elections were held in late 1993 amid tight security and official secrecy. Conté won with 51% of the vote, and in the elections of December 1998 was re-elected with 56%, a widely disputed result. Not long after, Conté's main rival was detained and imprisoned for alleged sedition. Opposition parties boycotted the 2002 parliamentary elections, which Conté's party won convincingly, of course.

Today, Guinea's economy relies heavily on a faltering mining industry. Conté's regime is widely condemned, but at least it has prevented a slide into civil war, an endemic regional problem that continues to add to Guinea's refugee woes. Modest gains of recent years in quality of life and standard of living have been threatened by violence in southern border areas, where some 1000 people died between 1998 and 2000. Peace has since been re-established, Guinea has made modest quality-of-life gains and, in theory, free enterprise is encouraged. At the time of writing, Conté, the diabetic billionaire-president, was rumoured to be on his deathbed. Without

him, the 2003 presidential elections could trigger the kind of turmoil that Guineans can hardly afford.

THE CULTURE
The National Psyche

'Le Guinéen est têtu' is a common refrain – the Guinean is stubborn. From the beginning of its short history as an independent nation, Guinea has done its own thing. It might have worked if the leadership had been more competent and humane, or if geography had not saddled the country with such a heavy refugee burden. Add to that the legacy of a cultural revolution marked by terror, xenophobia and paranoia, and it's little wonder that, on the surface, the Guinean psyche is marked by a weary reserve. Thankfully, Guineans are also stubborn about their national pride and their friendliness to guests.

People

Guinea's population is around 7.8 million, including 700,000 refugees from Liberia and Sierra Leone. The main groups are Susu in the coastal area, and Malinke and Peul in the centre and north. About 80% of the population is Muslim, about 5% Christian, and the remainder follows local religions.

PUSH & PEUL

Ethnically and linguistically related to the Wolof of Senegal and the Fula Jeeri of Mauritania, the Peul – also known as the Peuhl, Pulaar, Fulbe – are the biggest ethnic group in Guinea, representing 40% of the population. Traditionally nomadic herders, most Peul are now settled farmers (four in five Guineans are agricultural labourers today). Cattle still retain their cultural importance and herdsmen often put the safety of their stock above their own welfare. From the 12th century, Peul nomads were a key trigger to the spread of Islam across the region. At that time, the Peul didn't own cattle, but rather tended the cattle owned by farmers of other ethnic provenances. The peaceful cohabitation was perhaps not only due to an astute division of labour: Peul women are reputed for their beauty, and were highly coveted as wives.

ARTS

Socialism was an economic disaster, but the government's emphasis on nationalist *authenticité* in the arts, and state patronage of artistic institutions, was a boon. Notable Guinean musicians include Mory Kanté, famous for his 'kora funk' style, the guitarist Sékou Diabaté, aka Diamond Fingers. Camara Laye, author of *L'Enfant Noir*, is undoubtedly the country's literary giant.

ENVIRONMENT
The Land

Visitors – and Guineans – are constantly amazed that a country so naturally well endowed can be poorer than its parched northern neighbours. Guinea's geography ranges from humid coastal plains and swamps to the fertile and forested hills and plateaus of the interior. The dry season extends from December to May, but in the remaining months Guinea is one of the wettest countries in West Africa: Conakry receives an amazing 4 *metres* of rain, half of it in July and August.

National Parks

Guinea's national parks provide a fascinating insight into the country's ecological diversity. The Forêt Classé de Ziama, Parc Transfrontalier du Niokolo-Badiar and Parc National de Haut Niger are particularly significant. Fortunately Unesco has protected a section of the Nimba Mountains, where there is a rich variety of unique plant and animal life, including a rare species of frog.

Environmental Issues

Mining malpractice adds to the toll of deforestation: rainforests are being cut down by companies in search of bauxite, diamonds, iron, copper, gold, manganese and uranium. Guinea holds 30% of the world's bauxite reserves.

TRANSPORT

GETTING THERE & AWAY
Air

Within Africa, Conakry is connected to Bamako (Mali), Niamey (Niger) and all the capital cities along the West African coast. Most airlines have offices in the centre of Conakry on or near Ave de la République.

> **DEPARTURE TAX**
>
> For international flights, the departure tax is US$15 but this is usually included in the cost of the ticket. For domestic flights, the departure tax is around US$2.50.

European airlines serving Guinea include **Air France** (www.airfrance.com), **SN Brussels Airlines** (www.flysn.com) and **Aeroflot** (www.aeroflot.org). **Ghana Airways** (www.ghanaairways-us.com) and **Royal Air Maroc** (www.royalairmaroc.com) also have flights to/from Europe.

Land
CÔTE D'IVOIRE

Before services to Côte d'Ivoire were suspended due to the civil war, the most popular route was between Lola and Man either via Nzo and Danané or via Tounkarata, Sipilou and Biankouma.

Alternatively, you could go from Kankan to Odienné via Mandiana, or an even slower route by bush taxi to Mandiana, changing there for Mininian and again to Odienné. The roads are better on the Côte d'Ivoire side of the border.

GUINEA-BISSAU

The usual route to Guinea-Bissau goes via Labé and Koundara to Gabú. Getting from Conakry to Koundara is straightforward by bus or bush taxi. There's usually at least one morning bush taxi, but between Koundara and Gabú catching one can be chancy.

LIBERIA

There are border posts south of N'zérékoré and Guéckédou. They close intermittently according to political events, so check before starting out. When the Diéké border post is open (it wasn't at the time of research), daily bush taxis run from N'zérékoré to Ganta via Diéké, then on to Monrovia. At the time of research, this route was possible, but dangerous.

MALI

A barge carrying passengers goes once weekly along a major tributary and the upper reaches of the Niger River from Kankan to Jikuroni (upstream from Bamako) between July and November, or when the river is high enough (US$9, four days). However, most travellers go by road: the most frequent route to Bamako goes via Kankan, Siguiri and the border at Kourémalé. Buses to Bamako from Kankan cost US$7.50; from Siguiri US$3.50. Bush taxis on the same route charge about US$3 more. If you are in a hurry, bush taxis also go from Conakry to Bamako (US$30), but be warned that it's a long and totally exhausting journey.

SENEGAL
The usual route to Senegal goes via Labé and Koundara, from where vehicles head for Tambacounda or Vélingara via Diaoubé most days. Some may go all the way to Dakar (US$34, at least 25 hours) or Ziguinchor. Between Koundara and Kaliforou (the border town) the scenery is beautiful but the road is pitiful. During the wet season the stretch between Labé and Koundara is very slow or impassable for 2WD. In the dry, it is very dusty – bring a scarf to cover your nose and mouth.

SIERRA LEONE
A ferry between Conakry and Freetown runs every couple of days (US$20). There's no schedule; so ask at the port for more information. The alternative is to go by road, but the journey from Conakry to Freetown is often unsafe. Routes open and close intermittently, so check before starting out. The most common bush taxi route between Conakry and Freetown is via Pamelap (US$11, 10 hours); there's a sparsely travelled entry point from Faranah to Gberia-Fotombu and on to Kabala, another from Kindia to Medina Oula, then on to Kamakwie in Sierra Leone, and Guéckédou to Koindu, and on to Kenema and Freetown. Make sure you are well informed before any of these journeys, which are not to be taken lightly.

GETTING AROUND
Air
Paramount (☎ 454669) and **UTA** (☎ 453801) have domestic flights from Conakry to Siguiri, Kankan and Labé. There are usually one or two flights weekly to each destination, but schedules change constantly. For more information, see p334.

Local Transport
Private buses operate throughout the country and are more comfortable and cheaper than bush taxis. They're also slow and constantly breaking down.

Bush taxis (usually Peugeot 504s) are the main way of getting around Guinea's back country, which means most travellers will have to contend with two major hassles: terrible roads and severe overcrowding (12 or 13 passengers in a car made for seven, plus children, bananas, live goats and poultry and a few more people on the roof). Because the long-distance buses are cheap and regular, bush taxis do the relatively shorter runs between major towns. The upside is that these rides should leave an indelible impression on you.

Minibuses cover the same routes as bush taxis. They are cheaper, more crowded and significantly more dangerous.

In Guinea the term *gare voiture* is used, rather than *gare routière*, for the bus and bush-taxi park.

CONAKRY

☎ 013, 012, 011 / pop 1.5 million

After a long decline, Conakry is being put together again, and assuming a vibrancy and openness that is enhanced by its very African flavour.

It is a city with a split personality. On the one hand, Conakry has all the downsides of an African capital – and though less dangerous than some, it can be just as frustrating. On the other, it is an undeniably pulsating place: colourful, spontaneous, friendly, musical, a little wild, and always full of contrast.

Occasionally, Conakry is even beautiful – especially the idyllic islands a few miles offshore. It's a city tailor-made for a (long) weekend blast.

HISTORY
Conakry was one of colonial France's major ports in West Africa and was for a time known as the 'Paris of Africa'. Little of that glamour remains. What is now downtown Conakry was an island in the 19th century, until it was bridged at the site of the Palais de Peuple. During Sekou Touré's reign, Conakry was run down to such a state that it was one of the pits of Africa, a far cry from its colonial heyday, a decline that is slowly being reversed.

ORIENTATION

Conakry-G'bessia International Airport, 13km from central Conakry, is the country's only international airport. Domestic flights depart from the *aérogare nationale* next door.

Conakry is a long, narrow city, built on the Kaloum Peninsula. In the city centre are the banks, airline offices, several restaurants and some hotels. About 2km out of the centre the peninsula narrows, and at Place du 8 Novembre the road divides: Route de Donka to the north leads to the buzzing Camayenne neighbourhood; Corniche Sud to the south; and the Autoroute up the middle. About 10km north of the centre are the lively Rogbané and Taouyah *quartiers* (suburbs). Downtown Conakry recently changed its street names. The old names are more commonly used, and thus they're the ones we've used in this chapter. The Conakry map, however, lists both street names to help avoid confusion.

INFORMATION

Bookshops

Papeterie Hotimex (☎ 414791; 5th Ave) sells an expensive map of the city (US$25). **Soguidip Bookshop** (4th Ave) has some English-language magazines, as do street traders along Ave de la République.

Cultural Centres

The **Centre Culturel Franco-Guinéen** (La Corniche, near Place du 8 Novembre) programs French-language theatre and cinema, and houses a library and Internet facility. There's free live music on Wednesday night.

Internet Access

Internet facilities are easily found in Conakry. Connections can be slow, and rates are around the US$1 per hour mark.

Medical Services

Clinique Pasteur (☎ 412555; 5th Blvd) is recommended for emergency health advice, or try the **Hôpital Ignace Dean** (9th Blvd).

Money

Recommended for changing money is **Banque International pour le Commerce et l'Industrie de la Guinée** (Bicigui; Ave de la République), which accepts Thomas Cook, Visa and American Express (Amex) travellers cheques, and will give cash advances against a Visa card. Across the road, Ecobank is open on Saturday morning but charges a higher commission. You should change money in Conakry before venturing upcountry.

The exchange rate offered by black-market dealers is at best 8% higher than the bank rate; in Conakry these dealers operate at the airport, on Ave de la République and next to the main post office. It's not legal but it's tolerated. Provided one exercises the customary precautions, it should be safe.

Post & Telephone

The main post office (8th Ave) has post restante and holds items (US$0.25 per item) indefinitely. Next door, **Sotelgui** (Guinea Telecom; ☎ 450202; ⏰ 8am-8pm Mon-Sat) has cardphones. Rates for international calls are about US$2 per minute.

A complicated area code system exists in Conakry: ☎ 013 precedes numbers beginning with 21, 22, 23, 25, 26 and 27; ☎ 012 precedes numbers beginning with 66, 67 and 69; and ☎ 011 precedes numbers beginning with 40.

Tourist Offices & Travel Agencies

The **Office National du Tourisme** (2nd & 3rd fl, Karou Voyages, Ave de la République) is an administrative centre rather than an information point, but staff will endeavour to assist you if asked.

Karou Voyages (☎ 452042; Ave de la République) is recommended for domestic and international air tickets and runs trips to Îles de Los (about US$100 for two).

DANGERS & ANNOYANCES

As always, be careful around crowded public places such as the central Marché du Niger and at the Gare Voîture de Madina.

Conakry's chief annoyance, as in the rest of the country, is police checks, although tourists are far less of a target than locals. You'll always need your passport and paperwork handy. Some police officers may ask for a bribe, so factor such eventualities into your daily expenses.

SIGHTS & ACTIVITIES

The **Musée National** (☎ 415060; 7th Blvd; admission US$0.50; ⏰ 9.30am-5.30pm Tue-Sun), by the Corniche Sud, has a modest collection of masks, statues and musical instruments. The gigantic concrete **Grande Mosquée** in Camayenne

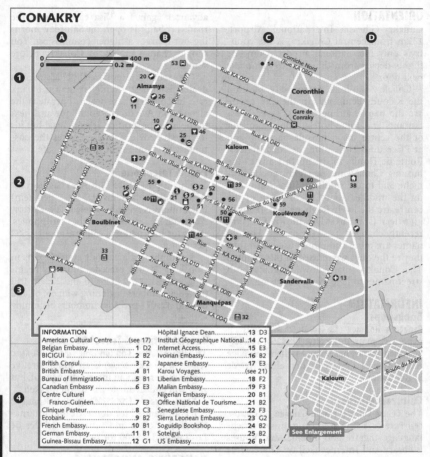

CONAKRY

can accommodate 10,000 worshippers; you may be able to see inside if you arrange it with the adjoining Islamic Centre. Sekou Touré's grave is in the mosque grounds.

Nearby, **Camp Boiro** (Route de Donka) in the Camayenne neighbourhood is not open to the public but is probably Conakry's most significant site: the military camp is where the worst atrocities of Touré's reign were carried out between 1960 and 1984.

The **Palais des Nations** (2nd Ave) was going to be the venue for the Organisation of African Unity conference in 1984, which was cancelled when Sekou Touré died. It now serves as the office of the president.

The beaches on **Îles de Los** (made up of Île de Kama and Île de Roume), about 10km

southwest of Conakry, were once used as a way-station for British slave traders. There are some good swimming beaches here that fill up on weekends.

SLEEPING

Conakry is surprisingly short of budget accommodation options.

Mission Catholique (☎ 442080; Route du Niger; r US$10-22; ✗) Imposing but friendly, well run, and close to downtown action. Good meals (US$2.50) are available on request. Rooms have showers.

Résidence Kaporo (☎ 216160; Route de Donka Extension; d US$15-22 with breakfast; ✗) Although 13kms from the centre, this is a very tidy, safe place. Facilities are shared. It's well signposted.

GUINEA

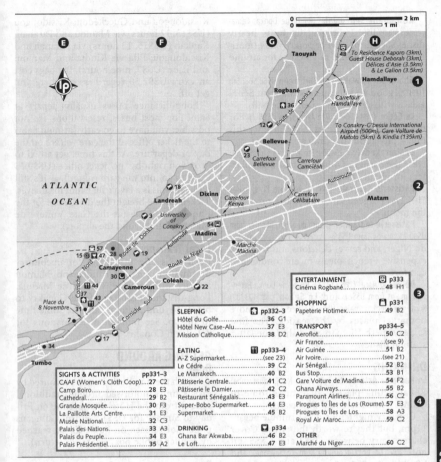

Guesthouse Deborah (☎ 421901; s/d US$17/20) Off the Route de Donka extension at the turn-off to the Ratoma Mariador hotels, this friendly guesthouse has spacious rooms and a rooftop restaurant.

Hôtel du Golfe (☎ 411394; s/d from US$22/30) Adequate but pricey rooms, distinguished by their cleanliness and the good service. Off Route de Donka extension.

Hôtel New Case-Alu (☎ 463707; Corniche Nord; d US$28; ❄) Good-value rooms in a pleasant part of town, although the cheaper rooms are scruffier and best avoided.

On the islands, accommodation on Île de Kassa is considerably cheaper than Roume – it's also closer to Conakry and small enough to walk around.

Close to Soro Beach on Île de Kassa are some rough-and-ready **bungalows** (☎ 415130; US$15); there's a restaurant nearby or you can order meals in advance.

EATING
Street food, such as grilled meat and maize, bread and cakes, is available in and around Marché du Niger.

On Route de Donka just south of Cinéma Rogbané, on 5th Ave opposite the petrol station, and at the intersection of the Corniche Nord and Blvd du Commerce, women sell bowls of rice and sauce for US$1 or less; it's cheap and very convivial. Several Lebanese places on or close to Ave de la République serve *shwarma* for around US$1.20.

Restaurant Sénégalais (Route de Donka, Camayenne; mains US$1-2) Serving up tasty, hearty dishes such as *poisson* or *poulet yassa* (marinated and grilled fish or chicken) for around US$1.50.

Ghana Bar Akwaba (4th Blvd; mains US$0.50-1.50) Just as good and cheap as Restaurant Sénégalais, with great cassava and rice balls.

Le Cèdre (☎ 414473; 7th Ave; mains US$5-7) For the best Lebanese dishes in Guinea, try this one – pity about the drab atmosphere.

Le Marrakech (☎ 294864; 5th Ave; mains from US$4) Near the corner of 4th Blvd, has lunch platters for about US$6.

Pâtisserie Centrale (☎ 411942; 6th Blvd; mains $3-5) Has burgers, sandwiches and pizzas on the menu.

Pâtisserie le Damier (Route du Niger; pastries from US$0.25, mains from US$5) Across from Marché du Niger, and serves delicious and relatively expensive French meals in air-conditioned comfort.

Délices d'Asie (☎ 412122; Route de Donka Extension; mains from US$6) and **Le Galion** (☎ 403282; Route de Donka; mains US$5-8) are two more upmarket places by the seaside. The first serves superb Vietnamese dishes, the latter seafood dishes.

DRINKING

La Paillotte Arts Centre (Corniche Nord, Camayenne) A happening place that features some of Guinea's most talented musicians.

Conakry nightclubs don't rumble before 11pm, but they're worth the effort. Cover charges vary between US$2 and US$5. Of note are **Le Loft** (Corniche Nord, Camayenne) and **L'Oxygène** (Rue RO 100, Ratoma; ☽ Wed-Mon).

GETTING THERE & AWAY
Air

Both **Paramount** (☎ 454669) and **UTA** (☎ 453801) operate services throughout the country. One-way flights are available to Siguiri (US$50), Kankan (US$45), Labé (US$30) and N'zérékoré (US$60). Return flights cost double, schedules vary constantly and routes are constantly changing.

Bus

Long-distance bus services leave from Gare Voîture de Madina, 6km from the centre, reached by city bus route 'A' from downtown. There are daily buses to Macenta (US$16, 16 hours) via Mamou, Faranah,

Kissidougou and Guéckédou; Kissidougou (US$13, 12 hours) via Mamou and Faranah; Kankan (US$15, 13 hours) via Faranah and Kissidougou; Pita via Kindia and Mamou; and Labé (US$7, nine hours). Big bags cost an extra US$2.50 regardless of where you get off.

Long-distance buses usually depart at 8am. For most buses, reservations are not possible; you have to go early (around 6am) to the ticket office at the *gare voîture* on the day of departure. At this time, get a taxi to drop you right by the ticket office (US$0.25 extra to go into the *gare voîture*), as it's still dark and this is a favourite haunt for thieves. Tickets can be bought the day before for the Kankan bus only (at the Gare Voîture de Matoto, 5km beyond the airport).

Local Transport

Bush taxis and minibuses for upcountry destinations such as Kindia and Mamou also leave from Gare Voîture de Madina. Long-distance bush taxis from Conakry to places beyond Mamou can take some time to fill up. See individual destinations for details on Conakry services.

GETTING AROUND
Boat

To reach the tiny Île de Roume, favoured by expats, hire a motorised pirogue (traditional canoe) from the Hôtel Camayenne on Friday to Sunday for US$12 return. Guineans prefer Soro Beach on Île de Kassa, reached by regular public boat (US$0.75 return).

Bus

To get around Conakry, Sogetrag has two main city bus lines: both start at the roundabout next to the port and go along Ave de la République and Route du Niger to Place du 8 Novembre, where the 'C' bus takes Route de Donka to Kaporo, out beyond Rogbané, and the 'A' bus either continues on the Autoroute or takes the parallel Route Nationale east to Matoto, out beyond the airport (US$0.15).

Taxi

To hail a shared taxi around town just stand at the side of the road appropriate to the direction you want to go and shout your destination as the taxi passes. It costs US$0.20 per zone; double for longer rides.

A private taxi costs about US$2.50 an hour. Private hire taxis from the city centre to Conakry-G'bessia International Airport (13km) cost from US$3 to US$5 depending on your bargaining powers. From the airport the fare should be around US$5. To hail a shared taxi (US$0.80) from the airport into town, just walk across the road and flag one down.

WESTERN GUINEA

Many travellers leaving Conakry stay on the bus as it rumbles along the main highway through Kindia and Mamou, heading for the delights of the Fouta Djalon, or the Guinea heartland around Kankan. But the towns of Western Guinea might be worth a stop, especially if you're heading back to Conakry on a late bus and want to avoid arriving in the capital at night.

KINDIA
Kindia, nestled beneath Mt Gangan, is a bustling market town just 65km from Conakry. The **Bridal Falls** (La Voile de la Mariée; admission US$0.50) are 12km beyond town, 2km off the road to your right, and are best seen during or just after the rainy season. There are **bungalows** (US$13) available at the falls, but bring your own food. Any bush taxi between Conakry and Mamou will drop you at the junction (US$0.30).

Near the *gare voiture*, **Hôtel Buffet de la Gare** (☎ 610143; d US$5-15; 🞶), has some cheap, scruffy but acceptable rooms.

On the other side of Kindia, **Hôtel Phare de Guinée** (☎ 610531; d US$5, with bathroom US$10-15), is better value, but located 3km south on the Conakry road.

For street food, look around the market and the *gare voiture*. **Restaurant Halimat** (mains US$1.50-3) has tasty African and French dishes. It's opposite the post office.

There are daily buses and bush taxis to/from Mamou (US$2.50), Conakry (US$1.25) and the Sierra Leone border (US$1.25).

MAMOU
Mamou is an important religious centre for the country's Peul population, but you wouldn't know it to look at it. For travellers, it's a dusty and grimy junction town, albeit with a couple of points of interest: several

vine bridges are nearby, as is the Peul centre of **Timbo**, and the Ecole Forestière is home to an attractive **nature reserve**.

On the Dalaba road, **Hôtel Luna** (☎ 680769; s/d $2.50/5, with bathroom US$8/10) is the cheapest place to stay. **Hotel Rama** (☎ 680430; s/d US$9/13) is a step up in comfort, serves tasty meals and even has a TV. There are a couple of basic eating houses near the *gare voiture* in the market. Across from Hôtel Luna, Restaurant Luna is a popular cheapie where filling meals cost as little as US$0.10.

Mamou is a major transport junction. Frequent bush taxis to/from Conakry, Dalaba, Faranah (US$6, three hours) and Labé (US$5, 2½ hours) depart from the *gare voiture*.

MARELLA
Marella is a small town roughly halfway between Mamou and Faranah. Readers have recommended Hôtel Mongo; tidy rooms are US$15 for a double.

FOUTA DJALON

Fouta Djalon's green rolling hills are more than a come-on for restless hiking boots, they're definitely must-see Guinea and among one of the most fascinating regions in West Africa. This green, undulant plateau is cooler than the lowlands, full of interesting villages and natural sites, and well worth the effort it takes to get there.

At the heart of the plateau are the towns of Dalaba, Pita and Labé, and these make ideal jumping-off points. The best time to visit is from November to January, as the rains have just ended, the air is clear, the landscape lush, and the weather pleasantly warm.

DALABA
While there's nothing special about the town, Dalaba's peaceful location, overlooking a sweeping valley, is impressive, and it's a great base for **hiking** and **mountain biking** (for those who bring their own) through this postcard-perfect region, with its many interesting villages. Its 1200m altitude makes life decidedly cooler than Conakry. For an idea of routes, drop in at the **tourist office** (Chargeur Quartier); it has guidebooks in English and French.

GUINEA

There are some good craft places in town, including the **Association des Couturières de Tangama** for tie-dyed clothes and batiks.

All the places to stay are on the southwestern edge of town, in the Chargeur Quartier. **Hôtel Tangama** (☎ 691109; d US$7.50, s/d with bathroom US$10/13) is the best pick, with clean rooms and good if pricey restaurant meals.

Auberge Seidy II (☎ 691063; d US$8) has acceptable rooms and serves good evening meals for US$2.50.

Near the *gare voître* are several simple cafés. The restaurant at **Hôtel SIB** (☎ 680626) is expensive; a cool drink, enjoyed with the view from the hotel terrace, is sublime.

Bush taxis to and from Labé (US$3) and Pita (US$1.75) pass through in each direction; they leave from the Pita and Labé taxi stand on the main road. Daily bush taxis also go to Mamou and Labé (both US$3) and Conakry (US$7, seven hours) from the *gare voître* near the market.

PITA

Roughly halfway between Dalaba and Labé, the small, interesting town of Pita is something of a peaceful haven.

Nearby are **Les Chutes du Kinkon**, reached by going north on the main road for 1km, then left down a dirt road for 10km. There are waterfalls above and below the hydroelectric power station, and both falls make for nice walks through villages and hills – you can easily walk there and back in a day. Camping is prohibited. A free police permit should be obtained beforehand from the police station. Check at the Cool & Cozy Café first.

Off the main road at the southern end of town is the **Auberge de Pita** (d US$8) with a bar-lounge area and a friendly atmosphere.

The **food stalls** on the main street where the buses stop are cheap and serve mainly grilled meat with onions and stock cube.

Cool & Cozy Café, to the west side of the road (opposite the Video Club Le Sapin), has excellent, inexpensive meals that should be ordered in advance. The owner willingly gives information on the Pita region, and organises local guides and accommodation.

Bush taxis leave from the Rex Cinéma to Labé (US$1) and Dalaba (US$1.50) throughout the day. Twice a week there's a service to Télimélé (US$5.50), on the primitive road back to Conakry.

LABÉ

Labé is at the northern end of the sealed road through the Fouta Djalon. It's Guinea's third-largest town and is not particularly attractive, but it is a major hub for traffic to/from Senegal and Guinea-Bissau.

Changing money in the bank can take an age; in the centre of town are black-market moneychangers in little stalls who'll give you a slightly better rate.

Near the main *gare voître*, **Hôtel de l'Indépendance** (☎ 511000; s/d with bathroom US$8/ 10) has basic rooms in an annexe with intermittent power and running water as well as better spacious rooms.

Hôtel Saala (☎ 510731; d US$3.50, d with bathroom US$7, villas US$9-11), 3km out of town on the Pita road, has clean, good-value rooms.

Italian-run **Hôtel Tata** (☎ 510540; r with breakfast US$15) is a splurge, but is the most comfortable accommodation in town. The restaurant food is relatively expensive.

Street food is plentiful and there are several cheap restaurants near the *gare voître*.

Keur Samba (☎ 510910; mains US$3) serves good if unimaginative fare at the Hôtel de Tourisme.

Air Guinée has a couple of scheduled flights each week to Conakry (US$30).

Vehicles for Koundara (US$8) and Senegal go from Gare Voître Dakar on the western outskirts of town. From the *gare voître* in the centre, the bus goes to Conakry three times per week (US$7, nine hours).

Bush taxis leave daily for Mamou (US$5, 2½ hours), Pita (US$1, 1½ hours) and, if there's no bus that day, for Conakry (US$10, nine hours).

SOUTHERN GUINEA

This is a very volatile area, where bandits, mercenaries, rebels, soldiers, gunrunners and diamond smugglers, not to mention refugees and displaced people, cross and re-cross the borders, and the forces of law and order are a long way away. Travellers are advised to check conditions on the ground before travelling to this region and to exercise extreme caution during their stay.

KANKAN

Kankan is Guinea's second city, and the main hub of transport in the south of the country, but it's a quiet place. Set on the banks of the Milo River (a tributary of the great Niger River), the city's principal sights are the **open market** (with its large arched entrances), the **covered market**, the **Grande Mosquée** (charging a small entrance fee) and the **old presidential palace** overlooking the river. Many Malinke (Mandinka) people regard Kankan as their spiritual home as it was the site of two famous victories – one against French colonial forces – by the famed Malinke warrior, Samory Touré.

Le Refuge Chez Marie (☎ 710541; d US$6), 2.5km from town on the Kissidougou road, has clean, basic rooms set around an inviting courtyard.

Centre d'Acceuil Diocesan (d US$10) is a step up. The newish, clean rooms have inclusive breakfast, fans, nets, showers and even power most nights.

Hôtel Baté (☎ 712686; r US$13-15; ✿) is a top-range place, but its annexe rooms are good value.

Le Calao (☎ 712797; d US$15; ✿), near the open market, has a great restaurant (mains US$2.50 to US$3). For cheaper fare, try **La Sympathie/Chez Mama** (mains US$0.50), where the owner's inspired cuisine is matched by her spunky personality.

Paramount runs flights to/from Conakry (US$45).

Kankan's main *gare voiture*, for all southbound traffic, is by the bridge over the river, where buses run to Conakry (US$15, 13 hours) and bush taxis to various destinations including Kissidougou (US$6, five hours) and Nzérékoré (US$12).

KISSIDOUGOU

Kissidougou (often called Kissi) is a friendly junction town where the main road from Conakry divides north to Kankan and south to Guéckédou and N'zérékoré. It lies next to the greatest area of remnant forest in this part of Africa, a lush expanse of thickly vegetated hills and streams – potentially a great hiking destination, about as far away from the beaten track as one could hope to be.

Hôtel Nelson Mandela (☎ 981305; d from US$8) is set on the Kankan road south of the main roundabout. It has decent double rooms, and a good, cheap restaurant (mains from US$1 to US$3).

Hôtel de la Paix (d US$5), reached by taking the road that runs north from the market, is

cheaper but probably not better value – the rooms are shabby.

For onward travel, bush taxis go to and from the *gare voiture* to Faranah (US$4.50, 2½ hours), Kankan (US$7.50, five hours), Macenta (US$3, four hours) and to Guéckédou (US$2.50, two hours).

There are also buses to Conakry (US$18, 12 hours).

GUÉCKÉDOU

Guéckédou is near the borders of Sierra Leone and Liberia (both of which can be reached from here) and is a major smuggling centre.

The town is quite unattractive, but the weekly **market** (Wednesday) is huge. Traders from all over Guinea, plus many more from Sierra Leone, Liberia, Mali and Côte d'Ivoire, come to do business. The town has long been populated with Sierra Leonean refugees.

The **Auberge Tomandou** (d US$20) is popular with aid workers and expats for its clean rooms and popular restaurant. The **Parawuie**, about halfway between the Kissidougou bridge and the spot where women sell indigo cloth, has fine cheap meals such as pea soup (peanut sauce) with 'cow beef', and yogurt and salad.

There are regular bush taxis to Macenta (US$3, two hours), N'zérékoré, Kissidougou (US$2.50, two hours) and Conakry.

MACENTA

The Toma people, known for their interesting ceremonies and dancing, inhabit Macenta, in picturesque southeast Guinea.

Hôtel Palm (d US$3), near the market, is cheap, but the rooms are dirty. **Hôtel Le Magnétic** (US$2.50) is even cheaper, no less grubby, but conveniently located near the *gare voiture*. If you're willing to pay a little more, **Hôtel Bamala** (d US$10-13; ✿), 3km from the town centre off the road to N'zérékoré, has much better rooms and provides meals on request.

Bush taxis run along the sealed road to N'zérékoré (US$5, six hours) departing from the *gare voiture* on the east side of town. All other traffic goes from the *gare voiture* on the west side.

Transport to and from Macenta to Guéckédou costs US$2.80 (two hours), and to Kissidougou costs US$3.

GUINEA

N'ZÉRÉKORÉ

In the far southeastern corner of the country, N'zérékoré is the major city in *Guinée forestière* (the forested part of Guinea, in case you didn't guess). It's a lively place – a smuggling base, a vital transport hub and a refugee centre for those fleeing the civil war in Liberia.

The **Musée Ethnographique** (Macenta Rd), between the stadium and the market, is small but interesting. About 35km from Nzérékoré, where the borders of Guinea, Liberia and Côte d'Ivoire meet, is **Mt Nimba**. You can hike to the top and back in a day from the small town of Lola, about 35km east of N'zérékoré, but check the security situation carefully before you set off.

Hôtel Bakoly (☎ 910734; s US$2.50/4), diagonally opposite the market, is as cheap as it gets. Avoid the more expensive annexe rooms.

The **Mission Catholique** (☎ 910793; d US$8), on the road to the airport, has simple and clean rooms that are worth paying extra for.

Chez Aïda (☎ 910747; d US$10, with bathroom US$18-23) is only small but it has excellent rooms, Senegalese dishes are served in its great little restaurant (US$2.50 to US$4).

N'zérékoré's *gare voiture* is on the Macenta road near the petrol station. There's a bus to Conakry on Monday (US$16), bush taxis to/from Macenta (US$4, six hours) and Conakry (US$21). If you're heading to Liberia, note that the Diéké border post closes intermittently, so check before setting out.

GUINEA DIRECTORY

ACCOMMODATION

There aren't a lot of budget hotels in Conakry. Outside of Conakry, most towns have at least one place to stay, often with quite basic, but cheap, facilities.

ACTIVITIES

Hiking opportunities abound in the Fouta Djalon area and (security permitting) in the forest area in the south. If you're touring Africa by mountain bike, the Fouta Djalon is also an excellent region to explore.

CUSTOMS

There's a theoretical restriction of the exportation of sums of GFr 5000 or more from the country, but it's rarely enforced. There are no such restrictions on foreign currencies.

DANGERS & ANNOYANCES

Outside the capital, Guinea is a safe country, other than in the southern border regions; street crime is a problem in Conakry. Visitors should take the normal precautions, particularly in markets and bus stations. It's more likely, however, that the only time you will be 'robbed' is at roadblocks and checkpoints manned by military and police officials. In Conakry, they're set up at night. In the countryside, travellers should expect frequent stoppages at all times. Have your papers in order and at hand and the only thing you should lose should be your time.

EMBASSIES & CONSULATES

Countries with diplomatic representation in Conakry:

Côte d'Ivoire (☎ 451082; Blvd du Commerce)
France (☎ 411605; cnr Blvd du Commerce & 8th Ave)
Germany (☎ 441506; cnr 2nd Blvd & 9th Ave, Kaloum)
Guinea-Bissau (☎ 422136; Route de Donka) 500m northeast of Carrefour Bellevue
Liberia (☎ 462059; Corniche Nord, Cité Ministérielle)
Mali (☎ 461418; Bloc des Professeurs, Camayenne)
Senegal (☎ 462834; Corniche Sud, Coléah)
Sierra Leone (☎ 464084; Carrefour Bellevue) Next to A-Z supermarket, Dixinn.
UK (☎ 455807; Blvd du Commerce, Almamya, Kaloum)
USA (☎ 411520; cnr 2nd Blvd & 9th Ave, Kaloum)

In West Africa, Guinea has embassies in Côte d'Ivoire, Gambia, Ghana, Guinea-Bissau, Liberia, Mali, Nigeria, Senegal and Sierra Leone.

FOOD & DRINK

In most towns, street food – grilled fish or meat (with onions and crumbled stock cube), peanuts and cakes – is available, and there are usually one or two basic eating houses doing cheap meals of rice and sauce. Only the larger towns have anything like a restaurant, where you might also find meat, chicken and chips. In northern Fouta Djalon, look for *gosseytiga*, a rice porridge with peanuts and sugar that's a regional speciality.

HOLIDAYS

As well as public holidays listed in the Africa Directory (see p1003), Guinea celebrates the following national holidays:

1 January New Year's day
3 April Declaration of the 2nd Republic
1 May May Day
27 August Market Women's Revolt
2 October Independence Day
1 November Armed Forces Day

INTERNET ACCESS

The Internet is widely available in Conakry and in some of the larger towns throughout the country. Connections are a little on the slow side in the capital; in the countryside, they're unreliable at best.

LANGUAGE

French is the official language and is widely spoken in all large towns and the less remote rural areas. The main African languages are Susu, Malinke and Fulani.

MAPS

The **Insitut Géographique National** (IGN; 5th Blvd) near Corniche Nord, Almamya, in central Conakry sells maps of Guinea as well as photocopies of maps (scales 1:50,000 to 1:500,000).

MONEY

Euros are the most widely accepted currency, then US dollars and CFAs. Guinean francs can't be changed back into hard currency when you leave – but moneychangers will help you out. Prices for transport and food, but not for accommodation in Conakry, are generally cheaper than in neighbouring countries. There's a bank at Conakry airport but the rates are low for travellers cheques. Credit cards are practically useless.

POST & TELEPHONE

The postal service is quite reliable between Conakry and Europe or the USA, although it's terrible to/from towns outside the capital.

Sotelgui is the national telecommunications carrier, but outside Conakry, post offices and Sotelgui offices are bundled together as PTTs. You can make domestic and international calls from these, although the line quality can be unreliable.

VACCINATION CERTIFICATES

Proof of immunisation against yellow fever is required of everyone coming into the country.

VISAS

Visas are required by all, except members of Ecowas countries, and cost between US$25 and US$50. You cannot get a visa upon arrival. Those issued in Africa are usually good for a one-month stay, but you can sometimes get longer.

Visa Extensions

For an extension, go to the **Bureau of Immigration** (☎ 441439; cnr 1st Blvd & 8th Ave, Conakry; US$40).

Visas for Onward Travel

Visas for the following neighbouring countries can be obtained in Guinea. See opposite for embassy and consulate information.

Côte d'Ivoire Tourist visas were not being issued at time of research.

Guinea-Bissau One-month single-entry visas cost US$20 and require two photos. Issued in two days. Open 8.30am to 2pm weekdays.

Liberia Three-month single-/multiple-entry visas cost US$25/37 (US$50 for US citizens), require two photos and are ready within two days.

Mali Issues one-month single-entry visas for US$8 and two photos.

Senegal One-month single-/multiple-entry visas cost US$5/10 and are issued within 48 hours.

Sierra Leone One-month single-entry visas cost from US$20 to US$50, depending on nationality. Open 9am-3pm Mon-Thu, 9am-1pm Fri.

GUINEA

Sierra Leone

SIERRA LEONE

FAST FACTS

- **Area** 72,325 sq km
- **ATMs** none
- **Borders** Liberia (can be crossed but was too dangerous at the time of research); Guinea open
- **Budget** US$50 per day
- **Capital** Freetown
- **Languages** English, Krio, Mende, Temne and others
- **Money** leone; US$1 = Le2000
- **Population** 5.5 million
- **Seasons** dry (mid-Nov–mid-May); wet (mid-May–mid-Nov)
- **Telephone** country code ☎ 232; international access code ☎ 00
- **Time** GMT/UTC
- **Visas** US$50 for 90 days; required by everyone except most West African citizens, and must be obtained in advance

WARNING

The end of the civil war has meant improved security in Sierra Leone. But many parts of the country remain unsafe to visit. We were unable to do on-the-ground research here, so some information in this chapter may be unreliable. Check the situation before travelling to Sierra Leone.

Sierra Leone was once a rather good place for travellers and, with a bit of luck and a following wind, it could soon be so again. But right now the country is a battle-scarred land, its people, places and infrastructure still recovering from over a decade of brutal civil war. The government and UN troops are now in total control of the country and despite the efforts of thousands of aid workers and expats it will take time for things to get back to normal.

Arriving in Freetown, the country's white sandy attractions are obvious: the beaches are magic and the stunning, tropical jungle enticing. Even the capital itself, though trashed during the war, has a happy-go-lucky and vibrant feel to it that seems somehow out of place; perhaps it's because this is gold-rush time in the capital, which is being pumped full of aid money (consequently the prices of accommodation and restaurants are more appropriate to the USA than West Africa). The interior was always a good, cheap place to travel, full of great lush landscapes, wildlife reserves and wonderfully friendly people.

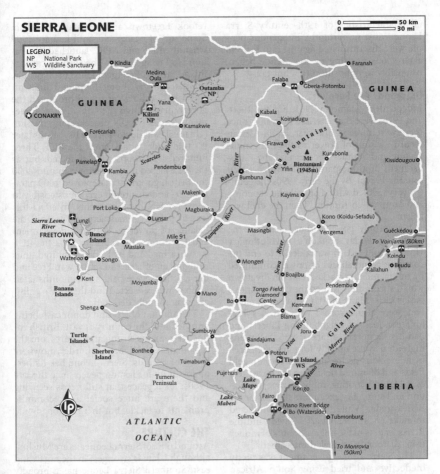

SIERRA LEONE

LEGEND
NP National Park
WS Wildlife Sanctuary

HISTORY

Sierra Leone has had an eventful 500 years. The country was a major player in the beginning and end of the slave trade, but inequalities between the Krio freed slaves who developed the modern nation and indigenous peoples caused bitterness and conflict. Krios have long ceased to rule the roost in Sierra Leone, but the same old inequalities between the Freetown elite and the poor of the interior remain alive, and were a factor in the recent, savage, decade-long conflict that left the country in ruins.

Slaves & Slavers

The American slave trade was effectively launched from Freetown in 1560, and by the 18th century Portuguese and British trading and slaving settlements lined the coast. In the late 1700s, freed slaves from places such as North America were brought to the new settlement of Freetown. Soon after, Britain abolished slavery and Sierra Leone became a British colony. Many subsequent settlers were liberated from slaving ships intercepted by the British navy. These people became known as Krios and assumed an English lifestyle together with an air of superiority, long dominating the government and trade of the country.

But things didn't all run smoothly in this brave new world. Black and white settlers dabbling in the slave trade; disease; rebellion; and attacks by the French were all characteristics of 19th-century Sierra Leone. Most importantly, indigenous people were discriminated against and in 1898 a ferocious uprising by the Mende began, ostensibly in opposition to a hut tax.

Diamonds Are Forever...

Independence came in 1961, but the 1960s and 1970s were characterised by coups (once there were three in one year, an all-African record), a shift of power to the indigenous Mende and Temnes peoples and the establishment of a one-party state (which lasted into the 1980s). By the early 1990s the country was saddled with a shambolic economy and rampant corruption. Then the civil war began.

It's entirely possible that buried in the depths of Foday Sankoh's Revolutionary United Front (RUF) was a desire to end the corruption and abuses of power committed by ruling, military-backed, elites in Freetown who'd successfully turned the country into a basket case. Many of RUF's founding members were also involved with Charles Taylor's conquest of neighbouring Liberia and had his support (see Liberia p351). But any high ideals were quickly forgotten, replaced by a ferocious desire for Sierra Leone's gold fields and diamond fields (see the boxed text on p24), with looting, robbery, rape, mutilation and summary execution all tools of the RUF's trade. While their troops plundered to make ends meet, Charles Taylor and the RUF's leaders made huge amounts of money from diamonds smuggled into Liberia.

The Sierra Leone government was pretty ineffective and tried using South African mercenaries the RUF who, bolstered by disaffected army elements and Liberian irregulars, were making gains across the country. In 1996 elections were held and Ahmad Tejan Kabbah was declared president, but a year later, after peace talks had brought hope then despair, the Armed Forces Revolutionary Council (AFRC) grabbed control of government and decided to share power with the RUF. By this time factionalisation and desertion on all sides had led to an utter free-for-all, with the civilian population suffering atrocities at every turn.

Hopes & Fears

In March 1998 Ecomog, a West African peacekeeping force led by the Nigerian army,

retook Freetown and reinstated Kabbah. Some sort of peace held until January 1999 when the RUF and AFRC launched 'Operation No Living Thing'. The ensuing carnage in and around Freetown killed 6000 people, mutilated many more (lopping a limb off was a RUF calling card) and prompted the government to sign the Lomé Peace Agreement. A massive UN peacekeeping mission (Unamsil) was deployed, but 10 months later it came under attack from the RUF. Three hundred UN troops were abducted, but as the RUF closed in on Freetown in mid-2000 the British government deployed 1000 paratroopers and an aircraft carrier, ostensibly to allow for UN reinforcements. In effect this was to prevent a massacre and to shift the balance of power to Kabbah's government and UN forces. By February 2002 the RUF was disarmed and its leaders captured, thus bringing an official end to the war. Free and fair elections were held a few months later; Kabbah was re-elected and the RUF's political wing soundly defeated.

The amount of UN and donor cash being pumped into the country is vast. British influence remains strong and, apart from the region near the Liberian border, nowhere is out of bounds. Sierra Leone has its best opportunity for lasting peace since the late 1960s; it's a peace that still needs securing and there are huge social and economic problems to tackle, but there is hope.

THE CULTURE

Around 60% of Sierra Leoneans are Muslim, although Islam is strongest in the north and east. Southern Sierra Leone has a broadly Christian flavour, but traditional religions are still followed by large numbers of people and exert significant influence over both Christian and Muslim traditions.

The country has various indigenous ethnic groups of whom the Temne (mainly in the north) and Mende (mainly in the south) comprise about 30% each. There are also small groups of Europeans, Lebanese and Krios (who make up 2% of the population) in and around Freetown.

The Mende and Temne operate a system of secret societies responsible for maintaining culture and tradition. If you see young children with their faces painted white, you'll know that they're in the process of being initiated. Masks are an important feature of some groups' ceremonies and are highly prized (copies are made for tourists, but local cloth is often a better buy).

ENVIRONMENT

Sierra Leone's fractured coast is lined with cracking beaches, mangrove swamps and islands. Coastal plains lead inland for some considerable distance, the mountainous Freetown peninsula being the exception to the rule. About 30% of the country is forest or woodland and much primary rainforest has gone (there are a few patches in the southeast). Central Sierra Leone is characterised by sweeping plains, while in the northeast are the Loma Mountains, which has Mt Bintumani (1945m) at its heart; check the security situation before trekking in this wildlife-rich environment (look out for pygmy hippos and chimpanzees).

Outamba-Kilimi National Park (which still has elephants) in the north and Tiwai Island Wildlife Sanctuary (great for primates) in the south are worth getting to if you can, but don't expect eco-lodges and ice cold beers – get the latest logistical information from the **Conservation Society of Sierra Leone** (☎ 022-229716; cssl@sierratel.sl; 2 Pike St, Freetown).

Sierra Leone is hot and very humid. The coast gets up to 3250mm precipitation per year and the wet season stretches from mid-May to November – the south may get a break in July and August. Sierra Leone doesn't really have a cold season, but December and January are the coolest and driest months, when the skies can be hazy from the *harmattan* (desert winds).

TRANSPORT

GETTING THERE & AWAY
Air

SN Brussels (☎ 226076; www.snbrussels.com) has twice-weekly flights from Brussels to Freetown and is your best bet from Europe and the US. **Red Air Airlines** (☎ 227112; www.flyredairlines.com) and **Sierra National Airlines** (☎ 224547) fly twice weekly from London direct to Freetown.

Gambia International Airlines (www.gia.gm) flies to Banjul, The Gambia (US$150; handy if you've picked up a cheap charter flight there from the UK); **Air Guinea** (☎ 227561) to Conakry, Guinea (US$100); **West Coast**

> **DEPARTURE TAX**
>
> Departure tax is US$25 payable in hard currency.

Airlines (☎ 227561) and **Paramount** (☎ 272006) to Bamako, Mali (US$300 to US$350); and **Ghana Airways** (☎ 224871) to Accra, Ghana (US$320; sometimes handy for European and US connections).

Land

There's a ferry from Conakry to Freetown roughly every two days, but it no longer continues to Monrovia (Liberia). Crossing into Liberia by land would be stunningly foolhardy. If things settle down and the border does open, you can cross at Fairo in the south, Kongo a little way north and Koindu further north again near the junction of Guinea, Liberia and Sierra Leone.

The main overland route to Guinea is via the Pamelap crossing; you may find transport going all the way to Conakry and the road is sealed for the most part. This is not the case for the Medina Oula and Gberia-Fotombu routes into Guinea, which are very rough. There's precious little traffic along the latter so you may have a long walk.

GETTING AROUND

It can be tricky to get around Sierra Leone without a vehicle. Travellers will need more than the usual African levels of patience and stamina for upcountry travel until the transport system recovers fully from the war.

It might be worth chatting up some aid agencies for a lift before heading out – certainly hitching around Freetown and environs is usually not a problem (everyone's aware of the country's transport problems).

West Coast Airways (☎ 227561; Wilberforce St, Freetown) flies from Freetown's Hastings airport to Bo and Kenema. Expect to pay less than US$70 one way. Flush shoestringers can also charter helicopters!

Bush taxis and *poda-podas* (minibuses) are the most common transport and leave Freetown for Bo, Kabala, Kenema, Makeni, Pamelap and Port Loko at least once a day (leaving very early). You may also have the somewhat safer option of taking a proper bus to these destinations. From upcountry towns, transport is more circumspect – leap on anything going your way and be prepared for some long roadside waits.

FREETOWN

☎ 022

Freetown used to have a dirty and decrepit air, and very little worth seeing. And then there was a war. Still, it is in a pretty nice setting for a sweaty, tumbledown town – and a town is really what Sierra Leone's capital feels like. The East End paid a high price in 'Operation No Living Thing', but while the effects of war can still be seen and felt, Freetown has undeniable pep and optimism. It is a vibrant and friendly place, hot as hell and pretty chaotic (you should see the traffic jams), but close to town are the fantastic beaches, focus of the country's tourist industry – many travellers don't bother leaving Freetown's mountainous peninsula.

ORIENTATION

Freetown's Lungi airport is on the other side of the bay. Paramount Airlines runs a helicopter service into town (US$20 one way), or take a taxi from the airport to Tagrin Ferry Terminal (US$5) from where fast ferries head to Freetown's Government Wharf in the centre of the city (US$10 one way; timed with arrivals/departures) and slow ones leave for Kissy Ferry Terminal 4km east of Freetown (US$1.50; once every two to three hours). Hastings airfield (for domestic flights) is about 20km east of central Freetown (US$15 in a taxi; allow at least 45 minutes).

Siaka Stevens St crosses the centre of town; close to the huge Cotton Tree that stands halfway along its length are the post office, markets, banks and offices. Away from the central area, winding streets climb the surrounding hills; Mt Aureol and Leicester Peak overlook the city. Kissy Rd leads east from the centre while Sanders St, Brookfields Rd and Main Motor Rd link together to lead 10km west to Aberdeen and Lumley Beach at the northeastern tip of the peninsula (the main areas where visitors stay).

INFORMATION
Medical Services

Sadly, **Choithram Memorial Hospital** (☎ 232598; Hill Station) and **Connaught Hospital** (☎ 224405; Percival St) are the best of Sierra Leone's medical facilities. However, for a good medical opinion see **Dr Anthony Williams** (☎ 231005; British High Commission, 5 Spur Rd). **Capital Pharmacy** (☎ 226751; 15 Siaka Stevens St) is pretty useful.

Money

Try **Standard Chartered Bank** (9-11 Lightfoot Boston St) or **Sierra Leone Commercial Bank** (29-31 Siaka Stevens St), but the forex bureaux on and around Siaka Stevens St and on Lumley Beach Rd usually give better rates.

Post & Telephone

The **main post office** is on the corner of Siaka Stevens and Gloucester Sts.

For international calls go to the **External Telecommunications Office** (☎ 222801; 7 Wallace Johnson St; ☼ 24hr) or use a cardphone in the main post office.

Tourist Offices

The **National Tourist Board** (☎ 272520; ntb info@sierratel.sl; Rm 100, Cape Sierra Hotel, Aberdeen Hill) is slowly getting its act together, but good tourist information is often available through your embassy or from a travel agent in town, such as **IPC Travel** (☎ 226244; ipctravel@sl.baobab.com; 10 Siaka Stevens St). Also contact the **Conservation Society of Sierra Leone** (☎ 229716; cssl@sierratel.sl; 2 Pike St).

DANGERS & ANNOYANCES

Freetown is pretty safe although robberies and burglaries do occur; approach the port and East End of town with caution, especially after dark. Diamond smuggling is big business, but fraught with scams and dangers – beware of anyone offering you stones and of bogus policemen and officials.

Freetown's beaches are pretty safe during the day, but keep an eye on your stuff, don't get too isolated and avoid the beaches at night. Persistent beach boys and would-be gigolos are becoming common on the most popular beaches.

Electrical supply can be pretty hit-and-miss in Freetown; if you're in a low-class restaurant or hotel it's mostly miss.

SIGHTS & ACTIVITIES

Don't hold your breath. The 500-year-old **Cotton Tree** (Siaka Stevens St), under which slaves were sold and the first emancipated slaves gathered in 1787, is the most famous landmark here. If you're up for sweating your way around town check out **State House** (closed to the public), the **Law Courts**, **Fourah Bay College** (on Mt Aureol) and the **National Museum**, which has a great collection of tribal masks.

The best views of the city are from **Hill Station** (take Pademba Rd south from the Cotton Tree and keep going uphill) while the cool villages of **Regent** and **Gloucester** (which also overlook the city) and the area east of Siaka Stevens Stadium are good places to gawp at interesting 19th-century wood-framed **Krio houses**.

Freetown Golf Club (☎ 272956; Lumley Beach Rd) offers some rare golfing experiences; the days when a landmine was found next to the eighth brown (no greens here, I'm afraid) and Nigerian peacekeepers had a machine-gun post in a bunker are over, but the course remains an adventure.

Lumley Beach is close to town (take a shared taxi); it is not the best on the peninsula, but does get packed on the weekend.

SLEEPING
Accommodation in Freetown is ludicrously overpriced. The cheapest places are in the East End of town, but it isn't a good idea to stay there; it's rough as a badger and not secure. The cheapest places, the **YMCA** (☎ 223608; 32 Fort St; dm US$12) and **Central Guest House** (Regent's St) are low, low quality so consider splashing out at the **Spur View Guesthouse** (26C Spur Rd; d US$42) or **Korean Guesthouse** (☎ 231016; 24 Lower Pipe Line; d US$60) which has an excellent Korean restaurant. One of Sierra Leone's best hotels, **Cape Sierra** (☎ 272272; Cape Rd; s/d US$135/160), is at the northern end of Lumley Beach.

EATING
Street-food vendors selling tasty fried pastries, dried meat and *suya* sticks (spiced beef or chicken on a kebab skewer) can be found throughout the city centre, especially on Siaka Stevens St, along Lumley Beach Rd and at the Aberdeen village roundabout.

For more-formal cheap eats try **Santanno House Cafeteria** (4th floor, Santanno House, 10 Howe St; dishes US$1) at lunchtime, **Crown Bakery** (6 Wilberforce St; sandwiches US$2.50, mains US$10) at any time and **Angel's Delight Restaurant** (Lumley Beach Rd; mains US$5-10) in the evening.

DRINKING & CLUBBING
Bars and pubs in Aberdeen attract expats and aid workers in search of bleary good times. Try **Alex's Beach Bar** (Cape Road, Aberdeen), **Paddy's** (Aberdeen Rd, Aberdeen) and **Buggies** (Lumley Beach, Aberdeen).

SHOPPING
The old **King Jimmy Market** down on the waterfront, nearby **Basket Market** (sometimes called the Big Market) and **Victoria Park Market** are fun places to wander around and check out everything from giant saucepans to monkey skulls. Victoria Park Market is a good place to buy 'country cloth' and *gara* (thin cotton tie-dyed or batik-printed fabric). Material is sold by the *lapa* (about 1.5m in length).

GETTING THERE & AROUND
Bush taxis, *poda-podas* and some private buses leave from various sites, depending on the destination: the corner of Free and Upper East Sts for Conakry; Dan St for Bo (US$6, seven hours) and Kenema; Ashoebi Corner (2km east of the central area on Kissy Rd) for Makeni, Kabala (US$8) and Kono (Koidu-Sefadu); and the Kissy Shell station (5km east of the centre) for numerous destinations.

Taxis in Freetown do not have meters, so for private hire the price must be negotiated. The official fare from the city centre to the beach area is about US$15. There are many private taxis gathered outside the Paramount Hotel (Independence Ave).

Shared taxis run to most destinations. A ride in a shared taxi costs about US$0.30 for a short trip in town. Make sure an empty taxi is a shared taxi before you get in.

AROUND FREETOWN

BEACHES
Some of the best beaches in Africa are found on the Freetown peninsula. Heading south from **Lumley Beach** and Freetown they include **Goderich Beach** (3km from Lumley and a nice fishing village), **Lakka Beach** (2km further south and a great long, tropical beach and weekend party destination), **River No 2 Beach** (probably the choicest beach of all – brilliant white sands backed by thickly forested, wildlife-filled hills) and **Tokey Beach** (an attractive launching point for trips to the Banana Islands; York and Black Johnson beaches are nearby).

Poda-poda transport is very infrequent and dries up after York Beach.

Accommodation is limited to what's reportedly a simple guesthouse on River No 2 Beach and **Pierre's Beach Bar & Resort** (☎ 030-207835; s/d US$30/60) on Lakka Beach. The latter is a big weekend party venue for expats and aid workers, with whom you may be able to hitch a ride.

While accommodation is limited, more beach bars and hotels are bound to spring up along this stretch of coast in the next few years.

BANANA ISLANDS

Diving and snorkelling are reportedly superb near these islands that lie off the southern tip of the peninsula. Kent is the nearest launching point, but without your own transport you may be better off bargaining hard for a boat at Tokey Beach (shoot for US$50; many captains will organise food for this). Near Dublin village in the north of the island are some interesting ruins of a church and slave centre.

BUNCE ISLAND

This intriguing destination is on the Sierra Leone River some 20km from Freetown. A British fort was established here in 1663, but the ruins are of a second fort from where various European powers traded in camwood (used to make dye), ivory and slaves.

TACUGAMA CHIMPANZEE RESERVE

Lying close to Sugar Loaf Mountain near the village of Bathurst you can watch rescued and rehabilitated chimps in a great little reserve. The area is also particularly profuse with birdlife (over 100 species have been spotted).

NORTHERN SIERRA LEONE

KABALA

This hill town is the largest settlement in the north and lies at the end of the sealed road, about 300km from Freetown. The surrounding hills are criss-crossed with cool streams and waterfalls, making for good and gentle hiking. One of the huge bald peaks close to town is where locals traditionally spend New Year's Day.

There's a simple guesthouse, plus a chop house and bar in town.

Bush taxis go to Freetown (US$8) and Makeni (US$3).

MT BINTUMANI

Also called Loma Mansa (King of the Lomas), Mt Bintumani lies at the centre of the Loma Mountains Forest Reserve, about 60km southeast of Kabala. At 1945m, this is the highest point in West Africa (not counting Mt Cameroon, 4095m, which is clearly Central Africa!) and the reserve protects an area of highland rainforest containing several primate species (you're quite likely to see chimpanzees). Above 1500m the forest gives way to open grassland where you can spot baboons, warthogs and buffaloes. After the rains, when the skies are clear, views from the summit are excellent.

The usual approach is from the village of **Yifin**, to the east of the dirt road that runs between Kabala and Bumbuna. It's at least a four-day walk to and from the summit. A shorter approach (at least three days) is from **Kurubonla**, north of Kono. The best time to attempt a climb to the summit is either side of the rainy season (go in April/May or October/November). Before setting out, get a briefing on the security situation in Freetown or Kabala.

Wherever you start from, you must carry enough food for at least five days, along with camping equipment. There are villages on the lower slopes where you might get a hut to sleep in, but you'll need a tent further up the mountain. A guide (and possibly a porter) is needed for the maze of forest paths (US$1 a day was recommended; prices are probably higher now) and remember to pay your respects to the chiefs in Yifin and Kurubonla.

OUTAMBA-KILIMI NATIONAL PARK

In the northwest close to the border with Guinea is a beautiful tract of savanna and jungle. The wildlife here is diverse: elephants, chimpanzees, colobus monkeys and sooty mangabeys can be seen and there are reportedly pygmy hippos, rare bongo antelopes, giraffes and even lions, along with over a hundred bird species.

The park has two sections. The northern Outamba section consists of rolling hills, grasslands, flood plains and rainforests, dissected by several rivers. By the park head-

SIERRA LEONE

quarters there's a basic camping ground and guides can be hired (although you need to sort this out through the Conservation Society of Sierra Leone in Freetown well in advance – see p343).

The Kilimi section is much flatter and not as interesting.

The park is easy to reach if you've got your own 4WD, and there's also public transport in the dry season. Once inside you'll be walking or taking canoe rides.

SOUTHERN SIERRA LEONE

BO
Close to the Tongo Field diamond-mining area, Bo is a vibrant trading centre. It was hit pretty badly during the war, but remains a lively little town and a good place to buy country cloth and gara.

There are a few ordinary hotels, a couple of restaurants and a supermarket for self-caterers.

You can fly up from Freetown with West Coast Airways or you could catch a bush taxi (US$6; seven hours). There are also regular daily services to Kenema (US$2).

KENEMA
Kenema, some 300km southeast of Freetown, at the end of the sealed road on the way to eastern Guinea, is something of a staging post full of the hustle and bustle of the diamond trade. There's no reason to rush through; the two large open **markets** to the east of the main drag are worth strolling around, and there's a small covered market near the town centre. The **Kambui Hills Forest Reserve**, on the edge of town, is a good place for hiking.

Lodging and eating options in Kenema are darned slim. Have a good look around before you commit to anything. Street-food vendors are plentiful and there's also a small handful of restaurants.

West Coast Airways flies between Freetown, Bo and Kenema. Bush taxis to Bo (US$2) and Freetown depart from the taxi park near the Maxwell Khobe St market. Although the journey to the capital should take about 6.5 hours this is very much dependent on the state of the roads and vehicles.

TIWAI ISLAND WILDLIFE SANCTUARY
This is a small reserve about 50km south of Kenema set on a small island (about 13 sq km) in the Moa River. It once had one of the highest concentrations of primates anywhere on the continent. Unfortunately, it has been out of bounds for many years although there have been rumours of rehabilitation, so you might just be able to see beautiful diana monkeys, crocodiles, pygmy hippos, electric fish, up to 120 bird species and hundreds of butterflies.

For more details contact the Conservation Society of Sierra Leone in Freetown (see p343).

SIERRA LEONE DIRECTORY

ACCOMMODATION
Thanks to free-spending aid workers and UN employees, accommodation in Sierra Leone is damned expensive. You're not yet going to find a nice, laid-back little backpacker lodge in this country. And you're not going to get much change from US$40 for a decent place to stay in Freetown. Upcountry places are cheaper, but good places are rare.

Accommodation varies in quality, with places at the lower end of the scale reflecting the style of British bed-and-breakfast establishments. This is a little odd, and thick carpet isn't the best floor covering for the tropics. Some of the major hotels have been completely taken over by aid agency staff.

DANGERS & ANNOYANCES
Sierra Leone is a recovering war zone. Government and UN troops are in complete control of the (now peaceful) country, but it's still a good idea to contact your embassy for an assessment of the current security situation before heading upcountry: most embassies will want you to register upon arrival in any case.

Very occasionally an unauthorised roadblock (basically a toll booth) appears outside Freetown, but the main security threat is found in the Liberian border and Moa River regions.

There have been incidents of armed hold-ups, but these are mercifully rare. However, watch your back at night.

SIERRA LEONE

Don't be drawn into the diamond smuggling business; it's nothing but a one-way trip to Miseryville.

EMBASSIES & CONSULATES

Countries with diplomatic representation in Freetown:

France (☎ 222477; 13 Lamina Sankoh St, north of Siaka Stevens St)

Germany (☎ 222511; Santanno House, 10 Howe St)

Ghana (☎ 223461; 13 Walpole St)

Guinea (☎ 232584; 6 Wilkinson Rd)

Mali (☎ 231781; 40 Wilkinson Rd)

UK (☎ 223961; 6 Spur Rd)

USA (☎ 226481; 1 Walpole St, near Siaka Stevens St)

Travellers from Commonwealth countries should apply to the British embassy.

In West Africa, Sierra Leone has embassies in Guinea, Ghana, Liberia, Nigeria and the Gambia.

FOOD & DRINK

You buy cheap eats from a *chop bar* (basic eating house), and most travellers reckon that the *chop* (food) in this country is some of the best in West Africa. You can nearly always find rice and *plasas*, which is a sauce made from pounded potato or cassava leaves cooked with palm oil and fish or beef.

Other typical Sierra Leonean dishes include okra sauce, groundnut stew and pepper soup. Street food (eg steamed yams, roasted corn and beef sticks) is also good and easy to find in most towns.

The local beer, Star, is reasonable. *Poyo* (palm wine) is light and fruity, but getting used to the smell and the wildlife floating in your cup takes a while. The spicy ginger beer sold on the streets is a nonalcoholic alternative, but you can easily get sick from it because the water is rarely boiled.

HOLIDAYS

As well as holidays listed in the Africa Directory chapter (p1003), these are the principal public holidays in Sierra Leone:

1 January New Year's Day

27 April Republic Day

29 April Day of Revolution

INTERNET ACCESS

Freetown has an increasing number of Internet cafés, but the connection speed is notoriously slow.

MONEY

You'll need wads of cash in Sierra Leone, which is complicated by the lack of ATMs. The local currency is the leone (Le), but US dollars are the notes of choice, with British pounds coming second and the euro third. At the time of writing, travellers cheques were accepted at very few places and you can forget about credit and debit cards.

Forex bureaux often offer better rates than banks (which can be a hassle), but shop around for the best rate. Remember that up north leones are sometimes called 'pounds'.

POST & TELEPHONE

The postal service in Sierra Leone is pretty lousy; if you're sending something important use **DHL** (☎ 225 215; 15 Rawdon St, Freetown).

Sierra Leone's telephone network is really pretty good and phonecards for domestic and international calls are on sale everywhere in Freetown and in the larger upcountry towns such as Bo and Kenema. You are best off making international calls from the **Sierra Leone External Telecommunications** (SLET; ☎ 222801; fax 224439; 7 Wallace Johnson St) office in Freetown. You can send and receive faxes here.

Of Freetown's three GSM mobile phone operators, Celtel has the best coverage (and covers Bo and Kenema) and temporary accounts are available.

VISAS

Everyone requires a visa. Single-entry, 90-day tourist visas cost around US$50.

A letter of invitation or accommodation reservation is often required, and application forms can be downloaded from the UK High Commission website (www.slhc-uk.org.uk).

Visa Extensions

Visas can be extended at the **immigration office** (☎ 227174, 223034; Rawdon St) in the centre of Freetown.

Visas for Onward Travel

Visas for the following neighbouring countries are available from embassies in Freetown: the Gambia, Ghana, Guinea, Liberia, Nigeria and Mali (see above for embassy and consulate information).

Liberia

FAST FACTS

- **Area** 111,370 sq km
- **ATMs** none
- **Borders** Côte d'Ivoire, Guinea and Sierra Leone; all open, but all dangerous
- **Budget** US$35 to US$40 per day
- **Capital** Monrovia
- **Languages** English and more than 20 indigenous languages
- **Money** Liberian dollar; US$1 = L$1
- **Population** 3.2 million
- **Seasons** dry (Nov–Apr); wet (May–Oct)
- **Telephone** country code ☎ 231; international access code ☎ 00
- **Time** GMT/UTC
- **Visas** US$40 to US$45; required and must be obtained in advance; a visitor's permit is also required

WARNING

At the time of writing, commercial air services to Liberia had been suspended and fighting between government troops and rebels was intensifying. We were unable to do on-the-ground research in Liberia, so information in this chapter may not be reliable. Check the situation before even considering travel to Liberia.

Liberia is, once again, at a crossroads. At the time of writing 15,000 UN peacekeepers were poised to enter the country. It's hoped that they'll establish countrywide the kind of security that the capital, Monrovia, has enjoyed since former president Charles Taylor was flown to Nigeria in August 2003. Rich in natural resources, Liberia's diamonds and timber have fuelled conflict for over two decades, despite various peace deals and periods of relative tranquillity. It's a depressingly common scenario of an African country transformed from a relative success story to an utter disaster area. Taylor's departure was hugely positive, but now a mammoth international effort is required to secure peace and sort out the mess he has left. One day travellers will again be able to explore this hot, wet and humid country, bask on beautiful beaches, trek across verdant hillsides and explore some of West Africa's last pockets of magnificent rainforest.

LIBERIA

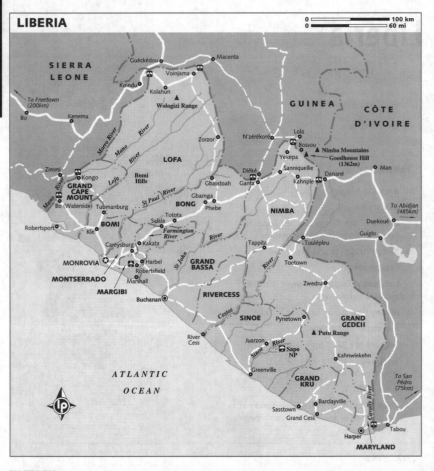

HISTORY

After being populated for a mere few thousand years, Liberia struck abolitionists in the USA as a spiffing place to resettle freed American slaves, the first group of whom were set up on Providence Island, Monrovia in 1822. Alas the settlers had to contend with tropical diseases and a rather hostile indigenous population, who greatly resented being lorded over by the prophesising Christian settlers. A few surviving settlers declared an independent republic in 1847 with Joseph Roberts as president, but the US-style constitution largely excluded the indigenous population, who had a form of forced labour thrust upon them – anywhere else it would have been called slavery. Decidedly dodgy labour practices continued into the 1960s.

Between the 1940s and 1970s Liberia had it good; foreign investment was high, but at the same time social inequalities and hostility grew between Americo-Liberians and indigenous peoples. In the early 1960s it was clear that things could soon go badly pear-shaped and indigenous peoples (97% of the population) were finally given political and economic rights. However, political opposition continued to be suppressed, while a dozen or so Americo-Liberian families continued to control government for their own ends. The corruption was obvious and during a series of demonstrations and food riots in 1979 a number of protesters were shot.

Then in April 1980 Liberia's two decades of terrible conflict began with a coup led by Master Sergeant Samuel Doe, a member of the indigenous Krahan tribe.

Doe!

Samuel Doe didn't mess around when he took power. President William Tolbert and many high-ranking ministers were killed and 13 ex-ministers were briefly 'tried' then shot on a Monrovian beach. The coup gave the indigenous population real political power for the first time since 1822, but capital flowed out of the country and the new crew simply redirected the corruption. Liberia's economy plummeted, anvillike, down the economic toilet.

The now-General Samuel Doe struggled to maintain his grip on power by holding a sham 'election' in late 1985 (largely to appease his major creditor, the USA, who backed him all the way to his downfall) and persecuting rival tribespeople – until early 1990 when the forces of Prince Johnson and Charles Taylor overran most of the country, which now lay in ruins. A West African peace-keeping force (known as Ecomog) tried to keep the warring factions apart, but to no avail. Refusing to surrender, Doe and many of his supporters were finally wiped out by Johnson's forces. There then began a power struggle between the various warlords and Ecomog, which was periodically suspended for the signing of a peace deal. The conflicts only ended after a particularly savage bout of carnage. In the subsequent elections of 1996, Charles Taylor and his National Patriotic Party (NPP) polled 75% of the vote. However, as the warring factions were disarmed, Taylor's loyalist army went about bullying and butchering his opponents. The 'peace' didn't last long.

Gun-slinging in the 21st Century

In the late 1990s Taylor's government was found to be supporting the Revolutionary United Front (RUF) rebels in Sierra Leone and the UN slapped a travel ban, arms embargo and diamond-trading ban on Taylor and his cronies (a ban on timber exports and UN charges of war crimes followed in 2003 and being linked to Al-Qaeda diamond trading didn't do Taylor any favours). At roughly the same time the catchily named LURD (Liberians United for Reconciliation

WHEN IS A REBEL NOT A REBEL?

That is the question people in Liberia had to ask themselves after some yellow T-shirts worn by the Liberian government's 'Navy Rangers' were captured and worn by rebels, causing utter confusion. T-shirts may not seem like decent military dress, but this is a conflict where gangsta-chic is as common as camouflage fatigues, and high-as-a-kite rebels have been known to wear pink bathrobes and shower caps. This wacky battle dress has as much to do with belief in the power of masks and the passage from boyhood to man (of which cross dressing is a symbol) as hallucinogenic drug use.

and Democracy, which Taylor accuses the US and Guinea of supporting) launched a series of attacks from Guinea, triggering a period of border skirmishes and raids. By the middle of 2003, LURD and the Movement for Democracy in Liberia (Model) appeared to control most of the country. Battles raged in and around Monrovia. Foreigners were evacuated, US warships anchored offshore and hasty negotiations between the government, rebels and West African mediators took place. Eventually Taylor agreed to go into exile (in Nigeria) and Nigerian troops flew in to secure Monrovia. They received a hero's welcome.

At the time of writing anywhere outside of Monrovia remained extremely dangerous. Officially the civil war is over, but it's anarchy out there. Looting, rape, torture, mutilation and casual execution (all characteristics of the civil conflict that has lasted two decades) are all concerns until the UN's 15,000-strong peacekeeping force has been deployed across the country. The UN and transitional government faces some stiff challenges, the first of which is to disarm nihilistic, drug-addled child soldiers used to the power of the gun.

THE CULTURE

Liberians are a people traumatised by war and the country is one of the worst places in the world to live – something that's pretty obvious on any sightseeing tour of Monrovia. Almost one in every two Liberians were displaced from their villages during the first civil war and now that the second is under

MASONS

Rather bizarrely, Americo-Liberian leaders embraced the Masonic Order, and five Liberian presidents have been Grand Masters. The Masonic Order is now banned in Liberia.

way power is guaranteed by only money, guns or both.

Liberia has a dozen major ethnic groups, including the Kpelle in the centre, the Bassa around Buchanan, the Krahn in the southeast, the Mandingo (also called Mandinka) in the north and the Kru along the coast. With the exception of the Krahn, a distinctive feature of these cultures is the secret societies in which strong hierarchies prevail, and rites and ceremonies aimed at educating young people in the customs and skills of the tribe. These processes sometimes involve as many as four years of training, and initiates are easily recognised by their white painted bodies and their shaved heads.

Half of Liberians are Christian, around 20% Muslim and the remainder follow traditional religions (sometimes with a mix of the previous two).

ENVIRONMENT

Liberia's coastal plain is intersected by marshes, creeks and tidal lagoons. Inland is a densely forested plateau with the mountainous Wologisi Range rising near the Guinean border. Rainforest covers about 40% of the country, primarily in the northwest and southeast, where Sapo National Park is found. The park covers some 1308 sq km of rare West African primary rainforest and supports forest elephants, pygmy hippos, chimpanzees and antelopes. Rampant logging and the bushmeat trade are the greatest threats to Liberia's fauna and flora, but the small and dedicated **Society for the Conservation of Nature of Liberia** (SCNL; ☎ /fax 227 058; scnlib2001@yahoo.com; Monrovia Zoo, Larkpazee) runs a variety of conservation projects

WEATHER FOR DUCKS

Monrovia is one of the wettest capitals in Africa with over 4500mm of annual rainfall and humidity of over 90% during the rainy season between May and October.

in Sapo and around the country, together with international partners. For more information also contact **Philadelphia Zoo** (www.phillyzoo.org) in the USA.

TRANSPORT

GETTING THERE & AWAY

Weasua Air Transport (☎ 227 544), offers reliable connections to Monrovia from Abidjan (Côte d'Ivoire; six times weekly), Accra (Ghana) and Freetown (Sierra Leone).

Flights between Monrovia and Conakry (Guinea) are provided by **Ghana Airways**, which also has flights to Accra and Freetown (note that at the time of writing, the airline was teetering on the brink of bankruptcy). **Air Ivoire** (☎ 227 436; cnr Ashmun & Mechlin Sts, Monrovia) offer flights to Abidjan. Departure tax is US$40.

If travelling overland, the main crossing with Sierra Leone is at Bo (Waterside). There's also a border post to the north at Kongo and one northwest of Kolahun, but the current governmental travel advice is not to go anywhere near the Liberia/Sierra Leone border area. For Guinea, there are border posts just north of Voinjama, Ganta and Yekepa. There's frequent transport on the other side to towns in Guinea. Border crossings with Côte d'Ivoire are just beyond Sanniquellie and east of Harper, towards Tabou.

Cargo boats occasionally make the two-day run between Conakry (Guinea) and Monrovia (inquire at Freeport, Monrovia) and fishing boats run sporadically between Harper and San Pédro (Côte d'Ivoire).

GETTING AROUND

Weasua Air Transport (☎ 227 544) offers air charters, but minibuses and bush taxis are the backbone of Liberia's transport system. In good times there are daily departures from Monrovia to the Sierra Leonean border and major towns across the country. Smaller destinations generally have a couple of departures per week. Bush taxies are safer and less crowded than minibuses. There's a surcharge for luggage, but it's usually not more than US$1.

Road conditions are generally bad. Some routes are impassable in the rainy season, although some are sealed (such as the ones from Monrovia to the Sierra Leonean border, Ganta, Tubmanburg and Buchanan).

For the adventurous, fishing boats or cargo ships can shift you along the coast, but other than a couple of semiregular services it's a matter of hanging out at Freeport in Monrovia and hoping for the best.

MONROVIA

Monrovia has suffered badly during the fighting of the past decade. Infrastructure has been largely destroyed and many buildings have been gutted. However, despite its initially depressing appearance, the city has pep. Pick a day when it's not raining, find some Liberian friends and soon you'll forget you're walking around what looks like a war zone.

ORIENTATION

Roberts International Airport is 60km from Monrovia in Robertsfield (take a taxi; US$30). The city is laid out along a coastal peninsula at the mouth of the Mesurado River. Inland of the city is a large area of swamp and estuary. Central Monrovia (which has most of the places of interest, and places to stay and eat) lies at the northern end of this peninsula. Embassies are liberally sprinkled around the city. Liberia's limited domestic and international boat traffic leaves from Freeport, north of the centre.

INFORMATION

Internet Access

Try **DataTech** (Broad St, near Cathedral) and the **Internet Café** (cnr Center & Carey Sts).

Medical Services

St Joseph's Hospital (☎ 226 207), south of town, is best for emergencies. **Charif Pharmacy** (Randall St; ⏰ 8am-7.30pm Mon-Sat) and the **American Drug Store & Pharmacy** (Benson St) are your best bets for good drugs.

Money

Try the banks and foreign exchange bureaux on Broad St.

Post & Telephone

You could try posting something from the **main post office** (cnr Randall & Ashmun Sts), but

that would be a huge leap of faith. Use the reliable, but expensive **DHL** (☎ 226 986; former Mandarin Bldg, cnr Broad & Lynch Sts).

Head to **Liberia Telecom** (Lynch St; ⏰ 8am-10pm) to make international telephone calls (to make collect calls and receive faxes, use the separate office on Nelson St). A GSM900 mobile phone system operates in Monrovia.

Tourist Offices

You could try the **Ministry of Information, Cultural Affairs and Tourism** (☎ 227 349; fax 226 544; United Nations Dr, Mamba Point), but tourism is not exactly a Liberian priority right now.

Travel Agencies

On Broad St **Weasua-KLM** (☎ 227 544), **Karou Voyages** (☎ 226 508) or **Gritaco Travel Agency** (☎ 226 854) can help you flee the capital.

DANGERS & ANNOYANCES

Monrovia has a high crime rate and there are numerous roadblocks, which can be good places to be relieved of cash and/or goods. The usual range of rip-off artists and con men operate in Monrovia, where there are few functioning political or judicial institutions. Don't get mixed up with the law in any way and show no interest in politics – human rights campaigners and journalists have been arrested and tortured.

Monrovia has had no reliable electricity supply for over a decade, so bring a torch (flashlight).

SIGHTS

The **Masonic Temple** (Benson St), once Monrovia's major landmark, is well trashed and the grand master's throne is now found in the looted **National Museum** (Broad St; admission free).

The **Waterside Market** (Water St, north city centre) is fun to walk around, as are the artisan stalls opposite the US embassy on Mamba Point.

Ellen's Beach is a popular weekend spot 10km north of the centre, just beyond the defunct Hotel Africa. Also popular is the attractive **Kendeja Beach**, 15km southeast of town on the Buchanan road. There's occasionally a good surf break at **Mamba Point**, but the sewage is terrible and, like on Monrovia's other beaches, the current can be a killer.

There are **swimming pools** at Coconut Plantation near Mamba Point, and at Cedar Club ('Lebanese Club') off Tubman Blvd, near Spriggs-Payne airfield.

SLEEPING & EATING

Good budget lodging is almost nonexistent and should the cease-fire hold prices are likely to soar as aid and UN personnel pour into the country. Expect to pay at least US$20/50 for a single/double.

There are some good eateries in the area around the cathedral, plus a couple of supermarkets for self-caterers, but expect more places to spring up to feed service personnel.

GETTING THERE & AWAY

Buses (☎ 226 588) to Abidjan, Côte d'Ivoire and Accra (Ghana) depart from Bong Mines Bridge on Bushrod Island Rd. Bush taxis and minibuses for most upcountry destinations leave from Red Light, 15km northeast of the centre, including Ganta (US$13, five hours) and Gbarnga (US$10, six hours). For Tubmanburg and the Sierra Leonean border head to the Duala motor park, 9km northeast of Monrovia.

Sam Kazouh (☎ 227 303; 1st fl, Association of Evangelicals of Liberia bldg, Randall St) runs a weekly boat to Greenville (US$30, deck seating only, 12 to 15 hours). The boat sometimes continues to Harper (from Monrovia US$50, 22 to 25 hours). There are also sporadic speedboats between Monrovia and Harper (US$60, 36 hours) from the 'fishing pier' at Freeport.

GETTING AROUND

Shared taxis trundle along routes around the city and prices range from US$0.10 to US$0.50. Private hire taxis around the centre cost US$1.50 to US$2.

AROUND MONROVIA

FIRESTONE PLANTATION

Firestone Plantation – the world's largest rubber plantation – is operating, although at greatly reduced capacity. There are no tours, but you may find employees who can show you around and explain the tapping process. Stick to the beaten path, as Firestone is one of several areas in Liberia where land mines have been found. The powerful oil corporationlike Firestone presence was one of the reasons the US backed Liberia's dodgy rulers for decades. In the era of banana republics, this country was even known as the Firestone Republic. The plantation is in Harbel, about 65km east of Monrovia, near Robertsfield airport. Take a taxi.

THE COAST

ROBERTSPORT

Once a relaxing beach town, now nothing more than a small fishing community, Robertsport has been completely destroyed by war. Only ruins and relics of a **WWII allied submarine base** remain, although the beaches are still beautiful and the **surfing** is the best in Liberia. The surrounding area is prone to flooding in the rainy season.

BUCHANAN

Liberia's second port is around 125km southeast of Monrovia. **Beaches** are good, but some areas are mined. Northwest of town is a lively fishing community set on a colourful cove.

GREENVILLE

Greenville (sometimes called Sinoe) was completely destroyed during the first civil war and captured by rebels early in 2003. The town is the centre of the country's logging industry and launching point for 4WD trips to **Sapo National Park** (see p352).

The road from Monrovia is rough, but there's an occasional boat service (see Getting There & Away, on this page).

HARPER

Harper, on the southeastern tip of Liberia, once had numerous sites of historical and architectural interest, including some fine old houses and the residence of the late President William Tubman. Nowadays it's a shell of its former self, although it's surrounded by beautiful countryside.

From Monrovia it's a hard three-day 4WD journey at best, but a speedboat runs sporadically between Harper and the capital (see Getting There & Away, on this page).

THE INTERIOR

GANTA

Ganta (Gompa City) is a pleasant, bustling town 2km from the Guinean border. There's an interesting **mosque** and there once was a good **craft shop** at the leper institution on Sanniquellie road.

There's one basic hotel in town, plus a couple of *chop houses* (local restaurants) with simple meals.

Frequent bush taxis leave from the main taxi stand to Gbarnga (US$3, 1½ hours), Monrovia (US$13, five hours) and Sanniquellie (US$3, one hour), with weekly departures to Tappita and Zwedru. Bush taxis from the centre to the Guinean border cost US$0.30.

GBARNGA

Gbarnga, Charles Taylor's headquarters during the first civil war, is Liberia's second city. It remains to be seen what will remain of the **Africana Museum** (Cuttington College in **Phebe**; 10km southwest of Gbarnga) after the latest spell of conflict; 30km to the northwest are the pretty **Kpatawe Falls**.

Villa de Via Classique (d US$25), a few kilometres towards Monrovia, is a decent place to stay.

Frequent bush taxis leave from Gbarnga to Monrovia (US$10, six hours), Ganta (US$3, 1½ hours) and Phebe Junction (US$0.60).

YEKEPA

War-torn Yekepa, set about 350m above sea level and north of Sanniquellie, has a pleasant climate, good views of the surrounding lush mountains and good trekking potential in the nearby Nimba range – **Goodhouse Hill** (1362m) is Liberia's highest peak. However, it's a very dicey place to be at present.

There's no regular transport to/from Yekepa, although Saturday, market day, is your best bet.

It's a walk of a few kilometres to the Guinean border from where there's transport to Lola (Guinea; US$1.50).

SANNIQUELLIE

Ironically, in this war-torn land, Sanniquellie is the birthplace of the Organisation of African Unity and the last major town before Côte d'Ivoire.

There's a basic hotel, a few undistinguished chop houses along the main road and a some reasonably well-stocked shops.

LIBERIA DIRECTORY

ACCOMMODATION

Any hotel with a generator and water will be expensive. There are few hotels upcountry and those that do exist have extremely basic facilities.

EMBASSIES & CONSULATES

Countries with diplomatic representation in Monrovia:

Côte d'Ivoire (☎ 227 436; 8th St, Sinkor, near St Joseph's Construction)
Ghana (☎ 227 448; 15th St, Sinkor)
Guinea (cnr 24th St & Tubman Blvd, Sinkor)
Sierra Leone (☎ 226 250; Hotel Africa compound, Villa 18)
UK, France & Germany (☎ 226 516; honorary consul at European Union Office, Mamba Point)
USA (☎ 226 370; http://usembassy.state.gov/monrovia; 111 United Nations Dr, Mamba Point)

Australians and New Zealanders are encouraged to register with the Canadian embassy in Cote d'Ivoire.

Liberia has diplomatic representation in Côte d'Ivoire and Guinea.

FOOD

Good chop bars (cheap street restaurants selling local food) are plentiful in Monrovia, but shortages of basic foodstuffs have been experienced. Expensive restaurants are reserved for the capital.

HOLIDAYS

As well as religious holidays listed in the Africa Directory chapter (p1003), these are the principal public holidays in Liberia:
1 January New Year's Day
March Decoration Day on the 2nd Wednesday
26 July Independence Day
November Thanksgiving Day on the 1st Thursday

MONEY

The Liberian 'unity' dollar (L$) is the national currency and is pegged to the US$ at a one-to-one rate, so US dollars are widely used and changed – Lebanese-owned shops are good places to do this. Travellers cheques are virtually useless, and accepted at only a small number of up-market shops and hotels. There are no ATMs.

POST & TELEPHONE

The Liberian postal service is not renowned for efficiency and customer service. Post stuff only from Monrovia, where the courier **DHL** (☎ 226 986; Broad & Lynch St) has an office. There is no poste restante in Liberia.

LIBERIA

There are no area codes in Liberia. Use the Liberia Telecom offices in Monrovia to make international calls. Collect (reverse charge) calls can be made through the branch on Nelson St, which also has an expensive fax service.

VISAS

Visas (US$40 to US$45) must be arranged in advance and are valid for 30 days.

After arriving in Monrovia, report to the **Bureau of Immigration** (Broad St) within 48 hours for a visitor's permit (US$25), it

is this permit that actually determines the length of your stay.

Visa Extensions

Visa extensions and exit visas (which are required for all those wishing to leave the country!) are also available from the Bureau of Immigration.

Visas for Onward Travel

Visas for onward travel to Sierra Leone, Guinea and Côte d'Ivoire are available at embassies in Monrovia (see p355).

Côte d'Ivoire

FAST FACTS

- **Area** 322,000 sq km
- **ATMs** found throughout the country, usually linked to Visa
- **Borders** Burkina Faso open; Guinea and Liberia borders closed
- **Budget** US$50 per day in Abidjan, US$15 to US$30 in the interior
- **Capital** Yamoussoukro; Abidjan is the biggest city and commercial hub
- **Languages** French and many local languages including Mande, Malinké, Dan, Senoufo, Baoulé, Agni, Dioula
- **Money** West African CFA franc; US$1 = CFA584
- **Population** 16.8 million
- **Seasons** wet seasons: in the south (May–Jul and Oct–Nov), in the north (Jun–Oct)
- **Telephone** country code ☎ 225; international access code ☎ 00
- **Time** GMT/UTC
- **Visas** required by all except citizens of the US and most West African countries; cost varies substantially depending on your nationality and where you apply; check before you go

WARNING

Following the attempted overthrow of the government in 2002, Cote d'Ivoire remains very unstable. Fighting continues in many parts of the country, and travel outside Abidjan is not recommended. We were unable to do on-the-ground research, so some information in this chapter may be unreliable. Check the situation before travelling to Cote d'Ivoire.

Mention Côte d'Ivoire (also known as Ivory Coast) to Africans in neighbouring countries and you'll get a sad shake of the head and a muttered 'What a shame'. Regarded as an economic miracle only a few years ago, with booming farm exports and a glittering high-rise city called the 'Paris of West Africa', Côte d'Ivoire has suffered a series of coups and violence-plagued elections in recent years and is now an ethnically divided and heavily armed country.

Which really is a shame. Before the current instability, Côte d'Ivoire was a travellers' favourite, known for its beaches, good surfing, traditional arts and crafts, national parks

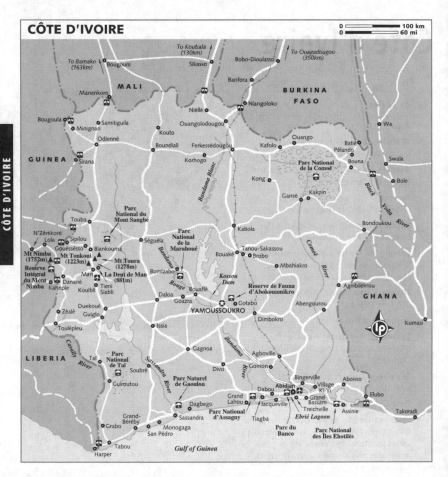

CÔTE D'IVOIRE

and friendly, outgoing people. These attractions are still here, though travel in the country is now strictly regulated and some areas are off-limits. Still, the peace process is ongoing and signs are promising that the country may return to relative stability and reopen to travellers.

HISTORY

Until the 1840s, the indigenous people of Côte d'Ivoire were protected from European colonialism by the inhospitable coastline and dense rainforest interior. In this relative isolation, kingdoms such as the Krou, Senoufo, Lubi, Malinké and Akan flourished. When the French began a big push towards colonial exploitation, they met fierce resistance from the interior tribes. But eventually the French took control of the entire area, trading for ivory and establishing coffee and cocoa plantations, which are still the backbone of the economy.

Independence & Boom Years

Born in 1905, Félix Houphouët-Boigny became the country's father of independence. A labour leader who turned his trade union into a pro-Independence political party, he was elected to the French parliament and eventually became the first African to be a minister in a European government. When independence became a reality in 1960 he was the obvious choice for the new country's first president.

Houphouët-Boigny's policies – maintaining close economic ties with France and relying on agriculture – were wildly successful. Côte d'Ivoire was the world's largest producer of cocoa, the economy maintained a 10% annual growth rate for 20 years and the country became known as the 'economic miracle of West Africa'.

The Downturn

But it couldn't last. A world recession, a drought, collapsing prices on agricultural products and over logging all contributed to Côte d'Ivoire's economic troubles. President Houphouët-Boigny initiated hardship measures, which sparked civil unrest. The 1990 elections were open to other parties for the first time, but Houphouët-Boigny won easily. He died in 1993 at age 88 after 33 years as the country's only president.

His hand-picked successor, Henri Konan-Bédié, inherited a mass of economic problems and civil unrest. He responded by scapegoating the northern workers, particularly immigrants and children of immigrants (mostly from neighbouring Burkina Faso), who had been the backbone of the agricultural economy during the good years. Under a policy of 'Ivoirité' these people were excluded from running in presidential elections and encouraged to leave the country.

The Current Crisis

In December 1999, Côte d'Ivoire suffered the first coup d'etat in its history. President Bédié was overthrown by forces loyal to General Robert Guéi, who promised free elections but in fact intensified Bédié's policies of Ivoirité.

While the country reeled from military rebellions and civil unrest, Guéi had the supreme court declare popular Muslim candidate Alasanne Ouattara ineligible to run for president because his parents were from Burkina Faso. This wasn't enough, however, as Laurant Gbagbo won the presidential election in October 2000. Guéi declared himself the official winner, but was quickly chased from power by massive popular uprisings. The following two years of Gbagbo's presidency were marked by attempted coups and tensions.

On 19 September, 2002, another mutiny attempt quickly escalated into a full-scale rebellion, with troops from the north gaining control of much of the country. Former president Guéi was killed early in the fighting and his death has never been investigated. Initially the government agreed to a cease-fire with the rebels, now known as the MPCI (Patriotic Movement of Côte d'Ivoire), who had the full backing of the mostly Muslim northern populace. But this truce was short-lived, and fighting over the prime cocoa-growing areas resumed. France sent in troops to maintain the cease-fire boundaries, and militias took advantage of the crisis to seize parts of the west. These militias included warlords and fighters from Liberia and Sierra Leone, veterans of some of the most savage and indiscriminate warfare in recent African history, who began full-scale looting and pillaging of the western border region.

In January 2003, President Gbagbo and leaders of the rebel factions met in Paris and signed accords creating a 'government of national unity', with representatives of the rebels taking up places in a new cabinet. This was slowly but peacefully implemented, curfews were lifted and French troops cleaned up the lawless western border. But the central problems remained, and neither side achieved its goals (the government wants to regain control of the north; the MPCI, now called the 'new forces', want new elections with their candidates eligible to run).

At the time of research, the rebels had pulled out of the new government amid allegations of fresh coup plottings, harsh words were exchanged and a return to conflict seemed likely. Sadly, the country remains divided and deadlocked.

THE CULTURE

Before times turned hard, Ivorians were known as extremely friendly and hospitable. Visitors would often be invited to someone's house for meals, or have free beers and travel advice offered at the local bars and markets.

ARTS

Côte d'Ivoire is known for the quality of its traditional artwork, particularly masks, but also dyed cloths, metalwork, woodcarvings, jewellery and more. You'll find good value on these items in markets and artisans' villages.

CÔTE D'IVOIRE

ENVIRONMENT

Côte d'Ivoire used to be dense rainforest, but most of it was cleared during the agricultural boom. What remains today is mostly in protected areas in the south. The north is now dry scrubland.

There's a network of national parks. Some are off-limits due to environmental research, but others are set up for visitors, especially package tourists.

TRANSPORT

GETTING THERE & AWAY

At the time of writing, most flights had been suspended. **Air Ivoire** (☎ 20 25 14 00) still has flights listed to major West African cities.

Buses run from Yamoussoukro to some of the nearby capitals, including Bamako, Ouagadougou and Niamey.

The optimistically named express train used to be a main way of getting from Abidjan to Ouagadougou, Burkina Faso, stopping in Bouaké. This has been suspended since the start of the current unrest, but check around when you get there.

GETTING AROUND

Air Ivoire no longer runs domestic flights; check with a travel agent for new options.

Buses run regularly throughout the country with fixed schedules and rates — even through the cease-fire border. Minibuses and bush taxis are the main means of getting around in remote areas.

ABIDJAN

Abidjan, the country's capital in all but name, has always had a mixed reputation with travellers. On one hand, it really is a glitzy, vibrant city of high-rise office buildings, fancy restaurants, budget-busting hotels and all the comforts of home (although the 'Paris of West Africa' moniker was a bit of an exaggeration, even during the boom years).

On the other hand, in addition to the high prices that go with these amenities, the city was known for rampant official corruption and especially for its high rate of petty and serious crime, often aimed at foreigners. It's not yet clear what effects months of curfew and tight police control will have on the crime situation.

ORIENTATION

The airport is in Port Bouët, 15km south of town; you'll have to bargain for a taxi into town. The main train station is in Treichville, on the south side of town. Most buses and bush taxis leave from and arrive at the chaotic Gare Routière d'Adjamé on the northern side of town.

Abidjan is spread out around a wide lagoon, which divides the city into very different districts. Le Plateau is the commercial and government centre, with the big buildings to prove it. Across a bridge, Treichville is the most active and 'African' *quartier*, with a reputation for being unsafe at night. To the east of Treichville is Marcory, with affordable hotels and dining spots. The exclusive residential *quartiers* east of Le Plateau have little of interest for budget travellers.

INFORMATION

Internet Access

Getting online is easy as Internet access is widely available in Abidjan.

Media

The weekly *Abidjan Sept Jours* has entertainment listings.

Medical Services

Abidjan Sept Jours also lists 24-hour pharmacies and doctors on call. **Polyclinique Internationale Ste-Marie** (☎ 22 44 51 32; Blvd de la Corniche) is recommended for medical treatment.

Money

Despite being the economic capital of the region, Abidjan can be a difficult place for a lowly traveller to change money or get cash from home. Banks will only change travellers cheques with proof of purchase and at bad rates (before waiting in line for hours, make sure they change your brand of cheques). Some of the larger banks have ATMs, usually linked to Visa. The big banks' main branches are all in Le Plateau.

Post & Telephone

The central post office is at the southern end of Le Plateau, across from the Place de la République.

CI Telecom in the EECI building in Le Plateau is the main communications centre, but calls from private telephone and Internet centres can be much cheaper. At Internet cafés in Treichville along Ave 16, rates for international phone calls can be as low as US$0.40 per minute.

Tourist Offices

There's a **tourist office** (☎ 20 25 16 10; Place de la République, Le Plateau) in the centre of town, which may be able to assist you with maps and general information.

DANGERS & ANNOYANCES

It's a good idea to be on guard in Abidjan. Though many travellers spend days here with no problems, incidents of robbery still occur. Areas with bad reputations include both bridges from Le Plateau to Treichville, most of Treichville at night and the Gare Routière d'Adjamé.

Depending on whether the police and soldiers are being paid, having bribes demanded at checkpoints around the city can be a major expense.

SIGHTS

A little more than 1km north of the market in Le Plateau, the **Musée National** (☎ 21 22 20 56; cnr Blvd Nangul Abrogoua & Av 13; admission free; 🕙 9am-noon & 3-6pm Tues-Sat) has over 20,000 artefacts, including wooden statues and masks, pottery, ivory and brass. It's a good introduction to Ivorian art. Some of the buses from Le Plateau to Adjamé pass by if you don't want to walk.

Nearby, the **Cathédrale St-Paul** (Blvd Angoulvant; 🕙 8am-7pm) is not as spectacular as Yamoussoukro's basilica, but it's still an impressive sight. Note the stained-glass windows with their Bible stories and historical events.

If you feel like a walking tour of the city, head south on Blvd de la République towards the skyscrapers of **Le Plateau** and stop and enjoy its café culture. For a change of pace, continue south to **Treichville** (watch your back on the bridge). It's a completely different scene, with cheap loud bars, restaurants and record shops. Check it out in the daytime, unless you're ready for serious nightlife and a lot of attention.

Outside of Abidjan you'll find some natural and cultural attractions, including **Parc du Banco** (admission US$5), with little wildlife but excellent hiking trails through the rainforest. It's about 3km northwest of town, and some buses north pass by. Or you can take a water taxi (US$0.50) to **Yopougon**, where the Rue de la Princesse lights up on weekends, with live music, street food, *maquis*, record shops and other cheap treats for travellers.

ACTIVITIES

The fancy hotels in town offer swimming pools, tennis, sailboarding and other activities, usually a reasonably priced splurge for nonguests.

SLEEPING

Hotels in Abidjan are generally a bad deal and not worth the expense. Cheap rooms range from US$8 to US$25, but anything under US$10 a night is almost invariably a brothel. The best options are in Marcory and Treichville. Le Plateau and Cocody are home to the expensive international hotels.

Abidjan's camping grounds are mostly tiny beachfront places surrounded by cement walls, a fair distance from the town centre.

EATING

Abidjan has a full range of eats, from street food stands to very fancy restaurants serving cuisine from around the world. Whatever your budget and tastes, you won't be disappointed.

Good places for inexpensive street food include Ave Noguès and Rue de Commerce in Le Plateau, Ave Victor Blaka in Treichville, Petit Marché in Marcory and Allocodrome in Cocody.

DRINKING

Abidjan is covered with cheap bars, especially in the *bouging* African sections of town, where a big Flag beer should cost less than US$1, and friendly Ivorians will usually strike up a conversation. Hotel bars are more expensive but can be fun places to meet other travellers. For live music try the fancy hotels.

CLUBBING

Months of a dusk-till-dawn curfew have made for tough times at Abidjan's clubs. But this is a city that loves to dress up and go dancing, so expect some clubs to be up and running. Check *Abidjan Sept Jours* for announcements.

ENTERTAINMENT

Abidjan has several cinemas that show French films and current Hollywood hits dubbed into French, which can be a fun way to spend a couple hours for about US$4. Traditional music and dance shows may also be staged in and around the city; check with one of the major hotels for details.

SHOPPING

Art

The **Marché de Cocody** (Blvd de France, Cocody) and the **Marché Plateau** (Blvd de la République, La Plateau) have African artwork in addition to the usual imported stuff. For more upscale shopping and high-quality goods check out the high-end hotels.

Clothing

There are fabric stores all over the city, often with tailors on-site or nearby for quick work on dresses, shirts etc. The markets mainly sell used clothing from the US, but you'll find some African goods in them as well.

Music

Abidjan, where many artists record, is one of the best places in West Africa to buy music. Look in the music shops in Treichville or Yopougon for the best deals.

GETTING THERE & AWAY

Air Ivoire (☎ 20 25 14 00) connects Abidjan with many Western capitals.

Buses that go to the borders with neighbouring countries leave from the Gare Routière d'Adjamé, except those for Elubo at the Ghanaian border, which leave from the Gare du Bassam, south of Treichville.

The train for Ouagadougou, Burkina Faso, is currently suspended.

Abidjan is connected by minibus and bush taxi to all major centres, including Bouaké (US$7, five hours), Grand Bassam (US$1, 40 minutes), Grand Lahou (US$3, two hours), Korhogo (US$8, eight to 10 hours), Man (US$9, nine hours), San Pédro (US$8, six hours), Sassandra (US$4, five hours) and Yamoussoukro (US$4, 3½ hours).

Buses leave whenever they're full, mostly in the morning.

GETTING AROUND

Abidjan, split by a lagoon, has several water taxis that connect its various *quartiers*. The fare across from Le Plateau to Treichville is US$0.70 and includes a new perspective on the city's layout.

Public buses run around the city on fixed routes, but unless you're planning on staying in Abidjan long enough to figure out the system, it's easier to take a taxi. Taxis are cheap (about US$0.50) for a shared cab or more to hire your own, but it's sometimes worth it. Make sure the meter is on if you hire your own.

THE EASTERN COAST

The eastern coast of Côte d'Ivoire includes the former capitals of Grand Bassam and Bingerville, with lots of colonial buildings fading in the salt air. Nowadays the coast is known primarily for its beach retreats, which in more peaceful times were packed with European vacationers.

GRAND BASSAM

Fading colonial glory and long stretches of beach lined with seafood restaurants are the main attractions at this popular getaway, 43km east of Abidjan. On the weekends, especially in the dry season, visitors pack the hotels and beaches. During the week the place is almost deserted, and good deals on hotel rooms are there to be had.

The city is laid out on a long spit of land with a quiet lagoon on one side and the turbulent Atlantic Ocean on the other. Most hotels and restaurants are on or near the beach.

Information

Around Place de Paix in Nouveau Bassam are a SGBCI bank with ATM, the post office and *commiseriat* (police station).

Dangers & Annoyances

The main danger is drowning in the Atlantic, which can be rougher than it looks from shore. Other than that Grand Bassam is a pretty laid-back place.

Sights & Activities

A walk through town will take you past the **colonial buildings** Grand Bassam is known for, some being restored, others slowly falling apart. The former post office and *mairie* are two of the most impressive. **Pirogue tours** of the lagoon and the mangrove swamps can be arranged with many of the local boatmen.

Festivals & Events
The Fête de l'Abissa is a week-long ceremony when the N'Zima people honour their dead, usually held in late October or early November.

Sleeping & Eating
The best hotels are found along the beachfront. Many hotels have different rates for different seasons and for weekends/weeknights.

Room prices range from about US$14 to US$35, but ask about discounts if the hotel is empty.

Seafood dining in *maquis* with views of the water is the mainstay of the dining scene here. The cheaper places front the lagoon, rather than the open ocean.

Shopping
Grand Bassam has a couple good spots for buying African art. At the entrance to Nouveau Bassam there's an **artisans market** with a wide range of goods. For more upmarket work, check out the **Masques Club** in Ancien Bassam, which is worth a look even if you don't buy.

Getting There & Away
Minibuses and bush taxis leave (mostly in the morning) from the *gare routière* by the Place de Paix to Abidjan (US$1, 40 minutes) and Assinie (US$2, 1½ hours).

ASSINIE
Like Grand Bassam, Assinie, 85km to the east, is a beach resort for well-off Ivorians and package tourists, but if you're there at the right time you'll have the place and the beaches to yourself.

Hotels in the area have rooms for around US$50 with full board, but smaller hotels in town may offer much, much lower rates during the off-season.

Bush taxis leave irregularly for Grand Bassam (US$2, 1½ hours). Ask around to put people in the know that you are looking for a ride.

THE WESTERN COAST
The western coast has some of the country's best beaches and seaside villages, with rainforest scenery and national parks.

GRAND LAHOU
This former colonial town is now a quiet seaside village at the mouth of the Bandama River. There's a modern town 1km from the road, but the old town is a further 18km south.

On the opposite side of the river, the **Parc National d'Assagny** has excellent rainforest hikes with observation decks for viewing the birdlife and possibly forest elephants. The park office in the modern town arranges trips and sells permits for US$3.50.

There are a couple of cheap places to stay and eat; ask around for recommendations.

Buses run from Grand Lahou to the Gare Routière d'Adjamé in Abidjan (US$3, two hours). Minibuses and ferries run between the modern town and the old town.

SASSANDRA
Sassandra is the jumping-off point for a string of beaches to the west, some with good surfing, and an interesting fishing village in its own right. It's also the gateway to the **Parc Naturel de Gaoulou**, 12km north. There's no accommodation, but for US$3.50 you can take a short tour and possibly see hippos.

There are plenty of places to stay and eat in town and along the beach road to the west. Prices range from US$9 to US$20. The best options for meals are the hotel restaurants and in-town *maquis*.

Buses run twice daily to Abidjan (US$4, five hours). Shared taxis and minibuses leave when full for San Pédro (US$2.50, 1½ hours). To get to the western beaches you'll need to hire a cab and make arrangements to be picked up later.

SAN PÉDRO
San Pédro, a major port, is also one of the most jumping cities in Côte d'Ivoire, with plenty of restaurants and nightclubs to keep travellers busy and happy. The Cité area is the hub of the action. There is also a nearby beach, though most of town is north by a lake.

CÔTE D'IVOIRE

Accommodation is reasonably plentiful, while cheap *maquis* and bars can be found along Ave Marché, just south of the market.

The best spot for clubs is **Le Triangle** in the eastern part of the Cité, with about half a dozen dance clubs blasting it out.

From San Pédro there are buses to Abidjan (US$8, six hours), Yamoussoukro (US$8, seven hours) and Man (US$10, 10 hours), as well as Sassandra (US$2.50, 1½ hours).

THE CENTRE & NORTHERN CÔTE D'IVOIRE

The central and northern parts of the country are home to a variety of ethnic groups and traditional cultures, as well as scenic mountains, hiking trails and national parks.

MAN

Rich in traditional culture and natural attractions, Man has long been a travellers' mecca. Unfortunately the region west of Man has been lawless since the rebellion, but stability is being restored.

Known as the city of 18 mountains, Man is surrounded by lush green hills and villages of the Dan and other tribes. It makes an ideal base for exploring and hiking, and is also a melting-pot city where various tribes come to sell their artworks and other wares. Since the covered market burned down, vendors set up shop all over town.

The **SGBCI bank** (Rue de l'Hôtel Leveneur) has a Visa-linked ATM.

Man has good accommodation options for all budgets, and you'll find plenty of street food around the *gare routière*. Cheap *maquis* with filling grilled meals also line the streets of downtown.

There are several bus companies that go to Abidjan (US$9, nine hours) and Yamoussoukro (US$7, six hours).

AROUND MAN

The area around Man has some of Côte d'Ivoire's most impressive scenery and is a good place to see dances and ceremonies in traditional villages.

La Dent de Man, 12km northeast of town, is a popular hike. Named for its molar shape, 'the Tooth of Man' is 881m at the summit, and a trip to the summit and back takes four or five hours, with a fairly gruelling ascent in parts. To get there, take a shared taxi to the village of Zobale, then head due east.

Another challenging hike is **Mt Tonkoui** (1223m), the second-highest peak in the country, with breathtaking views all the way to Liberia and Guinea if the weather allows.

The villages around Man are used to tourists and often stage dances and ceremonies; ask at the tourist office in Man to find out what's up. February is generally the best time to visit, as several villages have *fêtes des masques*.

YAMOUSSOUKRO

A capital city with no embassies, government ministries or significant commercial activity, Yamoussoukro is known mainly for its overwhelming basilica, presidential palace and other monuments, all the pet projects of former president Félix Houphouët-Boigny, who was born here. There's not a lot for travellers to do here except gawk at these unique buildings.

Information

The **SGBCI bank** (Ave Houphouët-Boigny) has an ATM linked to Visa cards; it's open 24 hours. The **tourist office** (☎ 30 64 08 14; Ave Houphouët-Boigny) can help arrange visits to local attractions.

Sights

The main attraction is the **Basilique de Notre Dame de la Paix** (Route de Daloa; admission US$3.50; ⏰ 8am-5pm Mon-Sat, 11.30am-5pm Sun), which resembles St Peter's in Rome. It's huge, ornate and strangely incongruous in this part of the world, but walking around the interior can be overwhelming. Bring your passport; you may be required to leave it with the guards at the gate.

The **presidential palace**, where Houphouët-Boigny is now buried, can only be viewed from afar. As well as the architecture, every day at around 5pm you can watch the feeding of the crocodiles that live in the lake.

Sleeping & Eating

Yamoussoukro has a number of reasonable accommodation options; check with the tourist office. There is cheap and abundant street food at the *gare routière* with dishes for about US$1, or try the *maquis* along the lake's edge in the Habitat *quartier*.

Getting There & Away

Yamoussoukro is a major transport hub, and buses leave in all directions. Some destinations are Abidjan (US$4, 3½ hours), Bouaké (US$3.50, 1½ hours), Korhogo (US$7, six hours), Man (US$7, five hours) and San Pédro (US$8, seven hours).

There are also buses to Ouagadougou, Burkina Faso (US$30, 24 hours), Bamako, Mali (US$20, 30 hours) and Niamey, Niger (US$43, four days).

BOUAKÉ

Côte d'Ivoire's second-largest city is known for its carnival and its market. It's a sprawling, modern city with plenty of amenities for travellers who've been on the road for a while.

The **SGBCI bank** (Ave Gabriel Dadié), as usual, has a Visa-linked ATM. You can make international phone calls from the CI Telecom centre, near the train station.

The Grand Marché on the north side of town is one of the most ethnically varied in all the country, with all kinds of artwork from various tribes on display.

In March, the **Carnaval de Bouaké**, one of Africa's largest Carnaval celebrations, is held here.

There are a couple of decent accommodation options in and around town. Try to get a recommendation from a local or other travellers. You can fill up for under US$2 at *maquis* in the Koko district.

There are buses to Abidjan (US$7, five hours), Yamoussoukro (US$3.50, 3½ hours), Korhogo (US$8, five hours), Man (US$9, seven hours) and San Pédro (US$10, eight hours).

At the time of writing, train service from Abidjan in the government-controlled south to Bouaké and possibly on to Ouagadougou was being re-established. Check around for the latest details.

KORHOGO

In Côte d'Ivoire's far north, Korhogo is the centre of the Senoufo culture, with its unique artwork, dance and traditions. Travellers come all the way out here to

visit the artisans' villages in the area and see the Senoufo artisans at work.

The **tourist office** (☎ 36 86 05 84; Route de Dikodougou), on the south side of town, can help arrange travel to the nearby villages. There are also many guides in town offering their services; you can to see their certification card before hiring them.

In town, the central market has all the wares of the surrounding villages, including Korhogo cloth – the dyed, coarse cotton that you'll see all over the country but which is produced here. There are also woodcarvings, pottery and other styles of artwork.

Accommodation in Korhogo is a real bargain; see the tourist office for information. Simple, cheap, local meals are also available.

Buses to Abidjan (US$8, eight to 10 hours) also stop in Bouaké (US$4, five hours) and Yamoussoukro (US$7, six hours).

PARC NATIONAL DE LA COMOË

Côte d'Ivoire's biggest and best-known national park has plenty of wildlife, including lions, elephants, hippos, many species of monkeys and antelopes, and abundant birdlife. In the far northeast of the country, the park is only open from 15 December until the end of May.

Unfortunately, it's a difficult place for budget travellers to fully enjoy. Accommodation is expensive, and you need a vehicle. Admission to the park is only US$5, but rooms in the **Comoë Safari Lodge** (r US$30-55, plus US$13/27 for half/full board) are expensive. There's also a **campement** at the southern end of the park with huts for about US$12, but you still have to get there somehow. The Lodge has 4WD safaris if there are enough clients, for US$31 per person for a full day.

It's much easier to get to the northern entrance at Kafolo than the southern ones at Gansé and Kakpin, especially if you're coming from Ferkessédougou (US$5, five hours) to the west.

CÔTE D'IVOIRE DIRECTORY

ACCOMMODATION

Hotels in Abidjan are expensive and not worth the money, although camping is available further out of town. Around the country good rooms cost under US$10.

ACTIVITIES

There's good cycling around the country, but for touring you'll need to bring all the gear from home. Grand Bassam and some other resort towns have rental bikes, which are good enough to get around town.

Côte d'Ivoire has great hiking. Popular spots are the hills around Man in the west, and the rainforest national parks in the south. The beaches west of Sassandra have good surfing, particularly around Niega.

DANGERS & ANNOYANCES

Before the current instability, the Côte d'Ivoire was known as a friendly place, with a few serious annoyances. Crime directed at foreigners was a big problem in Abidjan, and unpaid soldiers and police collected bribes at checkpoints all over the country. Government crackdowns and curfews may have improved things.

EMBASSIES & CONSULATES

Countries with diplomatic representation in Abidjan (all in Le Plateau):

Australia The Canadian embassy handles Australian affairs.

Burkina Faso (☎ 20 21 13 13; 2 Ave Terrasson de Fougères)

Canada (☎ 2032 2009; Immeuble Trade Centre, Ave Noguès)

France (☎ 2020 0505; Rue Lecoeur)

Germany (☎ 2021 4727; Immeuble Le Mans, Rue Botreau-Roussel)

Ghana (☎ 2033 1124; Résidence le Corniche, Blvd Général de Gaulle)

Guinea (☎ 2032 9494; Immeuble Crosson Duplessis, Ave Crosson Duplessis)

Liberia (☎ 2032 4636; 20 Ave Delafosse)

Mali (☎ 2032 3147; Maison du Mali, Rue du Commerce)

UK (☎ 2021 8209; Immeuble Les Harmonies, Blvd Carde)

USA (☎ 2021 0979; 5 Rue Jesse Owens)

Côte d'Ivoire has diplomatic representation in these neighbouring, or near-neighbouring, countries: Burkina Faso, Ghana, Guinea, Liberia, Mali, Nigeria and Senegal.

FESTIVALS & EVENTS

Cities and villages hold festivals, dances and all kind of traditional ceremonies, but few adhere to a fixed calendar; you'll have to ask around. These are some of the bigger, more regular events:

Fêtes des Masques Held in February in the villages around Man, with an impressive display of local art and dancing.

Carnaval Celebrated in the city of Bouaké in March, with the usual vibrant street celebrations.

Fête du Dipri Held in Gomon, northwest of Abidjan, in March or April. An all-night and all-the-next-day religious ceremony.

Fête de l'Abissa Held in October or November in Grand Bassam. A week-long ceremony honouring the dead.

Fête des Harristes Held in Bregbo, 15km east of Abidjan, on 1 November. A born-again religious gathering.

HOLIDAYS

As well as religious holidays listed in the Africa Directory chapter (p1003), these are the principal public holidays in Côte d'Ivoire:

1 January New Year's Day
1 May Labour Day
28 May Mothers Day
7 August Independence Day
15 November Fête de la Paix
7 December National Day

INTERNET ACCESS

Internet access is cheap and reliable in the big cities, and just as cheap but less reliable in remote areas.

MAPS

The Michelin map (No 957) is the best for the whole country if you can get it. The tourist office in Abidjan has a good, full-colour map of the city.

MONEY

There are ATMs at SGBCI banks throughout the country, linked to Visa cards only. Cash is the best while travelling, as credit cards and travellers cheques are virtually worthless outside the big cities. The local currency is the West African CFA franc. Changing cash money is easy if you have euros or dollars; anything else, including Central African CFA, will be difficult.

POST & TELEPHONE

Post offices are painted blue and white and are called SIPE. An airmail letter to the US costs about US$1, to Europe about US$0.75 and to Australia US$1.25.

You'll find there are good international phone connections at CI Telecom offices throughout the country, and phonecards are widely available.

RESPONSIBLE TRAVEL

You'll find bushmeat on the menu of many restaurants. Don't contribute to the loss of the country's wildlife just so you can say you ate gazelle when you get home.

VISAS

All visitors, except citizens of the US and the Ecowas West African community, require visas. These aren't available at the airport or the borders, so get them in advance. The price varies with your nationality and where you apply, so check around.

Visa Extensions

Visa extensions, which are valid for up to three months, are available from the *préfecture* in Le Plateau in Abidjan. They cost US$35 and can be processed the same day if you apply early.

Visas for Onward Travel

Visas for onward travel to Ghana (US$20 for 60 days, issued in 48 hours), Guinea (US$50 for 30 days, issued in 48 hours), Liberia (US$32 to US$40 for 30 days, issued the same day) and Mali (US$32 for 30 days, issued the same day) are available at embassies in Abidjan. See p366 for addresses of embassies.

CÔTE D'IVOIRE

Ghana

HIGHLIGHTS

- **Cape Coast** The dungeons inside the string of old coastal forts are a thought-provoking memorial to the slave trade (p381)
- **Kokrobite** On the sandy, palm-fringed beaches of Kokrobite you can chill out and drum with local musicians (p381)
- **Mole National Park** With baboons, antelopes and elephants marching past your window, this is Ghana's best wildlife reserve (p388)
- **Kumasi** The exquisite wooden sculptures of the fascinating Ashanti culture are on display in this ancient capital (p384)
- **Best journey** Take a boat trip up Lake Volta, the largest artificial lake in the world, and dance with the live band while admiring the rolling green hills (p389)
- **Off the beaten track** A boat ride along the Volta River into the hippo-infested Wechiau Community Hippo Sanctuary (p389)

FAST FACTS

- **Area** 238,537 sq km (about the size of Britain)
- **ATMs** in all big towns
- **Borders** Burkina Faso, Togo, Côte d'Ivoire
- **Budget** US$15 to US$20 per day
- **Capital** Accra
- **Languages** English, Twi, Ga, Ewe
- **Money** cedi; US$1 = C8500
- **Population** 19.8 million
- **Seasons** dry (Nov–Mar, Jul & Aug), wet (Apr–Jun, Sept & Oct); hot (Oct–May), cool (Jun–Sep)
- **Telephone** country code ☎ 233; international access code ☎ 00
- **Time** GMT/UTC
- **Visas** US$30 to US$60 single or multiple entry, required before arrival at all borders

Where do you begin when describing Ghana? It was home to West Africa's mightiest, gold-dripping empire; it was the first to drop colonialism and go it alone; it built the biggest artificial lake in the world; and it now produces some of Africa's best highlife music and most famous sculpture. Ghanaians have plenty to be proud of – and they know it. Yet you won't find a more chilled, stylish or polite people (they say 'sorry' even more than the British do!) who greet all foreigners with a genuine smile. So if you want to sample West Africa's modern and ancient cultures, explore its historic slave forts, toast yourself on its beautiful beaches – and do it all speaking English – it's got to be Ghana. They'll welcome you with open arms. '*Akwaaba*', as they say ('You are welcome').

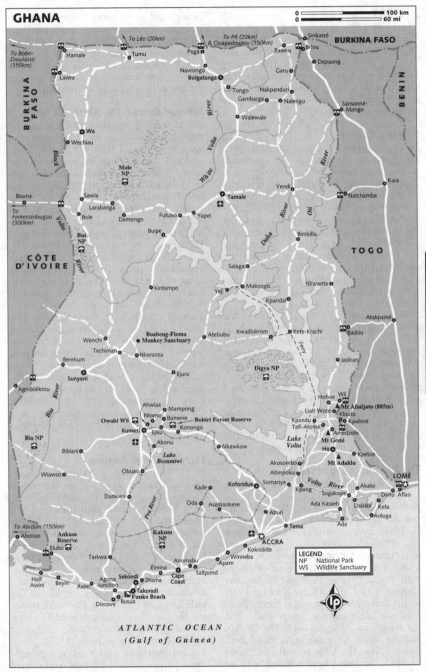

GHANA

GHANA

To Bobo-Dioulasso (150km)

BURKINA FASO

BURKINA FASO

CÔTE D'IVOIRE

CÔTE D'IVOIRE

TOGO

BENIN

Hamale
Lawra
Wa
Wechiau
Bouna
Sawla
Larabanga
Bole
Damongo
To Ferkessédougou (300km)

To Léo (20km)
Tumu
Paga
To Pô (20km) & Ouagadougou (150km)
Sinkassé
Bawku
Bitou
Garu
Dapaong
Navrongo
Bolgatanga
Tongo
Gambarga
Nakpanduri
Nalerigu
Sansanné-Mango
Walewale

Mole NP

White Volta
Black Volta
Volta River

Yendi
Natchamba
Kara

Tamale
Fufulso
Yapei
Buipe

Daka River
Oti River

Bimbilla

Bui NP

Volta River

Salaga

Kintampo
Yeji
Makongo
Kpandai
Nkwanta

Atakpamé

Boabeng-Fiema Monkey Sanctuary
Atebubu
Kwadiokrom
Kete-Krachi
Badou

Wenchi
Techiman
Nkoranza
Ejura

Digya NP

Ferry

Jasikan

Berekum
Sunyani
Agnibilékrou

Bia River

Ahwiaa
Mampong
Ntonso
Bonwire
Bobiri Forest Reserve
Owabi WS
Kumasi
Ejisu
Konongo
Abonu

Hohoe
Wli
Mt Afadjato (885m)
Liati Wote
Kpandu
Klouto
Kpalimé
Tafi-Atome
Amedzofe

Bia NP

Bibiani
Wiawso

Lake Bosumtwi

Nkawkaw

Lake Volta

Mt Gemi
Ho
Mt Adaklu
Kpetoe

LOMÉ

Obuasi

Pra River

Akosombo
Atimpoku
Volta River

Dunkwa
Kade
Oda
Asamankese
Aburi

Koforidua
Somanya
Kpong
Sogakope
Akatsi
Denu
Aflao
Dabala
Keta
Ada Kasseh
Anloga
Ada

To Abidjan (150km)
Aboisso
Elubo

Ankasa Reserve

Tarkwa
Kakum NP
Anomabu
Apam
Winneba
Saltpond

Kokrobite
ACCRA
Tema

Half Assini
Beyin
Axim
Agona Junction
Sekondi
Shama
Elmina
Cape Coast

Takoradi
Funko Beach
Busua
Dixcove

ATLANTIC OCEAN
(Gulf of Guinea)

LEGEND
NP   National Park
WS   Wildlife Sanctuary

0   100 km
0   60 mi

GHANA

HISTORY

There's now little to show for it, but present-day Ghana has been inhabited since 4000 BC, filled by successive waves of migrants from the north and east. By the 13th century several kingdoms had developed, growing rich from the country's massive gold deposits and gradually expanding south along the Volta River to the coast.

Power & Conflict

By the 16th century one of the kingdoms, the Ashanti, emerged as the dominant power, conquering tribes left, right and centre and taking control of trade routes to the coast. Its capital, Kumasi, became a sophisticated urban centre, with facilities and services equal to those in Europe at the time. And it wasn't long until the Europeans discovered this African kingdom. First the Portuguese came sniffing around the coast, and then came the British, French, Dutch, Swedes and Danes. They all built forts by the sea and traded slaves, gold and other goods with the Ashanti.

But the slave trade was abolished in the 19th century, and with it went the Ashanti's domination. By that time the British had taken over the Gold Coast, as the area had become called, and began muscling in on Ashanti turf. This sparked several wars between the two powers, which culminated in the British ransacking of Kumasi in 1874. The British then established a protectorate over Ashanti territory, which they expanded in 1901 to include areas to the north. The Gold Coast was now a British colony.

The Road to Independence

By the late 1920s the locals were itching for independence, and they set up political parties dedicated to this aim. However, parties like the United Gold Coast Convention (UGCC), formed in 1947, were too elitist and detached from those they were meant to represent – the ordinary workers. So the UGCC's secretary-general, Kwame Nkrumah, broke away in 1948 and formed the Conventional People's Party (CPP) in 1948, which became an overnight success. Nkrumah was impatient for change and called for a national strike in 1949. The British, anxious about his popularity, jailed him. Despite this, the CPP won the elections of 1951, Nkrumah was released and he became prime minister. When Ghana finally won its independence in March 1957, Nkrumah became the first president of an independent African nation. His speeches, which denounced imperialism and talked about a free, united Africa, made him the darling of the Pan-African movement.

Independence & the Nkrumah Years

But back home Nkrumah was not popular among traditional chiefs and farmers who were unimpressed with the idea of unity under his rule. Factionalism and regional interests created an opposition that Nkrumah tried to contain through repressive laws, and by turning Ghana into a one-party state.

Nkrumah, however, skilfully kept himself out of the fray and concentrated on building prestige projects, such as the Akosombo Dam and several universities and hospitals.

But things started to unravel. Nkrumah expanded his personal bodyguard into an entire regiment, while corruption and reckless spending drove the country into serious debt. Nkrumah, seemingly oblivious to his growing unpopularity, made the fatal mistake of going on a state visit to China in 1966. While he was away his regime was toppled in an army coup. Nkrumah died six years later in exile in Guinea.

Dr Kofi Busia headed a civilian government in 1969, but could do nothing to overcome the corruption and debt problems. Colonel Acheampong replaced him in a 1972 coup, but few things changed under his tenure.

Jerry Rawlings' Regime

By 1979 Ghana was suffering food shortages and people were out on the streets demonstrating against the army 'fat cats'. Jerry Rawlings came onto the scene – a good-looking, charismatic, half-Scottish air force pilot who kept cigarettes behind his ear and spoke the language of the people. Nicknamed 'Junior Jesus', Rawlings caught the public's imagination with his calls for corrupt military rulers to be confronted and held accountable for Ghana's problems. The military jailed him for his insubordination, but his fellow junior officers freed him after they staged an uprising. Rawlings' Armed Forces Revolutionary Council (AFRC) then handed over power to a civilian government (after a general election) and started a major 'house-cleaning' operation – that is, executing and jailing senior officers.

The new president, Hilla Limann, was uneasy with Rawlings' huge popularity, and later accused him of trying to subvert constitutional rule. The AFRC toppled him in a coup in 1981, and this time Rawlings stayed in power for the next 15 years.

Although Rawlings never delivered his promised left-wing revolution, he improved the ailing economy after following the orders of the International Monetary Fund (IMF). During part of the 1980s Ghana enjoyed Africa's highest economic growth rates.

The Democratic Era

By 1992, Rawlings was under worldwide pressure to introduce democracy, so he lifted the 10-year ban on political parties and called a general election. However, the hopelessly divided opposition couldn't get their act together, and Rawlings won the 1992 elections freely and fairly, with 60% of the vote. Still licking their wounds, the opposition withdrew from the following month's parliamentary elections, giving Rawlings' newly formed National Democratic Congress (NDC) an easy victory. In 1996 he repeated this triumph in elections that were again considered free and fair.

Post-Rawlings

In 2000, having reached the end of his two-term limit, Rawlings stepped down as NDC leader. His deputy, John Atta Mills, took over and contested the elections that same year, only to be defeated by John Kufuor, leader of the New Patriotic Party (NPP).

Kufuor, a mild-mannered, Oxford-educated lawyer known as the 'Gentle Giant', continued Rawlings' liberal economic policies and accepted a debt-relief scheme designed by the IMF. The subsequent removal of fuel subsidies sent petrol prices rocketing by 60%. Despite this rocky start, Kufuor's party remains popular. In 2002 the president inaugurated a South Africa-style truth and reconciliation commission to look into human rights abuses committed mainly under Rawlings' military rule. It is alleged that some 300 people 'disappeared' under that regime. Whether this investigation will heal the wounds of the past remains to be seen.

THE CULTURE
The National Psyche

There's an Ashanti saying: 'If you have something to say about me, first let me give you a stool to sit down'. That pretty much sums up the Ghanaian psyche. No need for fights, no need to disturb the peace – life is far too short for arguments.

Ghanaians are big on politeness, and no interaction is complete without a friendly greeting or a handshake (followed by the snapping of index fingers). Even the bus drivers are known to greet their customers at the start of journeys and the passengers reciprocate in a chorus.

Some might say that it's this politeness and calmness that has anchored Ghana through some pretty turbulent political times. Ethnic violence may have flared up recently in the north, but these incidences are a rarity in a country that has never collapsed into civil war – due partly to the fact that nearly 25% of the country was literate at the time of independence (compared to Mozambique's 1%). Such high levels of education have also spawned a free and vibrant press (replete with that special brand of Ghanaian English), where lively TV and radio talk shows discuss football and government corruption with equal fervour. No subject is taboo, which is why you'll feel the AIDS awareness campaign more strongly here than in most countries: even the major music stars sing about the virtues of safe sex. For more information see the boxed text on p27.

Lifestyle

If there's one feature of Ghanaian society that sticks out more than any other, it is religion. The country is 15% Muslim, 70% Christian and 100% obsessed with spiritual worship. This is the land of glory, gold and God, after all, and God is *everywhere*: 'God is Love Hair Salon', 'Jesus Loves Me Forex Bureau' and 'Forgiveness Communications' are just some of the pious names emblazoned across shop fronts in every town and city.

But that's not to say they can't have fun. Ghanaians will find any excuse to dance, and even the most sedate boat rides can turn into a massive party as young men and old grannies gyrate their hips to highlife rhythms. Ghanaians have produced

AKAN NAMES

After spending a couple of weeks in Ghana, you'll be wondering why half the men and women seem to have the same first names. This is because the Akan people (including the Ashanti and Ewe) name their new babies after the day of the week they were born. After eight days the parents give them a middle name, which is often the same name as an ancestor or senior relative.

Monday Kwadwo (male); Adwoa, (female)

Tuesday Kwabena (male); Abena (female)

Wednesday Kwaku (male); Akua (female)

Thursday Yao (male); Yaa (female)

Friday Kofi (male); Afua (female)

Saturday Kwame (male); Ama (female)

Sunday Kwasi (male); Akosua (female)

some of Africa's best and most well-known musicians and filmmakers, and this vibrant arts scene is a reflection of a society that is more culturally self-confident than most. Whether it's music, film, or exquisite Ashanti woodcarvings, Ghanaian products (and imitations of them) are scattered all over West Africa.

The ancient traditions of the Ashanti culture are particularly resilient and still going strong despite centuries of foreign influence.

The extended family is the foundation of a society that is unusually matrilineal, ie people belong to their mother's clan. But this has not necessarily created an equal society. Women's rights still have some way to go (particularly in the Muslim north and animist areas), although there is a relatively healthy representation of females in government and business.

ENVIRONMENT

Much of Ghana's terrain consists of wooded ranges, wide valleys and low-lying coastal plains. The damming of the Volta River in the mid-1960s created the world's largest artificial lake.

In the humid, southern coastal region the rainy seasons are from April to June and September and October. In the drier north, the rainy season lasts from April

to October. Temperatures are around 30°C throughout the year.

Logging, mining, the use of wood fuels and deforestation for agriculture have reduced Ghana's forests from over 8 million sq km in the early 20th century to less than 2million sq km now. Marine and coastal areas are threatened by high erosion and population concentration.

Population densities are highest within the Accra-Kumasi-Takoradi triangle, largely because of the timber-producing deciduous forests and cocoa-growing lands, which stimulate economic productivity.

On the other hand the Volta Basin is generally sparsely populated because of relatively infertile soil and scarcity of water during the harmattan season.

Out of Ghana's five national parks and nine protected areas, Mole National Park is the best place to see protected wildlife, including elephants, baboons and antelopes. Kakum National Park, just north of Cape Coast, is famous for its canopy walkway and is a good place to see rainforest habitat and birdlife. Bui National Park and the Wechiau Community Hippo Sanctuary are both relatively new and up-and-coming places to see hippos.

TRANSPORT

GETTING THERE & AWAY
Air
Ghana Airways, British Airways, KLM, South African Airlines, Alitalia and Lufthansa all have flights from Europe into Ghana. Ghana Airways also has flights from New York, while South Africa Airways links Ghana with Perth in Australia, via Johannesburg.

Regional airlines flying into Accra include Ghana Airways, Ethiopian Airlines and Air Ivoire, which have flights between Accra and the following cities (see p380 for airline contact information):

Abidjan (Côte D'Ivoire) Ghana Airways: US$170, one hour, five times a week; Air Ivoire: US$180, one hour, four times a week.

Cotonou (Benin) Ghana Airways: US$US170, one hour, weekly.

Lagos (Nigeria) Ethiopian Airlines: US$190; 50 minutes, twice a week.

Lomé (Togo) Ethiopian Airlines: US$140, 35 minutes, weekly.

Land

BURKINA FASO

The easiest way to enter Burkina Faso is via the border crossing at Paga. This is on the main road between Tamale and Ouagadougou, which is a safe and popular route. Regular transport from Accra, Kumasi and Bolgatanga passes here throughout the day.

A direct STC bus runs daily from Accra to Ouagadougou (US$11, 24 hours). *Tro-tros* from Bolgatanga regularly go to the border at Paga (US$0.90, 40 minutes), from where you can get onward transport to Po, 15km beyond the border, and Ouagadougou.

The other border crossing at Hamale is much harder to reach and cross because of scarce public transport.

You can also enter Burkina Faso from the northwest corner of Ghana, crossing between Tumu and Léo. Tumu can be most easily reached from Bolgatanga, but it's not as popular a crossing as Po.

CÔTE D'IVOIRE

The main border crossing is at Elubo on the main coastal road between Accra and Abidjan. Buses to the Ghana border post run from Accra via numerous coastal towns. At the border you'll have to walk across to the Côte d'Ivoire side (about 1km) and get onward transport from there.

Another border crossing lies between Bole and Bouna, though this involves a chartered canoe trip across the Black Volta River.

TOGO

The coastal border crossing at Aflao, just 2km west of Lomé, is by far the easiest and most popular, with dozens of vehicles plying the road. The border stays open until 10pm, but if you need a visa make sure you cross between 9am and 6pm. Public transport from Ghana doesn't actually cross the border, but stops 1km away at a parking station. From there you'll have to lug your baggage along the sandy road to the Ghana and Togo border posts (which are side by side), then another 2km into Lomé. If you don't want to walk, you can catch a taxi from the Togo side of the border into Lomé city centre.

GETTING AROUND

Air

At the time of research there were no domestic flights operating in Ghana.

Boat

The passenger boat **Yapei Queen** (☎ 021 665300) is a nice alternative to road travel (US$17/5 in 1st/2nd class, 24 hours, weekly) and departs 4am on Monday. It travels up Lake Volta from Akosombo and Yeji, passing through rolling hills and stopping at a few towns along the way (food and drinks are available on board). It makes the reverse journey on Wednesday. Try to book two weeks in advance as it's a popular form of transport.

Local Transport

STC runs the best bus service in the country. It has reliable, frequent and very popular services between the major centres in Ghana, including Accra, Kumasi, Takoradi, Cape Coast, Tamale and Bolgatanga among other places. Other companies include OSA and Kingdom Transport Services, which have cheaper fares but their buses are usually older and not as comfortable as STC's.

Minibuses, or *tro-tros*, as they're called, are the main form of transport around Ghana and connect every town daily.

Bush taxis are five-seater cars that run along the same routes as *tro-tros*. They fill up faster, but are slightly more expensive.

Hitching is possible, although public transport frequently runs along all main and secondary roads. If you find yourself in a remote rural area, you'll have to hope that the occasional mammy wagon (pick-up truck converted to carry passengers) comes along.

Train

Ghana's railway links Accra, Kumasi and Takoradi. At the time of writing the train system was suspended indefinitely. If normal service resumes a train from Accra to Kumasi should travel every evening in both directions (1st/2nd class US$2.50/2, 12 hours) but there is no sleeper. Between Accra and Takoradi (1st/2nd class US$2.50/2, 12 hours) a train also travels in both directions every evening, with a 1st/2nd-class sleeper (around US$3). Between Kumasi and

GHANA

Takoradi two trains travel daily in both directions (around US$2.50/2 in 1st/2nd class; US$3/1.50 with sleeper, eight to 11 hours).

ACCRA

☎ 021 / pop 2 million

Accra is a city of contrasts: vibrant shantytowns rub shoulders with suburbia's leafy avenues, and chop bars and food stalls vie with pizza joints and ice-cream parlours. Chauffeur-driven cars edge through streets congested with market stalls; immaculately coiffed women dressed in exquisite fabrics glide along dusty streets lined with sewers; and charismatic church services compete with lively nightclubs in the midnight noise stakes. There's not much for the traveller to do here, but what Accra lacks in sightseeing it makes up for in charm, great nightlife and the friendliest people.

Originally Accra was a scattering of villages controlled by Ga chiefs, who granted the Europeans trading rights at the ports. The Ga eventually lost control of these rights to the Ashanti, who were in turn overcome by the British in 1877. That same year Accra became the capital of the Gold Coast colony.

ORIENTATION

The action area of Accra is bounded by the West, Central and East Ring Rds, whose four major circles (roundabouts) and interchanges are Lamptey, Nkrumah, Sankara and Danquah. South of Danquah Circle lies Osu, the liveliest area. The commercial district extends along Nkrumah Ave (which runs south from Nkrumah Circle) through Adabraka, the budget hotel area.

Kotoka International Airport lies 3.5km northwest of the city centre. As soon as your flight arrives here you'll be ushered into a comfortable, private (or 'dropping') taxi, which has a fixed rate of US$7 for trips to central Accra. For a cheaper option, head to the small station within the airport where *tro-tros* (minibuses) and shared taxis (around US$0.50) depart for town.

INFORMATION
Bookshops
Books For Less (Map p375; ☎ 770770; 17th Lane) The best range of second-hand novels and nonfiction.
EPP Books (Map p376; ☎ 778347; Kinbu Rd)

Cultural Centres
Alliance Française (Map p375; ☎ 773134; alliance@ghana.com; Liberation Link) Local dance and theatre performances every Wednesday night.
Public Affairs, US Embassy (Map p375; ☎ 229179; African Liberation Square, off Independence Ave)

Internet Access
Internet centres have mushroomed all over Accra. A few of them have very fast connection. They usually charge around US$1 per hour.

Libraries
The **British Council Library** (Map p376; ☎ 244744; www.britishcouncil.org; Liberia Rd) is open to the public and holds British newspapers and magazines.

Media
Accra Life Quarterly is an entertainment listings magazine published by the Accra Visitor Centre and distributed through Accra's *Daily Mail*.

Medical Services
North Ridge Clinic (Map p375; ☎ 227328; eastern end of Ring Rd Central) Offers a general practitioner service.
37 Military Hospital (Map p375; ☎ 776111; near 37 Circle on Liberation Ave) Recommended for traumatic injuries.
The Trust Hospital (Map p375; ☎ 776787; Cantonments Rd) Has a laboratory if you need a medical test.

Money
Barclays Bank (Map p376; ☎ 228720; Nkrumah Ave, near Nkrumah Circle)
Standard Chartered Bank (Map p376; ☎ 669777; Liberia Rd) It is marked as No.18 on the Central Accra map.

Accra has dozens of forex (foreign exchange) bureaus, including:
Blessed Lady Forex Bureau (Map p376; ☎ 228159; Farrar Ave; ☽ 8.30am-5pm Mon-Fri)
City Main Forex Bureau Ltd (Map p376; ☎ 232368; Kojo Thompson Rd; ☽ 8.30am-5pm Mon-Fri)

Post & Telephone
The **Central Post Office** (Map p376; Lutterodt Intersection; ☽ 8am-5pm Mon-Fri, 9am-2pm Sat) has a reliable poste restante service; there's another branch on Nsawam Rd, just north of Nkrumah Circle.

The main telephone office is at **Ghana Telecom** (Map p376; High St; ☽ 7am-8pm), or you

ACCRA

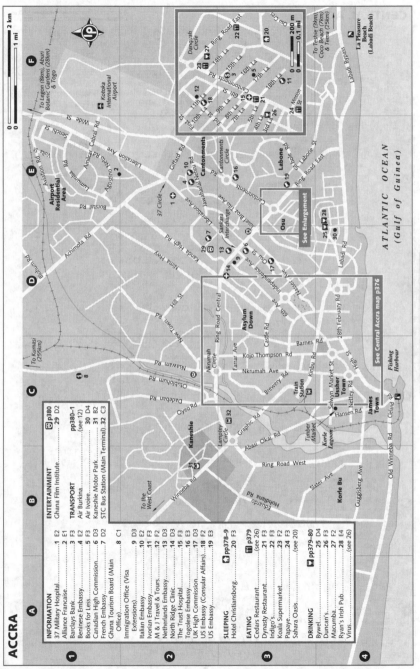

INFORMATION
37 Military Hospital...........................	1 E2
Alliance Française..............................	2 E1
Barclays Bank...................................	3 F3
Beninese Embassy.............................	4 E2
Books for Less..................................	5 F3
Canadian High Commission...............	6 D3
French Embassy................................	7 D2
Ghana Tourism Board (Main	
Office)...	8 C1
Immigration Office (Visa	
Extensions)..................................	9 D3
Italian Embassy................................	10 E2
Ivorian Embassy...............................	11 F3
M & J Travel & Tours........................	12 F2
Netherlands Embassy........................	13 D3
North Ridge Clinic............................	14 D3
The Trust Hospital............................	15 F3
Togolese Embassy............................	16 E3
UK High Commission........................	17 D3
US Embassy (Consular Affairs)......	18 F2
US Embassy.....................................	19 E3

SLEEPING 🛏 pp378–9
Hotel Christiansborg........................	20 F3

EATING 🍴 p379
Cedars Restaurant......................	(see 26)
Dynasty Restaurant.........................	21 F3
Indigo's..	22 F3
Koala Supermarket..........................	23 F2
Papaye...	24 F3
Sahara Oasis.................................	(see 20)

DRINKING 🍺 pp379–80
Bywel..	25 D4
Duncan's..	26 F3
Macumba.......................................	27 F2
Ryan's Irish Pub..............................	28 E4
Virus..	(see 26)

ENTERTAINMENT 🎬 p380
Ghana Film Institute........................	29 D2

TRANSPORT pp380–1
Air Burkina.....................................	(see 12)
Air Ivoire..	30 D4
Kaneshie Motor Park.......................	31 B2
STC Bus Station (Main Terminal).....	32 C3

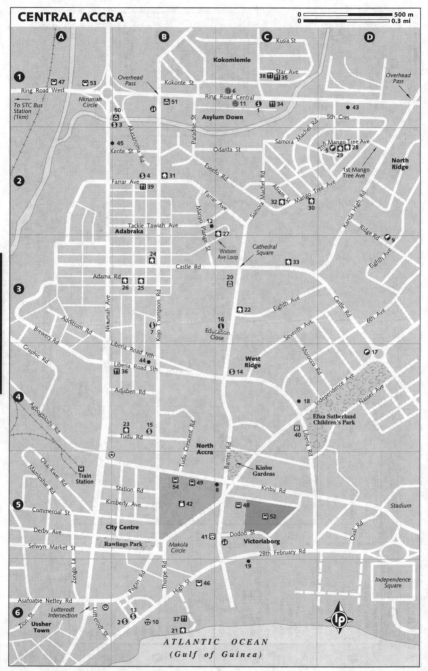

CENTRAL ACCRA

0 — 500 m
0 — 0.3 mi

Kokomlemle

Kusia St

Star Ave
38 35

Ring Road West
47   53

Overhead Pass

Kokonte St

Nkrumah Circle

Ring Road Central
@ 6
@ 11

Asylum Down

43

5th Cres

To STC Bus Station (1km)

51

50
3

Paradise St

Akaatonia Rd

Samora Machel Rd

2nd Mango Tree Ave
5   28
29

North Ridge

45
Kente St

Odanta St

Eseefo Rd

1st Mango Tree Ave

Kanda High Rd

4   31
Farrar Ave
39

Mango Plange St

Farrar Ave

Samora Machel Rd

Afram St

Mango Tree Ave

32

30

Ridge Rd
9

Tackie Tawiah Ave
Adabraka

12
27

Watson Ave Loop

Cathedral Square

Eighth Ave

24

Castle Rd

33

Castle Rd

6th Ave

Adama Rd
26   25

Nkrumah Ave

Kojo Thompson Rd

20

Additrom Rd

22

Eighth Ave

7

16
Education Close

Seventh Ave

Morocco Rd

Brewery Rd

Graphic Rd

Liberia Road Nth.

44

Liberia Road Sth
36

West Ridge

14

17

Independence Ave

Nasser Ave

Adjaben Rd

Agbogbloshi Rd

18

Efua Sutherland Children's Park

40

Liberia Rd

23   15
Tudu Rd

Tudu Crescent Rd

North Accra

Barnes Rd

Kinbu Gardens

Okai-Kwei Rd

Mamleshie Rd

Train Station

Station Rd
54   49
8

Kinbu Rd

Stadium

Commercial St

Kimberly Ave

42

48

52

Oval Rd

City Centre

Derby Ave

Rawlings Park

41

Dodoo St

Victoriaborg

Selwyn Market St

Makola Circle

28th February Rd

19

Zongo La

Pagan Rd

Thorpe Rd

High St

46

Independence Square

Asafoatse Nettey Rd

Lutterodt Intersection

Zion St

Ussher Town

Lutterodt St

13

2   10

37

21

ATLANTIC OCEAN
(Gulf of Guinea)

GHANA

INFORMATION		SLEEPING	pp378–9	ENTERTAINMENT	p380
Accra Visitor Centre	1 C1	Akuma Village	21 B6	National Theatre	40 C4
Barclays Bank (Head Office)	2 B6	Calvary Methodist Church Guest		Rex Cinema	41 B5
Barclays Bank	3 B1	House	22 C3		
Blessed Lady Forex Bureau	4 B2	Casa Nova Hotel	23 B4	SHOPPING	p380
Burkinabé Embassy	5 D2	Crown Prince Hotel	24 B3	Makola Market	42 B5
Busy Internet	6 C1	Date Hotel	25 B3		
City Main Forex Bureau	7 B3	Ghasom Hotel	26 B3	TRANSPORT	pp380–1
EPP Books	8 C5	Hotel de California	27 C2	Alitalia Office	43 D1
German Embassy	9 D3	Korkdam Hotel	28 D2	British Airways Office	44 B4
Ghana Telecom	10 B6	Lemon Lodge Hotel	29 D2	Ethiopian Airlines	45 A2
Mega Internet	11 C1	Mavis Hotel	30 C2	Labadi Lorry Park	46 B6
Speedway Travel & Tours	12 B2	Niagara Hotel	31 B2	Lufthansa Office	(see 43)
Standard Chartered Bank (Head Office)	13 B6	Times Square Lodge	32 C2	Neoplan Motor Park	47 A1
Standard Chartered Bank	14 C4	YMCA	33 C3	New Tema Station	48 C5
Standard Chartered Bank	15 B4			South African Airways Office	(see 43)
Tourist Office	16 C3	EATING	p379	STC Bus Station	
US Embassy, Public Affairs Section	17 D4	Assanka	34 C1	(to Ho and Aflao)	49 B5
		Champs Bar	35 C1	Taxi Station (for Labadi Beach)	50 B1
SIGHTS & ACTIVITIES	pp377–8	Elbi's Snack Bar	36 B4	Taxi Stop (to Labadi & Osu)	51 B1
British Council	18 C4	Home Point	37 B6	Tema Station	52 C5
Centre for National Culture	19 C6	Tasha Food	38 C1	Tro-Tro Park	53 A1
National Museum	20 C3	White Bell	39 B2	Tudu Station	54 B5

can make international calls can be made from one of the plethora of 'communication centres' around Accra.

Tourist Offices

Accra Visitor Centre (Map p376; ☎ 252186; Ring Rd Central; ☒ 8.30am-5pm Mon-Fri, 9am-1pm Sat) The young, friendly staff have travel information, plus the low-down on entertainment.

Tourist office (Map p376; ☎ 231817; Education Close, off Barnes Rd; ☒ 8am-4pm Mon-Fri) Has leaflets and some useful phone numbers, otherwise not a lot of practical information.

Travel Agencies

The following companies can organise international flights:

M & J Travel & Tours (Map p375; ☎ 236899; 11th Lane, Osu)

Speedway Travel & Tours (Map p376; ☎ 227744; Tacki Tawiah Ave)

DANGERS & ANNOYANCES

Accra is a very safe city to travel around. If you're on foot, dodging oncoming traffic as you cross the street is probably the most significant hazard you'll face.

As in any big city, be careful with valuables as there are pickpockets in busy areas such as the markets and bus stations. Also take care around Nkrumah Circle, James Town and Independence Square after dark.

SIGHTS & ACTIVITIES

National Museum (Map p376; ☎ 221633; Barnes Rd; admission US$1.20, camera fee US$0.60; ☒ 9am-6pm) This is a real eye-opener for those who know little about Ghanaian or West African

ethnography, history and art. The huge display includes royal stools, state umbrellas, swords, *akyeamepoma* (linguists' staves) and weights used by Ashanti goldsmiths for measuring gold. The whole place can be overwhelming, so perhaps do it in bits if you want to see the whole lot.

Centre for National Culture (Map p376; ☎ 602581; 28th February Rd; ☒ 9am-5pm) Also known as the 'Arts Centre', this place has an art gallery featuring a permanent national display, plus contemporary artists' work for sale. The maze of craft stalls sells beautiful wooden sculptures and beaded jewellery – prepare yourself for intense selling. Every Saturday the centre's '*Anansekrom*' programme (admission US$1) lays on drumming, dancing, drama, poetry and puppetry.

But for a dose of reality, take yourself to the corrugated shacks of James Town and see how the majority of Accra lives. A climb to the top of the old **lighthouse** there will give you great views of the city (smog and haze permitting). From the lighthouse walk back to the centre along Cleland Rd and find someone to take you around the **Timber Market**. The market's fetish section is full of *juju* (priests or priestesses who communicate with spirits) figurines, leopard skins and porcupine quills.

Akuma Village (see p378) is a hive of cultural activity and offers drumming, dance and lessons in *capoeira* (Afro-Brazilian martial art).

On Saturday and Sunday the whole of Accra seems to congregate on **Labadi beach** (La Pleasure beach; admission US$0.60), east of Accra.

GHANA

Sun-worshipping bodies lie on the sand and highlife tunes blare out from the outdoor cafés while boys with glistening pecs play football. The beach is between the luxury Labadi Beach hotel and La Palm Royal Beach Hotel, and is a 15-minute ride from Adabraka or the Labadi truck station to the eastern edge of Accra.

If you want to chill out without getting sand up your backside, sit among the palms and shrubs in the cool, relaxing **Aburi Botanic Gardens** (admission US$0.70; 🕑 8am-6pm). They were laid out by the British in the 1890s and are located about 35km northeast of Accra. At the southern entrance to the gardens you'll find **Aburi Bike Tours** (☎ 024 267 303; www.aburibike.ch), who offer hikes and cycling tours through bush and forested lands, remote Aburi villages and the colonial-style houses in the area.

SLEEPING
Most travellers wanting budget accommodation usually end up in the Adabraka district, where they can expect basic, cheerless rooms. But there are some much better options to be had.

Asylum Down
Times Square Lodge (Map p376; ☎ 222694; cnr Mango Tree Ave & Afram St; d US$5) It doesn't get better than this: bright, spotless rooms with fan and a shared bathroom that you won't dread using. Excellent value for money.

Lemon Lodge Hotel (Map p376; ☎ 227857; 2nd Mango Tree Ave; d US$6) Gorgeous pink and yellow exterior has contrastingly dull but clean rooms. Popular for good reason.

Korkdam Hotel (Map p376; ☎ 226797; www.kork damhotel.com; 2nd Mango Tree Ave; s/d US$7/9; 🖳) The bland rooms may have ancient carpets and lousy soundproofing, but this popular place is charming and clean enough to keep the guests coming.

Mavis Hotel (Map p376; ☎ 225426; Mango Tree Ave; s/d US$6/7) Clean but dull rooms with fan. There's a restaurant attached.

West Ridge
Calvary Methodist Church Guest House (Map p376; ☎ 234507; Barnes Rd; s/d US$4/7) Clearly cleanliness is godliness in this great-value guesthouse. Spotless rooms come with balconies and meals are available throughout the day. Make sure you behave yourself, though.

YMCA (Map p376; ☎ 224700; Castle Rd; dm US$1.20) Basic, cheap but clean dorms with a boarding-school feel.

Adabraka
Date Hotel (Map p376; ☎ 228200; Adama Rd; s/d US$3.70/ 4-5) This is one of the best options in Accra, with big, fresh rooms, clean bathrooms and a shady terrace bar and restaurant.

Ghasom Hotel (Map p376; ☎ 223876; Adama Rd; s/d US$4/4.50) This is a good alternative if the Date Hotel is full. The downstairs rooms are fresh with spotless bathrooms, but avoid the upstairs rooms.

Casa Nova Hotel (Map p376; ☎ 660536; Tudu Rd; s/d US$6/7) Formerly known as Gasotel, it's a matter of new name but the same old rooms (which let in lots of street noise). It's in a central location, though.

Crown Prince Hotel (Map p376; ☎ 225381; Castle Rd; s/d US$5/8) There's nothing princely about the somewhat dreary rooms and the shared facilities, but they are clean enough.

Hotel de California (Map p376; ☎ 226199; 11 Watson Loop Ave; s/d US$5/10) It's moved to a new location, so the rooms with fan and blue-felt carpets are clean, but the water supply still needs some work.

Osu
Hotel Christiansborg (Map p375; ☎ 776074; Dadebu Rd; s/d US$10/12) The huge rooms come with bathroom, a sitting area and a TV. One of the few cheap options in the lively Osu area, this is a real bargain. The downstairs restaurant (Sahara Oasis, see opposite) is fabulous.

City Centre
Akuma Village (Map p376; ☎ 660573; off High St; camp site per person s/d US$2/5/6) 'No herb smoking' signs hang everywhere, but there's still plenty of fun to be had at this lively hotel. Perched on a cliff overlooking the ocean,

> **SPLURGE!**
>
> **Niagara Hotel** (Map p376; ☎ 230118; Kojo Thompson Rd, Adabraka; s/d US$66/88) No more cold showers, no more old bed sheets, no more standing in the 'ski position' over the toilet. After weeks of budget trauma, the comfortable, modern rooms and the fantastic Lebanese restaurant is all the therapy you need.

the very basic rooms are clean, as are the shared showers and toilets.

Outside Accra

Olyander Guest House (☎ 0876 22058; d US$5-12) About 100m up the hill from the northern gates of the Aburi Botanic Gardens (see opposite) you'll find the peaceful, homely Olyander, which offers great meals.

EATING

When it comes to varied and delicious cuisine, Accra knows how to lay it on. The Adabraka neighbourhood is teeming with eateries serving delicious *fufu* (mashed cassava), *kenkey* (fermented maize meal) and *jollof* (West African paella). And after a week-long 'restaurant crawl' along Cantonment Rd in Osu you'll have sampled dishes ranging from Ghanaian, Ethiopian, Chinese and Mexican to Lebanese and Ivorian. There are also all the burger joints that exist to satisfy the local penchant for fast food.

African

For cheap local food head to the stalls that spring up around the transport terminals, Danquah Circle and Nkrumah Circle, where *fufu* dishes go for well under US$1.

White Bell (Map p376; Farrar Ave; mains US$2) A travellers' favourite, this upstairs restaurant has huge, tasty burgers and Ghanaian dishes that will have you walking out belly-first.

Sahara Oasis (Map p375; ☎ 776074; Dadebu Rd; mains US$2-3) This busily decorated restaurant is attached to the Christiansborg Hotel and serves generous portions of well prepared Ghanaian food.

Assanka (Map p376; Ring Rd Central; mains US$2) Accra's beautiful people congregate here at lunchtime for mouthwatering Ghanaian meals.

Home Point (Map p376; mains US$0.70) For those staying at Akuma Village, this is a great, nearby place for rice and fish dishes at rock-bottom prices.

Tasha Food (Map p376; Star Ave, Kokomlemle; mains US$1-2) Tucked away behind Ring Rd Central, this gem serves up full English breakfasts (sausages, at last!) as well as excellent Ghanaian dishes.

Elbi's Snack Bar (Map p376; ☎ 222718; Liberia Rd Sth, Adabraka; US$1) An old favourite with the locals, who bunch up at shared tables to get a lunchtime seat. The Ghanaian dishes are seriously flavoursome and ridiculously cheap.

Lebanese

Cedars Restaurant (Map p375; ☎ 782236; off Cantonments Rd; mains US$2-3) The wine rack and red tablecloths give this restaurant a classy feel, but the delicious Lebanese dishes are easily affordable.

Mexican

Champs Bar (Map p376; ☎ 228937; Paloma Hotel, Ring Rd Central; US$3) As if the wide-screen TV and comfortable pub seats weren't enough, the Mexican dishes here are simply awesome.

Vegetarian

Indigo's (Map p375; Ring Rd East, near Danquah Circle; US$2.50-7) With modern, colourful decor, Indigo's classy African dishes are pricey but there are pizzas and vegetarian dishes.

Western

Papaye (Map p375; cnr Cantonments Rd & Mission St, Osu) This is the place to eat burgers, fries and excellent charcoal-grilled chicken while watching the street below.

Self-Catering

Koala Supermarket (Map p375; ☎ 773455; cnr Cantonment Rd & 14th Lane) Extremely well stocked.

SPLURGE!

Dynasty Restaurant (Map p375; ☎ 775496; Cantonments Rd; mains US$10-15) The succulent Beijing dishes at this grand restaurant are worth the indignity of arriving wearing your last clean T-shirt.

DRINKING

Ghanaians love their booze, and practically every street in Accra seems to have places that start the day as a restaurant but transform into a bar at night.

Duncan's (Map p375; off Cantonments Rd; ☯ noon-10pm) Locals and expats pile into this popular bar to guzzle as many Bubra beers as possible, and to scoff even more kebabs, before the early closing time.

Bywel (Map p375; Abebresem St, off Cantonments Rd) On Thursday night it feels like half of

Accra has squeezed itself into the open-air courtyard for drinks and live entertainment (check out its nightly programme on the wall outside).

Ryan's Irish Pub (Map p375; off Cantonments Rd) The draught Guinness (unique in Ghana), large garden bar area and weekend live music make this a long-time favourite with expats.

Akuma Village (see p378) doubles as a happening drinking spot with live music every evening, including reggae on Friday.

CLUBBING

Accra livens up on Friday, Saturday and Sunday when the whole city lives out its 'highlife' aspirations. Osu is the centre of the action and things rarely get going until after 11pm. Most clubs have a cover charge of around US$3. You may be offered cocaine, lots of sex, smuggled gold and other deals – most best refused.

Macumba (Map p375; Ring Rd East, off Danquah Circle; entry US$3.50) One of Accra's longest-standing clubs, it still attracts a large European crowd with its mix of disco, techno, hip-life and R & B.

Virus (Map p375; next to Duncan's, off Cantonments Rd; US$3) Accra's newest and trendiest hangout that's popular with the both local and expat crowds.

Indigo's (Map p375; Ring Rd East, Danquah Circle; US$3.50) Take advantage of the free appetizers and occasional free entry for the ladies at this stylish joint beneath the restaurant.

ENTERTAINMENT

Accra hosts regular live music and theatre events featuring artists from around West Africa. For more information on what's going on, pick up a copy of *Accra Life Quarterly* magazine (see p374).

Theatre

Alliance Française (Map p375; Liberation Link) On Wednesday night people sit on the lawns here eating kebabs and popcorn while drinking and watching local performances.

National Theatre (Map p376; ☎ 663449; Liberia Rd) Regular dances and plays by West African playwrights, plus the new Ghana Jazz Heritage Festival held every February.

Cinemas

There is a handful of cinemas around town, including:

Busy Internet (Map p376; ☎ 258800; Ring Rd Central; admission US$1.20) Airs recent Hollywood movies on a wide screen DVD with surround sound from Friday to Sunday.

Rex Cinema (Map p376; Barnes Rd; admission US$1) Shows recent US releases.

Ghana Film Institute (Map p375; ☎ 228697; admission US$0.60) Plays Ghanaian and Nigerian films twice daily.

SHOPPING

Even a seasoned traveller can be overwhelmed by the size and energy of **Makola Market** (Map p376). Thousands of stalls have taken over the streets, making cars seem like intruders on the scene. As you get swept along by eddying currents of people, the market passes you by in a blur of pumpkin-sized bras, hair extensions, gaudy fake gold trinkets, piles of second-hand shoes, and the aroma of smoked fish and roast plantain. The vendors here take haggling very seriously, and the ensuing battle of wills might leave you exhausted (and a little bit poorer than you expected!).

GETTING THERE & AWAY

Air

Ghana Airways (☎ 221000; White Ave) and other airlines have flights into Accra's Kotoka International Airport, located about 2km from the city centre. **Ethiopian Airlines** (Map p376; ☎ 664857; Cocoa House, Nkrumah Ave) and **Air Ivoire** (Map p375; ☎ 761717; Sotrec Building, Abrebesem St) also have offices in Accra.

Local Transport

STC (Map p375; ☎ 221414) runs a daily service to Aflao at the Ghana-Togo border (US$2.60) from its station just north of Makola Market. Another local company is **KTS** (☎ 231 493; Ring Rd West).

From the main STC station in Kaneshie, buses leave for towns such as Kumasi, Cape Coast, Takoradi, Tamale and Bolgatanga. For Ho and Aflao, STC buses leave from the smaller station next to the Tudu bus station.

Other buses, *tro-tros* and bush taxis for points to the north (and sometimes to the east) depart from Neoplan motor park. Public transport to points west leaves from the chaotic Kaneshie motor park, and transport to the east leaves from the New Tema or Tema stations. Bush taxis and *tro-tros* for

Aflao and Akosombo also leave daily from Tudu station.

Train
Ghana's railway links Accra, Kumasi and Takoradi. For details see p373.

GETTING AROUND
Local *tro-tros* leave from Tema station, and also from the station just west of Nkrumah Circle. A typical journey costs about US$0.20. Transport to Labadi beach leaves from Nkrumah Circle and from Labadi truck station on High St.

Private taxis have no meters, but are still cheap: about US$1.60 is a standard fare across town.

COASTAL GHANA

It's no wonder some travellers never make it inland. Jam-packed with gorgeous beaches and historical forts, Ghana's coast is possibly the most exciting piece of shoreline in West Africa.

KOKROBITE
Travellers, rastas and musicians come to Kokrobite for two reasons: to learn traditional dancing and how to play drums, or to laze on the gorgeous beaches. The Academy of African Music & Arts Ltd (AAMAL) gives lessons and puts on live music on weekend afternoons.

Big Milly's (☎ 024 607998; bigmilly2000@hotmail. com; camp site per person s/d US$2-4/6/8) Travellers make a beeline for Milly's for good reason: fine beach, excellent restaurant, laid-back atmosphere, Friday night barbecues and live music on Saturday night.

Kokrobite Beach Resort (☎ 554042; d US$10-13) Run by AAMAL, in a tranquil seaside setting with abundant palms and frangipanis. It's a 2km walk west of Big Milly's along the main road.

Franco's, behind Big Milly's, has great Italian meals for US$3. However, if you're after a quick snack while you tan, Gasan cooks fresh pita bread on the beach nearby. For cheap Ghanaian dishes head to the small stall across the street from AAMAL.

Tro-tros leave regularly for Kokrobite from Kaneshie motor park in Accra (US$0.25, 45 minutes).

WINNEBA
☎ 0432 / pop 55,000
Winneba is a small town with beautiful, uncrowded beaches where huge groups of fishermen chant and drag in their nets in the mornings. Don't miss the **Aboakyaer** (Deer Hunt Festival) in May when two teams compete to catch an antelope for sacrifice to the tribal god Penkye Out.

The main bus station is in the centre of town, 1km from the beach. Winneba-bound *tro-tros* leave from Kaneshie park in Accra, or from Accra Park in Cape Coast (US$0.60). *Tro-tro* from Accra to Winneba is US$0.70 and takes 75 minutes. The Cape Coast to Winneba journey lasts one hour.

For a town of its size, Winneba has a good selection of hotels.

Lagoon Lodge (☎ 020 8162034; s/d US$5/7) This young upstart hotel is the best-value hotel in Ghana. The rooms have lemon-fresh walls and spotless bathrooms, and the upstairs terraces overlook the lagoon, which attracts migrating birds in the rainy season. It's about 500m west of the Sir Charles Tourist Centre.

Sir Charles Tourist Centre (☎ 22189; s/d US$3/4) The gloomy rooms with bathroom are starting to look their age, but the location, 500m southwest of the market by the beach and crashing waves is awesome.

Both hotels have good restaurants.

CAPE COAST
☎ 042 / pop 110,000
It's all happening here in this lively town. The majestic **Cape Coast Castle**, built in 1655, was headquarters for the British colonial administration until the capital was moved to Accra in 1876. It's now a Unesco World Heritage Site, and has a fantastic **museum** (admission guided/nonguided tours US$5/2.50; ☒ 9am-5pm) with lots of interesting artefacts and a screening room for a video about Ashanti culture.

The smaller **Fort William** and **Fort Victoria** are worth visiting for the great views, but they are off-limits to visitors.

Mighty Victory (☎ 30135; Aboom Close; s/d US$10/12) This beauty of a hotel sits just below Fort Victoria on a hill with magnificent views of the town and ocean. The rooms with fan are fresh, clean and well worth the extra cash.

Sammo's Guest House (☎ 33242; Jukwa Rd; s/d US$3.50/7) Popular with travellers, the rooms

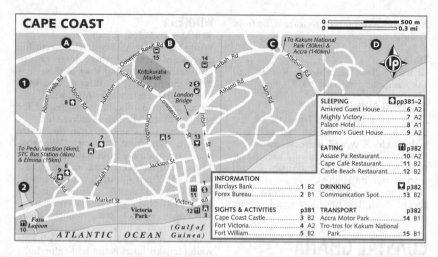

CAPE COAST

SLEEPING pp381–2
Amkred Guest House..............6 A2
Mighty Victory.......................7 A2
Palace Hotel..........................8 A1
Sammo's Guest House............9 A2

EATING p382
Assase Pa Restaurant.............10 A2
Cape Café Restaurant............11 B2
Castle Beach Restaurant........12 B2

INFORMATION
Barclays Bank........................1 B2
Forex Bureau.........................2 B1

DRINKING p382
Communication Spot..............13 B2

SIGHTS & ACTIVITIES p381
Cape Coast Castle..................3 B2
Fort Victoria.........................4 A2
Fort William..........................5 B2

TRANSPORT p382
Accra Motor Park...................14 B1
Tro-tros for Kakum National
   Park..................................15 B1

with fan are dark but clean. Dinner and drinks are available on the rooftop terrace.

Amkred Guest House (☎ 32868; d US$8) Hidden behind Sammo's Guest House, this place has light, spacious rooms with nice carpets, huge bathrooms, TV and food on demand.

Palace Hotel (☎ 33556; Aboom Rd; s/d with bathroom US$3/5) A palace this isn't. The rooms are drab but the shared facilities are actually not bad.

Cape Coast has a wide choice of eateries and, unusually for Ghana, is a vegetarian's paradise.

Cape Café Restaurant (☎ 34593; Commercial St; mains US$1.50-3.50) Trying to pick a dish from the large menu can seriously tax your brain. The women serve up excellent Ghanaian and Western dishes, including some vegetarian options and good breakfasts.

Castle Beach Restaurant (mains US$1.50-2.50) Located next to the castle and overlooking the sea, this place serves tasty seafood dishes and makes a great place for a relaxed evening drink.

Communication Spot (Commercial St) This is a cheerful and breezy place to sink a cold beer.

Assase Pa Restaurant has a fantastic location, on a promontory overlooking the sea just across the bridge over the lagoon. The extensive menu includes vegetarian versions of Ghanaian dishes.

For DIY, the Shell station shop further north from the Accra motor park is well stocked for self caterers.

The STC station in Cape Coast is at Pedu junction. There are four buses a day to/from Accra (US$2, three hours) and one a day to/from Kumasi (US$3.30, five hours). *Tro-tros* to Accra (US$1.40) and Kumasi (US$2) leave from the Accra motor park. For Elmina and Takoradi (US$1), take a *tro-tro* from Pedu junction.

Taxis around town cost about US$0.60.

KAKUM NATIONAL PARK

Tucked away in this small pocket of rainforest are endangered forest elephants, colobus monkeys, 300 species of bird and a staggering 600 species of butterfly. However, the main attraction is the canopy walkway suspended 30m above the forest floor. It makes for great viewing (or a trouser-wetting experience, depending on your point of view). Entry to the **park** (☎ 042 33278; adult/student US$7/3.50; 8am-5pm) includes a guided tour.

Most people visit Kakum as a day trip from Cape Coast, but if you want to stay, there's a **tree platform** (per person US$2) at the camp site near the park headquarters. They only provide mattresses, so you'll need to bring your own tent to be really comfortable.

Meals are available at **Kakum Rainforest Café** (mains US$1-2).

The entrance to the park is about 30km north of Cape Coast. *Tro-tros* (US$0.20, 45 minutes) that go past the entrance leave from a spot along Rowe Rd in Cape Coast. Alternatively, a chartered taxi will set you back US$5 for a round trip.

ELMINA

☎ 024 / pop 20,000

Elmina is a pretty town about 15km west of Cape Coast and home to two castles, both of which are Unesco World Heritage sites. Also known as Elmina Castle, **St George's Castle** (guided/nonguided tour US$5/2.50; ☼ 9am-5pm), built by the Portuguese in 1482, is Ghana's oldest and best-preserved fort. The smaller **Fort Jago** (admission free; ☼ 9am-5pm) was built by the Dutch 50 years later. It's pretty run-down these days, but still worth visiting for its panoramic views.

Nyansapow Hotel (☎ 33955; s/d US$6/7) At this friendly, quiet place, clean rooms with fan and bathroom open onto a courtyard. It's signposted off the main road into town.

Apart from the restaurants in the expensive hotels, the only budget place to eat at is **Gramsdel J** (mains US$1-2), opposite the Oyster Bay Hotel on the road to Cape Coast (about 2.5km from Elmina town centre).

Tro-tros to Takoradi (US$0.50, one hour) and shared taxis to Cape Coast (US$0.20, 15 minutes) leave from outside Elmina's Wesley Methodist Cathedral. In Cape Coast, shared taxis to Elmina cost US$0.30.

TAKORADI

☎ 031 / pop 270,000

There's nothing exciting to do in Takoradi, but it has several good restaurants and hotels. This makes it a good place to stay, as it is a staging post for trips to and from Côte d'Ivoire, and a base for day trips to nearby coastal towns. The well-restored **Fort Sebastian** lies 18km to the east in Shama.

Mosden Hotel (☎ 22266; Axim Rd; d US$9.50) By far the best budget option. Located within spitting distance of the STC bus station, the rooms with fan also come with TV, fridge and a clean bathroom.

Amenla Hotel (☎ 22543; Jon Sarbah Rd; s/d US$3/3.60) Although arranged around a brilliantly pink, open courtyard, the clean rooms with fan are not quite so exciting.

Zenith Hotel (☎ 22359; Kitson Rd; s/d US$3/3.60) 'Respect Yourself' signs hang over the clean, shared toilets. The big rooms are also spotless and surround a large courtyard that turns into a noisy club on Saturday night.

Super Hideout Catering Services (☎ 21086; Cape Coast Rd; mains US$2) This popular restaurant near the Sekondi Circle serves good-quality Ghanaian dishes.

SOS Restaurant & Bar (cnr Adhanti Rd & Market Circle; mains US$2) This small restaurant serves basic Ghanaian dishes and snacks. The breezy upstairs balcony overlooks the action on Market Circle.

There are also plenty of good food stalls around Market Circle and the motor parks.

STC buses leave for Accra several times a day (US$3.30, four hours), and regularly go to Kumasi (US$4, six hours) and Tamale (US$9, 14 hours). Most other forms of transport leave from the Accra motor park, opposite the STC station.

For information on trains between Takoradi and Accra or Kumasi, see p373.

FUNKO BEACH

At the time of research, cheap accommodation and a surfers' academy were being built on Funko Beach, about 3km west of Takoradi. For more details inquire at the Alaska Beach Bar in Dixcove.

BUSUA & DIXCOVE

These two small villages with fabulous stretches of beach used to be off the beaten track, but the new highway and streams of intrepid travellers have blown their cover. Still, the **beaches** are as gorgeous as ever – just be prepared for begging from the local children.

Most hotels line the main road in Busua, and range from very basic to comfortable.

Alaska Beach Club (☎ 024 460637; d from US$6) Unbeatable beachfront location, bonfire dinners on Saturday and boat trips to nearby Nanabokoa Island. The rooms with fan and mosquito nets have clean shared facilities.

Dadson's Lodge (s/d US$5/6) A converted private house with comfortable rooms, some with a sitting area, and bucket showers. Avoid the noisy rooms at the front.

Elizabeth's Guest House (d with breakfast US$3.60) Located at the village entrance, this place has clean rooms with fan, mosquito net, colourful walls, shared bucket showers and clean toilets. Lunch and dinner on the upper terrace are available on request. **Sabina's Guest House** (d with breakfast around US$3) on the main road is similarly priced, but the toilets are very basic.

In Dixcove the only accommodation is the **Quiet Storm Hotel** (d US$7.50), which has musty rooms.

All the hotels serve meals. Alternatively, some locals will cook some of their day's catch for you (it's lobster country here). There are also a few small places along the main road between Dadson's Lodge and Alaska Beach Club.

Daniel the Pancake Man has tasty, sweet and savoury pancakes, plus rice, seafood and vegetarian options for around US$2.

Tro-tros leave for Dixcove from Tema station in Takoradi. *Tro-tros* from Takoradi to Busua are infrequent, so it's best to walk here from Dixcove. Alternatively, take any transport along the coastal road to Agona junction, 20km west of Takoradi, and another *tro-tro* to Dixcove or Busua.

CENTRAL GHANA

KUMASI
☎ 051 / pop 1.2 million

Sssshhhh! Don't tell people in Accra, but Kumasi is Ghana's greatest city. Capital of the ancient and mighty Ashanti empire since 1695, and Ghana's second-largest conurbation today, Kumasi has always been a major player in the country's historical, cultural and economic life.

Whether it's the masterful sculptors, kente cloth weavers, Kotoko Olympic football team, colourful festivals, huge Kejetia market or the city's legendary traffic jams, Kumasi always does it on a grand and fascinating scale. Basically, if you haven't seen Kumasi, you haven' t seen Ghana.

Orientation
If you're arriving at the STC station you'll reach the central Adum district by turning left as you leave the station along a short, uphill road. Take the first right along Prempeh Rd. It 500m along Prempeh Rd until you reach a junction at the Shell station. Take a right turn and keep walking until you reach the busy Prempeh II Circle. As you approach it, Barclays Bank is on your right.

Information
INTERNET ACCESS
JCS Internet (Zongo Rd; US$0.80 per hr; ⊠) Located next to the Agricultural Bank of Ghana, JCS has a fast connection.

Internet Ghana Café (Harper Rd; US$1.20 per hr) Popular and central, located above the Shell service station.

MONEY
Barclays Bank (Prempeh II roundabout) Changes travellers cheques and has an ATM.

Standard Chartered Bank (Prempeh II roundabout) Changes travellers cheques and has an ATM.

Garden City Forex Bureau Limited (☎ 25046; Harper Rd; ⊙ 8am-6pm)

TOURIST OFFICES
The Tourism Board (☎ 34858; National Cultural Centre; ⊙ 9am-5pm Mon-Fri, 10am-2pm Sat) Provides useful information on transport, events, budget restaurants and hotels, and a not-very-detailed city map with restaurant locations for US$3.

Dangers & Annoyances
Kumasi is a pretty safe town. Just take the usual precautions in the busy market area where pickpockets lurk, and don't walk alone at night with valuables. The most annoying feature of the city is its roads, which seem to be in permanent gridlock. It can take a while to get from certain parts of town to others, so add an extra 20 minutes to your estimated journey time.

Sights
National Cultural Centre (☎ 34858; off Bantama Rd; admission free; ⊙ 8am-5pm) This is your one-stop shop for Ashanti culture. Visitors can watch woodcarvers and weavers at work, buy the artisans' products, or even learn some of those skills themselves. The art gallery features contemporary Ghanaian paintings.

To get a feel for the life and times of a modern Ashanti ruler, visit **Manhyia Palace & Museum** (off Antoa Rd; adult/student US$3/1.50; ⊙ 9am-noon & 1-5pm). On display are the palace's original furniture, including Ashantiland's first TV, a record player, silver ornaments and medals awarded to Prempeh II (a former Ashanti king) by various overseas governments. You will also see strikingly lifelike, life-size wax models of the two kings and Yaa Asantewaa (the Queen Mother), who led the revolt against the British and who died in exile in the Seychelles.

Another good museum is the **Prempeh II Museum** (admission US$0.50) at the National Cultural Centre. It is filled with fascinating historical artefacts, including the Ashanti king's ancient stool, his smoking pipes and the elephant tusks for resting his feet (the king's feet weren't allowed to touch the ground).

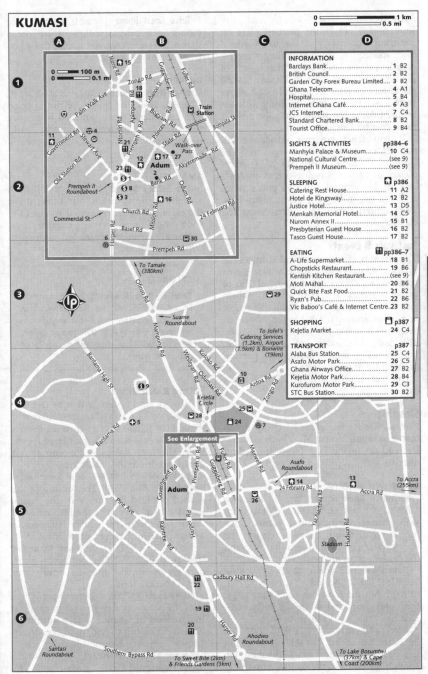

KUMASI

0 — 1 km
0 — 0.5 mi

0 — 100 m
0 — 0.1 mi

INFORMATION
Barclays Bank...........................1 B2
British Council.........................2 B2
Garden City Forex Bureau Limited....3 B2
Ghana Telecom.......................4 A1
Hospital...............................5 B4
Internet Ghana Café..................6 A3
JCS Internet...........................7 C4
Standard Chartered Bank............8 B2
Tourist Office.........................9 B4

SIGHTS & ACTIVITIES pp384–6
Manhyia Palace & Museum........10 C4
National Cultural Centre.........(see 9)
Prempeh II Museum...............(see 9)

SLEEPING p386
Catering Rest House...............11 A2
Hotel de Kingsway..................12 B2
Justice Hotel.........................13 D5
Menkah Memorial Hotel...........14 C5
Nurom Annex II.....................15 B1
Presbyterian Guest House..........16 B2
Tasco Guest House..................17 B2

EATING pp386–7
A-Life Supermarket.................18 B1
Chopsticks Restaurant..............19 B6
Kentish Kitchen Restaurant.......(see 9)
Moti Mahal.........................20 B6
Quick Bite Fast Food...............21 B2
Ryan's Pub..........................22 B6
Vic Baboo's Café & Internet Centre.23 B2

SHOPPING p387
Kejetia Market......................24 C4

TRANSPORT p387
Alaba Bus Station..................25 C4
Asafo Motor Park...................26 C5
Ghana Airways Office...............27 B2
Kejetia Motor Park.................28 B4
Kurofurom Motor Park.............29 C3
STC Bus Station....................30 B2

GHANA

Activities

Kumasi may not be the prettiest place on earth, but cycling is a great way to get around town and explore the surrounding villages – especially if you can't face another lungful of gas fumes in a mile-long traffic jam. Several places hire bicycles for around US$0.20 per hour. You'll find them along Zongo Rd, just north of Alaba bus station, and also around the corner on Odumasi Rd.

If you fancy wearing African cloth, you can create your own designs too. The National Cultural Centre (see p384) offers classes in batik tie-dyeing (expat students love it) for around US$3.50 per session, and you get to buy the fabric afterwards. The Cultural Centre also offers drumming classes.

Festivals & Events

The Ashanti calendar is divided into nine cycles of 42 days called Adae, which means resting place. There are two special days of worship within each Adae when a celebration is held and no work is done. The most important annual festival is the **Odwira festival**, which marks the last or ninth Adae. This festival includes lots of drumming, horn-blowing, food offerings and parades of elegantly dressed chiefs.

Contact the tourist office for exact dates.

Sleeping

Kumasi has its fair share of cheap hotels scattered around town. Most budget travellers end up in the Old Town and Adum districts.

OLD TOWN & ADUM

Presbyterian Guest House (☎ 23879; Mission Rd; d US$5-11) A lovely ramshackle colonial place with shaded verandas and gardens. It's hugely popular with travellers, despite the dodgy water supply. All rooms have fan and the pricier rooms are newly renovated.

Nurom Annexe 2 (mobile ☎ 024 271979; Nsene Rd; s/d US$2.40/3-4) Located on a noisy stretch of road, but the top-floor rooms are large, fresh and clean, and so are the bathrooms. Definitely the best value in town.

Hotel de Kingsway (☎ 26228; s/d US$8/10-15) Its looks are fading fast, but this old hotel still has decent amenities and bathrooms big enough for you and the odd cockroach.

Tasco Guest House (☎ 26547; d US$5-7) The rooms with private bathroom are pretty sparse, but clean enough to make this a better alternative to Kingsway.

BIMPEH HILL

Menkah Memorial Hotel (☎ 26432; 24 February Rd; s/d US$3/5) Don't be fooled by the exterior. The cool, dark, wood-panelled rooms are surprisingly comfortable and the bathrooms are clean. Stay in the back rooms if you want a quiet night's sleep.

AMAKOM

Justice Hotel (☎ 22525; Accra Rd; s/d US$5/6) It's a slight hassle to reach, but worth it for the excellent-value, renovated rooms (TV, fridge and new carpet). The cheaper, older rooms are clean with fan, but nothing to write home about.

SPLURGE!

Catering Rest House (☎ 23647; Government Rd; s/d US$20/25). At last! Hot water, clean floors and a bathroom of your very own in the modern, bungalow-style rooms. Go on, treat yourself. (Just make sure you avoid the old block rooms.)

Eating & Drinking

If it's African, Western, Asian or fast food you're after, Kumasi restaurants will have it, though you'll have to criss-cross the town to get it as the restaurants are scattered far and wide. However, there is a concentration of cheap eateries in the Adum area.

Friends Gardens (☎ 24611; South Suntreso Rd, off New Bekwai Rd; mains US$2-3) The locals love this shaded terraced restaurant in the South-Junction area, especially the dish *omo tuo*, the riceball specials on Sunday. It also makes a great place for having a quiet drink.

Sweet Bite (☎ 29333; Old Bekwai Rd, south of Ahodwo roundabout; US$1) The continental dishes here are pricey, but they do serve cheap, tasty Lebanese food.

Moti Mahal (☎ 29698; off Southern Bypass Rd; mains US$5) It's not every day you get to eat good Indian food in Ghana, so take advantage. Although difficult to find, most taxi drivers know where the restaurant is.

Kentish Kitchen Restaurant (☎ 21627; National Cultural Centre; mains US$1-2; ⏰ 8am-7.30pm) This is a good place to fill your stomach while spending a day at the Cultural Centre. The open-air restaurant serves cheap, tasty African and continental dishes within the centre's grounds.

> **SPLURGE!**
>
> **Chopsticks Restaurant** (☎ 23221; Harper Rd; mains US$5-7) It won't win any prizes for most imaginative name, but the Chinese dishes (and pizza too) here are second to none and well worth the extra dollars.

Vic Baboo's Cafe & Internet Centre (☎ 26757; Prempeh II Rd; mains US$1) This is a mecca for travellers. Its huge menu includes sandwiches, pizzas, burgers and vegetarian dishes.

Ryan's Pub (☎ 24072; Harper Rd; mains US$5-8) The continental dishes will lighten your wallet slightly, but it's a great place to have drinks and meet the local expats.

Quick Bite Fast Food (☎ 36180; Prempeh II Rd; mains US$0.80) They don't call it that for nothing. Located in the centre of Adum, you can fill your belly with burgers and fries at this fast-serving eatery.

If you're self-catering, **A-Life Supermarket** (Prempeh II Rd) is well stocked.

Jofel's Catering Services (on the airport roundabout) and Ryan's Pub (see above) are both lively places for an evening drink.

Shopping

Kejetia Market (Zongo Rd) Take a deep breath before you dive in – it'll be a head-spinner navigating your way through what is possibly Africa's biggest market. Vendors seem to outnumber shoppers here, selling everything from parrot wings, Ashanti sandals and kente cloth. Even if you don't want to buy anything, wander around anyway and absorb it all – you're unlikely to see anything like it again.

Getting There & Away

Kumasi's transport system can be confusing, so if in doubt, tell a taxi driver where you're headed and he should get you to the right station. Tro-tros to most regional destinations, including Accra (four hours), depart from the Kejetia motor park. Buses to Bolgatanga, Burkina Faso depart from Kurofurom motor park.

Minibuses to Tamale leave from the Alaba station. From the STC station buses to Accra leave every hour (US$4, five hours) between 6am and 7pm. STC also runs daily services to Bolgatanga (US$6, six hours), Cape Coast (US$3, five hours), Takoradi (US$4, five hours) and Tamale (US$5, six hours). OSA buses leave from the Kejetia motor park, and KTS buses leave daily for Accra and (less frequently) Bolgatanga and Tamale.

For information on trains between Kumasi and Takoradi or Accra, see p373.

AROUND KUMASI
Lake Bosumtwi

This 100m-deep crater lake is dedicated to the god Twi. It's a popular weekend spot for swimming (the water is safe) and motorboat trips. Take a tro-tro from Asafo motor park in Kumasi to Abonu (US$0.70, 45 minutes), the lakeside village.

Craft Villages

A number of craft villages are located within 30 minutes' tro-tro drive of Kumasi, including **Ahwiaa** (known for its exquisite woodcarving), **Ntonso** (cloth printing) and **Bonwire** (kente cloth). In Bonwire, ask for Fosu Francis, who offers lessons in weaving (expect to pay around US$10 per day).

To get to Bonwire you can take a tro-tro from Antoa motor park (US$0.30). But the easiest way to visit these villages is to hire a taxi from Kumasi for the day (around US$20 per half day).

NORTHERN GHANA

TAMALE
☎ 071 / pop 258,000

It's hot, it's busy, it's dusty and there's not much to do. But Tamale is a major transport hub, and it's a good base for visiting **Mole National Park** (see p388). Although it's the capital of the north, it's not as hectic as Kumasi and the widespread use of bicycles will make two-wheel travellers feel right at home.

At the time of writing the town was under indefinite military curfew (due to ethnic clashes following the murder of the Dagomba king), meaning the whole town has to be indoors by 10pm. Despite this, the daytime atmosphere is very relaxed.

Sleeping

Catholic Guesthouse (☎ 22265; Gumbihini Rd; d US$6-11; 💻) Your prayers have been answered! This hotel has clean, fresh rooms set in a leafy compound with a garden bar. The best value in town.

Atta Essibi (☎ 22569; Sir Charles Rd; s/d US$2/3) The good-value rooms with fan could do with a bit more daylight, but they are clean, tastefully decorated and quiet. The shared showers and toilets are also clean.

Macos Hotel (off Bolgatanga Rd; d US$4) The simple, clean rooms are arranged around a central courtyard, and the toilets are amazingly spotless.

Alhassan (☎ 23638; near Central Market; s/d US$2.70/3.30) Surprisingly popular, with hot, noisy, slightly dingy rooms with so-so bathrooms. Its central location is its main saving grace.

Eating & Drinking

Tamale has a good range of places to eat, but curfew starts at 10pm, so start your nights out early!

Giddipass Restaurant (Salaga Rd; mains US$2.50) This breezy, upstairs eatery has a long menu with good breakfasts, with Ghanaian and Chinese dishes thrown in. It also makes a good place for evening drinks.

Jalia Bar (mains US$0.20) Groups of women frantically prepare tasty northern specialties like TZ (the local millet-based staple) in a din of hissing steam and clanging pots and pans. You'll find Jalia Bar behind the central mosque.

Sparkles Restaurant (mains US$2) This place, in the National Cultural Centre, serves good Ghanaian and Chinese dishes.

Getting There & Away

From the STC station, two buses a day go to Kumasi and three a day depart for Accra (US$8, twelve hours). *Tro-tros* to Bolgatanga (US$1.80, two hours) and OSA buses to Mole National Park (US$2, four to six hours) leave from the main motor park next door to the STC station.

LARABANGA

The gateway to Mole National Park, Larabanga is also renowned for its famous **mosque**. Sahelian in appearance (with mud and pole construction), it is Ghana's oldest mosque, supposedly dating back to 1421. Women are not allowed to enter.

The tourist information centre in eastern Larabanga is a good place to get information about Mole National Park and to arrange accommodation at the guesthouse or in a room with a local family.

Daily buses from Tamale to Bole, Wa or Mole National Park stop at Larabanga.

MOLE NATIONAL PARK

☎ 0717

There aren't many places where you can wake up to see elephants, baboons and antelopes wandering past your bedroom window. **Mole National Park** (adult/student US$1.80/0.50; camera fee US$0.25) is one of them.

The park was established in 1971 and covers 5198 sq km. It's home to many bird species and to nearly 100 species of mammal, including lions and buffaloes.

The best time to visit is during the dry season (November to May). A three-hour guided tour on foot costs US$1.80 per person. A tour guide is compulsory.

At **Mole Hotel Lodge** (☎ 22045; camp site per person/dm/d per person US$2.50/4/15) the water supply is dodgy, but the views are fantastic and the restaurant is good. At the motel swimming pool area there's a viewing platform from where you can watch elephants, antelopes, baboons and waterbucks gathering around the water hole (although the sound of the generator nearby spoils the ambience a little bit). The motel arranges three-hour guided walks at 6.30am and 3.30pm daily (US$1.80 per person per hour).

This is the only place to stay within the park, so book well ahead as it gets very busy in the dry season. Alternatively, you can stay in nearby Larabanga.

The reserve is 135km west of Tamale along a dirt road. One OSA bus leaves Tamale every day at about 3pm (US$2, four to six hours) and heads right into Mole, via Larabanga.

The bus returns to Tamale the following morning at 5.30am. Alternatively, take a bus from Tamale towards Bole or Wa, jump off at Larabanga, then hire a taxi, or bike or walk 7km to the park entrance. Transport in these parts, however, is scarce.

The park entrance is about 4km north of the turn-off in Larabanga. The headquarters and the motel area are a further 2km into the park. There's infrequent public transport entering the park, so it's a question of waiting to hitch a ride with taxis that are heading for the park, or walking the 6km from Larabanga to the motel (this isn't advisable unless you're prepared to sweat a lot and walk for up to three hours).

WECHIAU COMMUNITY HIPPO SANCTUARY

Part of an ecotourism project, this sanctuary (a day tour costs US$6) protects a stretch of riverine habitat along the Black Volta River that is home to one of the last significant hippo populations in Ghana, as well as 250 bird species. Farmers and fishermen in the area traditionally compete with hippos for land, so this project aims to protect the species without compromising the locals' ability to earn a living. For more information contact the **tourist board** (☎ 75 622 431) in Wa.

Basic accommodation (US$10) and food is available at Tokali Lodge, 5km away from the sanctuary's nearest village, Wechiau. At Wechiau there is a tourist office where tickets can be bought and arrangements made for a guide and boat tour. The guide can take you to the lodge by car, or you can hire a bike at the office and cycle to the lodge.

Wechiau village is easily reached by *tro-tro* (US$1, one hour) from the main truck park in Wa. The sanctuary is about 20km from Wechiau – you can get here by hiring a bicycle for the day (US$1). If you're in a large group you can hire a bus for US$14.

To reach Wa, take an OSA bus from Tamale (US$3, seven hours), or a City Express bus from Bolgatanga via Tumu (US$2.50, six hours).

BOLGATANGA
☎ 072
Bolga, as it's known to the locals, is a pleasant town and the craft centre of the north. The **market** is filled with textiles, leatherwork and multicoloured baskets (woven from raffia) that are prized throughout Ghana. Bolgatanga is also a staging post for travel to and from Burkina Faso.

Sleeping
Black Star Hotel (☎ 22346; Bazaar Rd; s/d/tw US$5/10/13) This place is often full and for good reason. The rooms come with fan and are very comfortable and clean. The restaurant is not bad either.

Hotel St. Joseph's (☎ 23214; behind National Investment Bank; s US$3.70-8; 🐕) Located behind the National Investment Bank, this hotel's rooms are small, dark and unexciting, but some have air-con. The hotel redeems itself with a popular bar and a good restaurant serving kebabs and filling meals.

Sacred Hearts Catholic Mission (☎ 23216; off Bazaar Rd; dm/s/d US$1.30/4/5) Located across the street from the Black Star Hotel, with clean and comfy rooms and a quiet courtyard.

Eating & Drinking
Time Changes (STC bus station; mains US$1) Not your ordinary bus station canteen, its delicious, cheap Ghanaian dishes draw customers from across town.

Madam Rakia All Peoples' Canteen (Commercial Rd; US$2) Guinea fowl stew and TZ (the local millet-based staple) are some of the well-prepared dishes at this popular canteen.

The outdoor courtyard of the Sand Garden Hotel is a good place for a quiet drink.

Getting There & Away
Tro-tros to Tamale leave from the station near the southern end of Commercial Rd. From the STC station about 800m further south, buses go to Tamale (US$2, four hours) and Accra (US$9, fifteen hours). Minibuses and *tro-tros* to Paga on the Burkina Faso border leave from a station one block east of the post office.

EASTERN GHANA

AKOSOMBO
☎ 0251
Akosombo village is next to the dam that holds back Lake Volta, the largest artificial lake in the world. These days the huge expanse of water, surrounded by beautiful green hills, seems to generate as much tourist interest as it does electricity.

You'll find a wider selection of accommodation and eating options in the town of **Atimpoku** (3km south of Akosombo), where the Ho road crosses the Volta at an impressive suspension bridge.

Sights & Activities
The Volta River Authority arranges **tours** of the dam for US$3 (tickets are available at the visitor centre in the Volta Hotel). Even more fun is the Sunday cruise to **Dodi Island** (US$7), which has a restaurant, a live band

and beautiful scenery to occupy you for six hours. It leaves at 10.30am from a special jetty accessible only by private taxi from Akosombo (US$1).

Sleeping

Sound Rest Motel (☎ 20288; s/d US$4/5) This mini-paradise off the main road between Akosombo and Atimpoku has clean rooms with fan or air-conditioning. The rooms are arranged around a plant-filled courtyard and the shared showers are spotless.

Zito Guesthouse (☎ 20474; d US$8.50-10) Located 800m from the motor park, this is the only budget place in Akosombo. The clean rooms with fan have beds big enough for you to roll over in twice!

Benkum (☎ 20050; d US$6.50) This is the cheapest option in Atimpoku and can be found south of the suspension bridge. The old red carpets probably looked grand once upon a time, but the rooms come with fan and are big and clean enough.

SPLURGE!

Aylo's Bay (☎ 20093; aylosbay@hotmail.com; camp site per person/d US$3/14-28) Standing in the hotel's riverside gardens you'll be rubbing your eyes at the gorgeous views of the suspension bridge. After eating breakfast on the floating jetty you can swim in the bilharzia-free water, or rent a canoe and explore the river's islands nearby. Every April the hotel, located next to the Akosombo Continental Hotel, has a regatta where participants race their power boats, canoes and kayaks.

Eating & Drinking

The street food by the market includes the local specialities of fried shrimp and 'one man thousand' (tiny fried fish). Alternatively, 39 Steps, near the Benkum Hotel, is a good eating and drinking spot.

Getting There & Away

Tro-tros directly to Akosombo (US$1, 1½ hours) leave from Tudu station in Accra. Alternatively, get a bus or *tro-tro* from Accra to Ho, and a connection at the obvious turnoff to Akosombo at the bridge in Atimpoku. Akosombo village is 2km before the dam and 6km before the port for boats to Yeji.

For details about boats between Akosombo and Yeji, see p373.

GHANA DIRECTORY

ACCOMMODATION

Compared to neighbouring countries, cheap hotel rooms in Ghana are reasonably priced but generally decrepit. A decent budget-priced room with a fan and shared bathroom costs about US$4 to US$5 (more in Accra), while more-comfortable doubles with aircon and private bathroom start at about US$12. A twin room (with two single beds) is usually more expensive than a double room (with a double bed). A self-contained room includes a private bathroom.

Camping is possible at some of the beach resorts and national parks, but tents aren't always provided so bring your own.

ACTIVITIES

Ghana's coast is famous for its beaches, although the undertow makes some of them unsafe for swimming or surfing. Ghanaians are keen to spread their culture, so you'll have plenty of opportunities to learn batik dyeing, cloth weaving, dancing and drumming. For the latter contact the **Academy of African Music & Arts Limited** (AAMAL; ☎ 554042) in Kokrobite.

BUSINESS HOURS

Business hours are 8am to 12.30pm and 1.30pm to 5.30pm Monday to Friday, and 8.30am to 1pm Saturday. Government offices observe the same times during the week, but close on Saturday. Banking hours are 8.30am to 2pm or 3pm Monday to Friday.

DANGERS & ANNOYANCES

Ghana is one of the most stable countries in the region and, on the whole, very safe in which to travel. Having said that, ethnic violence flared up in 2002 in the north around Tamale, so check the latest news before heading up there.

EMBASSIES & CONSULATES

The following countries have representation in Accra.
Benin (Map p375; ☎ 774860; Switchback Lane)
Burkina Faso (Map p376; ☎ 221988; 2nd Mango Tree Ave)

Canada (Map p375; ☎ 228555; 46 Independence Ave)
Côte d'Ivoire (Map p375; ☎ 774611; 9, 18th Lane)
France (Map p375; ☎ 228571, fax 778321; 12th Rd, off Liberation Ave)
Germany (Map p375; ☎ 221311, fax 221347; 6 Ridge Rd)
Niger (☎ 224962; E104/3 Independence Ave)
Togo (Map p375; ☎ 777950)
UK (Map p375; ☎ 221665, fax 221745; 1 Osu Link)
USA (Map p376; ☎ 776601, fax 775747; cnr 10th Lane & 3rd St)

Ghana has diplomatic representation in Benin, Burkina Faso, Côte d'Ivoire, Guinea, Nigeria, Sierra Leone and Togo.

FESTIVALS & EVENTS

Ghana has colourful festivals and events, and Accra's tourist office sells a booklet with information on the festivals. Celebrations include Cape Coast's Fetu Afahye Festival (first Saturday of September), Elmina's Bakatue Festival (first Tuesday in July), the Fire Festival of the Dagomba people in Tamale and Yendi (dates vary according to the Muslim calendar) and various year-round Akan celebrations in Kumasi. Ghana's most famous festival – Aboakyer (Deer Hunt) – is celebrated in Winneba on the first weekend in May. Panafest is celebrated annually in Cape Coast, Accra and Kumasi.

FOOD & DRINK

Ghanaians take their tucker seriously, and there is no stretch of road in Ghana that doesn't have a 'chop bar' – a small roadside eatery serving meals consisting of a starch staple such as rice, *fufu* (mashed cassava) and *kenkey* (fermented maize meal). These come with stew or a sauce (called soups) made with okra or *palaver* (greens). Other menu regulars are fried rice with chicken or vegetables, and *jollof* rice (the West African paella). In the north there's plenty of opportunity to sample guinea fowl and grasscutter (a large rodent).

Cheap bars (known as 'spots') serve decent local brews and a popular millet beer called *pito*.

HOLIDAYS

As well as religious holidays listed in the Africa Directory chapter (p1003), these are the principal public holidays in Ghana:
7 January 4th Republic Day
6 March Independence Day
1 July Republic Day
December Farmers' Day (1st Friday)

MAPS

The best map of the country available outside Ghana is a 1:750,000 version of the country produced by International Travel Maps of Vancouver.

In Accra, the Survey Offices on Giffard Rd produce a series of four 1:500,000 maps (US$6 each) that cover the entire country. Other maps available in Ghana include the KLM-Shell map (US$5). There's also the *Tourist Map of Ghana* (US$7), which makes a nice souvenir. Both of these maps are available at the major hotels, the tourist office and at the Accra Visitor Centre.

MEDIA

Ghana's relatively free press has spawned a large number of newspapers. The national *Daily Graphic* is probably the best of them all, with reasonably good coverage of Ghanaian, African and international news. Ghanaian radio is excellent and its talk shows are popular. The National Radio has world news in English every hour. GTV is the national channel, available throughout the country.

MONEY
ATMs
Barclays Bank and Standard Chartered have ATMs in all major towns.

Credit Cards
Credit cards are accepted by major hotels and travel agencies.

Exchanging Money
Barclays Bank, Standard Chartered and Ghana Commercial Bank all change dollars, euros, pounds sterling and CFA. Forex bureaux are dotted around every town, although there are fewer in the north.

Travellers Cheques
Changing travellers cheques is quick and efficient in banks and bureaus. Barclays Bank and Standard Chartered cash Visa, MasterCard and Thomas Cook travellers cheques.

POST & TELEPHONE
Postcards cost US$0.20 to send anywhere. An airmail letter costs US$0.30 to the UK and Europe, and US$0.35 to Australia and

the USA. The main post offices in Accra and Kumasi have reliable post restante services.

Every town and city has plenty of private 'communication centres' where you can make national and international calls costing around US$0.80 per minute. They're slightly more expensive than cardphones, but very convenient. Phonecards can be purchased and calls made at telephone booths dotted around the streets of main towns or at Ghana Telecom offices.

If you have a mobile phone with you, SIM cards are available (with prepaid credit) from *Spacefon* for US$20. Top-up phonecards are available at many street vendors.

TOURIST INFORMATION

The tourist board has a network of offices in the major regional capitals, but their usefulness is generally limited. Most offices are closed on weekends.

VISAS

Everyone needs a visa, which must be obtained before arriving in Ghana. The 60-day visas can be single or multiple entry. Visas usually take three days to process and four photos are required. You also need to provide an onward ticket. In the UK, single/multiple entry visas cost £30/40. In the USA they cost US$20/50.

Visa Extensions

Visas can be extended at the **immigration office** (☎ 021 221 667) in Accra, near the Sankara interchange. Applications are accepted between 8.30am and noon Monday to Friday, and you need two photos, a letter explaining why you need an extension and an onward ticket out of Ghana. They keep hold of your passport during the two-week application process.

Visas for Onward Travel

Visas for the following countries are available from embassies in Accra (see p390):

Benin Visas cost US$25/50 for one-/three-month multiple entry and are issued within 48 hours.

Burkina Faso Visas cost US$40 for three months and are issued within 24 hours; three photos required.

Côte d'Ivoire Visas cost CFA20,000 (payable in CFA only), and are issued within 24 hours; two photos required.

Togo Visas cost US$20 cash (payable in dollars only) for multiple entry and are issued the same day if you apply in the morning; three photos required.

WOMEN TRAVELLERS

Ghana is probably the safest country in West Africa for single female travellers. Many women who have gone solo report few problems apart from the odd persistent flirting. In the northern Muslim areas it is worth dressing more conservatively so as not to offend local sensibilities.

Togo

HIGHLIGHTS

- **Aného** The crumbling, former colonial capital is set on a tranquil, blue lagoon where you can take boat rides with nothing but the sound of the waves to break the silence (p402)
- **Lake Togo** This bilharzia-free lake is the place for water-skiing and windsurfing (p401)
- **Voodoo** At the Marché des Féticheurs you can browse through dried animal organs and traditional voodoo medicines (p399)
- **Best journey** Hike through organic coffee plantations, rolling green hills and butterflies on the way to the impressive Akloa Falls near Badou, then cool off in the natural pool at the falls' bottom (p403)
- **Off the beaten track** The stunning, fortress-like *tata* houses in the isolated Tamberma region, where outsiders are still a rarity (p405)

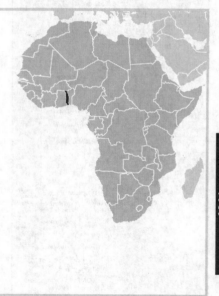

FAST FACTS

- **Area** 56,790 sq km (that's 1.3 of the Netherlands)
- **ATMs** in the capital and every major town
- **Borders** Benin, Burkina Faso, Ghana
- **Budget** US$20 to US$25 a day
- **Capital** Lomé
- **Languages** French, Ewe, Kabyé, Mina
- **Money** West African CFA; US$1 = CFA600
- **Population** 5.1 million
- **Seasons** wet (May–Oct), dry (mid-Feb–mid-Apr)
- **Telephone** country code ☎ 228; international access code ☎ 00
- **Time** GMT/UTC
- **Visas** US$20 for one month, issued at overseas embassies; US$17 if issued at Lomé airport

Togo is relatively obscure, and tiny – you could drive across it in less than two hours. But are you really going to let yourself miss out on the waterfalls, plate-licking cuisine, unique Tamberma architecture and beautiful countryside, peopled by the most diverse, easy-going folk this side of the Sahara? This bite-sized beauty used to be the pearl of Africa and the destination for thousands of travellers until recent political turmoil drove them all away. But now Togo has picked itself up, dusted itself off and is welcoming back travellers once more. Don't pass it over for its higher-profile neighbours. Stop for a bit, and discover an intriguing 'slice' of Africa.

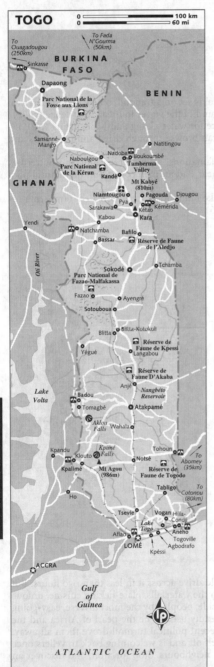

HISTORY

The coastal areas of what is now Togo were settled by the Ewe from Nigeria and Benin, and the Mina and the Guin from Ghana from the 13th century onwards.

By the 16th century, Togo's largest ethnic groups, the Ewe and the Kabyé, found themselves sandwiched between the slave-raiding empires of the Ashanti (in Ghana) and the Dahomey (in Benin), with the coastal town of Aného becoming a major slaving post. The slave trade continued until its abolition in the mid-19th century. The Europeans then turned their attention to important local commodities such as cacao and coffee. Britain and France vied for control of the trade, but it was the Germans who eventually snuck in and cornered the market.

The Colonial Era & Independence

In 1884 the German explorer Gustav Nachtigal signed a treaty with a village chief (see p401), turning Togo into a German protectorate. After Germany lost World War I, the French and British grabbed the German West African territory, dividing the spoils (and the Ewe tribe) between them. In a 1956 plebiscite the Ewe on the British (western) side voted to become part of soon-to-be-independent Ghana.

The French (eastern) half became independent in 1960, creating present-day Togo. Sylvanus Olympio was its first president, but the country's optimism and euphoria was short-lived. Olympio was assassinated in a 1963 coup (Africa's first ever) by a group of soldiers that included Gnassingbé Eyadéma, who handed power to a civilian government headed by Nicolas Grunitzky. But in 1967 Eyadéma pushed Grunitzky aside in another coup and decided to try the post of presidency for himself.

Eyadéma set up his political party, the Rassemblement du Peuple Togolais (RPT), and ruled Togo with an iron fist. Political dissenters scattered into exile or were imprisoned or run underground. However, in an ironic twist, Eyadéma styled himself as a regional peace-broker and intervened in several conflicts around West Africa.

The Uncertain Years

Years of oppression boiled over into massive protests and violent unrest in 1991. Eyadéma caved in to domestic and international demands, and made way for a transitional government headed by Joseph Koffigoh. But the new president lasted only one year. With forces loyal to Eyadéma breathing down his neck, Koffigoh agreed to form a 'government of national unity' with Eyadéma.

Back in the big chair once again, Eyadéma postponed the 1992 elections. Outraged trade unions called a general strike, sending Togo's economy into a tailspin, with major exports such as cocoa and phosphates lying stranded at the ports. Violence ensued and over 250,000 people fled into neighbouring countries.

In the middle of all this, Eyadéma announced elections to be held in August 1993, but not before he barred Gilchrist Olympio (the son of Togo's first president) from contesting. Opposition parties boycotted the elections, and although only a third of the electorate bothered to vote, 96% of them then voted for Eyadéma.

The following year's parliamentary elections were equally unsatisfactory. Several opposition members were killed, and the Union des Forces du Changement (UFC), Gilchrist Olympio's party, boycotted the proceedings. The opposition coalition managed to scrape up a parliamentary majority, but Eyadéma cleverly picked the leader of the coalition's junior partner, Edem Kodjo, to become prime minister, thereby creating divisions and resentment. When, in 1996, Eyadéma arranged by-elections without consulting Kodjo, the prime minister resigned, allowing Eyadéma to replace him with the more cooperative Kwassi Klutse.

By the 1998 presidential elections, the routine was familiar: voting irregularities, threats, intimidation and a ban on political rallies. Though Olympio was widely considered to be the winner, the RPT claimed victory and went on to repeat this success in the 2002 parliamentary elections.

Eyadéma for a Third Term?

Later in 2002, in what critics called a 'constitutional coup', the national assembly voted unanimously to change the constitution and allow Eyadéma to 'sacrifice himself again' and run for a third term during the 2003 presidential elections. Meanwhile, Gilchrist Olympio's attempts to beat the man who overthrew his father were scuppered yet again when he was banned from running for failing to provide a current tax ???.

Despite allegations of electoral fraud, Eyadéma won 57% of the votes in the elections, which international observers from the African Union described as generally free and transparent.

For many Togolese, there is little optimism for the future and there is a prevailing sense of *déjà vu* as Eyadéma extends his record as Africa's longest-serving ruler.

THE CULTURE

Out of 40 different ethnic groups, the two largest are the Ewe who are concentrated in the south, and the Kabyé who are concentrated in the north around Kara.

A third of the Togolese population is Christian, one fifth is Muslim and the rest are animists. But whatever their religion, the same age-old customs, rites and superstitions feature hugely in the national psyche. For the Ewe in particular, it's all about the afterlife: once a person dies their *djoto* (incarnated soul) may linger among the living, and funerals are an important way of freeing the soul and influencing its reincarnation. This is why death is celebrated above everything else – funerals are the most festive occasions, with plenty of dancing, singing and drumming to the sound of flutes, musical bows, *lithophones* (percussion instruments made of stone) and bells.

However, Christianity and Islam have made their mark, and after five decades of cheerless Eyadéma rule and economic decline, religious sects have sprouted all over the country. Fervent, evangelical, all-night worship is common, and in 1999 the reported appearances of the Virgin Mary to the town of Tsévié drew thousands of people who came rushing for her blessings and salvation.

But in Lomé and other cities, troubles haven't stopped them from living the good life. The young and the beautiful fill the bars and restaurants, dancing to salsa and R & B, downing palm wine, tucking into sauce *arachide* (peanut sauce) and *koliko* (fried yam) and engaging in cautious political conversation.

Their banter is loud and animated, and minor disputes can escalate into heated

TOGO

arguments that cool down just as quickly. But the Togolese are not nearly as brash or (in their own opinion) as flashy with their money as their Nigerian and Beninese neighbours to the east. They have an understated pride and a hospitality that extends to complete strangers, who are just as welcome in their homes as any member of their extended family.

Despite Togo's size and political climate, its creative juices have still run freely enough to produce notable stars. These include Tété-Michel Kpomassie (who wrote *An African in Greenland*, an autobiography containing his fascinating perspective on Arctic life); and Bella Bellow, Togo's biggest singing export, who dominated the local scene during the '60s and '70s.

High-profile women, however, are still a rarity in a country where human rights, never mind women's rights, are still a distant hope for most. While the government did ratify the 1979 Convention on the Elimination of All Forms of Discrimination against Women (Cedaw), Togolese women have a long way to go before they enjoy the same status as men.

ENVIRONMENT

Togo's coastline is only 56km across, but the country stretches inland for 540km. Mountainous, forested areas in the centre yield to savanna in the south and north.

Rain falls from May to October, but in the south there's a dry spell from mid-July to mid-September. In the north there is no such interlude, but on the whole the north is much drier. Mid-February (after the harmattan – dusty Saharan – winds lift) to mid-April is the hottest period throughout the country.

Togo is a densely populated country, with an average of 66 people per sq km. Many of them practise entrenched and damaging slash-and-burn agriculture, which, combined with the pressure for farmland, have taken a very heavy toll on Togo's environment. The problem is a low governmental priority and there is little money to deal with it.

The situation in Togo's national parks is particularly dire: poaching and deforestation have almost wiped animals off the map, and those mammals that do remain, including buffaloes, antelopes and deer, are limited to the far north.

TRANSPORT

GETTING THERE & AWAY

Air

If flying from Europe, Air France has three weekly flights to Lomé. There are three flights per week, costing around US$600 (one-way, low season).

Air Togo also operates a once-weekly flight between Lomé and Paris.

Ethiopian Airlines, Air Burkina and Air Togo all operate flights to West Africa (see p401 for airline contact information). There are twice-weekly flights from Lomé to Cotonou, Lagos and Ouagadougou.

DEPARTURE TAX

There is a departure tax of US$42, which is included in the price of the plane ticket.

Land

BENIN

The main border crossing is at Hilla-Conji. Plenty of bush taxis ply the road between Lomé and Cotonou all day, every day. The border is open 24 hours, but if you want a temporary visa you need to get there between 8am and 6pm. There are also border crossings at Tohoun (east of Notsé), Kémérida (northeast of Kara) and Nadoba (in the Tamberma Valley), but you'll have to wait half the day to get public transport, and visas for Benin aren't guaranteed at these borders.

BURKINA FASO

The main border crossing is at Sinkasse, north of Dapaong in northern Togo. Buses, minibuses and bush taxis run direct between Lomé and Ouagadougou (US$28, 36 hours) daily. To break up this long journey you could stop at Dapaong overnight, take a minibus from there to Sinkasse (US$6), and then a bush taxi from Sinkasse to Ouagadougou.

GHANA

The most popular route is via the coastal road. To Ghana it's best to take a taxi to the border (US$2, open 6am to 10pm), cross the border on foot and get onward transport on the other side.

Another frequently used border crossing is at Klouto (northwest of Kpalimé). There are bush taxis from Kpalimé to Klouto, as well as on the other side of the border.

There are other crossings at Badou, Natchamba (accessible from Sokodé) and at Sinkasse, northwest of Dapaong, but the roads are in bad shape and there's not a lot of public transport in these parts.

GETTING AROUND
Minibuses and bush taxis are the only forms of transport around Togo. The drivers will charge extra for your luggage, based on its size. There are bus companies in operation, but they run along international routes.

If you do find yourself in a rural area without transport, you will have to wait for the occasional truck to come rumbling past. Expect to make a payment, but don't expect a seat up front.

LOMÉ

pop 676,400

Cruising down the coastal boulevard, lined with palm trees, sandy beaches and blue sea, you can sense the former glory and tantalising potential of Lomé. Compared with the urban jungles of Lagos or Cotonou, Togo's capital feels more like a big town. But don't expect peace and quiet when you get here: Lomé is buzzing with the sounds of thousands of motorcycles, and morning rush hour looks like a bikers' convention has rolled into town. On top of that there's lively nightlife, great restaurants and possibly the best fetish (charm worn around the neck to ward off evil) market in the region.

ORIENTATION
Everything you'll need to see and do is located in, or just outside, the D-shaped central area defined by the coastal highway and the semicircular Blvd du 13 Janvier (often called Blvd Circulaire). The heart of town is around the intersection of Rue de la Gare and Rue du Commerce, which becomes Rue du Lake Togo beyond the market area.

Lomé's Tokoin International Airport lies 5km northeast of town. Arriving here, you will find a few *moto-taxis* (motorcycle taxis)

that can take you into town for US$1.60 (if you can handle juggling your backpack at the front). A more comfortable option is a private taxi – drivers charge US$3 for a ride into the city centre.

INFORMATION
Bookshops
Librairie Le Bon Pasteur (☎ 221 36 28; cnr Rue Aniko Palako & Rue du Commerce) City and country maps and a good selection of postcards.
Star Libraire (☎ 221 58 82; Rue du Lac Togo) Nonfiction and contemporary French-language novels, plus reasonably up-to-date British, German and Italian newspapers.

Cultural Centres
Centre Culturel Français (☎ 221 02 32; www.ccf.tg.refer.org; Ave du 24 Janvier) Weekly screenings of French and West African films. The centre also hosts arts performances.

Internet Access
Lomé is dotted with Internet cafés and there's a high concentration along Blvd du 13 Janvier.
CyberCafe (Blvd du 13 Janvier; per hr US$0.70)
Glory Internet (Ave Dr FJ Strauss; per hr US$0.70; 🔧) The fastest connection in town.
La Pointe (Blvd du 13 Janvier; per hr US$0.70)

Medical Services
Dr Noel Akouvi (☎ 221 32 46; Cabinet Dentaire NIFA 10, Rue Amouzou) For dental emergencies.
Polyclinique Internationale St Joseph (☎ 226 72 32; Blvd de Haho-Tokoin Hedjranawoé; ☽ 24 hrs) This private clinic offers the best medical help in Lomé.

Money
All the major banks change cash and travellers cheques.
BIA Togo (☎ 221 32 86; 13 Rue du Commerce) Changes Visa and Amex travellers cheques, but not MasterCard.
BTCI (☎ 221 01 79; Blvd du 13 Janvier) Located near the ECOWAS building, its ATMs accept Visa.
Ecobank (☎ 221 72 14; 20 Rue du Commerce)
UTB (☎ 221 77 01; Blvd du 13 Janvier) Can be found near L'Okavango.

Post & Telephone
Cabine Téléphonique (☎ 221 06 47; Rue 7ADK) Located behind the post office, this is the best place for international phone calls.
Main post office (Société des Poste du Togo; Ave de la Libération; ☽ 7am-5.30pm Mon-Fri, 8am-noon Sat) Runs an efficient poste restante service.

TOGO

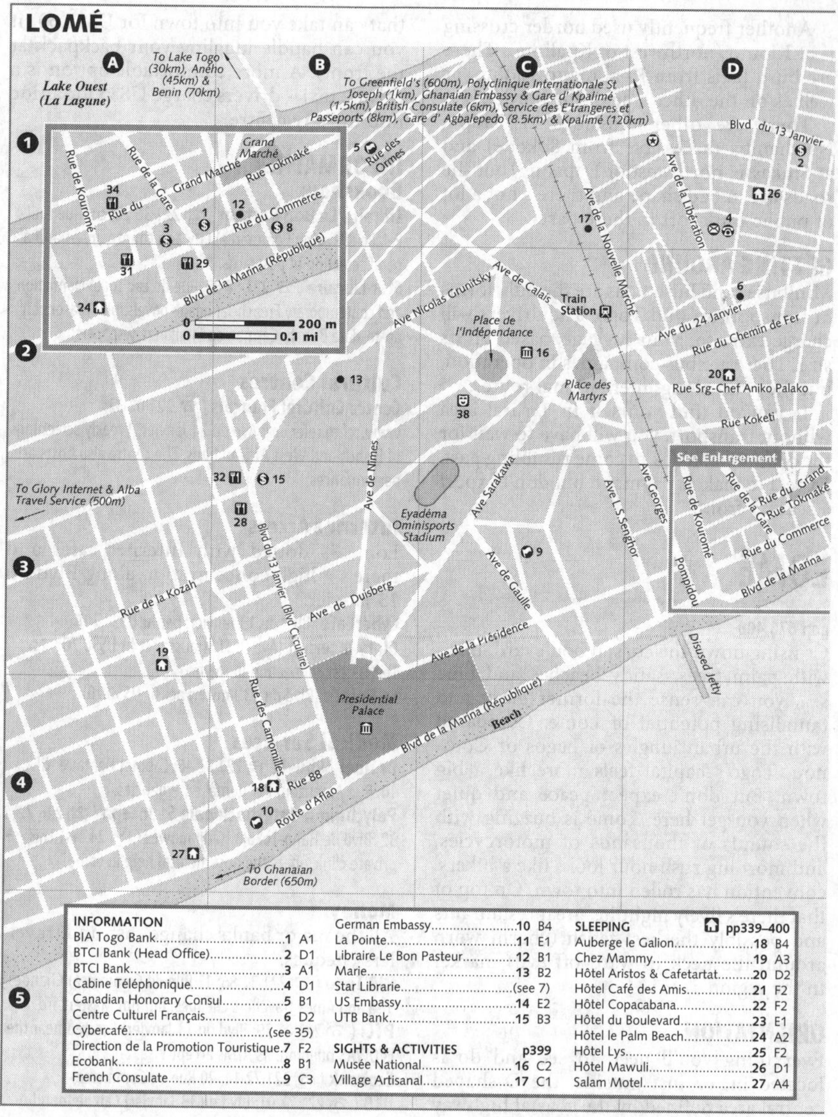

INFORMATION
- BIA Togo Bank ... 1 A1
- BTCI Bank (Head Office) ... 2 D1
- BTCI Bank ... 3 A1
- Cabine Téléphonique ... 4 D1
- Canadian Honorary Consul ... 5 B1
- Centre Culturel Français ... 6 D2
- Cybercafé ... (see 35)
- Direction de la Promotion Touristique ... 7 F2
- Ecobank ... 8 B1
- French Consulate ... 9 C3
- German Embassy ... 10 B4
- La Pointe ... 11 E1
- Libraire Le Bon Pasteur ... 12 B1
- Marie ... 13 B2
- Star Librarie ... (see 7)
- US Embassy ... 14 E2
- UTB Bank ... 15 B3

SIGHTS & ACTIVITIES p399
- Musée National ... 16 C2
- Village Artisanal ... 17 C1

SLEEPING pp339–400
- Auberge le Galion ... 18 B4
- Chez Mammy ... 19 A3
- Hôtel Aristos & Cafetartat ... 20 D2
- Hôtel Café des Amis ... 21 F2
- Hôtel Copacabana ... 22 F2
- Hôtel du Boulevard ... 23 E1
- Hôtel le Palm Beach ... 24 A2
- Hôtel Lys ... 25 F2
- Hôtel Mawuli ... 26 D1
- Salam Motel ... 27 A4

Tourist Offices

Alba Travel Service (☎ 222 13 43; Ave Joseph Strauss) A well-established travel agency that can organise tours and air travel.

Direction de la Promotion Touristique (☎ 221 56 62; Rue du Lac Togo; 🕐 7.30am-noon & 2.30-5.30pm Mon-Fri) One English-speaking member of staff, but not much useful information.

DANGERS & ANNOYANCES

Electricity cuts happen regularly during the day and at night, so remember to bring a flashlight.

It's not safe to walk along the beach or Blvd de la Marina (République) at night as muggings have occurred. Pickpockets around the Grand Marché and particularly

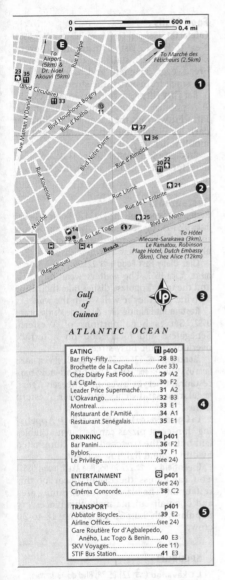

Gare de Cotonou are common at any time so be careful.

SIGHTS & ACTIVITIES

Marché des Féticheurs (Rue 3 AFM, Akodessewa; ☼ daily from around 8.30am-6pm) is the place to head if you want to sort out your lovelife, improve your memory or have good health. You'll smell the monkeys' testicles and snakes' heads as you approach. The *féticheurs* like to consult the spiritual 'juju man' for prices (and you can be sure the juju man will drive a very hard bargain!). It is located 4km north of the city centre in Akodessewa. A round trip by taxi from the city centre costs about US$3.20; a one-way *moto-taxi* trip costs about US$1.

Lomé's wide **beaches** and palm-fringed coastal **boulevard** give the place a romantic, almost 'Venice Beach' vibe. The locals sit under the shade of the palm trees just west of the disused jetty, while boys offer you bareback **horse riding**. On Sunday morning the beach comes alive with groups of students chanting and banging drums, Brazilian-style, as they jog along the beach and through the city.

The **Le Ramatou** (Route d'Aného; adult US$1.40) hotel owns the cleanest beach, with safe swimming. You can try using the next-door beach for free.

For salt-free swimming go to the Olympic-sized pool at **Hôtel Mecure Sarakawa** (☎ 227 65 90; Route de Benin; adult US$3.20).

The quiet, tree-lined avenues around the Place de l'Indépendance and the National Museum are free from noisy motorcycles and make a good place for a lazy cycle ride. Bikes can be bought from **Abbatoir** (Rue du Lac Togo) in front of Restaurant Mawulolo, diagonally opposite the US embassy.

SLEEPING

Lomé is full of cheap hotels, which are scattered all over town and in need of a facelift.

Hôtel Lys (☎ 222 63 62; Rue du Lac Togo; d US$7) This fresh, nicely decorated hotel has small, clean rooms with fan, and shared toilets that are clean enough to sit on.

Hôtel Café des Amis (☎ 221 06 18; Rue des Mauves; d US$12) The rooms in this new, Italian-themed hotel have freshly laid stone floors. The rooms come with fan but share a smelly bathroom. For the same price you can get a comfy space with fan and bathroom at the nearby **Hôtel Copacabana** (☎ 221 64 57; Rue Litimé).

Chez Mammy (☎ 222 44 80; Ave de Duisberg; dm US$6) This popular Peace Corps stopover has spotless rooms that are totally empty except for the beds and mosquito nets. The bathrooms, however, are a complete joy and there's a TV lounge downstairs.

TOGO

Hôtel du Boulevard (☎ 221 15 91; 204 Blvd du 13 Janvier; d US$6) Good, central location, popular with budget travellers. Rooms are large and quite clean, although the huge hallway lets in lots of street noise. Best choice in this price range.

Auberge Le Galion (☎ 220 00 30; Rue des Camomilles; d US$12) It's like rural France has been transplanted here. The spacious rooms have bathrooms and fans that can blow a hurricane. The pricey restaurant serves good meals.

Salam Motel (☎ 222 25 34; Route d'Aflao; d US$4) The small rooms, cluttered with furniture and fridges, are arranged around a courtyard. What the hotel lacks in charm it makes up for in a great sea location.

Hôtel Mawuli (☎ 222 12 75; off Rue Kadja; d US$6) The exterior may be pink and garish, but the rooms are dark enough to conceal the dirt. When we last visited the shared toilets were not clean.

Camping

Robinson Plage Hotel (☎ 947 00 17; robinsonplage@ hotmail.com; off Route d'Aflao; camp site per person US$3.50) Spend the night on some of Lomé's best stretch of beach.

Le Ramatou (☎ 227 43 53; off Route d'Aflao; camp site per person US$1.50) Right next door to the Robinson, but cheaper.

SPLURGE!

Hôtel Aristos (☎ 222 97 20; haristos@ub.tg; Rue Srgt-Chef Aniko Palako; d from US$59) Other hotels in town may be pricier, but the rooms here are the best. The TVs have 12 cable channels and there's a bedside phone for you to boast about to your friends.

EATING

They may have some of the best cuisine in West Africa, but eating out is not high up on the list of Togolese pastimes – foreign eateries tend to keep Lomé's restaurant scene alive. But cheap street nosh is in plentiful supply: you can't take more than a few steps along Blvd du 13 Janvier before hitting a food stall selling *koliko* (fried yams), fried plantain and *fufu* (fermented cassava). If you want snacks or to stock up for a picnic, head to **Leader Price Supermarket** (Rue du Commerce).

Food Stalls

Cafetartat (Rue Srgt-Chef Aniko Palako; mains US$1) Next to Hôtel Aristos, this is one of several cheap breakfast stalls in town. It serves bread, eggs, spaghetti and bacon that you can smell from across the street.

Bar Fifty-Fifty (Blvd du 13 Janvier; mains US$1.50-2) A popular evening-only restaurant, Bar Fifty-Fifty brings the pavement to life after dark, as people line up and sit down for mouthwatering *fufu* dishes.

Brochette de la Capital (Blvd du 13 Janvier) Head here for tasty chicken *brochettes* (kebabs) at US$1.50.

Restaurants

Restaurant Senégalais (☎ 222 34 20; Blvd du 13 Janvier; mains US$1-2) The Senegalese always know how to make delicious rice dishes. Here they've also thrown in a few Togolese dishes.

Chez Diaby Fast Food (☎ 221 75 11; Rue du Commerce; mains US$2) The waiters wear bow-ties, and the tasty Togolese dishes take their time arriving, but they're well worth the wait.

Restaurant l'Amitié (Rue du Grande Marché; mains US$2) Serves huge portions of Western, Senegalese and local food on a terrace overlooking the busy street.

Montreal (☎ 221 39 50; Blvd du 13 Janvier; mains from US$1.50; ☾ 4pm-3am) This brand-new bar-restaurant serves awesome cheeseburgers, vegetarian sandwiches and other Western dishes.

La Cigale (Blvd du 13 Janvier; mains US$7) Appetising thin-crust pizzas can be eaten at tables laid out on the stretched lawn, illuminated by dim ground lighting at night.

Greenfield's (☎ 222 21 55; Rue Akati; mains US$3) You can't miss the bright decor of this restaurant. The pizzas, outdoor dining area and open-air cinema make this place very popular with Lomé's expat and 18-to-30 crowd.

SPLURGE!

L'Okavango (☎ 221 05 78; Blvd du 13 Janvier; mains US$11) There's a Garden of Eden feel here, with lots of grass, lush foliage and even small deer wandering about! The inspiration may come from Botswana, but the tasty seafood dishes and pizzas are definitely more Western. The bar is very well-stocked but expensive.

TOGO

DRINKING

Lomé's nightlife has picked up again after years of keeping on the down-low. Blvd du 13 Janvier sees the lion's share of the action, although the whole city is dotted with lively drinking spots that tend to get going after 11pm.

Bar Panini (Blvd du 13 Janvier) Generally packed, with a mixed crowd that crams inside for snacks, cheap beers and occasional live music.

Le Privilège (Hôtel le Palm Beach; Rue Koumoré; US$3) Still going strong after 10 years, Lomé's beautiful people pile in here for some serious dancing to R & B and highlife (dance music) tunes.

Byblos (Blvd du 13 Janvier; admission US$4) Very chichi hangout blaring out salsa and highlife. If you can't afford the hideously expensive drinks, you can always try making friends with Lomé's jet set.

ENTERTAINMENT

Chez Alice (☎ 227 91 72; Route d'Aného; nonguests US$8) For live entertainment head to Chez Alice, about 12km from Lomé centre, on the road to Aného. Local bands and dance groups perform here on Wednesday evening.

There are a couple of good cinemas showing French-dubbed Hollywood films: **Cinéma Club** (Hôtel le Palm Beach; Rue Koumoré) shows recent Hollywood films four times a week and **Cinéma Concorde** (Hôtel du 2 Février, off Rue du Stade) also shows films a few times a week.

SHOPPING

Village Artisanal (Ave de la Nouvelle Marché) Artists sell and make batik T-shirts, dresses, leather bags and wooden sculptures for fixed prices in a quiet, secluded courtyard. Here you'll get less of the hard sell compared with the stalls near Rue du Commerce and the Grand Marché.

GETTING THERE & AWAY
Air

The airport is 7km northeast of the city centre. Among the airlines that connect Lomé with West Africa are **Ethiopian Airlines** (☎ 221 87 38), **Air Burkina** (☎ 220 00 83) and **Air Togo** (☎ 220 01 84). They all have offices at the Hôtel le Palm Beach complex on Rue Koumoré.

Cotonou (Benin) Air Togo: US$60, 50 minutes, weekly; Air Burkina: US$35, 45 minutes, twice-weekly.

Ouagadougou (Burkina Faso) Air Burkina: US$180, two hours, twice-weekly.

Local Transport

Minibuses and cars to all destinations north of Lomé depart from the Gare Routière du Nord d'Agbalepedo in northern Lomé, about 9km northwest of the centre.

Transport to Aného, Cotonou (Benin) and Accra (Ghana) departs several times a day from the chaotic market area, about 200m west of the STIF station.

STIF (☎ 221 38 48) buses depart daily from their depot on Blvd de la Marina to Ouagadougou (Burkina Faso, US$21, 40 hours), Bamako (Mali, US$38), Abidjan (Côte d'Ivoire, US$28, 15 hours) and Cotonou (Benin, US$5, three hours).

SKV Voyages (☎ 948 79 33) runs a weekly service to Ouagadougou (US$25, 40 hours) and Bamako (US$47, 48 hours), which departs from its office on Blvd du 13 Janvier.

GETTING AROUND

Shared taxis around town cost about US$0.15 for a short ride; private taxis charge about US$1 per journey. *Moto-taxis* (US$0.25) are a popular and convenient – if a little scary – way of getting around.

AROUND LOMÉ

LAKE TOGO & TOGOVILLE
☎ 331

Water-skiing and windsurfing in a shallow-ish lake that is bilharzia-free? It's an opportunity that cannot be missed, which is why Lake Togo is such a popular weekend getaway. On the lake's northern shore, Togoville is the home of voodoo. It's best to visit on Wednesday, market day. North of Togoville, the village of **Vogan** holds an impressive fetish-filled market on Friday.

Togoville's claim to fame is that Chief Mlapa III signed a treaty here with the German explorer Nachtigal, giving the Germans rights over all of Togoland.

Lake Togo is great for **water sports**, though the prices will have you eating bananas for a day or two. **Hôtel le Lac** (☎ 60 07) on the north side of the lake hires out water-skiing and windsurfing equipment for US$17 per day.

In Togoville stop and have a chat with **Chief Mlapa V Moyennant**, who (for a small fee) will show you his throne and some interesting pictures of his grandfather. His house is 100m west of the church. Otherwise you can wander around the back streets (with a guide if you like – US$2) and explore the many fetishes on display.

Hôtel Nachtigal (☎ 333 70 76; fax 221 6482; d with bathroom US$11) 100m west of the market, has comfortable, excellent-value rooms, plus a tennis court in the grounds. This Togoville hotel also offers cheap meals. Alternatively you can try the food stalls at the Togoville market.

From Lomé, catch a bush taxi to Aného (US$1, 45 minutes), then take another bush taxi to Togoville (US$0.90, 20 minutes). If you want to avoid backtracking you can jump off the taxi at Agbodrafo (about 10km before Aného) and get a local to take you across the lake to Togoville by canoe for about US$2.50.

SOUTHERN TOGO

Southern Togo is a narrow region that manages to squeeze in tranquil coastal lagoons, which rise into beautiful hills dotted with waterfalls that make up some of Togo's finest scenery.

ANÉHO
☎ 331 / pop 26,000

Aného is a sleepy town set on a beautiful blue **lagoon**, east along the coast from Lomé. It was the colonial capital of Togo until 1920, but is now a place where travellers come to sit back, relax and take lazy pirogue (traditional canoe) rides in the quiet waters.

Residence Antoinette (☎ 0110; Route de Togo-Benin; d US$10) The cheapest option in town, this hotel cuts a lonely figure on the roadside. The rooms are clean with fan, though nothing special. There's a restaurant, too.

La Becca (☎ 0513; Route de Togo-Benin; d US$14) The kitsch statues in the interior courtyard are a real eye-opener, and the rooms are fresh and clean with spotless bathrooms. It is also close to several eateries along the main road.

Hôtel de l'Oasis & Restaurant (☎ 0125; Route de Togo-Benin; d US$15) It's the priciest hotel in town, but you're paying for clean rooms, great lagoon views and a pet crocodile on the premises.

There's plenty of cheap *fufu* sold at the stalls near the defunct train station.

Bar 620 (off Rue de l'Hôpital) is a good place for cheap, local food for under US$1. At night it turns into a lively drink spot.

If you're self-catering, head for the **SGGG Supermarket** (Route de Togo-Benin). Bar Soprano next door is a popular place for evening drinks.

On Sunday make a beeline for **Hôtel de l'Oasis & Restaurant** (buffet US$10), where the international chef, Nicolas, lays on a mouthwatering buffet.

From the *gare routière* (bus or transport station) at the northeastern end of town, bush taxis and minibuses head to Lomé (US$1, 45 minutes), as well as the Benin (US$3, two hours) border and Cotonou (US$4, three hours).

KPALIMÉ
☎ 441 / pop 75,200

Kpalimé (pah-lee-may) is a small town plopped in the middle of some of Togo's finest scenery. You can take a hike in the beautiful surrounding countryside, or visit the Kpimé Falls. Other attractions include the **mountains** around Klouto (17km northwest of Kpalimé) with their various butterfly species, and **Mt Agou** (986m), Togo's highest mountain (20km southeast of Kpalimé).

After the wet season, the impressive **Kpimé Falls** crash onto the rocks from 100m above. The guide (US$1) will point out the monkeys that emerge in the evening. To get here, hire a bush taxi from Kpalimé (US$8, round trip). It's also possible to cycle here if you're reasonably fit. There are a few stalls in the market area that have bikes. Rental is around US$5 for a day (negotiable).

About 2km northwest of central Kpalimé, the **Centre Artisanal** (☺ 7am-5.30pm Mon-Sat, 8.30am-1pm Sun) sells pottery, macramé and batiks at fixed prices. A bush taxi here costs US$1.60 one way.

Hôtel Cristal (☎ 0479; Rue de Bakula; d US$10) Possibly the best-value accommodation in Togo. The plush lobby, classy restaurant and comfortable rooms might leave you thinking you've walked into the wrong hotel.

Hôtel Évasion (☎ 0185; d with bathroom US$6) Worth the trek up the long dirt path to get here. Located in a quiet part of town, the clean rooms are arranged in separate bungalows. The English-speaking owner also runs a good restaurant.

Hôtel Domino (☎ 0579; Rond-Point Texaco; d US$5) The rooms are dull and the bed sheets untrustworthy. But at least the *gare routière* is close by.

Cafeteria de Bel Air serves cheap European and Togolese meals and snacks 24 hours a day, every day. **Amical Bon Café** (Rue Singa) also serves cheap meals (including breakfast) for around US$2.

From the main *gare routière*, minibuses regularly go to Kara (US$6, seven hours) and Lomé (US$2.50, three hours).

ATAKPAMÉ
☎ 440 / pop 64,300

Atakpamé town is nestled in the mountains, with a pleasant climate that once made it a favourite hill station for German colonial administrators. Today it's more of an industrial hub and, for travellers, a good place to break the journey heading north or south. The town is famous for its **stilt dancers** and the colourful **market** on Friday.

Hôtel Delices des Retraites (☎ 0437; Route de Lomé; d US$5) This friendly place has fresh, clean rooms and a sitting area on the landing. The restaurant serves cheap African and European food. A popular choice with travellers.

Hôtel Le Kapokier (☎ 0284; d US$7) Located next to the post office, this hotel has spacious, clean rooms and shared toilets. The restaurant has a terrace overlooking the street and an extensive menu that includes vegetarian dishes.

Hôtel Relais des Plateaux (☎ 1105; Rue de la Station de Lomé; d US$11) A spacious, somewhat empty feel with forgettable but clean enough rooms.

Foyer des Affaires (☎ 0653, Rue de la Station de Lomé; d US$5) Rooms are bare but clean. Good value.

La Sagesse (Rue du Marché) is one of several places around the market where you can fill yourself with local food.

Bar-Restaurant Le Balafon (Rue du Gnagna) is popular eatery near UTB Bank. Those staying at the other end of town should try **Restaurant Chez Soi** (Route Internationale) where the no-nonsense women dole out ultra-cheap rice, *fufu* and tripe.

Transport to Lomé and Kara leaves from the Station de Lomé next to the Shell petrol station south of the Police Commissariat. There are minibuses to Lomé (US$3, 3½

hours), Sokodé (US$3, 3½ hours) and Kara (US$5, five hours). To get to Badou (US$2, 1½ hours) and Kpalimé (US$1.60, two hours), minibuses depart from Station de Kpalimé, just south of the market.

BADOU
☎ 443 / pop 21,600

Badou is one of the border crossings to and from Ghana and is the base for visiting Togo's best waterfall, the 35m-high Akloa Falls.

It's like something straight out of a shampoo commercial: water gushing down a cliff, and people frolicking in the pool below, surrounded by lush vegetation. The gorgeous **Akloa Falls** are accessible by taxi from Badou (about US$0.40) or a 40-minute walk from Tomagbé village. The entry fee (US$1.60) includes a local guide. The strenuous climb follows the Domi River, and passes through coffee fields, pineapple plantations and a butterfly garden. At the time of research, local artists were planning to sell their work by the waterfalls.

For cheap rooms head to **Cascade Plus Bar Hotel** (d US$4), by the petrol station, or the more comfortable **Hôtel Abuta** (☎ 0016; camp site per person US$3; r US$10). The latter has the town's only restaurant, but street food is available on the road leading to it.

There are regular minibuses between Badou and Atakpamé (US$2, 1½ hours), but you'll have to change at Atakpamé for transport to Lomé or points further north.

NORTHERN TOGO

Togo takes on a slightly more Islamic vibe as you travel further north. Here, the land's deep valleys and tall mountains peter out into flat savanna.

SOKODÉ
☎ 550 / pop 84,200

Driving along the main road you'd never guess that Sokodé is Togo's second-largest town. It has a low-key, distinctly Muslim feel, although the locals still maintain some pre-Islamic traditions. One of the most eye-boggling animist ceremonies, **Adossa**, takes place here one day after the Prophet's birthday (around April–May in 2004 and 2005). The town's menfolk slash each other with

TOGO

knives after drinking a specially prepared potion that supposedly makes their skin impenetrable.

Sleeping
In terms of finding cheap lodging that won't scar the memory, there's a wide choice in Sokodé.

Cercle de l'Amitié (☎ 0906; Route de Kara; d US$6) Will you be staying in Addis Ababa or Lagos tonight? Each of the clean, bamboo-walled rooms is named after an African city in this excellent-value hotel. The restaurant's cuisine is not so cosmopolitan, but damn tasty nevertheless.

Hôtel Essofa (☎ 0989; d from US$7) This gem of a hotel is located on a dirt path off Route de Kara (turn right as you go south past UTB Bank). The comfortable rooms are very good value and the (pricey) restaurant and bar brings in the locals every night.

Chez Macau (☎ 1641; d with bathroom US$4) Signposted off the main road to Lomé, the rooms here are dark and basic, but there's a popular restaurant attached.

Hôtel Le Manguier (☎ 1725; signposted off the main road to Lomé; d US$4) Ancient Janet Jackson posters decorate the walls of the simple but grubby rooms. Whoever cleaned the (pleasant) showers last time we stayed here forgot to do the toilets as well. The restaurant serves cheap meals in a huge courtyard. The main road to Lomé has signs to the hotel.

Eating & Drinking
Cafeteria Albarka (Route de Lomé; mains US$1-1.50; ☺ 24hr) by the Texaco petrol station serves cheap meals.

For local and continental dishes with a few vegetarian options, head for the locally recommended **Chez Macau** (mains US$1-3). The cheap beers also make it a good place for a quiet evening drink. **Prestige Bar & Restaurant** (Route de Lomé; mains US$2-3) serves tasty food.

Getting There & Away
From the *gare routière*, two blocks west of the market, minibuses regularly go to Kara (US$1.60, one hour), Atakpamé (US$3, 2½ hours) and Lomé (US$6, six hours).

KARA
☎ 660 / pop 49,800
Kara is the launch point for an unmissable trip to the **Tamberma Valley** (57km from Kara; see p405) and the scenic **Mt Kabyé** region (15km northeast of Kara). It is also a good stopover between Lomé and Burkina Faso. Despite its small size, Kara has some of Togo's best roads and facilities – thanks to its favourite son, Gnassingbé Eyadéma, whose photograph beautifies the walls of many of the hotels and restaurants.

Sleeping
Kara is as close to budget heaven as you can get in Togo.

Centre Communautaire des Affaires Sociales (☎ 6118; Route de Maman N'Danida; dm/s/d with bathroom US$3/6/13) By far the best value in Kara, there aren't any other hotels offering rooms with bathroom at such cheap rates. The internal windows and student lodgers make a noisy combination, though.

Hôtel Le Relais (☎ 0188; off Route de Maman N'Danida; camp site per person/d US$3/8) It's off the beaten track but the rooms, surrounding a plant-filled courtyard, are spotless and have a bathroom. The restaurant's menu serves vegetarian salads among its African and Continental dishes.

Hôtel de France (☎ 0342; off Rue de Chaminade; d with bathroom US$8) This hotel has relocated to no-man's land in the northern reaches of town. The rooms are brand new, spacious, but you might feel a bit stranded here.

Hôtel Sapaw (☎ 1444; off Rue de l'Hôtel de Ville; d US$5) The plain rooms with fan are clean and there's an atmospheric bar-restaurant attached. Across the street Hôtel Herzo has big, similar-priced rooms with fan.

Eating & Drinking
Cafeteria Mufet (Route Internationale) If you've been hanging out for Quaker oats, then this is the place for breakfast. This roadside eatery also serves Togolese food for less than US$1.50. Alternatively, try **Bar Columbia** (off Rue de l'Hôtel de Ville), where you'll have to fight for a seat before tucking into sublime pâté and *fufu*.

SPLURGE!

Hôtel Le Jardin (☎ 0134; off Rue de l'Hôtel de Ville; mains US$6) Whoever trained the chefs at Le Jardin ought to be congratulated. The pricey Asian and French cuisine practically borders on authentic and is worth a naughty splurge.

TOGO

Le Château (Ave du 13 Janvier; mains US$1) The popular Le Château prepares seriously tasty African and French meals on a terrace overlooking the street, and turns into a fun drinking spot at night.

Self-caterers can stock up at **SGGG Supermarket** (Ave du 13 Janvier).

Getting There & Away

From the main *gare routière* minibuses go to Sokodé (US$1.60, one hour), Atakpamé (US$5, five hours), Dapaong (US$4, four hours) and Kpalimé (US$6, seven hours). Transport to the borders of Ghana and Benin leaves from the Station du Grande Marché.

TAMBERMA VALLEY

It would be a crime to visit Togo and not check out this amazing valley. It has a unique collection of **fortified villages**, founded in the 17th century by people who fled the slaving forays of the Abomey kings (see the boxed text below).

Because the valley remained isolated until recently, the local culture is relatively intact and still suspicious of foreigners, although they are getting used to seeing

---

TAMBERMA COMPOUNDS

Still being constructed today, a typical Tamberma compound, called a *tata*, consists of a series of towers connected by thick walls with only one doorway to the outside. They are ingeniously built, using just clay, straw and wood – but no tools.

In the old days, the castlelike nature of these amazing structures helped ward off invasions by neighbouring tribes and, later, the Germans. Inside, there's a huge elevated terrace of clay-covered logs where the inhabitants cook, dry their millet and corn, and generally hang out in their free time.

The towers, which are capped with cone-shaped roofs, are used for storing corn and millet. The other rooms are used for sleeping, bathing and, during the rainy season, cooking. The animals are kept under the terrace, away from the rain.

If you're lucky enough to go inside you might see fetish animal skulls hanging on the walls and ceilings, and a tiny altar for sacrificing chickens.

---

travellers. **Nadoba** is a sizeable market town on the edge of the valley. The Nadoba-based **Association Général Voluntaire Pour le Développement Communautaire** (AGVDC; ☎ 667 20 11) can take you on a tour of Warengo, a small Somba village (US$10).

AGVDC (d US$3) in Nadoba offers very basic accommodation (no electricity). There's plenty of beer available, but food is on request. To arrange food in advance, call the AGVDC number.

There is nowhere to camp in the actual villages, but in Kandè there is a basic **campement** (☎ 667 00 73; bed US$3.50).

Bush taxis shuttle between Kandè and Nadoba on Wednesday (market day in Nadoba) and Friday (market day in Kandè), A chartered taxi for the day from Kara to visit the fortified villages costs around US$25 (after a lot of haggling).

DAPAONG

☎ 770 / pop 31,000

The flat, scrubby landscape makes you feel as though you're already in Burkina Faso (or are still there). Dapaong is Togo's most northerly town and sits in the middle of a major rice- and cotton-growing area. There's a lively Saturday **market** here, and it is also the jumping-off point for visits to the sadly depleted **Parc National de la Fosse aux Lions**. There aren't any lions in the park, just bushland and the occasional village.

Sleeping

Dapaong has plenty of cheap rooms, but nothing to get excited about.

Hôtel Lafia (☎ 946 22 41; Route de Kara; d US$6) Located within walking distance of the main *gare routière*, this spacious, breezy hotel has surprisingly pleasant rooms, and balconies that overlook the street (and a poor monkey tied to a tree).

Foyer des Affaires Sociales (☎ 8444; Route de Nasablé; dm/d US$3/4) Handily located about 2km north of the market, the rooms and their adjoining bathrooms are dull and a little grubby.

Hôtel Le Sahelien (☎ 8184; d US$8) This hotel in the market square has lost some of its value now that its restaurant has folded. It has darkish rooms and semiclean bathrooms, but it is right in the middle of the market and close to the Station du Grande Marché.

TOGO

Eating & Drinking

There are plenty of **food stalls** in the market. Also try the open-air **Bar-Dancing La Pléiade** (off Route de Korbangou) for cheap food and beer.

The **Hôtel Campement**, 500m south of the Commissariat, has the best meals, though they are expensive.

Getting There & Away

Transport to Sinkasse on the Burkina Faso border (US$1) and to Ouagadougou (US$7) regularly departs from Station de Korbangou, several blocks north of the market. Minibuses to Kara (US$4, four hours) and Lomé (US$10, 14 hours) leave from the main *gare routière*, 2km south of the town centre.

TOGO DIRECTORY

ACCOMMODATION

Places to stay in Togo are pretty cheap by West African standards. Most singles and doubles start at around US$6 (a bit higher in Lomé), though the rooms are often old and decrepit. Comfortable rooms with bathroom and air-con cost about US$16 to US$19. Prices include all taxes and tariffs are often listed somewhere prominent in the hotel entrance.

ACTIVITIES

Hiking

Togo's low mountains and beautiful scenery make it a good place for hiking, especially in the Kpalimé region. The best time to go is around late July and August, after the rains have stopped but before the waterfalls have run dry.

Swimming

There are some good beaches near Lomé and Aného, but the powerful currents can suck you under if you are not careful. Several of the top-end hotels have swimming pools.

Water Sports

The relatively shallow and bilharzia-free Lake Togo is one of the few places in the region where you can water-ski and windsurf. Equipment rental costs around US$17 for the day.

BUSINESS HOURS

Business hours are from 8am to 12pm and 3pm to 6pm Monday to Friday, and 7.30am to 12.30pm Saturday. Government offices are open from 7.30am to noon and 2.30pm to 5.30pm Monday to Friday. Banking hours are generally from 7.30am to 11am and 2pm to 3pm Monday to Friday.

DANGERS & ANNOYANCES

Togo is a generally safe and easy country for people to travel around, especially now that the ubiquitous police checks and roadblocks are a thing of the past. In Lomé, muggings and petty theft still do occur at night (especially along the beach) so it's best to take a *moto-taxi* after dark. Pickpockets are a real danger around the Grand Marché and the Gare de Cotonou, so you should avoid carrying valuables at all times.

EMBASSIES & CONSULATES

Togo has diplomatic representation in Ghana (see p391).

The following countries have representation in Lomé. For the location of these and other consulates, see the Lomé map.

Canada Honorary Consul (☎ 221 32 99; 1278 Rue des Ormes)
France (☎ 221 25 76; Rue de la Marina)
Germany (☎ 221 23 38; Route d'Aflao)
Ghana (☎ 221 31 94; Route de Kpalimé)
UK (☎ 226 91 81; Residence du Benin, Ave de l'Amitié)
USA (☎ 221 29 91; Rue Kouenou)

Visas for Burkina Faso and Côte d'Ivoire are issued by the French Consulate, and visas for Benin are issued at the border (see opposite for details).

FESTIVALS & EVENTS

Special events include Evala, the wrestling festival in the Kabyé region around Kara, in July; the Dzawuwu-Za harvest festival in Klouto and the Ayiza harvest festival in Tsèviè in August; and the Igname (yam) festival in Bassar in September.

FOOD & DRINK

The food in Togo is some of the best in West Africa and there are lots of places to try it, especially in Lomé. As in most of West Africa, meals are usually based on a starch staple accompanied by sauces. Sauces and starches come in many varieties. You'll find *riz sauce arachide* (rice with peanut sauce) almost everywhere. Togo also has its fair share of local brews. In the north, the preferred drink is *tchakpallo*, which is fermented millet with a frothy head, often found in the market areas. In the south, the most popular brews are palm wine and, to a lesser extent, *sodabe*. Distilled from palm wine, this is an incredibly strong, clear-coloured alcohol that can almost knock you out if you're not careful.

HOLIDAYS

As well as religious holidays listed in the Africa Directory chapter (p1003) the principal public holidays in Togo, these are:

1 January New Year's Day
13 January Meditation Day
27 April National Day
21 June Day of the Martyrs

MAPS

The best map of Lomé is the *Lomé city map* (1998) available at most bookshops and at the **Marie** (☎ 221 26 20; off Ave Sarakawa). It costs US$12.

MEDIA

The best bookshops and top hotels stock week-old British, American, German and Italian newspapers. There are several Togolese newspapers, but the biggest-selling are the government-run *Togo Presse* and the privately owned opposition daily, *Le Combat*. These are widely available in Lomé and in the larger towns.

Radio Togo, the national station, broadcasts news in French, Ewe and Kabyé, but Radio France Internationale (RFI) is by far the most popular station.

MONEY

Togo has ATMs operated by BTCI in every major town. They accept Visa cards, but not MasterCard. Credit cards are rarely accepted anywhere except in Lomé's large hotels. All the banks can change cash and travellers cheques. Black marketeers operate at the borders and around Rue de Commerce in Lomé and will change money at poor rates.

Travellers Cheques

All the main banks accept travellers cheques and they usually ask for the original receipts. Remember, however, that BIA Togo does not accept MasterCard travellers cheques.

POST & TELEPHONE

Postcards and letters per 10g cost US$1 to Europe and US$0.80 to North America and Australasia.

International phone calls can be made from official Telecom offices, or from the private telephone centres you'll find in every town. If you have a mobile phone, you can get a SIM card with prepaid credit from Togocel for about US$20. Additional cards start at US$5.

VISAS

Everyone is required to obtain a visa. Currently, one-month visas are issued at the airport, and one-week extendible visas (US$17) are available at the major border crossings.

Visa Extensions

Visas can be extended at Agbalepedo's **Service des Étrangeres et Passeports** (☎ 250 78 56; Rue des Tecks). Tell taxi drivers it's near the GTA building. A one-/three-month visa costs US$17/51. Bring three photos.

Visas for Onward Travel

Visas for most of the following countries can be obtained in Lomé. See opposite for embassy and consulate information.
Benin There is no Beninese embassy in Lomé, but temporary visas (US$17) are issued at the border; these can be extended at the Direction Immigration/Émigration in Cotonou within 24 hours for another US$20. Four photos are required.
Ghana One-month visas cost US$16/84 for single/multiple entry (depending on nationality) and are issued within 48 hours. Four photos are required.
Burkina Faso & Côte d'Ivoire The French consulate in Lomé issues three-month visas for both countries. Visas cost US$34, are issued within 48 hours and four photos are required.

WOMEN TRAVELLERS

In the predominantly Muslim northern towns of Sokodé and Kara, long dresses and sleeves are recommended as a mark of respect.

Benin

HIGHLIGHTS

- **Ganvié** The 'Venice' of Africa – the thatched-roof bamboo huts in this fascinating stilt village are perfectly viewed on a boat ride (p417)
- **Abomey** Huge walls, beautiful bas-reliefs and royal thrones (mounted on real human skulls) in one of Africa's largest palaces at the ancient capital of the Dahomey empire (p419)
- **Ouidah** In Benin's rich voodoo centre you can watch a spell-binding ritual, complete with animal sacrifices (p417)
- **Best journey** From the fetishes and tranquil stilt villages in Ouidah, retrace the last steps of the slaves along the Route des Esclaves, and finish up at the white-sand beach and the poignant Point of No Return memorial (p417)
- **Off the beaten track** Parc National de Pendjari, one of the best, but still low-key, wildlife reserves in the region with easy-to-spot hippos, lions and elephants (p420)

FAST FACTS

- **Area** 112,622 sq km
- **ATMs** none
- **Borders** Burkina Faso, Niger, Nigeria, Togo
- **Budget** US$23 to US$30 a day
- **Capital** Porto Novo
- **Languages** French, Fon, Bariba, Dendi
- **Money** West African CFA; US$1 = CFA600
- **Population** 6.7 million
- **Seasons** wet (Apr–Oct), dry (Nov–Mar)
- **Telephone** country code ☎ 229; international access code ☎ 00
- **Time** GMT/UTC + 1
- **Visas** US$20 to US$60 for one month, issued at most borders

You've heard about voodoo, you've heard about the Amazon female warriors, and you know about the Atlantic slave trade. But have you ever thought about where it all started?

Head to Benin to find out, and you'll get even more than you bargained for. You'll find remnants of vast palaces of the formidable Dahomey empire, boat rides through villages built entirely on stilts, hippos eyeballing you from murky rivers, deserted beaches where slaves once made their exit, and stunning indigenous architecture. There's even more to discover, but it takes time – Benin likes to keep its goodies hidden. So come and explore and let this country put a spell on you.

BENIN

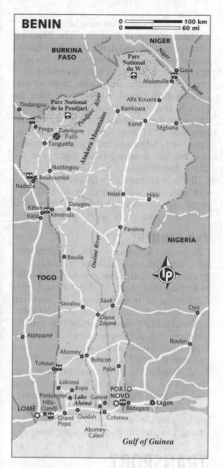

BENIN

0 _____ 100 km
0 _____ 60 mi

BURKINA FASO

NIGER

Parc National du W

Gaya

Malanville

Alfa Kouara

Tindangou

Parc National de la Pendjari

Banikoara

Porga *Tanougou Falls*

Kandi

Ségbana

Tanguiéta

Atakora Mountains

Pendjari River

Natitingou

Boukoumbé

Nadoba

Ndali

Nikki

Kétao

Djougou

Kara

Kémérida

Parakou

NIGERIA

Bassila

Ouémé River

TOGO

Savalou

Savé

Oyo

Dassa Zoumé

Atakpamé

Ibadan

Abomey

Bohicon

Tohoun

Pobè

Lokossa

Bopa

Possotomé

Lake Ahémé

PORTO NOVO

Hilla-Condji

Ganvié

Badagary

Lagos

LOMÉ

Grand Popo

Ouidah

Cotonou

Abomey-Calavi

Gulf of Guinea

HISTORY

Benin and the surrounding area was settled in the 13th century by Ewé-speaking people in the south, and by Voltaic-speaking people to the north.

By the 16th century the small space that is now Benin was dominated by large, prominent Fon states such as Allada, Porto Novo and, in particular, Dahomey. The Dahomian people fought and hacked their way to dominance over the southern region. At the same time, the Portuguese and other Europeans set up shop along the coast, hawking their cloth and guns in exchange for slaves, which Dahomians readily supplied. With their new-found wealth and military might, Dahomey kings built vast palaces and consolidated their political power.

But with the abolition of the slave trade and tightening of colonial controls, Dahomey's influence plummeted. By the late 19th century the French had taken over, incorporating the entire region into French West Africa in 1904. The locals were not happy about becoming French subjects, but soon went along with the takeover – Dahomians were a well-educated bunch (thanks to decades of missionary teaching) and ended up filling various administrative posts across the French West African colonies.

Independence

When Dahomey and some other French colonies gained their independence in 1960, some Dahomian expats returned home and formed an elite group of jobless, disenchanted intellectuals, whose discontent – along with traditional factionalism - spawned years of coups and power struggles in the country. Twelve years after independence, Dahomey (now called Benin) had already changed government nine times.

'Stability' eventually came in the form of the army's Major Mathieu Kérékou, who seized power in a 1972 coup that began almost two decades of military dictatorship. In an attempt to break from the colonial past, and distance itself from more 'moderate' neighbouring states, Kérékou's Benin took a sharp turn to the left, embracing Marxism and earning the nickname 'Africa's Cuba'.

Tensions with neighbouring Nigeria and Togo flared, often resulting in border closures and disruption of trade.

Kérékou's socialist agenda included major reforms in agriculture and education, but they left Benin virtually bankrupt by 1988. Matters were made even worse when the East European communist bloc (and the financial aid it provided) collapsed. France came to Benin's rescue – but on the condition that Kérékou introduce economic reform and accept multiparty democracy.

The Democratic Era

Unusually for a military dictator, Kérékou stepped down without a fuss in 1990 and accepted a new, provisional government that sidelined all members of his military government. Kérékou, however, remained nominal head of state, and basked in the

BENIN

glory of Benin's new reputation as a beacon of African democracy.

In March 1991 multiparty elections were held and won by Nicéphore Soglo, a former World Bank official. But his decision to devalue the CFA during a time of rising unemployment won him few friends among the Beninese people.

As a backlash, they voted Kérékou back into power in March 1996, and he went on to win the 2001 elections. Although the elections were tarnished by accusations of corruption, the withdrawal of two candidates and low voter turnout, discontent over the electoral process has not brought about any violence. Perhaps democracy has established solid roots. Kérékou may have his critics but – fingers crossed – it looks as though Benin's days of military coups may be over.

In 2003, parliamentary elections ran smoothly despite the opposition's accusations of government intimidation. The Union of Tomorrow's Benin (UBF – a new coalition of parties that support president Kérékou) won the elections, although their existing seat majority was narrowed somewhat.

THE CULTURE
Beninese society is so contradictory that it's difficult to sum it up. The mighty independent empire participated in some of the biggest slave markets; it painted itself deep red with Marxism before dancing to the tune of the International Monetary Fund (IMF); and then years of stubborn dictatorship were suddenly swept aside by stable democracy. Above all, Benin's sophisticated, intellectual postcolonial traditions have mixed with thriving animist undercurrents that ultimately govern the nation's psyche. Ask most Beninese and they'll tell you that it is, paradoxically, gri-gri (a curse) that brings rain and good fortune, destroys crops and ensures peaceful elections.

While 20% of the population is Christian and 15% worship Allah, the majority of them will still seek protection and favours from the voodoo spirits to which they are tied at birth. On Voodoo Day each year, thousands of country folk rub shoulders with urban sophisticates on Ouidah's beaches to pray for good health, and make sacrifices to their ancestors.

But if there's one Beninese face that never changes, it's the smiling one. The Beninese manage to laugh and dance through the most desperate poverty, welcoming outsiders with open arms. Perhaps it's their history of mixing with foreigners that makes them so welcoming: first it was the Portuguese, then the French, then the Brazilian freed slaves who came to these shores. Now Cotonou has become one of West Africa's major melting pots, with Nigerians, Senegalese, Togolese and Ivorians downing beers together in the city's ubiquitous bars and nightclubs.

Benin's attitude to women, however, is not quite so enlightened. Female literacy rates lag well behind those of men, and politics remain more or less a male affair.

ENVIRONMENT
The coastal lowlands rise to a central plateau and into the Atakora mountains in the northwest. In southern Benin, rainfall is highest from April to mid-July and mid-September to late October. The northern rainy season is from June to early October.

Despite rainy seasons, drought is a major problem for northern, marginal farmers, and deforestation and desertification have reduced the southern rainforests and farmland. Wildlife is threatened by poaching, though the Parc National de la Pendjari and Parc National du W provide decent protection for the animals. While the national parks provide some protection, it's not enough to prevent poaching completely.

TRANSPORT

GETTING THERE & AWAY
Air
There are four direct weekly flights between Paris and Cotonou on Air France. A standard return economy fare is about US$600/750 in the low/high season. Air Togo also flies between Cotonou and Paris twice weekly.

Airlines connecting Cotonou with West Africa include Air Ivoire, Air Burkina, Ghana

DEPARTURE TAX
There is a departure tax of US$10, which is included in the price of air tickets.

Airways, Cameroon Airlines, Air Togo and Nigeria Airways (see p415 for airline contact information).

Land

BURKINA FASO
The main border crossing is between Porga and Tindangou in the northwest corner of Benin.

There's a border crossing near Tanguiéta, also in the northwest. At least one bush taxi a day runs from Natitingou to Tanguiéta, but traffic is scarce along the dirt road between Tanguiéta and the border, except on market day (Monday). Minibuses and bush taxis from the border to Burkina's Fada-N'Gourma are infrequent and fill up slowly. There are regular connections between Fada N'Gourma and Ouagadougou by bus and bush taxi or minibus.

NIGER
The only border crossing is between Malanville and Gaya in northeast Benin. Malanville is easy to reach by bus direct from Cotonou or other parts of the country, then you cross the bridge over the Niger River (there are *moto-taxis* – motorcycle taxis) to Gaya. From Gaya, minibuses (six hours) and bush taxis (four to six hours) run to Niamey.

There are bush taxis from Malanville to Dosso (2½ hours), half-way between Niamey and Gaya.

NIGERIA
The only reliable border crossing is on the chaotic main road between Cotonou and Lagos (crossing open 24 hours). All sorts of regular public transport and daily STIF buses link the two cities.

TOGO
The main border crossing is at Hilla-Conji on the main road between Cotonou and Lomé. Bush taxis regularly ply this road and the border is open 24 hours, but temporary visas for Togo are only issued between 8am and 6pm. Another good crossing point from Togo into Benin is at Kétao, east of Kara. This border closes at 10pm.

GETTING AROUND
Car & Motorcycle
Because car rental in Cotonou is so expensive, and finding a taxi willing to negotiate a reasonable all-day rate is quite difficult, it's best to use the minibuses and taxis. The main north–south road through Parakou and Malanville is sealed and in good condition.

In towns you'll find *zemi-johns* (motorcycle/moped taxis). They are fast and convenient, but not as safe as regular taxis. In the larger towns and cities the drivers are recognisable by their yellow shirts. Expect to pay around US$0.30 per ride.

Local Transport
Buses are the most comfortable option for getting around in Benin. **Africa Lines** (☎ 30 85 85) operates separate services from Cotonou to Savalou (US$6, five hours), Parakou (US$11, seven hours), Natitingou (US$14, nine hours) and Malanville (US$19, 11 hours), each departing at 7am daily. Air-conditioned, with one bum for one seat, it's by far the most comfortable form of transport.

Minibuses and Peugeot bush taxis are the main form of transport. In the south, 'five-seater' cars will normally squeeze in about twice that number of passengers, while in northern Benin vehicles with nine seats are common on longer journeys. There is usually a negotiable surcharge for luggage. Some sample fares include: Cotonou to Abomey (US$4), Cotonou to Natitingou (US$14), and Cotonou to Ouidah (US$1).

In isolated rural areas, hitching is often the only option. You'll pay for a lift on a truck, but might get a free ride in the very occasional private car that passes.

Train
Benin's railway line links Cotonou with Parakou, via Bohicon (near Abomey). Trains leave daily in both directions, and another one furnished with couchettes (seats that convert to beds) departs twice weekly in both directions.

Tickets between Cotonou and Bohicon (about four hours) cost US$2.50/1.50 in 1st/2nd class, or US$5 for a sleeper; between Cotonou and Parakou (about 12 hours) is US$9/7 in 1st/2nd class and US$13 for a sleeper. There is also a daily express (nine hours) between Cotonou and Parakou. Food is available along the way.

BENIN

COTONOU

pop 762,000

Porto Novo may be the official capital, but Cotonou is where it all happens. It's large and chaotic: if the sound of hundreds of screeching *zemi-johns* doesn't bother you

the eye-stinging pollution may. But look past the smoggy haze and you'll find a city that's lively, friendly and full of things to do, with the region's best selection of eateries.

ORIENTATION

The heart of town is the intersection of Ave Clozel and Ave Steinmetz. Going northeast

COTONOU

INFORMATION
American Cultural Centre...........1 B5
Bank of Africa.........................2 A4
Belgian Consulate....................3 B2
Centre Culturel Français......(see 14)
Cyber Jonquet.........................4 B3
Cyber Laha.............................5 A2
Danish Embassy.......................6 A5
Direction de Tourisme et de l'Hotellerie
(Tourist Office)......................7 A4
Dr Richardier (dentist)..............8 C5
Ecobank (Main Office)...............9 E4
Ecobank...............................10 C4
Embassy of Niger....................11 B4
Financial Bank........................12 B3
French Consulate.....................13 B4
French Embassy.......................14 C5
German Embassy......................15 C5
Ghanaian Embassy...................16 A5
Nigerian Embassy....................17 B5
Polyclinique les Cocotiers..........18 B5
Sonaec................................19 B3
Star Navigation.......................20 B3
Telecommunications (OPT) Building.21 B3
Trinity Finance Forex Bureau........22 B2
US Embassy...........................23 C5

SIGHTS & ACTIVITIES   p414
Agence Africaine de Tourisme....24 A2
Cathedral............................25 E5
Concorde Voyages & Tourism......26 C3
Direction Immigration/Emigration (Visa
Extensions).........................27 D5
Eglise St Michel......................28 D4
Grand Marché de Dantokpa........29 E4
Librairie Nôtre-Dame................30 E5
Mosque...............................31 A3
Pharmacie Camp Ghezo............32 C5

SLEEPING   p414
Bénin Hôtel...........................33 A5
City Hôtel.............................34 B2
Hôtel Babo............................35 A2
Hôtel de la Plage.....................36 B4
Hôtel du Port.........................37 C5
Hôtel Le Concorde....................38 B3
Hôtel le Crillon.......................39 C3
Pension des Familles.................40 B2
Pension Souvenir.....................41 B3

EATING   pp414–15
Cafeteria Chez Nous..............(see 41)
Codiprix..............................42 B3
Fairouz...............................43 B2
Festival des Glaces..................44 B3
Hai King..............................45 B5
Le Petits Fours.......................46 C3
Mama Benin..........................47 D4
Maquis le Pili-Pili....................48 D4
Restaurant l'Amitié..................49 A2
Ylang-Ylang Bar & Restaurant..(see 35)

along Ave Clozel you pass over the Pont Ancien into the Akpakpa sector; the road eventually turns into the highway to Porto Novo and Lagos.

The main airport is on the western fringe of Cotonou, in Cocotiers district. Taxis into the centre of town as far as the Pont Ancien cost around US$5, or US$8 if you're going beyond the bridge. A *zemi-john* can usually juggle a backpack and will take you into town for around US$0.70.

The route de l'Aéroport leads straight from the airport into the heart of town. Hitching a lift along here is possible, but it isn't the safest option.

There are no direct buses, but if you don't have much to carry, you can walk from the airport along Route de l'Aéroport to Place des Martyrs (1km) and catch a shared taxi (US$0.25 to US$0.40) from there to the city centre.

INFORMATION
Bookshops

Librarie Nôtre Dame (☎ 31 40 94; Ave Clozel) Excellent selection of cultural and historical books on Benin (in French), as well as postcards and maps of Benin and Cotonou.

Sonaec (☎ 31 22 42; Ave Clozel) The best place for international newspapers and magazines.

Cultural Centres

American Cultural Center (☎ 30 03 12; off Blvd de la Marina) Has a large library with up-to-date copies of the *International Herald Tribune*.

Centre Culturel Français (☎ 30 08 56; Ave Jean Paul II) Good for French and German film screenings, concerts and dance shows, and art and photography exhibitions.

Internet Access

Cotonou has a large number of Internet cafés with reasonably fast connections, usually costing from US$0.70 to US$1.60 per hour:

Cyber Jonquet (Ave Proche; per hr US$0.80) Popular and has fast connections.

Cyber Laha (Rue 117; per hr US$0.70)

Star Navigation (per hr US$0.80) Located diagonally opposite Hôtel Le Crillon.

Medical Services

Dr Richardier (☎ 31 44 15) Opposite Pharmacy Camp Guezo; for dental care.

Pharmacie Camp Guezo (☎ 31 55 52; off Place de La Revolution; ☽ 24 hr) The best-stocked pharmacy.

Polyclinique Les Cocotiers (☎ 30 14 20; Carrefour de Cadjehoun) An efficient private medical clinic.

Money

Bank of Africa (☎ 31 33 13; off Ave Clozel)

Ecobank (☎ 31 00 75; Blvd St Michel)

Financial Bank (☎ 31 31 00; Rue de la Poste) Quick and easy advances on Visa, but charges a hefty 13% commission.

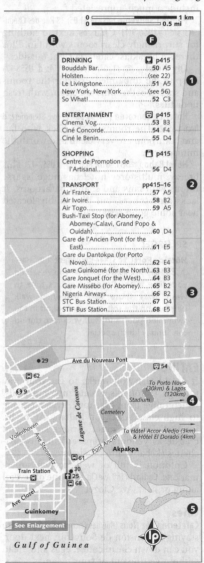

0 ————— 1 km
0 ————— 0.5 mi

E   F

● 29   Ave du Nouveau Pont   🚌 54

🚌 62

🚉 9

To Porto Novo (30km) & Lagos (120km)

Stadium

Cemetery

To Hôtel Accor Aledjo (3km) & Hôtel El Dorado (4km)

Laguse de Cotonou

Akpakpa

Pont Ancien

Vollenhoven

Ave Steinmetz

🚌 61

Train Station

🚌 30

🚌 25

🚌 68

Ave Clozel

Guinkomey

See Enlargement

Gulf of Guinea

BENIN

Cotonou has plenty of forex bureaus, including **Trinity Finance Forex Bureau** (☎ 31 79 38; Ave van Vollenhoven; ⊗ 8am-6pm Mon-Fri), which changes dollars, euros and CFA, and cashes MasterCard travellers cheques.

There's a large black market for the Nigerian naira around the Jonquet district, with rates similar to the banks.

Post & Telephone

The main **post office** (off Ave Clozel; ⊗ 8am-12.30pm & 3-6pm Mon-Fri) has a good poste restante service. The main **telephone office** (OPT; ☎ 31 47 82; Ave Clozel; ⊗ 7.30am-midnight Mon-Sat, 9am-1pm Sun) is the best place for international phone calls.

Tourist Offices

La Direction du Tourisme et de Hotellerie (☎ 32 68 24; tourisme@elodi.intnet.bj; off Place de l'Étoile Rouge; ⊗ 8am-6.30pm Mon-Fri) has English-speaking staff but little useful information. Reputable (but expensive) tour operators include **Agence Africaine de Tourisme** (☎ 31 54 14) and **Concorde Voyages & Tourisme** (off Av Steinmetz; ☎ 31 34 13).

DANGERS & ANNOYANCES

Unfortunately, muggings do occasionally occur along Cotonou's shoreline; the beachfront between Benin Hotel and Hôtel de la Plage is a particular no-go area, even during the day. If you do go, don't bring anything of value.

SIGHTS & ACTIVITIES

Grand Marché de Danktokpa (Ave du Nouveau Pont) This is a huge must-see market bordering the lagoon and Blvd St Michel. Everything is sold here, from food, radios, waxed cloth, pottery and baskets to bat wings and monkey testicles. Try to find *le fetiche d'amour* (a love fetish). Rub it on your hands, whisper to it seven times the name of the person you desire, then touch that person and he or she is yours!

There are a few beaches around Cotonou where you can swim without being sucked under. One of them is **Hôtel El Dorado** (swimming US$1.60), 4km east of the city centre, where the water is protected by a large jetty. At **Togbin beach,** 1km west of the airport, the German-run **Café Cauris** (☎ 90 04 72; swimming US$1.60) has a saltwater swimming pool.

SLEEPING

Most shoestringers end up in the Jonquet district, which has a concentration of cheap, if cheerless, budget hotels.

Pension des Familles (☎ 31 51 25; Ave Proche; s/d US$6/8) This is definitely the best accommodation choice in town. The rooms with shared bathroom are airy and clean and include a much-appreciated fan.

Pension Souvenir (☎ 39 11 05; 38 Rue des Cheminots; s/d/tw US$6/9/11) Charges next to nothing for surprisingly clean rooms with fan. Plus there's a breakfast cafeteria right outside.

City Hôtel (☎ 31 04 41; Rue 114; d US$8-17) Despite the unpainted exterior the rooms and shared bathrooms are clean, with fresh floor tiles.

Hôtel Le Concorde (☎ 31 55 70; Ave Steinmetz; d from US$12) The rooms at the back with fan and bathroom are very clean and worth the minisplurge.

Hôtel Babo (☎ 31 46 07; Rue 117; d US$7-12) This breezy, multistorey hotel has huge, sparse rooms with fans and shared bathrooms. It lacks atmosphere, but it's handily located near some good restaurants.

> **SPLURGE!**
>
> **Hôtel du Port** (☎ 31 44 44; w.demedeiros@firsnet.bj; Blvd de la Marina; d US$67-111) You've served your time in the fleapits. Now it's time to wash away those bad memories: walk barefoot on the soft carpets, cool off in the swimming pool, and stuff your face during the Sunday lunch special.

EATING

It would take you weeks to eat your way through Cotonou's restaurants and stalls, which range from first-rate African cuisine to high-class Asian or Italian. At night, Jonquet's smoky street corners sizzle and crackle as vendors prepare delicious brochettes (kebabs) and omelettes.

Cotonou is full of well-stocked supermarkets. **Codiprix** (off Ave Clozel) is one of several along or near Ave Clozel.

Cafés

Cafeteria Chez Nous (Rue des Cheminots) If you are staying at Pension de Souvenir, next door, you can down cheap coffee, eggs and bread without getting out of your pyjamas.

BENIN

Festival des Glaces (☎ 98 61 80; Ave Steinmetz; snacks US$1-2) Say goodbye to those ice-cream cravings! This popular expat eatery also serves cakes, éclairs and other pastries.

Quick Eats

Omelettes and brochettes can be found all over Cotonou from late afternoon, especially on Ave Steinmetz. Just look for the smoking grills piled with meat on sticks (around US$1).

Restaurants

Mama Benin (☎ 32 33 38; off Rue de Ouidah; mains US$1.50) This long-standing restaurant serves a variety of tasty Beninese dishes buffet-style from steaming pots.

Ylang-Ylang Bar & Restaurant (Rue 117; mains US$1.60) The menu doesn't offer a wide range, but it's always tasty and cheap. A handy place for those staying at the Hôtel Babo next door.

Restaurant l'Amitié (Rue 117; mains US$1.50) Also located near the Hôtel Babo, it knocks up large, tasty rice and meat dishes.

Hai King (☎ 30 60 08; off Carrefour de Cadjehoun; mains US$7) This Chinese restaurant gives friendly and amazingly fast service. You can eat mouth-watering Chinese meals on the upstairs terrace overlooking the city.

Fairouz (☎ 31 09 13; Ave Steinmetz; mains US$1-3) It makes king-size portions of Lebanese (the shwarmas are as long as your forearm!) and Western take-away dishes.

Les Petits Fours (☎ 90 30 25; Ave Steinmetz; mains US$3) This Peace Corps hang-out serves good pasta, pizzas and vegetarian dishes, and yummy burgers.

SPLURGE!

Maquis le Pili-Pili (☎ 31 50 48; off Ave Togbé; mains US$7) This classy restaurant with Afrochic decor serves monster portions from its extensive menu. The pricey dishes will fill your belly and empty your wallet, but you'll be glad you came.

DRINKING

The Beninese love a good party and a good drink – if you can't find a place to drink in Cotonou you've either lost your eyesight or your sense of smell. The city is cluttered with *buvettes* (small bars) and clubs, especially in the Jonquet district.

Holsten (Ave van Vollenhoven) This is one of dozens of cheap *buvettes* selling small beers for US$0.40.

Le Livingstone (☎ 30 27 58; Piste Amalco) Drinks cost US$3 to US$4. The drink prices are pretty sobering at this popular expat hangout, but it's worth paying for the chilled, outdoor atmosphere. Also try the trendy Bouddah Bar a few doors east.

So What! (☎ 01 14 64; off Ave Steinmetz; admission US$3) Every night it lays on live acts ranging from traditional drummers to African jazz artists to reggae bands, but things don't get started until after 11pm.

New York, New York (Ave Proche; admission US$7) For more-serious dancing head to the big apple, a long-time favourite for locals and travellers.

ENTERTAINMENT

There are a couple of cinemas in town showing newish French films, and Hollywood films dubbed in French:

Ciné Concorde (☎ 33 39 72; off Ave du Nouveau Pont, Akpakpa district; US$1)

Ciné le Benin (☎ 32 12 50; Blvd St Michel; US$0.80)

Cinema Vog (Ave Steinmetz; US$1)

SHOPPING

Centre de Promotion de l'Artisanal (☎ 30 38 59; Blvd St Michel) This is a good place to buy woodcarvings, batik T-shirts, leather knife sheaths and the famous Beninese appliqué banners. If your bargaining skills aren't up to scratch then head for the *bijouterie* (jewellers) and watch the men cutting and sculpting silver jewellery.

GETTING THERE & AWAY
Air

The main airport is on the western fringe of Cotonou, in Cocotiers. Departing from Cotonou is far less of a hassle than from some other West African cities. Most airline offices have reps in town. They include Ghana Airways, Air Ivoire and Air Burkina.

Air Burkina (☎ 31 37 06) US$200 one way, 90 minutes, three times a week.

Air Ivoire (☎ 30 17 61; Av Steinmetz) US$150 one way, two hours, five times a week.

Air Togo (☎ 30 92 95; Route de l'Aéroport) US$56 one way, 50 mins, weekly.

Ghana Airways (☎ 31 42 83; off Av Steinmetz) US$172 one way, one hour, weekly.

BENIN

Local Transport

Cotonou is the hub for transport to all destinations in Benin.

STIF, located just south of Eglise St Michel, runs daily services to Lomé (US$5, three hours), Abidjan (US$33, 12 hours) Ouagadougou (US$25, 30 hours) and Bamako (US$38, 48 hours). STC (off Rue de Ouidah) has buses to Abidjan in Côte d'Ivoire (US$20, 18 hours) departing three times a week.

Cotonou has a confusing number of stations for minibuses and bush taxis. It's best to ask a *zemi-john* or bush taxi driver to take you to the right station.

Gare Jonquet services places to the west (eg Lomé and Abidjan); Gare Guinkomé runs buses to the north (eg Parakou and Malanville); and Gare de l'Ancien Pont is for eastern destinations (eg Lagos in Nigeria).

Bush taxis to Porto Novo leave from Gare du Dantokpa; and to Abomey, from Gare Missébo. However, for Abomey, Abomey-Calavi (for Ganvié), Grand Popo and Ouidah, it's best to wait at the unofficial bush taxi stop about 100m southeast of Eglise St Michel on Blvd St Michel.

Train

For details of the train that goes from Cotonou to Parakou via Bohicon (near Abomey), see p411.

GETTING AROUND

Bush taxis cost US$0.25 for trips around town, but are relatively scarce. However,

Cotonou has no shortage of *zemi-johns*, all belting out their hideous fumes. They'll whiz you around town for about US$0.30.

SOUTHERN BENIN

PORTO NOVO

☎ 21 / pop 231,600

The quiet, well-ordered roads, devoid of traffic jams and screeching *zemi-johns*, make it hard to believe this is Benin's capital city. Feeling more like an overgrown village, Porto Novo is a refreshing antidote to hectic Cotonou. It has some interesting stilt villages and very good museums.

Musée Éthnographique de Porto Novo (☎ 21 25 54; admission US$1.60; ☒ open 9am-noon & 3-6pm) The museum traces the history of the Porto Novo kings and has a grand collection of masks of the Yoruba people, some from as far back as the 17th century.

The Songhai Centre (☎ 22 50 92) is the brainchild of Father Nzamujo, a Dominican priest. This experimental organic farm (1km northwest of Carrefour Catchi) is a centre for research, production and training for sustainable agriculture in Africa. There are vegetarian products for sale, such as soy milk. Call to arrange a visit.

Don't miss the unique **mosque** north of the market. It started off as a Portuguese-style church, but has been painted over several times and covered in Arabic script, giving it a multicoloured, schizophrenic look.

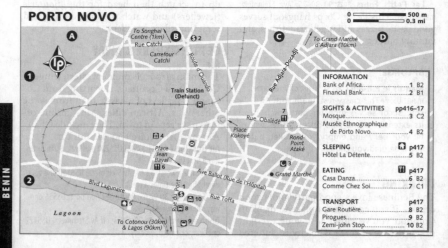

PORTO NOVO

0 _____ 500 m
0 _____ 0.3 mi

To Songhai Centre (1km)
Rue Catchi
Carrefour Catchi
Route d'Oluando
Rue Adjara-Docodji
To Grand Marché d'Adjara (10km)

Train Station (Defunct)

Rue Obalédé
Place Kokoyé
Rond-Point Ataké

Place Jean Bayal
Ave Ballot (Rue de l'Hôpital)
Grand Marché

Blvd Lagunaire
Rue du Pont
Rue Toffa

Lagoon

To Cotonou (30km) & Lagos (90km)

INFORMATION	
Bank of Africa	1 B2
Financial Bank	2 B1

SIGHTS & ACTIVITIES	pp416–17
Mosque	3 C2
Musée Éthnographique de Porto Novo	4 B2

SLEEPING	⌂ p417
Hôtel La Détente	5 B2

EATING	🍴 p417
Casa Danza	6 B2
Comme Chez Soi	7 C1

TRANSPORT	p417
Gare Routière	8 B2
Pirogues	9 B2
Zemi-john Stop	10 B2

BENIN

Take advantage of Porto Novo's beautiful **lagoon**, perfect for a pirogue (traditional canoe) trip to nearby villages. Ask around in the area 50m east of the bridge.

Hôtel La Détente (☎ 21 44 69; Blvd Lagunaire; d US$8) The turquoise walls and purple bed sheets aren't the prettiest sight, but the window views of the fishermen in the lagoon are gorgeous. Rooms come with fan, shower, shared toilet and a good, cheap restaurant.

Songhai (☎ 22 50 92; 1km northwest of Carrefour Catchi; d US$7) This hotel is attached to the Songhai agricultural centre. The rooms with fan are clean, and the restaurant serves some of the farm's produce with its meals.

Casa Danza (☎ 21 48 12; west of Place Jean Bayal; mains US$6) Patience is the order of the day here. The pricey Western and Beninese dishes take a while to come, but they are delicious. **Hôtel Détente** (Blvd Lagunaire; mains from US$1) and **Comme Chez Soi** (Rue Obalédé; mains from US$1) are the best options for cheap meals.

Plenty of minibuses and bush taxis leave for Cotonou (US$0.90, 45 minutes) from the *gare routière*, just north of the bridge. There is also frequent road transport to the Nigeria border.

GANVIÉ

Bamboo houses with thatched roofs overlook the water while residents glide past in pirogues on their way to the post office. Ganvié is a fascinating village of about 18,500 people, built on stilts raised 2m above **Lake Nokoué**. It is rightfully Benin's main tourist attraction, and it's best to visit in the late afternoon when the sun has died down.

Hôtel Te Moi de la Francophone (s/d US$7/10) Wake up to the sound of water underneath the floorboards at this hotel in Ganvié village. Food is available on demand. Staying at a stilt hotel is an exciting option, but remember there's the extra cost of taking a pirogue back to Abomey-Calavi.

Motel Djaka 1st (☎ 36 02 47; Route de Cotonou; r US$8-11.70; 🏊) For those who prefer dry land, this lovely hotel in Abomey-Calavi has clean, fresh rooms and a restaurant serving cheap African meals. It is located 70m east of the road to the jetty for Ganvié.

To get to Ganvié, catch a shared taxi from Cotonou to Abomey-Calavi (US$0.80), and walk or take a *zemi-john* down the signposted road to the jetty. Motorised pirogues to Ganvié can then be hired for US$12 return (for one passenger), or US$5 per person return for up to 10 passengers, but make sure you agree to the fee beforehand. Cheaper (US$10 for one person in a boat; US$3 per person return for up to ten passengers), un-motorised pirogues take 30 minutes longer.

OUIDAH
☎ 34 / pop 89,600

There's no underestimating Ouidah's cultural and historical significance in Benin. It is the centre of voodoo culture, and it was once a major exit point for thousands of slaves who took their music and religion with them to the Americas. Although Ouidah seems pretty quiet these days, underneath it all is a fascinating culture filled with voodoo fetishes, shrines, museums and temples.

Musée d'Histoire de Ouidah (☎ 34 10 21; admission US$1.60; 🕒 9am-noon & 3-6pm) Located two blocks east of the market, this fascinating museum focuses on the slave trade and Benin's cultural links with Brazil. It displays excavated slave chains, skulls, voodoo artefacts and ancient maps.

The Route des Esclaves is the road that slaves took to the coast to board ships to Cuba, Haiti and Brazil. On the beach you'll find the **Point of No Return memorial**. A *zemi-john* down here costs around US$3.20 return, otherwise you can take a long walk and recreate the slave experience for yourself.

If you haven't seen a voodoo ritual, check out the black-and-white photos at the **Casa do Brasil** (Ave de France; admission US$1.60; 🕒 7am-7pm). Of lesser interest in town are the **Temple des Pythones**, full of sleepy snakes, and the **Sacred Forest**, a small park with an array of bronze African deities.

If your brain can't absorb any more facts, try arranging a pirogue trip around the stilt village along the Route des Esclaves.

Ouidah has good-quality hotels, but they don't come cheap.

Buvette Ermitage (☎ 34 13 89; one block east of Rue Olivier de Montaguere; d US$10) The owner, Francois, wears a traditional African robe and has small, darkish rooms (with fan and bathroom) that get noisy at night.

Oriki Maquis Hôtel (☎ 34 10 04; Rue Maquis Moretel; d US$14-18) Audacious prices for rooms that come with fan only, but they are clean and big.

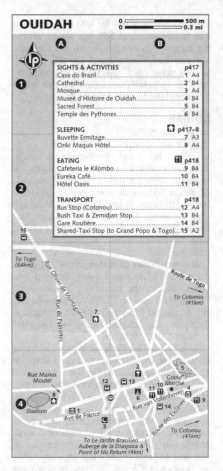

Le Jardin Brasilien Auberge de la Diaspora (☎ 34 11 10; Route des Esclaves; s/d US$12/15) You'll hear nothing but the sound of the waves at this gorgeous beachside hotel near the Point of No Return. The simple rooms have fan.

The best places to eat are **Oriki Maquis** (mains US$3) and **Hôtel Oasis** (mains US$2-4), but for cheaper fodder head to **Eureka Café** (Rue van Vollenhoven; mains US$2), or the outdoor **Cafeteria le Kilombo** (mains US$1.50-3) outside the Musée d'Histoire. Buvette Ermitage is still a popular drinking hole.

Bush taxis to Cotonou (US$1, one hour) leave from the *gare routière* opposite Hôtel Oasis, as well as the area south of the hospital. For rides to Grand Popo and Togo, wait along the main road northwest of town.

GRAND POPO
☎ 43

The deserted beaches, swaying palm trees and calm sea will make you want to stay forever. Once Benin's biggest port, it now feels more like a ghost town – which is just fine for a bit of peace and quiet.

To reach Grand Popo from Cotonou (US$2.50) catch anything heading towards Lomé in Togo.

The pricey hotels hog the best bits of beach, but they'll let you camp here cheaply. Nearly all the hotels are strung out along the main road.

Awalé Plage (☎ 43 01 17; awaleplage@yahoo.com; camp site per person US$7, s/d US$21/28) What more could you ask for in a hotel? An excellent beach bar, monthly full-moon parties, cheap boogie board rental and friendly staff. You'll never want to leave.

Plage Coin des Amis (☎ 43 03 98; s/d US$3/9) The rooms at this cheap and cheerful place are basic, but the staff are friendly and the restaurant is cheap.

Les Paillottes Bleues serves good meals. For something different, try asking locals about town to knock up some tasty seafood dishes for you. Prices are negotiable (around US$2 to US$3).

ABOMEY
☎ 50 / pop 120,700

Abomey was once the capital of the Fon Kingdom, Dahomey (which became the country's postcolonial name for a while), and its fearsome female fighters. The town won't win any beauty contests, but it is littered with fascinating traces of its glorious past.

Musée Historique d'Abomey (☎ 50 03 14; Rue du Palais Royal; admission US$2.50; 8am-6pm Mon-Fri, 8am-5pm Sat) Abomey's main, and seriously impressive, attraction, located 400m north of the market. For more on this see the boxed text on p419. Also check out the nearby village of **Dozoéme**, which hasn't changed for centuries. Here, the *forgerons* (blacksmiths) used to fashion implements exclusively for the Dahomian kings, although housewives and farmers are now the beneficiaries of their trade. A *zemi-john* there and back costs about US$1.

When it comes to budget accommodation in Abomey, the pickings are pretty slim.

Hotel Lutta (☎ 03 72 49; d US$6) Located 300m southwest of the market, this hotel

ABOMEY'S ROYAL PALACE

Once one of West Africa's most awesome indigenous structures, the royal palace at Abomey is now a humble version of its former self. The first building was constructed in 1645 by the third king of Dahomey. Each subsequent new king added his own palace, so that by the 19th century the compound was absolutely huge, with about 100 acres fitting a court of 10,000 people (it would take about 20 minutes to jog around the 4km fence). The inner complex consisted of a maze of courtyards, ceremonial rooms and a harem to fit 800 women. Following defeat by the French, the 10th king burned most of the palace as he fled their advancing forces.

The Musée Historique d'Abomey consists of the only surviving palaces of Ghézo and Glélé. The museum tells the history of the Dahomey kingdom and displays royal thrones and tapestries, human skulls that were once used as musical instruments, fetish items and the living quarters of the last king. Ghézo's throne is particularly large and mounted on four real skulls of vanquished enemies.

has hundreds of statues and paintings that clutter the lobby, and the basic rooms with bathroom are surprisingly fresh and clean. The owner has the low-down on voodoo ceremonies in the area.

Chez Monique (☎ 50 01 68; d from US$9) This is a great place to meet other travellers. There are monkeys in the courtyard, and even more wildlife inside the large rooms. The restaurant serves tasty meals in a nice garden. You'll find this place about 500m northwest of the police station.

Auberge le Guedevy (☎ 50 03 04; d from US$11) The friendly staff and good restaurant are about the only incentives to making the 2km schlep here (600 metres northeast of police station). We're not sure the gloomy rooms quite justify the price.

Hotel la Lutta (mains US$2.50-3), southwest of gare *routière*, and **Chez Monique** (mains US$3-4), northwest of police station, both offer good meals, but for something really cheap look around the street food at the market. Also, **Chez Ayato Adjara** (mains US$1), found behind the *gare routière*, serves tasty *pâte de mais* (mashed maize).

DJ Promav (formerly Aux Delices de France) is a well-stocked supermarket. For drinks, Confort Plus is a good place to rub shoulders with the locals.

Plenty of bush taxis run between Abomey and Cotonou (US$4, three hours), sometimes with a connection at Bohicon. Minibuses cost US$2.50. For details about the train between Cotonou and Parakou, via Bohicon, see p411.

Bush taxis and *zemi-johns* go back and forth all day (US$0.30) from early morning until early evening.

NORTHERN BENIN

PARAKOU

☎ 61 / pop 205,300

Parakou is Benin's most ethnically diverse town, thanks to its position as a centre of trading routes. In this bustling town the pavements disappear under the throng of market traders of the Dendi, Fon, Yoruba and Igbo tribes who sell everything under the sun. It is a popular overnight stop for travellers.

The centre of town is the area around the cinema at the intersection of Route de l'Aéroport, Rue des Cheminots and Route de Transa. There are three banks here. The market is three blocks away to the southeast.

Most of the hotels cater to a more moneyed crowd, but there are some good budget places dotted around.

Auberge Mon Petit Père (☎ 61 10 57; d US$7.50) This popular, friendly hotel about 1km northeast of the market has well-furnished rooms with fan and immaculate shared bathroom. The statue with a huge, erect penis (don't ask!) stands guard over the cheap restaurant and bar lounge.

Hôtel les Canaries (☎ 61 11 69; Route de l'Hôtel Canaries; s/d US$8/12) It scores low on the charisma front, but the clean, spacious rooms are the cheapest option in the town centre.

Maquis Aledjo (mains US$1) Located a few doors southeast of Hôtel OCBN, women here dish out food from behind bars, but it's cheap, tasty and very popular.

Maquis Amar (Rue du Marché; mains US$1) The food awaits you in steaming pots along the tables, making eating here a tasty, quick in-and-out affair.

Nearby, the **Le Miel bakery** (off Route de Transa; mains US$1-2) serves vegetarian sandwiches.

For drinks there are several *buvettes* around town. **Try Les 41 Collines** (Route de l'Hôtel Canaries) across from Hôtel les Canaries.

From the *gare routière,* just north of the market, bush taxis and minibuses regularly go to Cotonou (US$11, eight hours) and Malanville (US$7.50, six hours). Africa Lines buses depart for Cotonou three times a week at 7am (US$11, seven hours). For details about the train between Cotonou and Parakou, via Bohicon, see p411.

NATITINGOU

☎ 82 / pop 111,600

Situated at high altitude in the Atakora mountains, Natitingou is the base for visiting the Parc National de Pendjari and hiking and cycling in the surrounding area, including the Somba country. The Somba people are a traditional tribe renowned for their fascinating houses or 'tata sombas', which look like mini fortified castles.

Musée d'Arts et de Traditions Populaires de Natitingou (admission US$1.60; ☻ 8.30am-12.30pm & 3.30-6.30pm Mon-Fri, 9am-noon & 4-6.30pm Sat & Sun) Located behind Hôtel de Bourgogne, the museum has artefacts from the Somba region, including bells, flutes and armbands worn by women fighters to smash the faces of the enemy. Most interesting are the models of different types of *tata somba* (houses), two-storey huts that look like minicastles.

Also check out La Braiche de Nati, an amazing restaurant that's built in a replica-style with a rooftop terrace for drinking; 100m east of Hôtel Kantabourifa.

The surrounding area is great for **cycling** (ask around the market for rentals). Prices are negotiable, around US$3 for a day.

Auberge le Vieux Cavalier (☎ 82 13 24; d from US$8) Found 200m east of the gare routière, the bright, clean rooms with busy wall decor are a breath of fresh air. DVD movies are sometimes played in the lounge.

Hotel Nekima (☎ 82 10 46; d/bungalows US$10/8) A kitsch statue stands in the courtyard next to the tiny, round bungalows that come with fan and a clean bathroom. Located 500m west of Café Élevage.

Auberge Equied (☎ 82 10 83; d US$5) This quiet village hotel 500m east of the hospital has clean, basic rooms with traditional *banco*-coloured walls. Meals are available.

If you ask sweetly, the locals might let you camp, for a fee, in the open spaces away from the main road.

Red-skinned *wagasi* cheese is a northern speciality, and it goes surprisingly well in a tasty soup and pâté. You can sample some at the street stalls next to the mosque.

Café Élevage (mains US$1-2) Cheap and cheerful breakfasts, lunch and dinners are available at this roadside café, located on the main road 200m south of the market.

The tasty African dishes at the popular **Le Gourmet** (mains US$2.50) a few doors north of Financial Bank, will silence any grumbling tummies.

From the *gare routière* minibuses and taxis regularly go to Parakou (US$6.70, five hours). Minibuses go to Cotonou (US$14, 10 hours) and bush taxis go to the Togo and Burkina Faso borders. Africa Lines buses depart daily at 7am (US$14, nine hours). The Africa Lines bus goes to Cotonou. It departs from the OPT building just north of the market.

PARC NATIONAL DE PENDJARI

Pendjari is easily one of West Africa's best wildlife reserves. This tiny corner of Benin teems with hippos, lions, elephants, baboons and warthogs, and there's a very good chance of seeing them all – just keep your eyes wide open. The park is set up for visitors with cars, and walking is forbidden, so you have two options: stay in Natitingou and make day trips from there by car, although you'll have less chance of seeing the animals (the best viewing times are early in the morning and evening); or arrange a ride (or hitch) from Natitingou to one of the *campements* (guesthouses) in the park, base yourself there and hope to find people with cars who can take you out wildlife viewing.

Entry to the park costs US$10, plus a camera fee of US$5, and a surcharge of US$3.20 per night. The compulsory guides cost US$8 or you can hire a guide at Tanguieta, plus a car for US$25 per day. (The car rental in Tanguieta is much cheaper than in Natitingou).

In **Tanguiéta**, at the southern tip of the park, there are two very rustic *campements*. They're cheap, but very basic (US$5 per double room).

For more comfortable lodgings head to **Hôtel Campement de Porga** (d US$25) at the park entrance, or the cheaper **Campement** de Relais de Tanougou (☎ 82 11 24; d US$15) at Tanguiéta Falls.

There is daily, but infrequent, transport to Tanguiéta from Natitingou (US$3). If you're trying to hitch into the park, it's worth asking around at the larger hotels in Natitingou, such as Hotel Tata Somba.

MALANVILLE
Located near the point where Nigeria, Niger and Benin meet, Malanville is a border town filled with traders from across the region selling anything from *wagasi* cheese to radios.

Rose des Sables (☎ 67 01 25; d US$8), about 2km south of town, has reasonable rooms with fans.

The *gare routière* is full of stalls and *buvettes* selling cheap food and drinks.

Bush taxis to Parakou cost US$8 (five hours), minibuses cost US$6.70 (seven hours). Africa Lines buses depart three times a week for Cotonou at 10am (US$19, 11 hours).

BENIN DIRECTORY

ACCOMMODATION
Benin's tourist infrastructure is fairly limited, and though accommodation can be cheap, you rarely get good value for money. Basic singles/doubles cost about US$8/10, while comfortable air-con rooms with a private bathroom are around US$17. Tariffs include the tourist tax of US$0.80, and are often (but not always) listed somewhere in the hotel reception.

Booking ahead generally isn't necessary except during major festivals like Voodoo Day (see right).

ACTIVITIES
For swimming, the best beaches are west and east of Cotonou and around Grand Popo. Cycling is a great way to see flat, interesting towns like Abomey and Porto Novo (enquire at markets for bicycles; it's about US$5 per day for rentals). There are a few organised hikes, but you can just as easily walk on the fringes of Lake Nokoué, taking pirogue rides for some stretches.

BUSINESS HOURS
Business hours are 8am to 12.30pm and 3pm to 7pm Monday to Friday and 8am to 12.30pm Saturday. Government offices are open 7.30am to 12.30pm and 3.30pm to 6.30pm Monday to Friday.

Banks are generally open from 8am to 12.30pm and 3pm to 5pm Monday to Friday.

DANGERS & ANNOYANCES
Benin is a generally safe country with low crime levels, but it still pays for travellers to be vigilant.

EMBASSIES & CONSULATES
The following countries have representation in Cotonou. Visas for Burkina Faso, Côte d'Ivoire and Togo are issued by the French consulate.

France (☎ 31 26 38, 31 26 80; Rue 651A)
Germany (☎ 31 29 68; Patte d'Oie)
Ghana (☎ 30 07 46; Route de l'Aéroport)
Niger (☎ 31 56 71; Rue 651A)
Nigeria (☎ 30 11 42; Blvd de la Marina)
USA (☎ 30 06 50; Rue Caporal Anani Bernard)

In West Africa, Benin has diplomatic representation in Côte d'Ivoire, Ghana, Niger and Nigeria.

FESTIVALS & EVENTS
Apart from Benin's colourful annual Muslim celebrations in the northern towns (including Parakou and Kandi), the other main event is the annual Voodoo Festival, which is held in Ouidah on 10 January. Other low-key voodoo celebrations occur in Ouidah and in Abomey, but catching them is a matter of luck. To find out more, travellers should contact the **Direction de Tourisme et de l'Hotellerie** (☎ 32 68 24; tourisme@elodi.intnet.bj; off Place de l'Étoile Rouge, Cotonou).

FOOD & DRINK
The Beninese love their sauces, and meals are often smothered in *lamounou dessi*, a tomato-based stew containing seafood and vegetables mixed with the fiery *pilipili* sauce. The stew is accompanied by rice or (in the north) millet couscous. Other stews are made from the vegetable okra and eaten with staples such as yams, beans and rice.

For a country that loves drinking, the local beer, *La Beninoise*, is surprisingly average. If you're feeling adventurous you can try palm wine, *tchapallo* (a millet-based local brew) or

BENIN

sodabe (a distilled palm wine which is definitely *not* for lightweight drinkers!).

HOLIDAYS

As well as religious holidays listed in the Africa Directory (p1003), these are the principal public holidays in Benin:

1 January New Year's Day
10 January Vodoun or Voodoo Day
16 January Martyr's Day
28 February Liberation Day
26 October Armed Forces Day
4 December Republic Day

INTERNET ACCESS

The number of Internet centres has mushroomed in Cotonou, and there is at least one centre in every town of any size, although connections are slow. The average charge is US$0.70 per hour.

MAPS

A good city map is the 1:15,000 *Cotonou* produced by the Institute Géographique National de Benin, which lists the city's hotels, cinemas, banks and markets. It costs US$6 and is available in most bookshops.

MEDIA

You may be able to glean some football results and seesawing political accusations from Cotonou's dailies, which include *Le Nation* and *Le Soleil*. Foreign newspapers and magazines can occasionally be found at newspaper stands. The best bookshops and top hotels stock week-old British, American, German and Italian newspapers.

The state-run Radio Benin has occasional broadcasts in English, while the TV station LC2, also state-run, offers little beyond news, death announcements and a few hours of music videos each day.

MONEY

Financial Bank provides Visa card cash advances, but credit cards are rarely accepted outside the large hotels. Financial Bank, Bank of Africa and Ecobank are the best places to change travellers cheques – some large bureaux de change also provide this service. All the banks offer money-changing services, and black marketeers operate at the borders and in parts of Cotonou. The Cotonou black marketeers offer similar rates to the banks, but it's advisable to use them during daylight hours only.

POST & TELEPHONE

Postcards and letters cost US$0.40 per 10g to France, US$0.60 elsewhere in Europe, and US$0.80 to North America and Asia.

International telephone calls and faxes can be made at telephone offices and private telecom agencies throughout the country. The cost per minute is about US$2.50 to France, US$3 to elsewhere in Europe, US$2.50 to North America and US$4.50 to Australasia.

RESPONSIBLE TRAVEL

If you stop by the Songhai centre in Porto Novo, consider buying some of its organic produce such as syrups (pineapple, orange, ginger, mango), soy-bean yoghurt, meats and fruit juices. The proceeds go towards research into methods of agriculture that emphasis the use of local resources as well as modern and traditional methods.

VISAS

Visas for Benin are required of all visitors, and can be obtained at land borders (US$20, one photo, only valid for two days), but not at the airport. A one-month, multiple-entry visa costs from US$20 to US$60.

Visa Extensions

Visas can be extended in 24 hours for US$20 at the **Direction Immigration/Émigration** (☎ 31 42 13) in Cotonou. Extensions are only accepted from 11am Monday to Friday, and can only be picked up from 3pm to 5pm. One photo is required.

Visas for Onward Travel

Visas for the following neighbouring countries can be obtained in Cotonou. See p421 for embassy and consulate information.

Burkina Faso, Côte d'Ivoire & Togo Three-month visas (US$34) are issued by the French Consulate in 24 to 48 hours; two photos are required.

Ghana Visas cost US$34/50 for single/multiple entry, and are issued within two days.

Niger Multiple-entry visas valid for one/three months cost US$42/87 and are issued within 24 hours.

Nigeria Visas are required for all except nationals of most West African countries.

Nigeria

FAST FACTS

- **Area** 924,000 sq km
- **ATMs** none
- **Borders** Benin, Niger, Chad and Cameroon
- **Budget** US$10 to US$30 a day
- **Capital** Abuja
- **Languages** English, Hausa, Yoruba, Igbo, Edo, Efik
- **Money** naira; US$1 = N125
- **Population** 130 million
- **Seasons** wet (Apr–Oct in north; Mar–Nov in south); dry (Nov–Mar in north; Dec–Feb in south)
- **Telephone** country code ☎ 234; international access code ☎ 00
- **Time** GMT/UTC + 1
- **Visas** US$30 to US$65 for one month; required by all except West African nationals and best obtained in country of residence

WARNING

Nigeria is a chaotic, volatile country. Violent crime and robberies do happen throughout the country, and harassment by police still occurs. We were unable to do on-the-ground research in Nigeria, so some information in this chapter may not be reliable. Check the situation before travelling to Nigeria.

Nigeria has never had a particularly good press. Home to 20% of Africa's entire population, the country is notoriously volatile, corrupt and prone to outbreaks of violence, while Lagos, its largest city, has an unrivalled reputation as every traveller's nightmare. At the same time, however, the country is undeniably the heavyweight of the region, with an oil-rich economy, good education and considerable influence abroad. As a nation, it also seems to command the absolute devotion of its people: we regularly receive letters from Nigerian readers protesting vehemently at what they see as unfairly negative coverage of their country, and travellers themselves seldom have a bad word to say about the people they meet here, citing them as among the friendliest in Africa. Safety issues in Nigeria are still paramount, but if you take proper precautions, keep an open mind and learn who to trust, you may well find yourself enjoying your visit more than you expected.

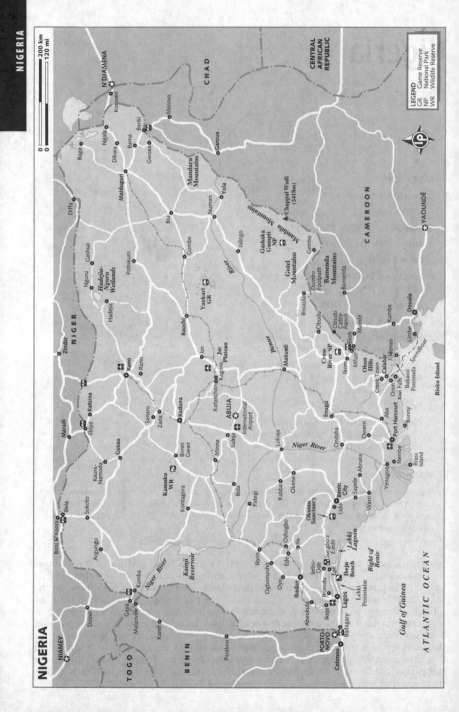

HISTORY

The territory now known as Nigeria has historically been split between three main tribal groups: powerful Hausa dynasties in the north, Yoruba empires in the southwest, and loose confederations of the Igbo people in the southeast. The divisions and enmities between these three groups have effectively determined the course of Nigeria's turbulent history ever since the first Europeans arrived in the 15th century.

Colonial Era

By the time slavery was abolished in the early 19th century, the coastal kingdoms had become dependent on the trade and were unable to adjust to the new circumstances. Around that time, the British were laying the foundations for direct political control of the hinterland in order to protect their commercial monopoly from a French challenge.

As demands for independence gathered force after WWII, the British attempted to put together a constitution taking into account the interests of the three main areas of the colony – the north, which was mainly Muslim with an ethnic majority of Hausa and Fulani; the east, Catholic and mainly Igbo; and the west, mixed Muslim and Anglican and mainly Yoruba. It proved to be an extremely difficult task.

Independence

When independence was granted in October 1960, Nigeria was essentially three nations, and the first six years were disastrous. National politics degenerated into a vicious power game, corruption became rampant and the elite accumulated wealth by any means possible. In early 1966, a group of young army officers, most of whom were Igbo, staged a coup. General Johnson Ironsi took over as head of state.

A few months later Ironsi was killed in another coup. A new regime was set up under the leadership of Lieutenant-Colonel Yakubu Gowon, a Christian from a minority group in the north. The coup was viewed with horror in the east, and the military commander of the area, Chukwuemeka Ojukwu, refused to recognise Gowon as head of state. His antipathy to the new regime was sealed when large-scale massacres of Igbo took place in the north, triggering a return to the east by thousands of Igbo from all over the country.

In May 1967, Ojukwu announced the secession of the east and the creation of the independent state of Biafra. Biafra was recognised by only a handful of African countries, and the civil war dragged on for three years as the Igbo forces fought for every inch of territory that the federal forces took back. By early 1970, as a result of the blockade imposed by the federal government, Biafra faced famine and its forces were compelled to capitulate. Up to two million Biafrans may have died, mainly from starvation.

Democracy & Generals

Gowon was overthrown by General Murtala Mohammed in a bloodless coup in 1975. Mohammed was assassinated in an attempted coup in early 1976 and succeeded by Lieutenant-General Olesegun Obasanjo, a Christian Yoruba, who did the unthinkable for an African military leader and stood down, retiring to his pig farm after paving the way for a civilian regime.

Political power was handed over following elections in 1979. Unfortunately Shehu Shagari's new government was no improvement and, almost inevitably, he was overthrown at the end of 1983 by General Muhammed Buhari.

In 1985, Buhari was overthrown by General Ibrahim Babangida, the army's chief of staff. Babangida made several promises, including that of free elections. The much-delayed presidential election finally went ahead in June 1993 with Moshood Abiola, a Yoruba from the south, claiming victory. Two weeks later, Babangida annulled the results and announced that another election would be held.

Seven years of planning went down the drain – but so did Babangida. He stepped down in August 1993 and appointed Ernest Shonekan as head of an interim civilian government. A new election date was set for February 1994.

The Abacha Years

Before elections could be held, General Sani Abacha, the interim defence secretary, seized control and forced Shonekan to announce his government's resignation. He then abolished all 'democratic' institutions, including the two political parties, the national and state assemblies and local governments.

Abacha is thought by some to be the most corrupt military leader in Nigerian politics. He had a particularly shady relationship with the transnational oil company that controls the oil reserves in the country. The execution in November 1995 of the outspoken playwright Ken Saro-Wiwa, on a spurious charge of plotting to overthrow the government, stunned the rest of the world and led to sanctions and Nigeria's temporary expulsion from the Commonwealth.

Abacha loosely promised a return to civilian rule, but died in June 1998 and was replaced by his defence chief, Abdulsalam Abubakar. He too promised democratic elections; much to the surprise of a sceptical population, he actually meant it! Free local elections were held in December 1998 and presidential elections in February 1999. The military stood aside and the successful presidential candidate was none other than Olusegun Obasanjo, who had recently been released from prison.

Obasanjo Returns

Nigerians were euphoric, as finally it seemed they were free from military rule. It was not long before things deteriorated as rival groups (religious and tribal) across the country, no longer threatened by army intervention, settled down to protracted conflict.

The worst manifestations of violence came in February 2000, when Sharia'a (full Islamic law) was introduced in the northern states, provoking widespread riots (see the boxed text). The move has also highlighted the huge political and cultural divide between the north and south of the country, an issue that still affects almost every aspect of Nigerian society.

The country was in turmoil, and the situation was exacerbated by fuel shortages and extended power blackouts. Obasanjo sacked the entire board of the power authority, NEPA, after weeks of darkness throughout the country.

Current Events

Little has improved under the new democracy. Obasanjo has consolidated Nigeria's position as West Africa's political heavyweight and a key player in the Commonwealth, as well as launching the New Partnership for African Development (Nepad) in conjunction with Algeria and South Africa, but the country is still beset by internal problems, with frequent outbreaks of ethnic and religious violence, explosions and gang war in Lagos and militant attacks on the southern oilfields during the 2003 Iraq war.

Presidential elections in April 2003 did nothing to quell international concerns about Nigeria's stability – while Obasanjo claimed an overwhelming victory, independent observers expressed reservations over 'serious irregularities' and intimidation in certain electoral districts, and his Muslim rival (and fellow former military leader) Muhammed Buhari rejected the result with veiled threats of violence. The result has been allowed to stand and so far Obasanjo has not encountered serious resistance, but with opposition parties just waiting for him to slip up, it seems this is once again a make-or-break time for Nigerian democracy.

THE CULTURE

Nigeria's already swollen population is estimated to be rising by about 3% a year.

MISSED WORLD

Kaduna, halfway between Kano and Abuja, has been the centre of some extraordinary religious violence in recent years. The rioting following the introduction of Sharia'a law in February 2000 was the worst in the country, described in the British *Guardian* as 'mind-boggling carnage'; over 300 people were killed in hand-to-hand struggles between Igbo Christians and Hausa Muslims, and tensions between the two communities are still palpable today.

Given this sensitive situation, you'd have to ask why no-one queried the bright spark who proposed holding the 2002 Miss World contest in Kaduna. Muslims were predictably outraged at this grotesque faux pas and riots broke out once again. The renewed carnage prompted the immediate relocation of the competition to the safer pastures of London – a victory for Muslim sensibilities, but another crushing blow to Nigeria's international standing.

About half the people are Muslim, 35% are Christian and the rest follow traditional religions. Juju, the native magic that was the original basis for Caribbean voodoo, is still an important element in many tribal cultures, and you'll find fascinating charms and potions in the markets in most towns.

Nigeria's rich art heritage is unequalled anywhere in West Africa. The oldest discovered sub-Saharan Africa sculptures are the 2000-year-old terracottas found near Nok village. Some tribal groups such as the Yoruba, Igbo and Ekoi still produce fine sculpture and masks.

ENVIRONMENT

Given the size if the country, Nigeria's topography is relatively unvaried. The north touches on the Sahel and is mostly savanna with low hills. Mountains are found only along the Cameroon border in the east, although there is also a 1500m-high plateau around Jos in the centre of the country. The coast is an almost unbroken line of sandy beaches and lagoons running back to creeks and mangrove swamps and is very humid most of the year.

The climate is generally hot and dry in the north and in the south it is wet and hot for much of the year.

The rainy season in the north is between April and September, while in the south it is from March to November. A long, dusty dry season stretches from December to March, when the *harmattan* wind blows in off the desert.

Nigeria's large population has contributed to widespread deforestation – 95% of the original forests have been logged. However, the oil industry has caused the greatest number of environmental problems: technological mishaps such as explosions and oil spills (which a leading transnational oil company has been reluctant to clean up) have damaged the fishing industry and rendered land in Rivers State unusable; farmers have been dislodged from their traditional lands; and the industry has also bulldozed local shrines and totems. When Nigerian playwright and novelist Ken Saro-Wiwa protested against the despoilment of his homeland in 1995, he was summarily tried and hanged, along with eight others.

TRANSPORT

GETTING THERE & AWAY
Air
Frequent flights connect Lagos with all the West African capitals; fares start around US$100. Ghana Airways is a major operator on these routes, and also serves the USA from around US$1000. Major international carriers serve key African hubs such as Addis Ababa (daily), Nairobi and Johannesburg (at least twice weekly), with fares generally around the US$500 mark.

Lagos's Murtala Mohammed International Airport is Nigeria's main gateway, but it's worth considering flying into Kano or Abuja instead of Lagos, which can be a real hassle.

The national carrier is the highly unreliable **Nigerian Airways** (☎ 490 0810; Tafawa Balewa Sq, Lagos), which flies to many African destinations, as well as Europe and the USA. See Getting There & Away (p430) for details of airlines that service Nigeria.

Departure tax for international flights is always included in the ticket price – double-check when booking, and on no account pay anyone who demands it in the airport!

Boat & Land
BENIN
The road from Lagos to Cotonou (120km) is excellent. Bush taxis (US$3, three hours) leave from the Mile-2 motor park, a short ferry trip west from Lagos Island. You can also enter Benin at Malanville via Kamba (Nigeria) and Gaya (Niger).

CAMEROON
There may be passenger speedboats from Oron, south of Calabar, to Idenao, a small place 50km northwest of Limbe (Cameroon), but these are often suspended due to clashes on the Bakassi Peninsula. Check the security situation before making any plans, and avoid the temptation to take one of the frequent cargo boats – these are almost all smugglers' vessels.

By road, the usual route is from Enugu or Calabar to Mamfé (Cameroon) via Ikom. From Calabar take a bush taxi to Ikom and another from there to Mfum on the Nigerian border. From Ekok there are taxis to most of the towns in western Cameroon via Mamfé. The border closes at 7pm. In the far east, the standard route is from Maiduguri to Maroua (Cameroon) via Banki.

CHAD
While Nigeria does share a small stretch of border with Chad around Lake Chad, this area is still under dispute and occasional armed clashes do occur here. The usual way to get to Chad is via Maiduguri to Kousséri (Cameroon), from where it is a short hop to N'Djaména (Chad).

NIGER
There are four main routes to Niger; the most popular is from Kano to Zinder (Niger), while the cheapest is Kamba to Gaya (Niger), as you spend less time on the more expensive Nigerien transport. The other routes are from Katsina to Maradi (Niger) via Jibiya, and Sokoto to Birni-N'Konni (Niger) via Illela.

There are innumerable checkpoints along the way on all these routes, and you can expect whatever vehicle you're in to be stopped at all of them.

GETTING AROUND
Air
Taking a domestic flight in Nigeria is like entering a madhouse: schedules (of a sort) are vague and constantly subject to delay or cancellation. The upside is that flights are impressively cheap (US$45 to US$55 for most journeys). The departure tax for internal flights is US$0.50; note that flights leave from a separate domestic airport in Lagos, about 10km north of the international terminal (see p430 for domestic airline details).

Hitching
You would have to be mad to hitch – the chances of being mugged (or worse) are very high. It's usually unnecessary anyway, given the low price of public transport.

Local Transport
The best and safest way to travel is by bus; however, these only leave when full, which can involve a wait of up to three hours. Bush taxis (usually Peugeot 504s) also go when full, but this usually means only five or nine passengers, so the waiting time is minutes instead of hours. The drawback is the dangerous speeds at which they travel. Fares are about the same over comparable distances (average US$1 per 100km) and they're both cheap compared with other West African countries – Nigeria's petrol is the cheapest in Africa, although there are sometimes shortages.

In large cities, there will usually be several motor parks for bush taxis servicing specific destinations. Virtually all of them will be on the outskirts of town and you'll have to take a taxi to get there.

Motorcycle-Taxi
If you're game, in many cities you can get around on the back of a motorcycle-taxi called an *okada* or 'machine'. They can manage a backpack on the handlebars and are a great way to cool off. Fares are never more than US$0.25 for a short trip.

Train
There are train services from Lagos to Maiduguri, Jos and Kano, all via Ibadan; they are an inefficient, slow and potentially dangerous way to get around, and never arrive on time.

LAGOS

☎ 01 / pop 13 million

Lagos takes its name from the Portuguese word for lagoons, but if it's secluded sandy bays you want this is definitely not the place. It's the second-largest city in Africa, with wall-to-wall people, bumper-to-bumper cars, noise and pollution beyond belief, a crime rate out of control, and public utilities that are simply incapable of coping with the demands of the huge population. Elevated motorways ring the city, jammed with speed freaks and snarl-ups ('go-slows') on top, and tin-and-cardboard shacks underneath. Power cuts are a daily fact of life.

Yet, while all that's true, particularly of Lagos Island, the city can be a buzz if you have the stamina and street savvy to survive this hot, steamy concrete jungle. The live music scene is superb, the street life is inimitable, and if you make some Nigerian friends you may see a whole different side to this lively metropolis.

ORIENTATION
For the traveller, there are four main areas of Lagos: Yaba on the mainland, south of

the international and domestic airports; Lagos Island, the heart of the city; Ikoyi Island, a smart suburb with some embassies and top-end hotels; and Victoria Island (VI) – an even smarter suburb facing the Atlantic Ocean with the bulk of the embassies and a number of top-end hotels. The islands are connected by elevated expressways and bridges.

It's a 20-minute ride from Murtala Mohammed International Airport to Lagos Island; head for the yellow taxis outside the departure lounge upstairs. Know your destination and expect to pay about half the official Nigerian Airports Authority (NAA) fare of around US$40.

Coming to the airport is much cheaper than leaving it – between US$10 and US$20, depending on your bargaining skills.

The domestic airport is 10km from the main terminal and is – if anything – more dodgy, with some very pushy staff. A taxi to the international airport should cost US$4.

INFORMATION
Internet Access
You can get online in Internet cafés all over Lagos; the usual price for access is around US$0.10 per minute.

Medical Services
Health services in Lagos include:
Medical Consultants Group (☎ 611 900, Eko Court Annexe, Kofo Abayomi Rd, VI)
St Nicholas Hospital (☎ 263 1739; 57 Campbell St, Lagos Island)

Money
In Yaba, the bureaux de change are on Oja Elegbu Rd between Western Ave and Murtala Mohammed Way. There are many others on Ikoyi along Awolowo Rd, or try the car parks of the larger hotels on VI. The black market for changing money is centred on the Bristol Hotel on Lagos Island.

Post & Telephone
The main **post office** (33 Marina St) is on Lagos Island. There are smaller branches on Ikoyi, about 200m east of the corner of Kingsway and Awolowo Rds, and on VI, on Adeola Odeku St. Many people prefer to use courier services, such as **DHL** (☎ 452 70861; www.dhl-ng.com; Sumbo Jibowu, Ikoyi).

For phone calls, your best bet is to dial through your hotel as the public phone network is pretty poor. Over the last couple of years, there's been an explosion in the mobile phone market, with increasing competition pushing prices down.

SIGHTS & ACTIVITIES
For street life during the day, take a stroll along the length of Broad St or dive into the labyrinthine **Balogun Market** on Lagos Island. It's worth considering hiring a guide to show you round Lagos's markets, as they're mazelike places and gang violence is not unknown. Look out for the dancing traffic policemen.

The **National Museum** (Awolowo Rd; admission US$0.80; ⏰ 9am-5pm) has some interesting displays and exhibits, including many fine works of ancient sculpture. It also has a nonprofit craft centre.

To get away to one of the fine **beaches** nearby, take a boat from Walter Carrington Cres on VI (up to US$5 return, 30 minutes). Palasides, Lekki and Tarkwa are all popular.

SLEEPING
The cheapest accommodation is generally found on Lagos Island, but standards are low and safety is a real concern. There are some slightly better options on the mainland and in Yaba. If you can afford it, though, the best place to stay is on Victoria Island.

EATING & DRINKING
Virtually the only places to eat on Lagos Island are the street stalls along Broad St and the good chop houses or suya stalls on King George St. Fast food is also available at outlets such as Mr Bigg's which can be found all over town.

Ikoyi has the best range of restaurants and snack places on offer, mostly concentrated around Awolowo Rd, while on VI there are food stalls and plenty of other cheap eateries at Bar Beach, as well as the best of Lagos's more expensive restaurants. Ask an expat for the current highlights.

There are plenty of bars and music on offer around town, wherever you go. Ask a trusted local for the best venues. Ikeja is one of the best districts for live music, while Apapa also has several clubs. Expect to pay US$0.80 to US$1.50 cover charge.

GETTING THERE & AROUND

Airline offices in Lagos include:

Cameroon Airlines (☎ 261 6270; Olosa St, VI)
EgyptAir (☎ 266 8344; 22B Idowu Taylor St, VI)
Ethiopian Airlines (☎ 263 2690; 20 Tafawa Balewa Sq)
Ghana Airways (☎ 266 1808; 130 Awolowo Rd, Ikoyi)
Kenya Airways (☎ 2616656; 5 Idowu Taylor St, VI)
Nigerian Airways (☎ 490 0810; Tafawa Balewa Sq)

Private airlines such as **Okado Air** (☎ 496 3881), **Kabo Airlines** (☎ 497 0449) and **Skyline** (☎ 493 4440) are generally less chaotic and more reliable than Nigerian Airways. They all have offices in Terminal 2 of Lagos domestic airport.

The Ojota motorpark, 10km north of Lagos Island, has bush taxi services to Ibadan (US$1, one hour) and Oshogbo (US$2).

Services to Benin City (US$3) and Calabar (US$6) leave from **Oju Elegba Junction Motor Park** (Western Ave, Surulere).

Iddo Motor Park (Murtala Mohammed Way) serves routes to Abuja (US$8, 12 hours), Jos (US$6, 12 hours) and Kano (US$7, 15 hours).

Private bus companies operate most of the same routes from their own offices near the motor parks.

Minibuses (US$0.08) serve points all over Lagos, but you'll have a job working out the routes unless you stay here for some time. Yellow private taxis can be found just about everywhere and require some haggling; a short trip should cost US$2.50 and a longer one US$4 (eg Lagos Island to VI or Ikoyi).

AROUND LAGOS

Only one hour away, **Sungbo's Eredo** is Africa's largest construction, a 160km-long, 1050-year-old, 20m-high linear boundary rampart that once surrounded the ancient kingdom of Ijebu. Built over two centuries, it's now largely covered by rainforest; use the guiding services of locals to explore, and respect the shrines and other crumbling remnants.

The site is signposted from the Ijebu–Ode road; take a bus from the CMS station on Lagos Island to Epe (US$1) and then a taxi (US$1).

NORTHERN NIGERIA

ABUJA

☎ 09 / pop 500,000

Construction on the new Federal Capital Territory (FCT) began in the 1980s, and Abuja took over as Nigeria's official capital in 1991. The rest of the world still thinks it's Lagos, and most Nigerians act that way too; many important ministries and embassies have yet to make the move from the old capital. The centre is squeaky clean with a smattering of imposing civic buildings, and you need your own transport to get around.

Most accommodation in Abuja is unreasonably expensive, and you'll have to look outside the centre for the best deals. There are a couple of good, moderately priced restaurants in the area around the Sheraton Hotel.

You can get bush taxis to Lagos (US$8, three hours), Kano (US$3, five hours), Jos (US$3, three hours) and Calabar (US$5, 12 hours) at the Karu motor park, 10km west of town. Several private bus companies operate 'night flights' to Lagos (US$16, 10 to 11 hours).

JOS

☎ 073 / pop 762,000

Scenic and relatively peaceful, the town of Jos is justifiably popular with travellers in Nigeria. It's at the heart of the green and shrubby Jos Plateau, 1200m above sea level, which has a relatively cool climate year-round and is surrounded by small undulating hills. The name Jos is said to derive from early missionaries who named it in honour of Jesus Our Saviour.

The town's main attraction is the outstanding **Jos National Museum** (admission US$0.08; ☼ 8.30am-5.30pm) off Gomwalk Rd. Exhibits in the main site include pottery, brassware, ornaments, carved doors and ceremonial headdresses. The attached **Museum of Traditional Nigerian Architecture** has some fascinating life-sized reproductions of Nigeria's historic and tribal buildings, which are best seen with one of the well-informed guides (tip US$1.25).

The town's large **covered market** and the nearby street scenes are also worth a look.

A bit of missionary zeal still survives in Jos, and the various centres run by religious organisations are your best bet for a cheap night's sleep. There are also some good private hotels around the centre of town.

Azikewe Ave (also known as Zik Ave) is a handy strip for cheap grub. There are also plenty of cheap chop houses near the stadium.

Long-distance bus lines serving points to the south and southwest stop at the stadium on Tafawa Balewa Rd. Buses east and minibuses/bush taxis to most destinations operate from the motor park on Bauchi Rd; minibuses and taxis to Abuja leave from the Zaria Rd car park.

KANO
☎ 064 / pop 2 million

Kano is the third-largest city in Nigeria, the largest in the north, and one of the country's most favoured tourist destinations. It has a history going back 1000 years and was once a very important trading centre, with a dominant position at the crossroads of the trans-Saharan trade routes.

Sharia'a law was introduced here relatively peaceably in June 2000. Bans on drinking, smoking and contact between the sexes are actively enforced; foreigners can get away with most things but should still behave discreetly.

The main drawback here is the air pollution. In combination with the *harmattan*, the vehicle fumes can quite literally choke you.

Information

Niger has a **consulate** (☎ 645274; 12 Aliyu Ave) here, which is a good place to get a visa if you're heading north and/or don't want to go to Lagos.

Internet access can be found at the **Motel la Mirage** (27 Enugu Rd) and several other places around town.

The private bureaux de change are the quickest places to change money officially. Black market moneychangers hang around outside the Central Hotel on Bompai Rd.

The post office is at the eastern end of Post Office Rd, but it has limited facilities. The Nigerian Telecom (Nitel) phone office is across the road.

There's an information office at the Kano State Tourist Camp; it's under-resourced, but is the best place to arrange tours (US$12 for three hours).

Sights

Any visit to the **old city** will probably involve hiring a guide. This isn't a bad idea – they know their way around, keep other would-be guides away and shouldn't pressure you to buy crafts or anything else. A tip of around US$4 per person is expected.

The crumbling **city walls** have mostly been allowed to fall apart, but some of the original **gates** on the southern edge of the old city remain. Inside the walls at Kofar Mata (Mata Gate) are the once-famous **dye pits**, said to be the oldest in Africa and still apparently in active use.

The huge old **Kurmi Market** is extensive and definitely worth visiting, but the range of craftwork, fabrics and artefacts doesn't always match up to the hype. You can find bargains here if you take your time.

The **Emir's Palace** is an outstanding example of Hausa architecture, but is still occupied by the Emir, so it's tricky to visit. Diagonally opposite is the excellent **Gidan Makama Museum** (admission US$0.40; ☯ 10am-4pm), a former palace which has been fully restored and also houses some interesting photographic displays.

Sleeping & Eating

Cheap accommodation is mainly concentrated around the northern Sabon Gari district. There's also a popular camp site and an overland truck stop near the centre.

In Sabon Gari there are a number of cheap chop houses at the western end of New Rd. They all serve comparable fare, mainly pepper soup and *gari*, for less than US$0.65.

Getting There & Away

Kano international airport is 8km northwest of Sabon Gari Market. A taxi to/from the airport is US$3; an okada (motorcycle taxi) is US$1.

The main motor parks are Naibowa motor park on Zaria Rd (for the south and east) and Kuka motor park on Katsina Rd (for the north, including Niger).

YANKARI GAME RESERVE

Yankari, 225km east of Jos, is Nigeria's best park for observing wildlife (admission US$0.80, photo permit US$0.80). It's possible to come across elephants, waterbucks, bushbucks, hippos, crocodiles and the occasional lion. Nigerian visitors are common, but you may find locals taking photos of you instead of the animals.

There's a wildlife-viewing truck (US$1.20 per person), which starts daily tours at 7.30am and 4pm. The other feature of interest in the park is the thermal **Wikki Warm Springs**. Their crystal-clear waters are free of bilharzia.

The best months to visit are the dry season (February to April), when wildlife gathers at the Gaji River.

The **Wikki Warm Springs Hotel** (☎ 077-41174; camp site/bungalow US$1.20/12; ✷), administered by the reserve, is set high above the spring and has a serene view over the lush area. The bungalow accommodation is often included in the price of overnight tours from Jos.

Make sure your gear (including the window of your bungalow) is secure, as the baboons are master thieves. The hotel has its own **dining room** (meals US$2).

Minibuses from Minivan motor park in Bauchi will drop you at the park entrance for US$4. From here you have to hitch the 40km to the lodge. This isn't too hard (Friday and Saturday are best), but if a taxi or one of the park's vehicles picks you up, expect to pay about US$1.

Alternatively, you may be able to arrange a tour from Jos.

SOUTHERN NIGERIA

IBADAN
☎ 022 / pop 8 million
Nigeria's second most populous city, Ibadan is not the prettiest (or cheapest) place, but at least it's not Lagos. The **Dugbe, Oje** and **Bode markets** are well worth exploring.

There are several cheap hotels south of the University of Ibadan on Bodija Rd, while street food can be found at stalls near Dugbe Market.

Bush taxis to Lagos (US$1, one hour) and points east leave from the New Garage and Challenge motor parks. Vehicles heading to the north leave from Sango motor park on Oyo Rd.

OSHOGBO
☎ 035 / pop 500,000
Located northeast of Lagos, Oshogbo is not much to look at, but it's quiet and the people are friendly. The main attraction is the **Sacred Forest**, covering a large area of rainforest about 2.5km from the centre. Inside the forest is the beautiful **Shrine of Oshuno**, the River Goddess. In addition to the natural beauty, there are many stunning sculptures, gates and walls put up by Suzanne Wenger (known locally as Aduni Olosa, the 'Adored

One'), an Austrian painter and sculptor who came here in the 1950s.

Oshogbo was once where the country's most famous artists made their homes, but seems to have lost much of its creative edge in recent years.

There aren't that many good cheap accommodation options in Oshogbo; try the area around Old Ede Rd and Old Ikurin Rd. You may find better deals outside the centre. Most of the chop houses are along Iwo Ibadan Rd.

The motor park for Lagos and Ibadan is on Oke Fia Rd in the town centre. There are regular bush taxis to Benin City (US$3) and Lagos (US$2).

BENIN CITY
☎ 052 / pop 1 million
Benin City is one of the old Yoruba capitals. The kingdom, which flourished here for centuries before the colonial period, gave rise to one of the first African art forms to be accepted internationally – the 15th-century 'lost wax' bronzes of Benin.

The **National Museum** (Ring Rd; admission US$0.10; ☺ 9am-6pm) is worth a visit. Note that many bronzes are on loan to other museums. The guides at the museum are good sources of information.

There are plenty of craft shops along Airport Rd close to the Oba's Palace.

The area around King's Square is a good place to start looking for cheap accommodation, and you could also try Akpakpava Rd.

Street food is found along Akpakpava Rd, especially in the Agbadan, Oba and New Benin Markets.

There are two motor parks, both quite a way from the centre. For vehicles going west (Lagos, Oshogbo etc) you need Uselu motor park; for destinations east (Onitsha, Aba etc) you need Aba motor park.

OKOMU SANCTUARY
Situated 72km from Benin City, this reserve has rainforest trails, a treehouse for bird-watching and interesting flora and fauna. It's run by the **NCF** (☎ 01-268 6163) in Lagos. You'll need your own transport or a taxi.

CALABAR
☎ 087 / pop 444,000
Calabar is one of Nigeria's oldest trading cities, with European connections going

back to 15th-century Portuguese mariners. Much of the old town remains, picturesquely sited on the hill overlooking the river, and it's a popular stopover for travellers heading to Cameroon.

Note that the ownership of the Bakassi Peninsula is still under dispute between Nigeria and Cameroon, and armed clashes do occur; check the security situation before you travel.

The **Cameroon consulate** (21 Ndidan Usang Iso Rd) issues visas and is a good alternative to the embassy in Lagos.

It is possible to send and receive emails at the university; ask at the main entrance.

The excellent **museum** (Leopard Town Rd; admission US$0.15; 9am-6pm) is housed in the former British governor's residence. It has a large exhibit on the history and effects of the slave trade.

Creek Town, a tiny village just upriver, and **Kwi Falls**, 35km south of Calabar, are worth day trips.

There's a reasonable range of accommodation available in Calabar; most of it not far from the town centre.

There are several chop houses on Edem St and Calabar Rd.

Bush taxis and minibuses are found at the motor park on Cameroon St. Cross Lines buses for Lagos (US$6) and Abuja (US$5, 12 hours) leave from the office just opposite.

THE EASTERN PARKS

The **Cross River National Park** (office: 3 Ebuta Cres, Ette Agbor Layout, Calabar) has a small population of gorillas. It's managed by the World Wide Fund for Nature (WWF) and the **NCF** (01-268 6163). Ask at the park office for an introductory letter; you can also get information about the American-run Drill Ranch & Rescue Centre. Bush taxis from Calabar will take you to Ikom, from where you can pick up a motorcycle taxi to the park.

The **Obudu Cattle Ranch**, northeast of Ikom, is in the 'Land of the Clouds' on the Cameroon border. It's not an official park, but it's a great place for hiking, swimming and horse riding. For information write to Obudu Cattle Ranch, PO Box 40, Obudu, Cross River State. Get a bush taxi from Ogoja to Obudu, then a motorcycle-taxi or bush taxi to the ranch (44km).

Gashaka Gumpti National Park is the country's largest park, has the highest mountain

in Nigeria (Chappal Wadi, 2418m), and contains the most diverse ecology of any park in Nigeria. Unfortunately, it's difficult to reach without your own transport.

NIGERIA DIRECTORY

ACCOMMODATION

Nigerian hotels, though usually cheaper than those in neighbouring countries, are generally 'squelched' – regardless of what facilities the hotels advertise, nothing works (air-con, water, fan, lights, door locks). Hotels in larger cities, notably Lagos, Abuja and Ibadan, start at much higher prices than elsewhere in the country.

Hotels often use the term 'single' for a room with one double bed and 'double' for one with two double beds. Many hotels in the mid- to high-price bracket demand a refundable deposit up front.

BUSINESS HOURS

Normal business hours are from 8.30am to 5pm Monday to Friday; government offices are open 7.30am to 3.30pm Monday to Friday and 7.30am to 1pm Saturday. Banking hours are 8am to 3pm Monday to Thursday and 8.30am to 1pm Friday.

The last Saturday of every month is 'sanitation day', when the streets are closed from 7am to 10am for a countrywide clean-up.

DANGERS & ANNOYANCES

Violent street crime and robbery happens throughout the country, often in broad daylight, and is the biggest threat to the traveller. Armed robbery occurs on roads from Lagos to the border with Benin, and on the Benin City and Ibadan expressways.

Current no-go areas include the oil-rich Niger Delta states, where there has been hostage-taking for ransom and local disturbances, while the northern Hausa cities have been the scene of prolonged violence following demonstrations over the implementation of Sharia'a law.

Other problems include: widespread scams and fraud at every level; piracy in Nigerian waters; doubts about the safety of local aircraft; an horrific death toll on the roads; international drug trafficking and money laundering; Chadian troop incursions in the northeast; and a dispute with

Cameroon over the Bakassi Peninsula in the southeast.

If all this hasn't put you off, and you need to travel here, contact the **British Deputy High Commission** (☎ 01-262 5930) or the **US Consulate** (☎ 01-261 0050) in Lagos for information on the current situation.

EMBASSIES & CONSULATES

The following countries have diplomatic representation in Nigeria:

Australia Abuja (☎ 413 5226; 2940 Aguiyi Ironsi St, Maitama)

Benin Abuja (☎ 413 8425; 2858 Danuba St, Maitama); Lagos (☎ 261 4385; 4 Abudu Smith St, VI)

Cameroon Lagos (☎ 261 2226; 5 Elsie Femi Pearse St, VI); Calabar (21 Ndidan Usang Iso Rd)

Chad Abuja (☎ 413 0751; 10 Mississippi St, Maitama)

European Union House Abuja (☎ 523 3144; 63 Usuma St, Maitama)

France Abuja (☎ 523 5506; www.ambafrance-ng.org; 32 Udi St, Maitama); Lagos (☎ 269 3427; 1 Oyinkan Abayomi Dr, Ikoyi)

Germany Lagos (☎ 261 1011; 15 Walter Carrington Cres, VI)

Niger Abuja (☎ 523 6205; 7 Sangha St); Lagos (☎ 261 2300; 15 Adeola Odeku St, VI); Kano (☎ 6452/4; 12 Aliyu Ave)

Sudan Abuja (☎ 413 9964; Katsina-Ala Cres, Maitama); Lagos (☎ 261 5889; 2B Kofo Abayomi St, VI)

UK Abuja (☎ 413 2010; consular@abuja.mail.fco.gov.uk; Shehu Shangari Way, Maitama); Lagos (☎ 262 5930; consular@lagos.mail.fco.gov.uk; 11 Walter Carrington Cres, VI)

USA Abuja (☎ 523 0916; usembassy.state.gov/nigeria; 7 Mambilla Dr, Maitama); Lagos (☎ 261 0050; uslagos@pd.state.gov; 2 Walter Carrington Cres, VI)

In West Africa, Nigeria has embassies in Benin, Cameroon, Chad and Niger.

FOOD & DRINK

Food in Nigeria is nothing to rave about. The best-known dish served in a local 'chop house' (cheap café) is pepper soup, a very hot sauce which comes with fish, beef or goat meat. It's served with rice or another grain-based staple such as *gari* or *eba* (manioc flour).

In the cities you'll find plenty of snack places serving stodgy chicken, meat or fish pies and doughnuts.

HOLIDAYS

As well as religious holidays listed in the Africa Directory (p1003) the principal public holidays in Nigeria are:

1 January New Year's Day
1 May Labour Day
1 October National Day
26 December Boxing Day

INTERNET ACCESS

Good, cheap connections are widespread in Lagos, Abuja and Kano, and can also be found in many other towns.

MONEY

There are no ATMs in Nigeria and credit cards are useless except at large international hotels; you're seriously advised not to use them at all because of widespread fraud. Changing travellers cheques is also difficult, except at the major hotels. If you have them stolen you'll wait forever to arrange a refund, usually via the UK. Bring cash and, if at all possible, avoid banks entirely as they offer poor exchange rates and service is very slow. Instead, change cash at either a bureau de change or with a black-market dealer, but be wary of the latter.

POST & TELEPHONE

Mail sent to/from Nigeria is notoriously slow. Forget about sending parcels (except by courier companies like DHL; see Post p429) – they'll never arrive.

You can phone or fax from Nitel offices in any regional capital. It's about US$3.50 per minute to Europe or North America.

VISAS

Visas are required for all except nationals of most West African countries. You cannot get visas at the border or at airports, and many embassies only issue visas to residents of the country in which that embassy is located (although this policy seems to have been relaxed in Chad, Mali, Ghana and Niger). As a rule it's best to get a visa before leaving for Africa.

The cost of a visa will depend on your nationality. For most, it's about US$30 to US$65.

You also need two or three photos, an onward airline ticket and either a letter of invitation or a letter detailing your reasons for visiting.

Visas allow for a stay of up to one month and remain valid for three months from the date of issue.

Visa Extensions

Extensions can be obtained in all the state capitals from the immigration department of the Federal Secretariat. The central Federal Secretariat is in Abuja, on Shehu Shagari Way. Extensions are free for most people, but UK nationals may have to pay a fee and supply one photo and a letter of recommendation from a citizen or resident.

Visas for Onward Travel

Visas for the following neighbouring and near-neighbouring countries are available from embassies and consulates in Nigeria

(see p434). Most visas require two or three photos.

Benin Fifteen-day visas cost US$5; you can extend them easily in Cotonou. Visa applications are accepted between 9am and 11am and issued at 2pm the same day.

Cameroon Free transit visas and 90-day, multiple-entry visas (US$50 in hard currency) are issued within 24 hours. You'll need an onward air ticket for the embassy in Lagos, but not always at the consulate in Calabar.

Chad One-month visas cost US$25; they're usually issued within a day or two, but you need a letter of application to get the forms in the first place.

Niger A one-month visa costs US$25 and is issued within 24 hours.

436

Cameroon

HIGHLIGHTS

- **Waza National Park** Cameroon's version of a safari: affordable, accessible and teeming with elephants, giraffes and much more (p458)
- **Mandara Mountains** Almost unlimited hiking opportunities through stunning landscapes and traditional villages (p458)
- **Kribi** A laid-back beach town where travellers and Cameroonians alike come to swim, relax, eat, drink and dance (p444)
- **The Northwest Province** Scenic mountainous region rich in history, with tribal chiefdoms, sultans and the challenge of the Ring Road (p452)
- **Mt Cameroon** The tallest peak in the region rising up from the foothill town of Buea and a rewarding challenge for climbers (p448)
- **Off the beaten track** The southeast town of Campo, with its nearby beaches and rainforest hikes (p445)

FAST FACTS

- **Area** 469,440 sq km (a little smaller than Spain, a little bigger than California)
- **ATMs** at banks in large cities, usually linked to Visa
- **Borders** Nigeria, Chad, Gabon, Equatorial Guinea all open; borders with Central African Republic and Congo often closed, check in advance
- **Budget** US$30 per day
- **Capital** Yaoundé
- **Languages** French, English and many local languages
- **Money** Central African CFA; US$1 = CFA600
- **Population** 16.2 million
- **Seasons** hot year-round; north: wet (Apr–Sep); south: heavy rain (Jun–Oct)
- **Telephone** country code ☎ 237; international access code ☎ 00
- **Time** GMT/UTC + 1
- **Visas** required by all, available in neighbouring countries for US$50

Cameroon has it all. Sure, other African countries might say that about themselves, but few could say it with the same confidence Cameroon can. Where else can you go from beach resorts through dense rainforests teeming with wildlife to bustling modern cities, then take a train to the arid, mostly Muslim north where you'll find traditional villages clinging to rocky cliffs, all in one country? The country's history has left a legacy of a diverse,

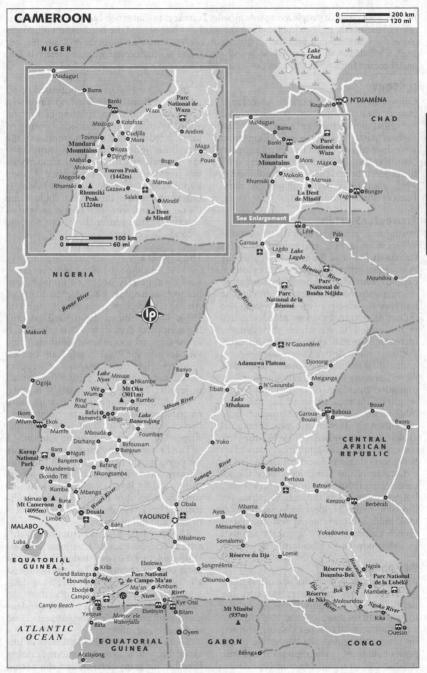

CAMEROON

0 ——— 200 km
0 ——— 120 mi

NIGER

Maiduguri
Bama
Banki
Waza
Kolofata
Mozogo
Oudjilla
Tourou
Mora
Mandara
Mountains
Koza
Maba
Djingliya
Mokolo
Mogodé
Tourou Peak
(1442m)
Rhumsiki
Rhumsiki
Peak
(1224m)
Gazawa
Salak
La Dent
de Mindif

Parc
National de
Waza
Andirni
Maga
Pouss
Bogo
Maroua
Mindif

0 ——— 100 km
0 ——— 60 mi

CHAD

Lake
Chad

Kousséri
N'DJAMÉNA

Maiduguri
Bama
Banki
Parc
National de
Waza
Mandara
Mountains
Mora
Maga
Rhumsiki
Mokolo
Maroua
La Dent
de Mindif
Yagoua
Bongor

See Enlargement

Léré
Pala

Garoua
Lagdo
Lake
Lagdo
Bénoué River
Moundou

NIGERIA

Benue River

Makurdi

Faro River
Parc
National de la
Bénoué
Parc
National de
Bouba Ndjida

N'Gaoundéré

Djonong
Adamawa Plateau
Meiganga

Ogoja
Lake
Nyos
Missaje
Nkambe
We
Mt Oku
Wum
(3011m)
Ring
Kumbo
Road
Bamessing
Ikom
Bafut
Mfum
Ekok
Bamenda
Sabga
Mamfe
Mbouda
Dschang
Bafoussam
Banjoun
Foumban
Korup
Baro
National
Nguti
Park
Bangem
Mundemba
Bafang
Ekondo Titi
Nkongsamba
Kumba
Mbanga
Idenao
Mt Cameroun
Buea
(4095m)
Limbe
MALABO
Douala
Luba
Edéa

Tibati
N'Goundal
Lake
Mbakaou
Banyo
Mbam River
Garoua-
Boulaï
Baboua
Bouar
Baoro

**CENTRAL
AFRICAN
REPUBLIC**

Yoko
Sanaga River
Bélabo
Bertoua
Batouri
Kenzou
Berbérati

Obala
Ayos
YAOUNDÉ
Mbama
Abong Mbang
Wouri River
Yokadouma

**EQUATORIAL
GUINEA**

Mbalmayo
Messamena
Somalomo
Réserve du Dja
Lomié
Ngola

Kribi
Grand Batanga
Ebolowa
Sangmélima
Réserve de
Boumba-Bek
Parc
National
de la Lobéké
Eboundja
Lobé
Parc National
de Campo-Ma'an
Olounou
Mambele
Ebodjé
Ma'an
Ambam
Ntem River
Réserve
de Nki
Moloundou
Campo
Kye Ossi
Ngoko River
Campo Beach
Ebebiyin
Bitam
Kika
Yengue
Menve'ele
Waterfalls
Mt Minébé
(937m)
Bata
Ouesso

**ATLANTIC
OCEAN**

**EQUATORIAL
GUINEA**
Oyem
GABON
CONGO
Acalayong
Bélinga

CAMEROON

multilingual range of people living side by side. Travellers to Cameroon can hike in the mountains of the north, explore the jungle in the south, or laze around the beaches and hill towns along the coast. All that plus there's the region's tallest mountain looming up from near sea level, a lethal lake, sultans, tribal kings and all-day and all-night ceremonies and festivals. Oh, and there are lions – wild ones in the bush and indomitable ones on the football pitch.

HISTORY

Cameroon is another example of colonial powers creating a country without regard for tribal boundaries or geography. The various parts of what is now Cameroon were divided and ceded between European countries throughout the colonial era until the modern boundaries were established in 1961, creating a part-Anglophone, part-Francophone nation.

Prawns for Starters

Portuguese explorers first sailed up the Wouri River in 1472, and named it Rio dos Camarões (River of Prawns). Soon after the Portuguese arrived by sea, Fulani pastoral nomads from what is now Nigeria began to migrate overland from the north, forcing the indigenous forest peoples southwards. The Fulani migration took on added urgency in the early 17th century as they fled the increasingly predatory attentions of Dutch, Portuguese and British slave-traders.

British influence was curtailed in 1884 when Germany signed a treaty with the well-organised chiefdoms of Douala and central Bamiléké Plateau, although for the local inhabitants the agreement meant little more than a shift from one form of colonial exploitation to another. After WWI, the German protectorate of Kamerun was carved up between France and Great Britain.

Local revolts in French-controlled Cameroon in the 1950s were brutally suppressed, but the momentum throughout Africa for throwing off the shackles of colonial rule soon took hold. Self-government was granted in French Cameroon in 1958, quickly followed by independence on 1 January 1960.

Wily Ahidjo

Ahmadou Ahidjo, leader of one of the independence parties, became president of the newly independent state, a position he was to hold until his resignation in 1982. Ahidjo, a man with a total lack of charisma, ensured his longevity through the cultivation of expedient alliances, brutal repression and wily if authoritarian regional favouritism.

In October 1961, a UN-sponsored referendum in British-mandated northwestern Cameroon ended up splitting it in two, with the area around Bamenda opting to join the federal state of Cameroon, and the remainder joining Nigeria. In June 1972 the federal structure of two Cameroons was replaced by the centralised United Republic of Cameroon – a move which is bitterly resented to this day by Anglophone Cameroonians, who believe that instead of entering a true union they have become second-class citizens.

The Biya Era

In 1982, Ahidjo's hand-picked successor, Paul Biya, quickly distanced himself from his former mentor, but adopted many of Ahidjo's repressive measures. In the late 1980s, Biya clamped down hard on calls for multiparty democracy. Diversions such as the national soccer team's stunning performance in the 1990 World Cup bought him time. But the demands for freedom would not go away and Biya was forced to legalise 25 opposition parties in 1991. When it became apparent that plurality placed limitations upon the president, these parties were quickly, though temporarily, suspended, along with the constitution.

The first multiparty elections in 25 years were grudgingly held in 1992 and saw the Cameroonian Democratic People's Movement – led by Biya – hanging on to power with the support of minority parties. International observers alleged widespread vote-rigging and intimidation.

The international anticorruption organisation, Transparency International, consistently ranks Cameroon among the world's most corrupt countries. This phenomenon affects every aspect of daily life, from dealings with petty government officials to the rampant destruction of the country's endangered rainforests by logging interests close to the government.

Today Cameroon exists in a state of uneasy calm, with a stagnant economy, causing hardship for many citizens, and simmering political unrest held down by tight government control.

THE CULTURE

Cameroonians are always on the job, ambitious and industrious, scrambling to make a better living. It's only a slight exaggeration when people say that if Cameroon closed its borders the rest of Central Africa would starve to death; Cameroon grows, produces and exports much of what you'll find at the market stalls in neighbouring countries. Of course this energy isn't always limited to strictly legal activities – Cameroonians have a reputation for being hustlers and scammers as well.

It's hard to pin down the Cameroonian population because it's made up of so many different elements – Anglophone in the west, Francophone in the east, Muslim in the north, Christian in the south, with all kinds of 'none of the above' mixed in. In general everyone gets along, but Cameroonians are keenly aware of their differences, and ethnic tension and discrimination are common.

ARTS

Cameroon has produced a few of the region's most celebrated artists. In literature, Mongo Beti, like many other Cameroonian writers, deals with the legacies of colonialism. Musically, Manu Dibango is the country's brightest star.

ENVIRONMENT

The land, like its people, contains a lot of different elements thrown together by colonial-era boundaries. The south is deep rainforest in a low coastal plain. In the cen-tre of the country the jungle gives way to a sparsely populated savanna. The north and extreme north are close to the Sahel, with arid, sandy conditions all the way up to Lake Chad. Mountains run up the west of the country, from Mt Cameroon near the Atlantic coast to the Bamenda Highlands to the Mandara Mountains in the north.

Cameroon has abundant wildlife, though it is threatened by habitat encroachment and poaching for the bushmeat trade. In the south there are gorillas, chimpanzees, forest elephants and a variety of rare Central African species, but they're almost impossible to see in the dense forest. In the scrublands up north the animals are much easier to find. Your best bet for wildlife-viewing is Waza National Park in the far north of the country. Many other national parks are being established and made accessible to visitors in hopes of developing an ecotourism industry while protecting endangered habitats.

TRANSPORT

GETTING THERE & AWAY

Air

Both Yaoundé and Douala have international airports linking Cameroon to major cities in Africa and Europe. Cameroon Airlines is the local carrier, with flights to major cities throughout Central and West Africa.

Flights to neighbouring countries can be surprisingly expensive: from Douala to Malabo (Equatorial Guinea) is US$230 return, Libreville (Gabon) US$300 and Abidjan (Côte d'Ivoire) around US$300 return.

FOOTBALL MADNESS

One thing visitors will notice right away: Cameroonians are absolutely, passionately mad about football (soccer). They play wherever there's an open space and enough people, attend all local matches in droves and rant and rave about the state of the game, especially after a few beers.

The national team (and the national obsession) are Les Lions Indomptables, the Indomitable Lions of Cameroon. Most male Cameroonians between the ages of 10 and 30 own and wear some version of their uniform, and anytime the Lions play a match the country comes to a standstill, as people gather wherever there's a television.

For Cameroonians the biggest event in football, even bigger than the World Cup, is the African Cup of Nations, held every two years (the last one was held in Tunisia in January 2004). At stake are bragging rights to the continent, and it doesn't hurt that the Indomitable Lions have won four times, including two recent tournaments.

CAMEROON

Land

There are borders open with all neighbouring countries.

CENTRAL AFRICAN REPUBLIC

To get to the CAR, head east to Garoua-Boulaï or Kenzou. These borders aren't always open. Again, check before you go. The crossing to Gabon takes you over the Ntem River in a pirogue (traditional canoe) from Kye Ossi, south of Ambam, to the Gabonese side where shared taxis leave for Bitam.

CHAD

For Chad, travellers head to Kousséri in the extreme north at the border near N'Djaména. Minibuses go to Kousséri from Maroua, but this area has a history of instability so check before setting out.

EQUATORIAL GUINEA

Border crossings are at Ebebiyin to the west side of Equatorial Guinea and Campo where you can hire a pirogue to take you across the border closer to Bata.

NIGERIA

To/from Nigeria the main crossing points are Ekok, west of Mamfé, where you cross to Mfum (Nigeria) for shared taxis to Calabar, and at Banki in the extreme north for crossings to Maiduguri.

GETTING AROUND
Air

Cameroon Airlines and several smaller companies have flights throughout the country, which are expensive but convenient and safe. A one-way fare from Yaoundé to Maroua is US$160, while shorter flights like Yaoundé to N'Gaoundéré are US$75.

Bus

Cameroon has an extremely competitive and well organised bus system connecting all major towns. Prices are low and fixed, and on some bus lines you can even reserve a seat. Some sample fares: Yaoundé to Douala US$5, Bamenda to Buea US$7 and N'Gaoundéré to Maroua US$10. However, some drivers are extremely reckless, and bus accidents occur all too frequently.

Train

There is a train service between Douala and Yaoundé and between Yaoundé and the northern city of N'Gaoundéré. See the Yaoundé Getting There & Away section (p443) for more details.

YAOUNDÉ

pop 1.1 million

Cameroon's capital city, Yaoundé, is a seemingly unplanned jumble of high-rise hotels and modern architecture side-by-side with shanty towns and crowded markets, all set on rolling hills. Most travellers end up spending some time here, getting visas or catching a plane, train or bus. It can be a relaxing place to stay, with comfortable accommodation and good, inexpensive restaurants.

ORIENTATION

The airport is south of town and taking a taxi in is the only option; the fare is negotiable.

Yaoundé's streets don't follow a pattern so it's easy to get lost. To get around the town centre orient yourself to the 'places' or 'rond-points' (squares or traffic circles) that are the main landmarks; this is how Cameroonians give directions. The four water towers, high on a hill and visible from much of the city, are also useful landmarks; if you're in the centre of town they're roughly north.

Most of the embassies and consulates, and the international restaurants that go with them, are in the affluent neighbourhood of Bastos on the north side of the city.

Buses from other cities stop at various *gare routières* (transport stop) around the city, usually a quick taxi ride away from downtown. The train station, however, is centrally located, and you can walk from there to some of the central hotels.

INFORMATION
Cultural Centres

British Council (☎ 223 3172; Ave Charles de Gaulle) Provides a listing of English-language events.

Centre Culturel Français (☎ 222 0944; Ave Ahidjo) Has a schedule of events in French.

CAMEROON

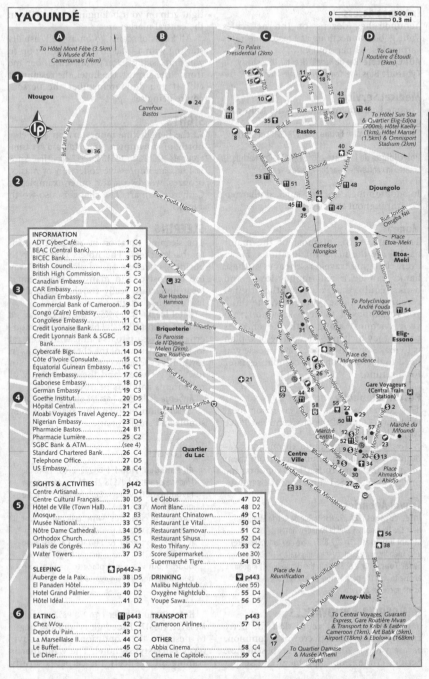

YAOUNDÉ

0 ————— 500 m
0 ————— 0.3 mi

To Hôtel Mont Fébe (3.5km) & Musée d'Art Camerounais (4km)

Ntougou

Carrefour Bastos

To Palais Presidential (2km)

To Gare Routière d'Étoudi (3km)

Bastos

To Hôtel Sun Star & Quartier Elig-Edjoa (700m), Hôtel Kaelly (700m), Hôtel Mansel (1.5km) & Omnisport Stadium (2km)

Djoungolo

Rue Fouda Ngono

Place Etoa-Meki

Etoa-Meki

Carrefour Nlongkak

Rue du 27 Août

Rue Hayabou Hammoa

Briqueterie

To Paroisse de N'Djong Melen (2km), Gare Routière

Rue Briqueterie

Blvd Manga Bell

Paul Martin Samba

Quartier du Lac

To Polyclinique André Fouda (700m)

Elig-Essono

Place de l'Independance

Gare Voyageurs (Central Train Station)

Marché du Mfoundi

Marché Central

Centre Ville

Place Ahmadou Ahidjo

Place de la Réunification

Mvog-Mbi

To Central Voyages, Guaranti Express, Gare Routière Mvan & Transport to Kribi & Eastern Cameroon (1km), Art Batik (5km), Airport (18km) & Ebolowa (168km)

To Quartier Damase & Musée Afhemi (6km)

Blvd de l'OCAM

Blvd Réunification

Ave Charles Atangana

INFORMATION
ADT CyberCafé............................1 C4
BEAC (Central Bank)......................2 D4
BICEC Bank..................................3 D5
British Council..............................4 C3
British High Commission.................5 C3
Canadian Embassy.........................6 C4
CAR Embassy...............................7 D1
Chadian Embassy...........................8 C2
Commercial Bank of Cameroon........9 D4
Congo (Zaïre) Embassy..................10 C1
Congolese Embassy.......................11 C1
Credit Lyonaise Bank....................12 D4
Credit Lyonnais Bank & SGBC
   Bank.....................................13 D5
Cybercafé Bigs.............................14 D4
Côte d'Ivoire Consulate.................15 C1
Equatorial Guinean Embassy...........16 C1
French Embassy............................17 C6
Gabonese Embassy.......................18 D1
German Embassy...........................19 C3
Goethe Institut.............................20 D5
Hôpital Central.............................21 C4
Moabi Voyages Travel Agency.........22 D4
Nigerian Embassy.........................23 D4
Pharmacie Bastos.........................24 B1
Pharmacie Lumière.......................25 C2
SGBC Bank & ATM...................(see 4)
Standard Chartered Bank...............26 C4
Telephone Office.........................27 D5
US Embassy................................28 C4

SIGHTS & ACTIVITIES   p442
Centre Artisanal..........................29 D4
Centre Cultural Français................30 D5
Hôtel de Ville (Town Hall).............31 C3
Mosque.....................................32 B3
Musée National............................33 C5
Nôtre Dame Cathedral...................34 D5
Orthodox Church.........................35 C1
Palais de Congrés.........................36 A2
Water Towers.............................37 D3

SLEEPING   pp442–3
Auberge de la Paix........................38 D5
El Panaden Hôtel..........................39 D4
Hotel Grand Palmier......................40 D2
Hôtel Idéal.................................41 D2

EATING   p443
Chez Wou...................................42 C2
Depot du Pain.............................43 D1
La Marseillaise II.........................44 C4
Le Buffet...................................45 C2
Le Diner...................................46 D1

Le Globus..................................47 D2
Mont Blanc................................48 D2
Restaurant Chinatown...................49 C1
Restaurant Le Vital......................50 D4
Restaurant Samovar......................51 C2
Restaurant Sihusa........................52 C2
Resto Thifany.............................53 C2
Score Supermarket...................(see 30)
Supermarché Tigre.......................54 D3

DRINKING   p443
Malibu Nightclub.....................(see 55)
Oxygène Nightclub.......................55 D4
Youpe Sawa................................56 D5

TRANSPORT   p443
Cameroon Airlines........................57 D4

OTHER
Abbia Cinema.............................58 C4
Cinema le Capitole.......................59 C4

Internet Access

Yaoundé has dozens of Internet cafés with good connections at reasonable rates (around US$1 per hour).

ADT CyberCafé (Rue de Narvik) Near the US embassy.

Cybercafé Bigs (Ave Kennedy) Centrally located.

Medical Services

For medical emergencies try the following clinics:

Polyclinique André Fouda (☎ 222 2612) In Quarter Elig-Essono.

Polyclinique de la Grace (☎ 222 4523; Rue Nachtigal) Located in Centreville, near the Abbias Cinema.

In addition there are well-stocked pharmacies throughout the city.

Money

There are ATMs at most of the major banks; see the maps for locations. However, changing travellers cheques at these banks can be a real money-loser, and banks require that you bring the original receipt of purchase (you know, the thing you're supposed to keep separate from your cheques) along with the cheques before they'll change them. The best plan is to make several photocopies in case you need to deal with cheque companies later for a refund.

Post & Telephone

The central post office is a major local landmark, south of the city centre at Place Ahmadou Ahidjo.

Teleboutiques are found throughout Yaoundé. You can buy phonecards from them or from the numerous street vendors, the price (US$5 to US$15) is about the same.

Travel Agencies

Inter Voyages (☎ 222 0361; Rue de Cercle Municipal) Near the US embassy and El Panaden Hotel.

Moabi Voyages (☎ 222 8737; Ave de l'independence) Very friendly, with English-speaking staff.

Safar Tours (☎ 222 8703; in the Hilton hotel) A good excuse to visit the posh Hilton, also good for plane tickets to other countries.

DANGERS & ANNOYANCES

Yaoundé has a bad reputation for petty crime. Pickpocketing in crowds is common, as are various distract-and-grab schemes. Serious crime is not a problem, but keep a tight grip on your belongings, especially in the central market area.

All kinds of scams go on as well, usually starting with a total stranger coming up to you and asking 'Don't you remember me from…the airport, the hotel, the restaurant etc'. If you don't remember the person, you're being set up.

SIGHTS

At the Benedictine monastery on Mt Fébé, north of downtown, the **Musée d'Art Camerounais** (admission US$1.75; ⏱ 3-6pm, Thu, Sat & Sun) has an impressive collection of masks, bronzes, woodwork and other examples of Cameroonian art. The chapel is also worth a look.

SLEEPING

The sleeping situation in Yaoundé is grim for backpackers. The hotels that cater to business travellers and diplomats are way too expensive, and many of the cheaper local hotels are really rough. There are a few options though.

Hôtel Idéal (☎ 220 9852; Carrefour Nlongkak; s/d US$10/12, superior r US$14) This clean and modern place lives up to its name, with a central location and some of the cheapest rooms in town. It's especially convenient if you're in town to get visas, and there are plenty of restaurants and bars nearby.

Auberge de la Paix (☎ 223 6502; Blvd de l'OCAM; r US$8.50) South of town, this place has very simple and small rooms.

SPLURGE!

El Panaden Hôtel (☎ 222 2765; Place de l'Independence; s/d US$18/22; ❄) A long-time favourite of travellers, El Panaden is a little pricey, but you get a lot for the money. The rooms are spacious with balconies, hot water and TV, and the staff are very helpful. The next-door restaurant **La Terrasse** (☎ 222 1262) is also a little tough on the budget but is a great place to have a cold beer and meet fellow wanderers.

Hotel Grand Palmier (☎ 220 9852; Rue Albert Ateba Ebé; s US$12) 'Faded glory' doesn't begin to describe the condition of this obviously once-stylish hotel. The wallpaper is coming off in sheets, the carpet is scruffy and the shower is a trickle. There's a restaurant and bar (without food or drink, though they'll run across the street and get you something), the rooms are big and reasonably priced, and the location is central to street food, bars and restaurants. If you decide to stay here bring a sense of humour and a torch for when the electricity goes out.

EATING

Yaoundés' restaurants are varied and generally very cheap. For a splurge head north to the embassy district in Bastos, where there are Chinese buffets, Italian restaurants and many other choices in all price ranges.

Restaurant Le Vital (☎ 763 6858; Ave de l'Independence; mains US$2-4) Le Vital is the place to go for veg food, mostly omelettes and sandwiches, with a convenient central location and extremely attentive staff.

SPLURGE!

If you want to splurge on Chinese food, **Chez Wou** (☎ 220 4679; rue Joseph Mbella Eloumden; mains from US$8) and **Restaurant Chinatown** (☎ 221 4514; rue Joseph Mbella Eloumden; mains from US$8), near each other in Bastos, both have lengthy menus and weekend buffets (US$15); popular with diplomats.

Le Buffet (Rue Joseph Mbella Eloumden; mains US$3) West of Carrefour Nlongkak, this popular restaurant is, not surprisingly, a buffet, where you pick what you want and pay by the item. The food is fresh, tasty and affordable, like chicken or fish with side dishes.

Le Diner (Rue Albert Ébé; mains US$5) Up towards the embassies, Le Diner has a *menu du jour* and tasty egg rolls to go. It's a bit more formal than it should be, but the food is worth it.

Le Globus (☎ 221 0281; Carrefour Nlongkak; mains US$4) Overlooking busy Carrefour Nlongkak, the Globus has a decent mid-range menu and good views.

Restaurant Sihusa (☎ 222 1764; Ave Kennedy; mains US$8-9) It's a little expensive, but the Sihusa has patio dining and great banana splits (US$4).

Restaurant Samovar (☎ 221 55 28; Rue Joseph Mbella Eloumden; mains US$7-8) The Samovar is an unusual dining experience, with very friendly staff and Italian and Russian dishes.

Depot du Pain (Rue Albert Ateba Ébé; snacks US$1) At the corner of the road to the embassies, this place has fresh, inexpensive bread and pastries to go.

Other popular inexpensive eateries, all with meals for around US$3, include **Resto Thifany** (Rue Joseph Mbella Eloumend), **Mont Blanc** (Rue Albert Ateba Ébé) and **La Marseillaise II** (Ave Foch), big with expats for breakfast.

DRINKING

Yaoundé isn't much of a party town, compared with Douala or other big cities. There are bars and game rooms all over, but they're pretty tame.

Most low-budget African restaurants double as beer halls in the evening.

Youpe Sawa (Blvd de l'OCAM) A lively bar that has live entertainment every night and promises 'spectacles' on weekends.

There are also a few nightclubs in town, including Oxygène and Malibu, both north of Place John Kennedy, where you can dance till dawn.

SHOPPING

The Marché Central and the area for blocks around it are the place to buy anything from socks to electronics.

It's a good idea to leave your valuables somewhere safe and only bring what you can afford to lose – this area is notorious for pickpockets.

For African art and handicrafts in a less high-pressure sales atmosphere, check out the Centre Artisanal on the north side of Place John Kennedy.

GETTING THERE & AWAY
Air

Several airlines connect Yaoundé to other major cities in Cameroon, including Maroua, Garoua, N'Gaoundéré and Bertua. This is quick and convenient, but it's expensive, ie US$160 to Maroua one-way, US$75 to N'Gaoundéré.

Yaoundé's international airport also has flights throughout the region; the main carrier is **Cameroon Airlines** (☎ 223 4001). International flights are also expensive: US$300 one-way to Libreville (Gabon), or around US$400 to major African cities like Abidjan (Côte d'Ivoire) or Lagos (Nigeria).

CAMEROON

Bus

There are buses between Yaoundé and all major cities in Cameroon. Buses leave from their companies' offices, spread out on the outskirts of town. Prices are fixed and generally quite low, for example US$6 to Douala or Kribi.

Train

The most popular and convenient way to travel north from Yaoundé is the train, which runs all the way to N'Gaoundéré. There are cheaper bench seats in cramped second class, and first-class airplane-style seats, but it's completely worth it to spend US$30 per person on a two- or four-person *couchette*. These are very small and basic, but the doors lock and there are bunk beds so you can sleep. (Unmarried couples may be told that it's against the rules for them to share a two-bunk couchette. This is yet another way of saying 'Give me a couple more dollars and your problem will be resolved', but in this case it may be worth it.)

The trip to N'Gaoundéré is scheduled for 12 hours, but usually takes 16 to 24 hours or longer. There's a dining car with simple meals, sandwiches and sodas, but no beer or wine, so you might want to discreetly bring your own supplies (22 hours on a slow-moving train with no beer can be a real endurance test).

You can reserve your seats the morning before departure at the station, the Gare Voyageurs, which is centrally located on the east side of downtown.

There is also service between Yaoundé and Douala, though this is used much less frequently, as buses are cheaper, faster and more convenient (though less safe).

GETTING AROUND

There are yellow taxi cabs all over the city. After dark you might want to hire one to yourself (US$1.75) rather than share a cab with strangers (US$0.25).

SOUTHERN CAMEROON

The area to the south of Yaoundé is mostly rainforest and includes Cameroon's number one beach destination, Kribi. It's also the route for overland travel to Gabon and Equatorial Guinea.

EBOLOWA

Not as glamorous as Campo or Kribi, Ebolowa is a crossroads city on the route from Yaoundé to the borders with Equatorial Guinea and Gabon. It's a fun, bustling city with cheap hotels, lively bars and other amenities for stranded travellers. During the day the whole city turns into a series of markets, with the usual clothes, food and imported appliances.

Several bus companies operate at all hours from Ebolowa to Yaoundé for about US$2.50.

KRIBI

For years Kribi has been a favourite spot for independent travellers to take some time off from the road and relax on the beach and enjoy the famous fresh seafood. Nowadays Kribi is also a popular weekend retreat for well-to-do Cameroonians and expats, but during the week, especially in the off-season, you may be one of the few travellers around.

The **Chutes de la Lobé**, 8km south of town (*moto-taxi* US$1), are a pretty impressive set of waterfalls that empty into a pool by the sea. Pirogue rides up the river can be arranged here.

Sleeping

There's a glut of hotels in town, and if they're mostly empty bargaining may get you a good deal.

Hôtel de la Paix (r from US$8.50) On a side road near the beach, this is one of Kribi's cheapest places to stay, with one of the better cheap restaurants in town and a bar.

Hotel Panoramique (☎ 461773; Route de la Poste; r US$8.50-34) This is a favourite haunt of travellers and aid workers for its in-town location, breezy outdoor bar and restaurant. The more expensive rooms on the second floor are larger and have balconies.

During the off-season you might get rooms at Le Croiserre Bleu for as little as US$12. This semifancy place is on the beach near the Chutes de la Lobé.

Eating & Drinking

The best spots for street food and local bars are the central market and nearby Carreour Kingué.

Hot & Cold Friterie Sandwicherie (☎ 999 7556; sandwiches from US$2) Across from the market, Hot & Cold is the best place in town to grab quick sandwiches and snacks, wrapped up to go for a tasty meal on the beach.

La Paillotte (☎ 956 4262; mains US$5-7) La Paillotte has outdoor tables that catch the sea breezes and it's a good place to meet travellers. Meals are the standard grilled fish fare.

Restaurant Italo Atlantique (☎ 999 77518; mains US$7-10) If you're tired of grilled fish, head for the Hotel Atlantique on the road out of town, where there's an Italian restaurant with pizza and pasta dishes.

There are a couple clubs for late-night dancing, including l'Escalier and Geraldine My Nightclub. These places don't get hopping until around midnight and stay open till dawn.

Getting There & Away

Buses for Douala (US$3.50, two to three hours) leave throughout the day. La Kribienne bus line runs to and from Yaoundé less frequently. Private taxi-buses leave from the *gare routières* at the market.

CAMPO

Campo, at the southwest corner of the country near the border with Equatorial Guinea, is developing a reputation as the new adventure travel destination in southern Cameroon. The main attractions are the new national park, the nearby undeveloped beaches and the opportunity to tour local villages and stay in local homes. If you're looking for a place to stay in Campo, try the **Auberge Bon Course** (r US$5) at the Bon Course Supermarché.

The recently opened Parc National de Campo-Ma'an is still in the developing stages but protects over 2500 sq km of rainforest and the wildlife that call it home. It's a lush place, but unfortunately you need to be self-sufficient in terms of equipment, supplies and a 4WD vehicle to get there. A place to try for lifts into the park might be the forestry office in Campo, where drivers have to get a park permit (US$9) and arrange for a guide (US$5 per day, mandatory).

WESTERN CAMEROON

Cameroon's predominately Anglophone western provinces include some of the country's most amazing scenery, including Mt Cameroon and the Ring Road. The northwest region is home to several tribal

kingdoms and sultanates, with all the pageantry you could ever ask for. The hectic city of Douala makes a good jumping-off point for exploring the area's many attractions.

DOUALA

pop 1.4 million

The largest city in Cameroon and the economic capital, Douala is a sprawling, dusty, honking traffic jam of a city. It's also swelteringly hot, with frequent downpours that do little to quell the heat or the dust. If you know that going in, and you're up for it, Douala can be a hell of a lot of fun. As the Cameroonians say, 'Yaoundé sleeps, Douala moves'.

Orientation

The airport is a couple kilometres south of town; a taxi fare is about US$5 to town, US$3.50 from town to the airport. Most hotels, restaurants, Internet cafés etc are in Akwa, towards the west end of town. Bonanjo is the city's financial hub, with the major banks and government offices.

Information

INTERNET ACCESS

There are Internet cafés all along Blvd de la Liberté, including Cyberix, Cyberbao and ICCNet, all with rates around US$1.50 per hour.

MEDICAL SERVICES

For medical emergencies try **Polyclinique Bonanjo** (☎ 342 7936; Ave de Gaulle).

For pharmacies try **Pharmacie de Centre** (Blvd de la Liberté) or **Pharmacie de Douala** (Blvd Ahidjo).

MONEY

Most of the city's banks are in Bonanjo. A couple have ATMs, but they may not be linked to your home account. In a pinch you can change money with the characters who hang around the Akwa Palace Hotel. You'll get good rates for cash, less for travellers cheques.

POST & TELEPHONE

The central post office is at the western end of Rue Joss in Bonanjo. There are *teleboutiques* all along Blvd de la Liberté that accept prepaid phonecards for international calls.

CAMEROON

DOUALA

INFORMATION
Amity Bank............................... 1 B5
BEAC (Central Bank)................ 2 B5
British Consulate...................... 3 D3
Commercial Bank of Cameroon
  (CBC).................................... 4 B5
Crédit Lyonnais........................ 5 B5
Crédit Lyonnais........................ 6 D3
Cyberbao................................. 7 D2
Cyberix.................................... 8 C4
Equatorial Guinean Consulate... 9 D4
French Consulate...................... 10 A5
ICCNet..................................... 11 D2
Nigerian Consulate................... 12 D2
Pharmacie de Douala................ 13 D4
Pharmacy Joss.......................... 14 B5
Polyclinique Bonanjo................ 15 B5
Saga Voyages.......................(see 40)
SCBC Bank (ATM)...................... 16 B4
SGBC.. 17 B5
Standard Chartered Bank........... 18 D3
Trans Africa Tours..................... 19 E2

SIGHTS & ACTIVITIES
Cathedral................................. 20 C4
Hôtel de Ville (City Hall).......... 21 B5

SLEEPING 🏠 pp447–8
Centre d'Accueil Missionaire...... 22 D3
Eglise Évangélique de Cameroon.23 C3
Foyer du Marin........................ 24 C4
Hotel Hila................................ 25 F4
Hotel le Combattant.................. 26 C5

EATING 🍴 p448
Boulangerie Zepol.................... 27 D3
Garmary Restaurant.................. 28 D3
Le Bistro Royal........................ 29 D3
Le Glacier Modern.................... 30 D3
Le Lido.................................... 31 C4
Restaurant Le PJ....................... 32 B5
Restaurant Le Pub..................... 33 C4

ENTERTAINMENT 🎭 p448
Echos de Bonanjo..................... 34 B5
Wouri Cinema.......................... 35 C4

TRANSPORT p448
Air France................................ 36 B5
Air Gabon................................ 37 B5
Cameroon Airlines.................... 38 B5
Cathay Pacific.......................(see 37)
Gare Routière de Yabassi (Transport to
  Yaoundé & Kribi).................... 39 F5
Kenya Airways.......................... 40 C4
Nigeria Airways........................ 41 C4
Shared Taxis to Gare Routière
  Bonabéri................................ 42 F1

Wouri River
Blvd Leclerc
Rue du Prince des Galles
Rue Joffre
Rue Sylvani
Rue Franceville
Blvd de la Liberté
Akwa
Rue de Lapeyrère
Rue Alfred Saker
Rue Pau
Blvd Ahidjo
Rue Galliéni
Rue Gare
Main Port
Rue Surcouf
Rue Kitchener
Rue Joss
Place du Gouvernement
Bonanjo
Rue Lugard
Rue French
Rue Pierre Loti
Bali
Rue Prince
Rue Koumassi
Rue Berlaut
Ave Douala Manga Bell
Ave des Cocotiers
Rue de Verdun
Ave de Gaulle
Rue de Trieste
Rue Ngoso
Bell
Rue de New Bell

To Marché des Fleurs, Centre
Artisanal de Douala & Swiss (1km),
& Airport (4km)
To Europcar

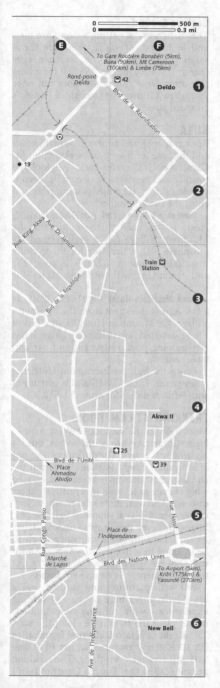

TRAVEL AGENCIES

Trans Africa Tours (☎ 342 8307), near Rond-point Deido, specialises in travel (mostly by air) to nearby African countries and represents several regional airlines.

Dangers & Annoyances

Douala has its share of petty crime, and it's not a good idea to walk around after dark unless you know your way.

For some people the chaos of Douala can be overwhelming. It's noisy, smelly, crowded and hot, and the action never stops long enough to let you catch your breath.

Sleeping

Most budget hotels are in Akwa, where there's a surprising range of prices for roughly the same quality of rooms. Hotels for business travellers charge more than US$40, but comparable rooms can be found for US$15.

Foyer du Marin (☎ 3422794; douala@seamannsmission. org; Rue Gallieni; r US$17-25) Also known as the German Seamen's Mission, the Foyer has a very refreshing pool and outdoor tables for the nightly sausage grill-up and beer fest. It's a good place to meet people from all over the world, even if some of them are doing their best to ignore the fact that they're in Africa.

Hotel Hila (☎ 342 1586; 15 Blvd de l'Unité; r US$15-22) A favourite of Cameroonian business travellers, the Hila has rooms with a variety of amenities, some of which are bound to be broken. But it's a fun place, with good views of the city from the top-floor rooms and a very friendly bilingual staff. There's a mosque on the second floor, and a downstairs bar where people lounge in the comfortable chairs and watch TV or just catch up on some shut-eye.

Centre d'Accueil Missionaire (☎ 342 2797; pro gemis.douala@camnet.cm; Rue Franceville; s/d US$12/20) This friendly place, housed at the Catholic mission, has basic, clean rooms and a swimming pool.

Eglise Évangélique de Cameroon (☎ 342 3611; Rue Alfred Saker; s/d/t US$14/17/26) Rooms here are a little rundown, but it's quiet and there's a kitchen.

Hotel le Combattant (☎ 342 5843; r US$17) In an out of the way location in Bonanjo, down the hill towards the autoroute, the Combattant has spacious rooms and an airy restaurant. The streets of this neighbourhood are very unsavoury after dark, and the gates of the hotel are locked at around 8pm (they'll let you in if you yell loud enough).

Eating

Douala has all kinds of restaurants in the budget range, mostly in Akwa.

Le Bistro Royal (Rue Franceville; mains US$4) In the heart of Akwa's restaurant district, Le Bistro serves authentic Cameroonian dishes like *poulet N'dolé* in a cramped but cosy space.

Restaurant Le Pub (Blvd de la Liberté; sandwiches from US$3.50) Despite its upscale appearance, the Pub is a great place for draft beer and cheap sandwiches, including lots of veg options.

Le Lido (Rue Joffre; mains US$3.50) The Lido has an amazing décor, draft beer and African dishes at very reasonable prices and very friendly staff. Rooms at the adjacent hotel are absolutely not recommended.

In Bonanjo, Restaurant Le PJ serves real African dishes for around US$2.50 with sandwiches for US$1.

Across the alley are a couple small bars and some of the best street food stalls in all of Cameroon. **Garmary Restaurant** (Blvd de la Liberté) has African and European dishes for under US$3.50.

Also recommended: **Le Glacier Modern** (Blvd de la Liberté) has ice cream, and **Boulangerie Zepol** (Blvd de la Liberté) sells pastries and has a small grocery store.

Entertainment

Echos de Bonanjo (☎ 342 6491; Rue Joss) Good for a cold drink in the afternoon, Echos de Bonanjo features karaoke-style singing and dancing in the evenings. They bill themselves as a restaurant-cabaret, but no-one seems to eat here.

Wouri cinema (Blvd de la Liberté) Shows recent Hollywood and European hits in French. It's a fun way to pass a couple hours, even if you can't keep up with the dialogue.

Getting There & Away

Douala has a major international airport with links to cities around the region. **Cameroon Airlines** (☎ 342 2525; Rue Joss, Bonanjo) is the main carrier.

Buses leave from and arrive at their offices scattered around the city. Buses to Yaoundé are US$6 (two to three hours) and to Limbe US$2.

Getting Around

The main ways of getting around are taxis and *moto-taxi*, of which there are thousands. *Moto-taxis* are cheaper than cabs (about US$0.20, maybe US$0.50 for a long ride after dark) and much more fun once you get past fearing for your life in Douala's crowded streets.

BUEA

Buea is a cool and breezy mountain town and the base for hiking and trekking on Mt Cameroon. It's a laid-back, Anglophone town spread over several steep hills. Even if you don't climb it's a nice place to relax and enjoy the cooler weather.

Mountain Village Hotel (☎ 322083; r US$8.50) Near the trailhead to the mountain, the Mountain Village has a very relaxed atmosphere with a fireplace for those chilly mountain evenings. There's a good bar and restaurant with outdoor tables for lounging.

Buea Mountain Hotel (☎ 322005; r US$15, ste US$34) Across the street from the Mountain Village, the Mountain Hotel has the feel of a long-deserted British hunting lodge. It has a swimming pool, restaurant and bar and table tennis.

Down the hill, the Paramount Hotel has clean rooms from US$15 and a restaurant with African dishes for around US$2.50.

TREKKING MT CAMEROON

Most treks to the summit of West Africa's highest peak take two or three days, but it's no stroll in the park. The difficulty stems not only from its height (4095m), but from the fact that you start from near sea level, making a big change in altitude in a relatively short distance. And then there's the weather: November to mid-May is supposed to be best for hiking, but even then it's still unpredictable. At any other time of the year you're likely to be trekking in a tropical downpour. And if that's not enough, throw into the mix the fact that Mt Cameroon is an active volcano.

But with planning and timing, and a bit of luck, a trek here can be a rewarding experience – with stunning views and endemic plant life to admire along the way. The **Mount Cameroon Ecotourism Organisation** (☎ 332 2038; mountceo@iccnet2000.com; PO 60, Buea SWP) will arrange everything. The trekking permit (called the 'Tourist Contribution') is US$5 per person per day. A mandatory guide is US$11 per day and a porter (optional) is US$8.50 per day. There are a few very simple huts where you can spend the night, but you'll need to bring all your provisions. The market in town has some simple gear, but it's best to bring your own sleeping bag and warm clothes. The ecotourism organisation can also set you up with anything from day-hikes to major eight-day expeditions.

LIMBE
pop 40,000

Seaside Limbe is one of Cameroon's most popular beach resorts, especially on weekends when hordes of vacationers come to town. The rest of the week it's a quiet town with relatively deserted sandy beaches and oceanfront restaurants.

Information

Along the beach road you'll find the town tourism office as well as the several banks that will change travellers cheques.

Head to **@Titi.com** (Rue Douala; US$1 per hr) for good Internet access.

Sights

Limbe's tranquil colonial-era **Botanical Gardens** (admission US$1.70; 6am-6pm) are a good start to a tour of the area. There's a small visitors centre and a cemetery with graves of British and African soldiers.

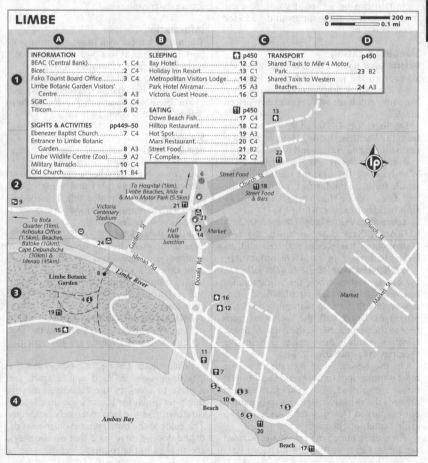

LIMBE

INFORMATION		SLEEPING		TRANSPORT	p450
BEAC (Central Bank)..........1 C4		Bay Hotel.........................12 C3		Shared Taxis to Mile 4 Motor	
Bicec.................................2 C4		Holiday Inn Resort..............13 C1		Park...............................23 B2
Fako Tourist Board Office....3 C4		Metropolitan Visitors Lodge...14 B2		Shared Taxis to Western	
Limbe Botanic Garden Visitors'		Park Hotel Miramar............15 A3		Beaches..........................24 A3
Centre.............................4 A3		Victoria Guest House..........16 C3			
SGBC................................5 C4					
Titicom.............................6 B2		EATING			
		Down Beach Fish................17 C4			
SIGHTS & ACTIVITIES pp449–50		Hilltop Restaurant...............18 C2			
Ebenezer Baptist Church.....7 C4		Hot Spot...........................19 A3			
Entrance to Limbe Botanic		Mars Restaurant.................20 C4			
Garden...........................8 A3		Street Food.......................21 B2			
Limbe Wildlife Centre (Zoo)...9 A2		T-Complex.........................22 C2			
Military Barracks................10 C4					
Old Church.......................11 B4					

The **Limbe Wildlife Centre** (admission US$1.70; ⏰ 9am-5pm) was originally set up to protect orphaned chimpanzees and is now an internationally renowned sanctuary for orphaned and abandoned chimps, gorillas, mandrills and other species. The admission price goes to support the animals' rehabilitation and the centre's antibushmeat campaign.

The best of Limbe's beaches are north of town and known by their distance from Limbe. While both Mile 6 and Mile 11 beaches are popular, there's a US$1 'gate fee' for each. The best beach of all is at the village of Batoké at Mile 8. It has a beautiful (free) beach from where you can still see the lava flows of Mt Cameroon's eruption a few years ago. Other lava flows further up the mountain can be visited if you hire a car from the gare routière for around US$5 for a couple hours.

Sleeping & Eating
Victoria Guest House (☎ 332446; r US$10-12) Up a hill from the main rond-point in town, the Victoria has simple rooms and its own bar and restaurant with reasonably priced meals.

Bay Hotel (☎ 332332; s/d US$11/20) Across from the Victoria, the Bay Hotel has similar undistinguished rooms and a restaurant.

Holiday Inn Resort (☎ 332290; r from US$14) Way back up the hill, off Church St, the semiluxurious Holiday Inn (not part of the well-known chain) has a range of rooms, all with bathroom and satellite TV.

Metropolitan Visitors Lodge (☎ 997 2012; Church St; r US$10-12) Back down in town, the new Metropolitan has rooms with fan and attached bathroom, in a convenient location.

Park Hotel Miramar (☎ 332689; s/d US$16/20) On the beach west of town, the Miramar has *boukarous* (open-sided circular mud huts) accommodation and a swimming pool and restaurant. Don't walk the back road from here to the popular bar at the Atlantic Beach Hotel, especially in the evening, as there have been reported robberies.

On the beach, Mars Restaurant is the most popular spot for weekend vacationers, meals are around US$5. Down the beach towards the fishing village, the aptly named but unmarked Down Beach Fish has cheap grilled catch-of-the-day.

There are a bunch of inexpensive African restaurants in town including Hilltop Restaurant, with good views, T-Complex and Hot Spot in the botanic garden, all with meals for US$3 to US$4.

Getting There & Away
The main *gare routières* is Mile 4, about 6km out of town. Minibuses and bush taxis leave approximately hourly to Buea (US$0.85, 30 minutes) and Douala (US$2, 1½ hours).

BAMENDA
pop 235,000

Bamenda, capital of the northwest province, is an interesting city and a good base for exploring the region. With an English-speaking population and wide choice of hotels and restaurants, it's a popular stop for weary travellers.

Information
The tourist office, with maps and information on the area, is in a pink building about three blocks from Commercial Ave.

There are a number of banks along Commercial Ave that change travellers' cheques.

For medical treatment, the **Mezam Polyclinique** (Bali Rd) is open 24 hours.

Sleeping
New City Hotel (☎ 336 22467; r from US$7) In a hard-to-find location down a dirt road in Old Town, New City has a bar, restaurant (order well in advance) and a nightclub, and at this price it's often full. The road is lined with bars and street food, so you don't have to venture far at night.

International Hotel (☎ 336 2527; s/d US$14/20) This is the place to stay for Cameroonian business travellers and vacationers, and even though it's a big, multi-storey building it's frequently full. There's a terrace bar and restaurant where you can cool off after your travels.

Def Hotel (☎ 336 3748; Nkwen St; r US$10-17) East of the city centre, the area around the Def isn't great, but the rooms are good for the money.

Holiday Hotel (☎ 336 1382; Commercial Ave; s US$8.50, 'big singles' US$10) If you're stuck for a place to stay, try the Holiday, but you don't get much for the money; the place is rundown and the staff extremely lethargic. The rules of the hotel, posted on the inside of the door, clearly state that no monkeys are allowed in the rooms.

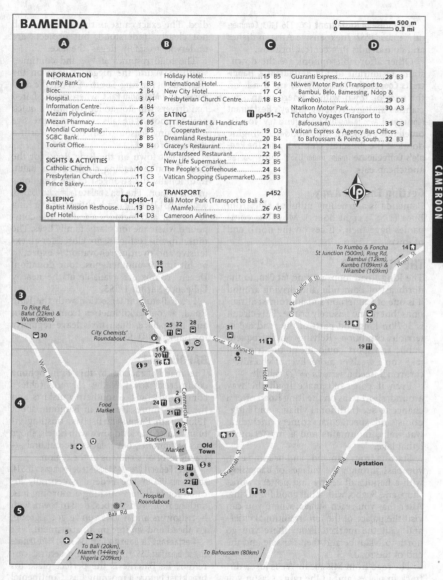

BAMENDA

0 ———— 500 m
0 ———— 0.3 mi

INFORMATION	
Amity Bank	1 B3
Bicec	2 B4
Hospital	3 A4
Information Centre	4 B4
Mezam Polyclinic	5 A5
Mezam Pharmacy	6 B5
Mondial Computing	7 B5
SGBC Bank	8 B5
Tourist Office	9 B4

SIGHTS & ACTIVITIES	
Catholic Church	10 C5
Presbyterian Church	11 C3
Prince Bakery	12 C4

SLEEPING	pp450–1
Baptist Mission Resthouse	13 D3
Def Hotel	14 D3

Holiday Hotel	15 B5
International Hotel	16 B4
New City Hotel	17 C4
Presbyterian Church Centre	18 B3

EATING	pp451–2
CTT Restaurant & Handicrafts Cooperative	19 D3
Dreamland Restaurant	20 B4
Gracey's Restaurant	21 B4
Mustardseed Restaurant	22 B5
New Life Supermarket	23 B5
The People's Coffeehouse	24 B4
Vatican Shopping (Supermarket)	25 B3

TRANSPORT	p452
Bali Motor Park (Transport to Bali & Mamfe)	26 A5
Cameroon Airlines	27 B3

Guaranti Express	28 B3
Nkwen Motor Park (Transport to Bambui, Belo, Bamessing, Ndop & Kumbo)	29 D3
Ntarikon Motor Park	30 A3
Tchatcho Voyages (Transport to Bafoussam)	31 C3
Vatican Express & Agency Bus Offices to Bafoussam & Points South	32 B3

To Kumbo & Foncha St Junction (500m), Ring Rd, Bambui (12km), Kumbo (109km) & Nkambe (169km)

To Ring Rd, Bafut (22km) & Wum (80km)

Longla St.

Cow St (Ndidfor III St)

City Chemists' Roundabout

Sonac St (Muna St)

Wum Rd

Hotel Rd

Food Market

Commercial Ave

Stadium

Old Town

Market

Savannah St.

Bafoussam Rd

Upstation

Hospital Roundabout

Bali Rd

To Bali (20km), Mamfe (144km) & Nigeria (209km)

To Bafoussam (80km)

The **Presbyterian Church Centre** (☎ 336 4070; dm US$3.50) and the **Baptist Mission Resthouse** (☎ 336 1285; r US$4) are both good budget options.

Eating

Dreamland Restaurant (☎ 336 1700; Commercial Ave; mains US$2.50) With stylish décor and second-floor balcony tables, the Dreamland comes across as upscale, and the food lives up to expectations. But what's most amazing is the price: you can get African dishes or a double cheeseburger for under US$3. There's a weekend breakfast buffet for US$2.50. Check it out before they change their mind.

CAMEROON

Mustardseed Restaurant (☎ 336 1403; Commercial Ave; mains US$2) Inexpensive African dishes and cold drinks in a central location.

Other affordable options are the downstairs restaurant at **CTT Restaurant & Handicrafts Cooperative** (mains US$3-5), up a hill on the east of town with Cameroonian specialities and great views, **Gracey's Restaurant** (Commercial Ave; mains US$2), legendary for its omelettes (look for the wooden swinging doors at the Prescraft Centre), and **The People's Coffeehouse** (mains under US$1) with coffee and cheap eats.

Getting There & Away

Bamenda is a gruelling minibus ride from Buea (US$7, eight hours). Most bus companies have their offices on the north end of town.

THE RING ROAD

The Ring Road loops around **Mt Oku**, to the northeast of Bamenda, and driving around it is one of Cameroon's major tourist attractions, but it's no leisurely cruise. This circuit is 367km long and parts of the road are in terrible condition. Relying on infrequent public transport could mean the trip will take you a week or more. Even if you hire a car, you'll need a serious 4WD vehicle.

Even if you can't make it all the way around, short trips on the Ring Road offer a chance to see traditional villages and kingdoms and spectacular scenery including waterfalls, mountains and a mysteriously lethal lake.

Starting from Bamenda and heading east, you pass through the villages of **Bamessing**, with a handicraft centre and pottery workshop, and Sagbo, with a hill good for hiking. After that you reach **Kumbo**, where you can visit the palace of the *fon* (traditional chief) and visit the market. From there you go north to Nkambe and then Missaje and the end of the road.

The road from Missaje to We is just a dirt track in places, and in the rainy season you might not even find that. Some travellers continue on foot, sometimes with help from Fulani herdsmen. It can take a couple days to get to We, so bring plenty of water.

Along this section of the road you pass **Lake Nyos**, which contains high levels of toxic carbon dioxide gas. In August 1986 gas was released and about 1700 people

died. The exact cause of the disaster is still not clearly understood, but projects are underway to safely 'degas' the lake.

The road resumes at We and continues south to Wum, the biggest village on the west side of the ring. South of Wum the road passes the **Metchum Falls**, where most shared taxi drivers will stop to let you have a quick peek or photo. The falls are most impressive in the rainy season (duh) but are worth a stop year-round.

The last town on the Ring Road (or the first, if you're heading clockwise) is **Bafut**, traditionally the strongest of the kingdoms in this region. The **fon's palace** (admission US$1.75, guide fee US$1.75) here is a highlight of the Ring Road tour and includes a tour of the compound where the fon's large family lives. The museum and resthouse are closed for an extensive and overdue renovation – expect to be hit up for another, post-tour donation. Decent rooms are available at the nearby Diligence Bar for US$5.

From Bafut's intersection with the Ring Road, a couple kilometres from the town and the palace, bush taxis leave regularly for Bamenda (US$1).

BAFOUSSAM

The main attraction in this Francophone commercial town is the *chefferie* (chief's compound) on the southern outskirts and the more impressive one in Banjoun, about 15km south. Bafoussam itself is a bustling, vibrant, dusty and loud town with hotels, shops and restaurants, but it lacks the cultural attractions of other towns in the region.

Hôtel Fédéral (☎ 344 1309; Rte de Foumban; r US$14, apartments US$16) The Fédéral is centrally located for travellers catching a morning bus, and the rooms are the best deal in town, with hot showers and TV. If you've got a group, go ahead and splurge on an apartment.

Restaurant La Bauxite (☎ 334 3297; Place Ouandé Ernest; breakfast US$2) Right at the central carrefour, La Bauxite is the perfect place for breakfast before a morning bus. Continental breakfast is US$2 and petit dejeuner bauxite, with omelette, fruit juice and the usual trappings is US$2.50. They do lunch and dinner as well, but breakfast is their speciality.

La Bonne Table de l'Ouest (☎ 344 1940; mains US$2.50-5) A travellers' favourite, La Bonne Table caters to foreign tastes with hamburgers and other exotica as well as African dishes, all washed down with lots of cold beer and fruit juice. It's right by the Bafoussam chefferie on the south road out of town.

La Fofani (☎ 334 2574; mains US$4) Up the hill from the Texaco station, La Fofani has excellent European-style food, but the setting and the service are a little too formal to be any fun.

Bush taxis run regularly to Foumban (US$1.35, one to two hours) from the carrefour near Hôtel Fédéral. Castor Voyages runs buses to Yaoundé (US$4, four hours).

FOUMBAN

Foumban is a fairly small town with more than its share of historical and cultural attractions. You can visit the palace of the sultan, bargain for local crafts at the artisans' village, check out the two museums, or just meet people and listen to the history and legends of the Bamoun sultanate. If you're anywhere near Foumban during a major Islamic holiday, head straight there for the most spectacular celebrations around (see the following Festivals & Events section for more information).

Sights

The must-see attraction of Foumban is the **Palais Royal** (Rue du Palais; admission US$3.50, camera fee US$2.50; ☺ 8:30am-6pm daily except during ceremonies), the sultan's palace, currently home to the 19th sultan of the Bamoun dynasty, which dates back to 1394. You may not see the sultan, but there's a hall of arms and a fascinating museum with the belongings of the previous sultans.

South of town, the **Village des Artisans** (Rue des Artisans), the artisans' village, is one of the best places in the country to buy Cameroonian handicrafts. Be ready for high-pressure sales tactics and hard bargaining.

Close by, the **Musée des Arts et Traditions Bamoun** (Rue des Artisans; donation expected; ☺ 9am-5pm) houses a private collection of art and historical artefacts.

Festivals & Events

During major Islamic holidays, especially the end of Ramadan and Eid al-Adha (known in French as the Fête de Mouton, Feast of the Sheep), Foumban attracts thousands and thousands of pilgrims for an extraordinary blend of Muslim and traditional Bamoun ceremonies.

It all starts before sunrise with the call to prayer blasting from loudspeakers at the mosque. Thousands of men and boys, dressed in their finest, climb the hill to the Sacred Mountain and kneel in prayer. Around dawn the imam arrives, followed by the sultan in his white Cadillac. There are sunrise prayers, a sermon from the imam, and a blessing from the sultan (on Eid al-Adha this is when the sheep is sacrificed). The heavy-set sultan then gets on his skinny little horse surrounded by his warriors in their full regalia, and everyone follows him in an enormous parade to the palace while the women and girls, so far absent from the proceedings, line the streets dressed all in white and ululate as the sultan passes.

After the parade there's a rest, and then horse races through the streets of town. Then another break until it gets dark, when the drumming and dancing start in front of the Royal Palace. Meanwhile (this is still Cameroon, after all) people pack the bars and clubs, and when these are full they set up speakers in the streets for heavy drinking and dancing until the sun comes up again.

Sleeping & Eating

For a place that attracts so many visitors and religious pilgrims, Foumban isn't really set up for tourism, though there are a couple of good hotels. If you arrive after dark, eat what you can find at the *gare routières*; the town's few restaurants may be closed.

Complexe Adi (☎ cellphone 743 1181; Rue de l'Hôtel Beau Regard; r US$12) This new hotel, across from the Hôtel Beau Regard, has clean, simple rooms and a popular restaurant and bar where locals and visitors gather.

Hôtel Beau Regard (☎ 348 2183; Rue de l'Hôtel Beau Regard; r from US$9) The Beau Regard is a Foumban institution and a landmark, but it's starting to show its age. Rooms are seriously run down, the water supply is erratic, and there's a bar and overpriced nightclub but no restaurant.

Mission Catholique (Rue de l'Hôtel Beau Regard; dm US$1-2) In a pinch try the Catholic mission down the street from the Beau Regard, which provides beds for a small donation.

Between the hotels and the Total petrol station, Restaurant Milanaise is a good inexpensive place for African meals and a cold soft drink.

Drinking

For a predominantly Muslim town, Foumban has a surprising number of local bars doing a pretty brisk business. There are also at least two nightclubs, one in the Beau Regard plus the Royal Club, which stays open late.

Getting There & Away

There are a few direct buses to Yaoundé and Douala, but most traffic stops at Bafoussam (US$2, 1½ hours), where you change buses; so get an early start if you want to make any headway.

NORTHERN CAMEROON

Cameroon's northern provinces are a world apart from the rest of the country; a mix of Muslim, Fulani and a number of other traditional animist cultures in an arid scrubland. This area draws adventure travellers from around the world for the hiking and wildlife-viewing opportunities, all conveniently reached from the town of Maroua.

N'GAOUNDÉRÉ

N'Gaoundéré is the northern end of the railroad line, and many travellers spend a night or two here enjoying the restaurants and bars before heading on. The town has a cool, breezy climate and there are a couple of cultural sites, including the palace of the *lamido* (traditional chief) and the ornate mosque next door.

The **Credit Lyonnaise** bank will change travellers cheques at good rates.

The **Ministry of Tourism** office on Ave Ahidjo is worth visiting for information on the surrounding area.

Globalisation Information, near Carrefour Tissu, has Internet access.

N'Gaoundéré has a reputation for being unsafe at night; hop on a *moto-taxi* if you need to go far.

BELLY-BUTTON MOUNTAIN

N'Gaoundéré reportedly gets its name, which means 'Navel Mountain', from the nearby landmark peak, also called N'Gaoundéré. Locals apparently believe that the round rock on top of the mountain resembles an 'outie'.

Sights

The **Palais de Lamido** (admission US$3.50, camera fee US$1.75, guide fee US$1.75), also known as the lamidat, is worth a trip inside for a taste of local culture. Next door is the **Grande Mosquée** with an impressive exterior.

Sleeping

Prices for hotel rooms here are definitely inflated by the number of visitors who pass through, but there are a number of simple *auberges* if you just want a night's sleep.

Hôtel le Relais (☎ 225 1138; r from US$17) Down a dark side street from the main drag, the Relais is a little expensive but worth it for spacious rooms (big enough for a group), central location near bars and restaurants, and friendly staff.

Cacia Auberge (r US$10) Outside of town off the bypass road, the Cacia Auberge is a quiet little place with signs all over town advertising 'tranquillity, security and comfort, but no prostitution'.

Auberge Pousada Style (☎ 225 1703; r from US$7) Northwest of the cathedral, the Pousada Style has simple, inexpensive rooms near the centre of the action.

Auberge de la Gare (☎ 225 2217; Rue de la Gare; r US$10) Rooms here are pretty basic, and the location (right by the train station) isn't much of a plus when you realise that the train leaves at 6.15pm and arrives whenever it wants.

Auberge al-Hilal (Rue de la Gare; r US$10) This *auberge* has simple rooms and is popular with Muslim travellers for its location, between the train station and the mosque.

Eating

Restaurants in the west (tourist) end of town have tourist-high prices, but some are well worth a splurge, and there are cheaper alternatives around as well. You'll find plenty of inexpensive street food across from the train station and at the intersection near the main market.

Marhaba Village (☎ 225 1893; Ave Ahidjo; mains US$4-7) In the centre of the action, the open-air Marhaba Village restaurant is at the back of a bigger complex with a snack-bar in the front and a 'salsateque' nightclub next door. It's a favourite of travellers and a good place to meet and trade stories. The food is excellent and very European, but may take some time to arrive at your table. The Marhaba Snack-bar in front is a great

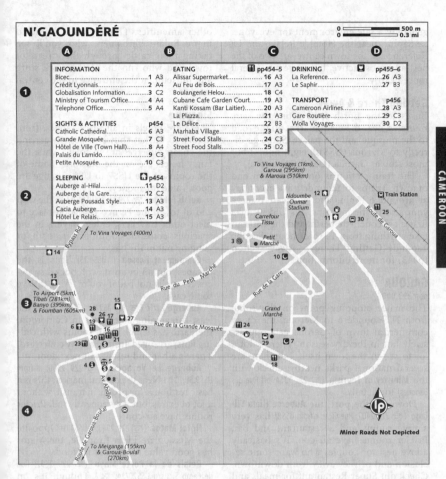

N'GAOUNDÉRÉ

INFORMATION	**EATING** pp454–5	**DRINKING** pp455–6
Bicec.....................................1 A3	Alissar Supermarket...............16 A3	La Reference...........................26 A3
Crédit Lyonnais.......................2 A4	Au Feu de Bois.......................17 A3	Le Saphir................................27 B3
Globalisation Information.........3 C2	Boulangerie Helou...................18 C4	
Ministry of Tourism Office.......4 A4	Cubane Cafe Garden Court.......19 A3	**TRANSPORT** p456
Telephone Office.....................5 A4	Kanti Kossam (Bar Laitier).......20 A3	Cameroon Airlines...................28 A3
	La Plazza...............................21 A3	Gare Routière.........................29 C3
SIGHTS & ACTIVITIES p454	Le Délice................................22 B3	Woïla Voyages........................30 D2
Catholic Cathedral...................6 A3	Marhaba Village......................23 A3	
Grande Mosquée......................7 C3	Street Food Stalls....................24 C3	
Hôtel de Ville (Town Hall).........8 A4	Street Food Stalls....................25 D2	
Palais du Lamido......................9 C3		
Petite Mosquée......................10 C3		
SLEEPING p454		
Auberge al-Hilal.....................11 D2		
Auberge de la Gare.................12 C2		
Auberge Pousada Style............13 A3		
Cacia Auberge........................14 A3		
Hôtel Le Relais.......................15 A3		

place for people-watching or catching a football match on TV.

Au Feu de Bois (☎ 225 1512; mains US$4; ✆ closed Sun) This is one of the best spots in town for large servings of authentic Cameroonian dishes like chicken N'dole with plantains. It's also a relaxing place to have a beer and watch American movies dubbed into French on the TV.

La Plazza (mains from US$5) This is one of the more expensive places in town, but the food is worth the splurge. If you're in town on Sunday, there's an all-you-can-eat brunch buffet (US$10). They also have an open-air bar with satellite TV.

For snacks and light meals, check out **Le Délice** (mains US$2), on the western end of the road to the mosque, and **Kanti Kossam** (Bar Laitier), which specialises in *dakkéré*, a local yogurt and rice concoction (US$1).

Early in the morning locals gather at the central Cubane Cafe Garden Court for coffee and bread. If you're on your way out of town in the morning, stop by the **Boulangerie Helou** (snacks US$0.50) across from the market and the *gare routières* to stock up on fresh pastries and bread for the road.

Drinking

N'Gaoundéré has no shortage of bars, particularly at the west end of town. Most are active by day and rowdy until the early hours of the morning. Foreign travellers may attract some attention and flirtation, but it's generally a safe environment for everyone. Le Saphir, near the Hôtel le Relais, and La Reference, in the town centre, are two of the best and most active, but there are several more nearby.

Getting There & Away
Buses to the north leave from the *gare routières*, near the main market on the road to the mosque and the palace. Some go directly to Maroua (US$10, eight hours) but most stop at Garoua (US$6, five hours).

The train station is on the eastern end of town. Trains to Yaoundé leave every day at around 6.15pm, and you can reserve your seat in the morning. It's US$30 for a first-class couchette berth, and the trip can take anything from 12 to 21 hours. See the Yaoundé Getting There & Away section (p443) for more information.

GAROUA
pop 293,000

The major stopping point on the route from N'Gaoundéré to Maroua, the dusty commercial town of Garoua gets oppressively hot in the dry season. There's not a lot to see in the town itself, but there are several national parks nearby; check with the **Ministry of Tourism** (☎ 227 1364; off Rue des Banques) for details.

Down by the port, the **Auberge Hiala Village** (☎ 227 2402; Rue Cicai; r from US$8) has very simple rooms and a restaurant and bar. Pricier rooms have air-con. It's basically a love nest for couples who want some seclusion and privacy away from downtown. Check out Super Restaurant for meals and fruit juices.

There are several bus companies that run day and night (avoid the night bus if you can) to Maroua (US$4, three hours), N'Gaoundéré (US$5, five hours) and other, closer destinations from their offices in the centre of town.

MAROUA
pop 214,000

Maroua is the hub for travel to some of Cameroon's most impressive natural attractions, including hiking in the Mandara Mountains and wildlife-viewing at Waza National Park. The town itself is well set up for travellers, with cheap hotels, good restaurants, banks, Internet access and

other amenities. This region is home to many Fulani herdsmen, who you'll see taking their cattle through the streets of town and who run the leatherwork store and museum at the entrance to the central market.

Sleeping
There are hotels in all price ranges, from luxury to bucket shower dives. In general the cheap *auberges* are in town, while the fancy hotels are on the outskirts. Some of the rooms in the US$7 to US$10 range are good value for money.

Relais Ferngo (☎ 229 2153; r US$10) On the west end of town, the Ferngo is a good place to meet other travellers, either staying in the spacious *boukarous* with private bath or hanging out in the bar.

Campement Bossou (r US$4.25) This is the cheapest option in town, with bucket showers. It's really not bad if you're trying to save some cash.

Auberge Faric (☎ 229 4521; r US$7) Down the least-threatening side street in Cameroon, the Faric has small, clean rooms with ceiling fans, arranged around a leafy courtyard. There's a bar and restaurant next door.

Auberge Le Voyageur (☎ 229 2100; r from US$9.50; 🕸) Near the central market, this is a basic resthouse for people in transit, without a lot of extras, but it's frequently full. Pricier rooms have air-con.

Hôtel Matos (☎ 229 2913; r US$11) Opposite the Mission de Plein Évangile, the Matos has good value rooms but no food.

Relais de la Porte Mayo (☎ 229 2692; Rue de Camp Sic; s/d US$20/24; 🕸) Though it's on the expensive side, this is Maroua's most popular and happening hotel. Rooms are in private *boukarous* with hot water, and there's a restaurant (see Eating) and travel agency on site.

Eating
La Comtesse de Mbam (mains US$2.50) Next to the Auberge Faric, this is the best place in town for cheap Cameroonian food and cold drinks. There's a very limited menu each day depending on what they feel like cooking; you should be prepared to wait a while for your meal.

Le Baobab (☎ 229 2720; mains US$4) Le Baobab is one of the nicest restaurants in town and surprisingly inexpensive. You'll be able to

MAROUA

CAMEROON

sit outdoors in thatched-roof booths, but for some reason there's more of a mosquito problem here than elsewhere in town.

Snack Bar Bimarva (Chez Emmanuel; mains from US$3) Conveniently located next to the CDG supermarket and across from the Wazanet Internet café. Unlike many snack bars, this one actually offers snacks and full meals. Or you can just sit in the comfy leather chairs and enjoy cold drinks and French pop videos on TV.

Relais de la Porte Mayo (☎ 229 2692; mains US$7, menu du jour US$9) Despite being the favourite dining spot for well-heeled travellers and aid workers, the Porte Mayo remains reasonably priced for a splurge. Relax and enjoy people-watching at the outdoor tables, along with the soothing music and the draft beer (US$1.75).

For light snacks and fresh juices, head to Chez Moussa, past the Cameroon Airlines office, or Restaurant de l'Artisanat, across from the entrance to the market.

Drinking
Maroua has a number of small bars, most near the river. Try the Bar Rondpoint, the always-animated Snack-bar El Cabalo or its quieter neighbour the Table Blanche.

Getting There & Away
There are daily flights to Yaoundé on Cameroon Airlines, but they cost a steep US$137 one-way. If you're in a big hurry you might

consider it, as the bus and train trip takes a couple days.

Buses to Garoua (US$5, five hours) and N'Gaoundéré (US$10, eight hours) leave from their company's offices, which are scattered around town. Woïla Voyages and Touristique Express are the best. Taxi buses to Mokolo and sometimes on to Rumsiki leave from Carrefour Parrah at the southern end of town.

MANDARA MOUNTAINS

Trekking in the spectacular landscapes of the Mandara Mountains west of Maroua is one of Cameroon's best and most popular attractions, especially for adventurous travellers. The whole region is full of traditional hillside villages of round huts, huge stone formations and wide green valleys. The standard arranged trek lasts two or three days, but you can just hike for a day if you want. Those who travel independently and stay a while will experience much more.

Rhumsiki is the starting point for treks, and it's consequently a hub for travellers. As soon as you arrive you'll be offered a tour of the village, which includes pottery-making, cotton-spinning, millet beer brewing and sampling, and a visit with the crab sorcerer (now quite old and near-deaf), who will answer questions about your future by consulting his bowl of crabs. At every stop you'll be asked for a small donation and pressured to buy something, but the tour is still an interesting, if prearranged, glimpse of local culture.

There are hotels, *auberges*, restaurants and bars in town, including the popular Chez Casserole, full of trekkers getting ready for the trip. Once past Rhumsiki the villages become more 'unspoiled' and the scale of the mountains and valleys becomes apparent. Local accommodation is available in some villages but you should bring all your provisions.

Prices for treks arranged in Maroua depend on your bargaining skills, but if you get to Rhumsiki and arrange your own tour (see the boxed text below) the standard rate is around US$15 per person per day, including guide, simple meals and accommodation.

PARC NATIONAL DU WAZA

Waza National Park (admission US$8.50, vehicle fee US$3.50, camera fee US$3.50, guide fee US$5; ☺ 6am-6pm daily, 15 Nov-15 Jun) is Cameroon's most accessible and rewarding wildlife-viewing experience. Visitors can reasonably expect to see large numbers of elephants, giraffes, hippos, many species of antelope and monkey, and abundant birdlife. There are lions in the park, but seeing them requires a very early morning start and some luck. The park is dry scrubland with a couple of waterholes that draw the animals. March and April are the best months to visit, before the rains come.

Waza is not set up for backpackers, and to get here you really need to hire a 4WD vehicle and driver. All the tour operators in Maroua will set this up for around US$60 to US$70 per car for a day trip, so try to get a group together – there are always travellers in Maroua looking for companions to Waza. You could get to the park entrance by public transport, but you can't get in without a car, and there are few suitable ones in the village of Waza.

RESPONSIBLE TRAVEL IN THE MANDARA MOUNTAINS

The high concentration of relatively rich tourists visiting the, until recently, very traditional villages of the Mandara Mountains (see p000) has brought prosperity to some but problems for others. Here are some ways you can minimise the negative impact of your visit.

Don't give money to child beggars. Rhumsiki and the road into it are full of kids asking for money, pens or anything else they see. They look like they're having fun harassing the strangers, but the problem is that parents are encouraging them to miss school for the more lucrative (in the short term, obviously) begging. Don't encourage this.

Arrange your own tour. Most trekkers arrange the entire tour while in Maroua, and most of their money stays with the tour operators in Maroua and doesn't get to the villages they're visiting. Independent travellers can easily (well, relatively easy for Africa) get to Rhumsiki and arrange tours and guides there. First get up early and take one of the many shared taxis to Mokolo (US$1.75, one hour) and then ask around for rides to Rhumsiki. Be aware that it's a rough ride on a *moto-taxi*.

If you want to stay near the park entrance in order to get a really early start, there are a couple options. The best, especially if you've got money and your own vehicle, is the **Campement de Waza** (☎ 229 1007 in Maroua; boukarous s/d US$25/27), up a steep hill across from the park entrance. The restaurant, bar, swimming pool and some of the rooms feature views overlooking the park.

Right at the park entrance the **mini-hotel** (r US$12) at the Centre d'Accueil de Waza has tiny *boukarous* and a restaurant if you order meals in advance. It's completely no-frills, and the only advantage is that you're at the park gate if you want to leave at 6am to chase lions.

EASTERN CAMEROON

Cameroon's eastern provinces are the country's least-visited, though their national parks and hiking opportunities are drawing more and more travellers who want an off-the-beaten path adventure. There's no tourist industry out here, and travel can be rough. This is also the route for crossing into the CAR, but the borders are sometimes closed, so ask around before getting all the way out here.

BERTOUA
The capital of East Province, Bertua has a few restaurants, hotels and bars. It's also the main town on the route to the border at Kenzou or Garoua-Boulaï.

Bertua's best place to stay is **Hôtel Mansa** (r US$25). Hôtel Montagne and Hôtel Alimentation both have cheap lodging as well.

There are several cheap eateries in town, including Café Moderne, Madame Lumere and Chez Odette; meals for around US$2.

MTA Travel in town can help with plane flights to Douala, via Yaoundé, and train travel on the Yaoundé to N'Gaoundéré line.

Buses to Yaoundé (US$8.50, seven hours), Garoua-Boulaï, and Bélabo, where you can catch the train, leave from the *gare routières* near the market.

GAROUA-BOULAÏ
Garoua-Boulaï is a seedy one-horse border town. The few *auberges* in town are not recommended; try the Mission Catholique, with dorm beds for a donation and a few rooms for around US$9.

At least one bus daily goes to N'Gaoundéré in the dry season, but check the local security situation as there have been incidents of banditry on this road. There are also daily buses to Bertua.

CAMEROON DIRECTORY

ACCOMMODATION
Cameroon has the full range of accommodation, from luxury hotels to dorm beds in religious missions. As a rule, decent single rooms with private bath go for around US$15. Larger rooms for two to four people are often just a couple dollars more.

ACTIVITIES
The whole country has great hiking opportunities, from rainforest walks in the south, to steep ascents of Mt Cameroon, to the unlimited trekking in the hills and valleys of the Mandara Mountains near Rumsiki. In the south the beaches are great for swimming and relaxing, but not surfing.

DANGERS & ANNOYANCES
The major cities, Douala and Yaoundé, both have reputations for petty crime, especially in the crowded central areas. In very remote parts of the country road bandits are a serious but infrequent hazard.

Scams and official corruption are a way of life in Cameroon; keep your guard up and maintain a sense of humour.

EMBASSIES & CONSULATES
The following embassies are located in Yaoundé unless otherwise indicated.
Australia Contact the Canadian embassy for diplomatic representation.
Canada (☎ 223 2311; Immeuble Stamatiades, Ave de l'Indépendance, Centre Ville)
Central African Republic (CAR; ☎ 220 5155; Rue 1863, off Rue 1810, Bastos)
Chad (☎ 221 0624; Rue Mballa Eloumden, Bastos)
Congo (☎ 221 2458; Rue 1815, Bastos)
Côte d'Ivoire (☎ 221 7459; Rue 1805, off Blvd de l'URSS, Bastos)
Equatorial Guinea Douala (☎ 342 2729; Blvd de la République); Yaoundé (☎ 221 0804; Rue 1805, off Blvd de l'URSS, Bastos)
France Douala (☎ 342 6250; Ave des Cocotiers); Yaoundé (☎ 223 6399; Rue Joseph Atemengué, near Place de la Réunification)

Gabon (☎ 220 2966; Rue 1816, off Rue 1810, Bastos)
Germany (☎ 221 0056; Ave de Gaulle, Centre Ville)
Nigeria Douala (Blvd de la Liberté); Yaoundé (☎ 222 3455; off Ave Monseigneur Vogt, near Marché du Mfoundi, Centre Ville)
UK Douala (☎ 442 3612; Blvd. de la Liberté); Yaoundé (☎ 222 0796; Ave Churchill, near the Place de l'Indépendance, Centre Ville)
USA (☎ 223 0512; Rue de Nachtigal, near Place de l'Indépendance, Centre Ville)

FOOD
Cameroon can boast excellent food, usually chicken, meat or fish with rice or plantain, sometimes with a starch like fufu, all with some kind of sauce. Street food is everywhere. Grilled meat, sandwiches, fresh fruits and other treats are all cheap and filling.

HOLIDAYS
As well as religious holidays listed in the Africa Directory (p1003), these are the principal public holidays in Cameroon:
1 January New Year's Day
11 February Youth Day
1 May International Workers' Day
20 May National Day

INTERNET ACCESS
Internet access is spreading rapidly to smaller cities throughout the country. In the big cities it's easy to find and cheap (under US$1 per hour).

MAPS
There are maps of Cameroon (US$6) and a two-sided Yaoundé/Douala (US$4) map available at bookshops and from street vendors in the bigger cities.

MONEY
Currency
Cash is king in Cameroon, especially in remote regions where it's the only way to pay, and you'll find yourself carrying lots of it.

Credit cards and travellers cheques are only accepted at the more upmarket hotels and restaurants, so don't count on them.

You can exchange cash or travellers cheques at banks in the bigger cities, but the process is long and uncertain, and the commissions and fees are painfully high.

Considering the hassles of changing money and the risks of carrying cash, one of the best solutions is to have money wired to you at any of the many Western Union offices throughout the country. There are charges on the sender's end, but you can quickly get cash CFA without standing in line at the bank.

Bargaining is a way of life in Cameroon and is always worth a try. If you pay the asking price at markets or craft centres you'll be regarded as an idiot.

PHOTOGRAPHY
Don't photograph anything connected with the military or the government. Ask before taking pictures of people; some will refuse or ask for money, others will gladly pose.

RESPONSIBLE TRAVEL
Cameroon is developing an ecotourism industry; your contributions at national parks and other attractions will help it get started.

The government is taking steps to halt the bushmeat trade, which is a huge threat to Cameroon's wildlife, but you may still find it on the menu; don't contribute to this.

See the Mandara Mountains section for specific tips for that region (p458).

TELEPHONE
There are private teleboutiques in all major towns. They take prepaid phonecards, available from shops and street vendors. International calls cost about US$5 per minute.

VISAS
Visas are required by all and must be bought prior to arrival in the country. At Cameroonian embassies in neighbouring countries, visas are issued quickly for about US$50. Getting a visa from an embassy in Europe or the US can take a week and may cost twice as much.

Visa Extensions
You can get a visa extension at the Ministry of Immigration in Yaoundé for US$30.

Visas for Onward Travel
Visas for Gabon (US$60 for 30 days), Equatorial Guinea (US$60 for 30 days) and many other nearby countries are available from embassies in Yaoundé; see p459 for address details. Visas to Nigeria are usually issued only to Cameroonian citizens.

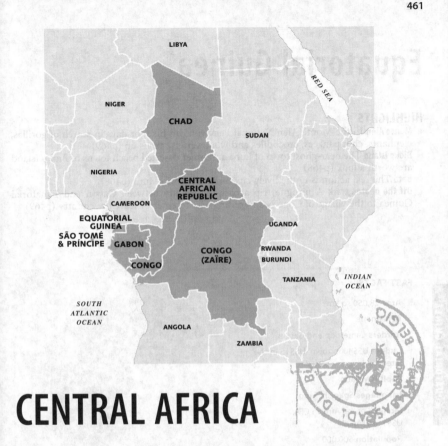

CENTRAL AFRICA

Central Africa – the heart of this great continent – pulsates at a hot, steamy and precarious pace. This is the Africa of dense virgin jungles, river highways bustling with trade, pygmies, forest elephants, chimpanzees and, sadly, a fair whack of wars.

Travelling in Central Africa is not for the faint-hearted. There are no luxury coaches here and no organised tours. This is the road less travelled. This is Tarzan territory, Bogey's *African Queen* and Joseph Conrad's *Heart of Darkness*. Here you'll be making like a missionary and cutting a path of your own. But your prayers will be answered with turquoise waters and deserted palm-fringed beaches, shouldered by tropical rainforests with volcanic highlands rising as a backdrop. Amid a sea of fascinating tribes, ethnicities and religions, Central Africa boasts islands that knock on heaven's door, giant turtles, blue lagoons and sparkling waterfalls. Get among the local lifestyle: bathing in mountain streams, camping in traditional villages, eating wild boar and chewing on crocodile. Take on some of Central Africa's peaks, paddle dugout canoes along equatorial rivers and gaze at gorillas (while avoiding guerrillas; remember this region is a hot spot in more ways than one).

When going troppo gets too hot to handle, hit the cities and party with the locals. You'd be mad to say no when the women in N'Djamena (Chad) take over a downtown bar. These parties are an institution. Just don't expect the same festivity in Abéché further north in the same country – it's a desert-locked Muslim town in the guts of the Sahara. A land of sand, turbans and camels – a long pirogue paddle from the Congo Basin, but Central Africa no less.

This region in Africa's hub can be hard core. It takes stamina and a sense of humour, but the rewards are real. Central Africa is for those who travel to feel alive.

Equatorial Guinea

HIGHLIGHTS

- **Monte Alen** In the Monte Alen National Park you can hike for days in search of gorillas, elephants, chimpanzees, crocodiles and whatever else turns up (p469)
- **Bioko Island** The near-ghost town of Luba and other deserted beach towns of Bioko Island are worth a look (p468)
- **Bata** The real action is in the lively city of Bata, on Rio Muni (p468)
- **Off the beaten track** A pirogue trip across the estuary between Gabon and Equatorial Guinea to the village of Cogo is an exciting way to enter or leave the country (p469)

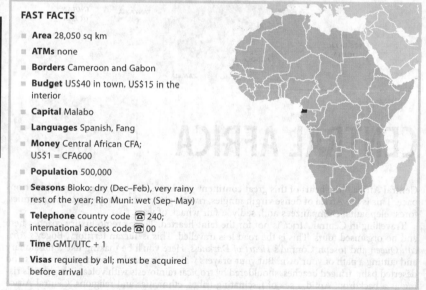

FAST FACTS

- **Area** 28,050 sq km
- **ATMs** none
- **Borders** Cameroon and Gabon
- **Budget** US$40 in town, US$15 in the interior
- **Capital** Malabo
- **Languages** Spanish, Fang
- **Money** Central African CFA; US$1 = CFA600
- **Population** 500,000
- **Seasons** Bioko: dry (Dec–Feb), very rainy rest of the year; Rio Muni: wet (Sep–May)
- **Telephone** country code ☎ 240; international access code ☎ 00
- **Time** GMT/UTC + 1
- **Visas** required by all; must be acquired before arrival

Equatorial Guinea is for explorers. Unless you're working for an oil company, the only way through the country is to hack and bribe and hold on tight to bush taxis through the jungle. Bioko Island has been thoroughly taken over by oil money and an influx of foreign workers, but the mainland (Rio Muni) is still one of the big challenges of African travel. It's a step back in time, to a country that hasn't whole-heartedly opened its borders to travellers, and if you decide to go, you're on your own. This is real adventure travel, with amazing rewards (rainforest, wildlife, beaches, traditional African villages and more) along with constant hassles. The main attraction for visitors is the Monte Alen National Park, where, with some hard hiking and luck you might get to spend some time with gorillas. Note that all travellers need a travel and photography permit, available in Malabo and Bata (see Visas p471). Your papers will be scrutinised often, so make sure you have them in order.

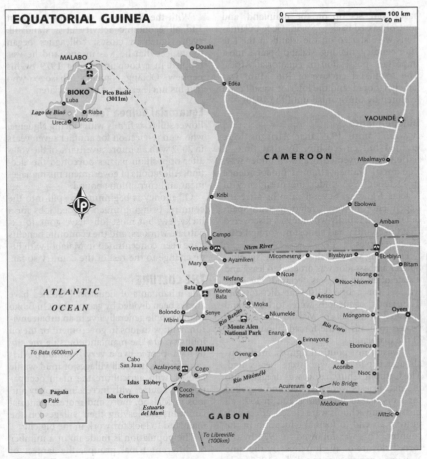

EQUATORIAL GUINEA

EQUATORIAL GUINEA

HISTORY

The original inhabitants of mainland Equatorial Guinea were Pygmies. The Ndowe people became the first wave of Bantu to migrate into the area in the 12th and 13th centuries. The final wave of Bantu migration came in the 13th century with the warlike Fang tribe, who quickly became the dominant and most numerous of the tribal groups as a result of war and intermarriage with the Ndowe. They made foreign occupation attempts a dangerous venture, but were forced to retreat from the coastal region during the centuries of slave trading by the British, Dutch and French. With the abolition of slavery they once again reoccupied the coast. Bioko Island was first settled by the Bubi between the 13th and 15th centuries.

Trade with Europe

The first part of the country to have contact with Europeans was the island of Pagalu, which was visited by the Portuguese in 1470. Portugal subsequently settled Pagalu and the other islands in the Gulf of Guinea (Bioko, São Tomé and Príncipe), but in the 18th century it exchanged Bioko and Pagalu, as well as parts of the mainland, with Spain for certain regions in Latin America.

Bioko became an important slave-trading base for several European nations, including Britain, during the early 19th century. Britain's interest in the island waned as naval bases were set up on the mainland, and control passed back to Spain. Cocoa plantations were started on the island in the late 19th century, making Malabo Spain's most important possession in equatorial Africa. The mainland enclave of Rio Muni was largely ignored, and the interior wasn't even explored by the Spanish until the 1920s.

Independence

It wasn't until 1959 that Africans were granted full citizenship. By that time, a nationalist movement was well under way. Equatorial Guinea attained independence in October 1968 under the presidency of Macias Nguema. Several months after independence, however, relations with Spain deteriorated rapidly when it was discovered that the country had almost no foreign currency reserves.

Following a stormy meeting with Nguema, Spain's ambassador was ordered to leave and a state of emergency was declared. The stage was set for a brutal 10-year dictatorship. Thousands of people were tortured and executed in the jails of Malabo and Bata, or beaten to death in the forced-labour camps of the mainland.

It wasn't just political figures, intellectuals and expatriates who were persecuted. The Catholic Church, too, was dragged into the net. Priests were arrested and expelled for plots real or imaginary, and in 1975 all mission-run schools were closed, effectively putting an end to formal education in the country. This was followed in 1978 by the forced closure of all churches. By the time Nguema's regime was toppled in 1979, only one-third of the 300,000 Guineans who lived there at independence remained.

With the country in shambles, bankrupt and all economic activity at a standstill, even Nguema's closest colleagues began to suspect that he was insane, and he was toppled in a coup in August 1979 by his nephew, Obiang Nguema Mbasogo, who had his uncle executed a month later.

Equatorial Guinea Today

Power still rests firmly with Obiang Nguema, who won re-election for another seven years in 2002 with an impressive 100% of the votes after opposition parties boycotted the election. Allegations of government mismanagement and corruption abound.

Oil money is beginning to spill into the country, bringing much-needed jobs for a lucky few, but most jobs have gone to expatriate workers, and the economic benefits have been concentrated in Malabo, with little change to the rest of the country so far.

THE CULTURE

The inhabitants of Equatorial Guinea have always been divided by geography. On Bioko Island people generally live in an urban environment, with jobs in government or the oil industry. On the mainland, outside the city of Bata, people live a very traditional African lifestyle, in small villages of mud-wattle houses, with agriculture the main occupation. Of course, with increasing money and jobs in Malabo, more and more Equatorial Guineans are leaving their villages on the mainland to look for work in the big city.

The population is made up of a number of different tribal groups, the largest of which is the Fang. You'll hear Fang spoken more often than Spanish if you travel around the interior.

POLICE & THIEVES

Pretty much all the readers' letters Lonely Planet gets about Equatorial Guinea say exactly the same things: the jungle is beautiful, the people are friendly, and yet the experience is ruined, or almost ruined, by the persistent hassles by corrupt officials demanding unreasonable amounts of money at checkpoints every few miles. There's no avoiding it; no matter how good you think you are at not paying bribes, there are going to be times in Equatorial Guinea when you either pay up or turn around and go back where you came from.

The best part is that at every checkpoint there's a sign saying that 'es prohibido' to pay money to the police/gendarmes/whatever. Don't bother pointing this out; you will be told that this sign applies to other people but not to you. Do not, under any circumstances, sit down and very conspicuously write down the phone number on the sign for reporting infractions; this will get you a ride to the *gendarmerie* plus payment of the original bribe.

ENVIRONMENT

Equatorial Guinea is made up of two very different parts. The small island of Bioko, off the coast of Cameroon, is formed from three extinct volcanoes. It's a rugged, jungle-covered island and its main products are petroleum, cocoa, coffee and madeira.

The mainland section, known as Rio Muni, is a roughly rectangular area of Central African rainforest with abundant wildlife, including gorillas, chimpanzees and forest elephants. Large sections of the interior have been set aside as protected areas, including Monte Alen National Park, which covers much of the centre of Rio Muni and offers amazing hiking opportunities. Logging is being more carefully controlled than in the past, but deforestation and the bushmeat trade that follows logging operations are still problems.

TRANSPORT

GETTING THERE & AWAY

From Europe the only direct flights are on Iberia Airlines from Madrid, Spain, twice a week. In Africa the usual way to Malabo is to depart from Douala (Cameroon) but the 25-minute flights are ridiculously expensive (about US$210 one way or US$220 return), but you don't really have a choice. There's

---

DEPARTURE TAX

There's a US$8.50 departure tax for international flights. If leaving the country overland you'll be charged around US$3.50 at customs and the same at immigration.

---

one flight from Douala per day on **Air Gabon** (☎ 91718) or the national airline **EGA** (☎ 94497), but they can fill up a week in advance so book early. The only other option is to go overland to Bata and take the much cheaper (US$50 one way) domestic flight to Malabo.

Rio Muni can be entered by land at Yengue from Campo (Cameroon), at Ebebiyin from Cameroon or, via a very rough road, from Gabon. Travellers going to or from Gabon can also take the pirogue crossing between Cocobeach and Acalayong. From Acalayong (customs) you head to Cogo (exit stamp), back to Acalayong (pick up passengers and

cargo) and over to Cocobeach in Gabon. It's a couple of hours, costs about US$10 and takes in everything from mangroves to the choppy waves of the open estuary. It's a pretty exciting way to leave a country.

GETTING AROUND

A number of local airlines fly daily between Malabo and Bata for about US$50 one way. **AGE** (☎ 50885) sometimes has advertised specials for around US$35.

Check at **MacGuinea** (Ave de la Libertad, Malabo) for information on the *Rio Campo*, a large passenger boat that makes the same trip about once a week, but it's not much cheaper than flying.

The usual means of getting around Bioko or Rio Muni is bush taxi, and the further you get from Malabo or Bata the more 'bush' they get. Travelling in the interior can be a real adventure.

MALABO

If you fly in to Malabo you'll know what it's all about before you even land; oil platforms are scattered around the harbour, tankers run back and forth from the port, and refineries on the coast shoot off flames night and day. Malabo is an oil town, where expatriates kick back at the end of the day before heading back to work on the platforms. Money flows freely, and everyone's looking out for the next big score.

Travellers arriving from other African cities may be surprised how small and quiet Malabo is; it's not the place to go for nightlife or excitement, though there are still bars and clubs where the drink flows freely. Also, despite the oil money, Malabo suffers frequent and lengthy outages of electricity and water, so be prepared.

ORIENTATION

Malabo is a small city on the north side of Bioko Island, centred on the new port. The airport is about 6km west of town and taxis meet most flights. Bush taxis and minibuses stop somewhat inconveniently by the central market, blocks away from the hotels in the centre of town, but nothing is too far of a walk in Malabo.

The heart of town is along Avenida de la Independencia, where you'll find the main bank, shops, hotels, restaurants, and, further east, the main square, which is undergoing major renovation including the building of a high-end hotel. Calle de Argelia, with the other big hotels in town, has some excellent views of the busy port and the harbour.

INFORMATION
Cultural Centres
The **Centro Cultural Hispano-Guineano** (Ave de la Independencia) in the heart of town sometimes has dance performances and other cultural events; look for posters in town. Further afield, the **French Cultural Centre** (Calle de Acacio Muñe) serves the city's Francophone population.

Internet Access
Malabo still has no reliable public Internet cafés, but this is likely to change.

Medical Services
Medical facilities are extremely limited; try the pharmacies in town.

Money
There are no ATMs in town and credit cards are not accepted. Cash and travellers cheques can be changed at the **SGBGE bank** (Ave de la Independencia) on the west end of town, but this is extremely time-consuming and the rates are poor, so try to bring enough cash to tide you over.

Post & Telephone
The **central post office** (Calle de Rey Boncoro) is near the centre of town.

Public telephones are rare; there's a GETESA telecommunications centre down the street from the post office where you can make calls.

Toilets
There are public toilets (available for a small fee) near the *mercado central*, but they're well patronised. It's a better idea to duck into one of the nicer hotels in town and use theirs.

Tourist Offices
The **Ministry of Culture, Tourism & Information** (Ave 3 de Agosto), south of town, doesn't have a lot in terms of maps or advice, but is a mandatory stop for tourists because of the travel and photography permit US$40,

which you'll need to show at the many roadblocks.

SIGHTS & ACTIVITIES
Malabo doesn't have a lot of must-see attractions; it's more of a place to walk and explore and maybe strike up a conversation with locals. The **mercado central**, on the south side of town, is a typically colourful and bustling scene in the mornings and a good place to meet people. The market has lots of fresh produce grown on the island, but everything else is imported from Cameroon and is relatively expensive.

SLEEPING
There are a couple of cheap *hostals* in town, mostly old and established, as well as an increasing number of new, modern (and expensive) hotels for foreign oil workers. Shoestring travellers will find that the cheapest, most popular *hostals* are often full. Prices vary widely and randomly; a US$50 room may not be much better than a US$10 room.

Residencia Ana Jose (☎ 92786; Avenida de la Independencia; r with shared/private bathroom US$12/17) In the centre of town, Ana Jose offers budget accommodation in an old house with a lot of character. Owned by an old Spanish lady who speaks no English, it's clean and pleasant.

Hostal Chana (☎ 93338; Avenida de las Naciónes Unidas; s US$8.50, d with bathroom & kitchen US$17) This is the cheapest option in town and is frequently full. It's reasonably clean.

Hostal Nely (BP 366, Avenida de las Naciónes Unidas; s US$43) Across the street from Hostal Chana, Nely has similar rooms but charges a fair bit more.

If you're stuck and willing to pay a bit more, the very friendly **Hostal Residencia Morenita** (☎ 91026; Calle de Mongomo 44; d with bathroom, air-con & fan US$55) has a quiet location and large, spotless rooms.

EATING
Restaurants in Malabo are either for locals or for foreigners, with very little crossover. African restaurants in the city are generally good and very cheap, but with the typical limited 'fish-or-chicken' menu. The spots that attract the expat crowd are more expensive but generally offer more variety. In the mornings, the area around the *mercado*

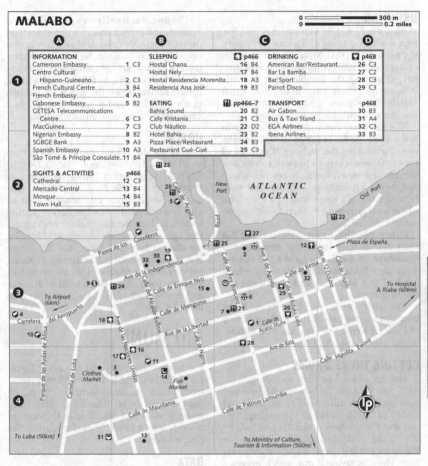

MALABO

0 _____ 300 m
0 _____ 0.2 miles

INFORMATION	**SLEEPING** 🛏 p466	**DRINKING** 🍷 p468
Cameroon Embassy...............1 C3	Hostal Chana..........................16 B4	American Bar/Restaurant.........26 C3
Centro Cultural	Hostal Nely.............................17 B4	Bar La Bamba........................27 C2
Hispano-Guineano.............2 C3	Hostal Residencia Morenita....18 A3	Bar Sport...............................28 C3
French Cultural Centre...........3 B4	Residencia Ana José................19 B3	Parrot Disco...........................29 C3
French Embassy......................4 A3		
Gabonese Embassy.................5 B2	**EATING** 🍴 pp466–7	**TRANSPORT** p468
GETESA Telecommunications	Bahia Sound...........................20 B2	Air Gabon..............................30 B3
Centre................................6 C3	Cafe Kristania.........................21 C3	Bus & Taxi Stand.....................31 A4
MacGuinea.............................7 C3	Club Náutico..........................22 D2	EGA Airlines............................32 C3
Nigerian Embassy....................8 B2	Hotel Bahia............................23 B2	Iberia Airlines.........................33 B3
SGBGE Bank...........................9 A3	Pizza Place/Restaurant...........24 B3	
Spanish Embassy..................10 A3	Restaurant Gué-Gué...............25 C3	
São Tomé & Príncipe Consulate.11 B4		
SIGHTS & ACTIVITIES p466		
Cathedral..............................12 C3		
Mercado Central....................13 B4		
Mosque.................................14 B4		
Town Hall..............................15 B3		

central is a good place for street food, including fresh fruit.

Up the stairs is the **Residencia Ana Jose**, but behind the residencia there's a no-name **restaurant** (meals US$5) that's an oasis of Central African fun and excitement in quiet Malabo; ask for 'the restaurant' or just follow your ears to the loud Cameroonian music. Fresh local specialties are prepared daily depending on what's on hand, and the beer, music and lively conversation never stop.

Restaurant **Gué-Gué** (Ave de la Independencia) is another African restaurant with a simple menu and low prices.

Cafe Kristania (☎ 91330; cnr Avenida de la Libertad & Calle de Rey Boncoro) This is a great place to go for coffee and pastries. You can get them to go or sit and relax in this European-style café.

Some of the other popular places with expats include the Lebanese-run **Pizza Place** (☎ 93450; Avenida de la Independencia), with pizzas from about $8, and **Club Náutico** (☎ 92641; mains around US$10), which serves excellent seafood down at the Old Port for expat prices.

The restaurant at Hotel Bahia and Mesa Verde at Bahia Sound, both on Calle de Argelia, are good stops for slightly expensive afternoon drinks and snacks with the best views in town, and if you're looking for a splurge these are the two nicest (and priciest) options.

DRINKING

With a steady supply of oil money and foreign workers coming and going constantly, it's no surprise that Malabo's got its share of bars and clubs. Most are safe and low-key, despite all the drinking that goes on. Women travellers should be aware that Malabo is definitely a boys' town, and any women will attract a lot of attention.

The most popular watering hole in town is the open-air **Bar La Bamba** (Ave de la Independencia) overlooking the harbour. It's where all the expat oilworkers go to swap stories and initiate the newcomers. Beers are cheap and there's a refreshing sea breeze and view. Be aware that it's also a major pick-up joint where local girls come to meet foreign workers and vice versa.

Other popular expat bars include **Bar Sport** (Calle de Acacio Muñe), the **American Bar/Restaurant** (cnr Avenida 3 de Agosto & Calle de Acacio Muñe), and **Bahia Sound** (Calle de Argelia) which is billed as a 'jazz' club and sometimes has live music.

The most popular nightclub is the **Parrot Disco** (admission free, beers US$2) near the junction of Calle de Kenia and Avenida 3 de Agosto. It gets going around 11 pm.

GETTING THERE & AWAY

A number of local airlines, including EGA, AGE and UTAGE, fly between Malabo and Bata daily with advertised rates of around US$35 to US$50 for the 40-minute trip. You can also travel between Malabo and Bata by sea on the passenger boat *Rio Campo*; see **MacGuinea** (Ave de la Libertad, Malabo) for information. The cost saving is minimal, however.

GETTING AROUND

Shared taxis and minibuses leave for villages all over Bioko Island from the mercado central. Shared rides cost about US$3 to Luba or US$5 to Riaba, and hiring your own cab can be cheap after some bargaining.

BIOKO ISLAND

LUBA

The oil boom in Malabo has left poor little Luba, formerly Bioko's second city, something of a ghost town. There's still a popular beach nearby, **La Reina Blanca**, but the town itself is increasingly deserted.

The owner at **Hotel Jemaro** (r US$8.50) speaks Spanish and French and also serves seafood meals if there are enough clients to warrant opening the restaurant. Nearby, the **Restaurante La Habana** has food and beers in a cozy garden atmosphere, but there's not a lot of action. **Bar Cleopatra** is the only place in town that's open late, and it sometimes draws a small crowd for music and conversation.

URECA

During the dry season, turtles come ashore at Ureca to lay their eggs. Since 1996, the Spanish conservation group **Los Amigos de Donana** (☎ /fax 94098; BP 962, Malabo) has employed people from this small village as guards to patrol the beaches during nesting season, and the local market for both turtles and eggs has gradually decreased. There's a guesthouse here and hikes into the jungle and along the beach can be arranged (phone before you leave Malabo). Ureca is on Bioko's southern coast, about 80km south of Malabo, and can be reached by shared taxi (US$5) or by hired cab.

RIO MUNI

Rio Muni is the mainland section of Equatorial Guinea, and is a very different world from Bioko, its island partner. The major (and only) city is Bata; other places are much smaller and described in this section roughly west to east, from the coast to the jungle interior.

BATA

The biggest city on the mainland of Equatorial Guinea, Bata feels a lot more lively than Malabo, with constant traffic and crowds on the sidewalks. It's a fun place to spend a couple days, planning for (or recovering from) hardy travel deep in the interior.

Although way behind Malabo, Bata also seems to be feeling the oil boom, with ambitious construction projects going up all over town. But just like Malabo, Bata has an infrastructure that can't handle the demands of the population, and water and power outages are common.

Orientation

Bata is a sprawling, unplanned African city where local residents and taxi drivers alike can find themselves lost. It's good to memorise some landmarks (the hospital, a big hotel etc) near where you want to go, because most streets aren't signed and many are unnamed.

Sleeping & Eating
Hotel Iberclima II (☎ 71438; r US$14) On the road to the hospital, Iberclima II has a very friendly staff, a bar and restaurant as well as small clean rooms with shared bath. Across the street, **Hotel Yessica** (☎ 83074; r with shared/private bathroom US$17/22) is very popular with local politicians and businessmen, but the rooms aren't much for the price.

Bata is a great town for street food and snack bars, particularly on the road to the hospital and around the various gares routieres, where you can stroll and sample to your heart's content for a dollar or two.

The best and most-popular breakfast in town (really) is at the outdoor tables next to the **Bar Restaurante Shanghai China**, where street vendors grill up chicken with tomatoes and fresh lime for US$0.85.

Dining splurges for visitors include **Pizza Mar** (☎ 74371) on the waterfront, serving seafood dishes for around $11, and **La Terraza** (☎ 83239; meals US$6-11), in the Hotel Panafrica, which has a seafront terrace bar complete with billiards table.

Getting There & Away
Bata has an airport outside of town that handles domestic flights, and several intersections where shared taxis leave for towns in the interior. Destinations include Mbini (US$4, one hour), and Ebebiyin (eight to 10 hours) for the Cameroon border crossing. Take a cab and tell the driver your destination and he should get you to the right place.

MBINI
About 50km south of Bata along the coast on the road to Acalayong, a quick ferry ride brings you to Mbini. It's a nice little town on the river with a couple of cheap hotels, restaurants and a nightclub, but it's no fun at all because of the drunken 'marines' who greet each boat demanding money and goods and getting drunker and more hostile as the day goes on. Even if your papers are completely in order, you'll be told that you're at 'the frontier' (the frontier of what?) and you need to

pay 'protection'. Avoid these people if you possibly can.

If you're planning on staying in town, head straight up the hill to the friendly **Hotel Parador** (r US$4, beers US$1), where you might escape the attention of the 'marines'. The other option is on your left as you get off the ferry where **Hostal Restaurant Pantala** (r US$5) has rooms available. Kerosene lamps and mosquito coils (you'll need them, it's bad down by the river) are provided, and cheap meals are available.

There are minibuses from Bata to Mbini ($3.50, one hour, including a ferry from Bolondo to Mbini) and others to Acalayong ($8, three to six hours).

ACALAYONG
Acalayong (ah-cah-lye-ong), the major southern border town, consists of a few bars, shops, houses, the police post, customs and a palm wine bar where you might find yourself drinking with the guy who just checked your bags. There is nowhere to stay in town. The best option is at isolated but charming **Cogo**, a former colonial capital a short ride across the estuary by boat, where **Hotel Bilogo** (r US$5) is on the main street. The hotel has cubicles partitioned by hardboard – it's a noisy place but there's a **restaurant** next door. You can enter Gabon from Acalayong via a lengthy but scenic and exciting pirogue ride (see Getting There & Away, p465) for details.

MONTE ALEN NATIONAL PARK
This park is one of Central Africa's best-kept secrets, a protected area covering 1400 sq km that's managed under the supervision of **Ecofac** (www.ecofac.org). Only 60km (usually one bus every morning from Bata, US$6, ask for 'Ecofac') southeast of Bata along the Evinayong road, it's an excellent place to experience the lush rainforests and wildlife of Rio Muni. There are well-maintained and accessible trails and a series of simple *campements* where hikers can spend the night. The trails lead to lakes where it's possible to spot gorillas, chimpanzees, forest elephants, crocodiles and many other species of wildlife.

Ecofac has also built the excellent **Hotel Monte Alen** (☎ 82817) in the village of Moka on the edge of the park (contact Ecofac to see it's still operating before making the trek out there). Run by locals from the village, the hotel has clean double rooms with views of the forest and bathrooms with hot water for US$30. There is a **restaurant** (meals US$10) in the hotel, but you need to order meals in advance.

Local guides are available through the hotel for either long or short hikes in the park (US$5 per day). Staying at the *campements* costs another US$3 per night. With a small group it could be a very affordable way to spend a few days seeing the rainforest and its wildlife up close, even if you splurge on a hotel room with hot shower, hot meal and cold drinks at the end of the hike.

Be aware that hiking in Monte Alen is hot, slippery and strenuous; it's a good idea to over pack on water, dry clothes and other supplies.

There are bush taxis and minibuses along the Bata to Evinayong route that pass through Moka, or you can arrange shared taxis from Bata to the hotel.

EBEBIYIN

Ebebiyin is the first village of any size in northeastern Rio Muni as you come across the border from Cameroon, 2km away. There are minibuses to/from Bata that take eight to 10 hours during the dry season, depending on the number of checkpoints.

The very friendly **Hotel Mbengono** (r US$4) on the western outskirts of town has rooms, as does **Hotel Nsi Ndogno** (r from US$5), near the market. **Hotel Central** (r US$6-8) and the new **Hotel Ruzmila** (r US$11-13) both have their own generators, which is always handy in this part of the world.

PAGALU

One of the most remote and untouristed destinations in all of Africa, the small island of Pagalu (as it's locally known; it's officially called Annobon) is about 600km southwest of Bioko and 160km southwest of São Tomé. The mountainous terrain of this island hides extinct volcanoes with crater lakes, and its beaches are largely deserted.

Hostal Memu Madze (r with bathroom & meals US$35) is the only hotel on the island and is in the village of San Antonio. To stay here call the proprietor, **Damian Segure** (☎ 95031, 93452), in Malabo. The hotel has 12 rooms (two with lights) plus a restaurant/bar.

It's a good idea to pay your respects to the **head of the village** (☎ 87401), who also owns the island's only ferry. Trips to/from São Tomé can be arranged through him.

EQUATORIAL GUINEA DIRECTORY

ACCOMMODATION
Cheap hotel rooms in the cities range from about US$8 to US$30 or more; in the interior very basic rooms go for as little as US$4.

ACTIVITIES
There are few organised activities in Equatorial Guinea, but there are good beaches for swimming. Hiking in the rainforest is also possible, especially at Monte Alen National Park.

CUSTOMS
Travellers leaving Equatorial Guinea, especially on international flights, can expect an extremely thorough search at customs. One of the things officials look for is currency, and if they find any there's a hefty fine (of course) for not filling out the 'currency declaration form'.

DANGERS & ANNOYANCES
The biggest annoyance is the constant hassling by corrupt officials looking for bribes, particularly at checkpoints in the interior. Apart from this, with normal precautions, Equatorial Guinea is a very safe country.

EMBASSIES & CONSULATES
Countries with diplomatic representation in Malabo include:
Cameroon (☎ 92263; Calle de Rey Boncoro)
France (☎ 92005; Carretera del Aeropuerto)
Gabon (☎ 93180; Calle de Argelia)
Nigeria (☎ 92487; Paseo de los Cocoteros)
São Tomé & Príncipe (Calle de Acacio Muñe)
Spain (☎ 92020; Parque de las Avdas de África)

The US embassy and British high commission in Yaoundé (Cameroon; see p459) handle USA and UK relations with Equatorial Guinea. The British high commission recommends the French embassy in Malabo for help. Equatorial Guinea has diplomatic representation in the following neighbouring or near-neighbouring countries: Cameroon, Nigeria and Gabon.

HOLIDAYS

As well as religious holidays listed in the Africa Directory (p1003), these are the principal public holidays in Equatorial Guinea:

1 January New Year's Day
1 May Labour Day
25 May OAU Day
5 June President's Birthday
3 August Liberation Day
12 October Independence Day
10 December Human Rights Day

INTERNET ACCESS

There is little or no public Internet access at present.

MEDIA

Radio, TV and newspapers are all in Spanish, and the media in Equatorial Guinea is tightly controlled by the government.

MONEY

The local currency is the Central African CFA franc. There are no ATMs in Equatorial Guinea and credit cards are not accepted.

Travellers cheques and cash can be changed at the banks in Malabo and Bata, but this can be very time-consuming, and the rates and commissions are steep. The best thing is to bring the cash you will need in Central African CFA.

Bargaining is expected at the markets but won't get you much in hotels or shops.

PHOTOGRAPHY

Film, equipment and developing are available in Malabo and Bata. All visitors taking pictures need a travel and photography permit from the Ministry of Culture, Tourism and Information, which has offices in Malabo (see p466) and Bata. Failure to get this permit can result in heavy fines.

Don't take photos of anything connected with the military, and steer clear of photographing government buildings as well.

POST & TELEPHONE

Postal services are reliable in Malabo and Bata; less so elsewhere. Sending a letter to most destinations costs around US$0.85.

RESPONSIBLE TRAVEL

Ecotourism projects in Equatorial Guinea, including the Monte Alen National Park and the turtle project at Ureca, are committed to employing local villagers while protecting the environment. Support them and more of these projects might take off. International phone services are limited to the cities of Malabo and Bata.

TOURIST INFORMATION

The Ministry of Culture, Tourism and Information isn't very helpful. Try asking at the hotels, which are used to explaining the country to foreigners.

VISAS

All visitors requre a visa which must be purchased before arriving in Equatorial Guinea. In most embassies, visas can be processed in a day or two for about US$50. They are good for 30 days. Visitors must also get a 'travel and photography permit' (US$40) from the tourist office in Malabo (see p466) or Bata.

Visa Extensions

Visa extensions are available from the tourist offices in Malabo and Bata, and cost US$17 for an additional 15 days.

Visas for Onward Travel

Visas for Cameroon and Gabon are available from embassies in Malabo (see p470 for addresses). Equatorial Guinea is one of the best places to get a Gabonese visa: 30-day visas cost US$60 and take about three days. Three-month visas for Cameroon cost US$50 and are issued the same day.

WOMEN TRAVELLERS

Travellers of any kind are rare in this country, and women travellers in particular will attract a lot of attention, especially in Malabo, which is teeming with (male) oil workers.

São Tomé & Príncipe

HIGHLIGHTS

- **The East Coast** Secluded white-sand beaches with a lush jungle backdrop, perfect for swimming, exploring or just relaxing (p478)
- **São Tomé town** A friendly, quiet capital city with scenic side streets and colonial architecture (p475)
- **Príncipe** A true tropical paradise; bring your mask and snorkel, rent a bike, and see if you ever want to leave (p478)
- **Off the beaten track** Ilhéu das Rolas, where you can straddle the equator (p478)

FAST FACTS

- **Area** 1000 sq km
- **ATMs** none at all
- **Borders** Gabon is the nearest neighbour
- **Budget** US$40 a day
- **Capital** São Tomé
- **Languages** Portuguese, Forro
- **Money** dobra; US$1 = 9000Db
- **Population** 170,000
- **Seasons** dry (Jun–Sep), wet (Oct–May)
- **Telephone** country code ☎ 239; international access code ☎ 00
- **Time** GMT/UTC
- **Visas** US$50; required by all

Never heard of this little slice of the Caribbean in the Gulf of Guinea? You're not the only one. The two islands of São Tomé and Príncipe comprise the smallest country in Africa and one of the newest. These sleepy islands are remote and rarely visited, at least for now. Tourists are starting to discover their attractions: miles of deserted beaches, crystal-blue waters with excellent and uncharted diving and snorkelling, rolling hills and jagged rock formations and lush rainforests. All this, plus they are home to a unique Portuguese-Creole island culture, which for visitors means a laid-back café lifestyle with real coffee, delicious fresh fruit and seafood, and the chance to sleep in refurbished plantation estates. If you're looking for a relaxing break from shoestring travelling, this is your chance for an island vacation. São Tomé and Príncipe is very different from its francophone mainland neighbours: quiet, calm and uncrowded.

SÃO TOMÉ & PRÍNCIPE

HISTORY

The islands were uninhabited when they were discovered by the Portuguese, who founded the town of São Tomé in 1485 and settled Príncipe in 1500. Seeing the islands' agricultural potential, the Portuguese set up sugar plantations and brought in slaves from Angola and Mozambique to do all the work. And that's how things stayed for hundreds of years. Coffee and cocoa replaced sugar as the main crops, and when slavery became illegal it was replaced with forced labour for low wages. The plantation economy under Portuguese control continued into the 1970s.

Not that it was always an easy ride. There were frequent uprisings and revolts, often brutally put down by the Portuguese. The last straw came in 1953, when a massacre of workers by Portuguese troops sparked a fully fledged independence movement. Portugal held on, however, until the fall of the fascist government in 1974, after which it got out of its colonies in a hurry. São Tomé & Príncipe achieved independence on 12 July 1975.

The Portuguese exodus left the country with virtually no skilled labour, a 90% illiteracy rate, only one doctor and many abandoned cocoa plantations. As such, an economic crisis was inevitable. Manual Pinto da Costa, who was the first president and, until then, a moderate, was forced to concede to many of the demands of the more radical members of his government. The majority of the plantations were nationalised four months after independence, laws were passed prohibiting anyone from owning more than 100 hectares of land and a people's militia was set up to operate in workplaces and villages.

The country remained closely aligned with Angola and communist Eastern Europe until the demise of the Soviet Union, when São Toméans began to demand multiparty democracy. The first multiparty elections were held in early 1991 and led to the inauguration of the previously exiled Miguel Trovoada as the new president in April of that year.

Elections in 2001 brought Fradique de Menezes to power. De Menezes has pledged to use revenues from increased tourism and exploitation of the country's off-shore oilfields to improve the standard of living and modernise the islands' infrastructure. So far, however, the effects have been limited to the development of a couple high-end tourist resorts. The government backed out of an initial agreement on oil exploration after discovering that most of the money would go to American and European oil corporations and some shady Nigerian companies, which led to a brief and bloodless coup attempt (peacefully resolved) while the president was out of the country. Meanwhile, rumours of American plans to build a military base to protect oil interests seem to be just that – rumours. The Americans says they have no plans to build a base, and would they lie to you? Big changes are definitely coming to these little islands in the next few years, but for now they're still tranquil and unhurried.

SÃO TOMÉ & PRÍNCIPE

THE CULTURE

Most São Toméans today are mixed-blood descendants of African slaves and Portuguese colonists, and 90% of the population is Roman Catholic. Many people identify themselves as *angolares*, as their ancestors were brought from Angola.

Outside the capital most São Toméans still live very simple island lives, with agriculture and fishing being the main occupations. There's a bit of activity early in the morning when the boats come in and the fish are distributed, a bustling market later in the morning and then a lazy siesta, a chance to avoid the afternoon heat and drink some imported boxes of *vino*. In the evenings people gather wherever there's a TV set and a generator.

ARTS

The main art form is woodworking; São Toméans produce intricately carved masks, boxes and wall hangings from locally harvested hardwoods. Visitors to the Roça São João (see p478) will see a wide variety of paintings and sculptures.

ENVIRONMENT

The islands are of volcanic origin and have towering eroded volcanoes. The highest peak (2024m) is Pico São Tomé. Partially cleared rainforests are a feature of both islands.

The driest and coolest months are from June to September, when temperatures hover around 28°C. The wettest month is March, when temperatures rise to around 30°C.

There are also many microclimates on São Tomé. The northeast, for instance, has a savannalike climate, whereas in the south it rains much more, even in the dry season.

The islands' isolation from the mainland means that many of their bird and plant species are endemic. Ecofac, the joint European and African conservation organization, has proposed that large areas of both islands be set aside as parks, and has also launched sea turtle protection programs.

TRANSPORT

GETTING THERE & AWAY

Air

Almost all travellers arrive by air from Libreville, Gabon. There are daily flights to and from Libreville on either Air São Tomé e Príncipe or Air Gabon; the round-trip fare is about US$250. Direct flights from Portugal are available from TAP Air Portugal and Air Luxor. Air Luxor is considerably cheaper with round-trip fares from Lisbon at around US$770.

> **DEPARTURE TAX**
>
> There's a departure tax of US$20, payable only in cash dollars, plus an additional fee of 3700 dobras, payable only in dobras. Which usually means a long line of passengers searching their pockets for the right amounts in the right currencies.

Boat

There is an occasional passenger ferry service from Libreville but the schedule is erratic; ask at the port in São Tomé or check at the offices at Port Môle in Libreville.

GETTING AROUND

Air

There are several flights a week between São Tomé and the island of Príncipe. Round-trip fares are about US$130.

Car

Rental cars are available from several spots in town, including Mistral Voyages (see p476), and with some bargaining you can get a jeep for around US$45 per day. This isn't a bad deal if you're planning to explore the island's hidden beaches.

In theory, a home-country driver's licence is required. In practice, cars are often rented out without checking licences and without insurance.

Hitching

Hitching is never entirely safe, and the usual common sense should be used when accepting rides. However, travellers sticking out their hand on the side of the road will have no trouble finding rides.

Local Transport

Taxis and moto-taxis are all around the Mercado Municipal in São Tomé. Rates are negotiable and very reasonable. In addition, taxi buses leave in the mornings for towns all over the island.

SÃO TOMÉ

The capital is São Tomé, on the island of the same name. It's a sleepy little town of fading Portuguese colonial buildings and shady parks facing the beach and the bay. All activity is in and around the Mercado Municipal, especially in the morning and at sunset.

ORIENTATION

The airport is about 4km north of town. Taxis meet all incoming flights, and you should be able to negotiate a fee of around US$5 to hotels in town (US$2 to US$3 from town out to the airport). The town itself curves along a sandy bay, so if you get lost just head for the water and you'll be able to orient yourself. Most hotels and shops are in a few compact blocks around the Mercado Municipal.

INFORMATION

Internet Access

There are a couple Internet cafés in town; the best is Café & Companhia, which has good Internet connection for US$3.25 an hour. They also serve sandwiches and snacks for around US$2 and have a full bar.

Medical Services

Medical services are quite limited. There's a hospital on the hill between town and the airport, but most serious cases are flown to Libreville, Gabon.

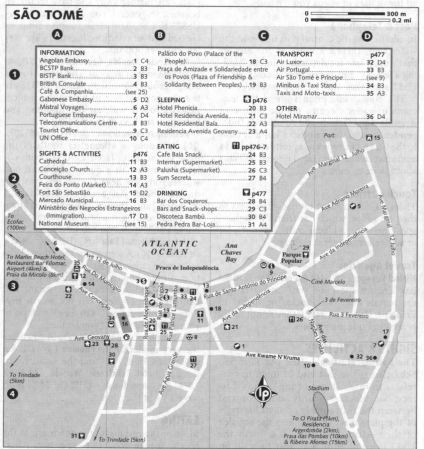

SÃO TOMÉ

0 ___ 300 m
0 ___ 0.2 mi

INFORMATION
Angolan Embassy.....................1 C4
BCSTP Bank..............................2 B3
BISTP Bank...............................3 B3
British Consulate.......................4 B3
Café & Companhia...............(see 25)
Gabonese Embassy....................5 D2
Mistral Voyages........................6 A3
Portuguese Embassy..................7 D4
Telecommunications Centre 8 B3
Tourist Office............................9 C3
UN Office 10 C4

SIGHTS & ACTIVITIES   p476
Cathedral................................11 B3
Conceição Church...................12 A3
Courthouse.............................13 B3
Feira do Ponto (Market)...........14 A3
Fort São Sebastião...................15 D2
Mercado Municipal..................16 B3
Ministério des Negocios Estrangeiros
(Immigration)........................17 D3
National Museum.................(see 15)

Palácio do Povo (Palace of the
People)..................................18 C3
Praça de Amizade e Solidariedade entre
os Povos (Plaza of Friendship &
Solidarity Between Peoples)....19 B3

SLEEPING   p476
Hotel Phenicia.........................20 B3
Hotel Residencia Avenida.........21 C3
Hotel Residential Baía..............22 A3
Residencia Avenida Geovany....23 A4

EATING   pp476–7
Cafe Baia Snack.......................24 B3
Intermar (Supermarket)............25 B3
Palusha (Supermarket).............26 A3
Sum Secreta.............................27 B4

DRINKING   p477
Bar dos Coqueiros...................28 B4
Bars and Snack-shops..............29 C3
Discoteca Bambú.....................30 B4
Pedra Pedra Bar-Loja................31 A4

TRANSPORT   p477
Air Luxor..................................32 D4
Air Portugal.............................33 B3
Air São Tomé e Príncipe.........(see 9)
Minibus & Taxi Stand................34 B3
Taxis and Moto-taxis................35 A3

OTHER
Hotel Miramar.........................36 D4

ATLANTIC
OCEAN

Ana
Chaves
Bay

Praça de Independência

Port

Ave Marginal 12 Julho

Ave Adriano Moreira

Ave Marginal 12 Julho

Parque
Popular

Ave da Independência

Ciné Marcelo

Ave 12 de Julho

Rua Do Municipio

Ave Conceição

Ave Geovany

Rua de Moçambique

Rua de Angola

Rua Patrice Lumumba

Rua de Santo António do Príncipe

Ave da Independência

3 de Fevereiro

Rua 3 Fevereiro

Rua Água Grande

Ave das Nações Unidas

Ave Kwame N'Kruma

Stadium

To
Ecofac
(100m)

To Marlin Beach Hotel,
Restaurant Bar Filomar,
Airport (4km) &
Praia da Micolo (8km)

To Trindade
(5km)

To Trindade (5km)

To O Pirata (1km),
Residencia
Argentimba (2km),
Praia das Pombas (10km)
& Ribeira Afonso (15km)

SÃO TOMÉ & PRÍNCIPE

Money

The main banks in town, BISTP and BCSTP, change dollars and euros (cash gets good rates; travellers cheques attract transaction fees). There are licensed money-changers in and around the Mercado Municipal who are open later than the banks and will change dollars and euros (cash or travellers cheques) for nearly the same rates as the banks, without all the waiting in line. Credit cards are useless except at the high-end hotels.

Travellers coming from mainland West or Central Africa should be aware that CFA francs are not accepted at banks, shops or hotels and can only be changed for very poor rates at the Mercado Municipal; bring all the dollars or euros you'll need.

Post & Telephone

In addition to the central post office on the waterfront, there's a kiosk at the airport that's open late for departing flights. Mailing a letter to Europe or the US costs about US$1 and takes only a couple weeks.

The only public phones are at the telecommunications centre on the corner of Avenida Aqua Grande and Avenida da Independencia, and they're often all in use. Calls to the US and Europe are a pretty steep US$4 a minute; calling from hotel phones will cost about twice as much.

Tourist Offices

There's a government tourist office next to the post office, which has friendly English-speaking staff and local crafts, but not a lot of advice for budget travellers.

Travel Agencies

Mistral Voyages (☎ 23344; Rua Padre Pinto da Rocha) has English-speaking staff and arranges car rentals and tours, including flights to Príncipe. However, again, they're not really geared to budget travellers.

SIGHTS & ACTIVITIES

The **National Museum** in the old Fort São Sebastião at the east end of town has artefacts from all stages of the islands' history, but it focuses mainly on the contrast between the ridiculously opulent lifestyles of the plantation owners and the squalor of their African workers. It's worth the US$3 price of admission just to walk on the ramparts of the old fort and catch the views of town.

The **Mercado Municipal** is a crowded, noisy, smelly adventure where you can have a great time without buying anything. It's a big change of pace from the islands' usual laid-back tranquillity.

There are no organised bicycle hire shops, but locals will rent out bicycles for around US$10 a day. Bikes are a great way to explore the outskirts of town, but once you get away from the ocean the roads become very steep very fast.

SLEEPING

Most of the budget hotels are in the centre of town, whereas the more expensive places are further away and have their own beaches. In general, you can expect to pay US$25 to US$30 for clean rooms with double bed and air conditioning; there are very few cheaper options.

Residencia Avenida Geovany (☎ 23929; fax 21709; Ave Geovany; r US$15-35) The stuffy rooms on the ground floor with fan for US$15 are the cheapest options in town. Much nicer upstairs rooms with air conditioning and balconies are US$25 to US$35.

Residencia Argentimoa (☎ 21941; s/d US$25/35; ✗) A couple of kilometres south of the town centre, this place has rooms with colonial furniture in a quiet neighbourhood where you can hear the waves crashing on the shore. An excellent breakfast is included, and there's a nightclub down the road, making it worth the extra couple bucks you'll spend on cab fare.

Hotel Residential Baía (☎ 21155; Ave Conceição 4; s/d US$30/55; ✗) A step above the other places in its price range, the Baía has a central location, air-con rooms with TV, bathtub and balconies, and an excellent restaurant and bar. Breakfast is great, but not worth anything near the extra US$10 they'll tack on to your room bill for it if you let them.

A couple of the nicer hotels in town are the very modern **Hotel Phenicia** (☎ 24203; Rua de Angola; r US$50-65; ✗) and the smaller, but homier **Hotel Residencia Avenida** (☎ 23912, 22368; Ave Independencia; r US$50-65; ✗). Both have TVs in the rooms.

EATING

Most of the restaurants in town are at the hotels; they're good but expensive. Alternatively, all over town you'll find bars and *petisquieras* (little bakeries selling filled pastries, ice cream and other small treats); there's a whole row of them on the east side of the Parque Popular. The area in front of the Mercado Municipal is good for cheap street food like fish and rice or the very popular sausage sandwiches.

Hotel Residential Baía (☎ 21155; Ave Conceição 4; mains US$6-7) One of the best places to eat in town. Considering that everything comes loaded with vegetables and side dishes and is easily enough food for two people, it's quite a deal. They'll also cook up traditional island dishes if you ask a day or so in advance.

O Pirata (☎ 90 45 15) Right on the beach road, about a kilometre south of the town centre, this is a classic pirate bar, complete with Jolly Roger flag flying high. Fresh fish goes for about US$5, and there's a full bar.

Restaurant Bar Filomar (☎ 21908; mains US$7) On the road to the airport, the Filomar is one of the most popular spots for seafood and cold drinks on a terrace overlooking the bay.

Café Baia Snack (Ave Aqua Grande) A decent snack bar with coffee, ice cream and pastries, and sea breezes off the bay.

Sum Secreta (Ave Kwame N'Kruma) A popular spot for ice cream and/or cold drinks where you can watch the kids play soccer at the school next door.

SPLURGE!

Marlin Beach Hotel, about 3km from town on the road north towards the airport, has European cuisine in a fairly formal setting. You can eat well for around US$10, and there are a lot more choices than the 'chicken-or-fish' menu found at most other spots.

DRINKING

São Tomé has a number of small hole-in-the-wall bars where (mostly) men drink boxes of imported wine or the local beer, Creola. Foreign women without male drinking companions will attract attention but usually no hassles.

Nightlife is pretty much nonexistent. Bars generally close early, and the few clubs in town aren't exactly hopping.

Bar dos Coquieros (Ave Geovany) has second-floor balcony tables that are good for people-watching, whereas Pedra Pedra Bar-Loja takes things in the other direction with a popular and very secluded basement bar.

Discoteca Bambú is one of the few in-town options for dancing, and it's small enough to feel busy with just a few people on the floor. South of town, down a side road behind the Residencia Argentimoa, the Club Argentimoa has an open-air disco with all the lights and effects you could ask for, but there's not a lot of dancing going on until late.

SHOPPING

The Mercado Municipal is *the* place in town for everything from fresh spices, fruits and fish to the usual cheap-quality clothes, kitchenware and appliances imported from Europe.

Somewhat surprisingly, the vendors who set up across from the ultra-fancy Hotel Miramar have the best prices on local handicrafts (after some bargaining, of course).

GETTING THERE & AWAY

Buses and taxis for other parts of the island leave from around the Mercado Municipal. Buses, with fixed rates of less than US$1 all the way to Neves or Ribiera Afonso, leave early (before 11am). Taxis are unmetered and you'll need to bargain.

AROUND SÃO TOMÉ

The town of São Tomé is a pleasant place to have lunch or spend the day walking around, but you'll have to venture a bit further for the island's real attractions: beaches, rainforests, reclaimed run-down plantations and the strange remnants of extinct volcanoes, which look like huge pillars, some of which rise 600m straight up out of the jungle. The whole coast is ringed with beautiful, deserted beaches of white sand, palm trees and turquoise water.

NORTH OF SÃO TOMÉ

Along the road north from the capital there is some stunning scenery but not too many good beaches. The road loops around and follows the west coast until it peters out in dense jungle just past Santa Catarina. There are minibuses every two to three hours

SÃO TOMÉ & PRÍNCIPE

WARNING

São Toméans are quick to point out how safe their island is, and it's true; you can walk around safely at night and expect no hassles. But it's possible to feel too safe. We've had several reports of break-ins of rental cars, usually on supposedly deserted beaches while the renters are camping or snorkelling nearby. Don't leave your valuables unguarded, and don't assume there's no-one around.

from São Tomé to Guadalupe. There's little traffic and hitching can be slow.

Go past Guadalupe to **Praia das Conchas** and **Praia dos Tamarindos**, both secluded beaches, a short walk off the road and on to **Lagoa Azul** (Blue Lagoon), where there is excellent snorkelling but only a rocky beach. The surrounding giant baobab trees are home to numerous species of birds.

From Lagoa Azul, you can continue to **Neves**, where there's a nice restaurant with cheap fish near the petrol station.

SOUTH OF SÃO TOMÉ

Taking the road south along the east coast will bring you to some of the island's best beaches. **Praia das Sete Ondas** is about 12km south of town and **Praia Grande** is a couple of kilometres south. However, almost any side road towards the ocean will bring you to a scenic and secluded beach; ask locals about where to go. Also worth seeing is the spectacular blowhole, **Boca de Inferno**, near Praia das Sete Ondas.

Minibuses to **São João dos Angolares** (US$2, 2½ hours) leave in the morning from near the market in São Tomé. Get off just before the town for the **Roça São João** (☎ 61140; s/d US$18/25), an old plantation that now operates as a cultural centre and guesthouse. It's a rambling, slightly run-down place with a bit of a haunted house feeling at night, and it's pretty damn romantic if you're into candlelight and mosquito nets. Large, colonial-style rooms open on to the surrounding balcony. There's a restaurant that specialises in island cuisine, and guides are available for excursions into the surrounding forests. The *roça* (plantation) is also the place where São Tomé's few independent travellers gather to laze around in hammocks and share stories.

From here you can head south to **Porto Alegre**, a dingy fishing village at the southern end of the island, where you can catch a motorised pirogue (dugout canoe, US$5) to **Ilhéu das Rolas**, a small islet off the coast that straddles the equator. It's an amazingly beautiful little island, home to the very upscale dive resort Equator's Line (see the boxed text opposite). If you're up for a splurge (like a US$33 lunch!) you can eat here and enjoy the beach, and they'll provide boat transport to and from their private dock north of Porto Alegre.

WEST OF SÃO TOMÉ

The road that runs southwest from the capital winds through coffee plantations, ramshackle villages and lush vegetation. It is also the way to Ecofac's forest research station at **Bom Successo** and the start of numerous walks into the national park.

Trindade is a pleasant little town from where you can continue to the well-known waterfall **Cascadas da São Nicolau** and the coffee plantation at **Monte Cafe**, an interesting place where coffee is still dried the same way it was a hundred years ago.

There are buses every two to three hours from São Tomé to Trindade (around US$2), or you can hitch. If you're hitching, stop on the edge of Trindade at the Bar Diamantina. To get to the waterfall hitch up past Monte Cafe to Pousada Boa Vista farm, then take the track on the right past the La Pousada da Boa Vista hotel. After about 3km you'll come across the Cascadas da São Nicolau.

PRÍNCIPE

Smaller and less populated than São Tomé, little Príncipe is a one-town island. Some small roads that lead into the interior are ideal for biking or hiking. The centre of action is the very upscale Bom Bom Island Resort (see the boxed text opposite) off the northern end of the island, which has brought improved infrastructure (between the resort and the airport) and some very well-off tourists. There is excellent snorkelling and fishing all around the island, and locals will negotiate renting boats or bikes or guiding you on pretty much any other kind of tour you want.

THE BIG DEEP SPLURGE

If you get yourself all the way to São Tomé and Príncipe, you owe it to yourself to get under the water. Unfortunately, this isn't easy to do on a shoestring budget.

Good snorkelling is possible all around the islands, and if you bring your own gear you avoid the high rental fees at local hotels. Those planning to do a lot of snorkelling should look into renting a car, as getting to and (especially) back from secluded beaches via public transport is unreliable.

There are only two options for scuba diving, both at very upscale resorts on opposite ends of the islands: Equator's Line on Ilhéu das Rolas off the southern tip of São Tomé and Bom Bom Island Resort off the north of Príncipe. Staying at Equator's Line is outside the price range of budget travellers at US$136/238 for a single/double room, and Bom Bom is outside the price range of normal human beings (US$270 a day for accommodation and US$500 to US$700 a day for sport fishing). However, both offer dive packages for around US$40 for a one-tank dive and US$190 for a five-dive package, and both offer NAUI certification classes.

On Príncipe you can easily stay at a cheap *pensão* and get to the resort for diving. On São Tomé it's probably best to rent a car, so you could stay somewhere like the Roça São João (see opposite) and get down to the boat launch for Ilhéu das Rolas in the morning.

SANTO ANTÓNIO

The island's capital is Santo António, which is about the size of a large European village. The architecture is similar to that of São Tomé town but more run-down.

Sleeping & Eating

Príncipe has a number of cheap pensãos which are ideal for budget travellers. Two of the best and most popular are Pensão Arca de Noé and Pensão Romar, both with restaurants and rooms for a negotiable rate of around US$8. The more expensive Pensão Residencial Palhota has a good restaurant as well.

Getting There & Away

For information on getting there and away, please see p474.

SÃO TOMÉ & PRÍNCIPE DIRECTORY

ACCOMMODATION

There are hotels in the towns charging US$25 to US$65; *roças* and *pensãos* outside towns are cheaper, as low as US$8 to US$10.

ACTIVITIES

Bikes are available for rent from locals around the islands – ask around. Snorkelling and diving are excellent, and the water is clear.

BUSINESS HOURS

Businesses and small shops close around noon for long siestas and might not reopen until 4pm in the afternoon or later.

DANGERS & ANNOYANCES

The islands are very safe by African standards, but unattended rental cars are broken into sometimes.

DISABLED TRAVELLERS

Modern hotels are wheelchair-accessible and can provide assistance for disabled travellers; older buildings are not disabled-friendly.

EMBASSIES & CONSULATES

The following countries have embassies or consulates in São Tomé:

Angola (☎ 22376; Ave Kwame N'Kruma)
Gabon (☎ 21280; Rua Damão)
Portugal (☎ 21130; Ave Marginal 12 Julho)
UK (☎ 21026; Praça de Independência)
USA (☎ 21814; c/o UN office, Ave Kwame N'Kruma)

São Tomé and Príncipe has diplomatic representation in both Gabon and Equatorial Guinea.

FESTIVALS & EVENTS

Independence Day celebrated across the islands on 12 July. Mardi Gras (Tuesday before Lent) is also a big party.

FOOD & DRINK

The island produces great fresh fruit and coffee. Local shops called *petisquieras* sell small baked goods, ice cream and cold drinks.

HOLIDAYS

Public holidays in São Tomé and Príncipe include:

1 January New Year's Day
March/April Good Friday, Holy Saturday and Easter Monday
1 May International Worker's Day
12 July Independence Day
25 December Christmas Day

INTERNET ACCESS

There are two Internet cafés in São Tomé town; they charge US$3 to US$4 per hour.

LEGAL MATTERS

Visitors should encounter no problems, no checkpoints, and helpful police if needed.

MAPS

A decent map of the islands is available for US$5 at hotels and tourist offices.

MEDIA

Local radio is in Portuguese and mixes local news with Afro-Portuguese music. Television is either Portuguese or African French, usually news or variety shows. The fancy hotels have satellite TV with CNN and other channels in English.

MONEY

There are no ATMs on the islands. Credit cards (Mastercard and Visa) are accepted only at the high-end hotels. Euros and US dollars, in cash or as travellers cheques, are widely accepted at hotels, shops and restaurants, and can be changed at banks and at moneychangers at the Mercado Municipal.

PHOTOGRAPHY

Film and photographic equipment are difficult to find outside São Tomé town, so bring what you'll need.

POST & TELEPHONE

The central post office is open during business hours unless they decide to go home early. Letters to the US or Europe cost about US$1.

Public telephones are available at the telecommunications centre in São Tomé and in some larger towns. They take prepaid phonecards.

RESPONSIBLE TRAVEL

Many craft shops sell souvenirs made of shells and coral and even turtle shell. However, if you buy them you will be contributing to the harvesting of these resources, and you might be arrested if you try to bring them into your country anyway.

TOURIST INFORMATION

Check the tourist information office or Mistral Voyages in São Tomé town (p476).

TOURS

Ecofac (☎ 23284), which has an office in town, and the **Roça São João** (☎ 61140) in São João dos Angolares both organise day hikes in the rainforest and to abandoned plantations.

These companies employ locals who have an excellent understanding of the islands' ecosystem and are definitely recommended.

VISAS

Visas are required by all and are available at the airport for US$50. They are valid for 30 days.

Visa Extensions

Visa extensions are available at the Immigration Ministry on Ave Marginal 12 de Julio near the Hotel Miramar in São Tomé.

Visas for Onward Travel

Visas for Gabon are available from the embassy in São Tomé (see p479 for address details). A 30-day tourist visa costs around US$50 and takes two to three days to issue.

Gabon

HIGHLIGHTS

- **Lambaréné** Island city with pirogue trips to visit wildlife-rich lakes region and Albert Schweitzer's jungle hospital (p491)
- **Mayumba** Untouristed beach town with great swimming, exploring, eating and relaxing possibilities (p492)
- **Réserve de la Lopé** Gabon's No 1 wildlife park, with elephants, buffalos and monkeys, and if you're lucky, forest walks to see the gorillas (p492)
- **Off the beaten track** Camping at the Cirque de Leconi, a spectacular red-rock canyon on the Bateke Plateau (p492)

FAST FACTS

- **Area** 257,670 sq km (about half the size of Spain)
- **ATMs** available in major cities
- **Borders** Equatorial Guinea, Cameroon and Congo
- **Budget** US$50 per day in Libreville, US$30 per day in the interior
- **Capital** Libreville
- **Languages** French, Fang, Bapunu, Geshira, Banjabi and other local languages
- **Money** Central African CFA ; US$1 = CFA600
- **Population** 1.2 million
- **Seasons** wet (Sep–May), dry (Jun–Aug)
- **Telephone** country code ☎ 241; international access code ☎ 00
- **Time** GMT/UTC + 1
- **Visas** required by all; must be acquired before arrival

Gabon has a lot to offer – outside the glitzy, air-conditioned capital city, Libreville, it's a laid-back, friendly country of small villages, steamy, dense rainforest, wide roaring rivers and imposing mountains. One of the richest and most stable countries in Africa, Gabon is a country in no hurry to get anything done, a place where people know the value of relaxation.

The jungle is full of the African wildlife travellers dream animals – elephants, leopards, gorillas, hippos, pythons and much more – but it takes some serious effort to find them. Fortunately, a new bunch of national parks is opening up the forest to ecotourism – and closing it to loggers.

The few travellers who do get here are usually passing through quickly on their way somewhere else, which is a shame. Gabon is a place that rewards patience. The longer you stay here, the more you'll find to explore and to like.

HISTORY

An African success story since independence in 1960, Gabon has avoided the coups, wars and poverty that have plagued the rest of the continent. Since the discovery of oil in the 1970s, it has been one of the richest countries in sub-Saharan Africa.

Early Inhabitants

Gabon appears to have been populated originally by Pygmies, whose descendants survive today only in the remote north of the country. The Pygmies were displaced between the 16th and 18th centuries by migrating peoples from the north, principally the Fang, who came from what are now Cameroon and Equatorial Guinea.

Contact with Europeans, starting with the arrival of the Portuguese in 1472, set in motion a train of events that had a profound effect on tribal social structures. British, Dutch and French ships called in along the coast regularly to trade for slaves, ivory and precious tropical woods. The coastal tribes established strong trading ties, but the tribes in the interior tried to protect their lands from European encroachment. Animosity still lingers between the coastal tribes and the rest of the country.

The capital, Libreville, was established in 1849 by freed slaves on an estuary popular with traders. From 1886 it was the capital of the French Congo until Brazzaville (Congo) became the capital in 1888.

Six years later Gabon became a territory of French Equatorial Africa.

Independent Daze

The country became independent in 1960 under the presidency of Léon M'Ba, who died in a French hospital in 1967. He was succeeded by the recently appointed vice president, Albert Bernard Bongo.

The newly independent nation got off to an extravagant start. With the money rolling in from the sale of oil, manganese ore, iron ore, chrome, gold and diamonds, the country sported a per capita income higher than that of South Africa and only slightly lower than that of Libya.

In 1976 an ambitious four-year plan with a budget of US$32 billion was announced. It aimed to create a modern transport system, encourage local industry and develop mineral deposits. Unfortunately, most of this money was squandered on misguided projects.

The downturn in the country's earnings did not prevent the completion of the US$140 million presidential palace, or the staging of one of the most extravagant Organisation of African Unity (OAU) summits ever held or ever likely to be held again.

Gabon has been ruled since 1967 by President El Hadj Omar Bongo (who changed his name when he adopted Islam in 1974). With a personal bodyguard composed of European mercenaries and Moroccan soldiers, 400 top-notch airborne troops from France, as well as numerous French political and military advisers, Bongo has been able to project a remarkable image of stability for the country.

From 1968 the country was a one-party state, and very lucrative ministerial posts were frequently shuffled between a small number of political faithfuls. However, in 1990, in response to the country's first real political unrest, Bongo ended more than two decades of one-party rule by legalising opposition parties. Today, the 120-seat elected National Assembly has acquired genuine political power and diversity, although it remains dominated by Bongo's ruling party, the Democratic Party of Gabon (PDG).

Allegations of massive government corruption continue, most recently in the trial of top executives of the Elf oil company, which caused a scandal in France but raised few eyebrows in Gabon, where they've seen it all before. Despite this, it's undeniable that Gabon has been an oasis of stability and prosperity in a very troubled region for more than 40 years.

THE CULTURE

With oil money continuing to roll in, and a small population enjoying one of the highest per-capita income rates in Africa, the Gabonese are living pretty easy. Even in tiny remote villages you won't find the kind of poverty seen in other parts of Africa. Everyone in Gabon has enough money for beer, and that's just what they spend it on. It's a bar culture, with endless arguments all day followed by the dancing the night away. Women are allowed to join in, but only after the wood is gathered, the food is prepared and the rest of the work is done.

If you're in a hurry to go somewhere or get anything done it's a frustratingly slow country. But if you just want to relax in the rainforest and drink and talk and drink and talk, Gabon is the place for it.

ARTS

Gabon has produced a number of musicians and groups who are big names in the Central African music scene; Oliver N'goma is probably the hottest Gabonese artist going now.

University students and other young people are very fond of writing and performing plays, usually morality tales, which are aired often on Gabonese TV and radio. They can be entertaining even if you don't speak much French.

ENVIRONMENT

Except for the far south, which is savanna, and the very far east around Franceville, which is savanna and high plateau, the country is made up of deep, dense, hot and sticky rainforest. Heavy logging is going on all over the place, but vast amounts of jungle remain. Wildlife, including gorillas, chimpanzees, forest elephants, leopards, hippos, antelopes and a lot more, is abundant but rarely seen in the thick forest. Trade in bushmeat and endangered species is a growing problem as new roads bring logging operations deeper into previously untouched jungle.

The good news is that President Bongo recently announced that 10% of the country will be set aside to form a system of national parks and protected areas. This is still in the early stages, but it's hoped that ecotourism can take the place of logging revenues. For more information check out the website gabonnationalparks.com.

TRANSPORT

GETTING THERE & AWAY
Air
Gabon is linked to most major cities in West and Central Africa by Air Gabon and other regional airlines. Libreville's Léon M'Ba Airport has daily flights to and from Abidjan, Brazzaville, Douala, Lagos, São Tomé and Johannesburg, among others. Travellers coming from outside Africa usually find it much cheaper to fly to a nearby country and travel on from there than to fly directly to Libreville from Paris or London, for example.

DEPARTURE TAX

There is no official departure tax, but you might be asked for 'a little something' by the immigration control.

Boat & Land
Occasionally you can find a passenger ferry service from Libreville to Cameroon, São Tomé, Benin and Togo for around US$60. Check around at Port Mole in Libreville for details. There are no organised bus lines between Gabon and neighbouring countries, so travel is by bush taxi and it's common to get stranded somewhere for a day or two.

CAMEROON
Travellers to and from Cameroon cross at the Ntem River between Bitam (Gabon) and Ambam (Cameroon). From the town of Ebolowa in Cameroon there's a regular bus service to Yaoundé and Douala. The trip between Libreville and Yaoundé can be done in three days and costs around US$80.

CONGO
The main crossing to Congo is via N'Dendé to Loubomo (Congo), where you connect with the Pointe Noitre to Brazzaville railway. Other land crossings to Congo are frequently closed; check before you get all the way out there.

EQUATORIAL GUINEA
The main routes to Equatorial Guinea are from Cocobeach, north of Libreville, to Acalayong (Equatorial Guinea) in a motorised pirogue (traditional canoe) across the estuary; or on a very rough road between Bitam (Gabon) and Ebebiyin (Equatorial Guinea). Via Cocobeach, it's possible to get from Libreville to Bata in two days for about US$35, the Bitam route is considerably longer, depending on the condition of the roads.

GETTING AROUND
Air
Air Gabon flies between all the major cities including Libreville, Oyem, Franceville and Port Gentil. Flights can be expensive, around US$100, but student discounts are often available.

Boat
There is passenger boat transport between Lambaréné and Port Gentil and between Port Gentil and Libreville.

Local Transport
Most travel outside Libreville is by bush taxi, usually an overloaded minibus or a ridiculously overloaded pick-up truck. There are no organised bus lines.

THE FUN OF FLYING AIR GABON

Air Gabon has a well-deserved reputation for lateness. Delays of up to six hours are common, and frequently after a long wait passengers are told: 'No flight today, come back tomorrow.' The most frustrating aspect of this is that airport staff won't tell you what's happening. If you politely ask when the plane is coming, you'll be politely told 'in an hour' or 'soon'. This is, of course, not true. But there's nothing you can do about it; you're still expected to show up early for check-in (if you show up at flight time you'll be told the flight's closed, even if it's six hours away). So you wait, and get to know your fellow passengers with that eternal Air Gabon airport lounge conversation starter, 'When do you think the plane will come?'

GABON

Train

The Transgabonaise train line runs through the centre of the country from Owendo, just south of Libreville, to Franceville in the east. If you're crossing the country train travel is a lot cheaper and faster than taking bush taxis. It's also the best way to get to the Réserve de la Lopé. The train schedule changes often and is printed in the newspaper *l'Union*. First-class (definitely worth the extra few dollars, 2nd-class is crushingly overcrowded) from Libreville to the end of the line in Franceville is about US$60 one way, US$40 to Lopé.

LIBREVILLE

Glitzy and glamorous in some spots, ramshackle and anarchic in others, Libreville is very likely to give you culture shock, especially if you've been slogging your way through the jungles of Central Africa. High-rise hotels line the beaches, European expats fill the shops and restaurants, and flashy cars speed down the wide boulevards. Meanwhile on the other side of town garbage is piled high and traffic slows to a crawl in the narrow, noisy streets.

It's a great place to stock up, resupply or just get a quick fix of the comforts you've been missing: car parts, cheeseburgers, quality clothes, English-language books and magazines, Vietnamese food, French wine and all the other comforts of home, all at imported-from-France prices. Libreville has everything you could ask for, at a price you probably can't afford.

But don't despair, you just have to look harder to find something affordable. The beach is free, and in the less ritzy parts of town you'll find snack bars and street food stands where a filling lunch will cost only a few dollars and a big beer is about US$0.60. If you explore a little and resign yourself to spending too much once in a while, Libreville can be a great diversion from the hassles of travel.

ORIENTATION

The airport is about 5km north of town. Taxi drivers will try to charge you big bucks, but you can walk across the parking lot, cross the highway and flag down a cab for about half the price (around US$3.50).

The train station is 8km south of Libreville; taxis meet the train and the fare to town is around US$8.

Bush taxis and minibuses coming from the interior will often drop you off at or near any address in town; make sure you're not paying extra for this service. Otherwise they stop at Marché Banane 8, 8km east of the centre of town, where you catch a cab.

Libreville is a big maze of a city, divided by major boulevards and ringed by the Voie Express freeway. Blvd de l'Indépendence runs along the seafront in the heart of the city. Blvd Omar Bongo runs through the middle of the city and passes by some of the most, um, unique oversized architectural experiments you'll ever see. The highest concentration of restaurants and nightspots is in Quartier Louis.

If you want to get to the shops in the city, just ask any taxi driver for 'la poste' and he'll drop you at the central post office.

The best beaches are north of the city, towards and past the airport.

INFORMATION
Bookshops

There are newsstands all over town. The larger ones, usually found in the indoor malls, have English-language books and magazines as well as maps and guidebooks.

Internet Access

There are Internet cafés all over Libreville, which charge around US$2 per hour to surf the web. One of the best and most convenient is **Club Internet Bord de Mer** (Blvd de l'Indépendence; 8am-10 or 11pm) across from Port Mole.

Media

The daily pro-government paper is *l'Union*, in French. There are a number of other papers with different political slants, all also in French.

Libreville is also the home of Central Africa's most popular (and jamming) radio station, Africa No 1, which broadcasts music and news throughout the region.

Medical Services

The most highly recommended of Libreville's medical centres is **Fondation Jeanne Ebori** (732771; Blvd Georges Pompidou) across from Port Mole in Quartier Louis.

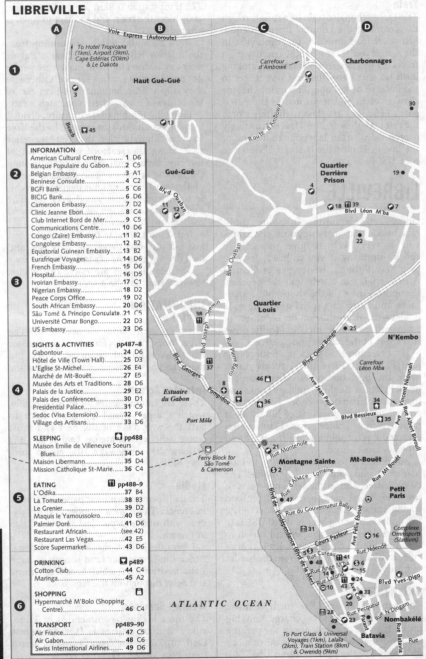

LIBREVILLE

INFORMATION

American Cultural Centre	1	D6
Banque Populaire du Gabon	2	C5
Belgian Embassy	3	A1
Beninese Consulate	4	C2
BGFI Bank	5	C6
BICIG Bank	6	D6
Cameroon Embassy	7	D2
Clinic Jeanne Ebori	8	C4
Club Internet Bord de Mer	9	C5
Communications Centre	10	D6
Congo (Zaïre) Embassy	11	B2
Congolese Embassy	12	B2
Equatorial Guinean Embassy	13	B2
Eurafrique Voyages	14	D6
French Embassy	15	D6
Hospital	16	D5
Ivoirian Embassy	17	C1
Nigerian Embassy	18	D2
Peace Corps Office	19	D2
South African Embassy	20	D6
São Tomé & Príncipe Consulate	21	C5
Université Omar Bongo	22	D3
US Embassy	23	D6

SIGHTS & ACTIVITIES	**pp487–8**	
Gabontour	24	D6
Hôtel de Ville (Town Hall)	25	D3
L'Eglise St-Michel	26	E4
Marché de Mt-Bouët	27	E5
Musée des Arts et Traditions	28	D6
Palais de la Justice	29	E2
Palais des Conférences	30	D1
Presidential Palace	31	C5
Sedoc (Visa Extensions)	32	F6
Village des Artisans	33	D6

SLEEPING	**pp488**	
Maison Emilie de Villeneuve Soeurs Blues	34	D4
Maison Libermann	35	D4
Mission Catholique St-Marie	36	C4

EATING	**pp488–9**	
L'Odika	37	B4
La Tomate	38	B3
Le Grenier	39	D2
Maquis le Yamoussokro	40	E5
Palmier Doré	41	D6
Restaurant Africain	(see 42)	
Restaurant Las Vegas	42	E5
Score Supermarket	43	D6

DRINKING	**p489**	
Cotton Club	44	C4
Maringa	45	A2

SHOPPING		
Hypermarché M'Bolo (Shopping Centre)	46	C4

TRANSPORT	**pp489–90**	
Air France	47	C5
Air Gabon	48	C6
Swiss International Airlines	49	D6

GABON

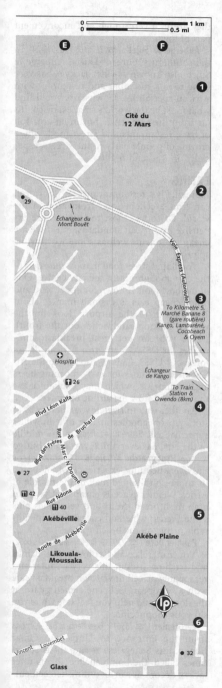

Money
Banks in Libreville will change cash and travellers cheques. For a better rate, here and around the country, find one of the many Lebanese merchants and ask discreetly about changing cash (they like to send money home in high-denomination US banknotes).

In central Libreville the BGFI bank has a money-changing office and a Visa-linked ATM, good for getting funds from home and conveniently located next to the new casino.

Post & Telephone
The main post office is in the heart of the city on Blvd de l'Indépendence.

Telephone offices are all over town, some advertising international calls. Make sure you get the rates up front or you could be in for an enormous shock when you get the bill.

Tourist Offices
The government tourist office, **Gabontour** (☎ 728504; Ave Col Parant), has a city office and staff who speak a little English. Most of their information is geared towards people with some money to spend on big tours.

Travel Agencies
Libreville has several reliable travel agencies, usually specialising in pricey arrangements for wealthy Gabonese and French business types but also helpful for travellers looking to book plane tickets.
Eurafrique Voyages (☎ 762787) Good for plane tickets to other countries.
Universal Voyages (☎ 724191) Specialises in tours of Gabon's national parks.

DANGERS & ANNOYANCES
Libreville is not a particularly safe city, especially at night, and 'insecurity' is the hot topic of the day. Taxi crime is a serious problem – everything from pick pocketing in crowded back seats to armed robbery with the driver's complicity. At night it's worth your while to find an empty cab and hire it for yourself (called a *course*).

SIGHTS
The **Musée des Arts et Traditions** (Blvd de l'Indépendence), in the former Elf Gabon building, has an interesting collection of Gabonese

masks and other artefacts, plus a re-creation of a traditional village house. It's a quick tour, and a small donation is expected.

The **Village des Artisans** (Ave Col Parant) is a fun place to wander and check out African art, but most of the goods (and the merchants) are imports. If you're going to be travelling in other African countries you'll find much better prices for the same stuff.

On weekends all of Libreville heads to the **beach** to swim, eat, drink, flirt and play a little football; it's a great opportunity for people-watching while relaxing in the sun.

SLEEPING

There's no shortage of very average, non-descript hotels, most in Quartier Louis, all charging around US$35/45 single/double – way beyond most backpacker budgets. And the fancy international chain hotels along the beach charge unreasonable amounts (more than US$100) for standard rooms. But don't panic – there are a few cheaper alternatives.

Mission Catholique St-Marie (Blvd Omar Bongo; dm US$12) Next to the church across from Port Môle, the mission has dormitory beds in a convenient location.

Maison Emilie de Villeneuve Soeurs Blues (☎ 747617; Blvd Bessieux; r US$12) and **Maison Libermann** (☎ 761955; Blvd Bessieux; r US$12) Directly opposite each other, these two Catholic missions are friendly, clean, quiet and comfortable, and have hot showers. However,

they are in a very rough and inconvenient part of town.

Auberge le Sujet (☎ 762646; r US$15-24) In the southern suburb of Lalala, Auberge le Sujet, also known as Chez Jacky's, has very basic rooms and a bar and restaurant with African specialities. Downstairs you'll find what must be the world's smallest disco. It's far from the city centre but in an area full of bars, restaurants and street food, where crowds of people party in the streets, especially on weekend nights.

EATING

Libreville is a restaurant mecca, where you can find excellent food from around the world. Of course most restaurants are expensive by African standards, but there are cheap options as well as some worthwhile splurges.

You'll find street food in most *quartiers* of the city, though not in the city centre. One of the best spots in town for street food and other cheap eats is a small market about 100m north of the airport (look for the women making sandwiches out the front), where you can get great breakfast sandwiches for US$0.75 and real African dishes for about US$3. This is also where the Air Gabon staff comes for early morning beers and arguments, which may explain a few things about how the airline operates.

Another way to stretch your budget is to stock up on goodies at one of Libreville's supermarkets. **Score** (Rue Laford), in the middle of the city, has everything you need, but go to the **Hypermarché M'bolo** (Blvd Omar Bongo) for the overwhelming experience of shopping in an air-conditioned mall in the middle of Africa. Neither place is cheap, but you can grab fresh bread, fruits and vegetables plus some French wine and cheese for a memorable picnic on the beach.

Palmier Doré (☎ 729839; Rue Cureau; snacks US$2-3) You can relax and enjoy coffee drinks and fresh pastries at this very popular and reasonably priced downtown breakfast café with a European feel. The armed guard at the door should help you feel safe while you sip your cappuccino.

Le Grenier (☎ 735619; Blvd Léon M'Ba) Across from the entrance to Université Omar Bongo, this Senegalese restaurant is sometimes called 'the bomb shelter' for its utter lack of décor – it's in an unfinished cement-

SPLURGE!

Le Tropicana (☎ 731531/32; tropicana@inet.ga; s/d US$27/41) North of town near the airport, the Tropicana's beachfront location alone makes it the winner in the budget (for Libreville) category. Rooms are nothing special, though they do have hot showers, and there's an excellent but expensive restaurant (main courses around US$10), which has outdoor thatched-roof palapa-style tables where you can have a couple of cold drinks while watching the sun set over the ocean. On weekends the beach here is the centre of Libreville's activity, and as a guest you can grab a beach chair and watch the action. The hotel is very popular with European expats and is often full; reservations are definitely recommended.

block building. Very affordable, delicious and authentic Senegalese specialities like *thiebou djenne* (US$2) or *riz poulet yassa* (US$2.75) are available to eat there or to take away. Cold soft drinks (there's no alcohol – they're Muslim) are US$0.50.

Maquis le Yamoussokro (☎ 377828; Rue Ndona) For cuisine from Côte d'Ivoire, head out to le Yamoussokro in Akébéville. It has reasonable prices and friendly staff.

Le Dakota (☎ 738984) Across from the airport, about 5km north of the city centre, Le Dakota has a menu that ranges all over, from breakfast to the best cheeseburgers in town (US$5) to overpriced African dishes (US$10). The atmosphere and location (on the highway and almost under the runway) aren't ideal, but the food makes up for it.

Among Libreville's cheaper splurges are **L'Odika** (☎ 736920; Blvd Joseph Deemin, Quartier Louis) and **La Tomate** (☎ 736477; Blvd Joseph Deemin, Quartier Louis), both with main courses around US$7. There are dozens of other restaurants in this area. Just make sure you check the prices; you might find main courses costing US$20.

SPLURGE!

Restaurant le Saigon (☎ 729842; Blvd de la Republique) The Saigon is a fun splurge for dinner, especially if you've gone a while without Vietnamese food, and it also has very affordable lunch specials that include soup, spring rolls, main course and rice for US$6.50. It's south of downtown, in Glass, across from Le Meridien Hotel.

DRINKING

You'll never have to go far to find a bar in Libreville. If the bar in your hotel is too expensive or dull, just walk down the street and see what turns up. There are 'restaurant-bars', 'bar dancings', 'snack bar-dancings' and variations on this theme everywhere. A big Regab beer typically costs around US$0.70. It's best to go with someone who knows Libreville well, if possible, or you'll never find the most happening spots. Women travellers, especially those without male company, will attract a lot of drunken attention that can get pretty annoying.

Libreville also has a number of glitzy nightclubs, full-on multistorey, mirror ball and strobe lights, dress-code–enforced clubs blasting European techno, African soukous, Caribbean zouk plus American rap and R&B. Standouts include the **Cotton Club** (Blvd Georges Pompidou; ☺ 9pm-dawn) and **Maringa** (Blvd Georges Pompidou; ☺ 9pm-dawn), both on the seafront. These places, and the others in town, are (surprise) very expensive. Entrance generally costs US$10 to US$12, more for special events. This gets you one free drink; after that all drinks are the same price as the door charge. That's right, US$12 for a small Fanta or a small beer. The real action doesn't start until 1am or so and continues until dawn.

Dancers of every race, gender and sexual orientation can expect to get hit on at these clubs. Yes, Libreville has a gay and lesbian scene, usually underground, but the dance clubs are a good place to look.

GETTING THERE & AWAY
Air
Air Gabon (☎ 779977; Rue Cureau) and several smaller airlines fly to all major Gabonese cities several times a day, including: Bitam (45 min, 11 flights a week), Franceville (one hour 20 minutes, 20 flights a week) and Oyem (45 minutes, 16 flights a week).

Flights to cities in nearby countries include: Douala, Cameroon (one hour, two Saturday, two Sunday), Malabo, Equatorial Guinea (one hour, one flight a day, no flight Wednesday), Pointe-Noire, Congo (one hour 10 minutes, eight flights a week), and São Tomé (one hour, four flights a week).

Local Transport
Buses and bush taxis to other parts of Gabon leave from Marché Banane 8, which is 8km from the city centre. Travel in the interior can be expensive, for example around US$17 from Libreville to Lambaréné or US$35 to Bitam.

Train
The train station is 8km south of the city centre in Owendo. It's worth an extra trip out there to purchase your ticket early, so you can avoid some of the chaos at boarding time.

GETTING AROUND
Libreville has a bewildering system of buses and minibuses that run various routes around the city with no destination signs or route numbers. The central hub is the

gare routière, where they leave from and eventually arrive back at. Unless you're very familiar with Libreville, it's best to stick to taxis, which are everywhere. Taxis can be flagged down and shared with other passengers (called a 'place') for about US$0.25, or you can hire it for yourself for US$1.50; prices double after nightfall.

AROUND LIBREVILLE

POINT DENIS
Point Denis is Libreville's nearest beach resort, directly across the estuary from the city. It makes a great day trip, and there are a couple new hotels and restaurants if you want to stay longer.

It's not always easy to get out to the beaches; check a day or two ahead at Port Glass south of the city for boats making the trip. Otherwise you'll have to charter one (which is way too expensive unless you can find a big group).

CAP ESTÉRIAS
For Libreville's expat community, Cap Estérias is a favourite getaway, a long stretch of beach with a couple of fancy restaurants. If you spend more than a lunch time there, however, you'll find an interesting local community and a thriving mangrove swamp.

The Auberge du Cap has rooms for around US$25, and they may let you camp there, especially if you spend some money at their beachfront restaurant. Le Nautic (☎ 375100) is where the expats head for Sunday brunch.

Shared rides from Libreville cost around US$3 and leave from an intersection on the main road about 5km north of the airport.

COCOBEACH
About 90km by road from Libreville, and the first town you hit in Gabon after crossing from Acalayong in Equatorial Guinea, Cocobeach is a fun place to spend a night and a great place get to know the country a little.

Football and beer drinking are the local passions, and you'll probably be invited to join in both.

There are a couple of hotels across from each other on the main drag, Hotel Iboga and **Beau Sejour Motel** (☎ 636046), both charging around US$9 for basic rooms. The cross-

roads bar past the football pitch is the only happening nightspot, with loud rap music and grilled food.

Shared bush taxi rides between Cocobeach and Libreville cost US$7.

NORTHERN GABON

NDJOLÉ
Ndjolé is a gritty port town, where the river, the railroad and the main road come together. The area down by the river has a bunch of very bustling bars, cheap African restaurants and a good market.

Nyadzane Papaye (☎ 593315; r US$10-50) is a centrally located hotel and has cheap fan-cooled rooms in its adjacent annex.

Hotel Kevazingo (☎ 080630; r US$17; ☒), 2km north of town on the road to Oyem, is much quieter, and there's a bar and restaurant with spectacular views of the rainforest.

Bush taxis and minibuses from Libreville (US$17) leave early in the morning and arrive at the central intersection in the afternoon; some continue north to Oyem.

The bars near the port are the best places to ask about boats leaving for Lambaréné or going all the way to Port Gentil. It's often possible to get rides on these boats for a negotiable fee, but they leave when they're ready, which might mean you're stuck in town for a few days.

OYEM
The largest city in the north, Oyem is a prosperous, sprawling place as well as being the centre of Gabon's Fang community and their opposition to the president. It's also home to a large number of Muslim traders from West Africa, who are referred to somewhat derisively by the Gabonese as 'the Arabs'.

There are cheap restaurants and bars all over the city, especially around the gare routière, where you'll also find street food and cheap hotels. **Hotel du Stade** (☎ 986429; s US$12) has decent rooms with fans, a restaurant and bar, and very friendly staff. You can also try the Mission Catholique and the Mission Protestante – both inexpensive places to stay.

Most public transport from Libreville to Oyem heads southeast through Ndjolé and Lalara and takes about a day. The route northeast along the border with Equatorial

Guinea doesn't get many travellers and can take several days, but it does pass through a beautiful and rarely visited part of the country if you've got the time.

The road from Oyem to Bitam is in good shape, but the Mitzic to Oyem stretch is miserable; expect slow going.

BITAM

Because it's so close to the border with Cameroon, Bitam has an excellent **market** with fresh fruits and vegetables at low prices. This is also where you find shared taxi rides to the border. If you're heading north to Cameroon, don't forget to stop at immigration here and get an exit stamp (no charge if your papers are in order) or you'll be turned back at the border checkpoint.

There are a couple of hotels in town, or you can ask whether you can stay at the Catholic mission.

From Libreville you'll need to get a bush taxi to Oyem (US$30) and change at the *gare routière* there for the trip to Bitam (US$5).

A shared taxi from Bitam to the river that forms the border with Cameroon costs US$3.50; the very quick pirogue ride across the river is US$5.

SOUTHERN GABON

LAMBARÉNÉ

Two big attractions draw Gabonese and foreign visitors alike to Lambaréné: **Albert Schweitzer's hospital** and boat tours of the **lake region**. The main part of town is on a hilly island in the Ogooué River, with *quartiers* sprawling across the river to the north and south. There's a row of cafeterias, shops, bars and teleboutiques along the river. This is also the place to arrange motorised pirogue trips to the lakes, where you're likely to see a wide variety of birds and possibly hippos and

other wildlife. The scale of the lakes is hard to believe – at times it's like being on an inland sea. The price of the trip depends on your bargaining skills, so it's best to have four or five people to share the cost.

Sleeping & Eating

The **Mission de l'Imaculée Conception** (dm US$11) is the best place to stay on the island. Across the southern bridge over the river in Quartier Isaac several hotels offer rooms for as little as US$3 to US$5, including Hotel Mathieu, La Solution and Hotel G Thytyss. Be aware that these are very basic sleeping quarters for transient workers; don't expect a quiet night or good security.

For cheap authentic African food try **La Touba** (dishes US$2-3) on the island in the market near the bridge to Isaac. For nightlife head to Quartier Isaac and the Beau Rivage disco.

SPLURGE!

Hotel Ogooué Palace (r US$43-60) Just down the street from the mission you'll find one of the best cheap splurges in Gabon. Even though it's ridiculously expensive to stay at the Ogooué Palace, it's just US$2.50 (US$4 on weekends) for nonguests to spend the day lounging around their riverside swimming pool. Cold beers are a reasonable US$1.75.

Getting There & Away

Bush taxis north to Libreville (three to four hours) and south to Fougamou (two to three hours) leave from the *gare routière* in Quartier Isaac across the bridge on the south end of town.

FOUGAMOU

Fougamou is a beautiful, sleepy town on the Ngounié River about 90km south of

---

ALBERT SCHWEITZER

In 1913 theologian, philosopher and musician Albert Schweitzer moved to Lambaréné and built a hospital in order to devote his life to serving humanity in what was then regarded as the heart of darkest, savage Africa. Today a more modern Schweitzer hospital still treats patients, and the old operating rooms, labs and living quarters have been preserved as a kind of museum. Tours are given for a small donation to the hospital.

There are many books by and about Schweitzer; the best place to start is his autobiography, *Out of My Life and Thought*.

Lambaréné. A spate of election-year construction projects has left a fancy hotel, a new indoor market, a nightclub and rows of housing for government employees, most of which are still empty or already closed. The town remains tranquil, and short trips in any direction will lead to traditional villages in the heart of the rainforest.

The **Auberge Tsamba Magotsi** (r US$14), named for the nearby *chutes* (rapids), has basic, comfortable rooms plus a bar, a restaurant (if you order well in advance) and a nightclub that heats up on weekends. Up the hill towards Mouila, the Roadhouse is a popular spot for cold beer and grilled brochettes.

N'DENDÉ

The last big town before Gabon's border with Congo, N'Dendé is where you get your exit stamp at the immigration bureau. If you don't, you'll be turned back at the border in typical Gabonese fashion. There are a few restaurants and palm wine bars if you're stuck waiting for immigration or for a ride.

MAYUMBA

Mayumba would be Gabon's premier beach resort if it weren't so hard to get to. Anyone who does get this far will discover miles and miles of deserted beaches, mangrove swamps and small fishing villages as well as the small town of Mayumba, where you'll probably be offered a place to stay in a private home. The town is at the end of a long spit of land with ocean on one side and a brackish lagoon on the other, and locals will offer to take you on fishing trips or boat tours of the region for a small price. It's a great place to spend a few lazy beach days enjoying the sun, the waves, fresh seafood, and peace and quiet.

Backpackers should check around the *gare routière* in Tchibanga, south of N'Dendé, for early morning bush taxis to Mayumba.

EASTERN GABON

RÉSERVE DE LA LOPÉ

The Réserve de la Lopé is Gabon's most accessible wildlife reserve, situated some 400km from Libreville by road or rail. You stand a good chance of seeing forest elephants, buffalos and a variety of primates. Recently the reserve has initiated gorilla

walks in an attempt to habituate the gorilla population to the presence of small groups of humans. Tours by pirogue, jeep and foot are also available.

Réserve de la Lopé isn't really set up for budget travellers. The usual way to visit is on a package tour arranged through one of Libreville's tour agencies. These typically include transport to and from Libreville, park fees, and meals and accommodation at the park's upscale hotel (rooms are a steep US$60 to US$150) or newer tent camping areas. If you show up on your own you'll need a vehicle to tour the park, and arranging tours and accommodation still won't be cheap for budget travellers.

FRANCEVILLE

At the end of the Transgabonaise train line, Franceville has all the city amenities, such as hotels, restaurants and shops, but unless you need something or you're waiting for the train, there's no real reason to stay here. It's a good place to find rides to the amazing natural and artificial attractions nearby.

AROUND FRANCEVILLE
Poubara Falls & Pont de Liane

About a half-hour drive south of the city, the **Poubara Falls** and the **Pont de Liane** are popular tourist spots in a rainforest setting on the Ogooué River. The Pont de Liane is a bridge made of vines, which locals still use to cross the river and tourists get their pictures taken on to prove they went to Africa and acted like Tarzan. Shared taxis to these spots leave from the *gare routière* in Franceville.

Bateke Plateau & Cirque de Leconi

East of Franceville the savanna rises up into the **Bateke Plateau**, a dry, cool and flat stretch of land that extends south and east into Congo. About 70km past Bongoville, birthplace of the president, you reach **Leconi**, a small, quiet town with a couple of bars and not much else. A few kilometres out of town is the spectacular **Cirque de Leconi**, a deep, circular red-rock canyon that looks like something from the American southwest.

You can get to the town of Leconi on infrequent bush taxis from Franceville, but then you'll still need to hire a 4WD in Leconi to get to the cirque. If you've got a vehicle of your own that's capable of handling the deep-sand road, you can camp overnight and enjoy the views of bush fires blazing miles away across the canyon.

GABON DIRECTORY

ACCOMMODATION
Hotels in Libreville charge from US$30, and in the interior US$15 to US$20 is average. Dorm accommodation in religious missions can be found in most big towns for around US$10.

DANGERS & ANNOYANCES
Libreville has its share of big-city crime: pickpockets, muggings, bag theft and taxi crimes are all problems. In the interior normal precautions, especially keeping your bags with you at all times, are recommended, but it's generally safe. Like other African countries, Gabon has some terrible roads and some even worse drivers. Inexperienced teenagers seeing how fast they can go, drivers who stop for palm-wine breaks, and completely neglected vehicles all contribute to the alarming number of serious traffic accidents.

EMBASSIES & CONSULATES
Countries with diplomatic representation in Libreville include:

Cameroon (☎ 732800; Blvd Léon M'Ba, Quartier Derrière Prison)

Congo (☎ 732906; just off Blvd Ouaban near Citibank, Gué-Gué)

Equatorial Guinea (☎ 732523; Route d'Ambowé, Haute Gué-Gué)

São Tomé & Príncipe (☎ 721527; Blvd de l'Indépendence)

Gabon has diplomatic representation in the following neighbouring countries: Cameroon, Equatorial Guinea, São Tomé and Congo.

GAY & LESBIAN TRAVELLERS
There is a small, underground gay and lesbian scene in Libreville; check out the dance clubs.

HOLIDAYS
As well as religious holidays listed in the Africa Directory (p1003), these are the principal public holidays in Gabon:

1 January New Year's Day
12 March Renovation Day
1 May Labour Day
17 August Independence Day
1 November All Saints' Day

INTERNET ACCESS
Internet access is widespread and cheap (US$1.75 per hour) in Libreville. Outside Libreville it's limited to the major cities and connections are unreliable, but this situation is improving.

MAPS
A map of the country produced by the Institut National de Cartographie is sporadically available in hotels and bookshops; grab one if you see it.

MEDIA
English-language magazines and books, and sometimes the *International Herald Tribune*, can be found at kiosks throughout the country. The daily pro-government paper is *l'Union*, in French. Local newspapers are mostly politics and commentary, in French, and not much use to the casual visitor.

Radio and TV are also in French, though many hotels have satellite TV and get CNN in English. The most popular radio station in Central Africa, the Libreville-based Africa No 1, broadcasts music and news throughout the region.

MONEY
There are ATMs in Libreville and a couple of the other big cities, but they're often out of service and are only linked to Visa; don't count on being able to get cash.

It's worth a try to ask for a lower price almost anywhere. You probably won't get anything at restaurants or shops, but it's expected behaviour at markets, and you never know at hotels.

Don't leave Central Africa with too many CFA, as they're nearly impossible to change in other countries.

Credit cards are accepted only at high-end hotels and restaurants in Libreville and other big cities. Getting a cash advance is not possible.

Changing money at the banks is time-consuming, the rates are bad and the commissions are worse. Try changing discreetly at shops selling imported goods – owners are always happy to have dollars or euros.

Travellers cheques are accepted in the more expensive shops, restaurants and hotels in Libreville but not in the interior. Cheques in euros are much preferred over those in dollars.

PHOTOGRAPHY
Quality film and equipment are available in Libreville but nowhere else in the country.

Never take pictures of anything connected with the military or the government, and that includes pictures of or in the airport.

POST & TELEPHONE
The postal service is not the most reliable, so don't risk sending anything of value to or from Gabon.

Rates for telephone calls outside of Africa are ridiculously high.

RESPONSIBLE TRAVEL
Despite the increase in ecotourism, Gabon's forests and wildlife are still under threat, and there are some steps you can take to avoid contributing to the problem.

Don't buy souvenirs made from endangered species, and don't eat bush meat, especially primates, which are seriously threatened.

TOURS & SAFARIS
The following organisations all offer travel information and arrange tours, mostly geared towards affluent tourists with enough money to afford a multi-day, all-inclusive tour of some of the wildlife parks. They generally have English-speaking staff on hand. Gabontour is state-run.

Equasud (☎ 768686; equasud@tourisme-gabon.com; Libreville)

Gabontour (☎ 728504; gabontour@gabontour.com; Ave Col Parant, Libreville)

Universal Voyages (☎ 724191; Libreville)

VISAS
Visas are required by all and must be obtained before arrival; they are not available at the airport or at border crossings. Getting a visa to Gabon is notoriously difficult and expensive. From countries outside Africa it can cost more than US$100, and perfectly valid visa requests are sometimes rejected without explanation or held up for weeks. Unless you're flying straight to Libreville from Europe, it is best to apply for one at the Gabonese embassy in a nearby African country, where it only takes a couple days and costs around US$50.

Gabon is one of the few countries with embassy staff that still insist on seeing an outgoing plane ticket or other proof of onward travel before issuing a visa. No 'proof of sufficient funds' or long excuses will be accepted. No ticket, no visa. End of story.

Visa Extensions
Visa extensions are available at the Sedoc office in Libreville, but they're quite expensive (US$100) and it's not guaranteed you'll get one.

Visas for Onward Travel
Visas for the following neighbouring countries are available from embassies in Libreville (see p493 for addresses): Cameroon, Congo, Equatorial Guinea, São Tomé & Príncipe.

WOMEN TRAVELLERS
Women travellers will quickly discover that Gabon is a sexist society, where unwanted attention from male admirers is the norm. The risk of real danger such as rape is low, but women often miss out on the fun of going to bars and dance clubs because the hassling is too persistent. On the other hand, women travellers have reported being 'looked after' and protected by local men who are surprised to see a woman travelling alone.

Congo

WARNING

Because of ongoing civil unrest, travel outside Brazzaville and Pointe-Noire is not recommended. We were unable to do on-the-ground research, so some information in this chapter may be unreliable. Check the situation before considering travel to Congo.

To visit Congo is to be assailed by Central Africa in all its glorious chaos, ingenuity and hopelessness. If you are prepared to wait a long time for everything and to be engaged in conversation by everyone, then you will be richly rewarded in this country. Congo boasts untamed jungle, elephants and Africa's largest lowland gorilla population, but its greatest asset is the Congolese themselves. Trawl the street markets for an intoxicating exhibition of Congolese food, culture and music. Venture into the streets for a game of *babyfoot* (table football) and a huge bottle of *Ngok* (crocodile) beer and you will never be short of interesting friends on a sultry evening under the equatorial stars – but be prepared to foot the bill at the end of the night. After three devastating civil wars in less than a decade, this is a nation of people eager for a good laugh. Be open and respectful and you will be invited to share the joke.

CONGO

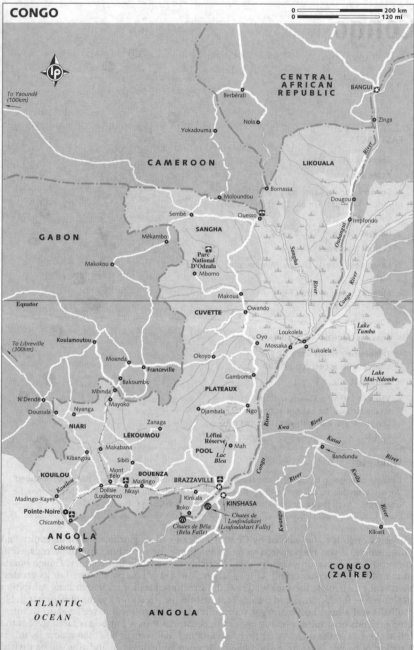

0 _____ 200 km
0 _____ 120 mi

CENTRAL AFRICAN REPUBLIC

BANGUI

Berbérati

Zinga

Nola

Yokadouma

To Yaoundé
(700km)

CAMEROON

LIKOUALA

Moloundou

Bornassa

Dougou

Sembé

Ouesso

Impfondo

SANGHA

Mékambo

GABON

Parc
National
D'Odzala

Mbomo

Makokou

Onangui River

Sangha River

Congo River

Makoua

Equator

CUVETTE

Owando

Lake
Tumba

To Libreville
(300km)

Koulamoutou

Loukolela

Oyo

Mossaka

Lukolela

Moanda

Okoyo

Lake
Mai-Ndombe

Franceville

Bakoumba

Gamboma

Mbinda

PLATEAUX

N'Dendé

Nyanga

Mayoko

Djambala

Ngo

Kwa River

Kasai River

Doussala

Zanaga

NIARI

LÉKOUMOU

Léfini
Réserve

Bandundu

Kwilu River

Makabana

POOL

Mah

Lac
Bleu

Kibangou

Sibiti

Mont
Bélo

Madingo

BOUENZA

BRAZZAVILLE

River

KOUILOU

Kouilou

Nkayi

Kinkala

Madingo-Kayes

Dolisie
(Loubomo)

KINSHASA

River

Kwango River

Pointe-Noire

Boko

Chutes de
Loufoulakari
(Loufoulakari Falls)

Kikwit

Chicamba

Chutes de Béla
(Béla Falls)

ANGOLA

Cabinda

**CONGO
(ZAÏRE)**

*ATLANTIC
OCEAN*

ANGOLA

HISTORY

Before the French turned up in the late-19th century, Congo was a group of separate but trading kingdoms comprising the Kongo, Lari, Mbochi, Teke and Vili peoples, among others. On his arrival in the early 1880s, the French explorer Pierre Savorgnan de Brazza set about busily getting local Onkoos (tribal leaders) to sign away their territorial rights to France. In return for their complicity, the Onkoos received paltry trinkets and fabric, but also a certain unexpected and controversial legitimacy. The French referred to Onkoos who had signed treaties as tribal 'kings' and a new distinction of rank among Onkoos was imported to Congolese culture. The French government then made free use of Congo's considerable natural resources such as ivory, tropical hardwood and rubber, as well as the local population who were used as forced labour. French colonial rule in Congo was easily as brutal as the notorious plunder of the Belgian Congo across the river, but received far less attention.

In addition, the French approach of simply corralling different tribes into one territory did not succeed in laying to rest tribal rivalries, and they failed to create a cohesive country over their 80-year rule. Successive Congolese governments haven't done any better since the country's independence in 1960 – instead, leaders from the northeast have used their time in office to let pals from back home pillage the country and subjugate southerners, and vice versa. Unsurprisingly, tensions between the north and south have caused three civil wars and a year of localised fighting in the southwest Pool region.

Self-Rule

Perhaps because he was widely perceived as a puppet of the French, Youlou, Congo's first president, lasted only three years in office. In 1963 Youlou was swept aside when he made the mistake of taking on the unions, which had become a focus for the struggle for independence from colonial rule. His successor, Massamba-Débat, tried to secure his position by founding the Mouvement National de la Revolution and declaring a one-party state, but he was in turn ousted by Captain Marien-Ngouabi in 1968. Ngouabi was one of a new generation of northern Congolese who would usher in an era of Marxism and greater ties with the Soviet Union. He would also establish a long dominance of Congolese politics by players from the north. However, not even his friends from the north were prepared to play fair, and in 1977 he was assassinated, allegedly by rivals within his own circle. The army chief of staff, Yhombi, stepped into the breach and ruled by means of a military commission. In 1979 Yhombi was ousted by an alliance of the unions with the Congolese Worker's Party (PCT), and Denis Sassou Nguesso, a rising star in the army, took power. Many Congolese see Sassou's monument to the 'Immortal Glory of Marien-Ngouabi' as confirmation that Sassou was the real orchestrator of the political intrigue surrounding Ngouabi's death. Sassou has certainly shown that he has the ruthlessness to survive at the top of Congolese politics where others have failed. He ruled with the PCT as the single party until 1992, a time referred to by the Congolese as Sassou I.

Civil War

In 1992, multiparty democratic elections were held and the unimposing academic Pascal Lissouba was voted in. A southerner, Lissouba promised to redress southern Congo's years spent exiled from development

---

BLACK GOLD & MURKY POLITICS

Oil has long dominated Congo's complex relationship with France. Pascal Lissouba, the country's first democratically elected president, accused the then state-owned French petroleum company Elf-Aquitaine of helping his rival and successor, Denis Sassou-Nguesso, seize power. And in a 2003 Paris trial the chief executive of the oil firm was accused of raking off hundreds of millions of dollars of company money. According to the Guardian, he is just one of 37 former top officials on trial for allegations that the company paid and received enormous commissions and used inflated bills and other devices to enrich a chosen few.

The towering Elf office block still dominates Brazzaville's skyline, a metaphor in concrete and glass.

and from access to the country's top jobs. Once in office he continued a fine tradition of pocketing the country's oil revenues and used his personal militia (known as the Cocoyes) to antagonise inhabitants of the capital who rallied around the ousted Sassou. In 1993 the situation erupted into civil war with Sassou's Cobra militia on one side, and the Cocoyes, together with the militia of Prime Minister Bernard Kolelas (the so-called Ninjas) on the other. Lissouba clung on to power until another – and this time decisive – civil war all but obliterated Brazzaville in 1997. Sassou took charge for the second time and Lissouba fled. But the real losers were Congo's civilians, who spent months hiding in the forests. Many children died – if not from bullets then from malnutrition. In 1999 the war started again on a smaller scale, this time fought predominantly between the Cocoyes and the Ninjas.

In 2002 Sassou bowed to international pressure and legitimised his presidency with multiparty elections. Although they were carried out with much fanfare, they have been called 'seriously flawed'. Sassou's election campaign was widely dubbed 'me or hell', a reference to the alternative of civil war if he was not elected. A resurgence of fighting between the Ninjas and government forces in the Pool region dogged Sassou's first year as president, but a peace agreement is now being bashed out between Sassou and the leader of the Pool insurgency, Pasteur Ntoumi. If both men make good on their promises Congo could be on the verge of a new era of peace and inclusive government. But not if history, and Sassou's own track record, is anything to go by.

THE CULTURE
Dress and manners are a sacred cow in the Congolese psyche and you will be judged on what you wear. A Congolese man will sleep on the floor rather than buy a mattress if it means he can save enough for a three-piece suit with hand stitching on the lapels. So go down to the market, buy a piece of bright cloth, choose a pattern at one of Congo's ubiquitous dressmakers and have yourself an outfit the same day for around US$10.

If you are lucky enough to be invited into a Congolese home, take a carton of Spanish table wine (US$3). It's Champagne to the Congolese and will be seen as prop-

erly respectful in a country obsessed with manners.

Do not kiss in public in Congo. The Congolese don't, and you will attract unwelcome attention at best and a lot of hostility at worst.

ENVIRONMENT
The plateau area around Brazzaville, the capital, bears a remarkable resemblance to Wales, with rolling hills, long grass and lush green trees. Further north, towards the equator, the scenery gives way to bright orange earth and dense tropical rainforest bristling with gorillas, chimps and monkeys of all kinds. Timber companies have long been busy making inroads into the rainforest around the northern-most town of Ouesso, and it has not been made public just how much of this unspoilt forest has already been sold. To the southwest is where Congo meets the sea and the Atlantic Ocean crashes onto some respectable pale yellow beaches. But be prepared, those aren't bright stars hovering low over the horizon but the lights of off-shore oil rigs.

TRANSPORT

GETTING THERE & AWAY
A number of international airlines fly into Brazzaville from other parts of Africa and from Europe (for details see p500). There is a ferry service between Kinshasa in Congo (Zaïre) and Brazzaville (see p500).

GETTING AROUND
From Brazzaville's MayaMaya airport, **Trans Air Congo** (☎ 81 1046) runs four flights a day to the coastal town of Pointe-Noire and two flights a day to the towns of Dolisie (Loubomo) and Nkayi, while flights to Imfondo leave once a week.

Passenger trains linking Brazzaville with Pointe-Noire via Dolisie (Loubomo) are not operating due to unrest in the Pool region. If stability returns, so might the rail service.

A good sealed road goes north from the capital as far as President Denis Sassou Nguesso's home town of Oyo. Beyond that the roads are increasingly bumpy until they disintegrate into sloshing mud lakes in the rain, and hard-set ridges with potholes of several feet after the rain. From Owando onwards the journey north can only be

CONGO

made in a convoy of 4WDs, stopping every 20 minutes for one vehicle to pull the other out of a hole. The coast also has a new road that reaches right down the coast to the Angolan enclave of Cabinda.

Shared taxis and minibuses run on an ad hoc basis between towns and villages. They are ridiculously cheap, great fun and crammed with Congolese villagers taking chickens and even goats to the capital.

Alternatively, barges follow the Oubangui and Congo rivers from the Central African Republic all the way to Brazzaville. However, they leave irregularly, and the journey can take anything from 10 days to three weeks depending on the vessel and whether the rains have come. Most barges are operated by the logging companies, so ask around at 'the Beach' – Brazzaville's river port.

BRAZZAVILLE

At first glance, Brazzaville looks like a sleepy French town plonked down in Central Africa. As a thriving river port that served as a trading post with the rest of Africa, Brazzaville was the obvious choice as the seat of French colonial rule. And it is in Brazzaville that the colonial legacy remains the strongest, with its tree-lined boulevards, parochial French architecture and street-side cafés serving fresh croissants. The city earned a certain cachet in Europe during World War II when it became the capital of Free France, the movement that opposed German occupation.

But the 1997 civil war wrecked Brazzaville, and the scars of mortar fire can still be seen. At one point most inhabitants fled into the surrounding forest, while militia men roamed the city with severed heads of their victims impaled on their car aerials.

That horrific chapter seems to be over, and Brazzaville is actually one of the safer cities in Africa to visit. With a little caution, you can venture into the rowdy suburbs of an evening to sample Brazzaville's pumping nightlife. Congolese music blares from roadside bars and nightclubs in the vibrant PotoPoto district with its candlelit night markets. It's a shame that the city was built with its back turned to the rapids that separate it from Kinshasa, but there are a few well-placed cafés where you can watch water hyacinths float down the Congo

River and the black marketeers paddle their pirogues (traditional canoes).

ORIENTATION

Brazzaville's MayaMaya Airport is just north of the city, a US$5 taxi ride to the centre. The 'Beach' – the river port where the ferry arrives from Kinshasa – is on the easterly edge of the town centre. The area between Ave Marechal Foch (which leads down to the town hall and the river) and the Elf Oil tower near the Beach is considered the city centre, with banks, ministries and international airline offices located here. But the beating heart of Brazzaville (and the markets) lies in the suburbs that splay off to the east and west.

INFORMATION
Cultural Centres
The **Centre Culturel Français** (☎ 81 1705; Rond Point de Bakongo) hosts exhibitions and performances of Congolese dancing and theatre through the year. On Sunday it turns into a cinema showing French films. Prices and opening times vary.

Internet Access
There are plenty of Internet cafés springing up in Brazzaville, although they are subject to the city's erratic Internet service providers and to periodic power cuts. You'll pay around US$1.50 per hour.

Medical Services
The French Government operates a free drop-in **clinic** (☎ 64 9979; Ave Patrice Lumumba) for foreigners, located next to the Belgian embassy. For more serious cases try the **Military Hospital** (☎ 66 3363; Rue Ecole Militaire).

Late-night pharmacies are located at Rond Point du City Centre.

Money
Exchange US dollars with moneychangers on the main road leading out of the Beach, or from any one of the Lebanese-owned cafés and Internet places on Ave Marechal Foch (at a slightly higher rate than moneychangers on the main road). They don't accept denominations lower than US$50 and can be fussy about the condition of notes.

Post & Telephone
The **post office** (Rond Point de la Poste; 🕑 8am-2pm Mon-Sat) is slow and also prone to theft. **DHL**

CONGO

(☎ 81 0103; Ave Marechal Foch; ◷ 8am-6pm Mon-Sat) is reliable and fast.

The cheapest option for local calls is the street stalls with mobile phones. For international calls try **CongoPhone** (Rond Point du City Centre) and **Basilio.com** (Ave Marechal Foch) although neither is cheap. Landlines are appalling in Congo and most businesses use mobile phones, which are often stolen so numbers regularly change. If you have a mobile you can buy a SIM card for US$15 at **Libertis** (Rond Point du City Centre) or **Celtel** (Ave Marechal Foch) and buy pay-as-you-go cards from street stalls.

Toilets
Clean toilets are near impossible to find in Brazzaville and soap and toilet paper largely unheard of, so come prepared.

DANGERS & ANNOYANCES
Avoid the Corniche (the road running between the city and the river) after dark, as it's a favourite hangout for soldiers (ie muggers with guns).

Be extremely careful when taking photos. The airport, government buildings and even the river are all considered national security zones so don't even try to photograph them.

SIGHTS & ACTIVITIES
Brazzaville's markets are its main attraction and provide an assault of local colour. At **Marche Total** (Ave de Loua, Bakongo; ◷ 8am-5pm) hawkers display popular foods such as fresh peanut butter, caterpillars, guinea pigs, bats and the ubiquitous manioc or cassava. You can trawl the stalls for everything from palm wine to Congolese fabrics and aphrodisiac charms.

Marche de Moungali (Blvd de Marechal Lyautey; ◷ 8am-5pm) is the home of Congo's West African community and is a great place for clothes and shoes, not to mention barbecued goat. The **Marche Touristique** (Plateaux; ◷ 8am-2pm) sells traditional weavings, carvings and masks from both Congos.

The rapids that separate Kinshasa and Brazzaville are best accessed for a swim or just to be appreciated over a local Ngok beer.

Table football, or *babyfoot* as it's known here, is very popular. While the tables might not be in mint condition, local players are always enthusiastic and it's a great chance

to make Congolese friends. Football tables are scattered liberally around all the neighbourhoods, but a favourite is located in the **Jane Vial market** (Ave de Trois Martyrs; ◷ 5-8pm Mon-Sat) in PotoPoto. It's best to go in the early evening when the market turns into a rabbit warren of stalls selling barbecued chicken and salted fish by candlelight.

SLEEPING
Budget accommodation in Brazzaville is pretty scummy and in most cases bathrooms equal a bucket of water and a drain. Console yourself with the fact that even for three times the price the city doesn't actually have much more to offer.

Budget hotels, often frequented by wealthy Congolese men and their mistresses in the afternoons, are springing up every day in the lively PotoPoto district. Water supply is irregular here but the hotels are well placed to enjoy Brazzaville's bustle by day and bars by night.

EATING
For cheap eats it's best to head into the suburbs. Here you can buy delicious *muboke* (river fish cooked with chilli and wrapped in manioc leaves) or barbecued goat for under US$1.50 from the street sellers. All over the city centre you can buy baguette sandwiches for under US$1 from stalls, but you might want to ask them to go easy on the dodgy margarine.

GETTING THERE & AWAY
International airlines flying to and from Brazzaville include **Ethiopian Airlines** (☎ 81 2646; Ave Marechal Foch), which flies from Addis Ababa to Brazzaville about twice a week; **Air France** (☎ 81 2719; Amilcar Cabral), which flies direct from Paris to Brazzaville once or twice a week; and Air Gabon, which flies from Libreville to Brazzaville a few times a week. However, flying into Brazzaville is very pricey. A far cheaper option is to fly into Kinshasa. From Kinshasa you can cross the river to Brazzaville.

Small fast boats cross from Ngobila Beach in Kinshasa to the 'Beach' in Brazzaville (US$15 one way). Alternatively, the big ferry only takes 20 minutes and it's an adventure, but keep an eye on your belongings and bear in mind service is often disrupted by fighting on either side of the river. Although the actual crossing is short, the bureaucracy involved at either side makes it a two-hour journey. Boats leave regularly and you can just turn up, although the last boat leaves at 4pm (noon on Sunday).

You can buy a 15-day, multiple-entry visa to Brazzaville on arrival for US$30, but you must have your yellow fever certificate with you.

GETTING AROUND
There is no public transport in Brazzaville, but privately owned buses spewing choking black smoke lurch around the capital regularly and are perfectly safe and cheap at under US$0.50.

Taxis are everywhere in Brazzaville and they're a real bargain. For a flat rate of US$1.30 you can go anywhere in town (or as little as US$1 if you can negotiate in French and there isn't a petrol shortage). You can also hire a taxi for US$6 an hour.

Note that even most Brazzavillois don't know the street names of their city and everyone makes reference to landmarks instead. When asking for directions, always first ask for the name of the place you're going, before the street name.

AROUND CONGO

DOLISIE (LOUBOMO)
This dusty red town used to be the weekend resort favoured by Brazzaville and Gabon's moneyed classes. Then it was destroyed in the 1997 war and now only chickens inhabit the wreckage of the once-plush Intercontinental Hotel, but the town's eerie charm remains. The one-hour flight from Brazzaville to Dolisie via Nkayi is well worth it, if only for the scenery.

POINTE-NOIRE
There are yellow sandy beaches, stretches of bars, and seafood restaurants humming with life in Congo's official tourist resort, but there's also a sinister edge to it all. Rich foreign oil company workers live next to – but completely apart from – the Congolese population here. The hard wood and oil shipped from this port has generated incredible wealth for some, but little evidence of it can be seen on the potholed streets of Pointe-Noire.

The cheap hotels are clean and of a much higher standard than in Brazzaville.

Although never 100% safe, you can also hitch up the coast to **Point Indien** for some unspoilt, deserted beaches and back to Pointe-Noire in the evening for some delicious, if pricey, seafood.

ODZALA NATIONAL PARK
Week-long trips to this haven of wildlife in the north cost US$600, including flight and accommodation, and can be booked at the offices of **Ecofac** (Ave Marechal Foch; www.ecofac.org /Ecotourisme/_EN/Odzala/Presentation.htm).

Visitors have reported seeing hundreds of lowland gorillas, monkeys and even elephants. However, an Ebola outbreak in 2002 devastated the gorilla population, so this may be a last chance to see the fast-dying-out animals – but it's also a hazardous trip. Check the situation at Ecofac before booking.

CONGO DIRECTORY

BUSINESS HOURS
Business hours are 8am to noon and 2pm to 3pm Monday to Friday, and 8am to noon Saturday.

DANGERS & ANNOYANCES
Scamming is an art form in Congo. The bald-faced cheek of those on the make is matched only by the elaborate manners and hospitality of the majority.

Don't give bribes at roadblocks just because you're asked; most soldiers are just trying it on. Instead say that you will buy them *un jus* (a juice) on the way back; this way they have more of a vested interest in letting you through.

EMBASSIES & CONSULATES
The following countries have diplomatic representation in Brazzaville.

Angola (☎ 81 1421)

Belgium (☎ 81 3712; Ave Patrice Lumumba, west of Place de la Poste)

Cameroon (☎ 81 1008; Rue Général Bayardelle)

Central African Republic (☎ 81 4721; Rue Fourneau)

Congo (Zaïre) (☎ 81 3052; Ave de l'Indépendance)

France (☎ 81 5541; Rue Alfassa)

Gabon (☎ 81 5620; Ave Monseigneur Augouard)

Germany (☎ 83 2990; Villa Marina, cnr Rue de Reims & Rue de Pavie)

Nigeria (☎ 81 1022; 11 Blvd du Maréchal Lyautey)
UK (honorary consul only; ☎ 51 3251; Ave de la Paix, video rental shop at Elf Tower end)
USA (☎ 81 1484) This embassy is temporarily operating from the US Embassy in Congo (Zaïre) (☎ 243 8843608; 310 Avenue des Aviateurs, Kinshasa)

In Central and West Africa, Congo has embassies in Cameroon, Gabon and Congo (Zaïre).

MONEY
CFA can be used in all countries within the Central African franc zone. These include Benin, Cameroon, Chad, Mali and Senegal. There are no ATMs in the country, and neither credit cards nor travellers cheques are accepted, so hard cash it is. If you need some money wired in, **Western Union** (☎ 81

4293; Rue Felix Eboue; ☺ 8am-4pm Mon-Sat) is reliable but takes a whopping percentage and uses ridiculous exchange rates. When shopping, always bargain – it's Congolese theatre.

POST & TELEPHONE
The postal system is unreliable throughout the country.

Mobiles are used rather than landlines. Phone coverage is limited to Brazzaville, Oyo, Owando and Pointe-Noire.

VISAS
All visitors to Congo need a visa. Visa applications from embassies abroad can be issued the same day or by the next day. You can also get a visa on arrival in Brazzaville if you come by boat from Kinshasa (see p500).

Central African Republic

FAST FACTS

- **Area** 624,980 sq km
- **ATMs** none at all
- **Borders** Cameroon, Congo, Congo (Zaïre), Sudan all open at the time of writing; Chad closed at the time of writing. Travellers are advised to contact the embassies of these countries to confirm the status of these borders prior to travelling, as borders may be opened or closed with little notice.
- **Budget** $US15 to US$50 a day
- **Capital** Bangui
- **Currency** Central African franc US$1 = CFA600
- **Languages** French, Sango, Arabic and tribal languages
- **Population** 3.6 million
- **Seasons** wet (May–Oct in the north; Jun–Sep in the south); dry (Nov–Apr in the north; Oct–May in the south)
- **Telephone** country code ☎ 236; international access code ☎ 19
- **Time** GMT/UTC + 1
- **Visas** US$30 for 30 days or US$155 for 90 days; required by most and must be obtained in advance

WARNING

The military coup in early 2003 led to widespread conflict and unrest. While things have improved in Bangui (even though the capital remains one of the most dangerous cities in Central Africa), the situation in other parts of the country, particularly in the north, is unpredictable and potentially very dangerous. We were unable to do on-the-ground research in this country, so some information in this chapter may not be reliable. Check the situation before travelling to CAR.

If it's the 'real' Africa you're looking for, Central African Republic (CAR) may be it. A country of staggering rare natural beauty, with some of the world's most amazing wildlife, it nonetheless remains underdeveloped, fragmented and poverty-stricken. It's a country that could and should be very prosperous; it's just that pesky 'government-that-doesn't-care-about-its-people' factor that gets in the way. The country has important mineral deposits and great natural resources, yet precious little of the wealth generated seeps down to the population. For centuries CAR has endured rapacity from invaders and then its own

CENTRAL AFRICAN REPUBLIC

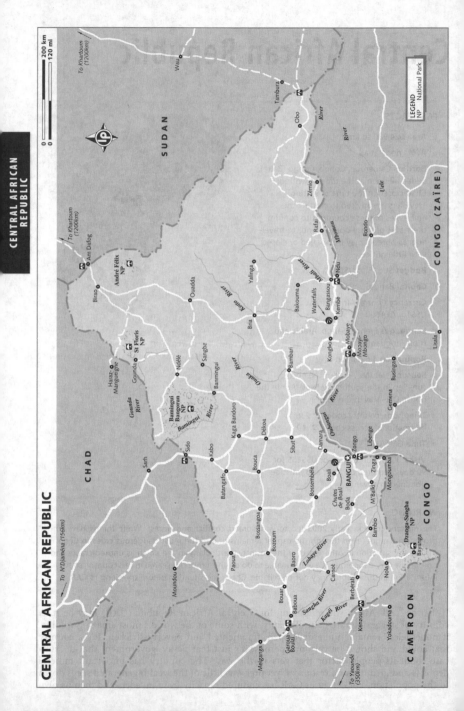

leaders. Sadly this is ongoing. So, why would the people of such a historically plundered nation be open, friendly and generous? As we said, that's the real Africa for you. However, travelling here is a backpacking bungee jump. At the time of writing the country was not considered stable or safe to travel through. Check the situation with your embassy before attempting to visit.

HISTORY

CAR was home to one of humanity's earliest civilizations. Thousands of years ago there was an advanced culture whose artisans and work found a ready market from nations far afield. They were extensively settled and relatively sophisticated even before ancient Egypt's time in the sun. However, beginning in the middle of the last millennium the slave trade gradually decimated this well-organised society. Tens of thousands were dragged westward to the Americas, while Arab conquerors from the north completed the devastation. As recently as the 19th century, 20,000 slaves were sold each year on the Egyptian market.

Colonial Days

France launched into CAR in the 1880s, finding a shattered society rich in agricultural potential. It divided the country into 17 parts and offered them to European companies in exchange for around 15% of profits reaped from the subsequent agricultural pursuits, plus a fixed annual payment. Vast cotton, coffee and tobacco plantations were established. In need of labour, these companies forcibly, often brutally, conscripted the local population. Resistance to the French was there from the outset and continued until the late 1920s. This resistance was finally broken as a combined result of French military action, famine and severe epidemics of smallpox.

The first signs of nationalism began to spring up after WWII via Barthlemey Boganda's Mouvement d'Evolution Sociale de l'Afrique Noire. In 1960, one year after Boganda was killed in a mysterious plane crash, his party forced the French to grant independence. CAR has had its fair share of instability ever since.

Brutal Leadership

The leadership was taken over by David Dacko, who became the country's first president. Dacko's rule quickly became highly repressive and dictatorial, but in 1966 he was overthrown by an army commander and close relative, Jean-Bédel Bokassa.

Then began 13 years of one of the most sordid, brutal and notorious regimes Africa has ever experienced, as Bokassa progressively took over the most important government portfolios and snuffed out all opposition. Offenders were publicly clubbed to death – often with Bokassa's personal involvement.

France, wanting the uranium deposits at Bakouma and the abundant big-game hunting grounds near the Sudanese border (which were personally sponsored by the former French president, Giscard d'Estaing), indulged Bokassa by supporting him and bailing out his floundering economy.

Using the country's mineral resources as carrots, Bokassa also negotiated loans from South Africa and private US banks. He then squandered virtually all this money on prestigious projects, many of which were never completed. Eventually he embarked on his final and most foolish fantasy – to have himself crowned 'emperor' of a renamed Central African Empire. Despite the worldwide derision that the 1977 coronation provoked, France picked up most of the tab of more than US$20 million – equivalent to CAR's annual earnings.

Such excess, together with news of a massacre of schoolchildren in Bangui, made Bokassa an embarrassment to his backers. And so France, with former president David Dacko as its front man, began to plot Bokassa's downfall. In 1979 they abruptly cut off aid to the 'empire' and while Bokassa was in Libya seeking still more funds, they flew in Dacko together with loads of French paratroopers.

Strangely (considering Bokassa's reputation), Dacko's takeover ultimately proved unpopular and he began to need to use the paratroopers as a personal army. He was overthrown in 1981 and replaced by André Kolingba, who in 1986 created a one-party state. All opposition groups were banned and their supporters jailed, harassed or forced to flee the country.

Believing that Kolingba wouldn't dare impeach him, the unstoppable Bokassa reared his head again and flew back to CAR. Surprise, surprise, he was convicted of treason, murder and cannibalism and sentenced to death. This was changed to life imprisonment and he was confined to a folly he had constructed at Berengo.

In 1993, Kolingba's 12 years of absolute rule ended when he was defeated in presidential elections and Ange-Félix Patassé became the country's leader of the first real civilian government. Patassé, however, immediately stacked the government with fellow tribesmen. In 1996 the army, dominated by officers from a southern tribe, instigated uprisings and general mutiny. The capital became a war zone. The Bangui Accords, a regionally brokered peace deal between Patassé and these rebels, was signed in January 1997, and an 800-strong African peacekeeping force was put in place. Elections were held in August 1998, and these saw Patassé gain a majority in the 109-seat parliament. He was re-elected in September 1999 amid claims of vote rigging.

Recent Developments
On October 25, 2002, the renegade former army chief-of-staff, General Francois Bozize, led ex-soldiers in an unsuccessful coup attempt. Civil war resumed. Bozize soon gained control of areas in the north and south. People were forced to flee their homes, villages and even the country. Tens of thousands fled over CAR's five borders as life became unbearable: women and young girls were raped by fighters allied to the government from neighbouring Congo (Zaïre), and towns that were held captive by government or rebel forces were cut off from outside supplies. When this happens, diseases – often in epidemic proportions – break out, as medical supplies get critically low. In Sibut, meningitis broke out in March 2003. A prolonged truck strike – protesting police extortion on the main roads – further exacerbated acute shortages of salt, sugar, kerosene, soap and other basic goods. Trucks were unable to pass checkpoints without giving police around 40L of petrol each.

The crises facing CAR have carried on largely unreported and get scant attention from the rest of the world. UN experts and Medecins sans Frontieres provide rape victims with psychological and medical care, and Unicef is looking after the many malnourished mothers and children. Similar missions are conducted wherever security conditions allow.

Meanwhile, the government has had a complaint filed against it by the International Federation of Human Rights. It is accusing President Patassé of war crimes and crimes against humanity in relation to his treatment of captives. Patassé's government has officially expressed 'surprise and indignation' at the accusations. And so it goes…

THE CULTURE
CAR's 3.6 million people comprise many tribes, ethnic groups and languages. Subsistence agriculture and forestry are the backbone of CAR and more than 70% of the population lives a rural existence. The main agricultural products are cotton, coffee, tobacco, tapioca, yams, millet, corn, bananas and timber. The average worker's annual income is US$310.

The national psyche has taken a battering due to ongoing political instability in the countryside, and to protracted moves by governments and rebels to force people from their homes (an act that perpetuates the poverty). In CAR life is tough and people hate Patassé. And so like all humans, the people of CAR are glad for a release. They like to drink banana and palm wine or beer and dance the gbadoumba, mambo and lououdou. Understandably, they also look to the afterlife – religion is paramount here, being evenly split between Catholics, Protestants, Muslims and indigenous beliefs. Ancient animistic convictions strongly influence Christianity here.

ENVIRONMENT
CAR is roughly the same size as France, and is landlocked and almost smack bang in the middle of Africa. It has virgin rainforests and some of the most pristine national parks in the world. The Dzanga-Sangha National Park is home to Baka (Pygmies), flowering tropical plants, beautiful butterflies, and some of the highest densities of lowland gorillas and forest elephants in Africa.

The country is one immense plateau varying in height between 600m and 700m, with scattered hills in the northeast and southwest. The closest thing to a real mountain is Mt Ngaoui, which at 1420m is the highest point in the country. Otherwise, the sweeping savanna grasslands are interspersed with lots of rivers. CAR has long had a reputation as one of the last great wildlife refuges, but increased poaching has diminished this standing in recent years. Logging forests also threaten animals and Baka, and open the forests to even more poaching.

Despite the enormous tourism potential and ample natural resources, CAR is one of the least developed countries on the continent.

The climate is tropical with hot, dry winters and mild to hot, wet summers. Natural hazards to the environment include hot, dry dusty winds affecting the northern areas, and flooding in the rainy season.

TRANSPORT

GETTING THERE & AWAY
Air
CAR is served by four airlines through Bangui airport: Air Afrique, Cameroon Airlines, Air France and Air Gabon.

DEPARTURE TAX

Airport departure tax is US$9.

Land
The following are the usual routes for getting to countries bordering CAR. They are well-worn paths, but check with embassies and other reliable sources before you go, as borders are all very prone to opening and closing. At the time of writing, the borders with Cameroon, Congo and Congo (Zaïre) were open. The border with Sudan was also open, but the Sudanese embassy said that this frequently changes. The border with Chad was closed, but its embassy indicated that this could change at short notice.

CAMEROON
The most popular crossing point is just east of the town of Garoua-Boulaï. Trucks and buses run from Bangui to Garoua-Boulaï, overnighting in Bouar. From Garoua-Boulaï, minibuses go to N'Gaoundal, and trains go from there to Yaoundé.

CHAD
The main border crossing is at Sido, on the route to Sarh. Trucks trundle most days

from Bangui to Kaga Bandoro, but from there only occasional trucks and minibuses go to Kabo (where there's a checkpoint) and on to the border. Once over the border, pick-ups go from Sido and Maro to Sarh.

CONGO
A riverboat managed by **Socatraf** (☎ 61 4315; Rue Parent Bangui, Bangui) steams between Bangui and Brazzaville every two or three weeks from late May to early December. The cabins are basic and the journey takes about seven days.

Alternatively, you can jump aboard one of the barges serving this route. They take twice as long, but are far less crowded; they depart every week, and the fare is around US$25.

CONGO (ZAÏRE)
The main border crossing between CAR and Congo (Zaïre) is over the Oubangui River from Bangui to Zongo. This (and the other border crossing at Mobaye) is currently closed to foreigners, and likely to remain that way while the war in Congo continues.

SUDAN
The route from Bangui to Juba, via Obo, was only ever for hardy travellers (or is that foolhardy?), but it's no longer viable due to unrest in CAR, southern Sudan and neighbouring Congo (Zaïre).

The only other option – and it's still a tough one – is from Bangui to Nyala via Birao in the northeastern corner of CAR, but this route is also currently closed to travellers due to poor security in CAR and western Sudan. Even if this route ever opens, you should expect to spend at least two weeks travelling here, as traffic is rare and the roads appalling.

GETTING AROUND
Overcrowded 24-seater minibuses connect Bangui with all major towns. Trucks and pick-ups are also a popular way to travel; their prices are similar to minibus fares. Some main roads are sealed, but pockmarked with wheel-swallowing holes. During the dry season, the dirt roads to major towns and the Cameroon and Chad borders are OK. But when the rains begin they become very muddy and can be closed for days.

BANGUI

pop 670,000

Bangui, the capital of CAR, is set beside the Oubangui River – the most important river in the country. It therefore follows that the city is the biggest trading port. Unfortunately, it is also one of Central Africa's most dangerous cities for petty thievery, pickpocketing and violence.

The French founded Bangui in 1880, deriving the name from the nearby rapids, and then constructed the city – à la France – with wide, shaded boulevards and a central market area from where everything radiated. These days, this area is considered the old town, but all public transport and activity still converges here.

ORIENTATION

You can take a public or private taxi from the airport – both are more expensive at night.

All major avenues radiate from the Place de la République, the centre of the capital. It is a desolate urban space as many of the buildings were shelled or torched during the 1996 army mutinies.

The heart of the African quarter is the unmarked K-Cinq intersection (Kilomètre 5) west of town (known variously and confusingly as Km 5, Kilo 5, Kam Cinq, or PK5 – pronounced 'payka sink'). It has the largest market and lots of bars and nightclubs. K-Cinq and Ave du Lt Koudoukou, which leads off it, are the city's liveliest areas for locals but also the most dangerous.

Muggers – sometimes drunk – are on the streets here day and night, so do not venture out alone.

INFORMATION

Cultural Centres

The **Martin Luther King Centre** (Ave David Dacko; 8.30am-1.30pm Mon-Fri), next to the US embassy, has an air-con library with magazines, newspapers and CNN.

The Maison de la Presse carries a good stock of French books and magazines and has a small range of international media.

Medical Services

The main hospital is called **Hospita Caumuomiter** (61 0600).

Money

At the UBAC bank, service is friendly and there's no commission for sums under US$835. Avoid the BIAO bank where the commission rates are vicious.

Post & Telephone

The mail service is very slow, although poste restante is efficient at the **post office** (6.30am-1.30pm Mon-Fri), located near the Socatel building on Ave des Martyrs. It charges a small fee per letter but only keeps letters for a limited period. You can send faxes and telexes from the post office, and phone calls from the nearby **Socatel office** (61 4268; BP 939 Ave des Martyrs, Bangui).

Tourist Offices

Try the **Ministère de l'Industrie, du Commerce, du Tourisme et de l'Artisant** (61 1055; BP 1988 Bangui).

SIGHTS & ACTIVITIES

The **Musée de Boganda** (Rue de l'Industrie) is well organised with helpful guides. There's an interesting collection of local musical instruments that you can try out, and good displays on the Baka and their culture.

Bangui has many markets. **Marché Central** in the centre of town is normally bustling, but is open mornings only. Avoid the market at K-Cinq; there are more thieves here than goods for sale. For artisan goods, head for the **Centre Artisanal** (until 6pm). You'll find ebony carvings, porcupine-quill bracelets, leather goods, batiks, appliqué, African costumes, malachite, grass dolls, woodcarvings and masks. Many of the artefacts are common to the whole Congo basin, but don't miss the butterfly-wing collages, which are common in CAR.

There's also the **Perroni Gallery** beside the port. Cyr Perroni came to CAR from Martinique over 40 years ago and has trained many of the artisans whose works are sold at the Centre Artisanal. Perroni's paintings are, however, very expensive.

SLEEPING

There are no inexpensive hotels in Bangui, but there's a camp site near the centre of the African quarter (ie the unmarked K-Cinq intersection west of town). It's a rough part of town, with the largest (and most threatening) market and lots of bars. Ave du Lt Koudoukou is also pretty action-filled and both these areas have the cheapest accommodation. But be on your guard because as with all 'lively' traveller-magnets, these areas also attract the dodgiest of locals. So don't venture out on your own – particularly at night.

EATING & DRINKING

For cheap but tasty food, check out the stalls along the river southwest of the port for fish or beef brochettes, and the stalls beside the taxi rank at the K-Cinq intersection – just don't risk the latter after dark. Other areas worth a look include Ave des Martyrs and Ave de la France.

GETTING THERE & AWAY

Transport for all towns except M'Baïki sets out from the *gare routière* around 6am. M'Baïki services depart from a lane beside Le Punch Coco. All vehicles then cruise up and down Ave de l'Indépendance looking for passengers. Once a vehicle has picked up as many passengers as possible, it heads for the control post at Kilomètre 12, which is the best place for catching a ride given all transport must wait there to complete formalities. Bus destinations from here include M'Baïki, Bossembélé, Sibut, Bossangoa, Bambari, Bouar, Berbérati, Sido, Bangassou and Garoua-Boulaï.

GETTING AROUND

There are cheap shared taxis and minibuses along all the main arteries. A private taxi costs US$2, even to the airport. It costs more after dark.

AROUND BANGUI

CHUTES DE BOALI

These waterfalls are 70km northwest of Bangui and tumble 50m – 1m higher than Niagara! They're spectacular in the rainy season (summer), but no more than a trickle when it's dry. There is a small entry fee.

To get here, take a minibus or shared taxi to Kilomètre 12, then a taxi or pick-up to the turn-off to the falls. From here it's a 5km walk to the chutes.

M'BAÏKI

Some 105km southwest of Bangui and surrounded by rainforest, M'Baïki is in a timber-, coffee- and tobacco-growing area. It's also the stopping-off point for visiting nearby Baka encampments.

One bus and several pick-ups leave Bangui each day from the lane beside Le Punch Coco nightclub at K-Cinq. At **Berengo** you'll pass another folly that Bokassa built on his tribal lands. It now functions as a rural development centre and chicken farm. About 10km northeast of M'Baïki is the village of **Sabe**, famous for its ebony sculptures.

AROUND CAR

The following towns are all regular stops on the routes from Bangui to either Yaoundé (Cameroon) or N'Djamena (Chad) and are reasonably set up for transit travellers, with basic places to stay and a few eateries.

Bossembélé is the second-largest town on the route between Cameroon and Bangui, but there isn't much to do here. Further northwest, **Bouar** is a more frequent stopping place for travellers. The area is dotted with megalithic stone monuments and it's also the site of a large French military base. Again, theft is a problem here.

Going north towards N'Djamena, **Sibut** marks the end of the sealed road and straggles around the junction where roads lead towards the Chad border and east to Bambari and Bangassou. **Kaga Bandoro**, about 120km further north, is also a regular stop-over town for bus travellers.

CAR DIRECTORY

ACCOMMODATION

Bangui doesn't have any cheap hotels rooms, but does have cheap dorm-style accommodation and a campground in the centre of the city. Hotels outside the capital are cheap.

DANGERS & ANNOYANCES

Watch out for thieves, armed rebels and the police – all are sinister enough to their own people, but they particularly target foreigners. And if they don't get you, the chloroquine-resistant malaria just might. AIDS is also a very serious problem with at least 14% of the population afflicted. Oh, and swimming is not safe anywhere because of bilharzia.

EMBASSIES & CONSULATES
The following countries have diplomatic representation in Bangui:

Canada (☎ 61 0973; PO Box 973, Quartier Assana)
Chad (☎ 61 4677; Ave Valéry Giscard d'Estaing, near Place de la République)
Congo (☎ 61 1877; Ave Boganda)
Congo (Zaïre) (☎ 61 8240; Rue Gamal Abdel Nasser)
France (☎ 61 3000; Blvd Général de Gaulle)
Germany (☎ 61 0746; Rue Gamal Abdel Nasser)
Nigeria (☎ 61 0744; Km 3, Ave Boganda)
Sudan (☎ 61 3821; Ave de la France)
USA (☎ 61 0200; BP 924 Ave David Dacko)

The British high commission in Yaoundé (Cameroon) deals with enquiries relating to CAR.

CAR has embassies in Cameroon, Chad, Congo and Congo (Zaïre).

HOLIDAYS
As well as religious holidays listed in the Africa Directory chapter (p1003), these are the principal public holidays in CAR:

1 January New Year's Day
29 March Anniversary of the Death of Barthélemy Boganda
12 April Easter Monday
30 June National Day for Prayer
13 August Independence Day
15 August Assumption
1 November All Saints Day
1 December National Day

MONEY
The unit of currency is the Central African franc (CFA), made up of 100 centimes (these notes are also legal tender in Chad and Cameroon). The import and export of local currency is limited to US$125. There

are no restrictions on the import of foreign currencies.

There are no ATMs in CAR and credit cards generally are not accepted. You can only exchange money in Bangui and Berbérati (banking hours are 7am to 11.30am Monday to Friday). Take travellers cheques in euros to avoid additional exchange rate charges. Even so, commission charges can be very high and the exchange rates very low – up to 25% below the current internationally accepted rate.

VISAS
Visas are required by most visitors and cost US$30 for 30 days or US$155 for 90 days. Where there is no CAR embassy, 30-day visas can generally be obtained from the French embassy. However, for certain nationalities (including Australians, New Zealanders and the Irish) the embassy may have no authority to issue visas, or may first have to radio Bangui for approval before issuing a visa. This takes time.

Visa Extensions
Because you pay the full price of a new visa, getting a visa extension is an expensive hassle. The immigration office is about 1km up the hill to the north of the Presidential Palace in Bangui. Ask for directions at the army post behind the palace.

Visas for Onward Travel
Visas for the following neighbouring countries can be obtained in Bangui: Chad, Congo, Congo (Zaïre), Nigeria and Sudan. See the listing above for embassy and consulate information.

Chad

HIGHLIGHTS

- **Zakouma National Park** One of the best places to see wildlife in Central Africa; hard to get to but worth the effort (p520)
- **Moundou** Perfect for chilling out in a bar by the Logone River with plentiful beers or an excellent smoothie (p520)
- **Abéché** Dramatic desert capital and gateway to Sudan for the adventurous (p521)
- **Off the beaten track** Mao, the frontier market town on the route to Niger is the place to spend some haggling time (p519)

FAST FACTS

- **Area** 1,284,000 sq km (12 times the size of Scotland)
- **ATMs** none at all
- **Borders** Cameroon, Central African Republic (CAR), Libya, Niger and Nigeria all open; land crossings to Libya, Sudan and CAR not recommended
- **Budget** US$20 to US$25 a day
- **Capital** N'Djaména
- **Languages** French, Arabic and more than 120 local languages
- **Money** Central African CFA; US$1 = CFA600
- **Population** 9 million
- **Seasons** dry (Nov–May), wet (Jul–Sep)
- **Telephone** country code ☎ 235; international access code ☎ 15
- **Time** GMT/UTC + 1
- **Visas** US$25 to US$80 for one month; easily obtained in West & Central Africa

Never a high point on the overland trail, Chad is still widely seen by travellers as a place to get through rather than visit. Few visitors do more than spend a few days in N'Djaména, the busy capital, and even fewer stay long enough to explore and do this struggling but fascinating country justice, but those who do discover a wealth of warmth and culture beneath the rough exterior. Physically you couldn't mistake Chad for anything except a Sahel country, though in the south the dusty expanses of the landscape are interspersed with incongruously green villages fed by small rivers, giving a welcome quasi-tropical break from the rigours of the road. Travelling here certainly poses many problems: the roads are unpaved, the transport uncomfortable and the policemen unreconstructed, but if you can take these things as challenges you may be surprised by the rewards.

CHAD

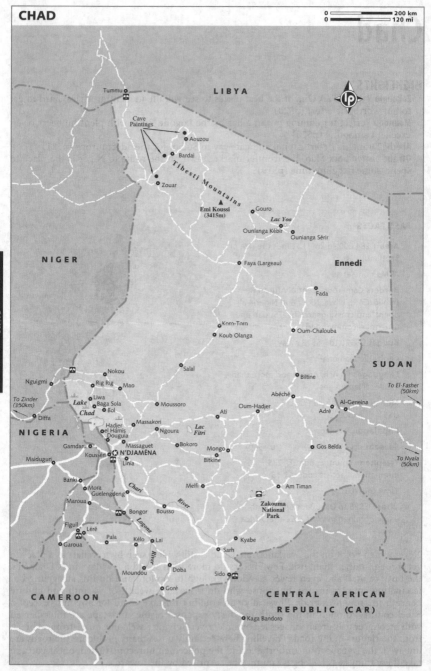

CHAD

0 — 200 km
0 — 120 mi

LIBYA

Tummu

Cave Paintings

Aouzou

Bardaï

Tibesti Mountains

Zouar

Emi Koussi (3415m)

Gouro

Lac Yoa

Ounianga Kébir

Ounianga Sérir

NIGER

Faya (Largeau)

Ennedi

Fada

Koro-Toro

Koub Olanga

Oum-Chalouba

Salal

SUDAN

Nguigmi

Nokou

Rig Rig

Mao

Biltine

To Zinder (350km)

To El-Fasher (50km)

Liwa

Lake Chad

Baga Sola

Bol

Moussoro

Ati

Oum-Hadjer

Abéché

Adré

Al-Geneina

Diffa

NIGERIA

Hadjer el Hamis

Douguia

Massakori

Ngoura

Lac Fitri

Bokoro

Mongo

Gos Beïda

To Nyala (50km)

Gamdaru

Massaguet

Koussén

N'DJAMÉNA

Linia

Bitkine

Maiduguri

Banki

Mora

Guelengdeng

Melfi

Am Timan

Maroua

Bongor

Bousso

Chari River

Zakouma National Park

Figuil

Léré

Pala

Kélo

Laï

Kyabe

Garoua

Sarh

Logone River

Moundou

Doba

Sido

CAMEROON

Goré

CENTRAL AFRICAN REPUBLIC (CAR)

Kaga Bandoro

HISTORY

Dominated historically by slave-trading Arab Muslims from the northern regions, Chad is primarily an agricultural nation, with 80% of the population living at subsistence level. Its recent history was shaped when the French began to take an interest in central and western Africa in the 1900s. By 1913 the country was fully colonised, and remained under French control for 47 years. Sadly the new rulers didn't really know what to do with their conquest, and investment all but dried up after a few years, leaving much of the territory almost entirely undeveloped.

Independence

When independence was finally granted in 1960, it was a southerner (see The Culture, p514) who became Chad's first head of state. Unfortunately, President François Tombalbaye, the former leader of the nationalist PPT, was not exactly the best choice for the job. By arresting opposition leaders and banning political parties he provoked a series of conspiracies in the Muslim north, the violent repression of which quickly escalated into full-blown guerrilla war. For the next quarter of a century, Chadian politics was defined by armed struggles, shifting alliances, coups and private armies, overseen and often exacerbated by France and Libya, who both took a keen interest in the area. In addition, the Sahel drought of the 1970s and early 1980s destroyed centuries-old patterns of existence and cultivation, causing large-scale migration to urban centres.

In 1975 Tombalbaye was assassinated and succeeded by General Malloum, a fellow southerner. Over US$1 million in cash was found in Tombalbaye's residence, along with plans to proclaim himself emperor.

National Unity?

The Government of National Unity was then formed by Malloum and Hissène Habré (a former northern rebel commander); it was a tenuous alliance between two men who shared little more than mutual distrust. The resulting internal power struggle in 1979 pitted north against south and Muslim against Christian or animist, all colliding with destructive force in the capital, where thousands of civilians were massacred. Eventually Malloum fled the country and Goukouni Oueddei – the son of a tribal chieftain from northwestern Chad and an arch-enemy of Habré – took over.

In 1980 Libyan forces supporting Oueddei briefly occupied N'Djaména. The French army drove them northwards, leaving Habré as the nominal ruler of Chad. A stalemate ensued with the country divided in half, with neither France nor Libya willing to risk an all-out confrontation.

In 1987, both foreign powers agreed to withdraw their forces. However, Libya, whose forces had occupied northern Chad and the uranium-rich Aouzou Strip since 1977, reneged and attacked Habré's army. Armed with little more than swords and machine guns, the Chadian forces pushed the well-equipped Libyans back across the border. It was a stunning victory, but, for Habré at least, a short-lived one.

The New Regime

In 1990 Idriss Deby, a northern Muslim warlord in self-imposed exile in Sudan, swept back into Chad with a private army of 2000 soldiers. Habré fled to Senegal, leaving Deby with a clear run to N'Djaména and the presidency of his war-ravaged country, which he consolidated by winning the first-ever presidential elections in 1996. While this ballot was widely regarded as rigged, the parliamentary elections a year later were considered much fairer. However, in 1998 a new rebellion broke out in the north, led by the Movement for Democracy and Justice in Chad (MDJT) under Deby's former minister Youssouf Togoimi.

In January 2000, former president Habré was placed under house arrest in Dakar and formally charged with crimes against humanity; however, in March 2001 the Court of Appeal ruled that the Senegalese courts had no jurisdiction to try him on these charges.

Current Events

Although Chad has enjoyed a period of relative peace and close relations with Libya over the past few years, conflict is never far away. Guerrilla raids are still common in the Tibesti region of northern Chad (despite accords signed in 2002 and 2003 with the MDJT and National Resistance Army rebel groups) and armed clashes with Nigerian forces occur occasionally around Lake Chad over ongoing demarcation issues.

Politically, little has changed: much to nobody's surprise, Deby won the May 2001 presidential elections by a comfortable margin, although results from a quarter of the polling stations had to be cancelled because of 'irregularities'. The MPS also confirmed its majority in the parliamentary elections in April 2002, winning 110 of the 155 seats.

After many years of NGO objections and environmental concerns, oil extraction is finally underway in the Doba Basin, where an estimated deposit of one billion barrels is located. According to the government and the three international companies involved, the first saleable supplies should hit the market in 2004; over its lifetime the project is expected to net over US$2 billion for the Chadian economy, although how much of this reaches the people who need it remains to be seen.

THE CULTURE

The black Africans of the south are in the majority and have traditionally dominated the government and civil service. The north is populated by people of Arab descent, as well as nomadic Tuareg, Peul Fulani and Toubou.

The difference between these two broad groups is profound. The animist or Christian southerners are mostly peasant farmers, tilling fertile land (ie people of the rains), while the northern Muslims are desert-dwelling pastoralists who live with the dry, dusty Saharan wind, the *harmattan*.

Surprisingly for such a subsistence economy, education is looked upon favourably, and literacy stands at 40% (compare this with around 16% in neighbouring Niger). Freedom of speech is also fiercely, if somewhat vainly, defended by various private newspapers and journals in N'Djaména; in particular the arrest of (and journalism ban on) the editors of *Notre Temps* in 2003 inspired vigorous protests.

ENVIRONMENT

Landlocked Chad has three distinct climatic zones. In the tropical south temperatures usually range from 20°C to 25°C, but can rise to 40°C just before the rains. The centre, where N'Djaména and Lake Chad are located, is a Sahelian blend of scrub and desert where prerains temperatures can rise to over 45°C. The arid north forms part of the Sahara desert and includes the Tibesti Mountains, which rise to the peak of Emi Koussi (3415m), the highest point in the Sahara.

Lake Chad was once one of the largest freshwater lakes in the world. Its dry season area of 10,000 sq km can rise to 25,000 sq km at the height of the rain. However, it is slowly drying up, and in 1984 disappeared completely during the worst of the Sahel drought.

TRANSPORT

GETTING THERE & AWAY
Air

The main airlines serving Chad are Sudan Airways, Ethiopian Airlines and Cameroon Airlines, which connect N'Djaména with major West and Central African cities at least once a week, including Khartoum (US$503) and Addis Ababa (US$548, twice weekly). Some European destinations are also covered, and Air France flies to Paris up to four times weekly (from US$920 return). See p430 for details of airlines that service Nigeria.

DEPARTURE TAX

The airport departure tax is officially US$8.50 for international flights, but you may be asked for twice that.

Land

Chad's borders with Libya and CAR are not currently considered safe for travellers.

CAMEROON

Minibuses run from the Rond-point de Demby in eastern N'Djaména to the Chadian border town of Nguelé (US$0.50) and, less frequently, directly to Kousséri in Cameroon; a motorcycle taxi between the two costs around US$1.30. From Kousséri there are regular minibuses to Maroua.

The border into Cameroon officially closes at 5.30pm. A 'departure tax' of around US$7 is pocketed by Chadian customs officials. You can also cross into Cameroon further south, via Léré or Bongor.

NIGER

The border between Chad and Niger runs roughly north through the Lake Chad area;

the main route between the two countries is a sandy track looping round to the north of the lake from N'Djaména to Nguigmi, via Mao. The quickest way to go is with one of the 4WDs that carry passengers from N'Djaména to Mao (US$21, 12 hours); there's usually a departure daily. Then from Mao, similar vehicles also do the run over the border to Nguigmi for around US$25.

Cheaper public transport in the form of pick-ups and big lorries is readily available, but you'll probably have to do the journey in stages, via Massakori, Nokou and Mao, which can take up to a week if you're unlucky.

Once in Niger, from Nguigmi take a pick-up to Diffa (US$350), from where there is plenty of public transport to Zinder; there is also a weekly SNTV bus between Nguigmi and Zinder, going on to Niamey.

Get your passport stamped in Mao (you'll be asked for US$5) and Nguigmi; you'll also be stopped at the two border posts in between, although for once the police will be more interested in African passengers than you (assuming you've got the right papers!). Remember that Niger uses West African CFA francs; you should be able to change your leftover cash unofficially at a rate of one to one (better for those coming from Chad than from Niger).

NIGERIA
To get to Nigeria from Chad you have to go through Cameroon. Follow the directions in the previous Cameroon section to reach Maroua, from where you can take a bush taxi straight to Maiduguri or a minibus to the border at Banki. Expect multiple checkpoints on the Nigerian side.

SUDAN
The overland route from N'Djaména to Khartoum is a real desert epic, often involving some hitching, and can easily take a week or more. There is no direct transport; the usual route is from Abéché via Adré, Al-Geneina, Nyala and El-Obeid. You should expect to change transport (and spend a day or two waiting for lifts) in each of these staging points.

Note that the area around the border, while not directly involved in Sudan's civil war, is still notoriously volatile; the northern road from Al-Geneina to El-Fasher was closed at time of research due to armed clashes and banditry, and you should seek local advice before attempting to cross by any route. Travellers are also often held up by officials at the border itself, sometimes for days at a time.

GETTING AROUND
In Chad, buses are nonexistent. Trucks, pick-ups and minibuses are your main choice for cross-country travel. Most of Chad's roads are not tar; they're mostly dirt tracks (pistes), making travel uncomfortable at the best of times and extremely difficult in the rainy season.

Within towns, taxis and minibuses are common; outside N'Djaména you'll also find fleets of *clandos* (motorcycle taxis).

N'DJAMÉNA

pop 610,000
Stretched out along the banks of the Chari River, N'Djaména is one of the more engaging Central African capitals, although it's by no means immune to the usual urban problems – the stark contrasts between modern and traditional are evident at every step. The atmosphere here is not always as friendly as elsewhere in Chad, but there's nowhere to beat it for life and activity, and at night the place is quite literally buzzing, as hundreds of generators struggle to take the strain off the city's beleaguered power grid and feed the sound systems of some of Africa's most vibrant bars.

ORIENTATION
The airport is under a kilometre from the northernmost tip of Ave Charles de Gaulle, the main street; despite the small distance involved, you'll have to bargain hard to get a taxi there or back for less than US$10, particularly at night. You can pick up shared taxis and minibuses from the Rond-Point de la Garde.

Having survived the devastation of the civil war, N'Djaména was subjected to a haphazard rebuild and is now split into two distinct sectors, highlighting its colonial roots. To the west of the Marché Central the smart commercial district is almost reminiscent of provincial France, sheltering well-to-do Chadians and a small expat community in its wide, leafy streets.

N'DJAMÉNA

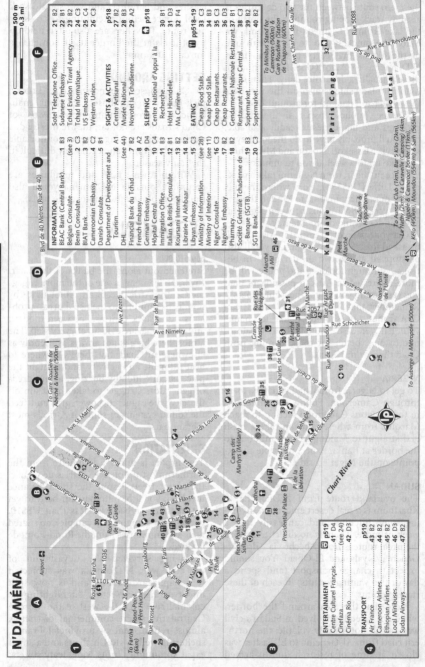

INFORMATION
BEAC Bank (Central Bank).................1 B3
Belgian Consulate........................(see 3)
Benin Consulate............................2 C3
BIAT Bank.....................................3 B2
Cameroonian Embassy....................4 C2
Danish Consulate..........................5 B1
Department of Development and
  Tourism...................................6 A1
DHL...(see 44)
Financial Bank du Tchad.................7 B2
French Embassy.............................8 A2
German Embassy............................9 D4
Hôpital Central............................10 C4
Immigration Office.......................11 B3
Italian & British Consulate.............12 B1
Koursami Internet.........................13 B2
Librarie Al Akhbaar.......................14 B2
Libyan Embassy............................15 C3
Ministry of Information.................(see 28)
Ministry of Interior......................(see 11)
Niger Consulate...........................16 C3
Nigerian Embassy.........................17 B2
Pharmacy....................................18 B2
Société Generale Tchadienne de
  Banque (SGTB)..........................19 B3
SGTB Bank..................................20 C3
Sotel Telephone Office..................21 B2
Sudanese Embassy........................22 B1
Tchad Evasion Travel Agency..........23 B2
Tchad Informatique.......................24 C3
US Embassy.................................25 C4
Western Union.............................26 C3

SIGHTS & ACTIVITIES   **p518**
Centre Artisanal...........................27 B2
Musée National.............................28 B3
Novotel la Tchadienne...................29 A2

SLEEPING   **p518**
Centre National d'Appui à la
  Recherche................................30 B1
Hôtel Hirondelle...........................31 D3
Ma Carrière.................................32 F4

EATING   **pp518–19**
Cheap Food Stalls.........................33 C3
Cheap Food Stalls.........................34 B3
Cheap Restaurants........................35 C3
Cheap Restaurants........................36 D3
Gendarmerie Nationale Restaurant...37 B1
Restaurant Afrique Central.............38 C3
Supermarket................................39 B2
Supermarket................................40 B2

ENTERTAINMENT   **p519**
Centre Culturel Français................41 D4
Cinefaza....................................(see 24)
Cinéma Rio.................................42 D3

TRANSPORT   **p519**
Air France...................................43 B2
Cameroon Airlines........................44 B2
Ethiopian Airlines.........................45 B2
Local Minibuses...........................46 D3
Sudan Airways............................47 B2

On the other side, the main residential areas are composed entirely of mud-brick houses with little in the way of modern amenities but plenty of character.

INFORMATION
Most amenities can be found towards the western end of Ave Charles de Gaulle.

Books
Librairie Al Akhbaar (Ave Charles de Gaulle) sells a good selection of books and journals in French, plus a few English-language newspapers and magazines.

Internet Access
Internet access is widely available: rates start at US$0.20 per minute, with some good deals available. **Tchad Informatique** (☎ 522519; t.info@intnet.td; per hr US$5), just off Ave Charles de Gaulle, offers one hour for US$2.50 between 4pm and 6pm on Saturday and 2½ hours for US$4.25 at the same times on Sunday, while **Koursami** (☎ 524043; Ave Charles de Gaulle; per min US$0.12) charges US$2.50 an hour all day Saturday.

Medical Services
Emergency medical services include the **ambulance service** (☎ 517725). The Hôpital Central is the largest medical facility in Chad, though conditions are not ideal. The pharmacy on Av Charles de Gaulle is a good place for medicines and advice.

Money
The best bank for travellers is the **Société Générale Tchadienne de Banque** (SGTB; just off Ave Charles de Gaulle), which changes cash plus travellers cheques quickly and easily and also does Visa cash advances for a fixed fee. At time of research, dollar rates were considerably better for Amex cheques than

for cash. The **Financial Bank du Tchad** (Ave Charles de Gaulle) may cash Eurocheques.

You'll find a limited black market in N'Djaména, particularly among the street traders on Ave Charles de Gaulle, where you can usually negotiate better rates for dollars than at the banks.

Post & Telephone
The **main post office** (Blvd de Paris; ⏰ 7-11.30am & 3.30-5.30pm Mon-Fri, 7-11.30am Sat) is next to the Sotel telephone office; private phone offices can be found all over town.

Tourist Information
N'Djaména's (and Chad's) only tourist office is the under-resourced **Department of Development and Tourism** (☎ 524420; cnr Rue de Farcha & Rue 1011).

Travel Agencies
The best of N'Djaména's travel agencies is probably the friendly **Tchad Evasion** (☎ 526532; Ave Charles de Gaulle), which runs a wide range of tours and expeditions, including to Lake Chad and the Ennedi region, and hires out cars for Zakouma National Park.

DANGERS & ANNOYANCES
Although N'Djaména is one of the safer cities in Central Africa, pickpocketing and petty street crime still occur, particularly when large groups of visitors hit town. Be very careful around the Marché Central; it's also best to avoid the western end of Ave Charles de Gaulle and the riverside area between the French embassy and the Novotel when there are few people around.

On the other side of the law, the city's many police and gendarmes (military police) can also be a problem, with regular ID checks on taxis and minibuses at major roundabouts in the evenings. Make sure you register with

---

NAME & NUMBER

Within 72 hours of arriving in N'Djaména you must register at the **sûreté** (Ave Félix Éboué); it's a relatively speedy process, requiring two photos. The **immigration office** (⏰ 8.30am-3.30pm weekdays) is on the right side of the compound at the back. You should also register with the police in each town in which you stay.

You'll also be required to register if entering Chad overland, particularly from Niger – almost every town between the border and N'Djaména has an army post and a police station, both of which will demand your details (and sometimes US$5 or so). Make sure you have plenty of passport photos for the registration forms.

the *sûreté* (security) office (Ave Félix Éboué) on arrival and carry your passport with you at all times if you don't want to have to argue your way out of nightly bribes.

SIGHTS

The small **Musée National** (Ave Félix Éboué; admission US$1.70; ☉ 8am-6pm Mon-Wed & Fri-Sat) displays recent palaeontological discoveries, including the record-breaking seven-million-year-old hominid skull (known as Toumai) found in the Djourab desert, northwest of N'Djamena in 2002.

To see local crafts being made, visit the **Centre Artisanal** (Rue de Marseille). The lively Marché Central and the surrounding streets have a great atmosphere during the day, while a walk by the river at sunset is much more relaxing.

SLEEPING

There is very little cheap accommodation in N'Djaména, so you'll have to take what you can get.

Hôtel Hirondelle (adjacent to Rue 2057; s/d US$12/15) There is no power or water during the day and the frequent comings and goings are a tad suggestive, but it's generally quiet here and the location, off Ave Charles de Gaulle right next to the market, is unbeatable. This place is really the best option in town. Insist on a terrace room rather than the grotty downstairs ones.

Ma Carrière (Blvd de Sao; r US$9) Southeast of the Paris Congo district, this dodgy joint is the only other cheap option around. It's more nightclub than hotel, with music til 2am at weekends and some distinctly unsubtle nocturnal activities.

Centre National d'Appui à la Recherche (☎ 522515; Rue de la Gendarmerie; r US$21; ✶) Over-priced but conveniently located near the airport; the surrounding *jardin scientifique* (botanical garden) makes up for the very basic rooms.

Auberge la Métropole (☎ 516292; r US$25; ✶) This upmarket pension is a bargain thanks to its out-of-the-way location, off Route de la Corniche in the Sabangali district. The ensuite rooms and wood panelling give a touch of class missing from many more expensive places, but it's often booked out. The restaurant here is also excellent.

La Caravelle (Ave Mobutu; camp site per person US$2.50-3.50) About 1km past the Rond-point du Pont, it's a decent camp site with a popular bar and restaurant, and can get pretty crowded when the overland trucks come through. Security is OK, but don't leave anything outside at night.

EATING & DRINKING

For a sit-down meal, the cheap restaurants around the Marché Central knock out some good standards, mainly for the lunchtime trade.

Restaurant Afrique Central (mains from US$1) One of several that stay open in the evening, this is a friendly eating house opposite the mosque.

Gendarmerie Nationale (Rue de la Gendarmerie; mains from US$0.40) If you're looking for something out of the ordinary, you could try eating with Chad's finest in their own cafeteria, where you'll certainly find yourself the centre of attention!

There's plenty of street food opposite the Place de la Libération and at the intersection of Ave Charles de Gaulle and Ave Gourang; at night you can get basic meals for around US$0.50 at any of the unlit stalls in Paris Congo or Moursal, or from the tiny kiosk outside the grand mosque.

Local nightlife is centred on the Paris Congo and Moursal districts, where the bars are generally the only places that have electricity.

SPLURGE!

Where most cities have a few good places to splash out, N'Djaména has an entire length of street – the western end of **Ave Charles de Gaulle** is a 1km strip straight out of small-town Europe, boasting banks, bookshops, Internet cafés, souvenir stalls, two Chinese restaurants, a French bistro, a Lebanese restaurant, half a dozen well-stocked supermarkets, several *caves du vin*, a good bar-pizzeria and two expensive nightclubs.

The real treat for budget travellers, however, has to be the wonderfully authentic French pâtisseries, which serve up delectable cakes, juices, milkshakes and real coffee for relatively reasonable prices in an almost scarily 'civilised' atmosphere. If you're looking for a brief escape from African life, this is the place.

There are also plenty of cheap joints near the gare routiére in Chagoua. Most close surprisingly early, but those that don't stay crammed until the early hours – try Bar 5 Kilo, Le Nathy or the Aurora Club on Ave Mobutu.

ENTERTAINMENT

Options are decidedly limited on this front in N'Djaména.

Centre Culturel Français (☎ 517705; Ave Felix Éboué) Hosts cultural events and exhibitions and also regularly screens films, usually of the arthouse variety.

Cinefaza (US$2) On the same site as Tchad Informatique, this informal picturehouse shows relatively recent DVDs on a big screen with a free soft drink thrown in.

Cinéma Rio (Rue du Marché; matinée/evening US$0.40/ 0.50) Screens Hindi films and third-rate action flicks.

GETTING THERE & AWAY

Airlines servicing Chad include:

Air France (☎ 522576; Ave Charles de Gaulle; ᛒ 7.30am-3pm Mon-Thu, 7.30am-12.30pm Fri, 8am-noon Sat)

Cameroon Airlines (☎ 517042; Ave Charles de Gaulle; ᛒ 7.30am-3pm Mon-Thu, 7.30am-12.30pm Fri)

Ethiopian Airlines (☎ 513027; Ave Charles de Gaulle; ᛒ 7.30am-3pm Mon-Thu, 7.30am-12.30pm Fri, 8am-noon Sat)

Sudan Airways (☎ 525148; Ave Charles de Gaulle; ᛒ 7.30am-3pm Mon-Thu, 7.30am-12.30pm Fri)

Land transport for most destinations can be found at the chaotic gare routière (called Station de Chagoua) on Voie de Contournement, 2km east of the centre. Minibuses run to Kélo (US$8, four hours), Moundou (US$13, eight hours) and Sarh (US$21, 12 hours); pick-ups and trucks are cheaper but take longer. In the rainy season, all prices and travel times can treble.

For Abéché (truck/pick-up US$21/42, two to three days) and Mao (US$21, 12 hours) you may have to head to the northern gare routière on Ave Nimeiry.

GETTING AROUND

Shared taxis and minibuses around town should cost around US$0.25 per seat. A taxi course (private hire) is negotiable, starting around US$2.50. Minibuses gather at the stand on Av Charles de Gaulle when empty.

AROUND CHAD

Travel in Chad is restricted to the south and east of the country, so we cannot cover the spectacular Tibesti Mountains of the north, or the truly vast stretches of desert of the centre. Places in this section are listed west to east, in order of distance from N'Djamena.

MAO

Anyone braving the rough desert crossing from Niger will pass through the white-washed trading town of Mao, capital of the once-powerful Kanem region of Chad. It's worth taking the opportunity to stretch your legs and spend a bit of time in this bustling town instead of jumping on the next vehicle out; the crammed central market in particular draws people from all over the district, and has much more of an outback feel to it than N'Djaména's Marché Central. One caveat: don't change foreign currency here if you can help it, as you'll get the lousiest rates in Chad.

If you're feeling hardcore, you could wander over to the thriving traditional **donkey and camel market** and try your hand haggling for a beast of burden. Doing the journey to Niger or N'Djaména on it is not something to undertake lightly or alone (and it certainly won't save you any money), but the trip would be absolutely the last word in adventure.

KÉLO

pop 36,0000

Once a tiny agricultural settlement, Kélo is now actually the fifth-largest town in Chad, but retains much of its small-town character, with a lively mazelike market and plenty of activity on the unlit streets after dark. It's a good place to break the journey between N'Djaména and Moundou or Sarh.

You can stay at the catholic mission or the basic Auberge Tandjilé for around US$5; the management at the latter seem sociable, but may try and stiff you with a 7.30am check-out. A bit further out of town, **Kélo Safari Hotel** (r US$17; ❄) is smarter but more expensive.

There are regular pick-ups to Moundou (US$3.50, three hours) from the main road past the auberge.

MOUNDOU
pop 282,000

Chad's second-largest town, set in a tranquil location on the bank of the Logone River, Moundou is probably best known for the **Gala brewery**, which famously stayed open throughout the civil war. It's not a bad place to spend a couple of days; almost everything you need can be found on the main street, Route de Doba, or just off it. The town has three banks, a post office and some very slow Internet access. You should register at the ST (immigration) office near the Prefecture.

Sleeping

Centre d'Acceuil La Fraternité (☎ 691578; r US$7-8.50) Run by a religious group, the centre has immaculate rooms with and without bathroom.

Hôtel Le Canari (r US$9) Not far from La Fraternité, the Canari has slightly rougher ensuites set around a small garden.

Catholic mission (Ave Charles de Gaulle; r US$14) This is one of the larger missions in Chad, located next to the cathedral near the river.

There are also several small, dubious auberges around the main street offering basic rooms from US$4.

Eating & Drinking

There are plenty of street stalls and cheap restaurants around Route de Doba, offering the usual staples and some good juices. Restaurant Oasis has some great outdoor seating, eccentric but friendly service and claims to do pizza. The Thursday night market in front of the Commissariat has a good range of fresh produce, including fish straight from the river.

Drinkers are spoilt for choice here, with countless seemingly identical bars strung out along the main road. There are also two nightclubs, **Climax** (entry US$2) and La Savane.

Getting There & Away

Frequent transport leaves for N'Djaména (12 hours) and Sarh (eight hours) from the parc des voitures, off the main road about 300m past the gare routière sign. Prices should be around US$10 for a pick-up, US$13 for a minibus and US$17 for the cabin of a 4WD; trucks are a little cheaper but a lot slower. Minibuses also go to Léré (US$13,

12 hours) and Figuil, over the Cameroon border (US$17).

Note that in the rainy season, the favoured route to N'Djaména cuts across Cameroon territory via Maroua, so make sure you have a Cameroon visa and a multiple-entry Chadian visa in your passport.

SARH
pop 194,000

An agreeably sleepy town shaded by enormous trees, Sarh was once constantly raided by Arabs from the north looking for slaves. These days it's not so well frequented, and apart from the good Centre Artisanal has little of interest for visitors: despite its status as Chad's cotton and sugarcane capital, local political opposition to the government has seen the city starved of resources. Even with the oil 'boom' set to transform the local economy in Doba, just 200km away, Sarh looks destined to remain little more than a provincial backwater.

There's very little accommodation available in Sarh.

Auberge Bolaou (☎ 681313; r with shared/private bathroom US$10/11; 🎛), near the eastern end of Ave Charles de Gaulle, has dim but decent rooms. They're not bad, but would be better value if the power was on during the day.

The **Catholic mission** (☎ 681232) is also a possibility.

For cheap food, head over to the Grand Marché in the centre of town, near the Cinéma Rex.

ZAKOUMA NATIONAL PARK

This national park, in the southeast of the country, is a major Chadian success story. After poaching and civil war ravaged local wildlife, the Chadian government and the European Union restocked the park with an eye on the affluent European tourist market.

Consequently, Zakouma is once again one of the best places in Central Africa to see large herds of elephants, as well as giraffes, wildebeests, monkeys, lions, and a wide variety of antelopes and birdlife.

Getting to the park can be expensive, although once inside costs are quite reasonable (park entrance fee US$9; vehicle entrance fee US$6; camera fee US$5). Accommodation is in comfortable **bungalows** (per person US$14) or you can **camp** (US$2).

Getting There & Away

Public transport to Zakouma, even from nearby Sarh and Am Timan, is practically nonexistent; the most realistic option is to organise a trip through one of N'Djaména's travel agencies. This is generally prohibitively expensive for the lone traveller, but can be quite good value if you can get a group of four or five together.

Tchad Evasion (see Information, p517) charges US$130 per day for a 4WD and driver, plus petrol (around US$40 to US$45 per day).

Although it is theoretically possible to reach Zakouma from N'Djaména in a day, expect a six-day round trip, including an overnight stop in Mongo in each direction and 2½ days in the park.

ABÉCHÉ

pop 188,000

Desert-locked, traditional and very, very hot, Abéché was once the capital of the powerful slave-trading Ouadaï sultanate and an important staging post on trading routes to Egypt, Sudan and the Indian Ocean. Plenty of more modern vehicles still head to and from Sudan – there's a Sudanese consulate here, although it's probably more prudent to sort out visas before getting this far. You may have problems trying to change US dollars in Abéché's banks.

Sleeping

Hôtel Jus de Fruits (r US$6, incl breakfast) Has simple rooms with fan and shared bathroom, but is often full.

Restaurant Etoile d'Afrique (US$3.50) If you're stuck for a bed, this place will let you sleep on the veranda.

There's also a Catholic mission.

CHAD DIRECTORY

ACCOMMODATION

Outside the capital, most hotels are fairly basic. Singles can usually be shared by two people for no extra cost.

The various Catholic missions around Chad also offer accommodation for travellers; they're generally more expensive than local hotels, but have good facilities and can provide full board.

BUSINESS HOURS

Banking hours are generally from 7.30am to 12.30pm weekdays, and most government offices, embassies and airlines close around 2.30pm; on Friday almost everything is closed by noon. Local businesses generally close between 1pm and 4pm, reopening in the evenings every day except Sunday.

DANGERS & ANNOYANCES

Simmering rebel activity and unexploded mines mean that travel to northern Chad's Tibesti region and along the border with Libya is off-limits. You should also check the current situation before heading to the northern province of Ennedi or to the Lake Chad area.

Crime is rarely a problem for visitors to Chad, although you should keep your eyes open in N'Djaména. However, the various police forces, particularly the ST or immigration, can be a nuisance anywhere you go, with checkpoints at every major town; you should register when requested to, but politely refuse all demands for payment if you can.

EMBASSIES & CONSULATES

The following countries have diplomatic representation in N'Djaména:

Cameroon (☎ 523473; Rue des Poids Lourds)
France (☎ 522576; off Ave Félix Éboué)
Italy & UK (☎ 523645; Rue 1035)
Niger (off Ave Gourang)
Nigeria (☎ 522498; Ave Charles de Gaulle)
Sudan (☎ 525010; off Rue de la Gendarmerie)
USA (☎ 516211; Ave Félix Éboué)

Chad maintains diplomatic representation in the following neighbouring countries: Cameroon, CAR, Libya, Niger, Nigeria and Sudan.

FOOD & DRINK

The food in Chad is typical of the region: tiny street stalls dish up cheap meals of rice, beans and soup or stew, while indoor restaurants offer omelettes, liver, salads, brochettes, fish and *nachif* (minced meat in sauce). Chicken and couscous appear frequently on menus, though less often on plates. To drink you have the usual range of *sucreries* (soft drinks), including the local Top brand, and excellent fresh *jus*, fruit concoctions with more resemblance to smoothies than normal juice.

CHAD

Mango and banana are the most common ingredients; bear in mind they're usually made with local water/ice. Beer is the favoured poison in bars, with a choice of local brews Gala and Chari or Cameroonian Castel.

HOLIDAYS

As well as religious holidays listed in the Africa Directory chapter (p1003), these are the principal public holidays in Chad:

1 January New Year's Day
1 May Labour Day
25 May Africa Freedom Day
11 August Independence Day
1 November All Saints' Day
28 November Republic Day
1 December Day of Liberty and Democracy

INTERNET ACCESS

Good connections are widely available in N'Djaména, but almost nonexistent elsewhere.

MONEY

There are no ATMs in Chad, but cash and travellers cheques can be changed easily enough, particularly in N'Djaména, but also in other regional towns. Cash advances on Visa cards are also available in N'Djaména, while most Catholic missions will also change cash at bank rates with no commission; ask for the *procure* (procurate).

PHOTOGRAPHY

Strictly speaking you should apply for a photo permit from the Ministry of Information; as this costs US$25 and can take up to a week to be issued, few people bother. Be discreet about taking photos, particularly in N'Djaména.

POST & TELEPHONE

The postal service is reliable, but can be slow outside N'Djaména. EMS rapid parcel services are available in major towns.

Sotel, the national telecoms company, has phone offices in most towns, charging US$3 per minute plus tax for calls to Europe (a five-minute call costs US$18 inclusive).

Private telephone offices are also common everywhere, operating with standard booths or mobile phones; charges vary but start at US$0.03 per unit in N'Djaména. There are no local telephone area codes in Chad.

VISAS

Everybody needs a visa to visit Chad. Costs for 30-day visas vary but can be as high as US$80 for some nationalities. You can obtain a visa at Chadian embassies in most countries in West and Central Africa. It can be worth getting a multiple-entry visa as some southern transport routes can cross international boundaries.

Visa Extensions

The **sûreté office** (Ave Félix Éboué) in N'Djaména issues visa extensions, usually on the same day; prices start at US$17 for up to 15 days.

Visas for Onward Travel

Visas for the following neighbouring and near-neighbouring countries are available from embassies in N'Djaména (see p521 for address details).

Benin A three-month tourist visa costs US$26 and requires two photos and a copy of your passport.
Cameroon One-month visas cost around US$35 to US$50; you'll need two photos. If you're just passing through, transit visas are free.
Niger The consulate issues one-month visas the same day for US$35 or two months for US$70; you need two photos.
Nigeria One-month visas cost between US$66 and an astounding US$155, depending on nationality; they require one photo and are usually issued within 24 hours.
Sudan Single-entry visas, valid for stays of one month from the date of entry, cost US$43. If you have an air ticket the visa is issued on the spot, but overland travellers will have to wait while the application is referred to Khartoum, a process that can take up to three weeks.
Other countries The French embassy issues visas within 24 hours for Burkina Faso, Côte d'Ivoire, Senegal, Togo (two days only), Djibouti (10 days only) and Gabon (apply one month in advance). Costs range from US$28 for 30 days to US$39 for a three-month, multiple-entry visa; all visas require two photos. At time of research the consular section was only open from 8am to 10am weekdays.

Congo (Zaïre)

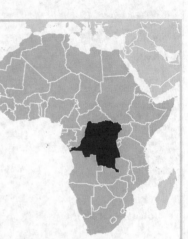

FAST FACTS

- **Area** 2,345,410 sq km
- **ATMs** none
- **Borders** Angola, Burundi, Central African Republic, Congo, Rwanda, Sudan, Tanzania, Uganda, Zambia
- **Budget** US$20 a day
- **Capital** Kinshasa
- **Languages** French, Lingala, Kiswahili, Kikongo, Tshiluba
- **Money** Congolese franc; US$1 = CDF420
- **Population** 57.2 million
- **Seasons** north of equator: wet (Apr–Oct), dry (Dec–Feb); south of equator: wet (Nov–Mar), dry (Apr–Oct)
- **Telephone** country code ☎ 243; international access code ☎ 00
- **Time** GMT/UTC + 1 (West); GMT/UTC + 2 (East)
- **Visas** US$60 for a single-entry, one-month visa; US$100 for a 60-day, multiple-entry tourist visa

WARNING!

Congo (Zaïre) has been at war since 1998, and the country is not safe to visit. We were unable to do on-the-ground research, so some information in this chapter may not be reliable. Check the situation before travelling to Congo (Zaïre).

Almost as large as western Europe, Congo (Zaïre) is a sprawling mass of rainforest, fast-running rivers, red clay and dust. Civil war, a lamentable lack of development, and a naturally impenetrable terrain means that Congo (Zaïre) remains the mysterious and intoxicating country that Joseph Conrad described as the 'Heart of Darkness'. Officially called the Democratic Republic of Congo (and increasingly referred to as DRC), Congo (Zaïre) is clinging to a fragile peace after decades of brutal civil war and neglect. If the situation stabilises, it has the potential to reclaim its mantle as Africa's most adventurous traveller destination. It offers the original Central African experience, and is worth a visit just for the vibrancy of the people and the music.

HISTORY

The country's history is a tragic story of an incredible potential that's been brutally dashed by foreign interference and home-grown oppression. The incredible richness of Congo (Zaïre) in terms of natural resources has been the country's downfall. First the population was horribly exploited by ivory and rubber traders during the country's private ownership by Belgian King Leopold II. And in recent years the mining of diamonds and coltan (used in mobile phones) has proved too lucrative to tempt foreign forces – most notably Uganda and Rwanda – to pull out of the civil war they are supporting in the country's northeast (see Civil War, opposite). However,

for the first time since independence, the future of Congo (Zaïre) is looking hopeful. In July 2003 a transitional power-sharing government comprising President Joseph Kabila and four vice-presidents (various rival rebel leaders and the civilian opposition) was sworn in to office. The aim of the power-sharing government is to bring an end to the civil war so that elections can be held by 2005 – the last elections were held in 1970. However, Uganda and Rwanda show no signs of ending their support of proxy armies, and even as the new government took power in Kinshasa, hundreds of civilians were still being murdered in fighting between ethnic militias in the Ituri Region.

'Dr Livingstone, I Presume'

The self-promoting adventurer and explorer Henry Morton Stanley allegedly spoke those words after his famous journey into Central Africa in search of the good Dr David Livingstone. Legend has it he was surprised to find he was ever considered to be missing. After this 'coup', broadly publicised in newspapers around the world, Stanley continued along the Congo River staking out the huge territory on its south bank for the Belgian King Leopold II in 1881. The area then enjoyed the dubious position of being the only colony ever to be owned by one man. Leopold II, monarch of one of Europe's smallest countries, proceeded to exploit one of Africa's largest, amassing a vast personal fortune without ever once visiting the country.

Hideous crimes were committed against the Congolese by Leopold's rubber and ivory traders. These included raiding villages and taking all the women and children captive as an incentive for the men to bring back ever-greater supplies of rubber from the forest. Those who did not bring back their quota often had their hands chopped off. All the while, in one of the earliest examples of a public relations campaign, Leopold passed off his Congo venture as a shining example of disinterested benevolent rule aimed at 'civilising the Negroes' and keeping the 'cruel Arab slave-traders' at bay. Eventually, the Belgian government agreed to buy the territory from the ailing King, but even then conditions for the Congolese scarcely improved. In a museum in Brussels dedicated to glorifying Belgian exploits in its former colony, documentation of these horrible atrocities is conspicuously absent.

Independence

The independence movement under the leadership of the charismatic revolutionary Patrice Lumumba gathered pace in the late 1950s at a rate that surprised the Belgian colonialists. The Belgians pulled out in 1960, leaving a population they had never bothered to school or to train to take over the reins of government. But Belgium's intervention was by no means finished. Together with the US, the country was instrumental in having Lumumba – who was seen as too pro-Soviet – overthrown in favour of army chief Joseph Désiré Mobutu. 'The cock who leaves no hen untouched' and 'the all-powerful warrior who because of his endurance and inflexible will to win will go from conquest to conquest leaving fire in his wake' are among the various translations of the name Mobutu Sese Seko gave himself after renaming the country Zaïre.

If Africa is a stain on the conscience of the world, then Belgium and the US are Lady Macbeth in this instance. By ensuring Mobutu's succession as leader they delivered newly independent Congo into the hands of a brutal dictator who proceeded to loot the country for personal gain for 32 years. Mobutu's institutionalisation of looting as a form of government caused Michela Wrong, author of *In The Footsteps of Mr Kurtz*, to dub his rule a 'kleptocracy' (see p29).

Civil War

'At least he kept the country together' is what Congolese weary of years of civil war often say of Mobutu. However, in 1997 Mobutu was toppled by rebel soldier Laurent Kabila who marched on Kinshasa from the east with the support of Rwanda and Uganda.

What hope he brought with him was soon dashed when Kabila outlawed political opposition while renaming the country (with no apparent irony) the Democratic Republic of Congo. Kabila then angered his former ally Rwanda by refusing to close down refugee camps where Hutus responsible for Rwanda's 1994 genocide were reforming. Anti-Kabila rebels with the support of Rwanda and Uganda then took control of several key border towns in the east of the country. But Angola and Zimbabwe waded in on the side of Kabila.

Thus began a civil war now fought ostensibly between rival Congolese militias, but in reality between the proxy armies of Uganda and Rwanda. Often called Africa's first world war, the conflict has caused the death of an estimated 2.5 million people.

The current president, Joseph Kabila, inherited this situation when he took control after his father's assassination in 2000. The young Kabila has repeatedly declared his intention to bring peace to the country, but the commitment of the new power-sharing government remains to be tested.

CONGO (ZAÏRE)

THE CULTURE

The Congolese are as unshakable in their faith as they are in their sense of style. And worshipping is a noisy business. A neighbourhood is far more likely to complain when a new church moves in (complete with sound system and huge speakers) than a brothel, which at least shuts down at 4am on a Sunday morning. Devout worship at one of the country's many imported churches – be it Protestant, Catholic or evangelical – is invariably accompanied by a strong belief in *fetishisme* or witchcraft. The two often meet in exorcisms, which are practically a national pastime and can be seen on TV, acted out like an alternative soap opera. It makes for surprisingly compelling viewing.

ENVIRONMENT

Congo (Zaïre) is the third-largest country in Africa, with much of it covered by impenetrable rainforest, and crisscrossed by huge rivers such as the Congo, Kasai and Oubangui, which flow into the Atlantic Ocean. The forests are home to all manner of primates, including Bonabo (or pygmy chimps – humans' closest relatives). The country includes the greater part of the Congo River basin, which covers almost one million square kilometres. To the east, Congo's borders run the length of the Rift Valley, opening up to the spectacular lakes of Albert (Mobutu), Edward (Rwitanzige), Kivu Tanganyika and Mweru, while mountains such as the Ruwensori range on the country's eastern border approach the 5000m mark. Congo (Zaïre) is also home to volcanoes; Mount Nyiragongo near Goma caused devastation when it erupted in 2002 covering much of the town in molten rock. There are vast, beautiful nature reserves in Congo (Zaïre) although most of them (including Kahuzi-Biéga and Virunga) are in the east, still patrolled by warring militias.

TRANSPORT

GETTING THERE & AWAY

You can fly to Kinshasa from Abidjan (Côte d'Ivoire), Bujumbura (Burundi), Douala (Cameroon), Johannesburg (South Africa), Lagos (Nigeria), Luanda (Angola), Libreville (Gabon) and Nairobi (Kenya). Although planes now fly from Kinshasa to the east of Congo (Zaïre), the east is more easily accessed via Kigali in Rwanda.

Most airlines have offices at Kinshasa's N'djili Airport. Alternatively, book through travel agents. Carriers include **Kenya Airways** (☎ 1221465; Hotel Memling, Ave Tchad, Gombé) and **SN Brussels Airlines** (☎ 8821346; Blvd 30 Juin, Gombé).

A ferry links Kinshasa with Brazzaville in Congo. You can catch a train from Lubumbashi to Johannesburg or Dar es Salaam.

GETTING AROUND

Flying is largely the only way to get around the vast territory that is Congo (Zaïre). However, airplanes are old and badly maintained and there have been several crashes. It is a wonder they don't happen more often. Domestic airlines include Hewa Bora Airways, Congo Airlines and Lignes Aeriennes Congolaises, all with offices at the airport or you can book through travel agents.

Train travel is possible from Kinshasa to Matadi, Lumbumbashi to Ilebo and Kalemie via Kabalo and Kisangani. You can also travel by road to Matadi, and then to Angola.

If you have enough time and aren't fussy about privacy you can travel by barge along the Congo River from Kinshasa to Kisangani. This is the real highway of Central Africa and a wonderful way to see the country. However, there is no fixed timetable for the departure of barges and they often break down or get stuck on sandbanks along the way.

KINSHASA

pop 5 million

Kinshasa is a huge, sprawling city, with more inhabitants crammed along its dusty roads than live in the whole country of neighbouring Congo. It is hectic, confusing and colourful, a sort of New York of Central Africa. But no-one could call it pretty. There are surprisingly deserted areas such as the once-grand (and now decrepit) colonial neighbourhood, or the centre of town on a Sunday. The general disrepair of Kinshasa and abundance of buildings in eternal stages of half-completion are as much due to a long-term lack of able government as to the ravages of war – Congo's various administrations have been too occupied trying to keep control of the country to develop it. The shanty towns of the suburbs are where you will find most of the population: hordes of begging children, women selling manioc, and men selling palm wine from huge, dusty plastic containers. Kinshasa is worth a visit for its traditional weavings and masks, such as those on display at the Académie des Beaux-Arts, and for the nightlife, where you can hear some of the best music on the continent. The country was, after all, the home of Africa's Elvis Presley, Papa Wemba.

ORIENTATION

N'djili international airport is 25km southeast of the city. Minibuses run to the city centre, but they are overcrowded, badly maintained and downright unsafe on the lawless, potholed roads. Opt instead for an unmarked taxi, which should charge US$10 for the drive into town – negotiate beforehand. The city centre branches off from the banks of the Congo River, looking directly across at Brazzaville on the other side. The diplomatic district of Gombé lines the riverbank with great views of floating water hyacinths and the skyline of Brazzaville.

INFORMATION
Internet Access
Prices are around US$3 per hour. A reliable, centrally located option is **Cybergd** (☎ 9903313; Ave Mobutu 18b, Masina).

Medical Services
Centre Privé d'Urgences (☎ 20 875; Ave du Commerce) is the best equipped of the emergency health centres in Kinshasa. There are several 24-hour pharmacies; the most central is **Maison de France** (Hal de la Gombé).

Money
Cash is king in Kinshasa, with travellers cheques and credit cards rarely accepted. US dollars are definitely preferred over Congolese francs, but they'll only be accepted if they're in good (or even mint) condition. You can change money at one of Kinshasa's banks or with black marketeers along the waterfront.

Telephone
Public phones consist of street hawkers who will let you use their mobile phones for a

fee. Alternatively, top-end hotels may let you make international calls.

Tourist Offices
Try the **Ministry of Tourism** (Ave Batetela, Gombé).

Travel Agencies
ICARE (☎ 8807608; Rwindi Building, Blvd 30 Juin) has extremely helpful staff.

SIGHTS & ACTIVITIES
If you are prepared to withstand lots of hassle and calls of 'mondele' ('white person'), head to the Central Market of Matongé for lots of local colour. Alternatively, the tourist market at **Marché de Valeur** (Pl de la Gare, Blvd 30 Juin) is great for everything from Congolese fabrics and masks to drums. Pay a third of the asking price tops, and keep an eye on your cash; it's locally known as Marché du Voleur (thieves' market). **Academy des Beaux-Arts** (Blvd 24 Novembre, Gombé) has beautiful gardens to stroll around and souvenirs of genuinely fine craftsmanship to buy in a more-relaxed setting.

SLEEPING
Kinshasa is expensive and real budget accommodation is hard to come by, but there are a few central and affordable options. Rather cheap but not especially clean hotels are also springing up in Matongé, but do take your own mosquito net.

EATING
Street-side vendors selling barbecued goat and manioc abound in Kinshasa and are your best bet for cheap eating. There are a couple of better-class places around town if you're sick of eating goat.

ENTERTAINMENT
Dancing and drinking beer pretty well covers the entertainment options in Kinshasa, although jazz and rumba can be found at some venues.

GETTING THERE & AWAY
Air France is the only airline with direct flights into Kinshasa (it flies from Paris to Kinshasa once or twice a week). KLM flies from Amsterdam to Kinshasa via Nairobi once or twice a week, and SN Brussels Airlines flies from Brussels to Kinshasa, usually via Douala, three times a week.

CONGO (ZAÏRE)

South African Airways flies between Kinshasa and Johannesburg about three times a week, and Ethiopian Airlines flies between Kinshasa and Addis Ababa around three times a week; you can also fly in from Nairobi on Kenya Airways.

Travelling overland, particularly from Uganda or Rwanda, is not recommended.

GETTING AROUND

There are no official taxis in Kinshasa, but you can hire unmarked taxis, known as 'taxi express', which tout for business outside the **Gallerie Presidentielle** (Blvd 30 Juin, Gombé). They cost from US$30 per day with driver. Alternatively, at much higher rates (from US$70), you can hire with **Avis** (Ave Batetela, Gombé) at the Intercontinental Hotel.

AROUND KINSHASA

A must-see while in Kinshasa is the **Chutes de Lukia**, 40 minutes by car or taxi from the centre of town, along the Matadi road. There is a decent restaurant, natural lakes to swim in and a Bonobo (pygmy chimp) orphanage, where you can play with the younger chimps. Beware if you are allergic to white 4WDs and walkie-talkies – it's a favourite haunt of resident UN and aid worker staff at weekends.

The fish market at **Kinkole**, 32km out of Kinshasa along the road to the airport, is worth a visit. The market was constructed by Mobutu to honour the country's fishermen as part of his 'authenticity' campaign. You can hire a pirogue for US$10 an hour and be paddled down the Congo River, drink intoxicating palm wine on the riverbank and try some of the country's best *liboke* (fish stewed in manioc leaves).

The botanical gardens of Kisanto are two hours' drive south of Kinshasa along the Matadi Road, or you can take the train. With a collection of 100-year-old trees from all over the world, and gentle rivers in which to swim, Kisanto is definitely worth a visit.

For an overnight stay, press on another two hours to the **Chutes du Zongo**, a nature reserve with waterfalls for swimming, and basic chalets with attached bucket-and-drain bathrooms. Take your own food to barbecue. Book via the **Ministry of Tourism** (Ave Batetela, Gombé).

AROUND CONGO (ZAÏRE)

GOMA

Once a popular stay-over for anyone going overland to or from Rwanda, Goma is now a base camp for the UN and other agencies trying to deal with the casualties of war – such as former child soldiers and people separated from their families. The town has changed beyond recognition with the eruption of Mt Nyiragongo, which covered it in molten rock.

KISANGANI

The major city along the middle reaches of the Congo River was once a fairly pleasant city, and a major hub for travellers. But it has never fully recovered from the 1997 fighting and remains in a state of disrepair.

LUBUMBASHI

In the heart of the copper belt, Lubumbashi was once a pleasant place, but (like so many cities in the south and east) was not spared the effects of rioting troops throughout the 1990s.

CONGO (ZAÏRE) DIRECTORY

BUSINESS HOURS

Businesses are usually open 8.30am to 3pm Monday to Friday and 8.30am to noon on Saturday.

DANGERS & ANNOYANCES

Avoid taking photos in public, especially of the river, government buildings and the airport, which are viewed as places of national security. Taking photos of these places can get you in serious trouble and even arrested.

Do not walk around at night. If you are involved in a car accident do not hang around; mobs can gather quickly. At roadblocks try to appear calm and get away quickly, showing photocopies of your documents if you have to, but don't hand over your originals or your passport.

Malaria remains rife (see p1032).

EMBASSIES & CONSULATES

The following countries have diplomatic representation in Kinshasa.

Belgium (☎ 8820109; Pl du 27 Octobre)
Canada (☎ 8841276; Ave Pumbu 17, Gombé)
Central African Republic (☎ 33 571; Ave Pumbu 11, Gombé)
Congo (☎ 34 028; Blvd du 30 Juin)
France (☎ 22 669; Ave Républic du Tchad)
Germany (☎ 27 720; Ave des Trois Z)
Kenya (☎ 33 205; Ave de L'Ouganda)
UK (☎ 8834775; Ave de Lemera 83, Gombé)
USA (☎ 8843608; 310 Ave des Aviateurs)
Zambia (☎ 21 802; Ave de l'École)

Congo (Zaïre) has embassies in Angola, Belgium, Congo, France, the UK and USA. Many of the country's embassies closed during 2003, but are likely to re-open.

MONEY

The local currency is the Congolese franc (CDF); it cannot be converted and cannot be taken out of the country.

It's hard to get to grips with the near-worthless notes, and if you change money on the street you will come away with a plastic bag full of them. An alternative is to use dollars, but only dollars in mint condition are accepted, and nothing below a US$20 note.

Travellers cheques and credit cards are rarely accepted; credit cards are only accepted in one or two upmarket hotels in Kinshasa. It is best to travel with a carefully concealed moneybelt containing US dollars.

You can change money around the port, but it's better to find a reliable contact (ask around where you are staying).

POST & TELEPHONE

The postal system ranges from unreliable to nonexistent.

Make calls from Internet centres or hotels. This is expensive, but land lines are rare. For local calls try using the street hawkers who rent out their mobiles at a fixed rate.

VISAS

All visitors need a visa. If flying into Kinshasa it is essential to get a visa beforehand. These cost US$60 for a one-month, single-entry visa, or US$100 for a 60-day, multiple-entry tourist visa. If crossing by land you can often get a visa at the border within 24 hours.

WOMEN TRAVELLERS

Exercise extreme caution if you are a female traveller. Do not drive alone after dark; instead drive in a convoy, if you can. Be very wary of the armed forces: rape has been used extensively as a weapon of war.

EAST AFRICA

East Africa is a natural wonderland. Terra firma: as wild as it gets. The original home of the safari – in the bad old days a magnet for Big Game hunters – the region is now as much a testament to our ability to restore as it once was to destroy. Nature here, in the cradle of civilisation, is dramatic, devastatingly beautiful and an antidote to concrete jungles. East Africa has the world's best national parks for wildlife – think Tanzania's Serengeti and Ngorongoro Crater, Kenya's Masai Mara and Uganda's Bwindi. Between them you can find every African animal you've ever dreamed of seeing and twice as many you've never even heard of.

From Addis Ababa to Dar es Salaam, East Africa seduces, inspires and throws up some mighty challenges: trek the rim of a live volcano, survive the streets of Mogadishu, climb the magnificent Mount Kilimanjaro. Indeed it's difficult not to go over the top when talking about East Africa: it has the nine highest mountains on the continent, Lake Victoria (which, as the largest lake on the continent, is bigger than some African countries), massive areas of tropical rainforest and mountain gorillas in between. Chimps, their more abundant cousins, compete for notoriety with breathtaking bird life in a region overflowing with lakes, waterfalls and rivers.

Dive into East Africa's coastline – from the Red Sea (one of the natural wonders of the world) to the Indian Ocean – and its world-class snorkelling reefs, endless sandy beaches and hot 'n' spicy islands such as Zanzibar. A great place to cut loose, Zanzibar is also a fine spot for culture vultures who love history and ancient architecture, although Ethiopia gives it a run for its shillings with her rock churches, island monasteries and ruined palaces. This is Africa at its most inspiring and beautiful – a veritable walk on the wild side.

Rwanda

HIGHLIGHTS

- **Parc National des Volcans** Scaling the slopes of the Virunga volcanoes to view the rare mountain gorillas of Parc National des Volcans (p542)
- **Kibuye** Soaking up the sun, sand and scenery at Kibuye, on Lake Kivu, Rwanda's new Mediterranean (p541)
- **Kigali by night** Checking the pulse of the nightlife in Kigali, which is slowly regaining its former reputation as a place to party (p537)
- **Best journey** Taking the ups and downs of the spectacular bus ride from Cyangugu to Kibuye along the shores of Lake Kivu (p541)
- **Off the beaten track** Getting up to monkey business in Nyungwe Forest National Park, the country's largest rainforest (p542)

FAST FACTS

- **Area** 26,338 sq km, just one-twentieth the size of France
- **ATMs** none
- **Borders** Uganda; Tanzania (open but not advisable); Congo (Zaïre) and Burundi (both open but dangerous)
- **Budget** US$25 per day
- **Capital** Kigali
- **Languages** French, English, Kinyarwanda
- **Money** Rwanda franc; US$1 = RFr350
- **Population** 7.4 million
- **Seasons** wet (mid-Mar–mid-May, mid-Oct–mid-Dec); dry (mid-May–mid-Oct, mid-Dec–mid-Mar)
- **Telephone** country code ☎ 250; international access code ☎ 00
- **Time** GMT/UTC + 2
- **Visas** US$60 for three months from embassy; two weeks only at most borders

Rwanda is known as Le Pays des Milles Collines (Land of a Thousand Hills), thanks to the endless mountains in this scenically stunning little country. Nowhere are the mountains bigger than the magnificent Virunga volcanoes in the northwest, and hidden among the dense forests here are some of world's last remaining mountain gorillas. The chance of an encounter with these noble creatures continues to draw visitors to Rwanda despite the country's painful past.

A beautiful yet brutalised country, Rwanda is known for the horrific events that unfolded here in 1994. It has been etched into the world's consciousness as the location

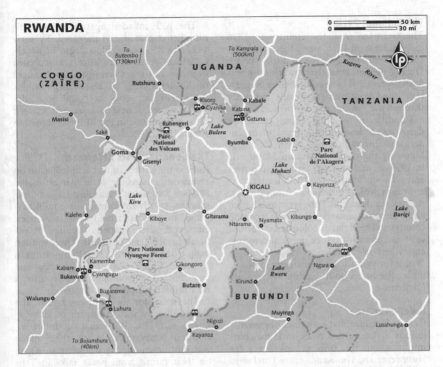

RWANDA

of one of the most vicious attempts at genocide in the history of mankind. What happened here is beyond belief, but the country has come a long way since. Forget the images of old, and start thinking of blissful beaches on Lake Kivu, primates galore in Nyungwe Forest and a lively night scene in Kigali. Coupled with good roads and efficient transport – not forgetting the thousand hills that slow things down – it really is a top spot for the independent traveller.

As long as security and stability persist, Rwanda is a refreshing country in which to travel, where travellers are a relative novelty and the rewards of the present outweigh the risks of the past.

HISTORY

The original Rwandans, the Twa Pygmies, were gradually displaced from 1000 onwards by migrating Hutu tribespeople who, in turn, came to be dominated by the Tutsi from the 16th century onwards. The authority of the Rwandan *mwami* (king) was far greater than that of his opposite number in Burundi, and the system of feudalism that developed here was unsurpassed in Africa outside Ethiopia.

The Rwandan *mwami* was an absolute ruler, with the power to exact forced labour and to allocate land to peasants or evict them from it. Tutsi overlordship was reinforced by ceremonial and religious observances; likewise, military organisation was the sole

preserve of the Tutsi, although intermarriage was blurring things by the time the Europeans arrived.

TRAVELLING TO RWANDA

Always inform yourself about recent developments in Rwanda before coming. Despite Rwanda's recent tragic history, it is currently safe to visit most of the country (including the Parc National des Volcans) and to travel overland to Rwanda from Uganda and Tanzania. Travelling overland to Burundi is very risky and it's downright dangerous to go anywhere near Congo (Zaïre).

RWANDA

The Colonial Period

The Germans took the country in 1890 and held it until 1916, when their garrisons surrendered to Belgian forces during WWI. During Belgian rule, the power and privileges of the Tutsi increased, as the new masters found it convenient to rule indirectly through the *mwami* and his princes.

Conditions for the Hutu peasantry deteriorated, leading to a series of urgent demands for radical reform in 1957, but following the death of Mwami Matara III in 1959, a ruthless Tutsi clan seized power and set about murdering Hutu leaders.

This provoked a massive Hutu uprising. A hundred thousand Tutsi were butchered, and many thousands fled into neighbouring countries. The Belgian colonial authorities were forced to introduce political reforms, and when independence was granted in 1962 it brought the Hutu majority to power under the prime ministership of Gregoire Kayibanda.

Independence

Certain Tutsi formed a number of guerrilla groups that mounted raids on Hutu communities, but this only provoked further Hutu reprisals. Thousands more Tutsi were killed, and tens of thousands of their fellow tribespeople fled to Uganda and Burundi.

The massacre of Hutu people in Burundi in 1972 reignited the old hatreds in Rwanda and prompted the army commander, Major General Juvenal Habyarimana, to oust Kayibanda.

In October 1990 the entire intertribal issue was savagely reopened when Rwanda was invaded by five thousand well-armed rebels of the Rwanda Patriotic Front (RPF), a Tutsi military front, from their bases in western Uganda. Two days later, at Habyarimana's request, France, Belgium and Zaïre (as it was then known) flew in troops to assist the Rwandan army to repulse the rebels.

With this support assured, the Rwandan army went on the rampage against the Tutsi and any Hutu suspected of collaborating with the rebels. Ugandan president Museveni was accused of encouraging the Rwandan rebels in an alleged attempt to repatriate the estimated 250,000 Tutsi refugees in western Uganda. The accusations were denied but the evidence is inconclusive.

The RPF invaded again in 1991, this time better armed and prepared. By early 1992 the RPF was within 25km of Kigali, at which point a ceasefire was cobbled together and the warring parties brought to the negotiating table. The negotiations stalled several weeks later and hostilities were renewed. A new peace accord between the government and the RPF was signed in August 1993.

The Genocide & Its Aftermath

In 1994 the entire conflict erupted again on an incomprehensible scale. An estimated 800,000 Rwandans were killed in just three months, mostly by Interahamwe militias – gangs of youths armed with machetes, guns and other weapons supplied by officials loyal to Habyarimana. Three million people fled the country to refugee camps in Tanzania, Congo (Zaïre) and Uganda, and an estimated seven million of the country's nine million people were displaced.

The spark for the rampage against the Tutsi minority was the death of Habyarimana (and his Burundian counterpart, Cyprien Ntaryamira) when their plane was shot down as it was landing in Kigali on their return from peace talks in Tanzania. The massacres that followed were no spontaneous outburst of violence but a calculated 'final solution' by extremist elements of Habyarimana's government to rid the country of Tutsi and Hutu reformists. Rwandan army and Interahamwe death squads ranged at will over the countryside killing, looting and burning, and roadblocks were set up in every town and city.

The government did not take into account the resistance of the well-disciplined forces of the Tutsi-dominated RPF, however, and by July 1994 the RPF had overrun the government forces and established a new Government of National Unity in Kigali.

Hutu extremists and their allies fled into eastern Congo (Zaïre) to regroup and launched cross-border raids into both Rwanda and Burundi from the refugee camps in the Goma and Uvira regions. Rwanda responded with raids into eastern Congo (Zaïre) and support for Tutsi rebels north of Goma.

The Hutu fought alongside the Zaïrean army, and the entire situation turned very ugly, as the million or so refugees were caught in the middle. But the RPF and their local allies proved too strong and swept across Congo (Zaïre), installing Laurent Kabila in power there and breaking the grip of the extremists on the camps. However, they soon decided Kabila was not such a reliable ally and became embroiled in Africa's biggest war to date, fighting over Congo (Zaïre) with nine other African states. Even today, the war there continues, and Rwanda remains committed through its local allies.

The International Criminal Tribune for Rwanda was established in Arusha (Tanzania), to bring to justice former government and military officials for acts of genocide. Several big fish have been sentenced in the past decade, but in Rwanda the prisons are still overflowing with smaller fish.

Rwanda Today

Rwanda has done a remarkable job of getting back on its feet under President Paul Kagame and has achieved an astonishing level of safety and security in a remarkably short time. The first parliamentary elections since 1994 were held in 2003 and the RPF won a convincing 74% of the vote, although this result was probably due in part to curbs on both the press and opposition. RPF leader Paul Kagame was again elected president, with 95% of the vote. However, as long as rebels remain at large in Congo (Zaïre), Rwanda's stability remains ephemeral. If the latest peace initiatives between Kigali and Kinshasa fail, Rwanda will no doubt continue the same strategy it has pursued the past four years: namely, keeping its problem exported, over the border in Congo (Zaïre).

THE CULTURE

Little Rwanda has one of the highest population densities of any country in Africa. Most Rwandaise speak at least some French, but increasing numbers of returnees in Kigali speak English, a legacy of their time as refugees in Uganda and Kenya. More than half Rwanda's population are Christians, about a quarter follow tribal religions and a small minority practise Islam.

Rwanda is home to two tribes, the Hutu and the Tutsi. The Hutu outnumber the Tutsi by more than four to one and, although the government is one of national unity with a number of Hutu representatives,

it is viewed by some as a Tutsi government ruling over a Hutu population. However, the government has done an impressive job of attempting to build a society with a place for everyone, regardless of their tribe. There are no more Tutsis, no more Hutus, only Rwandans. Idealistic perhaps, but it is also realistically the only road to the future.

ENVIRONMENT

Tiny and covered with a thousand hills, Rwanda has cultivated almost every unprotected piece of land, including sheer mountainsides edged with countless terraces, which some travellers say remind them of parts of Southeast Asia.

The average daytime temperature is 24°C, except in the highlands where the daytime range is between 12°C and 15°C. There are four discernible seasons: the long rains from mid-March to mid-May; the long dry from mid-May to mid-October; the short rains from mid-October to mid-December; and the short dry from mid-December to mid-March. It rains more frequently and heavily in the northeast, where the volcanoes are blanketed by rainforest.

Soil erosion caused by overuse of the land, anarchic terracing techniques and the lack of coordinated water management is the most serious problem facing the country. It could possibly create food shortages in future.

Wildlife in Rwanda for most people comes down to the mountain gorillas, the residents of Parc National des Volcans in the northwest, but there are also masses of monkeys in Nyungwe Forest National Park and a few lingering mammals in Parc National de l'Akagera in the east.

TRANSPORT

GETTING THERE & AWAY
Air

Within the region, Kigali is linked to Nairobi by Kenya Airways (US$260) and SA Alliance Air (US$215); to Kampala (Entebbe) by SA Alliance Air (US$190); to Bujumbura by Air Burundi (US$125) and Ethiopian Airlines (US$140); and with Air Tanzania to Dar es Salaam (US$245), via Kilimanjaro (US$155).

Land Transport
BURUNDI
We strongly advise against crossing by land into Burundi, as the situation in northern Burundi is extremely volatile. The main crossing point is between Butare (Rwanda) and Kayanza (Burundi). If for some crazy reason you want to do this, it's safer and quicker to take a minibus operated by **Yahoo Car** (☎ 085 41153 in Kigali), which travels to Bujumbura (US$8, 7am departure, six hours) daily. People are regularly killed on this road.

The road between Cyangugu and Bujumbura that goes via Bugarama (Rwanda), Congo (Zaïre) and Luhwa (Burundi) is very dangerous and should be avoided.

CONGO (ZAÏRE)
At the time of research, travelling overland to Congo (Zaïre) was extremely dangerous. If the situation improves, the two main crossings will again be between Gisenyi (Rwanda) and Goma in Congo (Zaïre); and also Cyangugu (Rwanda) and Bukavu in Congo (Zaïre).

TANZANIA
From Kigali, take a shared taxi or minibus to Kibungo (US$2, 1½ hours), and then a minibus (US$1, one hour) to the border town of Rusumo (there's cheap accommodation on the Tanzanian side). Once across the border, jump on any form of public transport – often a pick-up – to Ngara. From Ngara, catch a bus (US$10, 12 hours) to Mwanza. The road to Mwanza is mostly good but has some rough sections.

UGANDA
The main border crossing is located between Kigali and Kabale, via Gatuna (Rwanda) and Katuna (Uganda). Those travelling direct between Kigali and Kampala can travel with **Jaguar Executive Coaches** (☎ 086 14838; Place de l'Unité Nationale), which has a VIP bus (US$11) and a standard service (US$8), both depart 6am from the Okapi Hotel.

Between Kigali and Kabale there are lots of minibuses, but a change of vehicle at the border is involved. There are regular minibuses from Kigali to Gatuna (US$3, 1½ hours). Across the border in Katuna there are minibuses (US$0.50) and special hire taxis (US$4 for the car) to Kabale.

There's a second crossing between Ruhengeri (Rwanda) and Kisoro (Uganda), via Cyanika. From Ruhengeri to Kisoro via Cyanika is considered safe, but check the situation carefully in Kampala or Kisoro. Infrequent minibuses link either side of the border with Ruhengeri (US$1, 25km) and Kisoro (US$0.60, 12km).

GETTING AROUND
Air
There are no scheduled internal flights in Rwanda.

Boat
Before the latest civil war, there used to be ferries on Lake Kivu that connected the Rwandan ports of Cyangugu, Kibuye and Gisenyi, but these are still suspended at present. There is currently a speedboat available for charter between these ports, but at a price that hurts: Cyangugu–Kibuye costs US$160 and Kibuye–Gisenyi is US$120.

Hitching
Hitching around Rwanda is relatively easy because of the prodigious number of vehicles on the roads driven by expatriate aid workers. Drivers rarely ask for payment for lifts, because they're more interested in talking about mutual experiences in Africa.

Local Transport
Rwanda has an excellent road system, and plenty of modern, well-maintained minibuses serve all the main routes between dawn and about 3pm daily. Minibuses leave when officially full – which means when all the seats are occupied, unlike in Kenya and Tanzania, where many more are squeezed in.

The best minibuses are privately run, scheduled services operated by Okapi Car, Trans Express 2000, Volcano Express and Virunga Express. Destinations covered include Butare, Gisenyi, Kibuye and

Ruhengeri, and departures are guaranteed to leave – hourly in many cases. They are less crowded and drive more carefully than the usual minibuses, but cost a little more.

In Kigali and a few other places, you can use a 'taxi-motor'. It's just a motorcycle, but the driver can usually sling a pack across the petrol tank and they generally drive safely, if damn fast – but there's no helmet for the passenger.

Taxis

Taxis are necessary only in Kigali, but it is possible to find the occasional taxi in most other major towns.

KIGALI

pop 340,000

Rwanda was once eulogised as the 'Land of Eternal Spring', and Kigali, the capital, still mostly lives up to this description. Built on a ridge and cascading into the valley floors on either side, Kigali is small but beautiful in pockets, with superb views across the endless hills. It was quite badly trashed during the civil war in 1994, but following a long rehabilitation, it feels like a city looking ahead to the future, not back to the past.

ORIENTATION

Most minibuses arrive at Nyabugogo bus terminal, about 1.5km northwest of the centre. It's a long uphill walk, so catch a city minibus or a taxi motor (motorcycle taxi). The Jaguar bus from Uganda goes straight to the centre.

The Gregoire Kayibanda International Airport is at Kanombe, 12km from central Kigali. A private taxi to town costs about US$8, but it's much cheaper to catch a minibus (US$1) from outside the airport.

The low-rise capital sprawls over quite a large area. The commercial centre is on a hill to the southwest of the Place de l'Unité Nationale and is focused on Ave du Commerce and a network of streets that bisect it. To the south are several *grandes artères* leading into the diplomatic quarter where embassies and expensive restaurants are located. Quite a lot of night-time action is east of the centre in the suburb of Kacyiru.

INFORMATION

Bookshops

Most bookshops here stock mostly French-language publications.

Librairie Caritas (Ave du Commerce) A central bookshop for French titles.

Librairie Ikirezi (☎ 571314; Ave de la Paix) A wide range of English and French books on Rwanda and the world beyond.

Internet Access

Internet access is widespread and very cheap in Kigali.

Iposita Cybercafé (post office; per hr US$0.80) The cheapest place in town.

Okapi Hotel (off Blvd de Nyabugogo) There is a 24-hour Internet café in the lobby.

Medical Services

Kigali Hospital (☎ 71786) State hospital on Ave de la Paix.

Netcare King Faycal Hospital (☎ 82421) Swanky place in suburban Kacyiru, 7km northeast of the city centre.

Money

There are several banks around the city centre, but the best places to change money are the handful of bureaux de change near the main post office. **Banque de Kigali** (☀ 8am-3.45pm; Ave du Commerce) is the only place offering cash advances on credit cards.

Post & Telephone

The **main post office** (Ave de la Paix; ☀ 8am-5pm Mon-Fri, 8am-12pm Sat) has a poste restante service.

When it comes to making calls, there are plenty of kiosks opposite the post office. There are also public phone booths throughout the city.

Tourist Office

Office Rwandais du Tourisme et des Parcs Nationaux (ORTPN; ☎ 576514; ortpn@rwanda1.com; BP 905, Place de l'Indépendance; ☀ 8am-5pm Mon-Fri, 8am-noon Sat), the national tourist office, is just up from the Place de la Constitution. There's not a whole lot of information here, but this is where reservations should be made before visiting the Parc National des Volcans (see p542 for more details).

SIGHTS & ACTIVITIES

There are no sights and activities as such in Kigali, making it a good place to soak up the atmosphere of a real capital. Eat well,

KIGALI

Iposita Cybercafé	6 A2
Librairie Caritas	7 A2
Libraire Ikirezi	8 B3
Tanzanian Embassy	9 C2
Tourist Office (ORTPN)	10 B2
Ugandan Embassy	11 B4

SLEEPING   pp538-9
Belle Vie Lodgement	12 A2
Gloria Hotel	13 A2
Hôme d'Accueil Nazareth	14 B1
New Modern Guesthouse	15 B1
Okapi Hotel	16 B1

EATING   p539
Addis Ethiopian Restaurant	17 C1
Athenée Supermarket	18 A2
City 2 Shopping Centre	19 B1
Eden Garden	20 A2
L'Oasis	21 B2
La Sierra	22 B2
Le Glaçon	23 A3
Le Poseidon Bar & Restaurant	24 B2
Nile Grill	(see 25)
Pilipili	25 A2

DRINKING   p539
Bel Air Bar	26 A2
Travellers Bar	27 B1
Turtle Café	28 A3

SHOPPING   pp539-40
Cooperative des Artisans Rwandais	29 A2
Maison d'Objets d'Art Preferée	30 A2

TRANSPORT   p540
Air Burundi	(see 33)
Ataco Express	(see 38)
Ethiopian Airlines	31 B3
Jaguar Executive Coaches	32 B1
Kenya Airways	33 B3
Local Minibus Terminal	34 A1
Okapi Car	35 A2
SA Alliance Express	(see 33)
South African Airways	36 B2
Taxi Park	37 B1
Trans Express 2000	38 A1
Virunga Express	39 A2
Volcano Express	(see 27)
Yahoo Car	(see 32)

INFORMATION
Banque de Kigali	1 A2
Belgian Embassy	2 B3
Burundian Embassy	3 B2
Congolese (Zaïrean) Embassy (temporarily closed)	4 C3
French Embassy	5 C4
Internet Café	(see 16)

drink well and sleep well before diving into rural Rwanda.

SLEEPING

Compared with Kampala or Nairobi, the choice of budget accommodation is pretty poor. So Kigali is a good city to grit your teeth and splurge.

Kigali Hotel (☎ /fax 571384; s/d US$10/14), tucked behind the mosque on the road to Nyamirambo, remains by far the best budget deal in Kigali. It has large, clean rooms equipped with TV and bathroom. Great, if you can live with the early morning call to prayers from next door.

New Modern Guesthouse (☎ 574708; s/d US$6/10) is tucked down a small alley off Ave du

Commerce. It has some of the cheapest private rooms in the centre, but they are tatty, and the shared facilities hardly encourage ablutions.

Belle Vie Lodgement (☎ 557158; d US$10) is right opposite New Modern and offers slightly better rooms with a sink but shared shower and toilet. The shared toilets are passable and hot water sometimes dribbles out of the showers.

Gloria Hôtel (☎ 571957; fax 576623; cnr Rue du Travail & Ave du Commerce; s/d US$12/16) is the best of the uninspiring central places. It's pleasant and clean, but there are only cold water showers at present.

Hôme d'Accueil Nazareth (Blvd de l'OUA; dm US$1.50), behind the Église St-Famille church,

centre, offering such dishes as chicken, meat, sausages, fish and chips, as well as samosas and chapatis. Prices range from US$0.50 to US$1.75 for a meal, but be aware that grease features heavily in every dish.

Many of the markets around the city have local food stalls that are even cheaper than takeaways. For US$0.50, they usually offer a heaped plate of *matoke* (mashed plantains), Irish potatoes, groundnut sauce, beans, greens and meat or fish.

Fast food is growing in popularity in the capital. **Antonio's** (Map p554; Kampala Rd; meals US$1-2) is the best of the bunch, serving Indian, Mexican and Ugandan favourites at top speed. Curries and burritos are cheap, and portions are pretty large.

Nando's (Map p554) and Chicken Inn, both in the same building on Kampala Rd, turn out chicken in every size and shape at reasonable prices. Better is Vasili's Bakery (Map p554), serving perhaps the best range of pies and real cakes in the city, and located in the same strip.

Further west on Kampala Rd is Steers (Map p554), a South African clone of Burger King, plus Debonair's, a popular pizza parlour offering takeaways, in the same complex.

Restaurants

Fasika (Map p553; ☎ 268571; Gaba Rd; dishes US$3-4) is a decent Ethiopian restaurant in Kabalagala, just over the road from the ever-popular Capital Bar. The menu here includes a tasty Ethiopian platter with a splatter of everything.

Masala Chaat House (Map p554; ☎ 255710; 3 Dewinton Rd) is a popular little Indian place that serves a tasty *thali* (a traditional 'all-you-can-eat' meal) for US$3.

Chopsticks (Map p554; ☎ 250781; mains around US$4), at the Hotel Equatoria, is a sound option for a taste of the orient. It is big on

> **SPLURGE!**
>
> **Haandi** (Map p554; ☎ 346283; 7 Kampala Rd; dishes from US$5) is a classy eatery that offers North Indian frontier cuisine. The curries rank among the best in the world – seriously. The house vegetarian *masala* is excellent, as are the tilapia (fish) curries. Wine and dine well from about US$12 per person.

Chinese but has a few Thai and Vietnamese choices thrown in for good measure; and does promotional menus, such as four courses from US$6.

Le Petit Bistro (Map p553; Gaba Rd; steaks from US$4) is a must for steak lovers, an unpretentious little place that turns out mouthwatering meat at absurdly reasonable prices. It can take two hours for food to arrive – be patient and let the drinks flow.

DRINKING

Nightlife in Kampala is something to relish these days. Friday and Saturday are definitely the big nights out. Kampalans are a trendy, fickle bunch, and places that are in today are gone tomorrow – it pays to ask around on arrival.

All the most popular places to stay have bars: Red Chilli (Map p553) is one of the busiest that brings in expats as well as travellers; Backpackers (Map p553) is at it 24 hours a day and has a lush, leafy garden; and Blue Mango (Map p553) is classy, with fine furnishings and soft lighting guaranteed to make you stick around. The **Speke Hotel** (Map p554; Speke Rd) has a popular terrace bar out the front for those content to spend a little more for such surroundings.

Some of the best local bars with open terraces are along Kampala Rd. City Bar & Grill (Map p554) is set in one of the grandest Art Deco buildings in the city, while Slow Boat Pub & Restaurant (Map p554) is the place from which to people-watch on a busy afternoon.

On the Rocks (Map p554; Speke Hotel) is a major player on the nightlife scene. There is a covered bar and huge outdoor area, jammin' with people between 9pm and 4am. Drink prices are higher than elsewhere but fair, given that it is part of the Speke.

Just Kickin (Map p553; Cooper Rd) is a buzzin' sports bar up in the 'in' Kisementi district of town. It is a great place to start the weekend, as it shows all the big games of the sporting world, particularly rugby and football.

Nearby is **Wagadougou Bar** (Map p553; Bukoto St), which is more of a local joint. Its relaxed atmosphere makes it a good place to retreat to if Just Kickin is just too crowded.

Gaba Rd in Kabalagala is another popular late-night scene and is easy enough to get to by minibus or special hire taxi. **Al's Bar** (Map p553; Gaba Rd) is a legend in Kampala, although not always for the right reasons. You are guaranteed to find some people propping up the bar into the daylight hours of the morning. Right next door is the Half London, one of *the* places in Kampala for live music.

Drinkers with their dancing shoes can head to Ange Noir Disco (Map p553) or Club Silk (Map p553), both just off Jinja Rd in the industrial area of town. Entry costs from US$1.50 at either, and these are the spots to meet the local movers and shakers.

ENTERTAINMENT

Musicians Club 1989 (Map p554; National Theatre; admission free; ⏰ 7-10pm Mon), upstairs at the National Theatre, meets every Monday night for informal jam sessions. Drinks are cheap enough, and the place fills up with Ugandans letting off steam after a Monday back at work.

The Ndere Troupe performs Ugandan dances from 6pm every Sunday at the Nile Hotel, when they are in town; contact their **office** (Map p554; ☎ 341776; ntroupe@starcom.co.ug; Nile Hotel) to check the latest.

The best cinema is **Cineplex** (Map p554; Wilson Rd; admission US$2.30 at 2pm, 4.30pm, 7pm, 9.30pm), which shows mostly mainstream Hollywood movies. **Ciné Afrique** (Map p554; Kampala Rd) shows an eclectic mix of Hollywood, Bollywood and European arthouse films.

SHOPPING

Owino Market (Map p554) is a good spot to start sniffing about. It has a wicked selection of second-hand clothes and a maze of stalls selling everything but the kitchen sink – not very easy to fit in a backpack anyway. Craft shopping is less of a pull than in Kenya or southern Africa, but for the best browsing, try **Exposure Africa** (Map p554; 13 Buganda Rd).

GETTING THERE & AWAY
Air

Eagle Air (Map p554; ☎ 041 344292; www.eagleuganda .com; Kimathi Ave) has expensive flights from Entebbe to Pakuba airstrip in Murchison Falls National Park daily (US$85/170) and once a week to Kasese in the west (US$100/ 200). Other useful airline offices include:
Africa One (Map p554; ☎ 344520; 13-15 Kimathi Ave)
Air Tanzania (Map p554; ☎ 234631; 1 Kimathi Ave)
Ethiopian Airlines (Map p554; ☎ 254796; 1 Kimathi Ave)
Kenya Airways (Map p554; ☎ 344304; 1 Kimathi Ave)

SA Alliance Express (Map p554; ☎ 232555; Kimathi Ave)
South African Airways (Map p554; ☎ 345772; 1 Pilkington Rd)

Boat
See p551 for information about Tanzania Railways ferry services between Port Bell, near Kampala, and Mwanza (Tanzania).

Local Transport
From the chaotic bus station between Allen and Nakivubo Rds, buses go in all directions all over Uganda. Popular destinations include Fort Portal (US$6, six hours), Jinja (US$1.20, 1½ hours), Kabale (US$7, six hours), Masaka (US$2, two hours), Masindi (US$4, 3½ hours) and Mbale (US$4.50, three hours).

Post buses departs daily (except Sunday) at 8am from the main post office (Kampala Rd) to Kabale (US$7) via Masaka and Mbarara; Kasese (US$7); Fort Portal (US$7); Hoima (US$5) via Masindi; and Soroti (US$6).

For details on international bus services to Kenya and Rwanda, see p550.

Kampala has two parks for minibus taxis: the Old Taxi Park, on the triangle formed by Burton, Luwum and South Sts, which serves all parts of the city and country to the east; and the New Taxi Park, on the corner of Mackay and Namirembe Rds, which serves destinations in the countryside to the west and north. Prices and times for minibus taxis are pretty much the same as the buses.

GETTING AROUND
The ubiquitous white minibus taxis for trips around Kampala mostly leave from the Old Taxi Park. To find the minibus taxi you want, simply ask around – people are generally very helpful. Private taxis are unmetered and cost about US$2 for trips in the centre, more at night or into the suburbs. *Boda-bodas* offer a pillion seat for about US$0.50 around the city centre.

WESTERN UGANDA

BWINDI IMPENETRABLE NATIONAL PARK
Bwindi National Park, aka the Impenetrable Forest (331 sq km), is home to half of the world's known mountain gorillas, about

A WORD OF CAUTION!

Bwindi is very close to the border with Congo (Zaïre), which remains mired in a terrible civil war. In 1999, 14 tourists were kidnapped here – and eight killed – by Rwandan Hutu militia. Bwindi now has a large (mostly invisible) Ugandan army presence, so it is considered safe to visit. However, it never hurts to double check the security situation with the Uganda Wildlife Authority (UWA) office in Kampala or the backpacker pads in the capital.

320 of them – there's just one gorilla for every 20 million people! Penetrating the Impenetrable Forest is no picnic, as the terrain is steep and the foliage unforgiving, but what a reward. All the hardships are forgotten in an instant with the first glimpse of the gorillas in their mountain

kingdom. No bars, no cars – this is not a safari park but their world, and we are their privileged guests. Seeing the gorillas is one of Africa's magic moments so don't miss this chance, no matter how bad it looks for the budget.

Deep in the southwest of Uganda, the park is real rainforest and it rains a hell of a lot, so come prepared. As you might expect with a name like the Impenetrable Forest, it also gets pretty dark on a cloudy day, so bring fast film.

Activities

If US$275 to track gorillas makes you cringe, try a nature walk around parts of Bwindi forest to enjoy the birdlife, flora and other wildlife (perhaps chimps – but not gorillas). These guided walks cost US$3/6 per person for a half/full day, including a guide.

TRACKING GORILLAS

The chances of encountering gorillas are excellent, but the time spent with them is limited to exactly one hour. Only six people can visit each of the three habituated gorilla groups, so the demand for places can way exceed supply; head for Rwanda if the waiting list is long. All bookings should be made in advance through the UWA office in Kampala (see p555). There are sometimes no vacancies for months, so it might be necessary to shop around tour operators and backpacker hostels. If you just turn up at the park headquarters at Buhoma, and you're willing to hang around a few days, there might be last-minute cancellations – but there are no guarantees.

The cost of a permit to track gorillas is US$275 per person, including the park entry fee.

Rules of Engagement

Before meeting the mountain dwellers of East Africa, all visitors must observe the following gorilla etiquette:

- Anyone with any illness cannot track the gorillas. Shared biology means shared diseases. There's a full refund for those who are icky dick (common colds included).
- Eating and smoking anywhere near the gorillas is forbidden – they might take up the habit.
- Flash photography is another no-no – turn the autoflash off or you'll be mighty unpopular with both rangers and gorillas!

Also, remember:

- Speak quietly, and don't point at the gorillas – they might become paranoid.
- Leave *nothing* in the park; take out everything you bring in.
- Stay very close together, with the guide. Keep a few metres away from the gorillas.

And finally:

- As hard as it seems to stand still when faced by two tonnes of charging silverback, *never ever run away*... crouch down until he cools off.

UGANDA

Sleeping & Eating

Buhoma Community Rest Camp (camp site per person US$2.75, bandas per person from US$8), by the park headquarters, is part of a community tourism initiative to get locals more involved in tourist development here. There are twee little bandas set in spacious grounds. Hearty meals and cold drinks are available, plus hot water on request.

Most of the other places around Bwindi are upmarket lodges, but there are a few nameless canteens along the strip from the community camp, which churn out steaming mountains of *matoke*.

Some travellers end up spending a night in Butogota before walking to Buhoma the next day (see Getting There & Away, following). **Butogota Travellers Inn** (s/d US$11/17) has become a little ambitious with its pricing, so make for **Pineapple Lodge** (s/d US$3.50/ 4.50) – it's more basic, but they have a *basic* grasp of room pricing.

Getting There & Away

A direct Silverline bus travels every day in each direction between Kampala and Butogota (US$9, 12 hours), leaving at 4.30am!

Irregular pick-ups and minibus taxis connect Kabale with Butogota (US$4) on Tuesday and Friday, but other days are a nightmare; you have to persuade the driver to continue to the park headquarters for an extra US$4 per person.

From Butogota to the park headquarters at Buhoma (17km), public transport is scarce but is most likely to run in either direction on market day (Thursday). Pickups (US$11) or motorcycles (US$5) can be chartered for the run, which is money well spent to avoid a night in Butogota and a 17km walk.

FORT PORTAL

☎ 0493

Fort Portal, set amid rolling tea estates at the northern end of the Ruwenzori Mountains, is the base for trips into the Semuliki and Kibale Forest National Parks (p567 and p564, respectively) and a launching pad for exploring the crater lakes to the south.

Botex, overlooking the taxi park, offers not facial injections but Internet access.

Kabarole Tours (☎ 22183; ktours@infocom.co.ug; ⏰ 8am-6pm), signposted behind the Esso petrol station on Lugard Rd, is a useful agency in this part of the country for tours to most national parks in western Uganda. However, its prices aren't all that attractive.

Sleeping & Eating

Most people only pass through Fort, heading to the crater lakes or nearby national parks where more interesting accommodation awaits.

New Linda Lodge (☎ 22937; Balya Rd; s/d US$3/ 4.50) is the best of several basic cheapies just off the road to Kasese. Worth the little extra is the **Continental Hotel** (☎ 077 484842; Lugard Rd; s/d US$4.50/6, d with private bathroom US$11), right in the centre of town. Downstairs there are

---

FORT PORTAL

0 ————— 200 m
0 ————— 0.1 mi

INFORMATION
Botex Internet..............................1 A4
MTN..2 B4
Uganda Commercial Bank..............3 B4

SIGHTS & ACTIVITIES
Kabarole Tours............................4 B4
Mosque.......................................5 B3
Municipal Offices.........................6 B3

SLEEPING 🏠 pp560–1
Continental Hotel.........................7 B4
New Linda Lodge..........................8 B4
Rwenzori Travellers Inn................9 B4

EATING 🍴 pp560–1
Andrew Brothers Stores...............10 B4
The Gardens................................11 B3

TRANSPORT   p561
Bundibugyo Minibuses............(see 12)
Bus Stand...................................12 A4
Share-Taxis to Kamwenge &
    Rwaihamba.............................13 B3
Taxi Park....................................14 A4

To Mubende (150km)
& Kampala (322km)

To Semuliki
Valley (57km)
& Bundibugyo
(80km)

Toro Rd

Kaboyo Rd

Linon Rd

Kuhadua Rd

Rukidi III St

Babitha Rd

Lugard Rd

Kahinju Rd

Kasese Rd

Balya Rd

Market

To Crater
Lakes,
Rwaihamba
(23km), Lake
Nkuruba (25km)
& Kibale Forest
National Park
(35km)

To Kasese (74km),
Mbarara (155km)
& Kampala (400km)

clean rooms and a small restaurant, where they show films each night.

Ruwenzori Travellers Inn (☎ 077 500273; Kasese Rd; s/d US$8/14) is brand, spanking new, and at these prices it is serious value. Call ahead to check prices haven't risen – opening offers and all. Spotless, bright rooms and regular hot water.

The Gardens (☎ 22925; Lugard Rd; meals US$2-4) is one of the best restaurants in town. It serves some good Indian staples, including a filling vegetable curry, and all of the *mochomo* (barbecued meat) you could imagine and some you perhaps couldn't.

Self-caterers heading to Kibale Forest or the crater lakes must check out **Andrew Brothers Stores** (Lugard Rd), a little supermarket with pukka products for the provinces.

Getting There & Away
From the taxi park on Kahinju Rd, there are frequent departures to Kasese (US$2, two hours) and Kampala (US$6, six hours), among other places. From the bus station on Babitha Rd, a daily bus runs to Kabale (US$7, eight hours) via Kasese and Mbarara, and several buses go all the way to Kampala daily. The post bus leaves for Kampala daily (except Sunday) at 6.30am from the post office on Lugard Rd.

To Kamwenge (for Kibale Forest National Park) and Kasenda or Rwaihamba (for Lake Nkuruba), minibus taxis leave from near the bridge on Lugard Rd.

LAKE NKURUBA
A stunning crater lake among many great lakes in this area, Lake Nkuruba, 25km south of Fort Portal, is excellent for swimming and hiking.

Lake Nkuruba Community Camp Site (camp site per person US$2.20, bed in a banda US$4.50, lakeside cottage US$14) offers a tranquil setting for some serious R & R. Tents can be hired for US$1, as well a bike for US$2. Filling meals (US$3.50) and basic supplies are available in nearby Rwaihamba. For other accommodation around the crater lakes region, see the Kibale Forest National Park entry.

Minibus taxis that travel from Fort Portal to Kasenda and Rwaihamba (there are plenty on Monday and Thursday) pass Lake Nkuruba (US$0.60, 45 minutes). The lake is signposted on the left just before Rwaihamba.

KABALE
☎ 0486
Kabale is Uganda's highest town (about 2000m) and it gets a touch chilly at night – don't forget the winter woollies. This southwestern corner of Uganda is a stunner, with its intricately terraced hills and fjordlike lakes.

There are several foreign exchange bureaus in Kabale, including the banks near the post office and in the Highland Hotel, but rates are poor compared with Kampala – bring local cash. Western Union transfers are available from **Centenary Rural Development Bank** (Kisoro Rd). Internet access is available at **Kabale Computer Centre** (Kisoro Rd), next to Royal Supermarket.

The UWA maintains a **Gorilla Parks Information Office** (Kisoro Rd) here, but the staff cannot book gorilla trips and are not in direct contact with either Bwindi or Mgahinga. It is best to phone Kampala to stay on top of the situation.

Sleeping & Eating
Most budget places are in the noisy but central part of town near the bus and taxi station. Lake Bunyonyi is a much more satisfactory place to stay.

Visitours Hotel (☎ 077 443449; Kisoro Rd; s/d US$2.20/4.50) is impressive value for those striving to save the shillings. Rooms are grouped in threes, sharing a bathroom and small lounge.

Sky Blue Hotel (☎ 22154; Kisoro Rd; s/d US$4.50/ 6), opposite Visitours, is scrupulously clean, and service includes towels and soap. All rooms are named after the planets, so if you are suffering from the runs you might need to think about Uranus.

Trans Backpackers Hostel (☎ 071 149510; Kisoro Rd; per person US$3) is a budget place brought to you by the team who run Bunyonyi Overland Camp at nearby Lake Bunyonyi. Beds are certainly cheap and it might liven up as word spreads.

Lords Rest House (☎ 077 629492; Kisoro Rd; r US$9) is definitely the place to go for that little bit more comfort. The sparkling bathrooms include hot water and the rates include breakfast.

Little Ritz Restaurant (Nyerere Ave; meals from US$2.50) is one of the best restaurants west of Kampala. This surprisingly elegant place has good service and memorable food.

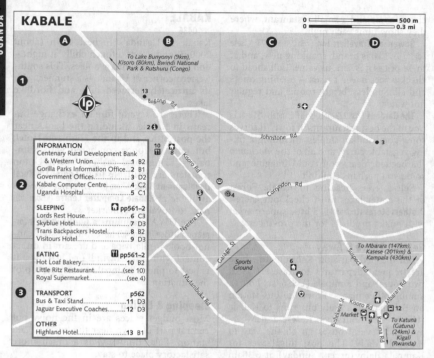

KABALE

To Lake Bunyonyi (9km),
Kisoro (80km), Bwindi National
Park & Rutshuru (Congo)

Bugongi Rd

Johnstone Rd

Kisoro Rd

Corydyon Rd

Nyerere Dr

Garage St

Sports
Ground

Mulambuka Rd

Budugwe St

Kisoro Rd
Market

Katuna Rd

Suspect Rd

Mbarara Rd

To Mbarara (147km),
Kasese (201km) &
Kampala (430km)

To Katuna
(Gatuna)
(24km) &
Kigali
(Rwanda)

INFORMATION	
Centenary Rural Development Bank & Western Union	1 B2
Gorilla Parks Information Office	2 B1
Government Offices	3 D2
Kabale Computer Centre	4 C2
Uganda Hospital	5 C1

SLEEPING	pp561–2
Lords Rest House	6 C3
Skyblue Hotel	7 D3
Trans Backpackers Hostel	8 B2
Visitours Hotel	9 D3

EATING	pp561–2
Hot Loaf Bakery	10 B2
Little Ritz Restaurant	(see 10)
Royal Supermarket	(see 4)

TRANSPORT	p562
Bus & Taxi Stand	11 D3
Jaguar Executive Coaches	12 D3

OTHER	
Highland Hotel	13 B1

Downstairs, Hot Loaf Bakery serves tasty samosas, as well as other delicious pastries and cakes, making it a good road stop before a long journey.

Among the hotels in town, Visitours does the business for guacamole fans and Sky Blue is a wise choice for those in need of a steak.

Those planning to do a bit of self-catering at Bwindi or Lake Bunyonyi should make for **Royal Supermarket** (Kisoro Rd), which holds a healthy stock.

Getting There & Away

Several buses go to Kampala (US$7, six hours) via Mbarara and Masaka early every morning from the main bus station. The post bus departs at 6.30am daily (except Sunday) for Kampala from the main post office on Kisoro Rd. For information about transport to Kigali (Rwanda), see p551.

Buses to Kisoro (US$4) depart at 10am and 4pm, passing over the Kanaba Gap with stunning views of Lake Bunyonyi and the Virunga volcanoes along the way.

LAKE BUNYONYI

Lake Bunyonyi looks like something straight out of *The Hobbit*, with terraced fields plunging into hidden bays and tiny islands dotted about. Guesthouses and locals have **dugout canoes** for rent, but practise before planning a *grand tour de Bunyonyi*, as many travellers end up going round and round in circles, known locally as the *muzungu* corkscrew.

Bunyonyi Overland Camp (☎ 23741; highland@ imul.com; camp site per person US$1.60, s/d tents US$6/9, cottages US$17) just keeps on growing, its sculpted gardens extending along a lovely stretch of lakeshore. It has steaming hot water and excellent toilets, and electricity is on the way. Go cheap or go in style, there is something for everyone here, but service at the restaurant can be slow, slow, slow.

Jasper's Campsite (Itambira Island; camp site per person US$1.40, dm/s US$2/3, house US$6) was hugely popular once but lost its way with the departure of the manager. It looks set to pick up with a new mentor. Big meals, board games and a basic bar make for an island hideaway. Catch a canoe from the mainland.

To get to Lake Bunyonyi from Kabale catch a minibus taxi (best on Monday and Friday), hitch, walk (about 9km), charter a motorcycle *boda-boda* or arrange a private taxi. The easiest is the shuttle service (US$1.50) from the Highland Hotel at 9.30am or 4.30pm.

KASESE
☎ 0483

Kasese is the uninspiring base for an expensive assault on the Rwenzori Mountains. Otherwise forget it, as it is a hot and dusty boom-and-bust town.

Rwenzori Mountaineering Services (RMS; ☎ 44235; rms@africaonline.co.ug), the appointed company for organising treks in the Rwenzoris (see right), is located beneath the Saad Hotel.

Rwenzori National Park Office (Rwenzori Rd) also offers information on climbing the mountains. Most punters pay their fees in advance at UWA headquarters in Kampala, but it is possible to pay here for those making the decision at short notice.

Centenary Rural Development Bank not only changes cash but also represents Western Union for those who suddenly decide they must conquer the mountains but lack the whopping US$480 required.

Sleeping & Eating

Kogere Modernised Lodge (Stanley St; s/d US$2.75/3.30) does not appear to be especially modernised but is a basic and decent enough little place.

Ataco Holiday Inn (Stanley St; s/d US$4/6) is clearly not part of the Holiday Inn hotel chain, but it is a clean and affordable option.

Saad Hotel (☎ 44139; Rwenzori Rd; d in old/new wing US$10/15) has for years been a popular travellers' hang-out for those venturing into the Rwenzoris. The new wing is worth the extra if only for the carpets. The restaurant has good service, but the menu is pretty basic.

Cheap eats are easy to find in Kasese. **Good Times Restaurant** (Stanley St; meals US$0.60), opposite the Saad Hotel, knocks together huge portions of cheap Ugandan standards and is great value.

Kasese Cafe (Rwenzori Rd) also has a reasonable menu of cheap, standard food, including some slightly more adventurous dishes than the average around town, plus fresh juices.

Titi's Supermarket (Rwenzori Rd) is the best stocked in Kasese for those heading up the Rwenzoris.

The nightlife scene is surprisingly interesting. Wednesday night is ladies' night in town, but the weekend is when it really gets going. The best bars are on Stanley St, including Comfort Zone and Friends Corner, but for a heavier night try **Club Atlas** (US$1; ♈ Wed & Fri), the only nightclub in town.

Getting There & Away

Eagle Air flies from Kasese to Kampala (US$100) once a week.

From the bus/taxi station, or from individual bus offices along the main streets in the town centre, buses go daily to Kampala (US$6, eight hours), via Masaka and Mbarara, and to Kabale (US$6, six hours). Minibus taxis frequently leave for Fort Portal (US$2, two hours) and Mbarara (US$2.75, three hours) from the roundabout to the southeast, near the Esso petrol station.

RWENZORI NATIONAL PARK

The fabled, mist-covered Mountains of the Moon, the Rwenzoris stretch for about 100km, and include several mountains that are permanently covered by snow and glaciers. The three highest peaks are Margherita (5109m), Alexandra (5091m) and Albert (5087m) – all on Mt Stanley.

Trekking the Rwenzoris has never been as popular with travellers as Mt Kilimanjaro and Mt Kenya because trekking conditions are tough, and the mountains have a well-deserved reputation for being very wet at times. As it says on the wall of Bujuku hut, 'Jesus came here to learn how to walk on water. After five days, anyone could do it'. But those who take up the challenge are rewarded with magnificent scenery, including tropical vegetation that soon yields to alien-like giant groundsel and the glistening glaciers that top the peaks. And unlike Kili or Kenya, you'll probably have it all to yourself; gazing over Congo (Zaïre) from the heights, you'll feel like Sir Edmund Hillary.

The park reopened in 2001 after closing for five years owing to rebel activity.

Trekking

Contact the UWA office in Kampala or the RMS office in Kasese: UWA administer the

US$480 charge for the seven-day climb, and RMS controls all facilities in the park and organises the treks.

A six-day trek is the absolute minimum set by park rules, but seven or eight days is better, including one or two days at the top huts. Starting in Nyakalengija, the route winds through the Guy Yeoman Hut (3450m), the Kitandara Hut (3990m), the Bujuk Hut (3900m) and John Mate Hut (3350m). The best times to trek are between late December and late February and from mid-June to mid-August. Even at these times the higher reaches are often enveloped in mist. Good all-weather clothing is required, but RMS rent a lot of gear.

KIBALE FOREST NATIONAL PARK

The **chimpanzees** are the stars at Kibale. There are hundreds and hundreds here, plus great hordes of monkeys, giving this small national park (just 560 sq km) one of the highest primate population densities in the world. It's not as strenuous as tracking the gorillas, but you don't get as up close and personal either. The chimps tend to keep a safe distance in the tall trees, chomping on fruit and defecating at will, but it's still a fascinating experience for the uninitiated. An excitable chimp makes mountain gorillas and monkeys look decidedly shy.

From the park headquarters at Kanyanchu, guided walks in search of the chimps (3km to 5km, two to four hours) can be arranged along well-marked tracks. The walks start at 8am (the better time) and 3pm and cost US$20 per person, plus park fees, making Murchison Falls National Park the cheaper place to track chimps these days.

BIGODI WETLAND SANCTUARY

A cheaper pursuit is the **Bigodi Wetland Sanctuary**, a community tourism project established to protect the Magombe Swamp, a haven for birds with 137 species. Guided walks (US$5.50) depart from the visitors centre on demand and take three hours. The sanctuary is just off the road between Fort Portal and Kamwenge, about 6km southeast of Kanyanchu.

Sleeping & Eating

Kanyanchu Park Headquarters (camp site per person US$6, banda s/d for US$6/8) is at the heart of things

and has smart *bandas*, a tree house and tasty food supplied by a local women's group.

Safari Hotel (camp site per person US$2, rooms US$3, bandas US$4.50) is a cheerful little spot in Nkingo village, about 6km from the park headquarters towards Bigodi village. Very basic, but a warm welcome is assured.

CVK Resort (☎ 077 792274; cvk.resortbeachlodge@ infocom.co.ug; campsite per bed US$3; bandas per bed from US$4, r with private bathroom US$20) occupies a fine ridge near Lake Nyabikere, about 18km on the road to Kamwenge from Fort Portal. It's also a good base from which to arrange hikes and other activities.

Getting There & Away

Minibus taxis travelling from Fort Portal to Kamwenge pass the park headquarters (signposted on the left about 6km before the village of Bigodi) at Kanyanchu.

KISORO

Kisoro is a one-horse town at the southwestern tip of Uganda and a base for trips to Mgahinga National Park (see opposite). Other reasons to come are few and far between. Exchange rates are poor in Kisoro so come armed with shillings.

Mgahinga National Park Office (☎ 30098) is the place to inquire about visiting the gorillas.

Rugagana Tourist Valley Camp Site (camp site per person US$2), popular with overland truckers awaiting gorilla permits, is about 1.5km from central Kisoro on the road to Congo (Zaïre). Tents are for hire at US$3.

In Kisoro, **Virunga Hotel** (☎ 30109; s/d US$3.50/6, d US$14 with private bathroom), just off the main road in town, is arguably the best place thanks to a healthy selection of rooms. Cheap local food is served.

Skyblue Hotel (☎ 30076; s/d US$4.50/7) is a not-so-distant relative of the Kabale outfit of the same name. Super service for these prices and one of Kisoro's better restaurants.

Horizon Coaches (☎ 077 469774) has three buses a day to Kampala (US$9, 4.30/6/8am). There are plenty of minibus taxis to Kabale (US$3, two hours).

LAKE MBURO NATIONAL PARK

This national park (260 sq km) is the zebra capital of Uganda. Midway between Masaka and Mbarara, the terrain is savanna with scattered acacia trees. There are five lakes, including Mburo, and some of the rarer mammals in Uganda, such as impalas, elands, roan antelopes, reedbucks, klipspringers and topis, as well as your bog standard buffaloes and hippos. Lake Mburo is one of the few national parks in which visitors are allowed to **walk**, accompanied by a ranger.

Rwonyo Rest Camp (park headquarters; s/d/tr bandas US$6/8/11) offers some of UWA's better bandas. Relatively expensive meals are available, or you can cater for yourself, buying fresh fish from locals. More serene for campers is the **camp site** (per person US$6) on the shores of Lake Mburo, just a short distance from Rwonyo.

There are three entrances to the national park from the main Masaka-Mbarara road, but for hitching into the park or chartering a vehicle, it's best to use the route from Sanga. A 4WD is recommended, but a trip around the park is possible in a 2WD car during the dry season.

MASAKA
☎ 0481

Masaka is not a place where travellers linger; for most it's just an overnight stop en route to the Ssese Islands in Lake Victoria (see p567), or for anyone travelling overland to Tanzania. In 1979 Masaka was razed by the Tanzanian army in the closing stages of the war that ousted Idi Amin. A lot of rebuilding has taken place, but there's still some way to go.

Masaka Backpackers (☎ 077 619389; camp site/ dm/bandas US$2/3/8) has a homely, rural feel thanks to the switched-on owner, but it is out of the way – 4km south of town just off the road to the Tanzanian border. Take a Kirimya taxi, get off at Kasanvu and follow the signs.

In Masaka proper, **Victoria End Guest House** (3 Elgin Rd; s/d US$6/8) is the cheapest but hardly an inspiring deal. The restaurant is more appealing than the rooms. Better to splash the cash and head to **Hotel La Nova** (☎ 21520; 12 Hobert Ave; s/tw/d US$14/17/20), which has smart rooms, a restaurant and bar.

Tropic Touch (Kampala Rd; dishes from US$2-3.50) has a top selection of Indian and Pakistani cuisine and some continental favourites to match. Portions are truly humungous.

Buses and minibus taxis run frequently to Kampala (US$2, two hours) and Mbarara (US$2.50, 2½ hours).

MBARARA
☎ 0485

There's not a lot to linger for in Mbarara as there was a lot of destruction during the war, but it's a useful place to stop on the way to or from southwestern Uganda. It's also a base for trips to **Lake Mburo National Park** (see opposite).

Standard Chartered Bank (☎ 20088; 24 High St) has an ATM and can change travellers cheques.

For reliable Internet access, head to the **Alliance Cybercafé** (High St) in the Alliance Française building.

Sleeping & Eating
Mayoba Inn (☎ 21161; 1 High St; s/d US$4/5, with private bathroom US$7/8) gets the vote among the cheaper places as it is well managed. There's also a restaurant and bar here.

Hotel Plaza (☎ 077 482159; 35 Mbaguta St; s/d/tw US$3/4/6) has the cheapest beds in town, and the eight simple rooms are acceptable enough for a night's sleep.

Pelikan Hotel (☎ 21100; fax 21704; Bananuka Dr; r US$5.50, s/d with private bathroom US$8/14, ste US$33), just south of Kabale Rd, is the best bet for those who want a large, clean and quiet room with a bathroom. Rates include breakfast.

For steaming heaps of local food for less than a buck, try Western Hotel or Friends Corner, both on Bremba Rd in the centre of town.

Mbarara Coffee Shop (High St; dishes US$2-3) has an excellent menu of pastas and curries, and inexpensive sandwiches and cakes – the vegie curry is particularly wholesome.

Getting There & Away
Buses and minibus taxis frequently go to Kampala (US$4, five hours), Masaka, Kabale and Kasese.

MGAHINGA NATIONAL PARK
Small park (34 sq km), big personality – this is the place for fans of big vistas and brooding volcanoes. Contiguous with Parc National des Volcans in Rwanda and Parc National des Virunga in Congo (Zaïre), together they form the Virunga Conservation Area (420 sq km), home to half of the world's mountain gorillas. When it comes to beautiful backdrops and gorillas in the mist, Mgahinga (and Parc des Volcans) leaves Bwindi

trailing as the jagged Virunga volcanoes are Africa at its biggest and best.

Activities

TRACKING GORILLAS

Reservations to visit the gorillas must be made at UWA headquarters in Kampala (see p555). The cost is US$220, including park fees, a ranger and armed guards. Six visitors per day leave the park headquarters at Nte-beko Camp, 12km from Kisoro, at 8am.

Although getting a booking at Mgahinga is usually easier than at Bwindi, the gorillas in Mgahinga sometimes cross into Congo (Zaïre) for a vacation. We can't follow, even with a passport, so chances of seeing the gorillas are lower at Mgahinga than in Bwindi or Rwanda. It's also a small family here compared with 35 gorillas in the Susa Group across the border in Rwanda.

HIKING

Mt Muhavura (4127m), Mt Sabinyo (3669m) and Mt Gahinga (3437m) can be climbed in a day for US$30 per person, including a ranger/guide. The 13km **nature trail** (per person half/full day US$3/6) offers the chance to spot some of the hundred or more species of bird, including the scarlet-tufted malachite sunbird – a blaze of colour. A number of other trekking options available in the area skirt the edges of the park, thereby saving you the entry fee.

Sleeping & Eating

Mgahinga Community Campground (camping per person US$1.70, banda beds US$3.50, twin/4-bed bandas US$7/13) is a fine little establishment near the main gate. It has top views of the volcanoes. There is a small canteen, and all proceeds from it are pumped back into the local community. Well worth supporting. Otherwise the nearest budget accommodation is in Kisoro (see p564).

Getting There & Away

There's no public transport between Kisoro and the park headquarters, so you'll have to walk (12km), hitch a ride (there is little traffic) or charter a pick-up (about US$15) from Kisoro.

QUEEN ELIZABETH NATIONAL PARK

Home to the greatest collection of mammal species in Uganda, this park (2000 sq km)

WARNING

There have been several armed robberies in the remote Ishasha area in the far south of the park. Ask around before venturing to this area.

is bordered to the north by the Rwenzori Mountains and to the west by beautiful Lake Edward. It once boasted massive herds of elephants, buffalos, kobs, waterbucks, hippos and topis but, like Murchison Falls, much of its wildlife was wiped out during the civil war. Still, it's worth visiting to see the huge numbers of hippos and some of the 500 species of bird.

Take a boat trip (US$8, two hours, 9am to 11am and 3pm to 5pm) up the **Kazinga Channel** between Lake George and Lake Edward to see hippos and pelicans.

The stunning **Kyambura (Chambura) Gorge**, in the eastern corner of the park, is home to a variety of primates, including chimpanzees. The best way to visit this little Eden is on a **walking safari** (US$20 per person, three to five hours), organised at the ranger post there.

Rangers are available for **wildlife drives** at US$5.50/8 per vehicle per half/full day.

Sleeping & Eating

The main places to stay are on Mweya Peninsula, overlooking Lake Edward. **Students' Camp** (dm US$3, camp site per person US$5) is the cheapest place, but is often full to the roof with Ugandan school parties, leaving camping the only option.

The **Ecology Institute** (dm US$5.50, r per person US$11) is an easier place to find a bed. Rooms are clean, if musty, but the shared bathrooms leave something to be desired.

Tembo Canteen (meals from US$1.50), at Students' Camp, is where the safari drivers hang out. Wholesome meals are served here, but you need to order in advance. There are also basic food supplies available in the nearby shop.

For something more sophisticated, the restaurant at the luxurious **Mweya Safari Lodge** (☎ 0483 44266; meals US$5-7) creates some fine flavours. Consider popping in for a sundowner cocktail on the terrace and an indulgent dinner. Forget the rooms – rates start at US$79.

Getting There & Away

The main gate is at Katunguru, accessible on any minibus taxi travelling between Kasese (US$1, one hour) and Mbarara (US$2, two hours). From the gate, it's 24km to the Mweya Peninsula. Try hitching at weekends or charter a vehicle in Katunguru (around US$10 to US$15) if traffic is light.

SEMULIKI NATIONAL PARK

Semuliki is part of the vast Ituri forest, where the steaming jungle of Congo (Zaïre) collides with the higher plateau that is Uganda. The main attractions of Semuliki are the **hot springs** near Sempaya and the (commercialised) **Pygmy villages** near the village of Ntandi, a few kilometres before Bundibugyo. The best part of any trip around the park, however, is probably the magnificent views over the rainforest and savanna of the Semuliki Valley and Congo (Zaïre) beyond.

At the park headquarters at Ntandi, there are **camp sites** (per person US$6). There are also two **bandas** (☎ 0493 22245; incl meals US$10), at Kichwamba/Nyankuku, located on the way to the nearby town of Bundibugyo. The money funds a local orphanage.

Minibus taxis travel between Fort Portal and Bundibugyo and can drop passengers at Ntandi. Otherwise, charter a vehicle with a driver from Fort Portal, rent a motorcycle or take an excursion offered by Kabarole Tours (see p560).

SSESE ISLANDS

☎ 0481

This is the number one spot for chilling out in Uganda, an idyllically beautiful group of 84 islands lying off the northwestern shores of Lake Victoria, east of Masaka and south of Entebbe. Beaches ring the islands, complete with swaying palms for that tropical touch, while inland lie rolling hills coated with lush rainforest. Locals live in villages along the shoreline and launch their fishing boats each evening at sunset. The principal islands are Buggala (with the largest town of Kalangala), Bufumira, Bukasa, Bubeke and Kkome.

Many spots afford beautiful views over the lake and across to the other islands. Negotiating with fishermen for a **boat trip** around the islands is easy, and **swimming** is also possible off most of the islands, as long as you observe the usual precaution about reedy areas (to avoid bilharzia).

There is nowhere to change money on any island.

Sleeping & Eating

The accommodation options are mostly limited to Buggala Island, usually in or near Kalangala.

Hornbill Camp Site (☎ 077 729478; camp site per person US$2, dm US$4, bandas US$11) is the most popular spot, about a 15-minute walk below Kalangala. It's a fun and friendly place to stay right on the lakeshore.

PTA Andronico's Lodge (☎ 255646; camp site per person/dm/d US$1/3/4.50) in Kalangala village is pretty basic and camping is a squeeze. However, the owner is a local character who welcomes guests as one of the family. There is a second branch near Scorpion Lodge in Liku.

Panorama Camping Safaris (☎ 077 406371; camp site per person US$1.60, bandas with shared/private bathroom US$11/17), below Kalangala near the water, is well set up with hot water on request and a generator.

Scorpion Lodge (camp site per person/s/d US$1/2/4) is about 500m from where the Bukakata ferry docks in Liku. It is hardly inspiring but might do at a push if you cross on the last ferry. Few travellers hang around Liku.

Getting There & Away

From the New Taxi Park in Kampala, catch a minibus taxi towards Masaka and get off at Nyendo (about 3km north of Masaka). Kalangala Express (US$2.30, 10am and 2pm, four hours) has two big buses a day from Nyendo straight through to Kalangala. There is also a regular ferry between Bukakata and Liku if you get to Bukakata under your own steam. Pick-ups go to Kalangala (US$1) from Liku.

EASTERN UGANDA

JINJA

☎ 043

Jinja, a charming town on the shores of Lake Victoria, is emerging as the Vic Falls of East Africa, with adrenaline activities galore at nearby Bujagali Falls. Check out the leafy 'suburbs' in the northwest to get an idea of how grand this town must have

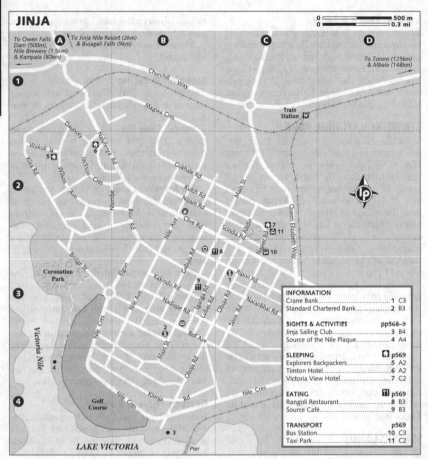

JINJA

0 _____ 500 m
0 _____ 0.3 mi

To Owen Falls (A)
Dam (500m),
Nile Brewery (1.5km)
& Kampala (80km)

To Jinja Nile Resort (2km) (B)
& Bujagali Falls (9km)

(C)

(D)

To Tororo (125km)
& Mbale (148km)

INFORMATION
Crane Bank...............................1 C3
Standard Chartered Bank............2 B3

SIGHTS & ACTIVITIES   pp568–9
Jinja Sailing Club.......................3 B4
Source of the Nile Plaque..........4 A4

SLEEPING   p569
Explorers Backpackers................5 A2
Timton Hotel.............................6 A2
Victoria View Hotel...................7 C2

EATING   p569
Rangoli Restaurant.....................8 B3
Source Café...............................9 B3

TRANSPORT   p569
Bus Station.............................10 C3
Taxi Park................................11 C2

been in its heyday. Jinja is the source of the mighty Nile, the world's longest river, which winds its way from here through Egypt and Sudan to the Mediterranean.

Information
Standard Chartered Bank (☎ 122661; 2 Grant Rd) changes travellers cheques and has an ATM. The **main post office** (cnr Main St & Bell Ave) has the usual postal and communication services. The **Source Café** (Main St) is a popular place to get online and one of the coolest coffee shops in the provinces.

Sights & Activities
The source of the Nile is one of the most spectacular white-water rafting destinations

in the world. There are three companies offering exhilaration without compromise: **Adrift** (☎ 041 252720; adrift@surfthesource.com), **Equator Rafts Uganda** (☎ 123712; rafting@utonline.co.ug) and **Nile River Explorers** (NRE; ☎ 120236; rafting@starcom.co.ug). You'll have a blast with any of them. The charge is US$65 at the time of writing. Credit cards are accepted and pick-up in Kampala is included.

The **Source of the Nile**, marked by a popular but uninspiring plaque, is all finished in garish reds and yellows thanks to official sponsorship by Bell Brewery. Nearby is a bronze bust of Mahatma Gandhi commemorating one of the spots where his ashes were scattered – was Gandhi perhaps the first to raft the Nile?

Bujagali Falls are more like a series of monstrous rapids than a waterfall, but the location is stunning. The falls are about 11km from central Jinja; find a minibus taxi or catch a *boda-boda* (motorcycle taxi). As well as the popular budget camps here, it is also possible to do some quad biking with **All Terrain Adventures** (☎ 077 377185; www.traveluganda.co.ug/ata), including a US$50 half-day trip for those who haven't aced all their cash on rafting or gorillas already.

Nile Hile Bungy (Jinja Nile Resort; ☎ 122190; bungy@surfthesource.com) is the newest fun in town, a 44m-high drop over the Nile. It is signposted 2km down the road to Bujagali Falls.

Sleeping

Explorers Backpackers (☎ 120236; rafting@starcom .co.ug; 41 Wilson Ave; camp site per person US$3, dm US$5, d US$15; 🖳) is a popular budget crashpad with a cheap bar, satellite TV and the obligatory pool table, as well as a new adventure centre for activities around Uganda. It also runs **Nile River Explorers** (camp site per person US$3, dm US$5, bandas US$15), a popular camp site above Bujagali Falls.

Speke Camp (☎ 075 584171; www.bujagali.co.ug; camp site per person US$2, dm US$5, d bandas US$15), is right next to Bujagali Falls themselves and has an attractive site. There's a small restaurant and bar area that fills up on weekends.

Timton Hotel (☎ 120278; 15 Jackson Cres; camp site per person US$2, s/d/ste US$10/17/28) offers camping in a well-manicured garden. The rooms could be worth the indulgence if you have had enough of your fellow travellers for a while.

Victoria View Hotel (☎ 122319; 36 Kutch Rd; tw US$6) is probably the best of the cheap hotels in central Jinja, although its name is purely wishful thinking. Rooms include a bathroom and it is conveniently located near the taxi park.

Eating & Drinking

Of the eateries along Main St, one of the best is Rangoli Restaurant, which has large vegetarian *thalis* (a mixed curry selection, including rice and poppadoms) at US$2.50 to keep the hunger at bay. The Source Café, with a wide selection of light meals and some of the best Ugandan coffee around, is also mighty popular here.

Jinja Sailing Club (below Nile Cres; mains US$3.50-5) has lush lawns that run right up to the edge of the lake. It's one of the best spots in town to sip a cold drink and watch the sun go down across the lake. Although generally pricey, it has a regular three-course lunch at US$4 – worth the trek across town.

Serious partying goes on at Explorers Backpackers when overland trucks are in town or out at Speke Camp if they are hosting one of their regular theme nights.

Getting There & Away

Buses and minibus taxis leave from the area along Kutch Rd and frequently travel to Kampala (US$1.20, 1½ hours), as well as Malaba (US$2.80, two hours), Busia (US$2.50, two hours) and Mbale (US$2.50, two hours).

MBALE

☎ 045

Mbale is a thriving provincial city with a superb setting at the bottom of Mt Elgon (4321m). It's an excellent base for expeditions to Mt Elgon National Park (p570) and Sipi Falls.

Information

Standard Chartered Bank (☎ 35141; 37 Republic St) can deal with major currencies and travellers cheques, and has an ATM. Internet access is available at **Serve Supermarket** (5 Cathedral Ave) and **Rocks Internet Café** (15 Republic St).

For information on trekking on Mt Elgon, visit the **Uganda Wildlife Authority office** (☎ 33720; uwaface@imul.com; Masaba Rd; ⏱ 8am-5pm) near Mt Elgon Hotel (not to be confused with the Mt Elgon View Hotel).

Sleeping & Eating

Mbale Tower Lodge (☎ 34620; 1 Pallisa Rd; s/d US$3.50/ 6, d with private bathroom US$7) is the pick of a pretty meagre bunch of cheapies, primarily as it is slap bang in the middle of town, overlooking the clock tower. Mull over the philosophical musings on the wall behind reception.

Apule Safari Lodge (☎ 077 502421; 5 Naboa Rd; s with shared bathroom US$4.50, d with private bathroom US$7) offers 'executive accommodation', although most corporations would disagree. Each of the well-tended rooms is named after one of Uganda's many lakes.

Mt Elgon View Hotel (☎ 34668; 7 Cathedral Ave; s/d US$7/8, d with private bathroom US$14) is the most traveller-friendly hotel in town. You can forget about misty-eyed views of Mt Elgon as there's no chance of seeing the peak from here. Beneath the hotel is Nurali's Café, an inspiring Indian restaurant, which offers a succulent fish tikka at US$3, plus some Ugandan dishes, a bit of Italian and a smattering of Chinese – almost a gastronomic grand tour. It's a popular drinking spot as well.

Many of the cheaper hotels have their own simple restaurants, such as the **Mukwano Restaurant** (6 Manafa Rd), conveniently located at the Mukwano Hotel opposite the taxi park and bus station.

Club Oasis (Cathedral Ave; admission US$0.60; ☺ Wed-Sun) is *the* late-night spot for pool, music and a dash of dancing.

Getting There & Away
Mbale is well connected by minibus taxi to Tororo (US$1, one hour), Jinja (US$2, two hours) and Kampala (US$4.50, three hours).

To Budadiri (park headquarters for Mt Elgon National Park) and Kapchorwe (for Sipi Falls), infrequent minibus taxis leave from the taxi park on Kumi Rd.

SIPI FALLS
Sensational Sipi Falls has three tiers, but the iconic lower one drops straight over a sheer cliff. Quite a sight, Sipi is 55km northeast of Mbale.

Guides are easy to arrange (about US$2) for short hikes around the falls, and are worthwhile because some trails are not well marked.

The **Crows Nest** (☎ 077 687924; thecrowsnest@ yahoo.com; camp site per person US$3, dm US$6, cabins US$12/15) offers some stunning views across to the falls. Cabins are sort of Swedish in style, and the restaurant turns out food with flair.

Moses' Camp Site (camp site per person US$2, bandas per person US$4.50), perched near a cliff, is set amid flourishing flower gardens with some big vistas. The basic restaurant serves simple but effective meals.

From Mbale, take a minibus taxi to Sipi or Kapchorwe (US$2, one hour) and jump off near the falls. Start early, as transport dries up later in the day. It might be more convenient to hire a private taxi if you're taking a day trip from Mbale.

MT ELGON NATIONAL PARK
Mt Elgon is an affordable alternative to the Rwenzoris, offering challenging but accessible wilderness trekking and wild scenery. The park encompasses much of Mt Elgon, which has one of the largest surface areas (80km by 50km) of any extinct volcano in the world, and runs right up to the Kenyan border. Wagagai is the highest peak at 4321m.

Trekking
Tourism on Mt Elgon is still in its infancy, so you need to be resourceful, patient and self-sufficient, and not expect the sort of well-worn paths found on Mt Kenya or Mt Kilimanjaro. The reward is fewer folk on the trails. The best time to trek is between December and March, and June and August. However, the seasons are unpredictable, so it can rain at any time.

The three main trekking routes are the **Sasa Trail**, which starts at Budadiri (US$1.50 from Mbale), the **Sipi Trail**, which starts at Sipi Falls, and the less-used **Piswa Trail**, which starts at Kapkwata. Allow four to five days return for a complete trek to the main peaks.

The best place to organise a trek is the UWA office in Mbale – see p569. The information centres at Budadiri, the Forest Exploration Centre (near Sipi) and Kapkwata can also help.

Trekking on Mt Elgon costs US$25 per person per day, including park entry fees, camping and ranger guide fees. It does not include porters (US$4.50 per day). These prices cover food for the guide and porters as well, but not tips, which are welcome. Fees can be paid in Mbale or at the information centres.

> **WARNING**
> Don't attempt to trek without a guide as it is illegal. It could also end in tears as Elgon is a big mountain.

Sleeping
With the new Sipi Trail, many trekkers start or finish at Sipi Falls – see that entry (left) for more details.

The park has several camp sites along the main trails. Basic tents and sleeping bags can be hired from the Forest Exploration Centre, but bring all cooking equipment, food and water.

In Budadari, **Rose's Last Chance** (camp site per person US$3, r US$4) is a popular place to stay before or after scaling the heights. Fun and friendly, it brings guests closer to the local scene, testing local brews being a favourite activity.

The **Forest Exploration Centre** (camp site per person US$4, dm US$6, s/d cottages US$11/16) has solid dorms and tasteful cottages. It is 1½ hours from Sipi on foot – contact the UWA office in Mbale for bookings (p569).

Those starting out on the less popular Piswa Trail can stay at the **Kapkwata Guesthouse** (r US$6), which is unsurprisingly in Kapkwata.

NORTHERN UGANDA

MURCHISON FALLS NATIONAL PARK

The best all-rounder in Uganda, Murchison (3900 sq km) is the largest park in the country. The Victoria Nile River flows through it on its way to Lake Albert. Wildlife was decimated by poachers, rebels and government troops during the civil war but is bouncing back. It's definitely one of the more backpacker-friendly parks in Uganda.

Murchison Falls is the most spectacular feature of the Nile along its 6700km length. The gorge is just 6m wide, making the falls one of the most powerful surges of water found anywhere in the world.

A must at Murchison is the three-hour **launch trip** from park headquarters at Paraa to the falls, passing hippos and crocs galore. The boats leave (if there's enough demand) at 9am and 2pm, and the cost depends on numbers (about US$85 per boat holding up to 10). Weekends provide the best chance of finding other punters, reducing the cost to US$11. It is possible to be dropped at the base of the falls for a spectacular trek to the top.

Chimp tracking in and around Murchison is much cheaper than at Kibale Forest or Queen Elizabeth National Parks. It costs just US$7 at either **Busingiro** or **Kaniyo Pabidi**, but the latter is inside the park boundaries, meaning a US$20 hit on top.

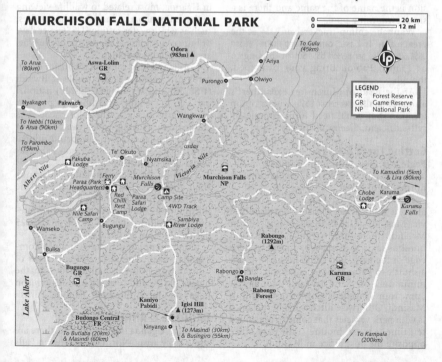

MURCHISON FALLS NATIONAL PARK

0 ——— 20 km
0 ——— 12 mi

To Arua
(80km)

Odora
(983m) ▲

To Gulu
(45km)

Aswa-Lolim
GR

Ariya

Purongo

Olwiyo

LEGEND
FR   Forest Reserve
GR   Game Reserve
NP   National Park

Nyakagot   Pakwach

Wangkwar

To Nebbi (10km)
& Arua (90km)

To Parombo
(15km)

Te' Okuto

asdas

Nile

Nyamsika

Victoria

Nile

Pakuba
Lodge

Murchison
Falls

Murchison Falls
NP

To Kamudini (5km)
& Lira (80km)

Ferry

Paraa (Park
Headquarters)

Chobe
Lodge

Karuma

Albert
Nile

Red
Chilli
Rest
Camp

Paraa
Safari
Lodge

Camp Site

Karuma
Falls

Nile Safari
Camp

4WD Track

Wanseko

Bugungu

Sambiya
River Lodge

Bulisa

Rabongo
(1292m)
▲

Bugungu
GR

Rabongo

Bandas

Karuma
GR

Lake Albert

Rabongo
Forest

Kaniyo
Pabidi

Igisi Hill
▲ (1273m)

Budongo Central
FR

Kinyanga

To Masindi (30km)
& Busingiro (55km)

To Kampala
(200km)

To Butiaba (20km)
& Masindi (60km)

Rangers are recommended for **wildlife drives** (available from the park headquarters) – the cost is US$6/8 per vehicle per half/full day. Red Chilli Rest Camp offers four-hour wildlife drives for US$14 per person (minimum US$55), including guide and ferry crossing.

The park is generally considered safe, but it is probably unwise to venture too far into the far northeast of the park as it is getting close to conflict zones.

Sleeping & Eating

Red Chilli Rest Camp (☎ 077 709510; chilli@info com.co.ug; camp site per person US$3, banda d/t US$8/11, with private bathroom US$16/22) brings Murchison to backpackers. This place is the old Paraa camp now run by the Red Chilli team from Kampala. Camping is on a grassy site with some Nile views, and the bandas are basic but improving fast. The restaurant and bar heave at weekends.

Sambiya River Lodge (☎ 041 233596; afritour@ africaonline.co.ug; camp site per person US$6, bandas from US$12, cottages from US$40) is just off the main track, beside the turn-off to the falls. Seclusion is the name of the game and there is a small swimming pool.

Wannabe chimp-trackers can stay at the great-value if basic **camps** (camp site per person US$1.60, bandas per person US$4.50) at Busingiro or Kaniyo Pabidi. Bring your own food, though.

At the head of Murchison Falls, there's also a **camp site** (per person US$6) with a tiptop location, but you'll need to be completely self-sufficient. Sleepwalkers stay away!

Getting There & Away

Eagle Air flies daily from Kampala to Pakuba Airstrip (US$85), a few kilometres northwest of Paraa.

By road, the usual – and safest – route is along a well-surfaced road from Kampala via Masindi (US$4, three hours). From Masindi there are irregular buses and minibus taxis to Wanseko, on the western edge of the park. Red Chilli Rest Camp run a shuttle to Paraa (US$6 per person, US$22 minimum) on Saturday and Monday at 3pm from Travellers' Corner restaurant in Masindi. Otherwise hitch – the best chance is with park vehicles that come to Masindi a few times a week. Inquire at the park office opposite the post office in Masindi.

The car ferry across the river at Paraa costs US$1/11 for passengers/cars, and leaves hourly in both directions (7am to 7pm).

Remember that most areas north of the park, particularly the roads to Lira and Gulu, are potentially dangerous.

UGANDA DIRECTORY

ACCOMMODATION

There are enough opportunities for camping in Uganda for it to be worth carrying a tent. Kampala has several options, as do most other popular towns and all the national parks. Camping usually costs from US$1 to US$6 per person, but in national parks you have to pay park fees on top.

Most towns have at least one basic hotel (rooms from US$3 to US$10). Some of these are pretty uninspiring, but in bigger towns and at parks there are backpacker lodges (dorms US$5, rooms from US$10).

ACTIVITIES

There are stacks of activities to choose from in Uganda, most related to wildlife viewing in the national parks, but adrenaline rushes, such as white-water rafting (US$65 per day) or bungee jumping at the source of the Nile, are also mighty popular.

Gorilla trekking is one of the major drawcards in Uganda – it is possible at Bwindi (US$275) and Mgahinga (US$220) national parks in the southwest. Almost as popular, particularly as it's a whole lot cheaper, is chimpanzee tracking, which can be done at Kibale Forest and Queen Elizabeth National Parks for US$20 or at Murchison Falls National Park for just US$6.50.

Trekking the big mountains of Uganda is another pull. The hardcore head for the Rwenzoris (US$480 for seven days), one of the toughest climbs in Africa, but for something more affordable, try Mt Elgon (US$25 per day for four to five days).

Other popular activities include community walks around forests and areas of outstanding beauty; wildlife drives in the bigger parks; and boat trips in Murchison Falls and Queen Elizabeth National Parks.

DANGERS & ANNOYANCES

Although Uganda is generally safe, there are some risky areas. North of Murchison Falls

National Park, and around some towns, such as Lira and Gulu, some fruitcakes in the Lord's Resistance Army (LRA) continue to cause havoc. It is also important to take care in the far northeast due to regular clashes between armed Karamajong people and anyone they don't like.

In addition, Rwandan rebels known as the Interahamwe occasionally make forays into western Uganda. They were responsible for the murder of eight foreigners and a Ugandan guide in Bwindi Impenetrable National Park in 1999.

It is *imperative* to make inquiries with knowledgeable local authorities before setting off to these areas.

EMBASSIES & CONSULATES

The countries listed below have diplomatic representation in Kampala. For information about obtaining visas for other countries, see p575.

Burundi (Map p554; ☎ 347823; 51 William St)
Congo (Zaïre) (Map p553; ☎ 233777; 20 Philip Rd)
Ethiopia (Map p553; ☎ 341885; 3L, off Kira Rd)
France (Map p554; ☎ 342120; 16 Lumumba Ave)
Germany (Map p553; ☎ 256767; 15 Philip Rd)
Italy (Map p554; ☎ 250450; 11 Lourdel Rd)
Kenya (Map p553; ☎ 258235; 41 Nakasero Rd)
Netherlands (Map p554; ☎ 346000; Rwenzori House, Lumumba Ave)
Rwanda (Map p553; ☎ 344045; 2 Nakayima Rd, off Kira Rd)
South Africa (Map p553; ☎ 343543; 2b Nakasero Hill Lane)
Sudan (Map p553; ☎ 243518; 21 Nakasero Rd)
Tanzania (Map p553; ☎ 256272; 6 Kagera Rd)
UK (Map p554; ☎ 078 312000; 10 Parliament Ave)
USA (Map p553; ☎ 259791; Gaba Rd)

FOOD & DRINK

Local food is pretty basic, usually involving *matoke* (mashed plantains) or *posho* (ugali or maize meal), but fish fans will enjoy the tilapia and Nile perch. Vegetarians can get by, but as local dishes are meat-based there is little choice – Indian restaurants offer the best selection of veg food beyond Kampala.

Popular local beers include light Bell and stronger Nile Special, and locally brewed Tusker and Castle are also available. The cost of a 500ml-bottle ranges from US$0.60 to US$1.50 depending on where you are drinking. Waragi is the local hard stuff and is a little like gin, so it's best with a splash of

tonic. The undistilled village version brings forth a memorable hangover.

HEALTH

If exploring Uganda's higher areas, be aware of the dangers of high-altitude sickness.

Bilharzia is a serious risk in Uganda's lakes. AIDS also continues to be a serious problem in Uganda and is worst in the southwest of the country. See the Health chapter (p1028) for further information about health issues.

A yellow fever vaccination certificate is sometimes required for entry or exit by air. If entering overland, immigration officials sometimes ask for them.

HOLIDAYS

As well as religious holidays listed in the Africa Directory chapter (p1003) the principal public holidays in Uganda are:
1 January New Year's Day
26 January Liberation Day
8 March Women's Day
1 May Labour Day
3 June Martyrs' Day
9 June Heroes' Day
9 October Independence Day

INTERNET ACCESS

Kampala has plenty of places to get an online fix from US$1 to US$2 an hour. More expensive access is available in Fort Portal, Jinja, Kabale, Mbale and Mbarara.

LEGAL MATTERS

Most travellers are very unlikely to end up having a brush with the law. Marijuana is illegal in Uganda, so if you are a smoker be discreet and be careful where you buy it in Kampala.

MAPS

The best available map of Uganda is the Macmillan 1:1,350,000 *Uganda Traveller's Map*, available in bookshops in Kampala. Macmillan also has a separate map of Kampala at 1:8000.

MEDIA

The daily *New Vision* is the government-owned newspaper, but it has its own voice. For gutsy, analytical journalism try *The Monitor*, a daily with broader coverage of international news.

UGANDA

The BBC World Service broadcasts on 103.7MHz in Kampala.

MONEY

The unit of currency is the Ugandan shilling (USh), a relatively stable currency.

Standard Chartered Bank has a network of ATMs that accept international credit cards, located at branches and Shell petrol stations in Kampala, as well as in Jinja, Mbale and Mbarara.

Bargaining is necessary in informal transactions such as at markets and roadside stalls, but not in most shops that display fixed prices. Souvenirs or handicrafts can usually be bargained for in the shops or markets.

For credit-card advances, the only realistic option is Barclays Bank in Kampala, which offers advances in US dollars or Uganda shillings. Some big expenses like white-water rafting can go on the card.

Cash can be changed easily at major banks and foreign exchange (forex) bureaus, sometimes called bureaux de change. For travellers cheques, banks in big cities are the better option, and using them in Uganda seems not to be the pain it is in some other countries.

The best banks are Standard Chartered, Crane and Barclays Banks. The forex bureaus offer slightly better exchange rates than the banks, and the rates among forex bureaus can vary by about 2%. At both banks and forex bureaus, small US dollar bills attract a much lower exchange rate than do US$50 and US$100 notes, and the rate for travellers cheques is about 2% lower than they are for cash. Exchange rates in Kampala are up to 15% better than is the case elsewhere in the country, so stock up on shillings in the capital.

PHOTOGRAPHY

Colour print film and APS film is widely available in Kampala but the supply dries up quickly elsewhere. Expect to pay around US$3.50 for a 36-exposure colour print film. Fast film is best for immortalising the gorillas at Bwindi.

POST

Sending a postcard/letter costs US$0.45/50 to the UK and Europe, and US$0.50/55 to North America, Australia and New Zealand.

There's an efficient poste restante service at the main post office in Kampala.

RESPONSIBLE TRAVEL

There have been numerous reports of illegal gorilla trekking during the past few years. When permits are selling like hot cakes, tourists have been known to cut corners by bribing rangers into multiple visits each day. This is not only illegal but also potentially life-threatening for the gorillas – it increases their stress levels, which in turn decreases their resistance to disease. Do not attempt to track illegally as you will be contributing to the demise of the highly endangered mountain gorilla.

There are many excellent community tourism initiatives underway across Uganda. For more on projects that plough proceeds back into the local community, visit the UCOTA office in Kampala (see p555 for details).

Beggars are a common sight in central Kampala, but they are not very persistent. However, if you do get harassed, try to be patient as there isn't much of a social security system in Uganda so some have no fall-back except to beg.

TELEPHONE & FAX

Local and international telephone calls can be made from UTL and MTN cardphones in towns throughout the country – try outside the post office if they aren't obvious. Calls can also be made from privately operated booths, which is useful for short calls if you don't want to buy a card. International calls cost from US$1.50 to US$2.50 per minute.

TOURIST INFORMATION

The Uganda Tourist Board (UTB) is the government-run tourist office in Kampala. Uganda Community Tourism Association (UCOTA) is a community tourism office in Kampala promoting local tourism initiatives. Uganda Wildlife Authority (UWA) promotes Uganda's national parks and, as well as its headquarters in Kampala it has offices in major towns and national parks. Other useful 'unofficial' tourist offices are budget hostels in Kampala, Jinja and beyond.

TOURS

A few reliable companies in Kampala and a few other towns offer tours and safaris to the major places of interest, but the budget safari industry in Uganda is not nearly as well established as it is in Kenya and Tanzania. Costs vary a great deal from one company to another, but are consistently high. Uganda Tourist Board (see p555) keeps detailed information on tour operators.

Afritours & Travel (Map p554; ☎ 041 233596; afritour@africaonline.co.ug) offer some of the cheapest organised safaris, including Murchison Falls, Bwindi Impenetrable and Queen Elizabeth National Parks. Otherwise, try Kabarole Tours in Fort Portal for Queen Elizabeth and Semuliki National Parks or Red Chilli Hideaway in Kampala for Murchison Falls National Park.

VISAS

The Ugandan authorities prefer that foreigners obtain visas at Ugandan embassies, high commissions or consulates before arrival, although visas are available at major borders and the international airport at Entebbe (near Kampala).

Single/double-entry visas valid for up to three months cost US$30/60 (US$20/40 if you have student ID); 48-hour transit visas cost US$15. Two photos are required and visas from Ugandan embassies or consulates are normally issued within 24 hours – sometimes while you wait.

Visa Extensions

Extensions are available at the **immigration office** (☎ 244899) on Jinja Rd, east of central Kampala.

Visas for Onward Travel

Visas for the following neighbouring countries are available from embassies in Kampala: Burundi, Ethiopia, Kenya, Rwanda and Tanzania.

Burundi

FAST FACTS

- **Area** 27,835 sq km
- **ATM** None at all
- **Borders** Congo (Zaïre), Rwanda, Tanzania; all borders are open but are unsafe to cross under any circumstances
- **Budget** US$20 a day
- **Capital** Bujumbura
- **Languages** Kirundi, French
- **Money** Burundi franc; US$1= BFr 750 approx
- **Population** 6.4 million
- **Seasons** rainy (Oct–May), dry (Jun–Apr)
- **Telephone** country code ☎ 257; international access code ☎ 00
- **Time** GMT/UTC + 2
- **Visas** US$40 for one month; must be obtained in advance

WARNING

Burundi remains engulfed in civil war, and fighting between the army and rebel groups continues. Although violence is rarely targeted at foreigners, travel in the country is not recommended. We were unable to do on-the-ground research, so some information in this chapter may not be reliable. Check the situation before travelling to Burundi.

Dwarfed by its huge neighbours Tanzania and Congo (Zaïre), Burundi is a tiny yet beautiful, mountainous country. Ask the old Africa hands about Burundi before the war, and it is the sort of place they go misty-eyed about and hark back to the life of the lotus-eaters. Sadly there has been no lotus-eating for most Burundians during the past decade of violence.

The country has a turbulent history of tribal wars and internecine rivalry between the ruling elites. A messy situation became messier with the arrival of the colonialists, first the Germans and later *les Belges*. Intertribal tensions have continued to plague Burundi since independence in 1962, culminating in the long civil war that engulfs the country today.

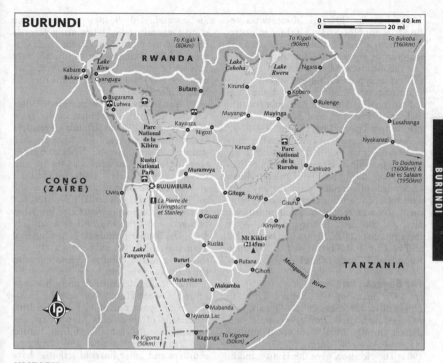

HISTORY

The original Burundi folk, the Twa Pygmies, were gradually displaced from about AD 1000 by the Hutu, mostly farmers of Bantu stock. In the 16th and 17th centuries, the country experienced another wave of migration: the tall, pastoral Tutsi from Ethiopia and Uganda. The Tutsi gradually subjugated the Hutu in a feudal system similar to that of medieval Europe. The Tutsi became a loosely organised aristocracy with a *mwami* (king) at the top of each social pyramid. Under this system, the Hutu relinquished their land and mortgaged their services to the nobility in return for cattle – a symbol of wealth and status in Burundi.

Colonial Period

At the end of the 19th century, Burundi and Rwanda were colonised by Germany, but they were so thinly garrisoned that the Belgians were easily able to oust the Germans during WWI. After the war, the League of Nations mandated Burundi (then known as Urundi) and Rwanda to Belgium.

Taking advantage of the feudal structure, the Belgians ruled indirectly through the Tutsi chiefs and princes, granting them wide-ranging powers to recruit labour and raise taxes. The Tutsi clearly were not averse to abusing these powers. The establishment of coffee plantations, and the resulting concentration of wealth in the hands of the Tutsi urban elite, further exacerbated tensions between the two tribal groups.

Independence Time

In the 1950s, a nationalist organisation based on unity between the tribes was founded under the leadership of the mwami's eldest son, Prince Rwagasore. But in the lead-up to independence he was assassinated with the connivance of the colonial authorities, who feared their commercial interests would be threatened if he managed to come to power.

Despite this setback, the Hutu challenged the concentration of power in Tutsi hands when independence was granted in 1962, and it appeared that Burundi was headed for a majority government. But in the

1964 elections, Mwami Mwambutsa refused to appoint a Hutu prime minister,
even though Hutu candidates attracted the
majority of votes. Hutu frustration boiled
over about a year later, and Hutu military
officers and political figures staged an attempted coup. Although it failed, the coup
led to the flight of the Mwambutsa into
exile in Switzerland, and he was soon replaced by a Tutsi military junta.

A wholesale purge of Hutu from the army
and bureaucracy followed, and in 1972 another large-scale revolt resulted in more than
1000 Tutsi killed. The Tutsi military junta
responded with selective genocide: any Hutu
with wealth, a formal education or a government job was rooted out and murdered,
often in the most horrifying way. After
three months, 200,000 Hutu had been killed
and another 100,000 had fled to Tanzania,
Rwanda and Congo (Zaïre).

The Bagaza Years
In 1976 Jean-Baptiste Bagaza came to
power in a bloodless coup. As part of a
so-called democratisation programme, candidates (mostly Tutsi) were voted into the
National Assembly during the elections of
1982. The elections gave the Hutu a modi-
cum of power in the National Assembly,
but it was limited. During the Bagaza years,
there were some half-hearted attempts by
the Tutsi government to remove some of
the main causes of intertribal conflict, but
these were mostly cosmetic.

Bagaza was toppled in September 1987 in
a coup led by his cousin Major Pierre Buyoya. The new regime attempted to address
the causes of intertribal tensions yet again
by gradually bringing Hutu representatives
back into positions of power in the government. However, there was a renewed
outbreak of intertribal violence in northern
Burundi in August 1988; thousands were
massacred and many more fled into neighbouring Rwanda.

Civil War Breaks Out
Buyoya finally bowed to international
pressure, and multiparty elections were
held in June 1993. These brought a Hutu-
dominated government to power, led by
Melchior Ndadaye, himself a Hutu. However, a dissident army faction staged a
bloody coup in late October the same year

and assassinated the new president. The
coup eventually failed when army generals
disowned the plotters, but in the chaos that
followed the assassination, thousands were
massacred in intertribal fighting and an
estimated 400,000 refugees fled across the
border into Rwanda.

In April 1994 the new president, Ntaryamira (a Hutu), was killed in the same
plane crash that killed Rwanda's President
Habyarimana and sparked the planned
genocide there. Sylvestre Ntibantunganya
was immediately appointed as the interim
president. Nevertheless, both Hutu militias
and the Tutsi-dominated army went on the
offensive. No war was actually declared, but
at least 100,000 people were killed in clashes
between mid-1994 and mid-1996. In July
1996, the former president, Pierre Buyoya,
again carried out a successful coup and
took over as the country's president with
the support of the army.

Since then, intertribal fighting has continued between Hutu rebels and the Tutsi-
dominated government and Tutsi militia.
Hundreds of thousands of political opponents, mostly Hutus, have been herded
into 'regroupment camps', and bombings,
murders and other horrific activities have
continued throughout the country.

Burundi Today
Peace talks have staggered on during the
conflict. They were stalled in late 1999 following the death of the convenor, former
Tanzanian president Julius Nyerere. His
replacement, the revered Nelson Mandela,
soon found trying to mediate between people
with such ingrained hatreds a daunting challenge, and ceasefires rarely lasted more than
days. However, a breakthrough came in April
2003, when President Buyoya handed over
power to Hutu leader Domitien Ndayizeye
and both sides promised to work towards
elections in late 2004. Despite the breakthrough, fighting continues to rage in the
countryside in a conflict that has killed about
300,000 Burundians in a decade. There's no
doubt about it, the people need peace.

THE CULTURE
Burundi's population comprises 84% Hutu,
15% Tutsi and 1% Twa Pygmies. Although
the stormy relations between Hutu and
Tutsi dominate the headlines, in many

ways it is the Twa who have had the roughest deal, with their forests stripped for agriculture by successive outsiders. The Catholic church plays a major role in the lives of most Burundians, although there is a small minority of Muslims.

ARTS

Burundi is famous for its athletic and acrobatic dances. Les Tambourinaires du Burundi are the country's most famous troupe and have performed in Berlin and New York. Their performances are a high-adrenaline mix of drumming and dancing that drowns the audience in a wave of sound and movement.

ENVIRONMENT

Burundi is mountains, mountains and more mountains. The capital, Bujumbura, is on the northern tip of Lake Tanganyika, which marks Burundi's western border.

Burundi has a variable climate; down near Lake Tanganyika it's hot and humid, with temperatures around 27°C, and in the more mountainous north the average temperature is around 20°C. The rainy season lasts from October to May.

TRANSPORT

GETTING THERE & AWAY
Air

There are very few international airlines serving Burundi due to the ongoing civil war. **Kenya Airways** (☎ 223542 in Bujumbura) flies to Nairobi (US$265). **Air Burundi** (☎ 223460 in Bujumbura; US$125) and **Ethiopian Airlines** (☎ 226820 in Bujumbura; US$140) take on the short hop to Kigali.

Land
RWANDA

It is not safe to enter or exit Burundi overland owing to the ongoing civil war. If the situation improves, however, the main crossing point is between Kayanza (Burundi) and Butare (Rwanda). Public shared taxis travel from Bujumbura to Kigali, via Butare, every day (US$4 or so, five hours). It's safer and quicker to take a minibus operated by **Yahoo Express** (☎ 085-41153 in Kigali, Rwanda), which heads between the two capitals daily (US$8, 7am).

The route between Bujumbura and Cyangugu (Rwanda), via Luhwa (Burundi) and Bugarama (Rwanda), is dangerous and should be avoided.

TANZANIA

Each week, the MV *Mwongozo* ferry sails along Lake Tanganyika between Bujumbura and Kigoma (Tanzania). Officially, the *Mwongozo* departs Bujumbura at 6pm on Tuesday and arrives in Kigoma at about 6am on Wednesday. Fares from Bujumbura to Kigoma are US$30/25/20 for 1st/2nd/3rd class, plus US$2.50 port tax. Tickets can be bought from the **office** (☎ 224904) on Place de l'Indépendance in Bujumbura, and must be paid for in US dollars.

ZAMBIA

On Lake Tanganikya, the MV *Liemba* used to link Bujumbura with Kigoma (Tanzania) and Mpulungu (Zambia), but lately it has been bypassing Bujumbura owing to the political situation. For more information about the *Liemba*, see Getting There & Away (p590).

GETTING AROUND

Air Burundi, the national airline, does not have regular internal flights.

Most major roads in Burundi are sealed and public transport is mostly minibuses. Destinations are displayed in the front window and they depart when full. They depart throughout the day from the *gare routière* (bus station) in any town. However, travelling around the countryside is potentially life-threatening owing to frequent rebel ambushes, so ask around before heading out of Bujumbura, even to the second city of Gitega.

BUJUMBURA

Bujumbura has a choice location, sprawling up the mountainside on the northeastern tip of Lake Tanganyika, overlooking the vast wall of mountains in Congo (Zaïre) across the waters. Swaying palms fringe the lakeshore, giving it something of a coastal feel.

The Burundian capital is a mixture of grandiose colonial construction – with wide boulevards and imposing public buildings – and the sort of dusty, anonymous suburbs found in many African cities. Buj, as many foreign residents refer to it, is also one of the most important ports on Lake Tanganyika.

Bujumbura has been under a curfew for a number of years now, and this has dampened the freewheelin' reputation it once enjoyed. The curfew is currently placed at midnight, but if you have access to a private or chartered vehicle it's not so rigidly enforced.

INFORMATION
Internet Access
Internet cafés have mushroomed in the past couple of years. Try **Face à Face** (Chaussée du Peuple Burundi), near the Novotel Bujumbura.

Money
There are no ATMs in town. Cash and travellers cheques can be changed at banks in the city centre, but charges can be steep (up to 7%); **Banque de la République du Burundi** (Ave de Révolution) is the best. You can also change travellers cheques at Bujumbura's large hotels, or there's an open black market – dealers hang around the market and near the **Dimitri supermarket** (Chaussée Prince Rwagasore). Rates vary according to the official exchange rates and the amount to be changed (large bills are preferred). At the time of writing, the street rate was double the bank rate.

Post & Telephone
The **main post office** (cnr Blvd Lumumba & Ave du Commerce; ☺ 8am-noon & 2-4pm Mon-Fri, 8-11am Sat) is also the place to find international card phones.

Tourist Offices
Office National du Tourisme (☎ 222202; Ave des Euphorbes; ☺ 7.30am-noon & 2-4.30pm Mon-Fri) has basic handouts. It's just off Blvd de la Liberté near the cathedral.

SIGHTS & ACTIVITIES
Forget sightseeing for the most part. The **Musée Vivant** (Ave du 13 Octobre; admission US$0.30; ☺ 9am-noon & 2.30-5pm Tue-Sun) is a reconstructed traditional Burundian village with exhibits about baskets, pottery and drums, plus some photographs.

The most popular beach around Bujumbura is **Plage des Cocotiers** (Coconut Beach), about 5km northwest of the city centre. Swimming is also possible at the Hotel Source du Nil pool (US$2).

SLEEPING
The cheapest hotels are generally in the suburb of Mbwiza, north of the city centre. However, this area is not particularly safe at night, so you may find that taxi fares add up considerably. Smarter, safer places are found in the city centre on and around Chausée du Peuҭ le Burundi.

EATING
Bujumbura's colonial past is evident in its cafés and restaurants, with pizza, pasta, pastries and other European dishes available, along with Chinese. Supermarkets are also well set up for self-caterers.

DRINKING
The choice of bars is reasonable, although most are primarily restaurants. Be aware of the city's midnight curfew. Good places can be found on the shores of Lake Tanganyika and in the city centre.

SHOPPING
Burundi is hardly famous for its handicrafts, but a lot of excellent work makes its way across the border from Congo (Zaïre) and is pretty cheap. The best place to browse is the small **craft market** (Ave du Stade). Haggle hard to get a good price, but there are bargains around.

GETTING THERE & AWAY
Air
Air Burundi (☎ 223460; Ave du Commerce) can issue tickets for the few remaining airlines serving Bujumbura. Other airline offices include **Kenya Airways** (☎ 223542; Place de l'Indépendance) and **Ethiopian Airlines** (☎ 226820; Ave Victoire).

Local Transport
Minibuses ply the major routes around the country, and leave from the minibus station in the market area southeast of Place de l'Indépendance.

AROUND BUJUMBURA

LA PIERRE DE LIVINGSTONE ET STANLEY
'Dr Livingstone, I presume?' The Tanzanians presume not. But the Burundians presume so. This large rock at Mugere, about 10km south of the capital, is alleged to mark the

spot where the infamous encounter between Livingstone and Stanley took place, but Ujiji in Tanzania is the more likely location. Some graffiti mark the date as 25 November 1871.

AROUND BURUNDI

GITEGA
Gitega, the second largest town in Burundi, is home to the **National Museum** and a limited number of accommodation and restaurant options.

A good day trip from Gitega is to the **Chutes de la Kagera**, near Rutana. These waterfalls are spectacular in the wet season (October to January), but there's no public transport there, so charter a taxi.

It is currently too dangerous to undertake a road trip from Bujumbura to Gitega, but if the situation improves, minibuses run throughout the day (US$2, one hour).

SOURCE DU NIL
This insignificant-looking little spring, southeast of Bujumbura, high up on the slopes of Mt Kikizi (2145m), is supposedly the southernmost source of the Nile as it's the furthest point from Lake Victoria, the Nile's main feeder. Naturally, the Ugandans dispute this, claiming the source as Jinja – where the Nile flows out of Lake Victoria. In Burundi 'le source' is no more than a trickle – not exactly a riveting sight – and access is impossible without a private or chartered vehicle.

NATIONAL PARKS
Burundi has no tourist infrastructure as such, and travelling to and around the forests and national parks while the civil war continues is madness.

If the situation improves, it might be possible to visit the **Parc National de la Kibira**, which is the largest rainforest in Burundi, and home to hundreds of colobus monkeys and chimpanzees; and **Parc National de la Rurubu**, the largest park in the country, with its wonderful hiking and views.

The most accessible national park – and the only one open – is the **Rusizi National Park** (admission US$1.50), 15km from Bujumbura. It's a wetland environment and provides a habitat for hippos, sitatungas

(aquatic antelopes) and a wide variety of birds.

BURUNDI DIRECTORY

DANGERS & ANNOYANCES
Tragically, Burundi is embroiled in civil war, so check the security situation carefully before making a trip or travelling around the countryside once here. Locals may undertake dangerous journeys as a matter of course, but are often unable to assess the risk for foreigners. Bujumbura is fairly safe these days due to the massive army presence, although it's wise to avoid walking between the docks and the centre of town at night.

Kigali (Rwanda) and Kigoma (Tanzania) are probably the best places to pick up reliable information about current events in Burundi.

EMBASSIES & CONSULATES
Countries with diplomatic representation in Bujumbura include:
Belgium (☎ 233641; Blvd de la Liberté)
Congo (Zaïre) (Ave du Zaïre)
France (☎ 251484; 60 Blvd de l'Uprona)
Germany (☎ 415729)
Rwanda (☎ 26865; 24 Ave du Zaïre)
USA (☎ 223454; 1 Ave des Etats Unis)

Neighbouring or near-neighbouring countries where Burundi has diplomatic representation are Kenya, Rwanda and Uganda.

HOLIDAYS
As well as religious holidays listed in the Africa Directory chapter (p1003) the principal public holidays in Burundi are:
1 January New Year's Day
1 May Labour Day
1 July Independence Day
5 August Assumption
18 September Victory of UPRONA Day
13 October Anniversary of Rwagasore's Assassination
1 November All Saints' Day

MONEY
There are no ATMs in Burundi. It's a cash economy and the US dollar is king, so come with cash unless you like handing over lots of money in commissions to banks, particularly for travellers cheques – some charge up

to 7%. Bujumbura is the best place to change money (see Money p580).

POST & TELEPHONE

The postal service is reasonably efficient, but the poste restante service at the main post office in Bujumbura is poorly organised.

Rates charged for international telephone calls are quite reasonable. Phonecards are available from the telecommunications office located behind the post office in Bujumbura; a card for US$5 should last about four minutes for an international call. There are no telephone area codes within the country.

VISAS

Visas are required by all, and they should be obtained from a Burundian embassy or consulate before arrival. Two photographs are

required and visas are often available in the afternoon if you apply early in the morning. One-month tourist visas cost US$40.

Usually, anyone who has arrived by air from a country without Burundian representation can get a transit visa on arrival at the airport – but not at the border. Transit visas, which must be extended within one working day, cost US$10.

Visa Extensions

Visas can be extended by going to the **immigration office** (Blvd de l'Uprona) in Bujumbura. Extensions cost US$1 per day at the time of research.

Visas for Onward Travel

Visas are available from the Rwanda and Congo (Zaïre) embassies in Bujumbura (see p581 for address details).

Tanzania

HIGHLIGHTS
- **Zanzibar** Wander among narrow streets, whitewashed Arab houses and fragrant spice markets in the old Stone Town (p599)
- **Serengeti** Watch vast herds of wildebeest, zebra and antelope migrating through the heat haze of the 'endless plains' (p612)
- **Dar es Salaam** Avoid the hustle of the big city by chilling out Robinson Crusoe style, with crystal-clear green water, palm-fringed white beaches and coral reefs on the coast (p597)
- **Kilimanjaro** Scale the heights with a trek to the glistening, snowcapped peak of Africa's highest mountain (p615)
- **Off the beaten track** Meet your cousins: the chimpanzee communities on the forested shores of Lake Tanganyika (p625)

FAST FACTS
- **Area** 945,087 sq km (twice the size of Sweden)
- **ATMs** Dar es Salaam, Arusha, Moshi and Mwanza only
- **Borders** Kenya, Malawi, Mozambique, Rwanda, Uganda and Zambia all open; Congo (Zaïre) and Burundi are considered unsafe, and not advised
- **Budget** US$15 to US$20 per day
- **Capital** Dodoma
- **Languages** Kiswahili, English
- **Money** Tanzanian shilling; US$1 = TS1000
- **Population** 36 million
- **Seasons** dry (Jun–Nov), short rains (Nov–Dec), long rains (Mar–May)
- **Telephone** country code ☎ 255; international access code ☎ 000
- **Time** GMT/UTC + 3
- **Visas** US$30 to US$50 for 30 days, issued at some borders.

Imagine a quintessential African image – the kind you saw in picture books when you were a kid – and the chances are it originates in Tanzania. In many ways the country really has got it all – wide golden plains occupied by wildebeest herds and lion prides, towering mountains, lush rainforests, glittering blue lakes and white beaches fringed by palm trees. All these natural attractions have been reasonably well-preserved by an enlightened

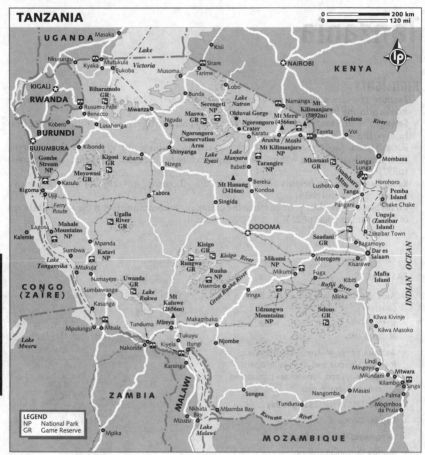

conservation policy, and rendered easy (though sadly not always cheap) to visit thanks to many years of political stability.

None of this is to say that Tanzania is some kind of African utopia: the roads are potholed in places, the city streets occasionally hot and hassle-filled. But all these minor annoyances are subsumed by something even more impressive than the scenery – the Tanzanians themselves, whose open, warm spirit and unfailing generosity are well-known throughout Africa. Look beyond the picture postcards, make some real Tanzanian friends, and you'll find this a country that's hard to leave.

HISTORY
First footprints

The history of Tanzania is also quite literally the history of humankind. Human beings are thought to have evolved in the area of the Great Rift Valley, which passes through modern-day Tanzania, Kenya and Ethiopia. The oldest set of hominid footprints ever

discovered (dating from over two million years ago) was found, enshrined in volcanic ash, near Laetoli in northern Tanzania in the 1970s.

Tanzania has been a travel destination since classical times. Ancient Egyptian and Greek mariners were visiting the East African coast to trade long before the Arabs,

Chinese, Indians and Persians who sailed in around the ninth century AD. These merchants, who came looking for gold, spices and ivory, often stayed and intermarried with the families of their local trading contacts. They formed a civilization known as the Swahili, with a common language (Kiswahili), and a chain of prosperous cities stretching from Mozambique to Somalia. The Arabic kingdom of Oman eventually gained control of the Swahili coast, installing its Sultan on Zanzibar and growing rich on the profits of slaving expeditions that penetrated far inland in search of booty.

Dr Livingstone, I Presume?

The Portuguese were the first Europeans to arrive in East Africa, doing battle with the Omanis for control of the lucrative trade routes to India. Later came English, Dutch and American merchant adventurers, all keen to exploit the riches of the interior. By the nineteenth century, European explorers (most famously Dr David Livingstone) were setting out from Zanzibar into the unknown, spurred on by reports of a mysterious snow-capped mountain (Kilimanjaro) and a giant lake (Victoria) far to the west. Dr Livingstone himself, searching for the source of the Nile, became so famously lost in the process that a special expedition headed by Henry Stanley was sent out to find him. Stanley caught up with Livingstone at Ujiji near modern-day Kigoma after a journey of more than a year, whereupon the only phrase he could utter was the famous inanity 'Dr Livingstone, I presume?'.

Livingstone was one of the chief opponents of the slave trade, whose suppression became the obsession of the Victorian British public and led to the downfall of the Omani Empire. British battleships blockaded the coast to prevent the slave ships escaping with their cargo, and the Omani sultan was reduced to no more than a puppet of the British Empire. Germany was doing a bit of empire building too, sending out quasi-officials like Carl Peters to persuade the illiterate petty chiefs of the region to put their marks on worthless 'friendship treaties'.

The new German colony was known as Tanganyika (Zanzibar, however, remained in British hands) and saw fierce fighting in WWI, with German forces under the legend-ary commander Von Lettow Vorbeck waging a highly successful guerrilla-style campaign in the thick bush of the modern-day Selous Game Reserve. When the war finally ended, the League of Nations mandated Tanganyika to Britain.

Independence

Soldiers returning from WWII helped fuel the rise of the independence movement. Julius Nyerere founded the Tanganyika African National Union (TANU) in 1954, and when the peaceful transition to independence occurred in 1961 he was installed as the first president of Tanganyika. Union with Zanzibar (which had just expelled the last of the Arab sultans) followed shortly afterwards. The new country was named Tanzania.

Nyerere inherited a country with few exploitable resources and fewer skilled workers. The problems this created eventually led to a policy based on the Chinese communist model, with a new system of co-operative farms known as *ujamaa* (togetherness) villages. In some areas this policy led to people being forcibly evicted from their homes and resettled elsewhere. Despite Nyerere's efforts, corruption remained widespread and Tanzania's socialist policies were an economic failure.

In 1978, Nyerere's outspoken condemnation of the murderous regime of Idi Amin in Uganda led to war – Uganda bombed Bukoba and Musoma, and sent ground troops over the border. Tanzania responded with an invasion of Uganda that ousted Amin from power.

Democracy

The war drained resources further and by the early 1980s Tanzania's economy was on its knees. In 1985 Nyerere decided to step down as President, openly discussing his failures as well as his successes.

Tanzania is now a multiparty democracy. The first elections were held in 1995 and 2000, and both were won by TANU's successor Chama Cha Mapinduzi (CCM) 'the Party of the Revolution', under the leadership of President Benjamin Mkapa. These days, economic growth is speeding up in Tanzania, and most political strife now centres around Zanzibar, where CCM holds a tenuous majority over its main rival the

Civic United Front (CUF). The 2000 elections in Zanzibar were condemned by CUF as fixed, and rioting followed the announcement of the new president, Amani Karume.

THE CULTURE
A Leader's Legacy
Very few African countries have been moulded in the image of their first president as closely as Tanzania. Always called Mwalimu (teacher) in Tanzania, and referred to as the 'conscience of black Africa' elsewhere, Julius Nyerere was one of Africa's elder statesmen. His policies didn't work but, crucially, he admitted it, and he was one of the few post-independence African presidents to leave office voluntarily. Nyerere's death in October 1999 caused monumental public grief throughout Tanzania. The former leader is never publicly criticised, and indeed politicians regularly quote selectively from his speeches in defence of their own policies. His kindly-looking face still gazes out of a photo frame in many businesses and even private homes.

One Big Family
Nyerere's policies of ujamaa may have been an economic failure, but his banning of tribal leaders and the adoption of Swahili as a single national language (Kiswahili in Swahili) have meant that Tanzania today is refreshingly free of the tribalism that has torn apart other African nations. Tanzanians are Tanzanian first and foremost, with little interest in promoting their tribal roots. This concept of togetherness is enshrined in the strong family values that rule life in Tanzania. A Tanzanian's idea of family applies not just to his or her many relatives – it includes the whole nation.

Tanzanians address perfect strangers politely as dada (sister) or kaka (brother), and even waiters and shop assistants are hailed with shouts of 'uncle!' or 'aunty!'. Marriage is sacred and seen as a duty – unmarried people are looked upon with puzzlement and pity. Educated or successful family or community members are expected to help out others less fortunate, and no one would willingly go against their parents' wishes. (Backpackers cheerily telling everyone they hate their parents or that the folks at home didn't want them to come to Africa won't make any new friends.)

Nyerere's ujamaa collective villages left a legacy of strong community organisation, with most villages and urban neighbourhoods in the charge of a sheha (leader) who co-ordinates the efforts of communities to work together – the idea of helping one's neighbour is enshrined in Tanzanian society. Again, this spirit of co-operation extends to perfect strangers – if you ask for directions, be prepared for someone to grab your hand and show you the way, however distant.

Common Cultural Courtesy
Tanzanian culture is also built on courtesy. Greetings are vitally important and can become highly complex. It is considered unbearably rude, for example, to walk into a shop and simply ask for what you want without at least a cursory enquiry into the health, wellbeing or general mood of the shopkeeper. Hospitality is equally important – most Tanzanians move freely in and out of their neighbours' houses. Instead of knocking, one pauses in front of an open door and shouts 'hodi' (may I enter?). The reply is always 'karibu!' (welcome!).

Tanzanians are conservative people (the government regularly bans pop songs that 'encourage immoral acts') and may look askance at piercings, tattoos, or very skimpy, dirty or ripped clothes. Most of the coastline is predominantly Muslim and women generally wear long skirts and headscarves. Public displays of affection are considered shocking, along with acres of leg or cleavage on display. It's also seen as fairly disgusting not to wash one's hands before starting a meal, and bowls of water are often brought to restaurant tables for this purpose. Likewise, no one eats or passes food with their left hand.

Where Women Fit In
Women in Tanzanian society have their own well-defined roles, the biggest of which is motherhood. Older women often drop their own names and become known as 'mama' followed by the name of their oldest child. In many traditional Tanzanian communities, adolescent girls are prepared for marriage with a period of segregation, during which they are coached by venerable older women in the arts of sex, etiquette and childrearing. Modern Tanzanian women, however, are subject to high levels of discrimination in

MZUNGU! MZUNGU!

The word *mzungu*, meaning 'white person' – and beloved of screeching urchins all over East Africa – was coined in the days of the early European explorers. It comes from the Kiswahili verb *kuzunguka*: 'to wander around aimlessly, like a mad person'. The Swahili word for a hangover, *kuzungu-zungu* ('my head's going round and round'), comes from the same root. Travellers wandering around aimlessly and nursing hangovers? Not much has changed…

education and employment, with few women holding positions in government or in trade unions.

ARTS

Music is the chief form of entertainment in Tanzania. The older generation on the coast adore *taarab*, a form of sung poetry with heavy Arab influences, usually accompanied by a full orchestra. Much more popular among younger people is Swahili rap, whose artists deliver hard-hitting lyrics about social issues such as AIDS or sexuality.

Communities, especially in rural areas, regularly come together for dancing and drumming sessions known as *ngomas* at which visitors are almost always welcome. Bigger *ngomas* can get pretty spectacular, with drummers leaping over and into a huge fire in the centre to keep the skins covering their drums warm.

The Makonde ethnic group of southern Tanzania and northern Mozambique produce highly sought after ebony carvings representing natural forms such as animals, or more abstract concepts like togetherness and family. The most popular are the so-called *shetani* sculptures, depicting fantastical and grotesque spirit creatures.

Tanzania's other principal art form is *tingatinga*, named after a 1960s painter named Edward Saidi Tingatinga, who began producing colourful naïve art works, executed on pieces of hardboard, in response to demand from tourists and expatriates. He was killed by the police in a case of mistaken identity in 1972, but he gave his name to a style of painting unique in that it was developed almost exclusively

for foreigners. *Tingatinga* paintings are on sale in shops all over Tanzania.

ENVIRONMENT
The Land

The Rift Valley, which runs down the spine of Tanzania, is an enormous fault in the earth's crust, created by volcanic activity when the world was formed. Lake Natron, Lake Manyara and Lake Nyasa (the Tanzanian name for Lake Malawi) all lie within the eastern Rift Valley. The western side of the Rift encompasses Lake Tanganyika, the second deepest lake in the world. Biggest of all the lakes is Lake Victoria, the source of the Nile River, which lies in the north of the country.

Wildlife

The massive Serengeti ecosystem, encompassing the Ngorongoro Crater Highlands (as well as the Masai Mara Reserve in neighbouring Kenya), is one of the biggest protected areas in Africa, and the site of one of the longest remaining animal migration routes in the world (see p612). In addition to the vast herds of wildebeest, zebra and antelope that migrate across the Serengeti plains, the savanna habitats of Tanzania also include a variety of other herbivores such as elephants, buffalos, giraffes and the rare black rhinoceros. Predators include lions, leopards, cheetahs and hyenas as well as smaller species such as servals, genets and jackals. The endangered African hunting dog is found in Ruaha National Park and the Selous Game Reserve, and crocodiles and hippos inhabit rivers and lakes all over the country. The forests of western Tanzania shelter several communities of chimpanzees, some of which are habituated to human contact and can be visited in the wild. Tanzania is also a birdwatcher's paradise, with over 33 species that can only be found here.

National Parks

An impressive 38% of Tanzania is allocated as a national or marine park or reserve. The most popular are probably the parks and conservation areas of the so-called 'northern safari circuit' – Serengeti, Ngorongoro, Lake Manyara and Tarangire, all of which are easily reached from the town of Arusha. The area around Mt Kilimanjaro is also designated as a National Park.

TANZANIA

Tanzania's southern and western national parks and game reserves are a bit harder to access but see far fewer tourists. The Selous Game Reserve, Mikumi National Park and Ruaha National Park are the most often visited wildlife destinations in the south, while Gombe Stream and Mahale Mountains on the shores of Lake Tanganyika attract visitors keen to watch chimpanzees.

For more information, contact Tanzania's **National Parks Authority** (Tanapa; ☎ 027 2503471; tanapa@habari.co.tz; PO Box 3134, Arusha).

PARK ENTRY FEES

Tanzania's National Parks may be spectacular, but cheap they aren't. The massive cost of maintaining conservation efforts (and the government's desire for tourist revenue) means that all foreigners (ie, non-Tanzanian citizens) must pay much more than locals to enter the parks and reserves. All fees must be paid in hard currency (usually US dollars, and preferably cash). See the individual National Park sections for entry fees.

On top of the entry fees, you have to pay if you stay overnight in a national park. Camping is only allowed at official camp sites within the park and costs US$20 per person per night. Other huts, hostels and resthouses inside the parks and reserves (and run by the park authorities) cost from US$20 to US$40 per person per night. Privately owned and run accommodation in national parks is usually a lot more than this – up to US$600 per person per night – so beyond most backpackers. Wildlife guides cost from US$10 to US$15 per day, and a guide for trekking is normally US$20. Foreign-registered cars must also pay an entry fee of around US$20, depending on the size of the car.

Environmental Issues

Tanzania's marine environment is at risk from overfishing – often to feed the demands of seafood-hungry tourists – and damaging practices such as dynamite fishing, which destroy coral and invertebrates on which fish live. Collecting shells from reefs also has an adverse effect on the health of the marine environment – so don't buy shells where you see them for sale.

On land, Tanzania's wildlife is in danger from human encroachment due to an expanding population and from poaching,

both for meat and for products such as ivory and rhino horn. Humans and animals frequently come into conflict, especially in areas bordering National Parks. Conservation efforts today are directed at including local populations in the planning of wildlife projects, and various schemes are in place to help locals benefit from the wildlife they are expected to preserve, mostly by setting up community-run tourist lodges and wildlife reserves.

TRANSPORT

GETTING THERE & AWAY
Air
KENYA

Dar es Salaam, Zanzibar and Arusha are linked to Nairobi and Mombasa by several airlines including **Air Kenya** (☎ 00254 20 605745; resvns@airkenya.com), **Kenya Airways** (☎ 022 2119376; www.kenya-airways.com), Air Tanzania and Precision Air (see p590 for contact details of these two). Some sample one-way fares are: Dar es Salaam–Nairobi US$200, Nairobi–Arusha US$135, Mombasa–Kilimanjaro US$107, Mombasa–Zanzibar US$100, and Nairobi–Zanzibar US$183.

Zanzibar, Dar es Salaam and Kilimanjaro airports handle international flights. Airlines such as British Airways, KLM and Gulf Air fly in from Europe. Zanzibar also sees a number of charter flights from Italy, Switzerland and France.

MALAWI

Air Tanzania flies three times a week from Dar es Salaam to Blantyre.

MOZAMBIQUE

Linhas Aéreas de Moçambique (☎ 00258 1465810/ 1/2/5-8; www.lam.co.mz) has flights from Dar es Salaam–Maputo, and Mtwara–Pemba.

UGANDA

Air Tanzania has flights four times a week between Kampala and Dar es Salaam, Kilimanjaro (near Arusha) and Zanzibar.

DEPARTURE TAX

Airport departure tax is US$20 for international flights and US$5 for regional flights.

Land
BURUNDI
It is not currently considered safe to travel from Tanzania to Burundi.

CONGO (ZAÏRE)
As for Burundi, it is not currently considered safe to travel from Tanzania to Congo (Zaïre).

KENYA
It may be possible to pick up a dhow (wooden cargo boat) in Mombasa to sail to Zanzibar or Pemba. The journey, in a dhow with a motor, takes around 16 hours, and you must bring all your food and water with you. The price, before bargaining, is around US$30.

The main border crossing between Tanzania and Kenya is at Namanga. Daily shuttle buses run between Nairobi and Arusha (four hours) and Moshi (five hours).

The shuttle services run by companies such as **Riverside** (☎ 027 2502639) are popular, but not cheap – foreigners are charged US$20 from Arusha and US$25 from Moshi (you should be able to get the residents' rate of US$10 if business is quiet). Normal buses only cost around US$8. Alternatively, catch a dalla-dalla (minibus) to the border, cross on foot or by bicycle taxi, and continue to Kenya by *matatu* (Kenyan minibus). Buses and dalla-dallas also run every day from Moshi to Voi in Kenya (three hours).

If you're travelling up the coast, it's easy to cross between Tanga and Mombasa at Horohoro. Buses leave from Tanga each morning for Mombasa (US$4, three hours), or you can do the journey in stages on dalla-dallas. There are also plenty of buses running from Dar straight through to Mombasa (US$15, 11 hours).

Buses run all day between Mwanza and the Kenyan border at Sirare (five hours). From here, minibuses and shared taxis run to Kisumu (US$6, five hours). A number of buses run direct from Mwanza to Nairobi, but they all arrive late at night, and are therefore best avoided.

MALAWI
An interesting route into Malawi (if you're not in a hurry) involves taking the bus from Mbeya to Kiyela, from where dalla-dallas and trucks run to Itungi on the shores of Lake Nyasa. From here you can board the VS *Songea*, a ferry that runs twice a week to Nkhata Bay in Malawi via Mbamba Bay in Tanzania, stopping in every village and taking around 14 hours. The ferry schedule is somewhat erratic, so check with the Sisi Kwa Sisi tourist office in Mbeya (see p623) before starting out.

The only border crossing is at Songwe, between Kiyela (Tanzania) and Karonga (Malawi) at the top of Lake Malawi. Dalla-dallas run from Mbeya to the border daily (US$2, 2 ½ hours). Beware of Mbeya's many bus touts, who will try to sell you tickets on this route at ridiculously inflated prices. From the Tanzania border post, it's a short walk across the bridge over the Songwe River to the Malawi border post, from where infrequent buses, and more frequent minibuses (US$1, one hour) go to Karonga and from there to Mzuzu (US$5). With an early start, it's easy enough to travel from Mbeya (Tanzania) to Mzuzu (Malawi) in one day. Buses from Mbeya also run overnight direct to Lilongwe (US$23) except on Monday.

To go the entire distance between Dar es Salaam and Lilongwe, several buses per week run via Mbeya and Mzuzu (US$35, 24 hours). It's *not* a comfortable ride – far better to do the journey in stages.

MOZAMBIQUE
Dhows connect Mozambique and Tanzania, but captains won't always take passengers. The best places to make arrangements are Mikindani, Mtwara or Msimbati. In Mozambique, try Moçimboa da Praia and Palma. Always travel with the wind (south to north from approximately April to September and north to south from approximately November to March), or choose a dhow with a motor.

The main border crossing is at Singa and the journey over is one of the most adventurous in Africa. From Mtwara, dalla-dallas go to the border post (three to four hours), on the banks of the Rovuma River. From here, it's a ride in a small boat or canoe across the river – a torrent in rainy season – to the Mozambican side. Note that you cannot buy Mozambican visas on this border, but must arrange them in advance in Dar es Salaam. From the Mozambican border post at Namuiranga to Moçimboa da Praia, the first major town, it's a good six hours

TANZANIA

in a pick-up truck along abysmal roads and through thick bush. The total cost from Mtwara is around US$15 and the journey time can be 10 to 12 hours. There is a vehicle ferry across the river, but check it's running before setting out.

RWANDA
The main border crossing is at Rusumu. Buses leave Mwanza daily for the town of Benacco, from where you can pick up a dalla-dalla for the last 15km to the Tanzania border post. It's a short walk across the bridge to the Rwanda border post, from where transport goes towards Kigali.

From Bukoba, a coach called 'Visram' leaves on Friday and goes straight to Kigali (US$6.50, 12 hours). Even the locals, however, say that this is a pretty rough ride.

UGANDA
The western route into Uganda follows the side of Lake Victoria between Bukoba and Masaka.

From Bukoba, take any form of transport (often a crowded Land Rover) along the appalling road to the border at Mutukula (five hours) – hitching is difficult because there's so little traffic. From the Ugandan side of the border, buses leave for Kampala (seven to eight hours). If you leave Bukoba early enough (for example if you're coming off the ferry from Mwanza), it's possible to get through to Kampala in one day. Alas, the big coaches that go directly from Bukoba to Kampala (US$10) only run three times a week – and not on the same days that the ferry arrives.

If you're travelling from Arusha to Kampala, there's a comfy Scandinavian Express overnight coach service via Nairobi (US$30, 18 hours). Remember that you'll also have to add your Kenyan transit visa (US$20, available at the border) to the fare.

ZAMBIA
The 90-year old steamer MV *Liemba* travels down Lake Tanganyika from Kigoma in Tanzania to Mpulungu in Zambia once a week. See p625 for timetable and fares. You can also get into northern Malawi from Mpulungu by catching a minibus to Mbala, from where it's a day's journey in pick-up trucks to Nakonde, then at Tunduma go back across the border into Tanzania to

reach Mbeya, where you can catch onward transport to Malawi.

There's frequent road transport (US$2, two hours) between Mbeya (Tanzania) and Nakonde (Zambia), via Tunduma. From Nakonde, there's frequent onward transport. You can also get direct buses from Dar es Salaam to Lusaka (US$35, 24 hours).

The best option is definitely the rather plush **Tazara railway** (☎ 022 28660340), with trains that run overnight between Dar es Salaam and Kapiri Mposhi in Zambia, via Mbeya and the border posts at Tunduma and Nakonde. (The station is called New Kapiri Mposhi – it's about 2km outside Kapiri Mposhi town.) This is a great journey to do as it passes through beautiful scenery including the Selous Game Reserve, where there's a very good chance of spotting animals from the windows.

Two 'express' trains leave Dar es Salaam for New Kapiri Mposhi each week; on Tuesday and Friday at 3.50pm and 3pm respectively. The journey takes between 30 and 40 hours. The fares are about US$53/37/29 in 1st/2nd/3rd class.

First and 2nd class will get you a bunk in a compartment, in 3rd you're sitting (or most likely standing).

Tickets should be booked at least a couple of days in advance for 1st and 2nd class at the Tazara train station in Dar es Salaam. Show your ISIC card when booking tickets for a 50% student discount.

GETTING AROUND
Air
Tanzania is criss-crossed by a comprehensive network of domestic flights. The principal carriers are **Air Tanzania** (☎ 022 2118424; www.airtanzania.com), **Precision Air** (☎ 027 2506903; information@precisionairtz.com), **Air Express** (☎ 022 2115672), who are generally the cheapest, **Zan Air** (☎ 024 2233670; www.zanair.com) and **Coastal Aviation** (☎ 022 2117959; www.coastal.cc). Some sample one-way fares are: Dar es Salaam–Zanzibar US$55, Dar es Salaam–Arusha US$145, Zanzibar–Pemba US$65, Dar es Salaam–Mtwara US$100 and Arusha–Mwanza US$145.

Boat
The ferry VS *Songea* runs twice a week to Nkata Bay in Malawi via Mbamba Bay in Tanzania, stopping in every village and

taking around 14 hours. Check with the tourist office in Mbeya (p623) for prices and schedules.

The MV *Liemba* connects Tanzania with Zambia, and stops at several Tanzanian ports along the way, including the Mahale Mountains National Park (see p626 for timetable).

The MV *Victoria* regularly travels between Bukoba and Mwanza (see p622).

The ferry FB *Santorini 3* plies the coast between Dar es Salaam and Mtwara, leaving Dar es Salaam at 4pm on Tuesday and arriving in Mtwara at 6am on Wednesday. It leaves Mtwara for the return journey at 4pm on Friday, arriving in Dar es Salaam at 6am on Saturday. It has a complex system of fares, ranging from US$45 for an air-conditioned cabin to US$19 for a seat in the 5th-class lounge. Since the road from Dar to Mtwara is one of Tanzania's worst, this is a pretty good deal. Bring your ISIC card when booking for a 20% student discount. Ticket booking offices are in the port in Dar es Salaam and on Uhuru Rd in Mtwara.

For information on ferry services to and from Zanzibar Island and Pemba, see the Getting There & Away sections under each destination later in this chapter.

Local Transport

Buses and passenger trucks or pick-ups (dalla-dallas) travel every conceivable route, no matter how potholed, in Tanzania. Quality varies wildly, and on long journeys it may well be worth paying a couple of extra dollars for the safer and more direct vehicles. The pride of Tanzania's bus system is the luxury company Scandinavian Express, with a gleaming new customer service centre in Dar es Salaam and an office in most major towns.

Scandinavian buses are streets ahead of the competition in terms of quality and punctuality, but they cost on average around US$5 more per journey than some of their more rickety competitors. Other reasonably reputable bus services are Dar Express and Akamba, with the ubiquitous Tawfiq (also known as Interstate 2000) being the least desirable of the big companies.

When choosing your bus or dalla-dalla at a bus station, remember that most only leave when full, so opt for the ones with the most people already in place if you're keen to get going.

Train

Tanzania only has two passenger train lines – the Central Line, which runs between Dar es Salaam and Kigoma, via Dodoma and Tabora, branching north to Mwanza, and the 'Tazara' line between Dar and Mbeya, which continues into Zambia.

Travelling by train, even in 2nd class, is safer and more comfortable than going by bus or dalla-dalla, but only the obsessively frugal would travel any long distance in 3rd class – it's *very* uncomfortable. As with bus travel, keep an eye on your gear at all times, particularly in 3rd class. Even in 1st and 2nd class, make sure that the window is jammed shut at night.

The main difference between 1st and 2nd class is that 1st class has two or four berths, while 2nd class has six. On both train lines, men and women can only travel together in 1st or 2nd class if they book the entire compartment. Some trains have restaurant cars, which serve good meals, soft drinks and beer. Bedding is available in 1st and 2nd class.

Tickets for 1st and 2nd class should be reserved at least five days in advance, though occasionally you'll be able to get a seat on the day of departure. (It's not unheard of for railway staff to claim that all seats are full just to get a bribe – be persistent.) If only 3rd-class tickets are available, you can always try to upgrade to 2nd or 1st class once you've boarded the train.

DAR ES SALAAM

☎ 022 / pop 2.5 million

Dar es Salaam, usually just known as 'Dar', is the capital of Tanzania in all but name. Dodoma may have the parliament, but all the biggest businesses and most of the government departments are based in Dar. Founded in the mid-19th century by the Arabic sultan of Zanzibar, it's a city that still has the feel of the Middle East or Asia about it. Shoeshine men, hawkers, beggars and con artists ply their various trades on potholed pavements, overlooked by shabby 1930 colonial façades.

Arriving from the sticks, Dar's big-city buzz is pretty exhilarating, but if the

TANZANIA

TANZANIA

CENTRAL DAR ES SALAAM

0 ————————— 500 m
0 ————————— 0.3 mi

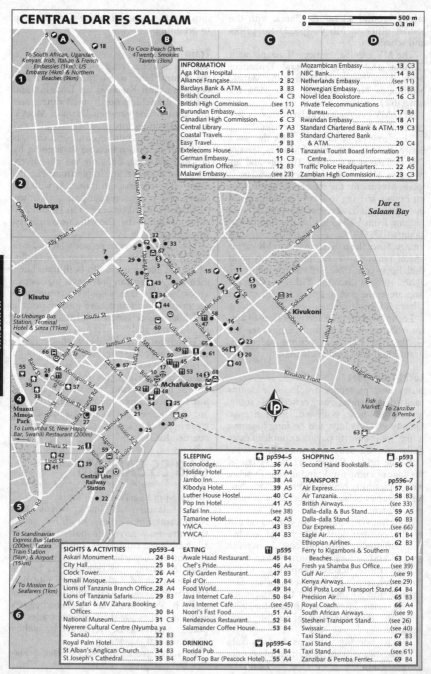

INFORMATION
Aga Khan Hospital..........................1 B1
Alliance Française...........................2 B2
Barclays Bank & ATM.....................3 B3
British Council.................................4 C3
British High Commission.........(see 11)
Burundian Embassy........................5 A1
Canadian High Commission...........6 C3
Central Library...............................7 A3
Coastal Travels..............................8 B3
Easy Travel....................................9 B3
Extelecoms House........................10 B4
German Embassy..........................11 C3
Immigration Office.......................12 B3
Malawi Embassy.....................(see 23)
Mozambican Embassy...................13 C3
NBC Bank.....................................14 B4
Netherlands Embassy...............(see 11)
Norwegian Embassy.....................15 B3
Novel Idea Bookstore..................16 C3
Private Telecommunications
  Bureau.......................................17 B4
Rwandan Embassy........................18 A1
Standard Chartered Bank & ATM..19 C3
Standard Chartered Bank
  & ATM.......................................20 C4
Tanzania Tourist Board Information
  Centre.......................................21 B4
Traffic Police Headquarters..........22 A5
Zambian High Commission...........23 C3

SIGHTS & ACTIVITIES   pp593–4
Askari Monument.........................24 B4
City Hall.......................................25 B4
Clock Tower.................................26 A4
Ismaili Mosque.............................27 A4
Lions of Tanzania Branch Office..28 A4
Lions of Tanzania Safaris.............29 B3
MV Safari & MV Zahara Booking
  Offices..30 B4
National Museum.........................31 C3
Nyerere Cultural Centre (Nyumba ya
  Sanaa)...32 B3
Royal Palm Hotel.........................33 B3
St Alban's Anglican Church..........34 B3
St Joseph's Cathedral..................35 B4

SLEEPING   pp594–5
Econolodge.................................36 A4
Holiday Hotel...............................37 A4
Jambo Inn....................................38 A4
Kibodya Hotel..............................39 A5
Luther House Hostel....................40 A5
Pop Inn Hotel...............................41 A5
Safari Inn................................(see 38)
Tamarine Hotel............................42 A4
YMCA...43 B3
YWCA...44 B3

EATING   p595
Awale Haad Restaurant...............45 B4
Chef's Pride.................................46 B4
City Garden Restaurant................47 B3
Epi d'Or..48 B4
Food World...................................49 B4
Java Internet Café.......................50 B4
Java Internet Café..................(see 45)
Noori's Fast Food.........................51 B4
Rendezvous Restaurant...............52 B4
Salamander Coffee House............53 B4

DRINKING   pp595–6
Florida Pub..................................54 B4
Roof Top Bar (Peacock Hotel)....55 A4

SHOPPING   p593
Second Hand Bookstalls...............56 C4

TRANSPORT   pp596–7
Air Express...................................57 B4
Air Tanzania.................................58 B3
British Airways........................(see 33)
Dalla-dalla & Bus Stand...............59 A5
Dalla-dalla Stand.........................60 B3
Dar Express............................(see 66)
Eagle Air......................................61 B4
Ethiopian Airlines........................62 B3
Ferry to Kigamboni & Southern
  Beaches.......................................63 D4
Fresh ya Shamba Bus Office.....(see 39)
Gulf Air.....................................(see 9)
Kenya Airways........................(see 29)
Old Posta Local Transport Stand.64 B4
Precision Air.................................65 B3
Royal Coach.................................66 A4
South African Airways.............(see 9)
Stesheni Transport Stand.......(see 26)
Swissair...................................(see 40)
Taxi Stand....................................67 B3
Taxi Stand....................................68 B4
Taxi Stand...............................(see 61)
Zanzibar & Pemba Ferries...........69 B4

steaming heat and the exhaust fumes get too much for you, just head up along the coast to the fantastic beaches north or south of the city for your fix of white sand and palm trees. Alternatively, wander into the green and pleasant area around Shaaban Robert St, or retreat into the grounds of the National Museum.

ORIENTATION
Dalla-dallas run into town from the end of the road outside the airport, or a taxi will set you back about US$12.

Dar's city centre, with most of the cheaper hotels and restaurants, lies around the harbour. Suburbs spread out west and north, and a ferry connects the centre with the southern beaches outside the village of Kigamboni. The main bus station lies in the suburb of Ubungo, 11km west of the harbour.

The Central Line railway station (from Dodoma or Mwanza) is on Sokoine Dr in the middle of town, and the Tazara railway station is about 5km away down Nyerere Rd – dalla-dallas marked 'Posta Vigunguti' go into central Dar.

INFORMATION
Bookshops
A Novel Idea (Steers food village, Samora Ave) The best bookshop in Dar, excellent selection of guidebooks and novels, plus cards and gifts. There's another branch in the Slipway shopping centre slightly out of town.
Bookstalls (cnr Sokoine Dv & Ohio St) Also worth checking out are these second-hand stalls.

Cultural Centres
Alliance Française (☎ 2119415; Ali Hassan Mwinyi Rd) is a good place to look for photographic and art exhibitions or the occasional French-language film.

Internet Access
Internet cafés have sprung up on almost every street corner in central Dar. The going rate is US$1 per hour.

Media
Dar has two entertainment guides, with lots of information about current events, transport timetables, useful addresses – and articles so bad they're good. Look for *What's Happening in Dar es Salaam* or the *Dar es Salaam Guide*.

Medical Services
Aga Khan Hospital (☎ 114096; Ocean Rd)
Regency Medical Centre (☎ 2150500; Ally Khan St, Upanga)

Money
For cash or travellers cheques, the best places to change money are the dozens of *bureaux de change* in central Dar (along Morogoro Rd and the central section of Samora Ave).
Barclays Bank (Ohio St) Has an ATM that accepts Visa.
Coastal Travels (☎ 2117959; Upanga Rd) Offers cash advances against Visa and MasterCard, but exchange rates are low and fees high.
Standard Chartered Bank (Shaaban Robert St) Also has an ATM that accepts Visa cards.

Post & Telephone
In addition to the **main post office** (Maktaba St), there's also a post office on Libya St, near many of the cheaper hotels.

International telephone calls can be made from the TTCL building (Extelecoms House) along Samora Ave, at various private telephone agencies, and in telephone boxes.

Tourist Offices
The **Tanzania Tourist Board** (☎ 2120373; www.tanzania-web.com; Samora Ave) have very helpful staff who can provide information on hotels in Dar and countrywide. They have a lot of useful stuff about bus prices and timetables too.

DANGERS & ANNOYANCES
Like any big city, Dar has its share of pickpockets and petty thieves – so keep a close eye on your possessions or, better still, leave them in the hotel safe. After dark, muggings are fairly common, so it's best to take a taxi over longer distances. Coco Beach in Oyster Bay, the closest beach to the city, is notorious for muggings, so it's better to head to Kunduchi Beach to the north or the beaches near Kigamboni to the south. See p597 for details.

SIGHTS
Dar is rather low on interesting sights. If you've just slogged in across country you'll probably want to head straight to one of the excellent **beaches** near the city instead. See p597 for details.

TANZANIA

THE BHANGI SCAM

Several travellers have fallen prey to hustlers in Dar who approach them offering *bhangi* (marijuana). Whether they say yes or no, and whether they manage to shake off the hustler or not, within a few minutes they're stopped by two 'undercover policemen' who claim to have caught them in the act of purchasing drugs.

They are then asked for a hefty fine on the spot to avoid going to the police station and/or jail. On several occasions the hustler has been packed into a car alongside the hapless tourists and beaten up.

This is a hard scam to avoid, no matter how streetwise you are, and a harder one to get out of, as the 'policemen' can sometimes be the real thing doing a bit of hustling of their own on the side. Insist on going to the police station, which will eliminate any fake police, and if you do end up negotiating a 'fine' with some corrupt real police, start low – locals caught like this will get away for around US$20.

The **National Museum of Tanzania** (☎ 2122030; Shaaban Robert St; admission US$3; ☼ 9.30am-6pm) is an attractive Arab-style building that nestles in gardens among the embassies of Dar's upmarket quarter. Inside, there's a rolling exhibition of photography, paintings and sculpture, plus exhibitions of skulls and bones from Olduvai Gorge, witchcraft and ritual items from all around the country, and a hall dedicated to the Swahili coastal civilisation. It's an excellent introduction to Tanzania if you've just arrived.

Nyerere Cultural Centre & Nyumbaa Ya Sanaa (☎ 2133960; Ohio St; admission free; ☼ 8am-7pm) comprises an art gallery, shop, theatre space and workshops all set around a pretty courtyard, next door to the Royal Palm Hotel. The cultural centre promotes crafts made by disabled people and sculptures carved from ebony grown in sustainable plantations. The café sells cheap and delicious Tanzanian dishes, and visitors are also welcome to look around the workshops and paper recycling plant which are on site. There are dance and theatre performances (US$2) by local groups every Friday at 7.30pm.

ACTIVITIES
Safaris
Several companies in and around Dar operate safaris to the southern parks of Mikumi, Ruaha and Selous Game Reserve, but its definitely more expensive to do a safari in the less-visited south than on the well-trodden northern circuit around Arusha. See p611 for more details on organised safaris within Tanzania, and see p627 for more Tanzania-wide safari options.

Swimming
There's a swimming pool at the **Mission to Seafarers** (☎ 0748 767625; Bandari Rd; admission US$2; ☼ daily), which also has a bar and restaurant. Take a dalla-dalla marked 'Mtoni/Mbagala' from outside the Central Line railway station.

SLEEPING
You won't have to look far in Dar to find a cheap hotel. Lindi St is the place to look for the real cheapies, while the area around Libya St has a few old backpackers favourites that are still doing sterling service. They can fill up, so book ahead to be sure.

Hostels
YWCA (☎ 2122439; ywca.tanzania@twiga.com; Azikiwe St; s/tw US$6/10) The best hostel in the city, with a great location, clean rooms with fan and a decent canteen. Prices include breakfast, and men are allowed, but book ahead as it's often full.

YMCA (☎ 2135457; Upanga Rd; s/tw US$10/13) Also clean and well located, but way overpriced for rather poky little rooms, although they do have fan and mosquito net. Women allowed.

Luther House Hostel (☎ 2126247; Sokoine Dr; s/tw US$20/25) The rooms here have bathroom, fan and net, but are ridiculously overpriced. The canteen, though, does excellent and very cheap Chinese food.

Hotels
Pop Inn Hotel (☎ 2126401; Lindi St; s/tw US$3/4) Clean rooms and friendly staff. Some rooms have fan, others net, some even manage both at once.

Tamarine Hotel (☎ 2120233; Lindi St; tw US$4) Also basic but sanitary, with fan but no net.

Holiday Hotel (☎ 2112246; Jamhuri St; s/tw US$6.50/ 7.50) Peaceful 2nd-floor hotel with rather hot rooms around an open courtyard. They'll also send emails for free.

Kibodya Hotel (☎ 2117856; Nkrumah St; tw US$8) Friendly staff and spacious, clean rooms with bathroom and fan but no net.

Safari Inn (☎ 2119104; safari-inn@lycos.com; s/d US$9/15; 🖳) The best of the Libya St joints, with a restaurant and smart but small rooms with bathroom, fan and hot water. Breakfast included.

Jambo Inn (☎ 2114293; Libya St; s/d US$9/15) Back to back with the Safari Inn, this place is another good bet. Rooms have fan, bathroom and sporadic hot water, breakfast is included, and they will store your bags for US$0.50 per day.

Econolodge (☎ 2116048; econolodge@raha.com; Libya St; s/d/t US$12.50/17/20) Down an alley off Libya St, this is nominally smarter, with big rooms, balconies, and a TV lounge, this costs a bit more but is roughly the same standard as Safari Inn or Jambo.

Terminal Hotel (☎ 2450228; rikihotel@raha.com; Ubungo Bus Station; s/d US$8/10) The bus station hotel is surprisingly smart, and a very good option if you're arriving in Dar late and/or exhausted. All rooms have their own bathroom, some have TV, or a balcony for those unforgettable views across the bus parking lot. It's often full, so book ahead to be sure of getting a room. There are restaurants outside, or they'll rustle you up some food.

EATING

As befits its status as a 'capital' city, Dar has restaurants featuring food from all around the world. Town specialities are Indian food (presumably due to its Asian population) and *mishkaki* (grilled meat on a skewer).

The cheapest food stalls and hole-in-the-wall cafés are to be found in the gardens opposite the SCB bank on Shabaan Robert St during the day, or at the bottom of Zaramo St Libya St in the evenings.

Epi d'Or (Samora Ave; snacks US$2) For snacks, lunches and pastries, head to this air-conditioned, brightly painted French bakery with an imaginative sandwich menu. They also do fresh juice and coffee, and every meal comes with a basket of free bread rolls.

Salamander Coffee House (cnr Mkwepu St & Samora Ave) Just around the corner; also has good sandwiches for the same price, as well as big breakfasts and a variety of hot dishes.

Awale Haad (Samora Ave) This restaurant, just opposite Salamander, also does lavish breakfasts along with 'Afro-Arab cuisine' curries, fish stew, spiced tea and ice cream.

Java Internet Café (Mkwepu St; mains US$2) Doesn't have Internet, but it does have extremely cheap *ugali* (maize porridge) with meat, fish or prawns, and an outdoor seating area.

Noori's (Mosque St; snacks US$1) Opposite the Ismaili mosque; recommended as the best place for Indian veg meals and snacks.

Food World (Azkikwe St; mains US$2) Near the Askari Monument; one of the few fast food joints that's open on Sunday.

Chef's Pride (Chagga St; lunch US$2) Deservedly a huge favourite with locals and travellers alike. Lunch here is a three-course meal of traditional dishes such as banana, ugali or curry, and they've got a vast menu of Chinese, Indian and Western food as well. To top it all off there's a *mishkaki* grill and a second-hand bookstall too.

Rendezvous Restaurant (Samora Ave; mains US$3) A great value place for a sit-down meal. It's got good décor, air-conditioning, great service and cheap steak dinners. Closed on Thursday evenings.

City Garden Restaurant (Garden Ave; mains US$5) Has a lovely outdoor seating area under the trees, and a big menu including a lunch buffet, cakes and snacks. No alcohol.

DRINKING

Many of the 'coolest' bars and clubs in Dar cater primarily for the city's huge expatriate population, and are located miles away in the remote suburbs. There are very few drinking places in the city centre, and most are pretty unexciting.

For sundowners, you could try climbing the stairs to the **Roof Top Bar** (Bibi Titi Mohammed Rd) at the Peacock Hotel. Alternatively head to **Florida Pub** (Samora Ave), a quaint British-style place behind the UN building. Florida also does meals for about US$3. Lumumba St, on the other side of the Mnanzi Moja Park, has a few interesting local pubs and restaurants – try New Happy Bar, or the Swahili Restaurant, a famous *mishkaki* joint. But beware – this area is NOT safe to walk around in after dark. Take one of the plentiful taxis, and don't carry too much cash.

A fun lunchtime drinking place is the bar on Coco Beach, out of town towards Msasani peninsular. This is the only beachfront place in central Dar, and sells very cheap prawns – but again, don't take too many valuables, or walk along the beach, as there have been robberies in this area.

If you're determined to have a big night out, and don't mind paying the US$5 taxi ride, head for **4Twenty** (420 Toure Dr) near the Sea Cliff hotel in the northern suburb of Oyster Bay – a combined bar/restaurant that is the latest trendy place to be seen. **Smokies Tavern** (Msasani Village) on the Msasani Peninsular is another expat favourite, with live music twice a week and occasional salsa classes.

GETTING THERE & AWAY

Air

Dar is the hub for most of Tanzania's domestic flights. See p588 for details.

Boat

Dar es Salaam is connected to Zanzibar and Pemba by ferries, operated by several different companies. Tickets can be booked in advance from the ticket offices by the port entrance – but don't buy from the touts who hang around outside.

The cheapest, and least comfortable, boat is the *Aziza*, which leaves at noon daily, arriving in Zanzibar at 3pm. The Pemba boat goes at noon on Tuesday and Friday, arriving next morning. The fare is US$15 one way to Zanzibar, or US$30 to Pemba.

The *Flying Horse* comes next in terms of price, leaving at 12.30pm daily and arriving in Zanzibar at 3pm. It costs US$20.

The other ferries are all of the speedy, 'luxury' variety, and make the journey to Zanzibar in around 90 minutes. *Sea Bus* leaves at 7am and 4pm, while *Sea Star* leaves at 10.30am daily. Both cost US$35.

For details of the FB *Santorini*, which sails overnight to Mtwara, see p591.

Bus

Buses to and from every conceivable part of Tanzania congregate at the enormous bus terminal in the suburb of Ubungo, inconveniently located 11km out of town along the Morogoro Rd. From here you can take a dalla-dalla marked 'Posta' to get you into the city centre, or grab a taxi for around US$10.

Scandinavian Express buses have their own very flash terminal (complete with smoked glass windows and 'customer serv-ice lounge') at the end of Sokoine Dr, past the Central Line railway station. For long distances, it's best to book in advance at one of the bus offices scattered around the Libya St in central Dar.

Dar Express, Royal Coach, Scandinavian, Tawfiq, and Freshi ya Shamba buses run several times a day to Arusha and Moshi (around US$10, 10 hours). Scandinavian, Tawfiq and Takrim go daily to Tanga (US$6, five hours) and Mombasa (US$12, 12 hours). Heading south, buses leave from Ubungo to Mbeya (US$14, 11 hours), Iringa (US$7, seven hours) and a few times a week to Lilongwe in Malawi (US$35, 24 hours). Scandinavian and Hood also go to Nairobi via Arusha (US$20 to US$30, 13 hours).

Train

Dar is connected via the **Central Line** (☎ 2117833; ccm_cserve@trctz.com) with Dodoma, Kigoma and Mwanza. Central Line trains leave Tuesday, Friday and Sunday at 5pm, supposedly taking 36 hours to Mwanza and 48 hours to Kigoma. In reality, though, trains are often up to 10 hours late arriving. Fares are US$45/33 in 1st/2nd class to Mwanza, and US$46/34 to Kigoma. It's probably worth getting first class, especially if you're going all the way to Kigoma. Men and women are not allowed to travel together in second class. Reserve in advance if you can – you might be able to get on a train at the last minute, but it could involve bribing the staff.

Trains on the much more comfortable Tazara railway run to Mbeya and on to Zambia. Trains leave on Tuesday and Friday at 3.50pm and 3pm respectively, arriving at Mbeya at 12pm on Wednesday and Saturday. There is also a slow train to Mbeya on Monday at 10am, arriving at 10am on Tuesday. Fares to Mbeya are US$25/17/11 in 1st/2nd/3rd class, with a 50% student discount if you show your ISIC card when booking. Again, if you want to travel with someone of the opposite sex, you'll have to book first class to be allowed to sleep in the same compartment. Tickets should be booked in advance at the Tazara station, 5km out of Dar on Nyerere Rd. For details of fares to Zambia, see p590.

GETTING AROUND

Dar's city centre is fairly compact, and if you can stand the relentless heat, you should have no problems getting around on foot. To get to outer suburbs like Msasani or Oyster Bay, or to reach the northern and southern beaches, look for city buses and dalla-dallas outside the post office on Azikiwe St or opposite NBC bank on Sokoine Dr.

There are taxis everywhere, and the standard fare within the city centre is US$1.50.

AROUND DAR ES SALAAM

DAR BEACHES

Dar is blessed with glorious tropical beaches just a few kilometres from the city centre. It's definitely a good option to stay out on the beach, as it's pretty easy to get in and out of town, especially from the slightly superior southern beaches.

South Beach

The stretch of coast that extends between the little fishing villages of Kigamboni and Gezaulole is always just known as 'South Beach'. To get there, take a ferry from the jetty on Kivukoni Front to Kigamboni, and pick up a dalla-dalla heading south. Just a few kilometres further on, the white sand beckons...

Kipepeo Campsite (☎ 2820877; info@kipepeo camp.com; camp site per person/dm/d US$2/5/8) A good setup for backpackers, although it gets very busy with a cliquey crowd of expats at the weekends. There's a bar, a restaurant selling burgers, chips and the like, and a noticeboard for travellers. The dorm's position between kitchen and bar makes it smelly and noisy – take a hut (the price of a double) on the beach instead if you can afford it. They can do airport transfers by prior arrangement for about US$10.

Gendayeka Beach Village (☎ 0741438957; camp site per person/s US$2/6) A locally owned place next door to Kipepeo, far scruffier, quieter and more relaxing. Don't expect fawning service or slick marketing, but the beach here is second to none. Breakfast included, and they can arrange evening meals. Recommended for serious chilling.

Akida's Garden (☎ 2112518; wcst@africanonline.co .tz; per person around US$4) A cultural tourism project in the tiny village of Gezaulole, a few kilometres further down the coast.

There's camping, or basic bandas in a shady garden, two minutes walk from the beach.

If you have your own tent you can camp at Kim Beach, the most stunning of all, which has a small camp site with water, toilets, and shade. You'll have to bring your own food, or make an arrangement with Akida's Garden for meals.

Kunduchi

The beaches around the village of Kunduchi, north of Dar, are also pretty good, although most of the best have been commandeered by upmarket hotels. To get there, take a city bus out to Mwenga, change onto a dalla-dalla to Kunduchi, then walk or take a bicycle taxi from there. Be careful if walking with valuables – there are frequent muggings along the more remote stretches of beach.

Silver Sands Campsite (☎ 2650567; relax@silver sands.co.tz; camp site per person/dm/d US$3/7/20) The only real budget option in Kunduchi has hot showers, a bar and an expensive restaurant. A firm favourite with overland trucks.

BAGAMOYO

☎ 023

Bagamoyo, perhaps more than any other town on the Tanzanian mainland, played a crucial role in shaping the history of the country. It was the site of a Swahili trading post and later the base for a bloody rebellion against the German colonial government. Bagamoyo was also the start and end point for the epic journeys into the interior made by slave traders and European explorers like Burton and Livingstone.

The town's name means 'lay down your heart', a reference to the relief the caravan porters felt when they arrived back at the coast after the hardships of the road, and to the despair of their slave captives, just about to embark for Zanzibar and a life of incarceration.

These days Bagamoyo is a sleepy and unspoilt fishing village, well worth a visit if you fancy some history with a bit of beach-time thrown in. It has a reputation for muggings, which is probably exaggerated, but take care when walking around with valuables.

Sights

The old **German Mission** (admission free; ☼ 10am-5pm) stands at the end of a beautiful avenue of mango trees a few hundred metres from the beach. There's an excellent museum, with explanations in English, setting out the role of Bagamoyo in Tanzania's history.

The **church** next door is one of the oldest in East Africa, with stained glass windows and bright naïve art paintings on the walls. Alongside, in another of the old mission buildings, is one of the most picturesque Internet cafés in Tanzania!

In the gardens of Badecco Beach Hotel, the **Hanging Tree** is a macabre reminder of the ill-fated Bushiri revolt of 1888, in which the people of this part of the coast rose up with brief success against the German colonialists. Their leaders were eventually strung up here for their pains.

The **Kaole Ruins**, about 5km out of town in the small village of Kaole, are the remains of an ancient Muslim settlement, with a mosque and a cemetery containing several Swahili gravestones. It's a pretty walk out to the ruins, but it's better to go along the dirt road rather than the beach because of the risk of robberies.

Sleeping

Old Market Guesthouse (☎ 0744 564909; Market St; s/d US$10/20) This beautifully restored house lies opposite the atmospheric Old Market and just a few minutes' walk from the beach. The brand new, well-furnished rooms mostly have their own bathroom. No breakfast, but you can buy food from the local stalls outside, or order food to be cooked in the evening. Highly recommended.

Bagamoyo Beach Resort (☎ 2440083; tw US$12) Bang on the beach, with few pretensions but plenty of character, especially if the eccentric French owner is in residence. The simple beach huts have a shared bathroom, or there are more upmarket rooms available for about US$25.

Double M Guesthouse (s US$5) A basic joint around the corner from the bus stop. Cleanish rooms have a bed big enough for a couple, and their own bathroom.

Getting There & Away

Buses and dalla-dallas (US$1, one hour) run to Bagamoyo from Ubungo bus terminus in Dar es Salaam. It is also possible to organise a dhow to sail from Bagamoyo to Zanzibar. If the wind allows, the journey should take four hours and cost less than US$10. But if the wind fails, you could be stranded – most dhows have no engines, and there will be no food, water or toilet facilities on board. Be warned – there are no lifejackets either.

THE ZANZIBAR ARCHIPELAGO

The name Zanzibar conjures up such exotic images that you might be forgiven for thinking it's not a real place at all, but just somewhere that appears in fairytales or stories from the *Arabian Nights*. But it's real all right – Zanzibar Island (known in Swahili as *Unguja*) and neighbouring Pemba island, plus a scattering of off-shore islets, together make up the state of Zanzibar, semi-independent from mainland Tanzania.

The good news is that Zanzibar is every bit as exotic as its name suggests – most of the time anyway. These days Internet cafés and fast food restaurants are springing up among the ancient minarets of the capital Stone Town, and package holiday beach

DRESS IN ZANZIBAR

Zanzibar is a conservative Muslim society and locals find it highly offensive to see visitors wearing skimpy clothing. To respect their customs, women should wear tops that don't show too much cleavage, and cover their legs to the knee. Men should not walk in the streets without shirts on. Swimwear (but not topless sunbathing) is fine on the beach, but cover up before walking into the villages.

resorts have appeared on some of the wide white beaches that ring the island.

But it doesn't take much effort to escape the traces of the modern world and plunge back several centuries into Zanzibar's heyday – it was once the capital of the Arab empire in East Africa, with its own sultan (complete with harem) and a flourishing trade in spices and slaves. The sultan and his slaves have gone, but the spices are still there, bubbling in fragrant pots of seafood curry or haggled over in tiny, dark markets.

And then, of course, there's the beach. Zanzibar's beaches are the kind of chocolate-box, picture-postcard fantasies you thought only existed in Bounty ads. The sea is impossibly turquoise, the sand is white and talcum powder soft, and it all stretches for mile after unbroken mile, punctuated only by the occasional seaweed farmer hauling in her crop.

'Zanzibar' officially refers to the whole archipelago, comprising Zanzibar Island and Pemba. The main town is also called Zanzibar, but the older, central part is usually referred to as Stone Town. To simplify things, we have referred to the island as Zanzibar, and the main town as Stone Town.

STONE TOWN

☎ 024

If you can resist the temptation to head straight for Zanzibar's perfect white beaches, it's well worth spending a day or two getting blissfully lost among Stone Town's narrow streets and hidden courtyards.

Orientation

Zanzibar's airport lies 7km from Stone Town, a US$6 taxi ride away. Haggle hard – taxi drivers start high here when quoting their prices. Alternatively, take the dalla-dallas marked U (US$0.50) from the airport car park, which run to Darajani Market on the eastern edge of the old town. If you're staying on the western side around Shangani, ask to be dropped off at Mnanzi Moja hospital, then walk straight ahead down Kaunda Rd to the old town centre.

If you're arriving by ferry, you'll come in at the main port in Malindi. After showing your passport at the immigration office in the port, go straight on across the roundabout for the Malawi Rd guesthouses, or turn right and walk along the seafront to get to Shangani and the main part of the old town. Don't worry too much about getting lost – by the time you've finished disembarking from the ferry, you will have gained a set of new 'friends' desperate to show you anywhere you want to go.

Information

BOOKSHOPS

2nd-hand bookstalls (Gizenga St) These stalls sometimes have the latest guidebooks.
Memories of Zanzibar (Kenyatta Rd) Has a good selection of books alongside curios and clothes.
Zanzibar Gallery (Kenyatta Rd & Gizenga St) Well-decorated and air-conditioned, with plenty of guidebooks, maps and novels.

INTERNET ACCESS

There are at least 20 Internet cafés in Stone Town, charging a standard rate of US$1 per hour. **Shangani Internet** (Kenyatta Rd) also has air-con and ice cream.

INTERNET RESOURCES

www.allaboutzanzibar.com Tour operator's site, but with excellent cultural articles.
www.earthfoot.org/guides/jumane.htm Local eco-guide.
www.encounterzanzibar.com Has a good list of dive sites.
www.zanzibar.net General tourist information.

MEDIA

Recommended in Zanzibar is a tourist magazine with tide tables, boat timetables and useful phone numbers. The *Swahili Coast Magazine* has hotel and restaurant listings.

MEDICAL SERVICES

Al Rahma Hospital (☎ 2236715) On the road to the airport.

TANZANIA

STONE TOWN

Ⓐ   **Ⓑ**   **Ⓒ**   **Ⓓ**

INFORMATION
Customs & Immigration..............1 F2
Dr Mehta's Hospital....................2 D5
Malindi Bureau de Change.......(see 67)
Memories of Zanzibar..............(see 5)
NBC Bank...................................3 B5
Shangani Bureau de Change.....4 B5
Shangani Internet Café..............5 B6
Telephone Office........................6 B5
Too Short Internet Café..............7 B5
Zanzibar Serena Inn....................8 A5
ZIFF Office...............................(see 24)

SIGHTS & ACTIVITIES   pp601–3
Aga Khan Mosque......................9 E3
Anglican Cathedral...................10 E4
Bahari Divers............................11 B5
Beit al Amani (Peace Memorial
   Museum).................................12 E6
Big Tree...................................13 E3
Coastal Travels.........................14 A6
Forodhani Gardens...................15 D3
Hamamni Persian Baths............16 E4
High Court...............................17 D5
Hindu Temple..........................18 E4
House of Wonders (Beit
   el-Ajaib)................................19 D3
Ijumaa Mosque........................20 E3
Institute of Swahili & Foreign
   Languages..............................21 E5
Mr Mitu (Spice Tours)..............22 F2

Msikiti wa Balnara (Malindi Minaret
   Mosque).................................23 F3
Old Fort..................................24 D4
Old Slave Chambers...............(see 43)
One Ocean...............................25 B5
Palace Museum (Beit al-Sahel)..26 E3
St Joseph's Cathedral...............27 D4
Tembo House Hotel..................28 B5
Victoria Gardens......................29 D6
Zanzibar Gallery (branch)..........30 D3
Zanzibar Gallery......................31 B5

SLEEPING   🏠 pp603–4
Annex Malindi Lodge................32 F2
Annex of Abdullah...................33 D4
Bandari Lodge..........................34 F2
Flamingo Guest House.............35 B5
Florida Guesthouse..................36 D5
Garden Lodge..........................37 D5
Haven Guest House..................38 D5
Jambo Guesthouse...................39 E5
Karibu Inn...............................40 B5
Malindi Lodge..........................41 F3
Manch Lodge..........................42 D5
St Monica's Hostel & Restaurant.43 E5
Victoria Guesthouse.................44 D5

EATING   🍽 pp604–5
Amore Mio...............................45 A6
Blues..46 D3
China Plate Restaurant.............47 B5

Dolphin Restaurant..................48 B6
Fany's Green Restaurant........(see 48)
Fisherman Restaurant..............49 B5
Green Garden Restaurant......(see 39)
Kiwengwa Tea Room................50 D4
La Fenice.................................51 A6
Paracuda Restaurant................52 C5
Passing Show Restaurant..........53 F3
Radha Food House...................54 B5
The Dhow Restaurant..............55 D3

DRINKING   🍷 p605
Africa House Hotel...................56 B6
Mercury's.................................57 E3
Starehe Club............................58 A5
Sweet Eazy..............................59 B5
The Garage Club......................60 B5

SHOPPING   🛍 p605
Chavda Street – Kanga Stalls.....61 E4
Zanzibar Curio Shop................62 D4

TRANSPORT   pp605–6
Air Tanzania............................63 E5
Bus Station..............................64 F4
Dalla-dallas to Airport..............65 D6
Ferry Tickets............................66 F2
ZanAir......................................67 F3

Zanzibar Channel

Shangani

Gizenga St

See Enlargement

Shangani

0   100 m
0   0.1 mi

To Al Rahma Hospital
(5km) & Airport (7km)

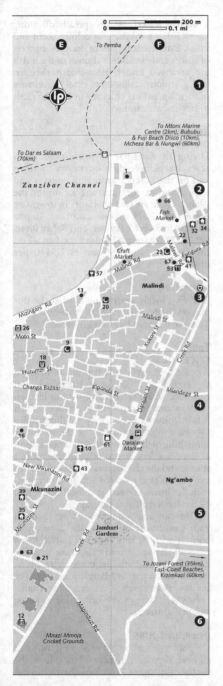

Dr Mehta's Hospital (☎ 0747 410099; Kenyatta Rd)
Opposite the High Court.

MONEY
There's no ATM in Zanzibar. The best
places to change cash or travellers cheques
are the various *bureaux de change* along
Kenyatta Rd or at the **NBC bank** (Kenyatta
Rd) near the Tembo Hotel. **Coastal Travels**
(☎ 2233489; Shangani St), which has branches
next to the Zanzibar Serena Inn and at the
airport, does cash advances on Visa cards,
but be prepared for a long wait and a high
rate of commission.

POST & TELEPHONE
The **'old' post office** (Kenyatta Rd) is the most
convenient one for travellers. You can
make phone calls from the telephone office
next door, and from **Too Short Internet café**
(Kenyatta Rd).

Dangers & Annoyances
Stone Town is generally safe, but tourists
wandering the back streets late at night
sometimes get mugged. Don't carry your
valuables around, or leave them in your
hotel room – lock them in the safe instead.

Sights
No one single attraction can beat an afternoon strolling through the narrow streets
and winding alleys of the old town. You'll
get lost – everybody does – but don't worry,
you'll emerge into the blinding sunlight of
the seafront eventually. In the meantime,
mingle with the coffee sellers, old men in
white skullcaps and women in black *bui-buis*
(veils) who bustle past the old Arab houses
with their magnificent brass-studded doors
and ornate latticed balconies. Remember to
keep looking up – below a blue strip of sky,
shutters are thrown open and neighbours
lean across the narrow gap between their
homes to swap gossip and jokes, hang out
washing, or just watch the world go by three
storeys below.

As well as the magic of the streets, Stone
Town has several historical buildings that
are worth a look.

Palace Museum (Mizingani Rd; admission US$3;
🕑 Mon-Fri 9am-6pm, Sat & Sun 8.30am-3pm) is a low-
rise white palace that was the residence of
the Sultans of Zanzibar until the revolution
toppled them in 1964. It includes a room

TANZANIA

PAPAASI

Zanzibar has an increasingly bad reputation for 'beach boys' (known as *papaasi* – ticks – in Swahili), the annoying touts who latch onto all newly arrived tourists and follow them endlessly, trying to sell various tours or fix up transport to the beaches. Some are drug addicts, unstable and potentially dangerous, while some are just local guys trying to earn a living as guides or 'fixers'. Whether you're happy to talk to them or not, remember to stay polite at all times, even when they're driving you mad – being rude will only lead to verbal abuse, or give offence. A few words of Swahili go a long way (see the Language chapter, p1039), or simply say you've arranged everything you want to do already. One area where the *papaasi* definitely come in handy is in arranging cheap shuttle buses to the beach – see p591 for details.

dedicated to Princess Salme, daughter of Sultan Said, who scandalously eloped with a German businessman in the 19th century. There are also oil paintings of various sultans and some rather dusty furniture.

House of Wonders (Beit al Ajaib; Mizingani Rd; admission US$3; Mon-Fri 9am-6pm, Sat & Sun 8.30am-3pm) got its name because it was the first building in East Africa to have electricity and a lift. This multi-storey ceremonial palace on the seafront was built by Barghash, one of the more ostentatious of Zanzibar's 19th-century sultans. It hasn't got much inside, but it's worth the entrance fee for the amazing view of the harbour and the town from the topmost balconies.

The **Old Fort** (8am-10pm) next door was built by the Portuguese in the 17th century, then taken over by the Arabs. It's free to enter, and there are a few craft shops, a travel agency, and a pretty café in the green space inside the walls, which makes for a welcome relief from the bustle and heat of the streets.

The **Anglican Cathedral** off Mkunazini Rd was built on the site of the old slave market, and has a crucifix made from the tree under which the explorer David Livingstone's heart was buried. Nearby are the **underground slave chambers** (8am-4pm Mon-Sat) in which slaves were kept, forced to crouch on stone shelves less than two feet high. Very moving.

Darajani Market, which spreads all along Creek Rd, is a mayhem of colour, scent and noise. Symmetrical piles of oranges, baskets of spices and enormous chunks of fresh fish are arranged under palm-thatch shelters, and garrulous stallholders extol the virtues of their squawking chickens or bolts of cloth to impassive customers.

Activities

DIVING

Diving in Zanzibar is world-class, with several reputable dive operators in town and on the beaches arranging courses and trips to various reefs and wrecks around the island. There are two operators in town: **One Ocean** (☎ 2238374; oneocean@zanlink.com; Kenyatta Rd) next to Sweet Eazy bar, and **Bahari Divers** (☎ 0742750293; Kenyatta Rd) near the tunnel on the seafront. Average cost is US$40 per dive.

SWIMMING

There's a lovely swimming pool at the upmarket **Tembo Hotel** (Shangani St; admission US$3). The entry fee isn't always enforced.

Tours

SPICE TOURS

A spice tour involves a trip out of town to the agricultural villages of Kizimbani and Kindichi, where spices are grown in kitchen gardens and government plantations. Even if horticulture's not really your thing, spice tours are worth doing for the chance to see something of the lives of the rural population of Zanzibar. You get to taste all the various spices, and the cheapest rate of about US$10 per person (for a shared trip in a minibus) includes lunch cooked in a local home and all the fresh fruit you can eat.

You can arrange a spice tour through your guesthouse or one of the *papaasi*, or book it with **Mr Mitu Tours** (☎ 2231020; Malawi Rd). Full day spice tours also take in some ruined Persian baths in the nearby countryside, and a trip to Mangapwani beach to see the 'slave caves' – underground chambers where slaves were kept prior to being shipped abroad.

DOLPHIN TOURS

Dolphin tours, also sold in Stone Town and all over Zanzibar, involve a bus ride to the southern village of Kizimkazi, then a trip out in a small boat to 'swim with dolphins'. The tours cost about US$25, and most people are disappointed – the dolphins don't always appear, and when they do the trip can turn into a bit of a circus, with tourist boats chasing the hapless dolphins around the bay.

Marine biologists are currently investigating whether the tours are harmfully disturbing the dolphins. In the meantime, if you really want to see dolphins, the best thing to do is to stay overnight in Kizimkazi – there are a number of local guesthouses in the village – then hire a boatman to take you out at first light, when there won't be anyone else around.

BOAT TRIPS

The two most common boat trips from Stone Town go to **Bawe Island** and **Changuu** (Prison Island). These can be arranged with any of the boat captains who hang around the so-called Big Tree opposite Mercury's Restaurant on Mizingani Rd on the seafront, or on the beach in front of Sweet Eazy bar.

Prison Island is the closest of the two, just 15 minutes away, with a small but perfectly formed beach and a rather grotty restaurant. It's chief attraction, though, is a pen full of wizened and enormous tortoises (you can buy bunches of spinach to feed them). A ruined prison also stands on the island, built by the British in the 19th century but never used. A trip to Prison Island and back in a boat should cost about US$12 per person, and there's an entry fee of US$5.

Bawe Island is further away – an hour by boat – and has stunning **beaches** and good **snorkelling**, but no food or drink facilities, so you'll need to bring your own. Boats here cost about US$20 per person for the return trip.

Festivals & Events

The **Festival of the Dhow Countries** (also known as The Zanzibar International Film Festival, or ZIFF) occurs in the first week of July every year, and is a celebration of arts, music, film and literature from Zanzibar, Pemba and the so-called dhow countries, a term which includes most of Africa, India and the Middle East.

If you're travelling in Tanzania around this time, definitely try to make it to Zanzibar for the festival – there's a real party atmosphere in town, and the open-air films and gigs inside the walls of the Old Fort are unforgettable. Some events are free; others cost US$5. Details of the exact programme can be obtained from the **festival office** (☎ 0747 411499; www.ziff.or.tz).

Sleeping

Stone Town has dozens of budget guesthouses, so you're unlikely to have much trouble finding a bed even in the high season. They're mostly quite basic, however, and much poorer value than the equivalent on the mainland, although you can usually reduce them a fair bit by bargaining.

There's not much to choose between the following – all have fan and net, but hot water is a rarity.

Malindi Lodge (☎ 2232359; Malawi Rd; s/d US$15/20) Handy for the port, plenty of character, clean, whitewashed rooms. Own bathroom, breakfast included.

Bandari Lodge (☎ 22379969; off Malawi Rd; s/d US$12/24) Also near the port, four poster beds, sunny rooms. Shared bathroom, breakfast included.

Annex Malindi Lodge (☎ 2230676; off Malawi Rd; s/d US$8/10) Opposite the fish market. Pretty rooms with shared bathroom, breakfast included in the rooftop restaurant.

Manch Lodge (☎ 2231918; maddybest@yahoo.com; s/d US$10/20) Deep in the heart of the old town, just off Vuga Rd. Small garden, own bathroom, breakfast included.

St Monica's Hostel (☎ 0741 352709; monicaszanzibar@hotmail.com; s/d US$12/24) Next to the Anglican cathedral, church-run and clean. Restaurant, shared bathroom, big balconies. Includes breakfast.

Jambo Guesthouse (☎ 2233779; jamboguesthouse@hotmail.com; off Mkunazini St; s/d/t US$ 10/20/30; ✂ ☐) Prices include breakfast, free tea and coffee, and an hour of Internet access. Shared bathroom. Close to the Green Garden restaurant.

Flamingo Guesthouse (☎ 2232850; Mkunazini St; s/d US$8/16) In a peaceful, genteel part of town, basic but cheap. Shared bathroom, breakfast included.

Haven Guesthouse (☎ 2235677; off Vuga Rd; s/d US$10/20) Clean and airy rooms, shared bathroom. Includes breakfast.

Annex of Abdullah (☎ 0747421845; off Sokho Muhogo St; s/d US$10/20; ✂ ☐) Discounts for longer stays. Breakfast and one hour of

SPLURGE!

Chumbe Island, a few miles off Stone Town, is one of the world's newest and most successful eco-tourism projects. In 1994 the reef surrounding Chumbe Island was created as Tanzania's first Marine National Park. The island itself, covered with lush mangrove forest, is a designated forest reserve and contains a lighthouse, a ruined mosque and the lighthouse keeper's house, now converted into a spectacularly built education centre and restaurant.

For an unforgettable night of Robinson Crusoe bliss, stay over in one of the seven **'eco-bandas'** (☎ 2231040; chumbe@zitec.org; per person per night US$200) that nestle in the forest. Each is a two-storey, private cottage built out of local materials and decorated with shells, driftwood and colourful local fabrics. Water and energy on Chumbe are self-sustaining – the roofs of the bandas and the education centre catch and filter rainwater, which is then heated by solar power. Beds are high in the palm-thatch roof, with a front wall that opens for a view of the stars. The price includes meals, most drinks, boat transfers, a snorkelling trip over the reef (one of the best in the world) and guided walks through the forest.

Internet, tea and coffee included. Shared bathroom.

Florida Guesthouse (☎ 2233136; off Vuga Rd; s/d US$10/20) Own bathroom, hot water, fridge in rooms, breakfast included, good value but poky.

Victoria Guesthouse (☎ 2232861; Victoria St; s/tw US$12/24) Good location overlooking Victoria Gardens. Airy twin rooms, own bathroom, includes breakfast. No unmarried couples in same room.

Garden Lodge (☎ 2233298; gardenlodge@zanlink .com; Kaunda Rd; s/d US$15/20) Very central, better rooms with own bathroom upstairs. A bit overpriced.

Karibu Inn (☎ 2233058; karibuinn@zanzinet.com; off Gizenga St; dm/s/d US$10/15/25) Central, but shabby and overpriced.

Eating

Worth the trip to Zanzibar on its own, and unquestionably the best place to eat in Stone Town, is the seafood market in Forodhani Gardens. The seafront comes alive at around 6pm every day, with stallholders setting up their wares of fried fish and chicken on skewers, piles of squid and octopus and mounds of chips.

The stalls go on until around 11pm, and the gardens, lit up by hurricane lamps, are a social meeting point for the entire town. Vegetarians are not left out and can feast on *bhajias*, falafels, samosas and 'Zanzibar pizza' – which is actually more like a combination of an omelette and a crêpe. A paper plate of seafood with chips, washed down with sugarcane juice and eaten with the fingers will cost about US$3.

For lunch, venture into the labyrinth of alleyways in the old town, where a number of local cafés do trays of rice with sauce, salad and spinach. Veggies (or those averse to eating goat) should ask for *maharagwe* – red beans cooked in coconut sauce. Try **Kiwengwa Tea Room** (Sokho Muhogo St; lunch US$0.30) or the locals' favourite **Passing Show Restaurant** (Malawi Rd; lunch US$0.50). If you're an ice-cream fan, head to **Amore Mio** (Shangani St) or nearby **La Fenice** (Shangani St; lunch US$5) for the real Italian McCoy. Both do pasta and pizzas of varying quality too. Kenyatta Rd, the main tourist street, has Fany's Green and Dolphin restaurants, both of which produce passable pasta, toasted sandwiches, and the like.

If you can tear yourself away from Forodhani in the evenings, **Paracuda** (Kenyatta Rd; mains US$3) and **Green Garden** (Mkunazini St; mains US$3) are highly recommended for good value local food. Service can be slow as they cook everything from scratch, but you'll get fantastic vegetable curries, grilled fish or steaks. Neither place serves alcohol. For vegetarians, Radha Food House, near Bahari Divers, does Indian *thalis* and fresh yoghurt for around US$3.

Stone Town has several upmarket restaurants, of which the best value is probably **Fisherman** (Shangani St; mains US$10) opposite the Tembo Hotel. It's a bit like a little French bistro inside, and does wondrous steaks, catch of the day and prawns, served in huge portions. Just around the corner, **China Plate** (Kenyatta Rd; lunch US$4), a stiff climb up hundreds of steps, has an attractive rooftop setting and does fantastic Chinese food. Evening meals are more expensive.

For a real splurge, there's the **Dhow Restaurant** (☎ 2250117; thedhow@zanzibar.cc; mains

US$25) on an old Arabic dhow moored just offshore in front of Forodhani Gardens (or the Zanzibar Serena Inn, depending on the tides). Guests are ferried over in a small motorboat at sunset and loll on cushions gorging on seafood, soups, vegetable dishes and fruit, followed by Arabic coffee. Hedonistically fantastic. Book by phone or email, or call at the stall in Forodhani Gardens. A bit cheaper is **Blues bistro** (Forodhani Gardens; mains US$4.50), on the jetty at Forodhani, which is a great place to get away from the crowds in town and loll around for the afternoon nursing a beer.

Drinking & Clubbing

Stone Town may not be the world's biggest party town, but there are a few atmospheric places for a sundowner. The upstairs bar at Africa House Hotel, off Kenyatta Rd, is the traditional place to watch the sunset, but it's so popular that you have to arrive early to get a spot by the edge of the terrace. There's an expensive pool table here, and they do pub snacks, but it empties out soon after sunset and is pretty dead later on.

Alternatively, try Sweet Eazy, at the bottom of Kenyatta Rd, or Mercury's near the port. These are the most popular bars in town, where locals and expats gather to drink too many cocktails and chat each other up. Both regularly have live music, and their restaurants serve pizza, pasta, and (at Sweet Eazy) Thai food.

A few kilometres out of town on the Bububu road, Mcheza Bar at Mtoni Marine Centre is a fun sports pub on the beach, with a good combination of locals and expats. They've got table football, TV and good-value pizza, hot dogs etc. This is the place to head for if there's a football or rugby match you want to watch.

As for discos, the Garage Club opposite the Tembo Hotel is the most central, but really only amusing if you're drunk, with 80s decor and a cheesy playlist. Starehe Club, a bit further up Shangani St, has cheap beer and occasional reggae nights, which involve enormous amplifiers and dozens of Rastas bobbing about in near-pitch darkness.

The best place to go dancing, if you can get there, is Fuji Beach Disco, a few kilometres out of town in the little village of Bububu. This is huge local place right on the beach, where the wide boys from town

RAMADAN

Zanzibaris observe the Holy Month of Ramadan every year by refraining from eating or drinking between sunrise and sunset. The dates of Ramadan change every year according to the Muslim calendar, and during this time all bars and discos are closed and most local restaurants shut during the day. Visitors are asked not to eat, drink or smoke in public during daylight hours.

mingle with country bumpkins down from the spice villages. It only happens on Tuesday, Friday and Sunday, with music varying from night to night. Before midnight, they generally play Taarab, the wailing semi-Arab music of the coast, but switch to Swahili and American rap and R'n'B later on. The dancefloor is always packed and heaving, and the beach makes a natural chillout area under the stars.

Taxis cost about US$3 each way.

Shopping

The main shopping street in town is Gizenga Street, with curio shops all the way up selling much the same thing – Tingatinga paintings, wooden carvings of every kind, spice baskets and sarongs.

Tucked in among all this tat are a few genuine antiques such as old clocks, chests and porcelain bowls dating from the days of the sultans. The back room of **Zanzibar Curio Shop** (Hurumzi St) is a good place to look for things like these.

Chavda St, behind Darajani Market, is the place to buy *kangas* – the colourful cotton wraps worn as headscarf and skirt by ladies all over East Africa. They come attached to each other in pairs, stiff with starch and decorated with a Swahili saying, which could be an advertising slogan, a riddle, or a barbed comment designed for a cheating boyfriend. *Kangas* cost around US$1.50, and you can take them to one of the little tailor's shops in the same area to be cut in half and hemmed. They get softer once you've washed them a few times.

GETTING THERE & AROUND
Air

Several airlines fly to Zanzibar from destinations within Tanzania. See p590 for details.

TANZANIA

Boat

Ferries run from the port in Stone Town to Dar es Salaam several times a day – see p596 for fares. The *Flying Horse* leaves at 10pm daily, arriving in Dar at 6am next day. The fast boats, *Sea Star* and *Sea Express*, leave at 7am, 1pm and 4pm.

To Pemba Island, the only options are currently the rather feral night boats. The *Serengeti* (US$20) leaves each evening from the port and arrives at Mkoani in Pemba next morning. The *Aziza* leaves on Friday at 9pm for Wete in Pemba, and also runs to Dar overnight six days a week, departing at the same time.

Car & Motorcycle

Renting a Suzuki 'jeep' is a very good way of exploring the island and saving on time spent sitting on dalla-dallas. Be aware though, that road rules are few and far between and accidents common.

Jeeps can be hired through any guesthouse or *papaasi* (see boxed text p602), or by approaching one of the drivers parked at the western end of Forodhani Gardens. Jeeps should cost about US$40 per day, not including fuel. You need an international driving licence, or a temporary permit (US$4) to drive on Zanzibar – and police checkpoints every few kilometres on the major roads mean you won't be able to get away without one or the other.

Vespas and Honda 250cc motorcycles are also available for hire at about US$20 per day – the main man in town for motorbikes is a colourful character called **Ally Keys** (☎ 0747 411797). He's not as disreputable as he looks, and his bikes are safe.

Local Transport

The principal mode of public transport in Zanzibar is the dalla-dallas – driving at high speed and bursting at the seams with baskets of farm produce, chickens and toddlers. They run all over the island and rarely cost more than US$0.50. The main terminus in Stone Town is on Creek Rd opposite Darajani market.

Each dalla-dalla is identified by a letter or a number – the best thing is just to ask for where you want to go. Dalla-dallas to the east coast villages of Bwejuu and Jambiani take at least two hours, and to Nungwi you could be rattling over the potholes for half a day.

The '*papaasi* bus' – a shuttle minibus service operated by 'beach boys' – leaves Stone Town every morning at about 8am for the beaches at Nungwi, Bwejuu or Jambiani. Arrange it the night before with any of the dudes who hang around Forodhani Gardens or Kenyatta Rd, and it'll come and pick you up from your hotel in the morning. The bus costs US$3, and when you arrive at the beach they'll drive you around a few selected hotels until you've made your choice. Be aware, however, that the *papaasi* only take you to the hotels that pay them commission – if you want to go to a different hotel, you might have to pay a higher fare.

NUNGWI
☎ 024

First views of the village of Nungwi, at Zanzibar Island's northern tip, are not inspiring. Rubbish lines the road into the village, and half-built guesthouses and bars sit cheek by jowl along the scruffy main street. But emerge onto the beach, and suddenly none of this matters – the water in Nungwi is startlingly turquoise, the tide is always in (meaning all day swimming), and the soft white sand goes on for miles.

Nungwi is the most visited of Zanzibar's beach villages, with several bars and restaurants and a fair number of people sunning themselves on the beach in high season. This makes it the best place on the island to meet other travellers. Kendwa, a couple of kilometres along the coast, is usually much quieter, except at full moon when there's a party on the beach.

There are Internet cafés and a *bureau de change* close to the beach guesthouses. It's not advisable to walk too far along the beach carrying valuables, or at night.

Sleeping

Many of the guesthouses in Nungwi burnt down in a fire in late 2002, and are in the process of being slowly rebuilt, but the following are still open. All prices include breakfast unless otherwise stated.

Cholos Bar (camp site per person/d US$5/20) Camp site on the beach (with shower and toilet); fun, but overpriced. A-frame sleeping platforms; no breakfast.

Morning Star Guesthouse (s/d US$8/16) In the village itself, away from the beach. Electricity and shared bathroom.

Union Guesthouse (s/d US$10/20) The Union is on the quietest stretch of beach in Nungwi, just past Cholos guesthouse. Own bathroom.

Jambo Guesthouse (s/d US$10/20) Next door to Union, also has decent en suite rooms.

Safina Bungalows (s/d US$10/20) Cramped in among the others in the village centre.

Kigoma Guesthouse (s/d US$10/20) Opposite Safina. Shared bathroom.

Amaan Bungalows (s/d US$10/20) A bit more upmarket, with own bathroom.

Kendwa is about two kilometres along the beach from Nungwi Village. You can walk (but not at night, and perhaps don't take valuables); or take one of the frequent boats which leave throughout the day. There are no fixed schedules or prices, just ask on the beach.

Kendwa Rocks (s/d US$8/16) Very basic palm-leaf huts, or extremely good wooden beach cottages for US$25. Camping allowed, rates negotiable.

Sunset Bungalows (s/d US$8/16) Next door to the Kendwa Rocks, and much the same – palm-thatch huts, or decent double rooms for US$20.

Eating & Drinking

There are a few restaurants on the beach and in the village itself, serving up fish, rice and pizza for about US$4. Those on the beach are slightly cheaper, and the best of these is Jambo Restaurant, on the other side of Union Guesthouse. Order a couple of hours in advance as they only have charcoal stoves.

As for drinking, there's no competition – the cult Cholos Bar, on the beach in the north of the village, is made of driftwood and mixes up ambrosial cocktails for an appreciative, mellow crowd of sun-worshippers. Cholos at sunset is worth the trip to Nungwi on its own.

THE EAST COAST
☎ 024

The beach that connects the east coast villages of **Bwejuu**, **Paje** and **Jambiani** is spectacular – white, wild and fringed by palm trees. There are far fewer tourists here than in Nungwi – you can walk for miles along the seashore and see only the occasional fishermen or seaweed harvesters. The only disadvantage is that the tide goes out a long way, so swimming is only

possible at certain times of the day. There's not much to choose between the three villages – Bwejuu perhaps has the most imaginatively designed guesthouses, many of which are run by the local Rastafarians. Nightlife, such as it is, centres around the guesthouse bars.

Sleeping

The east coast has literally dozens of budget guesthouses, all of which are sanitary and comfortable, and all costing roughly the same. The following is just a small selection of what's on offer. All prices include breakfast.

BWEJUU

Mustapha's Place (☎ 2240069; mustaphas@africamail.com; s/d US$10/20) Mustapha and friends have been living here for over 10 years, building rooms out of anything they could find – driftwood from the beach, coral rock, palm leaves, shells – and it still has more of the feeling of a commune than a hotel. Room prices vary as much as the rooms, but the cheapest have shared bathroom and mosquito net, plus mobiles, hanging baskets and wall paintings.

Bahari Guesthouse (☎ 0747 423101; hisdory@hotmail.com; s/d US$9/18) A great new beach house and cottages, with pretty decor and a laid-back atmosphere. Worth a visit for the friendly local manager, Hisdory. Shared bathroom.

Robinson's Place (☎ 0747 414561; robinsonsplace@hotmail.com; s/d US$15/30) Another wonderfully eccentric beach hang out, with beautifully furnished rooms and bathrooms that have to be seen to be believed. Evening meals available.

Twisted Palm (☎ 0747 438121; s/d US$15/25) An old favourite: spacious rooms with their own bathroom around a rooftop restaurant, right on the beach.

PAJE

Paje Ndame (☎ 0748 408948; s/d US$10/20) Scruffy rooms (own bathroom), but there's a good atmosphere and an occasionally lively bar. They hold beach barbeques on Saturday, and big discounts are negotiable in low season, or for long stays. Lots of dogs.

Kinasi Upepo (☎ 0748 334846; kinasi@hotmail.com; s/d US$15/35) Lovable eccentric Jamal presides over well-decorated rooms with their own

TANZANIA

bathroom, and a bright, friendly bar and restaurant. Cocktails a speciality; camping allowed (US$10).

JAMBIANI

Kimte Beach Inn (☎ 2240212; www.kimte.com; dm/d/t r US$10/20/30) A brightly painted and funky party place with a bar on the beach. Very friendly, great atmosphere. Shared bathroom, fan and hot water. Ask for 'Dr Mo' – the man in charge.

Red Monkey (☎ 2240207; standard@zitec.com; s/d US$10/20) Freshly painted, clean bungalows on the beach, each with its own bathroom and private veranda. Hot water and ceiling fan.

Gomani Guesthouse (☎ 2240154; s/d US$15/25) Pretty bungalows on a clifftop overlooking the beach. Some rooms have four poster beds, all have bathroom and fan.

Shehe Bungalows & Shehe Annex (☎ 2240149; shehebungalows@hotmail.com; s/d US$15/25) Huge place with bungalows with fan, net, own bathroom, hot water and fridge. Plasticky decor.

JOZANI FOREST

A tiny patch of pristine rainforest right in the centre of Zanzibar island, **Jozani Forest** (admission US$8; ⏰ 7.30am-6pm) is home to the extremely rare Red Colobus monkey, the Ader's duiker antelope, and numerous bird species. There's a mangrove boardwalk through the trees and a small education centre. Entry to the forest includes a guided tour. The monkeys have their own little ladder bridge across the road that runs through the middle of the forest, so if you're driving to the east coast, you may be able to see them without going into the park.

PEMBA

☎ 024 / pop 362,150

The island of Pemba is lusher and hillier than its sister island Zanzibar, and sees far fewer visitors. It was famed in the old days as a centre for the clove industry, with vast plantations of the glossy, dark-green trees and acres of fragrant buds laid out to dry in the sun.

Pemba's other claim to fame is as a hotbed of black magic – in the 1930s it was famous for the power of its sorcerers and magicians, with devotees coming from as far away as Haiti to be initiated into the rites of Pemban witchdoctors. The clove trees are still there, and by all accounts Pemba is still a centre of witchcraft today, but visitors will be unlikely to see any hint of the occult.

Pemba's lack of tourist facilities and infrastructure makes it a bit harder (and more expensive) to travel around than Zanzibar. You'll need at least a week to explore it fully. **Chake Chake**, the main town, is a pretty basic place, with a single main road, a bank (they change traveller's cheques), and an airport about 5km from the town centre (a taxi will cost US$5). The island's other towns of **Wete** and **Mkoani** are even smaller and less developed.

Sleeping

CHAKE CHAKE

Le Tavern (s/d US$15/30) Clean but rather noisy local guesthouse on the main road. Rooms have their own bathroom, and prices include breakfast. Evening meals are very good value – a big plate of local food is US$2.50. They'll also cook for non-residents by prior arrangement.

Old Mission Lodge & Swahili Divers (☎ 2452786; swahilidivers@intafrica.com; dm/d US$15/30) The only established backpackers lodge in Chake Chake is housed in an attractive old building, and has a dive centre on site, but it's overpriced – rates include breakfast, but dinner is US$7, and snorkelling or trips to the beach are US$45.

MKOANI

Jondeni Guesthouse (☎ 2456042; biir@zanzinet.com; dm/s/d US$8/15/20) A very well-run and good value backpackers lodge, which can arrange car or motorcycle hire (US$30 to US$60 per day), snorkelling, dhow trips (US$10) or canoeing (US$5). Breakfast included, excellent dinner is US$5. Turn left up the hill from the port.

WETE

Sharook Guesthouse (☎ 2454386; s/d US$15/30) A clean and friendly locally run place just behind the market. They can hire bicycles (US$3), motorcycles (US$25), or cars, and arrange boat trips, snorkelling, or very good diving (US$80 for two dives, including lunch on a yacht). Breakfast included, evening meals US$3.50. Suleiman Sharook and his French wife also plan to open a camp site on the beach near Wete, which will be the first budget beach place on Pemba.

Bomani Guesthouse (☎ 2454384; s/d US$10/20) Opposite Sharook, this is another local place with big clean rooms, some with fridges and their own bathroom. Breakfast included, but no evening meals – eat at Sharook instead.

Getting There & Around
AIR
There are daily flights to Pemba from Zanzibar and Dar with **Air Express** (☎ 022 2115672), **Zan Air** (☎ 024 2233670; www.zanair.com), **Coastal Aviation** (☎ 024 2233670; www.zanair.com) and **Precision Air** (☎ 027 2506903; information@precisionair tz.com). Fares are around US$65.

BOAT
Currently the only passenger boats running from Pemba to Zanzibar are the *Aziza*, which sails from Wete on Sunday mornings (US$15, five hours) and the *Serengeti*, which leaves Mkoani Tuesday, Thursday and Saturday at 10am (US$20, six hours). These are primarily cargo boats; their schedules vary wildly and they're very uncomfortable. There used to be a fast boat called the *Sepideh* between Dar, Zanzibar and Pemba – it's been suspended but may return to service in the future.

BUS
Dalla-dallas run from along the main street in Chake Chake to Wete (Nos 6 or 34, one hour) and Mkoani (No 3, two hours).

NORTHERN TANZANIA

ARUSHA
☎ 027 / pop 171,000
Arusha, centre of Tanzania's safari industry, is also the site of the United Nations Tribunal on Rwanda, as well as being home to the Meru people – who farm the slopes of the nearby hillsides – and the Arusha people – settled relatives of the nomadic Maasai. In the eclectic and potholed streets of Arusha town, battered safari buses mingle with the smart white Land Rovers of the UN lawyers, while herds of cattle are driven down the main road in dusty Wild West style.

UNITED NATIONS TRIBUNAL ON RWANDA

If you've got time to spare while waiting for your safari to depart, the **United Nations International Criminal Tribunal on the Rwandan Genocide** (Arusha International Conference Centre, Simeon Bouleva Rd; admission free; ⏰ 9am-noon & 2-6pm weekdays) is open to the public. You must show your passport to be allowed in.

The court sittings, which aim to prosecute those responsible for the Rwandan genocide of the 1990s, are conducted in French, but earphones are available for translations into any language.

Orientation
Arusha is served by two airports, Arusha and Kilimanjaro. Domestic flights often land at Arusha Airport, just 7km from the town centre along the Serengeti road. Kilimanjaro Airport, where most international flights land, is 30km away on the road towards Moshi. Coming from Kilimanjaro, your option is a taxi to Arusha (US$30), or a taxi to the end of the airport road (US$5), then a dalla-dalla into Arusha or Moshi from there.

Sokoine St and the market just north of it is the centre of town, with most of the cheaper hotels. Further east, around the clock tower, lie the tourist office, the post office and the Natural History Museum.

Buses come into the main bus station, deep in the chaos of the market area. Walking from here to any of the town's hotels is not a problem, but watch your bags – this area is notorious for pickpockets.

Information
BOOKSHOPS
The Bookmark (Jacaranda St), just off Sokoine Rd, has an excellent selection of novels and guidebooks on Africa, and a little café that does great banana smoothies.

INTERNET ACCESS
Arusha's town centre has dozens of Internet cafés, all charging the standard rate of US$1 per hour. If you'd like an éclair with your email, try the computers at Mac's or Dolly's Patisserie (See Eating & Drinking p612 for details).

TANZANIA

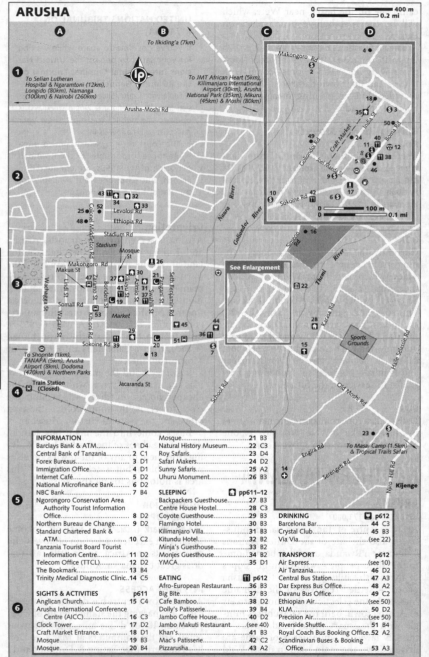

ARUSHA

0 — 400 m
0 — 0.2 mi

To Ilkiding'a (7km)

To Selian Lutheran Hospital & Ngaramtoni (12km), Longido (80km), Namanga (100km) & Nairobi (260km)

Arusha-Moshi Rd

To JMT African Heart (5km), Kilimanjaro International Airport (30km), Arusha National Park (35km), Mkuru (45km) & Moshi (80km)

Makongoro Rd

Craft Market

Colbondei Rd

Joel Maeda St

India St

Boma Rd

Sokoine Rd

0 — 100 m
0 — 0.1 mi

Naura River

Goliondoi River

Levolosi Rd

Ethiopia Rd

Stadium Rd

Stadium

Mosque St

Makongoro Rd

Makua St

Wachaga St

Lindi St

Wagare St

Zaramo St

Bondeni St

Kikuyu St

Azimio St

Somali Rd

Kitoua Rd

Market

Pangani St

Seth Benjamin St

Swahili St

Sokoine Rd

Jacaranda St

Train Station (Closed)

School Rd

Simeon Rd

Themi River

Kaloca Rd

Halle Selassie Rd

Sports Grounds

Old Moshi Rd

See Enlargement

To Shoprite (1km), TANAPA (5km), Arusha Airport (8km), Dodoma (470km) & Northern Parks

To Masai Camp (1.5km) & Tropical Trails Safari

Engira Rd

Serengeti Rd

Niru Hill Rd

Kijenge

INFORMATION
Barclays Bank & ATM	1 D4
Central Bank of Tanzania	2 C1
Forex Bureaus	3 D1
Immigration Office	4 D1
Internet Café	5 D2
National Microfinance Bank	6 D2
NBC Bank	7 B4
Ngorongoro Conservation Area Authority Tourist Information Office	8 D2
Northern Bureau de Change	9 D2
Standard Chartered Bank & ATM	10 C2
Tanzania Tourist Board Tourist Information Centre	11 D2
Telecom Office (TTCL)	12 D2
The Bookmark	13 B4
Trinity Medical Diagnostic Clinic	14 C5

SIGHTS & ACTIVITIES   p611
Anglican Church	15 C4
Arusha International Conference Centre (AICC)	16 C3
Clock Tower	17 D2
Craft Market Entrance	18 D1
Mosque	19 B3
Mosque	20 B4

Mosque	21 B3
Natural History Museum	22 C3
Roy Safaris	23 D4
Safari Makers	24 D2
Sunny Safaris	25 A2
Uhuru Monument	26 B3

SLEEPING   pp611–12
Backpackers Guesthouse	27 B3
Centre House Hostel	28 C3
Coyote Guesthouse	29 B3
Flamingo Hotel	30 B3
Kilimanjaro Villa	31 B3
Kitundu Hotel	32 B2
Minja's Guesthouse	33 B2
Monjes Guesthouse	34 B2
YMCA	35 D1

EATING   p612
Afro-European Restaurant	36 B3
Big Bite	37 B3
Cafe Bamboo	38 D2
Dolly's Patisserie	39 B4
Jambo Coffee House	40 D2
Jambo Makuti Restaurant	(see 40)
Khan's	41 B3
Mac's Patisserie	42 C2
Pizzarusha	43 A2

DRINKING   p612
Barcelona Bar	44 C3
Crystal Club	45 B3
Via Via	(see 22)

TRANSPORT   p612
Air Express	(see 10)
Air Tanzania	46 D2
Central Bus Station	47 A3
Dar Express Bus Office	48 A2
Davanu Bus Office	49 C2
Ethiopian Air	(see 50)
KLM	50 D2
Precision Air	(see 50)
Riverside Shuttle	51 B4
Royal Coach Bus Booking Office	52 A2
Scandinavian Buses & Booking Office	53 A3

TANZANIA

MEDICAL SERVICES
Trinity Medical Diagnostic Clinic (☎ 2544392; Engira Rd) Call ☎ 0744 318565 in an emergency.

MONEY
Standard Chartered Bank (Goliondoni Rd) and **Barclays** (Old Moshi Rd) have ATMs. There are a number of other banks in the centre of town. The best place to change travellers cheques is one of the *bureaux de change* at the end of Boma Rd.

POST & TELEPHONE
Main Post Office (Sokoine Rd) Just on the roundabout at the top of Sokoine Rd. There's another branch at the western end of Sokoine Rd.
TTCL Office (Boma Rd) International telephone calls.

TOURIST OFFICES
Tanzania Tourist Board (☎ 2503842; Boma Rd; ttb-info@habari.co.tz; ☷ Mon-Fri 8am-4pm, Sat 8.30am-1pm) The staff here maintain a list of blacklisted tour operators, and there's a noticeboard for travellers. This is a good place to come if you're looking for a safari group to join. The office of the **Ngorongoro Crater Conservation Area** (☎ 2537046; ncaa-info@africaonline.co.tz), which can provide information about getting to and from the crater, is just next door.

Dangers & Annoyances
The area around Arusha's central market and bus station is notorious for pickpockets during the day, and muggers during the night. It's not a good idea to walk around here with valuables – take a taxi instead.

Likewise, the stretch of Old Moshi Rd between Barclays Bank and the town centre has been the scene of several robberies in the past – if you're drawing cash out of the ATM, avoid walking back alone afterwards. If you're paying for a safari, ask the company to send someone to the bank with you.

Annoyance in Arusha comes in the form of the many touts or 'flycatchers' who wander the streets hoping to find customers for safaris. If you're looking for a safari group to join, these guys can be a good source of information – but only ever book directly with a reputable company like one of those listed in the following section.

Safaris
Almost all the tourists who visit Arusha are there for one reason – to arrange a safari

in the surrounding national parks of the so-called 'northern circuit'. Trips are generally four to six days long and combine a day or two in Lake Manyara, Tarangire and the Serengeti National Parks with a trip to the Ngorongoro Conservation Area. Many safari companies in Arusha can also arrange treks up Kilimanjaro. It is extremely advisable to book a safari with a reputable company such as one of the following:
JMT African Heart Expeditions (☎ 2548414; info@africanheart.com; Ilboru) Belgian-run.
Roy Safaris (☎ 2508010; roysafaris@intafrica.com; 44 Serengeti Rd) One of the best-known operators.
Safari Makers (☎ 2544446; safarimakers@habari.co.tz; India St) Very helpful and reliable.
Sunny Safaris (☎ 2507145; info@sunnysafaris.com; Colonel Middleton Rd) Well-established and good value.
Tropical Trails (☎ 2500358; info@tropicaltrails.com; Old Moshi Rd) Based at Masai Camp.

For further tips on arranging a safari, see p627, and for information on Kilimanjaro, see p615.

Sleeping
Most of Arusha's cheapest hotels are located around the central market area. Only the YMCA includes breakfast.

Masai Camp (☎ 2500358; info@tropicaltrails.com; camp site per person US$3) A very attractive camp site with a huge bar/restaurant 3km from the town centre. You can hire tents and bedding here for US$7, or bikes for US$1.50 per hour. The site is very popular with rowdy overland trucks, but it's so big you can usually find a quiet corner for your tent. The restaurant serves pizza, Mexican and big breakfasts for around US$3. To get here, take a dalla-dalla labelled Kijenge and ask to be dropped off.

Centre House Hostel (☎ 2502313; aidsuhai@cybernet.co.tz; Kanisa Rd; s/d/t US$6/12/18) A quiet, church-run place in pretty grounds, this is the most peaceful place to stay in central Arusha. Doors close at 10pm unless otherwise arranged. Secure parking.

Flamingo Hotel (☎ 2548812; flamingoarusha@yahoo .com; Kikuyu St; s/d US$8/10) This new, very clean and friendly guesthouse has well-furnished bedrooms with their own bathroom.

Backpackers' Guesthouse (☎ 0741 652158; back packguesthouse@hotmail.com; Mosque St; tw US$6; 🖳) Very welcoming staff, big rooms with shared bathroom, hot water.

Kitundu Hotel (☎ 2509626; Levolosi Rd; s/d US$4/8) Spick and span, tiled and recently renovated, good value. Monjes Guesthouse and Minja's Guesthouse around the corner are also basic but clean and reasonably safe.

Kilimanjaro Villa (☎ 0744 627492; Azimio St; s/d US$3.50/5) Old but clean rooms, some with balcony. The shared bathroom has hot water. There's a pretty courtyard in the middle for breakfast (US$1).

Coyote Guesthouse (☎ 0748 600252; Azimio St; d US$6) Big rooms with their own bathroom on a rooftop, very convenient for the town centre. Friendly, but local dogs bark ALL night.

YMCA (☎ 2544032; India St; s/d US$10/13) The YMCA has a good central location and clean but overpriced rooms, sharing bathroom.

Eating & Drinking

Arusha is definitely lacking in nightlife, but there are a few good restaurants.

Jambo Makuti Restaurant (Boma Rd; US$5) Very well-decorated and peaceful bar/restaurant serving pasta, sandwiches and evening meals. There's a coffee house next door, and a tiny art shop and gallery, as well as a noticeboard for travellers.

Café Bamboo (Boma Rd; US$5) Opposite Jambo Makuti, this very popular place is more of a tearoom, with slow service, especially when it's busy.

Mac's Patisserie (Sokoine Rd) Sells rolls, pies, cakes and fresh bread and also incorporates an Internet café. Dolly's Patisserie a bit further down Sokoine Rd provides exactly the same.

Afro-European Restaurant (Sokoine Rd) Nearby; has good pancakes and spiced tea.

Khan's (Mosque St; mains US$3; ☺ evenings only) Khan's is an Arusha institution – a car workshop by day, a street barbeque by night. Vegetarians get salad and lentil curry. No alcohol, but delicious juices.

Big Bite (Somali Rd; US$5-10) Cosy Indian restaurant with delicious vegetarian and meat dishes.

Pizzarusha, near Kitundu Guesthouse, is cheap, popular, and certainly convenient – but when we visited, they had run out of pizza...

Via Via Café behind the Natural History Museum is the best drinking option in central Arusha. It is a good place to meet locals and find out if there's any live music on around the town. They can also organise various cultural tours of Arusha and the surrounding area. For a beer during the day, try Barcelona Bar in the park off Sokoine Rd.

If you're self-catering, the gigantic Shoprite supermarket, just out of town past the old railway station, has anything you could possibly need.

Shopping

If you're buying souvenirs, the craft market, in an alley off Joel Maeda St, has the best selection.

Getting There & Away

All Tanzania's domestic airlines, plus a few international ones, fly to and from Arusha. See p588 for details. **Riverside Shuttle** (☎ 2502639; riverside_shuttle@hotmail.com; Sokoine Rd) run a shuttle bus to Kilimanjaro Airport from Arusha (US$8). Book in advance at their office. Air Express also runs a shuttle for passengers on its flights from Kilimanjaro Airport.

Buses leave daily from Arusha's central bus station near the market for Nairobi (US$10, four hours), Dar es Salaam (US$12, eight hours), Moshi (US$1, 1½ hours) and Tanga (US$6.50, seven hours). Scandinavian Express buses to Kampala (US$30, overnight) leave three times a week. The Ngorongoro Bus runs to the Conservation Area headquarters near the crater about four times a week; times are erratic, so it's best to ask around at the bus station.

SERENGETI NATIONAL PARK

Waving golden grasses, flat-topped acacia trees, distant blue hills. Herds of wildebeest sweeping majestically across the plain. Stately giraffes, indolent lions, stealthy cheetah. How do you describe the Serengeti without using every cliché in the book? Perhaps in the words of Alan Moorehead – 'Anyone who can go to the Serengeti, and does not, is mad.' Certainly, for the first time visitor to East Africa, a visit to the Serengeti will guarantee immersion in that quintessential African landscape immortalised in a million films, album covers and cheap aftershave advertisements.

It's worth remembering, however, that the Serengeti is not the same all year round. The wildebeest migration is not a single event but a continuous cycle of movement that varies from season to season. When planning your safari, it's wise to take account of this and realise it's not just the wildebeests who move, but zebras, antelopes and predators too. The southern Serengeti's teeming plains can seem eerily empty if you get there when the migration has moved on.

Generally speaking, the wildebeests breed on the southern plains during January and February, stay put during the long rains from March to May, then start heading northwards, arriving in the Maasai Mara in Kenya around September or October. From December until the following January they're in the eastern reaches of the Serengeti. So plan your visit accordingly – any safari company worth its salt will be able to advise on where the animals are and how easy they will be to reach on a short trip.

The park has numerous **public camp sites** (☎ 028 2621510; per person US$20), including those at Seronera, Kirawira, Ndabaka and Lobo. Facilities are minimal, so unless you're on an organised tour, you'll need to bring everything with you. The park is usually visited as part of an organised safari, starting from either Arusha or Mwanza. See p611 for safari companies. Park entry fees are US$30 per day.

For interesting information on the history and conservation of the Serengeti, take a look at the park's website: www.serengeti.org.

NGORONGORO CONSERVATION AREA

Ngorongoro Crater is a volcanic caldera – the collapsed upper cone of an ancient volcano. Its high walls contain a microcosmic ecosystem, with lakes, forests, and plains supporting hundreds of species of wildlife. The views from the misty highlands of the rim are spectacular, but they're nothing compared with the photo opportunities that await down on the crater floor – elephants grazing knee-deep in flowers, lions lying flat out on the sand by the lake, and rare black rhinos strolling casually across the grass. The crater's only drawback is that it is usually full of tourist vehicles, which can take away a bit from the wilderness feel.

The Maasai are partners in the management of the Conservation Area, driving their cattle to the crater floor for water and salt during the day, and returning to their

---

OLDUVAI GORGE

The Olduvai Gorge (also called Oldupai Gorge) made world headlines in 1959 following the discovery by Mary Leakey of fossil fragments of the skull of one of the possible ancestors of *Homo sapiens*. The fragments were dated back 1.8 million years.

In 1979 Mary Leakey made another important discovery in the form of footprints at nearby **Laetoli**. They were dated back 3.5 million years, and since they were made by creatures who walked upright, this pushed the origins of the human race much further back than had previously been supposed.

The gorge itself and the small, dusty museum at the site aren't of great interest unless you're archaeologically inclined. However, it has acquired a kind of cult attraction among those who just want to visit the site where the evolution of early humans may have taken place. To reach it, you'll need to be on an organised safari or in your own vehicle. All of the safari companies are mentioned on p627.

---

traditional homesteads – some of which can be visited – in the surrounding hills during the night. Entry fees are US$30.

Sleeping
NGORONGORO CRATER RIM
Simba Campsite (☎ 027 2537060; per person US$20) Most campers stay here, on the crater rim, about 2km beyond Ngorongoro village. The site is extremely dirty, but it is secure, and offers showers, toilets (which are not for the faint hearted!) and firewood. Remember that night time temperatures here can drop below freezing – so you will need warm clothing.

KARATU
Karatu (commonly known as 'Safari Junction') is about halfway between Lake Manyara and Ngorongoro Crater. It's just outside the Ngorongoro Conservation Area, but about 25km from the crater itself. Virtually all camping safaris out of Arusha stop overnight at Karatu in order to economise on entry fees.

Ngorongoro Safari Resort (☎ 027 2534287; camp site per person/s/d US$5/20/40) An upmarket hotel off the main road through Karatu, which also offers 4WD car hire for US$220 per day, including driver/guide.

Getting There & Around

A bus runs daily from the Arusha terminus to the Conservation Area Headquarters, from where you can arrange to hire vehicles for trips down into the crater. Most people, however, visit as part of an organised tour.

TARANGIRE NATIONAL PARK

Tarangire National Park is an excellent prospect for the budget traveller. It's easily accessible from Arusha (about two hours to the park gate) and it has wildlife in abundance. The catch? The wildlife viewing is only really good between June and November, as animals migrate into and out of the park. If you're into bird-watching, however, the park is a must at any time of the year.

Tarangire's huge herds of elephants rival the park's massive baobab trees as its most celebrated feature. Elephant populations are particularly dense during the dry season in the park's northern reaches, with herds of cows with calves and massive solitary bulls strolling casually across the roads in search of grazing, shade or water.

There are two public camp sites where you can pitch a tent for the usual price (US$20 per person). For a very good-value splurge, head for **Tarangire Safari Lodge** (☎ 027 2531447; sss@habari.co.tz; s/d US$54/62), set on a hill and with a beautiful terrace overlooking the Tarangire River – perfect for armchair wildlife watching.

Tarangire features on many organised tour itineraries, but if you want to visit the park on its own, the best thing is to hire a car with a driver from one of the safari companies in Arusha. See p627 for operators. Park entry fees are US$25.

LAKE MANYARA NATIONAL PARK

Lake Manyara National Park is very popular with safari companies; it features on almost all their itineraries due to its convenient location halfway between Arusha and the Serengeti. Manyara can provide very rewarding wildlife watching – thousands of flamingos congregate in the shallow waters of the lake, and the lions in Manyara are famous for climbing into trees. However, as often as not the park doesn't yield much in the way of wildlife sightings – you might

be lucky and see lots of animals on a brief visit, but the thickness of the bush, and the lack of roads down to the lake, often mean disappointment.

Some camp sites and simple bandas are located by the park gate, about 3km down the road from Mto Wa Mbu village. There are also camp sites, budget hotels and grocery stores in Mto Wa Mbu. Hitching into the park isn't really feasible, and the best way of seeing Manyara is as part of an organised safari. Park entry fees are US$25.

ARUSHA NATIONAL PARK

Although it's one of Tanzania's smallest parks (just 137 sq km), Arusha is one of the most beautiful. It's close enough to Arusha town for a day trip, and you're allowed to walk in the park if accompanied by a ranger. The park's main features are **Ngurdoto Crater** (often dubbed Little Ngorongoro), tranquil **Momela Lakes** and the rugged **Mt Meru** (4566m), a blue-grey mass that towers above the park. The animals in the park include zebras, hippos, antelopes, giraffes, the occasional leopard and more than 400 bird species.

It's possible to see Ngurdoto Crater, Momela Lakes and the lower slopes of Mt Meru in one day if you're in a vehicle. However, this won't give you the chance to walk around. A ranger's services are compulsory if you want to walk anywhere, and cost US$10 per day (US$15 for Mt Meru). Rangers can be organised at the park headquarters by Momela gate, on the northern side of the park. Note that rangers are not guides, and their level of performance varies. You may also have to wait some time at the gate for a ranger to become available. Park entry fees are US$25.

Mt Meru

The trek up Mt Meru passes through forest, heath, open moorland, and finally across bare powdery rock on the way to the summit. In the forest there's a very good chance of seeing animals. It's a steep trek, but once at the top, the reward is a sight of Mt Kilimanjaro, breathtaking in the sunrise.

The Momela route is the only way up Mt Meru. It starts at Momela gate on the eastern side of the mountain and goes to the summit along the northern arm of the mountain's horseshoe crater. The route can be done comfortably in four days (three nights), although experienced trekkers often do it in three days.

The best time to climb is from June to February. Porters can be hired from the park gate. As for Kilimanjaro, bring plenty of warm clothing and food from Arusha.

Sleeping

There's a **resthouse** (per person US$30) at Momela gate and three public **camp sites** (per person US$20) inside the park. On Mt Metu you can camp or use **Miriakamba Hut** and **Saddle Hut** (per person US$20), equally spaced a day's trek apart.

Getting There & Around

Momela gate is about 35km from Arusha, and about 24km north of the main Arusha–Moshi road. By public transport, take any dalla-dalla between Arusha and Moshi and get off at the park junction, about 1km east of Usa River village – look for the signs to the park. From the park junction, or from Usa River, there are pick-ups most days to Momela gate, but hitching is slow. An organised trek on Mt Meru with a safari company (see p611 for details) will save a lot of hanging around and doesn't work out to be much more expensive.

Gravel roads and tracks within the park go past all the main features and viewing points. Most are suitable for normal cars, though some of the tracks get slippery in the wet seasons (October and November, and March to May).

MOUNT KILIMANJARO

MT KILIMANJARO NATIONAL PARK

An almost perfectly shaped volcano that rises sheer from the plains, Mt Kilimanjaro is one of the continent's most magnificent sights. Snowcapped and not yet extinct, at 5892m it's the highest peak in Africa.

The name of Kilimanjaro is as shrouded in mystery as the mist-enveloped summit. 'Mountain of Light' is one of the several possible translations, although many locals refer to the snowy peak as Kipoo or Kibo. Daunting as it looks, its possible to scale the mountain without technical mountaineering skills – all you need is determination, warm clothing and a properly equipped guide.

There's no doubt you'll go through the pain barrier on the way to the top, but the reward is unforgettable – a sunrise view over what seems like half of Africa spread out below.

The surrounding National Park also offers great hiking opportunities on the lower slopes of the mountain. Entry fees are US$30.

Trekking

There are some things you should know before planning a trek.

First, independent trekking is not allowed – all treks must be organised through a tour company.

Second, the cost of most (but not all) treks includes park entry fees (about half of the trekking costs), hut fees, rescue fees, meals, guides, porters and, usually, transport to the park gate – but excludes the hire of camping gear, boots and clothing.

Standard five-day (four-night) return treks up and down the Marangu route cost about US$500 to US$650 per person, but better-quality trips start from US$750. For anything below US$500, don't be surprised if your hut is double booked, meals are on the small side and porters are desperate for tips. Some outfits allow you to save money if you provide your own food, do your own cooking and carry your own bag. You still need a guide though – and he needs a porter even if you don't!

Third, because trekking on Kilimanjaro is expensive, many people try to walk up and down in the shortest time possible. Never fall into this trap. You shouldn't feel that it's essential to reach Uhuru Peak (the summit) or that you have 'failed' if you don't – 50% of people who attempt Kili don't make it to the top. If you really want to sample Kilimanjaro, instead of stubbornly pushing for the summit, consider walking up to one of the midway huts to appreciate the splendour of the mountain before descending. If you're determined to make it to the top, a five night/six day climb will at least increase your chances of enjoying yourself en route.

Trekking is possible at any time of year, but there's usually a lot of rain during April, May and November, and it's also best to avoid the Christmas to New Year period, when most huts on the Marangu route are often booked out.

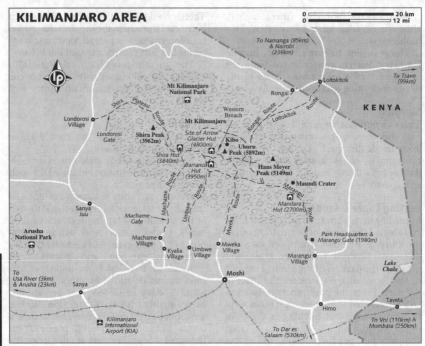

No specialist equipment is required to trek on Kilimanjaro, but you do need strong boots and plenty of warm clothing, including gloves, a hat and waterproofs. Even if you stay in the huts on the Marangu route, you will also need a sleeping bag and a small mattress. These can be hired from most trekking companies. If the huts are fully booked, you'll have to camp; make absolutely sure there are sufficient tents before setting off.

Two good topographical maps to take are *Map & Guide to Kilimanjaro* (1:75,000) by Andrew Wielochowski, and *Kilimanjaro Map & Guide* (1:50,000) by Mark Savage. Both of these maps are available in bookshops in Arusha or Dar es Salaam.

The guide and porters will expect tips at the end. You can even expect threats to abandon you on the summit unless you tip them before the descent – a lot of people have had nasty altercations about this. Make sure they understand that tips will be given only on completion of the trek, and don't compromise on this. About 10% of the trekking cost between all guides and porters is reasonable.

A few final tips: insist on inspecting the camping equipment, and make sure it is waterproof; go with a sizeable group that has proper radios and more than one licensed guide; bring trekking poles, and a headlamp rather than a torch; water containers and sterilising tablets will save money on porters or on buying expensive water on the mountain.

Sleeping

Accommodation on the Marangu route consists of three huts (actually groups of bunkhouses) spaced one day's walk apart. Hut fees should be included in the cost of the trek.

DRESS FOR THE OCCASION

If you're flying into Kilimanjaro International Airport from Europe just before your climb, wear your boots on the plane – and carry anything else likely to be vital – certain airlines on this route have a bad reputation for losing luggage.

Getting There & Away
From Moshi, take a dalla-dalla to Marangu village, from where there's usually some form of transport to the Marangu gate and park headquarters. Otherwise, it's a steep walk (5km) from the main junction in Marangu.

MOSHI
☎ 027 / pop 144,300
Moshi is an unmemorable little place with one memorable feature – the ethereal, snow-capped peak of Mt Kilimanjaro, 50km away, which appears in the evening – if you're lucky – like a vision among the clouds. Moshi is therefore the main jumping off point for most Kilimanjaro visitors, although treks can also be arranged in Arusha (see p611) and the village of Marangu, about 35km from Moshi (see p619).

Kiboroloni Market (☺ weekends only), a dalla-dalla ride out of town towards Marangu, is famous all over Tanzania for its excellent second-hand clothes. If you're sick of everything in your rucksack, this is the place to come – funky T-shirts are around US$0.50.

Information
Trust Bureau de Change, near the market, changes cash or travellers cheques without commission. There are numerous Internet cafés in the town centre, all charging US$1 per hour.

Trekking
Moshi is probably the cheapest place to arrange a trek on Kilimanjaro, but this is not always the case: if you want good accommodation the night before and the night after a trek, some safari companies in Arusha can offer discounted tariffs with good hotels. See p611 for recommended safari operators.

The following companies in Moshi are reputable and well established:
Mauly Tours & Safaris (☎ 2750730; mauly@kilionline.com; Mawenzi Rd)
Moshi Expeditions & Mountaineering (MEM; ☎ 2750669; info@memtours.com; Grenado Hotel)
Samjoe Tours (☎ 2751484; samjoetours@yahoo.com; Coffee Tree Hotel)
Shah Tours (☎ 27 2752370; kilimanjaro@kilionline.com; Mawenzi Rd)

Sleeping
The budget hotels in Moshi are of a slightly higher standard than those in neighbouring Arusha, and considerably better value than anything you'll get in Marangu. All prices include breakfast.

Hotel da Costa (☎ 2754054; wilfredmberesero@yahoo.com; Mawenzi Rd; s/d US$3/5) Excellent new budget hotel with very clean rooms and shared bathroom, a rooftop bar and a restaurant serving local dishes at US$1. Hot water. Towels. Soap. Fab.

New Kindoroko Hotel (☎ 2754054; kindoroko@eoltz.com; Mawenzi Rd; s/d/t US$10/20/30; 💻) Inside a pretty wooden complex that also contains a bar/restaurant, coffee shop, bureau de change and curio shop. Lovely decor in the rooms, some of which have their own bathroom as well as a TV and fridge. The rooftop bar here is the best for sundowners.

Grenado Hotel (☎ 0744 806769; Chagga St; s/d US$6/8) Clean tiled rooms with their own bathroom and hot water. MEM Tours is in the same building.

Buffalo Hotel (☎ 2750270; off New St; d US$6) An old favourite, with sunny, airy double rooms with a net and fan. Hot water, good restaurant and bar. Shared bathroom.

Coffee Tree Hotel (☎ 2752905; Old Moshi Rd; s/d US$4/7) Central but soulless, big on 1970s grey paint. The huge rooms can get noisy at weekends from Alberto's Pub opposite. Shared bathroom.

Climbers Hotel (Market St; s/d US$3/4) Only for the seriously broke. Small, hot rooms close to the bus station. Shared bathroom.

Eating
Buffalo Hotel and Kindoroko Hotel restaurants are both excellent for cheap local and vegetarian dishes (around US$2). Otherwise, try Big Bite near the market, or **Crispburger** (Kibo Rd) and EK Saturdays Stop 'n' Eat near the Clock Tower, which do excellent samosas, burgers and juices. If you're stocking up for a camping trip, **Safari Supermarket** (Riadha St) is the cheapest, and has some imported foods.

The most entertaining restaurant in Moshi is the **Salzburger Café** (Kenyatta Rd; mains US$3), also known as the Steakhouse, a little piece of the Alps in Africa. Owned by a Tanzanian who's spent time in Austria, it offers cheesy European decor along with grilled meat, chicken and fish dishes.

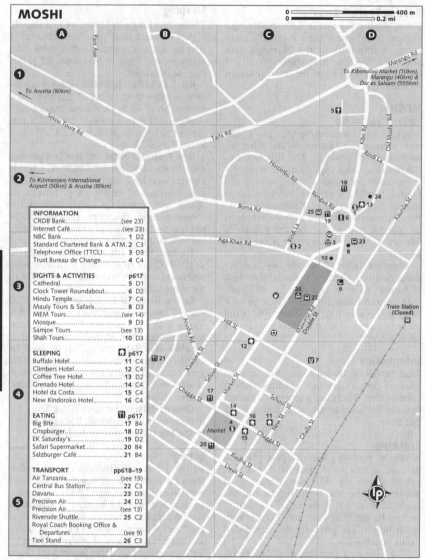

MOSHI

0 ———— 400 m
0 ———— 0.2 mi

INFORMATION
CRDB Bank..............................(see 23)
Internet Café...........................(see 23)
NBC Bank.................................**1** D2
Standard Chartered Bank & ATM.**2** C3
Telephone Office (TTCL)............**3** D3
Trust Bureau de Change.............**4** C4

SIGHTS & ACTIVITIES   p617
Cathedral.................................**5** D1
Clock Tower Roundabout...........**6** D2
Hindu Temple...........................**7** C4
Mauly Tours & Safaris...............**8** D3
MEM Tours...........................(see 14)
Mosque...................................**9** D3
Samjoe Tours.......................(see 13)
Shah Tours.............................**10** D3

SLEEPING   p617
Buffalo Hotel...........................**11** C4
Climbers Hotel.........................**12** C4
Coffee Tree Hotel.....................**13** D2
Grenado Hotel.........................**14** C4
Hotel da Costa.........................**15** C4
New Kindoroko Hotel................**16** C4

EATING   p617
Big Bite..................................**17** B4
Crispburger.............................**18** D2
EK Saturday's..........................**19** D2
Safari Supermarket...................**20** B4
Salzburger Café........................**21** B4

TRANSPORT   pp618–19
Air Tanzania........................(see 19)
Central Bus Station...................**22** C3
Davanu...................................**23** D3
Precision Air............................**24** D2
Precision Air........................(see 13)
Riverside Shuttle......................**25** C2
Royal Coach Booking Office &
    Departures........................(see 9)
Taxi Stand..............................**26** C3

To Arusha (80km)

Sekou Toure Rd

To Kilimanjaro International
Airport (50km) & Arusha (80km)

Parc Ave

Taifa Rd

To Kiboroloni Market (10km),
Marangu (40km) &
Dar es Salaam (555km)

Marangu Rd

Kibo Rd

Old Moshi Rd

Rindi La

Horombo Rd

Boma Rd

Rengua Rd

Kaunda St

Aga Khan Rd

Rindi La

Mawenzi Rd
Double St

Hill St

Arusha Rd

Kawawa St

Selous St

Market St

Chagga St

School St

Ghalla St

New St

Chagga St

Market

Riadha St

Liwali St

Train Station
(Closed)

Getting There & Away

Kilimanjaro International Airport is about 50km from Moshi town centre; a taxi will cost you about US$25, or take a dalla-dalla from the bus station and ask to be dropped off at the end of the airport road, from where it should be easy to find a lift. Airlines flying from Kilimanjaro to destinations all over Tanzania include Air Express and Precision Air – see p590 for details.

Buses run from Moshi's chaotic central bus station to Arusha (US$1, 1½ hours), Dar es Salaam (US$8, seven hours), Nairobi (US$4, three hours), Lushoto (US$6, five hours), and Tanga (US$8, seven hours).

Dalla-dallas also run from the bus station to Marangu (US$1, 45 minutes).

Davanu and Riverside operate minibuses to Nairobi (US$8) from their offices at the clock tower roundabout.

MARANGU
☎ 027 / pop 40,000
Marangu is a pretty, very English-looking village on the base of Mt Kilimanjaro. Many treks begin or end with a night here, but the village is so spread out that walking between places would be a good warm-up for Kili. To get to Marangu, take a dalla-dalla from Moshi to Marangu Mtoni in the centre of the village, from where you'll have to get a taxi, or try to hitch a lift.

Trekking
Several hotels in Marangu can organise treks up Kilimanjaro:
Babylon Lodge (☎ 2751315; babylon@africaonline.co.tz)
Marangu Hotel (☎ 2756594; marangu@africaonline.co.tz)

Sleeping
Sadly, budget accommodation in Marangu is generally overpriced and grotty.

Campers can pitch a tent in the lovely grounds of the upmarket **Marangu Hotel** (☎ 2756594; marangu@africaonline.co.tz; camp site per person US$3) at the beginning of the road through the village, or **Bismarck Hut Lodge** (☎ 0744 318338; camp site per person/s/d US$3/5/6), which also has basic rooms. **Mt Kilimanjaro Guest Wing** (☎ 0744 434075; s/d US$15/20), next door to Babylon Lodge, is easy to get to, if rather characterless. On the way to the National Park gate, **Coffee Tree Campsite** (☎ 0744691433; alpinetrekking@kilionline.com; camp site per person/dm US$8/12) has good facilities, but is overpriced.

NORTHEAST TANZANIA

TANGA
☎ 053 / pop 201,000
Tanga is a sleepy, quaint little town – its genteel colonial streets make it seem like a throwback to the 1950s. There's very little to do here, so if you decide to stay a few days in the area, try heading 30km down the coast to **Pangani**, where there are some great beaches. Ask about accommodation

and transport at the **Tourcare Tanzania** (☎ 0744 690495) information office in Tanga.

Sleeping
Inn by the Sea (☎ 2644614; Ocean Rd; d US$10) Definitely the best place to stay in Tanga, about 2km from the bus station, with whitewashed doubles overlooking the sea.

Ocean Breeze Hotel (☎ 2644545; off Independence Ave; d US$6) If you can't be bothered with walking that far, this has uninteresting decor but good-value rooms with their own bathroom.

Ferns Inn (s/d US$4/5) Around the corner from the Hindu Temple, Ferns has basic rooms with shared bathroom.

Eating
Raskazone Swimming Club next door to the Inn by the Sea does seafood for about US$3. It's US$0.50 to get in, and has a good beach for swimming. Patwas and **Food Palace** (Market St; lunch US$2) serve good Indian food.

Getting There & Away
Many buses travel daily to Dar es Salaam (US$8, five hours), Arusha (US$6, five hours) and Mombasa in Kenya (US$5, four hours). The bus station in Tanga is about 800m south of the clock tower on Independence Ave, and for some reason has a very high number of hustlers and hasslers – watch out.

For details of the border crossing into Kenya, see p589.

LUSHOTO & THE USAMBARA MOUNTAINS
☎ 027
Lushoto is a rugged little town in the Usambara Mountains, a range of high hills surrounded by sheer cliffs, just east of the main road between Dar and Arusha. Known as 'Africa's Switzerland' this is excellent hiking country, and Lushoto is a handy starting point for trips on foot into the beautiful hilly scenery. The Usambara are cheap and easy to get to, and the perfect place to visit *en route* between the northern safari circuit and Zanzibar. There's an Internet café and a market for basic provisions in town, but not many other facilities.

The Usambaras are hiking country, with endless possibilities for walks between the various villages and beauty spots hidden among the craggy hillsides. Local guides can be arranged through any of the hotels, or by contacting the helpful **tourist office** (☎ 2640132; usambaras2000@hotmail.com) near the bus stand. The tourist office also has camping equipment and mountain bikes for hire, and can help to arrange trips further afield to the Amani Nature Reserve or the eastern side of the Usambaras.

Karibuni Lodge (☎ 0748 403825; info@karibuni lodge.com; camp site per person/dm/d US$3/4/12) Definitely the best place to base yourself for an exploration of the area around Lushoto, this is a backpackers lodge in a lovely old house, with a big garden, home-cooked meals and stacks of local info. To get there, ask to be dropped at the 'Hospitali' on the way into Lushoto, then walk up the drive. Duvets, log fires, squashy sofas. Fantastic.

Maweni Farm (☎ 0748 379089; maweni@maneno .net; camp site per person/s/d US$5/20/35) About 2km above the village of Soni, just below Lushoto. Maweni is a stunning old farmhouse with beautiful gardens and a lake, simple but comfortable rooms, a restaurant and a peaceful camp site. It's run by the head of the local cultural tourism programme, who can help arrange village stays, hikes and guides in the area. Call or email in advance to arrange a lift from Soni.

Usambara Lodge (d US$3) Extremely cheap and convenient, this little guesthouse along the road from the tourist office has only five big, clean rooms with shared bathroom.

White House Lodge (☎ 2640177; s/d US$4.50/6) An old backpackers' favourite on the hill above the bus station that's looking a bit shabby round the edges these days. The blaring TV in the restaurant doesn't make for a good night's sleep, but the food is cheap and plentiful. Shared bathroom.

Dalla-dallas and buses run from Arusha (US$7, six hours), Tanga (US$3, three hours) and Dar es Salaam (US$7, six hours) to Lushoto.

CENTRAL TANZANIA

MWANZA
☎ 028 / pop 300,000
Mwanza, on the shores of Lake Victoria, is Tanzania's second-largest city. It receives hardly any visitors, making it a good place to kick back for a few days and see how

ordinary Tanzanians live, far from the tourist centres of Zanzibar, Dar es Salaam or Arusha. The rock formations in the lake on the west side of the town look spectacular at sunset, when great flocks of birds wheel over the water.

There are several Internet cafés and banks around Post St and Kenyatta Rd. The NBC bank on Kenyatta Rd, plus several *bureaux de change* in the town centre, change cash and travellers cheques. The post and telephone offices are next door to each other on Post St.

Orientation
The Central Line Railway station is about 10 minutes walk from the town centre – just turn right onto the main road and go straight ahead. If you're arriving on the ferry from Bukoba, just walk up the dirt road out of the port and you'll find yourself in the centre of town.

Most of the restaurants are situated around the roundabouts on Kenyatta Rd and Post St.

Safaris
Several tour companies in Mwanza can organise safaris into the nearby Serengeti, just a couple of hours' drive away. A safari from Mwanza is a particularly good idea if you're visiting between the months of June and August, when there's every possibility that the wildebeest migration will be in the western part of the park. Contact **Fourways Travel** (☎ 2501853; fourways.mza@mwanza-online.com) or **Masumin Tours** (☎ 2500192; masumins@thenet.co.tz) for prices.

Sleeping
Lake Hotel (☎ 2500658; Station Rd; s/d with bathroom US$8/9) If you're wearily dragging your bags from the station this is as good a place to deposit them as any. Get a room upstairs if possible, around the communal balcony. If there's football on at the stadium opposite, climb up onto the roof for a free grandstand seat. 'Breakfast' (cup of tea) is included.

Deluxe Hotel (☎ 240644; Uhuru St; s/d US$4/5) Hardly deluxe, but this is the best of the basic guesthouses on the road opposite the port. Avoid it at weekends, when there's a disco downstairs. Breakfast included, shared bathroom.

MWANZA

INFORMATION	
DBK Bureau de Change	1 B3
Hospital	2 D1
Karibu Corner Internet Café	3 B3
National Microfinance Bank	4 B3
NBC Bank & National Bureau de Change	5 D3
Telephone Office	6 B4

SIGHTS & ACTIVITIES	pp620
Fourways Travel Service	7 B4
Hindu Temple	8 C4
Hindu Temple	9 C4
Masumin Tours	10 C4
Mosque	11 C4
War Memorial & Speke Plaque	12 B3

SLEEPING	pp620-1
Deluxe Hotel	13 C3
Lake Hotel	14 B4

EATING	pp621-2
Chake Chake	15 C4
Fourways Restaurant	16 B4
Kuleana Pizzeria	17 B3
Szechuan Mahal	18 B3

TRANSPORT	p622
Air Express Office	19 B4
Air Tanzania	20 B3
Akamba Bus Office	21 C3
Bus Station	22 D4
Dalla-dallas to Nyegezi	23 D4
Ferries to Bukoba	(see 26)
Kamanga Ferry Terminal	24 A3
Local Transport Stand (Airport & Ilemela)	25 B3
Mwanza North Port	26 A3
Precision Air	27 B3
Taxis & Local Transport Stand	28 C4

If you're planning to be in Mwanza a few days, consider heading out of town to one of the following country retreats:

Ujamaa Camp (☎ 0744 589702; ujamaacamp@ yahoo.com; s/d US$10/20) Run by an affable Rasta called Japhet, this is an excellent cultural tourism centre in a small village outside Mwanza called Nyegezi. There's a camp site here and simple local huts; a kitchen and meals available. The emphasis is on education – classes can be arranged in dozens of subjects, from drumming to Third World economics. It is a very peaceful and friendly place. To get there, take a dalla-dalla from town to Nyegezi (US$3), then ask around for a lift. A taxi all the way will cost about US$9.

Serengeti Stopover (☎ 0748 406996; serengetiso@ yahoo.com; camp site per person/s/d US$5/30/40) Another camp site, this time owned by one of the Serengeti Veterinary Officers, this is two hours outside Mwanza on the road to the Kenyan border, just 1km from the National Park gate. Bandas are expensive but luxurious, or you can hire a tent for US$7. There's a restaurant and bar, and the friendly staff can help arrange lifts or cheap trips into the park. To get there, just get a bus going to Musoma or Kenya from Mwanza and asked to be dropped off.

Eating & Drinking

Kuleana Pizzeria (Posta Rd; mains US$5) is wildly popular, and does breakfast and sandwiches.

Fourways Restaurant (Kenyatta Rd) is cheaper still, with a big outdoor garden. **Szechuan Mahal** (Kenyatta Rd; US$10) is famous for Chinese, but expensive.

For street food, there are stalls opposite the post office and around the railway station and the port. Rock Beach Garden Bar on the lakeshore just outside the centre is a good place for a sunset drink. Imalaseko Supermarket sells tinned food, biscuits etc.

Getting There & Away
AIR
Precison Air, Air Express and Air Tanzania fly to Dar es Salaam (US$200) and Arusha (US$145) from Mwanza.

BOAT
The MV *Victoria* travels from Mwanza to Bukoba on Tuesday, Thursday and Sunday at 10pm, arriving at Bukoba at 7am the next day. Fares are US$18/16/13 for 1st/2nd/3rd class. First class gets you a two-bed cabin with a locking door and shared bathroom, 2nd class means a cabin shared with five others, and 3rd class is on the deck with the chickens. Book at the office in the port.

BUS
Akamba and Scandinavian buses run from the station opposite the market to Nairobi (US$13, 12 hours), Arusha (US$20, 17 hours) and Dar es Salaam (US$30, 26 hours). Buy tickets at the office on Liberty St. Roads in every direction from Mwanza are appalling and bus travel is generally a pretty bad idea. The exception is the road to the Kenya border at Sirare, which is tar all the way (five hours). See p589 for details of border crossings into Kenya and Rwanda from Mwanza.

TRAIN
Central Line trains leave Mwanza for Dar es Salaam and Kigoma on Tuesday, Thursday and Sunday at 6pm, and take about two days. To get to Kigoma, you'll have to change (and wait all day) at Tabora. Fares to Dar es Salaam are US$45/33/18 for 1st/2nd/3rd class, and to Kigoma US$31/23/9.

BUKOBA
☎ 028 / pop 81,200
Bukoba is principally just a ferry port and jumping-off point for the border cross-

ing into Uganda. If you need to stay the night, try the **Nyumba ya Vijana** (☎ 2220069; elct_nwd@twiga.com; s/d US$4.50/3), which has hot water and shared bathrooms, or the more upmarket **Spice Beach Motel** (☎ 2220142; s/d US$8/12), which is on the lakeshore near the port. The **Rose Café** on the main street has snacks and samosas, or if you're in Bukoba between December and March, ask around for the local delicacy *sanane* – fried grasshopper!

For details of the overland route from Bukoba to Uganda and Rwanda, see p580.

The MV *Victoria* ferry leaves Bukoba for Mwanza on Monday, Wednesday and Friday at 9.30pm, arriving at 6.30am next day. Fares are US$18/16/13 for 1st/2nd/3rd class.

DODOMA
☎ 026 / pop 174,000
Officially Tanzania's capital, Dodoma is in fact a very quiet and isolated town. There's little to see or do here, which might explain the plethora of bars – good for a night out with politicians (when Parliament is in session) or some of the many expat aid workers.

The following are all close to the railway station, clean and quiet: **CCT Hostel** (Njia Kuu; s/d US$5/7; 🖥), **Furaha Hostel** (☎ 2322393; Railway St; s/d US$3.50/5) and **Kilimanjaro Villa** (☎ 2353258; Boma Rd; s/d US$3.50/5).

Mnadani Market, a few kilometres out of town, happens on Saturday only and is the social highlight of Dodoma's week. Grilled meat, beer and fresh produce are all on sale. In town, Chick Villa and **Royal Taste** (Njia Kuu; snacks US$1) serve samosas, juices and chips. For drinking, the best local bars are Sunset Bar or Jacana Bar – find a local to show you the way.

Dodoma is connected by bus with Dar es Salaam (US$5, seven hours), and by train with Dar, Kigoma and Mwanza. Roads north and south of the town are appalling and travel very slow.

SOUTHERN TANZANIA

MBEYA
☎ 025 / pop 200,000
Mbeya is an attractive but vaguely seedy town, and is dominated by an enormous

bus station. It's the transport hub for any journey to Malawi or Zambia, whether on the Tanzam highway or the Tazara railway line. Most travellers only stop here overnight on their way into or out of the country, but if you've got time to stay longer, you'll be rewarded by superb hiking and a number of interesting cultural tourism projects in the rolling hills that surround the town. An afternoon is all you'll need to climb **Kaluwe peak** (2656m), which overlooks Mbeya to the north.

For information about hiking, village homestays or transport, visit the excellent **Sisi Kwa Sisi tourist office** (☎ 0477 463471; sisikwa sistours@hotmail.com), in the town centre near the Japan-Tanzania monument. This is a community-run initiative that can provide walking guides, organise accommodation and advise on bus, boat and train travel in the region.

The guesthouses on the hill opposite the bus station are all adequate, and have good views of the rolling hills beyond it. All three have restaurants.

New Millenium Inn (☎ 2500299; s US$4.50) is the newest and cleanest, with shared bathroom. Double beds in rooms.

Mkwenzulu Motel (☎ 2502225; d US$5) has fantastically bizarre concrete animals outside.

Annex no 3 of Mkwenzulu Motel (☎ 2502864; s/d US$4/4.50) is basic. Where are the other two?

The main bus terminus is at the bottom of the hill below the town. Dozens of buses go to Iringa (US$5, four hours) and Dar (US$11, 11 hours) every day.

Tazara 'express' trains to Dar es Salaam leave Mbeya station, a few kilometres from the town centre, on Wednesday and Saturday at 1.25pm; and a slow train to Dar leaves at 3pm on Tuesday. Tickets cost US$24/17/11 in 1st/2nd/3rd class. Make reservations well in advance if possible. Buses go past the station, or a taxi will cost about US$2. For more details on the Tazara train, see p596.

For details on crossing into Malawi and Zambia from Mbeya, see p589.

IRINGA
☎ 026 / pop 106,700

Architecturally nondescript, Iringa is nonetheless still a great place to use as a base for a few days exploring the surrounding Southern Highlands, whose dark-green hills glitter temptingly on all sides of the town. Opportunities for day trips or longer excursions abound – Iringa has Stone Age sites, tea farms, battlefields and the animal-filled Ruaha National Park right on its doorstep.

The best place to start looking for information about all this is at **Hasty Tasty Too** (☎ 2702661; shaffinhaji@hotmail.com), a lunch/breakfast café that also functions as an informal tourist information centre. Its jovial owner Shaffin Haji is able to provide details of local beauty spots and good hikes in the area. He also hires out his car, plus driver, for trips into the Ruaha National Park. These could work out to be very affordable if you're in a group – the car costs about US$230 for two days, including petrol.

Riverside Campsite (☎ 2725282; rvphillips@maf .org; camp site per person US$2.50) Campers should head straight for this gorgeous spot about 13km out of town. The site has toilets, hot showers, barbeques and firewood, and sells water, beers, soft drinks, eggs, milk and cheese. There's also a tent for hire (US$2.50). To get there, take a taxi from town (US$10), or take the dalla-dalla marked 'Ilula' from the bus station and ask to be dropped at the signpost, from where it's a 1.5km walk to the site.

Lutheran Centre Guesthouse (☎ 0744 5477429; iralutherancentre@yahoo.co.uk; Kuwawa St; dm/s/d US$2/ 2.50/3.50) Simple, clean rooms and a restaurant, 500m out of town. Shared bathrooms, no alcohol or cigarettes.

Staff Inn White House Lodge (☎ 27001611; off Pangani St; s/d US$4.50/5.50) Basic but clean guesthouse next to the bus station. Restaurant selling food of the goat/chips/ugali variety.

Buses run daily to Mbeya (US$5, four hours) and Dar es Salaam (US$7, seven hours).

RUAHA NATIONAL PARK
Ruaha National Park is Tanzania's second largest, a vast wilderness visited by only a handful of travellers each year. It's not the easiest park to get to if you're on a budget, but definitely worth a certain amount of effort or expense. At the park's heart is the Great Ruaha River, which dwindles to a mere trickle in dry season and turns into a bubbling torrent during the rains. Around the river is a dramatic, completely unspoilt

landscape of plains, rocky gullies, thick woodland and distant purple hills.

The banks of the Great Ruaha are a permanent hunting ground for lions, leopards, jackals, hyenas and the rare and endangered African wild dog. Ruaha's elephants are also recovering strongly from ivory poaching in the 1980s and remain the largest population in East Africa. Ruaha represents a transition zone where eastern and southern species of flora and fauna overlap – lesser and greater kudu co-exist with northern species such as Grant's gazelle. Rare sable and roan antelopes are also here in abundance.

The park's roads can become impassable during the rainy season, so check on latest conditions before setting out between March and June. The bandas at the park headquarters cost US$30 per person, with bedding, or you can camp for US$20 per person. There's a kitchen and a small shop for basic provisions. The best way to visit Ruaha is on an organised safari from Dar es Salaam, or by hiring a vehicle in Iringa (see p623 for details). The park entry fee is US$15.

SELOUS GAME RESERVE

Named after Frederick Courteney Selous, a British hunter and naturalist of the 19th century, the Selous Game Reserve is one of the earth's last great wild places: 55,000 sq km of untamed bushland, untouched forests, crocodile-filled lakes and emerald green floodplains. That is slightly larger than Switzerland, four times as big as the Serengeti, and the second biggest protected natural area in the world.

Most of the park is off-limits to tourists, the only accessible bit being the northern section above the great muddy sweep of the Rufiji River. Here you'll find hippos, elephants, wildebeests and zebras in abundance, together with predators such as lion (for some reason, the Selous lions don't have manes) or the rare African wild dog.

The Selous also is one of the few wildlife areas in Tanzania that you're allowed to explore on foot. Walking safaris are conducted from all the hotels in the reserve – they provide a fantastic opportunity to see Africa up close without the distractions of engine noise and diesel fumes. Boat safaris up the river are also on offer at the more upmarket lodges. Unfortunately, none of this is cheap,

and the Selous has no facilities for independent budget travellers. The best way to get in is on an organised camping safari from Dar es Salaam (see p627 for operators). The reserve entry fee is US$25.

MIKUMI NATIONAL PARK

In contrast to the other Southern parks, Ruaha and Selous, Mikumi is not only affordable but quite easy to access – it's only four hours' drive on a tar road from Dar es Salaam. The road runs right through the middle of the park, which takes away a bit from any feeling of wilderness, but there's a widespread network of vehicle trails away from the road, and plenty of observation points. The best animal viewing is in the western section. Once you get away from the road you won't see many other vehicles, and Mikumi's high animal concentrations mean that wildlife watching is generally good, with large numbers of elephants, hippos, lions and giraffes.

Dalla-dallas and buses from Dar es Salaam run to the small town of **Mikumi** just outside the park gate, where there's a comfortable guesthouse, **Genesis Motel** (d US$15). There is no vehicle rental, and efforts to hitch a ride are generally futile, so you'll really need your own car to get into the park. The easiest way to visit Mikumi is on an organised safari from Dar es Salaam (see p627 for operators). The park entry fee is US$15.

MTWARA
☎ 023 / pop 92,600
Mtwara is the jumping off point for the adventurous border crossing into Mozambique (see p589 for details). It's got a half decent beach, but it's a strangely spread out town, meaning that walking anywhere takes ages, so it's really preferable to stay at **Mikindani**, a little fishing village about 10km to the north of Mtwara on the main road towards Lindi and Dar.

In Mikindani there's an excellent backpackers lodge, **Ten Degrees South** (☎ 2334053; tendegreessouth@twiga.com; d US$15), which has cheap seafood and helpful staff. If you've just arrived from Mozambique, you can change money at the NBC bank on the main road in Mtwara before travelling on to Mikindani.

Buses to Mozambique leave around 8am from the bus station in Mtwara, so it might be best to spend the night before at one of the guesthouses nearby – try **Mabatini Inn Guesthouse** (☎ 0741 470115; s/d US$3/4). The journey to Mozambique takes around 10 hours.

Buses to Dar es Salaam also leave from the bus station, but the road is atrocious and the journey could take up to 15 hours – far better to take the FB *Santorini* ferry instead. See p591 for details.

LAKE TANGANYIKA

The oldest and largest of the African Rift lakes, Lake Tanganyika is incredibly deep (1470m) and stunningly beautiful. Uniquely interesting to biologists due to the endemic fish species that swim in its crystal clear waters, the lake is most famous for the colonies of chimpanzees that live in the steeply forested hills on its western shore. For travellers, Lake Tanganyika is a fantastic, off-the-beaten-track destination to explore if you have the time and patience.

KIGOMA
☎ 028 / pop 124,000

Kigoma is the most important port on Lake Tanganyika, and the terminus of the railway line from Dar es Salaam. It's also the starting point for journeys into Mahale Mountains or Gombe Stream National Parks, home to Tanzania's wild chimpanzee communities. Just out of town in the small village of **Ujiji** is the **Livingstone Memorial**, commemorating the explorer's famous meeting with Stanley in this very spot. It's free (a donation is appreciated), and definitely worth a visit just for the hilarious papier-mâché figures and comically appalling paintings in the small 'museum' next door. There are no fixed opening times – just turn up and ask around for someone to let you in.

Lake Tanganyika Beach Hotel (☎ 2802694; s/d US$9/12) Formerly the Railway Hotel, this is an atmospheric place with an attractive lakeshore setting, but we have received reports of thefts from the rooms. It's about 200m southwest of the main ferry dock. It has a decent restaurant, though the service is slow and prices high.

For a cheaper place to stay, head out about 2km out of town to the district of Mwanga, where there are several basic local guesthouses and plenty of food stalls. Try Zan-

zibar Lodge or Sebabille Lodge, which both have clean rooms for around US$4.

Roads to and from Kigoma are generally atrocious, so the only viable options for transport are the train and the boat.

The Central Line train leaves Kigoma for Dar es Salaam on Tuesday, Thursday and Sunday at 6pm, and takes around three days. See p596 for fares.

The 90-year-old lake steamer MV *Liemba* leaves Kigoma on Wednesday at 4pm and proceeds in a stately manner down Lake Tanganyika to Mpulungu in Zambia, arriving at 8am on Friday. It then turns round and heads back again at 6pm on Friday, arriving in Kigoma at 8am on Sunday. It costs US$44/40/35 in 1st/2nd/3rd class. It's probably worth taking a first class cabin to make sure your possessions are safe. In theory, you can reserve first class cabins on the *Liemba* at the Central Line railway station in Dar es Salaam before setting out on the train for Kigoma.

It's also possible to use the MV *Liemba* to visit the remote Mahale Mountains National Park – see p626 for details.

MAHALE MOUNTAINS NATIONAL PARK

Mahale Mountains is one of the most remote National Parks in Tanzania, a roadless forest reserve covering the spectacular peaks of the Malahe range and extending to the white beaches that line the shores of Lake Tanganyika. The stunning natural beauty of the area would be enough to make it a magical destination in its own right; but the park's chief draw is the community of chimpanzees that live in the forest. They've been studied by researchers for 40 years, meaning that they're totally habituated to humans, and allow visitors to approach to within just a few metres of them.

Trekking in the forest is sweaty, humid work. But an hour or two observing the chimpanzees – waiting breathlessly for the upshot of a monkey hunt, or jumping back into the bushes as a big male shoots by – is worth any amount of walking. And when you emerge from the forest you can plunge straight into the gin-clear waters of the lake, fringed with beaches pristine enough to rival any on earth.

Once in the park, there's a comfortable banda and cooking facilities, but you'll have to bring your own food supplies. Park entry

---

CHIMPS & DISEASE

Chimpanzees are susceptible to human diseases, and even a common cold can cause death. Visitors who have colds or flu are strictly forbidden from chimp tracking.

---

fees are US$50 per day, plus US$20 per group for the guide, and the banda costs US$20 per person per night. Walking in the park is only allowed with a guide and you can only spend two hours with the chimps in one go.

Mahale isn't as hard to get to as it seems – all you need is a willingness to spend a day or two in Kigoma.

Travel on the MV *Liemba* steamer (see p625 for timetable information) to the village of Lagosa (US$10, seven hours), whereupon a park boat will pick you up and take you to headquarters. It's best to arrange this in advance with the *Liemba* **office** (☎ 028 2802811) at the port in Kigoma. You can catch the *Liemba* three days later as it passes on its way back to Kigoma.

GOMBE STREAM NATIONAL PARK

Gombe Stream is a small strip of lakeshore forest, like Mahale Mountains primarily visited for chimpanzee watching. The entry fee of US$100 – yes, one hundred dollars! – per person per day puts off most budget travellers, but this only applies to time spent in the forest – if you stay two nights at the park headquarters either side of a day's chimp tracking, you'll only pay one day's fees. There's also a guide fee of US$20 per group. The chimps at Gombe – nowadays international celebrities thanks to the work of the famous primatologist Jane Goodall – are considered harder to find than those at Mahale, so you may have to walk several hours into the forest in search of them.

Accommodation at Gombe is in the hostel near the park headquarters at Kasakela, which costs US$10 per person. You can also camp on the beach for US$20. For either, you'll need to bring food from Kigoma. To stay in the hostel, you'll need to book in advance with the park warden – inquire at the upmarket Hilltop Hotel in Kigoma.

The only cheap transport options are lake taxis (US$2, two hours) that leave Kibirizi, 2km north of Kigoma, for Gombe daily. They return to Kigoma from Gombe early

in the morning – so it's not possible to do a day trip from Kigoma. Beware of local boat owners who claim there are no public boats and offer chartered trips for about US$60 one way!

TANZANIA DIRECTORY

ACCOMMODATION

There's an excellent range of budget accommodation in Tanzania, and a night in a decent guesthouse (known as a *gesti*) should cost on average around US$6 to US$10 per person. The exception is the huts and camp sites in the National Parks, which cost at least US$20 per person. It's worth noting that accommodation on Zanzibar is significantly more expensive than that on the mainland.

Most budget guesthouses have fans and mosquito nets, but not many have hot water. 'Shared bathroom' in the text indicates that the prices listed are for a room with a shared bathroom; there may well be rooms with private bathroom available for a slightly higher price.

Tanzania is also a good place to bring a tent – there are lovely camp sites scattered throughout the country, and it's a good way to save money.

ACTIVITIES
Diving & Snorkelling
The islands of Zanzibar and Pemba, together with various locations along the Tanzanian coast, provide world-class diving and snorkelling over pristine coral reefs, interesting wrecks and, at certain times of the year, the opportunity to spot species such as whale shark. The average price of a dive with one of the reputable PADI operations in the Zanzibar archipelago is US$35 to US$40. Rates for two dives per day are US$80, for six dives per day US$180.

Trekking
Tanzania's rugged and wild landscape provides endless opportunities for trekking and hiking. Mt Kilimanjaro and Mt Meru are the obvious destinations for serious trekkers, but other areas, such as the Usambara Mountains near Tanga and the Southern Highlands around Iringa, are also excellent places to do a bit of hiking. For trekking enthusiasts, the

Lonely Planet *Trekking in East Africa* guide will prove invaluable.

Wildlife Safaris

Tanzania's many national parks, reserves and conservation areas, as well as being some of the most spectacularly beautiful wild places on the planet, are home to a bewildering variety of animals. So a safari here is likely to be the highlight of any trip through Africa. For general details about safaris see p994 under Activities in the Africa Directory at the back of this book. Some Tanzania specifics worth bearing in mind are listed below.

You should expect to pay US$80 to US$100 per day for a good budget safari in Tanzania. Doing things under your own steam often works out no cheaper than taking an organised trip, and is often a lot more complicated.

It's usual for backpackers to team up and get a better price when arranging a safari. You can arrange things on the spot in towns like Arusha and Moshi, but most safari companies also take bookings in advance via email.

If you're being offered a ridiculously cheap deal by a safari operator, think again. Anything for US$75 a day or less is likely to have some compromises in quality – ask to see the TALA (government) licence of any operator you are booking with, as there are many disreputable companies in operation (particularly in Arusha).

Animals in the northern parks (especially Serengeti and Tarangire) move according to rainfall patterns and other seasonal factors, and may not be in the same place at all times of year. A good safari operator should be able to advise on which parks are best for the time of your trip – beware of those that offer the same packages all year round. For details on the wildebeest migration in the Serengeti, see p612.

The following tour companies, based in or around Dar es Salaam are recommended:

Easy Travel (Map p592; ☎ 2123526; easytravel@raha .com; Raha Towers, Bibi Titi Mohammed St) Well established operator offering budget camping and lodge safaris all over Tanzania. Student discount is 20%. They also have branches in Arusha and Zanzibar.

Fox Treks (☎ 0741/4/8 237422; fox@bushlink.co.tz) More upmarket outfit specialising in southern Tanzania. Their lodges and camps are good value for money, but not dirt cheap.

THE BIG FIVE & THE LITTLE FIVE

All of the 'Big Five' animal species (so called by old-time big game hunters because they were most sought after as trophies) are well represented in Tanzania's wildlife areas. Lions, leopards, buffaloes and elephants can be seen in many places, while the rare black rhinoceros is present in significant numbers only in the Ngorongoro Crater.

In addition to the obvious stars of the tourist circuit, many lesser-known but no less interesting species are worth seeking out. You'll know you've had a comprehensive tour of Tanzania's wildlife if your safari driver manages to find you the 'Little Five': ant-*lion*, *leopard* tortoise, *buffalo* weaver (bird), *elephant* shrew and *rhinoceros* beetle. Bring your magnifying glass as well as your binoculars!

Lions of Tanzania (Map p592; ☎ 2128162; lions@raha .com; Peugot House, Upanga St) This new company does cheap camping and guesthouse-based safaris to Mikumi, Selous, Ruaha and the northern parks. They also have a branch office in Libya St and operate a database for people looking to make up a group.

DANGERS & ANNOYANCES

Tanzania is generally a very safe country to travel around, but normal precautions apply: don't walk around with valuables in town centres after dark, or on deserted beaches, and lock your money in the safe when staying at a hotel. If you are stopped by the police for any reason, stay polite but insist on going to the police station and obtaining an official receipt for any 'fines' you might pay.

In tourist towns like Zanzibar Stone Town or Arusha, touts often follow visitors in an attempt to sell them tours or transport. If they're annoying you, don't lose your temper, and try a few words of Swahili: '*hapana, asante*' means 'no thank you'.

DRIVING LICENCE

An international driving licence, which needs to be shown together with the holder's own country's licence, is required by anyone driving themselves in mainland Tanzania or Zanzibar. In Zanzibar, temporary driving licences can be arranged – ask your vehicle's owner for help in obtaining these.

EMBASSIES & CONSULATES

The following embassies and consulates are located in Dar es Salaam:

Canada (☎ 2112831; 38 Mirambo St)
France (☎ 2666021; Ali Hassan Mwyini Rd, Kinodoni)
Germany (☎ 2117409; Umoja House, Garden Ave)
Ireland (☎ 2602355; Msasani Rd, Oysterbay)
Kenya (☎ 2701747; 14 Ursino, Old Bagamoyo Rd)
Malawi (☎ 2136954; 1st fl Zambia House, Ohio St)
Mozambique (☎ 2116502; 25 Garden Ave)
Netherlands (☎ 2110000; Umoja House, Garden Ave)
Rwanda (☎ 2115889; 32 Ali Hassan Mwinyi Rd)
South Africa (☎ 2601800; Mwaya Rd, Msasani)
Uganda (☎ 2666730; 25 Msasani Rd, Oyster Bay)
UK (☎ 2110101; Umoja House, Garden Ave)
USA (☎ 2668001; 686 Old Bagamoyo Rd)
Zambia (☎ 2118481; Zambia House, cnr Ohio St & Sokoine Dr)

For details on getting visas for neighbouring countries, see under Visas (p629) in the Directory at the end of this chapter.

Tanzania has diplomatic representation in the following neighbouring or near-neighbouring countries: Kenya, Uganda, Mozambique, Zambia, Zimbabwe, Ethiopia, Rwanda, South Africa and Malawi.

FOOD & DRINK

Tanzanians love to eat and drink – you haven't been properly entertained unless your host has produced at least a cup of *chai* (tea) or a 'soda' (fizzy drink). National favourite snacks include *keki* (vanilla cake), samosas and *maandazi* (donuts). Stews are popular, made with beef, goat or red beans. Chicken and chips is the staple menu item of cafés everywhere – vary your diet by asking for *ugali* (maize meal pap), *matoke* (cooked savoury banana) or *mishkaki* (meat or fish on a skewer). On the coast, the seafood is superb, and often served in spicy curries called *biryani* or *pilau*. Wash it all down with a bottle of Safari or Kilimanjaro lager or fresh fruit juice.

HOLIDAYS

As well as religious holidays listed in the Africa Directory chapter (p1003), these are the principal public holidays in Tanzania:
1 January New Year's Day
12 January Zanzibar Revolution Day
5 February Foundation Day
26 April Union Day
1 May Labour Day
7 July Saba Saba Day
8 August Farmers' Day
9 December Independence Day
26 December Boxing Day

INTERNET ACCESS

Even the smallest towns in Tanzania now mostly have well-functioning Internet cafés. The standard rate is US$1 per hour.

MONEY

Cash and travellers cheques can be changed for Tanzanian shillings at most of the numerous banks and *bureaux de change* in most cities and towns. *Bureaux de change* are quicker, open longer and offer slightly better rates than the banks.

At banks and forex bureaux, the rate for smaller bills (ie, less than US$50) is about 2% lower than for larger bills, and travellers cheques attract an exchange rate about 3% lower than for cash. In theory, foreigners must pay for a lot of things in hard currency (mostly US dollars in cash), such as entry fees to national parks and reserves, organised tours, upmarket hotels, international airline tickets, and ferries between Dar es Salaam, Zanzibar and Pemba.

ATMs

Standard Chartered Bank and Barclays both have ATMs that accept Visa cards. There are ATMs currently in Arusha, Moshi, Dar es Salaam and Mwanza.

Credit Cards

Some *bureaux de change*, particularly in Arusha, Dar es Salaam and Stone Town (Zanzibar), will provide cash (in Tanzanian shillings) against Visa or MasterCard. However, their exchange rates are very low, their fees are high, and you'll have to wait a long time, so use them only as a last resort.

POST & TELEPHONE

Post in Tanzania is cheap (US$0.40 for a postcard), but often unreliable.

Tanzanian public telephone bureaux are called TTCL, and charge upwards of US$3 per minute for international calls. You can also call abroad from public TTCL cardphone boxes if you have a card with enough money on it.

If you have your mobile phone with you, it's much cheaper to buy a SIM card for around US$8 from one of Tanzania's many phone companies (eg Vodacom, Celtel). You top up your account with cards that are sold in convenience stores everywhere.

VISAS

All visitors holding passports from European, North American and Australasian countries require a visa to enter Tanzania. Visas cost US$10 to US$50 depending on nationality, and can be bought on most major borders, or arranged in advance.

Visa Extensions

Because visas are valid for three months, extensions are rarely required, but they are available at immigration offices in any of Tanzania's major towns and cities. No fees or photos are required, and applications are often processed on the same day.

Visas for Onward Travel

Visas for neighbouring countries can be obtained at the following embassies in Dar es Salaam (see p628 for address details).

Kenya One-month visas cost US$50 and are issued within 24 hours. However, it's easier to obtain a visa at a Kenyan border or international airport.

Malawi Citizens of the USA, UK and Germany do not require visas. For other nationalities, visas cost up to US$70, require two photos and are issued within 24 hours.

Mozambique One-month visas cost US$30, require two photos and are usually ready within five days.

Rwanda One-month visas cost about US$50, require two photos and are issued within 48 hours.

Uganda Visas valid for up to three months cost about US$30, require three photos and are issued within 24 hours. You can also obtain visas at the border.

Zambia One-month visas cost up to US$43 (payable in local currency), require two photos and can be collected two days later.

Kenya

HIGHLIGHTS

- **Lamu** Laid-back locals, ancient Swahili culture, sand dunes and donkeys – chill! (p659)
- **Masai Mara National Reserve** Photography heaven with close-up big cats and wide-angle wildebeest migration (p654)
- **Mt Kenya National Park** A trek through bamboo forests and alpine moorlands leads to legendary peaks (p647)
- **Lake Bogoria National Park** Thousands of flamingos, a tranquil lake and some mighty hot springs (p647)
- **Off the beaten track** Kakamega Forest's sun-dappled rainforest walks among the birds and monkeys (p654)

FAST FACTS

- **Area** 583,000 sq km (that's two Italys)
- **ATMs** in all major towns
- **Borders** Ethiopia, Tanzania, Uganda all open; Somalia and Sudan border crossings not advised
- **Budget** US$15 to US$20 per day
- **Capital** Nairobi
- **Languages** English, Kiswahili
- **Money** Kenya shilling; 1US$ = KSh 75
- **Population** 31 million
- **Seasons** dry (Jun–Nov), short rains (Nov–Dec), long rains (Mar–Jun)
- **Telephone** country code ☎ 254; international access code ☎ 00
- **Time** GMT/UTC + 3
- **Visas** US$50 for 30 days issued at some borders; required by all but citizens of East African countries

For many years Kenya was the public face of the East African tourist trade. A million billboards, glossy magazines and badly made TV shows sold the idea of Kenya as the original home of man-eating lions, khaki-clad white hunters and fierce Maasai warriors. It worked, too – during the 1980s and '90s Kenya's tourism industry boomed, with prices going down and visitor numbers ever upward. Fleets of zebra-striped minibuses carried eager visitors into the Masai Mara National Reserve or Amboseli National Park, and the beaches of Malindi and Mombasa acquired a strip of cheap 'n' cheerful package-tour hotels.

But the real face of Kenya isn't the clichéd tableau sold by the travel agents. It's edgy, complicated, sometimes frustrating and always interesting. Step out the back of that cheesy curio shop filled with overdressed tourists and you'll find wide boys chomping on grilled goat, chewing narcotic herbs and slurping homemade hooch. Step in, pull up a chair, leave your preconceptions at home and keep your wits about you – and you'll be in for the ride of your life.

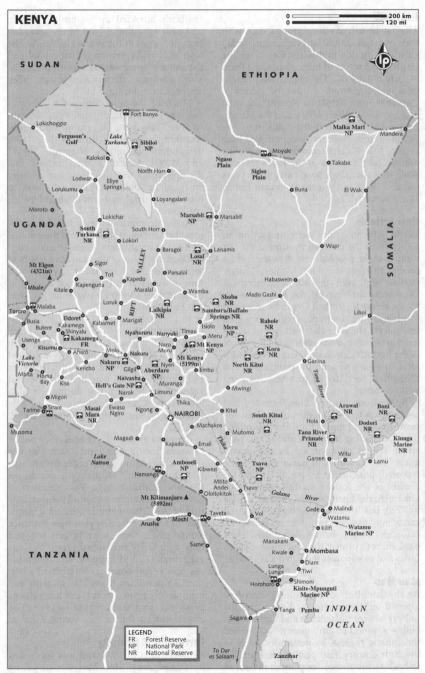

HISTORY

The patchwork of ethnic groups, each with their own culture and language, which today exist side by side in modern Kenya are the result of the waves of migration, some from as early as 2000 BC. The migrations brought groups from every corner of Africa – Turkanas from Ethiopia; Kikuyu, Akamba and Meru from West Africa; and the Maasai, Luo and Samburu from the southern part of Sudan. Kenya, however, was occupied long before this – archaeological excavations around Lake Turkana in the 1970s revealed skulls thought to be around two million years old and those of the earliest human beings ever discovered.

New Arrivals

While African tribes were migrating to Kenya from the interior, by around the 8th century other peoples were arriving from a totally different direction. Arabic, Indian, Persian and even the Chinese merchant ships were arriving on the Kenyan coast, blown across the Indian Ocean by monsoon winds and intent on trading skins, ivory, gold and spices. These new arrivals helped set up a string of commercial cities along the whole of the East African coast, intermarrying with local dynasties to found a prosperous new civilisation, part African, part Arabic, known as the Swahili.

By the 16th century, Europeans too had cottoned on to the potential of the East African coast, and most of the Swahili trading towns, including Mombasa and Lamu, were either sacked or occupied by the Portuguese. Two centuries of harsh military rule followed, punctuated by regular battles for control of the former Swahili empire. The Omani Arabs finally ousted the Portuguese in 1720, but it wasn't long before the coast came into the control of more European colonisers – the British, who used their battleships to protect their lucrative route to India and to suppress the hated slave trade.

Mau Mau

By the late 19th century the British had 'opened up' the interior of Kenya, and the railway between Mombasa and Uganda was built – a project so ambitious it was dubbed the 'lunatic express' by detractors. Early in the 20th century European settlers arrived to hack farms and coffee plantations out of the bush, attracted by the healthy climate and lush agricultural land of the area that became known as the White Highlands. The town of Nairobi grew up as their capital, and the antics of some settlers, including the dissolute lifestyle of the so-called Happy Valley set, became notorious.

Much of the land occupied by Kenya's new settlers was traditionally the domain of the Kikuyu ethnic group, and many resented the appropriation of their land, demanding its return. Returning WWI and WWII African soldiers helped fuel the opposition to British rule and a leader emerged in Jomo Kenyatta, who was to become the first president of an independent Kenya.

As the demands of the opposition movement became more strident, and the colonial authorities became less willing to make concessions, the seeds of the Mau Mau rebellion were sown. The Kikuyu-led revolt, by the time of its defeat in 1956, caused the deaths of more than 13,500 Kenyans and just over 100 Europeans.

Independence

Despite the ultimate failure of the Mau Mau rebellion, the movement finally achieved its goal. Independence came in December 1963, and Kenyatta, who had spent several years under house arrest during the Mau Mau crisis, assumed leadership of the new ruling party, Kenya African National Union (KANU).

Kenyatta assumed a conciliatory policy towards Europeans, and many former settlers stayed on after independence to take up Kenyan nationality and roles in the new administration. But members of Kenya's other tribes resented the domination of the Kikuyu and Luo ethnic groups, and the fruits of the new post-independence capitalist economy were largely enjoyed only by a fairly privileged group of Kenyans, many linked to powerful foreign investors. Tribal conflicts intensified when the Luo politician Tom Mboya, who had been widely tipped to succeed Kenyatta as president, was assassinated in 1969. The attack was attributed to a young Kikuyu.

Corruption & Disunity

Kenyatta died in 1978 and was succeeded by Daniel Arap Moi. Moi was unwilling to tolerate criticism of his regime, and his presidency was characterised by the arrest of dissidents, and frequent civil unrest. The obvious corruption of certain members of Moi's cabinet during his rule attracted widespread publicity, but ethnic divisions hampered the formation of effective opposition parties.

During the lead up to the elections in late 1992 and 1997, opposition disunity, together with widespread election fraud, led to KANU being returned to power. Strikes, demonstrations – many led by students – and political infighting marked the run-up to both elections. Demonstrations spiralled into violence, much of which was broadcast on international television, damaging the country's tourist industry and leading to the suspension of much foreign aid.

A New Beginning

In 2002, 71-year-old political veteran Mwai Kibaki – a one-time vice president of Moi's – assumed leadership of a coalition of 13 opposition parties known as the National Rainbow Coalition (NARC). NARC fought the 2002 general elections on an anticorruption platform, ending KANU's 40-year grip on power and winning a landslide victory against Moi's successor, Uhuru Kenyatta (the son of Jomo).

NARC faces a challenging task – Mr Kibaki has pledged to wipe out corruption and revive the country's crippled economy. Kenya's populace greeted the end of KANU rule with public jubilation, and hopes for the 'new Kenya' are higher than at any time since independence.

THE CULTURE
Tribal Patriotism

Between the four lanes of the highway that runs from Nairobi's international airport towards the skyscrapers of the city is a wide grass verge. There, covered in exhaust fumes and assailed by the roar of traffic, Maasai herdsmen, some clad in traditional bright red blankets, gaze contemplatively at the busily grazing mouths of their cattle, occasionally returning the stares of the tourists who whiz by in minibuses on the way to the next chain hotel.

This image is a potent symbol of life in Kenya. The many ethnic groups that make up the fabric of the country's society have adapted to the trappings of modern life without abandoning their traditional cultural practices or losing a sense of their origins. This sense of ethnic identity – or 'tribal patriotism' as one newspaper columnist recently called it – has positive and negative consequences. On the plus side, it has prevented the high level of foreign investment in Kenya from eroding the country's own cultural values and replacing them with an imitation of Western culture.

On the negative side, however, ethnic loyalties have often replaced any sense of belonging to the Kenyan nation as a whole, resulting in disunity and tension that regularly explodes into violence. Many accuse the KANU government, which ruled Kenya with an iron fist for more than four decades, of deliberately stoking inter-tribal resentment in order to sow disunity in its opposition parties.

Even in the optimistic mood that has followed the appointment of Kenya's new government, tribal loyalties have not been left behind. Kenyans meeting each other for the first time expect to ascertain each other's tribe at a very early stage in the conversation, and tribal generalisations are rife – Kikuyu are arrogant, Kalenjin are good runners, and so on.

Man Eat Man

The post-independence government of Kenya coined the word *harambee* (translates as 'self-help' or 'self-reliance') to encourage the country's citizens into greater efforts for the good of the new nation. When the term was first used, it served as a political call to prod wealthy people into donating funds for education, national disasters, health and medical care.

Like the government itself, the idea of *harambee* became corrupted, its ideals of national self-sufficiency changed into an unofficial doctrine of every person for themselves and an environment in which wealthy businesspeople used their assets to bribe their way to greater success. The socialist president of Tanzania, Julius Nyerere, once called Kenya a 'man eat man society'.

Kenya's government encouraged its fledgling tourist industry, cannily realising that foreign goodwill and foreign investment were essential for the growth of the nation. This long history of dealing with Western countries has led to parts of Kenya acquiring at least a veneer of Western development and Nairobi has more fast-food outlets, multiplex cinemas and giant supermarkets filled with imported goods than any other city in East Africa.

The tourist industry may have been good for Kenya's economy, but it has led to resentment among groups such as the Maasai, who assert that their complex culture is reduced to no more than camera fodder for tourists, given the same importance as a lion or a buffalo.

Cautious Optimism

The formation of the new government under Kibaki was greeted as a new *uhuru* (independence) and led to a mood of national euphoria and optimism that resulted in calls for a radical shift in national attitudes and an end to corruption, nepotism and deception in private as well as public life. Will the country's faith in the 'new Kenya' be justified? Early signs don't look entirely hopeful – one of the first acts of the new Members of Parliament was to pass a minibudget awarding themselves substantial pay rises and top-of-the-range cars.

The end result of four decades of tourism, capitalism and tribal loyalty is that Kenyans, in the eyes of some East Africans as well as many Western visitors, are cockier, more sophisticated and more arrogant than their Tanzanian or Ugandan neighbours, with an eye for a sharp deal, a ready sense of black humour and an irreverent attitude towards political figures, anyone in authority – and naive tourists.

SPORT

Since the 1960s, Kenya has produced more world-class athletes, more world-record holders and more Olympic medallists in long distance running than any other country. They haven't lost the steeplechase event at the Olympic Games since 1964, and account for 91 out of the 100 best times ever. The majority of Kenya's runners come from one ethnic group, the Kalenjin.

This athletic ability has attracted the attention of coaches, physiologists and even geneticists, none of whom have been able to agree on a reason for the Kenyan domination of running sports. In 1990 physiologist Bengt Saltin took some members of the Swedish national athletics team to a high school in Iten, near Eldoret. The local kids repeatedly trounced the national champions of athletics-mad Sweden, and Dr Saltin estimated that there were at least 500 schoolboys in the region who could beat Sweden's best adult athlete in a 2000m race.

ENVIRONMENT
The Land

Kenya is on the equator and its area of about 583,000 sq km (which includes around 13,600 sq km of inland lakes) can be divided roughly into four primary zones. The coastal belt, with its white beaches, coral reefs and palm trees, has hot weather all year round. The Rift Valley and central highlands are home to the salty 'soda' lakes Bogoria and Nakuru, as well as Mt Kenya, the continent's second-highest mountain.

Western Kenya, with pristine rainforest and bright-green tea plantations fading away to semidesert in the south, also includes the Masai Mara National Reserve, the tip of the Serengeti ecosystem.

Finally, the little-visited north and east regions of Kenya consist of vast semiarid bushland bordering Somalia and Ethiopia, where rainfall is sparse and cattle grazing is the main activity.

Wildlife & National Parks

Since its inception, Kenya's tourism industry has been defined by the country's wildlife. Most famous of the wildlife reserves is the Masai Mara, part of the Serengeti ecosystem, which witnesses part of the annual wildebeest migration, one of the largest mammal movements on the planet.

Amboseli National Park, also bordering Tanzania, has the stuff of a million photographs with its herds of elephants moving around and Mt Kilimanjaro as a stately backdrop. The best times for wildlife watching are the dry seasons – May to October and December to February.

Kenya's plant species include the distinctive flat-topped acacia tree, the squat, ancient baobab and the cabbage-like groundsel.

Offshore, the Watamu Marine National Park near Malindi provides spectacular opportunities for diving and snorkelling.

Environmental Issues

Illegal logging, human encroachment into wildlife habitats and destruction of marine life by unsustainable fishing practices such as dynamiting are all issues that affect Kenya's environment. Despite extremely stiff penalties, poaching of wildlife – mainly elephants and rhinos – continues, though on a smaller scale than in previous years.

Lake Victoria is suffering from a major environmental problem. Sewage from lakeside towns such as Kisumu flows directly into the lake, which is also under threat from the rapidly growing water hyacinth. This aquatic weed grows so prolifically that it chokes waterways, and is so dense that it stops light penetrating the lake surface, annihilating fish stocks.

On the positive side, Kenya has a well-known environmental campaigner, Dr Wangari Maathi, whose Green Belt Movement has facilitated the planting of over 17 million trees since its foundation in the 1970s. Several community-run wildlife lodges have also been set up throughout Kenya, giving local people a share of the revenues earned by the wildlife they are expected to help preserve.

TRANSPORT

GETTING THERE & AWAY
Air

Nairobi and Mombasa are linked to Tanzania's Dar es Salaam, Zanzibar and Arusha by several airlines. Some sample one-way fares include: Nairobi–Dar es Salaam US$200, Nairobi–Arusha US$135, Mombasa–Kilimanjaro US$110, Mombasa–Zanzibar US$100 and Nairobi–Zanzibar US$185.

Kenya Airways flies between Nairobi and Entebbe (Uganda) and operates flights from Nairobi to Addis Ababa (Ethiopia). Regional Air and Kenya Airways both operate flights from Nairobi to Khartoum (Sudan).

Nairobi is a major international hub and many airlines, such as British Airways, KLM and Swiss Air, fly there from Europe. Many

---

DEPARTURE TAX

Airport departure tax is US$20 for international flights and US$4 for domestic flights.

---

charter airlines also fly package tourists from various European countries to Mombasa.

Boat & Land
ETHIOPIA

There's only one reasonably safe crossing between Kenya and Ethiopia, at the dusty frontier town of Moyale. Public transport from Marsabit to Moyale is irregular, and the trip takes at least one whole day. The road is appalling in places and the area is sometimes politically unstable. Before using this crossing, seek reliable advice as to the current situation.

From the Ethiopian side of the border buses to the north, towards Addis Ababa, start very early, so this usually means staying overnight at a cheap hotel on either side of the border.

SOMALIA

Crossing between Kenya and Somalia is only possible if you are part of a refugee aid convoy. The entire border area is infested with well-armed Somali *shifta* (bandits), making any independent attempt to cross it a dangerous and foolhardy venture.

SUDAN

The border with Sudan is currently open but the area is not safe for travel. The only practical way to travel between the two countries is to fly.

TANZANIA

The main border crossing between Kenya and Tanzania is at Namanga. Daily tourist and shuttle buses run between Nairobi and Arusha (four hours) and Moshi (five hours). No need to change buses at the border.

The mini bus shuttle services run by companies such as **Riverside** (☎ 020-229618) are popular, but not cheap – foreigners are charged US$20 to Arusha and US$25 to Moshi (you should be able to get the residents' rate of US$10 if business is quiet). Normal buses cost only around US$8.

Alternatively, you can do the journey in stages: catch a *matatu* (minibus) from Nairobi to the border at Namanga, cross on foot or by bicycle taxi (it's about 1km between the Kenyan and Tanzanian border posts) and continue to Tanzania by *dalla-dalla* (pick-up truck or minibus).

In southwest Kenya, buses run all day from Kisumu (US$6, five hours) to the Tanzanian border at Isebania. From Isebania there's onward transport to Mwanza (five hours). A number of buses run direct from Nairobi to Mwanza – book at the Akamba or at the Scandinavian bus offices in Nairobi (see p644). The same companies also run overnight services to Dar es Salaam via Arusha and Moshi (US$20 to US$30, 11 hours).

If you're heading for Tanzania from the main road between Nairobi and Mombasa, buses and *matatus* also run every day from Voi to Moshi (four hours).

Travelling up the coast from Tanzania's Tanga, it's easy to cross the border at Horo Horo on the way to Mombasa. Buses also leave from Mombasa each morning (times vary) for Tanga (US$4, three hours), or you can do the border in stages on *matatus* and *dalla-dallas*. There are also plenty of buses running from Mombasa straight through to Dar es Salaam (US$15, 11 hours).

For another option on the coast it may be possible to pick up a dhow (wooden cargo boat) in Mombasa to sail to the islands of Zanzibar or Pemba. The journey, in a motorised dhow, takes around 16 hours, and you must bring food and water with you.

UGANDA
The two main border crossings are between Malaba (Kenya) and Tororo (Uganda), and between Kisumu (Kenya) and Busia (Uganda).

Bus companies such as Akamba, Tawfiq and Taqwa operate services between Nairobi and Kampala (US$10 to US$30, 12 to 14 hours, daily). The cost depends on the speed and comfort levels of the bus.

If you're doing the journey in stages from western Kenya through Malaba and Tororo, catch one of the frequent *matatus* from Kisumu, Kitale or Eldoret to Malaba. Walk (1km) or take a *boda-boda* (bicycle taxi) between the border posts to the minibus terminal in Tororo. From Tororo, minibuses (called 'taxis' in Uganda) frequently travel to Kampala via Jinja.

Less often used is the entry point via Busia. From Kisumu, *matatus* travel to Busia (US$3, 1½ hours), from where there's onward transport to Kampala. Akamba also has buses (from US$10, 24 hours, daily) between Kisumu and Kampala.

GETTING AROUND
Air
Kenya is covered by an efficient and usually reasonably cheap network of domestic flights operated by **Air Kenya** (☎ 020-605745; resvns@airkenya.com) as well as **Flamingo Airlines** (☎ 020-32074340; www2.flamingoairlines.com). Some one-way fares include: Nairobi–Mombasa US$55 and Nairobi–Lamu US$135.

Car & Motorcycle
Renting a vehicle to tour Kenya (or at least the national parks and reserves) offers flexibility and is sometimes the only way to reach more remote parts of the country. Most of the time, however, a self-drive safari will cost more than a safari organised by a tour operator, so most backpackers take the latter option. For safari company listings, see p665.

If you do team up with others and decide to rent a car, a 2WD vehicle is perfectly adequate in some parts of the country, including Amboseli and Tsavo National Parks and Masai Mara National Reserve – as long as it's not the rainy season. Most car rental companies insist, however, that you rent a 4WD vehicle if you're travelling outside major tourist areas or to more remote parks and reserves.

Base rates for a 2WD car are around US$90 per day excluding fuel. Many companies enforce a minimum driving age of 23 or 25, and unless you're paying by credit card you'll have to leave a (refundable) deposit – at least enough to cover the total rental.

International rental companies, such as **Avis** (☎ 020-336704) and **Hertz** (☎ 020-331973), have offices in Nairobi and Mombasa. For a cheaper deal on 4WD rental, contact **Roving Rovers** (☎ 051-343294; mm@africaonline.co.ke), near Nakuru, which hires out Land Rovers fully equipped for camping for US$105 per day (excluding fuel).

There's a charge of US$3 per day for vehicles entering Kenya's national parks.

Hitching
Simply standing by the side of the road and waving down a vehicle is the accepted mode of transport in many remote areas. In most cases, as this is often the only way to get around, payment is expected, so check this before setting off.

Hitching in the traditional sense (ie for free) is easiest around the coastal resorts of Malindi and Watamu. In these places many holidaymakers will often pick up hitchers.

Local Transport

Buses are slower than *matatus* (minibus taxis), but often more comfortable and safer over longer distances. For longer trips it's definitely better to travel with bus companies such as Akamba, Scandinavian Express (only from Nairobi and Mombasa to Tanzania) and Taqwa, which are usually quicker, more reliable and more comfortable than most others.

You'll always find *matatus* going to the next town or further afield, so long as it's not too late in the day. Simply ask around at the bus station, or let one of the touts lead you to the next departing *matatu*.

Matatus leave when full – and we mean *full* – and fares are fixed. However, this doesn't stop some *matatu* conductors engaging in a variety of practices, from simple overcharging to downright deception. Try, if possible, to establish the fare (and indeed the destination) from other *matatu* passengers before parting with any cash. There's very rarely room for luggage, so if you're travelling with a backpack you'll either have to sit on it or pay for an extra seat. Wherever possible, try to get the front seat.

Matatus are notorious for their involvement in horror road smashes (the Mombasa to Nairobi road is particularly bad), and robberies by ambush (mainly in and near Nairobi) are common. To avoid either, never travel by *matatu* at night.

Shared taxis are Peugeot cars that wait to fill up with six people and then take off at breakneck speed for their destination. Fares are extremely cheap, so if you're in a hurry you could probably buy up any remaining seats in your taxi and set off. However, the accident record of shared taxis is even more horrifying than that of *matatus*.

Train

The only passenger service still running in Kenya is the train between Nairobi and Mombasa. Once the main form of travel in Kenya under British colonial rule, the train these days is a pretty slow affair, with tickets being way more expensive than the bus, and not much less than a plane fare. See p645 for fares.

NAIROBI

☎ 020 / pop 2 million

At the end of the 19th century, Nairobi grew from a Maasai watering hole called 'Vaso Nyirobi' to a prominent settler town, due to its position as a stop on the new Kenya–Uganda railway, nicknamed the 'lunatic express'.

Your impression of today's Nairobi will depend on whether you've just slogged in overland from the wilds of Ethiopia, Tanzania or Uganda, or whether this is your first stop in Africa. If you've come from the sticks, Nairobi can seem like a welcome injection of first-world razzmatazz with its shopping malls, supermarkets and cinemas. If, however, you're fresh off the plane, it may seem like a seedy, scruffy city with an air of barely contained violence and scenes of shocking poverty. In fact, both pictures of Nairobi are true. If you're worried about the city's reputation for robbery, stay in one of the affluent suburbs, such as Westlands, full of young professionals, rather than the downtown dives with their Dickensian cast of hustlers, hookers, thieves and beggars.

ORIENTATION

Nairobi has two airports. Wilson airport, served by domestic flights, is just 2km from the outskirts of town, while Jomo Kenyatta International Airport, known as JKI, is 14km away. Metro Shuttle bus No 34 runs from both airports to Nairobi's city centre, from where it's a short walk to most of the hotels (but watch out for thieves on this bus). Alternatively, take a taxi to or from JKI (US$13, 30 minutes) or Wilson (US$6, 15 minutes).

Nairobi's main commercial district lies west of Tom Mboya St and north of Haile Selassie Ave. Most long-distance buses come in at various points along River Rd, a few blocks from the main business district. At all costs avoid arriving after dark, and if you do, wait in the bus or in the bus company office until morning – River Rd is one of Nairobi's roughest areas.

INFORMATION
Bookshops
Prestige Bookshop (Map p642; Mama Ngina St) A smaller place that also has a good selection of guides and novels.

KENYA

NAIROBI

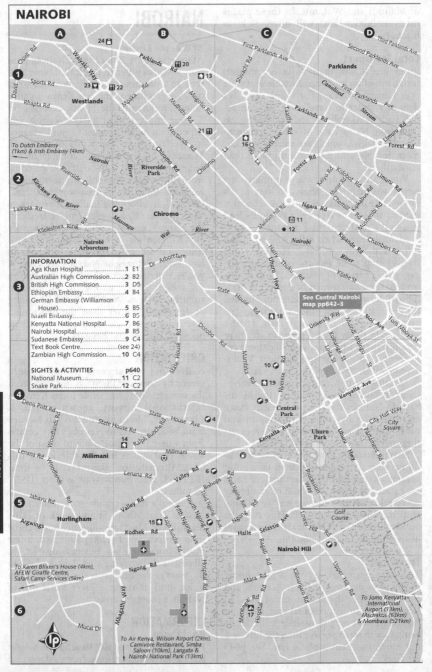

INFORMATION

Aga Khan Hospital	**1** E1
Australian High Commission	**2** B2
British High Commission	**3** D5
Ethiopian Embassy	**4** B4
German Embassy (Williamson House)	**5** B5
Israeli Embassy	**6** D5
Kenyatta National Hospital	**7** B6
Nairobi Hospital	**8** B5
Sudanese Embassy	**9** C4
Text Book Centre	(see 24)
Zambian High Commission	**10** C4

SIGHTS & ACTIVITIES p640

National Museum	**11** C2
Snake Park	**12** C2

See Central Nairobi map pp642–3

To Dutch Embassy (1km) & Irish Embassy (4km)

To Karen Blixen's House (4km), AFEW Giraffe Centre, Safari Camp Services (5km)

To Air Kenya, Wilson Airport (2km), Carnivore Restaurant, Simba Saloon (10km), Langata & Nairobi National Park (13km)

To Jomo Kenyatta International Airport (13km), Machakos (63km) & Mombasa (521km)

KENYA

SLEEPING	⬆ ⬆ pp640–1
Impala Hotel	13 B1
Nairobi Backpackers	14 B4
Nairobi Youth Hostel	15 B5
Plums Hotel	16 C2
Upper Hill Campsite	17 C6
YMCA	18 C3
YWCA	19 C4

EATING	🍴 pp641–4
Grapes Café	20 B1
Open House Restaurant	21 B2
Thali	22 B1
Wheels	(see 22)

DRINKING	🍹 p644
The Pavement	23 A1

ENTERTAINMENT	p644
Fox Cineplex	(see 24)

SHOPPING	🛍 p644
Sarit Centre	24 A1

TRANSPORT	pp644–5
Country Bus Station	25 F4

Text Book Centre (Map p638; Sarit Centre, Parklands Rd, Westlands) This huge emporium in the Sarit shopping centre has guidebooks, maps, phrasebooks and novels.

Cultural Centres
British Council (Map p642; ☎ 334855; Kenyatta Ave) Hosts occasional events.
Goethe Institute (Map p642; ☎ 211381; Loita St) German and English films and good information about events in Nairobi.
Maison Francaise (Map p642; ☎ 336263; Loita St) Hosts films, art exhibitions and cultural events, in English and French.

Internet Access
Nairobi has perhaps more Internet cafés than any other city in East Africa, with several on almost every street in the city centre. Access at all places is much the same speed, and all cost the same – US$1.50 per hour. Try **Capital Realtime** (☎ 219843; Conhro House, Standard St) or **Neutral Cyber Café** (☎ 342305; Kenya Cinema Bldg, Moi Ave).

Media
Nairobi has three listings magazines, *What's On*, *Having Fun* and *Going Out*, which all contain cinema and event listings. *What's On* also has transport timetables and useful telephone numbers.

Medical Services
Aga Khan Hospital (Map p638; ☎ 742531; Third Parklands Ave)
Nairobi Hospital (Map p638; ☎ 2722160; Ngong Rd)

Money
Standard Chartered Bank (Map p642; Kenyatta Ave; 🕐 9am-3pm) and **Barclays Bank** (Map p642; Moi Ave; 🕐 9am-3pm) both have numerous ATMs all over the city and at JKI airport that take Visa and MasterCard. There are also numerous *bureaux de change* in Nairobi, all of which will change cash and most travellers cheques, although proof of purchase is often required.

Post & Telephone
The **main post office** (Map p642; Kenyatta Ave & Haile Selassie Ave; 🕐 8am-6pm Mon-Fri, 9am-noon Sat) also has branches on Moi Ave and Tom Mboya St.

The main office of **Telkom Kenya** (Map p642; Haile Selassie Ave; 🕐 7am-midnight) is near the main post office. There are also many international telephone offices in the city centre.

KENYA

DANGERS & ANNOYANCES

Nairobi's well-worn nickname of 'Nairob-bery' is sadly well deserved, although walking around the main city centre during the day is generally pretty safe. The key is to carry nothing of value (not even a bag) and to wear no jewellery of any kind (not even a cheap watch).

The chances of being pickpocketed or having a bag slashed in central Nairobi seem to double when you enter the area east of Tom Mboya St, so take extra care when walking around this part of town. After dark, don't go anywhere in the city on foot – take a return taxi, even for short distances. The cheap hotels around River Rd, traditionally the haunt of backpackers, are now becoming a somewhat false economy – this area is notorious for violent robbery after dark.

See p665 for information on scams in Nairobi.

SIGHTS

National Museum (Map p638; off Museum Hill; admission US$2.50; 9.30am-6pm) Kenya's National Museum is definitely worth an afternoon as an introduction to the country if you've just arrived, or just to get away from the madness of downtown Nairobi and hang out somewhere cool, green and peaceful. The whole place is enlivened by extremely knowledgeable and enthusiastic guides (free).

The museum houses tribal portraits by Joy Adamson (of *Born Free* fame), various ethnic artefacts including circumcision knives and hair mudpacks, and reproductions of archaeological finds by the Leakey family. The **Bustani Cafeteria** round the back is a peaceful spot for a soda and samosa, with some interesting academic customers, but the **Snake Park** opposite is pretty depressing.

Nairobi National Park (www.kws.org; admission US$23; 6am-6pm) This is the most accessible park in Kenya, but its proximity to the city takes away the wilderness feel. Most of Kenya's major wildlife species – except elephants – are represented here, and it's a surreal experience to watch giraffes, impalas or rhinos grazing peacefully in front of a distant backdrop of skyscrapers.

Bus No 24 and *matatu* No 15 run right by the park entrance, and from there you'll have to hitch a ride through the park – this shouldn't be too difficult on Saturday and Sunday. Alternatively, rent a car or hire a taxi from Nairobi, or see what some of the safari companies (see p664) in town can offer. A trip through the National Park is a good way to get to JKI airport, which lies just the other side of it.

Karen Blixen's House (882779; Karen Rd; admission US$2.50; 9.30am-6pm) In the suburb of Karen, 10km from the city centre, the former home of the *Out of Africa* author was also in many scenes from the film. It's a lovely house and a peaceful spot for a picnic, with beautiful gardens and a gift shop with a good selection of books. To get here, take bus No 111 from outside the Hilton Hotel in town.

AFEW Giraffe Centre (890952; Koitobos Rd; admission US$7; 9am-5.30pm) A home for the endangered Rothschilds giraffe, the Giraffe Centre has a platform for feeding and offers a chance to get those close-up photographs that eluded you on safari. It's situated in the suburb of Karen, 10km from the city centre.

SLEEPING

Traditionally, the most popular area for backpacker accommodation in Nairobi was around River Rd, just east of Tom Mboya St. Nowadays, however, the area has become so rough that many travellers are opting for places further out of town. Unless otherwise stated, prices don't include breakfast. Never walk back to any hotel after dark – always take a taxi. See p992 for general advice on accommodation.

Hostels & Camping

Upper Hill Campsite (Map p638; 2720290; upperhill camp@africaonline.co.ke; Menengai Rd; camp site per person/dm/d US$4/4.50/11) This place is getting a fairly scruffy round the edges, and last time we visited the management was just a bit too laid-back, but Upper Hill remains the best value budget place in Nairobi – especially if you're on your own. Tents can be hired, meals are provided, the showers are hot (most of the time) and there are usually plenty of other travellers to meet. Upper Hill is about 3km from the bottom of Moi Ave – alternatively, take *matatu* No 34 from the city centre, then walk or grab a taxi (US$4). Security is good, and there's a car park. The dorm often gets full, so book ahead to be sure of a place.

Nairobi Backpackers (Map p638; ☎ 2724827; nbobackpackers@yahoo.com; Milimani Rd; camp site per person/dm/s/d US$4/7/14/16) Giving Upper Hill a good run for its money, this relatively new and very homely place is only 1km from the city centre, and can offer airport pickups by prior arrangement (US$13). There's a travel desk and food is served all day. All prices include breakfast, but still seem a little steep. Take *matatu* No 46 from the main post office and ask to be dropped off at Kenya Law School, 200m away.

Nairobi Youth Hostel (Map p638 ☎ 0722 656462; kyha@africaonline.co.ke; Ralph Bunche Rd; dm/s/d US$6/7/14) Spick-and-span, with big dorms but small bunk-bedded rooms, a cheap café and a self-catering kitchen. You need to join Hostelling International to stay here – one year's membership costs US$1.50. It's 3km east of the city centre; take *matatu* No 41, which goes past the end of the road. Metro Shuttle No 34 from the airport also passes close by.

YMCA (Map p638; ☎ 2724116; nationalym@net2000ke.com; State House Rd; dm/s/d US$7/13/19) The warren-like YMCA has small and unexciting rooms, some with private bathroom. It's within easy reach of the city centre (1km) and there's a pool (sometimes empty). There's also a cafeteria for breakfast and dinner, and staff can arrange taxis or laundry.

YWCA (Map p638; ☎ 724699; Mamlaka Rd; s/d US$17/32) The YWCA is only worth looking at if you're planning a long stay – its monthly prices are US$120 per person.

Hotels

Iqbal Hotel (Map p642; ☎ 220914; cnr Latema & Taveta Rds; dm/s/d US$4/6/8) Clean, safe (inside!) and good value, this old favourite is still the best of the River Rd area cheapies. The shared showers have hot water.

Danika Lodge (Map p642; ☎ 230687; Dubois Rd; s/d US$7/8) Readers have recommended this relatively clean, secure and odour-free place in the same dubious area as the Iqbal Hotel. Rooms on the quiet rooftop have their own bathroom and hot water.

Terminal Hotel (Map p642; ☎ 228817; Moktar Daddah St; s/d with private bathroom US$14/18) Pricier and a bit smarter than Danika Lodge, the Terminal is another old favourite in a marginally better area of town – although you'd still be advised to take a taxi around here after dark. The bathrooms have hot water.

Embassy Hotel (Map p642; ☎ 224087; hotel embassy@yahoo.com; Tubman Rd; s/d US$14/20) Exactly like the Terminal, but marginally more expensive, with a bar and restaurant. Get a room on the top floor – it's quieter.

Plums Hotel (Map p638; ☎ 3745222; Ojijo Lane; d with private bathroom US$18) Plums is located in the affluent suburb of Westlands, 1km from the shops and restaurants. Very quiet, big well-furnished rooms with TV and phone. Restaurant and bar.

Impala Hotel (Map p638; ☎ 3742346/7; Parklands Rd; s/d with private bathroom US$18/21) Mostly used by Kenyans, the Impala is becoming increasingly popular with tourists. Rooms are not beautiful, but are large and clean. There's a restaurant and bar, and the restaurants of Westlands are only 10 minutes' walk away. Breakfast is included. Matatu Nos 118 and 119 from the city centre run past the door.

EATING

There are dozens of little cafés and eating houses all over the city centre offering fairly uninteresting fare of the chips/toasted sandwich/burgers variety, along with *nyama choma* (barbecued meat), for around US$2. Cheapest of all are the Baker's Pies takeaways scattered everywhere, which have cakes, doughnuts and pies from US$0.50.

Some of the better lunch places include **Pasara** (Map p642; Lonrho House, Standard St; lunch US$4), which also has vegetable stir fries and salads, **Café Helena** (Map p642; Mama Ngina St; snacks US$2), possibly the only café in Kenya that *doesn't* serve Coca-Cola, and **Simmers** (Map p642; Kenyatta

---

SPLURGE!

For a lunch splurge in a very upmarket environment, head for the **Thorn Tree Café** (Map p642; New Stanley Hotel, Kenyatta Ave; lunch US$6). It provides an oasis of civilization amid the madness of the streets, although we think the food is very overpriced. The once famous travellers' noticeboard has been reduced to a shadow of its former self, presumably by the invention of email. **Trattoria** (Map p642; ☎ 340855; Kaunda St; mains US$6) is the traditional place for an end-of-holiday dinner splurge, with suitably plush decor, deferential waiters and homemade pasta.

KENYA

CENTRAL NAIROBI

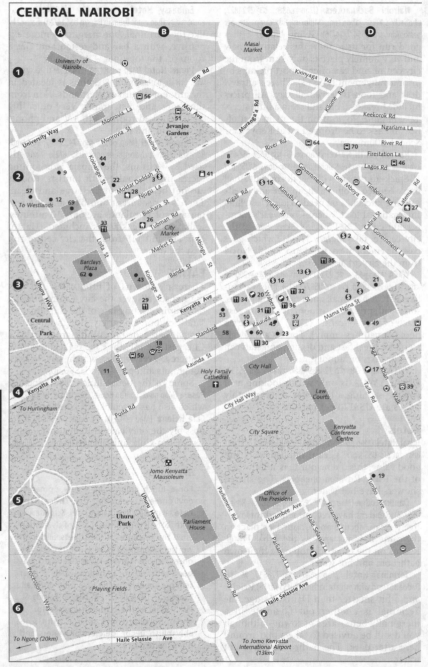

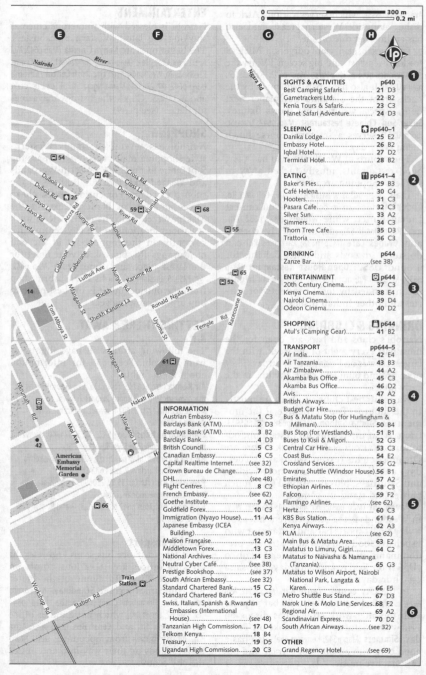

0   300 m
0   0.2 mi

SIGHTS & ACTIVITIES p640
Best Camping Safaris............... 21 D3
Gametrackers Ltd...................... 22 B2
Kenia Tours & Safaris.............. 23 C3
Planet Safari Adventure........... 24 D3

SLEEPING pp640–1
Danika Lodge........................... 25 E2
Embassy Hotel.......................... 26 B2
Iqbal Hotel............................... 27 D2
Terminal Hotel......................... 28 B2

EATING pp641–4
Baker's Pies............................. 29 B3
Café Helena.............................. 30 C4
Hooters.................................... 31 C3
Pasara Cafe.............................. 32 C3
Silver Sun................................ 33 A2
Simmers................................... 34 C3
Thorn Tree Cafe....................... 35 D3
Trattoria.................................. 36 C3

DRINKING p644
Zanze Bar................................(see 38)

ENTERTAINMENT p644
20th Century Cinema................ 37 C3
Kenya Cinema........................... 38 E4
Nairobi Cinema......................... 39 D4
Odeon Cinema.......................... 40 D2

SHOPPING p644
Atul's (Camping Gear)............. 41 B2

TRANSPORT pp644–5
Air India.................................. 42 E4
Air Tanzania............................ 43 B3
Air Zimbabwe.......................... 44 A2
Akamba Bus Office 45 C3
Akamba Bus Office.................. 46 D2
Avis... 47 A2
British Airways......................... 48 D3
Budget Car Hire....................... 49 D3
Bus & Matatu Stop (for Hurlingham &
  Milimani)............................. 50 B4
Bus Stop (for Westlands).......... 51 B1
Buses to Kisii & Migori............. 52 G3
Central Car Hire....................... 53 C3
Coast Bus................................ 54 E2
Crossland Services.................... 55 G2
Davanu Shuttle (Windsor House).56 B1
Emirates................................... 57 A2
Ethiopian Airlines..................... 58 C3
Falcon..................................... 59 F2
Flamingo Airlines....................(see 62)
Hertz....................................... 60 C3
KBS Bus Station....................... 61 F4
Kenya Airways......................... 62 A3
KLM..(see 62)
Main Bus & Matatu Area.......... 63 E2
Matatu to Limuru, Gigiri.......... 64 C2
Matatus to Naivasha & Namanga
  (Tanzania)........................... 65 G3
Matatus to Wilson Airport, Nairobi
  National Park, Langata &
  Karen................................... 66 E5
Metro Shuttle Bus Stand........... 67 D3
Narok Line & Molo Line Services..68 F2
Regional Air............................. 69 A2
Scandinavian Express............... 70 D2
South African Airways.............(see 32)

OTHER
Grand Regency Hotel..............(see 69)

INFORMATION
Austrian Embassy...................... 1 C3
Barclays Bank (ATM)................. 2 D3
Barclays Bank (ATM)................. 3 B2
Barclays Bank........................... 4 D3
British Council.......................... 5 C3
Canadian Embassy.................... 6 C5
Capital Realtime Internet........(see 32)
Crown Bureau de Change.......... 7 D3
DHL..(see 48)
Flight Centres............................ 8 C2
French Embassy......................(see 62)
Goethe Institute........................ 9 A2
Goldfield Forex........................ 10 C3
Immigration (Nyayo House)...... 11 A4
Japanese Embassy (ICEA
  Building)............................(see 5)
Maison Française...................... 12 A2
Middletown Forex..................... 13 C3
National Archives...................... 14 E3
Neutral Cyber Café................(see 38)
Prestige Bookshop.................(see 37)
South African Embassy............(see 32)
Standard Chartered Bank.......... 15 C2
Standard Chartered Bank.......... 16 C3
Swiss, Italian, Spanish & Rwandan
  Embassies (International
  House)...............................(see 48)
Tanzanian High Commission.... 17 D4
Telkom Kenya.......................... 18 B4
Treasury................................... 19 D5
Ugandan High Commission....... 20 C3

KENYA

Ave; mains US$3), which serves various African dishes alongside Western grease, and also has an Internet café on site.

For Caesar salad, giant burgers, a 'Michael Jordon Breakfast' and big screen TV, try the American-style **Hooters** (Map p642; Kaunda St; mains US$4). It also has a bar frequented by the hacks from the *Standard* newspaper next door, especially during big sports fixtures. **Silver Sun Chinese restaurant** (Map p642; Loita St; lunch US$4) serves a set three-course lunch menu every day.

The suburb of Westlands also has a few good restaurants, mostly tucked away in soulless shopping arcades.

Thali (Map p638; Westlands Arcade, Chiromo Rd; lunch US$4) does an excellent all-you-can-eat Indian buffet, while **Wheels** (Map p638; Chiromo Rd; mains US$2), just around the corner, and **Grapes Café** (Map p638; Parklands Rd) can do stews, gizzards and other delights for around US$2. **Open House Restaurant** (Map p638; Muthithi Rd; mains US$4) has been highly recommended by local residents for curries and other Indian dishes.

DRINKING & CLUBBING

Nairobi's clubs and bars are open for the most part every night of the week, with the largest crowds on Friday and Saturday. They open around 6pm and close anytime in the early hours.

Nairobi's best clubs and bars are mostly in the suburbs. Top of the tree at the moment is **Simba Saloon** (Map p638; ☎ 605933; Langata Rd) at the Carnivore Restaurant, out towards Nairobi National Park. There are DJs most nights (except Monday or Tuesday) and live music events most Fridays and Saturdays, plus occasional CD launch parties and stand-up comedy.

Pavement (Map p638; ☎ 4448444; Waiyaki Way) in Westlands is the other current hot spot, a very smart sports bar and restaurant with expensive food and beer and a trendy, predominantly Indian crowd. There's a disco (US$4) on Friday and Saturday, and salsa on Thursday.

In the city centre, **Zanze Bar** (Map p642; Moi Ave), a chilled-out and friendly bar popular with the after-work crowd, has discos on Friday and Saturday and karaoke on Tuesday. **Simmers** (Map p642; Kenyatta Ave) also has a good bar, with an outdoor terrace and occasional live music.

ENTERTAINMENT

Nairobi is blessed with numerous cinemas showing the latest Western blockbusters. The better ones are **Kenya Cinema** (Map p642; Moi Ave), **Fox Cineplex** (Map p638; ☎ 226981; Sarit Centre, Parklands Rd, Westlands) and the **20th Century Cinema** (Map p642; ☎ 226981; Mama Ngina St). Tickets cost about US$3. Check the listings magazines for details (see p639).

SHOPPING

Nairobi has several enormous Western-style shopping malls, best of which are the **Sarit Centre** (Map p638; Parklands Rd) in Westlands and **Village Market** (Map p638; Limuru Rd) in the suburb of Gigiri. For curios, crafts, cheap prices and lots of banter, seek out the Masai Market, which happens twice a week at various locations in the city centre – it's currently on the roundabout at the end of Muranga Rd, but ask at your hotel for the latest place and time. **Atul's** (Map p642; ☎ 225935; Biashara St) looks like a fabric shop from the outside, but it is the best place to buy or hire camping gear.

GETTING THERE & AWAY
Air

The following airlines all have flights to/ from Nairobi. See p635 for information about these flights.

Air Kenya (☎ 605745; resvns@airkenya.com) Based at the domestic Wilson Airport, 2km from town.

Air Tanzania (☎ 336224; www.airtanzania.com; Koinange St)

Flamingo Airlines (Map p642; ☎ 32074340; www2.flamingoairlines.com; Barclays Plaza, Loita St)

Kenya Airways (Map p642; ☎ 827029; www.kenya-airways.com; Barclays Plaza, Loita St)

Precision Air (☎ 00255 27 2506903 in Tanzania; information@precisionairtz.com)

Regional Air (Map p642 ☎ 311623; Grand Regency Hotel, Loita St)

Local Transport

Most long-distance bus stops and relevant booking offices are at various points on or around River Rd. Some of the better bus companies include **Scandinavian Express** (Map p642; Firestation Lane), **Akamba** (Map p642 ☎ 556062; Lagos Rd), which has another office on Kaunda St, and **Coast Bus** (Map p642; Accra Rd). Many buses from upcountry also stop in Westlands on their way into and out of the city centre.

Matatus to towns close to Nairobi leave from places in and around Accra, River and Cross Rds. Peugeot shared taxis to anywhere you can think of leave mainly from the streets around Latema Rd – but be very careful wandering around here with your luggage.

Train

Trains going to Mombasa leave from the central train station at the end of Moi Ave at 7pm, arriving at 8.30am the next day. However, there are often long delays. Fares are US$40/28/5 for 1st/2nd/3rd class. First class consists of two-berth compartments with a washbasin, drinking water, wardrobe and drinks service; 2nd class consists of four-berth compartments with a washbasin; and 3rd class is seats only. Sexes are separated in 1st and 2nd class unless you book the entire compartment.

Most trains have a dining car offering meals, but they're expensive, of average quality and the service is not great. All meals and bedding are included in 1st- and 2nd-class fares.

GETTING AROUND
Local Transport

KBS Metro Shuttle buses, much more comfortable and easier to fathom than the city buses, run from outside the Hilton Hotel on City Hall Way to destinations all over the city. Ask one of the uniformed staff which one to get on. For a more chaotic travelling experience, take a *matatu* or a city bus from the car park at the end of Tom Mboya St. Most *matatus* display their destinations on their windscreens, or you can just ask one of the drivers for directions. Needless to say, the bus stops of Nairobi are pickpocket heaven, so watch your stuff carefully.

Taxis

Private taxis operate from ranks all around the city. They're not metered, but the fares are remarkably standard – about US$3 around the city centre.

THE RIFT VALLEY

The lush, rolling hills of the Rift Valley combine with harsh, barren soda lakes to create one of Kenya's most spectacular natural areas. It's an easy area to get around and well worth a week or so to explore.

LAKE NAIVASHA
☎ 050

The shores of freshwater Lake Naivasha are a peaceful place to spend a few days – bird life is here in abundance, and hippos wander up out of the water to graze on the shore every night. There's probably nothing in **Naivasha** town itself that makes an overnight stay necessary – better to head straight to one of the excellent camp sites spread along the lakeshore, between 10km and 20km from town. When you get tired of lazing around by the lake, you can hike or mountain-bike through adjacent **Hell's Gate National Park** (see p646).

Sleeping & Eating
NAIVASHA TOWN

Heshima Hotel (Kariuki Chotara Rd; s/d US$3/4) This is the cheapest place in town but the rooms are cell-like. 'Any customer with huge sum of money to make agreement with the manager,' says the sign.

Othaya Annex (Kariuki Chotara Rd; s/d US$5/9) Quiet, with a bakery downstairs.

La Belle Inn (Moi Ave; mains US$4) A stately colonial restaurant in the middle of town. The veranda is a good place to watch the world go by.

ALONG THE LAKE

Lake Naivasha Lodge Campsite (☎ 20611; camp site per person US$5) The most beautiful camp site is at the end of sweeping lawns at this upmarket hotel. It has hot showers, a toilet, barbecue and sink. The hotel can organise boat rides and has an expensive restaurant.

YMCA (☎ 0733 989493; camp site per person/s/d US$2/4/8) This is definitely the cheapest option (the bedroom *bandas* – thatched roof huts – are very comfortable), and the nearest to Hell's Gate National Park, but it's far from the lake and rather scruffy. Friendly staff will cook to order. Theoretically, no alcohol is allowed.

Fisherman's Camp (☎ 30276; camp site per person/dm/s/d US$2.50/7/11/21) The traditional place for backpackers, on a stunning camp site right by the lake. It's very popular with overland trucks, so it's not always peaceful. The rooms and dorms are a bit overpriced, but Fisherman's is definitely the best place to meet other travellers. Members of the British army arrive for an adventure sports course every May or June, and the bar gets as rowdy as only a squadron of squaddies can make it. Tents, boats and mountain bikes can all be hired, and there's a full restaurant.

Burch's Camp (☎ 0733 660372; camp site per person/d US$2.50/4) A shady and well-equipped camp site, but no access to the lake. Sodas and water are for sale, and boats and bedding can be hired.

Getting There & Away
Most of the camp sites are at least 500m from the main road. Buses and *matatus* to Nairobi (US$1.50, one hour), Nakuru (US$1.50, one hour) and Kisumu (US$7, six hours) and a host of smaller destinations run from the bus stand near the covered market in the centre of town. *Matatus* along the lake depart from the stand on Kenyatta Ave – just tell them where you're going and they'll drop you off.

HELL'S GATE NATIONAL PARK
The towering red stone cliffs, weird volcanic rock formations and boiling hot springs of Hell's Gate are the source of the park's infernal name. You can hike or mountain-bike through Hell's Gate to the gorge at the far end, perhaps seeing buffalos, gazelles or some of the many resident vulture species along the way. True to its name, temperatures in the park soar to boiling point in the middle of the day, year-round, so make sure you set off early.

The usual access point is Elsa Gate, about 1km south of the road along Lake Naivasha. If you intend to walk the whole way through the park, allow a full day and take plenty of water. Alternatively, hire a mountain bike or try hitching. If you want to stay the night, camping in the park's camp sites costs US$8 per person. The entry fee is US$15.

NAKURU
☎ 051 / pop 200,000
Nakuru is one of Kenya's larger settlements, and the bus station is a fairly nerve-wracking place, with its jostling crowds and faint air of menace. The town itself is fine, though – a brash, cheery and colourful place. However, the best idea is to get out into the countryside as soon as possible: the lush green farmland

that surrounds Nakuru makes this region one of the most scenic parts of Kenya.

Amoody (☎ 211671; Nehru Rd; s/d US$2/3) This little place near the mosque is very good value, with small but clean rooms and hot water in the mornings.

Carnation Hotel (☎ 343522; Mosque Rd; s/d US$4/8) Clean and fairly quiet (apart from the mosque!) but dark.

Shik Parkview Hotel (☎ 212345/6; Kenyatta Ave; s/d with breakfast US$4.50/7) Central and clean but dark and noisy. Home to Nakuru's chess club!

Kembu Campsite (☎ 343203; kembu@africaonline.co.ke; camp site per person/d US$3/19) An excellent base for a visit to the Rift Valley, Kembu is a well set up farm camp site on the road between Nakuru (20km away) and Molo. The owners are an excellent source of information about the surrounding area and travel all over Kenya. The site hires out tents, Land Rovers and mountain bikes, and can organise horse riding, hikes or visits to local schools and community projects. There's a restaurant and bar on site. To get here, take a *matatu* towards Molo and ask to be dropped off at Kenana Farm. Wheelchair friendly.

Taidy's (cnr Gisii & Oginga Odinga Rds; mains US$3) The newest drinking and eating spot for Nakuru's young and upwardly mobile. There's an outdoor terrace, a disco on Friday and Saturday nights, and food of the roast chicken, burgers and pies variety.

Tipsy's restaurant (Gisii Rd; mains US$3) Recommended for vegetarians.

Buses, *matatus* and Peugeot shared taxis leave Nakuru's hectic central bus station, behind the central market, for Nairobi (US$3, 1½ hours), Naivasha (US$1.50, one hour), Eldoret (US$2, two hours) and Kisumu (US$4, three hours).

LAKE NAKURU NATIONAL PARK
Flamingos in their thousands often come to roost on the alkaline waters of Lake Nakuru, a shallow soda lake surrounded by woodlands. On land, the park is a good place to spot leopards, and waterbucks and buffalos are sure to be seen (along with zebras or even a huge python or two). Stately white pelicans join the rose-coloured flocks of flamingos on the lake.

The main gate is about 4km south of Nakuru, at the start of the road that circles the lake inside the park. The entry fee is US$30 per person.

The public camp site, just inside the park opposite the main gate, costs US$10 per person. Fresh water is available, and there are a couple of pit toilets. The **Wildlife Club of Kenya Youth Hostel** (☎ 051-850929; camp site per person/dm US$3.50/4), just off the road around the lake about 2.5km east of the main gate, is well maintained and friendly.

To visit the lake, walk or get a taxi from Nakuru to the main gate, and then try to hitch to the camp site. Once inside the park you'll need a vehicle to get around. You may get a ride with a safari vehicle (in which case you'll probably have to pay a share of the costs).

Alternatively, you can hire a taxi from Nakuru (about US$15 per hour), or go on a tour with an agency in town, such as **Pega Tours** (☎ 051-210379; pega@africaonline.co.ke; Mbua Gichua Rd; per car around US$90).

LAKE BOGORIA NATIONAL PARK

The bright turquoise expanse of the soda Lake Bogoria, 20km to Marigat, fringed with thousands of flamingos, stands out against a stark background of dry, barren hills. About 15km along the lakeshore from the park gate, a series of fearsome **hot springs** fling steaming water several feet into the air. Lake Bogoria is one of the few national parks in Kenya in which you're allowed to walk, and you're certain to see plenty of antelopes and buffalos as you hike along – you might even spot a rare greater kudu. The entry fee is US$15.

There's a basic camp site and a small local guesthouse at the park entrance gate. **Fig Tree Camp** (camp site per person US$8) at the far end of the lake is the most beautiful camp site in the park, and well worth the extra effort to get there. Both sites cost US$8 per person, and both have water and toilets.

To reach the park take a *matatu* to Marigat, then hitch or get a taxi to the Loboi park gate. From here, you can hike into the park, or wait for a lift. You're only allowed to hike alone as far as the hot springs – to go further you'll need special permission and an accompanying ranger.

LAKE BARINGO

Lake Baringo is freshwater, rather than a soda lake, so it's home to crocodiles and hippos as well as a mass of bird life – mak-

ing it one of the top bird-watching spots in East Africa. By far the best way to enjoy the lake is on an early morning boat trip, which can be organised at the camp site or with one of the numerous 'boat captains' touting for business. Take your camera – the boatmen throw bait into the air for diving fish eagles. Entry to the lake area costs US$3.

Roberts Campsite (☎ 051-51403; camp site per person/s/d US$4/7/14) Next to Lake Baringo Club on the lakeshore, this is the best budget place to stay. It has showers, toilets and a bar-restaurant, and can organise boat trips.

Buses and *matatus* run from Nakuru to Kampi ya Samaki, the nearest town to the lake, via Marigat (US$3, 2½ hours). Ask to be dropped off at Roberts Campsite.

CENTRAL KENYA

Central Kenya is truly a hiker's paradise. The slopes of Mt Kenya are the obvious challenge, but the little visited Aberdare National Park also offers fantastic trekking opportunities amid rolling moorland and stunning forest scenery.

MT KENYA NATIONAL PARK

Mt Kenya is Africa's second-highest mountain, and every bit as rewarding a trek as the better-known Kilimanjaro. Its gleaming snow-covered peaks, named after legendary Kikuyu spiritual leaders, can be seen for miles around until the late-morning clouds obscure the view. The mountain is so vast that it's easy to understand why the Kikuyu deified it, why their houses are built with the doors facing the peak and why it was probably never scaled until the arrival of European explorers.

Mt Kenya's highest peaks, Batian (5199m) and Nelion (5188m), can only be reached by mountaineers with technical skills. However, Point Lenana (4985m), the third-highest peak, can be reached by trekkers. The best times to go when you are more likely to have fair weather are from mid-January to late February and from late August to September. The park's entry fee for foreigners is US$15 per night.

Safety

Many trekkers do the ascent to Point Lenana much too quickly and end up suffering from headaches, nausea and sometimes more serious effects of altitude sickness.

Another problem can be the unpredictable weather; many go up the mountain without proper gear, unprepared for cold and wet conditions. Unless you're a regular mountain walker, and know how to use a map and compass, trekking anywhere other than the Naro Moru route without a competent companion or guide is asking for trouble.

In the last years, the final stretch of the ascent to Point Lenana has become quite dangerous, as the snow cover melts quickly and the exposed scree is steep and tricky to walk on. The best time to attempt it is early in the morning, when the stones are still frozen to the earth. In fact, most trekkers leave very early, and aim to be on the summit in time for sunrise.

Books & Maps

Before you leave Nairobi, try to buy a copy of *Mt Kenya 1:50,000 Map & Guide* by Mark Savage and Andrew Wielochowski. Keen trekkers looking for more informa-

tion should get hold of Lonely Planet's *Trekking in East Africa*.

Clothing & Equipment

You'll need a good sleeping bag (even if you're sleeping in the huts), warm clothes, a waterproof jacket (and over-trousers, if possible), a hat and gloves, a decent pair of boots or shoes, and some spare clothes (keep them dry during the day) and shoes or sandals to wear in the hut in the evening. You'll also need a water bottle (at least 1L), as well as water-purifying tablets and, ideally, a filter.

If you intend to camp, you'll obviously need a tent and items such as a stove and basic cooking equipment. Vegetation is protected within the park so lighting open fires is prohibited.

Surprisingly, mobile phones actually work on the mountain right up to the higher reaches, so if you have one, it could be useful to bring it in case of emergency (emergency number ☎ 999).

Trekking gear can be hired in Nairobi at Atul's (see p644) and from Mt Kenya Youth

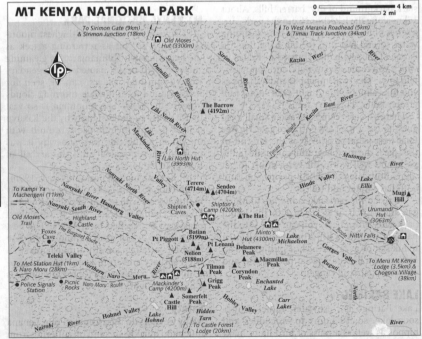

Hostel (see p650) or Naro Moru River Lodge (see p650), both beside the mountain.

Guides, Porters & Cooks

Licensed guides, porters and cooks can be organised at Mountain Rock Lodge, Mt Kenya Youth Hostel and the Mt Kenya Guides & Porters Safari Club (see below), all in or near Naro Moru village.

Guides charge around US$10 per day, while porters generally charge around US$6. These rates vary slightly according to the organisation you're using and the route you take. If you hire a local guide and/or porters, you'll have to pay their park entry fee (US$1.50 per person per night).

Organised Treks

The following are some of the more reliable outfits based in Naro Moru village:

KG Mountain Expeditions (☎ 062-62403; kgexpd@ arcc.org.ke)

Mt Kenya Guides & Porters Safari Club (☎ 062-62015; mtkguides@wananchi.com)

Mt Kenya Youth Hostel (☎ 062-62412; mtkenya hostel@wananchi.com)

Mountain Rock Kenya (☎ 062-62099; info@mountain rockkenya.com)

Trekking Mt Kenya

The three main routes from the lower slopes up to the summit area are the Naro Moru route, the Sirimon route and the Chogoria route. If you have trekking experience it's worth considering going up one route and down another. The details following are not enough for trekking safely on the mountain – they're just to get you started. If you're planning a trek, get full information from the sources listed above.

NARO MORU ROUTE

This is the most straightforward and popular route, with easy access on the southern side of the mountain. It's also the least scenic, though still a spectacular and enjoyable trail. Allow a minimum of four days return, or three days if you have transport between Naro Moru village and the Met Station Hut.

SIRIMON ROUTE

On the western side of the mountain, this is the least often used of the three main routes, but usually the driest. It's also the longest approach to Point Lenana, and involves some serious sections of trekking. If you're inexperienced in high mountain conditions, don't attempt to try this route without a local guide. Allow a minimum of five days return.

CHOGORIA ROUTE

This long route, on the eastern side of the mountain, is undoubtedly the most beautiful and certainly the easiest as far as gradients go. Facilities are limited, though, so it's ideal if you have a tent and some trekking experience. Allow five days return.

Sleeping & Eating

For details of places to stay before and after your trek, see the Naro Moru and Nanyuki sections, following.

There are many huts on the mountain, but not all are available to the general public. Several are owned by the Mountain Club of Kenya (MCK) and a few are reserved exclusively for use by members, while other huts can be used by the public but – apart from the recently refurbished **Austrian Hut** (US$14 per person), most are in bad condition. **MCK huts** (US$3 per person) can be booked either at the **MCK clubhouse** (☎ 020-501747; PO Box 4574, Nairobi) or **Let's Go Travel** (☎ 020-340331; info@letsgosafari.com) in Nairobi, or the Naro Moru River Lodge. There are also several bunkhouses along each route.

Camping may be a better option. Officially you can camp anywhere on the mountain, but it's usual to camp near one of the huts or bunkhouses, where there is often a water supply. Camping for trekkers costs US$8 per person per night.

Getting There & Away

For the Naro Moru route, the starting point is Naro Moru village, where there's a prominent signpost pointing to the Naro Moru park gate. There is an infrequent *matatu* from Naro Moru to Kiambuthi, 3km from the park gate. Otherwise from Naro Moru village to the park gate is an 18km walk. Look on it as a warm-up!

For the Sirimon route, take a *matatu* from Nanyuki towards Timau; the start of the route is signposted on the right about 15km northeast of Nanyuki. From the junction it's a 9km walk to the park gate.

To get to the Chogoria route, all *matatus* and buses between Embu and Meru stop at

KENYA

Chogoria village. From there, it's a 30km
uphill walk through the forest to the park
gate (although in Chogoria village you will
be able to hire Land Rovers to carry you up
this section).

For transport details to/from Naro Moru
and Nanyuki, see following.

NARO MORU
☎ 062

Naro Moru is a dusty little village on the
western side of Mt Kenya, but it's the most
popular starting point for treks up the
mountain, via the Naro Moru route.

Mt Kenya Youth Hostel (☎ 62412; mtkenyahost
el@wananchi.com; camp site per person/dm/d US$3/4/8)
A great place to arrange a trek or meet up
with a group, this very well equipped and
friendly hostel has a log fire in the sitting
room, and a bar. Meals can be ordered, or
there's a kitchen. It's 7km from Naro Moru
village on the track towards the park gate. To
get here, take a *matatu* towards the national
park gate and ask to be dropped off at the
hostel, or ring in advance for a pick-up.

Mountain Rock Lodge (☎ 62099; info@mountain
rockkenya.com; camp site per person US$5) About 7km
north of Naro Moru, the beautiful camp
site at this upmarket hotel has toilets, hot
water, firewood and cooking facilities. The
lodge is 1km off the main road, so if you're
coming by *matatu* from Nairobi, stay on at
Naro Moru village and ask the driver to drop
you at the lodge gates – easy to spot on the
right-hand side of the road as you're heading
north. The lodge may be 7km from the village but it's easy to reach by *matatu*.

Naro Moru River Lodge (☎ 62211; mtkenya@africa
online.co.ke; camp site per person /dm US$5/7) Another
very upmarket hotel, but with a curiously
scruffy camp site – although it does have
hot showers and toilet facilities. To get
there hire a taxi from the village (US$3) or
walk the relatively flat 3km.

Any bus or *matatu* travelling between
Nairobi and Nanyuki and Isiolo stops here.

NANYUKI
☎ 062 / pop 42,000

Prosperous and vaguely colonial in feel, the
small town of Nanyuki is the base for treks
up Mt Kenya using the Sirimon route. For
camp-food supplies and arguably the best
vegetable samosas in Kenya, head to Settlers Store on the main street. There's also

an ATM at the Standard Chartered Bank in
the town centre.

Nanyuki River Lodge (camp site per person/s/d with
private bathroom US$3.50/6/8) The camp site here
has a rustic feel, with cows grazing by the
river. The rooms are big and well furnished,
and there's a lively bar-disco and restaurant.
A pool is under construction, and there are
also plans for an Internet café. If this place
improves with the planned renovations it
will be lovely, but at the moment it's all
slightly haphazard, and the curio sellers,
guides and hustlers around the entrance are
very off-putting.

Sportsman's Arms (☎ 32347; Kenyatta Dr; info@
sportsmansarms.com; camp site per person US$5) This
upmarket hotel allows camping in a small
field next door, with hot showers, toilets and
a kitchen for self-catering. You can also hire
four-person tents with bedding for US$14.
Disconcertingly, the restaurant's stock of
goats shares the camp site. They are tethered
so that diners can inspect them, and then
pick one to become *nyama choma*…

Jambo House Hotel (☎ 31894; s/d US$3.50/6)
Right next to the *matatu* stage, this is a bog-
standard lodging with a noisy bar on the
first floor.

Nanyuki Guesthouse (☎ 31596; s/d US$3/4) The
cheapest of the lot, with comfortable enough
rooms despite the forbidding exterior. It's
1km from town on the Nyahururu Rd.

Matatus leave regularly for Nairobi (US$3,
2½ hours) and for all regional towns, such as
Nyahururu (US$3, 2½ hours).

ABERDARE NATIONAL PARK
Aberdare National Park has some spectacular highland-style scenery and is prime hiking country, with rocky gorges, waterfalls,
thick bamboo forests and mist-shrouded
moors. If you're lucky, you may unzip
your tent in the morning to see a line of elephants moving silently through the frosty
grass. If you're a true wilderness fan, it's
an excellent alternative to Mt Kenya for a
trekking and camping trip. The park entry
fee is US$30.

You can get to the park without your own
transport – take a taxi from the nearby town
of Nyeri to the Ruhurini Gate, just 11km
away (US$7). From here, you can camp at
the gate (US$10). The rangers can provide
firewood and water, but you must bring all
your food with you. You can safely leave

your stuff at the gate and do day hikes into the park, but you must take an armed ranger as a guide (US$7 for a half day, available at the gate) and also as protection in case you run into one of those elephants. For longer trips, there are several camp sites (US$10) in the park, but again you must arrange for an armed ranger to come with you.

NYAHURURU
☎ 065 / pop 25,300
Nyahururu, often called Thomson's Falls or 'T-Falls', the name given to the town by the British. The 72m-high **waterfall**, just off the main road about 1km north of the town centre, is the highest in Kenya. It's not as spectacular as you might expect though – a few of the waterfalls in the nearby Aberdare National Park are much more impressive.

Thomson's Falls Lodge (☎ 22006; camp site per person US$4) The falls are practically in the grounds of this upmarket hotel, which has a decent camp site around the back. The site has superbly hot and powerful showers, the cosy lounge and bar both have log fires, and meals in the restaurant start at about US$3. Get here by following the signs from the centre of town, or take a *matatu*.

Equator Lodge (☎ 32748; s/d US$4.50/8) Up the road from Barclays Bank, the Equator has dark but smart rooms behind a big restaurant.

Nyahururu Stadium Hotel (☎ 32772; s/d US$4/7) Located behind the stadium, this is a friendly and clean lodging but the beds are a bit saggy.

Matatus run from Nyahururu to Nakuru (US$1.50, one hour), Nanyuki (US$3, two hours) and Nyeri (US$2, one hour).

NORTHERN KENYA

The vast, arid regions of the north have always represented something of a frontier for Kenya travellers. Hard to reach, harder still to get around, this is an area that requires time, resilience and a taste for adventure.

ISIOLO
☎ 064 / pop 39,600
Isiolo is the gateway to northeastern Kenya, a vast expanse of mountains, deserts and scrub that's home to the Samburu, Rendille, Boran and Turkana peoples. This lively town is also a vital pit stop on the route towards the Ethiopian border, and is a good place to stock up on petrol, and food if you're self-catering. It's also the last place with Internet access if you're heading north.

Range Land Hotel (☎ 52340; camp site per person/d US$3/14) A few kilometres south of Isiolo along the main road, this has a big camping area and a few well-equipped stone cottages. There's also a decent restaurant and a bar.

Jamhuri Guest House (☎ 52065; s/d US$2/4) Just west of the main road, this is a basic lodging providing clean rooms with mosquito net. The café next door serves snacks and drinks.

One bus and several *matatus* go daily to Nairobi (US$4.50, four hours), via Nanyuki (US$2, two hours). Irregular trucks to Marsabit (US$6, seven hours) leave from the northern end of the main street. If you're heading to the Ethiopian border at Moyale, you'll need to stop in Marsabit first to establish if this route is currently safe.

MARALAL
☎ 065 / pop 21,100
Maralal is a rough and ready frontier-style place, with something of a Wild West atmosphere – in place of a rodeo, the whole town goes racing mad for the annual **Camel Derby**, a huge event usually held between June and October.

Yare Club & Camp (☎ 62295; yare@africaonline.co.ke; camp site per person/s/d US$3/15/23) Three kilometres south of central Maralal, this perennially popular place has camping, or you can stay in wooden *bandas* (thatched-roof huts) with their own bathroom. There's a bar and restaurant on site, and camel safaris can be arranged.

Jadana Guest House (☎ 62033; s/d with private bathroom US$3.50/6) In central Maralal, this place is very good value.

Minibuses regularly ply the route between Maralal and Nyahururu (US$3.50, three hours). There is also a fairly regular bus to Nairobi (US$6, eight hours), and a bus every other day to Isiolo (US$7, seven hours). Occasional trucks also go to Loyangalani on Lake Turkana.

KENYA

MARSABIT

☎ 069

The forested hills around the town of Marsabit stand in stark contrast to the surrounding desert plains and make the whole area an excellent spot for a bit of hiking. The main attraction of the area is **Marsabit National Park**. The park is dominated by the peak of Mt Marsabit, whose forests are home to good numbers of elephants and plentiful bird species. The park entry fee is US$15. This area is sometimes deemed unsafe for travel – check before heading out.

In the town itself, immigrant Somalis and Ethiopians mix with colourfully dressed Rendille tribespeople.

JeyJey Centre (s/d US$3/4), the biggest building in town, has decent rooms with a shared bathroom. Diku's Complex and Tulla's, next door to each other just along the road, both offer standard rooms for the same price.

If you want to stay overnight in the national park, and you're in a group, you can camp at a beautiful spot next to **Lake Paradise** (camp site per person US$15, set-up fee per group US$67). Otherwise, there's a public camp site (US$8) near the main entrance gate.

All vehicles (including buses) travelling between Isiolo and Marsabit, and Marsabit and Moyale on the Ethiopian border, must travel in convoy or carry an armed guard. Buses and trucks run irregularly from Marsabit to Isiolo (US$6, seven hours). The truck journey to Moyale on the Ethiopian border should take a day, but check this route is currently safe before setting off.

LAKE TURKANA

Formerly known as Lake Rudolf, and nowadays often evocatively called the 'Jade Sea', the expanse of Lake Turkana stretches all the way to Ethiopia. High salt levels render the sandy, volcanic area around the lake almost entirely barren, but in the water itself there's life in the form of the area's notorious giant crocodiles.

The two volcanic islands situated in the lake, **Central Island** and **South Island**, are both national parks (entry fee US$15) and are good places to watch crocodiles. To get there you can hire a boat from Ferguson's Gulf (for Central Island) or Loyangalani (for South Island).

Accommodation is available in various small settlements on the eastern and west-

ern shores of the lake, but most are inaccessible without a lucky hitch or a private vehicle.

At Ferguson's Gulf on the west side of the lake, **Lake Turkana Lodge** (☎ 020-760226; camp site per person US$10) has very limited facilities, but there's a bar and meals are available.

In Lodwar, southeast of the lake, the **New Suburb Tourist Lodge** (s/d US$4/6) east of the crossroads in the centre of town provides basic lodging.

At Loyangalani on the west shore of Turkana, **El-Molo Camp** (camp site per person US$3) is a shaded camp site with a swimming pool fed directly from a hot spring.

Mosaretu Camp, next door to the upmarket Oasis Lodge, is run by a local women's group and has accommodation in traditional huts (for around US$3).

Getting There & Away

A visit to the lake without your own transport will require huge reserves of time and patience. If you do decide to travel up to Turkana independently, you are probably better heading up the western side of the lake via Lodwar, as there's better transport on this route. Even if you usually object to organised travel, you might be better off visiting on an overland safari from Nairobi. And one last point – as logical as it might look on a map, going via Lake Turkana is not a route that can be used to get to Ethiopia, as the border crossing area at Fort Banya isn't safe for travellers.

LOCAL TRANSPORT

The best launch-pad for Turkana transport is the town of Kitale, northwest of Nairobi via Eldoret. *Matatus* and trucks travel daily from Kitale to Lodwar (US$8, five hours), the main settlement on the western side of the lake but still about 40km from the shore itself. From Lodwar you can take a *matatu* or hitch to Kalokol, and then pick up a lift or walk (1½ hours) to Ferguson's Gulf on the lakeshore.

Along the eastern side of the lake to Loyangalani, scheduled transport of any kind is very rare once you get beyond Maralal, and nonexistent beyond Baragoi, so you'll have to wait for a lift on a local truck – a process that could easily take three days of waiting and another two days of travel (expect to pay around US$10). With a huge dose of luck, you may find a ride with one of the very occasional adventurous tourists who might come this far in a rental 4WD.

TOURS
By far the most straightforward way to visit Lake Turkana is on the **Turkana Bus** (☎ 020-891348; safaricamp@kenyaweb.com) run by Safari Camp Services in Nairobi. This is actually an overland truck that departs once a month and passes through Nakuru, Nyahururu and Maralal on the way to Loyangalani on the eastern lakeshore, with a visit to Samburu Buffalo Springs National Reserve on the way back. Accommodation is in camp sites and equipment is provided. Prices are around US$500 for a nine-day round trip. Safari Camp Services can also organise **camel treks** (you walk, the camel carries your bags) as part of the Turkana Bus trip.

WESTERN KENYA

Western Kenya's main attraction is the Masai Mara National Reserve, site of the spectacular wildebeest migration and the best place in Kenya to see big cats. Further off the beaten track lie the sleepy lakeside town of Kisumu and the biologically rich Kakamega Forest.

KISUMU
☎ 057 / pop 275,000
Kisumu is Kenya's third-largest town, but it's something of a backwater, sweltering gently on the humid shores of Lake Victoria. There's virtually no tourist trade, which makes it a quiet and relaxing place in which to spend time. It has elegant colonial facades, tree-lined streets and genuinely friendly locals. Shops, banks and an Internet café are clustered around the attractive square in the centre of town.

Sleeping
Lodgers' Palace (☎ 21094; Paul Mbuya Rd; s/d US$4/5) Basic, but friendly and central. The big, quiet rooms have mosquito net and fan. There's a decent café downstairs.

YWCA (☎ 43192; Angawa Ave; dm/s/d US$3.50/4/8) A bit institutionlike, but handy for the bus station. There's a garden, meals are available and some rooms have their own bathroom.

New Victoria Hotel (☎ 21067; newvictoriahotel@ africaonline.co.ke; Gor Mahia St; s/d US$8/14) A bit grander than most budget hotels in Kisumu. Rooms have fan and mosquito net, and there's a good Indian restaurant in the same building.

Mona Lisa (☎ 45058; Oginga Odinga Rd; s/d US$3/4) Excellent position behind the restaurant of the same name, right on the central town square. It's cheap, but the rooms are drab and depressing.

Eating & Drinking
Kenshop Bakery (Oginga Odinga Rd; snacks US$2) and **Kenshop Internet Café** (Oginga Odinga Rd; snacks US$2) both sell fresh bread. The Internet café also has a good range of light meals and serves fantastic filled rolls (with real cheese – exciting if you've just come from dairy-free Tanzania!).

Kimwa Annex Café (off Oginga Odinga Rd; mains US$3) serves up cheap local food.

Getting There & Away
Train services to and from Kisumu have ceased, but there are buses to points all over Kenya. The bus station is just north of the town centre – it's a fairly easy walk, but there are also plenty of *boda-bodas* (bicycle taxis) whose riders will struggle manfully with your luggage if required. Buses, *matatus* and shared taxis go from Kisumu to Isebania on the Tanzanian border (US$6, five hours), Busia on the Ugandan border (US$2.50, 1½ hours), Nairobi (US$7, six hours), Kakamega (US$1.50, 45 minutes) and Eldoret (US$2, two hours).

ELDORET
☎ 053 / pop 250,000
Eldoret is a prosperous and bustling agricultural town with little to detain the visitor apart from a luscious **dairy** selling yogurt, ice cream and different kinds of cheese.

Sleeping
Mahindi Hotel (☎ 31520; Uganda Rd; s/d US$4/8) Handy for the bus station, with small but clean rooms. Some rooms have their own bathroom. The only problem is that there are no mosquito nets, or anywhere to hang one. Try to get a room on the 2nd floor – it's quieter. Big restaurant and bar.

Aya Inn (Oginga Odinga Rd; s/d US$6/8) Clean and friendly, with a lively bar and restaurant. Handy for local bars and restaurants – and discos, if you're up for a night out...

KENYA

Eldoret Lincoln Hotel (mobile ☎ 0722 247032; Oloo Rd; s/d with private bathroom & breakfast US$8/11) A vaguely colonial place, with big rooms and hot water. There's also a courtyard café.

Naiberi River Campsite (☎ 61195; campsite@ africaonline.co.ke; camp site per person/dm/d US$3/7/20) This is an extremely laid-back camp site, popular with partying overland trucks and a great place to meet other travellers. It's about 20km southeast of town – if you need a lift, ring the owner, Raj (☎ 32644) before 5pm Monday to Friday.

Eating & Drinking

'Come share our passion for food!' says the sign outside **Croydon Hotel** (Uganda St; mains US$2). Inside you'll find less passion and more porridge, toasted sandwiches and stews. Further along, **Otto Café** (Uganda St) and **Sizzlers** (Kenyatta St) serve up much the same sort of menu.

For more healthy options, **Doinyo Lessos Dairy** (☎ 63308; Kenyatta St), just outside the town centre, has cheese, ice cream and yogurt. To get here, walk straight over the roundabout at the bottom of Kenyatta St. You're allowed to taste the cheese before you buy, but the minimum amount is 250g.

Getting There & Away

Buses, *matatus* and shared taxis run from Eldoret's central bus station off Uganda Rd to Nairobi (US$4, 3½ hours), Kisumu (US$2, two hours), Nakuru (US$2, two hours) and Malaba on the Ugandan border (US$2, 1½ hours). Akamba buses also run to Kampala (US$10, six hours), leaving from next to the mosque on Arap Moi St.

KAKAMEGA FOREST

The Kakamega Forest, about 40km northeast of Kisumu, is a superb slab of virgin tropical rainforest in the heart of an intensively cultivated agricultural area. It is home to a huge variety of birds and animals, including the rare De Brazza's monkey. It is also an incredibly peaceful place to walk or to just chill out among the trees.

The forest has two sections, roughly east and north of the small town of Kakamega. There is no entry fee at present, although plans are afoot to introduce a charge of around US$6.

Forest Rest House (camp site per person/s/d US$2/5/10) A beautiful wooden house built on stilts in the heart of the forest, the rest house has a lovely camp site with showers and toilets, or your can stay in one of the house's four rooms. Guides for forest walks are always available, and you can probably find someone at the guide station to cook for you, if needed. To get here, take a *matatu* from Kakamega to Shinyalu, then hike or take a *boda-boda* (bicycle taxi) for the 8km into the forest.

Udo's Bandas & Campsite (☎ 20425; camp site per person/s/d US$2/10/20) A neat and well-kept place run by the Kenya Wildlife Service (KWS), with basic showers and toilets. To get here, take a *matatu* from Kakamega towards Kitale and ask to be dropped by the sign for the KWS. It's about a 2km walk from here.

MASAI MARA NATIONAL RESERVE

Virtually everyone who visits Kenya goes to the Masai Mara – and with good reason. The rolling plains are the Kenyan section of the Serengeti ecosystem, and the wildlife-watching opportunities are really second to none, particularly if you're looking to see big cats. The only downside is that as a result of the area's fame, tourist vehicles occasionally look as though they're set to outnumber the animals. Up to 20 Land Cruisers jostling for position around a torpid lion is not an unusual sight, particularly in the high season.

The highlight of the Mara is undoubtedly the annual wildebeest migration in July and August. Over a million of the comical-looking beasts, accompanied by zebras and antelopes, stream north from Tanzania in search of fresh pastures, before heading south again around October. The migration doesn't happen at exactly the same time every year, but it's well worth making the effort to see it, if you can. Decent safari companies in Nairobi (see p664) should be keeping track of the migration's progress and can tell you roughly where it is.

The three main gates are Talek Gate, on the road from Lemek; Sekenani Gate, along the road from Narok and Nairobi; and Oloolaimutiek Gate, on the road from Bakitabu. The park headquarters are near Sekenani Gate. The entry fee is US$30.

Sleeping & Eating

There is no budget accommodation within the reserve. To avoid the top prices at the upmarket lodges and tented camps, pitch

THE MAASAI

According to historian Charles Miller, 'During the 19th century, the Maasai were to East Africa what the Apache were to the southwestern United States'. Since their arrival in Kenya in the 17th century, the tribe who considered themselves the 'master race' had been conducting a series of scorched-earth campaigns as far afield as Mombasa. This was mostly to capture the cattle that they believed had been given to them by God at the beginning of time, and that other tribes had therefore 'stolen'.

A Maasai warrior, or *moran*, was a fighting machine, over 1.8m tall, armed with a buffalo-hide shield, a double-edged sword and a 2.4m spear, and 'totally impervious to physical pain ever since the day he stood erect and watched expressionlessly as his foreskin was flayed from his penis in the ceremony that elevated him from teenager to soldier', Mr Miller explains.

Today the Maasai have lost their traditional lands to the Masai Mara National Reserve (in return for 19% of the entry fees), and Maasai doctors, lawyers and government officials carry briefcases instead of spears. Despite this, the fearsome fighting reputation and colourful traditional costume of the *moran*, once calculated to instil fear in enemies, have persisted and are now used (both by the Maasai and government advertising campaigns) to attract the tourist trade.

your tent in a camp site just outside any of the gates for about US$3 per person. Alternatively, stay in one of several budget hotels in Narok, 69km away.

One of the better public camp sites is **Oloolaimutiek Camp Site** (camp site per person US$3.50), about 2km north of the gate of the same name. The best of the bunch near the Talek gate is the Maasai-run **Riverside Camp** (☎ 22128; camp site per person US$4), which has some permanent tents – some with bathroom and cooking facilities – from US$13 per person. Take care of your valuables when staying at these sites, as thefts have been reported.

Getting There & Away

There is no public transport to or within the reserve, but if you're patient and lucky you might be able to hitch a ride with other tourists from Narok (though be prepared to share the costs of the vehicle). However, the easiest way of seeing the reserve is on an organised safari from Nairobi (see p664).

THE COAST

At its best the coast of Kenya is a fantastic introduction to the eventful history of the Indian Ocean and a great place to immerse yourself in the culture of the Swahili – a coastal civilisation with a very distinctive way of life. Elegant old towns, sparkling beaches and spicy seafood are all best experienced away from the package-holiday atmosphere of the bigger resorts.

MOMBASA

☎ 041 / pop 700,000

Mombasa is Kenya's second-largest city, and the most important port in East Africa. For centuries, the old town and the harbour were the settings for desperate battles for control of the city (and thus of the entire Indian Ocean coastline), mostly fought between the Portuguese and the Omani Arabs.

Despite this bloody history, today's Mombasa is a far more laid-back place than the capital, Nairobi. This is largely due to the relaxed Swahili culture of the inhabitants, which renders the city closer in character to places such as Zanzibar or Lamu than to the brash towns of Kenya's interior.

Most of the population is Muslim, so modest dress is appreciated.

In November 2002, 10 Kenyans and three Israeli tourists were killed in a car bomb attack on the Paradise Hotel near Mombasa. Responsibility for the attack was claimed by the Al-Qaeda network.

Orientation

The bulk of the town sprawls over Mombasa Island, connected to the mainland by a causeway that carries the rail and road links, and by the Likoni ferry to the south. To get into town from the airport, take a taxi or walk the 1km to the *matatu* stop. From here, *matatu* run into town, stopping on Moi Ave. Alternatively, a taxi all the way will cost US$8.

Long-distance buses from Nairobi stop at various points up Jomo Kenyatta Ave, while

KENYA

buses from Malindi or Lamu stop on Abdel Nasser Rd. From either place, it's about 3km into the town centre (around Moi Ave and Digo Rd).

If you're arriving by train, the station is on Mwembe Tayari Rd, about 1km from the town centre.

An excellent landmark, to avoid getting lost when walking around Mombasa, is the 'tusks' – an enormous pair of steel elephant tusks that straddle Moi Ave on the outskirts of the town centre.

Information
INTERNET ACCESS
There are Internet cafés scattered liberally around Mombasa's town centre. The latest

craze appears to be fast food joints that also offer Internet and telephone services, so you can phone home, surf the net and eat greasy burgers at the same time. See p657 for listings.

MONEY
There are two branches of Barclays Bank in the city centre, both with ATMs. For cash or travellers cheques, try the many bureaux de change along Moi Ave.

TOURIST OFFICES
The **Mombasa Information Bureau** (☎ 311231; Moi Ave) next to the tusks has excellent information about transport, sights and hotels in Mombasa. These are the best people to

MOMBASA

0 ————————— 400 m
0 ————————— 0.2 mi

INFORMATION		SLEEPING	☐ p657	TRANSPORT	pp657–8
Akamba Office	1 A3	Berachah Hotel	9 B4	Air Kenya	(see 33)
Barclays Bank (ATM)	2 C4	Evening Guest House	10 A4	Buses & Matatus to Malindi	21 B2
Barclays Bank (ATM)	3 B3	Excellent Hotel	11 B3	Buses to Arusha & Moshi	22 B3
Fort Jesus Forex Bureau	4 D4	Lucky Guesthouse	12 A3	Buses to Dar es Salaam & Tanga	23 B3
Internet Café	(see 14)			Busscar Office	(see 26)
Mombasa Area Library	5 B4	EATING	☐ p657	Busstar Office	24 C3
Mombasa Information Bureau	6 A4	Baron Restaurant & Pub	13 D4	Coastline Safaris Office	25 A3
Mwembe Tayari Health Centre	(see 22)	Blue Room	14 B4	Falcon Office	26 C2
Telkom Kenya	7 B4	HD's Restaurant	15 B4	Gulf Air	27 C4
Telkom Kenya	8 C4	Mombasa Coffee House	16 A4	Interstate 2000 Office	28 B2
		Pistachio	17 B4	Kenya Airways	29 B4
		Rozina House Restaurant &		Matatus to Ferry	30 B4
		Café	18 A4	Matatus to Voi & Wundanyi	31 A3
		Splendid View Café	19 B4	Mombasa Raha (Mombasa Liners)	
				Office	32 A3
		DRINKING	☐ p657	Regional Air	33 B4
		Casablanca Restaurant & Club	20 A4	Scandinavian Express Office	34 C2
				TSS Express Office	35 C3

consult if you want to book a safari to nearby Tsavo National Park – they keep a list of recommended operators.

Sights

If you have any interest at all in the history of the East African coast, **Fort Jesus** (admission US$3; 🕑 8am-6.30pm), begun in 1593, is a must. The walls of the fort enclose a small museum that has a collection of objects salvaged from ships wrecked in the harbour. Objects include Chinese ceramic plates, glass perfume bottles and Persian chests dating back centuries. Outside there's an exhumed skeleton, a reminder of the fort's violent history. The inscription over the gate is especially chilling – a proud litany of the 'executions' and 'chastisements' inflicted on the locals by a past Portuguese commander.

Mombasa's **Old Town**, north of Fort Jesus, isn't really all that old – most of the houses were built in the last 100 years or so. But a stroll around this part of the town is a worthwhile introduction to the general architecture of the Swahili coast. Along the way you'll find plenty of characteristic **carved doors** and lacy fretwork **balconies** in among the narrow streets.

Sleeping

None of the budget options in Mombasa are much to write home about, but all have fan and mosquito net (essential in the boiling, mosquito-ridden hot season) unless otherwise stated.

Evening Guesthouse (🕾 221380; Mnanzi Moja Rd; s/d US$7/10) Cool, peaceful rooms in a quiet building. Don't be put off by the prisonlike wall outside.

Lucky Guesthouse (Shibu Rd; d US$7) Rooms have fan, but no mosquito net. The lively Mahaba bar and restaurant next door promises 'tension relieving activities'…so keep your door locked.

Excellent Hotel (🕾 227683; Haile Selassie Rd; s/d with private bathroom & breakfast US$10/14) 'Average hotel' might be a more appropriate name.

Berachah Hotel (🕾 224106; cnr Haile Selassie & Digo Rds; s/d with private bathroom US$6/8) Noisy, basic, but just about hygienic. Fan but no mosquito net.

YWCA (🕾 312846; ywcamsa@wananchi.com; Vanga Rd; s/d US$6/10) The usual basic hostel rooms, with a cafeteria for cheap meals.

Eating & Drinking

If you've just arrived on the coast, Mombasa is a good place to get acquainted with delicious Swahili cuisine. The best place is at **Recoda Restaurant** (Moi Ave; mains US$3), just past the crossed tusks. Here you can gorge on biryani and pilau curries with meat or fish, accompanied by coconut rice and fresh juice.

For an injection of Western food, you can pig out at one of the many Italian-style joints set up to catch the tourist market.

Pistachio (Maungano Rd; lunch US$4.50) and **Rozina House Restaurant** (Moi Ave; lunch US$4.50) both have pasta buffets and ice cream at lunch time. There's also a smaller **café** next door to Rozina selling snacks.

Baron Restaurant (Digo Rd; mains US$4) and **Splendid View Café** (Maungano Rd; mains US$4.50) both combine rather pretentious restaurants with garrulous beer halls, but the food is certainly edible and these are good places to meet locals.

If you'd rather chat with friends from home, **Blue Room** (Haile Selassie Rd; mains US$2), **HD's Restaurant** (Maungano Rd; mains US$2) and **Mombasa Coffee House** (Moi Ave; mains US$2) all provide Internet access to go with your chicken and chips. If you're lucky, you might get a free juice.

Casablanca Restaurant & Club (Mnanzi Moja Rd) is the place to go if you're after a night on the town. It has two floors of alcohol, music, table football and a plethora of overdressed local girls.

Getting There & Around

AIR

Kenya Airways (🕾 221251; Moi Ave) has daily flights to Nairobi for around US$80 one way, but at US$53, **Regional Air** (🕾 020-311623; Nkrumah Rd) is cheapest. **Air Kenya** (🕾 229777; Moi Ave) also has daily flights to Nairobi and flies most days to Lamu (US$100).

BOAT

It is theoretically possible to travel to Zanzibar or Pemba by dhow, but you must first sign an indemnity and get it stamped at the District Commissioner's office. A trip to Zanzibar should cost about US$30 and the journey in a dhow with a motor should take around 16 hours. Look for dhow captains around Fort Jesus or down by the harbour, but remember that dhows are cargo boats not designed for passengers – make sure you take all food and water with you.

KENYA

LOCAL TRANSPORT

To Nairobi (US$7, seven hours) buses leave from outside the bus company offices along Jomo Kenyatta Ave. Scandinavian Express is the best bus service, followed by Akamba, Mombasa Liners and Coast Bus.

Buses and *matatus* to Malindi (US$1.50, two hours) and Lamu (US$8, seven hours) leave from outside the New People's Hotel, on Abdel Nasser Rd. If going to Lamu, book ahead at one of the bus offices along Abdel Nasser Rd (try to get a window seat – they're more comfortable). Check with the tourist office whether the journey is currently safe – there have been recent incidents of armed robbery along this road.

Buses to Tanga (US$8, seven hours) leave from Jomo Kenyatta Ave. You can also catch *matatus* to Voi, Arusha and Moshi from here.

To get to the beaches south of Mombasa, take a Likoni-bound *matatu* from outside the post office on Digo Rd. Then simply walk on to the frequent (and free) Likoni ferry from Mombasa Island to the southern mainland, and catch another *matatu* to the south.

TRAIN

The train to Nairobi leaves Mombasa at 7pm every day, arriving the next morning. Fares are US$40/28/5 for 1st/2nd/3rd class. Make a reservation as far in advance as possible at the train station **booking office** (☎ 312220).

TIWI BEACH

Tiwi, about 20km south of the Likoni ferry, is a sweep of stunning beach that hasn't yet been spoilt by the package-tourist hotels that plague some other parts of the Kenyan coast. It's definitely a good place to head if you're looking for something a bit quieter than the tourist centres of Watamu and Malindi. To get here take a *matatu* from the far side of the Likoni ferry, then ask to be dropped off at the Tiwi Beach road junction. From here, it's a long and potentially dangerous walk (there have been numerous robberies in the area), so take a taxi to Tiwi itself. Buses to and from the Tanzanian border will also drop you off at the Tiwi junction.

Twiga Lodge (☎ 51257; camp site per person/s/d US$2/8/16) An old standby that's looking a bit scruffy these days, Twiga is still the place to

head if you're camping or on your own. It's smack on the beach, and the restaurant serves cheap seafood. Prices are very negotiable.

Coral Cove Cottages (☎ 51295; d US$14) Next door to Twiga Lodge and much smarter, Coral Cove has cottages, a rondavel and a bedsit, all beautifully decorated. Food is not provided, but there's an outside cooking area or you can eat in the Twiga restaurant. Coral Cove is a top choice if you're in a group.

MALINDI

☎ 042 / pop 46,800

If you're keen to get off the beaten track, Malindi may not be the place for you. The centre of Kenya's early tourist boom, the town has become a mecca for package tourists, many from Italy. There are some decent beaches not far away, but they are mostly the domain of the big hotels.

Malindi Marine National Park

This marine park, about 4.5km south of Malindi town centre, has an amazing variety of coral and fish. Boat trips cost about US$10 per person (if there are six passengers), which includes snorkelling gear and transport to/from the marine park – but not the park entry fee (US$5). Boat owners may approach you in the streets of Malindi about a trip to the park, or else you can ask at your hotel. Neighbouring Watamu also adjoins the National Park, so you may find it easier to arrange a snorkelling trip there.

Sleeping

Gilani's (☎ 0722 646872; Beach Rd; s/d US$8/16) The upstairs rooms at Gilani's are brightly painted and breezy, with four-poster beds, balcony and their own bathroom. There are some cheaper and dingier rooms downstairs. There's an attractive seafood restaurant on the ground floor.

Silver Sands Campsite (☎ 0733 802929; Beach Rd; camp site per person/d US$2/6) Two kilometres from town, Silver Sands is right on the beach, but the camping area is small and hot and the *bandas* (thatched-roof huts) are tiny. There's no real kitchen – just a corner for campfires – although there's a local restaurant nearby.

Dagama's (☎ 31942; Beach Rd; s/d US$7/10) More basic than Gilani's, but the rooms are light and some have fan. The restaurant downstairs serves decent food.

Eating

Many of Malindi's restaurants feature Italian signboards and menus, and serve only pasta and pizza. For cheap local food, check the streets closest to the market. But if you feel like a splurge, there are a couple of very classy restaurants down on the beach road.

The Old Man & the Sea (☎ 31106; Beach Rd; mains US$8) has beautiful decor and unusual food – try the smoked sailfish. Just along the road is **I Love Pizza** (☎ 20672; mains US$8), which is also expensive, but much posher than its name suggests and the pizza is excellent. **Gilani's** (Beach Rd; mains US$5) is the best-value place for seafood.

In town, **Stars & Garters** (☎ 31336; Lamu Rd; mains US$5) has an outdoor café that gets very lively in the evening. Even busier is **Palm Garden Restaurant** (☎ 20115; Harambee Ave; mains US$4), which serves relatively cheap, very good Indian food.

Getting There & Away

Buses run from the central market area to Mombasa (US$1.50, two hours) and Lamu (US$4, eight hours). If you want to avoid the long bus journey, you can fly from Malindi to Lamu (see p663 for details). *Matatus* run all day to Watamu (US$0.50, one hour).

WATAMU

☎ 042

An hour's *matatu* ride south of Malindi, Watamu is a bit cheaper and quieter than Malindi (although there are still no budget hotels on the beach) and is also an Italian resort village. The eerie and extensive **Gedi ruins** about 4km north of Watamu are a mystery – they're not mentioned in any Portuguese or Arab chronicles of the time. From Watamu, take a *matatu* to Gedi village; the ruins are about a 1km (signposted) walk.

Snorkelling trips to the coral reef that forms part of the **Malindi Marine National Park** can be organised in the village, or with one of the beach hotels. Prices are fairly fixed – US$15 per person for a shared boat, plus a national park fee of US$5.

Sleeping

Hotel Dante (☎ 32243; s/d with private bathroom US$4.50/10) Definitely the best of the village cheapies, with well-decorated rooms and a big restaurant. If you buy your own food in the village, they'll cook it here for you.

Villa Veronica (☎ 32083; s/d US$6.5/10.50), also known as Mwikali Lodge, offers basic doubles with fan and mosquito net, but has very grubby bathrooms.

Beach View Guesthouse (☎ 32383; d with private bathroom US$16) Spick-and-span German-run homestay, with a pool and self-catering kitchen. The rooms are beautifully furnished and have a small kitchen.

Getting There & Away

Matatus run all day to Malindi (US$0.50, one hour). If you want to get the bus to Mombasa, it may be better to go into Malindi first, as the buses that pass on the main road are always stuffed full. *Matatus* leave from the central market in Malindi.

LAMU

☎ 042

Lamu town is best seen from one of its many rooftops, sipping a juice in the faint breeze and gazing over a jumble of roofs, minarets and latticed balconies as donkeys pick their way along the impossibly narrow streets down below. A couple of days in Lamu generally turns into a couple of weeks as the infectious lethargy of the island sets in. After all, what have you really got to do that's more urgent than sipping black coffee and gossiping with the dhow captains on the waterfront, or heading to the beach at Shela to float in the crystal clear green water?

Orientation

If you arrive in Lamu by plane, you'll arrive on Manda Island opposite the town. A boat waits to meet each plane, and charges US$1.50 for the 10-minute trip across. Arriving by bus, you'll come in to Mokowe on the mainland, from where it's a trip to Lamu in a motorboat bus (US$0.50, 30 minutes).

Once on the jetty you'll be plagued immediately by touts offering to show you to a hotel – so if you don't want their services, plan a route on the map beforehand to get you to your chosen guesthouse, and thus avoid the need for a 'guide', who will demand commission once you arrive. For Shela and the beach, charter a boat on the jetty for the 10-minute ride up.

KENYA

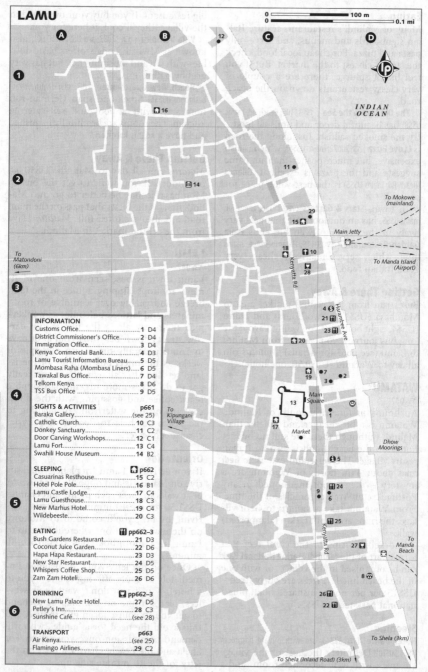

LAMU

0 — 100 m
0 — 0.1 mi

INDIAN OCEAN

To Mokowe
(mainland)

Main Jetty

To Manda Island
(Airport)

To Matondoni
(6km)

To Kipungani
Village

Main Square

Market

Dhow
Moorings

To Manda
Beach

To Shela (3km)

To Shela (Inland Road) (3km)

KENYA

INFORMATION
Customs Office.................................. 1　D4
District Commissioner's Office........... 2　D4
Immigration Office............................ 3　D4
Kenya Commercial Bank.................... 4　D3
Lamu Tourist Information Bureau....... 5　D5
Mombasa Raha (Mombasa Liners)...... 6　D5
Tawakal Bus Office........................... 7　D4
Telkom Kenya.................................. 8　D6
TSS Bus Office................................. 9　D5

SIGHTS & ACTIVITIES　p661
Baraka Gallery.............................(see 25)
Catholic Church.............................. 10　C3
Donkey Sanctuary........................... 11　C2
Door Carving Workshops................. 12　C1
Lamu Fort....................................... 13　C4
Swahili House Museum.................... 14　B2

SLEEPING　p662
Casuarinas Resthouse...................... 15　C2
Hotel Pole Pole.............................. 16　B1
Lamu Castle Lodge.......................... 17　C4
Lamu Guesthouse........................... 18　C3
New Marhus Hotel.......................... 19　C4
Wildebeeste................................... 20　C3

EATING　pp662–3
Bush Gardens Restaurant................. 21　D3
Coconut Juice Garden..................... 22　D6
Hapa Hapa Restaurant.................... 23　D3
New Star Restaurant....................... 24　D5
Whispers Coffee Shop..................... 25　D5
Zam Zam Hoteli.............................. 26　D6

DRINKING　pp662–3
New Lamu Palace Hotel................... 27　D5
Petley's Inn................................... 28　C3
Sunshine Café...........................(see 28)

TRANSPORT　p663
Air Kenya..................................(see 25)
Flamingo Airlines........................... 29　C2

Information
INTERNET ACCESS
The New Marhus Hotel, the Wildebeeste guesthouse (see p662) and the Tourist Information Bureau (see below) have Internet access for US$4 an hour.

MONEY
There's only one place to change money in Lamu – the small branch of **Kenya Commercial Bank** (☎ 632204; Harambee Ave) on the seafront. It changes travellers cheques and can perform cash advances on Visa cards.

TOURIST OFFICES
Lamu Tourist Information Bureau (☎ 633408; mbarak20mar@yahoo.com; Kenyatta Rd; ☼ 8.30am-noon Mon-Sat, 2-4pm Mon-Fri) The tourist bureau seems rather keen to promote its own dhow trips, but staff are a useful source of information nonetheless, and save you the hassle of having to deal with the dhow captains.

Sights & Activities
LAMU TOWN
The town of Lamu has some of the best-preserved **Swahili architecture** anywhere in East Africa – the old stone houses with their heavily carved doors and ornate balconies owe a debt to Arabic, Indian and colonial styles of building. Door carving is not a lost art – you can see **craftsmen** at work on new doors at the north end of Harambee Ave.

If you'd like to delve a bit deeper into the history of the place, visit the **Lamu Museum** (Harambee Ave; admission US$3; ☼ 8am-6pm) on the seafront. It's an excellent introduction to the boat-based culture of the Swahili, with detailed photographs of dhow building and the ceremonies that accompany the launch of a new boat. The explanations are in English, although some are confusing. For even more Swahili culture, find a local to show you the **Swahili House** (admission US$3; ☼ 8am-6pm), complete with antique furniture, buried deep in the back streets.

If you're an animal lover, the rather smart **Donkey Sanctuary** (Harambee Ave; admission free; ☼ 9am-1pm Mon-Fri) welcomes visitors, especially if you're willing to donate something to help aged or sick beasts of burden.

SHELA VILLAGE
The exquisite little village of Shela, 3km from Lamu Town, consists of a cluster of

BEACH WARNINGS
Be aware that there's a very strong current along the Lamu shore – don't go out too far even if you're a confident swimmer. It's also not a good idea to walk too far up the beach alone, or with valuables, as there have been muggings and assaults in the past.

whitewashed houses, an ancient mosque and one of the world's most spectacular beaches – 12km of gently undulating white sand dunes lapped by perfect turquoise water. It's still quite possible to find cheap accommodation here (the key is to arrive in the low season – outside July to August or December to January), and it's well worth decamping from town for a few days of blissful relaxation.

ISLANDS
The nearby islands of **Kiwayu**, **Paté** and **Manda** can be reached by dhow. To organise a trip, or to find a group to share costs, ask around the budget hotels; wait for someone to approach you along the streets; or visit the Tourist Information Bureau (p661). A day trip starts at about US$7 per person in a boat that has four or more people.

Kiwayu Island is part of the Kiunga Marine National Reserve, and offers some of the best snorkelling on Kenya's east coast. There is no public transport to Kiwayu, so charter a boat (from US$7 per person) or ask about the Air Kenya flight from Lamu (US$65). Some simple *bandas* (thatched-roof huts) and a camp site are the only accommodation options on the island.

To **Paté Island**, a boat leaves Lamu town every day but Friday to Paté village, a smaller version of Lamu town (if you can imagine that!). There's no official accommodation on the island, but camping at Mtangawanda village is allowed. Alternatively, organise a room with a local family (about US$3 per person). The Tourist Information Bureau can book this.

On **Manda Island** are the extensive **Takwa Ruins**, the remains of a 15th-century Swahili town. Entry to the ruins cost US$3, and you can only get to the island by chartering a boat (from US$5 per person). At Takwa, there are some simple *bandas* and a camp site.

Festivals & Events

Lamu Cultural Festival happens in August every year, and features music, traditional dancing and games. The **Maulidi** festival is also held yearly (dates vary) to celebrate the birthday of the Prophet Mohammed. Pilgrims arrive from all over Africa for songs and religious events, and accommodation is hard to find during this time. Contact the Tourist Information Bureau for details.

Sleeping

Budget accommodation in Lamu is plentiful, cheap and full of character. All prices are subject to bargaining – and the whim of the hotel management – so always negotiate.

The following places are some of the best.

LAMU TOWN

Wildebeeste (☎ 632261; wildebeestelamu@hotmail.com; apartments US$40; 🖳) If you're in a group, Wildebeeste should be the first place you head. It's a fantastically atmospheric warren of staircases, open-sided rooms, palm trees and courtyards, all decorated in traditional Swahili style. In among it all are two apartments, each sleeping four to six people, with a kitchen for self-catering. The management can provide food if required, and there's an art gallery on the premises.

Casuarinas Resthouse (☎ 633123; s/d US$3/6) One of the best places in town, smack on the seafront with great views of the ocean from a wide front balcony. The rooms are huge, of varying standards and prices, and all have fan and mosquito net. Lots of character, and a breezy rooftop restaurant – shame about the tacky cartoons painted on the outside.

New Marhus Hotel (☎ 633001; s/d US$4/5; 🖳) Rooms at Marhus are small, but there's plenty of outdoor seating on the roof terrace.

Lamu Castle Lodge (d US$4) No views, or decor to speak of, but this is a good cheap 'n' basic lodging – rooms even have a fan. It overlooks the market, so can get noisy.

Lamu Guesthouse (☎ 633338; s/d US$4/8) A friendly, family-run place with rooms that are nothing out of the ordinary, but clean, with fan and mosquito net. There's also a rooftop seating area.

Hotel Pole Pole (☎ 633344; d with private bathroom US$6) Lamu's tallest hotel (but well back from the sea), Pole Pole offers good views from its roof terrace and a nice breeze. Rooms have fan and mosquito net.

SHELA VILLAGE

In the high season – Christmas, New Year, Easter and August – the beautiful, white-washed holiday houses in Shela are let out to wealthy holidaymakers for big bucks. In the low season – lowest of all is March to June – they're yours for just US$6 to US$13 per double room. Each house has a breezy rooftop, four-poster Swahili beds with mosquito net, and a self-catering kitchen. There's no minimum stay, and you don't have to take the whole house – just ask to rent a room.

To find a place to stay, contact **Shella Royal House** (☎ 633091, 0722 698059; shella@africaonline.co.ke), the letting agency for three houses – Shela White House, Bongo House and Shela Resthouse. You can book in advance, or just drop into its office in the village and ask for Mr Mohamed, the manager. Alternatively, ask one of the beach boys to direct you to a local character called Abdul, or 'Stada', who rents a one-bedroom apartment with its own sitting room and kitchen for US$20 per night.

Eating & Drinking

LAMU TOWN

There is a plethora of cheap and authentic local restaurants in the backstreets of Lamu town, all serving up such Swahili delights as biryani, pilau, *bhajias* (spicy dough balls) or *maandazi* (coconut donuts), washed down with giant glasses of freshly squeezed juice. **Zam Zam Hoteli** (Kenyatta Rd; mains US$2) and **Coconut Juice Garden** (Kenyatta Rd; mains US$2) are particularly cheap and cheerful.

Along the seafront the restaurants are more touristy but still extremely cheap. Seafood is a speciality at all of them, with menus depending on what's been fished out of the sea that day. Vegetarians can order samosas or *maharagwe* (beans cooked in coconut). New Star, Hapa Hapa, Bush Gardens and Mangrove restaurants all do mains from US$3. For breakfast try the prettily decorated **Whispers Coffee Shop** (snacks US$2-4), next door to the classy Baraka Gallery shop.

The only places that serve alcohol to the public are Sunshine Café, on the ground floor of Petley's Inn, and the New Lamu

Palace Hotel. The standard price for a bottle of beer at these places is US$1.50.

SHELA VILLAGE

In Shela you can either hire a cook from the village, or buy your own food from the market. Alternatively, you can eat very cheaply at **Rangaleni Restaurant** (mains US$1.50) in the village centre. Stopover, Bahari and Bermuda restaurants are a bit more expensive, but still affordable.

The gorgeous and extremely expensive **Peponi Hotel** (☎ 33154) on the beach is a good place for a sundowner with the beautiful people.

Getting There & Away
AIR

Flamingo Airlines (☎ 633155) has daily flights to and from Nairobi (US$135), via Malindi (US$48); and **Air Kenya** (☎ 633445) has flights every day to and from Nairobi (US$135), Malindi (US$70) and Mombasa (US$100).

BUS

Bus tickets can be bought in Lamu town at the bus company offices listed on the map. Buses run to/from the jetty on the mainland, not far from Mokowe, to/from Mombasa (US$6, 10 hours), via Malindi (US$4, eight hours). See p658 for more information on buses to/from Lamu.

It's important to note that buses travelling between Lamu and Malindi have been attacked by bandits recently, so there is some risk if you travel by bus.

Getting Around

In Lamu your transport choices are limited to dhows or donkeys. There's only one car in Lamu, and it belongs to the District Commissioner (his driver cruises up and down the seafront every night to show it off). A motorised dhow from the jetty in town to Shela beach takes about 15 minutes.

SOUTHERN KENYA

Southern Kenya contains the excellent safari destinations of Tsavo East and West, with their red earth and endless horizons, watering holes and cliffs. Amboseli National Park, overshadowed by stately Mt Kilimanjaro, is perfect for elephant watching.

TSAVO NATIONAL PARK

The vast plains of Tsavo National Park are an excellent safari alternative to the well-trodden circuit of the Masai Mara or Lake Nakuru. Split into two sections, east and west, Tsavo is particularly good for watching elephants, who bathe in the red dust until they seem to be made of terracotta. There are also rhinos here. The park entry fee is US$27.

Tsavo East has the wide open spaces, while Tsavo West has a more varied terrain of rivers, pools and cliffs. Tsavo East, being more accessible, is an easier destination for budget travellers.

Tsavo East

The easiest way into the east section of the park if you don't have your own transport is via the town of Voi, close to the Voi Gate. There's no budget accommodation in the park, but you can sleep at one of the public camp sites (US$10), most of which have toilets and water.

Just outside the Voi Gate lies the up-market **Red Elephant Safari Lodge** (☎ 043-30543; camp site per person US$7), which allows camping in its grounds and will even give campers the use of a bathroom. If you're without a vehicle, you can rent a car and driver here for US$30 per person per day. In Voi itself, try the **Sunset Guest House** (s/d US$4/5), which has basic rooms.

Tsavo West

There are a few budget hotels here if you need to stay the night. There are four public camp sites (US$10) within the park, or you could stay at Kitani or Ngulia camps, both of which have basic *bandas* (thatched-roof huts) for around US$35. You'll have to bring food and cooking equipment with you.

Getting There & Away

Safaris to Tsavo can be arranged from Nairobi or Mombasa. See the safari company listings under Kenya Directory (p664). It's much more expensive to set up your safari in Mombasa – around US$200 per day for two people. For Tsavo East, *matatus* run daily from Voi to Mombasa (US$2, three hours) and Moshi in Tanzania (US$6, about four hours). To get into Tsavo West, take a bus to the small town of Mtito Andei, from where you should be able to hitch a lift into and around the park.

AMBOSELI NATIONAL PARK

The dusty grasslands of Amboseli feature on most standard safari itineraries, and the park scores instant photo opportunity points with its spectacular backdrop of Mt Kilimanjaro in neighbouring Tanzania. Be warned, though – 'Kili' is a notoriously bashful mountain, and remains shrouded in mist for much of the day.

A trip to Amboseli will give you a good chance of spotting hippos, antelopes and zebras, huge herds of buffalos and an incredible array of birdlife – all attracted to the park's permanent swamps. The star attraction, though, are the park's numerous elephants, many of which have been studied for years by biologists working in the area and are thus entirely unafraid of vehicles. The entry fee is US$30. Most people visit Amboseli on an organised safari – the best and cheapest way to do it.

The only camp site (US$10 per person) is on the southern boundary of the park. Elephants used to be a problem here, but since the site was fenced you're more likely to be approached by the local Maasai trying to sell you curios.

Kibo Slope Cottages (☎ 045-22091; s/d with breakfast US$20/35) is close to Oloitokitok village, and accessible by *matatu* from Emali. Prices are negotiable.

If you have your own car, the usual approach is from Namanga, but it's also possible to enter Amboseli from the east via Tsavo. To explore the park without a vehicle of your own, you'll have to try in Namanga for a lift, but it's much better to visit the park with an organised safari.

KENYA DIRECTORY

ACCOMMODATION

Some of the more expensive hotels listed in this chapter may increase their rates during the peak tourist seasons (Christmas, New Year, Easter and the July/August summer holidays).

Budget hotels in Kenya are often called 'boarding & lodging' and most are pretty basic. For about US$5 you can usually find somewhere with clean bedding, a lock on the door and a shared bathroom, but not all places have hot water, fans or mosquito nets. Unless otherwise stated, all rooms have a shared bathroom. Rooms with private bathroom may be available for a slightly higher price.

If you've got a tent, bring it – there are some lovely camp sites scattered over the country. All prices for camp sites in this chapter are per tent. If you don't want to carry camping equipment with you, it can be hired in various places.

ACTIVITIES

Kenya's Rift Valley, Central, Western and coastal regions are best visited in the dry season (May to October and December to March). At this time, roads in the national parks are easier to drive on, mountain paths less slippery and visibility is better for diving and snorkelling.

Diving & Snorkelling

Trips for diving and snorkelling can be arranged at Tiwi Beach near Mombasa, and Malindi or Watamu for the Watamu Marine National Park. Be sure to check the dive company's PADI or equivalent credentials before signing up for a dive. If you have your certificate already, a dive should cost around US$30, depending where you go. Some companies feed fish on snorkelling trips, which produces dramatic results for snorkellers but should not be encouraged, as it can promote aggressive behaviour and upset existing ecosystems.

Safaris

Kenya's many national parks and national reserves are home to a bewildering variety of animals. A trip into one of the parks or reserves is likely to be the highlight of any trip to Africa. For general details about safaris see p1009. Specific details about safaris in Kenya follow.

You should expect to pay US$60 to US$80 per day for a good budget safari in Kenya. Doing things under your own steam is often more costly than taking an organised trip, and is a lot more complicated. It's usual for backpackers to team up and arrange a safari as a group. You can arrange things on the spot in Nairobi, but most safari companies also take bookings in advance via email.

When shopping for a safari in Nairobi, don't be tempted by the offers of the safari company 'representatives' you meet on the streets – instead book through a well-known company such as those listed below.

If you're a student you are entitled to enter Kenya's parks for only US$10 – a substantial discount. Public camp sites in the park also give discounts to students, so make sure your safari company knows you have an ISIC card when calculating a quote for your safari. You may have to give them the card to show when making bookings for parks on your behalf. Some parks also give discounts to volunteers, so if you're working in Kenya, contact the **Kenya Wildlife Service** (☎ 020-602345; kws@kws.org) for details.

Nairobi is generally the best place to arrange a safari. Most safaris from Nairobi last four to five days and the most popular destinations are Masai Mara National Reserve, Amboseli National Park and Lake Nakuru. Check the details very thoroughly before parting with any money:

Best Camping Tours (Map p642; ☎ 229667; bestcamp@ africaonline.co.ke; Norwich Union House, Mama Ngina St)
Flight Centres (Map p642; ☎ 210024; fcswwat@form -net.com; Biashara St)
Gametrackers (Map p642; ☎ 338927; game@africa online.co.ke; cnr Koinange & Moktar Daddah Sts)
Kenia Tours & Safaris (Map p642; ☎ 223699; kenia@ africaonline.co.ke; cnr Kaunda & Wabera Sts)
Planet Safari Adventure (Map p642; ☎ 229799; planet@africaonline.co.ke; Moi Ave) This is one of the best-known companies in Nairobi, with the most consistently cheap prices for camping safaris. It also offers a 10% student discount and three nights' free accommodation in its dormitory for customers. However, reports about their services vary (some readers have had excellent safaris with Planet, while others tell tales of broken-down vehicles and disputes over payment).
Safari Camp Services (Map p642; ☎ 891348; safari camp@kenyaweb.com)

Trekking

Kenya's forests, hills and mountains provide plenty of opportunities for trekking and hiking. Mt Kenya is the obvious hiker destination, but other areas, such as the Aberdare National Park, are also excellent places to do a bit of walking. For full details, and more suggestions, see Lonely Planet's *Trekking in East Africa*.

SCAMS

Nairobi is notorious for scammers and conmen who pretend to be anything from hotel receptionists to refugees to secret police. The only sure way to avoid this problem is not to be drawn into conversation with anyone, however apparently friendly or genuine.

DANGERS & ANNOYANCES

If you apply a few commonsense rules, travelling in Kenya presents few serious dangers. When walking in urban areas such as Nairobi, avoid carrying valuables, and take a taxi after dark. For travel in the north of Kenya, take local advice before setting off on a route, as isolated incidents of banditry occur from time to time.

Annoyances come in the form of 'hustle'. Westerners are perceived as limitlessly wealthy, and the high numbers of rich tourists who visit Kenya every year back up this image. Expect to be routinely overcharged on *matatus*, in shops, and when negotiating taxi fares. Some parts of Kenya – notably the coastal resorts, Lamu and the Masai Mara area – are famous for the number of touts and souvenir vendors who hound tourists relentlessly in search of a sale.

The only way to deal with this and still keep your sanity is with good humour and politeness, but don't be afraid to stand your ground and insist when you feel you're being cheated. Equally, remember that most Kenyans are genuine and welcoming people – don't let the behaviour of a few colour your perception of the entire country!

EMBASSIES & CONSULATES

Countries with diplomatic representation in Nairobi include:
Australia (Map p638; ☎ 445034/39; Riverside Dr, off Chiromo Rd)
Canada (Map pp642; ☎ 214804; Haile Selassie Ave)
Ethiopia (Map p638; ☎ 723027; State House Ave; ⏱ 8.30am-12.30pm & 2-5.30pm)
France (Map p642; ☎ 339978; Barclays Plaza, Loita St)
Germany (Map p638; ☎ 712527; 4th Ngong Ave)
Ireland (☎ 562615; Owashika Rd)
Sudan (Map p638; ☎ 720883; Mamlaka Rd)
Tanzania (Map p642; ☎ 331056/7; Taifa Rd; ⏱ 8.30am-2pm)

Uganda (Map p642; ☎ 330975, 330899; Uganda House, 1st floor, Kenyatta Ave)
UK (Map p638; ☎ 714699; Upper Hill Rd)
USA (Map p638; ☎ 3636000; United Nations Ave, Gigiri)

Kenya has diplomatic representation in the following countries: Ethiopia, Tanzania, Uganda and Sudan.

FOOD & DRINK
Picture this: a couple of white plastic chairs and tables, a flickering fluorescent light, a glowing barbecue and a Coca-Cola fridge. You've just imagined the quintessential Kenyan restaurant. *Nyama choma* (barbecued meat – usually chicken, goat or beef) is a national obsession, and the consumption of it is the focus of much social activity.

Nyama choma restaurants are usually combined with butcheries (be prepared to eat while gazing at a suspended carcass), beer halls or pick-up joints. Even if the thought of consuming half-burnt goat fills you with horror, *nyama choma* is still the best way to meet locals on their own territory.

Slightly more vegetarian-friendly is the cuisine of the Swahili coast, which can be found in Mombasa, the coastal resorts (if you can get past the pizza restaurants) and Lamu. Here you can order such delights as biryanis and pilaus (coconut rice cooked with spicy fish or vegetables).

The best veggie dish in East Africa is *maharagwe* – red beans, onions and garlic cooked in a rich coconut sauce, and often served with *ugali* – the maize meal stodge that looks a little like mashed potato and tastes of nothing at all.

Kenya's favourite tipple is Tusker lager, while in Muslim areas delicious fresh juices are available along with the ubiquitous 'sodas' – bottled fizzy drinks. Only the truly brave would try *changaa*, a lethal and illegal home-brew made from anything from bananas to maize. For a truly Kenyan high, chew on some fresh *miraa* – a narcotic but legal herb that's sold on market stalls and in dodgy bars everywhere.

HOLIDAYS
As well as religious holidays listed in the Africa Directory (p1003) the principal public holidays in Kenya are:
1 January New Year's Day
1 May Labour/Workers' Day

1 June Madaraka Day
10 October Moi Day
20 October Kenyatta Day
12 December Independence Day

INTERNET ACCESS
Every decent-sized town in Kenya has at least one Internet café, and the going rate is around US$1.50 per hour. The exception to this rule is northern Kenya, where most places haven't yet gone on line.

MONEY
Barclays Bank and Standard Chartered Bank in all major towns have ATMs that accept Visa and MasterCard. Cash and travellers cheques can be exchanged for Kenyan shillings at banks and *bureaux de change* in all major towns. You may be asked for the original receipts when changing travellers cheques.

Hard bargaining is expected when buying goods from markets, curio sellers or smaller shops, or when negotiating taxi and transport fares.

POST & TELEPHONE
Letters abroad cost around US$1 – but could take weeks to arrive. Poste Restante is available in the main post office in Nairobi (p639).

International phone calls can be made from telephone offices, called Telkom Kenya, in most towns. Alternatively, you can buy a Telkom card to use in payphones. Calls to most countries cost about US$1.50 per minute. If you've got a mobile phone, you can save money by buying a SIM card from a phone company such as **Safaricom** (☎ 020-32723272), then topping it up with scratchcards, available at convenience stores everywhere.

VISAS
All visitors travelling to Kenya, except East African citizens, require a visa. European, North American and Australasian nationals can obtain a three-month tourist visa at most borders and international airports. Cost is US$50 for a single-entry visa.

If you will be making more than one entry into Kenya due to travel to Uganda or Tanzania, your single entry visa will allow you to travel to these two countries only and re-enter Kenya.

If you are travelling through Kenya for less than seven days you can obtain a transit visa at the border or airport for US$20. You may be asked for proof of onward travel (eg, a bus ticket showing your final destination).

Visa Extensions

Visa extensions can be applied for with the **Principal Immigration Officer** (☎ 020-222022) at Nyayo House in Nairobi or the immigration offices in Mombasa and Kisumu.

Visas for Onward Travel

Visas for the following neighbouring countries can be obtained in Kenya. See p665 for embassy addresses.

Ethiopia Single-entry visas cost US$63, require two photographs and take 48 hours to issue. Applications must be submitted before noon. You may also need to show a yellow fever vaccination certificate.

Sudan Visa requirements change constantly. Apply to the embassy in Nairobi and allow plenty of time.

Tanzania Visas cost US$20 to US$50 depending on your nationality. Two photos are required and visas often take only 30 minutes to issue. However, visas are easier to obtain at the border or airport.

Uganda The cost is US$15 for a one-day transit visa and US$30 for a single-entry visa, valid for up to three months. Applications are accepted between 9am and 1pm, and can be collected on the same day from 1.30pm to 4pm. You can also get a visa on the Ugandan border or on arrival in Kampala.

Somalia

FAST FACTS

- **Area** 637,657 sq km
- **ATMs** none at all
- **Borders** Kenya, Ethiopia and Djibouti (only the Djibouti and Ethiopian borders with Somaliland are open to travellers, and this on a hit-and-miss basis)
- **Capital** Mogadishu
- **Languages** Somali; numerous other languages including Arabic, Italian and English
- **Money** Somali shilling, US$1 = SSh 2600 approx; Somaliland shilling US$1 = SlSh 6800 approx
- **Population** 7.5 million
- **Seasons** wet (Mar–Jun & Sep–Dec), dry (Jul–Aug & Jan–Feb)
- **Telephone** country code ☎ 252; international access code ☎ 16
- **Time** GMT/UTC + 3
- **Visas** Somaliland US$35, obtained in advance; Somalia and Puntland approx US$40, available on arrival

WARNING

Most parts of Somalia remain unsafe to visit. We were unable to do on-the-ground research in this country, so some information in this chapter may be unreliable. Check the situation before travelling to Somalia.

Basket cases don't get much better than Somalia. Crammed uncomfortably into the Horn of Africa, much of the country is an unashamed gun-toting, foreigner-kidnapping, factional-fighting nightmare, where the rule of international law, the will of the UN and the might of the USA doesn't count for squat. In fact, since 1991 the country still known internationally as Somalia has effectively been three countries in one – Somalia in the south, Somaliland in the northwest on the Gulf of Aden, and Puntland (the eastern-most region in Africa) perched in the northeast corner. The security situation in each zone is very different, though. In the south, you'd be mad to go sightseeing without a truckload of armed guards, and Puntland, while a little more stable, is still run by a military junta and still sees a large number of armed clan clashes. Somaliland, remarkably, has managed to retain something close to peace and stability and offers the best hope for travellers. With a few ancient trading towns and some splendid natural and cultural attractions it has much to commend it, but it's unlikely to be overrun by backpackers anytime soon.

SOMALIA

HISTORY

Originally, Somalis probably hail from the southern Ethiopian highlands, and have been subject to a strong Arabic influence ever since the 7th century when the Somali coast formed part of the extensive Arab-controlled trans-Indian Ocean trading network.

In the 19th century much of the Ogaden Desert – ethnically a part of Somalia – was annexed by Ethiopia (an invasion that has been a source of bad blood ever since) and then in 1888 the country was divided by European powers. The French got the area around Djibouti, Britain much of the north, while Italy got Puntland and the south. Sayid Maxamed Cabdulle Xasan (known affectionately as 'the Mad Mullah') fought the British for two decades, but it wasn't until 1960 that Somaliland, Puntland and southern Somalia were united, which wasn't altogether a good idea.

Sadly, inter-clan tensions, radical socialism, rearmament by the USSR and the occasional (often disastrous) war with Ethiopia helped tear the country apart. Mohammed Siad Barre, Somalia's last recognised leader, fled to Nigeria in 1991 after the forces of General Aideed took Mogadishu. At the same time the Somali National Movement (SNM), moved quickly and declared independence for Somaliland. Puntland also broke away.

Restoration of Hope?

Fierce battles between warring factions throughout southern Somalia took place throughout the 1990s, but in 1992 the US led a UN mission (Operation Restore Hope) to distribute food aid to the southern population. Without much ado a nasty little conflict between the US-UN and warlord General Aideed began, during which it's estimated that thousands of Somalis died. The last UN troops pulled out in 1995 having alleviated the famine to some extent, but the nation was still a disaster area.

Thanks mainly to the predominance of a single clan (the Isaq), Somaliland has remained largely peaceful and stable since 1991. It has great oil and gas potential and voted for complete independence in 1997 before holding free presidential elections in 2003 (although opposition parties now don't recognise the victory of President Dahir Riyale Kahin). However, the fledgling

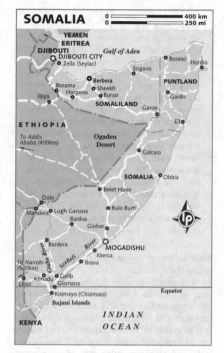

state is not officially recognised by the international community, which still hopes for a peace agreement covering all of Somalia.

Puntland is a different kettle of fish. It too did reasonably well up until 2001 when President Colonel Yusuf refused to stand down after losing an election, a point he reinforced by waging a little war.

Current Conditions

Designed to establish control across the whole of the country, Somalia's lame-duck Transitional National Government (TNG) was set up in 2000. Alas, it still only controls only about a third of Mogadishu and is periodically kicked out of its offices for nonpayment of bills. In 2002 the Somali Reconciliation and Restoration Council (SRRC) created a government for southwest Somalia; later that year 21 warring factions in the south and the TNG agreed to a cessation of hostilities for Kenyan-sponsored peace talks (which were continuing at the time of writing), although most of the delegates seemed more concerned with their private fiefdoms and quality of their

War-Zone Warning

All travel in the Sool and Sanaag regions of Somaliland is currently unsafe due to conflict in Puntland, which claims those provinces. The rest of Somaliland is relatively safe, and travelling in these former war zones can be an amazing, enlightening experience (in a sick sort of way). On the other hand, the rest of southern Somalia is very much a *current* war zone and the law of the gun means that things can go seriously wrong, even if you work for a well-protected aid agency. The whole of greater Somalia also has a huge problem of unexploded ordnance (check out www.mag.org.uk for details), particularly around the Ethiopian border and along arterial roads.

Kenyan hotel accommodation than creating a viable state.

So Somalia lurches on, somehow working within its own peculiar conditions; self-appointed Islamic courts sit whenever possible and Somalis are managing to create a reasonably vibrant economy in the harshest of capitalist environments. Hopefully a safe and stable country will emerge soon, but don't hold your breath.

THE CULTURE

Somalis are commonly tall and thin with aquiline features, and all hail from the same tribe, which is divided into four main clans and loads of sub-clans. The clan in particular and genealogy in general is hugely important to Somalis, who are more likely to ask a stranger 'Whom are you from?' than 'Where are you from?' This inter-clan rivalry has fuelled two decades of conflict.

Saving face is important to Somalis, so indirectness and humour are common in conversation, along with enthusiastic hand and arm gestures. Somalis can be quiet and dignified, with a tendency to ignore strangers, but have a tremendous oral (often poetic) tradition. Written Somali is a very young language – spelling variation, especially place names, is very common. English is widely used in the north, but Italian dominates in the south.

Well over a million Somalis are scattered across Europe, North America and the Middle East; together they send hundreds of millions of dollars back to Somalia each year.

ENVIRONMENT

Characterised by desert or semidesert terrain, Somalia is distinguished by three main topographical features: the Oogo, a mountainous highland region in the north dominated by the Gollis Mountains; the Guban, a relatively barren, hot and humid coastal region (dominating southern Somalia), and the Hawd, a sweeping area of rich, rainy-season pasture prone to overgrazing and desertification. Serious drought continues to plague the south of the country.

Unsurprisingly, Somalia has some of the longest beaches in the world. Coral reefs and the relatively pristine Saylac Islands lie in the Red Sea off the coast of Somaliland, but most of Somalia's waters are infested with sharks (and pirates).

Before civil war, Somalia boasted national parks with cheetahs, leopards, lions and antelopes. Today you'd be lucky to see any predator bigger than a mongoose.

TRANSPORT

GETTING THERE & AWAY
Air

Daallo Airlines (www.daallo.com) operates twice-weekly services from Dubai, London and Paris to Djibouti, from where there are connections to Hargeisa (Somaliland) and Mogadishu (Southern Somalia). They also have flights from Djibouti to other smaller Somali destinations. Ethiopian Airlines offers flights from Addis Ababa.

From Kenya the only traffic into southern Somalia are UN or European Union (EU) aid flights and daily shipments of *khat* (the shoots of the miraa bush, which produce amphetamine-like effects). It all comes from Nairobi's Wilson Airport.

Land

There's a large amount of dhow traffic from Djibouti and Kenya, but piracy is rife – major merchant ships get shanghaied in these waters so don't even think about sailing a yacht along Somalia's coast.

DEPARTURE TAX

Departure tax varies in different parts of the region, but does not exceed US$30.

SOMALIA

The land border between Somaliland and Djibouti is open, but it's a difficult two-day truck journey between Djibouti and Hargeisa. From Jijiga in Ethiopia there's bus and 4WD traffic to Hargeisa.

Although the southern border town of Liboi was once a fascinating little place, there's no way you can get overland from Somalia to Kenya at present. Moreover, the entire border area is infested with well-armed Somali *shifta* (bandits).

GETTING AROUND

In Somaliland there are a few sealed roads (like from Berbera to Hargeisa), so it's pretty likely that medium-sized buses and crowded 4WDs service routes between major Somaliland settlements. However, it's impossible to say what transport is currently running and how regular it is.

MOGADISHU

Although Mogadishu was founded in the 10th century AD by Arab merchants and was ruled by sultans until the 20th century, the city is now about as far from the glories of its 13th-century heyday as it's possible to get. Just before his overthrow, former president Siad Barre ordered his presidential guards to flush out rebels from the capital. As a result, they shelled Mogadishu continuously for four weeks, leaving 75% of it in ruins and an estimated 50,000 people killed. Mogadishu therefore has that *Mad Max*, post-apocalyptic feel, a city where heavily armed clans protecting their patches of turf prowl the ruins of a once beautiful city in 'technicals' – pick-up trucks with a dirty great machine gun mounted on the back. So don't worry about where you're going; worry about who's going to come with you – a gang of armed guards protects against kidnap.

As a result of the civil war all the old attractions probably don't exist any more, or at best are interesting ruins.

The **Hammawein**, or **Xamar Weyne**, is the original city of Mogadishu and was once one of the most beautiful sights on the east coast of Africa.

The ruins of the Roman Catholic **cathedral**, **museum** and **Al Aruba Hotel** are pretty remarkable, while the **Bakara Market** is the infamous location where US Rangers and special forces units were pinned down for over 15 hours (as documented in the Hollywood killfest *Black Hawk Down*). You might also like to visit the livestock market, **Suuqa Xoolaha**, early in the morning, but avoid the **Gun Market**, the most dangerous place in town.

Gezira Beach was once a popular beach with expats and Somalis, while further along the coast are a number of isolated **coves**; one is called Shark's Bay. Guess why?

No doubt there are a few hotels in which to stay, some of them probably quite nice, but as a rule of thumb stay in those recommended by Daallo Airlines.

There are many airports around the city, each controlled by a different clan. The international airport is no longer in use. Fly in with **Daallo Airlines** (☎ 01-215301; mogadishu@ daallo.com; No 30 St, Bakara Market) or on an aid flight from Kenya (see Transport, p670, for more information).

SOUTH OF MOGADISHU

MERCA

This wonderful old Arab town lies on the coast 100km south of Mogadishu. Some 5km from Merca you could once stay right on the beach in huts at **Sinbusi Beach**. The huts had basic bathrooms and the sea is calm, clear and warm with no sharks due to a sandbank further out. There was also a restaurant that served good grilled fish.

BRAVA (BARAAWE)

Another beautiful old Arab town 5km off the main Mogadishu–Kisimayo road, Brava is apparently now only popular with warring clans and Islamic fundamentalists.

KISIMAYO (CHISIMAIO)

Like much of southern Somalia, Kisimayo has been trashed. Optimists could look for the Hotel Quilmawaaye (which once had nice gardens), Hotel Africa or the Wamo Hotel, once the best and most expensive pad in town.

Of more interest to travellers are the largely isolated **Bajuni** (or Baajun) **Islands**, the beginning of the reef system that stretches from the equator down the East African coast. Apparently the diving is very good, but the lack of a decompression chamber would be the least of your worries.

SOMALILAND

BERBERA

There is nothing much of interest in the bustling commercial city-port of Berbera, which is a nice little earner for Somaliland thanks to land-locked Ethiopia's need for a cheap, friendly port. The journey from here to Hargeisa is beautiful and there are some majestic sea cliffs along the coast. Berbera also has a huge runway, built in the early 1980s as an emergency landing strip for the Space Shuttle!

Two of the cheapest places were Hotel Wabera and Hotel Saaxil, while more expensive is Hotel Sahel.

Close to the Djibouti border, the best reasons to visit **Zeila** (Seylac) are definitely the islands, coral reef and mangroves off the nearby coast.

The hill town of **Sheekh** and many other highland settlements in the **Sheekh Mountains** are a welcome refuge from the heat of lowland areas.

HARGEISA

The run-down capital of Somaliland, Hargeisa suffered hugely in 1988 when Siad Barre had it heavily bombed – up to 50,000 people died in the ensuing conflict.

There is nothing much of interest except perhaps the city's **war memorial** – a Somali Airforce MiG jet.

You can make some beautiful journeys in the mountains and along the plateaus, especially from Hargeisa to Berbera, and along the switchback ascent from the coastal plain to the central plateau on the Berbera–Burao road.

The following two hotels are up, running and popular with aid workers and businessmen. They are pretty good for a country with Somalia's reputation: **Ambassador Lion Hotel** (☎ 213 8895; ambassadorhotelhargeisa@hotmail.com; Airport Rd; s/d US$40/50) and **Maan-Soor Hotel** (☎ 285 3638, 252 7000; www.maansoor.com; s/d US$40-80).

Hargeisa has a number of restaurants (spaghetti is very popular) including the Chinese Ming Sing Restaurant. The London Bar used to sell a few soft drinks, and had pool and table-football tables.

Daallo Airlines (☎ 213 4460; hga@daallo.com; Rakuub Bldg, Main St) regularly flies into Hargeisa. Bus and 4WD transport leaves for Berbera, Borama and Burao.

PUNTLAND

Forming the tip of the Horn of Africa, Puntland is the eastern-most region of the continent. Raas Xaafuun should occupy a top spot but, alas, is fraught with danger. Not only is the political situation pretty fluid, the coast is renowned for piracy and kidnapping. There are also flashpoints in the Sool, southern and eastern Sanaag regions and Buhoodle district that currently lie in Somaliland, but are claimed by Puntland.

SOMALIA DIRECTORY

ACCOMMODATION

There's no telling what state the hotels in Somalia are currently like. Daallo Airlines (see Transport, p670) is a good source of current information, but you'll most likely end up paying US$40 to US$50 per night for something half decent and safe.

If you sleep out in the desert (as is often necessary on long truck trips) you need a sleeping bag or warm clothes as it gets quite cold at night.

DANGERS & ANNOYANCES

If you need to read this section you're heading to the wrong country. So few Westerners are found in Somalia that those who do turn up can be treated as cash cows and given a lot of hassle, so beware.

Armed robbery and acts of piracy against passing shipping are frequent and continuing. On land, aid organisations are not immune from attack or robbery.

EMBASSIES & CONSULATES

No countries have active diplomatic representation in Mogadishu at present. In theory there are Somali embassies in a number of African countries, including all neighbouring countries, but at the time of writing these were not operating.

FOOD & DRINK

The staples are rice, macaroni or spaghetti with a splash of sauce. With luck you may have a choice of mutton or goat. Endless cups of tea are obligatory. The standard breakfast throughout Somalia is fried liver with onions and bread. Camel is the preferred source of meat and milk (which is drunk by everyone). It's sometimes said of particularly tall Somalis that their height is a result of the great nutritious qualities of camel milk.

HOLIDAYS

As well as religious holidays listed in the Africa Directory (p1003), these are the principal public holidays in Somalia:

1 January Independence Day in Somalia
26 June Independence Day in Somaliland

MONEY

There are no ATMs anywhere in Somalia, so carry considerable amounts of US dollars that can be changed in hotels, shops and a few banks. There's no chance of changing your travellers cheques, and keep a little secret stash in case you need to buy your way out of trouble.

TELEPHONE

In Somalia, two competing telephone companies use different lines. However, much of the land network has been destroyed, while cheap wireless networks cover most major towns. International telephone calls made from Somalia are the cheapest in Africa.

VISAS

You will need a visa to enter Somaliland, but arrangements are much looser in Puntland and Mogadishu where entry probably will not cost more than US$40.

Note that onward visas are not available in Mogadishu.

Ethiopia

HIGHLIGHTS

- **Merkato** Get lost in one of Africa's biggest markets in Addis Ababa (p681)
- **Aksum** Dive into history and explore Aksum's tombs and ruined palaces (p685)
- **Lalibela** Take a step back in time and marvel at the rock-hewn churches (p689)
- **Harar** Witness the feeding of the hyenas in the Muslim walled city of Harar (p690)
- **Simien Mountains** Trek among the craggy peaks of the Simien Mountains (p688)
- **Off the beaten track** Catch a *tankwa* (open-ended papyrus canoe) and visit the island monasteries on Lake Tana (p686)

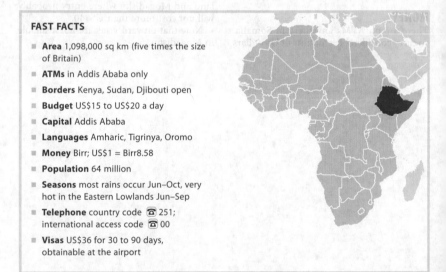

FAST FACTS

- **Area** 1,098,000 sq km (five times the size of Britain)
- **ATMs** in Addis Ababa only
- **Borders** Kenya, Sudan, Djibouti open
- **Budget** US$15 to US$20 a day
- **Capital** Addis Ababa
- **Languages** Amharic, Tigrinya, Oromo
- **Money** Birr; US$1 = Birr8.58
- **Population** 64 million
- **Seasons** most rains occur Jun–Oct, very hot in the Eastern Lowlands Jun–Sep
- **Telephone** country code ☎ 251; international access code ☎ 00
- **Visas** US$36 for 30 to 90 days, obtainable at the airport

Ethiopia has an image problem. The country is readily associated with famines, desert and war. But if you set aside what the media has portrayed, you'll discover that this country is a hidden gem. Though poor materially, Ethiopia boasts extraordinary cultural, historical and natural wealth. Endowed with such an amazing spectrum of wonders, it deserves the aura and fame of Egypt. Take the historical route, for instance. This circuit through northern Ethiopia includes all of the most famous historical and religious sites of the country and will enthral even the most jaded travellers. But the fact is, there seems to be a total disregard of its assets. This obscurity has positive consequences: the country is yet to be unveiled, ensuring that its culture has remained remarkably intact, and travel there is still tinged with a sense of discovery. You will often get the privileged impression of having the country all to yourself. After a visit to Ethiopia, you're bound to herald the following motto: 'forget the image, experience the reality'. It's Africa's 'dark side of the moon'. Get there before it's brought to light.

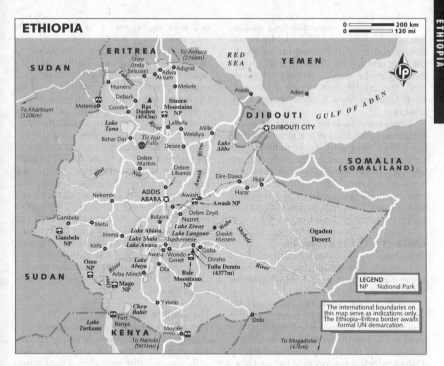

HISTORY

Ethiopia is part of the region that is known as the Cradle of Humanity as it is here that fossils of the earliest hominids have been found (dating from around six million years ago). Ethiopia is unusual among African countries for having never been colonised in the great European 'scramble for Africa' of the 19th and 20th centuries (the only other one was Liberia).

The Flourishing Aksumite Civilisation

At the beginning of the 1st millennium AD, there arose in the highlands of Ethiopia and Eritrea a unique African civilisation, known as the kingdom of Aksum. During seven centuries, it grew to number among the most powerful kingdoms of the ancient world, assisted by its favourable location on the edge of the Graeco-Roman world and with connections with the Indo-Persian-Arab people across the Red Sea. Early in the 4th century, Christianity was brought to Aksum. The Aksumite Kingdom gradually grew in power, extending as far as present-day Sudan and southern Arabia.

After the Prophet Mohammed's death in AD 632, the armies of Islam spread out of Mecca and drove the Aksumites back across the Red Sea into their natural highland strongholds. Here they remained unchallenged for several centuries. Even today the indigenous Orthodox church exists in Aksum and the country remains divided between the Christian highlands and the Muslim lowlands.

A Fragile Empire

According to tradition, the king of Aksum was overthrown late in the 10th century by the destructive Queen Judith (also known as Yodith or Esat). This pagan queen from the southern part of modern Ethiopia resisted Christianity. She fought against Christians, defeated the Aksumite ruling class and established a short period of terror. For nearly 300 years thereafter Ethiopia was ruled by the new Zagwe dynasty established in the capital at Roha (now known as Lalibela). Eventually the kingdom revived and its capital was moved south to the province of Amhara.

Islam gradually expanded into eastern Ethiopia between the 12th and 14th centuries, establishing short-lived kingdoms. In the 16th century, the Ottoman Turks began to support the various Muslim kingdoms. Only the intervention of the Portuguese in 1542 saved the Christian empire from collapse.

After a remarkable life span, the Aksumite kingdom, which had been in general decline since the 12th century, broke down into its constituent provinces in the 18th century, and 100 years of warfare between numerous warlords followed. The shattered kingdom was eventually reunified by Ras Kassa, who had himself crowned emperor at Aksum under the name of Tewodros in 1855.

Contacts with the Europeans

Tewodros had some British functionaries at this court but, an abrupt character, he soon became an enemy to the British, who sent an army to overthrow him.

His successor, Yohannes IV, fought his way to the throne using British arms. After him, Menelik II continued building up stocks of European arms, which he used in 1896 at Adwa to stop Italy's expansion from Eritrea, which it had occupied since 1889.

In 1936 the country was overrun by Mussolini's Italian troops, who remained until 1941 when they surrendered to Allied forces during WWII, after which Ethiopia resumed its independence.

Eritrea remained under British administration until 1952, when a UN resolution granted it self-government within a federal union with Ethiopia. However, in 1962 Emperor Haile Selassie unilaterally annexed Eritrea as a province of Ethiopia. This led to the outbreak of guerrilla warfare, since Eritreans regarded the annexation as colonisation by another African nation.

Haile Selassie's rule was a disaster for the country. He was finally deposed in 1974 and held under armed guard in his palace until his death several months later.

The Rise & Fall of the Derg

Overnight, a clique of junior army officers imposed a military dictatorship on the country. Mengistu Haile Mariam emerged as leader of the Derg, the new governing party. He threw out Americans, instituted a number of radical reforms, banned church

activities and appealed to the USSR for economic aid.

Months of chaos and excess followed. As the country slipped even further into disorder, the Eritreans stepped up their guerrilla campaign and the Somalis invaded the Ogaden desert, which they claimed.

The regime, on the point of collapse, retained power only with the massive intervention of Soviet and Cuban troops. However, despite the massive military support of his communist allies, in the 1980s Mengistu faced not only the Eritreans but several other regional guerrilla armies. Finally, with the Soviets withdrawing from all their Cold War fronts, the fall of Massawa (Ethiopia's principal port) to the Eritreans in 1990 and another major famine ravaging the country, the Derg collapsed. In May 1991, Mengistu fled the country and the government was taken over by a coalition of rebel groups, headed by Tigrayan rebel commander, Meles Zenawi.

The Road to Democracy

Though the new transitional government inherited six million people facing famine, a shattered economy and occasional clashes with the separatist guerrillas of the Oromo Liberation Front and the Ogaden National Liberation Front, they somehow managed to move the country towards democracy.

In May 1995, in Ethiopia's first ever parliamentary elections, regarded as free and fair, Meles Zenawi was confirmed as prime minister by the new parliament.

In the May 2000 elections, Meles Zenawi, the incumbent prime minister won another term in office.

The Dispute with Eritrea

Mounting tensions between Ethiopia and Eritrea over a disputed border escalated into a major military conflict in 1998. In June 2000 Ethiopia launched a major offensive and had not only won back 'occupied' territory but had also penetrated into Eritrea. A preliminary cease-fire was signed between the two sides on 18 June. The plan called for the creation of a 25km buffer zone along the border, to be patrolled by a UN peace-keeping force. The construction of boundary posts began in May 2003. Relations with Eritrea will remain tense until the border demarcation is completed, probably sometime in 2004.

THE CULTURE

Pride and a sense of formality are distinctive features of the national psyche. Remember that Ethiopians have never been colonised. Faith is also an extremely important part of an Ethiopian's life. Christian Ethiopians bring God into everyday conversation just as much as their Muslim counterparts. Roughly 45% of the population are Christian, another 35% are Muslim and the rest follow traditional faiths.

The Ethiopian highlanders attach great importance to etiquette, especially with greetings and dress.

There are more than 80 ethnic groups. The largest of these (some 54% of the population) are the Oromo. They live in the centre and south of the country. The Amhara and Tigrayans, who live in the north and west, together constitute some 29% of the population.

ARTS

Ethiopia is known for its ancient and rich culture. Dance forms an extremely important part of the lives of most Ethiopians. Ethiopia also boasts one of the most ancient, prolific theatrical traditions in Africa. Ethiopia's monumental architecture, almost wholly religious, is another dominant trait.

ENVIRONMENT

The high central plateau varies from 2000m to 3000m, with several mountains of over 4000m. It's dissected by numerous river valleys, the most important being the Blue Nile (the Abay River) flowing from Lake Tana, and split diagonally by the spectacular Rift Valley, which crosses East Africa. Although Ethiopia is relatively close to the equator, the central plateau enjoys a temperate climate, with an average annual temperature of 16°C. Only in the east, towards the Dankalia region, and west, near Sudan, does it get very hot.

Reflecting its geography, Ethiopia has a wide range of ecosystems, including deciduous forests, evergreen forests, desert scrubland, grassland and wetlands. Unfortunately, the high demand for fuel, demographic pressures, construction and fencing have led to the destruction of over 90% of Ethiopia's indigenous forests.

There are nine national parks, including the Simien and Bale Mountains National Parks.

TRANSPORT

GETTING THERE & AWAY
Air
Addis Ababa is the major gateway to Ethiopia. Airlines serving Ethiopia from other African countries include **Ethiopian Airlines** (☎ 511540; www.flyethiopian.com), **Djibouti Airlines** (☎ 633702), **EgyptAir** (☎ 564493), **Kenya Airways** (☎ 513018), **South African Airways** (☎ 511600) and **Sudan Airways** (☎ 504724). Ethiopian Airlines, the national carrier, offers an extensive network of flights to 35 African capital cities, including many West African cities as well as Djibouti, Egypt, Sudan, Kenya and South Africa.

It's also possible to fly to/from Europe: Paris–Addis via Frankfurt or London (return US$1000, four times a week), London–Addis (return US$700, four times a week) and Frankfurt–Addis (return US$1000). There are also connections with Rome, Stockholm and Amsterdam.

At the time of writing, all transport services between Eritrea and Ethiopia had been suspended but should resume when the situation normalises. The quickest way currently of reaching Eritrea from Ethiopia is via Djibouti.

DEPARTURE TAX

The departure tax for international flights is US$20, payable in US dollars only.

Land
There are six official points of entry by land into Ethiopia from neighbouring countries:
Djibouti – Galafi and, by train, Doualé.
Eritrea – Rama and Zala Ambessa (currently closed following the border dispute).
Kenya – Moyale.
Sudan – Humera (closed at the time of writing) and Metema.

DJIBOUTI
The quickest road is the new highway from Ethiopia to Djibouti via Awash, Mille, Logia and the border-crossing at Galafi then via Yoboki and Dikhil in Djibouti. Every day, countless trucks rattle along this road. The journey costs around US$30 and takes three days so you might want to do it in stages.

Alternatively you can go by rail. Though in urgent need of rehabilitation, the old Addis Ababa–Djibouti train still trundles along the old French-built tracks, passing through various small towns in Ethiopia before finishing the first leg at Dire Dawa. There travellers rest overnight and take the next leg to Djibouti City the next morning.

Trains leave three times a week. There are three classes; it costs about US$15 in first class to Djibouti. The quicker way is to take a bus from Addis Ababa to Dire Dawa, then to catch the train to Djibouti City.

ERITREA

There are three routes from Addis Ababa to Eritrea: north from Adwa, north from Adigrat and east to Assab. However, all border crossings between the two countries were closed following the recent border conflict. Go via Djibouti.

KENYA

The only border-crossing between Ethiopia and Kenya is the wild-west frontier town of Moyale. There are usually few problems travelling between the two countries, though vehicles on the Marsabit road travel in convoy for safety. From Addis, go to Shashemene (US$3, 5½ hours, daily), then take another bus to Moyale (US$5, 1½ days, daily).

From Moyale to Nairobi there are currently two routes: via the town of Wajir or via Marsabit. Both roads merge in Isiolo.

Between five and 20 trucks leave daily from Moyale for Nairobi, via Marsabit.

For Wajir, around four public Land Cruisers do the journey daily (four to six hours). From Wajir, two buses depart every morning for Nairobi (around eight hours).

Check the safety of these options when in Moyale, especially the Moyale–Wajir section.

SOMALIA

The border area between Ethiopia and Somalia is still officially declared unsafe and is closed. Check out the current situation before considering this route.

SUDAN

The usual overland route heading into Sudan (via Eritrea) is currently blocked since the Ethiopia–Eritrea border is closed. At the time of writing, the only border-crossing for Sudan is at Metema, 180km from Gondar. The best option is to take a bus to Gondar from Addis Ababa (US$10, 1½ days, daily). From Gondar, one bus leaves daily to Shihedi (US$6, eight to 10 hours). From there, pick-up trucks (US$1) cover the last 40km to Metema.

From Metema, you can walk across the border to the Sudanese town of Gallabat, and from there catch a truck to the nearest large town of Gedaref (SDD1500, eight to 10 hours).

GETTING AROUND
Air

Ethiopian Airlines (☎ 511540; www.flyethiopian.com), the national carrier, provides the only regular domestic air service and has a strong internal network. Flights include Aksum, Arba Minch, Bahar Dar, Dire Dawa, Gondar and Lalibela. Most flights leave from Addis Ababa, but a few connect other towns to each other.

For the more popular routes, there are departures at least three times a week, if not daily. Prices are reasonable.

One of the most useful flights for travellers is the 'historical circuit' – the planes do a loop from Addis to Bahar Dar, Gondar, Aksum and Lalibela, then back to Addis. It functions almost like a hop-on-hop-off bus service – and isn't too expensive.

There's one good-value discount, the 'Group Fair Discount', which offers 50% to 60% off the standard domestic fares. There must be three or more of you travelling together; your incoming international flights must have been with Ethiopian Airlines; and your domestic flights must be booked before leaving home.

There is a domestic departure tax of US$1.25 that can be paid in local currency.

Local Transport

A good network of buses connects all the major towns of Ethiopia. For the smaller towns and villages, light transport such as minibuses, shared taxis and truck services operate.

Buses are cheap (around US$1.50 per 100km) but dead slow.

Though their number is dwindling, *garis* (horse-drawn carts) are a popular local means of getting about town. They are very cheap (about US$0.20) and useful for travellers getting from hotels to bus stations.

On sealed roads you can expect to cover around 50km an hour or more, but on dirt roads 30km or less. They travel during daylight hours. Most long-distance buses set off early.

Train

The old Addis Ababa–Djibouti train passes through various small towns in eastern Ethiopia on its way to Dire Dawa at the end of the first leg. It takes about 14 hours (overnight only; no couchette). The bus option is swifter and scenically more varied.

ADDIS ABABA

☎ 01 / pop 5 million

On first impression, Addis Ababa (New Flower in Amharic) is noisy, dusty, sprawling and shambolic. But it's also a colourful and vibrant city that grows on you surprisingly quickly – helped undoubtedly by its gorgeous climate of seemingly perpetual blue skies and cool highland air. And after a couple of days, you'll start to feel its villagelike atmosphere, with donkeys trotting intrepidly through the red lights and snarling traffic, and goats grazing beside high-rise buildings.

Another compelling aspect of Addis Ababa is the strange mix of past and present. The old imperial statues coexist alongside the hammer and sickle placards of the former Marxist regime, as well as the slick advertisements for new private-sector banks. Wattle-and-daub huts stand a short distance from austere Fascist-era buildings and high-rise hotels. On the streets, priests in medieval-style robes mix with African diplomats, Western aid workers and young Ethiopian women with mobile phones.

It won't be long until you say 'Addis', as if you were talking about an old friend.

ORIENTATION

Bole International Airport lies 5km southeast of the city. Both international and domestic flights depart from here. Minibuses serve the airport from 6am to 8pm daily (about US$0.15). Taxis from the airport should cost US$4 to US$6. The railway station and the bus stations are right in the city centre.

There's no city centre per se. Most prominent landmarks are on Churchill Rd, with the train station at the southern end and St George cathedral at the northern end. Heading north on Churchill Rd, you'll arrive in Piazza, an area centred roughly around de Gaulle Square.

Most of the museums are dotted along Entoto Rd, running almost parallel to Churchill Rd in the east and eventually becoming Menelik Ave at its southern end. The huge Meskel Square in the centre is another landmark.

To the west, the open-air market, Merkato, can be found.

Most development is occurring on and around Bole Rd, between Meskel Square and the airport, and this is gradually shifting the focus of the city.

Note that few streets are signposted. Most residents go by local landmarks (usually larger buildings or major intersections).

INFORMATION
Bookshops

Bookworld (☎ 559010; Wavel St) In the Piazza, is the best place for books in English.

Mega Bookshop (☎ 518896) Off Meskel Square, has a good selection of books and has various branches in town.

Cultural Centres

Alliance Ethio Francaise (☎ 550213) West of the Piazza, puts on French films plus exhibitions of Ethiopian and international artists.

British Council (☎ 550022) Also in the Piazza, hosts regular talks on Ethiopia and has a library.

Internet Access

Internet access is relatively widely available in Addis Ababa, especially in the centre and along Bole Rd. Convenient outlets include Meseret Cafe & Business Centre in Arat Kilo, near the Natural History museum, and **Business Centre** (Bole Rd) on the 4th floor of Dembel Building, near the intersection with Meskel Flower Rd. Average prices are US$0.05 to US$0.10 per minute.

Media

Get a copy of the weekly *Time Out Addis* and the monthly *What's Up*, available in larger hotels and smarter restaurants. Ask also for the *Addis Guide* at the tourist office. It lists the main entertainment venues, restaurants, hotels and embassies.

ETHIOPIA

ADDIS ABABA

0 |———| 1 km
0 |———| 0.5 mi

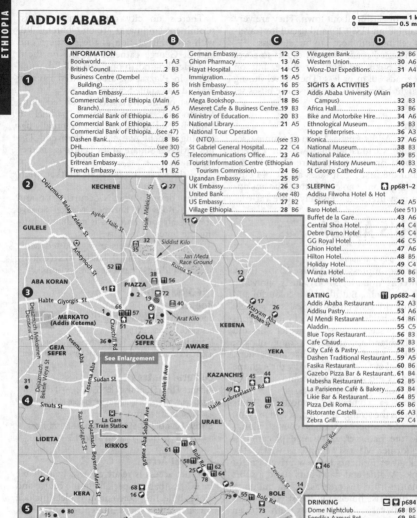

INFORMATION
Bookworld..............................1 A3
British Council.......................2 B3
Business Centre (Dembel
  Building).............................3 B6
Canadian Embassy..................4 A5
Commercial Bank of Ethiopia (Main
  Branch)..............................5 A5
Commercial Bank of Ethiopia......6 B6
Commercial Bank of Ethiopia......7 B5
Commercial Bank of Ethiopia....(see 47)
Dashen Bank..........................8 B6
DHL.................................(see 30)
Djiboutian Embassy..................9 C5
Eritrean Embassy....................10 A6
French Embassy......................11 B2
German Embassy......................12 C3
Ghion Pharmacy......................13 A6
Hayat Hospital........................14 C5
Immigration...........................15 A5
Irish Embassy.........................16 B5
Kenyan Embassy.....................17 C3
Mega Bookshop.......................18 B6
Meseret Cafe & Business Centre..19 B3
Ministry of Education................20 B3
National Library.......................21 A5
National Tour Operation
  (NTO)...............................(see 13)
St Gabriel General Hospital.......22 C4
Telecommunications Office.........23 A6
Tourist Information Centre (Ethiopian
  Tourism Commission)..............24 B6
Ugandan Embassy....................25 B5
UK Embassy...........................26 C3
United Bank.........................(see 48)
US Embassy............................27 B2
Village Ethiopia......................28 B6

Wegagen Bank........................29 B6
Western Union........................30 A6
Wonz-Dar Expeditions..............31 A4

SIGHTS & ACTIVITIES   p681
Addis Ababa University (Main
  Campus)..............................32 B3
Africa Hall.............................33 B6
Bike and Motorbike Hire............34 A6
Ethnological Museum................35 B3
Hope Enterprises......................36 A3
Konica..................................37 A6
National Museum......................38 B3
National Palace.......................39 B5
Natural History Museum.............40 B3
St George Cathedral..................41 A3

SLEEPING   pp681–2
Addisu Filwoha Hotel & Hot
  Springs..............................42 A5
Baro Hotel.........................(see 51)
Buffet de la Gare.....................43 A6
Central Shoa Hotel...................44 C4
Debre Damo Hotel....................45 C4
GG Royal Hotel.......................46 C5
Ghion Hotel...........................47 A6
Hilton Hotel...........................48 B5
Holiday Hotel.........................49 C4
Wanza Hotel...........................50 B6
Wutma Hotel..........................51 B3

EATING   pp682–4
Addis Ababa Restaurant.............52 A3
Addisu Pastry.........................53 A6
Al Mendi Restaurant.................54 B6
Aladdin.................................55 C5
Blue Tops Restaurant................56 B3
Cafe Chaud...........................57 B3
City Café & Pastry....................58 B5
Dashen Traditional Restaurant....59 A5
Fasika Restaurant....................60 B6
Gazebo Pizza Bar & Restaurant...61 B4
Habesha Restaurant.................62 B5
La Parisienne Café & Bakery.......63 B4
Likie Bar & Restaurant..............64 B5
Pizza Deli Roma......................65 B6
Ristorante Castelli...................66 A3
Zebra Grill............................67 C4

DRINKING   p684
Dome Nightclub......................68 B5
Fendika Azmari Bet..................69 B5
Fendika Azmari Bet..................70 B5
Memo Club...........................71 B6
Sunrise Cafe..........................72 B3
The Mask..............................73 C5
The Old Milk House..................74 B6
Topia Tej Bet.........................75 C4
Yegebawal Tej Bet...................76 B3
Yewedale Azmari Bet................77 B5

TRANSPORT   pp684–5
Daallo Airlines........................78 B5
Djiboutian Airlines...................79 C5
EgyptAir...............................80 A5
Ethiopian Airlines....................81 A6
Lufthansa.............................82 A6
Short-distance Bus Station.........83 A6
South African Airways...............84 B6
Sudan Airways.......................85 A5

KECHENE
GULELE
ABA KORAN
MERKATO
(Addis Ketema)
GEJA SEFER
PIAZZA
GOLA SEFER
AWARE
KEBENA
KAZANCHIS
YEKA
URAEL
LIDETA
KIRKOS
KERA
BOLE
Meskel Square

Dejazmach Belay Zeleke St
Ayele Halle St
Haile Melekot St
Atbeynoch St
Habte Giyorgis St
Churchill Rd
Tegesa Aba
Sudan St
Smuts St
Ras Luksegrad St
Dejazmach Beyene Merid St
Siddist Kilo
Jan Meda Race Ground
Russia St
Arat Kilo
Maryam Aba Techan St
Haile Gebreselassie Rd
Menelik II Ave
Beyene Aba Sebsib Ave
Bole Rd
Zewditu St
Ring Rd

See Enlargement

La Gare Train Station

Bole International Airport

Taitu St
Zewditu St
Yohannis St
Menelik II Ave
Tito St
Makonnen Ave
Ras
Bole Rd

La Gare Train Station

0 |———| 200 m
0 |———| 0.1 mi

Medical Services
The best hospitals are the private **St Gabriel General Hospital** (☎ 613622; ☯ 24 hr), east of the centre, and **Hayat Hospital** (☎ 624488) near the airport. Both have dental facilities. The centrally located **Ghion Pharmacy** (☎ 518606; Ras Desta Damtew St), northwest of Meskel Square, is well-stocked with supplies.

Money
Both government and private banks operate in Addis Ababa, and their exchange rates are pretty much the same. However, private banks usually have shorter queues.

The branch of the **Commercial Bank of Ethiopia** (Menelik II Ave; ☯ 6am-10.30pm) at the Hilton Hotel, keeps longer hours than normal. There's another branch at the Ghion Hotel with similar hours. At the time of writing, ATMs were being set up at various branches of the Commercial Bank of Ethiopia.

Private banks are also easy to find. They include **Dashen Bank** (Meskel Flower Rd) and **Wegagen Bank** (Meskel Sq), among others.

Post & Telephone
The **main post office** (Churchill Rd; ☯ 8am-6pm Mon-Fri, 8am-4pm Sat, 10am-noon Sun) is centrally located. It has a courier service called EMS.

The main **telecommunications building** (Churchill Rd; ☯ 8am-10pm) has phone and fax services available.

Tourist Offices
The **Tourist Information Centre** (☎ 512310; Meskel Sq; ☯ 8.30am-12.30pm & 1.30-5.30pm Mon-Thu, 8.30-11.30am & 1.30-5.30pm Fri) is on the ground floor of the Ethiopian Tourist Commission. Staff can speak English.

DANGERS & ANNOYANCES
Violence is uncommon but pickpockets and con artists operate particularly around the bus station, at minibus stands, in the Merkato and on the triangle of streets around the stadium in the centre. You're at risk walking around the city centre after dark. Also be vigilant near some of the larger hotels and the Piazza.

SIGHTS & ACTIVITIES
By far the best place to get bedazzled in Addis is the **Merkato** (☯ Mon-Sat). Even the most jaded traveller will be intimidated by the sheer size and fantastic ambience of this open-air

market – supposedly the largest in Africa. The Merkato is an immense conglomeration of stalls, shops, produce and people, where it's possible to find absolutely everything from a Kalashnikov to the most precious incense. The most impressive sections include the spice market (which is so pungent it'll make you sneeze), and the 'recycling market', where locals in open-air workshops turn old tyres into sandals, decrepit corrugated iron into metal buckets and olive-oil tins into coffee pots and tiny scoopers. Haggling is the order of the day. The Merkato is just west of the centre and the best time to visit is early on Saturday, when people from all over the country come in. The market has a terrific reputation for pickpockets, so be vigilant.

After a visit to the Merkato, you might want to recover at the **Addisu Filwoha Hot Springs** (Filwoha Hotel; Yohannis St; ☯ 6am-12.30pm & 2-7.30pm). A full massage with oil costs US$7 and a sauna bath US$3.

Do you want to meet a very remote relative? Head for the **National Museum** (☎ 117150; admission US$1.50; ☯ 8.30am-5.30pm Mon-Fri, 9am-5.30pm Sat & Sun) east of the Piazza, where you'll see Lucy, the star exhibit of the museum, on the basement level. Discovered in 1974 in northeastern Ethiopia, Lucy is the oldest known hominid in the world (about three million years old). The exhibit is in fact a plaster cast; the real bones are preserved in the archives of the museum.

Another must-see is the newly refurbished **Ethnological Museum** (admission US$2.50; ☯ 8am-noon & 1.30-5pm Tue-Thu, 8-11.30am & 1.30-5pm Fri, 10am-6pm Sat & Sun), on Addis Ababa University's main campus, north of the centre off Entoto Rd. It's undoubtedly the best museum in Ethiopia, with an attractive, modern layout. This is a great place to get your head around the culture and history of the country.

SLEEPING
There's a cluster of budget hotels in the Piazza area. Other venues are scattered around the city. Street names are mentioned when useful.

Baro Hotel (☎ 559846; barohotel@telecom.net.et; Piazza; s with private bathroom US$6-7, d US$8; ☐) The Baro is a perennial favourite with shoestringers and a good place to hook up with travellers. It is set in an attractive and leafy compound, and it's clean on the whole. Staff are clued up and can organise 4WD trips within Ethiopia. Facilities include free left-luggage and fax service.

Wutma Hotel (☎ 562878; wutma@yahoo.com; Piazza; s or d with private bathroom US$6-8) Opposite the Baro, this is another hang-out for budget travellers, with cramped but tidy rooms and left-luggage facilities. Management is well-informed and can help you organise 4WD rental.

Debre Damo Hotel (☎ 612630, 612921; Haile Gebreselassie Rd; s/d US$6, with private bathroom US$9/16; 🖳) Tucked off the main street, this place is more inviting than it looks from the outside. It offers cupboardlike but clean and tidy rooms set around a peaceful courtyard, and there's a relaxed vibe here. Facilities include a restaurant and bar.

Wanza Hotel (☎ 504893, 156177; off Bole Rd; s/d with private bathroom US$6/8) An excellent budget pick, with a great location, a short bag haul from the hurly-burly of Bole Rd and the city centre. It's low-key and kind of homey here, with compact but clean rooms.

GG Royal Hotel (☎ 292329; off Ring Rd; s/d with private bathroom US$17/34) Style-less but modern establishment featuring good-value rooms (especially the singles) in a handy location, only 2km away from the airport.

Buffet de la Gare (☎ 517888; s/d with private bathroom US$10/14) A few paces from the railway station, this one-storey joint is colourful and atmospheric, with light-filled, clean rooms. Added bonuses are the restaurant, the lively, if raucous, bar and an attractive, peaceful garden with lawn.

SPLURGE!

Ghion Hotel (☎ 513222; ghion@telecom.net .et; Ras Desta Damtew St; s/d US$55/68, bungalows from US$68; 🖳) The well-known Ghion is not exactly the place you would select for a honeymoon, but it does boast a special setting. The buildings are nestled in a large, lush park, right in the middle of the city. If you feel tired or stiff, this unexpected oasis of greenery might be the haven you're looking for. It also has banking facilities and several restaurants, including a one in a traditional *tukul* house. The rooms are nothing to write home about, but come with the usual mod cons. Tour groups throng to this place so it's wise to book.

Holiday Hotel (☎ 612081; Haile Gebreselassie Rd; s/d/tw with private bathroom US$16/18/21) In an expanding area east of the centre, the Holiday has simple but clean rooms, and a decent restaurant with a wooden ceiling. Prices include breakfast.

Central Shoa Hotel (☎ 611454; Haile Gebreselassie Rd; s/tw US$20/23) A well-managed place offering smallish but neat rooms, plus a cosy lounge and a restaurant. It's a good option if you need a modicum of comfort.

EATING

Good news for shoestringers: there's a wealth of options in Addis that won't break your budget, and you'll be surprised by the quality and diversity of the food.

Restaurants
ETHIOPIAN
There's a profusion of excellent Ethiopian restaurants offering a genuine culinary experience, with great food, costumed staff, traditional surroundings and music in the evening. They serve meat dishes and have good veggie options on fasting days (Wednesday and Friday). Most places also serve *tej* (mead).

Fancy something more adventurous? Try the *kitfo bets*, specialising in *kitfo* (chopped prime beef mixed with special spiced butter sauce).

Dashen Traditional Restaurant (☎ 529746; mains US$1-3) A welcoming classic behind the main post office, highly praised for its succulent food, cosy interior and relaxing closed courtyard.

Fasika Restaurant (☎ 514193; mains US$3.50-4) Off the northern tip of Bole Rd, the Fasika boasts delightful exotic decor with loads of character. It's a good starting point for the uninitiated.

Addis Ababa Restaurant (☎ 113513; Piazza; mains US$1.50-3) This long-standing favourite is housed in a former aristocrat's residence just north of the Piazza. Its nine rooms ooze ambience and the food is up to standard.

Habesha Restaurant (☎ 518358; Bole Rd; mains US$2.50-3) Tuck into some of the best Ethiopian fare in town. Sit at the round *mesob* and try the *zilzil tibs* (marinated beef cooked on clay) or *alicha firfir* (cubes of lamb meat in a mild sauce of ginger). The fairly classy Habesha draws an eclectic crowd of expats and wealthy returnees.

Karamara Restaurant (☎ 158053; Bole Rd; mains US$2-3) Set in a *tukul* (traditional mud house with conical thatch), off Bole Rd. A bit more touristy than its counterparts, but recommended for newcomers to Ethiopian food.

Likie Bar & Restaurant (☎ 517833; Bole Rd; mains US$1-2) One of Addis' best-kept secrets, about 150m from Habesha Restaurant (look for the orange canvas). A casual little place popular at lunchtime, Likie offers tasty veggie food on Wednesday and Friday, as well as meat dishes the other days.

EUROPEAN
Pizza Deli Roma (☎ 511204; Bole Rd; pizzas US$1.50-4.50) Near the northern end of Bole Rd, this joint is a tad impersonal but offers a selection of about 40 good pizzas, including some with vegetarian toppings.

Gazebo Pizza Bar & Restaurant (☎ 150766; Meskel Flower Rd; mains US$2.50-3) Hidden away, the cheap and cheerful Gazebo specialises in pizza cooked in traditional Italian ovens. The attractive garden provides a welcoming retreat from the hubbub of nearby Bole Rd.

Blue Tops Restaurant (☎ 550934; mains US$2.50-9) This well-known place north of the centre on Entoto Rd is a favourite haunt of expats and has two restaurants, one for lunch and snacks and a more formal Italian restaurant.

Zebra Grill (☎ 623630; mains US$2-3.50) Atmospheric place with thatched roof and subdued lighting, on the road to St Gabriel Hospital, serving good grilled food and various nibbles at purse-friendly prices.

Cafe Miru (mains US$1-2) Pastry shop on the ground floor and a small restaurant upstairs offering simple, hearty dishes. Very central, and crowded at lunchtime.

MIDDLE-EASTERN
Aladdin (☎ 615256; mains US$2-4) About 100m from Bole Rd, Aladdin gets rave reports from expats and well-heeled locals alike. Try the *mezze* and follow up with a kebab, and you'll understand why. It's a fairly voluptuous affair with an elegant decor, but it's anything but elitist.

Al Mendi Restaurant (☎ 512143; mains US$2-6) Off Bole Rd, the easy-going Al Mendi is an excellent Arabian-style eatery with a good selection of hearty dishes. Try *mendi* (sheep) or shish kebab, accompanied by *fetira* (bread with honey).

Cafés & Pastry Shops
There are oodles of pastry shops. These are great places for breakfast or just a treat in the afternoon. The following are recommended:

Tomoca (Piazza) An almost carbon copy of a 1960s Italian café (though the ambience is a bit marred by the loud TV), Tomoca is rated for its delicious coffee.

Cafe Chaud (off de Gaulle Sq) Unimpressive from the outside, but slick and almost trendy inside, with marble-topped tables and metal chairs. Good for pizzas, fruit juices and cakes.

Addisu Pastry (Churchill Rd) This cheap and cheerful pastry shop is standing room only. It has excellent fruit juices and savoury pastries.

Le Notre (Tito St) Need a fix of *viennoiseries*, cakes or croissants? Head for this large and trendily furnished French pastry shop serving enticing delicacies in fairly civilised surroundings.

Roby Pastry (Bole Rd) You'll feel at ease in this relaxed place, graced with a shady terrace where you can enjoy the usual suspects – cakes, juices and coffee.

La Parisienne Cafe & Bakery (Meskel Flower Rd) A mere stroll from Bole Rd in a civilised area, La Parisienne is – you guessed it – designed like a French café. When it's warm the outdoor tables fill up. The croissants are to die for.

Sunrise Cafe is a perfect spot to unwind after a visit to the National Museum nearby, with a large, open terrace from which to watch the world go by. Fruit juices, pastries and nibbles are available.

SPLURGE!

Ristorante Castelli (☎ 563580; mains US$4-9.50; ☾ closed Sun) In Addis' (limited) culinary hall of fame, the long-established Italian family who runs the place holds top honours.

If you need a break from Ethiopian fare, or if you're seeking sophistication in decor, food and atmosphere, this is the place to head to. Wait to be seated in one of the four fairly stylish rooms, and peruse the menu offering a small festival of Italian pleasures. The good selection of imported Italian wines is an extra thrill.

Self-Catering

Ethio Supermarket (Bole Rd; 🕑 24hr) will probably stock that special item you've been craving since you left home.

DRINKING

The cluster of bars in the Piazza around the Taitu Hotels are no-frills but very atmospheric places, where locals come for a beer or to dance to their favourite Amharic tunes. It's generally safe for women, although it's best not to wander around alone.

Another area great for bar-hopping is Kazanchis, east of the centre, with down-to-earth but authentic bars often turning to impromptu dance floors late in the evening.

You'll also find a host of typical, unpretentious but buzzing Ethiopian joints in Haya Hulet – follow the street leading from Bole Rd to St Gabriel Hospital and you'll stumble across them.

Other places worth investigating include:

Old Milk House (off Tito St) Near Africa Hall, this was a top spot among expats and trendy locals at the time of writing. It's a great place for socialising, with a welcoming shady courtyard and cheap tequila. Snacks and pizzas are available if you get peckish.

Mask (Bole Rd) A bit away from the hub of things, off the southern end of Bole Rd, The Mask is fairly sophisticated and filled with good vibes. It's renowned for its cocktails (from US$2).

JOY OF TEJ

If you're a male traveller, don't leave Addis without sampling a flask of tej in a tej bet. The traditional haunt of men, the tej bet is a kind of Ethiopian pub, serving tej instead of beer. It's rough and ready: prepare to be baffled by the raucous ambience. Ask for directions, there are no signs. The most central is the **Yegebawal Tej Bet** east of the Piazza, a few steps from the Mobil petrol station, near the Ministry of Education. Check also **Topia Tej Bet**, tucked off Haile Gebreselassie Rd, in a side street about 300m south of the Classic Hotel. Women travellers should be accompanied by a local if they wish to sample tej.

CLUBBING

Addis Ababa is known throughout East Africa for its nightclub scene. Many nightclubs tend to be 'Westernised' in terms of ambience and music. If that doesn't grab you, you can venture into more brash options where you will rub elbows with a wilder crowd. Most clubs get going on the weekend. Entrance generally costs US$2 to US$3. Most places are safe for women travellers. Male travellers should note that most single Ethiopian women encountered in nightclubs are prostitutes.

If you're in the mood for a genuinely Ethiopian experience, head for the row of bars and clubs in the area known as Datsun Sefer, north of the Piazza (ask for the Semien Hotel, it's very close to it). On Friday nights, the energy at these tiny places can rise to a fever pitch. Obvious tourists might get the occasional scowl but it's generally friendly.

South of Meskel Square, the Memo Club was the focal point of clubbers, expats and locals alike at the time of writing. It dishes up a mixture of African and Western music, and is crammed with bar girls.

Dome Nightclub (Debre Zeyit Rd) Of the same ilk as the Memo, the infamous Dome appeals to a mixed crowd of reckless expats and locals. The evening usually starts with a band playing Ethiopian music, then it turns to a regular dance club that goes off at weekends. It can get stiflingly crowded.

Don't forget to drop by an azmari bet – an azmari is a kind of Ethiopian stand-up comedian and an azmari bet is a traditional comedy club, and a very ancient tradition. Though performances are always in Amharic, it's still a merry thing to watch. Entrance is free; drinks cost just over US$1. Most azmari bets are dotted along Zewditu St. Pick of the bunch include **Yewedale Azmari Bet** (Zewditu St) and **Fendika Azmari Bet** (Zewditu St).

GETTING THERE & AWAY
Air

Airlines with offices in Addis include **Djibouti Airlines** (☎ 633702), off Bole Rd; **EgyptAir** (☎ 564493; Churchill Rd); **Kenya Airways** (☎ 513018), at the Hilton Hotel; **South African Airways** (☎ 511600; Flamingo Rd); and **Sudan Airways** (☎ 504724) in the city centre.

Ethiopian Airlines has about a dozen offices dotted around town. The **branch**

(☎ 511540) located at the Hilton has shorter queues.

Both EgyptAir and Ethiopian Airlines fly to Cairo once a week, and charge US$619 and US$738 one way, respectively.

Djibouti Airlines has three flights a week to Djibouti (US$102, one way); Ethiopian Airlines plies the same route four times a week (US$181, one way).

Sudan Airways flies to Khartoum once a week (US$360, one way).

Kenya Airways has two to three flights a week to Nairobi (US$350, one way).

Local Transport

There are two bus stations in Addis Ababa: the long-distance station (for any journey over 150km), at Merkato west of the Piazza, and the short-distance station, near La Gare in the centre.

Long-distance buses leave officially at 6.30am. They go to Aksum (US$13, 2½ days via Shire, Dessie and Mekele), Arba Minch (US$6, 12 hours), Bahar Dar (US$7, 1½ days), Dire Dawa (US$6, 11 hours) and Gondar (US$9, two days), among others.

Short-distance buses go to Shashemene (US$2.50, five hours).

Train

Trains leave three times a week from Addis Ababa's train station to Djibouti, and stop in Dire Dawa. The ticket office is open when the train is in, until 1pm. The train leaves at 2pm, in principle.

GETTING AROUND

The big yellow-and-red city buses are usually overcrowded and a haunt of pickpockets; it's better to avoid them. The white-and-blue minibuses follow defined routes and are safer. They cost US$0.10 to US$0.15 per journey. The two main minibus stations are on Meskel Square and Arat Kilo.

There are two types of taxi: the privately owned blue-and-white vehicles or the yellow NTO taxis. The former have no meters and prices should be negotiated beforehand. NTO taxis can be booked at any of the major hotels. They are more expensive than the little blue taxis hailed on the street. A reasonable rate to pay for blue taxis is from US$3.50 to US$5 for short trips around town.

NORTHERN ETHIOPIA

AKSUM
☎ 04

Sprawling, dusty, rural: Aksum is modest almost to a fault. At first sight, it's hard to imagine that the town was ever the capital of a great civilisation. Yet Aksum is one of Ethiopia's star attractions. If Egypt has Luxor, Ethiopia has Aksum, with the exception that you won't find pyramid-parking coaches or sound-and-light shows here.

The little town is littered with the ruins of palaces, underground tombs, stelae and inscriptions. Life continues here as it has for millennia, and you'll be graced by visions from another era. Around the crumbling palaces, farmers go on ploughing their land, women wash their clothes in the Queen of Sheba's Bath, and hurrying past towering stelae are the market-goers and their donkeys.

The **tourist office** (☎ 753924; ⏰ 8.30am-12.30pm & 1.30-5.30pm Mon-Sat) is in the heart of town.

You'll find several banks and an Internet café at the Africa Hotel.

Sights

Aksum is *the* place to get familiar with Ethiopia's amazing heritage. Sure, be prepared for a monument overkill, but it's worthwhile. The huge granite monoliths, or steles, of the **Stele Field** are symbols of this ancient grandeur. One, sadly broken, measures 30m, making it the largest monolith in the world.

Another highlight includes **St Mary of Zion church** (admission US$7), Ethiopia's holiest shrine, built in the 17th century on the site of a 4th-century Aksumite church. Every Ethiopian Orthodox Christian believes that the original Ark of the Covenant resides here; according to local tradition, it was smuggled from Jerusalem by Menelik I – but no-one is allowed to set eyes upon it.

To the northeast of the Stele Field is a modern reservoir, known as **Queen Sheba's Pool**. From here, a pleasant half-hour walk takes you to **King Kaleb's Palace**. It contains a number of underground chambers, a great example of the sheer sophistication of the Aksumite civilisation.

The underground **Tomb of King Basen**, hewn out of solid rock, is also awesome, as is the **Queen of Sheba's Palace**, which will give you a good insight into Aksumite civilisation.

In order to do these sites justice, hire an official guide (ask at the tourist office), who will explain all the ins and outs of Ethiopian history for around US$7 (plus tip).

Sleeping

Ghenet Hotel (☎ 752217; d/tw US$3/6, with private bathroom US$6) In the centre towards the market, this is the best bet for shoestringers.

Africa Hotel (☎ 753700; d/tw US$2.50/3.50, with private bathroom US$5.50/7.50) Another reliable, well-maintained option, east of the centre on the road to the bus station, with a garden/courtyard – perfect to chill out in the evening.

Ark Hotel (☎ 752676; s/d/tw with private bathroom US$8/9/11) A good pick if you want a new, comfortable and affordable mid-range place. It's close to the Africa Hotel.

Eating & Drinking

Axum Touring Hotel (mains US$2.50) It offers a quite respectable three-course, *faranji* (Western) food menu. The garden is a good place for breakfast or to enjoy a post-dinner tipple.

Café Abyssinia (mains US$1-1.50) In front of the hospital, this new venue has swiftly become a firm local favourite, serving as café/bar/restaurant. You can quaff a beer or chow down on Ethiopian or *faranji* food.

Mini Pastry is an ideal rest stop, near the telecommunications office, for pastries or a fruit juice fix. The little garden is a mellow spot for breakfast; at night it transforms into a bar.

Fancy something grittier or more authentic? Seek out the *tella bets* (local beer houses) in the tiny streets around town. They're great venues for Tigrayan dancing.

Getting There & Away

Ethiopian Airlines has one to two daily flights to Addis via Lalibela, Gondar and Bahar Dar (US$125, one way). For Gondar, Debark and the Simien Mountains, you'll need to go to Shire first. There are buses to Mekele, Adwa and Adigrat. A taxi to the new airport seven kilometres from town costs US$5. Taxis elsewhere charge from US$1 to US$3.

BAHAR DAR

☎ 08

Poised at the southern edge of the 3600-sq-km Lake Tana, Bahar Dar boasts a perfect scenic location. No wonder it's considered one of Ethiopia's most attractive towns. It makes an ideal base from which to explore the area's highlights: the Blue Nile Falls and the island monasteries of Lake Tana.

A little **Tourist Information Centre** (☎ 201112) can be found in the centre of town. There are Internet facilities at the Ghion and Papyrus Hotels. You'll also find several banks.

Sights

Bahar Dar has a vibrant Saturday market. This is where you can see stalls with colourful, striped woven cloth, as well as the delightful *agelgil*, a kind of leather-bound lunch box.

There are 29 **monasteries** (admission to each US$2.50) scattered over the 37 islands of **Lake Tana**. Dating from the 11th to 16th centuries, they are a must see (note that women are not allowed on some of the islands). Many are accessible by boat (about US$20 for up to four people, after negotiation, or US$35 for a half day).

South of the lake is the source of the Blue Nile, which feeds into Lake Tana and exits north of Bahar Dar to create the awesome **Blue Nile Falls** some 30km downstream.

They are impressive as much for their sheer width (measuring over 400m) as their depth (45m). Dropping into a sheer chasm, the thunderous noise can be heard long before arrival, and the spray that is thrown up can be felt up to a kilometre away. The ticket office is at the far end of Tis Abay village (US$1.50). To reach the falls you will need to take a bus to Tis Abay (US$0.50, one hour) or take a trip with a local tour operator (about US$22).

Sleeping

Camping (Ghion Hotel; US$3) You can camp in the grounds of the Ghion Hotel. Tents and mattresses can also be hired (US$5 per person, per night). It's fairly expensive, but its main asset is the picturesque location, in lovely gardens by the lake.

Tana Pension (☎ 201302; s/d US$2.50) Undoubtedly the best budget option in town, it's approximately midway between the bus station and Lake Tana, and has unpretentious but clean rooms.

Haddas Desta Hotel (☎ 200309; s or d without/with private bathroom from US$2.50/5) Another good-value place, northeast of the bus station.

Ghion Hotel (☎ 200740; s/d with private bathroom US$6/8) With its splendid gardens by the lake, the well-managed and friendly Ghion provides a perfect respite if you feel road-weary and it won't put too much strain on your wallet.

Papyrus Hotel (☎ 205100; s/d/tw with private bathroom US$11/16/22) If it's cosseting you're after, this more modern, newish hotel with a pool, close to the main market, may fit the bill.

Eating

Enkutatash Restaurant (mains US$0.50-2) and **Enkutatash 2** (mains US$0.50-2) are very popular options, with good fresh fish. The latter is a little more upmarket.

Tana Hotel (mains US$2-3) The restaurant inside the hotel is a good place to chow down on *faranji* food.

Tana Pastry is a welcoming place for sweet-tooths, with pastries, fruit juices or breakfast available.

The tiered terrace overlooking the lake is a boon. Mango Park is the place to head to for a drink at dusk.

Getting There & Around

Ethiopian Airlines (☎ 200020) has two to three flights daily to Addis Ababa (US$70), and one to two flights daily to Gondar, Lalibela and Aksum.

Two buses leave daily for Addis Ababa (US$7, 1½ days). One bus leaves daily for Gondar (US$2.50, four to five hours). For Debark (Simien Mountains) first go to Gondar.

Minibuses are good for getting around town. For the airport, taxis charge about US$5.

Various tour companies, including **NTO** (☎ 200537) based at the Tana Hotel, and the Ghion Hotel in Addis Ababa, rent cars and offer trips to the main attractions in and around Bahar Dar. A guide costs about US$35 for a small group (half-day). For transportation, count on US$16 per hour.

GONDAR
☎ 08

Gondar has been called Africa's Camelot. With its series of castles and churches, it is one of the major attractions of the historical route.

About 750km northwest of Addis Ababa, Gondar was the capital of Ethiopia from its foundation by Emperor Fasilidas in 1632 until 1886.

The piazza – a grandiose name for an unremarkable small square – is the heart of the modern town, where you'll find the post and telecommunications offices. A little tourist information centre, north of the Royal Enclosure, was closed at the time of writing, but is promising to reopen soon. There's no shortage of banks in Gondar.

Don't miss Gondar during the Orthodox festivals of Leddet and Timkat, both in January.

Sights

Monuments, that's what Gondar is all about. Like most towns in northern Ethiopia, the city is studded with superb historical remains testifying to the country's prestigious heritage. Don't skip them, they will enhance your trip.

Guides can give city tours for around US$18 per day for a small group. It can be organised through the tourist information centre if it's open or at the Royal Enclosure. Guided tours are free at the Royal Enclosure, but a tip is expected.

Start with the unmissable **Royal Enclosure** (admission US$6; ☼ 8.30am-12.30pm & 1.30-5.30pm), the first and most impressive castle within its surrounding walls built by Emperor Fasilidas around 1640. It's a massive complex housing several monuments, all worth a peek.

Your ticket also admits you to the **Bath of Fasilidas** (☼ 8.30am-12.30pm & 1.30-5.30pm), the emperor's bathing pool and pavilion, which is by the stadium about 2km out of town on the Bahar Dar road. Another highlight is the splendid **Debre Berhan Selassie Church** (admission US$1.50; ☼ 5am-6pm) with fine murals and painted ceiling, an easy 2km walk northeast of town.

The **merkato** in the south of town is a good place to soak up some local atmosphere. Traditional cloth, pottery and baskets can be bought here.

Sleeping

Belegez Pension (☎ 114356; s or d with private bathroom US$8) This newish place, northeast of the Royal Enclosure, is fairly commendable, with smallish but clean rooms set around a central courtyard.

Quara Hotel (☎ 110040; s/d US$8/9, with private bathroom US$9/10.50) The rooms of this Italian-built institution aren't much cop but the location is handy, right on the central square, and overall it's adequate.

Fasil Hotel (☎ 110221; d/tw US$3.50/5) An acceptable pick for penny-counting travellers, with basic but tolerable rooms.

Humera Pension (☎ 110787; s or d without/with private bathroom US$6/12) Though slightly overpriced, the rooms at this new pension are decent. Try to ask for a discount. It's on the northern outskirts of the town, on the road to Aksum.

Goha Hotel (☎ 110634; camp site per person US$6, s/d US$38/50) You might balk at the prices, but the prime location, 2km north of Gondar, makes this worth considering for a splash out. It's perched on a high natural balcony overlooking the town. And if you can't afford a room, you can still camp at moderate prices.

Eating & Drinking

Mini Fogera (also known as Zewditu Yilma) A local favourite turning out good Ethiopian and *faranji* dishes at simple prices.

Ras Bar & Restaurant (mains US$0.50-2) A well-rated eatery just next to the Shell station. Head for the bamboo-constructed tent at the back.

Decent pastry shops include the justly named Delicious Pastry, Sofa Juice and Member Café.

Bar Havana is an atmospheric venue on the main roundabout has live *azmari* performances nightly.

Hill Top Bar is American-inspired but irrepressibly Ethiopian. Try, if you dare, a *gin fir fir* (gin mixed with beer) or wine diluted with coke!

Getting There & Away

Ethiopian Airlines (☎ 110129) flies twice daily to Addis Ababa (US$93), and once daily to Lalibela, Aksum and Bahar Dar.

One bus leaves daily for Addis Ababa (US$9, 1½ days); two buses depart for Bahar Dar (US$2.50, four hours); for Aksum, go to Shire first (US$5, 12 hours).

For Sudan, one bus leaves daily to Shihedi (US$6, eight to 10 hours). From there, pick-up trucks cover the last 40km to Metema.

SIMIEN MOUNTAINS NATIONAL PARK

Debark, 101km from Gondar, is the access point for the Simien Mountains National Park. The park is easily accessible and excellent for trekking, with stirring views and a large variety of wildlife.

Most demands can be met, from casual strolls to several weeks' trekking, including an ascent of Africa's fourth-highest peak, 4620m Ras Dashen.

In two days you could walk from Debark to Sankaber and back; in five days you could get to Chenek, taking in Mt Bwahit; and in around seven to ten days you could bag Ras Dashen. All times include the return journey to Debark.

All treks can be organised in Debark, where the park headquarters are located. Daily fees, payable at the national park office in Debark, are US$8 per person per 48 hours, US$3.50 for a camp site per day and US$6 per day for an armed 'scout' (ranger). You pay about US$12 per day for a guide (including their park fees), plus US$6 for a mule and muleteer. You can hire a tent for US$3 per night.

In Debark, you can stay at the **Simien Park Hotel** (s/d/tw US$3/4/5).

One bus runs daily from Debark to Gondar (US$1.50, four hours). From there you can catch a bus to Debark (US$1.25, four hours).

LALIBELA

☎ 03

The Middle East has Petra, Ethiopia has Lalibela. Its rock-hewn churches are arguably Ethiopia's top attraction and they elicit an instinctive awe, whether you're a religious-architecture buff or not. Perched at an altitude of 2630m, Lalibela also remains a very isolated place and a centre of pilgrimage. Robed priests and monks still float among the dimly lit passageways and tunnels of the medieval churches; from hidden crypts and grottoes comes the sound of chanting, and in the deep, cool recesses of the interiors the smell of incense and beeswax candles still pervades. More than anywhere else in the world, you'll get the impression you've landed in a kingdom at least seven centuries behind your own.

The tourist office was scheduled to reopen at the time of writing. If closed, the hotels are also a good source of information.

There are still no banks in Lalibela, so come prepared. There are currently no Internet facilities.

Sights

What makes Lalibela's 11 **rock-hewn churches** (admission US$11) unique is that most are cut straight from the bedrock, so their roofs are at ground level. Originally called Roha, the town takes its present name from the 12th-century King Lalibela. Legend has it that the king established his capital here according to divine instructions revealed in a dream.

All 11 churches were built within one century; some, says another legend, with the help of angels. The churches have been kept alive by generations of priests who guard their treasures of ornamented crosses, illuminated Bibles and illustrated manuscripts.

An official guide is recommended (about US$11 – so at a dollar a church that's good value). Ask at the tourist office or a hotel. The best time to visit is during the country's major Orthodox festivals (p692).

Sleeping

Serkie Bar & Restaurant (☎ 390040; s/d US$3) The Serkie is probably Lalibela's best-kept budget secret, with unadorned but clean rooms.

Mini Roha Hotel (☎ 360094; s/d US$4/5) Also known as Private Roha, this place is simple but clean and welcoming and has a pleasant patio. Some rooms – and even loos – afford good views over town! It's west of the churches on the road to the Saturday market.

Alif Paradise Hotel (☎ 360023; d/tw US$10/14) A new, no-frills place, the Alif is a good deal, with a cosy compound and a homey feel. The helpful manager also does the place credit.

Eating & Drinking

Blue Nile Restaurant (mains US$1-3) One of the best bets in town for *faranji* food, with pizzas

> ### SPLURGE!
>
> **Jerusalem Guest House** (☎ 360047; camp site per tent US$6-10, s/d with private bathroom US$25/35) This pension gets consistently good reports. Prices might be off-putting for shoestringers, but it's peaceful and endowed with a traditional *tukul* restaurant which is worth blowing your budget for. Note that discounts of up to 30% are available in the low season.

and veggie options. It's north of the group of churches on the road to the bus station.

Helen Hotel, very close to the tourist office, brews its own *tej*, and *azmaris* usually perform here nightly. Its food has a good reputation too.

Serkie Bar & Restaurant is a local favourite serving decent and good-value nosh.

If you're in a mood for delicacies, Roha Snack & Pastry is the place to head to. It's south of the post office, near the football field. Come here for breakfast.

Askalech Tej House, close to the northern group of churches, is considered one of the best *tej* watering holes in town. From 7pm to 10pm *azmaris* often perform here.

Seven Olives Hotel is a lovely place for a drink at sunset or for breakfast.

Getting There & Away

Ethiopian Airlines flies at least once daily to Addis Ababa (US$95 one way, via Gondar and Bahar Dar) and to Aksum (US$65 one way). The new airport lies 23km from town. The NTO and various hotels offer an airport transfer service (US$3 to US$4 one way). Overland, the best approach is currently via Woldia. One bus leaves daily for Addis Ababa (US$9, two days).

EASTERN ETHIOPIA

DIRE DAWA

☎ 05

Dire Dawa is the second most populous town in Ethiopia. Its distinctive features include straight, tree-lined streets, neat squares and some interesting colonial architecture. For travellers, it's a convenient staging post to explore eastern Ethiopia. Don't miss the **market**, where Afar herders mix with Somali pastoralists and Oromo farmers; sometimes, around dawn, large camel caravans march in from the Somali desert.

Makonnen Hotel (☎ 113348; s/d US$3) Opposite the train station, this old Italian colonial hotel offers simple but spotless rooms. The manager, Nigatu, is a good source of local knowledge.

Tsehay Hotel (☎ 110023; d US$3, with private bathroom US$4-5) An adequate place to rest your head. This place has clean rooms, set in pleasant, hedged gardens. The restaurant is a local favourite.

Ethiopian Airlines has one to three flights daily to Addis Ababa (US$90 one way).

Trains head east for Djibouti City and west to Addis Ababa (US$9, 1st class). Four buses run daily to the capital (US$8.50, 12 hours). Minibuses run every 15 minutes to Harar (US$1, one hour).

HARAR
☎ 05

Harar is a must-see. At the crossroads of Christian and Islamic cultures, it's an awesome repository of culture and heritage. Who knows that it's the fourth-most holy city in Islam? It is tinged with a fascinating cosmopolitan aura and, as a merchant town, has atmosphere to burn. With Dire Dawa rising in significance, Harar has been a bit dwarfed by its neighbour and languishes somewhere in the past, but that's an inherent part of its pervasive charm. Try to get here, it's a jealously guarded secret.

Sights
With its 362 alleyways squeezed into just one square kilometre, Harar's **walled old town** is a treasure-trove of historical buildings and a fascinating place that begs exploration. With over 87 mosques in the old town alone, Harar is said to house the largest concentration of any city in the world – not to mention oodles of shrines.

Moseying down the maze of passages and alleyways is the best way to soak up atmosphere. You'll certainly come across Adare women, known for their very colourful traditional costumes – a fascinating sight.

Harar's most famous attraction are the **hyena men** of Harar. As night falls, the last remaining hyena men (just two) set themselves up just outside the city walls to feed the hyenas. Sometimes the hyena man risks feeding the animals from his own mouth – you can have a go at this, too, if you dare! This is a memorable spectacle, anchored in tradition, and not a touristy attraction.

Sleeping
Tewodros Hotel (☎ 660217; s or d US$2-3, with private bathroom US$4) This popular place near Harar Gate is unique in that you can watch hyenas stealing about in the shadows from the balconies at night. Your very own hyena show and an unforgettable experience. Ask

for rooms 13, 14, 15 or 16 (though they are sometimes renumbered).

Tourist Hotel (☎ 660824; d without/with bathroom US$3/3.50) In the new town. Clean rooms around a courtyard.

Dessie Hotel (☎ 660768; s or d without/with bathroom US$2/2.50) If the Tewodros is full, the peaceful Dessie, east of the new town, can also fit the bill.

Eating & Drinking
Hirut Restaurant is a cosy and intimate place, north of Ras Makonnen Square in the new town, serves excellent Ethiopian and *faranji* food.

Another reliable option, Belayneh Hotel, situated about 200m south of Shoa Gate, has a cool roof terrace yielding good views over the town.

Near the Harar Gate, Canal Cafeteria is a good spot to munch on cakes or sip smoothies. Try the Harari speciality, *hasher ka'ah*, a kind of tea made from coffee husks.

Central Café, close to the Harar Gate, is a good place to indulge in mouth-watering *fatira* (savoury pastries) and samosas.

Outside the Harar Hotel, you can find *fatira* sellers where *fatiras* are cooked to order on a griddle. They're cheap (US$0.50), filling and delicious.

Harar is well known for its beer. Hotspots to start a bar crawl include Samsun Hotel & Bar and the Cottage Bar, both inside the old town.

Getting There & Away
Two buses leave daily for Addis (US$7, 1½ days). Minibuses leave every 15 minutes for Dire Dawa (US$1, one hour).

SOUTHERN ETHIOPIA

RIFT VALLEY LAKES
If you're after the marvels of Mother Nature, the Rift Valley Lakes will be the highlight of your trip. If you come from northern Ethiopia, the Rift Valley Lakes will provide an escape from the monument circuit of northern Ethiopia. Everything here revolves around the joys of nature, with a string of lakes known for their birdlife. The wide valley through which the highway to Kenya slices is generally fertile and lush.

Lake Ziway is great for bird-watching.

Lakes Langano, **Abiata** and **Shala**, one brown, one silver and one blue, respectively, form a trio. Lake Langano is the only lake that is both bilharzia-free and safe for swimming. The latter two are designated as a national park. Lake Abiata is shallow and rich in birdlife, with up to 200,000 flamingos in season. Lake Shala nestles in a crater over 250m deep. There's a fine view from the hill above the narrow neck separating the two. Lake Langano makes a good base from which to visit these three lakes.

Lake Awasa is another outstanding natural site. Birdlife is the order of the day, but you can also indulge in **rowing** on the lake (US$6 per hour with rower). Awasa town is fairly large and has the best facilities – it's an ideal base for budget travellers, with all facilities.

Lakes Abaya and **Chamo** are regarded as the wildest of the group of lakes. The ridge between them is called the Bridge of Heaven and **Arba Minch**, a town nearby that you can fly to from Addis Ababa, means '40 springs'. Arba Minch is fairly unremarkable but is well-equipped and handy to both lakes. By Lake Chamo, don't miss the **crocodile market**, Africa's most impressive display of big crocs. You'll goggle at them sunning themselves on the warm sand of the lakeshore, south of Arba Minch.

Sleeping

LAKE ZIWAY
Park Hotel (☎ 412671; s or d with private bathroom US$2-5) and **Jemaneh** (s or d with private bathroom US$3-4) are the best options near Lake Ziway.

LAKE LANGANO
Bekele Mola Hotel (☎ 190011; camp site for 2 people US$4, tw from US$20) is by the bank of Lake Langano and has a beach. It can be packed at weekends. For cheaper hotels, head for the town of Arsi Negele.

AWASA
There's a profusion of budget accommodation in Awasa, including **Unique Park Hotel** (☎ 201318; d US$3), which has a prime location close to the lakefront. An attractive garden is an added bonus.

ARBA MINCH
There's plenty of choice when it comes to budget accommodation in Arba Minch,

including **Wubete Hotel** (☎ 811629; d without/with private bathroom US$3/4) and **Arba Minch Hotel** (☎ 810206; d US$3, with private bathroom US$5-7), both with acceptable rooms and a quiet location in Schecha settlement.

Getting There & Away
Being on the main road south the lakes are well served by buses, which stop at all the main towns including Ziway, Bulbula for Lakes Langano, Abiata and Shala, and Awasa. The trip from Addis Ababa takes about four to five hours (US$2). There are also daily buses between Addis Ababa and Arba Minch (US$6, 11 hours), and between Awasa and Arba Minch (US$3, six hours).

Ethiopian Airlines flies twice weekly from Arba Minch to Addis Ababa (US$72).

BALE MOUNTAINS NATIONAL PARK
This 2400-sq-km park is rich in endemic animals and birds, including the extremely rare Ethiopian wolf. Within the park you will find the **Sanetti Plateau**, Africa's highest moorland, and Tullu Demtu (4377m), southern Ethiopia's second-highest mountain. You can arrange one to five-day treks, on foot or by donkey, at the park headquarters at Dinsho Lodge in Dinsho, 46km west of Goba.

ETHIOPIA DIRECTORY

ACCOMMODATION
Hotels are plentiful and cheap at all levels, though facilities are lacking outside the larger towns. Cheap hotels (around US$2 to US$2.50 per night) consist of spartan rooms, little or no furniture and a shared toilet and bathroom. Note that a room with a double bed is usually called a 'single', and a room with twin beds a 'double'.

In the mid-range category, prices range from around US$15 to US$40. Facilities usually include a room with private bathroom, as well as an adequate restaurant. Though usually clean and quiet, the majority are looking tired and run-down, and rarely offer good value for money.

ACTIVITIES
Trekking is the most developed activity in Ethiopia. Both the Simien and Bale Mountains offer good trekking and good wildlife.

White-water rafting is increasingly popular, especially on the Omo River, but doesn't come cheap. Expect to shell out US$190 per person per day, all inclusive. Trips are organised by travel agencies in Addis Ababa (see p693 for agency details).

DANGERS & ANNOYANCES

Compared with many African countries, Ethiopia – even Addis Ababa – is a safe place. Serious or violent crime is rare. Outside the capital, the risk of petty crime drops still further. In bigger towns, especially Addis Ababa, beware of thieves, small-scale swindlers and pickpockets.

In the touristy places, you'll be approached by self-appointed and unofficial guides. Be polite but firm.

The most common annoyance is the 'faranji frenzy' or foreigner frenzy; expect lots of attention from howling mobs of children, especially in rural Ethiopia. Try to treat it with humour, never with anger.

EMBASSIES & CONSULATES

Embassies and consulates in Addis Ababa include the following. Street names for addresses being usually nonexistent, refer to the Addis Ababa map for locations.
Australia (see Canada)
Canada (☎ 713022)
Djibouti (☎ 613006)
Eritrea Currently closed
France (☎ 550066)
Germany (☎ 550433)
Kenya (☎ 610033)
Somalia (☎ 635921)
Sudan (☎ 516477)
UK (☎ 612354)
USA (☎ 550666)

Ethiopia has diplomatic representation in the following countries: Djibouti, Egypt, Kenya and Sudan, but not Eritrea.

FESTIVALS & EVENTS

Religious and secular festivals in Ethiopia are often colourful events with pageantry, music and dancing. The most outstanding ones include:
6-7 January Leddet (also known as Genna or Christmas)
19 January Timkat (Epiphany, celebrating Christ's baptism)
11 September Kiddus Yohannes (New Year's Day)
27 September Meskel (Finding of the True Cross)

HOLIDAYS

As well as religious holidays listed in the Africa Directory (p1003) the principal public holidays in Ethiopia are:
7 January Coptic Christmas
19 January Timket
2 March Battle of Adowa
2 May Moloud (Birth of the Prophet)
28 May Downfall of the Dergue
11 September Enkutatasha (New Year)
28 September Meskel (Finding of the True Cross)

MAPS

Of the maps currently available outside the country, the best is that produced by International Travel Maps (1998; 1:2,000,000).

MEDIA

The best-known English-language newspapers are the daily (except Sunday) *Ethiopian Herald*, the *Monitor* and the weekly *Addis Tribune*. Apart from the *Ethiopian Herald*, they are available only in Addis.

Radio Ethiopia broadcasts in six local languages, plus English, French and Arabic for around 1½ hours each per day. English-language radio can be heard from 1.30pm to 2pm and 7pm to 8pm weekdays.

Ethiopia's single television channel broadcasts every weekday evening from around 6pm to midnight (from noon on the weekend). From 10.30pm to midnight there is a broadcast in English. Some of the larger hotels, bars and restaurants have satellite dishes that receive CNN.

MONEY

At the time of writing, the Commercial Bank had just finished installing ATMs in several locations in Addis Ababa. The machines were undergoing a trial run.

Some of the larger hotels, some airlines (including Ethiopian Airlines) and a few travel agents now accept credit cards. A commission of up to 5% is sometimes charged. Some private banks (such as the Dashen Bank) can give cash advances with a credit card; there's a 5% commission charge. Outside the capital, credit cards are useless and you'll have to rely on cash.

US dollars are still the best currency to carry both in cash and in travellers cheques. Note that bank exchange receipts must be shown when changing birr back into dollars. All banks in the capital and the larger towns (but not the smaller ones) exchange travellers cheques. Like cash, travellers cheques are best carried in US dollars.

POST & TELEPHONE

Ethiopia has quite an efficient and reliable postal service. Airmail costs US$0.22/0.30/0.40 for a letter up to 20g to Africa/Europe/the Americas and Australia. Parcel post and courier services are available in the capital.

There are public telephone boxes in most of the larger towns. They accept both coins and cards, but international calls are best made from the telecommunications offices found in most towns.

International rates are calculated per minute: US$1.20 worldwide. Domestic calls cost from US$0.10 to US$0.25 per minute depending on the distance.

TOURIST INFORMATION

The **Ethiopian Tourist Commission** (ETC; www.ethiopia tourism.com) includes a tourism office in Addis Ababa, which is open to travellers. Independent tourist offices can be found in the regional capitals.

No national tourist office exists abroad.

TOURS

Organised tours in Ethiopia are useful for a specialist activity, such as white-water rafting or bird-watching or for access to remote regions with limited public transport.

Tours may be out of reach of most budget travellers, but you can try joining other tours to reduce costs.

There are at least 15 reputable travel agencies in Addis Ababa. They all offer tours in the country and have English-speaking staff. Try the following:

Ethio Travel & Tours (☎ 567150; www.ethiotraveland tours.com)

National Tour Operation (NTO; ☎ 514838; nto@telecom .net.et)

Village Ethiopia (☎ 523497; www.village-ethiopia.com)

Wonz-Dar Expeditions (☎ 757604; wonzdar@telecom .net.et) Located east of the centre, Wonz-Dar is hard to find. There's no street name. Go by taxi and say 'Jos Hansen, 3C'. It's inside 3C.

VISAS

All visitors need visas to enter Ethiopia. Nationals of 33 countries can now obtain tourist visas on arrival at Bole International Airport. These include most of Europe (including the EU countries), the United States, Canada, Australia and New Zealand.

Tourist visas cost US$36 for nationalities from Europe, the US and Australia. They are valid for between one to three months, depending on the application and special requests.

Visa Extensions

Tourist visas can be extended at the **Immigration Office** (☎ 553899), off Churchill Rd, near the post office in Addis Ababa, up to a maximum of three months.

Visas for Onward Travel

Visas for the following neighbouring countries are available from embassies in Addis Ababa (see p692 for details).

Djibouti You'll need your passport, two photographs and US$35. It takes one day to process.

Eritrea Closed.

Kenya You'll need your passport, one photograph and Birr438 (about US$50). It takes one day to process.

Somalia Addis is the only place in Africa where you can get a visa to enter Somalia. Bring your passport, US$30 and a photograph. It takes one day to process.

Sudan You'll need your passport, two photographs and US$70. You'll also be asked to mention an address in Sudan (eg, a hotel). It takes two to three days to process.

Djibouti

HIGHLIGHTS

- **Djibouti City** Strolling in the alleyways of Marché Central, teeming with life, colours and odours (p700)
- **Tadjoura** Dare to try a *qat*-chewing session with the locals (p705)
- **Goda Mountains** Take a walk to a refreshing waterfall and get away from it all in a *campement touristique* (p704)
- **Lac Assal** Descend to the lowest point on the African continent: 153m below sea level (p704)
- **Best journey** Crossing the Gulf of Tadjoura sitting on top of a dhow fully loaded with *qat* (p705)
- **Off the beaten track** Windsurfing on wheels across the great salty plain of Grand Barra (p703)

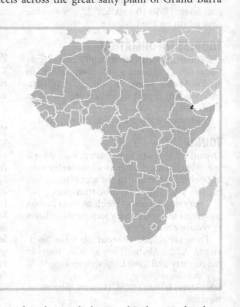

FAST FACTS

- **Area** 23,000 sq km
- **ATMs** only in Djibouti City
- **Borders** Eritrea and Ethiopia open
- **Budget** US$40 to US$50 a day
- **Capital** Djibouti City
- **Languages** Arabic, French, Afar, Somali
- **Money** Djibouti franc; US$1 = DFr175
- **Population** approx 650,000
- **Seasons** hot (Jun–Aug), cool (mid-Oct–mid-Apr), wet (Oct–Apr)
- **Telephone** country code ☎ 253; international access code ☎ 00
- **Time** GMT/UTC + 3
- **Visas** US$29 for 10 days, US$35 for 30 days; obtainable at the airport

If you're in search of something weird or strangely seductive, little-visited Djibouti is the place. Its geography says it all: the country consists of the port and town of Djibouti and an enclave of barren, but topographically dramatic, semidesert hinterland that offer scenery unparalleled elsewhere in the world. You'll be enthralled by the eerie, lunar, volcanic landscapes, such as the bizarre Lake Abbé or the vast salt Lake Assal, reminiscent of Dante's *Inferno*.

Djibouti is also a strange African anomaly filled with jarring cultural and social combinations. Traditionally robed Afar tribesmen, macho French legionnaires, exotic hennaed glamour-kittens, luscious French cuisine, nightly discos and seedy bars all jostle side by side, bearing out Arthur Rimbaud's pronouncement that 'the air of Djibouti will make you take leave of your senses'. Not to mention the ubiquitous *qat* (a mildly intoxicating herb) that sets the unhurried pace of the country and adds another touch of the bizarre.

So many things in such a tiny, raw patch of land. Djibouti could well be one of the best-kept secrets in East Africa.

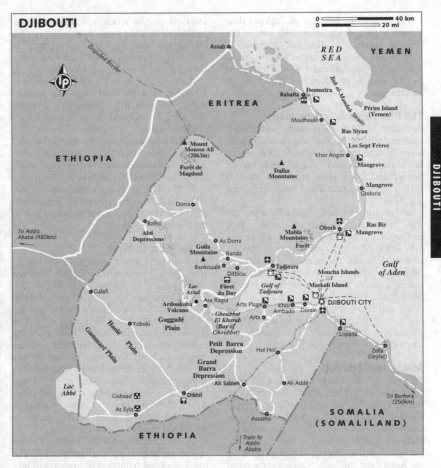

DJIBOUTI

DJIBOUTI

0 _____ 40 km
0 _____ 20 mi

RED SEA — YEMEN

Disputed Border

Assab

Rahaita — Doumeïra
ERITREA
Moulhoulé

Bab-al-Mandab Straits

Périm Island (Yemen)

Ras Siyan

Les Sept Frères

Khor Angor
Mangrove

Mount Moussa Ali (2063m)

Forêt de Magdoul

Dalha Mountains

ETHIOPIA

Mangrove
Godoria

Dorra

To Addis Ababa (480km)

Balho

Afol Depressions

As Dorra

Goda Mountains

Randa

Bankoualé

Dittilou

Mabla Mountains
Forêt

Obock — Ras Bir
Mangrove

Galafi

Lac Assal

Forêt du Day

Gulf of Tadjoura

Tadjoura

Moucha Islands

Gulf of Aden

Ardoukoba Volcano

Asa Ragid

Arta Plage

Maskali Island

DJIBOUTI CITY

Yoboki

Gaggadé Plain

Ghoubbet El Kharab (Bay of Ghoubbet)

Arta

Khor Ambado

Dorale

Hanlé Plain

Gammaré Plain

Petit Barra Depression

Hol Hol

Loyada

Grand Barra Depression

Ali Sabieh

Ali Addé

Zeila (Seylac)

Lac Abbé

Gobaad

Dikhil

As Eyla

Assamo

To Berbera (250km)

SOMALIA (SOMALILAND)

ETHIOPIA

Train to Addis Ababa

HISTORY
The Kingdom of Aksum

Around the 1st century AD, Djibouti made up part of the powerful Ethiopian kingdom of Aksum, which included modern-day Eritrea and even stretched across the Red Sea to parts of southern Arabia. It was during the Aksumite era, in the 4th century AD, that Christianity first appeared in the region.

The Arrival of Islam

As the empire of Aksum gradually fell into decline, a new influence arose that would supersede forever the Christian religion in Djibouti: Islam. It was introduced to the region around AD 825 by Arab traders from Southern Arabia, and consolidated after the fall of Constantinople (present-day Istanbul) in 1453, when the Muslim Ottoman Empire extended its control to the whole of the eastern coast of the Red Sea.

European Colonialism

In the second half of the 19th century, European powers competed to grab new colonies in Africa. The French, seeking to counter the British presence in Yemen on the other side of the Bab al-Mandab Strait, made agreements with the Afar sultans of Obock and Tadjoura that gave them the right to settle. In 1888 construction of Djibouti City began on the southern shore of the Gulf of Tadjoura. French Somaliland (present-day Djibouti) began to take shape.

France and the emperor of Ethiopia then signed a pact designating Djibouti as the 'official outlet of Ethiopian commerce'. This led to the construction of the Addis Ababa–Djibouti City railway, which remains of vital strategic and commercial importance to Ethiopia.

The Rise Towards Independence

As early as 1949 there were anticolonial demonstrations by the Issa Somalis, who were in favour of the reunification of the territories of Italian, British and French Somaliland. Meanwhile, the Afars were in favour of French rule. The French supported the Afars.

Major riots ensued, especially after the 1967 referendum, which produced a vote in favour of continued rule by France – a vote achieved partly by the arrest of opposition leaders and the massive expulsion of ethnic Somalis. After the referendum, the colony's name was changed from French Somaliland to the French Territory of the Afars and Issas.

On June 1977, the colony finally won its sovereignty from France. The country became the new Republic of Djibouti.

Ambivalent Djibouti

Djibouti quickly learnt to exploit its strategic position. When the Gulf War broke out in 1990, the country's president, Hassan Gouled Aptidon, while appearing to oppose the military build-up in the Gulf, simultaneously allowed France to increase its military personnel in the country, as well as granting the Americans and Italians access to the naval port. And he skilfully managed to retain the support of Saudi Arabia and Kuwait for the modernisation of Djibouti port, the country's most important development project.

During the Second Gulf War in 2003, Djibouti continued to play an ambivalent role, allowing a US presence in the country – to the great displeasure of France, who would have liked to be considered as the most privileged ally.

Ethnic Tensions, a Constant Dividing Line

Clan rivalries have always dogged Djibouti. The two main ethnic groups, Afars and Issas, have been jostling for power since the 1970s. These tensions came to a head in November

1991, when Afar rebels launched a civil war in the north, their traditional territory. Accusing the Issa-dominated government of favouring its own kind in the labour market, they demanded multiparty elections.

A peace accord was signed in December 1994 between the Afars and the government. However, this agreement is a fragile one and it will take time before ethnic hostility wanes.

In 1999 the moderate inter-ethnic People's Progress Assembly (RPP) retained power with a 74% majority and Ismaël Omar Guellah became Djibouti's second president.

At the last general elections in January 2003, the RPP won again. Seven women (out of 65 members of parliament) won a seat to the National Assembly.

A Confusing Outlook

Since its birth as a nation, Djibouti has always been poised rather uneasily between its larger and more powerful neighbours. The geographical position of the country, sandwiched between three stronger nations, and its strategic value as a port, as well as its limited natural resources, have made the maintenance of good international relations absolutely vital. This was obvious during the war between Eritrea and Ethiopia in the 1990s, though Djibouti didn't really manage to be the regional conciliator it aimed to be. Again, Djibouti's port proved to be strategic when Ethiopia diverted its foreign trade through it (and still does).

As for its relations with France, Djibouti continues to play an ambiguous part. The much-awaited reduction of French military personnel has been effective since 2000, but close links with France remain vital to Djibouti's economy.

There has been a flood of refugees arriving in the country since the early 1980s as a result of conflicts in Ethiopia, Eritrea and Somalia. About 200,000 refugees are estimated to have arrived during this time. Their future remains uncertain.

THE CULTURE

Djiboutians are charming, respectful and very hospitable people. It has to do with the traditionally nomadic culture of the two main ethnic groups, the Afars and Somalis. Despite an increasing tendency towards a more sedentary lifestyle, most Djiboutians living in towns retain strong links with their nomadic past. The nomadic tradition of hospitality has also retained its importance. Over 90% of the population is Muslim, yet the population is very tolerant and alcohol is widely available.

One of the most striking features in Djibouti is the overwhelming presence of *qat*. The life of most Djiboutian males seems to revolve entirely around the consumption of this mild narcotic. Every day, *qat* consumers meet their circle of friends in the *mabraz* (*qat* den) to *brouter la salade* (graze the salad). There, a minimum of five hours is spent reclining on cushions, smoking cigarettes and sipping tea, while 'grazing' on the leaves. If you're invited to partake a *qat* session, do not balk at the idea – it's an excellent insight into local life. *Qat* is said to be the reason behind numerous divorces. Only 10% of women are thought to consume the plant regularly.

ARTS

Dance is arguably the highest form of culture in Djibouti, along with oral literature and poetry. Some dances celebrate major events of life, such as birth, marriage or circumcision.

If you are looking for handicrafts, the traditional Afar and Somali knife and the very attractive Afar woven straw mats (known in Afar as *fiddima*) are among the finest products.

ENVIRONMENT

Djibouti's 23,000 sq km can be divided into three geographic regions: the coastal plains with white, sandy beaches; the volcanic plateaus in the south and central parts of the country; and the mountain ranges in the north, where the altitude reaches over 2000m above sea level. Essentially the country is a vast wasteland, with the exception of pockets of forest and dense vegetation to the north.

The climate is hot, with a cooler season (including occasional rain) from November to mid-April, when temperatures average 25°C. At the peak of the hot season, the thermometer can hit 45°C and the humidity is correspondingly high.

Livestock rearing is the most important type of agriculture. As demand for scarce grazing land mounts, the forests of the north are coming under threat, including the fragile Forêt du Day National Park, the country's only national park.

TRANSPORT

GETTING THERE & AWAY
Air
Djibouti is served by **Daallo Airlines** (☎ 353401) from Asmara (Eritrea) and Hargeisa (Somalia); by **Ethiopian Airlines** (☎ 351007) from Addis Ababa (Ethiopia); by **Djibouti Airlines** (☎ 351006) from Hargeisa, Addis Ababa and Dire Dawa (Ethiopia); and by **Regional Air** (☎ 250297) from Nairobi (Kenya). For more information see p703.

DEPARTURE TAX

The airport departure tax is US$17 for neighbouring countries and US$29 for further-flung destinations. It can be paid in Djibouti francs.

Land
ERITREA
Travel overland to Eritrea is now possible as the relations between the two countries have normalised, but there's no formal border post and traffic is limited to shared taxis from Obock to Moulhoule, the last town before the border. There should be other taxis plying the route from Moulhoule to Assab in Eritrea. It's about 3½ hours from Obock to the border (US$12) and from the border to Assab another 3½ hours (US$10).

ETHIOPIA
The border with Ethiopia is open and there's a lot of road traffic, but the old Djibouti–Ethiopia train link – though rather dilapidated and slow – presents the best and cheapest means of travelling between the two countries (at least as far as Dire Dawa in Ethiopia – continue by bus to Addis Ababa). It departs three times a week. See p703 for more information.

GETTING AROUND
The road network links all major villages in the country with the capital. The Route de l'Unité, a good sealed road, covers the 174km from the capital around the Gulf of Tadjoura to Tadjoura (which should be

extended as far as Obock by the time this book is published).

Public transport is pretty limited. By bus, you can go to Ali Sabieh and Dikhil in the south, and to Galafi at the Ethiopian border. Obock and Tadjoura are accessible by ferry or dhow from Djibouti City (see p703). The train linking Djibouti City to Addis Ababa in Ethiopia (see p703) makes several stops en route; Hol Hol and Ali Sabieh are of most interest to travellers.

The bad news is that the most spectacular attractions are way off the main roads, so to reach them you'll need to hire a 4WD and driver, or join an organised tour. Either way – be prepared for outrageous prices.

DJIBOUTI CITY

pop 400,000

The town of Djibouti, barely 100 years old, has an identity problem: it is the sedentary capital of a nomadic people, an African city designed like a European settlement in the Red Sea. For many travellers, Djibouti City is little more than a ramshackle little port village, with peeling colonial and modern buildings, a confusing mix of torpor and bustling activity. Unashamed *qat*-chewing men, sensuous women swathed in superb shawls, proud but desperate Somali refugees, gaunt-faced beggars and stalwart foreign legionnaires in their knee-length socks all roam the streets. This unusual, boisterous, sweltering cocktail of African, Arab, Indian and European influences is simply mind-boggling.

ORIENTATION

Djibouti City is small enough to explore on foot. The centre comprises the European Quarter to the north and the African Quarter to the south.

The place du 27 Juin 1977, still known by its former title, place Ménélik, marks the heart of the European Quarter.

South of place du 27 Juin 1977 lies place Mahmoud Harbi, which is also still known by its former name – place Rimbaud. Here the European Quarter ends and the African Quarter begins.

Northwest of town, a causeway known as L'Escale leads to a small marina, which is the point of departure for trips to Tadjoura

and Obock. Further north is the town's port proper.

Northeast of town is the Plateau du Serpent, where many of the foreign embassies can be found. It is connected to the centre by the Boulevard de la République.

There are no buses between town and Djibouti-Ambouli International Airport, 5km south of town, from where a taxi costs US$6 (after bargaining).

The train station is about 1km north of the centre. Flag down a minibus to get to the centre (US$0.25).

INFORMATION
Bookshops
Libraire Couleur Locale (☎ 352121; rue de Paris) Good for local literature and stocks English-French-Afar dictionaries.
Maison de la Presse (☎ 350223; off place du 27 Juin 1977) Good collection of international newspapers and magazines.

Internet Access
You'll find several Internet outlets in the centre. The cost is around US$3 per hour. The most useful for travellers include **Filga Foire Informatique** (rue de Paris) and **Dis-Pro** (rue Clochette).

Medical Services
Two European doctors keep a **surgery** (☎ 352724) in the building opposite Maison de la Presse, off place du 27 Juin 1977. They can speak English. **Dental services** (☎ 355278) are also available upstairs.

The best-equipped hospital is **CHA Bouffard** (☎ 351351; Boulaos), south of the city.

Pharmacie de l'Independance (☎ 352630; rue de Rome) is very well stocked and has knowledgeable staff.

Money
Most banks, including the **BCIMR** (☎ 350857; place Lagarde), can be found around the place Lagarde. They usually apply a 2% commission on travellers cheques and a service charge of about US$3 for each transaction, be it cash or travellers cheques.

Several authorised bureaux de change can also be found on the southeastern side of place du 27 Juin 1977. The bureaux de change don't charge any commission but their rates might be slightly inferior to the ones offered by banks. Banks keep regular

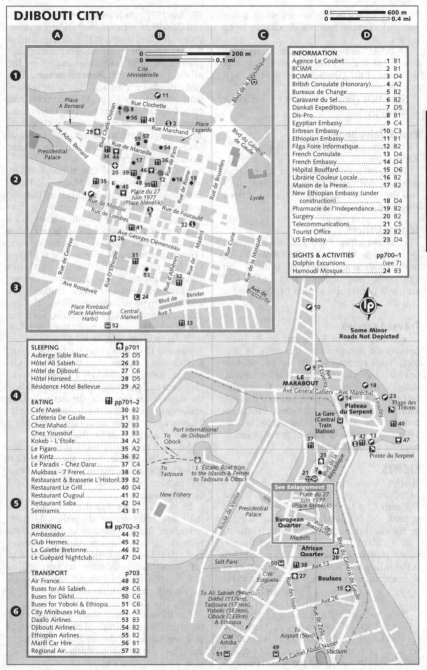

DJIBOUTI CITY

0 — 600 m
0 — 0.4 mi

DJIBOUTI

0 — 200 m
0 — 0.1 mi

INFORMATION
Agence Le Goubet	1 B1
BCIMR	2 B1
BCIMR	3 D4
British Consulate (Honorary)	4 A2
Bureaux de Change	5 B2
Caravane du Sel	6 B2
Dankali Expeditions	7 D5
Dis-Pro	8 B1
Egyptian Embassy	9 C4
Eritrean Embassy	10 C3
Ethiopian Embassy	11 B1
Filga Foire Informatique	12 B2
French Consulate	13 D4
French Embassy	14 D4
Hôpital Bouffard	15 D6
Librairie Couleur Locale	16 B2
Maison de la Presse	17 B2
New Ethiopian Embassy (under construction)	18 D4
Pharmacie de l'Independance	19 B2
Surgery	20 B2
Telecommunications	21 C5
Tourist Office	22 B2
US Embassy	23 D4

SIGHTS & ACTIVITIES pp700–1
Dolphin Excursions	(see 7)
Hamoudi Mosque	24 B3

Some Minor Roads Not Depicted

SLEEPING p701
Auberge Sable Blanc	25 D5
Hôtel Ali Sabieh	26 B3
Hôtel de Djibouti	27 C6
Hôtel Horseed	28 D5
Résidence Hôtel Bellevue	29 A2

EATING pp701–2
Cafe Mask	30 B2
Cafeteria De Gaulle	31 B3
Chez Mahad	32 B3
Chez Youssóuf	33 B3
Kokeb - L'Etoile	34 A2
Le Figaro	35 A2
Le Kintz	36 B2
Le Paradis - Chez Darar	37 C4
Mukbasa - 7 Freres	38 C6
Restaurant & Brasserie L'Historil	39 B2
Restaurant Le Grill	40 D4
Restaurant Ougoul	41 B2
Restaurant Saba	42 D4
Semiramis	43 B1

DRINKING pp702–3
Ambassador	44 B2
Club Hermes	45 B2
La Galette Bretonne	46 B2
Le Guépard Nightclub	47 D4

TRANSPORT p703
Air France	48 B2
Buses for Ali Sabieh	49 C6
Buses for Dikhil	50 C6
Buses for Yoboki & Ethiopia	51 C6
City Minibuses Hub	52 A3
Daallo Airlines	53 B3
Djibouti Airlines	54 B2
Ethiopian Airlines	55 B2
Marill Car Hire	56 B1
Regional Air	57 B2

business hours (see p706 for more information) whereas bureaux de change open longer.

Djibouti has two ATMs, one at the main branch of the BCIMR on place Lagarde, the other at the Plateau du Serpent BCIMR branch.

Note that there's no currency exchange at the airport.

Post & Telephone

The main post office is on blvd de la République.

The most convenient places to make an international call are the main post office and the various telephone outlets scattered around the city centre.

Tourist Offices

The **tourist office** (☎ 352800; rue de Foucauld; ⏰ 7am-1pm Sat-Wed & 4.30-6.30pm Sat, Mon & Wed), to the southeastern side of place du 27 Juin 1977, sells a map of the country for US$1.75 and will photocopy a map of the city for you free of charge.

Travel Agencies

In a country not really geared up for backpackers or independent travellers of any sort, travel agencies can be the only option to visit the spectacular sites of the hinterland. Reliable travel agencies include **Caravane de Sel** (☎ 356618; caravane@intnet.dj; place du 27 Juin 1977), **AECVETA** (☎ 354695; www.aecveta.com), **Dankali Expeditions** (☎ 350313; www.dankali.com; blvd de la République) and **Agence Le Goubet** (☎ 354520; goubet@bow.intnet.dj; blvd Cheik Osman).

SIGHTS

Historic buildings? Virtually nonexistent. Museums? Nope. At first sight, you'll find Djibouti City fairly decrepit and devoid of appeal, and for good reason. Most would-be colonial buildings are decaying. Djibouti City is a place of attitudes, mood, character, poses, glances, atmosphere. The pace of life is confusing for newcomers. It's buzzing in the morning and evening, while in the afternoon the centre looks like a ghost town, with most shops and offices closed.

If you go to the right place at the right time, Djibouti City will captivate you. Start your visit with a walk around the European Quarter in the early morning. Linger over a cup of coffee and a croissant at a terrace on place du 27 Juin 1977. With its whitewashed houses and Moorish arcades sheltering Parisian-style cafés and shops, it is a strange mix of the Arab and the European. To the south lies place Mahmoud Harbi, dominated by the minaret of the great **Hamoudi mosque**. This vast, shambolic, intimidating square is mayhem: market-goers with their donkeys and carts, itinerant peddlers hawking their wares, nomads exchanging news, pickpockets and street urchins, trundling minibuses and herds of sheep and goats trotting to and from the auction yards.

The chaotic **Marché Central** (Central Market), which extends from place Mahmoud Harbi eastward along and below blvd de Bender, is a must. Go there early morning or late afternoon, when it bursts with activity. It's a crisscross of alleyways where stalls and shops are lined cheek by jowl. Pungent odours, bright colours and loud noises will plunge you into another world. To the west, fruit and vegetables are sold. Eastward, women hawkers sell cooking spices, clothes dyes and every type of medicinal herb. The qat sellers, behind their rickety stalls, keep the precious leafy sprigs fresh and free from dust with damp towels and sacking.

Around 1pm, don't miss the arrival of qat, a fascinating slice of local life. The tension mounts swiftly. Suddenly, a cacophony of car horns and shouting breaks out, heralding the marvellous news: qat, the nation's daily addiction, has arrived, fresh from Ethiopia. Then a heavy torpor descends on the town and all activity ceases for the afternoon.

Another nice stroll takes you along the causeway to **L'Escale**, past the **presidential palace** to the small marina where you can see picturesque dhows, fishing skiffs and pleasure boats.

In the early evening the city resurrects itself and takes on an altogether different character. The lighted cafés and restaurants reopen, terraces fill up. Men are stoned and relaxed – a testimony to the effects of qat. Ethiopian prostitutes beckon sailors and legionnaires into sleazy joints. Locals previously ensconced in their houses flock towards the centre.

For those travellers ready for a big night out, there is a multitude of bars, restaurants and nightclubs to choose from. The neon lights give the town something of a down-at-heel, raucous Ibiza feel.

DIVING
There is excellent diving in the Gulf of Tadjoura, including around Musha and Maskali Islands, and in the Bay of Ghoubbet, a spot noted for its concentration of whale sharks from October to January.

Longer trips to the Sept Frères Archipelago are also available. It costs about US$100 for two dives at Musha Island, including boat transfer and picnic. Contact **Dolphin Excursions** (☎ 350313; www.dankali.com; blvd de la République) and **Breiz Izel** (www.multimania.com/breizizel). Some dive instructors can speak English.

SLEEPING
Budget travellers, a word of warning: staying in Djibouti City can leave you bankrupt if you come unprepared. Cheap, good-value budget accommodation is hard to come by in the capital. Let's call 'budget' any place where you can get a double room for less than US$40. The cheaper places invariably double as brothels and they will give you an unequivocal definition of the words 'sleazy' and 'dodgy'. Note that some mid-range options are only marginally more expensive than the budget places, and note also that between mid-April and late-October a room with air-conditioning is essential if you want to survive. Street names are given where appropriate.

Hôtel Ali Sabieh & Pizzeria Ali Sabieh (☎ 353264; ave Georges Clemenceau; s/d with private bathroom US$49/66; ❄) A choice location in the middle of the European Quarter; well-maintained, if smallish, rooms with prim bathrooms – what more could you want? It's relatively good value by Djiboutian standards. Prices include breakfast. An added bonus is the good pizza outlet on the ground floor.

Hôtel Horseed (☎ 352316; blvd du Général de Gaulle; r with shared bathroom US$29; ❄) Probably the most dependable option for budget travellers, for lack of serious competitors. It's a bit off the track but still within easy walking distance of the city centre. The 12 rooms, though nothing to rave about, are clean and the place is kind of homey.

Auberge Sable Blanc (☎ 351163; r without/with private bathroom US$35/40; ❄) A bit out of the way off blvd de la République, this converted villa with a relaxed atmosphere is a good haunt for travellers. Some rooms are more spacious than others, so ask to see a few. The proximity of a mosque guarantees that you'll be lulled by the muezzin prayer five times a day.

Hôtel de Djibouti (☎ 356415; ave 13; s/d US$29/40; ❄) Positioned in the African Quarter a short haul from the city centre, this outfit has a tarnished feel with slightly frayed rooms, but staff are amiable and prices can be negotiable for longer stays. The noise of ave 13 leaks right into the street-facing rooms – light sleepers should ask for a back room.

> **SPLURGE!**
> **Résidence Hôtel Bellevue** (☎ 358088; bellevue@intnet.dj; ave Saint Laurent du Var; s/d US$73/83, seaview US$88/98; ❄) The Bellevue isn't exactly the lap of luxury nor is it even slightly glam. So, what are its assets? Well, it's the best deal if you need an escape hatch from the sweltering heat and dust. Prices are high for what you get but, remember, you're in Djibouti and it matches the cost of living. What it lacks in style is made up for by an enviable location – bars, restaurants and nightclubs are just a skip away and it has a secure atmosphere. The bare modern but squeaky-clean self-contained rooms come with the usual mod-cons.

EATING
There's a dearth of budget hotels in Djibouti but a wealth of superb eating options at not-so-overwhelming prices. For sheer choice and quality of food, Djibouti ranks among the best places in Africa. No doubt, you'll be delighted by the eclectic amalgam of restaurants and cuisines. This is your chance to relish French cuisine, scoff absolutely fresh local seafood, savour tasty meat dishes, devour delicious pizzas and treat yourself to exquisite fruit juices or pastries. Most places listed below are open every day. *Bon appétit!*

Mukbasa – 7 Freres (☎ 351188; ave 13; fish dishes US$8.50-11.50) In the African Quarter, this is a cheery, authentic place to savour a truly finger-licking *poisson yemenite* (oven-baked fish). The chapatilike bread, along with *mokbasa* (puree of honey and either dates or banana), make a great accompaniment. Ask to see how it's all being prepared in the kitchen.

Chez Youssouf (☎ 351899; fish dishes US$8.50-11.50) Located in a back street east of place Mahmoud Harbi, the low-key Chez Youssouf may not impress at first sight but has earned a reputation for serving succulent grilled fish.

Le Figaro (☎ 353841; ave Administrateur Bernard; mains US$10-26) Attached to the Hôtel Plein Ciel, this upscale gourmet restaurant is justly revered for its refined and imaginative cuisine. Try the *carpaccio de bœuf* (slices of beef marinated in lemon and olive oil) and the excellently prepared grilled zebu fillet. If you're penny counting, go for the pizzas or the salads.

Restaurant Ougoul (☎ 353652; ave Georges Clemenceau; mains US$9-20) The fancy Ougoul is a long-standing institution and is regarded as one of the best fish and seafood restaurants in town.

Restaurant Saba (☎ 354244; ave Maréchal Lyautey; mains US$6-11.50) Close to the railway station, this joint is highly rated by expats. The extensive menu focuses on seafood, ranging from shrimps with coconut milk to fish dishes, including the famous *poisson yemenite* (US$8.50) – not to mention superb fruit juice cocktails (US$1.15). Vegetarians will opt for salads (US$2.30 to US$6).

Restaurant Le Grill (☎ 357293; Plateau du Serpent; mains US$6-11) At the Club des Cheminots (the old rail-workers club), Le Grill boasts a tranquil location. In the garden, the cool sea breeze and shade from the old acacia trees create a very welcome respite from the heat and dust. Try the delicious fish or beef *brochettes* (kebabs).

Kokeb – L'Etoile (☎ 350410; rue de Marseille; mains US$7-20) This Ethiopian restaurant is a good initiation to the cuisine of neighbouring Ethiopia, with all the classics, including vegetarian dishes. An exotic decor and a dance show (starting at 9.30pm) add to the pleasure of dining here.

Cafeteria De Gaulle (rue de Paris) Head to this hole-in-the-wall opposite Daallo Airlines office if you want a quick and cheap fix of vitamins (an excellent hangover cure). There's a wide assortment of refreshing fruit juices available (US$0.30 to US$0.85).

Chez Mahad (off rue de Madrid) Perfect for sipping a fruit juice after shopping in Marché Central, just a short stroll away. Grab a seat outside and watch the world go by.

Le Paradis – Chez Darar (mains US$2-6) A cheap and cheerful eatery with a large outdoor seating area, midway between the post office and the railway station, close to the seashore.

Pizzeria Ali Sabieh (☎ 353264; ave Georges Clemenceau; pizzas US$6-20; ☉ evenings only) If you're craving Italian tastes, this is the place to go, with a respectable selection of pizzas cooked in the oven.

Cafe Mask (place du 27 Juin 1977; mains US$6-16) A good eatery with a touch of sophistication in the setting – the walls are adorned with African masks and batiks. The menu runs the gamut from African dishes, such as *yassa* chicken, to more conventional fish or meat dishes, pancakes and pasta. It's also a good place for breakfast. The shaded terrace is a plus.

Restaurant & Brasserie L'Historil (☎ 354767; place du 27 Juin 1977; mains US$6-17) We've received good reviews for the restaurant upstairs, right in the heart of the European Quarter. Try the *émincé de poisson au basilic* (sliced fish with basil). The ground floor and the terrace are among the most popular spots in Djibouti City, but a beer costs a whopping US$4.

For those on a rock-bottom budget, the stalls and shops around place Mahmoud Harbi are groaning with colourful vegetables, fruits and spices at unbeatable prices.

Semiramis (rue Marchand) This supermarket is the best stocked in Djibouti.

SPLURGE!

Le Kintz (☎ 352791; rue de Marseille; mains US$11.50-20) Shiny 4WDs parked in front of the restaurant set the tone. No doubt, Le Kintz is a culinary reference in Djibouti and is one of the local elite's preferred meeting points. The rather chic interior and subdued style make this a very French place. Fish dishes, seafood, veal, beef and poultry make for a great dining experience, enhanced by an unflappable service. May we suggest you dress smart?

DRINKING & CLUBBING

If you are into clubbing you'll find Djibouti City very special. It offers a fascinating glimpse of local life. Yes, it is a sleazy scene but it's also a surprising social phenomenon that can still make for a fun night out, provided you don't take things too seriously. The underlying scenario is obvious: gorgeous Somali or Ethiopian 'princesses' strut around the dance floor to seduce mesmerised legionnaires and tentatively debauched male expats. This slightly surreal spectacle takes place in the nightclubs on and around rue d'Ethiopie, in the European Quarter, which are at their liveliest on Thursday and Friday nights. Entrance is free.

And if you're a solo female traveller? The Djibouti club scene may not be your thing, but it offers nonetheless a unique window into local culture – provided you come already accompanied.

Places to consider include the following: **Ambassador** (rue de Marseille), **La Galette Bretonne** (rue d'Ethiopie), **Club Hermes** (rue de Foucauld), **Le Guepard** (Sheraton Hotel, ave du Maréchal Lyautey, Plateau du Serpent) and the bar at **Brasserie & Restaurant L'Historil** (place du 27 Juin 1977). Note that many nightclubs are labelled 'Restaurant' to evade licensing laws, so don't be confused.

GETTING THERE & AWAY
Air
Airlines with offices in Djibouti City:
Air France (☎ 351010; place du 27 Juin 1977)
Daallo Airlines (☎ 353401; rue de Paris)
Djibouti Airlines (☎ 351006; place Lagarde)
Ethiopian Airlines (☎ 351007; rue de Marseille)
Regional Air (☎ 250297; place Lagarde).

Ethiopian Airlines flies four times a week to Addis Ababa (US$207 one way). Djibouti Airlines plies the same route three times a week (US$102 one way). Daallo Airlines flies twice a week to Asmara (US$145 one way).

To get to Dire Dawa in Ethiopia, Djibouti Airlines flies three times a week (US$77 one way). Regional Air flies once a week to Nairobi (US$420, one way) or try one of four flights a week with Ethiopian Airlines (via Addis Ababa; US$320 one way). Daallo Airlines and Djibouti Airlines also operate flights to Hargeisa (Somaliland; around US$130 return).

Boat
A ferry plies the Djibouti–Tadjoura and Djibouti–Obock routes three times a week, as well as speedboats and dhows carrying the precious *qat* and other commodities. All boats leave from L'Escale. See Getting There & Away under Tadjoura (p705) and Obock and Les Sept Frères (p706) for more information.

Car
Vehicle rental is extortionate in Djibouti but you can reduce the costs by joining up with other travellers to hire a car. For most off-road areas you'll need a 4WD. Try **Marill** (☎ 351150; rue Marchand). Expect to pay up to US$200 per day for a 4WD.

Local Transport
Minibuses leave from various departure points south of town (see Map p699). They connect Djibouti City to Ali Sabieh, Dikhil, Tadjoura and the Ethiopian border. There is no fixed schedule. Most buses leave early in the morning and when they are full. Most journeys cost about US$4.

There are no buses to Bankoualé, Dittilou, Forêt du Day or Obock.

Train
The Djibouti–Ethiopia train departs three times a week, on Wednesday, Friday and Sunday, and runs as far as Addis Ababa via Dire Dawa. You can take it and get off at Ali Sabieh (about US$15/7 in 1st/2nd class). Tickets can be bought 24 hours in advance at the railway station (morning only).

GETTING AROUND
The central hub for city minibuses (US$0.25) is on place Mahmoud Harbi. Taxis aren't metered; US$3 is a fair price for a journey within the town.

AROUND DJIBOUTI

DJIBOUTI CITY TO ALI SABIEH
The 95km road from Djibouti City crosses two spectacular desert plains: the **Petit Barra** and **Grand Barra**, the latter being 27km long and 12km wide. Believe it or not, at the eastern end there's a centre where you can windsurf on wheels on the great salty plain. Contact **AECVETA** (☎ 354695; www.aecveta.com). It costs US$71 for a full day, including one night's accommodation, food and transport from Djibouti City.

In Ali Sabieh, you can stay at **Hôtel la Palmeraie** (☎ 426198; r US$29) which has basic but tolerable rooms.

You can reach Ali Sabieh by train (en route to Ethiopia – see Djibouti City, p703) or bus (US$4) from the capital.

DIKHIL & LAC ABBÉ
pop 30,000 (Dikhil)

Situated at the junction of Afar and Issa territory, Dikhil, 118km west of Djibouti City on the sealed road to Ethiopia, is a starting point for 4WD expeditions west to Lac Abbé.

Lac Abbé, 35km from Dikhil, is thought to rate among the most desolate places on earth. The scenery is unique: the plain is dotted with hundreds of limestone chimneys, some standing as high as 50m, belching out puffs of steam. These spikelike chimneys are the result of calcareous deposits across time. It is often described as 'a slice of moon on the crust of earth', and for good reason. *Planet of the Apes* was filmed here. And it could form a perfect backdrop for a new version of *Mad Max*.

Though desolate, it is not uninhabited. Numerous mineral-rich hot springs feed the farms of local nomads who graze their camels and goats here. The banks of the lake are also where flamingos gather at dawn.

The best moment to visit the lake and the chimneys is at dawn or in the evening, when the sun sets behind the chimneys and the animals are driven home across the plain – the landscape takes on an eerie aspect.

A guide is essential to discover the area (organise one in Djibouti City).

Sleeping
Hôtel-Restaurant la Palmeraie (☎ 812204; r with shared bathroom US$29) This hotel in Dikhil has eight rooms and is an adequate place to stay. There is also a restaurant attached.

Campement Touristique de Koûta Boûyya (☎ 357446; full board US$40) A more traditional place 10km south of Dikhil, this *campement* offers accommodation in basic *daboyta* (traditional shelters of the nomadic Afar) or *tukul* (a sort of rondavel). Koûta Boûyya is popular with the French military at the weekend (Thursday night and Friday).

Campement Touristique d'Asbole (☎ 357244; full board US$46) This *campement* must surely be located in what must be the most surreal landscape you've ever imagined. It's on a plateau near Lac Abbé and overlooks the big chimneys. At dusk or at dawn, the scenery is other-worldly. As in all *campements*, accommodation is rudimentary but the traditional *daboyta* are in perfect harmony with the environment. Prices include a guided walk to the chimneys.

Getting There & Away
Buses (US$4) run from Djibouti City to Dikhil. Unsurprisingly, Lac Abbé is not accessible by public transport. You'll need to rent a 4WD or take a tour from the capital (see p700). *Campements touristiques* can arrange transportation if you can find a group of people (about US$80 per person, including accommodation and full board for two days).

LAC ASSAL
Just over 100km west of the capital lies one of the most spectacular natural phenomena in Africa: Lac Assal.

When it comes into view, be prepared to run out of superlatives. Here's the picture: situated 150m below sea level, this crater lake is encircled by dark, dormant volcanoes – a dramatic sight. It is three times more saline than the sea and represents the lowest point on the African continent. The aquamarine water is ringed by a huge salt field, 60m in depth. The salt field has been mined by the Afar nomads for centuries, and they can still be seen loading up their camels for the long trek south to Ethiopia. Numerous salt companies now have concessions on this salt shore and you will see a large number of manual labourers toiling throughout the day, in the stinging heat, bagging up the salt.

There's no public transport to Lac Assal. Most visitors come with tours (see p707) or hire their own vehicle from the capital. A tour should set you back US$60 – save up, it is definitely worth it.

GODA MOUNTAINS
Northwest of the Gulf of Tadjoura, the Goda Mountains rise to a height of 1750m and are a spectacular natural oddity. Although we've said that Djibouti is stark and arid, this area is unexpectedly lush and shelters one of the rare speckles of green on Djibouti's parched map, like a giant oasis – a real relief after the scorched desert landscapes. It sometimes rains and there's often mist. A real shock for some visitors, who find it inconceivable that **Dittilou** (a tiny settlement and a *campement touristique*) belongs to the same country as the one they left on the burning plain just one hour before.

The Goda Mountains shelter Djibouti's only national park, **Forêt du Day National Park**, which boasts good potential for hiking.

Sleeping

This area is favoured by expats and military men in search of cool air, and there's no shortage of traditional accommodation. Showers and toilets are communal. The prices quoted include guided walks.

Campement Touristique le Goda (☎ 822431; Randa; full board US$46) Nestled on the flank of a valley, about 1.5km from Randa town, at an altitude of 1000m, the Goda is a good spot to relax and breathe fresh air. There are six traditional *daboyta*, an Ethiopian *tukul*, three tents with beds and mattresses and a restaurant. It's spartan but very well run by the affable Ermano.

Campement Touristique de Dittilou (☎ 356618; Dittilou; full board US$46) If you want to get away from it all, this is the place. The 20 traditional huts, with shared showers and toilets, are set against a lush and totally quiet landscape, at the edge of Forêt du Day National Park. It's also a good base for hiking – don't miss the waterfall of Toha (three to four hours return).

Campement Touristique de Bankoualé (☎ 814115, 424154; Bankoualé; full board US$46) Another ideal camp where you can wonder at the marvels of Mother Nature, with good hiking possibilities. It overlooks a lush valley and there's an Afar village nearby.

Campement de Barra Bare (☎ 815346; Forêt du Day; full board US$46) Another good place with a wild location, perched at 1700m in Forêt du Day, west of Dittilou.

Getting There & Away

The most convenient way to visit the area is with a tour (see p707). Transport can also be organised by the *campements* if there's a group (from US$50 to US$80, including two days' accommodation and full board). If your budget doesn't stretch to it, contact the owners of the *campements*. They might offer you a lift from the capital when they take supplies to the camp. To Bankoualé, you can take the ferry to Tadjoura and asked to be picked up there.

TADJOURA

pop approx 25,000

Tadjoura is Djibouti's oldest town and as such it gave its name to the gulf separating the Afar and Issa lands. Originally a small Afar village trafficking in slaves, the white-washed town is now a quiet backwater. Poor and run-down, its setting is nevertheless attractive, nestled in the shadow of the green Goda Mountains with the bright blue sea lapping at its doorstep.

Plage des Sables Blancs, 7km east of Tadjoura, is the best beach in Djibouti, with a good string of white sand.

Sleeping

Hôtel-Restaurant Le Golfe (☎ 424091; hot.rest.le golfe@intnet.dj; r with private bathroom US$46; 🖵) A low-key but well-kept resort set in a relaxing waterfront setting, about 1.5km from the city centre. The 14 bungalows overlook the seashore. There's a good restaurant and a terrace where you can enjoy a drink at sunset. The owners can organise various tours as well as transfers to Plage des Sables Blancs (US$23 for two). Prices include breakfast.

La Brise de Mer (☎ 825199; bed US$9) The only budget option in town, next to the jetty where the boats from Djibouti City dock. Beds on the rooftop are basic but will do the trick. There's a restaurant.

Plage des Sables Blancs Campement (☎ 354520; Plage des Sables Blancs; full board US$46) Right on the beach, this is a good place to chill out for a couple of days. Accommodation is simple (beds and mattresses only), with well-maintained shared toilets and showers. Transfer can be organised from Tadjoura (US$29 flat fee) or from Djibouti City (US$23 per person if there's a group). Your best bet is to join a group from Djibouti at weekends. Contact Agence Goubet (see Tours, p707).

Eating

Mini-Cafe de Tadjoura (mains US$4-6) The best spot in town, right by the seafront. The inviting terrace is ideal for soaking up the atmosphere while sipping smoothies or filling up on simple but good dishes.

Getting There & Away

There is a good sealed road from the capital, but the best way to arrive in Tadjoura is by boat from L'Escale in Djibouti City. The ferry leaves every Thursday at 1pm and every Saturday at 9am from Djibouti City and takes 2½ hours (US$3.50, one way). It returns the same day. Or you can take one of the dhows that leave every day sometime between noon and 2.30pm from Djibouti to bring the much-awaited *qat* to Tadjoura (US$6, one way).

OBOCK & LES SEPT FRÈRES

The last significant town before the border with Eritrea, Obock lies 62km northeast of Tadjoura. Despite its run-down, forlorn appearance (or perhaps because of it), it exudes an intriguing aura. Its remote tranquillity and still palpable history also help create the distinctive spirit of this border town.

Obock is the place where colonisation of the region began in 1862, when the Afar sultans of Obock sold their land to the French. It was eclipsed after 1888, when the construction of Djibouti port began.

There is a kind of 'last frontier' feel about the place. Just off the coast, at **Les Sept Frères Archipelago**, the Bab al-Mandab Strait separates two worlds, the Red Sea and the Gulf of Aden.

There is really nothing of tangible interest in Obock, but visitors who want to experience this typical Red Sea atmosphere will enjoy the place. It is also a convenient staging post for those who want to travel to Eritrea.

If you do decide to stay, the **Campement de Ras Bir-Hougef** (☎ 816034, 811790; Obock; full board US$46) is a welcoming *campement* with several *daboyta* and *tukul*. The *campement* boasts a superb location right on a long, sandy beach, and it is a good place to sample seafood and *cabri* (kid).

The cheapest way to reach Obock is by ferry from L'Escale in Djibouti City. The ferry leaves on Wednesday and Monday morning (US$4, three hours) and returns the same day.

Another option includes the *qat*-carrying speedboats that leave every day from L'Escale around noon (US$9, two hours). If travelling by road, there are irregular bush taxis from Tadjoura (about US$5).

DJIBOUTI DIRECTORY

ACCOMMODATION

Djibouti's accommodation is limited: there are no formal camping grounds or hostels, and most hotels are in the capital, with few options outside. Hotel categories are also limited in range; most of them fit into the upper echelon and are expensive. At the lower end, the few budget options that exist are not really good value.

A rather popular option that is developing around the major attractions in the hinterland is the *campements touristiques*. These are privately owned traditional huts with shared showers and toilets. It's a good budget option, but there's no public transport to get there.

ACTIVITIES

The most prominent activity in Djibouti is diving. Most snorkelling and diving takes place off the islands of Maskali and Musha in the Gulf of Tadjoura, the Bay of Ghoubbet and Les Sept Frères Islands. Trips to Les Sept Frères Islands are expensive because of the distance and are usually organised in the way of live-aboards.

Hiking is also popular in the Forêt du Day and along the ancient salt route, led by the Afar nomads.

In the windy plain of Grand Barra you can windsurf on wheels.

BUSINESS HOURS

Most government offices, shops and institutions are open 7.30am to 1.30pm Saturday to Thursday. Private businesses reopen from 4pm to 6pm. Friday is the weekly holiday for offices and most shops, and Saturday and Sunday are normal working days.

DANGERS & ANNOYANCES

Djibouti is a relatively safe country, and serious crime or hostility aimed specifically at travellers is very rare. However, the presence of thousands of refugees in the capital has significantly pushed up the crime rate, particularly at night, so be on the lookout.

Djibouti's security services are known for being sensitive and active. There is no reason why travellers should attract the attention of the police, but if it happens, remain polite and calm, it's usually pretty harmless.

EMBASSIES & CONSULATES

Djiboutian diplomatic representation abroad is scarce, but there are embassies in the following neighbouring countries: Egypt, Ethiopia and Eritrea. Details are listed under Embassies & Consulates in the relevant country's Directory section. Elsewhere in the world, in countries without representation, travellers should head for the French embassy, which acts in lieu for the issuing of visas.

Most foreign embassies in Djibouti City are located on Plateau du Serpent, north of the city centre.

Egypt (☎ 351231; Ilot du Heron)
Eritrea (☎ 354951; rue de Kampala)
Ethiopia (☎ 350718; rue Clochette) Should be relocated in ave Franchet d'Esperey by the end of 2004.
France (☎ 352503; ave du Maréchal Lyautey, Plateau du Serpent)
UK (☎ 351709; Inchcape Shipping Office, rue de Geneve)
USA (☎ 353995; ave du Maréchal Foch, Plateau du Serpent)

For details on getting visas for neighbouring countries, see the next page.

HOLIDAYS
As well as religious holidays listed in the Africa Directory (p1003), these are the principal public holidays in Djibouti:

1 January New Year's Day
1 May Labour Day
27 June Independence Day
25 December Christmas Day

MAPS
The best map is the 1:200,000 map published in 1992 by the French Institut Géographique National (IGN).

MEDIA
Various local newspapers are available, all published weekly in French. They include *La Nation*, *Réalité*, *Le Renouveau* and *Liberté*.

Television broadcasts start at 6pm and last for between four and six hours. Programmes are in Somali, Afar, Arab and French. Radio Djibouti can be found at 92.25MHz FM 24 hours per day.

MONEY
There are plenty of banks and authorised exchange bureaus in the capital. They change cash and travellers cheques. Outside the capital, banking facilities are scarce and travellers are best advised to rely on cash.

There are only two ATMs in Djibouti City.

POST & TELEPHONE
International postal services from Djibouti City are efficient. A stamp for a letter weigh-

ing up to 10g costs US$0.65 for Europe, and US$0.75 for elsewhere. Courier services are also available in Djibouti City.

There are no area codes in Djibouti. International calls are best placed from the post office or from one of the phone shops in the city centre. Calls are expensive, varying from US$2.80 to US$5 per minute, depending on the country. For national calls, there are several phone booths around Djibouti City that accept coins or *télécartes* (phonecards). Phonecards are on sale in designated shops.

TOURIST INFORMATION
The only tourist office in the country is that found in Djibouti City. Travel agencies are also reliable sources of travel information (see Tours following).

Information for travellers is hard to come by outside the country. In Europe, the most knowledgeable organisation is the excellent **Association Djibouti Espace Nomade** (ADEN; ☎ /fax 01 48 51 71 56; aden@club-internet.fr; 64 rue des Meuniers, 93100 Montreuil-sous-Bois). Its director will do her best to inform you in English.

TOURS
Note that Djibouti is not yet properly geared up for independent tourism. The only way of getting to some of the country's principal attractions is by taking a tour. Some tour companies offer unusual trips, such as excursions in the bush to visit nomadic peoples. They're expensive (from US$60 per person), but the price includes food and accommodation and it can offer a fascinating experience. Besides, when there's no public transport, taking a tour is usually cheaper than hiring a 4WD. Try to be part of an existing group – the more people, the less you pay.

Reliable tour companies include **Caravane de Sel** (☎ 356618; place du 27 Juin 1977), **AECVETA** (☎ 354695), **Dankali Expeditions** (☎ 350313; blvd de la République) and **Agence Le Goubet** (☎ 354520; blvd Cheik Osman).

VISAS
All visitors, including nationals of France, need visas. Tourist visas cost US$35 and are usually valid for one month. Visas can be obtained at the nearest Djibouti embassy or, when there is none, from the French embassy. Note that it is also possible to get

a visa at the airport: leave your passport at the Immigration Officer and you get it stamped the next day (but it involves two more taxi rides).

Visa Extensions

Go to the **Immigration Services** (☎ 350023) at the Police Nationale building. Bring your passport, two photos and US$29 (in local currency). You'll also need to fill in a form and have it stamped by a *garant* (a hotel is fine). Make sure you extend your visa before your current visa expires.

Visas for Onward Travel

Visas for the following neighbouring countries can be obtained in Djibouti.

For information on embassies and consulates, see p707.

Eritrea You'll need your passport and two photos. It costs US$50. You might also be asked for an onward air ticket and an address in Eritrea. f this is the case, mention a hotel in Asmara.

Ethiopia A one-month visa costs US$64 (US$72 for US nationals). You'll need one photo.

Somalia The only place to get a visa is Addis Ababa, Ethiopia.

Eritrea

HIGHLIGHTS

- **Asmara** Safe and relaxed capital, oozing old charm, with great cappuccinos, perfect climate and enough colonial buildings to turn you into an architecture buff (p714)
- **Massawa** Strolling in the maze of little, dusty streets of this historical port with a distinct Arab influence (p721)
- **Dahlak Archipelago** Make the most of pristine reefs and snorkel among a dazzling array of colourful species (p722)
- **Keren** Exploring the alleyways of the silversmiths' market, or buying a camel at the seething Monday livestock market (p720)
- **Best journey** The spectacular winding descent from the central highlands to Massawa on the Red Sea Coast (p722)
- **Off the beaten track** Afar fishing villages in Dankalia, one of the most desolate areas on earth (p723)

FAST FACTS

- **Area** 124,320 sq km (about the size of England)
- **ATMs** none
- **Borders** Djibouti; the land borders with Sudan and Ethiopia are closed at present
- **Budget** US$15 to US$20 a day
- **Capital** Asmara
- **Languages** Tigrinya, Arabic and other regional languages
- **Money** Nakfa; US$1 = Nfa13
- **Population** 4.4 million
- **Telephone** country code ☎ 291; international access code ☎ 00
- **Time** GMT/UTC + 3
- **Visas** US$50 for 30 days, to be obtained in advance

Eritrea? Never heard of it? You may be forgiven, because this country must be one of the shyest on the continent. It shuns the limelight and avoids publicity. It has much to do with history and pride. History, because Eritrea is Africa's newest country, formed in 1993 when its people voted in a referendum to secede from Ethiopia – a final chapter in a war that had lasted for more than 30 years. Pride, because Eritreans have learnt to fend for themselves and won't let their country become anybody's client. You'll be astounded by the self-reliance, hospitality and genuine friendliness of its inhabitants. Worried about getting hassled? Rest easy: hustling is practically unknown here.

Sure, the statistics on this country are not particularly flattering nor optimistic. Eritrea is beset by economic problems, including serious droughts, and the funds are lacking to rebuild the country. And yes, there is a feeling of austerity. But you'll soon discover that beauty can

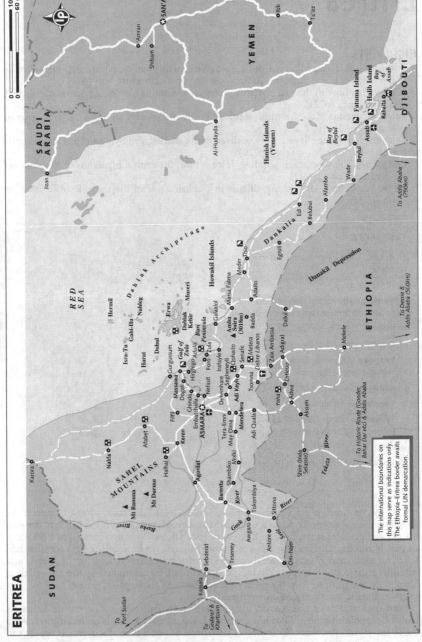

ERITREA

be austere and that austerity can be bewitching. Take the landscape – stark, arid, bleak and even bordering on the other-worldly in Dankalia – it will overwhelm you. After something more civilised? Relish Asmara, one of the most enchanting capitals in Africa. Can you believe it's like a film set from an early Italian movie, with old chrome espresso machines churning out cups of *macchiato*, *cinquecento* taxis putt-putting around town and outstanding Art-Deco architecture. For those with a penchant for the joys of ogling bright fish, there's the Red Sea coast and the Dahlak Archipelago, endowed with completely virgin reefs.

Though impoverished, the country is still a fascinating and rewarding place to visit. Be a pioneer. Get there before this gem unveils itself.

HISTORY

During the 1st millennium BC, tribes from present-day Yemen migrated to the southern highlands of Eritrea, settling on both sides of today's Eritrean–Ethiopian border. The descendant of their language, Ge'ez, is still used in church liturgy, and the contemporary Tigrinya and Amharic languages are still written in its script.

A Mythical Past

Since the dawn of history the Horn of Africa has been known to the outside world. Lying on the African side of the Red Sea, the area provided a crucial trade link, connecting Egypt and the Mediterranean with India and the Far East. But this wasn't the region's only asset. Known to the Egyptian Pharaohs as the Land of Punt (together with what is now Djibouti), the area yielded a seemingly limitless supply of precious commodities, including gold, frankincense, myrrh, slaves, ebony and ivory, all loaded onto foreign ships jostling in the region's port. Today, the Land of Punt still conveys a legendary aura.

A Period of Grandeur: the Aksumite Civilisation

The celebrated Aksumite kingdom flourished in Eritrea from the 1st to the 9th century AD. While the kingdom's capital city, Aksum, was in today's Ethiopia, important Aksumite towns were built in Eritrea (for more information on the Aksumite Civilisation, see p675). The ancient port of Adulis, south of Massawa, played a key role in the kingdom. Much foreign trade – on which Aksum's prosperity depended – was seaborne and came to be handled by the ancient port of Adulis.

One of the most significant imports into the region during the Aksumite period is Christianity, apparently brought by accident when Christian Syrian merchants travelling home from India were shipwrecked on the Red Sea coast. Christianity became the Aksumite state religion and exerted a profound influence on the country's culture.

Islam & the Decline of Aksum

After Islam's rise in the 7th century AD, Aksum's decline began. Adulis was destroyed in 710, and for centuries the dividing line between the Muslim Red Sea coast and the Christian Ethiopian highlands moved back and forth over what is now Eritrea. From the early 16th century to the late 19th century, the Egyptians and the Ottoman Turks fought each other for control of the Eritrean coast and its ports.

The Italian Colonisation

In the second half of the 19th century, the European powers undertook a massive colonisation process in Africa. Italy wasn't going to miss out on a piece of the pie, and wide-scale colonisation began in Southern Eritrea in 1882. The Italians invested heavily in Eritrea. All the architectural treasures in the country, especially in Asmara, date from this period.

In 1936 Mussolini invaded Ethiopia from Eritrea. When the Allied forces defeated the Italian army in 1941, Italy was forced to give up its three African possessions: Eritrea, Libya and southern Somalia. Eritrea was administered by the British until 1952, when a contentious United Nations (UN) resolution granted Eritrea self-government within a federal union with Ethiopia.

The Ethiopian Rule

Gradually more and more Eritreans turned against the Ethiopians who, they felt, were colonising their country. In 1961 a few Eritreans attacked an Ethiopian police station with two stolen pistols – an incident regarded today as the starting point of Africa's longest war in the 20th century. In 1962 Ethiopia's Emperor Haile Selassie annexed unilaterally, and in defiance of the UN, Eritrea as Ethiopia's 14th province.

A guerrilla war against the Ethiopians started, first with the Eritrean Liberation Front (ELF), then with the Eritrean People's Liberation Forces (EPLF, later Front), founded in 1970.

In 1974 Mengistu Haile Mariam, a communist dictator, rose to power in Ethiopia, and in 1977 the Soviet Union began its massive support of the Ethiopian army. As a result, in 1978 the EPLF, which had been on the point of overrunning the whole country, was forced to withdraw from the towns it controlled in the face of aerial raids, heavy artillery and tanks. This event is commemorated as the 'Strategic Withdrawal', crucial to the survival of the resistance.

From 1978 to 1986 the Ethiopian army carried out eight major offensives against the EPLF, all of which were repulsed. The fighting grew from hit-and-run guerrilla attacks to a war between two permanent armies, with frontlines and trenches in the style of WWI.

Towards Independence

In 1988 the EPLF inflicted major losses on the Ethiopian army. In 1990 the Ethiopians lost the port of Massawa and then blanket-bombed it. Finally, in 1991 the EPLF entered Asmara unopposed.

A Provisional Government of Eritrea (PGE) was established under the leadership of Isaias Aferwerki, a senior EPLF military commander, now president of the country.

In April 1993 the PGE held a referendum, regarded as clean and free by international monitors, in which Eritreans voted for independence by the resounding figure of 99.8%. The country is now run by the People's Front for Democracy and Justice (PFDJ), a political offshoot of the EPLF.

The Second War Against Ethiopia

After only five brief years of peaceful relations between Eritrea and its Ethiopian neighbours, the border dispute reared its ugly head again in 1998. What followed were two bitter years of conflict that saw tens of thousands killed, and sent over 250,000 refugees fleeing into Sudan. The relentless and uncompromising stance of both Isaias Aferwerki and Meles Zenawi dented the credibility of both governments as people starved to death, development floundered and internal problems escalated in both countries.

Towards Peace?

As Ethiopian troops swept over the Eritrean borders in May 2000, the conflict reached a head, and after tortuous negotiations a cease-fire was signed on 18 June 2000. According to the peace deal that followed, a UN peacekeeping force was deployed in Eritrean territory pending a final demarcation of the disputed border. A Temporary Security Zone (TSZ) between the two countries was established in 2001 and a UN mission was in charge of enforcing the ceasefire, planning future peacekeeping, and deploying de-mining experts throughout the dangerous border minefields. In April 2002, the Boundary Commission announced its decision on the demarcation of the border. Surveying and the construction of boundary posts began in May 2003. Relations with Ethiopia will remain tense until the border demarcation is completed – probably sometime in 2004.

THE CULTURE

Eritrea is one of the poorest countries in the world, but its people (and its government) are reluctant to ask anything for fear of being considered beggars. Eritrea's greatest resource is its people. Though impoverished, this young nation has from the outset shown self-reliance, vigour and independence. Eritrea is not about to become anyone's subordinate, an attitude that has provoked both passionate admiration and furious exasperation from visitors, aid workers and international organisations alike. Towards travellers, Eritreans show exceptional politeness, hospitality and friendliness. The harsh nature of the countryside, where most people live as nomads, may contribute to this keen sense of the importance of hospitality.

Another trait that will baffle you is the remarkable harmony that reigns between the various religious communities and ethnic groups. The population is equally divided between Christians, primarily Orthodox, and Muslims. Asmara epitomises this peaceful coexistence: apart from the Catholic cathedral, the city is home to 28 mosques, 12 Orthodox churches and a Jewish synagogue.

The status of women is also something to behold. Eritrean women have guaranteed representation in parliament. They enjoy their own national holiday, equal property rights and the right to divorce, and also have equal rights to the custody of their children in any settlement. Eritrean women have attitude. In Asmara, women that were soldiers during the war can be spotted wearing old jeans and T-shirts, and in the little villages women bark at men to form orderly lines outside their bakeries.

ENVIRONMENT

Eritrea has three climatic zones: the central highlands (the most densely populated area), the Red Sea coastal plain to the east and the western lowlands. The highland climate is moderate, with temperatures that never exceed 30°C. It is intensively cultivated. The eastern zone consists of desert or semidesert, and is inhabited by pastoralists or fishing communities. The driest part of the country is the low-lying southeastern Dankalia region, one of the hottest places on earth. The western lowlands, lying between Keren and the Sudanese border, are watered by the Gash and Barka Rivers and farming is practised.

Several mountains exceed 2500m, with the highest peak, Amba Soira, reaching 3018m. Offshore lie 350 islands, including the Dahlak Archipelago, the largest in the Red Sea.

Today, population growth is the biggest problem, placing increased demands on the land. Less than 1% of the country is covered by woodland, compared to 30% a century ago. The country is also affected by severe droughts that threaten food security. The 2003 drought was one of the harshest in the last 20 years.

No national reserve or park exists formally.

TRANSPORT

GETTING THERE & AWAY
Air
Asmara is served by Daallo Airlines and Regional Airlines from Djibouti, by EgyptAir from Cairo (Egypt), by Sudan Airways from Khartoum (Sudan) and by Regional Airlines from Nairobi (Kenya).

Boat
Eritrea has two ports, Massawa and Assab. Although there are no scheduled passenger

---

DEPARTURE TAX

The airport departure tax is US$15. It can only be paid in US dollars cash, so make sure you have some with you.

---

services, many cargo ships from other Red Sea countries use the ports, particularly the one at Massawa. It is sometimes possible to hitch lifts.

Land
DJIBOUTI
At the time of writing, the only border officially open is from Eritrea to Djibouti. Travel overland to Djibouti is now possible as the relations between the two countries have normalised. Only dirt roads lead south of the town of Assab to Djibouti. Very little traffic heads south, except for some shared taxis that go to Moulhoule, the first town after the border.

ETHIOPIA
At the time of writing, the border between Eritrea and Ethiopia was closed and all transport services were suspended.

SUDAN
The situation is fairly volatile with Sudan; check with the Sudanese embassy in Asmara.

GETTING AROUND
Air
Eritrean Airlines (☎ 125500; Harnet Ave), based in Asmara, flies to just one domestic destination: Assab.

Local Transport
There is a relatively good network of roads connecting Asmara with Keren, Massawa, Adi Quala and Barentu. The bus service is reasonably efficient, comfortable and extensive. There are usually at least two buses a day between the larger towns (Asmara, Massawa and Keren) and at least one bus a day between the smaller ones. Fares are cheap (about US$1 for the stretch Asmara–Massawa). Note that buses don't adhere to fixed timetables: they leave when they are full. For long-distance journeys, you need to be at the bus station by 6am to buy a ticket and be guaranteed a seat.

ERITREA

Train

At the time of research, the old railway line that stretches between Asmara and Massawa was under repair. There are no regular services as yet and the people in charge of the train are currently acquiring a new locomotive in Europe. Regular services should resume, but at the time of writing, the train only offered charter services. Check the current situation at the railway station in Asmara.

ASMARA

pop 500,000 / elevation 2356m

Believe it or not, Asmara is a capital for hedonists. It's not often that you feel enthusiastic about a capital city in Africa. But Asmara is unique. Okay, it's no wonderland, but it's still an oasis of comfort and convenience in a country besieged with economic problems. Your first impressions as you arrive in Asmara are likely to be unforgettable.

Asmara is a city that both time and much of the world forgot. The last three decades have literally passed it by in terms of business, technology and architecture. Having escaped the bombing experienced by many other towns, the city remains intact, and you'll think you've been time-warped into a small, 1960s southern Italian town. Old Fiats and bubble cars make up the majority of the traffic and the architecture is all pastel-coloured, Art-Deco monoliths. Most travellers succumb to the way of life they discover here – the morning cappuccino, the evening *passeggiata* (stroll) down the main artery and the relaxed pace. In addition to the Italian influence, the northern half of the city bears witness to the large Muslim population and the market square in front of the Al Khulafa al Rashidin mosque is pure oriental. This blend of Arabic and African influences is what makes this city so distinct.

In the morning you'll hear the sound of the cathedral bells and the footsteps of the Orthodox monks on their way to Mass as well as the Muslim call to prayer. And, tucked off Harnet Ave, the main artery, you'll even find the odd Jewish synagogue! And there's the climate: balmy and temperate, with cloudless blue skies for about eight months of the year. The average annual temperature is a temperate 17°C and from October to March gardens are a riot of jacaranda, hibiscus and bougainvillea. If you've just come from the coast or Djibouti, Asmara is a refreshing change.

With a population of around 500,000 Asmara remains uncrowded – a result of government policies seeking to prevent the rural exodus – unlike in Khartoum or Addis Ababa. It's also a safe city, even after dark; good news if you plan to revel all night in one of the lively bars or discos. You're sure to feel at ease in this capital that seems to be tailored to the expectations of budget-conscious travellers.

ORIENTATION

The airport is about 6km southwest of the city centre. A taxi ride should cost around US$5. You can also take the city bus No 1 (US$0.10); bear left at the airport exit and the bus stop is a two-minute walk from the far end of the airport compound. The bus service runs from 6am to 7.30pm.

The city centre encompasses the area just north of Harnet Ave, marked by Bahti Meskerem Square at the eastern end of Harnet Ave and the Governor's Palace to the west. To the south of Harnet Ave lies the Italian residential quarter. Many Art-Deco villas can be found in this area. To the northeast lies the residential quarter of the local population. To this day, it is still the poorest area.

INFORMATION
Bookshops

Awghet Bookshop (Bahti Meskerem Sq; ⏰ 7.30am-7pm Mon-Sat) has the widest selection of books on Eritrea and some novels by African writers, town maps and postcards.

Cultural Centres

Alliance Francaise (☎ 126599, off Nakfa Ave) Occasional exhibitions or concerts by local artists and, once a week, films in French (free).
American Cultural Centre (Felket Ave) Shows films every Friday at 6pm.

WHAT'S IN A NAME?

Note that there was a major renaming process at the time of writing; the old street names with Ethiopian references were being changed. In fact, most people go by local landmarks such as government buildings, hotels or bars. In this chapter, only the new, confirmed street names are mentioned.

ERITREA

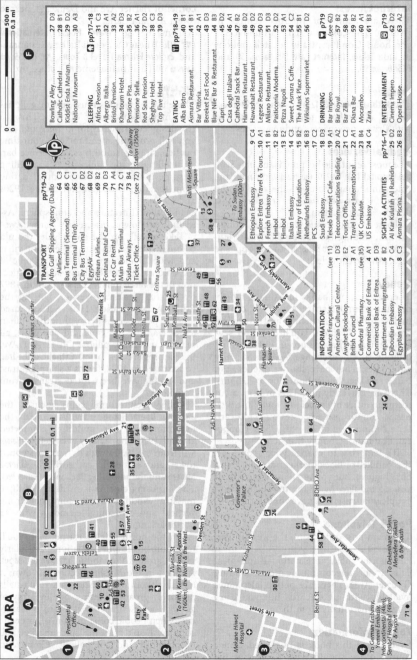

ASMARA

TRANSPORT pp719–20
- Afro Gulf Shipping Agency (Daallo Airlines).................. 64 C3
- Bus Terminal (Second)........... 65 C1
- Bus Terminal (Third)............ 66 C1
- City Bus Terminal................ 67 D2
- EgyptAir.......................... 68 D2
- Eritrean Airlines................. 69 B2
- Fontana Rental Car.............. 70 D3
- Leo Car Rental................... 71 A4
- Main Bus Terminal............... 72 C1
- Sudan Airways................... 73 B4
- Ticket Office.................(see 72)

INFORMATION
- Alliance Française...........(see 11)
- American Cultural Center......... 1 D3
- Awghet Bookshop................. 2 E2
- British Council................... 3 A1
- Cathedral Pharmacy..........(see 35)
- Commercial Bank of Eritrea...... 4 D3
- Commercial Bank of Eritrea...... 5 D3
- Department of Immigration....... 6 B2
- Djiboutian Embassy............... 7 C4
- Egyptian Embassy................ 8 C3
- Ethiopian Embassy............... 9 C4
- Explore Eritrea Travel & Tours...10 A1
- French Embassy.................. 11 B1
- Himbol........................... 12 B2
- Himbol........................... 13 E2
- Italian Embassy.................. 14 C3
- Ministry of Education............ 15 B2
- Netherlands Embassy............. 16 B3
- PCS.............................. 17 C2
- Saudi Embassy................... 18 D3
- TekseB Internet Cafe............ 19 A1
- Telecommunications Building..... 20 A2
- Tourist Office................... 21 C2
- Travel House International....... 22 A1
- UK Consulate.................... 23 B4
- US Embassy...................... 24 C4

SIGHTS & ACTIVITIES pp716–17
- Al Kar Kulafah Al Rashidin...... 25 D2
- Asmara Piscina.................. 26 B3

SLEEPING pp717–18
- Bowling Alley.................... 27 D3
- Catholic Cathedral.............. 28 B1
- Kiddist Enda Mariam............ 29 D2
- National Museum................. 30 A3

SLEEPING pp717–18
- Africa Pension.................. 31 C3
- Albergo Italia................... 32 A1
- Bristol Pension................. 33 A2
- Khartoum Hotel................. 34 D3
- Pensione Pisa................... 35 B2
- Pensione Stella................. 36 A1
- Red Sea Pension................ 37 D2
- Sheghay Hotel.................. 38 C3
- Top Five Hotel................. 39 D3

EATING pp718–19
- Alba Bistro..................... 40 B1
- Asmara Restaurant.............. 41 B1
- Bar Vittoria.................... 42 A1
- Bereket Fast Food.............. 43 D3
- Blue Nile Bar & Restaurant..... 44 B3
- Capri........................... 45 D2
- Casa degli Italiani............. 46 A1
- Cathedral Snack Bar............ 47 B2
- Hamasien Restaurant............ 48 D2
- Hawashait Restaurant........... 49 D2
- Legese Restaurant.............. 50 D3
- Milano Restaurant.............. 51 B2
- Pasticceria Moderna............ 52 D2
- Pizza Napoli.................... 53 A1
- Sweet Asmara Caffe............. 54 C2
- The Mask Place................. 55 B1
- Wikianos Supermarket........... 56 D2

DRINKING p719
- Bar Impero..................(see 62)
- Bar Royal....................... 57 B2
- Bar Zilli........................ 58 B4
- Diana Bar....................... 59 B2
- Mocambo........................ 60 A1
- Zara............................ 61 B3

ENTERTAINMENT p719
- Cinema Impero.................. 62 D2
- Opera House.................... 63 A2

Internet Access
There are scores of Internet centres in Asmara. The cost is usually around US$1 per hour. Good centrally located options include **Tekseb Internet Cafe** (Adi Hawsha St) and **PCS** (Denkel St).

Libraries
The **British Council** (☎ 123415), close to the presidential office, has a reading room stocked with British newspapers and magazines.

Medical Services
The most reputable hospital is the new **Sembel Hospital** (☎ 150230; Tiravolo district), near the Intercontinental Hotel on the road to the airport. It also offers dental services. Most doctors speak English.

There are numerous pharmacies around town, including the **Cathedral Pharmacy** (Harnet Ave; ☾ 8am-12.30pm & 3-8pm Mon-Sat), opposite the Catholic cathedral.

Money
There are various banks in Asmara, mostly on and around Harnet Ave. They change major foreign currencies and travellers cheques. In addition, you'll also find several foreign exchange bureaus in the centre, offering speedy exchange facilities at fairly good rates. They have shorter queues than banks and keep longer hours (up to 7.30pm). There are currently no ATMs in Eritrea but the main office of **Himbol** (☎ 120788; Bahti Meskerem Sq) can do cash advances on credit card for a commission of 7% plus US$2. Himbol can also handle money transfers.

It's tempting to change your money on the 'parallel' or black market (rates are about 60% higher), but you're taking a big risk. If you do indulge, make the transaction with people you trust, and never in the street.

Post & Telephone
The main post office is off the western end of Harnet Ave.

You can make international and local calls at the telecommunications building (Harnet Ave). There are public telephones available with phonecards but you can't ring internationally from them.

Tourist Information
By the time this book is published, a new tourist office should have opened at the corner of Harnet Ave and Denkel St, next to Sweet Asmara Caffe.

Contact also **Travel House International** (☎ 201881) near Casa degli Italiani Restaurant and **Explore Eritrea Travel & Tours** (☎ 125555; Adi Hawsha St). Their management is clued up.

SIGHTS
There are no tedious museums or galleries in Asmara. Heave a sigh of relief! This is a city designed primarily for *la dolce vita*, and you will probably spend most of your time outside, sipping smoothies at a terrace bar, or strolling in the back streets marvelling at some unusual historic buildings dating from the Italian occupation in the 1920s and 1930s.

In both architecture and atmosphere, Asmara is two towns, bisected by Harnet Ave.

Take a walk on the south side, the old colonial quarter; an area of elegant villas and wide, shaded streets. Another relic of the colonial era is the icing sugar confection of the old **Governor's Palace**, built in 1897 by the first Italian governor. During the Ethiopian occupation Haile Selassie used it as his personal residence. Another Italian extravagance is the splendid **post office**, all marble and Ionic pillars. On Harnet Ave, the impressive red-brick **Catholic cathedral**, constructed in 1922, forms a sharp contrast and could have been lifted straight from Lombardy.

Other architectural gems include the elegant **Opera House** (Harnet Ave), near the telecommunications building, completed around 1920; the **Ministry of Education** (Harnet Ave), from the 1930s, with its massive stepped tower; and, east of the cathedral, the **Cinema Impero** and the adjoining **Bar Impero** (Harnet Ave). The imposing cinema is made up of three massive windows which combine strong vertical and horizontal elements with 45 porthole lamps.

On the north side of Harnet Ave, you'll find more bustle and animation, particularly in and around the vibrant **market** (Eritrea Sq). Situated in the Muslim section of town, it has the flavour of an eastern souq with stalls positively groaning with a motley array of goods. The best time to visit is early on Saturday, when people come in from all over the country. Don't miss the spice market, full of powerful and compelling odours and colours.

Northeast is **Medebar market**, given over to the recycling and refashioning of unwanted metal into an astonishing array of household utensils, crosses and tools. If there's a fascinating place in Asmara, this is it. The air is filled with hammering, sawing and cutting; old tyres are made into sandals, corrugated iron is flattened and become metal buckets, and olive tins from Italy are made into coffee pots or tiny scoops.

Just south of Eritrea Square is the main mosque, **Al Khulafa al Rashidin**, around which the gold and silversmiths are concentrated.

East of Eritrea Square, you can't miss the Eritrean Orthodox **Kiddisti Enda Mariam**, built in 1938. This unusual-looking church is based on the traditional Ethiopian *tukul* (or rondavel; made of mud and wattle with a conical thatched roof). The whole building is covered in naive paintings illustrating scenes from the Coptic liturgy.

If you need to unwind, the **city park** (Harnet Ave) west of the centre is an excellent resting place. And you can enjoy an ice cream here.

A good place to meet young locals is the **bowling alley** one block south to the eastern end of Harnet Ave, opposite the Shell petrol station. It's one of the few genuine 1950s alleys left in the world. The reloading system is still manual. Come here late in the evening, when a young crowd gathers. Billiards is also available here.

The 1930s **Asmara Piscina** (Kohayto St) is just south of the Governor's Palace. It is another ideal place to meet and hang out with young Asmarans.

For a better understanding of the local culture, the **National Museum** (Mariam GMBI St; admission free; ☽ 9-11am & 3-5pm) includes exhibits on the ethnic groups of Eritrea and the main archaeological sites of the country.

SLEEPING

Asmara is a haven for shoestringers. There is a sprinkling of *pensions* (guesthouses) within easy reach of Harnet Ave and there's no trouble finding a budget port of call. Unless you're really determined to push your limits, avoid the cheapies around the market. They hover between the horrid and the seedy, and most of them double as brothels. You probably deserve better, mate.

Pensione Pisa (☎ 124491; Harnet Ave; s/d US$6.50/7.50) You'll feel at home at this friendly guest-

house located right in the thick of things, opposite the Catholic cathedral. It has seven spotless rooms and small but clean toilets. Need to stay in bed very late to recover from last night's frantic dancing effort? Ask for a room at the back.

Bristol Pension (☎ 121688; s/d with shared shower US$6/8.50) This well-kept *pension* near the telecommunications building is another good choice for shoestringers. Rooms are cupboardlike but very decent.

Top Five Hotel (☎ 124922; Marsatekly Ave; s/d US$13-26/15-30) In a mood for some creature comforts? This efficiently run establishment is for you. The Top Five is a reliable mid-range option with spic-and-span rooms not far from the gentle hubbub of Harnet Ave. An added bonus is the adjoining tastefully decorated restaurant, buzzing with a local crowd in search of a tasty meal at moderate prices.

Africa Pension (☎ 121436; s/d US$9/12) Back from rural Eritrea and tired of artless, stuffy shoe-box rooms? Opt for this huge Cubist villa built in the 1920s by a spaghetti millionaire, opposite the Italian embassy but still within walking distance of the city centre. Though slightly overpriced, it boasts a peaceful and attractive setting and has 10 rooms in which you can comfortably spread out all your belongings. You'll be welcomed by the bronze bust of Augustus Caesar in the once-formal garden. The shared toilets and showers are not as clean as the rooms.

Khartoum Hotel (☎ 128008; s/d US$15-17) One block south of Harnet Ave, this is a good alternative in the mid-range bracket. It's well-kept and offers cleanish rooms. The rooms with shower are unsurprisingly brighter.

Pensione Stella (☎ 120731; Adi Hawsha St; s/d US$4/5.50) Off the western end of Harnet Ave, this has hot showers and clean rooms. If you plan to stay out late in the neighbouring Mocambo nightclub, this place is a good base.

Red Sea Pension (☎ 126778; s/d US$3.50/4) Off the eastern end of Nakfa Ave; nothing inspirational here but it has unbeatable prices. The modest but tidy rooms are arranged around a roof terrace, where you'll probably meet other travellers. The hot communal showers are not exactly squeaky-clean.

Sheghay Hotel (☎ 126562; s/d US$10.50/12.50) A block south of the Catholic cathedral, Sheghay is good value, with unadorned but tidy rooms. It's also got a roof terrace with great

ERITREA

views over the town. Note that it can be noisy at night (but do you really care? You'll no doubt hang around at the bar downstairs).

SPLURGE!

Albergo Italia (Nakfa Ave; r US$40-80) At the time of writing, restoration works were still under way in this establishment ideally positioned a couple of blocks north of Harnet Ave. By the time you show up here to pamper yourself, it will feature 19 lavishly decorated suites with opulent bathrooms and other luxuries, as well as two high-class restaurants. Architecture buffs, this place will appeal to your sense of aesthetics: the Albergo Italia is housed in a historic, colonial-style building.

EATING

There's an array of excellent restaurants in and around the centre. They're very affordable by Western standards – about US$3 for a full meal. You'll find Italian food, such as pasta and pizza, as well as traditional Eritrean dishes, including the ubiquitous *tibsi* (fried meat with garlic and onion) and *zigni* (meat cooked in a hot sauce). If you're penny-counting, there's also an abundance of cafés and pastry shops where you can guzzle smoothies and feast on mouth-watering cakes for less than US$0.50.

The market area is home to a clump of little restaurants serving inexpensive and filling food.

One treat not to miss in Asmara is a cup of *macchiato* with a cake or pastry at one of the numerous cafés or pastry shops dotted on or around Harnet Ave. The best time is during *passeggiata* (between 5pm and 6.30pm), when the whole town seems to traipse around to check out what's new, catch up with friends, window shop and generally relax. Some cafés boast a terrace – a strategic spot for watching all the action. It's Asmara at its quintessence and a real slice of local life.

Restaurants

Pizza Napoli (Adi Hawsha St; pizzas US$1.50-3) A no-frills but authentic place well known for its tasty pizzas. Vegetarians will opt for the great *pizza vegetariana* (US$1.50).

Hamasien Restaurant (mains US$1.50-2.50) Tucked off Harnet Ave, this unpretentious

little joint with red tablecloths is a good place to sample Eritrean specialities as well as meat dishes, pasta and soups.

Asmara Restaurant (mains US$1.50-4) Near the post office, another recommended option popular with locals, with an emphasis on Eritrean food.

Hawashait Restaurant (Gindae St; mains US$1.50-3.50) A cheerful little place, with good pizzas and a selection of Eritrean dishes at moderate prices.

Milano Restaurant (Felket Ave; mains US$2-5) Milano is a long-standing favourite in Asmara. Don't be fooled by the name; it does serve some Italian dishes in the front room but also offers excellent Eritrean dishes in a room at the back, in great, traditional surrounds. Try the house speciality, *tibs zil zil* (sizzling lamb).

Legese Restaurant (☎ 120041; Mata St; mains US$3-5) The Legese is something of an institution in Asmara, with a well-entrenched reputation for quality cooking. The menu features meat dishes, pasta, fish and imaginative chef's suggestions in fairly formal but attractive surroundings.

Bereket Fast Food (Harnet Ave; mains US$1.50-3.50) The Bereket is a local joint and the best place in town for a fast feed (nothing to do with KFC). The menu runs the gamut from burgers to chicken to pasta, as well as excellent fruit juices and delicious yogurts. It's also a good spot for breakfast.

Cathedral Snack Bar (Harnet Ave; mains US$1.50-3.50) A modern eatery, just opposite the Catholic cathedral. Snacks, burgers, fruit juices and pastries are available.

Alba Bistro (Adi Hawsha St; mains US$1.50-4) Snazzy, busy place near Mocambo nightclub. Good spot for a comforting breakfast or a quick meal any time of the day.

Cafés & Pastry Shops

Most places listed here serve pastries and fruit juices, and are great for breakfast.

Bar Vittoria (Adi Hawsha St; snacks US$0.40-0.60) An unpretentious place with a good selection of cakes and great cappuccinos.

Casa degli Italiani (snacks US$0.50-1) Not far from the post office, and one of the most agreeable places in town. It has a peaceful, palm-shaded courtyard and is a great place to scribble a postcard over a coffee or a cocktail.

Sweet Asmara Caffe (Harnet Ave; snacks US$0.30-0.75) Almost opposite the Catholic cathedral.

This bright, wannabe sleek place attracts a local mix of teens and workers and offers a wide selection of tempting pastries.

Pasticceria Moderna (Harnet Ave; snacks US$0.50-1) and, a few doorsteps away, **Impero Bar** (Harnet Ave), are perfect spots to settle down during *passeggiata* and watch the world go by while sipping a *macchiato*. When it's warm the outdoor tables fill up quickly. Impero Bar is more traditional (look out for the zinc bar and the ancient *gelato* machine), while Pasticceria Moderna is an utterly hip hang-out.

Capri (Mata St; snacks US$0.40-0.60) is a large, unassuming place near the cathedral but comes recommended for its exquisite fruit juices (about US$0.75).

Self-Catering

Wikianos Supermarket (Harnet Ave) opposite the municipality has the best selection of products. For fresh fruits and vegies, the market is hard to beat.

SPLURGE!

Blue Nile Bar & Restaurant (☎ 117965; Semaetat Ave; mains US$3-15) This gem of a place serves the best Eritrean food in Asmara (not just the standard *tibsi* or *zigni*). It's just *tee-oom* (delicious)! The decor is another highlight, with a subtle blend of modern and traditional influences. If you want to stick to European food, there is also a respectable selection of pasta – accompanied with a drop of imported wine – and burgers. Bookings are essential for dinner.

DRINKING

Most bars stay open until 10pm or 11pm during the week, and until at least 2am at the weekend. Most of them are fairly safe for single women travellers (at least in comparison with other African cities), but expect to be the focus of attention.

Zara (Semaetat Ave) The most popular place at the time of writing, and for good reason – dimly lit interior, funky tables, couches to lounge on. It's a perfect place to while away the evening and meet clued up locals or expats. Zara boasts a blinding drinks list with unfailingly good cocktails (about US$3).

The Mask Place (Adi Hawsha St) Convenient hang-out to kick off the evening over a beer (or two).

Mocambo (Adi Hawsha St) Fairly hip and snappy bar/nightclub with a black and white decor draws a mixed crowd of expats and locals.

Diana Bar (Harnet Ave) Cheerful, down-to-earth little spot, popular for its lively atmosphere.

Bar Zilli (Semaetat Ave) Next to Blue Nile Bar & Restaurant, this is the place to head for a draught beer.

Bar Royal (Harnet Ave) This is a bit too Westernised but it's a good hang-out for a coffee or a beer.

ENTERTAINMENT

Cinema tickets cost about US$0.30. Cinema Impero, centrally located and housed in an historical building from the Fascist era, shows action-packed American, Italian and Saudi films (in the original English, Italian or Arabic).

GETTING THERE & AWAY
Air

Airlines with offices in Asmara:

Daallo Airlines (☎ 124848 Represented by Adulis Shipping Line/Afro Gulf Travel Agency).

EgyptAir (☎ 127492; Bahti Meskerem Sq)

Eritrean Airlines (☎ 125500; Harnet Ave; acts as an agent for Regional Airlines).

Sudan Airways (☎ 202161; BDHO Ave)

Dallo Airlines (US$145 one way, two weekly) and Regional Airlines (US$190 one way, weekly) fly to Djibouti. Regional Airlines also flies to Nairobi (US$508 one way, three weekly).

To Cairo, there's EgyptAir (US$583 one way, weekly). Sudan Airways (US$259 one way, two weekly) flies to Khartoum.

Bus

There are three long-distance bus stations, all located about 10 minutes' walk north of Harnet Ave. Buses to Massawa (US$1.50, 3½ to four hours), Barentu (US$2.50, five hours) and Assab (US$8, 1½ days, three per week) leave from the main bus station. There are numerous buses to Massawa until late in the afternoon.

Buses to Keren (US$1, 2½ to three hours, 30 daily) leave from the second bus station. Southbound buses (except Assab) leave from the third bus terminal.

There is no fixed schedule. Most buses leave early in the morning when they are full.

ERITREA

Car

Vehicle rental is not cheap in Eritrea but you can reduce the costs by joining up with other travellers to hire a car. Reliable agencies include **Fontana Rental Car** (☎ 120052; Mata St) and **Leo Car Rental** (☎ 125859; Semaetat Ave). Cars cost from US$20 to US$40 per day; a 4WD costs from US$75 to US$140 per day. A driver usually comes automatically with a 4WD. The first 50km to 90km are free, and each additional kilometre costs between US$0.10 and US$0.20.

GETTING AROUND

Central Asmara is so small that almost all places can be reached within 20 minutes on foot.

Red buses serve all parts of the town and cost about US$0.10. A taxi ride in town costs between US$1.50 and US$3.

NORTHERN ERITREA

Places in the rest of this chapter are listed roughly north to south.

KEREN

pop 75,000

Keren is the most important highland town after Asmara. It's a predominantly Muslim town with a large Christian minority. It doesn't have the aura of Asmara but it's a fairly bustling place, with plenty of character and atmosphere. Established by the Italians, who exploited the area's rich agricultural and fruit-growing land, the town's setting is extremely beautiful, surrounded as it is by farms and high mountains.

The bus station is in the premises of the former train station, on the Agordat road.

Sights

The heart of town is the small Giro Fiori, or Floral Circle, bordered by hotels, restaurants and cafés. These and the remaining run-down villas, as well as the **San Antonio cathedral**, a smaller cousin of the one in Asmara, still impart a distinct Mediterranean feel. It's a good area to settle down for a drink and watch the world go by.

Keren's colourful daily **market**, behind the Keren Hotel, is an experience not to be missed. You'll probably bump into people of various tribes from the surrounding area,

especially Bilen women, easily noticeable by their brightly coloured clothes and their gold, silver or copper nose rings.

The covered area sells fruits, vegetables, baskets and other household objects. Wander into the narrow alleyways branching off the covered market. They are filled with the whirring machines of tailors and cloth merchants. In another quarter off the covered market, the workshops and boutiques of the silversmiths are another highlight. They're easy to track – follow the tapping and hammering ringing in the street. Be prepared to bargain!

If you're in town on a Monday, don't miss the clamour of the small **camel market**, just to the south of town. Wandering around hobbled camels, among the crowds of men yelling as they haggle over the price of animals, is an unforgettable experience.

Sleeping

Sicilia Pension (☎ 401059; r US$3-6) This old colonial place with a leafy courtyard is a good budget pick. It's only a few minutes from the gentle hubbub of Giro Fiori.

Barka Hotel (☎ 401350; s/d US$2/4) Behind Sicilia Pension. This peaceful retreat with a shady courtyard is within easy walking distance of the city centre. The sign is in Tigrinya and in Arabic only.

Shege Hotel (☎ 401971; r US$7-13) On the outskirts of town on the Agordat road. The location is not exactly convenient, but it's a good choice if you're in search of some creature comforts. It has a small restaurant.

Eating

Most places to sleep have their own restaurant, but the menus tend to be standard and a little unimaginative.

Keren Hotel (mains US$1.50-3) This landmark hotel in the centre has a decent restaurant with a shady terrace. The menu mixes up Italian and local dishes.

Mackerel Seafood Restaurant (mains US$1.50-2.50) For those with a craving for *zigni* fish (fish stew) or other fish dishes, the Mackerel can oblige, in simple surroundings. You'll find it just off the Giro Fiori.

Heran Pastry (off the Giro Fiori; snacks US$0.50-1) Can't resist a sweet treat? Head for this pastry shop, off the Giro Fiori. The yogurt with honey is exquisite.

Getting There & Away
Keren lies about 90km northwest of As-mara. Between Keren and Asmara, there are about 30 buses daily (US$1, 2½ to three hours). There are also buses from Keren to Nakfa, Barentu, Agordat and Teseney.

MASSAWA
pop 35,000
For many travellers, it's not easy to form a judgment of Massawa. It's a contradiction in terms: while the outstanding history of the city is palpable, you can't help feeling a sense of dereliction about the place. Down on the coast, 115km east of Asmara, and not far from the former ancient port of Adulis, it was once known for its pearl-diving and salt-panning industries. During the Fascist build-up in the early 1930s it was the busiest port on the East African coast. However, the city was almost levelled by bombing raids in 1990, an act of vengeance by the Ethiopians after they lost the port to the EPLF.

Massawa, should be an architectural gem, but it is not. Almost every pre-1990 building bears battle scars, and the remaining ruins, empty lots and hillocks of rubble are a constant visual reminder of Massawa's blitz. But this predominantly Muslim city is being slowly reconstructed and becoming once again an active Red Sea port whose dusty alleys are fascinating to roam.

What is collectively called Massawa is really three entities. The mainland, with its new blocks of popular housing, is of little interest. Across the first causeway is **Taulud Island**. This was the old Italian quarter.

A second, much shorter causeway leads to **Massawa Island**, where lie the port and old town. It's an astounding blend of Egyptian, Turkish and Italo-Moorish architecture. Here each building, though decayed, oozes ambience and is centuries old, except for the ruined Banco d'Italia and the arched arcade along the wharf. The buildings are made of coral rock with *mashrabeya* (wooden screened windows).

If you want to lounge on a beach, head for **Gurgussum**, 12km north of town; take a taxi (about US$7) or, at weekends, a mini-bus (US$0.70).

Sleeping
There's a host of inexpensive hotels on Mas-sawa Island, but they are less-than-salubrious and utterly tattered. None of them come highly recommended.

Torino Hotel (☎ 552855; Massawa Island; d with shower US$17) While a bit scuzzy and over-priced, the Torino remains the only accept-able place on Massawa Island, and is right in the thick of things. If you're a nocturnal creature, you'll be wrapped to learn that there's a nightclub on the rooftop. If you want to sleep, this asset can turn into a nightmare.

The better hotels are all on Taulud Island. Though less central, it offers higher stand-ards. Good-value options include:

Corallo Hotel (☎ 552406; Taulud Island; s US$7.50-18, d US$10-24;) The Corallo is good value and hospitable, with three types of room to suit most budgets. The more expensive ones have bathroom, air-con and balconies with sea views.

Hotel Luna (☎ 552272; r with shower US$17;) Another reliable option, set back from the road, with unassuming but very tolerable rooms.

Eating & Drinking
As opposed to hotels, most restaurants are concentrated on Massawa Island. You'll find a row of cheap eateries and cafeterias on and around the main street.

Sallam Restaurant (Massawa Island; fish dishes US$4-6.50; dinner) A hop and skip from the big mosque, this place doesn't look like much from the outside and actually looks worse inside but, believe it or not, it is a culinary pleasure. Here you can splurge on fresh fish cooked Yemeni style, ie sprinkled with hot pepper baked in a tandoori oven – a delight to the palate. Have a seat on the informal ter-race, and ask to visit the kitchen at the back where the cooks sweat and toil.

Eritrea Restaurant (☎ 552640; Massawa Island; mains US$1.50-3) This is considered the most reputable place in Massawa Island. Indeed, you won't be disappointed by the rather eclectic menu, with local and Italian speci-alities as well as vegetarian options. The bar-becued fish kebabs are simply delicious. An added bonus is the airy, covered terrace.

Alba Bar Restaurant (Massawa Island; mains US$1.50-4) A few paces from the covered market, this is the most cheerful joint in Massawa, with a partially covered terrace, cosy atmosphere and background music. It's suitable for breakfast, lunch or dinner. The food's varied, with meat dishes, pasta and sandwiches, not to mention the usual suspects (fish). Also serves great, fresh fruit juices (US$1).

Banuna Bar and Restaurant (Massawa Island; mains US$1.50-6) Tired of *zigni*? Opt for the Banuna, closer to the seafront, and splash out on lobster, calamari or shrimps.

The Eritrean Supermarket is the best stocked if you're preparing for a picnic or a trip to the islands or through Dankalia.

Clubbing

Torino Hotel (Massawa Island; admission US$3) Massawa is not exactly the place you would think of clubbing, but the rooftop dance floor at the Torino is the closest thing Massawa has to a nightclub. To say it's tacky is an understatement, but it provides an authentic slice of harbour life. Depending on the day, it can be patronized by foreign seamen in search of exotic pleasures, locals in need of Western sounds or travellers looking for some thrills.

Getting There & Around

Buses leave from the bus station on the mainland for Asmara several times daily (US$1.50, 3½ to four hours). The road to Asmara is spectacular (read: hair-raising), beginning at sea level and winding its way up to 2300m above sea level.

The track of the old Italian-built railway linking Massawa to Asmara railway runs alongside or within view of the road for much of the journey. It's due to be functioning by 2004 and should make for a splendid journey.

At the time of writing an airport was being constructed on the outskirts of mainland Massawa.

Shared taxis and town minibuses are convenient for short hops around town (about US$0.20).

DAHLAK ARCHIPELAGO

The Dahlak Archipelago undoubtedly ranks among Eritrea's top drawcards, with 210 virgin islands sprinkled off the coast. The largest one, **Dahlak Kebir**, is just 9km across.

With its virtually unspoilt reefs, the Dahlak Archipelago is a haven for divers. However, this untouched world is not within everyone's reach. A trip to the islands is expensive and is quite tricky to organise. The only option available is to charter a boat. If

you manage to join up with other travellers and share the expenses, this becomes a more viable option, but expect to shell out about US$100 per person per day for the trip. Contact the **Eritrea Diving Centre** (☎ 552688) at the Ministry of Marine Resources on Taulud Island, or **Dahlak Sea Touring** (☎ 552489) on Massawa Island in Massawa, or one of the travel agencies in Asmara for more information.

On top of this, you have to pay a fee of US$20 for a three-day permit, which can be obtained from the **Eritrean Shipping Lines** office (☎ 552475) on Massawa Island.

A good, cheaper alternative day-trip is **Green Island**. This tiny island, little more than a large sandbank, is visible from Massawa. Sure, it can't really compete with a Polynesian atoll, but here you can still spend the day lazing on the empty, white beaches and snorkelling along reefs. A day excursion to Green Island costs about US$20 per person for four people. It costs about US$30 to US$50 for one to three people, depending on the boat. Contact **Eritrea Diving Centre** (☎ 552688; Taulud Island) or **Dahlak Sea Tourism** (☎ 552489; Massawa Island).

Apart from an expensive hotel on Dahlak Kebir, there are no places to stay on the islands, so if you head out there you will need to come prepared for camping.

SOUTHERN ERITREA

ASSAB

Situated at the southern tip of the country, over 500km from Asmara or Massawa, the coastal town of Assab was the first place to be settled by the Italians in the 19th century. It has remained an important trading town ever since and has kept its strategic value as a port. After the Ethiopian occupation, Assab expanded rapidly, developing into a modern port to handle Ethiopian trade. The Ethiopians took care not to damage the town and its industries during the War of Independence, believing that the city would remain in their hands. After independence, Ethiopia's access to this port was guaranteed. With recent hostilities, all harbour activity came to a halt. Its inhabitants seem now to feel nostalgic for the bygone Ethiopian era, when the city was bursting with activity.

For travellers, there is nothing of particular interest in Assab, but there is a pervasive ghost town feel that can be captivating. Its

IF YOU CAN'T STAND THE HEAT

Between Asmara and the highland towns and the distant port of Assab stretches the infamous **Dankalia region**, reputed to be one of the hottest places on earth and home to the famously hardy and fierce Afar people. There's little to see, nothing to do and no great destination awaiting you at the other end. But that's exactly what makes this area so exciting, with a genuine sense of exploration and a palpable mystique.

An inhospitable volcanic and rock desert, the region is best negotiable with a 4WD and the assistance of a guide. More adventurous-minded and penny-counting travellers will take the rickety old bus that plies the route from Asmara to Assab three times a week, a gruelling journey of one and a half days. For a break, you can stop off at an Afar fishing village, such as **Thio** or **Edi**, where you'll find ultra-basic facilities.

Although desolate and harsh in the extreme, Dankalia is truly uncharted territory, fostering an amazing way of life among the nomadic peoples who roam through it, and as such it is a unique experience.

sheer isolation is an attraction of itself. Not to mention some of the Red Sea's best and most unspoiled **beaches** nearby. Assab is also a convenient stopover for travellers heading for Djibouti; the border is just 112km south.

For a place to sleep, the **Kebal International Hotel** (☎ 661700; d or tw with shower US$4-13; 🔀) is a good bargain, with three types of spacious and well-kept room to suit most budgets. The more expensive ones come with air-con, TV and fridge. There's a restaurant on the premises. Or head for the **Aurora Restaurant** (mains US$1.5-2) – the best place to enjoy pasta or grilled fish.

You can reach Assab either by plane with the once-weekly flight from Asmara with Eritrean Airlines (US$42/84 one way/return) or by a taking the tough 1½ day bus journey (US$8, three per week) from Asmara via Massawa. The dirt track between Massawa and Assab has been much improved, but is still best traversed in a 4WD vehicle with local guidance if you're self-driving.

ERITREA DIRECTORY

ACCOMMODATION
Only Asmara and, to a lesser extent, Massawa, offer a good range of accommodation. Smaller towns have hotels and *pensions*, but they're often basic affairs. Many of the country's cheaper hotels have cold water only. There are no official campgrounds.

ACTIVITIES
The Dahlak Archipelago offers plentiful opportunities for scuba diving, although

it is still in its infancy. Snorkelling is also possible.

BUSINESS HOURS
In eastern Eritrea, government offices and privates businesses are usually closed between noon and 4pm. They reopen at 4pm until 7pm or 8pm.

DANGERS & ANNOYANCES
Eritrea is one of the safest countries in Africa to travel through, but there are still thousands of uncharted landmines around the countryside. Keep on the road. Also, follow the example of the locals and make sure you're off out-of-town roads by dusk.

EMBASSIES & CONSULATES
Countries with diplomatic representation in Asmara:
Djibouti (☎ 125990)
Egypt (☎ 120056; Marsa Fatuma St, Asmara)
Ethiopia (Franklin Roosevelt St, Asmara) Closed at the time of writing.
France (☎ 126599; off Nakfa Ave, Asmara)
Germany (☎ 186670; Saba Building, Andinet Ave, Asmara)
Sudan (☎ 120672; Hazemo St, Asmara)
UK (☎ 120145; BDHO Ave, Asmara)
USA (☎ 120004; Franklin Roosevelt St, Asmara)
Yemen (☎ 181399; off Andinet Ave, Asmara) Near the German embassy.

Eritrea has diplomatic representation in the following neighbouring countries: Djibouti, Egypt, Kenya and Sudan. For more details on getting visas for neighbouring countries, see p724.

ERITREA

HOLIDAYS

As well as religious holidays listed in the Africa Directory (p1003), these are the principal public holidays in Eritrea:

1 January New Year's Day
7 January Leddet (Christmas)
19 January Timkat (Epiphany)
8 March International Women's Day
1 May Workers' Day
24 May Liberation Day
20 June Martyrs' Day
1 September Start of the Armed Struggle
11 September Kiddus Yohannes (Orthodox New Year)
27 September Meskel (Finding of the True Cross)

MAPS

The best map currently available is the one produced by ITMB Publishing in Canada (2nd edition; 1:9,000,000).

MEDIA

The *Eritrea Profile* is published every week. Eritrean national radio broadcasts three times a day in at least four of Eritrea's national languages. Eritrean television broadcasts every evening from around 6.30pm. You can tune in to the English programmes at 9.30pm.

MONEY

There are no ATMs in Eritrea. Money (cash and travellers cheques) must always be changed at a bank or with an authorised dealer and a receipt obtained. You may be asked to present these receipts on your departure.

There's a black market in Eritrea. The rates offered are tempting (almost 70% higher than the official rates) but it's illegal. If you do indulge, make the transaction with people you know, and never in the street.

Credit cards are very rarely accepted outside a few of the top hotels in Asmara. If you are travelling around the country it is wise to change money before you leave Asmara.

POST & TELEPHONE

The Eritrean postal service is considered quite reliable, if not the speediest. Postage for the first 200g is US$0.20 worldwide, with the exception of neighbouring countries, which are cheaper. Courier services are available in Asmara.

For calls to Eritrea from abroad, phone numbers for the major towns must be prefixed by the number 1.

International calls are best made from the telecommunications building found in all the main towns. International rates vary from about US$1.50 to US$2.20 per minute depending on the country. For national calls, you can use phonecards.

TOURIST INFORMATION

There is currently no national tourist office in the country, though one is planned in Asmara. The best places to go for information are **Travel House International** (☎ 201881), near the post office, and **Explore Eritrea Travel & Tours** (☎ 121242; Adi Hawsha St), two leading travel agencies in Asmara.

VISAS

Tourist visas are for single entry only, valid for 30 days from the date of arrival in Eritrea. They cost about US$50, although requirements tend to vary arbitrarily from one Eritrean embassy to another. If there's no embassy in your home country, or in another country you're travelling though before arriving in Eritrea, contact one of the travel agencies in Asmara (see Tourist Information earlier); they can help you organise a visa.

Visa Extensions

Visas can be extended up to two times for a further 30 days at the **Department of Immigration** (☎ 200033; Denden St) in Asmara. It costs US$40. You'll need a photo.

Visas for Onward Travel

Visas for Sudan and Djibouti are available from embassies in Asmara (see p723).
Djibouti Travellers need their passport, two photos and US$30. It takes two days to process. The visa is valid for one month.
Ethiopia The embassy is closed and the borders between the two countries are still closed.
Sudan Travellers need a passport, a copy of the first pages of their passport, two photos and US$41 in cash. They might be asked also for a letter from their own embassy. The visa is valid for one month. Beware, it can take time to process (up to three weeks) as the application is treated in Khartoum (Sudan).

Madagascar

HIGHLIGHTS

- **Parc National de l'Isalo** Plunging into the waterfall and natural swimming pool at the end of a long hike through vegetated canyons that turn red in the sunset (p745)
- **Île Sainte Marie** Standing on the beaches of this island and watching the whales let off steam (p751)
- **Parc National de Ranomafana** Walking, Charles Darwin-style, past waterfalls and wild rivers, while spotting some of the most endangered lemur species hidden in the lush tropical foliage (p743)
- **Ifaty** Diving among the sharks in the clear blue waters off the beaches of this west coast village (p747)
- **Best journey** Seeing tuna fish throwing themselves out of the water, while crossing the sparkling blue seas between the mainland and Île Sainte Marie (p754)
- **Off the beaten track** Catching a wave with the surfers at Mahambo village, or toasting yourself on the white-sand beaches (p751)

FAST FACTS

- **Area** 587,401 sq km
- **ATMs** in all major towns
- **Budget** US$20 to US$25 per day
- **Capital** Antananarivo
- **Languages** French, Malagasy
- **Money** Malagasy Franc; US$1 = 6250 Fmg
- **Population** 16.9 million
- **Seasons** wet (Nov–Mar), dry (May–Oct), hot (Oct–Apr)
- **Telephone** country code ☎ 261; international access code ☎ 00
- **Time** GMT/UTC + 3
- **Visas** US$32 one-month, single entry; issued on arrival at the airport

What's this? People with Indonesian names and faces, speaking French and dancing to African-sounding music? No, you haven't accidentally swallowed a load of magic mushrooms. You've just landed in Madagascar – and there's no country on earth quite like it. Separated from the African continent by several hundred kilometres of ocean, and by millions of years on the evolutionary time-scale, this giant island has animal and plant species found nowhere else on the planet, crocodile-infested lakes, and thousands of miles of fabulous coastline with beaches, sunken ships and stunning coral. In a day's drive you might cross rocky mountains or rainforests teeming with lemurs and waterfalls. Fall asleep for an hour and you'll wake up to the sight of bald, rolling hills and impossibly bright, green rice paddies, all of it inhabited by a mad mix of dark-skinned Africans, straight-haired Asiatics, and every combination in between.

MADAGASCAR

0   200 km
0   120 mi

Moroni ○   **Grande Comore**
          Comoros
Fomboni ○   ○ Mutsamudu
    Mohéli **Anjouan**

          ○ Mamoudzou
        Mayotte

Cap d'Ambre
(Tanjon 'ny Bobaomby)

Parc National de   ○ **Antsiranana**
Montagne d'Ambre ⛺   **(Diego Suarez)**

Réserve Spéciale ⛺ ⛺ **Réserve Spéciale**
de l'Ankàrana   **d'Analamerana**

Nosy Be   ○ Ambilobe
Hell-Ville ○ ⓇⓃ6   ○ Iharana (Vohémar)
          ○ Ambanja

ANTSIRANANA

Tsaratanana   Maromokotro
Massif ▲ **(2876m)**   ○ Sambava

○ Béalanana   **Parc National** ⛺
                   de Marojejy
      ○ Antsohihy   **Marojejy** ○ Andapa
                    Massif   ○ Antalaha

Sofia ⓇⓃ6   **Masoala** Cap Est
        ○ Boriziny   **Peninsula**
        (Port Bergé)
Mahajanga   **Parc National** Maroantsetra ○ ⛺ **Parc National**
(Majunga) ○ **d'Ankarafantsika**   **Masoala**
Katsepy ○   **Réserve Forestière**   **Nosy**
Mitsinjo ○   **d'Ampijoroa**   **Mangabe** ○
          Marovoay ○   ○ Mananara
Soalala ○   ○ Ambondromany   **Parc National de**
Lac Kinkony   **Mananara-Nord** ⛺
      Réserve Naturelle   **Île Sainte Marie**
Besalampy ○ **Intégrale des**   **(Nosy Boraha)**
      Tsingy de Namoroka **TOAMASINA** Soanierana-Ivongo ○ ○ Ambodifotatra
          ○ Maevatanana   **Route des**
Tambohorano ○ **MAHAJANGA** **Contrebandiers** ○ Mahambo
                              ○ Mahavelona
                    Lac ○ Ambatondrazaka
Maintirano ○   **Alaotra** Vohijala ○   ⓇⓃ5 ○ Toamasina
                    ⓇⓃ4   **Parc National** (Tamatave)
Parc National   **de Zahamena**
des Tsingy de Tsiroanomandidy ○
Bemaraha ⛺   **ANTANANARIVO** ○ Ambohimanga Moramanga ○ ○ Ambila-Lemaitso
                ☆ **ANTANANARIVO**
          Miarinarivo ○   **Parc National**
Belo-sur-Tsiribihina ○ Miandrivazo ○ **Ankaratra** Vatomandry ○ **d'Andasibe-**
                    Massif   **Mantadia**
                Ambatolampy ○
      Réserve   Betafo ○ ○ Antsirabe   ○ Mahanoro
Morondava ○ **Forestière**
      de Kirindy   ⓇⓃ7
              ○ Ambositra   ○ Nosy-Varika
TOLIARA
      ○ Mandabe **FIANARANTSOA**
              Parc National
              de Ranomafana
Morombe ○ Beroroha ○ Fianarantsoa ○   ○ Mananjary
      Lac   ○ Ifandiana
      Ihotry   Ambalavao ○
          Parc   **Pic Boby** ○ Manakara
Ankazoabo ○ **National** ▲ **(2658m)**
          de l'Isalo Ihosy ○ **Parc National** ○ Vohipeno
              d'Andringitra ○ Farafangana
Ifaty ○   Ranohira ○
Sakaraha ○ ⓇⓃ7 ○ Ilakaka
      ○ Andranovory
Toliara (Tuléar) ○   ○ Betroka ○ Vangaindrano
Baie de Saint-Augustin ○ Onilahy
Anakao ○ Betioky ○ **Réserve Spéciale** ⓇⓃ13 **Tropic of Capricorn**
Beheloka ○ **de Beza-Mahafaly**
Réserve Naturelle Bekily ○ ○ Beraketa ○ Manambondro
Intégrale de
Tsimanampetsotsa Ampanihy ○ **Parc National**
Itampolo ○   **d'Andohahela**
          Réserve Privée ○ Manafiafy (Baie Sainte Luce)
          de Berenty
Androka ○   Ambovombe ○ ○ Lokaro Peninsula
      Beloha ○ Faux Cap **Taolagnaro**
                    (Fort Dauphin)
      Cap Sainte Marie

**INDIAN
OCEAN**

MADAGASCAR

HISTORY

It may only be a short hop from the mainland, but Madagascar remained uninhabited until about 1500 to 2000 years ago, when its first settlers sailed there from halfway around the world in Indonesia and Malaysia. This migration accelerated during the 9th century, when the powerful Hindu-Sumatran empire of Srivijaya controlled much of the maritime trade in the Indian Ocean.

How these first Indonesian settlers reached Madagascar is still a mystery. There's no way they could have crossed the Indian Ocean in their tiny out-rigger canoes. But one theory suggests that they reached the island by stopping en route at various points around the rim of the Indian Ocean. There's evidence of this in the distribution of Indonesian-style sailing vessels along the Indian Ocean's northern shoreline. These boats were coastal vessels rather than ocean-going craft, and they possibly skirted the Indian, Arabian and African shorelines, trading and perhaps settling in those areas, before finally arriving at Madagascar. The connection between Sanskrit (an Indian language) and Malagasy also supports this theory.

These settlers brought southeastern food crops with them, which is why Madagascar's farms seem so Asian in appearance. The settlers probably continued participating in the Arab-dominated trade and later the Swahili networks of eastern Africa, absorbing Bantu and Arabic influences along the way. Over the centuries, powerful kingdoms began to emerge on the island.

European Arrivals

The Portuguese were the first Europeans to arrive in Madagascar, naming it Ilha de Sao Lourenco, though the name didn't stick. How Madagascar got its present name is another mystery. Some say it's a derivation of Mogadishu (the Somalian capital), others say it's a corruption of the word 'Malagasy'.

The Portuguese, British, Dutch and French all, for various reasons, tried and failed to establish permanent bases on the islands. The French base at Taolagnaro lasted 31 years, before they abandoned it in 1674. Ironically, some of the most successful attempts were made by distinctly nongovernmental organisations – pirates. For several decades in the 17th century, pirates from Europe and the United States made Madagascar (and especially Île Sainte Marie) their base in the Indian Ocean.

As trade with the Europeans grew, several kingdoms began to gain dominance. The Menabe ruled the west, while in the east the Zana-Malata (people of mixed pirate and Malay-Polynesian descent) combined with other east coast peoples to form the confederation of the Betsimisaraka (Those Who Stick Together). At the same time in the central highlands the Merina grew into the most powerful of them all. Their chief, Ramboasalama, ascended the throne of Ambohimanga and took one of the longest names in history: Andrianampoinimerinandriantsimitoviaminandriampanjaka, which means 'Hope of Merina'. It was 'abbreviated' to Andrianampoinimerina.

Through his close trade relations with the Europeans, he acquired enough weaponry to dominate a major chunk of Madagascar. His son Radama became king in 1810 and, by marrying the daughter of a rival king, managed to fulfil his father's vow that his kingdom would have no frontier but the sea.

Radama became very cosy with the British, entering diplomatic relations with them in 1817 and allowing them to send over hundreds of missionaries to Christianise the Merina court. However, Radama's widow and successor, Ranavalona I, reversed her husband's policies. Nicknamed 'The Bloodthirsty', she had a passionate dislike of all things *vahaza* (white) and persecuted the missionaries. However, her son, Radama II, was a moderate like his father. He abolished forced labour, allowed freedom of religion, reformed the judicial system and re-opened trade links with the Europeans before he was assassinated in 1862. Christianity became the official religion for Madagascar's royal court.

Towards the late 19th century, British interest in Madagascar was waning, while the French became more interested. In 1890 the British handed the island over to the French in exchange for Zanzibar.

The Malagasies and the French rarely saw eye-to-eye. The French invaded Antananarivo in 1895 and turned Madagascar into an official colony the following year. In 1897, the first Governor-General, Joseph Gallieni, suppressed the Malagasy language and sent the then Queen Ranavalona III into exile in Algeria, thus ending the Merina monarchy.

MADAGASCAR

Autonomy

The French forged ahead with their development plans, constructing roads, transport systems and expanding the education network. Under their rule slavery was abolished, only to be replaced with a harsh tax system under which nonpayers became de facto slaves. A Malagasy elite began to emerge, and resentment of the colonial presence grew in all levels of society. Nationalist movements developed by the 1920s, and strikes and demonstrations became more frequent, culminating in a revolt in 1947. The French suppressed it, but only after killing an estimated 80,000 people and sending the rebel leaders into exile.

By 1958, the Malagasies had voted in a referendum to become an autonomous republic within the French 'community' of overseas nations. Philibert Tsiranana, leader of the Parti Social Democrate (PSD), became Madagascar's first president. Tsiranana, a *côtier* (non-Merina), preferred economic ties with South Africa, and allowed the French to keep control of most of Madagascar's trade and industry. The Merina elite, on the other hand, had Soviet leanings and were anti-French, even though they were the most Gallicised. Tsiranana was forced to resign in 1972, and was succeeded by army general Gabriel Ramantsoa.

Ramantsoa took Madagascar down a very socialist route, severing ties with South Africa and Taiwan, and making friends with China and the USSR instead. He closed down the French military bases and collectivised the farming system, which led to a mass exodus of French farmers. The economy took a nose dive and Ramantsoa was forced to resign. His successor, Richard Ratsimandrava, lasted just one week before being assassinated by rebel army officers. They were almost immediately routed by Ramantsoa loyalists, and a new government headed by Admiral Didier Ratsiraka came to power.

The Ratsiraka years were characterised by more socialist reforms, with even a Mao Zedong-style 'red book' of government plans and theories. A debt crisis in 1981 and 1982 forced him to abandon the reforms and obey the IMF instead.

In 1989 Ratsiraka was dubiously 'elected' to his third seven-year term, sparking riots that left six people dead. People were still demanding his resignation by 1991, and the ensuing demonstrations brought the economy to a standstill. But Ratsiraka refused to step down. In 1992 Malagasies voted in a referendum to limit the presidential powers. General elections were held that year, and Professor Albert Zafy thrashed Ratsiraka, ending his 17 years in power.

The Return of Ratsiraka

Years of communist-style dictatorship and economic mismanagement made it hard for Zafy to ignite the economy and gain the people's trust. Zafy refused to listen to the IMF and sought money from elsewhere. This led to accusations of money laundering. He was eventually impeached for abuse of constitutional powers (eg sacking his prime minister). Elections were called in 1996 and Ratsiraka surprised everyone by scraping a victory. Appealing for Madagascar to become a more 'humanist and ecological republic', Ratsiraka retook office in 1997.

Political Crisis

In 2001, Madagascans went to the polls for the general elections. During the first round Marc Ravalomanana, a former yogurtseller and businessman, claimed victory. But Ratsiraka was not going to give up his presidency without a fight, and he refused to accept the vote. Ravalomanana and his supporters mounted mass protests and a general strike at the beginning of 2002. A month later, Ravalomanana went ahead and declared himself president anyway, sparking off clashes between rival supporters that nearly brought Madagascar to civil war. Bridges were bombed, and Ratsiraka's supporters blockaded Antananarivo, cutting off its fuel and food supply for weeks.

After seven months of crisis, the Supreme Court held a re-count of the votes and declared Ravalomanana the winner. The OAU (Organisation of African Unity) refused to accept his victory. But when the US recognised Ravalomanana as the rightful president, Ratsiraka fled in exile to Paris.

Economic Change

Meanwhile, Ravalomanana's I Love Madagascar party sealed its popularity at the parliamentary elections in December 2002. The new president set about reforming the country's ruined economy, and announced salary increases for politicians in an effort to stamp out corruption. He generally made the right noises to the World Bank which, along with France and the US, pledged a total of US$2.3 billion in aid. They, like millions of Malagasies, are hoping that Ravalomanana, a self-made millionaire, can help to finally fulfil Madagascar's huge economic potential.

THE CULTURE

If there is one term that sums up the Malagasy mind, it is *mora mora* (nice and slow). It's *mora mora* that makes Malagasies so kind, friendly and generous. And it's *mora mora* that keeps them smiling through the droughts and cyclones that flood their rice paddies on a regular basis. Malagasies are so chilled and patient, it takes a lot for them to raise their voice. Outward shows of emotion are a rarity and, despite their friendliness, they can be extremely reserved and insular, keeping their innermost feelings and problems firmly hidden from family members and friends.

Traditional Beliefs

In the traditional rural areas, *razana*, or ancestor worship, is a big feature of Malagasy society, and one's ancestors are believed to exist in the present world in spiritual form. Ancestors are responsible for good and bad luck, and they are the owners of the land, which is sacred and can therefore never be sold (much to the chagrin of urban Indian businessmen!).

The belief in *fady* (taboos) is oriented towards maintaining good relations with the ancestors. These taboos vary widely from village to village and take on many forms – it may be forbidden to eat pork or eggs, to point at a sacred mountain, cross a certain river by boat, or hold a funeral on a Tuesday.

So entrenched are these belief systems that they have admirably withstood the onslaught of modernity, although this sometimes impacts negatively on Malagasy lives nowadays. Detrimental agricultural practices remain stubbornly in place, while traditional rites such as cattle-rustling (among the Bara people) has evolved into a corrupt business, now that the zebu (domesticated ox) population is dwindling.

Malagasies have a very strong sense of community, which is structured around the extended family and is often a source of entertainment. Traditional Malagasy society holds *kabary* competitions, *kabary* being a highly prized form of oral literature. The orator skilfully delivers a series of proverbs and introductions, using allegory, double entendre, metaphor and simile. The speaker continues for as long as possible while avoiding direct contact with the subject at hand.

Merinas & Côtiers

Tribal affiliations are a main source of Malagasy identity, but perhaps even more important is the distinction between the highlanders – specifically the Merina – and the so-called *côtiers* (everyone else). Centuries of precolonial Merina domination and favouritism under French colonial rule have given some of the very Gallicised (and Christianised) Merina highlanders a sense of superiority. In the minds of the snobbier set, the *côtiers* are backward, non-Francophone, country bumpkins with stubborn taboos, and old-fashioned ways.

The Bara people are tall, slender and dark, and have the most markedly African features of any Malagasy tribe. The members of this south-central tribe are pastoralists and well known for 'dahalo' (cattle rustling) as a test of manhood.

The Betsileo (The Invincibles) live around the Fianarantsoa region and are known for their rice cultivation skills and their woodcarving (especially the Zafimaniry sub-group).

The Betsimisaraka (Those Who Stand Together) constitute the second largest tribe in Madagascar. They count several important national political figures (such as Didier Ratsiraka) among their number, and they live along the east coast, as far south as Mananjary.

The Sakalava (and the Vezo), occupy western and northwestern Madagascar. They have a respect for a shared royal heritage, and their belief system centres around the 'tromba' (spirits of dead royalty).

The Mahafaly (Makers of Taboos) inhabit Madagascar's southern and southwestern regions. These agriculturalists arrived on the island less than 900 years ago and resisted Merina dominance until French colonial rule. They are known for their impressive, illustrated tombs.

The Antaimoro (Those From The Coast) live in southeastern Madagascar and have close ties with the Arab world. They are renowned for their paper-making techniques.

In urban areas such as Antananarivo and Fianarantsoa, the straight haired, light-skinned Merina elite fill the trendy bars, restaurants and cyber cafés, wearing the latest Western clothes while discussing world politics or their recent trips to Paris.

Still, whatever divisions exist, Malagasies are bound together by the land: they are an island race, with no strong allegiance to any other part of the world. They feel no connection with Asia, and they'll tell you they are most certainly not African, despite what the geopoliticians may say.

Social Problems

Gender equality in such a traditional society has yet to develop serious momentum, although there are currently several initiatives to empower rural women. In urban areas, however, the main problem facing women is prostitution, which is possibly Madagascar's most nagging social problem. Desperate poverty and high unemployment leads many girls, some as young as 11, to sell their bodies in hotels and bars where there's a thriving – and very visible – sex-tourism trade.

The government has strengthened its legislation dealing with sex offences involving minors, while several hotels pin up antiprostitution posters in an effort to deter the activity.

FOOTBALL SCORE OF 149–0 SETS NEW RECORD

Malagasy football put itself on the world map in 2002, but for all the wrong reasons. When Olympique l'Emyrne disagreed with a referee's decision, they deliberately scored an own-goal in protest. Following their coach's argument with the referee, the team began repeatedly kicking the ball into their own net, while Adema (the opposite team, and by now national champions) watched in bemusement. At the final whistle, Olympique had 'scored' 149 times.

The home crowd was so disgusted they threw their shoes onto the pitch.

RELIGION

Traditional beliefs aside, around 50% of the country will tell you that they are most definitely Christian and that religion plays a large role in their lives. On Sunday mornings, the cobbled streets of Antananarivo fill with the chimes of church bells and, increasingly, evangelical singing. Even President Ravalomanana is vice-president of a Protestant reform movement, and he expects employees in his private companies to attend prayer sessions before coming into work. All his company trucks are printed with the holy number seven, and he bases many of his political and business slogans on quotes from the Bible.

ENVIRONMENT
The Land

Madagascar's unique flora and fauna is one of its main attractions, yet it is in serious danger of disappearing. Madagascar has already lost 85% of its natural forest cover thanks to commercial logging and slash-and-burn agricultural methods. These methods, known as *tavy*, are used to open previously inhospitable regions to agriculture. However, without regular fertilisation, the land can become infertile within a year. In the dry western region, farmers burn large tracts of natural scrub to provide pasture for their cattle, and in the process end up destroying the habitat for hundreds of unique and endangered species. Although environmental awareness is on the up, the government has found it hard to enforce new laws and make people change culturally ingrained practices. However, the world's NGOs are on the case and several organisations have set up educational programs for Malagasy rural people (including the children) to help increase environmental awareness and find alternative ways of living off the land.

Wildlife

Visitors come from all over the world to check out Madagascar's world famous lemurs, which are found nowhere else on earth. They belong to the 'prosimian' group of primates, from which apes and humans are descended, and there are over 50 varieties of them. Because Madagascar split from the African mainland millions of years ago and remained isolated, it has a high percentage of endemic fauna, However, many of the island's large mammals are endangered, including the mongoose lemur and the broad-nosed gentle lemur (once thought to be extinct, but now protected). The zebu, or domesticated ox, is another well-known species – see the 'Zebu' boxed text on p744.

Nearly half of its 250 bird species are found nowhere else on earth, including the red-and-white kingfisher and the serpent eagle. The best-known reptiles, found only in Madagascar, include the chameleon and the huge ploughshare tortoise. Nearly all of the island's frogs are endemic and they are often brightly coloured, ranging from green, yellow and orange to grey, brown and black.

National Parks

National parks and reserves were first established under the French colonial government, some as early as 1927. Today there are several dozen parks and reserves, covering approximately 12% of the uninhabited land (or about 3% of Madagascar's total area). However, only a small number of these areas are actively protected, and many remain largely inaccessible to tourists.

TRANSPORT

GETTING THERE & AWAY
Air

Air Madagascar (☎ 22 222 22), **Air France** (☎ 22 223 21) and **Inter Air** (☎ 22 224 06) have flights into Madagascar. Air France flies direct from Paris.

Air Madagascar flies from both Johannesburg (South Africa) and Nairobi (Kenya), while Inter Air flies from Johannesburg.

Johannesburg Air Madagascar, US$550 return, 3½ hours, two per week; Inter Air, US$550 return, three hours, two per week.

Mauritius Air Madagascar, US$332 return, two hours, three per week.

Nairobi Air Madagascar, US$428 return, three hours, one per week.

Paris Air Madagascar, US$720 return, nine hours, two per week; Air France, US$900 return, nine hours, three per week.

DEPARTURE TAX

The airport departure tax is US$30 for international flights and US$4 for domestic flights, and is always included in the price of airline tickets.

Boat

Sea travel is possible, but it's not as easy as you might expect. Cargo boats from Mombasa (Kenya) or Zanzibar (Tanzania) often travel to the Comoros where several ships travel to Toamasina (Tamatave; Madagascar). Boats from South Africa are surprisingly infrequent. You'll need to ask around in Durban, try the **Port Authority** (☎ 27 31 361 8795).

If you're aiming to leave Madagascar by boat, it's best to head to Toamasina (Tamatave) and enquire at the port.

GETTING AROUND
Air

Air Madagascar flies between major cities. The poor roads and huge distances between cities mean that flying may be your only option if you are on a tight schedule.

Local Transport

Taxi-brousse (bush taxi) is the cheapest and most popular way to travel around Madagascar. *Taxi-brousse* is the generic term for any form of public transport that is not a big bus. The *bâché* is a small, converted pick-up truck with benches down each side. The *camion-brousse* is a larger truck where the passengers sit on the floor or on top of the cargo. Much more comfortable, faster (and therefore pricier) is the *taxi-be*, usually a Peugeot 504 or 505. Along the main roads (there aren't many) minibuses are the most common form of transport, though you won't see them elsewhere.

As an alternative to high car rentals, it's possible to hire taxis on the street. For direct journeys the fare should generally be the standard *taxi-brousse* fare multiplied by the number of passengers the driver would normally pick up.

The pirogue or 'lakana' (dug-out canoe) is the main form of local transport in many areas of coastal Madagascar. Hiring one is easy (the fee negotiable), but don't get in if the seas are rough or the boat overcrowded. Bring your own supplies and something waterproof to protect your luggage.

ANTANANARIVO

☎ 020 / pop 588,000

Welcome to one of the most unique capital cities in the world. The winding cobbled

MADAGASCAR

ANTANANARIVO

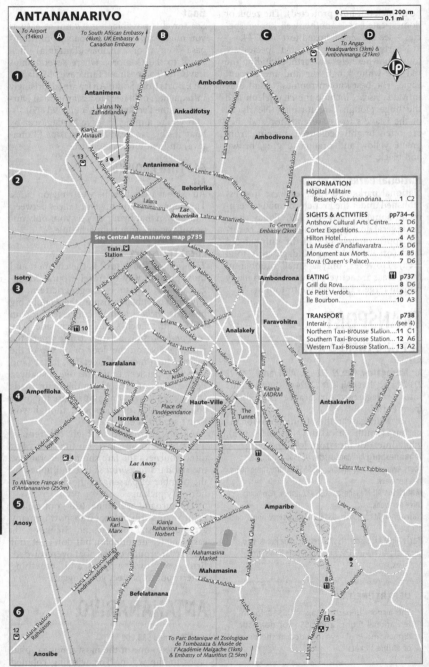

See Central Antananarivo map p735

INFORMATION
Hôpital Militaire
Besarety-Soavinandriana............1 C2

SIGHTS & ACTIVITIES pp734–6
Antshow Cultural Arts Centre......2 D6
Cortez Expeditions.....................3 A2
Hilton Hotel..............................4 A5
La Musée d'Andafiavaratra.........5 D6
Monument aux Morts.................6 B5
Rova (Queen's Palace)...............7 D6

EATING p737
Grill du Rova.............................8 D6
Le Petit Verdot.........................9 C5
Île Bourbon.............................10 A3

TRANSPORT p738
Interair................................(see 4)
Northern Taxi-Brousse Station...11 C1
Southern Taxi-Brousse Station...12 A6
Western Taxi-Brousse Station....13 A2

streets, narrow wooden houses and shuttered windows, the soaring church spires and high hills in the background – with the occasional horse-drawn cart rolling past – all give Antananarivo (or 'Tana') an other-worldly feel. And even though the centre of Madagascar's capital city may be polluted, crowded and full of traffic jams, a walk in the early morning or evening, when the surrounding hills turn blue and the sky is orange, is breathtakingly.

Antananarivo was originally called Analamanga ('Blue Forest') and is believed to have been populated by ancestors of the current population, known as the Vazimba. From 1610 the Merina king Andrianjaka conquered these villages and renamed the area Antananarivo, which means 'Town of the Thousand' (warriors). He then built his own *rova* (palace) on the highest hills, and by the 18th century Antananarivo had become an important Merina kingdom and the base for the various kings and queens.

In 1895 French forces captured Antananarivo, which subsequently became the seat of the colonial government, and renamed it Tananarive. Following independence it became Antananarivo.

ORIENTATION
The international and domestic airports are in Ivato, 14km north of Antananarivo. Taking a private taxi (US$10) is the easiest way of getting into town. But don't be tempted by the unofficial drivers – the prices may be cheaper, but their knowledge of the town is often poor and the cars are usually in terrible shape.

Alternatively you can take a taxi to the Ivato *taxi-brousse* station (US$1.60, five minutes) and from there get a minibus into town (US$0.25, up to 1½ hours).

The centre of Antananarivo's business district is along Araben'ny Fahaleovantena (Independence Ave), which runs through the centre of town from the northwest corner to the southeast.

The area at the southeast end of Araben'ny Fahaleovantena is called Analakely, from where a steep staircase leads into a small square (Place de l'Independence) in Haute-Ville. Here you'll find the main post office, banks, nightclubs, restaurants and Hotemore hotels.

INFORMATION
Bookshops
Librairie de Madagascar (Map p735; ☎ 22 22454; Araben'ny Fahaleovantena, Analakely) Best selection of French and English nonfiction books, magazines, international newspapers, maps and guidebooks.

Cultural Centres
Alliance Française d'Antananarivo (☎ 22 20856; Lalana Seimad, Andavamamba) Outside the centre; offers both French and Malagasy language courses.
Centre Culturel Albert Camus (CCAC; Map p735; ☎ 22 21375; ccac@dts.mg; 14 Araben'ny Fahaleovantena) Has a French library and an exhibition hall showing photographic and other displays, plus Malagasy language courses (for French speakers), and a program of concerts, dance, films and other events.

Internet Access
Antananarivo has several Internet cafés, particularly in the Haute-Ville area. All the post offices have Internet access. Connections tend to be rather slow. Prices are around US$1.50 to US$2.50 per hour:
Outcool Web Bar (Map p735; Lalana Andriamary Ratianarivo; from US$1.40 per hr) Fast connection and a bar serving alcohol.
Teknet Cybercafe (Map p735; 32, Ave Gal Ramantsoa Ambatonilika, Isoraka; US$1.20 per hr) Popular with students, and the big TV screen shows music videos.

Media
The biggest national newspapers are *Midi Madagasikara*, *Madagascar Tribune* and *L'Express de Madagascar*, and they are available across the city. They usually contain emergency numbers, pharmacies and entertainment listings.

Medical Services
Hôpital Militaire Besarety-Soavinandriana (Map p732; ☎ 22 39751; Lanana Razafindrakoto; ☾ 24 hr) French doctors and one of the best places for emergency treatment.
Pharmacie Métropole (Map p735; ☎ 22 20025; Lalana Ratsimilaho) A well-stocked pharmacy near Hôtel Colbert.

Money
Bank of Africa (Map p735; Lalana Ratsimilaho, Haute-Ville) Near Shoprite supermarket; does advances on MasterCard.
BFV-SG (Map p735; Lalana Ratsimilaho, Haute-Ville) Near Shoprite supermarket, does advances on Visa and MasterCard.

MADAGASCAR

BMOI (Map p735; Lalana Ratsimilaho, Haute-Ville) Opposite the post office; ATMs accept Visa.

BNI-CL (Map p735; Araben'ny 26 Jona 1960) East of the post office; advances on Visa and MasterCard; no commission on travellers cheques.

UCB (Map p735; Lalana des 77 Parlementaires Français) Near the Swiss Embassy; a 1% commission on travellers cheques; a flat rate commission of US$10/13 on Visa/MasterCard advances; and it has the least queues.

Outside the banks you can change money, at similar rates, at **SOCIMAD** Central (Map p735; ☎ 22 25246; Lalana Radama I; 🕓 8-11am & 1.30-4.30pm Mon-Fri, 8-11am Sat); Airport (☎ 033 113 6595).

Post
The **Central post office** (Paositra Malagasy; Map p735; Araben'ny 26 Jona 1960) offers a poste restante service and has a second branch on Lalana Ratsimilaho.

Telephone
All the post offices (paositras) have card telephones for domestic and international calls, and there are several card-phones dotted around town.

Tourist Offices
Angap office Representative (Map p735; ☎ 22 25999; off Place de L'Independence); Ambatobe Headquarters (☎ 22 41538; northeast of the city centre) If you plan on visiting several parks you can obtain an Angap 'passport' (which is available for six parks, including Isalo and Ranomafana). The passport itself costs US$3, plus the rates for however many number of parks you want to visit. The passport is only available in Antananarivo.

Maison du Tourisme (Map p735; ☎ 22 35178; LE Ravelontsalama; 🕓 8am-noon & 2-6pm Mon-Fri) The official tourist office, near UCB Bank, has English-speaking staff, useful information and free city maps.

DANGERS & ANNOYANCES
Antananarivo is no more dangerous than most large cities, and if you take standard precautions, you should not have any difficulties. Take a taxi at night if you go out, but if you walk, go in a group, and remember that many parts of the city don't have streetlights. Be alert for pickpockets in markets and on public transport and avoid carrying cash in bags and other obvious places.

Antananarivo is a seriously polluted city, so don't be surprised of you suffer from the odd headache and throat irritation in the first few days.

SIGHTS
The **Rova** (Palais de la Reine, Queen's Palace; Map p732; Lalana Ramboatiana) is the imposing structure that caps the highest hill overlooking Lac Anosy. It was Antananarivo's main attraction until it burnt down in a suspected arson attack in 1995. Plans for reconstruction are in the pipeline, though for now, it's just an empty shell. But after a few days in the city you'll be curious about this building that seems to be visible from every part of town (even from landing aeroplanes – if you've got beady eyes). Technically it's off limits, but the guard will show you around for about US$4. To get there take a taxi (about US$1.30), or walk – you can climb directly up the crag near Parc Botanique et Zoologique de Tsimbazaza, via a maze of winding paths and steep stairways.

About 50m east of the Rova you'll find **La Musée d'Andafiavaratra** (Map p732; admission US$2.50; 🕓 10am-5pm Tue-Sun), which will give you a taste of what was once inside the Rova. The museum is housed in the former prime minister's residence, and there is a fascinating collection of royal personal belongings that were rescued from the Rova, including King Radama's boots, oil paintings of successive monarchs, Queen Rasoherina's tiny throne, a clock indicating the exact time and date of her death, plus Ranavalona II's wigs. If you use the optional guide, he will expect a tip.

If, by a cruel twist of fate, you don't get to see a lemur in the wild, **Parc Botanique et Zoologique de Tsimbazaza** (off Arabe Rabozaka; admission US$4; 🕓 9am-5pm) offers a little consolation. In addition to lemurs, there are aye-ayes, crocodiles, chimpanzees, giant tortoises, egrets and rare plants species among other things. Within the zoo the **Musée de l'Académie Malgache** (admission free) has natural and cultural exhibits, including the vertebrae of a dinosaur found near Mahajanga in 1907, plus the skeletal remains of a preserved egg of the extinct 'elephant bird'. To get there a taxi from the city centre costs US$1.30, or take the No 115 minibus which runs from the main bus station (outside La Tulipe Restaurant) to the zoo (US$0.40).

ACTIVITIES
If you fancy a bit of swimming, head to the **Hilton Hotel** (Map p732; ☎ 22 260 60; Rue Pierre Stibe Anosy) where nonguests can use the pool for US$4.

CENTRAL ANTANANARIVO

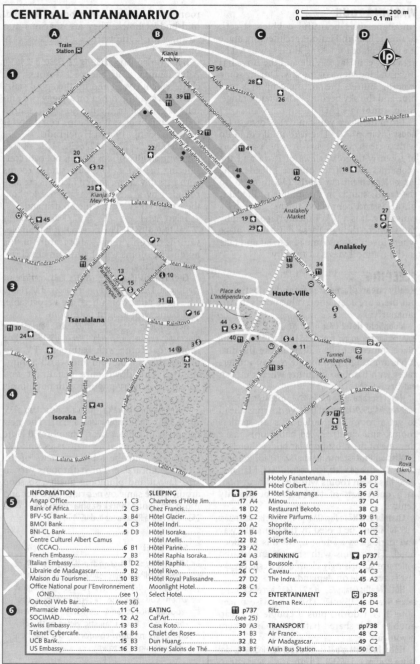

MADAGASCAR

WALKING TOUR

Antananarivo's beautiful cobbled streets, dramatic hills and unique architecture make it a good place for taking aimless walks. The area between Haute-Ville and the Rova has breathtaking views of the city. During some evening sunsets the surrounding hills turn blue and the sky becomes a brilliant orange. It's a stunning sight.

From the Rova you can walk down to **Lac Anosy** (Map p732). The lake itself could do with a clean, but it sits in a pleasant part of town with great views of Rova and the Mahamasina district on the hillside. The large **Monument aux Morts** (Monument to the Dead) stands in the middle of the lake, on an island connected to the shore by a causeway. It is a WWI memorial erected by the French, though these days it's a place where lovers often come just to sit and take in the tranquil views of the city.

SLEEPING

Really cheap places are few and far between, but there are a few good value hotels in Antananarivo.

Moonlight Hotel (Map p735; ☎ 22 26870; 52 Lalana Rainandriamampandry; dm/d US$4/12, s US$7-9) This place shines out like a diamond in the dirt. It has amazingly good-value rooms, and terraces with bamboo furniture where you can eat breakfast.

Hôtel Isoraka (Map p735; ☎ 22 65854; Arabe Ramanantsoa; s/d US$9/12) You'll have to ring ahead to get a room here. Friendly staff, spotless rooms, and clean, shared bathrooms make this one of the most popular budget hotels.

Mission Protestante (Map p732; ☎ 032 020 6265; off Rue RP Joseph de Villele, Faravohitra; d US$8) Madame Solo has clean rooms with shared bathroom in a quiet part of town, east of the city centre.

Chambres d'Hôte Jim (Map p735; Arabe Ramanantsoa; d US$10) Don't be fooled by the grim alleyway and dark steps leading up to this top-floor hotel. The rooms with shower and shared toilet are surprisingly clean and fresh. Breakfast is available on demand.

Hôtel Mellis (Map p735; ☎ 22 23425; htmellis@dts.mg; Lalana Nice; dm/d US$9/12) This otherwise pricey hotel has a dorm, plus a couple of cheap doubles with shared bathroom. Grab them if you can.

Hôtel Indri (Map p735; ☎ 22 20922; eindri@dts.mg; Lalana Radama I; d US$12) There are a few cheap

rooms with shared bathroom at this old, mid-budget hotel. They are spacious and clean, with Chinoiserie decor that's easy on the eye.

Hôtel Parine (Map p735; ☎ 22 23830; d US$6.50) After hauling your backpack through the cluttered courtyard and up the spiral staircase, you can flop down on a saggy bed and relieve yourself in the not-so clean, shared toilet – but at least it's cheap. You'll find it between Kianja 19 and Hotel Indri.

Hôtel Rivo (Map p735; ☎ 22 64630; 74 Lalana Rainandriamampandry; d US$6) This place is not bad, considering the price. The dull, simple rooms with passably clean, shared facilities are surrounded by a pleasant terrace overlooking the street. Food is available on demand.

Select Hotel (Map p735; ☎ 22 21001; 54 Araben'ny 26 Jona 1960; d US$13) The fact that it has an elevator is the only remarkable feature of this hotel. The rooms with bathroom are clean, but unexciting.

Chez Francis (Map p735; ☎ 22 61365; chezfrancis@vaniala.com; Lalana Rainandriamampandry; d US$14.50) The light, airy rooms here are very likable, and come with a clean bathroom.

Hôtel Glacier (Map p735; ☎ 22 20260; hotel.glacier@simicro.mg; Avenue du 26 Juin 1960; d US$15-18) For rooms that come with bathroom, TV and phone, this is a bargain and worth a mini-splurge. The downstairs restaurant and patisserie are very popular with both locals and tourists.

Hôtel Raphia Isoraka (Raphia Annexe; Map p735; ☎ 22 33931; Arabe Ramanantsoa; d US$15) The new rooms at this place near Chambres d'Hote Jim are very clean. The mattresses sink like hammocks, but the top-floor views of the city are unbeatable. The bathrooms vary in size, layout and plumbing quality, so shop around. The same owner runs the older and more spacious **Hôtel Raphia** (Map p735; ☎ 22 25313; off Lalana Ranavalona II; d US$15).

EATING

What Antananarivo lacks in budget accommodation, it makes up for in good cheap food.

Cafés & Quick Eats

Hôtel Colbert (Map p735; ☎ 22 20202; Lalana Printsy Ratsimamanga; dishes US$2) The excellent patisserie in this upmarket hotel does possibly the best chocolate éclairs in the Indian Ocean.

Le Sucre Sale (Map p735; Arabe Rabezavana; dishes US$1.50) Cheap and cheerful Chinese and Malagasy dishes are served here, along with some patisserie snacks.

Honey Salon de Thé (Map p735; ☎ 22 31858; 13 Araben'ny Fahaleovantena; dishes US$2) How civilised! A slice of cake washed down with a nice cup of tea. You can also get excellent ice-cream and pastries at this popular *salon de thé* (teahouse).

Hotely Fanantenana (Map p735; Araben'ny 26 Jona 1960; dishes US$0.90) Locals cram themselves into the tables at this small joint, which is the best of several *hotelys* around Analakely Market. The rice, chicken and *carot* (vegetables) are to die for.

Restaurants

Rivière Parfums (Map p735; ☎ 22 30714; off Arabe Andrianampoinimerina; dishes US$2) One of Antananarivo's oldest and best-kept secrets, this restaurant serves mouth-watering Vietnamese dishes at criminally low prices.

Dun Huang (Map p735; ☎ 22 66965; off Araben'ny Fahaleovantena; dishes US$4) For good Chinese in a large, comfortable dining room.

Restaurant Bekoto (Map p735; ☎ 22 31668; Araben'ny 26 Jona 1960; dishes US$2) This popular, central restaurant has a mix of filling Malagasy, Chinese and Western meals, plus a decent patisserie.

Le Minou (Map p735; Lalana Ranavalona II; dishes US$2.80) The extensive menu here offers sublime Malagasy and Chinese meals, although the child-sized dishes won't fill you up completely. It's near Hôtel Raphia.

Casa Koto (Map p735; Arabe Ramanantsoa; dishes US$1.50) A handy place for a quick Malagasy, French or Chinese meal, especially if you are staying at the Hôtel Raphia Isoraka a few doors away.

Caf'Art (Map p735; ☎ 22 67776; 68 Lalana Ranavalona II; dishes US$2) This place serves cheap snacks and Malagasy dishes in a great

atmosphere. There's occasional live music in the evenings.

Hôtel Sakamanga (Map p735; ☎ 22 35809; Lalana Andrianary Ratianarivo; dishes US$3) Everyone has this name on their list of favourite eateries. The French/Malagasy food is fantastic, but the service is complacently slow.

Le Chalet des Roses (Map p735; ☎ 22 64233; Rue de L'Auximad; dishes US$3.50) It's expat-central in here, and no wonder: they serve tasty pizzas and lovely desserts on a raised outdoor terrace overlooking the street.

Île Bourbon (Map p732; ☎ 22 27942; Rue Benyowski; dishes US$5; ☽ dinner) This is a rare chance to get yourself acquainted with Reunionnaise cuisine. It doesn't come cheap, but the mountainous portions will leave you bloated 'til lunchtime tomorrow.

Self-Catering

Shoprite Haute-Ville (Map p735; Arabe Ramanantsoa; ☽ 8.30am-7pm Mon-Sat, 9.30am-12.30pm Sun); Central Antananarivo (Map p735; Arabe Andriananpoinimerina) This is a well-stocked supermarket.

DRINKING

La Boussole (Map p735; 21 Lalana Docteur Villette, Isoraka) This French bar gets especially lively on Friday nights.

Hôtel Glacier (Map p735; Araben'ny 26 Jona 1960) The bar at this hotel is generally packed during the day and night for its relatively cheap drinks, lively atmosphere and live music (at least on weekends).

> **SPLURGE!**
>
> **Le Petit Verdot** (Map p732; ☎ 22 39234; Rue Samuel Rahamefy Ambatonakanga; dishes US$7) The wall plaques, the wine, the attentive service, the French guys invariably sitting at the bar – it all makes you feel like you're in Marseilles. And the French dishes are absolutely sublime.

CLUBBING

Indra (Map p735; Lalana Karija; admission US$1) This popular hangout plays a mix of European and Reunionnaise music. But be careful – even the men get their arses pinched here!

Le Caveau (Map p735; Lalana Ratsimilaho; admission US$1) This stalwart is still going strong, and with not so much of a lewd vibe. It's split

738 AROUND ANTANANARIVO •• Ivato

into two areas: one for the Western music and another for Malagasy tunes.

ENTERTAINMENT

Check the newspapers (*Midi Madagasikara, Madagascar Tribune* and *L'Express de Madagascar*) for city entertainment information.

Centre Culturel Albert Camus (CCAC; Map p735; ☎ 22 21375; ccac@dts.mg; 14 Araben'ny Fahaleovantena) The cultural centre holds regular concerts and theatre performances, and it's the best place to see films. Free monthly programmes are available at the entrance.

Grill du Rova (Map p732; ☎ 22 62744) Near the Rova, has traditional Malagasy music recitals and plays, often on Sunday evening.

Antshow Cultural Arts Centre (Map p735; ☎ 22 56547; Lot VK 67 Ter AC, Ambatolava, Morarano) This brand new centre promotes local Malagasy art and artists and lays on live musical events and exhibitions.

Cinemas around the city include the **Ritz** (Map p735; Araben'ny 26 Jona 1960), which sometimes shows Malagasy films, but you'll have to club, kick and claw your way to get a ticket, as lines of wannabe movie-goers will fill the entire street to catch a show. **Cinema Rex** (Map p735; Lalana Paul Dussac) screens French films throughout the year, including the ones selected for Cannes.

Hira Gasy is a traditional Malagasy performance of acrobatics, music and speeches that is held around Antananarivo most Sunday afternoons. The Maison du Tourisme (p734) can give you information on locations and times.

GETTING THERE & AWAY
Air

Air Madagascar (Map p735; ☎ 22 22222; 31 Araben'ny Fahaleovantena) has flights into Antananarivo's international airport in Ivato, 14km north of the city centre. The other airlines are **Inter Air** (Map p732; ☎ 22 22406; Hilton Hotel, Anosy) and **Air France** (Map p735; ☎ 22 26300; 29 Araben'ny Fahaleovantena).

Local Transport

Antananarivo is the hub for transport to all parts of the country, and *taxis-brousse* to most major cities leave throughout the day from three main *gares routière* (bus stations), which all have a chaotic plethora of minibuses and *taxis-be* (big taxis). You'll need to get a taxi to reach them:

Northern Taxi-Brousse Station (Gare Routière du Nord; Ambodivona) Located about 2km northeast of the city centre, transport to Toamasina (US$6.50) and Ambohimanga (US$0.30) departs from here.

Southern Taxi-Brousse Station (Gare Routière du Sud; Lalana Pastora Rahajason, Anosibe) About 1.5km southwest of Lac Anosy; vehicles for southern destinations such as Antsirabe (US$3), Fianarantsoa (US$8), Toliara (US$19) and Taolagnaro (US$32).

Western Taxi-Brousse Station (Gare Routière de l'Ouest) This station, about 400m northwest of the train station, is where you'll find *taxis-brousse* going to Ivato and the airport (US$0.25).

GETTING AROUND

The centre of Antananarivo is compact and it is possible to walk between Haute-Ville and the train station without getting tired (providing you avoid the steep staircase).

The local bus network is quite complicated, with a numbered route system. Each minibus has a number shown in the window. One route worth noting is the No 115 to the zoo – see p734 for details.

Antananarivo has no shortage of private taxis that will rattle you around town for about US$1.30 a ride.

AROUND ANTANANARIVO

IVATO

About 14km north of Antananarivo is Ivato, where the airport is located. If you're only changing planes here, there are a couple of decent places to stay nearby.

You could also take in the **Croc Farm** (☎ 22 23410; admission US$4; ◷ 9am-5pm), with crocodiles, fossas (primitive catlike mammals), boa constrictors, chameleons and ostriches in kitsch surroundings. If you want to see the crocodiles being fed, make sure you are here between noon and 2pm.

Hôtel Manoire Rouge (☎ 22 44104; www .madatana.com; camp site per person US$2, dm/d US$4/8) Located within spitting distance of the airport and set in beautiful gardens, this mecca for travellers has clean and comfortable rooms with shared bathroom, as well as a French restaurant (dishes from US$3). To get here from the airport, turn left out of the airport car park, and walk uphill past the military barracks following the traffic flow, which curves right into the village. Continue straight on to the hotel, which will be on your right.

A charter taxi from the airport to Ivato costs US$1.60. Between Ivato and Antananarivo is around US$6. Minibuses into Antananarivo leave every 20 minutes from the Ivato *taxi-brousse* station and cost US$0.25. The reverse journey departs from the western *taxi-brousse* station in Antananarivo.

AMBOHIMANGA

Ambohimanga (Blue Hill) was the original capital of the Merina royal family. Even after the seat of government was shifted to Antananarivo, Ambohimanga remained a sacred site, and was off-limits to foreigners for many years.

A large, traditional **gateway** marks the entrance to Ambohimanga, and it is one of the seven gateways to the eyrielike hilltop. At first sight of the enemy the stone would be rolled by up to 40 slaves to seal off the gate. To get there you'll need to walk 1km up the hill from the *taxi-brousse* station.

A few hundred metres uphill from Ambohimanga village is the walled **Rova** (☽ Mon-Fri), the palace compound of King Andrianampoinimerina who ruled from 1787 to 1810. It pales in comparison to Antananarivo's old *rova* before the fire. The king's home, the **Betavo**, resembles a black wooden shed, with spears, shield and eating utensils on the walls, and paintings and gifts from Queen Victoria. Today, it is a site of pilgrimage, and people come from all over the country to pray to the spirits of the queens.

Accommodation is limited, so it's best to visit Ambohimanga as a day trip.

Cheap snacks and drinks are sold outside the entrance to town. For something more substantial, try **La Colline Bleue**, just uphill from the *taxi-brousse* stop.

Ambohimanga is 21km north of Antananarivo. *Taxis-brousse* leave for Ambohimanga village throughout the day from just outside Antananarivo's northern *taxi-brousse* station (US$0.30).

CENTRAL HIGHLANDS

The central highlands (*haut plateaux*) is an area full of rolling hills and a quilted patchwork of brilliantly green paddy fields. It gets pretty cold here for a large part of the year.

The main tribes in the region are the Merina (around Antsirabe), and the Betsileo (around Fianarantsoa) who are major rice cultivators and, thanks to a Swiss company, wine-makers too.

ANTSIRABE

☎ 44 / pop 158,000

Antsirabe (Where There is Much Salt) is a lovely, chilled town with wide, noiseless, tree-lined avenues. There are few cars here, which makes a nice change from Antananarivo's traffic chaos.

The main form of transport is the *pousse-pousse* (see p741). Despite its tranquillity, the town is the region's industrial base, and a major trading centre for semiprecious stones and minerals. Don't be surprised if you're casually offered sapphire stones.

The town was founded by Norwegian missionaries in 1872 as a health retreat, and later became a popular getaway for French colonials.

Antsirabe and the surrounding area is excellent for cycling. **Tembike Tours** (☎ 032 04 444 68; tembike@yahoo.com), opposite BNI-CL Bank, rents bikes for excursions around Lac Andraikiba and Lac Tritiva (see Around Antsirabe, p741). Rates are around US$3/4 for a half/full day.

POUSSE-POUSSE

No description of Antsirabe would be complete without mentioning the *pousse-pousse* – the Malagasy version of the rickshaw. Brightly coloured, with an awning and cushioned seats, they are the main form of transport in this town. The drivers don't usually own them, but rent them from owners who charge almost US$2 per day. So the drivers are under pressure to make at least eight rides just to break even. The drivers are very skilful and strong, and will carry up to two grown adults through the streets, rain or shine, uphill, downhill and over potholes – usually without wearing any shoes! Taking this form of transport often makes travellers feel a bit guilty, but once you get used to it, it's an extremely fun and stress-free way of seeing the town.

Sleeping

Antsirabe has plenty of cheap, good-value hotels.

Green Park Tsarasoatra (☎ 032 075 3581; Rue Labourdonnais; camp site per person US$2.50, d US$11) This is paradise: you can pitch your tent on the beautiful green lawns, surrounded by banana trees, plants, a carp-filled artificial lake and streams arched by wooden bridges. Eat dinner under the wooden thatched huts, or at the next-door pizzeria.

Hôtel L'Entracte (Ex Kabary; ☎ 48768; entracte@ adsl.mg; off Ave de l'Indépendence; d US$5-8) Having undergone a recent facelift, the spotless rooms are light and nicely decorated, and the shared bathrooms will have you sighing with relief. Downstairs there's a restaurant that serves meals all day. The hotel's near Bourdon Voyages.

Hôtel La Joie (☎ 033 114 7423; d US$5-11) The lime green walls and orange curtains will give you a rude awakening, but the rooms and shared facilities are clean. The restaurant serves very cheap meals. It's signposted east off Ave de l'Indépendence, south of the Petit Marché.

Eating & Drinking

Eating is a real treat in Antsirabe, which has several good eateries.

Au Bon Coin (Ave Maréchal Foch) Offers cheap Malagasy breakfasts near the corner of Ave de l'Indépendence.

L'Oasis (dishes US$1.50) Easily the best restaurant in town. They serve divine Malagasy dishes in front of a TV showing French-dubbed Hollywood movies. To find it, turn west off Ave de l'Indépendence, south of the market.

Gaëlle (Ave Maréchal Foch; dishes US$2-3) A very popular Malagasy restaurant with delicious food and a lively atmosphere.

Le Tahiti (Hôtel Diamant) Located in the far north of town, this is the only real nightclub in Antsirabe. The music isn't great, but it's all you've got if you're desperate for some dancing.

Shopping

Even if you can't buy, you can look at and touch the precious gems at **Chez Joseph's Lapidarie** (☎ 032 024 8084; Lot 12 C80, Rue Kleber; ☼ daily). Chunks of unprocessed quarts, topaz and amethyst lie in piles, waiting to be polished on the premises (tree bark is used as a natural gem polisher). Another room is filled with polished gems that are sculpted in creative ways, such as bunches of 'grapes' and knives and forks.

Getting There & Around

Transport to Antananarivo (US$3) and other points to the north leaves from the northern *taxi-brousse* station. Vehicles heading for Ambositra (US$2.50) and Fianarantsoa (US$6.50) depart from the southern *taxi-brousse* station.

Pousse-pousse rides around town cost about US$0.30.

AROUND ANTSIRABE
Betafo

The Merina village of Betafo (Many Roofs) lies 22km west of Antsirabe and is one of the most interesting highland towns. **Lac Tatamarina** is a peaceful place, surrounded by rolling hills and cultivated terraces. Try catching tilapia fish here with the locals, using bamboo fishing rods.

Don't miss the **thermal baths**, 3km west of the road to Morondava. Hot, geothermal water pours out of a tap and into several stone basins that you can sit in for a relaxing bath. You will need to get local permission first, and pay a small fee.

From Antsirabe, *taxis-brousse* depart from the Asabotsy market on the western edge of town.

Lac Andraikiba & Lac Tritiva

In the hills west of Antsirabe are two volcanic lakes, both easily reached as day-trips from town. Lac Andraikiba (the larger one and a former retreat of Queen Ranavolona II), lies 7km west of Antsirabe, just off the Morondava Rd (RN34). It's a beautiful, tranquil place where local men play the guitar by the gem stalls on the shore.

Lac Tritiva (18km southwest of Antsirabe) is even prettier and mostly surrounded by a sheer cliff wall. Local 'fady' forbids swimming in this lake. There is no regular transport to either lake, so either go by bicycle or charter a taxi for around US$13, round-trip.

AMBOSITRA
☎ 47 / pop 26,900

Ambositra (pronounced am-boo-sh-tr) is set in beautiful hills, valleys and rice paddies,

and makes a good stop en route between Antsirabe and Fianarantsoa. The nearby **Zafimaniry villages** produce famous woodcarvings that you'll find in craft shops in town. There's also a cheese-making **Benedictine monastery** that's worth checking out.

Coming in from the north, the Rue Commercial passes the market before it forks. To the left the road continues past banks and several hotels. The branch to the right leads to the quieter part of town where the post office is located.

Ambositra has its fair share of dives, but there are a couple of good-value cheap places to stay and eat.

Hôtel Sympa (☎ 71343; d US$5-10) is on the main road, left after the fork. It has clean rooms with shared toilet and fantastic views of the surrounding valley. There's also a good restaurant downstairs.

Hôtel Prestige (☎ 71135; camp site per person US$2, d US$4) has clean rooms with shared bathroom set in a pretty garden. It's just south of the Grand Hotel and meals are available in the restaurant.

Hotely Tanamasoandro on the main road (look for the large 'Hotely Gasy' sign) serves the best meals.

Transport to points north, including Antsirabe (US$2.50) and Antananarivo (US$3), leaves from the northern *taxi-brousse* station 2km north of the fork in the road. Departures for Fianarantsoa (US$2.40, four hours) and other points south are from the southern *taxi-brousse* station.

FIANARANTSOA
☎ 75 / pop 137,700

Fianarantsoa means 'Place Where Good is Learned' and this academic town is the intellectual centre of Madagascar. The town itself isn't pretty, but it is surrounded by picturesque villages that lie in the heart of wine- and tea-producing country.

Fianarantsoa was founded in 1830 when Queen Ranavalona I decided to build an intermediate capital between Antananarivo and the remote southern provinces.

Information

The **Angap office** (☎ 51274; ⏰ 7am-5pm) is near Hôtel Soafia. All the banks line the same street in Nouvelle-Ville and they change money and travellers cheques.

MADAGASCAR

Chez Dom (Rue Ranamana, Basse-Ville; US$0.15 per hr) has an Internet connection, as does the **Zomatel Hotel** (Araben'ny Fahaleovantena, Nouvelle-Ville; US$3 per hr), but it's very slow.

Sights & Activities

The oldest and most interesting part of town is **Haute-Ville**, in the south, with its winding, cobbled streets and the imposing **Ambozon-tany cathedral**. The old *rova* is no longer standing, but the area has incredible views of the surrounding villages, where farmers bend over their rice paddies or cattlemen drive along herds of zebu.

Photography buffs should make a bee-line for Hotel Soafia to meet and chat with **Pierrot Men**, Madagascar's most famous photographer. Despite holding successful exhibitions in Paris and New York, Pierrot opted to 'keep it real' and stay in his home-town, selling high-quality postcards at the hotel.

It's possible to make a day-trip to the **vineyards** (per person US$30) near Fianarantsoa. Wine production started in the 1970s with funding and technical expertise from a Swiss company that saw the region's cultivation potential. The most popular and accessible vineyard is **Lazan'i Betsileo** (☎ 50275), about 15km north of Fianarantsoa. You can phone to arrange a visit, or go on an organised tour, arranged through the **Tsara Guest House** (☎ 50206; Rue Philibert Tsiranana).

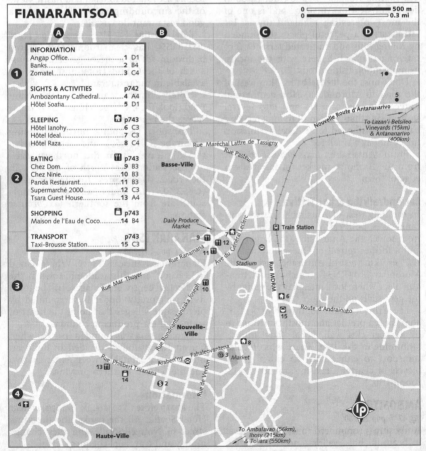

Sleeping

Hôtel Raza (☎ 51915; d US$8) This charismatic hotel, behind the Plazza Inn, has large, clean rooms filled with bamboo furniture. The shared toilet and bathroom are not bad, and the heavily decorated restaurant serves cheap Malagasy and French dishes.

Hôtel Ianohy (☎ 032 023 4881; d US$4-7) This is a real money-saver, opposite the *taxi-brousse* station. Simple, dark rooms with a clean but totally windowless shared shower. The top floor rooms are lighter, with bathrooms and hot water.

Hôtel Ideal (☎ 032 025 9405; Rue Printsy Ramaharo; d US$6-9) There's nothing ideal about the ageing rooms here, but they are large and well-furnished, and the top-floor terrace has nice views of the stadium.

Eating

Tsara Guest House (☎ 50206; Rue Philibert Tsiranana; dishes US$4-5) This is the best restaurant in town, with excellent French cuisine and an extensive menu.

Chez Ninie (Rue Rondriantsilanizaka Joseph; dishes US$0.80) This is a very popular *hotely* near Hotel Cotsoyannis, serving a wide selection of Malagasy dishes.

Chez Dom (☎ 51233; Rue Ranamana) has vegetarian dishes, and **Panda Restaurant** (☎ 50569; off Rue Ranamana; dishes US$2) has cheap, Chinese dishes.

Supermarché 2000 (Rue Ranamana, Basse-Ville) is the best place for self-caterers.

Shopping

For local handicrafts check out **Maison de l'Eau de Coco** (Rue Philibert Tsiranana; ☼ 8am-5pm Mon-Fri). It is run by a nongovernmental organisation that helps find housing, work and education for homeless families. The handicrafts on sale are made by women who have been released from prison in Fianarantsoa.

Getting There & Away

Air Madagascar, in the Zomatel Hotel, flies between Fianarantsoa and Antananarivo twice a week (about US$45/90 single/return).

Frequent *taxis-brousse* connect Fianarantsoa with Ambositra (US$4, four hours), Antsirabe (US$6.50) and Antananarivo (US$8). *Taxis-brousse* also go daily to Ranohira (US$8) and Toliara (US$12). They leave from the *taxi-brousse* station on Rue MDRM.

PARC NATIONAL DE RANOMAFANA

Parc National de Ranomafana is 400,000 hectares of lush rainforest, riddled with small streams that plummet into the Namorona River, and teeming with 12 lemur species, including red-bellied lemurs, diademed sifakas, red-fronted lemurs and rare broad-nosed gentle lemurs. With luck, you might even see the golden bamboo lemur, a species that was only discovered in 1986.

The park entrance, the Angap welcome office, the camping ground and the guesthouse are all at the tiny village of **Ambodiamontana**, about 6km west of Ranomafana.

Permits (adults US$8) last three days and are available at the park entrance. Guide fees depend on the route you take, but range from US$4 to US$13 per group per day. It's worth checking out the **Centre de l'Environnement** (admission free; ☼ 8am-5pm), 500m west of Ranomafana village, which has displays about the park and Malagasy culture in English and French.

The best time to visit the park is during the drier (but more crowded) July to October season.

Most travellers concentrate on the small section of the park known as Talatakely. There are two major walking trails through Talatakely. The short **Ala Mando trail** (Petit Circuit, two hours) can be done without a guide, and you'll spot lemurs along the way. Brochures are available at the park entrance (US$0.75). The same trail can be done at night, for easier lemur-spotting, but with a compulsory guide. The **Moyen Circuit** goes a bit further out and lasts three to four hours, during the day or at night.

At the park entrance is **Le Rianala** (camp site per person US$1.50-3, dm US$4), with showers and toilets, plus a restaurant. Alternatively, you can stay in Ranomafana village 6km to the east. **Hôtel Ravinala** (d US$5) has very basic accommodation with a cheap restaurant. **La Palmeraie** (d US$5-7) is a better choice, with hot showers. All the hotels in Ranomafana are strung out along the main road.

It is possible to visit the park on a day trip from Fianarantsoa, providing you start early. *Taxis-brousse* go daily from Fianarantsoa to Ranomafana (US$2.50), often continuing to Manakara. Ask the driver to drop you off at the park entrance and not at the village. To get back to Fianarantsoa from Ranomafana village or from the park entrance, you'll need to wait for an empty vehicle coming from Manakara or Mananjary.

AMBALAVAO
☎ 75 / pop 24,900

For a town of its size, Ambalavao (New Valley) has a lot going for it. Situated in the beautiful highlands, the buildings display the carved balcony balustrades characteristic of **Betsimileo architecture**. On Wednesdays the dusty streets come alive with the biggest **zebu market** in the country. Ambalavao is also famous for its production of elegant, traditional *lamba arindrano* (woven handspun silk scarves), which are used as burial shrouds, or fine dress for the living.

Ambalavao's biggest draw is **Fabrique de Papier Antaimoro** (admission free; ☼ daily), opposite the Fianarantsoa *taxi-brousse* station. The factory that makes the famous Antaimoro paper. You can take a free tour and watch the paper being made. The nearby souvenir shop sells very attractive cards, envelopes and other paper products.

Set in the grounds of the paper factory, **Hôtel aux Bougainvillees** (☎ 34001; ragon@dts .mg; d US$12) has clean shared facilities and fresh rooms that are just as colourful as the bougainvillea outside.

The rooms at **Hôtel Stop** (d US$4), on the main road, are basic and grubby, with shared facilities to match.

Hôtel Le Notre (d US$5), across the street from Hôtel Stop, puts up stiff competition in the dirty-room stakes. The shared toilets could bring on instant constipation, but the shared showers are OK.

Hôtel aux Bougainvillees and Hôtel Stop both have restaurants. There are also a couple of decent *hotelys* around the *taxi-brousse* station for Fianarantsoa.

Ambalavao is 56km south of Fianarantsoa, with which it has direct *taxi-brousse* connections (US$1.60, one hour). For transport heading further north or south, you'll need to get a connection at Fianarantsoa.

SOUTHERN MADAGASCAR

Southern Madagascar is a hugely diverse region, with a rocky, arid, Arizona-esque landscape to the southwest, rugged greenery to the southeast and various tribal groups. The main tribes are the Bara, around Ihosy and Parc National de l'Isalo, the Vezo along the coast, and the Mahafaly southeast of Toliara.

The region's unusual flora include the rosy periwinkle (a well-known treatment for leukaemia), the baobab tree, the carnivorous pitcher plant and the Mexican prickly pear cactus. Economically speaking, the south is the poorest region, and undeveloped infrastructure makes it hard to travel around these parts.

IHOSY
☎ 75

Ihosy is the traditional capital of the Bara tribe, the most African ethnic group in Madagascar, known for their cattle-rustling traditions and polygamy. There's not much reason to hang around in Ihosy, but it is an important transport junction where the RN13 from Taolagnaro meets the RN7 (which connects Antananarivo and Toliara).

The BTM bank beside the central market changes money.

The new **Hôtel Manambitsoa** (d US$6.50), 200m from the *gare routière* along the road to Ranohira, has immaculate rooms with clean toilets and bucket shower.

Hôtel Relais Bara (☎ 80017; d US$7-11) has comfortable rooms. For something cheaper try **Hôtel Galaxie** (d US$5), across the street from the petrol station, which has clean rooms, external toilets and a bucket shower.

Restaurant Nirina serves cheap Malagasy meals, and is a popular place for passing travellers to get fed and watered.

ZEBU

Together with the lemur and the chameleon, the zebu, or domesticated ox, is one of the most identifiable symbols of Madagascar. Zebu indicate wealth and power, are used for dowries and transport, and are sacrificed during important ceremonies. They are herded in vast numbers by the Bara and other southern tribes, and their meat often turns up in restaurant menus, though it feels very chewy to the uninitiated. The animals are almost identical to those in India, with the loose flap of skin under the throat and the humped back.

Taxis-brousse regularly ply the route between Ihosy and Fianarantsoa (US$5, four to five hours), as well as to Toliara (US$8). Vehicles depart for Taolagnaro (US$22) several times a week. The road is rough and the journey takes at least two days.

RANOHIRA
☎ 75

The small town of Ranohira is the base for exploring Parc National de l'Isalo (see below). There's nothing of interest within the town, but it sits in the middle of a grassy plain from which the **Isalo massif** rises up spectacularly.

Sleeping & Eating

Isalo Ranch (camp site per person/d US$2/12) This German-run hotel, located 3km southwest of Ranohira, has clean bungalows with shared shower, and the restaurant serves cheap Malagasy meals. There are free daily transfers to Ranohira at 7.30am.

Chez Momo's (☎ 80177; camp site per person with own/hired tent US$1.20/4, d US$7) Perched on the edge of town with stunning views of the Isalo massif, this hotel has traditional Bara-style mud huts with mosquito nets and clean, shared facilities. The sunset views from here are magical.

Chez Thomas (d US$5-6.50) This place, 50m south of the town centre, has dark, simple rooms with passably clean shared facilities. The upper balcony has views of the park's massifs.

All the hotels have restaurants. Before visiting the Parc National de l'Isalo, you can stock up on basic supplies at the shops in the centre of town near the Hôtel l'Orchidèe.

Getting There & Away

Only one or two direct *taxis-brousse* connect Ranohira and Ihosy, 91km to the east (US$2); get an early start if you want to catch these. Otherwise you'll have to hitch a ride or wait for a *taxi-brousse* with an empty seat to pass by. For Toliara and destinations south, it's much quicker to go to Ilakaka (US$0.50). There is frequent transport between there and Toliara (US$7).

To get to the park you and your guide need to take a taxi (around US$6 roundtrip, 15 minutes each way) which deposits you at the park and can arrange to pick you up when you have finished.

PARC NATIONAL DE L'ISALO

This national park has some of Madagascar's most unique and beautiful scenery. The topography is characterised by alternating flat, grassy plains and sandstone ridges, sculpted by wind and water into fanciful shapes: imagine the Grand Canyon, only shallower and filled with vegetation. In the old days, the Sakalava would bury their dead in caves 20m up in the cliffs. The park is also home to several lemur species.

The best time to visit is between April and October. For information on reaching the park, see Getting There & Away in the Ranohira section.

Three-day permits (US$8) are available from the **Angap office** (☉7am-5pm) in Ranohira. You need an official guide to visit the park. A few staff speak reasonable English (although many speak even better Italian!). Fees vary depending on the length of your route, but range from US$8 to US$20 per group per day.

There are several trails to follow in the park, all starting and finishing at Ranohira, which is about 20 minutes away by car. They range from one-day walks to seven-day treks, sleeping at camp sites along the way.

The **Canyon des Singes & Piscine Naturelle** is a relatively short, popular excursion that involves a hot, five- to six-hour walk from the Canyon des Singes, through hidden canyons and brilliantly coloured ranges. At the Piscine Naturelle, there's a natural stone cave overlooking a waterfall, which in turn tumbles into a pool surrounded by overhanging pandanus trees.

TOLIARA (TULÉAR)
☎ 94 / pop 101,900

When it comes to provincial capitals, Toliara is the new kid on the block, having been established only in 1895. It is the south's most significant port, and western Madagascar's only major town (the next big town on the west coast is 1000km north at Mahajanga). There's not much to see or do in Toliara, but the town has got excellent **beaches** and **snorkelling** to the north and south in Ifaty and Anakao.

Most commerce in the area is controlled by Indo-Pakistani traders, who have always been discriminated against in Madagascar, as a result they were the focus of Malagasy resentment in Toliara and consequently bore the brunt of Malagasy violence in 1987 rioting.

There's an **Angap office** (☎ 43570; off Rue Lieterand de Bridiers) in town. All the banks change money and travellers cheques, including **BFV-SG** (Rue du Marché), **BNI-CL** (Rue du Lieutenant Chanaron) and **Bank of Africa** (Rue Gouverneur Campistron).

Internet access is available at **Flash Video** (☎ 43432; cnr Blvd Philibert Tsiranana; per min US$0.15) and **Sancro Cybercafe** (Rue Estebe; per min US$0.12).

Musée Regional de l'Université de Toliara (Blvd Philibert Tsiranana; admission US$1.60; ⏱ 8-11.30am & 3-5pm Mon-Fri) has a small but interesting display of regional artefacts, including an egg from the prehistoric elephant bird and

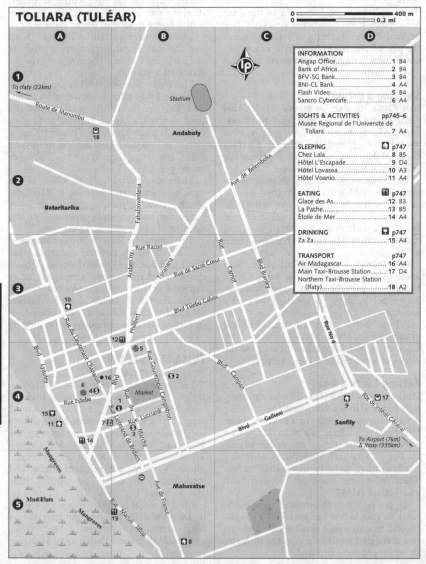

TOLIARA (TULÉAR)

INFORMATION	
Angap Office	1 B4
Bank of Africa	2 B4
BFV-SG Bank	3 B4
BNI-CL Bank	4 A4
Flash Video	5 B4
Sancro Cybercafe	6 A4

SIGHTS & ACTIVITIES	pp745–6
Musée Regional de l'Université de Toliara	7 A4

SLEEPING	🏠 p747
Chez Lala	8 B5
Hôtel L'Escapade	9 D4
Hôtel Lovasoa	10 A3
Hôtel Voanio	11 A4

EATING	🍴 p747
Glace des As	12 B3
La Pache	13 B5
Étoile de Mer	14 A4

DRINKING	🍷 p747
Za Za	15 A4

TRANSPORT	p747
Air Madagascar	16 A4
Main Taxi-Brousse Station	17 D4
Northern Taxi-Brousse Station (Ifaty)	18 A2

a Mikea (forager-farmers of southwestern Madagascar) mask with real human teeth.

Sleeping

Toliara has an excellent choice of hotels.

Hôtel L'Escapade (Ex Comme Chez Soi; ☎ 41182; Blvd Gallieni; d US$11) Rooms with private bathroom and hot water, arranged around a pretty courtyard for this price? Don't ask questions – just take the room! The excellent upstairs restaurant also has a bar and pool table attached.

Chez Lala (☎ 43417; Ave de France; d US$8) Newly refurbished in an unmissable pink building, this hotel has rather frosty staff, but it doesn't matter when you've got spotless rooms, clean, shared facilities and a good restaurant.

Hôtel Lovasoa (☎ 41839; Rue de Sacré Coeur; d US$6) The rooms with private shower and shared WC are basic and noisy, but it hasn't stopped the travellers from coming. Breakfast is available.

Hôtel Voanio (☎ 41660; Blvd Lyautey; d US$7) Arranged around a big courtyard, the rooms (with shared facilities) are dull, but clean enough. The hotel's main draw (or setback) is that it's near the Za Za nightclub.

Eating & Drinking

La Pache (Rue Marius Jatop; dishes US$2) A big menu filled with cheap Malagasy, French and Chinese dishes, as well as tasty desserts.

Étoile de Mer (Blvd Lyautey; dishes US$3-8) They've been dishing out excellent food for years here and are still going strong. There are also a few vegetarian dishes.

Hôtel L'Escapade (☎ 41182; Blvd Gallieni) Serves great meals from its long French menu in an open-air, upstairs terrace overlooking the street.

There are several food stalls by the market selling cheap Malagasy dishes. **Glace des As** (☎ 42693; Blvd Philibert Tsiranana) also offers cheap, filling snacks.

Za Za (Blvd Lyautey) is the place to head for some dancing. You'll love it if you've developed a taste for Malagasy pop and European techno.

Getting There & Away

Air Madagascar (☎ 94 415 85; Rue du Lieutenant Chanaron) flies from Toliara to Antananarivo three times a week (about US$146/292 single/return).

The **main taxi-brousse station** (Rte d'Intérél Général) is at the eastern end of town. Several vehicles leave for Antananarivo (US$19, 22 hours), but they fill up fast, so get there early or book the day before. Some sample *taxi-brousse* fares include: Ranohira (US$8), Ihosy (US$9), and Fianarantsoa (US$12). Trucks and other vehicles to Taolagnaro leave several times weekly (US$13, 40 to 60 hours).

The northern *taxi-brousse* station is on Route de Manombo.

IFATY
☎ 94

Ifaty is a quiet coastal village full of long, white-sand **beaches** and offshore **coral reefs**, which is why travellers come here in their droves for a spot of diving. New, expensive hotels are slowly filling up this part of the coastline, but there are still enough isolated spots to let you get away from it all. The beaches here are idyllic, and, if you're lucky, you might spot migrating whales passing by in July and August. Viewing the sharks is safe and is best done near a break in the reef known as the Northern Pass.

If you're willing to splash out, places such as **Hôtel Mora Mora** (☎ 42717) offer diving for US$20 to US$30.

Some locals are willing to rent out very basic **bungalows** in their family compounds for about US$3. Alternatively, try **Chez Micheline** (d US$5), five minutes' walk past the Bamboo Club, which has very basic accommodation.

Ifaty village lies 22km north of Toliara along a rough, sandy road. *Taxis-brousse* leave daily (until early afternoon) from the northern *taxi-brousse* station in Toliara (US$3, two hours).

TAOLAGNARO (FORT DAUPHIN)
☎ 92 / pop 38,700

Sandwiched between lush, green hills, fine beaches and blue sea, Taolagnaro (commonly known as Fort Dauphin) probably has the prettiest location (and best climate) of any major town in Madagascar, and is consequently a major tourist destination.

The Portuguese first landed here in 1504 and settled in until 1527 when the locals pushed them out. The French settled in the surrounding area in 1642, naming it after the then-six-year-old dauphin who was later crowned Louis XIV.

Information

The **Angap office** (☼ 7.30am-noon & 2-5.30pm) is on a hill 1km west of Ave du Maréchal Foch. You can change money at **BFV-SG** (Ave du Maréchal Foch), **BNI-CL** (Ave Flacourt) and **BOA** (Ave du Maréchal Foch).

Espace Telecom, on the main road north of town, diagonally opposite Motel Gina, has Internet access. There's also a **post office** (Ave Flacourt) and a **telecom office** (Ave Flacourt).

Sights & Activities

On Taolagnaro's northeastern tip is **Fort Flacourt**, built by the French in 1643. Today, there's not much left except a few cannons, but the views of the cape from here are good.

For good swimming and beautiful scenery, go to **Libanona beach**, on the southwestern side of the peninsula, but beware of strong tides and the occasional petty thief.

If you're feeling particularly energetic and fancy a bird's-eye view of all of Taolagnaro, climb **Pic St Louis**, the mountain that looms over the town. The half-day hike starts opposite the sisal factory (Usine Sifor) and the path is easy to follow. Taxis charge about US$3 one-way to the start of the hike.

Sleeping

Le Tournesol (☎ 21671; Route d'Aeroport; d US$11) A traveller's favourite with friendly staff and clean rooms. It's a short walk to the beach.

Chez Anita (☎ 21322; d US$8) Anita has good-value rooms in bungalows with bathroom and hot water. It's near the Cathedral.

Hôtel Mahavoky Annexe (☎ 21397; Ave du Maréchal Foch; d US$10) The rooms in this converted missionary school are basic, but clean. You'll have to fork out extra for the nice sea views.

Auberge Maison d'Or (off Rue Maréchal Lyautey; d US$5.50) This one is noisy and not totally comfortable, but the management is very friendly and helpful.

Eating & Drinking

The food in Taolagnaro's restaurants is generally excellent, the focus being on *fruits de la mer* (seafood).

Restaurant Miramar (☎ 21154; off Rue de la Corniche; dishes US$6) Miramar is the mother of all eateries in Taolagnaro, with tasty, but pricey, seafood and exquisite sea views. It's a good place for an evening drink, too.

Motel Gina (☎ 21266; Route d'Aeroport; dishes US$3) This is one of several hotel-restaurants that knock up seriously tasty fodder.

The usual cheap food is available at the *hotelys* around the *taxi-brousse* station. Chez Perline has a good reputation.

The Panorama, located right by the bay, is the most popular nightclub.

Getting There & Away

Air Madagascar (☎ 92 212 19) has daily flights between Taolagnaro and Antananarivo (about US$132/264 single/return).

Roads from Taolagnaro are rough in all directions, except for the short, sealed stretch to Ambovombe. *Taxis-brousse* travel to Toliara several times a week (US$13, 40 to 60 hours). Sample fares include: Ihosy (US$22), Fianarantsoa (US$27, 36 hours in the dry season) and Antananarivo (US$32). For Fianarantsoa and points further north, it's best to break up the journey at Ihosy where onward transport is frequent.

AROUND TAOLAGNARO

The **Lokaro Peninsula** is a beautiful area of inland waterways, green hills, barrier beaches and natural swimming holes. It is about 15km northeast of Taolagnaro along the coast, or about 40km by road.

To explore the area from Taolagnaro, take a taxi to the shore of **Lac Lanirano** (about US$1.30), then hire a pirogue (traditional canoe) from a local (around US$2) and go down the lake and on through the marshy passage that connects it to the next lake, **Lac Ambavarano**. On the northeastern end of this lake is the tiny fishing village of **Evatra**, from where it's around 3km over the hills to a good beach. If you want, you can continue to **Lokaro** island by pirogue.

EASTERN MADAGASCAR

Welcome to cyclone country. When it rains here it pours, but the wet skies and tropical humidity produce some of Madagascar's lushest, most densely forested areas, that are riddled with waterfalls and long rivers. They regularly wash away half the bridges, though, so the shoestring traveller should expect a certain amount of river-hopping by ferry in between long bus rides. The major tribe here is the Betsimisaraka tribe, which counts two former national leaders among its members.

TOAMASINA (TAMATAVE)

☎ 53 / pop 173,700

Wide boulevards and avenues, fringed with tall palm trees and shady flamboyants, a seaside promenade and a good selection of hotels and restaurants – you can get very comfortable here, so it's no wonder Madagascar's second city and largest port is a popular getaway for the Malagasy and a good place for travellers to stock up on creature comforts.

History

Toamasina started life as a pirate settlement and a French-controlled slaving port before being seized by the British after they abolished the slave trade. Toamasina was placed under the protection of Mauritius, kick-starting heavy trade which turned Toamasina into a big port. But by 1895 Toamasina fell under long-term French colonial rule.

Information

The Angap office is a few kilometres out of town on the road to the airport. **Librarie GM Fakra** (29 Blvd Joffre), near BNI-CL, sells French magazines and newspapers, the odd week-old British newspaper and Lonely Planet's French-language guide to Madagascar.

You can change money at **BFV-SG** (cnr Blvd Joffre & Araben'ny Fahaleovantena), **BNI-CL** (cnr Blvd Joffre & Rue Lattre de Tassigny) and **BOA** (Blvd Augagneur), a few blocks east of the train station.

Internet access is offered at a few places, including **Butterfly Internet** (Blvd Joffre; US$2.50 per hr), **CICOR** (US$1.30 per hr), above Musée Regional de l'Université de Toamasina; and **Le Cyber** (Rue Lattre de Tassigny; US$2.50 per hr), which has a reasonably fast connection and an English-speaking staff-member.

Sights & Activities

Parc Zoologique Ivoloina (admission US$2.50; ⏱ 9am-5pm) contains endangered lemurs (such as the diademed sifaka), radiated tortoises, tree boas and tomato frogs that will eventually be re-introduced to the wild. The park also has an education centre and captive breeding programs. Funded by the Durrell Wildlife Trust, this park is a good example of the local efforts being made

to protect and restore Madagascar's ailing flora and fauna.

The **promenade** (Blvd Ratsimilaho) along the coast is a great place for a lazy evening walk with views of the calm blue sea and ships in the background.

For swimming, Hôtel Miramar (off Boulevard Ratsimilaho) has a clean, 50m pool near the sea (US$1.60 for nonguests).

Sleeping

Hôtel Bouffe Rapide (☎ 31456; d US$5-10) The secret is definitely out! This absolute gem, hidden along a dirt road, has fresh, spotless rooms with mosquito nets. The upper-floor rooms with bathroom and TV have fantastic views of the Canal des Pangalanes. It's 100m northwest of the French Consulate.

Hôtel Beau Rivage (☎ 33085; 52 Rue Georges Clemenceau; d US$5-7) The rooms here are clean, with fan and a shared bathroom that won't make you squirm. There's a good restaurant attached too.

Hôtel National (☎ 32290; Ave de Tassigny; d US$10) The rooms and shared toilet are clean and comfortable, though they could do with more natural light.

Hôtel Eden (☎ /fax 31290; Blvd Joffre; d US$8) Colourful murals depicting the Canal des Pangalanes liven up the otherwise dull rooms and cleanish shared facilities. It's central location is a plus – as long as you don't mind traffic noise.

Hôtel Plage (☎ 32090; hotel-plage@simicro.mg; d without/with shower US$9/10) This place is well past its sell-by date. The rooms are musty, the toilets aren't great, but the showers just about pass the test.

SPLURGE!

Hôtel Joffre (☎ 32390; Blvd Joffre; d US$18) This is what it's all about! Toilet seats you could eat off, hot water, and firm beds that will give you the sweetest dreams. Better still, you can put it all on your credit card.

Eating

Toamasina is teeming with good restaurants.

Le Jade (☎ 33565; Rue Lattre de Tassigny; dishes US$4) Mouth-watering Chinese and Malagasy dishes in an upscale setting.

MADAGASCAR

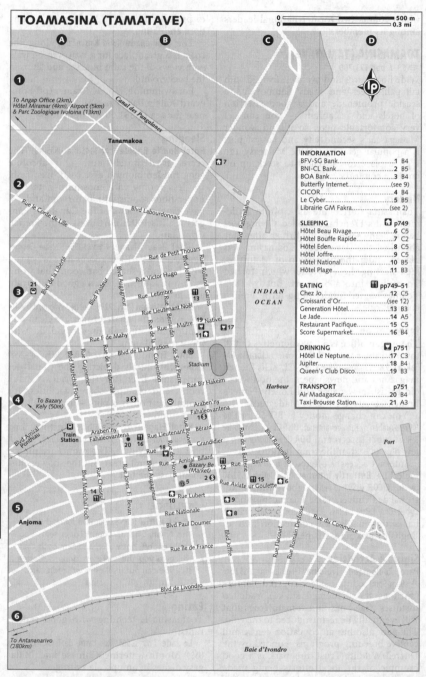

TOAMASINA (TAMATAVE)

To Angap Office (2km),
Hôtel Miramar (4km), Airport (5km)
& Parc Zoologique Ivoloina (13km)

Canal des Pangalones

Tanamakoa

INDIAN
OCEAN

Harbour

Port

To Bazary
Kely (50m)

Train
Station

Anjoma

Baie d'Ivondro

To Antananarivo
(280km)

Blvd Labourdonnais

Rue le Conte de Lille

Blvd de la Liberté

Blvd Pasteur

Rue de Petit Thouars

Rue Victor Hugo

Rue Letimbre

Rue Lieutenant Noël

Blvd Augagneur

Blvd Joffre

Rue Rolland Garros

Rue F de Mahy

Rue de la Fraternité

Blvd Marechal Foch

Rue Guyemer

Blvd de la Libération

de Saint-Pierre

Convention

Rue Bir Hakeim

Stadium

Araben'ny
Fahaleovantena

Araben'ny
Fahaleovantena

Rue Lieutenant Bérard

Rue Bouvet

Rue de Hovas

Rue Grandidier

Blvd Augagneur

Rue des Hovas

Rue Lubert

Rue Nationale

Blvd Paul Doumer

Rue Île de France

Blvd de Livondro

Blvd Ratsimilaho

Blvd Ratsimilaho

Blvd Joffre

Rue Elacourt

Rue Romain Desfosse

Rue du Commerce

Rue Aviateur Goulette

Rue Bertho

Rue de la Batterie

Bazary Be
(Market)

Amiral Billard

Blvd Amiral
Pontnau

Blvd Marechal Foch

Rue Chassol

Rue Jones F. Bevan

MADAGASCAR

INFORMATION
BFV-SG Bank	1 B4
BNI-CL Bank	2 B5
BOA Bank	3 B4
Butterfly Internet	(see 9)
CICOR	4 B4
Le Cyber	5 B5
Librairie GM Fakra	(see 2)

SLEEPING p749
Hôtel Beau Rivage	6 C5
Hôtel Bouffe Rapide	7 C2
Hôtel Eden	8 C5
Hôtel Joffre	9 C5
Hôtel National	10 B5
Hôtel Plage	11 B3

EATING pp749–51
Chez Jo	12 C5
Croissant d'Or	(see 12)
Generation Hôtel	13 B3
Le Jade	14 A5
Restaurant Pacifique	15 C5
Score Supermarket	16 B4

DRINKING p751
Hôtel Le Neptune	17 C3
Jupiter	18 B4
Queen's Club Disco	19 B3

TRANSPORT p751
Air Madagascar	20 B4
Taxi-Brousse Station	21 A3

Restaurant Pacifique (☎ 32223; 22 Rue Georges Clemenceau; dishes US$2) Delicious Chinese dishes that will pacify grumbling tummies without hurting any wallets.

Generation Hôtel (☎ 32105; Blvd Joffre; dishes US$3) Excellent Malagasy and French meals in a large, high-ceilinged dining room.

Chez Jo (☎ 32719; Blvd Joffre) Jo has pizzas and other cheap snacks.

Next door, try Croissant d'Or, which does good breakfasts.

Score Supermarket (Rue Lieutenant Bérard) This is the best place for self-caterers.

Drinking
Jupiter (Rue des Hovas) has live music on weekends. **Hôtel Le Neptune** (off Blvd Ratsimilaho) and **Queen's Club Disco** (off Blvd Joffre) are the most popular clubs in town.

Getting There & Away
Air Madagascar (☎ 323 56) is at Rue Lieutenant Bèrard.

Vehicles to Antananarivo (US$6.50, eight hours) leave all day from the *taxi-brousse* station off Boulevard de la Liberté. There are also vehicles all day heading to Soanierana-Ivongo (US$4, four hours), where you can catch a ferry to Île Sainte Marie.

NORTH OF TOAMASINA
Mahambo
☎ 57
The white-sand **beaches** of this small, coastal village are excellent for surfing. The waves are big, but safe. There is very basic accommodation in town, otherwise try **Le Recif** (☎ 30050; d US$11), on the beach. There is a restaurant here.

Early morning *taxis-brousse* heading north from Toamasina to Soanierana-Ivongo pass through Mahambo (US$2.50).

Soanierana-Ivongo
This small town is known mainly as the port for boats to and from Île Sainte Marie. Avoid staying here overnight as the accommodation is 'rustic', to put it politely. If you must stay, **Hôtel Escales** (d US$4) has very basic accommodation right by the boat launches. There's a decent, cheap restaurant downstairs.

Taxis-brousse head to Soanierana-Ivongo every morning from Toamasina, departing from around 6am (US$4, four to five hours).

However, they are not always co-ordinated with the ferry departure from Soanierana-Ivongo (which varies according to tides), so try to catch the earliest vehicle heading north. Going in the other direction, *taxis-brousse* heading to Toamasina will be waiting for the ferries from Île Sainte Marie.

ÎLE SAINTE MARIE
☎ 57
After a few weeks of hard-going on the mainland, it's time to put your feet up, laze on long sandy **beaches**, dive in the shallow, clear blue sea, go **whale watching** off the coast, or take a walk and explore remnants of this island's pirate past.

Île Sainte Marie lies 8km off the Madagascar mainland and despite its increasing popularity, it still retains an isolated, chilled vibe, unlike Nosy Be, its noisier, more developed counterpart on the western side of Madagascar. The island, however, is prone to cyclones, particularly from late August to late November.

Ambodifotatra lies on the west coast at the southern quarter of the island, about 12km from the airport. Most hotels and restaurants are along the coast south of Ambodifotatra. The northwestern part of the island is quieter, but more difficult to access. The east coast is relatively rugged and, until recently, undeveloped. It has some of the better beaches, particularly on the Ampanihy Peninsula.

Information

At the time of research the no-name **Internet centre** (per min US$0.15) was planning to move from just north of La Bigorne, to the south of it, next door to Aero Tours.

Located next to the boat harbour, **BFV-SG Bank** (Arabe la Bigorne, Ambodifotatra; 7.30-11am & 1.30-3pm Mon-Fri) is the only place to change cash and travellers cheques.

The post office is 200m south of BFV-SG bank. There are a few cardphones on the island, including in the centre of Ambodifotatra and at the airport.

Dangers & Annoyances

Many coastal areas north and south of Ambodifotatra have got sea urchins. Check locally before going swimming and always wear something on your feet.

Sights

Within Ambodifotatra you can check out Madagascar's oldest **Catholic Church**, which dates from 1857 and was a gift to the island from Empress Eugenie of France. The **Cimetière des Pirates** is an eerie, overgrown pirate cemetery located next to the Baie des Forbans, about 2km southeast of the southern end of the causeway. Most of the epitaphs aren't legible anymore, although there is supposed to be a visible pirate 'skull' symbol on one of them.

If Île Sainte Marie feels too crowded for you, **Île aux Nattes**, just off the southern tip of Île Sainte Marie, is the place to head. There are a few hotels on the island, though it can also be visited as a day trip – see the Getting Around section (p754).

Activities

Île Sainte Marie's coral is somewhat depleted, but it still offers good **diving**. The best time is from October to December (dive centres tend to close between February and May).

Popular dive sites include the two shipwrecks in the far north, and sites along the east coast near Sahasifotra. It costs around US$30 per dive.

The main dive centres in Ambodifotatra include **Il Balenottero** (40036), next to the boat harbour and **Mahary-Be Diving Centre** (/fax 40148; somasub@ifrance.com), opposite the same harbour.

Every year between July and September, hundreds of humpback whales come here to give birth or look for mates. **Whale watching** is pretty expensive (around US$40 per person), but it is possible to spot them from the shore at La Crique hotel to the north of the island.

Sleeping

You will find most of the cheap accommodation in Ambodifotatra and along the coastline stretching south of the town.

AMBODIFOTATRA

Hôtel-Restaurant Zinia (40009; d US$7.50) If your backpack feels like a bag of bricks, then stop at this hotel-restaurant, located right by the harbour. The simple, clean rooms have shower and shared toilets, and there is also a shared shower with hot water.

Le Drakkar (off Arabe Angleterre; d from US$7) The bungalows are dark and have no fans, but they are a clean-enough alternative if the Zinia is booked up.

SPLURGE!

La Bigorne (40123; off Arabe Angleterre, Ambodifotatra; bungalows US$13) The friendly owners run the best restaurant in town, plus the cushy, wood-panelled bungalows with private bathroom are an absolute treat.

SOUTH

Chez Alain (camp site per person US$2.50-3, d US$5-6) This rustic place, 3.5km south of Ambodifotatra, has zebus grazing among the beachfront bungalows under the shade of the palm trees. The bungalows have no electricity and the shared toilets are French-style crouch down affairs.

Le Palourde (032 021 5780; d US$6.50) The clean, simple bungalows here, 8km south of Ambodifotatra, come with bathroom and Lola, the resident tortoise. The restaurant serves cheap Malagasy meals.

Le Mangoustan (40135; d US$4) The high-season room rates here are somewhat excessive for the basic bungalows, but the manager is very friendly. It's 10km south of Ambodifotatra.

La Baleine (40134; d with/without private bathroom US$13/5) This place, 10km south of Ambodifotatra, has seen better days. The rooms are slightly run-down and the lemur tied to a tree nearby won't give you much

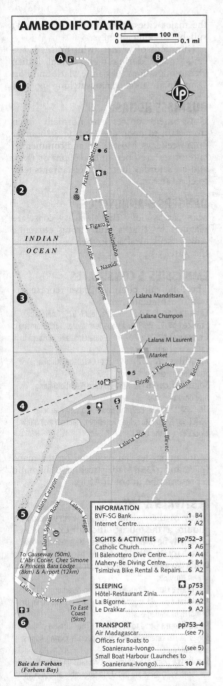

AMBODIFOTATRA

0 ———— 100 m
0 ———— 0.1 mi

INDIAN
OCEAN

Lalana Mandritsara
Lalana Champon
Lalana M Laurent
Market

*Baie des Forbans
(Forbans Bay)*

To Causeway (50m),
L'Abri Cotier, Chez Simone
& Princess Bara Lodge
(8km) & Airport (12km)

To East
Coast
(5km)

INFORMATION	
BVF-SG Bank...........................**1** B4	
Internet Centre.......................**2** A2	

SIGHTS & ACTIVITIES	pp752–3
Catholic Church.....................**3** A6	
Il Balenottero Dive Centre.....**4** A4	
Mahery-Be Diving Centre.......**5** B4	
Tsimiziva Bike Rental & Repairs....**6** A2	

SLEEPING	p753
Hôtel-Restaurant Zinia..........**7** A4	
La Bigorne...........................**8** A2	
Le Drakkar..........................**9** A2	

TRANSPORT	pp753–4
Air Madagascar.....................(see 7)	
Offices for Boats to	
Soanierana-Ivongo.............(see 5)	
Small Boat Harbour (Launches to	
Soanierana-Ivongo)............**10** A4	

peace. However, you can rent bikes here (US$5 per day).

NORTH
La Crique (☎ 40158; d US$13) Easily the best hotel on the island and worth a mini-splurge if you want to do some whale watching or enjoy urchin-free swimming. Lemurs also roam freely on the grounds. It's on the west coast, 1km north of Lonkintsy (or about 22km north of Ambodifotatra).

Hôtel Atafana (☎ 40154; camp site per person US$3, d US$7) This family-run hotel, 4km north of La Crique, occupies a lovely stretch of beach and serves very good meals. The best budget option in the north.

ÎLE AUX NATTES
La Bon Étoile (☎ 40131; d US$7) One of several hotels on the southwest section of Île aux Nattes. Simple, pleasant bungalows with clean shared bathrooms. The restaurant serves good seafood and breakfast.

Eating & Drinking
The main street in Ambodifotatra has several cheap places to eat.

La Bigorne (off Arabe Angleterre; dishes US$3) The restaurant here offers giant portions of delicious Malagasy dishes and tasty coco punch on the front porch.

Hôtel-Restaurant Zinia, by the harbour, has good meals, especially breakfast. Further south towards the airport, L'Abri Cotier and Chez Simone are popular. Princess Bara Lodge nearby does excellent pizzas.

Clubbing
Casa a Nono, 1km north of the airport, is where everyone comes for serious dancing (Zouk, a mix of French Caribbean and Western pop music, R'n'B and Malagasy).

Fotabe Disco has a great atmosphere on Thursday, Friday and Saturday, though there are more prostitutes here.

Getting There & Away
Air Madagascar (☎ 40046; ☿ 8am-5.30pm Mon-Fri) is located above Hôtel-Restaurant Zinia.

Four *vedettes* (launches) sail once daily between Île Sainte Marie and Soanierana-Ivongo. Departure times depend on the tide, but the first morning trips start from Île Sainte Marie. La Perigord (US$4 one way); La Madeleine (US$5.60 one way);

MADAGASCAR

Hyspaniola (US$4.80 one way) and La Ro-
zina (US$5.60 one way) are all *vedettes* that
sail between Ile Saint Marie and Soanierana-
Ivongo on the mainland. They all arrive and
depart from the Small Boat Harbour in
Ambodifotatra. All journeys take about
1½ hours. For all crossings, bring plastic
or something water-proof to protect your
luggage. All the launches have offices in
Ambodifotatra, near the Mahery-Be Diving
Centre, and Soanierana-Ivongo.

Getting Around

Bicycles can be a good, convenient way to
get around the island, given the scarcity of
taxis-brousse and the poor road conditions.
However, in the rainy season (November to
March) the roads can get very slippery.

Tsimiziva has a small bike-repair shop a
few metres north of La Bigorne hotel. They
rent out bikes for US$5 per day. Several
hotels hire bikes from US$3 to US$5 per
day. In the south, try **Hôtel Libertalia** (☎ 032
079 2634), 7km south of Ambodifotatra; **La
Baleine** (☎ 40134), 10km south of Ambodifotatra; and **Vanilla Café** (☎ 032 020 5213), 8km
south of Ambodifotatra.

Pirogues run to Île aux Nattes (US$0.80
each way), leaving from the beach just southwest of the airport runway.

MADAGASCAR DIRECTORY

ACCOMMODATION

It is almost always possible to find a decent,
relatively clean room with bathroom from
about US$12, or US$8 with shared facilities,
but don't expect a hot shower. Most hotel
rooms only have double beds – singles are
very rare. In the low season (January to July)
many hotels in the tourist areas offer significant discounts, so it's always worth asking.

ACTIVITIES

Madagascar offers some good diving, particularly along the southwest coast near Ifaty
and Île Sainte Marie where there are several
shipwrecks. Many companies offer diving
courses and trips for qualified divers.

Many travellers choose to travel by bicycle, due to Madagascar's poor roads and
excellent scenery. Bicycles can be hired in

the major cities, although the quality isn't
suitable for long journeys.

Hundreds of whales swim by Madagas-
car's shores during their annual Indian
Ocean migrations. Île Sainte Marie and Fort
Dauphin are good whale-watching spots.

BUSINESS HOURS

Government offices are normally open
from 8am to noon and 2pm to 3.30pm or
4pm weekdays. Most shops and commercial
enterprises are open until 5.30pm or 6pm,
and on Saturday morning. Restaurants tend
to close at 9pm.

DANGERS & ANNOYANCES

Many areas along the Malagasy coast are
plagued by sharks and strong currents.
Always seek local advice before going into
the water.

EMBASSIES & CONSULATES

The following countries have representa-
tion in Antananarivo:
Canada (☎ 22 42559; Villa Paule II M62C, Androhibe)
France (☎ 22 39898; 3 Lalana Jean Jaurès, Ambatomena)
Germany (☎ 22 23802; 101 Route Circulaire, Ambanidia)
East of the centre.
Mauritius (☎ 22 21864; Route Circulaire, Anjahana)
South of the centre.
South Africa (☎ 22 72303; Route d'Ambohimanga
Ambohitrarahaba)
UK (☎ 22 49378; Pullman House, Ivandry-Alarobia)
USA (☎ 22 20956; Lalana Rainitovo, Haute-Ville) A few
blocks east of the UCB Bank.

More embassies can be found on the maps
(p732 and p735). Madagascar has diplomatic
representation in South Africa.

FESTIVALS & EVENTS

Many of these dates change every year, so
enquire at the tourist office for exact dates:
Alhamady Be (March) The low-key Malagasy New Year.
Santabary (April/May) The first rice harvest.
Donia (May/June) A traditional music festival held annu-
ally on Nosy Be.
Fisemana (June) A ritual purification ceremony of the
Antakarana people around the town of Antsiranana in the
far north of Madagascar.
Famadihana (June to September) The 'Turning of the
Bones' burial ceremonies – held especially during August
and September.
Sambatra (June to September) Circumcision festivals – in
the southwest, these are usually in November and December.

Gasytsara (November/December) A contemporary music festival in Antananarivo. Ask at the Maison du Tourisme for the venue.

FOOD & DRINK

Eating in Madagascar is a real joy, especially if you like Asian dishes. *Vary* (rice) is the local staple and is often served with zebu, fish, chicken, duck or *ro* (a leaf-based broth). Favourite dishes include *romazava* (beef-and-vegetable stew) and *ravitoto* (pork stew with manioc greens).

The Vietnamese *mi sao* (vegetables with noodles) is very popular, as is the delicious Malagasy version of *soupe chinoise* (Chinese soup): noodles, vegetables and – in nicer restaurants – a blend of meat or seafood in broth seasoned with coriander. *Lasopy* (soup) of some type is easily found in most areas.

Vegetarian dishes are limited, but restaurants can always prepare egg and rice-based dishes for you if you ask.

Some restaurants produce their own rum and coconut punch called *punch coco*, which is delicious when well made.

The least expensive places are street stalls and *hotely*, which are small, informal roadhouses serving basic meals which vary in quality. Restaurants are much more expensive, although compared to other African countries they are still extremely cheap.

HOLIDAYS

As well as religious holidays listed in the Africa Directory (p1003), these are the principal public holidays in Madagascar:

1 January New Year's Day
29 March Insurrection Day celebrating the 1947 rebellion against the French
1 May May Day
26 June Independence Day
15 August Assumption Day
27 September St Vincent de Paul's Day
1 November All Saints' Day
26 December Boxing Day
30 December Anniversary of the Republic of Madagascar

INTERNET ACCESS

Internet access is expanding quite fast in Antananarivo, and now there are usually one or two Internet cafés in every sizable town. Most places charge from US$1 to US$3 per hour, but connections in smaller towns are very expensive (up to US$5 per hour), and extremely slow.

LEGAL MATTERS

Smoking and possessing marijuana and other recreational drugs is illegal in Madagascar. If you are arrested, ask to see a representative of your country. Madagascar is also strict in enforcing immigration laws, so don't overstay your visa.

MAPS

Official maps are produced by Foiben Taosarintanin'I Madagasikara (FTM) and are available at bookshops in Antananarivo and major towns. FTM also produces town plans for Antananarivo, Fianarantsoa, Toamasina, Antsirabe and Toliara.

MEDIA

The biggest national newspapers are *Midi Madagasikara*, *Madagascar Tribune* and *L'Express de Madagascar* and they are available in all the big towns. They usually contain emergency numbers, pharmacies and entertainment listings.

The main radio stations are Radio Nationale Malagasy 1 (RNM1) (FM 99.3), RNM2 (FM 101), Radio Lazan Iarivo, and Radio France Internationale (FM 92).

The government-run TVM broadcasts in Malagasy, but runs a half-hour BBC bulletin at 7pm every evening.

MONEY

Euros and US dollars are the best currencies to carry. Credit cards are accepted at some upmarket hotels in major cities and resorts, at Air Madagascar, and at some of the larger travel agencies. Most places levy a commission for credit card payments. The most useful card is Visa, followed by MasterCard. Amex is not accepted in many places. Visa and MasterCard can be used to obtain cash advances in Antananarivo and major towns.

Moneychangers will approach you at the airport and in the street. Their rates are almost the same as the banks, so avoid them. If you do use one, count the bills carefully before handing over your money. When leaving Madagascar make sure you don't have too much currency left on you, because you won't be able to change it outside the country. Bear in mind that the rates are terrible when changing back to dollars.

MADAGASCAR

The most widely accepted travellers cheques are Thomas Cook and American Express (Amex). Both can be readily changed in Antananarivo and all the provincial capitals.

POST & TELEPHONE

There are post offices in all major towns. Most are open from about 8am to noon and 2pm to 6pm weekdays, and until noon on Saturdays. The postal service is generally reliable. Post restante is available at the main post office in Antananarivo and in the provincial capitals.

The cheapest way to dial internationally is with a *telecarte* (phonecard). Cardphones are located at post offices and telecom offices and on street corners in big towns. Cards are sold at post offices, at Agence d'Accueil Telecom (Agate) offices and at some shops and hotels. If you have a mobile phone you can obtain SIM cards from Antaris or Madacom.

RESPONSIBLE TRAVEL

Madagascar is a poor country and relies heavily on its environmental tourism for foreign currency. So tourists can really benefit the country, providing they respect the communities and the environment.

You should always be conscious and respectful of local *fady* and keep in mind that these belief systems are connected to the ancestors who are highly regarded in Madagascar. Be conscious of Madagascar's ecological fragility and keep in mind a few simple points: don't touch or remove local plants; only light fires in designated areas; always use an official guide (part of their fee goes to local communities for development and education); and resist the temptation to throw your rubbish on the ground.

TOURIST INFORMATION

The official tourist office is the **Maison du Tourisme** (☎ 22 351 78; LE Ravelontsalama) in Antananarivo. Elsewhere in the country, the best sources of information on local tourist attractions are usually your hotel, or the local Angap office for information relating to parks and reserves. Angap is the Association Nationale pour la Gestion des Aires Protègèes (National Association for the Management of Protected Areas).

The Angap office holds information on the national parks, and it is the place to purchase permits for entering the parks.

TOURS

Organised tours can be arranged through the following:

Cortez Expeditions (Map p732; ☎ 22 21974; cortez md@dts.mg; 25 Lalana Ny Zafindriandiky, Antanimena) This American-based agency offers a wide range of itineraries for individuals and groups.

Michel Stephane Rakotomalala (☎ 032 02 56327; madagapscar@yahoo.com) A recommended English-speaking guide who organises tours across the country.

VISAS

Visas are required by all visitors and can be bought at the airport (one-month, single entry, US$32 payable in dollars – cash only). Make sure you have a return ticket. Alternatively, one- to three-month visas can be obtained in advance for US$25 to US$60.

Visa Extensions

Visas can be extended at the immigration office in any provincial capital. One-month extensions cost about US$25 and are issued in one to three days. Bring four photos and your return ticket, or documents for onward travel out of the country.

Visas for Onward Travel

Visas for travel to South Africa are available from their embassy in Antananarivo, see p754 for embassy and consulate address information.

SOUTHERN AFRICA

Southern Africa is a captivating cross-section of the best Africa has to offer with deserts, snow capped peaks, wildlife, grand rivers, cool cities, quiet villages, ancient kingdoms and monster surf. It's the Hollywood of the continent, home to many of Africa's celebrity sites and international stars. Think Victoria Falls (the world's biggest waterfall and seventh Wonder of the World), the Zambezi River, the Namib Desert, the Great Africa Plateau, Kruger National Park, Lesotho (the 'Kingdom in the Sky'), Soweto (Africa's most famous township) and Sun City (Africa's most famous casino).

Then there's a vast pool of dazzling unknowns awaiting your discovery: Chimanimani National Park where you can camp in caves and swim in waterfalls; the Bazaruto Archipelago for snorkelling in turquoise waters; and Monkey Bay on Lake Malawi for kicking back.

Travelling in Southern Africa – from backpacking to cruising in luxury buses on well-paved roads – suits solo explorers, female travellers, adrenalin junkies or group tours. It's a value-for-money, value-for-time, user-friendly place with more choices than voices. You can speak English… or learn to speak in clicks in the Kalahari. Indeed, your main problem here could be option-paralysis.

Even getting from one place to another is a trip worth telling: the train ride through Zambia is considered one of the world's great train journeys. The road trip from Windhoek to Cape Town is a beauty, and leaving Luanda any which way can be hairy.

Southern Africa is equally suited for adventure. Go nuts hiking, bungee jumping, white-water rafting, canoeing, drinking (sorry: 'sampling wine') and stay in traditional villages. Shop 'til you drop. No matter who you are or what turns you on, Southern Africa is simply one of the world's prime places to have a wicked time.

Mozambique

HIGHLIGHTS

- **Maputo** With cool pavement cafés and pumping salsa bars, Mozambique's capital is Africa's only Latin city and a red-hot place to party (p764)
- **Bazaruto Archipelago** Clear water, spectacular coral and well-protected marine life – including wild dolphins – make the waters around the Bazaruto islands a divers' and snorkellers' paradise (p770)
- **Tofo** Surf dudes and hippy chicks congregate among the white sand dunes to party, catch waves, or put in some quality hammock-time (p770)
- **Best journey** Night sailing on a wooden boat among the islands of the Querimba Archipelago, slipping along mangrove channels under the stars towards ruined colonial villas gleaming in the moonlight (p773)
- **Off the beaten track** Ilha de Moçambique, the former island capital of the Portuguese empire, is now a haunting town of pastel-painted mansions and whitewashed churches, set among waving palm trees (p772)

FAST FACTS

- **Area** 800,000 sq km
- **ATMs** available in all major towns
- **Borders** Malawi, South Africa, Swaziland, Tanzania, Zambia and Zimbabwe; all borders open
- **Budget** US$15 to US$20 per day
- **Capital** Maputo
- **Language** Portuguese
- **Money** Metical; US$1 = Mtc23,000
- **Population** 17.2 million
- **Seasons** dry (May–Nov), wet (Dec–Apr); during the rains, some roads in the north are impassable
- **Telephone** country code ☎ 258; international access code ☎ 00
- **Time** GMT/UTC+ 2
- **Visas** US$30 to US$40 for 30 days; issued at most border posts, except Tanzania

Mozambique has a public relations problem. If you've been watching television in the last 10 years, the only images of the country you'll have seen are probably Kalashnikovs, landmines and flood victims giving birth in trees. You'd be forgiven for expecting a nation on its knees, wracked by war and famine, and only good for charity appeals.

Here's the good news: Mozambique is on the up. After more than 10 years of peace, the spectres of the past are finally being laid to rest and the mood among the country's gentle, welcoming citizens is one of unbridled optimism. Best of all, most of the world's tourists

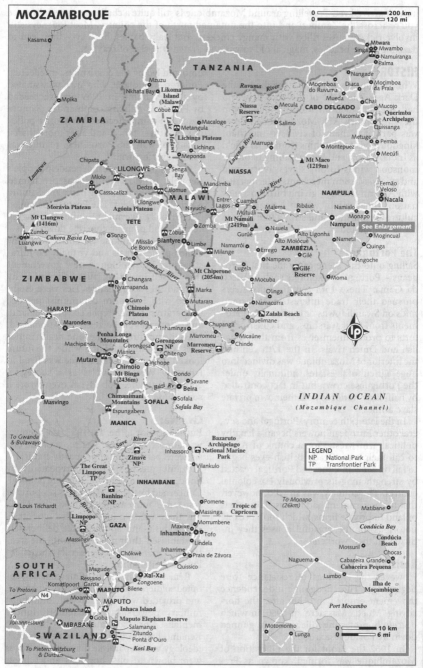

MOZAMBIQUE

0 ———— 200 km
0 ———— 120 mi

TANZANIA

Kasama

Mpika

ZAMBIA

Mzuzu
Nkhata Bay
Likoma Island (Malawi)
Cóbuè

Macaloge
Metangula
Lichinga Plateau
Lichinga
Meponda

Ruvuma River

Niassa Reserve
Mecula

Lugenda River
Marrupa

Mtwara
Mwambo
Singa
Namuiranga
Palma
Nangade
Moçimboa do Ruvuma
Diaca
Moçimboa da Praia
Mueda
Chai
Mucojo
CABO DELGADO
Macomia
Querimba Archipelago
Quissanga
Metuge
Pemba
Mecúfi

Salimo
Montepuez

Mt Maco (1219m)

NAMPULA

Fernão Veloso
Namialo
Nacala
Monapo
Nampula   See Enlargement

Chipata

Kasungu

LILONGWE

Mlolo
Cassacatiza
Dedza

Senga Bay
Calomue

Mandimba

NIASSA

Morávia Plateau
Mt Ulongwe (1416m)
Zumbo
Luangwa
Cahora Bassa Dam

Agónia Plateau
Ulongwe
TETE
Songo
Missão de Boroma

Entre Lagos
Nayuchi
Zomba
Zóbuè
Blantyre
Limbe

Cuamba
Mutuáli
Mt Namúli (2419m)
Gurúè
Namarrói
Milange

Malema
Ribáuè
Nauela
Alto Ligonha
Alto Molócuè
Errego
Nampevo
Lugela

Namialo
Nametil
Quinga
Angoche
Mogincual

ZAMBÉZIA
Gilé
Moma

ZIMBABWE

HARARE

Marondera

Machipanda

Mutare

Masvingo

Changara
Nyamapanda
Guro
Chimoio Plateau
Catandica
Penha Longa Mountains
Corongosa
Manica
Chimoio
Mt Binga (2436m)
Chimanimani Mountains
Espungabera

Tete
Zambezi River

Marka
Mutarara
Cala
Nicoadala
Chupanga
Inhaminga
Marromeu
Chinde
Dondo
Savane
Beira

Mt Chiperone (2054m)
Mocuba
Olinga
Namacurra
Zalala Beach
Quelimane
Micaúne

Gilé Reserve
Pebane
Moma

INDIAN OCEAN
(Mozambique Channel)

Gorongosa NP
Chitengo
Marromeu Reserve
Inchope
Búzi Rv
Sofala
Sofala Bay

SOFALA

MANICA

To Gwanda & Bulawayo

Save River

Inhassoro

Zinave NP

Bazaruto Archipelago National Marine Park
Vilankulo

LEGEND
NP   National Park
TP   Transfrontier Park

The Great Limpopo TP

Limpopo River

Banhine NP

INHAMBANE

Pomene
Massinga
Maxixe
Morrumbene
Inhambane
Tofo
Lindela
Inharrime
Praia de Závora
Quissico

Tropic of Capricorn

Louis Trichardt

Limpopo NP

GAZA

Massingir

Chókwè

SOUTH AFRICA

To Pretoria
N4

To Johannesburg

Magude
Ressano Garcia
Komatipoort
Moamba

Namaacha
MBABANE
Goba
SWAZILAND
To Pietermaritzburg & Durban

Xai-Xai
Zongoene
Bilene

MAPUTO
MAPUTO

Inhaca Island
Maputo Elephant Reserve
Salamanga
Zitundo
Ponta d'Ouro
Kosi Bay

Enlargement

To Monapo (26km)

Matibane

Condúcia Bay

Mossuril

Naguema

Lumbo

Condúcia Beach
Chocas
Cabaceira Grande
Cabaceira Pequena

Ilha de Moçambique

Port Mocambo

Motomonho
Lunga

0 ———— 10 km
0 ———— 6 mi

MOZAMBIQUE

haven't arrived yet. Travelling around Mozambique is still quite a challenge, especially once you're across the Zambezi and into the untamed north of the country. Most journeys still involve rickety buses filled with mangy chickens and leaky babies, but hey – they lead to dazzling white beaches, magical old towns and prawns the size of crayfish.

HISTORY

While Europeans were still struggling in the Dark Ages, the light of the ancient world had already fallen on Mozambique. From the 9th century AD, Mozambique's coast was part of a chain of civilised merchant kingdoms, visited by ships from as far afield as India, Arabia and Persia, sailing in on the monsoon winds to buy slaves, ivory, gold and spices. Muslim merchants intermarried with African families, giving birth to a new nation: the Swahili, whose language and culture are still alive and strong in northern Mozambique today.

The Portuguese

Sailing onto this scene came the first Europeans – Portuguese explorers such as Vasco da Gama. These 15th-century buccaneers pursued their trade interests with armed raids on Swahili towns or cannon bombardments from their warships, and constructed forts to protect themselves from their English and Dutch rivals. In the 17th century, the interior of Mozambique was divided into huge agricultural estates, nominally under the Portuguese crown but in fact controlled by half-caste warlords with their own private slave armies.

In the late 19th century, Portugal and several other European powers began a lengthy political arm-wrestle for a chunk of Africa to call their own. Beady British eyes began to fall on Mozambique, and Portugal reacted by strengthening its previously lax colonial control. The country was so wild, however, that the government had to lease large areas of land to private firms, which soon became notorious for the dreadful abuses they inflicted on their workers.

Resistance

However the stirrings of resistance were beginning. The fledgling independence movement erupted into life after the horrifying 'Mueda Massacre' in 1960, in which peacefully protesting villagers were gunned down by Portuguese troops.

In 1962 the Front for the Liberation of Mozambique was formed, known as Fre-

limo and led by the charismatic intellectual Eduardo Mondlane, who was assassinated by a letter bomb in 1969 and succeeded by Frelimo's military commander, Samora Machel. Frelimo decided early on a policy of violent resistance, and after more than a decade of war, the Portuguese regime was finally overthrown.

On 25 June 1975, the independent People's Republic of Mozambique was proclaimed with Frelimo as the ruling party and Samora Machel as president. The Portuguese pulled out virtually overnight – after sabotaging vehicles and pouring concrete down wells – and left Mozambique in chaos with few skilled professionals and virtually no infrastructure. Mozambique's new government threw itself into a socialist policy of hasty and radical social change. Ties were established with European communist powers, cooperative farms replaced private land, and companies of all sizes were nationalised. Mass literacy programmes and health initiatives were launched. For a while, the future looked rosy, and Mozambique was fêted in left-wing Western circles as a successful communist state. Bob Dylan even wrote a song about it.

Civil War

But it was not to be. By 1983, the country was almost bankrupt. The roots of the crisis were partly economic, partly natural – Mozambique was wracked repeatedly by flooding and drought – and partly political. Concerned by the government's support for resistance movements such as the ANC, the then white-minority ruled countries of Rhodesia and South Africa deliberately 'destabilised' their neighbour with the creation of a manufactured guerrilla movement known as Renamo.

Renamo was made up of mercenaries, co-opted soldiers and disaffected Mozambicans, and provided with funds by anticommunist military powers (and, incredibly, fundamentalist Christian churches) in the West. Renamo had no desire to govern – its only ideology was to paralyse the country. Roads were blown to bits, hospitals and schools destroyed, and atrocities committed on a scale barely matched anywhere in the world. 'Intellectuals' such as teachers and doctors were singled out for execution, children and adults tortured and murdered, occult practices encouraged and populations deliberately starved. The war raged on.

But by the late 1980s, change was sweeping through the region. The collapse of the USSR altered the political balance in the West, and new, more liberal policies in South Africa restricted Renamo support. Samora Machel died in a suspicious plane crash in 1986 (by a strange twist of fate, his widow, Graca, is now married to Nelson Mandela), and was succeeded by Joaquim Chissano. Frelimo switched from Marxist ideology to a market economy and Renamo changed too, evolving from a force with no political goals into a genuine opposition party. Their formal peace agreement was signed in October 1992.

21st Century

In October 1994, Mozambique held its first democratic elections. Frelimo won, but only by a narrow majority, with Renamo netting almost half the votes. The second election, in December 1999, produced a similar result. Mozambique has now enjoyed over 10 years of peace, and while the government has certainly not acquitted itself cleanly in all areas – recent scandals include bank fraud on a massive scale and the alleged murder of investigative journalist Carlos Cordosa – the country is enjoying peace and stability entirely unprecedented in its history. Still often hit by natural disasters such as the devastating floods of 2000, Mozambique is hugely dependent on foreign aid, and in an attempt to win the outside investment it badly needs infrastructure, and the tourism and education sectors are being improved rapidly.

THE CULTURE

When one Mozambican waves to another – whether it's truck passengers roaring along the Tete corridor in their eighteen-wheeler behemoths or local boatmen slipping their wooden dhows silently across a glassy-green expanse of water – they raise both hands, palms outward, towards one another in a gesture of surrender. This strangely helpless movement is a poignant reminder of Mo-

zambique's bloody recent past – raising two hands showed that the greeter was not concealing a weapon. But a history of war and devastation going back centuries seems to have lead only to a strengthening of the desire for reconciliation among Mozambicans – the two-handed wave is now interpreted as a message to say 'I mean you no harm'.

Mozambicans are shyer and more reticent than their ebullient Malawian or Tanzanian neighbours – their dealings with each other, and with visitors, are gravely courteous rather than exuberantly confident. Mozambican society is dignified, slow-paced, and based on a deep consideration for others. Religion, once banned under the communist regime, now flourishes, with any village, however small, having a catholic church, a mosque, or both.

But the Mozambicans, gentle as they are, are far from dull or bland. Gaggles of girls sashay along the pavement, high-heeled shoes clicking, hips swaying in flirty red dresses, and hands waving in the air to make their point. Centuries of Portuguese language and culture have led to a very Latin preoccupation with chic and style, clothes and accessories – even respectable businessmen can be seen sporting Elvis-style sideburns and discreet gold medallions well into middle age.

Mozambicans love to party – Sunday in particular is a day to gather on the beach or the village square, put on smart clothes, open a bottle of wine or a cask of home-brewed beer, and dance to the cracked Angolan pop music blasting from an ancient car stereo. Even travellers can join the fun: hawkers proffer bottles of wine, complete with long-stemmed glasses, through the windows of buses at the start of long journeys.

But alongside the gaiety, Mozambican culture has divisions and petty snobberies. Social upheaval and geographical separation have driven apart north and south, city and country. Social climbers in Maputo and the southern provinces openly despise the citizens of the north, dismissing them as nothing more than uneducated, unwashed peasants, an embarrassment to the modern state. Across the Zambezi river, northern Mozambicans, particularly in the province of Cabo Delgado, have a history of resistance to the *status quo* – it was here that the origins of Mozambique's independence movement

MARIA MUTOLA

One of Mozambique's greatest female role models is Maria Mutola, the rags-to-riches athlete known as the Maputo Express. She began her life playing football in an all-boys team in the shanty towns around Maputo, before being discovered by national poet (and football fan) José Craveirinha, and went on to snare the country's first ever gold medal at the 2000 Sydney Olympics. Mutola's victory in the 800m event sparked celebrations around the country that lasted for days, and a street in Maputo was even re-named in her honour.

lie. They cling closer to their ethnic roots – principally Makonde and Swahili – than their Mozambican nationality, protesting that the government, far away in Maputo, is interested only in the sophisticated, upwardly mobile denizens of the south.

Gender equality was one of the post-independence Frelimo party's strongest suits, with nearly a third of elected representatives being women. Women in today's Mozambique face the same challenges as elsewhere in the developing world – a struggle for independence in the face of a traditional culture that defines their roles narrowly and provides little legal recourse in the case of discrimination or abuse. Nonetheless, in urban areas especially, women are gaining access to education, employment and health care, with many programmes put in place by government and nongovernment organisations aimed at promoting the role of women in modern Mozambican society.

ENVIRONMENT

A wide coastal plain rises to mountains and plateaus on the borders with Zimbabwe, Zambia and Malawi. Three of Africa's major rivers – the Zambezi, the Limpopo and the Rovuma in the north – flow through Mozambique, and have played a major role in its economic history.

Mozambique has four national parks: Gorongosa, Zinave, Banhine and Bazaruto. The marine Bazaruto Archipelago National Park has well-developed tourist facilities, but wildlife in the others was decimated during the civil war, with soldiers on both sides shooting animals for target practice

as well as meat. Conversely, decades of war kept developers away from fragile beaches and coral reefs.

Hope for Mozambique's conservationists came recently in the form of the international initiative to establish a Transfrontier Conservation Area, or 'peace park', across the boundaries of South Africa, Zimbabwe and Mozambique. The new peace park is to be called the Great Limpopo Transfrontier Park, linking the Banhine National Park with the Kruger National Park in South Africa and the Gonarezhou National Park in Zimbabwe. To check the current status of the new park, go to www.peaceparks.org.

TRANSPORT

GETTING THERE & AWAY
Air

Linhas Aéreas de Moçambique (LAM; www.lam.co.mz) and **TAP Air Portugal** (☎ 303927; www.tap.pt) into Maputo. But if you're coming from Europe or a distant part of Africa, the cheapest option is often to fly to Johannesburg (Jo'burg, South Africa) and take the bus or train from there to Maputo.

LAM and **South African Airways** (☎ 420740; www.flysaa.com) fly between Johannesburg and Maputo, while **Pelican Air** (☎ 733649/2819; tta@ icon.co.za) plies the route between Jo'burg and Vilankulo.

If you're coming from Tanzania, LAM flies from Dar es Salaam to Maputo, and from Mtwara (in southern Tanzania) to the town of Pemba (in northern Mozambique), avoiding the adventurous land border crossing described later in this section.

DEPARTURE TAX

Airport departure tax is US$20 for international flights and US$10 for internal flights.

Land
MALAWI

There are literally dozens of road crossings between Malawi and Mozambique. Listed below are the main ones (which are theoretically the easiest).

The busiest border crossing is Zóbuè, on the main road through Mozambique linking Blantyre (Malawi) and Harare (Zimbabwe) known as the Tete Corridor. From Tete to the Mozambique border post there are daily chapas (minibuses). From here, you walk about 500 metres to the Malawian border post, from where minibuses run to Mwanza and on to Blantyre.

There's also a border-crossing point west of Cuamba, reached on the railway from Nampula. From Cuamba you can take a train (six to eight hours) or a pickup truck to the Mozambique border post at Entre Lagos, from where it's another pickup truck ride or a 20-minute walk to the Malawi border post at Nayuchi. From Nayuchi to Liwonde there's a daily train.

If you're aiming for southern Malawi, from Mocuba (north of Quelimane) there's a chapa or truck daily in the dry season to the small Mozambican town of Milange, from where it's about 3km to the Mozambique border post Muloza, then a short walk to the Malawi border post, from where minibuses run to the Malawian town of Mulanje and on to Limbe and Blantyre.

There's also a border crossing at Calomue, near the Malawian town of Dedza, closer to Lilongwe, but only very sporadic public transport on the Mozambique side.

If you're in northern Mozambique, and love a challenge, you can reach Malawi via boat. First, get to Lichinga; nearly all traffic here goes via Cuamba. From Lichinga, pick-ups go to Metangula (2½ hours, US$4) from where local boats sail slowly north along the Mozambican shore of Lago Niassa (what the Mozambicans call Lake Malawi) to Cóbuè. The ferry *Ilala* connects Likoma Island with Nkhata Bay mainland Malawi.

SOUTH AFRICA

The main border crossing is at Ressano Garcia, just east of Komatipoort. Buses run directly between Maputo and Jo'burg, Durban and Nelspruit, or you can do the trip in stages in minibuses, or you can hitch some of the way.

A train connects Maputo and Jo'burg, departing Maputo at 11am daily and arriving in Jo'burg the next day about 6am (US$25/20/11 for 1st/2nd/3rd class); you'll need to change trains at the border. There is also a train that runs twice weekly from Maputo to Durban via Swaziland.

There's also a border-crossing at Ponta d'Ouro, which you may be able to hitch to,

especially at weekends when many South Africans drive across the border to go to the beach, but it's a hard five- or six- hour journey to Maputo from there.

SWAZILAND

The crossing is at Namaacha. Minibuses between Maputo and Manzini cost US$4, or you can pick one up at Namaacha.

TANZANIA

Dhows (traditional Arab-style wooden boats) sail up and down the coast of the Indian Ocean, connecting Mozambique and Tanzania, and you might be able to arrange a ride, but captains won't always take passengers. The best places to try your luck are Moçimboa da Praia and Palma. In Tanzania, try Mikindani, Mtwara or Msimbati. Always travel with the wind (south to north from approximately April to September and north to south from approximately November to March), or choose a dhow with a motor.

If you're sticking to dry land (mostly), the border between Mozambique and Tanzania is the Rovuma River, and the journey across it is one of the most adventurous in Africa. The main border crossing point is at Namuiranga, from where you'll cross to the Tanzanian border post at Singa (also known as Kilamba). Chapas from Pemba run daily to Moçimboa da Praia (US$8, nine to 12 hours). From here, pickup trucks leave around 4am, bucketing through abysmal roads and thick bush (for up to six hours), to reach the border post on the edge of the Ruvuma River. After the border post, everyone gets into a dugout canoe, which is poled through thick reeds and across the river – a torrent in the rainy season – to the jetty at Singa on the Tanzanian side. From here, trucks go to Mtwara in Tanzania for around US$15, and the journey time can be 10 to 12 hours. There's also an occasional vehicle ferry across the river; it takes foot passengers and is a less precarious experience. But it's status is always uncertain, so if you're driving, check that it's running before setting out. Also note that you cannot buy visas for Mozambique on this border – you must arrange them in advance.

ZAMBIA

The main crossing is at Cassacatiza, north-west of Tete. From Tete, take any Moatize chapa over the bridge past the SOS compound to the petrol station, where you'll find chapas to Matema. From Matema, there is infrequent transport for the 200km to Cassacatiza.

ZIMBABWE

The main crossings are: Nyamapanda (southwest of Tete, on the main road linking Blantyre in Malawi and Harare in Zimbabwe, known as the Tete Corridor); and Machipanda (west of Chimoio) on the road between Mutare and Beira. Both are heavily travelled by private vehicles and buses.

GETTING AROUND
Air

Linhas Aéreas de Moçambique (www.lam.co.mz) and **STA Air Charters** (☎ 491765; sta.tta@tvcabo.co.mz) fly between all Mozambique's major cities. In the rainy season, flights might be your only option for getting around northern Mozambique.

Car & Motorcycle

If you're bringing in a car from South Africa (as some backpackers do) southern Mozambique's main roads can be negotiated in a 2WD vehicle, but for most other areas (and for the journey from Ponto d'Ouro to Maputo), you'll need a 4WD. Driving off-road is a seriously bad idea due to the thousands of landmines still in the country, and driving on beaches or sand dunes is an ecological no-no.

Hitching

Despite the possible dangers, hitching is often the only transport option, especially in rural areas. Vehicles that might give you a lift range from long-distance lorries to souped-up 4WDs driven by butch South African holidaymakers. Payment is often expected.

Pity the backpacker who was delighted to get a ride in the back of a farmer's pickup truck, only to discover he was about to sit for six hours on top of a slaughtered cow…

Local Transport

Buses are generally your best option for getting around Mozambique. Huge *machimbombos* (coaches) and smaller *chapacems* (minibuses, always known as 'chapas') connect almost every town daily. 'Luxury'

companies (it's a relative term!) are slightly more expensive, but faster and marginally more comfortable. The bigger bus companies are Transportes Oliveiras (in the south), TSL (countrywide) and Grupo Macula (in the north). For fares and times, see the individual town sections.

Buses and chapas leave early (between 3am and 6am), and – an anomaly in Africa – are often on time.

Train

A train service runs three times a week between Nampula and Cuamba. It costs US$17/4/2 for 1st/2nd/3rd class.

MAPUTO

☎ 01 / pop 1 million

Formerly called Lourenço Marques and famed as a 'prawns and prostitutes' mecca for apartheid-era South African tourists, Africa's only Latin city is a sociable and vibrant party town with flower sellers on every street corner, flame-tree-lined avenues, continental cafés, salsa bars, shops and markets galore. Make sure you're there at the weekend to sample beachlife and nightlife to the max.

ORIENTATION

Arriving at Maputo's Mavalane International Airport, about 7km from the city centre, your options are to catch a taxi (US$6), attempt to bag a lift on one of the courtesy buses sent out by the upmarket hotels, or one of the public chapas that run into town. Be warned, however – chapas will charge you extra for your backpack on this route.

Buses from Jo'burg stop at various points in the heart of the city, from where you can walk to any of the hotels. Most buses from the north arrive at the city bus terminal, about 3km west along the Avenida 24 de Julho from the centre. Hitching along here should be easy as it's the main route into town.

Maputo divides into two main districts – the Baixa and the Polana. Walking from the Avenida 25 de Septembro, the Baixa's main drag, to the Avenida 24 de Julho leading to the Polana, involves a steepish hill and will take about 20 minutes.

INFORMATION
Bookshops
The pretty **Europa-America Bookstore** (Ave José Mateus) is air-conditioned and sells English-language books and magazines plus gifts and greeting cards.

Cultural Centres
The **Centre Culturel Franco-Mozambicain** (☎ 420786; Praça da Indepéndencia) includes an art gallery with touring exhibitions, a cinema, theatre, Internet café and bar. The centre hosts regular gigs by Mozambican and foreign artists and holds drumming and music workshops – as well as showing films, some in English.

Internet Access
There are Internet cafés scattered liberally throughout Maputo. The going rate is about US$2 per hour. Try the Interfranca Shopping Centre, or the Polana Shopping Centre.

Media
Useful even if you don't speak Portuguese, *Que Passa* is an entertainment monthly that also contains discount vouchers for various restaurants, hotels and shops. Pick it up in travel agencies.

Medical Services
Clinic a Cruz Azul (☎ 305146/47/51; cnr Ave Karl Marx & Ave Zedequias Manganhela) is the best hospital to head to if you need any treatment and has English speakers.

Money
Banks in Maputo include:
Banco Austral (Ave 25 de Setembro) Near the telephone office; does advances on MasterCard.
Banco International da Moçambique (BIM) In several places in the city; ATMs accept Visa cards.
Hotel Polana Forex Bureau (Ave Julius Nyerere) Changes travellers cheques for 5% to 7% commission.
Hotel Rovuma Carlton BIM (Praça da Indepéndencia) Changes travellers cheques, for a US$20 flat fee irrespective of the amount you change.

There are plenty of foreign exchange bureaus in Maputo including:
Cota Câmbios (Polana Shopping Centre, Ave Julius Nyerere; ☽ Mon-Sun 9am-8pm)
Sarbaz Câmbios (Ave Julius Nyerere; ☽ Mon-Fri 8am-12.30pm, 2-5pm, Sat 8am-1pm)

Post & Telephone
The main **post office** (CTT; Ave 25 de Setembro; ☽ 7.45am-noon, 2-5pm Mon-Fri, 8am-noon Sat) also has a branch on Avenida 25 de Julho. The main **telephone office** (TDM; Ave 25 de Setembro) is best for international calls. There's also a TDM on Avenida 25 de Julho.

Tourist Offices
The National Tourism Organisation (ENT; ☎ 307323; 1203 Ave 25 de Setembro; ☽ Mon-Fri 8am-noon, 2-5pm) has friendly English-speaking staff, but not much information.

DANGERS & ANNOYANCES
Walking around most of Maputo city centre during daytime hours is hassle-free and safe. Avoid the areas of wasteland between Avenida Patrice Lumumba and Avenida 25 de Setembro, and between Avenida Friedrich Engels and Avenida Marginal.

Carry your passport (not a photocopy) at all times, as police frequently stop tourists, hoping to get a fine/bribe if you have no identification with you. After dark, take a taxi if you're going any distance.

SIGHTS & ACTIVITIES
The artists at **Núcleo Arte** (www.africaserver.nl/nucleo/eng; 194 Rua da Argélia; admission free; ☽ no fixed hours, closed Sun) turn arms into art. What better symbol of Mozambique's regeneration? The artists who work in this outwardly shabby villa have formed a co-operative that takes salvaged AK47s and landmines from rural farmers in return for tools. The arms are then welded into incredibly moving sculptures, on display in the gallery and the small garden. The artists on site are happy to talk about their work and other artworks by contemporary Mozambican artists are on display and for sale.

The beach at the little fishing village of **Catembe** comes alive with locals at weekends. A 10-minute ferry ride away from Maputo, it's a great place for a plate of prawns, a swim (if you fancy the rather dubious brown water) and some serious people-watching, as the town's fly girls and guys crank up their stereos and flirt, drink or play football on the sand with the skyscrapers of Maputo in the background.

The impressive domed **train station** on Praça dos Trabalhadores was designed by a pupil of Gustave Eiffel (of Tower fame) and has

MOZAMBIQUE

CENTRAL MAPUTO

been well restored, with a coat of pistachio-green paint, potted plants, and a couple of old-fashioned locomotives. Also worth a wander around is the **Praça da Independência**, flanked by the imposing **city hall** and the rather ugly **cathedral**.

SLEEPING
Most backpackers end up at one of the town's two excellent hostels; other budget options are basic, characterless, or both.

The **Base Backpackers** (☎ 302723; thebasebp@tvcabo.co.mz; 545 Ave Patrice Lumumba; dm/d US$5/13; 🖳) Maputo's newest backpackers' hostel is also its most central, with brightly painted dorms and doubles, a well-equipped kitchen, an outdoor terrace and fantastically helpful

staff. This place is an excellent mine of information about the town's attractions and a great place to meet other travellers.

Fatima's (☎ 302994; fatima@virconn.com; 1317 Ave Mao Tse Tung; dm/d US$5/15) Deservedly a long-standing budget favourite, comprising two houses next door to each other a little out of town. Very relaxed, with a garden, outdoor bar/kitchen, local food, squashed dorms and a travellers' noticeboard. It can get full, so book ahead.

Sadly your other budget accommodation options in Maputo are all unremarkable, shabby *pensãos* (cheap hotels). All prices are for rooms with a shared bathroom:
Pensão Central (Ave 24 de Julho; s/d US$8/12) The best option.

INFORMATION			Centre Culturel Franco-			ENTERTAINMENT	☺ p768
ATM	(see 66)		Mozambicain	23	B3	Ciné Africa	(see 43)
Australian Consulate	(see 21)		City Hall	24	B3	Ciné Gil Vicente	46 B4
Banco Austral	1	B4	Laurentina Beer Factory	(see 64)		Xenon Cinema	47 D3
British High Commission & British			Natural History Museum	25	D3		
Council	2	B3	Núcleo Arte	26	D3	SHOPPING	🛍 p768
Canadian High Commission	3	D2				Artedif Crafts	48 D1
Clínica Cruz Azul	4	B4	SLEEPING	🏠 pp766–7		Elefante	49 A4
Danish Embassy	5	B3	Base Backpackers	27	C3	Europa – America Bookshop	50 D3
French Embassy	6	D1	Fatima's Backpackers	28	B2	Interfranca Shopping Centre	51 B3
German Embassy	7	C1	Hotel Ibis	29	B4	Mozarte	52 A3
Italian Embassy	8	C1	Pensão Alegre	30	D1	Polana Shopping Centre	53 D3
Malawi High Commission	9	D1	Pensão Baixa	31	A4		
National Tourism Organisation			Pensão Central	32	B3	TRANSPORT	pp768–9
(ENT)	10	B4	Residencial Taj Mahal	33	A3	Chapas to Ponta d'Ouro	54 C4
Netherlands Embassy	11	D2				Ferry to Catembe	55 C4
Norwegian Embassy	12	D2	EATING	🍴 pp767–8		Greyhound	56 B3
Portuguese Embassy	(see 47)		Café Continental	34	B4	Intercape	57 C3
Sarbaz Câmbios	13	D2	Café Gil Vicente	(see 46)		LAM Office	(see 29)
South African High Commission	14	D3	Feira Popular	35	B4	LAM Sales Office	58 D2
Swaziland High Commission	15	C2	Fresco's	36	D3	Ponto Final	59 A3
Swedish Embassy	(see 3)		Mercado do Povo	37	B3	Ronil	60 A3
Tanzania High Commission	16	D3	Mercado Janeta	38	B2	South African Airways	61 B4
Telephone Office	17	C3	Pastelaria Nautilus	39	D3	TAP Air Portugal Office	(see 66)
Telephone Office	(see 21)		Pastelaria Wimbi	40	D3	Taxi Stand	62 C2
US Embassy	18	C1	Supermercado LM	41	C3	Translux	63 C3
Zambia High Commission	19	C1	Villa Itália	42	D3	Transport for Swaziland, South Africa,	
Zimbabwe High Commission	20	C2				Namaacha, Boane & Goba	64 A4
			DRINKING	🍷 p768			
SIGHTS & ACTIVITIES	pp765–6		Africa Bar	43	B3	OTHER	
33 Storey Building	21	B4	Gypsy's Bar	44	B4	Hotel Polana	65 D2
Cathedral	22	B3	Kaffé Mambo	45	A4	Rovuma Carlton Hotel	66 B3

Pensão Baixa (☎ 308190; Ave Fernão Magalhães; s/d US$12/14) Downtown.

Residencial Taj Mahal (☎ 732122; Ave Ho Chi Minh; s/d US$15/20) Bakery next door.

Pensão Alegre (☎ 307742; Ave 24 de Julho; s/d US$12/10) Basic but friendly.

SPLURGE!

If you're seriously in need of some comfort after the long slog south, try the brand new **Hotel Ibis** (☎ 352200; 1743 Ave 25 de Setembro; d US$38; 🏊). A business hotel with all the facilities you'd expect – satellite TV, air-con – that does very cheap rates at weekends. It has disabled facilities.

EATING

The gigantic prawns that made Maputo famous in the 1970s are still jumping out of the sea and into the pan in the city's many fantastic seafood restaurants. For lunch or all-day snacking, head straight for the many pavement *pastelarias* (cafés) around Avenida Julius Nyerere, which sell melt-in-your-mouth pastries and fresh bread, and are great places to while away a few hours watching the world go by.

If you're self-catering, try the **Supermercado LM** (Ave 24 de Julho) for imported goods.

For the cheapest eats, head to one of the city's markets – Mercado do Povo or Mer-

cado Janeta are the best for a plate of maize meal, cassava and peanut sauce that won't cost much more than US$1.

Cafés

Café Gil Vicente (Ave Samora Machel; snacks from US$1) Studenty, Art Deco café/bar next to Cinema Gil Vicente, with comfy sofas, cheap meals and a bohemian feel. Great for a precinema meal, or get a takeaway at lunchtime and eat it in the Jardim Tunduru opposite.

Of the many *pastelarias* in the uptown Polana district, two of the best are **Pastelaria Wimbi** (Ave Eduardo Mondlane) and **Pastelaria Nautilus** (Ave Julius Nyerere), which both sell a dazzling selection of cakes, bread and pastries and get packed with appreciative locals every lunchtime. In the Baixa in the city centre, there are fewer *pastelarias*, but the **Café Continental** (Ave 25 de Setembro) is one of the city's old favourites, and still a reliable spot for lunch.

Restaurants

City Fish Market (Ave Marginal; mains around US$6) Go straight to the source for your seafood meal – the catches come in around 6pm, so arrive early for dinner. You choose your fish or crustacean, take it to be weighed (garrulous questioning of everything from the weighing scales to the morals of the fishwife are *de rigueur*), then have it cooked by one of the restaurants next door. Tip: look for clear eyes, shiny scales, and red gills, or tip one

MOZAMBIQUE

of the urchins to tell you which fish are the freshest. Fantastic.

Feira Popular (off Ave 25 de Setembro; mains US$2-10) A cluster of restaurants and bars around a dusty fairground, this is one of Maputo's most popular eating – and drinking – spots, with a disco and bumper cars thrown in at weekends. Escorpio is the most upmarket, with enormous portions of steak alongside the seafood dishes, all served with mountains of chips. Cheaper is O Coqueiro, which specialises in the creamy chicken dishes of Mozambique's Zambezia province.

Fresco's (Ave Julius Nyerere; mains US$6-20) Lively and attractively decorated 'seafood eatery' that serves huge portions of wonderfully cooked calamari, prawns and fresh fish (starters are big enough for a main course). Very good value, and popular with groups.

Villa Italia (Ave Friedrich Engels; mains around US$5) An oasis of calm in the city centre, with a plunge pool (free to diners), a peaceful garden overlooking the sea, and a small bar.

Costa do Sol (Ave Marginal; mains around US$10) Art Deco seafood restaurant on the beach, famous for having stayed open all through the civil war.

DRINKING

Maputians love to drink and party – you can buy beer at swimming pools, newsstands, even bus stations. Most bars don't get going until after midnight, and are much busier at weekends, when many lay on live bands. Rua da Bagamoyo in the Baixa district is the city's disreputable but fun drinking centre; take a taxi from here when they finally kick you out.

Kaffé Mambo (Travessa de Palmeira) Off Rua da Bagamoyo and definitely Maputo's hottest spot – this extravagantly Latin-styled joint spills over onto the pavement outside on weekends, filled with beautiful young things dressed up to the nines, dancing to live salsa and quaffing *caipirinãs*.

Africa Bar (Ave 24 de Julho; admission US$2) Hyper-trendy hangout popular with expats and local media types. Beautiful decor, live jazz, cover charge (redeemable against drinks) at weekends.

Gypsy's Bar (Rua da Bagamoyo) Hilariously seedy, tiny bar with red-velvet walls and low lighting. One of a row of bars of varying degrees of seediness along this street, perfect for a pub crawl.

ENTERTAINMENT

Maputo hosts regular music events, often featuring artists from West and South Africa alongside local acts. Check the Centre Culturel Franco-Mozambicain (see p765) for a programme of their concerts, or pick up a copy of the entertainment listings magazine *Que Passa*.

There are three good cinemas in town:

Ciné Gil Vicente (Ave Samora Machel) The cheapest.

Ciné Africa (Ave 24 de Julho) Has concerts from time to time.

Xenon Cinema (Ave Julius Nyerere) Shows mainstream Western films, sometimes dubbed into Portuguese.

SHOPPING

Mozarte (Ave Felipe Samuel Magalia) A complex of workshops around a pretty courtyard, run by a project that also provides counselling, contraception and HIV education to young people in Mozambique. The crafts made here, including glassware and ceramics, are sold in a very smart shop, and there's a café and bar selling beer and snacks.

Elefante (Ave 25 de Setembro) The best place to buy the colourful wraps known as *capulanas* worn by many Mozambican women, which make excellent sarongs or bath towels.

Artedif (Ave Marginal) Run by a disabled persons' charity, this shop sells a good selection of locally made items, including sandals and leather bags.

There are craft sellers all over Maputo – some of the better ones are located outside the Polana Shopping Centre, or along the road outside the Polana Hotel. The best **craft market** (Praça 25 de Junho) takes place on Saturday mornings, with vendors selling basketwork, carvings, fabrics and malachite.

GETTING THERE & AWAY
Air

Linhas Aéreas de Moçambique (LAM; ☎ 465810/1/2/5; www.lam.co.mz; 225 Ave Karl Marx) has flights into Maputo from Beira: (US$130), Quelimane (US$160), Nampula (US$200) and Jo'burg (US$170).

Other airlines:

Pelican Air (☎ 733649/2819; tta@icon.co.za)

STA Air Charters(☎ 491765; sta.tta@tvcabo.co.mz)

Bus

Maputo is the main hub for bus services to all of southern Mozambique. Buses running north to Beira from Maputo stop overnight in Vilankulo before continuing their journey the next day.

The main bus lines from Maputo north is Transportes Oliveiras. Buses depart from the city bus depot, about 3km from the city centre on Avenida 24 de Julho, just beyond Praça 16 de Junho. Some Oliveiras buses from the north continue to the intersection of Avenidas 24 de Julho and Amilcar Cabral, near Pensão Alegre. Oliveiras buses north depart at 6am and 11am and take around six hours to Inhambane.

TSL buses also go north to Inhambane and Vilankulo from their depot at Praça dos Combatentes at the end of Avenida das FPLM in 'Xikelene'. Most buses coming into and out of town also stop at the Ponto Final transport stop, a 20-minute walk from the town centre.

Minibuses to Swaziland depart when full from outside the Laurentina Beer Factory on Avenida 25 de Setembro. To get to the South African border crossing at Ponta D'Ouro, you'll need to take a ferry to Catembe and pick up a chapa from there.

Translux, Greyhound, Intercape and Panthera Azul all run luxury coach services to Jo'burg, departing from different points along Avenida 24 de Julho. See map for their locations.

If you're travelling north from Maputo in the early morning, sit on the left-hand side of the bus to avoid being blinded and fried by the rising sun.

Train

Overnight trains to Jo'burg depart from the train station on Praça dos Trabalhadores. See p763 for times.

GETTING AROUND

Maputo's centre is reasonably compact, so if you're only here for a few days it's probably easier to walk than to try and negotiate the complex network of buses and chapas that whiz around the city.

City buses (US$0.10) are numbered, with destinations (not that you'll ever have heard of them) shown in the window. For the City Fish Market and Costa do Sol, take bus No 17 from the corner of Avenidas Mao Tse Tung and Julius Nyerere, or take a chapa from outside the National History Museum at the end of Avenida Patrice Lumumba. Chapas also run to the airport from here.

Private hire taxis cost about US$3 per journey during daylight, and can be found outside major hotels or along the Avenida 25 de Setembro.

SOUTHERN MOZAMBIQUE

The most accessible of Mozambique's regions, Southern Mozambique's tarmac roads and quick transport links make it a joy to get around, while a plethora of beachside hostels and hotels make finding accommodation easy too. Be warned though – in the high season (Christmas to New Year and Easter) Southern Mozambique can get chock-a-block with sunburned South Africans out to party, towing powerboats behind their 4WDs.

INHAMBANE & MAXIXE
☎ 023

The sleepy provincial capital of Inhambane, once an important trading centre, has a bit of a 'ghost town' feel these days, and most people only give it a couple of hours before heading to the fantastic beach at **Tofo**, 20km away. To get buses north, you'll need to cross the bay to Maxixe, pronounced 'Masheesh'.

Pensão Pachiça (☎ 20652; Ave Eduardo Mondlane, Inhambane; dm/d US$6/13) is the only place to stay in town. Although once popular, regrettably it's now an overpriced dive. If at all possible, head to the beach instead.

In Maxixe, **Campismo de Maxixe** (☎ 30351; EN1; camp site per person/tw US$3/16) is highly recommended, with good facilities and an excellent restaurant.

Hotel Oceano (☎ 30419; Rua Serpa Rosa; tw US$9) is cheery and convenient for the buses; there is a restaurant attached.

For cheap meals in Inhambane, try Ponto Final or Tic Tac near the market.

Stop Restaurant near the jetty in Maxixe is the best place for breakfast, or to pick up a lift north.

The ferry between Inhambane and Maxixe takes 20 minutes and runs all day, or you can take a dhow if the wind is up. Buses for Maputo (US$7, seven hours) leave Inhambane daily. For points north, you'll need to cross to Maxixe – chapas run all day from the post office, and a TSL bus to Vilankulo

(US$2, three hours) passes through around lunchtime.

TOFO

Tofo village is a backpackers' paradise – a massive sweep of white sand and rolling breakers, with a couple of excellent places to stay. It's the perfect place to kick back for a few days – or weeks – dive, surf or just hang with the hippy chicks and board dudes.

Tofo has superb diving and snorkelling as well as world-class surf. If you're interested **Tofo Scuba** (☎ 082 826 014; tofo.scuba@mantascuba .com) or **Diversity** (☎ 29002; info@diversityscuba.com) are the recommended operators.

Bamboozi Beach Lodge (☎ 082 459 056; bamboozi@teledata.mz; camp site per person/dm US$4/6) is Tofo's coolest backpackers, set among the sand dunes about 2kms up the beach. With its dive shop, tent rental, surfboards and restaurant, there are plenty of people who don't leave for months.

Fatima's Nest (☎ 01302944; fatima@vircom.com; camp site per person/dm US$2/4/10) has a kitchen available, or buffet food.

Nordin's Lodge (☎ 29009; dm/d US$5/20) has huge cabins with kitchens, but not many facilities – or guests.

If you're self catering, it's best to buy food in Inhambane before heading out to Tofo. To find some local flavour, head into the market in Tofo village, which has a couple of bars and a food stall.

Chapas for Tofo leave from outside the market in Inhambane; the journey takes about half an hour.

VILANKULO & THE BAZARUTO ARCHIPELAGO NATIONAL PARK
☎ 023

Despite being Mozambique's foremost holiday spot, Vilankulo (formerly Vilankulos) is an unspoilt and charming little town with a colourful market and a great beach. It's also the gateway to the islands of the Bazaruto Archipelago National Park, a divers' and snorkellers' paradise of turquoise water, pristine coral reefs and white sand dunes.

Sail Away (☎ 82385) near Campismo de Vilankulo offers two- to four-day dhow safaris to the Bazaruto Marine National Park for US$50 per day all-inclusive.

If you can't afford this, you can arrange something with one of the town's local dhow captains – ask at the helpful **tourist**

office (☎ 82228; margie@teledata.mz; beach road) for pointers.

For diving, contact **Vilanculos Dive Charters** (☎ 82393; mozzies@teledata.mz).at Aguia Negra Hotel.

All the best places to stay are along the beach road. **Zombie Cucumber** (☎ 082 804 941; dm/tw US$6/13) has everything a backpackers should have – comfy hammocks, garden, home-cooked meals and local info from the friendly English owners.

Casa Josef e Tina (☎ 82140; camp site per person/d US$5/26) has a pleasant shady garden with wooden chalets. You can hire a tent for US$13.

Campismo Vilankulos (☎ 0027 61427/8; www.vila nkuloscamping.co.za; camp site per person/d US$7/20) has grassy, shady camp sites with great facilities, and spacious en suite chalets.

Baobab Beach (☎ 82202; beach road; 2baker@bush mail.net; camp site per person/dm US$3/5) is cheap and right on the beach, but when we visited, the bathrooms looked dirty and the staff seemed surly.

The only budget place in Bazaruto Archipelago is on Benguerra Island. **Gabriel's Lodge** (☎ 82230; camp site per person/dm US$10/20) has a stunning beach, but the food we were served was horrid and the accommodation is a bit overpriced. They can arrange boat transfers for US$20.

Buses go to Maxixe (US$2, three hours) and Beira (US$13, six hours). It's best to get a chapa to Pambarra on the main road 20km east of Vilankulo and pick up a bus from there. **Pelican Air** (☎ 733649/2819; tta@icon.co.za) runs flights to Jo'burg.

CENTRAL MOZAMBIQUE

Central Mozambique encompasses Beira, the country's second city; Chimoio, which nestles in beautiful rolling hills, and Tete, which is...well, hot. Most travellers pitching up in these places are on their way to somewhere else – Malawi, Zimbabwe, or Mozambique's northern and southern regions.

BEIRA
☎ 03 / pop 350,000

Mozambique's second-largest city is very much the poor relation of Maputo. A few well-preserved colonial buildings and a decent **beach** (at Makuti, 5km out of town) sum up its attractions, and it's really only of interest as a transport hub.

Biques Restaurant and Campsite (☎ 312451; Makuti Beach; camp site per person US$5) may not have much in the way of facilities, but it is right by the sea. To get there take a chapa from near Hotel Embaixador.

Pensão Moderna (☎ 324537; 263 Rua Travessa de Igreja; s/tw US$4/15) has rooms with a fan in a quiet square near the cathedral. There's a café next door.

Hotel Miramar (☎ 322283; Villa Boas Trua; tw with private bathroom US$11) has very good value rooms and a terrace restaurant near the sea.

Bar Africa (☎ 324514; Rua Aires de Ornelas) is cosy with wood-panelling and a very kitsch disco next door.

On Praça do Município try Cafe Capri. Take-Away 2 + 1, near the buses, does good filled rolls.

If you're self-catering, head for Shoprite on Avenida Samora Machel.

Buses and chapas both leave from Praça do Maquinino, northwest of Praça do Município (Beira's main square) to Chimoio (US$4, three hours), Vilankulo (US$10, seven hours), Tete (US$8, eight hours) and Maputo (US$13, two days).

The journey from Beira to Quelimane used to be one of the country's hardest, but these days it's a doddle due to the nice new sealed road from Inchope to Caia, which then continues on to Quelimane. Get a chapa to Inchope or Dondo Balanca, just outside Dondo, then change to one marked Rio Zambeze or Quelimane. The whole process, including the Zambezi crossing, takes about 12 hours and costs around US$15. Hitching this road should be possible, but slow.

CHIMOIO
☎ 051
Despite being a truckers' stopover point on the way to Zimbabwe, Chimoio has a rather suburban feel to it, with tree-lined streets and a polite populace. The surrounding countryside is stunning, with green rolling hills perfect for hiking. However, there are still thousands of unexploded landmines in this area, so extreme caution is needed – ask around for a local guide to show you where it's safe.

Restaurant Chicoteca da Palhota (airport road; camping free) has an unofficial campsite in a gorgeous spot 3km out of town, with toilets

and water provided by the upmarket restaurant next door.

Residencial Flor de Vouga (☎ 22469; Ave 25 de Setembro; s/d US$7/13) has old-fashioned rooms and is above Banco Austral.

Pensão Atlantica (☎ 22169; s/d US$6/13) has bigger but shabbier rooms with shared bathroom. It's near the post office and there's a good bakery next door.

For a bite to eat, try Concorde or Elo 4, both on Avenida 25 de Setembro, or head to the market for the local food stalls.

TSL buses to Tete (US$5, eight hours), Beira (US$4, three hours), and chapas to Quelimane (US$13, 12 hours) and the border at Machipanda depart Chimoio daily from the train station.

TETE
☎ 052
Even the missionaries call it 'hell' – Tete is the hottest and most unpopular place in Mozambique. But you may well change transport or stop a night here. If so, sink a freezing cold beer at a bar overlooking the Zambezi River and it won't seem so bad after all.

All Tete's accommodation options are repulsive, so head for the ones with air-conditioning.

Pensão Alves (Ave 24 de Julho; tw US$13; ❄) is nearest the buses, but the shared bathroom is filthy. Much better is **Univendas** (☎ 22670; Ave Julius Nyerere; s/tw/d US$13/18/21; ❄) above the shop of the same name.

There's a cheap local food market opposite Univendas, or if that's just a bit *too* unhygienic, try Pic-Nic restaurant opposite. Complexo Pemba on the riverfront is the best place for beer.

Chapas for Zobué (US$1, one hour) and Nyamapanda (US$1, one hour) and buses to Chimoio (US$5, five hours) and Beira (US$7, eight hours) depart from along Avenida 25 de Junho.

NORTHERN MOZAMBIQUE

Mozambique's north is the least-explored area of the country and challenging to travel around. The rewards for those who do are spectacular – the haunting beauty of Ilha de Moçambique, the superb beaches of

LUÍS DE CAMÕES

Luís de Camões was Portugal's great national poet, author of the epic *Os Lusíadas*. He arrived on Ilha in 1657, after losing his eye during a skirmish with the locals. Despite this poor start, he described the island as 'a unique woman, lying sensuously in a state of abandon, in a sea of colours, sun-worshipping on the beach'. There's a statue of Camões, complete with eye patch, on Rua dos Combatentes, outside the Casa Branca guesthouse.

Pemba, and the unspoilt Swahili culture of the Querimba Archipelago.

QUELIMANE

☎ 04 / pop 170,000

Quelimane is a quiet, friendly town, ideal for a few days of peace on the hard slog north. There's a good beach at **Zalala**, about an hour's drive away through the coconut plantations.

Pensão Ideal (☎ 212731; Ave Samuel Magaia; tw US$7; ✳) is cheap but hot – it's worth paying more for a room with air-con.

Hotel 1 de Julho (☎ 215818; Ave Samuel Magaia; d US$13) is pick and span, and some rooms have a balcony.

Hotel Zambeze (☎ 215490; Ave Francisco da Mantenga; d US$16; ✳) has large rooms with an extra bonus – fresh condoms on the pillows!

Try the market for cheap food stalls. Bar Loucuras near the cathedral is a fun hangout with snack food, a swimming pool, and a disco at weekends.

Grupo Macula 'luxury' 'express' buses (don't get too excited about either of these terms) leave the Romoza train station at the edge of town at 5am for Nampula (US$12, nine hours). For details of the new route to Beira, see p771. For Zalala Beach, chapas leave from the market.

NAMPULA

☎ 06 / pop 300,000

The industrial centre of northern Mozambique, Nampula is one of Mozambique's scruffiest and least appealing towns. You'll probably only come here on the way to Ilha de Moçambique, or to catch the train to Cuamba for Malawi.

The **National Museum of Ethnography** (Ave Eduardo Mondlane; admission free; ☷ 2-4.30pm Tue-Fri & Sun, 10am-noon Sat) is good for a rainy afternoon, with explanations in English and a collection of ritual masks and marijuana pipes.

Budget options in Nampula are universally dire. Your choices include **Pensão Parque** (☎ 21230; s/tw US$7/13), **Pensão Estrela** (☎ 214902; tw US$15; ✳) and **Pensão Central** (☎ 212519; tw US$9) which are all on Avenida Paulo Samuel Kamkama.

There are cafés and bakeries along this road too.

Transport to Ilha de Moçambique (US$2, four hours), Quelimane (US$7, 11 hours) and Pemba (US$7, 11 hours) leaves from the train station. You can almost halve your journey time to Pemba if you're prepared to risk the roller-coaster 'Tanzaniana' minibuses that screech around the streets around 4am, playing thumping rap music to wake up their customers.

Trains to Cuamba leave Tuesday, Thursday and Saturday at 5am, costing US$18/5/3 in 1st/2nd/3rd class.

ILHA DE MOÇAMBIQUE

☎ 06

Tiny reed houses and pastel-coloured colonial mansions rub shoulders among the palm trees on tiny Ilha de Moçambique (Mozambique Island), the former capital of the Portuguese East African colony. It's haunting, magical, and a must-see.

Orientation

The 'Ilha' is attached to the mainland by a 1.5km causeway. Chapas and buses arrive at the southern tip of the island, from where it's a short walk north through the *makuti* (reed) town to the old colonial stone town. The island is tiny – just 2.5km long and 600m wide – so finding your way around is pretty easy.

Information

The very helpful **tourist office** (☎ 610081; ☷ 9am-noon & 2-5pm daily) in the Palacio de Sao Paulo, can organise guides and hire bikes. For an online guide, go to www.ilhademo.net.

Sights

To experience 'Ilha' at its best, get up early to beat the heat and wander through the reed town as it's waking up – with radios blaring and cocks crowing from the narrow streets. Then grab a breakfast of spicy *bhajias* from the food market, and walk up into the old colonial town as the museums open.

The bright red **Museu de Artes Decorativas** (admission free; ⏰ 8am-noon & 2-5pm Wed-Sun) in the Palacio de Sao Paulo is magnificently decorated with opulent furniture, tapestries, and portraits of sinister-looking colonial grandees.

The massive Portuguese **Fort of São Sebastão** (admission free; ⏰ 9am-5pm) is best visited at sunset, when it's bathed in glorious golden light, followed by a swim in the turquoise water beneath the battlements. Watch out for the bats that stream out across the sea at twilight.

In the southeast, the whitewashed **Catholic Cathedral** overlooks the glittering sea and the fishermen building their boats on the beach. Photo heaven.

Sleeping

There's no shortage of good accommodation on Ilha – all the places listed here belong to locals who have opened their homes to paying guests.

Casa Luís (Private Garden; ☎ 082 67 57; Travessa dos Fornos; s/d US$6/13) An Ilha institution – a friendly family-run place with a blissfully shady garden. Cute children, free drinking water and spicy prawn dinners. The small rooms have fans, nets, and shared bathrooms.

Casa Branca (☎ 610076; Rua dos Combatentes; s/d US$17/22) Worth a splurge, with beautifully decorated, cool rooms in a stunning old building overlooking the sea. Bathrooms are shared but prices include breakfast.

Residencial Meia Luia (☎ 610163; s/d US$8/15) Near the hospital. Very plush. Shared bathroom and kitchen, but no garden.

Eating

The cheapest restaurant is **Âncora d'Ouro** (mains US$2) near the museum. The best is the stylish **Relíquias** (mains US$4) nearby, which has good vegetarian options and local specialities. The night market near Casa Luís has fish and *chapatis*.

Getting There & Away

At least one bus and several chapas daily go to Nampula via Monapo (US$2, five hours).

CUAMBA
☎ 071

Cuamba is an important junction town on road and railway between Nampula and the Malawi border. If you have to stay the night, try the basic **Pensão Namaacha** on the main road.

Road transport leaves from Maçaniqueira market south of the railroad tracks. Trains leave for Nampula on Wednesday, Friday and Sunday at 5am, costing US$18/5/3 in 1st/2nd/3rd class. See p762 for information about crossing the border into Malawi.

PEMBA
☎ 072

The main draw of the sunny seaside town of Pemba is glorious Wimbe beach, 5km down the coast.

Russell's Place (Cashew Camp; ☎ 082 686 273; pembamagic@teledata.mz; camp site per person/dm/d US$3/6/20) is a chilled-out and friendly backpackers on Wimbe Beach, with useful travel info, a vehicle workshop and a lively bar. There's a kitchen, or they offer meals. Call to arrange a lift from Pemba.

In Pemba town centre, try **Residencial Lys** (☎ 20951; suleman@teledata.mz; s/d US$9/17) or **Pensão Baia** (☎ 20153; d US$11), both cleanish and friendlyish.

To get to Wimbe from the town centre, you can hitch along the beach road quite easily, or take a taxi (about US$2). Buses to Nampula (US$7, 11 hours) and Moçimboa da Praia leave from near the town market.

IBO ISLAND & THE QUERIMBA ARCHIPELAGO

Ancient wooden sailing dhows take Swahili fisherman around the Querimba Archipelago, one of Mozambique's remotest and most beautiful places. Ibo Island in particular, with creepers growing through its crumbling colonial mansions, seems to have been untouched for centuries.

By far the best place to stay on Ibo Island is **Bella Vista Lodge** (☎ 00 27 612235; sales@wildlifea dventures.co.za; camp site per person/dm/d US$5/10/30), a beautifully restored old house on the waterfront. The other option is charming **Casa Janine** (camp site per person/d US$2/7) next door.

Russell's Place in Pemba can arrange dhow trips to Ibo (US$26), or you can ask around at Paquitequete fish market. The journey in a motor dhow takes about 10 hours. Sailing, you'll need to camp on one of the other islands on the way.

Alternatively, get a chapa from Pemba to the tiny village of Tandanhangui for the two hour dhow crossing to Ibo (US$1). Dhows and chapas don't always co-ordinate, so prepare to spend some time in the village. If you need food or accommodation, ask for Sufu, who speaks English, and can arrange meals or a bed for a small fee.

MOÇIMBOA DA PRAIA
☎ 072

Mocimboa da Praia, a rusting, one-horse port town, is the last stop between Pemba and the border crossing into Tanzania.

Pensão Leeta (☎ 81147; d US$7) provides basic rooms and dinner.

Pickups to the border leave from in front of Pensão Leeta around 4am.

MOZAMBIQUE DIRECTORY

ACCOMMODATION

It's worth bringing a tent to Mozambique as there are some great camp sites. Cheap hotels aren't as cheap here as in neighbouring countries – most *pensãos* and *residencials* start at around US$8 and are comparatively overpriced. Nearly all only have rooms with shared bathrooms, and few have mosquito nets, so bring your own and some way of hanging it. When quoting prices, many establishments distinguish between a *duplo* (twin beds) and a *casal* (double bed).

Around Christmas and New Year the beach hostels and hotels in the south get very full – prices go up, and you'll need to book ahead to be sure of getting a bed.

ACTIVITIES

Mozambique, once described as 'a thousand mile long beach', is naturally a water sports paradise. Inland, the attractive hilly country around Chimoio, Tete or Nampula is great for hiking, but you'll need a local guide before going off the main roads because of unexploded landmines.

Diving & Snorkelling

There are operators all along the coast, with the most popular centres at Tofo, Vilankulo

(for the Bazaruto Archipelago) and Pemba. Visibility is best from March to July. Single-day dives cost between US$30 and US$50, a two-dive day trip costs between US$75 and US$85, five dives are about US$200, and PADI open-water courses are around US$300.

Surfing

There are also some spectacular surf beaches in Mozambique – try Ponta d'Ouro near Maputo, Tofo and Tofhino near Inhambane, or Wimbe near Pemba in the north.

DANGERS & ANNOYANCES

Mozambique is generally safe, with few hassles for travellers. It is, however, a very poor country, so keep a good eye on your possessions and don't leave anything valuable lying around hotel rooms. In cities such as Maputo and Beira, it's better to take a taxi rather than walk around after dark. If you're driving in a car, keep the doors locked.

Landmines – a legacy of the civil war – are still a danger in rural areas. Never walk into the bush, even close to a road, or approach abandoned buildings, airstrips, bridges or water tanks. Take advice from locals before venturing off the main roads.

Carry your passport at all times, and if stopped by the police, remain polite but don't surrender it – insist on going to the police station instead.

DRIVING LICENCE

If driving, it's obligatory to carry your driving licence (international permit *and* home country licence are safest) at all times, plus vehicle registration papers, temporary import permit (available at most borders), and third party insurance certificate. Driving on the beach is illegal, as is driving wearing sunglasses or without a shirt on. The latter two may be invented by police at roadblocks, but it's worth being prepared.

EMBASSIES & CONSULATES

The following embassies and consulates are in Maputo:

Australia (☎ 422780; 2nd floor, 33 Storey Bldg, Ave Zedequias Manganhela 95)
Canada (☎ 492623; 1128 Ave Julius Nyerere)
France (☎ 491774; 2361 Ave Julius Nyerere)
Germany (☎ 492714; 506 Rua Damião de Gois)
Ireland (☎ 491440; 213 Rua Dom Joao IV)

Malawi (☎ 491468; 75 Ave Kenneth Kaunda)
South Africa (☎ 491614; 41 Ave Eduardo Mondlane)
Swaziland (☎ 492451; Ave Kwame Nkrumah)
Tanzania (☎ 490110; 852 Ave Mártires de Machava)
UK (☎ 420111; 310 Ave Vladimir Lenine)
USA (☎ 492797; 193 Ave Kenneth Kaunda)
Zambia (☎ 492452; 1286 Ave Kenneth Kaunda)
Zimbabwe (☎ 490404; 1657 Ave Mártires de Machava)

For other embassies and consulates, see the Maputo map on p766. Mozambique has diplomatic representation in Malawi, Tanzania, South Africa, Swaziland, Zambia and Zimbabwe.

FOOD & DRINK

Near the coast, you won't have to go far before you're tucking into a plate of giant *camarão* (prawns), washed down with a cold *Dois M* (2M, Mozambique's favourite lager). Elsewhere the options include *xima* (maize porridge), *frango* (fried chicken) or *matapa* (peanut and spinach stew).

You don't necessarily get what you pay for – more expensive restaurants serve dull, overcooked food compared with the spicy fare served up at food stalls. Markets are always a good place to look for cheap local grub, which starts at around US$1. Even the smallest towns have bakeries turning out delicious fresh-baked bread and rolls.

It's easy to find bottled water, but it'll be cheaper to bring sterilisation tablets and treat your own.

HOLIDAYS

As well as religious holidays listed in the Africa Directory (p1003) the principal public holidays in Mozambique are:
1 January New Year's Day
3 February Heroes' Day
7 April Women's Day
1 May Labour Day
25 June Independence Day
7 September Victory Day
25 September Revolution Day

INTERNET ACCESS

These days even fairly small towns have well-functioning Internet cafés. The going rate is around US$2 per hour.

MONEY

Mozambique's unit of currency is the metical (plural – meticais).

Mozambique has a remarkably efficient network of ATMs operated by the Banco Internacional de Moçambique (BIM). There's one in every major town and they all accept Visa, but not MasterCard.

You can change US dollars cash into meticais at most banks without paying commission. Traveller's cheques don't work well in Mozambique – few banks are willing to change them, and when they do they always demand to see the original receipts, and charge enormous rates of commission.

POST & TELEPHONE

International mail takes about two weeks to reach Europe and costs a lot – US$1.10 for a postcard.

There are telephone (TDM) offices in all major towns. If you have a mobile phone handset with you, you can buy a prepaid line from the MCEL mobile company for about US$10, then top it up with scratch-cards sold in the gaudy yellow shops that have appeared on even the dustiest streets countrywide.

VISAS

Visas are required by all visitors and can be bought on most borders (but *not* the Tanzania border) or arranged in advance. One-month single-entry visas cost US$20 to US$40.

Visa Extensions

Visas can be extended at the immigration offices in provincial capitals.

Visas for Onward Travel

Visas for neighbouring countries are available from embassies in Maputo (see p774 for address details).
Malawi Visas cost US$15/40/55 for transit/single/multiple entry and are usually issued within 24 hours. Open from 8am to noon.
South Africa Visas are generally issued within 24 hours. Open from 7am to 11.45am.
Swaziland Visas cost around US$5 and are issued within 24 hours. Open from 8am to 11am.
Tanzania Visas cost US$20 to US$50 depending on nationality, and are issued within 24 hours. Open from 8 to 11am.
Zambia Visas cost US$25 and are generally issued within 24 hours. Open from 8am to noon and 2pm to 5pm.
Zimbabwe Visas cost US$30/45/55 for single/double/multiple entry, and are generally issued at point of entry only.

MOZAMBIQUE

Malawi

HIGHLIGHTS

- **Lake Malawi** A paradise of untouched, remote islands where you can paddle while listening to the shrill call of fisheagles floating across the waves (p797)
- **Nyika National Park** A rolling plateau filled with zebras and antelopes, and views down into the hazy plains of the Rift Valley (p786)
- **Mt Mulanje** Steep winding paths lead to cool, grassy plateaus speckled with wildflowers and hemmed in by rocky peaks (p793)
- **Liwonde National Park** On the Shire River you can cruise past hippos, or take a wildlife drive through the park to spot elephants, antelopes, hyenas and lions (p795)
- **Off the beaten track** The *Ilala* lake ferry is like a journey back in time, carrying its fascinating cargo and uncomplaining, squashed passengers to isolated lakeshore villages (p781)

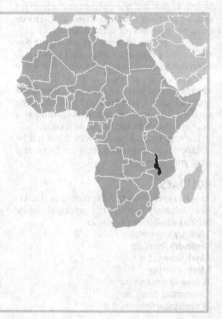

FAST FACTS

- **Area** 118,484 sq km
- **ATMs** only in main cities
- **Borders** Tanzania, Mozambique, Zambia; all main border crossings are open from 6am to 6pm
- **Budget** US$15 to US$25 a day
- **Capital** Lilongwe
- **Languages** English, Chichewa
- **Money** Malawi kwacha; US$1 = MK90
- **Population**: 11 million
- **Seasons** cool and dry (May–Aug); hot and dry (Sep–mid-Nov); hot and wet (mid-Nov–Apr)
- **Telephone** country code ☎ 265; international access code ☎ 101
- **Time** GMT/UTC + 2
- **Visas** free (for most nationalities) for 30 days, issued at point of entry

Malawi's ever-changing landscape takes you from the top of lofty mountains, down steep escarpments, through woodland, farmland and dry empty grassland, to the shores of a magnificent lake. Above the soft beaches fish eagles call from baobab trees, and bright tropical fish dart through the sparkling waves below. Fishermen balancing on their dugout canoes paddle home with their catch, calling across the water. Elsewhere, uniformed schoolkids skip home trailing their bags in the dust, and cyclists wobble past balancing precarious loads of firewood, furniture or struggling goats on their solid steel back-racks. Colourful crowds throng around marketplaces, and African music blares from pokey village bars.

HISTORY
Early Settlers
The settlement of Malawi began with the great Bantu migrations of the 14th century. In the 17th century several groups arrived from Central Africa including the Tumbuka who settled in the north, and the Maravi, or Chewa, who settled in the south. In the early 19th century Zulu people, now known as Ngoni, arrived from South Africa and settled in central and northern Malawi, and around the same time the Yao people from Western Mozambique settled in the south. Although the honour is usually attributed to the celebrated British explorer David Livingstone, the first Europeans to reach Malawi were Portuguese explorers in the 17th century. The 19th century brought with it the dark period of the East African slave trade when the inhabitants of Malawi were captured by slave traders and sold to Arabs at ports on the Indian Ocean.

Enter the British
In 1859, David Livingstone came tramping through the bush to Lake Malawi. When he pointed enquiringly at the lake, the local people told him it was called *nyasa*. Whether he realised that this simply meant lake in the local language isn't clear, but he promptly christened it Lake Nyasa. When the British later colonised Malawi, they called it Nyasaland.

Following in the footsteps of Livingstone came missionaries who brought the slave trade to an end and replaced it with the more 'civilised' principles of commerce and Christianity. It wasn't long before European settlers began arriving to establish tea and coffee plantations. Although the British had delivered the people from one form of slavery, in many ways they'd introduced another. Settlers took land away from locals, and when Nyasaland became a

WHAT'S IN A NAME?
During the autocratic rule of Dr Hastings Kamuzu Banda, it was easy to remember the names of landmarks as they all bore his ceremonial name: Kamuzu Bridge, Kamuzu Highway, Kamuzu Hospital, Kamuzu Airport, Kamuzu Academy, Kamuzu Dam, Kamuzu View. These days there's more variety.

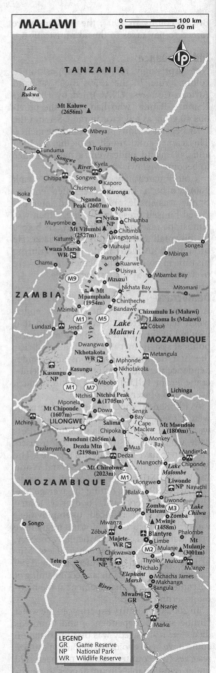

British colony in 1907, the Africans were forced to pay taxes to the administration.

Independence

Not surprisingly, this created opposition to colonial rule. In the 1950s the Nyasaland African Congress (NAC), led by Hastings Kamuzu Banda (who had spent the previous 40 years as a doctor in the USA and the UK), began a serious push for independence. This came, amid much rejoicing, in 1964 and Nyasaland underwent a name change to become Malawi.

Unfortunately, it became clear there wasn't going to be a 'happily ever after' ending. Banda was made president and later declared himself president for life, which was almost the case; he ruled for 30 years before his downfall and died three years later. He brought about many improvements during his time in power but his achievements were overshadowed by his stringent rule.

Democracy

A popular uprising in the early '90s ended when Banda agreed to a referendum that resulted in the introduction of a multiparty political system in 1993. The following year the first democratic elections since independence were held, and the United Democratic Front (UDF), led by Bakili Muluzi, acceded to power.

With Banda gone, the political prisons were closed, freedom of speech and print was permitted, and Banda's notorious dress code, which forbade women to wear trousers and men to have long hair, was repealed. The Muluzi government also made several World Bank and IMF-backed economic reforms, which, by 1996, were hitting the average Malawian citizen very hard. Food prices soared as subsidies were reduced; unemployment was officially recorded at 50% but might have been higher; and crime, particularly robbery, increased in urban areas. Nevertheless, Muluzi was re-elected as president in May 1999 despite opposition politicians complaining of corruption and mismanagement at the highest government levels.

In 2002 the country experienced the worst famine since independence, and hundreds died. The real tragedy was that the situation could have been avoided had Malawi's maize reserves (the country's staple) not been sold under questionable circumstances to neighbouring countries by a senior government official. While his fellow citizens were dying of hunger, the official was being promoted to a more senior position.

The next elections are due in 2004, and already democracy, which was so long in coming to Malawi, is looking very frail. The government seems determined to amend the constitution to allow for a third presidential term. It is believed that those in power are desperate to retain it to avoid charges of corruption and mismanagement. A further sign that all is not well is the order police have received to prevent all public demonstrations. Clearly, Malawi's freedom of expression is once again at stake.

THE CULTURE

Most Malawians have a light-hearted, easy-going nature and a great sense of humour. Laughter is the usual reaction to anything confusing or unusual. Needless to say, tourists are often a source of gleeful distraction, and their slightest faux pas is always cause for great mirth, albeit in the nicest possible way. Ever obliging, Malawians will go out of their way to please you.

Malawi's rapidly growing population and its population density (93 people per sq km) are a worry. The country's natural resources are struggling to support everyone, and the inadequate infrastructure means that schools, hospitals and other social institutions are overflowing.

Christianity and Islam are the dominant religions, but old habits die hard so traditional superstitions and beliefs are still strong.

Malawians, like most Africans, have a conservative dress code. No Malawian who

---

A HAIRY STORY   Tione Chinula

The first time I saw a man with long hair I was a young girl living in Malawi. I was watching planes come in to land from the observation deck at the new international airport in Lilongwe. There was an audible gasp as a man with his hair pulled back in a long ponytail stepped off a flight from Europe. When he walked into the arrival hall after clearing customs and immigration, his beautiful ponytail was gone; his hair had been chopped off at the top of his collar.

can afford a pair of shoes will go barefoot, yet often tourists will walk through town barefoot and male tourists will walk around in public bare-chested. You won't see any Malawians behaving in this way, so why should you? To avoid offending people, even at the lake when you're away from the beach, make sure nothing you wear is too short or transparent or not there at all!

ARTS

Malawi is especially known for skilful wood-carvers who turn out beautifully crafted chairs and coffee tables. Getting these in your backpack will be tricky, but you can always post them home – especially the chairs, which conveniently come in two flat pieces. Candlesticks, walking sticks, bowls, bracelets and figurines make much more portable options.

The carvers are often willing to swap their crafts for T-shirts, caps or interesting gadgets and a bit of money. Carvings are sold in many places, and you'll find particularly good roadside craft stalls in Nkhata Bay, Senga Bay, Lilongwe, Liwonde and Blantyre.

ENVIRONMENT

Malawi, roughly 900km long and between 80km and 150km wide, is wedged into the southern tip of the Great African Rift Valley. Lake Malawi takes up about 20% of the country's total area of around 18,000 sq km. The lake aside, much of Malawi is savanna plains, rolling hills and river valleys. There are some spectacular mountain areas too, including Mt Mulanje, Nyika National Park and Zomba Plateau. In the higher areas, the climate is pleasant, with temperatures averaging around 20°C between November and April, and 27°C from May to October. On the lakeshore temperatures are higher. The rainy season lasts from October to March.

For a relatively small country Malawi has a large number of protected wildlife areas and varied wildlife including elephants, antelopes, zebras, big cats, hippos and lots of birdlife. Lake Malawi National Park also has many freshwater tropical fish species. There are five national parks (Liwonde, Lengwe, Nyika, Kasungu, and Lake Malawi around Cape Maclear) and four wildlife reserves (Vwaza Marsh, Nkhotakota, Mwabvi and Majete). Of these, Malawi's flagship park is Liwonde, which has a wide range of animals. The Nyika National Park and nearby Vwaza Marsh Wildlife Reserve are also popular.

TRANSPORT

GETTING THERE & AWAY
Air

Most international flights from Europe or other parts of Africa use Lilongwe International Airport, although a few regional flights go to/from Blantyre.

Regional destinations with direct flights to/from Malawi include Harare (Zimbabwe; US$200, one hour), Nairobi (Kenya; US$400, 2½ hours), Lusaka (Zambia; US$184, one hour), Johannesburg (South Africa; US$540, 2½ hours), Dar es Salaam (Tanzania; US$375, two hours) and Maputo (Mozambique; US$230, 2½ hours). Fares are all one-way. Even when two airlines serve the same route, fares are pretty much the same. Airline offices are listed on p785. British Airways flies between Lilongwe and London once a week. There are daily flights to Nairobi from Tuesday to Sunday from where you can continue to Europe. You can also connect with flights to Europe and Australia from Johannesburg.

Boat & Land

Malawi's Mchinji border post (and the corresponding border post at Chipata in Zambia) is open 24 hours. All other Malawi border posts officially open from 6am to 6pm. Main border posts are Songwe (to Tanzania), Mchinji (to Zambia), Mwanza (to Mozambique and Zimbabwe via Mozambique's Tete Corridor) and Nayuchi, Chiponde, Muloza and Marka (to Mozambique).

MOZAMBIQUE

The Lake Malawi passenger ferry *Ilala* (see p781) stops at Cóbuè and Metangula on the Mozambican mainland twice a week. There's an immigration post on Likoma Island where you get an exit stamp. In Cóbuè

DEPARTURE TAX

All passengers flying out of the country must pay a departure tax of US$30 (payable at the airport in US dollars only).

you can get a lakeshore pass for US$1.30, which allows you to spend 10 days in Mozambique.

You can also sail from Likoma to Cóbuè by dhow (US$0.80). To carry on to Metangula you can catch a motorboat (US$5, six hours) or a dhow (US$2.50, 36 hours).

Travelling by land, you have many options. To reach Mozambique south of the Zambezi River, a bus between Blantyre and Harare can drop you at Tete, from where buses go to Beira and Maputo.

For central Mozambique, daily buses go from Wenela bus station in Blantyre to Nsanje (US$2.80) and the Malawian border at Marka (US$3.30). It's a few kilometres between the border posts, and you can change money on the Mozambique side. From here pick-ups go to Mutarara and Sena.

For northern Mozambique, buses go from Blantyre, via Mulanje, to the Malawian border at Muloza (US$2). From here walk 1km to the Mozambican border at Milange, from where it's another few kilometres into Milange town. In the dry season from Milange trucks go to Mocuba, where you can find onward transport to Nampula or Quelimane.

Your other option for northern Mozambique is a minibus or *matola* (pick-up truck) from Mangochi to Namwera (US$2). Then take a bicycle taxi 10km to the Malawian border at Chiponde (US$2). It's then 7km to the Mozambican border post at Mandimba. From Mandimba there's usually a daily pick-up to Cuamba.

Yet another option is a minibus from Liwonde to the Malawian border post at Nayuchi (US$3). From Nayuchi, walk to the Mozambican border post at Entre Lagos (1km), where you catch a freight train to Cuamba. If there's no train, you might find a battered old pick-up heading to Cuamba, but there are very few vehicles on this route. You can also travel the Malawian section of this route by train: a passenger train departs Liwonde for the Mozambican border at Nayuchi at 8am Monday, Wednesday and Friday (US$1, four hours). Whichever mode you use, nonconnecting trains and limited transport mean the journey can take several days.

SOUTH AFRICA
Several bus companies operate between Blantyre and Johannesburg.

City to City (☎ 01-621346; ⊙ 7am-5pm) buses, run by Translux, depart Monday, Wednesday, Thursday, Saturday and Sunday (US$35, 24 hours).

Linking Africa (☎ 01-677045; ⊙ 7am-5pm Mon-Fri, Sat morning) has comfortable coaches leaving from Blantyre Lodge in Blantyre at 9am on Tuesday, Thursday and Saturday (US$44, 24 hours).

Munorurama (☎ 01-724563; ⊙ 7am-5pm) buses depart from the Council Resthouse near the main bus station in Lilongwe (US$39, 28 hours) at 5.30am on Wednesday and Saturday and go via Blantyre's Wenela bus station at around 9.30am (US$33, 24 hours) to Johannesburg. However, these buses are less comfortable than those of other bus lines, and are prone to breakdowns.

Translux (☎ 01-621346; ⊙ 7am-5pm) has comfortable coaches departing from the Petroda filling station on Haile Selassie Rd at 9am on Monday, Tuesday and Thursday to Saturday (US$44, 24 hours).

TANZANIA
Malawi's only land crossing to/from Tanzania is at Songwe, north of Kaporo. Two bus companies go the entire way between Lilongwe and Dar es Salaam.

Taquabal (☎ 09-933505; ⊙ 7am-7pm) buses leave on Monday and Friday at 7am from behind the market in Lilongwe, via Mzuzu and Mbeya (US$33, 26 hours). Travel time is often much longer than the scheduled time.

Taqwa (☎ 08-302431; ⊙ 7am-7pm) buses leave on Tuesday and Saturday at 7am (all other details are the same as Taquabal).

You can also catch a Shire Bus Lines bus from Mzuzu to Karonga (US$4), then take a minibus between Karonga and the border at Songwe (US$1.30). It's 200m to the Tanzanian border post; from here buses go to Mbeya (sometimes looping to Kyela – about 5km off the road).

ZAMBIA
The main border post with Zambia is east of Chipata, on the road between Lusaka and Lilongwe.

Direct buses to Lusaka leave from behind the market in Lilongwe three times a week (US$12, 24 hours), but they are slow, so it's best to do it in stages. Regular minibuses run between Lilongwe and the Malawian border post, about 2km west of Mchinji (US$2).

From here, it's 12km to the Zambian border post. Shared taxis shuttle between them for US$1.20 per person. From the Zambian post minibuses run to Chipata for US$1.

ZIMBABWE
Malawi does not directly border Zimbabwe, but a lot of traffic between these countries passes through Mozambican territory via Tete.

Munorurama (☎ 08-858461; ⏰ 7am-5pm) buses leave Blantyre's Wenela bus station for Harare at 7am (US$13, 10 hours, daily) and from Lilongwe's **Munorurama** office (☎ 01-724563; ⏰ 7am-5pm) at the Council Resthouse near the main bus station on Wednesday, Saturday and Sunday at 5.30am (US$17, 13 hours).

Zupco (☎ 01-636561; ⏰ 7am-5pm) buses leave Blantyre's Wenela bus station for Harare at 7am (US$13, 10 hours, daily).

GETTING AROUND
Air
Air Malawi (☎ 01-750747; New Building Society Bldg, Mandala Rd, Lilongwe; ⏰ 8.30am-5pm Mon-Fri) has daily flights between Lilongwe and Blantyre, for around US$72 one way, and four flights a week between Lilongwe and Mzuzu for the same price. Domestic flights can be paid for in kwacha; there's a US$2 departure tax.

Boat
Every week, the *Ilala* passenger ferry chugs up and down Lake Malawi between Monkey Bay and Chilumba, stopping at a dozen towns and villages. Contact **Malawi Lake Services** (☎ 01-587311; ilala@malawi.net; ⏰ 7.30am-noon & 1-4.30pm Mon-Fri). As this boat is the only means of transport to many villages it also carries cargo so expect delays (which could stretch to many hours) if there's a lot to load or offload. The schedules are listed in the following tables (only main ports shown).

ILALA SCHEDULE
Northbound

Port	Arrival	Departure
Monkey Bay	–	10am (Fri)
Chipoka	8.15pm	10pm (Fri)
Nkhotakota	5.30am	7am (Sat)
Likoma Island	5.20pm	7.30pm (Sat)
Nkhata Bay	5am	7am (Sun)
Chilumba	6.30pm (Sun)	–

Southbound

Port	Arrival	Departure
Chilumba	–	2am (Mon)
Nkhata Bay	2.45pm	8pm (Mon)
Likoma Island	3.15am	6.15am (Tue)
Nkhotakota	5.45pm	7.20pm (Tue)
Chipoka	2.50am	4am (Wed)
Monkey Bay	2pm (Wed)	–

The *Ilala* has three classes: cabins, which are the most comfortable way to travel; 1st-class deck, which is generally quite spacious, with seats and a small area of shade; and economy – the entire lower deck – dark and crowded, with engine fumes permeating from below.

The full fares from Monkey Bay to Chilumba are: cabins without/with bathroom US$72/94, 1st-class deck US$46, economy US$10. There's a restaurant for cabin and 1st-class deck passengers. Meals such as chicken curry cost US$5, and you can request vegetarian meals. On the economy deck food is served from a galley where you'll pay less than US$1 for a plate of beans, rice and vegetables. Reservations are usually required for the cabins. For other classes, tickets are sold on the day and nobody is refused – it just keeps filling up!

Local Transport
Most buses around Malawi are operated by **Shire Bus Lines** (☎ 01-756229; ⏰ 7am-5pm) and come in several different types: Coachline, a luxury nonstop service between Blantyre and Lilongwe, and Lilongwe and Mzuzu; Express, fast buses between the main towns with limited stops; and long-distance buses (more commonly called 'local' and sometimes 'ordinary') covering long-distance routes but stopping everywhere, so they're very slow. Express buses charge between US$1.50 and US$2 per 100km, and local buses slightly less. For the Coachline you can buy tickets in advance and have a reserved seat.

Most routes served by buses are also served by minibuses. These usually cost slightly more than the bus and are slightly faster. There are also minibus services around towns and to outlying villages, or along the roads that big buses can't manage. In Blantyre, Shire Bus Lines also runs city buses between Blantyre and Limbe and some suburbs.

As well as buses and minibuses, pick-up trucks known as *matola* operate in rural

MALAWI

areas. Some remote areas, such as Cape Ma-clear, are only served by *matola*. The price is roughly the same as a bus fare.

Train

Passengers rarely use trains because road transport is quicker. The main railway line is centred on Blantyre, and passenger trains run to/from Liwonde (north of Zomba) three times a week (US$1.30, five hours). A service between Limbe and Nsanje, in the south of Malawi, runs three times a week (US$1.30, six hours). The service of most use to travellers runs between Liwonde and Nayuchi on the border with Mozambique (see p780).

LILONGWE

pop 450,000

Lilongwe is scattered over a wide, flat plain with a few slopes that don't quite qualify as hills. Purple splashes of bougainvil-lea grow by the roadside, and landscaped roundabouts adorn intersections. In the busy city areas, battered minibuses careen precariously down the streets, and dented cars putter and splutter through clouds of dirty fumes. High-heeled women with elaborate hairdos trip along the uneven sidewalks, and men walk by companion-ably hand in hand.

ORIENTATION

Lilongwe has two centres, about 3km apart: City Centre (or Capital City), where you find airlines, offices and embassies; and Old Town, which has cheap hotels, the market and the bus station. Despite its rather formal and deserted feel, City Cen-tre is, nevertheless, quite a pleasant place surrounded by trees and parks. Old Town, with its crowded dusty streets, is a different scene altogether.

There's an airport shuttle bus that will drop you at Le Meridien Capital Hotel, Lilongwe Hotel or Kiboko Camp for US$5.50. It meets most international flights and stops outside the airport arrival terminal.

Local minibuses run between Old Town and Lumbadzi, about 3km from the airport, for less than US$1. A taxi from the airport into town costs about US$10. The fare is negotiable.

INFORMATION

Internet Access

To access the Internet, make phone calls, send faxes or make photocopies, the best place to go is a business centre that usually offers all of these facilities. **Celtel Plus Cyber Café** (☎ 01-772199; World Travel Bureau, Bisnowaty Centre, Kenyatta Rd; US$3.50 per hr) and **Salephera Business Bureau** (☎ 01-771391; ADL house, off Africa Unity Rd; US$7 per hr) are both in City Centre and have a fast connection. In Old Town, **Licom.net** (☎ 01-758438; Mandala Rd; US$5 per hr) is next to Harry's Bar & Restaurant.

Medical Services

The **Seventh Day Adventist Health Centre** (☎ 01-775680; Presidential Way), near the Area 14 Baptist church, provides good health care. **MARS** (Medical Air Rescue Service; emergency ☎ 08-823590; Ufulu Rd East, Area 43) deals with emergency evacuations. Both addresses are not far from City Centre.

Money

You will often get a better exchange rate at a bureau de change than at a bank. Change Point Forex Bureau, at the top of Mandala Rd in Old Town, has good rates. The Na-tional Bank of Malawi and Commercial Bank of Malawi are on Kamuzu Procession Rd in Old Town.

Post

There are post offices in City Centre (off Independence Dr) and Old Town (cnr Kamuzu Procession Rd & Mandala Rd). To receive poste restante mail, ensure that your letters are addressed specifically to either the Old Town or City Centre post offices.

Tourist Information

The **Tourist Information Office** (☎ 01-757584; Murray Rd, Old Town; ⏲ 7.30am-5pm Mon-Fri) is at the National Parks & Wildlife office. It has a few maps and brochures.

Travel Agencies

For domestic and international air travel there are several travel agencies including **Rennies Travel** (☎ 01-774144; renniestravel@mw.celtel plus.com) in ADL House, off Africa Unity Rd in City Centre, and **Ulendo Safaris** (☎ 01-754950; reservations@ulendo.net; Old Town Mall), off Chilam-bula Rd. The latter is also an agent for the *Ilala* lake ferry.

LILONGWE

0 | 1 km
0 | 0.5 mi

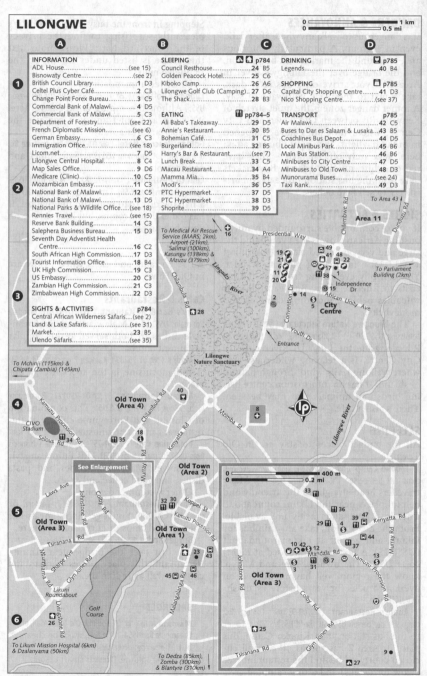

A

INFORMATION
ADL House..................................(see 15)
Bisnowaty Centre.......................(see 2)
British Council Library.................**1** D3
Celtel Plus Cyber Café................**2** C3
Change Point Forex Bureau.........**3** C5
Commercial Bank of Malawi.........**4** D5
Commercial Bank of Malawi.........**5** C3
Department of Forestry...............(see 22)
French Diplomatic Mission...........(see 6)
German Embassy........................**6** C3
Immigration Office.....................(see 18)
Licom.net.................................**7** D5
Lilongwe Central Hospital...........**8** C4
Map Sales Office.......................**9** D6
Medicare (Clinic)......................**10** C5
Mozambican Embassy................**11** C3
National Bank of Malawi.............**12** C5
National Bank of Malawi.............**13** D5
National Parks & Wildlife Office...(see 18)
Rennies Travel..........................(see 15)
Reserve Bank Building................**14** C3
Salephera Business Bureau.........**15** D3
Seventh Day Adventist Health
  Centre..................................**16** C2
South African High Commission...**17** D3
Tourist Information Office...........**18** B4
UK High Commission..................**19** C3
US Embassy..............................**20** C3
Zambian High Commission..........**21** C3
Zimbabwean High Commission....**22** D3

SIGHTS & ACTIVITIES   p784
Central African Wilderness Safaris....(see 2)
Land & Lake Safaris....................(see 31)
Market.....................................**23** B5
Ulendo Safaris..........................(see 35)

B

SLEEPING   p784
Council Resthouse......................**24** B5
Golden Peacock Hotel................**25** C6
Kiboko Camp............................**26** A6
Lilongwe Golf Club (Camping)....**27** D6
The Shack................................**28** B3

EATING   pp784–5
Ali Baba's Takeaway..................**29** D5
Annie's Restaurant....................**30** B5
Bohemian Café..........................**31** C5
Burgerland...............................**32** B5
Harry's Bar & Restaurant............(see 7)
Lunch Break.............................**33** D5
Macau Restaurant.....................**34** A4
Mamma Mia.............................**35** B4
Modi's.....................................**36** D5
PTC Hypermarket......................**37** D3
PTC Hypermarket......................**38** D3
Shoprite..................................**39** D5

C

DRINKING   p785
Legends...................................**40** B4

SHOPPING   p785
Capital City Shopping Centre......**41** D3
Nico Shopping Centre................(see 37)

D

TRANSPORT   p785
Air Malawi...............................**42** C5
Buses to Dar es Salaam & Lusaka...**43** B5
Coachlines Bus Depot.................**44** D5
Local Minibus Park.....................**45** B6
Main Bus Station.......................**46** B6
Minibuses to City Centre............**47** D5
Minibuses to Old Town...............**48** D5
Munorurama Buses....................(see 24)
Taxi Rank.................................**49** D3

MALAWI

DANGERS & ANNOYANCES

It is dangerous to walk anywhere after dark, even in a group. A particularly notorious area is around the market and bus station, and the bridge over the Lilongwe River in Area 2. If you arrive on a bus after dark, take a taxi to the place you want to stay. Another danger zone is the quiet stretch of Kenyatta Rd between Old Town and City Centre, where muggings have happened in broad daylight. Take a minibus or a taxi here. Take only official taxis – they have red-on-white number plates. Buy tickets only from the bus station office as con artists try to sell fake tickets.

SIGHTS & ACTIVITIES

If you're comfortable surrounded by noisy, bustling African crowds then you'll find the large and very animated **market** (Malangalanga Rd, Old Town) a fascinating place to wander. You can buy everything from roasted locusts to wheelbearings. But leave all your valuables behind, including cameras and moneybelts.

The **Lilongwe Nature Sanctuary** (☎ 01-773309; admission US$0.30; ⏰ 7.30am-5pm), off Kenyatta Rd, alongside the Lingadzi River close to City Centre, is a relaxing wilderness area where walking trails wind through natural bushland. It has an information centre listing birds and animals that may be seen. There's also a café.

SLEEPING

All the budget places to stay are in Old Town.

Kiboko Camp (☎ 08-828384; kiboko@malawi.net; camp site per person US$2.50, dm/d US$4/12) Many travellers head straight to this friendly and helpful place, near the Likuni roundabout. There's a bar, and meals are available. From the bus station, take any minibus for Likuni, and get off at Likuni roundabout (US$0.25). A taxi (recommended at night) costs US$2. The owners, Pim and Marga, know the region well having worked on overland trucks for years before establishing Kiboko.

Annie's Restaurant (☎ 09-930267; Conforzi Rd; camp site per person US$1.50, dm/d US$3/5.50) Closer to the bus station than Kiboko Camp, this place in Area 2 has rooms off a small enclosed courtyard behind the restaurant (see below for details) and a tiny camping area.

Stepping in from the busy street outside it's pleasantly surprising to find the privacy of the courtyard here. Please note that this venue is listed under Eating on the Lilongwe map.

Other recommendations:

Lilongwe Golf Club (☎ 01-753598; camp site per person US$5) Although camping is expensive here, it's clean and quiet and you can use the pool, bar and restaurant.

Golden Peacock Hotel (☎ 01-756632; Johnstone Rd; d with/without bathroom US$11/8) Safe, quiet and comfortable.

Council Resthouse (☎ 01-726820; d & tw from US$3, with bathroom from US$9) This large place is down a narrow dirt road opposite the market. It has old and new rooms, but keep an eye on your belongings.

EATING

All restaurants and cafés listed below are in Old Town.

Cafés & Restaurants

Harry's Bar & Restaurant (☎ 01-752201; Mandala Rd; mains US$1.50-4) Malawian and European-style dishes are both served at this popular restaurant and bar.

Modi's (☎ 01-757694; Kamuzu Procession Rd; US$3-5) Indian cuisine is the speciality at this place.

Macau Restaurant (☎ 01-750121; Portuguese Club, Selous Rd; mains US$3-5) The combination of Chinese and Portuguese cuisine at this restaurant might be unusual, but it works.

Bohemian Café (☎ 01-757120; Mandala Rd; snacks from US$1.50, mains from US$3) This European-style café serves salads, sandwiches and pasta dishes, and good coffee and cakes.

Other recommendations:

Annie's Restaurant (☎ 09-930267; Conforzi Rd; mains US$1.80-2.30) You'll get filling meals like chicken and chips or curry and rice here.

Burgerland (☎ 01-727294; Glyn Jones Rd; mains US$3-4) Just over the bridge near Annie's Restaurant, this place serves burgers and chips as well as Indian meals.

SPLURGE!

Mamma Mia (☎ 01-758362; Old Town Mall, off Chilambula Rd; US$4-10) It might not be cheap, but the excellent Italian meals here are worth the splurge. Dress is smart casual.

Quick Eats

Ali Baba's Takeaway (☎ 01-751523; Kamuzu Procession Rd; mains US$1-4) Serves pizzas and burgers for around US$3.

Delight Café (Kamuzu Procession Rd) Next to 7-Eleven by the Mchinji roundabout, this place is run by the people from Ali Baba's Takeaway and has similar fare and prices.

You can get cheap takeaways from **Lunch Break** (Kamuzu Procession Rd), a small place between Chilambula and Kenyatta Rds.

Around the market are several cheap food stalls selling hot potato chips and roasted meat. You might want to avoid the less-hygienic stalls.

Self-Catering

You can stock up on groceries at **Shoprite** (Kenyatta Rd), which has a wide selection of imported products, or the PTC Hypermarket in the Nico Shopping Centre across the street. There's another PTC Hypermarket in City Centre.

DRINKING

The **Shack** (☎ 01-759865; Chilambula Rd; ☽ 10am until late Tue-Sat) This busy bar next to the well-signposted Lingadzi Inn near Old Town attracts a happy mix of well-to-do Malawians and European expats (with many more of the latter). Wednesday evenings, when local teams meet to play volleyball on the outside court, are the best.

Legends (☎ 01-753612; ☽ 10am until late Mon-Sat) On the weekend, this popular bar and nightclub off Chilambula Rd is the best place to party. There's a pool competition and cheap beers on Wednesday night and a disco on Friday and Saturday night.

GETTING THERE & AWAY
Air

The following airlines have offices in the centre of Lilongwe:

Air Malawi (☎ 01-772132; www.airmalawi.net; ☽ 9am-5pm Mon-Fri)

Air Zimbabwe (☎ 01-772369; www.airzimbabwe.com; ☽ 8am-5pm Mon-Fri)

Kenya Airways (☎ 01-774227; www.kenya-airways.com; ☽ 8am-5pm Mon-Fri)

South African Airways (☎ 01-772242; www.flysaa.com; ☽ 8am-5pm Mon-Fri)

Shire Bus Lines runs luxury **Coachline** (☎ 01-758965; Kenyatta Rd, Old Town; ☽ 7.30am-5pm Mon-Fri, 8am-noon Sat) bus services twice a day between Lilongwe and Blantyre (US$16, four hours). There are three services a week between Lilongwe and Mzuzu (US$11, four hours). The Coachline leaves from the Shire Bus Lines main office opposite Shoprite in Old Town.

All other buses leave from the main bus station next to the market. **Shire Bus Lines'** (☎ 01-726334; main bus station, Mlangalanga Rd, Old Town; ☽ 7am-7pm) express buses run twice a day between Lilongwe and Blantyre (US$5, five hours) and Lilongwe and Mzuzu (US$6, five hours). A lakeshore bus between Lilongwe and Mzuzu (US$6, six hours) via Salima and Chintheche departs daily. A night bus to Karonga (US$8, 17 hours) via Mzuzu departs every evening. And there's a daily express bus to Monkey Bay (US$4, eight hours) via Mangochi.

Long-distance minibuses leave when full from behind the main bus station.

Several buses and international flights depart from Lilongwe (see p799).

GETTING AROUND

From Old Town, minibuses for City Centre (US$0.30) leave from Kenyatta Rd outside Shoprite supermarket. For other city areas, minibuses leave from the bus park near the market. In City Centre they leave from Independence Drive.

NORTHERN MALAWI

This section lists places north of Lilongwe beginning at the northern tip of Malawi.

KARONGA

This is the first town south of the border with Tanzania. The town is strung out for about 2km along the main street between a roundabout on the north–south road and the lakeshore. The **Cultural & Museum Centre** (☎ 01-362579; uraha@malawi.net) organises tours of local historical sites dating back to Karonga's slave trading and early missionary days. Payment is by donation.

The **Zgambota Resthouse** (s/d US$2.50/3), near the roundabout, has clean but basic rooms. Down by the lake, **Mufwa Lakeshore Lodge & Camping** (☎ 01-362390; camp site US$1, s/d US$3.30/5, with bathroom US$6.50/10) has clean simple rooms and a camp site with plenty of shade.

CHITIMBA

The beaches and clear waters of Lake Malawi at Chitimba are irresistible, especially if you've just travelled down from Tanzania. This is where you turn off the main north–south road to reach Livingstonia.

About 1km north of the Livingstonia turn-off is **Chitimba Beach Campsite** (kaya01@bushmail.net; camp site per person US$2, dm US$4, d with/without bathroom US$15/10; ❂), an overlanders' stop with a bar and restaurant.

About 5km north of Chitimba is **Mdokera's Beach Campsite** (camp site per person US$1.50, huts US$2). Cheap meals are available, and there's a visitors' book containing useful advice from previous travellers. If you want to wake up with the birds there are a couple of beds perched in trees overlooking the beach.

A minibus or *matola* between Chitimba and Mzuzu or Karonga will cost you around US$2.

LIVINGSTONIA

Perched on an escarpment about 800m above the lake, Livingstonia has some of the most spectacular views in Africa. This mission station and small town was founded by Scottish missionaries in 1894 and still exudes a quiet, bygone air.

Exhibits in the fascinating **museum** in the Stone House tell the story of early European exploration and missionary work. Nearby, the **church**, built in Scottish style, has a beautiful stained-glass window depicting Dr Livingstone and his African companions.

You can walk to the spectacular **Manchewe Falls**, which cascade down a 50m drop, about 3km from town. If you're after a bit of hair-raising fun contact **Mickey Wild** (mickmitchel2001@yahoo.com), who organises abseiling and similar activities up the escarpment near Livingstonia.

On the escarpment road, **Lukwe Permaculture Camp** (☎ 01-332201; ecologique2000@hotmail.com; camp site per person US$2.50, d cabins from US$10) is a friendly and restful place. Meals featuring home-grown produce cost between US$1.50 and US$3. Coming up from Chitimba, you'll see signs to the camp beyond the top of the zig-zags on the escarpment road; it's a further one-hour walk to Livingstonia. Tours to Nyika National Park and Vwaza Marsh

Buses run here from Lilongwe and Mzuzu (see p785 & p787).

Wildlife Reserve can be arranged from US$25 per person.

The **Stone House** (☎ 01-368223; camp site per person US$1.50, dm/d US$2.50/10) has original Victorian furniture and superb views. Meals are available for around US$2, or you can self-cater.

If you have just staggered up the escarpment road, the **resthouse** (camp site per person US$1.25, dm/d US$2/3.80) is about 15 minutes closer than the Stone House. It also has great views but is dirty.

At Falls Grocery, on the escarpment road opposite the path to Manchewe Falls, the friendly shopkeeper, Edwin Kamanga, lets you pitch a tent for US$0.80.

From Chitimba on the main north–south highway, a steep dirt road goes up the escarpment in a series of acute hairpin bends. There's no bus, but there are occasional *matolas*. You'll wait a very long time if you're hitching. Your alternative is to walk up: this is about 25km and steep in places, so it takes about five hours from Chitimba if you follow the road. There are short cuts that reduce it to about four hours, but these are even steeper. Walking down takes three to four hours. In the past there have been reports of muggings on this road. Although the situation has improved, get an update from one of the places to stay in Chitimba or Livingstonia before you set off.

NYIKA PLATEAU

Shrouded in peaceful solitude amid an expanse of waving grass and rolling hills, the Nyika Plateau is protected by the **Nyika National Park** (admission US$5 per day). The plateau is home to the rare roan antelope as well as many other antelope species and grazing animals. The air is pure, and there's a special kind of beauty in the barrenness of the plateau. On clear days, the views from the edge of the plateau are endless. Although you won't see the bigger animals you see in other African parks, the distinctive feature of Nyika is its romantic landscape. As you approach, antelopes and zebras will watch warily from a distance or gallop off into the safety of the tall pine forests around the camp. Other animals at Nyika include warthogs, jackals, hyenas and leopards, and more than 400 species of birds.

You are not allowed to enter the park on foot, but once inside hiking is allowed. You can arrange 'trails' (wilderness walks) with a ranger from a day to a week long. Routes to the western escarpment overlooking Zambia or to Nganda Peak, the highest point on the plateau, are popular. Many travellers recommend the three-day walk from Chelinda to Livingstonia; you can walk down to the lakeshore at Chitimba on the fourth day.

The **Nyika Safari Company** (☎ 01-330180, reservations@nyika.com; horse-riding US$15 per hr, mountain biking US$5 per hr, wildlife drives US$20) offers various activities. Two-day hiking trails cost US$30 for two hikers, plus US$5 for each extra hiker. A three-day hike from Chelinda to Livingstonia costs US$80 for two people plus US$10 for each extra person. On horseback you can get up close to the antelope and zebra.

The only budget place to stay is **Chelinda Camp** (see the Nyika Safari Company; camp site per person US$5, self-catering cottage US$120). The camp site here has hot showers and a few covered shelters. It's about 2km away from the cottages and main office, bar and restaurant. The cottages (sleeping up to four) overlook a small dam.

The main park entrance is at Thazima Gate, 54km from the small town of Rumphi. To Chelinda it's another 55km. There is no public bus. The nearest you can get is Rumphi (reached from Mzuzu by bus or minibus for US$1.10), from where *matolas* run once or twice per day to Katumbi, via Nyika Junction, which is 8km from Thazima Gate. You can try hitching at the gate – but be prepared for a long wait.

Another way of reaching Chelinda, especially if you're in a group, is to hire a taxi or *matola* in Mzuzu or Rumphi. In the rainy season the roads are usually impassable for conventional vehicles.

Several tour companies organise trips to Nyika (see p799). The Nyika Safari Company can organise charter flights into the park (Mzuzu–Nyika US$115 per person one way) Depending on when you travel, discounted fares may be available so make sure you enquire.

VWAZA MARSH WILDLIFE RESERVE

Lying in a rich flood plain south of the Nyika Plateau, **Vwaza Marsh Wildlife Reserve** (admission US$5 per day) attracts a wide variety of animals and birds, including elephants (don't be surprised if they wander past your cabin), buffaloes, hippos, antelopes and zebras. All

tourist activities and accommodation are operated by the Nyika Safari Company (see p786) and camping rates are the same as for Nyika. Several tour companies organise trips to Vwaza (see p799), which is easier to get to than Nyika.

MZUZU

There's a nice small-town feel about Mzuzu, Malawi's third city. In October, the main avenue through town is covered in a thick carpet of purple jacarandas. If you've just come down from the Tanzanian border, you might want to make use of its banks, post office and PTC supermarket, all on Orton Chirwa Ave, the main street. The **Tourist Information Office** (Viphya Dr; ☺ 7.30am-noon & 1-5pm Mon-Fri) opposite the High Court can give you brochures and sells maps. Visiting the **Tanzanian (Ataifa) market** (M'Mbelwa Rd), with its neat rows of timber stalls, is an interesting shopping experience. Tanzanian traders come here to sell clothes, lengths of colourful cloth, hair accessories, beauty products and various knick-knacks.

To access your email, make phone calls or send a fax go to **Mzuzu Business Centre** (☎ 01-334372; C@fe.com; New Commercial Area), where Internet access costs US$13 per hour. The cybercafé also serves coffee and cake.

Sleeping

Mzuzu has a limited choice of budget tourist accommodation.

Flame Tree Guesthouse (☎ 01-333053; camp site per person US$2.20, dm US$4.50, d with/without bathroom US$14/9; mains US$2-3) This friendly place is the best budget guesthouse in town. It sits securely behind a brick fence not far from the bus station. The welcoming rooms open on to a quiet garden and rates include breakfast. From the bus station the turn-off is the first left on the road to the airport. A taxi from town costs around US$2.

CCAP Resthouse (☎ 01-330335; Boardman Rd; camp site per person US$0.70, dm US$3, d with/without bathroom US$11/7; mains US$1.50) This place has long, echoing corridors and sparsely furnished rooms. Still, there are mosquito nets, and it's only a short walk into town. Take a taxi here at night, and don't leave valuables in your room.

Mphatso Investment Motel (☎ 01-334205; s/d US$6/8, d with bathroom US$10.50; mains US$2) About 1km out of town beside the airport road is this motel. It has clean but spartan rooms and a rather formal feel.

Eating

Sombrero (M'Mbelwa Rd; mains US$2-3) It may not be Mexican, but the chicken curry (US$2.20) is excellent. Sombrero is set back from the road opposite the Mobil station.

Obrigado Leisure Park (Boardman Rd; mains US$1.70-2.80) This garden restaurant is by the clocktower roundabout. You can order a plate of chambo (a Lake Malawi fish – a local speciality), chips and salad or beef stew and *nsima* for US$2.

Another favourite is **Auntie's Take Away** (Orton Chirwa Ave; takeaways US$1-2.50), which serves great samosas and other takeaway food.

Getting There & Away

The **bus station** (☎ 01-330256; ☺ 7am-5pm) is on the western side of town, next to the market. Shire Bus Lines' express buses run twice daily between Mzuzu and Lilongwe (US$5.50, five hours) via Kasungu. A daily lakeshore express runs via Nkhata Bay (US$0.80, one hour) and Salima (US$5.50, six hours) to Blantyre (US$10, 12 hours). A local bus goes to Karonga daily (US$3.10). Minibuses to Nkhata Bay and Karonga also leave from the bus station. They are slightly more expensive. Tanzanian Taquabal and Taqwa buses also leave from here for Dar es Salaam four times a week (US$25, 21 hours).

The luxury Coachline leaves for Lilongwe (US$11, four hours) three times a week from Mzuzu Hotel. Sometimes there aren't enough luxury coaches to go round so Mzuzu often gets an express bus, but it's never overcrowded and it's faster than the 'normal' express bus.

Taxis park outside the bus station.

NKHATA BAY

The small, bustling town of Nkhata Bay is cradled among the hills of the northern lakeshore. In front of the town a peninsula where the *Ilala* passenger ferry docks juts into the lake. Although local 'tour guides' are a nuisance, Nkhata Bay is a lovely place to visit as it offers a good balance of activities and relaxation. There are no banks in town. There's a PTC supermarket and large produce and craft **market** in the centre.

The friendly **Aqua Africa** (☎ 01-352284; andy@aqua-africa.com; half-day windsurf/canoe hire US$5)

runs five-day beginners NAUI dive courses that include six dives (US$150). A single dive is a real bargain at US$15, including equipment.

Monkey Business (half-day canoe hire US$2.50), based at Njaya Lodge (see the following entry), organises two- to five-day kayak excursions for US$30, including tented accommodation and meals. Day trips cost US$10, including lunch and snorkelling equipment.

There used to be a wide choice of places to stay in Nkhata Bay, but a slump in tourist numbers has affected the trade, and a couple of previously popular places were up for sale when we visited. With luck you'll find them reopened when you visit. There are a few small places to stay in town, but most tourists complain of the noise and lack of security. It's best to head on through town, across the bridge past the prison and police station, and up over the hill. In the past, travellers have been hassled here. If you're uncomfortable about walking alone ask the place you're staying at for a watchman to accompany you.

Njaya Lodge (☎ 01-352342; easymail@sdnp.org.mw; camp site per person US$1.50, chalets US$4-20; mains US$1.50-4.50) Perched serenely on a hilltop above the lake, this place is legendary on the travellers' grapevine. The chalets range from simple without bathroom, to comfortable with bathrooms. The bar and restaurant open on to a wide terrace with a magnificent view. Restaurant specials include a Saturday barbecue and Sunday roast (US$4.20). For activities see Monkey Business (see the previous entry). If you're on foot, ignore the Njaya signpost by the road, which takes you the long way. Instead, follow the signs to Chikale beach and cut across to the lodge.

Mayoka Village (☎ 01-352421; info@mayok a-village.com; camp site per person US$1.10, dm US$2.50, huts per person US$4; snacks & mains US$1-3) This friendly backpackers has rooms, modelled on traditional village huts, built into a terraced hillside sloping down to the lake. Above the beach there's a bar and restaurant serving tasty snacks and meals. To save yourself the hot walk up the hill, arrange for a boat pick-up from town.

Chikale Beach Resort (☎ 01-352368; camp site per person US$1.10, s/d US$11/20 with breakfast; mains US$2.80) This place sits in a grassy hollow opening on to a lovely beach, but it's somewhat lacking in soul. It has neat thatched brick chalets and a beach bar and restaurant with a local atmosphere. Traditional dances are organised on the beach every Saturday from 2pm.

Aqua Africa (tw US$20) This diving club's white-washed buildings on the peninsula past the *Ilala* wharf have a peaceful view across the bay. There are two pleasant twin rooms opening on to a balcony above the lake. See p788 for diving information.

Near the *Ilala* wharf, the **Safari Restaurant** (mains US$1-2) serves snacks and nice cheap meals, including chicken and fish with rice or chips. There might be a lengthy interval between ordering and eating.

All buses and minibuses go from the bus stand next to the market. The fare to Mzuzu or Chintheche is US$0.80. To reach Lilongwe, either take the lakeshore express or go to Mzuzu and transfer (see p785 and p788). Many travellers also come or go on the *Ilala* (see p781).

LIKOMA & CHIZUMULU ISLANDS
These peaceful islands sit in the middle of Lake Malawi cut off from the outside world. Missionaries settled here in colonial times, and their legacy – a huge **Anglican Cathedral** – is a major landmark on Likoma Island. With its beautiful beaches Chizumulu Island is the perfect hideaway where you'll meet few other tourists. The two islands are within the territorial waters of Mozambique but are part of Malawi.

When you walk around, remember that the people live a very traditional way of life, so keep your clothing and behaviour suitably modest.

Mango Drift (kaya01@bushmail.net; camp site per person US$1, dm US$3, s/d chalets US$4/8; mains US$3) sits on a beautiful sandy beach on the west side of Likoma Island. There's a bar and restaurant overlooking the lake. It organises four-day PADI Open Water diving courses for US$150 or a single dive for US$25.

Chikondano Restaurant near the market serves tasty Malawian dishes for less than US$1. Ordering in advance might prove rewarding, but don't expect a huge menu.

On Chizumulu, the main place to stay is **Wakwenda Retreat** (camp site per person US$2, dm/s/d US$2.50/4/6; mains US$2.50), with very friendly staff and a gorgeous beach. There's a bar and restaurant.

Likoma and Chizumulu are served by the *Ilala* passenger ferry, which also docks at a couple of Mozambican lake ports (see p781). Local boats sail between them, but if you want to visit both islands, it's best to go to Chizumulu first. Likoma is not far from the Mozambican shore and the town of Cóbuè.

CHINTHECHE
Kilometres of unspoilt beach stretch out along the serene Chintheche strand far from the bustle of Nkhata Bay. The tiny town of Chintheche is about 40km south of Nkhata Bay. Although the village sits beside the main road away from the lake, all the tourist establishments are right on the lakeshore.

Places to stay here are listed as you go south from Chintheche, where there is a small PTC supermarket. You can't go wrong with your choice as all the places have equally beautiful lakeshore settings.

Flame Tree Lodge (☎ 01-357276; camp site per person US$2.25, d US$17; mains from US$2) About 2km south of Chintheche village, and another 2km along a dirt track, this quiet lodge sits on a beautiful promontory jutting into the lake. It has chalets with bathrooms under large shady trees and an open bar and dining area that overlook the lake.

Nkhwazi Lodge (camp site per person US$2, d US$22) This is yet another lovely spot 1km further along the road from Chintheche Inn, then a few kilometres along a track. It has garden chalets and a bar and dining area overlooking a small sandy cove.

Makuzi Beach (☎ 01-357296; makuzibeach@sdnp.org.mw; camp site per person US$5, s/d US$29/46, with bathroom US$59/91; mains US$4) About 3.5km off the main road along a sandy track, this place has chalets dotted around a grassy garden. There are also a restaurant and bar opening on to a deck that overlooks a picturesque cove. It prides itself on its cuisine (mains US$4), and room rates include breakfast. Activities include kayaking, mountain biking and sailing.

Kande Beach Camp (☎ 01-357376; camp site per person US$2, dm US$3.80, chalet with/without bathroom US$20/11) This place, about 7km from the Makuzi turn-off, is popular with overland trucks. It's got a wide beach and an attractive thatched bar, restaurant, chalets and dorms. The evenings here are long and animated. Activities include sailing, kayaking and horse-riding. Aquanuts Dive School offers a four-day PADI Open Water course for US$180. A single dive costs US$25 including equipment.

The Lilongwe-Mzuzu express lakeshore bus passes through Chintheche (around US$1.50 from Mzuzu and US$5 from Lilongwe). Another way to get here is by minibus, from Mzuzu, Nkhata Bay or Salima. From Nkhata Bay it should cost less than US$1. *Matolas* also run along the lakeshore road.

SENGA BAY

This is a small town at the eastern end of a broad peninsula that juts into the lake from Salima. The clear water and wide sandy beaches are inviting, and you can go windsurfing, snorkelling and canoeing on the lake. You can also go hiking in the nearby Senga Hills. It's best to hire a local guide to show you the way, not least because of isolated incidents of robbery and harassment. Bird-watching in the area is excellent. However, note that this is one of the higher risk areas for bilharzia (see p1034).

All the following places to stay have nice sandy beaches.

Steps Campsite (☎ 01-263222; camp site per person US$5) At the end of the main street, next to the top-end Le Meridien Livingstonia Beach Hotel, is this gorgeous camp site. There's good security and spotless bathrooms (but no hot water). It sits peacefully at the end of a private beach where a rocky headland juts into the water. You can use the hotel bar and restaurant, but they are expensive.

Cool Runnings (☎ 01-263398; coolrunnings@malawi .net; camp site per person US$2, dm/d US$5/20) This comfortable, relaxed place has a cottage and

colourfully decorated dorms. It's all set in a garden with a thick lawn and lots of shade fronting on to the beach. There's a quiet bar and restaurant, and you can hire bicycles (US$5 per day) and windsurfers (US$2 per hour). Boat and catamaran tours can also be arranged. The turn-off is just before the Senga Bay shops.

Red Zebra Restaurant (snacks & mains US$1-4) This restaurant serves breakfast (US$1.50) and tasty meals, including burgers and omelettes (US$3) and fresh fish and chips (US$3.50). Tea is served in beautiful china cups and saucers. It's just before the Le Meridien Livingstonia Beach Hotel main gate.

Wheelhouse Marina (☎ 09-960266; camp site per person US$2, walk-in tents per person US$5) This tranquil place is on a secluded headland at the end of a dusty road. There's a large round bar over the water where you can order burgers and fish meals from US$1.50. The turn-off is on the right after the airfield before you reach Senga Bay. It's a very long walk over to the other side of the bay, past the army base, and hitching can be slow.

First, get to Salima – from Lilongwe it's easiest to take a minibus (US$1.50, 1½ hours). From Mzuzu and Blantyre, see p788 & p793. Minibuses run between Salima and Senga Bay for US$0.70.

SOUTHERN MALAWI

All places in this section are south of Lilongwe. Except for Mulanje, towns are listed heading north from Blantyre.

BLANTYRE
pop 490,000

Sitting tranquilly among the gentle contours of hills, Blantyre is surrounded by mountains and tall gumtree plantations. Although traffic trickles through crowded streets, its cheerful old buildings and tree-lined roads, coupled with the scent of eucalyptus and its cool climate, make Blantyre a relaxed and attractive city.

Orientation

Malawi's commercial capital, Blantyre was named after a town near Glasgow in Scotland, the birthplace of David Livingstone. The city is spread out along Chilembwe Hwy to the point where it merges into its

BLANTYRE CITY CENTRE

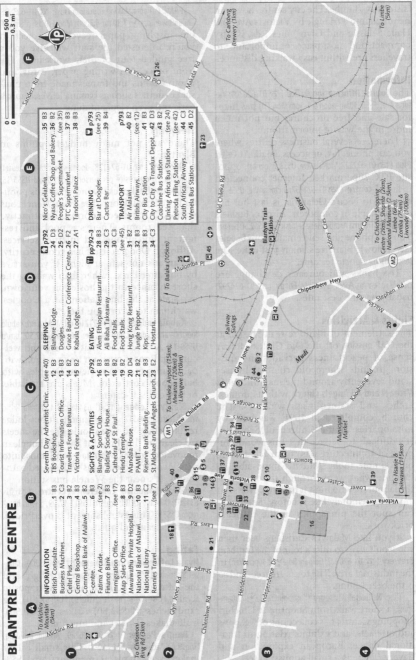

INFORMATION
British Consulate	**1** B3
Business Machines	**2** C3
Celtel Plus	**3** B2
Central Bookshop	**4** B3
Commercial Bank of Malawi	**5** B2
E-centre	**6** B3
Fatima Arcade	(see 2)
Finance Bank	**7** B3
Immigration Office	(see 17)
Map Sales Office	**8** B3
Mwaiwathu Private Hospital	**9** D2
National Bank of Malawi	**10** B3
National Library	**11** C2
Rennies Travel	(see 7)
Seventh Day Adventist Clinic	(see 40)
TBS Bookshop	**12** B3
Tourist Information Office	**13** B3
Travellers Forex Bureau	**14** B2
Victoria Forex	**15** B2

SIGHTS & ACTIVITIES (p792)
Blantyre Sports Club	**16** B3
Building Society House	**17** B3
Cathedral of St Paul	**18** B2
Hindu Temple	**19** B2
Mandala House	**20** D4
PAMET	**21** B2
Reserve Bank Building	**22** B3
St Michael and All Angels Church	**23** E2

SLEEPING (p792)
Blantyre Lodge	**24** D3
Doogles	**25** D2
Grace Bandawe Conference Centre	**26** F2
Kabula Lodge	**27** A1

EATING (pp792–3)
Alem Ethiopian Restaurant	**28** B3
Ali Baba Takeaway	**29** B3
Food Stalls	**30** C3
Food Stalls	(see 45)
Hong Kong Restaurant	**31** B2
Jungle Pepper	**32** B3
Kips	**33** B3
L'Hostaria	**34** C3
Nico's Gelateria	**35** B3
Nyasa Coffee Shop and Bakery	**36** B2
People's Supermarket	(see 35)
PTC Supermarket	**37** B3
Tandoori Palace	**38** B3

DRINKING (p793)
Bar at Doogles	(see 25)
Cactus Bar	**39** B4

TRANSPORT (p793)
Air Malawi	**40** B2
British Airways	(see 12)
City Bus Station	**41** B3
City to City & Translux Depot	**42** D3
Coachline Bus Station	**43** B2
Linking Africa Bus Station	(see 24)
Petroda Filling Station	**44** C3
South African Airways	**45** D2
Wenela Bus Station	**45** D2

'sister city', Limbe. The city centre, however, hemmed into a triangle by Victoria Ave, and Haile Selassie and Glyn Jones Rds, is very compact, and most places of importance to travellers are within easy walking distance.

Information

The **Tourist Information Office** (☎ 01-620300; Victoria Ave; ✆ 7.30am-noon & 1-5pm Mon-Fri) has maps for sale and free brochures but not much more in the way of information.

There are several business centres where you can phone, fax, or access email. At **Celtel Plus** (☎ 01-622222; Victoria Ave; US$3.50 per hr), opposite PTC supermarket, Internet connection is fast. **E-centre** (☎ 01-621157; Victoria Ave; US$5 per hr), next to Nico's Gelateria, is fast but has only a couple of computers. Also try **Business Machines** (Fatima Arcade, Haile Selassie Rd; US$2.50 per hr). You can phone and send emails from **Doogles** (see below). Blantyre's main **post office** (Glyn Jones Rd) has poste restante.

The banks and bureaux de change are on Victoria Ave. **Victoria Forex** (☎ 01-624799) usually has the best rates.

Sights & Activities

The settlement of Blantyre really began at the **CCAP mission** off the Old Chileka Rd. A sense of peacefulness pervades the mission grounds where old colonial houses stand reverently around the magnificent **St Michael and All Angels Church** with its domes, arches and stained glass windows. The church, completed in 1891, was built by missionaries of the Church of Scotland. It's difficult to believe that this wonderful piece of architecture was constructed using only simple tools. And it's impossible to imagine what went through the minds of the labourers who built it having never seen anything remotely like it before. See if you can spot the pineapples in the intricate brickwork.

If you like Malawi's Carlsberg beer then you won't want to miss a tour of the **Carlsberg Brewery** (☎ 01-670022; Gomani Rd; ✆ 2.30pm Wed) in the industrial area. The tours are free, and so is the beer tasting.

The **National Museum** (Kasungu Cres; ✆ 7.30am-5pm), a short walk from Shoprite at Chichiri Shopping Centre, has collections of weapons and artefacts, and exhibits relating to traditional dance, European exploration and slavery. There is a small admission fee.

PAMET (Paper Making Education Trust; ☎ 01-623895; Chilembwe Rd; ✆ 7.30am-4.30pm Mon-Fri) is a small but inspiring paper-recycling project. If you're interested the staff will give you a free guided tour of their workshop. The front office sells writing paper, cards, and photo albums and frames made from unusual materials such as banana leaves, baobab bark and even elephant dung.

Sleeping

There are not many budget options in Blantyre.

Doogles (☎ 01-621128; doogles@africa-online.net; Mulomba Pl; camp site per person US$3, dm/d US$5/15; 🖥) Most backpackers end up at this popular hostel next door to the main Wenela bus station. It has cheery dorms and attractive thatched rooms. There's a pool and restaurant, and phone and Internet services. Although Doogles itself has good security, the area is not safe at night. If you arrive by bus after dark, rather than walking the short distance to the hostel on your own, ask staff at the bus station for a Doogles' watchman to escort you there.

Kabula Lodge (☎ 01-621216; off Michiru Rd; kabula lodge@yahoo.com; camp site per person US$2.50, dm/d US$6/17) A quiet place that's warm and welcoming. Rooms open on to a veranda with panoramic mountain views. Doubles with bathrooms cost extra. Meals are available, or you can self-cater.

Blantyre Lodge (☎ 01-634460; Old Chileka Rd; d with bathroom US$12) This unpretentious lodge requires that 'no-one should use the sheets for cleaning the shoes'! It has tiny but clean renovated rooms with fans and mosquito nets. Avoid the old rooms with shared bathrooms. It's near the Wenela bus station.

Grace Bandawe Conference Centre (☎ 01-634267; Old Chileka Rd; dm/s/d US$11/17/29, d with bathroom US$33) This establishment is overpriced, but it's clean and quiet.

Eating

Nyasa Coffee Shop and Bakery (☎ 09-965200; Hanover St; mains US$1-6) The pastries are light and the coffee good at this relaxed café opposite Ryalls. It serves fresh quiche (US$2.50), big sandwiches (US$3.50), cakes (US$0.50), fruit shakes (US$2) and much more.

Jungle Pepper (☎ 08-826229; Apollo Building, Lingstone Ave; mains US$1.50-4) This small eatery makes excellent pizzas (medium from US$3, large from US$3.50). Other dishes include lasagne (US$3.50) and steak rolls (US$2). It's closed on Wednesday.

Ali Baba Takeaway (☎ 01-621560; Haile Selassie Rd; mains US$1-5) This takeaway serves great chicken shwarmas (US$2.50), pizzas (US$4.50), meat pies (US$1) and burgers (US$2).

Alem Ethiopian Restaurant (☎ 01-622529; Victoria Ave; ☽ lunch; mains US$2-4) For good Ethiopian food this is the place to go.

Kips (☎ 01-635247; Hanover Ave; mains US$1.50-5) A clean and friendly place, Kips serves breakfast (from US$1.50), chicken, fish, steak, burgers and chips (from US$2), and medium pizzas (US$4).

Nico's Gelateria (Victoria Ave; ice cream from US$2) This café next to People's supermarket has yummy but pricey Italian ice creams, cappuccinos (US$2.50) and milkshakes (US$4).

L'Hostaria (☎ 01-625052; Chilembwe Rd; mains US$3-12) You'll be served expensive but tasty Italian cuisine at this veranda restaurant set in a small garden.

Tandoori Palace (☎ 01-634508; Hanover Ave; mains US$1.50-4) This Indian restaurant is next to the Reserve Bank. You can order chicken tandoori (US$2) and naans and chapatis (US$0.50).

Hong Kong Restaurant (☎ 01-620859; Robins Rd; US$3-10) Malawi's oldest Chinese restaurant is a long-time favourite. These days, however, it gets mixed reviews.

For cheap eats and those not too fussy about hygiene, food stalls around the main bus station near Doogles; at the city centre bus station; and on Chilembwe Rd sell chips or grilled meat for less than US$0.50.

Shoprite (Chichiri Shopping Centre, Chilembwe Hwy) is a well-stocked supermarket.

PTC supermarket (Victoria Ave) and **People's supermarket** (Victoria Ave) are also good.

Drinking

The bar at **Doogles** (Mulomba Pl) is a popular local rendezvous (see p792). There's live music about once a week, and the Kiwi owners also organise cultural evenings with traditional dance and music.

Cactus Bar (Lower Sclater Rd) is another popular venue that's open late.

Getting There & Away

Blantyre's Chileka airport is about 15km north of the city centre. For details of flights to/from Blantyre see p779.

The luxury **Coachline** (☎ 01-623048; Hanover St; ☽ 7.30am-5pm Mon-Fri, 8am-noon Sat) bus runs twice a day between Blantyre and Lilongwe (US$16, four hours). It leaves from its booking office next to Ryalls Hotel.

Shire Bus Lines' (☎ 01-636561; Wenela bus station, Old Chileka Rd; ☽ 7am-7pm) express buses run to Lilongwe twice daily (US$5, five hours). There are also two daily express services to Monkey Bay (US$3.20, 6½ hours) via Zomba (US$0.90, 1½ hours), Liwonde (US$1.30, three hours) and Mangochi (US$2.45, 4½ hours), and to Mulanje (US$1.10, two hours). A daily lakeshore express runs to Mzuzu via Salima and Nkhata Bay (US$10, 12 hours). You can get local buses to Mulanje, Zomba and Monkey Bay from the Limbe bus station.

Long-distance minibuses depart when full from outside the Wenela bus station.

Getting Around

You can catch local minibuses to Limbe and various Blantyre suburbs from along Haile Selassie Rd or a **Shire Bus Lines** (City Bus Station, Browns Rd) city bus. There are taxi stands outside the main Wenela and City Bus Stations and at the big hotels.

MT MULANJE

Found near the southern tip of Malawi, Mt Mulanje rises regally above a rich green carpet of tea plantations. The mountain scenery is stunning, and the hiking here is relatively easy, although you need a reasonable level of fitness. After the initial ascent, which is quite steep, the tracks mainly follow rolling grassland plateaus unless you decide to climb to the higher peaks. On the plateaus there are clear mountain streams from which you can drink and swimming holes where you can cool off in the icy water.

Hiking

This is one of the finest areas for hiking in this part of Africa. There are clear paths up the mountain and several huts. Although you can hike up and down in two days, you'll appreciate it more if you spend at least three days hiking. Weather conditions can deteriorate rapidly so take warm, waterproof gear.

Mt Mulanje is a forest reserve so you need to register at **Likhubula Forest Station** (☎ 01-467718), about 15km from Mulanje town, at the foot of the main ascent path. There's no admission charge, but this is where you pay hut fees and arrange guides and porters if required. Porters cost US$6 per day and you'll need to supply food rations for them. The tourist attendant has a list of registered (and reliable) porters. For up-to-date information contact the **Mulanje Mountain Conservation Trust** (☎ 01-466282; mmct@malawi.net), a recently set-up environment and development trust.

Sleeping

At the foot of Mt Mulanje is Mulanje town, which has a few places to stay.

Mulanje Motel (☎ 01-466245; d with/without bathroom US$7/3) This is a simple establishment downhill from the bus station.

Mulanje Golf Club (☎ 01-466260; camp site per person US$3.80) You may camp at this club on the eastern side of town.

At the village of Likhubula, about 15km from Mulanje town, are two more options:

Likhubula Forest Lodge (☎ 01-467737; likhubula@cholemalawi.com; camp site per person US$5, s/tw US$12/15) This spotless lodge has a kitchen, lounge and twin bedrooms.

Likhubula CCAP Mission (camp site per person US$1, s/d US$7/13) The mission is not far from Likhubula.

On Mt Mulanje there are several **forestry huts** (camp site per person US$0.80, huts per person US$1.30), each with a caretaker. You provide your own food, cooking gear, candles, sleeping bag and stove (although you can cook on the fire – wood is provided). The only place you're allowed to camp on the mountain is outside the huts.

Getting There & Away

Buses and minibuses to Mulanje town go to/from Blantyre and Limbe (see p793). The dirt road to Likhubula turns off the main Blantyre-Mulanje road at Chitikali, about 2km west of the centre of Mulanje town. From Chitikali, irregular *matolas* run to Likhubula (US$0.50).

ZOMBA

This charming town is lined with beautiful old trees and is nestled at the foot of Zomba Mountain. Its old colonial buildings lend it character, and the cool climate and streams running down from the mountain give it a pleasant atmosphere. Until the mid-1970s it was the political capital of Malawi. You'll find banks, shops, a post office and a PTC supermarket along the main road. On the main road south of town is the striking brick **WWI memorial tower**. If you turn down the street beside the mosque, you come to the busy bus station and market. The colourful market, selling fresh produce, is an interesting place to wander. The rest of Zomba basks in peace and quiet.

The mist-shrouded **Zomba Plateau**, hovering protectively above the town, has fantastic views of the surrounding plains, hills and lakes and is a favourite with hikers. Queen's View and the Emperor's View are particularly impressive. There's no bus up here, so you'll have to hitch or take a taxi (around US$8). You can walk, but there have been reports of occasional attacks on lone hikers.

Caboodle Coffee Shop (☎ 01-524138; Main Rd; snacks from US$0.50, mains from US$3) If you crave a cappuccino or home-made meals, this café, opposite the Petroda petrol station on the main road, is the best place to go. It serves stuffed baked potatoes (US$0.50), toasted sandwiches (US$3.50) and cakes (US$1). It also sells crafts and has information on local accommodation and activities.

Ndindeya Motel (d US$4, s/d with bathroom US$4.50/5) This is a good, cheap place to stay near the bus station. With the bus station on your left, walk to the end of the road and turn left, then almost immediately turn right down the dirt road between the roadside stalls. It's clean, but the area is noisy. The restaurant serves chicken or beef stew and rice for US$1.

Avoid the Council Resthouse opposite the bus station, as it had filthy toilets on our last visit.

Up on Zomba Plateau, all the places to stay have hot showers, which is imperative in this cool mountain climate.

Chitinji Campsite (☎ 09-915143; njussab_2000@yahoo.com; camp site per person US$2.20, s/d US$4.50/9) Once you reach the top of the plateau, it's an 8km walk to this camp site. There's plenty of information on hiking on the mountain, and if you don't have a tent you can hire one for US$3.30.

Kuchawe Trout Farm (☎ 01-525271; tw US$18) This fish farm tucked into a mountain hollow has a small cosy cottage with two twin rooms overlooking the fish ponds. It has a sparsely equipped self-catering kitchen and a friendly caretaker to help with the cooking. There's also a nice picnic area beside a stream, which has covered shelters and tables. To visit the farm or picnic area, there's a US$0.50 admission fee per person plus US$1.10 if you have a vehicle.

As the name suggests, **Forest Campsite** (camp site per person US$0.80) sits in a forest near the top-end Le Meridien Ku-Chawe Inn.

Zomba is on the main road between Blantyre and Liwonde. There are frequent minibus services between Limbe and Zomba (US$0.90, 1½ hours). Buses and minibuses run to Liwonde several times a day (US$0.80, 1½ hours).

LIWONDE

This town flanks both banks of the wide Shire River where the river is straddled by a barrage. Liwonde, on the east side of the river, is 6km from the Liwonde National Park main gate. There's a PTC supermarket where you can stock up on groceries if you're heading into the park. If you need to stay the night, **Liwonde Park Motel** (☎ 01-542338; s/d US$9/9.50; mains US$1.50-4) on the main street through town, next to the shops, is convenient. It's enclosed by a brick wall. The rooms are plain but clean, and the restaurant mainly serves chicken. In a quieter location overlooking the river is **Warthogs** (☎ 01-542426; camp site per person US$2.20, s/d US$9/13; mains US$4). It's on the eastern riverbank, signposted from the barrage. It has two-storey brick thatched rondavels, a small pool and an upstairs thatched bar with a river view.

Riverboat River Safaris (☎ 01-542552; colin_sue@malawi.net), based on the western riverbank, runs river safaris to the national park. A 2½-hour cruise is US$28 per person. In the low season it offers reduced prices. Return boat transfers to Mvuu Camp (see below) cost US$120 per one or two persons. The more passengers, the cheaper the fare.

Liwonde is where you catch the train to Nayuchi at the Mozambique border (see p779).

LIWONDE NATIONAL PARK

A few kilometres south of Lake Malawi, **Liwonde National Park** (admission US$5 per day) is a fine wilderness area. A boat trip on the wide Shire River, which meanders lazily through the park, is a great way to explore. You can watch floating islands of weed slip past on the smooth current, birds building

their nests in the reeds, snorting hippos and snoozing crocs. As well as its river-dwelling creatures, Liwonde is known for its large elephant population. You'll also see plenty of antelope species (including sables, impalas, bushbucks and kudus) and warthog. If you're lucky you might even spot a lion or leopard. There's also a rhino-breeding programme close to Mvuu Camp. It's best to visit in the dry season (May to November), when the roads are more accessible and the animals easier to spot.

Sleeping

Mvuu Camp (☎ 01-771393; info@wilderness.malawi.net; camp site per person US$8, s/d US$50/70) Run by Central African Wilderness Safaris, who has an office in Lilongwe, this beautiful camp is perched on the riverbank in the northern part of the park. It has comfortably furnished chalets and roomy walk-in tents with bathrooms. There's a large thatched restaurant and bar overlooking the river, and the staff are welcoming. For an all-inclusive rate that includes all meals plus a wildlife-spotting drive and boat safari (but not the park admission fee) you'll pay US$170/260 per single/double per day. If you're not after the all-inclusive option, you'll save money by self-catering because the meals (breakfast US$8, lunch US$11, dinner US$15) aren't cheap. A fully equipped kitchen is available, and a cook is on hand to help. In the low season (mid-Jan–mid-Apr) the camp offers substantial discounts. Wildlife drives and boat safaris are US$18 per person.

Chinguni Hills Lodge (☎ 01-635356; chinguni@africa-online.net; s/d US$40/80) This friendly lodge is a more-affordable option than Mvuu Camp. It's just 3km inside the main gate. Room rates include meals but are cheaper if you are self-catering, and a kitchen is available. Between January and May rates are lower. The lodge is accessible in a conventional vehicle all year and the lodge runs transfers to/from Liwonde town for US$2.50 per person one way. Activities include wildlife drives (US$15) and river safaris (US$12.50).

Njobvu Cultural Village (US$50) To experience a night or two in a traditional Malawian village, stay with this friendly community, 6km from the western park boundary. There's a hut set aside for visitors, and the villagers organise traditional dances and prepare local dishes for guests. If you arrange the visit through Central African Wilderness Safaris (see p799), you'll pay US$50 per night. Although it's money well spent as it's then paid to the village, it's cheaper if you simply turn up as you can usually negotiate the price down to US$10. For more details on staying here you can also enquire at Mvuu Camp (see p795).

Getting There & Away

The main park gate is 6km east of Liwonde town. There's no public transport, but hitching is possible. From the gate to Mvuu Camp is 28km (although the road is impassable in the wet season).

The park's other entrance is reached via a dirt road (open all year) from Ulongwe, a village between Liwonde town and Mangochi. You can drive the 14km to the car park by the river, although you'll need a 4WD in the wet season. If you don't have wheels, take a minibus from Liwonde to Ulongwe (US$0.70, 20 minutes), then take a bicycle taxi (around US$2, one hour) to the jetty. You might have to hire two bicycles if you have a heavy pack. The car park is 1km beyond the park gate, near the riverbank and jetty; you hoist a flag, and a boat from Mvuu comes to pick you up. This service is free if you're staying at Mvuu Camp.

You can also get to Mvuu by boat from the Liwonde barrage. The camp does river transfers (US$20 per person) or you can go with Riverboat River Safaris (see p795).

MONKEY BAY

This small port, at the southern end of Lake Malawi, is home to a large and animated monkey population. It's also home to the esteemed *Ilala*, the trusty passenger ferry that's been chugging slowly up and down the lake for more than 50 years. Many travellers arrive in town or depart on the *Ilala*. From the deck you'll get a unique view of Malawi as the ferry calls at isolated villages, loading and offloading its intriguing cargo of fish, bicycles, goats and furniture.

Monkey Bay is also the gateway to Cape Maclear. If you're waiting in Monkey Bay, the people at Ujeni's Café, on the main street, will know when the next transport is due. They also serve drinks and snacks, and have information on accommodation and local tours in Monkey Bay. There's a PTC

supermarket but no banks – Ujeni's Café can advise on changing money.

Venice Beach (☎ 01-587250; camp site per person US$1.70, dm/s/d US$2.20/3.30/5.50; 🖳) This place, where you can lie in a hammock under a thatched bar and contemplate the beach, the sky and the water, is a 20-minute walk from town. Sociable travellers will like this place. The restaurant serves fish and chips, or fish or beef stew with rice, for US$2.80. If you're feeling too cut off from the world, you can access the Internet or use the phone.

K-Lodge (☎ 09-911723; camp site per person US$2.20, s/d US$8/17) in Nkhudzi Bay, 18km from Monkey Bay, is a more-tranquil place than Venice Beach, and is ideal for couples or families. It's set in a garden with a lush green lawn and plenty of shade. From the cool bar and lounge area above the beach you can watch the amusing antics of Bubu the diving dog, who's even appeared on German TV. Activities include sailing (US$4.50 per half day) and water biking (US$1.10 per hour), or you can use the snorkelling equipment for free. If you're arriving by minibus get off at the Nkhudzi Bay turn-off and walk the last 3km.

There are daily bus services between Monkey Bay and Blantyre and Lilongwe (see p785 and p793). Minibuses run between Monkey Bay and Liwonde several times a day (US$2, three hours). Minibuses also run to Blantyre (around US$3.50). You can also go to/from Monkey Bay on the *Ilala* ferry (see p781).

THE ILALA GETAWAY MAGAZINE

Each week, with the grace and style of yesteryear, the good ship *Ilala* steams out of Monkey Bay for the northern lake, village-hopping all the way. When we dropped anchor the scene was so saturated with metaphor and historical allusion it was difficult to believe it was real – and that we were in the 21st century.

CAPE MACLEAR

The view as you arrive at Cape Maclear is spectacular. A hilly landscape scattered with boulders and baobabs sweeps down to a long white beach and sparkling bay. At one end of the bay is **Chembe Village**, where fishing and tourism are the main activities. At the other end is Lake Malawi National Park. Although fewer tourists come here than in the past, it's still a must on many travellers' itineraries. It's easy to understand why as you watch the sun set across the lake, with islands silhouetted against a glowing sky.

Sights & Activities

Much of the lakeshore around Cape Maclear and several offshore islands are part of **Lake Malawi National Park** (admission US$5 per day). The road ends at the park headquarters. The bush in the park is home to shy rock dassies, monkeys, baboons, birds and also snakes. There's also an interesting museum explaining the formation of the lake and the evolution of its unique fish.

Cape Maclear has several traditionally sacred sites. One such site is the **Mwala wa Mphini** (Rock of Tribal Facial Scars), where a curious criss-crossed pattern of lines has been tattooed by the elements into a large weathered boulder. It is about 5km before the national park entry gate on the right-hand side, about 100m back from the main road. It's indicated by a small white sign.

Down a path to the left just before the park gate, several wooden crosses mark the **Missionary Graves** where a number of early evangelists who succumbed to malaria were buried.

You'll probably be besieged by young men calling themselves tour guides who try to sell you hikes in the bush or trips to nearby islands. If you're interested, they'll most likely quote you very high prices so be prepared for some tough negotiation. The Ministry of Tourism is conducting workshops to train the men as proper tour guides and might be establishing set prices for activities. So standards should improve. Some of the places to stay can recommend a guide so it's best to enquire at these places first.

You can hire or borrow snorkelling gear from most of the places to stay and tour

operators. **Otter Point**, in the national park, is a popular place to snorkel because of its dozens of small colourful fish.

Kayak Africa (☎ 09-942661; letsgo@kayakafrica.co.za; single/double kayaks US$5/10 per half/full day) You can hire kayaks here or do a guided day trip (US$30). This company also runs two- or three-day kayaking trips staying in tented camps on picturesque islands (US$120). Many travellers who have done the trip say it was the highlight of their Malawi holiday.

Kayak Africa Scuba Diving (☎ 09-942661; letsgo@kayakafrica.co.za), at Kayak Africa, and **Scuba Shack** (☎ 09-934220; scubashack@africa-online.net; Stevens Resthouse, Chembe Village) both run PADI Open Water four- or five-day beginners' courses for US$195. A single dive costs US$25, including equipment. This is one of the cheapest places anywhere in the world to go diving.

Sleeping & Eating

Places here are listed from west to east. You can walk to them either along the beach or along the main sandy street through the village, which runs parallel to the beach. They all have small simple rooms and usually serve fish or chicken meals with rice or chips for US$1.50 to US$2.

Emmanuel's (camp site per person US$1.10, s/d US$2.50/4.50) This is a small, pleasant place where you can relax in peace. The rooms are cramped, but it's a lovely camping spot. It has a small restaurant and bar on the beach. The owners also run **Thumbi Island Camp** (tents per person US$25) on the island across the bay. It has large walk-in tents. The price includes the US$5 park admission fee as the island is part of the national park.

Thomas's Grocery, Restaurant and Bar (mains US$1-2.50) Although there's a tranquil lake view at the back of the building, this place faces the village's main street, which is also quite tranquil in a different way. The menu has a tantalising choice of Italian and other Western dishes as well as Malawian specialities. They might not all be available, however, but you should be able to get a plate of fish and chips (US$1.50) or spaghetti fish salad (US$1.80).

Stevens Resthouse (☎ 01-587514; camp site per person US$0.50, s/d US$1.70/2.50) This was the first place in Chembe Village to open up to backpackers more than 20 years ago. These days it's looking very neglected. It has a shabby bar and restaurant.

Chikondi Resthouse (camp site per person US$1.20, dm US$1.70, s/d US$2.30/3.50) The rooms are set in a U-shape around a shady courtyard. You can laze in a hammock or a thatched beach lounge. It's run by a couple of young and motivated Israeli women who've set up a community AIDS education and orphan care programme. The profits from Chikondi (meaning love) are used to fund the programme. There's plenty of work for guests who want to volunteer.

Fat Monkeys (☎ 09-948501; camp site per person US$1.10, d US$5.50) This place is considerably larger than the others listed here. There's plenty of space for camping, although if you're staying in the rooms it's a bit of a hike to the bathrooms. It has a big bar and restaurant overlooking the lake, and it also hires kayaks (US$5/10 per half/full day).

Getting There & Away

Cape Maclear sits on the southern lakeshore, about 20km by road from the town of Monkey Bay. To go here, you first need to get to Monkey Bay (see p796). From Monkey Bay, *matolas* run to Cape Maclear a few times a day (US$0.90, one hour). In Monkey Bay, the people at Ujeni's Café can show you where to catch the *matola*.

MALAWI DIRECTORY

ACCOMMODATION

There aren't many backpackers hostels in the cities, but there are quite a few along the lakeshore. Prices range from US$3 for a dorm bed up to about US$8 per person for a room. Camping is about US$2.

Most towns have a choice of low-budget lodgings, although these are generally spartan and some are not very clean. Prices range from US$1 to US$5.

In national parks accommodation is usually more expensive; camping ranges from US$5 to US$8 and rooms cost around US$35 per person. Self-catering facilities are usually available at national parks and along the lakeshore.

ACTIVITIES

Active, adventurous travellers can try diving or kayaking in the lake; mountain-biking or horse-riding in Nyika National Park; and hiking on Zomba Plateau or, if you're feeling really energetic, on Mt Mulanje. To enjoy Malawi at a more leisurely pace you can go wildlife spotting on a driving safari, snorkelling among colourful fish in the lake or simply lazing in the sun on a soft beach.

DANGERS & ANNOYANCES

Although Malawi has long been regarded as one of the safest African countries in which to travel, this is gradually changing, especially in tourist areas such as Lilongwe, Zomba, Blantyre, Nkhata Bay and Cape Maclear. Lilongwe is particularly notorious. Crime has not yet reached alarming levels, but you do need to keep your wits about you. See the specific warning on p784.

EMBASSIES & CONSULATES

The following embassies are in Lilongwe:
Canada (☎ 01-651450; Accord Centre, Limbe, near Blantyre)
France (☎ 01-775265; off Convention Dr, German Embassy Bldg)
Germany (☎ 01-772555; germanemb@malawi.net; off Convention Dr)
Mozambique embassy (☎ 01-774100; off Convention Dr); consulate (☎ 01-643189; 1st floor Celtel Bldg, Rayner Ave, Limbe, near Blantyre)
South Africa (☎ 01-773772; sahc@malawi.net; Kang'ombe Bldg) Next to Capital City Shopping Centre.
UK (☎ 01-772400; bhc@lco.gov.uk; off Convention Dr)
USA (☎ 01-773166; consularlilongwe@state.gov; off Convention Dr)
Zambia (☎ 01-772590; off Convention Dr)
Zimbabwe (☎ 01-774988; zimhighcomllw@malawi.net; off Independence Dr)

For locations of other embassies, see the map of Lilongwe, p783.

In Africa, Malawia has diplomatic representation in the following countries: Kenya, Mozambique, Namibia, South Africa, Tanzania, Zambia and Zimbabwe.

HOLIDAYS

As well as religious holidays listed in the Africa Directory (p1003), these are the principal public holidays in Malawi:
16 January John Chilembwe Day
3 March Martyrs' Day
1 May Labour Day
14 June Freedom Day
6 July Republic Day

October Mother's Day, on 2nd Monday
December National Tree Planting Day, on 2nd Monday

LEGAL MATTERS

Although cannabis is widely available in Malawi, it is an offence to sell, purchase or consume it. There are severe penalties for its possession.

MEDIA

The *Daily Times* and the *Nation* are the main national daily newspapers. Major international papers and magazines are available in bookshops in the cities. The Malawi Broadcasting Corporation, the national radio station, broadcasts news and programmes in English, Chichewa and a few other Malawian languages. The national TV station broadcasts local news. Most of its programmes come from other African channels.

MONEY

The unit of currency is the kwacha (MK), which is made up of 100 tambala. The best foreign currencies to carry are US dollars, British pounds and South African Rands. You'll find a few ATMs at banks in Lilongwe, Blantyre and Mzuzu. Very few places outside main cities accept credit cards. Most banks and bureaux de change don't charge a commission for changing cash, but there's usually a 1% commission for changing travellers cheques. When enquiring about prices from restaurants, hostels and tour operators, make sure you ask whether the price you're quoted includes all taxes. Except for towns where there are no banks or bureaux de change, the black market is virtually nonexistent.

Bargaining

When buying crafts from roadside stalls, bargaining is part of the game. You can also negotiate with taxis, bicycle taxis and anyone you're hiring transport from before you accept the transport. In produce markets, however, the price is often not flexible so don't try to bargain too hard.

POST

Sending mail is more reliable if it's posted from cities. Some letters get from Lilongwe to Europe in three days, but others take three weeks. Poste restante is available in Blantyre and Lilongwe.

TELEPHONE & FAX

The best place to make a phone call is from a business bureau. These bureaus usually offer phone, fax, Internet and photocopying facilities. International calls (to destinations outside Africa) cost around US$8 for a three-minute minimum.

There are no telephone area codes within Malawi. However, when making national calls, all land lines are preceded by 01 unless you're calling a northern region number from within the northern region (areas north of Kasungu). This might change, however. Mobile phone numbers are preceded by 08 or 09. When calling from outside Malawi drop the initial 0.

TOURIST INFORMATION

There are tourist information offices in Mzuzu, Lilongwe and Blantyre that dispense a few brochures and sell maps but do not have much in the way of information. Most backpackers places have more-detailed information boards, and many can help guests to organise tours and activities.

TOURS & SAFARIS

Malawi's organised budget safari scene is much smaller than, say, Kenya's or Tanzania's, but backpackers do have a few options. The following operators are all based in Lilongwe.

Barefoot Safaris (☎ 01-707346; barefoot@malawi .net) This company, based in Likuni on the road to Mchinji, runs tailor-made tours to Malawi's national parks and to neighbouring countries. A four-day all-inclusive safari to South Luangwa National Park in Zambia costs US$350.

Central African Wilderness Safaris (☎ 01-771393; Bisnowaty Centre, City Centre; info@wilderness.malawi.net) As well as running several lodges, including Mvuu Camp in Liwonde National Park, this company organises tours in Malawi and to Zambia's South Luangwa National Park. A four-day camping safari to South Luangwa starts at US$250.

Kiboko Safaris (☎ 08-828384; kiboko@malawi.net) Specialising in budget tours, Kiboko's (see Kiboko Camp on p784) safaris include Nyika and Liwonde National Parks as well as Mt Mulanje. A one-week tour costs between US$275 and US$315. It also runs tours to South Luangwa National Park in Zambia.

Land & Lake Safaris (☎ 01-757120; Bohemian Café, Mandala Rd; landlake@africa-online.net) This company offers budget and mid-range safaris to South Luangwa National Park and various parts of Malawi. A four-day trip to Mulanje costs US$225. It also arranges car hire, sells hiking equipment and runs some forest resthouses.

VISAS

Citizens of Commonwealth countries, the USA and most European nations (except Switzerland) receive an automatic 30-day tourist visa at the point of entry at no cost.

Visa Extensions

Extensions are easy to arrange at the immigration offices in Blantyre (☎ 01-623777; Chilembwe Rd) or Lilongwe (☎ 01-753661; Murray Rd, Old Town). Visa extensions are free for most nationalities. A visa can be extended twice for up to a month at a time.

Visas for Onward Travel

Visas for the following neighbouring and near-neighbouring countries can be obtained in Lilongwe (see p798 for embassy and consulate information). All the embassies require visa applications and collections in the morning, although sometimes you can collect visas in the afternoon as well.

Mozambique Transit visas cost US$5 and are issued within 24 hours. One-month single-entry visas cost US$10 and take a week, although a four-day service costs US$15 and next day US$20. A three-month multiple-entry visa is US$30.

South Africa Visas are free and take two days to issue, or you can obtain them at the border.

Tanzania There is no diplomatic mission for Tanzania in Malawi. Visas are issued at the border or on arrival at the airport and cost US$50.

Zambia Visas are issued on the same day, if you come early, but costs depend on your nationality: British nationals pay US$42 for a single entry; most others pay US$25. Visa applications can be made only on Monday, Tuesday and Wednesday mornings. Passport collection is on Friday morning. You can also obtain them at the border at Chipata. If you'll be doing a tour or activity with a Zambian tour operator while you're in Zambia they can organise a visa fee waiver for you. These need to be arranged one to two weeks in advance. Some Malawi tour operators who offer trips to South Luangwa can also arrange them (see p799).

Zimbabwe Single-entry visas cost US$30 (US$55 for British nationals) and take a week to issue, but most nationalities can obtain a visa at the border, so it's not essential to go to the embassy.

Zambia

HIGHLIGHTS

- **Victoria Falls & Batoka Gorge** These mesmerising falls will get your adrenalin pumping for daring adventure activities on the Batoka Gorge below, or a more sedate option above the falls (p815)
- **South Luangwa National Park** One of southern Africa's best wildlife viewing experiences is in this beautiful national park, home to an impressive variety of wild animals (p811)
- **Lower Zambezi National Park** The tranquil Zambezi River is perfect for a paddle past yawning hippos and a close-up view of wildlife on the river bank (p815)
- **Kuomboka ceremony** This rich and colourful festival follows the Lozi as they accompany their king on an annual ceremonial journey (p819)
- **Off the beaten track** The serene lakes, hidden waterfalls and vast wilderness areas in north-eastern Zambia will take you away from the hectic pace of modern society (p813)

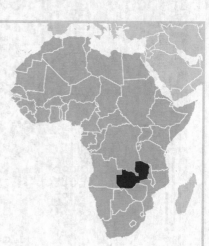

FAST FACTS

- **Area** 752,615 sq km (about three times larger than the UK)
- **ATMs** only in main cities
- **Borders** Tanzania, Malawi, Mozambique, Zimbabwe, Botswana, Namibia; Angola – risky because of land mines; Congo (Zaïre) – risky because of armed conflict;
- **Budget** US$15 to US$25 per day
- **Capital** Lusaka
- **Languages** English, Bemba, Tonga, Nyanja, Lozi
- **Money** Zambian kwacha; US$1 = ZK5000
- **Population** 10.4 million
- **Seasons** cool & dry (May–Aug), hot & dry (Sep–Nov), hot & wet (Dec–Apr)
- **Telephone** country code ☎ 260; international access code ☎ 00
- **Time** GMT/UTC + 2
- **Visas** US$25 for 90 days, issued at point of entry

Zambia's intrigue lies in its natural simplicity: its remote, untamed wilderness areas, tranquil scenery and friendly, easy-going people. Its most famous tourist attraction is undoubtedly the majestic Victoria Falls, which it shares with neighbouring Zimbabwe. But further inland lies a mysterious, isolated wilderness, which unravels itself to reveal hidden waterfalls, languid rivers that become swollen brown torrents, rich concentrations of wildlife and unending bush. Zambia's remoteness has preserved the strong culture of its

ZAMBIA

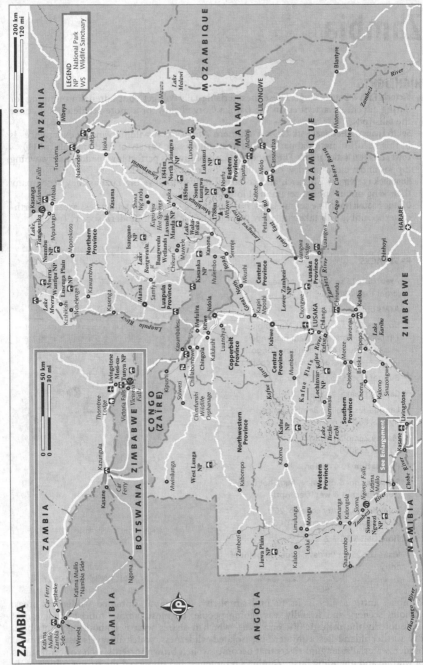

LEGEND
NP   National Park
WS   Wildlife Sanctuary

0   200 km
0   120 mi

0   50 km
0   30 mi

people, who still observe ancient traditional ceremonies. The transition from traditional to modern can be startling. A potholed road winding endlessly through deserted valleys and hills suddenly becomes a fast smooth highway whizzing you into a bustling city and a confusion of sounds and smells. The limited tourist infrastructure means there are bound to be a few hiccups, but it's all part of the fun and, in the likely event of a problem, Zambians always find a solution. When you arrive in this vast isolated country, the only thing you're guaranteed is an authentic African adventure.

HISTORY
Early Migrations
Zambia was originally inhabited by hunter-gatherer Khoisan people. About 2000 years ago Bantu people migrated here from the Congo basin and gradually absorbed or displaced the Khoisan. From the 14th century more immigrants came from the Congo, and by the 16th century various dispersed groups consolidated into powerful tribes or nations with specific territories and dynastic rulers.

The first Europeans to enter the area were Portuguese explorers in the 1790s. Centuries earlier, Swahili-Arab slave-traders had penetrated the region from the east coast of Africa.

The British explorer David Livingstone travelled up the Zambezi in the 1850s. He hoped to introduce Christianity and commerce to combat the horrors of the slave trade. In 1855 local people showed him a magnificent waterfall they called 'Mosi-oa-Tunya' (smoke that thunders). To Dr Livingstone, however, Victoria Falls seemed a more appropriate name.

The Colonial Era
In 1890 the area became known as Northern Rhodesia and was administered by the British South Africa Company, which empire-builder Cecil John Rhodes owned. In the late 1920s vast deposits of copper ore were discovered, and mines were established. Migrant labour was introduced and effectively became obligatory as taxes were imposed on local people, and their land was taken by European settlers for farming. Northern Rhodesia was put under direct British control in 1924.

Independence
In the 1950s African nationalism became more dominant, and the United National Independence Party (UNIP) was founded by Kenneth Kaunda. Northern Rhodesia became independent in 1964 when it assumed the name Zambia. Kaunda was made presi-

dent and remained in power for the next 27 years, largely because in 1972 he declared UNIP the only legal party and himself the sole presidential candidate.

Over the years, however, government corruption and mismanagement coupled with civil wars in neighbouring states left Zambia's economy in dire straits. This inevitably led to increased unemployment and crime. Violent street protests against increased food prices in 1990 were quickly transformed into a general demand for multi-party politics. Full elections were held in October 1991, and Kaunda and UNIP were resoundingly defeated by Frederick Chiluba and the Movement for Multiparty Democracy (MMD). Kaunda bowed out gracefully, and Chiluba became president.

A New Political Era
With backing from the International Monetary Fund (IMF) and World Bank, financial controls were liberalised to attract investors. But austerity measures were also introduced – and these were tough for the average Zambian. Food prices soared, inflation was rampant and state industries were privatised or simply closed, leaving many thousands of people out of work. For most Zambians, things were even worse than the 1980s.

By the mid-1990s, the lack of visible change gave Kaunda the confidence to re-enter the political arena. He attracted strong support but withdrew from the November 1996 elections in protest at MMD irregularities. Chiluba won a landslide victory and remained in firm control – sometimes too firm. Shortly after the election, two monitors who had claimed the elections were rigged were arrested, and some journalists were suspended from their jobs, apparently because their coverage of the MMD's victory had not been sufficiently enthusiastic. However, most Zambians accepted the result, in the hope that at least the country would remain peaceful.

ZAMBIA

Although Chiluba tried to amend the constitution to enable himself to run for a third term, he was unsuccessful. In 2001 Levy Mwanawasa, the new MMD leader, was elected Zambia's third president. Mwanawasa has set a strong precedent by supporting an investigation into alleged charges of corruption and misappropriation of funds against Chiluba. The former president is rumoured to have squirreled away millions in overseas bank accounts. Many Zambians see this as a positive step forward.

THE CULTURE

In Zambia anything that can go wrong usually will. But until it does, there's no point in worrying. Such is the calm philosophy you'll encounter among these friendly and laid-back people who live happily for the present. Zambians don't believe in becoming stressed, for what can be put off until tomorrow can wait. With this relaxed approach, they walk through life at a steady pace, meeting its joys with enthusiasm and its challenges with casual confidence.

Zambia has one of the lowest population densities in the world with only 14 people per sq km. More than 50% of Zambia's population lives in urban areas (mostly Lusaka and the cities of the Copperbelt). The majority of people are Christian, although many still adhere to traditional beliefs.

ARTS

Traditional ceremonies are still carried out in many parts of Zambia. They are usually loud and colourful events at which traditional dancers and musicians dress up in elaborate costumes made from animal skins or plant materials.

Lusaka galleries have fine collections of contemporary paintings. Wooden sculpture is another artistic outlet, and you'll see it exhibited in the southwestern part of Zambia around Livingstone. Since the sculptures are aimed squarely at the tourist market, you'll mainly find small wooden animals as well as towering giraffes.

ENVIRONMENT

Zambia is shaped like a contorted figure-of-eight, with an area of roughly 750,000 sq km. Much of the country is an undulating plateau, sloping to the south, which is broken by rivers and lakes.

Zambia has 19 national parks and 34 game management areas (GMAs). However, many are difficult to reach, and others don't contain much wildlife owing to decades of poaching, clearing and bad management. Since 1990, however, with the help of international donors, several of Zambia's parks have been rehabil.tated and the wildlife protected by projects that also aim to give local people some benefit from conservation measures. Zambia's parks are well known for walking safaris, and some, particularly South Luangwa, have a great diversity of wildlife.

TRANSPORT

GETTING THERE & AWAY

Zambia's main borders are open from 6am to 6pm. Chipata is open 24 hours and Victoria Falls to 10pm.

Most of the Zambian operators listed in this chapter can arrange a visa for you free of charge if you pre-book an activity with them. Contact them at least one to two weeks before you arrive. If you're arriving in Zambia via the Livingstone border this can be done at shorter notice. But as things can change, make sure you check the latest requirements before you arrive.

Air

Zambia's international airport is in Lusaka (about 20km from the centre of town), although some regional flights serve Livingstone (near Victoria Falls) or Mfuwe (South Luangwa National Park).

For information about airlines serving Zambia, see p810.

Boat & Land

Most border crossings are open from 6am to 6pm with the exception of Victoria Falls (to 8pm) and Chipata (open 24 hours).

BOTSWANA

The only crossing point between Zambia and Botswana is the vehicle pontoon (ferry)

DEPARTURE TAX

Passengers leaving on international flights must pay a departure tax of US$20 (payable in US dollars).

across the Zambezi at Kazungula, about 60km west of Victoria Falls. Pedestrians ride for free. Daily minibuses run between Livingstone and Kazungula (US$2.50).

CONGO (ZAÏRE)
The main border is near Chililabombwe, between Kitwe and Lubumbashi. However, owing to the conflict in Congo (Zaïre), this crossing is not considered safe.

MALAWI
The main border is 30km east of Chipata, between Lusaka and Lilongwe.

Buses travel on most days between the **CR Carriers** station (☎ 01-225633; ☼ 7.30am-5pm) in Lusaka and Lilongwe (US$12, 10 hours). These buses are slow, so most travellers do this trip in stages.

From Chipata regular minibuses run to the Zambian border post (US$1). The distance between the border posts is 12km, but shared taxis shuttle up and down for US$1.20 per person. From the Malawian border post, 2km west of Mchinji, minibuses run to Lilongwe (US$2.50).

MOZAMBIQUE
From Cassacatiza infrequent *chapas* (trucks) run to Matema. From there you can reach Tete.

NAMIBIA
The only border crossing is at the Zambian village of Katima Mulilo, on the west bank of the Zambezi River, near Shesheke. It's near the Namibian town also called Katima Mulilo. (Locals refer to 'Katima Mulilo Zambia side' and 'Katima Mulilo Namibia side'.)

Buses from Livingstone to Shesheke (US$7, four hours) depart in the mornings. You cross the Zambezi River by pontoon ferry (free for pedestrians) or canoe (US$0.20) to the west bank near the Zambian border post, then it's a short walk to the Namibian border post. From here to Katima Mulilo is 5km; a lift in a pick-up costs US$0.50.

SOUTH AFRICA
Although Zambia doesn't share a border with South Africa, several buses link Lusaka and Johannesburg.

CR Carriers (☎ 01-225633; ☼ 7.30am-5pm) leave from the CR Carriers station in Lusaka four times a week (US$37, 22 hours).

Linking Africa (☎ 01-234420; ☼ 7.30am-5pm) coaches leave five times a week from the distinctive Great China Wall complex by the South End Roundabout in Lusaka (US$41, 22 hours).

TANZANIA
If you're in northern Zambia, you can reach Tanzania by boat. A steamer called the MV *Liemba* on Lake Tanganyika departs Mpulungu on Friday, arriving at Kigoma (Tanzania) on Sunday, via other Tanzanian ports. Tanzanian visas are issued on the ferry and must be paid for in US dollars only (US$50). Fares from Mpulungu to Kigoma (US$55/40/35 in 1st/2nd/economy class) must be paid in Zambian kwacha, Tanzanian shillings or US dollars.

The main border crossing point to and from Tanzania is between Nakonde and Tunduma, on the Great North Road and the Tazara railway. Although buses do run from Lusaka to the border at Nakonde, the journey can be long, slow and uncomfortable, so most travellers take the train from Kapiri Mposhi in central Zambia to Dar es Salaam or to Mbeya in southern Tanzania. The Tazara station is called New Kapiri Mposhi, and is about 2km outside Kapiri Mposhi town.

There are two express services weekly each way. Trains depart from Kapiri Mposhi to Dar es Salaam at 3.10pm on Tuesday and Friday (US$34/24/15 in 1st/2nd/3rd class). The journey takes between 30 and 40 hours. In Lusaka, you can purchase your ticket in advance at **Tazara House** (☎ 097-884949; cnr Dedan Kimathi Rd & Independence Ave; ☼ 8.30am-12.30pm Mon-Fri, 2-3.30pm Mon, Wed & Thu). Students receive 50% discount. Buses from Lusaka to Kapiri Mposhi leave from the Intercity Bus station on Dedan Kimanthi Rd (US$4, four hours, daily) – make sure you catch one that goes all the way to the Tazara station; otherwise you'll be dropped in town and have a hot and hassled walk. Make sure you catch an early bus, too, or you might miss your train. When on the train, listen out in the wee hours for the immigration official coming through the carriages at the Tanzanian border, and make sure you get an entry stamp.

ZIMBABWE
Between Zimbabwe and Zambia are three border crossings. These are Chirundu, Kariba

and Victoria Falls. Most travellers cross at Victoria Falls (see p819). Buses leave from Lusaka's Intercity Bus Station for Harare (US$8.20, eight hours, daily) via Chirundu. They become crowded; arrive early.

At the Kariba dam, you can walk across the border to Kariba town in Zimbabwe.

GETTING AROUND
Air
A few small air companies, including **Zambian Airways** (☎ 01-271133; www.africa-insites.com/zambian airways), fly from Lusaka to Mfuwe (South Luangwa, US$140), Livingstone (US$135) and Kitwe or Ndola (US$100). Fares quoted here are one-way. Domestic departure tax is US$5.

Local Transport
All main routes are served by long-distance buses, either on a fill-up-and-go basis or with fixed departures (express buses). Fares are standardised: Lusaka to Livingstone is US$9 (475km), Lusaka to Chipata US$10 (605km) and Lusaka to Ndola US$7 (325km). If you have a big pack, it's not uncommon to be charged around US$1 extra.

CR Carriers and RPS run comfortable express buses on the main routes between Lusaka, Livingstone and the Copperbelt region. Fares are 10% to 20% more than ordinary buses.

Many routes in Zambia are also served by minibuses, which leave when full and in rural areas have very unpredictable journey times. In remote areas the 'bus' is often a truck or pick-up carrying goods as well as people.

Train
Express trains between Lusaka and Livingstone were suspended for refurbishment at the time of research. You can enquire at the Lusaka train station between Cairo and Dedan Kimathi Rds. Buses, however, are quicker. Between Lusaka and Kitwe, ordinary trains (only) go both ways daily (US$3/4 in economy/standard class).

LUSAKA

☎ 01 / pop 1.2 million
You haven't seen Lusaka unless you've been to Cairo Rd, the capital's nerve centre, where the pavement is a tangle of people and the street a cacophony of cars. It might be as flat as a pancake, but the colourful noisy crowds give the city plenty of character. If the clamour of central Lusaka gets too much, there are several sedate suburban shopping centres and malls with supermarkets, pharmacies, banks, shops, cyber cafés and restaurants.

ORIENTATION
The city centre lies along busy Cairo Rd, which runs in a north–south direction. This is where you'll find banks, shops, travel agencies, cafés and Internet cafés. East of the centre are the smarter suburbs, and west lie the poorer ones. Lusaka has several bus stations, which are all within walking distance of the city centre. The train station is also just east of Cairo Rd. Taxis run to the airport, 20km from the centre.

INFORMATION
Just about everything you need is on or near Cairo Rd, the city's main drag, including banks and bureaux de change, the main post and telephone office, a supermarket, bookshops, cafés and several travel agents.

Internet Access
Bwanji.com (☎ 223869; Central Park, Cairo Rd; US$2.40 per hr; ⏲ 8am-9pm), upstairs in the Central Park complex, has a large room full of computers, and connection is fast. **Digitech** (☎ 097-876655; Cairo Rd; US$1.80 per hr; ⏲ 8am-8pm Mon-Sat) is very crowded and has slower connection.

Money
To cash travellers cheques you must produce the receipt of purchase. Bureaux de change will generally give you a better rate than banks. There are banks and several bureaux de change on Cairo Rd. Mill Bureau

---

'GIVE ME ONE PIN'

If you hear children in the street calling out 'Give me one pin', they're not asking for help with their sewing. A 'pin' in Zambia is 1000 kwacha, because in the old days a pin was used to keep bundles of small notes together in thousands. So if a taxi driver says a ride across town is 'five pin' you say 'no, three pin' to show you know the local lingo – and the going rate.

de Change is next to the information office near Shoprite supermarket.

Post & Telephone
The **main post office** (Cairo Rd) has poste restante.

There are public phones outside the post office. Tokens are sold inside the building on the first floor where there are also card phones. If you buy tokens from the men selling them beside the phones you'll be charged twice the price.

Tourist Information
The **Zambia National Tourist Board** (ZNTB; ☎ 229087; www.zambiatourism.com; Century House, Cairo Rd; ✆ 8am-1pm & 2pm-5pm Mon-Fri, 8am-noon Sat), in the alley next to Shoprite, has a few brochures and maps. The staff can look up any extra information on a database.

Travel Agencies
The **Zambian Safari Company** (☎ 228682; reservations@zamsaf.co.zm; Central Park, Cairo Rd) can arrange domestic and international flights.

DANGERS & ANNOYANCES
As in any city, pickpockets take advantage of crowds, so be alert in Lusaka's markets and bus stations and on the busy city streets. In general, however, there are enough people around during the day to dissuade muggers from going for an outright attack. But at night it's best to take a taxi, even if you're on a tight budget.

SIGHTS & ACTIVITIES
To experience the colour, clamour and chaos of a lively African market go to the **Town Centre Market** (off Chachacha Rd). You'll find great bargains among the clothes, hardware, tapes, fruit and vegetables. It's relaxed, and tourists aren't hassled.

The **National Museum** (Nasser Rd; admission US$2; ✆ 9am-4.30pm) has an impressive display of contemporary Zambian paintings and sculpture. Upstairs are traditional exhibits; don't miss the display about witchcraft.

Munda Wanga (☎ 278456; Kafue Rd, Chilanga; admission US$2; ✆ 9am-4pm) This sanctuary for wounded or orphaned wild animals is about 15km out of town. It is surrounded by a beautiful botanic garden – the perfect setting for a relaxed picnic. To get there, catch a minibus from the South End Roundabout to Chilanga (US$0.75).

You can meet local artists who display their paintings and sculptures at the laid-back **Tayali Gallery** (Showgrounds, off Great East Rd; admission free; ✆ 9am-5pm Mon-Fri, 10am-4pm Sat).

SLEEPING
There isn't much choice of budget accommodation for tourists in Lusaka.

Chachacha Backpackers (☎ 222257; cha@zamtel.zm; 161 Mulombwa Close; camping per person US$3, dm US$6, s/d US$12/14; 🖳) Off Bwinjimfumo Rd, this place has a pool, bar, self-catering kitchen (meals are also available) and Internet, and offers free pick-ups from town. A range of budget safaris, pitched at backpackers, is also available. The only downside: it can be cramped and noisy. Wade, the Aussie owner, is helpful.

Kuomboka Backpackers (☎ 243771; kvkirkley@zamtel.zm; Mankanta Close; dm US$6, s/d US$14/15) The friendly owner of this spotless place off Makishi Rd, who comes from the Lozi tribe in Western Province, plans to organise trips to the annual Kuomboka ceremony (see p819). Meals or a self-catering kitchen are available; there's a quiet bar; a pool is planned.

YWCA (☎ 252726; ymca@zamnet.zm; Nationalist Rd; s/d US$10/20) A basic but clean and friendly place, popular with locals.

Hubert Young Hostel (☎ 254837; Lubwa Rd; s/d US$4/6, d with bathroom US$7) This place has rather gloomy rooms and is used mainly by civil servants.

For a more relaxed time away from the mayhem of the city, stay on the outskirts of Lusaka.

Pioneer Camp (☎ 096-432700; www.pioneercampzambia.com; Palabana Rd; camping per person US$5, d chalets from US$20) This friendly camp, off Great East Rd, 19km east of the centre, has a tranquil bush setting, swimming pool, tasty meals (US$7) and self-catering kitchen. It's convenient for the airport (9km), and management can arrange airport pick-ups. Free lifts into town are offered on weekday mornings. To get here from the city, take a minibus along Great East Rd to Chelston (US$0.30), from where a taxi costs about US$6.

Eureka Camp (☎ 272351; eureka@zamnet.zm; Kafue Rd; camping per person US$5, tw/d chalets US$20/30) A large property about 10km south of the city where zebras graze among the trees. Eureka Camp has a pool, a lounge and a bar serving snacks (burgers US$1). Minibuses to/from the city go past the gate.

ZAMBIA

ZAMBIA

LUSAKA

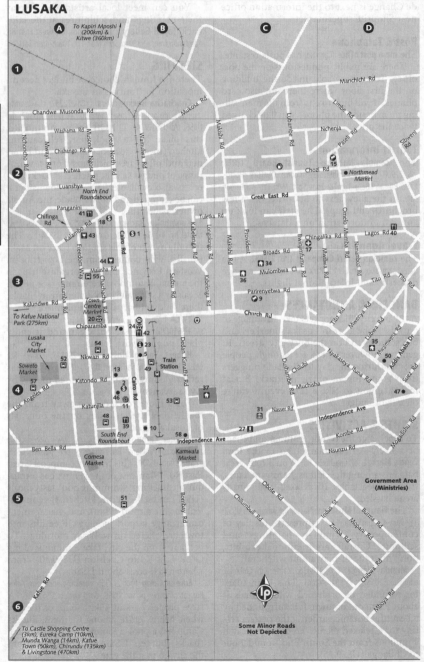

To Kapiri Mposhi
(200km) &
Kitwe (360km)

Manchichi Rd

Chandwe Musonda Rd

Washama Rd

Nchondo Rd
Mwayi Rd

Chishango Rd

Musonda Ngoza Rd

Great North Rd

Wamulwa Rd

Mukosa Rd

Makishi Rd

Limbe Rd

Nchenja

Paseli Rd

Siluweni Rd

Kutwa

Luanshya

North End
Roundabout

Great East Rd

Chozi Rd

• Northmead
Market

Panganini

Chifinga
Rd

41

18

43

Kalambo Rd

Cairo Rd

Freedom Way

1

Tuletka Rd

Kabelenga Rd

Longolongo Rd

Makishi Rd

Provident

Bwinjimfumu Rd

Chingalika Rd

Lagos Rd 40

17

Omelo Mumba Rd

Namambozi Rd

Lubambe Rd

Broads Rd

34

Mulombwa Cl

Tilo Rd

Malasha Rd

44

55

Chachacha Rd

59

36

Parirenyetwa Rd

9

Tilo Rd

Mwerya Rd

Lubwa Rd

Kalundwe Rd

To Kafue National
Park (275km)

Town
Centre
Market
20

Lumumba Rd

Chiparamba

7

24

42

Saidu Rd

Kabelenga Rd

Church Rd

Tilo Rd

Lusaka
City
Market

54

Nkwazi Rd

23

5

Train
Station

49

Dushambe Rd

Chilubi

Muchisha

35

Nyakaseya Iluna Rd

Wizimwoto Rd

50

Addis Ababa Dr

Suez Rd

Soweto
Market

52

57

Los Angeles Rd

13

Katondo Rd

2

46

11

37

47

Katunjila

48

39

10

South End
Roundabout

58

53

31

Nasser Rd

27

Independence Ave

Kombe Rd

Mogadishu Rd

Ben Bella Rd

Comesa
Market

Kamwala
Market

Independence Ave

Nsunzu Rd

Government Area
(Ministries)

51

Chilumbuli Rd

Obote Rd

Burma Rd

Indus St

Zimba Rd

Mopani Rd

Kafue Rd

Bombay Rd

Chibwa Rd

Mboya Rd

Some Minor Roads
Not Depicted

To Castle Shopping Centre
(3km), Eureka Camp (10km),
Munda Wanga (14km), Kafue
Town (50km), Chirundu (135km)
& Livingstone (470km)

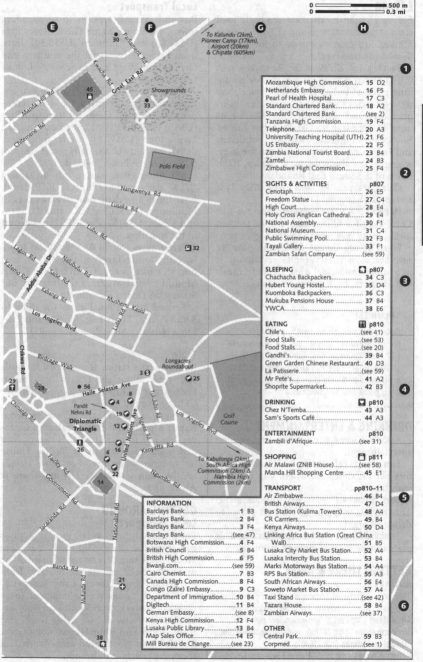

To Kalundu (2km),
Pioneer Camp (17km),
Airport (20km)
& Chipata (605km)

Showgrounds

Polo Field

Nangwenya Rd

Lusaka Rd

Longacres
Roundabout

Haile Selassie Ave

Pandit
Nehru Rd

**Diplomatic
Triangle**

Golf
Course

To Kabulonga (2km),
South Africa High
Commission (2km) &
Namibia High
Commission (2km)

Mozambique High Commission	15	D2
Netherlands Embassy	16	F5
Pearl of Health Hospital	17	C3
Standard Chartered Bank	18	A2
Standard Chartered Bank	(see 2)	
Tanzania High Commission	19	F4
Telephone	20	A3
University Teaching Hospital (UTH)	21	F6
US Embassy	22	F5
Zambia National Tourist Board	23	B4
Zamtel	24	B3
Zimbabwe High Commission	25	F4

SIGHTS & ACTIVITIES   p807

Cenotaph	26	E5
Freedom Statue	27	C4
High Court	28	E4
Holy Cross Anglican Cathedral	29	E4
National Assembly	30	F1
National Museum	31	C4
Public Swimming Pool	32	F3
Tayali Gallery	33	F1
Zambian Safari Company	(see 59)	

SLEEPING   p807

Chachacha Backpackers	34	C3
Hubert Young Hostel	35	D4
Kuomboka Backpackers	36	C3
Mukuba Pensions House	37	B4
YWCA	38	E6

EATING   p810

Chile's	(see 41)	
Food Stalls	(see 53)	
Food Stalls	(see 20)	
Gandhi's	39	B4
Green Garden Chinese Restaurant	40	D3
La Patisserie	(see 59)	
Mr Pete's	41	A2
Shoprite Supermarket	42	B3

DRINKING   p810

Chez N'Temba	43	A3
Sam's Sports Café	44	A3

ENTERTAINMENT   p810

Zambili d'Afrique	(see 31)	

SHOPPING   p811

Air Malawi (ZNIB House)	(see 58)	
Manda Hill Shopping Centre	45	E1

TRANSPORT   pp810–11

Air Zimbabwe	46	B4
British Airways	47	D4
Bus Station (Kulima Towers)	48	A4
CR Carrriers	49	B4
Kenya Airways	50	D4
Linking Africa Bus Station (Great China Wall)	51	B5
Lusaka City Market Bus Station	52	A4
Lusaka Intercity Bus Station	53	B4
Marks Motorways Bus Station	54	A4
RPS Bus Station	55	A3
South African Airways	56	E4
Soweto Market Bus Station	57	A4
Taxi Stand	(see 42)	
Tazara House	58	B4
Zambian Airways	(see 37)	

OTHER

Central Park	59	B3
Corpmed	(see 1)	

INFORMATION

Barclays Bank	1	B3
Barclays Bank	2	B4
Barclays Bank	3	F4
Barclays Bank	(see 47)	
Botswana High Commission	4	B4
British Council	5	B4
British High Commission	6	F5
Bwanji.com	(see 59)	
Cairo Chemist	7	B3
Canada High Commission	8	F4
Congo (Zaïre) Embassy	9	C3
Department of Immigration	10	B4
Digitech	11	B4
German Embassy	(see 8)	
Kenya High Commission	12	F4
Lusaka Public Library	13	B4
Map Sales Office	14	E5
Mill Bureau de Change	(see 23)	

0   500 m
0   0.3 mi

EATING

For very cheap meals there are basic food stalls at the bus stations and at Town Centre Market. Self-caterers can go to the **Shoprite** (Cairo Rd) supermarket.

Gandhi's (☎ 226735; off Cairo Rd; snacks & meals US$1-3) Down a small alley is this delightful little piece of India. The Indian spice shop serves delicious vegetarian meals (in thalli) on the veranda at lunch time. Despite its humble appearance, Gandhi's has hosted European diplomats, African politicians and Indian movie stars. Look for the alley, where there's also a dentist's surgery, 100m north of the South End Roundabout.

Chile's (Panganini Rd; meals around US$2) This restaurant has good local fare.

Mr Pete's (☎ 223428; Panganini Rd; meals from US$5) Come here for filling steak, fish or chicken meals, or its very rowdy Friday night disco.

Green Garden Chinese Restaurant (Lagos Rd; meals from US$4) This veranda restaurant is in a quiet residential area. Chinese meals include pork, beef, seafood and duck.

SPLURGE!

Going from north to south, your first stop for a splurge might be **La Patisserie** (☎ 224008; Central Park, Cairo Rd; snacks US$1-3) This smart café has good coffee (US$1), croissants and cakes, and a huge range of pies, pizza and sandwiches.

DRINKING & ENTERTAINMENT

Lusaka has some good venues for evening entertainment.

Sam's Sports Café (Malasha Rd) Travellers like this bar off Cairo Rd where you can mix with the locals.

Chez N'Temba (Freedom Way; admission US$1-2) This nightclub is one of the best places to dance all night.

Zambili d'Afrique (National Museum, Nasser Rd) This place organises good cultural evenings.

GETTING THERE & AWAY
Airlines

The main airlines (open 8am to 5pm Monday to Friday, 8am to 1pm Saturday) are:
Air Malawi (☎ 228120; www.airmalawi.net),
Air Zimbabwe (☎ 221750; www.airzimbabwe.com),
Ethiopian Airlines (☎ 236403)
Kenya Airways (☎ 255147; www.kenya-airways.com)

Local Transport

Bus and minibus services to surrounding towns, including Kafue (US$1), Siavonga (US$4.80) and Chirundu (US$3.50), leave from Kulima Towers (at the southern end of Freedom Way) and in front of Lusaka City Market.

CR Carriers (☎ 01-225633; ⏲ 7.30am-5pm) has express buses, departing from the company's station off Cairo Rd, run to Kitwe (US$8) via Ndola (US$7, 6½ hours, daily); Livingstone (US$9, 6½ hours, four times daily); Mongu (US$8, daily); and Chipata (US$10, seven hours, twice daily).

RPS (Freedom Way) runs a bus to Mongu (US$7, daily) and to Chipata (US$9, daily). Four times a week an ordinary bus goes to Mpulungu (US$16) via Kasama (US$14) and Mbala (US$15). Most RPS buses depart in the morning.

Tazara buses (Intercity Bus station, Dedan Kimathi Rd) going to the Tazara station (US$4, four hours), which is about 2km outside Kapiri Mposhi town, leave from the Intercity Bus Station on Dedan Kimathi Rd.

Several international buses travelling to South Africa, Zimbabwe, Malawi and Tanzania also use this station (see p805).

Train

Lusaka's **train station** (Dedan Kimathi Rd) deals with reservations and tickets for trains to Livingstone or Kitwe. For more details see Getting Around, p806.

Trains on the Tazara railway between Kapiri Mposhi and Dar es Salaam (Tanzania) do not run to Lusaka. However, you can make reservations at Tazara House on Independence Ave. For more details on the train service see Getting There & Away, p806.

GETTING AROUND
Local Transport

For getting around Lusaka, local minibuses run along the city's main roads, but there are no route numbers or name boards. The main routes of use to visitors are: from South End Roundabout, along Independence Ave to Longacres Roundabout (near most embassies); from South End Roundabout along Kafue Rd to Kafue town; and from North End Roundabout along Great East Rd, past Northmead and Manda Hill shopping centres to Chelston.

ZAMBIA

Taxi

Official taxis have numbers painted on their doors. There are ranks at the main hotels, near markets and outside the Shoprite supermarket on Cairo Rd.

For taxis without meters, fares are negotiable, but across town costs around US$1 and from the centre to the suburbs is between US$2 and US$4. Always check the fare first. **Dial-a-Taxi** (☎ 096-752233) has metered taxis that can be expensive if there's heavy traffic.

EASTERN ZAMBIA

CHIPATA
☎ 062

Chipata is a busy town near the border with Malawi and the main jumping-off point for South Luangwa National Park. Many travellers rush through, but as neat bus connections are unlikely, you might end up spending a night here. There's a big market, plus supermarkets, shops, banks and a telephone office.

Sleeping & Eating

On the outskirts of Chipata, **Mama-Rula** (2andrea@bushmail.net; camping per person US$5) has a tranquil setting in a large fenced property. The turn-off is 4km from town on the road to South Luangwa. It's a further 2km to the camp. Mama-Rula also has tidy rooms for US$35 including breakfast and dinner. There's a self-catering kitchen, or meals can be ordered for around US$7. A taxi from Chipata will cost US$3, or you could take a minibus to the turn-off and walk.

The **Kapata Resthouse** (☎ 222498; d US$7), near the bus station and market, 1km from the main street, is safe and fairly clean. A plate of rice or *nshima* (maize porridge) and stew is US$1.20.

The **Zambian Wildlife Conservation Society (ZWCS) camp site** (☎ 221382; wildchip@zamtel.zm; camping per person US$2), is about 1.5km from the bus station, off Parerenyatwa Rd. It's in a quiet area surrounded by a high wall and has friendly staff. Despite quite a few trees, the large property looks bare. To get here, turn off the main street at the BP station and continue east for two blocks.

Kamocho Guesthouse (☎ 222065; Msafunsa Rd; d without/with bathroomUS$18/19) is safe, clean

and quiet, and has a friendly local atmosphere. Simple but filling meals cost US$3.10. It's a block past the ZWCS camp site.

Getting There & Away

CR Carriers and RPS both run daily local and express buses to/from Lusaka (local/express US$8/10, six hours). Buses leave from behind the market at 5.30am. Minibuses run throughout the day to/from the Malawian border (US$1).

SOUTH LUANGWA NATIONAL PARK

Often considered the best park in Zambia because of the variety of animals and birds that you'll see and its (relatively) easy access for backpackers, **South Luangwa National Park's** (admission US$20 per day) woodlands and open grassy plains are home to lions, buffaloes, zebras, rare wild dogs, the endemic Thornicroft's giraffe and Cookson's wildebeest. There are also large herds of elephants, and even reclusive leopards are often spotted. Antelope species include bushbuck, waterbuck, impala and puku, and bird life is tremendous.

South Luangwa's high season runs from April–May to October–November, when the weather is dry, animals gater near waterholes and conditions are better for viewing wildlife. During the low (or 'green') season, some places to stay are closed, but others offer discounts.

The budget camps and lodges are all just outside the park boundary, within a few kilometres of **Mfuwe** village, where there's a small shop and a market. The park entrance is about 2km from the village. This part of the park can become quite busy

---

SOUTH LUANGWA ON A SHOESTRING

Although South Luangwa is hard to visit on the cheap, there are more options for the budget-conscious here than at other Zambian parks. Nevertheless, some shoestring travellers get a nasty surprise at the lack of real bargains. By the time you've paid for accommodation, park fees and a couple of wildlife-viewing drives, you're looking at a minimum of US$80. If you haven't got that, you won't get much from your visit.

with vehicles, but that's only because this is the best viewing area. And in Zambia everything is relative; if you've suffered rush-hour rally-style safaris in Kenya, you'll find it positively peaceful here.

Activities

All places to stay operate wildlife drives in the national park (morning US$25 per person, night US$30 per person). These rates are based on three or four people in the car, you'll pay extra if there are only two of you. Some also offer wildlife walks in the dry season (US$25).

If you have time, visit the **Chipembele Wildlife Education Trust** (www.chipembele.org; admission US$5), 16km from Mfuwe. The centre's main purpose is to educate local schoolchildren in wildlife and environmental awareness and conservation. Visitors are welcome to look at its interesting wildlife exhibits. Some of the lodges run tours here.

Sleeping & Eating

The following places to stay are listed roughly in order of distance from Mfuwe village.

Cobra Resthouse (s/d US$2/4) This basic but friendly resthouse in Mfuwe village is beside the main road opposite the petrol station and bus stop. The small rooms are spartan and have no mosquito nets. *Nshima* and chicken meals cost US$1. This place does not offer activities.

Camel House Co-op (meals US$5; ☺ 8am-11pm Mon-Fri, 8am-noon Sat) Buses and trucks stop at this café next to the petrol station. It serves burgers, chips and toasted sandwiches. It's a good place to wait for public transport to Chipata departing late at night.

For a complete safari feel, there is a good choice of budget accommodation at South Luangwa. All the places listed below are outside the park boundary, so you don't pay

fees until you enter the park. All overlook the river and have swimming pools.

Flatdogs (☎ 062-45136; flatdogs@campafrica.com; camping per person US$5, s/d chalets US$30/60) There's a social atmosphere at this long-standing and legendary camp, which has a lively bar and a lounge with pool tables and comfy couches. The mouth-watering choice of meals (from US$1.50 to US$9) includes nachos, kebabs and burgers.

Marula Lodge (☎ 062-45073; marula@zamnet.zm; self-catering s/d chalet US$20/40, with meals US$80/160) This simple and friendly lodge has chalets with bathroom, an open bar and restaurant (meals US$5).

Croc Farm (☎ 062-45074; mfucroc@super-hub.com; camping per person US$5, s/d US$12/24) Next to Marula Lodge, this place has a wide grassy camp site and simple cabins. There's a small bar where you can get tasty snacks (US$5) like burgers and chips.

SPLURGE!

Wildlife Camp (☎ 062-45026; wildlife@super-hub.com; camping per person US$3, s/d rooms US$17/33, s/d chalets with bathroom US$22/44) This beautiful and tranquil camp has a real bush feeling. The delightful chalets are built from local materials. The open thatched bar and restaurant have a magnificent river view. Vegetarian and meat meals, such as quiche and lasagne (US$3 to US$9), and self-catering kitchens are available. Ask your bus driver to drop you off here as it's too far to walk from the village. The camp can also arrange transfers for a small fee.

Getting There & Away

Local minibuses and pick-ups to Mfuwe leave from behind the market in Chipata from Monday to Saturday (US$4 plus backpack US$0.40). They usually leave in the morning and, depending on the road, the journey can take less than five and/or more than eight hours. The fare is negotiable – drivers will quote tourists more than what locals pay. For a little extra you can ask the driver to drop you at the place where you're staying, which saves a long walk and possible encounters with wildlife.

From Mfuwe to Chipata – you can find minibuses to Mfuwe from outside the

---

WARNING

If you're walking from Mfuwe village to one of the nearby camps, hippos, elephants and other wildlife can come out of the long grass – especially in the early morning and evening. Walking at night is out of the question. If you arrive late by bus and the driver won't drop you off at your accommodation, it's best to stay in Mfuwe village itself.

Camel House Co-op between 10pm and 11pm Sunday to Friday.

If you're in a group, consider chartering your own minibus or pick-up from Chipata to Mfuwe. Hitching with other tourists in their own vehicle is also a possibility. A final option for budget travellers is to join a tour. Several operators in Lilongwe (Malawi) run safaris to South Luangwa (see p799).

LUANGWA BRIDGE

On the long-haul journey between Lusaka and Chipata, the Great East Road crosses the Luangwa River on a large suspension bridge. On the west side of the river, 3km south of the main road, is **Bridge Camp** (☎ 01-290146; rshenton@zamnet.zm; camping per person US$3, s/d chalets US$15/25), an excellent place to break the trip. It sits on a steep slope and has an open bar and restaurant and simple thatched chalets overlooking the river. A three-course dinner costs a hefty US$12, but for US$3 you can have a filling plate of nshima and chicken stew.

Canoe and hiking trips (US$5/10 per half/full day) can be arranged. Three-day canoe trips to the spectacular **Lunsemfwa Gorge** cost US$100 per day between up to six people.

CR Carriers buses from Lusaka to Chipata or Lusaka to Luangwa can drop you at Luangwa bridge (US$6). From the turn-off at the main road, infrequent minibuses charge US$0.30 to run the 3km to the camp.

NORTHERN ZAMBIA

MPULUNGU

☎ 04

Mpulungu is a busy crossroads town between East, Central and Southern Africa. It's also very hot. The Lake Tanganyika ferry (see p805) docks here.

About 5km before Mpulungu, as you enter town on the road from Mbale, is the turn-off to **Tanganyika Lodge** (☎ 455130; camping per person US$5, chalets from US$12). It has a beautiful lakeshore setting and an open bar and restaurant.

Places to stay in town include a couple of local resthouses in the centre, but a long-standing favourite is **Nkupi Lodge** (☎ 455166; camping per person US$4, s/d rondavels US$10/20), east of town. The people here can also help

you find a boat to visit Kalambo Falls (see Around Mpulungu below) and if available they will find someone to act as your guide to the falls, staying with you at Luke's Beach the day before. Near the port is the **Harbour Inn** (s/d US$6/12), which has a popular bar and nice en-suite rooms.

Long-distance buses tie in with the ferry. The RPS bus goes from Lusaka to Mpulungu every Thursday and returns on Friday (US$16). CR Carriers also plans to start operating buses to Mpulungu. Minibuses are faster and go daily between Mpulungu, near the BP petrol station, and Mbala and Kasama, where you can get onward transport to Lusaka.

AROUND MPULUNGU
Kalambo Falls

About 40km northwest of Mbala you can also reach Kalambo Falls, on the border between Zambia and Tanzania. This is the second-highest single-drop waterfall in Africa. The people at the Old Soldier's Restaurant can drive you there (US$20 per person, negotiable). Many visitors also arrive by boat from Mpulungu.

From the boat there is also a hike up to the falls – start early as it gets hot! To do this hike you might have to arrive the day before you intend getting to the falls and stay at Luke's Beach (or any beach – Luke's is overpriced and not good value if you are just camping because there are no facilities). Check the times of the returning boats, and make sure you have enough food and water for the duration of your stay away from Mpulungu or Mbala. Local fishermen might row into the bay to sell fish, but don't rely on it.

About 20km further on is the **Kapishya Hot Springs** (☎ 04-370064; gameman@zamnet.zm; camping per person US$5, s/d chalets US$35/70), where you can soak in a warm pool fed by the hot springs. There are basic accommodation facilities, and you can order meals or self-cater. Canoe trips can be arranged.

To get here, take the northeast road (T2) from Mpika towards Nakonde. The signposted turn-off (about 87km from Mpika) is 13km from Shiwa House. From the house it's another 19km to the hot springs. Without your own transport it's difficult to get here. RPS buses run between Lusaka and Shiwa Ngandu (US$11).

MBALA

Mbala is a small town perched on the edge of the Great Rift Valley, from where the road north drops over 1000m in less than 40km down to Mpulungu and Lake Tanganyika.

The **Moto Moto Museum** (☎ 450098; admission US$5; ◷ 9am-4.45pm), located about 3km outside town, has a fascinating collection of artefacts relating to the Bemba tribe and surrounding area.

The **Grasshopper Inn** (☎ 450589; s/d US$7/10) has a bar and restaurant and clean rooms with bathroom. **Old Soldier's Restaurant** (main street; meals from US$1) offers good company and local food.

KASAMA

You might find yourself overnighting in this small busy town if you're travelling between Lusaka and Mpulungu or switching from Tazara train to local bus.

Places to stay close to the Tazara station (5km from the town centre) include the friendly **Elizabeth Guesthouse** (s/d US$6/12), which has rooms with shared bathroom, and the **Kapongolo Resthouse** (d US$12), where the rate includes bathroom and breakfast.

Shiwa Ngandu

Shiwa Ngandu is the name of the area around **Shiwa House** (☎ 04-370064; gameman@zamnet.zm; admission US$1; ◷ 9am-4pm), an imposing old colonial mansion built in the early 20th century by Sir Stewart Gore-Browne, an Englishman who was greatly respected by the local people. The rambling brick mansion (completed in 1933), with its antique furniture and formal gardens, is a surprising sight in such a remote place.

SAMFYA

On the western shore of beautiful **Lake Bangweulu** lies the small town of Samfya, a trading centre and hub of lake transport. It's about 10km east of the main road between Serenje and Mansa. There are a few restaurants and bars, but best of all is the wonderful white, sandy cabana beach, just outside town.

In Samfya, the **Transport Hotel** (s/d US$3/4, d with bathroom US$10) is a cheap place to stay at the port. **Bangweulu Lodge** (☎ 02-830124; camping per person US$5, s/d US$15/25) on the cabana beach is a lovely camping spot and has comfortable rooms with shared bathroom.

To get here, take a minibus from Serenje. Buses between Lusaka and Mpulungu go via Serenje.

THE COPPERBELT

KITWE & NDOLA

☎ 02 / pop 700,000 (Kitwe); 500,000 (Ndola)

These two cities are in the industrial Copperbelt region, and although rarely visited by tourists, you might pass through on your way to Chimfunshi Wildlife Orphanage (see below).

In Kitwe, the friendly **YMCA** (☎ 211710; Independence Ave; d without/with bathroom US$15/25), to the north of the city centre, has basic rooms. **Lothian House** (☎ 222889; Chandamali Rd; s/d US$15/20) has musty but clean rooms. Rates at both places include breakfast.

In Ndola, **Royal Hotel** (☎ 621841; Vitanda St; s/d from US$15/25), just north of the city centre, is good value with en-suite rooms and breakfast.

CR Carriers runs express buses between Lusaka and Kitwe via Ndola (US$8, 5½ hours, daily). Local buses between Lusaka and Ndola leave between 6am and 6pm when full. There are slow trains between Lusaka and Ndola and Kitwe (economy/standard class US$3/4).

CHIMFUNSHI

Chimpanzee mania reigns at **Chimfunshi Wildlife Orphanage** (☎ 02-311293; www.chimfunshi.org.za; camping per person US$5, s/d chalets US$10/20). The orphanage is home to various species of wildlife rescued from poachers and other distressing situations in Africa and all over the world but is most famous for its chimpanzees. It's 70km northwest of Chingola, a small town 50km northwest of Kitwe.

Chimfunshi also runs an education centre for local schoolchildren. Tourists can visit the chimp nursery (US$5) or tour the whole project (US$10). There are basic chalets with hot showers and a self-catering kitchen (bring your own supplies). Chimfunshi caters only for small numbers so it's imperative to book. There's no phone, but the people at the contact number will relay your message by radio.

Without private transport (ideally 4WD), it's not easy to get here. The most direct route from Lusaka is to take a CR Carriers bus to Solwezi via Chingola. These services operate daily. Get off at the Chimfunshi turn-off and trek the remaining 20km.

SOUTHEASTERN ZAMBIA

SIAVONGA
☎ 01

The small laid-back town of Siavonga sprawls along the banks of **Lake Kariba**. Just over the nearby Kariba Dam is Zimbabwe and the town of Kariba. From Siavonga, you can arrange houseboat trips on Lake Kariba and canoeing safaris on the Zambezi River.

Eagle's Rest (☎ 511168; eagles@zamnet.zm; camping per person US$7, s/d chalets US$30/60), east of town, has a shady camp site and chalets with bathrooms. There's a bar and restaurant serving snacks and meals. You can hire a canoe (US$7 per hour), and the management can organise houseboat cruises.

Sandy Beach (☎ 511353; camping per person US$6; s/d chalets US$30/60) is a secluded camp 14km west of the road between Siavonga and Chirundu. Transfer by car or boat can be arranged at Eagle's Rest.

Lake View Council Resthouse (d with bathroom US$7) has basic rooms but friendly management, a local feel and a good garden bar.

Minibuses from Lusaka leave for Siavonga in the morning (US$5). Minibuses also run to and from Lusaka and Chirundu several times a day (US$3.50). You can get off at the Siavonga junction and hitch the last 60km down to Siavonga from there. Another option is to take any bus between Lusaka and Livingstone and get off at the junction beyond Kafue town. From here, take a Chirundu minibus (around US$3).

LOWER ZAMBEZI NATIONAL PARK

The **Lower Zambezi National Park** (admission US$20 per day), bordering the wide Zambezi River with Zimbabwe's Mana Pools National Park on the opposite bank, is one of Zambia's top parks. The best way to view wildlife is from the river.

Western Side

Most of the up-market places to stay are in the western part of the park. On the western access road along the river bank from Chirundu are several more places, including a few budget options, but they're all impossible to reach without your own 4WD vehicle (which you'd also need to tour the park).

Chiawa Community Camp Site (camping per person US$5), a few kilometres before the main gate, has a lovely riverside setting. It's very basic so you need to take all your supplies.

Without your own wheels, the easiest way to reach the Lower Zambezi National Park is with an organised tour. Chachacha Backpackers (see p807) organises all-inclusive five-day camping safaris to the park (US$380) and four-day canoeing safaris on the Zambezi River (US$350). **River Horse Safaris** (☎ 01-511107; www.riverhorsesafaris.com) in Siavonga runs four-day canoeing safaris from Chirundu to Chongwe (from US$255). These trips end just outside the park boundary.

Eastern Side

There's no road link between the western and eastern sides of the park. Access to this area from Chipata is via Luangwa Bridge and Luangwa *boma* (town), on the bank of the Zambezi River, where the borders of Zambia, Mozambique and Zimbabwe meet.

Kingfisher Camp (☎ 01-290146; rshenton@zamnet.zm; camping per person US$3, chalets US$30) is on the banks of the Zambezi at the eastern end of the park. The chalets sleep three. It organises fishing, boating and walking safaris. You need to arrange accommodation in advance, which involves a boat transfer to the camp from Luangwa *boma* – the only way to get to the camp.

Buses run daily between Lusaka and Luangwa *boma* (US$7), but it's worth stopping off at Bridge Camp at Luangwa Bridge (see p813), as it's run by the same people. You could possibly organise a lift between the two camps if you arranged it with the Bridge Camp owners before leaving Lusaka.

WESTERN ZAMBIA

LIVINGSTONE & VICTORIA FALLS
☎ 03

People throw themselves off bridges, jump off cliffs and half-drown in rapids just a stone's throw away, but Livingstone lolls in sleepy contentment unfazed by the hype. It's hard to believe this humble, dusty town is Africa's adventure capital. Thousands of

ZAMBIA

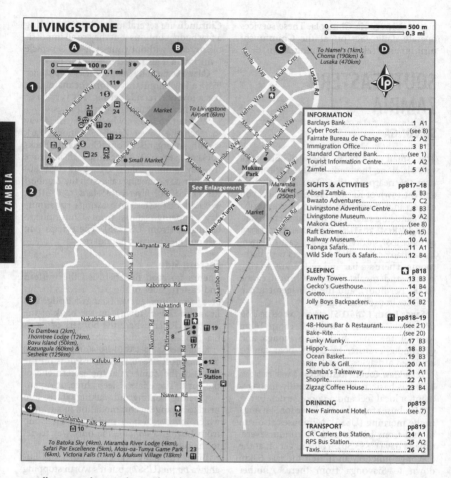

LIVINGSTONE

INFORMATION	
Barclays Bank	1 A1
Cyber Post	(see 8)
Fairrate Bureau de Change	2 A2
Immigration Office	3 B1
Standard Chartered Bank	(see 1)
Tourist Information Centre	4 A2
Zamtel	5 A1

SIGHTS & ACTIVITIES	pp817-18
Abseil Zambia	6 B3
Bwaato Adventures	7 C2
Livingstone Adventure Centre	8 B3
Livingstone Museum	9 A2
Makora Quest	(see 8)
Raft Extreme	(see 15)
Railway Museum	10 A4
Taonga Safaris	11 A1
Wild Side Tours & Safaris	12 B4

SLEEPING	p818
Fawlty Towers	13 B3
Gecko's Guesthouse	14 B4
Grotto	15 C1
Jolly Boys Backpackers	16 B2

EATING	pp818-19
48-Hours Bar & Restaurant	(see 21)
Bake-Rite	(see 20)
Funky Munky	17 B3
Hippo's	18 B3
Ocean Basket	19 B3
Rite Pub & Grill	20 A1
Shamba's Takeaway	21 A1
Shoprite	22 A2
Zigzag Coffee House	23 B4

DRINKING	pp819
New Fairmount Hotel	(see 7)

TRANSPORT	pp819
CR Carriers Bus Station	24 A1
RPS Bus Station	25 A2
Taxis	26 A2

travellers come here each year for adrenalin-pumping exhilaration and to stare at the mesmerising Victoria Falls thundering into the depth of a narrow gorge. The waterfall, on the mighty Zambezi River, spans nearly 2km and drops dramatically over a 100m cliff. In a place where so many foreigners converge, Livingstone's simplicity, in contrast to the magnificent falls, reminds us we are still in Africa.

Information

Aside from a few brochures, the **Tourist Information Centre** (☎ 321402; Mosi-oa-Tunya Rd; ☼ 8am-1pm & 2-5pm Mon-Fri, 8am-12pm Sat) doesn't have much in the way of information. **Wild Side Tours & Safaris** (☎ 323726; wild@zamnet.zm; 131

Mosi-oa-Tunya Rd; ☼ 8am-6pm Mon-Fri, 8am-noon Sat), which operates as a booking agent as well as running safaris, has loads of information on Livingstone and the rest of Zambia.

All the places to stay listed here can advise on tours and activities. All operators and places to stay can also arrange Zambian visa fee waivers with at least 24 hours notice.

You'll find most of what you need in Livingstone on Mosi-oa-Tunya Rd: shops, banks, bureaux de change, travel and tour agents, a post office and the Zamtel public phone office.

Cyber Post (☎ 321338; Internet US$3.70 per hr), at the Livingstone Adventure Centre, offers Internet access and phone and fax services. Overseas phone calls cost US$3 a minute.

Livingstone's main **produce market** (Maramba Township) is south of the town centre. **Shoprite** (Kapondo St) is a well-stocked supermarket.

Dangers & Annoyances

Don't walk from town to the falls as there have been a number of muggings here. Even people on bicycles have been attacked.

Sights & Activities

This waterfall is simply spectacular and must be seen, felt and heard to be understood as the experience can't be captured in words. You can see the falls up close at the Victoria Falls section of **Mosi-oa-Tunya National Park** (admission US$10; h6am to 6pm). The entrance is just before the Zambian border post (see the map on p911 in the Zimbabwe chapter). Mosi-oa-Tunya National Park also has a small wildlife reserve, **Mosi-oa-Tunya Game Park** (admission US$3; 6am-6pm), which has a good selection of animals including giraffes, zebras, antelopes and a few heavily guarded rhinos.

The range of activities on offer in and around Livingstone is mind-blowing (see Tour Operators below). If you want more for your money enquire about 'combos', which give you the opportunity to do a combination of different activities at a reduced rate. Also enquire about safaris to Chobe National Park (day safaris from US$136) – renowned for its enormous elephant population – in Botswana.

Mukuni village (entry US$3) is a traditional Zambian village 18km southeast of Livingstone. Many hostels and tour operators run tours here, but you can also go on your own by taxi (around US$8 return). You can do a guided tour that gives you the opportunity to take photos of the friendly villagers and observe how rural people live. The village also has an interesting history. At the end of your tour you'll be invited into the craft market where the pressure to buy something can be overwhelming.

Tours

Below is a list of some tour and activity companies that offer various activities around the Falls. They all act as agents for each other, so you can book anything with them or at your accommodation. It's rarely cheaper to go direct to a company, but it's always worth asking.

AIRBORNE ACTIVITIES

For the ultimate adrenaline rush you can bungee-jump (US$90), abseil, highwire or swing (half/full day US$80/95) into the Batoka Gorge below the falls. For a bird's-eye view of the falls take a microlight (15/30 minutes, US$75/125) or helicopter flight (15/30 minutes, US$75/150).

Abseil Zambia (321188; www.thezambeziswing.com; Mosi-oa-Tunya Rd) Operates the gorge swing across the Batoka Gorge and other wild airborne activities, including abseiling, rap-jumping and high-wiring.
African Extreme (324231; US$90) Gives you the chance to bungee-jump off the bridge over the Batoka Gorge just below the mighty falls.
Batoka Sky (320058; www.batokasky.com; Mosi-oa-Tunya Game Park road) Does microlight flights over the falls and/or Mosi-oa-Tunya Game Park and helicopter flights.

RIVER CRUISES & CANOEING

Booze cruises (noisy affairs involving a lot of alcohol), sunset cruises (more sedate) and morning cruises are run above the falls (from US$30). Canoeing trips also take place upriver from the falls (half/full day US$70/85).

Bwaato Adventures (324227; bwaato@zamnet.zm; New Fairmount Hotel, Mosi-oa-Tunya Rd) Runs booze and sunset cruises.
Makora Quest (324574; quest@zamnet.zm; Mosi-oa-Tunya Rd) Next to the Livingstone Adventure Centre, this place offers tranquil canoeing trips in Klepper canoes.
Taonga Safaris (324081; Mosi-oa-Tunya Rd) Runs booze and sunset cruises.
Wild Side Tours & Safaris (323726; wild@zamnet.zm; 131 Mosi-oa-Tunya Rd) Runs peaceful morning and sunset cruises.

SHOOTING THE RAPIDS

The Zambezi's legendary white-water rapids entice fun-seekers from across the world to go rafting (US$95), river-boarding (US$125) and jet-boating (US$60) in their seething turmoil.

Bundu Adventures (324407; www.bundu-adventures .com; 699 Industrial Rd) Offers river-boarding and rafting.
Jet Extreme (321375; www.jetextreme.com) Does jet-boating in the gorge.
Raft Extreme (323929; www.raftextreme.com; The Grotto, 2 Maambo Way) Does river-boarding and rafting.
Safari Par Excellence (321629; www.safpar.com) Offers rafting and river-boarding.
Touch Adventure (321111; www.touchadventure .com) Takes you white water rafting.

ZAMBIA

WILDLIFE VIEWING

To get in touch with nature take a wildlife drive (from US$30 for two hours) or guided wildlife walk (US$45) in Mosi-oa-Tunya Game Park or an elephant ride along the Zambezi (two-hour ride plus time petting the elephants US$100).

Bwaato Adventures (☎ 324227; bwaato@zamnet.zm; New Fairmount Hotel, Mosi-oa-Tunya Rd) Operates wildlife drives and walks.

Wild Side Tours & Safaris (☎ 323726; www.wildside safaris.com; 131 Mosi-oa-Tunya Rd) Offers wildlife drives.

Zambezi Elephant Trails (☎ 321629; www.zambezi safari.com; Thorntree Lodge) A 20-minute drive from Livingstone, this outfit offers elephant rides.

Sleeping

Livingstone has some great backpackers' accommodation.

Fawlty Towers (☎ 323432; www.adventure-africa.com; Mosi-oa-Tunya Rd; camping/dm per person US$5/8, d without/ with bathroom US$20/30; ☐) This lush oasis next to the Livingstone Adventure Centre has a large enclosed garden with a shady lawn, a pleasant pool and a popular bar and restaurant. It offers Internet access and free pick-ups from the Victoria Falls border.

Jolly Boys Backpackers (☎ 324229; jollybs@zamnet .zm; 34 Kanyanta Rd; camping/dm per person US$3/6, d US$15; ☐) Livingstone's first backpackers has moved to new premises with a swimming pool, bar and deck, which has a view over the treetops to the spray rising above the falls. It has great bargains on activities and offers Internet access and a free daily bus to the falls.

Grotto (☎ 323929; grotto@zamnet.zm; 2 Maambo Way; camping per person US$3; ☐) Overland trucks usually head here, but independent campers are also welcome. There's a big old colonial house with a pool, veranda bar and shady garden surrounded by a high wall. You can camp for one free night if you raft with Raft Extreme.

Gecko's Guesthouse (☎ 322267; gecko@zamnet.zm; 84 Limulunga Rd; camping/dm per person US$3.50/6, s/d US$14/21) This previously popular place was looking rather forlorn when we visited. It's surrounded by a quiet garden with a small pool, a bar and a kitchen for self-catering.

Outside town there are some camps with peaceful bush settings.

Maramba River Lodge (☎ 324189; www.maramba -zambia.com; camping per person US$5, s/d safari tents US$20/25, s/d chalets US$35/50; ☐) On the banks

of the Maramba River, 6km south of Livingstone on the road towards Victoria Falls, this stylish yet simple lodge with well-kept lawns, an attractive pool, a bar and restaurant has walk-in tents and thatched en-suite chalets.

Bovu Island (☎ 323708; jungle@zamnet.zm; camping per person US$5, s/d huts US$10/20) In the middle of the Zambezi, upstream from Victoria Falls, with village-style huts. Livingstone transfers (50km; US$20 including walking and canoe excursions) and meals (from US$3 to US$4) are available. The booking office is at Fawlty Towers.

Eating & Drinking

Most of the cafés and restaurants in Livingstone are along Mosi-oa-Tunya Rd. Unless otherwise stated, the places below are on this road.

Funky Munky (☎ 320120; meals US$1-5) This place, down from the Livingstone Adventure Centre, makes excellent pizzas (small/large US$2/3) and a selection of fresh snacks and mains, including pita bread, burgers and French bread sandwiches.

Hippos (☎ 323432; meals US$4-5) In the evenings there's always a great atmosphere at this bar and restaurant behind Fawlty Towers. It's open for dinner only and serves a set menu daily except Friday, when there's a barbecue.

Zigzag Coffee House (Mosi-oa-Tunya Rd; meals from US$3) There's a tempting selection of snacks and meals, including tacos, pizza and pancakes, at this café. It was in town, but you'll probably find it at new premises still on Mosi-oa-Tunya Rd but south of town after the railway crossing. The owners plan to open a craft village on the same premises.

Ocean Basket (☎ 321274; meals US$3-9) You can get fish and chips (US$4) or splash out on a seafood platter (US$9) at this seafood restaurant.

Rite Pub & Grill (☎ 320398; meals around US$4) This restaurant in the centre of town serves meat dishes and often has live music at the weekend. For cakes, doughnuts, samosas and pies (around US$0.50) go next door to Bake-Rite.

For cheap meals try the following:

Shamba's Takeaway (meals less than US$1), near the post office, serves burgers and meat and rice meals. Alternatively, try the smarter **48 Hours Bar & Restaurant** (snacks and meals from US$2) next door.

Hippos, Jolly Boys and the Grotto (see Sleeping, opposite) are popular places to socialise and have a few drinks. If you feel like a boogie, the **New Fairmount Hotel** (Mosi-oa-Tunya Rd) has a disco on Friday and Saturday nights.

Getting There & Away

RPS (Mutelo St) has two bus services a day to Lusaka (US$8, seven hours). **CR Carriers** (cnr Mosi-oa-Tunya Rd & Akapelwa St) runs four services a day to Lusaka (US$9, seven hours). Direct buses to Mongu (US$11) leave at midnight from Maramba market, but for safety reasons it's better to catch a morning bus to Shesheke and transfer to a Mongu bus. Buses to Shesheke (US$7) leave around 10am from Mingongo bus station next to the Catholic church at Dambwa (3km west of the town centre) and arrive in Shesheke early in the afternoon. (A taxi fare from town to Mingongo station is around US$0.50.) From Shesheke, buses to Mongu cost US$5.

Minibuses to the Botswana border at Kazungula (US$2.50) leave from Dambwa, 2km west of the town centre, on Nakatindi Rd.

Trains between Lusaka and Livingstone were under refurbishment at the time of research. For more information enquire at the **train station** (☎ 320001; off Mosi-oa-Tunya Rd).

Taxis from the Zambian border post at Victoria Falls to Victoria Falls town in Zimbabwe cost US$2. For details about getting to the border see Getting Around below.

Getting Around

It's 11km from Livingstone to Victoria Falls. Just beyond the entrance to the falls is the Zambian border post. From here you can walk across the bridge overlooking the falls to the Zimbabwean border post and Victoria Falls town on the Zimbabwean side.

A minibus between Livingstone and Victoria Falls or the Zambian border costs US$0.50. A taxi costs around US$3 to US$4 each way – not bad if you share with others. Walking is not advised as some people have been mugged on this road.

MONGU

☎ 07

This pleasant lively town is the capital of Western Province. From the outskirts of town, an 8km canal runs westwards to meet a tributary of the Zambezi. Around the **harbour** is a fascinating settlement of reed and

thatch buildings, where local fishermen sell their catch, and passenger boats take people to outlying villages.

Mongu comes alive once a year, around Easter, when thousands of people come here for the annual **Kuomboka ceremony**. This colourful ceremony takes place when the king of the Lozi people moves from his dry season palace out on the plains to his wet season palace on higher ground. The king is transported there on a decorated river barge. The wet season palace is at **Limulunga**, about 20km north of Mongu, where a museum contains exhibits about the Lozi people and the Kuomboka ceremony.

Near the bus station, the friendly **Lumba Guesthouse** (☎ 221287; Kanyonyo Rd; s/d US$7/10) has basic singles and en-suite doubles. A shoestringers' favourite is **Winters Resthouse** (Senanga Rd; d without/with bathroom US$6/9) at the northern end of town. Ask for a room away from the noisy bar.

CR Carriers buses run twice daily to/from Lusaka (US$8). To reach Mongu from Livingstone see above. Minibuses run between Mongu and Limulunga throughout the day for US$0.80.

ZAMBIA DIRECTORY

ACCOMMODATION

There isn't a great choice of budget tourist accommodation in Zambia. You'll find the widest selection in Livingstone, but Lusaka has only a couple of backpackers' hostels. However, there are lots of cheap local guesthouses in towns throughout Zambia, although they don't have special facilities for backpackers, such as dorms or information boards. In most places, camping generally costs US$3 to US$6 per person, dorm beds cost around US$6 and double rooms are around US$15.

ACTIVITIES

For adrenalin junkies, Livingstone offers an awesome choice of activities: rafting, microlighting, bungee-jumping, river-boarding, jet-boating, sunset and booze cruises, wildlife drives, helicopter flights and traditional village tours. When you've had your thrills and spills a great way to recover is to surround yourself with nature and wildlife in one of Zambia's many national parks. Most

ZAMBIA

tourists go to South Luangwa for its variety of animals or to Lower Zambezi for its canoeing safaris. Although we describe only a couple of national parks in this book, if you have time visit Lochinvar, northwest of Monze, renowned for its prolific bird life, and Kasanka, south of Lake Bangweulu, famous for its annual bat migration in late October. The latter can be reached by backpackers, and walking is allowed in Kasanka.

DANGERS & ANNOYANCES

Zambia is generally safe for travellers. There have been a few muggings in Livingstone between the town and Victoria Falls. You should also watch out for pickpockets on Lusaka's busy streets.

EMBASSIES & CONSULATES

The following embassies are located in Lusaka, most are situated along or near United Nations Ave. All open from 8 or 9am, usually until 2 or 4pm, but for visa applications it's best to go in the morning.

Botswana (☎ 250019; fax 253895; 5201 Pandit Nehru Rd)
Canada (☎ 250833; 5119 United Nations Ave)
Congo (Zaïre) (☎ 235679; fax 252080; 1124 Parirenyetwa Rd)
Germany (☎ 250644; 5209 United Nations Ave)
Malawi (☎ 265764; fax 265765; 31 Bishops Rd, Kabulonga)
Mozambique (☎ 239135; fax 220345; 9592 Kacha Rd, off Paseli Rd)
Namibia (☎ 260407; fax 263895; 30B Mutende Rd, Woodlands)
South Africa (☎ 260999; fax 263001; 26D Cheetah Rd, Kabulonga)
Tanzania (☎ 253222; fax 254861; 5200 United Nations Ave)
UK (☎ 251133; 5210 Independence Ave)
USA (☎ 250955; cnr Independence & United Nations Aves)
Zimbabwe (☎ 254006; fax 253582; 11058 Haile Selassie Ave)

Zambia has diplomatic representation in the following neighbouring or near-neighbouring countries: Angola, Botswana, Congo (Zaïre), Malawi, Mozambique, Namibia, South Africa, Tanzania and Zimbabwe.

HOLIDAYS

As well as religious holidays listed in the Africa Directory (p1003), these are the principal public holidays in Zambia:

1 January New Year's Day
March Youth Day (2nd Monday)
1 May Labour Day
25 May Africa Freedom Day
July Heroes' Day (1st Monday)
July Unity Day (1st Tuesday)
August Farmers' Day (1st Monday)
24 October Independence Day
26 December Boxing Day

INTERNET ACCESS

There are Internet bureaus in Lusaka (p806) and Livingstone (p816).

LANGUAGE

There are about 70 different ethnic groups, between them speaking many different languages of which seven are listed as official by the government. Main groups and languages include Bemba in the north and centre, Tonga in the south, Nyanja in the east and Lozi in the west. English is the official national language and is widely spoken across the country.

MEDIA

The *Daily Times*, *Daily Mail* and *Post* are the main national daily newspapers. Major international papers and magazines are available in bookshops in Lusaka. *The Lowdown* magazine has news and information on events around Lusaka and other useful tourist information. The Zambia National Broadcasting Corporation operates two radio stations and the national TV station, which broadcast news and programs in English and local languages.

MONEY
Bargaining

Bargaining is part and parcel of buying arts and crafts. You'll also need to negotiate before taking taxis or when hiring transport, which you might do in rural areas.

Exchanging Money

The best hard currency to carry is US dollars followed by British pounds and South African rand. You can exchange money at most banks – and they usually offer the best rates for travellers cheques. Most towns also have bureaux de change, which offer a quicker service and slightly higher rates for cash. In Livingstone and Chipata moneychangers operate on the streets, but to avoid rip-offs it's safer to avoid them. Most banks in the big towns have ATMs.

POST, TELEPHONE & FAX
Letters to countries outside Africa cost about US$0.45. The service from Lusaka is reasonably quick, but from elsewhere it's unreliable and slow.

There are public phone and fax bureaus in Lusaka and in most large towns. Calls within the country are about US$0.50 per minute. Public phones operated by Zamtel use a token, which are available from post offices (ZK500) or local boys (ZK1000) hanging around phone booths. These tokens last three minutes but are only good for calls within Zambia. International calls to Europe or Australia cost about US$3 per minute.

TOURIST INFORMATION
There are government funded tourist information bureaus in Lusaka and Livingstone, but they have limited information. Most backpackers' places have information boards and offer advice on activities and tours.

VISAS
All independent visitors to Zambia need a visa, except those from Australia or Ireland and some Commonwealth countries (visitors from the UK and New Zealand do need visas). Enquire about the latest visa requirements before you arrive in Zambia. Visas are available at most borders and ports of entry,

but if you're travelling by train or boat from Tanzania, you need to get one in advance.

Single/double/multi-entry visas (a maximum of three months) usually cost US$25/40/60. British visitors pay US$65/80/80.

If you book an organised tour with a Zambian operator in advance, they can arrange a visa fee waiver for you (see p799). Some Malawian operators can also do this. You need to arrange it one to two weeks before your arrival.

Visa Extensions
Once in Zambia, visa extensions are possible at the **Department of Immigration** office in Lusaka (Memaco House, Cairo Rd) and Livingstone (Mosi-oa-Tunya Rd).

Visas for Onward Travel
Visas for the following neighbouring countries are available from embassies in Lusaka (see p820 for address details). It is usually obligatory (and otherwise highly recommended) to make your visa applications before noon.

Malawi Most nationalities can obtain a visa free at the border.

Mozambique Transit and single entry visas cost US$24 and are issued the next day.

Tanzania Visas cost US$50 and are ready for collection later the same day.

Zimbabwe Single-entry visas cost US$30 (British citizens US$55) and take seven days, but most nationalities can obtain a visa at the border.

Angola

FAST FACTS

- **Area** 1,246,700 sq km
- **ATMs** none
- **Borders** Congo, Congo (Zaïre) and Zambia borders closed; Namibia open
- **Budget** US$100 per day
- **Capital** Luanda
- **Languages** Portuguese and various Bantu languages
- **Money** kwanza; US$1 = 70Kz (with 150% inflation rate)
- **Population** 14 million
- **Seasons** dry (Jun–Aug); wet (Oct–May, though Luanda gets far less rain than the rest of the country)
- **Telephone** country code ☎ 244; international access code ☎ 00
- **Time** GMT/UTC + 1
- **Visas** US$50 for 30 days; must be obtained in advance

WARNING

Although a ceasefire was signed in 2002, travel outside Luanda is still not recommended. Landmines remain uncleared and the crime rate is high. Luanda was thoroughly updated, but as we were unable to do on-the-ground research some information in the rest of this chapter may not be reliable. Check the situation before travelling to Angola.

For most outsiders Angola means bloody war, bloodier diamonds and bubbling crude – oil, that is. This, together with a history of a long, nasty marriage and messy divorce settlement from Mama Portugal, has more than a few labelling Angola as an African basket case. But don't underestimate this Sub-Saharan giant or its people. Angola stands on the cusp of a spectacular recovery, or even more murderous strife. Angolans are unshockable, resilient and resourceful. They're fighters – but they're lovers too. Portuguese is a great language for singing about love, which is perfect for these music-mad romantics. And for the visitor there's only one thing more breathtaking than being crushed in the clutches of a fast-moving kizomba dancer, sun-worshipping on your own stretch of beach, jamming with your new Rasta friends on makeshift drums, or cruising up a river in an *African Queen* lookalike – and that is being here for the new, peaceful chapter in Angola's history.

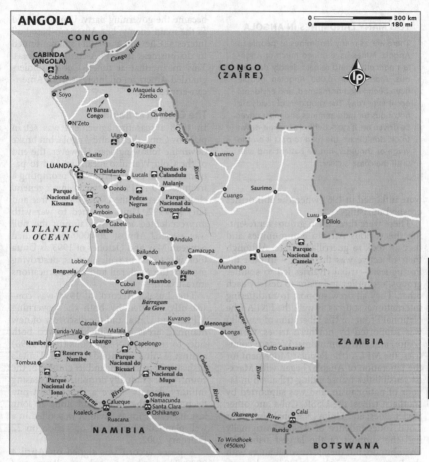

ANGOLA

CONGO

CABINDA (ANGOLA)
Cabinda

Soyo

Congo River

Maquela do Zombo

CONGO (ZAÏRE)

M'Banza Congo

N'Zeto

Quimbele

Uíge

Negage

Cuango

Luremo

Caxito

LUANDA

N'Dalatando

Lucala

Quedas do Calandula

Malanje

Saurimo

Parque Nacional da Kissama

Dondo

Pedras Negras

Parque Nacional da Cangandala

Cuango

Porto Amboim

Quibala

Luau

Dilolo

ATLANTIC OCEAN

Gabela

Sumbe

Andulo

Bailundo

Camacupa

Lobito

Kunhinga

Kuito

Luena

Parque Nacional da Cameia

Benguela

Munhango

Cubul

Huambo

Cuima

Barragam do Gove

Kuvango

ZAMBIA

Cacula

Matala

Menongue

Longa

Tunda-Vala

Lubango

Capelongo

Namibe

Reserva de Namibe

Parque Nacional do Bicuari

Cuito Cuanavale

Tombua

Parque Nacional do Iona

Cunene River

Parque Nacional da Mupa

Calueque

Ondjiva
Namacunda
Santa Clara
Oshikango

Okavango River

Calai

Koaleck

Ruacana

Rundu

NAMIBIA

To Windhoek (450km)

BOTSWANA

0 — 300 km
0 — 180 mi

HISTORY

Over the past 40 years Angolans have known more war than any other African country. Two major conflicts have devastated this Southern African giant: the War of Independence (1961–75), and the civil war (1975–2002). As a result, an entire generation has grown up in the context of death and destruction. The country's infrastructure is shattered and mines litter the land. One of the costs of the war is that four million people, or 30% of the population, have been separated from their families and homes.

A Grim Past

Angolans have long had a troubled history. The many ethnic groups and tribes – the main ones being Ovimbundu, Kimbundu and Bekongo – consider themselves very different and have rarely seen eye to eye. So when the Portuguese settled coastal Luanda in 1575, the warring tribes plundered and sold each other into slavery in return for food and booze, rather than grouping together against a common enemy.

Brazil was a far more lucrative colony than Angola, so for the next 300 years the Portuguese were content to milk Angola for slaves. It was only at the end of the 19th century, when the Portuguese were forced to stop the slave trade, that they settled inland.

Slavery did not endear the colonials to the people. Clashes began after WWII and

TOO MANY LANDMINES IN ANGOLA

There are as many landmines as people in Angola. Mines have ruined much of Angola's agriculture and remain deadly dangerous. More than 70,000 Angolan people have been killed or maimed, and accidents occur every day. The shoulders of roads are notorious for hidden mines and must never be driven on. If stuck behind a broken-down truck, don't leave the road to pass it on the verge or shoulder, but be patient and wait until the coast is clear.

were inflamed in 1961 when the authorities crushed uprisings.

There were three main groups representing the various African communities and they all took to guerrilla warfare. Although their objective was the same – to oust the Portuguese – tribal rivalries led to splinter groups, reshuffles and plans to destroy each other. They all drew support from differing international sources as well: the FNLA (the National Front for the Liberation of Angola) was supported by northern tribes, Congo (Zaïre) and anti-Communist Western countries; the MPLA (the Popular Movement for the Liberation of Angola) began with Marxist sensibilities transcending tribalism in favour of nationalism, and was supported by southern tribes, the USSR, Cuba and other Soviet allies; and Unita (National Union for Total Independence of Angola) originally had the support of the largest tribe, the Ovimbundu, but then formed alliances with the Portuguese right-wing, USA and apartheid South Africa.

In 1975, 400 years after colonisation, the Portuguese finally granted independence to Angola following the overthrow of the fascist government at home. Portugal then set up a transitional government representing themselves and the three different groups. But old tribal rivalries remained, the government collapsed, and Angola plunged into civil war. The Portuguese fled – half a million left in the biggest airlift in history, converting downtown Luanda into a ghost town and robbing the country of its administrative and technical expertise.

Angola quickly became a theatre for the playing out of the Cold War. The MPLA seized control of most of Angola and by early 1976

became the governing party. Unita emerged as the main enemy, but American-based oil interests (Chevron and Gulf) still continued to do business in MPLA-controlled areas. This meant that at times, Cuban soldiers guarded American oil interests from American-armed rebels!

The Ceasefires Begin

In 1988 a ceasefire agreement was set in place by Cuba, the US and Angola, but broke down the following year. However, the end of the Cold War also meant an end to patronage from the superpowers, prompting a fresh accord in 1991. After losing a general election (seen by the UN as largely free and fair) in 1992, Unita returned to war with unprecedented ferocity, claiming the poll was rigged. Almost 200,000 people died between May and October of 1993 as Unita took war to the provincial cities, destroying most of the road, rail and communications infrastructure.

The 'Lusaka Accord' of 1994 was consistently violated by both the governing MPLA and Unita, and the discovery of new diamond areas and oilfields allowed both sides to re-arm. UN sanctions (from 1998) against Unita diamonds caused Unita's cash supply to shrivel, and its control of the countryside gradually crumbled. Increasing military defeats drove a desperate Unita deeper into the hinterland and, at long last, its leader Jonas Savimbi was killed in a well-planned government operation on 22 February 2002.

A peace accord was signed on April 4 2002. Thin and exhausted guerrillas moved with their families (who had been travelling with them as they fought) to an agreed 35 'quartering areas' throughout the country. Senior Unita officials have emphatically declared their commitment to peace and have been absorbed (some may say 'bought off') into the government and army.

The Post-War Period

The northern enclave of Cabinda has been fighting for independence from Angola since 1975. It has 80% of Angola's oil, and now an Angolan army who can focus totally on the Cabinda Liberation Front (FLEC). The latter's chances of success are extremely slim.

The remaining threat to political stability and security in Angola is the reintegration

THE COST OF WAR

More than 2.5 million of those displaced by the recent civil war were children. Some witnessed their parents' deaths and more than a million lost the opportunity to attend school. Many young boys were abducted (by both sides) and forced to become child soldiers. In 1999 UNICEF declared Angola the worst country for children to grow up in.

The war in Angola claimed the lives of at least 1.5 million people. It was fuelled by Angola's natural wealth: intense exploitation of diamond mines and oilfields enabled both sides to heavily arm and re-arm. That same wealth could now power peace and prosperity – if the government so desired. New oilfields have helped Angola become Africa's third-largest producer behind Nigeria and Libya, and total export earnings are now US$8.8 billion a year. But little of this has any effect on employment or other sectors of the economy. Nor does it sway the government into investing in roads, health, housing or education. The government is corrupt, inefficient and not accountable for its spending. State finances are kept in secret offshore accounts and shadowy oil funds through systems that bypass Treasury and the budget. They are dealt with by President Dos Santos, the national oil company Sonangol (of which Dos Santos is the main shareholder) and the central bank. The IMF states that for the last five years, US$1 billion has gone unaccounted for each year.

of the 85,000-strong Unita army, and their 300,000 dependants. Failure to deal with these people properly, including finding them employment, could tempt the ex-soldiers into banditry. Many parts of the country are already violent, lawless places, particularly in the diamond areas of the northeast. This scenario may get worse, making much of the country an unknown and dangerous quantity.

But this is only a potential risk, not the writing on the wall.

For the first time in their lives, most Angolans are living without war. A collective sigh of relief reverberated around the country when Jonas Savimbi and his war were quashed. Reconstruction of the economy and social sectors must now begin with a strong partnership between UN agencies, NGOs and the government. The question is how to make the government contribute. It has promised the IMF that it will redirect spending to health, education and reconstruction, but progress has not been made and the 2003 budget did not indicate how it will.

Angolans are the first to tell you that things here take time. For now, the sphere of possibilities and opportunities is enough to keep the home fires of hope burning.

THE CULTURE

Angolans, at first, seem backwards in coming forwards. They will answer your questions but not ask any. This is a survival technique: every one of them has endured a lifetime with a government that doesn't listen or give a damn about them. You may be told Angolans are lazy – it's not true, it's just that they've grown up in a place where nothing is straightforward, where even the most basic task can be problematic. And so they have mastered the art of patience and an understanding of impermanence. What's not here today may reappear tomorrow: water, electricity, family, peace. In this post-war period, relief is tempered with continuing difficulties and the reality of dislocation. The answer is escapism and spirituality, and the vehicle is love. Angolans love going to church and they love romance. They go nuts for Valentine's Day and soap operas. But their favourite means of removal from reality is shaking their well-shaped and sexily clad booties at all-night parties. No wonder they have the highest fertility rate in the world!

ENVIRONMENT

Angola has 1600km of Atlantic-hugging coastline, with mountains in the central provinces of Huambo and Malanje. In the north, Cabinda is a small province located between Congo (Zaïre) and Congo. The countryside is green and fertile with many rivers, and is rich in natural resources. Major exports include oil, diamonds, minerals, coffee, fish, timber, cotton and sisal, but none of these crops feed the rural population and mines have reduced agriculture to subsistence levels. So Angola imports nearly all its food, making it very expensive

(Luanda is the fourth-most expensive city in the world) and meaning much of the population relies on foreign aid for food.

There are six large national parks in Angola, but most of the animals were eaten by hungry people during the recent war. The rest were shot by trigger-happy soldiers.

In a bid to boost tourism, wildlife from South Africa is being introduced in parks. Sadly the first four imported zebra (at US$10,000 a pop) were killed and eaten. However, Angolans spat the dummy over that, so there is hope for future wildlife.

TRANSPORT

GETTING THERE & AWAY
Air
Direct flights are possible from Paris (Air France), London (British Airways) and Lisbon (TAP). There's also a direct flight from Houston – 'The Houston Express' – check out www.houston-express.co for details.

You can also fly to Luanda from Addis Ababa (Ethiopia; US$820, weekly), Brazzaville (Congo; US$350, Wednesday and Saturday), Harare (Zimbabwe; US$440, Friday), Johannesburg (South Africa; US$600, daily), Kinshasa (Congo–Zaïre) and Windhoek (Namibia; US$445, Tuesday, Thursday and Sunday).

Land
The only border that's officially open is with Namibia. You can enter at Santa Clara from Oshikango (Namibia) or at Calai from Rundu (Namibia).

Forget trying to cross between Angola and Congo (Zaïre) or Zambia. And due to troubles in Brazzaville (Congo), the border into Cabinda closes without warning. Other borders may allow refugees through, but they are not officially open. Many illegals sneak through Dilolo to Luau (diamond country), hoping to find diamonds.

GETTING AROUND
Air
Air travel is the safest option, but **TAAG** (☎ 39 2541; 5th floor, Rua da Missão, 123, Luanda), the national airline, is often overbooked. **SAL Airlines** (☎ 35 0869) and **Sonair** (☎ 63 3543) both have offices at the Luanda airport or you can book through a travel agent.

Bus
Public transport in Angola is very limited. Although buses and trucks operate, they are often over-filled, unroadworthy, and prone to breaking down and crashing.

Car
Most visitors get around by car, but this is no joy ride. The roads are a disaster: badly potholed, often unpaved, frequently flooded and flanked by mines. Travel by road should only be undertaken in 4WD convoys along approved roads. Hitching is currently considered too dangerous.

Train
There are a few small trains on limited tracks: Luanda to Dondo (Tuesday and Friday, returns Wednesday and Saturday); Lobito to Benguela (daily); Lobango to Namibe (Monday, returns Wednesday); Lobango to Matala (Saturday, returns Friday). Prices range from US$1.40 to US$2.80.

LUANDA

☎ 02 / pop 3.5 million

Luanda is almost beautiful. Set on the coast with a harbour and open sea, its red-roofed colonial buildings offer shade from the belting sun. Pineapples and mangoes float by, balanced easily on heads of strutting fruit sellers with babies tied around their waists. Decayed footpaths and badly potholed roads swarm with street kids, shifting sand, fancy imported cars, cool dudes in wraparound shades, foxy girls in midriff tops, death-trap buses, businessmen, Rastafarians, and canary yellow kaftans with matching headscarves. All are eyed by vulture-like traffic cops.

The city was built for 500,000 people – it now heaves with 3.5 million. Once-lovely homes are now lush squats. Satellite dishes smother apartment blocks. Palm trees line main roads. Amputees beg at traffic lights. Scripture groups sing and sway outside 16th-century whitewashed churches. Art Deco meets the 1960s and old-world Europe in a tropical sweat.

One kilometre from the central business district is the Ilha, where the rich and penniless swim side by side. Ramshackle housing hits the ocean on one side, the harbour on the other. With its beach soccer, makeshift bars and barbecued bananas, it could be the Caribbean.

Luanda was spared any serious fighting, but its battle scars are everywhere. There are too many decayed buildings, too much festering rubbish, and far too many people for it to be beautiful. But it could be.

ORIENTATION
The airport is 4km south of Luanda, with the domestic terminal next to the international terminal. Catch a private taxi (Macontaxi) to the centre of town for around US$30. The city is set along a harbour overlooking a deceptively long skinny peninsula called the Ilha de Luanda, or just 'the Ilha'. The 2km promenade along the harbour, Avenida 4 de Fevereiro, is known as the Marginal and is the heart of the city. It hosts the reserve bank, head offices and international airlines. South along the Marginal is Mutamba where you are most likely to stay, play and get away – second only to the Ilha (900m away) with its endless beaches, bars and restaurants. North of the city and up the hill from the Marginal is Mirimar, home to the president, most of the embassies, rich oil expats and poor Angolans.

INFORMATION
Internet Access
Prices are around US$2.50 per hour. Good, centrally located options include **A Nave** (56 Rua da Missão), located at the back of a decent pizza joint, and **Correios CommCenter** (Largo de Pedro Alexandrino de Cunha, Mutamba) in the post office building.

Medical Services
Luanda's best clinics include **Clinica Sagrada Esperanca** (☎ 30 9034; Avenida Mortala Mohamed, Ilha de Luanda; ☽ 24hr), halfway down the Ilha behind the school; use the South African clinic opposite general admissions. Alternatively, try **Clinica da Mutamba** (☎ 39 3783, emergency ☎ 39 7222; Rua Pedro Felix Machado, 10/12), a one-stop medical facility that includes a pharmacy. There are also many 24-hour *farmacias* (pharmacies) in the capital.

Money
You can exchange money in banks and at major hotels, but you'll get better rates on the street. You'll need to know your numbers in Portuguese, and the current exchange

rate. The government periodically makes street exchanging illegal, so be discreet.

Post & Telephone
The **post office** (Largo de Pedro Alexandrino de Cunha, Mutamba) is in a large, renovated building, but its impressiveness belies a hopeless postal service. In case of urgency, **DHL** (☎ 39 5180; Kwamme Nkrumah, 274, Sagrada Familia) is fast and very reliable, if expensive.

The only public telephones that tend to work are located at the main post office and outside **Telecom** (Rua Congresso MPLA, 2) where you will also find telephone directories. You can buy phonecards from post office. You can make international calls. Note that telephone numbers change very frequently – for this and for cultural reasons, bookings are best made face to face.

Travel Agencies
Tropicana (☎ 44 8924; Avenida Comandante Valodia, 117; tropican@ebonet.net) is a travel agency and a private coach and car-rental company.

DANGERS AND ANNOYANCES
If travelling to the outer suburbs of Luanda or outside the city, you should travel with Angolans, where possible. Being robbed in Luanda is one of the biggest dangers you'll encounter. Be Smart. Don't walk far at night. Don't wear gold or silver jewellery (even imitation), watches or sunglasses. Keep money in a hidden money-belt. At the beach, don't take your eyes off your bags. See also Dangers & Annoyances, p830.

SIGHTS & ACTIVITIES
The best, safest market is Benfica, half an hour south of Mutamba by bus. It sells jewellery, artefacts and art from Angola and neighbouring countries (as well as ivory and leopard skins!). **Elinga Teatro** (Largo Tristao de Cunhu, 15, Mutamba) is an art gallery/fringe theatre where artists exhibit and hang out. Join them for drinks Friday, Saturday and Sunday nights or wander through (free) during the day and watch them work. The best beach is on Mussulo, an island accessed by boat from the marina at the end of Estrada da Samba, about 20km southwest of Luanda.

FESTIVALS & EVENTS
Carnival ain't Rio de Janeiro but it's something. Held in February and set along the

Marginal, it's a time for gays, gremlins and frustrated performers to come out of the closet. Amusingly, people dress up as the president, oil magnates, or their sexual fantasies. Dad and the kids dress in drag. But disturbingly, there are also a lot of half-dead cats (of which Angolans are very superstitious) tied to costumes and crucifixes.

November 11 is **Independence Day** and is also celebrated in the streets, with the added bonus of a public address and a few words from his nibs, the president.

SLEEPING

Most hotel rooms start at US$80 to US$100. A double room (or duplo) usually means two beds. If you forego air-conditioning and bathrooms you will cut costs.

Panorama Hotel (☎ 33 7843; Ilha de Luanda; s/d US$44/55) It's grubby and very rundown, but it's the cheapest joint in town by halves and in an excellent location: absolute water frontage onto the harbour, and views to the city, plus it's across the road from the beach. Bring your own mosquito net.

Hotel Avenida (☎ 33 4726; Rua Sequeira Lukoki, 120; s/d US$80/100) It's in the heart of Mutamba and has all the mod cons.

Residencia da Kianda (☎ 39 3394; Largo da Peixeiera; s/d US$80/100) Smack bang among Ilha local life, it has a roof terrace for sunset- and people-watching.

SPLURGE!

Hotel Tropico (☎ 37 0070; Rua da Missão, 103; s/d US$150/165) This is the most glamorous place in town where the tariff includes breakfast, use of hi-tech health club with the lot, a luxurious swimming pool and an outdoor bar with foreign newspapers.

EATING & DRINKING

You can eat and drink for around US$1 a pop from street vendors. Women sell fruit and baguette-like sandwiches; boys sell huge bags of fresh breadrolls. Street vendors sell beer for less than US$1 and, around the beach, bags of roasted nuts, barbecued chicken and corn. Hot-dog stands are everywhere. The best one is by the Telecom building – for US$0.75 you also get crunchy chips and mountains of mayo and ketchup.

Restaurants often double as bars, but they're expensive.

Rialto (☎ 39 1827; Largo Tristão Cunha, Mutamba) A landmark on the Marginal, it's a bar/restaurant with good pizza for US$10.

Restaurant So Tam 8 (☎ 30 9887; Chicala 2 do Ilha) This Vietnamese restaurant on the south end of the Ilha deliciously mixes mangoes and nuts with meat, fish and vegetables. Share a few dishes and pay US$16 each.

Cacuco, opposite Salina fish markets, 12km north on the main northbound road, is where you can experience great, authentic Angolan food. Eat under a thatched roof on the beach for US$20 a dish.

Miami, halfway down the Ilha, is a very popular beachclub-bar and often has parties on Saturday and live music on Sunday.

SPLURGE!

Veranda das Mangais (☎ 39 1653; Rua Major Canhangulo, 3b) If you want to 'pop the question' or simply celebrate the joy of being in Africa, then don't eat for two days and make the one-hour trip south of the city for a long, long lunch. Set on the River Kwanza and partially surrounded by jungle, this restaurant is an ode to Anglo-African architecture and the love of being laid-back. For US$50 or US$100 (with alcohol) dine on crayfish, steak, fish soup and more. Between courses take the complimentary boat ride up the river. It's an enchanting experience.

ENTERTAINMENT

Near Benfica market is **clube hipico** (admission free; ☾ 10pm-5am Fri, 8pm-5.30am Sat, 10pm-2am Sun), an outdoor place to listen to live jazz, semba, kizomba and kuduru.

There is one functioning cinema-theatre, the poignantly named **Karl Marx** (Rua de Oliveira Martins, 19), which is a large semi-outdoor bar-cinema screening Hollywood flicks with Portuguese subtitles. It occasionally hosts a performance group from Lisbon or Brazil. Check *Jornal de Angola* for daily listings.

GETTING THERE & AWAY
Air
Airlines servicing Angola include:

Aeroflot (☎ 33 0426; Avenida 4 de Fevereiro, 114)
Air France (☎ 33 5416; Avenida 4 de Fevereiro, 123)

Air Gabon (☎ 31 0614; Largo 4 de Fevereiro, 8)
Air Namibia (☎ 33 6726; Rua Assalto Q Moncada, 12)
Note that TAAG shares some routes.
Air Portugal (☎ 33 1692; Avenida 4 Fevereiro, 80)
British Airways (☎ 30 9270) You'll find this right near
Wimpy on the Ilha.
Ethiopian Airlines (☎ 31 0615; Largo 4 de Fevereiro,10)
South African Airways (☎ 39 1858; Rua Clube
Maritimo Africano, 2/4)
TAAG (☎ 39 2541; 5th floor, Rua Missão,123)

Land
You can hire cars from **Avis** (Hotel Tropical;
☎ 37 0070; Rua da Missão, 103) and **Equador** (Hotel
Continental, Rua Duarte Lopes, 2). Hire prices start at
US$70; drivers US$40 per day. The chaotic
nature of the Luanda traffic makes hiring a
driver highly recommended.

GETTING AROUND
For getting around Luanda, buses and 'taxis'
(blue-and-white Toyota Hiaces) start from
a terminus in Mutamba, in front of the
candy-pink Governo Provincial de Luanda
building. They go to most places within
Luanda and nearby (US$0.50 to US$1 per
ride). There are bus stops everywhere –
easily spotted by long queues. Private taxis
are 4WDs; try **Macontaxi** (☎ 47 0520), charging US$4 flagfall plus US$1 per kilometre.

AROUND ANGOLA

Travelling 'shoestring-style' outside the capital on trucks and buses is currently strongly
warned against. There are some fascinating
and beautiful places, however, if you have
the chance to fly or travel in 4WD convoys.

KUITO
The cooler climate, friendly faces and lush
surrounds make Kuito a pleasant escape
from Luanda. The city suffered terribly during the war and nearly all the grand colonial
buildings were ruined, making Kuito look
like the backlot for a WWII movie.

You can change money on the street at a
better rate than in Luanda.

Tambarino (Rua Principal; s/d US$30) has big,
clean rooms with TV. Along the same road
is **Esplanade** (Rua Principal), a restaurant-bar
with steak, eggs and chips for US$8.

An hour's bumpy-but-beautiful drive
north is **Kunhinga** (taxis leave when full;

hitching is possible), with a vibrant market
good for fruit and people-watching.

Kuito is 900km southeast of Luanda, two
days by car but only 90 minutes by plane.

LUBANGO
Largely unaffected by the war, Lubango
provides access to the coastal town of **Namibe**
and its excellent beaches. En route, watch for
the Tunda-Vala volcanic fissure, 20km from
Lubango, where you can climb to 2600km
above sea level. The view of a sheer drop to
sea level is quite spectacular.

Lubango has plenty of cheap hotels and
restaurants. Try the **Grande Hotel da Huila**
(☎ 061-20 512, Rua Deolinda Rodrigues) or the more-
upmarket **Hotel Imperio** (☎ 061-22 755).

Access to Lubango is by air with Air
Gemini (US$240) from Luanda. Namibe is
best accessed from Lubango by truck.

PARQUE NACIONAL DA KISSAMA
To the south of Luanda, Kissama (also spelt
Quiçama) is a stunning park of grassland,
amazing trees, and wildlife – giraffes, ostriches, and, unique to Angola, palanca
(antelope). The park is supported by various development organisations and is slowly
being re-established after years of war.

In the park, you can stay in a **bungalow** (s/d
US$60/80 with mosquito nets; 🔲) or a **tent** (US$25).
All bookings have to be made in advance
in Luanda at the **Hotel Forum** (☎ 32 4344; funda
caokissama@netangola.com or hotelforum@netangola.com;
Trevessa Hon Chemin).

The only way to get here is by 4WD.
Head south from Luanda along the coast
road. After about 70km (90 minutes' drive),
and 3km after the Barra do Cuanza (Kwanza
bridge), turn east then drive 40km inland.

ANGOLA DIRECTORY

ACCOMMODATION
Shoestring-budget accommodation is impossible to come by. You can expect to pay
upwards of US$30 for the most basic (bath-
roomless) room in the countryside and at
least US$80 in the cities.

BUSINESS HOURS
Most businesses are open 8.30am to 12.30pm
and 2pm to 6pm Monday to Friday, and
8.30am to 12.30pm Saturday.

DANGERS & ANNOYANCES

Travelling in 'shoestring mode' is considered too dangerous in Angola, as cheaper accommodation and transport modes have less security. And the guys in uniforms (police, army) are rarely the good guys – they are generally corrupt and keen for a *gasosa* (bribe).

EMBASSIES & CONSULATES

The following countries have diplomatic representation in Luanda:

Canada (☎ 44 8371; Rua Rei Katyavala, 113)
Congo (☎ 31 0293; Rua Fernando Pessoa, Vila Alice)
Congo (Zaïre) (☎ 31 0293; Rua Fernando Pessoa, Vila Alice)
France (☎ 33 4841; Rua Rev Agostinho Pedro Neto, 39)
Gabon (☎ 44 9289; Rua Eng Armindo Adrade, 149)
Germany (☎ 33 4516; Avenida 4 Fevereiro, 120)
Namibia (☎ 39 5483; Rua dos Coqueiros, 37)
South Africa (☎ 33 5869 or 39 8726; 31 Rua Kwamime Nkrumah)
UK (☎ 33 4582; Rua 17 de Setembro)
USA (☎ 44 7028; Rua Houari Boumedienne, 132)
Zambia (☎ 44 7496; Rua Rei Katyavala, 1618)

Angola has diplomatic representation in Namibia, Gabon and South Africa.

HOLIDAYS

As well as religious holidays listed in the Africa Directory (p1003), these are the principal public holidays in Angola:

1 January New Year's Year Day
4 February National Holiday
27 March Victory Day
1 May Worker's Day
1 August Armed Forces Day
17 September National Hero's Day
11 November Independence Day
10 December MPLA Foundation Day

MONEY

Angola's currency is the Kwanza (Kz). It is not convertible and cannot be taken out of the country. The largest note is 100Kz (about US$1.40), so be prepared for huge wads of cash. When drawing US dollars from banks, make sure you count the notes. There are many counterfeit dollars in circulation, best spotted by the smaller heads on the notes. Strangely, you can still exchange these outside of the capital; you just won't get as good a rate!

You can exchange money in banks and at hotels, but you'll get much better rates changing money on the streets – usually with women.

Angola is a cash economy, although there are no ATMs. Credit cards are rarely accepted (the major hotels and airlines being some exceptions) and travellers cheques are almost never accepted.

Bargaining is expected for some things, though vendors' starting prices are not wildly above what they will eventually settle for.

POST & TELEPHONE

The postal system is unreliable throughout the country. Angola Telecom often requires several attempts, but works in the main cities.

TOURS

Somitour (☎ 33 7965; Rua Manuel Ferreira Caldeira, 3a), opposite the Continental Hotel in Mutamba, is very helpful. The staff speak English and can organise safe tours to provinces.

VISAS

Tourist visas cost US$50 for 30 days (Americans get two years). Visa applications from embassies abroad are referred to Luanda, and can take up to two weeks to come through.

Visa Extensions

Visas can be renewed for 90 days in Luanda at the Department of Immigration (DEFA), adjacent to the British Embassy, for US$30.

Visas for Onward Travel

Visas for the following countries can be obtained in Angola. See above for embassy and consulate information.

Congo All visitors to Congo need a visa. Visa applications can be issued on the same or next day.
Congo (Zaïre) All visitors need a visa. It is essential to get a visa before you arrive; a one-month, single-entry visa costs US$60.
Gabon Visas are US$100 for 30 days and applications can be lodged 8.30am to 12.30pm Monday to Friday(air ticket and one photo required).
Namibia US$30 for one month and applications can be lodged on Friday from 8am to 2.30pm (two days processing time required).
Zambia Visas are US$25 for 30 days and applications can be lodged Monday to Friday 9am to noon and 2pm to 4pm (ready same day; two photos and a copy of air ticket required).

Namibia

HIGHLIGHTS

- **Sossusvlei** Get lost amid the towering red dunes and feel as if you've travelled to the ends of the earth (p847)
- **Swakopmund** Go wild in the adrenalin headquarters of Namibia, the place for skydiving, quad-biking, sandboarding and partying (p843)
- **Etosha National Park** Look for the Big Five amid the white dust of Etosha pan, then relax with a drink at sunset by a floodlit water hole (p851)
- **Damaraland** Explore vast spaces, desert species, mystical mountains and extensive rock art (p849)
- **Off the beaten track** Spend a few days relaxing on the banks of the Okavango River at Ngepi Camp in West Caprivi and enjoy the tranquillity of this lush and beautiful region (p855)

FAST FACTS

- **Area** 825,000 sq km
- **ATMs** in most large towns around the country
- **Borders** Angola, Botswana, South Africa, Zambia, Zimbabwe – all accessible overland except Zimbabwe, which has no direct border crossing with Namibia
- **Budget** US$20 to US$25 a day
- **Capital** Windhoek
- **Languages** English, Afrikaans, German, Owambo, Kavango, Herero, Khoikhoi (Nama/Damara), San dialects
- **Money** Namibian dollar; US$1 = N$8
- **Population** 1.8 million
- **Seasons** long rains season (Jan–Apr), dry (May–Oct), short rains season (Oct–Dec); note that it is very hot in Windhoek, Etosha National Park and Namib-Naukluft Park from Oct–Dec
- **Telephone** country code ☎ 264; international access code ☎ 00
- **Time** GMT/UTC + 2
- **Visas** none required for citizens of Australia, Canada, France, Germany, Ireland, New Zealand, UK, or USA

NAMIBIA

The only thing small about Namibia is its population. Everything else is larger than life: towering red dunes; bleak mist-shrouded coastlines of shipwreck lore; vast expanses of nothing; sky so big it swallows you up.

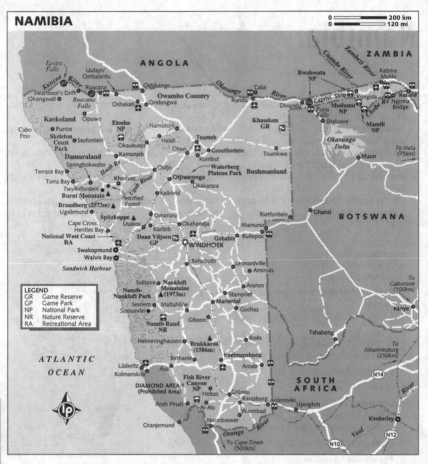

Namibia is one of those dreamlike places that make you question whether something so visually orgasmic could actually exist. Time and space are less defined here. Landscapes collide. Experiences pile up. Watch a lion stalking its prey on a never-ending plain in Etosha. Fly down a giant dune on a sandboard. Spend a night alone in the desert under a sky so thick with stars you can't differentiate between constellations. If you yearn to explore, get away from the crowds and lose yourself in a hauntingly beautiful place, then head to this safe, friendly nation wedged between the Kalahari Desert and the South Atlantic Ocean.

HISTORY

It's generally accepted that southern Africa's earliest inhabitants were San – nomadic people who adapted to even the severest terrain. San communities seem to have later come under pressure from Khoikhoi (Hottentot) groups, the ancestors of the modern Nama, with whom they share a language group (Khoisan).

The descendants of the Khoikhoi and San people still live in Namibia, but few of them have retained their original hunter-gatherer lifestyles. The so-called Topnaar Hottentots of the Kuiseb River area are an exception, maintaining ancient ways based on goat-herding.

Between 2300 and 2400 years ago, the first Bantu people appeared on the plateaus of south-central Africa. Their arrival marked the first tribal structures in Southern African societies.

Around AD 1600 the Herero people, who were Bantu-speaking cattle herders, arrived in Namibia from the Zambezi area. They occupied the north and west of the country, causing conflicts with the Khoikhoi over grazing lands and water holes. In what is now called Kaokoland, the more aggressive Herero displaced not only the Khoikhoi but also the remaining San and the Damara people (whose origin is unclear).

It is thought that the Nama people of present-day Namibia are descended from Khoikhoi groups who held out against the Herero despite violent clashes in the 1870s and 1880s. By then a new Bantu group, the Owambo, had settled in the north along the Okavango and Kunene Rivers. The Owambo were probably descended from people who migrated from eastern Africa more than 500 years earlier.

Colonial History

Because Namibia has one of the world's most barren and inhospitable coastlines, it was largely ignored by the European nations until relatively recently. The first European visitors were Portuguese mariners seeking a route to the Indies in the late 15th century, but they confined their activities to erecting stone crosses at certain points as navigational aids.

It wasn't until the last-minute scramble for colonies towards the end of the 19th century that Namibia was annexed by Germany (except for the enclave of Walvis Bay, which was taken in 1878 by the British for the Cape Colony). In 1904 the Herero launched a rebellion and, later that year, were joined by the Nama, but the rebellions were brutally suppressed.

The Owambo in the north were luckier and managed to avoid conquest until after the start of WWI, when they were overrun by Portuguese forces fighting on the side of the Allies. Soon after, the German colony abruptly came to an end when its forces surrendered to a South African expeditionary army also fighting on behalf of the Allies.

At the end of WWI, South Africa was given a mandate to rule the territory (then known as South West Africa) by the League of Nations. Following WWII, the mandate

was renewed by the United Nations (UN), who refused to sanction the annexation of the country by South Africa.

Undeterred, the South African government tightened its grip on the territory and, in 1949, they granted parliamentary representation to the white population. The bulk of southern Namibia's viable farmland was parcelled into some 6000 farms owned by white settlers, while indigenous families were confined by law to their 'reserves' (mainly in the east and the far north) and urban workplaces.

Nationalism & the Struggle for Independence

Forced labour had been the lot of most Namibians since the German annexation. This was one of the main factors that led to mass demonstrations and the development of nationalism in the late 1950s. Around this time, a number of political parties were formed and strikes organised. By 1960 most of these parties had merged to form the South West Africa People's Organization (Swapo), which took the issue of South African occupation to the International Court of Justice.

The outcome was inconclusive, but in 1966 the UN General Assembly voted to terminate South Africa's mandate and set up a Council for South West Africa (in 1973 renamed the Commission for Namibia) to administer the territory. At the same time, Swapo launched its campaign of guerrilla warfare. The South African government reacted by firing on demonstrators and arresting thousands of activists.

In 1975 the Democratic Turnhalle Alliance (DTA) was officially established. Formed from a combination of white political interests and ethnic parties, it turned out to be a toothless debating chamber, which spent much of its time in litigation with the South African government over its scope of responsibility.

The DTA was dissolved in 1983 after it had indicated it would accommodate members of Swapo. It was replaced by the Multiparty Conference, which had even less success and quickly disappeared. And so control of Namibia passed back to the South African–appointed administrator-general.

The failure of these attempts to set up an internal government did not deter South

Africa from maintaining its grip on Namibia. It refused to negotiate on a UN-supervised program for Namibian independence until the estimated 19,000 Cuban troops were removed from neighbouring Angola.

In response, Swapo intensified its guerrilla campaign.

In the end, however, it might not have been the activities of Swapo alone or international sanctions that forced the South Africans to the negotiating table. The white Namibian population itself was growing tired of the war and the economy was suffering badly.

The stage was finally set for negotiations on the country's future. Under the watch of the UN, the USA and the USSR, a deal was struck between Cuba, Angola, South Africa and Swapo, in which Cuban troops would be removed from Angola and South African troops from Namibia. This would be followed by UN-monitored elections held in November 1989 on the basis of universal suffrage. Swapo collected a clear majority of the votes but an insufficient number to give it the sole mandate to write the new constitution.

Independence

Following negotiations between the various parties, a constitution was adopted in February 1990. Independence was granted the following month under the presidency of the Swapo leader, Sam Nujoma. Initially, his policies focused on programs of reconstruction and national reconciliation to heal the wounds left by 25 years of armed struggle. In 1999, however, Nujoma had nearly served out his second (and constitutionally, his last) five-year term, and alarm bells sounded among watchdog groups when he changed the constitution to allow himself a third five-year term, which he won with nearly 77% of the vote.

In August 1999, a separatist Lozi faction in the Caprivi Strip launched a coup attempt – which was summarily put down by the Namibian Defence Force. In December of the same year the Caprivi Strip also suffered a spate of violent attacks on civilians and travellers, which were rightly or wrongly blamed on Unita sympathisers from Angola (see p823 for information on this group). These attacks destroyed tourism in the Caprivi Strip, but since Angola signed

a peace accord in April 2002, the region is slowly starting to come back to life.

Today, despite President Sam Nujoma's recent attacks on homosexuality and Christianity, and his open support of Robert Mugabe's disastrous policies in Zimbabwe (see p889), Namibia's economy remains relatively stable, corruption is somewhat under control and most Namibians harbour guarded hopes for the future of their fabulous country.

THE CULTURE

Despite only gaining independence less than 20 years ago, racism in Namibia is not as blatantly obvious as in South Africa. Whites, on the whole, are more open-minded, do not refer to their black countrymen in overtly negative terms and do not speak about apartheid in a positive manner.

Perhaps one of the most interesting differences between the two countries can be seen in the use of Afrikaans. Blacks in South Africa will tell you it is the language of apartheid, and although many were forced to learn the tongue in school, speaking it is considered insulting. In Namibia, where intermarriage between different tribes is common, Afrikaans has become a vital form of communication. Those of diverse ethnic backgrounds will tell you it is how their parents communicate with each other, and was the first language they learned at home as children.

With a population of barely 1.8 million, Namibia represents one of Africa's lowest population densities, with approximately two people per square kilometre. This number comprises 11 major ethnic groups, including Owambo, Kavango, Herero, Himba, Damara, Nama, Basters, Caprivians, German, Afrikaner and Tswana. About 75% of the population inhabits rural areas, but the uncontrolled urban drift for work or higher wages has resulted in increased homelessness, unemployment and crime in the capital and other towns.

ARTS

Although Namibia is still developing a literary tradition, its musical, visual and architectural arts are fairly well established. The country also enjoys a wealth of amateur talent in the production of material arts, including carvings, basketware and tapestry, along with simple but resourcefully designed and produced toys, clothing and household implements.

ENVIRONMENT
The Land
Namibia may be largely arid, but it encompasses broad geographical variations and can be divided into four regions: the dunes and desert coastal plains of the Namib and the Skeleton Coast; the Central Plateau; the Kalahari; and the bushveld of Kavango and the Caprivi Strip.

The whole country enjoys a minimum of 300 days of sunshine a year, but temperatures and rainfall vary considerably both seasonally and geographically. In the winter dry season (May to October) you can expect clear, warm and sunny days and cold, clear nights, often with temperatures falling below freezing. Generally, the mountainous and semi-arid Central Plateau (including Windhoek) is a bit cooler than the rest of the country. At this time the Kalahari region of eastern Namibia is usually hotter than the Central Plateau; it also receives less rain.

There are two rainy seasons, the 'little rains' (October to December) and the main rainy period (January to April). The latter is characterised by brief showers and occasional thunderstorms that clean the air.

January temperatures in Windhoek can soar to 40°C, and from December to March, Namib-Naukluft Park and Etosha National Park become hot and uncomfortable. From January to March, the northeastern rivers may flood, making some roads either impassable or hard to negotiate.

National Parks
Despite its harsh climate, Namibia has some of the world's grandest and most diverse national parks.

From the wildlife-packed Etosha to the often photographed Namib-Naukluft to the inhospitable Skeleton Coast, Namibia's parks offer something for everyone.

Namibian national parks are operated by the semi-private **Namibian Wildlife Resorts** (NWR; Map p840; ☎ 061-285 7000; www.namibiareservations.com/namibiawildliferesorts.html; 189 Independence Ave, Private Bag 13267, Windhoek; ☾ 8am-5pm Mon-Fri).

Unlike parks in East Africa and Botswana, which can cost a fortune to visit, parks in

Namibia, if you have your own vehicle, are a steal (entry fees are less than US$5). Of course the drawback is that you'll be your own safari guide, and searching for wildlife while driving can be quite an experience – but hey, when you spot the Big Five you'll be able to say you found them on your own! If you don't have a car consider joining an inexpensive tour. Most backpackers lodges can arrange these for you (or see p861 for tour operators).

Park camp sites and accommodation can be booked up to 12 months in advance, but this isn't usually necessary. Although pre-booking is advisable, especially for Etosha and Sesriem, it can easily be done just a few days in advance. Simply stop at the park offices in Windhoek or Swakopmund and see what's available. You may not get your first choice, but there's usually something. Even if you just turn up at the park gates without booking, accommodation is often available (as long as you're not travelling during major holidays). The exception to this is the camp sites in Sesriem, which usually fill up very quickly.

If you do wish to book ahead, you can do so by post or email. You'll need to give your passport number, the number of people in your group (including the ages of any children), your full contact details, the type of accommodation required and your date of arrival and departure – including alternative dates. Fees must be paid by bank transfer or credit card before bookings will be confirmed. In addition to fees for accommodation, parks charge a daily admission fee per person and per vehicle.

Environmental Issues
With a small human population spread over a large land area, Namibia is in better environmental shape than most African countries, but the country still lacks coherent environmental guidelines. The Ministry of Environment & Tourism (MET) is largely a holdover from pre-independence days and its policies reflect those of its South African counterpart.

Some major environmental issues facing Namibia involve offshore fishing policies, protection of desert rhinos, and proposed hydroelectric projects to provide water and power resources for the country's growing industrial and human needs.

TRANSPORT

GETTING THERE & AWAY

Air

Major airlines fly from Europe, Australia and the US to Windhoek; however, flights are limited and it is often cheaper to fly into South Africa and go overland or by plane into Namibia from there. **South African Airways** (www.flysaa.com) and **Air Namibia** (www.airnamibia.com.na) operate daily flights between Johannesburg (Jo'burg), Cape Town and Hosea Kutako International Airport, 42km east of Windhoek. One-way fares between Jo'burg or Cape Town and Windhoek start at US$200. Air Namibia also flies twice weekly between Windhoek and Harare, Victoria Falls, Lusaka, Maun and Gaborone.

Land

Namibia shares borders with Angola, Botswana, South Africa, Zambia and Zimbabwe. The two main border crossings with South Africa are Ariamsvlei in the southeast and Noordoewer on the west coast; both crossings are open 24 hours. You can also cross by train from Keetmanshoop.

There are three border crossings between Namibia and Angola, at Ruacana/Calueque (6pm to 10pm), Oshikango/Namacunda (8am to 6pm) and Nkurenkuru/Cuangar (7am to 5pm), but travellers need an Angolan visa permitting overland entry. These are best obtained at the Angolan consulate in Oshakati, in north Namibia, as the embassy in Windhoek tends to only give visas for air travel into Luanda. At Ruacana Falls, you can briefly enter Angola without a visa.

The Trans-Kalahari Hwy to Botswana crosses the border at Buitepos-Mamuno (open 8am to 1am). In the Caprivi Strip, you can cross the border into Botswana at Ngoma Bridge (8am to 6pm) or between Mahango and Mohembo (6am to 6pm). The border crossing between Mpalila Island and Kasane (7am to 12.30pm and 1.45pm to 4pm) exists mainly for guests of safari lodges on the island.

DEPARTURE TAX

At the time of writing there was no departure tax.

The only crossing between Namibia and Zambia is at Wenela, about 5km north of Katima Mulilo. On the Zambia side of the border you can continue along the west bank of the Zambezi towards Mongu, or cross the Zambezi on the pontoon ferry (US$10 per vehicle, pedestrians ride free) and head east to Sesheke, and eventually Livingstone.

There's no direct overland connection between Namibia and Zimbabwe. The most straightforward route is between Victoria Falls and the Caprivi Strip (via Botswana), which entails driving or hitching from the Namibian border at Ngoma Bridge through Chobe National Park (you won't be subject to Botswana national park fees unless you turn off onto the tourist route) and then to Kasane.

To bring a foreign-registered vehicle into Namibia, you must purchase a US$10 road-use tax certificate at the border. If the vehicle is rented from another country you must also present a letter from the car-hire company stating that you are allowed to take the vehicle out of the country. To take a Namibian-registered vehicle out of Namibia, you must first secure police clearance from any Namibian police station; you'll also need a 'Blue Book' sheet with the vehicle's engine and chassis number.

GETTING AROUND

Air

Air Namibia (☎ 061-298 2531; www.airnamibia.com.na) serves domestic routes out of Eros airport in Windhoek, including flights to and from Tsumeb, Katima Mulilo (Mpacha), Keetmanshoop, Swakopmund, Oshakati and Lüderitz, and to Alexander Bay in South Africa. One-way fares between Windhoek and Swakopmund begin at US$55. One-way fares between Windhoek and Lüderitz begin at US$130.

There is no domestic departure tax.

Car

An excellent system of sealed roads runs from Noordoewer in the south to Ngoma Bridge in the northeast, as well as spur roads to Lüderitz, Outjo, Kamanjab, Swakopmund and Walvis Bay. Most other towns and sites of interest are accessible on good gravel roads. Vehicles keep to the left, with a general speed limit of 120km/h on open roads. Extreme caution is required on gravel roads –

they look easy, but skidding into the ditch on corners can be surprisingly easy too.

RENTAL

If you really want to see Namibia, it's best to find a few friends, count all that small change you've been collecting in your pockets, pool your resources and splurge on a car. Due to a shortage of public transport to major sites (it's almost impossible to get to Sossusvlei without a vehicle) car hire is the best way. It's cheaper to hire a car in South Africa and drive it across the border (you'll need permission from the rental agency and may be charged a fee of about US$90) than to pick one up in Namibia. It's also worth checking out www.travelocity.com, as it often has good deals from major rental agencies – cars in Jo'burg and Cape Town were going for as little as US$13 per day at the time of research, with air-conditioning and unlimited kilometres. Many major credit cards carry rental insurance on them. A valid driving licence from your home country is sufficient to drive in Namibia.

If you are hiring from a company in Namibia, expect to pay US$45 to US$55 per day with unlimited kilometres for a compact car.

The following agencies offer car and/or 4WD hire. In addition, backpacker lodges with travel centres can often arrange car hire for you:

Avis Car Hire (☎ 061-233166; www.avis.co.za; Hotel Safari, Aviation Rd; Windhoek; ☎ 064-402527; Swakopmund Hotel & Entertainment Centre; Swakopmund)

Camping Car Hire (Map p838; ☎ 061-237756; www .campingcarhire.com.na; 36 Joule St, Southern Industrial Area, Windhoek)

Classic Car Hire (☎ 061-246708; www.carhireand tours.com; 30 Hendrik Hop St, Suiderhof, Windhoek)

Elena Travel Services & Car Hire (☎ 061-244443; www.namibweb.com/about.htm)

Imperial Car Rental (www.imperialcarrental.co.za; Tsumeb ☎ 067-220728; Travel North Namibia, 1551 Omeg Allee; Windhoek ☎ 062-540278; Hosea Kutako International Airport)

Triple Three Car Hire (☎ 064-403190; www.333.com .na; 28 Sam Nujoma St; Swakopmund)

To arrange car hire through any of these companies ring them and they will drop the vehicle off at your accommodation. If you're alone or cannot afford car hire, consider joining an organised tour (see p861).

Hitching

Although we do not recommend hitching, it is fairly easy, but even main highways see relatively little traffic and it is illegal in national parks. Your best option for finding lifts with other travellers is at backpacker lodges in Windhoek or Swakopmund. On the open road, truck drivers generally expect payment; the standard charge is about US$1.50 per 100km.

Local Transport

From Windhoek, **Intercape Mainliner** (Map p840; ☎ 061-227847; www.intercape.co.za) serves Swakopmund, Walvis Bay, Grootfontein, Rundu and Katima Mulilo, and also has international services. See p842 for fares.

Trans-Namib's **Star Line buses** (☎ 061-298 2030; www.transnamib.com.na – click on Starline) travel to Bethanie, Buitepos, Gobabis, Gochas, Grootfontein, Helmeringhausen, Henties Bay, Kamanjab, Khorixas, Lüderitz, Mariental, Opuwo, Oshakati, Outjo, Rundu, Walvis Bay and other destinations.

Fares on long-distance minibuses, which depart when full, work out as US$0.03 per km (but they also may charge US$1.80 per piece of luggage). Fares on minibuses generally work out to be cheaper than buses; however, they are not nearly as comfortable.

Train

Windhoek is the hub for the **Trans-Namib Rail Lines** (www.transnamib.com.na), with services south to Rehoboth, Mariental and Keetmanshoop; north to Tsumeb; west to Swakopmund and Walvis Bay; and east to Gobabis. See p842 for fares, and note that on weekend services (Friday to Monday) fares are about double what they are during the week. Book through the **Windhoek booking office** (☎ 061-298 2030). Rail travel in Namibia is slow, as all trains combine both passenger and freight services and trains tend to stop at every post. Rail travel in Namibia is not particularly popular, so trains are rarely fully booked. Most travellers opt to take the bus over the train.

WINDHOEK

☎ 061 / pop 240,000

Windhoek, Namibia's small and German-flavoured capital, is probably one of Africa's gentlest major cities. It's not at all typically

African – architecture is not cluttered, and the city centre is a mixture of colonial German architecture and modern steel-and-glass high rises.

At an elevation of 1660m, surrounded by low green hills and blessed with dry, clean air and a healthy highland climate, Windhoek lies at the crossroads of the country and you will most likely pass through it during your travels. Vibrant it is not, but it's a good place to join a tour of the country or to hook up with other travellers. And despite being tame by day, it has a wide range of excellent restaurants and decent nightlife.

Windhoek (the name means 'Windy Corner') has existed for just over a century. For

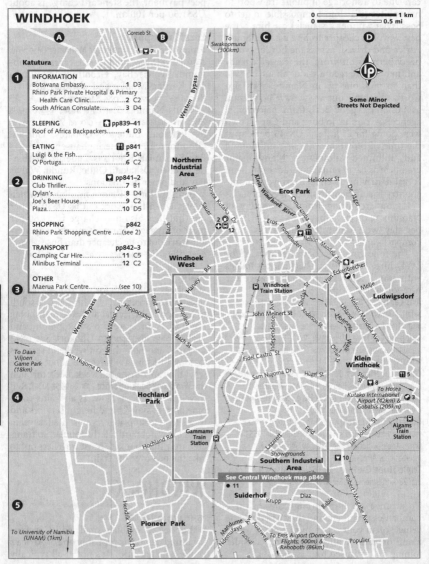

WINDHOEK

0 ———— 1 km
0 ———— 0.5 mi

Katutura

INFORMATION
Botswana Embassy...................1 D3
Rhino Park Private Hospital & Primary
    Health Care Clinic.................2 C2
South African Consulate.............3 D4

SLEEPING 🏠 pp839–41
Roof of Africa Backpackers.........4 D3

EATING 🍴 p841
Luigi & the Fish.......................5 D4
O'Portuga...............................6 C2

DRINKING 🍷 pp841–2
Club Thriller............................7 B1
Dylan's...................................8 D4
Joe's Beer House......................9 C2
Plaza.....................................10 D5

SHOPPING p842
Rhino Park Shopping Centre .....(see 2)

TRANSPORT pp842–3
Camping Car Hire....................11 C5
Minibus Terminal 12 C2

OTHER
Maerua Park Centre................(see 10)

Goreseb St

To Swakopmund (300km)

Some Minor Streets Not Depicted

Western Bypass

Northern Industrial Area

Pieterson

Heliodoor St

Eros Park

Klein Windhoek River

Eros Promenaden

Nelson

Windhoek West

Harvey St

Windhoek Train Station

John Meinert St

Ludwigsdorf

Metje

Von Eckenbrecher

Fidel Castro St

Sam Nujoma Dr

Hügel St

Klein Windhoek

Stein St

To Daan Viljoen Game Park (18km)

Sam Nujoma Dr

Hochland Park

Bach St

Schanzen

To Hosea Kutako International Airport (42km) & Gobabis (205km)

Gammams Train Station

Hochland Rd

Lazarett

Feld

Aigams Train Station

Showgrounds
Southern Industrial Area

See Central Windhoek map p840

• 11

Suiderhof

Krupp

Diaz

Robert Mugabe Ave

To University of Namibia (UNAM) (1km)

Hendrik Witbooi Dr

Pioneer Park

Mandume Ndemufayo Ave

Austweg

Pantval

To Eros Airport (Domestic Flights; 500m) & Rehoboth (86km)

Populier

NAMIBIA

more than 10 years at the beginning of the 20th century the city served as the administrative capital of German South West Africa. Its people reflect the country's ethnic mix; on the streets you'll see Owambo, Kavango, Herero, Damara, Caprivians, Nama, San and Europeans.

ORIENTATION

Central Windhoek is bisected by Independence Ave, where most shopping and administrative functions are concentrated.

Backpacker lodges, restaurants and bars are dispersed throughout the city, and not clustered in any one location. There are a number of shuttle services from Hosea Kutako International Airport, 42km east of the city, that cost about US$14 per person (see p842 for shuttle details).

INFORMATION

The **Windhoek Information & Publicity Office** (Map p840; ☎ 391 2050; Post St Mall; ☼ 7.30am-1pm & 2-4.30pm Mon-Fri) provides useful information about the city. **Namibia Wildlife Resorts** (NWR; Map p840; ☎ 285 7000; 189 Independence Ave; ☼ 8am-5pm Mon-Fri) is the booking agent for all national parks in Namibia.

Banks are concentrated along Independence Ave. The best places to change travellers cheques are the **Amex office** (Map p840; Post St Mall) and **Rennie's Travel** (Map p840; Levinson Arcade), the agency for Thomas Cook. Both places change their respective cheques without commission.

The main post office is on Independence Ave. Email and Internet access is available at most hostels, as well as at the **Namibia Information & Tourism Centre** (Map p840; Gutenberg Platz; US$2.50 per hr).

DANGERS & ANNOYANCES

Windhoek is generally safe by day, but avoid going out alone at night. Don't make yourself a target by walking around with a backpack or expensive camera and never leave anything of value visible in a rented vehicle. Windhoek's townships are generally safer than those in South Africa, but use caution and try to take take a local guide.

SIGHTS & ACTIVITIES

The whitewashed ramparts of **Alte Feste** (Map p840; ☎ 293 4437; Robert Mugabe Ave; admission by donation; ☼ 9am-6pm Mon-Fri, 10.30am-12.30pm Sat &

Sun), Windhoek's oldest surviving building, date from the early 1890s. It houses the historical section of the State Museum, and exhibits focus mainly on Namibia's independence struggle. Here you will see bizarre displays – the champagne glasses used by representatives from South Africa, Angola and Cuba to toast peace; the bottles of lager produced by Namibia for independence; and President Sam Nujoma's résumé.

At the affiliated **Owela Museum** (Map p840; ☎ 293 4358; 4 Lüderitz St; admission by donation; ☼ 9am-6pm Mon-Fri, 10.30am-12.30pm Sat & Sun), the exhibits focus on Namibia's natural and cultural history. The most interesting part of this museum is the big AIDS-awareness display at the entrance.

The heart of the Windhoek shopping district is the bizarrely colourful **Post Street Mall** (Map p840), which could have served as a set for the film *Dick Tracy*. At the eastern end is a display of Gibeon meteorites and the rest is lined with vendors selling curios, art, clothing and other tourist items, mostly from Zimbabwe.

The **National Art Gallery** (Map p840; ☎ 231160; cnr Robert Mugabe Ave & John Meinert St; admission free; ☼ 9am-5pm Tue-Fri, 9am-2pm Sat) features work by local artists in various mediums, some of which is for sale. It also houses a permanent collection of works reflecting Namibia's history and nature.

For details on beautiful Daan Viljoen Game Park see p843.

FESTIVALS & EVENTS

Windhoek's annual cultural bash is the September **/Ae//Gams** street festival, which features dancers and musicians in ethnic garb. Windhoek stages its own version of **Oktoberfest** in late October, and the German-style **Windhoek Karnival** is held in late April.

SLEEPING

Windhoek offers the best selection of backpacker accommodation in Namibia. Quality is high for the price, and rooms at most places are on a par with, or better than, their cheap hotel counterparts. Most lodges have a bar, Internet access and swimming pool and can arrange airport and bus pickups. Many serve meals too.

Chameleon City Backpackers (Map p840; ☎ 244347; www.chameleonbackpackers.com; 5 Voight St; camp sites per person US$3.75, dm/d US$7.50/18; ☐) This friendly

CENTRAL WINDHOEK

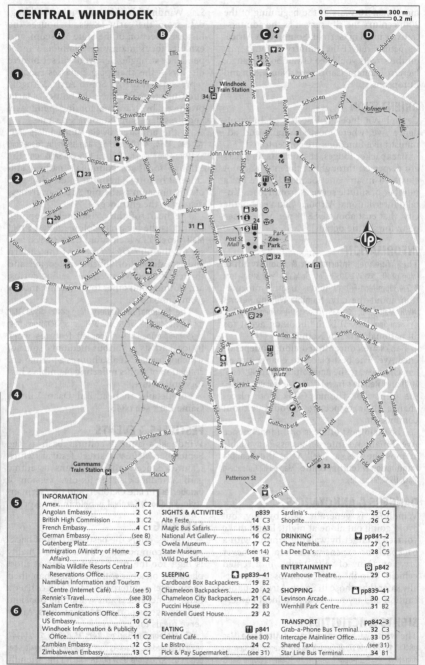

NAMIBIA

hostel is the best place to stay in town and convenient to the city centre. It has an inviting feel, immaculate facilities, brightly coloured walls and comfy couches for lounging. Staff members are well informed. They also run Chameleon Backpackers, a lodge in the suburbs (at 22 Wagner St), and do tours around the country.

Roof of Africa Backpackers (Map p383; ☎ 254708; www.roofofafrica.com; 124-126 Nelson Mandela Ave; camp sites per person US$5; dm/s/d US$7.50/36/43; 🖳) This place is trying to go more upmarket. It has done a substantial amount of renovating in the last few years and as a result doubles resemble what you'd find at a mid-range hotel, minus the antiseptic feel (doubles with air-conditioning cost US$49). These rooms are a good option for splashing out. Otherwise the dorms are standard and the place has a barnyard feel with goats and ducks in a pen by the pool. It's a 30-minute walk northeast of the city centre.

The Cardboard Box (Map p840; ☎ 228994; www.namibia.org; 15 Johann Albrecht St; camp sites per person US$3.75, dm/d US$6/18; 🖳) The Box is a perennial favourite, but dorms are cramped and can become stifling hot at night. Facilities are not super-clean, but it's only a 15-minute walk to the city centre, the bar is always lively and the Box runs an excellent travel centre giving unbiased advice about Namibian tours. The hostel also runs popular day trips to attractions in the area.

Puccini House (Map p840; ☎ 236355; puccinis@mweb .com.na; 4 Puccini St; camp sites per person US$3, dm/s/d US$6/10/18) This is the nearest backpackers to the city centre – it's only a few minutes' walk to Wernhill Park Centre (a shopping complex) – but the neighbourhood, especially around the Mozart St bridge, requires caution. The lodge has a sauna that costs US$4 per hour.

Rivendell Guest House (Map p840; ☎ 250006; www .rivendell-namibia.com; 40 Beethoven St; d/tr US$19/22) Head to Rivendell if you're looking for peace and quiet. Rooms are large and airy – try for one with floor-to-ceiling glass windows overlooking the pool area.

EATING

Windhoek has a varied selection of restaurants, some with excellent food. Residents love to eat out, so it's best to make reservations. For self-catering, try the **Pick & Pay** (Map p840) in Wernhill Park Centre. The cheapest

supermarket is the crowded **Shoprite** (Map p840) on lower Independence Ave.

Sardinia's (Map p840; ☎ 225600; 39 Independence Ave; mains US$5; 🕑 Wed-Mon) Sardinia's does above-average pizzas and good pastas, as well as excellent ice-cream-oriented desserts. It's close to Chameleon City Backpackers.

O'Portuga (Map p838; ☎ 272900; 151 Nelson Mandela Ave; mains US$4-8; 🕑 dinner daily) The best Portuguese and Angolan dishes in Windhoek are served here, including numerous seafood options. It also has an extensive wine list.

Le Bistro (Map p840; ☎ 228742; Post St Mall; breakfast US$2.50, sandwiches US$1.50, salads US$5) Located right on the edge of the Post Street Mall, Le Bistro is very popular at lunchtime. Grab an outdoor table and watch the world go by. Sandwiches, especially the mozzarella and pesto, are tasty and excellent value. There's also a large selection of salads.

Central Café (Map p840; ☎ 222659; Levinson Arcade; mains US$2.50-5) This is another breakfast and lunch option (it closes at 6pm) offering the usual selection of pizzas, pastas and more typical meat and fish fare.

Dial-a-Meal (☎ 220111; delivery charges US$2-3) If you're tired, lazy or lacking transport call this takeaway service. Order from a selection of local restaurants and have the food brought to you.

SPLURGE!

Luigi & the Fish (Map p838; ☎ 256399; 320 Sam Nujoma Dr, Klein Windhoek; mains US$4-10) The giant menu at this place includes a large selection of vegetarian dishes. Steak and calamari dishes are excellent, especially if ordered Cajun-flavoured. If you're partying with a group, order a 'fishbowl' – the concoction will set you back US$8.50, but you'll get to slurp down a giant blue bowl of alcohol. Luigi's is a little pricier than most Windhoek restaurants, but well worth the money. Try to get a table outside on the porch.

DRINKING

For such a sedate city, Windhoek is certainly not lacking in the nightlife department. Although what's hip is constantly changing (ask around at your hostel before venturing out), there are a few old standbys sure to be around for the long haul.

NAMIBIA

Joe's Beerhouse (Map p838; 160 Nelson Mandela Ave) This is Windhoek's most popular drinking establishment, and it's like no other bar in Southern Africa. You can sit outside under faux African huts or at the bar on stools made from toilet seats! Joe's is hectic and packed at all hours, but can be a whole lot of fun. It also has a restaurant serving large meat-oriented meals (US$6 to US$9).

Dylan's (Map p838; cnr Stein St & Sam Nujoma Dr, Klein Windhoek) Dylan's is one of the only places in Windhoek where you can hear live music on a regular basis. It's a small, tightly packed, smoky venue.

Chez Ntemba (Map p840; cnr Uhland St & Goethe St; admission US$1.25 Thu & Sun, US$3.50 Wed, Fri-Sat; ☿ Wed-Sun) Music from around the continent is played here – you'll hear Angolan, Zambian, Congolese and South African tunes. It's good for dancing.

Club Thriller (Map p838; Sam Shikongo St, Katutura; admission US$3) This is an old favourite, and the music is African and Western. The club's located in a rough neighbourhood in the Katutura township so avoid carrying valuables or wearing jewellery. You'll be searched for weapons at the door. Women travelling alone may not feel comfortable here.

Plaza (Map p838; Maerua Park Centre) This is a gay-friendly venue that plays a wide variety of music at less than ear-shattering levels.

La Dee Da's (Map p840; Ferry St near Patterson, Southern Industrial Area; admission before/after midnight US$2.50/3.50) This club was very popular at the time of research. Here you can dance to African, hip-hop, rave, rock and pop accompanied by a range of special effects.

ENTERTAINMENT

The Warehouse Theatre (Map p840; ☎ 225059; old South-West Breweries building, 48 Tal St; admission US$3.50) This is a delightfully integrated club staging live African and European music and theatre productions, but it's only open when an event is scheduled.

GETTING THERE & AWAY
Local Transport

Intercape Mainliner (☎ 061-227847; www.intercape.co.za) uses the **Grab-a-Phone bus terminal** (Map 000; Independence Ave). It runs on Monday, Wednesday, Friday and Sunday to and from Cape Town (US$45, 20 hours) and Jo'burg (US$58, 24 hours). There are also daily services to Swakopmund (US$13, 4½ hours). Monday

and Friday there are departures to Victoria Falls, Zimbabwe (US$52, 20 hours), via Okahandja, Otjiwarongo, Tsumeb, Grootfontein, Rundu and Katima Mulilo.

Star Line buses pick up and drop off passengers at the railway station.

Local minibuses can get you to most urban centres in Namibia. They leave when full from the terminal (Map p838) at the Rhino Park petrol station (just off Hosea Kutako Dr in the Rhino Park Shopping Centre) and are considerably cheaper (and not as comfortable) as regular buses. A few examples: Swakopmund (US$7, four hours), Tsumeb (US$8, seven hours), Rundu (US$10, 10 hours). Minibuses depart at least once daily. Be warned that minibus schedules are quite erratic, being subject to constant change.

Train

The station has a **booking office** (☎ 298 2030; ☿ 7.30am-4pm Mon-Fri). Tickets must be collected by 4pm on the day of departure. Note that on weekends, fares are about double those listed here. Overnight trains run daily except Saturday between Windhoek and Keetmanshoop, leaving Windhoek at 7.10pm and Keetmanshoop at 6.30pm.

Journey duration and weekday economy-class fares from Windhoek are: Rehoboth (US$3.50, 2¾ hours), Mariental (US$5, six hours) and Keetmanshoop (US$6, 10 hours). The Keetmanshoop run now offers sleepers on Monday, Wednesday and Friday.

On Sunday, Tuesday and Thursday, the northern-sector line connects Windhoek with Tsumeb (US$6, 16 hours) via Okahandja (US$3, 2½ hours). Other lines connect Windhoek with Swakopmund (US$7, 10 hours) daily except Saturday.

GETTING AROUND

To and from the Hosea Kutako International Airport, the **Elena Airport Shuttle** (☎ 244443, ☎ 0811-246286; elena@namibweb.com) provides 24-hour, door-to-door airport transport for US$17 per bus; they also meet international flights. Alternatively, try the **VIP Shuttle** (☎ 0812-563657), which costs US$12 per person. Advance bookings are required.

Airport taxis on the same trip cost a maximum of US$27.

City buses have been phased out in favour of inexpensive shared taxis and minibuses. Shared taxis from the main ranks at

Wernhill Park Centre (Map p840) follow set routes to Khomasdal and Katutura, and if your destination is along the way, you'll pay less than US$1. With private hire taxis from the main bus terminals or by radio dispatch, fares are either metered or are calculated on a per- kilometre basis, but you may be able to negotiate a set fare per journey. Plan on paying US$3 to US$4 to anywhere around the city centre. Try **Crown Radio Taxis** (☎ 211115, 0811-299116).

AROUND WINDHOEK

DAAN VILJOEN GAME PARK

Just arrived in Africa, and can't wait to see the wildlife? Then head to the beautiful **Daan Viljoen Game Park** (admission per person US$2.50 plus per vehicle US$2.50; ☉ sunrise-6pm), which sits in the Khomas Hochland about 18km west of Windhoek. Because there are no dangerous animals, you can wander freely through desert-like hills and valleys. You'll almost certainly see gemsboks, kudus, mountain zebras, springboks, hartebeests, elands and up to 200 bird species. The park has numerous hiking opportunities. For more information check with the NWR (see p839 for details).

Daan Viljoen Rest Camp (camp sites for up to 4 people US$15, s/d bungalows US$25/31) sits on the shores of Augeigas Dam; there's also a **restaurant** (☉ 7.30am-9am, noon-2pm & 7-10pm) further along the road. Prebook at NWR in Windhoek (p839).

There's no public transport to Daan Viljoen, but taxis charge around US$17 each way between the park and Windhoek, and persistent hitchers will eventually get a lift.

WESTERN NAMIBIA

A land of dunes and desolation that encompasses everything from the great Namib-Naukluft Park to the isolated Skeleton Coast (and includes the party town of Swakopmund), this section of Namibia must not be missed.

SWAKOPMUND

☎ 064 / pop 25 000
Fancy falling through the sky at 220km/h above out-of-this-world scenery? Think you've got what it takes to race a quad-bike straight down a giant orange dune? Want to test your sandboarding skills? Play Lawrence of Arabia on a camel? Feel the need to party like a rock star all night long? Then head to this little paradise on the sea. Okay, so the weather's not always great – it's often cold and grey. But if you're an adrenalin junkie this is *the* place to get your fix. Think Victoria Falls with sand instead of water.

Swakopmund (or Swakop, as the locals say) is one of those places you might arrive at for a night and end up staying a week or more. There's an energy here not found elsewhere in Namibia, and most travellers agree it's an absolute must.

Orientation
Swakopmund is small and compact. Bars and restaurants are concentrated within a few blocks' radius, and within easy walking distance of the most popular budget accommodation. Buses from around Namibia drop you off in town.

Information
The **Namib i Information Centre** (☎ /fax 403129; swainfo@iafrica.com.na; Sam Nujoma Ave; ☉ 8am-1pm & 2-5pm Mon-Fri, 9am-noon & 3.30-5.30pm Sat, 9.30am-noon & 3.30-5pm Sun) is helpful. Also useful is the **Namibia Wildlife Resorts** (NWR; ☎ 204172; Woermannhaus, Bismarck St; ☉ 8am-1pm & 2-5pm Mon-Fri), which sells Namib-Naukluft Park permits. Note that park permits are no longer available from petrol stations in Swakopmund – they must be purchased either from this office or the NWR office in Windhoek (p839).

There are numerous places throughout the town where you can surf the Internet. Try the **Swakopmund I-café** (Woermann & Brock Centre; US$2 per hr) or the **Talk Shop Internet Café** (☎ 461333; Roon St; US$2 per hr).

Sights
Beer lovers won't want to miss a tour of **Hansa Brewery** (☎ 405021; 9 Rhode Allee), brewers of Swakopmund's favourite beverage. The free tours allow ample opportunity to sample the product. Prebook at the office on Rhode Allee near the corner of Bismarck St. Tours run on Tuesday and Thursday at 10am and 2pm by appointment.

The **National Marine Aquarium** (Strand St; adult/child US$3.50/1.75; ☉ 10am-4pm Tue-Sun) is another option. It allows close-up views of rays and sharks. Don't miss the daily feeding at 3pm.

NAMIBIA

Rössing Uranium Mine (☎ 402046; admission US$2.50), 55km east of Swakopmund, is the world's largest open-cast uranium mine and certainly merits a visit. The scale of operations is staggering and at full capacity the mine processes about one million tonnes of ore per week. It's open to the public on the first and third Friday of the month; three-hour mine tours can be booked the previous day at the Swakopmund Museum on Strand St. The tours leave from Café Anton (inside the Hotel Schweizerhaus, 1 Bismarck St). Transport is included in the cost.

Activities

Swakopmund's main draw has to be adventure sports, and there are a host of companies offering numerous options. Most of the companies videotape the day's excursion; some include this video in the price, others charge extra. The videos are screened at various bars around town in the evening, which sets the scene for much hilarity and rehashing of events.

CAMEL RIDES

If you want to play Lawrence of Arabia in the Namib Desert, visit the **camel farm** (☎ 400363; 30min ride US$12; ⏰ 2-5pm) 12km east of Swakopmund on the D1901. To arrange transport to the farm phone and ask for Ms Elke Elb.

QUAD-BIKING

Outback Orange (☎ 400968; www.outbackorange.com; 15 Daniel Tjongarero St; 2hr ride US$50) offers stomach-dropping tours on quad-bikes (motorcycle-style 4WD). In two hours you'll travel about 60km, racing up and down dunes. The safety-conscious owners tailor trips to ability, but if you're feeling comfortable ask them to let you fly down one of the really big dunes.

Desert Explorers Adventure Centre (☎ 406096; swakadven@iafrica.com.na; 2 Woermann St; 2hr ride US$63) is more expensive, but the price includes a free video. The highlight of this trip is taking your bike over a jump at full throttle. You can catch some really big air! Desert Explorers also arranges bookings for other adventures.

SANDBOARDING

Alter-Action (☎ 402737; www.alter-action.com; lie-down/stand-up US$20/30) provides the most economical of the adventure sports. Sand-

boarding is truly a unique experience. Try the stand-up option, where you'll learn the basics of snowboarding before heading down the dunes. The lie-down involves much less finesse, but is equally fun. The highlight is an 80km/h schuss down a 120m mountain of sand with a big jump at the end – you'll fly about 4m into the air! There are no lifts, and trudging up the dunes in Swakopmund's heat can be taxing, so you need to be in moderate shape. Trips depart in the morning and last about four hours. The price includes board rental, transport to and from the dune, instruction and lunch, and beer or soda upon completion.

SKYDIVING

Ground Rush Adventures (☎ 402841; www.skydiveswakop.com.na; tandem jump US$160) provides the ultimate rush, and skydiving in Swakopmund is sweetened by the outstanding dune and ocean backdrop. The guys at Ground Rush have an impeccable safety record to date and make even the most nervous participant feel comfortable about jumping out of a plane at 10,000ft and freefalling for 30 seconds (5000ft) at 220 km/h! The price includes a 25-minute scenic flight.

Sleeping

Swakopmund has a small but growing number of backpacker options that are all of a high standard. You might want to book ahead as some places fill up quickly, especially when the overland trucks are in town.

Desert Sky Backpackers Lodge (☎ 402339; www.skakop.com/dsd; 35 Lazarett St; camp sites per person US$5, dm/s/d US$6.25/16/18; 🖳) Centrally located and very popular, Desert Sky is a good place to drop anchor in Swakopmund. Dorms are simple but comfortable, the lounge area is homey and the owner, Lofty, can give you lots of good advice on area excursions.

Alternative Space (☎ 402713; nam00352@mweb.com.na; 46 Dr Alfons Weber St; suggested donation d incl breakfast US$21) On the desert fringe is the innovative, and aptly named, Alternative Space. With whitewashed walls, hardwood floors and handmade furniture, Alternative Space has a stark industrial feel – it's well worth a stay for the architecture alone. Throw in the friendly owners, free Friday-night fish barbecue and free use of dune carts and you're in for something special. The only drawback is that it's a little way out of town, but owners

SWAKOPMUND

0 — 300 m
0 — 0.2 mi

SIGHTS & ACTIVITIES pp843-4
Alte Gefängnis (Old Prison)..........8 C1
Alter-Action........................(see 21)
Desert Explorers Adventure
Centre..............................9 B3
German Evangelical Lutheran
Church.............................10 C2
Ground Rush Adventures..........(see 21)
Hansa Brewery......................11 A4
Historic Railway Station............12 C2
Marine Memorial....................13 B2
National Marine Aquarium..........14 A4
Old German School.................15 C2
Outback Orange....................16 A1
Swakopmund Hotel & Entertainment
Centre..........................(see 12)
Swakopmund Museum...............17 A2
Woermannhaus......................18 B3

SLEEPING pp844-6
Atlanta Hotel........................19 A1
Desert Sky Backpackers.............20 B3
Hotel Grüner Kranz..................21 B3
Villa Wiese...........................22 C2
Youth Hostel.........................23 B3

EATING p846
Blue Whale Cafe...................(see 19)
Cape to Cairo.....................(see 21)
Model Supermarket..................24 A2
Out of Africa Coffee Shop..........25 A1
Swakopmund Brauhaus...............26 A1
The Tug.............................27 A3
Western Saloon Pizzeria.............28 A1

DRINKING p846
African Cafe.........................29 C2
Fagin's Pub........................(see 19)
Rafter's Action Pub................(see 9)
The Private Bar....................(see 21)

ENTERTAINMENT p846
Atlanta Cinema......................30 A1

TRANSPORT p846
Avis Car Hire......................(see 12)
Intercape Mainliner Bus Stop......(see 7)
Triple Three Car Hire...............31 A1

INFORMATION
Bismarck Medical Centre.............1 A3
Building/Bank of Windhoek.......(see 3)
Commercial Bank.....................2 A1
Historic Deutsche-Afrika Bank.......3 A2
Hospital.............................4 C1
Namib i Information Centre..........5 A1
NWR Office........................(see 18)
Swakopmund I-cafe..................6 A2
Talk Shop Internet Café.............7 B3

Sibylle and Frenus will drop off and pick up (at reasonable hours) if you ask. This is not a party place and there are no dorms.

Grüner Kranz (☎ 402039; swakoplodge@yahoo.com; 7 Nathaniel Maxuilili St; dm/s/d US$6/27/30; ☐) This budget hotel is at the epicentre of the action in Swakopmund. This is where many adrenalin activities leave from and where the videos are screened at night. The upstairs bar is popular with overland and adventure guides and there are a number of restaurants in the complex (see p846). The newly renovated rooms come with satellite TV.

Villa Wiese (☎ /fax 407105; villawiese@compuscan .co.za; cnr Bahnhof & Windhoeker Sts; dm/d US$6/17) This friendly and funky backpackers is also

popular with overland trucks. It's not a bad option though, and is housed in a historic mansion.

SPLURGE!

Beach Lodge B&B (☎ 400933; www.nat ron.net/tour/belo/main.html; Stint St; s/d US$40/55) Sitting right up on the beach sand this remarkable boat-shaped lodge offers some of the most unusual architecture and best sea views in the area. If that's not enough you can spoil yourself with direct service cable television, picture windows and huge portholes with spectacular ocean vista views in your room.

NAMIBIA

Youth Hostel (☎ 172503; old German Barracks, Lazarett St; dm & d per person US$3.50) The cheapest option in Swakopmund. There's no backpacker atmosphere, but the architecture is definitely different. Rooms are very simple. The bathrooms could use some cleaning – but you can't beat the price.

Eating

Thanks to its Teutonic roots, Swakopmund's restaurants have a heavy German influence. That said there are still a lot of choices serving everything from pizza to seafood.

Out of Africa Coffee Shop (☎ 404752; 13 Daniel Tjongarero St; breakfast US$1.50-4) Sit outside to people-watch and sip the best coffee in Namibia. Breakfasts are tasty and filling. There's also sandwiches and light lunches.

Cape to Cairo Restaurant (☎ 463160; 7 Nathaniel Maxuilili St; mains US$4-7.50) Fusing flavours and textures from all over the continent, Cape to Cairo serves traditional dishes in an atmospheric setting. Try one of the 'bellies' – chapatti stuffed with spicy vegetables and cheese – for something different. There are lots of vegetarian options, and plates are huge.

Swakopmund Brauhaus (☎ 402214; Brauhaus Arcade, 22 Sam Nujoma St; mains US$5-10) Popular with locals, this place serves up excellent German food. Try one of the steak dishes and a glass of German-style beer. There are few vegetarian options.

Western Saloon Pizzeria (☎ 403925; 8 Moltke St; pizza US$3-6; ⏱ 5-10pm daily) This tiny place has large, scrumptious pizzas. It's very popular with locals and always packed, so you might be eating on the street.

The Tug (☎ 402356; Arnold Shad Promenade; mains US$5-12) Housed in a beached tugboat, this restaurant has a wide selection of fresh seafood and is a good place to end your Swakopmund trip. It's very popular, so book in advance.

Blue Whale Café (☎ mobile 0811-294018; Atlanta Hotel, Roon St; salads around US$4, mains US$5; ⏱ Wed-Mon) This café has a creative lunch menu featuring lots of vegetarian dishes. Try to sit outside on the pavement.

Self-caterers should check out the Model/ Pick & Pay Supermarket on Sam Nujoma Ave near the corner with Roon St.

Drinking

Swakopmund likes to party. After chasing adrenalin rushes, drinking is the favourite pastime. The town is a major stop for over-land trucks so there's usually a crowd here. It's generally safe to walk around at night, and women travelling alone should not feel uncomfortable.

The Private Bar (upstairs in the Grüner Kranz hotel, see p845) This bar is very popular with adventure sport and overland truck guides. It's usually packed and rowdy, and someone is always buying a round of shots. There are a number of pool tables.

Rafter's Action Pub (cnr Moltke & Woermann Sts) The music is always pounding here, the strobes flashing and you can seriously strut your stuff on the dance floor. It draws a relatively young crowd and is always busy.

Fagin's Pub (Roon St) This down-to-earth watering hole is another drinking option. It draws a faithful clientele.

African Café (3B Schlosser St) Here you can listen to live music at the jazz bar or dance the night away at the adjacent disco.

Entertainment

Atlanta Cinema (Brauhaus Arcade; US$2.50-3) Tired of drinking? The Atlanta Cinema screens several popular films of an evening.

Getting There & Away

From the Talk Shop Internet Café on Roon St, the Intercape Mainliner bus travels to and from Windhoek (US$13, 4¼ hours) on Monday, Wednesday, Friday and Sunday, with connections to and from South Africa.

Minibuses between Swakopmund and Windhoek (US$7, three hours) stop at the Engen petrol station in Vineta. Phone Eddie (☎ 0812-420077) for a lift from your accommodation. Minibuses depart when full and make the trip at least once a day.

Overnight trains connect Windhoek with Swakopmund (US$7, 10 hours) daily except Saturday. Trains between Walvis Bay and Tsumeb (US$7, 17½ hours, three weekly) also pass through Swakopmund.

For rail information, phone **Trans-Namib** (☎ 463538). Both **Avis Car Hire** (☎ 064-402527; Swakopmund Hotel & Entertainment Centre; Swakopmund) and **Triple Three Car Hire** (☎ 064-403190; www.333.com.na; 28 Sam Nujoma St; Swakopmund) provide car hire in Swakopmund.

SKELETON COAST

The term 'Skeleton Coast' refers to northern Namibia's treacherous coastline, which has long been a graveyard for unwary ships and their crews. It is one of the world's most inhospitable waterless areas. Here white gravel plains and colourless dunes meet the chilly Atlantic Ocean. Mist swirls, perspectives lose tangibility and distances are skewed.

There is no public transport to the Skeleton Coast, but if you have rented a car, it's easy to visit the National West Coast Recreation Area on a day trip from Swakopmund. The stretch of coast road from Swakop to Cape Cross looks barren enough, then about 12km past the seal reserve the landscape turns to real desert.

National West Coast Recreation Area

This 200km-long and 25km-wide strip from Swakopmund to the Ugab River makes up the southern end of the Skeleton Coast. No permits are required to visit and the road is accessible to 2WD vehicles. The popular **Cape Cross Seal Reserve** (admission per person US$2.50, plus per vehicle US$2.50; ☉ 10am-5pm) is a breeding reserve for thousands of Cape fur seals. Be forewarned: the smell is putrid and will make even the tough nauseous.

Along the salt road up the coast from Swakopmund you'll find several bleak beach camp sites set up mainly for sea anglers. Sites at Myl 14, Jakkalsputz, Myl 72 and Myl 108 cost US$14 for up to four people. (Myl means 'mile' – the distance from Swakop.)

Skeleton Coast Park

At Ugabmund, 110km north of Cape Cross, the road passes into the **Skeleton Coast Park** (admission per person US$2.50, plus per vehicle US$2.50). UK journalist Nigel Tisdell once wrote in the *Daily Telegraph*, 'If hell has a coat of arms, it probably looks like the entrance to Namibia's Skeleton Coast Park', and the description is fitting.

Accommodation is available at **Torra Bay** (camp sites for 4 people US$12) and **Terrace Bay** (s/d incl 3 meals US$59/84), but the former is open only in December and January. Both resorts must be prebooked at the NWR office in Windhoek (p839) or Swakopmund (p843). If you are staying at either facility you must pass the Ugabmund gate before 3pm or the Springbokwater gate before 5pm.

Day visits are not allowed, but **transit permits** (US$2.50 per person, plus US$2.50 per vehicle) for the road between Ugabmund and Springbokwater gates are available at the Ugabmund and Springbokwater checkpoints. If transiting, you must enter through one gate before 1pm and exit through the other before 3pm the same day.

Skeleton Coast Wilderness

The Skeleton Coast Wilderness makes up the northern half of the Skeleton Coast Park, where seemingly endless stretches of foggy beach are punctuated by rusting shipwrecks and the cries of gulls and gannets. However, the area is closed to individual travellers. If you want to visit expect to shell out a cool US$3000 for four days to stay at the highly exclusive Skeleton Coast Wilderness Camp.

NAMIB-NAUKLUFT PARK
☎ 063

This is the Namibia of the picture books and movies, and it does not disappoint. The park is best known for Sossusvlei, a huge ephemeral pan set amid infamous towering red dunes that leave you speechless at first glance. The dunes are part of the Namib Desert, which stretches more than 2000km along the coast from Oliphants River in South Africa all the way to southern Angola. The Naukluft portion of the park is not as well known, but the craggy peaks here are almost (OK, not quite) as impressive as the dunes.

To leave the main park transit routes (the C28, C14, D1982 or D1998) you'll need a park permit (US$3.50 per person, plus US$2.50 per vehicle). These are available at NWR offices in Sesriem, Windhoek (p839) and Swakopmund (p843). Park roads are well maintained gravel, but 2WD cars with low clearance need to take it slow.

Camp sites in Sesriem and Naukluft must be prebooked through the NWR offices in Windhoek or Swakopmund. Permits for Sesriem-Sossusvlei and Naukluft hikes must be booked in Windhoek. There is no public transport to the area; you will need your own vehicle or to join a tour (see p861 for tour operators).

Sesriem & Sossusvlei

Despite being Namibia's No 1 attraction, Sossusvlei still manages to feel isolated. Hiking through the dunes, part of the 32,000 sq km sand sea that covers much of western Namibia, is a sombre experience. The dunes, which reach as high as 325m, are part of one of the oldest and driest ecosystems on earth.

NAMIBIA

The landscape here is constantly changing. Colours shift with the light, and wind forever alters the dunes' shape. If you can, visit Sossusvlei at sunrise when the colours are particularly breathtaking.

Sesriem is the gateway to Sossusvlei. Here you can pick up your park permit (which is needed to get to Sossusvlei). There is also a small food shop, the camp site and the pricey Sossusvlei Lodge (see below). If you want to view the dunes at sunrise, you must stay at either the camp site or the lodge, and drive the 65km from Sesriem to Sossusvlei (on a sealed road). The park gate opens at sunrise and closes at sunset.

On the way from Sesriem, you'll pass Dune 45, the most accessible of the red dunes along the Sossusvlei road. It's a good place to take a photo (or use up a couple of films). It is marked with a sign on the left side of the road driving towards Sossusvlei.

You will have to park at the 2WD car park before you reach Sossusvlei. The area is administered by a concession, **Hobas Tours** (☎ 240878), and vehicles cannot drive in. At the car park either hike the last 4km into the pan or take one of the shuttles (US$10). Unless you have plenty of water and good walking shoes, the shuttle service is worth the hefty fee. The driver will stay with you and take you on guided hikes. Ask to be taken to Dead Vlei. The walk is stupendous and you will feel as if you have reached the ends of the earth.

Sesriem Camp Site (camp sites for 4 people US$20) This camp site must be booked in Windhoek or in Swakopmund through the NWR, but arrive before sunset or they'll reassign your site on a standby basis; those who were unable to book a site in Windhoek may get in on this nightly lottery. A small shop at

the office sells snacks and cold drinks. The camp-site bar has music at night.

Naukluft Mountains

Rising steeply from the gravel plains of the central Namib, the Naukluft Massif is a high-plateau area cut around the edges by a complex of steep gorges. It is an ideal habitat for mountain zebras, kudus, leopards, springboks and klipspringers.

Hikers concentrate on the Waterkloof Trail or the Olive Trail; these day hikes need not be booked. There's also amazing four-day and eight-day loops with more restrictions attached; thanks to stifling summer temperatures and potentially heavy rains, they're only open from March to late October on Tuesday, Thursday and Saturday of the first three weeks of each month. The price (US$12 per person) includes accommodation at the Hikers Haven hut on the nights before and after the hike, as well as camping at trailside shelters and the Ubusis Canyon Hut. In addition, you'll have to pay US$3.50 per person per day and another US$2.50 per day for each vehicle you leave parked. Groups must be composed of three to 12 people.

Naukluft (Koedoesrus) Camp Site (camp sites for four people US$12). This camp site must be booked through the NWR in Windhoek or Swakopmund. It is pleasantly situated in a deep valley 2km past the entrance gate to the Naukluft portion of the Namib-Naukluft Park. It has running water and ablutions blocks. The maximum stay is three nights. The camp site also is the starting point for the Waterkloof and Olive Trails.

Solitaire

Solitaire is a lonely and aptly named settlement of just a few buildings about 80km north of Sesriem, reached on good gravel roads. **Solitaire Country Lodge** (☎ 061-256597; www.namibialodges.com; camp sites US$3.75 per site plus US$2.50 per person, bungalows per person US$6.75, flats per person US$12.50) is the cheapest noncamping accommodation option in the area. The tin-roofed bungalows are simple but have comfortable beds. The flats are spacious though not fabulous and have private bathrooms. Electricity is turned off at 10pm and there is a swimming pool and restaurant (US$9 dinner buffet). The affiliated Solitaire Country Store sells sandwiches

---

SPLURGE!

Sossusvlei Lodge (☎ 693223; www.sossusvlei lodge.com; Sesriem; bungalows with half board US$170-230) If you don't have a tent and want to see the dunes at sunrise, you'll be forced to stay here. It's not exactly worth the money, but your sunrise photos might be! It bears a strong resemblance to what happens when squabbling children topple a stack of coloured blocks. People either love it or hate it.

and beer, and Moose bakes excellent bread and creates delicious cheap breakfasts.

NORTHWESTERN NAMIBIA

Although tourism is increasing in Damaraland and Kaokoland, these areas still remain wild and free and take some serious effort to reach. There are no sealed roads and public transport is almost nonexistent. But if you do make it, you'll find a region of contrasts, quickly changing landscapes and friendly people. The predominant cultures include the hardy and enigmatic Damara and Himba.

To the east of Damaraland and Kaokoland is wildlife-packed Etosha National Park – one of the best in Africa, although the towns around the park tend to be little more than jumping-off points. The area around Etosha is accessible on good sealed roads; and public transport abounds in the region (but not in the park itself). The area also includes the less-known Waterberg Plateau Park, which is a hiker's paradise.

DAMARALAND
☎ 064

Damaraland, the territory between the Skeleton Coast and Namibia's central plateau, is named for the Damara people who populate it. It is home to a host of desert-adapted species including giraffes, zebras, lions, elephants and black rhinos. Here terrains collide and colours bleed. The red sands are interspersed with mountains and gravel plains. The endless open spaces are rich in both natural and cultural attractions, including Brandberg, Namibia's highest massif, and the rock engravings of Twyfelfontein.

Spitzkoppe
The 1728m **Spitzkoppe** (D3716, Groot Spitzkoppe village; admission per person US$1.75, plus per vehicle US$1; ☼ sunrise-sunset), one of Namibia's most recognisable landmarks, rises mirage-like above the dusty plains of southern Damaraland. The **camp sites** (☎ 530879; per person US$4) here are some of Namibia's best. The sites are spread out around the massif and not visible to one another; so you feel as if you're camping alone in the middle of nowhere.

Near the entrance, a small shop sells staples, but doesn't sell large quantities of water; so it's best to bring as much drinking water as you'll need for your entire stay with you.

There's no public transport here, and although several Swakopmund tour agencies run day trips you'll regret not allowing more time to explore this incredible place.

Brandberg
Brandberg (Fire Mountain) is named for the effect created by the setting sun on its western face, which causes the granite massif to resemble a burning slag heap. Its summit, Königstein, is Namibia's highest peak at 2573m. Its best-known attraction is the gallery of rock art in **Tsisab Ravine**, which features the famous *White Lady of the Brandberg*. The figure, which isn't necessarily a lady, stands about 40cm high and has straight, light hair. It's a 45-minute walk from the car park; guides charge US$2.70 per person.

Ugab Wilderness Camp (camp sites per person US$4 plus US$2.50 per vehicle, s/d tents US$18/26), 10km from Tsisab Ravine, organises guided Brandberg hikes or climbs for US$33 per person per day. The turn-off is signposted from the D2359.

Petrified Forest
This site, 40km west of Khorixas, is scattered with dozens of petrified tree trunks that date back 260 million years. Admission is free but the compulsory guides live only from tips; plan on US$1 per person for the 500m walking tour. Note that it's forbidden to take even the smallest scrap of petrified wood.

Twyfelfontein
Beautiful **Twyfelfontein** (admission per person US$0.75, plus US$0.75 per vehicle), with its fabulous 6000-year-old petroglyphs (drawings or carvings on rock), is one of the most extensive galleries of rock art in Africa.

Guides are available and expect tips of about US$1 per group, but the route is easy enough to walk alone.

Other nearby sites of interest include the **Wondergat sinkhole**, the volcanic **Burnt Mountain** and the **Organ Pipes** basalt columns. Access to these sites is only by private vehicle or organised tour from Windhoek or Swakopmund.

You can stay at the simple and rustic **Aba-Huab Camp** (☎ 697981; Khorixas; camp sites per person

US$4; d tents US$7; s/d chalets US$27/42), a popular stopover point for overland trucks. If you don't feel like camping, stay in one of the pre-erected open-sided A-frame shelters. There's not a lot going on here, but the new bar makes things a little more lively.

Another bonus to Twyfelfontein is that sometimes you can catch a glimpse of Namibia's desert elephants. They're attracted to the camp's water supply.

KAOKOLAND
☎ 065

You'll often hear Kaokoland described as 'Africa's last great wilderness', and even if that isn't exactly accurate, this faraway corner of Namibia is certainly a beguiling and primeval repository of desert mountains and fascinating indigenous cultures. Being so isolated, even the wildlife of Kaokoland has specially adapted to local conditions, the most renowned of which is the desert elephant.

There's no public transport anywhere in the region and hitching is practically impossible, so the best way to explore Kaokoland is with a well-outfitted 4WD vehicle or an organised camping safari (see p861).

In the dry season, the routes from Opuwo to Epupa Falls, Ruacana to Okongwati (via Swartbooi's Drift) and Sesfontein to Purros may be passable to high-clearance 2WD vehicles, but otherwise you'll need 4WD.

Opuwo
☎ 065

Although it's the regional 'capital', Opuwo is little more than a dusty collection of commercial buildings ringed by traditional rondavels (round huts). You'll see lots of Himba and Herero people here. The going rate for a 'people photo' is about US$1, but many people will ask for US$2. Please either respect local wishes or put the camera away.

To meet local artisans and purchase arts and crafts, head to the **Kunene Crafts Centre** (☎ 273209; 8am-5pm Mon-Fri, 9am-1pm Sat), which is located on the main road, the C43 on the northern edge of Opuwo's business district.

Opuwo (Power Safe) Guesthouse (☎ 273036; ☎ 0812-555088; camp sites per person US$4, dm US$8.50) offers camping on its green lawn, pleasantly cool dorms and kitchen facilities. Coming from the south, turn left at the BP petrol station, then take the next right; turn left after

the hospital and it's several houses down on the right; look for the large reeds and fence.

Uniting Guest House (☎ 273400; d without/with bathroom US$12/14), one block east of the church on the hill, is small and simple. Rates include breakfast and other meals are available.

Oreness Campsite (☎ 273572; camp sites per person US$4, bungalows per person US$14) occupies a compound immediately east of the centre.

You can get food at the **Oreness Restaurant** (snacks US$2.50, mains US$5.50-7) on the main road through town. Otherwise the Opuwo equivalent of quick culinary delights can be found at the bakery beside the petrol station on the main road, which sells doughnuts, yoghurt, beer, bread and renowned sausage rolls.

The best-stocked supermarket is the Power Safe, just off the main road, the C43, about midway through town. Drankwinkel next door sells soft drinks and alcohol.

Epupa Falls
☎ 065

At this dynamic spot, whose name means 'Falling Waters' in Herero, the Kunene River fans out and is ushered through a 500m-wide series of parallel channels, dropping a total of 60m over 1.5km. The greatest single drop – 37m – is commonly identified as *the* Epupa Falls, where the river tumbles into a dark, narrow cleft. During periods of low water, the pools above the falls make fabulous natural Jacuzzis.

You're safe from crocs in the eddies and rapids, but hang onto the rocks and keep away from the lip of the falls, where there's a real risk of being swept over; swimming here isn't suitable for young children. There's excellent hiking along the river west of the falls, and plenty of mountains to climb for panoramic views along the river and far into Angola.

There is no budget accommodation beyond camping. Bring a tent if you want to stay here, or visit on a budget safari. The **public camping ground** (camp sites per person US$4), right at the falls, can get very crowded. On the upside it has hot showers and flush toilets maintained by the local community.

Epupa village now boasts a real supermarket where visitors and locals alike buy staples or gather to socialise and drink a cold beer in the shade.

From Opuwo or Swartbooi's Drift, it's possible to drive to Epupa Falls via Okongwati in a high-clearance 2WD, but the route remains very rough. Via the Kunene River road, it's 93km to Epupa Falls from Swartbooi's Drift. Even with a 4WD vehicle it takes at least 12 hours, but this lovely stretch – known as the Namibian Riviera – serves as an increasingly popular hiking route.

ETOSHA NATIONAL PARK

The 20,000-sq-km Etosha National Park is undoubtedly one of the world's greatest wildlife-viewing venues. The park's name, which means 'Great White Place of Dry Water', is an apt moniker. Driving through the park one experiences endless flat expanses of greenish-whiteness as far as the eye can see. At first it may look barren, but this grandiose landscape is home to thousands of animals – the park protects 114 mammal species as well as 340 bird species, 16 reptiles and amphibians, one fish species and countless insects. The animals take shelter in the grass lands and bushes that surround the vast pan.

Unlike many other parks in Africa where you can spend days looking for animals across the plains, one of Etosha's charms is its ability to bring the animals to you. The usual routine here, if you've hired a car for a few days, is to park up by one of the many water holes with binoculars, zoom lenses, sandwiches and a cool box for water and beers and watch while a pantheon of animals comes by – lions, elephants, springboks, the whole lot – not two-by-two but in their hundreds.

The eastern part of the park is open to the public and the western portion is reserved for organised-tour operators. It is possible to drive through Etosha in a day, but to appreciate all the park has to offer, you need two or three days, and most visitors stay at one of the three public rest camps (see below). The staff at Andersson or Von Lindequist gates, where you pick up entry permits (US$3.50 per person, plus US$2.50 per vehicle), can provide maps and information.

Sleeping & Eating

All accommodation at Etosha should be prebooked at the NWR office in Windhoek (p839). All three of the rest camps, Namutoni, Halali and Okaukuejo, have a variety of accommodation options, swimming pools and floodlit water holes. The three camps are interspersed at 70km intervals.

All camps have restaurants and small shops, but you should stock up on food outside the park if you're self-catering, as park shops are overpriced and understocked. The restaurants only serve pricey buffet meals (breakfast US$4, lunch US$7.50, dinner US$10), but the food isn't too bad.

You must arrive in the rest camps before sunset and can only leave after sunrise; times are posted on the gates.

Okaukuejo Rest Camp (camp sites for 4 people US$20, economy rooms or bungalows US$33, 2-bed rooms US$41, 3-bed bungalows US$41, 4-bed chalets US$50;) The camping ground here is a giant dust hole but the self-catering facilities are the best in the park and there's a real bar and a pool table. There are two beds in the economy rooms and all the rooms come with air-con. The floodlit water hole is probably Etosha's best rhino-viewing venue, particularly between 8pm and 10pm.

Halali Rest Camp (camp sites for 4 people US$20, 2-bed rooms US$37; 4-bed economy bungalows US$42, 4-bed self-catering bungalows US$48-81;) In the centre of the park, this camp lies in a unique area between several incongruous dolomite outcrops that can be reached on the short Tsumasa Kopje hiking track. At the time of research it was the best wildlife-viewing camp in the park.

Namutoni Rest Camp (camp sites for 4 people US$20, 2-bed room without/with bathroom US$18/41, 2-bed economy flats inside/outside the fort US$38/27, 4-bed chalets US$45;) This camp, with its landmark whitewashed German fort, is the tidiest of the three camps. The tower and ramparts get crowded every evening when crowds gather to watch the sun go down. Also popular is the King Nehale water hole, with its throngs of frogs.

Getting There & Away

Etosha's two main entry gates are via Von Lindequist (Namutoni), west of Tsumeb, and Andersson (Okaukuejo), north of Outjo.

Bus and minibus routes extend to Tsumeb and Outjo, but from there Etosha is accessible only on tours or in private vehicles. The good news is that backpacker lodges in Outjo (p853) and Tsumeb (p853) can arrange economical safaris to Etosha. Travel North Namibia (p853) in Tsumeb

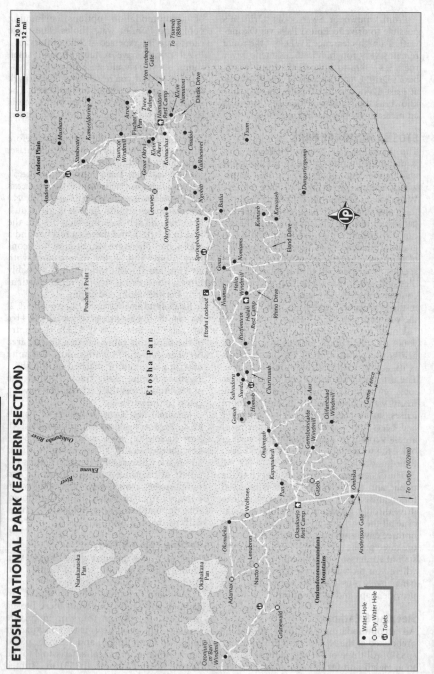

ETOSHA NATIONAL PARK (EASTERN SECTION)

NAMIBIA

0 ———— 20 km
0 ———— 12 mi

To Tsumeb (88km)

Von Lindequist Gate

Klein Namutoni
Dikdik Drive

Namutoni Rest Camp
Twee Palms
Fischer's Pan
Arve
Kameeldoring
Aroe
Mushara
Chudob
Kalkheuwel
Klein Okevi
Groot Okevi
Koinachas
Tsumcor Windmill
Stinkwater
Tsum
Andoni Plain
Andoni
Ngobib
Batia
Dungariespomp
Leeunes
Okerfontein
Springbokfontein
Kameeb
Noniams
Kawazeb
Eland Drive
Poacher's Point
Geras
Nuamses
Etosha Lookout
Helio Windmill
Rietfontein
Halali Rest Camp
Rhino Drive
E t o s h a   P a n
Salvadora
Genob
Sueda
Homob
Charitsaub
Aus
Oshigambo River
Ekuma River
Gemsbokvlakte
Olifantsbad Windmill
Ondongab
Kapupuhedi
Gaseb
Omhika
Wolfsnes
Okondeka
Natukanaka Pan
Okaukuejo Rest Camp
To Outjo (102km)
Andersson Gate
Leubron
Nacto
Adamax
Grünewald
Okahuka Pan
Ondundozonananandana Mountains
Ozonjuitji m'Bari Windmill

Legend
• Water Hole
○ Dry Water Hole
⊞ Toilets

also can arrange car hire. Out of Windhoek, one recommended Etosha safari is through Chameleon Safaris (p861), which offers four-day Etosha trips for US$250. Trips depart Windhoek every Friday.

OUTJO
☎ 067

Outjo is mostly a jumping-off place for Etosha National Park. Tourist information is available at the **African Curios Shop** (☎ 313513; corne delange@yahoo.com) on the main road through town. Internet access is available next door at the **Outjo Café-Backerei** (⏱ 7am-7pm Mon-Sat; US$4 per hr).

At the friendly **Outjo Backpackers** (☎ 313513; olabuschagne@yahoo.com; 84 Hage Geingob St; camp sites per person US$3.75, dm/d US$6/14) you can book great-value trips to Etosha and Kaokoland. Tours to Etosha cost US$93 per day per person, and include meals and tent; the price gets progressively cheaper the more people you have in your group (US$67 per person for two people, US$56 per person for three people).

Try the **Ombinda Country Lodge** (☎ 313181; mains US$5) for dinner and drinks (follow the signs in town). If it's stifling hot throw on a swimsuit, order a drink and no-one will say anything if you plunge into the pool. It's the town's local hang-out spot.

Minibuses connect Outjo with Otji-warongo (US$2.50, one hour) from the bakery and the OK supermarket on the main street, but at the time of research there was no public transport to Etosha.

TSUMEB
☎ 067

Although mineral-collectors rank Tsumeb among the world's greatest natural wonders, backpackers use it as another jumping-off point for Etosha. If geology is your passion, however, you'll be happy to know that of the 184 minerals discovered here, 10 are found nowhere else. The geological history is recounted in the **Tsumeb Museum** (☎ 220447; admission US$1; ⏱ 9am-noon & 2-5pm Mon-Fri, 9am-noon Sat), located in the 1915 Old German Private School on the corner of Main St and 8th Rd.

Travel North Namibia (☎ 220728; travelnn@tsu .namibia.com; 1551 Omeg Alee) provides nationwide tourist information, accommodation and transport bookings, as well as car hire any-

where in northern Namibia (with special rates for Etosha trips).

Sleeping & Eating
Mousebird Backpackers & Safaris (☎ 221777; www.mousebird.com; cnr 4th St & 8th Rd; camp sites per person US$4, dm/d US$7.50/16; ⛺ 🖳) Tsumeb's newest backpackers is also its friendliest. The owner, Sonic, goes out of her way to make you feel at home. Facilities are immaculate and the lounge is perfect for doing nothing (a good thing because there's not much to do in Tsumeb). If you don't have a car, Mousebird also organises three-day safaris to Etosha (US$160) that travellers are recommending. They also run two-day trips into Bushmanland (US$125).

Etosha Café & Biergarten (☎ 220826; Main St; s/d with shared bathroom US$13/22) This place has quaint, inexpensive accommodation and is good for breakfasts and light meals (US$1 to US$3.50). Sit outside in the garden amid caged tropical birds, leafy trees and a small fountain.

Makalani Hotel (☎ 221051; mains US$4-8) This is the best restaurant in town. Sit outside by the pool and order a steak – they're huge and cooked the way you ask (a rarity in Namibia). There are also pizza and pasta options for vegetarians. Head to the bar (on the corner of 3rd St and 4th Rd) after dinner.

Getting There & Away
The twice-weekly Intercape Mainliner bus between Windhoek and Victoria Falls stops in at the Travel North Namibia office. Minibuses travel frequently from the Bahnhof St terminus in Tsumeb to Grootfontein, Oshakati and Windhoek. One-way fares from Tsumeb to Windhoek are US$33. From Tsumeb to Victoria Falls a one-way trip costs US$45.

Rail services run three times weekly to and from Windhoek (US$7, 16 hours) and Swakopmund via Walvis Bay (US$7, 17½ hours). For more rail information, contact **Trans-Namib** (☎ 220358).

WATERBERG PLATEAU PARK
The **Waterberg Plateau Park** (admission per person US$2.50, plus US$2.50 per vehicle; ⏱ 8am-1pm & 2pm-sunset) is known as a repository for rare and threatened species, including sables, roans and white rhinos. Visitors may not explore the plateau in their own vehicles, but NWR

NAMIBIA

conducts three-hour wildlife drives (US$12) twice daily. However, the main attraction here is the range of walking and hiking options.

There are nine short walking tracks around Bernabé de la Bat Rest Camp (including one up to the plateau rim at Mountain View), which all take a day or less. A four-day, 42km, unguided hike around a figure-eight track (US$12 per person) starts at 9am every Wednesday from April to November. Groups are limited to between three and 10 people. Hikers stay in basic shelters and don't need a tent, but must otherwise be self-sufficient. Also from April to November, the four-day guided Waterberg Wilderness Trail (US$24 per person) operates every second, third and fourth Thursday of the month and is open to groups of six to eight people. Accommodation is in huts, but participants must carry their own food and sleeping bags. All hikes must be prebooked through NWR in Windhoek (p839).

Bernabé de la Bat Rest Camp (camp sites for 4 people US$12, d/tr bungalows US$39/43) offers a range of accommodation with fans, *braais* (barbecues) and outdoor seating areas. The camp restaurant serves meals during limited hours and a shop sells staples in the morning and afternoon.

There's no public transport to the park, but taxis from Otjiwarongo will get you there for around US$25 each way. Quite a few budget safaris include the park in their itineraries.

NORTHEASTERN NAMIBIA

This region, which includes the formerly dangerous Caprivi Strip, forms a stark contrast to the aridity of much of the rest of the country. Here water flows year-round. This is a tranquil area of stunning sunsets and lazy days. Spend some time relaxing on the banks of the mighty Okavango River, doing nothing more than listening to the hippos call. Although once an area whose name was synonymous with danger due to the intermittent civil wars in Angola, today the Caprivi Strip is perfectly safe. Angola signed a peace accord in April 2002 and problems in the area ceased.

RUNDU
☎ 066

Rundu occupies a beautiful setting on the bluffs overlooking the Okavango River and Angola. There is little of specific interest to travellers (other than lounging on the riverbank, or maybe crossing the river for a 'Cola in Angola'), but it does make a good stopping point between Windhoek and the Caprivi Strip. There's also the vibrant and authentic Kehemu market, selling mostly flip-flops, African music and used clothing. With its friendly and nonintimidating atmosphere, it's not a bad spot to spend a couple of hours chatting with the locals. There's even a bar and a few pool tables smack in the middle of the place!

Sleeping & Eating
Rundu has little in terms of budget accommodation. If you don't have a tent, expect to pay about US$22 per person. While all the lodges listed here are not bad value for money, N'Kwazi Lodge (see the boxed text opposite) really stands out and is worth the money.

Sarasungu River Lodge (☎ 255161; sarasungu@ mweb.com.na; camp sites per person US$4, s/d US$28/40) This place is a little pricey for what you get. The rooms in self-contained thatched huts are basic, but the lodge is in a quiet, secluded setting and its restaurant is known for its pizzas and pasta. It's 4km from town; phone for a pick-up from the Shell petrol station.

Kavango River Lodge (☎ 255244; kavlodge@tsu .namib.com; camp sites per person US$2.50, s/d US$31/45; ✕) The facilities here are looking a little run-down, but the views are still the best in town (it's perched right on the river). The self-contained rooms are clean, not shabby, and well equipped with TVs and direct-dial phones. To get here, follow the signs from town.

Ozzy's Beerhouse (☎ 256723; mains US$1-3) This restaurant has cheap, palatable food including vegetarian options. It also does takeaway and is open late. It's on the main road through town.

Getting There & Away
Intercape Mainliner's two weekly buses between Windhoek (US$36, nine hours) and Victoria Falls (US$36, 11 hours) stop at the Engen petrol station on Main St in Rundu. Minibuses to and from Windhoek,

---

CARING FOR KIDS

Right on the banks of the Okavango River, 20km down a dirt road from town, sits the gorgeously maintained **N'Kwazi Lodge** (☎ 255467; nkwazi@iafrica.com.na; camp sites per person US$3.75, African huts with bathroom US$25, d with breakfast US$55). This place blends into the environment, and rooms are beautifully laid out with personal touches like small hand-carved masks on the beds. This is as close as you'll get to one of Africa's top-end lodges for a fraction of the price. Excursions include sundowner cruises that feature drinking a 'Cola in Angola' (US$6.25) and horseback riding (US$12 for 1½ hours). Excellent home-cooked buffet-style meals are served in the open-air restaurant. Transfers from town cost US$29 per group.

The owners, Val and Wynand Peypers, are making a conscious effort at promoting responsible travel and have begun a partnership with a local school. Currently, 19 teachers are responsible for more than 565 children, most of whom will never advance beyond primary school because either their parents cannot afford the minimal school fees or they are needed to work the fields. The Peypers began bringing travellers to the school in 2002, and many who have visited have returned home and raised funds for supplies. Since the partnership began the school has been able to purchase a water-pump for drinking water and start a food program for hungry school children. A visit is a worthwhile experience – you'll get the chance to see how a Namibian school operates, talk to the teachers and take as many photos as you desire. No donation is required, or even expected, but after visiting you may feel compelled to help out.

Grootfontein and Katima Mulilo stop at the Shell petrol station on the corner of Main St and the Grootfontein road.

A car ferry and border crossing are expected soon between Rundu and Calai, across the river in Angola.

WEST CAPRIVI
☎ 066

The area surrounding the tiny town of **Divundu** is magnificent. It offers uncrowded wildlife viewing at the 25,400-hectare Mahango Game Reserve, serene hiking around Popa Falls and unparalleled relaxing at Ngepi Camp on the banks of the Okavango River. Before the 2002 Angolan ceasefire this area saw almost no visitors. Now that peace has returned, tourism is picking up. If you're looking to get off the beaten path, head to this area while it's still relatively undiscovered.

Travellers should note that Divundu is also marked as Bagani on some maps and road signs; technically they're separate places about 2km apart, but Bagani is little more than a petrol stop for most visitors.

Mahango Game Reserve (admission per person US$3.50, plus US$3.50 per vehicle) has been incorporated into the newly created Bwabwata National Park. It is the only national park in the country where visitors can leave their cars and walk at will. The best time for wildlife viewing is during the winter dry season when large concentrations of thirsty elephants gather.

Near Divindu and Bagani, the Okavango River tumbles down a broad series of cascades known as **Popa Falls** (admission per person US$2.50, plus US$2.50 per vehicle). They're not the most impressive falls in the world, but the area offers some decent hikes. During low water there is a 4m drop. **Popa Falls Rest Camp** (☎ 61-236975; camp sites for 4 people US$11, 4-bed huts US$26-28), operated by the NWR, is looking a little shabby these days but has eye-catching views of the cascades.

Looking to relax and experience genuine African hospitality? Head to **Ngepi Camp** (☎ 259903; getalife@getalifeplanet.com; camp sites per person US$5, d huts US$22, meals US$2-5). Travellers rave about this place and we agree: it's probably the best backpacker lodge in Namibia. Entire days can be spent sunbathing and reading on the green lawn or swimming in the 'cage' in the Okavango River (it keeps you and the crocodiles at safe distances from each other). When the sun sinks low head out on the river for a sundowner booze cruise (US$7.50), then spend the night drinking in the inviting bush bar. Go to sleep in a reed hut by the river and listen to the hippos splashing around nearby. Ngepi is not a luxury camp and doesn't pretend to be – showers are rough and there's no television or Internet – but all this just adds to its charm. You can also arrange Mahango wildlife drives (US$17) and inexpensive mokoro trips (three days from US$125) on the Okavango Delta Panhandle nearby in Botswana. The camp is 4km off the main road from Divundu. Note that the sandy access road may sometimes prove challenging for 2WD vehicles. Phone the lodge if you need a lift from Divundu.

All buses and minibuses between Katima Mulilo and Rundu pass through Divundu. The gravel road between Divundu and Mohembo (on the Botswana border) is accessible by 2WD; drivers may transit the Mahango park without charge.

EAST CAPRIVI
Katima Mulilo
☎ 066

Out on a limb at the eastern end of the Caprivi Strip lies remote Katima Mulilo, as far from Windhoek as you can get in Namibia. This pleasant and very African town features lush vegetation and enormous trees, and was once known for the elephants that marched through. Nowadays little wildlife remains, but the ambience remains pleasant.

Tourist information is dispensed at **Tutwa Tourism & Travel** (☎ 253048; tutwa@mweb.com.na), which also organises custom tours around the region. The office is located across the road from the Engen petrol station and the Mukusi Cabins. On weekdays, the Bank of Windhoek, beside the main square, changes cash and travellers cheques at an appropriately tropical pace. For fax, email and Internet access try **IWAY** (US$2.50 per hr; 8am-9pm Mon-Sat, 1-9pm Sun), in a nondescript building beside the Caprivi Arts Centre.

The **Caprivi Arts Centre** (Olifant St; 8am-5.30pm), run by the Caprivi Arts & Culture Association, is a good place to look for local curios and crafts such as woodcarvings, baskets, bowls and traditional weapons.

Mukusi Cabins (☎/fax 253255; mukusi@mweb.com.na; Engen petrol station; budget cabins US$14, s/d without bathroom US$20/28) is an oasis-like lodge providing excellent-value accommodation within easy walking distance of the centre. The lovely attached **bar-restaurant** (breakfast US$3.50, mains US$3.50-7) dishes up a range of unexpected options – calamari, snails, kingclip (a local fish) – as well as beef and chicken standbys.

Caprivi Travellers Guest House (☎ 252788; dm/s/d US$4.50/12/14) is a very basic backpacker

option 400m from the town centre just off Rundu Rd.

Mad Dog McGee's (☎ 252021; mains US$3.50-7) is a popular restaurant and bar serving a range of mainly meat, chicken and fish dishes. The bar stays open as long as there are patrons to prop it up. It's one block off Ngoma Rd.

Intercape Mainliner passes Katima Mulilo twice weekly en route between Windhoek and Victoria Falls (Zimbabwe). A one-way fare between Katima Mulilo and Victoria Falls is US$24. From Katima Mulilo and Windhoek the cost is US$55.

Minibuses run when full to and from Windhoek (US$15, 15 hours) and to various points in between.

SOUTHERN NAMIBIA

From the rugged walls of Africa's largest canyon, to the vast expanses of open road, to the surreal colonial relic of Lüderitz huddling on the barren, windswept Namib Desert coast, southern Namibia has something for everybody.

FISH RIVER CANYON
☎ 063

Nowhere else in Africa is there anything like Fish River Canyon. Fish River, which joins the Orange River at the mouth of the canyon, has been gouging out this gorge for thousands of years and the results are both dramatic and enormous. The canyon measures 160km in length and reaches up to 27km wide and 550m deep, but these figures don't convey the sort of response you're likely to have when you first gaze into its depths.

Most of the canyon and the surrounding area falls within the **Fish River Canyon National Park** (admission per person US$2.50, plus US$2.50 per vehicle). The two main camps are Hobas, at the northern end, and Ai-Ais Hot Springs Resort, in the south. Prebook all accommodation at NWR in Windhoek (p839).

The **Hobas Information Centre** (7.30am-noon & 2-5pm), at the camp site of the same name at northern end of the park, is also the check-in point for the Fish River hiking trail. This popular route begins at Hikers' Viewpoint, 10km from Hobas along a good gravel road; even if you're not hiking, you should definitely come here for the incredible view over the northern part of the canyon. The vista from Main Viewpoint, a few kilometres to the south, is also stunning. Both of these dramatic vantage points overlook the sharp riverbend known as Hell's Corner, which is featured in every Fish River Canyon tourist brochure ever published.

Trekking
The magical five-day, 85-km **Fish River Trail** (US$11 per person) between Hikers' Viewpoint and Ai-Ais is Namibia's most popular walk – with good reason. Due to flash flooding and heat in the summer months, it's open only from May to September. Groups of three to 40 people may begin the hike every day of the season, but it's very popular so you'll have to book well in advance. Bookings are made through the NWR in Windhoek or Swakopmund. Officials may also require a doctor's certificate as proof of fitness, issued less than 40 days before your hike, although if you look young and fit they may not ask for it. Hikers must arrange their own transport to and from the start and finish, as well as accommodation in Hobas and Ai-Ais.

Sleeping & Eating
The well-shaded **Hobas Camping Ground** (camp sites for 4 people US$15) offers a kiosk selling a few food items, a swimming pool and clean facilities, but there's no restaurant or huts, so you'll need camping gear. Drivers should note that petrol is not available here.

Ai-Ais Hot Springs Resort (camp sites for 4 people US$15, 4-bed bungalows US$27, 2-bed flat US$42, 4-bed flat US$36, mineral baths US$2.50; ☼ sunrise-11pm), whose name means 'Scalding Hot' in Nama, is known for its thermal baths that originate beneath the riverbed. They're rich in chloride, fluoride and sulphur, and are reputedly salubrious for sufferers of rheumatism or nervous disorders. The hot water is piped to a series of baths, Jacuzzis and an outdoor swimming pool.

Ai-Ais also has a **restaurant** (☼ 7-8.30am, noon-1.30pm & 6-8.30pm daily), petrol station, tennis courts, post office and a shop selling basic groceries.

Getting There & Away
There's no public transport to either Hobas or Ai-Ais, but from mid-March to October hitchers should eventually be successful. Alternatively, take the train from Keetmanshoop to the Hoolog rail halt, which

is within relatively easy hitching distance (43km) of Hobas. Be prepared for a long, hot wait though.

KEETMANSHOOP
☎ 063 / pop 15,000
Keetmanshoop is the main crossroads of southern Namibia, but it's not exactly a place to write home about. It's a small dusty town in the middle of nowhere with squat, nondescript buildings. But it's somewhere you might spend the night, and it's a good refuelling stop – especially if you're heading towards Sossusvlei. In fact if you're heading in any direction make sure you refuel here, or you'll find yourself stuck in the middle of the desert with no petrol.

The helpful **Southern Tourist Forum** (☎ 221266; fax 223818; ☼ 7.30am-12.30pm & 1.30-4.30pm Mon-Fri), located in the municipal building to the west of Central Park can give you information on historical attractions. The **town museum** (☎ 221256; admission free; ☼ 7.30am-12.30pm & 2.30-4.30pm Mon-Fri) in the 1895 Rhenish Mission Church outlines the town's history with a model of a traditional Nama home, early farming equipment and old photographs. The museum is on Kaiser St between 6th and 7th Avenue.

Sleeping & Eating
Rachel Guesthouse (☎ 223454; 12 Schmeide St; dm & d per person US$8.75) has friendly staff, and its biggest selling point is that you can stay in a double for the price of a dorm bed.

The budget **Schutzen-Haus** (☎ 223400; 8th Ave; s/d US$19/25; ✷) has clean, simple rooms. The grounds are ugly brown dirt, but there's a bar attached to drink away a night of boredom.

The **Municipal Camp & Caravan Park** (☎ 223316; camp sites per person US$5 plus US$2.50 per vehicle) has uninspiring, dusty camp sites; but it's the cheapest place in town. It's 200m north of Schutzen Haus.

For food, try **Lara's Restaurant** (☎ 222233; cnr 5th Ave & Schmeide St; breakfast US$3, light meals US$1.50-3, mains US$4-8), which has strange decor but palatable food, although it's very Germanic and very meat-oriented.

Getting There & Away
Intercape Mainliner buses between Windhoek (US$24, six hours) and Cape Town (US$32, 14 hours) stop at the Du Toit BP

petrol station (on the corner of 5th Ave and Hendrik Nel St) four times weekly in either direction; they also leave for Jo'burg (US$46, 17 hours) via Upington. The Engen station, opposite, serves as the bus terminal for minibuses to and from Windhoek, Lüderitz and Noordoewer. Star Line buses to Lüderitz (US$8, 4¾ hours) depart from the train station at 7.30am Monday, Wednesday and Friday.

Overnight trains between Windhoek and Keetmanshoop (US$9, 11 hours) run in either direction daily except Saturday. Trains to Upington in South Africa leave on Wednesday and Saturday morning (US$8, 12½ hours). For details phone **Trans-Namib** (☎ 292202).

LÜDERITZ
☎ 063

Lüderitz is a surreal colonial relic – a Bavarian village huddling on the barren, windswept Namib Desert coast, seemingly untouched by the 20th century (let alone the 21st). Here the icy South Atlantic Ocean is home to seals, penguins, flamingos and assorted marine life. To get here means a 700km return-trip detour from Keetmanshoop via the tarred B4, a long, lonely road through endless desert vistas between the desolate southern reaches of the Namib-Naukluft Park and the forbidden zone of Diamond Area 1, where stern signs forbid you to leave the road in case you should stumble across an uncut gem just lying in the sand.

In Lüderitz, the tourist office run by **Lüderitzbucht Tours & Safaris** (☎ 202719; Bismarck St; ludsaf@ldz.namib.com; ☼ 8am-1pm & 2-5pm Mon-Fri, 8am-noon Sat, 8.30-10am Sun) provides reliable tourist information, organises visitor permits for Kolmanskop and sells curios, books, stamps and phonecards. The helpful **NWR office** (☎ 202752; Schinz St; ☼ 7.30am-1pm & 2-4pm Mon-Fri) can help with national park information.

Several banks on Bismarck St change cash and travellers cheques. **Extreme Communications I-café** (☎ 204256; US$3.50 per hr; ☼ 8am-5pm Mon-Fri, 9am-1pm Sat) offers email and Internet access.

Sights & Activities
The architecture of Lüderitz is an intriguing mix of German Imperial and Art Nouveau styles. The bizarre **Goerke Haus** (Diamantberg St; ad-

mission US$1.25; ☼ 2-4pm Mon-Fri, 4-5pm Sat-Sun) is one of the town's most prominent buildings.

The **Lüderitz Museum** (☎ 202582; Diaz St; admission US$1.25; ☼ 3.30-5pm Mon-Fri) details Lüderitz' diamond-mining heritage and other aspects of its natural and cultural history.

The ghost town of **Kolmanskop**, 14km away, was once a substantial diamond-mining town. It boasted a casino, skittle alley and theatre with fine acoustics, but the slump in diamond sales after WWI and the discovery of richer deposits further south at Oranjemund ended its heyday. By 1956 it was deserted. Several buildings have been restored, but dunes have taken over many others. Tours of Kolmanskop (US$4) last 45 minutes and run at 9.30am and 10.45am Monday to Saturday and 10am Sunday; get a permit from the Lüderitzbucht Tours & Safaris office (see above) at least 30 minutes prior to each tour. Participants must provide their own transport from town. After the tour, you can eat lunch in the Ball Hall restaurant.

Sleeping
Lüderitz Backpackers (☎ 202000; luderitzbackpackers@hotmail.com; 7 Schinz St; dm US$6.50-8, d US$17) This place has all the usual backpacker amenities, including a kitchen, *braai* and good tourist information.

Kratzplatz (☎/fax 202458; kratzmr@iway.na; 5 Nachtigal St; dm US$5, s/d with breakfast US$19/28) A homely and informal B&B right in the town centre, Kratzplatz provides another option.

Shark Island (camp sites for 4 people US$12, 5-bed bungalows US$67) This camp site is operated by NWR and is beautifully situated but aggravatingly windy. It's connected to the town by a causeway but is no longer an island, thanks to the recent harbour reclamation project that attached it to the mainland.

Eating & Drinking
Fairies' Coffee Nook (☎ 0812-456158; Waterfront Complex; breakfast US$3.20, sandwiches under US$1) With a good sea view, Fairies' Coffee Nook serves up light meals, coffee and sweet snacks.

Badger's Bistro (☎ 202855; Diaz St; lunch US$2.50-5, mains US$3-7, lobster US$15) Try Badger's for lunch or dinner, but the attached bar can be noisy. Crayfish is available only in season.

Ritzi's (☎ 0811-243353; Diaz St; mains US$6-10) Book ahead if you want to eat here. Specialities include local oysters, kingclip and crayfish, as well as excellent venison, beef

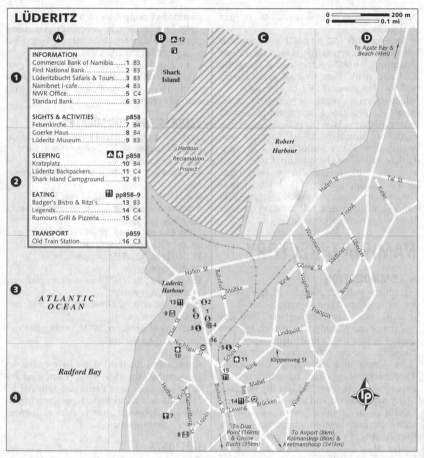

LÜDERITZ

0 ——————— 200 m
0 ——————— 0.1 mi

INFORMATION
Commercial Bank of Namibia.......1 B3
First National Bank......................2 B3
Lüderitzbucht Safaris & Tours......3 B3
Namibnet I-cafe..........................4 B3
NWR Office.................................5 C4
Standard Bank.............................6 B3

SIGHTS & ACTIVITIES   p858
Felsenkirche...............................7 B4
Goerke Haus................................8 B4
Lüderitz Museum.........................9 B3

SLEEPING   p858
Kratzplatz..................................10 B4
Lüderitz Backpackers..................11 C4
Shark Island Campground............12 B1

EATING   pp858–9
Badger's Bistro & Ritzi's.............13 B3
Legends....................................14 C4
Rumours Grill & Pizzeria.............15 C4

TRANSPORT   p859
Old Train Station........................16 C3

To Agate Bay & Beach (4km)

Shark Island

Harbour Reclamation Project

Robert Harbour

Hafen St

Tal St

Kiefer

Troost

Lübecker

Woermann

Stettiner

Bremer

Göring St

Ring

Vogelsang

François

ATLANTIC OCEAN

Lüderitz Harbour

Hafen St

Bahnhof

Moltke

Diaz St

Nachtigal St

Radford Bay

Lindquist

Schinz St

Ring

Klippenweg St

Mabel

Hother

Kirche

Diamantberg St

Leipzin

Bismarck St

Bay

Lessing

Brücken

Woermann

To Diaz Point (16km) & Grosse Bucht (35km)

To Airport (8km), Kolmanskop (8km) & Keetmanshoop (341km)

NAMIBIA

and vegetarian options. Entry is through Badger's Bistro.

Legends (☎ 203110; Bay Rd; mains US$5-10) This place specialises in seafood – especially crayfish – but you can also order pizza, beef and other mains, and takeaways are available. It also has a pub with billiards and a big-screen TV.

Rumours Grill & Pizzeria (☎ 202655; Kapp's Hotel; open for lunch and dinner daily; mains US$5-9, crayfish from US$15) This popular steak house is known for its beef, pizzas and seafood. You can choose between the sports bar and the beer garden.

Getting There & Away

Air Namibia flies five times weekly between Windhoek and Cape Town, stopping en route in Walvis Bay, Lüderitz and Oran-jemund. From Windhoek to Lüderitz a one-way fare costs US$130.

Star Line buses to Keetmanshoop (US$9, 4¾ hours) leave from the old train station on Bismarck St at 12.30pm on Monday, Wednesday and Friday.

AUS
☎ 063

Tidy, tranquil little Aus lies at the end of a long, empty stretch of road 125km east of Lüderitz, and is a popular stopping-off point for a cold drink and a loo – simply because there's nowhere else.

Namib Garage (☎ /fax 258029; Bahnhof St; camp sites per person US$2, s/d US$12/18) provides simple accommodation as well as snacks, burgers and grills.

Klein-Aus Vista (☎ /fax 258021; www.namibhorses .com; camp sites for 6 people US$4, 10-bed hut from US$40) occupies a 10,000-hectare ranch along the Lüderitz road, 3km west of Aus. Hikers will love the magical four-day hiking route, which traverses fabulous wild landscapes. Meals are available at the main lodge and accommodation is in the main lodge or one of the two wonderful hikers' huts: the dormitory hut Geister Schlucht, in a Shangri-La-like valley, or the opulent Eagle's Nest complex, with several chalets built right into the boulders. Beyond the hiking, activities include horse riding (US$20) and 4WD tours (US$38/76 for a half/full day) through their vast desert concession.

NAMIBIA DIRECTORY

ACCOMMODATION

Namibia is well equipped for budget travellers with backpacker accommodation found in most places, and camping areas throughout the country. Budget lodges are of high quality – you won't find many fleapits in Namibia. You can expect decent mattresses, clean sheets and impeccable bathrooms. Most backpacker lodges have Internet access, kitchen, pool, bar and laundry facilities. Many serve meals and run travel centres. Double rooms in most hostels are on a par with their cheap hotel counterparts, although they usually do not include private bathrooms. Most hostels offer camping on their lawns; prices are always per person, not site. Dorm rooms usually go for between US$6 to US$8, while doubles cost around US$20.

ACTIVITIES

Sparsely populated Namibia is an outdoor enthusiast's dream. There are endless opportunities for hiking and camping. Swakopmund (p843) serves as the adrenalin capital of the country with everything from skydiving to sandboarding available.

DANGERS & ANNOYANCES

Theft isn't particularly rife, but take care walking alone at night and conceal your valuables in Windhoek or towns around the country, and don't leave anything in sight inside a parked vehicle. Take the same pre-

cautions at camp sites in towns – although there's no problem at camp sites in national parks – not from humans anyway (just watch out for the monkeys).

East of Lüderitz, do not enter the prohibited diamond area, mainly south of the road to Keetmanshoop; well-armed patrols can be overly zealous.

EMBASSIES & CONSULATES

The following embassies are in Windhoek:

Angola (Map p840; ☎ 227535; Angola House, 3 Ausspann St, Ausspannplatz)

Botswana (Map p838; ☎ 221941; 101 Nelson Mandela Ave)

France (Map p840; ☎ 229022; 1 Goethe St)

Germany (Map p840; ☎ 223100; 6th fl, Sanlam Centre, 154 Independence Ave)

South Africa (Map p838; ☎ 205 7111; RSA House, cnr Jan Jonker St & Nelson Mandela Ave, Klein Windhoek)

UK (Map p840; ☎ 223022; bhc@mweb.com.na; 116A Robert Mugabe Ave)

USA (Map p840; ☎ 221601; www.usembassy.namib.com; 14 Lossen St, Ausspannplatz)

Zambia (Map p840; ☎ 237610; cnr Sam Nujoma Dr & Mandume Ndemufayo Ave)

Zimbabwe (Map p840; ☎ 228134; Gamsberg Bldg, cnr Independence Ave & Grimm St)

Canada and Australia don't have embassies in Namibia; the closest representation for those countries is in Pretoria, South Africa. Namibia has diplomatic representation in Angola, Botswana, South Africa, Zambia and Zimbabwe.

HOLIDAYS

Resort areas are busiest – often totally packed – over the Namibian and South African school holiday periods, which normally occur from mid-December to mid-January, around Easter, from late July to early August, and for two weeks in mid-October.

As well as religious holidays listed in the Africa Directory chapter (p1003), these are the principal public holidays in Namibia:

1 January New Year's Day
21 March Independence Day
April or May (40 days after Easter) Ascension Day
1 May Workers' Day
4 May Cassinga Day
25 May Africa Day
26 August Heroes' Day
10 December Human Rights Day
26 December Family/Boxing Day

INTERNET ACCESS

Email and Internet access is available at most backpacker lodges, tourist offices, Internet cafés and hotels in larger towns.

The rate per hour is usually between US$2 and US$4.

MAPS

The *Shell Roadmap – Namibia* is probably the best reference for remote routes; it also has an excellent Windhoek map (US$2). Shell also publishes the *Kaokoland-Kunene Region Tourist Map*, which depicts all routes and tracks through this remote area. It's available at bookshops and tourist offices for US$3.

The Macmillan *Namibia Travellers' Map* (US$3), at a scale of 1:2,400,000, has clear print and colour-graded altitude representation, but minor routes aren't depicted.

MONEY

The Namibian dollar (N$) equals 100 cents. In Namibia the dollar is valued the same as the South African rand (in South Africa, it fetches only about R0.70), and the rand is also legal tender at a rate of 1:1.

Major foreign currencies in cash or travellers cheques may be exchanged at any bank, but travellers cheques normally attract a better rate. Credit cards are widely accepted in shops, restaurants and hotels, and cash advances are available at banks and from BOB, First National Bank's ATM system.

Tipping is expected in restaurants if the service is good; 10% is the going rate.

POST & TELEPHONE

Overseas airmail post is normally faster than domestic post, and is limited only by the time it takes an article to reach Windhoek (which can be slow in the outer areas).

Namibian area dialling codes all have three digits that begin with '06'. When phoning from abroad, first dial the country code (☎ 264), followed by the area code without the leading zero.

Phonecards are sold at post offices and retail shops.

TOURS

Even if you normally spurn organised tours, camping safaris are often the best (or only) way to reach remote areas in Namibia. You'll find good value from the following:

Cardboard Box Travel Shop (☎ 061-256580; www .namibian.org; 15 Johann Albrecht St, PO Box 5142, Windhoek) This friendly, recommended agency offers bookings (including last-minute options) for all budget safaris. It can help with lodge, safari, car hire and transport bookings, national parks bookings and other travel services, and provides good advice to travellers.

Chameleon Safaris (☎ /fax 061-247668; www.cha meleonsafaris.com; 8 Voight St, PO Box 6107, Windhoek) This budget company is geared to backpackers and does a range of good-value safaris: six-day Damaraland/Skeleton Coast (US$400); three-day Sossusvlei (US$150); 18-day 4WD tour (US$950); seven-day northern or southern highlights (US$350 each); and 14-day northern and southern highlights (US$600).

Crazy Kudu (☎ 061-222636; fax 061-255074; www.crazykudu.com; 50 Van der Merwe St; PO Box 99031, Windhoek) One of Namibia's friendliest and most economical safari companies, Crazy Kudu does 10-day all-inclusive 'Namibia Explorer' adventures through northern and central highlights (US$440); a six-day northern highlights tour (US$275); and a three-day Sossusvlei Express tour (US$130), which may also be joined in Swakopmund; all departures are guaranteed. They'll also organise customised safaris, an Okavango Delta and Victoria Falls excursion, and Fish River or Kaokoland extensions for the best possible price.

Enyandi Safaris (☎ 061-255103; fax 061-255477; enyandi@iafrica.com.na) This recommended company runs budget tours mainly in northwestern Namibia, starting at US$245 per person for a seven-day trip.

Kaokohimba Safaris (☎ /fax 061-222378; www .natron.net/tour/kaoko/himbae.htm; PO Box 11580, Windhoek) Kaokohimba organises cultural tours through Kaokoland and Damaraland and wildlife-viewing trips in Etosha National Park.

Magic Bus Safaris (☎ 061-259485; magicbus@iafrica .com.na; 5 Grieg St, Windhoek) This small company runs budget trips from Windhoek to Sossusvlei (US$160 to US$190), Etosha (US$170), a seven-day combination (US$360) and other options.

Wild Dog Safaris (☎ 061-257642; www.wilddog safaris.com; 19 Johann Albrecht St, PO Box 26188, Windhoek) This friendly operation runs seven-day Northern Namibia Adventures and Southern Swings (US$340 each), three-day Etosha or Sossusvlei circuits (US$160 each, or US$350 for both), as well as longer participation safaris and accommodated excursions.

VISAS

Visas are not required for visitors from Australia, New Zealand, France, Germany, the UK, Ireland, Canada or the USA. Travellers receive entry for an initial 90 days (free).

NAMIBIA

Visa Extensions

Extensions on the initial 90-day visa are available from the **immigration office** (☎ 292-2111; mlusepani@mha.gov.na; cnr Kasino St & Independence Ave; Windhoek; ☼ 8am-1pm Mon-Fri). It's usually free to extend your visa; however, you are at the mercy of the immigration official. Another way of extending your visa is to simply leave the country for a few days and when you return get a new stamp.

Visas for Onward Travel

Visas for the following neighbouring countries can be obtained in Windhoek.

See p860 for embassy and consulate information.

Angola Travellers must apply for a visa in their home country (usually limited to fly-in visas for arrival in Luanda) or attempt to secure an overland visa from the Angolan consulate in Oshakati, northern Namibia.

Botswana No visa is required for citizens of Australia, New Zealand, France, Germany, the UK, Ireland, Canada or the USA.

South Africa No visa is required for citizens of Australia, New Zealand, France, Germany, the UK, Ireland, Canada or the USA.

Zambia Visas take one day to process and cost US$59/94 for a single/double-entry visa, and US$188 for a multiple-entry visa. Note that they're available at the border for considerably less (normally US$25 for US citizens and UK£45 for British subjects). However, they're free if you're 'introduced' to Zambia by a Zambian tour company – see the Zambia chapter (p821) for details.

Zimbabwe Visas cost US$30/45 for single/double entry (also available on the border). Multiple-entry visas cost US$55 and aren't available at the border.

Botswana

HIGHLIGHTS

- **Okavango Delta** Go looking for wildlife in this watery wilderness (p874)
- **Chobe National Park** Visit this largely undeveloped park with its mind-boggling numbers of elephants, and an arkful of other animals (p882)
- **Tsodilo Hills** Marvel at the 'Wilderness Louvre' of ancient San paintings in Botswana's most inspiring wild landscape (p881)
- **Off the beaten track** Do an inexpensive camping trip from Gweta to the Makgadikgadi Pans, an area like no place on earth (p884)

FAST FACTS

- **Area** 582,000 sq km
- **ATMs** found in large towns
- **Borders** South Africa, Namibia, Zambia, Zimbabwe (all can be crossed overland)
- **Budget** US$40 to US$70 a day
- **Capital** Gaborone
- **Language** English, Setswana
- **Money** pula; US$1 = P5
- **Population** 1.61 million
- **Seasons** wet (Nov–Mar), dry (May–Aug)
- **Telephone** country code ☎ 267; international access code ☎ 00
- **Time** GMT/UTC + 2
- **Visas** None required for citizens of Australia, New Zealand, France, Germany, the UK, Ireland, Canada or the USA

Botswana is like a good mystery – it takes a while to unravel its secrets. Most travellers on a budget rush through so fast they never get past the basic plot structure. Go this route and all you'll see is bland towns, thousands of donkeys, dust and a country bordering on psychotic paranoia about foot-and-mouth disease.

Good detectives, however, will uncover an African success story. Politically and ideologically enlightened, Botswana enjoys nonracial policies, and standards of health, education and economy almost unequalled in sub-Saharan Africa.

It takes some planning to traverse this largely roadless wilderness of savanna, desert, wetlands and salt pans. And to really unravel the mystery and to experience Botswana's giant skies, wildlife-packed plains and watery wonderlands you'll be forced to part with some cash in the process.

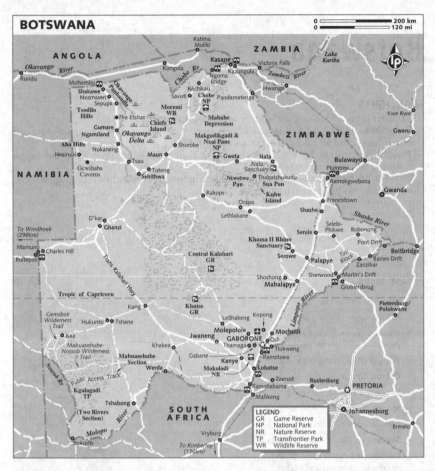

BOTSWANA

0 ——— 200 km
0 ——— 120 mi

HISTORY

It's widely believed that Botswana's first people were the San (also known as Bushmen,
although there is controversy over the use of
this name), who have inhabited the Kalahari
region for at least 30,000 years. The Khoikhoi
(Hottentots), thought to have originated
from a breakaway San group, came next.
A few thousand years passed, and some
time during the 14th century a Bantu group
known as the Tswana colonised the country's
southeastern strip. They stayed – Botswana
means 'Land of the Tswana' – and today are
the nation's largest population group.

Colonial History

In 1818 the confederation of Zulu tribes in
South Africa set out to conquer or destroy

all tribes and settlements in its path, causing waves of disruption throughout Southern Africa (see p943 for more information
on the *difaqane*, or 'the scattering'). Tswana
villages were scattered in the process and
some were pushed into the dead heart of the
Kalahari. In response to this aggression, the
Tswana regrouped and developed a highly
structured society.

From the 1820s the Boers began their
Great Trek across the Vaal River. Confident
that they had heaven-sanctioned rights to
any land they might choose to occupy in
Southern Africa, 20,000 Boers crossed into
Tswana and Zulu territory and established
themselves as though the lands were un-
claimed and uninhabited. At the Sand River
Convention of 1852, Britain recognised the

Transvaal's independence and the Boers informed the Batswana (people of Botswana) that they were now subjects of the South African Republic.

Prominent Tswana leaders Sechele I and Mosielele refused to accept white rule and incurred the violent wrath of the Boers. After heavy losses of life and land, the Tswana sent their leaders to petition the British for protection. Britain, however, was in no hurry to support lands of dubious profitability and offered only to act as arbitrator in the dispute. But by 1877, the worsening situation provoked the British annexation of the Transvaal and launched the first Boer War, during which violence continued until 1881. In 1882, Boers again moved into Tswana lands and subdued Mafeking (now Mafikeng), threatening the British route between the Cape and the suspected mineral wealth in Zimbabwe.

Again, the Tswana lobbied for British protection and in 1885, thanks to petitions from John Mackenzie (a friend of the Christian Chief Khama III of Shoshong), Britain resigned itself to the inevitable. Lands south of the Molopo River became the British Crown Colony of Bechuanaland and were attached to the Cape Colony while the area north became the British Protectorate of Bechuanaland.

A new threat to the Tswana chiefs' power base came in the form of Cecil Rhodes and his British South Africa Company (BSAC). By 1894 the British had all but agreed to allow him to control the country. An unhappy delegation of Tswana chiefs – Bathoen, Khama III and Sebele – accompanied by a sympathetic missionary, WC Willoughby, sailed to England to appeal directly to Colonial Minister Joseph Chamberlain for continued government control but their pleas were ignored. As a last resort, they turned to the London Missionary Society (LMS), which in turn took the matter to the British public. Fearing the BSAC would allow alcohol in Bechuanaland, the LMS and other Christian groups backed the Christian Khama. Public pressure mounted and the British government was forced to concede.

Chiefs now grudgingly accepted their rites and traditions would be affected by Christianity and Western technology. The capital of the protectorate was established at Mafeking – actually in South Africa – and

taxes were established. Chiefs were granted tribal 'reserve', jurisdiction over all black residents and the authority to collect taxes and retain a 10% commission on all moneys collected. In addition, the local economy was bolstered by the sale of cattle, draft oxen and grain to the Europeans streaming north in search of farming land and minerals.

The honeymoon didn't last. The construction of the railway through Bechuanaland to Rhodesia (now Zimbabwe) and an outbreak of foot-and-mouth disease in the 1890s destroyed the transit trade. In 1924 South Africa began pressing for Bechuanaland's amalgamation into the Union of South Africa, and when the Tswana chiefs refused, economic sanctions destroyed what remained of their beef market.

In 1923 Chief Khama III died and was succeeded by his son Sekgoma, who died after serving only two years. The heir to the throne, four-year-old Seretse Khama, wasn't ready for the job of ruling the largest of the Tswana chiefdoms, so his 21-year-old uncle, Tshekedi Khama, became regent of his clan.

Resident Commissioner Sir Charles Rey determined that no progress would be forthcoming as long as the people were governed by Tswana chiefs and proclaimed all local government officials answerable to colonial magistrates. So great was the popular opposition – people feared that it would lead to their incorporation into South Africa – that Rey was ousted from his job and his proclamation annulled.

During WWII, 10,000 Tswana volunteered for the African Pioneer Corps to defend the British Empire. After the war Seretse Khama went to study in England where he met and married an Englishwoman. Tshekedi Khama was furious at this breach of tribal custom, and the South African authorities, still hoping to absorb Bechuanaland into the Union, were none too happy. The British government blocked Seretse's chieftaincy and he was exiled from the protectorate to England. Bitterness continued until 1956 when Seretse Khama renounced his right to power and returned with his wife to Botswana to serve as a minor official.

Nationalism & Independence
The first signs of nationalist thinking among the Tswana occurred in the late 1940s, and in 1955 it had become apparent that Britain was

preparing to release its grip on Bechuanaland. University graduates returned from South Africa with political ideas, and although the country had no real economic base, the first Batswana political parties surfaced and began thinking about independence.

Following the Sharpeville massacre which took place in 1960, South African refugees Motsamai Mpho, of the African National Congress (ANC), and Philip Matante, a Johannesburg preacher affiliated with the Pan-Africanist Congress, along with KT Motsete, a teacher from Malawi, formed the Bechuanaland People's Party. Its immediate goal was independence for the protectorate.

In 1962, Seretse Khama and the Kanye farmer Quett Masire formed the more moderate Bechuanaland Democratic Party (BDP), soon to be joined by Chief Bathoen II of the Ngwaketse. The BDP formulated a schedule for independence, drawing on support from local chiefs and traditional Batswana.

They promoted the transfer of the capital into the country (from Mafeking to Gaborone), drafted a new nonracial constitution and set up a countdown to independence, to allow a peaceful transfer of power. General elections were held in 1965 and Seretse Khama was elected president. On 30 September 1966 the country, now called the Republic of Botswana, gained independence.

Sir Seretse Khama – he was knighted shortly after independence – was no revolutionary, adopting a neutral stance (at least until near the end of his presidency) towards South Africa and Rhodesia. The reason, of course, was Botswana's economic dependence on these countries. Nevertheless, Khama refused to exchange ambassadors with South Africa and officially disapproved of apartheid in international circles.

Botswana was economically transformed by the discovery of diamonds near Orapa in 1967. The mining concession was given to De Beers with Botswana taking 75% of the profits.

After the death of Khama in 1980, Dr Ketumile Masire took the helm. His popular presidency ended in March 1998, when Festus Mogae took over.

In 2000 the country suffered devastating floods that left 70,000 people homeless, while droughts in recent years have caused considerable suffering, especially in the western part

BATSWANA

In the predominant language, Setswana (which means 'language of the Tswana'), tribal groups are usually denoted by the prefix 'ba'. Thus, Herero people are known as Baherero, the Kgalagadi as Bakgalagadi, and so on. Collectively, all citizens of Botswana (which means 'land of the Tswana') – regardless of colour, ancestry or tribal affiliation – are known as Batswana (plural) or Motswana (singular), even if they are not strictly from the Batswana tribal group. The Batswana tribal group accounts for about 60% of the people living in the country.

of the country. Despite these challenges, Botswana remains a peaceful nation.

THE CULTURE

Botswana continues to be a shining light among its neighbours, with a nonracial, multiparty and democratic government that oversees the affairs of a peaceful and neutral state. Unlike in so many African countries, freedom of speech, association, press and religion, as well as equal rights, are all guaranteed under the constitution.

The greatest threat to Botswana's stability is the deadly AIDS virus (see p27). The country has the highest HIV infection rate in the world: according to a United Nations report, 19% of all people and 36% of young adults (aged 15 to 29) are infected. There is hope, however. The Botswanan government is tackling the virus head on, in contrast to governments of other African nations. Although discussion of AIDS, sexually transmitted diseases and contraception continues to be taboo in Botswanan society (especially in rural areas), the government increased health spending by 41% in 2001 and established the National Aids Council, which is conducting educational programs in schools and universities and highlighting the issue on billboards along the highway. It's also flooding newspapers with awareness articles. The government has purchased antiretroviral drugs to treat its infected populace, something traditionally unheard of in Africa.

ARTS

The original Batswana artists managed to convey individuality, aesthetics and aspects of Batswana life in their utilitarian implements. Baskets, pottery, fabrics and tools were decorated with meaningful designs derived from tradition. Europeans introduced a new form of art, some of which was integrated and adapted to local interpretation, particularly in weavings and tapestries. The result is some of the finest and most meticulously executed work in Southern Africa.

Botswana's most famous modern literary figure is South African-born Bessie Head (who died in 1988). Her works reflect the harshness and beauty of African village life and the Botswanan landscape. Her most widely read works include *Serowe – Village of the Rain Wind, When Rain Clouds Gather, Maru, The Cardinals, A Bewitched Crossroad* and *The Collector of Treasures* (the last is an anthology of short stories). Welcome recent additions to Botswana's national literature are the works of Norman Rush, which include the novel *Mating*, set in a remote village, and *Whites*, which deals with the country's growing number of expatriates and apologists from South Africa and elsewhere.

ENVIRONMENT
The Land
With an area of 582,000 sq km, landlocked Botswana extends more than 1100km from north to south and 960km from east to west. The Kalahari (Kgalagadi) Desert covers 85% of the country in the central and southwestern areas – but despite the name it's semidesert, and even surprisingly lush in places.

Botswana's rainy season runs from November to March, and the best season for wildlife viewing is during the dry winter months (late May to August), when animals tend to stay close to water sources.

Wildlife & National Parks
Unlike in East Africa parks, where carnivores are seriously affected by tourism (imagine trying to hunt and being trailed by an endless succession of minibuses), lions and other hunters in Botswana fare much better. Tourism numbers are lower so natural patterns are less altered by human onlookers. Most national parks in Botswana boast four of the Big Five, ie buffaloes, elephants, leopards and lions. Rhinos haven't fared so well and are virtually extinct outside of three private reserves – Gaborone Game

Reserve (p871), Mokolodi Nature Reserve (p874) and Khama II Rhino Sanctuary near Serowe (p886). Elephants have fared better. Chobe National Park (p882) alone has at least 60,000 elephants, and herds wreak havoc trampling bush and toppling trees.

About 17% of Botswana is designated as national parks or reserves. The major protected areas include the Central Kalahari Game Reserve, Chobe National Park, Khutse Game Reserve, Makgadikgadi & Nxai Pans National Park and Moremi Wildlife Reserve. The Kgalagadi Transfrontier Park is an amalgamation of Botswana's former Mabuasehube–Gemsbok National Park and South Africa's Kalahari–Gemsbok National Park. Most parks are characterised by vast open spaces with a few private safari concessions, next to no infrastructure and very limited amenities. Exceptions include Chobe National Park and Moremi Wildlife Reserve, which both see a lot of visitors.

Fees for parks (except for Kgalagadi Transfrontier Park) are US$22 per person per day, plus US$10 per vehicle per day. Camping costs another US$5.50 per person per night. Accommodation in the national parks must be prebooked. With the exception of the northern section of Chobe (which can be visited on a day trip from Kasane), you must have made a reservation for a camp site to enter a national park. Contact the office of the **Department of Wildlife & National Parks (DWNP) Reservation Office** (☎ 318 0774; dwnp@gov.bw; PO Box 131, Government Enclave, Khama Cres, Gaborone; 7.30am-12.45pm & 1.45-4.30pm Mon-Fri) for bookings. You can also book through the **Maun office** (☎ 686 1265) on Kudu St, beside the police station. For Chobe National Park, you can book at the **Kasane office** (☎ 625 0235) at the northern gate to Chobe.

Budget travellers may feel that Botswana's parks are beyond their reach due to high fees, exorbitant lodge rates, lack of public transportation and the fact that hitching along park roads is forbidden. But persistence pays off and anyone who really wants to enter the park cheaply usually does. If you want to get in, spend a few hours waving your thumb outside the park gate. It could very well work.

Environmental Issues
While much of Botswana is largely pristine, it does face several ecological challenges. The

BOTSWANA

main issue centres on its 3000km of 1.5m-high 'buffalo fence', officially called the 'veterinary cordon fence' – a series of high-tensile steel wire barriers that crosses some of the country's wildest terrain. The fences were first erected in 1954 to segregate wild buffalo herds from domestic free-range cattle and thwart the spread of foot-and-mouth disease, even though it hasn't been proven the disease is passed from species to species. Today the fences not only prevent contact between wild and domestic bovine species, but also prevent other wild animals from migrating to water sources along age-old seasonal routes. While Botswana has set aside large areas for wildlife protection, migratory wildlife numbers (particularly of wildebeests, giraffes and zebras) continue to decline. Cattle ranching is a source of wealth and a major export industry, but all exported beef must be disease-free, so understandably ranchers have reacted positively to the fences, and the government tends to side with the ranchers.

TRANSPORT

GETTING THERE & AWAY
Air
Botswana is not well served by international airlines, as most travellers use Johannesburg as the gateway to the region (and, to a lesser degree, Victoria Falls via Harare, Zimbabwe).

DEPARTURE TAX

The international air departure tax of US$9 is included in ticket prices.

Sir Seretse Khama International Airport in Gaborone is the country's largest airport. It's also home to the national carrier, **Air Botswana** (☎ 395 2812; www.airbotswana.co.bw), which flies to and from Johannesburg (Jo'burg; US$170) several times daily and Harare (US$300) three times weekly (with connections to Lusaka, Zambia). Air Botswana has an office on The Mall in Gaborone. The airline regularly offers special promotions between Gaborone and Harare, as well as between Jo'burg and Harare, Limpopo Valley, Maun and Kasane. These promotions

often include accommodation and car hire. See the website for the latest details.

Land
Overland travel to or from Botswana is pretty straightforward. Incoming travellers are often requested to clean their shoes (even those shoes packed away in their luggage) in a disinfectant dip to prevent them carrying foot-and-mouth disease into the country. Vehicles must also pass through a pit filled with the same disinfectant.

Border opening hours change all the time, but major crossings between Botswana and Namibia or South Africa generally open between 6am and 8am and close between 6pm and 10pm. The main crossings between Botswana and Zimbabwe are open from 6am to 8pm and the Kuzunguka ferry to Zambia runs from 6am to 6pm. Minor crossings, such as the many across the Limpopo and Molopo Rivers between Botswana and South Africa, are normally open between 8am and 4pm, but close in periods of high water.

NAMIBIA
The three main border crossings for Namibia are at the Ngoma Bridge, Mahango–Mohembo and Mamuno–Buitepos.

There's at least one daily minibus between Ghanzi and Mamuno (US$3, three hours), on the border, but from there, you'll have to wait for a minibus on to Gobabis or Windhoek. Unfortunately, on the Namibian side they only run when full, so you may have to wait for quite some time.

Although the Intercape Mainliner bus between Windhoek and Victoria Falls passes through Kasane, passengers may not embark or disembark in Botswana. There are no cross-border buses through the Mahango–Mohembo border crossing.

SOUTH AFRICA
Most overland traffic between Botswana and South Africa passes through the Ramatlabama, Tlokweng or Pioneer border crossings. Minibuses between Gaborone and Jo'burg (US$12, six hours) leave when full between 6am and 5.30pm from the northwest corner of Gaborone's main bus terminal.

The **Intercape Mainliner** (☎ Gaborone 357 4294; Kudu Shell, Queen's Rd; ☎ Pretoria 012-654 4774; 108 Klerk St) travels the route between Gaborone and Jo'burg (US$18, six hours) daily, leaving Gaborone at 6.30am and Jo'burg Station at 3.30pm.

ZIMBABWE

The two most commonly used borders are at Ramokgwebana–Plumtree and at Kuzunguka, west of Victoria Falls.

Between Francistown and Bulawayo buses leave from the main bus terminals five to seven times daily in either direction (US $3.50, three hours).

Between Kasane and Victoria Falls both Thebe River Safaris and Chobe Safari Lodge offer Victoria Falls transfers (US$28, two hours).

GETTING AROUND
Air

The national carrier, **Air Botswana** (☎ 395 2812; www.airbotswana.co.bw), operates scheduled domestic flights between Gaborone, Francistown, Maun and Kasane. The best fares are available with 14-day advance purchase (Apex) tickets, but the airline also offers occasional special packages between Gaborone and Maun that include accommodation and car hire; see the website for details. Note that one-way fares may be higher than return fares. The domestic departure tax of US$2.50 is included in ticket prices.

Car

Vehicle hire in Botswana is not cheap, but to get around much of the country you'll need a car. A valid driving licence from your home country is sufficient to drive here. Bear in mind that they drive on the left-hand side of the road. Most people hire a 4WD, as this allows you the freedom to more easily explore areas such as Chobe National Park, the Kalahari region and the Makgadikgadi Pans. We, however, managed to research much of this chapter in the cheapest car out there – a tiny Fiat. That said, we did spend quite a bit of time pushing it out of thick sand, and driving tough rocky roads we had no business being on in a car of this size.

As a guide, plan on paying around US$20 per day plus US$0.30 per kilometre (or US$32 per day with 200km free per day for a minimum of six days) for the least expensive Toyota or VW Golf. For a 4WD Toyota Hilux (the standard 4WD rental vehicle), you'll pay US$65 per day plus US$0.70 per kilometre (or US$120 per day with 200km free per day for a minimum of six days).

It is far cheaper to hire a car in South Africa (see p949 for details) and drive it across the border. However, you must tell the car-rental company you plan to take the car into Botswana, as you need a letter from the rental agency to get across the border. Most rental agencies will allow you to cross the border with the car, but will charge you an additional fee of about US$200 to do this. If you are planning on travelling to more than one country outside South Africa you will pay a flat rate of US$280. Good deals for rental cars in South Africa can be found at www.travelocity.com.

Many companies also will refuse to insure you if you drive on gravel roads. This means if you wreck the vehicle, you'll be responsible for all expenses.

If you're determined to rent a vehicle in Botswana, below are some reputable car-rental companies:

Avis (☎ 391 3093; fax 391 2550; www.avis.com; Sir Seretse Khama International Airport, Gaborone)

Budget (☎ 390 2030; www.budget.co.za; Sir Seretse Khama International Airport, Gaborone)

Holiday (☎ 686 2429; Maun, Maun Airport)

Imperial (☎ 390 7333; www.imperialcarrental.co.za; Sir Seretse Khama International Airport, Gaborone)

Tempest (☎ 390 0011; www.tempestcarhire.co.za; Sir Seretse Khama International Airport, Gaborone)

When driving anywhere look out for donkeys. At times main highways will be thick with these large-eared asses standing immobile in the roadway, with a few sheep and goats thrown in for good measure. In theory, livestock owners are responsible for keeping their animals off the road, but in practise they wander wherever they want. If you are driving anywhere close to the speed limit you may not have time to skid to a stop. Hitting a donkey will not only cause major damage to your vehicle but will also be compounded by a typically fruitless search for the owner and lots of red tape.

Other animals also wander onto major highways. The biggest problems are elephants and kudu (if you hit one of these you're screwed). So drive slow, keep calm and remember that the additional amount of time it will take you to get from point A to B is all just part of the journey.

Hitching

Because public transport is somewhat erratic, hitching is relatively safe and fairly common although it is still always a risk. On main routes there should be no major problems, but ascertain a price before climbing aboard. Most drivers expect the equivalent of the bus fare.

Hitching the back roads isn't as straightforward. If you're hitching along the Trans-Kalahari Highway, through the Tuli Block or from Maun to Kasane through Chobe National Park, be sure to carry camping gear and enough food and water for several days of waiting. For trips even further afield (eg through the Makgadikgadi Pans), remember that vehicles pass once or twice a day at most, so try to arrange a lift in advance through a nearby lodge.

Local Transport

Travelling by bus and minibus is the only cheap service in Botswana (costs normally work out at about US$1 per hour of journey time). Buses and minibuses travel regularly along all major highway routes in Botswana, but services are less frequent in the western part of the country than along the eastern corridor. With few exceptions, small villages are served only if they lie along major highways. On the most popular runs, minibus services operate according to demand and depart when full, while buses follow a fixed schedule. In both cases there are no advance bookings – tickets are sold only on board.

Train

Although it's slow, train travel is an inexpensive, relaxing and effortless way to traverse the vast and dusty scrublands of eastern Botswana. The domestic train line runs between Ramatlabama on the South Africa border and Ramokgwebana on the Zimbabwe border, and was once part of the now-defunct Johannesburg–Bulawayo train route. At the time of research, passenger services only extended between Francistown and Lobatse, with main stopping points in Palapye, Mahalapye and Gaborone. There's also a single-class commuter extension between Gaborone and Lobatse (US$1.50).

Botswana Railways (☎ 395 1401) runs two train services between Gaborone and Fran-

cistown – the quicker day train and the lumbering overnight train. Day trains have two classes, club and economy. Night trains have 1st- and 2nd-class sleepers and a cheaper economy section, but you don't get a bed. Timetables, reservations and tickets are available at Gaborone and Francistown; bookings are essential for 1st- and 2nd-class sleepers.

GABORONE

pop 250,000

This city's greatest claim to fame is as one of Africa's most expensive capitals. Gaborone is a sprawling village suffering from the growing pains, drabness and lack of definition that accompany an abrupt transition from rural settlement to modern city. Although it has a few interesting sights, it is certainly nothing to go out of your way for.

ORIENTATION

Gaborone lacks any central business district, and urban action focuses on the dispersed shopping malls. Downtown is The Mall, between Independence Ave and the government complex of ministries on Khama Crescent. The Mall is in need of renovations. Vendors line the street, and you can find a giant selection of mostly chicken-based fast food as well as many banks.

A little way southeast of town is the sparkling new Riverwalk Mall where you can choose from a plethora of restaurants, bars and shops. There also is a large (by Botswana standards) cinema. It's good for dousing culture shock.

Getting into town from the airport, 14km north of the centre, is a real pain. The only reliable transport is the courtesy minibuses operated by top-end hotels. If there's space, nonguests may talk the driver into a lift, but you'll have to tip at least US$6 or US$8. Taxis rarely turn up at the airport; if you do find one, you'll pay anywhere from US$3 to US$12 per person to the centre.

If you arrive by bus or train you'll be dropped off in town and from there it's easy to flag down a taxi to get to your hotel.

INFORMATION

The **Department of Tourism** (☎ 355 3024; botswana tourism@gov.bw; www.gov.bw/tourism; 2nd fl, Standard

Chartered Bank Bldg, The Mall; ☺ 7.30am-12.30pm & 1.45-4.30pm Mon-Fri) has greatly improved over the past couple of years and does its best to help with specific queries.

Major branches of **Barclays Bank** (Khama Cres) and the slightly better-value **Standard Chartered Bank** (The Mall) have foreign exchange facilities and ATMs.

The **main post office** (The Mall; ☺ 8.15am-1pm & 2-4pm Mon-Fri, 8.30-11.30am Sat) has coin and card phones. In shopping areas and around the train station, you'll find plenty of mobile phone stands charging competitive rates for phone calls.

There is an **Aim Internet Café** (The Mall; ☺ 8am-8pm; US$2.50 per hr) next to the Cresta President Hotel on the edge of The Mall. **Sakeng Internet Café** (☎ 397 5455; Broadhurst North Mall; ☺ 9am-9pm Mon-Sat, noon-6pm Sun; US$2.75 per hr) has new computers.

Botswana's best bookshop is **Exclusive Books** (Riverwalk Mall), with a range of literature, nonfiction and travel books.

SIGHTS & ACTIVITIES

There's not much to see or do in Gaborone, but you could spend an afternoon exploring the **National Museum & Art Gallery** (☎ 397 4616; 331 Independence Ave; admission free; ☺ 9am-6pm Tue-Fri, 9am-5pm Sat & Sun). It's not a bad option, especially if you're into stuffed wildlife. There are also and ethnographic and cultural exhibits, displays of San crafts and hunting techniques, and traditional and modern African and European art.

The **Gaborone Game Reserve** (☎ 358 4492; admission US$0.20 per person, plus US$0.40 per vehicle; ☺ 6.30am-6.30pm), 1km east of Broadhurst Mall, is accessible only by private vehicle. It's home to a variety of grazers and browsers (including rhinos in a guarded enclosure), and makes a nice break from the city bustle. Access is from Limpopo Dr; turn east immediately south of the Segoditshane River.

SLEEPING

You'll pay a bundle (compared to the rest of the continent) to stay in the cheapest hotels in Gaborone.

Lonaka Inn (☎ 313 3350; d US$36; ☒) This newly renovated, inviting place just off Tlokweng Rd is excellent value. Rooms come with great tiles, new furniture, spacious bathrooms and cable television. Lonaka is 500m off Tlokweng Rd; follow the signs.

Planet Lodge (☎ 390 3295; 514 South Ring Rd; s/d US$22/38; ☒) Rooms here feel lived in with homey touches like quilts. The best part about a stay is that you wake to breakfast in bed. Rooms come with TV, VCR and fridge, and guests can use the kitchen.

Boiketlo Lodge (☎ 355 2347; cnr Khama Cres & Kaunda Rd; s/d US$14/25) This is the cheapest option in town and it's convenient to the city centre. It's a little noisy (the front corner is a local hang-out spot) and poorly signposted, so you'll have to really look. You'll find it opposite the Botswana Post Building.

Brackendene Lodge (☎ 391 2866; felomena@it.bw; Tati Rd; s/d from US$19.50/36.50) Brackendene is more a collection of small houses than an organized lodge. The cheapest rooms are not the best value for money – they're small and have fans as opposed to air-con.

Citi-Camp Caravan Park (☎ 7244 6067; citicamp@info.bw; camp sites per person US$6, d US$30) A 15-minute walk north of the centre and within stumbling distance of the Bull & Bush Pub is this park, where frogs provide a riveting nightly performance. It's just off Francistown Rd.

EATING

Gaborone boasts a wide selection of Western and African fast-food chains, and has a special love affair with chicken.

Bull & Bush Pub (☎ 397 5070; mains US$3-10) The Bull & Bush is Gaborone's best and most popular eatery. It has an extensive menu, is always packed and is popular with expats. Sit outside in the thatched grass huts. Meal portions are large, there are vegetarian options and the pizzas are quite good. It's a 15-minute walk north of the city centre off Francistown Rd.

Fishmonger (Riverwalk Mall; mains from US$6) The seafood here is a little pricey, but generally delicious – it manages to taste fresh despite the fact you're nowhere near the ocean.

Equatorial Coffee Company (Riverwalk Mall; mains from US$2) The best espressos in town are served here, along with fruit smoothies, sandwiches with unique fillings, and real bagels. There's also a large selection of inexpensive gourmet takeaways – everything from Thai chicken to falafel.

Maharaja Restaurant (☎ 393 1870; mains US$4-8; ☺ closed Sun dinner) This large Indian restaurant has a giant selection of vegetarian options. The restaurant tries to be elegant

GABORONE

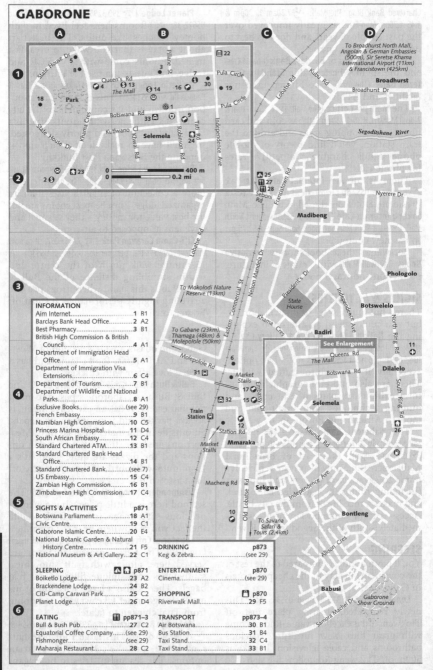

To Broadhurst North Mall,
Angolan & German Embassies
(500m), Sir Seretse Khama
International Airport (11km)
& Francistown (425km)

0 —— 400 m
0 —— 0.2 mi

INFORMATION

Aim Internet	1 B1
Barclays Bank Head Office	2 A2
Best Pharmacy	3 B1
British High Commission & British Council	4 A1
Department of Immigration Head Office	5 A1
Department of Immigration Visa Extensions	6 C4
Department of Tourism	7 B1
Department of Wildlife and National Parks	8 A1
Exclusive Books	(see 29)
French Embassy	9 B1
Namibian High Commission	10 C5
Princess Marina Hospital	11 D4
South African Embassy	12 C4
Standard Chartered ATM	13 B1
Standard Chartered Bank Head Office	14 B1
Standard Chartered Bank	(see 7)
US Embassy	15 C4
Zambian High Commission	16 B1
Zimbabwean High Commission	17 C4

SIGHTS & ACTIVITIES p871

Botswana Parliament	18 A1
Civic Centre	19 C1
Gaborone Islamic Centre	20 E4
National Botanic Garden & Natural History Centre	21 F5
National Museum & Art Gallery	22 C1

SLEEPING p871

Boiketlo Lodge	23 A2
Brackendene Lodge	24 B2
Citi-Camp Caravan Park	25 C2
Planet Lodge	26 D4

EATING pp871–3

Bull & Bush Pub	27 C2
Equatorial Coffee Company	(see 29)
Fishmonger	(see 29)
Maharaja Restaurant	28 C2

DRINKING p873

Keg & Zebra	(see 29)

ENTERTAINMENT p870

Cinema	(see 29)

SHOPPING p870

Riverwalk Mall	29 F5

TRANSPORT pp873–4

Air Botswana	30 B1
Bus Station	31 B4
Taxi Stand	32 C4
Taxi Stand	33 B1

BOTSWANA

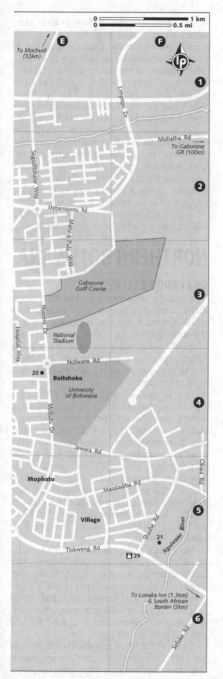

yet comes off feeling a little clinical, but the food is flavourful. It's right next to the Bull & Bush Pub, north of the city centre off Francistown Rd.

Caffe Prego (☎ 317 0227; Shop 30A, Broadhurst North Mall; mains from US$4) This little café does good breakfasts and home-made pastas.

DRINKING
The entertainment posters stuck to fences around town are the best source of information for what's happening in Gaborone. Clubs here go out of business much faster than guidebooks are printed.

Bull & Bush Pub (see p871) There is good ambience here and occasional live music.

Keg & Zebra (Riverwalk Mall) Come here for sing-along jam sessions whenever there is a live band on Sunday night. It draws a mixed-race crowd and has nightly meal specials.

Nightspark (Broadhurst North Mall; weekend admission US$2) This place is popular with middle-class Batswana youth and features all sorts of musical acts.

GETTING THERE & AWAY
The Sir Seretse Khama International Airport is 14km north of the centre.

Intercity buses and minibuses travelling to Serowe (US$4, five hours), Francistown (US$5, six hours), Ghanzi (US$10, 11 hours) and Jo'burg (US$12, six hours) use the main bus terminal, over the Molepolole flyover from the town centre. To reach northern destinations of Maun, Shakawe or Kasane, use the Francistown bus and change there. All buses and minibuses leave when full, and are usually more frequent in the morning.

The day train departs for Francistown daily at 10am (US$4 in economy, seven hours). There also is a night train that has 1st- and 2nd-class sleepers, as well as an economy section that does not include beds. The train leaves at 9pm (1st/2nd/economy US$24/20/5, eight hours). For current railway information, contact **Botswana Railways** (☎ 395 1401). The train station is to the west of the town centre.

There also is a night train with 1st- and 2nd-class sleepers as well as an economy section that does not include beds. It leaves at 9pm (1st/2nd/economy US$24/20/5, eight hours).

Locals stop regularly to pick up hitchers. To hitch north, catch the Broadhurst

4 minibus from any shopping centre along the main city loop, which passes all the main shopping centres except the new Riverwalk Mall and the Kgale Centre, and get off at the standard hitching spot at the northern end of town. Plan on paying around US$6 to Francistown, where you can look for onward lifts to Nata, Maun and Kasane.

GETTING AROUND

Packed white minibuses, recognisable by their blue number plates, circulate according to set routes and cost US$0.50. They pick up and drop off only at designated lay-bys marked 'bus/taxi stop'. The main city loop passes all the main shopping centres.

A number of companies operate conventional private hire taxis, known as 'special taxis', which charge around US$3 around the city and US$5 to the environs. Try **City Cab** (☎ 312 1031) or **Unique Cab** (☎ 391 6696). The 'special taxis' leave from the taxi stands marked on the map.

AROUND GABORONE

MOCHUDI

Best known for its museum and Batswana architecture, the village of Mochudi is about 35km northeast of Gaborone and makes a good day trip. The Kwena people, one of the three most prominent lineage groups of the Batswana tribe, first settled Mochudi in around the mid-1500s and evidence of this settlement is found in the few remaining walls in the hills. The Kwena are descendents of one of the 14th-century Chief Malope's sons: Kwena. The Cape Dutch-style **Phuthadikobo Museum** (☎ 577 7238; admission free, donations suggested; ☺ 8am-5pm Mon-Fri, 2-5pm Sat & Sun) is one of Botswana's best museums with displays on the village and its Kgatla history. In 1871 the Kgatla people came to the area after having been forced from their lands by northward-trekking Boers.

Buses to Mochudi depart from Gaborone's main bus terminal when full.

MOKOLODI NATURE RESERVE

The 5000-hectare **Mokolodi Nature Reserve** (☎ 316 1955; www.mokolodi.com; admission per person US$2, plus US$4 per vehicle; camp sites per person US$11, dm US$15 with breakfast; ☺ 7.30am-6pm), 12km

south of Gaborone, makes a nice (and rather cheap) break from the capital. This scenic reserve protects a full complement of Botswana's wildlife, including white rhino reintroduced from South Africa. Guided three-hour ranger walks cost US$44 per person; horse tours are US$11 per hour; two-hour day/evening wildlife drives are US$22/33; and special wildlife-tracking walks searching for rhinos are US$72. The reserve has an excellent restaurant and bar. Transfers from the centre/airport cost US$28/44 for up to four people and are organized by the reserve. Otherwise take a Lobatse minibus 12km south of Gaborone and get off at the turning 2.5km south of the Mokolodi village turn-off. From there it's a 1.5km hike west to the reserve entrance.

NORTHERN BOTSWANA

OKAVANGO DELTA

The watery wilderness of the Okavango Delta, sprawling like an open palm across northwestern Botswana, is certainly one of the most spectacular sights on earth. Travellers should spend some time cruising the Champagne-coloured waters in a *mokoro* (local dug-out canoe) – it's sure to melt your stress away.

The 1430km-long Okavango River rises in central Angola, then flows southward across Namibia's Caprivi Strip, where it tumbles through Popa Falls before entering Botswana near Shakawe. There the river's waters begin to spread and sprawl as the thirsty air and Kalahari sands swallow them. Eventually the water is lost in a vast 15,000-sq-km maze of lagoons, channels and islands. They never reach the sea, but the delta's waters attract countless birds and other wildlife, as well as most of Botswana's tourists.

For a place to stay, there are only a handful of (relatively) inexpensive delta lodges – two in the Inner Delta and one in the Panhandle. For anything else you will pay about US$600 per night for a double room, and that's at the low end. If you're willing to camp, however, inexpensive *mokoro* safaris can be booked out of Maun or Seronga.

Generally, the best months to visit the delta are July to September, when the weather is dry, the water levels are high – and the prices

MOKORO TRIPS

Most visitors to the Okavango spend at least some time travelling by *mokoro* (plural: *mekoro*), a shallow-draft dugout canoe hewn from ebony or sausage tree log (or, more recently, moulded from fibreglass). The mekoro are poled from a standing position and their precarious appearance belies their amazing stability.

While one-day trips are possible in the Eastern Delta (with a return drive of several hours from Maun), most people prefer a multiday trip. A *mokoro* normally accommodates the poler, two passengers and their food and camping equipment.

The importance of finding a competent poler cannot be overstated, especially when you're expecting them to negotiate labyrinthine waterways or lead you on bushwalks through wildlife country. The keenest polers can speak some English; warn you about dangers (never swim without first asking the poler!); identify plants, birds and animals along the way; explain the delta cultures; and perhaps even teach you how to fish using traditional methods.

When booking budget *mokoro* trips, inquire in advance whether you're expected to provide food for your poler. Even if they do bring their own supplies, many travellers prefer to share meals. The polers may, for example, provide a sack of *mealie meal* (ground maize) and cooking implements while travellers supply the relishes: tins of curries, stews and vegetables. If you have arranged to provide your poler's meals, the standard daily rations are 500g of mealie meal, 250g of white sugar, six tea bags and sufficient salt and powdered milk.

Although it's still possible to negotiate with independent polers, most backpackers organise *mokoro* trips through delta lodges or Maun safari companies (p879), or through the Okavango Polers Trust in Seronga (p878).

skyrocket. Because most people visit at this time, we've quoted these prices in this book. Decent deals for delta lodges can be found during the low season (December to March), but beware that *mokoro* trips out of Maun are often impossible at this time due to low water levels. *Mokoro* safaris still operate out of Seronga, where there is a permanent source of water.

The Okavango Delta is usually subdivided into four areas: Eastern Delta, Inner Delta, Moremi Wilderness Reserve and Okavango Panhandle.

Eastern Delta

The area normally defined as the Eastern Delta takes in the wetlands between the southern boundary of the Moremi Wildlife Reserve and the buffalo fence along the Boro and Santandadibe Rivers, north of Matlapaneng.

This part of the delta is more accessible – and therefore cheaper to reach – from Maun than the Inner Delta or Moremi. You can easily base yourself in Maun and enjoy viewing the delta by *mokoro* on a day or overnight trip for far less than the cost of staying in Moremi or an Inner Delta lodge. *Mokoro* trips are mostly organized by Maun lodges and safari operators. Trips usually require

a minimum of two people and the rule of thumb is the larger the group, the cheaper the price. The cheapest trips are self-catering, which means you must bring your own food and tent. Day *mokoro* trips cost about US$75 per person and three-day trips are about US$145. Audi Camp in Maun (see p879) rents tents for US$7 per night. You can also rent sleeping bags, mattresses and cooking utensils here.

Inner Delta

The area west, north and immediately south of Chiefs Island (part of Moremi Wildlife Reserve) is rich in wildlife. Accommodation here – with only a couple of exceptions – is in frightfully expensive camps and lodges and accessed only by expensive charter flights. Oddball's and Gunn's Camp are the only camps within a backpacker's budget.

Mokoro trips here are normally arranged through the camps, with their own pool of licensed polers. *Mokoro* trips operate roughly between June and December when water levels are high enough. To enter Moremi, where you'll see the most wildlife, you must pay park fees; advise your poler if you want to break the trip with bushwalks. In theory campers may carry food and other supplies from Maun, but charter airlines limit

OKAVANGO DELTA

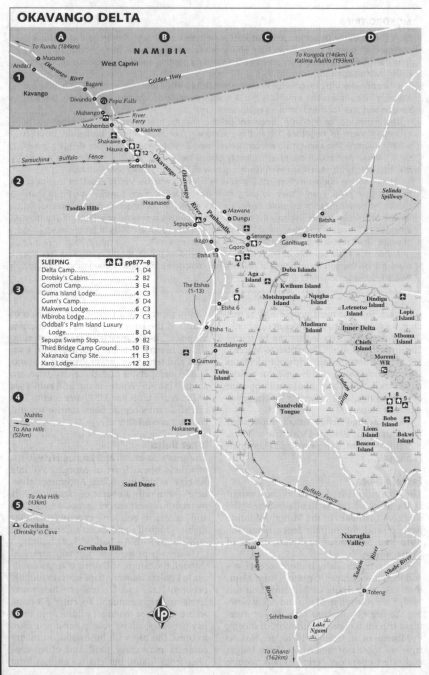

SLEEPING 🅐🅑 pp877-8

Delta Camp....................................1	D4
Drotsky's Cabins..........................2	B2
Gomoti Camp...............................3	E4
Guma Island Lodge......................4	C3
Gunn's Camp...............................5	D4
Makwena Lodge..........................6	C3
Mbiroba Lodge............................7	C3
Oddball's Palm Island Luxury	
Lodge.......................................8	D4
Sepupa Swamp Stop.....................9	B2
Third Bridge Camp Ground..........10	E3
Xakanaxa Camp Site....................11	E3
Xaro Lodge................................12	B2

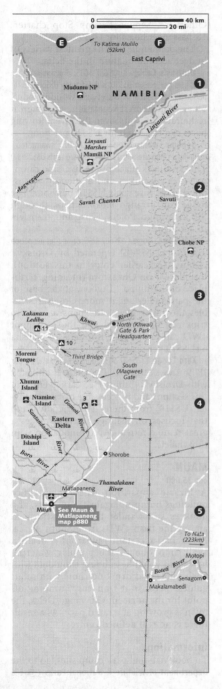

passengers to 10kg of baggage. So, most people buy some of their food at the camps, and also hire equipment from them.

The word inexpensive is relative, but the cheapest accommodation in the Inner Delta includes the following. Prices are inclusive of meals and *mokoro* excursions.

Oddball's Palm Island Luxury Lodge (☎ 686 1154; www.okavango.bw; Okavango Tours & Safaris, Mophane St, Maun; s/d US$240/400) There's no longer camping here, and the setting is less-than-exciting woodland beside an air strip, but it's within a short stroll of some nice delta scenery and remains less painfully priced than other nearby choices. Accommodation is in dome tents, and there is a bar on a raised viewing deck. The camp is only accessible by plane and air transfers cost US$140 per person from Maun.

Gunn's Camp (☎ 686 0023; gunnscamp@info.bw; Gunn's Camp Safaris, Maun; camp sites per person US$10, s/d luxury tents US$350/400) Beside the upper Boro River on palm-studded Ntswi Island is Gunn's Camp. The camping ground here has hot showers, flush toilets, braais (barbecues), a basic shop and bar. Rates for the 'luxury tents' include meals, drinks and wildlife-viewing. No-frills one-day *mokoro* trips are US$90 for two people and three-/four-/five-/six-day *mokoro* trips cost US$316/386/456/526 per person, with a minimum of two people (for one person, add 30%), including park fees and return flights from Maun. Those not on packages pay US$176 for return flights.

Moremi Wildlife Reserve

The 3000-sq-km Moremi Wildlife Reserve is the part of the Okavango Delta officially designated for wildlife protection. The park has a distinctly dual personality, with two large areas of dry land – Chiefs Island and the Moremi Tongue – rising between vast wetlands. The habitats range from mopane woodland and thorn scrub to dry savanna, riparian woodlands, grasslands, flood plains, marshes, waterways, lagoons and islands.

The entry gates at North and South Gate both have developed camping grounds. Rustically beautiful Third Bridge, 48km west of South Gate, is literally the third log bridge on the road and has a lovely camping ground. Be aware that swimming is extremely dangerous here due to crocodiles and hippos. At Xakanaxa Lediba, the camping ground occupies a narrow strip

BOTSWANA

of land surrounded by marsh and lagoon. With one of the largest heronries in Africa, it's a bird-watcher's paradise. All camping must be booked through the Department of Wildlife & National Parks (see p867 for contact details).

Besides the camping run by Botswana national parks, there is one budget option inside Moremi. **Santawani** (☎ 680 0664; santa wani@dynabyte.bw; Sankuyo Management Trust, Maun; camp sites or 2-bed chalets US$55) is a simple camp with shared ablutions and self-catering facilities. It's only accessible by 4WD. Self-drive wildlife-viewing costs US$9 per day. Book and pay at the Maun office.

There is no public transport to Moremi, but many companies out of Maun (see p879) run day trips. Generally the larger the group the cheaper the rates; for instance, with two people it will cost about US$140 per person, but with a group of six the price drops to US$75 per person.

Okavango Panhandle
In northwestern Botswana the Kalahari sands meet the Okavango Delta. Here, in the Okavango Panhandle, the river's waters spread across the valley on either side to form vast reed beds and papyrus-choked lagoons. The area is filled with clusters of fishing villages occupied by a cosmopolitan mix of people (Mbukushu, Yei, Tswana, Herero, European, San and refugee Angolans).

As the rest of the delta grows more expensive, the Okavango Panhandle is booming, thanks largely to the **Okavango Polers Trust** (☎ 687 6861; www.okavango.co.bw; Private Bag 109, Maun), in the small, traditional village of Seronga. The aim of this local cooperative is to allow clients to pay less for *mokoro* trips (US$28 per day for two people) and polers to earn more than they could through a lodge or agency. This part of the delta also has a permanent water supply, so *mokoro* trips are possible here year-round.

There's no longer a daily bus from Mohembo (on the Namibia border) to Seronga, but it's almost always possible to hitch from the free Okavango River ferry in Mohembo. Plan on paying about US$0.80 for a lift.

When they're running, water taxis operate along the Okavango between Sepupa Swamp Stop (see below) and Seronga (US$3, two hours); transfers from the Seronga dock to Mbiroba Lodge, 3km away, cost US$9.

Otherwise, Sepupa Swamp Stop charters 18-passenger boats for US$90.

The panhandle has the greatest variety of budget accommodation in the delta.

Drotsky's Cabins (☎ 687 5035; drotskys@info.bw; campsites per person US$10, s/d A-frames US$60/110, 4-person chalets US$120) A quiet and wooded lodge, set amid lush forest vegetation, it has a great restaurant on stilts over the river. Rowing boats can be rented for US$30 per hour.

Sepupa Swamp Stop (☎ 687 7073; swampstop@ maun.info; camp sites per person US$4, s/d tents US$28/37) This laid-back place offers riverside camping, clean facilities and a friendly atmosphere. Boat hire costs US$14 per hour. The lodge can arrange *mokoro* trips through the Okavango Polers Trust and transfers to Seronga.

Makwena Lodge (☎ 687 4299; camp sites per person US$6, s/d from US$30/45) Operated by Drotsky's Cabins (see earlier entry in this section), this place is on Qhaaxhwa (meaning 'birthplace of the hippo') Lagoon, at the base of the panhandle, but it more closely resembles the Inner Delta. Inexpensive *mokoro* trips can be arranged and those without 4WD can pre-arrange transfers from Etsha 6 (US$10 per person).

Xaro Lodge (☎ 687 5035; drotskys@info.bw; PO Box 115, Shakawe; s/d US$51/77) This place is affiliated with Drotsky's Cabins (see earlier entry in this section) and is accessible by river transfer (US$10) from there. It's a friendly camp that focuses on fishing, but also makes a great remote retreat. Accommodation is in tidy chalets.

MAUN
pop 35,000
A bizarre apparition where new office buildings bump up against mud huts, and donkeys still wander the dusty streets in among the flash 4WDs from South Africa, Maun has a certain raw frontier feeling. Walk into one of the popular watering holes and you'll be rubbing shoulders with bush pilots and drinking shots with safari guides. Because it's an easy jumping-off point for the adjacent Okavango Delta, the town is growing at a rapid pace. As a result there is no real defined centre.

Information
To book national park camp sites, go to the **Department of Wildlife & National Parks** (☎ 686

1265; 🕑 7.30am-12.30pm & 1.45-4.30pm Mon-Sat, 7.30am-noon Sun). The reservations office is housed in a caravan behind the main building on Kudu St, across from the police station.

The fastest banking exchange services, including credit card cash advances, are with **Sunny Bureau de Change** (☎ 686 2786; Ngami Centre; 🕑 7am-6pm) just off Sir Seretse Khama Rd.

Email and Internet access are available at the **Afro-Trek I-Café** (Shorobe Rd; 🕑 closed Sun; US$6 per hr) at the Sedia Hotel.

Sights & Activities

Almost everyone comes to Maun to book safaris. For activities, lounging in your lodge's pool is popular (Maun can get uncomfortably hot in the summer), as is drinking. If you're determined to do something you could head to the **Nhabe Museum** (☎ 686 1346; Sir Seretse Khama Rd; admission free, donations welcome; 🕑 9am-5pm Mon-Fri, 9am-4pm Sat), which features art exhibitions and outlines the natural history and cultures of the Okavango. It also sponsors theatre presentations and sells local curios and artwork.

Safaris

Almost all the companies running tours into the delta are based in Maun. From Maun it's also easy to book tours to other parts of Botswana, most notably to Chobe National Park. These excursions are often added to the end of delta tours. **Travel Wild** (☎ 686 0822; travelwild@dynabyte.bw), opposite the airport, on the corner of Airport Rd and Mathiba I St, serves as a central booking and information office for lodges, safaris and other adventures.

The following list includes major tour operators:

Afro-Trek (☎ 686 0177; www.afrotrek.com; Shorobe Rd) This popular, inexpensive option runs one-/two-/three-day *mokoro* trips in the Eastern Delta for US$55/85/110 with at least two people; clients must supply their own food and camping gear. It also does all-inclusive four-day camping safaris to Moremi Wildlife Reserve, Chobe National Park, the Central Kalahari Game Reserve or Makgadikgadi Pans (US$140 per day) and bird-watching hikes along the Thamalakane River (US$20 for two hours). The office is inside the Sedia Hotel.

Audi Camp Safaris (☎ 686 0599; www.audicamp.biz land.com; Mathiba I St) Audi Camp (see p881) offers budget *mokoro* trips in the Eastern Delta (three days, with/without meals US$220/145) and Okavango Pan-

handle fly-in safaris (two days with/without meals US$450/275). It also does several all-inclusive trips from Maun: day trips to Moremi (US$225); two-/three-day Moremi safaris (US$425/525), five-day Moremi and Chobe safaris (US$900); and two-/seven-day safaris in the Central Kalahari Game Reserve (US$325/1070).

Crocodile Camp Safaris (☎ 686 0265; www.botswana .com) Crocodile Camp (see p881) does one-/two-day trips to the Eastern Delta (US$75/120), fly-in day trips to the Inner Delta (US$185) and day trips to Moremi (US$80), as well as customised trips to Chobe, the Central Kalahari, Makgadikgadi and Nxai Pans, Kgalagadi Transfrontier Park etc. Participation safaris start at around US$150 per person per day. The office can be found at the camping ground.

Gunn's Camp Safaris (☎ 686 0023; gunnscamp@info .bw; Mathiba I St) This is the last budget option in the Inner Delta, and it also offers relatively inexpensive three-/four-/five-/six-day Inner Delta *mokoro* trips (US$316/386/456/526) from Gunn's Camp and its affiliated Bush Camp, near Chiefs Island. These include flights from Maun and park fees, but clients must provide their own food and camping gear.

Island Safaris (☎ 686 0300; island@info.bw) This company is run from Island Safari Lodge and operates *mokoro* trips in the Eastern Delta (one-day US$80/130 for one/two people, two days US$140/220, three days US$185/270).

Okavango River Lodge (☎ 686 3707; freewind@info .bw; Shorobe Rd) The friendly folks at this lodge (see p881) run good-value one-/two-/three-day *mokoro* trips in the Eastern Delta for US$60/90/120 with two people.

Okavango Tours & Safaris (☎ 686 1154; www .okavango.bw; Mophane St) This company's speciality is lodge-based tours in the delta. It is also the agent for Oddball's Palm Island Luxury Lodge and Delta Camp. The office is in the same group of buildings as the Power Station restaurant.

Phakawe Safaris (☎ 686 4377; www.phakawe.demon .co.uk; Sir Seretse Khama Rd) This recommended company, housed in the very orange building called the Pumpkin Patch, runs informal participation safaris through Botswana's wildest regions for US$135 per day, including meals and camping.

Sleeping

Most of the budget accommodation is about 9km northeast of Maun proper in the area called Matlapaneng. Accommodation, unless you have a tent, cannot be described as excellent value. Prices are high but, unlike in other parts of the country, most places do not have air-con. The good news is that even if it's stifling hot during the day, temperatures drop considerably at night. Most have pools and restaurants. All the camps and lodges listed here also run safaris into the delta (see p879).

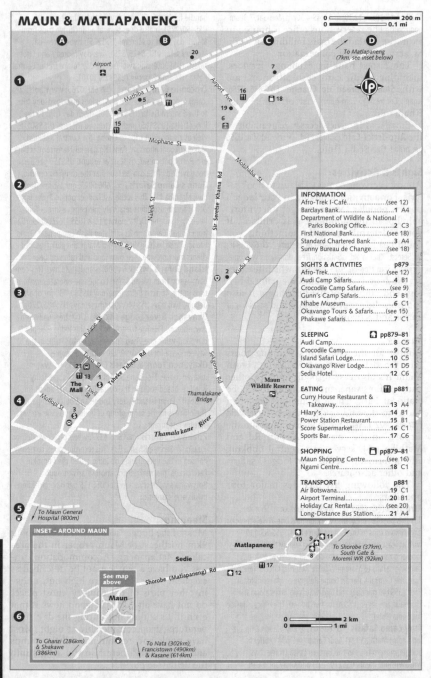

MAUN & MATLAPANENG

0 _____ 200 m
0 _____ 0.1 mi

INFORMATION
Afro-Trek I-Café......................(see 12)
Barclays Bank............................**1** A4
Department of Wildlife & National
　Parks Booking Office..........**2** C3
First National Bank.................(see 18)
Standard Chartered Bank...........**3** A4
Sunny Bureau de Change........(see 18)

SIGHTS & ACTIVITIES　　　　p879
Afro-Trek................................(see 12)
Audi Camp Safaris.....................**4** B1
Crocodile Camp Safaris............(see 9)
Gunn's Camp Safaris..................**5** B1
Nhabe Museum...........................**6** C1
Okavango Tours & Safaris......(see 15)
Phakawe Safaris.........................**7** C1

SLEEPING　　　　　　pp879–81
Audi Camp..................................**8** C5
Crocodile Camp..........................**9** C5
Island Safari Lodge...................**10** C5
Okavango River Lodge.............**11** D5
Sedia Hotel...............................**12** C6

EATING　　　　　　　　　p881
Curry House Restaurant &
　Takeaway..............................**13** A4
Hilary's....................................**14** B1
Power Station Restaurant........**15** B1
Score Supermarket...................**16** C1
Sports Bar................................**17** C6

SHOPPING　　　　　　pp879–81
Maun Shopping Centre...........(see 16)
Ngami Centre...........................**18** C1

TRANSPORT　　　　　　　p881
Air Botswana...........................**19** C1
Airport Terminal......................**20** B1
Holiday Car Rental...................(see 20)
Long-Distance Bus Station.......**21** A4

INSET – AROUND MAUN

Matlapaneng

Sedie

See map above

Maun

To Ghanzi (286km)
& Shakawe
(386km)

To Nata (302km),
Francistown (490km)
& Kasane (614km)

To Shorobe (37km),
South Gate &
Moremi WR (92km)

Shorobe (Matlapaneng) Rd

0 _____ 2 km
0 _____ 1 mi

To Matlapaneng
(7km, see inset below)

Airport

Mathiba I St

Airport Ave

Mophane St

Sir Seretse Khama Rd

Naledi St

Moeti Rd

Motshaba St

Moeti Rd

Pulare St

Tsaro St

Tsheko Tsheko Rd

The Mall

Tawi St

Motlopi St

Sekgoma Rd

Thamalakane
Bridge

Thamalakane River

Maun
Wildlife Reserve

To Maun General
Hospital (800m)

BOTSWANA

Audi Camp (☎ 686 0599; www.audicamp.bizland.com; camp sites per person US$4, s/d tents from US$20/26) This is the place to come to meet other backpackers and maybe find a group to head into the delta with. Doubles are in pre-erected tents with fans. There's not much grass, but lots of dust. However, the bar and swimming pool is reminiscent of more top-end places.

Crocodile Camp (☎ 686 0265; www.botswana.com; camp sites per person US$5, bedded tents US$40, chalets from US$80) The nicest of the Maun lodges. There actually is some grass and the bar occupies a superb spot right on the river. The chalets have fans and proper bathrooms. Camp sites are shady, and there are discounts during the low season.

Okavango River Lodge (☎ 686 3707; freewind@info .bw; camp sites per person US$3, s/d US$32/37) This quiet place has the best deals on chalets in town, which are roomy and clean with nice bathrooms. It's a friendly, unpretentious place, and the owners offer truthful advice about their *mokoro* trips.

Island Safari Lodge (☎ 686 0300; island@info.bw; camp sites per person US$5, s/d US$53/58) The property is looking a little shabby these days – it's barren and missing the atmosphere found at other places. It does enjoy a picturesque river setting, and can offer sizeable discounts if it's empty, so it's worth checking out.

SPLURGE!

So, you're planning to blow a lot of cash in the delta, and looking to spend some more in Maun? You could do worse than the **Sedia Hotel** (☎ 686 0117; www.sedia -hotel.com; Shorobe Rd; camp sites per person US$5, s/d US$72/84; ▨). Rooms are equipped with all the usual upscale hotel amenities and there's an inviting pool with an outdoor bar and restaurant. It's not the most spectacular place in the world, but it's not bad either.

Eating & Drinking

Self-caterers should check out the well-stocked **Score Supermarket** (Sir Seretse Khama Rd) in the Maun Shopping Centre.

Hilary's (☎ 686 1610; mains US$3; ⏰ 8am-4pm Mon-Fri, 8am-2pm Sat) Hilary's, off Mathiba I St, serves the best food in Maun, and possibly all of Botswana. The meals are home-cooked, healthy and not smothered in oil. There are lots of vegie options and

the bread is out of this world. Try one of the salads or sandwiches.

Power Station (☎ 686 2037; Mophane Rd; mains US$5.50-8) This bizarre industrial place (it used to be a power station) is trying to be new-age hip. The restaurant serves decent burgers, but it's best known as one of Maun's most happening nightspots.

Sports Bar (☎ 686 2676; Shorobe Rd; mains US$4-6) The pizzas here are excellent, but the other dishes border on mediocre for the price. It's a good drinking spot, however; expats congregate here and there are big-screen TVs showing sports.

Curry House Restaurant & Takeaway (☎ 686 2588; The Mall; mains US$1; ⏰ 8am-6pm) This tiny place is popular with locals and serves cheap Indian curries and rice. It's a little dirty inside.

Getting There & Away

At the long-distance bus station, which is in the car park of the centre where the Curry House is located, you'll find buses to Nata (US$6, three hours), with connections to Kasane (US$12, six hours) and Francistown (US$9, five hours); Shakawe (US$10, five hours); and Ghanzi (US$5, five hours).

Audi Camp (☎ 686 0599) runs a weekly shuttle between Maun and Windhoek (US$55, 10 hours). Shuttles leave Maun on Wednesday and Windhoek on Monday. Prebooking is essential.

For eastbound travellers, the best hitching spot is the Ema Reje Restaurant, on the Nata road.

Local minibuses between town and Matlapaneng (US$0.30) run when full from the long-distance bus station and airport, and the same journey in a taxi costs around US$4.

TSODILO HILLS

The four Tsodilo Hills (Male, Female, Child and North Hill – why didn't they name it 'Cousin'?) rise abruptly from a rippled, oceanlike expanse of desert and are threaded with myth, legend and spiritual significance for the San people. More than 2750 ancient rock paintings have been discovered at well over 200 sites. And as in most of Southern Africa, the majority of these are attributed to ancestors of today's San people.

There's now a **museum** near Main Camp, which extols the undeniably sacred nature of the hills. Normally, local San people will guide groups for around US$13 per group, per day.

Visitors can camp at the Main (Rhino), Malatso or Makoba Woods camping grounds or at wild camp sites around the base of the hills, but there are no shops or services.

Thanks to three notorious access routes from Samuchina, Nxamaseri and Sepupa (think excruciating 4WD tracks through deep sand), Tsodilo was once one of Botswana's most inaccessible wonders. The good news is that the middle (Nxamaseri) road was being upgraded at the time of research and by the time you read this will have turned a four-hour grind in low 4WD to a 30-minute 2WD jaunt through the bush. Note, however, that you'll still need a 4WD to explore the hills area.

There is no public transport to this area and hitching used to be nearly impossible, although it could become easier with the improved road.

CHOBE NATIONAL PARK

With 11,000 sq km of bush, grassland and forest, Chobe National Park is home to Botswana's most varied wildlife. The riverfront strip along the northern tier supports the greatest wildlife concentrations but, when they contain water, the lovely **Savuti Marshes** of the Mababe Depression in western Chobe also provide prime wildlife habitat and attract numerous water birds.

The riverfront area of Chobe National Park is the most popular area for visitors. Every Southern African mammal species (except the rhino) is represented here, and the abundance and variety of birdlife in this zone of permanent water is astonishing. The most obvious feature of the landscape is the damage done by the area's massive elephant herds.

The northern park entrance lies 5km west of Kasane and is accessible by conventional vehicles. However, to reach Savuti or other places in the interior of the park, or to approach from Maun, you need a high-clearance 4WD. Due to mud and flooding, Savuti is normally inaccessible from January to March.

There is no public transport inside the park, and lodges are expensive. If you have a vehicle and want to explore on your own, bring a tent, otherwise, try to join an organ-

ized tour from either Maun or Kasane. **Afro-Trek** (☎ 686 2674; www.afrotrek.com) runs trips to Chobe from Maun for US$140 per person per day. Trips last four nights and require a minimum of four people. **Audi Camp Safaris** (☎ 686 0581; www.audicamp.bizland.com) runs four-night Moremi and Chobe trips from June to October for US$900 per person if you have a group of three to four.

A great way to enjoy Chobe is on a river trip or wildlife drive. The best time to cruise is late afternoon, when hippos amble onto dry land and the riverfront fills with elephants heading down for a drink and a romp in the water. All hotels and lodges in Kasane arrange 2½- to three-hour wildlife drives and cruises in the morning and afternoon costing US$14 to US$22, plus discounted park fees. Note that if you take a morning wildlife drive you can also do an afternoon 'booze cruise' and pay park fees for only one day.

Sleeping

Ihaha Camp, inside Chobe National Park, is a lovely place about 15km west of the now-disused Serondela Camp, with toilets, cold showers and lots of wildlife. Unfortunately it has recently become a target for thieves from over the rivers. Book through the Department of Wildlife & National Parks (see p867 for details).

Buffalo Ridge Camping (☎ 625 0430; camp sites per person US$5.50) This camping area is immediately uphill from the Ngoma Bridge border crossing near the western end of the Chobe transit route.

KASANE & KAZUNGULA

The town of Kasane sits at the meeting of four countries – Botswana, Zambia, Namibia and Zimbabwe – and the confluence of the Chobe and Zambezi Rivers. It's also the gateway to Chobe National Park. Immediately to the east, the tiny settlement of Kazungula serves as the border crossing between Botswana and Zimbabwe, and the landing for the Kazungula ferry, which connects Botswana with Zambia.

Kasane's friendly **tourist office** (☎ 625 0357; President Ave; ⊙ 7.30am-12.45pm & 1.45-4.30pm Mon-Fri) dispenses basic information.

Kasane Bureau de Change (⊙ 8am-4.30pm Mon-Fri, 8am-1pm Sat) in the Audi Centre changes cash and travellers cheques. Also in the

Audi Centre, the **Kool Khaya I-Café** (☎ 625 0736; ✆ 8am-5pm Mon-Fri, 8am-1pm Sat, US$4 per hr) offers email and Internet access.

To book national park camp sites, go to the **Department of Wildlife & National Parks** (☎ 625 0235) at the northern gate to Chobe National Park, southwest of Kasane's town centre.

Thebe River Safaris (☎ 650 0314; www.theriver safaris.co.za), based at Thebe River Camping on Kazungula Rd, is one of Botswana's best-value companies. It organizes Chobe wildlife drives and cruises (US$35); custom overland safaris with varying degrees of luxury (US$100 to US$165 per day with at least four people) and one- to three-day Chobe camping safaris (US$80 to US$280 with at

least two people). An all-inclusive seven-day participation safari through Chobe and Moremi costs US$700.

Sleeping

All of the following places can organize Chobe wildlife drives and cruises, as well as other excursions.

Thebe River Camping (☎ 625 0314; thebe@info.bw; Kazungula Rd; camp sites per person US$8) Provides a green riverside setting, along with a bar, meals and Chobe wildlife drives and cruises (US$14).

Liya Guest Lodge (☎ 71-756903; liyaglo@botsnet .bw; 1198 Tholo Cres; s/d from US$38/56) This is a warm, friendly and very economical family-run option on the hillside.

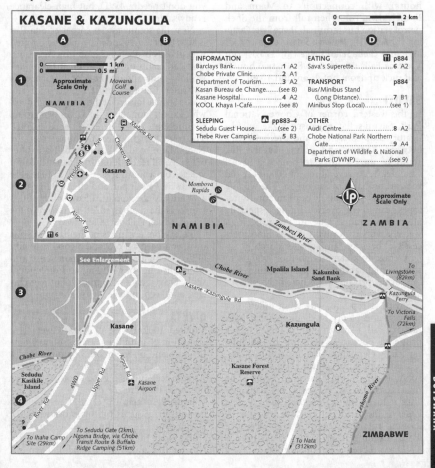

Sedudu Guest House (☎ 625 1748; President Ave; s/d US$37/51) This simple place along the main road serves meals on request (US$6 to US$8).

Eating
The Old House (☎ 71-425383; mains US$5-7; ☽ closed Mon) The Old House is Kasane's only real restaurant; here you'll find everything from steak and fish to chicken and vegetarian options.

Sava's Superette, diagonally opposite the petrol station, is the place to go if you're self-catering.

Getting There & Away
Minibuses travelling to Nata (US$8, three hours), with connections to Maun and Francistown, run when full from the Shell petrol station bus terminal. **Thebe River Camping** (☎ 625 0314), **Mowana Safari Lodge** (☎ 625 0300) and **Chobe Safari Lodge** (☎ 625 0336) run Victoria Falls transfers (US$40, two hours) and pick up from hotels around 10am.

SAVUTI
In the western corner of Chobe National Park, Savuti's flat expanses make an obligatory stop for safaris and overland trips between Kasane and Maun. **Gobabis Hill**, south of the Savuti gate near the Savuti Channel, bears several sets of 4000-year-old rock art probably of San origin. The wildlife populations, particularly elephants and antelopes, can seem overwhelming, especially after heavy rains. Due to potential high water, Savuti is normally closed (and inaccessible) between January and March.

Average folk can stretch their budget to spend a night at the national park camp site, but for the private camps here only millionaires need apply.

Savuti Camp Site, with flush toilets, hot showers and plenty of shade, is what park rangers call a 'rough camp', meaning it's prone to nocturnal invasion by wildlife, especially elephants, baboons and hyenas.

Under optimum conditions, it's a four- to six-hour drive from Kasane to Savuti. The road is passable by 2WD as far as Kachikau – after it turns south into the Chobe Forest Reserve the road deteriorates into parallel sand ruts that require a high-clearance 4WD. Coming from Maun, you'll need a 4WD to proceed north of Shorobe.

MAKGADIKGADI PANS
Botswana's great salt pans, Sua and Ntwetwe Pans, comprise the 80,000-sq-km Makgadikgadi Pans and are like no other landscape on earth. Especially during the sizzling heat of late winter days, the stark pans take on a disorienting and ethereal austerity. Heat mirages destroy all sense of space or direction, imaginary lakes shimmer and disappear, ostriches fly and stones turn to mountains and float in mid-air.

There is a beautiful 230-sq-km wildlife refuge at Sua Pan. The **Nata Sanctuary** (☎ 71-656969; admission US$5, fee includes camping; ☽ 7am-7pm) has a range of birdlife, as well as antelopes and other grassland animals. It's 15km southeast of Nata. In the dry season, you don't need a 4WD, but high clearance is advisable.

Near the southwestern corner of Sua Pan is **Kubu Island**, surrounded by salt and covered with ghostly baobab trees and Iron Age ruins. You can camp on the salt or at the otherworldly camp site on the island, but there's no water. Campers must register with the Game Scouts, located at the camping ground, who expect 'donations' of US$6 per group; get a receipt. To get here, you need a 4WD. The route is signposted 'Lekhubu' from the Nata–Maun road, 24km west of Nata; after 65km, you'll reach desultory Thabatshukudu village, on a low ridge. South of here, the route skirts a salt pan and after 15km passes a veterinary checkpoint; 1.5km south of this barrier is the signposted left-turn toward the island, which is about 20km away.

To explore any parts of the pans on your own, you need a 4WD and a good map and GPS system, as well as common sense and confidence in your driving and directional skills. Drive only in the tracks of other vehicles, and keep to the edges of the pan.

GWETA
Situated 100km west of Nata, Gweta is a collection of mud huts, and a solitary bottle store and phone booth operate out of a tin shack. It's a friendly place with a rural African feel and is a good spot to look for lifts onto the pans.

Gweta Rest Camp (☎ 621 2220; gweta@info.bw; camp sites per person US$4, huts without bathroom US$20) is a pleasant oasis in the middle of nowhere. Don't judge the place by the property's perimeter (it's much nicer inside). There's a large swimming pool, open-air restaurant and bar.

Planet Baobab (☎ 241 2277; www.unchartedafrica .com; camp sites per person US$4, s/d from US$19/29) is a novel, unpretentious lodge 4km east of Gweta. It's a funky place with beer-bottle chandeliers and cowhide chairs in the bar. Accommodation is in grass bushman huts (they're more comfortable than they sound) or, for a little more expenditure, in concrete huts modelled on traditional mud huts. These cost US$56 for a double, but are well worth it. You won't find décor like this elsewhere.

Planet Baobab's most appealing feature is its tours. During the dry season (usually April to September) there are overnight camping trips onto Ntwetwe Pan. You'll sleep on the salt in the middle of nothing with only a bedroll and thousands of stars for company. These trips cost US$70 and include rides on quad-bikes (motor-cycle-style 4WDs), breakfast and dinner. The lodge also does day excursions to the bizarre fossil formations of Nxasini Pan (US$25). To get to Planet Baobab turn off at the giant concrete aardvark and follow the rough road for about 1km.

All buses between Nata and Maun call in at Gweta.

NATA

This town is not much more than a dust hole full of petrol stations with attached bars, bottle stores and takeaway shops (if this doesn't promote drinking and driving we don't know what does). Most travellers use it as a refuelling stop between Kasane, Francistown and Maun.

Sua Pan Lodge (☎ 621 1263; camp sites per person US$5, s/d US$30/40) is the centre of action in town. There's the requisite bottle store, fuel pump and takeaway attached. Across the street is the **Northgate Shop & Takeaway** (☺ 6am-10pm), which serves up chicken and chips and charges US$2 to surf the Web. It also serves as the bus station.

EASTERN BOTSWANA

FRANCISTOWN
pop 95,000

Originally a gold-mining centre, industry and commerce have transformed Francis-

town into a repository for warehouses and shopping malls. There's no need to linger.

The only site of interest to travellers is the **Supa-Ngwao Cultural and Historical museum** (☎ 240 3088; New Maun Rd; admission free, donations suggested; ☺ 8am-5pm Mon-Fri, 9am-5pm Sat), which displays local and regional culture and history, as well as visiting art exhibitions.

Along Blue Jacket St you'll find most of the banks, the post office, the laundrette and several shopping centres.

Sleeping, Eating & Drinking

Grand Lodge (☎ 241 2300; cnr Haskins St & Selous Ave; s/d US$32/38; ☒) Here you can find large, clean, self-catering rooms. There's not much character, but it's suitable for a night.

Satellite Guest House (☎ 241 4465; s/d US$28/38) This quirky option is in a walled compound. From the Thapama roundabout, follow the Matsiloje turn-off for 2.5km and follow the signs.

Marang Hotel & Casino (☎ 241 3991; resmarang@ cresta.co.bw; camp sites per person US$5; budget s US$40; s/d US$92/105) This is the best deal in town for camping. The camp site is large and you have access to the hotel's luxury facilities. The budget accommodation (tiny rooms sleeping one) is in a trailer and could be considered a rip-off. The more-expensive rooms are what you'd expect from an upscale hotel.

Even if you're not staying at the Marang Hotel, it's still worth dropping by for a drink. The grounds are beautifully landscaped and there are two nice bars, one of which over-looks the lazy Tati River. On Friday nights there are happy hours with live entertainment, and the place has a casino (admission US$2 for nonguests). Fixed-menu dinners cost US$12. The Marang is 5km out of town on the old Gaborone Rd.

Milano Pizza & Chicken (☎ 241 0077) Located behind Barclays Plaza, there's not a lot of atmosphere here, but the food is tasty and cheap. Pizzas and pasta cost from US$4. It's off the Blue Jacket Plaza car park.

Getting There & Away

From the main bus terminal, between the train line and the Blue Jacket Plaza, bus and minibus services connect Francistown with Nata (US$3, two hours), Maun (US$8, five hours), Gaborone (US$7, six hours), Serowe (US$3, three hours) and Bulawayo (Zimbabwe; US$4, two hours). Minibuses depart when full but they usually run at least once daily.

The overnight train to Gaborone (US$5 economy, eight hours) leaves at 9pm and the day train (US$4 economy, six hours) leaves at 10am.

SEROWE
pop 38,000
Sprawling Serowe is the largest village in Botswana and has served as the Ngwato capital since King Khama III moved it from Phalatswe (Palapye) in 1902. Along with the Kwena and Ngwaketse tribal groups, the ancestry of the Ngwato tribe can be traced to the 14th-century Chief Malope. The reason to visit is the 12,000-hectare **Khama II Rhino Sanctuary** (☎ 463 0713; www.khamarhinosanctuary.org; admission US$2 per person, plus US$3 per vehicle; camp sites per person US$5, d chalets from US$40), 28km northwest of Serowe. It serves as a safe haven for 16 of Botswana's remaining rhinos. There are day and evening wildlife drives (from US$52) and rhino tracking (US$20).

There are direct bus services between Serowe and Gaborone. Once in Serowe call the sanctuary to arrange a lift. Buses run frequently from Gaborone to Serowe, and leave from the bus terminal at The Mall (US$4, five hours).

BOTSWANA DIRECTORY

ACCOMMODATION
Botswana is not geared towards budget travel. There are no hostels, and you'll pay about US$40 for a double in a cheap hotel, although this will usually include private

bathroom and TV. Many hotels will have air-conditioning and self-catering kitchens. To travel on the cheap, bring a tent. Camping costs about US$7 per person.

ACTIVITIES
Things to do in Botswana are centred on wildlife viewing, either by 4WD safari vehicle, boat or *mokoro*. There are inexpensive opportunities for quad-biking on the Makgadikgadi Pans. Hiking opportunities are limited to the Tsodilo Hills in the northwest and several small ranges in the eastern and southeastern parts of the country.

DANGERS & ANNOYANCES
Although theft occurs, Botswana enjoys a very low crime rate compared to other African (and many Western) countries. However, don't leave valuables in sight in your vehicle, especially in Gaborone.

The Botswana Defence Force (BDF) takes its duties seriously and is best not crossed. The most sensitive base, which is operated jointly with the US government, lies in a remote area off the Lobatse road, southwest of Gaborone. Don't stumble upon it accidentally!

EMBASSIES & CONSULATES
The following embassies are in Gaborone:
France (☎ /fax 397 3863; 761 Robinson Rd)
Germany (☎ 395 3143; fax 395 3038; 3rd fl, Professional House, Broadhurst)
Namibia (☎ 397 2685; BCC Bldg, 1278 Old Lobatse Rd)
South Africa (☎ 390 4800; Queens Rd)
UK (☎ 395 2841; fax 395 6105; Queensway, The Mall)
USA (☎ 395 3982; pausemb3@botsnet.bw; Government Enclave, Embassy Dr)

BOTSWANA TAKES MORE THAN A SHOESTRING

Travelling cheaply in Botswana isn't impossible, and a good way to cut down on expenses is to bring a tent. Camping is still more expensive here than in other African countries, but you'll save a bundle. Outside camp sites, Botswana has yet to discover backpacker hostels, and the cheapest accommodation costs about US$40 per double. Meals, alcohol, car hire and domestic flights are of comparable prices to Europe, North America and Australasia. Safari lodges – especially those in the Okavango Delta and Chobe National Park – are, for the most part, exclusive haunts of the wealthy; you'll rarely find anything for less than US$600 per double per night.

That said, there are some deals to be found in Botswana. If you want to see the Okavango Delta (and you really do), consider joining a tour of the country arranged in Windhoek – nearly all include a visit to the delta. Companies based in Maun also offer rather economical two- and three-day safaris in the delta and surrounding national parks; prices are still going to seem high if you're coming from South Africa or Namibia, but they're on par with East Africa.

Zambia (☎ 395 1951; fax 395 3952; Zambia House, The Mall)
Zimbabwe (☎ 391 4495; fax 390 5863; Embassy Dr)

Botswana has diplomatic representation in Namibia, South Africa, Zambia and Zimbabwe (see the relevant country chapters for information).

In countries where Botswana has no diplomatic representation, information and visas are available through the British high commission.

HOLIDAYS
As well as religious holidays listed in the Africa Directory chapter (p1003) the principal public holidays in Botswana are:
1 Janurary New Year's Day
2 January Day after New Year's Day
1 May Labour Day
April or May (40 days after Easter) Ascension Day
1 July Sir Seretse Khama Day
Third Friday of July President's Day
30 September Botswana/Independence Day
1 October Day after Independence Day

MAPS
The most accurate country map is the *Shell Tourist Map of Botswana* (US$3), which shows major roads and includes insets of tourist areas and central Gaborone. It's sold in a packet with a small tourist guide in bookshops all over the region.

MONEY
Botswana's unit of currency is the pula (P), which is divided into 100 thebe. 'Pula' means 'rain' – a valuable commodity in this desert land.

Full banking services are available only in major towns although ATMs are sprouting all over the country. Most credit cards are accepted at hotels and restaurants and cash advances are available at major banks (but not through ATMs).

VISAS
All visitors to Botswana need a valid passport but no visas are required by citizens of most Commonwealth countries, EU countries (except Spain and Portugal), Israel, Norway, South Africa, Switzerland and the USA. On arrival you'll get a 30-day entrance stamp.

Visa Extensions
Visa extensions are available at the small **Department of Immigration office** (☎ 395 2969) immediately north of Gaborone's Molepolole flyover. Extensions are available for up to three months.

Visas for Onward Travel
Visas for the following neighbouring countries can be obtained in Gaborone. See p886 for embassy and consulate information.
Namibia No visas are required for citizens of Australia, New Zealand, France, Germany, the UK, Ireland, Canada and the US.
South Africa No visas are required for citizens of Australia, New Zealand, France, Germany, the UK, Ireland, Canada and the US.
Zambia Visas are required by US, Australian and British citizens. In Gaborone, they take one day to process and cost US$59/94 for a single-/double-entry visa, and US$188 for a multiple-entry visa. Note that they're available at the border for considerably less (normally US$25 for US citizens and £45 for British subjects).
Zimbabwe Australians, New Zealanders and US citizens need a visa, which can be processed at the border (US$30/45 for single/double entry). However, you can also secure a visa in advance for the same rates; multi-entry visas cost US$55 and aren't available at the border.

Zimbabwe

HIGHLIGHTS

- **Victoria Falls** Psyche yourself up and get ready to join the adrenalin junkies at Africa's white-water run through the Batoka Gorge below the magnificent falls (p910)
- **Eastern Highlands** Climb Mt Nyangani or admire the mountain scenery in Chimanimani National Park, then bed down in a cave for the night (p903)
- **Great Zimbabwe** Walk among the dry-stone walls and whispering shadows of an ancient city at Africa's largest ancient stone structures south of the pyramids (p904)
- **Harare** Wander through stone sculpture gardens, treat yourself at a gourmet restaurant, then spend a night out on the town at a local gig (p898)
- **Mana Pools** Canoe gently down the placid Zambezi past hippos and crocs and walk unaccompanied in lion, elephant and buffalo territory in this remote wilderness (p900)
- **Off the beaten track** Mountain-bike through Matobo's surreal landscape of balancing boulders where rock paintings and cultural shrines lie hidden, and watch antelopes and zebras grazing (p908)

FAST FACTS

- **Area** 390,580 sq km
- **ATMs** only in main cities
- **Borders** South Africa, Botswana, Zambia, Mozambique
- **Budget** US$15 to US$25 a day
- **Capital** Harare
- **Languages** English, Shona, Ndebele
- **Money** Zimbabwe dollar; US$1 = ZW$825
- **Population** 13 million
- **Seasons** cool, dry (Apr–Sep); warm, wet (Oct–Mar)
- **Telephone** country code ☎ 260; international access code ☎ 00
- **Time** GMT/UTC + 2
- **Visas** 90 days (US$30 for most nationalities), issued at point of entry

SAFETY IN ZIMBABWE

Contrary to popular belief, there are no more safety concerns for travellers in Zimbabwe than in any of its peaceful neighbouring countries. Internal hostilities are not directed at visitors, although it's a good idea to keep your political views to yourself.

You've heard all about Zimbabwe's political scandals and economic crisis, but you might not know about all the wonderful things that make it an incredible tourist destination. Its groovy arts and music scene, rich cultural heritage, serene wildlife parks, friendly people and – best of all – the awesome Victoria Falls make visiting Zimbabwe an unforgettable experience.

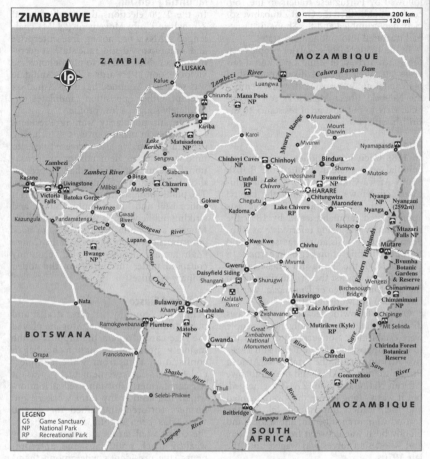

ZIMBABWE

0 — 200 km
0 — 120 mi

LEGEND
GS   Game Sanctuary
NP   National Park
RP   Recreational Park

At Victoria Falls, tourists converge from around the world to gaze at the mighty waterfall or to play on the wild Zambezi where it races through a narrow gorge below. In the east a spectacular mountainous region contrasts with the rock-studded plains and silent woodlands throughout the rest of the country.

Harare, the bustling capital, with its trendy bars, is a great place to catch a live gig or check out the arts scene. Zimbabwe's developed tourism and transport infrastructure gives you a wide choice of tours, activities and accommodation and makes getting around easy. And the best news for shoestringers is that it's one of the cheapest places in the region.

HISTORY

The wonderful ancient rock art that's dotted around Zimbabwe is testimony to the early Khoisan people, hunter-gatherers who inhabited Zimbabwe from the 5th century. They retreated to the southeast when Bantu settlers from the north began arriving in the 10th century.

In the 11th century a powerful and wealthy Shona dynasty rose at Great Zimbabwe in the vicinity of modern-day Masvingo, and Swahili traders began trading there. They were followed by Portuguese traders in the 16th century, but by then the Great Zimbabwe society had crumbled and the Shona dynasties had fractured into autonomous states.

In the 1830s Ndebele warrior people from the south arrived in Zimbabwe, and a few years later their chief, Mzilikazi, established his capital at Bulawayo. Later that century the Ndebele, under Mzilikazi's son Lobengula, were to put up a great resistance to the British settlers.

Rhodesia

In 1888 Cecil John Rhodes, an ambitious colonial entrepreneur, formed the British South Africa Company (BSAC) and colonised Zimbabwe, establishing the capital at Fort Salisbury (Harare). The colonists appropriated farmlands, and by 1895 the new country was being referred to as Rhodesia. A white legislature was set up, and European immigration began in earnest. In the late 1890s the Shona and Ndebele combined forces against the British pioneers in the first *Chimurenga* or *Umvukela* (war for liberation) but were defeated.

Over the following decades a series of laws discriminating against indigenous people were established. Not surprisingly, they led to black opposition. In the 1950s and 1960s two African parties, the Zimbabwe African People's Union (ZAPU) and the Zimbabwe African National Union (ZANU), emerged, but it wasn't long before they were banned and their leaders imprisoned. In 1966 the second *Chimurenga* began, and a long and bloody bush war between freedom fighters and Rhodesian forces was waged until the late 1970s.

Zimbabwe

Hostilities ended with independence in 1980. Rhodesia became Zimbabwe and Robert Mugabe, the ZANU candidate, its first prime minister (he later became the executive president). Very early on there were signs that all was not well when ZANU (mostly Shona) and ZAPU (mostly Ndebele) rivalries resurfaced. Mugabe sent his North Korean-trained Fifth Brigade to quash uprisings in Matabeleland. The result was horrific massacres in which tens of thousands of civilians, sometimes entire villages, were slaughtered. This was covered up, however, and eventually a peace deal was signed with ZAPU.

Mounting Tension

In the 1990 elections the newly formed Zimbabwe Unity Movement (ZUM) challenged ZANU, promoting free enterprise and a multiparty democratic state. A gerrymander enabled ZANU to post a landslide victory. Soon afterwards a ZUM candidate was seriously wounded in an assassination attempt. Other opposition candidates immediately sought a low profile.

With his popularity waning President Mugabe began making promises, including on land reform. He also increased taxes to fund war veterans' demands for compensation (government officials had ripped off the War Victims' Compensation Fund). The public protested, but the army and riot police beat and killed demonstrators, and striking public workers were sacked. When Mugabe sent Zimbabwean troops to back government soldiers in the war in Congo (Zaïre), the already crippled economy collapsed under the burden of the added military expenses.

The Land Fiasco

With the economy in dire straits and public outrage increasing, Mugabe played the race card. To gain the support of the majority peasant population he began confiscating land from white commercial farmers for resettlement by peasant African farmers. But land redistribution, which has seen many farm workers and farmers tortured and killed for several years, has been a total fiasco. Most of the confiscated farms are now owned by wealthy black politicians and entrepreneurs (the president's wife among them) who already have several substantial farms. Many farms have been abandoned by the peasants, who don't understand modern farming methods and can't afford to buy seed anyway, but commercial farmers who've tried to return have been beaten. Hundreds of farm workers have been left jobless and homeless, commercial farmers have fled the country, and the agricultural sector – the mainstay of the economy – is in total chaos.

Increasing Opposition

The odds were stacked against Mugabe going into the 2002 elections. There was a strong opposition, the Movement for

Democratic Change (MDC), led by Morgan Tsvangirai. Zimbabweans were confident the hour of change had come. But to everyone's stupefaction, Mugabe rigged the elections and managed to stay in power.

At the time of writing, Tsvangirai was on trial for treason for allegedly plotting to assassinate the president. The opposition leader claimed it was a set-up. Under cross-examination, the government's main witness eventually confessed that the government hired him to frame Tsvangirai.

The economy is a shambles and there are shortages of most basic commodities, including fuel, flour, dairy products, sugar – but Zimbabwe's octogenarian president is not yet ready to relinquish power. When you ask Zimbabweans why they put up with Mugabe, many will smile wryly and reply, 'He's an old man.'

THE CULTURE

Zimbabweans are convivial, spontaneous people who make great company. They love music and dance and will jump at any occasion for celebration – perhaps it's a form of escapism. They are gentle people who tolerate injustice and hardship in the hope that things will improve, rather than risk violent confrontation. Philosophical and patient, they talk optimistically about 'when things pick up again' as if it's just a matter of time.

There are 73 people per sq km. The two main ethnic groups are the Shona (76%), who occupy the north and east, and the Ndebele (18%), who live in the west. The majority are Christian, although traditional spiritual beliefs and customs are still practised, especially in rural areas.

ARTS

Festivals, literature, music, dance, art galleries, sculpture parks and roadside stalls all contribute to Zimbabwe's rich and varied arts scene. Contemporary Zimbabwean authors to look out for include Yvonne Vera, Chenjerai Hove, Charles Mungoshi, Tsitsi Dangarembga and Shimmer Chinodya. Traditional art plays an important role in society and continues to inspire contemporary artists. Artistic expression ranges from traditional dance and music to modern forms of art, such as abstract stone sculpture.

ENVIRONMENT

Zimbabwe sits mostly on highveld (high grassland) and middleveld (lower altitude grassland) plateaus between the Limpopo River to the south and the Zambezi River to the north. There are mountains and highlands along the eastern border. It has a pleasantly moderate climate. Temperatures are higher from November to April during summer and lower from May to October in winter.

Each of Zimbabwe's national parks has its own special attraction, such as Hwange's abundant wildlife (especially its high elephant population), Matobo's surreal landscape of smooth rocks and rounded boulders, Chimanimani's quiet mountain scenery and Mana Pools' riverside environment, where you can strike out on foot safari to meet animals. Park entry fees range from US$5 to US$20 per day, and accommodation is available (see p914).

TRANSPORT

GETTING THERE & AWAY
Air

Most international flights arrive in Harare, and there are also direct flights between Victoria Falls and Johannesburg. International flights link Zimbabwe to Johannesburg (US$130, 1½ hours), Gaborone (US$150, 1½ hours), Windhoek (US$301, 2½ hours), Maputo (US$146, 1½ hours), Lilongwe (US$131, 1 hour), Lusaka (US$121, 50 minutes), Dar es Salaam (US$425, 2½ hours) and Nairobi (US$225, 3½ hours). All fares are one way.

Land

Most of Zimbabwe's border posts are open from 6am to 6pm with the exception of Beitbridge (to South Africa, 6am to 10pm or later) and Victoria Falls (to Zambia, 6am to 10pm). Its other border posts are Plumtree and Kazungula (Botswana); Kariba and Chirundu (Zambia);

DEPARTURE TAX

The departure tax for international flights is US$30. It's usually included in your ticket but is otherwise payable in US dollars only.

and Mutare and Nyamapanda (Mozambique).

Most international bus services depart from Harare's **Road Port** (☎ 04-702828) terminal at the corner of Fifth St and Robert Mugabe Rd (Map p896). A few depart from the Mbare Musika Bus Terminal south of the city centre (Map p894).

FUEL CRISIS

There are major diesel and petrol shortages in Zimbabwe as a result of the country's inability to pay the fuel companies. This might affect bus schedules and will be a problem if you hire a vehicle because, when fuel is available, you often have to queue for hours and even days.

BOTSWANA
Chitanda & Sons (Renkini bus terminal, Bulawayo) runs daily buses to Francistown (three to six hours) and Gaborone leaving at 1pm.

MALAWI
The most direct route between Malawi and Zimbabwe is via Mozambique's Tete corridor. You'll need a transit visa to enter Mozambique if you're travelling through Mozambique side to Malawi.

Munorurama (☎ 751210; Mbare Musika Bus Terminal) has buses departing at 6am for Blantyre (US$8, nine to 12 hours, daily) and Lilongwe (US$10, 12 to 15 hours, three times a week).

ZUPCO (Map p894; Mbare Musika Bus Terminal) buses to Blantyre depart from the Mbare terminal (US$8, nine-12 hours, daily).

MOZAMBIQUE
You can go to Beira in Mozambique via Mutare. Take a minibus from Mutare to the border, then catch another bus on the Mozambique side. You can get to Malawi from Nyamapanda by minibus. Minibuses run infrequently between Nyamapanda and Tete (Mozambique) and more frequently between Tete and Zóbuè on the border with Malawi.

NAMIBIA
There's no direct overland connection between Zimbabwe and Namibia. The most straightforward route is between Victoria Falls and the Caprivi Strip via Botswana (see p913).

Intercape buses to Windhoek depart Victoria Falls on Sunday and Wednesday (US$65, 18 hours). Book at Backpackers Bazaar and Travel Junction (see p910).

SOUTH AFRICA
Greyhound (Map p896; ☎ 720801; Road Port) Buses depart at 10am Mon-Fri & 1pm Sun (US$44, 14 hr).
Minibuses (City Hall car park, Bulawayo) Buses leave Bulawayo for Jo'burg from the city hall car park when full.
Pioneer Coach (Map p894; ☎ 091-333615; Road Port) Buses depart at 9.30am Mon-Fri & 11am Sun (US$27, 14 hr).
Translux (Map p894; Mbare Musika Bus Terminal) Buses depart at 9am Mon, Wed, Fri & 1pm Sun (US$35, 14 hr). This company (☎ 66528; cnr Fourth Ave & Fife St, Bulawayo) also runs from Bulawayo to Jo'burg (US$20, 9 hr, daily).
Zimbabwe Travel (☎ 09-76208; www.gozimbabwe.co.za; Bulawayo) Runs a backpackers' bus/train service between Jo'burg & Victoria Falls (US$47) twice a week. The bus runs between Jo'burg & Bulawayo, & passengers continue to Victoria Falls by train or shuttle bus.

ZAMBIA
Chigubu (Map p894; ☎ 011-743449; Road Port) buses depart for Lusaka via Chirundu at 9am and 9pm (US$6, eight hours, twice daily).
ZUPCO (Map p894; ☎ 704933; Road Port) buses depart for Lusaka (via Chirundu) at 8.30am and 8.30pm (US$6, eight hours, twice daily).

To get to Zambia from Victoria Falls see p913. At Kariba, you can walk or catch a taxi across the dam wall into Zambia. Catch a minibus on the Zambian side to the town of Siavonga from where there are minibuses to Lusaka (US$4.80, daily).

GETTING AROUND
Air
Air Zimbabwe (Map p896; ☎ 04-253752; Eastgate Centre) flies domestic routes between Harare and Bulawayo (US$81/106 one way/return) and Harare and Victoria Falls (US$86/129 one way/hour). There's a domestic departure tax of US$5. Air Zimbabwe no longer flies to Hwange or Kariba.

Boat
Kariba Ferries (☎ 04-65476; Andora Harbour, Kariba) occasionally runs a ferry service between Kariba at the eastern end of the lake and Mlibizi at the western end. Because of the fuel shortage, there are no longer scheduled sailings. The ferry departs when there

is sufficient demand. To get to or from the Mlibizi ferry terminal, local buses between Bulawayo and Binga via Dete Crossroads pass within 15km of Mlibizi.

Bus
There are two types of buses: express and local. The relatively efficient express buses operate according to published timetables. Local buses normally depart when full from township markets outside the centre of a town.

Train
Zimbabwe's railway network connects Harare, Bulawayo, Mutare and Victoria Falls. Trains are very slow, and recently there have been a number of serious accidents. All major services travel at night, and sleeping compartments with bedding are available. Watch your belongings.

HARARE

☎ 04 / pop 2 million

There's a certain air of sophistication about Harare's busy but orderly streets and its high-rise buildings, and in September, when the jacaranda trees are in flower, the city is splashed with purple. The city centre is a kaleidoscope of people with smart office workers, dirty labourers, street hawkers and secret agents going about their busy agendas. In the crowded malls, tough street kids saunter past fast food restaurants and eye fashionable teens consuming greasy burgers. Street performers regale midday crowds with their slapstick comedy, and blind mothers send their toddlers begging among the throng. A colonial aura remains in Harare's quiet green suburbs, but there's a vibrant African feel in its crammed high-density areas (townships), although most travellers don't venture there.

ORIENTATION
The airport is 15 km from the city centre. Taxis cost around US$7.

Samora Machel Ave cuts from east to west through the centre of Harare; the main part of the city is to its south. About half way through the centre it's intersected by Julius Nyerere Way, which divides the crowded western part of the city and the less crowded

eastern side. Part of Second St, one of the main north–south streets, is also called Sam Nujoma St. In the eastern part of the city is Africa Unity Square, a calm shady spot for a rest.

INFORMATION
Aside from its free monthly publication, *What's on in Harare*, the **Harare Publicity Association** (Map p896; ☎ 781810; Second St; ◷ 8am-noon & 1-4pm Mon-Fri, 8am-noon Sat), at the southwest corner of African Unity Square, has very little practical information for travellers. You'll find more information at backpackers' hostels.

There are banks in the city centre on Samora Machel Ave and Second St, but before you change money at banks, read the boxed text on p915. Stamp sales and poste restante are upstairs at the **main post office** (Map p896; Inez Terrace; ◷ 8am-4pm Mon-Fri, 8-11.30am Sat).

The **National Parks Central Reservations Office** (Map p894; ☎ 706077; national-parks@gta.gov.zw; cnr Borrowdale Rd & Sandringham Dr; ◷ 8am-4pm Mon-Fri), near the northern end of the National Botanic Gardens, takes accommodation bookings for national parks.

Travelworld Budget Tours (Map p896; ☎ 253551; budget@travelworld.co.zw; green bridge, Eastgate, Second St), on the 5th floor of the Eastgate Centre, can book international and domestic air travel.

Most Internet centres in Harare also offer phone and fax services.

DC Africa Internet (Map p896; ☎ 708737; Mazowe St; US$0.90 per hr; ◷ 8am-8pm) is downstairs at the Travel Plaza. **Café Zimbabwe** (Map p896; ☎ 798201; Eastgate Centre; US$0.50 per hr; ◷ 24 hr) has a cheap, fast connection and funky Afro décor.

DANGERS & ANNOYANCES
Mbare Musika may be fascinating, but it's also notorious for muggings. Do not venture there without a local guide. Watch for pick-pockets in the busy city streets, and don't walk through parks and other secluded areas alone. At night take an official taxi and insist on being dropped right at your door.

SIGHTS & ACTIVITIES
Harare's sights are dotted around the city and its outskirts.

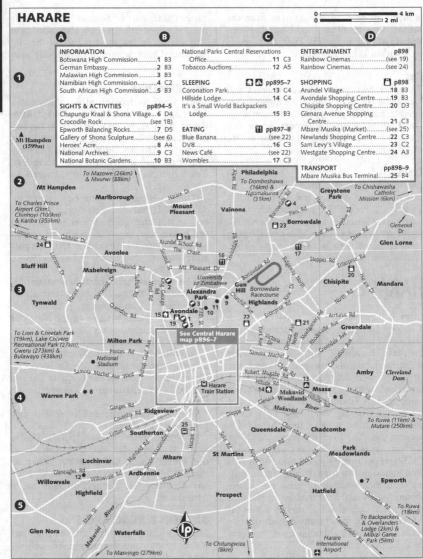

HARARE

0 ─────── 4 km
0 ─────── 2 mi

INFORMATION			
Botswana High Commission	1	B3	
German Embassy	2	B3	
Malawian High Commission	3	B3	
Namibian High Commission	4	C2	
South African High Commission	5	B3	
SIGHTS & ACTIVITIES		pp894–5	
Chapungu Kraal & Shona Village	6	D4	
Crocodile Rock	(see 18)		
Epworth Balancing Rocks	7	D5	
Gallery of Shona Sculpture	(see 6)		
Heroes' Acre	8	A4	
National Archives	9	C3	
National Botanic Gardens	10	B3	

National Parks Central Reservations		
Office	11	C3
Tobacco Auctions	12	A5
SLEEPING 🏕🏛 pp895–7		
Coronation Park	13	C4
Hillside Lodge	14	C4
It's a Small World Backpackers		
Lodge	15	B3
EATING 🍴 pp897–8		
Blue Banana	(see 22)	
DV8	16	C3
News Café	(see 22)	
Wombles	17	C3

ENTERTAINMENT		p898
Rainbow Cinemas	(see 19)	
Rainbow Cinemas	(see 24)	
SHOPPING 🛍 p898		
Arundel Village	18	B3
Avondale Shopping Centre	19	B3
Chisipite Shopping Centre	20	D3
Glenara Avenue Shopping		
Centre	21	C3
Mbare Musika (Market)	(see 25)	
Newlands Shopping Centre	22	C3
Sam Levy's Village	23	C2
Westgate Shopping Centre	24	A3
TRANSPORT		pp898–9
Mbare Musika Bus Terminal	25	B4

Mbare Musika (Market), 5km south of the city centre (Map p894), sheltering its stalls of sweet ripe fruit, bright vegetables, greasy motor parts and used clothing, is where traders and shoppers flock to the daily market. If you're feeling a little off-colour you probably won't want to consult one of the herbalists with their assortment of unlikely remedies: vile-looking liquids macerating in large jars, twisted roots and a horrifying collection of animal anatomy. Although it's a fascinating place to visit, tourists make easy pickings so don't bring any valuables, and get a local friend to accompany you. To get there, take the bus from the Angwa St bus terminal or get a taxi.

WARNING

Chancellor Ave, an extension of Seventh St, which eventually runs into Borrowdale Rd, is a no-go area between 6am and 6pm. The road passes between President Mugabe's Residence and the State House, which accommodates presidential guests and state offices. Guards weighed down by an impressive assortment of weaponry patrol this area 24 hours a day and have orders to fire without warning at anyone trespassing between the curfew hours.

At **Chapungu Kraal & Shona Village** (Map p894; Harrow Rd; admission US$0.20; 🕑 8am-6pm Mon-Fri, 9am-5.30pm Sat & Sun), 8km from the city centre, you can wander round a sculpture garden and a reconstructed Shona village. There are sculptors at work in the garden, and on Saturday and Sunday afternoons you can watch traditional dances.

Mukuvisi Woodlands Environmental Centre (Map p894; ☎ 747111; Glenara Ave South, Hillside Rd extension; admission US$1; 🕑 8am-5pm) is a peaceful native woodland area and wildlife park with zebras, giraffes and antelopes. The Greendale bus from the Rezende St terminal can drop you near Mukuvisi.

The **National Gallery of Zimbabwe** (Map p896; ☎ 704666; cnr Julius Nyerere Way & Park Lane; admission US$0.25; 🕑 9am-5pm) has interesting and insightful displays of Zimbabwean and African art including paintings, stone sculptures, masks and carvings. The attached shop sells crafts and books on art.

The **National Botanic Gardens** (Map p894; Fifth St; admission free; 🕑 dawn-dusk), with their extensive lawns and African plants, are a relaxing place to spend an afternoon. There have been muggings here, however, so be on your guard.

FESTIVALS & EVENTS

Harare International Festival of Arts (☎ 300119; www.hifa.co.zw) brings together an impressive gathering of artists of all genres from all over the world. Zimbabwean artists are present in force and there's always a good show of artists from other African countries. The performances by African traditional dancers accompanied by drums, *marimbas* (small instruments played with the thumb), shakers and other traditional instruments

are fantastic. If you're in the region at the beginning of May, head to Harare for this wonderful festival.

SLEEPING

There's a single backpackers close to the city centre and several cheap hotels, but the nicest places to stay for budget travellers are out of town.

Hillside Lodge (Map p894; ☎ 747961; 71 Hillside Rd; camp site per person US$1.50, dm US$2.50, s/d US$3.50/5; 🏊) This welcoming backpackers in an old colonial house is surrounded by a large garden full of jacaranda trees and has a lovely pool area. There's a bar, self-catering kitchen, bike hire and laundry service. Take the Msasa, Tafara or Mabvuku bus from the corner of Speke Ave and Julius Nyerere Way, get off at the Children's Home and walk up Robert Mugabe Rd to Helm Rd, which will take you to Hillside Rd.

Backpackers & Overlanders Lodge (Map p894; ☎ 575715; conxshon@mweb.co.zw; Twentydales Rd ext; camp site per person US$3, dm US$6, d from US$16; 🏊) This place is near the airport and has an idyllic bushland setting. There's a pool, bar and self-catering kitchen. Meals are available (from US$4). The lodge organizes day trips around Harare, and you can go horse-riding at the nearby Mbizi Game Park. During business hours it offers free airport pick-ups and two daily runs to the city centre.

It's a Small World Backpackers Lodge (Map p894; ☎ 335341; mail@backpackerslodge.com; 25 Ridge Rd; dm US$6, d US$15/20 without/with bathroom) Close to the Avondale shopping centre, this place is popular with travellers. It has a bar and a city view from its rooftop deck. It runs airport and town transfers (US$5/3).

Selous Hotel (Map p896; ☎ 727948; selhotel@mweb .co.zw; cnr Selous Ave & Sixth St; s/d US$8/9; 🖥) This hotel has rooms with bathroom and offers B&B. It has a comfortable guest lounge on the top floor where there's also a restaurant with a view (steak/pasta meals US$1.20 to US$2).

Palm Rock Villa (Map p896; ☎ 700691; palmrock villa@hotmail.com; 39 Selous Ave; dm US$1.50, s/d US$2/3) There's a mellow local atmosphere here, although it's dark and rather plain. It has a self-catering kitchen, shared bathrooms and a tiny front garden.

Horizon Inn (Map p896; ☎ 253851; 107 Fife Ave; s/d US$6/8) A large clean place with good security, this is popular with Zimbabwean

ZIMBABWE

CENTRAL HARARE

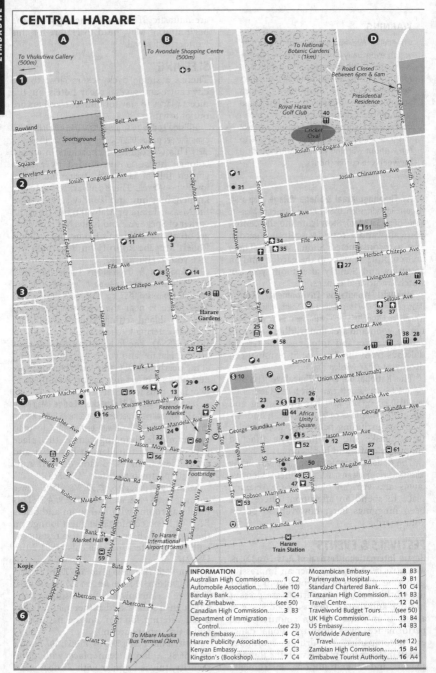

ZIMBABWE

businessmen. The rooms are plain but have bathroom and TV, and the rate includes breakfast.

The **Fife Avenue Hotel** (Map p896; ☎ 707031; 102 Fife Ave; s/d US\$5/6) Across from Horizon Inn, this hotel has unpretentious rooms with bathroom, a courtyard bar and a restaurant (traditional/European meals US\$1.50/2.50).

EATING

Backpackers lodges usually offer breakfast for around US\$1.50.

Cafés

Most cafés serve coffee for US\$0.30, cakes and snacks from US\$1 and light meals from US\$1.50.

The **Book Café** (Map p896; ☎ 792551; 1st fl, Fife Ave Shopping Centre; ☷ 10am-10pm) This café hosts popular local musicians, poets and writers, and it's crowded when there's a performance. There's a good selection of quality African literature in the attached bookshop. Its monthly program has details of poetry reading sessions, debates and live music.

Fournos (Map p896; ☎ 708348; 144 Samora Machel Ave; ☷ 7am-11pm) The veranda tables are a good place to watch the busy street scene. This café serves sandwiches, burgers and pasta dishes and is usually packed at lunch time. The bakery counter inside has a delectable selection of pastries, cakes, samosas, sausage rolls, fresh bread and doughnuts.

The **Hot Bread Shop** (Map p896; cnr Second St & Robson Manyika Ave) Serving freshly baked buns, doughnuts and cakes, this quiet café is a nice place for a coffee.

Sherrol's in the Park (Map p896; ☎ 705323; Harare Gardens; ☷ 10am-5pm) Enjoy a relaxed light lunch at this café, which serves salads, sandwiches and pies.

Quick Eats

If you're in a hurry, pick up a takeaway at the Mobil Fore Court (Map p896) where you can choose from several fast-food chains. The food court at Eastgate Centre (Map p896) has the usual fast-food outlets, including Eastern Deli, an Indian takeaway that makes excellent samosas.

Restaurants

Restaurants are open for lunch and dinner but are usually closed on Monday.

Roots of Africa (Map p896; ☎ 091-217146; cnr Seventh St & Livingstone Ave; mains US$1.50-2) There's a true traditional menu offering goat, fish or chicken dishes with *sadza* (maize meal porridge) or rice at this groovy African bar, restaurant and night club. Friday nights are *braai* (barbecue) nights and there's a group playing the *mbira* (a traditional Zimbabwean instrument) or there's a disco every Friday and Saturday night.

Cascais (Map p896; ☎ 704831; 139 Samora Machel Ave; mains from US$3) This place serves Portuguese specialities and has tables set around a covered courtyard.

DV8 (Map p894; ☎ 745202; Groombridge shops, cnr the Chase & Teviotdale Rd; mains US$3-5) The steaks here are divine. It also serves chicken and pasta dishes.

Wombles (Map p894; ☎ 870492; 19 Ballantyne Park Square; mains US$3-4) Feeling ravenous? Head to this popular restaurant which serves succulent steaks.

Gaby's Restaurant (Map p896; Travel Plaza, Mazowe St; mains US$1.50-3.50) This smart café and restaurant serves meat and pasta dishes. It's a nice place to stop for a coffee and cake.

The Keg & Maiden (Map p896; ☎ 700037; Harare Sports Club, off Fifth St; mains US$3-4) Tuck into bangers and mash or steak and chips in a cheerful pub atmosphere. You can also order a veg meal. Try this place for a pub meal. On Saturday nights there's live music.

News Café (Map p894; Newlands shopping centre; mains from US$2) You can order nachos or pasta at this relaxed café as you watch big sports matches on wide screens.

Blue Banana (Map p894; ☎ 705320; Newlands shopping centre; mains from US$3-4) For Thai, you can't beat this restaurant, which is next door to the News Café.

Self-Catering
There are TM supermarkets and OK supermarkets across the city, including on Nelson Mandela Ave between Second and First Sts, at the Fife Ave shopping centre (Map p896), Sam Levy's Village in Borrowdale, Avondale shopping centre, Chisipite and Westgate (Map p894).

DRINKING & ENTERTAINMENT
Harare's music scene rocks, and you can catch many traditional and contemporary music performances at bars and cafés around the capital where well-known local musicians play regularly. To see who's playing where, look at the entertainment page of the Friday and Saturday editions of the *Daily News* or the *Herald*.

The Book Café (see Eating above) has live performances a couple of times a week and at the weekend. The Mannenburg (Map p896; ☎ 730902), next door, has live jazz on Wednesday evenings. The trendy Jazz 105 (Map p896; ☎ 722516; cnr Second St & Robson Manyika Ave) has live Afro jazz performances on Sunday and Wednesday evenings. Famous musicians frequently play at Job's Night Spot (Map p896; Wonder Shopping Centre, Julius Nyerere Way, btwn Kenneth Kaunda & Robson Manyika Aves) and Anandas (Map p896; cnr Julius Nyerere Way & Nelson Mandela Ave).

The Harare Beer Engine (Map p896; cnr Samora Machel Ave & Park St) brews its own beers. You can see the workings of the brewery and sample its products.

SHOPPING
At the craft and flower stalls under the shady trees at the eastern corner of Africa Unity Square there's a wide selection of carvings, sculptures, paintings, batiks, wire model animals and bright bouquets. You'll probably be quoted outrageous 'tourist' prices so be prepared for some tough bargaining.

Crocodile Rock (Map p896; Travel Plaza, Mazowe St) and Spinalong (Map p896; Eastgate Centre) have a great selection of local music CDs, including Oliver Mtukudzi, Thomas Mapfumo, Simon Chimbetu and *mbira* groups.

GETTING THERE & AWAY
Air
Air Zimbabwe (Map p896; ☎ 253752; Eastgate Centre) operates flights to/from Bulawayo (US$80, one way, 45 minutes) and Victoria Falls (US$85, one way, one hour). Air Botswana, Air Namibia and South African Airways also have offices in Harare. See Map p896.

Bus
Most buses to destinations within Zimbabwe leave from the Mbare Musika Bus Terminal next to the market 5km from the city centre. To get there, hire a taxi or take a bus from the Angwa St bus terminal. A few buses leave from the Road Port terminal in town, which is also where international services leave from.

Blue Arrow (Map p896; ☎ 729514; barrow@africa online.co.zw; Chester House, Speke Ave) has daily comfortable coach services to Bulawayo (US$10, six hours) via Gweru (US$6, four hours). Coaches to Mutare leave three times a week (US$6, four hours).

Kukura Kurerwa (Map p894; Mbare) runs daily services to Victoria Falls (US$10, 11 hours).

Pioneer Bus (Map p894; Mbare Musika Bus Terminal) services depart from Mbare at 5am for Bulawayo (US$4, six hours), at 8am for Mutare (US$3, five hours), at 11am and 1.30pm for Kariba (US$3, four hours), and at 8am for Victoria Falls (US$9, 11 hours). Buses also run to Masvingo (US$3, five hours, daily).

Power Coach (Map p896; ☎ 702798; Road Port, cnr Fifth St & Robert Mugabe Rd) runs several services a day to Kariba (US$3.50, four hours).

Traveller (Map p896; ☎ 794231; Road Port) goes to Bulawayo at 11am (US$4, six hours, daily).

Train

The train station is near the corner of Kenneth Kaunda Ave and Second St. You can purchase tickets in advance at the **ticket office** (Map p896; ☎ 786034; ⏰ 7am-4pm & 7-9.30pm Mon-Fri, 8-11.30am & 7-9pm Sat, 7-9.30pm Sun). Daily trains depart at 8pm for Bulawayo (sleeper/standard/economy class US$4/2/2, nine hours) via Gweru (US$2/1/1, five hours), and 9.30pm for Mutare (US$2/1/1, 8½ hours).

GETTING AROUND

The crowded Harare city buses and 15-seat minibuses provide transport for the many masses. There are five central bus terminals: Market Square, Fourth St, Angwa St, Rezende St and Chinhoyi St. Buses to Mbare Musika leave from the Angwa St bus terminal. There is also a string of bus stops along Jason Moyo Ave, near Fourth St. Fares start at US$0.30.

There are taxi stands on the corner of First St and Nelson Mandela Ave; on Samora Machel Ave near First St; on Union Ave between Angwa St and Julius Nyerere Way; and in front of large hotels. All taxis are private hire. Official services include **Rixi Taxi** (☎ 753080). To or from anywhere in the city centre costs from US$1 to US$2 and to the suburbs costs from US$2 to US$3.

AROUND HARARE

For an interesting day trip, there are enormous rocks to climb, strangely shaped

boulders to inspect and ancient rock art to contemplate at both Domboshawa and Ngomakurira. **Domboshawa** (☎ 790044; admission US$2; ⏰ 6am-6pm) is 30km north of Harare. Bindura via Chinamora buses, from Mbare Musika bus station (Map p894), can drop you at the turn-off, and you'll need to walk 1km from there to the entry gate.

For **Ngomakurira** (☎ 790044; admission US$2; ⏰ 6am-6pm), also take the Bindura via Chinamora bus from Mbare Musika bus station and get off in Ngomakurira village (45km north of Harare). From the bus stop to the gate is a 2km walk.

NORTHERN ZIMBABWE

KARIBA

☎ 061 / pop 15,000

The small town of Kariba is spread out along the steep lake shore and across a hill (Kariba Heights) overlooking **Lake Kariba**. The road alongside the lake is, not surprisingly, called Lake Drive. From here another road winds up through the tree-covered hills to Kariba Heights. There are lovely lake views through the trees, and wildlife often can be seen in the town. Kariba has no real centre, although there is a lively township at Mahombekombe where Harare buses depart.

Information & Sights

The **Kariba Publicity Association** (☎ 2328; www .karibapa.co.zw; ⏰ 8am-5pm), a steep 15-minute walk uphill from Lake Dr, has an impressive view of the dam wall and the deep gorge below. The staff are friendly but can't help with much. However, it's still worth coming here for the view.

The main road leads to the **dam wall**, which straddles the Zimbabwe–Zambia border. You can walk or drive across the dam wall into Zambia. You can walk across the dam to have a look at the spectacular views even if you're not going to Zambia.

In Kariba Heights (known locally as the Heights) is the **Church of Santa Barbara**, built in the shape of a coffer-dam and dedicated to the 86 workers who perished during dam construction. The **Operation Noah Monument** nearby commemorates the 1959 rescue of wildlife from the rising waters of Lake Kariba.

Activities

There's not a lot to do in Kariba itself, but it's an ideal place to book a trip to Matusadona or Mana Pools National Parks or a Lower Zambezi canoeing safari. You can also arrange houseboat and canoeing trips on Lake Kariba.

Al Cove (☎ 3338; rstubbs@ecoweb.co.zw; the Heights Shopping Centre, Kariba Heights) operates houseboat trips (US$7 per person per day). **Kariba Houseboats** (☎ 2766; houseboats@zol.co.zw; Andora Harbour) is another operator. **Kariba Breezes Marina** (☎ 2237; karibamarina@mweb.co.zw; Chawara Marina) hires speedboats (from US$15/20 per half/full-day) and a driver, which is a great way to view the wildlife in Matusadona from the lake.

Several operators run canoeing safaris between Chirundu and Mana Pools (two/three days from US$120/300), and walking or driving safaris to Mana Pools and Matusadona National Parks (from US$80 per day). Rates for activities in national parks do not include park admission fees. Recommended companies include: **Buffalo Safaris** (☎ 3041; buffalo@ecoweb.co.zw; Kariba Kushinga Lodge, Kariba) and **River Horse Safaris** (☎ 2447; www.riverhorse.co.zw; Kariba Breezes Hotel, Kariba).

Sleeping & Eating

MOTH Holiday Resort (☎ 2809; Sable Dr; camp site per person US$0.15, dm US$0.20/person, d US$1, chalets US$4 with bathroom) This is the only place within walking distance of the shops and bus stop in Mahombekombe. The camp sites are quiet and shady and have pre-erected tents, and the simple but pleasant chalets accommodate from four to six people. It also sells *braai* packs and firewood.

Kushinga Lodge (☎ 2645; kushinga@zol.co.zw; camp site per person US$2, s/d chalets per person US$5, s/d self-catering rondavels from US$10/20 with bathroom; 🏊) This restful, secluded lodge on a hillside above the lake offers a great choice for all budgets. There's a flat shady camp site, a pool and access to the beach via stone steps leading down the terraced grounds. You can order meals at the bar and restaurant (meals from US$2).

Kariba Breezes Hotel (☎ 2433; breezes@mweb .co.zw; camp site per person US$1.50, dm US$6, s/d budget rooms US$1.50/3.10, s/d standard rooms US$ 7/9; 🏊 🍴) Amenities include a great restaurant, bar and two swimming pools, but the 1950s colonial-style architecture is unattractive. Rooms with lake views are more expensive.

Pagoma Grill (☎ 2894; Kariba Heights; mains from US$1.50) This thatched restaurant has a wonderful view of the lake and the islands from its terrace patio. It serves light snacks and grilled dinners.

Polly's Takeaways, at the turn-off to the Kariba Breezes Hotel, is a good place to find burgers, pasties, chips, chicken, pizza and ice cream.

For self-caterers, there's the Spar Supermarket in Mahombekombe.

Getting There & Around

Buses leave from outside the **Spar Supermarket** (Nhoro Cres, Mahombekombe). Power Coach buses link Kariba with Harare (see p899).

There are occasional ferry services across the lake between Kariba and Mlibizi (see p893).

Buses and minibuses run between Mahombekombe and Kariba Heights throughout the day.

MANA POOLS NATIONAL PARK

Mana Pools National Park (☎ 063-533; admission US$15; ☷ 6am-6pm) is covered with wide areas of grassland and thick woodlands, but is most scenic along the banks of the Zambezi River, which marks the northern perimeter of the park. The most exhilarating aspect of Mana Pools is that you can walk unaccompanied through the park among lions, buffalos and elephants. For your own safety, however, don't get too close! The best place to view wildlife is **Long Pool** just before dusk.

You need an entry permit for the park, which you must pick up at the **Mana Pools National Park Office** (☎ 063-512) in Marongora (on the main road, about 8km before the park turn-off) before 3.30pm on the afternoon of your first night in the park. You must then reach the park headquarters, near Nyamepi Camp, the main camp site, before 6pm.

Camping is available only between 1 May and 31 October. Lodges remain open all year, but access roads might be impassable, so check before setting out in the wet season (November to April). The **camps** (camp site per person US$1, four-/eight-bed lodge US$4/6) are run by National Parks.

Without your own transport (preferably 4WD), it's very difficult to reach the park, but tours can be easily arranged in Kariba. Another popular way to visit Mana Pools is by canoe safari; trips of three to nine days

between Kariba and Kanyemba are possible (see opposite). Trips operate mostly
between April and November, although
some companies operate all year round.

EASTERN ZIMBABWE

MUTARE
☎ 020 / pop 200,000
Mutare has a pretty setting in a bowl-like
valley surrounded by hills. It makes a convenient base for visiting the Bvumba region
and Nyanga National Park. Mutare is Zimbabwe's third-largest city, but it has a relaxed
rural town atmosphere.

The helpful **Manicaland Publicity Bureau**
(☎ 64711; fax 67728; cnr Herbert Chitepo St & Robert
Mugabe Rd; ☒ 8.30am-12.45pm & 2-4pm Mon-Fri) offers a book exchange and informal luggage
storage facility as well as accommodation,
activities and transport information. The
post office (Robert Mugabe Rd) is four blocks west.
To access your email, go to the **Internet Cyber
Café** (☎ 67939; 67 Fourth St; US$3 per hr).

Sights & Activities
The **Mutare Museum** (☎ 63630; Aerodrome Rd;
admission US$0.30; ☒ 9am-5pm) has interesting
exhibits on geology, history, anthropology,
technology, zoology and the arts.

The National Trust reserve on **Murahwa's
Hill** (admission free; ☒ always open) has great views
and natural landscapes. The complex encloses some **rock paintings** and the crumbled
ruins of an Iron Age village. Look for the
mujejeje (rocks that resonate when struck).

The 1700-hectare **Cecil Kop Nature Reserve**
(☎ 61537; admission US$2; ☒ dawn-dusk) wraps
around the northern side of Mutare and abuts
the Mozambique border. Part of the park that
can be reached without a vehicle is **Tiger's Kloof
Dam**. Try to visit Tiger's Kloof at feeding time
(about 4pm) when rhinos, antelopes, giraffes
and zebras congregate at the dam.

Sleeping & Eating
Most travellers stop in Mutare only briefly
on their way up or down the Eastern Highlands.

Homestead Guest House (☎ 65870; 52 Park Rd; s/d
US$2/3, US$3/4 with bathroom; ☒) This renovated
late-19th-century home is set in a pretty
garden with a pool. It has clean and comfortable rooms.

Anne Bruce's Backpackers' Lodge (☎ 63569; 99
Fourth St; dm US$1.50, d US$3) This homely place is
central but cramped.

Municipal Camping & Caravan Park (Harare
Rd; camp site per person US$1) This camp site is
next to the noisy highway, 6km from the
city centre. If you're arriving by bus from
Harare, buses stop at the Christmas Pass
summit from where it's 2km downhill to
the camp site. A taxi from Mutare will cost
around US$2.

Stax Steak House (☎ 62653; First Mutual Arcade,
Herbert Chitepo St; mains US$1-2) As well as suc-
culent steaks, this restaurant serves vegie
burgers, salads and delicious desserts.

Jenny's of Eighth Avenue (☎ 67764; cnr Eighth
Ave & Herbert Chitepo St; mains around US$1) You can
pop into this craft shop café for a coffee
or lunch.

Self-caterers can stock up at the **TM Supermarket** (cnr Herbert Chitepo St & B Ave) or visit
the large fruit and vegetable market at the
Sakubva Musika Bus Terminal.

Getting There & Around
Almost all long-distance buses leave from
the main Sakubva Musika Bus Terminal,
about 5km from town on the Masvingo
road. There are several daily buses travelling to Harare (US$3, five hours) and
Bulawayo (US$4, six hours), via Masvingo
(US$2, three hours). Chimanimani buses
leave between 5am and 1pm. **Blue Arrow**
(Holiday Inn, cnr Aerodrome Rd & Third St) runs services to Harare on Wednesday, Friday and
Sunday (US$6, four hours).

For the train to Harare, book at the **train
station ticket office** (☎ 62801; Railway St; ☒ 8am-
12.30pm & 2-4pm Mon-Fri). It departs Mutare
daily at 9pm (US$2/1/1 in sleeper/standard/
economy class, 8½ hours).

Green Travellers (☎ 61758; dennisborerwe@hotmail
.com; 1 Chaminuka Way, Palmerston) runs day excursions to the Bvumba Mountains (US$10)
and Nyanga National Park (US$20). It also
offers hiking trips to Chimanimani (from
US$15) and Nyanga National Park (from
US$25) and tailor-made tours around Zim-
babwe. All rates are based on a minimum
of four people.

AROUND MUTARE
The Bvumba
The mist-shrouded Bvumba Mountains
with their cool climate are unlike most

of Africa. Characterised by forested high-lands alternating with deep and almost junglelike valleys, the Bvumba, meaning 'mist' in Manyika, lie to the southeast of Mutare.

The **Bvumba Botanical Gardens and Reserve** (admission US$10; ☉ 7am-5pm), 30km from Mu-tare, are a peaceful place to stroll and admire the views over distant pale blue hills and valleys. There are 30 hectares of manicured gardens and 170 hectares of indigenous forest and bushland. Unfortunately, there's a hefty entry fee to get into the reserve. **Leopard Rock**, with its wonderful views, may be climbed via a track from the Bvumba Rd, 2km east of the botanical gardens turn-off. It has a **Game and Nature Reserve** (managed by the owners of Ndundu Lodge) where horse rides and walking trails are available.

SLEEPING & EATING
There is a good selection of holiday cottages and guesthouses scattered through the re-gion. Pick up the listings from the Manica-land Publicity Association in Mutare.

Drifters (☎ 62964; tents per person US$4, dm US$5, s/d US$6/8, d US$13/15 with bathroom; 🏊) If you don't have to stay in town, head for this friendly backpackers lodge on a small wildlife reserve 21km west of Mutare. There's a pool, bar and restaurant. Get off the bus at the turn-off on the Harare–Mutare highway.

National Parks Camp Site (camping per person US$0.10, four-bed lodges US$2; 🏊) Set in the lovely botanical gardens, the lodges and camp site have good amenities and a pool.

Tony's Coffee House (Bvumba Rd; coffees from US$1, gateaux from US$3; ☉ 10am-5pm Wed-Mon) This legendary little café next to Ndundu Lodge serves a delectable selection of cakes

and gateaux. There's a vast choice of cof-fees and hot chocolates laced with various blends of liqueur.

It's difficult to get to the Bvumba without your own transport. A couple of companies run tours from Mutare (see p901).

Nyanga National Park
Scenic and secluded Nyanga, which was for-merly one of Cecil Rhodes' private estates, has beautiful waterfalls and breathtaking views over the lush Honde Valley, into Mozambique.

Nyanga National Park (admission US$10; ☉ 6am-6pm) has its headquarters at Nyanga (Rhodes) Dam. Most people come here to hike on **Mt Nyangani**, Zimbabwe's highest peak. But we're not talking Kilimanjaro here – it takes 1½ to three hours to reach the summit from the car park, 14 km east of Nyanga Dam. Hikers should first reg-ister at park headquarters. Mists can roll in suddenly, and some locals believe the mountain devours hikers. For something more substantial, a three- to four-day hike continues from Mt Nyangani past Pungwe Drift and into Honde Valley.

There are a number of interesting sights near the park headquarters, including some **old ruins**, and the **Rhodes Museum**. **Nyangombe Falls** lies 5km west of Nyangombe camping ground and 2km from Udu Dam. At the southern end of the park the spectacular **Mtarazi Falls** and smaller **Muchururu Falls** plummet down a sheer cliff face into the Honde Valley.

For excitement on the Pungwe River, try **Far & Wide** (☎ 029-3011; farnwide@mweb.co.zw; Juliasdale; camp site per person US$1), whose activi-ties include raft and kayak trips, abseiling and mountain biking. It provides all meals, activities, guides, equipment and accom-modation for US$70 per day.

You can book **National Parks accommodation** (camp site per person US$0.40, lodges per person from US$2) at the park headquarters. Nyangombe Camp Site, set amid pine woods, lies be-tween the Nyangombe River and the high-way, 7km from Nyanga village, and Mtarazi Falls Camp Site is a basic but tranquil camp site. There are cosy National Parks lodges at Udu Dam, Nyanga Dam, Nyangwe Dam and Pungwe Drift.

Nyanga village, with its manicured gar-dens, village common and stone church,

SPLURGE!
The **Ndundu Lodge** (☎ 63777; www.ndundu .com; Bvumba Rd; camp site & dm per person US$1, s/d US$5/7) This delightful thatched cottage, 10 minutes' walk from Bvumba Botanical Reserve, has a library, an impressive CD collection, a well-stocked bar and a res-taurant offering veg and meat dishes. The enthusiastic owners have mapped out great walking and bike trails (for free) through the Bvumba. They run transfers to the Manica-land Publicity Association.

huddles beneath the towering Troutbeck Massif. **Mangondoza Hotel** (☎ 0298-588; s/d US$3/5), 3km north of Nyanga village, has simple rooms with grubby bathrooms, but the bar is cheap and friendly. The **Friary** (☎ 0298-713; r US$2-5), 4km from the village, is run by Franciscan brothers and usually caters for church groups. However, other guests are welcome. No room rate is set, but you should leave a donation of between US$2 and US$5.

From Mutare, buses leave from the Sakubva Musika Bus Terminal between 6am and 1pm for Nyanga village. They stop close to the main gate of the national park and in the centre of Nyanga village. From the Mbare Musika Bus Terminal in Harare, buses leave daily between 6am and 7am for Nyanga village, via Juliasdale.

CHIMANIMANI VILLAGE
☎ 026
In the Manyika language, Chimanimani means 'a place that must be passed single file', referring to a narrow gorge on an ancient trade route between what is now Zimbabwe and Mozambique. At the end of a long winding road that twists and turns through hills and forests is the mountain village of Chimanimani. The village faces the silent Chimanimani ranges in the national park, a beautiful hiking area with caves, waterfalls and breathtaking views. The village is a good place to aim for if you want to go hiking in the national park.

Information
There are information noticeboards at the Chimanimani Hotel, Blue Moon Bar and Msasa Café. There's a post office on the street past the village green. For information on hiking in the national park, see the Chimanimani National Park section below.

Sights & Activities
There are some nice walks in the vicinity of the village. The **Eland Sanctuary** is around 7km from the village. Unfortunately, the elands, Africa's largest antelopes, have all disappeared, but you might see duikers, waterbucks, klipspringers and baboons. From the village, turn left at the T-junction north of the post office, then take the first right. Continue north for 5km to the base of **Nyamzure** (Pork Pie Hill). Another good

walk is to the slender **Bridal Veil Falls**, 6km from the village.

Sleeping & Eating
Heaven Lodge (☎ 2701; camp site per person US$0.40, dm US$1.20, d A-frame huts US$2.30) This backpackers, about 400m from the village on the road to the park, has a magnificent mountain view, but the huts are cramped and the dorm is noisy. There's a bar, sauna (US$0.30 per hour) and good meals (including vegetarian dishes).

Frog & Fern Cottages (☎ 2294; s/d US$8/16, s/d US$10/20 with breakfast) These attractive, thatched cottages are about 1.2km west of the village. They're comfortable and peaceful, and the staff are adorable. Guests share a lounge and self-catering kitchen.

Chimanimani Hotel (☎ 2511; camp site per person US$0.80, s/d US$11/15; 🏊) This faded colonial wonder, surrounded by gardens, a pool and casino, has a fine mountain view. It's in the village, and room rates include breakfast.

Msasa Café (mains around US$1; 🕑 8am-5pm Mon-Sat) This place is the best spot in the village for eating out. It offers a wide variety of meals and snacks from local *sadza* and stew to delicious Mexican tortillas.

Blue Moon Bar (🕑 7am-late Mon-Sat) You can enjoy a couple of drinks and chat with some locals at this laid-back backpackers bar.

There's a supermarket selling basic items, next to the post office, but it's best to stock up on relevant supplies before you head to Chimanimani.

Getting There & Away
To get here from Mutare see p901. From Chimanimani, buses run to Mutare between 5am and 5pm. For Masvingo, get off at Wengezi junction and transfer to a Masvingo bus.

CHIMANIMANI NATIONAL PARK
Chimanimani National Park is a hiker's paradise. To go hiking in **Chimanimani National Park** (admission US$10; 🕑 6am-6pm), 19km from Chimanimani village, you must sign in and pay park fees at **Mutekeswane Base Camp**. There's a road leading to the base camp, but after that the park is accessible only on foot.

From base camp, Bailey's Folly is the shortest and most popular route to the mountain hut (around three hours). Another option is the gentler Banana Grove Track. From the mountain hut, it's an easy 40-minute walk to **Skeleton Pass**, a former guerrilla route between Zimbabwe and Mozambique. Go in the late afternoon for an unsurpassed view into Mozambique's **Wizard's Valley**.

The highest point in the Chimanimani Range is the 2437m-high **Mt Binga** on the Mozambique border, a stiff three-hour climb from the hut. Carry plenty of water. The last stream for a fill-up is less than halfway between the hut and the summit. **Hadange River Track** is a good but challenging exit route that comes out near the Outward Bound School. But you'll need to walk back along the road to sign out at base camp. Near Outward Bound is **Tessa's Pool**, a lovely swimming hole and a great place to cool off. Tessa's Pool is used by Outward Bound (☎ 026-2935) for some of its courses, and at these times it's closed to the public. So phone in advance to find out when it's available.

Chimanimani Bushwalking Company (☎ 2932; www.bushwalkingco.com; Chimanimani village) at the filling station in Chimanimani village, offers hiking and camping trips in the park (one/five days per person US$45/240). Rates include a guide, porter, transport, meals, camping gear and park admission fees. You camp in caves.

Sleeping & Eating
At Chimanimani National Park you can either camp at **Mutekeswane Base Camp** (camp site per person US$0.20), which is at the park entrance, or stay in the **mountain hut** (per person US$0.50), which is a long and steep half-day walk from the base camp. The Bundi Valley has several caves and overhangs where you can camp for free.

Getting There & Away
There's not much traffic along the road to the park, and hitching is difficult. You could ask around the village to see if someone's heading there or you can walk.

From the village, take the Tilbury road for 9km to Charleswood. Turn left at the coffee plantation, and immediately take the right fork. The Outward Bound School turn-off is 5km further, from where it's another 5km to Mutekeswane Base Camp.

CENTRAL ZIMBABWE

GREAT ZIMBABWE NATIONAL MONUMENT
☎ 039

Twenty-six kilometres to the southeast of Masvingo is the **Great Zimbabwe National Monument** (☎ 039-62080; admission US$5; ☻ 6am-6pm), an intriguing archaeological site where a powerful ancient city once stood. Today all that remains are old stone ruins and winding corridors. The ancient stone structures, also known as Great Zimbabwe Ruins or simply Great Zimbabwe, are the largest in Africa south of the Egyptian pyramids. The ruins are famous for their dry-stone architecture; the stones are wedged and piled on top of each other without any mortar to hold them together.

It's believed the name Zimbabwe is derived from *dzimba dza mabwe*, meaning 'houses of stone' in Shona. The ancient city was the capital of a wealthy Shona society. It was abandoned in the 15th century when the area's resources could no longer sustain the growing population.

The **Hill Complex** was a series of royal and ritual enclosures. The **Valley Enclosures** feature 13th-century walls and daga hut platforms. They have yielded such archaeological finds as metal tools and the Great Zimbabwe birds – soapstone sculptures that became the national symbol. The elliptical **Great Enclosure**, nearly 100m across and 255m around, with its 10m-high **Conical Tower**, was used as a royal compound. The walls are 11m high and, in places, 5m thick.

The site museum houses the soapstone Great Zimbabwe birds, which were probably Rozwi dynasty totems, as well as porcelain and glass goods brought by Swahili traders. Within the site there's also a reconstructed **Karanga village** where you can watch blacksmiths at work, consult a traditional doctor and learn to play a *mbira*.

The ruins are at their most beautiful at sunrise and sunset when the stones glow warmly in the still air.

In Masvingo, the helpful **Masvingo Publicity Association** (☎ 62643; mgpa@mweb.co.zw; Robert Mugabe St; ☻ 8am-5pm Mon-Fri, 9-11am Sat) distributes maps, brochures and the monthly publication *Masvingo Great Zimbabwe Bulletin*.

Sleeping & Eating

There are a few budget places to stay not too far from Great Zimbabwe. Other accommodation options are in and around Masvingo.

Great Zimbabwe Campground (☎ 7055; camp site per person US$1, dm per person US$1.50, s/d rondavels US$3.50/7) This camp, run by National Museums and Monuments, is inside the main gate within sight of the Hill Complex. Watch out for the thieving baboons and monkeys.

Inn on Great Zimbabwe (☎ 64879; iogz@innsofzimbabwe.co.zw; s/d US$1.50/3, s/d US$10/16 with bathroom) Tranquil and on a wooded hill above Lake Mutirikwe, 6km east of Great Zimbabwe. There are comfortable budget rooms, and rates for the more expensive rooms in self-catering cottages include breakfast.

Pa-Nyanda Lodge (☎ 63412; nrg-gr@icon.co.zw; Beitbridge Rd; camp site per person US$3, camp site US$5/8 with evening meal/wildlife walk, s/d cottages with bathroom per person US$9) This lodge, on an ostrich farm 11km south of Masvingo, is great value. The lovely cottages are built in a traditional style, and rates include breakfast and dinner. There's an attractive restaurant and bar.

Backpackers Rest (☎ 65503; Dauth Bldg, Josiah Tongogara Ave; dm US$1, r with breakfast & shared bathroom US$2) This place in Masvingo has dark and noisy rooms but is convenient and friendly. The entrance is along Robertson St.

Hidden Garden Café (39 Hughes St; mains around US$1.50) This café, in Masvingo, serves coffee and tasty snacks. The menu includes sandwiches, burgers, waffles and cakes.

Self-caterers can shop at **OK supermarket** (Josiah Tongogara Ave).

Getting There & Away

Long-distance buses use the Mucheke Musika Bus Terminal, 1.5km southwest of Masvingo centre (all buses also stop in town). Several buses and minibuses run to and from Harare (US$3, five hours, daily) between 6am and 5pm. There are a number of daily bus and minibus services to Bulawayo (US$2, three hours) and Mutare (US$2, three hours).

To reach Great Zimbabwe from Masvingo, take a minibus (US$0.20) from Mucheke Musika and get off at the Great Zimbabwe turn-off, 2km from the ruins. You can also take a taxi (US$5, negotiable).

ANTELOPE PARK

Just outside **Gweru**, a town 154km northwest of Masvingo, is **Antelope Park** (☎ 054-

52173; antelopepark.co.zw; camp site per person US$5, s/d US$15/24, river tents US$40/75, lodges US$50/90; mains US$5; ☒) – the only place in southern Africa where you can swim with elephants and walk with lion cubs (they're quite big, mind you!). You can also go horse-riding among the park's antelopes, zebras and giraffes, fishing on a dam, visit a flock of well-fed vultures or simply relax by the pool. Activities start at US$15.

The park's main activity is a lion-breeding program. The adult lions are kept away from the camp in large enclosures, but you can watch the amusing antics of the baby cubs in their play area at the camp. Overlooking a small river, the camp has thatched brick buildings surrounded by a lush lawn. The restaurant serves buffet meals, and there's a bar selling soft drinks. Guests can bring their own alcohol. The comfortable river tents and lodges have bathrooms, and room rates include breakfast.

The signposted turn-off is 6km south of Gweru, a town 160km north of Bulawayo on the Harare road. It's another 6km to the park gate. Harare-Bulawayo buses pass through Gweru from where the park does pick-ups. It also organizes day-trips to Great Zimbabwe (US$55 per person, minimum six people).

WESTERN ZIMBABWE

BULAWAYO
☎ 09 / pop 1 million
Formerly called Gu-Bulawayo ('Killing Place') by the Ndebele, Zimbabwe's calm second city shows no signs of its violent past. Peaceful parks, low colonial buildings and tree-lined streets give Bulawayo a laid-back atmosphere. Wide avenues divide the city into neat symmetrical blocks.

Information
The efficient **Bulawayo Publicity Association** (☎ 60867; bpa@netconnect.co.zw; off Leopold Takawira Ave; ◷ 8.30am-4.45pm Mon-Fri, 8.30am-noon Sat), in the City Hall car park, has information on accommodation, transport, tours, activities and events in Bulawayo. It sells the detailed *Bulawayo Mobil Street Atlas* (US$0.60) and distributes *Bulawayo This Month*, which lists upcoming events and useful addresses. Note that some Bulawayo phone numbers have five digits and others six.

CENTRAL BULAWAYO

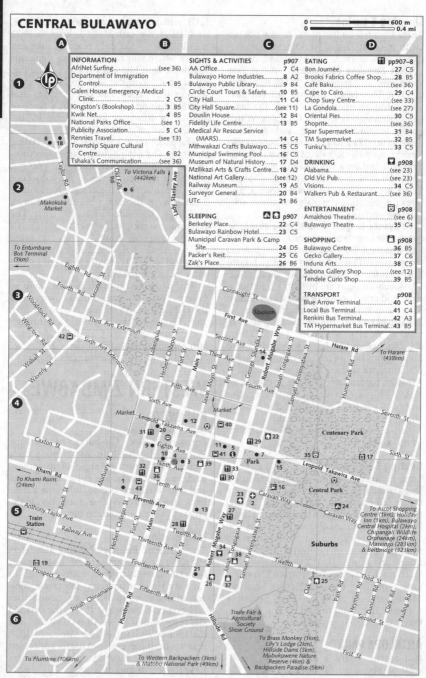

0 _____ 600 m
0 _____ 0.4 mi

INFORMATION
AfriNet Surfing....................(see 36)
Department of Immigration
   Control....................................1 B5
Galen House Emergency Medical
   Clinic......................................2 C5
Kingston's (Bookshop)...............3 B5
Kwik Net....................................4 B5
National Parks Office.............(see 1)
Publicity Association...................5 C4
Rennies Travel....................(see 13)
Township Square Cultural
   Centre....................................6 B2
Tshaka's Communication.......(see 36)

SIGHTS & ACTIVITIES   p907
AA Office....................................7 C4
Bulawayo Home Industries........8 A2
Bulawayo Public Library..............9 B4
Circle Court Tours & Safaris.....10 B5
City Hall..................................11 C4
City Hall Square....................(see 11)
Douslin House.........................12 B4
Fidelity Life Centre...................13 B5
Medical Air Rescue Service
   (MARS)................................14 C4
Mthwakazi Crafts Bulawayo.....15 C5
Municipal Swimming Pool........16 C5
Museum of Natural History.......17 D4
Mzilikazi Arts & Crafts Centre..18 A2
National Art Gallery.............(see 12)
Railway Museum......................19 A5
Surveyor General.....................20 B4
UTc..21 B6

SLEEPING   p907
Berkeley Place.........................22 C4
Bulawayo Rainbow Hotel..........23 C5
Municipal Caravan Park & Camp
   Site.......................................24 D5
Packer's Rest...........................25 C6
Zak's Place..............................26 B6

EATING   pp907–8
Bon Journée.............................27 C5
Brooks Fabrics Coffee Shop......28 B5
Café Baku...........................(see 36)
Cape to Cairo..........................29 C4
Chop Suey Centre................(see 33)
La Gondola..........................(see 27)
Oriental Pies............................30 C5
Shoprite..............................(see 36)
Spar Supermarket.....................31 B4
TM Supermarket.......................32 B5
Tunku's...................................33 C5

DRINKING   p908
Alabama..............................(see 23)
Old Vic Pub.........................(see 23)
Visions....................................34 C5
Walkers Pub & Restaurant....(see 36)

ENTERTAINMENT   p908
Amakhosi Theatre..................(see 6)
Bulawayo Theatre.....................35 C4

SHOPPING   p908
Bulawayo Centre......................36 B5
Gecko Gallery...........................37 C6
Induna Arts...............................38 C5
Sabona Gallery Shop............(see 12)
Tendele Curio Shop..................39 B5

TRANSPORT   p908
Blue Arrow Terminal.................40 C4
Local Bus Terminal....................41 C4
Renkini Bus Terminal.................42 A3
TM Hypermarket Bus Terminal..43 B5

The **National Parks Bulawayo Office** (☎ 63646; cnr Herbert Chitepo St & Tenth Ave; 🕑 8am-4pm Mon-Fri) takes accommodation bookings for Matobo National Park. For other parks you'll be better off booking at the Harare headquarters, where the system is more reliable.

Rennies Travel (☎ 880531; rtzim@africaonline.co .zw; Fidelity Life Centre, cnr Fife St & Eleventh Ave) can arrange international travel bookings.

The **main post office** (cnr Eighth Ave & Main St; 🕑 8am-5pm Mon-Fri, 8-11am Sat) has a poste restante service.

AfriNet Surfing (☎ 70324; Bulawayo Centre; US$0.30 per hr; 🕑 8am-5pm Mon-Fri, 8am-1pm Sat) has Internet access but is often full. **Tshaka's Communications** (☎ 66992; Bulawayo Centre; 🕑 8am-6pm) has a phone service. **Kwik Net** (cnr Ninth Ave & Main St; Internet US$0.30 per hr; 🕑 8am-10pm) has phone, fax and Internet facilities.

Sights

The **Museum of Natural History** (☎ 250045; Centenary Park; admission US$0.60; 🕑 9am-5pm) has displays on various wildlife, birds and bugs, and there's even a mounted elephant! There are also cultural, historical, geological and botanical displays.

Train enthusiasts must visit the **Railway Museum** (☎ 322452; cnr Prospect Ave & First St; admission US$0.10; 🕑 9am-4pm). It has an impressive collection of antique locomotives, rolling stock, Cecil Rhodes' extravagant carriage built in the 1890s and even a 'museum on wheels' – a 1904 passenger coach with original fittings.

The **National Art Gallery** (☎ 70721; Douslin House, cnr Main St & Leopold Takawira Ave; admission US$0.10; 🕑 9am-5pm Tue-Sun), in a beautiful hundred-year-old colonial building, has temporary and permanent exhibitions of contemporary Zimbabwean sculpture and paintings. There's also a souvenir shop, a café and studios where you can see artists at work.

Sleeping

Places listed below are all welcoming, clean and friendly. There are several less appealing budget hotels in the city centre.

Packer's Rest (☎ 251111; packers@mweb.co.zw; 1 Oak Ave, Suburbs; camp site per person US$3, dm per person US$4, s/d US$8/12; 🖳) Convenient to the city, this welcoming backpackers offers phone and Internet access, free bus and train station transfers, a self-catering kitchen and bike hire (US$2 per day). The entrance is off Twelfth Ave.

Backpackers Paradise (☎ 246481; allen@back packersparadise.org; 11 Inverleith Dr, Burnside; camp site per person US$2, dm per person US$3, s/d US$4/8; 🖳) On the outskirts of the city is this large property in a quiet bushland setting. The dorm opens on to a wide sunny balcony overlooking the garden. It's popular with travellers, and there's a sauna, pool, self-catering kitchen and video lounge.

Berkeley Place (☎ 67701; berkeley@ecoweb.co.zw; 71 Josiah Tongogara St; tw US$9) Right in the centre is this surprisingly calm hotel. The rooms with bathroom open off an interior courtyard, and there's a well-stocked craft shop.

Zak's Place (☎ 881130; 129 Robert Mugabe Way; d US$8) This tidy and central hotel has an attractive paved courtyard bar and *braai* area. Rooms overlooking the road are noisy, so request one on the courtyard side.

Western Backpackers (☎ 244100; tourzim@telconet .co.zw; 2 Dorset Rd, Hillside; s/d chalets US$5/9; 🖳) There's a wide lawn and a poolside bar at this place. It also offers tours to Great Zimbabwe, Matobo, Hwange and Victoria Falls.

Lily's Lodge (☎ 245356; nyararai@excite.com; 3 Masefield Rd, Malindela; s/d US$5/10) This large house has a local atmosphere. Lily organizes traditional evenings with food and dancing for guests.

Municipal Caravan Park & Camp Site (☎ 233851; Caravan Way, Central Park; camp site per person US$1 plus US$1, caravan per person US$2, s/d chalets US$2/3) In a corner of Central Park, a 10-minute walk from the centre. Take a taxi here after dark.

Eating

There's a nice choice of cafés and restaurants in the city.

La Gondola (☎ 62986; 105 Robert Mugabe Way; mains around US$2) The Italian cuisine is authentic in this restaurant with its 1970s décor, dim interior, mirror-lined walls, red carpet and vinyl chairs.

Brooks Fabrics Coffee Shop (☎ 66373; Fife St; snacks from US$1) You'll find good lattes and cappuccinos, irresistible cakes and filling snacks at this popular café in a fabric shop.

Bonne Journée (☎ 64839; Robert Mugabe Way, btwn Tenth & Eleventh Aves; mains US$2) Specialising in cappuccinos and ice cream, this popular choice also serves steaks, excellent peri-peri chicken and snacks.

Café Baku (☎ 883809; Bulawayo Centre, Main St; snacks from US$1) This small, trendy café serves coffee, cakes and sandwiches. It's open until late.

ZIMBABWE

Oriental Pies (☎ 72567; 85B George Silundika St; snacks & mains from US$0.50) The pies here are great. The shop also serves vegetable samosas, burgers and curries.

Cape to Cairo (☎ 72387; 77 Robert Mugabe Way; mains US$2.50) This colonial-theme restaurant and bar serves game dishes, steaks and seafood.

Tunku's and **Chop Suey Centre** (☎ 72828; Eighth Ave, btwn Robert Mugabe Way & George Silundika St; US$1-2) These neighbouring takeaways serve Chinese dishes.

There are several supermarkets in the city centre, including **Shoprite** (Bulawayo Centre, Main St). For cheap fruit and vegetables, the best place is Makokoba Market, northwest of central Bulawayo, or the **street market** (cnr Robert Mugabe Way & Eighth Ave) behind the Publicity Association.

Drinking & Entertainment

Amakhosi Theatre (☎ 62652; Township Square Cultural Centre, Basch St; admission US$1.50) This African theatre, off the Old Falls Rd, stages traditional and contemporary theatre, dance and music productions. It also organizes the annual Inxusa Festival, a traditional folk culture festival, around June and July.

Most Bulawayo pubs and clubs are fairly laid-back. **Walkers Pub & Restaurant** (☎ 69527; Bulawayo Centre, Main St) and the **Brass Monkey** (☎ 880495; Zonk'Izizwe Centre, Hillside Rd) are good pubs for a drink.

The **Old Vic Pub** (☎ 881273; Bulawayo Rainbow Hotel) has an Anglo-Zimbabwean atmosphere, and the Alabama, open Wednesday to Sunday at the same place, is a pleasant, casual bar with live jazz most evenings. **Visions** (Robert Mugabe Way) is a nightclub playing R&B and house music.

Shopping

Bulawayo is a good place to go shopping for curios. There are several art and craft galleries selling local jewellery, textiles, carvings, paintings and artefacts include: **Tendele Curio Shop** (☎ 52391; 90 Fife St), **Induna Arts** (☎ 69179; 121 Josiah Tongogara St) and the **Gecko Gallery** (☎ 72004; 129 Josiah Tongogara St).

Getting There & Away

The long-distance bus terminal at **Renkini Bus Terminal** (Sixth Ave Extension), opposite the Mzilikazi police station, is where buses depart for Harare, Masvingo, Beitbridge, Mutare and Kariba. There are several buses

daily from 6am, including **Kukura Kurerwa** (☎ 78806) buses to Harare, Masvingo and Mutare, and Tenda buses to Mutare (US$4, six hours). Buses to Victoria Falls via Hwange and Dete Crossroads leave daily from the Entumbane Bus Terminal near Luveve Rd, in the northwestern suburbs.

Blue Arrow (☎ 65548; Unifreight House, 73A Fife St) has daily services at 8am to Harare (US$10, six hours) via Gweru.

Buses also depart Bulawayo for South Africa and Botswana (see p892).

You can make train reservations at the **train station ticket office** (☎ 322210; Railway Ave; ☼ 7am-9pm Mon-Fri, 7am-2pm Sat & Sun). Trains depart nightly at 8pm for Harare (US$4/2/2 in sleeper/standard/economy class) and 7pm for Victoria Falls (US$4/3/1 in 1st/ 2nd/economy class).

Getting Around

For suburban buses, the **bus terminal** (Eighth Ave, btwn Robert Mugabe Way & George Silundika St) serves the northern, eastern and southern suburbs, and the **TM Hypermarket bus terminal** (Tenth Ave, btwn Fort & Herbert Chitepo Sts) serves the high-density western and southwestern suburbs.

Most Bulawayo taxis are metered, but for various reasons drivers don't necessarily use them, so make sure you negotiate the price. **Rixi Taxi** (☎ 231933) and **Skyork's Taxi** (☎ 72454) are reliable companies.

MATOBO NATIONAL PARK

Just 33km south of Bulawayo, **Matobo National Park** (☎ 083-8258; admission US$15; ☼ 6am-6pm) is a wild and beautiful landscape of weathered boulders balanced precariously on top of each other. Amid the jumbled boulders, rainbow lizards lie lazily in the sun and dassies (small fluffy rock-dwelling animals also known as hyrax) dart around busily. The best time to see the park is in the late afternoon when the lichen-covered rocks take on a soft golden glow. In the western corner of the park is **Whovi Game Park**, a small wildlife reserve where you can see white and black rhinos.

Dotted around the park are ancient rock paintings and old grain bins, where Lobengula's warriors once stored their provisions. Some hidden niches still shelter clay ovens that were used as iron smelters in making the infamous *assegais* (spears) to be used against the growing colonial hordes.

About 2km from the northwest entrance are the remains of Cecil Rhodes' rail terminus. When he died on 26 March 1902, his body was buried in the park, as he'd requested, at **Malindidzimu** (place of benevolent spirits), which Rhodes had called 'View of the World'.

From the Maleme Dam camp, it's an easy 7km walk to **Nswatugi Cave**, which has well-preserved rock paintings. Another easy walk is to **Pomongwe Cave**, where an early attempt to preserve the paintings resulted in their near obliteration. An onsite museum offers background information.

Activities
Several safari operators and some backpackers hostels offer walking and driving excursions to Matobo National Park and Whovi Game Park (day-trip/overnight from US$50/100). Safari operators offering day-trips or overnight trips to Matobo include: **Black Rhino Safaris** (☎ 09-241662; www .blackrhinosafaris.com), **Circle Court Tours & Safaris** (☎ 09-881309; www.cirtours.co.zw) and **Khangela Safaris** (☎ 09-289733; www.khangela.com).

Adventure Trails (☎ 09-242790; adventuretrails2000@ hotmail.com) offers mountain biking tours – an ideal way to explore Matobo (day trip US$60, two/three-day trip US$110/150). Rates include transfers to/from Bulawayo, accommodation and meals.

Sleeping & Eating
Matobo National Park (camp site per person US$0.10, tw chalets US$1, tw lodges US$2) There are several camp sites in the park, and there are chalets and lodges at Maleme Dam. You must book in advance at the parks office in Bulawayo (see p907).

Masiye Camp (☎ 09-60727; masiyeca@telconet .co.zw; village stay per person US$0.80, dm US$0.80, d chalet US$1.20, lodge US$5) This camp, just outside the southern boundary, offers traditional village stays, which include village meals. There's also a self-catering cottage and lodge overlooking a lovely dam. The surrounding bush has ancient rock paintings and great hiking trails. Profits fund education and vocational training for children and young people orphaned by AIDS.

Getting There & Away
Visiting Matobo is difficult without a vehicle, and hitching can be slow. You can take the Kezi bus from Renkini bus terminal in Bulawayo and get off at one of the three Matobo turn-offs. The easiest option is to take a tour with a safari company from Bulawayo.

HWANGE NATIONAL PARK
Hwange National Park (admission US$15 per day; ⊙ 6am-6pm) is particularly popular because it's the one of the easiest parks to reach and wildlife viewing is good, especially during the dry season (September and October), when animals congregate near waterholes. A good viewing spot is at **Nyamandhlovu Pan**, 10km from Main Camp. To really immerse yourself in the park's wild environment, try a walking safari in the more remote parts of the park. Two-hour walking safaris (US$30 per person) with armed guards to Sedina Pan can be organized at Hwange Main Camp, and to Mandavu Dam from Sinamatella Camp.

The main National Parks camps are **Main Camp**, **Sinamatella** and **Robins Camp** (camp sites per person US$1, two-/four-bed lodges US$2/4, two-/four-bed cottages US$1.50/3, tw chalets US$1-2). Each camp has a small shop, bar and restaurant.

Local buses stop at Safari Crossroads, 23km from the Main Camp park entrance (6km from Main Camp). From here you'll have to hitch to Hwange Main Camp, and you could be in for a long wait. The easiest way to see the park without your own transport is to book a trip with a safari company from Bulawayo or Victoria Falls. **Baobab Safaris** (☎ 42158; www.untamed-africa.com; Victoria Falls), **Khangela Safaris** (☎ 09-289733; www .khangela.com; Bulawayo) and **Leon Varley Walking Safaris** (☎ 45828; backpack@africaonline.co.zw; Victoria Falls) offer walking safaris in Hwange National Park (from US$100 per day). **Reedbuck Safaris** (☎ 011-407119; reedbucksafaris@ hotmail.com; Victoria Falls) operates wildlife drives (from US$85). At the park itself, **United Touring Company** (UTC; ☎ 018-393; fax 367; Hwange Safari

---

WALKING SAFARIS

Watching wildlife from a vehicle is pretty awesome, but watching it on foot – where you might come face to face with a herd of elephants or a pride of lions – is even better. When you're surrounded by the bush, with your senses sharpened against its smells and sounds, you slowly become part of it.

Lodge) offers wildlife drives from Hwange Main Camp (half/full day US$25/50).

VICTORIA FALLS

☎ 013 / pop 17,000

At Victoria Falls, the Zambezi River rushes over a sheer cliff almost 2km wide and plummets into the narrow Batoka Gorge, 100m below. When the water level is low the falls will sprinkle you with a fine spray, but when the Zambezi is in flood they will drench you in a torrential deluge, as this awe-inspiring waterfall sends clouds of spray up to 500m into the air. Below the falls, the Zambezi is renowned for its whitewater-rafting and above the falls for gentler canoeing. The nearby town, also called Victoria Falls, is a plethora of hotels, backpackers hostels, tour operators, restaurants and bars. You might be broke by the time you leave, but this is one place where you're guaranteed not to run out of things to do.

Information

The **Victoria Falls Publicity Association** (☎ 44202; vfpa@mweb.co.zw; 412 Park Way; ❧ 8.30am-4.30pm Mon-Fri & 8.30am-1pm Sat) gives out details of local accommodation and tour and activity providers and sells maps of Victoria Falls and the region. **Backpackers Bazaar** (☎ 45828; backpack@africaonline.co.zw; off Park Way; ❧ 8am-5pm Mon-Fri, 8am-4pm Sat & Sun) is a dynamic booking agency for activities, accommodation and tours in Victoria Falls and Livingstone (Zambia), as well as onward regional travel and safaris. **Travel Junction** (☎ 41480; junction@mweb.co.zw; Landela Centre, Livingstone Way; ❧ 8am-5pm Mon-Fri, 8am-4pm Sat & Sun) also books local activities, as well as accommodation and travel throughout the southern Africa region.

The post office and banks (see p915) are on Livingstone Way. There are shops, tour and activity operators, Internet centres and eateries along Park Way. **Telco** (☎ 43441; Phumula Centre; ❧ 8am-6pm; Internet US$1 per hr) has a fast connection, but most of the machines are out of order. You can surf the Web free of charge if you book an activity with **Shearwater Adventures** (☎ 45806; Sopers Arcade, Park Way; Internet US$1.20 per hr).

Raincoat & Camping Equipment Hire Services (☎ 44528; 307 Park Way) will come in handy if you're viewing the falls during high water when the spray is phenomenal.

Dangers & Annoyances

The street money-changers are insistent, but don't be tempted to change money with them. You'll usually be ripped off or arrested. Beware of muggers if you're walking in isolated areas.

Sights

The best place to see the falls is from **Victoria Falls National Park** (☎ 44310; admission US$20; ❧ 6am-6pm) just before the border post. You can also see them from across the border on the Zambian side (see p815). The falls are most visible during the low water period (September to November) but are magnificent at any time. During a full moon the park remains open after 6pm (admission US$40), which gives you the chance to see a magical lunar rainbow. There are fantastic views of the falls all the way along the sealed path that leads from the **Livingstone Statue** at the western end of the falls through lush rainforest, past **Cataract View** to **Danger Point**. Wrap your valuables in plastic, and be sure your camera equipment is protected.

The **Zambezi National Park** (admission US$10; ❧ 6am-6.30pm), 5km from town along the Zambezi River, has a good variety of wildlife, including elephants, lions, antelopes, zebras, buffalos and giraffes. Some Victoria Falls operators run wildlife drives and horse safaris here.

Victoria Falls Aquarium (☎ 40101; Livingstone Way; admission US$5; ❧ 9.30am-5.30pm) is home to around 70 fish species from the Zambezi, including electric cat fish, eels and tiger fish. The aquarium is small but very nicely presented with a high roof, plants and 25 tanks. There's a 200,000-litre tank waiting for a Zambezi shark, a species found close to the river mouth.

Falls Craft Village (☎ 44309; Adam Stander Dr; admission US$8; ❧ 8am-5pm) has a model traditional village that you can walk around. The **Zambezi Nature Sanctuary** (☎ 44485; Park Way; admission US$4; ❧ 8am-5pm) is primarily a crocodile farm but also has lion and leopard enclosures and an aviary (lion and croc feeding times are around 4pm). There's also a small café and curio shop.

Activities

There's a wide choice of exhilarating adventure activities (as well as more sedate

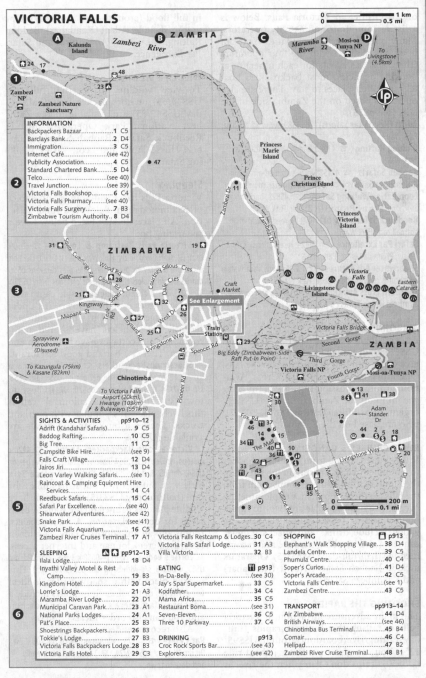

VICTORIA FALLS

0 _____ 1 km
0 _____ 0.5 mi

INFORMATION
Backpackers Bazaar.................1	C5
Barclays Bank.....................2	D4
Immigration.......................3	C5
Internet Café.................(see 42)	
Publicity Association.............4	C5
Standard Chartered Bank..........5	D4
Telco..........................(see 40)	
Travel Junction................(see 39)	
Victoria Falls Bookshop..........6	C4
Victoria Falls Pharmacy.......(see 40)	
Victoria Falls Surgery............7	B3
Zimbabwe Tourism Authority.. 8	D4

SIGHTS & ACTIVITIES   pp910–12
Adrift (Kandahar Safaris)..............9	C5
Baddog Rafting...................10	C5
Big Tree........................11	C2
Campsite Bike Hire............(see 9)	
Falls Craft Village................12	D4
Jairos Jiri........................13	D4
Leon Varley Walking Safaris.....(see 1)	
Raincoat & Camping Equipment Hire	
Services.......................14	C4
Reedbuck Safaris................15	C4
Safari Par Excellence...........(see 40)	
Shearwater Adventures.......(see 42)	
Snake Park..................(see 41)	
Victoria Falls Aquarium..........16	C5
Zambezi River Cruises Terminal.. 17	A1

SLEEPING   pp912–13
Ilala Lodge......................18	D4
Inyathi Valley Motel & Rest	
Camp.........................19	B3
Kingdom Hotel..................20	D4
Lorrie's Lodge...................21	A3
Maramba River Lodge............22	D1
Municipal Caravan Park..........23	A1
National Parks Lodges............24	A1
Pat's Place......................25	B3
Shoestrings Backpackers.........26	B3
Tokkie's Lodge..................27	B3
Victoria Falls Backpackers Lodge..28	B3
Victoria Falls Hotel..............29	C3

Victoria Falls Restcamp & Lodges..30	C4
Victoria Falls Safari Lodge.......31	A3
Villa Victoria....................32	B3

EATING   p913
In-Da-Belly..................(see 30)	
Jay's Spar Supermarket..........33	C4
Kodfather......................34	C4
Mama Africa....................35	C5
Restaurant Boma.............(see 31)	
Seven-Eleven...................36	C5
Three 10 Parkway...............37	C4

DRINKING   p913
Croc Rock Sports Bar..........(see 43)	
Explorers....................(see 42)	

SHOPPING   p913
Elephant's Walk Shopping Village.... 38	D4
Landela Centre..................39	C5
Phumula Centre.................40	C4
Soper's Curios..................41	D4
Soper's Arcade..................42	C5
Victoria Falls Centre...........(see 1)	
Zambezi Centre.................43	C5

TRANSPORT   pp913–14
Air Zimbabwe...................44	D4
British Airways...............(see 46)	
Chinotimba Bus Terminal.........45	B4
Comair........................46	C4
Helipad.......................47	B2
Zambezi River Cruise Terminal...48	B1

ones) on offer in Victoria Falls. Below is a list of some tour and activity operators. Many offer a variety of activities. You can book either direct with the tour operators (they all act as agents for each other) or at booking agencies, most backpackers hostels and other places to stay. There are also operators based on the Zambia side of the falls (see p815).

Adrift (Kandahar Safaris) (☎ 3589; www.adrift.co.nz; Park Way)

Baddog Rafting (☎ 41082; baddog@telcovic.co.zw; Park Way)

Baobab Safaris (☎ 42158; www.untamed-africa.com)

Kalembeza Safaris (☎ 45938; kalembeza@mweb.co.zw)

Leon Varley Walking Safaris (☎ 45828; backpack@ africaonline.co.zw; Backpackers Bazaar, Park Way)

Reedbuck Safaris (☎ 011-407119; reedbucksafaris@ hotmail.com; Park Way)

Safari Par Excellence (☎ 44424; reservations@safpar .co.zw; Phumula Centre, Park Way)

Shearwater Adventures (☎ 45806; www.shearwater adventures.com; Sopers Arcade, Park Way)

Southern Cross Aviation (☎ 44018; sca@zol.co.zw)

Zambezi Horse Trails (☎ 42054; www.horsesafari.co.zw)

AIRBORNE ACTIVITIES
A scenic flight over the falls (25/40 minutes US$55/80) in a small fixed-wing aircraft will give you a different perspective on the falls. Operators include Southern Cross Aviation. Another possibility is an 111m bungee jump off the Zambezi Bridge (US$95), organized by **African Extreme** (☎ 260-3-324231) who are based on the Zambian side.

RIVER CRUISES & CANOEING
River cruises lasting from a couple of hours to a number of days are run on the stretch of the Zambezi a few kilometres upstream from the falls (so there's no chance of plummeting over!). The most popular are two- to three-hour sunset or booze cruises (US$20–30), which include drinks and snacks. Longer canoeing and kayaking trips are also recommended (half/full-day US$65/75). Operators include Baobab Safaris, Adrift (Kandahar) and Kalambeza Safaris.

SHOOTING THE RAPIDS
The main adventure attraction in Victoria Falls is rafting the Zambezi rapids (full-day rafting/riverboarding around US$95/125). You can also try a faster jetboat ride (US$50). Trips don't run when the river is

in full flood (around April and May). Operators include: Adrift (Kandahar), Baddog Rafting, Shearwater Adventures and Safari Par Excellence.

WILDLIFE VIEWING
To view wildlife, drives (half/full day US$30/65) or horseback safaris (half/full day US$45/85) are available in the Zambezi National Park Operators include Reedbuck Safaris, Baobab Safaris, Zambezi Horse Trails and Leon Varley Walking Safaris.

Sleeping
Victoria Falls has a wide range and choice of accommodation. Below is a small selection. All places to stay listed below have a swimming pool.

Victoria Falls Restcamp & Lodges (☎ 40509; campsite@africaonline.zw; Park Way & West Dr intersection; camp site & caravans per person US$5 plus caravans US$6, dm US$5, s/d chalets US$15/20, s/d cottages from US$20/30; ⊠) This clean, spacious, safe camp with lawn and trees is right in town. It's under new management and has been renovated recently. The chalets have shared bathroom, and the cottages have bathroom and kitchen. There's a bar and good restaurant.

Shoestrings Backpackers (☎ 40167; sstring@mweb .co.zw; 12 West Dr; camp site per person US$3, dm US$5, s/d US$7/14, d with bathroom US$20; ⊠) Close to town surrounded by a colourful wall is this lively place. It's popular with overland trucks. There's a busy bar and meals are available (US$2).

Victoria Falls Backpackers Lodge (☎ 42209; matopo@mweb.co.zw; 357 Gibson Rd; camp site per person US$4, dm US$8, d US$20; 🖳 ⊠) This place is a little way out of town but it has bikes for hire (half/full day US$3/5). The rooms have wildlife pictures painted on the walls. A calm place for quiet relaxation. A-frame chalets, rooms and an attic dorm. There's a kitchen for self-caterers, lounge and Internet access.

Lorrie's Lodge (☎ 011-406584; 397 Reynard Rd; dm US$5, d US$18, s/d with bathroom US$15/20; ⊠) This relaxed place with a shady garden is ideal for couples or families. Room rates include a light breakfast, there's a self-catering kitchen and you can also order meals (US$3).

Also recommended:

Pat's Place (☎ 44375; twiga@telcovic.co.zw; 208 West Dr; dm US$6, s/d US$12/24; ⊠) Cramped but friendly and close to town.

Tokkie's Lodge (☎ 43306; tokkie@mweb.co.zw; 224 Reynard Rd; camp site per person US$3, dm US$8, s/d US$15/20; 🛪) Has a shady garden and is just a 15-minute walk away from town.

Villa Victoria (☎ 44386; villavic@telcovic.co.zw; 165 Courteney Selous Cres; s/d cottage from US$10/20; 🛪) A 10-minute walk from town with rooms in a house and cottage (self-catering kitchens).

Eating

In-Da-Belly (at Victoria Falls Restcamp & Lodges; mains US$2-4) Try the filled pita bread specialities at this large open-thatched restaurant. It's in the relaxed, quiet Restcamp grounds.

Ilala Lodge (☎ 44737; 411 Livingstone Way; mains US$3-4) Sample African wildlife dishes, including crocodile, antelope and ostrich, at this restaurant overlooking the bush.

Three 10 Parkway (☎ 43468; 310 Park Way; mains US$2-4) This relaxed café serves tasty snacks and mains.

At the **Kingdom Hotel** (cnr Livingstone Way & Mallet Dr), Panarottis serves Italian dishes (US$4), Spur Steak Ranches serves burgers, steaks and enchiladas (US$3), and White Waters Restaurant has buffet dinners (US$2.50).

Mama Africa (☎ 091-380430; behind the Landela Centre; mains US$5; 🕙 6pm-9pm) This restaurant exudes a trendy ethnic atmosphere and serves steak and local dishes on a wide veranda encircled by a small garden.

Boma (☎ 43201; Victoria Falls Safari Lodge, Squire Cummings Rd; mains US$2-4, buffet dinner US$9) You can have an African buffet or choose from the menu at this restaurant. Ndebele singers and dancers will entertain you.

For self-catering, there's a well-stocked **Jay's Spar Supermarket** (Clark Rd) and a **Seven-Eleven** (off Park Way, opp the Phumula Centre).

The **Kodfather** (☎ 43416; 307 Park Way; mains US$1.50-3) is a takeaway that serves pizza, barbecued chicken and burgers.

Drinking & Entertainment

Victoria Falls is a party town where tourists gather in busy pubs nightly to swap adventure stories.

The **Grid Bar** (Bulawayo Rd; 🕙 nightly) This is a relaxed shabeen-style open-air bar 10km out of town on the road to Bulawayo. You can bring your own meat to put on the *braai*. Go with a local friend.

Shoestrings Bar (at Shoestrings Backpackers; 🕙 nightly) For the backpackers scene, a laid-back backpackers' bar.

Explorers (Sopers Arcade, Park Way; 🕙 nightly) This bar is where you can meet up with people unwinding after a day's rafting.

Croc Rock (Zambezi Centre; 🕙 nightly) This is where the locals come. It's a bit sleazy but has a good variety of music.

Mama Africa (see Eating) has live music every night (usually reggae).

Falls Craft Village (☎ 44309; Adam Stander Dr; admission US$8) There's a dance show featuring traditional dances from Zimbabwe and neighbouring countries every night at this model African village.

Shopping

The craft market at the end of Adam Stander Dr has batiks, mats, wooden carvings and stone sculptures. The Jairos Jiri shop nearby has bags, wall hangings, crafts and jewellery made by disabled people. There are expensive craft shops in the **Elephants Walk complex** (Adam Stander Dr) and in the **Landela Centre** (Livingstone Way).

Getting There & Away

Kukura Kurerwa and other buses for Hwange, Bulawayo (US$5, five hours) and Harare (US$10, 11 hours) depart the **Chinotimba Bus Terminal** (Pioneer Rd, Chinotimba) near the market.

Overnight trains to Bulawayo leave the **train station** (🕙 7am-noon & 2-4pm Mon-Fri, 7am-noon Sat & Sun) at 6.30pm daily (US$4/3/1 in 1st/2nd/economy class).

If you're heading to Botswana, catch a taxi to the border (US$30) then take a local minibus to Maun. The most straightforward route from Zimbabwe to Namibia is between Victoria Falls and the Caprivi Strip via Botswana. Intercape runs buses to Windhoek (Namibia), departing from Park Way, and Zimbabwe Travel offers a train/bus package between Victoria Falls

---

DAY VISA TO ZAMBIA

If you decide to pop over to Zambia for the day you'll need a Zambian day visa (US$10). You don't need another visa to return to Zimbabwe as long as you don't stay overnight. It's essential that you tell the border officials you're only going on a day visit, however, or they might stamp you out for good!

and Johannesburg (South Africa; see p892). To get to the Zambian border post catch a taxi from town (US$2).

It's 11km from the Zambian border post to the town of Livingstone. Minibuses cost US$0.50 and taxis cost between US$3 and US$4. From Livingstone, buses head to Lusaka and other Zambian towns (see p819 for details).

Getting Around

Taxis stop by the information office on Park Way. You can hire bikes from **Camp Site Bike Hire** (Park Way; half/full day US$5/10 negotiable).

ZIMBABWE DIRECTORY

ACCOMMODATION

Zimbabwe has a well-developed tourism infrastructure with a good choice of budget accommodation from camping to backpackers' hostels and cheap hotels. Reservations for accommodation in Zimbabwe's national parks can be made through the national parks head office in Harare, and for Matobo National Park you can book at the Bulawayo office (see p893 for Harare and p907 for Bulawayo).

ACTIVITIES

Most activities centre around the country's natural highlights; hiking in the cool Eastern highlands and Chimanimani National Park, horse-riding, wildlife-viewing in national parks, canoeing safaris on the lower Zambezi River, boating and housebuilding on Lake Kariba and an enormous range of activities on offer at Victoria Falls.

DANGERS & ANNOYANCES

Harare has become notorious for muggings and theft, particularly in the suburb and bus station of Mbare. Be on your guard, and don't walk anywhere at night. Be careful in other towns and cities, too. Be discrete with your cash and other belongings. Leave your valuables in a safe at your accommodation. Use only official taxis, and insist on being dropped right at your door.

Don't change your money on the street. Some money changers might dob you in to the cops, and others will probably rip you off. For trustworthy money-changers, seek reliable local advice.

EMBASSIES & CONSULATES

The following embassies, consulates and high commissions are based in Harare. Most embassies are located along Samora Machel Ave, in the area just north of Harare Gardens and north of Josiah Tongogara Ave, in the vicinity of Second St.

Australia (☎ 253661; www.zimbabwe.gov.au; 29 Mazowe St)
Botswana (☎ 729551; 22 Phillips Ave)
Canada (☎ 252181; 45 Baines Ave)
France (☎ 703216; First Bank Bldg, 74-76 Samora Machel Ave)
Germany (☎ 308655; 2 Ceres Rd)
Malawi (☎ 798584; 9 & 11 Duthie Rd, Alexandra Park)
Mozambique (☎ 253871; 152 Herbert Chitepo Ave)
Namibia (☎ 885841; 69 Borrowdale Rd)
South Africa (☎ 753147; sahcomm@internet.co.zw; 7 Elcombe Ave)
UK (☎ 772990; 7th fl, Corner House, cnr Leopold Takawira St & Samora Machel Ave)
USA (☎ 250594; Arax House, 172 Herbert Chitepo Ave)
Zambia (☎ 773777; fax 773782; 6th fl, Zambia House, 48 Union Ave)

In Africa, Zimbabwe has representation in Botswana, Kenya, Malawi, Mozambique, Namibia, South Africa, Tanzania and Zambia.

FESTIVALS & EVENTS

See p895 for information about the Harare International Festival of Arts.

GAY & LESBIAN TRAVELLERS

You don't want to publicise the fact you're gay since, as well as a lot of other groups and individuals, President Mugabe dislikes gay men. Not surprisingly, it's illegal to be gay in Zimbabwe. As for lesbians, the powers that be pretend they don't exist. Ironically, Zimbabwe has quite a thriving gay and lesbian community, especially in Harare where there's even an annual drag queen pageant.
Gays and Lesbians of Zimbabwe (GALZ; ☎ 04-741736; galz@mweb.co.zw; 35 Coenbrander Rd, Milton Pk, Harare).

HOLIDAYS

As well as religious holidays listed in the Africa Directory chapter (p1003) the principal public holidays in Zimbabwe are:
1 January New Year's Day
18 April Independence Day
1 May Workers' Day
25 May Africa Day
11 August Heroes' Day

12 August Defence Forces' Day
22 December National Unity Day
26 December Boxing Day

INTERNET ACCESS
There are Internet centres in all the main cities and towns. Internet access is cheap (US$0.50 to US$1 per hour), although connections can be slow.

LEGAL MATTERS
In Zimbabwe, anything that's in short supply (the list is long) can usually be found on the black market. Quite often there's little choice, eg when changing money. Needless to say, it's an offence to trade on the black market, so make sure you don't get caught. One sure-fire way to get caught is to change money on the street. (See the boxed text below.)

MEDIA
The main print media cover national and international news. The *Financial Gazette* and the *Zimbabwe Independent* are weekly business papers. Independent newspapers include the *Daily News*, the weekly *Standard* and the weekly *Mirror*. The *Herald* in Harare and the *Chronicle* in Bulawayo are government-controlled papers. Some major international newspapers and magazines are available in bookshops. The Zimbabwe Broadcasting Corporation oversees the country's four radio and two TV stations. They broadcast national news (mainly government propaganda), international news and music programs in English, Shona and Ndebele.

MONEY
The unit of currency is the Zimbabwe dollar (ZW$). Although we quote prices in US dollars, you should always pay in Zimbabwe dollars except for visa fees at borders, national park entry fees, and some activity and safari operators who require payment in a major hard currency, usually US dollars.

Exchanging Money
The official bank rates listed below are what you'll get for your dollars or euros if you use a credit card and travellers cheques. The official rate at the time of research was US$1 to ZW$55, but it was officially devalued shortly after to US$1 to ZW$824. The parallel market rate constantly fluctuates,

but at the time of research US$1 was about ZW$1300 and it remained the same after the official devaluation. Despite this rate, the biggest note available is ZW$500. Prices in this book are based on the parallel rate (US$1=ZW$1300) at the time of research.

Because of the low exchange rate, using ATMs is not recommended.

POST & TELEPHONE
Poste restante services are available in all cities and larger towns, but the post offices at Harare and Bulawayo are the most efficient. An air mail letter to Europe and other overseas destinations costs less than US$0.10.

The best place to make calls is a communications bureau, which you'll find in most towns and cities. Internet centres often offer phone and fax services as well. Public phone booths are often vandalised or out of order. International calls from Zimbabwe cost less than US$1 per minute to anywhere in the world. Drop the initial 0 on the area code if calling from outside Zimbabwe.

TOURIST INFORMATION
The **Zimbabwe Tourism Authority** (Map p896; ☎ 758712; www.zimbabwetourism.co.zw; 1 Union Ave; ☻ 8am-4.30pm Mon-Fri) has general tourist information. There are Publicity Associations in Harare, Bulawayo, Victoria Falls, Kariba, Masvingo and Nyanga. Some are very efficient, helpful and have useful information, brochures and advice, but others just distribute a few maps and brochures.

CHANGING MONEY

In Zimbabwe, everyone changes money on the black market, more commonly called the 'parallel market'. If you change in banks you'll get the official rate and your money won't go far. So forget about travellers cheques, stow away your credit card and bring hard currency. Unhelpfully, at the time of research, the government had closed all bureaux de change, but whatever you do, don't change on the street. The people at your hostel, tour operators or other travellers can explain the ropes. The money situation is liable to change so get the latest update when you arrive. And be careful carrying that extra cash around.

VISAS

With a few exceptions, visas are required by nationals of all countries. They can be obtained at your point of entry. Single-entry/double-entry visas cost US$30/45 and multiple-entry visas (valid for six months) cost US$55, but are only issued at Zimbabwean diplomatic missions. The following neighbouring countries have Zimbabwe representation: Botswana, Malawi, Mozambique, South Africa and Zambia. British citizens pay US$55/70 for single/ double entry.

Visa Extensions

All tourist visas can be extended by one month, but three times is the maximum. Extensions cost US$30 and can be obtained at any office of the Department of Immigration Control, but you're more likely to be successful in **Harare Department of Immigration Control** (Map p896; ☎ 791913; Liquenda Hse, Nelson Mandela Ave).

Visas for Onward Travel

Harare is one of the best places in southern Africa to pick up visas for regional countries (for contact details see p914). Requirements constantly change, but nearly all require a fee (most in US dollars) and two passport-sized photos.

Visas for Zambia, Namibia, Malawi, South Africa and Botswana are easy to obtain on arrival in those countries for most visitors, so there is no need to obtain them in advance.

Mozambique For Mozambique, transit visas/single-entry visas/multiple-entry visas cost US$11/20/40. Visas are usually ready in 24 hr. Everyone needs a visa in advance for Mozambique, even if they're heading straight to Malawi. A 'border tax' of US$5 (hard currency only) is also payable.

Zambia Apart from Australian and Irish passport holders, most travellers need a visa for Zambia. Single/double/ multiple-entry visas cost US$25/40/60. For British citizens they cost US$65/80/80. However, if you book a tour with a Zambian operator in advance they can arrange a visa fee waiver. You can obtain a visa at most borders (see p821).

Lesotho

HIGHLIGHTS

- **Malealea** Be stunned by the mountainous region in Lesotho's rugged interior, with its breathtaking scenery and traditional Basotho villages (p924)
- **Thaba-Bosiu** Discover the mountain stronghold of King Moshoeshoe the Great, where the struggle for Lesotho was won (p923)
- **Quthing** See where fossilised dinosaur footsteps, San rock paintings and a cave house stand as landmarks of Lesotho's history (p925)
- **Off the beaten track** Explore Mokhotlong – it's Lesotho at its most remote, where you can step back into an older, more traditional Africa (p926)

LESOTHO

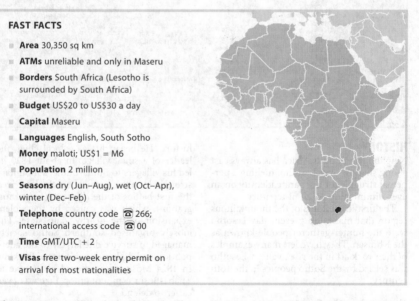

FAST FACTS

- **Area** 30,350 sq km
- **ATMs** unreliable and only in Maseru
- **Borders** South Africa (Lesotho is surrounded by South Africa)
- **Budget** US$20 to US$30 a day
- **Capital** Maseru
- **Languages** English, South Sotho
- **Money** maloti; US$1 = M6
- **Population** 2 million
- **Seasons** dry (Jun–Aug), wet (Oct–Apr), winter (Dec–Feb)
- **Telephone** country code ☎ 266; international access code ☎ 00
- **Time** GMT/UTC + 2
- **Visas** free two-week entry permit on arrival for most nationalities

The mountainous kingdom of Lesotho (le-soo-too) is a land of dinosaur footsteps, legendary kings, mountain hideaways – a hidden treasure for those who love the great outdoors. It's a chance to escape the clamour of South Africa, enjoy some spectacular scenery (either on foot or astride a pony) and experience life in traditional villages along the way.

LESOTHO

LEGEND
NP   National Park
NR   National Reserve

HISTORY

Neighbouring South Africa has always cast a long shadow over Lesotho, fuelling a perpetual struggle for a separate identity on an ever-diminishing patch of territory.

The first inhabitants of the mountainous region that makes up present-day Lesotho were the hunter-gatherer people known as the Khoisan. They have left many examples of their rock art in the river valleys. Lesotho was settled by the Sotho peoples in the 16th century.

Moshoeshoe the Great

King Moshoeshoe (pronounced mo-shwe-shwe but sometimes clipped to moshesh) is the towering father figure of Lesotho's

history. He began life as a local chief, the leader of a small village. In about 1820 he led his villagers to Butha-Buthe, a mountain stronghold in the north where they survived the first battles of the *difaqane* (forced migration), which was caused by the violent expansion of the nearby Zulu state. The loosely organised southern Sotho society managed to survive due largely to the adept political and diplomatic abilities of the king. In 1824 Moshoeshoe moved his people to Thaba-Bosiu a mountaintop that was even easier to defend.

From Thaba-Bosiu, Moshoeshoe played a patient game of placating the stronger local rulers and granting protection – as well as land and cattle – to refugees. These people and others like them were to form Basutholand, which by the time of Moshoe-shoe's death in 1870, had a population of more than 150,000.

As the *difaqane* receded a new threat arose. The Voortrekkers (Boer pioneers) had crossed the Orange River in the 1830s and established the Orange Free State. By 1843 Moshoeshoe was sufficiently concerned by their numbers to ally himself with the British Cape Colony government. The British Resident in Basutholand subsequently decided that Moshoeshoe was becoming too powerful and engineered an unsuccessful attack on his kingdom.

Treaties with the British helped define the borders of Basutholand but did little to stop squabbles with the Boers. The Boers pressed their claims on the land and increasing tension led to wars between the Orange Free State and the Basotho people in 1858 and 1865. After success in the first war, Moshoeshoe was forced in the second to sign away much of his western lowlands.

The Road to Independence

The continual war between the Orange Free State and Basutholand was not good for British interests, and in 1868 the British government annexed Basutholand and handed it to the Cape Colony to run in 1871. After a period of instability, the British government again took direct control of Basutholand in 1884, although it remained easier to give effective authority to local leaders than rule through British officers.

For many outsiders, modern Lesotho seems like an anomaly – a tiny kingdom entirely surrounded by the regional overseer, South Africa. Its existence is attributable to a quirk of history and fortuitous timing. In the 1880s, direct British rule was deeply resented by the local population as an infringement on Basutholand's freedom and sovereignty. Little were they to know that British occupation would, almost certainly without intending it, secure the future independence of Lesotho as other kingdoms fell under the South African umbrella. All because at the precise moment when the Union of South Africa was created, Basutholand was a British Protectorate and was not included in the Union.

In 1910 the advisory Basutholand National Council was formed from members nominated by the chiefs. In the mid-1950s the council requested internal self-government from the British; by 1960 a new constitution was in place and elections were held for a legislative council. The main contenders were the Basutholand Congress Party (BCP), similar to South Africa's African National Congress (ANC), and the conservative Basutholand National Party (BNP) headed by Chief Leabua Jonathan.

The BCP won the 1960 elections and demanded full independence from Britain. This was eventually agreed to, with independence to come into effect in 1966. However, at the elections in 1965 the BCP lost to the BNP and Chief Jonathan became the first prime minister of the new Kingdom of Lesotho, which allied itself with the apartheid regime across the border.

Big Brother

Stripping King Moshoeshoe II of the few powers that the new constitution had left him did not endear Jonathan's government to the people and the BCP won the 1970 election. After his defeat, Jonathan followed the example of many bad losers in African history by suspending the constitution, expelling the king and banning all opposition political parties. Jonathan changed tack, distancing himself from South Africa and calling for the return of land in the Orange Free State that had been stolen from the original Basutholand. He also offered refuge to ANC guerrillas and flirted with Cuba. South Africa closed Lesotho's borders, strangling the country.

Jonathan was deposed in 1986 and the king was restored as head of state. This was a popular move, but eventually agitation for democratic reform rose again. In 1990 King Moshoeshoe II was deposed by the army in favour of his son, Prince Mohato Bereng Seeisa (Letsie III). Elections in 1993 resulted in the return of the BCP.

In 1995 Letsie III abdicated in favour of his father. Five years after being deposed, Moshoeshoe II was reinstated, restoring calm to Lesotho after a year of unrest. Tragically, less than a year later he was killed when his 4WD plunged over a cliff in the Maluti Mountains. Letsie III became king for the second time.

A split in the BCP saw the breakaway Lesotho Congress for Democracy (LCD) take power. Elections were held in 1998 amid accusations of widespread cheating by the LCD, which won in a landslide. Tensions between the public service and the government became acute, and the military was also split over the result.

Following months of protests, the government appeared to be losing control. In late September 1998 it called on the Southern African Development Community (SADC) treaty partners, Botswana, South Africa and Zimbabwe, to help restore order. Troops, mainly South African, invaded the kingdom. Rebel elements of the Lesotho army put up strong resistance and there was heavy fighting in Maseru.

The government agreed to call new elections, but the political situation remained tense with the spectre of South African intervention never far away. Political wrangling delayed the elections until May 2002. The LCD won again and Prime Minister Mosisili began a second five-year term.

THE CULTURE

Lesotho has somehow held on as a redoubt of traditional culture for the Basotho people. Like their ancestors, they are proud that they're not South African. They intend to remain so – just ask any local.

Basotho culture centres on a belief in the power of ancestral spirits who act as conduits between themselves and the forces of good and evil. This is particularly important during the harvest time and during droughts. The Basotho are also great music lovers, and nothing gets them swaying more than their flutelike *lekolulo*, the stringed *thomo* (played by women) and the *setolo-tolo*, a stringed instrument played with the mouth by men. As herders, cattle also occupies an important role in traditional culture with cattle ownership a critical element of community identity, pride and status.

ENVIRONMENT

Lesotho's western border is formed by the Mohokare (Caledon) River. The eastern border is the rugged Drakensberg Range, and high country defines much of the southern border. In fact, all of Lesotho is over 1000m in altitude, with peaks reaching 3000m in the centre and east of the country.

Lesotho's climate is a mixture of temperate and sub-tropical influences, with surprising extremes of temperature ranging from January minimum temperatures which can drop five degrees below freezing up to July maximums of over 32. The best time to visit is in late April to May, when summer temperatures are yet to arrive but visibility is high after the rains. September to early October is another good time.

There are serious environmental concerns about the controversial Highlands Water Project, a series of dams on the Orange River in Lesotho, which will provide water and electricity to South Africa. Traditional Basotho communities have been disrupted (though compensation is promised) and the proposed Mohale Dam will flood some of the country's most fertile land – a resource already in short supply, as only around 10% of Lesotho's land is suitable for agriculture anyway. There are also the as-yet-unknown effects on the ecology of the Senqu and Orange Rivers and the impact on Namibia, a downstream user with its own water shortage problems. And in something of a test case for Africa, a number of Western companies involved in the project stand accused of bribery with cases currently before the courts.

Other key environmental issues include population pressure, resulting in overgrazing and soil erosion. About 18 to 20 tonnes of topsoil per hectare is lost each year and it has been estimated that there will be no cultivable land left in Lesotho by 2040.

TRANSPORT

GETTING THERE & AWAY
Air
Lesotho's Moshoeshoe International Airport is 18km southeast of Maseru. South African Airways (SAA) flies daily between Moshoeshoe airport and Johannesburg (Jo'burg) in South Africa for US$110, one way. The airport departure tax is US$4.50.

Local Transport
The main border crossings include: Maseru Bridge and Ficksburg Bridge (both open 24 hours); Makhaleng Bridge (open 8am–6pm weekdays, 8am–4pm on weekends); and Sani Pass (open 8am–4pm).

There are no direct buses between major South African cities and Maseru. You can get a bus to Bloemfontein or Ladybrand, then catch a minibus taxi into Lesotho from there. Minibus taxis run between Maseru and Jo'burg (US$10) and Bloemfontein (US$6).

GETTING AROUND

A good network of slow buses runs to many towns. Minibus taxis are quicker but tend not to travel long distances. In more remote areas you might have to arrange a ride with a truck, for which you'll have to negotiate the fare. Be prepared for long delays once you're off the main routes.

You'll be quoted long-distance fares on buses. It's better to just buy a ticket to the next major town as most of the passengers will get off there, you'll be stuck waiting for the bus to fill up again and other buses might leave before yours. Buying tickets in stages is only slightly more expensive.

MASERU

pop 288,950

Maseru has been a quiet backwater for much of its history and it remains an easy-going if unspectacular large town – one of Africa's less frenetic capitals. Kingsway, the city's main thoroughfare, was paved for the 1947 visit by the British royal family, and for many years remained the country's only nondirt road. As most of Maseru's population has arrived since the 1970s and the 1998 SADC invasion left many buildings scarred by torching and rampant looting, the city is undergoing a major rebuilding program.

ORIENTATION

Moshoeshoe International Airport is 18km from town, off Main South Rd. The Khali Hotel/Motel's shuttle bus runs to the airport. Minibus taxis cost about US$7.

Most places to stay, eat and shop are on or near Kingsway. It runs from the border post at Maseru Bridge right through the centre of town to the Circle, a traffic roundabout and landmark. At the Circle the street splits to become two important, though rather unimaginatively named, highways: Main North Rd and Main South Rd.

INFORMATION
Medical Services

The **Queen Elizabeth II Hospital** (Kingsway) is near the Lesotho Sun Hotel.

Money

Changing money is no hassle except for the short banking hours: 8.30am to 3pm weekdays (to 1pm on Thursday) and 8.30am to 11am Saturday. There are huge, slow-moving queues on Friday (pay day).

The main banks are all on Kingsway. The only (often unreliable) ATM is at Standard Bank.

Post

The main **post office** (Kingsway) is next to Standard Bank. Relying on poste restante may be risky.

Tourist Information

The **tourist office** (☎ 2231 2896; ltbhq@ltb.org.ls; Kingsway) is opposite the giant Basotho Hat building. The staff are friendly although they lack resources. The Lesotho accommodation price guide is handy.

SIGHTS

There are several good **walks** on the mountain ridges that skirt the city. Take the path from the gate of the Lesotho Sun Hotel to the plateau for great views over Maseru.

The impressive **Catholic cathedral** is near the Circle at the end of Kingsway.

Take some time to go into the 'urban villages' that surround Maseru. You can also visit the **rock paintings** near Roma as a daytrip – see p924 for details.

SLEEPING

Maseru is not really a budget destination. Most travellers don't linger for more than a night, especially those on a tight budget.

Anglican Centre (☎ 2232 2046; dm/tw US$6/12) Maseru's only cheap option has clean, austere rooms; meals are available if you give notice. The centre is about 500m north of Kingsway on the bend where Assisi Rd becomes Lancer's Rd.

Khali Hotel/Motel (☎ 2232 2822; d US$28) This large and comfortable hotel is the next closest thing you'll get to an affordable hotel. Take a Thetsane minibus on Pioneer Rd near Lancer's Inn and get off at the turnoff for the suburb of New Europa.

Lancer's Inn (☎ 2231 2114; fax 2231 0223; s/d US$30/55) This comfortable colonial-era hotel (with renovated rondavels) is located just off Kingsway. It's quite popular so make sure you book ahead.

LESOTHO

MASERU

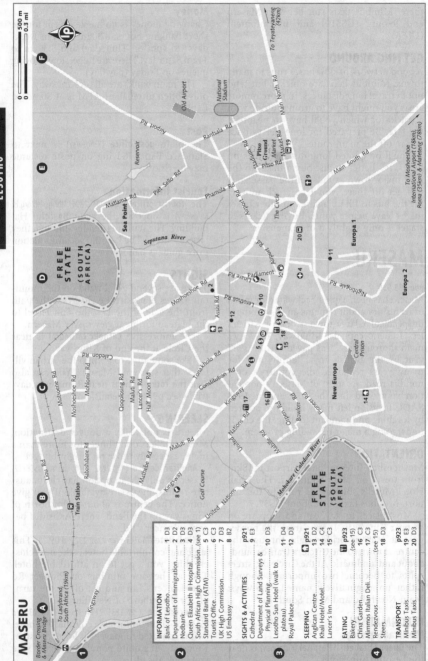

EATING

China Garden (Orpen Rd) This somewhat cavernous place off Kingsway serves uninspired but passable cuisine.

Mimmos Italian Deli (☎ 2232 4979; Maseru Club, United Nations Rd; dishes US$3.40) Mimmos is understandably popular, serving decent pasta and pizza primarily to ex-pats in the pleasant club surroundings.

All the hotels have restaurants. **Rendezvous** (Lancer's Inn) serves unexciting but reliable food.

There's a good bakery next to Lancer's Inn – try the freshly baked scones; the chicken and mushroom pies are also tasty. Fast-food choices include **Steers** (Kingsway).

There are plenty of central street stalls, mainly open during the day, along Kingsway selling grilled meat for about US$0.70. Servings of curry and rice cost US$0.60.

GETTING THERE & AWAY

Buses and long-distance minibus taxis congregate, haphazardly, in the streets around the Circle; minibus taxi destinations are displayed in the front window. Destinations include: Quthing (US$3.50, change at Mafeteng); Roma (US$1.50); Thaba-Bosiu (US$0.75); Semonkong (US$1.75); Morija (US$1); and Malealea (US$1.75, change at Motsekuoa).

GETTING AROUND

The standard minibus taxi fare around town is US$0.25. For private hire taxis try **Moonlite Telephone Taxis** (☎ 2231 2695) or **Planet** (☎ 2231 7777).

There are taxi stands on Main North Rd and Kingsway.

AROUND MASERU

THABA-BOSIU

East of Maseru is the evocative and historically significant mountain stronghold of Moshoeshoe the Great, who first occupied the place in 1824. **Thaba-Bosiu** (admission US$0.50) means Mountain at Night, perhaps a memory of when the sight was first occupied, but another legend suggests that Thaba-Bosiu is a hill in daylight, but transformed into a mountain after dark.

There's an information centre at the base of Thaba-Bosiu. An official guide will take you to the summit. Good views from here include those of the Qiloane pinnacle (inspiration for the Basotho hat), along with the remains of fortifications, Moshoeshoe's grave, and parts of the original settlement.

Melesi Lodge (☎ 2285 2116; s/d US$24/33) The only place to stay is a neatly kept lodge about 2km before the information centre. There's a terrific restaurant.

To get here from Maseru, look for a minibus taxi near the Circle; these go as far as the visitor centre (US$0.75).

SOUTHERN LESOTHO

ROMA

Getting to Roma is half the fun, reached as it is through a spectacular gorge south of town. After that, there's not a lot to do, but it's a relaxing place containing attractive sandstone buildings and, as a university town, it's a good place to meet students.

The important **Ha Baroana rock paintings** are just north of Roma. Although suffering from neglect and vandalism (including damage done by tourists who spray water on the paintings to produce brighter photos) they're worth seeing.

There are also dinosaur footprints; ask at the Trading Post Guest House for directions.

Trading Post Guest House (☎ 2234 0267; tradingpost@leo.co.ls; camp sites per person US$3.50, d US$18) This is a lovely, relaxing place 2km west of Roma off the Maseru road. The owners also run Trading Post Adventures a few kilometres away, offering more accommodation, tours, hiking trails and horse rides. There's no restaurant (try the Speakeasy Restaurant in Roma) but you can use the kitchen. Everything is provided except towels.

Roma is 35km southeast of Maseru. Minibus taxis run to/from Maseru (US$1.50).

If you want to visit the rock paintings on a day-trip from Maseru, take a minibus taxi (US$1.75) to Nazareth and get off about 1.5km before Nazareth. A signpost indicates the way to the paintings off to the left. Follow the gravel track 3km to the village of Ha Khotso then turn right at a football field. Follow this track a further 2.5km to a hilltop overlooking a gorge. A footpath zigzags down the hillside to the paintings inside a rock shelter.

To get to the paintings from Roma head back to the Maseru road and turn right onto the road to Thaba-Tseka. After about 12km turn off to the left, just after the Ha Ntsi settlement on the Mohlsks-oa-Tuka River.

SEMONKONG

The **Maletsunyane Falls** (also known as Lebehane Falls) are a 1½-hour walk from Semonkong (Place of Smoke). The 192m-high falls are at their most spectacular in summer and are best appreciated from the bottom of the gorge (where there are camp sites).

The remote 122m-high **Ketane Falls** are also worth seeing. These are a solid day's ride (30km) from Semonkong or a four-day return horse ride from Malealea Lodge (see below).

You can usually find a bed at the **Roman Catholic mission** for a small contribution.

The **Semonkong Lodge** (bookings in South Africa ☎ 051-933 3106; www.placeofsmoke.co.ls; camp sites per person/dm/s/d US$2.50/5/19/30) offers hiking and pony trekking.

Buses between Maseru and Semonkong (US$1.75) leave both places in the morning and arrive late in the afternoon.

MORIJA

This small village, about 40km south of Maseru on the Main South Rd, is where you will find the **Morija Museum & Archives** (☎ 2236 0308; admission US$0.70; ☎ 8am-5pm Mon-Sat, noon-5pm Sun). The collection includes archives from the first mission to Basutholand. As the missionary was associated with Moshoeshoe the Great, the collection is of great importance. There are some good displays of Basotho culture, some finds from the Stone and Iron Ages, and dinosaur relics.

Near the museum is the **Mophato Oa Morija** (☎ 2236 0308; camp sites per person US$3.25, dm US$5.20), an ecumenical centre.

There's also the pleasant **Ha Matela Guest Cottages** (☎ 2236 0306; cottages per person US$12). For bookings, call the museum and ask for Stephen Gill. Breakfast/dinner costs US$2.30/4.70.

A minibus to/from Maseru costs US$1.

MALEALEA

Set in truly stunning scenery, the village of Malealea, with its mountains and valleys, is one of the gems of Lesotho. The area has been occupied for a very long time,

and ancient **San paintings** hidden in rock shelters can still be seen. The best way to experience the spectacular landscape, and the people who call it home today, is to take a pony trek or wander on foot through the hills and villages. Even for the less energetic, Malealea is a wonderful place to stay – appropriately advertised as 'Lesotho in a nutshell'.

Activities
PONY TREKKING
Malealea Lodge (see Sleeping & Eating) is the best place in Lesotho to arrange pony trekking. It offers a great opportunity to meet with Basotho villagers and experience the awesome scenery of the mountains and deep valleys. The villagers act as guides and provide the ponies, and the business makes a significant contribution to the local village economy.

Pony trek prices start at US$18 per day. Overnight rides start at US$23 per person, plus US$4.50 for each night spent in one of the Basotho village huts.

WALKING
The owners of Malealea Lodge have put together a number of walking and hiking options, and also provide a map. Your packs can be carried on ponies if you wish to go for longer than one day.

The walks include a two-hour return walk to the Botso'ela Waterfall; a six-hour return walk to the Pitseng Gorge (take your swimwear); a short, easy one-hour walk along the Pitseng Plateau; a walk along the Makhaleng River; and a hike from the Gates of Paradise back to Malealea. The scenery along these walks is exceptional and all walks pass through local villages.

Sleeping & Eating
Malealea Lodge (bookings in South Africa ☎ 051-447 3200; www.malealea.co.ls; camp sites per person/dm US$4.50/7, rondavels per person US$9) Part of the original Malealea Trading Store established way back in 1905, today the trade is mainly catering for visitors and this lodge is a very friendly, well-run place. As well as comfortable rooms and a neat camp site, meals (breakfast US$3.50, lunch US$4.50 and dinner US$7) are available with prior notice. There are also self-catering facilities and the nearby shop is quite well-stocked.

Getting There & Away
From Maseru, 83km away, take a minibus to Motsekuoa, and from there another to Malealea (full trip US$1.75).

QUTHING
The southernmost town in Lesotho is often known as Moyeni (a Sephuthi word meaning 'Place of the Wind'). The town was established in 1877, abandoned three years later and then rebuilt at the present site.

Most of the town is in Lower Quthing. Up on the hill overlooking the dramatic Orange River Gorge is Upper Quthing, where there's a good hotel, a mission and sundry colonial-era structures. A minibus taxi between the two costs US$0.20. Off the highway, about 5km west of Quthing, is the five-roomed Masitise Cave House. This mission building was built into a San rock shelter in 1866 by Reverend Ellenberger. Inquire at the school about access to the cave house and someone will unlock it for you. There are San paintings nearby.

Probably the most easily located of the dinosaur footprints in Lesotho are close to Quthing and are believed to be 180 million years old. To get to them, go up the Mt Moorosi road from Quthing until you reach an orange, thatch-roofed building. The footprints are a short walk away.

Between Quthing and Masitise there is a striking twin-spired sandstone church, part of the Villa Maria Mission.

At Qomoqomong, 10km from Quthing, there's a good gallery of San paintings; ask at the General Dealers store about a guide for the 20-minute walk to the paintings.

Mountain Side Hotel (☎ 2275 0257; s/d US$20/30) This place, in Lower Quthing, is a basic pub with a restaurant and rooms. Breakfast/dinner is US$4/5.

Minibus taxis run daily between Quthing and Maseru (US$3.50), stopping at Mafeteng (US$1.75).

EASTERN LESOTHO

QACHA'S NEK
This pleasant town, on the border between Lesotho and South Africa, has a number of sandstone buildings. It was founded in 1888 near the pass of the same name. Oddly

enough, several California redwoods grow nearby, some more than 25m high.

The **Nthatuoa Hotel** (☎ 2295 0260; s/d US$17/23) offers adequate accommodation and serves meals.

There's also the **Farmer Training Centre** (☎ 2295 0231; s US$2.50) just off the main road (look for the 'Forestry Division' sign).

You can reach Qacha's Nek from Quthing (also called Moyeni) by daily bus (US$3.50, about six hours) – a slow but spectacular trip. There's also a bus to/from Sehlabathebe National Park.

SEHLABATHEBE NATIONAL PARK
Lesotho's first national park is remote and rugged – this sense of separation from the rest of the world is the main attraction. There are relatively few animals other than a rare Maloti minnow (thought to be extinct but rediscovered in the Tsoelikana River), rare birds such as the bearded vulture, and the odd rhebok or baboon. As well as hiking, the park has horse riding; guided horseback tours are US$5.80.

This is a summer rainfall area and thick mist is common. Winters are clear but cold at night, and there are sometimes light falls of snow.

Near the village of Sehonghong, to the northwest of the park, is **Soai's Cave**, named after the last chief of the Maloti San people, who was attacked and defeated here by Cape and Basotho forces in 1871.

For bookings contact the **National Parks Office of the Ministry of Agriculture** (☎ 2232 3600, ext 30; Raboshabane Rd; PO Box 92, Maseru 100).

Sleeping
You can camp in the park but there are no facilities except at **Sehlabathebe Lodge** (bookings ☎ 2232 3600, ext 30; camp sites per person US$2, s/d US$5/8). You can buy firewood and coal here, but for food (very limited) you'll have to rely on a small shop about 4km west of the park entrance.

Range Management Education Centre (dm US$4) This centre in Sehlabathebe Village, is modern and well equipped and serves meals. It's 1.5km down the road that heads to Sehonghong.

Getting There & Away
If you're in Lesotho, the usual way to reach the park is from Qacha's Nek, about 100km

by road southwest of the park. A daily bus (US$2.50, 5½ hours) runs between Qacha's Nek and Sehlabathebe village; it departs Qacha's Nek at noon and Sehlabathebe at 5.30am. This area can get snowed in during winter, so the bus won't run if the roads are blocked.

If you're in South Africa, the simplest way to reach Sehlabathebe National Park is to hike the 10km up the escarpment from the settlement of Bushman's Nek, which is about 40km by road from Underberg. From Bushman's Nek to Nkonkoana Gate, the park boundary and the Lesotho border crossing, takes about six hours. You can also take a horse up or down for US$5.

SANI PASS

This astoundingly steep road, at once arduous and beautiful, carves its way through the **Drakensberg Range** in a truly stunning fashion. It's the only dependable vehicle route between Lesotho and KwaZulu-Natal but the quality is pretty appalling even so – much of the 'road' is a rough jumble of gravel and broken rocks, especially tricky on the tight bends and 30% gradients. Just as well the views are worth it.

At the top of the pass is the Lesotho border post (the border between South African and Lesotho follows the highest point of the Drakensberg Range), and Sani Top Chalet – the base for several excellent day walks across the high parts of the Drakensberg. These include the walk to Hodgson's Peaks, 6km south, from where you get views over Sehlabathebe National Park and down to KwaZulu-Natal. There's also the long and strenuous hike to Thabana-Ntlenyana (3482m), the highest peak in Southern Africa. There's a path, but a guide is handy. Horses can also do the trip for around US$5 return.

Sani Top Chalet (www.sanitopchalet.co.za; camp sites per person/dm US$3.50/7, r per person with meals US$30) This is a great place perched dramatically at the top of the pass. There are self-catering facilities and a bar. In winter the snow is often deep enough to ski (a few pieces of antique equipment are available at the chalet) and horse trekking is available by prior arrangement. Book accommodation and tours through **Southern Drakensberg Tours** (☎ South Africa 033-702 1158; sanitop@futurenet.co.za).

At the bottom of the pass is the South African border post and two backpackers hostels

which arrange or advise on transport up and down (see p973 for details). To reach the top of Sani Pass from Mokhotlong or anywhere in Lesotho by public transport takes patience. Traffic is very sparse, and the route is very slow and bumpy. The easiest way to reach Sani Top is from South Africa – but even that's no stroll in the park. On the South African side the nearest towns are Himeville and Underberg. A minibus taxi from Underberg to Sani Top is US$2.50. A few minibus taxis, which cost much less, run Basothos into South Africa for shopping. You might have to wait a day or so for one of these.

Alternatively, if you want to try hitching up or down Sani Pass, it's best on weekends when there's a fair amount of South African traffic to and from the chalet.

MOKHOTLONG

Mokhotlong, about 270km from Maseru, is the coldest, driest and most remote place in Lesotho. With horses 'parked' outside the shops, the town could be the wild west. It's the first major town north of Sani Pass and Sehlabathebe National Park, so there are a few basic shops.

Molumong Guesthouse & Backpackers (per person US$7.50) Located about 15km southwest of Mokhotlong in Upper Rafolatsane village, this place is very basic – bring your own sleeping bag. There's no electricity or TV either, just the stars to look at. You should be able to arrange pony treks from here with the locals. There are three buses a day to the lodge from Mokhotlong.

In town, the **Farmer Training Centre** (per person US$1.75) has cold-water washing facilities and a kitchen. There's also the **Lefu Senqu Hotel** (☎ 2292 0330; s/d US$15/20).

NORTHERN LESOTHO

TEYATEYANENG

Teyateyaneng (Place of Quick Sands) is usually known as TY. The town has been developed as the craft centre of Lesotho and there are several places worth visiting. Some of the best tapestries come from Helang Basali Crafts in the St Agnes Mission, 2km before TY on the Maseru road.

The **Blue Mountain Inn** (☎ 2250 0362; s/d US$22/ 25) has comfortable, cosy cottages. There's also a restaurant.

LERIBE

A large town by Lesotho's standards, Leribe (also called Hlotse) is a quiet village serving as a regional shopping and market centre. It was an administrative centre under the British and there are some old buildings slowly decaying in the leafy streets. **Major Bell's Tower**, on the main street near the market, was built in 1879.

There's a set of dinosaur footprints a few kilometres south of Leribe at Tsikoane village. Going north towards Leribe from Tsikoane, take the small dirt road going off to the right towards some rocky outcrops. Follow it up to the church and ask someone to direct you to the *minwane* (dinosaur footprints). It's a 15- to 20-minute slog up the mountainside to a series of caves. The prints are clearly visible on the ceiling of the rock.

About 10km north of Leribe are the Subeng River dinosaur footprints. There's a signpost indicating the river but not the footprints. Walk down to the river from the road to a concrete causeway (about 250m). The footprints of at least three species of dinosaur are about 15m downstream on the right bank.

Sleeping options include the **Agricultural Training Centre** (☎ 2240 0226; dm US$3), just outside town; the **Catholic Mission** (10km past Leribe towards Butha-Buthe); and the **Leribe Hotel** (☎ 2240 0559; Main St; s/d US$18/24), an old-style place with a tea garden surrounded by well-established trees.

LESOTHO DIRECTORY

ACCOMMODATION

Cheap accommodation is hard to find but there are missions scattered around the country and Agricultural Training Centres in several places can provide a bed for a small fee.

ACTIVITIES

The main options in Lesotho are hiking and pony trekking. It's a wonderful experience, but as the climate is very changeable, you'll need to come prepared. Temperatures can plummet to near zero, even in summer, and during the wet many rivers flood, and fords become dangerous. Thick fogs can also delay you. By the end of the dry season, especially in the higher areas, water can be scarce. You'll

usually need to bring your own food, a sleeping bag, rainwear, sunscreen, warm clothing, a torch and water purification tablets. These are difficult to find outside Maseru.

Hiking

Lesotho's high country offers some of the most spectacular walking in Southern Africa. The crest of the Drakensberg Range (actually an escarpment, with the Lesotho plateau on the west, and the sheer drop down to South Africa on the east) is one of the most popular areas for serious hikers, but remote treks are also possible in many other areas. In much of the country there are scattered villages but in the south and east the rugged mountains are all but deserted. This makes for long treks and a great wilderness experience in a landscape reminiscent of the Tibetan plateau – but don't walk in this area unless you are very experienced, and in a party of at least three people. For more details see *A Backpackers Guide to Lesotho*, by Russell Suchet, available locally and in South Africa for around US$3.

Hikers' etiquette in Lesotho comes with a few unique twists. You should respect the mounds of stones (cairns) that mark graves. However, a mound of stones near a trail, especially between two hills, should be added to by passing travellers, who ensure their good luck by spitting on a stone and throwing it onto the pile. Note that a white flag waving from a village means that *joala* (sorghum beer) has just been brewed; a yellow flag indicates maize beer, red is for meat and green for vegetables.

Pony Trekking

Lesotho's tough, and thankfully sure-footed little Basotho ponies can take you to some remote and beautiful places in the highlands. The main centres are Malealea Lodge (p924), the Trading Post Guesthouse (p923) and Semonkong Lodge (p924). There are basic stores near all these centres but it's better to bring food and other supplies from Maseru. You don't need prior riding experience.

DANGERS & ANNOYANCES

There's little animosity towards South Africans, but if you're not one then it doesn't hurt to let people know.

Several lives are lost each year from lightning strikes. Keep off high ground during electrical storms and avoid camping in the open. The sheer ferocity of an electrical storm in Lesotho has to be seen to be believed.

On the last Friday of the month, when many people are paid and some of them get drunk, things can get a little boisterous. It can be fun, but as the day wears on some drinkers can become over-friendly or even aggressive.

Maseru is fairly safe but be on your guard at night, especially off the main street. Violent crime is unfortunately becoming more common but with common sense and precautions, you should be OK.

EMBASSIES & CONSULATES

The following consulates and embassies are in Maseru:

Canada (☎ 2231 6435; Block D, 5th floor LNDC Development House, Kingsway)
France (☎ 2232 7522) Inquiries handled by Alliance Française in Maseru, but all visas issued in Jo'burg.
Ireland (☎ 2231 4068; Tonakholo Rd, Maseru West)
Netherlands (☎ 2231 2114; Lancer's Inn) Off Kingsway.
South African (☎ 2231 5758; 10th floor, Bank of Lesotho Towers, Kingsway)
UK (☎ 2231 3961; Linare Rd) Opposite police headquarters.
USA (☎ 2231 2666; 254 Kingsway)

Lesotho has diplomatic representation in Mozambique and South Africa. Details are listed in the Directory section of those chapters.

HOLIDAYS

As well as religious holidays listed in the Africa Directory (p1003) the principal public holidays in Lesotho include:

1 January New Year's Day
11 March Moshoeshoe Day
4 October Independence Day
26 December Boxing Day

INTERNET ACCESS

At the time of writing, there was no Internet access in Lesotho.

MAPS

The **Department of Land Surveys & Physical Planning** (Lerotholi Rd), in Maseru, sells good topographic maps of Lesotho. Another good map of Lesotho is included on the *Republic of South Africa* (1:2,000,000) map by Cartographia.

MONEY

The unit of currency is the maloti (M), which is made up of 100 liesente. The maloti is fixed at a value equal to the South African rand, and rands are accepted everywhere – there's no real need to convert your money into maloti, particularly as maloti are not accepted back in South Africa. If changing travellers cheques you can usually get rand notes. The only foreign exchange banks (Bank of Lesotho, Nedbank and Standard Bank) are in Maseru.

PHOTOGRAPHY

You're better off bringing film into Lesotho and waiting until you're back home before getting it developed.

POST & TELEPHONE

Post offices are open from 8am to 4.30pm weekdays and 8am to noon Saturday. Delivery is slow and unreliable.

The telephone system works reasonably well. There are no area codes within Lesotho. Lesotho's country code is ☎ 266; to call Lesotho from South Africa dial the prefix ☎ 09 266. To call South Africa from anywhere in Lesotho, dial ☎ 00 27 and then the South African area code and phone number.

VISAS

Citizens of most Western European countries, the USA and most Commonwealth countries are granted a free entry permit at the border. The standard stay permitted is two weeks, although if you ask for longer you may be lucky.

For citizens of other countries, a single-entry visa costs US$3.50 and multiple-entry US$6. If you arrive at the Maseru Bridge border without a visa you *might* be given a temporary entry permit (but don't count on it) which allows you to go into Maseru and apply for a visa at the office of the **Department of Immigration** (☎ 2231 7339; PO Box 174, Maseru).

Visa Extensions

At most border posts you get two weeks' stay renewable by either leaving the country and re-entering, or by application at the Department of Immigration in Maseru.

For a longer stay, apply in advance to the **Director of Home Affairs** (PO Box 174, Maseru 100, Lesotho).

Swaziland

HIGHLIGHTS

- **Mkhaya Game Reserve** One of Africa's great wildlife experiences, with the chance to see rare black rhinos in the wild (p936)
- **Ezulwini Valley** The regal heartland of Swaziland; rich with symbolism, royal culture and home to the sacred *Incwala* ceremony (p935)
- **Best journey** Shoot the rapids or simply drift down the Usutu River through stunning gorges; white-water rafting at its best (p937)
- **Off the beaten track** Malolotja Nature Reserve, a genuine, unspoiled wilderness ideal for trekking and escaping the crowds (p938)

FAST FACTS

- **Area** 17,365 sq km
- **ATMs** only in Mbabane
- **Borders** South Africa, Mozambique
- **Budget** US$15 to US$30 a day
- **Capital** Mbabane
- **Languages** English, Swati
- **Money** lilangeni (plural emalangeni); US$1 = E6.9
- **Population** 1 million
- **Season** wet (Dec–Apr); winter (May–Aug) drier and cool; average temperature in Mbabane 12.2°C
- **Telephone** country code ☎ 268; international access code ☎ 00
- **Time** GMT/UTC + 2
- **Visas** not required for most nationalities

Swaziland might be among the smallest countries on the continent and one of Africa's last remaining monarchies, but there's more than novelty value on offer here. You can almost feel South Africa's undercurrents of tension fade away when you cross the border into friendly, easy-going little Swaziland, making it a relaxing stopover on the trip between Mozambique and South Africa. And it's surprising how much there is to do here – the royal ceremonies, excellent wildlife reserves and superb scenery should be more than enough reason to come.

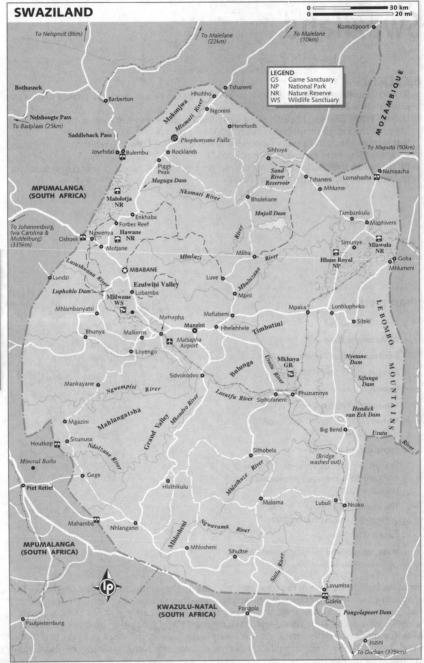

SWAZILAND

LEGEND
GS   Game Sanctuary
NP   National Park
NR   Nature Reserve
WS   Wildlife Sanctuary

0 —— 30 km
0 —— 20 mi

To Nelspruit (8km)
To Malelane (22km)
To Malelane (10km)
Komatipoort

MOZAMBIQUE

Bothasnek
Barberton
Tshaneni
Hhohho
Makonjwa
Mlumati River
Ngonini
Herefords

Nelshoogte Pass
To Badplaas (25km)
Saddleback Pass
Phophonyane Falls
Sihhoya
To Maputo (50km)

Josefsdal Bulembu
Rocklands
Piggs Peak
Sand River Reservoir
Tshaneni
Lomahasha
Namaacha
Mhlume

MPUMALANGA (SOUTH AFRICA)
Maguga Dam
Nkomati River
Bholekane
Mnjoll Dam
Tambankulu
Maphiveni

Malolotja NR
Enkhaba
Forbes Reef
Hawane NR
River
Mbuluzane River
Simunye
Mlawula NR

To Johannesburg, (via Carolina & Middelburg) (335km)
Oshoek Ngwenya
Motjane
Mbuluzi
Mliba
River
Hlane Royal NP
Goba
Mhlumeni

MBABANE
Luve
Mbuluzane
River

Lundzi
Ezulwini Valley
Lobamba
Mpisi
Mpaka
Lonhlupheko
Siteki
LEBOMBO MOUNTAINS

Luphohlo Dam
Mlilwane WS
Mhlambanyatsi
Matsapha
Mafutseni

Bhunya
Malkerns
Manzini Hhelehhele
Timbutini

Loyengo
Matsapha Airport
Bulunga
Usutu River
Nyetane Dam

Mankayane
Ngwempisi River
Sidvokodvo
Mkhaya GR
Sifunga Dam

Mgazini
Mahlangatsha
Lusutfu River
Siphofaneni
Phuzumoya
Hendick van Eck Dam

Houtkop Sicunusa
Ndolzane River
Grand Valley
Mkondvo River
Big Bend
(Bridge washed out)
Usutu River

Mineral Baths
Gege

Piet Retief
Hlathikulu
Sithobela
Mhlathuze River

Maloma
Lubuli
Nsoko

Mahamba
Nhlangano
Mhlosheni
Ngwavuma River

MPUMALANGA (SOUTH AFRICA)
Mhlosheni
Sihultse
Sitla River

KWAZULU-NATAL (SOUTH AFRICA)
Lavumisa
Golela
Pongolapoort Dam

Paulpietersburg
Pongola
Jozini
To Durban (375km)

HISTORY

In eastern Swaziland archaeologists have discovered human remains dating back 110,000 years, but the ancestors of the modern Swazi people arrived relatively recently.

During the great Bantu migrations into Southern Africa, one group, the Nguni, moved down the east coast. A clan settled near what is now Maputo in Mozambique, and a dynasty was founded by the Dlamini family. In the mid-18th century increasing pressure from other Nguni clans forced King Ngwane III to lead his people south to lands by the Pongola River, in what is now southern Swaziland. Today, Swazis consider Ngwane III to have been the first king of Swaziland.

The next king, Sobhuza I, withdrew under pressure from the Zulus to the Ezulwini Valley, which today remains the centre of Swazi royalty and ritual. When King Sobhuza I died in 1839, Swaziland was twice its present size. Trouble with the Zulu continued, although the next king, Mswazi (or Mswati), managed to unify the whole kingdom. By the time he died in 1868, the Swazi nation was secure. Mswazi's subjects called themselves people of Mswazi, or Swazis, and the name stuck.

European Interference

The arrival of increasing numbers of Europeans from the mid-19th century brought new problems. Mswazi's successor, Mbandzeni, inherited a kingdom rife with European carpetbaggers – hunters, traders, missionaries and farmers, many of whom leased large expanses of land.

The Pretoria Convention of 1881 guaranteed Swaziland's 'independence' but also defined its borders, and Swaziland lost large chunks of territory. 'Independence' in fact meant that both the British and the Boers had responsibility for administering their various interests in Swaziland, and the result was chaos. The Boer administration collapsed with the 1899–1902 Anglo-Boer War, and afterwards the British took control of Swaziland as a protectorate.

During this troubled time, King Sobhuza II was only a young child, but Labotsibeni, his mother, acted ably as regent until her son took over in 1921. Labotsibeni encouraged Swazis to buy back their land, and many sought work in the Witwatersrand mines (near Johannesburg) to raise money.

Independence

In 1960 King Sobhuza II proposed the creation of a legislative council, composed of elected Europeans, and a national council formed in accordance with Swazi culture. The Mbokodvo (Grindstone) National Movement, which was formed at this time, pledged to maintain traditional Swazi culture but also to eschew racial discrimination. When the British finally agreed to elections in 1964, Mbokodvo won a majority and, at the next elections in 1967, won all the seats. Swaziland became independent on 6 September 1968.

The country's constitution was largely the work of the British. In 1973 the king suspended it on the grounds that it did not accord with Swazi culture. He also dissolved all political parties. Four years later the parliament reconvened under a new constitution that vested all power in the king. Sobhuza II, at that time the world's longest-reigning monarch, died in 1982. In keeping with Swazi tradition, a strictly enforced 75-day period of mourning was announced by Dzeliwe (Great She-Elephant), the most senior of his hundred wives. Only commerce essential to the life of the nation was allowed. And that didn't include sexual intercourse, which was banned, punishable by flogging.

Choosing a successor wasn't easy – Sobhuza had fathered more than 600 children, thereby creating hundreds of potential kings. Prince Makhosetive, born in 1968, was finally chosen and crowned King Mswati III in 1986.

The king continues to represent and maintain the traditional way of life and to assert his pre-eminence, for better and often for worse, as absolute monarch. Following his predecessor's style, Mswati dissolved parliament in 1992 and Swaziland was again governed by a traditional tribal assembly, the Liqoqo. Since then, democratic reform has begun, but there is increasingly strident agitation for faster change, a struggle that has been met with ever more restrictive legislation.

Relations between the 9000 white farmers (who own 37% of the land, much of it the best) and the monarchy remain cordial. Swaziland's greatest challenge comes from the HIV/Aids pandemic, which here is almost beyond comprehension – 33% of Swazi adults are thought to be infected. In 2001 the

---

THE LION KING

When you're an absolute monarch you don't have to court popularity. Just as well for Swaziland's King Mswati III. In 2002 he decided to purchase a royal jet aircraft, against international objections and those of his own parliament. The price tag? A cool US$45 million at a time when many Swazis struggled to get enough to eat.

The other source of recent discontent with the king came after the 2002 *Umhlanga* (Reed Dance), during which (in keeping with tradition) he chose a young woman, 18-year-old Zena Mahlangu, to become his 10th wife. Zena's mother tried to take the king to court, accusing him of abducting and holding Zena against her will, something the king's aides strenuously denied. Refusing to let anyone speak to Ms Mahlangu, they blocked moves to try the king as unconstitutional. The chief justice and two other leading judges were told by the attorney general to resign for refusing to throw the case out. Soon afterwards lawyers and judges went on strike in protest at the king's refusal to subject himself to the rule of law.

Despite all that, the king is a highly revered figurehead; he is the *Ngwenyama* (the lion), a descendent of the great kings (and the occasional queen mother) who secured the independence of the Swazi nation. Looked on sympathetically, a Swazi king's power and the clan links, to which he is bound by marrying so many wives, might be seen as the source of Swaziland's relative stability and the foundation of its continued independence.

It's certainly a situation Mswati has used to his advantage as he resists pressure for constitutional reform. It's a licence, in fact, for him to do pretty much whatever he wants.

---

king provoked outrage by imposing a five-year ban on sex by unmarried women in an effort to curb the spread of AIDS.

THE CULTURE

Around 90% of the population are Swazi (although there are about 70 distinct groups). The dominant clan is the Dlamini – it's kind of equivalent to Smith, and you'll meet your fair share of them all over the country. With so many royal wives and offspring through Swazi history, it's hardly surprising that you'll probably also meet a prince. If you do, try out your Swati – *Sawubona* means 'I see you' (used as a greeting) and, like any good royal, the Swazi variety likes to be seen.

There's a strong sense of Swazi identity. Social and cultural cohesion is maintained by a system of age-related royal regiments. Boys graduate from regiment to regiment as they grow older, an arrangement that minimises the potentially divisive differences between clans while emphasising loyalty to the king and nation.

ENVIRONMENT

Swaziland, although tiny, has a wide range of ecological zones, from rainforest in the northwest to savannah scrub in the east. Western Swaziland is high veld, consisting mainly of short, sharp mountains. These

dwindle to plains in the centre and east of the country, where plantations of sugar cane dominate the landscape. To the east, the border with Mozambique is formed by the harsh Lebombo Mountains.

Try to avoid visiting rain-soaked Swaziland during the rainy season (December to April). The best time to visit is in May–June or October, but bring something warm.

Conservation can come from the most unlikely sources. The monarchy reserved some areas for hunting, and it is these that preserve the remnants of indigenous flora (including 14% of the recorded plant life in Southern Africa) and animals (such as elephants, warthogs, rhinos and lions) that have been reintroduced. The remoteness of parts of the countryside also means there are probably plant species that have not yet been brought to the attention of botanists. Swaziland has about a third of the non-marine mammal species in Southern Africa.

TRANSPORT

GETTING THERE & AWAY
Air
Swaziland's main airport is Matsapha Airport, southwest of Manzini. (Schedules and tickets often refer to the airport as Manzini.) **Swazi Airlink** (☎ 518 6192, 4043157)

DEPARTURE TAX

There is a departure tax of US$2.50, which is levied at Matsapha airport.

---

is a joint venture between South African Airways and the Swazi government. It operates daily flights to/from Johannesburg (US$72). **Swazi Express Airways** (☎ 518 6840; www.swazibusiness.com/steffenair) flies four times a week to Durban (South Africa, US$90).

Bus & Minibus Taxi
MOZAMBIQUE

The main border crossing between Swaziland and Mozambique is at Lomahasha-Namaacha (open 7am to 8pm). There is a twice-weekly bus service from Mbabane to Maputo (Mozambique); inquire at the tourist office in Mbabane (see below, right). Minibus taxis operate daily from Manzini to Maputo (US$4, 2½ hours).

SOUTH AFRICA

The main border crossings with South Africa are: Piggs Peak (open 7am to 8am); Josefsdal-Bulembu (open 8am to 4pm); Oshoek-Ngwenya; Houtkop-Sicunusa (open 8am to 6pm); Mahamba and Golela/Lavumisa (open 7am to 10pm).

The **Baz Bus** (in South Africa ☎ 021-439 2323) runs from Jo'burg/Pretoria to Durban via Mbabane and Manzini four times a week (US$30), returning the next day. For more details see Getting Around in the South Africa chapter (p947).

Generally speaking Manzini is best for transport to Durban and Mozambique, whereas Mbabane is best for Jo'burg and northern destinations. Minibus taxis operate three times a week to Johannesburg (US$10), Nelspruit (US$12) and Durban (US$12).

GETTING AROUND
Bus & Minibus Taxi

There are a few infrequent (but cheap) domestic buses, most of which begin and terminate at the main stop in the centre of Mbabane. Generally you'll find minibus taxis are the best public transport, although they often run shorter routes. There are also non-shared (private hire) taxis in some of the larger towns.

Hitching

Hitching is easier here than in South Africa, as the skin colour of the driver and hitch-hiker aren't factors in the decision to offer a lift. However, you have to wait a long time for a car on back roads, and everywhere you'll have lots of competition from locals.

MBABANE

pop 38,600

Mbabane (if you say 'mba-**baa**-nay' you'll be close enough) is a relaxed place to hang out. Use it as your introduction to Swaziland, a place to get your bearings before tackling the adjacent Ezulwini Valley. There's not much to see or do here, but the setting amid the Dlangeni Hills is picturesque, and in summer Mbabane is the place to be – the hills make it cooler than Manzini, which is why the British moved their administrative centre here in 1902.

ORIENTATION

Buses and minibuses from Mbabane to Manzini go past the turn-off to Matsapha Airport, from where it's a long walk to the terminal. The main street is Allister Miller St. Swazi Plaza, a large, modern shopping centre with most services and a good range of shops, is off Western Distributor Rd. The Mall, another shopping area, is across Plaza Mall St.

INFORMATION

The **tourist office** (☎ 404 2531; Swazi Plaza, off Western Distributor Rd) offers meagre brochure information and equally scarce staff. Pick up a copy of the free monthly *What's On in Swaziland?* for current information. Alternatively try the **tourist office** (☎ 442 4206) in the Ezulwini Valley.

Royal Swazi Big Game Parks (☎ 528 3944; The Mall; www.biggame.co.sz) has information on the main national parks.

There's a **Standard Bank** (Swazi Plaza, off Western Distributor Rd) with 24-hour ATM and a **First National Bank** (The Mall, Plaza Mall St).

The **post office** is on Warner (Msunduza) St, and medical services are offered at **Mbabane Government Hospital** (☎ 404 2111).

Internet access is available in a few places in town. The most convenient is **Real Image** (The Mall, Plaza Mall St).

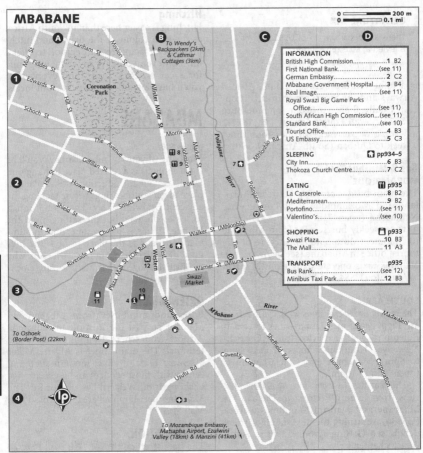

MBABANE

0 _____ 200 m
0 _____ 0.1 mi

INFORMATION	
British High Commission	1 B2
First National Bank	(see 11)
German Embassy	2 C2
Mbabane Government Hospital	3 B4
Real Image	(see 11)
Royal Swazi Big Game Parks	
Office	(see 11)
South African High Commission	(see 11)
Standard Bank	(see 10)
Tourist Office	4 B3
US Embassy	5 C3

SLEEPING	🏠 pp934–5
City Inn	6 B3
Thokoza Church Centre	7 C2

EATING	🍴 p935
La Casserole	8 B2
Mediterranean	9 B2
Portofino	(see 11)
Valentino's	(see 10)

SHOPPING	🛍 p933
Swazi Plaza	10 B3
The Mall	11 A3

TRANSPORT	p935
Bus Rank	(see 12)
Minibus Taxi Park	12 B3

DANGERS & ANNOYANCES

Mbabane is becoming unsafe at night, so don't walk around by yourself, especially away from the main streets. Always take precautions in the back streets even during the day.

SLEEPING

Cheap places to crash are hard to find, and none are central.

Wendy's Backpackers (☎ 404 3905; Lot 1120, Dalriach East; dm US$7, d US$18) This small but friendly place 2km from the city centre is probably the best of a limited bunch. Swimming pool and weekend walking tours are added bonuses, and prices include a light breakfast.

Thokoza Church Centre (☎ 404 6681; Polinjane Rd; d US$4, with bathroom US$5) Another good choice, the Thokoza has simple rooms. To get here from Allister Miller St, turn east on to Walker St, cross the bridge, turn left at the police station and head along a dirt road up the hill for about 250 metres. It's not safe to walk here at night.

Cathmar Cottages (☎ 404 3387; cathmar@africa online.co.sz; Pine Valley Rd; cottages US$7) For something a little different, the self-catering cottages here are cosy. There's also a pool. It's 3km north of Mbabane – follow the signs to Pine Valley, turn right into Fonteyn Rd, left into Mseni Drive and left into Lukhalo St.

City Inn (☎ 404 4278/2406; Allister Miller St; s/d US$14/16) This long-time travellers' favourite probably remains so only because there are no other cheap central options – it's pretty run down these days.

EATING

There are a few good restaurants in Mbabane if you know where to look.

Portofino (The Mall, Plaza Mall St; dishes US$2-3) A good breakfast option with large servings.

Mediterranean (Allister Miller St; dishes US$4.50) Indian, despite its name, but also has steaks and seafood.

Valentino's (☎ 404 7498; Swazi Plaza; dishes US$4.60) The place for a splurge (including a mean seafood platter).

La Casserole (Omni Centre) Serves a decent range of continental (especially German) cuisine, plus drinks.

GETTING THERE & AWAY

Minibus taxis to South Africa (mostly northbound) leave from the minibus taxi park near Swazi Plaza, where you'll also find buses and minibus taxis to destinations within Swaziland, including Manzini (US$0.50), Big Bend (US$1.25) and Piggs Peak (US$1). Any vehicle heading towards Manzini or Matsapha passes through the Ezulwini Valley. Non-shared taxis to the Ezulwini Valley cost at least US$6, more to the far end of the valley, and still more at night.

GETTING AROUND

Non-shared taxis congregate near the bus rank by Swazi Plaza. At night you can usually find one near the City Inn, or try calling ☎ 404 0965 or ☎ 404 0966.

AROUND SWAZILAND

EZULWINI VALLEY

The Ezulwini Valley is the homeland of Swazi royalty. As a natural landscape it's quite picturesque, with lush greenery and densely wooded, rolling hills, but is becoming less so as hotels and other developments crowd out the natural features. It begins just outside Mbabane and extends down past Lobamba village, 18km away. Most of the area's prime attractions are near Lobamba.

Lobamba

You can see the monarchy in action at the **Royal Kraal** in Lobamba during the *Incwala*

ceremony and the *Umhlanga* dance (see Festivals & Events on p939).

The **National Museum** (foreigners' admission US$1; ☒ daily) has some significant displays on Swazi culture and a traditional beehive village. The **National Trust Commission office** (☎ 416 1179), where you can make bookings for Mlawula Nature Reserve (p938) and Malolotja Nature Reserve (p938), is also here.

Next to the museum is the **parliament**, which is sometimes open to visitors. Across the road from the museum is a **memorial** to King Sobhuza II, the most revered of Swazi kings, and a small **museum** devoted to him.

Mlilwane Wildlife Sanctuary

This lovely sanctuary (adult/child US$2.50/1.25), near Lobamba, is a private reserve created by Ted Reilly on his family farm in the 1950s. The reserve is dominated by the precipitous Nyonyane (Little Bird) peak, and there are several attractive walks around it. Zebras, giraffes, many antelope species, crocodiles, hippos and a variety of birds can be seen; in summer, watch out for the black eagle (*Aquila verreauxii*).

There are plenty of guided trips through the reserve: **walks** cost US$1.75 per hour, **mountain biking** costs US$5 per hour and **horse-riding** is US$9 per hour. Watching the hippos from the restaurant is great entertainment, especially at feeding time (3pm).

The main entrance is 2km southeast of the Happy Valley Motel on the old Mbabane-Manzini road. You can get a sanctuary map at the gate.

Sleeping

Sondzela Backpackers (HI) Lodge (☎ 528 3117; dm US$6, s/d US$11/17) This hostel, just south of Main Camp, is great. It's roomy and has a large veranda that offers great views. A pickup shuttle runs to Malandela's restaurant in Malkerns, where the Baz Bus stops.

Mantenga Nature Reserve (beehive huts US$3.50, tented chalets US$21) Just down the dirt track from Mantenga Lodge, the reserve rents out beehive huts to campers and has some great tented chalets looking on to Excecution Rock (people really were once flung to their deaths from its jagged peak). Book through the Royal Swazi Big Game Parks office in Mbabane (p933).

Timbali Caravan Park (☎ 416 1156; timbali.co.sz; camp sites per person US$6, s/d US$32/52) Outside the

SWAZILAND

sanctuary you'll find this well-run place with a restaurant (closed on Monday) and swimming pool. There's a supermarket nearby.

Shonalanga Cottage (r per person with breakfast US$23) Shonalanga is in the sanctuary with spacious accommodation and a fully equipped kitchen. Book through the Royal Swazi Big Game Parks office in Mbabane (p933).

Inside Mlilwane Wildlife Sanctuary there are **camping and caravanning sites** (camp sites per person US$4), though there's no electricity. In the sanctuary's **Main Camp** (beehive huts per person US$11, camp huts per person US$16) there are also beehive huts and more luxurious rest camp huts with bathroom and fridge. Book through the Royal Swazi Big Game Parks office (p933).

Eating & Drinking
Calabash Continental (☎ 416 1187), next to Timbali Caravan Park, specialises in German and Swiss cuisine.

Malandelas (☎ 528 3115), next door to Gone Rural, is one of Swaziland's better restaurants and has a cosy bar.

Bella Vista Pizzeria at the Happy Valley Motel has large vegetarian pizzas for US$2.50 and hearty seafood pizzas for US$3.50.

Ezulwini Sun sometimes has music, food and drinks in the beer garden.

Martin's Bar & Disco near the Timbali Caravan Park is a basic but often busy watering hole.

House on Fire is a fantastically decorated space next door to Malandelas that often has music, live or otherwise.

Getting There & Away
During the day you could get on a Manzini-bound bus from Mbabane, but make sure the driver knows you want to get off in the valley. Even some nonexpress buses aren't keen on stopping. Non-shared taxis from Mbabane cost at least US$6. At night you'll have to negotiate.

MANZINI
pop 13,900
Manzini is the country's industrial centre. Downtown Manzini isn't large, but it feels like a different country from easy-going rural Swaziland. There are reckless drivers, city slickers and a hint of menace; be careful at night.

The **market** on Thursday and Friday mornings is excellent. Get there at dawn if possible when the rural people bring in their handicrafts to sell to retailers.

Sleeping & Eating
Swaziland Backpackers (☎ 518 7225; info@swazilandbackpackers.com; camp site per person US$3.50, dm US$6, r US$16; 💻) One of Swaziland's best backpackers is a well-run, clean place, just up the road from the lively locals' watering hole, the Salt 'n' Pepper Club. It has a bar and email facilities. The Baz Bus stops here.

Myxo's Place (☎ 5058363, camping US$4.60, dm US$7, d US$18) Just off the Big Bend Road is this chilled-out place. If you have time, Myxo runs two-day trips (around US$40 per person) to a local village where you can sleep and eat in the traditional Swazi way and spend some time among the villagers. It's a great experience.

Mozambique Hotel (☎ 505 2489; Mahleko St; s/d US$11/18) The rooms here are average, but there's a good bar and a popular Portuguese restaurant.

There are plenty of takeaways in Bhunu Mall, including Chicken Licken, King Pie and Steers.

Getting There & Away
A non-shared taxi to Matsapha airport costs US$7. The main bus and minibus taxi park is at the northern end of Louw St. Buses run up the Ezulwini Valley to Mbabane for US$0.30. Taxis to Mozambique leave from the car park next to KFC. Fares include Jo'burg (US$11), Durban (US$12) and Pretoria (US$11). Most long-distance taxis leave early in the morning.

MKHAYA GAME RESERVE
Mkhaya (☎ 528 3943/4) is a refuge for endangered species, including rare black rhinos – possibly your best chance of meeting a black rhino in Africa in the wild. Mkhaya takes its name from the mkhaya tree (or knobthorn, *Acacia nigrescens*), which abounds on the reserve. Mkhayas grow only on fertile land, and are valued not only for their fruit, from which Swazis brew beer, but also for the insects and birdlife that they support.

Although small, Mkhaya has a wide range of animals. In addition to the rhinos you'll find elephants and roan and sable antelopes. There are also herds of the indigenous and rare Nguni cattle that make the reserve economically self-supporting. The Nguni is an old breed, and centuries of natural selection have made it heat tolerant, disease immune, self-sufficient and, importantly, tick-resistant (rather like your ideal backpacker).

Activities

The reserve organises a couple of good-value **safaris**. A one-day drive (minimum two people) in a 4WD, with lunch, costs US$20; a half-day costs US$14.

One of Swaziland's highlights is **whitewater rafting** on the Usutu River. The river is usually sluggish and quite tame, but near Mkhaya Game Reserve it passes through the narrow Bulungu Gorge, which separates the Mabukabuka and Bulungu Mountains, generating rapids. At one stage you'll have to portage a 10m waterfall. The second half of the day is a sedate trip through scenic country with glimpses of the 'flat dogs' (crocodiles) sunning on the riverbanks. **Swazi Trails** (☎ /fax 416 2180; tours@swazitrails.co.sz; Mantenga Craft Centre, Ezulwini Valley) runs full-day trips in two-person 'crocodile rafts' for US$29 per person. Prices include lunch and all equipment.

Sleeping & Eating

Unlike the national parks in Swaziland, this is a private reserve, and the experience here doesn't come cheap. Note that you can't

visit without prebooking, and you can't drive in alone; you'll be met at Phuzumoya at a specified pick-up time.

Nkonjane (Swallow's Nest; cottage per person US$60) Nkonjane offers luxurious stone cottages. Rates are higher at weekends. Book through Royal Swazi Big Game Parks (p933).

> ### SPLURGE!
> **Stone Camp** (tents per person US$60) Stone Camp is like a comfortable 19th-century hunting camp. The floors of the tents are on sand, allowing you to see ant trails and the tracks of small nocturnal visitors. The price includes three meals, wildlife drives and walks.

HLANE ROYAL NATIONAL PARK

This **park** (adult/child US$2.50/1.25) – Hlane means 'wilderness' – in the northeast is near the former royal hunting grounds. It's a popular stopover for travellers looking for white rhinos en route to Mozambique via Lomahasha. Elephants and lions have also been reintroduced. There are guided walking trails (US$1.75 per person per hour). The park entrance at Ndlovu Gate (where there's a shop) is about 4km from Simunye.

RHINO WARS

In 1965 white rhino were re-established in the kingdom after an absence of 70 years. That was the easy part. Since then there has been an ongoing battle to protect them from poachers. At the forefront of this battle has been Ted Reilly and a band of dedicated, hand-picked rangers.

This defence hasn't been easy, especially as the poachers have received hefty financial backing from Taiwanese interests; after all, rhino horn is a lucrative prize on the Asian market. Poaching escalated in the late 1980s, and there were determined efforts to change rhino poaching laws in Swaziland. Rhinos were dehorned and confined to enclosures for their own protection. After Hlane Royal National Park was attacked in January 1992 by poachers with AK47s, the rangers armed themselves. With the rhinos dehorned at Hlane, the poachers shifted to Mkhaya Game Reserve. The battle commenced.

In April 1992 there was a shoot-out between rangers and poachers at Mkhaya, and some poachers were captured. Not long after there was another shoot-out at Big Bend in which two poachers were killed.

The last rhino (the majestic bull Mthondvo) was killed for horn in December 1992 while the Swazi courts still agonised over action relating to the Big Bend incident. The young king, Mswati III, intervened on behalf of Reilly's rangers, and the poaching of rhinos that were reintroduced declined dramatically. The rangers still wait with their rifles at the ready. You can help – your presence at any one of the big wildlife parks assists in rhino conservation.

A happy postscript was the donation by the Taiwanese government in 1996 of enough money to purchase six black rhinos; a gesture of good faith that was welcomed with open arms. Even better, the black rhinos, which were relocated from parks in KwaZulu-Natal, are breeding well.

SWAZILAND

There's **camping** (per person US$4), but no electricity.

Ndlovu Rest Camp (huts per person US$17) has thatched huts with communal facilities and no electricity.

Bhubesi Rest Camp (huts per person US$17) has self-contained huts with electricity. Book through the Royal Swazi Big Game Parks office in Mbabane (p933).

MLAWULA NATURE RESERVE

Taking in both plains and the Lebombo Mountains, **Mlawula** (admission per person/vehicle US$2.50/1.25) – pronounced something like mull-oo-way – is a 16,000-hectare reserve set in harsh but beautiful country in the country's northeast. Shy hyenas hide in remote areas as well as antelope species, and resident snakes include the deadly trio of black mamba, puff adder and spitting cobra. Aquatic dangers include both crocodiles and bilharzia. Watch out for ticks, too. Freaked out yet? That might seem like an awful lot to contend with, but the most important advice is that the park's well worth a visit.

The reserve's entrance is about 10km north of Simunye.

There's **camping** (camp sites per person US$2.30) and **tented accommodation** (tents US$14). Call for **bookings** (☎ 383 8885; mlawula@sntc.org.sz), or see the National Trust Commission in Lobamba (p935).

PIGGS PEAK

As well as its scenery, including the **Phophonyane Falls** about 8km north of town, this area in the hilly northwestern corner of the country is known for its handicrafts. The small town itself is the centre of the logging industry. There are huge pine plantations in the area, and some fine views are available from the ridges.

At the Highlands Inn in Piggs Peak, **Tintsaba Crafts** displays a good range; there are several other craft centres in the district, including a couple of excellent shops just up the main road from Piggs Peak Hotel (signposted from Phophonyane).

Highlands Inn (☎ 437 1144; s/d from US$19/36) About 1km south of the town centre on the main road, this is the only place to stay in town. The rooms are clean but aren't great value even if they do include breakfast. There's a pleasant garden area.

Getting There & Away

Roads in the northwest of the country are mainly dirt, but they're in reasonable condition. There's an express sprinter bus to Mbabane for US$1. The bus and minibus taxi rank is next to the market at the top end of the main street.

MALOLOTJA NATURE RESERVE

Malolotja is real wilderness – something hard to imagine in this tiny country, but much of this reserve is indeed rugged and largely unspoiled.

The **reserve** (☎ 442 4241; admission US$2.30; ☯ 6am-6pm) in the hilly northwest of the country is home to antelope species, more than 280 species of bird as well as wildflowers and **rare plants**. The **Komati River** cuts a gorge through the park and continues east in a series of falls and rapids until it meets the lowveld.

The reserve has one of the world's oldest known **mines**, where haematite and specularite were mined for cosmetic and ritual uses from 41,000 BC. You can visit the mine, but you must be accompanied by a ranger.

Hiking trails range from short day walks to a week-long trail, extending from Ngwenya in the south to the Mgwayiza Range in the north. For the extended trails, you must obtain a free permit and a map (US$0.60) from the reserve office. You need to bring all your own food and a camp stove as fires are not permitted outside the base camp.

There's camping at the established **camp sites** (sites per person US$4.50) and on the **trails** (sites per person US$2.30). There are also fully equipped **cabins** (d US$35). Book through the **National Trust Commission** (p935) in the National Museum, Lobamba.

The park entrance is about 35km from Mbabane on the Piggs Peak road. Take any transport between Mbabane and Piggs Peak.

SWAZILAND DIRECTORY

ACCOMMODATION
Many of the country's hotels are geared towards South African tourists and are expensive. If you're stuck for a room in rural areas, you could try the local school, where you'll probably be welcomed.

ACTIVITIES
Swaziland's wildlife reserves offer some terrific (rainy season) white-water rafting, horse-riding, walking and mountain biking.

EMBASSIES & CONSULATES
Neighbouring countries where Swaziland has diplomatic representation are Mozambique and South Africa. Details are listed in the Directory of those country chapters.

Countries with diplomatic representation in Mbabane include:

Germany (☎ 404 3174; 3rd Fl, Lilunga House, Gilfillan St)
Mozambique (☎ 404 3700; Princess Dr)
South Africa (☎ 404 4651; The Mall, PO Box 250)
UK (☎ 404 2581/2/3; 2nd fl, Lilunga House, Gilfillan St)
USA (☎ 404 6441; Central Bank Bldg, Warner St)

See the Visas for Onward Travel section (on the next page) for details on getting visas.

FESTIVALS & EVENTS
Colourful ceremonies (and traditional dress, which is still commonly worn) underline the Swazis' unique identity.

The *Incwala* ceremony is Swaziland's most sacred, celebrating the new year and the first fruits of the harvest in rituals of thanksgiving, prayer, atonement and reverence for the king. As part of the festivities the king grants his people the right to consume his harvest, and rains are expected to follow the ceremony.

The *Umhlanga* (Reed Dance), a great spectacle in August or September, is performed by unmarried girls who collect reeds for the repair and maintenance of the royal palace.

It is something like a week-long debutante ball for marriageable young Swazi women and a showcase of potential wives for the king. On the sixth day they perform the reed dance and carry their reeds to the queen mother. Princesses wear red feathers in their hair.

The venue for both festivals is near Lobamba in the Ezulwini Valley. Ask at the tourist office in Mbabane for exact dates.

Photography is not permitted at the *Incwala* but is at the *Umhlanga* dance.

HEALTH
Take precautions against malaria. Swimming almost anywhere in the country is risky because of bilharzia (for more information on how to avoid contracting these potentially deadly diseases, see Health in the Africa Directory – p1028). There are also crocodiles in some places.

If you need medical assistance there is the **Mbabane Government Hospital** (☎ 404 2111), the **Raleigh Fitkin Hospital** (☎ 505 2211) in Manzini and the **Piggs Peak Government Hospital** (☎ 437 1111).

HOLIDAYS
As well as religious holidays listed in the Africa Directory (p1003) the principal public holidays in Swaziland include:

1 January New Year's Day
9 April King Mswati III's Birthday
25 April National Flag Day
22 July King Sobhuza II's Birthday
August/September Umhlanga (Reed Dance Day)
6 September Somhlolo (Independence Day)
December/January Incwala Day

INTERNET ACCESS
Internet facilities are scarce outside Mbabane. A couple of places in Ezulwini Valley have Internet access.

MAPS
If you're serious about hiking, 1:50,000 scale maps are available from the Surveyor-General's office at the **Ministry of Works** (PO Box 58, Mbabane).

MEDIA
There are two English-language newspapers, the *Times of Swaziland* and the *Swazi Observer*. The former is a virtual mouth-piece for royalty and a would-be lurid tabloid. It's a

SWAZILAND

fascinating read as much for what it doesn't say as for what it does.

MONEY

The unit of currency is the lilangeni; the plural is emalangeni (E). It is tied in value to the South African rand. Rands are accepted everywhere in Swaziland, and there's no need to change them, although a few places don't accept South African coins. Emalangeni are difficult to change for other currencies outside Swaziland, even in South Africa. The bank at Matsapha airport, near Manzini, opens for flights.

Most banks ask to see the receipt of purchase when cashing travellers cheques. The First National bank charges a flat US$2.30 commission.

Only a few ATMs accept international credit or debit cards. The most convenient are at Standard Bank in Swazi Mall, Mbabane and inside the **Royal Swazi Hotel's casino** (☎ 416 1001).

TELEPHONE

To call Swaziland from South Africa dial the prefix 09-268. To call overseas from Swazi-land, use the code 00. The best way to make international calls is with E15 to E50 (US$2 to US$7) phone cards from post offices and shops.

TOURIST INFORMATION

Swaziland's only tourist offices are in Mbabane and the Ezulwini Valley.

VISAS

Most people don't need a visa to visit Swaziland. If you don't need a visa to enter South Africa, you won't need one for Swazi-land. Anyone staying for more than 60 days must apply for a temporary residence permit from the **Chief Immigration Officer** (☎ 404 2941; PO Box 372, Mbabane).

Visas for Onward Travel

One-month visas for Mozambique cost US$12 (considerably less than you would pay in Johannesburg) and require two photos. It can be done in a day at the Mozambique embassy in Mbabane (see p939 for address details). It is also possible to obtain a visa at the Swaziland–Mozambique border, although it is a little more expensive.

South Africa

HIGHLIGHTS

- **Cape Town** Spend some time exploring this majestic city, one of the most stunning in the world; witness history on a trip to Robben Island; sample the fruits of the Winelands (p950)
- **Transkei** Revel on secluded white-sand, warm-water beaches – a backpackers' paradise (p963)
- **The Drakensberg Escarpment** Experience the magic of this dramatic range either on foot or horseback (p972)
- **Johannesburg** Explore the centre of the nation's psyche – Jo'burg is vibrant and steeped in history; don't let its bad reputation put you off (p974)
- **Best journey** Travel down the Wild Coast in either the Baz Bus or your own vehicle starting in Port St Johns and ending in Cintsa (p965)
- **Off the beaten track** Hike through ancient rainforest near the quiet hamlet of Hogsback and you might spot a hobbit – legend has it that Hogsback inspired JRR Tolkien to write *Lord of the Rings* (p963)

FAST FACTS

- **Area** 1,223,404 sq km
- **ATMs** in most cities and large towns around the country
- **Borders** Namibia, Botswana, Zimbabwe, Mozambique, Swaziland, Lesotho
- **Budget** US$20 to US$25 a day
- **Capital** Pretoria (administrative), Cape Town (legislative) and Bloemfontein (judicial)
- **Languages** English, Afrikaans, Zulu, Xhosa, Pedi, Tswana, Sotho, Tsonga, Swati, Venda and Ndebele
- **Money** rand; US$1 = R7
- **Population** 44 million
- **Seasons** Cape Town: cold & wet (May–Aug), sunny & warm (Sep–May); Durban & Jo'burg: dry (May–Sep), wet (Oct–Apr)
- **Telephone** country code ☎ 27; international access code ☎ 09
- **Time** GMT/UTC + 2
- **Visas** free, 90-day entry permits issued on arrival to citizens of Australia, New Zealand, France, Germany, the UK, Ireland, Canada and the USA

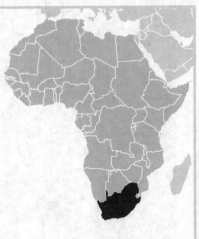

SOUTH AFRICA

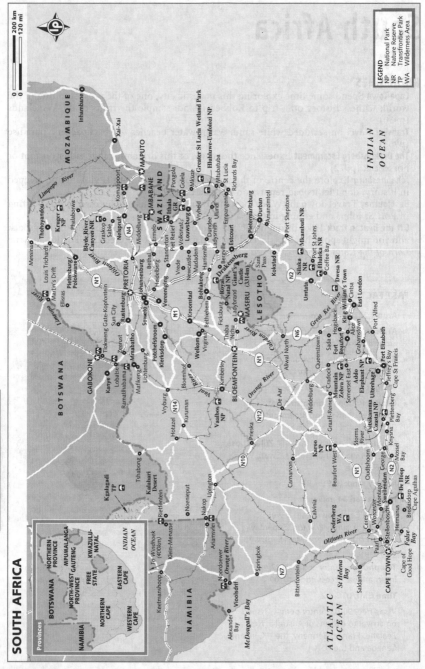

South Africa will nullify any stereotype you might hold about the African continent. An exhilarating, spectacular and complex nation, on the surface it's an easy introduction to Africa. Filled with world-class attractions and first-world amenities, it caters to backpackers like no other country on the continent. Whether you desire the snow-capped peaks of the Drakensberg range, the magnificent white-sand beaches of the Wild Coast, the picture-perfect beauty of Cape Town or the chance to view wildlife in Kruger, the 'rainbow nation' offers something for everybody. However, South Africa's beauty is somewhat diluted by its other face. Time has not yet healed the wounds of apartheid. Segregation is so deeply entrenched that it still predominates. Poverty and crime is rife among blacks and whites. Racist remarks are so ingrained that, sadly, they don't seem superlative. You will be forced to confront South Africa's appalling history on a daily basis, but if you are willing to immerse yourself in its psyche, and are ready to witness history in the making, then head to this fascinating country.

HISTORY

The earliest recorded inhabitants of this area of Africa were the San (Bushmen) and the closely related Khoikhoi (Hottentots). The next arrivals were Bantu-speaking tribes who, by the 11th century, had settled the northeast and the east coast and, by the 15th century, most of the eastern half of South Africa. These tribes were pastoral but they had trade links throughout the region. They were Iron Age peoples, and the smelting techniques of some tribes were not surpassed in Europe until the Industrial Revolution.

European Settlement

The Dutch East India Company established the first European settlement in South Africa at the Cape of Good Hope in 1652. The settlers developed a close-knit community with their own dialect (Afrikaans) and Calvinist sect (the Dutch Reformed Church). Slaves were imported from other parts of Africa and Southeast Asia.

Over the next 150 years, the colonists spread east, coming into violent contact with Bantu tribes. In 1779 the eastward expansion of the Boers (Dutch-Afrikaner farmers) was temporarily halted by the Xhosa in the first Bantu War.

Further Boer expansion was hastened after the British annexed the Cape in 1806. The abolition of slavery in 1834 was regarded by the Boers as an intolerable interference in their affairs, and led to migration across the Orange River two years later. This became known as the Great Trek.

Pressure on the Bantu from both the Boers and the British caused political and social changes among the tribes of the Natal area, resulting in the rise of the Zulu king Shaka in the early 19th century. His policy of total war

on neighbouring tribes caused immense suffering and mass migration in a period known as the *difaqane* (the scattering).

The Boers came into this chaos in search of new lands, and the British were not far behind them. The Zulu were eventually defeated, but relations between the Boers and the British remained tense – particularly after the formation of the Boer republics of the Free State and the Transvaal.

Diamonds were discovered in 1867 at Kimberley, followed by the discovery of gold in 1886 on the Witwatersrand in Johannesburg (Jo'burg). The Boer republics were flooded with British capital and immigrants, which created resentment among Boer farmers.

The British imperialist Cecil Rhodes encouraged a rebellion among the heavily taxed (but nonvoting) English-speaking miners in the Transvaal, with a view to destabilising the Boer republics and encouraging British intervention. The resulting tensions led to the 1899–1902 Anglo-Boer War.

The war ended with the defeat of the Boer republics and the imposition of British rule over the whole country. Britain had pursued a scorched-earth policy to combat Boer guerrillas, destroying homes, crops and livestock. During this time more than 26,000 Afrikaner women and children died in the world's first concentration camps.

Independence & Apartheid

In 1910 the Union of South Africa was created, which gave political control to the whites. Inevitably, this prompted black resistance in the form of strikes, and political organisations were formed. Despite the moderate tone of these early resistance groups, the government reacted by intensifying repression.

SOUTH AFRICA

The Afrikaner National Party won the election in 1948. It went even further in excluding nonwhites from having any political or economic power, and the security forces brutally enforced its laws. Violence was a routine method of supporting any opposition or protest. The suppression of black resistance ranged from the Sharpeville massacre of 1960 and the shooting of school children in Soweto in 1976 to the forcible evacuation and bulldozing of squatter settlements and the systematic torture – even murder – of political activists, such as Steve Biko.

One of the most important organisations to oppose the racist legislation was the African National Congress (ANC). As it became obvious that the white rulers were unwilling to undertake even the most cosmetic reforms, guerrilla warfare became the preferred option for the ANC. In the early 1960s many of ANC leaders were arrested, charged with treason and imprisoned for long periods; the most famous of those was Nelson Mandela.

The system of apartheid was entrenched even further in the early 1970s by the creation of the so-called Black homelands of Transkei, Ciskei, Bophuthatswana and Venda. These were, in theory, 'independent' countries. By creating the homelands, all blacks within white-designated South Africa were deemed foreign guest-workers and as such were without political rights. Any black person without a residence pass could be 'deported' to a homeland.

Meanwhile, South Africa was becoming an isolated case in the face of successful liberation struggles in Angola, Mozambique and Zimbabwe, which all brought Marxist-leaning governments into power. As a result, a war psychosis came to dominate government thinking, and resulted in the invasion of southern Angola by South African armed forces.

The South African Government also gave encouragement to counter-revolutionary guerrilla groups in both Mozambique and Angola, and refused to enter into genuine negotiations for the independence of Namibia.

The international community finally began to oppose the apartheid regime, and the UN imposed economic and political sanctions. The government made some concessions, including the establishment of a farcical new parliament of whites, coloureds (people of mixed race) and Indians – but no blacks.

The 'reforms' did nothing to ease sanctions. After the 1989 elections the new president, FW de Klerk, instituted a program that was aimed not only at dismantling the apartheid system but also at introducing democracy. The release of political prisoners on 11 February 1990 (including Nelson Mandela), the repeal of the Group Areas Act (which set up the homelands), and the signing of a peace accord with the ANC and other opposition groups all opened the way for hard-fought negotiations on the path to majority rule.

The Post-Apartheid Era

The country's first democratic elections took place in 1994, and across the country at midnight on 26–27 April, *Die Stem* (the old national anthem) was sung and the old flag was lowered. A new rainbow flag was raised and the new anthem, *Nkosi Sikelele Afrika* (God Bless Africa), was sung. In the past people had been jailed for singing this beautiful anthem.

In the first democratic election in the country's history, the ANC won 62.7% of the vote; 66.7% would have enabled it to overrule the interim constitution. The National Party won 20.4% of the vote, enough to guarantee it representation in cabinet. Nelson Mandela was made president of the 'new' South Africa.

In 1999, after five years of learning about democracy, the country voted in a more 'normal' election. Issues such as economics and competence were raised and debated.

There was some speculation that the ANC vote might drop with the retirement of Nelson Mandela. However, the ANC's vote increased to the point where the party came within one seat of the two-thirds majority that would allow it to alter the constitution. The National Party lost two-thirds of its seats, losing its official opposition status to the Democratic Party. Thabo Mbeki, who took over leadership of the ANC from Nelson Mandela, became president in the 1999 elections. Compared with Nelson Mandela, whose life has become the stuff of legend, Mbeki was not well known to the people. Still, he proved himself a shrewd politician, maintaining his political pre-eminence by isolating co-opting opposition parties (the most incredible example being a power-'sharing' deal with the New National Party – the rebranded architects of apartheid).

It has not all been plain sailing for Mbeki, however. In the early days of his presidency he invited global criticism for his effective denial of the AIDS crisis. Soon after, white South African land owners and foreign investors were spooked in 2001 and beyond as Mbeki conspicuously failed to condemn the chaotic, violent and forced reclamation of white-owned farms in neighbouring Zimbabwe. This tacit support for Zimbabwean president Robert Mugabe created fears for the future of white-owned land in South Africa and led to an alarming devaluation of the rand. The purchase in 2002 of a US$68 million presidential jet was seen as indulgent at a time when many citizens struggled to fill their stomachs.

THE CULTURE

'I don't know how to say this any other way,' a traveller said after spending a month in South Africa, 'but this country is fucked up. White people run all the hostels and bars for tourists, and some of them are telling me they wished apartheid had never died. I don't even feel like I'm in Africa – you can go for days without seeing the majority of the population.'

Despite the fact that there are only five million whites in South Africa, it's a sad reality that it's easy to travel a while on the backpacker circuit without seeing a black face in a position of authority. Hostels, bars and restaurants are almost exclusively run by whites who jumped on the budget bandwagon after the fall of apartheid.

Racism is so firmly entrenched in this country's psyche that it will take decades to reverse. The greatest hostilities exist between the Afrikaners and blacks. Other white South Africans, on the whole, are not as angry. Whites complain that the fall of apartheid negated economic stability and caused crime to skyrocket. For black South Africans the biggest gripe is economic inequality, as well as the reality of crime-ridden townships.

Poverty is not just a problem for the black population, but also for whites. Unlike other parts of the continent, South Africa has a large proportion of whites begging on the streets.

Although the outlook may seem glum at times, not every person in South Africa is a racist. Some white business owners do harbour backward views, others are employing blacks at fair prices and speaking positively and passionately about the new South Africa. At the same time, although positive race relations might still be in their infancy for many, intermingling does exist among the younger generation. Spend some time in Jo'burg, Cape Town and Pretoria, and your disillusionment might begin to dissipate.

ARTS

Although South Africa is home to a great diversity of cultures, most were suppressed during the apartheid years. Many artists, black and white, were involved in the anti-apartheid campaign, and some were banned. In a society where you could be jailed for owning a politically incorrect painting, serious art was forced underground and blandness ruled in the galleries and theatres. *Resistance Art in South Africa* by Sue Williamson gives an overview of South African art during these times.

It will take time for the damage to be undone, but there is hope. Many galleries are holding retrospective exhibitions of contemporary and traditional black artists, and musicians from around Africa perform in major festivals.

Jazz was about the only medium in which blacks and whites could interact on equal terms, and it remains tremendously important. Theatre also was important for blacks, both as an art form and as a way of getting political messages across to illiterate comrades.

ENVIRONMENT
The Land

South Africa extends nearly 2000km from the Limpopo River in the north to Cape Agulhas in the south, and nearly 1500km from Alexandra Bay in the west to beyond Durban in the east.

There are nine provinces: Gauteng, Northern Province, Mpumalanga, KwaZulu-Natal, Free State, North-West Province, Northern Cape, Eastern Cape and Western Cape.

The homelands ('independent' tribal territories established during the apartheid era) no longer exist, but there is still a perceptible change when you cross one of the old borders. The best-known homelands, Transkei and Ciskei, have mostly been absorbed into Eastern Cape. A small chunk of Transkei and much of the former Zululand is in KwaZulu-Natal.

The Western Cape has dry sunny summers with maximum temperatures around 26°C. It is often windy, however, and the south-easterly 'Cape Doctor' can reach gale force. Winters can be cold, with average minimum temperatures of around 7°C and maximum temperatures of around 17°C. There is occasional snow on the higher peaks.

The eastern plateau area has a dry, sunny climate in winter with days around 20°C and crisp nights with temperatures dropping to around 5°C. Between October and April there are late afternoon showers often accompanied by spectacular thunder and lightning, but it rarely becomes unpleasantly hot. Heavy hailstorms cause quite a lot of damage each year. It can, however, become very hot in the Karoo (the semidesert heart of all three Cape provinces) and the far north (the Kalahari).

The coast north from the Cape becomes progressively drier and hotter. Along the south coast the weather is temperate, but further north the east coast becomes increasingly tropical. KwaZulu-Natal and the Transkei region can be hot and very humid in summer, although the highlands are still pleasant; it's also a summer rainfall area. Mpumalanga and Northern Province lowvelds become very hot in summer, when there are spectacular storms. In winter the days are sunny and warm.

National Parks & Reserves

National parks and reserves are among South Africa's premier attractions as they have spectacular scenery, abundant fauna and flora, and reasonable prices. The South African National Parks Board runs all parks except those in KwaZulu-Natal, which are administered by a body called KwaZulu-Natal Wildlife (KZN Wildlife; www.kznwildlife.com). In addition, the provinces also have conservation bodies.

The national parks all have rest camps offering a range of good-value accommodation, from cottages to camp sites. Most have restaurants, shops and petrol pumps. Entrances to parks and reserves normally close around sunset.

Unfortunately there is no public transport inside park boundaries, so to visit you will need to rent a car or join an organised tour. Most backpackers lodges throughout the country either offer tours or act as booking agencies for tour companies.

Environmental Issues

South Africa is ranked as the third-most biologically diverse country in the world. A major environmental challenge for the government is to manage increasing population growth and urbanisation while protecting this diverse environment. With half of South Africa's people living in towns and cities, 30,000 hectares of farmland are being lost to the spread of urban centres annually. This is putting more pressure on agricultural land, and overuse of woody vegetation for fuel, livestock grazing and soil cultivation has caused vegetation and soil degradation, particularly in former homeland areas. Adding to the problem is water and wind erosion, which are responsible for the loss of 500 million tonnes of topsoil each year.

The (for now) rising population also contributes to an increase in the demand for water. To try to meet demand, all major rivers in South Africa have been dammed or modified – a practice that disrupts local ecosystems.

Conservation of native fauna is an active concern and, although we can only dimly imagine the extent of the loss since the arrival of Europeans, a significant amount remains. However, many species are threatened, and extinction rates are high. An estimated 37% of the country's mammals and 36% of its freshwater fish species are threatened with extinction. Protected areas assist conservation, but only 6% of natural land habitat and 17% of the coastline in South Africa is under formal protection. Provincial funding of many national parks and reserves has been recently cut, making it harder for parks to protect their inhabitants.

TRANSPORT

GETTING THERE & AWAY

Jo'burg is the most important gateway to the region for both land and air transport, although Cape Town and Durban are rapidly catching up.

Air

Most of the major European airlines fly to Jo'burg or Cape Town, with some flying via Nairobi (Kenya). South African Airways (SAA), Malaysia Airlines, Singapore Airlines and Qantas all offer connections with Australia and Asia.

The cheapest tickets to South Africa from Europe usually depart from London, although it's possible to fly out of almost any city in Western Europe. Cheap fares can also often be found out of Paris and Amsterdam. Air France, Egypt Air, South African Airlines and British Airways consistently offer the cheapest fares.

If you are staying in Africa for less than 30 days, tickets from London to Jo'burg can cost as little as US$600 roundtrip. Stays of more than 30 days hike the price up a couple of hundred dollars.

From the US roundtrip tickets to Jo'burg start at US$1100 from the east coast, although these deals are often hard to come by. Average tickets cost about US$1300 roundtrip from New York or Washington, DC. From Los Angeles and San Francisco tickets start at about US$1500 roundtrip.

From Australia roundtrip tickets to Jo'burg start at US$1300 for stays of 30 days or less and jump up to US$1900 for longer stays.

There are several flights to other countries within Southern Africa. Air Botswana has flights between Jo'burg and Gaborone. SAA flies between Jo'burg and Swaziland and between Jo'burg and Maputo (Mozambique) for about US$140 and from Jo'burg to Maseru (Lesotho) for about US$80. It also flies from Jo'burg to Harare for US$270. Comair flies between Windhoek (Namibia) and Jo'burg or Cape Town for about US$100.

DEPARTURE TAX

Airport departure and security taxes range from around US$9 for domestic flights to more than US$23 for international flights, although they are usually included in the ticket price.

Land

Some of South Africa's main bus companies have international services, including **Inter-** **cape Mainliner** (☎ 012-654 4182; www.intercape.co.za) and **Translux** (☎ 011-774 3333). The internal backpacker bus service, **Baz Bus** (☎ 021-439 2323; www.bazbus.com), also travels through Swaziland.

BOTSWANA

The main border crossings are Ramatlhabama, north of Mafikeng (open 6am to 8pm), Lobaste, northwest of Zeerust (6am to 10pm) and Tlokweng Gate-Kopfontein, north of Zeerust (6am to 10pm).

Intercape Mainliner runs daily from Jo'burg/Pretoria to Gaborone (Botswana; US$19). Minibus taxis run from Mafikeng (North-West Province) to Gaborone for about US$4.

LESOTHO

Lesotho is totally surrounded by South Africa, and there are numerous border-crossing points (see p920). For details see the Lesotho chapter. There are no direct buses between South African cities and Maseru – take a bus to Bloemfontein or Ladybrand and catch a minibus taxi from there. Bloemfontein to Maseru costs about US$3.

MALAWI

Malawi does not border South Africa, but many travellers go direct between these two countries. Translux runs from Jo'burg to Blantyre (US$60) three times a week.

MOZAMBIQUE

The main border crossing to Mozambique is at Komatipoort. **Panthera Azul** (☎ 011 337 7409), Translux and Intercape long-distance buses all make daily runs from Jo'burg/ Pretoria to Maputo (US$24).

The Komati train runs between Jo'burg and Komatipoort (US$20/14/9 in 1st/2nd/ 3rd class). From here you need to change trains for Maputo (about US$3.50, 150km). The Trans-Lubombo train runs between Durban and Maputo, but check for current schedules as this service has been disrupted recently.

NAMIBIA

The main crossings are between Nakop and Ariamsvlei, west of Upington (open 24 hours); and between Vioolsdrif and Noordoewer (7am to 7pm) on the west coast road. You can't cross the border between

Namibia and South Africa in the Kgalagadi Transfrontier Park; the nearest alternative is to cross between Rietfontein and Klein-Menasse (8am to 4.30pm).

Intercape runs between Cape Town and Windhoek (US$50) four times a week and between Windhoek and Jo'burg (US$65), changing at Upington.

SWAZILAND
Swaziland has four main border crossings with South Africa. The busiest is Ngwenya (open 7am to 10pm), which is a good place to pick up a lift. The Baz Bus runs from Jo'burg/Pretoria to Durban via Mbabane and Manzini (US$26) four times a week.

ZAMBIA
Zambia does not border South Africa, but many travellers go direct between these two countries. Translux runs to Lusaka from Pretoria (US$46) three times a week.

ZIMBABWE
The only border crossing between Zimbabwe and South Africa is at Beitbridge north of Messina on the Limpopo River (open 5.30am to 8.30pm). Lengthy waits are not uncommon. Translux runs four services each week from Jo'burg/Pretoria to Harare (US$40). Greyhound and Intercape Mainliner do the same run, but Greyhound also has a useful service six times a week from Pretoria to Bulawayo. Car drivers pay a toll at the border crossing to use the bridge over the Limpopo.

GETTING AROUND
Although public transport can be pricey compared with some other countries in Africa, the main backpacker routes (Cape Town to Johannesburg via the coast and the Drakensberg or Swaziland) are easy to negotiate. With a group, private car hire allows the most flexibility and rental is quite cheap. The Baz Bus is the next best option. If you don't have much money but do have time to spare, there's the extensive network of (moderately uncomfortable) minibus taxis and 3rd-class train seats.

Air
South Africa's no-frills airline, **Kulula** (☎ 0861 585852; www.kulula.com) offers good deals on domestic flights between Jo'burg, Durban, Port Elizabeth and Cape Town. Otherwise, **South African Airways** (☎ 0861 359722; www.flysaa.com) is a domestic as well as an international carrier. From Jo'burg to Cape Town one-way flights start at US$130; from Jo'burg to Durban costs US$60; and from Cape Town to Durban one-way flights start at US$100.

Bus
Translux (☎ 011-774 3333) and **Greyhound** (www .greyhound.co.za) provide 'luxury' services, which are a good but expensive way of getting from A to B. Intercape Mainliner is slightly cheaper and serves mainly the western half of the country. You'll find booking offices for these services in the big cities and agents in many towns along their routes.

City to City (☎ 011-337 6650) is another long-distance bus service, which is generally far cheaper than the major bus companies, but it's difficult to find current and reliable information.

The **Baz Bus** (☎ 021-439 2323; www.bazbus.com) is an excellent alternative to the major bus lines. Aimed specifically at backpackers, it offers hop-on hop-off fares and a door-to-door service between hostels in Cape Town and Jo'burg via the Northern Drakensberg, Durban and the Garden Route. It also does a very useful loop from Durban up through Zululand and Swaziland and back to Jo'burg, passing close by Kruger National Park. No other mainstream transport options cover this route. Fares include: Durban via Garden Route (US$160), Jo'burg via Northern Drakensberg (US$190) and Jo'burg via Swaziland (US$230).

Baz Bus receives mixed reviews from travellers, however. Some say it's too expensive; others complain that it's cramped and often overbooked. Booking ahead is essential, and most hostels take bookings. Despite the gripes, it's a convenient means of transport. If you're travelling solo it's the safest mode and a good way to meet other backpackers.

Car
A car in South Africa can be very useful despite high petrol prices and accident rates. If you don't have the cash to rent a vehicle, don't despair – South Africa has an excellent public transport network and there is even a bus (the Baz Bus) that caters specifically to backpackers.

CAR GUARDS

Parked cars are easy targets in crime-plagued South Africa, and you'll see car guards in most cities. Although probably incapable of actually stopping a band of armed robbers, they do act as a deterrent. The guards will ask to watch your car, and expect a tip of a few rands upon your return. Technically you could drive away without paying, but for most of these people tips are their only source of income. Supporting their entrepreneurial skills helps to keep them from begging on the street and could save you a smashed window.

That said, cars allow you to traverse the country more quickly than other modes of transport, and you will need a vehicle if you want to explore national parks. Rentals are generally inexpensive, so if you have a group this option might cost less than the Baz Bus. Most major roads are tar and in excellent condition, but if you get on to dirt roads, drive very carefully to avoid hitting people, animals or unexpected giant potholes.

Car theft is rampant in cities, and carjacking can be a problem in Jo'burg. Keep doors locked and windows wound up, and never leave anything visible inside. It's worth forking out the extra cash to put your car into a secure car park at night.

PURCHASE

Jo'burg is the cheapest place in South Africa to buy a car, but Cape Town is a nicer place to spend a week or two securing a deal. Many backpackers travelling in the same direction will team up and purchase a car to tour the region. If you're interested ask around at your hostel.

The main congregation of used-car dealers in Cape Town is on Voortrekker Rd between Maitland and Bellville Sts. (Voortrekker Rd is the R102, which runs west from Woodstock, south of – and pretty much parallel to – the N1.)

There are also dealers in Jo'burg who offer buy-back deals; most Jo'burg hostels can advise and explain how best to draw up a contract that should make the deal stick when the time comes to sell back. The *Star* newspaper has ads every day and a motoring supplement on Thursday.

RENTAL

First try checking out the Internet site www.travelocity.com as they often have good deals from major rental agencies. At the time of research cars in Jo'burg and Cape Town were going for as little as US$13 per day with air-conditioning and unlimited kilometres – a real bargain! Many major credit cards carry rental insurance on them. If your card does, you can waive the rental company's insurance policy (which will significantly lower your rates). You will need to have a decent amount of credit (about US$1000) free on your card, as the hire companies will hold a large amount on your card in case you are involved in an accident.

Otherwise, car hire in South Africa is cheaper than in many African countries. The major international companies, such as **Avis** (☎ 0800 021 111, toll free) and **Budget** (☎ 0800 016 622, toll free), are represented in most of the larger cities. Local companies, many of which come and go, currently include **Imperial** (☎ 0800 131 000, toll free) and **Tempest** (☎ 011-396 1080).

If you book a return internal ticket through www.kulula.com you can receive a discount on car rental. At the time of research their cars were going for US$20 a day with unlimited kilometres and insurance.

Hostels can often organise a hire-car deal through a broker with one of the major companies at far better rates than you would receive if you approached the company directly. For a small car (such as a Toyota Corolla) you can expect to pay around US$27 to US$32 a day, insurance etc included.

Local Transport

Minibus taxis are much more comfortable here than in other African countries. Their drawback is that they tend to run on relatively short routes, generally only to neighbouring towns, although you'll nearly always find a few running to a distant big city.

Away from the big cities, pickpocketing on taxis is not much of a problem. 'Taxi wars' between rival companies, involving often lethal shoot-outs, do occasionally happen, but, given the number of taxis, the incidence of attacks is very low. To be on the safe side, read the newspapers and ask around about the situation. The biggest problem you're likely to encounter on a long minibus taxi ride is driver fatigue.

SOUTH AFRICA

Train

Trains are a good way to travel long distances, and travel in 3rd class is quite cheap. Passenger services are all on 'name trains'. On overnight trips the fare includes a sleeping berth (more expensive private compartments can also be hired), but there's a charge for bedding hire (US$4). Meals are à la carte.

First- and 2nd-class tickets must be booked at least 24 hours in advance; you can't book 3rd class. Most stations and some travel agents accept bookings. Major routes are from Cape Town to Durban, Port Elizabeth and Jo'burg; from Durban to Bloemfontein and from Jo'burg to East London, Bloemfontein, Nelspruit, Port Elizabeth and Kimberley. The fare from Jo'burg to East London is US$16, Jo'burg to Cape Town US$23, Jo'burg to Durban US$12 and Cape Town to Durban US$33.

CAPE TOWN

☎ 021 / pop 2.6 million

Travel the world over and you'll agree – Cape Town is decidedly one of the world's most beautiful cities. Relaxed and genteel, the city is sure to invalidate any African stereotypes you might harbour. Cape Town exudes the aura of one of Europe's great cities – open-air cafés and markets abound, and the architecture dazzles.

Dominated by flat-topped Table Mountain with its virtually sheer cliffs, and surrounded by mountain walks, vineyards and beaches, Cape Town is the capital of the Western Cape province and the parliamentary capital of South Africa. Generally safe to walk around, racism is less inbred here, and progress in relationships between people formerly divided can be witnessed.

ORIENTATION

The airport is about 15km east of the city centre. A taxi costs about US$25. Alternatively, the **Homeland Shuttle and Tours** (☎ 426 0294) will pick you up from the airport and drop you off at your hostel for US$11. The more people you book with, the cheaper the service becomes. If you're on the **Baz Bus**, it stops at almost all hostels. Many hostels do free pick-ups from the bus and train station; just phone ahead.

Cape Town is easy to negotiate, and much of the city can be navigated on foot. The city centre lies to the north of Table Mountain and east of Signal Hill, and the inner city suburbs of Tamboerskloof, Gardens and Oranjezicht are within walking distance of it. This area is referred to as the City Bowl. On the western side of Signal Hill, Sea Point and Green Point are two inner suburbs, densely populated with high-rise apartments, hotels, restaurants and bars. Green Point is the heart of gay Cape Town.

Some suburbs and towns cling to the coast, such as exclusive Clifton and Camps Bay and, further south, Llandudno, Hout Bay and Kommetjie. The False Bay towns from Muizenberg to Simon's Town can be reached by rail from the centre.

Most of the population lives in sprawling suburbs on the eastern side of Table Mountain; whites close to the mountain and blacks and coloureds on the bleak plain known as the Cape Flats.

Long Street, in the city centre, could be considered Cape Town's Ko Sanh Road and caters to backpackers. It is filled with cheap restaurants, outdoor cafés, bars, clubs, shops and booking agencies for everything from car rental to overland trips. It's safe to walk around (but, as always, keep an eye out for pickpockets and don't flaunt your wealth) and you won't be hassled the way you are in many other African cities.

INFORMATION
Airline Offices

The following airlines have offices in Cape Town:

Air Namibia (☎ 936 2755; Cape Town Airport)
British Airways (☎ 936 9000; Cape Town Airport)
KLM-Royal Dutch Airlines (☎ 670 2500; Slade House, Boundary Terraces, 1 Mariendahl Lane, Newlands)
Lufthansa (☎ 934 8794; Cape Town Airport)
Malaysian Airlines (☎ 934 8534; Cape Town Airport)
SAA (☎ 936 1111, 24 hrs; Cape Town Airport)

Bookshops & Music

The main mass-market bookshop-cum-newsagency is CNA, with numerous shops around the city. **Clarke's Books** (☎ 423 5739; 211 Long St) has an excellent range of literature on South Africa from history to fiction to politics.

The **African Music Store** (☎ 426 0857; 134 Long St) specialises in music from the continent.

The helpful staff can help in the selection of genres and styles, and you can listen to everything before purchasing.

Internet Access
Cape Town Tourism has several Internet terminals and charges US$1.80 for 30 minutes, making it one of the cheapest places in town. Many hostels have email facilities, as do a number of places on Long St. The **Virtual Turtle** (☎ 423 7508; 303A Long St) is a good bet and stays open until midnight.

Medical Services
Doctors are listed under Medical in the Yellow Pages, and they generally arrange for hospitalisation, although in an emergency you can go directly to the casualty department of **Groote Schuur Hospital** (☎ 404 9111; cnr De Waal St & Eastern Blvd), to the east of the city.

Money
Money can be changed at any bank; they're open from 9am to 3.30pm weekdays, and on Saturday morning. ATMs are dotted all over town.

American Express has offices at **Thibault Square** (☎ 408 9700), **Victoria & Alfred Waterfront** (☎ 419 3917) and at the Cape Town Tourism office.

Rennies Travel has branches at **St George's St Mall** (☎ 418 1206), **Sea Point** (☎ 439 7529); and at the **Waterfront** (☎ 418 3744); it's the agent for Thomas Cook.

Post & Telephone
The **main post office** (cnr Darling & Parliament Sts; 🕒 8am-4.30pm Mon-Fri, 8am-noon Sat) has 24-hour public phones, but they're often busy.

There are plenty of privately run public phone businesses where you can make calls without coins.

You can rent mobile phones from the Vodacom and MTN desks at the airport. In town **Cellurent** (☎ 418 5656) offers mobile phone rental for US$1.75 a day. If you have your own mobile phone, consider buying a South African 'pay as you go' SIM card (around US$4.50).

Tourist Offices
There are two excellent tourism information centres in Cape Town, one in the City Bowl and one at the Waterfront.

Found in the city centre, **Cape Town Tourism** (☎ 426 4260; www.cape-town.org; cnr Castle & Burg Sts; 🕒 8am-6pm Mon-Fri, 8.30am-6pm Sat, 9am-1pm Sun, longer hours in summer) has an Internet café, information and booking desks for the Baz Bus, Western Cape Nature Conservation and South African National Parks, an American Express foreign exchange bureau and a good craft shop. Tours and car hire can also be booked here.

You can pick up maps of city walking routes here, such as the *Footsteps to Freedom* map for a self-guided walking tour through Cape Town's history. There are also maps of gay Cape Town, museums and markets, and restaurants.

Next door to the Robben Island departure point, the Waterfront **Cape Town Tourism office** (☎ 408 4500; The Clocktower Centre; 🕒 9am-11pm) is extremely helpful and especially good if you're seeking information on destinations in the Western and Eastern Cape and KwaZulu-Natal.

DANGERS & ANNOYANCES
Cape Town is one of the most relaxed cities in Africa, but common sense is still required. During the day it is safe to walk from Green Point to the City Bowl, but use caution at night.

There has been a substantial increase in street crime in recent years; that said, most tourists make it through a visit without being mugged. Take care in Sea Point late at night.

Walking to or from the Waterfront has been dangerous in recent years; however, the completion of the new Convention Centre theoretically means security should be much tighter. Seek local advice before walking around the city centre at night.

The townships on the Cape Flats have an appalling crime rate and are off limits without a trustworthy guide.

Swimming at all of the Cape beaches is potentially hazardous, especially for those inexperienced in surf. Check for signs warning of rips and rocks, and swim in patrolled areas.

The mountains in the middle of the city are no less dangerous just because they are in the city. Weather conditions can change rapidly, so warm clothing and a good map and compass are necessary. Also watch out for ticks here.

SOUTH AFRICA

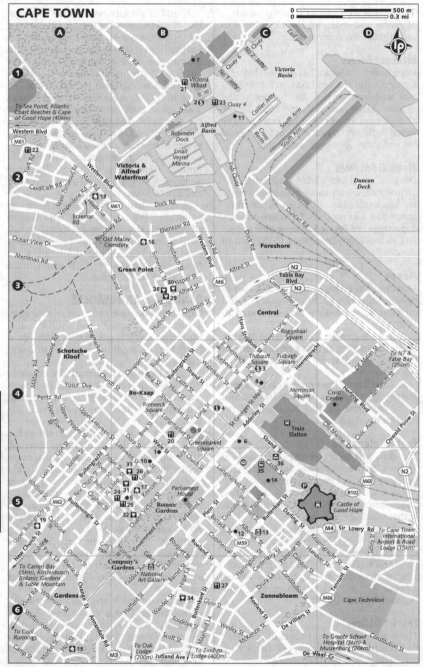

CAPE TOWN

0   500 m
0   0.3 mi

A   **B**   **C**   **D**

Beach Rd

☐ 7
Victoria Wharf
☐ 21

Victoria Basin

Quay 6
No 7 Jetty
Quay 7
East Pier

To Sea Point, Atlantic
Coast Beaches & Cape
of Good Hope (40km)

Dock Rd
2 ⓢ ☐ 23 Quay 4
☐ 11
Collier Jetty

Western Blvd
M61
☐ 22

York St

Cavalade Rd

Upper Portswood Rd
Main Rd
Beach Rd
Western Blvd
Palside Tce
☐ 18
Vesperdene Rd
Braemar Rd
M61

Victoria & Alfred Waterfront

Robinson Dock
Alfred Basin
Small Vessel Marina

Fish Quay
Cross Berth
South Arm
South Arm

Duncan Dock

Ocean View Dr

Boundary Rd
Old Malay Cemetery
☐ 16

Dock Rd
Ebenezer Rd
Port Rd
Dock Rd
Duncan Rd

Foreshore

Merriman Rd

Green Point

Strand St
Somerset St
Prestwich St
Western Blvd
Alfred St
M6

N2
Table Bay Blvd
N2

To N7 & False Bay (25km)

30 Napier St
28 ☐ ☐ 29
Alfred St
Dixon St
Chiappini St

Hans Strijdom Ave
Bree
Prestwich St
Lower Long St
Roggebaai Square
Thibault Square
Tulbagh Square

Central

Coen Styler Ave
Heerengracht

Schotsche Kloof

Military Rd
Vredehoek Rd
Longmarket St
Church St

Chiappini St
Rose St
Berg St
Buitengracht St
Castle St
Hout St
Long St
Loop St
Waterkant St
Lower Burg St

3 ☐
8 ☐

Merriman Square
Civic Centre

Hertzog Blvd
Jan Smuts St
DF Malan St

Oswald Pirow St

Bo-Kaap

Yusuf Drve
Pentz Rd
Upper Pepper St
Shortmarket St
Riebeeck Square
Longmarket St

ⓘ 4
@ 9
Greenmarket Square
St Georges Mall
Adderley St
☐ 6

Train Station

Old Marine Dr
Civic Ave

N2

Lion St
Jordan St
Dorp St
Bree St
Pepper St
Leeuwen St
Wale St
1 ☐
20

33 ☐
☐ 10
26 ☐
5 ☐
24 31
Keerom St
25 ☐
32 ☐

Longmarket St
Church St

☐ 36
35 ☐
☐ 14

Strand St
Castle St
Darling St

P
☐
Castle of Good Hope

M60
R102

Parliament House
Botanic Gardens

Queen Victoria St
Parliament St
Plein St
Burack St
Corporation St

M4 Sir Lowry Rd
To Cape Town International Airport & Road Lodge (15km)

Sidney St

Whitford St
Upper Buitengracht St
19 ☐
New Church St
Kohl Park La
M62
Buitensingle St

Grey's Pass
Mostert St

Buitenkant St

Keizergracht St

New Church St
Doman St

Company's Gardens

Government Ave
Gallery La
St Johns St
National Art Gallery
27 ☐

Alberts St
☐ 12 ☐ 13
M59

Harrington St
Canterbury St
Caledon St
Primrose St
Hanover St
Constitution St

To Camps Bay (3km), Kirstenbosch Botanic Gardens & Table Mountain

Paddock Ave
Bouquet St
Barnet St
Hope St
Roeland St
Commercial St
Drury La

Zonnebloem

M66
Tennant St
Cape Technikon

Gardens

Kloof St
Wilkinson St
Orange St
Annandale Rd
Hatfield St
Wandel St
Glynn St
34 ☐
Maynard La
Buitenkant St
Wesley St
Roeland St
De Villiers St

Constitution St
To Groote Schuur Hospital (3km) & Muizenburg (20km)

To Cool Runnings

Weltevreden
Camp St
Morkel St
Holt St
☐ 15
M3

To Oak Lodge (200m)
Jutland Ave
To Zindigo Lodge (400m)

Scott St
Roodehek St
McKenzie St
De Waal Cr

SIGHTS
District Six Museum

A visit to the small and simple **District Six Museum** (☎ 461 8745; cnr Buitenkant & Albertus Sts; donation requested; ☯ 9am-4pm Mon-Sat) is a moving experience. During the apartheid era the lively mixed-race suburb of District Six was bulldozed, and the government changed the street grid and the names of the few remaining roads. The museum was created as much *for* the former residents of this vanished area as it was for the public. Many visit and leave their stories behind. Walking tours of District Six's streets may be booked ahead for US$2.50, although tours take a minimum of five people.

Greenmarket Square

On 1 December 1834 more than 35,000 Cape slaves were emancipated in this historic square. Today it houses a bustling **market** that sells everything from clothing to traditional African crafts. You could easily spend an afternoon getting lost among the stalls. Prices are negotiable, although you should check the condition of clothing before purchasing; quality is often poor. When you tire of shopping, stop at one of the numerous cafés lining the square for drinks and people-watching. The square draws a cosmopolitan mix of people and many street performers.

Atlantic Coast

The Atlantic coast here has some of the most spectacular scenery in the world. The **beaches** include the trendiest on the Cape, but the emphasis is on sunbaking rather than swimming – the water comes straight from the Antarctic. If you have a car, it is definitely worth spending an afternoon exploring this area. Bring lots of film.

If you are reliant on public transport, buses and minibus taxis run along Victoria Rd from the city to Hout Bay, and minibus taxis run along Maid Rd to the end of Regent St in Sea Point, but no further.

SEA POINT

Sea Point is a bustling residential suburb, and Main Rd is lined with restaurants and shops (and often choked with traffic). The coast is rocky and swimming is dangerous, but there are four tidal swimming pools.

CLIFTON

There are four linked beaches at Clifton accessible by steps from Victoria Rd. They're the trendiest, busiest beaches on the Cape. **Fourth Beach**, at the Camps Bay end, is the most accessible and is popular with families. **First Beach** is the place to be seen.

CAMPS BAY

The spectacular **Twelve Apostles** of Table Mountain tumble into the sea above the broad stretch of white sand at Camps Bay. If swimming, watch out for strong surf. Although not as trendy as Clifton, it has **La Med** (☎ 438 5600; admission US$2 Sun) – the place to be

SOUTH AFRICA

ROBBEN ISLAND

A tour of **Robben Island** (☎ 419 1300/413 4200; www.robben-island.org.za; Nelson Mandela Gateway, Clocktower Precinct, Waterfront; adult US$18), where former president Nelson Mandela was held prisoner for 27 years, is an unforgettable and highly recommended experience.

The guides, ex-political prisoners many of whom were held here during Mandela's imprisonment, make the tours exceptional. Each has a story and will answer any questions about their personal experiences. Their answers are direct, personal and often shocking (one guide went into a trancelike state when telling about the electro-shock therapy he received while imprisoned).

Amazingly, the guides seem to be without bitterness and keep the memory of the prison's history and its criminal past alive out of a wish for reconciliation, not revenge. After the prison, a bus ride around the island reveals an interesting history, including the remnants of a leper colony, some WWII bunkers and two 19th-century churches. The view of Cape Town and Table Mountain from the island is stunning.

Tours to the island are hugely popular so booking ahead is essential.

among Cape Town's young and rowdy on a Sunday night. You'll have to fight for a spot of grass to watch that orange ball sink into the Atlantic, and drinks are overpriced, but it has the best sunset views in town. If you don't want quite so much chaos, visit on another night when there is no cover charge and fewer people.

False Bay

False Bay lies to the southeast of the city. Although the beaches on the eastern side of the peninsula are not quite as scenically spectacular as those on the Atlantic side, the water is much warmer. During October and November, False Bay is a favoured haunt for whales and their calves.

Sandwiched between the mountains and False Bay, picturesque **Simon's Town** with its tidy muted buildings and palm-tree lined streets is a nice place to spend an afternoon. Main Street is lined with curio and antique shops, and you can have a coffee or lunch at one of the outdoor cafés overlooking the bay. Don't miss the 3000-strong penguin colony 3km from the town centre around Boulder's Beach, part of the **Cape Peninsula National Park** (☎ 786 2329; ☉ 8am-6pm; admission US$1).

Trains run between Cape Town and Simon's Town at least once every hour. Cape Town to Simon's Town is US$0.60 in 3rd class.

Cape Flats

For the majority of Cape Town's inhabitants, home is in one of the grim townships on the Cape Flats. Visiting without a companion who has local knowledge would be foolish. If a black friend is happy to escort you, you should have no problems, and tours have operated safely for years. **One City Tours** (☎ 387 5351) and **Grassroute Tours** (☎ 706 1006) both get good feedback.

Kirstenbosch Botanical Gardens

Devoted almost exclusively to indigenous plants, **Kirstenbosch Botanical Gardens** (☎ 799 8800; www.nbi.ac.za; Rhodes Dr, Constantia; admission US$2; ☉ 8am-7pm Sep-Mar, 8am-6pm Apr-Aug) are among the most beautiful in the world. In 1895 Cecil Rhodes purchased the eastern slopes of Table Mountain and then bequeathed the property to the nation on his death in 1902. Today Kirstenbosch has about 9000 of Southern Africa's 22,000 plant species.

Rikki's (☎ 423 4888) runs taxis out to the gardens for US$7.

Table Mountain & Cableway

The **cableway** (☎ 424 8181; www.tablemountain.net; one way/return US$6/11; ☉ 8am-9pm daily) is such a clichéd attraction you might have difficulty convincing yourself it is worth experiencing – but it definitely is. The views from Table Mountain are phenomenal, and there are some excellent walks on the summit.

If you plan to walk, make sure you have warm waterproof clothing. Table Mountain is more than 1000m high, and conditions can quickly become treacherous. Note that cable cars don't operate when it's dangerously windy (which can be a problem if the weather turns after you've taken a cable car to the top, leaving you with a long, wet trudge home).

To get to the lower cableway station, catch the Kloof Nek bus from outside OK Bazaars in Adderley St to the Kloof Nek terminus and connect with the cableway bus. By car, take Kloof Nek Rd and turn off to the left (signposted).

Victoria & Alfred Waterfront
The Victoria & Alfred Waterfront is packed with restaurants, bars and at least a few interesting shops – you'll find it buzzing day and night.

One of the Waterfront's main charms is that the eating, drinking and shopping is done around a properly functioning (if small-scale) dock. Escape the mall muzak and wander around the dry dock, where fishing boats are scrubbed clean of barnacles, or just stand and watch yachts and liners coming and going.

Whatever else you do, don't miss a cruise into Table Bay. Try the **Waterfront Boat Company** (☎ 418 5806) or **Waterfront Boat Co** (☎ 418 0134; Port Captain's Bldg, Pier Head), across from Bertie's Landing, for a variety of cruises. Half-hour cruises start at around US$3.50.

SURFING
The Cape Peninsula has fantastic surfing possibilities: from gentle shorebreaks, ideal for beginners, to monsters made for experts only.

In general, the best surf is along the Atlantic side, and there is a string of breaks from Bloubergstrand through to the Cape of Good Hope. Most of these breaks work best in southeasterly conditions.

The **Surf Zone** (☎ 423 7853; cnr Castle & Berg Sts) in the city centre has a good stock of wetsuits and second-hand boards for hire or sale.

SLEEPING
Cape Town is jam-packed with budget accommodation. If you don't have a car try either Long St or the Gardens area. Much of Cape Town's nightlife centres on Long St, but the Gardens is an easy (and usually safe) walk. Green Point is a good bet if you have a car, as parking is easier (and safer) here. It's also convenient to the city bowl (about a 20-minute walk) and is the centre of gay Cape Town. Hostels cost more here than anywhere else in the country, and camping is almost nonexistent in town.

City Bowl
Ashanti Lodge (☎ 423 8721; www.ashanti.co.za; 11 Hof St, Gardens; camp sites per person US$7, dm US$10, d US$29; 🖳) Located in a rambling old mansion, Ashanti is one of the best – and most popular – hostels in town. Be sure to check out the second-floor bathroom, where you can view Table Mountain from the toilet with a pair of attached binoculars. This hostel sets itself apart from others by organising day trips to a local township to paint or pick up rubbish. Ask at the desk if you want to participate. Ashanti also has a great bar that specialises in prolonged drinking. It is also one of the only places in town with camping. Booking is essential, as spaces are minimal.

Long Street Backpackers (☎ 423 0617; www.longstreetbackpackers.co.za; 209 Long St; dm US$8; d US$20) This place has one of the best spots in town smack in the middle of Long St. There's a cool balcony for people-watching and beer-drinking, and funky mosaics in the bathrooms. It's well established and an old favourite.

Oak Lodge (☎ 465 6182; www.oaklodge.co.za; 21 Breda St, Gardens; dm US$8, d US$23) This well-maintained place lets travellers revert to the 1960s, and has a reputation for wild parties – it even brings in live bands! It gets good reviews from people for cleanliness.

Zebra Crossing (☎ /fax 422 1265; 82 New Church St; dm US$7, s/d US$13/18) Small, quiet and clean, Zebra Crossing is the best deal in Cape Town. There is secure parking.

Zindigo Lodge (☎ 461 4978; www.zindigolodge.com; 2 Vrede Hoek Ave; dm US$8, d US$28) This gay-friendly hostel is very clean and very quiet. There's no bar or loud music, but the owners can tell you what's happening on the city's gay and lesbian scene.

Green Point
St John's Waterfront Lodge (☎ 439 1404; www.stjohns.co.za; 6 Braemar Rd; dm US$10, d US$23) Don't come here to party wildly – the atmosphere is way too relaxed. It does have two pools and is fastidiously clean and within walking distance of the Waterfront and Green Point's nightlife.

Airport
Road Lodge (☎ 934 7303; Cape Town International Airport; d US$26) This place is clean, efficient and right next to the airport – stay here if you have an early morning flight to catch.

Camping

Brown Sugar (☎ 433 0413; 1 Main Rd; camp sites per person US$4; ⌨) It's hard to recommend staying here, but if you're set on camping in Cape Town, this is one of the few places you can do it. The fragment of brown dirt you'll be allocated to erect your tent on will be separated from a noisy main road only by a fence.

Zandvlei Caravan Park (☎ 788 5215; The Row; camp sites per person US$6) This is the closest proper caravan park. Located about 20km south of town in Muizenberg, it is about 2km from Muizenberg train station and about 1km from the beach.

EATING

Cape Town probably has the best selection (and quality) of food in Africa, although Jo'burg is in a pretty dead heat. Eating opportunities are varied – from five-star gourmet to roving falafel stands. There is a dominant café culture, and thanks to its seaside location Cape Town is an excellent place for fresh seafood. The largest concentration of restaurants is at the Victoria & Alfred Waterfront. Prices in Cape Town tend to be higher than in other parts of the country, but they're still a steal compared to Western cities.

City Bowl

Café Mozart (☎ 424-3774; Church St, near cnr of Long St; mains US$2-4) This place is popular with locals. You can listen to live music here and get tasty sandwiches, snacks and breakfast. Sit outside. It's open only for breakfast and lunch.

Long Street Café (☎ 424 2464; 259 Long St; mains US$2.50-5) This popular café is a good place to start or end an evening. They have the usual assortment of sandwiches and salads and a giant cocktail menu.

Lola's Café (☎ 423-0885; 228 Long St; mains US$2-3) The menu is entirely vegetarian, and the outside tables always buzzing. Try one of their saucy pastas.

Mr Pickwick's Deli (☎ 424-2696; 158 Long St; mains US$4-5) Always popular, this deli specialises in foot-long sandwiches.

Perseverance Tavern (☎ 461 2440; 83 Buitenkant St; mains US$4) Built in 1808, this place is a Cape Town pub gem that serves solid pub-style main courses.

Long Street also has a slew of cheap takeaway places. If you're hanging out at night, don't miss the roving falafel stands that serve up delicious Greek pita sandwiches for US$1.25 and stay open until 5am.

Green Point

Chariot's Coffee Bar (☎ 434 5427; 107 Main Road; mains US$3-6) Besides doing delicious breakfasts for US$4, Chariots does beautiful fresh pasta. Try the pesto or anything with calamari.

Wang Thai (☎ 439 6164; 105 Main Road; mains US$5-8) It's a little pricier than some places, but Wang Thai enchants the palate with excellent (and seriously spicy) Thai food. We loved the green curry.

Victoria & Albert Waterfront

Cape Town Fish Market (☎ 418 5977; Victoria Wharf; starters from US$1.75, mains US$4.60-7) This is another good fishy option with not bad sushi. It's near the cinemas at Victoria Wharf.

Hildebrand Restaurant (☎ 425 3385; Pierhead; mains US$5-8) With excellent service, white table clothes, an extensive wine list and a superb setting, the Hildebrand Restaurant is a great choice for a splash-out on seafood. Their calamari is the best we tried in South Africa. Come at sunset and sit outside.

DRINKING
Pubs & Bars

Cool Runnings (96 Station St) In the Observatory area, this is a hugely popular chain reggae bar. They've dumped sand outside to create a beachy feel. Inside it has island-hut decor.

Lounge (194 Long St) This has the best balcony in town. Sit outside to people-watch or dance the night away to pounding trance inside. It picks up after 11pm.

Stag's Head Hotel (71 Hope St, Gardens) A very popular grungy pub, it's one of the few English/Australian-style hotels in South Africa.

On the Waterfront try the always hopping **Quay 4** bar.

Clubs & Live Music

Wednesday, Friday and Saturday are the big club nights. The blocks around Bree, Loop and Long Sts – as well as Waterkant St a little further north – are incredibly lively all night long on summer weekends. There's a good buzz, although the music can be rather heavy on house and techno. Cover charges are about US$2.50.

Chilli 'n Lime (23 Somerset St, Green Point) is a lively, mainly straight bar and club in the heart of the gay district. Backpackers were gravitating towards this place at the time of research.

Mannenberg's (Clocktower Complex) attracts some of the best national and international performers and a refreshingly mixed black, white and coloured audience. Cover charges vary from US$3.50 up to US$12 depending on who's playing. You can sit and eat or just drink at the bar.

Rhodes House (60 Queen Victoria St, City Bowl) is the place to see and be seen. Cape Town's glam set parties here, and you'll pay Western prices (US$8 to US$10 cover charge) to party with them. However, it's a beautiful and imaginative venue, and worth it for a big night out.

Snap (6 Pepper St, City Bowl) plays lots hip-hop, has a small dance floor and pounding music, and is one of the few places near Long St where whites are still in the minority.

Gay & Lesbian Venues

There's an increasingly vibrant gay scene in Cape Town. Stop in at Cape Town Tourism upon arrival and pick up a copy of the *Pink Map* and *Detail*, the free monthly gay lifestyle newspaper. The folks at Zindigo Lodge can also help you out.

Bronx (cnr Somerset Rd & Napier St) is the city's premier gay bar. It's a lively place for dancing and mingling.

Club 55 (cnr Somerset Rd & Napier St), diagonally opposite Bronx, is the hot dance spot.

Entertainment

You can't do without the entertainment guide in the *Weekly Mail & Guardian* or the entertainment section of the *Cape Argus*. For bookings, contact **Computicket** (☎ 918 8910; www.computicket.com). It has outlets in the Golden Acre Centre on Strand St and the Waterfront.

GETTING THERE & AWAY
Air

Cape Town has an increasingly busy international airport. Domestically, SAA flies between Cape Town and major centres (see p948). There are many international airlines with offices in Cape Town. There's a short list on p950; for others, see the Yellow Pages.

Flights from London to Cape Town start at about US$800. From the east coast of the US to Cape Town expect to pay about US$1500. From the west coast flights start

at about US$1800. From Australia and Asia flights to Cape Town generally cost about US$2000.

For flights within South Africa check out www.kulula.com. From Cape Town to Jo'burg one-way flights cost US$130. From Cape Town to Durban one-way fares are about US$100.

Bus

All long-distance buses leave from the main Cape Town bus station across from the train station. **Intercape Mainliner** (☎ 386 2488; www.intercape.co.za) and **Translux** (☎ 449 3333) have offices there. Both companies run daily buses to Jo'burg (US$49 to US$52). Intercape does a direct run to Windhoek, Namibia (US$50) via Springbok (US$28).

The **Baz Bus** (☎ 439 2323) has hop-on hop-off service to Durban (US$175) and Jo'burg or Pretoria via the Drakensberg (US$205). It picks up from hostels, and you can stop in as many places as you want along its route.

Local Transport

Most long-distance minibus taxis start picking up passengers in a distant township and make a trip to the train station's taxi ranks only if they need more people, so your choices can be limited. Not all townships are off-limits, but the situation is volatile. A minibus to Jo'burg costs about US$21, but it's long and uncomfortable trip.

Train

All **trains** (☎ 086-000 8888 for information and bookings) leave from the main train station. Long-distance trains run to Pretoria via Kimberley and Jo'burg; Durban via Kimberley and Bloemfontein; and to Port Elizabeth via some Garden Route towns. The local area Metro service is the best way to get to the wineries area.

GETTING AROUND

The main local bus interchange is on Grand Parade, where there's an **information office** (☎ 461 4365). A bus (off-peak fares) to Sea Point costs US$0.30 and to Camps Bay for US$0.35. When travelling short distances, most people wait at the bus stop and take either a bus or a minibus taxi – whichever arrives first.

Minibus taxis cover most of the city with an informal network of routes, and these cost about the same as the municipal buses. The main rank is on the upper deck of the train station, which is accessible from a walkway in the Golden Acre Centre or from stairways on Strand St. In the suburbs, you just hail them from the side of the road – just point your index finger into the air.

Rikki's (☎ 423 4888) runs its tiny, open vans in the City Bowl and nearby areas for low prices. Telephone Rikki's or just hail one on the street – you can pay a shared rate of a few rand. They run between 7am and 7pm except Sundays and go as far afield as Sea Point and Camps Bay.

For private hire, try **Unicab Taxis** (☎ 447 4402). There are often taxis near Greenmarket Square and outside the Holiday Inn on Strand St. Taxis cost about US$1.20 per kilometre.

Hitching around Cape Town, although not recommended, is generally easy. For longer trips, either start in the city centre or catch public transport to one of the outlying towns – the idea is to miss the surrounding suburbs and townships.

AROUND CAPE TOWN

CAPE OF GOOD HOPE NATURE RESERVE

About 70km south of Cape Town, where the Atlantic and Indian Oceans merge, is the **Cape of Good Hope Nature Reserve** (☎ 780 9204; admission US$3; ☼ daily 6am-6pm summer, 7am-5pm winter). There are beaches and countless great walks offering a chance to see the Cape's unique flora up close, as well as antelopes and abundant birdlife. Beware of the belligerent baboons.

Maps are available at the gate, and there are picnic places, a kiosk and restaurant. The tip of the peninsula is a dramatic place to be on a clear day.

The only public transport to the peninsula Cape is with **Rikki's** (☎ 423 4888), which runs Asian-style tuk-tuk taxis from Simon's Town (accessible by train) and cost US$10 an hour.

Numerous tours include Cape Point on their itineraries; ask at your hostel. Much better, however, is to hire a car for the day, which will allow you to explore much of the peninsula.

THE WINELANDS

The Winelands region around Stellenbosch, sometimes known as the Boland, is the oldest and most beautiful wine-growing region in South Africa (dating from the 18th century). Franschhoek, Paarl and Stellenbosch, to the northeast of Cape Town, are all historically important towns. Each promotes a wine route around the surrounding wineries. Backpackers gravitate to Stellenbosch. From here you can join a day wine tour to the entire region.

Stellenbosch
☎ 021

Established in 1679 as a frontier settlement, Stellenbosch is the second-oldest town in South Africa, and the sense of history is palpable. There are some beautifully restored Cape Dutch buildings and interesting museums, all shaded by magnificent oaks. It also is home to a large university, so there's nightlife here.

The **Stellenbosch Tourism Bureau** (☎ 883 3584; 36 Market St) has Internet access for US$2 per half hour. Pick up *Stellenbosch & Its Wine Route*, which gives opening times and tasting information about dozens of nearby wineries.

Easy Rider Wine Tours (☎ 886 4651), run out of the Stumble Inn, are the cheapest and best for touring the wine region. The day tours depart at 10.30am returning after 5pm and cost US$28. Tours take in vineyards in Stellenbosch, Paarl and Franschhoek. The price includes lunch, a cellar tour, four wine tastings and a cheese tasting. Combine a wine tour with two nights in a dorm at the Stumble Inn for US$36.

If you don't want to pay for an all-day wine tour, and don't have your own transport, head to **Die Bergkelder** (☎ 886 3016), a short walk from the train station. They have tours and tastings at 10am, 10.30am and 3pm daily except Sunday. These cost US$1.50. Although better wines await your taste buds in the surrounding region, it's good value for money. The price includes a cellar tour and pour-your-own tastings of up to six wines.

Stellenbosch has a decent selection of places to sleep and drink, although food is not one of its strongest points.

Backpackers Inn (☎ 887 2020; 1st fl, De Wet Centre, cnr Church & Bird Sts; dm US$8, d US$20) This big place right in the centre of town caters mostly to students at the Afrikaans university.

Stumble Inn (☎ 887 4049; stumble@iafrica.com; 12 Market St; camp sites per person US$5, dm US$8, d US$20) The name is fitting. This is the most popular, hard-drinking hostel in town (they run the wine tours out of here). It's also within walking distance of nightlife and has a great terrace with grape vines woven through the rafters. Book a wine tour here and receive a discount on lodging.

Bohemia Restaurant (6B Andringa St) Bohemia is a laid-back place with lots of comfy couches to chill out on. The music is not deafening (you can actually hear yourself talk), and there's outdoor seating.

Decameron Italian Restaurant (☎ 883 3331; Plein St; mains US$4.50-7) Come here for genuine Italian food. Prices are high, but it's worth it.

De Soete Inval (☎ 886 4842; 5 Ryneveld St; mains US$4-5) Outstanding pancakes and some Indonesian fare can be found here. Try the *rystafel* with six dishes for US$7.

Nu Bar (51 Plein St) This swanky place with a small dance floor gets hopping after 11pm. The walls are covered with pictures of models, and the televisions show the fashion channels. It's full of college students, and they dress to impress.

With a car and a map from the tourist area you can explore the region on your own.

Buses to Cape Town are expensive (about US$2.30 with Translux), and you can't book this short sector. Translux stops here on the Mountain Route run between Cape Town and Port Elizabeth.

Metro trains run the 46km between Cape Town and Stellenbosch; 1st/3rd class is US$1.15/0.60 (no 2nd class), and the trip takes about one hour. For inquiries phone **Stellenbosch train station** (☎ 808 1111). To be safe travel in the middle of the day and not at weekends.

THE GARDEN ROUTE

The Garden Route is the beautiful stretch of coastline between Mossel Bay in the west and the Tsitsikamma Coastal National Park in the east. The region has some of the most significant tracts of indigenous forest in the country, and the narrow coastal plain is often forested and bordered by lagoons running behind dunes and superb beaches.

The climate is temperate, and the area is a favourite for water sports. Although it is beautiful, it is also heavily (and tackily) developed. Prices jump by at least 30% in mid-season (late January to May) and more than double over the high season (December, January and Easter).

Places are described west to east. Most travellers visit Oudtshoorn while traversing the Garden Route so, although this town is technically in the little Karoo, we've included it in this section.

Both **Translux** (☎ 021-449 3333) and **Intercape** (☎ 0861-287 287) run at least daily from Cape Town to Port Elizabeth via the main Garden Route towns. Translux also runs a service from Jo'burg to Knysna via some Garden Route towns. If you plan to travel around the area, don't forget the Baz Bus.

OUDTSHOORN
☎ 044

In Oudtshoorn it's all about the ostriches, the town bills itself as the ostrich capital of the world. It has a strong Afrikaner feel, with quiet tree-lined streets and shops and restaurants selling everything ostrich. The place was home to the rich 'feather barons' until the turn of the twentieth century, and many made a small fortune out of farming the strange birds. Today, the town capitalises on its past. You can visit ostrich show farms where you will learn everything you ever wanted to know about the birds, and probably a whole lot more.

Sights & Activities
Oudtshoorn has a number of show farms, and there's little to distinguish one from another. We liked **Oudtshoorn Ostrich Show Farm** (☎ 279 1861; Cango Caves Rd; admission US$3; ☉ 8am-5pm daily). They do informative tours and give you the opportunity to ride a ostrich.

If you're all ostriched out, head to the **Cango Wildlife Ranch & Cheetahland** (☎ 272 5593; admission US$4.50; ☉ 8am-5pm daily). It's got a bit of a zoolike feel, but has a good collection of wildlife and big cats (in rather small enclosures) including cheetahs, which you may pat for an extra US$3.50 (funds go to the Cheetah Conservation Foundation). The ranch is 3km from town on the road out to Prince Albert.

Otherwise, head out to the **Cango Caves** (☎ 272 7410; admission from US$5.75; ☉ 9am-4pm daily)

SOUTH AFRICA

HOW TO RIDE AN OSTRICH & SURVIVE

Ostriches cannot be trained. As Sakkie at the Oudtshoorn Ostrich Show Farm explained to us: 'Their eyes are larger than their brains and they have no capacity for learning.' So if you're expecting to hop in a saddle and grab the reins, forget it. Riding an ostrich is nothing like riding a horse. Instead someone will shove a bag over your bird's head, throw you up on its back and, just when you are rethinking the entire experience, will tell you to grab on to some feathers. The bag will be pulled off, and away you'll go.

There are three ways to stop: lose your balance and fall off as it makes a mad dash across the pasture; gracefully slide off its tail as it slows down; or wait for it to run into another ostrich, then hurl yourself off before it starts running again.

Whichever way befalls you, it's certainly an experience you can write home about.

30km from town. These heavily commercialised but impressive caves offer a variety of tours. Try one of the longer ones that involve crawling through tight damp places; it's lots of fun!

Sleeping & Eating

Backpackers Paradise (☎ 272 3436; paradise@isat.co.za; 148 Baron van Rheede St; camp sites per person US$4, dm US$8, d US$19) This place is quiet and clean, and offers discounts at area attractions. It has shady camping spots on a big green lawn, and the rooms are cool and dark. There is a nightly ostrich *braai* for US$5.

Backpackers' Oasis (☎ /fax 279 1163; backpackers oasis@yahoo.com; 3 Church St; camp sites per person US$4, dm US$6, d US$17) In a large relaxed house, this is another reasonable option.

Jemima's (☎ 272 0808; 61 Voortrekker St; mains US$4-10) For authentic Afrikaans cuisine head to sunny Jemima's. The food is painstakingly prepared and altogether delicious. It's a little pricey, but well worth it.

KNYSNA
☎ 044

Knysna is a bustling town with a holiday atmosphere that suffers a little from growing pains. The town is built on the side of a large lagoon some way from the nearest ocean beaches – **Brenton-on-Sea** (16km west) and **Noetzie** (11km east); so it's not the best place to come if you're just looking to lounge in the sand.

What Knysna lacks in sand it makes up for in water sports. The **Head Adventure Centre** (☎ 384 0831; adventure@cyberperk.co.za) is the place to go for diving or snorkelling. They offer PADI dive courses (open water US$235, advanced US$162) and do boat and short entry dives (US$10 to US$15) to some of South Af-

rica's best spots. Snorkelling equipment can be rented for around US$7. Ask the guides to point out the good snorkelling trails. They may go with you. To get to the Adventure Centre follow the road signs to the Heads.

Most accommodation, restaurants and nightlife are within easy walking distance of each other.

Highfield Backpackers (☎ 382 6266; highfields@ hotmail.com; 2 Graham St; dm US$9, d US$23) Located in a spacious old house, Highfield feels like a bed-and-breakfast. Its focus is on doubles, and these are well decorated with hard wood floors, brass beds and nice linen. The family rooms (US$45) sleep four, and are great if you are travelling in a small pack.

Peregrin Backpackers Lodge (☎ 382 3747; 37 Queen St; camp sites per person US$5, dm US$8, d US$21) This place has lots of character. Rooms are clean and the dorms not too cramped. All guests are given discount cards upon arrival for the area's bars and shops.

Woodbourne Resort (☎ 384 0416; woodb.kyn@ pixie.co.za; George Rex Dr; camp sites per person US$5, chalets from US$27) Here you'll find spacious, shaded camping and simple chalets with bathrooms and televisions. It's a quiet place a little way out of town. Rates more than double during high season and holidays. Follow the signs to the Heads.

Oyster Catcher (☎ 382 9995; Waterfront; tapas US$2.50-3.75) Here you'll find decent seafood tapas. It's a popular outdoor place with a great view of the marina.

Paquita's (☎ 384 0408; The Heads; mains US$2.50-10) If this place was any closer to the water it would be in it. The views are stupendous. Locals say the food isn't as good as other restaurants in town, but at least stop by for a drink. If you're lucky you might spot whales frolicking only metres away.

The **Waterfront** area, right on the marina, has a host of restaurants and shops. Most of the restaurants are seafood oriented. Knysna is known for its oysters.

For nightlife try the **Tin Roof** (Main St), a gritty bar with amazing black-and-white drawings of dead rock artists for wall art. It has a small stage and often brings in live local acts. **Zanzibar** (Main St), a trendy place with a large second-floor patio for people-watching over Main St, is another option. **Chilli Groove** (Queen St), a Mexican restaurant-bar at night, is a favourite with locals.

PLETTENBERG BAY

☎ 044

Plettenberg Bay is an upmarket resort town where the rich come to play. Expensive homes dot the hills above the ocean, and the town centre is filled with upmarket retail stores and fancy restaurants. It's on a beautiful beach with deep blue waters and a long coastline. If you're tired of the typical backpacker scene, come here and take a few days off; there are cheap places to stay.

Albergo For Backpackers (☎ 313 4434; www .albergo.co.za; 8 Church St; dm US$8, d with bath US$18) Near the town centre, this is a well-run, friendly place.

Northando Backpackers (☎ /fax 533 0220; mw deois@mweb.co.za; 3 Wilder St; dm US$8; d from US$20) This spotless and spacious place has a B&B feel.

The **Lookout** (mains US$5) On the beach near Lookout Rocks, this place is good for a meal by the surf; if you're lucky you might even see dolphins.

Buses and long-distance minibus taxis stop at or near the Shell Ultra City on the N2. The Baz Bus comes into town. Minibus taxis to Knysna (about US$1.75) leave from the corner of Kloof and High Sts. Other long-distance taxis stop at the Shell Ultra City.

SPLURGE!

If you want to live it up in this beach town, head to **Weldon Kaya** (☎ 533 2437; s/d in ron-davels from US$37/60), off the N2 at the corner of Piesang Valley Rd. It's a little way out of town, but worth the trip. The rondavels are beautifully appointed with huge comfort-able beds, and there is a bar and restaurant attached that serves contemporary food.

TSITSIKAMMA COASTAL NATIONAL PARK

☎ 042

Tsitsikamma Coastal National Park (admission US$2.30; ☼ 5.30am-9.30pm) occupies a narrow band of spectacular coast between Plettenberg Bay and Jeffrey's Bay, and extends 5km out into the sea. Here you can hike along steep cliffs where the pounding surf provides the musical soundtrack and whales and dolphins provide the visuals, or you could venture into the ocean to tackle the underwater snorkelling trail.

The park is traversed by one of the most famous hikes in the country – the **Otter Trail**, an easy five-day, 41km trail along the coast. Walking the trail costs US$48 per person and bookings should be made through the **National Parks Board** (☎ 012-428 9111; www.parks -sa.co.za). Unfortunately the trail is booked months in advance.

Even if you can't hike the Otter Trail, it's worth visiting Tsitsikamma for day walks. There are numerous trails that meander through tangled indigenous forests or along the scenic cliffs. When walking, keep an eye out for the elusive Cape clawless otter, ba-boons and small antelope.

The park gate is 6km of the N2. You can stay at the **Storms River Mouth Rest Camp** (camp sites for two people US$15, US$3 for extras, forest huts US$23, chalets/huts from US$34; office ☼ 7.30am-4.30pm) in the park. There are various types of cottages, with breakfast included in the rate; all are equipped with kitchens (includ-ing utensils), bedding and bathrooms. Book through the National Parks Board.

Buses running between Cape Town and Port Elizabeth will drop you at the sign-posted turn-off on the N2. From there it's a moderate 8km walk to the rest camp.

STORMS RIVER

☎ 042

Storms River is the adrenalin junkie head-quarters of the Garden Route. If you're itching to hang by your ankles at the world's highest bungee jump or take in some black-water tubing, then don't miss this tiny and scattered hamlet with tree-shaded lanes. The surrounding landscape isn't hard on the eyes, either – pointy green mountains roll right into the town.

Don't confuse Storms River and Storms River Mouth in the Tsitsikamma Coastal

National Park. The Storms River signpost is 4km east of the park turn-off (despite what some maps show) and leads to the village.

Storms River Adventures (☎ 281 1836; adventure@gardenroute.co.za) is based here and offers a huge range of activities, including **black-water tubing** (US$34), **abseiling** (US$14) and **snorkelling** (US$52).

The world's highest **bungee jump** (216m) is at the **Bloukrans River Bridge** (☎ 281 1458), 21km west of Storms River. The jump costs US$57; but don't be confused: it might be the world's highest jump but it is not the longest – you don't fall anywhere near the 216m.

Tube n Axe (☎ 281 1757; tube-n-axe@mweb.co.za; Storms River Village; dm US$7, d US$18) is a new place that was busy building a hot tub, bar and a giant multi-person hammock when we visited. It runs river tubing and other outdoor antics. Call for a pick-up from Tsitsikamma petrol station for US$2.30.

Storms River Rainbow Lodge (☎ 281 1530; 72 Darnell St; dm US$8, s/d US$11/22) has simple, clean rooms. The place feels homey and has wonderful gardens out back. There are a few self-catering cottages that sleep four and have bathrooms if you want a little more privacy. These cost US$53 for four people.

The Baz Bus stops at Storms River.

SUNSHINE COAST

This stretch of shoreline between the Garden Route and the Wild Coast is known as the Sunshine Coast, and is best known for the surfing Mecca of Jeffrey's Bay. We have also included the mystical mountain hamlet of Hogsback in this section because, although it's not actually on the coastline, it's often visited from East London.

JEFFREY'S BAY
☎ 042

J-Bay (as it is commonly known) is the quintessential surf town, and that's the main reason for stopping by. Few would disagree that J-Bay has the best waves in Southern Africa and among the best in the world. Supertubes can be better than a three-minute ride from Boneyards to the end.

If you don't want to surf, you can always shop. The town is centred on Da Gama Road, where you will find a myriad of surf shops, restaurants and pubs.

Island Vibe Backpackers (☎ 293 1625; ivibe@lantic.co.za; 10 Daageraad St; camp sites per person US$4, dm US$7, d US$18) is perched on a dune overlooking the beach and is quite the party spot. The dorm rooms are a little cramped, but camping is on a big grassy spot overlooking the sea. There's a pool table and a giant lounge area for nightly debauchery.

Jeffrey's Bay Backpackers (☎ 293 1379; backpac@netactive.co.za; 12 Jeffrey St; dm US$7, s/d US$8/15) is within a stone's throw of the centre of town. It's mellow, friendly and well run. Surf lessons can be arranged for about US$9/hour.

The **Sunflower** (☎ 293 1682, 20 Da Gama Rd; mains US$3-4) has huge filling breakfast baguettes. The menu is varied with a large emphasis on vegetarian food.

The Baz Bus stops at the hostels. **Sunshine Express** (☎ 293 2221) runs to Port Elizabeth for US$8, door-to-door. Minibus taxis depart from Bloch's supermarket.

PORT ELIZABETH
☎ 041 / pop 750,000

Port Elizabeth (PE) is a little generic. The suburbs are filled with strip malls, petrol stations and American fast-food chains. But the downtown area is less cluttered and run-down than in other African cities. The city is obsessed with pastel paint, especially the colour pink, and many of the buildings are done up in these hues. It's one of those places where you can't decide whether you want to stay a few days and dig beneath the surface or drive right through.

The beaches leave a lot to be desired. The good news is there is one; the bad news is if you're coming from the Wild Coast, or even Durban, disappointment awaits – you'll be sunbathing in full view of the shipping rigs, and the water is a little gritty.

Lungile Backpackers (☎ 582 2042; lungile@netactive.co.za; 12 La Roche Drive; camp sites per person US$5, dm US$8, d US$21) is in a quiet upmarket residential neighbourhood a little way from the city centre, but within walking distance of the beach. Their dorms are small but clean with sturdy wooden bunks.

Port Elizabeth Backpackers Hostel (☎ 586 0697; pebakpak@global.co.za; 7 Prospect Hill; camp sites per person US$5, dm US$9, US$20) Family-oriented, quiet and clean, it sits on top of a hill overlooking the lighthouse and sea. It's within easy walking distance of many bars and restaurants.

Angelos (☎ 585 2929; Parliament St; mains US$1.25-2) This is the place for cheap hearty food. The pastas are excellent, huge and a steal at US$2, and the wine is reasonably priced.

Up the Khyber (☎ 582 220; Macarthur Baths Complex; mains US$4) It's a bright modern curry house right on the beachfront.

Phoenix Hotel (Chapel St) A grungy little pub that sometimes gets rough, it has live music some nights.

Buses stop at the train station or the Greenacres shopping centre, which is a better place to disembark at night. PE has regular connections to the major South African cities. Most minibus taxis leave from the townships surrounding PE and can be difficult to find, although a very few do depart from the area under the flyovers around the station. **Norwich** (☎ 585 7253) runs shuttles to Cape Town (US$23, nine hours). **J Bay Sunshine Express** (☎ 581 3790) runs to Jeffrey's Bay (US$3.50) and other stops along the coast.

HOGSBACK
☎ 045

A trip to Hogsback is like leaving Africa. The only problem is you won't know where you've gone. There is something otherworldly about this magical mountain hamlet where the roads are still unpaved, wispy waterfalls tumble off craggy cliffs, and rainbows stretch across the sky. JRR Tolkien visited the area as a child, and legend has it the trip inspired him to write *Lord of the Rings*. It isn't hard to believe. Take a trip into the rainforest, where gnarled trees are tangled across the paths and the woods are singing with a multitude of insect voices, and at any minute you'll expect to encounter a hobbit or an elf as you traipse across the soft ground.

Away with the Fairies (☎ 962 1031; sugarsk@iaafrica.com; camp sites US$5 per person, dm US$8, d US$19) is a hostel – highly recommended by the travellers who've made it out here. The moniker fits the place; it looks like a fairy home. Tiny and tidy with a simple metal roof and white walls, it blends perfectly into the surrounding environment. Hikes in the region literally start in the hostel's backyard. The camping is spacious, in a big grassy area out the back, and there's a treehouse to sit in and watch the sun go down.

There's no public transport to Hogsback, but Sugarshack Backpackers in East Lon-don and Buccaneer's Backpackers in Cintsa run shuttles for US$4.50.

EAST LONDON
☎ 043

Although many backpackers just travel straight through East London, a stay here reveals a striking bay that curves around to huge sand hills, a good surf beach and a bustling port and family resort. **Tourism East London** (☎ 701 9600; cnr Longfellow & Aquarium Rd; ☉ 8am-4pm Mon-Fri) has loads of information on the area.

East London Backpackers (☎ 722 2748; 11 Quanza St; dm US$8, d from US$16) Very quiet and well maintained, this place has an excess of toilets and showers, a tiny plunge pool and a large terraced *braai* area.

Sugarshack Backpackers (☎ 722 8240; sugarsh@iafrica.com; Eastern Beach; dm US$7, d US$18) With a prime location right across the street from the beach, this is a party spot, and runs popular sand-boarding trips (US$9) to nearby dunes. Doubles don't leave much space to manoeuvre, but at least they're clean. The balcony is a great place to drink a beer and look out for frolicking dolphins or whales.

Buccaneers (☎ 743 5171; mains US$2.50-5) right next to the Sugarshack, is very popular for both meals and all-night partying.

Translux (☎ 700 1999) has buses to Umtata (US$10), Port Elizabeth (US$12), Durban (US$18.50), Jo'burg/Pretoria (US$33) and Cape Town (US$26). Intercape and Greyhound also run routes through East London at similar prices. All three companies depart from the Windmill Park roadhouse on Moore St. The Baz Bus also stops here.

Long-distance minibus taxis to points north of East London leave from near the corner of Buffalo and Argyle Sts. Destinations include Umtata (US$7), Port Elizabeth (US$9), Jo'burg (US$19) and Cape Town (US$23).

TRANSKEI & THE WILD COAST

Once a homeland, the Transkei no longer exists as a political entity (it is now in Eastern Cape). Today the region has become a big draw for backpackers, especially around the laid-back coastal settlements of Cintsa,

Coffee Bay and Port St Johns. Many travelling between Durban and Cape Town stop off to experience the spectacular Wild Coast with its miles of secluded warm surf beaches and lush subtropical vegetation.

The area is rich in history. The former Transkei was at the forefront of South Africa's independence struggle, and is home to many of the country's most renowned figures, including Nelson Mandela, Thabo Mbeki and Oliver Tambo. Nelson Mandela was born in the village of Mvezo on the Mbashe River, and spent most of his childhood in the village of Qunu, about 30km south of Umtata.

CINTSA
☎ 043

Tiny Cintsa is one of the best spots on the South African coast and a great place to hang out for a few days (or weeks).

Travellers can't get enough of **Buccaneer's Backpackers** (☎ 734 3012; camp sites per person US$5, dm US$8, s/d US$18/20; 💻). Some say it's the best hostel in South Africa, and it's easy to agree. The place almost feels like a summer camp with the next day's activities announced at dinner and a different free activity each afternoon. There is everything from sundowner booze cruises to volleyball. Dinners (US$5) are huge and often include T-bone steaks and fish. Guests stick around the bar afterwards and drink the night away. There's a long secluded swimming beach, and boogie boards and canoes are loaned free. There's opportunities for horseback riding, hiking, surfing lessons and popular one-day (US$29) and four-day (US$156) tours into the Transkei. The tours combine outdoor adventure sports with cultural experiences. The four-day trip includes a homestay in a traditional Xhosa

hut with a family. Travellers say these trips are educational and worth the cost.

The Baz Bus stops at Buccaneer's, and the hostel runs a daily shuttle to East London. If you're driving from East London, take exit 26 from the N2; coming the other way take the Cintsa/Cefani exit.

COFFEE BAY
☎ 047

There's not much to do in Coffee Bay except worship the sun, play in the surf and relax. If this is up your alley, head to this tiny village where the hostels are big on responsible tourism – both environmental and cultural. Coffee Bay's beaches are excellent and, except for locals fishing on rocks, mostly deserted. High-rise hotels or package tourists won't be found here. There are numerous hikes in the area, as well as opportunities to ride horses along the surf.

Bomvu Backpackers (☎ 575 2073; www.bomvu backpackers.com; follow the signs in Coffee Bay; camp sites per person US$4, dm US$8, s/d US$15/17; 💻) calls itself a holistic hostel. Situated on the banks of the Bomvu River right off the beach, it's simple and laid-back. You can sign up for yoga classes in the morning, or spend a few days building a traditional drum from scratch. This costs US$75 and was very popular at the time of research.

Next door to Bomvu is the **Coffee Shack** (☎ 575 2048; coffeeshack@wildcoast.com; camp sites per person US$4, dm US$8, d US$20), Coffee Bay's premier party spot. Music pumps at night, and the giant bar area is always full. Dorms and bathrooms are simple but clean. Don't stay here if you're looking for peace and quiet.

The Baz Bus, Translux and Greyhound all stop at the Shell Ultra City in Umtata. From here minibus taxis to Coffee Bay leave

---

RESPONSIBLE TOURISM IS A BUZZ WORD IN COFFEE BAY

You'll see the signs posted all over – in the toilets, by the bar – Bomvu and the Coffee Shack are pushing responsible tourism in a big way. One of the main points is not to encourage a begging culture among the locals. The hostels ask you not to give in to children's requests for sweets and small change, as this tells them it is OK not to work for a living. Instead help locals who are making an effort at entrepreneurial skills.

As a result of these efforts children will now approach you on the beach and offer to sing for small change. Old men are serving as fishing guides and women sell bracelets on the side of the road. Although begging has not been eradicated in the town, Coffee Bay is years ahead of much of the rest of the country.

To read more on this subject, see the Responsible Travel section on p990.

when full from the taxi park near Bridge St and cost about US$2.50. Hostels also run shuttles (phone ahead) for about US$6. The trip takes a little more than an hour.

UMTATA
☎ 047

Umtata lies on the N2 between Cape Town and Durban, and feels more like an over-grown African village than a city. There's something razor sharp and raw to it, and violent crime can be a problem. Many tourists pass through on their way to the coast. Most don't linger.

Wild Coast hiking trails can be booked here with the **Nature Conservation Department** (☎ 531 1191; ☼ 9am-5pm Mon-Fri).

If you have time to spare, head to the new **Nelson Mandela Museum** (☎ 532 5110; admission free; ☼ 9am-4pm Mon-Fri, 9am-noon Sat). It's a loving monument to the local boy who became a global statesman.

Umtata is lacking in budget accommodation. The **Savoy Hotel** (☎ 531 0791; Queenstown by-pass; s/d from US$21/24) is the best value in town. It's a big airy place.

Umtata is served by many bus lines; Translux, Greyhound and the Baz Bus stop at the Shell Ultra City outside town. Translux runs to Durban (US$16), Port Elizabeth (US$19), East London (US$11), Jo'burg/Pretoria (US$25) and Cape Town (US$11). A City to City bus service runs daily between Jo'burg and Umtata (US$23) via KwaZulu-Natal and Kokstad (US$12).

PORT ST JOHNS
☎ 047

The deliciously traditional Port St Johns is a magnet for hippies, both young and old. White hippies came here originally to escape the army draft in the apartheid days because Transkei was an 'independent' homeland. This idyllic little town at the mouth of the Umzimvubu River has tropical vegetation, dramatic cliffs, great beaches, a relaxed atmosphere and no traffic lights. It is about as close as you'll come to the new rural South Africa, with a dominant black population in town.

If you want to be within walking distance of **Second Beach** (the main swimming beach) head to **Amapondo Backpackers** (☎ 564 1344; Second Beach Rd, camp sites per person US$4, dm US$6.50, d US$15), which is a bright cheerful place with clean dorms and hammocks on a porch overlooking the water.

The **Island** (☎ 564 1958; theisland@wildcoast.co .za; 341 Bera Rd, First Beach; camp sites per person US$6, dm US$8, d US$20) is a great place to just chill out and take it easy. Delicious breakfasts and dinners (US$2 to US$4) are served at the Moroccan-style table by the stained glass window. If you're yearning to watch a movie, there is a large screen TV and a large DVD collection.

Next door is **Jungle Monkey Backpackers** (☎ 564 1517; camp sites per person US$3.75; dm US$7, d US$18). Here you'll find the best bar in town. It's more of a party spot than the Island. You also can book here to spend a night at **Mama Constance's Place** (US$10 including dinner, bed & breakfast) in the rambling Mtumbane township.

The Baz Bus, Translux and Greyhound all stop at the Shell Ultra City in Umtata, about 100km away. From Umtata, minibus taxis to Port St Johns leave from the taxi park near Bridge St and cost US$3. Hostels (phone ahead) run a shuttle service for US$6.

Wild Coast Hiking Trail

A community initiative aimed at promoting responsible tourism in the area has led to a revamp of the Wild Coast Hiking Trail. Once complete (it was almost done at the time of research) it will create a plethora of new options for visitors.

The trail network has five distinct sections that incorporate guided and catered horse, hiking and canoe trails. To walk the whole Wild Coast would take about three weeks; most people do only one section. The 100km hiking trail between Port St Johns and Coffee Bay takes about five days and includes some dramatic rugged coastline scenery.

One word of warning: in the last couple years there have been a few serious attacks on hikers on the trails south of Port St Johns. Be aware, but don't let this put you off, as attacks are very rare. Instead, seek local advice and take sensible precautions before heading off. If you're hiking, using local guides is a good idea; it's safer and you'll learn a lot more. As a guest, respect local traditions and cultures.

For bookings and current information on the trails and travel in the region contact **Wild Coast Trails** (☎ 039-305 6455).

SOUTH AFRICA

KWAZULU-NATAL

Despite being a relatively small province, KwaZulu-Natal manages to cram in most of the things visitors come to South Africa to see, plus a few things they might not expect. There's the spectacular Drakensberg range in the southwest, a long coast of subtropical surf beaches, the melting pot city of Durban and, in the middle of it all, Zululand, the Zulu heartland.

DURBAN
☎ 031
If asked to describe Durban (or Durbs as the locals say) in one word, fusion comes to mind – a mix of Africa, Europe and India. Durban is a place where the old meets the new; where crumbling peeling buildings bump up against slick skyscrapers. It has the feel of a real African city. It's at once gritty and posh. Located on a long surf beach, it's hot and sweaty and alive.

Orientation
The airport is 20km southwest of the city centre. A **bus** (☎ 465 5573) runs to the airport from near the corner of Aliwal and Smith Sts (US$3). By taxi the same trip costs around US$15. Many hostels offer airport pick-ups.

Marine Parade, fronting long surf beaches, is Durban's focal point. Many places to stay and eat are on the parade or in the streets behind it, and some of the entertainment is here as well. The neighbourhoods of Morningside and Berea also host restaurants, hostels and much of the city's nightlife. West St starts as a mall, but further west it becomes one of downtown Durban's main streets. The city hall and the centre of the downtown area are about 1.5km west of the beach, straddling West and Smith Sts.

A fair proportion of Durban's population, mainly black, lives in townships surrounding the city. These include Richmond Farm, KwaMashu, Lindelani, Ntuzuma and the Greater Inanda area.

Information
The main **information centre** (☎ 304 4934; cnr Pine & Gardiner Sts; ☻ 8am-5pm Mon-Fri, 9am-2pm Sat & Sun) is in the old train station in a complex known as Tourist Junction. Pick up a copy of *What's on in Durban* and a free Durban map.

Rennies Travel (☎ 305 5772), the Thomas Cook agent, has several branches including one at 333 Smith St, between Gardiner and Field Sts. **American Express** (☎ 301 5541, 10th Fl, Nedbank Bldg, Durban Club Place) is nearby just off Smith Street.

Sights & Activities
Durban's prime attraction is its long surf beach and warm water. North Beach is best for surfing and people-watching, although the entire beachfront is looking a little shabby nowadays. Paint is peeling and there's a general air of neglect. Fast-food chains have inundated Marine Promenade, which runs along the waterfront. But the surf breaks are still there, the shark nets are intact and the sun shines more days than not. To rent equipment try Surf Zone Surf Shop (Dairy Beach Pier).

Definitely worth a visit is the **BAT Centre** (☎ 332 0451; www.batcentre.co.za; 45 Maritime Place, Victoria Embankment; ☻ 10am-midnight), a venue for artists of various media (see the boxed text opposite). Spend some time wandering around the shops and studios in this funky place and chat with the artists. All the work is for sale and most of it is quality, so you'll have to fork over some cash if you want to purchase. There also is a restaurant and bar (see Drinking, p969).

The **Victoria Indian Street Market**, at the western end of Victoria St, has replaced the old Indian Market, which burned down. It is the main tourist attraction of the area, and you can pick up an amazing assortment of spices. A walk through the nearby bustling streets is equally interesting – but watch out for pickpockets. Grey St, between Victoria and West Sts, is the main shopping area. Prices are low and you can bargain. Most Muslim-run shops close between noon and 2pm on Friday.

Durban is home to the largest concentration of Indian-descended people in the country. The big **Juma Mosque** (☎ 306 0026; cnr Queen & Grey Sts) is open to visitors on weekdays and Saturday morning; call for a guided tour. The **Alayam Hindu Temple** (Somtseu Rd; ☻ 7am-6pm daily) is the oldest and biggest in South Africa. It's away from the main Indian area, north of the centre on Somtseu Rd, which runs between Snell Pde and NMR Ave.

The impressive **city hall** (1910), a facsimile of Belfast's own in Northern Ireland, is

CREATING CHANCES

The BAT Centre was started in 1995 to promote South African artists from the townships and rural areas. 'It's one of a kind,' said Njabulo Hlongwane, visual coordinator for the centre. 'We're trying to sell work at marketable prices.'

Up-and-coming artists without the cash flow to begin producing on their own are invited to come to the centre. Upon arrival they are given free studio space in a communal area. After their work begins to sell they can move on to private studios where they pay minimal rent.

'It gives them a foot in the door,' Hlongwane said. 'We are giving people a chance to get themselves established as professionals in their field. That's our vision.'

The centre, funded through a private trust, also runs programs for musicians. 'We train musicians in how to run a band as a business. We teach them what they need to know before signing a contract. They stay for eight months and then they go out on their own. What we're doing here is trying to give people a chance who wouldn't necessarily have one. To give them options in life.'

worth a look inside and out. In the city hall building is the **Natural Science Museum** (enter from Smith St; admission free; ☼ 8.30am-4pm Mon-Sat, 11am-4pm Sun). Upstairs is the **Art Gallery**, which houses a good collection of contemporary works; especially good are the arts and crafts of Zululand.

Sleeping

Durban has a good selection of budget accommodation, but no camping grounds. If you're itching to camp head to Tekweni, or one of the coastal resorts north or south of the city.

Banana Backpackers (☎ 368 4062, 1st fl, 61 Pine St; dm US$8, s/d US$10/20) This place gets mixed reviews; some hate it, others love it. Regardless, it's only 1km from the beach.

Hippo Hide (☎ 207 4366; michelle@hippohide.com; 2 Jesmond Rd, Berea; dm US$9, s/d US$13/21; 🖳) Hippo Hide has the best rock pool in South Africa. It's also centrally located, and provides guests with lists of what's happening around Durban every night.

Impala Holiday Flats (☎ 332 3232; 40 Gillespie St; flats from US$21) If there's a group of you, and you're tired of hostels, this is a good option. Impala has tidy three- or four-bed flats just off the main beachfront. Take care, however, as this area is slightly dodgy.

Nomads (☎ 202 9709; nomadsbp@mweb.co.za; 70 Essenwood Road, Berea; dm US$8, d US$20) Nomad's is big and friendly, although the place has a slight air of neglect. Try to grab a bed in the big dorm; it's much cooler.

Tekweni Backpackers Hostel (☎ 303 1433; www.tekweniecotours.co.za; 169 Ninth Ave, Morningside; camp sites US$6 per person, dm US$9, d US$21; 🖳) Don't head here if you're looking to sleep.

Tekweni folks say the hostel 'goes off', and it certainly appears to be Durban's party spot. There are large open areas for hanging out and drinking, and a Bob Marley lounge. Tekweni-Eco Tours also is here, and the hostel runs an excellent citywide taxi service (see Getting Around p970).

Eating

Durban has a huge Indian population and as a result an excellent array of Indian restaurants. The city's speciality is bunny chow (half a loaf of bread hollowed out and filled with curry), and you must try it at least once while in town. Costing about US$1, it's very cheap (and filling), and can be found at numerous take-away shops around the city. If you're looking for more upmarket seafood options head to the new **Wilson's Wharf** area.

Deck (☎ 368 3699; 139 Lower Marine Pde; breakfasts US$3, mains US$3-5) Arrive between 6am and 8.30am and catch the US$1.50 breakfast special – the best deal in Durban. Right on the beach and popular with surfers, the Deck has overstuffed, fluffy omelettes and a vast selection of salads.

Designer Diner (☎ 304 9235; 300 Smith St; US$1-2.50) Designer Diner is a take-away place where you can choose from a variety of pre-prepared pastas, sandwiches and curries.

Palki (☎ 201 0019; 225 Musgrave Rd, Berea; mains US$2.50-6) Huge portions of excellent Indian food are served here. Try one of the paneers. The ambience isn't bad, and it's within easy and safe walking distance of the Hippo Hide.

Papadum (☎ 368 4475; 1 Marine Parade; mains US$1) The bunny chow here is huge, spicy

SOUTH AFRICA

DURBAN

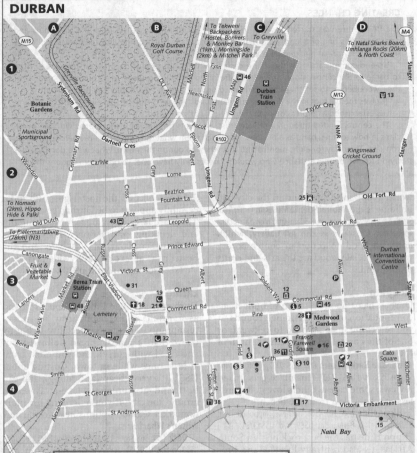

and filling. Right on the beach, it's a good option for cheap Indian food at lunch.

Zack's (☎ 305 1677; 18 Boatman Road, Wilson's Wharf; US$3-6) This is a trendy place where you can sit outside overlooking the harbour. There's a lot to choose from, including vegie options and seafood. Portions are big.

Drinking

Nightlife in Durban centres on the Berea and Morningside areas, especially Florida Road. There also are a few popular places on the beachfront and in downtown Durbs.

Bonkers (170 Florida Rd) North of the city centre, Bonkers draws a mostly white college crowd. Call ahead and ask when happy hour is happening. You'll pay US$1.25 to get in, but then get two-for-one drink specials for a few hours. The dance floor gets heated, and people dress to impress.

Cool Runnings (Milne St) This popular chain reggae bar stays open until 6am. There's a wooden motif and stumps for bar stools, and it draws a mixed-race crowd. The neighbourhood is dicey, so take a cab.

Joe Kool's (North Beach Promenade) The ever-popular Joe Kool's, right on the beach, is probably the most reliably lively place in town. It also does good recovery breakfasts for US$2.

Monkey Bar (258 Florida Rd) This place draws a slightly older crowd. It has a large cocktail menu and nice patio seating. There's a DJ on Thursday nights.

Riviera Hotel (cnr Victoria Embankment & Field St) This is probably the best place for gays and lesbians to meet people. The **Bar** (🕙 nightly) here is Durban's oldest gay club.

Trans-Africa Express (☎ 332 0451; BAT Centre, Victoria Embankment; mains US$3-6) On Fridays and Sundays there is live jazz and Zulu music, and on Tuesdays you can learn traditional drumming. There's also a concert hall where well-known acts from across the country play. The BAT Centre is a refreshing break from often segregated South African venues; you'll find a mixed crowd here. The restaurant bills itself as an 'African journey through music and food' and serves good-quality, well-presented dishes from all over the continent. It's well worth an evening trip.

Getting There & Away

Most long-distance buses leave from the rear of the train station. **Translux** (☎ 308 8111),

Greyhound (☎ 309 7830) and Intercape (☎ 307 2115) all have offices here. Sample fares include Bloemfontein (US$19), Cape Town (US$45), Jo'burg (US$18) and Port Elizabeth (US$23) via Umtata (US$18).

Panthera Azul (☎ 309 7798) runs to Maputo (US$25) Wednesday, Friday and Sunday at 7am, while the Baz Bus (☎ 304 9099) comes through Durban on its Cape Town to Jo'burg run.

Some long-distance minibus taxis leave from ranks in the streets opposite the Umgeni Rd entrance to the train station. Routes include Jo'burg (US$14) and the Swaziland border (US$12).

Other minibus taxis, running mainly to the south coast and the Transkei region in Eastern Cape, can be found around the Berea Rd station.

The *Trans Natal* train (Durban to Jo'burg via Newcastle and Ladysmith) runs daily except Tuesday and Saturday, and the weekly *Trans Oranje* (Durban to Cape Town via Bloemfontein and Kimberley) also runs from here. Contact the Durban train station (☎ 086 000 888; Umgeni Rd) for information on train travel.

Getting Around
Mynah (☎ 307 3503) is a small bus company that covers Berea, the Botanical Gardens and the central and beachfront areas roughly every 20 minutes on weekdays from around 6am to 8pm. All trips cost around US$0.50. There are also less-frequent full-size buses running more routes and travelling further from the city centre.

If there is more than one of you, Tekweni Eco-Tours taxi service (☎ 312 8727) is the cheapest way to get around town after dark. The cost is US$2.50 per trip for up to four people or US$0.60 per person for five or more. They will take you anywhere in the city and surrounding suburbs.

AROUND DURBAN
There are good beaches on the south coast between Durban and the old Transkei border. There are also resorts standing shoulder-to-shoulder, and in summer there isn't a lot of room to move.

Many of the towns along the coast have caravan parks where camping is possible, although even the cheaper municipal places can be expensive in summer.

The coast north of Durban up to the port city of Richards Bay isn't as developed as the south coast. The beaches are excellent, but most of the towns are quiet retirement villages and time-share resorts.

The Natal Sharks Board (☎ 031-566 0400; www.shark.co.za; admission US$1.75; ⊙ daily) in Umhlanga Rocks is a research institute dedicated to studying sharks. Call for the latest opening hours. The board is about 2km out of town, up the steep Umhlanga Rocks Drive (the M12 leading to the N3).

PIETERMARITZBURG
☎ 033
The capital of KwaZulu-Natal, Pietermaritzburg is an attractive old city, generally known as PMB. With its numerous historical buildings and British colonial air, it could be worth a day trip from Durban. Two of the town's best features are its avenues of huge old jacaranda trees and the maze of narrow pedestrian lanes running between Church and Longmarket Sts off the mall. Here you will find a number of impressive colonial-era buildings.

Information on the city, including a walking map, can be found at the publicity association (☎ 345 1348; 177 Commercial Rd).

You need to book most of the accommodation and walks for KwaZulu-Natal Parks in Pietermaritzburg. The office (☎ 845 1000; Queen Elizabeth Park; ⊙ 8am-4pm Mon-Fri) is a long way northwest of the town centre. You can make phone bookings with a credit card, but if you want to stop by, head out along Commercial Rd (which becomes Old Howick Rd) and after about 5km you'll come to a roundabout – don't go straight ahead (to Hilton), take the road veering to the right that has a very small sign directing you to 'QE Park', which is 2km further on. Some minibus taxis running to Hilton pass this roundabout.

Msunduzi Caravan Park (☎ 386 5342; 50 Cleland Rd; camp sites US$4) This place is about 5km from the train station. Head southeast on Commercial Rd, which becomes Durban Rd after the creek. Go left into Blackburn Road across the freeway, then take the first right.

Ngena Backpackers Lodge (☎ 345 6237; ngena@ sai.co.za; 293 Burger St; dm US$9; d US$25) Feeling like a guesthouse, it's fastidiously clean and well located.

Ristorante da Vinci (117 Commercial Rd; mains US$2-3.50) Cheap, decent Italian fare is on offer here. It also has a small, always crowded bar that's open late.

Greyhound, Intercape and Translux buses stop on Durban Rd. Book at the Publicity Association.

KWAZULU-NATAL RESERVES

As well as the parks in the Drakensberg, KwaZulu-Natal Wildlife (KZN Wildlife) has many other reserves. All accommodation, except camp sites, must be booked at the **head office** (☎ 033-845 1000; www.kznwildlife.com) in Pietermaritzburg or at the KZN Wildlife desk in the Tourist Junction in Durban. Below are a few of our favourites. As with so many parks in SA, it's best to visit with your own vehicle.

Hluhluwe-Umfolozi National Park

These magnificent twin **reserves** (US$3.50 per person plus US$4 per vehicle), dominated by wood-land savannah and flood plains, are a good place to spot 'the Big Five'. Travel to the northern reaches of the park, and forests full of mist, grassy hills and peaceful rivers will entrance you.

One of the main attractions is its 24,000-hectare wilderness area and walking trail sys-tem. Accompanied by an armed ranger, and donkeys to carry supplies, hikers spend four days walking in the reserve. You need a party of eight people, and bookings are accepted up to six months in advance. The cost is US$225 per person, including meals and equipment. On weekends there is a two-night trip that costs US$110 per person. Several tours arranged in Durban include Hluhluwe-Umfolozi Park. One inexpensive option is the three-day trip with Tekweni Eco-Tours (see Tekweni Backpackers p967), taking in the Greater St Lucia Wetlands. Isinke Bush Camp (near Umfolozi) and Bibs (St Lucia) also offer tours and day trips here.

The best place to stay in Hluhluwe is **Hilltop Camp** (self-catering chalets per person US$22, huts per person from US$44), which has stupen-dous views.

The main entrance to Hluhluwe, at Me-morial Gate, is about 15km west of the N2, about 50km northwest of Mtubatuba. Pet-rol is available at Mpila Camp in the park.

Ithala Game Reserve

In northern Zululand, **Ithala** (admission per person US$3.50 plus US$3.50 per vehicle) has all the trappings

of a private game reserve at much lower prices. It's a ruggedly beautiful place of steep riverbed valleys, sheer cliff faces and grass-land plateaus. Because it's a little way off the beaten path it doesn't attract the crowds that flock to Hluhluwe-Umfolozi. Animals include black and white rhino, elephant, buf-falo, baboon, leopard, cheetah and crocodile. This topographically diverse park supports more than 320 species of birds.

Ntshondwe (☎ 034-907 5105; camp sites per person US$2.70, units with shared kitchen from US$22, chalets from US$21) is the main centre, with superb views of the reserve below.

Itala is entered from Louwsburg, about 65km east of Vryheid on the R69, and about the same distance southwest of Pongola via the R66 and the R69.

Greater St Lucia Wetland Park

If you're looking to escape to a largely unspoiled part of South Africa, this watery wonderland, declared a UN World Heritage site in 1999, is well worth a visit. One of the world's great ecotourism destinations, this park stretches for 80km from Sodwana Bay, in the north of Maputaland, to Mapelane Nature Reserve at the southern end of Lake St Lucia. It protects five interconnected ecosystems: marine (coral reefs, beaches); shore (barrier between lake and sea); Mkuze reed and sedge swamps; the lake (the largest estuary in Africa); and western shores (fossil corals, sand forest, bushveld and grasslands).

One of St Lucia's highlights is the trip on a large boat called the *Santa Lucia*. It leaves from the wharf on the west side of the bridge on the Mtubatuba road at 8.30am, 10.30am and 2.30pm daily (US$8).

There is KZN Wildlife accommodation at several places, including the holiday vil-lage of St Lucia, where there also is privately run accommodation.

Bibs Hostel (☎ 035-590 1056; kgb@mega.co.za; dm US$7, d US$19; 🖳) At St Lucia Resort, this is a huge barn that's been converted into back-packer accommodation. It can get noisy. Bibs offers tours and day trips to Hluhluwe-Umfolozi.

African Tale Backpackers (☎ 035-550 4300; book ings@africantale.co.za; dm US$6, s/d US$8/17; 🖳) On the road between Mtubatuba and St Lucia Resort, this is a colourful place to hang out for a day or two. Accommodation options include genuine *umuzi* ('beehive' huts). It's a bit of a way outside the reserve, but the hostel runs a shuttle service to the park HQ at the St Lucia holiday village, and to the jetty where boat tours depart.

ZULULAND

Zululand covers much of central KwaZulu-Natal and is dominated by one tribal group, the Zulu. The name Zulu (Heaven) comes from an early chief. His descendants were known as *abakwaZulu*, or people of Zulu.

The capital of KwaZulu is **Ulundi**. The town is relatively new, but this area has been the stronghold of many Zulu kings. The **KwaZulu Legislative Assembly** has some interesting works of art and a statue of Shaka, but it isn't always open to visitors. Other than the expensive **Holiday Inn**, there is no accommodation.

Dumazulu Cultural Village is probably the best of the 'Zulu experience' villages. The nearby **Isinkwe Backpackers Lodge** (☎ 035-562 2258; isinkwe@saol.com; 104 Bush Road, camp sites US$4 per person, dm US$7, d US$17) gets rave reviews from travellers. Some say it's one of the top backpacker hostels in South Africa. Located on a large, beautiful patch of virgin bush, it has small but comfortable cabins, 'rustic' huts, tents and a dorm, all in a pleasant garden. There also is a good kitchen and bar. It's next to Dumazulu Cultural Village, off the N2 south of Hluhluwe (take the Bushlands exit).

In the Nkawalini Valley, north of Eshowe, **Shaka Land** is an upmarket fake craft centre, but the nearby **KwaPhekitungu Kraal**, a cooperative craft centre, is real, if not very scenic.

THE DRAKENSBERG

The Drakensberg is a land of sheer cliffs and jagged mountains, of green mosslike hills that seem to roll on forever, of giant skies and puffy clouds. Words don't do the dramatic landscape justice. It's the kind of place where fairytales must have been created. You can stretch your limbs here, breathe in the fresh mountain air and feel rejuvenated. The area, which was named a UN World Heritage site in 2000, is a mountainous basalt escarpment that forms the border between KwaZulu-Natal and Lesotho, and continues a little way into the Free State. The name means Dragon Mountains in Afrikaans. In

Zulu it's called Quathlamba, the Battlement of Spears. Both are equally fitting.

ORIENTATION

The Drakensberg (or the Berg, as it's often called) is usually divided into three sections, although the distinctions aren't strict. In this section, we describe a selection of places (ordered roughly north to south) that are relatively accessible by backpackers.

The northern Drakensberg runs from the Golden Gate Highlands National Park to the Royal Natal National Park. Harrismith and Bergville are sizeable towns in this area.

The central Drakensberg's main feature is Giant's Castle Game Reserve, the largest national park in the area. Northwest of Giant's Castle is Cathedral Peak wilderness area. The towns of Bergville, Estcourt and Winterton are all adjacent to the central Drakensberg.

The southern Drakensberg runs down to the Transkei. This area is less developed than the others but is no less spectacular. There's a huge wilderness area and the Sani Pass route into southern Lesotho.

INFORMATION

All the parks and reserves in the Drakensberg are administered by the KZN Wildlife organisation, except Golden Gate Highlands National Park, which is in the Free State. As well as the various KZN Wildlife offices in the reserves the **Drakensberg Tourism Association** (☎ /fax 036-448 1557), which covers the northern and central Drakensberg, is based in Bergville.

ROYAL NATAL NATIONAL PARK
☎ 036

Some of the Drakensberg's most dramatic and accessible scenery can be found at **Royal Natal** (admission US$1). Forming the park's southern boundary is the **Amphitheatre**, an 8km stretch of cliff, which is spectacular from below and even more so from the top. Here the **Tugela Falls**, Africa's highest cascades, drop 850m in five stages (the top one often freezes in winter). Looming up behind is **Mont-aux-Sources**, so called because the Tugela, Elands and Western Khubedu Rivers rise here – the latter eventually becomes the Orange River and flows all the way to the Atlantic. The **Rugged Glen Nature Reserve** adjoins the park on the northeastern side.

About 30 walks are available in the park, mostly day walks. Horse enthusiasts should not miss a day of horseback riding. Book through **KZN Wildlife** (☎ 438 6422); rides cost US$9 for two hours. Experienced riders will be able to partake in lots of galloping – just let the stables know your experience level ahead of time.

Inside the park there is camping at **Mahai** (☎ 438 6310; camp sites per person US$7) and **Rugged Glen** (camp sites per person US$6). Outside the park the best option is **Amphitheatre Backpackers** (☎ 438 6106; amphibackpackers@worldonline.co.za; camp sites per person US$4, dm US$8, d from US$17), a simple mountain place situated on a high plateau overlooking the Amphitheatre, with views that are out of this world. The owner is friendly and speaks fluent Zulu. Book ahead or you might find yourself sleeping in the back of the last pick-up truck (like a certain Lonely Planet writer).

The only road into Royal Natal runs off the R74, about 30km northeast of Bergville and about 5km from Oliviershoek Pass. The Baz Bus stops at Amphitheatre Backpackers, and the hostel runs a shuttle to Harrismith (US$7) where you can catch the Intercape Mainliner.

CENTRAL DRAKENSBERG
☎ 036

In some ways the Central Berg is the most attractive part of the range. It has some of the most challenging hikes: Cathkin Peak (3181m), Monk's Cowl (3234m) and Champagne Castle (3377m). The central area also includes the grand Giant's Castle Peak (3314m).

Giant's Castle Game Reserve (admission US$2.50) is located high in the mountains – the lowest point is 1300m and the highest tooth in the reserve juts up to 3280m. The reserve is rich in San rock paintings and has at least 50 sites. The most extensive examples of this art are **Main Cave** and **Battle Cave**.

There are a number of walking trails; most are round trips from either Main Camp or Injasuti, or one-way walks to various mountain huts. There are also walks between huts, so you can string together overnight hikes. Limited supplies (including fuel) are available at Main Camp, and there's a basic store near the White Mountain Lodge, but apart from these the nearest shops are in Estcourt, 50km away.

Main Camp (double bungalows from US$30) has a range of accommodation, but you can't camp here. **Injasuti Hutted Camp** (☎ 036-431 7848; admission US$2, camp sites per person US$5, 2-bed safari camp per person US$9) is a pleasant and secluded spot on the northern side of the reserve.

The best way into Main Camp is via the dirt road from Mooi River, although the last section can be impassable when wet. Infrequent minibuses run between Estcourt and the villages near the main entrance (KwaDlamini, Mahlutshini and KwaMankonjane), but these are still several kilometres from Main Camp. Injasuti is accessible from the township of Loskop, northwest of Estcourt.

SANI PASS
☎ 033

This steep rough road up the highest pass in South Africa is the only route for vehicles between KwaZulu-Natal and the mountain kingdom of Lesotho. It's also one of the most scenic parts of the Drakensberg, and many visitors drive or hitch a ride to the top just for the thrill of the journey, and then come back down to South Africa again. But if you're heading deep into Lesotho from this side of South Africa, Sani Pass is a possible jumping-off point. For more details see p926 in the Lesotho chapter.

Activities
The five-day, 60km **Giant's Cup Trail** runs from Sani Pass to Bushman's Nek (near Qacha's Nek – also described in the Lesotho chapter) and is one of the great long-distant hikes of South Africa. Any reasonably fit person can walk it, so it's very popular, and early booking (through the KZN Wildlife) is advisable. Camping is not permitted; there's accommodation in shared **huts** (US$7 per person). No firewood is available so you'll need a stove and fuel. The usual precautions for the Drakensberg apply – expect severe cold snaps at any time of the year.

If walking sounds too hard, **Khotso Horse Trails** (☎ 701 1502) has rides and treks in the area and has been highly recommended by readers.

Sleeping
There are two budget places at the bottom of the pass. **Sani Lodge** (☎ 702 1401; camp sites per person US$3, dm US$4.50, d US$12), 19km from Underberg, is small and quiet. It's near the

Giant's Cup Trailhead. **Mkomazana** (☎ 702 0340; camp sites per person US$4, dm US$4.50, d from US$12), another 5km along the road, is much larger. It's an old farm and in a beautiful spot, and there's good walking in the area. At the top of the Pass is Sani Top Chalet (see p926 in the Lesotho chapter).

Getting There & Away
Minibus taxis run between the small towns of Underberg and Himeville (US$0.40) and Pietermaritzburg (US$2.50). For a swifter service **Sani Pass Carriers** (☎ 701 1017) runs a shuttle bus daily between Underberg and Pietermaritzburg (US$12). To reach the foot of the pass from Underberg, there are occasional minibuses, or call Sani Lodge for a pick-up from Underberg or Himeville.

GAUTENG

Gauteng (Place of Gold, in Sotho) takes in the area once known as the PWV – Pretoria, Witwatersrand and Vereeniging. The Witwatersrand (literally, Ridge of White Waters) is often shortened to 'the Rand', and it contains the world's richest gold reef.

Gauteng is the smallest South African province (about 19,000 sq km), but with around 10 million people, and including the cities of Johannesburg (Jo'burg) and Pretoria, it has the largest population. It has been claimed that Gauteng accounts for 25% of the gross product of all Africa.

JOHANNESBURG
☎ 011 / pop 8 million

Here's a secret. Now tell all your friends. Jo'burg doesn't live up to its bad reputation.

By far the largest city in the country, and the heart of the new South Africa, many will tell you to fly through as quickly as possible. Don't listen. Yes, violent crime does happen here, but with the right precautions most travellers make it through their visit here without a problem. Stick to what feels safe, don't advertise your wealth, and ask around at your hostel about off-limit areas before heading out.

The townships around the city, in particular Soweto, played a crucial role in the struggle against apartheid and a government that routinely used bullets, tear gas, bombs, imprisonment without trial, torture, and

summary execution of men, women and children. Soweto was in a virtual state of war from 1976 when the first protesting school students were killed in defiance of a proposal to use Afrikaans as the language of instruction. This terrible era of violence continued as an internal political war in the dying days of apartheid, and many thousands perished in the years up to the 1994 elections.

Today, Jo'burg is a progressive city slowing letting go of its past. It's a vibrant place with top-notch restaurants, bars and shops. It even has a burgeoning art and music scene. Go on, don't be afraid – discover.

Orientation
Johannesburg International Airport is 25km east of the city centre. Between 5am and 10pm, buses run every half-hour between the airport and Park Station transit centre. The journey time is about 25 minutes, and the fare is about US$9. Buses also run from the airport to Pretoria (see Getting There & Away p983).

Two communication towers on the ridges to the north of the city centre make good landmarks: the JG Strijdom Tower in Hillbrow and the Brixton Tower, to the northwest of the city. The city centre is laid out on a simple grid.

Many people arrive in Jo'burg by bus or train at or near Park Station on the northern edge of the city centre. This is not an area you should walk with your luggage. Call a taxi or phone a hostel to be collected. If arriving by plane go the backpacker information desk at the airport and phone a hostel. All will collect travellers, although some will charge a fee.

Hostels are found almost exclusively in the affluent, white, middle-class northern suburbs.

Outside the city, the main township is Soweto (to the southwest), but there are also large developments at Tokoza (south of Alberton), Kwa-Thema and Tsakane (south of Brakpan), Daveyton (east of Benoni), Tembisa (to the northeast) and Alexandra (inside the N3 freeway to the north).

Information
The following airlines have offices in Jo'burg:
Air France (☎ 970 1526)
British Airways (☎ 921 6391)
KLM-Royal Dutch Airlines (☎ 961 6700)

JOHANNESBURG

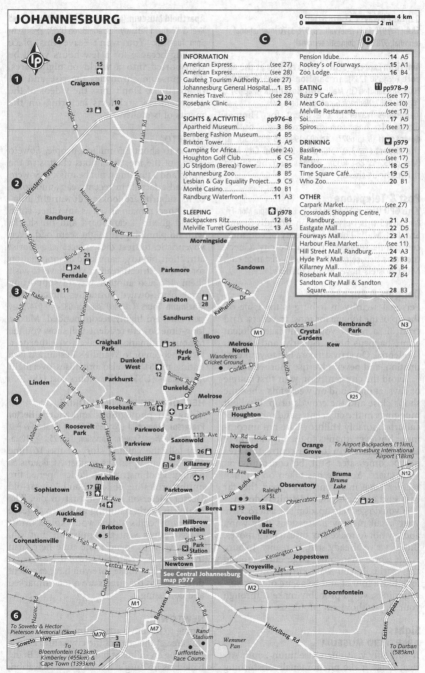

0 — 4 km
0 — 2 mi

INFORMATION
American Express.....................(see 27)
American Express.....................(see 28)
Gauteng Tourism Authority......(see 27)
Johannesburg General Hospital...1 B5
Rennies Travel..........................(see 28)
Rosebank Clinic............................2 B4

SIGHTS & ACTIVITIES   pp976–8
Apartheid Museum........................3 B6
Bernberg Fashion Museum.............4 B5
Brixton Tower...............................5 A5
Camping for Africa....................(see 24)
Houghton Golf Club.....................6 C5
JG Strijdom (Berea) Tower.............7 B5
Johannesburg Zoo........................8 B5
Lesbian & Gay Equality Project......9 C5
Monte Casino.............................10 B1
Randburg Waterfront..................11 A3

SLEEPING   p978
Backpackers Ritz.........................12 B4
Melville Turret Guesthouse.........13 A5

Pension Idube............................14 A5
Rockey's of Fourways.................15 A1
Zoo Lodge..................................16 B4

EATING   pp978–9
Buzz 9 Café...............................(see 17)
Meat Co....................................(see 10)
Melville Restaurants..................(see 17)
Soi..17 A5
Spiros.......................................(see 17)

DRINKING   p979
Bassline....................................(see 17)
Ratz..(see 17)
Tandoor......................................18 C5
Time Square Café........................19 C5
Who Zoo.....................................20 B1

OTHER
Carpark Market........................(see 27)
Crossroads Shopping Centre,
  Randburg................................21 A3
Eastgate Mall.............................22 D5
Fourways Mall............................23 A1
Harbour Flea Market.................(see 11)
Hill Street Mall, Randburg..........24 A3
Hyde Park Mall...........................25 B3
Killarney Mall.............................26 B4
Rosebank Mall............................27 B4
Sandton City Mall & Sandton
  Square....................................28 B3

SOUTH AFRICA

Qantas Airways (☎ 978 6414)
SAA (☎ 978 1111 reservations, 978 3370 international terminal, 978 3119 domestic terminal)

American Express (Amex) has offices at the **airport** (☎ 390 1233); in **Sandton** (Map p975; ☎ 883 9009; 78A Sandton City Mall); and **Rosebank** (Map p975; ☎ 880 8382; Nedbank Gardens, 33 Bath Ave).

Rennies Travel is the agent for Thomas Cook. It has foreign exchange outlets **downtown** (Map p977; ☎ 492 1990; 35 Rissik St), at the **airport** (☎ 390 1040) and **Sandton City Mall** (Map p975; ☎ 884 4035). ATMs can be found throughout the city.

Post & Telephone
The **GPO** (Map p977; Jeppe St; ☺ 8.30am-4pm Mon-Fri, 8am-noon Sat) is between Von Brandis St and Smal St Mall. There are plenty of commercial phone services around the city. Check the rates before making a long-distance call. Most hostels have email facilities.

Dangers & Annoyances
Personal security in Jo'burg is the issue on the tip of the tongue for most travellers. And crime is a reality you might face. Violent crime happens here, regularly, and caution is essential. On arrival, take a taxi to your destination, and never advertise your wealth.

Avoid the city centre on your first couple of days, at night and on weekends when the shops close and the crowds drop. Daylight muggings in the city centre and other inner suburbs, notably Hillbrow, are not uncommon; however, thanks to the installation of security cameras in the city centre, this area has become safer. Still, be constantly on your guard. Yeoville has taken on a much seedier edge in recent times, and the 'far east' end of Rockey St is definitely dodgy.

If you do get held up, don't be a hero. Give your assailants any possessions they want, and try not to make any threatening moves. But as we've already said, in reality, Jo'burg is no worse than most large cities around the world. If you walk confidently, don't look like a tourist and be aware of your surroundings, you'll probably make it through your stay without any problems.

Sights
APARTHEID MUSEUM
If you only visit one museum in South Africa, make it the phenomenally disturbing

Apartheid Museum (Map p975; ☎ 309 4700; cnr Gold Reef & Northern Parkway Rds; admission US$3; ☺ 10am-5pm Tue-Sun). You won't leave this place smiling because for a few hours you'll be transported into a world of nightmares. The museum chronicles the rise and fall of apartheid. Don't miss the videos of the apartheid-era architects lecturing on the merits of brutality.

SOWETO
Home to about 3.5 million people, Soweto is one of the most infamous ghettos in the world and a tour must not be missed. Soweto has had a facelift in recent years, and some of its suburbs are looking downright affluent. Others remain as sad as any other Third World ghetto – cardboard and tin shacks with no plumbing. It might seem odd, even voyeuristic, to treat these places as a tourist attraction, but to get any kind of appreciation for South African reality, you have to visit them. It's also another way of supporting local, black-owned businesses directly. **Max Maximum Tours** (☎ 469 3802 or 082-770 0247; day tours US$29) are highly recommended. Max, a long-time Soweto resident, will show you the famous landmarks and take you either to a local shebeen or to Wandie's Restaurant (see Eating p978). He also organises overnight homestays (US$39). Day tours cost US$29.

HECTOR PIETERSON MEMORIAL
Using old photographs and video, **Hector Pieterson Memorial** (☎ 536 2253; cnr Khumalo & Pela Sts, Orlando West, Soweto; admission US$1.25; ☺ 10am-5pm) tells the chilling story of the 16 June 1976 student uprisings against Afrikaans as a language of instruction. Police opened fire on the protesting children, and 13-year-old Hector Pieterson was the first to die. The exhibit is stark, haunting and sure to leave you with chills down your spine. Most Soweto tours visit this museum, but you might want to spend more time here than they allow. It's relatively safe to drive here on your own; just make sure you have excellent directions, as the streets are often unmarked and confusing.

NEWTOWN
Home to the city's arts community for years, this area at the edge of the city centre is now receiving an influx of billions of rands. Being hailed as Jo'burg's last hope of salvation,

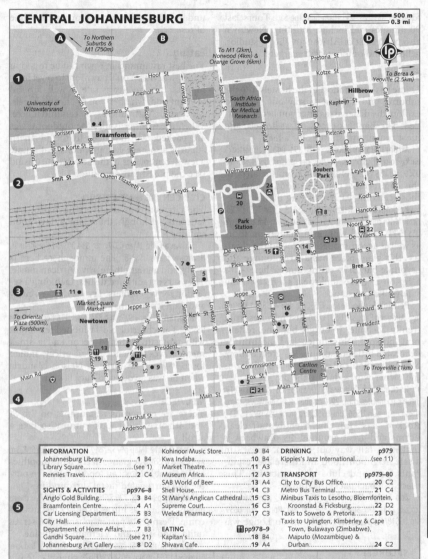

CENTRAL JOHANNESBURG

0 — 500 m
0 — 0.3 mi

INFORMATION		Kohinoor Music Store.................**9** B4	DRINKING	p979
Johannesburg Library................**1** B4		Kwa Indaba.....................**10** B4	Kippies's Jazz International........(see 11)	
Library Square.........................(see 1)		Market Theatre................**11** A3		
Rennies Travel.........................**2** C4		Museum Africa..................**12** A3	TRANSPORT	pp979–80
		SAB World of Beer............**13** A4	City to City Bus Office.............**20** C2	
SIGHTS & ACTIVITIES	pp976–8	Shell House.......................**14** C3	Metro Bus Terminal..............**21** C4	
Anglo Gold Building...............**3** B4		St Mary's Anglican Cathedral..**15** C3	Minibus Taxis to Lesotho, Bloemfontein,	
Braamfontein Centre..............**4** A1		Supreme Court...................**16** C3	Kroonstad & Ficksburg...........**22** D2	
Car Licensing Department......**5** B3		Weleda Pharmacy...............**17** C3	Taxis to Soweto & Pretoria........**23** D3	
City Hall................................**6** C4			Taxis to Upington, Kimberley & Cape	
Department of Home Affairs....**7** B3		EATING	pp978–9	Town, Bulawayo (Zimbabwe),	
Gandhi Square......................(see 21)		Kapitan's..........................**18** B4	Maputo (Mozambique) &	
Johannesburg Art Gallery.......**8** D2		Shivava Cafe.....................**19** A4	Durban.............................**24** C2	

city officials are hoping the renovations will
draw local and international tourists back to
a reinvigorated downtown. The area houses
Museum Africa (Map p977; ☎ 833 5624; 121 Bree St;
admission US$0.80; ⏰ Tue-Sun 9am-5pm), which has
some interesting exhibitions on Jo'burg's
recent history and a large collection of rock
art. The **Market Theatre** (Map p977; ☎ 832 1641; Bree

St) complex has live theatre venues, an art
gallery, coffee shop, some interesting shops,
a pleasant pub and **Kippie's Bar**, which is an excellent jazz venue (see Drinking p979). There
is always some interesting theatre – check the
Weekly Mail & Guardian entertainment section. Beer lovers can stop in for a tour of **SAB
World of Beer** (Map p977; ☎ 836 4900; 15 President St;

admission US$1.25; ⏰ 10am-6pm Tue-Sat). Tours last 90 minutes and include a tasting. Newtown also has a host of African art shops, studios, galleries and outdoor craft markets.

Sleeping

Crime has driven most of the hostels into the suburbs, and it's best to stay out here and explore the dicier areas after you become settled. The Baz Bus drops off at hostels, and most run airport shuttles for a fee.

Airport Backpackers (☎ 394 0485; airportback pack@hotmail.com; camp sites per person US$4.50, dm US$9, s/d US$19/24) Only 2km from the airport, this comfortable place is a good option for those catching early morning flights.

Backpackers Ritz (Map p975; ☎ 325 7125; ritz@iafrica.com; 1A North Rd, Dunkeld West; dm US$9, s/d US$16/23) Packed with information on tours as well as accommodation around the country, this giant place has a large lounge and cryptlike bar. Skip eating dinner here – it's a rip-off at US$6, and there's a mall within safe walking distance.

Pension Idube (Map p975; ☎ 484 4055; 11 Walton Ave, Auckland Park; s/d US$13/20) Just minutes from trendy Melville, Jo'burg's bar and restaurant hotspot, this quiet and beautifully decorated little guesthouse is a great option. Make sure you call ahead for a booking as the owner works during the day.

Rockey's of Fourways (Map p975; ☎ 465 4219; info@backinafrica.com; 22 Campbell Rd, Fourways; camp sites per person US$6, dm US$8, s/d from US$19/23; 🖳) Rockey's has a fun vibe, friendly staff, clean dorms and great grounds. Its drawback is that it's a fair way out of town, but it's in a safe neighbourhood and there are restaurants, bars and clubs in the vicinity. This place is a backpacker favourite.

Zoo Lodge (Map p975; ☎ 788 5182; www.backpack .co.za; 233a Jan Smuts Ave, Parktown North; dm US$9, s/d US$18/23) Another option, Zoo Lodge was

---

SPLURGE!

Melville Turrett Guest House (Map p975; ☎ 482 7197; turret@totem.co.za; cnr 2nd Ave & 9th St, Melville; d US$35) In a large, former residential house with lovely lime-green walls and a homely feel, this beautifully appointed place makes a nice break from the usual backpacker hostels. Rooms include televisions and phones, and it's just a safe few minutes' walk from Melville's bustle.

---

undertaking major renovations at the time of research.

Eating

The best restaurants in town can be found in trendy Melville. You'll pay more to revel in its hipness, but the area is safe to walk around at night and, whether you're craving bagels, Mexican or Vietnamese, you can find it here. When the weather is nice the outdoor tables are packed. All the malls in the northern suburbs also have eating options, with quite a few decent places in the new Monte Casino (see the boxed text opposite).

CITY CENTRE & NEWTOWN

The city centre is relatively devoid of restaurants, although there are a few good options left.

Shivava Café (Map p977; ☎ 834 8037; 1 President St, Newtown; mains US$3-8) The atmosphere here is lively, and at night there's live African music. They serve traditional dishes, including a selection for vegetarians. Try the chicken curry and pap; it's mouth-watering.

Kapitan's (Map p977; ☎ 834 8048; 11A Kort St; mains US$5-8) This cheerful, old-fashioned restaurant with fantastic cluttered décor and a small menu serves authentic, albeit pricey, Indian food. It was a favourite of Nelson Mandela when he was a young Jo'burg lawyer.

MELVILLE

There are numerous restaurants on 7th St and 4th Ave; most look yummy so take a stroll.

Buzz 9 Café (Map p975; ☎ 726 2019; cnr 7th St & 3rd Ave; mains US$5-8) A giant selection of smoothies and palatable Mexican food is served in purple and corrugated metal surroundings.

Soi (Map p975; ☎ 726 5775; cnr 7th St & 3rd Ave; mains from US$5) About as hip as Jo'burg's restaurants come. Despite its pretentiousness Soi serves quite good Thai and Vietnamese cuisine.

Spiros (Map p975; ☎ 482 1162; cnr 7th St & 2nd Ave; breakfast US$3, mains US$4-7) This cheery café is a good place for coffee and breakfast – there is a huge, varied selection. They also have an extensive menu of salads.

SOWETO

Soweto's eating options for travellers are very limited.

Wandie's Place (☎ 982 2796; 618 Dube; all-you-can eat buffet US$7) For the best traditional meal

---

SOMETHING SAFE

If Jo'burg terrifies you then head to the **Monte Casino** (Map p975; cnr William Nicol Dr & the N1). It's one of the safest places you can go in the city; they'll make you check your guns at the door and then frisk you to get in. Once inside you'll be transported into a faux (and slightly gaudy) Tuscan village complete with a never-ending sunset and canals. Besides the casino there are numerous restaurants, bars, clubs, live theatre, a cinema and shops. The place is a little cheesy (you'll either love it or hate it), but it's just down the road from Rockey's backpackers and it has one exceptional restaurant. The **Meat Co** is well worth the price (mains US$5 to US$8). Steaks melt in your mouth, and are cooked exactly the way you ask. You can choose from a large selection of sauces to place on top. Order a side of vegies (US$1.25); it's enough for two, and the creamed spinach is sumptuous.

---

in town, head to Soweto's best restaurant. The buffet is so good that Wandie's now sees as many white patrons as black. Make sure you have reliable directions, and visit during daylight in case you get lost.

Drinking

Melville is a good safe bet for a night of drinking. There are numerous bars (along with the restaurants) on 7th St and 4th Ave. Dress to impress here.

Bassline (Map p975; 7th St, Melville; admission US$2.50) Bassline is a small hip place with live jazz.

Horror Café/Rhythm of Africa (Map p977; 5 Becker St, Newtown) The name was in flux when we visited, but the garish green and purple monster-themed decor was still there. Go on the weekends for dancing to a DJ, or visit on a Sunday afternoon for live jazz. They also serve pizzas and food from around the continent (US$2.50 to US$5).

Kippie's Jazz International (Map p977; Bree St, Newtown; admission US$3.50) This is one of the best places to see South African jazz talent. Small, popular and cultural, it shouldn't be missed.

Ratz (Map p975; cnr 7th St & 3rd Ave, Melville) A popular night spot, this tiny place is packed when there is a DJ. Come for happy hour (5-7pm daily) when the extensive cocktail menu is up for grabs at US$1.75 per potent drink.

Stardust Palace (Map p977; 61 Jorissen St, Braamfontein; from 9pm Wed, Fri, Sat) Many Jo'burgers say this is their favourite gay bar. There are two dance floors, cabaret shows and strippers.

Tandoor (Map p975; east end of Rockey St, Yeoville) This is one of the best *kwaito* clubs in Jo'burg, and the only place in Yeoville worth going for live music. The neighbourhood is not the safest, so carry only what you're not scared of losing.

Time Square Café (Map p975; cnr Fortesque Rd & Rockey St, Yeoville) Another popular Yeoville haunt, the Time Square is a gathering place for intellectuals and artists, and a good place for a beer on a hot night.

Who Zoo (Map p975; Merrow Down Shopping Centre, Fourways) This big club is right around the corner from Rockey's and was popular with backpackers and locals. It draws a mostly black crowd, and you can dance to house music until the wee hours of the morning.

Getting There & Away

AIR

Johannesburg International Airport (JIA; 921 6262 for flight inquiries) is South Africa's major international and domestic airport (for details on domestic fares and destinations, see p948). Numerous international airlines also have offices in Jo'burg; for details see p974.

Roundtrip airfares to Jo'burg from London start at about US$600. From New York roundtrip fares to Jo'burg can be found for as little as US$1100, but generally cost about US$1300. From Los Angeles fares start at US$1500. From Australia and Asia fares start to Jo'burg start at US$1300 if you are staying less than a month and jump up to US$1900 for longer stays.

From Jo'burg to Cape Town one-way fares start at US$130.

BUS

International bus services leave Jo'burg for Botswana, Zambia, Mozambique and Zimbabwe.

The main long-distance bus lines (national and international) depart from and arrive at the **Park Station transit centre** (Map p977). There are booking counters for **Translux** (774 3333), **Greyhound** (249 8900) and **Intercape** (333 2312). City to City, the inexpensive government bus service, leaves from behind the Formule 1 hotel, also at the transit centre.

Don't forget the **Baz Bus** (☎ 021-439 2323) with its hop-on hop-off service.

There are at least daily buses to Beitbridge (US$14), Cape Town (US$46), Durban (US$21), East London (US$33), Mafikeng (US$9), Nelspruit (for Kruger National Park; US$15), Bloemfontein (US$26) and Port Elizabeth (US$37).

Intercape runs to Upington and from there to Windhoek (Namibia). There is no direct connection between the two cities.

HITCHING

We don't recommend hitching, especially around Jo'burg, but inevitably some people will do it. Heading north, a place to begin hitching is on the N1 near the Killarney Mall shopping centre, a couple of kilometres northwest of Yeoville. The N12 running east towards Kruger begins just east of Eastgate Mall. Heading south on the N1 (to Cape Town, for example) you could try your luck on one of the freeway on-ramps.

Also check hostel notice boards for details of free or shared-cost lifts.

LOCAL TRANSPORT

The main long-distance minibus taxi ranks cluster just inside the perimeter of the Park Station complex, where security is pretty tight. Be very careful, however, about venturing to the few taxis beyond the 'cordon' (such as the Lesotho-bound taxis). It might not seem far, but walking about laden with rucksacks is asking for trouble. Take a taxi around to these minibuses or use the left luggage facilities while you sort out a fare, and get one of the taxi guys help you with your bags if necessary.

Some destinations and approximate fares from Jo'burg include Bulawayo (Zimbabwe; US$23), Cape Town (US$34), Durban (US$14), Gaborone (Botswana; US$13), Kimberley (US$11), Manzini (Swaziland; US$11), Maseru (Lesotho; US$11), Nelspruit (US$11) and Pietersburg/Polokwane (US$11).

Getting Around

For inquiries about local bus services, call or visit the **information counter** (☎ 403 4300) on Gandhi Square. Most services stop by 7pm, and most fares are about US$0.60. Route

Nos 5 (Parktown, Houghton, Rosebank and Illovo), 22 (Yeoville and Bruma) and 67 (Braamfontein, Auckland Park and Melville) are useful.

Minibus taxi fares differ depending on the route, but US$0.80 will get you around the inner suburbs and the city centre. It's easy to get a minibus taxi into the city centre and, if you're waiting at a bus stop, a minibus will probably arrive before the bus does. Getting a minibus taxi back from the city is more difficult.

There has been a serious problem with violent crime on the metropolitan train system, mostly on lines connecting with black townships. In recent times the line between Pretoria and Jo'burg has been particularly bad. Be careful.

There are hire taxi ranks in the city centre and at the airport. Taxis have meters, but once you get an idea of distances and prices, try agreeing on a price rather than using the meter. **Maxi Taxi** (☎ 648 1212) is a reputable company.

PRETORIA

☎ 012 / pop 1.6 million

South Africa's administrative capital is only 56km from Jo'burg, but worlds away in most other respects. Relaxed and slightly bland, Pretoria is filled with students and is much safer than its big sister. If you're worried about crime, head here. It's just as easy to reach from Johannesburg International Airport, and most buses to points around South Africa originate here.

Orientation

Pretoria is served by Johannesburg International Airport (JIA). **Get You There** (☎ 346 3175) runs an hourly service from JIA day and night, dropping off at hotels and hostels for US$10. Many hostels offer airport pick-ups, some free, if you phone ahead.

The main east-west road is Church (Kerk) St. At 26km it's claimed to be one of the longest straight streets in the world. It runs through Church Square (although traffic is diverted), the historic centre of the city, and east to the suburb of Arcadia, home of most of the hotels and embassies, as well as the Union Buildings. Most cheap accommodation and nightlife is concentrated in the suburbs of Hatfield and Sunnyside. If you arrive by train or bus it's an easy walk down Church

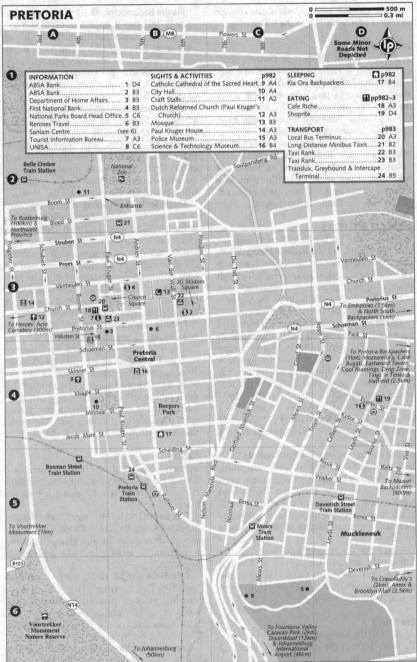

PRETORIA

Some Minor Roads Not Depicted

INFORMATION	
ABSA Bank..................................	1 D4
ABSA Bank..................................	2 B3
Department of Home Affairs.......	3 B3
First National Bank......................	4 B3
National Parks Board Head Office.5 C6	
Rennies Travel............................	6 B3
Sanlam Centre........................(see 6)	
Tourist Information Bureau..........	7 A3
UNISA..	8 C6

SIGHTS & ACTIVITIES	p982
Catholic Cathedral of the Sacred Heart.9 A4	
City Hall.....................................	10 A4
Craft Stalls.................................	11 A2
Dutch Reformed Church (Paul Kruger's	
Church).....................................	12 A3
Mosque......................................	13 B3
Paul Kruger House......................	14 A3
Police Museum...........................	15 A3
Science & Technology Museum........16 B4	

SLEEPING	p982
Kia Ora Backpackers................17 B4	

EATING	pp982–3
Cafe Riche.................................	18 A3
Shoprite.....................................	19 D4

TRANSPORT	p983
Local Bus Terminus....................	20 A3
Long Distance Minibus Taxis........21 B2	
Taxi Rank..................................	22 B3
Taxi Rank..................................	23 B3
Translux, Greyhound & Intercape	
Terminal..................................24 B5	

SOUTH AFRICA

St to the city bus ranks. Hostels can arrange to collect you from JIA or the bus stations.

Information

Pretoria's **Tourist Information Centre** (☎ 337 4337; Church Sq) is right in the centre of town. The **National Parks Board head office** (☎ 428 9111; www.parks-sa.co.za; 643 Leyds St, New Muckleneuk) is not far from the university, to the southeast of the city centre. Bookings may be made here, and some information is available.

For currency exchange, try **Amex** (☎ 346 2599; Brooklyn Mall). **Rennies Travel** (☎ 320 2240; Sanlam Centre, cnr Andries & Pretorius Sts) has a few branches. If you're flying in, there are also 24-hour Amex and Thomas Cook offices at JIA. ATMs are found throughout the city.

Sights & Activities

Pretoria is not particularly blessed with interesting sights, but the **National Zoological Gardens** (☎ 328 3265; cnr Paul Kruger & Boom Sts; admission US$3.50; ☉ 8am-5.30pm) is an impressive enough place to spend an afternoon. The highlight is the cable car that runs up to the top of a *kopje* (isolated hill) overlooking the city.

Church Square is the heart of Pretoria and surrounded by imposing public buildings. In the centre, Paul Kruger looks disapprovingly at office workers lounging on the grass. A short walk from Church Square on Church St, the residence of Paul Kruger (president of the Boer republics during the 1899–1902 Anglo-Boer War) has been turned into a museum, the **Paul Kruger House** (☎ 326 9172; 60 Church St; admission US$150; ☉ 8.30am-4.30pm Mon-Sat, 9am-4.30pm Sun).

The enormous **Voortrekker Monument** (☎ 326 6670; admission US$2.30; ☉ 9am-4.45pm), 6km south of the city, was begun in 1938 to commemorate the achievements of the Boers who trekked into the heart of the African veld. It's a striking temple to Afrikaner nationalism and an encapsulation of the Afrikaner mindset.

Catch the Voortrekkerhoogte or Valhalla bus on the southeastern corner of Church Square. Ask the driver to let you off at the entrance road to the monument; from there it is a 10-minute walk.

Sleeping

Almost all the backpackers hostels in Pretoria offer tours of the surrounding areas and national parks, including Kruger.

Kia Ora Backpackers (☎ 322 4803; hostel@absamail .co.za; 257 Jacob Maré St, dm US$8, s/d US$13/20) You'll love the long funky bar that looks like it's left over from a time gone by. The dorm rooms are a little cramped but clean. The restaurant serves an assortment of burgers and pasta for about US$3. It's within easy walking distance of the coach and train stations.

Mazuri Backpackers (☎ 343 7782; mazuri@lantic.net; 503 Reitz St, Sunnyside, dm US$7, s/d US$11/17) The rooms at this no-frills place are brightly painted and cheery, and there's a garage that's been turned into a reading lounge with comfy chairs and a small library. It's popular with American Peace Corps volunteers (their main office is just down the street).

North South Backpackers (☎ 362 0989; north south@mweb.co.za; 355 Glyn Street, Hatfield; camp sites per person US$5, dm US$9, s/d US$18/23) This popular place has the best mattresses in the city, warm showers and immaculate facilities. It's also within easy walking distance of the bars, shops and restaurants of popular Hatfield Square. There is a second lodge, for the same price, just up the street that offers more secluded and spacious accommodation.

Pretoria Backpackers (☎ 343 9754; ptaback@ netactive.co.za; 425 Farenden Street; dm US$10, s&d US$23) The double rooms are beautifully decorated with dark wood furniture and a safari motif. Stepping into the garden you feel as if you've been transported to a tropical rainforest – ducks and birds wander among giant palm trees, and the hidden tables in the garden are a good place for a quiet beer. The hostel also has a salon for facials and massages.

Eating

Burnett Road and the adjacent Hatfield Square have a huge selection of restaurants. For self-caterers there are also a few supermarkets here.

Café Bugati (☎ 362 5467; Shop 16, Hatfield Galleries, Burnett St; breakfasts & mains from US$3.50) Café Bugati serves fabulous coffee and giant salads and is a favourite among locals, especially for breakfast.

Café Riche (☎ 328 3173; 2 Church St; light meals from US$4) This swanky place, full of suit-wearing yuppies proudly comparing the latest in mobile phone technology, is the best place in town for people-watching. The food is pretty good.

Crawdaddy's (☎ 460 0889; cnr Middle & Dey Sts; Brooklyn; mains from US$5) Easily Pretoria's best steak house, this place is always packed. While you're there order one of the seafood and steak combos.

Eastwood Tavern (☎ 344 6534; cnr Eastwood & Park Sts; mains from US$6) Prices are a little high and you're unlikely to see any blacks in here, but excellent steaks abound. Televisions broadcast sports, and it's also a popular drinking spot.

Mozzarella's (☎ 362 6463; Hatfield Sq, Burnett St; mains US$4-5) Sit outside, order one of the excellent pizza or pasta dishes, and watch the beautiful people walk by.

Drinking

Again, Hatfield wins hands down when it comes to drinking. If the weather's nice head into the square and sit outside at one of the numerous bars. They'll be packed with students. Otherwise, **Cool Runnings** (Burnett St) and **Tings an' Times** (Hatfield Galleries off Burnett St) are two reggae places that draw friendly mixed crowds. **Drop Zone** (Hatfield Square) is Hatfield's pick-up place of choice and quickly gets packed.

Getting There & Away

Most interprovincial and international bus services commence in Pretoria, unless they are heading north. Most buses leave from the forecourt of Pretoria train station on Paul Kruger St. Most **Translux** (☎ 315 2333) and **Greyhound** (☎ 323 1154) services running from Jo'burg to Durban, the south coast and Cape Town originate in Pretoria. **Intercape** (☎ 654 4114) has services to Upington (US$29). From Upington you can then catch the Intercape bus to Windhoek (Namibia). Fares for these operators are identical to those from Jo'burg (see p979).

Long-distance minibus taxis leave from near the railway and bus stations just off Scheidling St.

Getting Around

The **inquiry office** (☎ 308 0839) and main terminus for local buses is on the southeastern corner of Church Square. Some services, including the one to Sunnyside, run until about 10.30pm. The standard minibus fare around town is US$0.30.

There are taxi ranks on the corner of Church and Van der Walt Sts, at Vermeulen and Andries Sts, and on the corner of Pretorius and Paul Kruger Sts. Alternatively,

call **Five Star** (☎ 320 7513/4). You'll pay about US$0.40 per kilometre.

HARTBEESPOORT DAM

Hartbeespoort Dam is a great day trip from either Pretoria or Jo'burg if you have your own transport (sadly there's no bus service here). Less than an hour's drive away, it feels like a different world. Gone is the city hustle, replaced by rolling hills, winding country roads and the green blue waters of the dam.

Although the surrounding countryside is lovely, the main reason to visit is for the **Welwitschia Country Market** (☉ 9am-5pm Tue-Sun). Here you can choose between 38 open-air stands selling African curios. Prices are reasonable, quality is fair to excellent (you can find some really nice pieces) and you can bargain.

If you're hungry afterwards, head to the **Upperdeck Restaurant** (mains from US$2) across the street from the market. There is a varied menu, including vegetarian dishes, and live music on the weekends.

SUN CITY

An extraordinary creation, **Sun City** (admission US$6) is an entertainment complex based on gambling, mildly risqué shows, Disneyesque interpretations of Africa, and Vegasstyle kitsch. There are also excellent golf courses, swimming pools, sports facilities, restaurants and high-quality accommodation. Such extravagance has always sat incongruously in such a relatively poor country, but these days it's also a refreshingly mixed place that's enthusiastically enjoyed by South Africa's affluent black as well as affluent white classes. It's also a substantial local employer.

Entry to Sun City includes 'chips' worth US$3.50. You don't have to use these for gambling; you could put them towards a meal or entry to the impressive beach and Valley of the Waves.

The enormous Lost City complex is worth a look if only for the scale of the thing. It's a sort of mega-amusement park in high-glitz style, with such attractions as the Bridge of Time, the Valley of Waves (US$7) and the Temple of Courage.

Several tour operators make the trip from Pretoria/Jo'burg; it's best to ask at a hostel.

MPUMALANGA

Mpumalanga is the province formally known as Transvaal – much of the area to the north and east of Gauteng. The area takes in both highveld and lowveld, with the dramatic Klein Drakensberg escarpment in between where the spectacular Blyde River Canyon is located. Down on the lowveld the world famous Kruger National Park is bordered by a host of luxurious private game reserves to the west and Mozambique to the east.

KRUGER NATIONAL PARK

Teeming with wildlife, this enormous **park** (admission US$3.50 per person plus US$3 per vehicle; ☼ gates open 4.30-5.30am & close 5.30-6.30pm depending on month) is a must-see in South Africa. Attracting close to a million visitors a year, the park stretches almost 350km along the Mozambique border to the east, the Northern Province to the west and Mpumalanga to the south, and it has earned its reputation as one of the most famous wildlife reserves in the world. Thanks to its immense size, the park swallows the crowds, and you're likely to see more wildlife than people on the roads. The landscape is varied here – sometimes the roads cut through thick vegetation, other times through endless plains interspersed with acacia thorn trees.

The park also is excellent value. Your biggest expense will be on car rental (there's no public transport inside the park so you'll need a vehicle), but otherwise you won't be forced to shell out US$100 a day or more in park fees and safaris as you would in some other countries. The main roads are tar, and you can drive yourself around looking for animals.

Kruger is said to have the greatest variety of animals in any wildlife park in Africa, including lions, leopards, cheetahs, elephants, giraffes and many varieties of antelope. The south of the park is the best place to see rhinos and hippos. Lions are most commonly seen on the plains north of Skukuza Camp. Elephants are common from Olifant's camp to the north to the end of the park.

Activities

Seven guided 'walking trails' offer a chance to walk through the park with knowledge-able and armed guides. Most trails take two days and three nights to walk, over a weekend. Accommodation is in huts. Trails cost US$195 per person, including meals, and must be booked well in advance.

If you don't trust your wildlife-spotting skills (it's a lot harder than it sounds) or you just want to know more about the place you've come so far to see, then join one of the organised wildlife drives. Drives leave from the rest camps at 5am and 5pm, last about three hours and cost about US$5 per person.

Sleeping & Eating

Accommodation (except for camp sites) can be booked through the **National Parks Board** (☎ 012-428 9111; reservations@parks-sa.co.za) in Pretoria. Offices in Cape Town and at the Tourist Junction in Durban also take bookings. You can make a phone booking with a credit card.

Except on weekends and peak times (school holidays, Christmas and Easter) you won't have trouble getting accommodation. Most people stay at rest camps. These have a wide range of facilities. The restaurants are good, and the prices are reasonable. Most have shops, phones and fuel. The accommodation varies, but usually includes huts and self-contained cottages on the low-price end. All huts and cottages are supplied with bedding and towels, and most have air-con and fridges. The cheapest huts cost between US$15 and US$23 for two people. Camping costs US$10 for two people plus US$3 for each additional person. Try the huts at Lower Sabie camp; they offer some of the cheapest accommodation in the park. The restaurant offers a stunning view of the Sabie River and is a prime wildlife-viewing spot. Cheap take-away food like burgers costs US$3.

Skukuza is the biggest of the camps and includes a visitors' centre, but often is crowded and lacks ambience. Other good camps include Olifants, for spectacular views down the Olifants River and great game-viewing territory, and Punda Maria, which is an old-fashioned place in an attractive setting that's good for exploring the unique northern end of the park.

Outside the park, near Nelspruit (15km from Numbi Gate), is the small village of Hazyview. You can stay at **Kruger Park Back-packers** (☎ 737 7224; huts around per person US$8), just past the White River turn-off, which has Zulu-style huts, organises tours of Kruger and will collect you from Nelspruit for US$15.

Getting There & Away

There is no public transport inside Kruger. Either join a tour (ask at North South Backpackers in Pretoria or the Backpackers Ritz in Jo'burg) or consider renting a car in Nelspruit, the most convenient large town near Kruger. It's well served by buses and minibus taxis to and from Jo'burg.

By car Skukuza is about 500km from Jo'burg and can be reached in five to six hours. Punda Maria is about 620km from Jo'burg and can be reached in about eight hours.

NELSPRUIT
☎ 013

Nelspruit, in the Crocodile River Valley, is the largest town in Mpumalanga's steamy southern lowveld. It is rather bland and hot but is a good jumping-off point for Kruger.

Funky Monkey Backpackers (☎ 310 4755; 102 Van Wijk St; dm US$8, d US$18) is like stepping into the Art Deco house you've always envied. The place is filled with modern artwork, bright colours and more than enough clean bathrooms. The owner knows the area and can direct you to the latest nightlife hotspot.

Laid-back **Nelspruit Backpackers** (☎ 741 2237; 9 Andries Pretorius St; dm US$8, d US$21) is the town's Rasta option.

For dinner head to the **Keg & Jock** (☎ 755 4969; cnr Ferriera & Van der Merwe Sts; mains US$3-5), which has a giant selection of food. Try the Dixie Pie.

Nelspruit is well served by buses and minibus taxis from Jo'burg, and even has a small international airport.

BLYDE RIVER CANYON

This immense gorge is one of South Africa's most spectacular sights. However, if you're not going to spend a day or two hiking around it's probably not worth the admission price of US$3 (at **Bourke's Lock Potholes** where most tourists enter the reserve) just to have a look.

If you're ready to stretch your legs, there are worthwhile self-guided day hikes. Stop at the **Bourke's Lock Potholes information centre** (☎ 013-759 5432) for maps. This is where you also can organise two-night camping trips

that take you into the canyon. The trip costs US$3.50 per person per night, is self-guided and is the only way to get on to the canyon floor. The trail covers about 20km in three days and transverses half of the nature reserve. Book well in advance.

God's Window is 5km off the main road from Graskop to Blyde River Canyon National Reserve and clearly marked. It's a bit of a tourist trap, but the view is worth a picture if you're heading that way already. You will need a car to reach this area as there is no public transport.

GRASKOP
☎ 013

At the edge of the Drakensberg escarpment, the sleepy mountain town of Graskop is a good jumping-off point for Blyde River Canyon and Kruger National Park. The region is filled with spectacular views and excellent hiking trails.

The **Green Castle Backpackers** (☎ 767 1761; 69 Eeufees St; camp sites per person US$4, dm US$7, s & d US$19) is packed with information on area hikes. Check out the walls – they're covered with political cartoons and interesting news stories about South Africa.

The **Summit Lodge** (☎ 767 1058; 8 Market St, camp sites per tent US$8, dm US$12) has the best bar in town and offers unique dorms; beds are in an old railway car! Quarters are a little cramped. The bar serves the usual pub grub for about US$2.50. There is more upmarket accommodation in bungalows for US$28 per person, including breakfast and dinner. Prices are negotiable, so ask for a deal if the place is empty.

NORTHERN CAPE

By far the largest, but one of the least populated of South Africa's provinces, much of Northern Cape Province is eerily beautiful. The mighty Orange River is a lifeline running through this area, which becomes desertlike on the fringes of the Kalahari and in the Karoo. The river forms the border between South Africa and Namibia, and this area is spectacularly harsh country. The roads stretch on endlessly; the solitary landscape is filled with vast fields of low scrub brush and punctuated only by small rocky hills. Namaqualand, world famous for its spring flowers, lies to the south. To the north lies the Kgalagadi Transfrontier Park.

KGALAGADI TRANSFRONTIER PARK

If you can make the considerable effort needed to get in and out of **Kgalagadi** (admission per person US$2.90 plus US$0.60 per vehicle; ☯ 6.30am-6.30pm) you'll be well rewarded as it is one of South Africa's greatest, but least known, national parks.

Established in 1999, when South Africa's Kalahari-Gemsbok National Park and Botswana's Mabuasehube-Gemsbok National Park merged, the area now is one of Africa's largest protected areas.

Although semidesert, the park supports large populations of birds, reptiles, small mammals and antelope species. These in turn support a large population of predators – lions, leopards, cheetahs, hyenas, jackals and foxes.

The best time to visit is in June and July, when the weather is coolest (below freezing at night) and the animals have drawn in to the bores along the dry riverbeds.

There are rest camps at **Twee Rivieren**, **Mata Mata** and **Nossob** (camp sites up to 6 people US$8.50, cottages for 3 people from US$38). All accommodation, including tent sites, must be booked through the **National Parks Board** (☎ 012-428 9111) in Pretoria.

There is no public transport, so those without private vehicles will need to join a tour. By car it's a five- or six-hour drive from Twee Rivieren to Kuruman (385km) or Upington (358km), and you have to cover a significant distance on gravel, although the road is being sealed.

No petrol is available between Upington and Twee Rivieren, so make sure you start with a full tank. It's important to carry water, as you might have to wait a while if you break down – you can rapidly become dangerously dehydrated when the temperature is over 40°C.

UPINGTON
☎ 054

Nestling on the banks of the Orange River, Upington is the principal town in the far north. It's an orderly, prosperous place, full of supermarkets and chain stores. It's a good starting point for the Kgalagadi Transfrontier.

Kalahari Junction Backpackers (☎ 332 7874; 3 Oranje St; camp sites per person US$4, dm US$8, d US$19) is a smallish place that runs tours into Kgalagadi Transfrontier Park.

Intercape (☎ 332 6091; Lutz St) has services to Jo'burg (US$29, nine hours) that connect with services to Windhoek (US$30, 10 hours). Intercape also runs to Cape Town (US$25, 10½ hours).

Minibus taxis can be found near Checkers supermarket on the corner of Mark and Basson Sts. Upington taxis can take a long time to fill, but there is generally at least one per day to major destinations.

SPRINGBOK
☎ 027

Hundreds of kilometres from another major town, Springbok is considered the capital of Namaqualand. It's a tidy, quiet place, and although there's not much to see or do, the surrounding landscape is stark, yet endearingly beautiful.

Visit during the spring when the place explodes with the colours of blooming flowers. It also makes a good overnight stop if you're heading between Cape Town and the Namibian border.

Richtersveld Challenge (☎ 718 1905; richtersveld .challen@kingsley.co.za; Voortrekker St; dm US$7, doubles US$29) is a peaceful place to stay. Try to snag the backpacker double. It's the same price as the dorms but beautifully appointed (you're given towels and soap upon arrival). This place runs 4WD adventure tours into the surrounding countryside.

Melkboschkuil Restaurant & Coffee Shop (☎ 718 1789; Voortrekker St; mains US$6-8) likes to experiment with various types of booze in their dishes, some with better results than others. They can cook a springbok more ways than you ever imagined.

Van Wyk's Busdiens (☎ 713 8559) runs a daily door-to-door taxi to Cape Town (US$19). Intercape's Windhoek to Cape Town service runs through Springbok. Springbok to Cape Town costs US$28; Springbok to Windhoek US$37.

FREE STATE

The Free State consists largely of the veld of the Southern African plateau and includes the college town of Bloemfontein.

BLOEMFONTEIN

☎ 051 / pop 109,000

Bloemfontein, or Bloem as it's called, is South Africa's judicial capital. As well as the legal community, there is a university and a large military camp, so you can meet a wide range of people. Most of the blacks still live in the enclaves they were shunted into during the apartheid days. The friendly **Bloemfontein Tourist Centre** (☎ 405 8490; 60 Park Rd) has excellent facilities, including cheap Internet access at US$1.75 per hour.

The **National Women's Memorial & War Museum** (Monument Rd; admission US$0.70; ☉ 9am-4.30pm Mon-Fri, 10am-4.30pm Sat, 2pm-4.30pm Sun), south of the centre, is devoted to the Anglo-Boer Wars and commemorates the Afrikaner women and children who died in British concentration camps.

Bloemfontein hosts important cricket and rugby games, and accommodation can be scarce on match weekends.

Two kilometres from the centre, **Reyneke Park** (☎ 523 3888; Petrusburg Rd; caravan sites US$9; chalets US$31) is well maintained.

Naval Hill Backpackers (☎ 430 7266; Delville St; descover@iafrica.com; dm US$8, s/d US$11/14) is in an old water-pumping station. The industrial decor is stylish but noise carries, there's not a lot of privacy and it's an oven on summer nights.

2nd Ave Café (cnr Tweedelaan & Kellner Sts; breakfast US$2.50-3.50) offers cheap, hearty breakfast deals.

There are loads of places to eat on the Waterfront. The lively **Jazztime Café** (mains US$4.50-5) stands out, although the music can be too loud. Try the *zivas* (US$3), a Yemeni-style dough stuffed with a variety of fillings (such as Cajun chicken, feta and avocado) rolled and toasted. The cocktails here pack a punch.

Forget what other South Africans tell you about this being a dull town – Bloemfonteiners party down with a passion. Being a university town, Bloem has always had fair range of places to drink, but there's a particular buzz about the half-dozen or so places on **Tweedelaan** and **Kellner Sts**.

The **Mystic Boer** (Zastron St) is a brilliantly decorated place. Technicolor Boer commandos glare from the walls while Bloem's party people sit and chat on ammo boxes.

Long-distance bus services arrive and leave from the tourist centre on Park Rd.

Translux (☎ 408 4888) runs to Durban (US$25), Jo'burg/Pretoria (US$21), Knysna (US$28), Cape Town (US$38) and other locations.

Most minibus taxis leave from near the train station. Long-distance taxis leave about 100m south of the covered local minibus taxi stand. Destinations include Kimberley (US$6), Maseru in Lesotho (US$6) and Jo'burg (US$11).

KIMBERLEY

☎ 053

Kimberley is synonymous with diamonds; it's where Cecil Rhodes and the Oppenheimers, among others, made their fortunes and where De Beers began.

The well-stocked **Diamantveld Visitors Centre** (☎ 832 7298) is near the corner of Bultfontein and Lyndhurst Rds.

The **Big Hole & Kimberley Mine Museum** (☎ 833 1557; admission US$2; ☉ 8am-6pm) is a reminder of the wild days when thousands of diggers flocked to the town and fortunes were made and lost. The museum incorporates entire streets of Victorian buildings and a **diamond museum**, all on the edge of the largest handmade hole in the world.

Gum Tree Lodge (☎ 832 8577; dm US$6, s/d US$11/19) is about 5km from town at the intersection of Hull St and the Bloemfontein road. It's a large, pleasant place with shady lawns, a pool and restaurant. Accommodation is in fairly basic flats with stove and fridge.

Stay-A-Day (☎ 832 7239; 72 Lawson St; dm US$5, s/d US$13/21) is an excellent, squeaky clean, central budget bet. Accommodation proceeds go towards a local orphanage.

Keg & Falcon (meals around US$3), conveniently located next to the Northern Cape Tourism office, has tasty, affordable meals.

Many bus services run to/from Jo'burg (about six hours). The cheapest is Greyhound's special service for US$13. Translux goes to/from Cape Town for US$33. There are also trains to Jo'burg and Cape Town.

SOUTH AFRICA DIRECTORY

ACCOMMODATION

South Africa has an excellent variety of backpacker accommodation and a bus that conveniently links many of the hostels together.

Accommodation is high quality for minimal prices. You can expect clean rooms and toilets, and linen on the beds. Most hostels are equipped with bars, swimming pools, some type of meal service and Internet access. Many also serve as booking agents or run their own tours around the country. Except in Cape Town, where camping is very scarce, most hostels allow you to pitch a tent on their lawn. Camping is charged per person and costs between US$3 to US$5. Dorms go for US$7 to US$10, and doubles cost about US$20. Doubles at backpackers often are beautifully appointed and nicer than their inexpensive hotel counterparts. They usually do not include bathrooms.

ACTIVITIES
Hiking
South Africa has an excellent system of hiking trails, usually with accommodation available. They are popular, and most must be booked well in advance.

There are many hiking clubs – contact the **Hiking Federation of South Africa** (☎ 012-327 0083; hanssteyn@yebo.co.za) – and several adventure travel outfits offer organised hikes.

The **National Parks Board** (☎ 012-428 9111; www.parks-sa.co.za) administers most trails. **KZN Wildlife** (☎ 033-845 1000; www.kznwildlife.com) controls most trails in KwaZulu-Natal.

Surfing
South Africa has some of the best and least-crowded surfing in the world. Jeffrey's Bay is famous, but there are myriad alternatives, particularly along the eastern and southern coasts. April to July offer the best surfing conditions.

Boards and surfing gear can be bought in most coastal cities. New boards cost about US$185 and good-quality, second-hand boards closer to US$100. If you plan to surf Jeffrey's Bay you'll need a decent-sized board – it's a big, very fast wave. **Wavescape** (www.wavescape.co.za) is worth a look online.

South Africa provides the adventure enthusiast with a host of activities. You can partake in the world's highest bungee jump in Storms River. Sky dive over Table Mountain in Cape Town. And go kloofing, sandboarding, shark diving and abseiling – not to mention hiking, swimming and biking – in spots throughout the country.

DANGERS & ANNOYANCES
Crime rates in the cities are soaring – be very careful at night. Even during the day, violent muggings are common in parts of Jo'burg. Avoid walking with money or valuables in the cities. Nearly all hostels have safes. If you are mugged, *do not resist*. The mugger might have a gun and will assume you have one too, and will be nervous. Don't scare him into shooting you first.

Most ATMs have security guards. If there is no guard around when you're withdrawing cash, watch your back or – better yet – get someone else to watch it for you.

If you've hired a car, *never* drive at night. Many vehicles travel without lights, and the consequences can be horrific.

Keep your windows up and doors locked when driving through cities, and consider hiring a mobile phone. Leave your car in a secure parking area at night, and don't leave anything valuable in the car when you're not in it.

It is unwise for an outsider of any race to venture into a black township without knowing the current situation and without a guide.

DISABLED TRAVELLERS
People with limited mobility might find the going a bit tough in South Africa, but it's one of most wheelchair-friendly countries in Africa. It will certainly be easier to travel with an able-bodied companion, but the good news is that there is a growing number of places with ramps, wheelchair access and wheelchair-friendly bathrooms. For information on travelling in South Africa with a disability, try the website www.access -able.com. The **National Parks Board Website** (www.parks-sa.co.za) has useful mobility information for all its parks.

Titch Tours (☎ 021-686 5501; www.titchtours.co.za; 26 Station Rd, Rondebosch, Cape Town) specialises in tours for visually impaired and physically disabled travellers. It has specialised equipment, including a coach with wheelchair lift, and hires cars fitted with hand controls for disabled people.

DISCOUNT CARDS
It is worth picking up a VIP Backpackers card. These can be purchased at most hostels and cost US$13. The cards are valid for one year and offer discounts of about 5% at

many hostels and discounts of 5-15% on long-distance buses, including the Baz Bus and Intercape.

EMBASSIES & CONSULATES

The following countries have diplomatic representation in South Africa:

Australia (☎ 012-342 3781; 292 Orient St, Arcadia, Pretoria; ☒ 8.45am-12.30pm weekdays)

Belgium (☎ 011-447 5495; Jan Smuts Bldg, 9 Walters Ave, Rosebank, Jo'burg; ☒ 9am-noon weekdays)

Canada (☎ 012-422 3000; 1103 Arcadia St, Hatfield, Pretoria; ☒ 8am-noon weekdays)

France (☎ 011-778 5600; fconsjhb@cis.co.za; 3rd fl, Standard Bank Bldg, 191 Jan Smuts Ave, Rosebank, Jo'burg; ☒ 8.30am-1pm weekdays)

Germany (☎ 012-427 8999; 180 Blackwood St, Arcadia, Pretoria; ☒ 7.30-11am weekdays)

Ireland (☎ 012-342 5062; 1234 Church St, Colbyn, Pretoria; ☒ 8.30am-1pm weekdays)

Lesotho (☎ 012-460 7648; 391 Anderson St, Menlo Park, Pretoria; ☒ 9am-4.30pm weekdays)

Mozambique (☎ 012-401 0300; 529 Edmund St, Arcadia, Pretoria; ☒ 8.30am-12.30pm weekdays)

Namibia (☎ 012-481 9100; 197 Blackwood St, Arcadia, Pretoria; ☒ 8.30am-12.30pm weekdays)

Netherlands (☎ 012-344 3910; 825 Arcadia St, Arcadia, Pretoria; ☒ 9am-noon weekdays)

Swaziland (☎ 012-344 1910; 715 Government Ave, Arcadia, Pretoria; ☒ 9am-12.30pm and 2.30pm-4pm weekdays)

UK (☎ 012-483 1200; 255 Hill St, Arcadia, Pretoria; ☒ 8.45am-noon weekdays)

USA (☎ 012-342 1048; 877 Pretorius St, Arcadia, Pretoria; ☒ 8am-noon weekdays)

Zimbabwe (☎ 011-838 5620; 17th fl, 20 Anderson St, Marshalltown, Jo'burg; ☒ 8.30am to noon weekdays, closed Wednesday)

South Africa has diplomatic representation in the following neighbouring and near-neighbouring countries: Botswana, Lesotho, Malawi, Mozambique, Namibia, Swaziland, Zambia and Zimbabwe.

GAY & LESBIAN TRAVELLERS

South Africa's new constitution guarantees freedom of sexual choice, and there are small but active and growing gay and lesbian communities and scenes in Cape Town, Jo'burg and Durban. However, the new constitution is a radical legislative move for this country, and it will be a while before the more conservative sections of society learn to accept it.

Check out the **GaySA website** (www.gaysouthafrica.co.za), which has entertainment and travel listings, but be warned that it also contains links to explicit erotic images.

In Cape Town, the **Mother City Queer Project** (www.mcqp.co.za) runs the hugely popular December party and festival.

HOLIDAYS

As well as religious holidays listed in the Africa Directory (p1003) the principal public holidays in South Africa are:

1 January New Year's Day
21 March Human Rights Day
17 April Family Day
27 April Constitution Day
1 May Workers' Day
16 June Youth Day
9 August Women's Day
24 September Heritage Day
16 December Day of Reconciliation
26 December Boxing Day

INTERNET ACCESS

Internet access (between US$2.50 and US$5 per hour) can be found almost anywhere in South Africa, and many hostels offer email facilities.

MAPS

Good maps are widely available. For a sturdy and helpful map of Cape Town, see Lonely Planet's *Cape Town City Map*. South African Tourism (formerly Satour) hands out a reasonable countrywide map, and the **Map Office** (☎ 011-339 4941) in Jo'burg sells government topographic maps for around US$7 a sheet.

The Michelin maps are excellent, and the Map Studio series is recommended. The **Map Studio** has offices in Cape Town (☎ 021-510 4311), Jo'burg (☎ 011 807 2292) and Durban (☎ 031-263 1203) and also sells government topographic maps.

MEDIA

Major English-language newspapers are published in the cities and sold across the country, although in Afrikaans-speaking areas and the ex-homelands they might not be available in every little town.

The *Sowetan* is the biggest-selling paper in the country and is worth reading as a contrast to the white perspective of many other papers.

The best newspaper or magazine for investigative journalism, sensible overviews and high-quality columnists, not to mention a week's worth of Doonesbury and a good entertainment section, is the *Weekly Mail & Guardian*. It also includes a shortened version of the international edition of the British *Guardian*, which includes features from *Le Monde* and the *Washington Post*.

MONEY

The unit of currency is the rand (R), which equals 100 cents. The import and export of local currency is limited to R500.

The Thomas Cook agent is Rennies Travel, a large chain of travel agencies. There are Amex offices in many cities too. Neither charges commission on its own travellers cheques. Nedbank is associated with Amex. First National Bank and Nedbank are associated with Visa and change Visa travellers cheques free of fees. Most other banks change travellers cheques in major currencies, but with various commissions.

Keep at least some of the receipts you get when changing money as you'll need to show them to reconvert your rands into hard currency when you leave.

Credit cards, especially Visa and Master-Card, are widely accepted and cards with the Cirrus logo occasionally also. Most ATMs give cash advances.

There is a Value Added Tax (VAT) of 14%, but foreign visitors can reclaim some of their VAT expenses on departure. This applies only to goods that you are taking out of the country, and the goods have to have been bought at a shop participating in the VAT Foreign Tourist Sales scheme.

To make a claim, you need the tax invoices (usually the receipt, but make sure that the shop knows you want a full receipt). They must be originals, and the total value of your purchases must exceed US$42. Upon departure, you'll have to fill out a couple of forms and show the goods to a customs inspector. At airports, make sure you have the goods checked by an inspector before you check in your luggage. You can pick up your refund cheque after you've gone through immigration.

POST & TELEPHONE

South Africa has reasonably good post and telecommunications facilities. Most post of-fices open from 8.30am to 4.30pm weekdays and 8am to noon on Saturday. Aerograms and internal letters cost R2.2 (US$0.25), postcards R3 (US$0.35) and airmail letters R3.3 (US$0.40) to send. Internal delivery can be very slow, and international delivery isn't exactly lightning fast.

Local telephone calls are fairly cheap. Phonecards are widely available. Long-distance and international telephone calls are very expensive. There are private phone centres where you can pay cash for your call without feeding coins into the slot of a public phone, but at double the rate.

To avoid high charges when calling home, dial your 'Country Direct' number, which puts you through to an operator in your country. You can then either place a call on your phone home account, if you have one, or place a reverse-charge call. To find out your Country Direct number, call a major telecommunications company in your country.

RESPONSIBLE TRAVEL

Many hostels are making an effort at promoting responsible travel, either by making travellers aware of the impacts they have on the local communities and the environment or by going so far as to organise volunteer projects in their community. Travellers can promote responsible tourism in South Africa by supporting entrepreneurial enterprise by locals – tip car guards or hire a local to be a fishing guide.

TOURS & SAFARIS

The boom in backpacker accommodation has brought with it a boom in good-value tours and activities. Most hostels take bookings. The most popular overland route in Southern Africa goes from Cape Town to Victoria Falls and could be a good option if you want to see Namibia and Botswana and don't have a car. There are also shorter trips just encompassing South Africa. Bear in mind that overland trips do not allow you the same flexibility as travelling solo, and you will be stuck with the same group of people in a small vehicle for weeks on end. This can get tedious, but if you're interested two such companies include **African Routes** (☎ 031-304 6358), based in Kwa-Zulu-Natal, and **Drifters** (☎ 011-888 1160), based in Gauteng.

VISAS

Entry permits, entitling you to a 90-day stay, are issued free on arrival to nationals of many Commonwealth countries and the majority of Western countries, including Ireland, France, Germany and the USA. Other nationalities might need a visa, which are usually free and multi-entry, but are not issued at the border, so get one in advance. South Africa has consular representation in most countries, but outside Southern Africa allow at least a couple of weeks for the process.

Visa Extensions

You can apply for a visa extension or a re-entry visa at the **Department of Home Affairs** (☎ 012-324 1860; Sentrakor Bldg, Pretorius St, Pretoria). Extensions cost about US$60.

Visas for Onward Travel

Visas for the following countries are available from embassies in Pretoria or Jo'burg: Lesotho, Mozambique, Namibia, Swaziland and Zimbabwe (see p989 for address details).

Angola Visas are hard to come by. You must apply in your home country (usually limited to fly-in visas for arrival in Luanda), or you could attempt to secure an overland visa in Oshakati in northern Namibia.

Botswana No visas are required by citizens of Australia, New Zealand, France, Germany, the UK, Ireland, Canada and the US.

Namibia No visas are required by citizens of Australia, New Zealand, France, Germany, the UK, Ireland, Canada and the US.

Zambia Visas are required by US, Australian and British citizens. In Gaborone, they take one day to process and cost US$59/94 for a single/double-entry visa and US$188 for a multiple-entry visa. Note that they're available at the border for considerably less (normally US$25 for US citizens and £45 for British subjects).

Zimbabwe Australians, New Zealanders and US citizens need a visa, which can be processed at the border (US$30/45 for single/double entry). However, you can also secure a visa in advance for the same rates; multi-entry visas cost US$55 and aren't available at the border.

DIRECTORY

Africa Directory

CONTENTS

Pan-continental information of a practical nature is briefly outlined in this Africa Directory. For more specific details, flip to the Directory sections at the end of each country chapter.

ACCOMMODATION

In the country chapters, we list mainly budget options, plus a pricey place we think is worth the splurge.

Prices are given for accommodation with a shared bathroom, unless otherwise stated.

If you're staying somewhere for a few nights, or at a quiet time, consider asking for discounts: some hotels will work out a deal; others will show you the door.

Camping

A tent usually saves you money, and can be vital in some national parks or wilderness areas, but it's not essential for travel in Africa. Official camp sites, of varying quality and security, charge around US$2 to US$5 per person, and most backpackers hostels also have a few spaces for tents. Many camp sites also have simple cabins (called *bandas*, *rondavels*, *paillottes* or some other local name) that cost US$5 to US$10 per person, often very good value.

'Wild' camping in Africa is fine if you're in a place where no-one will find you (or no animals trip over you).

Sleeping on beaches is another matter: unless it's really remote, there's a good chance your gear will be stolen, and you might even be attacked. In rural areas, if there's no camp site, you're often better off pitching your tent near a village. Seek permission from the village chief first, and you'll come to no harm. In fact, you'll probably be treated as an honoured guest and really get under the skin of Africa.

Homestays

In rural areas you can sometimes arrange informal 'homestays', simply by asking around politely in a village for a place to bed down and dish of local food in return for a payment. This is a great way for travellers to meet locals on their own turf, and a great way for locals to earn a bit of cash. And it's often the only option in more-remote places. But pay a fair fee – normally the cost a cheap hotel. Anyone who tries to

---

THE RATES THEY ARE A'CHANGING

Budget hotel rates are constant from day to day ('weekend specials' are rare), although they can drop when business is slack, and rocket when demand is high – like when there's a festival on in town. And things in Africa are always liable to change. So whether it's for hotels, tours or bus fares, be prepared for prices to be different to the ones we quote in this book. It may be the 'backpackers bible', but it ain't gospel.

save money by underpaying is a low-down parasite.

Hostels

Lodges and hostels aimed squarely at backpackers line the popular routes from Nairobi to Cape Town, although elsewhere in Africa they're less common. Most are run by South Africans or unfailingly cheery Aussies (you'll meet the occasional Brit, Kiwi or Belgian too), and they always come up with goods when you've had a few hard days on the road: hot shower, cold beer, clean bunk and the relaxing company of other travellers. A bed in a dorm costs around US$3 to US$5; a double room about US$10 to US$20. Backpackers hostels are also the best places to get information – from the management or other guests – on the hottest club in town, the coolest beach on the coast, the best exchange rates, the quickest bus or the easiest border crossing. There's only one downside: with their expatriate staff and backpacker clientele they can feel quite remote from Africa – the place you supposedly came to experience.

Hotels

Africa has numerous Hiltons and other dens of luxury, but in every town and city shoestringers can take advantage of cheap local-style hotels. These are no-frills joints, and quality ranges widely. At the top of the list are the gems that backpackers love: clean, safe, friendly and cheap. At the bottom are rat-holes with filthy rooms, surly staff and a lethal mix of leaking water and faulty electrics in the bathroom – those bare wires could knock out an elephant, so don't touch!

Depending on the country, a local hotel room costs from US$1 to US$10, maybe up to US$20 or more in some capital cities. At the cheap end of this range, it's rare to get a private bathroom (with the dodgy plumb-

ing you wouldn't want one anyway) and you can forget air-conditioning – a breeze blows though the broken window instead. Other 'extras' like fan or mosquito net can bump up the price by 50% or so.

In desert countries sleeping on the roof or in a central open-air courtyard is often an option at rural hotels. It's cooler, cheaper, and the views of the stars are unbeatable.

For the occasional splurge – or just to escape heat and bedbugs – there's a huge choice of mid-range hotels in towns and cities (plus safari lodges in the national parks). These usually cost around US$20 to US$50 for a double room.

Under the 'hotel' category you'll also be bedding down at a guesthouse, resthouse, *pensao* (in Mozambique), or *campement* (in West Africa). The latter is a simple rural hotel, not a camp site. Just to keep you on your toes, a cheap local hotel in East Africa is called a *gesti* or lodgings, while *hoteli* is Swahili for basic eating place – so you'll get tea and cake, but no bed here.

The distinction between cheap hotel and brothel is sometimes rather vague in Africa especially at the lower end of the market. The action is usually low key, and no cause for great concern, but you should expect some coming and going through the night.

Missions

Religious missions in remote areas (and in a few cities) have guesthouses, which may sometimes be open to travellers. These are usually well maintained, and cost about the same as a mid-range hotel. Some just ask for a donation, and you should pay what a hotel would cost. A few missions are choosy about guests because backpackers have abused their hospitality in the past, so if you're turned away, you'll know why.

ACTIVITIES

To enjoy the outdoors or work up a sweat, there's a great choice in Africa for energetic types. This section gives an overview; see the individual country chapters for more inspiration.

Adrenaline Pumping

Relaxation is for wimps. You want to get the blood pumping. You want to scare yourself witless. So how about white-water rafting, bungee jumping, jet boating, microlighting, abseiling, or kayaking past hippos and crocodiles while watching out for elephants on the river bank? All this, and more, is up for grabs at Victoria Falls – rightly billed as the adventure hub of Africa – and easily arranged on the spot (on both the Zimbabwe and Zambia sides).

South Africa is another great place for activities – some of them scary. Base yourself in Cape Town for mountain biking, paragliding or diving with sharks. Rafting and bungee jumping are on the menu too. Or head for Jinja in Uganda, the 'Vic Falls of East Africa', with adrenaline activities galore at nearby Bujagali Falls.

You can also raft and kayak on white water, or canoe on more gentle stuff, in Ethiopia, Kenya, Namibia, Zambia and Swaziland. Paddling around in a pirogue (dug-out canoe) on the streams and lakes of various West African countries is a great way to get off the beaten track – it's sometimes relaxing, and sometimes heart-stoppingly close to wildlife and waterfalls.

Cycling

Long-distance travel by bike is a great way to see Africa, but it's only for a hardy few. See the Transport chapter on p40 for some pointers. For shorter trips, you can often hire bikes by the day or week and tour some wonderful areas. Our favourites for relaxed peddling include Zanzibar, Malawi, the Cape region of South Africa and Casamance in southern Senegal. If you've got your own wheels, legs of steel and a sense of adventure other gems include the ancient trails through Morocco's Atlas Mountains, the Fouta Djalon plateau in Guinea and the mountain tracks of Ethiopia. For inspiration, see www.ibike.org/africaguide, the excellent website of the International Bicycle Fund.

Diving & Snorkelling

The east side of Africa is where you strap on goggles, snorkels or tanks, and slip into paradise. Egypt's Red Sea is world famous, while Kenya, Mozambique and Tanzania (especially Zanzibar) have some of the finest reefs in the Indian Ocean. And then there's Lake Malawi, idyllic freshwater diving and a cheap place to learn the skills.

Hiking

South Africa has a huge network of well-organised hiking trails – taking anything from a few hours to a few weeks – and Namibia has some desert specials, including the classic Fish River Canyon. But top of the list for most backpackers is Mt Kilimanjaro, the 'roof of Africa'; treks can be arranged in Moshi (Tanzania) and are a big draw for all outdoor types. Not far away, Mt Kenya is lower but more pleasing to the eye, while the remote Rwenzori range in Uganda is a more serious proposition. At the top of the continent, you could trek for literally months through the Atlas Mountains of Morocco, while the Drakensberg peaks between Lesotho and South Africa offer countless routes and views to die for, and in West Africa a hike along the Dogon Escarpment (Mali) is a journey to another world.

Skiing

Skiing and snow-boarding in Africa? Surely not? But yes – this activity is available during winter in the high mountains of South Africa and Morocco. If snow's in short supply, don't worry. Head for the dunes of Namibia and South Africa, and go sand-boarding instead. It's just what it says, and easier than the Alpine variety. The landing is softer too.

Surfing

Get off the bus in South Africa and get your baggy shorts on. Jeffrey's Bay is classic Surfville RSA, but there are other options on the south and east coasts, with some of the best and least-crowded waves in the world. Neighbouring Mozambique is also pretty good, while at the other end of Africa, the Atlantic swell produces good breaks on the coast of Morocco.

Wildlife Safaris

Africa's many national parks, reserves and conservation areas are some of the most spectacularly beautiful places on the planet, and home to a bewildering variety of wild animals. You could watch lions stalk their prey in the dry savanna, see hippos wallowing in magnificent mud or track gorillas through rainforest. Wherever you go, a safari to see Africa's wildlife will undoubtedly be a major highlight of your trip.

Full information on the safari scene in every country is given in the individual chapters.

PLAYING THE GAME

Wild animals in Africa – especially the bigger ones that roam the savanna – are often called 'game'. It's a hangover from hunting days, but still a common (and perfectly acceptable) term throughout East and Southern Africa. We use the term 'wildlife' throughout this book, but don't be shocked when your hear people talk about game-viewing, game-spotting, game-tracking, game park, game fence or game trail. It doesn't mean you need a gun.

ORGANISED SAFARIS

Vast distances (some parks are bigger than some European countries) and the unpredictable nature of large animals usually mean you need a vehicle to visit, so in countries like Kenya and Tanzania it's usual for backpackers (and most visitors – however wealthy) to join an organised safari. There are options to suit all budgets, but even the cheapest rates might be too much for some shoestringers. You should expect to pay US$50 to US$100 per day for a basic all-inclusive experience. Doing things yourself (taking the bus, using your own tent, carrying your own food) is often no cheaper, and is a lot more complicated. Public transport rarely goes into parks, and even if it does, you still need to rent a vehicle or arrange lifts to tour the park itself. And the main expense – park entry fees – has to be paid however you get there.

It's usual for backpackers to team up into groups and get a better price when arranging safaris (although make sure you like the people you're going with). Safari companies in Nairobi and Arusha will help you find other travellers; some have regular departures where you can just rock up, pay, and head for the wilds the next day. Many safari companies also take bookings in advance via email.

One factor that can make or break a safari is the driver. A good driver is a guide too, and can turn even the most mundane trip into a fascinating one; a driver's experience in spotting animals and understanding their behaviour is paramount. A bad driver does just that – drive. Always try to meet your driver-guide before booking a safari, to gauge their level of knowledge and enthusiasm.

Tips are an important part of the income of safari employees, so if your driver-guide and cook have given good service, tip them around 10% of the total cost of your safari (ie about 5% for the driver, 5% for the cook). If the service has been poor, tip less, and explain why.

If you're offered a ridiculously cheap deal by a safari company, think again. Anything less than the norm may compromise in quality – vehicles break down, food is substandard, park fees are dodged or fuel is skimped on, meaning your driver won't take detours in search of animals.

The best way to avoid the sharks and find good guides is to get advice from other backpackers who've recently returned from a safari. It's well worth holing up in Nairobi or Arusha for an extra day or two, and doing some asking around, rather than joining the first trip you find – which could well turn out to be a disaster.

DIY SAFARIS

In some countries, there's less of an organised backpacker safari set-up, and the usual way of doing things is to get to the park under your own steam, stay at a lodge or camp site (either inside the park, or just outside to save on park fees) then arrange activities on the spot to suit your budget and interest. You can join wildlife-viewing drives, walking safaris, boat trips or visits to nearby villages – all normally for a half-day

---

WALK ON THE WILD SIDE

Walking safaris are a fantastic experience. Nothing heightens your senses more than a stroll in the bush when lions and elephants are nearby. But on foot you don't get as close to animals as you do in a vehicle, and for most visitors (especially first-timers) proximity is the key. If you have the chance, do a drive *and* a walking safari.

DIRECTORY

or full day, although longer options may also be available. National parks where this is possible include Liwonde (Malawi) and South Luangwa (Zambia). Note that doing things this way can cost more than fully organised trips, but generally you're paying for a more exclusive experience.

BORDER CROSSINGS

Every backpacker's heart beats a little faster when an African border post comes into view. And in a continent of 50 countries, there are a lot of borders – and a lot of border posts. Crossing a border is always a bit of a lottery. Sometimes the process is quick and straightforward, but at other times it can take several hours to get through the queues at Immigration or Customs desks (even assuming that your visas are in order and your paperwork is pristine), not to mention possible checks of medical certificates, or a detailed search of your backpack. At all times it's essential to remember that patience and politeness will see you through. Getting shirty with a guy in uniform is one sure-fire way for 'discrepancies' to be discovered, or delays to be even longer.

Although the borders between countries in Africa are often thousands of kilometres long, the number of border-crossing points can be surprisingly small. Official border-crossing points, that is. Locals who live in border areas come and go at will, just as they did before the colonials drew arbitrary lines through their territory. Throughout this book we list the main border-crossing points – usually those on more-frequented roads and transit routes.

Don't forget that there's usually a border post on each side of the border crossing (ie one belonging to each country). Sometimes, the border posts are just 100m apart, such as at the Namanga crossing between Kenya and Tanzania; sometimes they can be 100km apart, with a 'no-man's-land' in between, such as those on the route between Algeria and Niger. If you're catching a bus 'to the border', check exactly how far it goes. Does it take you just to the first border post (from where you have to walk or take a taxi to the second one)? Or does the bus go across the border all the way to the second border post, before you have to change to onward transport?

BUSINESS HOURS

Across Africa, official places like embassies, tourist bureaus and travel agencies open from around 8am or 9am to around 5pm or 6pm, Monday to Friday (although most embassies are only open to the public during the morning – so that's when you need to apply for visas).

In most countries in Africa, shops keep similar hours and are usually open on Saturday too (as are some travel agencies). Smaller shops and market stalls don't keep strict business hours at all. When there are customers around, they open. In fact, often when there isn't any custom they still stay open. In most cities, many shops and supermarkets stay open until late in the evening and on Saturday too, although only the largest are open on Sunday.

SWAHILI TIME

When asking about times – of buses, boats or anything else – in Tanzania, be aware that in Swahili speakers have a different system for telling the time. Their clock begins at sunrise (6am) rather than midnight, so 7am becomes 1 o'clock, 8am becomes 2 o'clock and so on. Many Swahili speakers translate their time directly when speaking English, so always double-check when you're being given a time.

In East and Southern Africa, shops and offices close for an hour or so around noon. In North, West and Central Africa the noon break can be two to four hours long, and businesses may stay open until 7pm or 8pm, sometimes later. Places such as phone and Internet bureaus keep much longer hours.

Banks in most African countries open Monday to Friday, from 8am or 9am to around 2pm or 3pm. Some banks even shut at noon.

In Islamic countries, businesses (especially banks and embassies) may close all day on Friday, or have an extended lunch break (prayer-break, actually). Most cafés and smaller restaurants offer lunch from around noon to 2pm (for locals it's the main meal of the day) and dinner in the evening from around 5pm to 7pm. Larger restaurants catering for locals and tourists keep the same lunch hours but open later in the evening, usually from around 7pm to 10pm or later. Many restaurants open all day.

Throughout this book, we don't repeat main opening hours for every place listed unless it has 'unusual' habits – such as a restaurant that opens lunch time only, or a bar that doesn't serve drinks until midnight.

CLIMATE

Most backpackers tie in their trip with Africa's dry seasons. This is because travel is easier, especially once you get off the main roads – dirt tracks become a sea of mud when it rains. And it's also because lounging on the beach in a downpour just doesn't cut the mustard.

There are regional variations but essentially it goes like this: East Africa has two dry seasons – December to February/March and June to October – with rainy seasons in between.

In Southern Africa it's dry from May/June, gets really hot in October, then rains November to April/May.

In West Africa the dry season is October/ November to April/May, and it gets very hot at the end of this period.

In Central Africa, June to September is the dry time.

In North Africa, rain isn't the main issue: it's temperature. The best time to travel is the cooler period from October to March.

Although dry seasons are usually the popular times, don't avoid the rainy season everywhere. In some countries it only rains for a few hours each day (often at night) and then the air is crystal clear, views go on for ever, photographers soon run out of film. It's also a good time for bird-watching, if that's your thing. Hotel rates are cheaper and popular tourist haunts much quieter too. And generally the local people are also happier because good rains mean good crops, so traditional festivals are often held at this time.

SHOULD I STAY OR SHOULD I GO?

Before fine-tuning your trip, note that weather patterns all over Africa have been unpredictable in the last few years, with rainy seasons coming early or late – or sometimes not at all. So try to find out from people on the ground what it's like before ruling out any place for certain.

CUSTOMS

At some borders you may have your bag searched, but serious shakedowns are rare. Nevertheless, every backpacker has a favourite horror story, but as long as you leave the drugs at home, you should be fine.

Stuff like turtle shell, or anything made from an endangered animal, is likely to get you in trouble. And you'll need a permit from the Ministry of Antiquities or a similar office if you're exporting valuable cultural artefacts (no, not that 'ebony' hippo carving you bought on the beach with the shoe polish that comes off on your hands).

Some countries limit the local currency you can bring in or out, although a small amount is unlikely to be a problem. You can carry large amounts of CFA francs between countries in the CFA zones (see Money on p1004), but there's still officially an upper limit of the equivalent of about US$3000.

A few countries have restrictive exchange regulations, and occasionally you may need to fill in a declaration form with details of your dollars or other 'hard' currencies.

DANGERS & ANNOYANCES
Crime

Travel in Africa is remarkably safe most of the time, but you need to be alert in some cities. Dakar can be a bit edgy, and Nairobi is often called 'Nairobbery', while Lagos and Johannesburg are no joke at all. Snatch-theft and pick-pocketing are the most common crimes, but violent muggings can also occur, so it pays to read – and heed – the tips below, and the warnings in country chapters.

- Don't make yourself a target on the streets. Carry as little as possible.
- Don't wear jewellery or watches, however cheap. Strolling with a camera or Walkman is asking for trouble.
- Don't walk the backstreets, or even some main streets, at night. Take a taxi – a few bucks for the fare might be a sound investment.
- Do use a separate wallet for day-to-day purchases. Keep the bulk of your cash hidden under loose-fitting clothing.
- Do walk purposefully and confidently. Never look lost (even if you are!).
- Do be discreet with your possessions, especially in dorms. Keep your gear in your bag. Out of sight, out of mind.

DIRECTORY

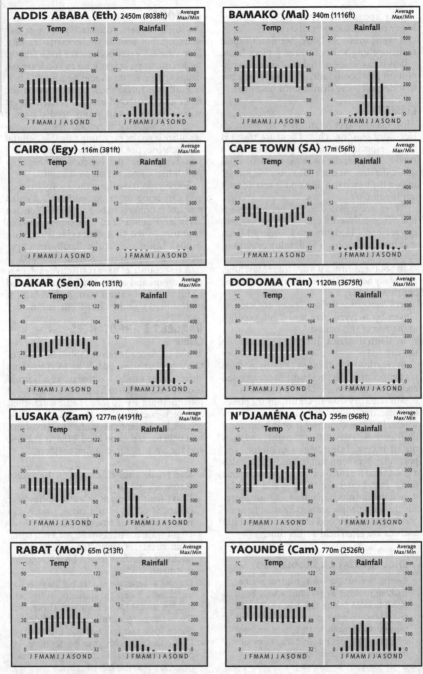

UNSAFE SAFE

Some travellers have left money in a hotel safe, where less-reputable members of staff with a spare key have helped themselves. Often this trick involves taking just a few notes, in the hope that you won't notice. To avoid this, store your valuables inside a pouch with a lockable zip, or in an envelope sealed with tape.

Drugs

It's very straightforward: the buying, selling, possession and use of all recreational drugs is illegal in every country in Africa. Having said that, cannabis (grass or resin) and other drugs are easily found just about anywhere you find backpackers. If this is your scene, take care. In 1999, two Kiwi travellers in Zambia got busted with a relatively small amount of dope, and did six months in jail with hard labour.

Scams & Con Tricks

The main annoyance you'll come across in Africa are the various hustlers, touts, con men and scam-merchants that always see tourists as easy prey. Although these guys are not necessarily dangerous, some awareness and suitable precautions are advisable, and should help you deal with them effortlessly. See the 'Surviving Scams' boxed text on p1000 for advice.

War Zones

It's an unhappy fact that there's always a major conflict going on somewhere in Africa. Corrupt dictators and power-crazed warlords scrap over turf (and the oil or diamonds it contains) while ordinary people end up as refugees – or worse. Going to a war zone as a backpacker is, to put it bluntly, bloody stupid. Sure, you'll get deep under the skin of the continent, and may even get to understand something about anarchy and suffering, but you'll be no help to anyone, and you'll quite likely get yourself kidnapped or killed.

Things change fast in Africa, so be aware that just because a place is listed in this book there's no guarantee that it's secure. Likewise, places we list as dangerous might become safe in the shelf life of this book. The message here is to keep yourself up to date with what's happening on the ground.

DISABLED TRAVELLERS

There are more disabled people per head of population in Africa than in the West, but wheelchair facilities are virtually nonexistent. In some capitals, a few official buildings are constructed with ramps and lifts – but not many, and probably not the ones you want to visit. And don't expect things like specially graded walkways, all-terrain wheelchairs, park or museum signs in brail, or any other facilities that are available in tourist areas in other parts of the world. They just don't exist here. It has to be said that most disabled travellers find travel much easier with the assistance of an able-bodied companion.

A key attraction of Africa is a wildlife safari, which often involves simply sitting in a vehicle and is therefore suitable for those in wheelchairs or on crutches. However, you'll still need to be pretty intrepid, and ideally arrange things in advance with a safari company. A final factor to remember, which goes some way to making up for the lack of facilities, is the friendliness and accommodating attitude of Africans. In most situations, people will be more than happy to help if you explain to them exactly what you need.

DISCOUNT CARDS

A student or youth identity card (eg ISIC) is only occasionally good for discounts on

JUST BECAUSE YOU'RE PARANOID...

Having read the safety tips, don't get too paranoid. Instead, remember this: considering the wealth of most tourists, and the unimaginable levels of poverty suffered by most Africans (a backpacker's budget of US$10 a day is more than a local labourer makes in a month), robbery rates are incredibly low. When you sit in a bus station and you see an old woman selling cakes for a tenth of the price of the Coke you're sipping, or a teenage youth trying to earn a few coins by cleaning shoes, remember that the vast majority of people are decent and hard-working, and want from you only respect and the chance to make an honest living.

SURVIVING SCAMS

Dud Sounds
You buy some cassettes from the market, but back at the hotel you open the box and it's got a blank tape inside, or music by a different artist. The solution: always try to listen to the tapes first.

Phone Home
You give your address to a local kid who says he wants to write. He asks for your phone number too, and you think 'no harm in that'. Until the folks back home start getting collect calls in the middle of the night. And when it's the kid's big brother making false ransom demands to your worried ma and pa, then things can get serious. The solution: stick to addresses, and even then be circumspect.

Police & Thieves
If you're unwise enough to sample local narcotics, don't be surprised if dealers are in cahoots with the local police who then come to your hotel room and find you 'in possession'. Large bribes will be required to avoid arrest or imprisonment. The solution is easy – don't buy drugs from strangers.

Remember Me?
A local lad comes up in the street and says, 'Hello, it's me, from the hotel, don't you remember?'. You're not sure. You don't recognise him, but then you don't want to seem rude, either. So you stop for a chat. Can he walk with you for a while? Sure. Nice day. A few more pleasantries. Then comes the crunch: 'How about a visit to my brother's souvenir shop? Or do you wanna buy some grass? Need a taxi? A tour?' By this time you're hooked, and you probably end up arranging something. To avoid the trap be polite but firm: you don't remember anyone, and you'd really like to be alone.

Welcome, Friend
You're invited to stay for free in someone's house, if you buy meals and drinks for a few days. Sounds good, but your new friend's appetite for food and beer makes the deal more expensive than staying at a hotel. More seriously, while you're out entertaining, someone else will be back at the house of your 'friend' going through your bag. This scam is only likely in tourist zones – in remote or rural areas you'll often come across genuine hospitality.

trains and museum entries – although they are recognised more in some countries than others. They're more useful for international flights, as some airlines give sizable discounts to under-26s or full-time students. In South Africa, a 'VIP backpackers' card is useful (ISIC much less so) – see p988.

EMBASSIES & CONSULATES
In the Directory section of each country chapter we list embassies of neighbouring states and other useful countries (UK, Australia, USA etc). In this book, the term 'embassy' often includes consulates and high commissions; for practical purposes they're pretty much the same thing.

If you need to find an embassy of an African country in your own country (to get some visas), it's easy to look them up in your capital city's phone directory or on the web with a good search engine.

EMERGENCY
Generally speaking, following decades of under-funding, the emergency services in most African countries are stretched to the point of torpor, and not at all what you'd be used to at home. Essentially, if you're in trouble, you have to take the initiative and do more for yourself. For example, if you're robbed or attacked, don't expect the police to respond when you dial an

THE HONORARY CONSUL
In some parts of Africa, countries are represented by an honorary consul who's not a full-time diplomat, but usually an expatriate with limited duties, and who often has more idea of what's happening locally than full-on embassy staff in air-conditioned ivory towers.

emergency number: the chances are their phones won't work or the squad car won't have fuel. However, you will have to visit the police to report the offence – otherwise your insurance won't be valid – but expect an all-day form-filling process. Likewise, if you're sick or injured, don't waste time phoning an ambulance – get a taxi straight to a hospital or clinic. And if you want a private medical service or an English-speaking doctor, ask for directions at an embassy or a top-class hotel. Better still, use common sense and stay out of trouble!

FOOD & DRINK

Even on a tight budget, you won't go hungry in Africa – there's a vast selection of weird and wonderful dishes to tempt your tastebuds, although the range varies considerably from place to place. In the desert areas like Mauritania or Sudan ingredients are limited, while rainfall on the coast of countries like Ghana or Kenya means bountiful crops and an enticing menu.

Each region has its staples: in East and Southern Africa, the base for many local meals is a stiff dough made from maize flour, called – among other things – *ugali* and *nsima*.

In West Africa millet is common, and served in a similar way, while staples nearer the coast are root crops such as yam or cassava (*manioc* in French) – served as a near-solid glob called *foufou*. In North Africa bread forms a major part of the meal, and the cornerstone of Ethiopian cuisine is a sour-dough pancake called *injera*. All over Africa, rice is an alternative to the local specialities. In some countries, plantain is also common – either fried, cooked solid or pounded into *foufou*.

Whatever the carbo base, to it is added a sauce of meat, fish, beans or vegetables – depending on the locality. If you're eating local style, you grab a portion of bread or dough or pancake (with your right hand, please!), dip it in the sauce and enjoy!

THE FUTURE'S BRIGHT, THE FOOD IS ORANGE

In West Africa, don't miss *sauce arachide*, a thick brown paste made from groundnuts (peanuts), either on its own or mixed with meat or vegetables. Sometimes palm oil is also added. Your fingers turn bright orange but the taste is great.

Drink

Tea and coffee are the standard drinks, and countries seem to follow the flavours of their former colonisers. In (former British) East Africa, tea and coffee tends to be weak, grey and milky. In much of (former French) West Africa tea is usually served black, while the coffee from roadside stalls contains enough sugar and sweetened condensed milk to keep you fully charged for hours. In North Africa and some Sahel countries, mint tea and strong Arab-style coffee are the local delights. Other variations include Swahili tea or coffee spiced up with lemongrass or cardamom in East Africa, or flavoured with a woody leaf called *kinkiliba* in West Africa.

International fizzy drinks, such as Coke and Pepsi, are widely available, while many countries have their own local brands that

---

WHEN TO STORM THE EMBASSY

If you get into trouble on your travels, it's important to realise what your embassy can and can't do to help. Remember – you're bound by the laws of the country you are in, and diplomatic staff won't be sympathetic if you're jailed after committing a crime locally, even if such actions are legal at home.

In genuine emergencies you might get some assistance, but only if other channels have been exhausted. For example, to get home urgently, a free ticket is exceedingly unlikely – the embassy would expect you to have insurance. If all your money and documents are stolen, staff might assist with getting a new passport, but a loan for onward travel is way out of the question.

On the more positive side, some embassies (especially US embassies) have notice boards with 'travel advisories' about security, local epidemics, dangers to lone travellers etc. If you're heading for remote or potentially volatile areas, it might be worth registering with your embassy, and 'checking in' when you come back so they don't send out search parties.

DIRECTORY

are cheaper and just as good (and great if you're in an anti-globalist mood). You can also get locally made soft drinks, sold in plastic bags, or frozen into 'ice-sticks', but these are worth avoiding unless your constitution is strong, as the water they're made from can be unclean.

In bars you can buy local or imported beer in bottles, and a range of spirits. Alcohol allegedly kills the bugs, so no health worries here. Well, not of the stomach. Traditional beer is made from millet or maize, and drunk from communal pots with great ceremony at special events, and with less ado in everyday situations.

West Africa's most popular brew is palm wine. The tree is tapped and the sap comes out mildly fermented. Sometimes yeast is added and the brew is allowed to ferment overnight, which makes it much stronger yet still deceptively sweet. So beware!

SCRAPING THE BARREL

Bottled water is available in most African countries, though not remote rural areas. But check that the cap seals are unbroken. In some places bottles are refilled with river water and sold to unsuspecting tourists. It's cheaper and more environmentally sound to drink local water – as long as you filter or add purifying tablets to suspect supplies.

Food Stalls
If you're looking for budget bites, all over Africa most towns have a shacklike stall or two (or 10) serving up local staples for the bargain price of US$1 or so, or fill-you-up deals like tea, milk and bread for even less. Furniture is usually limited to a rough bench and couple of upturned boxes, and hygiene is rarely a prime concern. However, this is the place to save money and meet the locals. Good places to seek out these no-frills joints include bus stations or markets.

Restaurants
For something more comfortable, most towns have cheap restaurants where you can buy traditional meals for about US$2 to US$3. In cities and larger towns, the restaurants might be a bit smarter, with meals around US$3 to US$4. However, the price rise is often determined by the quality of

the surroundings rather than the quality of the food. Up another level are the smarter restaurants with meals from about US$3 to US$5, and facilities such as tablecloths, waiters and menus. They serve traditional food, and straightforward standards like chicken and chips, as well as more elaborate options such as steaks, pies and fish in sauce. Towns that receive a lot of visitors have restaurants specifically catering to the tourist trade, where you can get all the goodies you miss from home, like cheese toasties and – that eternal backpacker favourite – banana pancakes.

Street Food
At bus stations or markets, or just on the roadside, vendors sell 'street food' – portable snacks like grilled meat, deep-fried potato or cassava chips, roasted corn cobs, boiled eggs, peanuts, biscuits, cakes and fried balls of flour-paste that sometimes come close to tasting like doughnuts. Street food rarely involves plates or knives – it's served on a stick, wrapped in paper, or in a plastic bag. Prices are always dirt cheap.

Takeaways
If you want food on the go, or just yearn for a taste from home, many African towns and cities have Western-style takeaways alongside the local eateries. Some are small and basic, offering greasy sausage and chips for US$1 to US$2; others are more glitzy, with neon signs, plastic furniture and staff in baseball caps serving burgers, hot dogs, pizzas and so on, all for about US$2 to US$3.

Vegetarian & Vegan
Some people may think a meal is incomplete unless half of it once lived and breathed, but across African many cheap restaurants serve rice and beans and other meals suitable for vegans simply because it's all the locals can afford. Eggs are usually easy to find, and fish is often available. Beware that in many places chicken usually is not regarded as meat, and may be served to strict but unsuspecting vegetarians. Also, even the simplest (and seemingly innocuous) vegetable sauce may have a bit of animal fat thrown in.

GAY & LESBIAN TRAVELLERS
African societies are very conservative towards gays and lesbians; same-sex rela-

tionships are a cultural taboo, and there are very few openly gay communities. Officially, homosexuality (male, female or both) is illegal in many African countries, even attracting the death penalty in Nigeria, Sudan and a few other areas. However, prosecutions rarely occur. (For more see www.sodomylaws.com.) In most of Africa, public displays of affection show insensitivity to local feelings, whatever your orientation.

HOLIDAYS

Public holidays such as Independence Day or President's Day are listed in the country chapters. The other main holidays are Christmas and Easter in largely Christian countries, while in Muslim countries the main events are: Eid al-Moulid, the birthday of the Prophet Mohammed; Eid-al-Fitr, marking the end of Ramadan – the annual 30-day fast; and Eid al-Adha (also called Eid al-Haj, Eid al-Kebir or Tabaski), which commemorates Abraham's readiness to sacrifice his son on God's command and coincides with the end of the pilgrimage to Mecca. Spellings may vary from country to country, and since the Islamic year has 354 or 355 days, these holidays fall about 11 days earlier each year in the Western calendar.

INSURANCE

Travel insurance to cover theft and illness is highly recommended. Although having your camera stolen or your backpack eaten by lions can be a problem, the medical cover is by far the most important aspect because hospitals in Africa are not free, and the good ones are not cheap. Simply getting to a hospital can also be expensive, so ensure you're covered for ambulances (land and air) and emergency flights home.

There are many policies available, including several pitched at backpackers on

long trips. Some forbid unscheduled boat or plane rides, or exclude dangerous activities such as white-water rafting, canoeing, or even hiking. Others are more sensible and understand the realities of travel in Africa. Ask your flight agent, try a student travel service, or search on the web, but shop around and read the small print to make sure you're fully covered.

INTERNET ACCESS

The Internet can be a great source of information while you're travelling, and web-based email – such as Hotmail, Yahoo or Lonely Planet's ekno – is the perfect way to stay in touch with folks back home or friends elsewhere on the road.

There are cybercafés and Internet bureaus in most capitals and major towns, while many hotels and backpackers hostels also offer this service. There's even an Internet café in Timbuktu! Phone lines are pretty good in the main centres, but often shaky elsewhere, so you can lose connection now and again. Expect to pay anything from US$1 to US$10 per hour.

Internet services in Africa are not totally reliable. If you're trying to contact a hotel or tour company by email, don't expect your messages to arrive, and don't expect to receive replies, either. Anecdotal evidence suggests that only about 90% of email messages get through to the recipient. If anyone finds the other 10% please let us know.

MAPS

For continental coverage, you can't go wrong with Michelin maps of Africa – No 741 *North & West*, No 745 *North-East* and No 746 *Central & South*. The detail is incredible, given the limitations of scale (1:4,000,000). Buy them before you leave home, but do make sure you get a recent

ISLAMIC HOLIDAYS

Hejira Year	New Year	Eid al-Moulid	Lailat al-Mi'raj	Ramadan Begins	Eid al-Fitr	Eid al-Adha
1425	22.02.04	01.05.04	10.09.04	14.10.04	13.11.04	21.01.05
1426	10.02.05	19.04.05	31.08.05	03.10.05	02.11.05	10.01.06
1427	31.01.06	11.04.06	20.07.06	24.09.06	24.10.06	31.12.06

Please note that dates can vary slightly.

MICHELIN 153

The Michelin *Africa North & West* (sheet No 741, formerly No 953 and No 153) is one of few maps in the world to achieve classic status. The routes across the Sahara, showing oases, lonely outposts, and even the site of a single tree, are particularly evocative. There's even a 153 Club for desert aficionados.

version. Even so, expect a few discrepancies, particularly with regard to roads, as rough tracks get upgraded and smooth highways become potholed disasters.

MONEY

In many African countries, inflation is high and exchange rates unpredictable. Quoting prices in local currencies is not helpful as these will have changed by the time you arrive, so throughout this book we have quoted in US dollars (US$). Although prices in dinars, shillings, rands, kwachas, pulas or whatever may rise from month to month, exchange rates normally keep pace, so what you pay in 'hard currency' (eg US dollars or euros) remains pretty much the same. Quoting prices in US dollars also assists with budgeting, and helps you avoid nasty surprises – at least to do with money – when you're on the ground. We outline travel costs in the Getting Started chapter (see p20), and give more specific details in the country chapters.

ATMs

Along with email, the automated teller machine (ATM) is the greatest invention for travellers since the backpack. Instead of having to take enough money for your whole trip, you can draw local cash as you go with

a credit card or – even better – a debit card. Charges are low and exchange rates usually good. The downside for travellers in Africa is that ATMs are located only in capitals and major towns, and even then not in every country. What's more, due to dodgy phone lines they frequently malfunction – so you'll still need a pile of hard cash or travellers cheques as backup.

Bargaining

In many African countries, bargaining over prices – often for market goods – is a way of life. Visitors may be used to things having a fixed value, but in Africa they're worth whatever the seller can get. Once you get the hang of bargaining, it's all part of the fun.

Black Market

In countries with controlled exchange rates, you can get more local money for your hard currency by dealing with unofficial moneychangers on the so-called black market, instead of going to a bank or bureau. This helps with costs, but it's illegal, morally questionable and sometimes dangerous – so think twice before you do it.

You may have to resort to unofficial methods if you're stuck with no local cash when banks and bureaus are closed. Hotels or tour companies may help, although rates are lousy. Try shops selling imported items. Be discreet though: 'The banks are closed, do you know anyone who can help?' is better than a blunt 'D'you wanna change money?'.

Even in countries with free exchange rates (and therefore no black market), moneychangers often lurk at borders where there's no bank. Although illegal, they operate in full view of customs officers, so trouble is probably unlikely.

There's more chance of trouble from the moneychangers themselves, so make sure

ROUNDING UP, ROUNDING DOWN

Prices throughout this book are quoted in US$, even though you'll usually pay in local currency on the ground. Likewise, it's pointless giving you figures that were accurate to the nth degree when we researched a place, but that will have changed undoubtedly when you pass through. We've rounded most prices to the nearest US$0.50 or US$1 for things under US$10, to the nearest US$1 or US$5 for things between US$10 and US$50, and to the nearest US$5 or US$10 for things over US$50. For really minor items, we have quoted the exact price (stamp US$0.15, plate of cheap grub US$0.35). But whatever prices we quote, they should always be regarded as guidelines – not guaranteed costs. Change and the unexpected are constant features of travel in Africa... Enjoy you know the exchange rates, and count all local cash carefully, *before* you hand over your own money. Watch out for old or folded notes. A calculator ensures you don't miss a zero or two on the transaction. And beware of 'Quick, it's the police' tricks, where you're panicked into handing over money too soon. Use common sense and you'll have no problem, but it's best to change only what you'll need until you reach a more reliable bank or bureau.

> **BLACKMARKET STING**
>
> In countries with free exchange rates, there's no black market. You may be offered a few shillings or kwacha more than the bank by shady-looking characters on the street but it's likely to be a con. If they offer a lot more than the bank, you *know* it's a con.

Credit Cards

Credit or debit cards are handy for expensive items such as tours and flights, but most agents add a hefty 10% surcharge. It's therefore usually cheaper to draw local cash from a bank and pay with that, although this still attracts charges of around 5%. The cheapest and easiest option is to use your card to draw cash from an ATM, if they exist. Withdrawing money from a bank can be an all-day process at times, so go early.

Before leaving home, check with your own bank to see which banks in Africa accept your card (and find out about charges). You'll also need to arrange for someone to pay off your monthly card bills if you're away for more than four or five weeks. Debit cards generally have no monthly bills (if you have money in your account, of course), so are more suited to longer travels.

Throughout Africa, cards with the Visa logo are most readily recognised, although MasterCard is also accepted. Whatever card you use, don't rely totally on plastic, as computer or telephone breakdowns can leave you stranded. Always have cash or travellers cheques, too.

Currencies

Whether you're carrying cash or travellers cheques, or both, give some thought to the currency you take before you leave home. This will depend on the countries you

visit. In East and Southern Africa, by far the most readily recognised international currency is the US dollar (US$). Also accepted are UK pounds (UK£) and South African rands (ZAR). Currencies from other European countries or Canadian dollars may occasionally be accepted, but don't rely on this.

Many countries in West and Central Africa use a common currency called the CFA (Communauté Financière Africaine) franc (usually shortened to 'CFA' – pronounced say-eff-aah in French), and here the euro is much more readily recognised by banks and bureaus. US dollars or other currencies are often not accepted at all. There are actually two CFA zones: the West African (or BCEAO) zone, which includes Mali, Senegal, Niger and Burkina Faso; and the Central African (or BEAC) zone which includes Chad, Cameroon, Gabon and Equatorial Guinea.

Until 1999 the CFA was pegged to the French franc at exactly 100:1. With the advent of the euro, the West African CFA is now pegged at exactly 655.957 to 1 euro. If you're changing cash euros into West African CFA that's always the rate you'll get (although there will be charges for travellers cheques). In the Central African countries, things are slightly different: there is some flexibility, and the Central African CFA seems to fluctuate between about 590 and 690 to the euro.

Technically, you should be able to exchange West African CFA for Central Africa CFA, and vice versa, at one-to-one, but in reality you'll pay a bit over or under the odds, depending on the rates – and especially if you're dealing with traders at remote border posts a very long way from the nearest bank!

> **THE RULE OF THIRDS**
>
> As a rule of thumb, divide your travel budget into thirds: carry one-third as hard cash (usually in US dollars or euros), one-third as travellers cheques, and leave one-third in your bank account, which you'll access via ATMs. These ratios will change depending on the number of ATMs (and the security situation) in the countries you visit, and your own attitude to risk.

In non-CFA West African countries, the handiest currencies for travellers are euros and US dollars. It's the same for North Africa, where UK pounds are also accepted in some places.

Wherever you go, remember to carry a mix of high and low denominations; in some countries US$100 bills get you better rates, in others they're not accepted. Smaller denominations (cash or travellers cheques) are handy if you need to change money to last just a few days before leaving a country. And US$1 bills are useful for tips or minor palm-greasing.

Exchanging Money

You can exchange your hard cash or travellers cheques into local currency at banks or foreign exchange bureaus in cities and tourist areas. For cash, bureaus normally offer the best rates, low (or no) charges and the fastest service, but what you get for travel-

---

A BIG HEAD IS GOOD FOR YOU

Due to counterfeiting, old US$100 and US$50 bills are sometimes not accepted, so you're much better off with new-style bills – 'big head dollars', as they're called locally.

---

lers cheques can be derisory – if they're accepted at all. Travellers cheques are more readily accepted at banks, but while rates may be OK, the charges can be as high as 10% or 20%.

Travellers Cheques

Although ATMs are handy, they sometimes don't work. Cash is widely accepted and gets good rates, but cannot be replaced if lost. That's where travellers cheques come in. They can attract poor rates and slow service, and are often a pain to deal with,

---

THE FINE ART OF BARGAINING

Everyday Goods

Market traders selling basic items such as fruit and vegetables may raise their prices when they see a wealthy foreigner (that's you), so some minor bargaining could be called for. But away from cities or tourist areas, many sellers will quote you the same price that locals pay. It is very important not to expect *everybody* to rip you off. If nothing else, thinking this way will ruin your trip.

After a couple of days in a new country (when you'll inevitably pay too much a few times) you'll soon learn the standard prices for basic items. But don't forget that these can change from place to place – a soft drink in a remote village can cost three times what you'll pay in a city. Conversely, fruit and vegetables can be bought more cheaply in the rural areas where they're grown.

Souvenirs

At craft and curio stalls, where items are specifically for tourists, bargaining is very much expected. The vendor's aim is to get the highest price. Your aim is to get a good deal.

Some vendors may ask a price four (or more) times higher than what they're willing

to accept. You decide what you want to pay, and your first offer might be about half this. The vendor may feign outrage, while you plead abject poverty. Then the price starts to drop, and you make better offers until you arrive at a mutually agreeable price.

And that's the crux – *mutually agreeable*. You often hear travellers moaning about how they got 'overcharged' by souvenir sellers. But when things have no fixed price, nobody gets overcharged. If you don't like the price, it's simple: don't pay it.

And Finally...

Something to remember when bargaining is your own self-respect. Souvenir-sellers normally give as good as they get, but if their 'final' price is close to what you're prepared to pay, consider accepting it. Buying food in markets, the same might apply; some backpackers will happily spend US$100 on white-water rafting then sternly barter with an old lady selling bananas to save a truly minuscule amount. It's worth being relaxed in such situations. You'll avoid stress, and most locals need that money more than you do.

but they do have a major advantage of being replaceable.

When exchanging travellers cheques, most banks also check the purchase receipt (the paper you're supposed to keep separate), so make sure you have this. You can pay for items such as safaris and activities directly with travellers cheques, but most operators add a surcharge – usually 10%, but sometimes up to 20%, because that's what banks charge them.

PHOTOGRAPHY

Photos – what better way to remember your trip? But what camera to take? A simple point-and-shoot is fine for mementos of people, landscapes, market scenes and so on, but for better-quality shots, especially of animals, you'll need a zoom lens, and maybe a camera with changeable lenses. A good camera shop can advise you on this.

If you buy a new camera for your trip, get used to its workings at home – otherwise you'll waste film or find yourself lurching around in a safari bus frantically reading the manual. For more advice, see Lonely Planet's *Travel Photography: A Guide to Taking Better Pictures* by Richard I'Anson.

You can buy film at camera stores and supermarkets in major capitals and large towns, but check the expiry date and remember that film may not have been kept in ideal conditions. Depending on the country, 36-exposure print films (Fuji or Kodak) cost US$4 to US$10. Other brands are slightly cheaper. Developing and printing costs around US$8 to US$15. If you have specialist requirements (slides, high ASA etc), it's usually best to bring your own film.

PHOTOS FROM HOME

Female backpackers may be regarded with suspicion in places unused to tourists – especially if alone. You should be at home rearing families or tending the crops, not engaged in frivolous pastimes like travel. To show you do have a home life, you could carry photographs of family or friends, or even a mythical husband (unless you've got a real one, of course). Photos of yourself at work do the same trick. For everyone, men and women, photos from home are also perfect conversation-openers.

Useful photographic accessories include a small flash, a cable or remote shutter release, filters and a cleaning kit.

Also, remember to take spare batteries, and a good padded bag to protect your camera from dust, humidity and jolting on bad roads.

POST

With the advent of email, few backpackers use post these days, but if you do want to send a letter to a lover left behind, or a postcard to your granny, it's always better doing this from a capital city. From some countries, the service is remarkably quick (just two or three days to Europe, a week to the USA or Australia). From others it really earns the snail-mail tag, but it's still more reliable than sending stuff from the sticks.

If your granny wants to reply, you can use the *poste restante* service at any post office where mail is held for collection. Letters should be addressed clearly with surname underlined and in capitals, to '(Your Name), Poste Restante, General Post Office, Lusaka, Zambia' (for example). In French-speaking countries, send it to 'Poste Restante, PTT', then the name of the city.

To collect mail, you need your passport, and to pay about US$0.50 per item. Letters sometimes take a few weeks to arrive, so have them sent to a town where you'll be for a while, or will be passing through more than once – although in some places mail is only held for a month, then returned to the sender.

For sending home those carved rhinos from Kenya, or that beautiful cloth you bought in Mali, you'll need parcel post. Price, quality and speed vary massively from place to place – so see the individual country chapters for more details.

Sometimes, lugging a souvenir for a few extra days from one country to another before posting it home can mean the difference between US$50 and US$10 postage.

TELEPHONE & FAX

In most capital cities and major towns, phone connections are good. Thanks to satellite technology, it's often easier to make an international call than to dial someone 20km up the road. Rates vary

PRACTICALITIES

Newspapers & Magazines

For continental coverage you can't go wrong with *BBC Focus on Africa* magazine. Published quarterly, the writing is sharp, and the overview of politics, sport, arts and music perfect for travellers. It's available worldwide on subscription from www.bbc.co.uk and from shops in English-speaking countries in Africa. Other current affairs mags include monthly *New African* and *Africa Today*. Look out too for *West Africa*, available in most English-speaking West African countries and a few in East Africa. Also in West Africa, if your French is well-oiled, *Jeune Afrique* is a highly regarded weekly news-magazine.

Radio

All countries in Africa have national radio (the choice is normally commercial music stations or state-sponsored talk), but for continental coverage locals and travellers tune into international broadcasters; most have dedicated Africa slots. A compact radio is great for keeping in touch with events while you're on the road – for many travellers, scratchy shortwave is as much a sound of Africa as drums and roaring lions. Favourite stations include the BBC World Service (also available in some cities on FM), Voice of America and Radio France Internationale.

Time

Africa is covered by four time zones, from UTC (formerly GMT) in the west to UTC+3 in the east. Crossing from Chad to Sudan there's a two-hour difference, but elsewhere it's one hour or none at all. Watch out at the town of Katima Mulilo in Namibia, where the locals have their watches set to Zambia time,

and at borders such as Songwe between Malawi and Tanzania, where the Malawi guards cheerfully stamp you out at 5.30pm, but when you get to the Tanzania side it's 6.30pm, and the border post is already shut for the night. And you can't go back to Malawi because the guards won't let you in again. Africaaagh!

Electricity

Take care before you plug in to recharge your fancy MP3 player or some other electrical device. Most countries use a 220/240V current, but some mix 110V and 240V (Libya, Madagascar, Mauritania, Morocco and Senegal), while a few (Eritrea, Liberia) use 110V only. The choice of sockets can also be a shock. Generally, in English-speaking countries, they're the British type. In Francophone parts of Africa they're the French type. South Africa has yet another system. In some countries you'll find whatever people can get hold of – British, French, American, Chinese, whatever. And if all that hasn't put you off, don't forget that power cuts or vicious surges are a part of life in many African countries.

Weights & Measures

Metric units (metres, kilos, litres etc) are officially used in most African countries. But nobody told the market traders, so fruits and vegetables are simply displayed in small piles – and sold that way too – while in many countries a bottle anywhere between 300mL and 500mL is called a 'pint'. You'll quite likely buy peanuts by the cup-full, or strips of colourful fabric according to the length of the tailor's arms.

from country to country, ranging from US$5 to US$15 for a three-minute call to Europe, USA and Australia. Calling home from the cheaper places can therefore ease the strain on your budget – especially as collect calls are rarely possible. In each country chapter we give details of rates, and in the Fast Facts box we give the country code and the access number for international calls.

Bureaus

To call long distance you're usually better off at a public phone bureau than a booth in the street. (To call local, it's often easier to use a bureau too.) In each city, there's normally a bureau at the main post office, plus numerous privately run bureaus where rates can be cheaper and the service faster. In the absence of these, try upmarket hotels as they often have a business

> **TELEGRAMME**
>
> This archaic method of communication is often overlooked, but if you just want to send an 'All OK' message, it can be cheaper than phone or fax, although a 10-word minimum is sometimes imposed. Inquire at main post offices.

centre. At most bureaus you can also send or receive faxes.

Mobile Phones

In some countries you can take your own mobile phone (cell phone) handset and get a local pay-as-you-go SIM card. To check whether your phone will work in the African countries you plan to visit, contact your network provider. Ask about charges as well – and don't forget that if anyone rings you while you're overseas, the bulk of the cost goes on *your* bill. See www.mobilephonesabroad.com for more details.

Phonecards

In some countries you can buy phonecards that let you dial a local number then make cheap international calls. You can also buy phonecards to top up mobile phones, and phonecards to use in public booths instead of coins. Just make sure you get the right one!

TOILETS

There are two types of toilet in Africa: the Western style, with a bowl and seat; and the African style – a hole in the floor that you squat over. Standards vary tremendously, from pristine to nauseating. In rural areas, squat toilets are built over a deep hole in the ground and called 'long-drops'; the crap just fades away naturally, as long as the hole isn't filled with too much other rubbish (such as tampons – these should be disposed of separately). Toilet paper is OK – although you'll inevitably need to carry your own. In Muslim countries, a jug of water or hosepipe arrangement is provided for the same task.

Some travellers complain that African toilets are difficult to use, but it only takes a little practice to accomplish a comfortable squatting technique. We'd draw you a diagram, but there just isn't space...

TOURIST INFORMATION

Much of Africa isn't geared for tourism, and decent tourist offices are rare. For information before you leave home, a few countries have small tourist offices at their embassies, and a call may elicit brochures or help with specific travel details – although these are usually of the mainstream variety. While you're on the road, some countries have a tourist information office in the capital, but apart from a few tatty leaflets and vague advice from the remarkably little-travelled staff, you're unlikely to get much here. Notable exceptions are listed in the country chapters. Tour companies, hotels and backpackers hostels that provide information for independent travellers are also listed.

TOURS

Overland truck tours did much to open up cheap travel in Africa, blazing overland trails where no tourist had boldly gone before. Today there are a huge number of overland trucks chugging around East and Southern Africa (Arusha in Tanzania and Nairobi in Kenya are common starting points), but fewer range across West Africa. There are a number of trucks heading all the way from London and Istanbul to Cape Town, a trip that can last seven months.

Truck tours don't suit everyone, but it can be a real laugh travelling in a close group (especially if you'd otherwise be travelling alone) and the truck and its staff take away many of the hassles of travelling in Africa (something you'll appreciate if you're crossing through Nigeria, Chad and Sudan). You'll also get to experience a full range of cultures, landscapes and attractions in a relatively short time and for relatively little cash (like under US$200 a week).

There are, of course, downsides: you don't always get time to explore a place in depth, and sightseeing can end up being a terrible rush; it's much harder to meet locals; getting stuck with a bunch of morons for months might send you crazy; some trucks take up to 30 passengers, not exactly an intimate travel experience; group chores and vehicle security can be a pain.

Whatever you decide, go through company brochures with a fine-tooth comb and remember to ask what you're required to do (on most tours you'll have to do the

OVERLANDING ON THE CHEAP

Because most people prefer to travel north to south, overland truck companies sometimes drive empty trucks back from Cape Town, Victoria Falls and Harare, and will sometimes transport travellers back up to Arusha or Nairobi (Harare to Nairobi costs around US$100, transport only), with a pleasant two-day stop by Lake Malawi sometimes thrown in.

washing up at least), how many people are on the truck (loads of people equals cheaper prices) and how much flexibility is in the itinerary.

The truck tour business is dominated by British companies (see the following list), but they often have representatives in North America and Australasia (check out the websites for more information).

Acacia Expeditions (☎ 020-7706 4700; www.acacia-africa.com) Concentrates on East and Southern Africa with their quality truck tours.

African Trails (☎ 01772-330907; www.africantrails.co.uk) Offers truck tours through East Africa plus a seven-month, trans-African route.

Dragoman (☎ 01728-861133; www.dragoman.co.uk) Includes a hardcore loop through the Sahara and West Africa plus Kathmandu to Cape Town; quality.

Economic Expeditions (☎ 020-8995 7707; www.economicexpeditions.com) Small but quite hardcore; trans-African and Kenya to South Africa routes.

Encounter (☎ 01728-862222; www.encounteroverland.com) Dragoman's budget brother; runs a huge variety of stuff across Africa including the west.

Exodus (☎ 020-8675 5550; www.exodus.co.uk) Runs well-respected truck tours mostly in East and Southern Africa; one includes the Middle East.

Guerba (☎ 01373-858956; www.guerba.com) Well respected with tours in West, East and Southern Africa, including Mozambique.

Kumuka (☎ 0800 068 8855; www.kumuka.co.uk) Offers adventurous overland truck tours of all sorts, but concentrating on East and Southern Africa.

Nomadic Expeditions (☎ 0870 220 1718; www.nomadic.co.uk) A small company specialising in Morocco and West Africa.

Oasis Overland (☎ 01963-363400; www.oasisoverland.com) Runs overland truck tours mostly through East and Southern Africa.

Phoenix Expeditions (☎ 01509-881818; www.phoenixexpeditions.co.uk) Budget truck tours in East and Southern Africa, plus Istanbul to Cape Town.

Truck Africa (sales@truckafrica.com; www.truckafrica.com) Concentrates on adventurous London to Dar es Salaam or Cape Town routes.

VISAS

A visa is a stamp in your passport giving you permission to enter a country. They are available from embassies before you arrive, and *sometimes* on the spot at borders and airports – although if you're flying from outside Africa most airlines won't let you board without a visa for the destination country.

Not all countries require visas, but many do, and the fees involved can take a sizable chunk from your budget: expect to pay US$10 to US$25 for standard one-month single-entry visas, and up to US$200 for three-month multiple-entry visas. If you want to stay longer, extensions are usually available – for an extra fee, of course.

Rules vary for different nationalities: British and Aussie citizens don't need visas for some Southern African countries; French don't need them in much of West Africa; Americans need them nearly everywhere. The price varies according to your nationality, and where you actually buy the visa.

Most visas are issued in one to two days (and it always helps to go to embassies in the morning) but occasionally the process takes a week or longer. You may have to show you have enough funds to cover the visit, or prove that you intend to leave the country rather than settle down and build a hut somewhere. (An air ticket home does the job.) For most visas you also need two or three passport photos; take what you'll need, although you can get new supplies from photo-booths in most capitals. Some embassies ask for a photocopy of your passport data page – it's always worth carrying a few copies anyway.

NO VISA? NO GO

Whatever you do, don't turn up at a border without a visa (where one is required) unless you're absolutely sure you can get one at the border. Otherwise, you may well find yourself trekking back to the nearest embassy – and, in some countries, this can be a long, long way.

For a short trip through Africa you might get all your visas before you leave home. For a longer trip, it's easier to get them as you go along. Most countries have an embassy in each neighbouring country, but not all – so careful planning is required. Some visas are valid from when they are issued, so you may have to enter the country pretty soon after getting it. On other visas you say when you plan to enter the country and arrive within a month of that date. Sometimes it's convenient (and relatively cheap) to get several visas in one place – South Africa or Kenya, for example.

If you're travelling in West Africa, ask about a Visa Touristique Entente – a five-country visa covering Benin, Burkina Faso, Niger, Togo and Côte d'Ivoire. It costs around US$38 and is usually valid for two months. You should be able to get it in any embassy of the five countries covered, but in practice embassies of Benin seem the best

bet (when we passed through Chad, the Niger embassy hadn't even heard of it).

A final note: if you have Israeli stamps in your passport, this may prove problematic when you enter Sudan and some North African countries. Israeli border officials may stamp a piece of paper, which you can then remove, but if you're travelling overland your Egyptian entry-point can still be a giveaway.

Specifics on visas are given in each country chapter, but regulations can change so it's always worth checking before you enter the country. For general details see www.lonelyplanet.com, which also has links to other visa sites.

VOLUNTEERING
There are very few openings for ad hoc volunteer work in Africa. Unless you've got some expertise, and are prepared to stay for at least a year, you're unlikely to be much use anyway. What Africa needs is people with skills. Just 'wanting to help' isn't enough. In fact, your presence may be disruptive for local staff and management, and you'll just be a drain on resources.

For formal volunteer work, which must be arranged in your home country, organisations such as VSO (in the UK) and Peace Corps (in the USA) have programmes throughout Africa, where people, usually with genuine training (eg teachers, health workers, environmentalists), do two-year stints. Similar schemes for 'gap-year' students (between school and university) tend to be for shorter periods, and are of questionable benefit to the host country.

The following can provide more information:

Australian Volunteers International www.ozvol.org.au
Coordinating Committee for International Voluntary Service www.unesco.org/ccivs
Gap Activity Projects www.gap.org.uk
Global Volunteer www.globalvolunteer.com, www.globalvolunteers.org
Peace Corps www.peacecorps.gov
Timebank www.timebank.org.uk/givetime/overseas
Voluntary Service Overseas (VSO) www.vso.org.uk
Volunteer International www.volunteerinternational.com
Volunteer Work Information Service www.workingabroad.com
Worldwide Volunteering www.worldwidevolunteering.org.uk

WOMEN TRAVELLERS

It's no use pretending otherwise – women travelling in Africa (alone or with other women) will occasionally encounter specific problems, most often harassment from men.

North Africa can be particularly tiresome from this perspective. And in places where an attack or mugging is a possibility, women are seen as easy targets, so it pays to keep away from these areas (they're listed in the individual country chapters). But don't panic! On a day-to-day basis, compared to many places, travel in Africa is relatively

---

Tam Tam Femme

An international women's organisation, can put you in touch with local women who are happy to have you to stay – www.tamtamfemme.org.

---

safe and unthreatening, and you'll meet friendliness and generosity far more often than hostility.

Having said that, when it comes to evening entertainment, Africa is a conservative society and in many countries women don't go to bars without a male companion. However distasteful it may be to liberated Westerners, trying to buck the system could lead to trouble.

Because of these attitudes, it can be hard to meet and talk with local women. It may require being invited into a home, although because many women have received little education, sometimes language barriers can be a problem. However, this is changing to some extent because a surprising number of girls go to school while boys are sent away to work. This means that many of the staff in tourist offices or government departments are educated women, and this can be as good a place as any to try striking up a conversation. In rural areas, a good starting point might be teachers at a local school, or staff at a health centre.

POSITIVE VIBES
Amy Marsh

Much advice for women travellers concentrates on negative aspects, reinforcing the stereotyped view that it's really only men who can do 'adventurous' things in Africa. The following observations form a refreshing and very welcome antidote:

I'm a 22 year-old white female, and I spent three months in Senegal, Mali, Niger, Benin, Ghana, Côte d'Ivoire and Guinea, travelling mostly alone, eating street food and sleeping in the most cockroach-laden hotels. I always wore a skirt and covered my hair, but often found myself surrounded by men, especially young men – often simply because men are more likely to be in a situation to interact with foreign travellers – Just the sheer numbers can be daunting! It was a lengthy learning process – understanding how to recognise innuendos, separate nice boys from those with ulterior motives, and generally how to raise the red flags at the appropriate time.

Eventually, though, I *did* learn, and felt very comfortable going solo. I went to Agadez, and hiked 100km through the villages of the Fouta Djalon. Wherever I went, people took excellent care of me. Fellow bus passengers brought me coffee or got my passport back for me from awkward border guards. They brought me home, showed me around, and gave me unlimited supplies of manioc and bananas. Once I'd learnt how to react, it seemed that locals knew I'd been travelling for a while, and I certainly found it increasingly easy and enjoyable to be in Africa.

Some expatriates you meet may be appalled at the idea of lone female travel and will do their best to discourage you with horror stories, often of dubious accuracy. Others have a far more realistic attitude. (If you happened to be African, and travelled far alone, your family would be just as concerned.) When you're on the road, the best advice on what can and can't be undertaken safely will come from local women. Use common sense and things should go well.

Sexual Harassment
Unwanted interest from male 'admirers' is an inevitable aspect of travel in Africa, especially for lone women. This is always unpleasant, but it's worth remembering that although you may encounter a lewd border official, or a persistent suitor who won't go away, real harm or rape is very unlikely. If you're alone in an uneasy situation, act cold or disinterested, rather than threatened. Stick your nose in a book. Or invent an imaginary husband who will be arriving shortly.

Part of the reason for the interest is that local women rarely travel long distances alone, and a single foreign female is an unusual sight. And, thanks to imported TV and Hollywood films (not to mention the behaviour of some tourists), Western women are frequently viewed as 'easy'.

What you wear may greatly influence how you're treated. African women dress conservatively, in traditional or Western clothes, so when a visitor wears something different from the norm, she will draw attention. In the minds of some men this is provocative. In general, look at what other women are wearing and follow suit. Keep your upper arms and legs covered.

Sanitary Protection
You can buy tampons and pads in most cities and major towns from pharmacies or supermarkets – prices are about the same as in Europe (from where they're imported) but you seldom have choice on type or brand. They're rarely found in shops in the sticks, so you might want to bring supplies if you're spending a lot of time in remote areas.

WORKING
It's hard for outsiders to find work in most African countries, as high unemployment means a huge number of people chase every job vacancy. You'll also need a work permit, and this is usually hard to get as priority is given to qualified locals – fair enough.

If you're skilled in computing, teaching, journalism or safari guiding you might be lucky, but you're unlikely to see such jobs advertised (except maybe for teaching), and the only way to find out about them is by asking around among the expatriate community.

Transport

CONTENTS

THINGS CHANGE...

The information in this chapter is particularly vulnerable to change. Check directly with your airline or a travel agent to make sure you understand how a fare (and ticket you may buy) works and be aware of the security requirements for international travel. Shop carefully. The details given in this chapter should be regarded as pointers and are not a substitute for your own careful, up-to-date research.

'Nothing in Africa is adjacent to anywhere.'

James Cameron, Point of Departure:
Experiment in Biography
(Grafton Books, 1969)

GETTING THERE & AWAY

AIR

Few African countries are devoid of intercontinental air links. The bulk of traffic is to/from Europe, but there are a handful of direct flights between Africa and North America, the Middle East and Asia. A few flights link Australia with Africa and there's one route between South Africa and Brazil. Many North American travellers pass through Europe on their way to Africa. For Australasian travellers it's often cheaper to pass through a Middle Eastern and/or Asian hub before arriving, but thanks to the Eurocentricity of Africa's international air links and numerous airline code-share agreements they too often pass through a European 'hub' (airports located in London, Amsterdam, Paris and Frankfurt for example) before arriving in Africa. This can mean a long haul but can give you a little more flexibility in your point of arrival – just remember that flying into the continent's main hubs is going to be your cheapest option wherever you are coming from.

The main gateway into East Africa is Nairobi (Kenya), although Dar es Salaam (Tanzania) is also busy. Cheap deals into Addis Ababa (Ethiopia) occasionally pop up. Thanks to the country's political troubles Harare (Zimbabwe) receives fewer international flights and tourists than it did, so Johannesburg (South Africa) is the Southern African hub offering the most options (flights arrive from the Americas, Asia and Australasia as well as Europe) and biggest bargains – also look out for cheap deals into Cape Town (South Africa). In West Africa, Accra (Ghana) and Lagos (Nigeria) are the busiest gateways (and receive flights from North America), but Dakar (Senegal) is often a cheaper option. In North Africa flying into Casablanca (Morocco) and Cairo (Egypt) can cost peanuts from Europe and the national carriers of both countries can easily transport you to other destinations across Africa. If you're travelling from Europe, Tunis (Tunisia) is often the cheapest African city in which to arrive. However, it's surrounded by Algeria and Libya, which can make for tricky onward overland travel (see those chapters for details).

Flying into places like Lilongwe (Malawi), Windhoek (Namibia), Ouagadougou (Burkina Faso) and Conakry (Guinea) can cost you 30% more than flying into, say, Nairobi, Dakar or Johannesburg. You can add 60% to a Nairobi fare for out-of-the-way Antananarivo (Madagascar) and there is no cheap or easy way to get into Central Africa or former war zones like Kinshasa (Congo: Zaïre), Luanda (Angola) and Freetown

(Sierra Leone). If you really want a more unusual destination, then a cheap flight into a regional hub followed by a local continental flight may hit the spot (many of these 'add-on' flights can be booked through a decent travel agent at home – see Air on p1020 for more information).

Tickets

Wild climatic variations across Africa, and differing holiday seasons in the northern and southern hemispheres, means that it's tricky to pin down the cheapest times to fly to Africa. Using milewide brush strokes it could be argued that flying in June to September or around Christmas (a 'peak season' that can last from November to March if you're coming from Australasia) is going to hit your budget hardest. But you don't need generalities if you've a well-defined trip in mind, so get the low-down on costs from a travel agent well in advance.

It's easy to become totally focused on basic return fares when planning any big trip, so ditch the blinkers and consider open-jaw tickets. These tickets allow you to fly into one city, then out of another, and can save you cash, time and hassle. Rarely more expensive than a bog standard return into the most expensive of your entry/departure points, open jaws let you travel in a continuous general direction, which can actually give you more flexibility, especially if you can get a deal where your departure point can be changed. All manner of combinations are available, enabling some great overland journeys: think about a ticket into Cairo and out of Cape Town (fares from here can be amazingly cheap), or into Nairobi and out of Cape Town, or even into Dakar and out of

USE THE BACK DOOR
Looking for a quirky way into Africa? Well, you could get a dirt-cheap European charter flight to the Canary Islands or Cape Verde and then grab a flight to Dakar (Senegal), Nouakchott (Mauritania) or from there to Casablanca (Morocco).

Cape Town. Even if you're set on exploring one country, open jaws can still be worth considering. How else would you experience the great, gruelling, enlightening train journey between Bamako (Mali) and Dakar, for example?

Next up on the 'things-not-to-forget list' are stopovers. Due to the complexities of airline alliances, code shares and routings, many flights to Africa stop at least once before arriving at the main destination. On some tickets (sadly not always those at the bottom of the barrel) you'll have the chance to get off, and on some happy occasions taking advantage of these stopovers can effectively save the cost of an internal flight. For example a Kenya Airways flight from London to Addis Ababa goes via Nairobi, allowing you to explore Kenya first. Likewise, flights on Ethiopian Airways from Europe to Kenya or several other Africa countries go via Addis Ababa and allow for a stopover there. Middle Eastern stopovers are common on some routes and if you're coming from North America or Australia even a stop in Europe can be handy if you need to pick up an obscure visa in Paris or Amsterdam or just fancy getting your travel legs somewhere vaguely familiar.

Jumping on a charter flight can sometimes save you a bundle if you're travelling from or via Europe, especially if you pick something up at the last minute. Short-date returns are common, but there is sometimes some flexibility. From the UK charter flights leave for The Gambia, Morocco, Tunisia, Egypt and Kenya, destinations that are also serviced by French operators. Charter flights to Senegal, Mali, Burkina Faso, Togo and Benin also leave from France and November to May **Point Afrique** (☎ 00 33 4 75 97 20 40; www.point-afrique.com) offers cheap flights (from €150 one way) to these and other Saharan countries from Paris and Marseille. Heaps of other charter flights leave from across Europe.

TRANSPORT

HIGH FLYERS

For many travellers reading this book the final leg into Africa will be with a European (and occasionally Middle Eastern) carrier. In this world of giant alliances and code-share agreements, ticketing via Europe is possible from across the globe. **Air France** (www.airfrance.com) boasts some of the best connections to French-speaking West and Central Africa, but coming from Europe **SN Brussels Airlines** (www.snbrussels.com) cheerfully undercuts them, and the rest of the competition, here and there. Air France forms part of **Skyteam** (www.skyteam.com), which includes US airline **Delta** (www.delta.com).

British Airways (BA; www.ba.com) has good connections across Africa (especially East and South-ern), but not always the cheapest fares. However, it is part of the oneworld alliance (www.oneworld.com), which includes **American Airlines** (www.aa.com) and **Qantas** (www.qantas.com.au).

KLM (www.klm.com) has a huge African network, consistently offers deals and has a strong partnership with **Northwest Airlines** (www.nwa.com) and **Kenya Airways** (www.kenya-airways.com). Also check out **Lufthansa** (www.lufthansa.com), **Swiss** (www.swiss.com) and **Emirates** (www.emirates.com), which is good for cheap deals with stopovers in the Middle East. Lufthansa is part of the **Star Alliance** (www.staralliance.com), which includes **United** (www.ual.com) and **Air New Zealand** (www.airnewzealand.com).

Using an African airline to get to the continent is not always the cheapest option, but these carriers often offer the only direct routes from Australasia and North America, plus easy access to the continent's air network. **Ethiopian Airlines** (www.flyethiopian.com) has a good African network (with decent links between West and East) and a sound reputation. Kenya Airways has a very useful network that links its hub in Nairobi with Cairo, East, Southern and West Africa.

South African Airways (SAA; www.flysaa.com) operates a massive domestic and Southern African network, but almost entirely out of its hub in Johannesburg (which can mean long journey times). **Royal Air Maroc** (www.royalairmaroc.com) offers some useful flights from North America and has good connections to North and West Africa. **Egypt Air** (www.egyptair.com) also flies from North America but has a rather limited African network (good for the Middle East though).

COURIER FLIGHTS

These tickets offer you cheap passage in exchange for you carrying documents or (increasingly rarely) giving up your baggage allowance. It's not always easy to get to Africa on one of these beauties, but cheap fares to Cape Town, Jo'burg and Mauritius are not unheard of. Transatlantic flights for under US$250 and one-way fares between Sydney and London for under US$300 can be had if your plans take you through Europe. The common drawbacks are fixed dates and two-week returns.

Based in the USA, the **International Association of Air Travel Couriers** (IAATC; ☎ 308-632-3273; www.courier.org) are a good first stop for information, but you must join the organisation before taking advantage of any courier flights The organisation also has a **UK Office** (☎ 0800 0746 481; www.aircourier.co.uk), although for courier flights to Africa (commonly Cape Town and Johannesburg) contact **ACP Worldwide** (☎ 020-8897 5130; www.acpww.com) – its flights can be a little expensive, but six- and 12-week returns are offered.

ROUND-THE-WORLD (RTW) TICKETS

On the cheapest RTW tickets Nairobi and Johannesburg are the usual stops, but stopping in these major hubs will cut down your options once you leave the continent. If you want more stops look at the Global Explorer or oneworld Explorer RTW tickets offered by the **oneworld alliance** (www.oneworld.com), which includes Aer Lingus, American Airlines, BA, Cathay Pacific, Finnair, Iberia, LanChile and Qantas. The former gives you between 29,000 and 34,000 miles to circumnavigate the world and allows three or four flights within Africa. The oneworld Explorer is similar, but allows you to visit between three and six continents. Four flights are allowed in Africa, or you can buy two more. Coming from Europe with BA can get you to a variety of interesting African destinations, but flights within Africa are limited to BA's African franchises **Regional Air** (based in Nairobi) and **Comair** (based in Johannesburg), essentially limiting travel to East and Southern Africa.

The trick with RTW tickets is to decide where you want to go first and then talk to a travel agent, who will know the best deals, cunning little routes and pitfalls of the various packages.

TICKET HUNTING

It's not rocket science, but take your time; shop around; double-check all restrictions and date/route-change penalties on your ticket; look out for credit card surcharges; and book well in advance. The classifieds in the travel sections of weekend broadsheet papers are full of useful travel leads; you may not pick up the cheap fares advertised, but you'll find the names and numbers of numerous budget travel agents. Talk to as many travel agents as possible. Internet fare generators are great for getting rough quotes, but they cannot tell you about little add-ons and shortcuts, nor can they custom-build itineraries from a cluster of domestic and regional flights.

If you're under 26 or a student you'll occasionally be able to turn up some juicy deals. There are many specialist student travel agents, but many 'normal' travel agents offer student fares, just as student travel agents can serve older travellers. Student fares may not always be cheaper, but they can be sweeter, offering more flexibility and fewer penalties should you wish to change your itinerary (for example, it may cost you between nothing and around US$20 to US$30 to change the return date on the ticket compared with the US$50 that many airlines will sting you for).

After taking over USIT in the US, **STA Travel** (www.statravelgroup.com) became a truly global student/backpacker travel agent. It has hundreds of potentially useful offices and affiliates around the world, but service can vary and it's vital that you shop around.

Travel agents that recognise the **International Student Identity Card** (ISIC; www.isic.org) scheme are another possibility – the contact details of thousands of agents are available on their website.

From the Americas

Flights to Africa from North America are not cheap. Direct flights to Accra (Ghana), Lagos (Nigeria), Addis Ababa (Ethiopia), Cairo (Egypt), Casablanca (Morocco) and Johannesburg (South Africa) are possible. The latter two destinations are serviced by Royal Air Maroc (from New York and Montreal) and SAA (from New York and Atlanta) respectively and are reliable options. As well as efficient trans-African networks, both these carriers have good connections inside the USA. Accra and Lagos are serviced by rather flaky national carriers, but the Ethiopian Airlines flight to Addis Ababa (from New York or Washington) and Egypt Air's Cairo flight (from New York or Montreal) are worth considering. Although through ticketing via Europe is a very popular option it might be cheaper to get a supersonic deal across the Atlantic and then sort out a deal to Africa (or book over the Internet).

SAA has a flight between Johannesburg and São Paulo (Brazil) that continues to Buenos Aires (Argentina). Just think of the possibilities…

Lonely Planet (www.lonelyplanet.com) Part of this excellent website is a US RTW fare generator.

STA Travel (☎ 800-329-9537; www.statravel.com) Now the biggest student/under-26 flight agent in North America.

Travel CUTS (☎ 800-667 2887; www.travelcuts.com) Canada's primary student and discounted travel agent.

www.onetravel.com A comprehensive North American fare generator.

BRINGING YOUR BIKE

You could cycle all the way into Africa or you can save your legs for Africa's rough roads and stick your wheels in the hold of a plane. There are two ways of doing this; you could partially dismantle your bike and stuff it into a large box or just simply wheel your bike to the check-in desk, where it should be treated as a piece of baggage (although you might need to take the pedals off, turn the handlebars sideways and wrap it in cardboard and/or foam). Don't loose too much sleep about the feather touch of baggage handlers – if your bike doesn't stand up to air travel it won't last long in Africa.

Some airlines don't include sports equipment in the baggage allowance; others may charge around US$50 extra because your bike is not standard luggage size; others, however, will take it with pleasure.

TRANSPORT

From Australasia & Asia

Most flights head to Africa via the Middle East, often with Emirates or **Gulf Air** (www.gulfairco.com); Cairo with Egypt Air; direct to Johannesburg with Qantas or SAA; and even via Mauritius with **Air Mauritius** (www.airmauritius.com) from Perth (Australia). Other fares go via Europe. Many of these flights, including those going via the Middle East, often allow a nice Southeast Asian stopover.

Of course, you could head straight to Europe and then root around for a bargain to Africa (or sort it out over the Internet first), but either way, you'll go via a combination of airlines so it may be worth considering a RTW ticket.

In Southeast Asia the only options at the time of writing were from Bangkok, Hong Kong, Kuala Lumpur and Singapore. Most of these only fly into Johannesburg. However, **Kenya Airways** (www.kenya-airways.com) runs services from Nairobi to Bangkok and Hong Kong. Flights leave Nairobi for Bangkok on Wednesday, Friday and Sunday and then continue to Hong Kong. The returning flight leaves Hong Kong on Thursday, Saturday and Monday, stopping in Bangkok en route to Nairobi.

Flight Centre Australia (☎ 133 133; www.flight centre.com.au); New Zealand (☎ 0800 23 35 44; www.flightcentre.co.nz)

STA Travel Australia (☎ 1300 733 035; www.statravel.com.au); New Zealand (☎ 0508 782 872; www.statravel.co.nz)

www.travel.com.au Good Internet-only fare generator for Australasia.

From Europe

If you are coming from Europe, then Africa is your oyster. London, Paris and Amsterdam probably have the greatest selection of flights, but whatever country you start from there's almost nowhere that a good travel agent can't get you into even if you have to go via a hub in a different country or in the Middle East.

El Al (www.elal.co.il) Offers a few flights into East Africa from Tel Aviv (Israel).

Africa Travel Centre (☎ 020-7387 1211; www.africatravel.co.uk) A highly experienced UK operator offering flights and tours.

Air Fare (☎ 020-620 5121; www.airfair.nl) A well-respected Dutch travel agent.

CTS Viaggi (☎ 06-462 0431; www.cts.it) A reliable Italian student travel agent.

ISSTA (☎ 3-5210 555; www.issta.co.il) One of many Israeli ISIC-affiliated travel agents.

Nouvelles Frontières (☎ 08 03 33 33 33; www.nouvelles-frontieres.fr) A good French option with adventure tours and charter flights.

OTU Voyages (☎ 0825 004 027; www.otu.fr) Has branches across France.

STA Travel UK (☎ 0870 1600 599; www.statravel.co.uk); Germany (☎ 01805-456 422; www.statravel.de) There are loads of other offices across Europe.

Trailfinders (☎ 020-7938 3939; www.trailfinders.com) Excellent, reliable UK travel agent with huge experience.

From the Indian Subcontinent

There is a stack of traffic between Mumbai (Bombay) in India and East Africa; flights to/from Nairobi can be pretty darn cheap. Many other Middle Eastern carriers (connections from Dubai and Muscat are pretty common) service North and East Africa.

LAND & SEA

If your starting point is Europe you can hitch, drive or even get the train to the northern Mediterranean (where modern ferries ply many routes to North Africa) or head through the Middle East, where Africa's only land border divides Israel and Egypt in the Sinai. Sadly, the continuing troubles in Israel and the Palestinian Territories mean that the direct route via Rafah is dodgy, so go via the Eilat–Taba border crossing on the Gulf of Aqaba – it's a little

---

NO-FRILLS EUROPE

Cheap carriers (and major international airlines trying to recoup market share – very handy if you're transferring directly from a North American or Australasian flight!) can help you get within spitting distance of North Africa from across Europe – book online and well in advance:

- Air France (www.airfrance.com)
- Basiq Air (www.basiqair.com)
- British Airways (www.ba.com)
- bmibaby (www.bmibaby.com)
- easyJet (www.easyjet.com)
- Germanwings (www.germanwings.com)
- Ryanair (www.ryanair.co.uk)
- Virgin Express (www.virgin-express.com)

easier and gets you to a nicer part of Sinai in any case. However, note that if your passport has an Israeli stamp in it you won't get into countries such as Libya, so if this is going to be a problem take the ferry from Jordan.

If you're planning to enter North Africa by land or sea and need to cross Europe first, there are a few cheap tricks. Firstly, consider using a 'no-frills' carrier to get you to southern Europe (US$40 for a one-way ticket from London to southern Spain is pretty common; see p1018 for details).

Secondly, investigate the possibility of taking to Europe's excellent train network either with a rail pass (Inter-Rail tickets are available to EU residents, Eurail passes for other nationals – some variations of these will get you as far as Istanbul; check out the details at www.raileurope.com) or standard one-way train ticket – they're often quite cheap in continental Europe, and good-value student/under-26 **EuroStar** (www.eurostar.com) tickets from London to destinations across France are often available.

A third (cheaper, but less comfortable) option is to go by bus. **Eurolines** (www.eurolines.com) runs a huge European network that includes Morocco and you can (if you're a masochist) get a bus directly to Casablanca from London.

Hitching down through Europe is feasible, but it's never 100% safe. Happily, there are lift-sharing organisations in many European countries (especially France and Germany) that can connect you with vehicles going your way – contact local tourist or student organisations or search the web for information.

The days of working your way to Africa aboard a cargo ship are, alas, over. Now towering car ferries (always the cheapest boats to take), sleek powerful 'fast ferries' and hi-tech catamarans ply the routes across the Mediterranean and Red Sea.

Egypt & Sudan
There are daily ferries and a catamaran between Nuweiba in Sinai (Egypt) and Aqaba (Jordan), which is a stone's throw from Eilat in Israel. Regular boats also ply the routes between Suez (Egypt) and Ammam (Saudi Arabia) and between Hurghada (Egypt) and Duba (Saudi Arabia).

There are regular ferry services between Suakin (Sudan, just south of Port Sudan) and Jeddah (Saudi Arabia).

If you're a real adventurer you could hunt down some informal cargo and local boat traffic; there's traffic from Saudi Arabia and Yemen in the Middle East to Eritrea, Djibouti and Somaliland, the safe(ish), northern breakaway region of Somalia on the Gulf of Aden (see p670).

Morocco
The two main companies propelling travellers across the Strait of Gibraltar from Spain to Morocco are **Trasmediterránea** (www.trasmediterranea.es) and **EuroFerrys** (www.euroferrys.com). Boats leaving Algeciras (Spain) for Ceuta (a Spanish North African enclave) are the cheapest and fastest. Boats to Tangier are also very common (from Algeciras and occasionally Cadiz, Tarifa or Gibraltar), but arriving here can be a nightmare of hassle and hustle. If you want real tranquillity arrive in Melilla (another Spanish enclave) or Nador further east (from Málaga or Almeria).

In addition to these relatively short hops, **Comanav** (www.comanav.co.ma) runs ferries to Tangier and Nador from Séte (France) and to Tangier from Genoa (Italy).

Most services increase in frequency during the summer months, when other routes are sometimes added. Cars can be taken on almost all services.

Tunisia, Algeria & Libya
Compagnie Tunisienne de Navigation (CTN; www.ctn.com.tn) runs ferries from Marseille (France) to Tunis (Tunisia), and a host of companies offer services from Italy to Tunis (Genoa is a year-round point of departure; summer services leave from La Spezia, Napoli and Trapani).

From Malta there are ferries going to both Tripoli and Benghazi in Libya and a few ferries heading to Algeria (the north of which remains unsafe) from Nice and other French ports.

GETTING AROUND

Travelling around much of Africa often requires time, patience and stamina, but logistically it's often simply a matter of catching a bus between towns, cities and tourist resorts. African public transport *sometimes* leaves/arrives roughly on time and off the beaten track transport is more circumspect and unreliable, but there are few interesting places that you cannot reach, even if you have to wait for a few days.

AIR

Africa's internal air network is pretty comprehensive and can save you considerable time and hardship on the roads; certainly flying over the Sahara, Congo (Zaïre) and the often chaotic and difficult Chad and southern Sudan is really quite a good idea. Some airlines are first-class operations; others are about as reliable as a chocolate fireguard (see p1016). Check flight details carefully (many tickets are really quite flexible), but be prepared for delays, cancellations and bureaucratic pantomimes, especially when travelling on state-owned enterprises. Don't expect to be put up in a four-star hotel should your flight get canned.

If you're serious about taking a few African flights, consider sorting it out when booking your main ticket. Any half-decent

---

AIR MAYBE   *by Matt Fletcher*

Air Mali had a reputation for cancellations, over subscribed seats and general chaos. My plane from Timbuktu to Bamako was late and the passengers were getting restless. Finally we were called to board and there was a huge surge for the door. One of the airline staff, getting desperate, started shouting, 'Don't worry, there are seats for everyone!' but the panic in his voice made things even worse.

---

travel agent should be able to book a host of African flights and possibly find fares that allow a little date flexibility. These 'add-ons' are often sold at a discount overseas, so forward planning can save you a small fortune.

Air Passes

This section is something of a misnomer. All products purporting to be Africa air passes are just cheapo deals on domestic and continental flights available to travellers flying into Africa with certain airlines. The following schemes operate on a tailor-made basis – routes are usually divided into price bands or sectors and you pick 'n' mix to make an itinerary. Most schemes are fairly limited and usually dictate that your flights include arrival/departure at one or two hubs. The airlines mentioned in this section won't always offer the cheapest flights into Africa, but if you're planning to take a few African flights some 'air pass' schemes offer great value in the long run – the best offer savings of well over 50% on domestic and continental fares (see opposite). Do your homework before approaching an airline – have a pretty definite idea of where and when you want to travel (route networks can often be found on airline websites) and fix a budget. With most schemes you'll need to buy at least two continental or domestic flights, and remember that booking an open-jaw ticket into Africa to begin with can broaden your options and avoid costly backtracking.

The 'air pass' scheme being run by SAA concentrates on Southern Africa but offers a cheap way into Madagascar. **Virgin's** (www.virgin-atlantic.com; through ticketing is available from North America with Continental) scheme is really limited to Southern Africa, as is the one offered by **Air Namibia** (www.airnamibia.com),

---

SAMPLE AFRICAN AIR FARES

These fares give a rough idea of what to expect:

Continental

- Accra–Addis Ababa US$900
- Cairo–Tunis US$300
- Casablanca–Dakar US$415
- Casablanca–Johannesburg US$630
- Dakar–Accra US$450
- Dakar–Bamako US$135
- Dar es Salaam–Johannesburg US$330
- Douala–Nairobi US$600
- Johannesburg–Maputo US$140
- Nairobi–Dar es Salaam US$200

Domestic

- Bamako–Timbuktu US$165
- Cairo–Aswan US$165
- Dar es Salaam–Zanzibar US$55
- Johannesburg–Cape Town US$75
- Kampala–Murchison Falls National Park US$85
- Nairobi–Lamu US$135

but the **Indian Ocean Pass** (one-way fares cost between US$50 and US$240) run by **Air Seychelles** (www.airseychelles.net), Air Mauritius or Air Austral allows great exploration of the Indian Ocean including Madagascar.

The **oneworld Visit Africa Pass** (www.oneworld .com) is one of two comprehensive schemes (one-way fares costing between US$62 and US$200), but is constrained to East and Southern Africa in the same way as oneworld RTW tickets (basically only short-haul routes from Johannesburg and Nairobi are offered); see p1016.

KLM's **Passport to Africa** (www.klm.com) is a little more like it (one-way fares cost between US$60 and US$250). The scheme hooks into the African network of Kenya Airways (see p1016), enabling links between Nairobi and West, North and Southern Africa as well as a good range of flights in East Africa. However, some routes on Kenya Airways' network (Nairobi to Accra and Nairobi to the Seychelles for example) are not available for some reason.

BICYCLE

Cycling around Africa is predictably tough. Long, hot gruelling journeys are pretty standard, but you'll be in constant close contact with the peoples and environments of the continent, and get to visit small towns and villages that most people just shoot through. In general, the remoter the areas you visit, the better the experience, but you've got to be fully prepared; a tent is standard issue, but remember to ask the village headman where you can pitch a tent when camping near settlements in rural areas.

Touring bikes aren't the best choice for Africa, a continent not exactly blessed with smooth tarmac roads. Adapted mountain bikes are your best bet – their smaller 660mm (26-inch) wheel rims are less likely to be misshaped by rough roads than the 700mm rims of touring bikes, and mountain-bike frames are better suited to the rigours of African travel. Multipurpose hybrid tyres with knobbles on their edges for off-road routes and a smooth central band for on-road cruising are useful in Africa, but your tyre choices (along with the types of components, number of spares and the like) should depend on the terrain you want to tackle.

You may encounter the odd giraffe or zebra while cycling, but motorists are more of a threat to cyclists than rampaging wildlife. Cyclists lie at the bottom of the transport food chain, somewhere below mules, so if you hear a vehicle coming up from behind you be prepared to bail out onto the verges. That said, many of Africa's roads are pretty quiet, but be very cautious about cycling in busy towns and cities.

The heat can be a killer in Africa, so carry at least 4L of water and don't discount the possibility of taking a bus, truck or boat across some sections (bikes can easily be transported, but it might cost you).

The **International Bicycle Fund** (IBF; www.ibike .org) is a one-stop shop for information and recommended reading for cycling in Africa, although some stuff is out of date.

BIKE HIRE

If you haven't got a bike of your own, don't fear: steel steeds can be rented across the continent in tourist areas. Prices vary across Africa; you can pay US$2 to hire a cheap, Chinese bone-shaker or over US$7 for a half-decent mountain bike.

BOAT

Lakes Malawi, Tanganyika and Victoria in Southern and East Africa, as well as Lake Volta (Ghana) and Lake Nasser (Egypt and Sudan), all have ferries operating on them. There are even more fantastic journeys to be had along the Niger, Congo, Nile, Senegal, The Gambia and Zambezi Rivers, to name but a few.

On simple river boats you'll be sat on mountains of cargo, the bows of the craft sitting just above the water line, but on some major river routes large ferries and barges are used. Generally speaking, third class on all ferries is crammed with people, goods and livestock, making it hot and uncomfortable. Happily there is usually a better way: at a price, semiluxurious cabins and with bar and restaurant access can be yours.

Seafaring travellers might be able to hitch a lift on cargo boats down the West African coast (and there's a passenger ferry from Conakry in Guinea to Freetown in Sierra Leone) and on the Red Sea, but this will take some work. Down the east coast there's a little cargo traffic and ferries from Dar es Salaam to Zanzibar, but mostly you'll find small Arabic-style dhow sailing vessels ply the coastal waters (certainly this is the way to get to beautiful isolated islands off Mozambique and Kenya). Similar to dhows are feluccas, the ancient sailing boats of the Nile. Tiny canoes, or pirogues, ferry people across remote waterways where small, diesel-powered (and often unreliable), pontoon-style car ferries are not available. No ferries or boats take vehicles, but you can get a motorbike onto some.

Travelling by boat can be hazardous in Africa. For the most part you can forget about safety regulations and lifeboats, and overloading is very common. To make matters worse, on some ferries third-class passengers are effectively jammed into the hold with little opportunity for escape.

If you're planning lots of boat travel, think about bringing your own life jacket. It won't keep off the sharks, but at least you won't drown.

CAR & MOTORCYCLE

In a few places backpackers often club together to hire a vehicle. However, by and large few backpackers spend much time driving around Africa, and vehicle-bound travellers are going to need much more driver-related information than we can or should offer here. Cheap African travel is much more about gloriously chaotic boats, buses and trains, so this book concentrates on these forms of transport.

Travelling in your own vehicle enables exploration of Africa at your leisure, but it takes some doing. The itineraries described in the Destination Africa chapter (see p15) all avoid the chaos of Congo (Zaïre) and either include the challenge of crossing the Sahara and then toughing it out across Nigeria, Chad and Sudan (the bureaucratic hurdles in these last two states can be just as daunting as the logistical ones) or arriving in Tunisia and crossing Libya (which also takes boxes of paper work) and navigating Lake Nasser, which if you're in a 4WD means hiring an expensive barge to transport your vehicle into Sudan (up to four motorbikes can go on the regular ferry). See all those chapters for further details.

You could well ship a vehicle to Mombasa or Cape Town, but what's the point? You're much better buying something in

South Africa before exploring Southern and East Africa (see p948). Public transport in South Africa is appreciably more expensive than elsewhere, so consequently backpackers buying and selling vehicles are more common. Handily, cars registered in South Africa don't need a *carnet de passage* for travel in Southern Africa, but you will need an international driving licence, your home licence, insurance and registration, and you'll have to get a new set of plates made. The **Automobile Association** (www.aasa.co.za) in South Africa offer vehicle checkups, insurance, travel advice and loads more besides.

ROAD TIPS

■ Watch out for kamikaze cyclists/pedestrians/livestock and massive potholes.

■ Night-time road travel can't be recommended; day-time hazards won't be illuminated.

■ Driving skills are generally nerve-shatteringly poor, especially in rural areas; moderate your speed.

■ Tree branches placed in the roadway signal a stopped vehicle or other problem ahead.

■ Reckless overtaking on blind bends, hills and other areas with poor visibility is standard operating procedure; head-on collisions are common.

■ Keep your fuel tank full and carry a jerry can. Fuel sold on the roadside is unreliable, it's often diluted.

■ Expect frequent stops at checkpoints; police, customs and border officials will want to see all your documentation.

■ Mechanical knowledge and a collection of spares are essential. A winch can get you out of trouble in the rainy season.

■ Desert roads may be just tracks in the sand; red lines drawn on maps are often deceptive. Many roads are impassable in the wet season.

■ Most trips off the beaten track require a 4WD.

■ Motorcycles generally aren't permitted in national parks.

Carnets

A *carnet de passage* (sometimes known as a *triptyque*) is required for many countries in Africa, with the notable exceptions of Morocco, Algeria and Tunisia. A *carnet* guarantees that if you take a vehicle into a country, but don't take it out again, then the organisation that issued it will accept responsibility for payment of import duties (up to 150% of its value). *Carnets* can only be issued by national motoring organisations. They'll only issue the document if they're certain that if ever duties arose you would reimburse them. Essentially this means you have to deposit a bond with a bank or insure yourself against the potential collection of import duties before getting a *carnet*.

You don't need to pre-arrange a *carnet* for many West and Southern African countries (most Southern African countries issue a Temporary Import Permit at the border, which you must buy), but if you're driving through Africa, you're going to need a *carnet*, which sadly doesn't exempt you from the bureaucratic shenanigans encountered at numerous borders. Also consider the following:

- Insurance companies can be a little paranoid in their designation 'war zones' in Africa so watch out; no insurance company will insure against the risks of war, thus denying you a *carnet*.
- If you intend to sell the vehicle at some point, arrangements have to be made with the customs people in the country in which you plan to sell the car for the *carnet* entry to be cancelled.
- If you abandon a vehicle in the Algerian desert, you'll be up for import duties that are twice the value of your car when it was new.

Insurance

Legislation covering third-party insurance varies considerably from one country to another – in some places it isn't even compulsory. Where it is, you generally have to buy insurance at the border (a process that is fraught with corruption), but the liability limits on these policies are often absurdly low by Western standards; this means if you have any bad accidents you'll be in deep shit, so it's a smart plan to insure yourself before heading out. If you're starting from the UK, one company highly recommended

> **ROADBLOCK**
>
> The time taken at army/customs/police roadblocks is one of the biggest variables in much African travel. Sometimes these checkpoints can take two minutes, sometimes 42. Africans often joke it depends on how hungry the officers are feeling.

for insurance policies and for detailed information on *carnets* is **Campbell Irvine Ltd** (☎ 020-7937 6981; www.campbellirvine.com).

Rental

Hiring a vehicle is usually only an option to travellers over 25. This isn't too much of a disaster as for the most part vehicle hire is darned expensive (2WD vehicles commonly cost over US$75 a day in sub-Saharan Africa; you're looking at over US$100 a day for a 4WD) and rental often comes with high insurance excesses and bundles of strings. On a brighter note, car hire in South Africa can be an utter bargain (less than US$20 a day), especially if booked from overseas; start with **Travelocity** (www.travelocity.com), **Expedia** (www.expedia.com) and **Holiday Autos** (www.holiday autos.com). Some vehicles can then be taken into Namibia and Botswana, which is great if you get a group together. Also consider hiring a car for exploring southern Morocco and taking a 4WD to explore Kenya's wildlife parks at your leisure.

HITCHING

Hitching is never entirely safe in any country, and we don't recommend it. But in some parts of Africa it's a recognised form of transport – there is often simply no other option to grabbing lifts on trucks, 4WDs, dumper trucks or whatever vehicle happens to come down the road first. Trucks are the most common vehicles, but you'll generally have to pay. In the more developed countries, such as Ghana, Kenya, Morocco, South Africa, Tunisia and Zimbabwe, where there are plenty of private cars on the road, it's not only possible to hitch for free, but in some cases it's very easy indeed; you may also be offered somewhere to stay the night!

On the other hand, don't expect much in the way of lifts from expatriate workers. Occasionally a nice air-conditioned 4WD will

TRANSPORT

Road Distances (km)

	Abidjan	Accra	Addis Ababa	Asmara	Bamako	Banjul	Bujumbura	Cairo	Cape Town	Conakry	Cotonou	Dakar	Dar es Salaam	Djibouti City	Gaborone	Harare	Kampala
Abidjan (Côte d'Ivoire)	---																
Accra (Ghana)	560	---															
Addis Ababa (Ethiopia)	6710	6150	---														
Asmara (Eritrea)	6510	5950	1060	---													
Bamako (Mali)	1160	1710	6860	6670	---												
Banjul (The Gambia)	2490	3210	8200	8010	1340	---											
Bujumbura (Burundi)	7090	6530	2980	4040	8190	9530	---										
Cairo (Egypt)	7800	7240	3270	2210	7950	9290	6250	---									
Cape Town (South Africa)	8900	8340	8830	9890	9320	10660	6000	12250	---								
Conakry (Guinea)	1700	2260	7780	7580	920	1230	8780	8870	10600	---							
Cotonou (Benin)	910	360	5790	5600	2020	3360	6170	6880	7990	2610	---						
Dakar (Senegal)	2790	3350	8280	8090	1420	300	9610	9290	11420	1530	3360	---					
Dar es Salaam (Tanzania)	8120	7570	2510	3560	9580	10910	2070	5770	5280	10860	8250	11690	---				
Djibouti City (Djibouti)	7620	7060	910	1210	7780	9110	3890	3420	9740	8690	6710	9200	3420	---			
Gaborone (Botswana)	8600	8040	6300	7350	10020	11330	3460	9570	1500	10300	7680	11440	3780	7210	---		
Harare (Zimbabwe)	8220	7670	5150	6200	9330	10670	2310	8560	2530	9920	7310	10750	2630	6060	1150	---	
Kampala (Uganda)	6520	5970	2230	3280	7630	8970	760	5500	6750	8550	5610	9050	1600	3140	4220	3060	---
Khartoum (Sudan)	5550	4990	1720	960	5710	7040	4700	2250	10700	6630	4640	7040	4230	2170	8170	7020	3950
Kigali (Rwanda)	7430	6880	2750	3800	8380	9720	230	6020	6230	9130	6360	9810	2300	3660	3700	2540	520
Lagos (Nigeria)	1030	480	5670	5480	2140	3480	6050	6760	7860	2730	120	3560	8120	6590	7560	7190	5500
Libreville (Gabon)	3580	3030	6760	6020	4690	6030	3830	7300	5480	5280	2670	6120	5900	7670	5180	4800	4540
Lilongwe (Malawi)	8450	7900	4180	5240	8880	10220	1840	7450	3490	10150	7540	10310	1670	5090	2120	970	2590
Lomé (Togo)	760	200	5950	5760	1870	3220	6330	7040	8150	2460	160	3290	8400	6870	7840	7470	5770
Lusaka (Zambia)	7740	7190	4810	5870	8850	10190	1830	8080	3010	9440	6830	10270	1990	5720	1640	480	2580
Malabo (Equatorial Guinea)	2220	1660	6450	5640	3430	4770	4790	6730	6600	4710	2100	5540	6860	6550	6300	5930	4230
Maputo (Mozambique)	9550	9000	6810	7850	10980	12290	4460	10080	1900	11250	8960	12400	3910	7720	960	1650	4710
Maseru (Lesotho)	9290	8740	7000	8700	10720	12030	4380	10270	1170	11000	8380	12140	4200	7910	700	1560	4920
Mbabane (Swaziland)	9310	8760	7020	8070	10740	12050	4300	10290	1090	11020	8400	12160	4130	7930	720	1400	4940
Nairobi (Kenya)	7180	6630	1570	2620	8290	9670	1530	4840	5630	8880	6270	9710	940	2480	4090	2940	660
N'Djaména (Chad)	3010	2450	3700	3500	3170	4500	4300	4780	7820	4080	2100	4500	5150	4610	7770	6610	3550
Niamey (Niger)	1570	1390	5470	5270	1410	2750	6070	6550	9020	2320	1040	2740	6920	6380	8720	8350	5320
Nouakchott (Mauritania)	2800	3360	8510	8320	1650	870	9840	9610	10030	2100	3670	570	10890	9430	11670	10980	9280
Ouagadougou (Burkina Faso)	1070	970	5970	5770	900	2240	6580	7050	9100	1820	1120	2240	7420	6880	8800	8430	5820
Rabat (Morocco)	5000	4910	8660	8470	4350	3580	9510	4590	12450	4810	4470	3270	10110	9580	12160	11570	8510
São Tomé (São Tomé & Príncipe)	3010	2450	7080	6060	3750	5200	4150	7150	5800	4450	1830	5280	6220	6970	5500	5120	4860
Tripoli (Libya)	6260	5090	5410	4350	4940	6280	7560	2140	10800	5850	4560	6080	8410	5560	11020	9860	6160
Tunis (Tunisia)	4960	4860	6170	6760	4420	6180	8310	2900	11840	5710	4440	5330	9160	6320	11780	10620	7560
Windhoek (Namibia)	7430	6880	6460	7520	8540	9890	3480	9730	1460	7510	4900	9970	3635	9740	1160	2030	4230
Yaoundé (Cameroon)	2650	2100	5280	5280	3760	4410	4430	6370	6240	4350	1740	5180	6500	6190	5940	5570	3870

stop for you, but sadly most of the time you'll be left eating their dust.

Travellers who decide to hitch should understand that they are taking a small but potentially serious risk. People who do choose to hitch will be safer if they travel in pairs. Remember that sticking out your thumb in many African countries is an obscene gesture; wave your hand vertically up and down instead.

LOCAL TRANSPORT

Bus travel is the way to go where there's a good network of sealed roads. International bus services are pretty common across the continent, and in the wealthier African states

TRANSPORT

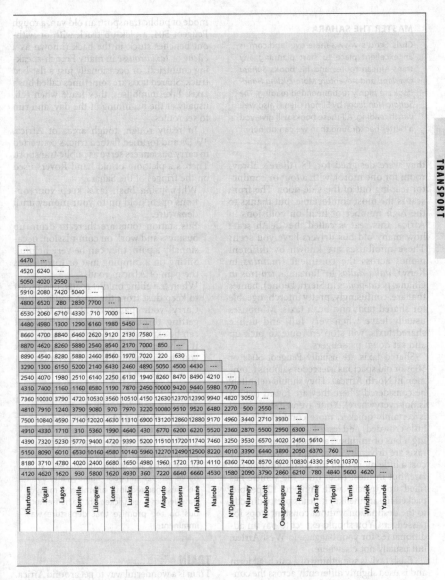

	Khartoum	Kigali	Lagos	Libreville	Lilongwe	Lomé	Lusaka	Malabo	Maputo	Maseru	Mbabane	Nairobi	N'Djaména	Niamey	Nouakchott	Ouagadougou	Rabat	São Tomé	Tripoli	Tunis	Windhoek	Yaoundé
Khartoum	---																					
Kigali	4470	---																				
Lagos	4520	6240	---																			
Libreville	5050	4020	2550	---																		
Lilongwe	5910	2080	7420	5040	---																	
Lomé	4800	6520	280	2830	7700	---																
Lusaka	6530	2060	6710	4330	710	7000	---															
Malabo	4480	4980	1300	1290	6160	1980	5450	---														
Maputo	8660	4700	8840	6460	2620	9120	2130	7580	---													
Maseru	8870	4620	8260	5880	2540	8540	2170	7000	850	---												
Mbabane	8890	4540	8280	5880	2460	8560	1970	7020	220	630	---											
Nairobi	3290	1300	6150	5200	2140	6430	2460	4890	5050	4500	4430	---										
N'Djaména	2540	4070	1980	2510	6140	2250	6130	1940	8260	8470	8490	4210	---									
Niamey	4310	7400	1160	1160	8580	1190	7870	2450	10000	9420	9440	5980	1770	---								
Nouakchott	7360	10030	3790	4720	10530	3560	10510	4150	12630	12370	12390	9940	4820	3050	---							
Ouagadougou	4810	7910	1240	3790	9080	970	7970	3220	10080	9510	9520	6480	2270	500	2550	---						
Rabat	7500	10840	4590	7140	12020	4630	11310	6900	13120	12860	12880	9170	4960	3440	2710	3930	---					
São Tomé	4910	4330	1710	310	5360	1990	4640	430	6770	6200	6220	5520	2360	2870	5500	2950	6300	---				
Tripoli	4390	7320	5230	5770	9400	4720	9390	5200	11510	11720	11740	7460	3250	3530	6570	4020	2450	5610	---			
Tunis	5150	8090	6010	6530	10160	4580	10140	5960	12270	12490	12500	8220	4010	3890	2050	6370	760			---		
Windhoek	8180	3710	4780	4020	2400	6680	1650	4980	1960	1720	1730	4110	6360	7400	8570	6020	10830	4330	9610	10370	---	
Yaoundé	4120	4620	1620	930	5800	1620	4930	360	7220	6640	6660	4530	1580	2090	3790	2860	6210	780	4840	5600	4620	---

you may get a choice of 'luxury' air-con buses with movies (of the trashy Hollywood action variety) on tap, as well as rough old European rejects with nonfunctioning air-con and questionable engineering.

In poorer countries you just get the latter. Out in the sticks, where there are very few or no sealed roads, ancient buses tend to be very crowded with people, livestock and goods; buses tend to stop frequently, either for passengers or because something is broken.

Small minibuses are taking up the slack in many African transport systems. All too often they are driven at breakneck speed and rammed with nearly 30 people, when

MASTER THE SAHARA

Chris Scott's www.sahara-overland.com is an excellent place to start planning any trans-African routes and his books *Sahara Overland* and *Adventure Motorcycling Handbook* are highly recommended reading. *The Sahara Handbook* by Simon Glen is also well worth reading. All these books will give you a better background than we can do here.

they were designed for 18 (there's always room for one more), with a tout or conductor leaning out of the side door. The front seat is the most comfortable, but thanks to the high number of head-on collisions in Africa, this seat is called the 'death seat': how many old bus drivers have you seen? These minibuses are known by different names across the continent (*matatus* in Kenya, *dalla-dallas* in Tanzania, *tro-tros* in Ghana, *poda-podas* in Sierra Leone), names that are, confusingly, pretty interchangeable for shared taxis and bush taxis. Minibuses usually leave when very full, and unlike shared taxis, will stop en route to pick up and set down passengers.

Shared taxis are usually Peugeot 504s or 505s or old spacious Mercedes saloons (common in North Africa). They should definitely be considered where they are found (which is not everywhere). Your average shared taxi is certainly quicker, more comfortable (if a little crowded) and less of a palaver than taking a bus or minibus, although many shared taxis are driven by lunatic speed freaks. They cost a little more than the corresponding bus fare, but in most cases once the vehicle has filled up (usually with nine to 12 people, packed in sardinelike) it heads pretty directly to the destination without constant stops for passengers. You should expect to pay an additional fee for your baggage in West Africa, but usually not elsewhere.

'Bush taxi' is something of a catch-all term and is used slightly differently across the continent. Basically, a bush taxi is a multiperson

WARNING

When travelling around the continent on public transport, remember that time certainly isn't money.

mode of public transport: an old van, a rough Peugeot 504, a pick-up truck with or without benches stuck in the back (known as a *bâché* or *taxi brousse* in many French-speaking countries), or occasionally just a flat-bed truck. Shared taxis are sometimes called bush taxis. Like minibuses, they leave when full, usually at the beginning of the day, and run to set routes.

In really rough, tough areas of Africa, 4WDs and fortified flatbed trucks converted to carry passengers serve as public transport. There's a plethora of old Land Rovers used on the fringes of the Sahara.

- When using bush taxis keep your options open; hold on to your money until departure.
- Bus station touts are there to drum up business and work on commission; occasionally a pain, they can be very helpful.
- Sitting on a camping mat or towel eases the pain of African roads.
- When travelling on dirt roads, use a scarf to keep dust from the nose and mouth.
- Carry your passport at all times – getting through roadblocks without it can be expensive and complicated.
- It's always a good idea to try and book your bus/minibus ticket in advance.

BUS STATIONS   *by Matt Fletcher*

'Stay calm and don't talk to anyone', was the sage advice of a bus station tout as we were ushered through the chaos towards a waiting bus. Slightly overstated perhaps, but inside many of Africa's chaotic, noisy bus stations it's important to keep your nerve, temper and good humour, and don't be press-ganged into anything – many a traveller has been tricked onto a half-empty bus on the promise that departure was imminent.

TRAIN

Train is a wonderful way to get around Africa. Even the shortest rail journey can be a classic experience, full of cultural exchange, amazing landscapes and crazy stations where all kinds of food, drinks and goods are hawked at train windows. Train travel is safer and usually more comfortable than travelling by road, although outside Southern and North Africa the trains are generally slow, often very slow. Long delays while the train or track is repaired en route aren't uncommon. Second-class fares weigh in about the same or less than the corresponding bus fare.

Much more expensive are sleeping compartments and 1st-class or 2nd-class carriages, which take the strain out of long journeys and occasionally allow you to travel in style – Zimbabwe's high-class train carriages are like little wood-panelled museums of colonialism. The flip side is that security on trains can be poor, especially in 3rd class, which, although novel and entertaining at first, soon becomes simply crowded and uncomfortable. Keep an eye on your baggage at all times and lock carriage doors and windows at night.

CLASSIC TRAIN JOURNEYS

- Cairo to Aswan (Egypt)
- Dakar (Senegal) to Bamako (Mali)
- Dar es Salaam (Tanzania) to Kapiri Mposhi (Zambia)
- Harare (Zimbabwe) to Gaborone (Botswana)
- Johannesburg (South Africa) to Maputo (Mozambique)
- Nairobi to Mombasa (Kenya)

TRUCK

In many out-of-the-way places, trucks are the only reliable form of transport. They may primarily carry goods, but drivers are always keen to supplement their income, so

---

RAIN EQUALS PAIN

Main roads throughout North, East and Southern Africa are sealed and in reasonable states of repair. However, in rural areas and much of West and Central Africa, roads range from decent to terrible, with potholes that would swallow a truck, washed-out bridges etc. And things get worse in the rainy season, when many secondary routes become mud baths. In the rainy season, bus and bush taxi fares can double and even triple. For more about climate, see p997.

---

there's always room for paying passengers. Most folks are stuck up on top of the cargo, but a few more expensive spots are often available in the cab.

Sitting high and exposed on top of a truck chugging through the Africa landscape can be a great experience; just take precautions against the sun, dust and uncomfortable cargo! Also remember that trucks are even slower than buses.

On many routes you'll be able to wave down a truck, but lifts can often be arranged the night before departure at the 'truck park' – a compound or dust patch that you'll find in almost every African town of note. 'Fares' are pretty much fixed and expect to pay a little less than an equivalent bus fare, but make sure you're paying what the locals reluctantly cough up; certainly make sure to agree on the price before climbing aboard. If the journey is going to take more than one night or one day, ask about the availability of food and/or water.

Health by Dr Caroline Evans

As long as you stay up to date with your vaccinations and take some basic preventive measures, you'd have to be pretty unlucky to succumb to most of the health hazards covered in this chapter. Africa certainly has an impressive selection of tropical diseases on offer, but you're much more likely to get a bout of diarrhoea (in fact, you should bank on it), a cold or an infected mosquito bite than an exotic disease such as sleeping sickness. When it comes to injuries (as opposed to illness), the most likely reason for needing medical help in Africa is as a result of road accidents – vehicles are rarely well maintained, the roads are potholed and poorly lit, and drink driving is common.

Health care in Africa is varied: it can be excellent in the major cities, which generally have well-trained doctors and nurses, but it is often patchy off the beaten track. Medicine and even sterile dressings and intravenous fluids might need to be purchased from a local pharmacy by patients or their relatives. The standard of dental care is equally variable, and there is an increased risk of hepatitis B and HIV transmission via poorly sterilised equipment. By and large, public hospitals in Africa offer the cheapest service, but will have the least up-to-date equipment and medications; mission hospitals (where donations are the usual form of payment) often have more

reasonable facilities; and private hospitals and clinics are more expensive but tend to have more advanced drugs and equipment and better trained medical staff.

BEFORE YOU GO

A little planning before departure, particularly for pre-existing illnesses, will save you a lot of trouble later. Before a long trip get a check-up from your dentist and from your doctor if you have any regular medication or chronic illness, eg high blood pressure and asthma. You should also organise spare contact lenses and glasses (and take your optical prescription with you); get a first aid and medical kit together; and arrange necessary vaccinations.

It's tempting to leave it all to the last minute – don't! Many vaccines don't take effect until two weeks after you've been immunised, so visit a doctor four to eight weeks before departure. Ask your doctor for an International Certificate of Vaccination (otherwise known as the yellow booklet), which will list all the vaccinations you've received. This is mandatory for the African countries that require proof of yellow fever vaccination upon entry, but it's a good idea to carry it anyway wherever you travel.

Travellers can register with the International Association for Medical Advice to Travellers (IMAT; www.iamat.org). Its website can help travellers to find a doctor who has recognised training. Those heading off to very remote areas might like to do a first aid course (contact the Red Cross or St John's Ambulance) or attend a remote medicine first aid course, such as that offered by the Royal Geographical Society (www.wildernessmedicaltraining.co.uk).

If you are bringing medications with you, carry them in their original containers, clearly labelled. A signed and dated letter from your physician describing all medical conditions and medications, including generic names, is also a good idea. If carrying syringes or needles be sure to have a physician's letter documenting their medical necessity.

How do you go about getting the best possible medical help? It's difficult to say – it really depends on the severity of your illness or injury and the availability of local help. If malaria is suspected, seek medical help as soon as possible or begin self-medicating if you are off the beaten track (see p1032).

INSURANCE
Find out in advance whether your insurance plan will make payments directly to providers or will reimburse you later for overseas health expenditures (in many countries doctors expect payment in cash). It's vital to ensure that your travel insurance will cover the emergency transport to get you to a hospital in a major city, to better medical facilities elsewhere in Africa, or all the way home, by air and with a medical attendant if necessary. Not all insurance covers this, so check the contract carefully. If you need medical help, your insurance company might be able to help locate the nearest hospital or clinic, or you can ask at your hotel. In an emergency, contact your embassy or consulate.

Membership of the African Medical and Research Foundation (Amref; www.amref .org) provides an air evacuation service in medical emergencies in some African countries, as well as air ambulance transfers between medical facilities. Money paid by members for this service provides grass-roots medical assistance for local people.

RECOMMENDED VACCINATIONS
The World Health Organization (www.who .int/en/) recommends that all travellers be covered for diphtheria, tetanus, measles, mumps, rubella and polio, as well as for hepatitis B, regardless of their destination. Planning to travel is a great time to ensure that all routine vaccination cover is complete. The consequences of these diseases can be severe, and outbreaks of them do occur.

According to the Centers for Disease Control and Prevention (www.cdc.gov), the following vaccinations are recommended for all parts of Africa: hepatitis A, hepatitis B, meningococcal meningitis, rabies and typhoid, and boosters for tetanus, diphtheria and measles. Yellow fever is not necessarily recommended for all parts of Africa, although the certificate is an entry requirement for many countries (see p1035).

MEDICAL CHECKLIST
It is a very good idea to carry a medical and first aid kit with you, to help yourself in the case of minor illness or injury. Following is a list of items you should consider packing.

- Antibiotics (prescription only), eg ciprofloxacin (Ciproxin) or norfloxacin (Utinor)
- Antidiarrheal drugs (eg loperamide)
- Acetaminophen (paracetamol) or aspirin
- Anti-inflammatory drugs (eg ibuprofen)
- Antihistamines (for hayfever and allergic reactions)
- Antibacterial ointment (eg Bactroban) for cuts and abrasions (prescription only)
- Anti-malaria pills
- Steroid cream or hydrocortisone cream (for allergic rashes)
- Bandages, gauze, gauze rolls
- Adhesive or paper tape
- Scissors, safety pins, tweezers
- Thermometer
- Pocket knife
- DEET-containing insect repellent for the skin
- Permethrin-containing insect spray for clothing, tents, and bed nets
- Sun block
- Oral rehydration salts
- Iodine tablets (for water purification)
- Syringes and sterile needles
- Acetazolamide (Diamox) for altitude sickness (prescription only)
- Sterile needles, syringes and fluids if travelling to remote areas

If you are travelling through a malarial area – particularly an area where falciparum malaria predominates – consider taking a self-diagnostic kit that can identify malaria in the blood from a finger prick.

ONLINE RESOURCES
There is a wealth of travel health advice on the Internet. For further information, the Lonely Planet website at www.lonelyplanet.com is a good place to start. The World Health Organization publishes a superb book called *International Travel and Health*, which is revised annually and is available online at no cost at www.who.int/ith/. Other websites of general interest are MD Travel Health at www.mdtravelhealth.com, which provides

complete travel health recommendations for every country, updated daily, also at no cost; the Centers for Disease Control and Prevention at www.cdc.gov; and Fit for Travel at www.fitfortravel.scot.nhs.uk, which has up-to-date information about outbreaks and is very user-friendly.

It's also a good idea to consult your government's travel health website before departure, if one is available:

Australia: www.dfat.gov.au/travel/
Canada: www.hc-sc.gc.ca/pphb-dgspsp/tmp-pmv/pub_e.html
UK: www.doh.gov.uk/traveladvice/index.htm
USA: www.cdc.gov/travel/

FURTHER READING

- *A Comprehensive Guide to Wilderness and Travel Medicine* by Eric A Weiss (1998)
- *Healthy Travel* by Jane Wilson-Howarth (1999)
- *Healthy Travel Africa* by Isabelle Young (2000)
- *How to Stay Healthy Abroad* by Richard Dawood (2002)
- *Travel in Health* by Graham Fry (1994)
- *Travel with Children* by Cathy Lanigan & Maureen Wheeler (2004)

IN TRANSIT

DEEP VEIN THROMBOSIS (DVT)

Blood clots can form in the legs during flights, chiefly because of prolonged immobility. This formation of clots is known as deep vein thrombosis (DVT), and the longer the flight, the greater the risk. Although most blood clots are reabsorbed uneventfully, some might break off and travel through the blood vessels to the lungs, where they could cause life-threatening complications.

The chief symptom of DVT is swelling or pain of the foot, ankle or calf, usually but not always on just one side. When a blood clot travels to the lungs, it could cause chest pain and breathing difficulty. Travellers with any of these symptoms should immediately seek medical attention.

To prevent the development of DVT on long flights you should walk about the cabin, perform isometric compressions of the leg muscles (ie contract the leg muscles while sitting), drink plenty of fluids, and avoid alcohol.

JET LAG & MOTION SICKNESS

If you're crossing more than five time zones you could suffer jet lag, resulting in insomnia, fatigue, malaise or nausea. To avoid jet lag try drinking plenty of fluids (nonalcoholic) and eating light meals. Upon arrival, get exposure to natural sunlight and readjust your schedule (for meals, sleep, etc) as soon as possible. Antihistamines such as dimenhydrinate (Dramamine) and meclizine (Antivert, Bonine) are usually the first choice for treating motion sickness. Their main side effect is drowsiness. A herbal alternative is ginger (in the form of ginger tea, biscuits or crystallized ginger), which works like a charm for some people.

IN AFRICA

AVAILABILITY & COST OF HEALTH CARE

Most drugs can be purchased over the counter in Africa, without a prescription. Many drugs for sale in Africa might be ineffective – they might be counterfeit or might not have been stored under the right conditions. The most common examples of counterfeit drugs are malaria tablets and expensive antibiotics, such as ciprofloxacin. Most drugs are available in capital cities, but remote villages will be lucky to have a couple of paracetamol tablets. It is strongly recommended that all drugs for chronic diseases be brought from home. Also, the availability and efficacy of condoms cannot be relied upon – bring all the contraception you'll need. Condoms bought in Africa might not be of the same quality as in Europe or Australia, and they might have been stored in too hot an environment. Keep all condoms as cool as you can.

There is a high risk of contracting HIV from infected blood if you receive a blood transfusion in Africa. The BloodCare Foundation (www.bloodcare.org.uk) is a useful source of safe, screened blood, which can be transported to any part of the world within 24 hours.

The cost of health care might seem very cheap compared to first world countries, but good care and drugs might be not be available. Evacuation to good medical care (within Africa or to your own country) can be very expensive indeed. Unfortunately, adequate – let alone good – health care is available only to very few residents of Africa.

INFECTIOUS DISEASES

It's a formidable list but, as we say, a few precautions go a long way...

Cholera

Cholera is usually only a problem during natural or artificial disasters, eg war, floods or earthquakes, although small outbreaks can also occur at other times. Travellers are rarely affected. It is caused by a bacteria and spread via contaminated drinking water. The main symptom is profuse watery diarrhoea, which causes collapse if fluids are not replaced quickly. An oral cholera vaccine is available in the USA, but it is not particularly effective. Most cases of cholera could be avoided by close attention to good drinking water and by avoiding potentially contaminated food. Treatment is by fluid replacement (orally or via a drip), but sometimes antibiotics are needed. Self-treatment is not advised.

Dengue Fever (Break-bone Fever)

Found in Sudan, Cameroon, Congo (Zaïre), Senegal, Burkina Faso, Guinea, Ethiopia, Djibouti, Somalia, Madagascar, Mozambique and South Africa. Dengue fever is spread through the bite of the mosquito. It causes a feverish illness with headache and muscle pains similar to those experienced with a bad, prolonged, attack of influenza. There might be a rash. Mosquito bites should be avoided whenever possible. Self-treatment: paracetamol and rest.

Diphtheria

Found in all of Africa. Diphtheria is spread through close respiratory contact. It usually causes a temperature and a severe sore throat. Sometimes a membrane forms across the throat, and a tracheostomy is needed to prevent suffocation. Vaccination is recommended for those likely to be in close contact with the local population in infected areas. More important for long stays than for short-term trips. The vaccine is given as an injection alone or with tetanus, and lasts 10 years. Self-treatment: none.

Ebola & Marburg Viruses

Found in Sudan and Uganda. These viruses cause haemorrhagic fever, which is usually fatal. The route of infection is not yet known. It is rare in travellers. Self-treatment: none.

Filariasis

Found in most parts of West, Central, East and Southern Africa, and in Sudan in North Africa. Tiny worms migrating in the lymphatic system cause filariasis. The bite from an infected mosquito spreads the infection. Symptoms include localised itching and swelling of the legs and or genitalia. Treatment is available. Self-treatment: none.

Hepatitis A

Found in all of Africa. Hepatitis A is spread through contaminated food (particularly shellfish) and water. It causes jaundice and, although it is rarely fatal, it can cause prolonged lethargy and delayed recovery. If you've had hepatitis A, you shouldn't drink alcohol for up to six months afterwards, but once you've recovered, there won't be any no long-term problems. The first symptoms include dark urine and a yellow colour to the whites of the eyes. Sometimes a fever and abdominal pain might be present. Hepatitis A vaccine (Avaxim, VAQTA, Havrix) is given as an injection: a single dose will give protection for up to a year, and a booster after a year gives 10-year protection. Hepatitis A and typhoid vaccines can also be given as a single dose vaccine, hepatyrix or viatim. Self-treatment: none.

Hepatitis B

Found in all of Africa. Hepatitis B is spread through infected blood, contaminated needles and sexual intercourse. It can also be spread from an infected mother to the baby during childbirth. It affects the liver, causing jaundice and occasionally liver failure. Most people recover completely, but some people might be chronic carriers of the virus, which could lead eventually to cirrhosis or liver cancer. Those visiting high-risk areas for long periods or at social or occupational risk should be immunised. Many countries now routinely give hepatitis B as part of the routine childhood vaccination. It is given singly or can be given at the same time as hepatitis A (hepatyrix).

A course will give protection for at least five years. It can be given over four weeks or six months. Self-treatment: none.

HIV

Present in all of Africa. Human immunodeficiency virus (or HIV), the virus that causes acquired immune deficiency syndrome (AIDS), is an enormous problem throughout Africa, but is most acutely felt in sub-Saharan Africa. The virus is spread through infected blood and blood products, by sexual intercourse with an infected partner and from an infected mother to her baby during childbirth and breastfeeding. It can be spread through 'blood to blood' contacts, such as with contaminated instruments during medical, dental, acupuncture and other body-piercing procedures, and through sharing used intravenous needles. At present there is no cure; medication that might keep the disease under control is available, but many countries in Africa do not have access to it for their own citizens, let alone for travellers. If you think you might have put yourself at risk of HIV infection, a blood test is necessary; a three-month gap after the exposure and before testing is required to allow antibodies to appear in the blood. Self-treatment: none.

Leishmaniasis

Found in North Africa. This disease spreads through the bite of an infected sandfly. It can cause a slowly growing skin lump or ulcer (the cutaneous form) and sometimes a serious life-threatening fever with anaemia and weight loss. Dogs can also be carriers of the infection. Sandfly bites should be avoided whenever possible. Self-treatment: none.

Leptospirosis

Found in West and Southern Africa; in Chad, Congo and Congo (Zaïre) in Central Africa; in Algeria, Morocco and Sudan in North Africa; and in Ethiopia and Somalia in East Africa. It is spread through the excreta of infected rodents, especially rats. It can cause hepatitis and renal failure, which might be fatal. It is unusual for travellers to be affected unless living in poor sanitary conditions. It causes a fever and sometimes jaundice. Self-treatment: none.

Malaria

Endemic in Central, East, West and Southern Africa; slight risk in North Africa (except for Sudan, where the risk is significant). The risk of malarial transmission at altitudes higher than 2000m is rare. The disease is caused by a parasite in the bloodstream spread via the bite of the female Anopheles mosquito. There are several types of malaria; falciparum malaria being the most dangerous type and the predominant form in Africa. Infection rates vary with season and climate, so check out the situation before departure. Unlike most other diseases regularly encountered by travellers, there is no vaccination against malaria (yet). However, several different drugs are used to prevent malaria, and new ones are in the pipeline. Up-to-date advice from a travel health clinic is essential as some medication is more suitable for some travellers than others. The pattern of drug-resistant malaria is changing rapidly, so what was advised several years ago might no longer be the case.

Malaria can present in several ways. The early stages include headaches, fevers, generalized aches and pains, and malaise, which could be mistaken for flu. Other symptoms can include abdominal pain, diarrhoea and a cough. Anyone who develops a fever in a malarial area should assume malarial infection until a blood test proves negative, even if you have been taking antimalarial medication. If not treated, the next stage could develop within 24 hours, particularly if falciparum malaria is the parasite: jaundice, then reduced consciousness and coma (also known as cerebral malaria) followed by death. Treatment in hospital is essential, and the death rate might still be as high as 10% even in the best intensive-care facilities.

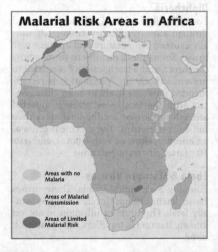

Malarial Risk Areas in Africa

Areas with no Malaria

Areas of Malarial Transmission

Areas of Limited Malarial Risk

THE ANTIMALARIAL A TO D

A Awareness of the risk. No medication is totally effective.

B Bites – avoid at all costs. Sleep in a screened room, use a mosquito spray or coils, sleep under a permethrin-impregnated net at night. Cover up at night with long trousers and long sleeves, preferably with permethrin-treated clothing. Apply appropriate repellent to all areas of exposed skin in the evenings.

C Chemical prevention (ie antimalarial drugs) is usually needed in malarial areas. Expert advice is needed as resistance patterns can change, and new drugs are in development. Not all antimalarial drugs are suitable for everyone, particularly people with depression or epilepsy; children; or pregnant women. Most antimalarial drugs need to be started at least a week in advance and continued for four weeks after the last possible exposure to malaria. No drug is 100% effective, but protection of up to 95% is achievable with most drugs, as long as other measures have been taken.

D Diagnosis. If you have a fever or flu-like illness within a year of travel to a malarial area, malaria is a possibility, and immediate medical attention is necessary.

Many travellers are under the impression that malaria is a mild illness, that treatment is always easy and successful, and that taking antimalarial drugs causes more illness through side effects than actually getting malaria. In Africa, this is unfortunately not true. Side effects depend on the drug being taken. Doxycycline can cause heartburn and indigestion; mefloquine (Larium) can cause anxiety attacks, insomnia and nightmares, and (rarely) severe psychiatric disorders; chloroquine can cause nausea and hair loss; and proguanil can cause mouth ulcers. Side effects are not universal, and can be minimized by taking medication correctly, eg with food. Also, some people should not take a particular anti-malarial drug, eg people with epilepsy should avoid mefloquine, and doxycycline should not be taken by pregnant women or children younger than 12.

People of all ages can contract malaria, and P. falciparum causes the most severe illness. Repeated infections might result eventually in less serious illness. Malaria in pregnancy frequently results in miscarriage or premature labour. Adults who have survived childhood malaria have developed immunity and usually only develop mild cases of malaria; most Western travellers have no immunity at all. Immunity wanes after 18 months of non-exposure, so even if you have had malaria in the past and used to live in a malaria-prone area, you might no longer be immune. One million children die annually from malaria in Africa.

If you decide that you really do not wish to take antimalarial drugs, you must understand the risks, and be obsessive about avoiding mosquito bites. Use nets and insect repellent, and report any fever or flu-like symptoms to a doctor as soon as possible. Some people advocate homeopathic preparations against malaria, such as Demal200, but as yet there is no conclusive evidence that this is effective, and many homeopaths do not recommend their use.

If you are planning a journey through a malarial area, particularly where falciparum malaria predominates, consider taking standby treatment. Emergency standby treatment should be seen as emergency treatment aimed at saving the patient's life and not as routine self-medication. It should be advised only if you will be remote from medical facilities and have been advised about the symptoms of malaria and how to use the medication. Medical advice should be sought as soon as possible to confirm whether the treatment has been successful. The type of standby treatment used will depend on local conditions, such as drug resistance, and on what antimalarial drugs are being used before standby treatment. This is worthwhile because you want to avoid contracting a particularly serious form such as cerebral malaria, which affects the brain and central nervous system and can be fatal in 24 hours. As mentioned on p1032, self-diagnostic kits, which can identify malaria in the blood from a finger prick, are also available in the West.

The risks from malaria to both mother and foetus during pregnancy are considerable. Unless good medical care can be guaranteed, travel throughout Africa when pregnant – particularly to malarial areas – should be discouraged unless essential. Self-treatment: see standby treatment (above) if you are more than 24 hours away from medical help.

Meningococcal Meningitis

Found in all areas of Central, Western and Eastern Africa; only in Sudan in North Africa; and only in Namibia, Malawi, Mozambique and Zambia in Southern Africa. Meningococcal infection is spread through close respiratory contact and is more likely in crowded situations, such as dormitories, buses and clubs. Infection is uncommon in travellers. Vaccination is recommended for long stays and especially towards the end of the dry season, which is normally from June to November. Symptoms include a fever, severe headache, neck stiffness and a red rash. Immediate medical treatment is necessary.

The ACWY vaccine is recommended for all travellers in sub-Saharan Africa. This vaccine is different from the meningococcal meningitis C vaccine given to children and adolescents in some countries, and it is safe to be given both types of vaccine. Self-treatment: none.

Onchocerciasis (River Blindness)

Found in all of Central, West and East Africa; Sudan in North Africa; and Malawi in Southern Africa. This is caused by the larvae of a tiny worm, spread by the bite of a small fly. The earliest sign of infection is intensely itchy, red, sore eyes. Travellers are rarely severely affected. Treatment in a specialised clinic is curative. Self-treatment: none.

Poliomyelitis

Found in all of Africa. Generally spread through contaminated food and water. It is one of the vaccines given in childhood and should be boosted every 10 years, either orally (a drop on the tongue) or as an injection. Polio can be carried asymptomatically (ie showing no symptoms) and could cause a transient fever. In rare cases it causes weakness or paralysis of one or more muscles, which might be permanent. Self-treatment: none.

Rabies

Found in all of Africa. Rabies is spread by receiving the bites or licks of an infected animal on broken skin. It is always fatal once

the clinical symptoms start (which might be up to several months after an infected bite), so post-bite vaccination should be given as soon as possible. Post-bite vaccination (whether or not you've been vaccinated before the bite) prevents the virus from spreading to the central nervous system. Animal handlers should be vaccinated, as should those travelling to remote areas where a reliable source of post-bite vaccine is not available within 24 hours. Three preventive injections are needed over a month. If you have not been vaccinated you will need a course of five injections starting 24 hours or as soon as possible after the injury. If you have been vaccinated, you will need fewer post-bite injections, and have more time to seek medical help. Self-treatment: none.

Rift Valley Fever

Found in Kenya. This fever is spread occasionally via mosquito bites. The symptoms are of a fever and flu-like illness, and is rarely fatal. Self-treatment: none.

Schistosomiasis (Bilharzia)

This disease is spread by flukes (minute worms) that are carried by a species of freshwater snail. The flukes are carried inside the snail, which then sheds them into slow-moving or still water. The parasites penetrate human skin during paddling or swimming and then migrate to the bladder or bowel. They are passed out via stool or urine and could contaminate fresh water, where the cycle starts again. Avoid paddling or swimming in suspect freshwater lakes or slow-running rivers. There might be no symptoms. There might be a transient fever and rash, and advanced cases might have blood in the stool or in the urine. A blood test can detect antibodies if you might have been exposed, and treatment is then possible in specialist travel or infectious disease clinics. If not treated the infection can cause kidney failure or permanent bowel damage. It is not possible for you to infect others. Self-treatment: none.

Schistosomiasis can be a problem in the following countries:
North Africa – Egypt, Sudan
Central Africa – Chad, Congo, Congo (Zaïre), Equatorial Guinea, Gabon, Sao Tome & Principe
West Africa – all countries
East Africa – all countries
Southern Africa – all countries

Tuberculosis (TB)

Found in all of Africa. TB is spread through close respiratory contact and occasionally through infected milk or milk products. BCG vaccination is recommended for those likely to be mixing closely with the local population. It is more important for long stays than for short-term stays. Inoculation with the BCG vaccine is not available in all countries. It is given routinely to many children in developing countries. In some countries, for example the UK, it is given to babies if they will be travelling with their families to areas of high-risk TB, and to previously unvaccinated school-age children if they live in areas of higher TB risk (eg multiethnic immigrant populations). The BCG gives a moderate degree of protection against TB. It causes a small permanent scar at the site of injection, and is usually given in a specialised chest clinic. It is a live vaccine and should not be given to pregnant women or immunocompromised individuals.

TB can be asymptomatic, only being picked up on a routine chest X-ray. Alternatively, it can cause a cough, weight loss or fever, sometimes months or even years after exposure. Self-treatment: none.

Typhoid

Found in all of Africa. This is spread through food or water contaminated by infected human faeces. The first symptom is usually a fever or a pink rash on the abdomen. Sometimes septicaemia (blood poisoning) can occur. A typhoid vaccine (typhim Vi, typherix) will give protection for three years. In some countries, the oral vaccine Vivotif is also available. Antibiotics are usually given as treatment, and death is rare unless septicaemia occurs. Self-treatment: none.

Trypanosomiasis (Sleeping Sickness)

Found in most of West, Central, Eastern and Southern Africa; only in Sudan in North Africa. Spread via the bite of the tsetse fly. It causes a headache, fever and eventually coma. There is an effective treatment. Self-treatment: none.

West Nile Fever

Found in Egypt. This rare disease is spread via mosquito bites. The symptoms are of a fever and flu-like illness; it is very occasionally fatal. Self-treatment: none.

Yellow Fever

Travellers should carry a certificate as evidence of vaccination if they have recently been in an infected country, to avoid any possible difficulties with immigration. For a full list of these countries visit the World Health Organization website (www.who.int/wer/) or the Centers for Disease Control and Prevention website (www.cdc.gov/travel/blusheet.htm). There is always the possibility that a traveller without a legally required, up-to-date certificate will be vaccinated and detained in isolation at the port of arrival for up to 10 days or possibly repatriated.

Yellow fever is spread by infected mosquitoes. Symptoms range from a flu-like illness to severe hepatitis (liver inflammation) jaundice and death. The yellow fever vaccination must be given at a designated clinic and is valid for 10 years. It is a live vaccine and must not be given to immunocompromised or pregnant travellers. Self-treatment: none.

MANDATORY YELLOW FEVER VACCINATION

- **North Africa** – Not mandatory for any areas of North Africa, but Algeria, Libya and Tunisia require evidence of yellow fever vaccination if entering from an infected country. It is recommended for travellers to Sudan, and might be given to unvaccinated travellers leaving the country.

- **Central Africa** – Mandatory in Central African Republic (CAR), Congo, Congo (Zaïre), Equatorial Guinea and Gabon, and recommended in Chad.

- **West Africa** – Mandatory in Benin, Burkina Faso, Cameroon, Côte d'Ivoire, Ghana, Liberia, Mali, Niger, Sao Tome & Principe and Togo, and recommended for The Gambia, Guinea, Guinea-Bissau, Mauritania, Nigeria, Senegal and Sierra Leone.

- **East Africa** – Mandatory in Rwanda; it is advised for Burundi, Ethiopia, Kenya, Somalia, Tanzania and Uganda.

- **Southern Africa** – Not mandatory for entry into any countries of Southern Africa, although it is necessary if entering from an infected country.

Yellow Fever Risk Area

Endemic Zones

TRAVELLERS' DIARRHOEA

Found in all of Africa. Although it's not inevitable that you will get diarrhoea while travelling in Africa, it's certainly very likely. Diarrhoea is the most common travel-related illness – figures suggest that at least half of all travellers to Africa will get diarrhoea at some stage. Sometimes dietary changes, such as increased spices or oils, are the cause.

To help prevent diarrhoea, avoid tap water unless you're sure it's safe to drink (see p1037). You should also only eat fresh fruits or vegetables if cooked or peeled, and be wary of dairy products that might contain unpasteurised milk. Although freshly cooked food can often be a safe option, plates or serving utensils might be dirty, so you should be highly selective when eating food from street vendors (make sure that cooked food is piping hot all the way through).

If you develop diarrhoea, be sure to drink plenty of fluids, preferably an oral rehydration solution containing (lots), and some salt and sugar.

A few loose stools don't require treatment but, if you start having more than four or five stools a day, you should start taking an antibiotic (usually a quinoline drug, such as ciprofloxacin or norfloxacin) and an antidiarrheal agent (such as loperamide) if you are not within easy reach of a toilet. If diarrhoea is bloody, persists for more than 72 hours or is accompanied by fever, shaking chills or severe abdominal pain, you should seek medical attention.

Amoebic Dysentery

Contracted by eating contaminated food and water, amoebic dysentery causes blood and mucus in the faeces. It can be relatively mild and tends to come on gradually, but seek medical advice as soon as possible if you think you have the illness as it won't clear up without treatment (which is with specific antibiotics).

Giardiasis

This, like amoebic dysentery, is also caused by ingesting contaminated food or water. The illness usually appears a week or more after you have been exposed to the offending parasite. Giardiasis might cause only a short-lived bout of typical travellers' diarrhoea, but it can also cause persistent diarrhoea. Ideally, seek medical advice if you suspect you have giardiasis, but if you are in a remote area you could start a course of antibiotics.

ENVIRONMENTAL HAZARDS
Heat Exhaustion

This condition occurs following heavy sweating and excessive fluid loss with inadequate replacement of fluids and salt, and is particularly common in hot climates when taking unaccustomed exercise before full acclimatisation. Symptoms include headache, dizziness and tiredness. Dehydration is already happening by the time you feel thirsty – aim to drink sufficient water to produce pale, diluted urine. Self-treatment: fluid replacement with water and/or fruit juice, and cooling by cold water and fans. The treatment of the salt loss component consists of consuming salty fluids as in soup, and adding a little more table salt to foods than usual.

Heatstroke

Heat exhaustion is a precursor to the much more serious condition of heatstroke. In this case there is damage to the sweating mechanism, with an excessive rise in body temperature; irrational and hyperactive behaviour; and eventually loss of consciousness and death. Rapid cooling by spraying the body with water and fanning is ideal. Emergency fluid and electrolyte replacement is often also required by intravenous drip.

Insect Bites & Stings

Mosquitoes might not always carry malaria or dengue fever, but they (and other insects) can cause irritation and infected bites. To avoid these, take the same precautions as you would for avoiding malaria (see p1032). Use DEET-based insect repellents. Excellent clothing treatments are also available; mosquitos that land on treated clothing will die.

Bee and wasp stings cause real problems only to those who have a severe allergy to the stings (anaphylaxis.) If you are one of these people, make sure you carry an 'epipen' – an adrenaline (epinephrine) injection, which you can give yourself. This could save your life.

Sandflies are found around the Mediterranean beaches. They usually only cause a nasty itchy bite but can carry a rare skin disorder called cutaneous leishmaniasis (see p1032). Prevention of bites with DEET-based repellents is sensible.

Scorpions are frequently found in arid or dry climates. They can cause a painful bite that is sometimes life-threatening. If bitten by a scorpion, take a painkiller. Medical treatment should be sought if collapse occurs.

Bed bugs are often found in hostels and cheap hotels. They lead to very itchy, lumpy bites. Spraying the mattress with crawling insect killer after changing bedding will get rid of them.

Scabies is also frequently found in cheap accommodation. These tiny mites live in the skin, particularly between the fingers. They cause an intensely itchy rash. The itch is easily treated with malathion and permethrin lotion from a pharmacy; other members of the household also need treating to avoid spreading scabies, even if they do not show any symptoms.

Snake Bites

Basically, avoid getting bitten! Do not walk barefoot, or stick your hand into holes or cracks. However, 50% of those bitten by venomous snakes are not actually injected with poison (envenomed). If bitten by a snake, do not panic. Immobilise the bitten limb with a splint (such as a stick) and apply a bandage over the site, with firm pressure – similar to bandaging a sprain. Do not apply a tourniquet, or cut or suck the bite. Get the victim to medical help as soon as possible, when antivenom can be given if needed.

Water

Never drink tap water unless it has been boiled, filtered or chemically disinfected (such as with iodine tablets), except in South Africa. Never drink from streams, rivers and lakes. It's also best to avoid drinking from pumps and wells –some do bring pure water to the surface, but the presence of animals can still contaminate supplies.

Traditional Medicine

At least 80% of the African population relies on traditional medicine, either because they can't afford conventional Western-style medicine, because of prevailing cultural attitudes and beliefs, or simply because (in some cases) it works. It might also be because there's often no other choice: a World Health Organization survey found that although there was only one medical doctor for every 50,000 people in Mozambique, there was a traditional healer for every 200 people.

Although some African remedies seem to work on malaria, sickle cell anaemia, high blood pressure and some AIDS symptoms, most African healers learn their art by apprenticeship, so education (and consequently application of knowledge) is inconsistent and unregulated. Conventionally trained physicians in South Africa, for example, angrily describe how their AIDS patients die of kidney failure because a *sangoma* (traditional healer) has given them an enema containing an essence made from powerful roots. Likewise, when traditional healers administer 'injections' with porcupine quills, knives or dirty razor blades, diseases are often spread or created rather than cured.

Rather than attempting to stamp out traditional practices, or simply pretend they aren't happening, a positive first step taken by some African countries is the regulation of traditional medicine by creating healers' associations and offering courses on such topics as sanitary practices. Although it remains unlikely that even a basic level of conventional Western-style medicine will ever be made available to all the people of Africa (even though the cost of doing so is less than the annual military budget of some Western countries), traditional medicine will almost certainly continue to be practised widely throughout the continent.

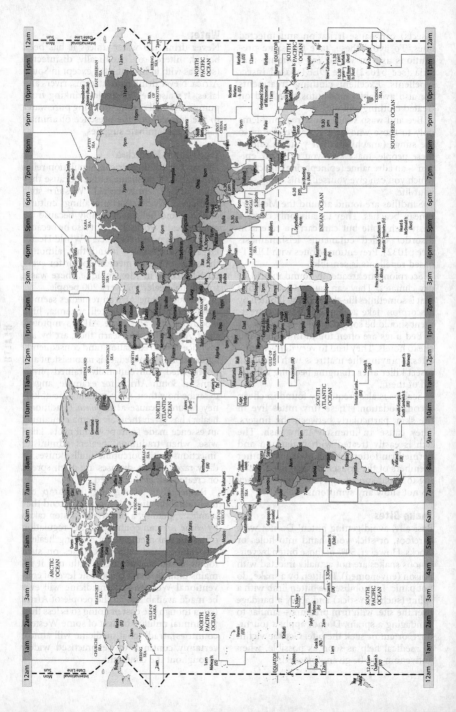

Language

CONTENTS

Across Africa, the region's myriad ethnic groups speak several hundred local languages, many subdivided into numerous distinct dialects. The people of Nigeria, for example, speak no less than 350 languages and dialects, while even tiny Guinea-Bissau (population just over one million) has around 20 languages.

Consequently, common languages are essential, and several are used. These may be the language of the largest group in a particular area or country, such as Hausa, or a language which has spread beyond its original geographical boundaries due to trade, such as Swahili. The former colonial languages (French, English and Portuguese) also serve well as common languages. In some areas, the common tongue is a creole – a combination of African and European languages.

WHO SPEAKS WHAT WHERE?
Algeria
Main languages: Arabic, French and Berber. Very little English is spoken.

Angola
Official language: Portuguese (first language of much of the population, especially in Luanda). At least some Portuguese is needed to get by in Angola. In the villages various Bantu languages predominate.

Benin
Official language: French, but many in the tourist industry speak reasonable English. Fon is the main indigenous language in the south; Bariba and Dendi are spoken in the north.

Botswana
Official language: English. Setswana is the principal spoken language (first language of more than 90% of the population).

Burkina Faso
Official language: French, spoken by most Burkinabé. Major African languages are Moré, Dioula, Gourma, Fulfuldé and Lobiri.

Burundi
Official languages: Kirundi and French, although Swahili can be useful. English isn't common, but a few people in Bujumbura speak it.

Cameroon
Official languages: French and English, but English is rarely heard, except in larger towns in the far west of the country.

Central African Republic (CAR)
Official language: French, though Sango is known as the national language and is spoken by most people. The CAR has over 100 languages. Originally a trading language along the Oubangui River, Sango is, however, the mother tongue of few. Very little English is spoken.

Chad
Official languages: French and (since 1996) Arabic, but there are more than 120 local languages. The main ones include Sara, spoken primarily in the south, and Turku (often referred to as Chadian Arabic), in the north.

Congo
Official language: French. The main African languages are Lingala and Munukutuba.

Congo (Zaïre)

Official languages: French (official language of government); and Lingala, spoken in Kinshasa and along the rivers (official language of the armed forces). Other major spoken languages are Swahili, Tshiluba and Kikongo.

Côte d'Ivoire

Official language: French. Major African languages include Baoulé and Agni in the south; Mandé, Malinké and Senoufo in the north; and Dioula, the language of trade.

Djibouti

Official languages: French and Arabic. Afar and Somali are also spoken. Few speak English outside Djibouti town.

Egypt

Official language: Arabic. English and, to a lesser extent, French are widely understood in the cities.

Equatorial Guinea

Official languages: Spanish and French. Local languages such as Fang and Bubi are widely spoken, as is Pidgin English on Bioko Island.

Eritrea

Official languages: Arabic (common in coastal areas) and Tigrinya (used widely in the highlands). Each of the nine ethnic groups speaks its own language: Afar, Bilen, To Bedawi, Kunama, Nara, Arabic, Saho, Tigre and Tigrinya. Amharic, a legacy of Ethiopian rule, is also still widely spoken. English is also surprisingly useful, not least because during the war most families had at least one member abroad, and most returnees from Western Europe or North America speak it fluently.

Ethiopia

Official languages: Amharic (spoken predominantly in the central highlands and to the north), Tigrinya (spoken in northern areas) and Oromo (spoken in the south). Amharic is probably understood in most of the main cities (see the Amharic section on p1046). English is the language of schools and many people manage more than a smattering. Arabic is spoken in parts of the east and west.

In Ethiopia there are almost as many indigenous languages (from a variety of families: Semitic, Hamitic, Nilotic and Omotic) as there are peoples.

Gabon

Official language: French. In the interior there are many local languages spoken, including Fang, Bandgabi and Bapunu.

The Gambia

Official language: English. Indigenous languages include Wolof (the main trading language), Mandinka and Fulani.

Ghana

Official language: English. There are 75 or so African languages and dialects spoken in Ghana, including Akan, Mole-Dagbani, Twi and Ga.

Guinea

Official language: French, widely spoken in all large towns and the less remote rural areas. The main indigenous languages are Susu, Malinké and Fula (Pulaar).

Guinea-Bissau

Official language: Portuguese, but Kriolu is the common tongue. Many other regional indigenous languages are spoken (mainly Wolof) and French is widely understood.

Kenya

Official languages: English and Swahili. There are many major tribal languages, including Kikuyu, Luhia, Luo and Kikamba. Although English is spoken by most people in Kenya, a working knowledge of Swahili is useful, especially outside urban areas and in remote parts of the country (see the Swahili section on p1048).

Lesotho

Official languages: South Sotho and English. (For all-important greetings, see the South Sotho section on p1048).

Liberia

Official language: English. Major indigenous languages include Kpelle, Bassa and Kru.

Libya

Official language: Arabic. All road, shop and other public signs are in Arabic, so some working knowledge of the language is extremely useful. Outside Tripoli and Benghazi, where some English or Italian is spoken, few people speak a foreign language. The exceptions are Ghadhames and Ghat, where some older people speak French.

Madagascar

Official languages: Malagasy and French. Malagasy is the everyday spoken language while French is often used for literary, business and administrative purposes, and in more upmarket sectors of the tourism industry. English is taught in schools, but it's uncommon outside the middle to top-range hotels and restaurants in Tana, Nosy Be and Île Sainte Marie. (For a few key Malagasy phrases, see the Malagasy section on p1048.)

Malawi

Official language: English – very widely spoken. All the different ethnic groups in Malawi also have their own language or dialect. The Chewa are the dominant group and Chichewa is the national language and is widely used throughout the country as a common tongue.

Mali

Official language: French, but Bambara is the most widely spoken tongue (especially south of Mopti). Other indigenous languages spoken in various areas of Mali are Fulfuldé, Songhaï and Tamashek (Tuareg language).

The Dogon language is spoken in a relatively compact area, but there are 62 dialects. Sanga is a major one, but even this is not understood by many Dogon.

Mauritania

Official language: Arabic. The Moors speak an Arabic dialect known as Hassaniya, whereas the black Africans of the south speak Pulaar, Soninké and Wolof.

Morocco

Official language: Arabic. Berber and French are widely spoken. Spanish is spoken in former Spanish-held territory (particularly the north) and some English is spoken in the main tourist centres. Arabic and French are taught in schools and French is important in university education and commerce. Moroccan Arabic and French

are generally the only languages heard beyond the main cities and tourist spots.

Darija (spoken Moroccan Arabic) is different from the Arabic you hear in the Middle East. Various Berber dialects are spoken in the countryside, particularly in the mountains. For more detail, get a copy of Lonely Planet's *Moroccan Arabic phrasebook*.

Mozambique

Official language: Portuguese. There are numerous indigenous languages, all belonging to the Bantu language family. Outside southern resorts and areas bordering Zimbabwe and Malawi, English is not widely spoken.

Namibia

Official language: English (since independence in 1990), but the most widely used European language is Afrikaans (first language of over 100,000 Namibians of diverse ethnic backgrounds). German is also widely spoken and, in the far north, many people also speak Portuguese.

As a first language, most Namibians speak either a Bantu language, such as Owambo, Kavango, Herero and Caprivian, or a Khoisan language, including Khoikhoi (Nama), Damara and San dialects, which are characterised by 'click' elements that make them difficult to learn and pronounce for non-native speakers.

Niger

Official language: French. Each ethnic group has its own customs and language, but the main spoken languages are Hausa (see the Hausa section on p1047), Djerma (Jer-mah), Fulani and Tamashek (Tuareg language).

Nigeria

Official languages: English and French (the language of commerce for most of the region). The main indigenous languages are Hausa (see the Hausa section on p1047), Yoruba, Igbo, Edo and Efik.

Rwanda

Official languages: French, English and Kinyarwanda (the most widely spoken tongue). Some French will be enough in most areas, though English is not far behind as the major European language, especially in Kigali. Swahili is also useful in some areas.

São Tomé & Príncipe
Official language: Portuguese. Forro, a creole language, is widely spoken.

Senegal
Official language: French. Many people speak at least two indigenous languages. Some of the native tongues spoken as a first language by a significant proportion of people are: Diola (also called Jola), in the Casamance region; Fulfulde/Pulaar, mainly in the north and south; Futa Fula (also known as Fuuta Jalon), in the east; Malinké, in the northeast; Mandinka, in the south; Wolof (spelt *ouolof* in French), in central areas, north and east of Dakar, and along the coast. Wolof is the most widely spoken African language.

Sierra Leone
Official language: English. There are also about 14 indigenous tribal languages, including Mende, Limba and Temne. The usual spoken language is Krio, which has its roots in English and various African tongues.

Somalia
Official language: Somali. English is widely used in the north but Italian dominates in the south. Written Somali is a very new invention and there are many variations – Hamar and Xamar, for example, both refer to Mogadishu (which can also be spelled Moqdishu). Somali is written using the Roman alphabet. Arabic script is only used for religious purposes.

South Africa
Official languages (in order of spoken predominance): Zulu, Xhosa, Afrikaans, Pedi, English, Tswana, Sotho, Tsonga, Swati, Venda and Ndebele. Most people speak Afrikaans, English, or both, as well as their mother tongue. Xhosa and Zulu both use a variety of 'clicks', which are very hard to reproduce without practice.

Sudan
Official language: Arabic (the lingua franca spoken almost everywhere and the mother tongue of about half the population, mainly in the north and centre). There are more than 100 languages spoken in Sudan. Nilotic and Nilo-Hamitic languages are spoken in the south, and Darfur is spoken in the western provinces of the same name. English is also widely spoken.

Swaziland
Official languages: Swati and English. Swati is similar to Zulu (see the Swati section on p1050).

Tanzania
Official languages: Swahili and English. Many local African languages are also spoken. Outside the larger towns and cities, fewer people speak English than in comparable areas of Kenya, so a smattering of Swahili is useful (see the Swahili section on p1048).

Togo
Official language: French. Many people working in the tourism industry in Lomé also speak passable English. The main indigenous languages are Ewé, Kabyé and Mina.

Tunisia
Official language: Arabic (the language of education and government), but almost everyone speaks some French. English speakers are uncommon outside the main tourist centres.

Uganda
Official language: English (spoken by most Ugandans). The other major languages are Luganda and Swahili (see the Swahili section on p1048), though the latter isn't spoken much in Kampala.

Zambia
Official language: English (widely spoken across the country, even in quite remote areas). There are about 35 different ethnic groups, all with their own language. Main groups and languages include Bemba (in the north and centre), Tonga (in the south), Nyanja (in the east) and Lozi (in the west).

Zimbabwe
Official language: English. Most people speak Shona or Ndebele as a first language.

EUROPEAN LANGUAGES

FRENCH

Visitors to West and Central Africa will find that a working knowledge of French is more or less essential. English is not widely spoken and you'll find yourself struggling if you don't have at least the basics in French. There are a number of other countries – such as Algeria, Burundi, Djibouti, Rwanda and Tunisia, where French comes in very handy.

African French varies quite widely from 'pure' French, and while you should have no difficulty making yourself understood, you may find it hard to understand other people.

Though we have used the polite verb form *vous* in the following phrase list, the informal form *tu* is used much more commonly in Africa; you'll hear *s'il te plaît* more than *s'il vous plaît*, which may be considered impolite in France unless spoken between good friends. If in doubt in Africa (when dealing with police, border officials or older people) it's always safer to use the polite *vous* form. If both forms are given in this guide the polite form is indicated by 'pol', the informal by 'inf'.

For a more in-depth guide to the language, pick up a copy of Lonely Planet's *French phrasebook*.

Greetings & Civilities

Hello/Good morning.	*Bonjour/Salut.* (pol/inf)
Good evening.	*Bonsoir.*
Goodbye.	*Au revoir.* (pol)
	Salut or *A bientôt.* (inf)
Good night.	*Bonne nuit.*
How are you?	*Comment allez-vous?* (pol)
	Ça va? (inf)
Fine, thanks.	*Bien, merci.*
Yes.	*Oui.*
No.	*Non.*
Please.	*S'il vous plaît.* (pol)
	S'il te plaît. (inf)
Thank you (very much).	*Merci (beaucoup).*
You're welcome.	*De rien.*
Excuse me.	*Excusez-moi.*
I'm sorry.	*Pardon.*
What's your name?	*Comment vous appelez-vous?* (pol)
	Comment tu t'appelles? (inf)
My name is ...	*Je m'appelle ...*

Useful Words & Phrases

Do you speak English?	*Parlez-vous anglais?*
I understand.	*Je comprends.*
I don't understand.	*Je ne comprends pas.*
I want to go to ...	*Je veux aller à ...*

When does (the) ... leave/arrive?	*À quelle heure part/arrive ...?*
bus	*le bus*
train	*le train*
boat	*le bateau*

Where is ...?	*Où est ...?*
a bank	*une banque*
the market	*le marché*
the post office	*la poste*
a public telephone	*une cabine téléphonique*

Where are the toilets?	*Où sont les toilettes?*
Go straight ahead.	*Continuez tout droit.*
Turn left.	*Tournez à gauche.*
Turn right.	*Tournez à droite.*
Do you have any rooms available?	*Avez-vous des chambres libres?*
I'd like a single/ double room.	*Je cherche une chambre (à un lit/ double).*
How much is it?	*Ça coûte combien?*

Health

Where's the (nearest) ...?	*Où est ... (le/la plus proche)?*
hospital	*l'hôpital*
doctor	*le médecin*
pharmacy	*la pharmacie*

I feel dizzy.	*J'ai des vertiges.*
I feel nauseaous.	*J'ai des nausées.*
diarrhoea	*la diarrhée*
medicine	*le médicament*
sanitary napkins	*des serviettes hygiéniques*

Food & Drink

breakfast	*le petit déjeuner*
lunch	*le déjeuner*
dinner	*le dîner*
market	*un marché*
banana	*banane*
beer	*bière*
the bill	*l'addition*
bread	*pain*
chicken	*poulet*
fish	*poisson*
meat	*viande*
potato	*pomme de terre*
vegetables	*légumes*

Numbers

0	*zéro*
1	*un*
2	*deux*
3	*trois*
4	*quatre*
5	*cinq*
6	*six*
7	*sept*
8	*huit*
9	*neuf*
10	*dix*
11	*onze*
12	*douze*
13	*treize*
14	*quatorze*
15	*quinze*
16	*seize*
17	*dix-sept*
18	*dix-huit*
19	*dix-neuf*
20	*vingt*
21	*vingt-et-un*
22	*vingt-deux*
30	*trente*
40	*quarante*
50	*cinquante*
60	*soixante*
70	*soixante-dix*
75	*soixante-quinze*
80	*quatre-vingts*
90	*quatre-vingt-quinze*
95	*quatre-vingt-dix*
100	*cent*
200	*deux cents*
1000	*mille*
2000	*deux mille*
one million	*un million*

PORTUGUESE

English isn't widely spoken in African countries where Portuguese had colonial links (Angola, Guinea-Bissau and Mozambique), so at least some Portuguese is essential; in Mozambique it is still the official language.

Note that Portuguese uses masculine and feminine word endings – usually '-o' and '-a' respectively – to say 'thank you'; a man will therefore say *obrigado*, a woman, *obrigada*. These differences are noted in this guide by the abbreviations 'm' and 'f' respectively.

Greetings & Civilities

Good morning.	*Bom dia.*
Good afternoon.	*Boa tarde.*
Good evening.	*Boa noite.*
Goodbye.	*Adeus/Ciao.*
How are you?	*Como está?*
I'm fine, thank you.	*Estou bem/Muito bem, obrigado/a.* (m/f)
What's your name?	*Como se chama?*
My name is ...	*Chamo-me ...*
Please.	*Por favor.*
Thank you.	*Obrigado/a.* (m/f)
Excuse me. (sorry)	*Desculpe.*
Excuse me, can you help me?	*Desculpe, podia ajudar-me?*

Useful Words & Phrases

Yes.	*Sim.*
No.	*Não.*
I don't understand.	*Não compreendo/Não entendo.*
I don't speak Portuguese.	*Não falo Português.*
How much is it?	*Quanto custa?*
cheap	*barato*
expensive	*caro*
very/too expensive	*muito caro*
When does the ... leave/arrive?	*A que hora chega/parte o ...?*
boat	*barco*
bus	*bus/machibombo*
converted passenger truck	*chapa/chapa-cem*
plane	*avião*
train	*comboio*
airport	*aeroporto*
stop (eg bus)	*paragem*
station	*estação*
ticket	*bilhete*

Where is ...?	Onde é ...?
the bank	o banco
a hotel	um hotel/uma pousada
the post office	o correio
a public phone	um telefone público
the police	a polícia
the tourist office	o posto de turismo

How do I get to ...?	Como é que se vai para ...?
Is it near/far?	É perto/longe?
Go straight ahead.	Vá em frente.
on the left	à esquerda
on the right	à direita

Do you have a ... available?	Tem algum ... disponivel?
single room	quarto simples
double room	quarto duplo
double bed room	quarto com cama de casal

toilet/bathroom	casa da banho
shower	chuveiro
bucket of (hot) water	balde de agua (quente)

Food & Drink

breakfast	pequeno almoço
lunch	almoço
dinner	jantar
market	mercado
menu (list)	cardápio
menu (a set meal)	menu
the bill	quanto
beer	cerveja
tea	chá
water	aqua
mineral water	agua mineral
bread	pão
chicken	frango/galinha
eggs	ovos
fish	peixe
fruit	fruta
potatoes	batata
meat	carne
rice	arroz
salt	sal
steak	bifel
sugar	açucar
vegetables	legumes

I'm a vegetarian.	Sou vegetariano/a. (m/f)

Health

I'm sick.	Estou doente.
I've been vomiting.	Tenho estado a vomitar.

I feel ...	Estou ...
feverish	com febre
nauseous	com naúseas

Where's the (nearest) ...?	Onde fica ... (mais próximo/a)?
doctor	o médico
hospital	o hospital
pharmacy	a farmácia

condoms	preservativos
sanitary napkins	pensos higiénicos
sunblock	protector do sol

Numbers

1	um/uma
2	dois/duas
3	três
4	quatro
5	cinco
6	seis
7	sete
8	oito
9	nove
10	dez
11	onze
12	doze
13	treze
14	catorze
15	quinze
16	dezasseis
17	dezassete
18	dezoito
19	dezanove
20	vinte
21	vinte e um/uma
30	trinta
40	quarenta
50	cinquenta
60	sessenta
70	setenta
80	oitenta
90	noventa
100	cem
1000	mil

EMERGENCIES – PORTUGUESE	
Help!	Socorro!
Call a doctor!	Chame um médico!
Call the police!	Chame a polícia!
Go away!	Deixe-me em paz!/
	Vai-te embora! (inf)
I'm lost.	Estou perdido/a.

LANGUAGE

REGIONAL LANGUAGES

See the 'Who Speaks What Where?' section on p1039 for information on the countries where these regional and indigenous languages are spoken.

AMHARIC

Amharic word endings vary according to the gender and number of people you're speaking to, indicated in this guide by the abbreviations 'm' (to a male) and 'f' (to a female). Note that **gn** is always pronounced as the 'ni' in 'onion'. For a more comprehensive guide to the language, get a copy of Lonely Planet's *Ethiopian Amharic* phrasebook.

Greetings & Civilities

Hello/Greetings/ Goodbye.	*teanastellen*
How are you?	*dehna neh?* (m)/*dehna nesh?* (f)
(response)	*dehna*
OK.	*eshi*
Please.	*ebakeh* (m)/*ebakesh* (f)
	ebakon (polite)
Thank you.	*amesegenallo*

Useful Words & Phrases

Yes.	*owo* (very breathy)
No. (not true)	*ie*
No. (not available)	*yellem*
I want ...	*afellegallo*
I don't want ...	*alfellegem*
How much is it?	*sint no wagaw?*
That's expensive.	*wedd no*
Do you have anything cheaper?	*rekash alle?*
What is it?	*minduno?*
One tea please.	*ante shai ebakeh* (m)/ *ante shai ebakesh* (f)
tomorrow	*nege*
tomorrow morning	*nege twat*

Food & Drink

I'm vegetarian	*sega albellam*
banana	*mooz*
bread	*dabbo*
bread-like pancake	*injera*
egg	*encular*
raw minced meat & herbs	*kitfo*
saucy stew	*wat*
vegetables with bread	*atkilt-b-dabbo*

water	*wuha*
soda water	*ambo wuha*
tea	*shai*
coffee	*buna*
milk	*wetet*

Getting Around

left	*gra*
right	*kagn*
main road	*wanna menged*
Where are you going?	*wadyet te-hedaleh?*
Where is the ...	*yeat ... no?*
Which is the road to ...?	*ye ... mengad yet no?*

Numbers

1	*and*	21	*haya and*
2	*hulett*	25	*haya amist*
3	*sost*	30	*salassa*
4	*arat*	31	*salassa and*
5	*amest*	40	*arba*
6	*sedest*	50	*hamsa*
7	*sebat*	60	*selsa*
8	*sement*	70	*seba*
9	*zeteny*	80	*semanya*
10	*asser*	90	*zetena*
11	*assra and*	100	*meto*
20	*haya*	1000	*and shi*

ARABIC

While written Arabic (MSA or Modern Standard Arabic) is universally understood by literate speakers of all Arabic dialects, the spoken language is subject to considerable variation. For example, 'camel' is gamal in Egypt but jamal in Sudan. The words and phrases included here should be understood in most of the Arabic-speaking regions covered in this book. For a more detailed guide to Arabic for travellers, get a copy of Lonely Planet's *Egyptian Arabic* and *Moroccan Arabic* phrasebooks. Even if you don't have the time or inclination to learn Arabic, you need to be familiar with at least some of the numerals.

Useful Words & Phrases

Greetings.	*salaam aleikum*
Greetings. (response)	*wa aleikum as-salaam*
Thank you.	*shukran*
You're welcome.	*afwaan*
madam (polite)	*lalla*
sir (polite)	*mansoor*
sir (very polite)	*sidi*
I don't speak Arabic.	*ma-atkallam arabi*

Do you speak ...?	*tatkallam ...?*
	wash kt'aref ...? (in Morocco)
English	*ingleezi*
French	*faransi*

How much?	*kem?*
Yes.	*naam*
No.	*ley*
camel	*jamal*
market	*souq*
mountain	*jebel*
river bed	*oued/wadi*
sand	*ramia* (*ramla* in Egypt and Sudan)
fork	*mtaka*
knife	*mus* (*sekkin* in Egypt and Sudan)
spoon	*tobsi*
bread	*khobz* (*a'aish* in Egypt and Sudan)
coffee	*gahwa*
tea	*atai*
water	*mey/ma*

HAUSA

Dialectal variation in Hausa is not extreme so the phrases included in this language guide will be universally understood, and will prove useful in Benin, Burkina Faso, Côte d'Ivoire, Gabon, Niger, Nigeria and northern Ghana (where it is the principal language of trade). Some knowledge of numbers in Hausa is especially useful.

The Hausa greetings don't translate strictly into their English equivalents. *Ranka/Ranki ya dade* means 'may your life be long' and is said to seniors or those deserving of respect. *Sannu* is the universal greeting and means 'gently'.

Greetings & Civilities

Greetings. (polite)	*ranka ya dade* (*ranki* for women)
Hello. (greeting)	*sannu*
Hello. (response)	*yauwaa sannu*
Good morning.	*eenaa kwanaa*
(response)	*lapeeyaloh*
Good evening.	*eenaa eenee*
(response)	*lapeeyaloh*
Goodbye.	*sai wani lookachi*
Please.	*don allaah*
Thank you.	*naa goodee*
Sorry, pardon.	*yi hakurii, ban ji ba*
Yes.	*ii*
No.	*aa'aa*
How are you?	*inaa gajiyaa?*
I'm fine.	*baa gajiyaa*

What's your name?	*yaayaa suunanka?*
My name is ...	*suunaanaa ...*
Can you help me, please?	*don allaah, koo zaa ka taimakee ni?*

Useful Words & Phrases

Do you speak English/ French?	*kanaa jin ingiliishii/ faransancii?*
I speak only English.	*inaa jin ingiliishii kawai*
I understand.	*naa gaanee*
I don't understand.	*ban gaanee ba*
Where is ...?	*inaa ...?*
Is it far ...?	*da niisaa ...?*
straight ahead	*miiKee sambal*
left	*hagu*
right	*daama*
How much is this?	*nawa nee wannan?*
That's too expensive.	*akwai tsaadaa ga wannan*
Leave me alone!	*tafi can!*

Food & Drink

food	*abinchi*
chicken	*dantsako*
cola nut	*goro*
eggs	*kwai*
fish	*kifi*
meat	*nama*
milk	*madara*
okra	*guro*
onions	*albasa*
rice	*shinkafa*
salt	*gishiri*
water	*ruwa*

Numbers

1	*d'aya*
2	*biyu*
3	*uku*
4	*hud'u*
5	*biyar*
6	*shida*
7	*bakwai*
8	*takwas*
9	*tara*
10	*gooma*
11	*gooma shaa d'aya*
12	*gooma shaa biyu*
13	*gooma shaa uku*
14	*gooma shaa hud'u*
15	*gooma shaa biyar*
16	*gooma shaa shida*
17	*gooma shaa bakwai*
18	*gooma shaa takwas*
19	*gooma shaa tara*

LANGUAGE

20	ashirin
30	talaatin
40	arba'in
50	hamsin
60	sittin
70	saba'in
80	tamaanin
90	casa'in
100	d'arii
1000	dubuu

one million	miliyan d'aya

MALAGASY

Good day. (any time)	Salama.
Hello. (How are you?)	Manao ahoana ianao.
Thank you (very much).	Misaotra (indrindra).
I'm good/bad.	Tsara/Ratsy.
I'm fine.	Salama tsara aho.
Very well, thank you.	Tsara fa misaotra.
Goodbye.	Veloma/Manorapihaona.
See you soon.	Vetivety.
See you later.	Mandram pihaona.
My name is ...	... no anarako.
Cheers!	Ho ela velona!
Bon voyage!	Tongava soa!
Yes.	Eny/Eka.
No.	Tsia.

SOUTH SOTHO

Greetings are an important social ritual in Lesotho, so it's useful to know some. If you think the person you are greeting is older than you then use mother/father; if younger use sister/brother.

Greetings father.	Lumela ntate.
Peace father.	Khotso ntate.
Greetings mother.	Lumela 'me.
Peace mother.	Khotso 'me.
Greetings brother.	Lumela abuti.
Peace brother.	Khotso abuti.
Greetings sister.	Lumela ausi.
Peace sister.	Khotso ausi.
Thank you.	Kea leboha.

There are three ways to say 'How are you?' (the first in each pair applies to one person, the second to a group of people). All the questions and responses listed below are interchangeable.

How do you live?	O phela joang/Le phela joang?
How did you get up?	O tsohele joang/Le tsohele joang?

How are you?	O kae/Le kae?
I live well.	Ke phela hantle/Re phela hantle.
I got up well.	Ke tsohile hantle/Re tsohile hantle.
I'm here.	Ke teng/Re teng.

When parting, use the following phrases:

Go well.	Tsamaea hantle/Tsamaeang hantle.
Stay well.	Sala hantle/Salang hantle.

SWAHILI

Swahili has become the lingua franca of Tanzania (though educated people still speak English). Much the same thing is happening in Kenya, though the process there will be much slower since English is far more entrenched. Swahili is also useful in parts of Uganda, eastern Congo (Zaïre), Malawi and Zambia. This is especially so in the rural areas where the local people may only have had a smattering of education or none at all, and so are unlikely to be able to speak any English or French.

If your time is limited, concentrate first on the all-important greetings, and then on numbers (very useful when negotiating with market vendors, taxi drivers etc). For a more comprehensive guide to the language get a copy of Lonely Planet's *Swahili phrasebook*.

Greetings & Civilities

Jambo is pidgin Swahili, used to greet tourists who are presumed not to understand the language. There are two possible responses, each with different connotations: *Jambo* (Hello, now please speak to me in English), and *Sijambo* (Things aren't bad, and I'm willing to try a little Swahili).

If people assume you can speak a little Swahili, greetings may involve one or a number of the following exchanges:

How are you?	Hujambo? (to one person)
I'm fine.	Sijambo.
How are all of you?	Hamjambo?
We're fine.	Hatujambo.

The word *habari* (meaning 'news') can also be used for general greetings. Among other 'habari' greetings, you may hear *salama* substituted for *habari*, or the habari may be dropped altogether.

How are you?	*Habari?*
What's the news?	*Habari gani?*
Good morning.	*Habari za asubuhi?*
Good day.	*Habari za leo?*
Good afternoon.	*Habari za mchana?*
Good evening.	*Habari za jioni?*
(including night)	
Goodbye.	*Kwa heri.*
Good night.	*Usiku mwema.*

Useful Words & Phrases

Please. (if asking	*Tafadhali.*
a big favour)	
Excuse me.	*Samahani.*
Can you help me,	*Tafadhali, naomba msaada.*
please?	
Thank you (very	*Asante (sana).*
much).**	
Yes.	*Ndiyo.*
No.	*Hapana.*
What's your name?	*Jina lako nani?/Unaitwa nani?*
My name is ...	*Jina langu ni .../Naitwa ...*
Do you speak English/	*Unasema Kiingereza/Kiswahili?*
Swahili?	
I understand.	*Naelewa.*
I don't understand.	*Sielewi.*

(Remember to always exchange greetings before asking for help or information.)

What time does	*... inaondoka saa ngapi?*
the ... leave?	
bus	*basi*
minibus	*daladala* (Tanzania)
	matatu (Kenya)
train	*treni*

I'd like to hire a ...	*Nataka kukodi ...*
bicycle	*baisikeli*
car	*gari*
motorcycle	*pikipiki*

I want to go to ...	*Nataka kwenda ...*
Is it near?	*Ni karibu?*
Is it far?	*Ni mbali?*

Go ...	*Kata/Pita/Chukua ...*
left	*kushoto*
right	*kulia*
straight ahead	*moja kwa moja*

Where is a/the ...?	*... ni wapi?*
bank	*benki*
chemist/pharmacy	*duka la dawa*

market	*soko*
police station	*kituo cha polisi*
post office	*posta*
telephone centre	*mahali pa kupiga simu*

guesthouse	*gesti*
hotel	*hoteli* (note: *hoteli* also means restaurant)
Do you have a room?	*Je, kuna nafasi ya chumba hapa?*
How much is it?	*Ni bei gani?*
That's very expensive.	*Ghali sana.*

Food & Drink

Is there a restaurant	*Je, kuna hoteli ya chakula hapo*
near here?	*jirani?*
I'm vegetarian.	*Nakula mboga tu.*

bananas	*ndizi*
beef	*ng'ombe*
bread	*mkate*
chicken	*kuku*
egg(s)	*(ma)yai*
fish	*samaki*
food	*chakula*
goat	*mbuzi*
meat	*nyama*
milk	*maziwa*
rice	*mchele*
salt	*chumvi*
vegetables	*mboga*
water	*maji*

Health

Where can I find a ...?	*Naweza kupata ... wapi?*
doctor	*daktari/mganga*
hospital	*hospitali*

I'm sick.	*Niko mgonjwa.*
diarrhoea	*harisha/hara/endesha*
fever	*homa*
headache	*umwa kichwa*
nausea	*tapika*
vomiting	*tapika*
medicine	*dawa*
sanitary napkins	*Kotex*
water purifier	*chombo cha kusafisha maji*

Numbers

0	*sifuri*
1	*moja*
2	*mbili*
3	*tatu*
4	*nne*
5	*tano*
6	*sita*

LANGUAGE

7	saba
8	nane
9	tisa
10	kumi
11	kumi na moja
12	kumi na mbili
20	ishirini
21	ishirini na moja
22	ishirini na mbili
30	thelathini
40	arobaini
50	hamsini
60	sitini
70	sabini
80	themanini
90	tisini
100	mia (or mia moja)
200	mia mbili
300	mia tatu
1000	elfu
10,000	elfu kumi
100,000	laki
one million	milioni

EMERGENCIES – SWAHILI

Help!	Nisaidie!Jamaani!
It's an emergency.	Ni jambo la haraka.
Call a doctor!	Muite daktari!
Call the police!	Muite polisi!
I've been robbed!	Nimeibiwa!
Go away!	Toka!
I'm lost.	Nimepotea.

SWATI

Tonality (raising and lowering the pitch of the voice within words) plays a part in Swati and there are some clicks to contend with, but people are pleased (and often amused) with your attempts to speak their language.

Greetings & Civilities

Hello. (to one person)	Sawubona. (literally: 'I see you')
Hello. (to more than one person)	Sanibona.
How are you?	Kunjani?
I'm fine.	Kulungile.
Goodbye. (to one staying)	Sala kahle. (literally: 'stay well')
Goodbye. (to one leaving)	Hamba kahle. (literally: 'go well')
Please.	Tsine.
I thank you.	Ngiyabonga.
We thank you.	Siyabonga.

Useful Words & Phrases

Yes.	Yebo.
No.	Ha. (click)
Sorry.	Lucolo.
Do you have ...?	Une ... yini?
How much?	Malini?
Is there a bus to ...?	Kukhona ibhasi yini leya ...?
When does it leave?	Isuka nini?
morning/afternoon	ekuseni/entsambaba

Yebo is also often said as a casual greeting. It is the custom to greet everyone you meet. Often you will be asked *U ya phi?* (Where are you going?).

Glossary

For a list of food and drink terms used in this book, see p1053.

adobe building – building made of sun-dried bricks
albergos (Eritrea) – inns
ANC – African National Congress
animism – the base of virtually all traditional religions in Africa; the belief that there is a spirit in all natural things and the worship of those spirits that are thought to continue after death and have the power to bestow protection
asantehene (Ghana) – Ashanti king
askari (Kenya) – guard
auberge (mainly West & Central Africa) – traditionally a simple guesthouse, though some auberges are quite smart hotels
auberge de jeunesse (West & North Africa) – youth hostel

bab (North Africa) – Islamic gate
baché (West Africa) – bush taxi or truck
baksheesh (Egypt) – tip
banda (East Africa) – hut
BIAO – Banque International pour l'Afrique Occidentale
bijou (Egypt) – service taxi
boda-boda (East Africa) – bicycle taxi
boîte – nightclub
boîte postale (BP) – post office box
boksi (Sudan) – pick-up
boukarous (Cameroon) – open-sided, circular mud huts
braai (Southern Africa) – barbecue that normally includes lots of meat grilled on a braai stand or pit
Burkinabé (Burkino Faso) – adjective for Burkino Faso
bush taxi (West Africa) – public transport (usually pick-up or Peugeot 504/505)
buvette (West Africa) – refreshment stall

cadeau – gift of money
caleche (Egypt) – horse-drawn cart used for public transport; also called *hantour*
camiões (Mali, Mozambique) – truck
camion see *camiões*
campement (West Africa) – guesthouse
cãna (West Africa) – rum
car, grand car (Côte d'Ivoire, Mali) – bus
caravanserai – courtyard inn
careta (Egypt) – donkey-drawn cart
carnarval – festival
carte jaune (West Africa) – vaccination certificate
chambre d'hôte – guesthouse
chapa (West Africa & Mozambique) – bush bus

chop bar/house (West Africa) – streetside restaurant or bar selling inexpensive local food
chotts (Tunisia) – salt lakes
colectivo (São Tomé & Príncipe) – share taxi
commissariat – police station
cundonga – black market; also called *mercado paralelo*

dalla dalla (Tanzania) – pick-up or minibus
dash (West Africa) – bribe
dey (Algeria) – commander or governor
dhow (East Africa) – traditional sailing boat
dolomite – white mineral found in sedimentary rocks
douche – public shower
duka (Kenya) – shop

ECOWAS – Economic Community of West African States
ergs – sand seas

feira – market
felucca (Egypt) – Nile River sailing boat
forex – foreign exchange bureau
foro – musical instruments
funduq (Tunisia & Libya) – see *caravanserai*

gara (Sierra Leone) – thin cotton material, tie-dyed or batik-printed either with synthetic colours or natural dyes
garage (West Africa) – bus & taxi station
gare lagunaire (West Africa) – ferry terminal
gare routière (North & West Africa) – bus or transport station
gare voiture (Guinea) – bus or taxi station
gargotte (West Africa) – cheap restaurant
ghibli (Libya) – dry, dusty Sahara wind
gité (Morocco) – hiker's accommodation
grand taxi (Morocco) – bus
guichet automatique (West Africa) – automatic teller machine (ATM)

haj, the (Islamic countries) – pilgrimage to Mecca
hammam (Morocco) – Turkish-style bathhouse
hantour (Egypt) – horse-drawn carriage
harmattan – dry, dusty Sahara wind that blows towards the West African coast, particularly from November to March
hôtel de ville – town hall

IMF International Monetary Fund
impluvium – large, round mud house
ISIC – International Student Identity Card
Ivoirian - of or relating to the Côte D'Ivoire and its inhabitants

jawwazat (Libya) – security office where visitors to Libya have to register
jebel – mountain range
juju – object used as a charm or fetish

kandonga (Equatorial Guinea, Guinea-Bissau) – small pick-up
kasbah (North Africa) – fort or citadel, often outside the administrative centre; also spelt *qasba*
kente cloth – probably the most expensive material in West Africa, made with finely woven cotton, and sometimes silk, by Ghana's Ashanti people
kimbanda (Angola) – cult based on magic, from which Brazilian umbanda was based
kinguila (Angola) – woman who changes money on the black market
kizomba (Angola) – African-style nightclub with local music and traditional food
kopje – prominent, isolated hill or mountain
koubba (North Africa) – Islamic tomb
kraal (Southern Africa) – livestock enclosure or hut village
ksar (Tunisia) – (plural ksour) fortified stronghold
kwasa kwasa music – rhythmic, driving and repetitious music that originated in Congo (Zaïre)
KWS (Kenya) – Kenya Wildlife Service

lista de correos (Equatorial Guinea) – poste restante
lokanda (Sudan) – basic lodge
louage (Tunisia) – share taxi
lycée – high school

Maghreb – west (literally 'where the sun sets'); used to describe the area covered by Morocco, Algeria, Tunisia and, sometimes, Libya
mahdis (Tunisia) – Fatimid rulers
mairie (West Africa) – town hall
makonde (Tanzania) – ebony carving
maquis (West Africa) – small open-air restaurant with low, wooden tables, sandy floors and good music
marabout – religious saint (animist) or holy man (Muslim)
marché (West Africa) – market
marginal – waterfront (Angola); coast road (Mozambique)
matatu (Kenya) – minibus
matola (Malawi) – vehicle, usually a pick-up van, acting as an unofficial public transport service
medersa (Morocco) – college for teaching theology, law, Arabic literature and grammar
medina (North Africa) – old town, usually Arab
mellah (Morocco) – Jewish quarter of a *medina*
mercado paralelo (Angola) – black market, also see *cundonga*
mestiço (Angola) – people of mixed race
MET (Namibia) – Ministry of Environment & Tourism
mihrab – prayer niche in a mosque
mobylette (Burkina Faso) – moped

mokoro (Botswana) – dugout canoe
moto-taxi (West Africa) – motorcycle taxi
muezzin – mosque official who does the call to prayer from the minaret
musika (Zimbabwe) – bus station
musseque (Angola) – shanty
mwalimu (Tanzania) – teacher

NGO – Non-Governmental Organization

OAU – Organisation of African Unity
occasions (Central African Republic) – trucks

pagnes (Togo) – traditional strips of cloth
PAIGC – African Party for the Independence of Guinea-Bissau and Cape Verde
paillotte (West Africa) – straw awning
palmeraie (North Africa) – oasis-like area around a town where date palms, vegetables and fruit are grown
particular (Angola) – truck
pensão – cheap hotel
petroglyph – drawing or carving on rock
pinasse (Mali) – motorised boat
pirogue – dugout canoe
pont (West Africa) – bridge
pousada (Mozambique) – better-grade cheap hotel
praça – square
préfecture – administrative headquarters
processos (Angola) – share taxis
PTT – post office
pungwe (Zimbabwe) – beer hall

qasba – see *kasbah*
qat (East Africa) – leaves chewed as a stimulant

Ramadan – ninth month of the Islamic year, a period of fasting
RMS – Ruwenzori Mountaineering Services
rondavel (Southern Africa) – circular building, often thatched
rond-point – roundabout

Sahel – dry savanna area
shari'a – Islamic law
sharia (Arabic) – street
shifta (Kenya & Somalia) – bandit
souk/souq (North Africa) – outdoor market
sûreté – police station or place for registration
SWAPO – South-West African People's Organisation
syndicat d'initiative – government-run tourist office

tamanan (Egypt) – 80-octane (regular) petrol
taxi-brousse (West Africa) – bush taxi
télécentre, téléboutique, cabine téléphonique (West Africa) – private-sector telephone centre

tisa'en (Egypt) – 90-octane (super) petrol
toiles – rough, painted textiles
torgokaha – baskets and hats
tro-tro (Ghana) – small wooden bus/minibus
tukul (Eritrea) – type of hut/architectural style

UNITA – National Union for the Total Independence of Angola

ville nouvelle – 'new city', towns built by the French alongside existing towns and cities of the Maghreb
voodoo – the worship of spirits with supernatural powers, widely practised in southern Benin and Togo

waraniéné – woven shirts and trousers

ZANU – Zimbabwe African National Union
zaouia (Tunisia) – religious fraternity based around a *marabout*
ZAPU – Zimbabwe African Peoples' Union
zawiyya (Morocco) – shrine
zemi-john (Benin) – motorcycle taxi

FOOD & DRINK GLOSSARY
attiéké – grated manioc, not unlike couscous

bassi-salété – millet covered with vegetables and meat
brochettes – kebabs
briq (Tunisia) – crisp, very thin pastry envelope that comes with a range of fillings (always including egg)
bush meat – meat prepared from indigenous wildlife

capitaine – fish
chai (Kenya & Somalia) – tea
chapati – Indian-style bread
chwarma – see *shwarma*
couscous – semolina grains

felafel – chickpea burger
feuille (Central Africa) – manioc leaves
foutou – boiled and pounded yams or plaintains eaten as a staple food with sauce
fufu (West Africa) – fermented cassava
fuul (Egypt) – fava beans with a variety of ingredients added to spice them up, eg oil, lemon, meat, egg

harissa (Maghreb, Tunisia) – spicy chilli sauce
hummus – chickpea paste mixed with sesame puree (tahina), lemon and garlic

igname – pounded yams baked into a bread-like mix
injera (Ethiopia & Eritrea) – unleavened bread

karkaday (Egypt & Sudan) – hibiscus tea
kedjenou – chicken and vegetable stew served with rice or *foutou*

konjo (Mali) – millet beer
kushari (Egypt) – popular and cheap dish; oil-based mixture of noodles, rice, black lentils, fried onions, chickpeas and spicy tomato sauce

mafé – peanut-based stew
makhroud (Tunisia) – honey-soaked pastry stuffed with dates
mandazi (East Africa) – semi-sweet African doughnut
meis (Eritrea) – mead
moza (Egypt) – roast lamb on rice

nai tsom (Eritrea) – vegetable dishes
nsima (Malawi) – maize porridge, the regional staple

palava sauce – sauce made from pounded leaves, palm oil and seasonings, generally eaten with *fufu* or rice
pâté (Niger) – cornmeal stodge
plat du jour (West Africa) – dish of the day
poisson yassa – see *poulet yassa*
poulet braisé – fish or chicken cooked over the embers of a low fire
poulet yassa – marinated and grilled chicken or fish

riz sauce – very common basic meal (rice with meat sauce)

sadza (Zimbabwe) – maize meal porridge
sahleb – sweet, milky drink made from rice flour, grapes, coconut and nuts
sanbousak (Egypt) – pies filled with meat, cheese or spinach
shwarma – popular snack of grilled meat in bread, served with salad and sesame sauce, originally from Lebanon; also spelt *chwarma*
suya/soya (Nigeria/Cameroon) – spiced brochette

ta'amiyya – Egyptian version of *felafel*
tabouna (Tunisia) – traditional flat Berber bread
tajine – stew, usually with meat as the main ingredient
t'ej (Ethiopia) – mead
t'ella (Ethiopia) – home-brewed beer
tiéboudienne – rice baked in a thick sauce of fish and vegetables with pimiento and tomato sauce
tô (Burkina Faso) – millet or sorghum-based pâté

ugali (East Africa) – maize meal

xima – maize- or cassava-based staple, usually served with a sauce

yaourt (West Africa) – yogurt

Behind the Scenes

THIS BOOK

This is the 10th edition of *Africa on a shoestring*. The 1st edition, then called *Africa on the Cheap*, was written by Geoff Crowther in 1977. Geoff subsequently wrote, then became the coordinating author for, the next five editions of *Africa on a shoestring*, before handing over the reins to Hugh Finlay, who coordinated the next four editions. As the scope of the book grew, so did the need to share the load: this edition is the work of 18 authors. Coordinating author David Else led the team of authors: Kevin Anglin, Becca Blond, Jean-Bernard Carillet, Tione Chinula, Jane Cornwell, Pascale de Lacoudraye, Caroline Evans, Matt Fletcher, Anthony Ham, Abigail Hole, Alex Landragin, Tom Parkinson, Gemma Pitcher, Liza Power, Nick Ray, Noo Saro-Wiwa, Nicola Simmonds and Vincent Talbot.

THANKS from the authors

David Else Firstly   a big thank you to my wife Corinne, who joined me for many research trips through Africa, and kept me fired up with encouragement and coffee while I was writing at home. For advice, help, friendship and good company, thanks go to the many people who I met along the way – a marvellous mix of expats, VSOs, Peace Corps, gappies, backpackers, overlanders, hikers, bikers and global travellers. Your thoughts and feedback made this book what it is today. For initial inspiration, my thanks go to Geoff Crowther, a larger-than-life figure and the first author of this book, which I carried on my early visits to Africa. On subsequent trips I took the 3rd, 4th, 5th and 6th editions, and also had the dubious pleasure of spending several evenings with Geoff in disreputable Nairobi bars. Despite this, I hooked up with Lonely Planet and wrote various chapters for the 7th to 9th editions of *Africa on a shoestring*. It is a particularly satisfying achievement to be coordinating author of this book – the all-new landmark 10th edition. Although I was the coordinator, this book would not have been possible without the hard work and dedication of the authors who covered the ground, everywhere from the deep Sahara to the jungles of Johannesburg, to bring home the latest information on bars, beaches, bus fares and backpackers hostels – expertly handling bouts of malaria and dodgy borders along the way. So end-

less thanks to: Abi, Alex, Anthony, Becca, Gemma, Jean-Bernard, Kevin, Liza, Nicola, Matt, Nick, Noo, Pascale, Tom, Tione and Vincent. Our thanks also go to Commissioning Editor extraordinaire, Hilary Rogers, who kept the whole show on the road. Lastly, to all the citizens of Africa that I've met over the years: a heartfelt *asante*, *shukran*, *zikomo*, *merci* and thank you for providing insights and never-ending cheerfulness, often in the face of profound adversity. It was a great pleasure and a humbling experience travelling in your land. *Nkosi sikalele Afrika*. God bless Africa.

Kevin Anglin Big thanks to all my new friends and old friends who showed me around their home towns in Africa: Aba Enko Richard, Augustin Gansou, Prince Ibrahim, Alain Moungengui, Deb Pires, JG Collomb and the WCS, Mamadi at Waza, the staff of the Hotel Hila, Bradley Hodges, Melanie Szulczewski, and all the PCVs in Cameroon and Gabon who taught me that some things never change. At Lonely Planet thanks to Tasmin Waby and Hilary Rogers for all their hard work, and to Vivek Waglé for reminding me about all that 'art and felicity' stuff. Oh, and Doves. At home, thanks to TGOS, to Joy Hucklesby for all her kindness and support, and to my sister Kathy, who came through for me when I needed her.

Becca Blond First I have to thank my best friend and map-reader extraordinaire Alana Houseman who put her life on hold to join me for a while in Southern Africa. Similarly, I have to thank Bill, Gina, Haley and Brooke Hethcock without whose support I would have never made it to Lonely Planet in the first place. I'm also indebted to my family – David, Patricia, Jessica, Jennie, John and Vera who have always fully supported my not-so-lucrative writing career. And to Jo and Daniel in London for always offering a couch. In South Africa thanks go to John and Andrea Martin (Pretoria), Lisa Mason (Cape Town); Evan and Colleen (Jo'burg), Max Lentsoane (Jo'burg), Brawny Dube (Jo'burg) and to travellers Ben Macauley (thanks for spending the day wandering around Central Jo'burg when no-one else would), Dave Kilimnik, Aditi Rao, Linda Raven, Alison Silverglad and Ovidio Perez (who came over from Afghanistan just to visit) – all of whom provided invaluable insight. In Namibia, thanks in

Swakopmund go to Dave Richards, Craig Milne (who convinced me jumping out of aeroplanes was fun), Beth Sarro and Uys De Vos. Thanks to Jackie in Windhoek; Sonic in Tsumeb; Val and Wynand Peypers in Rundu; and Rob Ven Rensberg. Finally I am indebted to Hilary Rogers and Cathy Lanigan at Lonely Planet, who gave me the opportunity of a lifetime when I least expected it.

Jean-Bernard Carillet A big thank you to Frances Linzee-Gordon who offered assistance and guidance when needed, and for having opened doors in the Horn of Africa during the superb project *Ethiopia & Eritrea 2*. Our baby is in good shape! I'm also indebted to HE Yusuf Sukkar, Menbere Girma and Messeletch Tsige, Dominique Lommatzsch, Bruno Pardigon, Ali Liaquat, Paul Mandl, Guy Delile and Nadege, Pierre Montaigne, Said Baragoita, Mohammed Abdillahi Wais, Solomon Abraha, Tedros Kebbede, Annabel Hart and Thomas Fitzsimmons. At Lonely Planet, a big thank you to the editors and cartographers for their ongoing trust and support during this mammoth project, as well as David and Matt for their coordinating job. No thanks would be complete without a mention of Eva, my little daughter who tries to understand what makes her father so passionate about travel.

Matt Fletcher Thanks to David, Hilary and Robert for comments on numerous rough drafts and for making my life so much easier. Thanks to the rest of the authors of various contributions; Tony Irvin for great, insightful wildlife information; to Clare for proofreading; and Ag and Bando for leading me astray when I should have been proofing.

Anthony Ham Thank you to Jan for sharing a special Moroccan journey, Clinton and Stephanie for again bringing Morocco alive and Marina for making each day so wonderful. Thanks also to Hilary Rogers and Shahara Ahmed at Lonely Planet for their patience during the writing period.

Abigail Hole Many thanks to Hilary Rogers, David Else, Matt Fletcher, Andrew Rebold, Robert Reid, Alan Murphy and Anthony Ham at Lonely Planet; Whitney F Floyd, Violet Diallo, Beth Brogaard, Aly Tembely, Karen Crabbs, Kate Joyce and Boubacary Ouologuem in Mali; the Peace Corps, Elboya Cheikh, Lori Mitchell and Whitney Rokui in Mauritania; Wahid Chebbi and Hemantha Perera in Tunisia; Mohammed Dora, Ibrahim, Sherif Salama, Siona Jenkins and Henry the New Zealander in Egypt; California heart-throbs Eric Teran and Nolan Sambrano everywhere; Stephane Dahan for help

with Mauritania; all the readers who wrote in with comments and suggestions; as well as superstars Omi, Ginnie, Anthony, John, Morag, Sumeet, Sophie, Ben, Joe, Kelda and Esther.

Alex Landragin My thanks to Hilary Rogers for giving me the opportunity, and to David Else for his thoroughness; to Adrien for putting me up and putting up with me in Dakar; to Paul, John and Will in Burkina Faso; to Boris in Bobo; to the countless locals who helped me along the way; and to my parents.

Tom Parkinson Special thanks to Greg Campbell, Elizabeth McGrath, Colin and Karen, Eric, Mat and Beate and the Oasis/Economic lot for Nigeria info. Limited-word-count thanks: Algeria – Mike Tiney, the Bahedis; Niger – Reinhard, Rolf and the Domagalas, Franco, Fati, Sidi Mohammed, Kyrzika, Ibou and family, Moustaffa, Zara, Moktar, Marco, Manuel and Mousse, Delphine, Nicolas, the Zinder Francophones, Martino; Chad – Yoshi, God's Gifts and Abani, Sebastian and Charlotte, Blaise (vive Meg Ryan!); Sudan – Eric, Tajami, Asim Ahmed and Mazir, the British embassy; UK – Jeremy Keenan. Cheers also to Hilary Rogers for giving a new author a chance (or two)!

Gemma Pitcher The biggest thanks of all are reserved for the anonymous Mozambican who gave me his rain jacket on the road from Moçimboa da Praia to the Tanzanian border. He will never read this, but he saved me from breakdown, pneumonia or possibly both. Other people who deserve special thanks for their kindness and useful information are Mandla, Monica and Luis in Maputo; John and Steph in Vilankulo; Zito in Beira; Russell in Pemba; John on Ibo; Jools, Dominic, Isabelle and Matthew in Dar; Dory, Pascal and Anita in Zanzibar; Junior in Lushoto; Bart and Sarah in Nairobi; and Andrew and Zoe in Njoro. Thanks also to Colm McCarthy, Marc Douma and the many other travellers, volunteers and locals who went out of their way to help with information on the road and once I returned home. Lastly, thanks as always to my family for their unstinting support.

Liza Power Thanks go to Ala Elshabi, who introduced me to all things Libyan. Sand dunes, apple tobacco and *bohka* have filled many daydreams since.

Nick Ray First up a huge collective thanks to the good folk of Uganda, Rwanda and Burundi, and a loving thanks to my wife Kulikar Sotho who joined me for part of the adventure. In Uganda, thanks to: Dr Mugisha at UWA; all the crew at Backpackers, Blue Mango and Red Chilli; Bingo at NRE; and the Kampala night shift, Simon, Steve, Henry and Sat. In Rwanda, thanks to Patrice; Emmanuel Werabe and Mugisha Davidson at ORTPN; and John Kayihura of Primate Safaris. In Burundi, thanks to Adrien Nihorimbere and Aly Wood.

Noo Saro-Wiwa I'd like to give extra special thanks to Richard Hamilton, Lailana Rajohnson, Christian Randrianarison, Kayode Iposu, Olivier, Dana Mc-Donald, Elisha Delate-Moore, Mike Jacob, Abubakar, Mia, Rob Vissers, Ninie Bringmann, Le Bao and Maggie Koopman for all your invaluable help during my research.

Nicola Simmonds All the thanks in the planet to my husband, James, for his patience, his technical support in the face of chaos, his fact-finding missions, his proofreading and, very importantly, his well-timed and most delicious coffees with Baileys.

Vincent Talbot & Tione Chinula Our thanks to Lewis and Catherine Chinula; Ida Manjolo and the family at Likuni; Pim and Marga at Kiboko Camp in Lilongwe; Wade at Chachacha Backpackers and Stewart Sutherland at VSO in Lusaka; Karien at Wild Side Tours and Safaris in Livingstone; Mags, Suzanne, Lorrie, and the team at Backpackers Bazaar in Victoria Falls; Mike and Anna Scott in Bulawayo; Val Bell and James Hadebe at the Bulawayo Publicity Association; Kerina Zvobgo; Tony and Heather Freeman in Harare; Ruth Mthawanji in Blantyre; and June and Brian Walker in Monkey Bay. And thanks to people and travellers everywhere who helped with information. We dedicate our chapters to Brian Walker who loved Malawi, *yendani bwino*.

CREDITS

Series Publishing Manager Robert Reid oversaw the redevelopment of the shoestring guides series, and Regional Publishing Manager Virginia Maxwell steered the development of this title. The series was designed by Maria Vallianos, with mapping development by Paul Piaia. The series development team included Shahara Ahmed, Anna Bolger, Jenny Blake, Erin Corrigan, Nadine Fogale, Virginia Maxwell, Dave McClymont, Leonie Mugavin, Rachel Peart, Lynne Preston, Howard Ralley, Kalya Ryan, Paul Smitz and Vivek Waglé.

This title was commissioned and developed in Lonely Planet's Melbourne office by Hilary Rogers. The cartography was developed by Shahara Ahmed. Tasmin Waby coordinated the editing of this book

and Amanda Sierp coordinated the new and improved cartography. Pablo Gastar laid the book out, with assistance from Yvonne Bischofberger, Indra Kilfolye, Katherine Marsh, Andrew Ostroff and Tamsin Wilson. Overseeing the whole production were Ray Thomson (project manager), Brigitte Ellemor (managing editor) and Shahara Ahmed (managing cartographer) – their support and guidance throughout has been tremendous! Quentin Frayne compiled the language chapter and Gabrielle Green provided content advice during layout.

A cast of thousands (well, almost) helped behind the scenes, including a talented list of editors, proofers and indexers: Carolyn Bain, Carolyn Boicos, Cathryn Game, Cecilia Thom, Danielle North, David Andrew, Evan Jones, Fionnuala Twomey, Francesca Coles, Helen Christinis, Joanne Newell, Kalya Ryan, Kate James, Kim Hutchins, Linda Suttie, Martine Lleonart, Maryanne Netto, Melanie Dankel, Monique Choy, Paul Harding, Pete Cruttenden, Piers Kelly, Suzannah Shwer and Tony Davidson. Assisting with mapping were Marion Byass, James Ellis, Daniel Fennessy, Louise Klep, Mike Mammarella, Julie Sheridan, Sarah Sloane, Chris Thomas and Natasha Velleley. The fabulous colour map was created by Wayne Murphy. The gorgeous cover artwork was created and designed by Maria Vallianos. Technical assistance was provided by David Burnett, Ben Handicott and Nicholas Stebbing. Thanks also to Adriana Mammarella and Kate McDonald for their layout checks. And last but not least, a massive thank you to our brilliant team of authors, without whom there'd be no *Africa on a shoestring*.

THANKS from Lonely Planet
Many thanks to the travellers who used the last edition and wrote to us with helpful hints, useful advice and interesting anecdotes:

A Mohamed Abdulaziz Mohamed, Leslie Abramson, DK & Sue Adams, Janet Adams, Jodi Adams, Leah Adams, Gomez Adekunle, Maarten Adelmeijer, Giuliani Adolfo, Albert Afolabi, Mike Agerton, Morten Agri, Debbie Ait-Kaci, Enrico Alberti, Belinda Alborough, Brooke Aldrich, Charles Allen, Elizabeth Allman, Tradian Almasanu, Olivia Almeida-Duque, Luis Ambrosio, Tore Rye Andersen, Amanda S Anderson, Dave Anderson, Yiannis Andredakis, Sarah Andrews, Anita Montvazski, Sarah Annetts, Michelle Antici, Nikke Ariff, Dave & Louise Armstrong, Rik Arnoudt, Hilmir Ásgeirsson, Ruth Ash, Cathy Atkinson, Jeffrey Austin **B** MJ Bache, Charles Bailey, Jerry Baker, Monica Baker, Dr Rolf D Baldus, Jamie Baldwin, Shubha Banerjee, Shiriin Barakzai, Gord Barentsen, Bierta Barfod, Gabi Barkay, Lisa Barnes, Aaron &

Karen Barnett, Phil Barnett, Rosa Maria Perales Barrero, Frank Barresi, Eileen Barrett, Richard Bartlett, Mark Bartolo, Geoff Barton, Andrea Barucchello, Andrea & Alessandra Barucchello, Carolyn Baxter, Tonya Beck, Oliver Becker, Rüdiger Beckert, Helen Beecher Bryant, Henk Bekker, George H Bell, Keith & Bronwen Bell, Kate Belton, Gali Ben, Gunnar Berggren, Andrew Bergwald, Rose Bernfried, S Bertholin, Andrzej Bielecki, Peter Birch, Michael Birrell, Sarah Bisi, Sarah & Gianluca Bisi, Haralampos Bizas, Leila Blacking, Arnaud Bocquier, Julien Bodart, Geert Boeije, Paolo Boglietti, Martin Bohnstedt, Michael Boller, Rory Bolton, Marcel Bon, Marc Bond, Joerg Bongen, Mies Bono Mas, Christopher Borgmann, Ellen Bork, Frans Borst, Dr Stuart Borthwick, Adam Boryniec, Piero Boschi, Kees Bouman, Inge Bouwman, Bob & Anne Bown, Lucienne Braam, Lucila Bracco, Kerry Bradford, Marijana Brajac, Pamela Bregman, Bob & Sally Brennand, Kate Bretherton, Zella Bridle, Claudio Brigati, Eldad Brin, Ron Broadfoot, Matt Brocklehurst, Sjoukje Broer, Julie Bromley, Steve Brooks, Justin Brown, Christiane Bruno, Ang Bryans, Steve Bryant, Mary Buchalter, Lisa Bucovaz, Peter Budd, Martin Buekers, Kathleen Burke, Annaliese Burleigh, Rowland Burley, Didier Buroc, Ian Burton, Maret Busch, Michelle Bush, Ben Buston **C** Gerald Cadieux, Tricia Callender, Antonello Calvi, Simone Candido, Joseph Capaldi, Paul S Cariker, Michaela Carnaffan, Rob Carr, Milton Cassidy, Hedvig Castberg Tresselt, Nick Cawthon, Luigi Ceccarini, Maria Cecilia Macatangga, Mark Chambers, Myriam Champagne, Colleen Chan, Alan & Lynne Charlton, Dorothy Chatwin, David Chaudoir, Stephen Cheng, Yee Cheng, Alison Cheung, Cindy Choua, Flavio Ciferri, Nat Ciferri, Sheldon Clare, Ian Clements, Mieke Clerx, April Coetzee, Lynne Cole, Jo Coley, Bryant Collins, Elvio Colombino, Laurel Colton, Ross Connell, Stephen Cook, Gary Cooper, Dan Coplan, Etelka Corten, Giles Cory, Jane & Colm Cosgrove, Marie Cousens, Emily Cowan, Helen Cowan, Mavis Coxon, Ben Craig, Marnie Cranwell, Benedict Croell, Christian Crolla, Joseph D Crowley, Zsolt Cseke, Jody Culham, Sam Culpin, Monique Cuthbert **D** Johan & Lyn Dackner, Kristin Daley, Trish Daly, Nikki Dalziel, Uwe Danapel, Cora Dankers, Rob Davidowitz, Julie Davies, Tyron Davies, Carey Davis, J Day, Doc Dayal, Laury de Jong, Andrea de Laurentiis, Katie De Meerleer, Dietrich De Roeck, Tom De Schauwer, Zelna de Villiers, Eimear Deady, Marieke Dekker, John Delaney, Philippe Delesalle, Peter Demey, Elissa Dennis, Pam Dennison, Joanna Depledge, Walter Derks, Claude Desaintjan, Andre DeSimone, Robin Deweeerdt, Kelly Dewett, Stefano Di Marino, Bronwyn Dicker, Karlheinz Dienelt, Johan Dippenaar, Rob Dirven, Dave Dissette, Jan Ditheridge, David & Alison Dixon, Charly Dolman, Ivo Domburg, Rudolf Doppler, Sandrine Dossou-Yovo, Kelly Douglas, Naomi Doumbia, Simon Dowse, Jeff Doyle, Sigrid Drage, Dave Drake, Andreas Drechsler, Crystal Dreisbach, Niels Drent, Lunay Dreyer, Lorrie Drumm, Tilman Duerbeck, Kate Duffy, Nick Duke, Alistair Duncan, Hamish Duncan, Maria-Louise Dungworth, Clay Durham, Marie Durrant, Sonya Dykstra **E** Moray Easdale, Anne Easterling, Matt Ebiner, Gary Edgar, Dave Eggelton, Roderick Eime, Emmanuel Ekong, Ian Emerson, Angie Eng, Pieter Engelbrecht, Jacyntha England, Kerrieann Enright, Aurelia Erhardt, Andrew Esiebo, Andrea Evans **F** Tewabe Fanta, Bernard Farjounel, Jake Farnum, Jane Federman, Jonathan Feinn, Elijah Feinstein, Jerry Felix, Suzie Fendick, Rashida & Alexis Ferrand, Ornella Ferrari, Andrew Ferrone, Joey & Dianne Field, Hanne Finholt, D G Finley, Amy Colleen Finnegan, Tammy Fladebo, Elier Flagraklett, Mary Fletcher, Agner Fog, Cait Fogarty, Marco Fornier, Lars Erik Forsberg, Jordi Fortia-Huguet, Mark Foster, Richard Foster, Stephane Foucaud, Angela Fountain, Alastair Fraser, Bryan & Sonja Fraser, Kevin Fraser, Andrea French, Mike French, Anja Frensen, Laura Frew, Alex Friedman, Flynn & Jo Ellen Fuller, Julianne Fuller, Garrett Fulton, Scott Furness, Werner Furrer **G** Heiko Gabriel, Tomasz & Anna Galka, Michael Gallagher, Marzia Gandini, Alexander Garcia, Maribel Garcia, Vibhor Garg, Rob Garner, Stefan Gasser, Ewan Gatherer, Robert Gathu, Audrey Gaughran, Anne Gaven, Mark Gazia, Maria G-Beato, Jane Geary, Ev Gerson, Megan Gibbons, Bruno Gilissen, Lee Gillyon, John Gimblett, Paul W Gioffi, Ben Giola, Rebecca Glancy, Ian Glennon, Christian Glossner, David Godfrey, Jane Golding, Christian Goltz, Miguel Alvim Gonzalez, Maria Gonzalez-Beato, David Goodman, Barry Gore, Tom Graham, David Grant, Hamish Grant, Adin Greaves, Marion Green, Sian Green, William Greenberg, Sarah Greenfield, Bryan Grenn, Gwendoline Griffiths, Nicole Grima, Daniel Groeber, Tony Grooms, Benghazi Gross, Paul Gross, Emerson Grossmith, Brian Grove, Marc Grutering, Matteo Guidotti, Jeff Gunn, Kumar Gupta, Peder Gustafsson **H** Edwin Haagen, Arne Haaland, Stefan Haberl, Hugh Hadley, Guy Hagan, Ole Peder Hagen, Sally Hagen, Stephen Haines, Angela Hale, Ken Haley, Sue Hall, Suzanne Hall, Ben Hallett, Andrew Hamling, Maria Hannon, Lars Folmer Hansen, Thor Hanson, Katherine & Christoph Hantel, Angus Hardern, John Hardy, Kathleen Hardy, Steven Harlow, Donna Harris, Veronica Harris, Robin Hartle, Sonke Hartman, Charles Hartwig, Kate Harvie, Erica Hastings, Rex Haught, Stefan Havadi-Nagy, Jan Havranek, Matt Hawkins, Vanessa Hayes, John Hayman, Dana Hearn, Theresa Heasman, Trevor Heath, Janelle Heine, Kirsten Hellevang, Arnold Helmig, Cherifa Hendriks, Consuela Hendriks, Consuela & Vincent Hendriks, Sharon Herkes, Helma Hesse, Rona Hiam, Jalna Hickey, Max Hickey, Gary W Hickman, Maria Hidalgo, Kristin Higgins, Laura Higgins, Art Hilado, Sarah Hilding, Richard Hill, Michiel Hillenius, Peter Hiller, Edward Hillman, Dr Steffen Himmelmann, Nick Hind, John Hindson, Anthea Holland, Lawana Holland, Lee & Mei Hook, Teresa Horscroft, Sarah Horton, Jenny Horwood, Rhoda Houge, Brent Hourd, Sean Howell, Monika Hoyer, Wei-hsiang Huang, Derek Huby, Patrick Huddie, Matt Huddleston, Glenda Hudson, Kevin Hudson, Clephane Hume, Mary Hunt, Matt Hunter, Rachel Hunter, Aline Huppi **I** Christine Ingemorsen, Corey Innes, Adam Issa **J** Trygve Jackson, Tone Jacobsen, Jessica Jacobson, Bridgett James, Sir Jan, Patrick Jansen, Rogier Jaspers, Tansy Jefferies, Michael Jennings, Ove Jensen, Asa Johansson, BJ Johnson, Brian Johnson, Ken Johnston, Marissa Johnston, Evan Jones, Kirsten Jones, Laura Jones, Mark Jones, Nick Jones, Virginia Jones, Cara Joos, Ingo Jorgensen, Beate Josephi, Sandra Jouravlev, Catherine Junor, Kerry Just **K** Oscar Kafati, Niki Kalogiratou, Aziz Kara, Cynthia Karena, Karen Kavnar, Pavla Kazbundova, Tim Kealy, Edwina Kearney, Wendy Keeney, Peter Kell, Kevin Kelleher, Chris Kelly, Nick Kennedy, Colin Kenworthy, Ben & Paul Keown, Clare Kerr, John Kerrigan, Yvon Kersten, Svensson Kerstin, Ralph & Ute Kettritz, Paul Kilfoil, Brian King, Paul Knudsen, Karl Kociper, Otto Koene, David Koetsier, Olka Kolker, Vesa Komssi, Rudolf Konecny, Andreas Konieczny, Adriane Krapp, Barbara Kreijtz, Joost Kremers, Lucas Krezdorn, Blaz Krhin, Jennifer Krischer, Mia Kristiansen, Roger & Cecilie Kristiansen, Arnout Kroezen, Marjan Kroone, Mike Kruchten, Dale & Debbie Krumreich, Jon E Krupnick, Felicia Kruse **L** Chrissy Labenz, Michel Lacroix, Noshir Lam, Sandy Lam, Tony & Judy Lamborn, Gilles Lamere, John Lam-Po-Tang, Radka Langhammerova, Chris Lanyon, Mary-Justine Lanyon, Mike Lapetina, Giavi Lara, Rocco Lastella, Johan Le Roux, Tim Leary, Gordon Lee, Simon Lee, Marc Lees, Veronique Lefebvre, Sophie Lefever, Anna Leggett, Jessaca Leinaweaver, Paul Lelievre, Eugene Lemaire, Ruud Leukel, Adam Levine, Glyn Lewis, Rebecca Lewis, Anja Lieder, Edo Lin, Paul Lindsay-Addy, Mary Lindsey, Jennie Lindwert, Debbie Ling, Matt Link, Bob Lipske, Willem & Joany Lisman, Harriet Little, Ellen Livermore, Dorothea Loefler, Peter Loeskow, E Loman, Gustaf Lorentz, Andre Lotz, Gerd Lotze, Helen Louise, Fiona Lovatt Davis, Serena Love, Christophe Lucet, Erich Ludwig, Mikael Lundmark, Patrizio Luntini, Catarina Lyden, Carrie Lyle **M** Tarek Maalouf, Pam & Bob Macauley, Brian MacCormaic, Andrew MacDonald, Alanna MacDougall, Jonny Macintosh, MJ Mackay, Jim Mackie, AJ Mackinnon,

Bernard Madigan, Diana Maestre, Mike Maglalang, Greg Magnus, Maureen Maguire, Katherine Majors, Raffael Mallepell, Mary-Ann Malloy, John Mamone, Sanjay Mandhare, Fiona Mann, Oscar Mann, Mike Mannion, Barbara Mansvelt, Susan Mares-Pilling, Dr Mario Mariani, Monika & Alex Marion, Helen Marsh, David Marshall, Tadzio Martin Kolelb, Clara Mindy Martone-Boyce, Audrey Mason, Herb Masters, Melissa Matheny, Peta Mathias, Lois Mativo, Paul Mattock, Nick Matzke, Claire Mawdsley, Geoff & Hilary May, David Mayer, Andrew Maynard, Silvia & Stefano Mazzocchio, Neal McCall, Ann McCarthy, Gordon Mcewan, Bill T McFarlane, Charles McFeely, Delia McInerney, Heather McIntyre, Jim McIntyre, Ross McKenzie, Amy Lee McKeon, Kelvin McKinstry, RN McLean, Ian McLeod, Paul McLoughlin, Elizabeth McSweeney, Jan Mecklenburg, Basia Meder, A Meier, Sharon Meieran, Silvia Meli, Koen Mertens, Pierre Messier, Hub Metry, Scotty Meyers, Petra Meyr, Markella Mikkelsen, Natasha & Paul Pellizzari Milijasevic, P AP Miller, Rachel Miller, Claire Missing, Judith Mitchel, Chris Mitchinson, Roos Molendijk, Kai Monkkonen, Jesse Monsour, Ilse Monsted, Dore Montes, Sumaiyah Moola, David Moore, Mike Moore, Stuart Moore, Guy Moorhouse, Carolina Moreira, Jonathan Morgan, Paul Morley, David Morris, Pedr Morris, Tom Morris, Doug Moseley, Inge Mossige, Heather Mothershead, Nelly Moudime, Katie Mountford, Chris Mueller, Claudia Mueller, K Mulzer, Sonja Munnix, Jane Munro, Ana Murillo, Jasper & Vincent Murphy, Diane Murray, Strother Murray, Marco Mwaniki **N** Anneke Naerebout, Oscar Nagtegaal, Ramsay Napier, Alf Nathoo, Inger Nelson, Ross Nelson, Eva Nerga, Rainer Neumann, Carlyle Joy Newman-Eden, Jean Nicca, Nigel Vere Nicoll, Brad Nilson, Kwame Nkrumah-Boateng, Jon Noble, Mick Nolan, Boerma Nooiji, Bjorn Norheim, Paul Norrish, Elizabeth Norton, Sabine Nouvet **O** Stephan Oberuck, Padraig O'Blivion, Christine Louise Oddy, Paul S Odendaal, Kevin O'Donovan, Carrie Oelberger, Tobias Oettl, Brigid O'Hagan, John Oldham, Jan Olver, Stefanie Opper, Jenny Orchard, Finbarr O'Reilly, John Osman, Wanda Ot, Ivo Oud, Len Outram, Leonard Outram, Irene Ouwens, Lynne & Wayne Oxenham **P** Nick Pace, Michael Padua, Vittorio Paielli, Rebecca Painter, Iris Palmer, Anita Paltrinieri, Ellen Pansegrau, John Papageorgiou, Les Parkes, Mary-Lou Penrith, Alfredo Perez, Jane Perry, Ann M Pescatello, Katja & Henry Petzold, Johann Pfenninger, Chris Phillips, Mark Pickens, Nick Picton, RC Pietri, S A Pietsch, Shiobhaun Pilbeam, Claudia Alice Pinkas, Sophie Pitcher, Geert Pladet, Dr Sunthorn Plamintr, Markus Planmo, Shawn Plummer, Charlie Pointer, Adam Pollock, Robert Portais, Jessica Posner, Isabel Posthuma, Marisca Postma, Jim

Potter, Cameron Poulton, Deborah Pownall, Cristina Pratas, Luigi Prati, Claudio Predan, Glenn Pressnell, Vicky & Martin Pringle, James Prior **Q** Jacob Quarcoo, Paul Quenby **R** Bethan Rand, Peter Ras, Birgitte Rask, Goolzaar Rattanshi, Andrea Rausch, Sarah Ravaioli, Helen Ray, Anne Rees, Sue Rees, Helen Reeves, Claire & Kodjikeka Reindorp, Jacqueline Remmelzwaal, Howard Richards, Sara Richelson, Lorraine Ridgwell, Steven Riley, Judith Ripoli, Caterina Rizzo, Maurice Roberts, John Robertson, Leslie Robin, Mary Robinson, Jenny Roche, Anna Rockert, Dusseaux Rodolphe, Daniel Rodriguez, Keith Rodwell, Kathryn Roe, Nick Rooker, Diana Rose, Kerstin Rosen, Marvin Rosen, Nicolas Rosenbaum, Darren Ross, Miga Rossetti, William Rowden, Angela Rowe, Alison Rowlands, Stephen Rowlands, Synnove Roysland, Nerea Rozas, Carol Ruddock, Poitr Rudzki, Anny Ruesink, Richard & Caroline Rule, Marguerite Rummery, Katherine Rushby, Vic Russell, Monika Rutishauser **S** Marta Nguessa Sabbadini, Aimee Sacks, Nahla Saleh, Errol Salvador, Stefan Samuelsson, Malin Sanden, Aidan Santer, Amelia Savino, Keith Savory, Elie Schecter, Michael Scheiwein, Gisela Scherz, Tina Scheutz, Dana Schiffner, Lisa Schipper, Reinhard Schmidt, Polly Schmincke, Josette Schoenmakers, Monique Schoone, Holger Schulze, Fiona Scully, Nancy Seigel, Oliver Selwyn, Michael Seto, Nadeem Shah, Robert & Ruth Shannon, Sherin Sharawy, David Sharp, Hussein Shatry, Mark Sheard, Jim Shelley, Kim Shockley, Emily Shults, Bilal Sidani, Stephan Siemer, Steve Signal, Julie Silva, Karolina Simmons, Ezra Simon, J Simonis, John Simpson, Gerald Sing Chin, Cheryl Singer, Barun Sinha, Vica V Sissoko, Laura Sisti, Boris Skoric, Mirjam Skwortsow, Betania SL, R & VA Slack, Ryan Slimmon, Peter Sloth Madsen, Julia Smailes, Gavin Smith, Jonathan Smith, Kathryn Smith, Martin Smith, Heleen Snoep, Joost & Conny Snoep, Krzysztof Sobien, Saskia Soeterbroek, Jennifer Solomon, Jo Somers, Ralph Somma, Nienke Sonneveld, Zoe Sowden, Paul Spaans, Ken Sparkes, Andy Sparrow, Jim R Speirs, Tim Spicer, Ann & Frank Spowart Taylor, Manuela Stahl, Mike Stapleton, Marc Steegen, Paul Steele, Morini Stefano, Krista Stegink, Urs Steiger, Peter Stein, Chris Stephenson, Nan Stevens, Simon Stevens, Tracy Stewart, Richard Stokes, Ruth C Stoky, Eduard Stomp, Terrilee Stone, Bill & Ann Stoughton, Garry & Marita Stout, Dr Mohar Subbiah, Bridget Sudworth, Richard Sudworth, Tarren Summers, Paul Sutton **T** Jean-Francois Tackoen, Jouko Tahvanainen, Joe Taschetta, Heidi Tavakoli, Jon Taylor, Liz Taylor, Ingrid Teige, David Teli, David & Evonne Templeton, Martin Terber, Sue Thomas, Steven Thompson, Jesper Thomsen, Michel Thuriaux, Kristien Thys, Mel Tilkicioglu, Sandra Timmermans, Liz Tinney, Michel Tio, Ivar Tjernberg, Bruce Toman, Carol Tompkins, Jaume Tort, Alex & Becca Tostevin, Stephen Totterman, Chiara Trapani, Shane Trembath, Jon Tringham, Elizabeth Trybek, Jonathan Tsou, Konrad Tuchscherer, Jeff Tucker, Iain Turner, Jo Turner, Jenny Turunen, Daniel Twentyman **U** Pauline Ubels, Christine Ungruh, Helix F Union, Urmen Upadhyay **V** Marc Valliant, Jerry van Beers, Francien van de Moosdijk, Liselotte Van de Perre, Reijco Van De Pol, Pim van de Werhen, Kim van den Berg, Edda-Nathalie Van den Bergh, Patrick van der Hijden & Saskia van Grinsven, Anthony van der Hooft, Sylvia van der Oord, J van der Velden, Wouter van der Westhuizen, Corne van Dongen, Johannes van Eeden, Erwin van Engelen, Caren van Halen, Nathalie van Leeuwen, Caroline van Moorsel, Marieke van Schaik, Slavica & Jilles van Werkhoven, Erwin van Wijk, Marcel van Zonneveld, Robin Vandenberg, Vera Vandervelde, Kim Vaughan, Thomas Vaughan, Harmen Venema, Jan Venema, Bart & Linda Verhaak, Hans Verhoef, Vikki Vermod, Viktor Kaposi, Manuel Villanueva, Marte Villegas, Kimmo Virta, Esther Visser, Amy Vogt, Hayco J Volkers, Joost Vollaard, Sally von Holdt, Sylvia von Minden, Jens von Scheele, Jan Voorhagen, Carmel Votano, Bas Vriesema, Esther Vusser **W** Charlie Wade, Chelly Wael, Bill Wagman, Tom Walker, Kerry Wallace, Kerry & John Wallace, Malcolm Wallace, Kelly Walton, Ian Ward, Stephen Ward, Vanessa Ward, E Warmer, Alex Watt, Nathan Weber, Claude Wechenk, Steph Weeks, Suzanne Wehl, Jason Weigold, Ana Weil, Denise Werner, Kerrin Werner, Thomas Werner, Roger Wesson, Mike Westerhaus, David Westland, Johan Westman, Guy Westoby, Phi Weyers, Peter White, Ruben Wickenhauser, Camilla Wickstrom, Jose Wiechmann, Vincent Wiegers, Klaas Wiersema, Jeroen Wijkamp, Sanne Wijnhorst, Eddie Wild, Eddie Wilde, Brita Wilfling, Brian Wilkes, Aled Williams, Jeff Willner, Jean A Wilsen, Ron Wilson, Sean & Dympna Wilson, Shane Wilson, Joseph Winter, Debra Winters, Jan Witkiewicz, Andreas Wladis, Karin Wohlgemuth, Danielle Wolbers, Ross Wold, Arielle Wolfe, Lisa Womersley, Geoff Wood, Keith Wood, Viv Wood, Paul Woodward, Robert Wotton, Natalie Wray, Jane Wright, Mark Wright, Susan Wright, Mary Wynn **Y** Najim Yassine, Pablo Yee, Pablo & Fremon Best Yee, Jim Ying, Ian Young, Lisa Young **Z** Bianca Zegers, Julie Zeitlinger, Maya Zeller, Andrea Zeus, Jan A Zijlstra, Felix Zimmermann, Rene Zorn, Nicolien Zuijdgeest.

ACKNOWLEDGMENTS

Many thanks to the following for the use of their content.

Mountain High Maps® Copyright © 1993 Digital Wisdom, Inc.

Index

INDEX

INDEX

INDEX

INDEX

INDEX

INDEX

THE LONELY PLANET STORY

The story begins with a classic travel adventure: Tony and Maureen Wheeler's 1972 journey across Europe and Asia to Australia. There was no useful information about the overland trail then, so Tony and Maureen published the first Lonely Planet guidebook to meet a growing need.

From a kitchen table, Lonely Planet has grown to become the largest independent travel publisher in the world, with offices in Melbourne (Australia), Oakland (USA), London (UK) and Paris (France).

Today Lonely Planet guidebooks cover the globe. There is an ever-growing list of books and information in a variety of media. Some things haven't changed. The main aim is still to make it possible for adventurous travellers to get out there – to explore and better understand the world.

At Lonely Planet we believe travellers can make a positive contribution to the countries they visit – if they respect their host communities and spend their money wisely.

SEND US YOUR FEEDBACK

We love to hear from travellers – your comments keep us on our toes and help make our books better. Our well-travelled team reads every word on what you loved or loathed about this book. Although we cannot reply individually to postal submissions, we always guarantee that your feedback goes straight to the appropriate authors, in time for the next edition. Each person who sends us information is thanked in the next edition – and the most useful submissions are rewarded with a free book. See the Behind the Scenes section.

To send us your updates – and find out about LP events, newsletters and travel news – visit our award-winning website: **www.lonelyplanet.com**.

Note: We may edit, reproduce and incorporate your comments in Lonely Planet products such as guidebooks, websites and digital products, so let us know if you don't want your comments reproduced or your name acknowledged. For a copy of our privacy policy, email privacy@lonelyplanet.com.au.

Published by Lonely Planet Publications Pty Ltd
ABN 36 005 607 983

© Lonely Planet 2004

© photographers as indicated 2004

Cover montage by Maria Vallianos. Cover photographs by Lonely Planet Images: David Else, Dennis Jones, Oliver Strewe, Ariadne Van Zandbergen; back cover: Ngorongoro Conservation Area, North Eastern Tanzania, Steve Davey. Many of the images in this guide are available for licensing from Lonely Planet Images: www.lonelyplanetimages.com

Printed by SNP SPrint (M) Sdn Bhd, Malaysia.

LONELY PLANET OFFICES

Australia
Head Office
Locked Bag 1, Footscray, Victoria 3011
☎ 03 8379 8000, fax 03 8379 8111
talk2us@lonelyplanet.com.au

USA
150 Linden St, Oakland, CA 94607
☎ 510 893 8555, toll free 800 275 8555
fax 510 893 8572, info@lonelyplanet.com

UK
72–82 Rosebery Ave,
Clerkenwell, London EC1R 4RW
☎ 020 7841 9000, fax 020 7841 9001
go@lonelyplanet.co.uk

France
1 rue du Dahomey, 75011 Paris
☎ 01 55 25 33 00, fax 01 55 25 33 01
bip@lonelyplanet.fr, www.lonelyplanet.fr